Birds of Venezuela

STEVEN L. HILTY

Birds of Venezuela

PRINCIPAL ILLUSTRATORS

John A. Gwynne and Guy Tudor

ADDITIONAL COLOUR PLATES BY

Alejandro Grajal, Larry B. McQueen and Sophie Webb

LINE DRAWINGS BY

Michel Kleinbaum and John A. Gwynne

CHRISTOPHER HELM   LONDON

Published by Christopher Helm, an imprint of A & C Black Publishers Ltd., 37 Soho Square, London W1D 3QZ

Copyright © 2003 by Steven L. Hilty (text and maps) and Guy Tudor and John Gwynne (illustrations)

ISBN 0-7136-6418-5

A CIP catalogue record for this book is available from the British Library

A & C Black uses paper produced with elemental chlorine-free pulp, harvested from managed sustainable forests.

Printed and bound in Italy by Eurografica

10 9 8 7 6 5 4 3 2 1

Artists' credits

Plates
Alejandro Grajal—15, 16
John A. Gwynne—1 (part), 2, 4, 5 (part), 18, 19, 31, 33–36, 43, 47 (part), 48, 51, 54–67
Larry B. McQueen—52
Guy Tudor—1, 3, 5–14, 17, 20–23, 28–30, 32, 37–42, 44–47, 49, 50, 53
Sophie Webb—24–27

Line drawings
All drawings by Michel Kleinbaum, except those on pages 245, 442, 464, and 595, by John A Gwynne

Range Maps
Steven L. Hilty, assisted by Dimitri Karetnikov

Contents

List of Figures, Photographs, and Table

National Parks

1. Sierra del Perijá
2. Ciénegas del Catatumbo
3. El Tamá
4. Chorro El Indio
5. Páramos Batallón y La Negra
6. Sierra Nevada
7. Sierra de la Culata
8. Guaramacal
9. Dinira
10. Cerro Saroche
11. Yacambú
12. Terepaima
13. Sierra de San Luis
14. Médanos de Coro
15. Cueva de la Quebrada El Toro
16. Morrocoy
17. Yurubí
18. San Esteban
19. Henri Pittier
20. Macarao
21. El Avila
22. Guatopo
23. Laguna de Tacarigua
24. Archipiélago Los Roques
25. Mochima
26. Laguna de la Restinga
27. Cerro Copey-Jóvito Villalba
28. Península de Paria
29. Turuépano
30. El Guácharo
31. Mariusa
32. Aguaro-Guariquito
33. Cinaruco-Capanaparo
34. Yapacana
35. Duida-Marahuaca
36. Serranía de la Neblina
37. Parima-Tapirapecó
38. Jaua-Sarisariñama
39. Canaima

The Northwest: Zulia and Falcón

40. Adicora, Falcón
41. Catatumbo, Río, Zulia
42. Cedro, Alto de, Zulia 450m
43. Chichiriviche, Falcón
44. Coro, Falcón 20m
45. Curimagua, Falcón
46. Encontrados, Zulia
47. Kaimare Chico, Zulia
48. Lagunillas, Zulia
49. Machiques, Zulia
50. Maracaibo, Zulia
51. Mene Grande, Zulia
52. Mirimire, Falcón,
53. Misión, Cerro, Falcón 50–300m
54. Negro, Río, Zulia
55. Olivitos, Los, Zulia
56. Paraguaipoa, Zulia
57. Pejochaira, Cerro, Zulia
58. Piritú, Falcón
59. San José de La Costa, Falcón
60. San Luis, Sierra de, Falcón 1200m

61. Tacarigua, Embalse de, Falcón
62. Tucacas, Falcón
63. Zulia, Río, Zulia

Andes and Northern Cordilleras East to Miranda

64. Águila, Páramo del, Mérida 4100m
65. Altamira, Barinas 700m
66. Azulita, La, Mérida 1100m
67. Barinas, Barinas 200m
68. Barquisimeto, Lara 550m
69. Betijoque, Trujillo 550m
70. Boconó, Trujillo 1100–1300m
71. Burgua, Táchira 350–500m
72. Cabudare, Lara 450m
73. Caracas, Distr. Federal 900m
74. Cendé, Páramo, Trujillo/ Lara 3550m
75. Cerrón, Cerro El, Falcón/Lara 1900m
76. Chama, Río, Mérida
77. Chiquito, Río, Táchira
78. Choroní, Aragua 0–10m
79. Cogollal, Cerro El, Lara/Falcón 1600m
80. Copas, Cerro Las, Táchira
81. Delicias, Las, Táchira 500m
82. Frailes, Hotel Los, Mérida 3000m
83. Fria, La, Táchira 100m
84. Golfo Triste, Cerro, Aragua 1200m
85. Izcaragua, Miranda 1000m
86. Maracay, Aragua 400m
87. Misisí, Páramo, Trujillo
88. Mitisús, Mérida 1550m
89. Mucubají, Páramo de, Mérida 3500m
90. Negro, Cerro, Miranda 1000m
91. Ocumare, Aragua 150m
92. Palmichal, Carabobo 1000m
93. Rancho Grande Biol. Station, Aragua
94. Platillón, Cerro, Aragua/Guárico 1900m
95. Pregonero, Táchira 1260m
96. San Isidro Road, Barinas 1450–1500m
97. Santa Elena, Mérida 100m
98. Seboruco, Táchira 900m
99. Tamá, Páramo de, Táchira 1800–3350m
100. Tovar, Colonia, Distr. Federal 1400–2100m
101. Univ. de Los Andes forest, Mérida 2100m
102. Valencia, Carabobo 430m
103. Zumbador, Páramo, Táchira 2600m

The Northeast Sucre and Monagas

104. Azul, Cerro, Sucre 1500m
105. Barrancas, Monagas
106. Caripe, Monagas 800m
107. Colorado, Caño, Monagas 25m
108. Cumaná, Sucre
109. Guaraunos, Sucre 100m
110. Humo, Cerro, Sucre
111. Maturín, Monagas 75m
112. Negro, Cerro, Sucre/Monagas 2400m
113. Peonía, Cerro, Sucre 1500m
114. Turumiquire, Cerro, Sucre 2600m

Llanos South to Río Orinoco

115. Acarigua, Portuguesa 200m
116. Boconoito, Portuguesa 200m
117. Calabozo, Guárico 100m
118. Cantaura, Anzoátegui 250m
119. Cedral, Hato, Apure 150m
120. Frio, Hato El, Apure 150m
121. Guanare, Portuguesa
122. Guasdualito, Apure
123. Indios, Hato Los, Apure 100m
124. Masaguaral, Hato, Guárico
125. Páez, Pto., Apure 100m
126. Piñero, Hato, Cojedes 150m
127. San Fernando de Apure, Apure
128. Santa Bárbara, Barinas
129. Santa María de Ipire, Guárico
130. Sombrero, El, Guárico
131. Zuata, Río, Guárico

State of Amazonas

132. Alechiven Camp
133. Asisa, Río
134. Ayacucho, Pto. 100m
135. Calentura, Cerro 2300m
136. Camturama Lodge
137. Capuana, Caño
138. Carmelitas, Las
139. Carmen, El
140. Cataniapo, Caño 100m
141. Cuao, Caño
142. Duida, Cerro 2250m
143. Guanay, Cerro 1800m
144. Huachamacari, Cerro
145. Junglaven
146. Kabadisocaña, 550m
147. Mavaca, Río
148. Neblina, Cerro de la 3045m
149. Ocamo, Río and Misión
150. Padamo, Río
151. Parú, Cerro, 1600m

152. Samariapo,
153. San Carlos de Río Negro 100m
154. San Francisco de Atabapo
155. San Juan de Manapiare
156. Simarawochi
157. Sipapo (Paraque), Cerro 2100m
158. Yapacana, Cerro 1250m
159. Yavi, Cerro 2400m
160. Yavita-Pimichín

State of Bolívar and Delta Amacuro (DA)

161. Acopán-tepui
162. Aprada-tepui
163. Araguaimujo, Misión de, DA
164. Auyán-tepui 2560m
165. Caicara
166. Canaima 400m
167. Carabobo
168. Carún, Río
169. Caurama Lodge
170. Chimantá-tepui 2000m
171. Cuchivero, Río
172. Cuquenán, Cerro 2680m
173. Curiapo, DA
174. Dorado, El 150m
175. Grande, Río 250m
176. Guaiquinima, Cerro 2100m
177. Guasipati 200m
178. Icabarú
179. Imataca, Serranía de 500m
180. Jaua, Meseta de and Cerro 2250m
181. Km 84 and 88
182. Lema, Sierra de
183. Maijía, Salto (Falls)
184. María Espuma, Salto (Falls)
185. Maripa 100m
186. Negro, Cerro El 1200m
187. Nicharé, Río
188. Nieves, Hato Las
189. Nuria
190. Ordaz, Pto. 50m
191. Palmar, El 250m
192. Paragua, La
193. Paurai (Parai)-tepui 2000m
194. Pijiguaos
195. Ptari-tepui 2650m
196. Roraima, Cerro 2800m
197. Santa Elena de Uairén, 900m
198. Sarisariñama, Cerro 1400m
199. Sororopán-tepui 2000m
200. Tucupita, DA
201. Tumeremo
202. Uaipán (Uaipá)-tepui 1900m
203. Uei-tepui 2670m
204. Upata
205. Urbana, La
206. Urutaní, Cerro

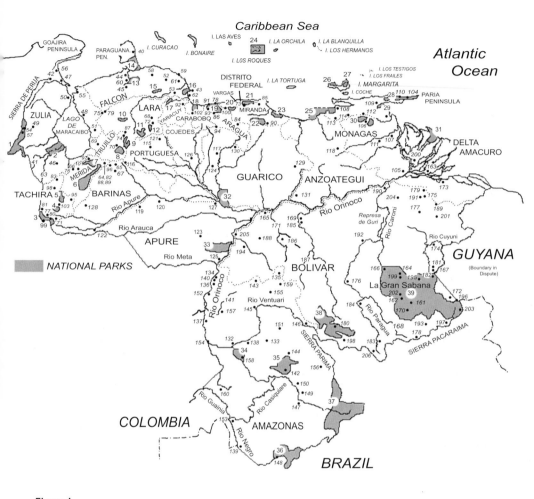

Figure I

Venezuelan locations.

Symbols and Abbreviations

Range Map Symbols

Solid black dot: Specimen record
Open circle: Sight record, tape or photo documentation
Solid gray: Breeding range
Vertical hatch: Northern (Boreal) migrant
Horizontal hatch: Southern (Austral) migrant
For other details see Key to Map Symbols on page 178.

Abbreviations

ad(s).	adult(s)
adj.	adjacent
Amaz.	Amazonian
amt(s).	amount(s)
approx.	approximate(ly)
assoc.	association, associated
BC	breeding condition
c	central
ca.	about
C Amer.	Central America(n)
Carib.	Caribbean
cf.	compare
cm	centimeter(s)
conspic.	conspicuous(ly)
Distr. Federal	Distrito Federal (Federal District)
distrib.	distribution, distributed
e, w, n, s,	east or eastern, west or western, etc.
E, W, N, S	East, West, etc. (compass points)
el(s).	elevation(s), elevational
esp.	especially
freq.	frequent(ly)
g	gram(s)
gd(s).	ground(s)
ha	hectare(s)
hd.	heard
hr	hour(s)
ht(s).	height(s)
imm(s).	immature(s)
incl(s).	include(s), including
inconspic.	inconspicuous(ly)
info.	information
infreq.	infrequent(ly)
intermed.	intermediate
introd.	introduced
irreg.	irregular(ly)
isl(s).	island(s)
juv(s).	juvenile(s), juvenal (plumage)
kg	kilogram(s)
km	kilometer(s)
loc(s).	location(s)
m	meter(s)
max.	maximum
med.	medium
mid.	middle
min	minute(s)
mm	millimeter(s)
mt(s).	mountain(s)
N Amer.	North America(n)
ne, se, sw, nw	northeast, southeast, etc.
no(s).	number(s)
occas.	occasionally
Pen.	Peninsula
PN	Parque Nacional (National Park)
pop(s).	population(s)
poss.	possible, possibly
pr(s).	pair(s)
predom.	predominant(ly)
presum.	presumed, presumably
prob.	probable, probably
prom.	prominent(ly)
Pto.	Puerto (Port)
publ.	published
rec(s).	record(s), recorded
reg.	regular(ly), regularity
S Amer.	South America(n)
sec	second(s)
ser.	series
sim.	similar(ly)
sp.	species (singular)
spp.	species (plural)
subad(s).	subadult(s)
subsp.	subspecies (singular)
subspp.	subspecies (plural)
unrec.	unrecorded
US	United States
Venez.	Venezuela(n)
W Indies	West Indies
wk	week(s)
yr	year(s)

Abbreviations for months are Jan, Feb, Mar, Apr, May, Jun, Jul, Aug, Sep, Oct, Nov, Dec.

**Abbreviations for Museums
and Institutions**

AMNH	American Museum of Natural History, New York
FMNH	Field Museum of Natural History, Chicago
USNM	United States National Museum, Washington, D.C.

Acknowledgments

Author's Acknowledgments

I thank foremost my wife, Beverly Hilty, who has been my companion and confidant during the years of work on this project, for her effort in almost single-handedly running our household and raising our daughters during my many absences, and for always being there when I needed her. I could not have completed this book without her. I also thank my daughters, Dru Hilty and LaRae Hilty, for their support during the many times when I was away in the field or working in museums, and Dru Hilty for preparation of the relief, vegetation, and rainfall maps.

Several people have been enormously generous with their time and expertise, and I owe them a debt of gratitude. David Ascanio has been an almost constant companion on field trips for several years. He has provided much information on the distribution and songs of Venezuelan birds, updated some Spanish names, and aided this project in innumerable ways. Albert Boggess cheerfully tackled the enormous task of computerizing much of the distributional data, especially the tens of thousands of specimen records, which form the backbone of the range maps. Peter Boesman provided a large number of new distributional records, many of them unpublished at the time, as well as several useful regional lists. Margaret Bullock (deceased) provided much assistance in the early stages of computerization of the maps and the development of an electronic gazetteer of localities. Mary Lou Goodwin introduced me to some little-visited corners of Venezuela. Miguel Lentino placed the facilities of the Colección Phelps in Caracas at my disposal, and his tremendous knowledge of the Venezuelan avifauna provided a sounding board for innumerable questions. Christopher Parrish allowed me to use his meticulously detailed field notes and tape-recordings spanning his nearly 13-year residence in Venezuela, and these yielded a treasure of information on distribution, behavior, and voice. Robert S. Ridgely provided detailed field notes from several field trips, co-led two trips with me, and gave helpful advice on many taxonomic issues.

Mark B. Robbins read portions of the manuscript and also offered helpful insight into taxonomic questions. Clemencia Rodner provided transportation and help with various aspects of work at the Colección Phelps. Kevin Zimmer co-led several trips to Venezuela with me, read portions of the manuscript, and provided much information on foraging behavior and vocalizations of furnariids, antbirds, and flycatchers. Krzysztof Zyskowski read portions of the manuscript and added much useful information, especially on the nesting of furnariids.

For assistance in providing computerized printouts of Venezuelan bird specimens in their care, I thank Phil Angle at the United States National Museum, Kenneth C. Parkes at the Carnegie Museum, and David Willard at the Field Museum of Natural History. David Wege of BirdLife International in England generously sent maps and information on rare and endangered species in Venezuela. I also extend my appreciation to Kathleen Deery de Phelps (deceased) for her encouragement of this project from its inception, and for granting me permission to work at the Colección Phelps in Caracas.

During the several years of work on this project many people have shared their knowledge, assisted in travel, or helped in innumerable ways. To all of them I am grateful. They include Peter Alden, Alan Altman, Eduardo Alvarez-Cordero, Gustavo Añez, Gregorio Aquilino L., José Aquilino L., John Arvin, Ramón Aveledo H., Alejandro Bacouros, Gian Basili, Robert A. Behrstock, Francisco Bisbal, Paul Blair, Carlos Bosque, Ignacio Branger, Richard Buchholz, Irving Carreño, Clark L. Casler, Henry Cleve, Magali Cleve, Javier Colvée, John Coons, Dan Cooper, Paul Coopmans, Maria Rosa Cuesta, Philip Desenne, Peter English, Fenix Fernández, Ernesto Fernández B., David Fisher, Donald Forbes, Jorge Freitas, Leopoldo Garcia B., Fabio Garcia H., Ramón Gil, Federico Giller, Gustavo Giller, Hernán Giménez C., Luis Gonzalo M., Alejandro Grajal, John Gwynne, Cecilia Herrera, Morton L. Isler, Phyllis R. Isler, Ned K. Johnson, Kenn Kaufman, Jeff Kingery, Jeri Langham, Juan Pablo López, Ellen Luce, Raymond J. McNeil, Heriberto

Merchán B., Claus Müller, Tony Myer, Ramón Nieves S., Henri Ouellet (deceased), Theodore A. Parker III (deceased), Gilberto Pérez C. (deceased), Luis A. Pérez C. (deceased), Jan Pierson, Brian G. Prescott, Rick O. Prum, Robin Restall, Gustavo Rodríguez, Iokine Rodríguez, Lorenzo Rodríguez, Ricardo Rodríguez, José Gregorio Rojas (deceased), Tom Ryan, Richard Schofield, Thomas Schulenberg, Paul Schwartz (deceased), Christopher Sharpe, Raúl Sojo, Dave Stejskal, Levi Stofkin, Stewart Strahl, Paul Sweet, Alfredo Tellez, Ivan Tepedino, Betsy Thomas (deceased), Guy Tudor, Ani Isabel Villanueva, Bret Whitney, and Andrew Whittaker.

For opportunities to guide and travel extensively throughout Venezuela for more than a decade and a half I thank Victor Emanuel of Victor Emanuel Nature Tours, Inc. I also thank the Victor Emanuel staff, and especially Linda Carrell, for superb logistic support on more than 60 birding tours to Venezuela, and the hundreds of people who traveled with me on those trips. I also thank Ira Joel Abramson for travel opportunities in Venezuela in the late 1970s, at a time when ecotourism was in its infancy.

The following people provided access to museum collections in their care: Townsend Peterson, Rick O. Prum, and Mark B. Robbins at the Museum of Natural History, University of Kansas, Lawrence; Frank Gill and Robert S. Ridgely at the Academy of Natural Sciences, Philadelphia; Miguel Lentino, Ramón Aveledo H., Luis A. Pérez C., Clemencia Rodner, and Robin Restall at the Museo de Phelps in Caracas, and Francisco Bisbal at the Coleccíon PROFAUNA in Maracay, Venezuela.

I am indebted to copyeditor Elizabeth Pierson for superb editing skills and her efforts to bring consistency to a large manuscript. The Princeton University Press staff, including Tracy Baldwin, Nicole E. Lokach, and in particular Ellen Foos, Sam Elworthy and Senior Life Sciences editor Robert Kirk, have helped in many ways. Dimitri Karetnikov provided helpful advice with the range maps and oversaw their production.

Artists' Acknowledgments

Sophie Webb expresses her appreciation to Guy Tudor and Robert A. Behrstock for the loan of photos and to Steve Howell for comments on the plates. Christine Blake and Mary LeCroy of the American Museum of Natural History packaged and sent specimens to Sophie Webb, and Carla Cicero and Ned Johnson provided access to the Museum of Vertebrate Zoology, University of California, Berkeley. Robert A. Behrstock, Miguel Lentino, and Guy Tudor provided slide photos, and James Dean provided digital photos to John Gwynne. George Barrowclough, Christine Blake, Joel Cracraft, and Paul Sweet of the American Museum of Natural History aided John's work in many ways, and Al Gilbert provided assistance with reference material, as did Robin Restall at the Coleccíon Phelps in Caracas. John Gwynne also thanks Alejandro Grajal, Michel Kleinbaum, Larry McQueen, and Kathleen Deery de Phelps for assistance in various artistic matters.

Financial Contributors

The following people provided financial assistance with the publication of this work. Among other things, their generosity has helped make possible the publication of the color maps and color photos in the introductory chapters. Major contributors include Peter Jennings, Robert Kleiger, Alexander Power, Richard and Juanita Ritland, and Mona Webster. Other contributors (alphabetically) include Sherrill Boardman, Curtis Burger, Duane and Patricia Carmony, Erwin D. Cruce, Neil Currie, George Hall, Joseph and Jeannette Herron, Thomas Keesee, Jr., Richard and Dorcas Koenigsberger, Ken and Louise Martin, Bill and Donna McGowan, Susan McGreevy, Norman and Maggie Mellor, John and Ruth Moore, Francis Newton, Ben Olewine IV, George and Jean Perbix, Sara Simmonds, Phoebe Snetsinger (deceased), Edward Thayer, Julia Tullis, Alan Weeden, Robert and Liza Weissler, Florence Wiltamuth, and Jeannie B. Wright.

I thank the International Council for Bird Preservation, Pan American Continental Section at Washington, D.C., for a generous grant which helped support field work and weeks of museum work in Caracas and Maracay. The WCS (Wildlife Conservation Society) in New York, and Margaret Schwartz, administrated contributor funds.

Birds of Venezuela

Plan of the Book

This book treats 1382 species of resident and migrant birds reported in Venezuela or on its island possessions as of January 2001. Several species as yet unrecorded but likely to be found in Venezuela are described in footnotes.

Family Accounts

Avian taxonomy is currently in a dynamic state. Classification and nomenclature in this volume borrow from recent literature in journals and several other sources[10,403,544,545,606]. The order of families follows the American Ornithologists' Union's (AOU) Check-list[10] with a few exceptions. Family accounts discuss distribution, physical appearance, habits, breeding behavior, and sometimes taxonomic problems, with the emphasis varying from family to family.

Genus Accounts

A brief summary is given for most genera, especially of features that might be important to a field observer. Emphasis varies but may include physical features, behavior, and taxonomic issues.

Species Accounts

Species accounts contain up to seven sections—Identification, Similar species, Voice, Behavior, Status and habitat, Range, and Notes. Sections are omitted when not applicable or when information is unavailable. All information that is not from the author is followed by a bibliographic reference (superscript) or citation. For brackets around a species' name, see under "Hypothetical" in "Status and Habit" section below.

Identification

A species' average length from bill tip to tail tip is given in English and then in metric units. This is followed, if available, by an average weight in grams (g) or kilograms (kg). Weights are from Venezuelan birds when available[737,740] (M. Lentino) but are sometimes derived from birds outside Venezuela[130,222,253,274,385,706]. Key identification features—for example bill length, bill shape, soft-part colors, general aspect of shape—or additional measurements may follow. Sexually mature males, females, and in some cases immatures usually are described in that order except for some North American breeding species that are present in Venezuela mainly in their nonbreeding or immature plumages. Minor racial variation is mentioned (e.g., olive to olive green), but if differences are more clearly observable in the hand or in the field, the subspecies is also given. Color names are generally from Ridgway[546] and Smithe[659]. Measurements are from the author unless noted. Wing-length measurements are flat; tail lengths are from the feather insertion point to the tip of the longest feather; bill lengths are the chord of the culmen from the feathering at the base of the culmen to the tip.

Similar Species

This section lists similar-looking species that overlap in range and may cause confusion in the field. In many cases, key points useful in separating them from the species in question are given. The emphasis is biased heavily toward features useful in field identification, including unique features of a bird's plumage, behavior, voice, habitat, and distribution. The emphasis and length of this section vary with the difficulty of the species and may be omitted.

Voice

Onomatopoeic transcriptions of songs, calls, and mechanical sounds are given in italics whenever known and believed to be useful. Terms such as "high,""low,""rising,""falling," etc., apply to pitch. Vowels are generally sounded according to English rules of pronunciation. The following are used to describe songs or vocalizations.

Accent: an emphasized but not otherwise unusually loud note.

Apostrophes separating letters (i.e., i'i'i'i'i): these represent trills, which are fast, or rattles, which usually have fewer notes per unit of time.

Capital letters: loud notes or phrases.

Comma between notes (ti, ti, ti): a brief pause between notes, e.g., a slower series.

Dash (-) between notes (ti-ti-ti): a series of notes without a pause.

Exclamation note at end of song or call (!): an abrupt, emphatic, or explosive ending.

Series of periods at end of phrase (. . .): the notes continue more or less uninterrupted, as indicated.

Series of periods between notes or phrases (. . or . . . or . . . . , etc.): pauses or progressively longer pauses between notes.

Transcriptions are from the author's tapes and notes and are of birds from Venezuela unless noted. Published or unpublished transcriptions or tape-recordings from other sources are acknowledged. Calls or songs of species not normally heard in Venezuela, e.g., some seabirds and north and south temperate migrants, are not given.

Behavior

The information in this section varies with the family—for instance, flight characteristics in parrots, display in manakins, or specialized foraging behavior in flycatchers. Attention is given to food choices, foraging behavior, and social behavior, as well as behaviors that would aid an observer in finding and identifying the species. A summary of breeding information— breeding months, nests, eggs, etc.—is given if known. Breeding information is brief and not intended to be exhaustive. Some foraging-behavior terms (especially for raptors and flycatchers) include the following.

Aerial hawking: sallying in which prey is pursued and captured in flight.

Hover-gleaning: locating prey or food item while perched. This is followed by a short, direct flight to a leaf or other substrate, with the prey or food taken during a momentary hover, after which the bird falls away and continues to a new perch. Outward hover-gleaning and upward hover-gleaning are specific flight-approach directions that terminate in a hover-glean.

Perch-gleaning: various foraging maneuvers and prey captures that are executed while perched. Food captures may be from twig, foliage, bark, etc., but from a place the bird can reach while perched. There are many variations; antbirds often pause to peer in

various directions before moving; vireos, warblers, some tanagers, and others move steadily and at times scarcely pause at all. Some birds typically look upward; others, such as *Tangara* tanagers, lean far downward and peer beneath twigs and branches.

Perch-to-ground sallying: sallying from a stationary perch to the ground for prey capture.

Perch-to-water sallying: sallying from a stationary perch to water for prey capture.

Sally-stall: resembles hover-gleaning, but fruit or animal prey is taken at the end of an upward swoop followed by a momentary "stall" with wings outstretched (and slotted like an airplane). Typical of trogons and fruitcrows.

Sally-strike: prey is taken from an exposed surface, usually the underside of a leaf, during a direct flight that is slightly upward, horizontal, or downward, but there is little or no pause or hovering at the moment of prey capture.

Still-hunt: foraging by waiting on a perch for a variable length of time, then moving some distance and waiting and watching again. Mainly seen in forest-dwelling raptors.

Stoop: prey-capture attempt at conclusion of a dive; may be powered by wing flapping or be free-fall. Mainly applies to raptors of open terrain.

Status and Habitat

This section gives a species' seasonal status; relative abundance *in its main habitat(s)*; and major habitat(s). Locations where the species is readily seen or where specimens have been collected are sometimes discussed, as well as additional comments on seasonal and/or migratory behavior. Other comments may include notes on contact zones and overlap with congeners.

Seasonal status is defined using one or more of the terms below. Most of the terms are not mutually exclusive. For example, the Fork-tailed Flycatcher, as a species, would fit at least three of the following categories. A few Fork-taileds breed in Venezuela and are permanent residents; a much larger group breeds in austral latitudes of South America but migrates north to Venezuela during the "southern" winter; and a third group of intratropical migrants moves northward to breed in Central America but returns to northern South America for part of the year. In another example, the Orange-throated Sunangel is resident in Venezuela but is also a seasonal elevational migrant in the Andes and thus may also be regarded as a short-distance migrant and intratropical migrant. Finally, many species are resident in Venezuela but undertake some minor population shifts annually or irregularly. Examples include many waterbirds, waders, and hummingbirds. Most of these species are here considered residents, but the likelihood of seasonal movement is usually mentioned.

Resident: a species that breeds and resides at the same locality throughout the year. Examples: tinamous and antbirds. Also includes species that may undertake daily elevational movements traveling to and from feeding areas, e.g., White-collared Swifts. In a broader sense, also includes species that carry out their entire life cycle in Venezuela but may undertake minor seasonal or local movements within the country. Examples: Groove-billed Toucanet, quetzals, and many hummingbirds.

Breeding-season resident: a species that breeds in Venezuela but migrates out of the country for part of the year. Example: Lined Seedeater.

Nonbreeding resident: a generalized category for nearctic (northern) and austral migrants. Present for varying periods of time up to a year or more but do not breed. Examples: Osprey and many shorebirds.

Northern winter resident (or North American breeding migrant): a species that breeds in north temperate latitudes (usually North Amererica) and is present for part of the year in Venezuela but does not breed there. Examples: Spotted Sandpiper and Blackburnian Warbler. A few species have both migratory nonbreeding populations present and presumably resident breeding populations. Examples: Green Heron and Black-whiskered Vireo.

Austral winter resident: a species that breeds in south temperate latitudes of South America and is present for part of the year in Venezuela but does not breed there. Examples: Small-billed Elaenia and Crowned Slaty Flycatcher. In some species, both austral breeders and resident populations occur. Examples: Streaked Flycatcher, Swainson's Flycatcher, and Brown-chested Martin.

Intratropical migrant: a generalized term for species that breed in tropical latitudes but migrate, wholly or in part, to other areas in the tropics on a seasonal or periodic basis. Migrations vary from local movements of a few kilometers to hundreds of kilometers and are not necessarily confined to Venezuela. Still poorly documented. Examples: Azure Gallinule, Dwarf Cuckoo, Greater Ani, and Swallow-Tanager. This category includes short-distance and elevational migrants.

Short-distance migrant: a species that migrates short distances seasonally or irregularly, mostly within Venezuela. Examples: Scarlet Ibis and Pinnated Bittern. Elevational migrants are usually short-distance migrants, but not necessarily vice versa.

Elevational migrant: a species that regularly migrates from one elevation to another on at least an annual basis and within the same biogeographic realm. Most can also be classified as short-distant migrants. Examples: Sword-billed Hummingbird, Orange-throated Sunangel, and Masked Flowerpiercer. Called altitudinal migrant by Hayes[254].

Passage migrant or transient: a species that passes through Venezuela during the northern (boreal) or southern (austral) spring and fall migratory periods (mainly Aug–Oct and Apr–May) and is present for varying periods but does not breed and is not normally present as a nonbreeding resident. Examples: White-rumped Sandpiper, Eastern Kingbird, Connecticut Warbler, and Scarlet Tanager.

Vagrant or Wanderer: used more or less interchangeably to denote a species that moves at irregular or erratic intervals.

Most species of birds are "common" somewhere, and they are most likely to be common in their optimum habitat or at certain times of the year. Consequently, the relative abundance terms used in this book often are biased, reflecting to some extent the locations and times of the year the author or contributors have visited, the openness of the habitat, the amount and seasonality of vocalization, and the location of the bird with respect to its overall range. The locations one visits also affect the chances of finding even some "common" birds. In an absolute sense, however, "common" small birds are almost always more numerous than "common" large birds, and some common birds are seen much more often than others (Tropical Kingbirds are seen much more often than Buff-breasted Wrens, yet both are "common" and widespread). With this in mind, abundance guidelines are used to suggest not so much a bird's actual abundance as an observer's likelihood of encountering it, at least by voice, in proper habitat and during a favorable season.

Common: recorded on virtually all field trips, often in numbers.

Fairly common: recorded on at least half of field trips.

Uncommon: recorded on about a quarter of field trips.

Rare: recorded on fewer than a quarter of field trips; often there are only a few records for the country.

Accidental: recorded only 1–3 times in the country.

Local: real or apparent absence from apparently suitable habitat.

Irregular or erratic: used interchangeablly to denote a migrant or wanderer with strong or unpredictable fluctuations in numbers.

Hypothetical: denotes a few species for which well-documented evidence of occurrence in the country is lacking (e.g., no specimen, recognizable photograph, or tape-recording).

Brackets [ ] on a species' name denote a species for which there is no specimen, photo, or tape recording for Venezuela. Bracketed species may be documented by a published sight record, or written description of a sight observation.

Range and Range Maps

Highest and lowest elevations of a species' occurrence are based on specimen evidence unless noted. Supplemental sight records, shown in parentheses, may give higher or lower elevations. Where elevations differ north and south of the Orinoco, these are shown separately. If only one elevation is given (e.g., to 500m), it may be assumed that the species occurs from sea level or the lowlands up to the stated elevation. Also note that a highland species may occur at a lower elevation in a very humid region than in a dry region, and vice versa, and occasionally this may be denoted by a second set of elevations. Other factors, such as the size of a mountain mass (Massenerhebung-effekt), prevailing winds, cloud cover, historic factors, and recent human activity also affect local elevational distributions, and in all cases the stated elevations should be viewed primarily as guidelines rather than as absolute limits.

Elevations are followed by the range of the species in Venezuela. Distributions are given for all subspecies, although the validity of some subspecies is questionable. If no subspecies are listed, it may be assumed that the species is monotypic (has no subspecies). In a few cases where subspecies have not been recognized, the source for the change is given. Ranges in general, and the sequence of subspecies in particular, are described from west to east and then north to south. The Andes, however, orient along a diagonal from southwest to northeast, and Andean distributions are described in an easterly direction, beginning at the southwesternmost point and continuing to the northeasternmost. A bird's range in Venezuela is followed by a brief outline of its world range if applicable.

Endemic species are noted in capitals under Range. Endemic is here applied, in a narrow sense, to species found only within the political boundaries of Venezuela. Many additional species are endemic to the tepui region but not strictly to Venezuela, or to the Sierra de Perijá, the northwestern deserts, etc., but also occur to a limited extent in adjacent Guyana, Brazil, or Colombia.

Range maps were prepared for all species except long-tailed Jaeger, Rock Pigeon, White-crowned Pigeon, Green-tailed Trainbearer, and five introduced species. A list of locality records with coordinates was stored as a text file for each species and then plotted using Range Mapper 2.3, a coordinate-based mapping program. Plotted coordinates were then exported into Adobe Illustrator 9.0, from which the final maps were produced.

Topography

Shaped like a broad letter T, Venezuela sits astride the northern end of South American. The country's long shimmery coastline is bathed in balmy Caribbean waters, and the southernmost frontier stretches deep into Amazonia. Most of the northern coast lies between 10° and 11° north latitude, whereas the southernmost equatorial tip of Amazonas state is less than 1° north. A scattering of island possessions lie varying distances offshore, mostly between about 10.5° and 12° north. The largest island possession is Isla Margarita. The northernmost—tiny Isla de Aves, at 15°42′ N, 63°38′ W—lies a little over 200km west of Dominica in the Lesser Antilles. Venezuela's international boundary along it's western and southern border with Colombia and Brazil is defined mostly by rivers or their watersheds. All of the north is bounded by the Caribbean, the east by an as yet not fully resolved accord with Guyana.

The topography from northern to southern Venezuela is complex but divides broadly into three regions—mountains and deserts in the north, a wide belt of flat grassland across the middle section, and a broad expanse of rain forest dotted with savannas and overshadowed by great vertical-walled, flat-topped mountains known as tepuis in the south (Figs. 3 and 4). The total area of Venezuela is a little over 900,000km^2 (351,000 sq miles), or slightly more than Texas and Oklahoma combined.

Northwestern Venezuela is dominated by mountains. The axis of Colombia's Eastern Andean range bifurcates at the border with Venezuela, sending the left arm—the Sierra de Perijá—westward around Lago de Maracaibo and the other arm northeastward toward the coast. The Sierra de Perijá forms Venezuela's westernmost boundary with Colombia. This region is remote and plagued with internal problems, and there has been little ornithological exploration of it in more than two decades. Lago de Maracaibo is a large, mostly freshwater lake that exits through a narrow neck to the Caribbean. The lake and the flat, low terrain surrounding it overlie vast petroleum reserves.

The right-hand arm of the Andean bifurcation crosses the border of Colombia into Venezuela and is abruptly severed by an unusually deep and arid valley formed by the Río Uribante and its tributary, the Río Torbes. This valley, forming the Táchira Depression, drops to between 300 and 1700m but is flanked on either side by Andes mountains soaring to more than 3300m. This valley is so deep that biogeographically it isolates the Andes to the north from those to the south.

The Andes then run northeastward as the Cordillera de Mérida, occupying most of the states of Táchira, Mérida, Trujillo, and southern Lara. The Andes, together with the Sierra de Perijá, comprise the highest relief in the country. Pico Bolívar in the state of Mérida rises to more than 5000m; nearby Pico Espejo and several others are nearly as high. In the Sierra de Perijá several peaks rise to more than 3000m, but the Perijás overall are somewhat lower in elevation and less massive than the Cordillera de Mérida. The Andes terminate just south of Barquisimeto in southeastern Lara, but isolated remnants reappear in the northwestern corner of Lara at Cerro El Cerrón and Cerro Cogollal.

Northward from the Andes, isolated mountains reappear in the Sierra de San Luis in central Falcón, Sierra de Aroa in Yaracuy, and Coastal Cordillera extending eastward from the state of Carabobo to Miranda. A smaller, lower, and less contiguous Interior Cordillera lies immediately southward. The highway from Caracas to Valencia follows the valley between these two ranges. Most of the coastal uplift has been produced by friction between the Continental and Caribbean plates moving in opposite directions. The low Sierra de Chichiriviche and Cerro Misión are old karstic limestone sea ridges situated immediately north of the Coastal Cordillera in southeastern Falcón. Cerro Santa Ana, on the Paraguaná Peninsula, is the remnant throat plug of an ancient volcanic.

A final wrinkling of the geologic tapestry occurs in northeastern Venezuela, beginning with the Serranía de Turumiquire on the Anzoátegui-Sucre border, the southward-running Serranía de la Paloma which terminates in Cerro Negro, and the mountains of the Paria Peninsula. Average elevations throughout are less than 2000m, often considerably less. East of the Serranía de la Paloma the terrain descends to flat, swampy, mangrove-dominated lowlands with extensive tidal inflow bordering the Gulf of Paria.

South of Venezuela's mountainous northern rim is a large flat basin, only slightly above sea level and tilted ever so slightly from west to east and north to south. With relief amounting to only a few millimeters per kilometer, this slowly draining region known as the llanos, or grasslands, partially floods for several months every year. The llanos are drained principally by the Ríos Meta, Arauca, and Apure, all of which flow into the Río Orinoco. The Orinoco itself loosely marks the southern boundary of the llanos.

The remote southern third of the country, a mixture of lowland and mountain terrain, is pristine and largely uninhabited. The lowlands are mostly flat—a mixture of hot, steamy, redolent jungles and grasslands. But from them arise magnificent vertical-walled, flat-topped mountains—great sheer blocks of Precambrian sandstone—that spring thousands of meters upward into the clouds. These are the tepuis—a Pemón Indian name for these mountains. Often shrouded in fog and seldom visited (few have been thoroughly explored), the tepuis, remnants of a once great sandstone plateau, have been isolated for millions of years. Much of the plant and animal life on or near their summits is unique, and our knowledge of the tepuis is, even today, almost as much fiction as fact. The tepuis and associated massifs dominate much of the landscape of northern, eastern, and extreme southern Amazonas state, as well as the southern two-thirds of Bolívar state. Waterfalls abound in this rainy, cloud-filled region, and Angel Falls, the world's highest, plunges from the top of Auyán-Tepui, one of the largest of more than 100 tepuis in Canaima National Park alone. Although difficult to access except by air, Angel Falls is an important tourist destination, and it offers visitors a glimpse of this vast pristine wilderness.

The geologic history of the tepuis is one of the longest in earth's history. Sands from ancient seabeds and highlands repeatedly covered an igneous-metamorphic base of granites and gneisses about 1.6 to 1 billion years ago.

These sedimentary layers of sand were compressed and cemented with silica, eventually growing to more than 1000m in thickness. The resulting quartzite and sandstone rocks, along with igneous intrusions forced into fissures in the sandstone, comprise what is broadly referred to today as the Guyana Shield. These are some of the oldest continually exposed rocks to be found anywhere on earth. There are no fossils here, an indication of the rocks' very old origin. As ancient Gondwanaland broke apart and the South American continent separated, stress fractures and repeated local uplift set the stage for cycles of erosion. Today we see only remnants of this ancient, eroded land, the isolated "table mountains" with their hard sandstone tops and sheer, fissured walls[43].

Soils of the regions are complex, but visitors are always struck by the virtually pure white sand that comprises the "soil" beneath most savannas, and beneath many forests south of the Orinoco as well. White sandy soils are very poor in nutrients and very acidic, whereas soils originating from parent igneous rock have better nutrient content and lower acidity. Forest cover is more likely to thrive on the latter soils. Soil types and the resulting vegetation over them importantly influence bird distributions.

Several low mountain ranges in southern Venezuela are composed primarily of granitic material, their overlying sandy sedimentary layers already having been lost to erosion. Among them are the Serranía de Imataca, Sierra Parima, the many granitic hills and low ranges in northwestern and northcentral Amazonas, and the Sierra de Maigualida[43]. Most of these mountainous regions are low in elevation and lack the characteristic table-mountain shape of the tepuis.

Most rivers in southern Venezuela flow into the Orinoco, the major exceptions being the Río Negro which drains a corner of southwestern Amazonas and flows southward into the Amazon, and the Río Cuyuní which flows eastward from Bolívar state into the Essequibo River of Guyana. Rivers flowing from very nutrient-poor, white sandy soils are typically "blackwater" rivers with little suspended material. Their water is the color of strong tea, is highly acidic, and is discolored by high amounts of humic and tannic acids dissolved in groundwater[278]. The majority of rivers in southern Venezuela are blackwater rivers. Rivers flowing from more nutrient-rich regions carry high sediment loads and are known as whitewater rivers; however, they usually look turbid and brownish or muddy. Most rivers draining the Andes and the llanos are whitewater rivers that carry heavy loads of silt.

The Orinoco is primarily a whitewater river, although many of its south-bank tributaries are blackwater rivers. During the rainy season the Orinoco carries high silt loads and becomes very muddy. The river ends in a broad, flat, fan-shaped delta that breaks up into hundreds of tributaries. The outermost part of the delta is permanently flooded, areas inland progressively less so. Most rivers in southern Venezuela are free flowing, but the Caroní has been dammed in several places. The largest hydropower project is the immense Guri Dam which floods almost $4250km^2$.

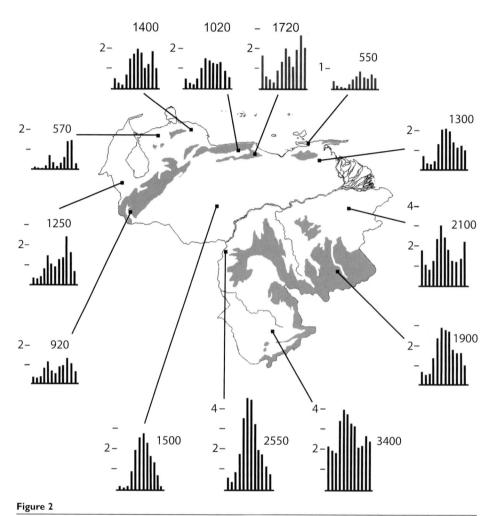

Figure 2

Annual distribution of rainfall in 13 regions of Venezuela. Vertical lines in millimeters (×100), annual totals in millimeters, from data collected 1931–1960. Figure adapted from Schwerdtfeger[588]. Gray areas > approx. 500m.

Climate

Venezuela enjoys a classic warm and humid tropical climate. Two global influences dominant this climate: the northeast trade winds, which bring moisture onshore, and the twice-annual passage of the sun, which strongly affects general atmospheric circulation. Regionally the coastlines, mountains, and prevailing vegetation also play important roles and can result in dramatic climatic changes in rainfall and average wind speed in a matter of a few kilometers. Arriving international passengers witness this dramatic change in rainfall and vegetation during the short drive from the arid coast to the humid mountains surrounding Caracas.

Seasonal change in Venezuela is marked by differences in rainfall, not temperature. Average rainfall (Fig. 2) is strongly bimodal, resulting in a dry season from about December through April and a rainy season from May through November over much of the country. There are local exceptions to this pattern. In addition, rainfall generally increases linearly from north to south. Thus, with the exception of the northern cordilleras which are very wet at high elevations, the most arid regions are on or near the coast, and rainfall increases southward, becoming heaviest in southern Amazonas.

Temperature and day length show relatively minor changes during the year. Day length changes by little more than an hour, and average temperatures vary more during the day than from month to month. Average temperatures decrease about 6°C for each 1000-m increase in elevation, and it is changes in temperature and rainfall regimes up mountain slopes that are the main physical factors affecting flora and fauna at higher elevations in the tropics. Temperatures are hottest in the Maracaibo Basin, with an annual average of about 28.5°C. The second warmest region is the llanos, averaging about 28°C. The Caribbean coast, moderated slightly by the adjacent sea, averages about 27°C. Caracas, at about 900m elevation, has cool evenings and warm days; Mérida, at about 1400m, has still cooler evenings and pleasant balmy days. At

treeline in the Andes, especially in the dry season, temperatures regularly drop below freezing at night. Above treeline, snow occasionally falls in August or September, the peak of the rainy season.

Four broad climate zones in Venezuela are described below.

Northern Maracaibo Region, Caribbean Coast, and Islands

Most of the Caribbean coast of Venezuela is hot and arid with a long dry season lasting from November through April and a slightly cooler rainy season from May through October. Most of the annual rainfall falls during only a few days during the rainy season. At Coro, Falcón, for example, about 90% of the rainfall falls on only 10% of the days. Trade winds blow most strongly during the dry season. At this time most trees lose their leaves, vegetation becomes dry and parched, and few birds breed. Average rainfall is about 400 to 700mm along the coast, and even less locally and on offshore islands. As one progresses inland and upward in elevation, rainfall increases dramatically, such that just a few kilometers inland lush cloud forests at barely 1000m in elevation may overlook stark desert scrub vegetation fringing the seacoast.

Andes and Northern and Northeastern Cordilleras

The northern Maracaibo Basin is very hot and arid, but rainfall increases southward and with increasing elevation on the slopes of the Sierra de Perijá and the Andes. Rainfall reaches a maximum of about 2000 to 2500mm per year in the Andes, generally between elevations of 500 and 1500m, but occasionally at lower elevations on northwest-facing slopes. On east-facing slopes, rainfall is highest at about 1000m elevation. Everywhere above 2000m, rainfall totals diminish; some of the lowest annual rainfall totals anywhere in the country probably occur at very high elevations in the Cordillera de Mérida.

The exposure and orientation of mountain slopes are important in determining local rainfall distribution. Windward-facing slopes, such as the San Isidro Valley in northwestern Barinas, receive high annual rainfall totals. By contrast, lee-facing slopes or valleys in the rainshadow of a high mountain barrier, such as the Río Chama in Mérida, are quite arid, whereas dripping cloud forest can be found only a short distance away.

The Coastal and Interior Cordilleras of northern Venezuela are climatically diverse. Trade winds desiccate the coast but dump copious amounts of water as they ascend the northern slope of the Coastal Cordillera, resulting in a spectacular band of cloud forest extending virtually the length of the north slope of the cordillera. By contrast, the interior slope and valley, which are among the most heavily populated regions of the country, are relatively dry. Almost everywhere in the Interior Cordillera, rainfall is less than on corresponding slopes of the Coastal Cordillera. Coastal northeastern Anzoátegui and the Araya Peninsula of western Sucre are very arid, partly because of a lack of orographic relief and because they lie within the lee of mountains to the east and north. Eastward the mountainous backbone of the Paria Peninsula receives abundant rainfall on the windward north side from inbound, moisture-laden trade winds, but lee-side totals are lower. Inland across southern Sucre and northern Monagas, rainfall is strongly affected locally by the mountainous relief but is generally moderate to fairly high.

Llanos

The vast grasslands that occupy the entire central portion of Venezuela experience a strongly "monsoonal" type of climate—months of blistering hot days with sunny skies and not a drop of rain. Then almost overnight thunder rumbles, the skies darken, and the rains arrive, quickly transforming the land from a scorched landscape of dust and drying pools to emerald fields and silt-laden, swollen rivers overflowing their banks. Annual rainfall averages about 1500mm over most of the llanos, climbing to almost 2000mm at the base of the Andes and near the Orinoco Delta. Annual totals drop to about 1000mm on the lee side of the coastal mountains, in southern Guárico, and locally in a few other places.

July is typically the wettest month, January, February, and March the driest. Rainfall is slightly higher in the south and somewhat lower eastward. More than 90% of all rain falls between May and the end of October or early November. A long dry season from late November through late April ensues, and at the end of the dry season most pools are dry and parched, grass is brown, and trees any distance from watercourses have lost their leaves. The llanos flood locally in many areas, but flooding is most extensive in the southern drainage basins of the Ríos Meta and Apure. During the long dry season most of the grassland of the llanos is deliberately burned, and the resulting haze and smoke are widespread. The practice of annual burning is deeply entrenched, but its value is controversial.

Orinoco Delta and South of the Orinoco

These regions, encompassing the states of Delta Amacuro, Amazonas, and Bolívar, experience a hot and humid climate in the lowlands. Rainfall averages about 2000 to 2500mm a year in Bolívar, but locally annual totals may be considerably less, e.g., around Tumeremo (with 1250mm) and on the Gran Sabana. In general rainfall is highest in Amazonas, averaging about 3000mm a year. The rainiest area in the country is the vicinity of the Río Orinoco headwaters and the Río Negro of extreme southern Amazonas, where average annual totals exceed 3500mm and there is no clear-cut-dry season, although March and September average slightly drier.

Biogeography

Venezuela's deserts, swampy basins, mountains, grasslands, and southern forests and tepuis divide rather broadly and naturally into seven biogeographic regions. They are (1) the arid northwest and Caribbean coast, (2) the southern Maracaibo Basin swamplands, (3) the Andes and northern mountains, (4) the llanos, (5) the Amazonian lowlands of Amazonas state, (6) the Guianan lowlands of Bolívar state, and (7) the tepui highlands spanning portions of Amazonas and Bolívar. A glance at the range maps of birds in this text shows that many distributions lie within just one or two of these seven regions. Physical barriers such as mountains, climatic barriers past and present, and interactions with competing allies all work in concert to limit or define the ranges of birds and, in turn, the seven regions outlined below. Repeating patterns such as these are of great interest to biogeographers attempting to understand the history of avifaunas. A brief discussion of each of the seven regions follows.

Arid Northwest and Caribbean Coast

Birds of this region often have a continuous distribution extending westward into arid regions of northern Colombia. Examples include many desert-scrub specialists of relatively limited distribution, such as Bare-eyed Pigeon, Yellow-shouldered Parrot, Buffy Hummingbird, Chestnut Piculet, White-whiskered Spinetail, Black-backed Antshrike, Slender-billed Tyrannulet, Ultramarine Grosbeak, Vermilion Cardinal, and Tocuyo Sparrow. They have probably evolved from ancestral stocks that were present during an earlier and somewhat different climate regime. Secondly, there are many scrub-inhabiting species that are more widespread in dry habitats across northern South America; examples of such species are Rufous-vented Chachalaca, Blue-crowned and Brown-throated parakeets, Black-crested Antshrike, White-fringed Antwren, Pearly-vented Tody-Tyrant, Tawny-crowned Pygmy-Tyrant, Mouse-colored Tyrannulet, Tropical Gnatcatcher, and Tropical Mockingbird.

Southern Maracaibo Basin

The Maracaibo Basin is a large, flat, low-level region bounded by the Caribbean on the north and by mountains on the remaining three sides. Almost a quarter of the basin is occupied by Lago de Maracaibo, the largest lake in South America. The northern end of the basin is arid, and biogeographically it shares its affinities with the northern deserts and dry Caribbean coast. Southward, rainfall increases steadily and the southern part of the basin is, or was, mostly covered with humid forest, swamps, and marshes, parts of which are periodically inundated. Several notably arid valleys on the western slope of the Andes open into this generally humid region. As a consequence of the basin's isolation by mountains and the sea, its avifauna is heavily derived from adjacent regions. Although few species are endemic, there are many endemic subspecies, and the ranges of many Central American and northern Colombian species terminate in or on the slopes immediately above the Maracaibo Basin. Species with a substantial proportion of their range in the basin include Northern Screamer, Pygmy Palm-Swift (endemic), Citron-throated Toucan, Russet-throated Puffbird (several endemic subspecies), One-colored Becard, and Crimson-backed Tanager.

Andes and Northern Mountains

Birds of this region are mostly derived from ancestral stocks living in the Andes to the south. Diversity is greatest near the Colombian border, and with each successive filtering barrier northward, such as the Táchira Depression and Yaracuy Depression, diversity decreases. Thus, the remote mountains of the Paria Peninsula, the most distant outlier of the northern Andes, are, not surprisingly, the least diverse and contain, as a proportion of the avifauna, the greatest degree of endemism of species and subspecies.

Llanos

With its wide open spaces and watery habitats, this central grassland plain draws its avifauna from a wide array of sources but especially from widespread and historically ancient lineages such as waders and waterfowl which are present in large numbers here. Many of these species are good colonizers, tolerant of an array of environmental conditions, and capable of migrating away during unfavorable times. Many of these widespread species are shared with distant grassland and marshy regions such as the pantanal of Brazil and the Beni of Bolivia. Passerines in the llanos also are varied in origin. Some are widespread species, such as Vermilion Flycatcher, Brown-crested Flycatcher, and Grayish Saltator, or are derived from formerly widespread taxa. Others are derived from nearby arid or semiarid regions, such as Scrub Greenlet, Glaucous Tanager, and Gray Pileated-Finch; several others, such as Rusty-backed Spinetail, Striped Woodcreeper, and Red-capped Cardinal, are of Amazonian origin.

Amazonian Lowlands

To a large extent, birds of the lowland forests of the state of Amazonas share their ancestral affinities with allies of the Amazon Basin. Some examples include White-throated Tinamou, Colbalt-winged Parakeet, White-fronted Nunbird, Reddish-winged Bare-eye, and Flame-crested Tanager. As a group, this avifauna is a slightly less diverse subset of Amazonia with a sprinkling of species from the Guianas. This is particularly true in far southern Amazonas, but northward and eastward the number of Guianan species increases. There also are a few habitat specialists, most notably species of white sandy soil regions such as Bronzy Jacamar, Yapacana Antbird, Pale-bellied Mourner, and Red-shouldered Tanager, that seem to have evolved in scrub regions outside humid Amazonia. Others, such as Yellow-crested Manakin, Black Manakin, Blackish-gray Antshrike, and Cherrie's Antwren, were probably derived from ancestors living in humid Amazonia but appear to have secondarily adapted to drier, scrubbier, sandy soil habitats outside Amazonia. Mountains along the entire eastern and most of the

northern boundary of Amazonas act as a blockade to the dispersal of some lowland species eastward into Bolívar, and vice versa.

Guianan Lowlands

As a consequence of repeated isolation from Amazonia by a broad band of savanna in drier periods of the historical past, a distinctive avifauna has evolved in the Guianan region and eastern Venezuela. Remnents of this grassland separation are still evident today in the form of savannas scattered across southern Venezuela, Guyana, and Suriname. The state of Bolívar in southeastern Venezuela thus shares a majority of its lowland forest species with the Guianan region rather than Amazonia. Among them are Red-fan Parrot, Guianan Toucanet, Ferruginous-backed Antbird, Capuchinbird, White Bellbird, Rose-breasted Chat, Blue-backed Tanager, and Red-and-black Grosbeak. A marked Amazonian influence in still evident, however, in the Río Caura region of western Bolívar.

Tepui Highlands

Of great interest to biogeographers are the tepui highlands, which are most extensive in the state of Bolívar but also occur in Amazonas. The origins of this distinctive and highly endemic avifauna remain somewhat obscure. Almost all of these endemic species are found at elevations above 900 to 1000m, and they are usually numerous only at higher elevations. Some taxa with distinctive subspecies in the tepuis, such as Sierran Elaenia, several *Turdus* thrushes, and Black-headed Tanager, certainly seem to share ancestors from the distant Andes; others may also share a similar ancestry, although time and history have erased obvious links. Many, such as Tepui Tinamou, Streak-backed Antshrike, Roraiman Antwren, Flutist Wren, and Tepui Greenlet, appear to be derived from ancestors in the adjacent lowlands, the closest species-rich pool. However, the Andes and northern cordilleras, which are much farther away and separated by a large lowland barrier, appear to have contributed almost as many species. Among them are Velvet-browed Brilliant, Roraiman Barbtail, Chapman's Bristle-Tyrant, and Red-banded Fruiteater.

Vegetation Zones and Habitat Descriptions

Natural plant communities are affected by physical and biological factors such as temperature, rainfall, evapotranspiration, soil moisture, flood regimes, fire, the structure of the plant community, and the succession of plant species over time. Major vegetation zones (sometimes also called plant formations) are shown in Figure 4. These loosely follow Holdridge[264] and Huber and Alacron[272,535]. They are (1) desert scrub and thorn woodland, (2) tropical dry forest, (3) tropical moist forest, (4) tropical humid forest, (5) premontane and montane dry and moist forests, (6) premontane and montane humid and wet forests, (7) savanna, and (8) paramo. Each of the eight vegetation zones is discussed below and shown in Fig. 4.

Vegetation Zones

Desert Scrub and Thorn Woodland

Rainfall ca. 200–750mm/yr. This is the vegetation of the Caribbean coast from northern Zulia to western Sucre. It consists of desert scrub, often with columnar cactuses. This vegetation is particularly well developed across northern Zulia and much of Falcón, culminating in its most extreme in extensive sand dunes at the base of the Paraguaná Peninsula. Along the northern base of the Coastal Cordillera, desert scrub is confined to a narrow strip, often no more than a few kilometers inland, but is again extensive eastward across northern Anzoátegui and on the Araya Peninsula of western Sucre. Common shrubs and bushes include *Acacia, Calotropis, Mimosa,* and *Prosopis.* In some areas cactuses are common, especially *Opuntia, Cereus,* and *Armatocereus.* Where rainfall increases, desert scrub gives way to a denser thorn woodland and eventually to tropical dry forest.

Tropical Dry Forest

Rainfall ca. 750–1500mm/yr. Tropical dry forest, also called deciduous forest, occurs where rainfall is strongly seasonal, causing most trees to lose their leaves for up to half the year. Tropical dry forest is, or was, widespread in the interior of Falcón and northern Lara, at lower ele-

vations around the Coastal and Interior Cordilleras, locally across much of the llanos from Barinas to Anzoátegui, and south of the Río Orinoco in northern Bolívar. Gallery forests along streams in the llanos are either tropical dry or moist forest. Large areas of interior Falcón and Lara states are now highly degraded and little more than acacia scrub, the result of overgrazing by goats.

Tropical Moist Forest

Rainfall ca. 1000–2000mm/yr. Moist forest, also known as semideciduous forest, is somewhat restricted in extent, being found especially in or near the base of the Andes, the northern cordilleras, along streams in the llanos, and south of the Orinoco in northern Bolívar. It is found where there is a moderately pronounced dry season and usually within a matrix of other forest types ranging from deciduous to evergreen. Moist forest is most apt to occur on slopes or hilltops in undulating terrain where the water-retention capacity of soils is poor. It is thus less defined by rainfall than by edaphic and other factors. Dominant trees in moist forests in the vicinity of Upata and Tumeremo, Bolívar, are *Tetragastris planamensis, Pouteria egregia, Sterculia pruriens, Protium* sp., *Chaetocarpus schomburgkianus, Aspidosperma marcgravianum, Licania densiflora, Manilkaria bidentata,* and *Erisma uncinatum.*

Tropical Humid Forest

Rainfall ca. 2000–4000mm/yr. This is the dominant forest in the southern Maracaibo Basin, in or around the base of the Andes, northern cordilleras, and almost all of the forested lowlands south of the Orinoco. Most of the tall stately forests at the southern end of the Maracaibo region have been destroyed. Those south of the Orinoco are largely intact.

Under the umbrella of the tropical humid forest formation there is a daunting array of forest types in Venezuela that vary in stature and tree composition depending on soils, inundation, and other factors. Those on rich floodplains (várzea forest) are tall and floristically diverse, those on well-drained upland soils (terra firme forests) diverse but somewhat less statuesque, and those growing on white sandy soils notably shorter, scrubbier, and with fewer species.

Humid forests of the Orinoco Delta and Amacuro plains are strongly influenced by flooding regimes. Forests of the coast and outer delta are rather short, evergreen, permanently flooded, and composed primarily of the mangrove *Rhizophora mangle* in high-salinity water and *Avicennia schaueriana* and *Laguncularia racemosa* in more brackish water. Inland within the delta there is progressively less flooding, and mangroves are mixed with *Euterpe* palms and *Pterocarpus*, a buttress-rooted legume. Here, harvesting of palm hearts (*Euterpe oleracea*) is an important business. These forests in turn give way to areas that do not flood or are only briefly flooded and are dominated by *Ceiba, Ocotea, Mora excelsa, Erythrina, Tabebuia, Spondias, Triplaris, Gustavia,* and *Licannia,* among others. Many of these same trees are dominant in the forests of the Sierra de Imataca immediately south of the delta and in other areas of high rainfall in Bolívar. Large areas of seasonally flooded grassland can be found in the middle and upper portions of the Orinoco Delta.

The Río Caura and Río Paragua basins are covered by extensive tall evergreen forest on upland or terra firme sites and by partially flooded or várzea forest near the rivers. Locally there are many *Oenocarpus* and *Euterpe* palms, and palm-dominated forests also occur on some slopes above the floodplain of the Río Caura.

The lowlands of Amazonas in Venezuela are covered by an unusually complex mosaic of humid forests mixed with savannas, which almost invariably grow on zones of pure white sandy soil. Savannas are commonest in the vicinity of large rivers. The great variability of humid forest types here is due mainly to different soils, ranging from rich alluvial floodplain deposits to yellowish and reddish soils to pure white sandy soils. Other factors influencing the forest type are the length of seasonal flooding and gradients of rainfall. Flooded forests of Amazonas are notable for their many species of palms, especially *Mauritia, Euterpe,* and *Manicaria.* Dominant tree families in rich floodplains include Apocynaceae, Fabaceae,

Mimosaceae, Lecythidaceae, Myrtaceae, and Sapotaceae.

In the Ríos Negro, Casiquiare, Guainía, and Atabapo region of southwestern Amazonas, even where rainfall is very high, trees growing on white sandy soils are stunted and often no more than 20–25m high. They have thin trunks, small, open crowns, and pale sclerophyllous gray green leaves. This region, known as the Río Negro Caatinga, has relatively low tree diversity, but many families and species are endemic or unusual. **Tropical wet forest** where rainfall exceeds 4000mm/yr, is very restricted in extent in Venezuela, being found locally at or near the base of some tepuis. These forests are very tall and contain a well-developed layer of emergent trees that may exceed 45m in height.

Premontane and Montane Dry and Moist Forests

Rainfall 500–2000mm/yr but mostly less than 1500mm. Dry forest and moist forest are not widespread in montane regions in Venezuela but are most readily seen in the Andes. Several large valleys lie in rainshadows, being blocked from prevailing moisture-laden winds, and thus receive greatly reduced amounts of rainfall. The middle and upper Río Chama of Mérida and the Río Torbes in Táchira are the most dramatic examples. Several smaller river valleys on Trujillo's western slope are also rather dry. The original vegetation in almost all of these valleys was long ago removed and replaced by small-scale agriculture. The foothills on the northern slope of the Coastal Cordillera contain dry premontane and moist premontane forests; both forests types are extensive on both slopes of the Interior Cordillera and locally in the mountains of Sucre. Deforestation is extensive in all of these areas as well.

Premontane and Montane Humid and Wet Forests

Rainfall 1000–4000mm/yr. These are mature forest formations of mountain regions. They vary greatly in amount of rainfall, seasonal distribution of rainfall, and soils. Those of the Andes and northern cordilleras share many features in common and also share many tree species or genera. In general, at middle elevations in the

Andes these forests are tall and stately, and in certain areas trees carry heavy burdens of mosses, ferns, bromeliads, and other arboreal epiphytes. Tree ferns are characteristic components of the forest understory, and small palms are also often common. At higher elevations the trees are shorter, more gnarled, and their crowns more flattened and dense. Undergrowth often increases and bamboo (*Chusquea*) becomes an important component of the forest. At treeline, and locally on ridgetops, wax palms (*Ceroxylon* spp.) tower high over the surrounding forest. At treeline woody vegetation is often stunted and elfinlike and gives way in patches to open paramo. In the tepuis south of the Orinoco this forest formation contains mostly very different tree species, many of which are endemic.

Savanna or Grassland

Rainfall 1200–2000mm/yr. The best known of the tropical grasslands in Venezuela are the llanos, a vast, almost ruler-flat region that extends in a broad belt from the Andes eastward to Monagas and locally into northern Bolívar. All told, the llanos compose some 40% of the country and are used heavily for cattle ranching and agriculture. The llanos, and scattered grasslands south of the Orinoco, are believed to result from or be maintained by fire, seasonal flooding, and varying degrees of soil porosity, aeration, and fertility rather than climate. Singly or in concert, these factors effectively deter forest development. Most natural grasslands in Venezuela occur on flat terrain. Broadly speaking, the llanos of Venezuela divide into two regions. A "high" region forms the western, northern, and eastern boundary rim of the llanos. Here the terrain is flat but relatively well drained, not subject to extensive flooding, and often supports extensive areas of dry forest. In the more central and southerly portion of the llanos, especially in southern Portuguesa, eastern Barinas, and most of Apure, heavy clay soils predominate, drainage is poor, and larger areas quickly flood to shallow depths at the onset of the rainy season and remain flooded for many months. *Trachypogon* grasses predominate in well-drained terrain, *Andropogon* grasses and *Sorghastrum* in areas subject to flooding. Common trees and shrubs,

especially of well-drained savannas, include *Pithecellobium, Copaifera, Cochlospermum, Psidium, Davilia, Caesearia, Eugenia, Xylopia, Genipa, Jacaranda, Mikania, Pavonia, Rudgea, Vismia,* and *Annona.*

In contrast to the rather impermeable soils underlying the llanos, most grasslands in Amazonas and southern Bolívar occur on extremely porous white sandy soils which retain very little water despite high rainfall. Here grasses are high in silica, and scattered scrubby trees such as *Curatella, Brysonima,* and *Vochysia* predominate.

Paramo

This is a specialized high-elevation wet grassland. It occurs mainly in the Andes and extends from treeline at 2800–3400m to the upper limit of plant growth. In Venezuela paramo is distributed in the form of high-elevation islands on the tops of massifs and mountain peaks and is most extensive in northern Táchira and Mérida. Páramo de Tamá of southern Táchira is contiguous with a much larger area of paramo vegetation in Colombia. Other paramos occur in the Sierra de Perijá, and in Trujillo northward as little isolated mountaintop stepping-stones to southern Lara. Paramo vegetation presents a dramatic spectacle because of the many unusual plants that occur in it, but it accounts for less than 1% of Venezuela's land area. The most characteristic group of paramo plants are in the genus *Espeletia*, a rosette-shaped, densely woolly group of composites with at least 45 species in Venezuela. *Senecio*, another group of composites with about 12 species, is also common. Paramo plants flower mostly from September to November in one of the most spectacular floral tapestries to be seen anywhere in the world. Most visitors delight to *Espeletia schultzii*, a common species on Páramos de Mucuchíes and Mucubají. *Espeletia*, also widely known as *frailejón* in Spanish, are extremely hardy and occur to 4600m elevation, or within 100m of the upper limit of plant growth in Venezuela[767]. At lower elevations within paramo, ravines are often filled with various woody shrubs, among them *Escallonia, Polylepis, Weinmannia, Alnus,* and various species of Euphorbiaceae, Ericaceae, and

Melastomataceae. At high elevations *Espeletia* and many grasses, sedges, cushion plants, and bryophytes predominate, especially around small lagoons and acid bogs.

Habitat Descriptions

Tropical Wet Forest

Mature canopied, tall, and evergreen forest of lowland areas with rainfall near or in excess of 4000mm/yr. Confined to a few small regions in Amazonas and Bolívar and similar to Holdridge's[264] "very humid" zone. Includes tropical rain forest, a term not used here because of ambiguity in popular usage.

Humid Forest

Tall, canopied, and largely evergreen forest. Resembles tropical wet forest but rainfall lower, ca. 2000–4000mm/yr in the lowlands, less in the highlands. There is usually a moderate dry season and a longer wet season. This is the dominant lowland forest south of the Orinoco. Also found in foothill and montane zones in the Andes and northern cordilleras. Usually prefaced in text as tropical humid forest, premontane humid forest, or montane humid forest.

Moist Forest

Slightly drier forest than previous categories (above). Moderate height, semievergreen forest in which many trees are deciduous and vines become more numerous. Transitional between evergreen humid forest and deciduous dry forest. Rainfall ca. 1000–2000mm/yr. Foothills above Ocumare de La Costa on north slope of Coastal Cordillera; west of El Palmar; and vicinity of Guasipati, Bolívar. Usually prefaced in text as tropical moist forest or premontane moist forest.

Dry Forest

Low to moderately high, deciduous forest in which the dry season is marked and severe. Most trees lose their leaves for up to half the year. Rainfall averages ca. 500–1000mm/yr and falls during a few "wet" months of the year. Examples: Morrocoy National Park; locally west of El Palmar; and vicinity of Guasipati, Bolívar.

Usually prefaced in text as tropical dry forest or montane dry forest depending on elevation in which it occurs.

Desert Scrub or Arid Scrub

Permanent scrub zone that occupies much of Caribbean littoral and locally inland in rain-shadow valleys in mountains (e.g., Río Chama, Mérida). Rainfall ca. 400–700mm/yr or less and falls only during a few months. Characterized by low thorny bushes, small drought-resistant trees, and several kinds of cactus.

Terra Firme Forest

Humid or wet lowland forests not subject to inundation. The designation is applied mainly to lowland forests of the Amazonian and Orinocan region to distinguish them from várzea forest.

Várzea Forest

Humid or wet lowland forest that is seasonally flooded to depths of ca. 1–6m, often for several months, one or more times a year. Found in floodplains of major rivers and their tributaries, including one (or occasionally both) banks of the Ríos Negro, Casiquiare, Orinoco, Caura, and Caño Colorado. Most gallery forests (below) in the llanos flood for several months each year, but they are not comparable to these tall, floristically complex várzea forests of south of the Orinoco.

Cloud Forest

Popular but somewhat ambiguous term that refers to any very humid or wet mountain forest that is frequently enveloped in clouds and whose trees are heavily burdened with mosses and epiphytes. Most premontane and montane wet forests (below) are, in a popular sense, cloud forest.

Premontane Wet Forest

Specific designation for wet forest found at low elevations in mountain areas. Elevational limits vary but are mostly ca. 1000–1600m, rarely as low as 400m. Rainfall is high; the forest is frequently enveloped in clouds, especially in the afternoon; and trees carry abundant loads of epiphytic plants, including mosses and orchids.

In popular terminology this and montane wet forest are often called "cloud forest."

Montane Wet Forest

Specific designation for wet forest found at middle or upper elevations in mountain areas. Elevational limits vary but are mostly ca. 1600–3000m. Abundant rainfall and foggy conditions prevail. Trees are tall at middle elevations, shorter in stature at high elevations, and always heavily festooned with mosses and epiphytes. Along with premontane wet forest, often called "cloud forest" in popular terminology.

Elfin Forest (Dwarf Forest) and Elfin Woodland

Elfin forest is a stunted or dwarf forest growing at high elevations, typically near tree line and often where exposed, as on ridges or slopes. Formed under constant exposure to wind and fog and is characteristically gnarled, mossy, and miniature in size (ca. 2–8m high). Elfin woodland is similar but refers to vegetation where the trees and shrubs are more widely spaced.

Paramo

Wet to moderately dry tropical alpine grassland or shrubland that occurs from treeline (ca. 3000–3300m) to the upper limit of vegetation or snowline. Characterized by large expanses of bunch grass mixed with rosette-shaped *Espeletia* shrubs of the Compositae family. Quaking bogs and cold lakes dot poorly drained regions of the paramo. Rainfall in the paramo is highly seasonal in Venezuela, with a spectacular display of flowering from September to November.

River-edge Forest

Zone of *Cecropia, Erythrina, Ficus*, and vines along the banks of the Orinoco, Caura, etc. May or may not flood seasonally.

Sandy-belt Forest

Humid forest growing on white sandy soil. Resembles terra firme forest but is less luxuriant, usually having a lower canopy and containing a high proportion of trees with tannins, phenols, and strong defensive chemicals in their leaves. Rivers flowing through sandy-belt forest are always black. Vast areas of sandy-belt forest are found in the upper Orinoco and upper Río Negro drainage of Amazonas, as well as spottily throughout much of Bolívar. A few sandy-belt forests are subject to seasonal inundation, then usually resembling a dense, stunted, and low-stature scrub forest.

Savanna Woodland

Resembles sandy-belt forest but is scrubbier, shorter (about 3–15m), and more open. In its extreme form resembles Brazilian cerrado, with short, well-spaced shrublike trees and a low semiclosed canopy. In appearance intermediate between sandy-belt forest and savanna.

Gallery Forest and Riparian Woodland

These are more or less interchangeable terms for bands of trees confined to and dependent on watercourses in otherwise largely open or shrubby country. They border virtually all rivers in the llanos (unless removed by people).

Light Woodland and Thinned Woodland

These habitats include parklike areas. They are forests thinned by human activity (e.g., for coffee plantations or by lumbering) where a more or less continuous canopy is maintained but much undergrowth is removed. Important habitats for wintering North American migrants.

Second-growth Woodland (Regrowth Woodland)

Relatively advanced regrowth stage of forest that in time will become mature forest. Differs from mature forest in species composition, absence of emergent trees, usually lower canopy height, and more open canopy (older stages largely closed) with well-lighted, bushy undergrowth.

Forest or Woodland Border

Edge of a forest or woodland along a road, stream, treefall, etc., and usually dense and shrubby. Older stages become a solid wall of vegetation. Common plants include *Cecropia, Heliconia, Miconia, Piper*, and vines. This is the most frequently "birded" habitat in most tropical areas, and it usually contains a mixture of both forest and nonforest bird species.

(Habitat descriptions continued on page 29)

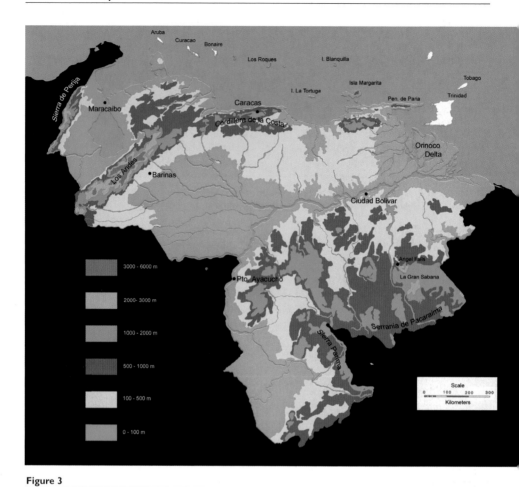

Figure 3

Relief map of Venezuela. Graphics by Dru Hilty.

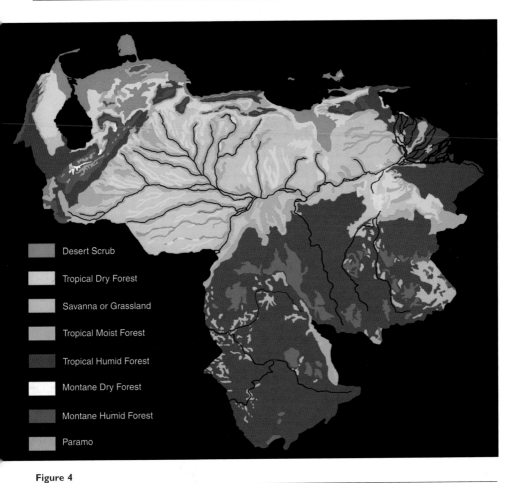

Desert Scrub

Tropical Dry Forest

Savanna or Grassland

Tropical Moist Forest

Tropical Humid Forest

Montane Dry Forest

Montane Humid Forest

Paramo

Figure 4

Major vegetation zones of Venezuela. Adapted from Huber and Alarcon[272] and Mapa Ecologica[535]. Graphics by Dru Hilty.

Paramo vegetation with *Espeletia* (Compositae). Mucubají, Mérida. 3600m. Photo S. Hilty.

Espeletia schultzii in paramo. Pico Águila, Mérida. 4000m. Photo S. Hilty.

Partially deforested elfin woodland/paramo ecotone above Santo Domingo, Mérida. 2900m. Photo S. Hilty.

Below left
Stunted upper montane wet forest, 2500m, Táchira/Mérida border. Photo S. Hilty.

Below
Paramo near Pico Bolívar, Mérida. Photo R. Sojo.

Flowering immortelle (*Erythrina*) in disturbed premontane humid forest. Henri Pittier National Park, Aragua. 800m. Photo S. Hilty.

Deforestation in Andes, northern Táchira. Photo S. Hilty.

Montane wet forest (cloud forest) above Bramón, southern Táchira. 1800m. Photo S. Hilty.

Montane humid forest, Guaramacal National Park, Trujillo. 2300m. Photo S. Hilty.

Premontane humid forest on south slope of Coastal Cordillera, Henri Pittier National Park, Aragua. 1000m. Photo S. Hilty.

Desert scrub near Barquisimeto, Lara. 700m. Photo S. Hilty.

Médanos de Coro National Park, Falcón. 20m. Photo S. Hilty.

Degraded desert scrub west of Barquisimeto, Lara. 700m. Photo S. Hilty.

Tree-bordered pastures and cattleland, eastern Falcón. Formerly tropical moist forest. 50m. Photo S. Hilty.

Tropical dry forest, Hato Cedral, Apure. 200m. Photo S. Hilty.

Caribbean coast at Choroní, Aragua. Photo R. Sojo.

Archipiélago Los Roques National Park. Photo R. Sojo.

Red mangrove (*Rizophora mangle*) community, Morrocoy National Park, Falcón. Photo S. Hilty.

Marine estuaries, Morrocoy National Park, Falcón. Photo S. Hilty.

Grasslands and lagoons, dry season, Hato Cedral, Apure. 150m. Photo R. Sojo.

Grassland and samán (*Pithecellobium*) trees. Formerly tropical dry forest. 200m. Guárico. Photo R. Sojo.

Lagoon and *Copernicia* palms. Wet season, Guárico. 200m. Photo S. Hilty.

Copernicia palms, Hato Piñero, Cojedes. 200m. Photo S. Hilty.

Caño Matiyuri, Hato Cedral, Apure. 150m. Photo S. Hilty.

Flooded grassland in rainy season, Apure. 150m. Photo S. Hilty.

Scarlet Ibis. Photo S. Hilty.

Marshes, Hato Cedral, Apure. 150m. Photo S. Hilty.

Tropical dry forest and grassland, Cojedes. 200m. Photo S. Hilty.

Mixed sandy-soil savanna and tropical humid forest, middle Río Orinoco near Río Ventuari. 250m. Photo S. Hilty.

Tropical humid forest (terra firme) on reddish soil, Junglaven. 300m. Photo S. Hilty.

Mixed savanna and *Curatella-Byrsonima*-dominated woodland on sandy soils with quartzite outcrops, Pto. Ayacucho. 150m. Photo S. Hilty.

Tropical humid forest (várzea or floodplain forest on left bank), middle Río Ventuari. 250m. Photo S. Hilty.

Granitic quartzite outcrop and open woodland and savanna on white sandy soil, Pto. Ayacucho. 150m. Photo S. Hilty.

Scrubby white sandy-soil forest and savanna along middle Río Ventuari. 250m. Photo S. Hilty.

Tropical wet forest, north base of Sierra de Lema, Bolívar. 300m. Photo S. Hilty.

Granitic quartzite mountains west of Middle Río Ventuari, Amazonas. Tropical humid forest in lowlands. Xerophytic scrub on slopes and summit. Photo S. Hilty.

Moriche palms (*Mauritia flexuosa*), lower Río Caura, Bolívar. 150m. Photo S. Hilty.

Ptari-tepui in Gran Sabana, Bolívar. 2650m. Tropical humid forest and savannas in foreground. Photo S. Hilty.

Savanna and moriche palms (*Mauritia flexuosa*). Santa Elena de Uairén, Bolívar. 900m. Photo S. Hilty.

Classical tepui formation near Auyán-tepui. Photo S. Hilty.

Auyán-tepui. 2560m. Photo R. Sojo.

Grasslands of Gran Sabana and tepui formations. 1300m.
Photo R. Sojo.

Cerro Roraima. 2850m. High tepui shrub woodland on
slopes. Photo R. Sojo.

Auyán-tepui and Angel Falls in rainy season.
Photo R. Sojo.

(Text continued from page 17)

Shrubby Areas and Clearings

Any regrowth vegetation, with or without scattered trees, that follows deforestation and precedes woodland. Mostly composed of shrubs, thickets, grass, and small trees. Later stages give way to large trees.

Scrubby Areas

Relatively permanent plant community (not a regrowth stage) found chiefly in drier regions. Characterized by scrubby bushes and small trees, often *Acacia*. In some cases forested areas become so permanently altered as a result of human activity (erosion, overgrazing, wood-cutting, etc.) that forest regeneration is unlikely and they become scrubby areas.

Melastome-dominated Forest

Highly characteristic, mostly regrowth vegetation stage found at middle elevations on tepuis. Mostly low to moderately high (to ca. 15m) and dominated by dense stands of various species of Melastomataceae. Widespread in disturbed areas along the highway ascending Sierra de Lema, Bolívar.

High Tepui Shrub Woodland

Scrubby mixture of herbs, grass, and dense leathery-leafed shrub vegetation peculiar to upper elevations of most tepui mountains. Composed mostly of highly range-restricted, endemic plants. Specific plant associations are often unique to each major tepui.

Marshes

Areas with more or less permanent standing water dominated by various kinds of grasses, sedges, and non-woody emergent vegetation, but not trees. Fresh or brackish water. Widespread in llanos. In forested areas found mainly around oxbow lagoons, rivers mouths, and on river islands.

Swamps

Similar to marshes but dominated by trees and woody vegetation.

Mangroves

Forest community of a few species of evergreen trees and shrubs that grow in salt or brackish water of the tidal zone. Several species of mangroves are characterized by shiny, dark green foliage and a tangle of aerial or stiltlike roots. Locally distributed along the coast. Largest expanses in Venezuela occur in the Orinoco Delta.

Coastal, Offshore, and Pelagic Zones

These habitats are, respectively, within sight of land, beyond sight of land but over the continental shelf, and open ocean beyond the continental shelf.

Savanna or Grassland

Savanna is a general term for grassland, although the word grassland is sometimes reserved for areas lacking shrubs or trees, while savanna is reserved for areas with shrubs or trees. They are used interchangably here, and often grade into open savanna woodland (above), especially in white sandy soil areas. The Venezuelan-Colombian llanos is the largest grassland in northern South America.

Morichales

Areas dominated almost exclusively by moriche palms (*Mauritia*). Found in savanna or forest but always where the soil is poorly drained, wet, and/or permanently water-logged. Palms often grow in shallow water. A grove of these palms is known in Spanish as a *morichale* and represents a specialized kind of swamp forest.

Cultivated Areas, Residential Areas, Parks, Gardens, and Ranchlands

More or less self-descriptive terms; all are created and maintained by human activity.

Conservation and National Parks

Most of Venezuela's population is spread across the northern third of the country, and this is where the greatest environmental modification and degradation have occurred. Nevertheless, even within this settled region there are numerous protected and unprotected areas that are still relatively pristine. Some of the most heavily populated and degraded areas lie in the corridor between Caracas, Maracay, and Valencia and in the vicinity of other large population centers such as Maracaibo, San Cristobal, Mérida, Barquisimeto, Barinas, the coast from Chichiriviche to Tucacas and Puerto Cabello, the coast of eastern Anzoátegui and western Sucre, the mountains of southern Sucre and northern Monagas, and from Puerto Ordaz southeastward through Guasipati and Tumeremo.

As in many developing countries, the problems derive from a failure to treat land as a renewable resource and from a lack of enforcement of policies designed to deal with problems such as air, water, and soil pollution, misuse of toxic chemicals by industry and agriculture, uncontrolled burning, forest destruction, and unregulated urban development. In general, the Andes and mountainous areas across the northern and eastern sector of the country are at greatest risk.

Across the llanos and south of the Orinoco the population density is extremely low, and large areas are either uninhabited or harbor low numbers of humans. The discovery of gold has led to much uncontrolled mining in the southeastern part of the country, with the consequence that many rivers are now highly polluted with mercury, and deforestation and erosion are severe in a few areas.

Venezuela has a fine system of parks and reserves, but bureaucracy and budgetary constraints limits the park service's ability to administer or protect these areas. Furthermore, there are few voices of advocacy for conservation in Venezuela. At the present time the number of bird species in serious trouble is still not large. BirdLife International[127] identified 19 threatened species in Venezuela, but unfortunately more than half of these are endemic or nearly endemic to the country. Several other species

with greatly restricted ranges also could be added. Examples of threatened species include Andean Condor, Northern Helmeted Curassow, Plain-flanked Rail, Rusty-faced Parrot, Yellow-shouldered Parrot, Great Antpitta, Hooded Antpitta, Scalloped Antpitta, Venezuelan Flower-piercer, Paria Redstart, Gray-headed Warbler, Slaty-backed Hemispingus, and Red Siskin.

Parks and natural monuments now account for more than 7 million ha, or about 8% of the total land surface of Venezuela. This is substantially more than in most countries, yet almost 70% of this total is in the southern half of the country, which has a tiny, mostly indigenous population and relatively minor and sporadic threats to the environment. Responsibility for park management is under the Instituto Nacional de Parques (INPARQUES) which has insufficient budget and staff to provide adequate services and protection for the park system.

The following annotated lists of national parks, national monuments, and faunal and biological reserves[765] account for most of the protected land in Venezuela. The areas are listed here in order of when they were granted protection. Rainfall amounts given are annual averages.

National Parks

1937 Henri Pittier. 107,800ha (266,374 acres). 0–2435m. 700–2000+mm rainfall. Northern Aragua. Arid scrub, tropical dry and moist forest; premontane humid and wet forest; montane wet forest. Largest protected area of cloud forest in Coastal Cordillera. Important watershed, beaches, recreational areas. Spectacular mountains, beautiful forests, incredibly rich flora and fauna, including more than 500 species of birds.

1952 Sierra Nevada. 190,000ha (469,490 acres). 600–5007m. 2000+mm rainfall. Eastern Mérida. Humid and wet premontane and montane forest, paramo and glacier-covered high Andean mountain peaks. Protects important watersheds, Andean birds; valuable for recreation.

1958 Guatopo. 92,640ha (228,913 acres).
200–1450m. 1400–2800mm rainfall. Interior Cordillera in Miranda and extreme
northern Guárico. Tropical dry and moist
forest; smaller areas of tropical humid
forest. Notable for large mammal fauna,
including Jaguar. Very diverse avifauna.
Protects endemic Blood-eared and
Venezuelan parakeets; large raptors,
cracids, Military Macaw, Black-and-white
Owl, and others.

1958 El Avila. 85,192ha (210,510 acres).
120–2765m. 600–1400mm rainfall. Distrito Federal. Mostly humid premontane
and montane forest. Important watershed and recreational site at outskirts of
Caracas. Deforestation and regrowth
stages of woodland predominate in all
but uppermost elevations.

1960 Yurubí. 23,670ha (58,489 acres).
500–1950m. Ca. 1500–1600mm rainfall.
Tropical dry forest, premontane dry and
moist forest; montane humid forest at
headwaters of Río Yurubí; critical watershed to city of San Felipe. Includes Cerro
El Tigre and mountains of central
Yaracuy. Flora and fauna bridge Andes
and northern cordilleras.

1962 Canaima. 3,000,000ha (7,413,000 acres).
400–2700m. 1200–1600mm rainfall
(locally higher). Eastern Bolívar. One of
the largest national parks in the world
and a world-class heritage. Poorly protected and facing numerous threats.
Savannas on white sandy soils; moist,
humid, and wet forest; spectacular tepui
(mesa) mountains; waterfalls and blackwater rivers. Unusually high number of
endemic or near-endemic plants and
birds.

1962 Yacambú. 14,580ha (36,027 acres).
500–2300m. 1400–2400mm rainfall.
Andes of southern Lara in Sierra de Portuguesa. Beautiful humid and wet premontane and montane forest (cloud forest). Protects important watershed for
agriculture and water for Barquisimeto.
Northern Helmeted Curassow, guans,
Bearded Bellbird, and many tanagers.

1969 Cueva Quebrada del Toro. 8500ha
(21,004 acres). 400–1100m.

1100–1200mm rainfall. Southeastern Falcón. Tropical dry forest. Protects an Oilbird colony and forest watershed.

1972 Archipiélago Los Roques. 225,153ha
(546,388 acres). 0–250m. Ca. 425mm
rainfall. Barrier reefs and marine islands.
Dry scrub vegetation, mangroves, abundant coral formations. Nesting sites for
Green and Hawksbill turtles; large
seabird breeding colonies.

1973 Macarao. 15,000ha (37,065 acres).
1000–2200m. 1000–1400mm rainfall.
Northwestern Miranda. Humid and wet
montane forest in Coastal Cordillera. Preserves an important watershed for Caracas. Rich montane flora and fauna.

1973 Mochima. 94,935ha (234,584 acres).
0–1150m. 250–1000mm rainfall. Northeastern Anzoátegui. Coastal islands,
including Islas Caracas, Chimanas, and
Lechería west to Isla Borrachas in Golfo
de Santa Fe; also seacoast, xerophytic
coastal plains, and low mountains. Mangroves, beaches, desert scrub, and tropical dry and moist forest. Some coral formations. Important fish fauna and
seabird colonies.

1974 Laguna de la Restinga. 10,700ha
(26,440 acres). 0–280m. <500mm rainfall. Northern coast of Isla Margarita.
Lagoons, extensive mangroves, and
some desert scrub vegetation. Important
coastal habitat for waterfowl, herons,
egrets, flamingos, and especially migratory shorebirds.

1974 Médanos de Coro. 91,280ha (225,552
acres). 0–20m. 200–250mm rainfall.
Northern Falcón. Spectacular shifting
beach dunes, desert scrub vegetation,
and seacoast. Harbors several species of
birds confined to arid zones of northern
Venezuela and adjacent Colombia.

1974 Laguna de Tacarigua. 18,400ha (45,466
acres). 0–10m. 1000–1500mm rainfall.
Miranda. Valuable coastal estuary habitat, including mangroves and beaches.
Important region for wintering migratory
shorebirds, migratory waterfowl, and
flamingos.

1974 Cerro Copey-Jóvito Villalba. 7,130ha
(17,576 acres). 100–1000m. 500–1000mm

rainfall. Isla Margarita. Desert scrub, thorn woodland, dry and moist (semideciduous) hill forest. Much of vegetation disturbed or modified by human activity. Protects island's only semipermanent or permanent source of water.

1974 Aguaro-Guariquito. 169,000ha (417,560 acres). 35–225m. 1200–2000mm rainfall. Southcentral Guárico. Llanos grassland, gallery forest (tropical dry forest), and sand dunes. Great diversity of birds, mammals, and reptiles.

1974 Morrocoy. 32,090ha (79,294 acres). 0–285m. 1000–1800mm rainfall. Eastern Falcón. Extensive coastal islets (cays), white sandy beaches, mangroves, estuaries, shallow seas, desert scrub, tropical dry forest, and tropical moist (semievergreen) forest. Land area is dominated by Cerro Chichiriviche. Rich fish fauna, important frigatebird breeding colony, very diverse avifauna, and scenic and important recreation area.

1975 Cueva del Guácharo. 45,500ha (112,431 acres). 900–2324m. 1200–1800mm rainfall. Northern Monagas. Premontane and montane moist and humid forest. Centerpiece is Cueva del Guácharo, which harbors 10,000–18,000 Oilbirds. Extensive deforestation in park. Oilbirds are heavily dependent on remaining primary forest. An important recreational site.

1976 Terepaima. 18,650ha (46,084 acres). 300–1500m. 800–2000mm rainfall. South of Barquisimeto in southern Lara. Desert scrub, tropical dry (deciduous) and moist (semideciduous) forest; humid forest, including cloud forest at higher elevations. Numerous endemic plants. Northern Helmeted Curassow. One of the largest butterflies in the world, *Thysania agripina*, occurs here.

1978 Serranía de Neblina. 1,360,000ha (3,360,560 acres). 500–3045m. Ca. 3000mm rainfall. Southern Amazonas bordering Brazil. Highest mountain in Amazonas. Tropical humid forest, premontane and montane wet forest (cloud forest), and elfin forest. High plant and bird endemism.

1978 Yapacana. 320,000ha (790,720 acres). To 1345m. Ca. 2350mm rainfall. Central Amazonas. Tepui (mesa) formation within humid tropical forest and savanna, much of it on white sandy soil, and seasonally inundated savanna and forest. High species diversity.

1978 Duida-Marahuaca. 210,000ha (518,970 acres). 250–2880m. Ca. 2500mm rainfall. Tepui (mesa) formation in southcentral Amazonas. Access difficult. Savannas, palm swamps, tropical humid forest, and montane humid and wet forest. High diversity and endemism of birds and plants.

1978 Península de Paria. 37,500ha (92,663 acres). 0–1370m. 1000–2000mm rainfall. Northeastern Sucre. Coastal mountains. Desert scrub to cloud forest vegetation. Endemic plants, several endemic species and subspecies of birds.

1978 Sierra de Perijá. 295,288ha (729,657 acres). 300–3400m. 1500–2400mm rainfall. Western Zulia in Sierra de Perijá. Park borders Colombia. Extensive *Podocarpus* forest, cloud forest, and paramo. Lower elevations heavily deforested. Spectacled Bear; numerous endemic or near-endemic birds.

1978 Jaua-Sarisariñama. 330,000ha (815,100 acres). 1000–2400m. 2800–3600mm rainfall. Located at headwaters of Río Caura in southwestern Bolívar in wild and remote region with no access. Humid to very wet (pluvial) premontane and montane forest and herbaceous and shrub zones. Much of park occupied by Meseta de Jaua and several other tepuis. Highly endemic flora and fauna.

1978 El Tamá. 139,000ha (343,470 acres). 330–3350m. 2000–4000mm rainfall. On Colombian border in southern Táchira. Premontane and montane wet forest and paramo. Harbors several endemic birds and many Andean species found nowhere else in Venezuela.

1987 San Esteban. 44,050ha (108,848 acres). 0–1830m. 700–1800mm rainfall. Northern Carabobo. Mangroves, desert scrub near coast; dry forest changing to moist/humid forest with increasing elevation. Rich flora and fauna (similar to Henri Pittier National Park), historical sites, and pre-Colombian archeological sites.

1987 Sierra de San Luis. 20,000ha (49,420 acres). 200–1500m. 1000–1400mm rainfall. In Sierra de San Luis, northern Falcón. Desert scrub, tropical dry and moist forests, premontane humid forest. Valuable watershed. Isolated populations of many Andean and northern cordilleran birds.

1988 Cinaruco-Capanaparo. 584,368ha (1,443,973 acres). 30–200m. Ca. 1500mm rainfall. Southeastern Apure. Open savanna, seasonally inundated savanna, marshes, scattered lagoons, morichales, gallery forest, tropical dry forest, and shifting sand dunes. Avifauna includes Festive Parrot, Lesser Razor-billed Curassow. Orinoco Crocodile, caiman, many mammals. Park threatened.

1988 Guaramacal. 21,000ha (51,890 acres). 1000–3200m. 900–3200mm rainfall. Andes of eastern Trujillo and western Portuguesa. Exceptionally beautiful humid and wet montane forests, steep forested valleys, paramo, and diverse northern Andean flora and fauna.

1988 Dinira. 42,000ha (103,782 acres). 1800–3585m. Ca. 1300mm rainfall. Overlaps borders of Lara, Trujillo, and Portuguesa. Primarily humid mountain forests and Páramo Cendé. Several important caves. Preserves biological, geological, and cultural features of national importance.

1989 Cerro Saroche. 32,294ha (79,800 acres). 500–1300m. 800–1600mm rainfall. Central Lara. Xerophytic (desert scrub) vegetation and intermittent streams. Protects an array of desert mammals, reptiles, and birds, including Vermilion Cardinal and Venezuelan Troupial.

1989 Sierra de la Culata. 200,400ha (495,188 acres). 800–4750m. 800–1900mm rainfall. Central Mérida. Paramo and humid upper montane forest communities. Lower zones heavily disturbed. Spectacled Bear; endemic *Espeletia* plants.

1989 Páramos Batallón y La Negra. 65,000ha (160,615 acres). 1800–3300m. 800–2300mm rainfall. Southern Mérida

and northern Táchira. Wet upper montane forest and paramo. Sword-billed Hummingbird, Ocellated Tapaculo, many high-elevation birds and mammals.

1989 Chorro El Indio. 10,800ha (26,687 acres). 1100–2600m. Ca. 2300mm rainfall. Northeastern Táchira. Small mountain park in Sierra La Maravilla. Humid montane forest, heavily deforested. Chorro El Indio waterfall; trails used by indigenous people.

1991 Mariusa. 265,000ha (654,815 acres). 0–40m. 2000–2500mm rainfall. Delta Amacuro. Mangroves, vast palm swamps, and marshes. Protects colonies of ibises, herons, egrets, and Blue-and-yellow Macaws.

1991 Parima-Tapirapecó. 3,500,000ha (8,648,500 acres). 250–1800m. Ca. 2800mm rainfall. Enormous park in extreme southeastern Amazonas on Brazilian border. Mostly humid lowland and lower montane forest. Region of exceptional beauty. Protects numerous Indian communities and diverse Alto Orinoco-Casiquiare flora and fauna.

1991 Turuépano. 72,600ha (179,395 acres). 0–40m. Ca. 1800mm rainfall. Southeastern Sucre. Coastal river delta region of mangroves, swamp forest, and seasonally inundated forest centered on Caño Ajíes and Caño Guariquén. Varied fish fauna. Protects rich avifauna, including waterbirds and parrots. Important migratory shorebird stopover and wintering area.

1991 Ciénegas del Catatumbo, Zulia. 269,000ha (664,439 acres). 0–60m. Ca. 3550mm rainfall. Fresh- and saltwater marshes, estuaries, and evergreen humid forest at southwestern end of Lago de Maracaibo. Waterfowl, both screamers, raptors, and psittacines.

No information is available on the following newer parks: 1992, **El Guache**, 16,700ha (41,249 acres) in Lara; 1992, **Río Viejo**, 68,200ha (168,454 acres) in Apure; 1992, **Tirgua**, 91,000ha (224,770 acres) in Cojedes; **Santos Luzardo**, 584,604ha (1,443,973 acres) in Apure and Bolívar states; and **Juan Crisóstomo Falcón**, 19,838ha (49,400 acres) in Falcón state. These are not plotted on Figure 1.

National Monuments (partial list)

1949 Alejandro de Humboldt-Cueva del Guácharo. 181ha. 1070m. 1200–1400mm rainfall. Northern Monagas.

1949 Morros de San Juan. 2755ha. 630–800m. 600–800mm rainfall. Northern Guárico.

1960 María Lionza. 11,712ha. 1400–2000mm rainfall. Southern Yaracuy.

1972 Cerro Santa Ana. 1900ha. 0–450m. <450mm rainfall. Paraguaná Peninsula of Falcón.

1974 Laguna de Las Marites. 3674ha. 0–40m. Ca. 425mm rainfall. Southeastern coast of Isla Margarita.

1974 Las Tetas de María Guevara. 1670ha. 0–135m. 125–250mm rainfall. South coast of Isla Margarita.

1974 Cerros Matasiete and Guayamurí. 1672ha. 80–685m. Ca. 600mm rainfall. North coast of Isla Margarita.

1978 Piedra de Cocuy. 15ha. 400m. 3000–3500mm rainfall. Extreme southwestern Amazonas.

1978 Cerro Autana. 30ha. 250–1250m. 2400–2800mm rainfall. Northwestern Amazonas.

1978 Morros de Macaira. 99ha. 1000–1250mm rainfall. Northeastern Guárico.

1978 Cueva Alfredo Jahn. 58ha. 60–300m. Ca. 2000mm rainfall. East central Miranda.

1979 Laguna de Urao. 29ha. 1135m. 2000–4000mm rainfall. Southern Mérida.

1980 Chorrera Las González. 126ha. 1700–2400m. 2000–2400mm rainfall. West of city of Mérida.

1987 Cerro Platillón. 8000ha. 600–1930m. 1000–2000mm rainfall. Northern Guárico.

1989 Loma de León. 7275ha. 1300m. 600mm rainfall. South of Barquisimeto, Lara.

1991 Formación de Tepuyes. 1,750,000ha. >2500mm rainfall. Includes 25 sites in Amazonas and Bolívar.

1991 Pico Codazzi. 11,850ha. 600–2430m. 1000–2000mm rainfall. North of Colonia Tovar. Parts of Aragua, Miranda, and Distrito Federal.

Faunal and Biological Reserves

1972 Isla de Aves. 54ha. 0–3m. <150mm rainfall. Isla de Aves in Caribbean. Breeding site for Green Turtle and many seabirds.

1972 Cuare. 11,852ha. 0–280m. Ca. 1000mm rainfall. Golfo de Cuare west of Chichiriviche. Estuary.

1974 Estero de Chiriguare. 32,170ha. 50–55m. Ca. 1450mm rainfall. Northern Portuguesa, Tropical dry and moist forest.

1986 Los Olivitos. 25,727ha. 0–7m. 250–500mm rainfall. Northeastern coast of Zulia. Flamingo colony.

1989 Laguna Boca de Caño. 453ha. 0–1m. 500–1000mm rainfall. Eastern Falcón, Mangrove estuary.

1989 Caño Guaritico. 9,300ha. 60–70m. 1000–1600mm rainfall. Western Apure, Gallery forest.

1989 De la Tortuga Arrau. 17,431ha. 1700–2000mm rainfall. Southeastern Apure. Gallery forest (tropical dry and moist forests).

Biosphere Reserves

Two areas are designated as biosphere reserves, Delta del Orinoco in the Orinoco Delta region of Delta Amacuro, and Alto Orinoco-Casiquiare in southeastern Amazonas state.

Protected Zones

The Ciénagas de Juan Manuel de Aguas Blancas y Aguas Negras Faunal Reserve, Zulia, and Sabanas de Anaro Faunal Reserve, Barinas, are listed as protected areas. Additionally, 47 other sites are designated by law as protected zones. Many of these encompass small watersheds and lakes or impoundments that are used for urban water supplies.

Migration

The movement of birds within Venezuela and to and from areas outside the country is far greater than has been previously recognized. Tropical avifaunas in general are more dynamic than has been acknowledged, although documentation of these movements, especially of species that are resident in the country, has barely begun. This will be evident to readers from the numerous notations in the species accounts indicating that movements are known to occur but are poorly documented.

The greatest number of long-distance migrants comes from North America, with about 135 species (List 1). Three or four additional species, primarily vagrants on List 1, may come from Europe or other northern latitudes. As a group northern migrants are better documented in Venezuela than other migrants. Less well known is the extent of long-distance migration from southern South America; presently at least 16 species have been identified as austral-breeding migrants to Venezuela

List 1. North American-breeding migrants that are resident or transient in Venezuela during the northern winter.

An asterisk (*) denotes species that also have breeding populations in Venezuela.
A dagger (†) denotes a species in which northern populations, including a few European breeders, appear to be vagrant to Venezuela rather than regular migrants.
A question mark (?) denotes a species whose status as a northern migrant to Venezuela is uncertain.

American Wigeon	Sanderling	Common Tern*	Magnolia Warbler†
Northern Pintail	Semipalmated Sandpiper	Least Tern*	Cape May Warbler
Blue-winged Teal	Western Sandpiper	Black Tern	Black-throated Blue
Northern Shoveler	Least Sandpiper	Black Skimmer*	Warbler
Lesser Scaup	White-rumped Sandpiper	Black-billed Cuckoo	Yellow-rumped Warbler
Ring-necked Duck	Baird's Sandpiper	Yellow-billed Cuckoo	Black-throated Green
Least Bittern*?	Pectoral Sandpiper	Common Nighthawk	Warbler
Great Blue Heron	Dunlin	Chuck-will's-widow	Palm Warbler†
Cattle Egret?	Stilt Sandpiper	Chimney Swift	Bay-breasted Warbler
Green Heron*	Buff-breasted Sandpiper	Belted Kingfisher	Blackpoll Warbler
Turkey Vulture	Ruff†	Eastern Wood-Pewee	Blackburnian Warbler
Osprey	Short-billed Dowitcher	Western Wood-Pewee	Cerulean Warbler
Swallow-tailed Kite*	Common Snipe	Olive-sided Flycatcher	Black-and-white Warbler
Northern Harrier†	Wilson's Phalarope†	Willow Flycatcher	American Redstart
Broad-winged Hawk	American Oystercatcher*†	Alder Flycatcher	Prothonotary Warbler
Swainson's Hawk†	Gray Plover	Great Crested Flycatcher	Worm-eating Warbler†
Peregrine Falcon	American Golden-Plover	Gray Kingbird*	Swainson's Warbler†
Merlin	Semipalmated Plover	Eastern Kingbird	Ovenbird
American Kestrel?	Wilson's Plover?	Red-eyed Vireo*	Northern Waterthrush
Sora	Snowy Plover?	Yellow-throated Vireo	Louisiana Waterthrush†
Common Gallinule*?	Killdeer	Purple Martin	Kentucky Warbler
American Coot	Great Skua†	Tree Swallow	Connecticut Warbler
Greater Yellowlegs	Pomarine Jaeger	Bank Swallow	Mourning Warbler
Lesser Yellowlegs	Parasitic Jaeger	Barn Swallow	Common Yellowthroat†
Solitary Sandpiper	Long-tailed Jaeger	Cliff Swallow	Hooded Warbler
Willet*	Lesser Black-backed Gull†	Gray-cheeked Thrush	Canada Warbler
Spotted Sandpiper	Great Black-backed Gull†	Swainson's Thrush	Summer Tanager
Upland Sandpiper	Herring Gull	Veery	Scarlet Tanager
Whimbrel	Ring-billed Gull	Cedar Waxwing†	Rose-breasted Grosbeak
Long-billed Curlew	Laughing Gull	Blue-winged Warbler†	Indigo Bunting†
Hudsonian Godwit	Franklin's Gull†	Golden-winged Warbler	Dickcissel
Bar-tailed Godwit†	Gull-billed Tern?	Tennessee Warbler	Bobolink
Marbled Godwit†	Caspian Tern	Northern Parula†	Baltimore Oriole
Ruddy Turnstone	Royal Tern*	Yellow Warbler	Orchard Oriole
Red Knot	Sandwich Tern*	Chestnut-sided Warbler	Lincoln's Sparrow

List 2. Austral-breeding migrants to Venezuela.

Those with a question mark (?) need further verification as migrants and/or breeders. Those with an asterisk (*) also have breeding populations in Venezuela. Those with a dagger (†) are rare or vagrant to Venezuela.

Peregrine Falcon?	Nacunda Nighthawk?	Crowned Slaty Flycatcher	Fork-tailed Flycatcher*
Speckled Crake?	Small-billed Elaenia	Variegated Flycatcher*?	Tropical Kingbird*?
Dark-billed Cuckoo	Greenish Elaenia?	Swainson's Flycatcher*	Southern Martin†
Short-tailed Nighthawk*?	Slaty Elaenia	Streaked Flycatcher*	Lined Seedeater

List 3. Central American- or Caribbean-breeding migrants to Venezuela.

All also breed in Venezuela or its island possessions except those with an asterisk (*). A dagger (†) denotes a species that is rare or vagrant to Venezuela.

Turkey Vulture	Plumbeous Kite	Greenish Elaenia?	Gray-breasted Martin
Black Vulture	Snowy Plover	Piratic Flycatcher	Caribbean Martin†
Swallow-tailed Kite	Mangrove Cuckoo?	Fork-tailed Flycatcher	Yellow-green Vireo*?
	Common Nighthawk?	Gray Kingbird	Black-whiskered Vireo

(List 2). Several of these species, unlike their North American counterparts, also have resident populations breeding in Venezuela, thus complicating the identification of specific populations. A few of them even have austral-breeding populations, resident breeding populations, and populations that migrate northward into Central America to breed. A third group of migrants consists of several essentially tropical species that migrate from northern South America into Central America to breed each year (List 3). These populations, shuttling varying distances back and forth mostly within tropical latitudes, often are virtually identical in appearance, or differ only slightly, from true stay-at-home resident forms. Consequently, arrivals, departures, and distributions of these varying migratory forms are often much more difficult to detect than in long-distance migrants from North America or austral South America. Proper documentation may require collecting or sophisticated field identification of sub-species coupled with careful long-term field notes. For example, there are three subspecies of Fork-tailed Flycatchers in Venezuela, two migratory and one resident, but only one can be separated in the field. By contrast, resident and migratory forms of Streaked Flycatcher can be distinguished relatively easily in the field. A fourth, small group of species breeds in Venezuela and migrates away to other areas within tropical latitudes for the remainder of the year (List 4). It is likely that this group is

List 4. Species that breed in Venezuela but migrate away from the country to other tropical latitudes during the nonbreeding season.

Bridled Tern	Brown Noddy
Sooty Tern	Lesson's Seedeater

much underreported and that several additional species, among them Greater Ani and Azure Gallinule, may eventually be included.

In general, long-distance migrants from North America are numerous and fairly conspicuous in northern Venezuela, the Andes, the northern cordilleras, and along the coast. Relatively few occur south of the Orinoco. Two important exceptions to this are Gray-cheeked Thrush and Blackpoll Warbler, both of which spend the northern winter in numbers in southern Venezuela. Conversely, austral migrants tend to be most numerous south of the Orinoco, especially species such as Swainson's Flycatcher, Streaked Flycatcher, and Brown-chested Martin.

Many resident breeding species undertake minor migratory movements almost entirely within Venezuela. Some of this movement is normal postbreeding dispersal of juveniles and adults rather than regular migration. This undoubtedly accounts for the growing number of observations of vagrant waders crossing the Andes. Other migratory movements, however, such as those seen in parrots in responses to changes in food abundance, are well known, but there is little quantitative documentation of them. Almost all parrots in the Andes and northern cordilleras, and many lowland psittacines as well, are highly nomadic or undertake seasonal migratory movements. Bronze-winged and Scaly-naped parrots, for example, are notoriously unpredictable in occurrence. Rose-headed and Barred parakeets follow seeding bamboo, which is unpredictable in occurrence, and Scarlet-fronted Parakeets show dramatic seasonal population shifts within the Andes, as do Tepui Parrotlets in the southeastern highlands. Few groups are more migratory or responsive to changing food supplies than hummingbirds, and their migrations are swift and dramatic. These migrations are nowhere more evident than in montane areas, where entire populations virtually disappear or reappear overnight. Some populations of Oilbirds are migratory—perhaps more so now as deforestation has greatly reduced food supplies and forced seasonal movements. The movements of some interior forest species occur year-round but are difficult to detect, such as the "floater" populations of manakins. Others, such as periodic migrations of Ruddy Quail-Doves (documented in Brazil), are poorly understood. *Sporophila* seedeaters also provide dramatic evidence of intratropical migrations. Among Venezuelan species, all except Gray Seedeater are migratory or nomadic, but the migrations of only a few have been examined in any detail[583].

Not surprisingly, some of the most dramatic seasonal migratory movements occur in the llanos, where seasonal droughts and floods impose drastic environmental changes on the inhabitants. An indication of the extent of migration has been presented for the Colombia llanos[260], and it is no less remarkable in the contiguous and even larger Venezuelan portion of this grassland. A list of species that are migratory or undertake some seasonal movements would include the majority of the waders and waterfowl present, as well as most rails and crakes, and at least some raptors such as Slender-billed Kite and Long-winged Harrier. Seasonal movements of small landbirds in and out of the llanos have as yet been little

reported, but there is qualitative evidence that, here too, several species may be affected, among them Nacunda Nighthawk, Glaucous and Hooded tanagers, and the yellow-finches (*Sicalis*).

Seasonal migrations of this magnitude need careful consideration when juxtaposed against the needs of agribusiness. This is perhaps nowhere better illustrated than with the vexing problem of the recent alteration in winter distribution of the northern migrant Dickcissel. Wintering Dickcissels formerly spread widely across northern South America's grasslands with minimal impact, but recently the entire population of the species, numbering into the millions, has begun concentrating in a few key rice-growing regions, especially in Portuguesa and Guárico, with disastrous economic results for rice growers and birds alike. It is perhaps surprising that in the llanos, which hosts one of the greatest spectacles of wildlife on the continent, and upon which the intertwined economies of agribusiness and ecotourism are so dependent, that so much still remains to be learned.

The extensive seasonal flooding of the Río Orinoco and its tributaries affects the species that nest and feed on sandbars and riverbanks. Riverine passerines simply move vertically with the flooding, but waders and others closely time their breeding to dry seasons, when water levels drop, and apparently migrate away during high water. Among this latter group are Pied Lapwing, Collared Plover, Yellow-billed and Large-billed terns, Black Skimmer, and Sandcolored and Nacunda nighthawks. The migratory movements of these species when they leave their riverine nesting sites or colonies are still largely unknown.

The dynamic nature of bird populations in Venezuela, and the relative infancy of our knowledge of these seasonal migrations, illustrate the urgency with which information is needed. As human activities increasingly come into conflict with those of wild birds, informed decisions can only be made if there is an understanding of the needs of bird and wildlife populations throughout the changing seasons.

History of Ornithological Exploration in Venezuela

One of the earliest scientific accounts of birds in Venezuela comes from the notes of Baron Nicolas Joseph Jacquin of Holland, who visited the coast and interior of Venezuela in 1784. Descriptions of birds from his notes were later published by his son Joseph[472]. The first scientific collection of birds in Venezuela was made by Alexander von Humboldt during his travels in Venezuela in 1799 and 1800. Although most of his specimens were lost in a shipwreck, descriptions of his travels and many of his scientific findings survive, including accounts of the Oilbird cave at present-day Caripe. During the remainder of the 1800s numerous scientists visited Venezuela, although mostly for short periods of time. Many of them made collections. Among them were Johann von Natterer, who made large collections in Brazil and also collected in southern Venezuela. Others included Richard Schomburgk, Auguste Sallé, Alfred Russell Wallace, M. Levraud, Adolf Ernst, and James Spence. From about 1856 to 1888 C. F. Starke and his son Augusto Starke, working near San Esteban, Carabobo, sent bird collections to the University of Munich and to other overseas institutions. From 1866 to 1872 Anton Goering made small collections in Mérida and Táchira and in the vicinity of Caracas and Carabobo for the Zoological Society of London. Many new species and subspecies were described from his collections. From 1881 to 1884 Henry Whitely, Jr., made collections in the vicinity of Cerro Roraima from which numerous new species and subspecies were described, including pan-tepui endemics such as Tepui Parrotlet, Tepui Spinetail, and Roraiman Barbtail.

The Briceño family of Mérida collected professionally from about 1872 to as late as 1944, selling many of their specimens to the Rothschild Collection in Tring, England. From the early 1900s onward, several large collections were made, beginning with those of George Cherrie during three separate expeditions in 1897–1899, 1905–1907, and 1918–1919, mostly to the Orinoco region. Cherrie's collections were important for the number of new

taxa described, and his 1916 publication[115] contained much valuable information on breeding birds of the Orinoco region. Eugene André collected at least 1600 bird specimens between 1897 and 1901, as well as orchids, butterflies, and mammals. Most of his specimens went to the Rothschild Collection, but on André's last expedition, in 1901, six men died and all of André's specimens were lost in an accident at a falls on the upper Río Caura. Samuel M. Klages made three expeditions to Venezuela, the first in 1898–1900, the second in 1909, and the last in 1913. Working in the Río Caura, Río Orinoco, Distrito Federal, and Carabobo, he took more than 5000 specimens; those from the first expedition went to the Rothschild Collection, and those from the next two were acquired by the American Museum of Natural History (AMNH). In 1912–1913 Leo Miller, working for the AMNH, took 1000 specimens from the Amazonas region of Venezuela. One of the most prolific collectors of all, M. A. Carriker, worked in northern and western Venezuela from 1909 to 1911, then returned again in 1922, making collections for the Carnegie Museum. In the 1920s mammologist G. H. H. Tate also began collecting for the AMNH, taking nearly 1000 specimens in 1925 and more than 800 in 1927–1928 near Cerro Roraima. The AMNH Tyler Expedition of 1928–1929, headed by Tate and numerous assistants, took more than 6400 specimens in the vicinity of Cerro Duida, the Río Casiquiare, and the Río Negro. Alfonzo M. Ollala, one of the collectors on the Tyler Expedition, continued to collect for some time in Venezuela, selling his specimens of birds and mammals to many institutions.

Many ornithologists visited Venezuela during the first two decades of the twentieth century, among them J. F. Ferry, Wilfred H. Osgood, Boardman Conover, and Emmet R. Blake. Several of them made or acquired small collections for the Field Museum of Natural History (FMNH) in Chicago. In 1908, 1922, and 1942, William Beebe visited Venezuela to undertake zoological studies, and in 1922 Jean Delacour of France visited to obtain live birds for his collection in Clères Park. In 1930 and 1931 Ernest G. Holt, working for the United States National Museum (USNM), Smithsonian, obtained more than 3000 specimens in Amazonas[185]. Between 1944 and 1948 F. D. Smith made a small but important collection in Anzoátegui and Monagas[186,187]. In 1937–1938 the AMNH Phelps Expedition, assisted by William Coultas, E. Thomas Gilliard, Félix Cardona, William H. Phelps, and W. H. Phelps, Jr., visited Auyán-tepui, taking more than 2000 specimens between early December 1937 and mid March 1938. A small number of specimens were also obtained near Caracas. The following year William H. Phelps established the Colección Phelps in Caracas. This private collection has grown into one of the largest and finest bird collections in all of South America, the legacy of a single family, William H. Phelps, his son W. H. "Billy" Phelps, Jr., and Billy's wife, Kathleen. The Phelps family made at least forty-nine expeditions to the Caribbean islands, fifteen to the tepuis, fifteen to Amazonia, ten to the llanos, and four to the Sierra de Perijá. Over the years many collectors worked for the Museo de Phelps, among them Alberto Fernándo Yépez, Ventura Barnés, Ramón Urbano, and more recently Gilberto and Luis Pérez. By 1944 the collection comprised some 28,000 specimens, by 1995 more than 77,000 specimens, and from it have been described more than 300 new species or subspecies and the authoritative distributional lists of birds of Venezuela[480,486,489]. These annotated lists formed the basis for the *Guide to the Birds of Venezuela* by Rodolphe Meyer de Schauensee and William H. Phelps, Jr., in 1978. The Coleccíon Phelps remains today at the

center of Venezuelan ornithology. Under the direction of Miguel Lentino, it serves as an invaluable resource for students and professionals, as well as a meeting place and focal point for current ornithological research and conservation efforts. Thanks to Kathleen Phelps, head of the Phelps Foundation, and to Miguel Lentino, this collection has also served as the primary base of research for the present author's work. Other important but smaller collections are maintained at the Universidad Nacional and Universidad La Salle in Caracas, at PROFAUNA in Maracay, and at the Universidad de Zulia in Maracaibo. Numerous Venezuelan ornithologists, among them Carlos Bosque, Miguel Lentino, Luis Gonzalo, and others, are at work at universities and public and private organizations throughout the country today, and their works are acknowledged in this text. The author's own work began in Venezuela in 1975 and continues to the present.

Today, at the onset of the twenty-first century, we are witness to environmental changes that threaten to overwhelm us. Deforestation, water and air pollution, and an expanding population place ever greater burdens on the land and on natural resources. The need for solid biological and ecological information has never been greater because information is the currency of biologists, conservationists, and government policy makers. This book brings together such a base of information for the birds of Venezuela, but it owes its foundation to the efforts of all of the people who have gone before it. Without their collective efforts, spanning nearly two centuries, this guide could never have been written.

Plates

Preface to Plate Notes

The facing-page names and accompanying information mention all native described species in Venezuela, including those not illustrated. In order to compress information into limited space, only the first part of the English name of species in polytypic genera is usually mentioned; likewise the genus is usually designated only by an initial following its introduction. For scientific names, the subspecies mentioned is the one illustrated. If a subspecies is not listed, the species is monotypic.

All illustrated species are numbered; species not illustrated are indicated in bold-face print following a related congener and followed by the word "text" in parentheses. Letters modifying numbers (1a, 2b, etc.) refer to additional plumages (i.e., age, subspecies, color phase, etc.) but not to sexual differences. Gender symbols (σ, φ) are used on the plates to denote sexual differences in plumage. A horizontal line dividing a plate indicates two different size scales.

Following a species' English and scientific names, letters and letter combinations (see below) and a few geographical place names (i.e., Perijá Mts., Andes, etc.) and states (i.e., Amazonas) are used to roughly indicate ranges. If none is indicated, the species is widespread in Venezuela.

- N: generally north of the Río Orinoco
- S: generally south of the Río Orinoco
- E: states of Sucre, Monagas, and Delta Amacuro
- SE: mainly Bolívar state
- N mts.: some or all mts. north of the Río Orinoco
- NE mts.: mts. of Sucre and Monagas
- S Táchira: mts. of southern Táchira state
- Tepuis: mountains south of the Río Orinoco

Definitions

Juv. (juvenal plumage): first true plumage following natal down

Immature: any plumage following the juvenal plumage

N migrant (N migr.): nonresident wintering bird from N Amer.

S migrant (S migr.): nonresident wintering bird from southern S Amer. (also austral migr.)

Overlap: indicates overlap in distributional sense, i.e., range

1. **Highland Tinamou**   *Nothocercus b.*
bonapartei   p. 180
N mts. Fairly large, brown with slaty cap, variable
amt. of buff dotting on rearparts, pale fulvous
throat, rufescent tinge to underparts. Terrestrial;
inside humid mt. forest.

Tinamous   *Tinamus*
Med. to large sized; dark, somber colors; mostly humid lowlands; terrestrial; retiring, suspicious, and
difficult to see; hd. far more than seen. Inside humid
forest.

2. **Gray**   *T. tao septentrionalis*   p. 179
N mts. Large; overall *much grayer* than allies;
dark neck stripe separates white speckling.

3. **Great**   *T. m. major*   p. 179
Large and brownish; few good marks, but note
size, usually pale throat, variable amt. of barring
(sometimes almost none).

Tinamous   *Crypturellus*
Small, mostly lowlands (except 4); terrestrial; often
vocal but challenging to see. Note overall coloration
(grayish, brownish); presence or absence of barring;
color of underparts and legs.

4. **Brown**   *C. obsoletus cerviniventris*   p. 182
N mts. Reddish brown with dark gray head. Less
common than lowland allies.

5. **Little**   *C. soui andrei*   p. 181
Small, quail-sized tinamou; plumage variable but
usually with whitish throat; ♀ brighter rufous
below than ♂.

6. **Undulated**   *C. undulatus manapiare*   p. 183
Amazonas. Grayish brown above with whitish
throat and *gray-tinged underparts;* lacks
good markings, but note wavy bars on
flanks.

7. **Red-legged**   *C. e. erythropus*   p. 184
N. Usually some barring on upperparts (variable
but less in ♂); chest gray, flanks barred, legs
salmon. **Gray-legged** *C. duidae* (text). Amazonas. Sim. to 7 (no overlap) but barring often
faint; head, neck, and breast rufous; lower underparts crisply barred black; legs gray.

8. **Variegated**   *C. v. variegatus*   p. 183
S. Boldly barred black and deep buff above;
most of head black, neck and underparts rufous;
legs grayish olive.

9. **Tawny-breasted Tinamou**   *Nothocercus*
julius   p. 181
S Táchira. Crown chestnut, upperparts barred
black; throat whitish turning bright cinnamon on
lower underparts. Inside humid mt. forest, usually at higher els. than 1.

10. **White-throated Tinamou**   *Tinamus*
guttatus   p. 180
Amazonas. Recalls 3 but smaller; rearparts and
wings thickly dotted buff. Humid lowland forest.

11. **Barred Tinamou**   *Crypturellus*
casiquiare   p. 185
S Amazonas. Handsome but poorly known. *Back
coarsely barred black and rufous*; head rufous,
foreneck and *chest and sides gray*, mid. belly
whitish.

12. **Cinereous Tinamou**   *Crypturellus*
cinereus   p. 181
S. Unmarked smoky gray brown; little contrast
on throat or belly. Low-lying areas near rivers.

13. **Tepui Tinamou**   *Crypturellus*
ptaritepui   p. 182
Tepuis of SE. Small and almost uniformly dark
brown; *white eyes.* Limited distrib.; seldom seen.

14. **Crested Bobwhite**   *Colinus cristatus*
sonnini   p. 265
Plumage variable. Face buff to rufous; ♀ duller,
crest shorter. Common in open country.

Wood-Quail   *Odontophorus*
Larger, more robust than *Colinus*; bushy crest; small
bare ocular area; cryptic plumage; shy forest dwellers;
prs. or groups. Rollicking duets often hd. at dawn.

15. **Black-fronted**   *O. atrifrons navai*   p. 266
Perijá Mts. *Black foreface and throat*; chestnut
crown.

16. **Marbled**   *O. g. gujanensis*   p. 266
Plain with bright orange red ocular area.

17. **Venezuelan**   *O. columbianus*   p. 267
S Táchira; Coastal Cordillera. *White throat*, black
crescent, *white spotted breast.*

Least Grebe and **Pied-billed Grebe**: see figure in
text, page 186.

1. **Magnificent Frigatebird**   *Fregata magnificens*   p. 193
Large, angular, buoyant seabird; long pointed wings, forked tail; long hooked bill. Ad. ♂: black with red gular pouch (inconspic. unless inflated); subad. ♂ may show some white on belly. Ad. ♀: white chest. Imm. has white head and chest.

2. **Brown Pelican**   *Pelecanus occidentalis carolinensis*   p. 191
Familiar bird of seacoasts and isls. Large pouched bill. **2a.** Ad.: mainly gray, black, and brown; head mostly white. **2b.** Imm.: browner above, paler below.

3. **Anhinga**   *Anhinga a. anhinga*   p. 192
Lakes and rivers. Slender, blackish bird with stiletto bill, snakelike neck, long tail. ♂ silvery gray shoulders. ♀ buff brown head, neck, and chest. Imm. duller than ♀. May swim with only head above water. Solitary or prs.

4. **Neotropic Cormorant**   *Phalacrocorax brasilianus olivaceus*   p. 192
Widespread and common. Slender, blackish, and long-necked; narrow hooked bill. Floats low in water. Often in groups. **4a.** Ad. **4b.** Imm.

Boobies   *Sula*
Sleek, aerodynamic seabirds with pointed, angular bill; pointed wings; small wedge-shaped tail. Gregarious, plunge-dive for fish; pelagic but often rest on land. Ads. of most spp. are white, often with black or brown on wings.

5. **Masked**   *S. d. dactylatra*   p. 190
5a. Ad.: white with black flight feathers and tail; ♂ has yellowish bill, ♀ greenish yellow. **5b.** Imm.: brownish above; upper wing coverts and rump whitish; nuchal collar whitish. **Red-footed** *S. sula* (text). *Bluish bill, red legs.* Plumage variable: white with black flight feathers and black wrist; all brown; or with white tail or white head and tail.

6. **Brown**   *S. l. leucogaster*   p. 191
Commonest booby along coast. **6a.** Ad.: brown with *sharply separated white lower underparts*; yellowish bill and feet. **6b.** Imm.: duller.

7. **Pomarine Jaeger**   *Stercorarius pomarinus*   p. 304
Powerfully built seabird with long *"forearm"* and pointed wing tips; smallish, rounded head; fairly heavy bill *pale at base*. **Light-phase ad.:** 2 projecting central tail feathers; pale hindneck and underparts with nearly complete dark chest band; *pale patch at base of primaries*. Rare dark-phase ad. retains pale wing patches and pale bill with dark tip. Imm. (Pl. 19:6), incl. light, dark, and intermed. forms, generally brownish; uniform head and nape and pale barring on upper tail coverts unique; note whitish barring on under wing coverts, bicolored bill. **Parasitic** *S. parasiticus* (text). Ad. like Pomarine but more slender with smaller, all-dark bill and spiky projecting central tail feathers. Rare dark phase not reported in Venez. waters. Imm. illus. Pl. 19(5). **Long-tailed** *S. longicaudus* (text). Like above spp. but a little smaller and slighter and *essentially lacking white under wing patch*. Ad. has stubby black bill, long projecting central tail feathers. Imm. usually gray-toned; tail coverts and under wing coverts crisply barred white (paler than body); often unmarked grayish breast and whitish belly. Presum. rare in Venez. waters.

8. **Red-billed Tropicbird**   *Phaethon aethereus mesonauta*   p. 189
White ternlike seabird with long white tail streamers (hard to see); *black outer primaries*; gray-barred back and upper wing coverts (hard to see); bill red (yellow in 1st-yr imm.). Flight more direct, less buoyant than most terns. Carib. isls.

9. **Audubon's Shearwater**   *Puffinus lherminieri loyemilleri*   p. 188
Small shearwater; short winged and long tailed for genus; dark under tail coverts; up close note dark supraloral spot; at rest wings do not reach tail tips. **Greater** *P. gravis* (text). Large; dark gray above; sharp black cap and tail; white nape and ring over tail; underwings white with dark *"braces"*; thin black bill. **Cory's** *Calonectris diomedea* (text). Large; brownish above, whitish below (unmarked); heavy yellowish bill.

10. **Wilson's Storm-Petrel**   *Oceanites oceanicus*   p. 188
Dark "sea swallow" with *white rump extending to sides of under tail coverts;* feet project behind tail. Few recs. **Leach's** *Oceanodroma leucorhoa* (text). Small white rump often partially divided by dark bar in center; no white on under tail coverts; toes *do not project behind notched tail;* pale carpal bar more extensive than on Wilson's. Rare.

♀

♂

1

2b

2a

3

♀

4b

4a

5b

5a

6a

6b

6a

7

8

9

10

JAGwynne

1. Limpkin *Aramus g. guarauna* p. 279
Brown with white-streaked neck; long legs; slight droop to bill; stiff wing beats with obvious up flick.

2. Glossy Ibis *Plegadis f. falcinellus* p. 219
Long legs project in flight. Usually in flocks. **2a.** Ad.: glossy reddish maroon; no red facial skin; nonbreeding ad. duller. **2b.** Imm.: brownish flecked white.

3. Scarlet Ibis *Eudocimus ruber* p. 219
Imm. rump and belly white in 1st yr; pinkish by start of 2d yr. Ad. (Pl. 4:13) all deep scarlet with black wing tips.

4. Buff-necked Ibis *Theristicus c. caudatus* p. 216
Dry-land ibis. Buff neck; large whitish wing patch. Mostly in prs. or 3–4.

5. Green Ibis *Mesembrinibis cayennensis* p. 217
Solitary in or near forested streams. Dull, chunky, short-legged; bushy hackles on rear of neck; dark oily green iridescence shows only in good light.

6. Bare-faced (Whispering) Ibis *Phimosus berlepschi infuscatus* p. 217
Small and short-legged (in flight legs do not project behind tail); facial skin and bill dull pinkish. Often in flocks.

7. Sharp-tailed Ibis *Cercibis oxycerca* p. 217
Large, lumbering ibis; long tail, short legs; facial skin bright red; malar patch orange. Prs. or 3s (not flocks).

8. Orinoco Goose *Neochen jubata* p. 196
Large and chesty; whitish foreparts, rufous rearparts; white wing speculum conspic. in flight. Prs. walk with proud, upright attitude.

9. Masked Duck *Nomonyx dominicus* p. 204
Small, secretive duck. ♂ has bright blue bill; ♀ has double-striped facial pattern. Both show white wing patch in flight.

10. Brazilian Teal *Amazonetta b. brasiliensis* p. 203
Dull at rest but can be striking in flight. *Iridescent greenish black wings and white speculum;* ♂ has *dull reddish bill,* pale face, raspberry legs; ♀ has spotted head. Mostly prs. but often with whistling-ducks and waders.

11. Blue-winged Teal *Anas discors* p. 200
N migr. Pale blue shoulders in flight. ♂ has white crescent on face, white patch near rear end. ♀ has pale foreface, spotted sides. N migrs. (text): **American Wigeon** *A. americana;* **Northern Pintail** *A. acuta;* **Northern Shoveler** *A. clypeata;* **Ring-necked Duck** *Aythya collaris.*

12. Andean Teal *Anas andium altipetens* p. 199
Andes. Darker and grayer than ♀ 11; buff-edged wing speculum; speckling not obvious at distance. Paramo lakes. **Cinnamon** *A. cyanoptera* (text). Accidental from Colombia.

13. White-cheeked Pintail *Anas b. bahamensis* p. 200
Coastal lagoons; mangroves. Dapper and clean-cut; red on bill; sharp white cheeks; pointed buff tail. Sexes sim.

14. Torrent Duck *Merganetta armata colombiana* p. 198
Andean streams. Sexes very different; both inconspic. when swimming. Juv. like ♂ but dull gray above, no neck stripes. Alone or prs.; loafs on boulders in rushing streams.

Whistling-Ducks *Dendrocygna*
Large and gangly; long necks and long legs; erect posture. Gregarious; often active at night.

15. Black-bellied *D. autumnalis discolor* p. 196
Bright rosy bill, black belly, *large white wing patch.* Juv. has much duller bill and plumage.

16. White-faced *D. viduata* p. 195
White face (often dirty); all dark in flight.

17. Fulvous *D. bicolor* p. 195
Tawny buff with white fringes on side; in flight white ring at base of tail; no white on wings. Uncommon and declining.

Southern Pochard, Lesser Scaup, Muscovy Duck, Comb Duck: see figures in text, pages 198 and 202.

1. American Flamingo   *Phoenicopterus r.*
ruber   p. 204
Familiar coastal sp.; tall, slender, elegant, pink; in
flight note black wing tips on wings that seem
too small. Imm. grayish above, buff tinge on
head and neck, dull white below; bill grayish
with black tip. Subad. whitish with pink blush;
bill pale with black tip.
2. Black-crowned Night-Heron   *Nycticorax*
nycticorax hoactli   p. 214
Also Pl. 5(2). **2a.** Ad.: crown and *entire back*
black; wings grayish, below whitish; strong,
pointed black bill. **2b.** Imm.: *large white spots on*
wing coverts, broad blurry streaking below;
heavy, pointed bill mostly greenish yellow to
yellowish.
3. Yellow-crowned Night-Heron
Nyctanassa violacea cayennensis   p. 215
Also Pl. 5(1). **3a.** Ad.: bold head pattern, white
cheeks, iron gray body. **3b.** Imm.: like 2b but
darker, white spots on wing coverts tiny; streaks
on underparts narrower; *bill black.*
4. Reddish Egret   *Egretta r. rufescens*   p. 210
4a. Dark-morph ad.: pinkish rust foreparts, gray
body; dark legs; pink bill with black tip. Dark juv.
chalky gray with tinge of rusty; bill and lores all
dark. 2d-yr imm. like ad. but bill variable, usually
with some pink; lores dark. **4b.** White-morph ad.:
all white with gray legs; bill pink with black tip;
white juv. has dark legs, bill, and lores; imm. (2d
yr) like juv. but shows some pink on bill.

Herons   *Ardea*
Long neck and long legs; overall larger and more robust than *Egretta*, bill heavier. Stand or wade slowly;
mostly solitary when foraging (but 6 sometimes gregarious); breed in colonies.
5. Cocoi   *A. cocoi*   p. 208
Crown and sides of head black, *neck and breast*
white; *thighs gray to whitish;* in flight upper wing
coverts extensively white. Imm. much duller.
Great Blue *A. herodias* (text). Much like 5, esp.
imm., but duller, neck and upper breast always
grayish, *thighs tinged rufous* incl. juv. of 1st yr.
6. Great Egret   *A. alba egretta*   p. 209
Black legs, long yellow bill. Young birds sim.
7. Cattle Egret   *Bubulcus i. ibis*   p. 211
Stout yellow bill, thick neck, dusky legs. Bill orange yellow and legs reddish when breeding.
Young birds show mostly dark bill, but note
body shape and behavior.

Egrets   *Egretta*
Smaller and generally more slender than *Ardea;* more
likely to be gregarious; some forage in active manner.
8. Snowy   *E. t. thula*   p. 210
Ad.: black bill, yellow lores, blackish legs with
pale yellow feet. Imm. (2d yr) like ad. but lower
mandible may show some yellow; legs greenish
with black on forepart of legs. Juv. (1st yr) has
bill dull yellow with dusky tip; lores dull yellow
green; legs dirty green.

9. Little Blue Heron   *E. caerulea*   p. 210
9a. Ad.: bicolored bill, dull greenish legs. **9b.**
Imm.: white; bill usually as in ad. but duller and
paler, occas. pinkish; older imms. mottled or
pied dark gray and white; bill obviously bicolored but still paler than ad.
10. Tricolored Heron   *E. tricolor ruficollis*   p. 211
Also Pl. 5(13). White belly and wing linings.
Breeding ad.: bill gray with dusky tip. Nonbreeding ad.: has bill yellowish. Juv. (1st yr) may show
rusty on neck and shoulders; old imms. more
like ad.
11. Roseate Spoonbill   *Ajaia ajaja*   p. 220
Spatulate bill distinctive. **11a.** Ad.: quite pink;
deep red shoulders. **11b.** Juv.: nearly white with
dusky on wing tips; 2d-yr birds pinkish but lack
red shoulders and black on head.

Ibises   *Eudocimus*
Larger, heavier, and bill thicker than in many allies.
12. White   *E. alba*   p. 218
12a. Ad. **12b.** Imm. (1st yr): brown; rump and
underparts mostly white; neck streaked brown
and white; bill and legs dull red; by beginning of
2d yr plumage mostly white; wings and neck
brownish. Juv. (not shown) dark brown with
white belly and underwings.
13. Scarlet   *E. ruber*   p. 219
13a. Ad. **13b.** Imm.: stages sim. to those of 12.
Acquires pinkish rump and abdomen by beginning of 2d yr. Imm. also Pl. 3(3).

Storks   *Euxenura, Jabiru,* and *Mycteria*
Large and long-legged; long, heavy neck; rather slow
moving but wary; all with bare heads and heavy,
slightly upturned bill (or slightly downturned—
Mycteria).
14. Maguari Stork   *Euxenura maguari*   p. 221
Large and white; *black on shoulders and flight*
feathers; basal half of bill and facial skin orange
red; yellow eyes. Notably solitary.
15. Jabirú   *Jabiru mycteria*   p. 221
Largest wader in Venez.; *all-white wings;* bare
black head; red ring at base of inflated bare
neck. Prs. or varying-sized groups.
16. Wood Stork   *Mycteria americana*   p. 220
Ad. white with *black flight feathers;* bare grayish
to blackish head. Imm. dull brownish and
homely. Often gregarious.

4

1. **Yellow-crowned Night-Heron**
   Nyctanassa violacea cayennensis   p. 215
   Ad.: bold head pattern, white cheeks. Ad. and
   imm. also Pl. 4(3).
2. **Black-crowned Night-Heron**   *Nycticorax*
   nycticorax hoactli   p. 214
   Ad.: black cap and back; underparts all white.
   Also Pl. 4(2). Often abroad by day, esp. imms.
3. **Boat-billed Heron**   *Cochlearius c.*
   cochlearius   p. 215
   Ad. *mainly white;* crown and band across upper
   mantle black; forehead broadly white; *belly
   chestnut;* thick, broad bill. Strictly nocturnal
   when foraging. Roosts by day in colonies in trees
   near water.
4. **Capped Heron**   *Pilherodius pileatus*   p. 214
   Baby blue facial skin and bill; black topknot and
   "French vanilla" tinge to foreparts. Imm. lacks
   buff tinge; facial color duller. Solitary when
   foraging.

Tiger-Herons   *Tigrisoma*
Named for bold "tiger barring" of imm. plumages;
heavy, sharp-pointed bills; rather short legs. Mostly
solitary or prs.

5. **Fasciated**   *T. fasciatum salmoni*   p. 208
   Ad. mainly dark gray; fine etchlike barring on
   upperparts hard to see. Imm. almost identical to
   better known 6 but bill stouter, underparts whiter
   and less barred. *Only foothill rivers.*
6. **Rufescent**   *T. l. lineatum*   p. 207
   Somewhat bitternlike. **6a.** Ad.: rufescent
   foreparts; finely barred rearparts. **6b.** Imm.: bold
   buff and black barring on upperparts (cf. 5 and
   7). Widespread in lowlands, esp. llanos.
7. **Pinnated Bittern**   *Botaurus p. pinnatus* p. 205
   From imms. of 5 and 6 by streaking on back,
   dense streak-like barring on wings. Note dusky
   cap, fine buff barring on long, thick neck. Blackish flight feathers. Marshes.
8. **Stripe-backed Bittern**   *Ixobrychus*
   involucris   p. 206
   Small and seldom seen. Larger and decidedly
   paler than 9; grayish buff with bold black-striped
   back. Note small black cap, buff-tipped wings.

9. **Least Bittern**   *Ixobrychus exilis*
   erythromelas   p. 206
   N. Shape of 8 but more richly colored and a bit
   smaller; sides of head and neck pale rufous;
   back solid black (♂) or chestnut (♀), *large contrasting buff shoulder patch;* flight feathers black;
   no buff tips. Local.
10. **Striated Heron**   *Butorides striatus*   p. 212
    Small, chunky, and common. Short legs. **10a.**
    Ad.: *obviously gray foreparts* and contrasting
    shaggy black crown. **10b.** Imm.: duller; some-
    what streaked below; not as obviously gray as
    ad. **Green** *B. virescens* (text). N migr. Sim. shape
    but dark maroon rufous neck and foreparts.
    Imm. in youngest stage probably indistinguish-
    able from imm. 10; older imms. show brownish
    to dull rufous on neck and foreparts; somewhat
    streaky below; wing coverts pale edged.
11. **Zigzag Heron**   *Zebrilus undulatus*   p. 207
    Small and secretive. Chunky shape. **11a.** Ad.:
    sooty above with fine buff barring; below paler,
    more buff densely vermiculated black. **11b.**
    Imm.: foreparts strongly rufous, barring dark ru-
    fous. Swampy or seasonally flooded places in-
    side forest.
12. **Whistling Heron**   *Syrigma sibilatrix*
    fostersmithi   p. 213
    Colorful face; buff neck; wing patches; white
    rump and tail conspic. in flight. Dry to damp
    grasslands of llanos.
13. **Tricolored Heron**   *Egretta tricolor*
    ruficollis   p. 211
    Coastal. Contrasting white belly and wing lin-
    ings. Long bill, thin neck. Also Pl. 4(10).
14. **Agami Heron**   *Agamia agami*   p. 213
    Slow and stealthy; *unusually long stiletto-like bill.*
    14a. Ad.: breathtaking in favorable light; wispy
    blue neck plumes highlight bottle green and
    chestnut plumage. **14b.** Imm.: duller, somewhat
    brownish. Retiring and difficult to find in shad-
    ows of vegetation-covered lagoon and stream
    edges.

5

1. **Yellow-headed Caracara** *Milvago*
chimachima cordatus p. 251
1a. Ad.: creamy head and underparts; whitish
wing patches in flight. **1b.** Imm.: recalls imm. of
7. Note slighter build, pale wing patches, profusion of blurry streaks, esp. on very young birds
which are dingy, mainly brown. In flight Pl. 8(7).

2. **Plumbeous Kite** *Ictinia plumbea* p. 230
Short legged; long pointed wings extend beyond
tail; up close note reddish eyes, orange legs, rufous in wings, white tail band from below. Ad. in
flight and perched imm. Pl. 14(4).

Vultures *Cathartes*
Blackish with bare, colored head; longish narrow tail.
Flight silhouettes Pl. 8

3. **Turkey** *C. aura ruficollis* p. 223
Bare reddish head with white nape patch (resi-
dent race); solid red head (N migr. *meridionalis*).
In flight Pl. 8(4). **Black** *Coragyps atratus* Pl. 8(2).

4. **Lesser Yellow-headed** *C. b.*
burrovianus p. 224
Bare dull yellow head tinged blue on crown, orange on front and sides. Damp grassland. In
flight Pl. 8(5).

5. **Greater Yellow-headed** *C.*
melambrotus p. 224
Larger and blacker than 4 and head brighter,
contrasting yellow. Always near or over humid
forest. In flight Pl. 8(6).

6. **Laughing Falcon** *Herpetotheres c.*
cachinnans p. 254
"Panda Bear" face, short legs, long tail. Sits motionless and looks downward. Loud, rhythmic,
long-sustained call.

7. **Gray Hawk** *Buteo n. nitidus* p. 240
Imm. buffier on head and underparts than allies;
spotting bold; bold wing patches in flight. Ad.
Pl. 7(6), in flight Pl. 9(5).

8. **Slate-colored Hawk** *Leucopternis*
schistacea p. 234
S. Chunky, gray, unsuspicious hawk of swampy
backwaters; red orange cere, orbit, and legs.
Short tail has 1 band; eyes yellow. Ad. in flight
Pl. 10(4).

9. **Crane Hawk** *Geranospiza c.*
caerulescens p. 232
Acrobatic, "double-jointed" hawk of open or
forested regions. Long orange red legs, long 2-
banded tail; gray cere; ruby eyes. Narrow white
crescent on underside of primaries from below.
Ad. in flight Pl. 10(1).

10. **Collared Forest-Falcon** *Micrastur s.*
semitorquatus p. 253
Imm. whitish, tawny, or dark below; note facial
pattern, collar, coarse barring below; long tail.
Ad. bust Pl. 7(14); dark phase in flight Pl. 13(1).

11. **Snail Kite** *Rostrhamus s. sociabilis* p. 228
Marsh dweller with thin sicklelike bill. **11a.** Ad.
♂: *large white base to square tail,* narrow white
tip; *red orange cere, orbit, and legs.* **11b.** Imm.:
brown, *heavily streaked below;* tail as in ♂; soft
parts duller. ♀ sim. to imm. but less streaky below; soft parts brighter. ♂ and imm. in flight
Pl. 10(6).

12. **Slender-billed Kite** *Helicolestes*
hamatus p. 228
Locally distrib. swamp dweller. Recalls 11 but *all
gray with white eyes.* Sexes sim. Imm. Pl. 10(5).

13. **Hook-billed Kite** *Chondrohierax u.*
uncinatus p. 226
13a. Ad.: *overly large hooked bill; yellow to
greenish supraloral spot and whitish eyes* impart
peculiar vacuous look. Note short legs. ♂ usually grayish; ♀ brownish to rusty. **13b.** Dark
phase (both sexes blackish); rare. In flight
Pl. 10(2). Normal-phase ad. ♀ Pl. 9(8).

14. **Rufous Crab-Hawk** *Buteogallus*
aequinoctialis p. 236
NE coast. Miniature of 16 but much *darker, grayer
above;* note *all-gray head and throat;* limited
white in tail; richer soft-part colors. Mangroves.

15. **Harris's Hawk** *Parabuteo u. unicinctus* p. 238
Rufous shoulder and thighs; white at base and
tip of tail (above and below); mostly dry semiopen country. Imm. in flight Pl. 10(8).

16. **Savanna Hawk** *Buteogallus*
meridionalis p. 236
Sluggish, mostly rufous hawk of open country;
notably long-legged; *wings unusually long and
broad;* tail short and narrow. Imm. in flight Pl.
11(3).

17. **Black-collared Hawk** *Busarellus n.*
nigricollis p. 238
Fishing hawk with broad wings and short,
fanned tail. Ad. rufous with whitish head and
black bow tie; black flight feathers. Imm. dull
brown, streaky, and confusing, but note shape as
in ad. Near water. Imm. in flight Pl. 11(4).

6

Falcons *Falco*

1. Bat *F. r. rufigularis* p. 256
Small, dark; perches on high stubs; wide black vest finely barred white; rufous lower underparts. Imm. duller below; thighs barred but usually a suggestion of vest. Ad. in flight Pl. 14(9).

2. Orange-breasted *F. deiroleucus* p. 256
Rare (spotty). Compared to 1, black on breast narrower, more U-shaped across top, *white barring coarser,* crissum barred black; feet larger, head larger and more squarish, torso longer. Overall larger (esp. ♀); throat always white; wings extend to tip of tail. See text.

3. Aplomado *F. f. femoralis* p. 256
Open terrain. Fairly large but slender and long-tailed. *White headband; dark moustache; narrow vest.* In flight shows *white on trailing edge of wing.* Imm. darker above, streaky below, vest lacking or incomplete; belly and thighs tawny. In flight Pl. 14(8).

4. American Kestrel *F. sparverius isabellinus* p. 255
Small, slender falcon with longish tail. Bold face pattern, rufous back and tail. ♂ has bluish wings; ♀ barred above, somewhat streaked on breast. ♂ in flight Pl. 14(11).

5. Pearl Kite *Gampsonyx swainsonii leonae* p. 227
Tiny, almost toylike kite with speedy flight and open-country habits; mainly black above, white below; tinge of cream on cheeks, dark pectoral patch, rufous thighs. In flight Pl. 14(6).

Hawks *Buteo*

Small to med.-sized raptors; fairly broad wings and tail; barred underparts and banded tails in ad.

6. Gray *B. n. nitidus* p. 240
Obviously gray with *blackish eyes;* entirely barred below; faintly barred above (inconspic.); contrasting black and white banded tail. Note narrow white inner band. Imm. Pl. 6(7); ad. in flight Pl. 9(5).

7. Roadside *B. m. magnirostris* p. 241
Handsome little hawk, ad. usually darker (in Venez.) than 6. Mostly unbarred gray brown chest, rufous in wings; uniform tail bands. Commonest raptor in Venez. Ad. in flight Pl. 9(7a); imm. Pl. 9(7b).

8. Broad-winged *B. p. platypterus* p. 242
N migr. Ad. brown above (cf. 6 and 7); entirely barred rusty below; quite pale then below in flight (see Pl. 9:6). N migrs. (text): **Swainson's** *B. swainsoni;* **Red-tailed** *B. jamaicensis.*

9. Double-toothed Kite *Harpagus b. bidentatus* p. 229
Small with *1 black throat stripe;* rufous chest (more extensive in ♀) becomes barred below; short legs; *long, fluffy white under tail covert feathers protrude on sides of tail;* longish tail. In flight Pl. 9(9). **Rufous-thighed** *H. diodon* (text). S migr.

Hawks *Accipiter*

At rest likely to sit somewhat hunched; note long tail; *lack* bare facial skin of *Micrastur.*

10. Bicolored *A. b. bicolor* p. 233
Never barred below. **10a.** Ad.: light to dark gray below; *note rufous thighs.* **10b.** Imm.: variable; whitish to rufous below, usually with pale collar; thighs often darker.

11. Plain-breasted *A. ventralis* p. 232
Dark gray above; highly variable below; all have rufous thighs. **11a.** Ad.: coarsely barred rufous and white below. **11b.** Ad.: mainly white below. Others may be mostly dark chestnut below (sim. to 11c but without streaky effect) or melanistic. **11c.** Dark-morph imm. In flight Pl. 9(10).

12. Gray-bellied *A. poliogaster* p. 234
12a. Ad.: closely resembles 10 but larger, underparts usually lighter gray, cheeks darker, no rufous thighs. **12b.** Imm.: remarkably like larger Ornate Hawk-Eagle but note *bare (not feathered) legs, absence of crest.*

13. Tiny *A. s. superciliosus* p. 233
Tiny forest *Accipiter.* **13a.** Ad.: *ruby eyes, fine barring* below in all plumages (cf. *Micrastur*). Rufous phase (rare) mostly rufescent above; barring rusty. **13b.** Imm.: occurs in normal brown phase and less numerous rufous phase. Best told by tiny size. **Semicollared** *A. collaris* (text). N mts. Rare montane *Accipiter.* Ad. much like 13a but somewhat larger; eyes yellow (not red). Imm. much like 13b but larger.

Forest-Falcons *Micrastur*

Recall *Accipiter* but all with *extensive bare facial skin* surrounding eyes; roundish head, tail also somewhat rounded; fairly long legs; rounded wings; *long, narrowly banded tail;* stealthy but often vocal.

14. Collared *M. s. semitorquatus* p. 253
Largest in genus. Greenish facial skin. Ad.: white collar and underparts; prom. black crescent below eyes. Tawny- and dark-phase darker below respectively. Imm. Pl. 6(10). **Buckley's** *M. buckleyi* (text). Like 14 but has 4 instead of 6 white tail bands; voice differs; smaller in size.

15. Slaty-backed *M. mirandollei* p. 252
S. Confusing. Ad.: *fairly large;* uniform gray cheeks; no pale collar; yellowish facial skin; underparts unmarked white (cf. 12 and 14). Imm. scaled or streaked below (not barred).

16. Lined *M. gilvicollis* p. 252
S. Much like 17 but no rufous phase. Note *white eyes, red orange facial skin, and vocal differences.* In Venez. known primarily from lowland forest s of Orinoco (17 mainly in N mts). Imm. much like imm. of 17.

17. Barred *M. ruficollis zonothorax* p. 251
Mainly N mts. **17a.** Ad.: *rich yellow facial skin; dark red eyes* (all areas?); finely barred underparts; narrow white tail bands (cf. *Accipiter*). Rufous phase, with rufous barred underparts, not reported in Venez. but possible. **17b.** Imm.: pale collar, widely spaced barring; pale buff below, less often darker buff.

7

1. **Osprey**   *Pandion haliaetus carolinensis*   p. 225
   N migr., but some individuals present yr-round;
   large size, crooked wings, whitish underparts
   with black "wrists"; labored flapping flight. All
   els.; usually near water.
2. **Black Vulture**   *Coragyps atratus
   brasiliensis*   p. 223
   Widespread and common in settled areas. Broad
   wings angle forward; whitish patch at base of primaries; tail very short (almost tail-less). May alternate flapping with gliding.
3. **King Vulture**   *Sarcoramphus papa*   p. 222
   Long broad wings white with black flight feathers (cf. Wood Stork) and black tail; bare, highly
   colored, wattled head best seen up close. Solitary; soaring steady, often very high. Imm. mainly
   dusky brown; older imms. show paler or dingy
   whitish wing linings echoing ad. pattern.

Vultures   *Cathartes*
Tail relatively long; wings long; bare colored head appears neckless; most spp. hold wings up in slight V;
flight tippy (4 and 5) or more steady (6).

4. **Turkey**   *C. aura*   p. 224
   Upper wing (shown). 2-toned underwings as in
   5; from above *primary quills not obviously pale;*
   head dull red (dusky—imm.) with small but
   conspic. *white patch on bare nape* (or no white
   on nape—N migrs.); soars high, infreq. low,
   often teeters, appearing unsteady. N migrs.
   commonest in llanos. Head (resident subsp.)
   Pl. 6(3).
5. **Lesser Yellow-headed**   *C. b.
   burrovianus*   p. 224
   5a. Upperwing: whitish primary quills from
   above. **5b.** Ad.: mostly dull yellow head (often
   not obvious at a distance); plumage duller, more
   faded than 4. Imm. even duller than ad.; head
   dusky. Soars low over damp grassland and
   marshes, also over dry fields. Flight notably tippy.
   Head Pl. 6(4).

6. **Greater Yellow-headed**
   C. melambrotus   p. 224
   S. **6a.** Upperwing: whitish primary quills from
   above. **6b.** Ad.: larger and much deeper black
   than 4 or 5; flight feathers not as pale and contrasting; from below *several blackish inner primaries* form obscure dark zone (distinctive once
   learned); head deep yellow (dusky—imm.).
   Flight steadier than 4 or 5. Head Pl. 6(5). **Andean Condor** *Vultur gryphus* (text). See figure
   in text.
7. **Yellow-headed Caracara**   *Milvago
   chimachima cordatus*   p. 251
   Smaller and more lightly built than 8 but in flight
   shows sim. pale areas on wings and rump. Note
   pale head and underparts. Perched Pl. 6(1).
8. **Northern Crested-Caracara**   *Caracara
   c. cheriway*   p. 250
   Numerous in grasslands. Robust with fairly long
   neck and legs. **8a.** Ad.: *bare red face* (skin color
   somewhat changeable); bushy crest, thighs, and
   lower underparts black. **8b.** Imm.: whitish areas
   replaced by buff, blackish areas by brown; mantle and neck somewhat streaked.

Caracaras   *Daptrius* and *Ibycter*
Mainly black, forest-based caracaras with bare skin
on face and throat. *Ibycter* is larger, heavier, broader-
winged, also differs in diet and social behavior.

9. **Black**   *Daptrius ater*   p. 249
   Lanky with narrow white rump band; facial skin
   bright red orange. Imm. has yellowish facial skin,
   barring on white tail band.
10. **Red-throated**   *Ibycter americanus*   p. 250
    Belly and crissum white; facial skin dull reddish,
    less extensive than 9; cere gray, bill yellowish; ro-
    bust shape with roundish wings; travels in
    groups; voice extremely loud and raucous.

8

Hawks *Buteo*
In general chunky with broad wings and broad, moderate-length tail. Often soar; more often seen aloft than perched. Forest or open country.

1. Zone-tailed *B. albonotatus*   p. 243
Imm. spotted below; long, parallel-width, 2-toned wings; longish tail; soars with dihedral and tilting, closely mimicking *Cathartes* vultures. Ad. Pl. 10(3).

2. Short-tailed *B. b. brachyurus*   p. 242
Compact with fairly short fanned tail. **2a.** Light-phase ad.: mostly white underwings contrast with dark flight feathers and dark "hood" over head. Usually seen soaring, rarely perched. All ads. have small inconspic. white foreheads. **2b.** Dark-phase ad.: reverse image of light phase; black with pale flight feathers.

3. White-throated *B. albigula*   p. 243
Andes. Rare *Buteo* of high mts. Rather small, compact, short-tailed. Dark hooded look to head; blackish armpits; overall streaky, esp. sides of body; some rusty on thighs. Imm. like imm. of 2 but streakier on sides; no range overlap.

4. White-rumped *B. leucorrhous*   p. 241
N mts. Ad.: small, short-winged *Buteo*; pale wing linings contrast sharply with blackish flight feathers; white rump can be difficult to see. Imm. streaked on head, mottled tawny below; wing linings barred; chestnut thighs as in ad.

5. Gray *B. n. nitidus*   p. 240
Ad.: (also Pl. 7:6) pale gray with sharply contrasting black and white banded tail. Imm. (Pl. 6:7) has head and underparts buff boldly spotted and marked with black.

6. Broad-winged *B. p. platypterus*   p. 242
Chunky with broad, fanned tail. **6a.** Ad. (also Pl. 7:8): underwing mostly whitish; underparts densely barred rusty; contrasting black and white banded tail. **6b.** Imm.: streaky below, underwings flecked and barred more than ad.; tail with numerous narrow bars. Listen for high thin whistle.

7. Roadside *B. magnirostris insidiatrix*   p. 241
Small *Buteo*; rather long tailed for genus. **7a.** Ad. (also Pl. 7:7): grayish above and on chest; bars on breast; eyes and cere yellow; rufous patch on base of primaries conspic. in flight from above or below. **7b.** Imm.: differs from allies in streaks on chest and some barring on lower breast; prom. whitish eyebrow; broad but sometimes poorly defined dusky malar.

8. Hook-billed Kite *Chondrohierax u. uncinatus*   p. 226
Normal-phase ad. ♀ (flying ♂ and dark phase Pl. 10:2) below barred like many allies; note lanky shape; *long-projecting head;* boldly barred wings *rounded and broad at tip, narrowed at base;* long tail; underparts barred rufous; up close pale eye and supraloral spot. Also ♂ and ♀ Pl. 6(13).

9. Double-toothed Kite *Harpagus b. bidentatus*   p. 229
Small; secondaries broad but rear edge of wing angled inward and narrowed at base; tail long. **9a.** Ad.: rufous on chest; *fluffy white under tail coverts protrude on sides* (visible from above). **9b.** Imm.: streaked below. Ad. ♂ and ♀ also Pl. 7(9).

10. Plain-breasted Hawk *Accipiter ventralis*   p. 232
Relatively short wings and long, square-tipped tail typical of genus; occas. soars for short periods, but usually in or near cover. Also Pl. 7(11).

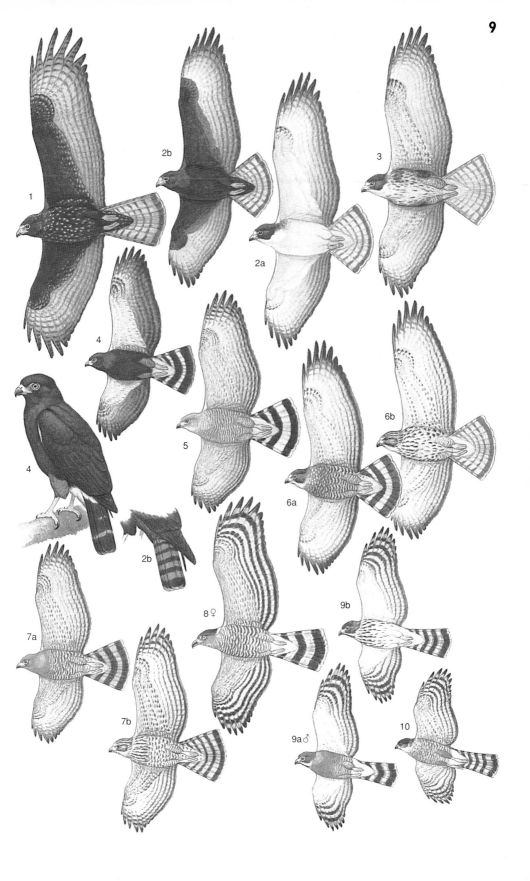

9

1. **Crane Hawk**   *Geranospiza c.*
   caerulescens   p. 232
   Lanky and nimble raptor. Ad. dark bluish gray;
   long orange red legs; gray cere; ruby eyes; white
   underwing crescent conspic. in flight; long tail.
   Imm. (not shown) brownish but *underwings and
   tail much like ad.*; below heavily streaked; lower
   underparts mottled and banded paler. Perched
   ad. Pl. 6(9).

2. **Hook-billed Kite**   *Chondrohierax u.*
   uncinatus   p. 226
   Long oval wings, long narrow tail. **2a.** Ad.: complex plumage (text) but ♂ usually grayish,
   ♀ brownish. In all plumages note unusually long
   hooked bill, pale supraloral spot, pale eyes. **2b.**
   Rare black-phase ad.: mostly dark below with 1
   broad tail band. ♀ in flight Pl. 9(8); perched
   ads. Pl. 6(13).

3. **Zone-tailed Hawk**   *Buteo albonotatus*   p. 243
   Ad.: 2-toned wings held in dihedral and teetering
   flight recall Turkey Vulture. Cf. heavier black-
   hawks Pl. 11(5–6) and dark-phase Short-tailed
   Hawk Pl 9(2). Imm. in flight Pl. 9(1).

4. **Slate-colored Hawk**   *Leucopternis*
   schistacea   p. 234
   Amazonas. Imm. resembles ad., incl. red soft
   parts and yellow eyes, but with close whitish barring on wing linings and lower underparts, often
   a 2d white tail band. Perched ad. Pl. 6(8).

5. **Slender-billed Kite**   *Helicolestes*
   hamatus   p. 228
   Imm. resembles ad., incl. broad wings, red soft
   parts, and white eyes, but shows weak white barring on flight feathers, 2 narrow tail bands visible
   on short, square tail. Swampy terrain. Perched
   ad. Pl. 6(12).

6. **Snail Kite**   *Rostrhamus s. sociabilis*   p. 228
   6a. Ad. ♂: recalls 5 but longer winged, longer
   tailed, lankier in shape. All plumages told by
   thin hooked bill, red cere and legs, white tail
   base. **6b.** Imm.: brownish above; heavily streaked
   below; rump and tail as in ♂. ♀ like imm. but
   darker brown above, less streaked below.
   Perched ad. ♂ and imm. Pl. 6(11).

7. **Gray-headed Kite**   *Leptodon*
   c. cayanensis   p. 225
   Dark-phase imm. confusing and infreq. seen.
   Head and upperparts usually dark, underparts
   broadly streaked, outer primaries barred. Note
   small head, bluntly rounded wings. Ad. and
   light-phase imm. perched and flying Pl. 12(4).

8. **Harris's Hawk**   *Parabuteo u. unicinctus*   p. 238
   Imm. dark and somewhat buteonine in shape
   but wings and tail longer; flight feathers dark
   above with chestnut shoulders; from below
   shows large pale window on outer primaries and
   dark wing linings mixed chestnut and sooty; underparts heavily mottled sooty and whitish; tail
   grayish to dusky, finely barred, broad base and
   narrow tip whitish; often soars. Perched ad.
   Pl. 6(15).

9. **Long-winged Harrier**   *Circus buffoni*   p. 231
   9a. Ad. ♀: slender with long wings and long narrow tail. **9b.** Dark-phase imm.: harrier shape variable depending on behavior, ranging from almost buteonine when soaring to falconlike when
   gliding with wings bent back. Note owl-like facial disk. All plumages show some white on
   rump and multibanded tail. Dark-phase ad. ♀
   shows pale gray window on upper flight feathers, dark chest, pale lower underparts. Imms. resemble respective ads. but are heavily streaked
   below with light or dark according to phase.
   Northern *C. cyaneus* (text). Accidental N migr.

10

Large, long-legged, heavily built raptors of mostly open terrain (except 7). Short tailed, sluggish when perched, but reg. soar.

I. Black-chested Buzzard-Eagle
Geranoaetus melanoleucus australis   p. 239
Andes. Imm. longer tailed than ad.; tail wedge-shaped. Streaked and mottled plumage confusing, but note large size, paramo habitat, long primaries. Legs not long. Ad. flying Pl. 14(1).

2. White-tailed Hawk   *Buteo albicaudatus*
colonus   p. 244
Large, pale raptor of grasslands and open terrain. **2a.** Light-phase ad.: slate above, incl. *"hooded effect"* on head, with rufous shoulders; white wing linings contrast; *tail all white above and below* with narrow black subterminal band. Cf. light-phase Short-tailed Hawk. Dark-phase birds (not shown) common in se Bolívar; usually show rufous on shoulders; *white tail as above*. **2b.** Imm.: mottled and variable, but look for some rufous on shoulders, whitish on tail; wing linings darker than flight feathers.

3. Savanna Hawk   *Buteogallus meridionalis* p. 236
Imm. predom. buff and variably mottled with dusky above and below (text); older imms., at least, usually show some rufous; note *long pale yellow legs*, prom. eyebrow on older imms. Ad. mainly rufous; unusually long, broad wings and short, narrow tail in all plumages. Grasslands and open terrain. Perched ad. Pl. 6(16).

4. Black-collared Hawk   *Busarellus n.*
nigricollis   p. 238
Exceptionally broad winged, short tailed; usually near water. Imm. mostly dark buff *streaked and blotched with black; patchiness* of black on underparts sometimes a good mark; most individuals show slightly paler head, hint of black collar; in flight note *contrasting blackish outer wing*; only older imms. show rufous in plumage.

Perched ad. Pl. 6(17) mainly rufous with creamy white head.

Black-Hawks, etc.   *Buteogallus*
Strong, heavily built raptors; broad rounded wings, short fanned tail; 2 spp. (in Venez.) mainly black with yellow cere and white at base of tail; 2 others mainly rufous. Most spend considerable time on or near gd.

5. Common   *B. a. anthracinus*   p. 237
Mostly near coast. Ad. all black; note *rich butter yellow cere, single median white tail band* and narrow tip; up close faint white barring on thighs. Imm. very different and much like imm. of 6; mainly brownish to dark buff heavily mottled and streaked blackish; buff eyebrow; tail has *5–8 narrow blackish bars* and broader subterminal band (cf. 6b).

6. Great   *B. u. urubitinga*   p. 237
Larger and more "common" than 5 and with very different voice (text); *legs much longer*, tail longer. **6a.** Ad.: *cere usually dull yellow* (color variable, sometimes quite dull); basal half of tail and upper tail coverts white. Widespread and common across central grasslands. **6b.** Imm.: much like respective ages of 5 but note larger size, *long legs*, tail with many more narrow blackish bars (10–14).

7. Solitary Eagle   *Harpyhaliaetus s.*
solitarius   p. 239
Superficially like 5 and 6 but with massive, eagle-like proportions. Enormously broad wings; short fanned tail barely protrudes behind wings (much shorter and more fanned than shown). Look for projecting aquiline head (bushy crest up close), narrow median tail band, and *slate gray* (not black) plumage. Imm. very dark, mottled and blotched black and buff below, some individuals almost solid black on chest.

11

1 imm

2a

2b

3

4 imm

5

6a

6b

5

6a

7

Generally long-tailed forest raptors, dark gray to black-ish above; usually white or nearly white below. Most reg. soar (except 2). Also cf. Laughing Falcon on Pl. 6(6) and various forest-falcons on Pl. 7(14–17), most of which are smaller.

Hawks   *Leucopternis*
Chunky and *Buteo*-like in proportions; broad rounded wings and short fanned tail (very short in 1); plumage mainly black and white. Imm. much like ad.

  1. White   *L. a. albicollis*   p. 235
    In flight a large, broad-beamed raptor with widely fanned tail barely protruding behind wings; tail mostly black with white base and tip (*albicollis*) or with black of tail less extensive (Perijá); *cere gray*; legs yellow. Imm. has crown usually streaked as in 2 but tail sim. to ad.

  2. Black-faced   *L. melanops*   p. 235
    Superficially a miniature of 1 but tail black with a *narrow white central tail band* (more or less the reverse of 1); best mark is *bright orange cere*. Crown and nape streaking hard to see at a distance. Imm. like ad. but tinged buff; less streaking on upperparts. Does not soar.

  3. Hook-billed Kite   *Chondrohierax u.*
    uncinatus   p. 226
    Normal (light-phase) imm. mostly white below with some barring on sides. Note protruding head and bill, lanky, bluntly rounded, elliptical wings, and long tail like ad.; up close note pale collar. Reg. soars. Perched ads. Pl. 6(13). In flight ♀ Pl. 9(8). Ad. ♂ and black-phase ad. Pl. 10(2).

  4. Gray-headed Kite   *Leptodon c.*
    cayanensis   p. 225
    Broad elliptical wings and longish tail recall a small hawk-eagle. **4a.** Ad.: *black wing linings* contrast with paler flight feathers; small, all-dark bill; head small, almost dovelike. Reg. soars. **4b.** Imm.: white-headed with black yarmulka. In all plumages note *dull cere, dark eyes*, and lack of crest (cf. ad. of 5 and imm. of 6). Imm. in flight Pl. 10(7).

  5. Black-and-white Hawk-Eagle   *Spizastur*
    melanoleucus   p. 246
    Always scarce. Small hawk-eagle with muscular, almost buteonine proportions (wings broad, tail not esp. long) and short thick legs feathered to toes; black above, white on head and under-parts; look for *white on leading edge of forewing* (narrow "headlights") as soars; from imm. of 4 by black crest, *orange cere, black lores*. Cf. larger imm. of 6.

  6. Ornate Hawk-Eagle   *Spizaetus o.*
    ornatus   p. 248
    Imm. looks like imm. of 4 and ad. of 5. From either by barring on sides of body and on wing linings (but very young birds nearly immaculate); from 5 by yellowish (not orange) cere, paler lores, and long loose crest white in young birds but blackish in older birds. Ad. Pl. 13(2). Also cf. imms. of Harpy and Crested eagles (Pl. 13).

12

1. Collared Forest-Falcon   *Micrastur s.*
semitorquatus   p. 253
Does not soar, but note short-winged, long-tailed
shape typical of genus. Dark phase (shown) rare
but distinctive; cf. 3a (below); also ad. of 4 on
Pl. 12. Perched imm. Pl. 6(10). Ad. Pl. 7(14).

Hawk-Eagles   *Spizaetus*
Large, rangy, but muscular raptors with elliptical-
shaped wings, occipital crest, legs feathered to toes,
and protruding aquiline head; they have fierce, commanding presence at rest or in flight. Reg. soar mid
mornings; often vocal.

2. Ornate   *S. o. ornatus*   p. 248
Glorious ad. with spiky black crest, *rufous sash
on sides of neck*, long black malar, and *immaculate underparts and wing linings crisply barred
and spotted white* should be unmistakable. Cf.
smaller Gray-bellied Hawk (Pl 7:12) which has
bare yellow legs and no crest. Imm. flying
(Pl. 12:6) is mostly white below but has proportions and commanding presence of ad.; look for
its white crest (white in youngest birds, darker
with age).

3. Black   *S. tyrannus serus*   p. 247
Notably oval wing shape; long tail. **3a.** Ad.: all-
black body and *checkered* barring on outer flight
feathers unique. Overall a littler slighter and
longer-tailed than 2. **3b.** Imm.: heavily mottled
and streaked below, esp. on sides and flanks,
with *strong facial pattern* (white eyebrow, black
cheeks).

4. Black-and-chestnut Eagle   *Oroaetus
isidori*   p. 248
Large, muscular eagle of Andes. Imm.: ragged,
unkempt appearance; short occipital crest;
heavy streaking on chest, sides, and flanks; pale
ovals at base of flight feathers. Early stages quite
pale, older imms. darker and streaked, gradually
acquiring rusty chestnut; tail retains barring until
last imm. stage. Ad. Pl. 14(2).

5. Crested Eagle   *Morphnus guianensis*   p. 245
Rarely encountered. Large, long-tailed eagle but
more lightly built and slender-legged than 6. **5a.**
Normal ad.: gray head and chest; *whitish wing
linings* (all ages); whitish underparts with faint
barring; *black lores* (all ages); small, single-
pointed crest; amber eyes. **5b.** Barred ad. (less
common): dusky chest; *heavy, coarse barring on
wing linings and underparts*. Imm. much like
imm. of 6, but note smaller bill and feet, more
finely barred tail, usually paler chest. Also see
figure in text, page 245.

6. Harpy Eagle   *Harpia harpyja*   p. 246
Rarely encountered. **6a.** Ad.: enormous size, esp.
ad. ♀; exceptionally broad wings, moderately
long tail, massive bill, tarsi, and feet. Long, somewhat bifurcated black crest; black chest band acquired relatively early; eyes dark (esp. younger
birds; lighter, more grayish with age). **6b.** Juv.
(shown) and imm.: much like comparable ages
of 5; early stages whitish to pale gray with little
black, but soon acquire black crest, hint of dark
chest band; often also some barring on thighs;
upper wing coverts remain gray with only some
black mottling until near ad. Note Harpy's *gray
lores* (all ages); in flight look for broad black
line and narrow barring on wing linings. Cf. various New World hawk-eagles, all with feathered
tarsi and less robust proportions. Also see figure
in text, page 245.

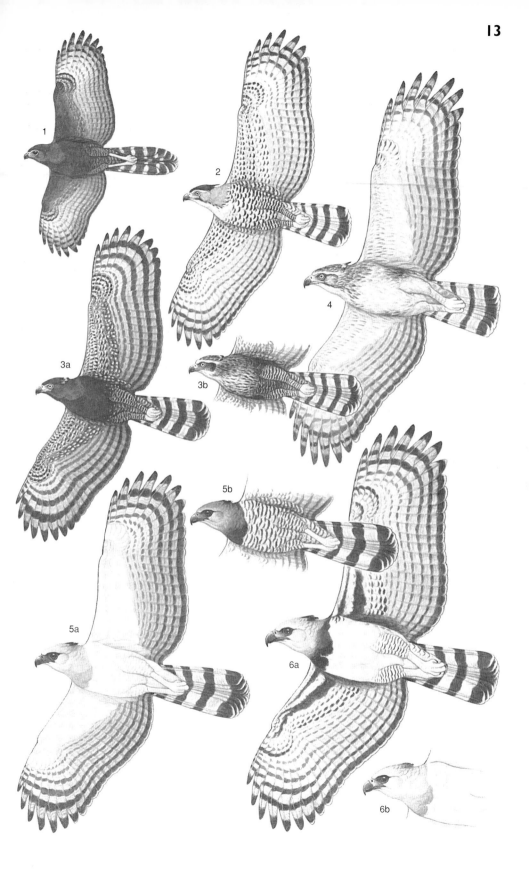

13

1. Black-chested Buzzard-Eagle
Geranoaetus melanoleucus australis   p. 239
Ad. a flying wing with barely protruding tail.
Flight silhouette, pale shoulders, and black chest
unique in high-Andean paramo. Imm. (Pl. 11:1)
much duller and mottled; tail decidedly longer
and *distinctly wedge-shaped.*

2. Black-and-chestnut Eagle   *Oroaetus
isidori*   p. 248
Richly colored ad. mainly black on head, upperparts, and thighs; breast chestnut streaked black;
tail pale gray with black band near tip; always
shows *large, pale, oval windows at base of outer
primaries.* Reg. soars mid mornings, often quite
high. Imm. Pl. 13(4).

3. Swallow-tailed Kite   *Elanoides forficatus
yetapa*   p. 227
Highly social and aerial kite of lowlands and
lower montane regions. Imm. sim. to ad.

4. Plumbeous Kite   *Ictinia plumbea*   p. 230
Long, pointed, almost scimitar-shaped wings and
narrow tail. **4a.** Ad.: red eyes; mostly dark gray;
rufous at base of primaries. Perched ad. Pl. 6(2).
At rest long wings extend well beyond tail. **4b.**
Imm.: mottled brownish above; head and underparts whitish heavily mottled and streaked dark
gray and brown; some barring on sides. Always
note distinctive long-winged shape.

5. White-tailed Kite   *Elanus leucurus*   p. 227
Angular, med.-sized raptor; often hovers. **5a.** Ad.:
whitish with pointed wings, black shoulders,
white tail, red eyes. **5b.** Imm.: tinged buff, esp. on
head and underparts; some streaking on crown
and nape; brownish back but retains black
shoulders and underwing wrist mark.

6. Pearl Kite   *Gampsonyx swainsonii leonae* p. 227
Tiny, almost toylike kite with speedy flight and
open-country habits; mainly black above, white
below; tinge of cream on cheeks, dark pectoral
patch, rufous thighs. Perched ad. Pl. 7(5).

Falcons   *Falco*
Long pointed wings and torpedo-shaped body; dashing flight and powerful rowing wing beats; to some
extent all have dark moustachial streak. ♀♀ decidedly larger. Genus contains both resident and migr.
spp.; residents (shown perched) Pl. 7.

7. Peregrine   *F. peregrinus anatum*   p. 257
N migr. Large, fast-flying falcon. Imm. brownish
above, heavily streaked below; indistinct eyebrow and moustache. Ad. (not shown) above
dull bluish gray, cap and moustache blackish;
pale below with some barring and spotting on
lower underparts.

8. Aplomado   *F. f. femoralis*   p. 256
Fairly large but slender and long-tailed; *white
headband, dark moustache, narrow vest;* in flight
shows *white on trailing edge of wing.* Imm.
(shown) darker above, streaky below, vest lacking or incomplete; belly and thighs tawny. Open
terrain. Perched ad. Pl. 7(3).

9. Bat   *F. r. rufigularis*   p. 256
Small and dark; perches on high stubs; wide
black vest finely barred white; rufous lower underparts. Perched ad. Pl. 7(1). Imm. duller below; thighs barred but usually a suggestion of
vest. Cf. ad. with larger, rare Orange-breasted
Falcon (Pl. 7:2) which has narrower vest more
U-shaped across top; coarser white vest barring;
rusty orange of chest always clearly outlining
white throat; usually some black barring on
crissum; larger head and feet; longer torso.

10. Merlin   *F. c. columbarius*   p. 255
N migr. Small size, faint moustache; *pale brow;
quite streaked below.* ♂ dull bluish above; tail
banded gray and blackish. ♀ and imm. unbarred
brownish above; tail dusky banded buffy white.

11. American Kestrel   *F. sparverius
isabellinus*   p. 255
Small, slender falcon with longish tail. Bold face
pattern; rufous back and tail. ♂ has bluish
wings, almost solid rufous tail; ♀ wings and
back all rufous and barred; rufous tail densely
barred; breast somewhat streaked. Perched
Pl. 7(4).

14

1. Hoatzin *Opisthocomus hoazin*   p. 357
Disheveled crest, bare blue ocular area, and
loose rufous feathers enhance prehistoric appearance. Note buff shoulders and tail tips. Always near water.

Chachalacas *Ortalis*
Slender with gallinelike appearance, bare red throat,
strong legs, and long tail. Thickets, wooded borders.
Noisy at dawn.

2. Rufous-vented *O. r. ruficauda*   p. 258
N. *Head grayish*, under tail coverts rufous; broad
tail tips rufous (or buff to white in Goajira region).

3. Little *O. m. motmot*   p. 258
S. Smaller than 2; head rufous.

Guans *Penelope*
Med.-sized to large, dark forest guans, usually with
white streaking on foreparts; bare bluish facial skin
and small red dewlap. Most spp. quite sim. (cf.
ranges).

4. Band-tailed *P. a. argyrotis*   p. 259
N mts. Med.-sized *Penelope* guan; frosty white
eyebrow and sides of head; prom. red dewlap;
outer tail feathers with broad but *inconspic. buff
to dull rufous tips*. Mid. els.

5. Andean *P. m. montagnii*   p. 259
Andes. Small guan; strong grizzled grayish streaking on face imparts *"wizened" appearance;*
foreparts streaky; red dewlap rudimentary.
High els.

6. Marail *P. m. marail*   p. 260
SE. Almost a miniature of 7b and often not easily
separated. Note *very short tarsi and small size.*
The two widely overlap in range. Canopy of humid forest.

7. Spix's *P. jacquacu*   p. 260
S. Med.-sized dark guan; streaky foreparts, red
dewlap. **7a.** *P. j. orienticola:* smaller and more
olive above than 7b; size of 6 but not known to
occur with it. **7b.** *P. j. granti:* larger than 6 and 7a.
Occurs with 6, but note *larger size, longer tarsi,
different vocalizations*. Humid forest.

8. Crested *P. purpurascens brunnescens*   p. 261
N mts. Large size, bushy crest, relatively little
grayish streaking on head; all-dark tail. Local; humid forest; lower montane els.

9. Common Piping-Guan *Pipile pipile* p. 261
S. Slender, elegant-looking guan; mainly black
with white crown; bright blue facial skin,
dewlap, and wattle; large white wing patches;
shaggy white crest. Canopy of humid lowland
forest.

10. Wattled Guan *Aburria aburri*   p. 262
Andes. Large black guan with *mostly bright blue
bill and rich yellow legs;* unusually long yellow
wattle dangles from throat. Andes.

15

Curassows   *Crax*
Large; ♂♂ mainly black, ♀♀ often cryptically patterned. Most spp. with some combination of white or chestnut belly and/or tail tips; usually crested, some with curly crests; bill, cere, and forehead often adorned with colorful wattles, knobs, or swollen protuberances. Mainly terrestrial.

1. Black   *C. alector*   p. 263
   1a. *C. a. erythrognatha*: white belly; tail all black; conspic. swollen cere orange red (Amazonas and W Bolívar). **1b.** *C. a. alector:* sim. but cere bright yellow (E Bolívar). Sexes sim. Humid forest.
2. Yellow-knobbed   *C. daubentoni*   p. 264
   N. White belly and tail tips. ♂ has yellow knobs and cere. ♀ has white scaled breast, no yellow adornments. Dry forest.
3. Nocturnal Curassow   *Nothocrax urumutum*   p. 262
   S (Amazonas). Rarely seen (day or night); vocal high in forest at night; smaller than *Crax;* mainly reddish chestnut; bare colorful facial skin. Sexes sim.

Curassows   *Mitu* and *Pauxi*
Both sometimes incl. in genus *Crax; Mitu* differs in deep bladelike red bill; *Pauxi* has large grayish casque on crown and is mainly montane in distrib.

4. Crestless   *Mitu tomentosa*   p. 263
   SE Apure and Amazonas. Chestnut belly and tail tips; bladelike red bill; no crest. Sexes nearly alike. Low-lying forest, várzea, and riverbanks.

5. Northern Helmeted-   *Pauxi p. pauxi* p. 264
   N mts. (now local). Both sexes black with white lower underparts and tail tips; fig-shaped gray casque on crown. Rare rufous-phase ♀ has head and neck black, rest of body rufous finely barred black, lower underparts and tail tips white.

Screamers   *Chauna* and *Anhima*
Large gooselike birds, mainly black, white, and gray; sturdy legs and long unwebbed toes; dense short feathers not in feather tracts; thick spongy skin. *Anhima* differs most notably from *Chauna* in long, unicornlike quill projecting from forehead.

6. Northern   *Chauna chavaria*   p. 194
   Maracaibo Basin. Bare red ocular area, white "muffler," and black neck band distinctive. Marshes.
7. Horned   *Anhima cornuta*   p. 194
   Mainly N. Mainly black with white belly; ruffled scaly gray neck; black face and whitish on crown; up close note long quill (the "horn") on forehead. Marshes.

Trumpeter   *Psophia*
8. Gray-winged   *P. c. crepitans*   p. 279
   S. Hunched and guineafowl-like in aspect; large gray lower back feathers, tertials, and inner flight feathers conceal rearparts. Often shy; varying-sized groups on floor of humid forest.

16

1a

1b

2

♂

♀

3

4

5

6

7

8

AG

1. Pied Plover *Hoploxypterus cayanus*   p. 282
Bold black and white plumage; coral eyering and legs. Sandbars along rivers, lagoons.

2. Southern Lapwing *Vanellus chilensis cayennensis*   p. 281
Fairly large; ornate head; black breast; flashy black-and-white wing pattern. Noisy and bold.

Rails *Rallus*
Fairly large rails with long, slender, slightly decurved bills and barred flanks (most spp.); fresh and salt water.

3. Spotted *R. m. maculatus*   p. 274
N. Heavily spotted and streaked; yellowish bill; pink legs. Marshes, rice fields. **Blackish** *Pardirallus nigricans* (text). S Maracaibo region.

4. Plain-flanked *R. wetmorei*   p. 273
Coastal E Falcón to Aragua. Ad. *uniform and unmarked;* no barring on flanks. Dark phase sim. but *dusky blackish brown.* Highly localized and threatened; mangroves. **Clapper** *R. longirostris* (text). Carib. coast. Occurs with 4; differs in orangish bill, dusky barring on flanks and lower underparts. Salt marshes and mangroves.

Wood-Rails *Aramides*
Large and rather colorful rails, bill fairly long and thick; all have yellowish green bills, red eyes, coral legs, rufous primaries, and black posteriors; cackling calls (as far as known); mostly swamps and wooded streams and lagoons.

5. Gray-necked *A. c. cajanea*   p. 275
Widespread. Mostly gray head and neck; note putty orange breast. Colorful, engaging sp., often shy in forested regions but much bolder along gallery forests in llanos.

6. Rufous-necked *A. axillaris*   p. 274
Mainly on or near coast. Head, neck, and underparts rich rufous chestnut. Imm. much duller; brownish gray neck and foreparts. Rare and local.

Crakes *Porzana*
Small to med.-sized; short thick bill has flat culmen, blunt point. Secretive; hide in vegetation near water.

7. Sora *P. carolina*   p. 270
N migr. Yellow bill, black face, iron gray underparts. Lagoons, wet areas, rice fields.

8. Ash-throated *P. albicollis olivacea*   p. 270
Recalls 7 but larger, plainer. Streaked back; dull greenish to yellowish green bill; gray below; barred flanks; legs dull. Wet grass, marshes.

9. Yellow-breasted *P. f. flaviventer*   p. 271
Small. Yellow buff foreparts; bold flank bars; Dangling yellow legs when flushed. Marshes.

10. Ocellated Crake *Micropygia s. schomburgkii*   p. 272
Very small. *Ochraceous below;* white ocelli on upperparts; *coral red legs.* Dry grass. Locally common in SE Bolívar. **Speckled** *Coturnicops notatus* (text). Size of 10 but dark brownish slate, speckled and barred white; white patch in secondaries. Few recs. Wet fields.

11. Paint-billed Crake *Neocrex erythrops olivascens*   p. 271
Uniform brown above; barred flanks; *base of bill red;* legs pinkish. Migratory, erratic, local.

Crakes *Laterallus*
Small and secretive. Most spp. (elsewhere) have black barring on white flanks (except 13 and 14); hd. much more than seen. Marshes and wet grass; some spp. favor dry grass or partly wooded regions.

12. Gray-breasted *L. exilis*   p. 268
Gray underparts paler than 11. *Nape and upper mantle rufous chestnut;* rearparts barred. Erratic and local in marshes, wet grass, fields.

13. Rusty-flanked *L. levraudi*   p. 268
Rufous below with white median underparts. *No barring on flanks.* Local in marshes of N central region. **Rufous-sided** *L. melanophaius* and **Uniform** *Amaurolimnas concolor* (text).

14. Russet-crowned *L. v. viridis*   p. 269
Recalls 13 but note *gray cheeks and entirely rufous underparts* (no barring). *Rosy legs;* gray blue bill. Tall wet to dry grass.

Gallinules *Porphyrula*
Large, colorful, gallinelike rails with bright yellow legs; ads. usually have white crissum; imms. buffy below. Marshes and lagoons.

15. Azure *P. flavirostris*   p. 276
Delicate proportions. Bill, frontal shield, and legs bright yellow; foreparts azure. Imm. resembles 16b but smaller, back more streaked, rump blackish. Imms. seem to outnumber ads. Migratory. Marshes.

16. Purple *P. martinica*   p. 275
16a. Ad.: *bright bluish purple;* yellow-tipped bill. **16b.** Imm.: *predom. buff below; white on throat and belly;* yellow legs; blue wash on mantle and wings (like imm. of 15). Marshes. **Common** *Gallinula chloropus* and **Caribbean Coot** *Fulica caribaea* (text and text figure, page 277).

17. Sunbittern *Eurypyga h. helias*   p. 278
Delicate appearance; graceful, balletlike movements. Ornate pattern provides superb camouflage. Gives startling "Navajo-rug-sunburst" wing display as threat or distraction. Terrestrial; wooded streams, lagoons.

18. Sungrebe *Heliornis fulica*   p. 277
Grebe- or ducklike. Small, brown; floats low. Bold head and neck stripes. ♂ has white cheeks, ♀ buff. Small white tail tips visible in flight. Vegetation bordering streams.

19. Wattled Jacana *Jacana jacana intermedia*   p. 286
Lilly trotter with *extremely long toes; bright yellow flight feathers.* **19a.** Ad.: overall dark; red wattles, chestnut back and wings. **19b.** Imm.: often mistaken for a rail. Striped head, white underparts. Conspic. around lagoons.

Double-striped Thick-knee: see figure in text, page 281.

17

Plovers *Charadrius*

1. **Snowy**   *C. alexandrinus tenuirostris*   p. 284
   Sandy beaches. Thin black bill, grayish legs; black smudgy bar on pectoral region forms incomplete band in breeding ad. Nonbreeding ad. and imm.; no head markings; pectoral bar brown.

2. **Semipalmated**   *C. semipalmatus*   p. 283
   2a. Breeding ad.: orange yellow legs; orange base to short bill. **2b.** Nonbreeding ad.: sim. but duller; bill mostly dark; black band over forehead reduced or lacking. Mainly coastal. N migr. **Killdeer** *C. vociferus* (text).

3. **Wilson's**   *C. wilsonia cinnamominus*   p. 283
   Large stout bill always black (much larger than allies); broad black chest band (brown in ♀). Legs dull dusky pink. Coastal.

4. **Collared**   *C. collaris*   p. 284
   Only *Charadrius* reg. inland. Black bill; *cinnamon hindcrown*; narrow chest band; legs dull yellow.

5. **Ruddy Turnstone**   *Arenaria interpres morinella*   p. 293
   N. migr. Short, thin bill. Bold plumage of breeding birds usually not seen in Venez. Nonbreeding ad. (shown) duller, only hint of pattern, little or no rufous.

6. **Gray Plover**   *Pluvialis squatarola*   p. 282
   N migr. Beaches. White wing stripe, white base to tail; black "armpits." **6a.** Nonbreeding ad.: plain gray, paler below, little pattern. Juv. more speckled above; note pale eyebrow; black axillaries. **6b.** Breeding ad.: whitish speckled black above; face and underparts black; white eyebrow extends to sides. N migr. **American Golden-Plover** *P. dominica* (text).

7. **Common Snipe**   *Gallinago gallinago delicata*   p. 300
   N migr. mainly to Andes. Not separable in field from South American Snipe (little overlap); smaller than Noble Snipe. **South American** *G. paraguaiae.* Resident in lowlands. Essentially identical to 7 (text). **Giant** *G. undulata*, **Andean** *G. jamesoni*, and **Noble** *G. nobilis* (see figure in text, page 301).

8. **Short-billed Dowitcher**   *Limnodromus g. griseus*   p. 299
   N migr. Long straight bill, relatively short legs; triangular white rump. Nonbreeding ad. grayish with pale eyebrow, finely streaked face, weak speckling on breast, irreg. coarse gray barring on flanks; legs dull yellow. Breeding ad. (text).

9. **Sanderling**   *Calidris alba*   p. 294
   N migr. Nonbreeding ad. (shown) pale gray above, white below; black bill and legs. Juv.: some black speckling on upperparts. Breeding plumage (text). Chases waves on beaches.

10. **Solitary Sandpiper**   *Tringa s. solitaria*   p. 288
    N migr. White spectacles; sides of tail barred; wings all dark above and below; greenish legs.

11. **Spotted Sandpiper**   *Actitis macularia*   p. 289
    N migr. Nonbreeding ad. smudgy brown on chest; bill and short legs pale yellow. Juv.: some buff and black barring on wings and rearparts. "Spotting" visible prior to migration.

Sandpipers *Calidris*
Small; short bills and legs; plumages all quite sim. Bill shape important; leg color an aid for 13. N migrs.

12. **Western**   *C. mauri*   p. 295
    Slightly drooped bill; black legs. **12a.** Breeding ad.: rufous on shoulders, crown, and cheeks. **12b.** Nonbreeding ad.: gray above, whitish below. Juv.: uppermost scapulars edged rufous, lower ones gray edged black. N. migrs. (text): **Red Knot** *C. canutus;* **Baird's Sandpiper** *C. bardii;* **Dunlin** *C. alpina;* **Buff-breasted Sandpiper** *Tryngites subruficollis;* **Ruff** *Philomachus pugnax;* and **Wilson's Phalarope** *Phalaropus tricolor.*

13. **Least**   *C. minutilla*   p. 296
    Thin-tipped, almost straight bill and yellowish legs. Nonbreeding ad. shown. All stages are *brownish* (not gray), incl. breast; juvs. show much rufous edging on brown upperparts. Breeding ad. quite mottled brown above.

14. **Semipalmated**   *C. pusilla*   p. 294
    Gray nonbreeding ad. (shown) much like 12 but *bill straighter, thicker, blunter.* Juv. gray brown and scaly (no rufous) above with brownish cheeks, vague brownish streaking on breast. Breeding ads. more gray brown than allies.

15. **Black-necked Stilt**   *Himantopus m. mexicanus*   p. 286
    Stiltlike red legs. Shallow lagoons, sandbars.

16. **Willet**   *Catoptrophorus semipalmatus inornatus*   p. 289
    N migr. to coast; resident on Islas Los Roques. Long, thickish, slightly upturned dusky bill; bold white stripe on mostly black wing. Nonbreeding ad. (shown) and juv. mainly gray; juv. shows whitish forehead.

17. **Whimbrel**   *Numenius phaeopus hudsonicus*   p. 291
    N migr. to coast. *Striped head*, gray legs, and *long decurved bill.* **Long-billed Curlew** *N. americanus* (text).

18. **Hudsonian Godwit**   *Limosa haemastica* p. 291
    Rare. N migr. to coast. Pointed wings. *In all plumages shows white tail base, broad black tail tip, black wing lining, and narrow white wing stripe.* Nonbreeding ad. (shown) gray with blackish base, short whitish eyebrow, slight upturn to long thin bill, orange basally on lower mandible. Juv. and breeding ad. (text). N migrs. (text): **Bartailed** *L. lapponica* and **Marbled** *L. fedoa.*

19. **Greater Yellowlegs**   *Tringa melanoleuca*   p. 287
    N migr. Large; long blackish bill gray basally with slight upturn (cf. thinner, straight, all-black bill of Lesser Yellowlegs). Nonbreeding ad. (shown) plain gray above. Juv. more speckled above; breeding ad. (text).

White-rumped, Least, Western, Pectoral, and Stilt sandpipers; Sanderling; Greater and Lesser yellowlegs; Upland Sandpiper; and American Oystercatcher: see figures in text, pages 288, 290, 295.

2a

1

2b

3♂

♀

4

5

6a

6b

7

8

9

10

11

12a

12b

13

14

15

16

17

18

19

Gwynne 11·85

Gulls   *Larus*

All except 4 are vagrants to Venez. coastal waters.

1. Herring   *L. argentatus smithsonianus*   p. 306
N migr. 1st winter large and brownish; legs pink, bill all black; plumage variable but look for coarse checkering on wing coverts, mottled scapulars, smudged brown on sides. Older stages progressively paler, base of bill pink. Ad. (text). **Lesser Black-backed** *L. fuscus*, and **Great Black-backed** *L. marinus*, both vagrant (text).

2. Ring-billed   *L. delawarensis*   p. 306
N migr. Subad. *always paler above than Laughing Gull;* pink bill with black tip (yellow with black ring in ad.); variable amt. of brownish on head, vague barring on sides and chest; may show dark centers on pale wing coverts. Vagrant.

3. Franklin's   *L. pipixcan*   p. 307
N migr. Nonbreeding ad. dusky half hood, narrow black wing tips bordered on each side by white; tail all white; 1st-winter birds show black tail tip (outermost feather white). Vagrant.

4. Laughing   *L. a. atricilla*   p. 307
Common resident. **4a.** Nonbreeding ad.: limited gray streaking on rearcrown; all-dark wing tips and extensive black on underside of primaries. **4b.** Breeding ad.: black head, narrow white arc above and below eye, red bill. **4c.** 1st.-yr imm.: brownish; breast smudged brown; dark legs, black bill; tail white with black terminal band.

Jaegers   *Stercorarius*

5. Parasitic   *S. parasiticus*   p. 305
Imm. *cinnamon wash on plumage,* nape streaky; upper tail coverts and under wing coverts less barred (little contrast with adj. body) than on Pomarine, but very pale imms. show contrasting pale rump. Prob. commoner than the few recs. indicate. Ad. Pl. 2(7). **Long-tailed** *S. longicaudus.* See Pl. 2(7) and text.

6. Pomarine   *S. pomarinus*   p. 304
Imm., incl. light, dark, and intermed. forms, brownish; uniform head and nape, pale barring on upper tail coverts unique; whitish barring on under wing coverts and flanks; bicolored bill. Ad. Pl. 2(7). **Great Skua** *Catharacta skua* and **South Polar Skua** *C. maccormicki* (text).

Terns   *Sterna*

7. Common   *S. h. hirundo*   p. 309
N migr. **7a.** Breeding ad.: black cap, red bill, tail usually shorter than wing tips; slightly paler gray below than above. **7b.** Nonbreeding ad. and 1st yr: whitish forehead, all-black bill, *prom. dark carpal bar,* outer primaries dusky.

8. Roseate   *S. d. dougallii*   p. 310
Breeding ad. black cap, thin black bill, tail longer than wing tips; faint pink blush on breast. Nonbreeding ad. has white forehead; no dark carpal bar; only 2–3 outer primaries dark.

9. Royal   *S. m. maxima*   p. 308
9a. Breeding ad.: black cap, bright orange bill. **9b.** Nonbreeding ad.: *white forehead,* bill paler orange.

10. Caspian   *S. c. caspia*   p. 308
Coast. Nonbreeding ad. thick reddish bill with faint dark tip; *entire crown streaked blackish.*

11. Large-billed Tern   *Phaetusa s. simplex*   p. 314
Heavy yellow bill; flashing black and white wings. Mostly freshwater rivers and lakes.

12. Gull-billed Tern   *Sterna nilotica aranea*   p. 308
Coast; locally inland. Nonbreeding ad. *stout black bill,* tail short and *only slightly forked;* long outer primaries somewhat dusky; pale head with small dusky eye patch. Breeding ad. has solid black crown, whiter outer primaries.

13. Sandwich Tern   *Sterna sandvicensis*   p. 309
13a. *S. s. acuflavidus:* nonbreeding ad. *pale gray above* (only Gull-billed Tern is so pale); white forehead, black fringe from eye rearward; *black bill tipped yellow.* Breeding ad. sim. but crown all black. **13b. Cayenne** type, *S. s. eurygnatha:* breeding ad. sim. to breeding *S. s. acuflavidus* but *bill all yellow.*

14. Brown Noddy   *Anous s. stolidus*   p. 313
White forehead blends to gray hindcrown; bill almost straight; plumage brown-tinged. **Black** *A. minutus.* (text). Smaller and blacker; bill thinner, straight. See text figure.

15. Least Tern   *Sterna a. antillarum*   p. 311
Breeding ad. *bill yellow with small black tip.* In nonbreeding ad. white of forehead becomes finely streaked black on mid. crown; *bill all black.* Imm. carpal bar darker than in imm. of 16. Breeds on offshore isls.; wanders to coast.

16. Yellow-billed Tern   *Sterna superciliaris*   p. 311
Mainly inland. Breeding ad. very like 15 but bill all yellow; nonbreeding ad. bill yellow, tip and small patch at base of upper mandible black. Imm. much like 15 but carpal bar not as dark. Freshwater rivers and lakes; infreq. on coast.

17. Sooty Tern   *Sterna f. fuscata*   p. 312
Slaty black upperparts; tail looks mostly dark with narrow white edges; all-dark primaries, from below, contrast with white wing lining. **Bridled** *S. anaethetus* (text). Much like 17 but paler gray above, *white tail edges broader,* less underwing contrast. See text figure.

18. Black Tern   *Chlidonias niger surinamensis*   p. 314
Short, slightly forked tail. **18a.** Molting ad.: variable amt. of black shows. **18b.** Nonbreeding ad.: white head with dusky half-hood; smudge of gray on chest. Breeding ad. has foreparts to lower breast black, belly white.

19. Black Skimmer   *Rhynchops n. niger*   p. 315
Large red, bladelike bill with "underbite" (esp. ♂). Breeding ad. black above, white below. Nonbreeding ad. has white hindneck.

Brown Noddy, Sooty Tern, Black Noddy, and **Bridled Tern**: see figure in text, page 312.

1

2

3

4a

4b

4c

5

6

7a

7b

8

9a

9b

10

11

12

13a

13b

14

15

16

17

18a

18b

19

J.P.Gwynne

Pigeons   *Columba*

Large and plump; rounded tail; primarily arboreal; occupy broad spectrum of habitats; most spp. rather plain and sim. to each other.

1. Bare-eyed   *C. corensis*   p. 317
N deserts. Large and pale; bare blue ocular area ringed black (like goggles); large white wing patches.

2. Pale-vented   *C. cayennensis andersoni*   p. 318
Reddish on shoulders and mantle, white belly, dark bill. Widespread and common in semiopen terrain and along rivers in forested areas; gathers in flocks. In flight cf. 3.

3. Scaled   *C. speciosa*   p. 317
Most colorful New World pigeon. Neck and underparts scaled; strong reddish on shoulders and mantle; red bill with white tip. Widespread in forest and semiopen terrain but solitary and never as numerous as 2.

4. Ruddy   *C. subvinacea purpureotincta*   p. 318
Olive brown above, vinaceous below with overall ruddy tone; black bill and *red eyes;* solitary in forest. **Plumbeous** *C. plumbea* (text). E slope Andes; S. Much like 4 but slightly larger and grayer. Note *yellowish white* (not red*)* eyes and vocal differences. Also **White-crowned** *C. leucocephala* and **Scaly-naped** *C. squamosa* (text).

5. Band-tailed   *C. fasciata albilinea*   p. 316
Highlands. Large and dark, white neck band, 2-toned tail, yellow bill; often in flocks.

6. Scaled Dove   *Scardafella squammata ridgwayi*   p. 320
N. Heavily scaled; long, narrow, white-edged tail; rufous in primaries. Common in dry areas.

Ground-Doves   *Columbina*

Small; short, slightly rounded tail; rufous at base of flight feathers; terrestrial; often loosely gregarious. Semiopen areas; settlements.

7. Common   *C. passerina albivitta*   p. 320
Scaly neck and breast; base of bill pinkish or yellow. Widespread but seldom numerous.

8. Ruddy   *C. talpacoti rufipennis*   p. 321
Mainly rufous with gray crown. ♀ much duller and nearer 9 but larger; lacks latter's gray tones to crown and back, and has black under wing coverts. Widespread; common.

9. Plain-breasted   *C. m. minuta*   p. 321
Small. Bill black (cf. 7); no scales or spots on neck. ♂ shows subtle gray tone to crown and back, less obvious on ♀ which is much like ♀ of 8 but smaller and no black under wing lining.

10. Eared Dove   *Zenaida auriculata stenura*   p. 319
Wedge-shaped tail tipped rufous; up close note 2 black lines across face. Widespread; common in agricultural areas.

Ground-Doves   *Claravis*

Larger, tail longer than *Columbina;* bars on wings (both sexes); reclusive forest-dwellers, mainly alone or in prs.

11. Blue   *C. pretiosa*   p. 322
♂ blue gray with pale foreface, purple spotting on wings; ♀ has 2 chestnut bands on primaries, rufous rump and tail. Both sexes have black outer tail feathers but no white tips.

12. Maroon-chested   *C. m. mondetoura*   p. 322
♂ dark gray with maroon breast and white-edged tail. ♀ like ♀ of 11 but no rufous; outer tail feathers tipped white. Follows maturing bamboo seed crops in mts.

Doves   *Leptotila*

Fairly large, robust doves, uniform above and below; forehead and belly usually paler; colored bare eyering; rufous wing lining; tail tipped white. Feed on ground but otherwise arboreal.

13. White-tipped   *L. v. verreauxi*   p. 323
Most widespread of genus. Overall paler than 14 and lacks blue gray tone on crown; prom. white tail tips; *orbital skin blue.* Dry woodland; semiopen areas (minimal overlap with 14).

14. Gray-fronted   *L. rufaxilla dubusi*   p. 323
Only *Leptotila* in most of its range; note pale forehead, gray crown, *red orbital skin.* Voice somewhat different from 13; mainly inside humid lowland forest.

Quail-Doves   *Geotrygon*

Plump and short-tailed; no white tail tips; colored orbital skin, often with iridescence on hindneck and mantle; solitary or in prs.; terrestrial; retiring; difficult to see.

15. Ruddy   *G. m. montana*   p. 325
Buff cheek stripe and darkish malar mark (more obvious in ♂). ♂ mainly rufous chestnut above. ♀ and imm. olive brown above. Terrestrial but flies fast, low and erratically through forest; perhaps partially migratory. Most widespread of genus.

16. Violaceous   *G. violacea albiventer*   p. 324
Local and scarce in foothills and lower montane els. *No moustachial stripe* (cf. other *Geotrygon*); whitish forehead, glossy mantle. ♀ duller above, grayish below, belly pale buff.

17. Lined   *G. l. linearis*   p. 324
Montane. Large. Rich russet brown; note cinnamon forehead, gray nape, long black malar line. ♀ and imm. duller.

20

Macaws   *Ara*
Med. to large; some spp. colorful; long pointed tail; *bare cheeks and facial area*; thick bill; mainly humid forest, but 3 and 4 also occur in dry forest.

1. Blue-and-yellow   *A. ararauna*   p. 326
Unmistakable up close. Note blue flight feathers as in 2, 3, and 4, and at a distance surprisingly easily confused with them. Quite local in Venez.

2. Red-and-green   *A. chloroptera*   p. 327
NW; S. Much like 3 but median upper wing coverts green. Note facial lines, deeper red plumage.

3. Scarlet   *A. m. macao*   p. 327
Yellow median upper wing coverts (cf. 2). Unlined face; lighter, more scarlet color; proportionately longer tail than 2. Most widespread large macaw.

4. Military   *A. m. militaris*   p. 326
N. Large, all green; red forecrown; blue primaries and yellowish underwings (cf. 1). Local; mostly drier regions.

5. Chestnut-fronted   *A. s. severa*   p. 328
Med. sized. Chestnut frontlet; whitish facial skin. In flight note *red underwings* and undertail. Widespread and common, often in settled and urban areas.

6. Red-bellied Macaw   *Orthopsittaca manilata*   p. 328
Mainly SE. Med. sized; yellow gold underwings and undertail (cf. 7); red belly patch often visible in flight; pale yellowish facial skin. Local around moriche palms.

7. Red-shouldered Macaw   *Diopsittaca n. nobilis*   p. 328
Small. Yellow gold underwings and undertail as in 6, but note *red wrists*. Told from 4 (Pl. 22) by blue forecrown, dark bill, no yellow under bend of wing.

Parrots   *Pionus*
Med. sized; rather dark; red crissum; deep, mostly under-the-body wing beats; lowlands and highlands.

8. Bronze-winged   *P. chalcopterus*   p. 343
Dark with brownish shoulders; ultramarine flight feathers. Note yellowish bill. Local in W foothills.

9. Red-billed   *P. s. sordidus*   p. 342
N mts. Pinkish to red bill (usually); overall much duller, paler than 11 and with unkempt mottled appearance, esp. head. Foothills and lower montane regions.

10. White-capped   *P. seniloides*   p. 343
Andes. Whitish forecrown; heavily mottled head; bright green wings, red crissum.

11. Blue-headed   *P. m. menstruus*   p. 340
Handsome with blue head, bright green body, red crissum. Widespread, esp. S of Orinoco.

12. Dusky   *P. fuscus*   p. 343
SE. Much darker than 11; mainly violet brown (no green), usually some whitish mottling on head; flight feathers deep blue. Uncommon.

13. Red-fan Parrot   *Deroptyus a. accipitrinus*   p. 347
S. Hawklike. Whitish forecrown; long tail. Expressive fanlike ruff freq. raised. Striking red and blue underparts often difficult to see. Dipping flap-and-sail flight. Uncommon.

Parrots   *Amazona*
Large, mainly green, often with red patch in secondaries, a few also with red on shoulder; rapid but *shallow and stiff wing beats*; most spp. in lowlands.

14. Orange-winged   *A. a. amazonica*   p. 346
Note *yellow cheeks*. Shows yellow and blue on crown (cf. 15 and 17); red orange to orange wing patch on secondaries. Widespread in semiarid to humid regions. **Blue-cheeked** *A. dufresniana* (text). SE. Forehead and lores yellow; *cheeks blue*, wing speculum orange.

15. Yellow-crowned   *A. o. ochrocephala*   p. 346
Large yellow crown patch (yellow occas. extends down to, even around, eyes); red patch on secondaries *and on shoulders*. Note voice. Widespread, esp. gallery forests of llanos.

16. Yellow-shouldered   *A. b. barbadensis*   p. 345
N deserts. From 14 and 15 by *extensive yellow on crown and foreface*, incl. lores; *yellow on shoulders* (prom. in flight); scaly neck. Local, threatened, declining.

17. Mealy   *A. f. farinosa*   p. 347
S. *Large.* Lacks good marks. Note *2-toned tail, large bare ocular ring, and size.* Small circular crown patch present or absent. Humid forest. **Red-lored** *A. autumnalis* (text). Maracaibo region. Red frontlet; red wing patch.

18. Scaly-naped   *A. mercenaria canipalliata*   p. 347
Andes. Large; mainly all green. Usually no red patch in secondaries; obvious scaly appearance on hindneck and mantle. Higher els.

19. Festive   *A. festiva bodini*   p. 345
Río Apure; lower Río Orinoco to Delta Amacuro. No red on wings; *large blaze of red up rump and back* (difficult to see). Note *red forehead* and bluish cheeks. Local; riverine.

21

Parakeets   *Aratinga*
Med. sized; *long, pointed green tail;* steady, fast flight, often quite high in some spp.
1. **Brown-throated**   *A. pertinax venezuelae*   p. 331
Face and chest dull and brownish (dirty); upperparts can look bright green in good light. Widespread and common in dry semiopen terrain.
2. **Sun**   *A. solstitialis*   p. 330
Orange head and underparts, yellow shoulders and back. Only one rec. (?); doubtless formerly occurred. Guyana; N Brazil.
3. **Blue-crowned**   *A. acuticaudata haemorrhous*   p. 329
N. Large parakeet. Blue crown; base of undertail reddish (hard to see). Local; dry semiopen.
4. **White-eyed**   *A. l. leucophthalmus*   p. 330
E. Large parakeet. All green with conspic. red at bend of wing, yellow on under wing coverts (flashes red and yellow in flight); flight feathers and tail dull yellowish from below.
5. **Scarlet-fronted**   *A. wagleri transilis*   p. 329
N mts. Large parakeet. Look for red frontlet, flecks of red feathering on head and neck; noisy, high-flying flocks.

Parakeets   *Pyrrhura*
Smaller than *Aratinga;* tail long, dark red, narrowing to bluntly rounded point; blue primaries; fast, erratic flight through forest canopy.
6. **Blood-eared**   *P. h. hoematotis*   p. 333
N mts. Small red ear patch, bright blue primaries, dark red tail. Local.
7. **Venezuelan**   *P. emma auricularis*   p. 332
N mts. Much like 8; no range overlap with 6 or 8. Note *whitish auriculars; broad, rounded scaling on chest;* red belly patch. In flight blue primaries and dark red tail. Local.
8. **Painted**   *P. p. picta*   p. 331
S. Colorful. Pale auriculars; *broad V-shaped scaling on chest.* Humid forest. **Perijá** *P. caeruleiceps* (text). Perijá Mts. Formerly subsp. of 8.
9. **Fiery-shouldered**   *P. e. egregia*   p. 333
Tepuis. Bright *orange red under wing coverts extend to bend of wing.* Flashes blue primaries and dark red tail in flight. **Maroon-tailed** *P. melanura* (text). S. Much like 9 but under wing coverts green; *small red patch on primary coverts.*
10. **Rose-crowned**   *P. rhodocephala*   p. 334
Andes. Crown rose orange (cf. larger 5); conspic. white wing patch in flight.

Parrotlets   *Forpus*
Tiny, bright green; ♂♂ blue in wings; ♀♀ much alike, green with brighter rump. Forest, semiopen.
11. **Green-rumped**   *F. passerinus viridissimus*   p. 335
Bright green with pale bill. ♂ light blue wing patch; ♀ brighter than allies (cf. Dusky-billed). Widespread. **Spectacled** *F. conspicillatus* (text). Río Meta. ♂ has blue on wings and rump. **Dusky-billed** *F. sclateri* (text). S. ♂ dark blue on wings and rump; overall rather dark green; *bill dusky* (cf. 11 and 12).

12. **Tepui Parrotlet**   *Nannopsittaca panychlora*
p. 337
SE tepuis. Dark green with curving yellowish mark below eyes; slightly wedge-shaped tail. Often in large, high-flying flocks.
13. **Barred Parakeet**   *Bolborhynchus lineola tigrinus*   p. 334
Mainly Andes. Dark green; short, wedge-shaped tail; high flying flocks; barring hard to see.

Parakeets   *Brotogeris*
Larger than *Forpus; wedge-shaped tail;* buzzy calls.
14. **Orange-chinned**   *B. jugularis exsul*   p. 336
N. Brownish shoulders; yellow under wing coverts. Up close note chin spot. Dry areas.
15. **Golden-winged**   *B. c. chrysopterus*   p. 337
SE. Orange wing patch (often not visible at rest), short wedge-shaped tail. Humid forest. **Cobalt-winged** *B. cyanoptera* (text). Amazonas. Smallish green parakeet with short wedge-shaped tail, blue primaries. Small orange chin spot.

Parrotlets   *Touit*
Small, compact parrotlets; tail coverts almost cover short square tail; colorful tail inconspic.
16. **Sapphire-rumped**   *T. p. purpurata*   p. 339
S. Brownish scapular band; mostly red outer tail feathers; sapphire rump difficult to see. Uncommon. **Scarlet-shouldered** *T. huetii* (text). Green; extensive red at bend of wing, on under wing coverts and axillaries. Cf. 9 and 22.
17. **Lilac-tailed**   *T. batavica*   p. 338
N mts. Colorful up close. Note yellowish head, black upperparts, yellow in wing. Flies high and fast in compact flocks.
18. **Blue-fronted**   *T. dilectissima*   p. 339
Andes. Blue frontlet; extensive red band across upper wing. Scarce.
19. **Rusty-faced Parrot**   *Hapalopsittaca amazonina theresae*   p. 341
Andes. Foreface brownish red; shoulders and bend of wing red; flight feathers dark blue. Local; prs. or small groups.

Parrots   *Pionopsitta*
Med. sized, chunky parrots; short, square tail; often with contrasting color on head and/or red under wing coverts. Fast, twisting flight through forest canopy.
20. **Saffron-headed**   *P. pyrilia*   p. 340
Andes. Bright yellow head, red on under wing coverts. Local; prs. or small groups.
21. **Caica**   *P. caica*   p. 340
SE. Black head and *"old gold"* nuchal collar. Humid forests.
22. **Orange-cheeked**   *P. barrabandi*   p. 341
S. Black head with orange malar patch; red under wing coverts; fast, twisting flight through canopy. Lowland forest.
23. **Black-headed Parrot**   *Pionites m. melanocephala*   p. 340
S. Bold pattern; black cap, apricot collar and lower underparts, white breast. Lowland forest.

Cuckoos   *Coccyzus*
Slender and well groomed; long graduated tail with
white spots visible from below; slightly decurved bill.
  1. Yellow-billed   *C. a. americanus*   p. 349
    N migr. White below; rufous in primaries; lower
    mandible yellow. **Pearly-breasted** *C. euleri*
    (text). Very like 1 but no rufous in wings. **Black-
    billed** *C. erythropthalmus* (text). N migr. Also
    much like 1 but bill all black, eyering red, no ru-
    fous in wings; white tail spots small and narrow.
  2. Dark-billed   *C. melacoryphus*   p. 351
    Deep buff below; black mask bordered below by
    band of gray; no rufous in wings. At least par-
    tially migratory. **Mangrove** *C. minor* (text). Much
    like 2 but larger and heavier; bill stouter, yellow
    at base of lower mandible; no gray band below
    mask. Rare. Mangroves (?).
  3. Gray-capped   *C. lansbergi*   p. 351
    Darker, richer brown than allies; gray crown,
    deep buff below. Rare.
  4. Dwarf   *C. pumilus*   p. 348
    Grayish above; rufous throat; tail-tipping obscure.
    Partially migratory.
  5. Striped Cuckoo   *Tapera n. naevia*   p. 355
    Quail-like head pattern; expressive crest; flexes
    black alula feathers at bend of wing; striped
    above (cf. 7 and 8); black whisker mark. Imm.
    rather spotted above, faint barring below.

Cuckoos   *Dromococcyx*
Hunched and brown; small headed; flat, pointed
crest; long, broad tail; spotted upper tail coverts
nearly as long as tail. Suspicious and retiring.
  6. Pavonine   *D. p. pavoninus*   p. 356
    Unspotted fulvous neck and breast. Cf. larger 8.
    Uncommon, local, difficult to see.
  7. Pheasant   *D. p. phasianellus*   p. 355
    Scaly above; *speckled neck and chest.* Note
    chestnut cap; tail longer and broader than 6 but
    equally uncommon, local, and difficult to see.

Cuckoos   *Piaya*
Long graduated tail; plumage mostly reddish chestnut.
  8. Little   *P. m. minuta*   p. 352
    Much smaller and shorter-tailed than 9; red eye-
    ring; underparts mainly rufous chestnut. Low in
    wet thickets.

  9. Squirrel   *P. cayana mehleri*   p. 351
    Bill and eyering greenish yellow; *lower under-
    parts pale gray* (cf. 8 and 10). Widespread.
  10. Black-bellied   *P. m. melanogaster*   p. 352
    S. Red bill; colorful blue and yellow orbital skin;
    gray cap; plumage rufous with black belly. Forest
    canopy.
  11. Rufous-winged Ground-Cuckoo
    Neomorphus rufipennis   p. 356
    S. Nothing quite like it (but cf. 3 on Pl. 15). Be-
    havior and appearance recall a roadrunner of N
    Amer. Forest floor.

Greater, Smooth-billed, and **Groove-billed anis**:
see figure in text, page 353.

  12. Black-collared Jay   *Cyanolyca armillata
    meridana*   p. 682
    Andes. Rich deep blue, crown and throat
    brighter; note black mask and inconspic. collar.
    Cloud forest.

Jays   *Cyanocorax*
Black on throat and chest; short plushy tuft on forehead; most with patches of colored skin around eyes.
  13. Black-chested   *C. a. affinis*   p. 683
    NW. White lower underparts and white tail tips;
    only jay in its range. Dry forest and scrub.
  14. Inca   *C. yncas guatimalensis*   p. 684
    N mts. Colorful and not likely mistaken. Blue
    crown, green upperparts; yellow underparts; yel-
    low outer tail feathers.
  15. Violaceous   *C. v. violaceus*   p. 682
    S. Foreparts black; nape pale; body dull, faded
    brownish violet to brownish blue (duller than
    shown). Widespread. **Azure-naped** *C. heilprini*
    (text). Local in Amazonas. Much like 15 but note
    white eyes; mostly white crown; white tail tips.
  16. Cayenne   *C. cayanus*   p. 683
    SE. Boldly marked. White crown, white lower
    breast and belly; white tail tips.

23

1. **Barn Owl** *Tyto alba hellmayri* p. 357
Very pale, almost ghostly; note heart-shaped face, dark eyes; minute dotting on plumage; underparts white to rich buff.

2. **Short-eared Owl** *Asio flammeus pallidicaudus* p. 367
Med.-sized, open-country, diurnal owl; *boldly streaked below;* yellow eyes in dark eye sockets; inconsequential ear-tufts. *Black wrist patch* in flight.

3. **Burrowing Owl** *Athene cunicularia apurensis* p. 363
Appealing little owl with *long legs* and perpetual stare. *Coarse white spotting above;* scattered coarse barring on chest. Terrestrial. Open terrain.

4. **Striped Owl** *Asio c. clamator* p. 366
Bold crisp streaking, close-set ear-tufts, *dark eyes.* Open terrain, grasslands.

Screech-Owls *Otus*
Mostly small owls with short ear-tufts; eyes yellow or brown, plumages quite sim. and often confusing; inconspic. habits; nocturnal; best told by combination of voice and range.

5. **Tropical** *O. choliba crucigerus* p. 359
Yellow eyes; *narrow black streaking on underparts and fainter horizontal hatching;* black rim on facial disk. Widespread; common. **5a.** Gray form. **5b.** Rufescent form.

6. **Foothill** *O. r. roraimae* p. 358
N; SE mts. Recalls 5b but plumage pattern denser, more vermiculated; voice differs. Humid foothill forest.

7. **White-throated** *O. albogularis meridensis* p. 360
Andes. Large *Otus;* dark brown with *white throat;* contrasting buff belly streaked dusky; inconsequential ear-tufts.

8. **Rufescent** *O. ingens venezuelanus* p. 359
N mts. Large *Otus;* dark eyes, rufous to dark brown plumage with few good marks; note *whitish eyebrows; absence of facial rim.*

9. **Tawny-bellied** *O. w. watsonii* p. 360
Perijá Mts.; S. Fairly large, dark *Otus;* plumage variable; black ear-tufts and facial rim; usually quite tawny below with weak streaking and cross-hatching. Humid forest.

Pygmy-Owls *Glaucidium*
Tiny, "earless," rather long tailed, and with alert demeanor; largely diurnal; 2 black "false eyespots" on hindneck (as if looking in both directions); bold streaks on underparts.

10. **Andean** *G. jardinii* p. 361
Andes. Much like commoner 11 but markings finer, more muted; crown dotted. **10a.** Grayish form (commonest). **10b.** Rufescent form. **10c.** Mixed plumage. **Amazonian** *G. hardyi* (text).

11. **Ferruginous** *G. brasilianum phalaenoides* p. 362
Plumage varies from grayish brown to bright rufous; crown with fine dotlike streaks; boldly streaked below. Widespread in lowlands. **11a.** Rufescent form. **11b.** Grayish brown form.

12. **Buff-fronted Owl** *Aegolius h. harrisii* p. 367
Mts. Unmistakable buff and black plumage. Note black-rimmed facial disk and unmarked deep buff underparts. Rare.

24

J WEBB '97

1. **Great Horned Owl**   *Bubo virginianus nacurutu*   p. 361
   Large, powerful owl; black-rimmed facial disk; prom. ear-tufts; *close, even-spaced barring below.* Common in llanos.

2. **Crested Owl**   *Lophostrix c. cristata*   p. 363
   Med. sized; appears unmarked below; long white crest typically flattened and not conspic.; raised almost vertical in alarm or threat.

Owls   *Strix*
Med. sized, "earless" forest owls.

3. **Black-and-white**   *S. nigrolineata*   p. 364
   N. No other Venez. owl has black upperparts, and neck and underparts white finely and evenly barred black. Local.

4. **Black-banded**   *S. h. huhula*   p. 365
   S. Smaller, darker version of 3; black above and below; narrow white lines (sometimes faint above).

5. **Stygian Owl**   *Asio stygius robustus*   p. 366
   Dark enigmatic owl with close-set ear-tufts; note whitish patch on forehead; coarse herringbone streaks on underparts. Very rare.

6. **Spectacled Owl**   *Pulsatrix p. perspicillata*   p. 364
   Large and "earless." **6a.** Ad.: chocolate brown above, *white facial markings; dark brown chest band.* **6b.** Juv.: white with black mask. Widespread in lowland forest, gallery forest, etc.

7. **Rufous-banded Owl**   *Strix albitarsis*   p. 365
   Andes. Resembles 8 but markings coarser on hindneck and mantle; bolder facial outline, *decidedly rufous chest band and pale squarish markings on lower underparts.*

8. **Mottled Owl**   *Strix v. virgata*   p. 365
   Med. sized. Local. **8a.** Ad.: note *dark eyes and absence of ear-tufts;* plumage densely mottled

brown, more streaky below. Facial disk outlined pale. **8b.** Juv.

9. **Oilbird**   *Steatornis caripensis*   p. 368
   Resembles a giant nightjar (*Caprimulgus*). *Rufous with white spotting;* yellowish bill. Long winged and long tailed in flight. Nocturnal; in caves.

Potoos   *Nyctibius*
Nocturnal, solitary, and cryptic; sit erect and motionless in trees by day. Eyes reflect orangish yellow at night. Note vocalizations.

10. **Great**   *N. g. grandis*   p. 369
    Large and robust; *usually quite whitish* (some variation); no dusky malar but may show sprinkling of dark spots on chest. Tail-bar pattern diagnostic if seen (text); at night, when foraging, usually perches higher than 13. Gruff voice on moonlit nights. Widespread.

11. **Long-tailed**   *N. aethereus longicaudatus* p. 369
    S. Almost as large as 10 but plumage nearer 13 (even *darker and browner*); note *long, pale malar stripe; wedge-shaped tail extends well beyond tail.* Low inside humid forest.

12. **Andean**   *N. maculosus*   p. 370
    S Táchira. Rather small, rare montane potoo; overall rather dark; ♂ has whitish wing coverts (not always obvious).

13. **Common**   *N. griseus panamensis*   p. 370
    Pale grayish to brownish; lacks strong markings; look for dusky malar, dark mottling on chest; much smaller than 10 and at night normally perches lower than 10 when foraging. Wailing, descending voice on moonlit nights. **13a.** Foraging. **13b.** Resting.

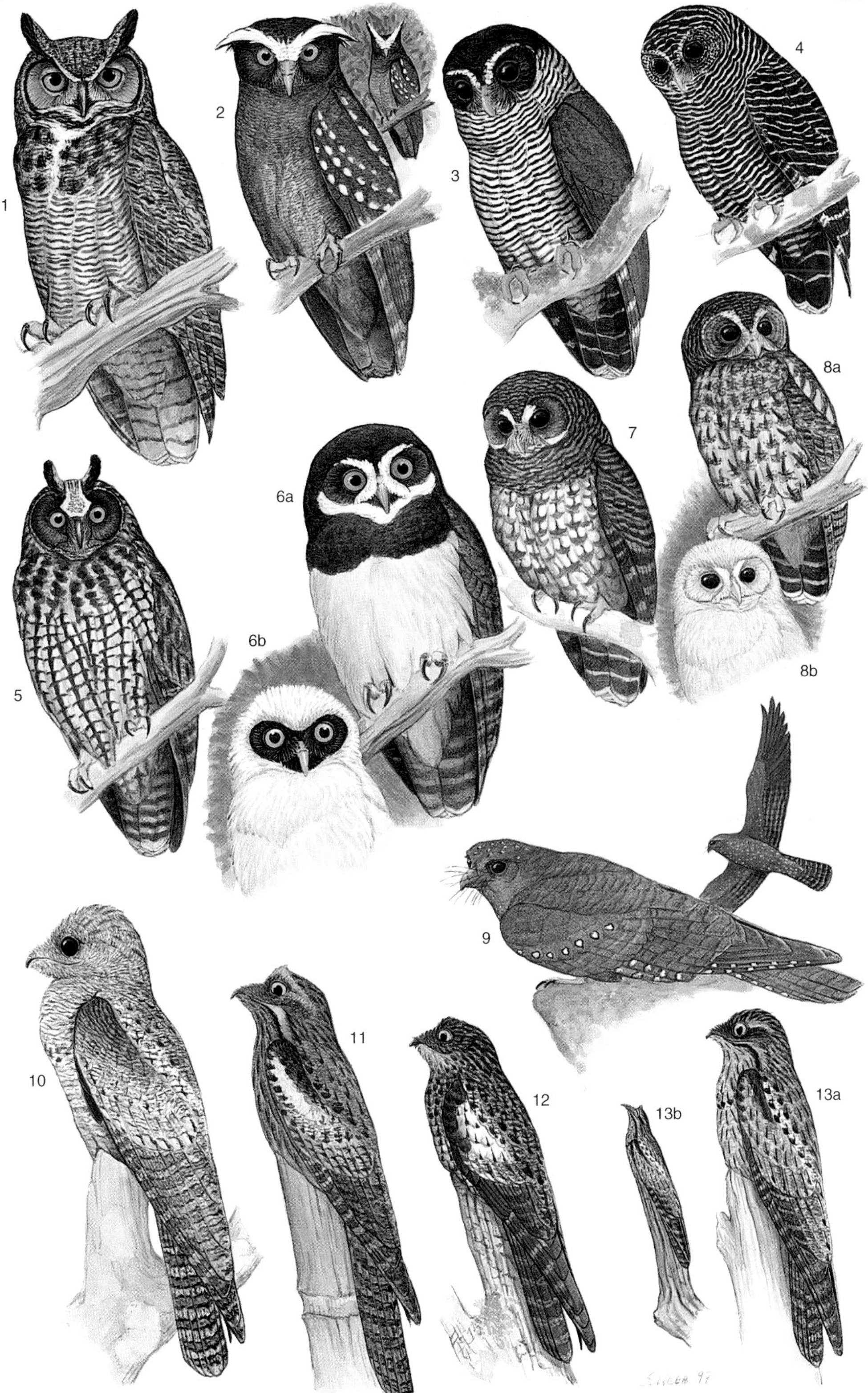
1
2
3
4
8a
7
6a
5
6b
8b
9
10
11
12
13b
13a

25

1. **Nacunda Nighthawk**   *Podager nacunda*
   minor   p. 375
   Resembles *Chordeiles* (below) but much larger,
   wings broader and rounded. Note white wing
   linings and belly; short tail. Bounding flight high
   overhead. Rests in open on gd.

Nighthawks   *Chordeiles*
Open zones, sandbars, or in migration, over humid
forest; narrow, pointed wings; hunt in sustained, stiff-
winged flight, high or, in some spp., rather low.
   2. **Sand-colored**   *C. r. rupestris*   p. 374
      S. Flashing black-and-white wing pattern; no
      wing bands; smaller, paler, and longer-tailed than
      1; mechanical flight. Social, small to large flocks,
      often in vicinity of water. Rests on river sandbars.
   3. **Least**   *C. pusillus septentrionalis*   p. 372
      S. Much like 4 but smaller and darker; *crissum*
      white; from above note *white trailing edge on
      secondaries*. Rests under bushes in savanna.
      Grasslands.
   4. **Lesser**   *C. a. acutipennis*   p. 373
      Resident. Med. sized; prom. white wing band
      (buff—♀) nearer wing tip than 5; shows white
      subterminal tail band from below as flushes. Of-
      ten rests on unpaved roads shortly after dark.
   5. **Common**   *C. m. minor*   p. 373
      N migr. Much like 4, but note placement of *white
      wing band about midway between wrist and tip*
      (instead of nearer tip).

Nighthawk   *Nyctiprogne*
Small, dark *Chordeiles* ally. Peculiar voice and social
habits.
   6. **Band-tailed**   *N. leucopyga pallida*   p. 374
      Small and uniformly dark; *no white wing bands*.
      From below shows narrow white band across
      mid. tail (hard to see). Varying-sized flocks flut-
      ter low to high over water, less over land, at
      dusk.

Nighthawks   *Lurocalis*
Solitary, fast-flying nighthawks without wing bands.
Emerge moments before dark; swerve and dart
among treetops. Rest on high tree branches in forest.
   7. **Short-tailed**   *L. s. semitorquatus*   p. 371
      Fairly large and all dark but with blackish barring
      on belly and under wing coverts (cf. 8); *very
      short tail* (almost a "flying wing"); fast, notably
      erratic treetop flight. Lowlands and foothills. Pre-
      sum. resident, and austral migrs.
   8. **Rufous-bellied**   *L. rufiventris*   p. 372
      Andes. Much like 7 but larger; *belly rufous, wing
      linings rufous; note montane distrib.*

26

Nightjar *Uropsalis*
Resembles *Caprimulgus* but ♂ with greatly elongated
tail; elaborate aerial courtship display.
 1. **Lyre-tailed**   *U. l. lyra*   p. 381
    Andes. Cryptic plumage. Note ♂'s long, white-
    tipped, somewhat lyre-shaped tail. Both sexes
    quite dark; *densely barred below*; *rufous nuchal
    collar*. ♀'s tail not elongated.

Nightjars *Caprimulgus*
Cryptic plumage; long, rounded wings, slightly
rounded tail; rather large head and wide gape; rest by
day on gd. or low branch; flush with bounding,
floppy flight, wings bowed and raised high; sally for
flying insects or (some spp.) forage in low, slow, rambling flights on shallow wing beats; forage and call
only after dark. Often difficult to identify, esp. ♀♀; always note voice.
 2. **Blackish**   *C. nigrescens*   p. 377
    S. Very blackish (cf. 3 and 4) with grayish area
    on tertials; *wings reach tip of short tail*. ♂ has
    small, inconspic. white bar on wing; tiny white
    tail corners. ♀ all dark (text). Boulders in rivers;
    small openings in humid forested lowlands and
    foothills.
 3. **Band-winged**   *C. longirostris*   p. 377
    N mts. Very dark. **3a.** *C. l. ruficervix:* boldly
    marked ♂ has prom. white wing band, rufous
    nuchal collar; all but central tail feathers broadly
    tipped white. ♀ sim. but white markings re-
    placed by buff. **3b.** *C. l. roraimae:* tepuis (higher
    els. than 4). Sim. to 3a but larger and blacker;
    tail tipped buff.
 4. **Roraiman**   *C. whitelyi*   p. 378
    A few tepuis in S Bolívar. Much like 2 and 3. *Very
    dark;* tail short; note ♂'s *white-spotted wing
    coverts*, small white wing band. ♀ may show a
    few rufous dots on wing coverts; no white wing
    band. Belly buff (♂ and ♀) with variable gray
    barring. ♀ from 2 or 3 by white tail tips. Very
    rare and little known. Moderate els.
 5. **Spot-tailed**   *C. maculicaudus*   p. 379
    Small, handsomely marked nightjar. Dusky
    crown; underparts mostly gray and buff; *dusky
    ocular area* (blackish "eye sockets"); *rufous
    nuchal collar, no white band in wing; rather spotty
    below; broad white tail tip* (or grayish—♀). Local
    in weedy, grassy, and damp semiopen areas.
 6. **Little**   *C. parvulus heterurus*   p. 380
    Notably small and grayish; *wings reach tips of
    short tail*. White throat; prom. *white wing band,
    broad white tail tips*; inconspic. rufous nuchal
    collar. ♀ sim. but buff wing bands, no tail band.
    Near or in forest.

 7. **White-tailed**   *C. c. cayennensis*   p. 379
    Slender and pale. ♂ has conspic. *cinnamon ru-
    fous nuchal collar, white wing bands, mostly
    whitish underparts* with a few buff markings;
    longish tail white-edged from above, *mostly
    white from below*. Confusing ♀ like ♂ above
    (incl. nuchal collar) but darker, underparts mot-
    tled and barred buff; *no white* in wings or tail.
    Often forages in long-sustained low, rambling
    flights. Grasslands; open slopes in foothills.

Nightjar *Hydropsalis*
Much like *Caprimulgus* but wings narrow; long tail
double-notched (trident shaped).
 8. **Ladder-tailed**   *H. c. climacocerca*   p. 380
    S. Fairly large, slender, and lanky. ♂ flashes
    much white in wings and notably long, triple-
    pointed tail. ♀ essentially uniform but note slen-
    der, long-winged, long-tailed shape as in ♂. Sal-
    lies from low stub or gd. Sandbars and
    riverbanks.
 9. **Pauraque**   *Nyctidromus a. albicollis*   p. 375
    Long rounded tail extends well beyond wings. At
    rest look for *chestnut cheek patch*, prom. row of
    buff-encircled black scapular spots. In flight ♂
    shows bold white wing band and much white on
    inner webs of outer tail feathers (conspic. when
    flushed). ♀ has narrow buff wing bands; white
    only on tips of outer tail feathers. At times wary,
    at other times can be approached closely. Often
    sits on quiet roadsides. Widespread; common.
    Two phases. **9a.** Gray phase (commonest).
    9b. Rufous phase (local).
10. **Rufous Nightjar**   *Caprimulgus rufus
    minimus*   p. 376
    Nearly identical to 11, but voice differs and this
    sp. is often vocal in Venez. (unlike 11). *Quite
    large, uniform dark rufous to rufous brown, incl.
    crown;* lacks good marks but everywhere densely
    mottled and vermiculated blackish; buff white
    inner web of outer third of outer tail feathers
    forms large oval patch (from below). Wide-
    spread but local in forested lowlands and
    foothills.
11. **Chuck-will's-widow**   *Caprimulgus
    carolinensis*   p. 376
    N migr. Rufous ads. practically identical to 10
    (text). Grayish ads. (none reported in Venez.)
    more easily recognized. In all forms note *grayish
    (not rufous) crown;* white inner webs on outer
    tail feathers more extensive, extending nearly full
    length of tail. Few recs.; does not vocalize in
    Venez.

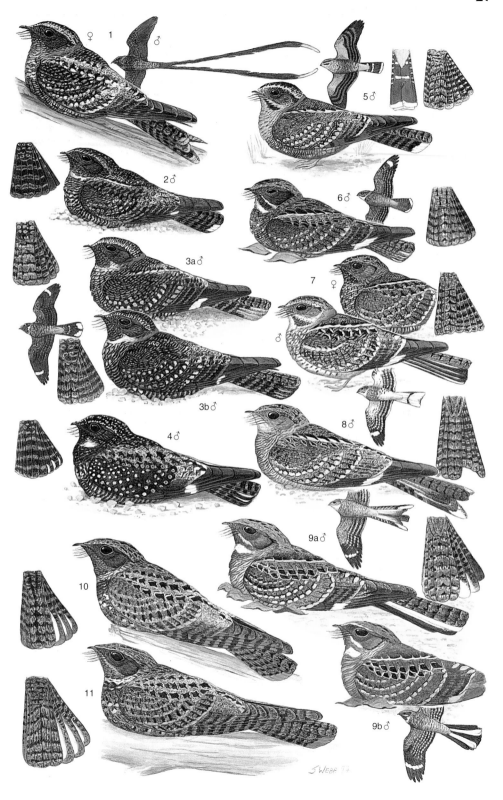

♀ 1

♂

5♂

2♂

6♂

3a♂

7 ♀

♂

3b♂

8♂

4♂

9a♂

10

11

9b♂

J. WEBB

NOTE: Many swifts are difficult to identify with confidence. Learn the plumages, flight patterns, habits, and distributions of the commonest and most distinctive spp. first (1, 3, 6, 8, 11, 14). Especially note the effect of differing light levels on pale and dark areas. Experience and careful observation are essential, and even then many spp. can be identified with certainty only under ideal conditions.

1. White-collared Swift   *Streptoprocne zonaris albicincta*   p. 382
Large, powerful, fast-flying swift. White collar usually visible (except at great distance) but often incomplete on young birds. Large, noisy flocks of its own, less often joined by smaller spp.; often sails upward in vortex of thermals. Widespread.

Swifts   *Cypseloides*
Larger and blacker than *Chaetura*, and with more swept-back wings and faster flight that includes more gliding. Wings, rump, and tail always virtually uniform (no contrast); underparts usually uniform, or with chestnut or white on throat. Imms. have gray scaling on belly.

2. Tepui   *C. phelpsi*   p. 383
Tepuis. Much like more widespread 3 but *rufous collar of ♂ more extensive on underparts* (entire chin and throat). ♀ little or no rufous. Wings longer and tail decidedly longer and more forked than allies.

3. Chestnut-collared   *C. r. rutilus*   p. 383
N mts. Blackish and rather long tailed. ♂ has chestnut collar but chestnut difficult to see except against dark background. ♀♀ (and young?) lack or have incomplete rufous collars (usually look all black in field).

4. White-chinned   *C. cryptus*   p. 384
SE. Uniformly blackish; large robust body, notably short square tail. Tiny white chin spot a useful mark in hand. Status uncertain because sp. is so difficult to identify with confidence in field. Rare.

5. Spot-fronted   *C. cherriei*   p. 384
N mts. Very sim. to 3. Another large, all-blackish swift. White loral and postocular spot diagnostic but rarely, if ever, visible in field. Few recs.

Swifts   *Chaetura*
Small with twittery, stiff-winged flight (little gliding); many are difficult to identify with confidence; all have, to a greater or lesser degree, contrasting rumps and pale throats, slight differences in which are important in field identification. Experienced observers will realize that many sightings should remain unidentified.

6. Band-rumped   *C. spinicauda latirostris*   p. 387
Small, slender, relatively long tailed. From all others by *narrow whitish rump band*; tail blackish; throat quite pale; speedy, veering flight.

7. Gray-rumped   *C. cinereiventris lawrencei*   p. 387
Small; *obviously gray (never whitish) rump and upper tail coverts* (cf. narrow band of 6) contrast with blackish back. Relatively small; no brown in plumage. **Chimney** *C. pelagica* (text). N migr. *Larger* than most of allies; sooty black, rump a little paler, more dark grayish brown; contrasting whitish gray throat. Few recs., prob. in part because of identification difficulties. At present, inseparable in field from 10 (text).

8. Vaux's   *C. vauxi andrei*   p. 386
Mainly N mts. Notably small; overall rather dark, lacking strong contrast on rump; throat markedly paler than rest of underparts. Common resident in N; local along lower Orinoco.

9. Chapman's   *C. c. chapmani*   p. 385
A bit larger than most allies and very like 8 and 10; dark, glossy blue black above, blackest on crown and mantle, turning grayish brown on rump but with minimal contrast; throat hardly paler at all than rest of underparts (some virtually concolor below). Difficult to identify with confidence. Recs. widely scattered; range uncertain.

10. Ashy-tailed   *C. m. meridionalis*   p. 385
Presum. S migr. Large and essentially identical in field to Chimney Swift (see 7 and text), a N temperate migr. Prob. the 2 occur in Venez. with little or no temporal overlap. So far definitely known only from 1 specimen in Venez.

11. Short-tailed   *C. b. brachyura*   p. 386
Med. sized; *notably pale rump and upper tail coverts* completely cover *very short tail* (looks tail-less). Notably broad secondaries impart floppy aspect to wing beats. One of more easily identified *Chaetura*. Mostly over humid lowland forest, occas. dry semiopen zones.

12. White-tipped Swift   *Aeronautes m. montivagus*   p. 388
Slender, speedy swift with fairly long squarish to slightly forked tail; note *white bib, small white flank patches, white tail tips*. Flocks in foothills and mts.

13. Lesser Swallow-tailed Swift   *Panyptila c. cayennensis*   p. 388
Recalls 14 but *plumage contrasting black and white;* long, deeply forked tail (no white tips), more white on throat and neck. *Solitary or in prs.* (never flocks) in lowlands and foothills.

14. Neotropical Palm-Swift   *Tachornis s. squamata*   p. 389
Slender, dingy brownish swift that usually holds long forked tail closed in needle point. Note narrow wings, buzzy flight. May fly low over open areas, high over forest, usually not far from palms. Lowland forest and semiopen areas. Common S of Orinoco; local northward.

15. Pygmy Palm-Swift   *Tachornis furcata nigrodosalis*   p. 389
S Maracaibo Basin. Not as tiny as name would suggest, although smaller than 14 (no range overlap) which it closely resembles. Reduced whitish on underparts; up close note white at base of tail. Reg. over towns and villages where there are palm trees.

28

Coquettes   *Lophornis*
Beelike; white or buff rump band (both sexes).
1. **Spangled**   *L. stictolophus*   p. 406
   N. ♂ bushy black-dotted crest (cf. 2); ♀ forecrown rufous; buff throat speckled blackish.
2. **Tufted**   *L. ornatus*   p. 406
   ♂ much like 1 but crest solid rufous; tufts on
   neck. ♀ rufous frontlet; throat and chest rufous
   (no speckling).
3. **Peacock**   *L. p. pavoninus*   p. 407
   Tepuis. ♂ fanlike cheek plumes. ♀ *streaked
   below.*
4. **Festive**   *L. chalybeus verreauxii*   p. 407
   S. ♂ recalls 3; overall quite dark. ♀ Pl. 31(1).
5. **Black-bellied Thorntail**   *Popelairia
   langsdorffi melanosternon*   p. 408
   S. White rump band ♂ spiky tail. ♀ white malar;
   underparts green and black. Cf. ♀♀ of 1 and 2
   (Pl. 31).
6. **Racket-tailed Coquette**   *Discosura
   longicauda*   p. 408
   S. ♂ racket tail. ♀ (also Pl. 31:2) buff rump
   band, black throat and white malar; belly buff.
   Cf. ♀ of 1 (Pl. 31) and ♀ of 5.

Woodstars   *Calliphlox* and *Chaetocercus*
Beelike; white (♂) or buff (♀) crescent on chest;
white flank patch (no rump band).
7. **Amethyst**   *Calliphlox amethystina*   p. 434
   ♂ rosy throat, forked tail. ♀ dingy throat, whitish
   across chest; belly cinnamon.
8. **Rufous-shafted**   *Chaetocercus jourdanii
   andinus*   p. 435
   ♂ forked tail shows rufous (cf. 9). ♀ cinnamon
   below; outer tail rufous (cf. 9). Mts. W, N.
9. **Gorgeted**   *Chaetocercus h. heliodor* p. 435
   Andes. ♂ flared gorget. ♀ like ♀ of 8 but tail all
   rufous with black subterminal band.

Emeralds   *Chlorostilbon*
♀♀ white postocular, dusky cheeks, grayish underparts. All Venez. *Chlorostilbon* illus. Pl. 31.
10. **Blue-tailed**   *C. mellisugus caribaeus*   p. 409
    ♂ straight black bill; forked tail. Pl. 31(6).
11. **Narrow-tailed**   *C. s. stenura*   p. 410
    Andes (high els.). Also Pl. 31(11). ♂ spiky outer
    tail feathers. Cf. 9 and 10 (lower el) on Pl. 30.

Emeralds   *Amazilia*
12. **White-chested**   *A. c. chionopectus* p. 417
    E; S. Also Pl. 31(15). *Bill black* (cf. 13, 14). **Plain-
    bellied** *A. leucogaster* Pl. 31(13).
13. **Versicolored**   *A. versicolor hollandi*   p. 417
    S. Also Pl. 31(12). Pinkish red on mandible; S
    race bluer on head.
14. **Glittering-throated**   *A. fimbriata
    elegantissima*   p. 418
    Wedge of white up belly. ♀ duller. Common.
    Sapphire-spangled *A. lactea* Pl. 31(16).
15. **Blue-chinned Sapphire**   *Chlorestes n.
    notatus*   p. 409
    Blue glitter on throat; unforked tail. ♀ underparts
    grayish disked green.

16. **Shining-green Hummingbird**
    Lepidopyga goudoti phaeochroa   p. 413
    NW. ♂ all green; forked tail. ♀ below dingy
    white speckled green.
17. **Wedge-billed Hummingbird**   *Schistes g.
    geoffroyi*   p. 433
    N mts. *Coppery rump.* ♀ gorget duller.
18. **Speckled Hummingbird**   *Adelomyia
    melanogenys aeneosticta*   p. 421
    N mts. Brown; *Phaethornis*-like plumage.

Hummingbirds   *Amazilia*
19. **Rufous-tailed**   *A. t. tzacatl*   p. 420
    NW. Bill quite red; *rufous tail;* underparts dull.
20. **Green-bellied**   *A. viridigaster iodura*   p. 420
    Andes. Brownish rump. **Copper-tailed** *A. cupre-
    icauda* (text). S tepuis. Tail rufous.
21. **Copper-rumped**   *A. tobaci caudata*   p. 420
    Rump brown; crissum brown. Widespread.
22. **Steely-vented**   *A. saucerrottei braccata*   p. 419
    Much like 21. Narrow reddish copper band
    across upper tail coverts; bluish crissum.
23. **Fork-tailed Woodnymph**   *Thalurania
    furcata fissilis*   p. 412
    E; S. ♂ emerald gorget; purple belly; forked tail.
    ♀ gray below; gray tail tips. **Violet-crowned** *T.
    colombica* (text). N mts. Forecrown violet blue.
24. **Golden-tailed Sapphire**   *Chrysuronia o.
    oenone*   p. 414
    Golden rufous tail. ♂ blue head. ♀ spotty below.

Sapphires   *Hylocharis*
25. **Rufous-throated**   *H. sapphirina*   p. 413
    SE. ♂ red bill, rufous chin and tail. ♀ chin ru-
    fous, throat and breast spotted.
26. **White-chinned**   *H. cyanus viridiventris*   p. 413
    Narrow coppery rump band. ♂ all dark with red
    bill. ♀ grayish and speckled below.
27. **Buffy Hummingbird**   *Leucippus f. fallax*   p. 416
    N deserts. Faded green; underparts buff.
28. **Ruby-topaz Hummingbird**   *Chrysolampis
    mosquitus*   p. 404
    Short decurved bill. ♂ dark with rufous tail.
    ♀ gray below; rufous in white-tipped tail.
29. **Violet-headed Hummingbird**   *Klais g.
    guimeti*   p. 405
    N mts. *Small.* Conspic. *white eyespot; white tail
    tips.* ♂ violet head. ♀ gray below.

Goldenthroats   *Polytmus*
30. **Green-tailed**   *P. theresiae leucorrhous*
    S. Smaller, greener than 31. No white in tail.
    ♀ mottled white underparts. Semiopen.
31. **White-tailed**   *P. g. guainumbi*   p. 416
    Decurved bill, stronger facial pattern than 30;
    white at base and tip of tail. Grasslands.
32. **Tepui**   *P. milleri*   p. 415
    Tepuis. Large size; white in tail; note distrib.
33. **White-vented Plumeleteer**   *Chalybura
    buffonii aeneicauda*   p. 415
    N mts. ♂ large and dark; decurved bill; ample
    tail, white crissum. ♀ gray below.
34. **White-necked Jacobin**   *Florisuga m.
    mellivora*   p. 400
    ♂ white belly and tail. ♀ duller, or scaly below;
    tail with or without white. ♂ Pl. 31(22).

29

Sunangels   *Heliangelus*
Short bill; buff or white crescent on chest. ♀ buff gorget speckled green; med.-long tail.

1. Orange-throated   *H. mavors*   p. 428
Andes. ♂ dazzling orange throat; buff crescent. ♀ rusty buff below; crescent band duller.

2. Longuemare's   *H. clarisse spencei*   p. 428
Perijá Mts.; Andes. Amethyst throat; white crescent on chest.

3. Tyrian Metaltail   *Metallura tyrianthina oreopola*   p. 431
N mts. Small with short bill; longish tail. ♂ all dark with reddish to wine to purple tail. ♀ speckled rufous throat. **Perijá** *M. iracunda* (text).

4. Bronze-tailed Thornbill   *Chalcostigma heteropogon*   p. 431
S Táchira. Large; short bill; reddish bronze rump.

5. Purple-backed Thornbill   *Ramphomicron microrhynchum andicolum*   p. 430
Andes. Tiny. ♂ purple back. ♀ spotted below; long white-tipped tail.

Pufflegs   *Eriocnemis*
Greatly enlarged, puffy leg-tufts; colorful crissum.

6. Coppery-bellied   *E. cupreoventris*   p. 429
Andes. Coppery orange belly; white leg puffs; violet crissum (shared with 7).

7. Glowing   *E. vestitus*   p. 429
Andes. Glittery green; white leg puffs. ♂ blue throat patch; violet crissum (as in 6). ♀ mixed buff and green below.

Brilliants   *Heliodoxa*
Rather large; bill stout; crown flat; ♀♀ and imms. often show whitish malar stripe.

8. Violet-fronted   *H. l. leadbeateri*   p. 422
Andes. Very dark. ♂ violet frontlet; ♀ speckled below.

9. Velvet-browed   *H. xanthogonys*   p. 423
Tepuis. Very dark. ♂ emerald frontlet.

Lancebills   *Doryfera*
Dark; unusually long, thin, straight bill.

10. Blue-fronted   *D. johannae guianensis*   p. 398
Tepuis. ♂ blackish; blue-violet frontlet. ♀ as in 11.

11. Green-fronted   *D. l. ludovicae*   p. 397
Andes. ♂ frontlet green.

Violetears   *Colibri*
Violet ear patch; dark subterminal tail band; slight decurve to bill (except 12).

12. Brown   *C. delphinae*   p. 401
Mts. Dull and brownish; bill short; rump rusty orange.

13. Green   *C. thalassinus cyanotus*   p. 401
N mts. Chin and underparts entirely green.

14. Sparkling   *C. c. coruscans*   p. 401
Mts. *Large;* violet blue "chin strap," *blue breast patch.*

Mangos   *Anthracothorax*
Slightly decurved bill; magenta in tail. ♀♀ distinctive but all sim.

15. Black-throated   *A. nigricollis*   p. 403
♂ central underparts solid black. **Green-throated** *A. viridigula* Pl. 31(28).

16. Green-breasted   *A. prevostii viridicordatus*   p. 402
N. ♂ black confined to center of throat; breast mainly green (cf. 15).

17. Long-billed Starthroat   *Heliomaster l. longirostris*   p. 434
Long straight bill; ruby throat; white stripe up lower back (usually). ♀ usually lacks ruby on throat.

18. Mountain Velvetbreast   *Lafresnaya lafresnayi greenewalti*   p. 424
Andes. Decurved bill; tail mostly white (buff—S Táchira).

Sabrewings   *Campylopterus*
Large, slightly decurved bill.

19. Lazuline   *C. falcatus*   p. 400
N mts. Decurved bill. ♂ tail mostly *dark rufous chestnut.* ♀ grayish below; less rufous in tail.

20. Gray-breasted   *C. l. largipennis*   p. 398
S. Large; gray below; large white tail corners.

21. White-tailed   *C. ensipennis*   p. 399
NE. Mostly white tail. ♀ duller.

22. Rufous-breasted   *C. hyperythrus*   p. 399
Tepuis of Bolívar. Underparts and tail all rufous. Cf. **Buff-breasted** *C. duidae* Pl. 31(24).

23. Violet-chested Hummingbird   *Sternoclyta cyanopectus*   p. 424
N mts. ♀ has violet chest; like ♀ of 8 but belly buff.

24. Buff-tailed Coronet   *Boissonneaua f. flavescens*   p. 427
Andes. Short bill; ample, mostly buff tail.

Incas and Starfrontlets   *Coeligena*
Long, straight to slightly upturned bills.

25. Collared Inca   *C. torquata conradii*   p. 425
Andes. ♂ white chest and bold flashing white in tail. Plumage blackish in S Táchira. ♀ sim. but speckled green and buff below.

26. Bronzy Inca   *C. c. coeligena*   p. 424
N mts. Mainly brownish wine; throat speckled.

27. Golden-tailed Starfrontlet   *C. eos*   p. 426
The Andes. **Golden-bellied** *C. bonapartei* (text). Perijá Mts. Both spp. show prom. buff wing band and golden rufous rearparts.

28. Blue-throated Starfrontlet   *C. helianthea tamae*   p. 426
S Táchira. Very dark; glittery patches of color may show, incl. glittery aqua rump. ♀ duller belly.

30

Coquettes   *Lophornis*
Tiny; ♂♂ ornate; white or buff rump band.
  1. Festive   L. *chalybeus klagesi*   p. 407
    S (local). ♀ underparts mixed buff, green, and
    black; much like ♀ of 5 (Pl. 29) but smaller
    malar patch. Also cf. ♀ of 2. ♂ Pl. 29(4).
  2. Racket-tailed Coquette   *Discosura*
    longicauda   p. 408
    S. ♀ black throat bordered on sides by white
    malar, more or less by white below. Cf. ♀ of 1;
    also ♀ of 5 (Pl. 5). ♂ Pl. 29(6).
  3. Spangled Coquette   *Lophornis*
    stictolophus   p. 406
    ♀ rufous forecrown; throat speckled black; chest
    smudged blackish. Cf. ♀ of 2 (Pl. 29).
  4. Gorgeted Woodstar   *Chaetocercus h.*
    heliodor   p. 435
    N mts. Tail *all rufous* with only narrow black
    band (cf. ♀ of 8 on Pl. 29); tail not deeply
    forked.
  5. Booted Racket-tail   *Ocreatus*
    underwoodii polystictus   p. 429
    ♀ white speckled green below; large white tips
    on long tail.

Emeralds   *Chlorostilbon*
♂♂ small and glittery; differ mainly in bill color, tail
color and length. ♀♀ all very sim.; white postocular,
blackish cheeks, grayish below. Not safely separated
in field (text).
  6. Blue-tailed   *C. mellisugus caribaeus*   p. 409
    ♂ very glittery; straight black bill; steel blue tail.
    ♂ and ♀ Pl. 29(10).
  7. Red-billed   *C. gibsoni nitens*   p. 410
    N deserts. ♂ like 6 but with partly red bill.
  8. Coppery   *C. russatus*   p. 410
    Perijá Mts. ♂ coppery tail; mainly green; faint
    chartreuse tinge on throat.
  9. Short-tailed   *C. poortmani*   p. 411
    Andes. ♂ green tail much shorter than tail tips.
  10. Green-tailed   *C. alice*   p. 411
    N mts. ♂ like 9 but tail about as long as wing
    tips; outer tail feathers normal (cf. 11).
  11. Narrow-tailed   *C. s. stenura*   p. 410
    Andes. ♂ like 10 but outer tail feathers narrow
    and spiky. ♂ also Pl. 29(11).

Emeralds   *Amazilia*
Avg., med.-sized hummers; all (except 15) with some
red on lower mandible.
  12. Versicolored   *A. versicolor*   p. 417
    12a. *A. v. hollandi:* E; S. Head *strongly tinged blue*
    (also Pl. 29:13). **12b.** *A. v. milleri:* NW Bolívar; n
    Amazonas. Glittering aqua green crown.
  13. Plain-bellied   *A. l. leucogaster*   p. 417
    SE Sucre to Delta Amacuro region.
  14. Táchira   *A. distans*   p. 418n
    Now considered a hybrid. See Note 4 (text) un-
    der Glittering-throated Emerald.

  15. White-chested   *A. c. chionopectus*   p. 417
    E; S. Coppery bronze rump and tail; clean white
    central underparts. Also Pl. 29(12).
  16. Sapphire-spangled   *A. lactea zimmeri*   p. 418
    S. Bolívar. Dull; throat spangled blue (usually
    looks dull and grayish); median breast whitish.
    Poorly known.
  17. Sword-billed Hummingbird   *Ensifera*
    ensifera   p. 426
    Andes. ♀ bill even longer than ♂. **Great Sap-**
    phirewing *Pterophanes cyanopterus* (text).
  18. Scissor-tailed Hummingbird
    Hylonympha macrocerca   p. 423
    E Sucre. No other long-tailed hummer in its
    range. ♀ deeply forked tail; outer feathers ru-
    fous.
  19. Long-tailed Sylph   *Aglaiocercus kingi*
    margarethae   p. 432
    N mts. ♂ long glittery violet blue tail. ♀ white
    throat; rufous belly; white tail tips. **Venezuelan**
    A. berlepschi (text). W Sucre; N Monagas. ♂ like
    19 (no overlap); ♀ nearest ♀ of 19. **Green-**
    tailed Trainbearer *Lesbia nuna* (text). Doubtful
    rec.

Topazes   *Topaza*
  20. Crimson   *T. p. pella*   p. 404
    SE. Large; note heavy bill with slight droop. *Ru-*
    fous outer tail feathers (cf. 21).
  21. Fiery   *T. pyra*   p. 405
    S Amazonas. Much like 20 but *outer tail feathers*
    black.
  22. White-necked Jacobin   *Florisuga m.*
    mellivora   p. 400
    ♂ white nape band; mostly white underparts
    and tail. ♀ usually scaly below; Pl. 29(34).
  23. Black-eared Fairy   *Heliothryx a. aurita*   p. 433
    E; S. Snowy underparts and outer tail feathers;
    dances in front of leaves.
  24. Buff-breasted Sabrewing   *Campylopterus*
    d. duidae   p. 399
    Tepuis of S Amazonas. Pale ally of 22 on Pl. 30.
  25. Bearded Helmetcrest   *Oxypogon guerinii*
    lindenii   p. 432
    Charming little character of Andean paramo.
    Tiny bill. ♀ duller but retains pattern (no beard).
  26. Fiery-tailed Awlbill   *Avocettula*
    recurvirostris   p. 403
    E Bolívar. ♂ and ♀ much like 28 but smaller; bill
    upturned.
  27. Gould's Jewelfront   *Helidoxa*
    aurescens   p. 422
    S Amazonas. Rufous crescent on chest; rufous in
    tail.
  28. Green-throated Mango   *Anthracothorax*
    viridigula   p. 402
    ♂ throat entirely green. See other mangos Pl. 30
    (15, 16). ♀ (text).

JAGwynne·97

Hermits *Phaethornis*
Long decurved bill; marked facial pattern (except 6);
3 sizes: large with prom. elongated white-tipped central tail feathers; med. with less obvious white in tail;
tiny with only slightly elongated, white-tipped central tail feathers and mostly rufous plumage.

1. Pale-bellied *P. a. anthophilus* p. 394
N. Fairly large; lacks submalar; above faded brownish tinged green; below grayish; lower mandible orange red. Dry woodlands.

2. Green *P. g. guy* p. 392
N mts. Large. *Dark green above*, dark gray below; buff facial lines. Local.

3. White-bearded *P. hispidus* p. 392
Large, *very grayish*. Prom. throat streak; yellow lower mandible.

4. Sooty-capped *P. a. augusti* p. 395
Foothills and mts. Large hermit. The darling of group. Impish, curious; *long wiggling white tail and rufous rump.*

5. Eastern Long-tailed *P. s. superciliosus* p. 393
S. Large and brownish. **Western Long-tailed** *P. longirostris* (text). Perijá region. **Great-billed** *P. malaris* (text).

6. Straight-billed *P. bourcieri whitelyi* p. 394
S. Fairly large. Bill straight. Weak face pattern; 3-syllable call.

7. Rupurumi *P. r. rupurumii* p. 395
S. Med. sized. Dull and dingy; grayish below with dark mottling on throat.

8. Stripe-throated *P. striigularis ignobilis* p. 397
N. Med. sized. Buff below; usually speckled dusky on throat. **Little** *P. longuemareus* (text). E. Local. Much like 8 but no overlap.

9. Gray-chinned *P. g. griseogularis* p. 396
NW; S. Tiny. Rich buffy rufous below with gray chin. ♂ narrow black breast band.

10. Reddish *P. ruber episcopus* p. 396
E. Tiny. Much like 9 (no overlap) but lacks gray on chin; throat mottled dusky.

11. Rufous-breasted Hermit *Glaucis h. hirsuta* p. 390
Long decurved bill; dull rufous below; rufous in tail.

Barbthroats *Threnetes*
Resemble hermits in behavior and appearance; black throat and chest separated by orangish bar.

12. Pale-tailed *T. niger leucurus* p. 391
S. Black and orange throat; large whitish V on underside of tail.

13. Band-tailed *T. ruckeri venezuelensis* p. 391
NW. Much like 12 (no overlap). Whitish V on undertail.

Quetzals *Pharomachrus*
Also Pl. 34 (5–7). Larger than *Trogon*; plumage glittery; long, lance-shaped wing coverts extend to sides of breast; long upper tail coverts conceal tail.

14. Golden-headed *P. auriceps hargitti* p. 437
Andes. ♂ rear crown a bit bushy but no obvious crest; eyes dark; undertail black. ♀ sim. but head duller, bronzy olive, more contrasting; undertail black or with a few whitish bars. Tail illus. Pl. 34(7). **Pavonine** *P. pavoninus* Pl. 34(6).

15. Crested *P. antisianus* p. 436
Andes. Eyes red (♂), dark (♀). ♂ bushy frontal crest partly covers bill; undertail white. ♀ head and breast greenish brown; undertail barred white. Occurs only with 14. **White-tipped** *P. fulgidus* Pl. 34(5).

Trogons *Trogon*

16. Amazonian White-tailed *T. v. viridis* p. 438
S. Large trogon. ♂ undertail mostly white. ♀ full bluish white eyering, barred undertail (cf. 17).

17. Amazonian Violaceous *T. v. violaceus* p. 441
S. Small. ♂ undertail densely barred; eyering yellow; shoulder patch vermiculated gray. ♀ like 16 but smaller; broken whitish eyering. **Northern Violaceous** *T. c. caligatus* (text). NW. Much like 17 (no range overlap); voice somewhat different.

18. Black-tailed *T. m. melanurus* p. 438
NW; S. Large trogon. Undertail black. ♀ is only gray-bodied trogon with red belly; tail often faintly barred.

19. Masked *T. p. personatus* p. 439
Mts. ♂ much like 20 but eyering bolder; mask more obvious; undertail barring finer. ♀ from 20 by conspic. black face mask, all-yellow bill, barred undertail. Occurs mostly above el. of allies.

20. Collared *T. collaris exoptatus* p. 439
Mainly lowlands. ♂ coarse tail barring. Brownish ♀ has black face faintly indicated (cf. 19); only lower mandible yellow; tail rufous chestnut above.

21. Black-throated *T. r. rufus* p. 440
S. ♂ like 17 but bottle green. No other ♀ is brown with yellow belly.

32

1. **Swallow-winged Puffbird**   *Chelidoptera t. tenebrosa*   p. 454
Chunky; broad wings, short tail; note white rump, rufous belly; sits in open treetops and sallies.

Puffbirds   *Notharchus*
Mainly black and white; lowland forests.

2. **White-necked**   *N. macrorhynchos hyperrhynchus*   p. 448
Large; white forecrown (less in E subsp.); no white on wings (cf. smaller 4).

3. **Brown-banded**   *N. ordii*   p. 449
Amazonas. Med. sized; recalls 2 but little white on frontlet; lower part of breast band brown; lower underparts barred. Rare.

4. **Pied**   *N. t. tectus*   p. 449
Small with long narrow white eyeline; spotted crown; white patch on inner wing; no white on hindneck (cf. 2).

5. **Russet-throated Puffbird**   *Hypnelus ruficollis bicinctus*   p. 451
N. Double-banded form (some have incomplete 3d band) with whitish throat typical of birds E of Andes. Single-banded, russet-throated birds of arid NW Pl. 34(2).

Puffbirds   *Malacoptila*
Streaky plumage; "walruslike" whitish tufts; bill thinner than allies; inconspic. in forest understory; usually quiet.

6. **Moustached**   *M. m. mystacalis*   p. 452
Andes; N mts. Brownish with fulvous bib; spotted wings.

7. **White-chested**   *M. fusca venezuelae*   p. 452
Amazonas. Quite streaky; narrow white crescent on chest; partly orange bill. Scarce.

8. **Rusty-breasted Nunlet**   *Nonnula rubecula duidae*   p. 452
Amazonas. Small and plain; large heavy bill; buff wash on chest; bold eyering encircles large eye. Inconspic. in forest.

Puffbirds   *Bucco*
Inconspic.; med. sized; often with bold pattern on head and foreparts.

9. **Spotted**   *B. t. tamatia*   p. 450
S. Head pattern recalls that of 10 (esp. from rear); note *coarse-barred underparts*, large black malar patch. Perches low.

10. **Chestnut-capped**   *B. m. macrodactylus*   p. 450
S. Smaller than 9; crown chestnut, throat white; 1 black chest band; low, often near water.

11. **Collared**   *B. c. capensis*   p. 451
S. Bright cinnamon rufous head; orange bill, black chest band. Forest.

Jacamars   *Brachygalba*
Small; bill unusually long but tail rather short; overall brownish.

12. **Pale-headed**   *B. goeringi*   p. 445
N. Frosty head, chestnut belt; occurs only with very different 16.

13. **Brown**   *B. l. lugubris*   p. 445
S. Dull dark brown with white belly; low or high in forest borders; no overlap with 12.

Jacamars   *Galbula*
Highly alert birds with long, sharp-pointed bills; glittering green upperparts; long narrow tail; short weak legs. Execute looping sallies from semiopen perch for flying insect prey.

14. **Bronzy**   *G. l. leucogastra*   p. 447
S. Local in wooded borders in white sandy soil; dark glossed plumage; white belly. ♀ throat buffy white.

15. **Green-tailed**   *G. galbula*   p. 447
S. Resembles 16 but tail shorter and all dark below. ♀ throat buff.

16. **Rufous-tailed**   *G. r. ruficauda*   p. 446
N. Tail longer than 15; undertail rufous. ♂ throat white; ♀ throat buff. Widespread.

17. **Yellow-billed**   *G. a. albirostris*   p. 446
S. Small; all rufous below; yellow bill. ♀ throat buff. Low in forest.

18. **Paradise**   *G. d. dea*   p. 447
S. Blackish and pointed at both ends; white throat (both sexes). Forest canopy; often sits in open.

19. **Great Jacamar**   *Jacamerops aureus ridgwayi*   p. 448
S. Large and robust; stout, slightly decurved bill; rufous underparts; ♀ throat cinnamon rufous; forest subcanopy or lower.

Kingfishers   *Chloroceryle*
Four spp. with dark oily green plumage (cf. *Megaceryle*), differ in size. Rufous chest band (♂) or irreg. green band (♀).

20. **Amazon**   *C. a. amazona*   p. 442
Little or no white spotting on wings; tail dark (cf. smaller 21).

21. **Green**   *C. a. americana*   p. 443
Quite small; prom. white spotting on wings; white in outer tail base conspic. in flight.

22. **American Pygmy**   *C. a. aenea*   p. 444
Sparrow sized. Almost a miniature of 23 but note white mid. belly. ♀ narrow green chest band. Shady stream borders and small pools.

23. **Green-and-rufous**   *C. i. inda*   p. 443
Larger than 22. *All rufous below incl. belly;* minute white dotting on wings. ♀ has speckled green chest band. Heavily shaded forest streams.

Ringed and **Belted kingfishers**: see figure in text, page 442.

33

1. **Blue-crowned Motmot** *Momotus momota* p. 444
   1a. *M. m. momota:* large with long racquet-tipped tail; widespread S of Orinoco. **1b.** *M. m. osgoodi:* NW. Smaller; breast rusty; local.
2. **Russet-throated Puffbird** *Hypnelus ruficollis coloratus* p. 451
   N. Single-banded, russet-throated form (shown) typical of arid NW region and Maracaibo Basin. Double-banded form Pl. 33(5).

Nunbirds *Monasa*
Rather large and long-tailed; mainly gray; colorful bill; often noisy and conspic. esp. in early morning and late afternoon; sometimes notably unsuspicious. Humid wooded areas.
3. **Black** *M. atra* p. 453
   S. Large and slaty; white on shoulders; heavy reddish bill; humid forest.
4. **White-fronted** *M. morphoeus peruana* p. 453
   S. Amazonas. Like 3 but paler gray; white around bill, none on shoulders.

Quetzals *Pharomachrus*
Also Pl. 32(14–15).
5. **White-tipped** *P. f. fulgidus* p. 437
   Only quetzal in N mts. ♂ bold white tail tips. ♀ much duller; reduced white on tail tips.
6. **Pavonine** *P. p. pavoninus* p. 437
   Only quetzal in Amazonas. Bill usually reddish; undertail black. ♀ undertail usually with some white barring.
7. **Golden-headed** *P. auriceps hargitti* p. 437
   Andes. Only tail shown. Small frontal crest; dark eyes (cf. Pl. 32:15); undertail all black (♂) or mostly black (♀). See head, Pl. 32(14).

Barbets *Eubucco* and *Capito*
Sturdy, colorful, and heavy-billed; sexes differ. *Eubucco* typically with yellowish to greenish yellow bills and greenish backs; *Capito* larger with dusky to grayish bills, varied plumage.
8. **Red-headed** *Eubucco bourcierii* p. 455
   Andes. Heavy yellow bill. ♂ all-red head; ♀ mainly green but head multicolored.

9. **Black-spotted** *Capito niger* p. 454
   E Bolívar. *Red forehead and throat.* ♂ all-yellow breast (no spots); ♀ heavily spotted below.
10. **Gilded** *Capito auratus* p. 455
    Amazonas and W Bolívar. ♂ *orange throat;* crown "brownish gold"; flanks spotted. ♀ sim. but more streaked, esp. below.

Toucanets *Aulacorhynchus*
Rather small, mainy green toucans; montane in distrib.; in some areas 2 spp. occur together; note bill color and pattern, and presence or absence of chestnut tipping on tail.
11. **Groove-billed** *A. s. sulcatus* p. 456
    N mts. Small toucanet. Dark bill lacks contrast. Overlaps only with 15.
12. **Chestnut-tipped** *A. derbianus whitelianus* p. 457
    Tepuis. No other "green" toucanet in range. Chestnut tail tips.
13. **Crimson-rumped** *A. h. haematopygus* p. 458
    Perijá Mts.; SE Táchira. Large toucanet; upper mandible mostly reddish; throat green, tail tips chestnut, rump red.
14. **Emerald** *A. prasinus albivitta* p. 456
    Andes. Yellow on upper mandible; crissum and tail tips chestnut; throat pale gray (cf. 15).
15. **Yellow-billed** *A. calorhynchus* p. 457
    Andes. More yellow on bill than 14; crissum green. Interbreeds very locally with 11 (text).

34

1. **Black-billed Mountain-Toucan**   *Andigena n. nigrirostris*   p. 461
Andes. Colorful high-el. toucan; black bill, whitish foreneck, gray underparts.

Toucans   *Ramphastos*
Colorful tropical icons; noisy, conspic., sometimes social; sit in open to call; large, banana-like bill longer in ♂♂ than ♀♀. Note bill pattern, bib color (yellow or white), and rump color. Extensive hybridization blurs species limits of some taxa.

2. **White-throated**   *R. tucanus*   p. 463
E; S. Two subspp. formerly considered separate spp., both with *yellow rumps*. **2a.** *R. t. cuvieri:* mainly "black-billed" birds of Amazonas and W Bolívar (formerly Cuvier's Toucan). **2b.** *R. t. tucanus:* reddish-billed birds (formerly Red-billed Toucan) of Bolívar E of Río Caura. Most reliably told from allied Channel-billed Toucan by yelping calls; in E Venez. also by white bib.

3. **Channel-billed**   *R. vitellinus*   p. 462
Two subspp. formerly considered separate spp., one with *red rump*. **3a.** *R. v. culminatus* with black bill, yellow culmen, and *yellow rump* (formerly Yellow-ridged Toucan) mainly W of Río Caura. **3b.** *R. v. vitellinus* with *all-black bill, yellow on bib, and red rump* (Channel-billed Toucan) mainly E of Río Caura. Both forms give croaking calls (cf. 2).

4. **Citron-throated**   *R. citreolaemus*   p. 461
Maracaibo Basin. Much like 3a (no overlap) but with suffusion of pale yellow on bib. Uncommon and declining.

5. **Black-mandibled**   *R. ambiguus abbreviatus*   p. 462
Andes. Colorful "yelping" toucan. Note bicolored bill, yellow bib. Wide ranging and often erratic in occurrence.

6. **Keel-billed**   *R. sulfuratus brevicarinatus*   p. 461
Perijá foothills. Colorful "Fruit Loops" bill, croaking call. Limited distrib. in Venez.

Toucanets   *Selenidera*
SE. Small, dark toucans; mid. level or subcanopy in humid lowland and foothill forest. Solitary or in prs. Sexes differ. Grinding, froglike calls.

7. **Guianan**   *S. culik*   p. 458
SE. ♂ black head and underparts; golden ear patch, bicolored bill. ♀ gray below (cf. 8).

8. **Tawny-tufted**   *S. nattereri*   p. 458
Amazonas; S Bolívar. ♂ much like 7 but bill dull red with blue spots. ♀ chestnut below. Local. No known overlap with 7.

Araçaries   *Pteroglossus*
Med.-sized black toucans with yellow lower underparts, red rump, long bill and tail; often colorful bare ocular area. Fairly conspic. Differ in pattern and color of bill, and banding pattern (or lack of) across underparts. Social; fly "single file."

9. **Green**   *P. v. viridis*   p. 460
S. Smallest of genus. Unbanded yellow underparts. ♀ foreneck tinged sooty chestnut.

10. **Ivory-billed**   *P. azara flavirostris*   p. 460
S. Ivory bill unique. Note broad red chest band, yellow confined to belly.

11. **Black-necked**   *P. aracari roraimae*   p. 459
SE. Primarily Guianan in distrib., just reaching E Venez. Single red breast band; bicolored bill.

12. **Collared**   *P. torquatus nuchalis*   p. 459
NW. Large for genus. Single black breast band mixed with red; bicolored bill (no overlap with any other of the genus in Venez.); note eye pigments.

13. **Many-banded**   *P. pluricinctus*   p. 460
Andes; S. Two black bands across yellow underparts form "bumblebee" pattern. Bicolored bill.

35

JAGwynne 2.98

NOTE: ♀♀ usually resemble ♂♂ but lack red moustache and/or red forecrown.

Woodpeckers *Celeus*
Hammerheaded; greenish yellow bill; chestnut to cinnamon plumage (except 5); mainly lowland forests.
 1. **Chestnut** *C. elegans deltanus* p. 468
    E; S. Large; unbarred dark chestnut; rump unbarred yellow buff; crest color varies with subsp.
 2. **Scale-breasted** *C. g. grammicus* p. 469
    S. Med. sized; chestnut narrowly barred black above and below; rump unbarred yellow buff.
 3. **Waved** *C. u. undatus* p. 469
    E; S. Much like 2 but head paler, chest often blackish; rump concolor with back; rump and tail barred. May hybridize with 2.
 4. **Ringed** *C. t. torquatus* p. 470
    E; S. Large; pale head contrasts with rufous upperparts; black breast band; Amaz. subsp. heavily barred above and on lower underparts.
 5. **Cream-colored** *C. f. flavus* p. 470
    Unmistakable chamois color; color of wing coverts and flight feathers varies with subspp.
 6. **Spot-breasted Woodpecker** *Chrysoptilus punctigula punctipectus* p. 466
    Deceptively like 7; note barred upperparts, black dots on soft yellow underparts. Nonforest.

Woodpeckers *Piculus*
Med. sized; most spp. plain olive above with bars or scallops below; head pattern distinctive.
 7. **Golden-olive** *P. rubiginosus meridensis* p. 467
    Mostly mts. White cheeks (cf. 6); plain olive above, densely barred below. ♀ has gray crown, red nape.
 8. **Golden-green** *P. chrysochloros* p. 468
    8a. *P. c. capistratus*: S. Long yellow gape stripe diagnostic. Barred throat (and olive crown—♀).
    8b. *P. c. xanthochlorus:* N. Mustard yellow throat (and crown—♀).
 9. **Yellow-throated** *P. f. flavigula* p. 468
    S. Yellow face and bold scalloping below. ♀ red confined to nape.
10. **Crimson-mantled** *P. rivolii meridae* p. 467
    Andes. White cheeks; *mostly crimson upperparts;* high montane forest to treeline.

Woodpeckers *Veniliornis*
Small and inconspic.; olive to mustard olive above; finely banded below (except 12).
11. **Yellow-vented** *V. dignus abdominalis* p. 474
    S Táchira. Strong whitish facial lines border dusky cheeks; belly yellow; high els.

12. **Smoky-brown** *V. fumigatus reichenbachi* p. 472
    N mts. Uniform "smoky" brown; in flight note barred flight feathers (from below).
13. **Red-rumped** *V. kirkii continentalis* p. 474
    Red rump usually visible in either sex.
14. **Little** *V. passerinus modestus* p. 472
    S. Fairly prom. grayish white facial lines; no yellow on nape (cf. with 15). Local.
15. **Golden-collared** *V. cassini* p. 473
    S. Yellow gold on nape and dots on shoulders.
    Red-stained *V. affinis* (text). S. Much like 15 but little or no yellow on nape or shoulders; obscure red staining on shoulders.

Woodpeckers *Melanerpes*
Conspic. and vocal in lowland and foothill forest; white rump.
16. **Red-crowned** *M. r. rubricapillus* p. 472
    Zebra-barred back; dingy grayish white below.
17. **Yellow-tufted** *M. cruentatus* p. 471
    Colorful, clownlike plumage; mainly black with red belly; presence or absence of nape band varies geographically.

18. **Lineated Woodpecker** *Dryocopus l. lineatus* p. 471
    Much like *Campephilus* woodpeckers but sexual differences less pronounced; throat streaked; *white facial stripe narrow;* white scapular bands do not converge on back.

Woodpeckers *Campephilus*
Large, lanky woodpeckers; solid black throat; ♂♂ of most spp. have all-red heads (except 20); ♀♀ have less red on head than ♂♂; white scapular stripes (if present) meet in center of back; all spp. best told by head pattern differences.
19. **Crimson-crested** *C. m. melanoleucos* p. 475
    ♂ all-red head, small white cheek spot; white at base of bill. ♀ *broad white facial stripe.*
20. **Powerful** *C. p. pollens* p. 475
    S Táchira. Only high els. (little overlap with 18 or 19). ♂ much like either sex of 18 but note black throat and broad white facial stripe. Also cf. ♀ of 19 (black forehead). ♀ monochromatic and unique in range.
21. **Red-necked** *C. r. rubricollis* p. 475
    S. Red head and *all-rufous underparts and underwings.* ♀ white slash across face.

36

Piculets   *Picumnus*
Tiny woodpeckers; short tail not used for support.
♀♀ all with white-dotted black crown.
 1. Chestnut   *P. c. cinnamomeus*   p. 466
   Arid NW. Chestnut plumage distinctive.
 2. Olivaceous   *P. olivaceus tachirensis*   p. 466
   W. Olive breast; streaky lower underparts. Local.
 3. Scaled   *P. squamulatus rohli*   p. 465
   Profusely scaled above and below (except *apurensis* subsp. almost unmarked below). **Black-
   dotted** *P. nigropunctatus*: see figure in text, page
   464.
 4. White-bellied   *P. spilogaster orinocensis* p. 465
   Lower Orinoco. Much like *apurensis* subsp. of 3
   but larger, bill heavier, underparts whiter; note
   ♂'s contrasting red and black crown. Local.
 5. Golden-spangled   *P. exilis undulatus*   p. 464
   S. Spotlike scales above; densely barred below.
   See very sim. **Orinoco** *P. pumilus* (text note under 5) which has unmarked upperparts; not yet
   reported in Venez. but likely.

Woodcreepers
 6. Olivaceous   *Sittasomus griseicapillus
   griseus*   p. 505
   Small and short billed; *unmarked* dark olive
   foreparts, rufous rearparts.
 7. Wedge-billed   *Glyphorynchus s. spirurus* p. 504
   Small with thick stubby bill; spotting confined to
   throat and chest.
 8. Long-tailed   *Deconychura longicauda
   connectens*   p. 503
   S. Confusing (see text); med. sized; shortish,
   straight bill; tail a bit long. **Spot-throated** *D.
   stictolaema* Pl. 43(1).

Woodcreepers   *Dendrocincla*
Unmarked plumage; straight bill; 9 and 10 reg. follow
army ants.
 9. Plain-brown   *D. fuliginosa phaeochroa*   p. 502
   Very plain; E subspp. show more evident facial
   markings (dark malar, grayer cheeks, buff chin).
   Tyrannine *D. tyrannina* (text). Rare; high els. in
   Andes of Táchira.
 10. White-chinned   *D. merula bartletti*   p. 502
   S. Much like 9 but slightly smaller, darker; small
   white chin patch but no evident facial markings;
   eyes dark (in Venez); wings contrast little with
   body; notably wary; local.
 11. Ruddy   *D. homochroa meridionalis*   p. 503
   NW. Darkest, most uniform woodcreeper in its
   range.

Woodcreepers   *Lepidocolaptes*
Smallish and slight; bill thinner, more decurved than
larger allies.
 12. Streak-headed   *L. souleyetii littoralis* p. 512
   Paler than 13, streaking lacks crispness; thin, decurved bill reddish; light woodland and drier areas. Cf. with 2 on Pl. 43.
 13. Montane   *L. l. lacrymiger*   p. 513
   N mts. Crown dotted; crisp linear streaking below; thin bill. **Lineated** *L. albolineatus* Pl. 43(2).

Woodcreepers   *Xiphorhynchus*
Med. to large sized; most spp. streaked; bill strong,
straight to slightly decurved.
 14. Olive-backed   *X. triangularis hylodromus* p. 512
   Andes; N mts. Prom. eyering; obviously spotted
   below.
 15. Buff-throated   *X. guttatus polystictus*   p. 511
   S. Large; streaked to mid. back; long, nearly
   straight bill pale to mostly dark. **Cocoa** *X.
   susurrans* (text). N. Sim to 15; bill darker; some
   vocalizations differ.
 16. Chestnut-rumped   *X. pardalotus
   caurensis*   p. 510
   S. Resembles 15 but smaller, *much darker; bill
   shorter and blackish*. **Ocellated** *X. ocellatus*
   (text). S. Smaller than 15; back essentially unstreaked; throat and chest more spotted than
   streaked.
 17. Striped   *X. obsoletus notatus*   p. 509
   Bill almost straight; profusely streaked above and
   below; favors low-lying riverine forest.
 18. Straight-billed   *X. picus phalara*   p. 509
   Straight, pale, daggerlike bill. N subspp. (incl.
   phalara) face and throat whitish. S subspp.
   darker and confusing (see text and Pl. 43:3).

Woodcreepers   *Dendrocolaptes*
Large, moderately robust; strong bill.
 19. Amazonian Barred-   *D. c. certhia*   p. 508
   S. Pale brown; barring weak (obscure at a distance)*; bill reddish*. **Northern Barred-** *D. sanctithomae* (text). N. Richer brown than 19, more
   distinctly barred; *bill dusky*.
 20. Black-banded   *D. picumnus seilerni*   p. 508
   Foreparts streaked, lower underparts barred light
   (subsp. shown) to dark; bill strong and straight.
 21. Strong-billed Woodcreeper
   Xiphocolaptes promeropirhynchus procerus p. 507
   Large with long, heavy, slightly decurved bill;
   plumage streaked (no bars); dusky malar usually
   evident.
 22. Red-billed Woodcreeper   *Hylexetastes p.
   perrotii*   p. 506
   E. Large and rare; no streaks or bars; prom. dark
   malar; large reddish bill. **Cinnamon-throated**
   Dendrexetastes rufigula. Pl 43 (4).
 23. Long-billed Woodcreeper   *Nasica
   longirostris*   p. 505
   S. Long, slightly downcurved, whitish bill and
   long neck impart reptilian look.

Scythebills   *Campylorhamphus*
Long, slender, scythelike bill.
 24. Red-billed   *C. trochilirostris venezuelensis* p. 514
   Widespread; bill reddish; mostly lighter woodland and forest edges in lowlands; wet forest in
   mts. (cf. 25). **Brown-billed** *C. pusillus* (text). Perijá Mts.; S Táchira. Bill brownish; rare.
 25. Curve-billed   *C. procurvoides sanus*   p. 514
   S. Bill brownish; plumage more finely streaked
   (obscure at a distance) than 24. Humid forest in
   lowlands; minimal overlap with 24.

1. **Bar-winged Cinclodes**   *Cinclodes fuscus heterurus*   p. 476
Andes. Terrestrial; whitish eyebrow and throat; cinnamon wing stripe conspic. in flight. Above treeline.
2. **Streak-backed Canastero**   *Asthenes wyatti mucuchiesi*   p. 486
Andes. Terrestrial or in low bushes in paramo; streaked above; rufous wing band and outer tail.
3. **Ochre-browed Thistletail**   *Schizoeaca coryi*   p. 485
Andes. Long, frayed tail; rufous eyebrow and face. **White-chinned** *S. fuliginosa* (text). S Táchira. Gray eyebrow, whitish chin. **Perijá** *S. perijana* Pl. 43(5). All 3 spp. in paramo.
4. **Andean Tit-Spinetail**   *Leptasthenura andicola certhia*   p. 477
Andes. Heavily streaked whitish; tiny bill; long double-pointed tail. Paramo.

Spinetails   *Synallaxis* and *Hellmayrea*
Long graduated tail (except 6); skulk in thickets; note crown color, presence or absence of throat patch, color of tail. Occur in wide variety of habitats.
5. **White-whiskered**   *S. candei venezuelensis*   p. 481
NW deserts. Bright rufous; bold forepart markings; semiterrestrial.
6. **White-browed**   *Hellmayrea gularis cinereiventris*   p. 482
Andes. Short tail, white eyebrows and chin; wrenlike behavior.
7. **Black-throated**   *S. castanea*   p. 481
Coastal Cordillera. Bright rufous; black lores and throat. **Rufous** *S. unirufa* (text). Andes. Like 7 but lacks black throat; voice differs.
8. **Stripe-breasted**   *S. cinnamomea bolivari*   p. 480
N mts. Heavily streaked below (no overlap with 18); stays in thick cover.
9. **Pale-breasted**   *S. albescens trinitatis*   p. 479
Dull plumage; brownish tail. Widespread in shrubby semiopen areas. **Azara's** *S. azara* Pl 43(6).
10. **McConnell's**   *S. m. macconnelli*   p. 478
S. Dark gray; tail shorter than 9. Low along dense forest borders.
11. **Plain-crowned**   *S. g. gujanensis*   p. 479
S. Plain brownish head; rufous wings and tail.
12. **Ruddy**   *S. rutilans dissors*   p. 481
S. Chestnut foreparts, black throat and tail; forest undergrowth.
13. **Plain Thornbird**   *Phacellodomus i. inornatus*   p. 487
Plain and dull; thickish bill, rounded tail. Large stick nest. Semiopen.

14. **Yellow-chinned Spinetail**   *Certhiaxis cinnamomea orenocensis*   p. 482
Dark loral line; dingy white underparts; low in open areas near water.

Spinetails   *Cranioleuca*
Shorter tailed than *Synallaxis;* arboreal and easier to see.
15. **Crested**   *C. s. subcristata*   p. 483
N mts. No obvious crest; rufous wings and tail; usually high in trees; follows mixed-spp. flocks. **Streak-capped** *C. hellmayri*. Perijá Mts.
16. **Rusty-backed**   *C. vulpina alopecias*   p. 484
Somewhat like 14 but darker below; near water but always arboreal.
17. **Tepui**   *C. d. demissa*   p. 484
Tepuis. Rufous cap, gray eyebrow; follows mixed-spp. flocks.
18. **Speckled**   *C. gutturata hyposticta*   p. 484
S. Entirely speckled below (obscure at a distance); humid forest and overgrown light gaps.
19. **Orinoco Softtail**   *Thripophaga cherriei* p. 486
Amazonas. Pale streaking and orange chin. Local.

Xenops   *Xenops*
Small and mechanical-acting; rufous wing stripe; some with upturned bill.
20. **Plain**   *X. minutus ruficaudus*   p. 498
Streaking largely confined to chest; unstreaked above. **Streaked** *X. rutilans* Pl. 43(9).
21. **Slender-billed**   *X. t. tenuirostris*   p. 498
S. Thin bill and white malar mark. Cf. 22.
22. **Rufous-tailed**   *X. milleri*   p. 499
S. Much like 21 but tail all rufous; no white malar mark.
23. **Pearled Treerunner**   *Margarornis squamiger perlatus*   p. 488
Andes. Rich, dark coloration and ornate spotting.

Barbtails   *Premnoris, Premnoplex,* and *Roraimia*
24. **Rusty-winged**   *Premnoris guttuligera venezuelana*   p. 490
S Táchira. Faintly scaled throat; profuse buff streaking above and below.
25. **Spotted**   *Premnoplex brunnescens rostratus*   p. 489
N mts. (except NE). Dark, quiet, and unassuming; rich buff spotting below. Low in forest. **White-throated** *P. tatei* Pl. 43(7).
26. **Roraiman**   *Roraimia a. adusta*   p. 489
Tepuis. Quiet. Black mask, white throat, streaked underparts.

38

1. **Streaked Tuftedcheek**   *Pseudocolaptes*
boissonneautii striaticeps   p. 487
N mts. (except NE). Large, streaky, rufous; *bold buff white cheek tufts.* Forages in bromeliads.

Treehunters   *Thripadectes*
Large and robust; most spp. heavily streaked; low in forest. All 3 spp. occur in S Táchira.
2. **Streak-capped**   *T. virgaticeps klagesi*   p. 497
N mts. (except NE). Large; fine buff streaking confined to foreparts.
3. **Striped**   *T. h. holostictus*   p. 497
Andes. Heavily streaked brown and buff above and below (cf. 4).
4. **Flammulated**   *T. f. flammulatus*   p. 496
Andes. Boldly streaked black and buff (S Táchira subsp. shown); less streaky in Mérida.
5. **Caribbean Hornero**   *Furnarius l. longirostris*   p. 477
NW. Bright cinnamon rufous above; short tail; semiterrestrial.
6. **Lineated Foliage-gleaner**   *Syndactyla subalaris olivacea*   p. 491
Andes. Rather like 3 but smaller, thinner-billed, upper throat unstreaked buff white; mainly at lower els. **Guttulated** *S. guttulata.* Coastal Cordillera. Pl. 43(8).
7. **Montane Foliage-gleaner**   *Anabacerthia striaticollis venezuelana*   p. 491
N mts. Prom. "spectacles," rufous tail; note lack of streaking. Common.

Foliage-gleaners   *Philydor*
Slender; strong eyestripe; long rufous tail; much more arboreal than *Automolus.*
8. **Buff-fronted**   *P. rufus columbianus*   p. 494
Mts. Bright ochraceous buff eyestripe, throat, and underparts; contrasting gray crown; rufous wings. Local.
9. **Cinnamon-rumped**   *P. pyrrhodes*   p. 493
S. Rich ochre below; black wings; bright cinnamon rufous rump and tail. Shy.
10. **Rufous-tailed**   *P. r. ruficaudatus*   p. 493
S. Yellow buff eyestripe and throat; chest obscurely streaked; wings olive brown like back (cf. 11).
11. **Chestnut-winged**   *P. e. erythropterus*   p. 492
S. Grayish above with contrasting rufous wings and tail.

Foliage-gleaners   *Automolus*
Larger, more robust, and duller than *Philydor;* understory or near gd.; all are hd. much more than seen.
12. **Chestnut-crowned**   *A. rufipileatus consobrinus*   p. 495
S. Quite uniform; crown slightly darker, throat slightly paler than rest of plumage. Hd. more than seen. **Ruddy** *A. rubiginosus* (text). S. Táchira foothills (scarce). Very dark.
13. **Buff-throated**   *A. ochrolaemus turdinus*   p. 495
S. Prom. buff eyering and eyeline; contrasting buff throat. A common voice.
14. **Olive-backed**   *A. infuscatus badius*   p. 495
S. Obscure eyering and eyeline; contrasting white throat; olive gray underparts.
15. **Tepui**   *A. r. roraimae*   p. 494
Tepuis. Contrasting face pattern and throat; raspy voice like *Syndactyla* (but plumage nearer *Automolus*).
16. **Eastern Striped Woodhaunter**
Hyloctistes s. subulatus   p. 492
S. Proportions sim. to *Automolus*, but note fine buff streaking on foreparts and back, more diffuse below.

Leaftossers   *Sclerurus*
Long, slender bill; plumages of all spp. rather sim.; semiterrestrial.
17. **Gray-throated**   *S. a. albigularis*   p. 500
N mts. Upper throat pale gray (difficult to see).
18. **Tawny-throated**   *S. mexicanus andinus*   p. 499
Local. Cheeks darker, throat deeper, richer tawny rufous than allies; bill has slight droop at tip.
19. **Black-tailed**   *S. caudacutus insignis*   p. 500
S. A bit larger, chin whiter, and bill longer than most allies; best told by voice. **Short-billed** *S. rufigularis* (text). S. Much like 19; bill shorter.
20. **Sharp-tailed Streamcreeper**   *Lochmias nematura chimantae*   p. 501
Coastal Cordillera; tepuis. Very dark; spotting often not esp. evident. Streambanks.
21. **Point-tailed Palmcreeper**   *Berlepschia rikeri*   p. 488
S; E. Rakish black-and-white streaking, pointed bill, rufous rearparts; local; harder to find than identify. Moriche palms in lowlands.

39

Antshrike

1. Black-throated Antshrike   *Frederickena*
viridis   p. 516
SE. *Very large;* long flat crest. ♂ black hood and
slate gray body (no wing spots). ♀ nearest ♀ of
3; note rufous upperparts.

2. Great Antshrike   *Taraba major*
semifasciata   p. 516
Either sex by bicolored plumage and red eyes.

3. Fasciated Antshrike   *Cymbilaimus lineatus*
intermedius   p. 515
Heavy bill; either sex by fine, dense barring.
Mid.-level vine tangles.

4. Barred Antshrike   *Thamnophilus doliatus*
fraterculus   p. 518
Yellow eyes. ♂ coarsely barred (finer barring in
W subsp.); disheveled crest. ♀ rufous and buff;
streaked face. **Bar-crested** *T. multistriatus* (text).
Perijá foothills. ♂ much like ♂ of 4. ♀ underparts barred black and white.

5. Black-crested Antshrike   *Sakesphorus*
canadensis intermedius   p. 517
♂ black foreparts and impressive crest (or face
streaked with white in W subspp.). ♀ rufous
crest; breast lightly streaked (least in W).

6. Black-backed Antshrike
Sakesphorus melanonotus   p. 517
N. ♂ mainly black, incl. back; white bars and
edgings on wings and lower underparts. ♀ crown
dusky brown; prom. buff eyering. Dry zones.

Antwrens   *Herpsilochmus*
Flashy patterns; long spotted or white-tipped tail;
black crown (♂); canopy.

7. Rufous-winged   *H. rufimarginatus frater* p. 533
Rufous flight feathers. Only *Herpsilochmus* in N.

8. Todd's   *H. stictocephalus*   p. 532
S. ♂ best told by voice or ♀ (white-spotted
crown). **Spot-tailed** *H. sticturus* Pl. 43(10).

9. Spot-backed   *H. dorsimaculatus*   p. 532
S. ♂ much like 10 on Pl. 43; note voice and see
text; little or no overlap with ♂ Todd's Antwren.
♀ buff on forecrown; buff wash on chest.

10. Roraiman   *H. r. roraimae*   p. 533
Tepuis. Occurs above el. of sim. allies; tail longer
and with more spots. ♀ white-dotted crown.

Antwrens   *Terenura*
Colorful and warblerlike; black cap (♂); rufous lower
back and rump; high in canopy.

11. Ash-winged   *T. s. spodioptila*   p. 536
S. Small and whitish below; look for rufous
chestnut on back. **Rufous-rumped** *T. callinota*
Colorful Andean (43:14).

Antwrens   *Myrmotherula*
Small, short-tailed, fidgety, often difficult to identify.
Near gd. to canopy. Note throat pattern, wing and tail
markings, dorsal coloration in some; 3 groups (text);
many ♀♀ very sim. to each other (text).

12. Pygmy   *M. b. brachyura*   p. 525
S. Streaked above; yellow below with white
throat. ♀ buff on foreparts. **Yellow-throated** *M.
ambigua.* S Amazonas. Illus. on Pl. 43(13).

13. Guianan Streaked-   *M. surinamensis*   p. 526
S. ♂ streaked black and white. ♀ foreparts orange rufous finely streaked black (amt. of streaking may vary). **Amazonian Streaked-** *M. multostriata* (text). NW Amazonas. Nearly identical to
13 but voice differs. **Cherrie's** *M. cherriei* Pl.
43(12).

14. Rufous-bellied   *M. guttata*   p. 528
S. Rufous belly; large tawny orange wing bars
and tertial spots; tail tipped tawny orange. ♂
mainly gray, ♀ brownish.

15. Brown-bellied   *M. gutturalis*   p. 528
SE. Brown with dotted buff wing bars. ♂ checkered throat. ♀ unmarked below; throat and chest
ochraceous; wings sim. to ♂.

16. Stipple-throated   *M. haematonota*
pyrrhonota   p. 528
S. More colorful than 15. Rufous back in ♂ and
♀.

17. Slaty   *M. schisticolor sanctaemartae* p. 528
N mts. ♂ dark gray; black throat; 3 white wing
bars. ♀ dark and plain (text).

18. White-flanked   *M. a. axillaris*   p. 529
S. Flashing white flank plumes (both sexes).
Long-winged *M. longipennis* Pl. 43(11).

19. Gray   *M. menetriesii cinereiventris* p. 531
S. ♂ clean light gray; 3 white wing bars. ♀ paler,
more blue gray above than allies.

20. Plain-winged   *M. behni inornata*   p. 530
Tepuis. ♂ solid gray (no white) with black
throat. ♀ darker rufescent above than allies.

Antwrens   *Formicivora*

21. Northern White-fringed   *F. i.*
intermedia   p. 534
N. ♂ unusual brown over black coloration; long
white stripe. ♀ streaky below. Dry regions.

22. Southern White-fringed   *F. grisea*
rufiventris   p. 534
S Amazonas. ♂ as in 21. ♀ orange rufous eyestripe and underparts. Voice differs from 21.

Miscellaneous formicariids

23. Plain Antvireo   *Dysithamnus mentalis*
cumbreanus   p. 523
Foothills. ♂ dusky cheeks, whitish median underparts. ♀ rufous crown; eyering, yellow tinge
below.

24. Russet Antshrike   *Thamnistes anabatinus*
gularis   p. 523
S Táchira. Heavy bill; buff eyebrow; contrasting
dark chestnut crown and tail. Arboreal.

25. Long-tailed Antbird   *Drymophila caudata*
klagesi   p. 535
N mts. Rather garishly patterned (for an antbird).
Note streaking, rufous rearparts; long, graduated,
white-tipped tail. Favors bamboo.

26. Warbling Antbird   *Hypocnemis cantator*
flavescens   p. 538
S. Streaked foreparts; soft yellow underparts,
rusty flanks.

40

1. **Pearly Antshrike**   *Megastictus*
margaritatus   p. 522
S. Large, round wing and tail spots; ♀ spots and
underparts buff.

Antshrikes   *Thamnophilus*
2. **Guianan Slaty-**   *T. p. punctatus*   p. 520
S. Gray with conspic. white wing and tail markings; ♀ crown rufous chestnut. **Western Slaty-**
T. atrinucha (text). NW. Much like 2 but voice
differs.
3. **Amazonian**   *T. amazonicus cinereiceps*   p. 521
S. ♂ much like ♂ of 2. Smaller ♂ of Amazonas
subsp. has gray crown. ♂ of e Bolívar subsp.
nearly identical to 2; ♀ has *head and breast
bright orange rufous.*
4. **Streak-backed**   *T. i. insignis*   p. 521
Tepuis. Both sexes much like ♂ of 2 but even
more decorated with white; ♀ has chestnut
crown. Higher els.
5. **Mouse-colored**   *T. m. murinus*   p. 520
S. ♂ faint dots on brownish wings; ♀ like ♂ but
brownish.
6. **White-shouldered**   *T. aethiops*
polionotus   p. 519
S. Strong bill. ♂ dark gray; crown blackish; abundant white dots on shoulders; ♀ uniform dark
reddish chestnut. Cf. 17 on Pl. 43.
7. **Blackish-gray**   *T. nigrocinereus*
cinereoniger   p. 519
S. ♂ much more white on wings than 6; ♀ uniform dark rufescent brown above (no spots or
edgings), orange rufous below. Scrubby white
sandy soil woodland.
8. **Spot-winged Antshrike**   *Pygiptila stellaris*
occipitalis   p. 522
S. Chunky and bobtailed; heavy bill. ♀ rufous-
edged wings.

Antbirds   *Schistocichla* and *Percnostola*
Bill relatively long and slender.
9. **Spot-winged**   *Schistocichla l. leucostigma* p. 541
S. Two very different forms and song types
(surely 2 spp.). Neat white (buff—♀) wing dots.
Pink-legged birds occur in lowlands. Darker,
gray-legged birds occur in E Táchira and tepui
highlands. ♀ underparts orange-rufous in lowlands, dark rufous in highlands. Cf. **Caura** *S. caurensis* Pl. 43(17).
10. **Black-headed**   *Percnostola rufifrons*
minor   p. 543
S Amazonas. ♂ black crown and throat; white-
fringed shoulders. ♀ brownish above, pale rufous below; shoulders fringed buff.

Antbirds   *Cercomacra*
Rather slender and long-tailed; bill thinner than allies.
Most skulk in thick lower growth.
11. **Jet**   *C. nigricans*   p. 537
N. ♂ jet with bold white tipping on wings and
tail. ♀ dark gray, throat densely streaked with
white. Local; vines near water.

12. **Dusky**   *C. t. tyrannina*   p. 536
S. ♂ dull med. gray (no black on crown); shoulders and tail narrowly edged white. ♀ above
brownish, crown tinged gray; tawny orange below. **Gray** *C. cinerascens* Pl. 43(18).
13. **Scale-backed Antbird**   *Hylophylax p.*
poecilinota   p. 540
S. Wings and back scaled. ♀ rufous head and
buff scaling; or (in S Amazonas) ♀ all rufous below; scaling white.
14. **Black-chinned Antbird**   *Hypocnemoides*
m. melanopogon   p. 539
E; S. Thin, longish bill; short tail. ♂ black throat,
white-fringed shoulders and tail tips. ♀ clouded
gray white below. Near water.
15. **Venezuelan Antvireo**   *Dysithamnus*
tucuyensis   p. 524
Coastal Cordillera. ♂ quite dark, white markings
not prominent; ♀ reddish brown crown; profusely streaked underparts. Montane forest.

Antshrikes   *Thamnomanes*
Med. sized; lack strong markings; longish tails.
16. **Cinereous**   *T. caesius glaucus*   p. 525
S. Also Pl. 43(19). ♂ all gray; no white markings.
♀ pale grayish throat and chest sharply separated from orange rufous lower underparts.
17. **Dusky-throated**   *T. ardesiacus*
obidensis   p. 524
S. ♂ all gray with inconspic. black throat. ♀ pale
ochraceous below, throat paler.
18. **Silvered Antbird**   *Sclateria n. naevia*   p. 524
E; S. Long slender bill, longish pale legs. Races
vary from extensively streaked below (♂ and ♀)
to whitish median underparts and no streaking.
♀ always somewhat brownish above. **18a.** *S. n. argentata*: Amazonas.

Antbirds   *Myrmeciza*
19. **Black-throated**   *M. a. atrothorax*   p. 545
S. Rather small. ♂ black throat, white-dotted
shoulders; *brown upperparts.* ♀ whitish throat,
dull orange rufous breast. Common in grass at
forest edge. **Yapacana** *M. disjuncta* Pl. 43(16).
20. **Gray-bellied**   *M. pelzelni*   p. 546
Amazonas. ♂ like 19 but cheeks mottled, wing
spots larger and buff, tail shorter. ♀ whitish
throat and chest; breast scaled black. Local.
21. **White-bellied**   *M. l. longipes*   p. 544
Bright rufous above; long pale legs. ♂ black
foreface (some subsp. variation). Dry forest; borders. **Ferruginous-backed** *M. ferruginea* Pl.
43(15).
22. **Dull-mantled**   *M. laemosticta*
palliata   p. 547
Perijá Mts. ♂ recalls 19 but larger, chunkier. ♀
throat checkered. Limited distrib. in Venez.
23. **Immaculate**   *M. i. immaculata*   p. 546
Perijá Mts.; Andes. Large with broad tail; bare
bluish white orbital area. ♂ all black; ♀ dark
chocolate.

41

1. **Ocellated Tapaculo**   *Acropternis o.*
   orthonyx   p. 561
   Andes. Rich chestnut with exotic alabaster-
   spotted pattern.
2. **Recurve-billed Bushbird**   *Clytoctantes*
   alixii   p. 542
   Perijá foothills. Thick, curiously upturned bill;
   chunky; short tail.

Antthrushes   *Chamaeza*
Terrestrial; fairly large and sturdy; short cocked tail,
bold pattern on underparts.
3. **Short-tailed**   *C. campanisona*
   venezuelana   p. 551
   Much like 4; best told by song. Some el. and
   habitat separation (text). S subspp. tinged buff
   below.
4. **Schwartz's**   *C. turdina chionogaster*   p. 551
   N mts. (except NE). A bit more scalloped below
   than 3 (see); tail lacks pale tips. Note song, habitat, and el. (usually higher than 3).

Antpittas   *Grallaria*
Rotund "egg-on-legs" shape; long legs; mostly terrestrial except when singing; challenging to see.
5. **Plain-backed**   *G. h. haplonota*   p. 554
   N mts. (local). Large and plain; dark submalar.
   Other "plain" allies (13 and 14) are much
   smaller.
6. **Scaled**   *G. guatimalensis regulus*   p. 553
   Mts. Obscurely scaled above; buff white malar,
   narrow white crescent across chest. **Variegated**
   G. varia (text). S lowlands. Much like 6, slightly
   streakier below. **Táchira** *G. chthonia* Pl. 43(21).
7. **Rufous**   *G. r. rufula*   p. 555
   Andes. Dark rufous, paler below. Perijá subsp.
   (not shown) paler, duller.
8. **Gray-naped**   *G. g. griseonucha*   p. 555
   Andes. Dark rufous; gray crown and nape; larger
   than 7.
9. **Chestnut-crowned**   *G. ruficapilla avilae* p. 554
   N mts. Widespread. Large; striking pattern.
10. **Great**   *G. e. excelsa*   p. 552
    Andes; Coastal Cordillera. Huge antpitta; gray
    crown; below ochraceous scalloped black. **Un-
    dulated** *G. squamigera* Pl. 43(22).
11. **Spotted Antpitta**   *Hylopezus m.*
    macularius   p. 556
    SE. Large buff eyering, bold necklace.

12. **Thrush-like Antpitta**   *Myrmothera c.*
    campanisona   p. 556
    S. Blurred breast streaking on whitish under-
    parts. Devilishly hard to see. **Tepui** *M. simplex*
    Pl. 43(20).

Antpittas   *Grallaricula*
Small, elfish versions of *Grallaria*; understory but not
terrestrial.
13. **Rusty-breasted**   *G. f. ferrugineipectus*   p. 557
    Andes; Coastal Cordillera. Plump, cartoonish as-
    pect to appearance; whitish lores and eyering;
    throat orange rufous, slightly paler than chest;
    median underparts white.
14. **Slate-crowned**   *G. n. nana*   p. 558
    N mts. Recalls 13 but darker; crown gray.
15. **Hooded**   *G. cucullata venezuelana*   p. 558
    S Táchira. Orange bill; contrasting rufous head.
    Rare; little known.
16. **Scallop-breasted**   *G. loricata*   p. 558
    Coastal Cordillera. Another rarely seen little
    antpitta; ornate pattern.

Antthrushes   *Formicarius*
Terrestrial; walk with jaunty, self-assured manner.
17. **Black-faced**   *F. analis saturatus*   p. 550
    Black face, blue white eyering; smoky gray be-
    low. Widespread, common, vocal.
18. **Rufous-breasted**   *F. rufipectus lasallei* p. 550
    Perijá Mts.; S Táchira. Dark rufous crown and un-
    derparts; local; a challenge to see.
19. **Rufous-capped**   *F. c. colma*   p. 549
    S. Rufous cap; black foreparts. ♀ whitish lores
    and throat often somewhat mottled black.
20. **Reddish-winged Bare-eye**   *Phlegopsis e.*
    erythroptera   p. 548
    S Amazonas. Exotic-looking. ♂ bare red ocular
    area, white fringed upperparts; rufous wing
    band. ♀ rich brown above, rufescent below,
    tawny buff wing bars and primary band.
21. **Wing-banded Antbird**   *Myrmornis t.*
    torquata   p. 548
    S. Oddly proportioned. Long bill, stub tail; ornate
    pattern of subdued colors; buff wing band. ♀
    throat and chest rufous.

42

1. **Spot-throated Woodcreeper**
Deconychura stictolaema secunda   p. 504
S. Rather small and short-billed. Easily confused
(see text). **Long-tailed** D. longicauda Pl. 37(8).
2. **Lineated Woodcreeper**   Lepidocolaptes a.
albolineatus   p. 513
S. Small; thin bill; crisp, linelike streaking below.
Forest canopy. E and S subspp. differ in voice
and crown pattern. See other Lepidocolaptes
Pl. 37 (12–13).
3. **Straight-billed Woodcreeper**
Xiphorhynchus picus duidae   p. 509
Much duller than N forms Pl. 37(18). Note
straight, pale, dagger-shaped bill.
4. **Cinnamon-throated Woodcreeper**
Dendrexetastes r. rufigula   p. 506
SE. Large; thick yellowish green bill; unpatterned
except for small necklace; often clambers in foliage like a Philydor.

Miscellaneous furnariids
5. **Perijá Thistletail**   Schizoeaca perijana   p. 486
Perijá Mts. White eyering, tawny orange throat
patch; long, frayed tail. Restricted distrib. and
little known.
6. **Azara's Spinetail**   Synallaxis azarae
elegantior   p. 478
Andes. Contrasting rufous crown and shoulders;
long rufous tail. Common; shrubby forest borders.
7. **White-throated Barbtail**   Premnoplex tatei
pariae   p. 490
NE mts. Throat and breast white thickly scalloped dusky (look spotted); short tail. Cf. 8 on
Pl. 38.
8. **Guttulated Foliage-gleaner**   Syndactyla g.
guttulata   p. 491
Mainly coastal Cordillera. Heavily streaked; no
overlap with allies in Andes.
9. **Streaked Xenops**   Xenops rutilans
heterurus   p. 497
N mts. Heavily streaked above and below; upper
els. Cf. 20 on Pl. 38.

Antwrens
10. **Spot-tailed Antwren**   Herpsilochmus s.
sticturus   p. 531
S. Best told from Todd's Antwren (Pl. 40:8) by
voice. ♂ solid black crown; ♀ rufous streaking
in crown.
11. **Long-winged Antwren**   Myrmotherula l.
longipennis   p. 530
S. ♂ from lowland allies by black throat and
white on wing; ♀ confusing; belly whitish.
12. **Cherrie's Antwren**   Myrmotherula
cherriei   p. 527
Amazonas. ♂ coarsely streaked to belly. ♀ all
buff below. Cf. 13 on Pl. 40.

13. **Yellow-throated Antwren**   Myrmotherula
ambigua   p. 526
S Amazonas. Much like 12 on Pl. 40 but throat
yellow.
14. **Rufous-rumped Antwren**   Terenura
callinota venezuelana   p. 535
W mts. Tiny and colorful; 2 yellowish wing bars;
rufous rump. Cf. 11 on Pl. 40.

Antbirds, Antshrikes, and Antpittas
15. **Ferruginous-backed Antbird**   Myrmeciza
ferruginea   p. 545
SE. ♂ bright ferruginous above; bare blue ocular
area; black throat, white postocular. ♀ throat
white. Delicate looking; delightful, winsome
manners. Semiterrestrial.
16. **Yapacana Antbird**   Myrmeciza
disjuncta   p. 544
Amazonas. Long thin bill; pale legs; underparts
white (♂) or buff (♀). Cf. argentata subsp. of Silvered Antbird, Pl. 41(18). Very local; habitat specialist (text).
17. **Caura Antbird**   Schistocichla caurensis   p. 542
S (bouldery hills). Easily confused; best told by
voice and peculiar habitat specialty. Large size;
long heavy bill. ♂ blackish with white wing
spots; ♀ gray head, buff wing dots, rufous underparts.
18. **Gray Antbird**   Cercomacra cinerascens immaculata   p. 536
S. ♂ gray with white tipping on long graduated
tail. ♀ sim. but dull ochraceous below. Canopy
vines.
19. **Cinereous Antshrike**   Thamnomanes
caesius glaucus   p. 525
S. Also Pl. 41(16). Longish tail; erect posture. ♂
plain gray; ♀ bicolored below. Noisy in lower
forest levels.
20. **Tepui Antpitta**   Myrmothera s. simplex   p. 557
Tepuis. Found above el. of most allies. White
throat, brown chest, grayish white belly.
21. **Táchira Antpitta**   Grallaria chthonia   p. 554
S Táchira. Enigmatic sp. much like Scaled
Antpitta (Pl. 42:6); slightly smaller, more scaled
below, median underparts paler more buff white.
No recent recs.
22. **Undulated Antpitta**   Grallaria
squamigera   p. 552
Andes. Upper-el. ally of nearly identical Great
Antpitta (Pl. 42:10). Mid. crown and nape gray;
bold scalloping on ochraceous underparts.

Tapaculo
23. **Rufous-rumped**   Scytalopus griseicollis
fuscicauda   p. 561
Andes. Much like other Scytalopus; see
Pl. 53(1–3). Unbarred bright rusty rearparts.
Very local.

43

Antbirds *Myrmoborus*
Small; short tailed; ♂♂ gray and black with prom.
pale eyebrows. Undergrowth.
1. **White-browed** *M. leucophrys*
   angustirostris   p. 538
   Andes; S. ♂ white eyebrow, black face. ♀ cinnamon eyebrow, black mask, white below.
2. **Black-faced** *M. myotherinus elegans*   p. 538
   S. ♂ black face outlined gray; 3 white wing bars.
   ♀ much like 1 but breast and belly buff.
3. **Rufous-throated Antbird** *Gymnopithys*
   rufigula pallida   p. 547
   S. Army-ant follower; bare bluish ocular area. Rufous throat.

Antbirds *Hylophylax*
Small and cute; ornate patterns; short tails. ♀♀ have
black malar but lack black throat of ♂♂.
4. **Spot-backed** *H. n. naevia*   p. 540
   S. ♂ dark gray cheeks; buff spots on central
   back (cf. 5). ♀ buff below, necklace reduced.
5. **Dot-backed** *H. p. punctulata*   p. 540
   S. ♂ pale gray cheeks; extensively white-dotted
   back and rump. ♀ white below, thickly spotted.
6. **Banded Antbird** *Dichrozona cincta*   p. 541
   S. Small; long bill, insignificant tail. Plumage recalls 4 and 5. Note white rump band, buff wing
   band. Quirky, semiterrestrial behavior.
7. **White-plumed Antbird** *Pithys a.*
   albifrons   p. 547
   S. Shaggy plumes on foreface. Blue gray upperparts; orange yellow legs. Army-ant follower.

8. **Lance-tailed Manakin** *Chiroxiphia*
   lanceolata   p. 666
   N. Fairly large. ♂ crimson cap; sky blue back;
   tail spikes. ♀ and imm. ♂ olive with dark eyes;
   retain short tail spikes. **Blue-backed** *C. pareola*.
   SE. No tail spikes.
9. **Wire-tailed Manakin** *Pipra f. filicauda* p. 668
   ♂ distinctive. ♀ olive with *white eyes and yellowish belly*; tail "wires" a bit shorter than ♂.
10. **White-bearded Manakin** *Manacus mana-
    cus interior*   p. 665
    ♂ black and white. ♀ olive with *orange legs*.
11. **Golden-winged Manakin** *Masius c.*
    chrysopterus   p. 663
    Andes. ♂ yellow in wings in flight; ♀ dark olive;
    raspberry legs; longish tail

Manakins *Dixiphia, Pipra,* and *Lepidothrix*
♂♂ with colored caps or heads. ♀♀ plain olive, quite
sim. and confusing.
12. **White-crowned** *Dixiphia. p. pipra*   p. 670
    N (local); S. ♀ more gray green than allies; gray-
    ish head, red eyes. NW subsp. brighter.
13. **Golden-headed** *Pipra e. erythrocephala* p. 669
    N (mts.); S. ♀ a bit duller, dingier than allies;
    note pale bill (but not as pale as ♂). Imm. ♂♂
    olive but soon acquire pale eyes and bill.
14. **Crimson-hooded** *Pipra a. aureola*   p. 668
    NE. White eyes. ♂ foreface and median under-
    parts mixed orange and red. ♀ ochre tinged
    throat.

15. **Scarlet-horned** *Pipra cornuta*   p. 669
    Tepuis. ♀ and imm. ♂ much like 20; slight
    nuchal tuft; paler legs shorter wings.
16. **Orange-bellied** *Lepidothrix suavissima* p. 670
    E. ♀ green above; *bluish tinge on forehead and
    rump*; belly yellow. Cf. ♀ of 17. Mainly foothills.
17. **Blue-crowned** *Lepidothrix coronata*
    carbonata   p. 670
    ♀ like 16 *above* but no blue; paler belly. Primar-
    ily lowlands.
18. **White-throated Manakin** *Corapipo*
    gutturalis   p. 666
    E. ♀ dull olive; whiter below than allies, breast
    smudged olive. **White-ruffed** *C. leucorrhoa*
    (text). N mts. Quite sim. but no overlap. ♀ yel-
    lowish lower underparts (cf. ♀♀ of 12 and 13).
19. **Black Manakin** *Xenopipo atronitens* p. 664
    S. Longish tail. ♂ very sim. to 6 on Pl. 48; note
    habitat and vocal differences (text). ♀ very like
    20 but smaller; little overlap.
20. **Olive Manakin** *Chloropipo u. uniformis* p. 662
    Tepuis. Found at els. above most allies (cf. ♀ of
    15). Uniform olive; longish tail; weak eyering.

Manakins *Machaeropterus*
Tiny. ♂♂ snappy pink and white stripes; flame caps.
21. **Striped** *M. regulus zulianus*   p. 663
    Andes; S. ♂ solid red cap. ♀ vague streaking;
    blush of pink below. Local.
22. **Fiery-capped** *M. pyrocephalus*
    pallidiceps   p. 664
    S (local). ♂ flame coronal stripe surrounded by
    yellow gold. ♀ hint of streaking below.

Tyrant-Manakins *Tyranneutes*
23. **Dwarf** *T. stolzmanni*   p. 672
    S. Pale eyes (usually grayish). Best told by song.
24. **Tiny** *T. virescens*   p. 672
    SE (local). Much like 23 (text). Song quite
    different.
25. **Cinnamon Neopipo** *Neopipo c.*
    cinnamomea   p. 603
    S Amazonas, Bolívar. Cf. Ruddy-tailed Flycatcher,
    Pl. 46(48). Legs bluish gray; voice, habitat differ.
26. **Saffron-crested Tyrant-Manakin**
    Neopelma chrysocephalum   p. 673
    S. Flycatcherlike. Semiconcealed yellow coronal
    stripe; "bloodshot" eyes; yellow belly.
27. **Wing-barred Piprites** *Piprites chloris*
    chlorion   p. 640
    Bold wing bars; yellowish face; large black eyes.

Schiffornis *Schiffornis*
28. **Thrush-like** *S. turdinus olivaceus* p. 639
    Robust, brown, longish tailed; big, dark, liquid
    eyes. Solitary and reclusive.
29. **Várzea** *S. major duidae*   p. 639
    Amazonas. Like 28 but gray on head; relatively
    bright cinnamon body; yellowish on belly.
30. **Yellow-crested Manakin** *Heterocercus*
    flavivertex   p. 671
    S. ♂ white bib; ♀ slaty cheeks, fulvous on belly.

44

1. **Cinnamon Flycatcher** *Pyrrhomyias*
cinnamomea vieillotioides p. 607
N mts. Perky; cinnamon rufous below.

Chat-Tyrants *Ochthoeca*
Long narrow eyeline; flattish crown. High els.
2. **Brown-backed** *O. fumicolor superciliosa* p. 614
Andes. Long rufous eyebrow (or white—S
Táchira), rufous breast.
3. **Rufous-breasted** *O. rufipectoralis*
rubicundula p. 613
Perijá Mts. White eyeline; rufous breast band.
4. **Yellow-bellied** *O. diadema meridana* p. 614
N mts. Long yellow eyeline. Retiring.
5. **Blackish** *O. nigrita* p. 613
Andes. All slaty; narrow white eyeline. **Slaty-
backed** *O. cinnamomeiventris* (text). S Táchira.
Belly reddish chestnut.
6. **Vermilion Flycatcher** *Pyrocephalus rubinus*
saturatus p. 612
♀ streaky below (usually); strawberry belly.
7. **Drab Water-Tyrant** *Ochthornis*
littoralis p. 615
S. Whitish eyeline; pale rump; dark wings and
tail. Riverbanks.

Flycatchers *Myiobius*
8. **Tawny-breasted** *M. villosus schaeferi* p. 605
N. Tawny breast and sides.
9. **Whiskered** *M. b. barbatus* p. 604
S. Grayish olive breast; clear yellow belly. **Black-
tailed** *M. atricaudus* (text). N Bolívar. Much like 9.
10. **Agile Tit-Tyrant** *Uromyias agilis* p. 580
Andes. Streaked; long narrow eyebrow and tail.
11. **Rufous-tailed Tyrant** *Knipolegus poecilurus*
venezuelanus p. 617
Shape recalls *Contopus*; red eyes, fawn belly.
12. **Tropical Pewee** *Contopus cinereus*
bogotensis p. 607
Also Pl. 47(29). Pale eyering; grayish lores.
13. **Euler's Flycatcher** *Lathrotriccus euleri*
flaviventris p. 611
Close to *Empidonax*; buffy wing bars. N migr.
Empidonax **Willow, Alder,** and **Acadian flycatchers** (text).
14. **Fuscous Flycatcher** *Cnemotriccus fuscatus*
cabanisi p. 611
Flat crown, long narrow eyeline, long tail.

Flycatchers *Myiophobus*
15. **Flavescent** *M. flavicans venezuelanus* p. 606
N mts. Olive above; streaky below; buff bars.
16. **Roraiman** *M. r. roraimae* p. 606
Tepuis. Rich brown above; yellow below; buff bars.
17. **Bran-colored** *M. f. fasciatus* p. 606
Reddish brown ("bran colored"), streaked below.

Flatbills *Tolmomyias*
Confusing and difficut genus; broad flat bill, pale
lower mandible; sharp yellow wing edgings. Vocal differences critical to field identification.
18. **Yellow-olive** *T. sulphurescens exortivus* p. 598
Gray-tinged crown; grayish eyes. **Zimmer's** *T. assimilis* (text). Much like 18; slightly smaller; dark
eyes; voice differs.

19. **Gray-crowned** *T. p. poliocephalus* p. 599
S. Slightly smaller, grayer crowned than 18; dark
eyes.
20. **Ochre-lored** *T. flaviventris collingwoodi* p. 600
Bright yellow below; ochre loral spot.
21. **Olivaceous Flatbill** *Rhynchocyclus olivaceus*
flavus p. 597
Wide, flat bill; lower mandible pale. Streaky underparts. **Fulvous-breasted** *R. fulvipectus* (text).
S Táchira. Tawny ochre wash on breast.

Flatbills *Ramphotrigon*
Bill moderately wide.
22. **Bamboo** *R. megacephala pectoralis* p. 596
Short eyebrow mark; buff wing bars; lightly
streaked below. Bamboo.
23. **Rufous-tailed** *R. ruficauda* p. 597
S. Streaky breast; rufous wings and tail.
24. **Northern Scrub-Flycatcher** *Sublegatus*
arenarum glaber p. 574
N. Dapper and clean-cut. Recalls a miniature
Myiarchus; stubby black bill. **Amazonian** *S. obscurior* (text). Orinoco drainage. Dingier, slightly
smaller, and itself prob. comprising 2 spp. (text).

Elaenias *Myiopagis*
Smaller than *Elaenia;* few distinguishing marks. Also
Pl. 48(7).
25. **Greenish** *M. viridicata restricta* p. 570
No wing bars; yellow crown patch.
26. **Forest** *M. gaimardii bogotensis* p. 569
Yellowish wing bars; white crown patch; vague
breast streaking. **Yellow-crowned** *M. flavivertex*
Pl. 48(7).
27. **Gray** *M. caniceps cinerea* p. 568
♂ gray; white bars on black wings. ♀ different
(text).
28. **Amazonian Royal-Flycatcher**
Onychorhynchus c. coronatus p. 603
S. Crest normally laid flat. Finely barred. **Northern** *O. mexicanus fraterculus* (text). NW foothills.
Lacks barring. No overlap with 28.

Elaenias *Elaenia*
Challenging genus; many sim. spp. Also Pl. 48(8–10).
29. **Yellow-bellied** *E. f. flavogaster* p. 571
Large; bushy unkempt crest shows white
(usually); yellowish belly.
30. **Small-billed** *E. parvirostris* p. 572
S migr. Clean white eyering (faint in 1st-yr birds);
no crest. **Mountain** *E. frantzii* Pl. 48(8); **Lesser**
E. chiriquensis Pl. 48(9); **Plain-crested** *E. cristata*
Pl. 48(10).
31. **Rufous-crowned** *E. ruficeps* p. 574
Mainly S. Rear-projecting crest with rufous
showing.
32. **Sierran** *E. pallatangae olivina* p. 572
Tepuis. Yellowish underparts.
33. **Great** *E. d. dayi* p. 570
Tepuis. Large and dark.
34. **Slaty** *E. strepera* p. 574
Rare S migr. Slaty; white belly.

45

1. **Black-chested Tyrant**   *Taeniotriccus a.*
   andrei   p. 592
   Mainly Orinoco delta region. ♀ duller.

Spadebills   *Platyrinchus*
2. **White-crested**   *P. p. platyrhynchos*
   griseiceps   p. 601
   S. Gray head; buff breast. **Cinnamon-crested**
   P. saturatus (text).
3. **Golden-crowned**   *P. coronatus gumia*   p. 602
   S. Strong facial pattern; yellowish underparts.
4. **White-throated**   *P. mystaceus insularis*   p. 601
   Strong facial pattern; whitish underparts.
5. **Yellow-throated**   *P. flavigularis vividus*   p. 601
   NW mts. No facial pattern; yellow underparts.

Tody-Flycatchers   *Poecilotriccus* and
Todirostrum
6. **Rufous-crowned**   *Poecilotriccus r.*
   ruficeps   p. 593
   Andes. Rufous crown; complex facial pattern.
7. **Ruddy**   *Poecilotriccus russatum*   p. 593
   Tepuis. Gray crown; rufous face and wing bars.
8. **Common**   *Todirostrum c. cinereum*   p. 594
   Widespread. **Maracaibo** *T. viridanum* (text). NW.
9. **Black-headed**   *Todirostrum nigriceps*   p. 596
   Andes. Contrasting black crown.
10. **Painted**   *Todirostrum p. pictum*   p. 596
    S. Black crown and necklace.
11. **Spotted**   *Todirostrum maculatum*
    amacurense   p. 594
    E. Gray foreparts; finely streaked breast.
12. **Slate-headed**   *Poecilotriccus sylvia*
    griseolum   p. 593
    Gray head, white spectacles; yellow wing bars.

Tody-Tyrants   *Hemitriccus*
13. **Black-throated**   *H. granadensis andinus* p. 593
    N mts. Whitish face. **White-eyed** *H. zosterops*
    and **Snethlage's** *H. minor* (text).
14. **Pearly-vented**   *H. margaritaceiventris*
    impiger   p. 590
    Brownish tone to upperparts. Orangish eyes.

Pygmy-Tyrants   *Lophotriccus*
15. **Pale-eyed**   *L. pilaris venezuelensis*   p. 590
    Olive tone to upperparts (cf. 14). Dry zones.
16. **Helmeted**   *L. galeatus*   p. 589
    S. Black-streaked crest; obscure breast streaking.
17. **Scale-crested**   *L. pileatus santaeluciae*   p. 589
    N mts. Rufous in crest; obscure breast streaking.
18. **Short-tailed Pygmy-Tyrant**   *Myiornis*
    ecaudatus miserabilis   p. 588
    N mts. Rufous in crest; obscure breast streaking.
19. **Bearded Tachuri**   *Polystictus pectoralis*
    brevipennis   p. 580
    ♂ blackish throat. ♀ whitish throat. **Crested**
    Doradito *Pseudocolopteryx sclateri* (text).
20. **Tawny-crowned Pygmy-Tyrant**
    Euscarthmus meloryphus paulus   p. 581
    N. Faded brown; black eyes; peaked crest.
21. **Mouse-colored Tyrannulet**   *Phaeomyias*
    murina incompta   p. 567
    Dingy; flat crown; long eyeline; longish tail.
22. **Southern Beardless-Tyrannulet**
    Camptostoma obsoletum venezuelae   p. 567
    Peaked crest, pinkish bill.

Inezias   *Inezia*
23. **Slender-billed**   *I. tenuirostris*   p. 578
    Arid NW. Smaller than 22; no crest; thin bill.
24. **Pale-tipped**   *I. caudata intermedia*   p. 578
    N. Spectacles. **Amazonian** *I. subflava* (text). S.
25. **Torrent Tyrannulet**   *Serpophaga c.*
    cinerea   p. 577
    Andes. **River** *S. hypoleuca* (text). **Lesser Wag-**
    tail Tyrant *Stigmatura napensis* (text).

Tyrannulets   *Mecocerculus*
26. **White-banded**   *M. stictopterus*
    albocaudatus   p. 575
    Andes. Conspic. white eyebrow and wing bars.
27. **White-throated**   *M. leucophrys*
    palliditergum   p. 576
    Mts. **Sulphur-bellied** *M. minor* (text). S Táchira.

Tyrannulets   *Ornithion*
28. **Brown-capped**   *O. brunneicapillum*
    dilutum   p. 566
    Sepia crown; no wing bars; yellow below.
29. **White-lored**   *O. inerme*   p. 566
    S. White-spotted wing bars.
30. **Yellow Tyrannulet**   *Capsiempis flaveola*
    cerulus   p. 579

Tyrannulets   *Zimmerius, Phyllomyias*
31. **Golden-faced**   *Z. c. chrysops*   p. 565
    N mts. Yellow on face.
32. **Venezuelan**   *Z. improbus petersi*   p. 565
    N mts. Slaty cap; strong facial markings.
33. **Black-capped Tyrannulet**   *Phyllomyias*
    nigrocapillus aureus   p. 564
34. **Slender-footed Tyrannulet**   *Zimmerius g.*
    gracilipes   p. 566
    S. Gray eyes; yellow wing edgings; canopy.
35. **Yellow-crowned Tyrannulet**   *Tyrannulus e.*
    elatus   p. 568
    Stubby bill, gray face; wing bars.
36. **Sooty-headed Tyrannulet**   *Phyllomyias*
    griseiceps cristatus   p. 563
    Tawny-rumped *P. uropygialis* Pl. 48(12).
37. **Urich's Tyrannulet**   *Phyllomyias urichi* p. 563
38. **Rufous-lored Tryannulet**   *Phylloscartes*
    flaviventris   p. 586
    Coastal Cordillera. Rufous spectacles. **Rufous-**
    browed *P. superciliaris*. Perijá Mtns. (text).

Bristle-Tyrants   *Pogonotriccus*
39. **Venezuelan**   *P. venezuelanus*   p. 587
    N mts. Yellow wing bars; black coverts. Cf. 40.
40. **Marble-faced**   *P. ophthalmicus purus*   p. 587
    N mts. Wing coverts dull, wing bars weaker than
    39. **Variegated** *P. poecilotis* (text). Andes.
41. **Chapman's**   *P. chapmani duidae*   p. 586
    Tepuis. Cinnamon buff wing bars.

Tyrannulets   *Phylloscartes*
42. **Black-fronted**   *P. nigrifrons*   p. 585
    Tepuis. Black forehead; grayish underparts.

Flycatchers   *Mionectes*
43. **Olive-striped**   *M. olivaceus venezuelensis* p. 582
    Dark olive; finely streaked below.
44. **Ochre-bellied**   *M. oleagineus chloronotus* p. 582
    Cf. **McConnell's** *P. macconnelli* Pl. 48(13).

Plate 46 (continued on page 136).

46

Plate 46 continued

Flycatchers *Leptopogon*
45. Rufous-breasted *L. rufipectus*
venezuelanus   p. 584
46. Slaty-capped *L. superciliaris*
venezuelensis   p. 583
N mts. Long bill and tail; higher els. than 47.
47. Sepia-capped *L. amaurocephalus*
obscuritergum   p. 584
48. Ruddy-tailed Flycatcher *Terenotriccus*
erythrurus venezuelensis   p. 604

Plate 47

1. Cattle Tyrant *Machetornis rixosus*
flavigularis   p. 619

Bush-Tyrants *Myiotheretes*
Large; high els.; hooked bills; rufous wing patches.
2. Smoky *M. fumigatus lugubris*   p. 615
Andes. Large and dark; watch for rufous in
wings; W subsp. has pale eyebrow.
3. Streak-throated *M. s. striaticollis*   p. 616
Andes. Large. Streaked throat. Open terrain.
4. Cliff Flycatcher *Hirundinea f.*
ferruginea   p. 616
Mts. Grizzled face; rufous in wings.
5. Yellow-browed Tyrant *Satrapa*
icterophrys   p. 618
Broad yellow eyebrow, blackish mask. Llanos.

Kingbirds *Tyrannus*
Conspic.; semiopen; most spp. have migratory pop.
6. Gray *T. d. dominicensis*   p. 637
N. Gray with whitish underparts; prom. mask;
large bill. **Eastern** *T. tyrannus* (text). N migr.
7. Tropical *T. m. melancholicus*   p. 636
Head dull gray, back olive gray. Note olive wash
chest.
8. White-throated *T. albogularis*   p. 637
SE. Much like 7. Pale gray head *contrasts with
dusky mask*; white throat meets yellow underparts (no olive on chest); back *greenish olive*.
9. Sulphury Flycatcher *Tyrannopsis*
sulphurea   p. 636
E; S. Darker, dirtier than 7; bill short; white central throat. Fond of moriche palms.
10. Dusky-chested Flycatcher *Myiozetetes l.*
luteiventris   p. 631
S. Blurry streaking on chest. Forest canopy.

Flycatchers *Conopias*
11. Lemon-browed *C. cinchoneti*
icterophrys   p. 632
Andes. Long yellow eyestripe; noisy; canopy.
12. Yellow-throated *C. p. parva*   p. 632
S. White eyebrows encircle crown; noisy in
canopy. **Three-striped** *C. trivirgata* (text). S.

Flycatchers *Myiozetetes*
Short bill; strong facial pattern (except 10, above).
13. Social *M. similis columbianus*   p. 630
Crown and cheeks dusky gray; back tinged olive. S
subsp. has blacker head, browner back, nearer 15.

14. Gray-capped *M. granadensis obscurior* p. 631
S. Whitish forehead extends rearward as *short
eyebrow*; grayish head. Local.
15. Rusty-margined *M. cayanensis*
rufipennis   p. 630
Head markings blackish; back brownish (olive in
W subsp.); flight feathers edged rufous. W and S
subspp. show little rufous and are very like 13.
16. White-bearded Flycatcher *Phelpsia*
inornata   p. 629
Llanos. Large head, puffy white throat; stubby
bill. White eyebrows meet on nape.

Flycatchers *Myiodynastes*
17. Streaked *M. maculatus difficilis*   p. 633
Heavy bill; plumage streaked with brown, rufous
in tail. Austral migr. has blackish streaking.
18. Golden-crowned *M. chrysocephalus*
cinerascens   p. 634
N mts. Dark malar; blurry streaking on chest.

Miscellaneous large flycatchers
19. Boat-billed Flycatcher *Megarynchus p.*
pitangua   p. 629
Oversized bill, decurved culmen; olive-tinged
back; no rufous in wings. Cf. 20.
20. Great Kiskadee *Pitangus sulphuratus*
trinitatis   p. 627
Brown back; rufous wing edgings. Widespread.
21. Lesser Kiskadee *Philohydor l. lictor* p. 628
Smaller, longer-billed version of 20; voice differs.
Always near water.
22. Piratic Flycatcher *Legatus l.*
leucophaius   p. 634
Stubby bill; unstreaked back; no rufous in tail.
23. Variegated Flycatcher *Empidonomus*
varius rufinus   p. 635
Larger than 22; back streaked; stronger wing
edges; longer, rufous-edged tail. Migr. more
streaked.
24. Crowned Slaty Flycatcher *Griseotyrannus*
a. aurantioatrocristatus   p. 635
S migr. Black crown; smoky gray below. Treetops.
25. Eastern Sirystes *Sirystes sibilator*
albocinereus   p. 623
SE Táchira. Blackish crown, wings, and tail.

Flycatchers and Pewees *Contopus*
Dull; erect posture, slight crest; short legs, long wings;
note vocal differences.
26. Olive-sided Flycatcher *C. cooperi*   p. 609
N migr. Chunky, short-tailed; dark vest on white
median underparts; white behind wing.
27. Smoke-colored Pewee *C. fumigatus*
cineraceus   p. 609
Mts. Crested, slaty; pale lower mandible. Treetops.
28. Eastern Wood-Pewee *C. v. virens*   p. 607
N migr. Dull; no eyering (cf. *Empidonax*). **Western** *C. sordidulus* (text). N. migr.
29. Tropical Pewee *C. cinereus bogotensis* p. 607
Smaller than 28; pale loral spot; lower mandible
pale; short primary extension. Also Pl. 45(12).

47

1. **White-headed Marsh-Tyrant**
Arundinicola leucocephala   p. 620
♂ unmistakable. ♀ above pale; foreface and underparts whitish; tail black.
2. **Pied Water-Tyrant** *Fluvicola p. pica*   p. 619
Pied plumage. Imm. hindcrown and back tinged brownish (cf. ♀ of 1).
3. **Black Phoebe** *Sayornis nigricans angustirostris*   p. 612
N mts. Much white wing edging; white belly. Near water.
4. **Long-tailed Tyrant** *Colonia colonus poecilonotus*   p. 618
Pale crown; long central tail feathers. Imm. lacks long feathers.
5. **Riverside Tyrant** *Knipolegus o. orenocensis*   p. 617
Dull blackish; ♀ paler, grayer. Erect posture, semiopen habitat.
6. **Amazonian Black-Tyrant** *Knipolegus poecilocercus*   p. 617
♂ glossy blue black (cf. 19 on Pl. 44); wings short. ♀ dark brown; rufous edgings on wings and tail; rather large headed (cf. 17 on Pl. 45). Semihorizontal posture; flooded forest.

Elaenias *Myiopagis* and *Elaenia* (also Pl. 45)
7. **Yellow-crowned** *Myiopagis flavivertex* p. 569
E; S. Yellow crown patch; unstreaked grayish olive breast; swamps.
8. **Mountain** *Elaenia frantzii browni*   p. 573
N mts. Dingy; roundish head; no white in crown.
9. **Lesser** *Elaenia chiriquensis albivertex* p. 571
Much like **Small-billed** Pl. 45(30); slight crest, *no eyering*.
10. **Plain-crested** *Elaenia c. cristata.*   p. 573
Dull; crested; no white in crown; little to no yellowish tinge below.

Tyrannulets *Phyllomyias*
11. **White-fronted** *P. zeledoni*   p. 562
N mts. Grayish tinged crown; short eyebrow broadest in front, narrow and curved over eyes; vaguely streaked on chest. Local.
12. **Tawny-rumped** *P. uropygialis*   p. 564
Andes. Grayish foreparts, buff wing bars, tawny rump. Local. **Ashy-headed** *P. cinereiceps* (text).
13. **McConnell's Flycatcher** *Mionectes macconnelli roraimae*   p. 583
S. No wing bars; foothills and tepuis. Cf. 44 on Pl. 46.

14. **Fork-tailed Flycatcher**   *Tyrannus savana monachus*   p. 638
Ad. distinctive. Imm. brownish cap; tail much shorter.

Flycatchers *Myiarchus*
Numerous confusing spp. (text).
15. **Brown-crested** *M. t. tyrannulus*   p. 627
More brownish and crested than allies; rufous-edged tail. Common.
16. **Great Crested** *M. crinitus*   p. 627
N migr. Brightest of the genus in Venez.; tail quite rufous.
17. **Swainson's** *M. swainsoni*   p. 624
17a. *M. s. phaeonotus:* resident subsp., much like 18 (text). **17b.** *M. s. swainsoni:* S migr. Rather distinctive (for a *Myiarchus*); *pale and faded; notably reddish bill.*
18. **Short-crested** *M. ferox brunnescens* p. 625
N subsp. (shown) palest; best told by voice (text).
19. **Pale-bellied Mourner** *Rhytipterna immunda*   p. 623
Amazonas. Much like *Myiarchus;* note short bill, rounded head (text).
20. **Venezuelan Flycatcher** *Myiarchus venezuelensis*   p. 625
Avg.-looking *Myiarchus*. Little or no rufous in tail; dry zones.
21. **Dusky-capped Flycatcher** *Myiarchus tuberculifer pallidus*   p. 624
Smaller, darker headed than allies. Soft whistles.
22. **Pale-edged Flycatcher** *Myiarchus cephalotes caribbaeus*   p. 626
N mts. Upper els. Whitish edges to tail.
23. **Panama Flycatcher** *Myiarchus p. panamensis*   p. 626
NW. Best told by voice and range (text).
24. **Tropical Mockingbird** *Mimus gilvus melanopterus*   p. 714
Lanky and long-tailed; white wing edges and tail tips. **Pearly-eyed Thrasher** *Margarops fuscatus* (text). **Cedar Waxwing** *Bombycilla cedrorum* (text).
25. **Black-capped Donacobius** *Donacobius a. atricapillus*   p. 692
Creamy buff underparts; golden eyes. Always near water. Cf. 5 on Pl. 53.
26. **White-capped Dipper** *Cinclus leucocephalus leuconotus*   p. 702
Andes. Plump; short tailed; on rocks in rushing mt. streams.

48

Tityras *Tityra*
Robust and heavy-billed; mainly black and white;
duller ♀♀ show brown on back, streaking on breast.
 1. **Masked**   *T. semifasciata columbiana*   p. 648
    N. ♂ most of bill and facial skin red; narrow
    black mask; broad white tail tips. ♀ sim. but
    tinged brownish (no streaking).
 2. **Black-tailed**   *T. c. cayana*   p. 648
    ♂ bill and face like 1 but crown all black; tail all
    black. ♀ tinged and streaked brown.
 3. **Black-crowned**   *T. inquisitor*
    erythrogenys   p. 647
    ♂ solid black crown and bill. ♂ rusty cheeks.

Becards *Pachyramphus*
♂♂ of 4, 5, and 6 all quite sim.
 4. **White-winged**   *P. polychopterus tristis*   p. 644
    ♂ slaty to blackish below. ♀ brownish crown;
    broken eyering; buff edging on wings and tail
    tips.
 5. **Black-and-white**   *P. a. albogriseus*   p. 645
    N mts. No overlap with 6. ♂ plain pale gray back
    and underparts. ♀ chestnut crown outlined
    black.
 6. **Black-capped**   *P. marginatus nanus*   p. 644
    S. ♂ much like 5 (no overlap); streaked back. ♀
    like ♀ of 4 but crown chestnut. **Glossy-backed**
    P. surinamus (text).
 7. **Cinereous**   *P. r. rufus*   p. 645
    N. ♂ mostly plain gray (no prom. white wing
    edgings). ♀ much like 8 but whiter below; prom.
    black primary covert patch.
 8. **Cinnamon**   *P. cinnamomeus magdalenae* p. 646
    W of Andes. Sexes sim. Dusky lores and buff
    supraloral. Note range.
 9. **Chestnut-crowned**   *P. castaneus*
    intermedius   p. 646
    Sexes sim. From any other by gray band around
    head.
10. **Barred**   *P. v. versicolor*   p. 643
    N mts. Smallish in size; yellowish face; light bar-
    ring below. ♀ rufous on wings.
11. **Green-backed**   *P. viridis griseigularis*   p. 642
    SE. ♂ black cap, olive body; yellowish chest
    band. ♀ sim. but crown olive like back; small ru-
    fous patch on shoulders.

12. **White-naped Xenopsaris**   *Xenopsaris*
    albinucha minor   p. 642
    Miniature of 7 (♂); note small bill; brownish-
    tinged wings; white underparts. Local, mainly
    llanos.
13. **Pink-throated Becard**   *Platypsaris*
    minor   p. 646
    S. Large. ♂ paler below; pink throat diagnostic.
    ♀ gray crown and nape; rufous wings. **One-
    colored** *P. homochrous* (text). Maracaibo Basin.
    ♂ like 13 but no pink. ♀ much like 8 and ♀ of 7,
    but note large size, heavy bill.

Attilas *Attila*
14. **Bright-rumped**   *A. s. spadiceus*   p. 620
    Color phases range from rufous to olive (in-
    termed. shown); note wing bars, streaky breast;
    yellow rump.
15. **Citron-bellied**   *A. citriniventris*   p. 621
    Combination of *gray head and throat* and lack of
    wing bars diagnostic. **Rufous-tailed** *A. phoenicu-
    rus* (text). S (rare). Much like 15 but bill shorter;
    gray of head much less extensive (extends only
    to just below eyes and to nape); throat and un-
    derparts cinnamon.
16. **Cinnamon**   *A. cinnamomeus*   p. 622
    Rich rufous; *no wing bars*; no obvious contrast
    on rump.
17. **White-browed Purpletuft**   *Iodopleura i.*
    isabellae   p. 653
    Stubby little bird; *white facial markings and
    rump*. Treetops. **Dusky** *I. fusca* (text). SE (few
    recs). White only on median lower underparts
    and rump band.
18. **Ringed Antpipit**   *Corythopis torquata*
    anthoides   p. 588
    S. Mostly terrestrial; *dark above with white throat*;
    bold fused necklace. Often snaps bill in authori-
    tative manner.

1. Pompadour Cotinga   *Xipholena
punicea*   p. 655
S. ♂ wine red; white eyes and wings. ♀ plump
and gray; white eyes and wing edges.

Cotingas   *Cotinga*
Round, dovelike shape; ♂♂ various shades of blue;
♀♀ grayish to brownish and scaly. Sedate and serene
countenance; forest canopy.
2. Purple-breasted   *C. cotinga*   p. 654
S. ♂ deep cobalt blue; note extensive purple on
breast. ♀ quite dark; heavily scaled and spotted.
3. Spangled   *C. cayana*   p. 655
S. ♂ metallic turquoise spangled with black. ♀
much paler, less spotted and scaled than 2. **Blue**
C. nattererii (text). SW base of Andes. Somewhat
like 3; nothing sim. in range.
4. Red-crested Cotinga   *Ampelion
rubrocristatus*   p. 649
Andes. High els. Plump and gray; flat maroon
crest; whitish rump; white tail band (from below).
5. Cinereous Mourner   *Laniocera
hypopyrra*   p. 641
S. Cinnamon buff wing spots; orange rufous
(yellow—♀) pectoral tufts occas. visible. Imms.
and some ads. may show variable amt. of rufous
spotting on underparts. Never as numerous as
6 and 7.
6. Grayish Mourner   *Rhytipterna simplex
frederici*   p. 622
S. Plain gray. Much like 7 but smaller (text).

Pihas   *Lipaugus*
7. Screaming   *L. vociferans*   p. 640
S. Larger, more robust than 6. Can always be told
by call.
8. Rose-collared   *L. streptophorus*   p. 641
Tepuis. ♂ magenta collar. ♀ and imm. cinnamon rufous collar.
9. Andean Laniisoma   *Laniisoma buckleyi
venezuelensis*   p. 653
Andes. ♂ black crown; black scaling on sides of
yellow underparts. ♀ olive crown; more scaled
below. Rare.

10. Scaled Fruiteater   *Ampelioides tschudii* p. 652
Andes. Odd patchy plumage. ♂ scalloped above
and below; black crown. ♀ sim. but crown olive;
bolder black-edged scalloping below. Very scarce.

Bellbirds   *Procnias*
♀ and imm. dark olive; heavily streaked yellow and
olive below. Young ♂♂ look like ♀♀; gradually acquire ad. ♂ plumage in stages.
11. Bearded   *P. averano carnobarba*   p. 656
♂ unique. ♀ sim. to ♀ White Bellbird but head
darker than back, more streaked below (text).
White *P. alba* Pl. 51(3).

Fruiteaters   *Pipreola*
Rotund; some shade of green above; most with bright
bills and legs; high-pitched songs; inconspic. habits.
12. Green-and-black   *P. riefferii
melanolaema*   p. 650
N mts. ♂ black hood with yellow border. ♀ olive
hood with yellow border.
13. Barred   *P. a. arcuata*   p. 650
Andes. Large; ♂ black hood; barred underparts;
large yellow tertial spots. ♀ olive above; all
barred below incl. throat.
14. Handsome   *P. f. formosa*   p. 651
Coastal Cordillera; NE mts. Bright green. ♂ not
likely confused; note large white tertial spots. ♀
mostly green; finely barred yellow below.
15. Golden-breasted   *P. aureopectus festiva* p. 651
N mts. ♂ rich yellow to chin. ♀ broadly streaked
green and yellow below.
16. Red-banded   *P. whitelyi kathleenae*   p. 652
Tepuis. ♂ grayish below with red cummerbund;
tawny bands on head and neck. ♀ head and upperparts duller than ♂; below white sharply
streaked black.
17. Sharpbill   *Oxyruncus cristatus phelpsi* p. 649
Tepuis and cerros S of Orinoco. Densely spotted
below; orangish eyes; pointed bill. Flame crest
often mostly hidden. Inconspic. in forest canopy.

1. **Andean Cock-of-the-rock**   *Rupicola peruviana aequatorialis*   p. 661
Andes. Large as a hen. ♂ could hardly be mistaken. ♀ dull dark reddish brown; crest small. Wet forested mt. ravines with cliffs or boulders. Local.

2. **Guianan Cock-of-the-rock**   *Rupicola rupicola*   p. 661
S. A bit smaller than 1. Bright ♂ a fiery ball of orange in flight. ♀ lumpy and dusky brown with small crest. Lowland and foothill forest, always near rocky outcrops.

3. **White Bellbird**   *Procnias alba*   p. 656
SE. ♂ all white with black vermiform wattle. ♀ and imm. much like 11 on Pl. 50 but olive crown concolor with back; underparts streaking broader (text). Some vertical migr. within tepuis but always low density.

4. **Capuchinbird**   *Perissocephalus tricolor*   p. 659
S. Large, oddly proportioned cotinga. **4a.** Ad.: rufescent with bare bluish crown, large bill, and bobtail. **4b.** Display posture when calling.

5. **Amazonian Umbrellabird**   *Cephalopterus ornatus*   p. 659
Amazonas. Large; a bit woodpecker- or jaylike. ♂ large crest and pendant wattle. ♀ crest and wattle reduced.

6. **Purple-throated Fruitcrow**   *Querula purpurata*   p. 657
S. Large and round-winged; strong, pale bill. ♂ magenta throat. ♀ all black.

7. **Red-ruffed Fruitcrow**   *Pyroderus scutatus*   p. 658
7a. *P. s. granadensis:* N mts. Large, black, and crowlike; crinkly orange chest. **7b.** *P. s. orenocensis:* E Bolívar. Sim. but has dull chestnut breast. **Crimson** *Haematoderus militaris* (text).

8. **Bare-necked Fruitcrow**   *Gymnoderus foetidus*   p. 657
Amazonas. Vulturine head with pale gray blue wattles and lappets. ♂ silver wings flash conspic in high flight. ♀ less ornamented head; wings almost concolor with body. Imm. scaled whitish below.

Red-cotingas   *Phoenicircus*
Size of a plump *Turdus*. ♂♂ red and black; ♀♀ duller, mainly olive brown above; crown and tail maroon red; belly dark pinkish red.

9. **Black-necked**   *P. nigricollis*   p. 660
S Amazonas. ♂ glistening red and velvet black. ♀ duller; throat and rump olive brown like back. Rare and local.

10. **Guianan**   *P. carnifex*   p. 660
SE. Duller than 9. ♂ glistening red and blackish maroon. ♀ raspberry crown; brownish olive back and wings; brownish pink breast. Rare and local.

JAGwynne

1. **White-thighed Swallow**   *Neochelidon*
tibialis griseiventris   p. 689
S. Tiny and batlike. Above dusky brown, rump
and underparts paler; white leg tufts (mainly visible at rest). Scarce and local.
2. **Blue-and-white Swallow**   *Notiochelidon c.*
cyanoleuca   p. 688
Mts. Common in N. **2a**. Ad.: dark glossy blue
above, snowy below; crissum black. **2b.** Imm.:
brownish above; brownish wash on chest. S
migr. *N. c. patagonica* (not illus.) sim. but *larger*,
less black on crissum.
3. **Barn Swallow**   *Hirundo rustica*
erythrogaster   p. 691
N migr. Ad. dark glossy blue above; throat bright
rusty; underparts rich buff; white band forms inverted V on underside of long, deeply forked
tail; in flight note bicolored underwing. Imm.
(shown) duller and paler, esp. below. **Cliff**
Petrochelidon pyrrhonota (text). N migr. Wings
broader than allies; short squarish tail; white
forehead; chestnut face and blackish throat bordered by pale collar.

Swallows   *Notiochelidon*
4. **Pale-footed**   *N. flavipes*   p. 688
High els. in Andes. Closely resembles 2 but
smaller, voice differs, and usually at higher els.
Look for cinnamon tinge on throat, more blackish on sides and flanks. Low over forest. Local.
5. **Brown-bellied**   *N. murina meridensis*   p. 687
High els. in Andes. *Large, dingy swallow.* Gloss
on upperparts usually not apparent in field. Over
forest or paramo.
6. **Tawny-headed Swallow**   *Alopochelidon*
fucata   p. 690
Mainly SE. Small and pale; tawny rufous brow
and collar surprisingly bright but not always conspic.; rump usually pale. Low over open areas
and grassland. Local.

Swallows   *Atticora*
Steely blue black above; *long, deeply forked tail.*
7. **Black-collared**   *A. melanoleuca*   p. 689
S. Glossy bluish black; note narrow black band
across snowy underparts; mostly over blackwater
rivers.
8. **White-banded**   *A. fasciata*   p. 689
S. All glossy blue black with white cummerbund.
Mostly over blackwater rivers.
9. **Southern Rough-winged Swallow**
Stelgidopteryx ruficollis aequalis   p. 690
Plainly attired; brown with *whitish rump;* at rest
note *dark forecrown*, slight peaked crest.

10. **Bank Swallow (Sand Martin)**   *Riparia r.*
riparia   p. 691
N migr. Resembles 13 but much smaller and
quite pale, esp. back and rump. Narrow chest
band; notched tail. White of throat extends up
behind dusky auriculars. In llanos often with 3
but scarcer.
11. **White-winged Swallow**   *Tachycineta*
albiventer   p. 687
Large white wing patches; white rump. Widespread, usually near or over water. **Tree** *T. bicolor* (text). Accidental N migr. Much like 11 but
no white on wings (except tertials) or rump.

Martins   *Progne*
Large; identification of some spp. difficult, but only 13
and 14 are common.
12. **Southern**   *P. elegans* (subsp. prob. *elegans*)   p. 686
Rare or accidental S migr. (1 sight rec.). Largest
martin. ♂ essentially identical to ♂ of 15 but
slightly larger, tail more deeply forked (longer-
tailed appearance). ♀ forehead occas. pale;
nuchal collar never pale (cf. ♀ of 15); only ♀
Progne almost all dark below; note *coarsely
scaled and spotted underparts.*
13. **Brown-chested**   *P. tapera*   p. 684
13a. *P. t. tapera*: resident. Clean horizontal chest
band; note *long fluffy white under tail coverts*
projecting on sides of tail. **13b.** *P. t. fusca*: S migr.
Chest band as above but also with short row of
vertical spotting down median breast.
14. **Gray-breasted**   *P. c. chalybea*   p. 685
Resident; prob. also S migr. Sexes essentially sim.
and ♀-plumaged (cf. other *Progne*). Grayish
brown throat and chest blend to whitish belly.
Widespread and common.
15. **Purple**   *P. s. subis*   p. 685
N migr. (few recs.). ♂ all glossy blue black;
forked tail. ♀ *gray nuchal collar;* forehead narrowly grayish; dingy gray brown throat and
chest fade to paler lower underparts. Imm.
much duller; mainly grayish above but retains
pale nuchal collar. **Caribbean** *P. dominicensis*
(text). Rare or accidental vagrant from Carib.
(sight recs.). ♂ glossy blue black with sharply
demarcated white lower breast and belly. ♀ and
imm. throat and breast tinged brownish; white
belly less sharply defined.

Tapaculos   *Scytalopus*
Complex Andean genus. Scamper and hop mouselike
on gd. or low in thickets. Slaty black, some with black
barring on brownish flanks and rump. Juvs. dark
brown, heavily barred.
1. **Unicolored**   *S. unicolor latrans*   p. 559
   S Táchira. Uniform bluish slate.
2. **Northern White-crowned**   *S. atratus*
   nigricans   p. 560
   Andes. White crown spot; rusty-barred flanks.
3. **Mérida**   *S. meridanus*   p. 560
   Andes. Mouse gray with barring on brownish
   rear end. **3a.** Ad. **3b.** Imm. **Caracas** *S. caracae*
   (text). Like 3; loud, angry voice; Coastal
   Cordillera. **Rufous-rumped** *S. griseicollis fusci-*
   cauda Pl. 43(23). Paler than 3; *rusty rearparts*
   brighter and unbarred.

4. **Rufous Wren**   *Cinnycerthia u. unirufa*   p. 694
   Perijá Mts.; S Táchira. Much like Rufous Spinetail
   (7 on Pl. 38) but tail shorter; wings faintly barred;
   often in groups; some have whitish foreheads.

Wrens   *Campylorhynchus*
Largest wrens; barred, spotted, or with contrasting
plumage; dry to humid semiopen areas, forest borders.
5. **Bicolored**   *C. griseus minor*   p. 693
   Large and "bicolored."
6. **Stripe-backed**   *C. n. nuchalis*   p. 693
   Unique in its limited range.

Wrens   *Thryothorus*
Small or med. in size; most spp. brown above, paler
or white below; pale eye stripe and streaky face; bars
on tail; thicket dwellers; hd. much more than seen.
7. **Rufous-breasted**   *T. r. rutilus*   p. 696
   N mts. Speckled face and throat; *bright rufous*
   chest.
8. **Whiskered**   *T. mystacalis consobrinus*   p. 695
   N mts. Large and skulky; brownish gray tones to
   foreparts; contrasting facial markings, bold black
   "whisker."
9. **Coraya**   *T. coraya caurensis*   p. 696
   S. Very dark; E tepui race (not illus.) extensively
   black on sides of head to neck; rufescent below.
   Lowlands and tepuis.
10. **Rufous-and-white**   *T. rufalbus*
    cumanensis   p. 697
    Large; clean-cut rufous and white plumage;
    crissum barred; sneaky, "peek-a-boo" habits.
11. **Buff-breasted**   *T. leucotis venezuelensis* p. 697
    Widespread; thickets, often near water; *buff*
    underparts.

Wood-Wrens   *Henicorhina*
Small; white eyestripe; streaky face; short, cocked tail.
12. **Gray-breasted**   *H. leucophrys*
    venezuelensis   p. 700
    N mts. Iron gray below; skulks and fidgets in
    thickets.
13. **White-breasted**   *H. l. leucosticta*   p. 699
    S. Undergrowth in humid lowland forest.

Wrens   *Troglodytes*
Small, brownish, and plain, but eyestripe usually evident; short cocked tail.
14. **Mountain**   *T. solstitialis solitarius* p. 698
    Andes. Buff eyestripe; overall buffier than 15; ar-
    boreal in forest.
15. **House**   *T. aedon albicans*   p. 698
    Widespread and familiar. Always paler than 14 or
    16; crissum unbarred.
16. **Tepui**   *T. rufulus fulvigularis*   p. 699
    Tepuis. Rich ruddy brown (paler in Amazonas);
    confiding and gifted singer but most pops. re-
    mote and inaccessible.

Wrens   *Cistothorus*
Tiny; stubby tail; Venez. spp. densely barred on wings
and tail; easily overlooked.
17. **Grass**   *C. platensis alticola*   p. 694
    Local in wet grass; much buffier in Táchira;
    some buff white streaking on back.
18. **Mérida**   *C. meridae*   p. 695
    Paramo (local). Fidgety; prom. eyestripe and
    white streaking on back; bubbling song.
19. **Musician Wren**   *Cyphorhinus arada*
    urbanoi   p. 700
    Bolívar. Rufous foreparts, streaky neck, bare blue
    ocular area; odd bill shape. Forest "spirit" with
    enchanting song.

Wrens   *Microcerculus*
Small and dark; long, thin bill; longish legs; short,
cocked tail.
20. **Southern Nightingale-**
    M. marginatus   p. 701
    Often on gd.; hd. far more than seen. **20a.** *M. m.*
    squamulatus: dark with long bill, stubby tail; cen-
    tral underparts whitish heavily scaled and scal-
    loped brown. **20b.** Amaz. subsp. *M. m. margina-*
    tus: median underparts white.
21. **Flutist**   *M. ustulatus duidae*   p. 701
    Tepuis. Plain rufescent brown (no eyestripe); wet
    forest undergrowth; fifelike song quite variable.
    Behavior as in 20.
22. **Wing-banded**   *M. bambla caurensis*   p. 701
    Mainly bases of tepuis. Bold wing band. Behav-
    ior as in 20.
23. **Collared Gnatwren**   *Microbates c.*
    collaris   p. 703
    S. Tiny with notably long bill; stub tail; bold
    black markings. Thickets; can be devilishly diffi-
    cult to see.
24. **Long-billed Gnatwren**   *Ramphocaenus*
    melanurus trinitatis   p. 703
    Plain with unusually long bill, long wiggling tail;
    arboreal in vines.

Gnatcatchers   *Polioptila*
Mostly clean-cut gray and white; tail black with white
edges; highly arboreal and sprightly.
25. **Tropical**   *P. plumbea innotata*   p. 704
    Widespread, esp. in dry regions. ♂ black cap;
    ♀ gray cap, white cheeks.
26. **Guianan**   *P. guianensis facilis*   p. 704
    Very local. Much like ♀ of 25 but note eyering;
    gray cheeks and breast.

1. **Orange-billed Nightingale-Thrush**
Catharus a. aurantiirostris   p. 706
N mts. Orange bill, eyering, and legs; gray underparts. Shy.
2. **Slaty-backed Nightingale-Thrush**
Catharus f. fuscater   p. 706
Andes. Slaty with blackish head; white eyes; orange bill, eyering, and legs; central belly usually yellowish. Timid.
3. **Spotted Nightingale-Thrush**   *Catharus dryas maculatus*   p. 706
Andes. Recalls 2 but almost all yellowish and spotted below. Scarce and local.
4. **Swainson's Thrush**   *Catharus ustulatus swainsoni*   p. 707
N migr. Cold grayish olive above; prom. buff eyering and lores; buff wash on spotted throat and chest.
5. **Gray-cheeked Thrush**   *Catharus m. minimus*   p. 707
N migr. Much like 4 but note gray around eyes, *lores, and on cheeks, and no buff;* breast more densely spotted; flanks with more olive.
6. **Veery**   *Catharus f. fuscescens*   p. 708
N migr. Much ruddier above than 4 or 5; indistinct pale eyering; pale unspotted throat bordered by faint narrow submalar; chest weakly spotted, buff wash confined mainly to chest; lower underparts more gray-white than 4 or 5.
7. **Rufous-brown Solitaire**   *Myadestes leucogenys gularis*   p. 705
Tepuis of SE. Slender and long-tailed. Warm brown; central throat pale rufous; belly light grayish brown; yellow lower mandible. Erratic.
8. **Andean Solitaire**   *Myadestes ralloides venezuelensis*   p. 705
N mts. Timid. **8a.** Ad.: warm gray above; most of head and underparts iron gray; white tail tips show in flight. **8b.** Juv.
9. **Chestnut-bellied Thrush**   *Turdus fulviventris*   p. 711
Andes. Black head, gray chest sharply separated from bright ferruginous lower underparts. Mid.-el. forests.
10. **Pale-eyed Thrush**   *Platycichla leucops*   p. 709
♂ glossy black with white eyes. ♀ confusing: mainly dark brown, paler on lower underparts; eyes grayish (to light brown?); note lack of streaking on throat (cf. ♀♀ of 11, 12).
11. **Yellow-legged Thrush**   *Platycichla flavipes venezuelensis*   p. 708
Mts. ♂ body gray; head, foreparts, wings, and tail black; soft parts yellow. ♀ difficult, paler than allies (10, 12, 14, 15); throat vaguely streaked, belly pale grayish.

Thrushes   *Turdus*
12. **Glossy-black**   *T. serranus atrosericeus*   p. 710
N mts. Large thrush. **12a.** *T. s. atrosericeus:* ♂ all glossy black; orange eyering, bill, and legs. ♀ *darkest ♀ Turdus in Venez.* (cf. 10, 11, 13, 14); note size, inconspic. yellowish eyering. **12b.** *T. s. cumanensis:* NE mts. ♂ a bit duller. ♀ underparts darker, sooty gray.
13. **Great**   *Turdus fuscater gigas*   p. 709
Andes. Much larger than allies. ♂: dark grayish brown to sooty; yellowish eyering, orangish bill and legs. ♀: sim. but duller, paler; eyering narrow and inconspic. or lacking. Juv.: much like ad. ♀; no evident eyering. Open areas near treeline.
14. **Black-hooded**   *T. o. olivater*   p. 710
Mts. ♂ N of Orinoco (subsp. shown) black hood; yellow eyering, bill, and legs; lower underparts olive gray to pale brownish. S of Orinoco black of hood confined to head; rest of plumage varies with subspp. (text). ♀ duller, black of hood replaced by brown but usually retains hint of ♂'s pattern.
15. **Black-billed**   *T. ignobilis*   p. 712
15a. *T. i. murinus:* tepuis. Bill black; no eyering; dull dark grayish brown, grayer below; throat streaked; belly dirty grayish white. **15b.** *T. i. debilis:* Andes. Paler and browner; more distinct dark streaking on whiter throat; belly whiter.
16. **White-necked**   *T. albicollis phaeopygoides*   p. 714
Rich dark brown above; throat thickly streaked black (white scarcely evident); narrow inconspic. white crescent on chest; underparts mostly gray.
17. **Pale-breasted**   *T. leucomelas albiventer*   p. 713
Widespread and common. *Gray head contrasts with brownish back;* breast pale, belly whitish.
18. **Cocoa**   *T. fumigatus*   p. 713
18a. *T. f. aquilonalis:* richer rufescent above and below than allies. Richer and darker still in E Bolívar race (not shown). **18b.** *T. f. orinocensis:* more southerly subsp. sim. but darker, more brownish; belly whitish.
19. **Bare-eyed**   *T. n. nudigenis*   p. 711
Rather plain but from any other by *large yellowish ocular ring.*
20. **Lawrence's**   *T. lawrencii*   p. 712
SE. Best told by remarkable mimetic song. Otherwise another dull thrush, paler brown below. ♂ *bright yellow bill* tipped black; yellow eyering; whitish belly. ♀ plainer, duller; bill dusky; retains yellow eyering.

JAGwynne 7·97

1. **Rufous-browed Peppershrike**   *Cyclaris*
gujanensis parvus   p. 673
Strong, hooked bill; crown and cheeks gray,
brow rufous, chest yellow. S birds (not illus.)
head darker and grayer; brow reduced.

Shrike-Vireos   *Vireolanius*
Strong, hooked bill; yellow eyebrows.
2. **Slaty-capped**   *V. l. leucotis*   p. 674
S. Contrasting gray crown; yellow eyestripe, facial markings, underparts. Forest canopy.
3. **Yellow-browed**   *V. e. eximius*   p. 674
Perijá; SE Táchira. Bright green above; yellow
eyebrow and throat.

Vireos   *Vireo*
4. **Brown-capped**   *V. leucophrys mirandae* p. 676
N mts. Small size; rufescent brown crown;
whitish eyebrow, *"beady" black eyes.*
5. **Red-eyed**   *V. o. olivaceus*   p. 675
N migr. Rather flat, dark-edged gray crown; white
eyestripe; dark red iris shared with 6 and 8; yellow-tinged crissum on freshly molted birds.
6. **Yellow-green**   *V. flavoviridis*   p. 675
C Amer. migr. Much like 5; gray crown lacks dark
border (blurry look); cheeks and sides of neck
tinged yellow; brighter, more extensive yellow on
crissum, yellow extending to flanks. Rare.
7. **Yellow-throated**   *V. flavifrons*   p. 676
N migr. Prom. yellow spectacles; yellow of breast
sharply separated from white belly.
8. **Black-whiskered**   *V. altiloquus*
bonairensis   p. 676
Carib. migr. Sim. to 5 but duller, paler (a bit
faded), lacking crispness. *Dark whisker mark;*
light yellow tinge on flanks.

Greenlets   *Hylophilus*
Small, active; pale bill (most spp.); songs very helpful
in identification.
9. **Golden-fronted**   *H. aurantiifrons*
saturatus   p. 679
N. Cinnamon gold forecrown turns reddish
brown on hindcrown; *"beady" black eyes.*
10. **Dusky-capped**   *H. h. hypoxanthus*   p. 680
S Amazonas. Dull and confusing. Brownish
crown; no other in range has entire breast and
lower underparts yellowish (pale).
11. **Brown-headed**   *H. b. brunneiceps*   p. 679
S. Dull. Brownish crown and nape; gray below.
12. **Buff-cheeked**   *H. m. muscicapinus*   p. 680
SE. Also dull. Grayish crown, weak buff wash on
cheeks, sides of neck, and vaguely to chest;
lower breast whitish.
13. **Rufous-naped**   *H. semibrunneus*   p. 681
Perijá foothills. Dark rufous crown and nape;
face and throat grayish white.
14. **Tawny-crowned**   *H. ochraceiceps*   p. 681
14a. *H. o. ferrugineifrons*: S. Forecrown tawny rufous, turning rufous on rearcrown; eyes pale.
14b. *H. o. luteifrons*: extreme E Bolívar. A bit
darker and more uniform; eyes dark.

15. **Scrub**   *H. flavipes*   p. 677
15a. *H. f. galbanus*: mainly N. Uniform; almost
featureless; buff wash on chest; *bill and legs
pinkish; eyes pale to dark.* Dry scrubby areas.
15b. *H. f. acuticauda*: vicinity of Orinoco. Sim. but
underparts faintly tinged yellowish.
16. **Lemon-chested**   *H. thoracicus*
griseiventris   p. 678
SE. Rearcrown and nape gray; upperparts olive;
broad yellow chest band; pale eyes.
17. **Gray-chested**   *H. semicinereus viridiceps* p. 677
S. Mainly olive above; *gray below;* hint of yellow
on sides of breast; *pale eyes.*
18. **Ashy-headed**   *H. pectoralis*   p. 678
Delta Amacuro. Much like 16; *entire crown and
sides of head ashy gray; eyes dark.* Note range
and vocal differences.
19. **Tepui**   *H. sclateri*   p. 679
Tepuis; above el. of allies; much like 16–18. Note
gray wings and tail; pale eyes.

Warblers   *Vermivora*
20. **Tennessee**   *V. peregrina*   p. 717
N migr. **20a.** Ad.: smaller, thinner-billed, more delicate than greenlets; contrasting gray crown, white
eyestripe and underparts. **20b.** Imm.: duller, more
olive; thin bill. **Blue-winged** *V. pinus* (text).
21. **Golden-winged**   *V. chrysoptera*   p. 717
♀ sooty gray of face and throat replaced by
black in ♂.
22. **Black-and-white Warbler**   *Mniotilta*
varia   p. 724
♀ much less streaked below than ♂.

Warblers   *Dendroica*
N migrs.; mainly N mts. (except 26). Not illus. (text):
Chestnut-sided *D. pensylvanica;* **Magnolia** *D. magnolia;* **Cape May** *D. tigrina;* **Black-throated Blue** *D.
caerulescens;* **Yellow-rumped** *D. coronata;* **Black-
throated Green** *D. virens;* **Palm** *D. palmarum.*
23. **Cerulean**   *D. cerulea*   p. 723
N migr. mainly to E slope of Andes and n
cordilleras. ♂ cerulean blue above; black line
across chest. ♀ *contrasting blue gray cap;* yellowish white eyestripe; olive-tinged back; *white wing
bars;* faint streaking on sides. Imm. like ♀ but
duller, yellower.
24. **Blackburnian**   *D. fusca*   p. 723
Mainly N mts. **24a.** ♀ and imm.: duller than ad.
♂; markings yellow and often restricted to face
and throat. **24b.** Ad. ♂: fiery orange markings
on head, throat, and chest. Ad. ♂♂ often winter
at higher els. and in more mature forest than ♀♀
and imms.
25. **Bay-breasted**   *D. castanea*   p. 722
N migr. **25a.** Imm.: *blackish legs* (cf. 26a); see
text. **25b.** Ad. plumage (mostly prior to northward migr.).
26. **Blackpoll**   *D. striata*   p. 722
Mainly S of Orinoco. **26a.** Imm.: straw yellow
legs (cf. 25a); see text. **26b.** Ad. plumage (mostly
prior to northward migr.).

JAGwynne 96

Warblers   *Basileuterus*
Rather large, sturdy warblers; proportions much as in *Hemispingus* tanagers.

1. **Golden-crowned**   *B. culicivorus cabanisi*   p. 734
Head and upperparts mainly gray; black crown stripes; yellow coronal stripe. More slender, delicate looking, and sprightly than allies.

2. **Russet-crowned**   *B. coronatus regulus*   p. 736
N mts. Quite dark. Dark gray head and throat; orange coronal stripe; black crown stripes obscure.

3. **Roraiman**   *B. roraimae*   p. 734
SE tepuis. Rather dark. Dark olive upperparts; dark orangish coronal stripe; yellowish eyestripe.

4. **Rufous-capped**   *B. rufifrons mesochrysus*   p. 735
Perijá foothills. Chestnut on head, white eyestripe. Slender, active (like 1).

5. **Gray-throated**   *B. c. cinereicollis*   p. 735
Perijá Mts.; W slope of Andes (local). Dark (cf. 2); *dark gray head and chest* (throat paler) sharply divided from yellow lower underparts; crown stripes obscure.

6. **Mourning Warbler**   *Oporornis philadelphia*   p. 728
N migr. Smaller, more delicate looking, not as sim. to 5 as it seems. Gray hood to mid. chest (with black crepe bib—♂); no white eyering. **Connecticut** *O. agilis* (text). N migr. Much like 6; prom. white eyering (all plumages); elongated shape.

7. **Gray-headed Warbler**   *Basileuterus griseiceps*   p. 735
NE mts. Very rare and local. Gray head, short white supraloral streak; throat and underparts yellow. Overlaps only 1 and 8.

8. **Three-striped Warbler**   *Basileuterus tristriatus besserei*   p. 733
N mts. Much geographical variation in plumage. Dusky crown stripes and cheek patch; drab underparts (never bright yellow).

9. **Black-crested Warbler**   *Basileuterus nigrocristatus*   p. 732
N mts. Sharp black stripe on forecrown (no crest); large yellow eyestripe; crisp black line through eyes.

10. **Citrine Warbler**   *Basileuterus l. luteoviridis*   p. 732
Andes. *Short yellow eyebrow*; blackish line through eyes; *rounded tail*; brownish legs (cf. esp. 15 on Pl. 57).

11. **Flavescent Warbler**   *Basileuterus flaveolus*   p. 733
N mts. *Short narrow eyeline;* pale legs. Sweeps tail side to side. Mainly foothills.

12. **Masked Yellowthroat**   *Geothlypis a. aequinoctialis*   p. 728
♂ gray crown, *black mask.* ♀ plain; inconspic. yellowish eyering; head often tinged brownish gray. **Common** *G. trichas* (text).

13. **Kentucky Warbler**   *Oporornis formosus*   p. 727
N migr. Olive above; *yellow spectacles; black "sideburns."* ♀ sim. but duller. Imm. dull; often a hint of black on neck. Rare.

14. **Canada Warbler**   *Wilsonia canadensis*   p. 729
Mts. N migr. *Uniform gray above;* white eyering; *black necklace.* ♀ necklace reduced. Imm. necklace obscure. **Hooded** *W. citrina* (text). Rare.

15. **Yellow Warbler**   *Dendroica a. aestiva*   p. 719
N migr. ♂ yellow; rusty breast streaking. ♀ yellow, incl. tail. Wings relatively long (cf. 16, 17).

16. **Golden Warbler**   *Dendroica petechia cienagae*   p. 719
Coast (Paraguaná Pen. eastward); isls. ♂ chestnut crown; ♀ sim. to ♀ of 15 (see text).

17. **Mangrove Warbler**   *Dendroica erithachorides paraguanae*   p. 719
Coast (Zulia to central Falcón). ♂ chestnut head; ♀ like ♀ of 15 but slightly larger; primary extension shorter; bill thinner; some also show flecks of chestnut on crown and tinge of chestnut on throat. Little overlap with 16.

18. **Tropical Parula**   *Parula pitiayumi elegans*   p. 718
Blackish face *lacks* broken white eyering; smudgy chest band. ♀ no chest band. **Northern** *P. americana* (text). Rare N migr. *Broken white eyering;* less yellow below.

19. **Prothonotary Warbler**   *Protonotaria citrea*   p. 725
Mainly near coast. Golden head and underparts; white crissum; white in spread tail.

20. **Riverside Warbler**   *Basileuterus rivularis mesoleuca*   p. 736
S. Brownish; buff eyebrow; dingy below. On or near gd.; sweeps tail.

21. **Northern Waterthrush**   *Seiurus noveboracensis*   p. 726
N migr. Dark brown; narrow pale eyebrow; narrow streaks on creamy underparts. Not illus. (text): **Louisiana Waterthrush** *S. motacilla*; **Ovenbird** *S. aurocapillus*; **Worm-eating Warbler** *Helmitheros vermivorus;* and **Swainson's Warbler** *Limnothlypis swainsonii*.

22. **Rose-breasted Chat**   *Granatellus p. pelzelni*   p. 737
S. ♀ buff face and throat; rose crissum.

23. **American Redstart**   *Setophaga ruticilla*   p. 724
N migr. ♀ yellow patches on chest, wings, and tail. ♂'s black and orange plumage unique. 1st-yr ♂ (not illus.) Like ♀ but pectoral patches richer, more orange yellow.

Whitestarts   *Myioborus*

24. **Slate-throated**   *M. miniatus ballux*   p. 729
Mts. Rufous cap, *slaty throat;* only breast and belly yellow.

25. **White-fronted**   *M. albifrons*   p. 730
Andes. White frontlet and bold spectacles; all yellow below.

26. **Paria**   *M. pariae*   p. 731
NE mts. Yellow spectacles; all yellow below.

27. **Tepui**   *M. c. castaneocapillus*   p. 731
Tepuis. Inconspic. broken white eyering; *all yellow below* (cf. 24).

28. **Golden-fronted**   *M. o. ornatus*   p. 730
S Táchira. *Yellow forecrown* and underparts; *white face.*

29. **White-faced**   *M. albifacies*   p. 732
N Amazonas cerros. Black crown; large white face.

30. **Guaiquinima**   *M. cardonai*   p. 731
Cerro Guaiquinima. Much like 29 (no overlap) but crown black.

J.Gwynne 11·95

Flowerpiercers   *Diglossopis*
Larger and bill not as modified as *Diglossa*. Mainly forest and forest borders, feed heavily on fruit.

1. Bluish   *D. caerulescens saturata*   p. 781
N mts. Dull grayish blue; black lores; dark red eye; thin bill.

2. Masked   *D. c. cyanea*   p. 782
N mts. Rich deep blue; small black mask; bright red eyes.

Flowerpiercers   *Diglossa*
Smaller than *Diglossopis*; bill upturned, hooked at tip; mainly forest borders and shrubby areas; feed heavily on nectar.

3. Greater   *D. major gilliardi*   p. 782
Tepuis. Large; frosty streaking, pale malar stripe; chestnut crissum. Other subspp. less streaked.

4. Scaled   *D. d. duidae*   p. 783
Tepuis of Amazonas. Very dark; belly scaled and spotted grayish.

5. White-sided   *D. a. albilatera*   p. 784
N mts. ♂ gray. Conspic. white flank tufts (both sexes).

6. Venezuelan   *D. venezuelensis*   p. 785
NE mts. ♂ much like 5 (no overlap) but all black. ♀ like 5 but more yellowish olive.

7. Rusty   *D. sittoides dorbignyi*   p. 785
N mts. ♂ cinnamon underparts. ♀ lacks good marks; note obscure breast streaking.

8. Black   *D. h. humeralis*   p. 783
Perijá Mts.; S Táchira. Black; small gray patch on shoulders; rump dark gray. Imm. grayish brown; obscure streaking below.

9. Glossy   *D. l. lafresnayi*   p. 783
Andes. Very like 8 but overlaps it only in S Táchira. Often not separable from 8 but slightly larger, glossier, all black (incl. rump), and bill slightly larger.

10. Mérida   *D. gloriosa*   p. 784
Andes. Chestnut lower underparts; gray flanks; small blue gray patch on shoulders.

Conebills   *Conirostrum*
Small; quite active; arboreal; warblerlike but sturdier; thin, sharp, pointed bill; mainly in canopy foliage.

11. Capped   *C. albifrons cyanonotum*   p. 740
N mts. ♂ white cap in S Táchira; blue cap in Coastal Cordillera. ♀ bluish cap, olive body. Local.

12. Rufous-browed   *C. rufum*   p. 739
S Táchira. Forehead and underparts rusty. Treeline.

13. Blue-backed   *C. sitticolor intermedium*   p. 740
W mts. Black head and foreparts; blue back; rusty breast.

Hemispinguses   *Hemispingus*
Mostly rather small, thin-billed tanagers; morphologically (but not vocally) close to *Basileuterus* warblers.

14. Gray-capped   *H. reyi*   p. 745
Andes. Gray cap; olive yellow body. Often in bamboo.

15. Superciliaried   *H. superciliaris chrysophrys*   p. 744
Andes. Look for long, narrow, yellowish eyestripe; squarish tail; slaty legs. Cf. closely 10 on Pl. 56. Often at forest edges.

16. Black-capped   *H. a. atropileus*   p. 743
S Táchira. Black head; long whitish eyestripe; yellow below.

17. Oleaginous   *H. frontalis*   p. 744
17a. *H. f. hanieli*: Coastal Cordillera. Dull brownish olive above; *buffy ochre below*; long, narrow, rather weak eyeline. **17b.** *H. f. flavidorsalis*: Perijá Mts. Sim. but overall more olive. Low inside forest.

18. Slaty-backed   *H. goeringi*   p. 745
Andes. Bold white head stripes; bright orange rufous below. Local.

19. Black-eared   *H. m. melanotis*   p. 745
S Táchira. Small black mask, cinnamon underparts.

20. Black-headed   *H. verticalis*   p. 746
S Táchira. **20a.** Ad.: black sides of head and neck; sandy crown stripe; pale eyes; gray below. **20b.** Imm.: dark eyes.

21. Gray-hooded Bush-Tanager
Cnemoscopus r. rubrirostris   p. 743
S Táchira. Pinkish bill; gray hood; moves with crouching gait; flicks tail up. Forest canopy.

Bush-Tanagers   *Chlorospingus*
Rather dull-plumaged group, mainly gray, olive, and yellow; dominant in many montane mixed-spp. flocks in forest and at borders.

22. Common   *C. ophthalmicus jacqueti*   p. 742
N mts. Geographically variable. Race shown is most widespread in Venez. Contrasting head; white eyepatch. Montane forest and borders.

23. Ashy-headed   *C. c. canigularis*   p. 742
S Táchira. Quite like 22; note dark eyes, pale gray on throat.

J Gwynne 4·97

Tanagers *Piranga*
♂♂ usually reddish; ♀♀ olive to yellow; heavy bill.
1. **Summer**   *P. r. rubra*   p. 754
   N migr. Pale bill. ♂ rosy red. ♀ yellowish olive to
   a bit orangish; paler, yellower below. Lighter
   woodland.
2. **Highland Hepatic-**   *P. lutea faceta*   p. 753
   Mts. Bill dark above, pale below. ♂ darker, more
   brick red than 1. ♀ darker than ♀ of 1; breast
   washed olive.
3. **White-winged**   *P. leucoptera venezuelae* p. 755
   Mts. ♂ black lores; white wing bars. ♀ white
   wing bars. **Scarlet** *P. olivacea* (text). ♂ much
   like 3 but no black on lores; no white on wings.
   ♀ rather olive; blackish wings and tail. Forest
   canopy.
4. **White-capped Tanager**   *Sericossypha*
   albocristata   p. 742
   S Táchira. Large; snowy cap, crimson bib
   (darker—♀). Noisy groups in treetops. Scarce.
5. **Blue-capped Tanager**   *Thraupis*
   cyanocephala   p. 758
   5a. *T. c. auricrissa*: N mts. Head blue, underparts
   dark gray. **5b.** *T. c. olivicyanea*: Coastal
   Cordillera. Underparts blue like head. **5c.** *T. c.
   subcinerea*: NE mts. Crown blue, sides of head
   black; pale freckled malar line; underparts gray.
   Favors second growth; often common.
6. **Fawn-breasted Tanager**   *Pipraeidea*
   melanonota venezuelensis   p. 761
   Mts. Widespread but not numerous. ♂ sky blue
   crown; red eyes; fawn below. ♀ crown duller,
   smoky gray blue.
7. **Buff-breasted Mountain-Tanager**
   Dubusia t. taeniata   p. 761
   W mts. Frosty eyebrow; black head and throat;
   buff chest band inconspic. Often rather low; broken mt. forest.

Mountain-Tanagers   *Buthraupis*
Large, robust, high-el. tanagers; mosty yellow underparts; humid forest.
8. **Black-chested**   *B. e. eximia*   p. 759
   S Táchira. Entire crown blue; upperparts rich
   dark mossy green.
9. **Hooded**   *B. montana gigas*   p. 758
   Perijá Mts.; S Táchira. Large and rotund. Red
   eyes; black head; blue above, yellow below. Note
   conspic. *"garters."*

Mountain-Tanagers   *Anisognathus*
Colorful group of fairly large tanagers; rather thick
stubby bill; most with blue wing edgings (or blue on
shoulders). Often social.
10. **Lacrimose**   *A. lacrymosus melanops*   p. 760
    W mts. Slaty to dark gray blue above; yellow be-
    low; flecks of yellow on head. Common.
11. **Blue-winged**   *A. somptuosus*
    venezuelanus   p. 760
    S Táchira; coastal mts. Bold black and yellow
    pattern; blue on wings. Or back dark green
    (Táchira; Interior Cordillera).
12. **Scarlet-bellied**   *A. igniventris lunulatus* p. 759
    S Táchira. Red ear patch and belly; watch for
    blue rump.
13. **Golden-crowned Tanager**   *Iridosornis r.*
    rufivertex   p. 761
    S Táchira. Dark tanager. Rich glowing purplish
    blue; golden yarmulka. Dense, wet, elfin forest
    near treeline.
14. **Orange-eared Tanager**   *Chlorochrysa*
    calliparaea (bourcieri?)   p. 768
    Andes. Glistening emerald green; dark throat, or-
    ange ear patch and rump band. Mossy forest.
    Very local.

Tanagers   *Thlypopsis*
Slender, active, and warblerlike; thin bill; many spp.
with orange, yellow, or rust in plumage.
15. **Fulvous-headed**   *T. f. fulviceps*   p. 746
    N mts. ♂ gray with rufous chestnut head; below
    paler. Up in forest edge vines.
16. **Orange-headed**   *T. sordida orinocensis*   p. 746
    Shrubs on lowland river banks and isls. of Río
    Orinoco. Gray with orange yellow head; pale
    gray to whitish below.
17. **Rufous-crested Tanager**   *Creurgops*
    verticalis   p. 750
    S Táchira. Dull bluish gray above; pale rufous be-
    low. Crown patch (♂ only) inconspic. Forest
    canopy.
18. **Plushcap**   *Catamblyrhynchus d. diadema* p. 786
    N mts. Yellow forehead patch; sides of head and
    underparts dark chestnut. Bill stubby; tail
    rounded. Mainly in bamboo. Local.

1 ♂ ♀

2 ♂ ♀

3 ♂ ♀

4 ♂

5b

5a 5c

6 ♂ ♀

7

8

9

10

11

12

13

14 ♂ ♀

15♂

16 ♂

17♂ 18

J. Gwynne

1. Hooded Tanager   *Nemosia pileata*
hypoleuca   p. 748
Mainly N. Porcelain blue above; white below.
Note bright yellow eyes and legs. ♂ black crown
extends down to chest. Semiopen areas; local.

Conebills   *Conirostrum*
Small; quite active; arboreal; warblerlike but sturdier;
thin, sharp, pointed bill; mainly canopy foliage (except 2).

2. Bicolored   *C.b. bicolor*   p. 739
Mangroves on coast. **2a.** ♂: dull gray blue, dingy
below. Reddish eyes; pink legs. **2b.** Imm.: olive
above; often buff yellow on face.

3. White-eared   *C. l. leucogenys*   p. 739
N. Very small. ♂ black cap and white ear patch;
chestnut crissum. ♀ rather nondescript; dull
blue gray above; buff eyebrow, face, and underparts; whitish rump seldom visible.

4. Chestnut-vented   *C. speciosum*
amazonum   p. 738
Mainly N. ♂ much *darker blue gray* than 3; chestnut crissum. ♀ blue gray crown, yellowish olive
upperparts, buff white to whitish below; crissum
buff. Llanos and dry woodlands.

Honeycreepers   *Cyanerpes*
Long, thin, decurved bills; bright legs; short tails. ♂♂
bluish, ♀♀ greenish. Social; often in canopy of flowering trees.

5. Red-legged   *C. cyaneus eximius*   p. 781
♂ azure cap, red legs. ♀ face and throat grayish
(cf. 6 and 7); blurry streaking on dingy grayish to
pale yellowish underparts.

6. Purple   *C. caeruleus microrhynchus*   p. 780
♂ rich purple blue; bright yellow legs. ♀ rusty
on face and throat; breast streaking more prom.
than 5.

7. Short-billed   *C. nitidus*   p. 780
S. Bill obviously short (cf. 5 and 6). ♂ legs dull
pinkish red. ♀ rather like ♀ of 6; note short bill;
buff (not rusty) on throat; sides of head greenish; blue malar streak.

8. Green Honeycreeper   *Chlorophanes spiza*
subtropicalis   p. 779
♂ unique. ♀ all plain green with sharp-pointed,
slightly decurved bill.

Dacnises   *Dacnis*
Active and arboreal; thin, sharp, pointed bill; ♂♂
usually colorful; ♀♀ drab (note eye colors).

9. Blue   *D. c. cayana*   p. 777
♂ turquoise; narrow black throat patch; black on
back. ♀ a little dull green bird with bluish head.
Forest canopy and borders.

10. Black-faced   *D. l. lineata*   p. 778
S. ♂ golden eyes embedded in black mask; no
black on throat; white belly. ♀ yellowish eyes;
otherwise drab olive brown, paler below, whitish
belly. Canopy.

11. White-bellied   *D. albiventris*   p. 779
S. ♂ mainly dark cobalt blue; angular black
mask; golden eyes. ♀ brownish, median lower
underparts dull yellowish; eyes dark. Rare in
canopy and emergent trees.

12. Yellow-bellied   *D. flaviventer*   p. 778
S. ♂ mainly black above, yellow below; yellow
"suspenders"; black throat patch. ♀ brownish
with red eyes (cf. 10 and 11). Forest canopy and
borders.

13. Bananaquit   *Coereba flaveola*   p. 737
Energetic busybody. Sharp, pointed, decurved
bill. **13a.** *C. f. lutea*: typical of mainland subspp.;
white eyestripe and wing spot; gray throat; yellow rump. **13b.** Sooty black forms on coastal
and offshore isls.

Tanagers   *Hemithraupis*
Smallish and active; ♂♂ colorful; ♀♀ duller and
quite sim.

14. Guira   *H. guira nigrigula*   p. 747
♂ black face outlined yellow; burnt orange on
chest. ♀ like 15 but with weak yellowish eyeline
and eyering; lower underparts paler. Forest
canopy borders.

15. Yellow-backed   *H. flavicollis aurigularis*   p. 747
S. ♂ black; *yellow throat, rump, and crissum*;
breast grayish white. ♀ olive above, yellowish below; no facial pattern (cf. 14). Forest canopy.

Gwunne '94

Chlorophonias   _Chlorophonia_
Plump, bobtailed, and emerald green. ♀♀ duller. Fond
of mistletoe and other small berries. Forest canopy.
1. **Chestnut-breasted**   _C. pyrrhophrys_   p. 768
Andes. ♂ green; narrow chestnut belt and chestnut median underparts. ♀ blue crown; chestnut
brow; hint of "divided" underparts. Cf. ♀ of 10 on
Pl. 61. Scarce.
2. **Blue-naped**   _C. cyanea longipennis_   p. 767
Mainly mts. ♂ blue on nape and rump; cleanly
"divided" underparts. ♀ duller; blue nape; green
throat merges into dull yellowish underparts.
3. **Swallow Tanager**   _Tersina viridis_
occidentalis   p. 787
♂ turquoise with black face; white belly; black
barring on flanks. ♀ mainly green; flanks barred.
Often sits high and in open.

Tanagers   _Tangara_
Large genus; complex, mostly colorful plumages;
sexes sim. or ♀ slightly duller. Highlands; also lowlands S of Orinoco. Active, fast moving.
4. **Golden**   _T. a. arthus_   p. 769
N mts. Golden yellow head; angular black patch
on cheeks; chestnut below. Or yellow below
(Perijá Mts.).
5. **Flame-faced**   _T. p. parzudakii_   p. 770
S Táchira. Flame face; black back, silvery underparts.
6. **Saffron-crowned**   _T. xanthocephala_
venusta   p. 769
Andes. Bright yellow head; body mainly
turquoise green; belly cinnamon.
7. **Blue-and-black**   _T. v. vassorii_   p. 771
Andes. Mainly at higher el. than other _Tangara._
Dark blue; black wings and tail.
8. **Rufous-cheeked**   _T. rufigenis_   p. 770
Coastal Cordillera. Shining bluish green; _cheeks
rufous;_ belly fawn.
9. **Black-capped**   _T. heinei_   p. 771
N mts. ♂ dark with black cap; pale aquamarine
face and throat. ♀ much duller; greenish; retains
hint of dark cap and aqua throat. Note slight
scaled effect on breast.
10. **Beryl-spangled**   _T. nigroviridis cyanescens_ p. 770
N mts. Crown straw to opal; mask and back
black; _spotted below._ Often quite common.
11. **Blue-necked**   _T. cyanicollis hannahiae_   p. 773
N mts. Turquoise head on black body; burnished
gold shoulders. Forest edges.

12. **Burnished-buff**   _T. c. cayana_   p. 772
♂ _crown rufous;_ black mask; _body straw to burnished greenish gold_ (varies with light); blue gray
throat. ♀ and imm. often much duller. Dry, semiopen areas.
13. **Black-headed**   _T. c. cyanoptera_   p. 772
N mts. ♂ opalescent with black head, wings,
and tail. ♀ a bit like 9 but face and throat mottled grayish and white; belly yellowish. Tepui
subsp. darker, duller. ♂ lacks blue edging on
wings. ♀ yellower below.
14. **Bay-headed**   _T. g. gyrola_   p. 777
N. Bright green with brick red head. S of
Orinoco underparts with varying amts. of blue.
15. **Turquoise**   _T. mexicana media_   p. 773
E; S. At any distance looks blackish with yellow
belly. Up close note blue pattern; azure shoulder.
Lively little flocks.
16. **Speckled**   _T. guttata chrysophrys_   p. 775
Mts. Green above; _yellow on face;_ black spotting
on _white underparts._ Cf. 17 and 20.
17. **Spotted**   _T. p. punctata_   p. 775
S. Green above; grayish face; black spotting on
white median underparts and yellowish green
sides.
18. **Green-and-gold**   _T. schrankii_
venezuelana   p. 775
S. Bold green and yellow pattern; _large black
patch on cheeks._ ♀ crown and rump more green
than yellow.
19. **Masked**   _T. nigrocincta_   p. 773
S. Pale lavender head surrounds small black
mask; black breast; white median underparts.
20. **Yellow-bellied**   _T. x. xanthogastra_   p. 776
S. All green spotted with black; yellow center
belly. Cf. 16 and 17.
21. **Dotted**   _T. varia_   p. 776
S. _Easily confused._ Unmarked green. ♂ bluish-
edged wings. ♀ slightly paler; wings edged
greenish. Rare. Cf. carefully with ♀♀ and imms.
of several other species (text).
22. **Paradise**   _T. chilensis coelicolor_   p. 774
S. Like no other in Venez. _Scaly apple green
head; turquoise underparts._ Watch for scarlet in
rump (usually more evident than the yellow).
23. **Opal-rumped**   _T. velia iridina_   p. 774
S. Dark blue to black; _rufous chestnut belly and
undertail coverts._ Opalescent rump often difficult
to see.

Euphonias   *Euphonia*
Small, plump, and short-tailed. Three basic plumage types (text): commonest is standard black and yellow of many ♂♂, but differences between many of these spp. are complex. ♀♀ usually drab and confusing.

1. Thick-billed   *E. laniirostris crassirostris*   p. 762
N. **1a.** Ad.: ♂ *all yellow below incl. throat and under tail coverts.* ♀ yellowish below, brightest on throat and undertail coverts; lores gray. **1b.** Subad. ♂: like ♀ but with blackish mask.

2. Violaceous   *E. violacea rodwayi*   p. 763
S. ♂ same pattern as 1 but *much darker, richer orange yellow on throat and chest;* less yellow on forecrown. ♀ *very uniform;* olive above (no gray); olive yellow below, slightly darker yellow on belly.

3. White-vented   *E. m. minuta*   p. 764
S. Small. ♂ dark throat; small yellow frontlet; *white lower underparts.* ♀ dull but with *white lower underparts.*

4. Trinidad   *E. trinitatis*   p. 764
Mainly N. Small. ♂ large yellow crown patch; throat dark, rest of underparts yellow. ♀ plain olive above; *center of breast and belly grayish.*

5. Purple-throated   *E. chlorotica cynophora*   p. 765
Mainly S. ♂ essentially identical to 4 (text). ♀ perhaps differs in less gray on median underparts (cf. ♀ of 4), but the 2 spp. are prob. not reliably separable except by range (and prob. not at all in narrow zone of overlap).

6. Finsch's   *E. finschi*   p. 765
SE. ♂ rich "burnt orange" below; white patch in wings (prom. in flight). ♀ forehead slightly yellowish; lower underparts yellowish. Very local.

7. Orange-bellied   *E. xanthogaster*   p. 763
7a. *E. x. exsul:* N mts. ♂ *forecrown chestnut;* underparts rich orange yellow. ♀ *forecrown chestnut; nape gray.* **7b.** *E. x. brevirostris:* tepuis. ♂ forecrown and underparts yellow. ♀ retains some rufous on forecrown; underparts more yellowish.

8. Rufous-bellied   *E. rufiventris carnegiei*   p. 766
S. ♂ all dark steel blue (no yellow); dark rufous lower underparts. ♀ rufous on belly and crissum.

9. Golden-sided   *E. cayennensis*   p. 766
SE. ♂ steely midnight blue with golden yellow pectoral tufts (usually visible). Central underparts and all of belly extensively gray.

10. Golden-rumped   *E. cyanocephala intermedia*   p. 762
Mts. ♂ sky blue crown. ♀ blue crown; rufous frontlet, *uniform olive* below. Cf. ♀ of 1 on Pl. 60.

11. Plumbeous   *E. plumbea*   p. 766
S. ♂ upperparts and throat to chest bluish gray; *no yellow on forecrown.* ♀ echoes pattern of ♂; head dull gray; upperparts olive; below duller. Scrub woodland.

12. White-lored   *E. chrysopasta nitida*   p. 767
S. ♂ rather dull, ♀-plumaged; bill thick; white across frontlet and around bill; belly yellowish. ♀ duller.

13. Blue-backed Tanager   *Cyanicterus cyanicterus*   p. 758
SE. Large bill; red eyes. ♂ rich cadet blue and yellow. ♀ paler, tinged greenish blue; face and throat buff. Uncommon and local. Canopy of tall humid forest in lowlands.

Tanagers   *Thraupis*
Most spp. common and widespread; moderately large; strong bill; thrive in settled areas.

14. Palm   *T. palmarum melanoptera*   p. 757
Rather drab; often shows yellowish forecrown; outer half of wing black forming black "triangle." ♀ slightly paler.

15. Blue-gray   *T. episcopus*   p. 756
15a. *T. e. cana:* pale gray head contrasts with darker back; flight feathers edged blue (cf. 16). **15b.** Imm. flying. **15c.** *T. e. mediana:* S Amazonas. Sim. but white lesser wing coverts and 1 white wing bar.

16. Glaucous   *T. glaucocolpa*   p. 757
N (dry areas). Obviously *gray head concolor with back;* primary coverts black forming small patch at base of flight feathers; *wings edged aquamarine* (cf. 15); *belly white.*

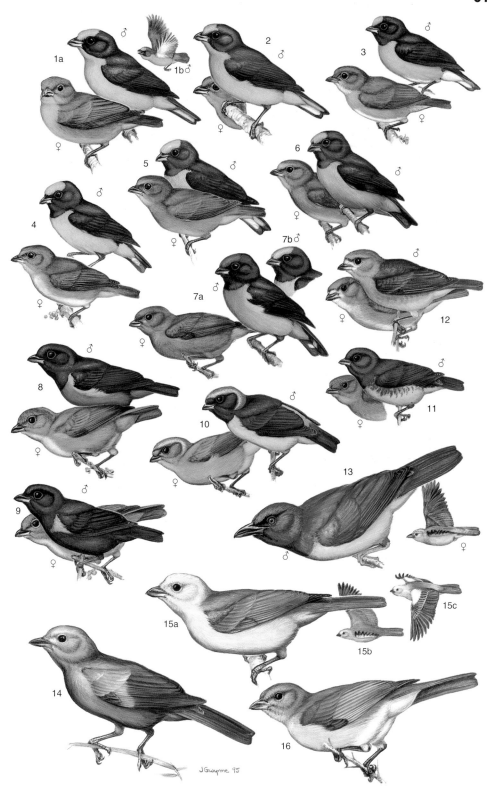

1. **Rosy Thrush-Tanager**   *Rhodinocichla r. rosea*   p. 748
N (local). ♂ begonia rose eyestripe and under-parts like no other. ♀ sim. but caramel below; eyestripe white behind eyes.
2. **Red-crowned Ant-Tanager**   *Habia rubica crissalis*   p. 753
Mainly N. Robust and heavy-billed. ♂ rosy red throat and chest; bright red coronal stripe. ♀ rather drab; tawny crown stripe, ochraceous buff throat and chest. Shy and retiring.

Tanagers   *Ramphocelus*
♂♂ velvety black and red; *expanded chalky white lower mandible.* ♀♀ usually duller; bill usually more or less normal.
3. **Silver-beaked**   *R. carbo venezuelensis*   p. 755
♂ blackish crimson (looks mainly black), redder on throat; white on bill. ♀ dark reddish brown above, brick red below; heavy blackish bill.
4. **Crimson-backed**   *R. d. dimidiatus*   p. 756
W of Andes. ♂ rather like ♂ of 3 (no range over-lap) but rump and lower underparts bright crim-son. ♀ mainly sooty brown to reddish brown; rump, lower breast, and belly dark red.

Tanagers   *Tachyphonus*
Slender and long-tailed; ♂♂ mostly black, usually with white on or under wings; ♀♀ brownish to olive.
5. **White-lined**   *T. rufus*   p. 750
♂ all black; in flight flashes a bit of white under wings; bill gray blue. ♀ all rufous; slightly paler below.
6. **Red-shouldered**   *T. phoenicius*   p. 752
S. ♂ shiny black; in flight flashes white and tiny bit of red under bend of wing. ♀'s dark head im-parts hooded look; whitish throat. Scrub on white sandy soil.
7. **Fulvous-crested**   *T. s. surinamus*   p. 751
S. ♂ coronal patch and rump yellow buff; may show white and chestnut on flanks. ♀ olive above with *contrasting gray head;* buff below; *note pale spectacles.* Often low around forest borders.

8. **Flame-crested**   *T. cristatus intercedens* p. 751
S. ♂ rather like 7 but small buff patch on throat; look for red or orange crest. ♀ rufescent above, face tinged gray; underparts yellowish brown (or ochraceous buff—Amazonas and W Bolívar). Forest canopy.
9. **White-shouldered**   *T. l. luctuosus*   p. 752
Rather small. ♂ black with bold white shoulder patch. ♀ gray head and yellowish body (cf. larger 12). Subcanopy vines.
10. **Fulvous Shrike-Tanager**   *Lanio. f. fulvus*   p. 750
S. ♂ oriole-like plumage. Dark *"burnt orange"* with black head, wings, and tail. Tawny patch on chest. ♀ resembles ♀ of 8 but larger; bill heavier, crissum darker rufous.
11. **Olive-backed Tanager**   *Mitrospingus oleagineus obscuripectus*   p. 749
Tepuis. Large and undistinguished. Yellowish olive with gray face; gray eyes. Forest understory.
12. **Gray-headed Tanager**   *Eucometis penicillata cristata*   p. 749
Mainly N. Gray head, slight crest (sometimes raised as shown); quite yellow below. Cf. smaller ♀ of 9. Understory and thickets.
13. **Magpie Tanager**   *Cissopis l. leveriana*   p. 741
Andes; S. Large pied tanager; shaggy hood; yel-low eyes, long, graduated tail with white tips. Shrubby forest clearings.
14. **Black-faced Tanager**   *Schistochlamys melanopis aterrima*   p. 741
Savanna with scattered bushes: **14a.** Ad.: gray with black foreface, throat, and chest. **14b.** Imm.: olive green above, yellowish below; note *narrow broken eyering* and habitat.

Saltators *Saltator*
Large; arboreal; thick bill; most have white eyestripe
and black malar bordering pale throat. Fine singers;
some regularly sing duets. Sexes sim.
  1. Buff-throated   *S. m. maximus*   p. 787
  Look for eyestripe, black malar, and *olive upperparts;* unstreaked below (cf. 4). Buff throat often
  hard to see.
  2. Grayish   *S. coerulescens brewsteri*   p. 787
  Rather like 1 but all gray above. Median throat
  whitish (not buff).
  3. Orinocan   *S. o. orenocensis*   p. 788
  N. Handsomest of genus. *Bold white eyestripes
  on black head; rich cinnamon buff lower underparts.* Subsp. in NW desert more extensively buff
  below.
  4. Streaked   *S. striatipectus perstriatus*   p. 788
  N. *Above olive* like 1 but *underparts streaked.*
  Mainly dry zones.
  5. Slate-colored Grosbeak   *Saltator g.
  grossus*   p. 789
  S. Thick, pinkish red bill; slaty plumage. ♀ lacks
  black around white throat; even duller imm. may
  lack white.

Grosbeaks *Pheucticus*
Large, robust finches; massive bills; plumage (at least
♂♂) bold and colorful. Sexes sim. or different.
  6. Black-backed   *P. aureoventris meridensis* p. 790
  Andes (Mérida). ♂ *black hood and upperparts;
  bold white wing bars.* ♀ echoes pattern of ♂ but
  heavily mottled and spotted brownish.
  7. Southern Yellow-   *P. chrysogaster
  laubmanni*   p. 789
  N mts. (local). ♂ mainly yellow; black wings,
  white wing bars. ♀ head mainly yellow (cf. 6);
  back streaked.

Grosbeaks *Caryothraustes, Periporphyrus,* and
Pheucticus
  8. Yellow-green   *Caryothraustes c.
  canadensis*   p. 792
  S. Mainly olive yellow with small black face;
  thick gray bill. Flocks in forest canopy.
  9. Red-and-black   *Periporphyrus
  erythromelas*   p. 789
  SE. ♂ unique. ♀ like ♂ but yellow replaces red.
  Rare and local.
  10. Rose-breasted   *Pheucticus ludovicianus* p. 790
  N migr. Winter-plumage ♂ and imm. often heavily mottled, but black and white markings and
  rose bib usually evident. ♀ streaky and brown;
  thick bill, whitish eyebrows; fine streaking on
  buff-tinged breast.

Sparrows *Arremonops*
Resemble *Arremon* but duller; bill dark; songs differ
markedly.
  11. Black-striped   *A. conirostris umbrinus*   p. 813
  Mainly N. Black stripes on *gray head.* Cf. 12
  which it overlaps minimally in E Falcón.

12. Tocuyo   *A. tocuyensis*   p. 813
  NW deserts. Whitish eyebrows separate black
  crown stripes; smaller than very sim. 11.

Sparrows *Arremon*
Elegantly patterned, colorful, semiterrestrial finches
of lowlands and foothills; larger than most "sparrows,"
smaller than allied *Atlapetes* of highlands.
  13. Pectoral   *A. taciturnus*   p. 813
  13a. *A. t. axillaris:* E base of Andes. Bold head, *bicolored bill;* yellow on shoulders; *black pectoral
  patches.* **13b.** *A. t. taciturnus:* S. Bill black; *belt on
  chest almost complete.* ♀♀ of both subspp.
  tinged buff below; patch on chest grayish and
  faint.
  14. Golden-winged   *A. s. schlegeli*   p. 812
  N. Very attractive. Black head, yellowish bill, yellow shoulders; Local; often difficult to find; dry
  to moist woodland borders.

Brush-Finches *Buarremon*
Much like *Atlapetes* but more secretive; mostly terrestrial; songs extremely high and thin.
  15. Stripe-headed   *B. torquatus*   p. 812
  15a. *B. t. phygas:* Coastal Cordillera eastward.
  White crown stripes. **15b.** *B. t. larensis:* Perijá
  Mts.; Andes. Gray crown stripes.
  16. Chestnut-capped   *B. brunneinuchus
  frontalis*   p. 811
  N mts. Quietly handsome. *Chestnut cap* bordered
  cinnamon; *puffy white throat.* No chest band in
  Sierra de San Luis. Forest undergrowth and on gd.

Brush-Finches *Atlapetes*
Midsized montane finches; short, conical bill; head
patterns and color of underparts distinctive though
racial variation rampant in some spp. pools.
  17. Slaty   *A. schistaceus castaneifrons*   p. 810
  Perijá Mts.; Andes. Slaty with chestnut cap, white
  moustache.
  18. Moustached   *A. albofrenatus meridae*   p. 809
  Andes. Bright olive green above; chestnut cap,
  white malar, yellow below (cf. 19).
  19. Pale-naped   *A. p. pallidinucha*   p. 809
  S Táchira. Cinnamon median stripe turns white
  on hindcrown; yellow underparts.
  20. Rufous-naped   *A. latinuchus phelpsi*   p. 811
  Perijá Mts. Most like 19 (no overlap); crown and
  nape all chestnut.
  21. Ochre-breasted   *A. semirufus denisei*   p. 809
  N mts. Head and underparts orange rufous. Note
  racial variation (text).
  22. Tepui   *A. personatus*   p. 810
  22a. *A. p. personatus:* tepuis. Much racial variation in amt. of chestnut on head and underparts.
  Subsp. shown typical of SE Bolívar. **22b.** *A. p.
  duidae:* found on some cerros in Amazonas.

JAGwynne 99

Seedeaters   *Catamenia*
Small, plain finches of high els.; chestnut crissum; back often streaked.
  1. Plain-colored   *C. inornata minor*   p. 804
  Andes. Stubby *pink bill*. ♂ gray with streaky back; chestnut crissum. Ad. ♀ pale and buff; upperparts streaked; underparts variable, ranging from unstreaked to finely streaked; crissum buff. Imm. sim. but usually more extensively streaked above and below, esp. ♀. Paramo.
  2. Páramo   *C. homochroa duncani*   p. 804
  Mts. ♂ slaty; yellowish bill; chestnut crissum. ♀ dark and streaked above and below. Imm. much like ♀ but more coarsely streaked. Older imms. gradually look more like respective ad. plumage. High-el. forest. Local.
  3. Plumbeous Sierra-Finch   *Phrygilus unicolor nivarius*   p. 805
  Andes. Larger than allies (1, 2, 4). Bill small and stubby. ♂ uniform gray. ♀ heavily and coarsely streaked throughout.
  4. Slaty Finch   *Haplospiza r. rustica*   p. 808
  Mts. *Slender, pointed bill*. ♂ uniform gray. ♀ brown; obscure streaking below. Follows seed crops of bamboo in mts. Local and erratic.

Seed-Finches   *Oryzoborus*
Massive bill broad at base; culmen straight (cf. *Sporophila*). ♂♂ mostly black; ♀♀ dark brown. Not esp. social (cf. *Sporophila*). Taxonomic confusion abounds.
  5. Lesser   *O. a. angolensis*   p. 797
  ♂ black with chestnut belly; small white wing spot. ♀ dark brown; note large bill (cf. *Sporophila*).
  6. Large-billed   *O. c. crassirostris*   p. 798
  Widespread but local. ♂ massive bill smooth, white; ♀ bill black; no white in wing. Cf. 7.
  7. Great-billed   *O. maximiliani magnirostris*   p. 798
  Delta Amacuro region. Very like 6 but larger; bill of ♂ has rough texture. ♀ sim. to 6 but bill larger.

Grosbeaks   *Cyanocompsa*
  8. Blue-black   *C. c. cyanoides*   p. 791
  Massive bill. ♂ frontlet and short eyebrow azure; ♀ very dark brown. Distinctive song and calls. Humid regions.
  9. Ultramarine   *C. brissonii minor*   p. 791
  N. ♂ much like 8; a bit more azure on head and shoulders; rump always contrasting brighter blue. ♀ sandy to cinnamon below, much paler than 8. Mainly dry areas; little or no overlap with 8.
  10. Indigo Bunting   *Passerina cyanea*   p. 793
  Accidental N migr. ♂ bright methyl blue. ♀ warm brown; buff wing bars; paler, slightly streaked below. Molting imm. ♂ shown.
  11. Blue-black Grassquit   *Volatinia jacarina splendens*   p. 794
  Ubiquitous. **11a**. Ad. ♂ (far right in jump display) glossy blue black; tiny white mark on shoulder. ♀ dull and brownish above; buffy white streaked dusky below. **11b**. Subad. ♂ brown with varying amts. of black; older birds progressively blacker.

Grassquits   *Tiaris*
Bill more slender than *Sporophila*. Buzzy songs; dry brushy habitats; shrubs and clearings in humid zones.
  12. Yellow-faced   *T. olivacea pusilla*   p. 796
  S Táchira. ♂ black foreparts; yellow brow and throat. ♀ pattern of ♂ faintly indicated. Shrubby or grassy wooded borders.
  13. Black-faced   *T. bicolor omissa*   p. 795
  Arid N. ♂ olive above; black foreparts. ♀ plain and dull; overall grayish tinge.
  14. Sooty   *T. fuliginosa*   p. 795
  N. ♂ all sooty; ♀ much like 13 but little range overlap. Local.
  15. Dull-colored   *T. obscura haplochroma*   p. 796
  N. Well named. Sexes sim. Note bicolored bill (more than half of birds); flocks of pure ♀-plumaged birds a tip-off.

Seedeaters   *Sporophila*
Thick stubby bills with curved culmen; social; flocks in grasslands, etc. ♀♀ usually much alike (and unlike ♂♂). See Table 1, page 803.
  16. Gray   *S. i. intermedia*   p. 799
  Common. ♂ uniform med. gray; bill pale yellowish to pinkish. ♀ bill blackish. Cf. 17.
  17. Slate-colored   *S. schistacea longipennis*   p. 799
  ♂ darker gray than 16; usually shows small white spot on neck and/or narrow white wing bar. Rare; erratic. ♀ see text and Table 1, page 803.
  18. Plumbeous   *S. plumbea whiteleyana*   p. 800
  S. ♂ gray; chin and subloral area white; bill black. ♀ bill somewhat bicolored.
  19. Yellow-bellied   *S. n. nigricollis*   p. 802
  ♂ blackish hood; creamy belly. ♀ belly buffy yellow.
  20. Ruddy-breasted   *S. m. minuta*   p. 803
  Small. ♂ rump and underparts cinnamon rufous. ♀ smaller and buffier than most.
  21. Chestnut-bellied   *S. castaneiventris*   p. 804
  Amazonas. ♂ maroon chestnut median underparts. ♀ much like 20 (text).
  22. Lined   *S. l. lineola*   p. 801
  ♂ *large white malar patch;* narrow white coronal line (often difficult to see). ♀ contrasting buff white central belly.
  23. Lesson's   *S. bouvronides*   p. 801
  ♂ white malar patch much smaller than 22; solid black crown. ♀ like 22.
  24. Wing-barred   *S. a. americana*   p. 800
  Delta Amacuro region northward. ♂ white nape and wing bars.
  25. Black-and-white   *S. luctuosa*   p. 802
  Andes. ♂ white belly; large white wing speculum; bill pale. ♀ olive brown; belly buffy yellow.
  26. White-naped Seedeater   *Dolospingus fringilloides*   p. 797
  S Amazonas. Larger, longer-tailed than *Sporophila*. ♂ pale conical bill; 1 broad wing bar; narrow white collar partially encircles neck. ♀ uniform warm cinnamon brown. Local.

1. Rufous-collared Sparrow *Zonotrichia capensis venezuelae* p. 815
"Sparrow backed." **1a.** Ad.: black streaks on gray, slightly crested head; narrow rufous nuchal collar. **1b.** Juv.: finely streaked, esp. below.

Siskins *Carduelis*
Small, gregarious, seed-eating finches; short conical bill; ♂♂ bold yellow (most spp.), white, or red wing band; ♀♀ and imms. dull, often quite sim. Note ranges.

2. Andean *C. s. spinescens* p. 831
N mts. ♂ sharp black cap; olive green above, yellower below. ♀ (text).

3. Yellow-faced *C. yarrellii* p. 831
N. Like 2 but *much yellower* (no overlap). No reliable recent recs.; perhaps an introd. sp.

4. Hooded *C. magellanica longirostris* p. 830
Mainly SE. ♂ black head extends to chest. No other in range.

5. Red *C. cucullata* p. 830
N. Unique. Relentlessly pursued for cage traffic; now rare, local, and declining.

6. Lesser Goldfinch *C. psaltria columbiana* p. 832
N. ♂ glossy black head to below eyes; black upperparts; white wing band. ♀ white wing band.

7. Yellow-bellied Siskin *C. x. xanthogastra* p. 832
N mts. ♂ only lower breast and belly yellow; yellow wing band. ♀ dull but ♂'s pattern faintly indicated.

8. Red-capped Cardinal *Paroaria gularis* p. 792
Ad. distinctive. **8a.** *P. g. gularis*: S subsp. N subsp. (across llanos) has *throat and chest red.* **8b.** Imm.: buffy brown head and throat.

9. Vermilion Cardinal *Cardinalis phoeniceus* p. 793
NW deserts. ♂ rose red with long, spiky upstanding crest. ♀ same crest; gray face, buff below.

10. Gray Pileated-Finch *Coryphospingus pileatus brevicaudus* p. 808
N. ♂ gray with white eyering; black crown conceals spectacular flame crest. ♀ duller; no crest; vaguely streaked below. Dry zones.

Sparrows *Ammodramus*
Rather large headed; flat crowned; short tailed; intricately streaked head and back patterns; many allies in N Amer.

11. Yellow-browed *A. aurifrons apurensis* p. 814
Yellow lores and brow; quite pale below (cf. 12).

12. Grassland *A. h. humeralis* p. 814
Grayish face and neck; narrow white eyering; touch of yellow over lores (cf. 11); inner flight feathers heavily edged chestnut. **Lincoln's** *Melospiza lincolnii* (text).

13. Dickcissel *Spiza americana* p. 793
N migr. ♂ yellow brow; small black V on yellow chest; rufous shoulders. ♀, nonbreeding ♂, and imm. all duller to much duller; little or no black bib. Abundant very locally.

Pipits *Anthus*
Streaky; thin bill; white outer tail feathers; long hind claw.

14. Páramo *A. bogotensis meridae* p. 716
Andes. Larger than 15 (no overlap); quite buffy; streaking on underparts reduced. Paramo.

15. Yellowish *A. l. lutescens* p. 715
Necklace across pale yellow to whitish underparts. Grasslands.

Grass-Finches *Emberizoides*
Long, graduated, spiky tail.

16. Wedge-tailed *E. herbicola sphenurus* p. 816
Bill black above, yellow below; long spiky tail. Grasslands; stays out of sight much of time.

17. Duida *E. duidae* p. 816
S (Cerro Duida). Larger, darker than 16. Unknown in life.

18. Saffron Finch *Sicalis f. flaveola* p. 806
N. **18a.** Ad.: ♂ *mostly bright yellow;* golden orange forecrown extends to mid. crown. ♀ duller. **18b.** Imm.: pale and streaked; broad yellow chest band. Common.

Yellow-Finches *Sicalis*
Mostly bright yellow below; often in flocks in open country.

19. Orange-fronted *S. c. columbiana* p. 806
Smaller than 18. ♂ obviously greenish; small dark orange forecrown (cf. 18). ♀ grayish brown; darkish ocular area; yellowish olive wing edging. Common locally and seasonally in S llanos.

20. Stripe-tailed *S. citrina browni* p. 807
Local. ♂ *unstreaked yellow forecrown; white in tail.* ♀ underparts tinged yellow and broadly streaked, unlike ♀ of 21.

21. Grassland *S. l. luteola* p. 807
♂ *finely streaked crown; yellow lores, eyering, and ocular area.* ♀ yellow on face reduced; fine streaks on crown; *unstreaked* yellowish underparts (cf. ♀ of 20). Grasslands.

J.A.Gwynne '00

Orioles   *Icterus*

Slender; long tailed; sharp, pointed bills; yellow- or orange-and-black plumage; sexes sim. in resident spp.; loud, sweet, whistled songs.

1. **Yellow-tailed**   *I. mesomelas carrikeri*   p. 824
   NW. *Black back* and wings; yellow shoulder band; *yellow undertail.* Faint narrow white edging on tertials.
2. **Yellow-backed**   *I. chrysater giraudii*   p. 823
   N mts. Yellow with black bib, wings, and tail. Note *black on forecrown; never shows white on wing* (cf. 4). Clearings, semiopen areas in premontane and montane zones.
3. **Orange-crowned**   *I. auricapillus*   p. 824
   N. Basic pattern sim. to 1 but *crown extensively orange;* tail all black. Wide range of broken or disturbed habitats; dry to humid regions.
4. **Yellow**   *I. n. nigrogularis*   p. 824
   N. **4a.** Ad.: basic pattern sim. to 2, but note *white edging on wings* (amt. of white varies, sometimes obscure); black of face and bib restricted; *no black on forecrown.* **4b.** Imm.: duller and greenish; black restricted or mottled.
5. **Moriche**   *I. chrysocephalus*   p. 822
   Mainly E and S. Slender, long-tailed, mostly black; note *yellow crown, shoulders, rump, thighs.* Breeds in moriche palms.
6. **Orchard**   *I. s. spurius*   p. 822
   N migr. Rare in Venez. **6a.** Ad.: ♂ chestnut and black. ♀ olive above; white wing bars; narrow white edgings on inner flight feathers; yellowish below. **6b.** Imm. ♂ (1st yr): like ♀ but *bib black.*
7. **Baltimore**   *I. galbula*   p. 822
   N migr. ♂ black hood and back; white wing bar; orange outer tail feathers. ♀ head and throat light brownish; underparts tinged orange (cf. 6).
8. **Venezuelan Troupial**   *I. icterus ridgwayi*   p. 823
   N. National bird; not likely confused. Shaggy black hood; bare blue ocular area; large white wing patch. Arid areas; llanos.

9. **Golden-tufted Mountain-Grackle**
   Macroagelaius imthurni   p. 819
   Tepuis. Long tailed, short billed; watch for yellow flank tufts. Social and quite vocal; forest canopy.

Grackles   *Lampropsar* and *Quiscalus*

10. **Velvet-fronted**   *Lampropsar tanagrinus guianensis*   p. 819
    SE Sucre to Orinoco delta. Small grackle. Short conical bill; dark eyes; tail flat, somewhat rounded. Swampy riverbanks, mangroves.
11. **Carib**   *Quiscalus l. lugubris*   p. 820
    N. ♂ smaller, shorter-tailed than 12 (little or no overlap) but full of strut and swagger. Longish bill; yellow eyes; keel-shaped tail. ♀ brownish. Cf. 13. Locally abundant. Villages and ranches.
12. **Great-tailed**   *Quiscalus mexicanus peruvianus*   p. 820
    Zulia coast. Long stout bill; yellowish eyes. ♂ glossy; long keel-shaped tail. ♀ dusky brown above; head, eyestripe, and underparts buffy brown. Juv. brownish eyes.

Cowbirds   *Molothrus*

Two brood parasites in Venez. Glossy, small-headed ♂♂ sport ruff (esp. obvious in 14). ♀♀ dull; no ruff.

13. **Shiny**   *M. bonariensis venezuelensis*   p. 821
    Smallish. ♂ glossy, a bit short tailed; eyes dark; bill fairly short, almost conical. ♀ dingy grayish brown; faint paler eyebrow. Parasitizes large no. of mostly passerine spp.
14. **Giant**   *M. o. oryzivora*   p. 821
    Large. ♂ glossy; orange red eyes; flat-shielded bill extends straight onto forehead. Note ruff. ♀ smaller, duller; eyes yellowish. Lays eggs in nests of caciques and oropendolas; often seen at their colonies.

Oropendolas *Psarocolius*
Large, active, noisy icterids; outer tail feathers yellow
(tail may look all yellow from below); bill large, often
colorful, sharp pointed (excellent nest weavers), and
conical with shield extending onto forehead; many
spp. have icy blue eyes; breed in colonies; long, hanging, well-spaced nests conspic. in large, isolated trees.
Display vocalizations of ♂♂ notable for amazing
complexity. ♂♂ much larger than ♀♀.
  1. Russet-backed   *P. angustifrons*
    oleagineus   p. 828
    N mts. Large and dingy; bill dusky horn, fore-
    head somewhat yellowish. Travels in noisy flocks.
  2. Olive   *P. y. yuracares*   p. 829
    S. Largest icterid in Venez. Black bill tipped red;
    bare pink facial skin. Obviously bicolored with
    olive yellow foreparts, reddish chestnut rearparts.
    Tall humid forest.
  3. Green   *P. viridis*   p. 829
    E and S. Grayish green bill *tipped bright orange;*
    blue eyes. Mostly yellowish olive; rearparts chest-
    nut. Tall humid forest.
  4. Crested   *P. d. decumanus*   p. 828
    Mostly black with *creamy bill.*

Caciques *Cacicus*
Mid-sized icterids; black with varying amts. of red or
yellow on rump, or yellow on wings. Pointed bill as in
Psarocolius; eyes icy blue (brownish in juvs.); breed
in compact colonies, often with nests clumped, even
fastened together in isolated trees or branches. ♂♂
much larger than ♀♀ (up to twice weight of ♀♀).
Lowlands and mts.
  5. Red-rumped   *C. h. haemorrhous*   p. 826
    S (local). Black with ivory bill; diagnostic red
    rump often hard to see.
  6. Subtropical   *C. uropygialis*   p. 826
    Andes (no overlap with 5). Larger, slightly duller,
    red less extensive than 5.
  7. Yellow-rumped   *C. c. cela*   p. 825
    Widespread, often common. Note yellow on
    wings, rump, undertail coverts, and most of tail.
    Lowlands and foothills.
  8. Northern Mountain-   *C. l.*
    leucoramphus   p. 827
    S Táchira. Yellow on wing coverts and rump (no
    yellow on tail). High mt. forests.

  9. Solitary   *C. solitarius*   p. 827
    SE base of Andes. All black; *dark eyes.* Prs. (not
    colonies) in undergrowth.
10. Yellow-billed Cacique   *Amblycercus*
  holosericeus australis   p. 827
    N mts. All black; pale bill. Eyes yellowish white.
    Solitary or prs. in montane forest undergrowth.
    Shy.
11. Bobolink   *Dolichonyx oryzivorus*   p. 817
    N migr. Nonbreeding ad.: yellow buff head and
    underparts; narrow black crown stripes; crisp
    black streaking on back; line of streaking on
    sides and flanks. ♂ in transitional plumage like
    breeding ad. but buff feather-tipping shows;
    breeding ♂ (only in northward passage) mainly
    black; yellow buff nape; white scapulars and
    rump. Uncommon.

Meadowlarks, etc. *Sturnella*
Long, sharp, pointed bill; grasslands. Two subgroups:
(1) sexually dimorphic, primarily S Amer. group; ♂♂
mostly black and red, ♀♀ streaky and brown; and (2)
"meadowlarks," a sexually monomorphic group;
streaky upperparts; black V-shaped bib on yellow
breast.
12. Red-breasted Blackbird   *S. militaris*   p. 818
    ♂ black with bright red breast; heavily buff-
    scaled in fresh plumage. ♀ head streaked; buff
    underparts may be somewhat streaked or
    stained rose.
13. Eastern Meadowlark   *S. magna*
  paralios   p. 818
    Long bill; streaky above, yellow below with black
    V. Look for white in outer tail as flushes up in
    spurting flight. Grasslands.
14. Oriole Blackbird   *Gymnomystax*
  mexicanus   p. 825
    Large; easily recognized. Golden yellow head
    and underparts. Often on gd. in open areas.
15. Yellow-hooded Blackbird   *Agelaius i.*
  icterocephalus   p. 817
    ♂ yellow hood. ♀ retains enough of ♂ pattern
    for recognition. Note yellowish eyebrow and
    foreparts. Marshes in open terrain; riverbanks.

Gwynne. 7.97

Key to Map Symbols

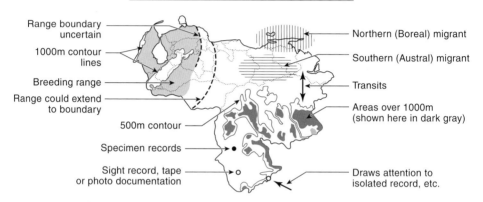

Range boundary uncertain

1000m contour lines

Breeding range

Range could extend to boundary

500m contour

Specimen records

Sight record, tape or photo documentation

Northern (Boreal) migrant

Southern (Austral) migrant

Transits

Areas over 1000m (shown here in dark gray)

Draws attention to isolated record, etc.

Species Accounts

TINAMIFORMES

Tinamidae: Tinamous

Gallinas de Monte, Gallinetas y Ponchas

Tinamous are plump, fowl-like birds confined to the New World. Related to flightless ratites, one of the oldest lineages of modern-day birds, tinamous are characterized by slender necks, small heads, short rounded wings, very short tails, and terrestrial habits. In Venezuela they are furtive birds of forested regions. Their plumages are cryptically patterned, and when alarmed tinamous prefer to walk away quietly or occasionally crouch, but they can fly rapidly for short distances. They eat a mixed diet of seeds, roots, insects, and some fruit. Tinamou breeding systems include monogamy, polygyny, and serial polyandry; in those species studied, however, polygyny prevails, with the sex roles reversed and the male incubating the eggs and caring for the young. The beautiful eggs are glossy and porcelainlike, varying from gray, greenish, turquoise, and pinkish vinaceous to dark brown. The chicks leave the nest within a few hours after hatching and follow the adult male, who looks after them for several weeks. The taxonomy of some species, especially of the genus *Crypturellus*, is still not well understood.

Tinamus

Med. to large size; plump but neck slender and head small; bill slightly decurved; legs and feet strong; rear toe rudimentary; rasplike posterior tarsal surface; mostly in lowlands; terrestrial but roost on low branch; nest on gd.; glossy eggs incubated by ♂ as far as known.

Gray Tinamou   PLATE I
Tinamus tao   Gallina Azul
Identification: 18″ (46cm). 2kg. Large and grayish. Eyes dark brown; legs dull bluish gray. *Crown and hindneck dark sooty brown*, crown finely spotted white; *white-dotted line from eyes down sides of neck*; otherwise above olive gray obscurely etched black, *the barring sometimes a little more evident on wings, lower back, and rump*; upper throat white, lower throat tinged buff, chest gray turning buffy or brownish gray on breast and pale rufous on under tail coverts; flanks olive gray vermiculated black. ♀: above more olive, *barring more prom.*, underparts grayer. Or sim. but both sexes grayer above (less olive), barring more distinct, below more extensively olive gray (*septentrionalis*).
Sim. species: Looks *gray* above and below (esp. *septentrionalis*). From Great or Highland tinamou by gray appearance, neck stripe, contrasting under tail coverts, and near absence of barring.

Voice: At Rancho Grande, at dawn and dusk, a penetrating, uninflected whistle, *whuuuu*, at well-spaced intervals (P. Schwartz recording).
Behavior: Sim. to others of genus (see Great Tinamou). Nest a leafy depression at base of tree or to 1m up in rotten stump or palm base; 2–9 shiny greenish blue eggs; Jun nest (1500m), Rancho Grande, Aragua.
Status and habitat: Uncommon and local resident in humid forest in hilly lowland and lower montane els. There are more recs. from PN Henri Pittier and PN Guatopo than elsewhere.

Range: 50–1900m. Sierra de Perijá (Alto de Cedro southward); w slope of Andes in Mérida (La Azulita) and nw Lara, e slope in Táchira, Apure, nw Barinas (hd.—P. Boesman), and Lara (Cabudare; Cerro El Cogollal[60]); hd. at Cerro Misión, se Falcón[60]; mts. of Yaracuy, Coastal Cordillera in Carabobo, Aragua, and Distr. Federal e to Pto. La Cruz (*larensis*); Interior Cordillera in s Miranda (sight, PN Guatopo—C. Parrish), Sucre (Cumaná and Paria Pen.), and n Monagas on Cerro Negro (*septentrionalis*). Guyana; mts. of Colombia s to Bolivia and locally in Amaz. Brazil and e Bolivia.

Great Tinamou   PLATE I
Tinamus major   Gallina de Monte
Identification: 18″ (46cm). 1.1kg. *Large and brownish*. Eyes large and dark brown; legs dark gray to dark bluish gray. Crown and short bushy crest on rearcrown dark rufous brown, *throat white, sides of head and foreneck cinnamon rufous flecked buff* (imparts a blond or pale look to head); head and neck *otherwise unmarked*; rest of upperparts brown varying from virtually unbarred to occas. rather heavily barred dusky; chest grayish brown, rest of underparts buff (light to dark), flanks and thighs with variable amt. of blackish barring; under tail coverts cinnamon rufous mottled dusky. Or sides of head and neck brighter rufous (*zuliensis*). Imm.: sim. but above unmarked, below with a few buff spots.
Sim. species: Larger than other lowland tinamous. Plumage variable but always brownish to buffy brown, usually with no markings on neck and little or no barring above. In foothills and mts. see Gray and Highland tinamous; in Amazonas cf. smaller White-throated Tinamou.

Voice: Song variable but always loud, very rich, and resonant (cf. Little Tinamou); typically 1–2 short tremulous whistles, then a longer one that rises slightly, then falls, the whole phrase repeated once or up to 6 times, e.g., *wuu, wuu wooouuuuuuuooo, wuuu wuuuuuuuoo, wuuu wooouuuuuuuooo*, etc., or a ser. of long tremulous whistles, each fractionally higher than the preceding. Song seems to grow louder and more tremulous and urgent as it continues. Most often hd. at dusk, the hauntingly beautiful song is one of the most memorable of lowland rainforest. Caution: Almost all song patterns are closely duplicated by Little Tinamou, but Little's songs are weaker, flatter, and lack full-bodied resonance.
Behavior: A shy, terrestrial, and solitary bird, usually encountered accidentally. Avoids detection by quietly walking away, but if surprised may rise with a roar, a whistling sound, and a rush of wings, accelerating away, sometimes noisily crashing into vegetation before landing a short distance away. Wary when hunted, but where unmolested may become habituated to humans. Roosts on branch or vine above gd. Nest a leafy depression on gd. between tree buttresses; up to 7 large, porcelainlike, turquoise eggs.
Status and habitat: Fairly common resident (by voice) in humid lowland and lower montane forest. Generally characteristic of mature, relatively undisturbed forest. Now rare and local where hunted for food.

Range: To ca. 200m n of Orinoco; to 1500m s of Orinoco. E base of Sierra de Perijá (Ríos Aricuaisa, Negro, and Catatumbo), Zulia, e to w base of Andes in Mérida; e base of Andes; n cordilleras from Tucacas, Falcón to Cerro Negro, se Miranda; ne Monagas (Caripito); generally in Amazonas; nw Bolívar e to lower and mid. Río Caura at Salta Pará (*zuliensis*); Delta Amacuro and rest of Bolívar (*major*). Se Mexico to n Bolivia, Amaz. Brazil, and the Guianas.

White-throated Tinamou   PLATE I
Tinamus guttatus   Gallineta Chica
Identification: 13.5″ (34cm). 600g. Eyes brown; legs dull greenish. Med.-sized tinamou with spotted rearparts. *Crown sooty black*, sides of head and neck cinnamon buff flecked black; *back, wings, and tail dark brown thickly dotted buff* to whitish and coarsely and inconspic. barred black; *throat white*, chest buffy brown turning buffy white on lower underparts; thighs and flanks barred dusky (often faint), under tail coverts dull rufous.

Sim. species: Looks like a small version of Great Tinamou with conspic. pale spotting on rearparts. Contrasting cap, throat, and spotting are the marks. See Undulated, Variegated, Gray-legged, and Barred tinamous.
Voice: Song at San Carlos de Río Negro a slow, mournful, 2-noted whistle, *whuuuUUU, uuuuuuaaaa* (ca. 3.5 sec), 1st note stronger at end and barely separated from 2d; song of 2d bird (♀?) sim. but higher pitched, a single, long whistle, weaker or with faint quaver in middle (suggests 2 notes) and last note rising slightly at end (C. Parrish recording).
Behavior: Sim. to others of genus. Four BC birds, late Mar–late Apr, Cerro Yapacana[185].
Status and habitat: Floor of mature, humid lowland forest. Judging from no. of specimens in Colección Phelps (8 near San Fernando de Atabapo), at least locally fairly common.

Range: To 200m. W half of Amazonas from Río Sipapo and Cerro Yapacana s to Río Negro and Cerro de la Neblina. Se Colombia to n Bolivia and Amaz. Brazil.

Nothocercus

Med. size; humid and wet forest in Andes.

Highland Tinamou   PLATE I
Nothocercus bonapartei   Gallina Cuero
Identification: 15–16″ (38–41cm). 810g. Bill dusky brown, base of lower mandible flesh; legs dark brown. *Rather large, dark, uniform-looking highland tinamou. Crown and nape sooty black*; otherwise above rich dark brown, back, wings, and tail dotted buffy white (or occas. almost no spots), flight feathers obscurely barred dusky, *throat contrasting buff*, neck dark chestnut brown becoming rufescent brown to tawny brown on breast, paler on belly; lower underparts with fine wavy black lines.
Sim. species: Slaty crown and buff throat are good marks. Tawny-breasted Tinamou has chestnut crown, barred upperparts, and *white* throat. Gray Tinamou is larger and grayer. Also cf. Brown Tinamou.
Voice: Song a loud, bisyllabic, and nasal *tuy-onk*, or *ca'wow*, ca. 1/sec, with honking or barking quality; repeated 3–5 times, then a pause, or given over and over for up to 1 min or longer.
Behavior: Like most forest tinamous, shy, solitary, and terrestrial and usually only encountered accidentally. Walks away quietly to avoid detection. Rarely flies unless startled. Feeds on fallen seeds and fruit

and some animal matter. Nest a slight leafy depression on gd., usually between buttress roots of large tree; up to 7 (usually 2–3) turquoise eggs; Jan–Jun breeding in Panama[788].
Status and habitat: Uncommon and infreq. seen resident on floor of humid and wet montane forest (cloud forest), esp. near ravines and other areas of dense second growth.

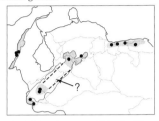

Range: 1300–2500m (once to 1000m in Distr. Federal?). Sierra de Perijá, Zulia; Andes of Táchira, s Mérida, n Trujillo, and Lara (n to Cubiro); Coastal Cordillera in n Carabobo, Aragua, and Distr. Federal (*bonapartei*). Costa Rica and w Panama; Colombia s in Andes to Peru.

Tawny-breasted Tinamou   PLATE 1
Nothocercus julius   Chócora de Tamá
Identification: 15–16″ (38–41cm). Bill blackish; legs dark gray. Forecrown chestnut, otherwise brown above *evenly and densely barred black throughout*; sides of head cinnamon rufous, *chin and throat white* (conspic.), neck dark gray faintly barred dusky and becoming *bright cinnamon rufous on breast and belly*; thighs and flanks olive brown barred black.
Sim. species: See duller Highland Tinamou which lacks barring above, is much duller below, and has buff (not white) throat. Also see larger Gray Tinamou.
Voice: In Ecuador a chantlike ser. of short, fluttery trills, *t'r'r'r'a, t'r'r'r'a, . . .*, fairly high in pitch, for up to 30 or more sec at ca. 3 per 2 sec[247]; song fades at end, often with lower-pitched trill near end[541].
Behavior: As in Highland Tinamou.
Status and habitat: A poorly known sp. found mostly outside Venez. Wet montane forest (cloud forest). Occurs mainly above range of Highland Tinamou.

Range: 2400–2800m. S Táchira at headwaters of Río Táchira (Páramo de Tamá; Villa Páez) and upper Río Chiquito at Cerro El Retiro. Colombia s in Andes to s Peru.

Crypturellus

Small; mostly in lowlands; taxonomically complex genus; sp. limits of many pops. still uncertain.

Cinereous Tinamou   PLATE 1
Crypturellus cinereus   Poncha
Identification: 12″ (30.5cm). 480g. Bill dark gray, base of lower mandible orangish gray; eyes dark brown; legs gray to yellowish gray. *Essentially unmarked.* Crown and nape rufous brown, otherwise above uniform brown, below smoky gray brown paler than above; wings sometimes faintly barred buffy brown; a few birds show obscure dark barring (hard to see in field) on flanks, thighs, belly, and crissum.
Sim. species: Best told by small size, uniform plumage, and voice. Cf. Little, Red-legged, and Gray-legged tinamous.
Voice: Song a single pure-tone whistle (easily imitated) at 4- to 5-sec intervals, often for extended periods of time. May countersing (same or different sexes) on different pitches. Occas. sing from a log or other slightly elevated perch. Cf. very sim. song of Sunbittern.
Behavior: Learn voice well. This sp., like other *Crypturellus*, is furtive and difficult to see. Walks on gd., usually alone, picking here and there in gallinelike manner for seeds and fruit. Crouches, walks, or scurries away if frightened, rarely flies. Nest in thick vegetation on forest floor; 2 (more?) salmon violet eggs[253].
Status and habitat: Uncommon and local resident in Venez. Floor of várzea forest, esp. near streams and other low-lying, seasonally inundated or damp areas in forest.

Range: To 200m. N Amazonas from Caño Cataniapo and lower Río Ventuari (Las Carmelitas) s to San Carlos de Río Negro; nw Bolívar (hd., Hato Las Nieves, Feb 1991—R. Ridgely and Hilty) and n Bolívar in lower Río Caura (Río Suapure). E Colombia to n Bolivia, Amaz. Brazil, and the Guianas.

Little Tinamou   PLATE 1
Crypturellus soui   Ponchita
Identification: 8.5–9.5″ (22–24cm). 220g. Bill blackish, lower mandible dark greenish gray; legs dull dark yellowish green. *Plumage variable but ♀♀ generally brighter and more tawny rufous below than ♂♂*. ♂: crown and hindneck dark gray, sides of head grayish brown, rest of upperparts dark rufescent brown, throat white to buffy white, foreneck grayish

brown, breast dull grayish clay to dull rufous, paler more buffy white on belly; flanks with or without a few obscure brown bars. ♀: darker, more rich rufous brown above and with strong tawny wash below. Or ♀ rich dark rufous on foreneck, breast, and sides (*soui*). Or more rufescent overall, esp. above, than any other subspp. (*mustelinus*). Or both sexes overall gray brown, paler below (*andrei*). Juv.: sim. but somewhat spotted dusky above; irreg. barred dusky below.

Sim. species: Smallest tinamou, but this is not always obvious given a glimpse in field. Points to note on ads. are *virtual lack of barring anywhere* (but cf. Cinereous and Undulated tinamous), warm rufescent to buff (not grayish) body tones, leg color (cf. Red-legged Tinamou), voice, and habitat. In Andean foothills and n cordillera may meet larger Brown Tinamou which has contrasting gray head and neck and barring on flanks. Also see Marbled Wood-Quail and quail-doves.

Voice: Several song types as well as sexual differences in songs complicate song recognition. At dawn and dusk both sexes give long song, a slightly quavering ser. of ca. 5–6 slow whistles, each a half-step higher in pitch (much like that of Great Tinamou but without its rich resonance and quaver). Commoner, esp. during day, are various shorter whistles, either singly or *often doubled*, e.g., each whistled note sliding a quarter tone lower and quavering a little at end, *weeeeuuuu*, or a single, long whistle sliding up a quarter tone in middle, trembling, and then down again, *wuuueeeeeeuuu*. ♂♂ and ♀♀ often countercall using these different calls (P. Schwartz). Or ♀ (?) gives single short whistle on same pitch, ♂ answers immediately with longer quavering whistle that descends slightly.

Behavior: Like others of genus, furtive and difficult to see. Calls freq., esp. at dusk, but rarely ventures into open. Feeds on gd. by walking quietly, hunched in gallinelike fashion, pecking at seeds, small fruits, and some animal matter, and constantly raises head to watch. Roosts (reportedly) and nests on gd.; 2 glossy vinaceous lavender eggs, blunt on both ends; in Costa Rica breeds almost yr-round[706].

Status and habitat: Uncommon to locally fairly common resident (by voice) in humid forest borders, overgrown pastures, bushy plantations, damp thickets, and young regrowth vegetation. Mostly replaced in drier regions by Red-legged Tinamou.

Range: To 1700m n of Orinoco; to 1600m s of Orinoco. Ne base of Sierra de Perijá to w base of Andes

in nw Táchira and w Mérida (*mustelinus*); rest of w and n Venez. from e base of Andes in Táchira, w Apure, w Barinas, Portuguesa, and s Cojedes to nw Lara (Cerro El Cogollal), c and e Falcón (Sierra de San Luis eastward), mts. of Yaracuy, Carabobo, Aragua, Distr. Federal, and Miranda (e to Cerro Negro); Sucre and Monagas s to Maturín. Monagas (*andrei*); Delta Amacuro[342] (subsp.?); generally in Amazonas and Bolívar (*soui*). S Mexico to n Bolivia and s Brazil.

Tepui Tinamou   PLATE 1
Crypturellus ptaritepui   Poncha de los Tepuis
Identification: 11–12″ (28–30.5cm). *Eyes creamy white* (or grayish, yellowish, or brownish, esp. in ♀♀; or young birds?); bill black, lower mandible yellowish tipped black; legs brownish olive. *Overall very uniform and dark with no barring or spotting.* Crown and hindneck dark chestnut brown, back dark rufescent brown, wings smoky gray brown; sides of head, throat, and foreneck gray, rest of underparts dark smoky gray brown tinged rufescent. Or darker more violet gray above; underparts smoky gray turning brown on belly (on Auyán-tepui).

Sim. species: Likely overlaps only with Little Tinamou which has dark eyes and is overall much paler, more rufescent. Also see Red-legged Tinamou.

Voice: Song a long (ca. 4 sec) high-pitched, pure tone whistle on same pitch, last half fading away; much like song of Wing-banded Wren (D. Ascanio recording).

Behavior: Terrestrial. Apparently much like others of genus. Two BC birds, Feb, Auyán-tepui[26].

Status and habitat: Resident in humid and wet montane forest. Known from 6 specimens on Ptari-tepui and Sororopán-tepui and 4 on Auyán-tepui[26]. Fairly common at high els. on Auyán-tepui (M. Lentino). Prob. more numerous than the few recs. suggest. May occur on Chimantá-tepui and others.

Range: ENDEMIC. 1350–1800m. Se Bolívar. Known only from Auyán-tepui, Ptari-tepui, Sororopán-tepui; also sight/tape, Sierra de Lema, 1450m (D. Ascanio).

Brown Tinamou   PLATE 1
Crypturellus obsoletus   Poncha Montañera
Identification: 10–12″ (25–30.5cm). 480g. Eyes yellowish to yellowish brown; bill black, lower mandible grayish; legs olive gray. *Crown and nape dark gray, rest of head and neck med. gray contrasting with uniform brown upperparts*; chest warm rufescent brown turning buffy brown on lower breast and

belly; *flanks and belly barred dusky*. Or sim. but paler below, lower underparts buff barred dusky (*cerviniventris*). ♀: sim. but usually more rufescent.
Sim. species: *In Andes and mts. e to Distr. Federal* a rather small, reddish brown tinamou with contrasting gray head and neck, and barring on flanks, will likely be this sp. Highland Tinamou is larger and essentially uniform (lacks obvious barring on flanks). Also see Little Tinamou and much larger Gray Tinamou.
Voice: Song, not often hd., a long ser. (up to 40 notes in 30 sec) of tremulous "police whistles," starting slowly then gradually accelerating, rising in pitch, and building almost to frantic hysteria at end, the last 2–3 notes flattening or dropping in pitch, e.g., *eEEeert . . . . . . eEEeert . . . eEEeert . . eEEert, eEEert, eEEert, eEEert-eEEert-eEEert-eEEert-eEEert-eert, eert*; once hd., not likely forgotten.
Behavior: As with most tinamous in Venez., hd. far more than seen. Usually alone. Walks on floor of humid mt. forests and is retiring and difficult to see. Nest in w Brazil a depression on gd.; 4 dark glossy brown eggs[188].
Status and habitat: Uncommon and low-density resident of moist and humid premontane and montane forest (usually not cloud forest), esp. in steep ravines. Has been found with some reg. above La Azulita, Mérida.

Range: 1200–2200m. W slope of Andes in Mérida (La Azulita), e slope in nw Barinas (hd. above Altamira at ca. 800m), and ne end in Lara at Cabudare (*knoxi*); nw Lara (Cerro El Cerrón), mts. of Falcón (Sierra de San Luis), and Coastal Cordillera in Aragua (Colonia Tovar) and Distr. Federal (*cerviniventris*). Colombia s in Andes to n Argentina, Paraguay, and Brazil s of the Amazon.

Undulated Tinamou
PLATE 1
Crypturellus undulatus Gallineta Ondulada
Identification: 11–12.5″ (28–32cm). 540g. Eyes brown; bill dusky; legs dingy greenish yellow. Crown dusky brown, rest of upperparts brown, wings grayish brown, all of upperparts finely vermiculated blackish (visible mainly in hand); *upper throat white*, lower throat gray densely freckled whitish, rest of foreneck gray; chest brown becoming pale brownish buff to dirty buffy white on breast and belly; under tail coverts buffy white to pale rufous; *flanks, thighs, and under tail coverts coarsely barred black*.
Sim. species: A med.-sized, gray brown tinamou, noticeably pale below, with barring on flanks. Occurs

near or within range of several other *Crypturellus*, but unlike all others, except Cinereous Tinamou, shows distinct preference for low-lying, swampy, or seasonally flooded areas. Whitish throat and flank barring are good marks.
Voice: Often calls incessantly, a rhythmic, melancholy, 4-parted whistle, *oóo, oo-oóóuu*, last phrase sliding upward (some geographic variation). Recalls first 3 notes of Barcarolle in Offenbach's opera *The Tales of Hoffman*[403].
Behavior: Shy and retiring but generally easier to see than others of genus and more likely to wander out into little open spaces along trails and riverbanks. Occas. flies across rivers and readily reaches river isls. Can be attracted by a whistled imitation of its song, and when breeding sings all day and periodically at night. Nest a depression on gd.; 3 glossy vinaceous pink eggs[433].
Status and habitat: Local in Venez. but doubtless more widespread than the few recs. suggest. Várzea forest and swampy, low-lying, or transition forest, esp. along wooded borders and vicinity of streams. In w Amazon Basin also found locally (in absence of competing *Crypturellus*) in terra firme areas such as second growth in wet pastures and thickets along forest borders.

Range: To 200m. Amazonas on lower and mid. Río Ventuari (sight/tape, 1998, at mouth of Ventuari at Alechiven—K. Zimmer; sight/tape at Junglaven; specimens from Caño Negro, San Juan de Manapiare) (*manapiare*). E Colombia to n Bolivia, w Argentina, Paraguay, Amaz. Brazil, and Guyana.

Variegated Tinamou
PLATE 1
Crypturellus variegatus Gallineta Cuero
Identification: 11–12″ (28–30.5cm). 350g. Eyes brown; bill blackish horn; legs grayish olive. *Boldly marked. Crown, nape, and sides of head black, neck and upper mantle deep rufous, rest of upperparts black boldly barred ochraceous buff*; throat white, chest rufous turning pale yellowish buff on breast and pale buff on belly; *sides, flanks, and crissum coarsely barred black and buff*. Juv.: above russet brown with broad black-bordered buff eyebrow and median crown stripe; below bright yellow buff.
Sim. species: Not likely confused if seen well. Note mostly black head, rufous neck, and bold barring on upperparts, sides, and flanks.
Voice: Song, mostly a dawn or vespertine performance, is slightly quavering ser. of whistles, *tuuuoo . . . . tuuuoo . . . tuu, tuu, tuu, tuu, tuu*, 1st 2 notes long

drawn and downward inflected, 2d after a 2- to 3-sec pause, last 5 or so after a 1-sec pause, then hurriedly upscale.

Behavior: Much as in others of genus. Terrestrial, shy, and hard to see as almost always attempts to sneak away quietly on foot. When surprised flushes almost straight up and flies off in a panic of furious whirring wings and drops back to gd. out of sight and some distance away. Eats small fallen fruits, many seeds, and a few arthropods. Roost on gd. or log; polyandrous breeder, Mar–Oct and Dec (prob. all yr) in n Guyana; nest a leafy depression on gd.; 1 egg was light glossy purplish vinaceous[32].

Status and habitat: Uncommon to fairly common resident (by voice) where not persecuted by hunting; floor of moist and humid terra firme forest.

Range: To 1300m. Throughout Amazonas; n Bolívar from Pijiguaos, lower Río Caura, and Río Grande southward. E Colombia to e Peru, n Amaz. Brazil, and the Guianas.

Red-legged Tinamou   PLATE 1
Crypturellus erythropus Soisola Pata Roja

Identification: 11–12″ (28–30.5cm). Eyes brown to grayish yellow; bill black, lower mandible flesh tipped dusky; *legs dull rose red to salmon*. Crown dusky to gray brown to gray (see below); sides of head usually cinnamon rufous, rest of upperparts brown tinged rufescent and densely but obscurely vermiculated and barred buff and dusky (often barred mainly on wings with only a few inconspic. bars on lower back and rump); throat whitish to occas. buff; *chest gray contrasting with buffy clay breast*; lower underparts pale buff, *flanks barred black (spencei)*. Or crown grayish brown (*idoneus*); or dusky (*erythropus*); or grayish (*cursitans*); or slightly *smaller*, darker, more richly colored, and chest gray contrasting sharply with deep buff lower underparts (*margaritae*). Note: subspp. all rather sim., with variation within each subsp. virtually as great as between them.

Sim. species: This small tinamou is best told by its rosy legs, but also note contrasting gray chest, barred flanks, and if close, obscure barring on wings and back. Known to overlap with only 2 other *Crypturellus* (Little and Variegated tinamous), neither of which has rosy red legs.

Voice: ♂♂ sing a flat, whistled *whuu, whúu-whu?* or *whuu, whu-wheúu?* on same pitch, with slight downward inflection in mid. of each note. Individual ♂♂

apparently sing 1 of the 2 song types (note difference in length of whistled mid. or last note) but rarely both. ♀♀ seldom sing[585]. A shorter, slightly higher pitched *whuu-whuu?*, trailing off on last note, is also occas. hd. (♂ or ♀?). Most vocal Apr–Aug in ne Venez.[186].

Behavior: Sim. to that of Little Tinamou but inhabits drier and somewhat more open habitats so easier to see. Eggshells found 28 May, Guárico[734]; eggs pale grayish lavender tinged brown, more pinkish in some races[585].

Status and habitat: Uncommon to locally fairly common resident, by voice, in dry and moist forest, thickets along forest borders, and gallery forest. Some seasonal movement in and out of flooded gallery forest regions.

Range: To 1300m n of Orinoco; to 700m s of Orinoco. Throughout s to Orinoco and in n Bolívar. Sierra de Perijá, Zulia (*idoneus*); se Táchira (*cursitans*); w Mérida, Lara, Falcón, and generally in n cordilleras and e of Andes to Anzoátegui (*spencei*); Sucre (Paria Pen.) and n Monagas; n Bolívar s to lower Río Caura, lower Río Paragua, and Río Cuyuní (*erythropus*); Isla Margarita (*margaritae*). N Colombia to the Guianas and n Brazil n of the Amazon.

Note: Taxonomy follows Schwartz and Lentino[585]. Some subspp. have been placed with other spp., or considered separate spp. Does not incl. *atrocapillus* of e Peru and n Bolivia.

Gray-legged Tinamou
Crypturellus duidae Soisola Pata Gris

Identification: 11–12″ (28–30.5cm). Eyes brown to orangish (?); bill blackish above, dull dingy yellowish tipped dusky below; legs gray. Recalls better-known Variegated Tinamou. *Entire head, neck, and mantle rufous*, back blackish *finely barred buff* (or occas. with little or no buff barring above); throat white turning *rufous on chest and rich ochraceous buff on breast*, paler on belly; sides, flanks, and crissum barred black. Or occas. with dusky crown (both sexes?).

Sim. species: A med.-sized tinamou with rufous foreparts, very fine barring on back, and bright yellowish buff underparts. Variegated Tinamou has black head, much coarser, bolder barring above and below, and darker rufous chest. Cinereous, Little, and Undulated tinamous are duller, lack contrasting underparts, and show little or no barring. In s Amazonas see Barred Tinamou.

Voice: Song a slow, monotone whistle with brief pause or break near beginning, *whu-uuuuuuuuuh* or *aah-aaaaaaaaah*[585].
Status and habitat: Poorly known in life. The few Venez. specimens are mostly from humid lowland forest and forest borders in c and s Amazonas. Found in more humid forest than Red-legged Tinamou.

Range: To 200m. Nw Bolívar (Pijiguaos) and w Amazonas (Caño Cuao; Samariapo; San Fernando de Atabapo; Cerro Yapacana; Cerro Duida; San Carlos de Río Negro). E Colombia.
Note: Has been regarded as a subsp. of Yellow-legged Tinamou (*C. noctivagus*) of Brazil.

Barred Tinamou   PLATE 1
Crypturellus casiquiare   Soisola Barreteada
Identification: 10″ (25cm). Bill blackish above, pale below; eyes brown; legs yellowish olive. *Head rich rufous*, hindneck dark gray, *back boldly and coarsely barred black and buffy rufous*, throat whitish, *foreneck, chest, and sides iron gray*, sharply contrasting with white center of breast and belly; under tail coverts buffy rufous, sometimes with obscure dusky barring on flanks and under tail coverts.
Sim. species: A small tinamou with rufous head, boldly barred back, and strongly "divided" underparts. Gray-legged Tinamou lacks conspic. barring above; Variegated Tinamou has black head. White-throated Tinamou is larger with spotted rearparts.
Voice: Long song of ca. 32 notes over 40 secs, a ser. of med.-pitched, pure whistles (no tremolo), 1st note a little longer, rest *very slightly* rising and accelerating, then gradually slowing and dropping fractionally in pitch, notes at end labored and coming slowly (P. Schwartz recording).

Status and habitat: Another poorly known tinamou of lowland sandy soil forests of upper Río Orinoco,

Río Casiquiare, and upper Río Negro drainage basins. Hd. several times 10–19 Aug 1985, San Carlos de Río Negro, Amazonas (C. Parrish).
Range: To 300m. Sw Amazonas (Yavita-Pimichín trail s to San Carlos de Río Negro). E Colombia.

PODICIPEDIFORMES

Podicipedidae: Grebes
Zambullidores

Grebes are a small family of worldwide distribution and uncertain taxonomic affinity. Venezuelan species occur in freshwater from the lowlands to high mountain lakes. They have lobed toes and swim and dive expertly using only their feet for propulsion. Their legs are positioned so far to the rear of the body that they can hardly walk on land; they do so only to climb up on their nests, which are soggy floating rafts of reeds located at water level and anchored to emergent plants. The young swim immediately upon hatching but are carried under the parents' wings most of the time. Grebes eat fish, aquatic insects, and crustaceans by pursuit in the water or gleaning from plants. All Venezuelan species are resident and relatively sedentary, although they move locally, become flightless during molt, and may gather in groups during this period of time.

Least Grebe   Illus. p. 186
Tachybaptus dominicus   Patico Zambullidor
Identification: 8.5″ (22cm). 145g. *Small, roundish, and dull*; blackish *bill slender and pointed*; eyes *golden yellow*. Above dark brownish gray, crown dusky, sides of head and neck grayish, median throat black, chest brownish, rest of underparts white heavily mottled grayish brown, under wing coverts and *speculum on inner flight feathers white* (conspic. from above in flight). Nonbreeding: sim. but throat whitish, head paler and dingier. Imm.: paler and grayer than ads.; crown dusky, sides of head whitish; below grayish white with dusky brown chest band; eyes dark.
Sim. species: Easily confused with larger Pied-billed Grebe which differs in having dark eyes, thick, chalky, "ringed" bill, and paler head.
Voice: Call (advertising?) a loud, churring whinny, much like that given by many *Laterallus* rails. Groups may simultaneously give long, quavering, gabblelike call. Occas. a little hornlike *beek*.
Behavior: Most often seen alone or in prs. swimming in small ponds but occas. in groups of 20 or more when breeding. Sometimes with Pied-billed Grebe but also on bodies of water too small for that sp. Prefers to dive or hide in aquatic vegetation and rarely seen in flight. Jun nest, ne Venez.[186]; floating platform of weeds anchored to live or dead plants; 3–6 dirty white eggs.

Pied-billed Grebe (left), Least
Grebe (right)

Status and habitat: Common locally. Resident on
freshwater lakes, ponds, and marshes in forested or
open areas. Usually found where there is abundant
aquatic vegetation and sometimes on remarkably
small bodies of water. Movements (seasonal?) need
documentation. Many recs. up to ca. 2250m on both
slopes of Mérida Andes; prob. occas. to treeline or
higher.

Range: To 1950m (sight to ca. 2250m). Widespread n
of Orinoco (but absent from most of c Venez. From
Apure e to Anzoátegui); e Bolívar s to Gran Sabana;
Isla Margarita (*speciosus*). S Texas to n Argentina.
W Indies; Trinidad and Tobago.

Pied-billed Grebe   Illus. above
Podilymbus podiceps   Buzo
Identification: 13″ (33cm). 440g. Eyes dark; *thick,
blunt, chickenlike bill chalky white with dark "ring."*
Breeding plumage: throat and foreface black; sides
of head and foreneck grayish, rest of body grayish
brown; breast and sides somewhat paler and mottled
with brownish white; belly and *under tail coverts
whitish.* Nonbreeding plumage: browner and dingier,
no black on foreface or throat; ring on bill faint. Juv.:
sides of head with several whitish stripes, throat whitish, underparts yellowish buff.

Sim. species: See smaller Least Grebe.
Voice: Usually quiet. Occas. a loud frog- or cuckoo-
like ser. of notes that may start as a whinny, then
gradually slow.
Behavior: Usually seen swimming, alone or in prs.,
rarely several together. Floats lightly on water, but if
disturbed can slowly sink until only head and neck
remain visible. When frightened dives in an instant
(folds in middle), swims underwater, and reappears
some distance away. Despite grace and speed in
water, walks awkwardly and with difficulty on land,
and rarely leaves water except to nest. Feeds on fish,
large arthropods, and crustaceans. Tiny young often
ride on back of an ad. Nest a floating platform of
vegetation; 3 white eggs.
Status and habitat: Uncommon and local resident;
also migrant from N Amer. (many more recs. mid
Aug–Mar), mainly on freshwater ponds and lagoons.

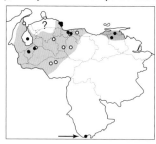

Range: To 500m (once to 3600m at Laguna Mucubají, Mérida[60]). Spottily throughout n of Orinoco (no
recs. from c Guárico e to n Monagas); once in s Amazonas (*antarcticus*). Canada to s Argentina. W Indies. Trinidad and Tobago.

PROCELLARIIFORMES

Procellariidae: Shearwaters and Petrels

Petreles

Petrels and shearwaters are mostly small to medium-sized, tube-nosed birds of the open seas. Found worldwide, they are characterized by long, narrow, and pointed wings and usually short legs and tails. There is little age or sexual difference in plumages, but some species have color morphs. Smaller species flutter erratically at the surface of the ocean or flap and glide, holding their wings slightly bent at the wrist, and often bank and swing erratically, sometimes arcing high above the water. They eat mostly squid taken from the surface of the water. Larger petrels and shearwaters skim rapidly just above the water, alternating a few fast, stiff flaps with long, directional glides. They take food from the ocean surface or in shallow dives. Petrels and shearwaters spend 5–6 months each year nesting in burrows or holes on sea cliffs on small oceanic islands. Around the nesting colony they are mainly nocturnal. Incubation periods are very long, up to 60 days or more. Both sexes incubate for up to 2 weeks before they are relieved by their mate. When not breeding they migrate away or wander widely. So far only shearwaters have been recorded in Venezuelan waters. Identification of members of either group is difficult and requires careful attention to flight patterns, shapes, plumage, and soft part colors.

[Cory's Shearwater]

Calonectris diomedea   Petrel de Cory

Identification: 18–21″ (46–53cm). Large shearwater. Resembles Greater Shearwater but lacks its distinct "capped" appearance; ashy brown upperparts *merge gradually* (blurry separation) into white underparts; white band on upper tail coverts variable, usually not obvious or lacking; in flight black and white underwing pattern decidedly sharper, with *larger black wing tips*; up close *bill yellowish* tipped black. More identification details on these 2 spp. are available[49].

Behavior: Follows ships. Glides and arcs fairly close to waves. Holds wings angled down at wrist.

Status and habitat: Known only from sight recs. of 2 seen n of Paria Pen. (no photo documentation) 27 Feb 1997 at ca. 10°59′ N, 62°29′ W, by W. Murphy

and others[424]. A 3d bird was seen on same date w of Tobago. Further documentation desirable. Inhabits deep offshore waters.

Range: Breeds on isls. in e N Atlantic incl. Azores, Madeira, Canary, Berlenga, and many Mediterranean isls.; postbreeding dispersal is into mid.-latitude waters of Atlantic, occas. to coastal N Amer., isls. in Carib., Trinidad, Guyana, and off nw Africa. Scattered recs. elsewhere.

Note: Sometimes placed in genus *Puffinus*.

Greater Shearwater

Puffinus gravis   Petrel Cauicho

Identification: 19″ (48cm). 850g. Black bill. Large with long slender wings, distinct dark brown cap, *crisp white band across upper tail coverts*, and short, blackish, wedge-shaped tail. Plumage mainly scaly grayish brown above and white below with distinctive mottled *grayish brown patch on belly; prom. white collar across hindneck sets off sooty crown, which extends to bottom of eyes.* In flight from below, wings mostly white narrowly outlined blackish; irreg. dark "strut" bar extends from wrist to rear wing base. From above, outer half of wing is darker.

Sim. species: As yet most other sim.-looking shearwaters are unrec. in Venez. waters (but see Note). Cf. smaller Dusky-backed Shearwater.

Behavior: A large, powerful shearwater that flies with quick, stiff wing beats and relatively straight (not bowed) wings. Follows trawlers, where often noisy, sounding like fighting cat[248].

Status and habitat: Rare migrant. 1 ♀ taken 19 Jun 1971 ca. 8km off Islas Los Roques; 1 (sex?) 20 Aug 1971 off Isla La Blanquilla. N transequatorial migration off e S Amer. begins in Apr, passing Bermuda May–Jul[248], with birds continuing past Greenland to ne Atlantic. Most return to breeding gds. by Oct–Nov[248].

Range: Venez. isls. of Los Roques and La Blanquilla. Breeds on isls. in s Atlantic (Nightingale; Inaccessible; Tristan da Cunha; Gough), possibly Falklands. Winters (austral winter) to n Atlantic.

Note: Sooty Shearwater (*P. griseus*) is likely in Venez. waters; 17″ (43cm), almost all dark brown with narrow lengthwise band of white (variable in extent) flashing on underwing. Austral-latitude breeding birds migrate northward off both coasts of SA. Does not follow ships.

Audubon's Shearwater   PLATE 2
Puffinus lherminieri   Petrel Garrapatero
Identification: 12″ (30.5cm). 170g. *Small, clean-cut,
black and white shearwater.* Slender black bill; pink
feet. Head to just below eyes, and entire upperparts,
dark brown ("capped" appearance) sharply set off
from pure white underparts; *under tail coverts* and
tail dusky brown. In flight underwings white broadly
outlined dusky. No seasonal or sexual differences.
Sim. species: Smaller and more sharply patterned
than any other shearwater likely in Venez. waters;
looks a little "short winged" in flight and has thicker
body and broader wings than most.
Behavior: Gregarious at sea, with singles or small
groups scattered but loosely assoc. in favorable,
deep-water feeding areas, and often seen sitting on
water. Patters across surface to get airborne. Does
not usually follow ships and seldom seen from shore.
Flight a ser. of quick flutters followed by sail low
over waves.
Status and habitat: Breeds on Venez. isls., and prob.
resident, but seasonal nos. poorly documented; offshore and pelagic waters. Some W Indies (Venez.?)
birds disperse n in Gulf Stream off e N Amer. in late
summer, reaching peak nos. in Sep[248]. Coastal and
offshore recs. incl. a few seen 2 Jul 1976 near Ocumare de la Costa, Aragua (B. Zonfrillo and others); 3
seen after heavy winds off Cata, Aragua (C. Parrish);
1 seen 6 Jan 1996 w of Isla La Tortuga; and 2 on 7
Jan 1996 nw of Isla Margarita[424].

Range: Breeds on Venez. isls. of Los Roques, La Or-
chila, and Los Hermanos (*loyemilleri*). Also breeds in
Bermuda, W Indies, off Panama, Tobago, Galápagos
Isls., and isls. in tropical Pacific and Indian oceans;
reported n to Costa Rica and in Guyana.
Note: Also called Dusky-backed Shearwater[403].

Hydrobatidae: Storm-Petrels

Golondrinas de Mar

Storm-petrels are a worldwide group of small, swallowlike seabirds. All are brownish to blackish, often
with varying amounts of white on the upper tail coverts or underparts. They are shorter winged and
longer legged than shearwaters, and they flutter
close to the water. Those of the genus *Oceanites* patter or skip across the water on dangling webbed feet
and constantly beating wings, looking for all the
world as if they are walking on the water's surface.

Despite this, they are unable to walk on land. Larger
species swoop and dive more like gadfly-petrels.
They eat planktonic crustaceans, tiny fish, squid, and
oil droplets from the surface of the water. They differ
from gadfly-petrels in having the tube nostrils united
into one opening. Storm-petrels sometimes follow
ships. Nesting is colonial in burrows or rock crevices
on oceanic islands. Both adults incubate the single
white egg, typically for 2 days or more, while their
mate is feeding at sea. Field identification of the various species is difficult, even with the aid of flight
and feeding characters.

Wilson's Storm-Petrel   PLATE 2
Oceanites oceanicus   Petrel de Tormentas
Identification: 7″ (18cm). 32g. Black legs extend beyond slightly forked tail; webs of feet yellow (rarely
visible even up close). Small dusky black storm-
petrel with pale brownish white diagonal band
across upper wing coverts; *white C-shaped band
across rump extends to sides of under tail coverts* and
is almost always visible from sides or below. In flight,
wing shorter than in Leach's Storm-Petrel and with
rounded tip and little or no carpal bend.
Sim. species: See Leach's Storm-Petrel.
Behavior: Notable for habit of feeding by "walking
on water," skipping and fluttering over sea surface
with wings up and legs dangling. Flight otherwise
tends to be direct (contra Leach's), steady, and with
fewer glides than in other storm-petrels. Usually gregarious, occas. singly at sea, and may follow ships or
fishing boats.
Status and habitat: Accidental. 1 ♂ taken 25 Jul
1958 off La Guaira, Distr. Federal, is only rec. Breeds
Nov–Apr in subantarctic and Antarctic regions; postbreeders undertake transequatorial migration, spending austral winter (Apr–Sep) in n Atlantic, c Pacific,
and Indian oceans.

Range: Coast of Distr. Federal; Islas Los Roques (?).
Rec. off Guyana and Suriname. Breeds in Antarctic.
Migrates or wanders n to ne US, Labrador, and En-
gland; in Pacific n to Japan.

Leach's Storm-Petrel
Oceanodroma leucorhoa   Golondrina de Mar
Identification: 8″ (20.3cm). 39g. Much like Wilson's
Storm-Petrel. Differs in smudgy white rump less extensive (does not extend around to underside of tail),
diagnostic *dark division down center of rump* (visible
up close), and slightly deeper fork to tail; in direct

comparison wings longer, more angular. Amt. of white in upper tail coverts varies (s Mexican pops. entirely dark rumped).
Sim. species: See Wilson's Storm-Petrel.
Behavior: Unlike Wilson's, does not "walk on water" freq. Flight bouncy and swerving and with erratic course. A few deep wing beats alternate with short glides with wings held up steeply at angle and "bent" at wrist. Occurs singly or in small parties. Apparently seldom follows ships.
Status and habitat: Rare or accidental. Known from 4 specimens: 1 on 5 Apr 1955 from mouth of Río San Juan in Gulf of Paria, Monagas; 2 on 9 Feb 1950 off Curiapo, Delta Amacuro; and 1 on 29 Jan 1965 at mouth of Río Amacuro, Delta Amacuro. Sight rec. off coast[227]. A few seen between Bonaire and Trinidad on 3 different Jan passages, mid 1990s[424]. Breeds May–Jun in n latitudes; to be watched for passing through tropical Atlantic and Carib. waters mainly before or after these dates (except nonbreeders).

Range: Venez. coast of Monagas and Delta Amacuro (*leucorhoa*); Islas Los Roques (sight) and Isla de Aves (sight). Breeds in n Atlantic, n Pacific, and w Mexico. Migrates s in Atlantic to e Brazil and cape of S Africa; in Pacific s to equator or beyond.

PELECANIFORMES

Phaethontidae: Tropicbirds

Chíparos

This family comprises 3 species that are highly pelagic away from their breeding sites and are found worldwide in warmer oceans. All 3 are beautiful, mostly white seabirds, graceful in flight and best known for their 2 long, thin, central tail feathers that stream behind like ribbons. The sexes are similar, and the bills are strong and usually reddish or yellowish. Tropicbirds are mostly solitary. As in many diving seabirds, a network of tiny air sacs beneath the skin of the foreparts cushions the impact of the dive. These birds nest in small, loose colonies on ledges or in crevices on or near rocky sea cliffs, often beneath vegetation. A single brownish egg is incubated for about 45 days in shifts of 3–5 days by both sexes.

Red-billed Tropicbird PLATE 2
Phaethon aethereus Chíparo
Identification: 20–24" (51–61cm). 725g. With *long, flexible, central tail streamers*, length reaches 40" (102cm). Heavy red bill. *Mostly white, outer primaries and line through eye black*; back, rump, and wing coverts barred with black (not visible at a distance). Imm.: lacks long tail feathers; bill yellowish, barring coarser, and eyestripes meet on nape. Juv: bill yellowish.
Sim. species: At a distance looks like a tern, esp. Royal Tern. Also see Note below.
Behavior: Usually seen flying alone, although several may be visible in air near breeding colonies. Flight is graceful and direct with strong, rowing wing beats, much like that of a large tern (e.g., Royal Tern). Hovers momentarily before plunging with half-closed wings, usually from quite high (10–20m up), for fish or squid. Sometimes rapid wing beats are interrupted by short glides. Feet fully webbed (all 4 toes); swims well, holding tail cocked up out of water, but cannot stand or walk on land.
Status and habitat: Breeds Feb–Apr (earlier?) on offshore isls. of Los Hermanos and Los Roques. Apparently no reg. migration but may disperse when not breeding. Imms. wander more widely than ads. Three seen 5 Feb 1984 on Isla. Margarita–Pto. La Cruz ferry crossing (S. Whitehouse et al.) are closest recs. to coast.

Range: Venez. isls. of Los Roques, La Orchila, La Blanquilla, Los Hermanos, and Isla de Aves (*mesonauta*). In Carib. on Curaçao, St. Giles, and Little Tobago. Also from Baja California to Malpelo Isl., Colombia; Galápagos Isls. and isls. off Peru. Widely in tropical Pacific and Indian oceans.
Note: White-tailed Tropicbird (*P. lepturus*) is unrec. but prob. occurs reg. in offshore and pelagic Venez. waters. Like Red-billed but smaller (to 31"; 79cm with tail streamers) and more slender, with thinner orange yellow bill, bold black patch at base of outer primaries, and broad diagonal black bar across wing coverts. Shaft of tail streamers black. Imm.: much like imm. Red-billed but lacks bold black wing tips (only shows small amt. of black on outer web of outer feathers).

Sulidae: Boobies

Bobas

Boobies occur mainly in warm tropical waters, whereas gannets, their temperate-latitude allies, are birds of cool waters. Sulids are large, sociable seabirds, rather angular in appearance, with pointed bills, narrow pointed wings, and wedge-shaped tails. Boobies differ from gannets chiefly in having a bare rather than mostly feathered throat pouch. Female sulids are a little larger than males, but otherwise the sexes are similar. When breeding the sexes may differ markedly in eye and soft-part color. These species are veritable diving machines, plunging obliquely into the sea from considerable heights for fish they may pursue and swallow beneath the surface. Boobies breed colonially on the ground or build a small stick nest in a low tree.

Masked Booby   PLATE 2
Sula dactylatra   Boba Borrega

Identification: 32–36″ (81–91cm). 1.5kg. *Larger and heavier* than its allies. Bill yellowish (♂) or greenish yellow (♀). *Bare facial skin dark gray blue* (looks black), legs yellowish to yellowish olive. *Looks pointed at both ends.* Slender, pointed wings. Pure white with *black flight feathers* (incl. long black-tipped tertials) and *pointed black tail.* Juv.: recalls imm. Brown Booby; above brown with inconspic. white collar across hindneck; head and neck brown sharply demarcated from white underparts; wing linings white with narrow black band from carpal zone to axillaries; flight feathers blackish. Imm.: paler than juv.; upper wing coverts and rump whitish; *white collar more conspic.* Ad. plumage acquired in ca. 2 yr.

Sim. species: Ad. is nearest white morph of Red-footed Booby which differs in white tail and distinct black carpal patch on underwing. Cf. juv. and imm. plumages with those of Brown Booby.

Voice: Silent at sea. At colonies greets with reedy, piping, gooselike whistle; also a lower, harsh call.

Behavior: Loosely gregarious at sea. Flight is strong and fast on deep, powerful wing beats that alternate with occas. glides. Executes shallow, diagonal dives into deep oceanic waters for fish, esp. flying fish; does not follow ships. Nests in small colonies on gd. on sandy isls. and beach dunes; 2 chalky white eggs, incubation ca. 45 days; both sexes incubate and feed young; normally only 1 fledges.

Status and habitat: Rec. breeding Feb–Nov on Islas Los Roques, Los Monjes, and Los Hermanos; 1–15 nests on Isla Selesquí in Los Roques. Reg. and conspic. between offshore isls. and coast, esp. near Islas Los Hermanos[403]. Prob. present yr-round in deep offshore waters, and occas. wanders to coast: more than 30 seen 31 Jul 1983 off Cabo Codera, Miranda (C. Parrish); 3 seen 4 Feb 1984 from Pto. La Cruz–Margarita ferry, and 14 seen 5 Feb 1984 on same ferry (S. Whitehouse and others). Least numerous booby in s Carib.; very scarce e of Isla Margarita[424].

Range: Coastal and offshore isls. incl. Los Monjes, Los Roques, La Blanquilla, Los Hermanos, and Isla de Aves (*dactylatra*); sightings near Isla Margarita

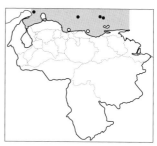

and off coastal Aragua and Cabo Codero, Miranda. Coastal isls. from w Mexico to Peru and Chile, Greater and Lesser Antilles s to Brazil; throughout warmer parts of Atlantic, Pacific, and Indian oceans.

Red-footed Booby
Sula sula   Boba Rabo Blanco

Identification: 26–29″ (66–74cm). 985g. *Bill and facial skin pale blue, base of bill pink; legs and feet bright red.* Plumage polymorphic (1st two most likely in Venez. waters). White morph: *all white with black flight feathers;* black patch on carpal area of underwing. White-tailed brown morph: all brown or grayish brown with *white rump, belly, and tail.* Brown morph: all more or less brown or grayish brown; crown and hindneck tinged yellowish. White-headed, white-tailed morph: brown with *white head, neck, rearparts, and tail.* Juv.: ashy brown to dusky gray brown, bill dusky brown, legs yellowish gray; plumage always streaked at first; imms. lose streaks but can be told by dusky bill and dingy yellowish legs. Subad.: underwings mottled whitish without clear pattern; bill dull blue, legs dull reddish.

Sim. species: *Smaller* than others with which it occurs, but variety of plumages confusing. All ads. have red legs and feet. Cf. Masked and Brown boobies.

Voice: Loud, quacking *ghaaow*! when pursued; at nest low grunts, snoring growls, or hisses[706].

Behavior: Breeds colonially on many offshore Venez. isls. Dives from fairly high up, esp. for flying fish, its main food, and freq. feeds at night. May follow and alight on ship riggings, etc., and overall the most highly pelagic booby in Venez. waters. May be active at night. Roosts and nests in bushes or low in mangroves, not on rocks. In Cocos Isls., Costa Rica, small stick platform nest in top of tree, usually near shore or ridge; 2 eggs[706].

Status and habitat: Resident in offshore and pelagic waters, rarely seen (recs.?) near coast. Nests (starting in Oct) on Islas Las Aves, Los Roques, Los Testigos, and Los Hermanos; largest colony occupied yr-round, on Las Bubíes in Los Roques, has up to 5000 birds[403]. Younger birds may disperse at sea, but details of dispersal unknown. White morphs much commoner (50:1) than brown ones in waters w of Isla Margarita[424].

Range: Coastal isls. from Golfo de Venezuela (Los Monjes) to Miranda (Cabo Codera); most offshore isls. from Las Aves to La Blanquilla, Los Hermanos, and Margarita (*sula*). Breeds on many isls. of Carib.

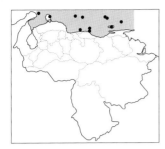

(incl. Tobago) and s Atlantic, w coast of Mexico, Cocos Isls., Galápagos Isls., and isls. of Pacific and Indian oceans.

Brown Booby   PLATE 2
Sula leucogaster   Boba Marrón
Identification: 26–30" (66–76cm). 1kg. *Bill and feet yellowish*; bare facial skin pale yellow (or grayish— nonbreeding). Upperparts and head to upper breast chocolate brown *sharply separated* from white lower underparts; white wing linings broadly outlined dark brown. Juv.: pattern echos that of ad. but much paler, dingy brown; white wing linings mottled with brown.
Sim. species: Juv. and imm. Masked Booby are superficially sim. but larger with white cervical collar and distinctive dark band through white wing linings.
Behavior: A familiar bird, often seen along coastal waters, even in harbors. Alone or in small loose groups, but may gather in larger groups over favorable fishing areas at sea, where plunges for fish. Flies in lines low over water, feeds mostly in shallow, inshore waters. Prefers to perch on rocks and buoys rather than settle on water. Leaf- or twig-lined nest in depression on gd.[788]; usually 2 eggs.
Status and habitat: Fairly common resident in coastal and inshore waters. Breeds on Islas Los Monjes, Las Aves, Los Roques, La Orchila, and Los Hermanos; nesting reported Feb–Oct; 1st recs. for Zulia are 1 taken 30 Nov 1976, another seen 9 Mar 1977 at Kaimare Chico[353]. Often around frigatebird colony off Tucacas, Falcón, and off Ocumare de la Costa, Aragua. Everywhere imms. seem to outnumber ads. Specimens from Cabo Codera, Miranda; Bahía de Guanta, Anzoátegui; and Isla La Tortuga.

Range: Coast and all offshore isls. of Venez. (*leucogaster*). Breeds on isls. of Carib., incl. Aruba to Trinidad and Tobago, and warmer waters of Atlantic and Indian Oceans.

Pelecanidae: Pelicans
Alcatraces

There are up to 8 species of pelicans worldwide, all of them large, social birds, best known for their enormous pouched bill with a huge extensible gular pouch. They regularly fly in stately formation with slow, heavy wing beats and long glides that keep them just above the water's surface. In flight or at rest the head is drawn back with the bill resting on the neck. Pelicans often forage cooperatively and are quite social when breeding. Nesting birds are very sensitive to human disturbance and readily abandon their eggs[248], so great care should be exercised when visiting colonies.

Brown Pelican   PLATE 2
Pelecanus occidentalis   Alcatraz
Identification: 45–55" (114–140cm). 3kg. Huge, unmistakable bird with *enormous pouched bill*. Breeding ad.: above grayish, flight feathers blackish; hindneck chestnut brown, most of head and narrow stripe down sides of neck white to yellowish white, foreneck and underparts brown; orbital skin reddish, bill and pouch tinged reddish. Nonbreeding ad.: neck mostly whitish; bill brownish; pouch and facial skin dull gray. Imm.: dull brownish above incl. head and neck; below dingy grayish white. Ad. plumage in ca. 3 yr.
Behavior: Small groups scale low over coastal waters in long, silky smooth glides with wing tips mere inches above waves. In shallow water feed by swimming, often in cooperative groups, herding small fish; in deeper water dive from various hts., transforming their ungainly shapes into precision, arrowlike diving machine just before entering water. Breed Nov–Jun with Jan–Feb peak; 2–3 white eggs stained brown; rough stick nest in mangroves (77%), edge of dry to moist forest (22%), or thorn woodland (1%). In 1983 at least 21 colonies on continental Venez. shoreline and 4 more on offshore isls. (3369 nests); largest colony exceeded 400 nests; more than half of all Venez. colonies are on coast of Sucre[232].
Status and habitat: Common resident along entire coast; occas. strays inland. Pop. apparently relatively stable, in 1982 estimated at 17,500 birds[232]. Breeding colonies widely scattered from s end of Lago de Maracaibo (Lagunetas) and Falcón (Maraguey) to Miranda (3 colonies), Anzoátegui (Isla Chimanas), e end of Golfo Cariaco, Sucre, entire n coast of Sucre (11 colonies), Golfo de Paria, Sucre (2 colo-

nies), and n Delta Amacuro (Caño Macareo); also breeds on offshore isls. of Los Roques (3 colonies) and Islas Margarita (1 colony); reported nesting on Isla La Tortuga and Las Aves[784], but in 1983 no colonies noted there[232]. N migrants occas. (reg.?) reach Venez.

Range: Coast and all offshore isls. (resident *occidentalis*); coast of Aragua, Sucre, and Isla Margarita (n migrant *carolinensis*). Coasts of w and s US s to s Chile and nw Brazil. W Indies.

Phalacrocoracidae: Cormorants

Cotúas

Cormorants are a widespread and evolutionarily old lineage of birds characterized by large size, totipalmate toes, long hooked bills, and long stiff tails. Most species are black or gray, and several Southern Hemisphere species are white below. Soft-part colors are much brighter during the breeding season. Cormorants eat mostly fish captured in underwater chases. They float low in the water and taxi long distances to get airborne but are very strong fliers, often forming long strings or Vs in the air. Cormorants are very sociable and nest and roost colonially, sometimes in large numbers, on sea cliffs or in trees. They are valued producers of guano in Peru and, at least formerly, were well-known servants of humans, being trained for fishing in the Orient.

Neotropic Cormorant   PLATE 2
Phalacrocorax brasilianus   Cotúa Olivácea
Identification: 25–28" (64–71cm). 1.3kg. Tail fairly long. Long, narrow black bill hooked at tip; eyes blue green; legs black. *Plumage black* with oily green gloss; *gular pouch and facial skin dull yellow* (color varies somewhat with season) *outlined behind by narrow white line.* Juv. and imm.: all brown to dusky brown above, paler brown below, no white gular line; throat, foreneck, and breast whitish in older imms. Homely chicks covered in black down. Ad. plumage attained in 3–4 yr.
Sim. species: Anhinga has longer, thinner neck and tail, longer and stiletto-shaped bill (not hooked), and gray wing patches.
Voice: Usually silent, but often noisy around nest or roost. Utters croaks and low, guttural, belching *uuraack.*
Behavior: Often seen in long straggling lines or V-shaped wedges, sometimes flying low over water; more often singles, prs., or small groups along forested rivers. Like all cormorants, floats low in water, may submerge with only head, neck, and uptilted bill visible. Flies with neck slightly withdrawn, bill and head raised, body inclined, and wings beating steadily. Dives while swimming and pursues fish; propels itself rapidly underwater with feet. May fish in cooperative groups. Plumage not waterproof, and after swimming perches on dead snags, bushes, etc., with wings and tail spread to dry. Large stick nest 1–10m up over water; usually nests in colonies, mostly containing its own sp.; 3–4 blue green eggs; incubation ca. 30 days.

Status and habitat: Common and widespread resident wherever there are bodies of water. More numerous inland than on coast, and mainly in lowlands, but wanders widely, often over high mt. passes with some reg. seasonal movements.

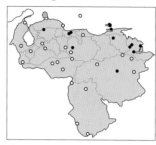

Range: To 3600m (sightings at Laguna Mucubají, Mérida). Throughout incl. Islas Margarita, Los Roques, and Coche (*olivaceus*). Breeds from s US to s S Amer.; also Bahamas, Cuba, and Aruba to Trinidad.
Note: Also called Olivaceous Cormorant[403]; scientific name follows Browning[84].

Anhingidae: Darters

Cotúas Agujitas

Darters are a small but widespread group of aquatic birds closely related to cormorants. They are found mainly in freshwater lakes and rivers in warmer parts of the world. Superficially like cormorants, they differ in having a longer, broader tail and much slimmer neck, among other things. Darters fly well and often soar, but they take off from the water only after a long splashing taxi across the surface. They swim underwater, propelled by their short, fully webbed feet, and spear fish with their pointed bill rather than grasp them. At the surface they often swim submerged with only the head and neck visible, a habit that has earned them the name "snakebirds."

Anhinga   PLATE 2
Anhinga anhinga   Cotúa Agujita
Identification: 32–36" (81–91cm). 1.2kg. Long pointed bill. Facial skin and eyering brownish, or both bright blue green when breeding. *Small head, long neck; long fan-shaped tail.* ♂: glossy greenish black; *upper wing surface densely dotted silver, large silvery gray patch on wing coverts.* ♀: sim. but head, *neck, and chest pale buffy brown.* Imm.: like ♀ but browner and duller. Ad. plumage in ca. 2 yr.
Sim. species: Most likely confused with a cormorant, but note long snakelike neck and head, longer tail, and silvery wing patches.
Behavior: As in cormorants, plumage is not waterproof, and Anhingas are often seen hanging out to dry on low branches or shrubs. Alone or in prs. (no migratory flocks reported in Venez.). Swims well, often with only head and neck above surface. In normal flight, flapping alternates with gliding, and soars well on flat wings. Stick nest a flat platform 1–4m up over water; often nests in small colonies or scattered among larger nos. of egrets and ibises; 3 or more

pale blue eggs with glaucous coating, soon stained brown; incubation ca. 30 days; ads. feed by regurgitation; nestlings may drop into water if frightened[706].
Status and habitat: Fairly common resident along sluggish freshwater rivers, swamps, lagoons in llanos, and forested streams, occas. brackish water. May wander into mts.; highest rec. (below) at PN Yacambú, Lara[60].

Range: To ca. 300m (sight to 1400m). Throughout (*anhinga*). Breeds from se US to w Ecuador, n Argentina, and Uruguay; also Cuba, Grenada, Trinidad and Tobago.

Fregatidae: Frigatebirds

Tijeretas de Mar

Frigatebirds, or "man-o'-war birds," are a small group of 5 sexually dimorphic marine birds that ply warmer oceans of the world. Remarkably, they do not walk or swim and never intentionally settle on the water. For their weight they have the largest wingspread of any birds, and they are exceptionally agile and buoyant. They catch flying fish and squid and also pirate prey from other seabirds, steal eggs and chicks from seabird nests, or snatch carrion, hatchling sea turtles, and other items from beaches. Nesting is colonial on oceanic islands. During the breeding season males inflate and display a spectacular, balloonlike, red gular pouch.

Magnificent Frigatebird   PLATE 2
Fregata magnificens   Tijereta de Mar
Identification: 38–42″ (97–107cm). 1.3kg. Large and kitelike. *Long slender wings* with prom. "bend" in middle (wingspan up to 7.5'; 2.25m). *Long, deeply forked tail.* All toes webbed. ♂: all black with bare red throat pouch (usually visible only in display). ♀: black with broad band of white on *sides of neck and across breast*; no throat pouch; band on upper wing coverts brown. Imm.: like ♀ but *head and neck also white*; imm. plumage retained for several yr.
Sim. species: Much like Lesser Frigatebird (see Note).
Voice: At nesting colony a continuous, nasal cackling; aggressive call a rapid rattle descending in pitch and accelerating[427]; silent away from colonies.
Behavior: Soars effortlessly and lazily high overhead. Often alone at sea but may congregate in large groups in coastal areas. Strictly diurnal; roosts in groups in small bushes or trees near ocean at night. Stick nest in mangroves, low bush, or on rocks; 1–2

white eggs. In PN Morrocoy breeding is protracted with approx. 14-month cycle; ♂♂ breed annually (Oct–Apr, then gradually depart colony, with fewest present Jul–Oct), ♀♀ breed biennially with 2 breeding pops. present simultaneously for part of yr (Oct–Jan). Sex ratio skewed almost 2:1 in favor of ♀♀. Courtship Oct–Jan; nest building Feb–Apr; nestling stage May–Jul; fledgling stage Jul–Oct with some fledglings to Jan of following yr[429]; 1 white egg may be incubated by both sexes; fed (entirely?) by ♀; 5–6 months to fledge, dependent for many more; reaches breeding age in ca. 5 yr.[706].
Status and habitat: Common resident along coast and over coastal waters, isls., estuaries, and beaches, occas. a short distance inland (e.g., over Caracas and Maracay). Breeds on Islas Los Hermanos and Los Testigos, and little islets near Tucacas and Chichiriviche, Falcón (Isla de Pájaros); in last colony breeds with Brown Pelican, Great, Snowy, and Cattle egrets, and Tricolored Heron in mixed colony. No known breeding colonies in Golfo de Venezuela where sp. is a yr-round visitant[353].

Range: To ca. 1200m. Venez. coastline and all offshore isls. Generally along Carib. and Atlantic coasts. Tropical Atlantic and Pacific.
Note: Lesser Frigatebird (*F. ariel*) breeds on Trinidade and Martin Vaz off coast of s Brazil and is vagrant as far n as se US. ♂ smaller than Magnificent Frigatebird; *spurlike white axillary patch.* ♀ has U-shaped white chest patch with spur extending onto axillar region (cf. closely with ♀ Magnificent Frigatebird).

ANSERIFORMES

Anhimidae: Screamers

Arucos, Chicagüires

This small group of anatomically peculiar, aquatic birds is found only in South America. Heavy bodied and superficially gooselike, they have many unusual anatomical features that suggest an ancient lineage. Among other things, they lack feather tracts; the feathers on the head and neck are very short, soft, and downy; and the skin is thick and spongelike. They possess a shaggy crest or long frontal spike on top of the head, 2 sharp-pointed spurs on the bend of each wing (both sexes), and perforate nostrils which form a hole completely through the bill. The legs and unwebbed toes are unusually large and strong, the middle toe is exceptionally long, and screamers walk easily over floating vegetation despite their great weight. Their powerful voice, a gulping hoot or yelping scream, is among the loudest of all birds.

Horned Screamer   PLATE 16
Anhima cornuta   Aruco
Identification: 33–37″ (84–94cm). 3.1kg. Enormous, corpulent bird with small chickenlike bill hooked at tip. *Long "unicorn" quill projects forward from fore-crown* (hard to see unless close). *Upperparts, throat, foreneck, and chest mostly black,* crown speckled and scaled with white; large silvery white shoulder patch conspic. in flight; under wing coverts and *belly white.*
Sim. species: See Northern Screamer.
Voice: Not likely forgotten. Powerful, far-carrying call unlike any other; typically several throaty *U-WHO's,* a few *GULP-HOO's,* and a more raucous (honking) *QULK-QUOO, QULK-QUOO, YOIK-YOK, YOIK-YOK,* etc., with variations in sequence. Prs. give duet calls (context?); 1 bird calls *U-WHO,* the 2d a *cluck* and deep resonant *uuh,* combined result being a rhythmic 3- or 4-note call. With some calls head is jerked rather violently back, then forward.
Behavior: A sedentary vegetarian that feeds in marshy grass or in floating vegetation. Eats a variety of small shoots and buds. When not feeding, single birds, prs., family groups, or occas. several loosely assoc. individuals loaf on tops of highest nearby vegetation, usually a low bush or tree, although if alarmed they may fly ponderously away to top of a tall tree. Once fully airborne, they fly buoyantly and soar well. Nest a large pile of floating marsh vegetation in shallow water and partially anchored to brush or grass; 2–3 olive brown eggs[195].
Status and habitat: Vegetation-choked lagoons and riverbanks in forested areas; shallow marshes and ponds in open regions, but everywhere usually with some bushes and taller trees nearby. Locally distrib. in Venez., but a sizable pop. occurs in San Pablo marshes of n Carabobo. S of Orinoco only at Pto. Ordaz (Hilty); prob. elsewhere.

Range: To 300m. S end of Maracaibo Basin; se Falcón (incl. Cerro Misión) and n Carabobo (sight, San Pablo); prob. nw Yaracuy; e of Andes from Táchira, Apure, Barinas, and Portuguesa e locally through s Aragua (formerly) to Monagas (Barrancas), Sucre

(Caño La Brea), Delta Amacuro (Tucupita), and ne Bolívar (sightings since 1978, Pto. Ordaz). Colombia and the Guianas s through Amazonia to e Bolivia and Brazil; w Ecuador. Formerly Trinidad.

Chauna

Differs from *Anhima* in bare facial skin, no frontal quill, red legs; different plumage.

Northern Screamer   PLATE 16
Chauna chavaria   Chicagüire
Identification: 33–37″ (84–94cm). Large, corpulent bird like previous sp. *Bare orbital skin and legs coral red;* bill black. Crown gray, ragged occipital crest black, *throat and broad white band sweep up behind eye* (white "scarf" tied around head); neck black, narrow *white collar encircles base of neck,* otherwise blackish above, brownish gray below; under wing coverts white.
Sim. species: From Horned Screamer by white "scarf" on upper neck and red facial skin and legs. Also note white ring around base of neck. Both occur together in s Maracaibo Basin.
Voice: Recalls that of Horned Screamer but not as loud or powerful; a high-pitched, almost yelping scream that rises. Often quiet for long periods. A calling bird is usually answered immediately by a mate.
Behavior: Like Horned Screamer, a sedentary and rather sedate vegetarian, most often seen standing alone or in prs., occas. several loosely assoc. together, in a marsh, perched atop a bush, or on large open branches of a high tree. Not shy but generally does not allow an observer to approach closely before flushing off in powerful but ponderous flight. Consumes green parts of aquatic plants. Nest a pile of aquatic vegetation just above water in marsh; 2–7 eggs, May[452].
Status and habitat: Uncommon and local resident. Vegetation-choked lagoons in swampy forest, and in marshes and grassy ponds in open country, but always where there are trees and bushes nearby. Easily overlooked as often forages or rests out of sight in tall marsh grass. Can usually be seen near Encontrados, s Zulia. Nos., now estimated at ca. 2000, have declined with settlement and ranching[127].

Range: S half of Maracaibo Basin in Zulia (Río Catatumbo) to w Mérida and w Trujillo (Altamira); prob. nw Táchira. N Colombia.

Anatidae: Ducks and Geese

Patos

Ducks and geese are a large family of "game" birds found the world over. Venezuelan species include migrants from the north, a few residents, and 1 that may undertake short-distance migrations within tropical latitudes. One or more can be found at any elevation from the lowlands to treeline in Venezuela, although for the most part they compose a relatively small proportion of the total avifauna. All members of the family have the 3 anterior toes webbed, a broad bill, and a fleshy tongue with corneous lamellae along the edge which is useful for straining items from water. Wing and tail feathers are molted simultaneously, during which time both sexes become flightless for a month or so. Whistling-ducks are numerically the most abundant ducks in Venezuela and are best known for their gangly appearance, reedy whistling calls, and in some cases, habit of perching in trees. The Orinoco Goose is the only "sheldgoose" in Venezuela, and like its allies in the Old World, males lack a courtship display but fight with each other for a mate. Most of the dabbling ducks (*Anas*) are migratory. They are notable for shiny or iridescent wing speculums and their habits of "tipping up" at the surface to feed and of springing directly into the air to fly. By contrast, diving ducks such as pochards, *Aythya*, and *Oxyura* lack iridescent speculums, dive expertly, and patter across the water's surface to get airborne. Tree or perching ducks such as Muscovies and Comb Ducks are notably arboreal, whereas the little Torrent Duck is one of the few members of the family anywhere to spend its entire life amid raging mountain torrents. For new views on waterfowl taxonomy, see Livezey[360,361].

Dendrocygna

Long legs and necks; some spp. reg. perch in trees; formerly called tree-ducks.

Fulvous Whistling-Duck   PLATE 3
Dendrocygna bicolor   Yaguaso Colorado
Identification: 18–21″ (46–53cm). 730g. Long legged and long necked. Bill and legs ash gray. Mostly rich cinnamon brown; crown and narrow line down hind-neck rich dark brown; back and wings blackish broadly scaled buff, inconspic. patch of small whitish striations on neck; *at rest shows creamy white stripes on sides*. In flight *wings all blackish* (no white on wings); *narrow, curved white band across base of black tail*.
Sim. species: Cf. other whistling-ducks. In flight look for a duck with all-dark wings and narrow white ring at base of tail. See Northern Pintail.
Voice: Call a high, reedy *kur-dúr*, mostly in flight and constantly repeated.
Behavior: Gregarious and formerly in flocks mixed with other spp. of whistling-ducks but now in serious decline in Venez. and seen mainly as singles, 2s, or 3s within large flocks of other whistling-ducks. Often

feeds at night, esp. by tipping up. Usually stands on gd. (rarely in trees) to rest. Eats mostly seeds and is esp. fond of rice (more so than other whistling-ducks) but has suffered from pesticides and from rice harvesting during nesting period. Loosely woven nest (no down lining) built in dense vegetation (or rice), almost always over water; 9–12 eggs; 2d or 3d clutch laid if previous one destroyed; breeds early Apr–late Sep, peak in Jul. Flightless for 2–3 wk during postbreeding molt, Sep–Nov, after which flocks form until next breeding season[206].
Status and habitat: Formerly relatively common, now a rare resident, and by far the least numerous whistling-duck in Venez. Freshwater marshes, grassy lagoons, wet pastures, and occas. brackish water. Fond of areas with extensive emergent vegetation, esp. rice fields, which are used for feeding, roosting, and nesting. Concentrates in available wetlands during dry season; disperses to breed at start of rainy season.

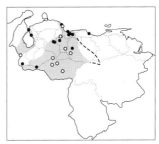

Range: To 300m (prob. occas. higher). Maracaibo Basin, Zulia, and nw Táchira; coast from e Falcón e to Miranda (Laguna de Tacarigua); generally e of Andes from Táchira, Apure, Barinas (sight), Portuguesa, Cojedes, and Yaracuy e to Guárico (eastward?); Isla de Aves (sight). S US locally to Honduras; c Panama s spottily to Bolivia and c Argentina, occas. Chile. Trinidad. E Africa and se Asia.

White-faced Whistling-Duck   PLATE 3
Dendrocygna viduata   Yaguaso Cariblanco
Identification: 16–18″ (41–46cm). 655g. Bill black. *Smaller and darker than allies and with conspic. white foreface* (but face often stained somewhat brownish), rear part of head and neck black, mantle brown narrowly streaked buff, back, wings, and tail *all blackish* (in flight shoulders maroon), chest maroon, rest of underparts black, sides and flanks barred with white. Imm.: face and upper foreneck grayish brown.
Sim. species: White face (often dirty) is the mark. In flight *no white* in wings or tail.
Voice: High, reedy whistle a hurried *WEE-te-de*, often repeated incessantly in flight day or night.
Behavior: A gregarious sp. that spends most of day standing alert and wary in dense flocks in marshy areas or near water. When alarmed stands very tall and freezes, watching intently, or springs directly into air. Readily mixes with other spp. of whistling-ducks but seldom perches in trees. At night flies out to foraging areas to feed by wading, swimming, or

tipping up in shallow water and is capable of diving. Feeds heavily on grass seeds in dry season, more on tubers and insects in rainy season; commonest plant spp. (seeds and tubers) eaten are *Caperonia, Echinochloa, Cyperus, Oriza,* and rice[207]. Breeds Apr–Sep; nest on gd., often near water; 8–12 eggs (range 2–19), whitish cream; incubation 31 days; renests if early clutch destroyed. Ads. flightless for several wk approx. Nov–Jan during molt[206,374].

Status and habitat: Common to locally abundant resident in freshwater marshes, grassy lagoons, and flooded fields, occas. brackish water, and in all habitats usually near bodies of open water. This and next sp. are 2 most numerous ducks in Venez. Gathers in large nos. in suitable areas, e.g., Hato Cedral, in dry season; disperses to nest during rainy season.

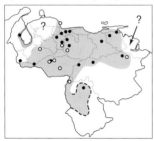

Range: To 300m (prob. occas. higher). Prob. throughout n of Orinoco (few recs. w of Andes or in Falcón; Delta Amacuro?); n Amazonas (San Juan de Manapiare) and n Bolívar. Costa Rica spottily to n Argentina and Uruguay. Trinidad. Tropical Africa and Madagascar.

Black-bellied Whistling-Duck   PLATE 3
Dendrocygna autumnalis   Guirirí
Identification: 20–22″ (51–56cm). 740g. *Bill coral red; legs pinkish red.* Mostly rufescent brown, sides of head and upper foreneck and chest grayish brown, breast and belly black. In flight wings black with *large white shoulder patch.* Imm.: much duller and grayer but with suggestion of ad.'s pattern, incl. white eyering; bill and legs grayish to dusky. Flies with long neck slightly drooped and legs protruding behind tail.
Sim. species: Largest whistling-duck and only one with red bill and white on wings. Beware dull imms. (grayish bill) which can be confused with Fulvous Whistling-Duck.
Voice: Call, mostly in flight, a single reedy, whistled *wee,* varying to *weeree* or *wissree,* or up to 5 notes, *wee-tee-Wée-te-re.*
Behavior: Disperses in prs. when breeding, but otherwise gathers by day in ponds and lagoons in small flocks that grow to immense nos. in dry season. Feeds mostly at night, foraging in water, in ricefields, or by grazing for seeds, some green shoots, and invertebrates. Active and noisy both day and night. This is only whistling-duck in Venez. that reg. perches and roosts in trees, esp. on large, high, dead limbs, and is overall less closely tied to water than the other 2 spp. Breeds May–Sep, peak in Jul; nest in hollow

tree, marsh, or flooded field, occas. far from water; 9–18 eggs (large clutches incl. eggs of more than 1 ♀); elsewhere known to use nest boxes; eggs white; incubation ca. 28 days. Ads. are flightless during postbreeding molt, ca. Nov or Dec–Jan[206,374], possibly earlier.
Status and habitat: Common to locally abundant in freshwater ponds, marshes, and flooded fields, occas. brackish water and mangroves. With White-faced Whistling-Duck, the commonest resident duck in Venez. Shows strong seasonal movements, congregating in enormous nos. at favorable sites Jan–Apr (dry season), e.g., Hato Cedral and Hato El Frio, and dispersing widely May–Dec to breed.

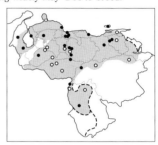

Range: To 600m (prob. occas. higher). Prob. throughout n of Orinoco; nw Amazonas and n Bolívar; Isla Margarita (*discolor*). S Texas, Mexico, W Indies, and Bahamas to n Argentina, Paraguay, and se Brazil. Trinidad.

Neochen

Large; thick-necked and barrel-chested; allied to Old World *Tadorna* (shelducks and sheldgeese); walk more than swim.

Orinoco Goose   PLATE 3
Neochen jubata   Pato Carretero
Identification: ♂ 27″ (69cm), 1.7kg. ♀ 23″ (58cm), 1.3kg. Barrel chested. Thick stubby bill blackish above, red below (red "lips"); legs dull red orange. *Foreparts incl. head, neck, upper back, and breast dull buff,* otherwise mostly chestnut becoming dark green on lower back and tail; under tail coverts white; wings glossy greenish black with *squarish white patch on secondaries* (conspic. from above in flight). Both sexes have knoblike spurs on wings. Downy juv.: yellow buff with cap, large cheek spot, line down hindneck, shoulder bar, and back black.
Sim. species: Two-toned appearance (buff foreparts, dark rearparts) distinctive. Overall larger, more robust, and with different habits than other waterfowl with which it occurs (e.g., whistling-ducks). In flight Black-bellied Whistling-Duck has large white area on forepart of wing. Also cf. Buff-necked Ibis.
Voice: ♂♂ give a shrill whistled *zree* and ser. of hollow reedy whistles, *preep, preep . . .* (1/sec or faster), like whistling into a barrel, given esp. when alarmed or disturbed; ♀ utters a low guttural honking or braying *gur'rump, gur'rump, gur'rump.* In display (?) or aggression both fly or circle and give a loud purring

pur'r'r'ra over and over (sound of "wookie" in Star Wars movies); in flight (disturbance call) a low *puu puu* . . . like muffled bugle.

Behavior: Barrel chest of ♂ imparts a rather proud attitude as it walks alertly with head high. Forms prs. when breeding (permanent?), but at other times gathers in small, loosely assoc. groups, esp. during eclipse molt in last 3 months of yr. ♂♂ fight with wings at onset of breeding[115]. Feeds mostly by grazing for vegetable matter (grasses) and takes some insects and other animal matter while walking on land near rivers or lagoons. Rather confiding and does not fly much, but readily takes to water for safety and often perches on high tree branches. Some nest in dry season (as early as Dec or Jan), but peak nesting activity prob. Jul–Aug; cavity at almost any ht.; down lined, 6–10 or more eggs, pale brownish cream[146,206]; competes with Yellow-crowned Parrots and Barn Owls for nest cavities.

Status and habitat: Once fairly numerous, now a very local resident in wetter portions of llanos, surviving mainly on a few large ranches, e.g., Hato Cedral and Hato El Frio, in Río Apure, Río Meta, and lower and mid. Río Orinoco drainage basins. Freshwater marshes, lakes, muddy river banks, river sandbars, and short grass fields, usually not far from water. Wanders widely when not breeding. Southernmost Venez. rec. is near Samariapo (sight, Hilty).

Range: To 300m. W Apure and Barinas e to s Anzoátegui and Delta Amacuro; n Amazonas and n Bolívar (lower Río Caura). Spottily e of Andes s to n Argentina and Paraguay.

Note: Also called Orinoco Sheldgoose. More closely allied with Old World shelducks (Taborninae) than with New World geese[360].

Muscovy Duck
Illus. p. 198

Cairina moschata Pato Real

Identification: ♂ 33″ (84cm), 3kg. ♀ 26″ (66cm), 1.7kg. Ad. ♂ has gray bill with broad diagonal black band around center; red caruncles on bare black ocular region and at base of bill. ♂: glossy greenish black with slight bushy crest, *large white shoulder patches* (conspic. in flight), and *white wing linings*. ♀: smaller and duller, no caruncles or crest, less white on wing. Imm.: dark brown with *white on wing reduced or often absent*.

Sim. species: Ad.'s white wing patches and large size are diagnostic. Cf. smaller Black-bellied Whistling-Duck. All dark imms. could be mistaken for a cormorant or Anhinga.

Voice: ♂ a hiss, rarely hd.; ♀ a weak quack.

Behavior: Usually in 2s or 3s or small groups up to 12; larger groups up to a 100 or so are occas. encountered during dry season. Feral birds, unlike domesticated ones, are wary and usually do not associate with other waterfowl. Reg. perch and roost in trees, often in nos. (communal roosts). Feed by tipping up in shallow water or by grazing when on land. Feed opportunistically on a wide variety of plant or animal matter. Breeding promiscuous, apparently with ♂-dominance system; all nesting by ♀; ca. 8–15 greenish white eggs; nest mainly in tree cavities or crown of palms. Nesting Jul and Nov, Guárico[734].

Status and habitat: Uncommon and somewhat local resident along wooded rivers, lakes, and swampy lagoons in lowlands. Generally everywhere in or near forested areas. Shows marked local and seasonal migratory movements, concentrating in nos. in open wetlands of llanos in dry season. Prefers freshwater but occas. in salt or brackish water and mangroves along coast during Dec–Apr dry season. Pop. now much reduced by hunting and other human activities. Uses nest boxes in Mexico.

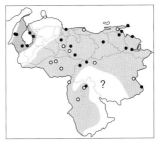

Range: To 300m. Prob. throughout incl. Delta Amacuro (no recs. In Falcón, Lara, Yaracuy, or Portuguesa). W Mexico locally to sw Ecuador, n Argentina, and Uruguay.

Comb Duck
Illus. p. 198

Sarkidiornis melanotos Pato de Monte

Identification: ♂ 30″ (76cm), 2.9kg. ♀ 22″ (56cm), 1.1kg. Gooselike. ♂: *fleshy rounded comb on upper mandible*; line down center of crown and hindneck black, the feathers slightly curly; rest of *head, neck, and most of underparts white*, head and neck irreg. *spotted black*; back, wings, and tail black strongly glossed green and purple. ♀: sim. but noticeably smaller and lacks comb; also profusely spotted on head. Imm.: crown and upperparts dark brown; white of ad. replaced by buffy brown; dark eyeline and inconspic. mottling on flanks. In flight both sexes show all-dark wings.

Sim. species: A large (esp. ♂), homely duck that looks white-headed at a distance. Unkept appearance more likely to recall a domesticated Muscovy Duck, which often shows much white below. Ad. Muscovies usually have white patch on front of wing (sometimes faint or lacking in ♀).

Behavior: Usually only scattered individuals or prs., infreq. small groups (often of same sex), rarely up to 40 (C. Casler). Often consorts with large groups of

Large perching ducks: Comb Duck
(upper left) (female left, male right),
Muscovy Duck (lower right) (male
left, female right)

whistling-ducks around grassy lagoons in llanos. Notably wary. Readily perches in trees and shows strong
seasonal movements, esp. during dry season. Apparently breeds in early wet season; ♂♂ take "harems"
of 2 or more ♀♀; tree-cavity nest, but despite much
breeding info. from Old World, almost nothing has
been reported on New World pops.
Status and habitat: Uncommon and local resident.
In dry season concentrates at large permanent wetlands such as those at La Yé and at Hato Cedral in
w Apure, but even there occurs mainly as singles or
2s or 3s amidst flocks of 1000s of whistling-ducks.
Scatters widely during May–Oct rainy season, e.g., to
nw of Barquisimeto and to Maturín, Monagas (P.
Boesman); present Apr–Dec, peak nos. in Jul in
Anzoátegui and nw Monagas[186].

Range: To 300m. E of Andes from Apure, Barinas
(sight), and Portuguesa e to Guárico, Anzoátegui,
and Monagas (sight, Maturín); occas. n to ne Lara
and e Falcón (*sylvicola*). E Panama locally (mostly e
of Andes) to c Argentina. Africa; se Asia.
Note: New World birds may be a separate sp., South
American Comb-Duck, *S. sylvicola*[361].

Merganetta

Monotypic genus. Numerous superb adaptations for
life in cascading mt. streams incl. narrow, elongate
body; large feet; long, stiff, rudderlike tail; and soft,
pliable bill.

Torrent Duck   PLATE 3
Merganetta armata   Pato de Torrentes
Identification: 15–17″ (38–43cm). 320g. Rather small,
streamlined duck with rubbery *rosy red bill and long,
stiff tail.* Red legs; *very large red feet.* ♂: *head and
neck white; crown, stripe down hindneck, and line
down side of neck black;* rest of upperparts black
streaked with gray and pale brown; underparts grayish white faintly streaked sandy brown. ♀ very different; crown and hindneck blue gray, rest of upperparts gray streaked black and brown like ♂; *sides of
head and underparts orange cinnamon.* Juv: above
like ♀ but grayer, tail narrowly barred with black;
below white with wavy blackish barring on sides, bill
dusky, base of lower mandible orange yellow; legs
and feet pale yellowish orange, mostly dusky in very
young birds.
Voice: Usually quiet. Loud, high-pitched *wheek
wheek* in flight, softer in display[407].
Behavior: Prs. or families (never flocks) spend much
time loafing on large boulders in middle of swift,
cold-water streams where they stand rather upright
and often nod heads. Swim and dive expertly in fast-
flowing turbulent water, or skitter across fastest sections. Often use small eddies behind boulders when
foraging or moving upstream. Inconspic. as float low
with head submerged to forage. Food is mostly
caddis-fly larva, mayflies, stoneflies, and mollusks,
incl. gastropods, taken by diving or occas. by dabbling in shallow water. Fly well but infreq. do so,

and most often simply swim rapidly up or down river if pressed. Down-lined nest on rock ledge near torrent; 2 dull buff eggs have 43–44 days incubation, one of longest of family; only ♀ incubates[407]; in Venez. breeds mainly Nov–May (dry season) or longer.

Status and habitat: Fairly common resident, but now local, in highly oxygenated cold-water mt. streams where there are rapids, falls, and abundance of large emergent boulders. Max. density is ca. 1 pr./0.8–1km of river[67,407]. Type of vegetation adj. to river unimportant (forest or open), and prs. may live in close proximity to human habitation if unmolested (e.g., at Mitisús, Mérida; and at Hotel Los Frailes, Mérida). Water pollution, and deforestation and subsequent river siltation, which destroys sp.'s food, are major threats. Introduced insectivorous fish competitors may also be a threat.

Range: 2000–3000m (sightings to 1700m). Andes from s Táchira to n Mérida (*colombiana*). Colombia s in Andes to Tierra del Fuego.
Note: Nearest affinities possibly with New World steamerducks (*Tachyeres*) and New Zealand's Blue Duck (*Hymenolaimus malacorhynchos*)[358].

Anus

Largest waterfowl genus; very social; float high in water, feed by dabbling on water surface, tipping up (seldom dive), or grazing; occur mostly in shallow freshwater; sprint directly into air; walk well on land; colorful speculum on secondaries; n spp. all highly migratory.

Andean Teal   PLATE 3
Anas andium   Pato Serrano
Identification: 15–17″ (38–43cm). 405g. Small, brown, ♀-plumaged duck of high-Andean lakes. Heavily speckled. *Bill blue gray.* Ad.: head buffy brown densely dotted brown, above dark brown with pale edgings (looks scaly); *chest and sides buff white conspic. spotted brown*, lower underparts uniform brownish gray. In flight speculum mostly iridescent black (inner part green) bordered buffy rufous in front, buffy white behind. Imm.: less spotted.
Sim. species: Small size, blue gray bill, and speckling on chest are good marks for either sex. ♀ Blue-winged Teal differs in light blue upper wing coverts.
Voice: ♂ a mellow whistle; ♀ a cackle[67].
Behavior: A rather wary but social little duck that occurs in prs. when breeding, otherwise in families or small groups of up to a few dozen on highland lagoons or along lakeshores. Tips up to feed in shal-

low water and springs directly into air when flushed. Pairing may be permanent (?) or semipermanent. Nest on gd. in marshy paramo, small isl. on lake, or hole in bank, but usually near water; sometimes several nest close together. Eggs 5–8, creamy white; incubated by ♀; breeds at least Mar–Sep[206].
Status and habitat: Fairly common resident in small nos. on ponds and lakes, or around wet, boggy areas in paramo. Move readily (seasonally?) between highel. lakes.

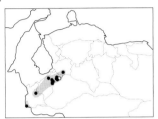

Range: 3200–3800m (sight to 3000m). Andes from s Táchira (Páramo de Tamá) n to Niquitao, Trujillo (*altipetens*). Andes of Colombia and Ecuador.
Note: Does not incl. Speckled Teal (*A. flavirostris*) of n Peru s to Tierra del Fuego.

American Wigeon
Anas americana   Pato Calvo
Identification: 17–20″ (43–51cm). 750g. Bill blue gray. ♂: *crown white* with small green mask behind eyes; throat and neck buff speckled black (look gray at a distance), otherwise above brown, chest and flanks pinkish brown, central underparts white; *prom. white flank patch in front of black rear end.* ♀: mostly reddish brown with *grayish head and neck*, below like ♂ but duller. In flight both show *conspic. white wing coverts* (above and below) and green speculum.
Sim. species: ♂ easily told by white cap; in flight Blue-winged and Cinnamon teals and Northern Shoveler have sim. pale wing patches. Andean Teal lacks white wing-covert patch.
Voice: ♂ a clear, piercing, whistled *wheeooo* in flight; ♀ a low growled *krrr* as it flushes[371].
Behavior: A dabbler that is wary and highly social away from breeding gds. In Venez. most often found assoc. with other n migrant waterfowl.
Status and habitat: Known from a leg-band recovery in Apr at Lago de Maracaibo[9]. An irreg. n winter visitant to Chichiriviche, Falcón, with sight recs. 14 Jan–

14 Mar of 2–2000 or more almost annually in salt and brackish water lagoons (many observers) since first reported there in Jan 1970 by P. Alden. Also reported from Islas Los Roques[347]. In Colombia there are more recs. from inland than on coast.

Range: NW Zulia; e Falcón (several sightings); inland in Carabobo (sight, Lago de Valencia); Islas Los Roques (sight). Breeds in nw N Amer.; winters from s and coastal US s to n Colombia and W Indies. Trinidad.

White-cheeked Pintail   PLATE 3
Anas bahamensis   Pato Malibú
Identification: 16–18″ (41–46cm). 480g. Bill blue gray, *base of maxilla red*. A slender brown duck with *bold white cheeks and throat*. Mainly fulvous brown, crown and hindneck browner and *sharply contrasting with white sides of head, throat, and foreneck*; underparts speckled black; tail rather pointed, pale buff. In flight shows narrow green speculum bordered buff and *pale rear end contrasting with darker back*.
Sim. species: White cheeks are the mark.
Voice: Usually quiet. ♂ a low whistle, ♀ a soft ser. of quacks.
Behavior: Most often seen in prs. or small groups up to about 12 (very rarely to 100) that dabble and tip up in shallow water or rest on mudflats. During n winter often assoc. with migrant ducks. Eats mostly seeds, a few insects. Nest in W Indies concealed in grass near or under mangrove root; 5–12 buff eggs[65]; may breed Jun–Dec in Venez. (info. scanty); Aug–Nov in Trinidad and Tobago[206].
Status and habitat: Uncommon resident (breeder?) and wanderer in small nos. in brackish water, tidal flats, and mangroves, infreq. inland on freshwater ponds and sloughs near coast. May be resident yr-round at Chichiriviche, Falcón, but not always reliably found there.

Range: Prob. entire Carib. coast; rec. from n Falcón (San Juan de Los Cayos) and Aragua e to Anzoátequi (Laguna de Unare) and Sucre (Cumaná; sight e of Carupano—C. Parrish); Islas Los Roques (sight); Isla Margarita (*bahamensis*). Bahamas, s Texas, and s Florida (rare), W Indies, Netherlands Antilles, most of coastal S Amer. (w coast only from s Ecuador to Chile); nw Argentina and e Brazil s to Patagonia. Galápagos Isls.
Note: Also known as Bahama Pintail.

Northern Pintail
Anas acuta   Pato Rabudo
Identification: 22–26″ (56–66cm). 975g. Fairly large, slim duck with long slender neck and *long pointed tail with needlelike central tail feathers* (much shorter in ♀). Bill gray. ♂: head and hindneck brown, *underparts white extending up on foreneck to point behind eye*; upperparts and sides gray; creamy white patch on flanks in front of black rear end. ♀: head buffy brown, almost unmarked, otherwise all brown, lighter below, mottled and spotted dark brown throughout. In flight both sexes show green speculum bordered white behind.
Sim. species: Undistinguished ♀'s best marks are size (larger than most allies), *pointed tail*, and company she keeps. Cf. several smaller ♀ teal, and Northern Shoveler.
Behavior: A fast-flying, streamlined, highly social duck. Look for it among large flocks of migratory ducks.
Status and habitat: Very rare or accidental. Known from 1 old specimen in Nov from Carabobo (El Paíto) and from wings of 2 (also old) from Anzoátegui (Mesa de Guanipa). Colombian recs. (none recent) are from both fresh and brackish water.

Range: Breeds throughout N Hemisphere; winters s in New World, rarely to n Colombia (*acuta*); accidental in Guyana and Suriname.

Blue-winged Teal   PLATE 3
Anas discors   Barraquete Aliazul
Identification: 14–16″ (36–41cm). 370g. Bill gray; eyes dark. ♂: head blue gray, crown dusky with *narrow white "quarter moon" crescent across foreface*; otherwise mainly brown, underparts paler and thickly spotted blackish; white rear flank patch in front of black rear end. ♀: all buffy brown spotted and mottled dark brown; faint pale loral patch; cap and narrow line through eyes dusky. In flight both sexes show *large pale blue patch on front of wing* and small green speculum.
Sim. species: Breeding-plumage ♂ distinctive but crescent often faint on early-arriving migrants. In flight cf. Northern Shoveler and Cinnamon Teal, both also with blue wing patches. ♀ barely separable from ♀ Cinnamon Teal but latter is darker, has decidedly larger and more spatulate bill, more sloping forehead, and even fainter pale loral spot and eyeline. Andean Teal lacks blue shoulders.
Voice: ♂ a thin whistled *whuee*, often doubled; ♀ a high-pitched quack.

Behavior: A small speedy flier given to some twisting and turning in flight. Very social, typically found in compact small to moderate-sized flocks (up to a few hundred) with ♀-plumaged birds predominating, and often with other spp. of ducks. Dabbles and tips up to feed, more at night than by day.

Status and habitat: Commonest and most widespread migrant and n winter resident duck in Venez., early Sep–early May (rarely to Jun), in both coastal estuaries and brackish lagoons, and inland in freshwater marshes and ponds. Up to 20,000 may winter at Chichiriviche, Falcón; large concentrations in wetlands of Apure, Portuguesa, and Guárico, smaller nos. e to e Anzoátegui; 1 ♂ examined in Jun[186].

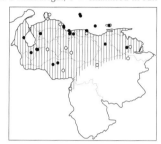

Range: To 3600m. Throughout n of Orinoco; Islas Margarita, La Tortuga, and Los Roques; s of Orinoco from nw Amazonas and n Bolívar (sightings, lower Río Caura; Upata) e to Delta Amacuro (sight, Tucupita). Breeds in N Amer.; winters from s US to n S Amer., rarely to c Argentina and Uruguay.

Cinnamon Teal

Anas cyanoptera   Barraquete Colorado

Identification: 15–17″ (38–43cm). 390g. Rare migrant. Bill large and blackish; *eyes yellow to red* (♂) or dark (♀). *Mostly reddish chestnut*, back streaked blackish, underparts unmarked; rear end black. ♀: very sim. to ♀ Blue-winged Teal (see). In flight both show blue shoulder patch and green speculum.

Sim. species: Breeding ♂♂ easily told; non-breeding plumaged ♂♂ from ♀ Blue-winged Teal by eye color (always red or yellow); either sex by longer and more spatulate bill, flatter forehead, somewhat warmer rufous tone to plumage, and more uniform head pattern (loral spot and eyeline faint or obscured by darker mottling). N Amer. migrants acquire breeding dress by Dec or Jan.

Behavior: Social but usually alone or in small groups (not large flocks) in S Amer. Otherwise much like Blue-winged Teal.

Status and habitat: Accidental. Known from 1 imm. ♂ (migrant from N Amer.) taken in Oct on Páramo Conejos, Mérida. Resident subsp. (*borreroi*), known from as close as Boyacá, Colombia, is as yet unrec. in Venez.

Range: Once at 4000m. Mérida (*septentrionalium*). Breeds in w N Amer. s to c Mexico, spottily to Colombia; generally in Andes from c Peru southward, and from se Brazil to Tierra del Fuego; n and s pops. migratory, n ones casually s to n S Amer.

Nothern Shoveler

Anas clypeata   Pato Cuchareta

Identification: 17–20″ (43–51cm). 630g. *Long spatulate bill* imparts "top-heavy" look in flight. ♂: *head and neck glossy bottle green*, center of back black, *chest and breast white*, belly and sides chestnut, white patch on rear flank. ♀: mottled brownish. In flight both sexes show *large light blue patch on front of wing* and small green speculum.

Sim. species: Best mark for either sex is "spoonbill." Looks long necked and short tailed in flight, as if wings placed too far to rear of body. Shares blue wing patches with Blue-winged and Cinnamon teals.

Behavior: A highly social dabbling duck, most often seen in flocks of its own or with other spp., where sifts in shallow water. Floats low in water with long bill angled down. Flight is fast and direct.

Status and habitat: Rare and irreg. winter visitant from N Amer. to shallow fresh- and saltwater habitats. One specimen (Coleccíon. PROFAUNA) from Mirimire, Falcón (M. Lentino). Rec. 15 Jan–14 Mar; at least 8 sight recs. of flocks of 8–40 at Chichiriviche, Falcón, as follows: 11 seen 11 Mar 1970 (P. Alden); 8 ♀-plumaged birds 15 Jan 1976 (P. Alden); ca. 40 on 6 Mar 1976 (C. Parrish); 30 on 14 Mar 1981 (R. Ridgely and A. Keith); 18 on 18 Feb 1987 (M. Van Beirs); flocks seen twice in Feb 1988 (J. Pierson); ca. 25 seen at Refugio Curari (near Mirimire), Falcón, 24 Jan 1993 (P. Boesman); and 20–21 Feb 1993[64]. Also 3–4 observed (no details) ca. 1982 in Falcón[206]. In n Colombia reported Oct—Mar.

Range: To 100m. E Falcón (Mirimire to Chichiriviche); Islas Los Roques[347]. Breeds in n part of N Hemisphere; in New World winters s to n Colombia, occas. Venez.

Southern Pochard   Illus. p. 202

Netta erythrophthalma   Pato Negro

Identification: 19–20″ (48–51cm). 800g. Rather large dark duck with *long blue gray bill* and slight peak to

Southern Pochard (top) (male left, female right), Lesser Scaup (bottom) (male left, female right)

crown; *eyes red* (♂) or brown (♀). ♂ *all dark*; upperparts and wings very dark brown, head, neck, and most of underparts black somewhat glossed purple, *sides and flanks dark chestnut*. ♀: uniform dark brown with white under tail coverts; *white patch at base of bill and on throat, the white curving up behind eyes to form a broken crescent*. In flight rather long necked; both sexes with conspic. white band (from above) across base of flight feathers.
Sim. species: No other ♂ duck in Venez. is so dark. Cf. ♂ Lesser Scaup which is white on sides; also ♂ Andean Duck and very rare Ring-necked Duck. Patchy-faced ♀ is nearest ♀ Lesser Scaup, but latter has white confined to area around bill. Also cf. small ♀ Brazilian Teal.
Behavior: Not well known in S Amer. Reported in prs. and groups up to 7–10 in small bodies of water[107]. Floats high in water when resting, lower and with tail down when feeding. Patters across water to get airborne. Feeds by diving or up-ending, mostly for seeds, plant matter, and a few insects. In Africa (apparently also in S Amer.) undertakes extensive seasonal movements; nest on gd., close or relatively far from water. ♂ with large testis, Jul, Payara, Portuguesa; prob. breeds in rainy season as most recent recs. are during this period[108].
Status and habitat: Very rare, local, and in serious decline. Freshwater marshes, lagoons, and esp. rice fields. Resident (seasonal?) or irreg. visitant. Possibly undertakes reg. seasonal migrations (mostly seen 1st half of rainy season). Formerly relatively common in vicinity of Lago de Valencia (Carabobo) and near Chichiriviche, Falcón[201]. Observed 4 times early May–Sep 1977 and 1978 in rice farms in Portuguesa[108]; other recs. incl. several sightings (early 1980s) near Calabozo, Guárico (C. Parrish); 1 near Pto. de Nutrias, Barinas, Jun 1994 (D. Ascanio); sight at Módulo Experimental de la UNELLEZ, w of Mantecal near La

Yé (C. Casler) and at nearby Hato Cedral[206]. Reasons for decline and rarity are unknown.

Range: To 500m. Zulia (Lagunillas), e Falcón (Chichiriviche); w Apure (sight), Barinas (sight), Portuguesa, s Carabobo, s Aragua (Lago de Valencia), and Calabozo, Guárico (*erythrophthalma*). Spottily from Venez. to s Chile, most recs. in or near Andes; also e Brazil. E and s Africa.

Lesser Scaup   Illus. above
Aythya affinis   Pato Zambullidor del Norte
Identification: 15–18″ (38–46cm). 820g. Bill bluish, slightly curved throughout length; eyes yellow (♂) or dark (♀). A short-bodied diving duck. ♂: head, neck, and chest black (head glossed purple, but this hard to see), rearcrown shows distinct "bump" or peak; otherwise *back gray, sides white*, rear end black. ♀: all brown with distinct *white patch encircling base of bill*. In flight both sexes show *white band on secondaries*, fading to gray on inner primaries.
Sim. species: ♂ is black on each end and white in middle. See ♂ Ring-necked Duck and Southern Pochard. ♀ easily picked out by white encircling bill.
Behavior: Individuals or small flocks occur alone or with other waterfowl. Favors open, deeper freshwater where dives to feed (N Amer.) on aquatic plants, in-

sects, fish, and mollusks. Patters across water to get airborne.

Status and habitat: Vagrant to Venez. Rec. early Dec–mid Mar, mostly to freshwater ponds and lakes with smaller no. of recs. along coast. There are at least 4 recs. from Laguna Mucubají, Mérida (3600m), as follows: 22 Jan 1973 (P. Alden); date? (C. Parrish); 1 Jan 1991 (P. Boesman); 20 Feb 1994 (R. Behrstock).

Range: To ca. 400m (sight to 3600m). Spottily along Carib. coast from e Falcón (San Juan de Los Cayos, Mirimire) to Aragua, e Miranda, Anzoátegui (coast and inland), and Monagas; Mérida Andes (sightings, Laguna Mucubají); Isla Margarita. Breeds in nw N Amer.; winters from e and c US to n Colombia, accidental to w Ecuador and Suriname. Trinidad.

Ring-necked Duck
Aythya collaris   Pato Zambullidor de Collar
Identification: 15–18″ (38–46cm). 705g. Bill blue gray with *white ring* and black nail; eyes yellow (♂) or dark (♀). Distinct "bump" or peak to rearcrown. Both sexes resemble respective sex of Lesser Scaup. ♂: head, chest, *entire back*, and rear end black, sides white. ♀: mainly brown, darker on back; *narrow white area almost encircling bill* (forehead usually dark), vague broken white eyering and whitish postocular streak. In flight both sexes show grayish band on secondaries.
Sim. species: Black back separates ♂ from ♂ Lesser Scaup. First-winter ♂♂ have brownish sides and look much like ♂ Southern Pochard but differ in yellow eyes, ring on bill, and chunkier shape (incl. shorter bill). ♀ is nearest ♀ Lesser Scaup but shows much less white.
Status and habitat: Accidental. Known from 3 recs.: an ad. ♀ taken 6 Dec 1952 at El Paíto (near Valencia), Carabobo; 1 bird on Isla Margarita; and 1 sight (?), Embalse Suata, Aragua.

Range: Breeds in n N Amer.; winters from US s to Panama and in W Indies.

Brazilian Teal
PLATE 3
Amazonetta brasiliensis   Pato Brasileño
Identification: 14–16″ (36–41cm). 470g. Small, brownish duck with *raspberry red bill and legs* (*bill dark blue gray to dusky*—♀). ♂: mostly brown, crown and hindneck darker with *conspic. gray area on rear cheeks and sides of upper neck*; chest warm rufescent brown; rump and tail black, pale brown band across rump; sides speckled black. ♀: sim. but with large white spot on sides of forecrown, behind eye, at base of bill, and on throat. In flight both sexes show *brilliant metallic black and green wings* (upper surface) with *triangle of white on axillaries and inner secondaries*. Pale rump ring is conspic. as bird flies directly away.
Sim. species: Not likely confused if seen well. Good marks for hen-plumaged ♂♂ are reddish bill and pale sides of head. If in doubt, flush this little brown duck and note brilliant wings. ♀'s head more spotted than that of larger Southern Pochard.
Voice: In flight ♂ (?) gives a reedy whistled *pueep-pueep-pueep* or *tuwee* or *tuu-ree* with shrill quality; ♀ a low raspy or grunty *grak* or *unk*.
Behavior: Prs. or groups of up to ca. 6, rarely more, are confiding as they dabble in shallow water or loaf on shore. Often loosely assoc. with other waterbirds such as ibises, egrets, and whistling-ducks. Flight is fast and low. Eats mostly seeds (*Sagittaria, Brachiaria, Luziola, Panicum,* and *Paspalum*) supplemented by invertebrates, esp. beetles, in dry season[373], taken by dipping head below water. Small flocks break up at onset of rainy season when breeding begins. May form permanent pr. bonds; the few nests reported have been on gd. near water (1 nest 2.5m up in abandoned blackbird nest in tree); ca. 6–8 white eggs[206,373].
Status and habitat: Common resident in small nos. in shallow ponds, marshes, flooded fields, and damp grass in wetter southern portions of llanos, esp. Apure and Barinas. There are local seasonal movements. A few austral birds may reach Venez. during austral winter[53].

Range: To 300m. Río Apure and its tributaries in Táchira, Apure, Barinas, c Cojedes (rare), and Guárico; sight in e Falcón[60]; mid. Orinoco from mouth of Río Meta e to Ciudad Bolívar (*brasiliensis*); prob. n Amazonas. E Colombia to Guyana; e Bolivia and s Brazil s to c Argentina.
Note: Also called Brazilian Duck[403].

Masked Duck   PLATE 3
Nomonyx dominicus   Patico Enmascarado
Identification: 12–14″ (30.5–36cm). 365g. Chunky
with bright blue bill (duller—♀) and narrow blue
eyering; stiff spiky tail cocked up or depressed.
Breeding-plumage ♂: forepart of head black, *rest of
body dark rufous chestnut*, belly paler, back and sides
speckled with black. ♀ and nonbreeding ♂: above
dark brown, sides of head buffy white with *dusky
stripe through eye, another below eye*; underparts
buffy white mottled dark brown. In flight both sexes
show *large white patch on rear of wing*.
Sim. species: ♀-plumaged birds more often seen than
breeding ♂♂, but "double-striped" face always diagnostic.
Voice: Displaying ♂♂ spread cocked tail, raise head,
thrust bill forward, and inflate neck as utter a soft,
throaty, pigeonlike *ouu-goo-goo-ouu*; several ♂♂ and
♀♀ may be present during courtship calling and displays.
Behavior: Rather reclusive and inconspic., everywhere occurring in prs. or small loosely assoc. colonies of its own. Often confiding. Floats rather low in
water and tends to stay hidden in reeds, marsh vegetation, and water lilies. Feeds mainly by diving for
vegetable matter. Springs directly into air, but often
reluctant to do so, instead escaping by hiding in tall
vegetation. Flies well with fast buzzy wing beats,
then rears up and splashes down heavily. Rather sedentary, but seasonal and/or periodic dispersal movements occur (often after several yr of residence), although these movements are not well documented.
Nest a bowl of reeds just above water in marsh; 3–4
buffy white eggs with granular shells[175].
Status and habitat: Somewhat spotty or local resident in freshwater marshes, small ponds with dense
reeds, emergent vegetation (esp. water lilies and
water hyacinth), and rice fields. Groups may reside
permanently at some lagoons for yrs. Perhaps resident at Hato Cedral, Apure, but nos. erratic and seasonal or irreg. movements likely.

Range: To 2100m. Locally throughout n of Orinoco
and in e Bolívar (El Palmar to Río Icabarú); no recs.
Delta Amacuro. S Texas and Mexico to Chile and s
Argentina. W Indies; Trinidad.
Note: Often placed in genus *Oxyura*[359].

PHOENICOPTERIFORMES

Phoenicopteridae: Flamingos
Flamencos o Tococos

Flamingos are a small family with species scattered
in discontinuous populations in both the New and
Old Worlds. All show a distinct preference for brackish or alkaline water. They are pinkish wading birds
with extraordinarily long necks, long stiltlike legs,
and short webbed toes. Their remarkable lamellate
bill is thick and bends sharply downward at the mid-
point. When feeding, the bill is held in an inverted
position with the head immersed in shallow water.
Food, obtained by sifting and straining water and
mud, is mostly minute crustaceans, algae, diatoms,
saltfly larvae, and occasionally small fish.

American Flamingo   PLATE 4
Phoenicopterus ruber   Flamenco o Tococo
Identification: 40–48″ (102–122cm). 3kg. *Pink wader
on stilts*. Thick boomerang-shaped bill pink with
black tip. *Extraordinarily long pink legs. Plumage rosy
pink* (intensity varies) *with black flight feathers* (conspic. in flight, concealed at rest); eyes yellow. Imm.:
dull grayish white, upperparts and flight feathers
brownish.
Sim. species: Nothing quite like it. See Roseate
Spoonbill. In flight flamingo's wings look too small
for size of bird (wingspan is barely a third of bird's
total length).
Voice: Rather noisy. A variety of gooselike honking
notes on different pitches in flight; at other times an
incessantly repeated, gabbling *hu-HU-hu*.
Behavior: Breeds, forages, and loafs in groups of
varying size, often numbering in 1000s, although individuals may wander alone. When feeding wades actively in shallow water for small mollusks or sifts
plankton through bill. Typically somewhat wary.
Flight is swift and strong with fast steady wing beats,
neck and legs fully outstretched. Nest a truncated
cone of mud with saucerlike top; at Los Olivos,
Zulia, breeds (up to twice) early Feb–late Jul when
water levels are favorable (not every yr); in Bonaire
some breeding activity yr-round; 1 egg. Flightless
young pullets up to 2.5 months old gather in crèches
of up to 3000 birds or more. Ads. flightless for a few
wk each yr during molt.
Status and habitat: Large numbers (250–5000) concentrate locally on coast of Zulia (Paraguaipoa) and
Falcón (Paraguaná Pen.; San José de La Costa; near
Chichiriviche). Nos. peak Aug–Oct at Chichiriviche.
Breeders in Bonaire commute to Venez. coast to
feed. Also often in nos. at Boca de Uchire, Anzoátegui; and at Araya Pen., Sucre[231]. Rare inland (1 juv.
at Hato Cedral, 1 at Hato El Frio, Apure, 1994; also
w Lara). Formerly bred on Isla La Orchila (ca. 50
nests in 1952). Large colony with max. 4015 nests
and 3000+ pullets rediscovered 20 May 1987 at Ciénaga de Los Olivitos, Zulia (first reported in 1834),
and breeding there through 1989[106] and in Aug 2000

(D. Ascanio). Human predation on eggs and young, pollution, and high storm tides (at nests) are threats.

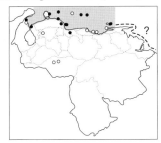

Range: Carib. coast from Zulia locally e to Sucre and inland near coast; a few may reach Orinoco Delta (recs.?); Islas Margarita (Laguna de la Restinga), La Orchila, Los Roques, and Las Aves (*ruber*); accidental inland (Lara and w Apure). Presently known to breed at only 6 major colonies in W Hemisphere (Bahamas; Cuba; Yucatán Pen., Mexico; Bonaire; Galápagos; Isls.; w Venezuela); formerly bred in ne Colombia (presently?) and elsewhere; disperses across Greater Antilles; very local from coastal ne Colombia to ne Brazil; Galápagos Isls. Rarely to Gulf coast of US.

CICONIIFORMES

Ardeidae: Herons, Egrets, and Bitterns

Garzas

Members of this well-known and worldwide family are characterized by long thin necks, usually a straight pointed bill, and concealed powder down. Most are found in or near fresh or salt water where they stand or wait patiently, or wade in shallow water for fish and other aquatic animals. Two Venezuelan species are regularly found in dry grassy areas. Many herons roost and nest communally, often in mixed-species heronries. Tiger-herons, bitterns, the *Butorides* herons, and perhaps a few others nest solitarily or in small loose groups. Recent studies have realigned some taxa in Ardeidae. The present taxonomy follows McCracken and Sheldon[388]. There are several important references on the family[148,239,240].

Botaurus

Large, streaky brown bitterns; legs short; wings somewhat pointed; "freeze" in classic upright posture when alarmed.

Pinnated Bittern   PLATE 5
Botaurus pinnatus   Mirasol
Identification: 25–29″ (64–74cm). *Looks like an imm. tiger-heron, but back is streaked.* Eyes and lores yellow; bill and legs greenish yellow. Forecrown dark brown, hindcrown and sides and back of neck buff *narrowly* and evenly barred black; *rest of upperparts buff streaked and variegated blackish*; throat white, foreneck and underparts buffy white streaked light brown; *flight feathers blackish* (strong contrast in flight), *inner primaries and secondaries broadly tipped buff.* In flight pale band on tip of secondaries contrasts with blackish flight feathers. Imm.: paler; barring on head and neck more obscure.
Sim. species: From imm. tiger-herons by streaked (not barred) wings and back, finer barring on hindneck, and *uniformly blackish* (not barred) flight feathers; look for pale band on trailing edge of wing. If in doubt, flush bird. Cf. imm. night-herons which have more rounded and uniform wings and never any barring.
Voice: Infreq. hd. song, produced during a retching spasm, is much like deep, rhythmic, pumping *oong-ka-choonk* of American Bittern (*B. lentiginosus*) but a little higher and less resonant. Song not loud but far carrying; mostly at dawn and dusk.
Behavior: Solitary and secretive in tall marsh vegetation; usually attempts to escape notice by "freezing" with bill pointed skyward, or by crouching, but also may slowly creep away. Flushes only at last moment, flies slowly, and unlike tiger-herons, rarely or never alights in trees. Forages by waiting patiently and ambushing small aquatic prey and rodents. Shallow rush-stem platform nest just above water in marsh; 2–3 olive eggs[175,706].
Status and habitat: Local in brackish and freshwater marshes and taller emergent vegetation in drainage ditches, lagoons, flooded pastures, and rice fields. Resident but shows marked seasonal movements with nos. becoming increasingly concentrated in shrinking wetlands in dry season, e.g., at Hato Cedral, Apure, where commonest Jan–Apr, and in coastal areas such as Chichiriviche, Falcón (most recs. Jan–Mar). Disperses in wet season; breeds Jul–Oct in Trinidad[175].

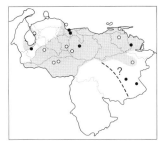

Range: To ca. 400m. Maracaibo Basin of Zulia and w Mérida; spottily e of Andes from w Apure (sight), w Barinas, s Cojedes (sight) e across llanos to e Monagas (Maturín)[60], Delta Amacuro, ne Bolívar (sight, Tumeremo), and se Bolívar (Gran Sabana); e Falcón (sight, Chichiriviche), occas. n Aragua (*pinnatus*). Se

Mexico to Costa Rica; Colombia and w Ecuador to the Guianas; s of Amazon Basin from s Brazil to n Argentina and Uruguay.

Ixobrychus

Small, tawny bitterns; slight crest; tibia feathered; marshes; notably secretive.

Least Bittern   PLATE 5
Ixobrychus exilis   Garza Enana
Identification: 10–11″ (25–28cm). 85g. Bill dusky above, yellowish below; eyes yellow; legs brownish yellowish. *Crown and entire back and tail black* with narrow buff stripe ("suspender") on each side of back; *hindneck and sides of head rufous*, foreneck and underparts buffy white, *shoulders tawny buff* (conspic., esp. in flight), *flight feathers rufous*. ♀: sim. but crown and back dark chestnut brown; a few black shaft streaks on underparts. Imm.: like ♀ but somewhat scaled above (feathers buff-edged) and streaked below.
Sim. species: See Stripe-backed Bittern and Zigzag Heron.
Voice: In ne Monagas a low, almost guttural, cooing, *gruua* or (*cuuua*), rather like call of Zigzag Heron but lower pitched, repeated several times a min. In comparison, Zigzag's call sounds forced or strained. Also reported (*erythromelas*, in Brazil) a deep *rro-rro-rro* and croaking *raaahb* and *gheh-eh*[611].
Behavior: Shy, solitary, and inconspic., and like other bitterns, when closely approached usually attempts to hide by "freezing" in reeds with elongated neck and bill pointing skyward. Runs or climbs among reeds and flushes reluctantly, but flies well, albeit in rather bewildered, loose-jointed manner, before dropping back into cover. Food incls. small fish, other small vertebrates, and aquatic insects. Trinidad breeding Jul–Oct; twig nest low in reeds or mangroves; 3 buffy white eggs[175].
Status and habitat: Fairly common resident very locally in emergent vegetation, incl. cattails, rushes, and large masses of water hyacinth, in freshwater marshes in llanos. Seasonal movements need documentation; n migrants possible.

Range: To ca. 300m. Marshes spottily throughout s to n Bolívar. Specimens from s Zulia (Laguna Estrella), e Guárico (Santa María de Ipire), and e Miranda (Río Chico)(*erythromelas*); sightings from w Apure (Mar–Jun, Hato Cedral; Hato El Frio[259]), s Cojedes,

Carabobo (Laguna Guataparo), e Monagas[60], ne Bolívar (Feb, El Palmar[259]), and Delta Amacuro[343]. Breeds from N Amer. to ne Argentina and se Brazil. N and s pops. migratory.

Stripe-backed Bittern   PLATE 5
Ixobrychus involucris   Garza Enana Amarilla
Identification: 12–13″ (30.5–33cm). 85g. Tiny bittern. Bill yellowish green; eyes yellow; legs pale green. Above mostly ochraceous to sandy buff; *broad coronal stripe black; back boldly striped black, ochre, and buff*; throat white, rest of underparts buff (paler than above) more or less streaked with brown and white; bend of wing rufous chestnut, shoulders and wing coverts pale sandy buff (not in strong contrast with back), *flight feathers black with broad rufous tips*; pectoral tufts mixed black and dark rufous.
Sim. species: Easily confused with Least Bittern which has solid black (♂) or chestnut (♀) back, rufous sides of head and neck. In flight Least shows conspic. pale tawny shoulder patch and *rufous* flight feathers (not mostly black tipped rufous). Both spp. flush from marsh with slower, more labored wing beats than rails. Also cf. Zigzag Heron.
Voice: Call, from concealment, 4 low, abrupt *huu* notes (lower pitched than those of Least Bittern), ca. 1 note/1.5 sec; also a low, slowly gargled *g'u'u'u'a'a*, both calls given by day or night.
Behavior: Much like Least Bittern.
Status and habitat: Uncommon to locally fairly common but easily overlooked resident; prob. also a local or short-distant migrant. Cattails (*Typhus*) and other emergent marsh vegetation in both fresh and brackish water, rice fields and irrigation ditches. Rec. almost all months Jan–Nov but recs. too few and scattered to establish seasonal movements (if any). Breeds Jul–Sep in Trinidad[175]. Has been seen with some reg. near mouth of Río Tocuyo, Falcón. At least formerly quite numerous (many specimens) at Embalse de Suata, s Aragua.

Range: To 500m. W Apure (many sight recs.[259]), w Barinas (sight, s of Barinas—P. Alden), and Portuguesa n to e Falcón (sight[259]), nw and s Carabobo, n and s Aragua, and Distr. Federal. Prob. more widespread in llanos. N pop. breeds from e Colombia to Trinidad, Guyana, and Suriname; s pop. from se Bolivia and c Chile e to se Brazil and c Argentina; e Peru (sight). Southernmost breeders (Argentina) migratory, but no evidence of movement between n and s groups.

Zebrilus

Diminutive, pocket-sized heron; chunky; bull headed but bill and feet small; dark plumage; tibia feathered; rare and never seen often enough.

Zigzag Heron   PLATE 5
Zebrilus undulatus   Garza Cebra
Identification: 12–13″ (30.5–33cm). 125g. *Tiny dark-backed heron with chunky shape.* Bill blackish (ad.) or yellowish green (juv.); eyes yellow; bare loral skin dark gray; legs dull yellowish green. Crown and bushy occipital crest black, *sides of head and upperparts blackish finely barred with narrow wavy buff lines*; flight feathers and tail unbarred black; *below buff to ochraceous densely vermiculated black on foreneck and chest* (♂ more heavily marked than ♀), vaguely on lower underparts; under wing coverts white. Imm. sim. *but strongly rufous on foreparts*; forecrown and ocular area chestnut, rest of upperparts black finely barred with wavy rufous buff bars; sides of head, neck, and sometimes breast rufous chestnut to rufous buff, with or without scattered wavy black bars (usually none—♀) on throat and chest; bill and legs yellowish green.
Sim. species: Most likely confused with Least or Stripe-backed bitterns which are sim. in size; both *lack* fine barring and show *contrasting buff patches on wings*. Also cf. Striated Heron.
Voice: Call of ad. a low, hollow, hooting or grunting *oooop*, singly or up to 7–8 in ser. at rate of ca. 1/sec or less (recalls Least Bittern); also a nasal, slightly higher pitched *ahnnn*. Calls with bill pointed upward slightly.
Behavior: Solitary and secretive, calling from a concealed or partly concealed perch ca. 1–3m up, but forages on gd., esp. in moist soil and leaf litter at wet places inside forest or along wooded streams[143]. Moves through vegetation with springy hops, and late in evening may venture into small, partially open areas along streams. Tends to perch somewhat hunched over, and if disturbed, twitches tail to side or up. Best located by listening for call along small, forest-lined creeks at dusk. Imm. (rufous) birds may behave territorially. Nest in Ecuador a shallow twiggy platform in or at edge of clump of thorny *Bactris* palms; 1–3m up over water; 1 white egg; downy young yellowish cream to whitish[168].
Status and habitat: Very local resident (easily overlooked). Increasing no. of recs. at Junglaven in Amazonas, in Delta Amacuro, and in llanos suggest sp. may be patchy in distrib. but locally fairly common. First rec. at Hato Piñero, 24 Feb 1993 (K. Zimmer and D. Wolf); at Hato Cedral Aug 1996 (G. Rodríguez). Favors dense, shady vegetation along forested streams, lagoons, and ponds; also wet areas inside gallery forest and seasonally flooded or perennial swamp forest.
Range: To 800m. N of Orinoco in s Cojedes (sight), w Apure (sight), Monagas (sight, Caripito), and Delta Amacuro (several areas); s of Orinoco in Amazonas (sight, Junglaven; El Carmen; San Carlos de Río

Negro) and n Bolívar (lower and mid. Río Caura; Río Paragua s to Salto Guaiquinima; near Ciudad Bolívar). Spottily from se Colombia to n Bolivia, Paraguay, Amaz. Brazil, and the Guianas.

Tigrisoma

Distinctive buff- and black-barred imm. plumage (the "tiger" in English name); neck feathers loose and fluffy, imparting massive look to long neck; short legs; behavior and habits bridge those of herons and bitterns; nest solitarily.

Rufescent Tiger-Heron   PLATE 5
Tigrisoma lineatum   Pájaro Vaco
Identification: 26–30″ (66–76cm). 840g. Long thick neck. Stout yellowish bill; eyes and bare loral area yellow; narrow loral line dusky; legs dull green. *Head, neck, and chest deep reddish chestnut*; median white stripe on foreneck, rest of underparts buffy brown, flanks narrowly banded black and white; back, wings, and tail buffy yellowish brown vermiculated black (has gray look at a distance). Imm.: *mainly bright cinnamon buff coarsely and thickly barred with black*; throat, median underparts, and belly whitish; tail black narrowly banded white; blackish flight feathers tipped white from above, boldly barred black and white below; bill somewhat dusky above, orangish yellow below; legs very pale greenish white. Attains ad. plumage in 4–5 yrs.
Sim. species: Slightly smaller ad. Fasciated Tiger-Heron has mainly slate gray neck (not rufous chestnut), but confusion unlikely as the 2 spp. almost never overlap in habitat (Fasciated only along fast-flowing foothill rivers). Imm.: very like imm. Fasciated Tiger-Heron. Latter differs in *shorter, thicker bill* and less barring on flanks (barring not obvious even in hand), but the two doubtfully separable in field. Also see Pinnated Bittern, easily confused with imm. tiger-heron, esp. in flight.
Voice: Song, often hd. at odd intervals, esp. at dusk and even at night, a low, rhythmic ser. of muffled barks, *WOO-HOO, WOO-Hoo, Wóo-hoo, wóo-hoo, wóo-hoo, wóo-hoo, wú-hu*, slowing and decreasing in volume at end; sometimes just *huu-huu-huu-huu . . .* (10 notes or so), winding down in pitch and tempo. Flushes off with guttural *gwalk* alarm or ser. of rough *uuk-uuk-uuk-uuk-uuk . . .* notes, louder and more frantic at end.

Behavior: In wooded areas rather furtive and inconspic., customarily freezing without elevating bill when disturbed, or flushing up into high branches and cover. In llanos, however, forages in open, often far from trees or cover, and very conspic. Everywhere solitary, hunting alone by standing patiently in shallow water (sometimes belly deep), then striking with quick thrust of bill for small vertebrates and invertebrates. Flight is labored. Breeds Jul–Sep in Guárico; frail stick platform high in tree; nest alone or up to 13 nests together[734]; 1 bluish white egg blotched pale violet[253].

Status and habitat: Resident. Banks of forest streams, vegetation-choked lagoons, and freshwater ponds and lakes in forested or open terrain. Thinly spread and easily overlooked in forested areas. Very common and conspic. in llanos, esp. in Dec–Apr dry season at drying lagoons and streams, but much dispersed in May–Oct rainy season.

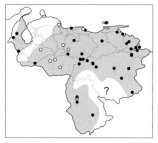

Range: To 300m. Locally throughout (no recs. for Andean region; Lara; w and c Falcón); Isla Margarita (*lineatum*). Se Mexico; Honduras to w Ecuador, n Argentina, s Brazil, and Uruguay.

Fasciated Tiger-Heron   PLATE 5
Tigrisoma fasciatum   Pájaro Vaco Oscuro
Identification: 24–27″ (61–69cm). 850g. Bill dusky above, yellowish below, base of lower mandible and lores greenish; bill *shorter and heavier* than in other tiger-herons and with slightly arched culmen. *Crown black, sides of head slaty gray, neck and upperparts slaty black finely vermiculated pale buff*; medial line down foreneck white, abdomen grayish cinnamon to rufescent brown, flanks gray. In flight wings slaty with *narrow white trailing border*, often the leading wing edge also narrowly bordered white. Imm.: not safely separated from juv. Rufescent Tiger-Heron but whiter below, less distinctly barred on flanks and under wing coverts, and with *shorter, stouter* bill; in hand imm. Fasciated has 3 vs. 4 narrow white tail bands[541].
Sim. species: See Rufescent Tiger-Heron and Pinnated Bittern. Little overlap with either.
Behavior: Stands on boulders in rivers or along gravelly riverbanks where conspic. but somewhat wary. Watches and waits patiently, with neck partly extended, for prey (mostly fish?) which is snapped with quick thrust of bill. Occas. relocates to a new spot a short distance up or down river. Solitary, but in favorable areas several may station themselves at intervals of only a few hundred meters along rivers.

Status and habitat: Uncommon and local resident of gravel bars and boulders along fast-flowing wooded streams in foothills; usually, but not always, in humid regions. Look for it in small rivers above Choroní and Ocumare de La Costa in Aragua and along Río Santo Domingo near Barinitas, Barinas.

Range: 300–800m (sight to 1200m, Río Quinimarí, Táchira—G. Rodríguez). Spottily in foothills of Sierra de Perijá; nw Lara (Río Jordan), e base of Andes in e Táchira (sight); e Barinas (sight, Barinitas); Coastal Cordillera in n Aragua and Distr. Federal; e Sucre (*salmoni*); Cerro de la Neblina, s Amazonas (sight)[801]. A specimen, reportedly from Guayabal, s Guárico[486], is prob. an error. Mts. from Costa Rica to nw Argentina and se Brazil; Guyana.

Cocoi Heron   PLATE 4
Ardea cocoi   Garza Morena
Identification: 40–50″ (102–127cm). 2.1kg. Resembles Great Blue Heron but *with much more white*. Bill dull mango orange, basal half of upper mandible grayish; eyes yellow. Differs mainly in *crown as well as sides of head to below eyes black* (when breeding has long black occipital plumes tipped white); *neck and upper breast white* (not gray), a few black streaks on foreneck, lower underparts black, *thighs white* (*not* rufous). In flight *upper wing surface mostly white with blackish flight feathers* (not gray with slaty flight feathers). Imm.: sim. to ad. but duller.
Voice: Guttural *gawk, uuk, uuk*, sometimes in longer ser. as bird flushes.
Behavior: A solitary fisherman and paradigm of patience. This sp. stands motionless and waits, in or near water, for long periods, or occas. wades slowly in shallow water and watches for fish and a variety of other small vertebrate prey from water or shore. Rather wary except around breeding colonies. Flight is powerful with slow, labored wing beats and head

held back between shoulders. Nests in small colonies; large stick nest platform well above gd.
Status and habitat: Common resident in almost all brackish and freshwater habitats, incl. mangroves, estuaries, lakes, marshes, and rivers. Local movements, esp. in llanos, occur in response to changing water levels.
Range: To 1200m. Throughout. C Panama to s Chile and s Argentina.
Note: Also called White-necked Heron[403].

Great Blue Heron
Ardea herodias   Garzón Cenizo
Identification: 40–50″ (102–127cm). 2.4kg. Large, slender, and long-necked. Eyes yellow; bill dusky yellow; legs dusky olive. *Head and throat white; black band on side of crown extends rearward as narrow pointed occipital plume* (longer when breeding); *neck grayish,* foreneck streaked with black, rest of upperparts and *wings bluish gray;* underparts more or less streaked black and white; *thighs chestnut.* Imm.: duller, crown gray to dusky; no occipital plumes; sides of head whitish, neck grayish brown, narrow black streaking on foreneck obscure; often with *little or no rufous* on thighs. White phase birds (resident on Islas Los Roques) considered a separate sp. by some.
Sim. species: See Cocoi Heron. Imms. of the 2 spp. are easy to confuse, and many Great Blues in Venez. are imms. or very dull-plumaged birds. In any plumage Great Blue is grayer, and ad. always has rufous (not whitish) thighs.
Voice: Croak sim. to that of Cocoi Heron.
Behavior: A solitary sp. that employs a stand-and-wait method of foraging in shallow water, or occas. wades slowly. Typically somewhat wary and does not allow close approach. In Costa Rica reported to maintain winter feeding territories[706].
Status and habitat: Reg. winter visitant in small nos., mid Aug to mid Mar, to Carib. coast from N Amer. Nos. increase Feb–Mar, prior to n migration, with up to 25 seen daily at Chichiriviche, Falcón. Earliest rec. is 1 photographed 10 Aug 1972, El Palmar, Bolívar (P. Alden). A few sight recs. inland s to nw Táchira (P. Alden), w Apure (Hilty), Cojedes (many observers), Guárico, and PN Guatopo, Miranda (P. Alden). Only seen Oct and Mar at Kaimare Chico, nw Zulia[353]. Resident breeder on Esparquí in Los Roques (where 20% are white, 20% gray and white, and 60% gray).

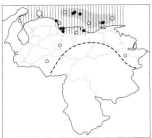

Range: To ca. 300m (sightings). Migrant from N Amer. to coast of Venez., occas. inland s to Táchira, Apure, and ne Bolívar (*herodias*). Resident on Islas Los Roques, Las Aves (sight), La Tortuga (sight), Los Testigos (sight), and La Orchila (*occidentalis*). Breeds in N Amer., Mexico, Greater Antilles, and Galápagos Isls.; winters s to n S Amer.
Note: Gray Heron (*A. cinerea*) of Eurasia and Africa has been rec. in Trinidad, Lesser Antilles, and as far n as Greenland and may stray to Venez. waters. Head as in Great Blue Heron, *neck and entire underparts unstreaked grayish white,* back and wings pale gray, flight feathers blackish. Imm. duller; crown all black.

Great Egret   PLATE 4
Ardea alba   Garza Real
Identification: 36–40″ (91–102cm). 885g. Large, slender, long-necked egret. *All white with yellow bill* (always) *and long black legs and feet.* Breeding birds have long conspic. scapular plumes.
Sim. species: Large size and combination of yellow bill and black legs are diagnostic. White-phase Reddish Egret has blue gray legs and bicolored bill. Snowy Egret and imm. Little Blue Heron are both smaller with black or bicolored bills. Cattle Egret is smaller, stockier, and with dingy greenish legs.
Voice: Usually quiet. Flushes with coarse or raspy *guuk* or *guuk-uuk-uuk* or extended *gruuuuuuk,* 1 to several times, in alarm.
Behavior: A patient fisherman, waiting immobile for long periods, often with neck more or less fully extended. Forages alone or in loose groups, but typically maintains individual spacing. Along coast occas. gathers in nos. in assoc. with other egrets and waders at rich tidal flows. Breeds in mixed colonies with other waders, Jul–Nov, in Guárico; up to 140 nests in heronry[734]; twiggy platform nest ca. 2m up or higher, in mangroves, cactus, or broadleaf tree; 2–3 blue gray eggs.
Status and habitat: Common breeding resident. Some seasonal movements occur, incl. birds occas. noted crossing Andean passes. Present in varying nos. all yr in llanos. Perhaps somewhat seasonal on coast of Zulia[353].

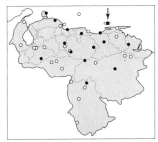

Range: To 300m (occas. to 3000m). Throughout incl. Isla Margarita; sightings from Islas Las Aves and Los Roques (*egretta*). Virtually worldwide in warmer latitudes. In New World from s Canada to s Chile.
Note: Sometimes placed in genus *Casmerodius*[403].

Egretta

Long-billed, long-necked, long-legged waders, several of which have been placed in various monotypic genera; all with shaggy plumes on head, neck, or back, at least when breeding.

Snowy Egret   PLATE 4
Egretta thula   Chusmita
Identification: 20–24″ (51–61cm). 330g. Rather small and dainty. Entirely pure white with *black bill and legs; feet bright yellow*; bare loral skin yellow. Breeding birds have long, lacy, recurved aigrettes arising from crown and back and elongated plumes on breast. Imm.: sim. but no plumes; rear and inner surface of legs dull greenish yellow (feet not in strong contrast).
Sim. species: Contrasting yellow feet are diagnostic if seen. Great Egret is much larger with longer neck and yellow bill. Imm. Little Blue Heron has bicolored bill and greenish legs, is also differently proportioned (longer legged and lanky).
Voice: Occas. a soft *gwah*.
Behavior: Solitary or in small, loosely assoc. groups, occas. in nos. with other waders at drying pools, feeding actively by taking advantage of feeding action of larger waders and storks. Solitary birds also are sometimes fairly active foragers, walking elegantly in shallow water, sometimes stirring water with a foot while walking, or occas. even dashing around, these active bouts alternating with periods of inactivity. Roosts communally, often at large rookeries with other egrets. Breeds Aug–Oct in Guárico[734]; stick platform nest in mixed colony of egrets and herons; 2–4 pale blue green eggs[175].
Status and habitat: Common resident in mangroves, estuaries, and coastal mudflats; less numerous inland in freshwater marshes and along rivers and lagoons, where usually alone; present throughout yr in llanos, although nos. may fluctuate seasonally. Nos. may be augmented during n winter by migrants, esp. on coast.

Range: To ca. 500m (occas. much higher). Throughout (*thula*); sightings from Islas Las Aves. Breeds from s US to c Chile and n Argentina; Greater and Lesser Antilles; Trinidad and Tobago.
Note: Little Egret (*E. garzetta*) of Eurasia and Africa is known from numerous New World localities, incl. several recs. in Trinidad, and is prob. overlooked in Venez. Very like Snowy Egret. Differs in *lores and or-*

bital skin gray to bluish gray (pale yellow to orangish at peak of breeding).

Little Blue Heron   PLATE 4
Egretta caerulea   Garcita Azul
Identification: 20–25″ (51–64cm). 320g. *Base of bill pale blue gray, distal two-thirds black*. Legs dull greenish. *Mainly dark slate blue* with head and neck deep maroon (subads. lack maroon). Imm.: pure white, usually with dusky tips on flight feathers, or pied and mottled dusky to varying degrees as molts to ad. plumage; bill as in ad.; legs duller.
Sim. species: Imms., which are all white, are easily confused with white-phase Reddish Egret which has basal half of bill pinkish (not basal third blue gray) and slate blue (not greenish) legs. Egret's larger, heavier body, shaggy-headed appearance, and erratic behavior are often helpful. Also cf. other white waders, i.e., Great and Snowy egrets and Capped Heron.
Behavior: Most often seen alone or in well-spaced 2s or 3s standing in shallow water, body somewhat bent and bill pointing downward. Occas. with groups of waders. Mainly a stand-and-wait forager, but sometimes also wades actively. Flight is rather loose jointed with deep wing beats and slight side-to-side rolling at times. Breeding reported Jul–Oct in Guárico[734]. In Trinidad, nest platforms 1–3m above water; 2–5 blue eggs[175].
Status and habitat: Fairly common resident in small nos. on coast and inland. More numerous in coastal areas, least numerous s of Orinoco. Some seasonal movements occur, esp. in llanos (need more documentation). N Amer. birds likely as there are Nov–Mar recs. of banded birds in Colombia.

Range: To 1600m. Throughout (mainly n of Orinoco); once to s Amazonas at Cerro de la Neblina[801]; sightings from Islas Las Aves, Los Roques, La Orchila, and La Tortuga. Breeds from e US (wanders n to Alaska and Canada) and winters s to Mexico, c Peru, n Chile, se Brazil, and Uruguay. W Indies, Netherlands Antilles, Trinidad and Tobago.
Note: Has been placed in genus *Florida*.

Reddish Egret   PLATE 4
Egretta rufescens   Garza Rojiza
Identification: 29–31″ (74–79cm). 475g. *Bill pinkish flesh, distal third black. Legs slate blue*. Dark phase: dull pastel rufous head and neck very shaggy and disheveled; rest of plumage slate gray to reddish

brown. Light phase: plumage entirely white, otherwise sim. Imm.: white-phase birds have blackish bills; dark-phase imms. are grayish brown, usually with suggestion of ad.'s rufous head and neck (but not very shaggy looking); bill, legs, and feet dark. **Sim. species:** Key mark is bill. Cf. white-phase birds with imm. Little Blue Heron. Imm. light-phase birds told from other white waders by uniformly dark bill, legs, and feet; erratic behavior helpful but not diagnostic alone.
Behavior: Usually quite active when feeding. Runs, lurches, and staggers around in shallow water, almost as if intoxicated, often with wings held open (canopy feeding) or flicked open as it chases fish. Alone or loosely assoc. with other waders.
Status and habitat: Uncommon resident (presum. breeds, but no recs.) in small nos. in shallow brackish and saltwater lagoons along coast; in larger nos. during n winter when n migrants are present. Yr-round at Chichiriviche, Falcón; all months but Dec at Kaimare Chico, Zulia[353]. First Zulia rec. (photo), Paraguaipoa, 31 Jul 1969 (P. Alden). White-phase birds outnumber dark ones.

Range: Coast from Zulia and Falcón to Sucre; Islas Margarita, Los Roques, La Orchila, La Tortuga, and Las Aves; n migrant once on Los Roques (*rufescens*). Breeds in Baja California, coast of s US, Mexico, Bahamas, Greater Antilles, Bonaire, and prob. n Colombia and Venez. Winters s to El Salvador, Netherlands Antilles, and coastal Venez.
Note: Has been placed in genus *Dichromanasa*.

Tricolored Heron
PLATES 4, 5
Egretta tricolor   Garza Pechiblanca
Identification: 22–26″ (56–66cm). 320g. Slender and long-necked. Bill bluish tipped black, legs salmon when breeding (or bill and legs greenish yellow—nonbreeding). *Mostly slate blue with contrasting white belly, under wing coverts, and rump*; long narrow white line bordered or mixed maroon down foreneck; base of foreneck maroon; long white occipital plumes when breeding. Imm.: above dark gray to brownish, below duller than ad.; no occipital plumes.
Sim. species: In flight contrasting white belly and wing linings are diagnostic. Cf. all-dark Little Blue Heron and reclusive Agami Heron.
Behavior: A solitary sp. that feeds by standing and waiting or by wading actively, but occas. is loosely assoc. with other waders. Freq. fishes by partly raising and spreading wings and holding head partially

under a wing ("under wing" foraging technique) as it walks around rather erratically in shallow water. Breeds colonially in mixed heronries in mangrove or freshwater areas. In Trinidad, stick platform in tree; 2–4 eggs[175].
Status and habitat: Uncommon and local resident (presum. breeds) in brackish water along coast, even less numerous inland in freshwater where prob. seasonal. Rare or vagrant to some coastal areas (only a single Jan sighting during a 2-yr census in Zulia[108]). N breeders migrate s to Panama.

Range: Entire coast and locally inland in llanos from w Apure (sight) to Cojedes and Guárico; also s Zulia and Delta Amacuro; Isla Margarita; sight, Islas Los Roques and La Orchila. Breeds from se US to coastal n S Amer. (*ruficollis*); coastal s Peru; e Brazil; Greater Antilles and Trinidad (*tricolor*).
Note: Has been placed in genus *Hydranassa*.

Cattle Egret
PLATE 4
Bubulcus ibis   Garcita Reznera
Identification: 17–20″ (43–51cm). 340g. *Small, hunched, white egret with thick neck, heavy jowls, and rather short greenish yellow legs. Bill and eyes yellow.* Breeding birds have buff to cinnamon tinge on crown, back, and breast and reddish bill, eyes, and legs. Imm.: sim. to nonbreeding ad. but legs blackish.
Sim. species: Smaller and chunkier than other white egrets or herons in Venez., and ads. are only ones with combination of yellowish bill and yellowish tinge to legs. Snowy Egret is lankier, has *black* bill and legs, and has shaggy-headed appearance; look for its contrasting yellow feet.
Voice: Usually quiet except at nest, where greets with low *rick-rack*; in courtship a harsh *roo* and muffled *thonk*.
Behavior: Gathers in large nos. to roost, then fans out each morning in long streaming lines. Flocks often fly far in search of cattle, which they follow, 1 or 2 birds to a cow, to watch for disturbed insects, esp. grasshoppers, and some small vertebrates flushed by cattle. Also follow farm implements, capybaras, etc., in search of disturbed prey, or forage alone. Breeds colonially but usually not with other herons or egrets; in Guárico mainly Jun or Jul–Oct[734] (Hilty). Stick platform nest in small- to med.-sized tree.
Status and habitat: Common resident of farms, ranchland, and settled areas. Forages in dry or wet pas-

tures, marshes, and fields, nearly always in partial assoc. with cattle. An emigrant from Old World that may have arrived on ne coast of S Amer. as early as the 1870s (first reported in Colombia in 1917). Date of arrival in Venez. unknown; 1st specimen taken in 1943 in Guárico.

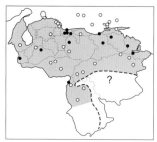

Range: To ca. 2000m (sight to 3600m). Prob. throughout, but recs. spotty s of Orinoco (none in s Bolívar); nw Amazonas s to Río Ventuari (*ibis*); sightings, Islas Las Aves, prob. all offshore islands. E and s US and Canada to n Chile, n Argentina, and se Brazil. W Indies. Trinidad and Tobago. S Europe, Africa, Asia, and Australia.

Butorides

Squat, hunched little herons; relatively short legs; worldwide; sp.-level taxonomy controversial[408].

Striated Heron   PLATE 5
Butorides striatus   Chicuaco Cuello Gris
Identification: 15–17″ (38–43cm). 175g. Much like Green Heron but *sides of head, neck, and chest gray* (not maroon chestnut); white stripe down center of foreneck wider on chest. Imm.: may not be safely separable in field from imm. Green Heron but *sides of head and neck grayer*.
Voice: Sharp *keoup!*, esp. when flushed.
Behavior: Usually seen alone, standing at edge of water or on a branch just over water, where it waits patiently for small fish and other aquatic items which it takes with quick stabs of bill; seldom wades. Flies with wings slightly cupped. Often perches in trees, and when alarmed flicks tail down and raises and lowers bushy crest. Known to fish from logs floating down rivers, periodically flying upriver in search of new logs. Solitary breeding, Jul–Oct, Guárico[734]. Stick platform 1 to several m up, often over water; 3 pale greenish eggs[115].

Status and habitat: Common resident in all kinds of fresh- and saltwater habitats; mostly lowlands. Very common along muddy rivers and streams in Amazonas.
Range: To 1000m n of Orinoco; 250m s of Orinoco. Throughout; Islas La Tortuga and Margarita. C Panama to c Chile, c Argentina, and Uruguay. Trinidad and Tobago.
Note: Taxonomy follows Blake[53]. Sometimes 1 or more subspp. are recognized.

Green Heron
Butorides virescens   Chicuaco Cuello Rojo
Identification: 17″ (43cm) migrant *virescens*; 210g. Or 15″ (38cm) resident *maculatus*. *Small and dark. Short orange yellow legs*. Crown and bushy crest (not always apparent) black, *sides of head, neck, and chest rich maroon chestnut* with narrow black line bordered white down foreneck; rest of plumage mainly greenish black above, soft gray below. Imm.: greenish brown above, white heavily streaked brown below; several rows of white dots on wings; dull yellow legs.
Sim. species: See Striated Heron.
Voice: As in Striated Heron.
Behavior: Sim. to Striated Heron.
Status and habitat: Rare migrant and n winter resident along coast and inland; recorded 15 Aug–10 Jan (prob. later); not known to breed in Venez. (*virescens*). Uncommon yr-round resident on coast (breeds?), and fairly common breeding resident on several offshore isls. (*maculatus*). Some of numerous inland sight recs. (up to 2300m in Mérida Andes) need verification, or may refer to resident *maculatus*.

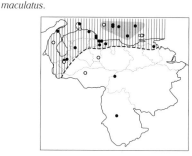

Range: To 600m (to 2300m?). Entire Carib. coast incl. Delta Amacuro[343] and inland in Mérida, Lara, Falcón, Aragua, and ne Monagas (*virescens*); sight recs. s to Zulia, w Apure, s Cojedes, and c Aragua; vagrant s to n Bolívar and s Amazonas (subsp. prob. *virescens*); offshore isls. of Las Aves (breeds), Los Roques, La Orchila, La Blanquilla (breeds), La Tortuga (*maculatus*). Breeds from s Canada to n S Amer. W Indies; s Carib. isls.[774]; Trinidad and Tobago. N migrants s to n and e Colombia and e Ecuador (Río Napo).
Note: Taxonomy follows Blake[53]. Resident birds sometimes not considered a separate subsp.

Agamia

Short-legged, stiletto-billed heron with reclusive photophobic habits.

Agami Heron

PLATE 5

Agamia agami Garza Pechicastaña

Identification: 26–30″ (66–76cm). 580g. Long neck and *extraordinarily long, rapierlike, grayish green bill*, lower mandible pale yellow; eyes amber to dark red; facial skin yellowish green (red briefly when breeding—♂). Rather short, dull yellow legs. Mainly deep glossy gray green to deep bluish above (varies with light); scapulars maroon; head black with long blue gray occipital crest; *neck and underparts deep chestnut*; throat and median line down foreneck silvery white; numerous long wispy silvery blue feathers crisscross foreneck (like "Chinese painting"); patch on chest silvery blue. Imm.: above dull dark brown, crown and flight feathers blackish, throat and median line on foreneck white, lower underparts streaked brown and white; eyes amber.

Sim. species: A lovely heron—breathtaking in good light—but marvelous colors are seldom seen to advantage. Cf. imm. Tricolored Heron with white belly, white wing linings, and shorter bill.

Voice: Seldom vocalizes. Prs. or families utter a guttural, clattering *kur'r'r'r'r'r* in mild alarm; also a rattling or snoring *ku'd'd'd'd'd*, almost froglike; and a low raspy *ka-da-dik* to each other.

Behavior: A solitary and reclusive anchorite that crouches in shallow water at edge of well-shaded stream banks where there is abundant overhanging vegetation. Relies on stealth, disruptive coloration, and very slow wading movements to avoid detection and to capture fish (often surprisingly small ones for size of bird) which it grasps or more often spears with forward thrusts of unusually long bill while creeping forward. May crouch "frozen" for lengthy periods, belly deep in water. When alarmed flicks tail up mechanically and may attempt to creep away by slowly climbing through or up into shrubby vegetation. On rare occas. when flushes, flies with head reared slightly. Rarely or never wades in open water, but families (up to 3) may hunt together in shady backwater pools. Nests semicolonially; in Barinas 6 stick platform nests 1.5–2m up in bushes in small seasonal marsh surrounded by forest; Jun–Sep[523]; eggs bright blue; in Costa Rica breeds Jun–Sep[706].

Status and habitat: Uncommon and very local resident (easily overlooked). Generally a low-density sp. of small forested streams, oxbow lagoons, wet and muddy areas inside humid lowland forest, streamsides in gallery and seasonally inundated forest, and sometimes mangroves. In a few areas seen with reg., e.g., sluggish gallery forest streams at Hato Piñero and Hato Cedral, and Camani area of Amazonas. Scarce or absent in blackwater areas of Bolívar.

Range: To 1000m. W base of Andes in Mérida; generally (but recs. widely scattered; none in nc Venez.) from e base of Andes, s Carabobo, and Aragua e to Sucre (Caño San Juan) and Monagas; Delta Amacuro[343]; throughout Amazonas and Bolívar. S Mexico

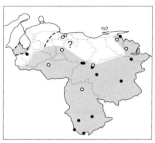

to nw Ecuador, n Bolivia, and Mato Grosso, Brazil. Trinidad.

Note: Also known as Chestnut-bellied Heron.

Whistling Heron

PLATE 5

Syrigma sibilatrix Garza Silbadora

Identification: 21–23″ (53–58cm). 370g. Rather thick *bill pink with black tip*; bare *facial skin and skin encircling eyes baby blue*. Legs rather short and greenish. Crown and long loose occipital crest feathers slaty, *sides of head, neck, breast, and broad scapular area golden buff*; upperparts blue gray; *lower back and rump* white forming broad band; *belly and under tail coverts white*. Imm.: dull gray above, darker on crown and flight feathers; wing coverts faintly streaked tawny, below light gray, *rump, belly, and tail white*.

Sim. species: Striking, and not likely confused if seen well. In flight note chamois upper wing coverts and white rearparts. Cf. Tricolored Heron, in flight imm. Scarlet and White ibises.

Voice: Freq. hd. call, on gd. and esp. in flight, a high, reedy, complaining whistle, often doubled or uttered in a ser., *wueeee, wueeee, ...*, easily imitated.

Behavior: Mostly seen alone or in well-spaced prs., less often loosely assoc. groups of up to ca. 6 (rarely more), but roosts in small groups. Individuals or prs. maintain foraging territories (unique call may aid spacing). Forages mostly in dry pastures by standing erect in 1 place for up to several min at a time, or walking very slowly taking insects, earthworms, other soft-bodied invertebrates, frogs, small snakes, and flying insects (i.e., dragonflies), the last snapped from air. Almost never wades in open water. May sway neck before striking[308]. Solitary nest (Argentina) of loose sticks, 4m up in eucalyptus; 4 pale blue and speckled eggs[239].

Status and habitat: A dry-land heron. Common resident in tall dry grass and pastures, occas. tall damp

grass, flooded fields, and drainage ditches. Some seasonal wandering[596].
Range: To 500m (sight, 2300m, w Mérida). Nw Zulia; e of Andes from Apure, Barinas, Cojedes, s Carabobo, and s Aragua e to n Monagas, and s to n Bolívar at Pijiguaos (sight—P. Boesman), lower Río Caura (sight), Caicara, and vicinity of Upata (*fostersmithi*). E Colombia and c Venez.; s of Amazon Basin from n Bolivia and s Brazil s to c Argentina and Uruguay.

Pilherodius

Chunky, short-legged heron with long foppish occipital plumes, "french-vanilla" tinge to plumage, and antisocial behavior; bill long, sharp-pointed.

Capped Heron   PLATE 5
Pilherodius pileatus   Garciola Real
Identification: 22–24″ (56–61cm). 550g. Heavyset and short legged. *Bare lores and facial skin bright cobalt blue*; bill gray blue. Legs gray. *Peaked crown black*, forehead white, *2–3 very long white occipital plumes*, otherwise plumage white, most ads. *strongly tinged creamy buff on neck and breast* (esp. prom. when breeding). Imm.: no buff; crown somewhat mixed with gray. Chunky flight profile. Flies with labored wing strokes mostly below horizontal and wings cupped downward.
Sim. species: Easily mistaken for an egret, but note black crown, colorful face, and long floppy occipital plumes. In flight has chunky, hunched profile.
Voice: Usually silent. Occas. a short croak when flushed. ♂(?), in pretty display to ♀ (?) high in bare tree, stretches neck up, ruffs feathers (esp. neck), and bows repeatedly as gives soft, low, almost hesitant *ca-huu, ca-huu, ca-Huu, ca-huu, ca-huu* (louder in middle).
Behavior: In all areas generally a loner, wary and quick to flush, but in swampy forested areas infreq. congregates in loose groups of up to 12 or more, and a few may roost a few meters apart in open bare trees. Feeds on muddy banks, in shallow flooded areas, or occas. wades belly deep along riverbanks. Not esp. active but does not usually wait patiently for long periods of time. Typically holds a pose a few sec while it slowly moves a foot to begin a new step. Often retraces path, and freq. flies off 100m or so to a new site. Eats mostly small fish and a few insects, occas. other items. Doubtless breeds in Venez (no recs.).
Status and habitat: Uncommon to fairly common resident of freshwater habitats but typically in low density. Muddy, grassy, or rocky riverbanks in forested regions; also small shallow pools in forested areas, occas. ponds in open savanna, but seldom strays far from vicinity of forested riverbanks. Some seasonal movements; present in n Guárico only in dry season, Nov–May[734]; 1 at 2300m, Laguna Miraflores, w Mérida[596].
Range: To 500m (sight to 2300m). Spottily throughout n of Orinoco and in nw Amazonas (sight) and n

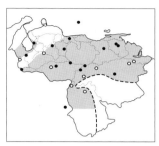

Bolívar s to lower Río Paragua; vagrant to Islas Los Roques. C Panama to n Paraguay and se Brazil.

Nycticorax

Stocky heron with short neck and legs; rather heavy bill; imm. very different; often active at night.

Black-crowned Night-Heron   PLATES 4, 5
Nycticorax nycticorax   Guaco
Identification: 24–27″ (61–69cm). 770g. Chunky and hunched with short neck, heavy black bill. Eyes bright red; legs greenish yellow (reddish when breeding). *Crown and back glossy black*; long occipital plumes white; *wings and tail gray; forehead, sides of head, and underparts whitish*. Imm.: very different; eyes orangish; upperparts brown *streaked and spotted whitish throughout* (markings usually somewhat blurry); below dull white streaked light brown; bill and legs dull yellowish green, bill yellow green tipped dusky. In flight feet (but not legs) protrude beyond tail. Attains ad. plumage in ca. 3 yr.
Sim. species: Ad. most resembles Boat-billed Heron, but that sp., aside from distinctive juglike shape, has *all-white back* (overall looks much whiter at rest and esp. in flight), chestnut belly, and *much more massive, flat bill*. Black-crowned's body shape, by comparison, is more tapered with smallish head. Cf. imm. with imm. Yellow-crowned Night-Heron.
Voice: In flight and when alarmed a low, forced, *wuuk!* or *quock!*, singly or in ser.; reminiscent of call of Boat-billed Heron (and of alarm of capybara, *Hydrochaeris hydrochaeris*). Local name, Guaco, suggests call.
Behavior: Roosts by day in varying-sized groups in swampy woodland or mangroves or trees near streams. Is abroad mainly after dark, then often seen silhouetted in flight commuting to nighttime feeding areas. Prey incls. fish, other small vertebrates, and crustaceans. Ads. are occas. abroad by day, and imms. are much more freq. active by day. In Guárico breeding reported Jul–Oct[734]; colonial; twig platform nest 1–7m up; 2–3 pale bluish eggs[175].
Status and habitat: Common and widespread resident (also n migrants?) although easily overlooked because of partially nocturnal habits. Mangroves, forested rivers, savanna with gallery forest, and fresh- or saltwater marshes. Esp. common in wet and swampy areas in llanos.

Range: To ca. 500m (sight to 1400m, Trujillo and Lara). Generally n of Orinoco and s to n Amazonas and n Bolívar (prob. throughout); Islas Margarita, Las Aves, La Orchila, and Los Roques (*hoactli*). Virtually worldwide except holoarctic regions and Australia.

Nyctanassa

Robust, med.-sized heron with stout bill; neck and legs longer than in *Nycticorax.*

Yellow-crowned Night-Heron
PLATES 4, 5
Nyctanassa violacea   Chicuaco Enmascarado
Identification: 24–28″ (61–71cm). 640g. Shape recalls Black-crowned Night-Heron but lankier, with thicker bill and longer legs; in flight feet *and part of legs* protrude behind tail (only feet in Black-crowned). Bill black; eyes black; legs orange yellow. *Head black with broad white crown stripe and long white stripe behind eye* (yellowish forehead not conspic.), otherwise light bluish gray; back blackish, the feathers edged whitish. Imm.: much like imm. Black-crowned Night-Heron but *bill thicker and all dark, legs longer,* upperparts darker, more slaty brown; *spotting and streaking much finer and more sharply defined.* On gd. stands taller and slimmer, without Black-crowned's stocky, hunched appearance.
Voice: Short *qwok*, singly or in laughlike ser.; higher, not as throaty as in Black-crowned Night-Heron.
Behavior: Not as nocturnal as Black-crowned Night-Heron and can be seen feeding by day as well as night. Most often seen alone, and often even roosts alone. Varied diet incls. many crustaceans. Oct breeding (2 nests in colony) in Guárico[734]; 3 pale green eggs[788].
Status and habitat: Chiefly in mangroves, estuaries, and tidal flats along coast and on offshore isls., where a fairly common resident; less numerous and

local inland along sluggish tree-lined streams and shallow freshwater ponds in llanos. In Guárico reported only Apr–Oct[734]; at Hato Cedral, Apure, present at least Dec–Jul (prob. yr-round). Some n temperate breeders may reach Venez.
Range: To ca. 500m (once, Páramo La Culata, ca. 4000m). Generally n of Orinoco (no recs. for inland Falcón or Lara), Delta Amacuro, n Bolívar (sight, lower Río Caura), and spottily throughout Amazonas (*cayennensis*). Offshore isls. of Las Aves, Los Roques, La Orchila, La Blanquilla, Los Testigos, and Margarita, with vagrants on coast of Distr. Federal and Sucre (*bancrofti*). Breeds from s US and Baja to nw Peru and e Brazil (everywhere mainly coastal). W Indies, Galápagos Isls.; Bermuda (introd.).
Note: By some placed in genus *Nycticorax.* Subsp. *bancrofti* may not be recognizable.

Cochlearius

Most closely allied to *Nycticorax*; notable for broad, heavy, touch-sensitive bill; large eyes and nocturnal habits; breeds in colonies of its own (not mixed).

Boat-billed Heron
PLATE 5
Cochlearius cochlearius   Chicuaco Cajeto
Identification: 18–20″ (46–51cm). 600g. Thick, *jug-shaped,* whitish heron with *broad,* black, shovel-like bill. Unusually large, glistening black eyes. Gular pouch yellowish (black when breeding). Forehead white, *crown and nape black,* the occipital feathers lengthened; otherwise *white above with broad black bar across mantle;* cheeks and underparts white; *lower breast and belly chestnut* (usually not conspic.); *sides, flanks, and under wing coverts black* (last often conspic. in flight). Imm.: above *pale brown to rufescent brown,* below paler brownish white turning dull white on belly; older birds have sooty crown.
Sim. species: Easily confused with Black-crowned Night-Heron; Boat-billed is *much whiter* (almost ghostly in spotlight at night). As bird stands, tilted forward with neck extended and bill down, broad head and massive bill impart a distinctive jug or bowling-pin shape to body, unlike bulbous, tapering, squat shape of Black-crowned.
Voice: Low, guttural *guuk* or *uuk.* At day roost flushes heavily and awkwardly with chimpanzeelike *o-o-ou-ou-ah-ah-aa* as it takes flight.
Behavior: Roosts by day in groups of its own of up to 100 or more in thick mid. or upper canopy foliage of trees along watercourses. Leaves roost only after full darkness to fly to muddy feeding sites in open or wooded terrain, where usually seen standing at edge of shallow water, or wading slowly; once noted stirring water with a foot, then stabbing quickly into water with bill. Also often walks in very short grass some distance from water. Once noted regurgitating a large fish (D. Ascanio photo). Foraging behavior appears rather sim. to Black-crowned Night-Heron but more wary than Black-crowned and flushes quickly at night. Touch-sensitive foraging not verified

in Venez. Breeds Aug–Sep in Guárico[734], Jun–Sep in Apure; in small colonies; 2–3 bluish white eggs faintly spotted reddish at large end, on frail stick platform 1–5m up over water[706]. Typically a high percentage of imm.-plumaged birds are seen yr-round. Day roost sites and attendance at them vary seasonally. **Status and habitat:** Widespread but somewhat local resident; easily overlooked because of nocturnal habits. Mangroves, brackish lagoons, shallow freshwater lagoons, pools, borrow pits, and wooded streamsides. Common locally in llanos (e.g., Hato Cedral and Hato El Frio, Apure). Some dispersal prob. occurs (skull found at 3600m, Laguna Mucubají, 15 Aug 1977—D. Ascanio).

Range: To 300m (once to 3600m). Generally throughout (*cochlearius*); no recs. in arid Falcón and n Lara. W Mexico locally to w Ecuador and n Argentina. Trinidad.
Note: Sometimes placed in family Cochleariidae.

Threskiornithidae:
Ibises and Spoonbills

Corocoros, Garzas, Paleta

Ibises and spoonbills are another ancient lineage of birds found virtually throughout warmer regions of the world. Ibises have long, decurved bills and fairly short legs; spoonbills have straight, spatulate bills and fairly long legs. All species are characterized by bare facial skin, and all lack powder down. Like storks, they fly with the neck outstretched, typically in Vs or lines, and with wing flapping interrupted by occasional short glides. Ibises mostly probe soft mud for crustaceans, insects, and other small items; spoonbills strain shallow water through their bills by using a rapid back-and-forth sweeping motion. Nesting is colonial or solitary, and both adults incubate the 2–5 eggs. There are several important recent references to the family[148,241].

Theristicus

Dry-land ibises; large; bold plumage pattern; prs. or small groups; noisy; complex vocalizations and displays.

Buff-necked Ibis   PLATE 3
Theristicus caudatus   Tautaco
Identification: 28–32" (71–81cm). 1.6kg. Long, decurved bill; eyes bright red; bare face black; legs

pinkish red. *Head, neck, and chest pale creamy buff* stained rusty on crown and lower chest; otherwise dark gray above; *wings black with silvery white upper wing coverts* (conspic. in flight); lower underparts and tail black. Imm.: head and neck streaked brownish.
Sim. species: Heavy bodied and gooselike at a distance, although can always be told by long bill. Cf. Orinoco Goose.
Voice: Flight call a loud, nasal *KNACK-KNOCK*. Also gives same call over and over in predawn darkness from roost trees. Before leaving roost, groups may chant in loud, rhythmic chorus, 1 bird starting, *ca-ca-ca-cu-cu-cu-nac-nac-NAC-NAC-* . . . , softly at first but rapidly building as others join with high- and low-pitched calls in long-sustained pulsating chorus that reaches a frantic crescendo before dying away. At large roost, several groups may chant more or less simultaneously in an unforgettable display of vocal power.
Behavior: Forages alone, in prs., or in small loosely assoc. groups, in short grass in dry or burned pastures, or infreq. in damp areas near water. Individuals are often well separated from each other. Roost in isolated groves of tall trees, palms, etc., esp. around ranch buildings. Often noisy in flight and at roost at dawn, where prs. (maintained for life?) engage in extended choruses, bill fencing, and comical bowing displays (pr. maintenance?). Nests mostly in small loose groups; stick platform quite high and near end of branch; 2–3 greenish eggs spotted brown. Breeds in wet season.
Status and habitat: Common resident in savanna and ranchland of llanos. Occurs in almost any open terrain where there is short grass or dry pastures; also occas. around drying pools and in damp grass. Local and seasonal movements occur in response to flooding.

Range: To 300m. S Zulia; generally e of Andes from Táchira, Apure, Barinas, Cojedes, and s Aragua to ne Monagas, and s to n Bolívar (Cerro Tigre on Río Paragua) (*caudatus*). E Panama (rare); n and e Colombia; Guyana.
Note: Formerly incl. birds of Andes from Ecuador to Patagonia and Tierra del Fuego, Black-faced Ibis (*T. melanopis*).

Cercibis

Large; long tail and short legs; bill as in other ibises; prs. or families, not large social flocks.

Sharp-tailed Ibis   PLATE 3
Cercibis oxycerca   Tarotaro
Identification: 28–32″ (71–81cm). *Large, long-tailed ibis*. Decurved dark reddish bill; *bare throat orange, facial skin and legs bright red orange.* Plumage glossy greenish black, short bushy nuchal crest. In flight legs *do not* protrude beyond *long* tail.
Sim. species: Recalls Bare-faced Ibis but *much larger, heavier, and longer-tailed*. Up close note colorful throat and facial skin; in flight note Bare-faced's fast wing beats. Also cf. Green Ibis.
Voice: Loud, nasal, bugled *TUUR-DEEE* or truncated *TUT-TOOT* (like French ambulance, 2d note higher), often repeated constantly in flight. Call, most often given in flight, is sometimes antiphonal, with 1 bird (♂?) uttering the *TUUR* or a *TUUR-TUUR*, the other (♀?) the *DEEE* call. Variations occur, esp. when trios call in flight. Local name, Tarotaro, suggests call.
Behavior: Almost always in prs. or 3s, occas. up to 5, but not large flocks. Walk in soft muddy places that are bare and relatively open, often near water but usually not in it, and probe deeply with long bill. Flight is slow and labored. Normally fly rather low, and will be hd. before coming into view, as they make their way across long open expanses of savanna to a roosting or feeding site.
Status and habitat: Uncommon to fairly common resident locally, but always in small nos. and the least numerous ibis in llanos. Muddy shores of small pools, lagoons, rice fields, and damp grass. Roosts in gallery forest. Found mainly in drainage basins of Ríos Apure, Meta, and Orinoco.

Range: To ca. 300m. W Apure, w Barinas, and Portuguesa e across s Cojedes to Guárico and s to nw Bolívar (Caicara; Altagracia; Río Cuchivero). E Colombia and c Venez.; Guyana; w Amaz. Brazil n of the Amazon; sw Brazil.

Mesembrinibis

Med.-sized, short-legged, all-dark ibis; solitary in or near forest.

Green Ibis   PLATE 3
Mesembrinibis cayennensis   Corocoro Verde
Identification: 19–22″ (48–56cm). 720g. *Short legs (feet do not project beyond tail in flight)* and slender decurved bill dark jade green; legs dark greenish gray; bare face slaty. Plumage dark bronzy green; hackles on hindneck and mantle speckled with iri-descent green; inconspic. bushy nuchal crest. Imm.: sim. but duller, no gloss.
Sim. species: No other New World ibis is so uniformly dark (shows little color on soft parts), but in good light glittery green hackle spots are distinctive. Bare-faced Ibis is smaller with pinkish bill and legs and faster, smoother wing beats. Glossy Ibis is shiny bronze maroon but may look black at a distance, then best told by less robust shape and long projecting legs.
Voice: Distinctive voice a loud, rapid, and rolling *co'ro, co'ro . . .* or *kr'u'u'u'u'u'u'u'a . . .*, often over and over with scarcely a pause. Often given from a high snag, or in flight at dusk as birds fly to roost, or briefly as they flush.
Behavior: Notably solitary and wary, usually seen alone or in prs., rarely 3–4 together. Does not associate closely with other ibises. As a general rule, if there are more than 2 together, they prob. are not Green Ibises. A water-edge specialist that walks slowly in damp and muddy places or occas. in very shallow water, usually along shady forested streams or open shores of lagoons near forest, and probes into soft mud. Most active and vocal at dusk. Wing beats are jerky with quick, stiff upflicks of wings like a Limpkin. Jul nest, Guárico[734]; frail twig platform high in tree[253].
Status and habitat: Fairly common resident locally in swampy lagoons or wet areas in low-lying forest, along muddy stream banks, shady gallery forest streams; occas. in marshes or other open muddy pools, but usually not far from woodland. S of Orinoco along small streams and forested backwaters. May vacate some portions of llanos during dry season[182].

Range: To 500m. W Zulia (El Rosario); generally e of Andes from w Apure, Portuguesa, and Cojedes e to Delta Amacuro, Río Orinoco, locally in n and e Bolívar s to upper Río Cuyuní (sight, km 88), Santa Elaena de Uairén, and Amazonas. Costa Rica to n Argentina and Paraguay.

Phimosus

All-dark ibis; short legs; small size; very social.

Bare-faced (Whispering) Ibis   PLATE 3
Phimosus infuscatus   Zamurita
Identification: 19–20″ (48–51cm). 575g. *Small, dull ibis*. Decurved bill dull pinkish red to reddish brown; bare face and legs pinkish red; *legs rather short*; in

flight feet do not project beyond tail. Plumage black glossed bronze to green above; head and neck may show purplish red reflections.
Sim. species: No other ibis in Venez. has such short legs, and it is only all-dark ibis with pinkish to reddish bill, facial skin, and legs, but colors often dull, obscured by mud, and difficult to see. Glossy Ibis is larger, glossier, and longer legs project in flight. Larger, heavier Sharp-tailed Ibis has long tail, labored flight, and up close, orange throat.
Voice: Rather quiet. Call, hd. mostly at roost or nest, a soft, somewhat whispery (hence sp.'s old name), and slightly pulsating *cua-cua-cua-cua-cua* . . of 12 or more brisk notes, the ser. swelling in volume then fading, often given over and over, like a soft chant, for several min by 1 or several birds.
Behavior: Usually seen in fairly compact groups varying from a few to several hundred individuals. Walk in damp grass or wet areas and probe into mud with bills. Often with other spp. of ibis, esp. Scarlet and Glossy ibises, and freq. forage around cattle or horses but rarely with non-ibis waterbirds[182]. Often permit fairly close approach before flushing off with fast, steady wing beats and less gliding than Glossy Ibis. On longer flights form long stringy lines or Vs like cormorants. Nest in small colonies; small twig platform; Jul–Oct in Guárico[734]; 1–6 light greenish blue eggs[750].
Status and habitat: This and Scarlet Ibis are 2 commonest ibises in llanos where, in dry season, every little pond or lagoon seems to have some of these birds. Resident in damp pastures, marshes, rice fields, and muddy or grassy borders of ponds, lakes, wetlands, also canals and ditches in urban areas. Some seasonal and local movements, with much dispersal to breed during rainy months of May–Oct.

Range: To 500m (vagrant to 3600m). Maracaibo Basin, Zulia; river valleys in Andes (sight, Mérida; Barinas), e Falcón to n Aragua (Ocumare de la Costa; Maracay), Miranda, and generally e of Andes from Táchira, Apure, Barinas, and Guárico to n Bolívar (sight e to lower Río Caura) and nw Amazonas (*berlepschi*). N Colombia and generally e of Andes (except Amazon Basin) s to c Argentina and Paraguay; e Ecuador (rare).

Eudocimus

Red or white plumage; forehead, sides of face, and throat bare; long legs; very social.

White Ibis   PLATE 4
Eudocimus albus   Corocoro Blanco
Identification: 22–24″ (56–61cm). 750g. *Decurved bill and bare facial skin red* (bill blackish briefly when breeding); eyes bluish; legs pink. Plumage *white with narrow black wing tips.* Imm.: above brown, sometimes mottled with white; rump white; head, neck, and chest light brown streaked whitish, sharply separated from white lower underparts; bill and legs pinkish to dusky.
Sim. species: Other white waders are much larger or show much more black on wings (cf. Wood Stork, Maguari Stork, and Jabirú). Imms. for 1st yr virtually identical to imm. Scarlet Ibis; older imm. Scarlet Ibis show pink.
Voice: Nasal grunting *urnk* on gd. or in flight.
Behavior: Notably gregarious. In dry season in llanos, foraging behavior is very sim. to that of Scarlet Ibis. Walks in shallow water and probes in mud. Prey captures are based mostly on tactile probing and incl. a wide variety of soft-bodied items and small crabs[307]. In wet season freq. forages out of water, walking in muddy areas with grass[182]. When not breeding congregates at communal roosts, often commuting long distances between feeding areas and roosts. Almost always with flocks of Scarlet Ibises and breeds in mixed colonies with them on coast and inland; in Apure, shallow, compact twig and leaf platform in small tree; or cactus (on coast); 2 white to buffy white eggs blotched and finely speckled brown[788]; breeds in wet season.
Status and habitat: Mainly coastal, where an uncommon to locally fairly common resident in brackish and saltwater marshes, mangroves, and other tidal areas (always much less numerous than Scarlet Ibis). Scarce and local resident in llanos; some seasonal movements prob. occur. Generally outnumbered ca. 100 to 1 by Scarlet Ibis in llanos (Hilty), but occas. composes up to 10% of birds in a Scarlet Ibis colony. Interbreeding between the 2 spp. is rare; less than 0.3% of pairs[10,528].

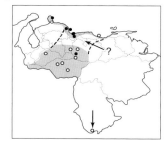

Range: To 300m. Carib. coast from n Falcón (Adícora) e to Anzoátegui and s to Ríos Meta and Orinoco; vagrant to s Amazonas (Cerro de la Neblina)[801]. Se US and Mexico s to Pacific coast of Panama, w Ecuador, and nw Peru; e Colombia. French Guiana. Greater Antilles.
Note: Has been considered conspecific with Scarlet Ibis.

Scarlet Ibis
PLATES 3, 4

Eudocimus ruber   Corocoro Colorado

Identification: 22–24" (56–61cm). 650g. Ad. unmistakable. Decurved bill, facial skin, and legs pinkish red (bill blackish when breeding). Plumage all *intense scarlet with narrow black wing tips.* Imm.: sim. to imm. White Ibis (prob. inseparable for 1st yr) but gradually acquires pink on rump. Older imms. show pink on back, wings, and underparts. Coastal birds redder than inland birds.

Voice: Usually quiet. Nasal *urunk* as in White Ibis.

Behavior: Few sights in nature are as memorable as one's first views of the breathtaking red color of a flock of Scarlet Ibises, whether the birds are at rest, flashing past a line of mangroves, or illuminated against an evening sky. Most often seen in flocks, sometimes 100s, feeding in open shallow water (esp. in dry season; muddy places with grass, or in lines or Vs overhead, peddling away on commutes to feeding or roosting areas. Large flocks often contain a sprinkling of White Ibises. Take larger prey items (mostly arthropods) than other ibises (except Buff-necked), often quarrel over prey captures, and along with White and Bare-faced ibises, regularly follow cattle or horses, even whistling-ducks, and watch for disturbed insects[182]. On coast breeds in colonies, incl. at least 1 site in e Falcón; near Pto. Cabello, Carabobo; Laguna de Unare, Anzoátegui; and at least 3 colonies (prob. many more) in Delta Amacuro; inland breeds mainly in w llanos of Cojedes, Portuguesa, Barinas, Apure, and w Guárico; Apr–Nov breeding on coast not synchronized with rains; May–Sep breeding in llanos is synchronized with rains. Pop. in *sharp decline* on coast and in Orinoco Delta; 95% of pop. bred inland, only 5% on coast in early 1980s[93,527]; frail stick platform 2–12m up in mangrove; 2–3 dull grayish olive eggs spotted and blotched brown.

Status and habitat: Common resident locally on coast and in Apure and Barinas where found in freshwater marshes, shallow lagoons, and rice fields. On coast most numerous where there are extensive mangroves, e.g., e Falcón and outer reaches of Orinoco Delta. At Chichiriviche, Falcón, occurs yr-round but nos. variable, usually highest Sep–Oct (C. Parrish and P. Alden recs.). In llanos some move to higher gd., i.e., to w perimeter of llanos, during rainy season.

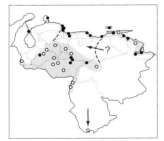

Range: To 300m (sight to 1500m, San Cristobal, Táchira). Carib. coast and locally throughout s to n Bolívar (sight, lower Río Caura), Río Meta, and nw Amazonas (sight, Pto. Ayacucho); once to s Ama-

zonas (near Cerro de la Neblina)[801]; Isla Margarita. Colombia to the Guianas and e Brazil. Trinidad. Stragglers to e Ecuador and Panama; W Indies; formerly n to se US.

Glossy Ibis
PLATE 3

Plegadis falcinellus   Corocoro Castaño

Identification: 22–24" (56–61cm). 610g. Decurved bill brownish olive; eyes brown; facial skin and legs greenish gray; *legs very long; in flight feet and legs project beyond tail.* Breeding plumage *glossy bronzy maroon to chestnut maroon,* the feathers, esp. above, with purplish reflections; wings and lower back tinged greenish; narrow white border around facial skin when breeding extends back to eye (not behind). Nonbreeding plumage: head and neck somewhat streaked whitish; short pale supraloral line from bill to eye. Imm.: like nonbreeding ad. but duller, foreneck and underparts dingy grayish white to brown.

Sim. species: Very glossy but may look black in poor light. Green Ibis is chunkier, shorter legged (feet don't project in flight), often shows "hackles" on neck, and occurs alone or in prs. in or near forest (never in flocks like Glossy). If in doubt, note Glossy's long trailing legs in flight. Also cf. smaller Bare-faced Ibis which has very short legs and pinkish tinge to bill, face, and legs.

Behavior: Gregarious, feeding in groups of 6–100 or more, and often assoc. with Scarlet and White ibises. Probes in soft mud in marshy areas or around lagoons, often pausing to spend much time probing in a small area before moving. Flies in long skeins, flapping alternating with gliding. In Costa Rica, nest a compact platform of dry rush stems 2–5m up in mangrove tree; 3 dark blue green eggs; rainy season[706].

Status and habitat: Fairly common to common resident in freshwater marshes and wetlands, occas. in dry grass but generally not far from damp areas or water. There seem to be few recs. of this sp. prior to 1950s. Seasonal movements occur. Thousands concentrate in wetlands of w Apure during Jan–Apr dry season. Occas. on coast. Migrants from N Amer. possible.

Range: To 300m. Apure, Barinas, and Portuguesa n to e Falcón (Chichiriviche) and e to Aragua (Maracay) and w Guárico (Calabozo). Coast of s US to Costa Rica; Greater Antilles; n S Amer.; locally in warmer parts of Old World and Australia. Mid. Amer. and some n S Amer. sight recs. may refer to this sp. or to White-faced Ibis.

Note: White-faced Ibis (*P. chichi*) of w N Amer. and s S Amer. may wander to Venez. Much like Glossy Ibis but legs slightly shorter, eyes red, *bill and legs reddish, bare facial skin red*; when breeding, facial skin completely outlined by a feathered white border extending around eye and under bill. Nonbreeders lack Glossy's pale line from bill to eye. Imms. are brown eyed and inseparable in field from imm. Glossy; older imms. have red eyes.

Roseate Spoonbill   PLATE 4
Ajaia ajaja   Garza Paleta
Identification: 28–32″ (71–81cm). 1.5kg. *"Spoonbill"* unmistakable in any plumage. Bald grayish head; whitish neck and upper back; *otherwise pink*, brightest on wings and lower back, *with blood red bar across shoulders* (reddest when breeding); legs red. Imm.: whitish incl. feathered head; bill yellow, legs dusky red; older imms. pinkish. Ad. plumage attained in ca. 3 yr.
Behavior: Small groups wade in shallow water and sift for plankton-sized organisms by rapidly swinging submerged bill from side to side as they walk and stir water with feet. In dry season often gather with other waders at drying pools. Flight is steady and strong without gliding. In Costa Rica, sturdy nest cup of sticks lined with green vegetation, 1.2–5m up in dense colony; 2–4 dull white eggs blotched with brown; mainly early dry season[706].
Status and habitat: Common in brackish and saltwater habitats along coast, mainly where there are mangroves. Smaller nos. occur inland (seasonal?), esp. in dry season in lower, wetter parts of llanos. Breeds on coast (inland?). Noted May–Aug in ne Venez.[186]

Range: To 300m; vagrants to 3600m at Laguna Mucubají, Mérida. Carib. coast from Zulia to Delta Amacuro and s to n Amazonas (sight, s of Pto. Ayacucho; prob. rivers throughout) and nw Bolívar (sight, lower Río Caura). Coastal se US and Mexico s locally to Uruguay and c Chile. Greater Antilles; Aruba, Bonaire, Curaçao; Trinidad and Tobago.

Ciconiidae: Storks
Gabanes y Cigüeñas

Storks are a small but very ancient group of birds found throughout warmer parts of the world. There are many more species in the Old World than in the Americas. Storks are long-legged birds somewhat re-

sembling herons but much less dependent on water. They differ from herons in lacking powder down, having heavier bills, flying with the neck fully extended, and in their habit of soaring to great heights. They are omnivorous, feeding in shallow water or in dry grassy areas where they take fish, amphibians, snakes, and a variety of arthropods. Many species are essentially voiceless but make bill-clapping sounds, especially near the nest. Nests are large stick platforms in trees; some Old World species nest atop buildings. Eggs are incubated and young are fed by both parents. The young hatch naked but soon acquire down.

Wood Stork   PLATE 4
Mycteria americana   Gabán Huesito
Identification: 34–39″ (86–100cm). 2.5kg. Blackish bill thick at base and decurved. Legs black. Large white stork with *bare blackish head and neck and black flight feathers.* Imm.: sim but dingier; head and neck partially feathered and brownish; bill dirty gray to yellowish.
Sim. species: Maguari Stork has white head and neck (not black) and less white in wings (only outer half of feathers black). In flight cf. larger Jabirú, which has all-white wings, and smaller King Vulture.
Voice: Mostly quiet. Grunting sounds and bill clapping around nest colonies.
Behavior: Notably gregarious and almost always seen in groups ranging in size from a few to 100s. Given to wandering widely when not breeding, and apt to turn up almost anywhere there is suitable habitat. Walks on gd., perches on large dead snags in trees, flies with slow wing beats alternating with glides, and soars well, often ascending to great hts. Sometimes feeds cooperatively, wading together in shallow water and stirring bottom with a foot and sweeping partly opened bill back and forth, but in dry season in llanos obtains ca. 30% of food by stealing it from conspecifics or other waders[208]. Eggs 2–4, rough and whitish; nests colonially; at Hato Cedral half to nearly grown young present Jan–Feb.
Status and habitat: Fairly common and widespread resident and prob. short-distant migrant or wanderer. Marshes, lagoons, shallow savanna pools, sandbars, and mudflats along rivers, also coastal mangroves and brackish lagoons. Commonest in llanos, irreg. and unpredictable elsewhere. Follows rivers through forested lowlands of Amazonas.

Range: To 400m (prob. higher). Locally throughout. Breeds from s US to s Argentina. Greater Antilles. Trinidad.

Maguari Stork   PLATE 4
Euxenura maguari   Gabán Pionio
Identification: 38–40″ (97–102cm). 4kg. Large, straight, dagger-shaped bill gray with dark reddish tip; *base of bill and bare facial skin orange red*; eyes pale yellow; *legs orange red*. A large *white* stork with *black greater wing coverts and outer half of flight feathers black*; short forked tail black (long white under tail coverts extend beyond tail and round it out). Juv: white down (to 2–3 wk), then all black down and feathers (to 10 wk); by 12–14 wk juv. sim. to ad. but eyes brown[733].
Sim. species: Up close, colorful head and glaring yellowish eyes are unique, but there is tendency for head or foreparts of this sp. to look dirty or stained. On gd., at any distance, black rearparts are diagnostic. In flight cf. Wood Stork, Jabirú, and King Vulture.
Voice: Usually silent. Rarely a wheezy, bisyllabic whistling[288]; also clatters bill.
Behavior: Typically rather solitary, and when not breeding found alone, in prs., or in small loose groups of 3–4, infreq. up to several dozen. May dig or stab into mud with bill, and is sometimes with other storks around drying ponds where they may feed cooperatively. Soars well and may range far from water, occas. wandering widely. In flight long legs and extended neck and head hang beneath body line (as though bird is suspended in middle). Nests colonially (usually) in llanos, mostly Jun–Nov, a few to Mar; stick nest in low bush or reeds, near or over water; 2–4 white eggs[288,734,826].
Status and habitat: Local. Resident in dry open savanna and ranchland with scattered gallery forests, ponds, and temporary pools. Forages in dry grassy fields as well as damp areas and shallow water. Most numerous in wetter low llanos s of Río Apure.

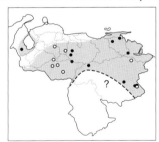

Range: To 1400m (sight in Feb, Gran Sabana). Spottily throughout n of Orinoco from Zulia to Sucre, Monagas, and Delta Amacuro[343]; s of Orinoco from n to se Bolívar. Colombia to the Guianas, s Chile, s Argentina, and Uruguay.

Jabirú   PLATE 4
Jabiru mycteria   Garzón Soldado
Identification: 48–55″ (122–140cm). 6.1kg. Wing span more than 8 ft. (2.4m). *Enormous Pleistocene-like bird with large, slightly upturned black bill and almost macabre appearance*. Long, stiltlike, black legs. *Plumage entirely white; bare head and bare swollen neck black, basal third of neck red*. Imm.: mostly brownish gray, becoming whiter with age.

Voice: Usually quiet. Bill clacking at nest.
Behavior: Occurs alone, in prs., or in varying-sized groups, occas. up to a 100 or more, that feed and loaf in groups of their own or with other waders. Walk with slow stately tread, flush with short lumbering taxi, and soar well, often very high and far from water. Hunt in dry grassy areas or wetlands, and in dry season gather with other large waders at small drying pools that contain an abundance of trapped fish and other aquatic organisms. Prey incls. fish, eels, amphibians, snakes, and other small vertebrates and invertebrates. More than 20% of fish taken by Jabirús in mixed-spp. flocks in late dry season is from intra- or interspecific piracy[208]. Solitary nest in palm, *Ceiba*, or other large, open tree, and may be reused; mostly Jul–Dec, but some nesting continues through Feb or Mar; 2–5 dull white eggs[736].
Status and habitat: Fairly common resident across low llanos, esp. in Río Apure, Río Meta, and lower and mid. Orinoco drainages; more local and spotty in forested regions s of Orinoco. Freshwater marshes, dry savanna, ranchland, ponds, lagoons, and riverbanks; wanders to coastal estuaries, (e.g., Turiamo) and large forested rivers. Scarce or absent in arid parts of w Falcón. Imm. and postbreeding ads. wander widely.

Range: To 400m. Locally throughout. S Mexico (accidental n to s Texas) s locally to n Argentina and Uruguay.

FALCONIFORMES

Cathartidae: New World Vultures

Zamuros

The American vultures are a small group of mostly carrion feeders found in the Western Hemisphere. Their greatest diversity is in tropical latitudes and in extreme southern Argentina and Chile. They most resemble hawks and eagles and have traditionally been placed with them in the Falconiformes, but much evidence now suggests a close relationship with storks[10]. Unlike the accipitrine hawks and eagles, vultures have unfeathered heads, slit nostrils, and much weaker bills, and their feet and toes are better suited for walking then for grasping. All of them soar with great proficiency and find most of

Andean Condor (adult ♂)

their food through keen eyesight. Evidence suggests that cathartid vultures also are capable of locating carrion by a keen sense of smell. The family contains the two largest flying birds in the world, the Andean and California condors.

Andean Condor
Illus. above

Vultur gryphus   Cóndor

Identification: 40–50″ (102–127cm). ♂ 12.5kg, ♀ 10kg. Enormous size. Long broad wings (spread ca. 10 ft.; 3m) with *prom. "fingers" that bend upward* as bird soars. Bare wrinkled head dull reddish. ♂ has prom. flat-topped comb on forehead and dewlap on throat. Plumage black with *large silvery white patch on upper wing surface and conspic. white neck ruff.* ♀: sim. but comb and dewlap smaller. Imm.: all dusky brown incl. ruff; no caruncles; older birds blackish; upper wing surface increasingly pale, but ruff brown.

Sim. species: Ad. told by size, white ruff, and silvery white patches on upper wing surface; all ages by prom. wing tip "fingers" that bend up, and rearmost finger that sweeps back at angle to rear edge of wing (imparts a squared-off look to wing tip).

Voice: Silent. Rarely a hissing sound.

Behavior: Single birds, prs., or several soar effortlessly and magnificently, if a little ponderously, on flat wings and with no tilting or teetering. Roost and nest on inaccessible cliffs and seldom aloft until well after sun up, even midmorning. Range over very large area on daily foraging rounds. In suitable areas several may gather at carcasses to feed.

Status and habitat: Two free-flying birds were rec. ca. 1912 in Andes[486,724], thereafter none until 2 ads. and 1 imm., prob. vagrants from Colombia, were seen 7 Jul 1976 at La Chorrera ca. 30km w of Mérida[835], and subsequently by other observers for a few wk. More recently 1 seen 27 Aug 1985, another 23–24 Jul 1986 above Torote-Jopa peak (3250m) in Páramo de Tetarí, PN Sierra de Perijá, Zulia (L. Lanier), and 2 seen there 30–31 Oct 1989 (3400–3600m) by A. Viloria[98]. In early 1990s a few condors

were reintroduced near Apartaderos, Mérida, and this proud symbol of the Andes again soars over its birthright. Sadly, this effort has faced local resistance. **Range:** 2000–5000m. Locally in Sierra de Perijá, Zulia. Formerly s Táchira to Mérida; recently reintroduced in ne Mérida. Andes from Colombia s to Tierra del Fuego.

King Vulture
PLATE 8

Sarcoramphus papa   Rey Zamuro

Identification: 28–32″ (71–81cm). 3.3kg. *Large.* Wingspread to 6.5 ft. (ca. 2m). Wrinkled and folded skin of *colorful bare head* orange, yellow, red, and bluish purple. Bill black tipped red; base of cere orange red; eyes white (narrow eyering red). A *white vulture with black flight feathers, rump, and tail;* neck ruff dusky. Imm.: sooty brown; under wing linings paler, echoing pale pattern of ad., and becoming increasingly white with age. In flight all ages show broad wings, almost squarish at tips; *soars with flat wings.*

Sim. species: Ad. likely confused only with Wood Stork. Imm. recalls Turkey or Greater Yellow-headed vulture but holds wings flatter and wing linings nearly always paler than flight feathers, or with some white mottling.

Behavior: Single birds, occas. prs. or 3–4, typically soar high, usually not assoc. for prolonged periods with other vultures. Soaring is steady and sustained, heavier than small vultures, and without teetering or flapping. Often alone at small carcasses inside forest. From great hts. also watches other vultures, esp. Turkey Vultures, and follows them to carcasses, dominating them but also better able to open carcasses than smaller, weaker spp. Usually perches in canopy of isolated trees or inside forest, hence infreq. seen perched. Nest in large tree cavity, tree stump, or base of spiny palm; eggs dirty white blotched brown, esp. at larger end; mainly dry season[526,706].

Status and habitat: Uncommon and low-density sp. over dry, moist, or humid forest and partially

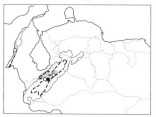

open or cleared terrain; typically away from settled areas.

Range: To 1200m (doubtless occas. higher). Virtually throughout. S Mexico s to nw Peru (not Pacific Colombia), n Argentina, and Uruguay.

Coragyps

Smaller, stockier, and longer-billed than *Cathartes*; bill depressed slightly at tip, nostrils linear; lacks keen sense of smell of *Cathartes*.

Black Vulture   PLATE 8
Coragyps atratus   Zamuro
Identification: 22–26″ (56–66cm). 1.1–1.8kg. Entirely black incl. bare wrinkled head and neck; *whitish patch at base of primaries* conspic. in flight from below (only white outer primary quills from above). In flight profile, wings broadest at base, pulled forward somewhat, and held flat to slightly raised; tail short, squarish, barely protruding behind wings. May alternate flapping with soaring (instead of mostly soaring), but also soars well with little or no teetering. On gd. a bald black bird in white spats (legs often whitish from defecation).
Sim. species: One of commonest soaring birds over n half of country and one whose flight profile is worth learning well. No other "raptorial" bird its size has such a short tail (looks almost tail-less); up close note white patch in wing.
Voice: Occas. grunts or hisses.
Behavior: Feeds voraciously on carrion, incl. putrefying carrion too old to be accepted by other vultures; also eagerly scavenges fruit, vegetables, palm fruits, almost anything remotely edible. More often at larger carcasses than Turkey Vulture. Widespread in settled areas; often roosts in trees or buildings in towns and may become quite bold and assertive around garbage dumps, congregating in throngs and serving as de facto garbage collectors. Roosts and usually soars in groups, and the only vulture likely to be abroad at or even before sun up. Olfaction not important in location of food. Lays 1–2 bluish white eggs heavily spotted brown, in hollow log, cavity at base of tree, between rocks, etc., usually in forest[788]; prob. in dry season.
Status and habitat: Very common resident around villages, towns, and all kinds of settled areas, ranchland, open or semiopen regions, and along coast. Scarce in extensively forested regions, there mainly along large rivers. Migratory movements possible but

not documented. Daily movements occur over Portachuelo Pass, Aragua[33].
Range: To ca. 3000m (usually much lower). In suitable habitat throughout, incl. Isla Margarita, Coche, and Cubagua (*brasiliensis*). US to c Chile and s Argentina. Trinidad.

Cathartes

Bare colored head; narrow wings and longish tail; nostrils oval; well-developed sense of smell.

Turkey Vulture   PLATES 6, 8
Cathartes aura   Oripopo
Identification: 26–30″ (66–76cm). 1–2kg. *Bare head and neck dull reddish with broad whitish band or patch across nape* (resident breeders). *Or head and neck all dull red* (N Amer. breeders). Plumage brownish black, *wings 2-toned* with dark under wing linings and *light gray flight feathers*. Imm.: duller and browner with bare brown head and neck. In flight tilts unsteadily from side to side, wings held well above horizontal.
Sim. species: Shares 2-toned under wing pattern with other *Cathartes*, but latter have yellow heads (head color often difficult to discern in field). Lesser Yellow-headed Vulture is slightly smaller, has pale area at base of primaries from above (because of whitish quills), and different habits (see). Greater Yellow-headed Vulture is larger, heavier, overall blacker, and *innermost primaries* are distinctly blacker than other flight feathers.
Voice: Essentially silent; rarely weak aspirated hisses and grunts.
Behavior: May be seen alone or in nos. taking advantage of rising thermals. Usually scatters widely and soars high with almost unequaled, if slightly teetering, mastery of air, tilting constantly as light body adjusts to changing air currents. A carrion feeder at carcasses of all sizes but more often seen at smaller ones and may concentrate in large milling groups with Black Vultures over suitable large carcasses. Olfaction important in locating food. Lays 1–2 creamy white eggs[589] in stump, under boulder, cave entrance, even abandoned hawk nest.
Status and habitat: Common resident throughout, and transient and winter migrant from the north, mid Oct–late Feb (prob. later). Movements and status of migratory n birds not well documented. Wintering N Amer. migrants may be quite localized (e.g., up to 25 seen daily in early Jan at Hato El Frio, but almost

none at nearby Hato Cedral in same yr. Migratory flocks of up to 160 individuals seen over Hato El Frio, w Apure, on 31 Oct 1983 (R. W. Andrews). Resident forms outnumbered migrants ca. 10:1 in early Feb at Hato Los Indios, se Apure (Hilty).
Range: To 3600m (Laguna Mucubají). Resident *ruficollis* throughout. Migrant from N Amer. to c Venez. (*septentrionalis*) and prob. throughout. Partially migratory w N Amer. and C Amer. birds (*aura*) may reach Venez. S Canada to Falkland Isls. and Tierra del Fuego. Greater Antilles. Trinidad.

Lesser Yellow-headed Vulture   PLATES 6, 8
Cathartes burrovianus   Oripopo Cabeza Amarilla Menor
Identification: 23–26″ (58–66cm). 950g. Much like more common Turkey Vulture (incl. 2-toned underwings) but slightly smaller and with *distinct whitish area at base of primaries* from above (because of white quills); up close note *bare pale yellow head* with orangish red forecrown and nape and blue gray central crown. Imm.: sim. but browner, head dusky, nape whitish. S subsp. (mostly s of Orinoco?) is larger.
Sim. species: See Turkey Vulture; also Greater Yellow-headed Vulture, which almost always soars over lowland forest (not grasslands).
Behavior: Single birds or well-spaced prs. hold wings in strong dihedral and tilt and teeter even more than Turkey Vultures, but unlike latter, usually soar quite low, often over marshes and wet fields; very infreq. high, and more apt to be seen perched on fence posts or other low sites. Feed at small carcasses and seldom assoc. with Turkeys, Blacks, or other vultures at large carcasses. Few nest recs.; 1 in Panama in hollow in tree; 2 whitish eggs with dark markings[706].
Status and habitat: Fairly common to common resident (and short-distant migrant?) over damp open fields, wet pastures, and marshy terrain; also may wander over dry fields and clearings and perch in trees around ranch buildings in llanos. In dry season in w Apure (Hato Cedral, Hato El Frio) often as numerous as Turkey Vulture, or even more so; less numerous n in llanos. Quite numerous Dec–Mar in ne Anzoátegui[186]. Seasonal changes in abundance (local movements?) need documentation.

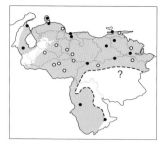

Range: To ca. 1000m. Locally throughout n of Orinoco from Zulia and Falcón to Sucre and s to mid. and lower Orinoco; Delta Amacuro[343] and n Bolívar (sight, lower Río Caura) (*burrovianus*); spottily throughout in savannas s of Orinoco (prob. *urubi-*

tinga) but distrib. of subsp. s of Orinoco uncertain. E Mexico locally s to n Bolivia, n Argentina, and Uruguay.

Greater Yellow-headed Vulture   PLATES 6, 8
Cathartes melambrotus   Oripopo Cabeza Amarilla Mayor
Identification: 29–32″ (74–81cm). 1.4kg. *Bare wrinkled head butter yellow*, loral area pinkish; crown tinged blue, nape pale grape to red (age/sex?); diagonal black line through dark red eyes. Plumage deep black, wings 2-toned with under wing linings black and flight feathers silvery gray; *inner primaries blackish* (from below), *forming a conspic. dark patch that contrasts with rest of flight feathers*; primary quills white from above.
Sim. species: Rather like Turkey Vulture, but once learned can be told easily, even at a great distance. Compared to Turkey, and Lesser Yellow-headed Vulture (which it rarely overlaps in habitat), this sp. is larger, blacker, broader winged, and shows prom. blackish area (smudge) on central flight feathers. Also, flight is heavier and steadier (less teetering), and wings are held nearly flat to only slightly above horizontal. At close range yellow head diagnostic.
Voice: Usually silent; rarely a hiss or grunt.
Behavior: Much like that of Turkey Vulture. Hunts mainly alone (occas. several together in thermals) by soaring at moderate hts. over lowland rain forest. Apparently searches by combination of olfaction and keen eyesight for carcasses inside forest. Flight is steady and sure with solid mastery of air. Up to 6 may roost together on high, exposed bare stubs and may not leave until well after sunrise.
Status and habitat: Common resident over extensively forested humid lowland regions, greatly outnumbering or virtually replacing Turkey Vulture; wanders over grassland, but seldom far from tall humid forest. Most common vulture away from settled areas s of Orinoco.

Range: To ca. 500m. E Monagas (incl. sight, Caño Colorado)[58], Delta Amacuro, and forested areas throughout Amazonas and Bolívar. E Colombia and the Guianas s to n Bolivia and Amaz. Brazil.

Pandionidae: Osprey
Aguila Pescadora

The Osprey is a large, nearly cosmopolitan raptor closely allied to hawks, eagles, and kites (Accipitridae) but differing from them in its leg musculature, more compact plumage, equal-length toes, reversible outer toe (as in owls), and sharp spines (spicules) on the soles of the feet.

Osprey   PLATE 8
Pandion haliaetus   Aguila Pescadora
Identification: 21–24″ (53–61cm). 1.4–1.7kg. *Long narrow wings bent at wrist* (form broad letter M). Above dark brown, head and underparts white, *broad black mask through eyes*; hindcrown narrowly streaked brown; tail shows several narrow brown bands; underwings *mostly white with conspic. black patch on wrist*; tail rather short. ♀: usually a little brownish streaking on breast. Imm.: crown streaked brown; some white edging above and brownish streaking below.
Voice: Ser. of high, clear, upward-inflected whistles, *curlée, curlée, curlée . . ,* or high, thin *chur, chee chee, chee,* 3–5 notes in a ser. in flight or perched.
Behavior: Perches on high stubs overlooking water. Feeds mostly on fish taken by flying out rather high over water, hovering momentarily, then plunging feet first into water. Flies with deep, measured wing beats, usually flapping more than gliding. Wanders widely and likely to turn up almost anywhere.
Status and habitat: Fairly common *nonbreeding* resident (imms. may remain more than a yr?) from N Amer. to coast and inland around large rivers and lakes, or wandering between bodies of water from lowlands to above treeline. Present yr. round, but more recs. in n winter months.

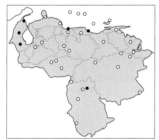

Range: To 3600m. Throughout incl. offshore isls. of Las Aves, Los Roques, La Orchila, La Tortuga, and Isla de Aves (*carolinensis*). Breeds almost worldwide except in S Amer.; New World birds breed s to Guatemala, Belize, and Greater Antilles; winter (and oversummer) to s S Amer.

Accipitridae: Kites, Hawks, and Eagles
Gavilanes, Aguilas

The Accipitridae is a large, well-known family of diurnal predators found throughout the world. They all possess a strong hooked bill and strong feet with sharp claws, but they are heterogeneous in appearance and behavior. English names for some groups are rather misleading and do not always reflect natural groupings. Kites in particular denote an artificial

collection of birds, some with pointed wings, others with blunt round wings, and with diverse habits and appearance. The Buteonine subfamily, including the buteos, black-hawks, and hawk-eagles among others, comprises mostly broad-winged species, but many do not soar, and hunting behavior, diet, and habits vary widely. In contrast, accipiters and harriers are well-defined natural groups. Accipiters are short-winged, long-tailed woodland hawks notable for speedy maneuverable pursuit of prey, often birds. Harriers are best known for their lanky shape, facial ruffs, and quartering flight over open country. Venezuela's raptors are adversely affected by human activities and deforestation, and the use of chemicals in agriculture continues to pose threats. Raptors are particularly vulnerable as they sit atop a food chain of increasingly concentrated toxins.

Kite

Vernacular name applied to numerous small- to med.-sized raptors of diverse habits and anatomical structure; the name does not characterize a specific group of closely related spp. Many are graceful, buoyant fliers.

Gray-headed Kite   PLATES 10, 12
Leptodon cayanensis   Gavilán Guacharaquero
Identification: 18–21″ (46–53cm). 410–605g. Broad, bluntly rounded wings and long accipiter-like tail. Bill black; bare lores and short tarsi and feet blue gray; eyes dark blue gray. Rather small *head pale gray, contrasting with slaty upperparts* and merging smoothly into white throat and underparts; tail black, 2 visible white bars (occas. 3) from above and narrow white tip; *under wing coverts black, flight feathers white boldly and coarsely barred black*. Light-phase imm.: head, neck, and underparts all white, or head with dusky med. crown patch and short blackish streak over eye; upperparts dusky brown, tail blackish banded grayish brown; underwing surface mostly white (*shows as large white "window" in each wing*), tips of primaries coarsely barred black, secondaries lightly barred black; cere, lores, and feet yellow. Subad.(?): as in imm. but with broad dusky area across underwing near tip. Dark-phase imm.: variable but usually brownish black above *incl. sides of head*; below dirty white, lightly to heavily streaked blackish, streaking ranging from breast nearly solid black to breast white with only a few fine dusky marks on center of throat and chest; underwings, tail, and soft parts as in light-phase imm.
Sim. species: Note wing shape, small gray head, and black wing linings (often hard to see). Light-phase imm. easily confused with ad. Black-and-white Hawk-Eagle. Up close note eagle's orange cere, black lores, black crest (patch on crown), and blacker upperparts. In flight, at any distance, eagle best told by *white on leading edge* of forewing. Also cf. larger Crested Eagle, imm. Ornate Hawk-Eagle, and imm. Hook-billed Kite, all with different flight profile, last 2 with some barring on underparts and wing linings. Dark imms. the most difficult (memorize flight pro-

file), but most have distinct "black-headed" look. Cf. smaller imm. Double-toothed Kite, imm. Gray Hawk, Roadside Hawk, Common Black-Hawk, and larger *Spizaetus* eagles.

Voice: As circles in flight gives an odd, nasal, slurred *eed-lée-er* that slowly rises in pitch, then trails off (Hilty); also a loud cackling ser. of *caw* notes, beginning slowly then accelerating rapidly, lasting ca. 3 sec[746].

Behavior: Most often seen in flight. Perches in tree canopy where easily overlooked, although sometimes sits in open in early morning or evening. Soars on flat wings with accipiter-like flapping and gliding; displays with short "butterflylike" wing strokes with wings held above body, but seldom stays aloft long or soars high. Hunts from a ser. of perches in or below canopy. Preys heavily on reptiles and has strong reptilian odor, but diet also includes wasp larvae, insects, honeycomb, bird eggs, small vertebrates, even mollusks; twig nest high (22–26m up) in top of tree; 1–2 eggs; dirty white mostly purplish at one end, otherwise heavily spotted rusty brown[746].

Status and habitat: Thinly spread resident in humid terra firme and várzea forest, swampy areas, second growth, and larger gallery forests (i.e., sight, Hato Cedral); also occas. in dry wooded areas and occas. in foothills (i.e., nw Barinas). Scarce or absent in arid regions and very local in llanos, but likely to turn up in a wide variety of places, and at unpredictable times. Seen with some reg. in Río Grande area of ne Bolívar.

Range: To ca. 800m (once to 2000m). Locally throughout (*cayanensis*) but no recs. In arid zones of Falcón and Lara. E Mexico to w Ecuador, n Argentina, and s Brazil.

Bare loral area and supraloral spot; strongly hooked bill; oval wings; rounded tail.

Hook-billed Kite   PLATES 6, 9, 10, 12
Chondrohierax uncinatus   Gavilán Pico Ganchudo
Identification: 16–18″ (41–46cm). 250–300g. Broad lanky wings oval shaped, bluntly rounded, and *obviously narrow at base*. Rangy profile emphasized by rather long tail. Pale eyes, eyespot, and large hooked bill on head that seems too small for body all impart odd visage. Plumage variable but conspic. *hooked bill, greenish facial skin, orange spot above and forward of lime green eye*, and short yellow legs are consistent. Normal- (light-) phase ♂: slate gray, below paler and usually coarsely barred whitish, sometimes barred rusty, or uniform gray; upper tail coverts whit-

ish, tail slaty with 2 broad white to grayish bands and narrow white tip. In flight from below, wing linings grayish, flight feathers barred black and white (or occas. more or less uniform below). Normal- (light-) phase ♀: dark brown above with *rusty nuchal collar* and gray sides of head; underparts rusty to brownish coarsely barred white, tail as in ♂. In flight from below, wing linings grayish white, flight feathers barred black and white. Rare melanistic phase (both sexes): entirely brownish black, incl. unbarred underwings; tail with 1 broad white band. Imm.: brownish black above with *narrow whitish nuchal collar*; underparts creamy white becoming progressively barred with age; 3–4 narrow grayish (or brownish–♀) bands on tail. Melanistic imm.: all black with 1 broad white tail band and narrow white tip.

Sim. species: Normal ads. (barred ones) recall several buteos (e.g., Gray Hawk) but are rangier in profile and have heavier bill and coarser pattern on underparts and flight feathers. Melanistic birds (rare) are more confusing; see esp. Slate-colored Hawk with red orange cere and legs, ♂ Snail Kite with very broad white band at base of tail, and ad. black-hawks with broader, rounder wings and tail and much different countenance (no eyespot, bill thicker, less hooked, etc.). Cf. imm. to imm. of Collared Forest-Falcon, Gray-headed Kite, and Bicolored Hawk.

Voice: In Panama a rapid chuckling *wi-i-i-i-i-i-i-uh!*[818].

Behavior: Rather lethargic, often perching alone and out of sight inside canopy, or in open when disturbed and about to take flight. Reg. goes aloft mid-mornings to soar in small circles, usually with some slow flapping, but seldom goes high or stays up long. Diet incls. many terrestrial and arboreal snails. Occas. in migratory groups[460].

Status and habitat: Uncommon, low-density resident and short-distance migrant of forested terrain from humid lowland forest and swamp forest to wet montane forest (cloud forest), semideciduous gallery forest, wooded borders, and occas. patches of moist riparian woodland in arid zones (e.g., near San Juan de la Costa, ne Falcón). Migratory groups of 8 and 20 moving north on 14 and 16 Jun 1996, e of Pto. Ayacucho, Amazonas[259]; rec. only irreg. Apr–Nov at Caicara, ne Monagas[186]. Movements need documentation.

Range: To 2500m n of Orinoco; to 2200m s of Orinoco. Locally throughout n of Orinoco; n and c Amazonas (Pto. Ayacucho; Cerro Yapacana), throughout Bolívar (*uncinatus*). Mexico (rarely s Texas) to n Argentina and se Brazil. Trinidad. Cuba and Grenada.

Swallow-tailed Kite   PLATE 14
Elanoides forficatus   Gavilán Tijereta
Identification: 22–26″ (56–66cm). 390–445g. Unmistakable. *Narrow pointed wings and long, deeply forked black tail*. Above black with head, neck, underparts, and *under wing linings white*; upper back glossed oily green; eyes dark red; bill and feet dark gray. Imm.: sim. but head to upper breast narrowly streaked dusky.
Voice: Usually rather quiet; occas. a high, thin *k'weep, k'weep, k'weep-weep-weep-eep*, uttered rapidly as swoops in air.
Behavior: Notably gregarious. Prs. or several, occas. up to 30 or more, drift gracefully along mt. ridges or above lowland forest on sunny days. Perch and roost on high exposed bare limbs. One of only 2 "flycatching" raptors in Venez. (other is Plumbeous Kite); catches flying insects or snatches large insects, small vertebrates, snakes, nestling birds, etc., from canopy and devours them in flight; also occas. snatches fruit from canopy. Breeds in loose groups; Jan–May in Costa Rica; nest high and exposed[642].
Status and habitat: Fairly common resident (migrant?) in humid forests, but often local or seasonal. Presum. breeds; migratory movements prob. occur but are as yet undocumented (9 over Portachuelo Pass 15 Aug[33]; only Apr–Sep in nw Monagas, with flocks up to 50[186]). It is not known if migratory C Amer. birds (*yetapa*) are transients or nonbreeding seasonal residents in Venez., but there are marked movements into Panama late Jan–Feb and out of Panama late Jul–early Sep[543]. Migrant *forficatus* of se US also may reach Venez. as it is reported in w Ecuador and apparently winters mainly in Brazil. It differs in glossy dark purplish blue (not glossy dark green) shoulders and is not safely separated in field.

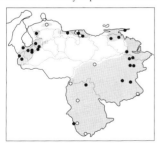

Range: To 1800m (prob. higher). Locally throughout but mainly montane areas n of Orinoco; no recs. in arid coastal regions or llanos (*yetapa*). Se US to n Argentina, Uruguay, and se Brazil. N birds migrate s apparently to Panama, Colombia, and nw Ecuador. Transients or wanderers reported in Cuba, Jamaica, and elsewhere.

Pearl Kite   PLATES 7, 14
Gampsonyx swainsonii   Cernícalo
Identification: 8–9″ (20.3–23cm). 80–95g. *Tiny kite* with pointed wings and square-tipped tail. *Mostly blackish above and white below*; forehead and cheeks creamy yellow; narrow rufous-edged nuchal collar (inconspic.); *black patch on sides of chest*; *thighs rufous*, also sometimes rufous on flanks. In flight *rear edge of wing edged white*. Imm.: crown dotted and back scaled russet.
Sim. species: So small it will not likely be confused, but cf. Aplomado Falcon and American Kestrel, both larger and with "sideburns."
Behavior: A confiding little raptor usually seen perched alone in open on utility wires, poles, or tops of scrubby trees. Hunts from a perch, giving chase in dashing, falconlike manner, but may pause to hover before stooping on lizards, insects, or occas. small birds. Nest a frail twig platform in small tree.
Status and habitat: Uncommon and somewhat local resident throughout its wide range. Found in drier semiopen terrain with scattered trees and patches of forest or brush; also dry to arid desert scrub, even vacant lots in towns if there are a few trees. Readily invades humid regions following deforestation. Chief requirements seem to be open areas with a few trees, high poles, or wires for lookouts. Scarce or absent in llanos. Readily found along highway between Upata and Tumeremo in ne Bolívar. Some local movements likely; reported only Jan–Sep in ne Anzoátegui[186].

Range: To ca. 1000m. Locally throughout (few recs. in llanos, Amazonas, or s Bolívar) incl. Isla. Margarita (*leonae*). Nicaragua; Panama; w Ecuador and nw Peru; n Colombia and e of Andes spottily from the Guianas to n Ecuador, e Peru, and s to nw Argentina and Paraguay. Trinidad.

Elanus

Med. size; lightly built; long pointed wings reach to tail tip; long tail; open areas.

White-tailed Kite   PLATE 14
Elanus leucurus   Gavilán Maromero
Identification: 15–17″ (38–43cm). 250–305g. Eyes orangish to red; bill black; feet yellow. Lanky *pointed wings* and rather long, square tail. *Mostly pearl gray above and white below*; *tail white, shoulders black*; in flight from below shows small curved black wrist mark; small black area partly encloses eye. Imm.:

sim. but more or less streaked and tinged brown above and on breast and tail.

Sim. species: No other med.-sized raptor has sim. shape. At a distance rather gull-like. Cf. larger Cinereous Harrier which has black wing tips and black on tail.

Voice: Not very vocal. Greets with whistled or chirped *kewp*; also *eee-grack*, 1st note whistled, 2d guttural and raspy[83].

Behavior: Attractive and demure, and most often seen alone, perched in tree tops in open country, or hovering for extended periods of time with body angled upward. May then drop to gd. in a controlled fall with wings held up in V to pounce on prey, incl. small rodents and insects. Nest a small twig platform in top of small to fairly large isolated tree; 3–5 white eggs heavily marked brown[706].

Status and habitat: Fairly common and widespread resident of drier open grassland, cultivated areas, ranchland with scattered trees, and gallery forest borders. Has profited from deforestation and now found in many new, recently opened areas in both lowlands and highlands. Reg. in open highlands (e.g., near Santo Domingo, Mérida), even above treeline.

Range: To 3000m (prob. higher). Locally throughout n of Orinoco; s of Orinoco across n Bolívar (sight, Maripa, Feb 1982–J. Pierson; sightings, El Palmar, Upata, and Tumeremo) and s Gran Sabana (Cerro Roraima; sight, Santa Elena de Uairén, Feb 1995– Hilty and D. Ascanio); prob. Amazonas (*leucurus*). S California locally to c Panama; n Colombia to Suriname and s locally into w Amazonia; c and e Brazil, Uruguay, n Argentina, e Bolivia, and Chile. Aruba, Bonaire, Curaçao, Trinidad.

Rostrhamus

Long, strongly hooked bill; ♂♂ have predom. dark gray plumage; sexes alike or different; show fondness for vicinity of water but otherwise habitat and hunting techniques differ.

Snail Kite   PLATES 6, 10
Rostrhamus sociabilis   Gavilán Caracolero
Identification: 16–18″ (41–46cm). 305–385g. Rangy wings broadest toward tips; tail sharply squared off. *Slender black bill strongly hooked; cere, facial skin, and legs orange red.* ♂: uniform slaty black, *upper and under tail coverts and basal half of tail white,* narrow tip white; eyes red. ♀: above dusky brown with *whitish forehead and eyestripe;* below incl. under-

wings *creamy buff heavily mottled and streaked dark brown; tail as in* ♂. Imm.: like ♀ but browner above, more sharply streaked below, and soft parts orangish. In flight wings somewhat bent down at wrist.

Sim. species: Any age or sex told by combination of red facial skin, thin hooked bill, and white on base of tail. Slender-billed Kite has white eyes but *no white* in plumage (imm. has narrow white tail bands). Long-winged Harrier is larger with white rump.

Voice: Raspy, clicking *crik-ik-ik-ik—ik—ik—ik*; also a nasal, almost hissing *ca'ca'ca'ca'a'a'a'aaa*, descending (recalls Black-collared Hawk).

Behavior: Typically social, with several beating low over open wetlands in characteristic floppy and rather disjoined flight, body often angled sideways and head looking downward. Occas. soar. Heaps of *Pomacea* snail shells, an important food item, accumulate beneath favorite perches which are usually low. In Guárico reported eating many freshwater crabs (*Dilocarcinus dentatus*). Nests colonially; 6 nests 4.3–6.7m up in *Copernicia tectorum* palms 19 Sep, w Guárico; frail nest platform in bush or tree low over water; 2–3 whitish eggs spotted and blotched brown[369].

Status and habitat: Fairly common resident very locally in freshwater marshes and wetlands; replaced in swampy woodland by next sp. Some short-distance migratory movements occur, but seasonal pop. changes need documentation. Concentrate around rice fields, presum. when snail pops. are high.

Range: To 500m. Locally throughout n of Orinoco (no recs. in arid Falcón or Lara); n Bolívar (sight, lower Río Caura)(*sociabilis*). S Florida, Cuba, Mexico locally s to w Ecuador, c Argentina, and Uruguay. Austral pops. migratory.

Slender-billed Kite   PLATES 6, 10
Rostrhamus hamatus   Gavilán Pico de Hoz
Identification: 14–16″ (36–41cm). 375–485g. Broad wings; very short square tail; slender, sharply hooked black bill. *Cere, facial skin, and legs orange red.* Ad.: uniform slate gray with *yellowish white eyes.* Imm.: sim. but faint buff to whitish scaling below; 2–3 narrow white bands and narrow white tip on tail; flight feathers lightly and obscurely mottled grayish and rusty. Shows chunky flight profile with short tail barely protruding beyond rear of wings.

Sim. species: Broader beamed and shorter tailed than allied Snail Kite and with no white on rear end or tail. Larger Slate-colored Hawk shares same swamp and riverine habitat but seldom soars, has single prom. white band across roundish tail and heavy bill. Also cf. dark-phase Hook-billed Kite, always with prom. eyespot and white tail band.

Voice: Commonest call a buzzy, kazoolike *wheEEaaaaaah*, nasal, rising a little then falling; very unlike that of Snail Kite. At nest greets with buzzy *ah-ah*, often repeated several times. Both calls, esp. latter, given as duets, with calls overlapping in syncopated fashion or immediately following that of a mate[45].

Behavior: Single birds or several loosely assoc. individuals hunt from low to med.-ht. perches around shallow pools and swampy lagoons. Reg. soar in groups, but usually not high or for extended periods. Display with ser. of undulating swoops. A snail specialist with diet of ca. 90% *Pomacea doliodes* snails, 10% freshwater crabs (*Dilocarcinus dentatus*), both captured by flying directly out from a perch (still-hunt method) in wooded area (cf. foraging behavior of Snail Kite). Takes smaller snails than Snail Kite. Nest 9–20m up in trees in flooded forest; minimum distance between nests 1–1.2km; breeding Jul–Oct; both sexes attend nest; 1–2 quiet young fledge in 35 days, fly by 40 days[45]; 2 brownish cinnamon eggs splotched darker[369].

Status and habitat: Uncommon and *very local* resident in swampy forest and around shallow, stagnant lagoons and drying pools in low-lying forests. Readily found in swampy areas ne of Tucupita, Delta Amacuro. Local in llanos in flooded or low-lying forests along major rivers. Reported only in rainy season, about May–Oct, when breeds, at Hato Masaguaral, Guárico (B. Thomas); 1 seen 6 Sep 1999, Pto. Concha, s Zulia, is only rec. w of Andes (D. Ascanio and J. del Hoyo)

Range: To 400m. S Zulia (sight); locally from w Apure e through Guárico and Río Orinoco to n Bolívar (Caicara); se Sucre (sight/tape, Guaraunos), e Monagas, and Delta Amacuro s to e Bolívar (upper Río Cuyuní). E Panama locally to Suriname and s to n Bolivia and Amaz. Brazil.

Note: Has been placed in genus *Helicolestes*[10].

Harpagus

Two small, compact raptors; longish tail; oval wings narrow at base; in hand show "double tooth" (not single) on cutting edge of maxilla.

Double-toothed Kite PLATES 7, 9
Harpagus bidentatus Gavilán Bidente
Identification: 13–15″ (33–38cm). ♂ 170g, ♀ 220g. Looks like a chunky accipiter. Fairly long tail and short legs; rather short wings *angle inward on trailing edge near body.* Cere greenish yellow; *eyes red*; legs yellow. ♂: head bluish gray, rest of upperparts brownish gray, *throat white with distinct blackish median stripe; chest rufous*, breast and belly rufous thickly barred gray and white; tail dusky with 3 ashy white bands and narrow white tip. In flight from below, under wing linings whitish contrasting with dark body and barred flight feathers; *prom. fluffy white under tail coverts puff out on sides of base of tail, this esp. visible from above in flight.* ♀: sim. but much less rufous below. Imm.: sim. but dark brown to brown above; breast and belly unmarked creamy white with a few fine streaks on throat, varying to heavily streaked brown. Older imms. have dark throat stripe, streaked chest, and coarsely barred lower underparts.

Sim. species: Apt to be mistaken for an accipiter or small buteo in air, but easily told at any distance by beveled wings at base and conspic. fluffy white under tail coverts; at close range by diagnostic throat stripe; in hand by blunt bill with 2 small "teeth" on cutting edge of maxilla. Combination of gray head and rufous chest often helpful even in flight. See Roadside, Broad-winged, and Plain-breasted hawks and esp. Rufous-thighed Kite.

Voice: Occas. a high, thin, weak ser. of slightly tremulous *peeeea* or *peeeawe* notes in flight (Hilty); a thin *tsip-tsip-tsiptsip-wheeeooip* and long-drawn, flycatcher-like *wheeeooo*[83].

Behavior: A rather unsuspicious little hawk that usually perches at mid. level or subcanopy hts. inside forest, or somewhat lower when with primates, and is occas. along forest borders. Flies out to snatch principally lizards but also takes bird nestlings, large insects, even butterflies. Reg. follows troops of monkeys, esp. capuchins and squirrel monkeys, typically sitting a little behind and below them to watch for prey disturbed by their activities. Single birds or prs. soar for short periods during midday, either low or sometimes riding thermals to great hts. Nest a shallow twig saucer high up (to ca. 35m) and near end of branch; 1 white egg speckled brown[328].

Status and habitat: Fairly common resident in humid and wet forest, forest borders, and tall second-growth woodland. Prob. absent from most of llanos; gener-

ally numerous only in fairly extensive tracts of humid forest, e.g., s of Orinoco.

Range: To 1800m n of Orinoco; to 900m (sight 1200m, Sierra de Lema—C. Parrish) s of Orinoco. Throughout in extensively forested areas (*bidentatus*) but n of Orinoco mainly in montane areas. S Mexico to w Ecuador, e Bolivia, and se Brazil. Trinidad.

Rufous-thighed Kite
Harpagus diodon   Gavilán Calsón Rufo
Identification: 13–15″ (33–38cm). Size and shape of Double-toothed Kite and very like it in flight profile. At rest plumage nearer Bicolored Hawk (incl. yellow eyes and soft-part colors). Above gray, head, wings, and tail darker more brownish gray, sides of head gray, *central throat white with narrow black medial line; rest of underparts iron gray, thighs rufous,* sometimes with rufous wash on belly and crissum; *under wing coverts bright ferruginous;* tail dusky with several rather narrow diffuse ashy bands.

Sim. species: Ferrugineous under wing coverts are the key. Larger Bicolored Hawk is uniform gray below (no throat stripe) with white underwings. Additionally, Bicolored is longer tailed and shorter winged. Also cf. Double-toothed Kite.

Behavior: In s part of its range a rather inconspic. little forest hawk that perches well up in trees. Individuals or prs. reg. soar up over forest for short periods on warm sunny mornings. Possibly a rare migrant from austral region.

Status and habitat: Known from 2 specimens: 1 ♀ (Coleccíon Phelps) 18 Aug 1947 (180m) at San Carlos de Río Negro, Amazonas; and 1 ♀ (Coleccíon PROFAUNA) 16 Apr 1950 at Guamitas (ca. 900m) in PN Henri Pittier, Aragua (M. Lentino).

Range: To ca. 900m. N Aragua (once); s Amazonas (once). Guyana (once). Breeds from Suriname s along coast to s Brazil and s Amaz. Brazil s to Paraguay and n Argentina.

Ictinia

Long curved wings extend well beyond tail at rest; legs short; take mostly insect prey in air; often feed aloft.

Plumbeous Kite   PLATES 6, 14
Ictinia plumbea   Gavilán Plomizo
Identification: 13–15″ (33–38cm). 190–280g. *Unusually long curved and pointed wings.* Eyes red; cere dusky; short legs reddish orange. Plumage mainly

slate gray, head and underparts slightly paler; from below 2–3 narrow white bands across rather short squarish black tail. In flight from below shows *prom. rufous patch at base of primaries.* At rest *folded wings extend well beyond tip of tail.* Imm.: above slate gray heavily scaled and streaked whitish; cere yellow; short indistinct white mark over eye; below white streaked and mottled dusky, sides coarsely and indistinctly barred; wings and tail more or less as in ad. (less rufous in wing).

Sim. species: No other raptor in Venez. has such long curving wings in flight, or wings that project beyond tail at rest. Note short-legged posture when perched. Also see note below.

Behavior: A "flycatching" kite (1 of 2 in Venez.) that captures insects in air or occas. flies from a perch to take mostly insects, occas. small vertebrates, from foliage or branches. Everywhere a highly visible bird that soars alone, in prs. or in flocks of its own and sometimes with other raptors. Reg. soars quite high, esp. in migratory groups. Perches on high exposed bare branches. Building nest, Feb, lower Río Caura (Hilty); Mar nest, ne Monagas[186]; small stick platform high on outer tree branch. Breeding starts late in dry season in Guatemala; 1 dull white egg; ads. share incubation and catch own food; nests ca. 0.5km apart at forest opening[592].

Status and habitat: Fairly common to common resident and intratropical migrant in humid forest, forest borders, tall second growth, and extensive gallery forest. Also in mangroves; occas. wanders over open (but not arid) areas. Rec. Mar–Sep, ne Monagas[186]. C Amer. birds migratory; flocks up to several 100 move n early Feb–mid Mar and early Aug–late Sep in Panama, absent mid Oct–Jan[543]. Migratory flocks in Venez. may be C Amer. breeders (e.g., 19 moving nw over Hato Los Indios, Apure, 10 Feb 1994—Hilty; 3 at 2400m in PN Guaramacal 20 Feb 1996; scattered individuals Feb–Mar at e base of Andes near Boconoito, Portuguesa—Hilty and D. Ascanio); origin or destination of large Jun–Jul flocks (up to 40 individuals) in Río Grande unknown.

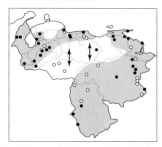

Range: To 2400m n of Orinoco (sight, PN Guaramacal); to 1400m s of Orinoco. Throughout but n of Orinoco mainly in montane areas. Breeds from e Mexico to w Ecuador, n Argentina, and se Brazil. Some or all C Amer. and austral birds migratory.

Note: Mississippi Kite (*I. mississippiensis*), breeding in N Amer. and wintering s to Paraguay, is unrec. but possible in Venez. Very sim. to Plumbeous Kite, differing in contrasting *pale gray secondaries* (from above look whitish), *longer all-dark tail* (wings only reach tail tip), and *very contrasting pale gray head.* Up close legs darker; less rufous in wings. Imm. is browner above, has broader more rufous brown (not dusky) streaking below.

Circus

Long, narrow, "crooked" wings; long tail; long legs; rather owl-like facial disk; hunt low over open areas with much wing flapping and quartering back and forth.

Northern Harrier
Circus cyaneus   Aguilucho Pálido
Identification: 18–21″ (46–53cm). 435g. Typical harrier shape. *Conspic. white rump in both sexes.* ♂: *mostly pale gray with black wing tips*; tail gray with narrow black subterminal band and several *narrow very indistinct bars*; lower breast and belly dotted and lightly barred buffy rufous. In flight from below, underwings white, primaries tipped black. ♀: above dark brown, short white eyebrow and white line below eye; underparts buff heavily streaked brown; *tail with ca. 3 broad dark bands (incl. tip).* In flight underwings buff heavily barred dusky. Imm.: like ad. ♀ but underparts mostly uniform dull rufous, throat and chest streaked brown.
Sim. species: See Long-winged Harrier which is not known to overlap in range. Imm. told from imm. Long-winged by *lack* of contrasting gray areas on flight feathers from above.
Behavior: Sim. to that of other harriers.
Status and habitat: Accidental winter visitant from N Amer.; 1 rec. 14 Dec 1903 from Montañas Sierra, ca. 20km e of Mérida.

Range: Ca. 2500m. Andes of Mérida (*hudsonicus*). Breeds in N Amer. and Old World. Amer. birds winter mostly from w US to Panama, casually to Colombia.
Note: Cinereous Harrier (*C. cinereus*) of e Andes (Cundinamarca) in Colombia to Tierra del Fuego is unrec. in Venez. but may occur. ♂ very like Northern Harrier but lower breast and belly coarsely barred rufous; tail more distinctly barred. ♀ like ♀ Northern but lower underparts heavily barred (as in ♂). Imm. sim. to imm. Northern but with buff or rufous collar.

Long-winged Harrier   PLATE 10
Circus buffoni   Aguilucho de Ciénaga
Identification: 18–24″ (46–61cm). ♂ 410g, ♀ 610g. Typical harrier shape but *large*. Plumage rather vari-

able; all show white rump and *contrasting gray primaries barred black from above.* Light-phase ♂: upperparts and sides of head black with white forehead and eyestripe; below white with *contrasting black chest band*; lower underparts white sparsely dotted black; tail with several light gray and black bands and narrow white tip. In flight underwings pale brownish gray barred black, primaries tipped black. Light-phase ♀: like ♂ but brownish above; facial markings and throat buff, breast and belly lightly streaked brown, thighs tawny. Dark phase (both sexes): *body sooty black*, browner below; rump barred white; facial markings, underwings, *and tail as in respective sex of light phase*; wing from above with large pale "window" near tip. Light-phase imm.: like light-phase ♀ but more broadly streaked below. Dark-phase imm.: like dark-phase ad. but thighs and under tail coverts rufous; rest of underparts sooty streaked whitish.
Sim. species: Contrasting black, white, and gray plumage of ad. ♂ (either phase) and dark-phase ♀ should be distinctive, but cf. Zone-tailed Hawk which lacks facial markings and usually flies higher. Light-phase ♀ and imm. much like Northern Harrier, but latter only accidental in Venez. Note Long-winged's *gray patches on flight feathers* from above (lacking in Northern Harrier).
Behavior: Like other harriers, a hard-working raptor usually seen quartering back and forth low over wetlands, its almost continual wing beating interrupted only occas. by short buoyant glides or tilting and doubling back. When hunting often abruptly pulls up and plunges feet first into tall grass. Prey incls. mostly small vertebrates, occas. birds. When not foraging may fly higher, where soars well. Nest on gd. in tall grass; bluish white eggs[175].
Status and habitat: Uncommon and local resident in grasslands, wet pastures, and marshy areas. Everywhere scarce, but most numerous in more extensively flooded s parts of llanos. Likes to hunt over wet or marshy areas.

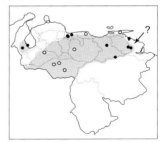

Range: To 600m. Maracaibo Basin, Zulia; e of Andes from Apure (sight), Barinas (sight s of Barinas, Jul 1969—P. Alden), and Carabobo e through Anzoátegui and Monagas to se Sucre, Delta Amacuro, and Río Orinoco. E Colombia to the Guianas; e Brazil s of Amazon Basin to e Bolivia and s Argentina, rarely c Chile. Trinidad and Tobago.

Crane Hawk
Geranospiza caerulescens   Gavilán Zancón

PLATES 6, 10

Identification: 17–20″ (43–51cm). 330g. Rather rangy-looking raptor with large, bluntly rounded wings and small dovelike head. Narrow med.-length tail; *long, "double-jointed," reddish legs.* Bill small and black; cere and lores slaty; *eyes ruby red.* Mostly dark bluish slate with narrow but conspic. *white crescent across underside of outer primaries* (visible in flight); lower underparts often indistinctly barred with white or buff; tail black with 2 broad white bands and narrow white tip. Wing linings gray finely mottled and barred white. Imm.: sim. to ad. but brownish; head more or less streaked white; below extensively mottled and barred chamois and white; white tail bands wider. Unique "double-jointed" legs can bend backwards ca. 30° beyond normal 180° extension. In flight note uniformly broad wings (not narrowed at base), bluntly rounded tips; wings angle forward somewhat.

Sim. species: When flying, in any plumage, white wing crescent (from below), long red legs, and long-ish tail are diagnostic. Perched birds look small headed and long legged, then most like a black-hawk or Slate-colored Hawk, but note Crane Hawk's lighter frame and differing soft-part colors. Also cf. Slender-billed Kite, Snail Kite, and Zone-tailed Hawk.

Voice: Infreq. a ser. of soft bleating and downslurred whistles, *ueeoo* or *ueeoo-ueeoo.*

Behavior: Usually seen singly. For a med.-sized raptor, surprisingly active and agile and a versatile hunter. Takes a wide variety of food and apt to be seen at almost any ht., from gd., where it walks around, to treetops. Can often be seen reaching a long leg deep into tree holes or holes in posts to capture lizards or small prey, clings to trunks for lizards, checks deep cracks in mud along riverbanks. In n Bolivia noted attempting to take roosting bats by inserting a leg between dead hanging fronds of *Copernicia* palms. Infreq. soars. In Guárico, 7 nests 23 Jul–28 Sep, 4 with eggs, 3 with downy chick; 2 eggs; 3 prs. in 7km² home range[369].

Status and habitat: Uncommon resident in wide variety of habitats from dry deciduous woodland to humid forest, tall second growth, swamp forest, gallery forest, and savanna with marshes and ponds. Often near water. Despite catholic choice of habitats, nowhere very numerous. Most readily found in llanos.

Range: To 300m. Spottily throughout except arid nw (*caerulescens*). W Mexico to nw Peru; e of Andes s to n Argentina and Uruguay.

Accipiter

Mostly med. to small raptors; secretive habits; rather short blunt wings, long tails, small bills, and long thin legs; ambush mostly birds in speedy dashes, weaving rapidly through forest; occas. soar; ♀♀ much larger than ♂♂. Several are quite sim. in appearance, complicating field identification.

Plain-breasted Hawk
Accipiter ventralis   Gavilán Arrastrador

PLATES 7, 9

Identification: ♂ 11.5″ (29cm), 105g. ♀ 12.5″ (32cm), 175g. Small *Accipiter*; plumage variable. Above dark gray, tail blackish with 4 gray bands (at least 3 usually visible), *thighs rufous* (except melanistic phase); *underparts highly variable* but generally fall into 1 of 3 broad groups: (1) throat whitish finely streaked darker, rest of underparts cinnamon rufous more or less barred and spotted white, and thighs rufous; (2) white with only a few faint dark shaft streaks or light barring on sides, and thighs rufous; or (3) mostly chestnut to tawny rufous below shading to deep rufous on thighs and belly. Melanistic birds (blackish below) have been reported in Colombia but apparently not in Venez. Imm.: above dark brown, *below whitish heavily streaked brown; thighs rufous*; tail as in ad. Melanistic imm. is heavily streaked dark chestnut and brown below.

Sim. species: Very pale birds resemble Bicolored Hawk which is *decidedly larger* and usually grayer and more uniform below. Also see Double-toothed Kite (different shape, prom. throat stripe), Tiny Hawk (smaller, no rufous thighs), and imm. Semicollared Hawk (cinnamon collar). Imm. is only *Accipiter* in Venez. that is "streaked" below.

Voice: Harsh, cackling *kra-kra-kra-kra* while soaring.

Behavior: Inconspic. and infreq. seen but occas. soars briefly. Perches alone, inside forest or occas. at forest borders, and mostly at low to moderate ht. Dashes rapidly through cover in pursuit of small birds.

Status and habitat: Uncommon resident of humid foothill and montane forest, patches of woodland in partially cleared areas, and older second growth. Most numerous at high els. in Andes.

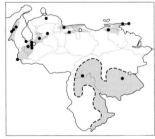

Range: 300–3000m n of Orinoco (sight to 4000m, Páramo del Águila, Mérida); 1200–1800m s of Orinoco. Throughout in hilly and mountainous terrain n and s of Orinoco. Andes from Colombia to Bolivia.

Note: Sometimes considered a subsp. of Sharp-shinned Hawk (*A. striatus*).

Semicollared Hawk
Accipiter collaris   Gavilán Acollarado
Identification: 12–14″ (30.5–36cm). Very rare. Much like Tiny Hawk but *eyes yellow*. Sexes sim. Above brownish black, *broken whitish nuchal collar*, *sides of head sharply mottled black and white*, throat white, rest of underparts white *rather coarsely and conspic. barred dusky*; tail blackish brown with 4–5 broad pale bands. Imm. (brownish phase): sim. but duller, incomplete rufous collar; throat white, rest of underparts buffy white coarsely barred rufous. Imm. (rufous phase): dark rufous above with conspic. rufous nuchal collar; throat whitish, rest of underparts tawny coarsely barred dark rufous (barring broad).
Sim. species: Ad. or imm. told from Tiny Hawk by yellow (not red) eyes, nuchal collar, mottling on cheeks, and coarse (not fine and narrow) barring on underparts. Also see larger forest-falcons. Any imm. told from Plain-breasted Hawk by rufous nuchal collar.
Status and habitat: Rare and little known anywhere in range. In Venez. known from 1 specimen from Montañas de Morro, Mérida[53], another from Táchira. There are 2 sight recs., reportedly this sp.: 1 on 12 Sep 1990, Río Chiquito, Táchira (M. Pearman), and 1 on 14 Jan 1993, San Isidro Rd., nw Barinas (G. Green), both in *Cotinga* 1994 (1): 29. All recs. are from regions of humid mt. forest.

Range: 1300–1800m. Andes of Táchira and Mérida; nw Barinas (sight). Colombia s in mts. to w Ecuador and Peru.

Tiny Hawk   PLATE 7
Accipiter superciliosus   Gavilán Enano
Identification: ♂ 8.5″ (22cm), 75g. ♀ 10.5″ (27cm), 120g. Tiny forest accipiter with usual shape of genus. *Eyes bright red (grayish yellow—imm.)*; cere and legs yellow. Above slaty gray, crown blackish, *underparts white finely barred throughout with dark gray* except throat; tail blackish with 3–4 (usually 3) visible grayish bands. Rufous-phase ♂ (♀?): sim. but upperparts *rufous brown* indistinctly barred dusky; underparts *buff barred rufous.* Normal-phase imm.: above dusky brown, below buff finely barred cinnamon; tail with 6–7 dusky brown and ashy brown bands. Rufous-phase imm.: above chestnut barred black, tail brighter rufous, head dusky, underparts buff barred rufous brown.
Sim. species: Usually can be told by size alone as no other Venez. accipiter is so small, but closely resembles rare and slightly larger Semicollared Hawk of higher els. Also cf. Plain-breasted Hawk and larger Lined and Barred forest-falcons.

Voice: Call (context?) a slightly quavering ser. of 20–30 notes, accelerating at first, then steady but pitch uneven, *caucau-ca-ca-ca . . . .* (4–5 sec), shrill, fairly high pitched, and insistent at end.
Behavior: A secretive and infreq. seen little predator that still-hunts from perch from undergrowth to canopy, and occas. even perches fairly exposed for brief periods. Often changes perches in quick succession as hunts through lower growth, and is known to capture hummingbirds[638]. Flies fast, typically a few quick wing flaps, then closes wings momentarily and hurtles forward, bringing to mind a large thrush. In Venez. a pr. nested in abandoned Black-collared Hawk nest; 1 white egg[788].
Status and habitat: Uncommon and infreq. seen (easily overlooked) resident of lowlands and lower montane els. Found in a surprisingly wide range of humid and wet forest habitats, also young and old second growth in lowlands and lower montane els.

Range: To 1800m (most recs. below 1000m). E base of Andes in Táchira, Mérida, and Barinas; Coastal Cordillera in Carabobo (San Esteban), Aragua (sight), and Distr. Federal; throughout Amazonas and Bolívar (*superciliosus*). Nicaragua spottily to w Ecuador, e Peru, n Bolivia, n Argentina, Paraguay, and s Brazil.

Bicolored Hawk   PLATE 7
Accipiter bicolor   Gavilán Pantalón
Identification: ♂ 14″ (36cm), 230g. ♀ 17″ (43cm), 395g. Rather long tail with rounded corners. Cere and legs yellow; eyes orange. Above slate gray, blacker on head, wings, and tail; below *very light to dark gray* (throat always paler) with *conspic. rufous thighs*; wing linings whitish, tail with 3 narrow ashy bars and tip. Imm.: above blackish brown, usually with narrow indistinct buff or whitish collar and spotting; below uniform buffy white varying to whitish or rufous; thighs normally darker or mottled rufous.
Sim. species: Ad. distinctive if seen well but easily confused with smaller *ventralis* subsp. of Plain-breasted Hawk which usually shows some barring below. Caution is urged in identification of imm. which is notably variable. Imm. Plain-breasted Hawk is smaller, faintly barred below, and has solid rufous thighs (often mottled in imm. Bicolored). Ad. of very rare Gray-bellied Hawk is somewhat larger (esp. ♀) and paler below (whitish to pale gray) with darker cheeks and *thighs never rufous.* Light- and tawny-phase ads. of Collared Forest-Falcon have longer graduated tails and black mark protruding onto

cheek. Slaty-backed Forest-Falcon is always whitish below (never rufous on thighs) and lacks pale collar. **Voice:** Scolding or barking *kra-kra-kra-kr-kr-kr-ka*, much like Cooper's Hawk (*A. cooperi*) of N Amer., esp. near nest.
Behavior: Rather shy and secretive. A solitary sp. that still-hunts from perches, mainly on inner branches. Watches carefully, then dashes boldly and rapidly after prey, mostly birds, or flies fast, low and quietly, through lower growth. Occas. soars, even quite high, but not for long. Nest ca. 20–25m up in tree in tall riparian growth in dry forest, 25 Mar, Cumboto, Aragua (Hilty and K. Kaufman); pr. building nest 2 Apr fledged young 4 Jul, also pr. building nest 5 May, both at Hato Masaguaral, Guárico[369]; small leaf-lined, cup-shaped nest near end of branch, 12–18m up; 2 white eggs with slight rusty streaks[788].
Status and habitat: Rare to uncommon resident in dry, moist, or moderately humid forest, gallery forest, riparian woodland, open second growth, and light woodland in lowlands and foothills. More recent sight recs. from wooded regions of llanos of Cojedes (Hato Piñero) and Guárico (Hato Masaguaral, Hato Flores Moradas) than elsewhere; everywhere seems to favor drier woodland.

Range: To 2000m n of Orinoco (most recs. below 400m); to 1000m s of Orinoco. Prob. throughout. Maracaibo Basin of Zulia, locally in Andes of Mérida, n cordilleras in Carabobo and Aragua, and very locally from w Apure (sight, La Yé, 1982—C. Parrish) e to w Sucre and nw Monagas; n and c Amazonas (s to Río Asisa) and Bolívar (*bicolor*). E Mexico spottily to Tierra del Fuego.

Gray-bellied Hawk   PLATE 7
Accipiter poliogaster   Gavilán Vientrigris
Identification: 17–20″ (43–51cm). Large accipiter with sharply contrasting upper- and underparts. Cere and legs yellow; eyes reddish orange. *Crown blackish*, sides of head and upperparts slate gray (cheeks may be paler), throat and under tail coverts white, *rest of underparts and all of underwing uniform pale gray to grayish white* (no barring); tail dusky with 3 broad grayish bands and narrow pale tip. Imm.: very different; *looks like a miniature Ornate Hawk-Eagle*, crown black, rest of upperparts blackish with *broad chestnut nuchal collar continuing onto sides of head and on sides of chest*; white throat bordered by black malar stripe; remaining underparts white with *coarse broken black barring*; tail as in ad.; eyes yellow.

Sim. species: Ad. looks much like Slaty-backed Forest-Falcon but lacks bare facial skin, has more distinct "capped" appearance, darker cheeks (dusky reaches throat), and different proportions (shorter and squarish, not graduated, tail; shorter legs). In flight wing linings and flight feathers more or less unbarred (forest-falcon has boldly barred flight feathers). Imm. is a half-size version of Ornate Hawk-Eagle lacks latter's crest and has bare (not feathered) legs.
Voice: In flight a rapid cackling *kek-kek-kek-kek-kek—kek*, rather like that of Bicolored Hawk, slowing or trailing off at end.
Behavior: Sightings have been of single birds well up inside or at edge of moist to humid forest. When hunting often perches high, reg. in semiopen crown of emergent tree in forest. Perches for a few min, watches alertly with freq. head movements, then flies rapidly to another emergent tree some distance away. May move to several emergent trees in succession, then flies fast and dives into midst of mixed-spp. flock. In ne Peru observed to circle and dive twice into same flock, then gave cackling call as it flew off.
Status and habitat: Very rare resident with recs. scattered Jan, Feb, and Mar–Nov. Humid lowland forest and occas. at forest borders. Austral birds believed to be migratory[780].

Range: To 400m (sight to 900m). Known from se Táchira (Burgua), w Amazonas (Caño Cataniapo; Cerro Yapacana; Río Casiquiare), and c Bolívar (Río Paragua; Auyán-tepui). Locally from ne Colombia e to Guyana; e Ecuador, ne Peru, Amaz. Brazil e of Rios Negro and Madeira and s to ne Bolivia, n Argentina, and Paraguay.

Leucopternis

Wings and tail even broader than in *Buteo*; plumage mostly white or mostly slaty; tail short; some soar (others never seem to); all prey heavily (mostly?) on reptiles and amphibians.

Slate-colored Hawk   PLATES 6, 10
Leucopternis schistacea   Gavilán Azul
Identification: 16–17″ (41–43cm). 460g. Chunky, broad winged, and short tailed. *Conspic. orange red cere and legs; yellow eyes.* Plumage *uniform, dark bluish slate incl. underwings*; tail slaty black with *1 narrow white median band* and narrow white tip. Imm.:

sim. but lower underparts, underwings, and upper tail coverts barred with white; tail sometimes with a 2d white band.

Sim. species: Combination of red cere and legs and single white tail band is diagnostic. Cf. Slender-billed Kite which has long, slender, hooked bill and small, squarish, all-dark tail. Black-phase Hook-billed Kite has rangier shape (wing profile different), blacker plumage, larger and more prom. hooked bill, and greenish "false" eyespot. Larger black-hawks have yellow to gray ceres and yellow legs.

Voice: Call a loud, piercing whistle, *wEEEeeeeeeeeer*, not harsh, rather long sustained and slightly melancholy. Sometimes over and over.

Behavior: A bird of flooded backwaters, swamps, and quiet forested streams. Typically sluggish and unsuspicious, perching on open branches from fairly low to high along wooded borders of lagoons and rivers. When hunting may drop very low, even to gd., but not known to dive into water. Rarely or never soars, although may be seen in rather languid flight flapping high over openings or along rivers.

Status and habitat: Swampy or várzea forest, river and lake edges, and swampy river isls. in humid forested regions in lowlands. Few recs. in Venez., but relatively common s in Amazon Basin. Possible sight rec. from lower Río Caura, Bolívar[596].

Range: To 200m. Nw and w Amazonas at Caño Capuana, San Fernando de Atapabo, and Pto. Yapacana; n Bolívar (?). E Colombia s to n Bolivia and Amaz. Brazil.

White Hawk   PLATE 12
Leucopternis albicollis   Gavilán Blanco
Identification: 18–22″ (46–56cm). ♂ 650g, ♀ 840g. Very broad wings; broad but *extremely short tail. Bill black, cere dark gray; lores and eyes black*; legs orange yellow. *Plumage mainly white, wings* (from above) *and upper back black* lightly scaled white, shoulders scaled white; tail mostly black, base and terminal band white (*albicollis*). Or with streaklike spots from midcrown to upper back; wings and upper back heavily scaled white (*williaminae*). In flight from below, all subspp. look mostly white with dark cere and lores, black wing tips, narrow black rim on trailing edge of wing, and broad black central tail band. Also in flight note bluntly rounded wing tips, slightly bulging (long) secondaries which make tail seem even shorter, and wings strongly angled forward. Imm.: sim. but crown and nape heavily streaked blackish.

Sim. species: See smaller but very sim. Black-faced Hawk. Other "black-and-white" raptors have different proportions (e.g., Black-and-white Hawk-Eagle), incl. longer tail, and several tail bands.

Voice: Call (e Bolívar) when perched a rather high, short scream, *screeea*, tinny sounding (recalls whistle of Piratic Flycatcher).

Behavior: Usually seen alone, occas. prs., soaring fairly low or less freq. high over humid forest, or perched on a bare exposed stub. A still-hunter that watches from a perch inside forest, then moves and resumes vigil, mainly for snakes or other reptiles. Often rather confiding, allowing close approach. A Trinidad nest was placed atop a bromeliad; 1 bluish white egg marked brown[175].

Status and habitat: A local and generally not very numerous resident of humid and wet lowland and foothill forest and forest borders. Readily seen around biological station in PN Henri Pittier, also freq. in foothills of Sierra de Lema, Bolívar. Rec. at many lowland sites s of Orinoco (incl. sight recs. s to San Carlos de Río Negro, 1985—C. Parrish and A. Altman) but more often in broken hilly terrain or foothills of tepuis.

Range: To 1500m. Sierra de Perijá, Zulia (*williaminae*); Andes of se Táchira (Santo Domingo), se Falcón (sight, Cerro Misión), n cordilleras from Carabobo and Aragua e to Anzoátegui and Sucre; throughout Amazonas; e Bolívar (*albicollis*). S Mexico to e Bolivia, Amaz. Brazil, and the Guianas. Trinidad.

Black-faced Hawk   PLATE 12
Leucopternis melanops   Gavilán Carinegro
Identification: 15–17″ (38–43cm). ♂ 310g, ♀ 340g. Almost a miniature of White Hawk. *Cere and legs bright orange or orange yellow*; bill and *lores black*; eyes dark red. Head, neck, and underparts pure white, *crown and hindneck finely streaked black* (streaks inconspic., occas. virtually absent); upper back mostly white with a few black bars, wings and rest of upperparts black; scapulars and back somewhat edged and spotted with white; *tail black with single white median band and very narrow white tip*. Imm.: white of ad. tinged buff, streaks on head less prom.; tail black with 2 white bands and narrow white tip.

Sim. species: Very like White Hawk but differs in bright orange (not gray) cere, smaller size, streaked rearcrown, and mostly black tail with only 1 narrow white band (White Hawk has very *broad white tip*

and base). Generally shows more white markings on back and less on wings. In flight slightly longer tailed than White Hawk.
Voice: Call a single reedy downslurred whistle, *peeeeea* (D. Brooks recording from n Peru).
Behavior: Occas. perches up alone on a high bare branch at dawn on sunny mornings, otherwise stays mostly low inside forest where still-hunts by moving from perch to perch, pausing a few min at each. Unlike White Hawk does not soar, and seen much less often.
Status and habitat: A genuine rarity. Resident at very low density inside swampy or várzea forest in humid lowlands and along creeks and wooded riverbanks in low-lying areas in hilly terra firme regions. A specimen from Sierra de Lema is from foothill terrain. Perhaps less confined to floodplains in Venez. and the Guianas than in w Amazonia.

Range: To 1000m. Throughout Amazonas (Caño Cataniapo, Cerro Yavi, and Cerro Camani s to San Carlos de Río Negro) and Bolívar (lower Río Caura; Río Grande; Auyán-tepui; Sierra de Lema; Canaracuni). E Colombia to the Guianas and s to e Peru and Amaz. Brazil (most recs. n of Amazon).

Buteogallus

Robust raptors; broad wings and chunky profile; yellow cere; long yellow legs.

Savanna Hawk   PLATES 6, 11
Buteogallus meridionalis Gavilán Pita Venado
Identification: 18–24″ (46–61cm). 845g (sexes sim. in size). *Unusually long broad wings* (almost too large for size of bird) and short tail; *very long yellow legs*; eyes orange amber; bill small. *Mostly dull cinnamon rufous*; back tinged grayish, underparts narrowly and rather indistinctly barred dusky; rump and tail black; single median white tail band and narrow white tip. In flight *wings mostly rufous above and below*; flight feathers tipped black. Imm.: variable and confusing. In all stages note long pale yellow legs. Very young birds show buffy head with dark line through eyes; underparts pale buff with darker mottling; with age become dusky brown above with *buff eyestripe* and buff or white mottling on back and wings; below dark buff heavily mottled and streaked dusky; *shoulders and thighs usually with some rufous edging*; tail with several dark bars. Older birds gradually acquire more rufous.

Sim. species: In any plumage, distinctive shape and habitat of this large, handsome hawk are good clues. Likely confused only with Black-collared Hawk.
Voice: Infreq. a shrill *keeeeeeru*.
Behavior: A conspic. open-country raptor that perches in open, soars reg., and still-hunts from low open perches on trees, fence posts, shrubs, even gd., or less often stoops on prey in flight. Often walks on gd. where it uses long legs to capture some prey while afoot. Follows agricultural machinery (esp. where earth is plowed), and groups up to 12, occas. to 30 or more, gather at dry-season grass fires. Wet-season prey items incl. eels, frogs, crabs, and birds. Also rodents in dry season. Shares grassy habitat with White-tailed Deer, hence Spanish name, meaning "deer lookout." Nest in top of low shrub, small tree, palm, etc.; 1 white egg (all nests) at Hato Masaguaral, Guárico; eggs laid Feb–Sep with most breeding activity Apr–Oct (79 nests), peaking in early wet season; young fledge in 6.5–7.5 wk.[370].
Status and habitat: Widespread, common, and conspic. resident in dry ranchland, savanna, and other mostly open regions with scattered trees and shrubs. Less numerous in desert scrub; occas. along coast.

Range: To 500m (prob. higher). Throughout n of Orinoco; n and c Amazonas s to San Juan de Manapiare (sight, s to mouth of Río Ventuari); n Bolívar in lower Río Caura, La Paragua, Upata, and sightings to Brazil border. W Panama s to n Argentina and Brazil.
Note: Formerly placed in genus *Heterospizias*[403] based primarily on long wing length; now in *Buteogallus*[8,10].

Rufous Crab-Hawk   PLATE 6
Buteogallus aequinoctialis Gavilán de Manglares
Identification: 16.5–18″ (42–46cm). 700g. Looks like a small, dark edition of Savanna Hawk with gray head. Cere and legs yellow orange. *Head and throat gray*, rest of upperparts gray more or less heavily edged and scaled rufous, inner primaries and secondaries dull rufous basally (forms broad band) and tipped black; underparts (except throat) dull cinnamon rufous finely and rather obscurely barred black, *tail very short* and blackish with *single ill-defined median white band* and narrow whitish tip. Imm.: above mainly brown; narrow whitish eyebrow; dusky line through eyes; cheeks whitish mixed brown; in flight *wings show large pale tawny patch at base of primaries* (from above); underparts dirty buffy white to dark buff, throat and chest somewhat streaked and spotted dusky, breast with long, heavy black streak-

ing (or sparse streaking and spotting on younger? stages); thighs narrowly barred brown (only older stages?); tail dirty whitish mottled dusky, central feathers with numerous narrow dark bars. Cere and lores dusky; legs very pale yellow.

Sim. species: Ad. told from Savanna Hawk by small size, contrasting gray head and throat, and restricted range. Overall crab-hawk looks dull and dark compared to Savanna Hawk. Also see Black-collared Hawk which has whitish head. Imm.'s best marks are tawny wing patches (in flight).

Voice: Call (by imm.) a harsh, shrill *ke-KEE-KEE-ka-ca*, 2d and 3d notes higher and louder.

Behavior: Single birds or scattered prs. perch at low to med. hts. in mangroves. Feed heavily on crabs.

Status and habitat: Uncommon resident of mangroves and swampy coastal vegetation. More numerous and better known eastward in coastal regions of the Guianas.

Range: To 100m. Sucre (sight, Ajies)[596] and ne Monagas s to n Delta Amacuro (Pedernales and Isla Corocoro). Coastal Guianas and Brazil.

Common Black-Hawk   PLATE 11
Buteogallus anthracinus   Gavilán Cangrejero

Identification: 17–21″ (43–53cm). 930g. Very broad wings and short tail (in flight or at rest tail barely protrudes). *Bare loral area, cere, and basal half of bill bight yellow; cere more orange yellow; legs yellow.* Mostly black with *single rather broad, median white tail band* and narrow white tip; thigh feathers uniform black (cf. Great Black-Hawk). In flight from below, wings black with *whitish area at base of primaries* (usually fairly conspic.). At rest wings reach to tip of tail or slightly beyond. Imm.: very different; above blackish brown with buff streaking and spotting on head; indistinct buff eyestripe and dusky line through eye; *below rich dark buff streaked and blotched dusky* (teardrop-shaped spots form streaks), thighs barred black; *grayish buff tail crossed by 5–8 narrow dark bars and broader subterminal band.* Subad.: occas. pale buffy to clay color, esp. on head which is finely streaked. In flight from below, wing linings more or less unmarked buff, flight feathers darker and tipped black.

Sim. species: Easily confused. Ad. Great Black-Hawk differs in *larger* size (not always that apparent), *much duller yellow (not rich orange yellow) cere and lores*, longer tail (esp. apparent at rest), basal half to two-thirds of tail entirely white (Common Black-Hawk shows less white), and *longer legs* (in hand tarsus ca. 110 vs. 100mm); up close note Great Black-Hawk's barred thighs. Imm. even more sim. to imm.

Great Black-Hawk. Latter usually has more tail bars (10–14 vs. 5–8) which give tail a more fine-barred look. Also cf. dark-phase Hook-billed Kite, Slate-colored Hawk, Crane Hawk, dark-phase Short-tailed Hawk, and larger, rarer Solitary Eagle.

Voice: Commonest call, usually hd. in flight, a high, thin, piping *spink-speenk-speenk-spink-spink-spink-spink*, urgent, rising then descending slightly.

Behavior: Unlike Great Black-Hawk, reg. soars, sometimes in prs. or up to 6 at once which display by gliding in roller-coaster loops and circles as they call. Tends to perch within trees where inconspic., hence less often seen perched than larger Great Black-Hawk. Hunts mostly by watching from a fairly low perch, and freq. also on gd. around mangroves, esp. for crabs but also a wide variety of small vertebrates, eggs, even carrion. Bulky stick nest usually high in a mangrove[788]; 1 egg, dull white sparsely spotted with brown[706].

Status and habitat: Less numerous and much less widespread in Venez. than Great Black-Hawk. Locally fairly common resident in mangroves, tidal and estuarine habitats, and adj. dry to humid woodland, mostly within a few km. of coast. Easily seen around Cerro Misión, Falcón, Guaraunos, Sucre, and on Paria Pen. Very local inland, mostly near base of Andes (both sides) and in Coastal Cordillera.

Range: To 1100m (mts. of Carabobo). Base of Sierra de Perijá; s end of Lago de Maracaibo (sight), Zulia; nw Táchira; e Andean foothills in Barinas (Barinitas); otherwise mainly on or near Carib. coast (occas. inland in Coastal Cordillera) from e Falcón very locally e to Sucre and Delta Amacuro (*anthracinus*). Sw US to nw Peru and coastal Guyana. Trinidad. Lesser Antilles.

Great Black-Hawk   PLATE 11
Buteogallus urubitinga   Aguila Negra

Identification: 22–25″ (56–64cm). 1.1kg. Very broad wings and rather short tail. Bill black, *cere and lores dull yellow*; legs dull yellow. Plumage entirely black with *basal half of tail and upper tail coverts white*, narrow tail tip white; thighs barred white. In flight from below shows small whitish patch at base of outer primaries (not as obvious as in Common Black-Hawk). Imm.: sim. to imm. Common Black-Hawk but larger; tail with more dusky bands (10–14 vs. 5–8); bill blackish, cere grayish black. At rest tail projects somewhat beyond wings (unlike Common Black-Hawk).

Sim. species: See Common Black-Hawk. Larger, rarer Solitary Eagle, also quite sim., differs as follows: more massive proportions with longer and broader wings, longer attenuated primaries (usually bent up like those of a condor when soaring), shorter tail (barely protrudes behind wings), single median tail band, overall dark *blue gray* (not black) plumage, and more projecting aquiline head; up close an inconspic. bushy crest and no whitish at base of primaries.

Voice: Perched or in flight a high-pitched whistled scream, *wheeeeeeeuur.*

Behavior: Large and rather sluggish. Usually seen alone, on gd. in pastures, on sandbars, open areas, or perched atop low shrubs or in small to med.-sized trees. Soars well, but in llanos seldom seems to do so; in forested areas somewhat more freq. noted soaring. Spends much time on gd., esp. near water, where it hunts on foot. In llanos seen eating fish, frogs, lizards, snakes, and rodents. Bulky stick nest in palm or tree near water; eggs 28 Aug[369]; juvs. Jul and Nov, Guárico[734].

Status and habitat: Common resident along rivers and oxbows in humid lowland forest; also ranchland, open areas with scattered trees, gallery forest, riparian woodland, and mangroves. Often but not invariably near water, and much more a bird of interior than mainly coastal Common Black-Hawk. This is *the* common, widespread "black-hawk" n of Orinoco.

Range: To 500m; once to 1700m (Auyán-tepui). Throughout n and s of Orinoco, incl. Delta Amacuro[343] (*urubitinga*); no recs. in n Zulia, w Falcón, or Lara. N Mexico s to Bolivia, n Argentina, and Uruguay; w Ecuador and nw Peru. Trinidad.

Harris's Hawk   PLATES 6, 10
Parabuteo unicinctus   Gavilán de Hombros Rufos
Identification: 19–22" (48–56cm). ♂ 690g, ♀ 1kg. Cere and legs yellow. Rangier than *Buteo* and with longer, narrower tail. Mostly sooty brown with *prom. chestnut shoulders* and thighs; tail blackish, *rump, basal half of tail, and narrow tip white.* In flight from below, *wing linings chestnut,* flight feathers black. Imm.: above rather like ad. but scaled and streaked buff and white; *rufous chestnut shoulders usually faintly indicated* (rufous edgings), underparts buffy white with varying amts. of dusky streaking and spotting, heaviest on breast and belly; tail dingy grayish with numerous narrow dark bars and broader bar near tip; in flight from below, wing linings pale ru-

fous with *prom. dark patch on wrist;* flight feathers (esp. *base of primaries*) *whitish.*

Sim. species: Lanky blackish appearance, chestnut shoulders, and white at base of tail are good marks. Imm. usually enough like ad. to be recognized; in flight from below resembles imm. Snail Kite but wing linings pale rufous (not creamy buff mottled brown) with dark wrist patch, tail with less white at base, and bill not as strongly hooked.

Voice: Call a short, wheezy *hu'u'u'u'u,* like exhaling air.

Behavior: A fairly active raptor that still-hunts from a perch or stoops while soaring low. Sometimes groups of 3 may hunt cooperatively, stooping from air, and prs. or families are often seen soaring together, but usually rather low and not for extended periods of time. Prey items include birds, mammals, and reptiles, and reported taking carrion. Perches at almost any ht., sometimes quite low or even on gd. In Costa Rica breeds Dec–Apr; stick platform, usually high in tree at edge of woodland; 2 eggs, white or lightly marked with brown[706].

Status and habitat: Uncommon to locally fairly common resident. Desert scrub and dry semiopen savanna with brush and scattered woodlots; borders of dry and moist woodland, gallery forest, ranchland with scattered trees, even in trees around ranch buildings. Mainly in dry to moist regions.

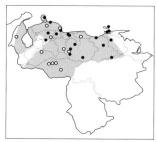

Range: To 800m. W Zulia (sight, Machiques—P. Alden); generally in Falcón, n Lara, and e of Andes from w Apure (sight), Yaracuy, and Aragua e to n Anzoátegui, w Sucre, nw Monagas, and n Bolívar; Isla Margarita (*unicinctus*). Sw US locally to w Ecuador, Bolivia, and s Argentina.

Busarellus

Monotypic genus; extraordinarily broad wings and short tail; mostly rufous plumage; bottom of feet covered with spiny papillae as in Osprey.

Black-collared Hawk   PLATES 6, 11
Busarellus nigricollis   Gavilán Colorado
Identification: 18–20" (46–51cm). ♂ 650g, ♀ 815g. Broad wings, short fanned tail, and projecting head impart aquiline shape. Legs bluish slate; eyes brownish amber. *Mostly bright rufous with buff white head and thick black crescent across upper chest* (the "collar"); tail narrowly barred rufous and black; broader black band near tip. In flight from below, *wing linings and flight feathers rufous, primaries broadly and*

secondaries narrowly tipped black. Imm.: upperparts mottled rufous brown and dusky; head, neck, and throat whitish more or less streaked dusky, rest of underparts buffy white streaked and irreg. mottled with black, often heaviest on belly; may show *traces of black forecollar;* older birds also show patches of rufous; tail as in ad. but dingy buff. In flight from below, *outer third of wing blackish contrasting strongly with paler and mottled inner part*.

Sim. species: Ad. with mostly rufous plumage likely confused only with Savanna Hawk which lacks whitish head and black collar, has more prom. banded tail and, in flight, proportionately longer wings. In ne cf. smaller but confusingly sim. Rufous Crab-Hawk.

Voice: Imms. and ads. utter a slow rising whistle, rather plaintive, *wuuueeeeeeeeEEE,* and a clear downslurred whistle, *shreeeuur.* Ads. also a low nasal and guttural *na-a-a-a-a-a-a* (like mechanical vomiting).

Behavior: A rather "unsuspicious" fishing hawk usually seen perched at low to med. hts. on a stub, bush, or branch overhanging water, esp. by quiet water. Hunts by jumping feet first into midst of floating vegetation or shallow open water, mostly for fish; also occas. frogs, tadpoles, and other aquatic life, or while in flight snatches fish from water surface. A fine soarer and often seen cruising low over swampy terrain. Pr. with 2 juvs., Apr, Guárico[734]; Jun–Sep nests in Suriname; large stick platform 12–15m up in mangrove or tree at edge of swamp; 1 grayish white egg blotched brown[253].

Status and habitat: Fairly common to common locally in mangroves, and in any forested or semiopen region where there are lagoons, old oxbows, and other bodies of sluggish water, esp. with emergent or floating vegetation. In llanos common around small tree-lined ponds, or almost any body of water where there are elevated perches nearby. Rare or absent in blackwater river regions s of Orinoco. No Amazonas recs.

Range: To 300m. Throughout n of Orinoco (except arid nw), Delta Amacuro, and n Bolívar (lower Río Caura) s to lower Río Cuyuní (sight) at El Dorado (*nigricollis*). W and s Mexico s locally to e Bolivia and s Brazil.

Solitary Eagle
PLATE 11

Harpyhaliaetus solitarius   Aguila Solitaria

Identification: 26–28″ (66–71cm). 3kg. Massively proportioned eagle; unusually broad wings and extremely short tail (a "flying wing"). When soaring, fanned *tail barely protrudes beyond trailing edge of*

wing. Bill black, basal half yellowish; cere, lores, and legs yellow. Entirely *dark slate gray to bluish slate*. In flight underwings all dark (up close note faint whitish barring at base of outer primaries). Imm.: brownish black above with rufous feather edgings; sides of head and underparts buff heavily streaked, blotched, and mottled black, becoming almost solid black on chest and thighs; tail buffy gray mottled dusky and *becoming blacker on terminal half*. In flight from below, wing linings mottled yellowish buff and dusky; flight feathers dark.

Sim. species: Easily confused with Great Black-Hawk. Imm. from imm. Great Black-Hawk by larger size, more extensive black mottling below, esp. on chest and thighs (little or no spotting), and lack of prom. narrow tail barring.

Voice: Not very vocal. Rarely, when soaring, a piercing *pipipipipip* and an arresting *yeep . yeep . yeep . yeep . yeep . yeep,* unlike scream of Great Black-Hawk[654].

Behavior: As name implies, usually alone or occas. in prs., soaring ponderously but impressively on broad, flat wings. Soars at low to moderate hts., and without much wheeling or circling, as it cruises over hill or mt. forest, crosses low over sharp ridges from one valley to the next, or undertakes long slow glides down steep valleys. Territories prob. immense as single birds or prs. cover large areas when aloft. Usually perch on open limbs inside canopy of large tree, hence infreq. seen perched. Huge conical nest of sticks high in fork of large tree in mts. (in s Peru).

Status and habitat: Very uncommon to rare and local resident of humid foothill and mt. forest. A low-density sp. most reliably seen (not on daily basis) near Choroní Pass, Aragua, and over hilly terrain in PN Guatopo, Miranda.

Range: To 1700m. N cordilleras in Carabobo, Aragua, Distr. Federal (sight, Turgua), and s Miranda (sight, PN Guatopo, 1980s—C. Parrish); s Amazonas at Cerro de la Neblina[801] (*solitarius*). Nw Mexico very locally s in mts. to Bolivia and nw Argentina.

Black-chested Buzzard-Eagle
PLATES 11, 14

Geranoaetus melanoleucus   Aguila Real

Identification: 24–27″ (61–69cm). 2.3kg. Large raptor with *massive proportions. Wings long, extremely broad at base, tapering near tips* (like a "flying triangle"); tail short, slightly wedge shaped and *barely protruding behind wings*. Cere and legs yellow. Above slate gray, *shoulders contrasting silvery gray,* throat pale gray, *broad chest band black,* rest of underparts pale gray finely barred black (barring not visible at a distance); tail black very narrowly tipped white. In flight from below, wing linings white; flight feathers blackish. Imm. (1st yr): above somewhat mottled slaty and brownish, no contrasting gray shoulders; *eyebrow pale*; below tawny buff, throat and chest somewhat *spotted and streaked black, lower breast and belly heavily mottled and barred blackish; tail decidedly longer than in ad. and with prom. wedge shape*; gray with numerous black bars. In flight from above, base of primaries often pale. 2d yr: more like ad. but heavily mottled and splotched blackish; overall darker than ad.

Sim. species: In its cold high-Andean habitat not likely confused. Note broad-beamed shape, pale shoulders, and very short tail. Dark chest and flight feathers, and wing shape narrowing near tip, recall Swainson's Hawk but latter is smaller and longer-tailed. Imm. best told by size, broad wings, and peculiar tail shape. Cf. imm. Black-and-chestnut Eagle (bigger; protruding head), imm. Solitary Eagle (usually lower el.), and Black Vulture.

Voice: Occas. a high, reedy whistle.

Behavior: Almost always seen alone or in prs. soaring over rugged terrain or sweeping back and forth over rolling paramo. Soars majestically but a little heavily on flat or slightly upbent wings and with much wheeling. Perches on boulders, rock ledges, or on gd., occas. shrubs. Hunts on wing, stooping on prey, incl. a variety of small mammals and birds, and has occas. been reported eating carrion. Bulky twig nest on rock ledge or cliff; 2 white eggs[280].

Status and habitat: Uncommon to fairly common resident over humid paramo, but pop. density low. Rugged paramo terrain, mountain canyons, and stunted high temperate and treeline forest, occas. at lower els. in dry open intermountain valleys. Reg. seen in vicinity of Páramo del Águila and Laguna Mucubají, Mérida.

Range: 3300–4500m (once to 1600m, Lagunillas, sw Mérida—P. Alden). Andes of Mérida (*australis*). Colombia s in Andes to Tierra del Fuego.

Buteo

Mostly med.-sized, rather heavy-bodied raptors; broad wings with several short "fingers" at tip and slightly curved trailing edge; tail usually broad and rounded; plumage sometimes variable or with color phases; often soar; characteristic of open or lightly wooded regions or forest edge more than forest interior.

Gray Hawk   PLATES 6, 7, 9
Buteo nitidus   Gavilán Gris
Identification: 15–17″ (38–43cm). 475g. Rather small gray hawk with clean-cut pattern. Cere and legs yellow; *eyes black*. Above light gray obscurely barred darker gray (most obvious on wings and back); *below white, narrowly and closely barred gray*; under tail coverts white; *tail contrasting black with 2 white bands* (3d concealed at base) and narrow white tip. In flight from below, wing linings light gray barred darker gray (barring not conspic.), flight feathers paler. Imm.: very different; above dark brown with varying amts. of buff and whitish edging; head and *underparts whitish to rich creamy buff*, head and hindneck heavily streaked brown, some with dusky area on sides of head and prom. pale eyebrow; *chest and breast with numerous large drop-shaped dusky spots*, sometimes also with suggestion of a dusky malar; tail blackish with 4–6 narrow pale bands. In flight from above shows *prom. pale patches at base of primaries*.

Sim. species: Ad. likely confused only with Roadside Hawk which is browner overall with unbarred throat, coarser rufous (not gray) barring on breast, and in flight always shows rufous in wings. Imm. rather like many other med.-sized imm. raptors but overall buffier, esp. on head, and with much bolder, irreg.-placed spotting (instead of streaking) on underparts; in flight note pale wing patches. Cf. esp. imm. Roadside and Broad-winged hawks; larger, heavier black-hawks (more tail barring); and imm. Yellow-headed Caracara.

Voice: Call when perched a loud, shrill whistle, descending in pitch, *PREEEEEEeeeea* or *PREEEEEEyuurr*, usually at long intervals.

Behavior: Fairly active buteo, sometimes even pursuing prey through trees. Freq. soars for short periods but usually not high. Still-hunts from partially exposed perch, and often sits in open when calling. Observed prey incls. birds and lizards (incl. *I. iguana*). Nest, May, Cantaura, Anzoátegui; ca. 10m up in leafless tree[186]; 1–3 pale bluish eggs.

Status and habitat: Fairly common resident in forest borders, scattered trees in forest clearings, gallery and riparian forest, and semiopen or lightly wooded areas in both dry and humid zones.

Range: To 1600m (Betijoque, Trujillo) n of Orinoco; to 250m s of Orinoco. Throughout s to c Amazonas (Cerro Duida) and Bolívar from lower Río Caura s to Brazilian border at Santa Elena de Uairén (*nitidus*); prob. throughout. Sw US to Bolivia, n Argentina, and s Brazil.

Note: Some consider birds from se Costa Rica to s Brazil, with light barring on upperparts, a separate sp. (Gray-lined Hawk, *Asturina nitida*) from unbarred n birds; both often placed in monotypic genus *Asturina*[10]. They are essentially identical vocally.

Roadside Hawk   PLATES 7, 9
Buteo magnirostris   Gavilán Habado
Identification: 16–19" (41–48cm). 265g. *Learn this common and widespread raptor well.* Med.-sized and proportionately longer tailed and shorter winged than others of genus. *Eyes and cere yellow.* Upperparts, head, throat, and chest dingy grayish, lower underparts thickly barred rusty and white, tail dusky with 4–5 ashy gray bands (*insidiatrix*). Or overall more brownish gray; underparts white barred cinnamon brown (*magnirostris*). In flight *always shows conspic. rufous patch at base of primaries.* Imm.: above dull brown somewhat mottled whitish; dull whitish eyebrow; usually an ill-marked dusky malar; below buff white somewhat streaked brown on chest and breast; older birds also with some dark barring on lower underparts.
Sim. species: Nearest is Gray Hawk which is always "grayer" (if there is doubt, it is a Roadside Hawk) with more clean-cut appearance (incl. crisper black-and-white tail pattern) and *black* (not yellow) eyes. Also cf. imm. Broad-winged Hawk.
Voice: Commonest call a nasal, angry-sounding *kzeeeeeer*, buzzy and descending in pitch. Single birds, prs., or 4–5 circle overhead (territory advertisement?) and give a nasal annoying ser. of *kee* notes, often over and over for several min. as if in fits of peevishness.
Behavior: A rather sluggish and guileless little raptor, usually seen perching on low open branches, fence posts, or other exposed places. Flies rather slowly, usually several rapid wing beats followed by a short glide, to cross small clearings, but seldom flies far. Often shakes tail side to side as alights. Occas. soars, usually with a ser. of flaps and glides and lots of noisy calling as prs. or families wheel in small circles at moderate hts. Preys heavily on frogs, also insects, reptiles, bats, rodents, occas. unwary birds. Eight stick nests at med. hts. (6 with eggs) May–mid Aug, Guárico; 1–2 largely white eggs speckled or lightly streaked brown[369].
Status and habitat: Commonest and most freq. seen raptor in Venez. Resident in almost all kinds of dry to humid forest, wooded river borders, plantations,

and open or shrubby areas with trees. Scarce in arid coastal regions.
Range: To 2500m n of Orinoco; to 2200m s of Orinoco. Throughout n of Orinoco, incl. Isla Patos (*insidiatrix*). Delta Amacuro (possibly also Paria region) and s of Orinoco (*magnirostris*). E Mexico to c Argentina and se Brazil.
Note: Some incl. subsp. *insidiatrix* in *magnirostris*.

White-rumped Hawk   PLATE 9
Buteo leucorrhous   Gavilán Rabadilla Blanca
Identification: 13–15" (33–38cm). 290g. Small buteo of Andes and n mt. forests. Rather short winged and long tailed; narrowed base and tips of wings and narrow tail impart lanky shape; cere and eyes yellow. Mainly black with *white rump and under tail coverts;* black tail shows *1 whitish band from above,* 2–3 visible from below; thighs barred rufous (not conspic. in field). In flight from below, *white wing linings contrast sharply with black flight feathers.* Imm.: above dark russet brown mottled rufous, head, neck, and underparts creamy buff heavily and coarsely streaked dark brown, belly sometimes barred; *upper and under tail coverts white;* tail like ad., or with only 1 ashy bar above, 2 below, and whitish tip; thighs barred rufous. In flight from below, *underwing shows more white than in ad.,* secondaries often pale; primaries dusky or somewhat barred black.
Sim. species: In mt. forests this small buteo should be easily recognized by contrasting underwing pattern, white rump, and white under tail coverts.
Voice: In display flight (Ecuador) a high, metallic, quavering *pee-ee-ee-ee* or more drawn-out *eeEEeeee-ee-ee-ee*[412]. Call a short, clear whistle, *SPEEaa* (like call of Golden-crowned Flycatcher), often over and over in flight.
Behavior: Rather infreq. seen little hawk of montane cloud forests. Single birds or prs. occas. soar in tight circles rather low over forested slopes for short periods of time during morning hr.; perch in forest mid. level or lower part of canopy, occas. on a high, exposed bare branch.
Status and habitat: Uncommon resident of humid and wet montane forest and forest borders; esp. broken-canopy forest on steep slopes; most freq. noted at forest borders or near clearings. Seen with some reg. over San Isidro Rd. in nw Barinas and upper els. of PN Guaramacal, Trujillo.

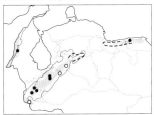

Range: 1400–3000m. Sierra de Perijá, Zulia; Andes of s Táchira n to Mérida and Trujillo (sight, PN Guaramacal); Coastal Cordillera in Distr. Federal. Colombia s in Andes to n Argentina; se Brazil and Paraguay.

Broad-winged Hawk
PLATES 7, 9
Buteo platypterus   Gavilán Bebehumo

Identification: 15–18″ (38–46cm). 450g. Stocky, med.-sized buteo. Above dark grayish brown, throat white bordered dusky, *rest of underparts white thickly barred and spotted brownish rufous*; broad tail black with 2 wide white bands and narrow white tip (3d band may show at base). In flight *from below, wings mostly white rimmed dark*. Imm.: above brown, below dull white broadly streaked dark brown; tail narrowly and evenly barred dusky and whitish.

Sim. species: Ad. Roadside Hawk is grayer and always shows rufous in primaries (if in doubt, flush bird). Imm. easily confused with several small buteos, esp. imm. Gray Hawk which is creamy below and more spotted than streaked, and imm. Roadside Hawk which shows prom. eyebrow, moustachial mark, and tends to be barred (not streaked) below. Also cf. Double-toothed Kite.

Voice: Freq. hd. call, by ad. and imm., a high, pure whistle, *w'eeeeeeEEE*, last part penetrating.

Behavior: Usually alone, perched on a semiopen branch or stub along forest borders, or soaring at low to moderate ht. over forest or clearings. Hunts by changing perches, then waiting varying amts. of time before moving again or ambushing prey. Individuals seem to hold nonbreeding territories.

Status and habitat: Common transient and n winter resident, late Aug–early May (most recs. Oct–early Apr), to humid montane forest, forest borders, and highland pastures with scattered trees in Andes and n cordilleras (seldom lowlands); progressively less numerous in highlands of e and s Venez.; uncommon in lowland forests s of Orinoco (scattered recs. mostly from Amazonas, lower Río Caura, and Río Grande area). No large migratory flocks reported in Venez.

Range: To 3000m n of Orinoco, to 1450m s of Orinoco. Throughout, mostly in mts. (*platypterus*). Breeds in N Amer. Winters from s Florida and s Mexico to Bolivia, n Brazil, occas. Trinidad. Resident birds (*antillarum*) breed in Lesser Antilles and Tobago.

Short-tailed Hawk
PLATE 9
Buteo brachyurus   Gavilán Cola Corta

Identification: 15–18″ (38–46cm). 490g. Rather small with compact proportions; wings broad but narrower near tips; tail *somewhat shorter* than in other buteos. An often confused sp. Light phase: above slaty black, *incl. sides of head to well below eyes* (looks

"hooded"); forehead and *underparts pure white in sharp contrast with upperparts*; tail grayish brown above, whitish below with several narrow black bands and broader black subterminal band. In flight from below, *wing linings whitish*, flight feathers grayish (lacks a strongly 2-toned look), primaries tipped black and with narrow blackish rim to trailing edge of wing. Dark phase: all sooty black with narrow white forehead (inconspic. in field), tail as in light phase. In flight from below, *wing linings black contrasting sharply with paler flight feathers*. Imm.: above rather like respective phase of ad. plumage but tail with more barring. Light-phase imm. shows some whitish mottling above; head and underparts creamy buff to whitish, lightly to heavily streaked and spotted brown, esp. on head and neck. Dark-phase imm. has underparts boldly spotted white.

Sim. species: Widespread. Good marks are compact proportions and lack of prom. tail bands. On light-phase birds note dark "hood," contrasting upper- and underparts, and wing linings in only moderate contrast with flight feathers (cf. Swainson's Hawk). On dark-phase birds note shape, size, and strongly 2-toned underwing. Cf. esp. imm. and dark-phase White-tailed Hawk which is considerably larger, also rare dark-phase Swainson Hawk which is slightly larger and has all-dark underwings incl. flight feathers and paler tail. Also cf. Zone-tailed Hawk (different shape; longer, strongly banded tail) and black-hawks; both of latter have heavier profile and much more white at base of tail.

Voice: Usually quiet. Occas., when soaring, a short nasal *keeer*, almost like distant meow of kitten.

Behavior: Infreq. seen *except* when soaring, then usually quite high and at a distance. Typically alone or in prs.; sometimes stoops from great hts. to capture birds, small mammals, and reptiles. One of few tropical raptors that reg. hunts over wooded terrain (as well as open areas) by stooping from air to snatch birds, reptiles, etc., from canopy rather than ambushing prey from a perch. Florida nest (no Venez. recs.) a bulky stick platform lined with green leaves, high in large tree; 2 whitish eggs, plain or with dark markings[706].

Status and habitat: Widespread resident but nowhere common or numerous; few recs. in llanos or ne. Dry, moist, and humid lowland and premontane forest and partially open or lightly wooded terrain. More numerous in humid regions; most recs. below ca. 1500m. Light-phase birds outnumber dark ones by a wide margin.

Range: To 2200m. Virtually throughout (many sight recs.) except arid regions (*brachyurus*). S Florida. Mexico s to n Argentina, Paraguay, and se Brazil. Trinidad.

White-throated Hawk PLATE 9

Buteo albigula Gavilán Gargantiblanco
Identification: 16–19″ (41–48cm). Longer-tailed upper-el. ally of Short-tailed Hawk. *Blackish brown above and on sides of head to below eyes* (looks "hooded"); *sides of neck and sides of breast chestnut brown*, rest of underparts white; necklace of brown streaks across chest; varying amt. of streaking on wing linings and rest of underparts, forming *a patch of brown on flanks*; thighs barred rufous; tail brown above, grayish below, with numerous indistinct dark bars. Imm.: sim. but breast and flanks also with large brown spots and blotches.
Sim. species: In any plumage told by combination of hooded appearance, flank patch, dark area along sides of neck and breast, and more or less streaky underparts. Cf. esp. imm. and subad. Short-tailed Hawk which is usually at much lower el. Imm. also much like imm. Broad-winged Hawk, but note dark smudge on sides and dark flank patch.
Behavior: In Andes of Peru individuals or prs. go up to soar on sunny midmornings for short periods of time. Wheel in rather small, tight circles at moderate hts. Occas. perch in open in high tree, but apparently hunt by ambushing prey from concealed perch inside forest.
Status and habitat: Prob. a rare resident, but no recent recs. Known from 1 specimen taken 10 May 1927 at Escorial, Mérida. Humid upper montane forest and stunted treeline forest.

Range: 3000m. Andes of Mérida (Táchira?). Colombia (1700–3600m) s in Andes to c Argentina and Chile.
Note: Once considered a subsp. of Short-tailed Hawk[334].

Swainson's Hawk

Buteo swainsoni Gavilán Langostero
Identification: 19–22″ (48–56cm). 1kg. Rather rangy med.-sized buteo with *noticeably pointed, slightly upturned wings*. Pale-phase ad.: above dark brown, below whitish with *broad reddish brown chest band*; *tail whitish basally* (looks pale-rumped) becoming grayer toward tip and crossed by numerous narrow inconspic. dark bars and broader subterminal band. In flight *from below, white wing linings contrast with dusky flight feathers.* Dark-phase ad. (rare): entirely brownish black, *incl. underwings*; foreface and chin

whitish; *tail pale* as in normal ad. Intermediates show varying amts. of tawny brown mottling or barring on lower underparts. Pale-phase imm.: above dark brown, hindcrown, sides of head, and upper back mottled whitish, below buff streaked and spotted brown; some show large dark patch on either side of chest.
Sim. species: Ads., with contrasting chest band, should be distinctive. Dark-phase birds are confusing, but most sim.-sized buteos in Venez. show some contrast between under wing lining and flight feathers, also rufous on shoulders, more white in tail (e.g., Zone-tailed, dark-phase Short-tailed and White-tailed hawks). In all plumages Swainson's usually looks pale rumped.
Behavior: In Venez. most likely encountered singly or in small migrating groups. A fine soarer on wings that are slightly upswept and angled forward. Feeds by stooping from considerable hts., but rarely feeds on migration.
Status and habitat: Very rare passage migrant from N Amer. Only recs. are 1 bird, doubtless a migrant, taken in Sep along Río Chama, Mérida; and 5 birds (3 light phase, 2 dark phase) seen 10 Jan 1976 at a fire in rice field 12km s of Calabozo, Guárico (P. Alden). Latter may have been early returning migrants or "wintering" birds. Migrating groups of 1000s reg. pass through Panama and Andes of Colombia.

Range: To 1600m (prob. higher). Known from s Mérida; w Guárico (sight). Breeds in w N Amer.; migrates mostly through C Amer. and n S Amer. to wintering gds. in s S Amer.

Zone-tailed Hawk PLATES 9, 10

Buteo albonotatus Gavilán Zamuro
Identification: 18–22″ (46–56cm). ♂ 600g, ♀ 885g. Long wings of uniform width. *Shape and soaring behavior closely mimic that of Turkey Vulture. Cere and legs yellow.* Plumage all black with 3 grayish white tail bands (2 always visible), outermost broadest. In flight *from below, wings 2-toned* with black wing linings and grayish flight feathers; tail proportionately longer and narrower than in most buteos. Imm.: sim. but browner; underparts mottled and speckled whitish; tail grayish brown above, whitish below with several narrow dark bars; distinctive shape sim. to ad. but no yellow cere.
Sim. species: Easily passed over as a Turkey Vulture because of 2-toned wings and teetering flight with wings held in dihedral, but note dark head, *yellow cere and legs* (if close), and *white bands* on tail.

Smaller, dark-phase Short-tailed Hawk has white forehead and broader, more typical buteo-shaped wings and tail. Black-hawks are heavier and show much more white on tail (esp. at base). Also cf. dark-phase Swainson's Hawk (rare) and imm. White-tailed Hawk.

Voice: Infreq. call a squealing whistle.

Behavior: Single birds or scattered prs. are active and usually seen soaring at moderate hts. over open or partially open terrain. Their teetering flight and plumage are sim. to that of Turkey Vulture, a convergence that may permit them to approach closer to potential prey before eliciting an alarm response. Prey incls. birds and small mammals. Large stick nest high in tree (mostly in dry season?); 1 downy chick, May, San Mateo, Anzoátegui[186]; 2 pale bluish white eggs.

Status and habitat: Uncommon resident. Dry open or semiopen terrain, cattle land, gallery forest, and areas with scattered trees and lighter woodland; locally over humid lowland forest (e.g., at PN Guatopo). Everywhere a sp. of low pop. density.

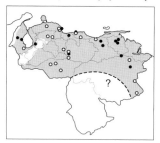

Range: To ca. 600m. Maracaibo Basin e to Monagas and se Bolívar (sight, El Palmar; El Dorado; Santa Elena de Uairén); prob. Amazonas. Sw US to Venez., e Ecuador, e and w Peru, nw and e Brazil, Bolivia, Paraguay, and the Guianas. N pops. migratory.

[Red-tailed Hawk]

Buteo jamaicensis   Gavilán Colirrojo

Identification: 20–25″ (51–64cm). 1–1.2kg. Above dark brown, rump paler, *broad tail bright rufous from above* (grayish below but rufous usually shows); underparts white, typically with *band of coarse hatched streaking across mid. and lower breast*, but underparts vary from very pale to very dark. Imm.: sim. but tail grayish brown, usually with numerous narrow dusky bars; whitish chest and streaked lower underparts as in ad.

Sim. species: Ad. should be unmistakable if seen well; imm.'s best mark is its unmarked white chest.

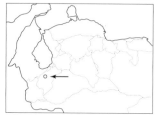

Status and habitat: Accidental. Known in Venez. from 1 publ. sight rec. (no specimen or photo) of a fully ad. "red-tailed" bird soaring over entrance of Universidad de Los Andes forest w of Mérida, 2100m, 16 Jan 1992, by Hilty, K. Zimmer, and several others[259]. No previous recs. for S Amer.

Range: Breeds from Alaska s to n Mexico, locally to w Panama; winters s to Canal Zone.

White-tailed Hawk   PLATE 11

Buteo albicaudatus   Gavilán Tejé

Identification: 20–24″ (51–61cm). 870g. Large buteo with broad wings (primaries long and attenuated) and short rounded tail. Light phase: above slate gray *incl. sides of head;* conspic. *rufous shoulders;* underparts, rump, and *tail white; tail with single broad black band near tip;* throat sometimes black. In flight from below, wing linings white; flight feathers grayish. Dark phase: all slate gray with white-barred under tail coverts; usually some rufous on shoulders; *tail as in normal ad.* Imm.: brownish black with varying amts. of white mottling and streaking below; may show fine barring on shoulders and crissum; younger birds show prom. pale eyebrow; shoulders often tinged rufous; rump whitish barred brown; tail brownish to light gray crossed by numerous fine darker bars and often with ill-defined black subterminal band; tail becomes whiter with age. From below, wing linings blackish, darker than flight feathers.

Sim. species: In flight from above, white rump and mostly white tail of ad. are diagnostic (either phase). Short-tailed Hawk is superficially sim. and has sim. "hooded" look to head but is smaller, has less contrasting underwings, and is *uniformly dark from above.* Imms. can be confusing, but most show enough rufous on shoulders and/or white at base of tail to be recognized. Note habitat.

Voice: High whistled *klee* and nasal *kleewee*, over and over.

Behavior: Seen alone or in prs. soaring to hts. over open or scrubby country. Only buteo in Venez. that reg. hunts by hovering, often facing into wind on almost motionless wings, scanning gd., then stooping in spectacular fashion on mostly gd.-dwelling prey. Often attracted to grass fires, with up to 16 (more than half dark phase) seen at a fire 1 Mar 1998 in Gran Sabana. Noted eating rodents, iguanas, and birds. Large bulky nests in bush, small tree, palm, or occas. human-made structure (i.e., windmill); 4 nests (3 in dry season) mid Feb–Aug; density of 4 prs./ 32km² in w Guárico[369]; several nests Jan–late Mar, w Apure (Hilty); 1–2 dull white eggs.

Crested Eagle (left, light-phase adult), Harpy Eagle (right, adult)

Status and habitat: Fairly common resident in dry open savanna and ranchland, occas. broken, partially wooded terrain. Most easily found on ranches in llanos, also reg. over Gran Sabana and grasslands of Monagas.

Range: To ca. 2000m (once to 4000m?) n of Orinoco; to 1500m s of Orinoco. Maracaibo Basin and Sierra de Perijá, Zulia; Andes of Mérida and Lara (*hypospodius*); elsewhere throughout n of Orinoco, grasslands s of Orinoco in Amazonas and Bolívar; Isla Margarita (*colonus*). Sw US to the Guianas, se Peru, c Argentina, and s Brazil. Netherlands Antilles. Trinidad.

Crested Eagle   Illus. above, PLATE 13
Morphnus guianensis   Aguila Monera

Identification: 31–35″ (79–89cm). ♂ 1.3kg, ♀ 1.8kg. *Very large but rather lightly built eagle.* Broad bluntly rounded wings; *very long tail.* Small pointed occipital crest black. Cere and lores slaty. Light phase: above brownish black, *head, neck, and chest pale gray* vaguely tinged brown, *sharply contrasting with white breast and belly*, both sometimes with faint brownish barring; *tail black with 3 broad ashy gray bands*. In flight from below, wing linings creamy white, flight feathers *boldly barred black and gray*. Barred phase: sim. but head, neck, and chest dark gray, *rest of underparts and wing linings white boldly and coarsely barred black*. Intermediate plumages and almost all-black plumage are known. Imm.: upperparts blackish mottled white; *entire head, neck, and underparts white*, lores slaty, crest white tipped black, *long tail grayish with 7–8 narrow dusky bands*. Several yr required to attain fully ad. plumage.

Sim. species: All plumages much like respective plumages of Harpy Eagle, and field identification often not easy. In general Crested is slightly smaller, slighter, and with proportionately longer tail. Also note, if possible, smaller, weaker bill; longer but thinner tarsi (bare in both spp.); and single-pointed crest. Crested never shows ad. Harpy's broad dark chest band (but beware imm. and subad. Harpies which lack black band); light-phase birds also differ in unmarked wing linings and more or less unbarred thighs (barred in ad. Harpy). Barred phase easily told by heavy barring below. Also cf. smaller Gray-headed Kite. Imm. very like imm. Harpy, but note latter's more massive proportions, heavy bill, and double-pointed crest. Also cf. imm. Ornate Hawk-Eagle, and ad. Black-and-white Hawk-Eagle, both much smaller and with legs feathered to toes.

Voice: Call reportedly resembles that of Great Black-Hawk[333].

Behavior: Overall much less well known than Harpy Eagle. Apparently still-hunts inside forest and rarely or never soars. Birds in Peru, presum. to be hunting, were seen alone at mid. level to subcanopy hts. inside forest, where they flew rapidly between perches, then remained for ca. 1 min before moving again (Hilty). Preys on mammals (occas. birds) up to size of small monkey. Ad. bringing green twigs to large, stick platform nest 20m up in tall forest tree, e Bolívar, Mar 1981 (R. Ridgely, G. Tudor, and others).

Status and habitat: Resident. Rarely seen, low-density raptor with highly dispersed distrib. in humid lowland and lower montane forest. Most recent recs. are s of Orinoco, but an imm. seen and photographed on s slope of Choroní Rd. in PN Henri Pit-

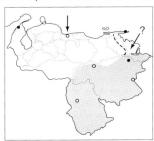

tier 11 Jan 1986, ca. 900m, is exceptional (Hilty, R. Ridgely, and others); there are a few recent sightings from lower Río Caura.
Range: To 1600m. Nw Zulia (Cerro Alto del Cedro); n Aragua (specimen and photo); Paria Pen., Sucre (wing specimen)[297]; c Amazonas (sight, mouth of Río Ventuari, Feb 1998—K. Zimmer and D. Wolf); n Bolívar in lower Río Caura (sightings) and e Bolívar (nesting pr., late 1970s, Guyana Trail). Honduras to w Ecuador, Bolivia, Paraguay, ne Argentina, and se Brazil.

Harpy Eagle
Harpia harpyja Aguila Harpía
Illus. p. 245, PLATE 13

Identification: 35–40″ (89–102cm). ♂ 4.5kg, ♀ 7.5kg. World's most powerful bird of prey. *Rounded wings unusually broad and massive*; tail fairly long; massive yellow tarsi (almost as large as a man's wrist). Cere and very heavy bill black; eyes dark amber. Head and upper throat gray with *conspic. double-pointed black crest* (usually raised); upperparts blackish; feathers indistinctly edged gray; entire *chest black forming broad band*, rest of underparts white, thighs barred black, tail black with 3 broad ashy gray bands and faint grayish white tip. In flight from below, wings are extremely broad, esp. secondaries, and long; wing linings barred black and white, flight feathers grayish white *boldly* barred black. Juv.: eyes dark brown; head and entire underparts whitish (incl. divided crest), above brownish gray to light gray, the feathers heavily pale-edged; tail gray with several narrow dusky bands; underwings much as in ad. Imm.: darker above; crest dusky (acquires dark crest early); chest band med. gray. Older imms. acquire blackish patches on wing coverts and scapulars; ultimately entire upperparts become blackish as in ad. birds; broad chest band med. gray, chest darkening with age.
Sim. species: Ad. or imm. likely confused only with Crested Eagle.
Voice: Ads. at or near nest utter rather weak but penetrating scream, *screeeeeaaae*, with melancholy quality, typically in ser. of 7–10 or so notes. Juv. gives shrill, grating *jaaeee!*
Behavior: Normally keeps within forest canopy, displaying remarkable agility as it glides and swerves among branches and around tree crowns. Does not soar, and rarely flies much above canopy, then only briefly at ht. of canopy or emergent trees (never high above canopy). Despite enormous size, not conspic. and usually seen only when crosses rivers or other forest openings. Not esp. wary in presence of people, hence a tempting target for hunters. Hunts by watching from perches inside forest, then flying out with remarkable speed and agility for so large a bird to ambush large arboreal mammals such as monkeys, sloths, and coatis, large birds, snakes, and occas. terrestrial mammals. Large stick-and-leaf nest high in sturdy fork in canopy or emergent tree may be reused; 1–2 white eggs. Asynchronous nesting begins in any month and lasts approx. 9 months; ads. do not renest for 9 months or more, resulting in 1.5- to 2-year breeding cycle[537].

Status and habitat: Low-density resident of tall, humid lowland and hill forest. Infreq. encountered because of enormous size of territory over which it hunts. Requires large tracts of lowland forest with large mammalian prey, but pop. densities vary, even in prime lowland forest; one of highest densities of Harpies is in Río Grande Forestry Reserve where logging is extensive (E. Alvarez study). No recent verifiable recs. of this sp. in n cordilleras.

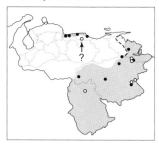

Range: To 1800m. Coastal Cordillera in Carabobo (Cumbre de Valencia), Aragua (Rancho Grande), Distr. Federal, and Miranda (Río Chico); Delta Amacuro[343]; s of Orinoco in Amazonas (sight) and Bolívar. Se Mexico to n Argentina and s Brazil.

Spizastur

Smaller and more compact than other hawk-eagles, with proportions intermediate between *Buteo* and *Spizaetus*; wing shape less oval than in *Spizaetus*; occipital crest short; feathered tibia longer than tarsus.

Black-and-white Hawk-Eagle
PLATE 12
Spizastur melanoleucus Aguila Blanquinegra
Identification: 22–24″ (56–61cm). 815g. Smallish, compact eagle with muscular *buteo*-like proportions. *Cere red orange*; eyes yellow. *Above all black with head, entire underparts, and feathered legs white*; small mask and short bushy crest black; *tail relatively short*, black with at least 3 broad grayish bands and narrow tip. In flight from below, mostly white with a few blackish bars on tips of primaries; *white wing linings wrap up over leading edge of forewing* (like long narrow "headlights") *in sharp contrast to black of upper wing.* Imm.: sim. but upperparts duller, browner, and somewhat scaled whitish; may *lack or show only partly developed white* on leading edge of forewing.
Sim. species: Often confused with several other superficially sim. raptors, e.g. Ornate Hawk-Eagle, pale-phase imm. Gray-headed Kite, White Hawk, and Short-tailed Hawk, but told from any by distinctive narrow white "*headlights*" along leading edge of forewing. Also note that Black-and-white Hawk-Eagle's head projects more than in buteos (looks like a "stretched" buteo) but less than in larger hawk-eagles. Wings are broad, but shape is nearer that of a buteo than of oval wings of Black and Ornate hawk-eagles. Up close note colorful cere and feathered legs.

Voice: In flight occas. a shrill, whistled *wheEEeer*, or ser. of whistles; unlike that of Ornate Hawk-Eagle.
Behavior: Single birds are sometimes aloft for short periods on sunny mornings, soaring in slow circles on ruler-flat wings with primaries curled up slightly at tips. Perch and still-hunt, mostly for birds and mammals, in forest canopy or lower, where inconspic. and rarely seen; also may pursue prey rapidly through forest. In Panama reported building nest 40m up in large tree, 24 Sep[720].
Status and habitat: Rare to uncommon and local resident, although increasing no. of recent recs. suggests the sp. has been underreported. Tall humid and wet forest in lowland and lower montane regions. Can be seen with some reg. near Rancho Grande Biol. Station, Aragua, and near n base of Sierra de Lema in e Bolívar; also seen with some reg. in early 1980s in forested valley below San José de Los Altos sw of Caracas (C. Parrish).

Range: To 1500m n and s of Orinoco. Distrib. spotty. W slope of Andes in Mérida, e slope in Táchira (sight, La Fundación, 26 Nov 1982—C. Parrish) and ne Barinas (sight, La Soledad, 11 Aug 1983—C. Parrish); n mts. in Carabobo (sight, Palmichal), n Aragua, Distr. Federal, and Miranda (e to Santa Lucia); e Sucre (sight, Guaraunos, 5 May 1996—R. Ridgely et al.) and ne Monagas (sight[58]) s to Delta Amacuro; nw Amazonas (Capuana) and e Bolívar s to Sierra de Lema area (sightings). S Mexico locally s to Bolivia, n Argentina, Paraguay, and s Brazil.

Spizaetus

Rounded, butterfly-shaped wings (like heliconid butterfly) noticeably narrow at base; long tail; feathered tarsi; long occipital crest (unlike *Spizastur*); advertise territories by soaring and calling for short periods on sunny mornings.

Black Hawk-Eagle   PLATE 13
Spizaetus tyrannus   Aguila Tirana
Identification: 25–28″ (64–71cm). 1kg. Large with *bluntly rounded wings conspic. narrowed at base* (butterflylike in shape) and slightly swept forward; *long tail*; cere slate gray; eyes amber to yellowish. *Mostly black* with short bushy occipital crest spotted white at base; thighs and under tail coverts barred black and white; tail with 3 broad grayish bars (whitish from below). In flight from below, wing linings mottled black and white, *flight feathers boldly "check-*

ered" black and white. Imm.: above brown with varying amts. of whitish mottling; prom whitish eyestripe and white throat; cheeks blackish, underparts buffy white heavily streaked blackish, becoming almost solid black on sides and flanks; thighs and belly barred with black. Subad.: like ad. but retains white eyebrows and white mottling on head.
Sim. species: Flight profile much like that of Ornate Hawk-Eagle, but wings rounder, tail longer, and all plumages much darker (note imm.'s strong facial pattern). No other large dark raptor has such bold black-and-white checkered flight feathers and such obviously rounded wings that are pulled forward and narrow at base.
Voice: Advertises during brief midmorning periods aloft, a loud, clear, whistled *wheep-wheep-wheep-waHEEE-er*, last note slurred downward; may call once or several times without clear pause. Also may give only 1 *wa-wHEEEer*, varying to *puwheér*; accented note at middle or near end of call is diagnostic (reverse of Ornate Hawk-Eagle).
Behavior: Reg. soars, often to great hts., during midmorning or midday, where it may circle for 10 min or so, calling freq. and occas. displaying with slow "butterflylike" wing flapping as it calls, before returning to forest. Still-hunts by moving from one perch to another in or at edge of forest, then flying out with surprising speed to ambush birds and mammals up to size of a large toucan or small cracid. Occas. perches rather low. Usually alone and seldom seen except when soaring. Mar nest 14m up in tree in Panama; 1 or more young[83].
Status and habitat: Uncommon to locally fairly common resident in humid lowland forest and along forest borders and tall second-growth woodland. May favor, or at least tolerate, more open or broken woodland than allied Ornate Hawk-Eagle. Rec. virtually throughout n of Orinoco, but few recs. along e base of Andes or llanos.

Range: To 1500m (sight, 1800m). W and s Zulia and w Mérida; e slope of Andes in nw Barinas (sight, Altamira, 9 Mar 2000—Hilty and D. Ascanio); c Falcón (sightings, Sierra de San Luis); se Falcón (sight) and Coastal Cordillera in w Carabobo (sight)[60]; Aragua (sight), Miranda (sight) and Distr. Federal (sight)[259]; Sucre, Monagas, and Delta Amacuro; throughout s of Orinoco (*serus*). E Mexico s to ne Argentina, Paraguay, and se Brazil. Trinidad.

Ornate Hawk-Eagle
PLATES 12, 13

Spizaetus ornatus Aguila de Penacho

Identification: 23–25″ (58–64cm). 1.2kg. Lanky eagle with *bluntly rounded wings narrowing at base.* Tail relatively long; cere yellow; eyes yellow to amber; lores gray; legs feathered. Crown and *long pointed crest black* (crest usually held flat). Upperparts black, *sides of head, hindneck, and sides of chest bright rufous,* throat and center of chest white bordered by black malar stripe; *rest of underparts incl. thighs white coarsely barred black,* tail black with 3 broad grayish bands. In flight, under surface of wings white, wing linings spotted, and flight feathers barred black. Imm.: above dusky brown, *head and underparts white, thighs and flanks barred black* (mostly white in very young birds); *tail* blackish with broad grayish brown bands. Underwing sim. to ad. but less spotted and barred (nearly all white in very young birds). Soars with *flat wings pulled slightly forward,* aquiline head protruding noticeably.

Sim. species: Handsome ad. shouldn't be confused except with rare imm. Gray-bellied Hawk, an *Accipiter,* which has remarkably sim. plumage (but not shape) but differs as follows: smaller size, no crest, bare legs, slighter build, short rounded wings, and not likely to be seen soaring. Imm. told from imm. Black-and-white Hawk-Eagle by shape (lankier, longer tailed), extensive black flank and thigh barring, usually spotted wing linings (except very young birds), yellow (not red orange) cere, no black mask, and all-dark leading edges of forewing. Also see Crested Eagle and ad. and imm. Gray-headed Kite.

Voice: Mainly hd. midmorning. May call more or less continually for 1 min or more, a loud whistled *whit, wheEEeuuu, whep whep, whep whep* (1st note faint, 2d downslurred), often repeated several times. Cf. call of Black Hawk-Eagle (pattern reversed).

Behavior: Reg. aloft on sunny mornings, ca. 9:00–10:00 A.M., where it circles leisurely, calls loudly to announce presence, and occas. displays with short bouts of butterflylike wing flutters (as though shaking wings) while calling. May ascend very high, sometimes almost out of sight, but also often soars closer to canopy than Black Hawk-Eagle. Hunts by moving from one inconspic. perch to the next at med. hts. inside forest or along borders, but occas. power dives with awesome speed into colonies of roosting egrets, troops of monkeys, etc. Almost always seen alone. Bulky stick nest high in branch fork or near trunk of large canopy tree; building nest, 2 Mar, Rancho Grande, Aragua; pr. incubating, Dec, Trinidad.

Status and habitat: Uncommon and low-density resident of tall humid forest, gallery forest in lowlands, foothills, and lower montane forest. More often seen when perched along natural openings in forest, high in trees along rivers, or in broken hill forest than inside unbroken forest. Less numerous (or less often seen) than Black Hawk-Eagle, esp. where the two occur together.

Range: To 1200m (prob. higher). Locally throughout n and s of Orinoco. Sierra de Perijá, Zulia; w base of

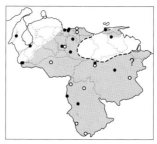

Andes in w Mérida; e base of Andes in Táchira, n cordilleras in Carabobo, Aragua, Distr. Federal (sight, El Avila), and s Miranda (Mar 1979, Charallave— C. Parrish); and llanos from w Apure (sight, Hato Cedral, 1999), Cojedes, and Guárico; Sucre and n Monagas; throughout Amazonas and Bolívar (*ornatus*). S Mexico to w Ecuador, n Argentina, and s Brazil. Trinidad.

Oroaetus

Large highland eagle; differs from *Spizaetus* and *Spizastur,* etc., in dark, coarsely marked plumage, larger size, more robust proportions, and less oval wing shape.

Black-and-chestnut Eagle
PLATES 13, 14

Oroaetus isidori Aguila de Copete

Identification: 25–29″ (64–74cm). Large, robust eagle with projecting head. Eyes golden yellow. Broad wings recall *Spizaetus* but are longer and with slight point to tips; tail short and rather narrow (seems too small for size of bird). Legs feathered. Mainly black incl. spikelike crest (often held elevated even in flight); *breast and lower underparts chestnut streaked black;* thighs black, tarsal feathers chestnut; *tail pale gray with broad black band near tip.* In flight from below, wing linings chestnut, flight feathers grayish with a few dusky bars and black tips, *outer primaries with large pale "window" at base* (above and below). Imm.: above brown with buff edgings, crest tipped black, forehead and eyestripe buffy white, sides of head and underparts whitish *stained and streaked dusky and chestnut, esp. on sides of head and sides of breast;* tail longer than in ad., brownish gray with 3–4 narrow black bands. In flight from below, wing linings mottled, flight feathers banded, base of primaries with *large pale "window"* (above and below). Young birds become progressively darker with maturity; subads. quite dark but blotchy and mottled as chestnut coloration of ad. appears; retain pale panel in wing.

Sim. species: Handsome ad. distinctive, undistinguished imm. confusing. Latter from imm. *Spizaetus* hawk-eagles by larger, more robust proportions; longer, less oval wings; shorter tail; and more ponderous flight. In *all* plumages, *pale windows on wings are good mark.* Imm. Black Hawk-Eagle has more distinct facial pattern and blacker underparts and sides; imm. Ornate is whiter without mottled "dirty" appearance. Imm. Solitary Eagle shows more contrast between black chest and striped lower underparts. Also see Black-chested Buzzard-Eagle.

Voice: Call a low-pitched, gull-like *quaAAaa*, drawn out; also a reedy *kreee, kee-kee*.

Behavior: A large, spectacular, and often unsuspicious mt. eagle that reg. goes aloft on sunny mornings or at midday to soar, sometimes for 15–20 min or more at a time, mostly at low to moderate hts. over mt. forest or along forested ridges, but occas. quite high. Perches mostly in canopy of large trees where not too conspic. Hunts by watching from perches in forest, then flies out to ambush prey. Reported to prey on arboreal birds and mammals ranging in size from squirrels to guans. Flight is heavier than in *Spizaetus*. In flight occas. drops legs and holds wings up in strong dihedral or flaps slowly (wing-flutter display?). Stick nests in large tree forks are reused for many yrs and may reach enormous size.

Status and habitat: Uncommon and low-density resident in large tracts of relatively undisturbed humid and wet montane forest (cloud forest) of Andes. Reg. over San Isidro Rd. (nw Barinas) and PN Guaramacal, Trujillo, Feb 1995–1999 (Hilty and D. Ascanio).

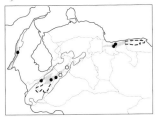

Range: 600–2500m (mostly above 1200m). Sierra de Perijá, Zulia; Andes of Mérida and Trujillo (sight); Coastal Cordillera in Carabobo and Aragua (PN Henri Pittier). Colombia in Andes s to nw Argentina.

Falconidae: Falcons and Caracaras

Halcones y Caricares

One or more members of this family can be found on all continents except Antarctica and some oceanic islands. They differ most obviously from hawks, eagles, and kites (Accipitridae) in having a "tooth" or notch on the upper mandible, as well as in many osteological features. The caracaras, a New World group, have bare facial skin, rather long wings and tail, and with the exception of the Red-throated Caracara, are rather omnivorous. The Laughing Falcon is a New World species notable for its puffy-headed appearance and remarkable voice. Nidification has been reported only a few times for the Laughing Falcon and for only a few of the for-

est-falcons. True falcons (*Falco*) are a worldwide group of streamlined, pointed-winged predators capable of fast flight and tremendous speed when stooping. The open-country species occasionally soar briefly and also regularly hover. Higher level taxonomy of the family follows Griffiths[225,226].

Daptrius

Predominantly black; large area of bare facial skin; lanky shape; rather long tail.

Black Caracara PLATE 8
Daptrius ater Chupacacao Negro

Identification: 17–19″ (43–48cm). 350g. *Long, narrow wings and tail.* Bill black; *large area of bare facial skin bright orange* becoming yellowish on throat. Plumage glossy black with *conspic. white band across base of tail.* Imm.: facial skin lemon yellow; underparts indistinctly barred and speckled buff; basal two-thirds of tail white with 3–4 black bars.

Sim. species: Orange (or yellow) face and white at base of tail are diagnostic. See Red-throated Caracara, a forest bird of heavier proportions.

Voice: Harsh, scratchy scream, *kraaaaaaaa*, descending somewhat, hoarser than respective call of Yellow-headed Caracara; in flight a harsh, screaming *sqeeoow, sqeeoow, . . .* repeated over and over when excited.

Behavior: Most often seen in families of 3–4 but occas. alone. Stands or walks on river sandbars, perches high in open in trees along rivers or forest borders, or flies high over forest. Flight is straight with almost continuous flapping. Rarely soars but may glide short distances. Scavenges a variety of food, from carrion and nestlings to insects and palm fruits. Nests Mar–Jun in Guyana; 2–3 buff eggs spotted brown[83].

Status and habitat: Uncommon to fairly common resident locally; almost always in rather low density. Tall moist to humid forest borders, river borders, sandbars along *large* rivers, and other semiopen areas in forested zones, but most often along forested river edges. Invades partially deforested areas (e.g., w of El Palmar, Bolívar).

Range: To 300m. Maracaibo Basin, Zulia, and w base of Andes from nw Táchira n to Trujillo (sight, 1970s at Llanos de Monay—P. Alden; 1980s at La Ceiba—C. Parrish); e base of Andes n locally to Portuguesa (Guanare); se Sucre, Monagas, and Delta

Amacuro; throughout Amazonas and Bolívar. The
Guianas s to n Bolivia and Amaz. Brazil.

Ibycter

Differs from *Polyborus* in less raptorial bill, bare
throat, longer tail, black plumage, and habits.

Red-throated Caracara   PLATE 8
Ibycter americanus   Chupacacao Ventriblanco
Identification: 19–22″ (48–56cm). 570g. Long and
ample tail, chickenlike bill, and black and white
plumage bring to mind a curassow. Mostly glossy
black with *bare red throat and red facial skin*; cheeks
somewhat grizzled whitish; *belly and under tail coverts white*; bill yellow, base gray; legs dull red.
Imm.: sim. but duller; throat and facial skin dusky
(little or no red).
Sim. species: Cf. Black Caracara which has bright orange to lemon yellow face and white band across
base of tail.
Voice: Often incredibly noisy as prs. or groups suddenly burst into loud, raucous chorus, *AH-AH-AH-
AAou* (a common Spanish rendition is *CO-ME CA-
CAO*), over and over while perched or in flight.
When several mob simultaneously, 1 may utter *AH-
AH-AAou*, another a harsh *GRA'OU*, and a 3d a loud
GRAAHEE'ow, all simultaneously in cacophony of
quarrelsome sound. At a distance vocalizations resemble those of macaws.
Behavior: A social forest caracara almost always
seen traveling in prs. or noisy groups of 3–6 that
range over very large areas and are highly territorial.
Normally perches high in tree crowns along river
edges, forest borders, or in canopy of tall forest, but
occas. descends much lower, even to forest floor.
Preys on wasp and bee larvae, apparently raiding
nests of even the most vicious spp. with impunity.
Also eats fruit (esp. palms). Flight is slow and labored, usually with much flapping, occas. a short
sail; seldom flies far and does not soar. Members of
prs. display to each other with alternate wing raises.
Nest reportedly of twigs high in tree; 2–3 white or
buff eggs spotted brown[83].
Status and habitat: Uncommon to fairly common resident, but always in low density. Lowlands in moist
and humid terra firme and várzea forest, along forest
borders, and in small clearings with scattered trees.
Most numerous in areas of extensive forest, but wanders through gallery forest on grasslands of Gran Sa-

bana. Occas. in dry forests (i.e., w of El Palmar,
Bolívar).
Range: To 500m (sight recs. to 1450m, Gran Sabana).
Maracaibo Basin of Zulia and w base of Andes in
nw Táchira and w Trujillo (sight, n of Llanos de
Monay—P. Alden); e base of Andes n to Portuguesa
(Turén); nw and se Monagas, Delta Amacuro, and
throughout Bolívar and Amazonas. Se Mexico to
w Ecuador (now virtually extinct in C Amer.), e of
Andes from e Colombia to ne Bolivia, Amaz. Brazil,
and the Guianas.
Note: Here placed in genus *Ibycter*[83,225], but by most
earlier authors in *Daptrius*[10,403]. Slightly larger C Amer.
birds have been recognized as a separate subsp.

Caracara

Robust scavengers; rather long lanky wings with prom.
white patch; moderately long tail; bare facial skin.

Northern Crested-Caracara   PLATE 8
Caracara cheriway   Caricare
Identification: 20–24″ (51–61cm). 920g. Imposing
countenance with bushy crest and powerful bill.
*Bare facial skin and base of bill red to yellowish or-
ange*; eyes grayish white; long legs yellow. *Crown
and occipital crest black*; rest of head, neck, and
throat white; breast white narrowly scalloped with
black and becoming solid black on thighs and belly;
mantle barred black and white, back black, *upper
tail coverts and tail white* with numerous narrow
wavy black bars (faint at base) and broad black subterminal tail band. In flight note *lanky shape* (for-
ward-projecting head, longish tail) and conspic.
patch of white at base of primaries. Imm.: much
duller and brownish; foreparts dirty buff white
streaked brown.
Sim. species: At least superficially like Yellow-headed
Caracara, esp. from above in flight (both show conspic. pale wing patches and sim. tail pattern).
Crested can always be told by black cap, black
lower underparts, and greater size; up close note its
red facial skin.
Voice: Occas. several very grating *kra'a'a'ak* rattles.
Behavior: Alone or in prs. patrolling open country
for almost anything edible. Perches on fence posts or
tops of small or large trees and also spends much
time on gd., esp. along roads, where it walks gallinelike. An opportunistic scavenger and predator, gathering in nos. at grass fires in savannas, and often given
to piracy. Flies strongly with steady, rowing wing
beats and bill pointed downward slightly. Occas.
glides on strong updrafts in mts. but rarely does so in
lowlands. Six dry-season nests, w Guárico, Mar–
May[369]; other breeding evidence there Sep–Dec[734].
Stick nest in open ranchland, often atop *Copernicia*
palm or in shrub; 2–3 eggs, white clouded with
shades of brown and dark blotches[706].
Status and habitat: Common resident of dry open
country, ranchland with scattered trees, agricultural
areas, and along borders of large rivers in forested
zones.

Range: To 850m. Throughout n of Orinoco; Amazonas s to mouth of Río Ventuari (sight); n Bolívar s to lower Río Caura, lower Río Paragua (Cerro Tigre), and s border at Santa Elena de Uairén; Islas Margarita, La Blanquilla, and Los Roques (*cheriway*). Sw US and s Florida s to Ecuador, nw Peru, and Brazil n of the Amazon.
Note: Formerly placed in genus *Polyborus*[23].

Milvago

Much like *Caracara* but smaller and slighter; bill weaker.

Yellow-headed Caracara
PLATES 6, 8
Milvago chimachima   Chiriguare
Identification: 16–18″ (41–46cm). 325g. Rather long wings; long tail rounded at tip. Bill and feet small; bill greenish ivory; cere orangish; eyes amber brown; orbital ring deep yellow. Above mostly blackish brown; *head, neck, and underparts creamy white to rich buff with narrow blackish streak behind eyes*; tail with numerous narrow wavy dark bars (faint at base) and broad subterminal band. In flight shows *conspic. whitish patch at base of outer primaries*. Imm.: sim. but upperparts dull brown; head, neck, and underparts buff with profusion of blurred brown streaks; wings and tail as in ad.
Sim. species: Ad. is nearest Northern Crested-Caracara (see) and Laughing Falcon but smaller and slighter than either. Imm. somewhat like several imm. hawks, esp. Gray Hawk.
Voice: Often hd. call a loud, coarse (unpleasant scratchy sounding) scream that slowly descends, *SCREEEEEEEEEa*; also a grating *kraa-kraa-kraa*.
Behavior: A conspic. bird of open country and ranchland. Usually seen alone or in scattered prs. perched in tops of trees or afoot along roadsides, in pastures, or on riverbanks, patrolling with great diligence. Scavenges carrion and almost any edible plant or animal matter, incl. insects, bird nestlings, mice, etc., and rides backs of cattle and capybaras where watches for prey disturbed by their activities. Flies slowly but buoyantly with steady wing beats and occas. sweeping glides but no sustained soaring. Two nests, Aug, Guárico[369]; stick nest in tree, esp. palm, usually high; 1–2 buff eggs marked rufous brown[83].
Status and habitat: Common resident in agricultural areas, ranchland, and other open or semiopen country with scattered trees; also along larger rivers in forested areas. Very common in llanos.

Range: To 900m (vagrant to 3000m or higher in Andes). Maracaibo region and generally n of Orinoco; n Amazonas s to mouth of Río Ventuari (sight) and n and e in Bolívar (*cordatus*). Sw Costa Rica to n Argentina and Uruguay. Trinidad.

Micrastur

Long legs; very long, full tail with rounded corners; bare lores and facial skin encircle unusually large eyes which are set in slight facial disk; reclusive forest-dwellers; fast-flying, rapacious predators; often vocal at dawn or dusk; downy young are white. Two groups: (1) large spp. with strong legs and feet; tend to be found higher in forest and prey heavily on birds; and (2) small spp. with weaker legs and feet; more often in mid. strata of forest and with more varied diet that incls. fewer birds.

Barred Forest-Falcon
PLATE 7
Micrastur ruficollis   Halcón Palomero
Identification: ♂ 13″ (33cm), 168g. ♀ 15″ (38cm), 219g. Small. Usual long-tailed, *long-legged Micrastur* shape. Cere, lores, and facial skin deep butter yellow; eyes dark red. Above slate gray (occas. rich rufescent brown); below white *very narrowly and evenly barred black*; tail black with 3 (occas. 2 or 4) narrow white bars and narrow white tip. Imm.: eyes brown; upperparts dark brown, below buffy white with widely spaced narrow black bars, *usually with prom. whitish nuchal collar*; occas. with buff collar and underparts and almost no barring below; tail as in ad.; yellowish cere, lores, and facial skin. Imm. usually has white spotting on upper tail coverts, but this often concealed (best noted in hand).
Sim. species: Handsome, crisply patterned ad. likely confused only with Lined Forest-Falcon which has *bright orange* cere, lores, and facial skin, *white* eyes (conspic.), usually only 2 narrow white tail bands, and weaker barring on lower underparts. Imm. *easily confused*; told from larger imm. Slaty-backed Forest-Falcon by pale nuchal collar; from imm. Collared Forest-Falcon by decidedly smaller size, yellow (not olive green) lores and facial skin, and whiter (usually) nuchal collar. Also cf. imm. Bicolored Hawk which lacks bare facial skin and is usually buffier and unbarred below (an occas. juv. Barred Forest-Falcon is deep buff below and essentially unbarred). Also see nearly identical imm. Lined Forest-Falcon.
Voice: Often vocal at or *well before* dawn, occas. in late evening. Commonest song, given from perch, is

a succession of single *KELP* notes (rising and falling inflection) like bark of small dog, often tirelessly repeated at ca. 1 note/2 sec; less often songs varied to 2–6 notes with ca. 1-sec interval between notes and several-sec interval between songs[582]. In songs of 3 or more notes there is usually a distinct pause after 1st note. When excited, songs may change to short bursts of cackling barks. May call from roost, but calling birds typically change perches several times while giving dawn chorus. No aerial song or display[748].

Behavior: Like others of genus, furtive and solitary. Territories tend to be small, and individuals keep concealed in forest mid. levels and are seldom detected unless calling. Mainly active early mornings and evenings. Relies on stealth, surprise, and agile pursuit for prey captures. Has been noted (esp. juv. birds) at army ant swarms and even on gd. Eats insects, arachnids, crabs, lizards, small opossums, and nestling and ad. birds[582]. Avoids crossing openings and does not perch in open. Nest in natural cavities 10–30m up in live trees, occas. in holes excavated by other animals or in dead trees; ♂ brings all food to incubating ♀; 2–3 eggs dark reddish brown with small dark spots; breeds mostly Mar–Jun or early Jul in Guatemala; young fledge in 35–44 days; 54% of nests fledge an offspring; nests may be only 600m–1km apart[748,749].

Status and habitat: Uncommon to fairly common in humid and wet premontane and montane forest, incl. cloud forest n of Orinoco; also reg. in moist semideciduous forest (unlike Lined Forest-Falcon). Reported in foothills (150m) at La Misión, Falcón[60]. S of Orinoco known only from humid lowland and foothill forest in 2 river valleys, but surely more widespread.

Range: 1200–2500m (locally to 150m) n of Orinoco; ca. 1000m s of Orinoco. Sierra de Perijá, Zulia; Andes from Táchira to Lara; se Falcón[60] and Coastal and Interior cordilleras from Carabobo to Miranda (*concentricus*); s of Orinoco on Cerro Tabaro in upper Río Nicharé, Bolívar; se Amazonas in Sierra Parima (*zonothorax*). S Mexico to w Ecuador; e of Andes s to nw Argentina and s Brazil.

Lined Forest-Falcon   PLATE 7
Micrastur gilvicollis   Halcón Palomero del Sur
Identification: ♂ 12″ (30cm), 185g. ♀ 14″ (36cm), 230g. Much like Barred Forest-Falcon. *Cere, lores, and bare ocular area reddish orange; eyes white.* Above slate gray, below white finely and evenly

barred blackish; *flanks weakly barred; belly and under tail coverts usually unbarred pure white,* tail blackish *with 2* (occas. only 1) *narrow white bars* and narrow white tip. Imm.: almost identical to imm. Barred Forest-Falcon except for orange red (not yellow) soft parts; eye color ?. In hand upper tail coverts uniformly dark (no white spotting or barring as in imm. Barred); perhaps only 1–2 (vs. 3–4 in Barred) visible whitish tail bands from above[541].

Sim. species: Overall, proportionately longer winged and shorter tailed than Barred Forest-Falcon, but most easily told by *white* eyes, orange red facial skin, fewer white tail bars (2 vs. 3 or 4), and weaker barring on lower underparts. See discussion of imms. under Barred Forest-Falcon. Occas. ads. or imms. with little ventral barring might be confused with larger Slaty-backed Forest-Falcon.

Voice: Reg. sings for a short period at dawn or even in predawn darkness (like most *Micrastur*). Commonest dawn song is 3 slow, lamenting notes, *cunk, . unk, unk,* 1st note halting and lower in pitch than the rest (Hilty). However, some dawn song sessions begin with a few (occas. up to 20) single notes, the ser. slowly accelerating then changing to a slow, lamenting 2-noted call that continues for some time, or progresses to 3 notes or even 4- or 5-note songs intermingled; longer songs have distinct pause after 1st note. Calling birds often change perches several times while calling. In Río Negro region, song may begin with 2-noted song[582].

Behavior: Sim. to Barred Forest-Falcon. Stays mostly in low or mid. levels inside tall forest where hunts by changing perches freq. and ambushing small vertebrates. Calling birds difficult to track down.

Status and habitat: Uncommon resident of relatively undisturbed humid terra firme and várzea forest in lowlands and on lower slopes of tepuis. Minimal range overlap with mainly highland Barred Forest-Falcon.

Range: To 1100m. Throughout Amazonas and Bolívar. E Colombia to e Bolivia, Amaz. Brazil, and the Guianas.

Slaty-backed Forest-Falcon   PLATE 7
Micrastur mirandollei   Halcón de Lomo Pizarreño
Identification: ♂ 16″ (41cm), 420g. ♀ 18″ (46cm), 550g. Long legs and tail. *Cere, lores, and facial skin yellowish;* bill black; *eyes yellowish brown.* Crown and upperparts slate gray (no pale collar), cheeks light gray (paler than crown), gray extending out onto sides of chest somewhat; *below unmarked white*

to white tinged buff, some birds (young?) showing a few narrow dark shaft streaks on chest; tail black with 3–4 narrow gray or white bands and narrow white tip; wing linings white, flight feathers dark brown coarsely barred pale gray (from below). Imm.: browner above, bill mostly yellow; underparts white *broadly scaled dusky*; cere, lores, and facial skin yellowish.

Sim. species: Looks a lot like very rare Gray-bellied Hawk, and a good look is required to tell the two apart. Key marks for ad. forest-falcon are extensive yellow facial skin surrounding eyes, dark (not reddish) eyes, and usually whiter (not gray) underparts. Gray-bellied Hawk has contrasting black cap, darker cheeks, shorter legs, and broader gray (not white) tail bands. Some imm. Barred Forest-Falcons lack barring below (older imms. usually show some barring), and these closely resemble buffy ad. Slaty-backed Forest-Falcons (most Slaty-backs are pure white below) but are smaller with paler sides of head. Imm. Bicolored Hawk is about same color as buffiest ad. Slaty-back but has conspic. buff nuchal collar and much shorter legs. Imm. from imm. Collared Forest-Falcon by yellowish facial skin and no nuchal collar.

Voice: Call in e Bolívar a nasal ser. of ca. 5–8 notes, *aw-aw-aw, auw, auw . . auw . . . auu*, 1st 3–4 notes rising slightly in pitch, middle notes strongest, last note or 2 slower and descending. Tone quality of notes very sim. to that of Collared Forest-Falcon (K. Zimmer recording). In se Peru in late afternoon a very slow, hesitant 5-note ser., *aw . aw . awu . . aw . . . aw*, 3d note higher, last 2 successively lower in pitch and slowing; repeated over and over for several min. Most often hd. at dawn or late in afternoon.

Behavior: Sim. to Barred and Lined forest-falcons. Usually seen alone at low to mid. heights *inside* forest. Calls from low to mid.-level perch inside forest. Prey believed to be mostly birds, some lizards, ambushed from concealment, pursued in air, or even on gd.[706]

Status and habitat: Very uncommon or rare resident of undisturbed humid lowland forest. Like other large spp. of *Micrastur*, occurs in low density, and territories perhaps much larger than those of smaller spp. Seldom encountered in same place repeatedly.

Range: To 300. Prob. throughout s of Orinoco. Rec. in Amazonas s of Río Ventuari; n Bolívar from lower

Río Caura and ne Bolívar (Río Grande) s to upper Río Cuyuní (km 72, sight/tape, Feb 1992—K. Zimmer); Delta Amacuro[343]. Costa Rica to Bolivia, Amaz. Brazil, and the Guianas.

Collared Forest-Falcon
Micrastur semitorquatus Halcón Semicollarado

PLATES 6, 7, 13

Identification: ♂ 19″ (48cm), 535g. ♀ 24″ (61cm), 700g. Largest of genus; tail long and rounded; legs long. *Cere, lores, and facial skin dull green*; eyes very large and dark brown. Ad. with 3 phases. Light phase: above blackish, the *black of hindcrown extended diagonally forward as narrow wedge across lower part of cheek*; narrow collar around hindneck, cheeks, and entire underparts white, tail black with several narrow whitish bands. Tawny phase: sim. but white replaced by buff to tawny. Dark phase (rare): mostly sooty black (no nuchal collar) with grayish white tail bands and usually minor white barring on rump, flanks, and abdomen. Imm. (variable): above like ad. but brownish, the feathers scaled buff; *whitish to tawny nuchal collar* (sometimes indistinct or lacking); below white to tawny *coarsely barred brown or black*; chest washed cinnamon or chestnut; tail blackish banded buffy brown to white. Older imms. gradually lose buff scaling on upperparts. Dark-phase imm.: entirely dark brown with white barring on thighs and belly; tail as in ad.

Sim. species: Greenish facial skin, pale nuchal collar, and dark crescent across cheek are diagnostic marks for most plumages of this *large* forest-falcon. Smaller imm. Bicolored Hawk usually has tawny nuchal collar but lacks bare facial skin and black cheek mark and has shorter legs, shorter and more banded tail, and yellow lores. Dark phase best told by shape, ventral barring, and greenish facial skin. Imms. also best told by shape, green facial skin, and wide-spaced barring below.

Voice: Call, from high, concealed, or partly exposed perch near forest edge or along river and usually *in predawn darkness* or after sundown, a loud, hollow, slowly repeated *cow . . . . . . cow . . .* , drawn out as if in distress, 1 to up to 15 notes, each 10–15 sec apart; quality of Laughing Falcon but much slower and does not accelerate. Also a slow, low-pitched ser., *auk, auk, uuk, uuk, cuuk, cuuk, calk, calk . . auuk . . . . auk*, slowing and descending at end and overall rather like Slaty-backed Forest-Falcon and some vocalizations of Laughing Falcon. Cf. sim. but faster call of Slaty-backed Forest-Falcon. Imm. Collared gives a 5- to 6-noted *cooou, cow, cow, cow, cow* (1st note lower and sliding up), much like call (incl. tempo) of Barred Forest-Falcon.

Behavior: A furtive forest hawk that perches concealed at low or mid. hts. in forest but more likely seen only as a silhouette when it takes a more prom. perch at dawn or dusk to call, then moving out into open somewhat. When hunting moves from perch to perch, watching carefully, then attacks birds and other vertebrates by bold ambush and pursuit, even to gd. Nest 12–21m up in tree cavity; Aug nest with nearly fledged chick in gallery forest of Guárico[368,747,749].

Status and habitat: Uncommon (seldom detected except by voice) resident of dry, moist, and humid forest, along forest and wooded river borders, gallery forest, and older second-growth woodland.

Range: To 1500m. Prob. throughout in forested regions (no recs. in nw or ne). Maracaibo Basin of Zulia and Mérida e locally through Falcón (Cerro Chichiriviche), Coastal Cordillera in Aragua and Distr. Federal, and Guárico to Delta Amacuro; throughout s of Orinoco (*semitorquatus*). Mexico to nw Peru, n Argentina, and s Brazil.

[Buckley's Forest-Falcon]
Micrastur buckleyi   Halcón de Buckley
Identification: 16–18″ (41–46cm). Very like light-phase Collared Forest-Falcon *but smaller and with 4 instead of 6 white tail bands* (incl. tip). ♀ shows white spotting on scapulars and secondaries. Imm.: like imm. Collared but darker, upperparts almost black, breast uniform cinnamon buff and almost completely devoid of black markings. Flat wing of unsexed bird 219mm or less vs. 244 or more for Collared; tarsus proportionately much shorter[53].
Voice: Normal territorial advertisement a slow, rather low-pitched, hollow *coowa-cow . . caw*, last note characteristically coming after a distinct pause or occas. omitted; sometimes over and over (A Whittaker). At a distance song is quite sim. in quality (but not pattern) to that of Collared Forest-Falcon. Also reported is a longer ser. of 15–16 notes, like Slaty-backed Forest-Falcon but given more quickly, and up to 25 *ko* notes with 2 longer nasal notes at end[541].
Behavior: Poorly known. Presum. sim. to that of Collared Forest-Falcon.
Status and habitat: In Venez. known from 1 sight rec. 16–18 Feb 1998 with tape (tape verified by A. Whittaker) at km 74 s of El Dorado, e Bolívar (D. Stejskal). A rare sp. (or rarely detected) throughout its range[798] and a significant range extension.

Range: Venez. (sight/tape, e Bolívar). E Ecuador, se Colombia (sight), and e Peru.
Note: Has been considered a subsp. of Collared Forest-Falcon.

Herpetotheres

Monotypic; short, rounded wings; long tail rounded at tip; no tooth on bill; legs short; legs and feet covered with notably thick rough scales (note diet); crown feathers stiff and pointed.

Laughing Falcon   PLATE 6
Herpetotheres cachinnans   Halcón Macagua
Identification: 18–22″ (46–56cm). 500–625g. *Large headed* with "Panda Bear" appearance. Cere and legs yellow. Head and entire underparts whitish to deep creamy buff; *conspic. black mask extending from eyes around hindneck*; upperparts dark brown, *tail blackish with several narrow white bands and pale tip*. In flight shows large pale buff patch at base of primaries.
Sim. species: Not likely confused if seen well. Cf. ad. Yellow-headed Caracara which is slimmer with only a narrow black line through eyes.
Voice: Well named for its tireless, laughlike call hd. mostly in early morning or late evening, occas. even after dark. Typically a long, far-carrying, and lamenting tirade, *gúa-co, gúa-co, . . .* or sim. variation lasting several min, often increasing somewhat in tempo and becoming more rhythmic as it goes along. Less freq. a shorter ser. of chuckling *gwa* or *hah* notes suggesting muffled laughter. A calling bird is often joined by mate, the notes of the 2 alternately syncopated, simultaneous, or out of sequence in a long-drawn, slowly accelerating cacophony suggesting maniacal laughter. Most vocal in wet season.
Behavior: Sluggish and often confiding, reg. perching for long periods of time at med. hts. or higher in large bare or open trees that afford good visibility. Characteristically perches very upright with tail down and head slightly bowed, as if in prayerful attitude, as it watches gd. for snakes, its main prey. Flies rather slowly with stiff, rapid wing beats, as if churning air, followed by a short glide. Does not soar. Tail flicked stiffly to side when disturbed. Nest in bare tree hole (no nest material) or occas. an old hawk's nest; 1 Guárico nest 19 Sep; 1 egg; 4 prs. in ca. 13.4km^2 in w Guárico[369].
Status and habitat: Fairly common resident. Forest borders, forest clearings with scattered trees, gallery

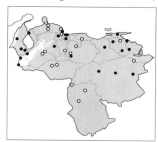

and riparian forest in dry, moist, or humid regions. Generally most numerous in humid zones; readily found in wooded or partially wooded areas in llanos. **Range:** To 500m (prob. higher). Throughout n and s of Orinoco (*cachinnans*). Mexico to w Peru, n Argentina, and s Brazil.
Note: Also called Laughing Hawk.

Falco

Streamlined shape; long, pointed wings swept back at wrist; longish tail; *eyes dark* (cf. *Accipiter*); ♀♀ larger than ♂♂; almost worldwide; do not build nests.

American Kestrel
PLATES 7, 14
Falco sparverius Halcón Primito
Identification: 9–11″ (23–28cm). 115g. Small falcon with russet upperparts and "double whiskers." ♂: *crown and wings bluish, back and rump rufous* with short black barring; throat and sides of head white; *2 vertical black marks on sides of head* (the "whiskers"), 1 beneath eye, 1 behind eye; large black spot on side of nape; sides of neck and rest of underparts whitish buff to deep buff to pinkish cinnamon sparsely spotted black on breast and sides; *tail rufous with broad black subterminal band* and white tip. ♀: above like ♂ but wings and back rufous brown barred black; below paler buff with some brown streaking and spotting.
Sim. species: No other small raptor in Venez. has such prom. facial markings and rufous tail.
Voice: Sometimes rather vocal, esp. at nest; a high, thin *killy-killy-killy* or *kleé-kleé-kleé*, much like that of Bat Falcon but thinner. Also cf. song of Red-stained Woodpecker.
Behavior: Familiar little falcon of open country. Sits alert and erect on utility poles, wires, or tops of trees (it requires high perches), flies out over grassy areas, hovers freq., then stoops on mostly insect prey. Almost always alone (sexes hold separate territories except when breeding). Nesting Jan and Apr in Anzoátegui; uses tree cavity, termite nest, or hole in building[186]; 3–4 buff eggs mottled rufous brown.
Status and habitat: Fairly common resident, esp. in mts., local in lowlands where possibly does not overlap with Aplomado Falcon. Grasslands, roadsides, agricultural fields, and other open or semiopen terrain with scattered trees from lowlands to well above treeline (sight to 3600m, Mucubají—P. Boesman). Profits

from deforestation. N temperate migrants possible but unrec.
Range: To 3000m n of Orinoco (sight, 3600m); to 950m s of Orinoco. Andes from Táchira n to Trujillo (*ochraceus*); elsewhere n of Orinoco; Isla Margarita; n Amazonas; n and e Bolívar s to Brazilian border (*isabellinus*). Breeds from n N Amer. s to Tierra del Fuego. N temperate birds winter s to e Panama, prob. n S Amer.

Merlin
PLATE 14
Falco columbarius Halcón Migratorio
Identification: ♂ 10″ (25cm), 160g. ♀ 13″ (33cm), 215g. Compact little falcon with pointed wings and rowing, pigeonlike flight. Cere yellow. ♂: above dark grayish blue, forehead and weak eyestripe buffy white; *sides of head and underparts whitish to buffy white profusely streaked dark brown*; slight indication of dark "sideburns"; tail dusky with 3–4 broad gray bands and pale tip. ♀ and imm.: sim. but brown above, often more cinnamon buff below. Subad.: above mixed blue gray and brown, forecrown weakly streaked, pale collar on sides of neck buff mixed brown, underparts may show a combination of streaks with coarse irreg. barring on sides and flanks.
Sim. species: Can be confusing. Small size, streaked underparts, evenly banded tail, and no obvious face pattern are good marks. Cf. imm. Plain-breasted Hawk and American Kestrel.
Voice: Rarely vocalizes on wintering gds. On breeding gds. a strident cackling.
Behavior: Perches on fairly open, low branches or snags where inconspic. and easily overlooked, but occas. sits on high open stubs. As in others of genus, flight is fast and fluid with rowing wing beats. Typically flies rather low, then accelerates dramatically in powerful pursuit of prey, sometimes rapidly gaining speed in a ser. of shallow stoops. Preys heavily on small birds, also dragonflies and other large flying insects.
Status and habitat: Uncommon migrant and n winter resident, early Oct–early May, to mostly open terrain with scattered trees from lowlands to highlands. Reg. in agriculture fields near Santo Domingo, Mérida, and around Dickcissel flocks in llanos.

Range: To 1800m (sight to 3000m, ne Mérida). Locally throughout n of Orinoco; s of it at Caicara, nw Bolívar; Islas La Tortuga, Los Roques (sight), and Las Aves (*columbarius*); other subspp. (*richardsoni*, *suckleyi*) possible. Breeds in n N Amer. and Old World; N

Amer. birds winter from s US to n Peru, Colombia, W Indies, and Trinidad.

Aplomado Falcon
PLATES 7, 14

Falco femoralis   Halcón Aplomado

Identification: ♂ 14" (36cm), 240g. ♀ 17" (43cm), 350g. Slender and *"faded-looking"* with *white "sweatband and black sideburns."* Tail unusually long for genus. Cere, orbit, and legs bright yellow. Above pale bluish slate with *conspic. buffy white eyestripe from forehead encircling crown;* cheeks, sides of neck, and chest whitish to pale buff with *prom. black mark* below eyes (the "sideburns"); sides and band across upper belly black finely barred white; lower underparts pale rufous; tail dull slate with several narrow white bars. In flight from above shows *prom. white trailing edge on secondaries;* underwings blackish checkered white. Imm.: sim but duller; above tinged brownish; lacks yellow soft-part colors on head; broad band across breast brownish to brown coarsely streaked and mottled with buff.

Sim. species: Bat and Orange-breasted falcons are darker, shorter tailed, lack prom. head markings, and occur in forested terrain. Cf. Merlin.

Voice: Rather quiet. Occas. a scolding cackle, *ke-ke-ke-ke-ke.*

Behavior: A bird of open country. Usually seen alone or in scattered prs. perched very upright (hence name) on top of a small tree, shrub, fence post, or utility pole. Hunts by watching from perch, then flying out very fast and low to gd., often long distances, in surprise attacks on birds (incl. jacanas, plovers, nighthawks, yellow-finches), bats, etc.; also hovers for insects. Reg. follows large grass fires, sometimes with several in attendance; prs. may hunt cooperatively. Nest 17 Mar, Guárico, 3 chicks; appropriates old stick nest of other raptor; 1–3 bluish or cream eggs with reddish brown blotches.

Status and habitat: Fairly common resident but always in low density. Open grasslands with a few widely scattered trees and shrubs; also scrub, tree-lined borders of fields, and patches of light woodland in arid and moist regions. Everywhere favors areas of predominantly open terrain.

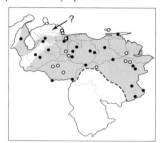

Range: To 600m n of Orinoco; to 1800m s of Orinoco. Locally throughout n of Orinoco (no recs. in Falcón); n and e Bolívar s to Gran Sabana; Isla Margarita (*femoralis*). Sw US (now reintroduced in Texas) s locally in open areas to Terra del Fuego.

Bat Falcon
PLATES 7, 14

Falco rufigularis   Halcón Golondrina

Identification: ♂ 9" (23cm), 110–150g. ♀ 12" (30.5cm), 180–240g. Small dark falcon with long, pointed wings and squarish head. Cere, orbit, and legs yellow. Upperparts and sides of head to below eyes black; *throat, chest, and crescent on sides of neck buff to whitish but most often tinged rufescent; breast and upper belly black* (broad "buttoned-up vest") finely barred white; lower underparts dark rufous; tail black with several narrow white bars. Imm.: sim. but throat buffier; under tail coverts barred with black. Downy nestlings white.

Sim. species: Easily confused with very rare Orange-breasted Falcon (see). Larger, paler Aplomado Falcon has white "headband," whitish sides of head, and prom. black "sideburns" below eyes. Also cf. Merlin and American Kestrel.

Voice: Shrill, high-pitched *ke-ke-ke-ke* in flight or perched; much like call of American Kestrel and Red-stained Woodpecker!

Behavior: A well-dressed and speedy little falcon. Single birds or more often prs. spend most of time perched very high on open snags or branches above canopy, occas. flying out in little sorties and calling or pursuing bats, birds, and insects, incl. moths, butterflies, and dragonflies (♂♂ take more insects, ♀♀ more birds and larger bats), taking them by stooping or in direct pursuit. Flight is swift, fluid, and very powerful. Often most active at dusk, just as bats emerge. Nest an unlined hole in tree or building; 2–3 umber brown eggs speckled darker[83].

Status and habitat: Fairly common resident of dry to humid forest, forest borders, river edges, and large trees in forest-bordered clearings. Most numerous s of Orinoco. Absent or very local in arid regions of n Zulia, Falcón, and nw Sucre; absent or very local in llanos.

Range: To 1450m. Maracaibo Basin; c and e Falcón e to Guárico; e Monagas to Delta Amacuro; se Táchira; generally s of Orinoco. (*rufigularis*). S Mexico to n Argentina and se Brazil. Trinidad.

Orange-breasted Falcon
PLATE 7

Falco deiroleucus   Halcón Pechinaranjado

Identification: ♂ 13" (33cm), 350g. ♀ 15" (38cm), 550–650g. Closely resembles smaller Bat Falcon. Aside from *larger size* (but large ♀ Bat Falcon almost as big as small ♂ Orange-breasted), *single best mark* is *coarse and rather widely spaced whitish and slightly scalloped barring on black vest* (not fine, closely spaced, and linear barring). Also helpful is more robust shape with broader-based wings, longer and more graduated tail, and squarish head. Overall Orange-breasted has lankier look with "longer torso." Orange-breasted Falcon *always has white throat* surrounded by buffy orange on chest and sides of neck; Bat Falcon (in S Amer.) often has *entire throat as well as chest and sides of neck buffy orange*. Other points to ponder are *narrower black vest* (usually) with top U-shaped (top of vest straighter in Bat Falcon); *larger, stronger feet; black barring* on under tail coverts; and wings as long as or longer than tail (vs. as long as or shorter in Bat Falcon)[269]. All of these differences are subjective and difficult to verify in field, and great care should be exercised in documentation of Orange-breasted Falcon, esp. in lowlands where it is apt to occur with Bat Falcon.

Sim. species: See Bat and Aplomado falcons.

Voice: ♂ gives a hard *kip-kip-kip* (cf. much higher, thinner call of Bat Falcon); also a faster, longer ser. or piercing *ki* notes.

Behavior: Prs. spend most of time perched on rocky cliff edges or on high exposed stubs that overlook forest. Nest on cliffs or rock ledges in mts., prob. large high tree holes in lowlands. Stoop mostly on birds. Noted attacking a kiskadee along a riverbank in ne Bolivia.

Status and habitat: Very rare resident. Most records and specimens are from humid foothill or mt. locs. where there are suitable cliffs and rock ledges for roosting and breeding, but also occurs in lowlands away from mts., a habitat in which it may be somewhat overlooked. Most known prs. are in remote locs. Reasons for low density and spotty occurrence are unknown, but sp. prob. occurs on or near most tepuis. Recent recs. incl. 1 seen s of Maripa, lower Río Caura, 1992 (D. Stejskal); sight, near Río Cuyuní, early 1990s (Hilty) and early 2000 (D. Fisher); sight, 25 Nov 1980, Sierra de Lema (R. Webster); photo at n end of Gran Sabana, 1996 (T. Barksdale); sight, Cerro Roraima, 2200m, Mar 1982 (C. Parrish), and Sep 1999 (D. Ascanio).

Range: To 1700m n of Orinoco; to 1500m (sight to 2200m) s of Orinoco. Known from Mérida (at 1700m), Carabobo (s of Pto. Cabello), and n and se Bolívar s to Cerro Roraima. Se Mexico very locally s to Bolivia, n Argentina, Amaz. and s Brazil; the Guianas.

Peregrine Falcon
PLATE 14

Falco peregrinus Halcón Peregrino

Identification: ♂ 15″ (38cm), 600g. ♀ 20″ (51cm), 950g. *Robust* falcon with pointed wings and tapered tail. Cere, orbit, and legs yellow. *Crown, nape, and "sideburns" black*, rest of *upperparts and tail blue gray* more or less barred dusky; auricular area, sides of neck, and underparts white, breast and belly tinged buff and coarsely spotted and barred dusky. In flight from below, wing linings whitish barred black, flight feathers coarsely barred black (*anatum*). Austral-breeding *cassini* (as yet unrec. in Venez.) differs as follows: above slightly smaller and darker blue gray, sides of head entirely black (no white auriculars), below buffier, and with heavier barring above and heavier spotting below. Nearctic-breeding *tundrius* (wintering s to Peru, Chile, and Trinidad, also unrec. in Venez. but likely), differs as follows: smaller and paler than either of above, and with less barring and spotting.

Sim. species: Told by large size, facial pattern, and black crown. Cf. esp. Merlin, Aplomado Falcon, and American Kestrel, all of which are decidedly smaller and slighter.

Voice: Occas. a sharp repeated *hek*; also a bisyllabic note.

Behavior: Usually alone, either in air or perched high on an open branch, stub, tower, or building. Flight is fluid, graceful, and deceptively swift. Short, quick, and powerful wing strokes interspersed occas. by short glides may impart choppy aspect to flight. Occas. soars. Stoops on prey, esp. shorebirds, ducks, and other spp. of birds of open areas, also bats, with breathtaking bursts of speed and may also give aerial chase. Prey killed in flight.

Status and habitat: Uncommon migrant and n winter resident, early Oct–mid Apr. Earliest rec. is 1 on 30 Sep, PN Henri Pittier (C. Sharp); latest is 1 on 18 Apr 1992, Caicara, Bolívar (P. Boesman). Open or semi-open habitats; dry to humid areas from lowlands to above treeline. Reg. seen in vicinity of concentrations of shorebirds and waders in llanos and on coast.

Range: To 3600m. Throughout n of Orinoco (sight recs. from many states); Isla Margarita (*anatum*); sight recs. from Islas Los Roques, La Orchila, and Los Hermanos (subsp.?). N Amer. breeders (*anatum*) and nearctic breeders (*tundrius*) winter s to Chile and Argentina; austral breeders (*cassini*) winter n from Argentina and Chile to sw Colombia.

Note: Both *tundrius* and *cassini* unrec. but possible.

GALLIFORMES

Cracidae: Chachalacas, Guans, and Curassows

Guacharacas, Pavas, y Paujiés

Cracids are a homogeneous and historically old group of Galliforme birds found mainly in the New World tropics. They are fowl-like in appearance with large, strong legs and feet. Most species are predominantly arboreal, although all can run well on the ground; curassows spend most of their time foraging on the ground but seek safety in trees. All cracids eat mostly fruits, seeds, and young shoots. Most species live in humid lowland forests with smaller numbers in the mountains; 1 even reaches the cold Andean treeline. In most humid forests of Venezuela at least 2 species coexist; in some areas south of the Orinoco as many as 4 species are found together. All of them are considered game birds, and curassows in particular are much persecuted for food. Chachalacas, despite noisy and sometimes conspicuous habits, may flourish near humans and expand into brushy regrowth areas. By contrast, guans and especially curassows seem to require large areas of natural forest, do not thrive under hunting pressure, and are strongly affected by human activities[613].

Ortalis

Small, slender, and dull colored with bare red throat skin (no knobs, wattles, or dewlaps). Dwell in brush, thickets, or forest borders at low els.; arboreal but occas. on gd.; loud raucous dawn chorus; no flight display.

Rufous-vented Chachalaca   PLATE 15
Ortalis ruficauda   Guacharaca del Norte
Identification: 21–23″ (53–58cm). ♂ 640g, ♀ 540g. Slender, long-tailed, and long-necked. *Bare malar stripe red*; facial skin and *legs slaty. Head and upper neck gray*, otherwise mostly olive brown, foreneck darker, belly grayish buff becoming *rufous on under tail coverts*; tail greenish black, *outer feathers broadly tipped chestnut (ruficauda).* Or white *(ruficrissa).* Birds with buff tail tips, intermediate between the 2 subspp., occur in w Zulia.
Sim. species: Little Chachalaca, only slightly smaller (despite name), has conspic. rufous chestnut head and neck, pinkish red legs.
Voice: Like most chachalacas, greets dawn with loud chorus, sometimes brief or lasting hrs, as groups shout back and forth to each other from leafy treetops. Typically once 1 pr. begins calling, others are quickly galvanized into song activity. Calling is typically antiphonal, with ♂ (?) giving a lower-pitched, grating *OTRA MAS* and ♀ (?) completing sequence with much higher-pitched *WATCH-a-läk*, result being a loud, syncopated song with distinct "beat" or rhythm, esp. if several birds join the chorus (also

sounds like *Puerto Rico*—D. Ascanio). Also clucking notes and a soft rising whistle, *woooooouuuuueee.*
Behavior: Very social, occurring in prs. when breeding but otherwise in family groups (esp. Sep–Jan), flocks up to ca. 12 or so. Highly arboreal but reg. in low bushes or trees and drops to gd. to drink. Walks nimbly along branches, and when frightened threads way rapidly through dense thickets. Flies with a few quick flaps and a flat-winged glide. Not esp. shy but usually does not perch conspic. in open. Becomes extremely suspicious and wary when hunted. Shallow saucer nest of twigs and leaves mostly 1–3m up, occas. on gd. or quite high; 3–4 rough-shelled white eggs; nesting begins in Apr, sometimes earlier[572]; Jun–Jul fledglings, Anzoátegui[186].
Status and habitat: Common and widespread resident across n Venez., esp. in dry to moist woodland, gallery forest, desert scrub, and second growth and disturbed vegetation. Often in woodlots and brushy areas in urban areas, e.g., Caracas. Most numerous in dry regions.

Range: To 1600m. Extreme nw Zulia at base of Goajira Pen. *(ruficrissa)*; rest of Venez. n of Orinoco, Delta Amacuro (Misión Araguaimujo), and Isla Margarita *(ruficauda).* Ne Colombia. Lesser Antilles. Tobago.

Little Chachalaca   PLATE 15
Ortalis motmot   Guacharaca Guayanesa
Identification: 18–21″ (46–53cm). ♂ 510g, ♀ 385g. *Slender little chachalaca with contrasting dark rufous head and upper foreneck.* Bare facial skin and center of throat slaty; broad bare malar stripe red; legs pinkish red. Rest of upperparts mainly olive brown, paler grayish brown below; under tail coverts rufous brown, tail dark bronzy olive, the *outer feathers broadly tipped chestnut.*
Sim. species: Only chachalaca s of Orinoco. Along Orinoco cf. slightly larger Rufous-vented Chachalaca which has gray (not rufous) head; also cf. slightly larger Marail Guan which has prom. red dewlap and liberal dose of whitish streaking on foreparts.
Voice: Dawn chorus a loud, coarse, and rhythmic *WATCH-a-läk*, over and over; recalls that of Rufous-vented Chachalaca but shriller, less raucous. Not as vocal as latter.
Behavior: Sim. to Rufous-vented Chachalaca; favors humid zones.
Status and habitat: Fairly common resident in thick vegetation along humid forest borders, river edges,

and patches of second growth of various ages in Bolívar; only a few recs. in Amazonas.

Range: To 1700m. Throughout Amazonas and Bolívar (*motmot*). The Guianas and Brazil e of Rio Negro and n of the Amazon.
Note: Has been considered a subsp. (smallest and darkest) of Variable Chachalaca (*O. motmot*) complex[147].

Penelope

Large, dark, forest guans with liberal doses of white-splattered streaking; rather grizzled ("old") faces with bare, dull blue skin around eyes; red dewlap; longish crest feathers; arboreal habits; noisy rattling flight display enhanced by stiff, strongly bowed outer 3 primaries that are very narrow at tip; wing-rattle display of ♂ (mainly during breeding season) functions to attract ♀ and strengthen pr. bond; barrage of very loud, honking calls in alarm.

Band-tailed Guan   PLATE 15
Penelope argyrotis Camata
Identification: 21–24″ (53–61cm). ♂ 840g, ♀ 775g. Dark, med.-sized forest guan of n mts. Bare ocular area dull bluish; dewlap red; legs pinkish. Head with slight bushy crest; *sides of head frosted whitish forming pale eyebrows, moustache, and pale rear cheeks*; rest of plumage mainly brown to rufescent brown, foreneck, mantle, shoulders, and breast streaked and daubed white (sides of feathers edged white); 4 central tail feathers dark rufescent brown, rest duskier, all with *rather broad but inconspic. dull rufous tips* (or whitish—*albicauda*).
Sim. species: Easily confused. Despite name, diagnostic tail band is dull and difficult to see. Smaller, squatter Andean Guan has grayish face (lacks distinct frosty look), duller and grayer streaking, tiny red dewlap, and no terminal tail band. Crested Guan is dramatically larger with more prom. bushy crest, *no whitish* feathers around bare face, and no tail band.
Voice: Noisy during Feb–Apr territory establishment, otherwise rather quiet. Wing-rattle display is *two* 1- to 2-sec bursts (like canvas ripping forward, then in reverse) given during short predawn flight in a tree or more often between 2 nearby trees. Alarm a few soft, piping whistles; panic alarm (used to startle or distract predator) a *frighteningly loud* crowing or shrieking *GUEEEA!* over and over (recalls wail of Limpkin), interrupted by gruff or harsh notes.

Behavior: In prs. when breeding but at other times usually in families or groups of 3–6. Quiet and secretive except early in breeding season. Like others of genus, mainly arboreal, somewhat wary, and seldom on gd. except for fallen fruits or briefly to drink. Loose nest 1–7m up in dense foliage[570].
Status and habitat: Uncommon to fairly common resident but infreq. seen. Humid and wet mt. forest, tall second-growth woodland, occas. coffee plantations. In decline because of deforestation and hunting pressure.

Range: 300–2400m (mostly 900–2100m). Sierra de Perijá, Zulia (*albicauda*); both slopes of Andes from Táchira to Lara, Sierra de San Luis, Falcón, n cordilleras from Carabobo to Miranda, and mts. of ne Anzoátegui, w Sucre, and n Monagas (*argyrotis*). Ne Colombia.
Note: Subspp. *mesaeus* (sw Táchira) and *olivaceiceps* (Sucre and Anzoátegui) not recognized[403].

Andean Guan   PLATE 15
Penelope montagnii Pava Andina
Identification: 20–23″ (51–58cm). 460g. Only at high els. in Andes. Throat more feathered than in most guans; *red dewlap small and inconspic.*; bare ocular area dull bluish; *short legs pinkish. Head, neck, and chest grayish brown, head finely streaked and neck and breast feathers edged* (scaled) *pale gray*; otherwise above bronzy brown, lower back and rump dull rufous chestnut, lower underparts rufescent.
Sim. species: Found mostly above range of Band-tailed Guan, which has much more prom. dewlap and facial markings, brighter and whiter streaking on foreparts, and inconspic. rufous tip on tail. Crested Guan, usually at lower els., looks twice the size.
Voice: Esp. vocal Feb–Mar during territorial establishment; flight display in predawn darkness is a *single* (not double) short, wing-rattle burst as bird glides between trees. Infreq. at dawn a very loud, squawking honk, somewhat gooselike.
Behavior: Usually seen in prs. or, when not breeding, groups of 3–7. Primarily arboreal, foraging mostly in mid. or upper levels of forest, walking stealthily out along branches and reaching out with long neck for ripe or unripe fruit. Sometimes spends long periods of time in a favorite fruiting tree; reg. feeds on *Ceroxylon* palm fruit. Rarely on gd. except to eat fallen fruit. May wander into second growth or isolated trees away from forest.
Status and habitat: Where unmolested a fairly common resident in humid and wet mossy forest (cloud

forest), wooded borders, and second growth. No other *Penelope* in Venez. occurs at such high els. Thrives even in small fragmented patches of woodland if not persecuted. Reg. near Zumbador, Táchira, Mucuy entrance to PN Sierra Nevada, Mérida, and PN Guaramacal, Trujillo.

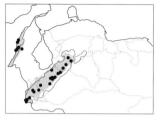

Range: 1800–3200m (most recs. above 2000m). Sierra de Perijá, Zulia; Andes from s Táchira n to extreme ne Trujillo at Páramo Cendé (*montagnii*). Colombia s in Andes to nw Argentina.

Marail Guan
PLATE 15
Penelope marail   Pava Bronceada
Identification: 24–27″ (61–69cm). ♂ 895g, ♀ 825g. Rather small dark guan; crest bushier than most in genus. Bare facial skin dull blue; prom. dewlap red; *short* legs pinkish. Head, neck, upperparts, and breast dark glossy olive green; head faintly streaked and *feathers of neck, mantle, and breast edged white imparting streaky look*; lower underparts gray brown to dark rufescent brown.
Sim. species: Essentially sim. in plumage to larger, leggier Spix's Guan and easily confused with it. Note Marail's squat, *short-legged* appearance and decidedly smaller size (only a little larger than a chachalaca). In hand, tarsus of Marail (♂ and ♀) 51–65 mm, of Spix's (♂ and ♀ of subsp. *granti*) 70–84mm[53].
Voice: Flight displays increase ca. Mar, but some displays may be given throughout yr. In predawn darkness ♂♂ perform a 3- to 4-sec double wing-whirring rattle (rattle seems to roll forward then backward) as bird sails from one tree to next, but rattle displays often cease even before it is light enough to see. At dawn, dusk, or even after dark, gives a low, muffled, and rough chachalaca-like *racha, racha, racha, . . . ,* usually mixed with other harsh and high notes. Apparently lacks loud "honking" of Spix's Guan.
Behavior: A highly arboreal bird of tall rain forest that rarely descends to gd. Occurs in prs. when breeding but at other times of yr in little families or groups up to ca. 6 that are alert and suspicious and tend to move away from observers. Displaying ♂♂ (predawn) are often close enough together that up to 4 can be hd. simultaneously. Feeds mostly on fruit, incl. *Cecropia*, sometimes coming into trees to feed very late in evening, almost in complete darkness.
Status and habitat: Fairly common resident in areas remote from human disturbance but easily overlooked unless hd. at dawn or dusk. Humid lowland and foothill forest. Can still be found in forest e of Río Grande, ne Bolívar; in many areas seems outnumbered by larger Spix's Guan. Interspecific rela-

tionships between Marail and Spix's guans need investigation.

Range: To 600m. Bolívar from lower and mid. Río Caura (Pto. Carretico, Salto Pará) and Sierra de Imataca s to Cerro Roraima (*marail*). Guianas and adj. n Brazil.
Note: Presence of slightly smaller, paler subsp. *jacupeba* in Venez. (upper Río Caura) needs verification[53].

Spix's Guan
PLATE 15
Penelope jacquacu   Úquira
Identification: 30–32″ (76–81cm). ♂ 1.6kg, ♀ 1.4kg. *Very like* Marail Guan but *larger* (subsp. *granti*) in zone of overlap from Río Caura e; *legs noticeably longer* than in Marail Guan. Mostly bronzy bluish green, primaries pale brown, rump brown, lower underparts dull dark rufescent brown, feathers of head, neck, mantle, and breast edged whitish imparting streaky look; tail dusky green, outer feathers darker. Or sim. *but smaller*, 26–28″ (66–71cm) and darker, mostly dark bronzy olive instead of bluish green; flight feathers dusky (*orienticola*). In Venez. Spix's Guan is largest in regions where it occurs *with* Marail Guan, smaller where it occurs alone.
Sim. species: See Marail Guan. Spix's *usually* looks decidedly larger (heavier) and longer-legged.
Voice: At dawn or dusk a powerful honking or crowing, *QUOOEEEL! . . QUOOEEL!* several in ser., almost gooselike. Like others of genus, gives a few loud, "ripping" double wing rattles during short display flights in predawn darkness, esp. during breeding season. When alarmed or annoyed, a low muffled ser. of grunting or barking sounds; high-intensity alarm a very loud, crowing *CA-OU, CA-OU* mixed with honking and grunting sounds. In general, noisier than others of genus.
Behavior: Arboreal, and most often seen in prs. or groups high in canopy. Walks stealthily along high limbs or leaps from one to another, sometimes with wing-assisted hops, and reaches out with long neck for small ripe or unripe fruit. Presence is often betrayed by falling fruit, dropped while feeding. When alarmed may call softly or take flight silently and glide away. If surprised likely to take flight with extraordinarily loud, crowing alarm calls sure to startle and confuse predators temporarily, this accompanied by crashing of wings and foliage as bird flees to safety, but then often pauses some distance away, wobbling on branch and bobbing head foolishly, and peering curiously back through foliage toward

source of danger. Occas. descends to gd. to feed on fallen fruits. Nest mostly of leaves was ca. 5m up in a tree in Colombia[260].

Status and habitat: Fairly common to common, when not persecuted by humans, in humid lowland and foothill forest, along forest borders, scattered trees in slashed clearings, and locally in gallery forest. Generally more numerous than Marail Guan.

Range: To 1600m. Nw Amazonas (Caño Cataniapo) and throughout n and c Bolívar (*granti*); rest of Amazonas (Cerro Yavi; Caño Parucito southward) to Brazil border (*orienticola*); s Bolívar (subsp.?). E Colombia to Guyana, and s to n Bolivia and w and c Amaz. Brazil.

Note: Larger *granti* has been considered a separate sp.[486].

Crested Guan   PLATE 15
Penelope purpurascens Pava Culirroja
Identification: 30–36″ (76–91cm). ♂ 1.9kg (?), ♀ 1.5kg. *Large dark guan with bushy crest.* Bare facial skin dull blue; *large red dewlap*; pinkish legs. Mostly dark brownish olive to bronzy olive with slight gloss; feathers of head, neck, upper back, and breast broadly edged white forming conspic. streaking; rump and lower underparts unmarked dark brown to rufescent brown. Or sim. but wings and rearparts more rufescent (*brunnescens*).
Sim. species: Band-tailed Guan is overall very sim., differing principally in smaller size, shorter legs, and frosty marking on sides of head. Up close note Band-tail's broad but inconspic. rufous tail tips. Cf. even smaller Andean Guan.
Voice: Call a loud, honking *quonk*; in high-intensity alarm a ser. of extraordinarily loud, honking squawks, *quonk, quonk, quonk, rrrrrr* (Hilty); these become higher pitched and more rapid with excitement[290]; when disturbed, little whistles, grunts, and a ser. of low, muffled barks, *wof, wof, wof, . . .* varying to a loud *cawcák* or muffled *auwuk*[654]. Dawn song a powerful "steam-whistle" call, ending in a low growl, *kuLEEErrr!*[706]. Like Spix's Guan, often quite noisy.
Behavior: Sim. to others of genus (see Spix's Guan). Bulky leaf and twig nest in broken stump or well up in tree; ca. 3 white eggs[147].
Status and habitat: Despite fairly widespread distrib. across n Venez., an uncommon and local resident. Humid lowland and premontane forest but mainly in foothill and lower montane els. There are more recs. from base of Sierra de Perijá and from Delta Amacuro than elsewhere.

Range: To 1100m. Sierra de Perijá, Zulia, and e around Lago de Maracaibo to w Mérida (Capaz); e base of Andes in se Táchira and w Apure n to Portuguesa (upper Río Tucupido); hills of se Falcón (near Sanare), mts. of Yaracuy, n cordilleras from Carabobo e through Aragua to n and s Miranda; ne Anzoátegui and Sucre s to Delta Amacuro (*brunnescens*); no Monagas recs. Mexico to w Ecuador and Colombia.
Note: Treatment of subspp. varies[53,559].

Pipile

Large forest guans; long slender neck, small head, shaggy crest, bare face, large colored dewlap, and ample tail enhance oddly "prehistoric" (reptilian) appearance; noisy, rattling flight display (often hd., infreq. seen) aided by stiff, bowed, deeply emarginate 4 outer primaries.

Common Piping-Guan   PLATE 15
Pipile pipile Pava Rajadora
Identification: 24–27″ (61–69cm). 1.2kg. Long slender neck and small head. Bill powder blue tipped black; throat and *conspic. dewlap cobalt blue*; legs rose red. Plumage mostly black glossed bluish green; *large shaggy white crest extending down nape and bare white facial skin* impart white-headed look; *large white wing patch* (greater wing coverts); rest of wing coverts and breast streaked and flecked with white.
Sim. species: Wing patches, mostly white head, and odd shape render this sp. unmistakable. Note head and neck seem too small and slender for body, and tail too large.
Voice: Call ca. 6 slow, clear, "piping" whistles (hence name), the ser. slightly ascending in pitch, *püüeee, püüeee, püüeee, . . .* ; recalls song of Scale-backed Antbird and often hd. in predawn during breeding season. Also at dawn or intervals during day performs a whirring flight display, 2 quick wing-claps (often barely audible), then 2 whirring rattles with wings, *prrrrrrrip-purrrrr*, as bird glides out from one tree to another. Rattles seem to fan forward, then backward in reverse (like shuffling deck of cards). Rattle display of *Pipile* very sim. to those of *Penelope* and difficult to distinguish, but *Penelope* may lack 2 introductory wing-claps, and rattle perhaps slower. Unlike *Penelope*, piping-guans reg. perform wing-rattle displays during day, esp. during breeding season.

Behavior: A handsome guan that occurs in prs. when breeding, otherwise in various-sized groups. Up to 12 or more may gather in a favorite tree to eat fruits or flowers. Walks lightly and with agility along large high branches, or moves with wing-assisted hops high in canopy. Rarely descends low. Often crosses large open spaces such as clearings, rivers, or airstrips by launching out into space with a flurry of wing beats, then a long, flat-winged glide alternating with more boosts from wing beats to maintain altitude across large openings. Twig nest in dense canopy foliage; 3 yellowish white eggs[147].

Status and habitat: Fairly common resident in areas where not persecuted. Humid terra firme and várzea forest and along river and forest edges in lowlands.

Range: To 1000m (mostly below 600m). Throughout Amazonas and w and c Bolívar e to Río Caura (*cumanensis*); Delta Amacuro[343] and sight n to ne Monagas[58] (prob. *cumanensis*). E Colombia to n Bolivia, Amaz. Brazil, and the Guianas.

Note: Some split numerous piping guan taxa into more than 1 sp.[606] *Pipile* has been merged into *Aburria*[147].

Aburria

Large, dark, montane relative of *Pipile*; long wattle but no dewlap; noisy rattling flight display as in *Pipile*; buzzy vocalizations unique.

Wattled Guan   PLATE 15
Aburria aburri   Pava Negra

Identification: 28–31″ (71–79cm). 1.3g. Long, slender, serpentlike neck and head. Bill powder blue tipped black; *legs bright butter yellow*. Plumage *entirely black* strongly glossed bronze green; small bare yellow throat patch and long *yellow vermiform-shaped dangling wattle*. Wattles lacking or vestigial in young birds.

Sim. species: A large dark guan of wet montane forests that will not likely be confused if conspic. yellow wattle and legs are seen.

Voice: Song a long, rising buzz, *baaaarreeeeeeeeeeee-eer* (trilled r's), dry, sustained, and snapping over at end. Repeated incessantly, esp. at dawn and dusk, also irreg. throughout day and at night during breeding season. Most vocal Dec–Apr in s Táchira[147]. Wing-rattling flight display is 1–2 brief wing-claps (barely audible at a distance), then 2 short rattles that seem to fan forward then backward (much like that of *Pipile*), given 1 or a few times in predawn darkness.

Behavior: Found alone or in prs. or little families of 3–4, mostly from forest mid. level to canopy. Tends to keep in dense foliage where difficult to see, but very noisy during breeding season, then easily located. Nest undescribed; eggs (this sp.?) in Colombia dirty white, smoother shelled than in most cracids[589].

Status and habitat: Resident in humid and wet montane forest (cloud forest), occas. into wet foothill forest. Common in s Táchira in late 1960s (P. Schwartz). Uncommon at Universidad de Los Andes forest w of Mérida. Has declined significantly with deforestation and hunting and now local and difficult to find.

Range: 450–1850m (once to 20m; sight to 2200m, w Mérida). Sierra de Perijá, Zulia; both slopes of Andes of s Táchira and in w Mérida; e Mérida (?); possibly se Lara (PN Yacambú and PN Terepaima)[612]. W Venez. s to s Peru.

Nothocrax

Small guan-sized curassow; colorful facial skin; bushy crest of long spatulate-shaped feathers; plumage rich brown (not black); deep humming song hd. only at night; differ most obviously from *Crax* and *Mitu* in cryptic plumage, small size, and nocturnal behavior.

Nocturnal Curassow   PLATE 16
Nothocrax urumutum   Pauji Nocturno

Identification: 23–26″ (58–66cm). 1.25kg. Small curassow. *Long expressive black crest of slightly recurved feathers. Bill reddish orange*; bare multicolored ocular area *yellow above*, blue in front, and slaty below eye. *Plumage mainly rich reddish chestnut*, lower underparts paler; back, wings, sides of breast, and central pr. of tail feathers vermiculated with wavy black lines; rest of tail feathers black with broad buff tips.

Sim. species: No other sp. of its size is mainly reddish chestnut.

Voice: Song, hd. irreg. (song bouts of 30 min–1 hr) throughout night from ca. 9:00 P.M. onward, and esp. in the 2- 3-hr. period before dawn (moonlight or dark) from partly concealed perch high in tree, is ser. of deep, sepulchral humming notes, *hoou, hu-hu, huu-hu-hu . . wUUT!* given about 1/min, sometimes followed by a thin, rising, and complaining *whooooouu*; not loud but very far carrying in stillness of night and extremely difficult to track down. All singing birds have been ♂♂.

Behavior: As name implies, a "nocturnal" curassow. Poorly known and something of an enigma. Well-separated birds sing from high in canopy trees at night and also may feed at night or in dim crepuscular light of dawn and dusk. When singing tends to perch near trunk or in areas of high dense vegetation where difficult to see. Sings from same tree or same group of trees night after night. Remarkably, only a very few observers have ever seen this sp. by day. Reports, mostly from native hunters, are of single birds or up to 3–4 together on gd. during day, but rarity of such reports suggests sp. is not reg. abroad by day. In Brazil 1 nest with 2 white eggs 4m up in viny tree in upper Río Negro[566]. In Brazil hunters reportedly pursue this sp. during daylight, using dogs to flush it from hollow logs or other hiding places (A. Whittaker).

Status and habitat: Locally a fairly common resident in humid lowland forest in white sandy soil and blackwater regions of s Amazonas, but very difficult to track down. In Jan 1972 up to 4 singing birds at a time could be hd. a few km s of where Ríos Guainía and Casiquiare join to form upper Río Negro[147].

Range: To 200m. S Amazonas from Cerro Duida, Caño Casiquiare, and Río Guainía southward. E Colombia to e Peru and w Amaz. Brazil.

Crax and Mitu

Largest cracids; ♂♂ predom. black; ♀♀ sim. or cryptically patterned; usually crested (some curly); bill, cere, and forehead often adorned with colorful wattles, knobs, or protuberances; most terrestrial of family. Song of most spp. a ser. of deep, sepulchral humming notes (no flight display), usually from perch above gd.; a few whistle. Nest a small, coarse, stick-and-leaf saucer at low to med. ht. in tangle, on stump, or at palm frond base; 2 white eggs incubated by ♀; both sexes care for young. Nests of some spp. undescribed. Unlike other cracids, do not regurgitate to feed young. *Mitu* differ in laterally compressed, rosy bills, feathered lores, pinkish legs, and no curly tips on crest feathers, but all spp. often placed in *Crax*.

Crestless Curassow   PLATE 16
Mitu tomentosa   Pauji Culo Colorado
Identification: 33″ (84cm). ♂ 2.4kg, ♀ 2kg. *No crest.* Feathers of head and neck short, dense, and plushy. Arched, laterally compressed *bill pinkish red*, paler and almost colorless at tip; legs pinkish red. Plumage mainly black, upperparts strongly glossed blue; *belly, under tail coverts, and broad tail tips rufous chestnut.*

Sim. species: In parts of range overlaps Black and Yellow-knobbed curassows, both of which have white (not chestnut) bellies and yellow (not red) around bill.

Voice: Song a booming or humming *uuut . . . . uu-UU-uu-uhoot . . .* or, a common variation, *uuút . . . . ,UU-a-uu-uhuút . . . .*, 2d part of song after a pause of ca. 3 sec, usually given from a perch ca. 1–5m up. Often fairly long pauses between songs. Alarm a ser. of sharp, reedy *queet* whistles, much as in other *Crax*. When breeding sings mornings, evenings, moonlit nights, and intermittently during day; some song prob. hd. yr-round.

Behavior: Like others of genus, forages mostly inside or at edge of forest. Prs. or little groups walk on gd. but seek shelter in trees, often ascending quite high if pressed. In Orinoco region 2 nests with eggs, Jun[115].

Status and habitat: Resident. Where it overlaps with Black Curassow, confined to várzea forest, esp. palm-dominated (*Bactris*, etc.) swamps on riverbanks and in adj. floodplain forest. N of Orinoco (in absence of Black Curassow) also in gallery forest and open, upland deciduous woodland, often some distance from streams (e.g., at Hato Los Indios, Apure).

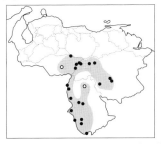

Range: To 600m. E Apure (formerly n to San Fernando de Apure), nw and c Bolívar (e to Salto Guaiquinima), and generally in w Amazonas. E Colombia, nw Brazil, and Guyana.

Note: Previously called Lesser Razor-billed Curassow and placed in genus *Crax*[147,403].

Black Curassow   PLATE 16
Crax alector   Pauji Culo Blanco
Identification: 34–37″ (86–94cm). ♂ 3.4kg, ♀ 2.8kg. Large. Short curly crest extends to nape. Slightly swollen cere and base of bill orange red (*erythrognatha*) or rich butter yellow (*alector*), tip black; legs gray. Plumage entirely glossy black, *belly, thighs, and under tail coverts white.* ♀: sim. but crest barred white at base (not visible in field).

Sim. species: See Crestless Curassow. The 2 spp. broadly overlap in range but are largely kept apart by preference for different habitats. Also see Yellow-knobbed Curassow.

Voice: Song of ♂ a low, sepulchral humming or booming *umm-um . . . umm, um-um,* hd. esp. mornings and evenings but in breeding season at any time of day or night. As in others of genus, song never sounds loud and is difficult to locate and usually much farther away than one imagines. When annoyed a brief *pit pit peer;* alarm a whistled *peep.*

Behavior: Most often seen in prs. or small groups, and typically rather unsuspicious in areas where not hunted. Looks very elegant walking with head up, legs together ("knock-kneed"), and fanned tail bowed down in manner typical of all *Crax*. Forages by walking on gd., and likes to come out along forest borders or onto gravel roads at dawn, but always just a few steps from forest. Seeks safety in trees, and if highly alarmed will go into canopy, ascending quickly in ser. of wing-assisted hops. ♂♂ sing from perches 1–5m up or so, occas. from gd. Complex but rarely observed display toward rivals and ♀♀ involves exaggerated posturing, incl. a dramatic tail-up and fluffed-crissum display, wing-claps, a variety of vocal noises, and booming song.

Status and habitat: Fairly common to common in areas where not disturbed. Resident on floor of humid terra firme forest and tangled forest borders in lowlands and humid and wet foothills. Locally (e.g., w of Tumeremo, ne Bolívar) in dry forest and dry gallery woodland, but replaced by Crestless Curasow in most riverine areas and s llanos.

Range: To 1500 m. Throughout Amazonas; Bolívar e to Río Caura (*erythrognatha*); rest of Bolívar and Delta Amacuro (*alector*). E Colombia to the Guianas and n Brazil.

Yellow-knobbed Curassow   PLATE 16
Crax daubentoni   Pauji de Copete
Identification: 34–37" (86–94cm). ♂ 3kg, ♀ 2.3kg. *Large curly crest extending to nape.* Eyes orange amber to pale orange red. ♂: glossy black with *base of bill, large knob on cere, and large knoblike wattles on lower mandible bright yellow*; belly, *thighs, and under tail coverts white; tail tipped white.* ♀: sim. but *breast,* sometimes also wing coverts, *barred white,* crest feathers white basally (seldom visible in field), bill black (no knobs).
Sim. species: Only curassow found over most of its range, but in s Apure meets Crestless Curassow. In Andean foothills approaches or meets Northern Helmeted-Curassow.
Voice: Territorial song of ♂, hd. mainly Feb–Jul in llanos, a loud, clear, and leisurely whistle that rises slightly then descends and fades (like a "falling bomb" with no explosion at end), *wheeeeeeee-uuuuuuuuu,* ca. 4 sec, usually given from 1 or more traditional calling trees. ♂♂ give wing-flap display, also possibly as aggressive signal toward other ♂♂, by striking wings together over back 4–10 times in 1–2 secs, typically the 1st 2 *wapp!* sounds spaced,

rest in rapid succession. Some ♂♂ boom (hd. in Jun), a weak *Gmp! Gmp!* followed shortly by a deep *uuumh . . . uhh,* higher pitched than in other *Crax* and barely audible[88].
Behavior: ♂♂ scatter on territories when breeding, but at other times, esp. in dry season, ♂♂ and ♀♀ gather in groups of 3–20 or more, usually near a water source[718]. Forage on gd. by walking but seek safety by hopping or flying up into trees. Call and display with raised fanned tail from trees. Like to venture out along gallery forest borders and into little openings or onto narrow shady roads in early morning and late afternoon where dust bathe or forage for gravel. Breed in early rainy season (Apr–Jun); 2 white eggs[147]. Some polygyny occurs[87,719].
Status and habitat: Formerly a relatively common resident in dry, deciduous forest, gallery forest, and isolated patches of dry woodland. Now somewhat local in llanos; very spotty away from llanos, and locally extirpated where hunting pressure is high. Can still be found in nos. on large ranches where not hunted (e.g., Hato Cedral, Hato Piñero).

Range: To 500m. Maracaibo Basin, Zulia, and w Mérida; w Falcón, hills of se Falcón (incl. Tucacas); lowlands and foothills of Yaracuy and Carabobo e through Aragua to Miranda and generally from e base of Andes in Táchira, Apure, Barinas, and Cojedes to Guárico, locally to e Sucre and Monagas. Ne Colombia.

Pauxi

Formerly placed in genus *Crax*[147,260,403]; differ in large casque; feathers of crown only slightly curly; montane distrib.

Northern Helmeted-Curassow   PLATE 16
Pauxi pauxi   Pauji Copete de Piedra
Identification: 34–37" (86–94cm). ♂ 3.6kg, ♀ 2.7kg. *Large fig-shaped iron gray casque on forehead* (casque smaller and glossed brownish violet in Andes; or small, more pointed, and brown in Sierra de Perijá). Bill and legs dull red. ♂ and normal-phase ♀: *mostly black,* upperparts glossed bluish to greenish, feathers scaled dull black; *belly, under tail coverts, and tail tip white.* Rufous-phase ♀ (rare): head and neck blackish *contrasting* with rest of plumage which is rich rufous brown finely barred and vermiculated black; wing coverts narrowly tipped white, belly and under tail coverts white; tail black prom. tipped buffy white.

Sim. species: Unique in limited range. See Crested Guan.

Voice: Song, as in allied *Crax* and *Mitu*, an exceptionally low-pitched humming, typically *uum. . . . uUH a uum . . uum . . uUH . . um-uUH . . . . . um . .* and so on; louder and more emphasized *uUH* notes usually follow 1–3 or more slow humming notes. Song resonates for long distances even through dense cloud forest, and singing ♂♂ are difficult to track down. Alarm a high, reedy whistle, *fweet*, over and over.

Behavior: Sim. to *Crax* and *Mitu*. Prs. or family groups forage by walking on forest floor, feeding on fallen fruits, seeds, and some green material. Seek safety by flushing into trees. Relatively confiding where not hunted. Breeds Dec–Jul with peak ca. Mar or Apr; nest building Mar, 2 eggs; nest 4–6m up on horizontal branch[570]; 2 ads. with chicks, Jun, Rancho Grande Biol. Station (Hilty); Aug juv., Sierra de Perijá, Colombia[260]; juvs. remain with ads. several months.

Status and habitat: Resident in humid and wet premontane and montane forest (cloud forest), esp. humid ravines with thick undergrowth incl. *Heliconia* and Araceae. Formerly fairly numerous; now rare, local, and declining because of deforestation and hunting in and out of parks. Rugged terrain limits access to habitat. Present distrib. mostly within existing national parks[612]. Roads in PN Henri Pittier and PN Yacambú provide access to habitat, but there are few recent recs. elsewhere in Andes or Coastal Cordillera; status of pop. in Sierra de Perijá unknown.

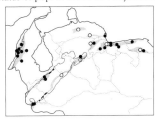

Range: 500–2200m (mostly 1000–1800m). Sierra de Perijá (Río Tocuco southward), Zulia (*gilliardi*); both slopes of Andes from s Táchira to s Lara; adj. nw Portuguesa?; n Falcón (Sierra de San Luis), e Falcón (formerly in PN Morrocoy; Tucacas?), mts. of n Yaracuy, Coastal Cordillera from Carabobo e to Distr. Federal (to El Calvario), and Interior Cordillera in sw Miranda at Cerro Negro (*pauxi*). Formerly Sucre (?). Ne Colombia.

Note: Taxonomy follows Sibley and Monroe[606].

Odontophoridae: Wood-Quail and Bobwhites

Perdices

Formerly the Odontophoridae were considered a subfamily of the Phasianidae, but the group has been elevated to family status based on skeletal studies[265] and more recent DNA-DNA hybridization work[504]. As currently defined, the Odontophoridae are found only in the New World. They are generally robust terrestrial birds with strong legs. Venezuelan species, in particular, are reluctant to fly and are mostly secretive forest-dwellers, much better known by their loud, rhythmic songs than by sight. Only the Crested Bobwhite is found in open areas and frequently seen. It behaves and sounds rather like its familiar and widespread northern allies. All Venezuelan species are granivorous and nest on the ground.

Colinus

Chunky with thick bill; bushy crest; strong legs; short rounded wings; cryptic plumage; sexes differ slightly; terrestrial.

Crested Bobwhite   PLATE I
Colinus cristatus   Perdiz Encrestada

Identification: 8–9″ (20.3–23cm). 130g. Thick black bill. Much geographical variation in plumage. ♂: head buffy white with *conspic. pointed crest smoky grayish white*, throat and broad postocular rufous, sides and back of neck spotted black and white; upperparts brown somewhat vermiculated black and gray, wings and back speckled black; chest uniform smoky gray tinged pinkish, *lower underparts rufous boldly spotted black and white*, incl. under tail coverts (*sonnini*). ♀: sim. but head darker smoky gray, underparts buff broadly scaled black (*sonnini*). Or both sexes sim. to *sonnini* but ♀ finely spotted and dotted brown below (*mocquerysi*). Or ♂ *rather different* with forehead, eyebrow, and throat buff to rufous, crest gray brown, upperparts mostly blackish somewhat scaled white, throat mottled, underparts dark brown, flanks and lower underparts spotted black and white; ♀ sim. above but entirely spotted black and white, throat streaked black, chest finely spotted black (*barnesi*). Or ♂ sim. to *sonnini* but crest pale rufous, upperparts heavily marked black and white, eyebrow and throat buff, rest of underparts boldly reticulated black and white, center of belly mostly rufous (*parvicristatus*).

Sim. species: Only bobwhite in its range. Easily recognized everywhere despite geographical variation.

Voice: ♂ sings flat *bob-white* (1st note weak, 2d rising) from gd. or low perch. Call resembles that of Northern Bobwhite (*C. virginianus*) of N Amer. but faster and without that sp.'s richness. Less vocal than n ally, but song can be hd. most of yr. Contact call a soft, low *turée-burr-burr*; alarm a sharp *tick* or *tick-tick* over and over.

Behavior: Found in prs. when breeding, but during rest of yr in coveys of 3–20 or more that forage by walking through grass or weeds or other open areas. Peck at gd. for seeds, fruits, and insects or scratch with one foot, then the other. Generally stay within cover, freeze to avoid detection, or run rapidly. If pressed, a covey may explode upward in a blur of wing beats and noise as birds fly off low in various directions, gliding and veering erratically and soon dropping out of view to run. Breeding starts in mid or late dry season or later; flying chicks mid Nov[787];

nest a grassy bowl, usually concealed from above by grass; up to ca. 15 eggs.

Status and habitat: Fairly common to locally common resident in grassland or grassy and weedy areas with scattered brush and thickets, also in dry scrubby areas. During May–Oct rainy season when much of low llanos is flooded, congregates in large nos. wherever there is high gd., esp. along dikes and roadbanks.

Range: To 1500m n of Orinoco; to 1000m s of Orinoco. Throughout s to n Amazonas and se Bolívar. Goajira region of nw Zulia e to Falcón, Lara, and Trujillo (*cristatus*); Andes of Mérida (*horvathi*); w Barinas to n Portuguesa (*barnesi*); ne Anzoátegui, Sucre, Monagas, and Isla Margarita (*mocquerysi*); most of rest of nonforested Venez. n of Orinoco (*sonnini*); Apure e to s Anzoátegui, n Amazonas (Caño Cataniapo), and Bolívar locally to Santa Elena de Uairén (*parvicristatus*). W Panama; Colombia to the Guianas and n Brazil. Aruba and Curaçao.

Note: Subsp. *continentis*[403] incl. in *parvicristatus*. Validity of some other subspp. in doubt.

Odontophorus

Large, robust, forest-dwelling quails; most with slight bushy crest.

Marbled Wood-Quail   PLATE I
Odontophorus gujanensis Perdiz Colorada
Identification: 11″ (28cm). 260g. Large and dark. *Lacks prom. markings except for conspic. bare orange red ocular area and postocular stripe. Crown and short bushy crest dark chestnut contrasting* (in good light) *with gray nape, mantle, and foreneck;* face tinged rufescent, rest of upperparts chestnut brown with a few buff to white dots on wing coverts and back and a few darker streaks; tertials edged *buffy rufous;* underparts pale rufescent brown tinged ochre with small inconspic. buff and black barring. ♀: sim. but head paler, face rufescent; above more coarsely mottled brown, buff, and black; below more extensively barred (*gujanensis*). Or sim. but ♂ paler, more ochraceous to tawny below; ♀ almost unmarked below (*medius*). Or sim. but underparts grayish (esp. ♂); both sexes more extensively barred below (*marmoratus*). In flight all races show buff barring on primaries.

Sim. species: Plainer and browner than others of genus, and generally found at lower els. Best marks are *bold orange eyering*, rufescent face, contrasting

crown and mantle, and prom. buff-edged tertials (but none of these marks easy to see in dark forest understory).

Voice: Prs. sing antiphonal duets a few times at dawn and dusk, even after dark. Song s of Orinoco a loud, mellow *koo-KEE-poo;* 1st bird gives *koo-KEE,* 2d adds *poo* note, the phrase *repeated rapidly over and over in rhythmic chant,* often answered by other prs. (or groups) nearby. In nw Barinas (Altamira) duet has different cadence, a rapid, rollicking *buba-WINKkle, buba-WINK-kle* . . . ; single birds sing a hollow, burry *koo-KEE.* When alarmed, soft peeping notes as runs away.

Behavior: Prs. or coveys of up to 8–10 birds call softly as they scratch and forage on shady forest floor for seeds, fruits, and insects, or move off in single file. Not esp. wary but tend to remain within cover, and habit of crouching and freezing, or running off hurriedly when pressed, makes them difficult to observe. Reluctant to fly unless surprised or hard-pressed. When groups flush off in a blur, 1–2 may remain crouched and "frozen" rather than fly. Roost a few meters up in vine tangles. Nest in Costa Rica a roofed structure with side entrance, or a deep depression in fallen leaves; 4–5 white eggs[706]; chick 7 Apr, Cerro Urutaní, Amazonas[157].

Status and habitat: In most areas an uncommon and infreq. noted resident except by voice; even then groups may be rather widely separated. Floor of humid forest, old second-growth woodland; in nw Barinas in wooded ravines and patches of humid forest mixed with coffee plantations.

Range: To 1500m n of Orinoco, to 1800m s of Orinoco. Base of Sierra de Perijá, Zulia; both sides of Andes from Táchira to Lara (*marmoratus*); hd. in Sierra de San Luis, Falcón (P. Boesman); throughout Amazonas; w and c Bolívar e to Río Paragua and Cerro Guaiquinima (*medius*); e Bolívar from Sierra de Imataca southward (*gujanensis*). Costa Rica to e Bolivia, Amaz. Brazil, and the Guianas.

Black-fronted Wood-Quail   PLATE I
Odontophorus atrifrons Perdiz Frentinegra
Identification: 11–12″ (28–30.5cm). 305g. Large and dark. Bill thick. Bare ocular ring slaty. *Forehead, sides of head, and throat black,* crown and short bushy crest chestnut brown; upperparts brown vermiculated buff, gray, and black; *wing coverts coarsely streaked and blotched black and buff;* below grayish brown finely vermiculated gray and brown, center of breast and belly buff somewhat dappled

and mixed with dusky and white. ♀: sim. but center of lower underparts more extensively mottled buff and white.
Sim. species: Only wood-quail with prom. black face and throat (no white collar), otherwise very plain in field. Cf. Venezuelan Wood-Quail which has white throat.
Voice: In Santa Marta Mts. of Colombia a whistled *bob-white*, much like call of Santa Marta Antpitta (*Grallaria bangsi*) (T. B. Johnson); also apparently a rollicking call like others of genus, or sim. to Gray-necked Wood-Rail[750].
Behavior: Poorly known but apparently sim. to others of genus (see Venezuelan Wood-Quail).
Status and habitat: Floor of humid and wet montane forest almost up to treeline. Known from at least 10 localities (incl. Cerros Yin-Taina, Jurustaco, and Viruela) in upper Río Negro, Zulia (1952–1978), where prob. fairly common. May also occur in s Táchira (occurs in adj. Colombia).

Range: 1650–3100m. Sierra de Perijá, Zulia (*navai*). Ne Colombia.

Venezuelan Wood-Quail
PLATE I
Odontophorus columbianus   Perdiz Montañera
Identification: 10–11″ (25–28cm). 315g. *Looks dark-headed.* Crown and nape dark reddish brown, otherwise above brown streaked and mottled black, buff, and white; pale forehead and eyebrow faintly dotted white, cheeks and subocular area black, *throat white speckled black and bordered below by broad crescent of black*; rest of underparts rich rufescent brown sparsely but boldly spotted white. ♀: sim. but underparts grayer.
Sim. species: Dark head and white throat are the marks for this dark, cryptically patterned sp. Cf. Marbled Wood-Quail (minimal range overlap).
Voice: Prs. (coveys?) sing 1–several times at dawn (not during day), a very loud rollicking and *rapidly repeated* antiphonal duet, *chúrdole-chúr-it, chúrdole-chúr-it* . . . (lasts up to 10 sec); 1st bird sings *chúrdole*, 2d (♀?) answers with *chúr-it*, rhythmic and with resonant yodeling quality, gradually winding down with only 1 bird finishing. May also be transcribed as *go-hurry right now*. Singing prs. (groups?) often answered by other groups.
Behavior: Hd. far more than seen. Occur in prs. when breeding, otherwise in small coveys that move quietly, with individuals keeping very close together and constantly uttering soft contact calls (audible to a few meters away). Walk a few steps, then pause to scratch industriously in forest floor litter, sometimes 2 birds hunched side by side with tails down. Often

travel more or less single file through forest. Generally rather confiding (if observer is very quiet); when alarmed crouch and hide, or run; fly only if surprised or hard-pressed. Breeding reported May–Jul[571].
Status and behavior: Uncommon to fairly common resident (by voice) in humid and wet premontane and montane forest in n mts.; also reg. found in forested pass between Bramón and Las Delicias in s Táchira. Prob. occurs in adj. Norte de Santander, Colombia.

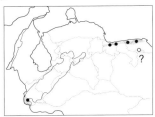

Range: ENDEMIC. 900–2400m. S Táchira (Río Chiquito; sight, above Las Delicias); Coastal Cordillera from Carabobo (Cumbre de Valencia) e to n Miranda (e of Caracas at Curupao).

GRUIFORMES

Rallidae: Rails and Coots
Cotaras, Pollas de Agua, y Gallinetas

This worldwide family has a good representation of species in Venezuela. Notorious for their secretive habits and often enigmatic behavior, they are found in a variety of habitats, but most species favor damp grass or marshy vegetation. A few occur in dry grasslands far from water, and some occur in damp areas or stream banks inside tall humid forest. Some are crepuscular or at least partially nocturnal in habits and are difficult to see except when calling. Distribution records for several species are very spotty, and their true distribution is incompletely known. "Typical" rails are characterized by narrow, laterally compressed bodies, fairly long bills, short wings, a short tail, and rather long legs. Crakes are similar but usually have shorter bills. Gallinules and coots are specialized for more aquatic habits and are excellent swimmers. Coots, with the addition of lobed toes, also are good divers. Most rails are quite omnivorous, a fact that has undoubtedly contributed to their success worldwide. All nest on or near the ground or on floating vegetation. There are two important monographs on the family[547,729].

Laterallus

Small rails (known as crakes) with short stubby bill and short rounded wings; tail often cocked; sexes sim.

Gray-breasted Crake
PLATE 17

Laterallus exilis   Cotarita Cuellirrufa

Identification: 6″ (15cm). 34g. Small brown and gray rail with *conspic. bright rufous patch on nape and mantle.* Short bill glossy black; *basal two-thirds of lower mandible and basal corner of upper mandible pale fluorescent green;* legs yellowish buff. Eyes red; narrow eyering yellow. Upperparts wood brown, wing coverts blackish narrowly barred white, crown dark gray, *rest of head, foreneck, and breast iron gray,* center of throat and belly white, *flanks and under tail coverts sharply barred black and white.* Under wing coverts whitish barred and mottled black.

Sim. species: No other small crake has bright rufous patch on upper back. Cf. Paint-billed Crake, larger Ash-throated Crake, and Sora.

Voice: Commonest call (ne Bolivia and Costa Rica) when alarmed or disturbed 2–4 sharp, tinkling, and penetrating notes, 1st slightly higher pitched, *Peee-dee-deet* or *Peee-dee-dee-deert*, often answered by another bird. Territorial song (?) a dry rattle with sharp "ticking" quality and of varying length[705].

Behavior: A shy and extremely skulking rail of tall dry or damp grass. In Costa Rica interspecifically territorial with other *Laterallus,* but does not respond strongly (by song playback) to territorial churring calls of other *Laterallus.* Pops. undergo marked habitat shifts during yr[705]. Trinidad nest (Jul) a grassy sphere with side entrance; near sugarcane root; 3 cream-colored eggs spotted dark brown at larger end[175].

Status and habitat: Occurs in damp or seasonally flooded grass, marshes (seasonal?), and tall dry grass in pastures and around clearings. The small no. of recs. in Venez. are widely scattered, and pop. is prob. highly dynamic as in Costa Rica. Interspecific interactions with other *Laterallus,* and seasonal and successional changes in water level and vegetation, result in dynamic pop.

Range: To ca. 1700m (most recs. below 500m). Rec. from Mérida, w Apure (sight and specimen, Hato Cedral, 1994, 2000—D. Ascanio), Portuguesa (Aparición), e Falcón (Cuare), Carabobo, Aragua (juv., 1968, Rancho Grande), Miranda (Caucagua), and Monagas (Caripito). Belize and Guatemala locally to e Bolivia, Paraguay, and Brazil; the Guianas. Trinidad.

Rufous-sided Crake

Laterallus melanophaius   Cotarita Pechiblanca

Identification: 6″ (15cm). 52g. *Small, dark* rail with short greenish bill, yellowish green legs, red eyes. Above dark brown, lores grayish, *sides of head, fore-*neck, and breast bright rufous;* center of throat and belly white, *flanks boldly and coarsely barred black and white,* under tail coverts rufous chestnut. Under wing coverts barred black and white.

Sim. species: Both Rusty-flanked and Russet-crowned crakes look rather sim. but lack bold barring on flanks.

Voice: Territorial song an abrupt, loose churring gradually descending or settling down but not slowing much, *thur'tr'tr'tr'tr'tr'tr'tr'tr'tr'tr'tr'tr'tr'—tr,* often given almost simultaneously by mate, or answered by another bird. Song sim. to others in genus.

Behavior: In most areas extremely skulking and furtive. Runs through grass and is almost impossible to flush. Prs. may call almost from beneath an observer's feet yet remain invisible, although often they can be lured into partial view with patience. Grassy ball nest with side entrance a little above water; in grass or bush; 3–5 pale buffy white eggs sparsely dotted reddish brown[589].

Status and habitat: Only 2 definite recs. in Venez., where perhaps only a vagrant. Elsewhere in damp grassy pastures, drainage ditches, and tall marsh grass around lake edges; most often found in vicinity of water, but occas. well away from it. Replaced in n Venez. by Rusty-flanked Crake.

Range: To 900m. Known only from Distr. Federal (near Caracas) and Cumaná, Sucre (*melanophaius*). E Colombia, Guyana, Suriname, and locally s to c Argentina and Uruguay.

Rusty-flanked Crake
PLATE 17

Laterallus levraudi   Cotarita de Costados Castaños

Identification: 6.5″ (16.5cm). Looks like Rufous-sided Crake but whiter below and *without* flank barring. Short dull greenish bill; legs yellowish brown. Above dark olive brown, *supraloral area, sides of head, and sides of neck continuing to sides of body and flanks bright ferruginous;* center of throat and all of central underparts pure white, belly buff, under tail coverts dark rufous chestnut. Under wing coverts dull rufous.

Sim. species: Only small crake in Venez. with rufous and white underparts and *no flank bars.* Cf. Rufous-sided Crake.

Voice: Territorial song sim. to those of other *Laterallus,* a long churring whinny that starts fast and furious, then seems to gradually slow and descend; often given simultaneously by both members of a pr. Most vocal Jun–Jul[59] but can be hd. yr-round. Contact calls (or territorial defense) a slow, irreg., squeaky *E—E—E, da, da, da;* also *squEEE. . . squEEE . . . SKE-a . . . SKE-a,* reedy *week* and *wit,* scraping

chirp notes, and other odd, tinkling, and rough notes, some rather like those of Gray-breasted Crake.
Behavior: Sim. to other *Laterallus*. A furtive denizen of marsh vegetation. Occas. walks into open briefly but mostly lurks in tall vegetation. Difficult to flush. Prob. breeds May–Jul with young fledging Aug–Sep[59].

Status and habitat: Resident in tall wet grass, reeds, and marshy vegetation around natural or human-made ponds and lagoons in forested and open areas. Despite being listed as vulnerable[127], it remains locally fairly common. Rec. (sight and specimens) from more than 25 localities, it thrives in small ponds in e Falcón, Carabobo, s Aragua, and Lara (PN Yacambú). Colonies recently found at several new areas in w Carabobo, e.g., Embalse de Canoabo; Bejuma; Hacienda Guataparo[59]; also Boconoito, Portuguesa, Feb 1998 (D. Ascanio).

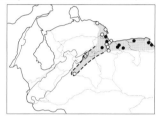

Range: ENDEMIC. To 1350m. Sw Portuguesa (sight, Boconoito) and Lara (sight, PN Yacambú) e through Yaracuy, e Falcón (w to San José de la Costa, sight, 6 Feb 1990—Hilty), Carabobo, Aragua (Lago de Valencia; Embalse de Taguaiguai; Bella Vista), Distr. Federal (vicinity of Caracas), and extreme e Miranda (San José de Río Chico).

Russet-crowned Crake
PLATE 17

Laterallus viridis Cotarita Corona Rufa
Identification: 6.5″ (16.5cm). 64g. Small dark-colored crake *without* barring. Short greenish bill a little heavier than others of genus; eyes red; legs reddish pink. Crown rufous chestnut *contrasting with gray lores and sides of head*; rest of upperparts dark olive brown; throat whitish tinged cinnamon, otherwise cinnamon rufous below becoming darker rufous chestnut on lower underparts. Under wing coverts rufous.
Sim. species: In e Venez. a small dark crake with uniform rufous underparts (no barring) is likely to be this sp. Cf. Rufous-sided Crake which is barred black and white on flanks and is not known to overlap in range.
Voice: Territorial song a long, loose, whinnying churr rather like many others of genus, but slower, the notes more tinkling and distinctly separated, esp. toward end. Most vocal mornings and evenings.
Behavior: Furtive and skulking in tall dry grass. Stays beneath cover as walks lightly on gd. or climbs or runs through grass, thickets, even on low branches, but rarely flushes. Spherical grass ball nest with side entrance, sometimes with extended runway; up to 1m up in dense vegetation; 1–3 eggs[589].
Status and habitat: Fairly common resident locally in tall dry grass, bushy pastures, grassy manioc gardens,

and overgrown roadsides. A grass rail, not assoc. with water. Commonest in grasslands on sandy soils, e.g., Gran Sabana (esp. n end at Monumento de Soldado Pionero) and in grasslands around bases of tepuis.

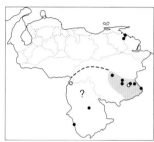

Range: To 1450m. Amazonas (tape, Pto. Ayacucho, Jun 1996; Cerro Duida; San Carlos de Río Negro); n Delta Amacuro (Capure; Pedernales), and e Bolívar from Río Paragua to Gran Sabana (*viridis*). N and e Colombia to the Guianas and s locally to e Peru and s Brazil.
Note: By some placed in genus *Anurolimnas*[435,606].

Amaurolimnas

Monotypic genus; rather small; unbarred, all-dark forest crake; short bill rather like *Porzana*.

Uniform Crake

Amaurolimnas concolor Cotara Unicolor
Identification: 8–8.5″ (20.3–22cm). 115g. Local. *Small, dark rufous brown rail. Short, thick, greenish yellow bill*; dull reddish legs. Upperparts dark ruddy brown, flight feathers dull brown, face and throat cinnamon buff, neck and underparts rufous brown, ruddier than above; throat pale.
Sim. species: A very plain, dark little rail with few good marks. Look for pale greenish yellow bill, and note habitat. Other spp. most sim. to it occur in marshes (e.g., Rusty-flanked Crake) or are not known to overlap (Russet-crowned Crake).
Voice: In Costa Rica territorial call a ser. of clear whistles, loudest in middle then speeding up and fading away, *tooeee toooeee TOOOEEE TOOOEEE TOOEE tooee-tuee-tui*. Alarm note a sharp nasal *kek*. Low clear whistles as contact or aggressive notes[706].
Behavior: A wood- or thicket-rail that seldom leaves safety of dense cover. Like other small rails, walks with jerky but alert movements and tends to flick short tail, esp. when disturbed. In Costa Rica reported to peck in leaf litter and hanging debris for seeds, berries, invertebrates, and small vertebrates and to dig in soft mud with beak; nest a loose cup of leaves and stems in top of stump; 4 eggs, pale buff blotched shades of brown and gray near large end; wet season[706].
Status and behavior: Only rec. is 1 specimen taken from humid forest 21 Aug 1968 at Hacienda La Encantada, near Boquerón, Carabobo, but surely more widespread. In Costa Rica found in wet forest, streamside thickets, and old wet second growth[699,706].

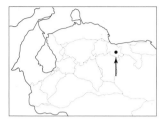

Range: 700m. Carabobo (*castaneus*). S Mexico spottily to w Ecuador, e Bolivia, Guyana, Amaz. and se Brazil. Jamaica (formerly?).

Porzana

Short bill with thick base; culmen flat, tapering to blunt point; small to med. size.

Sora   PLATE 17
Porzana carolina   Turura Migratoria
Identification: 8″ (20.3cm). 70g. Small, plump rail with thick stubby bill and greenish legs. Above brown, back streaked and mottled with black and white; *small black face* ("dipped in ink") *surrounds yellow bill*, sides of head, foreneck, and breast gray, *lower underparts white narrowly barred black*; under tail coverts a fluff of white beneath short, cocked tail.
Sim. species: Best mark is yellow bill encircled by black. Also cf. Ash-throated, Paint-billed, and Gray-breasted crakes, all of which also are small and gray below.
Voice: Song a distinctive, whinnylike ser. of ca. 12 high, thin notes that fall in pitch; when disturbed a sharp *kee*.
Behavior: Skulks in tall marsh grass but more easily seen than some rails. Walks into openings along edges of reeds and grass in early morning and late evening, but never far from cover. Tail is normally cocked up, and twitched when bird is nervous or alarmed. Flushes readily, sometimes also swims.
Status and habitat: Uncommon to locally fairly common (easily overlooked) n winter resident, early Oct–end of Apr, to fresh- and saltwater marshes, flooded rice fields, irrigation ditches, and tall grass around ponds and lakes.

Range: To ca. 500m (once to 2500m, Mérida). W Zulia (Río Anaure), Mérida, Portuguesa, Falcón, Carabobo (Lago de Valencia), Aragua, Distr. Federal, Miranda, and Guárico (Calabozo) to Anzoátegui (Pto.

La Cruz) and Delta Amacuro; once in s Amazonas (s of Cerro Duida at Esmeralda); once in Bolívar (Río Carapo); Islas Margarita, Los Roques, and La Orchila and Isla de Aves. Breeds from Canada to Mexico; winters from s US to c Peru and Guyana. Trinidad.

Ash-throated Crake   PLATE 17
Porzana albicollis   Turura Gargantiblanca
Identification: 8″ (20.3cm). 105g. *Dull greenish bill* longer and more slender than bill of Sora; legs grayish to purplish brown; eyes red. Upperparts brown, hindneck finely and back broadly streaked black; *sides of head and underparts gray*, median throat white (not very conspic.); *flanks dusky barred narrowly with white, under tail coverts coarsely barred black*.
Sim. species: Gray-breasted and Paint-billed crakes are smaller and unstreaked above, latter also with red legs and red on bill. Sora has yellow bill and black face.
Voice: Easily recognized and often hd., a loud, fast ser. of vibrating rattles, *d'd'd'd'd'd'-ou, d'd'd'd'd'd'-ou* . . . (ca. 18 phrases in 20 sec), reminiscent of bursts from a machine gun. Call a sharp *tuk*.
Behavior: Another rail that skulks in tall grass but flushes readily, flies a short distance with dangling legs, then drops into cover. Not often seen in open or away from cover, although occas. appears briefly at edges of marshes or damp grass or when crossing roads or small openings. In Guyana breeds Feb–Jul, peak in May; woven grassy bowl on gd. in grass; 2–3 eggs, pinkish cream to white, finely spotted brown and lilac at larger end[37].
Status and habitat: Widespread but local resident in damp grass and sedges, rice fields, drainage ditches, also sometimes marshes. More of a damp-grass than a marsh rail. In Gran Sabana in wet grass around moriche palm groves. Seasonal movement between habitats needs documentation; perhaps only found in w llanos in wet season; occas. in wet grassy roadside ditches in lowland forest regions but not in forest.

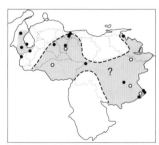

Range: To 1200m. Maracaibo Basin, Zulia; e of Andes from w Apure (sight/tape, Hato Cedral, Jun 1993—Hilty), n Portuguesa, Cojedes, Carabobo, and Aragua to se Sucre and Delta Amacuro[343]; nw Bolívar (Caicara) and e Bolívar from El Palmar to Santa Elena de Uairén (*olivacea*). Colombia to c Argentina, e Brazil, and the Guianas. Trinidad.
Note: Subsp. *typhoeca*[53,403] apparently invalid[148].

Yellow-breasted Crake PLATE 17
Porzana flaviventer Polla Enana
Identification: 5.5″ (14cm). 26g. *Tiny, buffy yellow crake.* Short bill dusky; *legs orange yellow. Crown and stripe through eyes black*, short white eyebrow; hindneck and rest of upperparts buffy brown *streaked black and white on mantle and scapulars*; median upper wing coverts and tertials black barred white and partly covered by a few long pale brown wing coverts that obscure most of wing; *underparts rich yellow buff*, throat whitish, *flanks and under tail coverts barred black and white.*
Sim. species: Perched or in flight over a marsh, a tiny yellowish crake with black cap and boldly barred lower underparts will be this sp. Ocellated Crake lacks head pattern and flank barring and does not occur in marshy habitat.
Voice: In e Colombia a hoarse, slow, slightly downscale *zeee-eee-eee-eee*, ca. 1 note/sec (W. McKay); in Costa Rica a harsh, churring, scratchy *je-je-je-jrr*, sometimes introd. by a rolling note; a squealing *kweer* and high, whistled *kleeer*[706].
Behavior: Difficult to see because of small size and habit of staying out of sight as it walks or climbs through floating vegetation or grass and reeds growing in water. Flushes readily, with dangling legs, and soon drops back into marsh. In Panama noted perching and foraging out in open in early morning, but withdrew to cover later in morning[788]. In Greater Antilles, loosely built nest in water plants; 3–5 pale cream eggs sparsely spotted brown[65].
Status and habitat: Widespread but easily overlooked local resident and short-distance migrant in freshwater marshes and floating vegetation, esp. water hyacinth in choked pools and lagoons. Prob. seasonal in some areas; trans-Andean dispersal may occur. Numerous sight recs. since ca. 1995 at Hato Cedral, Apure.

Range: To ca. 500m (rarely to 2500m, Mérida). E of Andes from w Apure, Portuguesa, e Falcón, s Carabobo, Aragua (Embalse de Suata), Distr. Federal, and Miranda (Río Chico) to Guárico (Santa María de Ipire), Delta Amacuro (Río Amacuro), and ne Bolívar (*flaviventer*). S Mexico spottily to n Argentina and c Brazil. Greater Antilles. Trinidad.
Note: Has been placed in genus *Poliolimnas*.

Paint-billed Crake PLATE 17
Neocrex erythrops Polla Pico Rojo
Identification: 7.5″ (19cm). 53g. *Bill chartreuse green; basal half bright red;* eyes scarlet orange; *legs peach*

red. Crown and upperparts dark olive brown, *sides of head* (from above eyes), *foreneck, and underparts* gray, throat whitish, *flanks and under tail coverts black coarsely barred white.* Downy young black.
Sim. species: Nearest is Gray-breasted Crake which has rufous patch on upper back and no red on bill. Also cf. Ash-throated Crake and Sora.
Voice: Call a high *keek*; also a froglike note followed by a trill. Song a long accelerating and descending ser. of notes ending in 3–4 churring trills that drop in pitch, last note often a longer flat trill (P. Schwartz recording).
Behavior: Furtive and difficult to see, although single birds can occas. be flushed short distances. Grassy nest found in cornfield[186].
Status and habitat: Rare and local. Wet grass in pastures, overgrown grassy and bushy areas, and marshes. Mainly a "grass and thicket" rail. Notably migratory, but seasonal movements/dispersal poorly understood; 36 specimens in Colección Phelps were all taken late May–early Nov (mostly Sep–Oct), with more than half near Calabozo, Guárico; only Sep–Dec at Hato Masaguaral, Guárico[734]. One taken 14 Jun 1945, another (and 4 more seen) 23 May 1946, at night lights at Rancho Grande Biol. Station[33] suggest seasonal movements. Common in Aug (no other months) in nw Monagas at puddles along a dirt road[186]; 1 found by soldiers 7 Jul 1997 on rainy evening at Fort Luepa (1400m), n end of Gran Sabana[596].

Range: To 1000m (sight, 1400m). Spottily in Mérida, Barinas, Portuguesa, Carabobo (sight), Aragua, Distr. Federal, Miranda, Guárico, and nw Monagas (Caicara de Maturín); Delta Amacuro[343]; e Amazonas; e and s Bolívar from Upata to upper Río Caura (*olivascens*). Guyana, Surinam, e Brazil, e Bolivia, ne Argentina, and Paraguay; w Peru. Galápagos Isls.

Speckled Crake PLATE 17
Coturnicops notatus Cotarita Moteada
Identification: 5.5″ (14cm). Small blackish crake heavily speckled with white. Bill dusky; legs dusky olive; eyes red. Above mostly black somewhat mixed brown, wing coverts, lower back, and rump black narrowly barred white; *head, neck, mantle, and breast black speckled white*, throat whiter, breast also streaked with white, *flanks black narrowly barred white.* In flight a *large, conspic. white patch shows in center of pale gray secondaries;* under wing coverts mixed black and white.
Sim. species: No other small crake in Venez. is mainly speckled black and white. White wing patch

should be conspic. in flight. Cf. larger Sora. Spotted
Rail is more than twice the size.
Voice: During day austral birds give a weak
kooweee-caak, 1st note high, 2d louder and dry;
alarm a whistled *keeee* and high *kyu*[730].
Behavior: Has been taken at night with lights. Secretive in tall grass where runs and is reluctant to fly.
Stomach contents included mainly grass seeds, a few
insects[127].
Status and habitat: Very rare; 3 recs. in Venez.: a ♀
from Mérida, 14 Jun 1914 (or 1916?), and 2 ♀♀ Aug
1954 (or 1960?) from Aparición, Portuguesa. Presently known only from ca. 16 specimens throughout
its range. The 5 specimens from n of Amazon Basin
were all taken Mar–Sep and are possibly postbreeding dispersers. Found in wet or inundated grass and
marshes, dense vegetation in flooded rice fields,
flooded *Spartina* mashes, and wheat stubble[127].

Range: Mérida (1500m) and Portuguesa (200m). E
Colombia (Macarena Mts.), ne Guyana, se Brazil, e
Paraguay, Uruguay, Argentina; Falkland Isls. (once?).

Ocellated Crake   PLATE 17
Micropygia schomburgkii   Cotarita de Ocelos
Identification: 5.5" (14cm). 32g. Small yellowish
crake spotted white above. Short dusky gray bill;
eyes red; *legs coral red.* Above warm buffy brown,
*crown, hindneck, and entire upperparts incl. upper
wing coverts with large black-encircled white spots*
(the "ocellations"); forehead rufous (inconspic.),
*sides of head and most of underparts bright ochre yel-
low,* center of throat and center of breast and belly
white. Bill (in hand) very narrow and laterally compressed with high culmen. Tail short.
Sim. species: Yellow-breasted Crake is streaked and
barred (not spotted), but the two do not occur in
same habitat. When flushed, ocellations on upperparts are not conspic.
Voice: Freq. hd. song, esp. mornings and late afternoons, a high, thin, almost fragile ser. of wee
tinkling notes, sometimes accelerating a little at first,
t-t-t-t-t-t-t- . . . (ca. 2–3 sec), on same pitch. Easily
overlooked.
Behavior: An extremely shy and furtive rail of dry
grasslands. On rare occas. when this sp. flushes, it
flies off low over grass, legs dangling or raised, and
soon drops back out of sight in grass. An egg from
Guyana was buff with fine and coarse light brown
spots[573].
Status and habitat: Fairly common to locally common resident (by voice) in dry grass in s part of

Gran Sabana and in grasslands surrounding tepuis.
Possibly seasonal or vagrant to n part of country.

Range: To 1400m. Distr. Federal (Caracas), Miranda
(Baruta; Los Teques), n Monagas (Caripe), Delta
Amacuro[343], c Amazonas (Cerro Duida), se Bolívar
(Auyán-tepui to Roraima), and sightings s to Brazil-
ian border at Santa Elena de Uairén and El Pauji
(*schomburgkii*). Sw Costa Rica; the Guianas, e Peru,
e Bolivia, and c and se Brazil.
Note: Has been placed in genus *Coturnicops*[547].

Rallus

Long, slightly decurved bill (longer than in crakes);
legs usually pinkish to reddish (but often quite dull);
fairly large; fresh- or saltwater marshes.

Clapper Rail
Rallus longirostris   Polla de Mangle
Identification: 13" (33cm). 290g. Rather large *dingy
gray brown* rail of salt marshes. *Fairly long bill
slightly decurved,* mostly dull orange, culmen dusky;
legs orangish gray; eyes reddish brown. Above dull
smoky gray brown with short ill-defined buff eyebrow and dull whitish lower eye-arc; back streaked
dark brown; throat dull white, malar area buff, foreneck and breast pinkish buff; *flanks, belly, and under
tail coverts dull white barred light brown.* Birds from
w are palest (*phelpsi*), those in e darker and with
much bolder barring (*margaritae*).
Sim. species: Large size, rather "faded" gray brown
appearance, and prom. barring on flanks are best
marks for this coastal dweller. Cf. esp. Plain-flanked
Rail which *lacks* barring on lower underparts.
Voice: Call, occas. at dawn and dusk, a loud clattering *kek-kek-kek* . . . accelerating then slowing; some
calls have bellowing quality; a low, drawn-out *raaaa*
. . . *raaaa.* . . .
Behavior: A saltwater sp. that is shy and usually stays
hidden in coastal marsh grass or mangroves. Usually
in prs., but individuals may be well separated. If
pressed or startled, may flush heavily, fly a short distance with legs dangling or up, and soon drop back
into cover. Forages most actively at low tide and
preys heavily, at least in some areas, on fiddler
crabs. In Trinidad breeds Apr–Dec, mostly May–Jun;
twig nest in mangroves and near water; 3–7 pale buff
eggs spotted and blotched deep purple[175].
Status and behavior: Local resident of brackish and
saltwater marshes and mangroves along coast. Easily
overlooked except when vocalizing, and prob. more

numerous than scattered recs. indicate. Apparently interspecifically territorial with allied Plain-flanked Rail.

Range: Locally on coast of Zulia (Paraguaipoa), Falcón, Carabobo, and e Miranda (*phelpsi*); Isla Margarita (*margaritae*); coastal Sucre at Chacopata (*dillonripleyi*). Coastal s US s to Belize; ne Colombia e spottily on coast through the Guianas to e Brazil; sw Colombia s on coast to nw Peru.

Plain-flanked Rail   PLATE 17
Rallus wetmorei   Polla de Mangle Negro
Identification: 13″ (33cm). Poorly known. Large, uniform-looking rail of salt and brackish water, apparently with 2 color phases. *Fairly long, slightly decurved bill almost entirely dusky*; eyes dark brownish red; legs dull dark straw yellow. Pale phase: crown dark brown, rest of upperparts pale smoky brown, back somewhat streaked dusky; below light smoky buff, *throat, center of belly, and under tail coverts whitish; no barring on lower underparts.* Dark phase: above uniform *sooty blackish brown* (unstreaked), below uniform dark smoky brown, throat very slightly paler, lower underparts tinged grayish, *no barring on flanks or under tail coverts*; sexes sim. Note: More study is desirable to confirm unequivocally that light and dark individuals represent ad. color phases and are not related to age or sex.
Sim. species: Should be identified with caution. Dark ad. birds are completely unmarked and should be distinctive; neutral-colored birds look very like dull Clapper Rails but have absolutely *no barring* on lower underparts. Note Clapper's longer bill.
Voice: Recalls that of Clapper Rail but with rhythmic pattern. Typical territorial call a fast ser. of harsh, grating, and metallic-sounding triplets, *tak-tak-TZAK, tak-tak-TZAK*, . . . repeated 10–20 times; excited birds (after playback) may repeat shorter or longer phrases, e.g., *tak-TZAK* or *tak-tak-tak-tak-tak-TZAK*, some of which take on bellowing quality reminiscent of Clapper Rail. Often prefaces a ser. of calls with 1 or more low, guttural, and drawn-out *gumma* notes (D. Ascanio recordings). Prs. may respond to playback with antiphonal calling, i.e., *chak-chak-chat, ru'u'u'r* (1st 3 notes by ♂, rattle by ♀), over and over.
Behavior: Single birds or prs. walk cautiously, with tail cocked and sometimes twitched, peering intently and occas. running forward or to side a few steps to grab prey by reaching or stabbing with bill. Notably confiding and may spend much time foraging in a

small area. Highly territorial; apparently interspecifically territorial with Clapper Rail.
Status and habitat: Rare, sedentary, and little-known resident of mixed red and black mangrove communities, esp. with a few small, semiopen muddy areas. First taken in 1943 in Aragua, but not refound there[828]. Subsequently known from a small no. of specimens, mostly near Pto. Cabello, Carabobo (11 taken Sep 1945), and Tucacas, Falcón (9 taken May 1951), none since. Relocated in May 1999 near Tucacas where up to 11 were hd., tape-recorded, and videotaped (D. Ascanio and R. Ridgely); others hd. at e end of peninsula of PN Morrocoy in Jun 1999 (D. Ascanio). There are a few other unverified reports[127]. Two BC birds Apr and May; juv. in Sep. *Seriously threatened* by coastal development.

Range: ENDEMIC. Carib. coast from vicinity of Morrocoy Pen. (videotapes and sound recordings, D. Ascanio) and Tucacas, Falcón, se to Pto. Cabello, Carabobo, and Aragua (mangroves on w shore of bay of La Ciénaga at Turiamo).

Pardirallus

Recall *Rallus* but bill brightly colored (usually with green), underparts gray or black, and voices differ.

Blackish Rail
Pardirallus nigricans   Polla Negra
Identification: 11″ (28cm). 215g. Large, dark rail with *long yellowish green bill.* Eyes red; *legs coral red.* Upperparts dark brown; *sides of head, foreneck, and underparts dark iron gray*, throat whitish, center of belly, under tail coverts, and short tail black. Imm.: sim. but brown, esp. on posterior upperparts.
Sim. species: Combination of *long greenish* bill, *red* legs, and lack of barring is diagnostic. Cf. Sora, Spotted Rail, and Paint-billed and Ash-throated crakes.
Voice: Unusual territorial call a few loud (big sound) bellowing growls followed by rising squeal, *gr'r'R''R''R'R keeEEEEE!*, the *keeEEEEE* squeal often repeated over and over, sometimes with several loud metallic *kick* notes at end. Throaty (mammal-like) growls loud and disconcerting when close.
Behavior: In se Peru a furtive marsh dweller that runs or occas. flushes up a short distance, then drops in again. Runs quickly when crossing open spaces, e.g., narrow roads. Prob. sedentary as long as habitat does not change, but like many other rails, a good disperser as it finds isolated marshes that form around newly created oxbow lagoons. Nest 30 May, Colombia; shallow, woven cup with wild-rice stem; base of cattail clump in marsh; 3 creamy white eggs with irreg. chestnut marks on larger end.

Status and habitat: Resident (?); 1 specimen 15 Feb 1981 and 4 more 17–18 Aug 1981 at Laguna de Estrella in the Ciénega de Juan Manuel protected area in sw Zulia[95]. Found in tall wet grass and emergent vegetation around ends of lagoons and oxbows.

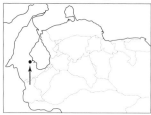

Range: Sea level. Sw Zulia (subsp.?). Colombia, e Ecuador, e Peru, Paraguay, and Brazil.
Note: Has been placed in genus *Rallus*. Subsp. not determined[95].

Spotted Rail   PLATE 17
Pardirallus maculatus   Polla Pintada
Identification: 10″ (25cm). 165g. *Boldly spotted black and white.* Bill rather long, greenish yellow with red at base of lower mandible; *legs rosy red*; eyes yellow (or red?). *Head, neck, upper back, and breast black heavily streaked and spotted white; lower underparts barred black and white*; back, wings, and tail brownish somewhat streaked with black and more narrowly with white. Imm.: black replaced by brown; underparts with only faint whitish spotting and barring.
Sim. species: No other rail is so boldly spotted. See smaller Sora which has short yellow bill, greenish yellow legs, and more or less uniform foreparts.
Voice: In Costa Rica a repeated groaning screech, each note preceded by a grunt, *g'REECH g'REECH* . . or *pum-KREEP pum-KREEP* . . . , possibly territorial or aggressive; also an accelerating ser. of *pum* notes; a sharp *gek*[706].
Behavior: Secretive and not easily flushed, but often leaves cover to feed partially in open in early morning. Runs rapidly, crosses open spaces, occas. even roads. In Costa Rica, under favorable conditions, territories are small and birds occur in locally high densities of 8–9/22ha[50]. Sim. high densities have been noted in rice fields in Cauca Valley of Colombia (P. Jennings). Open rush-stem nest just above water; 2–7 pale buff eggs marked dark purple mainly at larger end[175].
Status and behavior: Resident very locally in flooded rice fields, marshes, and along irrigation ditches.

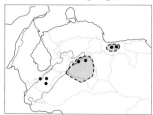

Prob. more numerous than the few scattered recs. suggest.
Range: To 1700m. Maracaibo Basin in w Mérida (Lagunillas; Mérida; El Valle) and locally e of Andes in Portuguesa (Finca El Porvenir; Zanjon), Carabobo (Lago de Valencia), and near Maracay, Aragua (*maculatus*). Se Mexico, Belize, Costa Rica spottily to Bolivia, n Argentina, and Uruguay. Cuba; Trinidad.
Note: Has been placed in genus *Rallus*.

Aramides

Large colorful rails with bold red legs; med.-length bill; wide variety of habitats near or away from water but usually in wooded areas.

Rufous-necked Wood-Rail   PLATE 17
Aramides axillaris   Cotara Montañera
Identification: 13″ (33cm). 290g. Large. *Bill greenish yellow; legs coral red. Head, neck, breast, and sides rufous chestnut*; central throat whitish, belly gray, under tail coverts and short cocked tail black; *patch on nape and upper back contrasting gray*; rest of upperparts dark olive; axillaries and under wing coverts barred black and white.
Sim. species: Much like Gray-necked Wood-Rail and easily confused. Rufous-necked is *all rufous* from head to belly (lacks "divided" underparts of Gray-necked). Both share black rear ends and red legs. Other Venez. rails with rufous underparts are much smaller.
Voice: Call a long sharp ser. *Keulp, Keulp,* . . . . . ca. 2 per sec. (D. Ascanio recording); elsewhere reported to recall that of Gray-necked Wood-Rail, a loud, incisive *pik-pik-pik* or *pyok-pyok-pyok*, repeated ca. 8 times, mostly at dawn and dusk; often antiphonal[175].
Behavior: Secretive and difficult to see in mangroves, but at low tide may leave cover to forage in open on mudflats. In Trinidad breeding evidence Jul and Oct; nest and eggs sim. to Gray-necked Wood-Rail[39].
Status and habitat: Fairly common resident on offshore isls., locally along coast (e.g., Falcón), and very locally inland; both salt- and freshwater habitats, incl. mangroves, swampy riverbanks, and damp wooded areas in dry regions; infreq. seen. Sp. has been collected at numerous localities across n Venezuela but remains poorly known.

Range: To 1800m (mostly below 500m). Very locally in w and n Zulia (incl. Cerro Alto del Cedro), w and e Lara (Cerro El Cerrón; Cabudare), Falcón (incl. Sierra de San Luis; Tucacas), Carabobo (Pto. Cabello),

Aragua, Miranda (inland and on coast), and Monagas (mouth of Río Guarapiche); Delta Amacuro[343]. Islas Patos and Los Roques. W Mexico and Yucatán s locally (mainly on or near coast) to w Ecuador and the Guianas. Trinidad.

Gray-necked Wood-Rail
PLATE 17
Aramides cajanea   Cotara Caracolera
Identification: 15″ (38cm). 410g. Large and impeccably groomed. *Legs coral red* with matching *ruby red eyes* and pinkish coral eyering. *Head, neck, and chest gray*, crown darker, throat whitish, the *gray in sharp contrast to cinnamon rufous* (dull brick red) *breast*; wings and back olive brown; belly, *under tail coverts, and short, cocked tail black*; under wing coverts barred rufous and black.
Sim. species: Shares red legs and black rear end with Rufous-necked Wood-Rail, but always told by gray head and "divided" gray and rufous underparts.
Voice: Often hd. at dawn or dusk or even 1–2 hr before dawn or after nightfall, a loud, cackling, rhythmic duet, *KEE-KAULK, KEE-KAULK . . .* and so on with variation, as 2d bird sings a simple *KAULK-KAULK-KAULK . . .* or *KOOK-KOOK-KOOK . . .* on slightly different pitch; often several in a chorus that lasts several min, gradually winding down with only 1 bird calling at end.
Behavior: In lowland forested regions rather secretive, suspicious, and difficult to see, although often hd., but in llanos, esp. in dry season, concentrates along stream banks and around waterholes, and then often very easy to see, sometimes in nos. Forages by walking on gd., usually with tail cocked and nervously twitching. May venture into open but usually just a short dash from cover. Feeds at water's edge on a variety of small animal matter incl. crabs, some seeds and fruit; roosts in bushes above gd. In alarm runs fast but rarely flies. Breeds Jul–Sep, Guárico[734]; deep twiggy bowl 1–7m up in vines or bush; 3–7 eggs pale cream spotted and blotched brown[175].
Status and behavior: Widespread resident along forested river and stream banks in dry to humid regions, seasonal pools in or near gallery woodland, and mangroves. In almost all areas generally near water or damp areas and in or near woodlands. Common in llanos where reg. ventures into semiopen; less numerous and generally in or near cover in wooded regions.

Range: To 1900m n of Orinoco; to 650m s of Orinoco. Throughout but no recs. in arid nw (*cajanea*). C Mexico to n Argentina and Uruguay. Trinidad.

Porphyrula
Rather sim. to *Gallinula* but plumage much brighter; bill colorful.

Purple Gallinule
PLATE 17
Porphyrula martinica   Gallito Azul
Identification: 13″ (33cm). 220g. Elegantly dressed marsh dweller. *Frontal shield pale blue; thick wedge-shaped bill bright red with yellow tip.* Eyes dark red to reddish brown; legs rich yellow. Plumage iridescent. *Head, neck, and entire underparts brilliant bluish purple;* back and wings bronzy green; under tail coverts fluffy and white. Imm.: brown above, wings bronzy blue; sides of head, foreneck, and chest buffy white, chest washed gray; throat and lower underparts white; bill dusky olive, frontal shield and legs as in ad.
Sim. species: Imm. easily confused with ad. and imm. Azure Gallinule. From ad. Azure by decidedly larger size, extensive buff on neck and underparts, unstreaked back, and more or less dingy brown (not blackish) rump and tail. Up close note Azure's red eyes. Imm. from imm. Azure Gallinule by larger size, mostly buffy gray (not white) underparts, and heavier bill.
Voice: Low, nasal *uuuah*? and guttural notes and reedy cackles sim. to those of Common Gallinule; a hard, nasal *kek* or ser. of *kek* notes; also a Limpkin-like wail.
Behavior: Walks over floating vegetation or climbs around in taller marsh vegetation. Swims less than Common Gallinule and usually avoids open water. Often perches up in marsh grass, on a bush, low branch, or even occas. on post in water. Flies rather slowly and in straight line with rapid wing beats and dangling legs; raises legs on longer flights. Bulky open nest of grass or rice stems a little above water in marsh or rice field; often roofed and may have entrance runway; 3–7 eggs, cream to buff spotted brown and pale purple[706,788].
Status and habitat: Common resident, but nos. show strong seasonal fluctuations; small resident pop. prob. augmented by short- or long-distance intratropical migrants (from Amazonian and/or austral region?). Freshwater marshes, flooded rice fields, and other areas near water. Common Jun–Nov, Hato Ma-

saguaral, Guárico, uncommon in other months[734]; sim. pattern elsewhere in llanos. Breeds Apr or May–Oct or Nov (need verification). Very scarce during Dec–Apr dry season. Most numerous in broad-leaved marsh vegetation, e.g., *Thalia* (cf. Azure Gallinule); also locally very common in rice fields[357].

Range: To 500m (doubtless occas. higher). Throughout n of Orinoco; a few scattered recs. s of Orinoco. Se US and Mexico to n Argentina, rarely Chile and Uruguay. W Indies. Trinidad.

Note: By some placed in genus *Porphyrio*.

Azure Gallinule   PLATE 17
Porphyrula flavirostris   Gallito Claro
Identification: 9.5–10″ (24–25cm). 92g. Small and delicately proportioned. *Plumage looks faded.* Bill and small frontal shield pale greenish yellow; eyes bright red; *legs bright lemon yellow.* Crown, hindneck, and back pale brownish olive tinged aquamarine and *somewhat streaked dusky;* wing coverts pale azure blue; rump and tail brownish black, tail feathers tipped white; *sides of head, foreneck, and sides of breast faded azure blue, center of breast and lower underparts immaculate white.* Under wing coverts white. Imm.: sim. but duller; below mostly white; bill greenish yellow, culmen black; legs bright yellow.

Sim. species: Should be recognized by distinctive faded, or "stonewashed," appearance and pale azure on sides of head, neck, and breast. Cf. esp. larger, heavier imm. Purple Gallinule. Imm. also rather like ad. Ash-throated Crake but legs bright yellow (not purplish to grayish brown).

Voice: Quieter than allied Purple Gallinule; occas. a short trill (J. V. Remsen).

Behavior: Skulks in tall grass and other marshy vegetation much more than Purple Gallinule, seldom swims, and is rarely or never in open water. Flushes somewhat reluctantly, flies a short distance with dangling legs, and typically holds wings up momentarily upon alighting. Reg. perches up exposed for short periods of time atop marshy or floating vegetation, then climbs down out of view. In Suriname dry reed cup nest in marsh, May–Aug; 4–5 eggs, creamy, thickly dotted red brown[253].

Status and habitat: Uncommon to locally common resident and intratropical migrant (from Amazonia?), mainly May–Nov, to flooded short to tall grass, freshwater marshes, rice fields, and grass-choked edges of lagoons, mainly in llanos. Small nos. are resident but generally very scarce or absent during Dec–Apr dry

season. Breeding not yet reported in Venez.[533]. Few recs. s of Orinoco.

Range: To 300m. Prob. spottily throughout. W of Andes in nw Táchira (sight, La Fria, 24 Jan 1974—P. Alden); e of Andes from w Apure and w Guárico (Calabozo) to Delta Amacuro; n Amazonas (Río Ventuari) and Bolívar (Río Chanaro on upper Río Caura). E Colombia and the Guianas s to Paraguay and n Argentina. Trinidad.

Note: Has been placed in genus *Porphyrio*.

Gallinula

Bill thinner than in *Fulica*; prom. frontal shield; long lobed toes unwebbed.

Common Gallinule (Moorhen)   Illus. p. 277
Gallinula chloropus   Gallineta de Agua
Identification: 13–14″ (33–36cm). 320g. *Frontal shield and thick wedge-shaped bill bright red tipped yellow.* Legs greenish with red "garters" (hard to see). Mainly slate gray, blacker on head and neck; wings and back tinged brownish; *long conspic. white stripe on sides and flanks;* "divided" white under tail coverts (black in center). Imm.: *pale gray* to brownish gray, browner above; throat, foreneck, and chest mottled with white, bill dull yellowish brown (dingy).

Sim. species: Resembles a smaller, paler version of imm. Purple Gallinule (see).

Voice: Deep *kuk* and higher *kip*, sim. to but lower pitched and more hesitant than Caribbean Coot; a cackling *ker-ker'r'r-ker-ker-ker-ca-ca*, slowing, and clucking notes.

Behavior: Unlike Purple Gallinule, usually seen swimming, both in open water and along edges of tall marsh vegetation. Pumps head back and forth like a coot as swims, and picks food items from surface of water or below, and seeks cover in marsh vegetation if alarmed. Walks well on gd. or on floating vegetation, but reluctant to fly, then pattering on surface to get airborne. Open reed nest at edge of water, often with reeds bent over top of nest; 3–6 dark buff eggs spotted and blotched brown and lilac; imm. helpers may assist ad. prs. feeding young[706].

Status and habitat: Common resident locally. Marked seasonal movements need documentation; nos. possibly augmented by n migrants. Freshwater ponds and marshes. Large nos. seasonally (esp. Jan–Mar, other months?) at Laguna Tacarigua, e Falcón; wanders to lagoons in Andes (e.g., at PN Yacambú). Small nos. s to El Palmar and Guasipati in n Bolívar.

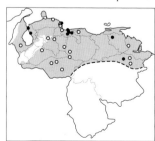

Common Gallinule (left),
Caribbean Coot (right)

Range: To 500m (occas. to 1350m). Throughout n of Orinoco and in ne Bolívar (*galeata*). Virtually worldwide except Australia and New Zealand. In New World breeds from s Canada s locally to n Chile and Argentina. West Indies. N birds migratory.

Caribbean Coot   Illus. above
Fulica caribaea   Gallineta Pico Plata
Identification: 13–14″ (33–36cm). Robust and rather ducklike in water. *Thick wedge-shaped bill and enlarged bulbous frontal shield* (extends to crown) chalky *white* (shield often faintly tinged yellow); inconspic. dusky ring near bill tip. Mostly slate gray, head and neck blackish; white on sides of under tail coverts. In flight shows white rear border on secondaries. Imm.: paler gray below, throat and foreneck mottled white.
Sim. species: See Common Gallinule which has mostly red bill and shield.
Voice: Variety of cackles, clucks, and grating sounds. Commonest are sharp, explosive *Kik!*, low *grup*, grinding *raakup*, and ser. of piping whistles[60].
Behavior: Usually seen swimming in ponds and small lagoons, alone or in prs. Dives well, tips up to feed, and walks easily on shore. Like most coots, sometimes reluctant to fly, preferring to patter across surface with a great commotion to safety of far shore. Nest a large pile of aquatic vegetation in reeds, open or partly roofed; ca. 6 eggs light brown marked darker brown[280,706].
Status and habitat: Uncommon to locally fairly common resident in small nos. Ponds, lagoons, and

sloughs bordered by aquatic weeds and rushes. Few specimens but many sight recs. across n Venez., esp. in e Falcón.
Range: To 500m (sight to 1350m). Ne Zulia (Lagunillas) to Falcón (Coro eastward), Lara (sight, Yacambú), Carabobo, Aragua (Suata Reservoir), and Miranda (specimens and sightings) e to Monagas (sight, El Guamo). W Indies; Curaçao. Trinidad and Tobago (sight). Casual to Florida.
Note: Often considered a subsp. of American Coot (*F. americana*) which breeds in N Amer. s to Nicaragua (*americana*) and in Andes of Colombia (*columbiana*). N migrants may reach Venez. Sim. to Caribbean Coot but frontal shield small, chestnut, and not bulbous. Mixed prs. reported in Cuba, Hispaniola, and Virgin Isls.[10].

Heliornithidae: Finfoots
Zambullidor de Sol

Finfoots are a small pantropical family of waterbirds related to rails but somewhat grebelike in appearance. There is 1 species each in the New World, Africa, and Asia. They have short legs and fleshy lobed toes and swim and dive very well. Their food is small aquatic life and some seeds. Males are unique in possessing folds of skin, or pockets, under their wings where the young can be carried.

Sungrebe   PLATE 17
Heliornis fulica   Zambullidor de Sol
Identification: 11–12″ (28–30.5cm). 130g. Looks like a small brown duck with longish tail. Eyering and short grebelike bill dull red (brightest when breeding), lower mandible paler than upper. ♂: *crown and hindneck black with white postocular stripe bordered below by black stripe through eyes; sides of neck with bold black and white stripe*; remaining upperparts olive brown; *tail blackish* narrowly tipped white (inconspic.); foreneck and underparts white, sides tinged buff. ♀: sim. but cheeks buff. Both sexes show gaudily banded black and yellow feet (seldom visible in field).

Sim. species: Striped head and long slender body are diagnostic. When flushed resembles a small, weak-flying brown duck or grebe. Note broad blackish tail (pale tips hard to see).

Voice: Usually quiet. Unusual and seldom hd. advertisement a low-pitched, honking *eeoó, eeoó, eeoó, eeoó*; (2–4 notes) with froglike or echolike quality.

Behavior: Usually wary and solitary. Swims along shady riverbanks and secluded streams, keeping near or under overhanging shoreline vegetation. Floats low and somewhat flattened in water, dives quickly, sometimes partly submerged with only head and neck above water. If alarmed, capable of almost explosive pattering takeoff like a little coot, then showing white tail corners, but flies low and seldom far. Occas. rests on a low, semiconcealed branch overhanging water. Eats a variety of small aquatic life and picks grasshopper nymphs from water hyacinth. Small, loose groups (to ca. 12) reported. Panama nests, Jun–Jul[788]; small, frail, twig platform lined with leaves; in bush ca. 1m over water; 3–4 pale cinnamon eggs spotted reddish brown; short 11-day incubation[7].

Status and habitat: Uncommon to fairly common but easily overlooked resident on slow-moving streams, almost always where trees, vines, and vegetation overhang bank; also occas. freshwater ponds and lagoons. Recs. spotty n of Orinoco; 1 dead on shore of Laguna Mucubají (3600m) Oct 1994 suggests dispersal (D. Ascanio).

Range: To 400m (once, 3600m). Maracaibo Basin, Zulia (Caño Aguas Negras); Apure (Río Meta; sight, Hato Cedral), s Cojedes (sight), and w Carabobo (sight, Represa Cachinche[60]); locally e to Sucre (Caño La Brea), Monagas, and Delta Amacuro; throughout Amazonas and Bolívar (recs. spotty). S Mexico to ne Argentina and s Brazil.

Eurypygidae: Sunbittern

Tigana

The single species in this family is exquisitely patterned and possessed of an elegance rivaled by few other birds. It is a sedate bird of shady forest streams in warmer parts of the New World tropics. It has a long, slender neck, moderately long legs and tail, and unwebbed toes, and it moves with a dainty, halting gait. The somber colors belie a "sunburst" of color on the flight feathers, which can be seen to advantage

during spectacular courtship and threat displays with spread wings, fanned tail, and lowered head.

Sunbittern   PLATE 17

Eurypyga helias   Tigana

Identification: 18–19″ (46–48cm). 220g. Bustard-like appearance, but proportions delicate and slender. Rather *long straight bill* dusky above, orange yellow below; eyes red, legs butter yellow. *Small head black with long white stripe above and below eyes*; throat and foreneck white, rest of neck and upperparts brown densely vermiculated and barred white, black, gray, and chestnut; *wing coverts spotted with white*; breast brown vermiculated black and fading to plain buffy white on lower underparts; tail vermiculated gray and black and crossed by 2 black-bordered chestnut bands. In flight (or display) shows *spectacular sunburst* ("Navajo rug" pattern) *of rufous, chestnut, and black at base of primaries*.

Voice: Vocal early morning and late in evening; song a high, penetrating whistle (pure tone), *wuuuuuuuuuu*, melancholy, ventriloquial, and either rising or falling slightly in pitch at end or swelling then fading in volume (recalls song of Cinereous Tinamou). When disturbed high, soft, vibrating trills, *td'td'td'td'td'td'td'td'td'td*, as if complaining. Trills may ascend or descend or be combined with bill clatters and vocal rattles in alarms and threats (also raises and spreads wings in "threat"); alarm a louder *cra-cra-cra . . .*, up to 6 notes. A loud *kak-kak-kak-kak* may be advertisement.

Behavior: Solitary birds or prs. walk lightly and gracefully along shady, leaf-littered stream banks or damp places in forest, but seldom wade in water. If disturbed fly up buoyantly on broad wings to a low branch, or around a corner and out of sight, typically alternating a few quick stiff wing beats below horizontal, with glide that reveals startlingly bold wing patches ("ocelli"). Young and ads. also flash these "falso ocelli" on wings in "startle" defense. Usually rather wary, preferring to maintain a discrete distance from observer. Picks, gleans, or jabs for small, mostly aquatic life (incl. fish) from near edge of water. Large, circular, and truncated cone nest of leaves, mud, and twigs; on low, bare branch 2–6m up in woodland or tree in clearing; both ads. participate; 1–2 pinkish buff eggs with irreg. purplish spots at large end; breeds May–Aug, juvs. Oct–Dec in Guárico[734,744,745].

Status and habitat: Fairly common to common in llanos; elsewhere an uncommon and local resident

along quiet forest streams, shady riverbanks, small forest pools, and damp thickets near water; humid and wet lowland forest and gallery forest.
Range: To 1800m (Sierra de Perijá, Coastal Cordillera); to 500m s of Orinoco. Sierra de Perijá, Zulia; Coastal Cordillera in Aragua; generally from Portuguesa, Cojedes, Sucre, and Delta Amacuro southward (*helias*). S Mexico to n Bolivia and Amaz. Brazil.

Aramidae: Limpkin

Carrao

The Limpkin is a large marsh-dwelling bird that resembles an ibis but is more closely related to cranes (Gruidae). It is the only member of its family. Found in warmer parts of the New World, it eats mostly large *Pomacea* snails, also insects, frogs, and other aquatic life. The outer primary feather is bent with a portion of the inner web incised.

Limpkin   PLATE 3
Aramus guarauna Carrao
Identification: 24–28″ (61–71cm). 1–1.4kg. Shape and plumage recall an ibis. Broad rounded wings, slender neck, long legs, and slightly drooped bill. Plumage *mainly unmarked* dark sooty brown, *hindneck and upper mantle densely streaked and spotted white*; throat mostly white, a few inconspic. white spots down center of underparts. Bill and legs dark. Shows *much less* white streaking than N Amer. birds.
Sim. species: Ibises have thinner, more decurved bills, bare facial skin, and a smooth, sustained flight (except Green Ibis). See nonbreeding and imm. Glossy Ibis and imm. Black-crowned Night-Heron.
Voice: Noisy, esp. at dusk and at intervals during night, giving a loud, far-carrying cry, a harsh, reedy, rolling *kreEEEooou* or *carrEEEooou* repeated several times. At a distance, call has wailing or lamenting quality, almost like a human in distress. May call in response to any sudden noise, e.g., splash of a canoe paddle.
Behavior: Usually seen alone, a little hunched and partly hidden in marshy vegetation, or standing at edge of a wooded stream. During dry season may concentrate in small loose groups at drying pools, then often standing in open. Walks slowly and carefully, searching for snails which it seizes with long bill, or probes for other items in shallow water or muddy places. When not feeding may retire to top of a low bush. Flight is buoyant with stiff upward jerks of wings, this often followed by a short sail. Breeding Sep–Oct, Guárico[734]; platform nest of twigs, leaves, and dry rushes, usually less than 3m up in marsh vegetation; 3–6 eggs, cream with brown blotches and spots[175,706].
Status and behavior: Fairly common resident in freshwater marshes, flooded pastures, and gallery forest streamsides in llanos (abundance depends on snail pops.); more local in forested regions s of Orinoco and in coastal mangroves. Some local movements; in

llanos most numerous Jun–Oct[734]; absent from areas where water levels are regulated and snails cannot breed (e.g., Hato Cedral).

Range: To 300m (sight to 550m, Represa Guamo, n Monagas[60]). Throughout (*guarauna*), but no recs. in arid nw; few recs. in s Amazonas and s Bolívar. S Florida and Mexico s to Bolivia, n Argentina, and Uruguay. Greater Antilles; Trinidad.

Psophiidae: Trumpeters

Grullas

This small but interesting family of terrestrial birds is confined mainly to Amazonia. They are believed to be most closely related to cranes (Gruidae) and rails, but in life they more closely resemble large, long-legged guineafowl. They have a distinct humped carriage and short, fowl-like bill. The feathers of the head and neck are very short, extremely dense, and velvety. They eat both plant and animal matter, including reptiles and amphibians, fly weakly, and are known to swim across small rivers.

Gray-winged Trumpeter   PLATE 16
Psophia crepitans Grulla
Identification: 19–22″ (48–56cm). 1.3kg. *Hunchbacked and guineafowl-like* with *long legs*, short greenish yellow bill, and large dark eyes. Plumage mainly black with *long gray inner wing feathers* (secondaries and tertials) *covering entire back*. Feathers of head and neck are short, plushlike, those on foreneck and chest *highly glossed* purple, violet, and greenish (iridescent in good light). Gray inner flight feathers are exceptionally long, loose, and hairlike or fuzzy at tips; innermost somewhat ochraceous.
Voice: "Song," by 1 or several together, a low, almost guttural, humming that accelerates then gradually slows and descends, *um-BUM-Bum-umm umm, umm, umm, umm, um um*, hd. during day, also occas. at roost. Alarm a very loud, discordant, grating *JZZAK!* or *JEEK!* as well as other loud grunts and harsh or strident notes as birds run away.
Behavior: Very social and usually encountered in prs. or groups up to several dozen (flocks of 50 or more reported). Forage by walking in open formation through forest, picking up fallen fruit and a variety of small animal matter. When alarmed flee by running rapidly, but if pressed will fly laboriously to mid.-story branches or higher. Not unusually wary if

observer is quiet, but hunted groups become very suspicious and difficult to observe. Much sought as pets by Amerindians, as captive young birds become tame and affectionate and are prized for their habit of "sounding the alarm" at the least disturbance day or night, and for their prowess as snake hunters. At night groups gather in communal roosts 3–6m up in a tree. Allied White-winged Trumpeter (*P. leucoptera*) has cooperatively polyandrous breeding (all ♂♂ copulate with 1 breeding ♀); groups contain a dominant ♂ and ♀ plus 2 subordinate ♂♂, 1 subordinate ♀, and offspring of previous season; a few fugitive prs. or trios breed apart from groups; territories avg. ca. 72ha. Acrobatic displays involve "play" or territory defense (not courtship). All members of groups incubate eggs and feed young; eggs white, 3 (rarely 4) in unlined hollow tree cavity 8–13m up[599,600].

Status and behavior: Uncommon and low-density resident (groups range over large areas) in humid terra firme forest, also seasonally in low-lying floodplain forest along rivers, esp. if there are fruiting fig trees. Typically only found well away from settled areas.

Range: To 700m. Se Sucre (Guanoco) and ne Monagas (sight, Caño Colorado[58]); s Monagas (Barrancas); Delta Amacuro[343]; throughout Amazonas and Bolívar (*crepitans*). Colombia to ne Peru, n Amaz. Brazil, and the Guianas.

CHARADRIIFORMES

Burhinidae: Thick-knees

Daras

Thick-knees are a small but almost worldwide family, notably absent from North America, New Zealand, and the Pacific. Usually only 1 species is found in a region. They are robust, cursorial birds that with their long heavy legs and strong bills somewhat resemble oversized plovers. Their large eyes are well adapted for night vision but in bright light are partly hidden by the heavy brow and eyelids. Most live in dry, open country and spend much of the day crouched unobtrusively on the ground. They eat a variety of animal matter.

Double-striped Thick-knee   Illus. p. 281
Burhinus bistriatus   Dara

Identification: 18″ (46cm). 785g. *Large, robust, and somewhat ploverlike. Big yellow eyes* (often partly cut off by frowning brow on bright, sunny days). Heavy dusky-tipped bill; long sturdy greenish gray legs. Upperparts, head, and breast dark brown streaked fulvous and white, throat and belly white, *broad white eyebrow bordered above by narrow black line.* In flight shows *broad white wing stripe* and white subterminal patch on either side of short tail.
Voice: Quiet during day but often noisy at night; loud strident calls, *kee-kee-kee* . . . (or shrill *da-ra*, hence Spanish name), sometimes accelerating into noisy cacophony, resemble those of Southern Lapwing. In general, noisy lapwinglike calls at night will be this sp., by day a lapwing.
Behavior: Single birds, prs., or occas. small loose groups are vigilant and suspicious but may allow fairly close approach before moving away with graceful, fluidlike steps, maintaining a minimum "safe" distance. Diurnal or nocturnal though usually most active at dusk or at night. During day rest in sun or shady place and crouch to avoid detection. Run swiftly; taxi when taking off, and in flight long legs trail far behind slender tail. Breed Jan or Feb–Apr; nest a scrape on gd.; 2 eggs olive buff prom. marked dark[184]. During rainy season may concentrate in nos. (up to 40–50) in remaining dry areas such as on dikes in low llanos.
Status and habitat: Fairly common to common resident but sometimes difficult to locate. Dry pastures and dry open areas, with or without scattered trees and shrubs. Less numerous and local in arid scrub near coast and savannas of nw Amazonas.

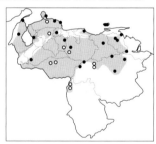

Range: To 200m (sight, 550m, nw of Barquisimeto). Goajira Pen., Zulia e across n Falcón (*pediacus*); Apure, Barinas, and s Lara (sight) e to Anzoátegui, Sucre, and Delta Amacuro; n Amazonas (sight s to Samariapo) and n Bolívar (sight, lower Río Caura; lower Río Paragua at Cerro Tigre); Isla Margarita (*vocifer*). S Mexico to Costa Rica; n and e Colombia to Guyana and ne Brazil. Curaçao. Hispaniola.

Double-striped Thick-knee

Charadriidae: Lapwings and Plovers

Alcaravanes y Playeros

Plovers and lapwings are a large worldwide family that differs from sandpipers in having a proportionately shorter and thicker bill and more robust proportions. They favor seashores and edges of bodies of freshwater, but they wade little. Some also are found in grassy fields and dry savannas. Most of the plovers seen in Venezuela breed in the Arctic and spend the remainder of the year on their neotropical or austral wintering grounds. Lapwings differ in having rounded spurred wings and slower, more bounding flight; and the species in Venezuela are resident.

Vanellus

Mostly rather large; wings rounded; wing spurs and hind toe present; some spp. (not S Amer. spp.) have wattles; majority are sedentary tropical inhabitants.

Southern Lapwing   PLATE 17
Vanellus chilensis   Alcaraván

Identification: 13–15″ (33–38cm). 295g. *Bold black and white wings in flight.* Bill pinkish with black tip; longish legs pink. Above mostly brownish gray, shoulders iridescent bronzy green, long pointed occipital crest black, *forehead, throat patch, and breast black*, belly white. In flight note broad, rounded black wings with large white patch on wing coverts; white rump and black tail.

Sim. species: Handsome at rest and boldly patterned in flight, this impetuous, sharp-eyed inhabitant of plains areas could hardly be mistaken or overlooked.

Voice: Very loud, rather metallic scolding *keek, keek, keek . . .* and *kee, kee, kee . . .* and other calls at slightest disturbance. Cf. calls of Double-striped Thick-knee.

Behavior: A noisy neighbor, usually found in prs., families, or seasonally in groups up to several dozen

that gather to loaf in open pastures. Nesting prs. are notorious kibitzers, shrill of voice, vigilant and quick to rise up and mob persistently. Because territories are often clumped close together, more than 1 pr. often join forces to mob and harass predators. Flight is rather slow and heavy, but wing beats are springy; at times flight highly aerobatic. Feeds by run-and-wait method, mostly at night. May–Jun nests[734]; 2–3 olive brown eggs spotted and blotched darker in small depression in gd.

Status and habitat: Widespread, common, and conspic. resident of grassland and open pastures, occas. in marshy areas. Prefers short dry grass, hence often in pastures grazed by cattle. In llanos some seasonal movements occur, esp. as birds move to high gd. during rainy season.

Range: To 300m n of Orinoco (occas. to 3000m); to 1400m s of Orinoco. Open areas throughout (*cayennensis*); no recs. in s Amazonas. C Panama locally to Tierra del Fuego. Trinidad.

Pluvialis

Fairly large, dumpy, and pot-bellied; thick blunt bill; toes unwebbed; no hind toe; arctic-breeding migrants; spangled above, black below when breeding.

Gray Plover
PLATE 18

Pluvialis squatarola   Playero Cabezón

Identification: 12″ (30.5cm). 215g. Thick-set with rather large head and peglike black bill. Nonbreeding plumage: above light brownish gray *inconspic. mottled white*; eyebrow white, below white somewhat flecked and mottled gray (heaviest in juv.) on breast; rump and tail whitish, tail lightly barred black. Breeding plumage: *sides of face and most of underparts black; white forehead extends as broad stripe along side of head down to side of chest*; upperparts densely marbled black and white. In flight in any plumage shows *black axillars* ("armpits"), white wing stripe, white rump, and mostly white tail. Molting birds with black mottled underparts are often seen in Mar–Apr.

Sim. species: See American Golden-Plover.

Voice: Plaintive, whistled *clee-er-ree*, lower pitched than American Golden-Plover.

Behavior: Scattered individuals, not flocks, occur in coastal habitats. A few may gather with other shorebirds to rest near mangroves.

Status and habitat: Fairly common transient and n winter resident in small nos., late Aug–early Apr, to mudflats, beaches, and coastal lagoons. Poss. inland rec. of 3 nonbreeding-plumage birds at Hato El Cedral, Feb 1992 (R. ffrench and D. Ascanio). A few oversummer.

Range: Carib. coast from Zulia to Sucre; Delta Amacuro[343]; Apure (?); Islas Margarita, Los Roques, La Orchila, La Blanquilla. Circumpolar breeder; in winter s in New World on coasts from s US to s S Amer.; throughout Old World.

Note: Widely known in New World as Black-bellied Plover.

American Golden-Plover

Pluvialis dominica   Playero Dorado

Identification: 9–11″ (23–28cm). 150g. Resembles Gray Plover. Nonbreeding plumage: above brownish flecked with gold; cap darker; weakly indicated buff eyebrow; below grayish buff somewhat mottled dusky, belly paler. Breeding plumage: above dark brown *thickly spotted and flecked with gold and white*, sides of face and most of underparts black, broad white forehead extends as stripe from behind cheeks down neck to sides of breast. In flight from above in any plumage looks uniformly dark.

Sim. species: Smaller and decidedly darker above than Gray Plover. In flight from above shows no

white; from below note pale axillaries (cf. Gray Plover).

Voice: Clear, high *queedleet* or *que-e-e-a* (dropping at end), unlike plaintive call of Gray Plover.

Behavior: On migration generally travels in small flocks.

Status and habitat: Uncommon to locally common fall transient, Sep–Dec, from N Amer.; possibly a rare winter resident inland in grassy pastures, less freq. beaches and mudflats (reverse of Gray Plover). Common Oct–Nov in grasslands of ne Anzoátegui and nw Monagas with flocks of 10–40 and peaks of 200/day[186]. Only offshore rec.: 1 taken 14 Oct 1976, Islas Las Aves.

Range: To 1200m (sight to 3600m, Laguna de Mucubají, 10 Nov 1980—R. Webster). Carib. coast from Aragua to Sucre; inland in Mérida (sight), Guárico (sight), Apure (sight), Anzoátegui, Monagas, and e and se Bolívar; Islas Los Roques. Breeds in N Amer. and n Asia; in New World migrates chiefly e of Andes to wintering gds. in Argentina, occas. Chile.

Hoploxypterus

Small size; pied plumage; small spur on wing; no hind toe.

Pied Plover
PLATE 17

Hoploxypterus cayanus   Alcaravancito

Identification: 9″ (23cm). 74g. *Striking black and white pattern.* Eyering and *legs coral red.* Crown sandy brown ringed by white; forecrown, sides of head, hindneck, upper mantle, and broad collar across breast black, *scapulars black bordered white and forming conspic. black V on back*; otherwise mainly sandy brown above and white below. In flight outer half of wings and tail black, most of inner half of wings, rump, and base of tail white.

Sim. species: Ploverlike, but none is so boldly marked. Southern Lapwing is much larger and with very different distribution of black and white.

Voice: Rather quiet. Occas. a soft, reedy *whee-whuu* (1st note higher) as flushes, or nasal clattery *calee-calee-calee . . .* with soft clicking and complaining quality.

Behavior: A charming and handsome little shorebird. Usually seen alone or in scattered prs. standing quietly and in dignified manner on a sandbar or along shore. Runs ahead a short distance, then stops abruptly with a dip. Typically somewhat wary and reluctant to allow close approach. Teeters rear end when alarmed. Nest an unlined scrape in sand; 2–3 eggs, olive buff speckled darker brown, more heavily at larger end; nest 22 Mar, Hato Cedral. Stands over eggs, stamps feet, and raises wings to divert slow-moving capybaras.

Status and habitat: Uncommon to fairly common resident on sandbars and bare shores of freshwater ponds and rivers from Apure (low llanos) e to Orinoco. Requirement is some sand and bare muddy areas. Vagrant or seasonal wanderer to high llanos of s Cojedes. Some local or short-distance migratory movements to higher gd. occur in rainy season; noted on coast of Aragua Oct and Nov.

Range: To 450m. Maracaibo Basin, Zulia; e of Andes from Apure, Barinas, s Cojedes, n Guárico, and n Anzoátegui s locally to Amazonas and Bolívar; irreg. n to Carabobo (Lago de Valencia), Aragua (Turiamo), and Sucre (San Antonio del Golfo); Delta Amacuro[343]. E Colombia and the Guianas s to e Bolivia, Paraguay, and se Brazil; rarely nw Argentina.
Note: Called Pied Lapwing by most previous authors; often placed in genus *Vanellus*.

Charadrius

Large, varied, and cosmopolitan group; typically with long legs and short, peglike bill; basal web connects outer and mid. toe; some breed in very high temperate latitudes and migrate; others are tropical and sedentary; collars, breast bands, and patterns on head common to many.

Semipalmated Plover
PLATE 18
Charadrius semipalmatus Playero Acollarado
Identification: 6.5–7.5″ (16.5–19cm). 45g. Rather large headed. *Short yellow bill tipped black*; legs yellow (often dull). Brown above with blackish face; white forehead bordered black behind; short white eyebrow mark; *white collar on hindneck continuous with white underparts*; *narrow black breast band*. Nonbreeding plumage: sim. but bill dusky; black markings on head, and black chest band, replaced by brown; white of forehead continues as whitish eyestripe. As name implies, toes partially webbed.
Sim. species: Easily confused with Collared Plover which *lacks* white collar around hindneck.
Voice: Plaintive slurred *chu-reép*, 2d note higher. Song in Costa Rica a ser. of short notes accelerating into chuckling trill[706].

Behavior: Individuals scatter along mudflats when feeding but gather in groups up to 20–50 when resting; larger groups during Sep and Apr migratory periods.
Status and habitat: Fairly common transient and n winter resident, mainly late Aug–May, in small nos., with most birds arriving by about 2d wk Sep (C. Parrish recs.); small nos. all year on nw coast of Zulia[353] and on offshore isls. (1 taken 7 Jul 1895 on Isla Margarita). Sandy beaches, tidal flats, rocky shores, and mangroves. The few inland recs. incl. single birds in nw Monagas (prob. also ne Anzoátegui) in Oct–Nov[186]; 1 seen 1 Dec 1980, Río Caroní near Ciudad Guyana, Bolívar (R. Webster). Perhaps overlooked inland because of similarity to Collared Plover.

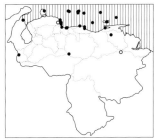

Range: To ca. 100m (once to 800m in Táchira). Carib. coast; offshore isls. of Las Aves, Los Roques, La Orchila, La Tortuga, La Blanquilla, Margarita, and Los Testigos; inland in Táchira (Colón), sw Guárico (Camaguán), ne Anzoátegui, Monagas, e Bolívar (sight); Delta Amacuro[343]. Breeds in arctic N Amer.; winters mostly on coasts from s US to Chile and Argentina.

Wilson's Plover
PLATE 18
Charadrius wilsonia Playero Picogrueso
Identification: 7–8″ (18–20.3cm). 57g. *Long and heavy black bill* (a "can opener"). Dusky pink legs. ♂: above sandy brown, broad forehead, short eyebrow, collar on hindneck, and underparts white; lores and short black bar across forecrown black; *single broad black chest band*. Or crown and sides of head tinged rufous (resident *cinnamominus*). ♀: no black on head; breast band brown (or tinged rufous—*cinnamominus*). Juv. and nonbreeding ♂: sim. to ♀.
Sim. species: Looks like an overgrown version of Semipalmated or Collared plover but from either by much larger, heavier bill. Also from Semipalmated by pinkish legs (not yellow), from Collared by *presence of white collar encircling neck*.
Voice: Call an emphatic whistled *phit* or *pheet*.
Behavior: Generally found alone, in prs., or as scattered individuals, infreq. small groups. Eats many tiny crabs (hence strong bill). In Trinidad breeds May–Jun; 2–3 grayish white eggs heavily spotted dark brown; bare scrape on pebbly beach or near mudflat[175].
Status and habitat: Uncommon to locally fairly common resident (*cinnamominus*) and n migrant (*wil-*

sonia) in small nos. to pebbly or sandy beaches, usually not mudflats and rarely inland; 3-km transect counts at Chichiriviche, Falcón, Aug–Nov 1976–1978 yielded mostly 1–4 (max. 11) birds (C. Parrish and A. Altman).

Range: Carib. coast in Zulia (specimens and sightings), Falcón (many sightings), and Carabobo to Sucre; offshore isls. of Las Aves, Los Roques, La Orchila, and Margarita (*cinnamominus*). Winter resident from coastal Anzoátegui to Sucre; Islas Las Aves, Los Roques, and Margarita (*wilsonia*); once (accidental) at Barcelona, Anzoátegui (*beldingi*). Breeds on Pacific coast from Mexico to Peru, se coast of N Amer., and W Indies to Suriname and ne Brazil. Aruba; Trinidad. N birds winter s to Ecuador and Bahía, Brazil.
Note: Also called Thick-billed Plover.

Snowy Plover

PLATE 18

Charadrius alexandrinus   Frailecito
Identification: 6.5″ (16.5cm). 40g. *Slender black bill and blackish legs.* Above pale sandy gray brown (slightly darker in nonbreeding garb) with *blackish band across forecrown and another on ear coverts;* broad *forehead, sides of head, and underparts* "*snowy*" *white; prom. black smudge on sides of chest* forms incomplete chest band. Imm.: black markings replaced by pale brown; juv. birds retain hint of brown smudge at side of chest.
Sim. species: Nearest is Collared Plover, but in all plumages Snowy has black (not yellowish) legs and breast band always incomplete. Collared has decidedly stubbier, thicker bill.
Voice: Soft, whistled *puweea.*
Behavior: May gather in very small groups on wintering gds.
Status and habitat: Reg. on coast of Falcón in Sep and Oct (recorded 30 Aug–16 Oct 1976–1978 with 1–10 seen on weekly 3-km transects at Chichiriviche; A. Altman and C. Parrish); 1 seen 18 Jan, Chichiri-

viche, Falcón (P. Alden). Sandy flats and beaches. On offshore isls., scatter of recs. throughout 1st half of yr suggests breeding: Los Roques (Feb–Mar), La Orchila (Apr and Jul), Las Aves (sight in May), Margarita (Jul).
Range: Carib. coast of Falcón and Miranda (Tacarigua); Islas Las Aves, Los Roques, La Orchila, La Blanquilla, and Margarita (*nivosus*). Breeds in s and w US, Mexico, W Indies, coastal Peru, Chile, and much of Old World; also Curaçao and Bonaire. Winters s to Panama, w Ecuador, and Greater and Lesser Antilles; in Old World to Africa, s Asia, and Australia.
Note: Subsp. *tenuirostris*[403] incl. in *nivosus*[53].

Collared Plover

PLATE 18

Charadrius collaris   Turillo
Identification: 5.5–6″ (14–15cm). 27g. *Slender all-black bill; flesh pink to yellowish legs.* Above brown with rather large white forehead bordered behind by broad band of black, *hindcrown and nape strongly tinged cinnamon, sometimes forming distinct cinnamon* (not white) *nuchal collar;* below white with black breast band. Imm.: duller with little or no cinnamon on head.
Sim. species: Easily confused with Semipalmated Plover but slightly smaller, daintier, and with thinner black bill (winter Semipalmated also has blackish bill) and no white nuchal collar. Usually shows some cinnamon on back of nape. Also cf. larger Thick-billed Plover.
Voice: Quiet. When disturbed a short *dreep* or 2-noted *keedup*, 2d syllable lower (K. Kaufman).
Behavior: Most often in prs. scattered along sandbars or edges of lagoons; in rainy season prs. concentrate in higher and drier areas in llanos. Does not gather in large flocks. Rather confiding but can run rapidly. Prob. breeds in Dec–Apr dry months; nest a scrape on gd.; 2 eggs, cream with many black spots and scrawls[280].
Status and habitat: Locally common breeding resident on sand and gravel bars along larger rivers, in short grass fields, and on mudflats and beaches. Short-distance seasonal movements need documentation; e.g., along larger rivers such as Orinoco and Apure occurs mainly during dry season (absent during high water); in w Apure (Hato Cedral) concentrates on human-made dikes and other high gd. during Jun–Sep high water; disperses in dry season. At Chichiriviche nos. dropped from 90 in Aug to 1–2 by Nov (A. Altman and C. Parrish census recs.) and remained low throughout dry season; flocks up to ca.

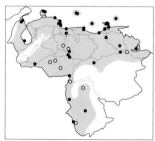

50 seen only Jul–Aug at Urica, Anzoátegui[186]; 1 in roadside grass near Portachuelo Pass (1100m), Aragua[33], is highest rec.

Range: To 200m (sight to 1100m). Carib. coast and lagoons and rivers inland throughout s to s Amazonas and n Bolívar; Islas Las Aves, Los Roques, La Tortuga, Margarita, Los Testigos, and Los Frailes. W and s Mexico to c Argentina. Netherlands Antilles; Trinidad.

Killdeer

Charadrius vociferus   Playero Gritón

Identification: 9–11″ (23–28cm). 95g. *Double black breast bands diagnostic.* Bill black; narrow eyering red; legs pinkish. Above brown, *rump and most of tail orange rufous,* subterminal tail band black tipped white; forehead, short white mark over eye, collar on hindneck, and underparts white.

Sim. species: Combination of breast bands, rump, and voice is unmistakable.

Voice: Loud *kil-dee* or *kil-deéa*; nonbreeding birds rather quiet.

Status and habitat: Rare vagrant from N Amer.: 1 taken 11 Nov 1949 at Páramo de Mucuchíes, Mérida (4150m); another in Dec from Golfo de Cariaco, Sucre. Sight recs. of 1 on 13 Feb 1980 at Laguna Los Tanquecitos (near Coro), Falcón (C. Bosque); 2 seen 17 Mar 1981 at edge of pond w of Coro, Falcón (R. Ridgely and A. Keith); 1 near Coro, Falcón (P. Boesman); and 1 in Jan (between 1945 and 1948) near Cantaura, Anzoátegui[186].

Range: Known from Mérida, Falcón, Anzoátegui, and Sucre (*vociferus*). Breeds in N Amer., W Indies,

coastal Peru, and nw Chile. N birds winter s to Ecuador, Greater and Lesser Antilles and n Colombia (rare).

Haematopodidae: Oystercatchers

Caracoleros

This is a small family whose members are found mostly on coastlines and throughout the world except in high latitudes and on oceanic islands. One species breeds far inland in Patagonia. All are rather large, stout shorebirds with short necks, fairly long legs, and unique coral-colored bladelike bills with a chisel tip. There is no hind toe. Along coastlines the bill is used to pry open oysters and shellfish and to chisel limpets from rocks. Breeding is monogamous; nests are shallow depressions in sand or gravelly areas.

American Oystercatcher   Illus. below

Haematopus palliatus   Caracolero

Identification: 16–18″ (41–46cm). 590g. Large chunky shorebird with bold pattern and *bright coral red bill* flattened laterally; pale yellow eyes (red eyering); *pink legs.* Head, neck, and chest black; otherwise dark brown above; pure white below, a small "finger" of white extending up in front of bend of wing. In flight shows conspic. *white band across base of tail and broad white wing stripe.*

Sim. species: See Black Skimmer.

Voice: Can be quite noisy both day and night, giving loud whistled *wheep* with piping, insistent quality.

Behavior: Prs. are conspic. but wary and usually keep somewhat apart from other shorebirds. Breeding not yet reported in Venez.; nest in Panama a depression in sand, sometimes lined with shells or pebbles; 3 pale buff eggs evenly spotted grayish brown[788].

Status and habitat: Resident in small nos. on sandy beaches and on muddy or rocky tidal areas. Migrants from N Amer. possible.

American Oystercatcher

Range: Coast from Zulia to Aragua and e Miranda; Cayo del Medio (Falcón); Islas Margarita, Las Aves, Los Roques, La Orchila, La Tortuga, La Blanquilla, and Los Testigoes (*palliatus*); once (sight) on coast of Sucre (C. Parrish). Breeds locally on Pacific coast from Baja California to Chile; Galápagos Isls.; on Atlantic locally from New Jersey and e Mexico to Argentina. W Indies. Trinidad.
Note: Subsp. *prattii*[403] not recognized[53].

Recurvirostridae: Stilts

Playeros Patilargos

Stilts and avocets are a small group of graceful waders widespread locally in both warm and temperate regions of the world. Stilts are notable for their extremely long legs and long, almost needlelike bills; the bills of avocets are recurved. All members of the family are boldly patterned, mostly pied or with shades of buff on the head and neck. Only 1 of the 3 New World species occurs in Venezuela.

Black-necked Stilt   PLATE 18
Himantopus mexicanus   Viuda Patilarga
Identification: 14–16″ (36–41cm). 165g. Slim, long-necked, *mainly black and white* shorebird. *Extraordinarily long, stiltlike, rosy red to pink legs* trail far behind tail in flight. Long needle bill. Above black, lower back, rump, and tail white, forehead, large patch over eyes, foreneck, and underparts immaculate white.
Voice: Often noisy. Sharp ternlike *yip* and *ruk*; a long-sustained, high-pitched, unmusical *kii-kii-kii-kii* . . . and other strident yelping or barking notes.
Behavior: A lovely sp. that occurs in small elegant flocks that are easily aroused to a noisy excited state. Individuals may scatter somewhat to forage in muddy areas or wade belly-deep in water, but are usually in water less than "knee" deep where actively pick items from surface of mud or water, probe in soft mud, or occas. chase prey. Sometimes sit on gd. as if on nest, and tend to bob head and scold if closely approached. Usually nest in loose groups, much less often singly. Small, loose groups of 4–5 build dry reed-stem nests on gd. and near water in Ecuador[379]; in Trinidad breed May–Jun; 3–4 olive buff eggs blotched and spotted black[175].
Status and habitat: Common and widespread resident in brackish and saltwater lagoons, shallow freshwater ponds, and marshes. Sensitive to seasonally changing water levels, and local migratory movements cause sharp fluctuations in nos. Small nos. only Jan–Jun (dry season), Hato Masaguaral, Guárico[734]; 4 flying s over Portachuelo Pass (1050m), Aragua, 21 May[33].

Range: To 400m (sight to 1050m). Throughout n of Orinoco; n Bolívar (s to La Paragua) and c Amazonas; Islas Margarita, Las Aves, Los Roques, La Orchila, and La Tortuga (*mexicanus*). Breeds from w and s US to c Chile and Argentina. Galápagos Isls.; W Indies; Trinidad (sight). N temperate and austral birds migratory.
Note: Often merged with Old World forms from Africa to Australia. W Hemisphere birds (3 subspp.) differ in having black on hindneck and sides of head. Birds of s S Amer. also may be a separate sp., *H. melanurus* (White-backed Stilt).

Jacanidae: Jacanas

Gallitos de Laguna o Gallitos de Agua

Jacanas comprise a small family of delicately proportioned marsh birds found throughout warmer parts of the world. All have extraordinarily long toes and nails that enable them to walk over floating vegetation with ease. They have a leathery frontal shield above the bill and a sharp spur on the carpal joint of the wings. Jacanas eat small aquatic plant and animal life. The New World species are polyandrous breeders.

Wattled Jacana   PLATE 17
Jacana jacana   Gallito de Laguna
Identification: 9–9.5″ (23–24cm). ♂ 90–120g, ♀ 140–150g. *Bill yellow* with bilobed raspberry red frontal shield and small drooping lappets at corner of bill. Long gray green legs and exceptionally long spidery toes. Head, neck, and underparts black; back and *most of closed wing rich chestnut maroon, flight feathers pale yellow*, conspic. in flight (*intermedia*). Or sim. but back and most of closed wing purplish maroon (*melanopygia*). Imm.: very different; above brown, crown and hindneck blackish with *long white eyestripe* and blackish postocular stripe, *underparts entirely white*; *wings as in ad.*
Sim. species: Imm. often mistaken for a rail, but no rail has such a boldly striped head or such long toes.
Voice: Often noisy, giving a loud, complaining *kee-kick, kee-kick* . . . as flushes off over marsh; a nasal complaining *chúff-fit, chúff-fit.* . . . while on gd.

Behavior: Occurs alone or occas. several loosely assoc. and scattered along vegetation-choked shorelines. Forages by walking in jerky manner across floating vegetation (almost literally "walking on water") and pecking rapidly at vegetation for insects, etc. Often lifts and flashes yellow flight feathers when disturbed. If alarmed may fly off low across water with vocal protest and flurry of quick stiff wing beats, alternating with short glides, scattering like bright butterflies to a far shore. In flight usually carries long legs and toes raised and trailing behind. Can swim but rarely does. Noisily mobs snakes, caimans, etc. Nest a small depression in pasture or aquatic vegetation; 4 olive brown eggs streaked and scrawled black. Slightly larger, polyandrous ♀ (usually) lays for 2 or more ♂♂ within her territory in resource-defense polyandry breeding system. ♂♂ incubate their separate clutches in sex-role reversal[46,451]; Aug and Nov breeding, Guárico[734].

Status and habitat: Common resident and characteristic bird of shallow freshwater ponds, marshes, lagoons, and sluggish streams with floating and emergent vegetation. Nos. fluctuate seasonally, and some local migratory movements or postbreeding dispersal likely (need documentation); e.g., 2 at night (1 very fat bird collected) 22 Jun at Rancho Grande Biol. Station, Aragua[33].

Range: To 1000m n of Orinoco; to 300m s of Orinoco. Maracaibo Basin (*melanopygia*); rest of Venez. n of Orinoco; n Amazonas and n Bolívar (*intermedia*); rarely (few recs.) s Amazonas and s Bolívar (*jacana*?). W Panama to n Argentina and Uruguay; also w Ecuador and nw Peru, rarely to c Chile.

Scolopacidae: Sandpipers and Snipes

Playeros y Becasinas

The scolopacids are a worldwide family with members closely related to plovers but differing, among other things, in having more slender proportions, longer necks and legs, and often thinner and somewhat decurved bills. Most are solitary when nesting in the high Arctic but highly gregarious during migration and on their wintering grounds, where they concentrate along seacoasts or near lowland bodies of water. Venezuela is an important wintering area for nearctic shorebirds, with an estimated 130,000, or 4.5% of the South American total, spending the northern winter months on Venezuela's coastline. They are most heavily concentrated near the mouth of Lago Maracaibo, Gulf of Coro, east side of the Paraguaná Peninsula, coast of Anzoátegui, north coast of the Araya Peninsula, southeastern shore of the Paria Peninsula, and north and south ends of the Orinoco Delta[415]. Most important are the large regional concentrations of Red Knots near the mouth of Lago de Maracaibo, Short-billed Dowitchers at Laguna de Chacopata, and Sanderlings in the outer Orinoco Delta. The family as a whole presents numerous identification problems, and accurate identification of many shorebirds requires that the observer first recognize the plumage stage, i.e., breeding, nonbreeding, or juvenile, before a specific identification can be made. In many cases the three differ substantially. First-year birds often oversummer.

Tringa

Mostly med.-sized spp.; long legs (often brightly colored); slender bill as long or longer than head; actively peck visible prey but do little probing.

Greater Yellowlegs
Illus. p. 288, PLATE 18

Tringa melanoleuca Tigüi-Tigüe Grande

Identification: 12–14″ (30.5–36cm). 165g. Almost identical to Lesser Yellowlegs in all plumages but *larger* (most noticeable when the two are together); *bill decidedly heavier* (greater thickness esp. apparent near base of bill), *longer* (obviously longer than length of head instead of about equal to length of head), and *distinctly 2-toned with basal third grayish, distal two-thirds blackish*. In flight note that Greater's blackish secondaries and inner primaries are *barred* (or notched) pale brown (Lesser's uniform blackish).

Sim. species: See Lesser Yellowlegs. In addition to bill and size differences, the two usually can be separated by vocalizations and by Lesser's daintier, more springy behavior when foraging.

Voice: Call a loud, clear 3- or 4-noted *teu-teu-teu*, slightly descending; or a longer or shorter ser. of *teu* notes. More emphatic and ringing than otherwise sim. call of Lesser Yellowlegs.

Behavior: As in Lesser Yellowlegs. Usually wades in shallow water, sometimes up to belly. More apt to dip bill in water or skim or probe than Lesser, and more wary and noisy.

Status and habitat: Transient and n winter resident along coast, less numerous inland, mid Aug–Apr; scattered oversummer recs., e.g., 22 Jun 1991, San

Greater Yellowlegs (left), Lesser
Yellowlegs (right), Solitary
Sandpiper (center)

Juan de Los Cayos, Falcón (P. Boesman); Apr and
Jul–Nov in ne Anzoátegui[186]. Common but generally
less numerous than Lesser Yellowlegs.
Range: To 4100m. Carib. coast and inland throughout; Islas Margarita, Las Aves, Los Roques, La Orchila, La Tortuga, La Blanquilla, and Los Testigos.
Breeds in n N Amer. Winters from s US s to Chile
and Argentina. Trinidad.

Lesser Yellowlegs   Illus. above
Tringa flavipes   Tigüi-Tigüe Chico
Identification: 10–11″ (25–28cm). 85g. Rather pale,
slender, and long-bodied; *bright yellow legs. Thin,
straight black bill about as long as head.* Above grayish brown freckled, dotted, and notched with white;
short, ill-defined whitish eyeline; below white lightly
streaked and spotted brownish gray on neck and
sides of breast. In flight note *dark wings* (no stripe,
no pale barring on flight feathers), square whitish
rump and tail. Breeding plumage: sim. but above
more crisply patterned, underparts more distinctly
dotted and freckled.
Sim. species: An elegant shorebird, easily confused
with larger Greater Yellowlegs (see). Solitary Sandpiper has dark legs, dark rump, and strong barring
on sides of tail. Stilt Sandpiper has prom. eyestripe,
greenish legs, and longer bill (longer than length of
head). Smaller nonbreeding Wilson's Phalarope,
somewhat sim. in flight, is immaculate below with
needlelike bill.
Voice: Much like that of Greater Yellowlegs. Lesser
has softer whistle, generally an inflected 1- or 2-noted
yew or *you-you.* Cf. louder, more forceful call of
Greater Yellowlegs. Both spp. occas. give calls similar to that of the other.
Behavior: Feeds actively by picking at water surface
or dipping bill in water. May occur in rather loosely
assoc. flocks or with peeps. Not very social on wintering gds. when feeding, but may rest in large groups.
Wades up to belly, occas. even swims. More social

and less wary on wintering gds. than Greater Yellowlegs.
Status and habitat: Common transient and n winter
resident, mostly early Aug–late Apr, to tidal flats,
mudflats, lake shores, fresh- and saltwater marshes,
and mangroves n of Orinoco; smaller nos. inland;
only a few recs. s of Orinoco (seen Feb 1992 at
Maripa, Bolívar—J. Pierson). Scattered oversummer
recs. in Jun and Jul along coast. At Chichiriviche, Falcón, nos. peak (900–4600 in 3-km transect) mid
Sep–early Nov (1976–1978—A. Altman and C. Parrish).

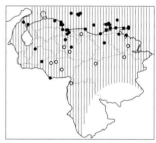

Range: To 400m. Carib. coast and inland throughout
(mainly n of Orinoco); Islas Las Aves, Los Roques,
La Orchila, La Tortuga, Los Testigos, Margarita.
Breeds in Canada and Alaska; winters inland and on
coasts from s US s to Chile and Argentina. Dutch and
Venez. isls. Trinidad.

Solitary Sandpiper   PLATE 18
Tringa solitaria   Playero Solitario
Identification: 7.5″ (19cm). 47g. Slender dark sandpiper. *Thin black bill; long dusky green legs; conspic.
white eyering.* Above dark olive *finely streaked and
dotted white,* below white lightly streaked dusky on
chest; center of tail blackish, outer feathers white
barred black. In flight note *barred sides of tail, dark
rump, and lack of wing stripe.*

Sim. species: Good marks are thin, straight bill, eye-ring, and barred tail. Spotted Sandpiper is more tee-tery and in flight shows prom. wing stripe. Yellowlegs are paler and grayer above with white rumps and "yellow" legs.

Voice: Flushes off with emphatic *peet!* or *peet-weet-weet!*, higher pitched and sharper than that of Spotted Sandpiper.

Behavior: True to its name, a loner, usually encountered singly, sometimes 2–3 scattered birds. Does form small, loosely assoc. flocks up to 20 or so during migration. Nods head continually as it wades in shallow water or along margins of small ponds. Flight is rapid but erratic, almost tern- or swallowlike with deep, quick wing strokes.

Status and habitat: Common transient and n winter resident, mostly Aug–early May, but a few return very early. Earliest sight recs. 23 Jul 1977, Hato Masaguaral, Guárico[734]; 25 Jul, Laguna Mucubají, Mérida, and 31 Jul, Maturín, Monagas (P. Boesman); 6–17 Aug 1985, San Carlos de Río Negro, Amazonas (C. Parrish); 1 on Sierra de Lema at 1450m, 8 Mar 1999, is highest rec. s of Orinoco.

Range: To 3600m n of Orinoco; to 500m s of Orinoco (sight to 1450m). Throughout; sightings on Islas Margarita, Los Roques, and La Tortuga (*solitaria*); once at Caicara, Monagas (*cinnamomea*). Breeds in n N Amer.; winters from s Mexico to Bolivia and c Argentina.

Willet

PLATE 18

Catoptrophorus semipalmatus   Playero Aliblanco

Identification: 14–16″ (36–41cm). 225g. Rather heavyset. *Flashes bold black-and-white wing pattern in flight* but nondescript at rest. Rather long, thick, blackish bill; strong legs blue gray. Nonbreeding plumage: above brownish gray to pale gray, below dull egg-shell white, breast tinged gray, belly whitish; ill-defined whitish eyestripe; rump white, tail pale gray. Breeding plumage: above grayish brown mottled and freckled dusky on back; head and neck densely streaked, flanks somewhat spotted and flecked dark gray, rump and tail as above. In flight in any plumage note *large size* and *broad white wing stripe contrasting with black flight feathers and black wing linings*.

Sim. species: Long heavy bill and bold black-and-white pattern in wings are diagnostic, but cf. Hudsonian Godwit.

Voice: Noisy and quick to "sound the alarm," a loud, clamorous, and reedy *klee*, *wree-wree-wree* or sim.

variation; also a loud, ploverlike *kuik-kuik-kuik* and more melodious song.

Behavior: Often rather wary and quick to take wing with noisy outburst of shrill calls. Occurs alone or in small loose flocks, often with other shorebirds. Feeds by walking on sand, mudflats, or in shallow water where probes in mud, picks items from surface, or chases larger prey. May loaf or sleep in flocks.

Status and habitat: Common transient and n winter resident (*semipalmatus*) in small nos. on coast and offshore isls., mainly late Jul–May, on sandy beaches, mudflats, and fresh- and saltwater lagoons. Largest nonbreeding concentrations reported in Golfo de Araya, Sucre[415]. Resident breeder (*inornatus*) on Islas Los Roques, May–Jun[494], elsewhere(?). A few oversummer; present all yr at Kaimare Chico, nw Zulia[108].

Range: Carib. coast from Zulia to Sucre; Delta Amacuro[343]; Islas Margarita, Los Roques, and Las Aves (*semipalmatus*); 1 specimen 4 Aug near Ocumare de La Costa, Maracay, another 26 Aug on Isla Coche (*inornatus*). Breeds in N Amer., Bahamas, W Indies (s to Hispaniola and St. Croix), and Los Roques, Venez.; winters from s US s mainly on coasts to Peru and n Brazil, occas. to n Chile.

Spotted Sandpiper

PLATE 18

Actitis macularia   Playero Coleador

Identification: 7–8″ (18–20.3cm). 40g. Rather short-legged, low-slung sandpiper that teeters. Bill dull yellowish tipped black, legs dull yellow (color of both varies in nonbreeding birds). Nonbreeding plumage: above plain grayish brown with weakly indicated whitish eyeline; below white with gray brown smudge on sides of chest. Breeding plumage: sim. but obscurely barred with black above; *thickly spotted black below* (large, round spots). In flight in any plumage note *white wing stripe* (mostly across primaries) and stiff, shallow, quivering wing beats interspersed with short glides with wings bowed downward.

Sim. species: Solitary Sandpiper lacks wing stripe, has outer tail feathers barred white, and bobs head more and teeters less.

Voice: Clear, tittering *peet* or *peet-weet-weet!* (cf. Solitary Sandpiper) as flushes, often the first indication of its presence.

Behavior: A cheerful little sandpiper notable for its habit of compulsively nodding head and teetering rear end as if unbalanced. Inconspic. and usually found alone, individuals typically scattering uniformly throughout suitable habitat and defending feeding territories, but several may roost together. Feeds on insects and other small aquatic life at water's edge. May occur in almost any area where there is water, but favors river and stream borders or bodies of water that are not used by other sandpipers. Flushes off in jerky, stiff-winged flight, low over water, and may perch on stones, posts, boats, etc. Migrates alone or in small groups up to 6 or so. By Apr most birds are obviously "spotted" below.

Status and habitat: Very common transient and n winter resident, mainly late Jul–late Apr, to all kinds of coastal and inland waters. Birds with and without spots seen 7 Jul 1982, Hato El Frio, Apure (C. Parrish).

Range: To 1600m n of Orinoco; to 1800m s of Orinoco. Carib. coast and inland throughout; Islas Margarita, Las Aves, Los Roques, La Orchila, La Tortuga, and Los Testigos and Isla de Aves. Breeds in N Amer.; winters from US to Chile, Argentina, s Brazil; Aruba and Trinidad.

Upland Sandpiper   Illus. below
Bartramia longicauda   Tibi-Tibe
Identification: 11–12″ (28–30.5cm). 135g. Looks like a small curlew with long neck, short straight bill, and longish tail. *Long yellow legs. Small head with eyes large for size of head; long slender neck; tail* graduated and pointed. Upperparts, head, neck, and breast

dark brown streaked and mottled buff, rump and central tail feathers blackish, belly white.

Sim. species: Best clues are pigeonlike head and finely streaked plumage which lacks strong pattern. See smaller Buff-breasted Sandpiper, Ruff, and larger Double-striped Thick-knee.

Voice: Mellow, tremulous *quip-ip-ip-ip* or *que-lee-lee*, musical; short, bubbly *b-bip* in flight. Long-drawn, haunting song not likely hd. in Venez.

Behavior: Solitary or in small loose groups, and usually not with other shorebirds or near water. Most often seen standing in fields or open areas. May taxi a little before flying. Rather upright and formal stance, stiff movements, and habit of holding wings raised momentarily upon alighting are characteristic. Flight is stiff, on wing tips. Tends to be wary on migration.

Status and habitat: Transient from n in small nos., mainly Sep–Oct and early Mar–end of May, to short grass pastures, burned fields, airports, rough grassy fields, and other open areas in interior of country. Earliest rec. is 1 taken 15 Aug 1910 at Páramo Los Conejos, Mérida. No. of Mar–Apr recs. from Amazonas and w and n Bolívar suggests substantial movement through s part of country. Earliest northbound recs. are 1 seen 28 Feb 1999, Caurama Lodge, Bolívar (J. Posner), and several seen 2 and 5 Mar 1992 near Camani, Amazonas (K. Zimmer and R. Ridgely). Scattered birds there throughout much of Mar and Apr (R. Prum and J. Kaplan); 5 seen 4–5 Apr 1985 at Pto. Ayacucho, Amazonas, 25–30 between 7 and 17 Apr 1985 at San Carlos de Río Negro, Amazonas, and 3 on 12 May 1981 at Hato Pedregosa, Barinas (C. Parrish); rather common migrant in Mar and Sep–Oct in ne Anzoátegui[186]; 1 in early Mar, El Palmar, ne Bolívar.

Range: To 300m (twice to 4000m in Mérida). Prob. throughout; rec. from Mérida, Apure (sight), Barinas, Aragua, Distr. Federal, Miranda, Anzoátegui, Monagas, Delta Amacuro (sight), n Bolívar, and Ama-

Upland Sandpiper

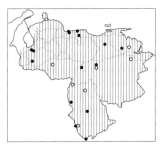

zonas. Breeds in N Amer.; migrates through n S Amer.; winters mostly in s S Amer.

Numenius

Brown plumage with little seasonal change; very long, decurved bill; some spp. among largest shorebirds; probe in mud or feed from surface of mud or gd.

Whimbrel
PLATE 18
Numenius phaeopus   Chorlo Real
Identification: 16.5–18″ (42–46cm). 380g. Bill long, 3–4″ (76–102mm) decurved at tip; legs grayish. Above mostly dark brown, the feathers edged buff imparting a scaled and streaked look, head dull whitish, 2 black crown stripes and stripe through eye; underparts dull buffy white; foreneck and breast somewhat streaked and dotted brown. In flight from above shows inconspic. pale area on lower back and rump, otherwise unpatterned. Juv.: sim. but more distinctly scaled above; streaking on underparts finer.
Sim. species: Only curlew likely in Venez.; easily recognized by long decurved bill. Cf. godwits.
Voice: Most freq. call a far-carrying and rippling titter, *bibibibibibibi . . .* , with flat tone and even emphasis[255].
Behavior: Mainly forages alone. Grasps prey, esp. tiny crabs, or probes in mud for marine worms. Roosts and loafs in small groups, often perching with larger plovers and Willets on tree roots or branches of mangroves.
Status and habitat: Transient from n in small nos., mainly early Aug–early Nov and late Feb–late May; prob. small nos. throughout n winter months but few recs.: 6 seen 30 Nov and 8 seen 2 Dec 1980 at Boca de Uriche, Anzoátegui, were prob. wintering (R. Webster and E. Copper). Mudflats, beaches, and man-

groves; occas. inland. Scarce at Chichiriviche but reg. in small nos. in mangroves at Tucacas, Falcón (A. Altman and C. Parrish censuses). Latest spring date 27 May 1977, Kaimare Chico, Zulia[354].
Range: Carib. coast from Zulia (sight) and Falcón to Sucre and s Delta Amacuro; scattered recs. inland in Monagas and n Bolívar s to Río Carapo; Islas Margarita, Las Aves, and Los Roques (*hudsonicus*). Breeds in arctic N Amer. and Eurasia; winters from s US coastally s to s S Amer.; in Old World s to Africa and Australia.

Long-billed Curlew
Numenius americanus   Chorlo Pico Largo
Identification: 22–26″ (55–66cm). 590g. *Unusually long decurved bill, 5–8″ (127–203mm)*, but beware juv. birds which have bill length about same as Whimbrel. Bill dusky above, mostly pinkish below. *A large curlew with distinctive cinnamon-colored plumage, esp. wing linings.* Above buffy brown heavily marked dusky, below mainly buffy cinnamon finely streaked dusky.
Sim. species: From Whimbrel by larger size, absence of that sp.'s bold head stripes, and by *bright cinnamon under wing linings* (no dark patches above or below on wings). Whimbrel has brownish underwings.
Status: Accidental. Known only from sight recs. as follows: 1 seen and photographed 7 Feb 1984 at Laguna de Chacopata on s side of Araya Pen., Sucre[394]; also seen (presum. same bird) 20 Feb 1984. Earliest sight rec. (no photo verification) is 1 bird seen Oct 1982 by R. Navarro, and on several occas. between Aug 1983 and Jan 1984 by G. Marin and R. Rodríguez.

Range: Rec. in w Sucre. Breeds in w N Amer.; winters from s US to Mexico, rarely s to Costa Rica; accidental in Panama; possibly Tobago.

Limosa

Large waders; very long, slightly upturned bill; marked seasonal change in plumage; ♀♀ larger than ♂♂.

Hudsonian Godwit
PLATE 18
Limosa haemastica   Becasa de Mar
Identification: 14–16″ (36–41cm). 270g. Large wader with *long slender bill, 2.6–3.8″ (66–97mm), slightly upturned, basal half dull pinkish*, rest brown (pink changes to orangish when breeding); legs dark blue

gray. Nonbreeding plumage: *mainly uniform dark gray above*, pale gray below, with *prom. white eyestripe* and *broad white rump band* separating black of lower back and tail. Juv.: brownish version of nonbreeder; above dark brown scaled buff, scapulars vaguely barred; eyebrow and underparts pale brownish buff; rump band white. Breeding plumage: above dark brown sparsely flecked and spotted buffy white; *head and neck grayish white*; prom. white eyestripe; breast and lower *underparts rich reddish chestnut*. In flight in any plumage shows *black wing linings*, white rump, black tail, and short white wing stripe contrasting with *blackish wings*.

Sim. species: Very long, slightly upturned bill is the key. In flight black and white wing and tail pattern recall Willet, but note *white rump* and, up close, white eyebrow.

Voice: Usually silent on migration; call a clear, high *toe-wit* or *whit*[255].

Behavior: A strong, powerful flier. Most southbound migrants congregate in Hudson and James bays area of Canada and fly direct to s Argentina. Stragglers appear in coastal areas of n S Amer. In n passage rarely seen s of US.

Status and habitat: Rare migrant from n, late Jul–late Oct. Three specimens: 2 (1 in Oct) at Lago de Valencia; 1 on 20 Oct 1941 at Barcelona, Anzoátegui. Sight recs. as follows: 1 photographed 20 Oct 1971 at Chichiriviche, Falcón (P. Alden); 2 seen 1976–1978 at Chichiriviche, Falcón (C. Parrish and A. Altman); 1 on 5 Sep 1983 at El Hatillo, Laguna de Unare, Anzoátegui (C. Parrish and T. Parker); 1 on 24 Sep 1983, Laguna de Unare, Anzoátegui (C. Parrish); 1 on 25 Jul 1993 over Caño Colorado, Monagas, another 19 Oct 1994 at Boca de Macareo, Delta Amacuro[60]. Coastal mudflats during southward migration.

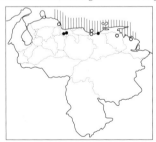

Range: Carib. coast from e Falcón (sight) to Anzoátegui; inland in Carabobo (specimen), e Monagas (sight), and n Delta Amacuro (sight). Breeds in arctic N Amer.; winters in s S Amer. s to Tierra del Fuego.

Bar-tailed Godwit
Limosa lapponica Aguja Cola Rayada
Identification: 16″ (41cm). 375g. Rather short-legged godwit, at rest much like nonbreeding Hudsonian Godwit but different in flight. Bill long, slightly upturned, dowitcherlike, pinkish on basal half, dusky on tip; legs black. *Two races, both accidental to S Amer.* Breeding ♀ also differs from ♂, thus *identifica-*

tion of this sp. is complex and confusing. Nonbreeding ad.: *prom. whitish eyebrow*; rest of upperparts pale brownish gray, the feather edges pale giving scaled and streaked appearance; foreneck grayish tinged brown, lower breast and belly whitish. In flight from above, wings brownish gray, tips darker; *lower back and rump mainly white, tail whitish with ca. 5 narrow black bars; wing linings and most of underwing white in w Palearctic* (form most likely in S Amer.); or *back brown, rump heavily barred brown, under wing coverts grayish barred dusky in e Palearctic*. Juv.: sim. but browner, esp. on foreneck and breast; mantle and scapulars edged bright buff. Ad. ♂: head, neck, and entire underparts rich brick red. Ad. ♀: sim. to juv. and nonbreeding ad., some with a small amt. of brick red in plumage.

Sim. species: Look for barred tail. Hudsonian Godwit has prom. white slash along base of primaries and secondaries (above or below), black wing linings, and *solid black tail* contrasting with white rump; breeding ♂ has chestnut breast and belly. See smaller Short-billed Dowitcher.

Status and habitat: Accidental. Known only from sight recs. (with photos, Colección Phelps) of 1 bird seen 17 Nov 1985 through Apr 1986 at Laguna de Chacopata, Sucre[397]. No other S Amer. recs.

Range: Rec. in w Sucre. Breeds in Alaska and n Eurasia; winters in Old World s to s Europe, Africa, India, and s China to Australia; vagrant s in New World to California, e US, Venez., and isls. in c and s Atlantic.

Marbled Godwit
Limosa fedoa Aguja Moteada
Identification: 17–19″ (43–48cm). 370g. Large with *long slender bill*, 4–5″ (102–130mm), *slightly upturned; basal half pink to orangish, distal half black*; legs gray. Mainly rich buffy brown heavily mottled dusky above; lightly mottled on breast and sides. In flight from below shows *cinnamon wing linings*; from above *uniform brown* (no contrasting black or white on tail); outer primaries and primary coverts dusky.

Sim. species: Godwits have bills that turn up slightly, and none is so uniform rich brown as this sp. Also see Whimbrel which has striped crown and long decurved bill.

Status and habitat: Known from publ. sight recs. and photos of 7 seen 20 Feb 1984 at Laguna Bocaripo (part of Laguna de Chacopata) on n side of Araya Pen., Sucre[395]; also from 2–7 seen reg. between 21 Jul

1984 and mid Oct 1984 by F. Mercier; 1 banded 9 Dec 1984 was seen repeatedly until 30 Aug 1986 on Araya Pen.[397]; unpubl. recs. 28 Jan 1983 (G. Marin and R. Rodríguez) and 26 Mar and 5 Apr 1982 in Laguna El Peñon, 3km e of Cumaná, Sucre (G. Marin and R. Egañez).

Range: Breeds in w N Amer. (*fedoa*); winters on both coasts of s US s to Panama; rarely to Chile, scattered recs. on many Carib. isls., vagrant to n Colombia. Trinidad (recent recs.).

Ruddy Turnstone
PLATE 18
Arenaria interpres   Playero Turco
Identification: 8–9″ (20.3–23cm). 205g. Stocky with *short orange-red legs*; fairly slender bill wedge-shaped, slightly upturned at tip. Breeding plumage: *upper back and wings bright rufous chestnut*; head and underparts white; *broad black chest band* spreads up sides of head to forehead; narrow black band extends narrowly around sides of neck, another wraps over shoulders and onto back; *lower back, rump, and most of tail white; base and subterminal tail band black*. Nonbreeding plumage: much duller but retains enough of ad. pattern for recognition; head and upperparts mostly brown; broad dusky chest band spreads onto sides of neck and lower breast; throat and lower underparts white. In flight in any plumage note *boldly striped black, white, and rufous pattern on back, wings, and tail*.
Voice: Sharp, rather metallic *tut-e-kut*.
Behavior: On wintering gds. scattered individuals or small groups often assoc. with other shorebirds. Strong neck muscles, heavy legs, and unusual bill shape are adaptations for curious foraging behavior of busily turning over pebbles, seaweed, and jetsam on beaches to search for prey hidden beneath. Also digs in sand. Loafs with others of its kind on rocks, boats, or other places well above high tide.
Status and habitat: Uncommon and local transient and n winter resident along coast; much commoner and more numerous on offshore isls., mostly Sep–late Apr. Oversummer birds rec. 28 Jun (Islas Las Aves), 5 Jul (Islas Los Roques), and 7 Jul 1895 (Isla Margarita). Reported yr-round at Kaimare Chico, nw Zulia[108,353]; a few on Aug–Nov censuses at Chichiriviche, Falcón (A. Altman and C. Parrish). Only inland recs. are 1 on 16 Mar 1995 and 2 on 24 Nov 1995, both at Hato El Frio, Apure[207].
Range: Carib. coast from Zulia to Sucre; Delta Amacuro[343]; virtually all offshore isls. incl. Isla de Aves

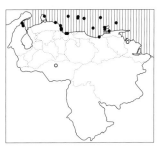

(*morinella*); w Apure (sight). Circumpolar breeder; Amer. birds winter s on both coasts of C and S Amer. to Chile and Argentina; in Old World s to s Africa and s Asia.

Calidris

Small to med. size; compact bodies with long slender wings; med. to longish legs; usually no hind toe; nonbreeding plumages often quite sim. Bill tips have many sensory neurons, and most spp. forage using rapid pecking and probing motions; high-arctic breeders; all are migrants to Venez.

Red Knot
Calidris canutus   Playero Pecho Rufo
Identification: 9–10″ (23–25cm). 135g. Bulky and *short-legged. Largest* calidrid in Venez. Straight black bill somewhat thickened at base; *dull greenish legs*. Nonbreeding plumage: above pale gray with *fairly prom. white eyeline and white wing bar*; flight feathers blackish; *below white*, chest often slightly streaked and smudged grayish, sides often with a few brownish gray flecks. Breeding plumage: above densely mottled dusky, gray, and buff; sides of head incl. eyebrow and entire underparts brick red; center of belly and under tail coverts whitish. In flight in any plumage shows *narrow white wing stripe and scaly grayish white rump*.
Sim. species: Breeding ad. resembles a dowitcher but bill much shorter (dowitcher has long snipelike bill). Nonbreeders can be confusing, but note large size (almost as large as Gray Plover), bill shape, chunky, oval body with short legs, faded gray plumage, and lack of strong contrast between back, rump, and tail.
Voice: Usually rather quiet. Low, rough *knutt* and softer, disyllabic *knuup-knuup* in migration[255].
Behavior: On wintering gds. tends to concentrate in large, spectacular, wheeling flocks of its own sp. at a few coastal sites, but Venez. recs. are mostly of scattered individuals on tidal flats or coast. May assoc. with other spp. such as Ruddy Turnstone and Gray Plover. Probes in sand.
Status and habitat: Rare or uncommon spring and fall transient and uncommon and local n winter resident, mostly late Aug–early May, to sandy beaches, less often mudflats; earliest fall arrivals are 4 seen 22 Aug 1983 and 2 more 5 Sep 1983 at Unare, Anzoátegui (C. Parrish and T. Parker); latest spring rec. is 1

♀ taken 20 May 1925 at Cumaná, Sucre, but scattered recs. reported yr-round (mostly Oct–Mar) at Kaimare Chico, nw Zulia[353]. Beaches of nw Venez. are important wintering area for this sp., with flocks up to 520 reported in Feb[415].

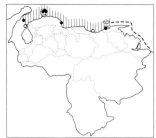

Range: Carib. coast of Zulia, Falcón, Anzoátegui (sightings), and Sucre (*roselaari, rufa*). Breeds in circumpolar regions; migrates s mainly along Atlantic coast of S Amer. Winters on coasts of s US and C Amer. s to Straits of Magellan; in Old World s to s Africa, Asia, Australia, and New Zealand.

Sanderling
Illus. p. 295, PLATE 18
Calidris alba   Playero Arenero
Identification: 7.5–8.5″ (19–22cm). 48g. Compact, thick-set shorebird with sturdy, blunt, black bill and black legs. Nonbreeding plumage: above pearly gray, almost unmarked or with light dotlike streaking on upperparts; below white, *shoulders and primaries blackish*. Juv.: like nonbreeder but crown buff mixed brown; weak whitish eyestripe; dusky lores and ear coverts; rest of upperparts mottled and spangled with black and white (somewhat scaly), chest tinged buff. Breeding plumage: *upperparts, head, and breast bright rusty with black mottling on upperparts*, head, neck, and breast; lower underparts white. In flight in any plumage shows *broadest, boldest white wing stripe* of any peep.
Sim. species: In nonbreeding plumage the palest shorebird in Venez. Combination of white appearance, contrasting black bill and legs, and black shoulder (carpal) bar should preclude identification problems. Also note distinctive behavior.
Voice: Distinctive *trick* or *tuit*.
Behavior: Mechanical and toylike as scattered individuals or small groups run rapidly on twinkling legs, chasing receding waves, and then are chased themselves by incoming waves. Feed on small marine crustaceans exposed by wave action. Usually tame and do not fly far when disturbed. Loaf in large groups of their own high up on sandy beaches.
Status and habitat: Uncommon transient and n winter resident, mainly mid Sep–mid Apr, on sandy and pebbly beaches and sandier outer zones of estuaries; no inland recs. Largest concentrations (up to 460, or ca. 70% of total estimated winter pop. on coast of Venez.)[415]. Fairly numerous on offshore isls., with a few oversummering birds: 1 taken 7 Jul 1895 on Isla Margarita; present yr-round with peak nos. Sep–Dec at Kaimare Chico, nw Zulia[108].

Range: Carib. coast from Zulia (Paraguaipoa) to Anzoátegui (Barcelona) and Delta Amacuro; isls. of Margarita, Las Aves, Los Roques, La Orchila, and Los Testigos. Breeding circumpolar; winters on both coasts of US s to s S Amer.; in Old World from s Europe and Asia southward.

Semipalmated Sandpiper
PLATE 18
Calidris pusilla   Playerito Semipalmeado
Identification: 6–6.5″ (15–16.5cm). 24g. Small, dull, grayish brown peep. Bill black, *rather deep at base* and blunt tipped; legs blackish. Breeding plumage: above more or less streaked grayish brown, feathers of mantle and back dark-centered giving scaled and streaked look; crown, cheeks, and scapulars faintly tinged rufous; below white washed buff and indistinctly streaked dark on neck and breast. Nonbreeding plumage: sim. but grayer and more uniform above; faint whitish eyeline; chest washed brownish (little or no streaking). Juv.: above much like breeding birds but facial pattern stronger (whitish eyeline, dusky cheeks); little or no streaking below. In flight shows pale wing stripe and white sides on rump.
Sim. species: Easily confused, and a good view is required to separate it from Western Sandpiper. Western usually has longer bill with droopy tip; in breeding plumage it is rustier on mantle and scapulars and has V-shaped flecking on sides and flanks. Grayish nonbreeding Westerns usually retain rusty edges on scapulars, and birds with either bill droop or rusty scapular edges are prob. Westerns. But because short-billed ♂ Western may lack droopy bill tip, and in fall plumage will often lack rusty scapulars, reverse is not true for confirming Semipalmated Sandpiper. Most Semipalmated Sandpipers are safely identified by voice and bill measurements[504]. (In hand exposed culmen lengths of unsexed birds <20mm are Semipalmated; from 20 to 22 either sp.; ≥23 prob. Western; and >24 definitely Western.) Also in hand note partial webbing of toes (lacking in Western).
Voice: Call a rather low-pitched *cherk* or *chrup*, extended to *chirrup*, which can be told (with practice) from that of Western Sandpiper.
Behavior: Likes to gather in large flocks on coastal mudflats. Flushes nervously, "fine-grained" flocks wheeling and banking, turning silver one instant, then dark or almost disappearing the next. Forages more by picking from surface of sand or mud, less by probing and wading than other peeps.
Status and habitat: Common to very common transient and n winter resident (but note identification

Small sandpipers (all in nonbreeding plumage): Stilt Sandpiper (upper left), White-rumped Sandpiper (middle left), Least Sandpiper (lower left), Pectoral Sandpiper (upper right), Sanderling (middle right), Western Sandpiper (lower right)

problems above), late Jul–early May, on coastal mudflats and tidal areas, smaller nos. on beaches; few inland recs. (southernmost is a specimen 29 Aug 1963 at Pto. Páez on Río Meta, s Apure). Only oversummer rec. is 6 seen 24 Jun 1994 at Represa Tacarigua, e Falcón.

Range: To 400m (higher?). Carib. coast from Zulia to Delta Amacuro; inland s to se Apure. Islas Las Aves, Los Roques, Margarita, and Los Testigos. Breeds in arctic N Amer.; winters mostly on coasts of Panama and S America, rarely n to Florida.

Western Sandpiper   Illus. above, PLATE 18
Calidris mauri Playerito Occidental
Identification: 6.5″ (16.5cm). 26g. Rather long black bill *thick at base*, often *drooped at tip*. Legs blackish. Breeding plumage: above grayish brown with *rusty on crown and cheeks and much rusty on scapulars*; below white with *narrow blackish streaking on neck and upper breast* and little Vs or arrowhead flecking on sides, flanks, sometimes even on under tail coverts. Nonbreeding plumage: almost identical to that of Semipalmated Sandpiper except for differences in bill, call, and absence of toe webbing (in hand). Juv.: plain below, but upperparts *usually show rusty on mantle and esp. scapulars* (upper 2 rows). In flight like Semipalmated Sandpiper.

Sim. species: See Semipalmated and Least sandpipers.
Voice: Usual call a thin, high-pitched *squeep* or slightly rough *jeet*. Some calls, which are lower pitched and rougher, are almost identical to those of Semipalmated Sandpiper.
Behavior: Like Semipalmated, often gathers in large, mixed sandpiper flocks, esp. along coast. With longer bill, tends to forage nearer water and probe more deeply than allies. May allow close approach.
Status and habitat: Common transient and n winter resident, late Aug–mid Mar, with small nos. of oversummering birds, e.g., a few 22 Jun 1991, San Juan de Los Cayos, Falcón (P. Boesman); 1 taken 7 Jul 1895 on Isla Margarita. Mainly tidal mudflats and shallow lagoons, smaller nos. on beaches; rarely inland. Nos. of fall migrants peaked in Sep at Chichiriviche, Falcón (A. Altman and C. Parrish census).

Range: Carib. coast from Zulia to Delta Amacuro; Islas Margarita, Las Aves, Los Roques, La Blanquilla, and Los Testigos. Breeds in w Alaska and ne Siberia; winters along coast from s US to n S Amer.

Least Sandpiper
Illus. p. 295, PLATE 18
Calidris minutilla   Playerito Menudo
Identification: 5.5–6" (14–15cm). 21g. *Smallest peep.* Fairly short bill *thin near tip. Yellowish or greenish yellow legs.* Breeding plumage: crown finely streaked dark brown and whitish, rest of upperparts dark brown, the feathers edged buff and rufous forming streaks on mantle; tertials blackish edged rufous; below white, *chest to mid. breast washed buffy brown and finely streaked.* Juv.: brighter, more crisply patterned than ad. Nonbreeding plumage: above grayish brown, the feathers dark-centered and paler toward edges (dull scaly look); below whitish, *chest smudged and streaked brownish.*
Sim. species: Only small peep with *yellow* legs (color varies and often difficult to see; legs muddy, etc.). Always looks *dark chested* compared to nonbreeding Semipalmated and Western sandpipers which are white chested. Note that rufous edging on back wears away quickly after breeding. Also see Baird's and Pectoral sandpipers.
Voice: Typically a high, shrill *treeed,* slightly trilled or blurred, often repeated several times, esp. as flush.
Behavior: Occurs singly or more often in small scattered groups when foraging, but gathers in larger groups with other peeps to rest. Typically rather confiding. Flushes off in rather erratic manner.
Status and habitat: Common transient and fairly common n winter resident on coast and inland; much more numerous mid Aug–Nov and Feb–mid May, with smaller nos. oversummering on or near coast. Sandy beaches, mudflats, mangroves, and muddy places in or near fresh and salt water. Fall transient nos. peak 1st 2 wk Sep at Chichiriviche, Falcón (A. Altman and C. Parrish census data); nos. gradually increase from Feb through late Mar at Hato Cedral, Apure.

Range: To 400m. Carib. coast and inland throughout; virtually all offshore isls. Breeds in arctic N Amer.; winters from s US s to s S Amer. on both coasts and inland s to n Chile and c Brazil. W Indies. Trinidad and Tobago.

White-rumped Sandpiper
Illus. p. 295
Calidris fuscicollis   Playero de Rabadilla Blanca
Identification: 7.5" (19cm). 35g. In flight in any plumage note *all-white rump;* at rest *long wings extend beyond tail tip.* Legs dark greenish; med.-length black bill fractionally drooped at tip (longer and more obviously drooped in ♀). Nonbreeding plumage: *above*

almost uniform brownish gray, rather weak whitish eyestripe; below white lightly shaded and streaked grayish on upper breast. Breeding plumage: feathers of upperparts dusky brown edged gray, buff and rufous (sometimes with noticeable rufous edging on shoulders); narrow whitish eyeline; below white, chest to mid. breast streaked dusky; distinct line of *streaks and flecking down sides and flanks.* In flight wing stripe indistinct.
Sim. species: Only small peep with all-white rump (if in doubt, flush bird). Only Baird's Sandpiper has such long wings, but that sp. is always buffier (not gray) above, generally more scaly-backed, and lacks prom. flank streaking of breeding White-rumps. Smaller than Pectoral Sandpiper; larger than Least, Semipalmated, and Western.
Voice: Flushes off with high, thin, metallic, almost scraping *skreet* or squeaking *jeeet;* highest pitched of any peep in Venez.
Behavior: Gregarious and on migration often forms small to fairly large flocks of its own, or more often assoc. with other *Calidris.*
Status and habitat: Uncommon transient from the north, 1 Sep–10 Nov and 10 Mar–30 May (specimens); scattered inland sight recs., mainly from Apure and Guárico (C. Parrish; P. Boesman; B. Thomas). Highest nos. at Chichiriviche, Falcón, in mid to late Oct (A. Altman and C. Parrish census); 1 seen 30 Nov and 2 Dec 1980 at Boca de Uriche, Anzoátegui, may have been wintering (R. Webster). No definite oversummer recs.

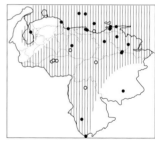

Range: To 400m. Carib. coast from Zulia, Falcón, Aragua, Miranda, Anzoátegui, Sucre, and Delta Amacuro; Islas Los Roques, La Orchila, and La Tortuga. Scattered inland recs. in Apure, Guárico (sight), Anzoátegui, Monagas, Amazonas (sight), and Bolívar. Breeds in arctic N Amer.; winters mainly e of Andes in s S Amer.

[Baird's Sandpiper]
Calidris bairdii   Playero de Baird
Identification: 7–7.5" (18–19cm). 41g. Short, straight bill, *short black legs; very long wings extend beyond tail.* Breeding plumage: *above buffy brown,* the feathers pale-edged imparting a *scaled* appearance (most conspic. in juv. birds); very faint whitish eyebrow (blank look to face); breast light buffy brown finely and obscurely streaked dark brown; rest of underparts white (no streaking on sides or flanks). In flight shows inconspic. narrow white wing stripe and white

on sides of rump. Nonbreeding plumage (plumage most likely seen in Venez.): sim. but duller.

Sim. species: Confusing and prob. often overlooked, but note long wing tip extension (only White-rumped Sandpiper has wings extending beyond tail). Nearly as large as White-rumped but told from it by mostly dark rump (white narrowly on sides), more scaly and uniformly buffy (not grayish) upperparts; usually also by unmarked flanks (cf. breeding-plumage White-rumped). Larger, more portly Pectoral Sandpiper differs in streaked (not so scaly) upperparts, thinner bill, and yellowish legs. Other sim. small peeps—Least, Semipalmated, and Western—are grayer, esp. nonbreeders which are the ones usually seen in Venez. Spring-plumage Sanderlings are rusty buff on head and breast and rarely found away from sandy beaches.

Voice: Usual call a rather low-pitched *krrek* or slightly rolling *preeet,* unlike call of sim. White-rumped Sandpiper.

Behavior: Likely to be seen alone or with other sandpipers such as Least and Pectoral that frequent flooded rice fields, grassy borders of small ponds, and lagoons.

Status and habitat: No specimens or photos. Known from sight recs. as follows: a few seen 27 Oct near Ocumare de La Costa, Aragua[787], and 1 seen 11 Aug 1991 at Chichiriviche, Falcón (P. Boesman). More documentation desirable. Prob. a rare n fall transient (no spring recs.).

Range: Carib. coast of e Falcón and Aragua. Breeds in arctic N Amer. and e Siberia; in New World winters in high Andes from Peru s and on both coasts of s S Amer.

Pectoral Sandpiper

Illus. p. 295

Calidris melanotos Tin-Güín

Identification: ♂ 9″ (23cm), 75g. ♀ 8″ (20.3cm), 57g. ♂ larger than ♀ but both *long necked* and more portly than their allies. Bill thin, vaguely decurved at tip. *Legs greenish yellow.* Above brown heavily streaked black; weakly indicated whitish eyestripe; head, neck, and breast buffy *finely streaked* brown, *the brown of breast sharply cut off from white lower underparts.* In flight shows little or no white wing stripe, narrow whitish edge on tip of secondaries, and dark-centered rump with white on sides.

Sim. species: From any other peep by fine breast streaking, "squared-off" and *sharply separated from white lower underparts.* In coloration closest to Least

Sandpiper, but note "pot-bellied" shape enhanced by longish neck, more erect carriage (Least is typically very hunched), and much larger size. Also cf. Baird's Sandpiper.

Voice: Harsh, reedy *tr'r'r'k* or *ch'r'r't,* often doubled, grating and coarser than that of other sandpipers.

Behavior: Most often seen singly or in very small flocks in Venez., often loosely assoc. with other waders, esp. Least Sandpiper. Tends to feed in drier areas away from water's edge and is often in grass. Rather confiding as it pecks and probes to feed, esp. on insects. Zigzag flight somewhat snipelike when flushed.

Status and habitat: Passage migrant from the north in small nos., rec. (specimens) 15 Aug–25 Oct (sight rec. of 27 on 30 Oct 1976 at Chichiriviche, Falcón—A. Altman and C. Parrish), favoring grassy edges rather than open mudflats; fairly common in small nos. inland around freshwater ponds, grassy lagoons, and flooded fields, also sandbars on rivers. Perhaps less numerous as northward passage migrant: 1 specimen 16 Mar 1943 (San Fernando de Atabapo, Amazonas); sight recs. of up to ca. 15 reported 7 Feb–13 Mar (various observers).

Range: To 500m n of Orinoco (once to 4000m?); to 1300m s of Orinoco (Misión de Kabanayén, Bolívar). Carib. coast and spottily inland throughout; offshore isls. of Los Roques, La Orchila, Los Frailes. Breeds in arctic N Amer. and nw Siberia; winters mostly in s S Amer.

[Dunlin]

Calidris alpina Correlimos

Identification: 7–8.5″ (18–22cm). 55g. *Long, sturdy black bill distinctly drooped near tip; legs black.* Notable variation in bill length and body size. Compact hunched appearance. Nonbreeding plumage: above plain brownish gray with short ill-defined pale eyebrow; underparts white, face, throat, foreneck, and chest tinged gray. Breeding plumage: above gray brown streaked black, scapulars and back blackish edged rusty; sides of head (incl. above eyes) and underparts white narrowly streaked black; large black belly patch. In flight shows *narrow* white wing stripe; *center of upper tail coverts and tail dark,* whitish at sides of base of tail. Juv.: sim. to ad. but upperparts crisply scaled rufous, foreparts tinged buff, belly spotted with black.

Sim. species: In any plumage, bill is the key; also note black legs and "neckless" appearance. Non-

breeders easily confused, esp. with nonbreeding Sanderling which is quite sim. but paler and shorter-billed; and nonbreeding Stilt Sandpiper which has thinner bill, *all-white rump*, pale tail (no dark center), and longer greenish legs. Also cf. nonbreeding Wilson's Phalarope which has straight, needlelike bill.
Status and habitat: Only recs. are 1 nonbreeding-plumage bird seen and documented by notes on 30 Nov 1980 at Boca de Uriche, Anzoátegui (R. Webster and E. Copper), and 3 breeding-plumage birds seen at tidal lagoon at Chichiriviche, Falcón, 25 Apr 1995 by N. Addey (*Cotinga* Vol. 6, p. 37; 1996). Coastal mudflats.

Range: Coast of Anzoátegui. Breeds in n N Amer. and Eurasia; winters mostly in s US and Mexico; vagrants to Costa Rica and Panama; accidental in w Peru.

Stilt Sandpiper   Illus. p. 295
Calidris himantopus   Playero Patilargo
Identification: 8–9″ (20.3–23cm). 55g. *Slender, long-necked* wader with dowitcherlike head. *Long, rather thin, and fractionally decurved bill* often droops at tip. *Long, usually dull greenish legs* (occas. greenish yellow). Nonbreeding plumage: above mostly plain gray with *narrow white superciliary; unmarked white rump patch*; below white, foreneck and sides of chest smudged gray. Juv.: sim. but upperparts somewhat scaled buff, foreneck and sides with fine grayish streaking. Breeding plumage: above grayish brown somewhat scaled paler; *conspic. white rump* streaked with white; *crown and cheeks smudged rufous; narrow white eyestripe*; below dirty white, foreneck streaked, rest of underparts narrowly barred blackish, more coarsely on lower underparts.
Sim. species: Nonbreeders and juvs. resemble larger short-billed Dowitcher but bill shorter and thinner, legs longer (looks like it's on "stilts," but this often not apparent when wading in water), and underparts whiter; dowitcher has long wedge of white up back (not just on rump). Nonbreeders from both yellow-legs by more uniform gray upperparts, usually greenish legs, slightly decurved bill (never looks upturned as in Greater Yellowlegs), and different feeding habits. Also cf. nonbeeding Dunlin.
Voice: Single *kuew* or *huee*, lower and hoarser than in Lesser Yellowlegs; raspy *tri'i'i'nk.*
Behavior: Often with dowitchers, and feeds with sim. sewing-machine motion, or sweeping bill side to side. Usually in small, scattered, loosely assoc. flocks. Like to wade belly-deep in water.

Status and habitat: Common transient and n winter resident, mainly late Aug–end of Apr, to shallow freshwater pools, flooded agricultural fields, and muddy fields, generally less numerous on mudflats and beaches but occas. in large nos. on coast, e.g., 750 on 18 Jan 1974 and 500 on 16 Jan 1975 at Chichiriviche, Falcón (P. Alden). At Chichiriviche nos. usually peak ca. 10–30 Oct with counts of up to 1200 on 3-km censuses, 1976–1978 (A. Altman and C. Parrish); 2 oversummer recs. in Jul (Colección Phelps); 2 breeding-plumage birds seen 1 Aug 1969 near Coro, Falcón, may have been early arrivals (P. Alden). Along with Least Sandpiper, one of most numerous flocking shorebirds wintering inland in c Venez.

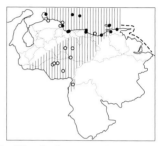

Range: To 400m. Carib. coast and locally inland throughout (mainly llanos); Islas Margarita, Las Aves, and Los Roques. Breeds in arctic N Amer.; winters in S Amer., rarely in s US and Mexico.

Buff-breasted Sandpiper
Tryngites subruficollis   Playerito Dorado
Identification: 8″ (20.3cm). 57g. Small head, long neck, and erect carriage recall Upland Sandpiper. Black bill short and thin; legs ochre yellow. Above dusky, the *feathers broadly edged buff giving a spotted or scaled appearance; sides of head incl. eyebrow, foreneck, and underparts uniform buff*; black eye in uniform face imparts wide-eyed innocent expression. In flight wings are dark above, *mostly white below with dusky wrist mark.*
Sim. species: Nearest are juv. and nonbreeding Ruff, but Buff-breasted is smaller with bright yellow (not greenish to pinkish yellow) legs, shorter bill, and prom. black eyes (Ruff has faint eyebrow). In flight Ruff shows inconspic. narrow white wing stripe, *diagnostic white ovals on sides of base of tail*, and entirely white underwings. Larger Upland Sandpiper has streaked and barred underparts.
Voice: Rather quiet. Occas. a low *pr-r-r-reet* in flight or high *paWEEea* on gd.
Behavior: Very social and almost always in small flocks on migration. Often "freezes" rather than flies, allowing close approach. When flushed tends to turn and bank sharply, often circling once or twice in tight little flocks, showing white underparts, before flying off. Erect posture and wide-eyed facial expression impart dignified, if somewhat innocent, countenance.
Status and habitat: Scarce n spring transient, mid Mar–early May (11 specimens from Amazonas, 2

from Zulia). Also a small no. of sight recs. Mar–early May as follows: flock of 8 at Hato Cedral, Apure, 21 Mar 1994 (Hilty); 1 at Santa Cruz de Mora, Zulia, 20 Mar 1970 (P. Alden); 6 on 24 Apr 1993 at Represa Tacarigua, Falcón (P. Boesman); small flock 26 Apr 1982 at Hato Masaguaral, Guárico (C. Parrish); 3 groups at Hato Cedral, largest with 32 birds, 5 May 2000 (G. Rodríquez); and up to 300 seen late Apr–early May 2000 (several observers). No fall recs. Mostly short grassy areas, rain pools, fields, and river sandbars.

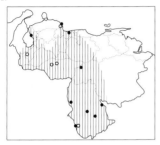

Range: To 220m. Known from coast of e Falcón and inland in Zulia, Mérida, Apure, Aragua, Guárico, Amazonas, and Bolívar. Breeds in w arctic N Amer.; winters mainly on pampas of s S Amer.

[Ruff]
Philomachus pugnax   Rufo
Identification: ♂ 11.5″ (29cm), 165g. ♀ 9″ (23cm), 100g. Straight med.-length bill paler at base, slightly drooped; legs vary in color, greenish in juvs., usually somewhat yellowish on older birds. Nonbreeding plumage: upperparts mottled grayish brown, scapulars and tertials unusually long, lax, and vaguely pale edged; center of rump and tail dusky; *large oval area of white on each side of base of tail* (distinctive in flight); *whitish loral area*; underparts dull white, foreneck and breast somewhat mottled grayish brown. Juv.: sim. but with buffy wash below; more distinct buff-edged wing coverts, scapulars, and tertials impart scaly look; *lores whitish*. Breeding-plumage ♂ (unlikely in Venez): mostly bare face and large erectile neck ruff colored black, white, or chestnut. Breeding-plumage ♀ (also unlikely): variable but usually sooty gray above, some feathers dark-centered; below dark gray spotted and blotched black, belly white. In flight in any plumage shows *all-white underwings*; from above a narrow white wing stripe.
Sim. species: Despite complex plumages and size variation, readily recognized by large size and curious shape (rather deep bodied, humpbacked, and long necked). Tail pattern is diagnostic in flight, and all birds should be flushed.
Behavior: Large, powerful flier, to be watched for among flocks of waders such as yellowlegs and dowitchers. Probes in shallow water and mud. ♀ often called Reeve.
Status and habitat: One publ. Venez. rec.: 1 seen 18 Nov 1977, Chichiriviche, Falcón[5]. Several recs. from Trinidad and Tobago. Can occur in a wide variety of freshwater habitats incl. damp grasslands, shallow la-

goons, flooded rice fields, coastal lagoons, and mangroves. Prob. a reg. but rare visitor to Venez. coast.

Range: Coast of e Falcón. Breeds in n Eurasia; winters from s Europe to Africa; casual visitant to N Amer. and Lesser Antilles. Trinidad and Tobago. Presum. Colombia ("Bogota" specimen).

Limnodromus

Med. sized and chunky; very long straight bill (snipelike) slightly broader at tip; fairly short legs; probe rapidly in water.

Short-billed Dowitcher   PLATE 18
Limnodromus griseus   Becasina Migratoria
Identification: 11″ (28cm). 95g. Long, straight, snipe-like bill, 2.5–2.7″ (64–69mm); rather short greenish legs. At all seasons *tail whitish closely and narrowly barred black and extending up back as conspic. wedge of white*. Nonbreeding plumage: above brownish gray, *distinct white eyestripe* and dark gray line through eyes; below white, foreneck tinged gray; *a few bars and spots on flanks*. Breeding plumage: crown dark brown flecked buff, rest of upperparts blackish streaked and edged buff; whitish eyebrow and narrow dusky line through eyes; *foreneck and chest washed pale rufous*, rest of underparts white, chest and upper breast densely spotted black, flanks usually boldly barred black; rump and tail as above. Juv.: sim. to breeders but feather edgings on upperparts *brighter buffy rufous*; below buff turning white on mid. breast and belly; faintly barred and spotted buff on flanks. In flight note pale tail continuing as *white wedge to mid. back*; also white rear edge of secondaries.
Sim. species: Nonbreeding Stilt Sandpiper is smaller with longer legs, thinner and slightly drooped bill, and white *only* on rump (not also lower back). Also cf. Ruff and both yellowlegs.
Voice: Usual call as flushes, or in flight, a rapid, emphatic *tu-tu-tu*. Seldom calls on gd.
Behavior: Notably gregarious and usually in compact flocks. Rests on mudflats and feeds by wading up to belly in shallow water and probing with distinctive up-and-down sewing-machine motion, or sweeping bill side to side; submerges head completely at times. Occurs in large flocks, of its own or with other shorebirds.
Status and habitat: Common transient, less common n winter resident, mainly mid Aug–late Apr, on coastal mudflats; largest wintering concentrations

were w of Barcelona, esp. Laguna de Chacopata[415].
Rare inland: 1 on 8 Aug 1993 at Maturín, Monagas
(P. Boesman). Sight recs. of oversummering birds as
follows: 22 Jun 1991, San Juan de Los Cayos, Falcón
(P. Boesman); 2 Aug 1969 at Chichiriviche, Falcón
(P. Alden). Fall transient nos. peak late Aug–late Sep
with max. of 250–700 in mid Sep on 3-km transects
at Chichiriviche, Falcón (A. Altman and C. Parrish
census data).

Range: Carib. coast from Zulia (sight) and Falcón e
to Sucre; sightings inland in Apure and Monagas;
Islas Margarita, Las Aves, and Los Roques (*griseus*).
Breeds in Alaska and Canada; winters from s US to
Peru, c Brazil, and the Guianas.
Note: Long-billed Dowitcher (*L. scolopaceus*), unrec.
in S Amer., is possible (winters in s US and C Amer.,
rarely s to Panama). In any plumage most safely told
by voice, a high, thin *keek*, 1 or 5–6 in rapid ser. Juv.
is darker above (with rufous edgings) and has much
grayer foreneck than Short-billed. Breeding plumages
very sim., but Long-billed has foreneck streaked and
spotted, flanks more barred, and unlike e *griseus*
subsp. of Short-billed also has white scapular tips
and all rufous belly. Nonbreeding-plumage birds inseparable except by voice.

Gallinago

Very long, straight bill (soft, flexible tip); parallel
buff stripes down back; large eyes high and posterior
on crown; tarsus short, toes long; no. and shape of
tail feathers vary between spp.; notable for aerial
displays.

Common Snipe   PLATE 18
Gallinago gallinago   Becasina Chillona
Identification: 10.5–11.5" (27–29cm). 115g. *Long slender bill*, 2.5–3" (64–78mm). *Short* greenish yellow
legs. Above mainly dark brown, mantle streaked and
barred buff; *eyebrow and crown stripes whitish*,
below whitish *mottled buff and brown on foreneck
and breast*; short orange rufous tail (sometimes conspic.); primaries unbarred (hard to see).
Sim. species: See South American Snipe. Andean
Snipe is larger and heavily barred below. Giant Snipe
is much larger. Noble Snipe overlaps only in extreme
s Táchira.
Voice: Flushes with nasal, throat-clearing *khatch*;
flight display not performed on wintering gds.
Behavior: As in South American Snipe. A tight sitter,
freezing then flushing off in zigzag flight at last mo-

ment. Occas. encountered in small, loosely assoc.
groups of 2–5 in Andes.
Status and habitat: Transient and n winter resident
15 Sep–18 Apr to wet or boggy areas with grass
cover from paramo (where most numerous) to e lowlands; often in areas of scant cover in paramo. Because it cannot be separated with confidence from
lowland South American Snipe in field, true status is
unknown. Greatest no. of recs. is from highlands
(where South American Snipe does not occur), but
smaller no. of recs. are widely scattered across
lowlands.

Range: To 3600m. Maracaibo Basin, Zulia; Andes of
Táchira and Mérida; e Falcón, Carabobo, and s Aragua (Embalse de Suata) to e Miranda; scattered recs.
from Apure to Anzoátegui; Amazonas and Bolívar
(*delicata*). Breeds in N Amer. and Eurasia; winters s
to n S Amer.

South American Snipe   Illus. p. 301
Gallinago paraguaiae   Becasina Paraguaya
Identification: 10.5–11.5" (27–29cm). 110g. *Prob. not
safely distinguished in field from Common Snipe*
(often difficult even in hand). In hand South American differs as follows: *black bars on axillary feathers
narrower than white bars* (reverse in Common
Snipe); bill averages longer (69–84 vs. 64–78mm);
wing length (arc) shorter (117–128 vs. 129–140mm);
width of outer tail feather narrower (4–6 vs. 6–
9mm). Other helpful features for South American
incl. buffy gray upper tail coverts (instead of rich
deep buff); *black barring on tertials narrower or
about as wide as pale barring between* (instead of
black bars wider to much wider); pale barring on innermost tertials pale buff to grayish buff (instead of
rufous); general upperparts color blacker with fewer
vermiculations and bars. *In general, birds seen in lowlands between May and Sep are prob. South American, those during rest of yr either sp.*, although most
specimens of Common Snipe are from high els.
Voice: In aerial display, mostly May–Jul, circles and
dives endlessly, producing a winnowing or vibrating
sound, much like that of Common Snipe, made by vibration of widely spread tail feathers during shallow
dives.
Behavior: A solitary bird that usually "freezes," rely-
ing on cryptic coloration to avoid detection. Flushes
off at last moment with nasal call and zigzag flight
but generally does not fly far. Holds bill somewhat
downward at rest and in flight. During early and
mid. part of rainy season, May–Sep in llanos, air is

Snipes: Giant Snipe (upper left),
Noble Snipe (upper right), South
American Snipe (lower left),
Andean Snipe (lower right)

often filled with winnowing sounds of this snipe in overhead display flights which continue throughout day. Forages by probing rapidly and deeply in soft mud. In Trinidad breeds May–Oct; a depression in gd.; 2 buff eggs blotched brown[175].

Status and habitat: Apparently resident, but seasonal or local movement, or even austral migrants, possible. Relatively common in llanos and at least locally fairly common in grasslands of se Bolívar. Wet grass, boggy areas, marshes, and muddy areas with grass cover. Only noted May–Jul at Hato Masaguaral, Guárico[734].

Range: To 300m n of Orinoco (once to 1100m in w Mérida); to 1300m s of Orinoco. Táchira (Santo Domingo), w Mérida (Laguna de Urao at 1100m), Barinas, and Aragua e to Sucre, Monagas, and Delta Amacuro; spottily in Amazonas and Bolívar s to Santa Elena de Uairén (*paraguaiae*). E of Andes s to Tierra del Fuego.

Note: By some considered a subsp. of Common Snipe (*G. gallinago*). Called Magellanic Snipe (*G. magellanica*) by some. Also Paraguayan Snipe.

Noble Snipe
Illus. above

Gallinago nobilis Becasina Paramera

Identification: 12″ (30.5cm). 195g. *Long, slender bill*, 3.2–3.8″ (81–97mm), *pale at base and dusky at tip*. Closely resembles Common Snipe, differing as follows: larger size, broader wings, longer and distinctly *2-toned bill*, and *dark trailing edge to secondaries*. In direct comparison foreneck and breast are darker, more tawny buff heavily streaked and mottled with black, and only central belly uniform white.

Sim. species: Andean Snipe is darker, all *barred* below, and has heavier, all-dark bill. In flight Noble's *toes project beyond tail* (Andean's do not).

Voice: Flushes with nasal grating note. In crepuscular dawn and dusk display flight (or at night on moonlit nights), circles and dives repeatedly, producing a whistling or winnowing sound like others of genus. Simultaneously ♀ (presum.) gives a loud chipping from gd. Flushes with raspy call.

Behavior: Like other snipes, a close sitter, depending on camouflage for protection. Flushes off in heavy but somewhat zigzag flight. Nest a depression on gd.; prob. breeds mainly in rainy season; eggs brownish olive spotted several shades of dark brown, esp. at larger end[589].

Status and habitat: Resident in boggy meadows, wet grass, and lake edges in temperate and paramo zone. Found with Andean Snipe, but center of abundance is at lower el. Fairly numerous with many specimens from within its small range in Venez. **Range:** 2700–3300m. Páramo de Tamá and Cerro Las Copas, s Táchira. Extreme nw Venez. s in Andes to s Ecuador.

Andean Snipe
Illus. p. 301
Gallinago jamesoni   Becasina Andina
Identification: 11″ (28cm). 165g. *Large, bulky, and dark. Bill long,* 4″ (102mm), *decidedly heavy and slightly drooped at tip.* In flight note *very broad, strongly rounded wings.* Above mainly dark brown, mantle streaked and barred buff; central crown stripe and eyebrow deep buff (neither in strong contrast); sides of head, throat, and chest brownish buff speckled and streaked with brown, *rest of underparts buff coarsely and heavily but somewhat irreg. barred and marked dusky,* no rufous or white in tail.
Sim. species: Larger and much darker, esp. below, than other snipes in Venez. Good marks are large size, heavy bill, weakly contrasting head stripes, more or less *fully barred underparts* incl. belly. As flushes, tail brownish (little or no rufous), *wings notably broad* with no white trailing edge; *feet do not project beyond tail.* Cf. Noble and Common snipes.
Voice: In aerial display at dusk, a jetlike whine or winnowing (swelling dramatically as bird passes overhead) accompanied by a loud, rapid *wic-a, wic-a, wic-a* . . . in dive; display repeated several times as bird circles overhead. On gd. a soft, froglike *whik-ick-ick-ick* . . . ; when flushed a louder *whit,* several times (C. Parrish).
Behavior: Like most snipes, a close sitter, but favors areas with tall grass and vegetation, hence often attempts to creep or scamper away on foot, running from one clump of grass to next, then freezing momentarily behind each clump and uttering a faint ser. of calls. Flushes off in straight, rather heavy flight (C. Parrish). Breeds May–Sep in E Andes of Colombia[260].
Status and habitat: Uncommon to locally fairly common resident (seasonal movements?). Wet or boggy areas in paramo, esp. where water trickles over mats of moss, tall sedges, and grass, but avoids open boggy areas that lack cover. As many as 4 have been flushed from small areas of Páramo de Mucubají, Mérida, on 25 Oct (C. Parrish) and mid Jan (Hilty); 2 seen at Páramo Batallón, nw Táchira, on 1 May 1966

(R. Ridgely and others); possibly as low as 2500m on Lara/Trujillo border[60].
Range: 3200–3300m (sight to 3600m). Locally in paramos of Táchira and Mérida n to Páramo de Las Rosas, ne Trujillo (*jamesoni*). Colombia in Santa Marta Mts.; Andes s to La Paz, Bolivia.
Note: Previously called *Chubbia jamesoni*[403]. Often regarded as a subsp. of Cordilleran Snipe (*G. stricklandii*) of s Chile and s Argentina.

Giant Snipe
Illus. p. 301
Gallinago undulata   Becasina Gigante
Identification: 14–15″ (36–38cm). 320g (♀ larger than ♂?). Large but otherwise resembles other snipes. *Long bill,* 4–4.5″ (102–114mm), *deep at base and joining high on forehead* (imparts flat-headed look). Above dark brown streaked and barred buff, *markings bolder than in other snipes;* throat and belly whitish; foreneck streaked and breast and sides barred black (white spaces twice width of brown bars). In flight wings unusually broad and rounded, the *flight feathers barred* (most apparent on secondaries but unique among snipes), trailing edge of wing narrowly white, and *no white tips on tail.*
Sim. species: Bulks larger than Common and South American snipe but this not always apparent in field. Look for barring on flight feathers, lack of white tail tips, bolder markings, and thick base to bill.
Voice: In flight display a sonorous, winnowing *HO-go, go* or *GA-ga, ga* (humanlike) 2–5 times, the ser. weakening in volume; also various buzzing sounds, *bzz, sch,* some lasting up to 4 sec (*gigantea* in Brazil)[611]. Hd. and seen calling from gd. 30 Dec 1990 in n Gran Sabana (P. Boesman); 3 hd. predawn, Dec, 16km n of Santa Elena de Uairén, Bolívar (C. Parrish and T. Parker).
Behavior: Much more nocturnal than Common Snipe. A close sitter, flushing only at last moment. Usually squats and freezes, or may attempt to creep away slowly. Aerial displays given mostly at night or before dawn. BC birds, Suriname, Dec–Feb[251].
Status and habitat: Poorly known. Very local resident; possible short-distance seasonal migrant to some areas. Flooded grasslands, damp fields, and moist areas. Damp or wet heathlike scrub and grassland in Gran Sabana.

Range: To 300m n of Orinoco; to 1400m s of Orinoco. Scattered recs. from s Carabobo (Valencia area), s Monagas, nw and se Bolívar (Caño Maniapure; Auyán-tepui se to Cerro Roraima), and Río Asisa, Amazonas (*undulata*). Locally from e Colom-

bia to the Guianas and ne Brazil; Paraguay, se Brazil, and prob. Uruguay. Río Grande, Argentina (?).
Note: S form (*gigantea*) of s of the Amazon is larger and perhaps a separate sp.

Phalaropus

Thin bill; dainty proportions; lobed, partly webbed toes; ♀♀ brighter than ♂♂ and sex roles reversed. Most aquatic of family and only ones that seem comfortable swimming at sea. Sometimes placed in family of their own.

[Wilson's Phalarope]
Phalaropus tricolor   Falaropa de Wilson
Identification: ♂ 8.5″ (22cm), 45g. ♀ 9.5″ (24cm), 62g. Distinctive S-shaped neck and black *needlelike bill*; legs greenish yellow (nonbreeding) or blackish (breeding). Nonbreeding plumage: above *unmarked gray*, below pure white with blurry gray smudge through eyes and pale eyestripe. Breeding-plumage ♀: above dark gray; short white eyeline; *broad black mask through eyes narrows behind, then broadens and turns dark reddish chestnut down sides of neck and across scapulars* (forms little "suspenders"); 2d chestnut band crosses lesser wing coverts; below mostly white, chest tinged brown. Breeding-plumage ♂: like ♀ but much duller and browner. On land looks small headed and pot-bellied. In flight in any plumage both sexes show *solid gray wings* (no stripe) and *white rump and tail*.
Sim. species: Should be easily recognized by distinctive shape, behavior, needle bill, and pale plumage. Cf. nonbreeders (the ones likely in Venez.) with nonbreeding Stilt Sandpiper, Sanderling, and Lesser Yellowlegs. Other phalaropes (not yet rec. in Venez.) have wing stripes.
Behavior: Gregarious in small to large flocks and most often seen on water, swimming and spinning as buoyantly as corks. Take tiny invertebrate life from water's surface by spinning daintily on water, stirring it, and dabbing with bill. Often distinguishable as phararopes on these behaviors alone. On land walks hurriedly, almost frantically, picking rapidly at muddy surface.
Status and habitat: Very rare[392]. One publ. rec. in Venez. of 1 winter-plumage bird seen 5 Nov 1977 and again 7 Nov in Refugio de Fauna Silvestre de Cuare near Chichiriviche, Falcón[5].

Range: Breeds in high Arctic of w N Amer.; winters on coast from Peru to Chile, in c Argentine pampas,

and on high Andean lagoons; vagrant to isls. of Jamaica, Guadeloupe, Martinique, and Barbados; also Mato Grosso, Brazil.

Laridae: Skuas, Jaegers, Gulls, Terns, and Skimmers
Gaviotas y Tiñosas

The Laridae here includes the subfamilies Stercorariinae, Larinae, Sterninae, and Rynchopinae, each considered a separate family by some authors.

This large group of birds is found mostly along seacoasts or at sea, with only a few species regularly found inland. Many are gregarious and strong fliers. Gulls are characterized by a fairly heavy hooked bill, rounded wings and tail, predominantly gray and white plumage, gregarious habits, and easy, buoyant flight. Most gulls seen in Venezuela breed in northern latitudes and spend the northern winter offshore or along coastlines. Terns have slender, pointed bills and pointed wings, and many have forked tails. They dive into the water for prey but seldom swim. Terns seen in Venezuela include northern-latitude breeders, some that breed on offshore islands, and 2 species that breed inland. Skuas and jaegers are large, powerful predatory seabirds well known for aerial piracy. Jaegers breed in north polar regions, skuas are bipolar breeders, and both are highly migratory on the open sea outside the breeding season. Skuas and jaegers have wings that are sharply flexed at the wrist; those of jaegers are long and falconlike, and both groups easily outdistance gulls and terns, harassing them until they give up their food. Adult jaeger plumages are distinctive but are not acquired for several years; immature plumages pose special identification problems requiring comparative experience.

Finally, the 3 species of skimmers (only 1 in the New World) look like long-winged terns and are distinguished by their large, laterally compressed bills which are knifelike with the lower mandible longer than the upper. They "skim" low over the water, cutting the surface with the bill, and seize fish and other prey the bill touches.

[Great Skua]
Catharacta skua   Salteador Mayor
Identification: 21″ (53cm). 1.14kg. Large and muscular. Ad.: mostly brown with *cinnamon, rufous, or ginger brown shaft streaking, esp. on neck and back*; cap dusky, underparts warmer brown and more uniform than above. In flight note white at base of primaries (above or below); tail short, slightly rounded. Juv.: like ad. but with less cinnamon and rufous on neck.
Sim. species: See South Polar Skua.
Status and habitat: HYPOTHETICAL. Sight recs. (no dates given) of *Catharacta skua* (Great Skua) from Chichiriviche, Falcón, and Golfo de Venezuela, Zulia[503], were believed to be of this sp.; also, sight recs. of 1 on 7 Jan 1996 n of Paria Pen. (11°15′ N, 62°38′ W); 7 more later same day with a large group of Brown Boobies near ne tip of Paria Pen. (11°02′

N, 61°54' W); and 1 on 8 Jan 1996 e of Isla Margarita and n of Paria Pen. at 10°56' N, 62°44' W[424]. Specimens or photographs needed for verification. To be watched for Aug–Mar.

Range: Coast of Zulia and Falcón; waters off coast of Sucre and Isla Margarita. Breeds in N Atlantic and Eurasia; disperses s in Atlantic to nw Africa and w Mediterranean, rarely to e coast of N Amer.

South Polar Skua

Catharacta maccormicki Salteador Polar Antártico
Identification: 21" (53cm). 1.15kg. Both this sp. and Great Skua (see Note) are likely off coast, and any skua identification should be made with care and preferably accompanied by good photos. Both spp. are large, robust seabirds with broad wings showing *white wing patches above and below*, rather short wedge-shaped to roundish tails, and conspic. hunchback appearance in flight. Ad.: above uniform brown, below plain cold grayish brown, usually with pale collar on hindneck; may show minimum of gold to cinnamon streaking on foreneck. South Polar Skua has light and dark phase but shows no streaking in either and is uniform brown to flat cold gray brown. Dark phase: much like Great Skua. Light phase: has blondish gray head, neck, and underparts. Juv.: pale bluish bill with black tip; much like ad. but head grayer, throat paler, body overall grayer, wing coverts narrowly edged buff; usually less white on underwing. Imm.: less streaky but retains ginger brown color. Imm. of either phase darker than respective ad.
Sim. species: Great Skua differs from South Polar in *overall more reddish brown or ginger brown color* (esp. upperparts) and *dusky streaking on back, wing coverts, and underparts* (not conspic. unless close). South Polar also recalls Pomarine Jaeger but is heavier in all proportions, incl. bill.
Behavior: Will most likely be seen alone at sea. Flight is fast and powerful, and skuas easily overtake and harass gulls, terns, and other seabirds, forcing them to disgorge their food. May occas. follow ships. Readily alights on water.
Status and habitat: Rare or vagrant in Carib. waters. Known from 1 specimen taken 2 Jul 1976 at mouth of Caño Sagua, nw Zulia[354]. Identified as this sp., but further verification desirable. This is prob. most likely skua in Carib.[10], esp. May–Sep.
Range: Coast of Zulia. Breeds in S Shetland Isls. and Antarctica (dark morph mainly on outer pen., light

morphs elsewhere); disperses n (mostly juvs.) into Indian Ocean and n latitudes in Atlantic and Pacific oceans.
Note: Skua taxonomy is reviewed in AOU Check-list[10].

Pomarine Jaeger   PLATES 2, 19

Stercorarius pomarinus Salteador Pomarino
Identification: 21" (53cm). 700g. Largest and most robust jaeger. Bill bicolored (tip dark). *Pointed wings show conspic. white patch at base of primaries from above and below*. Tail wedge-shaped with *2 twisted feathers protruding* up to 4" (102mm) but these sometimes broken or missing. Light phase (commonest): cap blackish; *white collar around hindneck*; rest of upperparts dark brown, below whitish, cheeks tinged yellowish (looks pale headed at a distance), usually with *narrow brownish chest band* and dusky barring on sides. Dark phase (rare): all sooty brown with pale wing patches; pale bill tipped black. Imm.: like dark phase, or mottled and barred above and below; no projecting central tail feathers; all juv. and imm. birds show *pale rump* with strong dark barring on rump and lower underparts.
Sim. species: Much like Parasitic Jaeger, but ads. with full tails are distinctive. Imm. not safely told from Parasitic even with size comparisons, but Pomarine is bigger framed and has more primaries with white shafts (5–8 vs. 3–6). Central tail feathers are bluntly rounded in Pomarine, pointed in Parasitic.
Behavior: Flight heavier than in other jaegers but more buoyant and graceful (less stiff) than skuas; flapping often alternates with short glides. Usually solitary or in prs., but migrates in flocks and reg. assoc. with gulls and terns. Eats fish and squid taken from surface or stolen from other seabirds. Often settles on water.
Status and habitat: Prob. reg. nonbreeding transient in nearshore and offshore waters, occas. in nos. along coast: 9 specimen recs. from Miranda 28 Dec–1 Mar (Colección Phelps). Sight recs. incl. 7 seen along coast 11 Feb 1987 at Laguna de Unare, Anzoátegui (M. Van Beirs); up to 20 seen off Macuto coast, Distr. Federal, 28 Feb 1999 (R. Schofield); 1 imm. seen 20 Apr 1977 and others seen Sep 1976–1978 at Kaimare Chico, nw Zulia[354]; 1 seen in Sep, "La Guaira," 18km off coast[403]; numerous in s Carib. (vicinity of Venez. isls.) with Pomarine accounting for ca. 90% of all identified jaeger sightings during 3 sea crossings in Jan[424].
Range: Carib. coast from Zulia to Anzoátegui; Islas Los Roques (sight). Breeding circumpolar in Arctic;

winters s at sea, mostly in New World, to Peru and Guyana.

Parasitic Jaeger PLATE 19
Stercorarius parasiticus Salteador Parásito
Identification: 19″ (48cm). 465g. Both color phases and imm. much like respective forms of Pomarine Jaeger, but slightly smaller, slimmer, and with *short, pointed tail feathers* projecting up to 3″ (76mm) beyond tail. Light phase usually has paler breast band (occas. lacking) than Pomarine.
Sim. species: See Pomarine Jaeger.
Behavior: As in Pomarine Jaeger but faster, more agile, and more aggressively harries other seabirds in flight.
Status and habitat: Four specimens, early Feb–early Jul 1977–1979, and several seen in Sep, all near Caño Sagua, nw Zulia[108]; also 1 specimen (Colección Phelps) from Islas Los Roques (M. Lentino). Sight recs. Jan–Sep, as follows: 2 seen 2 Jan 1986 near Ocumare de la Costa, Aragua (A. Altman); 1 dark-phase subad. 16 Jan 1975, 5km s of Tucacas, Falcón (P. Alden); and Parasitic Jaegers estimated to account for ca. 8% of all identified jaeger sightings during 3 crossings of s Carib. between Bonaire and Isla Margarita in Jan 1996–1998[424].

Range: Carib. coast of Zulia; sight recs. off coast of Falcón and Aragua; Islas Los Roques. Breeding circumpolar in Arctic; migrates s at sea in New World to s S Amer.

[Long-tailed Jaeger]
Stercorarius longicaudus Salteador Colilargo
Identification: 15″ (38cm); 300g. Smaller and trimmer than previous 2 jaegers. *Long central tail feathers* project up to 10″ (25.25cm) beyond tail, less white in primaries (3 or fewer white shafts), proportionately smaller bill (but some Parasitics have small bill), and

lighter, more graceful, gull-like flight. Light-phase ad.: differs from other jaegers by immaculate cheeks, complete white collar on hindneck setting off black cap, paler gray back, no breast band, and usually darker abdomen. More identification details available[434].
Status and habitat: No photos or specimens: 1 seen with long projecting tail feathers during 1 of 3 crossings of s Carib. (Bonaire to Isla Margarita) in Jan 1996–1998; a few others, possibly this sp., during same crossing; max. of 1/day[424]. Expected as a rare visitant.
Range: Offshore Venez. waters. Breeding circumpolar in Arctic; winters mostly at sea in Pacific off s S Amer. and in s Atlantic.

Larus

Large, worldwide genus with most spp. in cold temperate latitudes; ads. mostly white and gray, often with black on wings, wing tips, and/or tail; reach maturity in 2–4 yr; terms such as 1st yr, etc., (used here) refer to a plumage type, not a definite age; field identification, esp. of younger birds, challenging; some individuals best left unidentified; 1 sp. breeds on offshore Venez. isls., none on mainland.

[Lesser Black-backed Gull]
Larus fuscus Gaviota Dorsinegra Menor
Identification: 22″ (56cm). 715g. Breeding-plumage ad.: resembles Herring Gull but *entire back and upper wings* blackish (*fuscus*) or *dark gray* (*graellsii*); in flight from below, underwing shows *black tip and rather broad dusky trailing edge to rest of flight feathers* (Herring has black wing tips, rest of flight feathers all white from below); legs yellowish (breeding) to flesh (winter). Juv.: not separable from juv. Herring. All other age stages progressively darker backed than Herring.
Status and habitat: Known from 1 sight rec. (with photos) of a 1st-yr bird (subsp.?) 9 Feb 1983 at Laguna de Unare, Anzoátegui (R. Fairbanks and S. Gautlett). There is 1 additional rec. (Colección Phelps files), presum. this sp. (specimen not located). Sandy beaches.

Range: Coast of Anzoátegui. Breeds from Iceland to Norway and s to Britian and Netherlands. Three subspp: *fuscus* wintering s to Nigeria, Red Sea, and Kenya; *graellsii* wintering from Europe to w Mediterranean and Nigeria; and *intermedius* wintering over both of above zones. Reg. in N Amer. s to Florida and Texas. Guyana. Trinidad and Tobago.

[Great Black-backed Gull]
Larus marinus   Gaviota Dorsinegra Mayor
Identification: 30″ (76cm). 1.7kg. *Huge 4-yr gull with massive yellow bill*; red spot near bill tip. Breeding plumage: head, underparts, and tail white, upperparts *deep black*, eyes pale, legs pink. In flight *tip of outermost primary and spot near tip of next primary white*. 3d-yr plumage: like ad. but with some black near bill tip and brown on wing coverts, sometimes also a little on tail. 1st winter: above heavily mottled and *checkered* brownish and white; *head and underparts whitish* with a little brown mottling and streaking, bill and eyes dark; rump and base of tail whitish broadly tipped blackish. 2d summer: like 1st winter but with *some black on back*; bill may only be black at tip.
Status and habitat: Prob. casual visitor. No specimens. Only publ. S Amer. rec. is of 2 ad.-plumage birds seen 20 Mar 1990 at Los Olivitos estuary on e shore of El Tablazo Bay (27km ne of Maracaibo), ne Zulia[103].

Range: Coast of Zulia. Breeds on coasts of ne N Amer. and Palearctic; winters inland to Great Lakes and s to Florida. Vagrant in W Indies from Cuba, Bahamas, and Puerto Rico s to Aruba and Barbados; Colombia (once, Buenaventura).

Herring Gull   PLATE 19
Larus argentatus   Gaviota Argéntea
Identification: 22–25″ (56–64cm). 1kg. Large 4-yr gull. Nonbreeding plumage: bill yellow with red spot on lower mandible; legs pink. Plumage mainly white, back and wings pearl gray, *wing tips black with several white spots at tip*; narrow white rear border to wings; head, neck, and sides of breast streaked and mottled brown (amt. variable, often heavy). Breeding plumage (4th yr): sim. but head and breast all white. Juv. (1st yr): mottled grayish brown, slightly paler below; dusky flight feathers and tail; legs dusky pink; bill blackish. 2d-winter imm.: mantle grayer; head, neck, and rump white mottled with brown; tail dusky, base white; underparts whitish; legs pink; bill tipped or ringed black. 3d-winter imm.: recognizably sim. to ad. but with traces of brown above and below, and band near tail tip; bill yellowish but with at least vestiges of dark ring across both mandibles.
Sim. species: Large size and pink legs of ad. are distinctive. Both imm. and ad. much like Ring-billed Gull but decidedly larger.
Status and habitat: Known from 1 specimen in Colección Phelps (juv.?), 18 Apr 1954 from Isla de Aves (M. Lentino). Sight records as follows: a 3d-yr bird

seen 19 Feb 1983 at Laguna de Unare, Anzoátegui (C. Parrish); an imm. 19 Feb 1987 at same loc. (M. Van Beirs); 1 at Los Olivitos, Zulia (C. Casler); 1 on coast of e Falcón[503]; and 1 on 1 Feb 1995, Laguna de Unare, Anzoátegui (P. Boesman). Sandy beaches.

Range: Carib. coast in Zulia (sight), Falcón (sight), and Anzoátegui (sight); Isla de Aves (presum. *smithsonianus*). Breeds in N Amer. and n Eurasia; winters in New World s to Mexico and W Indies, rarely to Panama and Trinidad.

[Ring-billed Gull]   PLATE 19
Larus delawarensis   Gaviota de Pico Anillado
Identification: 17″ (43cm). 495g. Typical, med.-sized 3-yr gull. Bill of ad. *yellow with black ring around tip*. Breeding plumage: pale gray mantle and upper wings; black wing tips with 2 white outer spots; head and underparts white, eyes and legs yellow. Nonbreeding ad.: sim. but some light brownish streaking on head and hindneck. Imm. (2d yr): like nonbreeding ad. but *bill pinkish ringed black*, legs dull pink, wing tips with more black, tail with more or less distinct black subterminal band. Juv. (1st yr): above dingy white mottled grayish brown; below whitish somewhat mottled brown, flight feathers dusky, outer primaries blackish; upper and under tail coverts weakly barred dusky, tail heavily mottled brown with broad dusky terminal band; bill pinkish with broad blackish tip.
Sim. species: Older birds always told by "ringed" bill. Note intermed. size and rather lightly built proportions. Young birds would require good photos or specimen for confirmation in Venez. See Harrison[248] and Grant[215] for more details.
Behavior: To be looked for in company of gulls and terns loafing on coast. Slightly larger than Laughing Gull.
Status and habitat: No specimens. Known from several sight recs.: a 2d-yr bird seen 1 Feb 1983 at La-

guna de Unare, Anzoátegui (R. Fairbanks and S. Gautlett) and again 19 Feb 1983 (C. Parrish); an ad. seen 16 Mar 1993 (M. Van Beirs) and 2 ads. seen 1 Feb 1995 (P. Boesman), all at Laguna de Unare, Anzoátegui. A rec. from Laguna de Píritu, Anzoátegui, is cited by M. Lentino[503].

Range: Coast of Anzoátegui. Breeds in s Canada and n US; winters from US s to Mexico and Greater Antilles, rarely to Panama and Colombia. Trinidad and Tobago. Tefé, Brazil (once).

Laughing Gull   PLATE 19
Larus atricilla   Guanaguanare
Identification: 15–17″ (38–43cm). 275g. Med.-sized 3-yr gull. Bill and legs blackish (dusky red in breeding plumage). Nonbreeding plumage: above gray *darkening to black on wing tips* (no white separating black); rear border of wing white; head, underparts, and tail white, *ear coverts and rear crown mottled brownish* (not a distinct "half hood" as in Franklin's Gull). Breeding plumage: sim. but *head black with conspic. white eyelids*. Subad. (2d yr): like nonbreeding ad. but brownish above; black subterminal band on tail. Juv. (1st yr): mostly dark grayish brown, throat and belly whitish; trailing edge of wing, *rump, and tail white; black subterminal tail band*.
Sim. species: Ad. Franklin's Gull always separable by white band separating black wing tip. Nonbreeding and subad. Franklin's have distinct "half hood" of dark mottling on back of head (Laughing has only a little brown). Beware occas. subad. Franklin's with developing hood, white tail like ad., and all-dark wing tips (like imm.). If in doubt, note tail pattern. Laughing has complete black tail band, Franklin's has outermost pr. of tail feathers white (band incomplete).
Voice: Loud, strident, laughing *ka-ka-ka-ka-kaa-kaa-kaa* and shorter *ka-wick*.
Behavior: Reg. gathers in large flocks along coast. An opportunistic forager, pirating food from pelicans, dipping for fish, or scavenging from ocean or beach.
Status and habitat: Common transient, nonbreeding resident, and n winter resident along coast, occas. inland (Lago de Valencia); small no. of imms. and nonbreeders present yr-round. Rec. all months except Apr at Kaimare Chico, nw Zulia[108]. Very common breeding sp. May–Jul on offshore isls. of Las Aves, Los Roques, La Orchila, and other isls. On Trinidad most numerous Mar–Nov[175].

Range: To 400m. Carib. coast from Zulia to Delta Amacuro; once inland in Aragua (Maracay); Islas

Margarita, Las Aves, Los Roques, La Orchila, La Tortuga, La Blanquilla, Los Frailes, and Coche (*atricilla*). Breeds locally on Atlantic and Gulf coasts of N Amer. s to Belize, W Indies, Trinidad and Tobago; Pacific Mexico s to Sinaloa. Winters in s part of breeding range, Carib., Pacific coast s to n Chile, Atlantic s to mouth of the Amazon.

[Franklin's Gull]   PLATE 19
Larus pipixcan   Gaviota Rosada/Guanaguanare de Franklin
Identification: 14″ (36cm). 265g. Much like Laughing Gull. Bill and legs reddish (brightest in breeding season). Nonbreeding plumage: mantle gray, paler than in Laughing Gull; *black wing tips bordered white and separated from gray mantle by white band*; rear border of wing and rest of plumage white; *dusky black "half hood" from midcrown to nape and over sides of head to below eyes and ear coverts*. Breeding plumage: sim. but head black with conspic. white eyelids; breast tinged pink. Subad. (2d winter): like nonbreeding ad. but less white separating black wing tips (occas. white absent); tail with dusky subterminal band. Imm. (1st winter): mainly brownish gray with contrasting white rump and underparts; head with "half hood" like nonbreeding ad.; tail white with *partially complete* black subterminal band (outer pr. of feathers white).
Sim. species: Ad. from Laughing Gull by white on either side of black wing tips; nonbreeders by wing-tip pattern and conspic. partial hood; 1st-winter birds by more contrasty partial hood, whiter breast, and only partial black tail band.
Behavior: Notably social and may occur with Laughing Gull, its closest ally. Flight more graceful and buoyant than Laughing Gull.
Status and habitat: No specimens or photos. Sight recs. from Laguna de Unare and Laguna de Píritu, Anzoátegui (M. Lentino)[503]; and 2 breeding-plumage ads. seen (no photos) 31 May 1992 at Hato Cedral Apure (J. Kingery and B. Finch).

Range: To 200m. Carib. coast and inland. Breeds in interior plains of w N Amer.; winters mostly on Pacific coast of S Amer. from Guatemala to c Chile.

Sterna

Long, pointed wings; long, often deeply forked tail (except Gull-billed Tern); plumage and soft-part colors mostly very sim. and confusing; some are champion long-distance migrants. Most imm. *Sterna* terns, and some other terns, have a 1st-yr and 2d-yr plumage that is broadly equivalent to juv. and imm. plumages of gulls. Birds in these plumages are most likely to be seen on or near their wintering gds. (most imm. terns do not migrate northward their 1st yr, sometimes not the 2d summer). In general these plumages resemble those of the respective nonbreeding ads.[248,290]

Gull-billed Tern   PLATE 19
Sterna nilotica   Gaviota Pico Gordo
Identification: 13–14″ (33–36cm). 170g. "Whitebacked" tern with thick black bill and gull-like proportions; wings rather broad; *tail short, slightly forked*; legs black. Nonbreeding plumage: mostly white with very pale grayish white mantle, blackish area in front of eyes, and dusky ear patch. Breeding plumage: crown and nape jet black; no dusky ear patch. Imm.: may have obscure yellow bill tip. Juv.: also mottled dark brown on crown and back.
Sim. species: Palest Venez. tern; at a distance looks white, and gull-like tail only slightly forked. See Sandwich Tern.
Voice: Call a rasping *jeep* and *ra* note; also *chey-ráck*, repeatedly.
Behavior: In flight tends to carry bill forward, not downward in manner of most terns. Flies with smooth, buoyant strokes, more leisurely than other large terns. Swoops to surface for prey but seldom dives. Prey ranges in size from insects (incl. some captured in flight) to small crabs and other crustaceans and fish. Loafs with other terns, gulls, skimmers, etc., on sand spits.
Status and habitat: Fairly common to common yr-round transient or visitant on coast and locally inland, but nos. may vary markedly. Breeding unproved but likely. Specimens (May and Oct) from Barcelona, Anzoátegui, 1 in Mar from Laguna de Tacarigua, Miranda; also Aragua and Falcón. In varying nos. (sight recs.) in every month at Chichiriviche, Falcón (many observers), with counts ranging from 28 to 165 in same month in successive yr (P. Alden); resident all yr at Kaimare Chico, nw Zulia, with peak nos. Sep–Oct[353]. Inland at permanent water approx. Dec–Apr or May in w Apure, but disperses in rainy season. Shallow saline and brackish coastal waters, beaches, and lakes; inland on larger bodies of freshwater.

Range: Carib. coast from Zulia to Anzoátegui (prob. entire coast); inland in Falcón and Apure (*aranea*); doubtless elsewhere inland. Breeds locally on coast

of s US and w Mexico, in W Indies, w Ecuador, and from the Guianas to Argentina. Nonbreeders range s to Peru and more widely inland. Also breeds in Old World, wintering to s Africa and s Asia.
Note: Often placed in genus *Gelochelidon*.

Caspian Tern   PLATE 19
Sterna caspia   Gaviota Cáspica
Identification: 21–23″ (53–58cm). 655g. *Robust, broad-winged tern with short, slightly forked tail and very heavy red bill*; legs blackish. Nonbreeding plumage: slight bushy crown and nape black streaked with white; rest of upperparts and upper wing light gray, underparts and tail white. In flight primaries very broadly tipped black (esp. from below). Breeding plumage: crown all black (only on breeding gds.). Imm.: mottled brown back.
Sim. species: Large size and heavy red bill are the marks. Royal Tern has thinner orange bill, white forehead (all plumages), and is more crested. In flight note Royal's longer, deeply forked tail and mostly white under wing surface (Caspian has very broad black tips).
Voice: Deep, rough, almost croaking *karr-aa* or *karr*.
Behavior: In Venez. usually found singly in assoc. with other terns, esp. Royal and Gull-billed.
Status and habitat: Reg. visitant in small nos. First reported 20 Mar 1970 with 20 seen and photographed at Santa Cruz de Mara, Zulia; another same day at Laguna Sinamaica, Zulia; 3 more 30 Jan 1971 at Laguna Sinamaica (P. Alden); 5 specimens on 24 Oct 1975; present all yr with highest nos. Feb–Apr (max. of 225 in Mar 1978) at Kaimare Chico, nw Zulia[351]; scattered recs. elsewhere on shores of Lago de Maracaibo[351], at Boca de Uriche and Laguna de Unare, Anzoátegui (R. Webster; C. Parrish), and numerous sightings from e Falcón.

Range: Carib. coast from Zulia and Lago Maracaibo, and Falcón to Anzoátegui (sight). Breeds locally in N Amer. and Old World. Winters along coast of s US and Mexico sparingly s to Panama, W Indies, and n S Amer.

Royal Tern   PLATE 19
Sterna maxima   Tirra Canalera
Identification: 19–21″ (48–53cm). 450g. Large white tern with black crest. *Stout bill reddish orange to orange.* Nonbreeding plumage: mainly white with black hindcrown and nape (sometimes lightly streaked white); back and wings pale gray, outer primaries somewhat dusky from above; tail moderately

forked. In flight from below, wings mostly white, most of primaries tipped dusky showing only as dark trailing edge on wing. Breeding plumage: crown solid black (of very short duration and rarely seen on coast of Venez.).

Sim. species: Closely resembles Caspian Tern which differs in larger size, thicker, redder bill, dark forehead (never all white), and different underwing pattern (broad blackish tips from below).

Voice: Shrill *keer* or *keerlep*, unlike low, raspy note of Caspian Tern.

Behavior: Rather gull-like in flight, with slow, steady, rowing wing beats. Usually flies rather high and fishes, often singly, by plunging into sea. Dives from greater hts. than Caspian Tern. Otherwise quite sociable; breeds in colonies; rests on sandbars in varying-sized groups (cf. Caspian Tern) or with other terns and gulls.

Status and habitat: Fairly common visitant and nonbreeder along entire Carib. coast. Breeds on offshore isls. of Islas Las Aves (Barlovento; Sotavento) and Los Roques. First Falcón rec. is 1 seen 2 Aug 1969 at Chichiriviche (P. Alden), and in varying nos. in all months since then (many observers). Present all yr at Kaimare Chico, nw Zulia, with peak nos. Mar–Apr and Sep[108].

Range: Carib. coast from Zulia and Lago de Maracaibo e to Anzoátegui Sucre (recs.?) and Delta Amacuro; Islas Margarita, Las Aves (Barlovento and Sotavento), Los Roques, La Orchila, La Tortuga, La Blanquilla, and Los Hermanos (*maxima*). Breeds locally on both coasts of s US, Mexico, Dutch and Venez. isls. off coast of S Amer., and in e S Amer. s to Argentina (Chubut); also w Africa. Nonbreeding birds wander coastally to Peru and Argentina.

Sandwich Tern
(Includes Cayenne Tern)   PLATE 19
Sterna sandvicensis   Gaviota Patinegra

Identification: 15–16" (38–41cm). 190g. Med.-sized tern that *looks very white and has black slender bill tipped yellow* (yellow tip often difficult to see at a distance and occas. lacking); all-white tail with small white fork. Nonbreeding plumage: midcrown to nape black with some white streaking; slight crest on rearcrown; back and wings pale gray; outer primaries edged dusky. Breeding plumage: solid black cap briefly while breeding. Imm.: sim. but back and upper wing coverts mottled with black; primaries and tail dusky (*acuflavidus*). Or as above but bill all

lemon yellow (*eurygnatha*) or almost any variation between all yellow and all black with yellow tip.

Sim. species: Nearest is Gull-billed Tern. Up close note *slender, yellow-tipped bill*. At any distance note longer and much more deeply forked tail, slender frame, and narrow pointed wings which give a more buoyant, graceful flight (Gull-billed has stocky, gull-like proportions). At least during northern breeding period, Sandwich has outer 3–4 primaries black forming a wedge; Gull-billed has only tips of outer 6–8 dusky[248].

Behavior: Feeds by diving from fairly high up for small fish, and usually gregarious in little groups of its own or with other spp. of terns. Flight is strong, fast, and light. Often rests in groups that crowd together on sand spits, piers, or rocks. May fish well offshore.

Status and habitat: Uncommon to fairly common locally as visitant along coast and on all offshore isls. Seasonal movements poorly known. Specimens from Miranda and Monagas. Numerous coastal sight recs. virtually yr-round from e Falcón (Tucacas, Chichiriviche), Aragua, and Anzoátegui. Breeds on Islas Los Roques and Las Aves. Breeding colonies are mostly *eurygnatha* (Cayenne Tern), but both forms (*eurygnatha* and *acuflavidus*) breed on Soldado Rock off sw tip of Trinidad. Also rec. on Isla La Orchila.

Range: Carib. coast and offshore isls. Breeds locally on coast of se US, e Mexico, Belize, Virgin Isls., Lesser Antilles, and Curaçao to Trinidad; winters coastally from se US s to Peru, s Brazil, and Uruguay (*acuflavidus*); also breeds in Old World, wintering to Africa. Breeds in Puerto Rico, Virgin Isls., Netherlands Antilles, isls. off Venez., n Trinidad, French Guiana, se Brazil, and Argentina (*eurygnatha*); nonbreeders from coastal Colombia to Argentina.

Note: Cayenne Tern (*S. eurygnatha*), often regarded as a separate sp., interbreeds with Sandwich Tern in Virgin Isls., Bonaire, and Curaçao[286] off Suriname[253], and prob. elsewhere. Individuals showing intermed. bill characters are freq. seen in Venez. waters. Birds from Curaçao e are progressively more "yellow billed" (true Cayenne type), those w and n more typical of black-billed *sandvicensis* (Sandwich Tern).

Common Tern   PLATE 19
Sterna hirundo   Tirra Medio Cuchillo

Identification: 13–15" (33–38cm). 115g. Slender, med.-sized tern with long, forked tail. Ad. bill usually orange red tipped black (coral red only when breeding), but bill color variable, occas. blackish, and not

a reliable field mark. Legs reddish to dull orange. Nonbreeding plumage: forecrown white, hindcrown and nape black bordered on sides of head by narrow band of white below eyes; mantle and upper wing surface pearl gray; underparts gray white, rump and tail white, sides of tail edged blackish. In flight from above, outer *5–6 primaries to bend of wing blackish forming dark wedge*; from below, 5–6 primaries broadly tipped black forming V-shaped area enclosing a wedge of white (forms narrow black border on both leading and trailing edge of wing) visible in field; only small area of *translucence* on inner primaries. Breeding plumage: sim. but crown and nape solid black and bend of wing not dusky. In flight at any season note distinct shape (side profile) with wings approx. centered between long bill and head and relatively short tail. At rest folded wing reaches to tail tip.
Sim. species: Caution. Med.-sized *Sterna* terns are very difficult to identify and often not safely separable in nonbreeding season. Comparative experience, esp. with shapes, is essential. Much like Roseate Tern which differs in side profile (wings set forward with long tail trailing behind) as well as longer, much more deeply forked tail (beware of worn or growing feathers) which is *all white* (no dark edge). In flight Roseate looks more "white-winged" than Common Tern, showing, from above, black only on outer 3 (vs. 5–6) primaries (black distinct but narrow); in flight from below, leading edge of primaries is black but almost all of trailing edge is white and *very translucent*. At rest wings noticeably *shorter* than tail tips. Also see Arctic Tern (Note) and Sandwich Tern.
Behavior: Likes to gather in flocks to loaf or roost, and is apt to be seen in groups when foraging over schools of fish. Flight is buoyant with deep wing strokes and freq. hovering. Dives into water for fish.
Status and habitat: Breeds May–Jul on Islas Los Roques and Las Aves (Barlovento); uncommon along coasts of Zulia and Falcón, with only a small no. of recs.: 3 seen 2 Aug 1969 at Chichiriviche, Falcón, another 18 Jan 1974 (P. Alden); only Sep–Oct at Kaimare Chico, nw Zulia[108], but much commoner and with more recs. from Miranda e to Sucre and Delta Amacuro, e.g., ca. 20 seen 30 Nov and 10 seen 2 Dec 1980 at Boca de Uriche, Anzoátegui (R. Webster). Both long-distance migrants (banded individuals rec. Sep–May) and presum. residents of nearby offshore isls. occur on coast.

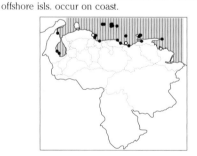

Range: Carib. coast from Lago de Maracaibo, Zulia, e to Sucre; Delta Amacuro[343]; isls. of Las Aves, Los

Roques, La Orchila, La Tortuga, and Margarita and Isla de Aves (*hirundo*). Breeds across s Canada and n US, locally in W Indies and on isls. off coast of Venez. Winters mostly on Carib. and Atlantic coasts of S. Amer., a few in W Indies and both coasts of C Amer. Also in Old World.
Note: Arctic Tern (*S. paradisaea*) is unrec. but could occur as a vagrant to Venez. waters. Breeds in Arctic; presum. winters s to antarctic waters by moving s along w African coast and Pacific coast of W Hemisphere. N movement presum. occurs along both coasts of S Amer. (reg. off Peru and Ecuador), but no Carib. recs. Breeding birds told by blood red bill (no black tip). At other times very like Common Tern but dark tail edge usually not as apparent; in flight from above, *upper wing almost uniform pale gray* (only leading primary and very narrow tips on trailing edge are dark); from below all flight feathers translucent admitting much light, and most of primaries (8–9) narrowly tipped black (vs. outer 3–5 with broad dark tips). In side profile in flight, wings are positioned far forward (not equidistant from front and back) and bill is short, giving round-headed look. Gray-tinged underparts (hard to see) separated from black crown by more distinct white facial stripe (mainly breeding season). At rest wings do not reach to tail tips, and legs very short[290].

Roseate Tern   PLATE 19
Sterna dougallii   Tirra Rosada
Identification: 15″ (38cm). 110g. Bill black (red at base only when breeding); feet orange (more red when breeding). Nonbreeding plumage: forecrown white spotted black; rearcrown and nape black; mantle pale gray (paler than Common Tern), underparts, rump, and *long, deeply forked tail pure white* (tail projects well beyond closed wing, and no blackish edge on outer tail feathers). Breeding plumage: crown and nape all black; breast tinged pinkish. In flight from above, most of wing light gray, *outer 3 primaries dusky* forming very narrow but sharply contrasting dark leading edge; in flight *from below, wing shows almost no dark tip at all* (except leading primary) *and trailing edge of wing entirely white and translucent*[290].
Sim. species: See Common and Arctic terns (latter in Note). Sandwich Tern, also very light colored, has slender black bill usually with yellow tip, black legs (not orange or red), and only moderately forked tail.
Voice: Flat, tinny, almost scraping *keer* or *keeer-karl* and thin *quit* over and over in flocks.
Behavior: Often in little groups of 3–12 or so, foraging well out to sea or resting on a buoy or flotsam, but the few coastal recs. are of solitary individuals, prob. mostly young birds.
Status and habitat: Breeding resident on Islas Los Roques and Las Aves; very scarce visitant along coast. Long-distance migrants may occur (?). Tends to forage farther offshore and over deeper water than Common Tern, hence scarcity of coastal recs.
Range: Carib. coast of Falcón and Anzoátegui (Bahía de Guanta, Pto. La Cruz); Islas Margarita, Las Aves, Los Roques, La Tortuga, and Coche (*dougallii*).

Breeds on Atlantic coast of N Amer., Dry Tortugas, off Belize and Honduras, Bahamas, W Indies, Netherlands Antilles, and a few isls. off Venez. Spends nonbreeding time at sea, mainly in e Carib. and adj. Atlantic coastal waters; a few to n Colombia and e Brazil.

Yellow-billed Tern
PLATE 19
Sterna superciliaris Gaviota Pico Amarillo
Identification: 10″ (25cm). 46g. Small tern. Rather slender, *pointed bill all yellow when breeding*; nonbreeders and imms. usually have dark bill tip and dark area at base of upper mandible (dark area larger in juv. and imm. birds). Legs dull yellow. Breeding plumage: above pale gray with *3 outer primaries (rarely 2–4) blackish* forming narrow black wedge on wing tip (prom. from above); crown, nape, and line through eyes black; forehead and short eyebrow projecting back to eyes white; underparts white. Nonbreeding plumage and imm.: head mainly whitish to gray streaked black on nape and around eyes; upperparts tinged and smudged brownish, bend of wing mottled dusky; usually more than 3 outer primaries dark. Juv.: head whitish with dusky ear coverts and brownish gray spotting on back.
Sim. species: Closely resembles Least Tern; the two may overlap to a limited extent along Carib. coast. Best separated by bill differences: when breeding both have yellow bills but Least has dark bill tip; in other ages and plumages Least has all-dark bill; Yellow-billed has yellow bill with dark tip and dark base on upper mandible.
Voice: In flight a nasal *yank* and reedy, blurred *tee-le-le*.
Behavior: Scattered individuals, prs., or small parties, seldom exceeding 12 birds, dive from moderate hts., mostly for small fish which are taken from surface or during shallow splash. Not as social as larger terns. Flight is quick with rapid wing beats and freq. hovering. Nests during low water (dry season) on sandbars in larger rivers such as Ríos Meta and Orinoco; 2 dark brown eggs with blackish markings[141].
Status and habitat: Widespread resident on river systems and freshwater lakes throughout. Rare or infreq. along coast: specimens from coast of Zulia (Lago de Maracaibo), Aragua (Turiamo), and Miranda (Laguna de Tacarigua) are mostly from saltwater lagoons or bays separated or somewhat apart from open seacoast. Generally less numerous than Large-billed Tern with which it shares sim. mostly inland distrib.

Range: Virtually throughout (no recs. from Lara or Falcón) s to s Amazonas and n and c Bolívar; Isla Margarita. E Colombia and the Guianas to n Argentina and Uruguay. Trinidad.

Least Tern
PLATE 19
Sterna antillarum Gaviota Filico
Identification: 9″ (23cm). 45g. Small marine tern. Very sim. to Yellow-billed Tern, differing as follows: overall slightly smaller; *bill even more slender and usually all dusky* (yellow tipped blackish only for short period when breeding); *only outer 2 (rarely 3) primaries blackish* (vs. 3 in Yellow-billed Tern); tail proportionately longer and more deeply forked in fresh plumage. Imm.: sim. but forewing heavily mottled blackish, primaries extensively black from bend of wing to tip.
Sim. species: See Yellow-billed Tern.
Voice: Shrill *kip-kip-kip* and grating *krid-ick, krid-ick*.
Behavior: Like other small terns, occurs alone or in small, loosely assoc. groups. Plunges from moderate hts. for small fish.
Status and habitat: Uncommon migrant from N Amer. to offshore isls. (specimens Apr, May, Jul, and Oct); also a breeding resident on at least 2 offshore isls. Rare and local on coast with only 1 rec., none inland in Venez. (unlike N Amer.). Sight recs. along coast should be confirmed by photos because of great similarity to Yellow-billed Tern.

Range: Carib. coast of Zulia (Lago de Maracaibo), Falcón, Aragua (Turiamo), and Anzoátegui (Barcelona); Delta Amacuro[343]; breeds on Islas Margarita and Los Roques; recorded on Las Aves, La Orchila, La Tortuga, and Coche (prob. *antillarum* and *athalassos*). Breeds from s US to Mexico, Carib. (locally), Netherlands Antilles; prob. Trinidad; winters s coastally to e Brazil; rarely Hawaii and Canada.
Note: Taxonomy follows AOU[10].

Pantropical terns: Brown Noddy (upper left), Sooty Tern (upper right), Black Noddy (lower left), Bridled Tern (lower right)

Bridled Tern

Illus. above

Sterna anaethetus   Gaviota Llorona

Identification: 14″ (36cm). 98g. Slender black bill and black legs. *Above grayish brown*, primaries slightly darker and *tail decidedly paler than upperparts* (looks almost whitish), deeply forked *outer tail feathers white*; forehead and short eyestripe white; black cap and black stripe through eye merge behind eye; narrow white nuchal collar and white underparts. Nonbreeding ad.: streaked white on crown and back; forecrown white. Imm.: crown grayish brown streaked and smudged white; prom. black stripe through eye; upperparts dark brown scaled whitish; below dull white.

Sim. species: Closely resembles Sooty Tern. Bridled's best marks are dark grayish (not sooty) back, *pale tail contrasting with back*, and broader white edges on tail. Up close or in hand note longer white eyestripe and white nuchal collar (both very hard to verify in field). Imm. Sooty Tern is all dark (not white) below.

Voice: Locally called *Llorona* ("cry baby"), a reference to its low-pitched, often-repeated call[403].

Behavior: Occurs singly, in prs., or in small to moderate-sized groups. Often rests on pieces of driftwood or flotsam in drift lines, and forages more by dipping to surface for small fish and squid than by diving. Nest a scrape on gd.; often partially hidden but near water; 1 egg.

Status and habitat: Fairly common but irreg. visitant along coast; breeds Feb–Jun on Islas Las Aves and Los Roques and prob. present most of yr around offshore isls. In early Mar 1966 there were an estimated 1000 nests on Islas Las Aves[329]. First sight recs. (Apr–Jul) on coastal Aragua incl. 23 seen 25 Apr 1980 on islet at entrance to Ocumare Bay (C. Parrish) and 30 at same loc. 29 Apr 1980 (C. Parrish and A. Altman); 1st for Miranda are 40 or more off Cabo Codera, 31 Jul 1983 (C. Parrish). Numerous sightings off coast of Aragua subsequently. When not breeding forages mainly over deeper, pelagic waters but closer to shore than Sooty Tern.

Range: Carib. coast in Falcón (Cayo Borracho; Chichiriviche), Aragua (sight), Distr. Federal (La Guaira), Miranda (sight); offshore isls. of Las Aves, Los Roques, La Blanquilla, La Tortuga, Los Testigos, and Coche (*recognita*). Breeds locally on many isls. in tropical oceans incl. W Indies, off Mexico, Costa Rica, Colombia, and possibly Panama; also Netherlands Antilles (Aruba and Curaçao); Trinidad. Ranges widely near coasts and at sea when not breeding.

Sooty Tern

Illus. above, PLATE 19

Sterna fuscata   Gaviota de Veras

Identification: 16″ (41cm). 180g. Contrastingly patterned "black-and-white" tern. *Above mainly black* incl. tail; underparts white; white forehead and eyebrow just reach eyes (useful mainly in hand); tail deeply forked, outer feather *narrowly edged white*; bill and feet black. Imm.: *mainly dusky brown*, belly dirty white; upperparts and upper wing coverts scaled and barred white, this lost with wear.

Sim. species: Much like Bridled Tern but blacker above, tail same color as back, tail edges only narrowly white. Bridled's white nuchal collar and longer eyestripe are useful marks in hand or up very close. Imm. is only all-dark, fork-tailed tern. Brown Noddy has long, wedge-shaped tail.

Voice: Noisy day and night; loud *kay-arak* or *wide-a-wake*, the latter an old sailor's name.

Behavior: Pelagic and often wanders far from breeding colonies. Flight sim. to Bridled Tern, more buoyant than Black Tern. Typically flies low and fairly near surface of water, splashing for small fish.

Status and habitat: Breeds on offshore isls. of Los Roques, Los Hermanos (Morro Fondeadero, La Horquilla), Las Aves, and La Orchila, then disperses widely at sea. In early 1950s there were an estimated 500,000–1,000,000 breeding birds (mostly Sooty Terns) in mid Apr at Isla de Aves[836]. In early Mar 1966 there were only ca. 4000–5000 Sooty Tern nests[329]. Large nos. also on La Orchila[403]. Rare visitant on coast (no specimens) with 2 sight recs.: 20 or more seen 2 Jul 1976 near Ocumare de la Costa, Aragua (B. Zonfrillo and others); several seen 31 Jul 1983 off Cabo Codera, Miranda (C. Parrish). Away from breeding colonies found mostly over deep pelagic waters.

Range: Carib. coast off Aragua and Miranda (sight); most offshore isls. incl. Margarita, Las Aves, Los Roques, La Orchila, and Los Hermanos and Isla de Aves (*fuscata*). Breeds in W Indies, Panama (?), Trinidad, Little Tobago, Dry Tortugas off Florida, and locally almost worldwide in tropical and subtropical waters; wanders widely at sea when not breeding.

Anous

All-dark plumage with pale cap; long, slender bill; wedge-shaped tail with small notch; more pelagic than *Sterna*.

Brown Noddy   Illus. p. 312, PLATE 19
Anous stolidus   Tiñosa

Identification: 15–16" (38–41cm). 185g. Med.-sized dark tern; long slender black bill; black legs. Entirely *plain brown* with *conspic. white forehead and forecrown* fading to gray on midcrown and nape and merging smoothly onto brown of back; white of forehead sharply separated from black lores; flight feathers and long wedge-shaped tail dark brown (darker than rest of plumage) imparting *2-toned look in flight*. Juv.: all dark brown (incl. cap); white feather tips and linelike white streaking on upperparts.

Sim. species: See very sim. Black Noddy.

Voice: Guttural *kaark*.

Behavior: Gregarious and often with other terns at sea. Flight is strong and fast but erratic, heavier, and less graceful than in other med.-sized terns. Swims

well and often settles on water or flotsam. Usually flies close to surface, hovers, then splashes or swoops for small fish (esp. sardines and anchovies), but seldom dives and submerges. Often active at night. Nods and bows extensively during courtship, hence name. Nests in large colonies; nests of sticks, shells, seaweed, etc., are mostly on gd. or in low fork of tree; 1 pale buff egg spotted darker brown[175].

Status and habitat: Common, nesting in large nos. Feb–Jul on many offshore isls. and recorded, at least seasonally, around most Venez. isls. Very small nos. nesting in mid Apr 1954 on Isla de Aves[836], but most numerous breeder there in 1967 with 10,000–12,000 nests[329]. Ranges widely at sea when not nesting. An infreq. visitant to coast. One juv. taken 2 Jul 1976 and an ad. 26 Oct 1978, both at Kaimare Chico, nw Zulia[354], are 1st mainland Venez. recs.; ca. 10 seen 31 Jul 1983 off Cabo Codera, Miranda (C. Parrish); also reported off La Vela and Cayo Sal, Falcón; and La Guira, Dist. Federal.

Range: Carib. coast and offshore isls.; breeds on Islas Los Roques, Las Aves (Barlovento; Sotavento), Los Hermanos (Morro Fondeadero, La Horquilla), and Isla de Aves; rec. off Margarita, Los Testigos, and La Orchila; sight at Los Monjes (*stolidus*). Breeds in Dry Tortugas off s Florida and locally on isls. from Belize to Curaçao, Trinidad, and Suriname; also widely elsewhere in tropical oceans. Disperses far at sea when not breeding.

Black Noddy   Illus. p. 312
Anous minutus   Tiñosa Chocora

Identification: 13–14" (33–36cm). 110g. Very sim. to Brown Noddy. Mostly *dark brown* with white cap sharply separated from black lores but fading to gray on nape; flight feathers and rather long wedge-shaped tail *concolor with rest of plumage*.

Sim. species: Very sim. to Brown Noddy and not always easily distinguished. Comparative experience or direct comparison very helpful. Differs from Brown Noddy by longer, thinner bill that is slightly decurved and more extensive white cap extending to nape. In flight underwings uniform with rest of plumage. Other points to ponder, under favorable conditions, are overall somewhat darker plumage; loral line separation (between white cap and black lores) ruler straight in Black Noddy (usually S-curved in Brown); overall smaller size (in direct comparison); more slender proportions; and white of head more sharply defined. In flight Brown Noddy a little broader winged.

Behavior: As in Brown Noddy.

Status and habitat: Fewer recs. than for previous sp.; 4 taken 18 Apr 1962 at Los Roques (Isla Sarquí); 3 taken at Los Roques (Isla Bequevé) in May and Jul were breeding among a large colony of Brown Noddies[486]. Only definite coastal rec. is 1 ♂ collected 6 Nov 1974 off Cuyagua, Aragua.

Range: Carib coast (Aragua); offshore isls. of Las Aves, Los Roques, and Isla de Aves (*americanus*). Breeds locally in Carib., tropical Atlantic and Pacific; disperses at sea when not breeding.

Note: Some incl. Lesser Noddy (*A. tenuirostris*) of Indian Ocean with present sp.

Black Tern
PLATE 19

Chlidonias niger   Gaviota Negra

Identification: 9–10″ (23–25cm). 58g. Small tern with notched tail. Bill and legs black. Breeding plumage: above dark gray; *head and underparts black* with white under wing and under tail coverts. Nonbreeding ad.: above gray; head, nuchal collar, and underparts white with *dusky patch on back of head and smaller patch around eyes and on ear coverts*. Juv.: like nonbreeding birds but upper wing surface and back strongly mottled dusky; sides of chest smudged dusky. 1st winter: sim. to juv. but back paler gray like nonbreeding ad; white below. Confusing birds in molt with pied or blotched black and gray plumage are commonly seen during summer months.

Sim. species: Unmistakable in breeding plumage. Others best recognized by small size, notched tail, and white nuchal collar bordering black rearcap.

Voice: Sharp *keep* or *kee-ip*.

Behavior: Gregarious and often in large flocks when not breeding. Flies with erratic fluttery flight like a nighthawk, with many pauses and dips, as swoops to surface of water for small fish, but rarely plunges.

Status and habitat: Vagrant or erratic visitor to mudflats, beaches, and coastal lagoons: known from Isla

Coche off coast of Sucre, 1 ad. collected 23 Sep 1975 at Kaimare Chico, nw Zulia[354] and in Falcón. Seen irreg. throughout yr at Kaimare Chico, Zulia, peak nos. Jul–Oct[108]; scattered recs. off Paraguaná Pen. (Salinas del Infierno), Falcón (C. Parrish); at Chichiriviche, Falcón, incl. 4 breeding-plumage ads. seen 2 Aug 1969, ca. 45 seen 20 Oct 1971, and 55 seen 15 Jan 1976 (P. Alden); and Cayo Sal, e Falcón (C. Parrish).

Range: Carib. coast of Zulia, Falcón, and Sucre; Isla Coche off Margarita (*surinamensis*); doubtless entire coast. Breeds in N Amer. and Europe; N Amer. birds winter s on Pacific coast to Peru (accidental in Chile), on Carib. coast s to Suriname.

Large-billed Tern
PLATE 19

Phaetusa simplex   Guanaguanare Fluvial

Identification: 15″ (38cm). 240g. Large river tern with flashy wing pattern and *thick yellow bill*. Legs lemon yellow. Breeding plumage: crown black, mantle and notched tail dark gray, narrow frontlet and underparts white. In flight primaries and primary coverts black *contrasting with conspic. white triangular area on secondaries extending forward to carpal area*. Nonbreeding plumage: sim. but forehead and crown mottled with white.

Sim. species: Black and white wing pattern and heavy, pointed, yellow bill are distinctive.

Voice: Often noisy. A loud, reedy *kaay-rak* and other sim. notes.

Behavior: A boldly patterned tern usually seen flying fairly high up and down rivers or over lagoons. Occurs alone or more often in loosely assoc. groups when foraging. Gathers in varying-sized groups to rest or roost on river sandbars, often with cormorants, skimmers, and other terns. Dives from moderate hts. to pick small fish from surface of water. Nests in colonies, often mixed with skimmers, Yellow-billed Terns, and Sand-colored Nighthawks, on river sandbars; 2 olive brown eggs, blotched and spotted darker, on scrape in sand. In mid. Orinoco breeds Dec–Feb[115].

Status and habitat: Fairly common breeding resident along Orinoco, most of its larger tributaries, and on lagoons in llanos; less numerous or scarce on blackwater rivers (fewer fish). Erratic visitant to coast (where does not breed) with recs. scattered throughout yr, but more reg. and in greater nos. during rainy months of May–Oct at Chichiriviche, Falcón; May–Jul and Sep at Kaimare Chico, nw Zulia[108]. Inland wanders seasonally, but movements not docu-

Black Skimmer

mented. A sp. in decline because of molestation of breeding colonies.

Range: To ca. 400m. Large rivers and estuaries throughout. Lago de Maracaibo, Río Orinoco and its tributaries to vicinity of Pto. Ayacucho, Amazonas s to San Carlos de Río Negro (sight, 20 Dec 1979—C. Parrish); n Bolívar in lower Río Caura (s to La Prisión) and Río Paragua to Salto Arebuchi; Isla Margarita (*simplex*). C Panama (rare), n Colombia, and generally e of Andes s to c Argentina; w Ecuador.

Rynchops

Long, laterally compressed, knifelike bill; lower mandible longer than upper; eyes dark with slit, catlike pupils; resemble long-winged terns; 3 spp. worldwide.

Black Skimmer

Illus. above, PLATE 19

Rynchops niger Pico de Tijera

Identification: 16–18" (41–46cm). ♂ 325g, ♀ 235g. *Long bladelike bill bright red tipped black*; lower mandible longer than upper. Legs very short. Plumage *black above*; forehead, trailing edge of wing, and *underparts white*; tail slightly forked, mostly dark gray with little or no white edging (*cinerascens*). Or central feathers light gray broadly edged white (n migrant *niger*). Nonbreeding ads.: bill duller; ill-defined whitish nuchal collar. Imm.: like ad. but browner and above somewhat streaked or scaled with white.

Voice: In flight occas. a nasal barking *CAaa*.

Behavior: Sociable and mostly seen in prs. or groups up to ca. 20, occas. more. Often loafs with gulls and terns on sandbars during day. Primarily nocturnal when feeding but also active at dawn and dusk and occas. for brief periods during day. When foraging flies low, slicing water surface with bill as it courses back and forth, and snaps up small fish and inverte-

brates the instant bill touches them. Flight unusually buoyant and agile. Breeds in loose groups on sandbars during low water (dry season).

Status and habitat: Widespread and fairly common on large rivers, lagoons, and seacoast. Seasonal movements not documented; present Feb–May and Oct–Nov at Hato Masaguaral, Guárico[734]. N migrant recorded once, 14 Jan 1904 in Golfo de Cariaco, Sucre[53]; prob. overlooked. First Falcón rec., ca. 200 seen 2 Aug 1969, Chichiriviche (P. Alden).

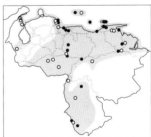

Range: To 500m (sight to 550m in n Monagas). Carib. coast from Zulia to Delta Amacuro; inland throughout incl. entire Orinoco, Río Meta, Río Apure, and most large tributaries; Islas Los Roques, La Orchila (sight), La Tortuga, and Margarita (*cinerascens*). Gulf of Cariaco, Sucre (n migrant *niger*); no recs. in se Bolívar. N birds breed on se coasts of US, both coasts of Mexico s to Guatemala; winter southward. S races breed or wander over coasts and interior rivers of most of S Amer.; on Pacific coast from Ecuador to Chile.

Note: By some placed in separate family, Rynchopidae.

COLUMBIFORMES

Columbidae: Pigeons and Doves
Palomas y Tortolitas

The Columbidae is a worldwide family of old ancestry. The family has no close relatives, and Old and New World groups are not especially closely related. In Venezuela this family is represented by both terrestrial and arboreal species in almost all major habitats. Pigeons and doves are typically fast-flying birds with plump bodies, small heads, weak bills, and bare skin across the cere. The plumpness is due primarily to large flight muscles which comprise 31 to 44% of the total body mass. In general the name "pigeon" is applied to large species, "dove" to smaller species, but popular usage is inconsistent. In all New World species the plumage is soft, dense, and mostly subdued shades of brown or gray, sometimes with a metallic gloss on the head, neck, or back. Sexes are similar in most species except ground-doves. Pigeons and doves include both arboreal and terrestrial species, but almost all of them feed mostly on fruits and seeds. Their cooing calls are not especially varied, but advertising songs are more complex than calls. Differences in pitch, speed, rhythm, and tone among the species' vocalizations are useful in identification. Almost all species form pairs for breeding; nests are frail platforms in trees or bushes, or little scrapes on the ground, usually holding only 1–2 eggs. The young at first are fed a secretion regurgitated from the crop and known as "pigeon milk."

Columba

Arboreal; largest, heaviest members of family in New World; broad squarish to rounded tail; upper part of tarsus feathered; ♂♂ slightly larger than ♀♀.

Rock Pigeon
Columba livia   Paloma Doméstica
Identification: 12″ (30.5cm). 300g. *Common feral pigeon* of urban areas. Plumage highly variable but always with *white rump and black tail tip*. Cere grayish white; eyes orangish; legs dull pink. Generally dark gray glossed green and purple on neck, wings with 2 broad bars. Plumage often with large irreg.-shaped areas of white, rusty, black, or brown.
Voice: Song a low, moaning *uu, cu-cuu, cuUUUuua.*
Behavior: This non-native sp. is confined mostly to cities and towns, and groups are often seen on gd. in parks, plazas, streets, and outdoor food markets, or in flocks flying overhead. Readily assoc. with domesticated pigeons which are often allowed to fly free during day. Feed on seeds and edible scraps. Perch and nest on buildings and other human-made structures. Frail stick platform nest on ledge of building, church, bridge, warehouse, etc.
Status and habitat: Widespread in vicinity of people, mainly in urban areas. Pops. range from completely feral to domesticated.

Range: To ca. 3000m. Widespread n of Orinoco; locally in towns s of Orinoco. Native to Eurasia and n Africa; now worldwide as a commensal of humans.
Note: Often called Rock Dove.

Band-tailed Pigeon   PLATE 20
Columba fasciata   Paloma Gargantilla
Identification: 14″ (36cm). 315g. *Bill, eyes, and legs yellow.* Large, broad-tailed, highland pigeon. Head and underparts vinaceous gray, nape glossed greenish, *band on nape white*, back and wings smoky brown; rump gray, tail *2-toned, dusky at base, rest light gray.* ♀: duller vinaceous below. Or sim. but above brown glossed green, underparts darker (*roraimae*).
Sim. species: Only highland pigeon normally found in flocks. See Ruddy Pigeon.
Voice: Deep, mellow cooing, *co' oooh, co' oooh . . .* (2–several times); occas. a grating or croaking *grrrak.*
Behavior: Prs. or fast-flying flocks of varying size are often seen perched on high snags or in fruiting trees at high els. in Andes. Eat acorns (in N and C Amer.) and small fruits and are normally somewhat wary. In display solitary ♂♂ fly out in wide semicircles over mt. forest and alternate quick shallow wing beats with short glides while holding wings up in a V. Nest a frail stick platform high in tree; 2 creamy white eggs[750].
Status and habitat: Locally common resident and short-distance migrant in humid montane forest, clearings with scattered large trees, and scrubby slopes. Shows marked seasonal movements and may move far above or below "normal" range. Deforestation has greatly reduced nos.

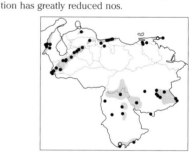

Range: 900–3200m n of Orinoco; 900–2000m s of Orinoco. Sierra de Perijá, Zulia, Andes, mts. of Falcón (Sierra de San Luis), Yaracuy, and n cordilleras from Carabobo e to Sucre and n Monagas (*albilinea*); tepuis of Amazonas and Bolívar (*roraimae*). W N Amer. to w Panama; Colombia s in Andes to nw Argentina; tepuis of nw Brazil and Guyana.

[White-crowned Pigeon]
Columba leucocephala   Paloma Cabeciblanca
Identification: 13.5″ (34cm). 260g. Eyes whitish; orbital skin white; bill dusky red with white tip; legs red. A large, square-tailed pigeon. Plumage *slaty black with blue gray tinge*; *crown snowy white*, narrow band on hindcrown black (inconspic.), nape glossed iridescent green. ♀: crown duller. Juv.: crown grayish brown.

Sim. species: No other pigeon has "snow" cap.
Voice: Slow, deep 2- or 3-parted *coo-curoo-coo* or
coo-croo.
Behavior: In Antilles and keys of s Florida generally
in varying-sized flocks that nest in mangroves but
commute inland to feed on fruit. A strong flier that
easily moves between isls. in Carib.
Status and habitat: Known from 1 bird captured in
Oct on Isla de Aves[224]. Vagrant.
Range: Isla de Aves. S Florida, Bahamas, Greater and
Lesser Antilles s to St. Lucia, locally on isls. off coast
of C Amer. s to Panama, occas. on mainland from
Quintana Roo, Mexico, to w Panama.

Scaled Pigeon   PLATE 20
Columba speciosa   Paloma Guacoa
Identification: 12.5″ (32cm). 290g. Eyes white; narrow orbital ring red; *bill red tipped white*. Most colorful pigeon in Amer. tropics. Crown dusky, sides of
head, neck, and underparts whitish *boldly and
densely scaled dusky*, belly less heavily scaled, under
tail coverts white; *back and wings glossy reddish
chestnut*, wings and tail dusky. ♀: sim. but back and
wing coverts duller.
Sim. species: See Pale-vented Pigeon which is remarkably sim. in flight.
Voice: Song a low-pitched, very slow, drowsy *coo-
OOOOaa cook, cooOOOOaa cook, cooOOOOaa
cook* . . . (ca. 4 phrases), 1st note halting; repeated
every 15–30 sec.; a guttural purring *coo* much like
other *Columba*.
Behavior: Notably solitary, usually seen perched
alone or in prs. in treetops or flying in a long straight
course over open areas. Occas. in parties of 3–4,
rarely more (unlike Pale-vented Pigeon) at fruit trees.
Feeds mostly on small fruits and berries in forest canopy and usually wary. Nest a flimsy stick platform
1–18m up; 1 white egg[640].
Status and habitat: Fairly common resident in humid
forest borders, tall old regrowth forest, and gallery forest. Often seen in flight high over savanna and open
country as it commutes between wooded areas. Also
sometimes locally inside forest (when Plumbeous Pigeon is absent?). Local or seasonal movements need
documentation. Distrib. somewhat patchy.

Range: To 1400m n of Orinoco; to 950m s of Orinoco. Maracaibo Basin, Zulia, e to nw Lara (Cerro El
Cogollal); e base of Andes in e Táchira; n cordilleras
from Carabobo and Miranda e to Sucre and Monagas; throughout Amazonas and Bolívar. S Mexico to
w Ecuador, n Argentina, and s Brazil.

Scaly-naped Pigeon
Columba squamosa   Paloma Isleña
Identification: 14″ (36cm). 250g. Eyes red; bill yellow
with red base; prom. red eyering. *Large dark pigeon.*
Above dark blue gray, nape and mantle pinkish lilac
heavily scaled maroon, below blue gray, chest dark
vinaceous. Legs unusually large and strong.
Sim. species: Only on offshore isls. Looks all dark at
a distance.
Voice: Song an emphatic *cruu, cruu-cru-cruuu*, 1st syllable brief, 4th strongest and drawn out; last 3 sound
like *who are yoou!*[520]; overall much like song of
White-crowned Pigeon[148].
Behavior: Single birds or small flocks fly high over
forest or open areas and feed opportunistically, often
on gd. Nest Mar–Jun, in trees, palm, bromeliad; apparently on gd. on uninhabited Carib. isls.[520]
Status and habitat: Known from a few taken in Sep
and Oct from Islas Los Frailes and Los Testigos[486].
Elsewhere in Carib. in mt. forests, lowlands, and locally in towns and villages. Reported from Islas Los
Roques[347] without documentation.

Range: To 100m. Islas Los Frailes and Los Testigos;
Los Roques(?)[347]. Cuba to Curaçao and Bonaire (formerly Aruba) and Lesser Antilles.

Bare-eyed Pigeon   PLATE 20
Columba corensis   Paloma Ala Blanca
Identification: 13.5″ (34cm). Large pale pigeon of
arid regions. Eyes yellowish brown; *large blue ocular
ring* (wears "goggles") surrounded by narrow black
ring. Bill pinkish flesh (bill paler—♀). *Prom. white
wing patches show in flight*. Above sandy brown,
back of neck pale gray turning pink on mantle and
finely scaled black; lower back and rump pale gray;
lower edge of wing coverts and inner secondaries
white *forming white line* at rest, rest of flight feathers
dusky; head and underparts pale vinaceous, belly
and crissum white.
Sim. species: Only pigeon with conspic. white wing
patches. See Pale-vented Pigeon.
Voice: Song a slow pigeonlike *coooo, chuck-chuk,
cooouu*, mid. notes brief.
Behavior: A rather wary pigeon that occur in prs.
when breeding but otherwise gathers in small to
large flocks of its own to loaf, feed, or roost (100s
may gather at roosts). Primarily arboreal and most
often seen in flight or when perched in open atop a
large columnar cactus or on a bare branch. Feeds
on a variety of seeds and berries, incl. ovaries or
imm. seeds of *Agave*. In Anzoátegui mostly prs.

Dec–Mar, fledglings mid Apr–late Jul[186]. On Curaçao and Bonaire nests alone in trees, shrubs, and esp. mangroves[773].
Status and habitat: Uncommon to locally common resident in desert scrub, esp. with columnar cactus; also mangroves and dry, disturbed, or abused semiopen brushland. Shows seasonal movements in desert scrub s of Coro and in mangroves at Chichiriviche; often scarce Dec–Mar but numerous (in prs.) May–Jul. Large roosting flocks (unpredictable) have been seen in Feb w of Chichiriviche. Some wandering to n llanos occurs, with sightings at Camatagua, s Aragua, 9 Feb 1978 (P. Alden); El Sombrero, ne Guárico, sight 18 Apr 1992 (P. Boesman); 1 in Nov 1978 at Hato Masaguaral, sw Guárico[734]. Present yr-round in ne Anzoátegui with increasingly large flocks Mar–Nov[187]. Reported to reg. cross between Netherlands Antilles and Venez. coast[148].

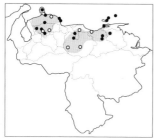

Range: To 400m. Disjunct. C and e Falcón and Lara; s Aragua (sight) s to c Guárico; n Anzoátegui to w Sucre and Monagas (s to Caicara); Islas Margarita, Los Frailes, Los Testigos. Ne Colombia; Netherlands Antilles.

Pale-vented Pigeon
PLATE 20

Columba cayennensis   Paloma Colorada
Identification: 12.5″ (32cm). 230g. *Eyes* and eyering *bright red*, bill black. Crown glossed light green, otherwise upperparts brownish vinaceous with *conspic. vinaceous rufous shoulders and mantle*; rump gray, underparts pinkish vinaceous, whitish on throat and turning *white on lower underparts*. Legs and feet pinkish. Or sim. but overall slightly darker, lower underparts grayish (*cayennensis*).
Sim. species: In flight resembles Scaled Pigeon, also with rufous shoulders and pale lower underparts, but differs in scaly plumage, red bill with white tip, and solitary habits (Pale-vented often in flocks).
Voice: Song slow and drowsy, a low, mournful cooing (3–8 phrases), *ooouu . . co-woo, tu-cooo, tu-cooo*, sometimes followed by display flights.
Behavior: Large, conspic. pigeon. May occur alone or in prs. but likes to gather in sizable groups high in trees along riverbanks or around waterholes, esp. in late afternoon where it descends to bare shore to drink. Displaying ♂♂ fly in wide semicircles and periodically sail with wings held up stiffly in a V. In lowlands this and Scaled Pigeon are only pigeons likely to be seen flying in open well away from forest. Along Orinoco small to large flocks roost on river

isls. Seeds and small fruits of *Byrsonima, Solanum,* and *Trema* and melastome berries reported in diet[148]. Mar–Aug breeding, w Guárico and Anzoátegui[186,734]; nest a frail twig platform in tangle, spiny palm, etc., a few meters up; 1 white egg[789].
Status and habitat: Common and widespread resident along forest borders, riverbanks, gallery forest, and partially or mostly open areas with scattered trees. Moist to humid areas; over much of country one of commonest and most freq. seen pigeons. Esp. numerous in llanos but minimal overlap with Bare-eyed Pigeon.

Range: To 1400m n of Orinoco (mostly below 800m); to 1300m s of Orinoco. Generally n (except arid nw) and s of Orinoco (*andersoni*); e Bolívar (cayennensis?). S Mexico to n Argentina, Uruguay, and se Brazil.

Ruddy Pigeon
PLATE 20

Columba subvinacea   Paloma Morada
Identification: 11.5″ (29cm). 155g. *Short* black bill; *eyes red. Uniformly dark.* Above ruddy brown tinged vinaceous, head and underparts dull rufous vinaceous; under wing coverts and most of flight feathers (from below) rufous. Or above darker smoky purple brown; head and underparts purplish vinaceous; bill even shorter (*purpureotincta*).
Sim. species: Med.-sized, dark, forest pigeon, easily confused with Plumbeous Pigeon which bulks larger and is a little more 2-toned (darker above, paler below), but s of Orinoco the two are almost indistinguishable. Plumbeous Pigeon tends to be grayish, not ruddy. Best clues are *vocal* (listen to pitch) and, up close, note *eye color* (yellow in Plumbeous Pigeon). In open areas and along riverbanks see Pale-vented and Scaled pigeons.
Voice: Song, more or less sim. in all areas, resembles that of Plumbeous Pigeon but faster and ca. 1 octave higher in pitch. Typically a 4-noted whistle, *what do-yoóou know?* (or *Hit the FOUL pole!*), 3d syllable emphasized and longer. In a few areas (e.g., e Bolívar) rhythm varies slightly with last syllables truncated, i.e., *wut wood-woóhoo.* Also a loud, purring *purrr-r-r-r*, sim. to other *Columba.*
Behavior: A forest pigeon usually seen alone or in prs. inside canopy. Often quite vocal and territorial but otherwise rather inconspic. Feeds mostly on small fruit (esp. *Ficus*) and seeds of trees, epiphytes, mistletoe, and *Cecropia* catkins in forest canopy. Generally does not perch in open (occas. on high open branches at forest edge) and not apt to be seen fly-

ing across large open areas. In Costa Rica, frail loosely stacked twig platform in fork of branch 5m up at forest edge; 1 white egg[706].

Status and habitat: Fairly common resident in a wide range of moist to wet lowland and premontane (mt) forests and tall second growth. N of Orinoco mainly in foothill and montane regions; s of Orinoco also in lowlands, and most numerous in areas with slightly less rainfall than those preferred by Plumbeous Pigeon. Largely sedentary; some seasonal, postbreeding downslope movements may occur.

Range: To 2200m n of Orinoco; to 1100m s of Orinoco. Sierra de Perijá, Zulia, both slopes of Andes from Táchira to nw Lara at Cerro El Cerrón (no recs. in w and c Falcón or Yaracuy); n cordilleras from Carabobo e to Miranda (*zuliae*); Sucre and n Monagas (*peninsularis*); Delta Amacuro and throughout Amazonas and Bolívar (*purpureotincta*). Costa Rica to n Bolivia and s Brazil.

Plumbeous Pigeon
Columba plumbea   Paloma Plomiza

Identification: 13.5″ (34cm). 180g. Bill black; *eyes yellowish white to yellowish* (sometimes reddish brown—young?); narrow eyering red. *Large, dark, forest pigeon.* Above dull dark brown vaguely tinged olive; head and *underparts paler*, pinkish vinaceous, darkest on crown, chest, and crissum. Under wing coverts and flight feathers (from below) gray. Or sim. but head and underparts dark putty brown below with no pink tones (*delicata*).

Sim. species: See very sim. Ruddy Pigeon. Best points are differences in size, eye color, and voice.

Voice: Unlike in Ruddy Pigeon, song varies geographically (also individually?). Usually a deep, drawled, 4-noted phrase (upper Río Cuyuní), *whook, a-cóok-huuuu*; or 3- or 4-noted phrase in Sierra de Imataca. In nw Barinas foothills, 3-noted *whut, wub, whooooa* (1st note rises, last downslurred). In all areas *about an octave lower in pitch* than that of Ruddy Pigeon, and slower and drawled, esp. last note. Occas. intermed.-pitched songs of birds of uncertain identity are hd. In Guyana all singing birds collected have been ♂♂ (M. B. Robbins); a growling *purrr-r-r-r-r-r* sim. to others of genus.

Behavior: Solitary or in prs. but several may gather in canopy fruiting trees, esp. *Ficus*, or at seeps or mineral licks on gd. inside forest. Also eats many mistletoe berries. Generally in canopy where hard to see; occas. perches on edge of tree but not on high

exposed stubs. Flies rapidly across small rivers and clearings and directly into forest. Does not cross large areas of open grassland. Notably territorial when breeding.

Status and habitat: Locally fairly common resident (easily overlooked unless calling) in tall humid to wet forest in lowlands and foothills. More numerous in lowland regions with high rainfall than allied Ruddy Pigeon, e.g., close to base of Sierra de Lema in e Bolívar.

Range: To 1900m n of Orinoco; to 300m s of Orinoco. Sierra de Perijá, Zulia e to w Mérida; e base of Andes in Táchira (sight/hd., 1000m, 3 Apr 1980, Cerro El Teteo—C. Parrish) and nw Barinas on San Isidro Rd. (sight/tape, Feb 1997); very locally throughout (?) s of Orinoco (*delicata*). E Colombia to e Bolivia, Amaz. Brazil, and the Guianas; Paraguay and se Brazil.

Note: Sometimes other subspp. recognized. Subsp. *delicata* may be a synonym of *bogotensis* (P. Coopmans).

Eared Dove
PLATE 20
Zenaida auriculata   Paloma Sabanera

Identification: 9.5″ (24cm). 112g. *Common med.-sized dove of open areas.* Crown and nape gray, upperparts pale brown with 2–3 black spots on tertials; 2 narrow black lines on cheeks; below pinkish brown to buffy vinaceous, *tail wedge-shaped, pointed, all but central pr. of feathers broadly tipped rufous.* Bill narrowed near base.

Sim. species: Ground-doves are smaller with short *rounded* tails and no rufous tips.

Voice: Low-pitched cooing *ooo-cú-ooo*, not loud; also a rising *coooo*.

Behavior: Prs. when breeding, otherwise gregarious, congregating in large flocks in agricultural areas where sometimes destructive to grain crops. Often perch in open treetops or on electric wires. Feed mostly on seeds taken from gd. Marked local or long-distance dispersal occurs, prob. in response to food levels. Flies very fast and direct, without sailing. Breeds mainly Apr–Nov in ne Venez.; 2 white eggs on flimsy stick platform[186,734].

Status and habitat: Fairly common to seasonally abundant resident in dry open or semiopen country, agricultural areas, and light woodland borders. Large nos. and flocks in dry season (Jan–Apr); nos. dramatically lower in May–Oct rainy months in llanos of Apure. The reverse in ne Anzoátegui where very scarce Jan–Feb, building to peak of 1000s late May–early Jun, then decreasing sharply to end of yr[186].

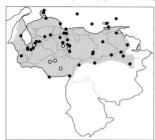

Range: To 3000m (sight to ca. 3700m, ne Mérida). Andes (*ruficauda*); coastal Falcón; rest of Venez. n of Orinoco (no recs. Sucre; Delta Amacuro) and locally s of it in n Bolívar; Islas La Tortuga, Los Testigos, Los Roques, and Margarita (*rubriceps*). Colombia to the Guianas and s locally (open terrain) to Tierra del Fuego. Netherlands and Lesser Antilles; Trinidad; Panama (twice).
Note: Arrangement of subspp.[148] varies.

Scardafella

Recall *Columbina* ground-doves but plumage scaly, tail long and pointed, and voice and displays differ; lack signal spots on wings of true *Columbina*. Sometimes placed in *Columbina*[10,283].

Scaled Dove   PLATE 20
Scardafella squammata   Palomita Maraquita
Identification: 8.5″ (22cm). 54g. Eyes red (♂) or reddish brown to yellow (♀; imm.?). *Short legged and scaly with long pointed tail.* Above pale sandy brown, below pinkish white, palest on belly, heavily scaled black throughout; primaries dusky, *inner webs rufous* (shows in flight), 4 central feathers of long tail brown, rest black increasingly *tipped with white*, outer pr. almost entirely white.
Sim. species: A long-tailed, scaly little dove of dry open areas will surely be this species. In flight from other small doves with rufous in wings by pointed, white-tipped tail.
Voice: Song, often hd. continually even during heat of the day, a monotonously repeated, rhythmic whistle, *aaaw, c'mon!*, 1st note drawled; other renditions are *ál, co'hol!* and *there's, no-hope!* During bow-coo display (lacking in *Columbina*) tail is raised vertically and spread slightly as head and body rock forward with each call. Also a loud purring *crrrruu* over and over. Local names, *Maraquita* and *Maraquera*, are onomatopoeic.
Behavior: Prs. or little groups are confiding and charming as they walk around on gd., pecking at trifles and shuffling along with bellies almost scraping gd. When disturbed flush off in a rush with dry rustling whir of wings to safety of a nearby tree. Feed mostly on small seeds. Sing and loaf in scrubby thickets and trees. Breed Jan–Jun and Aug–Nov (prob. most of yr), ne Anzoátegui; twiggy cup nest more substantial than that of most doves; 1–3m up, occas.

on gd.; 2 white eggs[115,186]; 7 nests in Jun, 5 in Aug–Nov, w Apure[137].
Status and habitat: Very common resident in arid scrub and dry semiopen areas, gallery forest borders, waste areas, around habitations, urban areas, or wherever there are a few trees and shrubs. Locally into humid areas (e.g., Tucupita, Delta Amacuro).

Range: To 1100m n of Orinoco; to 200m s of Orinoco. Throughout n of Orinoco incl. Delta Amacuro, and s to nw Amazonas and n Bolívar; Isla Margarita (*ridgwayi*). N Colombia to n Venez.; French Guiana; e Brazil to Paraguay and n Argentina.

Columbina

Smallest members of family in Venez.; short, squarish tail; ♂♂ brighter than ♀♀; widespread.

Common Ground-Dove   PLATE 20
Columbina passerina   Tortolita Grisácea
Identification: 6.3″ (16cm). 32g. *Bill pinkish to orange with dusky tip* (or bill all dark—sw Amazonas). Upperparts pale brown (color of damp sand), wings tinged vinaceous, shoulders with numerous dark spots; head, neck, and chest pinkish vinaceous scaled dusky (feathers have dark centers), lower underparts pinkish white; tail gray brown above, black below, all but 2 central feathers with broad black terminal band; *under wing coverts and base of flight feathers rufous* (shows in flight). Some ♀♀ almost whitish below.
Sim. species: Plain-breasted Ground-Dove has all-dark bill (but in sw Amazonas, Common Ground-Dove also has dark bill), *no scales*, and ♂ is distinctly grayish with faint blue tinge (not brown) above (Common Ground-Dove always browner). ♀ Ruddy Ground-Dove is larger, lacks scaly appearance; all Ruddy's show black (not rufous) under wing coverts and more rufous in flight feathers.
Voice: Song, sometimes rather infreq. hd., a simple *caaOOP!* usually repeated at ca. 1/sec for 10–15 sec.
Behavior: Prs. or small groups feed on gd. where they walk in a jerky mechanical manner and peck at soil for seeds and occas. fallen berries; rest and sing from a perch a few meters up in shrub or tree. More wary than Ruddy Ground-Dove and quick to flush off rapidly to cover. Small matlike nest of grass and twigs on gd. or low in shrub; 2 white eggs. Nests Jan–Jun, Sep, and Nov, ne Anzoátegui[186].
Status and habitat: Fairly common resident in scrubby forest borders, brushy and weedy areas,

abandoned fields, and grassland with overgrown
fence borders in dry to arid regions. Common on offshore isls. Mainly lowlands. Occurs locally with
Plain-breasted Ground-Dove but prob. interspecifically territorial with it and in most of llanos replaced
by it.

Range: To 1600m n of Orinoco; to 500m s of Ori-
noco. Throughout n of Orinoco (few recs. in Apure,
none in Barinas, Portuguesa, Cojedes, or most of
Guárico); n Amazonas; n Bolívar s to lower Río
Caura, lower Río Paragua, and El Callao (*albivitta*);
sw Amazonas along Río Negro (*griseola*); Islas La
Tortuga, La Orchila, Los Roques, La Blanquilla, Los
Hermanos, and Margarita (*tortugensis*). S US to Costa
Rica; Colombia to the Guianas and spottily in ne and
e Brazil; high els. in Ecuador. Netherlands Antilles;
Trinidad.

Plain-breasted Ground-Dove PLATE 20
Columbina minuta Tortolita Sabanera
Identification: 6" (15cm). 32g. *Bill dusky, base often
vaguely yellowish. Head to mantle gray with faint bluish tinge,* this turning pale grayish brown on rest of
upperparts; shoulders and wing coverts with several
dark spots; below vinaceous, all but 2 central tail
feathers with broad terminal black band, outermost
pr. narrowly tipped white, *under wing coverts and
base of flight feathers rufous,* tips of flight feathers
dusky. ♀: sim. but brownish above, paler brown
below fading to buff white on belly.
Sim. species: Much like ♀ Ruddy Ground-Dove but
smaller, tail shorter, under wing coverts rufous (not
black or mostly black). Also cf. Common Ground-
Dove.
Voice: Song, sometimes infreq. hd., *whoop, whoop,
whoop, . . .* (or *haOOP*), a little faster than 1/sec
without pause for 20–40 sec, often repeated at short
intervals.
Behavior: Rather like other *Columbina* but generally
less conspic. Mainly in prs. in wet season and in little
groups up to ca. 12 in dry season. Forage on gd.,
flush off to trees or drop back into cover again. ♂♂
sing from low perches in trees or shrubs and display
by sailing out from low perches on stiffly spread
wings. Jun–Nov breeding, Apure and Guárico[137,734];
shallow grass and twig nest cup, gd. to 3m up,
occas. higher; 2–3 white eggs.
Status and habitat: Fairly common resident in s portion of llanos (s of Río Apure); nos. decreasing
sharply n of Apure; also declining again s of Orinoco. Dry brushy areas with scattered bushes, weedy

pastures, abandoned fields, borders of dry forest. Absent or very local in coastal zone.

Range: To 850m n of Orinoco; to 500m s of Orinoco.
Locally in Zulia (Río Socuavo; Mene Grande), e Falcón (sight, Cerro Misión), Aragua (Maracay area),
Distr. Federal (Caracas), and Miranda; generally from
Apure, Barinas, c Guárico, and Delta Amacuro s
across Amazonas and Bolívar (*minuta*). Se Mexico
locally to the Guianas, c Argentina, and s Brazil;
w Peru. Trinidad.

Ruddy Ground-Dove PLATE 20
Columbina talpacoti Chocolatera
Identification: 6.7" (17cm). 47g. Bill grayish; eyes reddish brown (or red to orange). Common small dove
of open areas. ♂: *pale gray head contrasts with rufous body;* numerous black spots on wings; under
wing coverts black. ♀: duller and lacks ♂'s contrast;
head dull brownish gray, upperparts *olivaceous
brown,* below grayish brown (paler than above),
outer tail feathers dusky; under wing coverts black,
base of flight feathers rufous (conspic. as flush), tips
dusky.
Sim. species: Cf. ♀ Common and ♀ Plain-breasted
ground-doves, both of which are *smaller* and shorter-
tailed. ♂ Ruddy's contrasting gray head is distinctive;
♀ Ruddy is browner above (no gray tones), with
black under wing coverts (if in doubt, flush bird).
In hand ♀ Ruddy's tail 60–65mm vs. 50–55 for
Plain-breasted.
Voice: ♂ sings a hollow, rather drowsy, monotonous
ca-HUU, ca-HUU, ca-HUU . . . , up to 10 phrases, from
perch above gd. Slower than advertising song of
Common and Plain-breasted ground-doves.
Behavior: Confiding and social, often allowing close
approach. Feeds mostly in open on gd., walking
alone, in prs. or in groups of various sizes, pecking
for seeds. Walks mechanically with short, rapid steps
and bobbing head. Flushes suddenly with an audible
wing-whir and flies away rapidly a short distance.
Not always a harbinger of peace; ♂♂ freq. threaten
and quarrel with each other by flashing up a raised
wing. Lunges and pecks may knock opponents over.
Nov breeding, w Guárico[734]. Frail shallow nest 1m or
more up in bush; 2 white eggs.
Status and habitat: Common to abundant resident in
all kinds of partially open country, fields, ranches,
gardens, urban areas, and along forest or woodland
borders; dry to humid areas. Clearings or river edges
in forested zones. S of Orinoco mostly in forest openings and villages.

Range: To 1600m n of Orinoco; to 900m s of Orinoco. Throughout except in area of next subspp.; Islas Margarita and Patos (*rufipennis*); Delta Amacuro s to se Bolívar (*talpacoti*). Sw US and Mexico to nw Peru (rarely n Chile), n Argentina, Paraguay, and Uruguay (sight). Trinidad.

Claravis

Larger than *Columbina*; strong sexual dimorphism; square tail; glossy signal spots on wings; forest dwellers; feed on gd.

Blue Ground-Dove   PLATE 20
Claravis pretiosa   Palomita Azul
Identification: 8″ (20.3cm). 65g. Bill gray green; eyes reddish brown (yellow—age?); legs flesh color. ♂: above *blue gray, below pale gray*; foreface and throat whitish; wing coverts spotted black, *2 rather widely spaced vertical black bars on wings*; tail squarish, central feathers blue gray, rest with progressively more black. ♀ very different: above ruddy brown, below pale brown, throat and belly whitish, *rump and tail rufous* (outer tail feathers black), wing coverts with a few obscure dark spots, tertials crossed by 2 irreg. chestnut bars.
Sim species: ♂ unique, ♀ confusing. Note ♀'s rufous rump and tail, and habitat. Larger than other ground-doves.
Voice: ♂'s song a rather soft, abrupt *boop* or *whoop*, repeated 4–5 times at ca. 1 note/sec., then often a lengthy pause before song is repeated. Sings from well up in trees, and at unpredictable times, usually not for very long.
Behavior: Usually seen singly or in loosely assoc. prs., infreq. 3–4 together. Feeds on seeds and a few insects taken on gd., sometimes in shady clearings or roadsides, but otherwise perches above gd. and in shady cover where infreq. seen. Walks along a branch, nods head, and moves to partial cover when aware of an observer. Most often seen shooting by in flight as it crosses a road or clearing, or as it flies from one wooded area to another. Flies higher above gd. than other ground-doves and invariably disappears from view before stopping. Nov breeding, w Guárico[734]; frail twig nest 1–6m up in tangle; 2 white eggs[640].
Status and habitat: Widespread but generally not very numerous. Dry to humid forest, wooded borders, gallery forest, and light or scrubby woodland.

Most numerous in dry woodland (e.g., around Canoabo, Carabobo) in n part of country. Least numerous and local in humid forested regions s of Orinoco where found mostly near edges or in lighter woodland (not inside tall humid forest). Seasonal movements occur in drier regions.

Range: To 1000m n of Orinoco; to 300m s of Orinoco. Throughout n of Orinoco (few recs. in llanos); locally in Amazonas; n Bolívar s to Gran Sabana. S Mexico s to nw Peru, n Argentina, and s Brazil. Trinidad.

Maroon-chested Ground-Dove   PLATE 20
Claravis mondetoura   Palomita Pechirroja
Identification: 8.5″ (22cm). 92g. Bill black; eyes red; legs coral red. ♂: above dark gray with *whitish forehead and whitish sides of head and throat; chest and breast maroon chestnut*, lower breast gray, belly and under tail coverts whitish; central pr. of tail feathers dark gray, base black; rest of tail *white* (conspic. as flushes), tail looks all white from below; 2 blotchy to diamond-shaped purplish black bars cross flight feathers; variable number of black spots on wing coverts. ♀: above brown, *rump and upper tail coverts* (but not tail) *cinnamon rufous*, forehead, face, throat, and belly tinged buff, breast gray, central tail feathers ruddy brown, rest black *tipped white* (watch in flight). Juv.: like ♀ but browner; wing coverts edged and spotted rusty.
Sim. species: ♂ unique in highland range. ♀ much like ♀ Blue Ground-Dove (range overlap?) but lacks latter's rufous tail and has white outer tail tips.
Voice: Song 6–45 or more deep resonant *hwoop* notes at rate of ca. 1/sec; recalls song of Blue Ground-Dove but may continue without pause for nearly 1 min. Sometimes notes slightly bisyllablic.
Behavior: A nomadic bamboo specialist, rarely seen except when singing in patches of seeding bamboo. ♂♂ sing from perches well above gd. Ads. feed heavily (exclusively?) on bamboo seeds. During peak bamboo seed production may form loose breeding colonies with several ♂♂ singing only short distances apart. Nesting undescribed.
Status and habitat: Rare. Almost invariably found in dense patches of seeding bamboo (*Chusquea* spp.) in montane cloud forests. Seeks bamboo die-offs when bamboo seed crops are produced, breeds rapidly, then disperses, presum. in search of new patches of seeding bamboo, which are unpredictable in occurrence. Disappears for yrs., then reap-

pears during maturation of bamboo seed crops. Perhaps most numerous in Táchira. Everywhere local and threatened by deforestation.

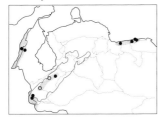

Range: 1300–2600m. Sierra de Perijá, Zulia; Andes of Táchira and Mérida (prob. Trujillo and Lara); Coastal Cordillera in Aragua, Distr. Federal, and Miranda (*mondetoura*). Se Mexico to w Panama; Andes from Colombia to Bolivia.

Leptotila

Large and plump; rufous wing linings; rounded, fan-shaped tail with white tips; white belly; very narrow red or blue orbital skin and loral line; legs coral; told by subtle differences in color of crown, head, and underparts, and orbital skin color; feed on gd. on seeds, fallen berries, grit, occas. small insects; flush with obvious wing noise.

White-tipped Dove
PLATE 20

Leptotila verreauxi Paloma Turca

Identification: 11″ (28cm). 155g. Bare loral line and *narrow eyering blue*; eyes yellow. *Forehead dull grayish to brownish white*, crown vinaceous gray, rest of upperparts grayish brown; throat whitish becoming pinkish vinaceous on sides of head and chest; belly white; tail brown, outer feathers increasingly black with broad white tips (black below); wing linings and all but tips of flight feathers *chestnut rufous*.

Sim. species: Gray-fronted Dove has *gray* forehead in strong contrast to warm brown head, and *buff* (not pinkish vinaceous) sides of head; note habitat differences. Despite White-tipped Dove's name, tail tipping much like others of genus.

Voice: Deep, hollow, *ub'uOOOOu*, 1st note faint at a distance; much like sound produced by blowing across top of a bottle; 2-noted pattern is diagnostic (cf. Gray-fronted Dove). In n Aragua song less distinctly 2-noted.

Behavior: Single birds or prs. forage on gd. by walking rather mechanically with much head-nodding and pecking at trifles. Typically rather wary and when disturbed walks away quietly or flushes off with audible wing-whir to a nearby low or mid-level perch where it nervously nods head and dips tail, as if to obtain a better view, before walking along branch a few steps to concealment. Jul–Nov breeding in sw Guárico[734]; usual dove nest platform low in bush or tree, occas. on gd.; 2 white eggs.

Status and habitat: Common resident in dry forest, light woodland, open second growth, tangled borders, plantations, and shady pastures in dry to fairly

humid areas. Primarily a nonforest bird (cf. Gray-fronted Dove). Small migratory movement through Portachuelo Pass, Aragua, 23–24 Apr and 10 Jul[33].

Range: To 3000m n of Orinoco (mostly below 1500m); to 1200m s of Orinoco. Throughout s to n Amazonas (Samariapo); Bolívar s to Río Cuyuní and s end of Gran Sabana at Santa Elena de Uairén; Islas Los Patos, Los Testigos, and Margarita (*verreauxi*). S Texas and Mexico to w Peru, c Argentina, and Uruguay. Aruba to Trinidad.

Gray-fronted Dove
PLATE 20

Leptotila rufaxilla Paloma Pipa

Identification: 10.5″ (27cm). 155g. Narrow bare *loral line and eyering red*. Eyes yellow. Much like previous species. *Forecrown to midcrown gray, sides of head buff*, rear crown, nape, and rest of upperparts dark umber brown, back tinged olive; upper throat whitish, lower throat buff turning vinaceous on chest and white on belly; underwings and tail as in White-tipped Dove, white tail tips not as large. Or sim. but entire crown gray, forecrown paler (*rufaxilla*).

Sim. species: See White-tipped Dove which does not occur inside humid forest. In all subspp. note gray forecrown and buff face; up close note red eyering.

Voice: Hd. much more than seen. Call a deep, resonant, and abrupt *wooOOOou*, expanding and contracting quickly, and much like sound made by blowing across a bottle top. Given every 5 sec or so. ♀ (presum.) gives a sim. but higher pitched call; the two (or sometimes several) often countercall in lazy, hypnotic serenade on warm sunny afternoons. Cf. 2-noted call of previous sp.

Behavior: Sim. to that of White-tipped Dove. Most often seen when it flushes noisily from beside a forest trail or flies low and fast across a forest opening. Usual dove nest platform in bush or top of rotten stump or log; 2 white eggs; breeds yr-round in Trinidad[175].

Status and habitat: Common resident in terra firme and várzea forest, second growth of various ages, and gallery forest in humid lowlands; less numerous and local n of Orinoco where mostly replaced by White-tipped Dove which favors drier areas and lighter or scrubby woodland.

Range: To 600m n of Orinoco; to 1450m s of Orinoco. Maracaibo Basin of Zulia, nw Táchira, and w Mérida; e base of Andes in w Apure and nw Barinas (Barinitas) and sw Portuguesa (*pallidipectus*); recs. in n mts. from Yaracuy (Finca El Jaguar) and Carabobo

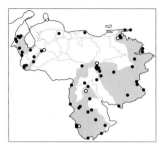

to Distr. Federal (Acarigua) need verification; se Sucre (Guanoco) and n Monagas; generally in Amazonas, Bolívar (except se), and Delta Amacuro (*dubusi*); Paria Pen. of Sucre (*hellmayri*); se Bolívar at Cerro Roraima (*rufaxilla*). Generally e of Andes from Colombia and the Guianas to ne Argentina and Uruguay.

Geotrygon

Plumper and shorter-tailed than *Leptotila*; no white tail tips; colored bare skin forms narrow loral line and narrow eyering; feathers on back of neck and upper mantle usually iridescent; short coral legs; terrestrial but roost and nest above gd.; flush *without* obvious wing noise (unlike *Leptotila*).

Lined Quail-Dove   PLATE 20
Geotrygon linearis   Paloma Perdiz Rojiza
Identification: 12" (30.5cm). 245g. Loral line and eyering red; eyes yellow. *Prom. facial pattern.* Forecrown *buff*, large area behind eyes and band across nape gray, *cheeks and throat pale buff separated by long black malar line*; short white streak on rear border of cheeks; otherwise above rich dark brown, back glossed purple (or glossed bronzy green—*trinitatis*), throat whitish, chest light gray turning tawny buff on breast and lower underparts. ♀: duller.
Sim. species: Largest quail-dove and only one at high els. Smaller Ruddy Quail-Dove lacks multicolored head. Smaller Violaceous Quail-Dove has no facial pattern.
Voice: Song a deep, hollow, pigeonlike *ooUUoo*, repeated ca. 20 times/min. Some birds (different sex or age?) give sim. but higher pitched call, and both may countercall together. Song resembles that of Ruddy Quail-Dove and *Leptotila* doves but is shorter and lacks booming resonance (at least up close) of latter. Most vocal Jan–Jun (later?) at intervals throughout day.
Behavior: Like others of genus, walks on floor of shady forest, shuffling along with waddling gait and exaggerated pumping of head. Usually seen alone or in loosely assoc. prs., and when spotted typically hustles out of view with surprising facility. Eats seeds and fruits from forest floor, but sings from perch well up in trees (ca. 8–20m up). If disturbed while singing, falls silent and glides back to forest floor. Trinidad nest a deep twig and dead leaf cup ca. 4m up in branch fork; 2 eggs, rich cream[175].

Status and habitat: Fairly common resident (by voice) in humid and wet mt. forest (incl. cloud forest) and tall second-growth woodland. Generally found at higher els. and in wetter forest than Ruddy Quail-Dove.

Range: 400–2500m (mostly 900–2200m); sight to 2800m[60]. Sierra de Perijá, Zulia, both slopes of Andes from Táchira to Lara; mts. of Falcón (Sierra de San Luis, Curimagua) and Yaracuy and n cordilleras from Carabobo to se Miranda (*linearis*); mts. of Sucre and n Monagas (Cerro Negro); doubtful rec at El Merey, s Monagas. N Colombia. Trinidad.
Note: Goodwin[210] incl. *G. albifacies* (White-faced Quail-Dove) of Mexico to Nicaragua and *G. chiriquensis* (Rufous-breasted Quail-Dove) of Costa Rica and w Panama with this sp.

Violaceous Quail-Dove   PLATE 20
Geotrygon violacea   Paloma Perdiz Violacea
Identification: 9.5" (24cm). 120g. Bill, loral line, and narrow eyering red; eyes yellow. ♂: *forehead whitish*, rest of crown grayish vinaceous, *rearcrown, nape, and back rich dark chestnut strongly glossed purple*; rump and tail dull rufous; central throat white, edges tinged buff, chest glossy purplish vinaceous turning white on lower breast and belly. ♀: overall much duller; above olive brown, rump and upper tail coverts dark chestnut rufous, *chest vinaceous gray* (grayer than ♂), throat and belly pale buff.
Sim. species: Only Venez. quail-dove with *no facial stripe*. Iridescent back color of ♂ difficult to see in field. ♀ recalls Ruddy Quail-Dove but underparts grayish. In mts. see Lined Quail-Dove.
Voice: Call (Paria Pen.) a low *HOOou* (last part drops in pitch, as if swallowed), higher pitched and more mellow than that of Ruddy Quail-Dove, repeated every few secs for up to 1 min or more.
Behavior: Shuffles along shady forest floor like other *Geotrygon* and is adept at quickly moving out of view if pursued. Flushes quietly, unlike *Leptotila*. Usually calls from perch 2–8m up but drops silently to gd. if approached. Perhaps somewhat more arboreal than other *Geotrygon*. In Panama frail stick nest 2–3m up; 2 buff eggs[818].
Status and habitat: Uncommon and local resident inside humid and wet lowland and foothill forest. Prob. more widespread, esp. in Andean foothills, than the few recs. suggest. Seasonal or periodic movements likely. Only Coastal Cordillera rec. is an unsexed bird netted in Aragua[130].

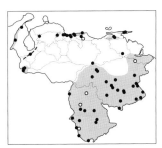

Range: 400–1400m n of Orinoco; to 500m s of Orinoco. Sierra de Perijá, Zulia; locally along w base of Andes in Mérida (La Azulita) and nw Lara (Cerro El Cogollal), e base of Andes in se Táchira and se Lara; Coastal Cordillera in Aragua (Portachuelo Pass); mts. of e Sucre (e to Cristóbal Colon); ne Bolívar in Sierra de Imataca (*albiventer*). Locally from Nicaragua to Colombia; Guyana; Suriname; e and se Brazil to Bolivia, n Argentina.

Ruddy Quail-Dove   PLATE 20
Geotrygon montana   Paloma Perdiz Cara Roja
Identification: 9″ (23cm). 110g. Most widespread member of genus. Bill, narrow loral line, and eyering red; eyes yellow. ♂: *crown, sides of head, and upperparts rich rufous chestnut*; crown and mantle glossed reddish violet (visible in hand); *broad buff stripe below eyes*; throat pale buff, *prom. dark malar streak*; chest pinkish vinaceous turning buffy ochraceous on belly; under wing coverts and underwings mostly rufous. ♀: much like ♂ but above brownish olive (no gloss), face pattern duller, chest rich brown.
Sim species: ♂'s overall ruddy color and double cheek stripes are distinctive in flight or at rest. ♀ is darker and has less distinctive facial pattern. In mts. cf. Violaceous Quail-Dove (no face stripes).
Voice: Call a low, resonant, almost moaning *oooOOoou*, much like that of Gray-fronted Dove but slightly longer and with less resonance; repeated at intervals of 3–5 sec.
Behavior: Shy and unobtrusive forest dove. Chiefly terrestrial, walking with rapid steps and bobbing head, although if surprised may flush to a low branch. Flushes quietly and flies fast and low with abrupt batlike swerving. Reg. on forest floor beneath fruiting trees where it eats fallen seeds and fruits. Frail dove-type twig platform ca. 2–3m up in bush or top of stump; 2 buff or cream eggs[621]; early Feb nest, 2 naked young, e Bolívar.
Status and habitat: Uncommon resident (infreq. seen) on floor of humid lowland and premontane forest, tall second growth, open woodland, and coffee plantations. Small migratory movement reported through Portachuelo Pass, Aragua, 22 Apr–3 May, mostly at night[33]. Dramatic but unpredictable migratory movements reported in Amaz. Brazil.
Range: To 1900m. Base of Sierra de Perijá, Zulia, w slope of Andes in Mérida n to nw Lara (Cerro El Cogollal); e slope in Táchira; n cordilleras from Yaracuy and Carabobo e to Distr. Federal and Miranda

(Santa Lucia); Sucre and n Monagas (Cueva del Guácharo); Delta Amacuro[343]; throughout Amazonas; Bolívar from lower Río Caura and lower Río Cuyuní southward (*montana*). W and s Mexico s to ne Argentina and s Brazil. Greater and Lesser Antilles. Trinidad.

PSITTACIFORMES

Psittacidae: Macaws, Parrots, and Parakeets
Guacamayos, Loros, Cotorras, y Pericos

From garish to sublime and enormous to tiny, macaws, parrots, and parakeets are strikingly varied in appearance but an anatomically homogenous group of birds most diverse in New World tropical latitudes and in Australia. They are noisy, intensely social, and well known for their thick, hooked bills that form crooked grins and for their yoke-toed feet, and their lives and fates are, for better or worse, thoroughly entwined with that of modern human history. Venezuelan species are mostly green and range from sparrow-sized parrotlets to gargantuan macaws. They have adapted to almost every habitat from steamy rain forests to cold, wind-ravaged treeline vegetation but are most numerous in the warm lowlands. Most are seed predators, but they also eat substantial quantities of fruit and some blossoms and nectar. They nest in tree holes, woodpecker cavities, or even a hole they dig in a termite nest, but such sites are relatively scarce and one of the major factors that may limit populations. Larger species are believed to mate for life but may take another mate if a partner is lost. Small-bodied species tend to gather in larger flocks and favor low-lying or river-edge habitats more than large-bodied species. Many are kept as pets or for entertainment in a tragic burlesque of misguided anthropomorphism. Anyone witness to the stirring sight of these wild and magnificent birds winging through dawn's rising mists, or anyone who stands mute to their raucous cries echoing overhead, is unlikely ever again to view these same creatures in captivity with anything but sadness. They are symbols of wildness that belong in the rain forests and savannas of their ancestors. Tragically, unabated demand for

captive psittacines continues. Coupled with inexora-
ble loss of habitat, many of these birds now fly into
a future of greatly dimmed hope.

Ara

Med. to very large in size; long pointed tail; all with
bare cheeks and facial area; enormously thick bill;
mainly seed predators; plumage colorful; formerly
incl. several spp. now usually placed in *Orthopsittaca*
and *Diopsittaca*.

Blue-and-yellow Macaw   PLATE 21
Ara ararauna   Guacamayo Azul y Amarillo
Identification: 30–33″ (76–84cm). 1.1kg. Spectacular
macaw of swampy lowlands in extreme e and s.
Long pointed tail; eyes yellow, bill black. Upperparts
mainly *bright cerulean blue, below orange yellow incl.
underwings and undertail*; up close forehead green,
upper throat black, sides of head white with narrow
lines of tiny black feathers.
Sim. species: Despite striking plumage, easily confused with Scarlet or Red-and-green macaws in flight
at a distance because all spp. have blue flight feathers (beware low evening light).
Voice: Typical flight call a guttural *rising* note, *raaak*
(C. Munn), raucous but less so than that of other
large *Ara*; also other semimusical calls, mostly
weaker, more nasal and mellower than those of
other large macaws.
Behavior: Like others of genus, noisy and gregarious.
May spend long periods of time during day resting,
arguing among themselves, or allopreening on high
branches or in palms in forest canopy. Fly in pairs or
in 3s (ad. pr. with offspring) that are maintained
within larger flocks. In the few areas where they
occur in Venez. (e.g., Delta Amacuro) generally
closely assoc. with palms, which they use for roosting, feeding, and nesting (unlike other *Ara*). May
commute long distances between roosting and feeding areas each morning and evening, and likely to
be noted by call long before they appear in view.
Perhaps eat more fruit and fewer seeds than others
of genus. Flight is strong, steady, and leisurely, with
long tail streaming behind. Nest in high cavity in
large, dead, and usually rotten palm trunk; reuse
same cavity; 2 eggs.
Status and habitat: Fairly common resident locally in
várzea forest and low-lying or swampy regions with
many palms or mangroves. Still relatively numerous

in remote parts of palm-rich Delta Amacuro; small
nos. in vicinity of Caño Colorado, e Monagas, where
perhaps occurrence is seasonal. Resident in low
numbers in swampy and seasonally flooded forests
in c and s Amazonas. Occas. wandering individuals
or prs. are reported well away from main pop.
centers.
Range: To 500m (prob. higher). N Monagas (Río
Guarapiche) s through mid. Delta Amacuro; c
Amazonas (Pto. Yapacana) s locally to San Carlos de
Río Negro and Río Siapa on Brazilian border. E Panama locally to c Bolivia, Paraguay, and c and e Brazil. Trinidad (extinct).

Military Macaw   PLATE 21
Ara militaris   Guacamayo Verde
Identification: 30″ (76cm). 1.1kg. Long pointed tail.
Bill black; eyes yellow. *Mainly green* with *bare rosy
pink face* and red forehead; blue lower back and
rump; flight feathers dark blue, tail brownish red
tipped blue; bare whitish face has several feathered
black lines. In flight from below, *wings and tail
brassy gold*.
Sim. species: Larger than any mostly green parakeet in
its range. See Red-and-green Macaw, smaller Chestnut-
fronted Macaw, and Blue-crowned Parakeet.
Voice: Raucous, guttural *kraaak*.
Behavior: Sim. to other large *Ara*. Prs. or groups up
to ca. 30 (at least formerly) commute between feeding and roosting areas. Flight is strong and direct on
slow, shallow wing beats. Nests in large natural tree
cavities, prob. in dry season.
Status and habitat: Uncommon and now very local
resident in dry, moist, and moderately humid forest
and in riparian woodland in arid regions. Lowlands
and foothills. Local and seasonal movements need
documentation. In nos. in roosting flocks near Cumboto, Aragua, in rainy season, early 1990s (P. Boesman), but absent in dry season. Most readily found
in PN Guatopo, Miranda (to 1000m). May have formerly occurred (seasonally?) in PN Morrocoy, e Falcón, but recs. need confirmation. Habitat destruction
and recent cagebird trafficking are serious threats[150].

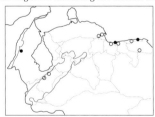

Range: To 600m (sight to 1000m). Nw Zulia (La Sierra); w Mérida (sightings); se Falcón (sightings, La
Misión)[297]; locally in Coastal Cordillera of Aragua and
Distr. Federal (formerly to San José de Caracas); Interior Cordillera in Miranda (sightings, PN Guatopo)
and adj. n Guárico (*militaris*); unconfirmed recs. in n
Cojedes[150]. Three in e Apure may have been escaped
cagebirds[297]. Isolated pops. from w Mexico to Bolivia
and nw Argentina.

Scarlet Macaw   PLATE 21
Ara macao   Guacamayo Bandera

Identification: 32–37″ (81–94cm). 1kg. *Long, pointed, mainly red tail.* Bill whitish above, black below. Eyes yellow to whitish. *Plumage mostly scarlet, median upper wing coverts yellow* (conspic. when perched, sometimes also in flight), *flight feathers blue,* rump and under tail coverts light blue; *tail red,* outer feathers tipped blue, short outermost ones all blue; bare facial skin whitish and *unlined.*

Sim. species: Red-and-green Macaw bulks larger but has shorter tail, is darker red, and has green wing coverts and prom. facial lines (visible up close). In flight note tail differences and voice. Compared to Red-and-green Macaw, Scarlet has *longer, all-red* tail, and tail wiggles as bird flies (C. Munn).

Voice: Flight call a loud, harsh *RAAAAH* which sounds like "white noise" with no note inside (C. Munn), much louder and harsher than that of Blue-and-yellow Macaw, and lacking "falsetto" note of Red-and-green Macaw. In general the coarsest and most grating call of the 4 large macaws in Venez.

Behavior: Most sim. to that of Red-and-green Macaw but (in Peru) feeds more on ripe fruits and mature seeds (less on unripe fruit and seeds). Found in prs., or 3s, latter consisting of ad. pr. and offspring, or when not breeding may gather in larger flocks. Nest in tree cavities 10–25m up; in dry season in llanos.

Status and habitat: Fairly common resident in llanos in gallery forests, tree isls., and where unmolested, even in large trees around ranch buildings. In c and s Amazonas also in humid lowland forest and forest borders, esp. in white sandy soil areas. In general favors drier or more strongly seasonal habitats (e.g., llanos) in Venez. than does Red-and-green Macaw, and the two (unlike in much of w Amazonia) do not overlap widely in Venez.

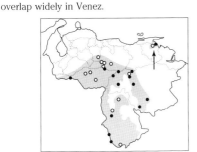

Range: To 500m. W Apure, Barinas, Cojedes (sight), and Guárico (sight) s to Amazonas and w Bolívar (e to Río Caura); se Sucre and n Monagas (*macao*). Se Mexico to c Bolivia and Amaz. Brazil. Trinidad (old sight recs.).

Red-and-green Macaw   PLATE 21
Ara chloroptera   Guacamayo Rojo

Identification: 33–37″ (84–94cm). 1.25kg. Resembles Scarlet Macaw. Bill whitish above, black below, *larger* and heavier than bill of Scarlet Macaw; eyes yellowish white. Plumage mainly deep crimson, *upper median wing coverts green* (fairly obvious

when perched, not in flight), *flight feathers, rump, and most of outer tail feathers blue*; bare facial skin crossed by *several narrow lines of red feathers.* Juv.: sim. but eyes dark, face more heavily feathered.

Sim. species: See Scarlet Macaw. In flight Red-and-green's *tail looks dark* (not red as in Scarlet although there is red in center of tail from above), tail is proportionately shorter than in Scarlet, and it is steady (no wiggle) in flight (C. Munn).

Voice: Flight calls harsh and much like those of Scarlet Macaw but slightly higher pitched and with a falsetto note in middle, or less often (listen) with slightly musical hic-up added quickly at end, e.g., *kaarRRRR UL-a* or *kaaarRRRR O-E-a,* last 2–3 notes high pitched and slurred. Song a rambling ser. of argumentative gurgles, semimusical glides, and harsh notes.

Behavior: Gregarious and noisy. In prs. when breeding but otherwise almost always in varying-sized flocks. In lowlands sometimes up to 30 or more; on forested slopes of tepuis generally only 2–3 prs. together. Roost communally and commute out to distant feeding trees each day to eat fruit and esp. seeds (they are principally seed predators) of many kinds of large forest trees. Flight is strong and direct. Often spend long periods of time during day resting, garrulously arguing among themselves, or allopreening on large high limbs in forest canopy. Nest in large cavity high in mature live tree; in Peru cavities used repeatedly for yrs., and nest cavities are often re-visited and guarded even when birds are not nesting; 1–2 eggs (C. Munn).

Status and habitat: Fairly common resident in humid lowland and foothill forest and in partially deforested areas. Now very local and in decline (or extirpated) in many areas of north and west (e.g., Zulia, Táchira, Carabobo, ne Bolívar). Small nos. persist in vicinity of Cerro Misión, Falcón. Pop. prob. stable in Delta Amacuro and s of Orinoco. In Venez. found in more humid and heavily forested regions than Scarlet Macaw, and much more in upland or terra firme forests than Blue-and-yellow Macaw.

Range: To ca. 500m n of Orinoco; to 1530m s of Orinoco. Maracaibo Basin, Zulia (n to Mene Grande), and nw Táchira; e base of Andes in w Apure and w Barinas; n Carabobo and se Falcón (sight, Cerro Misión); nw Bolívar (Hato Las Nieves) and Amazonas; s Delta Amacuro and e Bolívar. E Panama to n Argentina, Paraguay, and s Brazil.

Note: By some called Green-winged Macaw.

Chestnut-fronted Macaw   PLATE 21
Ara severa   Maracaná
Identification: 19″ (48cm). 335g. *Half the size of large
macaws.* Bill black, eyes orange to yellow. Long
pointed tail. Mainly green with *underside of wings
and tail dull red*; bend of wing bright red, *primaries
blue* above (conspic. in flight), secondaries green
above; up close shows narrow chestnut frontlet and
bluish crown; bare facial skin *whitish but often looks
yellow in low light.*
Sim. species: Slightly larger than largest parakeets, all
of which lack bare face typical of macaws. In flight
from other small macaws by *red underwings* (color
of facial skin unreliable).
Voice: Flight call a grating, scratchy (like fingernails
on a blackboard) *jaiiit,* shrill and without deep harsh
gruffness of large macaws. When perched gives a liquid or gurgling *kurrit.* Remarkable song, often given
when a pr. perches together in evening, a long rambling ser. of gurgles, liquid slides, falsettos, and
occas. rough notes that may continue intermittently
for several min.
Behavior: Usually in prs. or small groups up to ca. 20
that may commute long distances from roosting to
feeding areas. In some areas (e.g., llanos) gather in
large roosting groups for a few months (Nov–Jan).
Most active mornings and evenings, less so during
midday. Jun nests in tree cavity in w Apure; also use
cavity in dead palm. Nest in May, Suriname, over
water[253].
Status and habitat: Fairly common resident in a
wide variety of forested or partly forested habitats
incl. gallery forest and dry to moist woodland in
llanos, morichales (groves of *Mauritia* palms) in wet
grasslands, and humid lowland forest. Also in urban
areas (most are escaped cagebirds) where may roost
and nest in royal palms, e.g., Valencia, Caracas, etc.
In general thrives even in relatively settled areas,
e.g., nw Táchira.

Range: To 1000m n and s of Orinoco. Maracaibo
Basin and w base of Andes in Táchira and Mérida;
e of Andes from Apure, Barinas, Portuguesa, Carabobo, and e Falcón (sight, Cerro Misión) to coastal
foothills in Aragua (Turiamo); locally (introd.?) in
Distr. Federal and Miranda; Cojedes s to Amazonas
and in nw Bolívar se to Brazilian border (*severa*).
E Panama to w Ecuador, n Bolivia, and se Brazil
(Bahía).

Red-bellied Macaw   PLATE 21
Orthopsittaca manilata   Guacamayo Barriga Roja
Identification: 18″ (46cm). 370g. Eyes reddish brown;
large bare area of yellowish facial skin. Bill black; tail
long and pointed. Mainly green with bluish head
and *red belly* (often visible even in flight); *primaries
from above blue, underwings and undertail brassy
gold.*
Sim. species: Smaller, quicker Red-shouldered
Macaw has conspic. red wrists from below. Chestnut-
fronted Macaw has red (not greenish gold) underwings. Smaller Blue-crowned and White-eyed parakeets lack bare face.
Voice: Flight call a reedy, strained *neeareek* with urgent, complaining, not raucous, quality.
Behavior: Prs. when breeding, otherwise in varying-
sized groups up to 100 or more. Most often seen in
flight during morning and evening commutes to feeding and roosting sites. Flight is fast and steady with
fairly rapid wing beats, suggesting a large *Aratinga*
more than a macaw, but with rather swept-back
wings. In all areas strongly assoc. with *Mauritia* (moriche) palms which are used for nest sites (cavities),
roosts, and seeds for food. In Guyana breeds Feb–
Jun, cavity in palm that often is standing in water[389].
Status and habitat: Locally common resident in extensive groves of *Mauritia* palms, esp. in areas of
mixed savanna and forest. Also moriche swamps in
lowland forest. Large nos. roost and feed in moriche
palms ne of Santa Elena de Uairén. Destruction of
these palm trunks for posts and palm fronds in arte-
sian industry (hammocks, baskets, etc.), extensive deforestation for cattle grazing, and trapping for cage
traffic have resulted in a significant decline in this
sp.[150]. Seasonal movements likely but not
documented.

Range: To 500m; sight to 900m (se Bolívar). Ne Anzoátegui and Sucre (Caño La Brea) s through Monagas to Delta Amacuro n and e Bolívar (lower Río
Caura s to Santa Elena de Uairén); sight, nw Amazonas (Pto. Ayacucho)[259]. Locally e of Andes s to
Bolivia and Amaz. Brazil.
Note: Taxonomy follows Juniper and Parr[287].

Red-shouldered Macaw   PLATE 21
Diopsittaca nobilis   Guacamayo Enano
Identification: 13–14″ (33–36cm). 150g. *Very small
macaw* (size of *Aratinga* parakeet). Eyes reddish
orange. Long pointed tail. Mainly green; *bend of
shoulders red, primaries green,* under wing coverts

and undertail brassy yellow green; forecrown blue; *bare facial skin much restricted in size, pinkish white.* **Sim. species:** Best marks are very small size, red shoulders, bare face, and lack of red on belly. In flight from Red-bellied Macaw by *green primaries* (it is only *Ara* with essentially all-green flight feathers) and red underwrists; from White-eyed Parakeet by facial skin, blue crown, and in flight, lack of red and yellow under wing coverts. Also see Blue-crowned Parakeet.

Voice: Flight call a soft, nasal, and rather high *neee* given constantly by flock members, not harsh and guttural as in large *Ara*. At a distance calls of a flock have a gabbling, gooselike quality.

Behavior: Prs. or small to large groups up to ca. 40 (occas. to 100 or more) are usually found around *Mauritia* palms where they roost and nest and are reg. seen in flight, commuting between palm groves. Often "freeze" in palms and allow close approach before flushing. Sometimes loosely assoc. with Red-bellied Macaws. Flight is fast but somewhat weaving. Flocks usually do not fly high. Reported feeding on *Cordia* and *Erythrina* seeds[829]; also on *Mauritia* palm seeds. In Guyana breeds Feb–Jun, hole in live or dead palm or arboreal termitarium[389].

Status and habitat: Uncommon to fairly common resident in small nos. in palm-dotted (*Mauritia*) savannas and gallery forests of s portion of Gran Sabana. Wanders seasonally to humid forest and forest borders but generally near *Mauritia* palms. Almost always less numerous than allied Red-bellied Macaw and declining for similar reasons (loss of moriche palms).

Range: To 1400m. N Monagas s through Delta Amacuro; locally along mid. and lower Orinoco in Bolívar from Río Caura e and s to Gran Sabana (*nobilis*). The Guianas; ne, e, and se Brazil.
Note: Taxonomy follows Juniper and Parr[287].

Aratinga

Large (some as large as small macaws); long pointed tail; conspic. bare white ocular ring; high, fast-flying flocks. Called conure instead of parakeet by some.

Blue-crowned Parakeet   PLATE 22
Aratinga acuticaudata Carapaico
Identification: 13.5" (34cm). Bill yellowish white above, grayish below; eyes yellow to orange to brown, surrounded by *conspic. bare whitish ocular*

ring. Long pointed tail. Plumage mainly green with *blue forecrown;* underwings and undertail yellow green, outer tail feathers dull red on inner webs (inconspic.). Or smaller (12"; 30cm); eyes whitish (*neoxena*).
Sim. species: A large, entirely green parakeet of dry regions. Up close watch for blue on head. White-eyed Parakeet has red and yellow under wing coverts, no blue on head. Brown-throated Parakeet is much smaller, brownish on face and underparts. Also see Red-shouldered Macaw and slightly larger Red-bellied Macaw.

Voice: Flight call a smooth, gabbling *c'r'r'a,* almost musical but with blurred roughness; in tone quality nearest that of Red-bellied Macaw.

Behavior: Travels in varying-sized flocks of 8–50 or more, rarely up to 200, usually flying fairly low, often over savanna or semiopen areas. Regularly commutes long distances between roosting and feeding sites each morning and evening. Feeds on seeds and fruit. Nest (in Argentina) in tree cavity.

Status and habitat: Fairly common resident but quite local, mainly in dry forest and savanna, dry scrubby vegetation, and gallery forest in dry to moist regions. Shows marked seasonal movements; at Cantaura, Anzoátegui, mostly absent Feb–Jul but nos. increased from Aug to peak in late Jan[186]. Formerly much commoner but in decline because of extensive cultivation, deforestation, and settlement of former habitats. In severe decline on Isla Margarita[150]. Still occurs in some nos. locally in c Falcón (s of Sierra de San Luis) and Tumeremo, ne Bolívar.

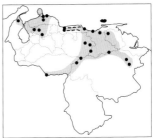

Range: To 600m. Nw Zulia (Río Socuy) e through Falcón and n Lara; Aragua (below Rancho Grande), se Miranda, e Guárico, Anzoátegui, and n Monagas to nw and ne Bolívar (Tumeremo); Río Meta (Cararabo) in s Apure; prob. entire mid. Orinoco (*koenigi*); Isla Margarita (*neoxena*). Ne Colombia and Venez.; e and s Brazil to Bolivia and c Argentina.
Note: Subsp. *haemorrhous*[403] is now *koenigi*[287]. Subsp. *neoxena* not recognized by some[180].

Scarlet-fronted Parakeet   PLATE 22
Aratinga wagleri Chacaraco
Identification: 13.5" (34cm). 190g. Bill brown; eyes orange to yellow; large bare whitish ocular ring. Long pointed tail. *Mainly green, forecrown red;* under wing coverts green, *underwings and undertail brassy yellow green.* Some individuals have small patches of red on neck, chest, bend of wing, or around legs.

Sim. species: In Andes and n mts. the only large green parakeet with red forecrown (red not conspic. at a distance). Note habits and distrib. (only in foothills and mts.). See smaller Brown-throated Parakeet; also Rose-crowned and smaller Barred parakeets.
Voice: Loud strident *skreek*! flight call is high pitched and discordant; at a distance resembles calls of Red-billed Parrot.
Behavior: A large parakeet of Andes and n cordilleras. Gregarious, noisy, and most likely seen in large flocks flying high overhead. Where unmolested roosts in flocks of 1000s, e.g., Jan–Feb below La Azulita and at Caripe, Monagas. Flocks break up by May or Jun at onset of rains to breed early in rainy season. Wander widely in search of fruits and seeds and are occas. destructive in cornfields. Nest (in Colombia) in crevices in rock cliffs.
Status and habitat: Fairly common resident but now somewhat local. Shows marked seasonal movements and pops. may disappear for months; moist to humid mt. forest, coffee plantations, and partially forested regions. Sometime seen flying long distances high over largely deforested regions. Present nos. doubtless much reduced. Large flocks Jan–May or Jun above Maracay, but few in latter months of year. Once (vagrant or escaped) in w Guárico (P. Alden).

Range: Mainly 700–2000m (occas. almost to sea level). Sierra de Perijá, Zulia; both slopes of Andes in Mérida n to nw and s Lara (*wagleri*); mts. of Falcón (Sierra de San Luis) and Yaracuy, and n cordilleras e to Distr. Federal; mts of Sucre and n Monagas at Caripe (*transilis*). Colombia s in Andes to Peru.

White-eyed Parakeet   PLATE 22
Aratinga leucophthalmus   Perico Ojo Blanco
Identification: 13.5″ (34cm). 160g. Bill cream colored; eyes orange to light brown. Conspic. bare whitish ocular area encircles eye (the "white eye"); long pointed tail. Mainly green, *lesser under wing coverts and bend of wing red, median and greater under wing coverts yellow* (conspic. in flight), rest of underwing and undertail brassy greenish yellow.
Sim. species: In flight from any other long-tailed parakeet in Venez. by conspic. red and yellow under wing coverts. Name is misleading as most *Aratinga* have bare ocular rings, but ocular ring is larger and more conspic. in this sp.
Voice: Flight call a harsh grating *geeit* or *jeeit*, sometimes over and over, coarser and raspier than corresponding calls of other *Aratinga*.

Behavior: Very social and usually in noisy flocks, sometimes up to 100 or more, that commute to and from feeding and roosting areas each morning and evening. Fly long distances high over forest or partially open country. Flight is fast and straight. Like to feed in treetops in river- or forest-edge trees, esp. flowering trees (e.g., *Erythrina*), where they eat blossoms as well as fruit and seeds. In Peru nest in cavities in trees (often in dead palms).
Status and habitat: Fairly common to locally common resident in humid terra firme and várzea forest, *Mauritia* palms (morichales), and mangroves; also over partially deforested or semiopen terrain in humid regions. Marked seasonal movements in nw Monagas where present mainly Jan–Jun[186].

Range: To 500m. N Anzoátegui, se Sucre (sight, Guaraunos, 1996—R. Ridgely), Monagas, and Delta Amacuro s to ne Bolívar on Río Paragua, Sierra de Imataca, and La Bomba on Río Yuruarí (*leucophthalmus*). E Colombia and the Guianas to n Argentina and Uruguay.

[Sun Parakeet]   PLATE 22
Aratinga solstitialis   Perico Dorado
Identification: 11″ (28cm). No unequivocal recs. in Venez. Eyes brown; bill and legs dusky gray. *Upperparts mainly yellow, below orange yellow*, forecrown and sides of head bright orange; lesser and median upper wing coverts yellow, greater upper wing coverts green, *flight feathers blue* with patch of green at base of wing; tail olive tipped blue. Brightness of ad. plumage varies. Juv.: duller, upperparts marked with green; underparts more orange.
Sim. species: No other parakeet in Venez. is mostly yellow and orange.
Voice: Flight call is unparrotlike, high pitched and repetitive, like wheezy yapping of Boat-billed Flycatcher[284].
Behavior: In Brazil occurs in flocks of various sizes which may fly rapidly over open savanna or partially wooded terrain. Between 1840 and 1844 reported in *Malpighia* trees, and in immense flocks in forested valley of Rio Cotinga (= Contigo) near Mt. Curatakie, Brazil, by Schomburgk. Flock movements reported by several observers may represent nomadism or reg. seasonal responses to food abundance. Nests in Feb, s Suriname; cavity in a *Mauritia* palm[253].
Status and habitat: HYPOTHETICAL. No specimen. 1 distant flying bird (prob. this sp.) 20 km ne Santa Elena de Uairén, late 1970s (C. Parrish). Specimen at-

tributed to Venez. from near Cerro Roraima by Schomburgk in 1848 appear to have been taken in Brazilian territory[284]. Found in tree-dotted savannas in s Suriname; in Brazil in savanna and savanna woodland, forest edges, secondary forest, cultivated regions, and carnauba palm groves. If it occurs in Venez., it is (or was) prob. only a *very rare* seasonal or sporadic migrant along se border. Has been heavily trapped in Guyana; birds from sector of Rupununi Savanna in Guyana (the pop. nearest Venez.) apparently extirpated by trapping in early 1980s (M. B. Robbins).

Range: 1200m. Possibly se border with Guyana and Brazil. S Guyana, s Suriname, and ne Brazil (Sierra Pacaraima and s of Roraima) s to s of the Amazon.

Brown-throated Parakeet
PLATE 22
Aratinga pertinax Perico Cara Sucia
Identification: 10″ (25cm). 85g. *Above bright green, flight feathers blue* (often not conspic.), narrow frontlet powdery white mixed brown, rest of crown dull gray blue, large feathered eyering dull orangish to yellowish to whitish, *sides of head to chest dull brown* turning greenish yellow on lower underparts, central tail feathers blue distally, rest green; *under wing coverts greenish yellow* (greater under wing coverts yellowish), rest of underwing from below gray (*venezuelae*). Or in arid nw, frontlet and forehead brown, little or no eyering, no yellowish on belly (*aeruginosa*). Or frontlet brownish (*chrysophrys*). Or eyering unusually large and bold (ne Venez. and offshore isls.). Or eyering and cheeks dull yellowish (*surinama*).
Sim. species: Shares its dry habitat with Blue-crowned Parakeet. Note med. size, green upperparts, and brownish underparts. Watch for contrasting yellow under wing coverts in flight. Spanish name, meaning "Dirty-faced Parakeet," is a reference to appearance.
Voice: Flight call a rough, harsh *chzak* or *cherr-chzek*, given constantly and often the first indication of approach of a group.
Behavior: Very social and usually in small flocks of 3–15 or so that fly fast and low in tight twisting formation through scrubby semiopen country. Groups rest in tops of small trees, even bushes, but are suspicious and apt to flush off noisily when approached. Eat a wide variety of seeds, fruits, and blossoms, incl. nectar-rich blossoms of legume *Gliricidia*; locally a high percentage of food comes from domesticated

plants or those planted by humans. Nests Feb–Apr in ne Anzoátegui; hollowed-out termite nest; 3–4 eggs[186].
Status and habitat: Widespread and common resident in dry to arid regions. Desert scrub, esp. with columnar cactus which provide nest cavities; also mangroves, dry forest, gallery forest, ranchland, savanna, and dry semiopen areas with scrubby or abused vegetation. Occurs widely s of Orinoco in white sandy soil savannas with scattered trees. Some local seasonal movement.

Range: To 1500m n of Orinoco; to 1600m s of Orinoco. Nw Zulia (*aeruginosa*); most of rest of n Venez. (*venezuelae*); Delta Amacuro and se Monagas (*surinama*); se Bolívar from Gran Sabana (Cerro Roraima) to upper Río Caroní (*chrysophrys*); w Amazonas (*lehmanni*); Isla Margarita (*margaritensis*); Isla Tortuga (*tortugensis*). Sw Panama to the Guianas and n Brazil; Netherlands Antilles. Introd. on St. Thomas in Virgin Isls.

Pyrrhura

Slender; med. sized; long, tapering, bluntly rounded and reddish tail; primaries mostly blue above; often with patches of red on forehead, cheeks, or shoulders; scaly chest; bare orbital ring; fly in fast-flying, tight flocks in forest. Distrib. of various spp. complex; those in Venez. largely or wholly allopatric. Called "conure" by some.

Painted Parakeet
PLATE 22
Pyrrhura picta Perico Pechiescamado
Identification: 9″ (23cm). 63g. Eyes yellowish to yellowish brown; bill dusky; small pale eyering. Generally much like Maroon-faced Parakeet. Frontlet and sides of head maroon bordered by round *silvery white patch on rear cheeks*; crown dull blue, brownish behind; rest of upperparts green, *tail mostly dark red, throat and chest dusky broadly scaled dull whitish to cream color (scales distinctly V-shaped)*, green below, red belly patch; bend of wing red, *primaries blue*.
Sim. species: Minimal overlap with Fiery-shouldered Parakeet which is on slopes of tepuis (not lowlands) and has flashy red and yellow under wing coverts, green head, and few scales. Maroon-tailed Parakeet is much plainer (no head pattern, no belly patch, no color on shoulders, and few scales) and mainly in lowlands.

Voice: Flight call a coarse *pik-pik* or *pik-pik-pik*, rather forceful but less harsh than flight calls of most others of genus.
Behavior: As in other *Pyrrhura*. In tepuis see Fiery-shouldered Parakeet.
Status and habitat: Fairly common resident in tall humid forest and scattered trees in forest clearings in lowlands and foothills. Distrib. s of Orinoco is complex—in Amazonas and in w and s Bolívar most recs. are from slopes of tepuis (e.g., above range of Maroon-tailed Parakeet); in e Bolívar occurs in lowlands, and in vicinity of Gran Sabana in se Bolívar it is replaced on slopes of tepuis by Fiery-shouldered Parakeet.

Range: To ca. 1000m (to 1800 on Cerro Yavi, Amazonas). Amazonas (mostly slopes of tepuis) and Bolívar; s Delta Amacuro at Manoa (*picta*). The Guianas and locally from ne Brazil to e Ecuador, e Peru, and n Bolivia.
Note: Formerly incl. Perijá Parakeet (*P. caeruleiceps*) and isolated pops. in Panama and n Colombia.

Perijá Parakeet
Pyrrhura caeruleiceps   Perico de Perijá
Identification: Sim. to Painted Parakeet but eyering dull (not maroon), cheeks maroon (not bicolored maroon and blue), and with broad dusky bars (not chevrons) on chest.
Sim. species: No other *Pyrrhura* in its range. Cf. smaller Barred Parakeet.
Status and habitat: Little known. Considered a distinguishable phylogenetic sp. by Joseph[285] and here tentatively raised to sp. level to emphasize its isolated range. Its status as a biological sp. seems questionable. Both subspp. (below) have been considered subspp. of Painted Parakeet (*P. picta*), a sp. found primarily in lowland regions of Amazonia but ranging well up into lower montane els. on some tepuis of s Venez. The few specimens from Venez. are from humid montane forest in the Sierra de Perijá. Behav-

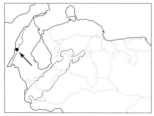

ior presum. sim. to that of Painted Parakeet. Highland cloud forest.
Range: 2000m. Sierra de Perijá (headwaters of Quebrada Ponjía), Zulia (*pantchenkoi*). Colombia (100–1300m) in foothills at w base of Sierra de Perijá in s César and w base of E Andes in Magdalena (*caeruleiceps*).
Note 1: The 2 subspp. (above) differ little if at all.
Note 2: This sp. (and isolated pops. in Colombia and sw Panama) are closely allied to Venezuelan Parakeet (*P. leucotis*).

Venezuelan Parakeet   PLATE 22
Pyrrhura emma   Perico Pintado
Identification: 9″ (23cm). Eyes orange to yellow; bill dusky. Frontlet and sides of head maroon bordered behind by *prom. whitish fringed patch on rear cheeks*; crown dull blue, rear half mixed brownish, rest of upperparts green, tail mostly dull red, *chest olive broadly scalloped yellowish white* (scalelike bars), otherwise green below, large dull red patch on lower breast and belly; *primaries blue* (conspic. in flight). Some birds (mainly *emma*) show red at bend of shoulders.
Sim. species: Blood-eared Parakeet lacks strong head pattern and scaling.
Voice: Flight call a loud, harsh *KIK-KIK-KIK-KIK* with hard edge (unlike whining call of allied Blood-eared Parakeet). Angry or distress call of perched bird a nasal, *Synallaxis*-like *wa-Ké-Ké-Ke-ka*.
Behavior: Sim. to that of Blood-eared Parakeet. Seen eating balsa (*Ochroma*) flowers and nectar at PN Guatopo (C. Parrish).
Status and habitat: Fairly common resident but distrib. complex and disjunct. Humid and wet forest and forest borders, mostly in hilly terrain at low els. Little or no range overlap with allied Blood-eared Parakeet.

Range: ENDEMIC. 250–1700m (to sea level in e Sucre). Mts. of Yaracuy and Carabobo (e to Río Morón); mts. of Distr. Federal, interior mts. of s Aragua (Aricagua; Cerro Golfo Triste) and Miranda (s to PN Guatopo) and w Anzoátegui (sight—C. Parrish) on Cerro Tucusito (*emma*); mts. of e Anzoátegui (Bergantín), Sucre, and n Monagas s to Caripe (*auricularis*).
Note: Previously called Maroon-faced Parakeet (*P. leucotis*)[403], a name now applied to birds of se Brazil[285].

Fiery-shouldered Parakeet PLATE 22

Pyrrhura egregia   Perico de Pantepui

Identification: 10″ (25cm). *Med.-sized green parakeet of se tepuis.* Eyes brown; *conspic. bare eyering whitish.* Flashes *brilliant blue primaries* in flight and *bold red and yellow (mixed) under wing coverts* as it flies. Chest patch scaled with gray, tail dark maroon red, bend of shoulders red. Up close shows narrow maroon frontlet and brownish tinged crown; lower mandible dusky.

Sim. species: No other parakeet in tepuis flashes red and yellow underwings in flight. Smaller Tepui Parrotlet lacks these colors. In lowlands see Painted, Maroon-tailed, and Golden-winged parakeets.

Voice: Flight call an unusually harsh, grating *jjaaEEK!*, often the first indication a flock is approaching.

Behavior: Flies in small, tight, fast-flying flocks of 3–25 (usually ca. 6–10) that thread and twist their way through forest canopy or lower with amazing speed and agility, then suddenly settle into a canopy tree and "disappear." Typically very silent and watchful when feeding on fruit or seeds, but usually utter a few scratchy calls immediately before taking flight. If surprised when feeding may freeze and watch carefully. Noted eating *Cecropia* catkins.

Status and habitat: Resident in humid and wet (mossy) premontane forest and tall dense second-growth forest on tepui slopes. More in flocks Dec–Mar. Common above 1000m on Sierra de Lema.

Range: 700–1800m. Tepuis of se Bolívar from upper Río Caroní (incl. Auyán; Aprada; Chimantá; Paurai; and Uei-tepui) e to forests on Gran Sabana (*obscura*); slopes of Cerro Roraima (*egregia*). W Guyana.

Blood-eared Parakeet PLATE 22

Pyrrhura hoematotis   Perico Cola Roja

Identification: 10″ (25cm). 70g. Eyes brown; bill dull horn gray; eyering dull whitish blue. Mainly coastal mts. Mostly dark green, crown tinged blue, *small elongated red patch on ear-coverts* ("the blood ears"), underparts tinged brownish, sides of neck, throat, and chest with obscure dusky scaling; *primaries blue*, under wing coverts green, *tail dull dark red above and below*; central belly red. Or sim. but greener below and no scaling (*immarginata*).

Sim. species: Venezuelan Parakeet (not known to overlap in range) differs in dark maroon face, white cheek patch, and red at bend of wing. Scarlet-

fronted Parakeet is larger, all green with red frontlet, and usually not inside forest.

Voice: Flight call a grating squeal, lacking harshness of some in genus.

Behavior: Much like other *Pyrrhura* (see). Travels in tight, fast-flying flocks of ca. 6–25 (occas. much larger groups) that swoop through forest canopy then alight suddenly and disappear. Just as abruptly may burst into flight with a volley of screeching and fly off swerving through canopy. When foraging climb about quietly and slyly among branches and foliage; eat a variety of fruit and seeds, esp. *Heliocarpus* seeds. Aug breeding[571].

Status and habitat: Common resident in humid and wet forest (cloud forest), along forest borders, and in tall second-growth woodland. Some seasonal movements (local and el.) during yr. Usually around Rancho Grande Biol. Station, Aragua.

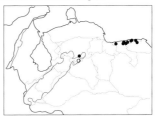

Range: ENDEMIC. 800–2000m (Once to 420m, Miranda). Se Lara at Cubiro; sight at Yacambú (*immarginata*). Coastal Cordillera from Aragua e to Miranda at Curupao and Guarenas (*hoematotis*).

Maroon-tailed Parakeet

Pyrrhura melanura   Perico Cola Negra

Identification: 9″ (23cm). 68g. Eyes brown; bare ocular area whitish; bill dusky horn. Only s of Orinoco. *Mostly green*, crown tinged brown, *throat and chest dusky brown narrowly scaled buff and white* (forms obvious band of scaling extending across chest and up to sides of neck), *tail dark maroon*, primaries dull blue green, often also with small *patch of red or yellow at base of primaries* (on primary coverts); sometimes shows red at bend of wing; under wing coverts green.

Sim. species: Resembles others of genus but no red belly patch, primaries *much duller*, tail darker. Note lack of head markings (cf. Painted Parakeet). Look for red or yellow on primary coverts.

Voice: Flight calls are among harshest and most grating of genus; silent when perched and foraging.

Behavior: Sim. to others of genus but usually only in small groups of 5–9. Fly rapidly, weaving their way through canopy, calling as they go, or fly low across narrow rivers and small forest openings. When in fruiting trees very quiet and watchful, climbing around slowly and feeding methodically, but occas. falling fruit or soft notes prior to taking flight give away their presence.

Status and habitat: Uncommon to fairly common resident (easily overlooked except for loud flight calls) in humid lowland forest in Amazonas.

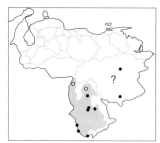

Range: To 300m (prob. higher). Throughout Amazonas; e Bolívar from lower to upper Río Paragua (*melanura*); no recs. in Río Caura. Se Colombia to ne Peru and w Amaz. Brazil; locally in Andes from s Colombia to n Peru (latter perhaps a different sp.).

Rose-crowned Parakeet   PLATE 22
Pyrrhura rhodocephala   Perico Cabecirrojo
Identification: 10″ (25cm). Eyes brown; prom. bare ocular ring whitish; bill pale pinkish white. *Crown peachy red*, tiny red patch on ear coverts, otherwise mainly green, *primaries bright blue; conspic. white patch at base of primaries* (primary coverts); tail dark red, breast tinged olive and vaguely scaled dusky; red belly patch variable in size.
Sim. species: Crown and wing patch are the marks, but latter often hidden when bird is at rest. In restricted mt. range see Rusty-faced and Speckle-faced parrots, both with different habits, shapes, etc.; also Scarlet-fronted Parakeet.
Voice: Flight calls are softer, less harsh than notes of most *Pyrrhura*. When perched a clear *clee*, sharp *kik!*, and rapid, angry-sounding *kik-kik-kik-kik*.
Behavior: Most often seen in noisy flocks flying low over mt. forests, but unlike many others of genus reg. wanders over open areas away from forest, often perching in isolated trees, on fence posts, even wires along pasture borders. Feeds on a variety of small seeds incl. *Heliocarpus* (Tiliaceae) and esp. *Chusquea* bamboo.
Status and habitat: Fairly common resident in humid and wet montane forest, wooded borders, and highland pastures with scattered trees. Wanders widely, esp. to lower els. during rainy months of late May–Nov.

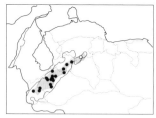

Range: ENDEMIC. 800–3100m (mostly 1500–2500m). Andes of n Táchira, Mérida, nw Barinas, Trujillo (n to Páramo de Cendé on Lara border), and s Lara (sight, PN Yacambú).
Note: Previously called Rose-headed Parakeet[403].

Bolborhynchus

Small, green, highland parrotlets with blunt bill swollen on sides; *short, wedge-shaped* tail; in hand note pointed tail feathers.

Barred Parakeet   PLATE 22
Bolborhynchus lineola   Perico Barreteado
Identification: 6.3–6.7″ (16–17cm). 54g. Small and barred. Bill pinkish horn. Plumage all green, darker above; bright apple green below; neck and back finely scaled and barred black; rump coarsely barred black; *entire sides of underparts narrowly barred black*; shoulder patch and 2 narrow wing bars black. ♀ and juv.: sim. but duller; barring less prom.
Sim. species: Black barring and wing markings can be hard to see. Most likely confused with a *Touit* parrotlet, e.g., Blue-fronted Parrotlet which overlaps in Andes and Lilac-tailed Parrotlet which overlaps in n cordilleras, but in flight told from either by pointed (not squarish) tail, and different flight calls. Also see various spp. of *Pyrrhura*, all slightly larger, and Green-rumped Parrotlet.
Voice: Flight call a soft, mushy *chewuuee* (or *whuweee*) uttered quickly and with breezy, whining quality. Given constantly in flight. At a distance flock calls have soft chattery sound.
Behavior: Usually seen in prs. or fast-flying flocks of 3–100, occas. more, commuting long distances in *straight* purposeful flight *high* over mt. forest or partially wooded terrain. Flight is rapid and buzzy with no pause in wing beats. Before landing apt to circle an area for several min and call repeatedly. Feed on many small fruits, seeds, buds, and esp. bamboo seeds, in mt. forest canopy or edges, where quiet, conservative of movement, and very difficult to detect. Other *Bolborhynchus* are known to nest in colonies in rocky cliffs[280].
Status and habitat: Uncommon and unpredictable resident or nomad, often locally and/or seasonally numerous (e.g., many at 2100–2200m over PN Guaramacal, Trujillo, Feb 1996); possibly somewhat affiliated with bamboo seeding (R. Ridgely). Able to disperse long distances rapidly and may wander over immense areas.

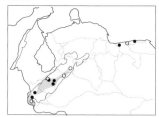

Range: 900–1500m (sight to 2200m). Andes of Táchira, Mérida, and Trujillo (*tigrinus*); Coastal Cordillera in Aragua (specimen, Rancho Grande—M. Lentino; Hilty[259]; subsp.?) and Dist. Federal (sight e of Colonia Tovar—P. Alden). S Mexico locally in mts. to c Peru.

Forpus

Very small, chunky, green parrotlets; short, somewhat wedge-shaped tail (shorter than in *Bolborhynchus*), all spp. very sim.; ♂♂ have blue in wings. In hand, tail feathers very pointed; flight jerky and erratic, buzzy wing beats alternating with closed wings.

Green-rumped Parrotlet   PLATE 22
Forpus passerinus   Periquito Mastrantero
Identification: 5″ (12.7cm). 23g. *Bill pinkish white to ivory. Sparrow sized and very bright green*, brightest and lightest on rump and underparts; lower part of *median and greater upper wing coverts and all under wing coverts blue* (not conspic. when perched); primary coverts dark blue (show as small patch at base of flight feathers). ♀: sim. to ♂ but all green; sometimes with yellow on forecrown (amt. varies, often not conspic.) or tinged yellow around eyes.
Sim. species: Few others of genus in its range. ♂'s green rump is very bright but hard to see unless bird flushes. Dusky-billed Parrotlet, mainly in e forests, is darker green with obvious dusky (not whitish) bill. ♀ prob. often not separable from others of genus but may show yellow around eyes. Also cf. Spectacled Parrotlet.
Voice: Constant ser. of shrill, chattery *chee* and *cheet-it* and *chee-sup* notes when foraging and in flight (like notes of little finches). Song a much longer, sustained, and complex ser. of sputtery notes.
Behavior: Prs. or chatty and twittery groups of 5–50 or more call incessantly but can be difficult to locate if perched in foliage. Fly in little dipping spurts, a few buzzy wing beats then a free-fall as wings are closed tightly for a moment. Feed on small fruits, buds, and flowers and eat many grass and weed seeds by perching on bending stems, or from gd. Nest in hollow limbs, termitary, stub, or old hornero nest; or many excavate a hole; 5 eggs and 2 young in late-Apr nest in Orinoco region[115]; breeding May–Nov, sw Guárico and ne Anzoátegui[186,734].
Status and habitat: Widespread. Common to locally abundant resident in dry to arid scrub, deciduous woodland, gallery forest, ranchland with scattered shrubs and trees, urban parks, and cultivated areas. Dry to moist regions, small nos. expanding into humid zones following deforestation. Abundant over much of llanos.

Range: To 1800m (mostly below 1000m). Throughout n of Orinoco incl. Delta Amacuro; s of Orinoco in n Bolívar from Caicara and lower Río Caura e to Río

Grande and Río Cuyuní (sight, 2001) (*viridissimus*). E Colombia to the Guianas and ne Amaz. Brazil. Trinidad. Introd. on various isls. in Carib. incl. Jamaica, Curaçao, and Barbados.

Spectacled Parrotlet
Forpus conspicillatus   Periquito Ojiazul
Identification: 4.8″ (12.2cm). 26g. *Bright green*. Bill pale gray. ♂: plumage mostly green, lightest and brightest on head; *rump glistening cobalt blue, leading edge of upper and under wing coverts and part of upper wing coverts glistening cobalt blue*, small patch or line of blue over and behind eyes. ♀: rump and tail pale emerald green (contrast with darker body), forehead tinged yellow, no blue on wings or head.
Sim. species: ♂ from previous sp. by blue rump and blue near eyes; ♀ best told by accompanying ♂ but consistently shows a little yellow on forehead, and note paler, more apple green rear parts (♀ Green-rumped Parrotlet has dark emerald rear end concolor with body). In hand this sp. is slightly smaller, shorter-tailed, and has smaller bill than Green-rumped. Also cf. Dusky-billed Parrotlet.
Voice: Shrill jangling ser. of chatters and twitters, like little finch notes, given incessantly. Almost identical to calls of Green-rumped Parrotlet.
Behavior: Sim. to that of Green-rumped Parrotlet.
Status and habitat: Dry semiopen ranchland, brushy pastures, and gallery forest borders in llanos. Known only from a few localities in Venez. but common there (many specimens). Possibly overlooked (very like Green-rumped Parrotlet). Common in adj. Colombia.

Range: To 100m. W Apure on Río Meta at Cararabo and Frontera (*metae*). E Panama and Colombia (to 2600m).

Dusky-billed Parrotlet
Forpus sclateri   Periquito Pico Oscuro
Identification: 5″ (12.7cm). 25g. *Bill dusky above, slightly paler gun metal gray below. ♂: overall dark green, and paler, more apple green below; rump glistening blue*; patch of blue at base of wing, part of greater and median upper wing coverts, and under wing coverts blue. ♀: sim. but no blue in plumage.
Sim. species: Obviously *dark bill* is the mark. Plumage darker green than others of genus, and various patches of blue are inconspic. in field. See esp. Green-rumped Parrotlet. ♀ from other ♀ *Forpus* by dark bill; from Tepui Parrotlet by smaller size, different bill shape, and ♂ also by blue on wings and rump.

Voice: Flight call a buzzy *bzeeet*, lacking jangling quality of others of genus. Also gives a soft, thin *jeeea* and *weeenk*, doubled or trebled. Song, by prs. when perched, a soft ser. of 5–8 chittery *chet* notes.

Behavior: Prs. when breeding, otherwise in small twittery groups that are usually noisy in flight but become very quiet and furtive when perched in forest canopy. Occas. in *Cecropia* trees along forest borders but in general much less conspic. than nonforest allies such as Green-rumped Parrotlet. Flight is dipping, erratic, and usually not long sustained.

Status and habitat: Uncommon to fairly common resident in humid lowland forest and along forest borders. Easily overlooked. Not known to wander widely or commute long distances between roosts and feeding areas.

Range: To 300m. N Bolívar in lower Río Caura (?); Sierra de Imataca (Río Grande), upper Río Cuyuní, and Sierra de Lema; sw Amazonas (specimen and sightings) at San Carlos de Río Negro (*eidos*). Se Colombia to n Bolivia, Amaz. Brazil, and the Guianas.

Brotogeris

Small; rather short, wedge-shaped tail; wings pointed; buzzy wing beats alternate with closed wings, producing jerky erratic flight; mainly lowlands; often active throughout heat of the day. In hand tail feathers very pointed.

Orange-chinned Parakeet   PLATE 22
Brotogeris jugularis   Perico Ala Marrón
Identification: 7″ (18cm). 61g. Bill maroon pink. Entirely green, crown often faintly tinged bluish, back tinged olive to brownish; below brighter, more yellowish green; bend of wing and *shoulders bronzy brown*; small chin spot orange, primary coverts dark blue (inconspic.), under wing coverts and axillaries bright yellow.

Sim. species: See Green-rumped Parrotlet and Brown-throated Parakeet. No overlap in range with others of genus.

Voice: Noisy, esp. in flight, where keeps up a shrill chatter mixed with many buzzy notes. In fruit trees may be quiet or noisy, uttering a variety of buzzy, grating, and shrill notes.

Behavior: Prs. when breeding, otherwise in small chattery and well-coordinated flocks. Fly in fits and starts, spurting ahead with buzz of wing beats, then a free fall with wings closed for a sec, and with freq. lit-

tle erratic changes of direction. Stay fairly high in tall trees, eat fruits, seeds, and blossoms of many spp., i.e., *Bombax, Byrsonima, Ceiba, Ficus, Cecropia, Muntingia*[148], and are sometimes destructive to cultivated fruit. Nest in cavity of dead stub or excavated in termitary, usually high; clutch 4–5, up to 8 reported[789]; Feb breeding, sw Guárico[734].

Status and habitat: Common resident in fairly dry to moist regions; woodland, partially deforested or cultivated areas, edges of gallery forest, ranchland, and parks and gardens in towns. Not in arid vegetation but in tall riparian woodland in arid zones. Sightings, Parque Cachamay, Pto. Ordaz, Bolívar, 1998–2001 (D. Ascanio; Hilty), may be of escaped cagebirds or natural expansion.

Range: To 1000m. Maracaibo Basin, Zulia, and w base of Andes in Táchira and Mérida (*jugularis*); rest of n Venez. from Trujillo, Falcón (sight), and Lara e through n cordilleras to Distr. Federal (vicinity of Caracas), and generally e of Andes from w Apure, Barinas, Portuguesa, and Cojedes e to Guárico at Santa María de Ipire (*exsul*); sight, Pto. Ordaz, Bolívar. Sw Mexico to Colombia.

Cobalt-winged Parakeet
Brotogeris cyanoptera   Periquito Azul
Identification: 8″ (20.3cm). 65g. Bill pinkish horn. Plumage mainly green, crown tinged dull blue, *forehead usually yellowish; small orange chin spot* (inconspic.); *primaries bright cobalt blue above*, dull blue below; tail short, wedge-shaped, mostly green. In hand central tail feathers green edged blue, rest green with yellowish inner webs.

Sim. species: See Dusky-billed and Sapphire-rumped parrotlets, both smaller with different tail shape and no yellow on forehead; ♂ of latter also has blue rump. Cf. Golden-winged Parakeet and Scarlet-shouldered Parrotlet.

Voice: Buzzy flight calls much like other *Brotogeris*, and given constantly by chattery groups, a shrill *jeek!* or buzzy *jiip-jiip . . .* , screechy and unpleasant. Song, sometimes more or less simultaneously by both members of a pr. when perched, a shrill, chattery, but patterned *jéek'ja che-cha JIL'da* or shorter *JEEK'ker-KEE'jur*, over and over in rhythmic pattern.

Behavior: Generally sim. to Orange-winged Parakeet. Mostly in prs. when breeding, otherwise in lively flocks of 5–30, sometimes in much larger groups. Feed in treetops or at edge of forest canopy. Fly high over canopy of lowland forest, chattering constantly as they go. Compact, well-coordinated groups fly in little fits and starts, with jerky erratic flight typical of genus. Flocks reg. descend to large bare riverbanks to drink, but frighten easily, flushing off in a shrill blur of blue and green. Nest in tree hole cavity or hole excavated in arboreal termite nest.

Status and habitat: Common resident in canopy of humid terra firme and várzea forest, along forest and river borders, in clearings with scattered trees, and in areas of mixed savanna and sandy soil forest. A characteristic species of lowland rain forest regions of Amazonas. Sight recs. of *Brotogeris* from lower Río Caura, Bolívar, may be this or previous sp.

Range: To 300m (prob. higher). N Amazonas from Caño Cataniapo (sightings), Samariapo, and upper Río Ventuari southward (*cyanoptera*). E Colombia to n Bolivia and Amaz. Brazil e to Rio Negro.

Golden-winged Parakeet PLATE 22
Brotogeris chrysopterus Periquito Ala Dorada
Identification: 7″ (18cm). 55g. Bill pale. *Short pointed tail.* Plumage almost entirely green, crown tinged bluish, narrow frontlet brown; *bright orange patch at base of flight feathers* (primary coverts), but this spot occas. small or *absent* and often concealed or difficult to see at rest; small orange chin spot; primaries bluish edged green.
Sim. species: Lilac-tailed Parrotlet, usually at higher el., has squarish tail, flies very high, fast, and straight, and up close shows yellow on face and black on wings. Also cf. Tepui, Green-rumped, and Dusky parrotlets and Orange-chinned Parakeet.
Voice: Often noisy, esp. in flight. Calls, perched or in flight, resemble those of other *Brotogeris* but buzzier and even more energetic.
Behavior: Prs. or small lively groups feed on small fruits, berries, buds, and blossoms, mostly in forest canopy[180]. Flight is jerky and erratic with much chattering. Digs cavity in arboreal termite nest or nest in tree cavity, Nov, Feb, and Apr[253]; 3–4 eggs[464].

Status and habitat: Uncommon to fairly common resident in humid lowland forest and forest mixed with savanna (e.g., e and s of Tumeremo). Commonest in areas where forest has been disturbed or where there are natural openings; nos. decline in areas of very high rainfall (e.g., n base of Sierra de Lema); few in tepui foothills. Some seasonal wandering.
Range: To 1200m (mostly below 300m). Sucre (Paria Pen.) and ne Monagas; Delta Amacuro[343]; nw Bolívar (Pijiguaos) e through lower Río Caura to Sierra de Imataca and s to Sierra de Lema (*chrysopterus*). The Guianas and e and c Amaz. Brazil.

Nannopsittaca

Small with short, slightly *wedge-shaped to almost squarish* tail with very pointed feathers; bill not strongly hooked but laterally compressed (thinner than in *Forpus*), culmen not as strongly decurved as in other small parrots; lacks tooth on cutting edge of upper mandible (present in *Forpus* and *Brotogeris*); flight is straight but wing beats not continuous.

Tepui Parrotlet PLATE 22
Nannopsittaca panychlora Chirica
Identification: 6.2″ (15.7cm). 44g. Bill dusky gray. Eyes yellowish orange. *Tail short and slightly wedge shaped.* Entirely dark green above, lighter and brighter green below; very narrow dusky eyering; ocular area tinged yellow with short curved *yellowish line below eye* that flares rearward. ♀ (or imm.?): forehead slightly tinged grayish to yellowish.
Sim. species: Easily confused when seen in flight high overhead. Note tail shape, flight pattern, and vocalizations. Up close narrow dark eyering and flaring yellow mark below eye impart sleek appearance. Cf. esp. Lilac-tailed and Sapphire-rumped parrotlets, both chunkier and square-tailed. Also see Dusky-billed and Green-rumped parrotlets, both smaller and with erratic flight, ♂♂ also with blue on wing coverts and rump. Also cf. Golden-winged Parrotlet.
Voice: Flight call a tinkling chittering *seize'la* or *tseez'zip*, like jangling a small metal chain or metallic scraping; high pitched, given constantly in flight; resembles flight calls of *Forpus* but more continuous and musical.
Behavior: Most likely seen only in flight as tight-knit, very high-flying flocks of 6–150 pass high overhead. Often commute in dramatic waves as flock after flock moves long distances between roosting and feeding sites. Fly fast and straight with no swerving. Wing beats rapid and buzzy, typically a buzz of wing beats, then a beat or 2 are missed as birds close wings momentarily, but unlike *Forpus*, pause in wing beats is not long enough to produce undulations or affect course of flight. Quiet and stealthy in fruit trees. Noted in prs. or small groups in *Clusia* trees in gallery forest (in Mar) at s end of Gran Sabana.
Status and habitat: Mature humid and wet lowland and montane forest around tepuis. Resident, but seasonally or sporadically may commute long distances out over lowlands, thus pop. nos. show dramatic swings (patterns need documentation). Periodically

absent from Sierra de Lema and adj. lowlands, then in other months 100s pass overhead daily. Roost (and presum. breed) high in tepuis and fan out daily over Gran Sabana and lowlands to feed.

Range: 750–950m n of Orinoco; 100–2200m (sight) s of Orinoco. W and e Sucre (Cerro Humo; Cerro Papelón); prob. n Monagas; Amazonas (Cerros Duida and Marahuaca; Cerro de la Neblina), and most tepuis of e Bolívar and forests of Gran Sabana s to Santa Elena de Uairén. Possibly in Sierra de Imataca, ne Bolívar. W Guyana.

Touit

Small, chunky parrots; long upper and under tail coverts almost completely cover short, square and usually highly colored tail; some with colorful wing patches; flight straight and sustained with continuous wing beats; highlands (mostly) and lowlands.

Lilac-tailed Parrotlet   PLATE 22
Touit batavica   Perico Siete Colores
Identification: 6.5″ (16.5cm). 58g. Eyes gray. Bill yellow green. Small and colorful, but colors difficult to see in field. Head yellowish green, nape scaled dusky, *wings and tail black, broad band of yellow across greater wing coverts and tertials*; underparts pale green, sometimes tinged powdery blue on chest; under wing coverts dark blue, small inconspic. patch of rose at bend of shoulder; *tail mostly vivid rosy lilac* (color hard to see) with narrow black band on tip.
Sim. species: See Dusky-billed Parrotlet and Golden-winged Parakeet, both with pointed tails and different flight and voice. Also easily confused with Tepui Parrotlet, but note that sp.'s more shrill calls and wedge-shaped tail. Sapphire-rumped Parrotlet may not overlap in range.
Voice: Flight call a soft nasal *naaaee*, typically slurred up, producing a rather high whining sound that does not immediately bring to mind a psittacine. Groups vocalize almost continuously in flight. Usually very quiet when foraging but may give weak nasal calls prior to taking flight or flying within tree.
Behavior: In prs. when breeding, otherwise in compact, fast-flying flocks of 10–40, occas. up to 100 or more, and commute long distances high overhead (specks in sky) to distant feeding trees and roosting sites. Flight is straight, steady, and with soft, continuous chatter. Once in canopy of a fruit tree, they become very quiet and stealthy, climbing around

slowly with aid of bill. Often fan tail widely, showing lilac, as clamber around in trees; do not perch in open and usually not in isolated trees. In Trinidad may roost in same tree, at least seasonally, for yrs. Nest in tree hole or excavate hole in termitary; breed Jan–Mar (prob. longer); 5–6 white eggs.
Status and habitat: Uncommon and erratic resident in humid and wet montane forest and forest borders. Wanders widely (seasonally or irreg.) in mts. and very locally over lowlands, but movements not well documented. Most vocal at PN Henri Pittier in early wet season. Prs. in early Mar and large groups flying NNE late Jun–early Jul 1994 over lowland forests of Río Grande in ne Bolívar (Hilty). Sight recs. over lowlands and hills of ne Monagas[60]. Prob. more widely distrib. than recs. show.

Range: 400–1700m (occas. to ca. 100m). Se Falcón on Cerro Misión[60]; n cordilleras from Aragua to Distr. Federal and Miranda (Cerro Negro); mts. (occas. lowlands) of Sucre and n Monagas (sightings, Caripe and Caño Colorado[58]); n Bolívar in Sierra de Imataca (sight). Guyana; Suriname. Trinidad.

Scarlet-shouldered Parrotlet
Touit huetii   Periquito Azul Alirrojo
Identification: 6.3″ (16cm). 60g. Eyes brown. Bill greenish yellow. Mainly dark green, *greater wing coverts sapphire blue, bend of wing, under wing coverts, axillaries, and patch on sides of breast bright red* (conspic. in flight); primaries black; up close note dark blue forehead and lores; central feathers of short, square tail green, outer ones magenta to purplish lilac tipped black; under tail coverts greenish yellow, *as long as tail.* ♀: sim. but tail feathers green tipped black above, pale yellow to greenish yellow tipped black below.
Sim. species: *Easily confused* with larger Orange-cheeked Parrot which *also has red under wing coverts.* Also cf. much larger White-eyed Parakeet.
Voice: Flight call a soft, bisyllabic *touit*[142] or nasal, whining *reenk*[61], over and over; much like flight call of Lilac-tailed Parrotlet.
Behavior: Flies in compact flocks up to 50 or so and gives soft calls, but very quiet in fruiting trees, where birds climb around, moving slowly and stealthily within concealment of foliage in canopy, or suddenly burst from tree and fly away, either silently or with a few calls[142]. BC ♂ early Apr, San Fernando de Atapabo, Amazonas[180].
Status and habitat: Not well known. Most recs. are from canopy of várzea forest. Relatively numerous

May–Jun along Caño Colorado, e Monagas, but rare or absent rest of yr (P. Boesman). Prob. a resident breeder locally, but nomadism and unobtrusive habits contribute to scarcity of recs.

Range: To 200m. Ne Monagas (Maturín; sight, Caño Colorado); w Bolívar (upper Río Parguaza, Caño Bejuco); nw Amazonas (San Fernando de Atabapo; sight, Junglaven). E Colombia, n Guyana, e Ecuador, e Peru, n Bolivia, and Brazil.

Blue-fronted Parrotlet
PLATE 22
Touit dilectissima   Churiquita
Identification: 6.7″ (17cm). 65g. Bill yellow green. Plumage mainly green; *part of upper wing coverts and shoulders red, under wing coverts, axillaries, and patch on sides of breast bright yellow* (flashes red and yellow in flight); black band at base of flight feathers, central tail feathers green tipped black, rest yellow tipped black. Up close note dull blue forecrown and sides of head, small red loral spot, red spot below eyes. ♀: crown brownish, little or no red under wings.
Sim. species: In range few others show bold red and yellow on wings. See Barred Parakeet and larger Rusty-faced and Saffron-headed parrots.
Voice: Flight call a nasal, whining *tuueet*, soft and somewhat bisyllabic. Call does not bring to mind a parrot. Very quiet at rest and when foraging but noisy bursting into flight.
Behavior: Prs. or little flocks of up to 15 or so perch or climb quietly in canopy or lower inside forest; not in open or in isolated trees in clearings. Fly in compact groups and call softly as skim low over treetops or through canopy of forest, and sometimes circle back and forth repeatedly before alighting. Flight is fast and direct or somewhat swerving, and with smooth rapid wing beats. Roost communally in canopy. Feed on fruit; in w Colombia also seen nibbling on thin layers of moss on mid-level limbs. Dig nest cavity in arboreal termitary.
Status and habitat: Rare and local resident of humid and wet premontane forest (cloud forest) and tall

second-growth forest. Recs. very scattered; not well known in Venez.
Range: 1000–1800m (to 2000m? in Sierra de Perijá). Sierra de Perijá, Zulia; w slope of Andes from Mérida (loc.?) to Trujillo (Escuque); e slope in ne Táchira (possible to nw Barinas?). E Panama to nw Ecuador.
Note: Sometimes incl. with *C. costaricensis* (Red-fronted Parrotlet) of C Amer., the two then called Red-winged Parrotlet[403].

Sapphire-rumped Parrotlet
PLATE 22
Touit purpurata   Periquito Rabadilla Púrpura
Identification: 6.7″ (17cm). 60g. Eyes gray to brown. Bill greenish yellow. *Chunky, square-tailed, and small. All green* with brownish tinged head and *brownish scapular band* (or head green—*viridiceps*); *rump sapphire blue* (hard to see in field); central tail feathers green, rest magenta with black tips (or green tips—♀). Underwings green.
Sim. species: Brownish scapular bands a good mark at rest. See Dusky-billed Parrotlet and Cobalt-winged Parakeet, both with pointed tails. Easily confused with Tepui Parrotlet; in flight that sp. has shrill calls, wedge-shaped (not square) tail, and is likely to be seen in high-flying flocks (contra Sapphire-rumped).
Voice: Unusual flight call (and also occas. when perched) a low, nasal, horn- or gooselike *áá-neck* (or *náy-neck*), rising on 1st syllable then dropping; or call varied to more trisyllabic *áá-a-neck*, given at rate of ca. 1/1.5 sec.
Behavior: Prs. or small flocks fly low over forest canopy or cross rivers and streams at treetop ht. Flight is swift and direct with fast, but not buzzy, wing beats. Perch quietly in forest canopy, then seldom noticed. Dig nest cavity in dead tree or arboreal termite nest.
Status and habitat: Humid terra firme and várzea forest in lowlands. Known from a no. of widely scattered localities but uncommon and very locally distributed.

Range: To 1200m (most recs. below 400m). N Amazonas from Junglaven (sight/tape), San Fernando de Atapabo and lower Río Ventuari s to Cerro Yapacana, San Carlos de Río Negro, and se slopes of Cerro Duida (*viridiceps*); ne side of Cerro Duida, upper Río Caura (Sabana Canaracuni) e to Auyántepui, upper Río Cuyuní (Sierra de Lema), and Gran Sabana s to Cerro Roraíma (*purpurata*). E Colombia to the Guianas, e Ecuador, ne Peru, and Amaz. Brazil (mainly n of the Amazon).

Pionites

Chunky med.-sized parrots; short, stout bill; short square tail; rather short, rounded wings; unusual voice; lowland forests; some incl. genus *Pionopsitta* in *Pionites*[287].

Black-headed Parrot   PLATE 22
Pionites melanocephala   Perico Calzoncito
Identification: 9" (23cm). 150g. Eyes yellow orange; bill blackish. Unusual color pattern. *Crown to below eyes black*; otherwise green above with *sides of head, throat, and broad collar encircling neck apricot in front, cinnamon orange behind*; breast and belly white, *thighs and under tail coverts apricot*.
Sim. species: Caica Parrot is mostly green below and has black head. Also cf. Orange-cheeked Parrot.
Voice: Flight call a high, squealing *SKEEEEEa, SKEEEEEa* (typically doubled); when perched a variety of whistled, piping , and slurred notes, some musical, others as if produced by an electronic synthesizer, none particularly parrotlike.
Behavior: Small flocks of 3–10 fly fast and straight with moderately deep wing beats, usually at or just above canopy ht. In early morning prs. or groups like to rest on open bare branches or stubs projecting above canopy and give high *kleee* or *kleek* calls, occas. spreading wings as they call. Sometimes unsuspicious, but when foraging for fruit and seeds in canopy may be very quiet and stealthily.
Status and habitat: Fairly common to common resident in humid lowland forest; esp. numerous in blackwater/white sandy soil forests where often seen in flight crossing little savannas from one forest to another.

Range: To 1100m. Se Sucre and ne Monagas (sight[58]) s to Delta Amacuro (Caño Guayo); forested regions throughout Amazonas and Bolívar (*melanocephala*). E Colombia to e Ecuador, ne Peru, n Amaz. Brazil (s to n bank of the Amazon), and the Guianas.

Pionopsitta

Chunky and med. sized; short, square tail; wings fairly short and rounded; mostly lowland forests; merged into *Pionites* by some[287], although the 2 genera differ vocally.

Saffron-headed Parrot   PLATE 22
Pionopsitta pyrilia   Perico Cabecidorado
Identification: 8.5" (22cm). Eyes dark reddish brown; *prom. pale ocular ring (surrounded by narrow black ring*—nw Barinas; elsewhere?); bill greenish yellow with narrow black line around base of lower mandible. *Head, neck, and shoulders bright yellow*, otherwise mainly green with broad mustard-olive chest band that extends onto sides of neck and to nape; *bend of wing, under wing coverts, and axillaries red* (conspic. in flight), greater wing coverts blue, flight feathers blackish; squarish tail green tipped blue; legs greenish olive. Some birds in nw Barinas (imm. or subsp.?) show *light to dark reddish mustard frontlet* and varying amts. of green mottling on rearcrown and nape.
Sim. species: Only parrot in Venez. with contrasting yellow head. Flashes red and yellow in wings in flight.
Voice: Flight call a scraping *skweek* or *cheeweek* (recalls Orange-cheeked Parrot). Perched, a single high, unparrotlike *keek*!
Behavior: Singles, prs., or little groups of 3–10 fly fast, mostly threading their way through canopy, or lower along forest edges, calling constantly as they go. Flight somewhat rolling as birds pitch from side to side. Perch mostly inside foliage where very quiet and inconspic. and move slowly. In nw Barinas noted feeding on small green fruits and chewing discolored leaves of mistletoe; 3 juvs., Jul, Sierra de Perijá, Colombia[260].
Status and habitat: Resident in humid and wet foothill and lower montane forest, tall second growth, and forest borders. Recs. in Andes are spotty; most recent sightings are from San Isidro Rd. in nw Barinas, but not seen with reg. and perhaps only seasonal to higher els. Many specimens from Río Negro region (ca. 1200m) of Sierra de Perijá suggest sp. was (at least formerly) fairly common there.

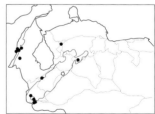

Range: 150–1650m. Sierra de Perijá, Zulia (near Río Negro); w slopes of Andes in Mérida (El Vigía) and nw Lara (Cerro El Cerrón); e slope of Andes in Táchira (several areas), nw Barinas (sightings), and se Lara (Guárico). E Panama and Colombia; nw Ecuador.

Caica Parrot   PLATE 22
Pionopsitta caica   Perico Cabecinegro
Identification: 9" (23cm). 130g. Eyes yellow; bill yellowish olive. Plumage mainly rich dark green with *black head and broad band of dull tawny orange across nape continuing as larger band of tawny olive across chest and lower throat*; leading edge of wing deep blue, flight feathers dusky, underwings dull green; tail yellowish below. Juv.: head mostly ochre.
Sim. species: See Black-headed and Orange-cheeked parrots.

Voice: Generally rather quiet. Flight call an odd, nasal (mechanical or hornlike) *queek!* or *skrek*. When perched in treetop a nasal, hornlike (like child's plastic horn) *kunk* or nasal *aank*, every 5–10 sec or so. **Behavior:** Prs., 3s, occas. up to 8, fly rapidly through forest at mid. levels or higher or at treetop ht. Flight is tippy with side-to-side rolling as birds weave between trees, but less so than flight of Orange-cheeked Parrot. Singles or prs. may perch briefly in open on top of high tree but mostly stay inside forest when resting or feeding. Recorded food plants incl. fruits and seeds of *Dracoides*, *Protium*, and *Brosimum*[148].
Status and habitat: Uncommon resident in humid lowland forest. Most numerous in high-rainfall areas, e.g., lowlands near bases of Sierra de Lema and Sierra de Imataca.

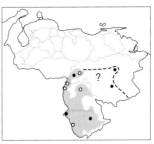

Range: To 1100m. E Bolívar from lower Río Caura and Sierra de Imataca s to tepuis (Kabanayén, Paurai-tepui) at s end of Gran Sabana. The Guianas and adj. ne Brazil.

Orange-cheeked Parrot   PLATE 22
Pionopsitta barrabandi   Perico Cachete Amarillo
Identification: 10″ (25cm). 140g. Entire head and throat black with *large tawny orange malar patch*, otherwise plumage mainly green, shoulders tawny (usually not conspic. in field), *bend of wing and under wing coverts red*, flight feathers black; rather broad, inconspic., mustard yellow band across chest; up close note yellow orange thighs.
Sim. species: Most likely confused with smaller Scarlet-shouldered Parrotlet, esp. in flight as both show red in wings, but that sp. has green (not black) head and lacks orange malar patch. Also cf. Black-headed and Caica parrots.
Voice: Flight call a distinctive mushy or reedy *chewit* or *choyet*, somewhat bisyllabic.
Behavior: Prs. or groups up to ca. 12 (rarely larger) forage from mid. level to canopy. Fly very fast with deep wing beats and slightly twisting or rolling flight, generally at treetop ht. or lower (not above canopy), sometimes skim low along forest borders. Hd. or glimpsed in flight far more often than seen perched. Recorded food plants incl. fruits and seeds of *Ficus*, *Pourouma*, *Pseudolmedia*, *Heisteria*, and legumes[148].
Status and habitat: Uncommon to locally common resident in humid terra firme and várzea forest; most numerous in white sandy soil regions of mixed forest, forest isls., and savanna across w Amazonas. Largely replaced e of Río Caura by allied Caica Parrot.
Range: To 300m. Generally in Amazonas; nw Bolívar (Serranía de Pijiguaos) s to upper Río Paragua (*barra-*

bandi). E Colombia and e Ecuador to n Bolivia and w Amaz. Brazil.

Hapalopsittaca

Chunky and med. sized; short, square tail, the feathers noticeably pointed (in hand); bill not as large or heavy as in allied *Pionopsitta*; fairly deep wing beats; highlands.

Rusty-faced Parrot   PLATE 22
Hapalopsittaca amazonina   Perico Multicolor
Identification: 9.5″ (24cm). 105g. Bill blue gray; eyes reddish brown to greenish yellow(?). Smudgy colors of foreparts give dull, unkept appearance. *Front half of head brownish red* turning yellow brown behind, rest of upperparts green; throat and chest mustard olive (sometimes stained reddish) turning green on lower underparts; *shoulders and bend of wing red*, greater upper wing coverts blue, under wing coverts dull blue green, *flight feathers dusky blue; tail red basally*, dark blue distally. Or sim. but foreface redder, no reddish on underparts (*amazonina*).
Sim. species: In limited high Andean range likely confused only with Speckle-faced Parrot, which has head mottled white, and much larger Scaly-naped Parrot, which has different flight profile.
Voice: Flight call a loud, metallic (almost screeching) *jiink* or *jeenk* (or *shrEEnk*); when perched a metallic and bisyllabic *EEareek* (like metal scraping metal).
Behavior: Recent (1990s) Venez. sightings are mostly of prs. or flocks up to 6 (in Colombia flocks up to 25 reported) perching in open in tops of trees at edge of forest or flying over montane forest. Fly high over forest with deep, loose wing strokes. Reported eating *Clusia* arils and mistletoe berries[127]. Like most parrots, feed inside canopy. Daily commutes between roosting and feeding sites are common.
Status and habitat: Rare and threatened. Resident in humid to very wet, epiphyte-rich montane forest, esp. at high els. Deforestation and fragmentation of forest at high els. doubtless are factors in severe decline as this sp. is seldom pursued for cage traffic. Most recent recs. are from Táchira, extreme s Mérida, and Trujillo (no info. from Perijá region) incl.: Queniquea Rd. (2200m), s Mérida, Mar 1981 (R. Ridgely); 3 above Zumbador, n Táchira, Jan 1993; 1 above Betania, Táchira, Jan 1996; 2 on Pregonero Rd., Táchira, 23 Mar 1999 (Hilty); up to 6 at PN Guaramacal, Trujillo, 2200m, Jan and Feb 1999 (Hilty and D. Ascanio). Other Mérida recs. (old) are primarily on e-slope drainage near city of Mérida[127]. Seasonal movements likely.

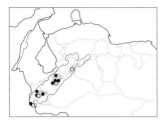

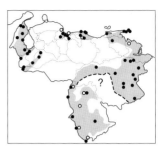

Range: 2300–3000m (sighting to 2200m). S Táchira on Páramo de Tamá (*amazonina*); n Táchira n to c Mérida (*theresae*); c Trujillo (sight, prob. *theresae*). Andes of Colombia[221] to Peru.

Pionus

Med. size; short, square tail; *red under tail coverts*; bare whitish ocular ring; several spp. dark and unkept in appearance; deep wing beats mostly below horizontal; widespread.

Blue-headed Parrot   PLATE 21
Pionus menstruus   Cotorra Cabeciazul
Identification: 10.5″ (27cm). 245g. Bill dark gray, rose spot at base of maxilla. *Solid blue head, neck, and chest*; blackish spot on ear coverts, otherwise mostly green, *under tail coverts and base of underside of tail red*; flight feathers green above and below. Note "bobtailed" appearance in flight.
Sim. species: Much like Red-billed Parrot (overlap only in mts.) which usually has reddish bill (color variable and difficult to see), duller and unkept plumage, and dingy bluish brown head. Red-billed normally occurs above range of Blue-headed.
Voice: Flight call a raucous, shrieking *schweenk!* or *chuweenk!* with metallic quality; calls are characteristically doubled or given in longer ser.
Behavior: Single birds, prs., or raucous free-wheeling flocks of 5–15, occas. up to 100 or more, fly with deep wing strokes that impart a "floppy" aspect to flight. In general, flight is rather slow and flocks seem loosely organized and "undisciplined," with members and subgroups constantly changing positions, separating, rejoining, or leaving. Roost in large groups, fan out in smaller day groups to feed. Perch in treetops, often on exposed palm frond spikes or bare exposed branches, but move slowly and feed quietly within canopy, only an occas. contact note or dropped fruit giving away their presence. Rec. food plants incl. seeds of *Albizia, Anacardium, Caraipa, Dialium, Hevea, Hura, Clusia, Ocotea, Inga, Brosimum,* and *Micropholis*; fruit of *Inga, Ficus,* and *Euterpe,* also flowers[148]. Venez. nest, upper Orinoco, 13 Mar; 3 young of different sizes[115]; 3–4 eggs; palm stub or hole in live or dead tree.
Status and habitat: Fairly common but local resident n of Orinoco; common s of Orinoco. Humid lowland and foothill forest, light woodland, and scattered trees and palms in clearings. Scarce or absent in dry and arid regions; largely absent from llanos.
Range: To 1000m (once to 1500m s of Orinoco). Sierra de Perijá and Maracaibo lowlands of Zulia, in or near Andes and n cordilleras e to Sucre and n Monagas; Delta Amacuro; generally in Amazonas and Bolívar

(*menstruus*). Costa Rica to n Bolivia, Amaz. Brazil, and the Guianas; se Brazil.

Red-billed Parrot   PLATE 21
Pionus sordidus   Perico Pico Rojo
Identification: 11″ (28cm). 250g. *Bill red*, tip and base of maxilla dusky. *Ragged, unkept appearance.* Head mixed dusky brown and dirty blue green, back olive brown somewhat scaled gray, flight feathers and tail green, central throat and chest bluish with a few white feathers showing through, rest of underparts scaly dull olive; *under tail coverts red.* Or head brighter greenish blue, back olive green, breast purplish blue mixed green (*ponsi*).
Sim. species: See Blue-headed Parrot. In mts. of Zulia cf. much darker Bronze-winged Parrot.
Voice: Much like Blue-headed Parrot but thinner and higher pitched.
Behavior: Sim. to allied Blue-headed Parrot of lowlands. Gathers in shrieking flocks up to 40–50, eats fruits and blossoms, and flies with labored but deep and free wing strokes raised just to horizontal. Apr breeding reported[148].
Status and habitat: Resident in small nos. in moist and humid forest, older second growth, partially deforested areas with scattered trees, and lighter woodland over coffee in foothills and lower mt. els. (usually not lowlands). In general found in slightly drier areas than Blue-headed Parrot and at slightly higher els. Pops. now small, somewhat fragmented, and persist in areas subject to extensive burning, deforestation, or alteration[150]. Daily movements up and down valleys and seasonal nomadism greater than in Blue-headed Parrot.

Range: 100–3000m (mostly 450–1850m). Sierra de Perijá, Zulia (*ponsi*); nw Lara (Cerro El Cerrón); se Lara (Cubiro); Falcón (Sierra de San Luis); n cordilleras from Carabobo e to Miranda at PN Guatopo (*sordidus*); mts. of ne Anzoátegui, s Sucre, and n Monagas (*antelius*). Colombia s in mts. to n Bolivia.

White-capped Parrot PLATE 21
Pionus seniloides Cotorra Cabeciblanca
Identification: 11″ (28cm). 210g. Eyes orange; bill greenish yellow. *Looks ragged and unkept. Forecrown white, feathers of hindcrown, nape, sides of head, and throat dusky violet speckled and mottled with white* and a little pink, chest purplish gray, rest of plumage green, wings green above and below; under tail coverts red.
Sim. species: In flight watch for whitish crown. Shares high-mt. habitat with Rusty-faced Parrot which has reddish face, red shoulders, and red under wing coverts. Also cf. Bronze-winged and larger Scaly-naped parrots.
Voice: Flight calls incl. a smooth *reenk* and *careenk* with laughing quality; also a harsher *kiaank*. When perched a nasal *ra-aaa*. Calls generally rather nasal and unlike those of other *Pionus* parrots.
Behavior: Like most highland parrots, rather nomadic, wandering widely in search of fruit and seeds (perhaps more so now as a result of extensive deforestation). Usually in rather high-flying flocks of 3–25, infreq. larger. Feed very quietly in canopy. Flight silhouette recalls an *Amazona* but with deeper wing beats.
Status and habitat: Uncommon and local resident in small, seasonally shifting pops. Seldom very numerous. Humid and wet montane forest and forest borders, or in flight over deforested highland areas. Doubtless in decline because of deforestation and alteration of its Andean cloud forest habitat.

Range: 1900–3000m. Andes of Táchira and Mérida; sightings in Trujillo (PN Guaramacal) and Trujillo/Lara border (PN Dinira)[60]. Colombia s in Andes to n Peru.
Note: Taxonomy not resolved[443]. May be only a subsp. of Plum-crowned Parrot (*P. tumultuosus*) of s Andes[148].

Bronze-winged Parrot PLATE 21
Pionus chalcopterus Cotorra Negra
Identification: 11″ (28cm). 210g. Eyes orange brown; bill yellowish green. *Dark.* Plumage mainly dusky midnight blue, throat whitish with a few salmon-colored feathers; upper wing coverts and tertials bronze brown, *flight feathers rich ultramarine blue above,* pale verditer blue below; *under tail coverts red,* undertail light blue.
Sim. species: Like others of genus, a little unkept looking on head and throat. See Rusty-faced, Red-billed, and Speckle-faced parrots, none of which are so dark.
Voice: Flight calls resemble those of Blue-headed Parrot but are shriller and higher pitched, *she'lank* or *she'l-'lank.*
Behavior: Like many highland parrots, nomadic and wanders widely in search of fruit and seeds. Usually in

small flocks up to ca. 8 or so (larger?). Flies with very deep wing strokes with most of stroke below horizontal. Mar nest in tree cavity, Colombian side of Sierra de Perijá[821].
Status and habitat: Very uncommon, local, and unpredictable in Andes (still no specimens?); more numerous and widespread in Sierra de Perijá (many specimens from Río Negro watershed at 1200–1400m). Humid montane forest and borders, and partially deforested terrain with scattered tall trees; also gardens and orchards. Quite nomadic, wandering widely when not breeding. Movements (seasonal or nomadic?) not documented. In w Mérida (La Azulita) seen Nov, Dec, Jan, and Jun (several observers). Rec. at higher els. (to 2800m) in Colombia.

Range: 120–1400m (most recs. 900m or higher). Sierra de Perijá, Zulia; Andes of e Táchira (sight, Cerro El Teteo, 3 Apr 1980—P. Schwartz, C. Parrish); sightings in w Mérida at La Azulito and Río Perdido (subsp.?). Colombia to nw Peru.

Dusky Parrot PLATE 21
Pionus fuscus Cotorra Morada
Identification: 10″ (25cm). 205g. Eyes brown; ocular ring gray blue; bill blackish, base of upper mandible pale yellow; nasal area red. Plumage overall *dark and dingy.* Head dull dusky blue, cheeks dusky; buffy yellow mottling below and behind cheeks; most of upperparts dusky gray brown, *below lavender brown somewhat scaled dusky, most birds with strong raspberry wash on lower breast and belly;* flight feathers and tail deep midnight blue, under wing coverts dark blue, rest of underwings bright blue, *under tail coverts red.*
Sim. species: Occurs only in humid forests of e Bolívar where likely confused only with Blue-headed Parrot which has bright blue head and green body. Dusky Parrot's head is darker than its body.
Voice: In flight or perched, call a rather high, nasal *tellit, tellit tellit* . . or *feelit, feelit* . . with hard, ringing quality. Calls typically doubled or trebled, then a pause.
Behavior: A rather unsociable parrot, most often seen singly or in prs., occas. up to ca. 12, but not large flocks. Occurs mostly in forest but reg. perches up in open at forest edge or in isolated trees in clearings. Flies like others of genus but swerves or rolls side to side somewhat. Most of wing stroke is below horizontal; wing strokes smoother and shallower than in Blue-headed Parrot. Eats fruit and seeds, incl. *Eschweilera* and *Micropholis*[148], also seen eating red flowers of Gesneriaceae vines. Apr cavity nest, Guyana; ca. 12m up in tall dead tree; 4 young of different sizes[29].
Status and habitat: Uncommon to fairly common resident in tall humid lowland forest and forest borders. Seasonal or local movements occur.

Range: To 1000m. N Bolívar in lower Río Caura; and Sierra de Imataca s to upper Río Cuyuní and Sierra de Lema. The Guianas and ne Brazil. W slope of Sierra de Perijá, Colombia.

Amazona

Large and bright green; with or without showy red to orange speculum in secondaries (visible in flight); a few with red on shoulders; bare whitish orbital ring variable in size; wings and tail somewhat rounded; *wing beats stiff, shallow, and rapid* (like ducks); often fly high and straight, keeping in prs. within flocks; most spp. in lowlands. Familiar talking "polly" parrots. Some authors use "Amazon" as an English name.

Red-lored Parrot
Amazona autumnalis   Loro Frentirrojo
Identification: 13″ (33cm). 415g. Eyes orange; bill dull yellowish above, horn gray below. *Forehead and lores red* (hard to see in field), crown green scaled lavender blue, otherwise plumage all green, *prom. red speculum in secondaries* (shows in flight); flight feathers otherwise dusky, central tail feathers green, rest with concealed red at base and broad yellowish tips; outer feathers yellowest.
Sim. species: Easily recognized as an *Amazona*, but at a distance the various spp. are not always easy to separate. May occur with Yellow-crowned and Orange-winged parrots in small Venez. range. Told from either by absence of yellow on cheeks or crown and by voice. Red forehead is diagnostic if seen.
Voice: Flight call shrill and more discordant than in most *Amazona*, a loud *chikák chikák* or *oorák oorák*, typically doubled or in longer ser. This and many other vocalizations given when perched.
Behavior: Noisy and often perches in open in treetops, flying in prs., or in prs. within small to large flocks. Flight and other habits typical of genus (see Yellow-crowned Parrot). Forms communal roosts when not breeding. Eats a wide variety of fruits and seeds incl. palms, and may damage cultivated fruits. Nest in unlined tree cavity or palm stub; in Costa Rica 3–4 eggs in dry season, young fledge early in rainy season[706].
Status and habitat: Resident in humid forest and partially forested lowland and foothill regions. Known only from a few specimens from a restricted area of Venez. Deforestation within its small range is extensive, and unknown nos. of young and adults are captured for illegal transport to Colombia[150]

Range: 100–400m. Base of Sierra de Perijá from Río Negro s to Río Socuavo, Zulia (*salvini*). E Mexico to w Ecuador; nw Brazil.

Blue-cheeked Parrot
Amazona dufresniana   Loro Cariazul
Identification: 14.5″ (37cm). 565g. Eyes yellow orange; maxilla dark reddish, tip pale, mandible all black. *Forehead yellow*, lores dark yellowish orange, *sides of head blue*, rest of plumage green, *wing speculum orange* (no red on shoulder), tail green *broadly tipped greenish yellow*. In hand inner webs of base of tail feathers red to orange, throat mixed green and blue, some birds with traces of blue on entire breast.
Sim. species: Resembles Orange-winged Parrot, incl. orange in wings, but larger and cheeks blue (not yellow).
Voice: One of noisiest *Amazona* parrots. Flight call (also when perched) a loud, raucous, and throaty *queenk-queenk-queenk* (the triplet characteristic) with distinctly nasal quality. When perched also harsher notes and a gurgling, babbling song.
Behavior: Much like others of genus (see Yellow-crowned Parrot). Flies in prs. or in prs. within small flocks, usually not more than 4–8 birds. Flight is deceptively strong with fast, shallow wing strokes. Gathers in groups to roost, and commutes varying distances, often many km, to fruiting trees each morning and returns in evening. Noisy and gregarious in flight but becomes very quiet, slow moving, and stealthy when feeding, then easily overlooked.
Status and habitat: Resident in a restricted area of e Bolívar where fairly common but with some irreg. or seasonal movements. Humid and wet lowland and foothill forest ranging up onto plateau of Gran Sabana. Can usually be found in tall lowland forest around Las Claritas and San Isidro (El 88). Most recs. are in or near hilly terrain or on slopes of tepuis.

Range: To 1700m. E Bolívar from vicinity of Sierra de Lema (sightings from ca. 80km s of El Dorado southward) and Gran Sabana, incl. Kabanayén and Sororopán-tepui (*dufresniana*). The Guianas (prob. adj. n Brazil); coastal e Brazil from Alagoas s to Rio de Janeiro.

Festive Parrot

PLATE 21

Amazona festiva   Loro Lomirrojo

Identification: 14″ (36cm). Bill dusky; very narrow bare eyering; eyes yellowish orange to brown (imm.?). Mainly green with *rump and elongated blaze of red up lower back* (red often not easily seen even in flight); lores and narrow frontlet dark red (like dark frown line); up close note sides of head tinged (scaled) bluish. *No red on wings.* Imm.: less blue on head; red on rump variable, usually much less than in ads.

Sim. species: Only *Amazona* parrot in Venez. with *no red on wings.* Look for red on rump. Note limited range and distinctive calls.

Voice: Flight call an odd, nasal, almost laughing *ooínk* (or *raank*) over and over; sim. but higher pitched when perched, often doubled; also a wide variety of gurgling and caroling notes, many very humanlike.

Behavior: Much like other *Amazona* (see Yellow-crowned Parrot) but with distinct preference for vicinity of swampy terrain, large rivers, etc. Noisy at dusk as prs. gather in flocks and fly to roost. In Delta Amacuro roosts apart from Orange-winged Parrots. In captivity an accomplished talking parrot.

Status and habitat: Fairly common *but very local* resident. Always closely assoc. with várzea forest, swamps, large rivers, and river-isl. vegetation; also large gallery forests in s part of llanos. Fairly widespread in Delta Amacuro and readily found ne of Tucupita (nos. vary seasonally); increasingly captured and transported illegally for sale in Guyana[150]. Small nos. in gallery forests s of Hato Los Indios, Apure; prs. seen (through 1999) near Caurama Lodge (n of Maripa), Bolívar (R. Behrstock, Hilty). Formerly very common along Orinoco from Caicara to Altagracia[115].

Range: To 100m. S Apure along Río Meta (Cararabo) n to Río Capanaparo and e along Orinoco from mouth of Río Meta to Caicara, Altagracia, and lower Río Caura (sight); Delta Amacuro from ne of Tucupita s to Piacoa (*bodini*). Nw Guyana, se Colombia, e Peru, and w Amaz. Brazil.

Yellow-shouldered Parrot

PLATE 21

Amazona barbadensis   Cotorra Cabeciamarilla

Identification: 13″ (33cm). Eyes orange to yellow; bill whitish. *Forecrown, face, cheeks, and chin yellow* (throat sometimes yellow), rest of plumage green narrowly scaled black above, faintly below (visible in

hand); *shoulder extensively yellow; prom. red wing speculum;* underwings dull blue, thighs yellow, tail broadly tipped yellow (in hand, base of outer feathers red). Birds of offshore isls. may show blue malar area and throat and have shoulder mixed yellow and red.

Sim. species: Only *Amazona* in arid scrub of nw and ne. In humid ravines meets or overlaps minimally with Orange-winged Parrot, which lacks yellow shoulders and has much less yellow on face, and with Yellow-crowned Parrot, which *usually* has only a yellow crown spot.

Voice: Flight call a throaty, rolling *cu'r'r'r'ak, cur'r'r'ak . . .* ; at roost, calls higher, less rolling, and more varied.

Behavior: Usually seen in prs. or prs. within flocks. When not breeding, roost communally, sometimes in flocks of 100s, and fan out in smaller flocks over desert countryside during day in search of fruits, seeds, and nectar-rich flower blossoms, esp. of cardon cactus (*Ritterocereus*), a critical yr-round resource; also fruit and seeds of *Lamaireocereus* cactus and fruits of many spp. of trees (fruits of 22 tree genera reported in diet). Near Coro breeds Mar–Aug; nest in tree holes (esp. *Bulnesia arborea* and *Prosopis juliflora*) or cavity in cliff; 3–4 eggs[127].

Status and habitat: Uncommon to locally fairly common resident in n Falcón but *in decline.* Xerophytic scrub (rainfall to ca. 1000mm) where mesquite (*Prosopis*), cacti, and other thorny vegetation predominate. Greatly diminished on mainland but still in some nos. locally; e.g., 500–600 at roost Jan–Mar near Coro, Falcón, in 1993 and 1994 (Hilty); very rare in e Falcón. In serious decline on Isla Margarita with nos. presently estimated at 200–800 where formerly 100s seen in a morning[127,366]. Only 100–200 remain on Isla La Blanquilla[150,561]. Threats are internal cagebird sales, habitat degradation (e.g., tourism on Isla Margarita), and overgrazing by goats. Protected by Venez. law, but no reserves protect significant nos. of this sp. Pop. movements need documentation.

Range: Disjunct. To 450m (mainland and Isla Margarita). Throughout Falcón (near Zulia border e to Sanare); formerly s to vicinity of Barquisimeto, Lara (sight, early 1980s—C. Parrish); n Anzoátegui (Lago Píritu) e to Araya Pen., Sucre; Islas Margarita and La Blanquilla. Bonaire; Aruba (extinct).

Note: Carib. subsp. *rothschildi* invalid[148].

Yellow-crowned Parrot   PLATE 21
Amazona ochrocephala   Loro Real

Identification: 14″ (36cm). 500g. Eyes orange; bill pale gray. Mainly green with *large yellow central crown patch* (extent of yellow varies, sometimes incl. fore-crown and lores, occas. even encircling eyes); *bend of wing red, speculum on secondaries red*, distal half of tail yellowish, thighs yellowish. In hand outer tail feathers red at base.

Sim. species: Much like Mealy Parrot which may or may not have small yellow crown patch; that sp. is larger, more robust, has *larger* orbital ring and *no red* on shoulders. Also cf. Orange-winged Parrot.

Voice: Flight call a loud, throaty *curr-ouw* (or *bow-wow*), over and over. Song sim. to that of other *Amazona*, a long, rambling ser. of gurgles, babbles, and trills mixed with musical and harsh notes, some of which sound quite humanlike. Sings from exposed branch at dawn or dusk, otherwise seldom vocalizes until it flies; however, perched birds will answer flying birds. Unfortunately, because of its uncanny ability to mimic human sounds, it is highly prized as a cagebird.

Behavior: Usually seen in prs. or prs. within small flocks, but gathers in larger groups at communal roosts when not breeding. During long evening and morning commutes to and from roosts, prs. or flocks fly fairly high in steady, straight-line flight with shallow, stiff wing-beats and call freq. During midday fan out to feeding trees, often many km distant from roost, and there spend day in quiet vigilance. Move slowly and silently when feeding in tree canopy, and climb using bill. Eat a wide variety of fruits, seeds, some buds and flowers, and are generally very wasteful of food. Nest in unlined cavity in tree, palm, or termitary; breeding late Feb–May, ne Anzoátegui[186]; ca. 3 eggs.

Status and habitat: Widespread but now somewhat local and in decline in many areas n of Orinoco. Still fairly common in moist to moderately humid forest, gallery forest, and various semiopen areas with woodland, even mangroves (e.g., s of Chichiriviche) and urban areas, but this sp. is the most widely sought *Amazona* in Venez. by trappers. Most readily found on large ranches in llanos where trapping is prohibited. Least numerous in very humid areas, esp. lowland forests of s Amazonas (absent?).

Range: To 500m. Resident locally throughout s to s Amazonas and n Bolívar (*ochrocephala*); not arid regions of nw and ne. W Panama to e Peru, c Bolivia, Amaz. Brazil, and the Guianas. Possible in Trinidad; introd. on Puerto Rico.

Note: Formerly incl. Yellow-headed Parrot (*C. oratrix*) of se Mexico to Belize and Yellow-naped Parrot (*C. auropalliata*) of sw Mexico to nw Costa Rica[10]. All pops. prob. best considered conspecific.

Orange-winged Parrot   PLATE 21
Amazona amazonica   Loro Guaro

Identification: 13″ (33cm). 340g. Eyes orange yellow; bill pale with dusky horn tip. Mainly green with *yellow crown patch and yellow cheeks* separated by blue lores and small blue area above eyes; *speculum on secondaries red-orange*, outer tail feathers broadly tipped yellow.

Sim. species: Best mark is yellow cheek patch. In arid nw see Yellow-shouldered Parrot, s of Orinoco see esp. Yellow-crowned, Blue-cheeked, and Mealy parrots. In Maracaibo area see Red-lored Parrot.

Voice: Noisy. Distinctive flight call a high-pitched (higher, more screeching than in most *Amazona*), often repeated *cm'quick* or *cm'quick-quick*. Fight call perhaps higher and more varied in Falcón, e.g., *ca'le-ca'le-caLEEK*.

Behavior: Sim. to Yellow-crowned Parrot. At least in dry nw, groups tend to fly higher than those of Yellow-crowned and Yellow-shouldered parrots. Food plants incl. fruits and seeds of many native trees as well as cultivated spp. such as oranges, mangoes, and cocoa. Breeds Mar–Jun in ne Venez.[148]; in Trinidad peaks in Mar; nest in unlined tree hole or palm stub cavity; 2–5 eggs[431].

Status and habitat: Resident and generally the commonest and most freq. seen *Amazona* over much of Venez. (except llanos). Occurs in a wide variety of habitats ranging from dry to humid forest and in urban areas; often commutes over extensively deforested areas. Overlaps with Yellow-crowned Parrot in many areas but not llanos. In Falcón, Yellow-crowned occurs in pockets of humid vegetation and riparian areas (e.g., c and se Falcón) within desert, Yellow-shouldered in desert scrub, and Orange-winged in areas of intermed. rainfall, e.g., at e base of Sierra de San Luis.

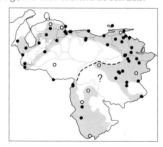

Range: To 600m n of Orinoco; to 1500m s of Orinoco. Sw Maracaibo Basin, Zulia, w and e base of Andes from Táchira n to Lara, locally in Falcón, and e through n cordilleras to Anzoátegui, Sucre, Monagas, and Delta Amacuro; w Apure (sight e to Hato Cedral); throughout Amazonas and Bolívar; to 800m on Cerro El Copey, Isla Margarita (*amazonica*). Colombia and the Guianas s to e Peru, Amaz. Brazil, and ne Bolivia.

Scaly-naped Parrot   PLATE 21
Amazona mercenaria   Loro Verde
Identification: 13″ (33cm). 340g. Eyes red; bill pale,
sides dull yellowish. Large *Amazona* of high Andes.
Mostly green, crown and nape *scaled blackish* (usually
not conspic. in field), bend of wing and underwing yellow, wings otherwise dusky; *red speculum on secondaries often small or absent*, central tail feathers green
broadly tipped yellowish, rest sim. with red at base
and broad subterminal band of red. In hand outer web
of outermost pr. of tail feathers dark blue.
Sim. species: Only *Amazona* in highlands. Large size
and characteristic stiff-winged flight unlike that of
other highland parrots. Up close note scaly nape and
tail pattern.
Voice: Flight call reminiscent of Mealy Parrot but
higher pitched, shriller, and uttered at faster rate, *kalee*
or *chalák*, sometimes in long ser.
Behavior: Sim. to Yellow-crowned Parrot. Flies in prs.
or prs. within groups, sometimes up to 30 birds or
more, but generally more wary than other *Amazona*.
Most often seen when commuting to and from roosting areas at dusk and dawn.
Status and habitat: Low-density resident of humid and
wet high montane forest (cloud forest) and in flight
over partially deforested terrain. Marked local or seasonal movements occur, prob. in response to food resources. Even in prime habitat, abundance varies from
common to rare to temporarily absent. Most numerous
in wilder, more remote Andean regions with large
tracts of undisturbed forest on steep terrain, i.e., PN Yacambú and Guaramacal. Loss of mt. forest is a serious
threat, and nos. are in decline[150].

Range: 1700–2900m (prob. occas. lower). Sierra de
Perijá, Zulia; Andes in n Táchira (sight); Mérida, Truji-
llo (sight, PN Guaramacal), and se Lara (sight) at PN
Yacambú[259] (*canipalliata*). Colombia s in Andes to n
Bolivia.

Mealy Parrot   PLATE 21
Amazona farinosa   Loro Burrón
Identification: 15″ (38cm). 620g. Eyes yellow to
orange; bill dusky above, olive below. *Very large bare
whitish ocular ring.* Largest *Amazona*. Plumage mainly
green, hindcrown and nape with powdery blue
bloom; *often has small patch of yellow on crown* (or no
yellow—*inornata*); red speculum on secondaries;
small red patch at bend of wing; *distinctly 2–toned tail*
green basally, *distal half pale greenish yellow.*
Sim. species: Largest and dullest of genus and not always easy to separate from other *Amazona*. Mealy has
few good marks, but in flight or at rest note large bare
eyering, 2–toned tail, and deep throaty voice. Up close

note large size, and sometimes small yellow patch on
crown. Cf. esp. Blue-cheeked, Orange-winged, and
Yellow-crowned parrots.
Voice: Commonest flight call a deep throaty *CHOauk*
or *CHO-op*, often doubled or repeated many times.
Song, when perched, an astonishing repertoire of whistles, clucks, gurgles, and babbles that ramble on for up
to several min.
Behavior: Sim. to Yellow-crowned Parrot. Usually in
prs. or a few prs. flying together in groups, infreq. large
flocks, although may gather in nos. at a roost. Feeds
on wide range of fruits, seeds, arils, some buds, and
flowers, mostly of large canopy trees, e.g., palms, figs,
*Brosimum, Inga, Dussia, Cecropia, Helicostylis, Pou-
teria, Sloanea, Virola*, etc.[148]. Nest high in unlined cavity in tree or palm.
Status and habitat: Locally fairly common but in small
nos. Humid and wet forest and forest borders. A bird
of tall lowland forest, surviving in areas with moderate
deforestation. Nos. have greatly declined
n of Orinoco where now rare or no longer occurs in
much of former range. Strong seasonal movements in
Colombia[258].

Range: To 500m. Base of Sierra de Perijá and s end of
Maracaibo Basin, Zulia, w base of Andes from nw Táchira and w Mérida n to e Zulia (Mene Grande);
e base of Andes in Táchira (Burgua); throughout
Amazonas; s Delta Amacuro; and Bolívar from lower
Río Caura e to Sierra de Imataca and Río Cuyuní
(*farinosa*). S Mexico to c Bolivia, c Brazil, and the Guianas.
Note: Kawall's Parrot (*A. kawallii*), a recently described sp. from upper Rio Negro, Brazil (n to San Gabriel de Cachoeira), may occur in s Amazonas. Like
Mealy Parrot but eyering smaller and grayer, narrow
white line along each side of base of bill, and more
red at base of tail. Flight call a rolled *e'raaaup*, more
2–noted than in Mealy (A. Whittaker recording).

Deroptyus

Large blocky head with erectile fanlike crest; unusually long tail; undulating flight.

Red-fan Parrot   PLATE 21
Deroptyus accipitrinus   Jía-Jía
Identification: 14″ (36cm). 240g. Eyes yellow; bill
black. *Unusually long, slightly rounded tail. Forecrown
buffy white*, rear crown, sides of head, and throat light
brown finely streaked white; *long crimson feathers of
nape fringed blue* (usually held depressed but can be

raised to form spectacular fan-shaped ruff); back, wings, and tail green, feathers of underparts mostly dull red to reddish brown broadly edged blue, flight feathers and undertail black.

Sim. species: Oddly proportioned parrot easily recognized by large hawklike head, long tail, and undulating flap-and-sail flight. At rest could be mistaken for a small bird of prey, but note prom. whitish forecrown and remarkable rufflike crest which it raises when excited.

Voice: Distinctive. Flight call several noisy *chack* notes followed by 1–5 high-pitched, almost squealing *tak, tak, KEEya, KEEya* phrases (*KEEya* notes much louder). At rest a variety of musical and unmusical chatters and whistles; buglelike and raspy *yaag*, a nasal honking *naaaaaa-unk* (2d note much higher), and musical whistles prob. assoc. with pr. maintenance and courtship.

Behavior: Prs. or small groups of 3–7 (rarely more) often perch exposed on dead treetop branches. Fly rather low over forest, usually skimming treetops, a few shallow flaps followed by a short descending glide with wings held angled slightly downward, tail slightly spread, and head raised (like swimming breast stroke) in distinctive undulating flight. Reported feeding on buds of *Bombacopsis*, unripe *Dialium guianense* fruit, and *Euterpe* palm seeds in Venez. Nest in cavity in dead trunk, limb, or woodpecker hole; breeding evidence Feb–late Jun in Río Caura[716]; in Guyana Jan–late Mar[389].

Status and habitat: Uncommon and rather low-density resident (perhaps also local) in tall humid forests in lowlands and hilly regions in soils ranging from alluvial floodplain to lateritic upland and white sandy-belt soils. Local seasonal movements reported in Nicharé watershed, ne Bolívar[716]. Survives in areas of moderate forest disturbance, but in ne and e Bolívar nos. now greatly reduced as settlement increases. Sought for cagebird trade but does not thrive in captivity.

Range: To 200m. Ne Bolívar from lower Río Caura and Sierra de Imataca s to upper Río Cuyuní and base of Sierra de Lema (*accipitrinus*); prob. sw Amazonas (in adj. Colombia and Brazil on Cerro de la Neblina). Se Colombia to the Guianas, e Ecuador, ne Peru (Loreto), and n Amaz. Brazil (both banks of the Amazon s to n Mato Grosso).

CUCULIFORMES

Cuculidae: Cuckoos and Anis

Cuclillos, Garrapateros, y Piscuas

Cuckoos are a group of anatomically similar but behaviorially diverse birds found in tropical and temperate latitudes worldwide. On the basis of DNA-DNA hybridization studies, cuckoos have been separated into 6 families, including 3 families—American cuckoos, anis, and ground-cuckoos—in the New World[604]. It does appear that New and Old World groups are distinct, although family limits are not yet resolved and a traditional taxonomy is maintained here. In general cuckoos are slim bodied, long tailed, and soft plumaged, and many have inconspicuous and unobtrusive habits. All species have a zygodactyle foot with 2 toes forward, 2 backward. Venezuelan cuckoos occur in a wide variety of lowland and lower montane habitats and include both terrestrial and arboreal members. Their breeding habits are diverse, often unconventional, and notable for varying degrees of brood parasitism, a behavior that may have arisen more than once within the broad cuckoo lineages. Two groups, *Tapera* and *Dromoccyx*, are parasitic, whereas *Crotophaga* are generally communal nesters. *Coccyzus* and *Piaya* build their own nests and mostly rear their own young, although the young of some species in these genera leave the nest well before they are able to fly. Nestlings of many, especially *Coccyzus*, secrete a repugnant-smelling, black cloacal liquid when disturbed. A majority of Venezuelan *Coccyzus* are north- or south-temperate breeders or short-distance intratropical migrants; the movement patterns of some species remain largely unknown. Cuckoos eat chiefly insects and caterpillars, although the large terrestrial species also eat small vertebrates.

Coccyzus

Lithe and slender; slightly decurved bill; long graduated tail usually with pale tip or large pale spot at tip; some spp. feed mostly on hairy and noxious caterpillars and periodically shed stomach lining; some occas. parasitize other species by laying eggs in their nests; young have black leathery skin; feather sheaths remain almost until fledging.

Dwarf Cuckoo   PLATE 23
Coccyzus pumilus   Cuclillo Gusanero
Identification: 8.5″ (22cm). 36g. Feathers of head often somewhat ruffed (looks fuzzy headed). Eyes and narrow eyering red; bill black, rather thin. *Tail rounded. Does not look like others of genus.* Smooth brownish gray above, grayer on crown; *throat and chest dull rufous*, rest of underparts light buff to whitish; tail graduated, moderately long, dusky above, gray below, each feather with *black subterminal band and white tip* (visible from below). Imm.: above light brown, throat gray (no rufous), tail tipping obscure, eyes dark, eyering yellowish.

Sim. species: Size, shape, and rounded tail with pale tips suggest a mockingbird or thrush. Note rufous throat and chest and med.-length tail (short for genus).
Voice: Rather quiet. Occas. a *churr*; and grating *trrr trrr trrr . . . carrack, carrack . . .* of 4–25 notes at ca. 1/sec; also a low *cluck* or *tock*[521]; rarely hd. dawn song a mellow *köööa köööa* (P. Schwartz).
Behavior: Like other *Coccyzus*, sluggish, inconspic., and solitary. Forages at almost any ht. but usually not too high. Peers slowly at both inner and outer foliage, then flies a short distance. Occas. drops to gd. near cover. Eats many caterpillars (nestling diet almost entirely caterpillars), and apparently periodically sheds stomach lining as do other *Coccyzus*. Home ranges of ca. 10ha broadly overlap, and prs. may nest near each other. Both monogamy and simultaneous polyandry (1♀ mated with 2 ♂♂) occur. Very flimsy twig, tendril, and leaf nest platform 1–7m up (avg. 2.6m) in canopy of small tree; 2–3 white eggs; black-skinned nestlings leave 4–11 days before full flight; ad. may molt while nesting[521]; breeding reported Jul–Aug, w Guárico[732], but prolonged in Colombia.
Status and habitat: Gallery forest borders, woodlots, tree-lined fence rows, and bushes and scattered trees in wet pastures; also parks and gardens in towns; most often seen in llanos. Resident and perhaps short-distance intratropical migrant (?). Relatively common (local) in small nos. in rainy season from ca. May–early Nov in llanos; scarce or locally absent late Nov–Apr dry season.

Range: To 400m n of Orinoco; to 200m s of Orinoco. Locally distrib. in Zulia and Lara; e of Andes from Táchira, w Apure, and Cojedes (sight) e to Monagas (no recs. in Sucre) and Delta Amacuro; s of Orinoco in w Amazonas (s to San Fernando de Atabapo); nw Bolívar (lower Río Caura). Isla Margarita. Colombia and Venez.

Black-billed Cuckoo

Coccyzus erythropthalmus   Cuclillo Pico Negro
Identification: 10″ (25cm). 47g. *Bare eyering red* (or yellow—imm.). *Bill black.* Much like Yellow-billed Cuckoo. Above entirely brown, below white or occas. with vague brown tinge on throat and chest; *long graduated tail below with narrow white tips* (mainly visible from below). No rufous in wing.
Sim. species: Yellow-billed Cuckoo has yellow bill, rufous primaries, and larger tail spots. Also see rare Pearly-breasted Cuckoo and austral migrant Dark-billed Cuckoo.

Behavior: Much like more numerous Yellow-billed Cuckoo. Rather retiring, even furtive, and seldom away from cover except when migrating. Not known to sing on wintering gds.
Status and habitat: Rare transient from n temperate latitudes (n winter resident?), recorded 28 Oct– mid. Feb from a few scattered locs. in Andes and mts. of Aragua as follows: Táchira (18 Nov at Burgua); Aragua (5 Nov 1951 at Maracay; 18 Nov at Hacienda Santa Rosalia near Tiara; 28 Oct 1963 at Rancho Grande Biol. Station); sight rec. in Mérida (2km s of La Azulita, Feb 1985—C. Parrish). To be watched for esp. during n fall and spring migratory periods when may funnel through mt. passes or gaps, e.g., Portachuelo in Aragua, Mucubají in Mérida, and San Cristobal (Río Torres) in Táchira.

Range: 350–1100m (doubtless much higher). E Táchira, w Mérida (sight), and Aragua. Breeds in N Amer.; transient and n winter resident in w S Amer., mostly Colombia to n Peru, rarely to n Argentina, Paraguay, and Bolivia. Trinidad (once in Sep).

Yellow-billed Cuckoo   PLATE 23

Coccyzus americanus   Cuclillo Pico Amarillo
Identification: 11–12″ (28–30.5cm). 50g. Eyes brown; bare eyering yellow. Bill brown above, *yellow below*. Slender and long-tailed. Upperparts brown, *inner webs of primaries rufous* (conspic. in flight, difficult to see at rest), below white vaguely tinged gray on chest. Tail long and graduated, all but central feathers black with *large terminal white spots* (mainly visible from below).
Sim. species: Very sim. to Pearly-breasted Cuckoo, but latter has uniform brown wings (Yellow-billed's rufous can be very difficult to confirm on resting bird). Also see Black-billed, Dark-billed, and Gray-capped cuckoos.
Behavior: Quiet and rather furtive on wintering gds. Usually stays within cover, although locally in nos. and relatively conspic. when migratory groups funnel over high mt. passes. Flies with deep, loose wing beats. Forages slowly and deliberately with much peering, and occas. sudden sallies or scrambling runs into foliage for larger, slower-moving arthropods, esp. bristly caterpillars.
Status and habitat: Fairly common to common but very local transient and rare winter resident from the north, late Aug–early May; most recs. Sep–early Nov and late Mar–mid May; latest recs. are 7 Jun (5 specimens) and 9 Jun at Carora, Lara. Dry to humid areas in a wide variety of vegetation types incl. desert scrub, mangroves, gallery forest, humid montane forest, and

paramo. On migration in mid to late Oct crosses high mt. pass at Mucubají, Mérida (prob. elsewhere), in nos. Known from a large no. of localities, mainly in north and west, and mainly during n fall and spring migratory periods; few llanos records (2 seen 1–2 Nov 1981, Hato El Frio, Apure—C. Parrish; Apr–May recs., Hato Masaguaral, Guárico[734]). Migrants in arid scrub of nw (e.g., Falcón and Zulia) may remain until end of rainy season (Nov), then continue southward.

Range: To ca. 1400m (migrants over mt. passes to 4200m). Spottily throughout n of Orinoco; s of Orinoco s to c Amazonas (Pto. Yapacana) and nw Bolívar at Caicara and Altagracia; Islas Los Roques, Los Testigos, La Orchila, and Las Aves. Breeds in N Amer., Mexico, and n W Indies; winters mostly in S Amer. s to Brazil and Argentina; rarely C Amer.

Pearly-breasted Cuckoo
Coccyzus euleri   Cuclillo Ventriblanco
Identification: 10–11″ (25–28cm). 53g. Eyes brown, bare eyering gray (?). Bill brown above, *yellow below*. Very sim. to Yellow-billed Cuckoo, differing in *slightly smaller size*, darker upperparts (noticeable in hand), *no rufous in primaries* (hard to see in field), and *throat and chest silvery gray* forming faintly indicated broad band that contrasts slightly with white lower underparts; thighs also silvery gray.
Sim. species: Very like Yellow-billed Cuckoo but much less numerous; best marks are smaller size and *absence* of rufous in wings. Black-billed Cuckoo has all-dark bill, red eyering, and narrow white tail spots (not large and round). Cf. Dark-billed Cuckoo (rich buff below) and Gray-capped Cuckoo.
Voice: Song 5–15 (occas. up to 20 or more) deliberate *kuoup* notes (sounds bisyllabic), 1/sec or slower, esp. at end; recalls slow terminal notes of Yellow-billed Cuckoo; less often a short ascending and guttural ser. followed by 4–9 accented notes almost identical to those of Yellow-billed Cuckoo, *tuctuctuctuctuctuc, tówlp, tówlp, tówlp, tówlp* (P. Schwartz recording). Migrant Yellow-billed is normally silent in Venez.
Behavior: Like Yellow-billed Cuckoo, sluggish, usually within cover and easily overlooked. One in Jun with a small mixed-spp. flock in dry forest (ne Bolívar) sat almost unmoving in overhead foliage for a min, then with upflick of tail flew off abruptly. Oct breeding, Roraima, n Brazil[148].
Status and habitat: Erratic and local (breeding or migrant from austral region?). May be present in low nos. 1 yr, then absent for 1 or more yr. Abundance perhaps tied to caterpillar outbreaks (P. Schwartz). Easily over-

looked because of confusion with commoner and very sim. Yellow-billed Cuckoo.

Range: To 700m n of Orinoco; to 350m s of Orinoco. Spottily in Mérida, Distr. Federal (San José de Los Caracas), se Apure (Pto. Páez), n Bolívar (Caicara; upper Río Caura; Ciudad Bolívar; Upata; sight, Guasipati), and w Amazonas (Caño Cuao; El Carmen); Isla Margarita. Very locally in Suriname, Guyana, Colombia, se Peru, e and s Brazil, and n Argentina.

Mangrove Cuckoo
Coccyzus minor   Cuclillo de Manglar
Identification: 12″ (30.5cm). 65g. Large, slender, and long-tailed. Eyering yellow; bill black, *base of lower mandible yellow*. Crown grayish, rest of upperparts grayish brown, prom. *dusky mask through eyes; below buff*, graduated tail blackish below with large white terminal spots.
Sim. species: Heavier billed than other *Coccyzus* cuckoos. Much like austral-migrant Dark-billed Cuckoo which is smaller, has *all-dark bill* and, up close, shows gray band across lower cheeks. See other *Coccyzus* cuckoos.
Voice: Song a grating, slightly hurried *ke-ke-ke, ka ka kra, kra, kra*, last few notes lower in pitch and slowing; briefer than that of most others in genus.
Behavior: No information from Venez. Elsewhere a notably furtive sp. found at various hts., mostly in mangroves. Breeding birds seem more retiring, less vocal, and generally even more difficult to see than other *Coccyzus*. Forages in very deliberate manner, with much peering around, then an abrupt pursuit of slower-moving prey. Rare breeder (Jul and Sep) in mangroves in Trinidad.
Status and habitat: Rare. Two specimens, 1 at Capure, n Delta Amacuro (1966); 2d from an unknown locality[486]. One seen in red mangroves (*Rhizophora mangle*) 10 Jun 1998, Caño Macareo, Delta Amacuro (M. Lentino and D. Ascanio). Once (sight?) in Islas Los

Roques[347]. Often in mangroves but elsewhere also in light dry woodland and scrubby areas.
Range: E Venez. in Delta Amacuro; Islas Los Roques (*minor*). Breeds in s Florida, W Indies, and locally in C Amer. The Guianas and ne Brazil. Netherlands Antilles; Trinidad and Tobago.

Dark-billed Cuckoo PLATE 23
Coccyzus melacoryphus Cuclillo Grisáceo
Identification: 10.5″ (27cm). 48g. Narrow bare eyering yellow (or gray?). *Bill all black.* Slender and long-tailed. Crown grayish, rest of upperparts brown, prom. dusky mask through eyes; long, rather *inconspic. silvery gray area beneath cheeks* continues onto sides of neck; *underparts entirely rich buff*, tail from below black with large terminal white spots.
Sim. species: Remarkably sim. to Mangrove Cuckoo but smaller, bill all black, and upperparts plain brown (not *gray* brown). Gray-capped Cuckoo is obviously darker with contrasting gray crown and darker fulvous (not buff) underparts. Cf. other *Coccyzus*.
Voice: Song, only during rainy season (May–Oct or Nov), a low, guttural *cu-cu-cu-cu-cu-cu-kolp, kolp, kulop*, or with last 3–4 notes omitted; song tends to drop in pitch; not loud and typically given only at intervals of several min. Recalls song of Yellow-billed Cuckoo but shorter and weaker. Calls incl. a purring *grrrr* and *graa-ak*.
Behavior: Like others of genus, a slim, graceful bird of calm, unperturbed demeanor. Usually solitary, perching at low to moderate hts. in leafy vegetation or occas. out in open. Moves quietly, often rather furtively, and on the whole is easier to see than most others of genus. Noted eating caterpillars (C. Parrish), also grasshoppers, beetles, and ants[148]. Aug breeding, w Guárico[734]; nest a flat twig platform; 2–3 eggs, green to pale blue[148].
Status and habitat: Dry and partly open ranchland, shrubby pastures, woodlots, scattered trees along fence rows, gallery forest, occas. borders of humid forest and mangroves. Fairly common breeding resident and prob. also austral migrant during rainy season (May–Oct) in llanos, but rare or absent Dec–Apr. E of Andes in Colombia only reported May–Oct[260].

Range: To 500m n of Orinoco; to 950m s of Orinoco. Spottily from w Zulia and nw Táchira to Sucre and Delta Amacuro; n and s Amazonas (Pto. Ayacucho; sight, San Carlos de Río Negro, 1978—C. Parrish) and n and e Bolívar (Ciudad Bolívar to Santa Elena de Uairén); Islas Margarita and Patos. Colombia to the Guianas, w Peru, n Chile, c Argentina, and Uruguay.

Gray-capped Cuckoo PLATE 23
Coccyzus lansbergi Cuclillo Acanelado
Identification: 10.5″ (27cm). Usual *Coccyzus* shape. Narrow bare eyering yellow (?). Bill black, base of lower mandible grayish to yellow. *Head to below eyes dark gray contrasting with rich ruddy brown upperparts*; primaries edged rufous; *below rich tawny buff*, darkest on chest; tail dusky above and below, underside with large terminal white spots.
Sim. species: Much darker above and below than any other *Coccyzus*.
Voice: Song faster than others of genus, a rapid, hollow *cucucucucucu-cu* (6–8 notes), last note slower; sometimes repeated several times at short intervals (P. Schwartz recording).
Behavior: Like other *Coccyzus*, solitary and sluggish. Often remains low in vegetation and out of sight.
Status and habitat: Rare and local. All of scattered recs. are from nw part of country. Possibly a migrant from w S Amer. (no definite breeding recs. in Venez.). Reasons for its rarity are unknown, but like Pearly-breasted Cuckoo, its nos. may fluctuate with caterpillar infestations or other factors. Rec. Jun–Aug, Hato Masaguaral, Guárico[734]; recent recs. incl. singles 23 Jul and 14 Aug 1996, Canoabo, Carabobo[60], in dry to moist semideciduous woodland.

Range: To 1400m. Known from Zulia (Laguna Tule), Mérida (Culata), Lara (Terepaima), Carabobo (Pto. Cabello; sight Canoabo[60]); Aragua (Rancho Grande; Cata), and w Guárico (sight). N Colombia; sw Ecuador and nw Peru.

Piaya

Bill shape and long graduated tail like *Coccyzus*, but overall more robust; plumage mostly rich reddish chestnut.

Squirrel Cuckoo PLATE 23
Piaya cayana Piscua
Identification: 17″ (43cm). 95g. Large with long, loose-jointed tail. Eyes red; narrow bare eyering red. *Bill greenish yellow. Upperparts rufous chestnut*; throat and chest pale pinkish buff turning light gray on breast and black on rear of belly and under tail coverts; *long graduated tail chestnut*, from below distal half of tail feathers dusky with large white tips.
Sim. species: Closely resembles Black-bellied Cuckoo of s of Orinoco, but that sp. has gray cap, red bill, colorful skin around eyes, and *dark* underparts. Little

Cuckoo is half the size, mostly rufous below, and usually low in wet thickets.

Voice: Has a wide variety of odd vocalizations, many of which are very different from one another; commonest a loud, abrupt *gweep, caweer!* and dry *chickawraaaa* (kiskadeelike); also a short buzzy or jangling *djet!* or *djet-djet-djet!*; a raspy *wa' ditch-e-er*; in disputes or when disturbed an odd nasal and glottal *eee' ga'da'da*. Song a long ser. of rather sharply inflected whistles, *wheep, wheep, wheep, wheep, wheep, . . .*, often for several min without interruption.

Behavior: Alone or in loosely assoc. prs., and with mixed-spp. flocks or away from them about equally. Forages in vegetation from mid. levels upward, mostly by peering slowly and carefully, then reaching or lunging for static prey (katydids, many spiny caterpillars), or occas. leaping or sallying for fast-moving or flying prey incl. wasps. Can be surprisingly unobtrusive for such a large bird. Hops along limbs or bounds up through vine tangles in a ser. of rather squirrel-like leaps and runs (hence name), then sails out across a small clearing or forest opening in long descending glide, sometimes with a few quick wing beats, to a lower perch. Occas. at army ant swarms. Very furtive at nest site. Frail coarse twig platform with cuplike lining of live or dead leaves, ca. 1–12m up (but often rather low) in dense or tangled vegetation in bush or tree; 2–3 white eggs; young leave prior to flying[643].

Status and habitat: Common resident in a wide variety of habitats incl. fairly dry forest, riparian and gallery woodland, tall humid lowland forest, second growth, and clearings with scattered trees. Reg. along forest and woodland borders. May be interspecifically territorial with Black-bellied Cuckoo.

Range: To 2500m (usually below 1200m) n of Orinoco; to 1800m s of Orinoco. Throughout. S end of Maracaibo Basin in Zulia, nw Táchira, w and c Mérida, and w Apure (*circe*); rest of Venez. n of Orinoco (*mehleri*); se Monagas, Delta Amacuro, s Apure along Río Meta, and throughout Amazonas and Bolívar (*cayana*). W Mexico to n Argentina and Uruguay.

Black-bellied Cuckoo   PLATE 23
Piaya melanogaster   Piscua Ventrinegra

Identification: 15" (38cm). 100g. Much like Squirrel Cuckoo. *Bill red*; eyes red, *prom. bare orbital area blue*, *loral spot yellow*. *Crown gray*, rest of upperparts rich rufous chestnut, below rufous turning *black on lower breast, belly, and under tail coverts*; long graduated tail

chestnut, from below showing broad blackish subterminal band and large white tips.

Sim. species: See Squirrel and Little cuckoos.

Voice: Many vocalizations recall those of Squirrel Cuckoo but are harsher or higher pitched; generally much less vocal. A loud *jjit, jjit-jjit-jjit* and scratchy, descending *yaaaaa* followed by a dry jaylike rattle.

Behavior: Rather like Squirrel Cuckoo but stays high in forest canopy where often somewhat obscured by foliage, hence difficult to see. Single birds, occas. prs., are most often seen with canopy mixed-spp. flocks. When foraging, a few hops or scrambling runs along high branches alternate with immobile periods when bird peers around carefully. Stays within foliage cover and seldom glides out across light gaps like allied Squirrel Cuckoo.

Status and habitat: Uncommon resident (easily overlooked) in humid lowland forest, esp. sandy-belt forest, and occas. at forest borders. Infreq. in scrubby, savanna woodland.

Range: To 500m. Amazonas and Bolívar. Colombia to the Guianas and s to e Peru, n Bolivia, and w Amaz. Brazil.

Little Cuckoo   PLATE 23
Piaya minuta   Piscuita Enana

Identification: 10.5" (27cm). 40g. Miniature of Squirrel Cuckoo. Differs in *much smaller size*, proportionately shorter tail, rufous chestnut (not buff) throat and chest, and paler rufous brown (not black) belly. Birds from w Venez. and w llanos (*barinensis*) are paler below, gray from mid. breast to belly, and even more closely resemble Squirrel Cuckoo, except for size.

Sim. species: Cf. larger Black-bellied Cuckoo.

Voice: Commonest call (contact note) a low, brief *czek!* (like crackle of static electricity); also an odd nasal chattering, *nyaa-nyaa-nyaa*, and soft *geep*, like muted Squirrel Cuckoo.

Behavior: Alone or in prs. but members of a pr. forage independently of each other and are usually not close together. Stays low, usually within ca. 5m of gd. and within cover, where carefully peers about before hopping short distances or lunging after prey, incl. caterpillars and other arthropods. Trinidad nest, Jul, a deep twig cup in thick shrubbery; 2 white eggs[175].

Status and habitat: Fairly common but local resident. Normally near water and most numerous around lagoons or other damp areas with dense shrubby vegetation mixed with small openings; also along humid forest borders and in damp thickets. Very common in swampy terrain around Tucupita, Delta Amacuro, else-where generally much less numerous; rare or absent in arid nw and ne.

Range: To 700m n of Orinoco; to 950m s of Orinoco. S Maracaibo Basin, Zulia, w base of Andes in Táchira, Mérida, and Trujillo; e base from Táchira to Barinas; Yaracuy (*barinensis*); sight in se Falcón (subsp.?); rest of Venez. e and s of previous subsp. (*minuta*); no recs. in Guárico or Anzoátegui. E Panama locally to the Guianas and s to n Bolivia and s Brazil.

Crotophaga

Loose black plumage; deep, laterally compressed bill with high, arched, bladelike culmen; long, narrow, loose-jointed tail; social, but members of a flock typically fly in single file, one after another; skin or feathers may have unpleasant odor.

Greater Ani   Illus. below
Crotophaga major   Garrapatero Hervidor
Identification: 19″ (48cm). 170g. *Large and glossy*. Conspic. yellowish white eyes (or brown—imm.). Bill black, laterally compressed with culmen thin and arched, forming distinct hump ("broken nose" profile). All glossy blue black, somewhat scaled glossy green on back; *very long, loose-jointed tail* rounded, glossy purplish black.
Sim. species: Other anis are smaller, duller, have dark eyes, and generally favor different habitat. Caribbean Grackle is much smaller and has different proportions (thin bill, shorter tail).
Voice: Often noisy with an astonishing variety of sounds; commonest a guttural gobbling or bubbling *kro-koro* . . . rapidly repeated, sometimes for 30 sec or more, and often by several birds in chorus (the "pot-boiling sound," hence Spanish name); a drawn-out reptilian growl; a variety of croaks, grates, hisses, and whirs.
Behavior: Prs. or loose groups up to 20 or more stay rather low and sneak around mostly out of sight or sit out in sun at edge of dense shrubbery along a creek or lagoon. When alarmed stream out 1 by 1, flying low along a lagoon or across a small stream, and dive into vegetation on opposite shore. Hop rather heavily and somewhat clumsily as search foliage, often lunging awkwardly to grasp prey, esp. small frogs, katydids, caterpillars, and other arthropods. May follow and forage in vicinity of troops of monkeys along river edges. Breed communally, Sep–Oct in w Guárico[734]; bulky leaf-lined and flat cup in tree or shrub surrounded by water (usually); 6–7 greenish blue eggs covered with chalky coating; up to 8 birds may participate in nest construction. Five-day-old young may leap into water if frightened, but swim and climb back to nest[327].
Status and habitat: Fairly common migrant (from Amazonia?) approx. late Apr–Nov (rainy season) to llanos where apparently breeds. Small nos. linger to Jan, a few very locally throughout dry season. Rec. only Aug–Dec in ne Anzoátegui[186]. Forested river edges,

Smooth-billed Ani (left), Greater Ani (center), Groove-billed Ani (right)

flooded low-lying woodland, shrub-bordered lagoons, and marshland; occas. wet riparian woodland in dry to arid regions.

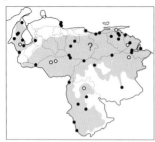

Range: To 200m. Widely but locally distributed throughout n of Orinoco incl. Delta Amacuro; Amazonas and n Bolívar in lower Río Caura, along Orinoco, and upper Río Caroní (once, near Chimantátepui). C Panama and Colombia (to 2600m) to the Guianas and n Argentina.

Smooth-billed Ani   Illus. p. 353
Crotophaga ani   Garrapatero Común
Identification: 13″ (33cm). 95g. *Black bill arched and laterally compressed with raised hump on basal half of maxilla* (forms a distinct notch between forehead and bill). Eyes dark. Plumage flat black, vaguely scaled glossy bronzy purple (sometimes apparent in good light), long loose tail rounded at tip.
Sim. species: See smaller Groove-billed Ani.
Voice: Commonest call a smoothly rising squeal, *oooeeEEENK?*, querulous and often repeated over and over, esp. when alarmed and in flight.
Behavior: Gregarious and almost always seen in loose unkept groups up to ca. 15 that roost and forage together and are conspic. and familiar over most of country, esp. because this sp. often sits in open. Perches in bushes, small trees, or lined up in disheveled rows on fences, esp. to dry out after a rain. Flight is weak and barely utilitarian, typically a few quick flaps and a wobbly sail as members of a group straggle across an opening and land with long tail flipped up. Run well on gd. and reg. forage on gd., often alongside cattle, catching insects they disturb. Occas. pick ticks from cattle, hence Spanish name, and occas. eat berries and catch small vertebrates. Large bulky cup nest, sometimes with several layers, each with unincubated eggs; well-concealed 2–6m up in dense shrub or thorny vegetation; built by a pr. or by several cooperating individuals (prs.?); ca. 9 chalky white eggs (max. 29 reported but seldom more than 15). Jul–Aug breeding, Guárico and Anzoátegui[186,734]; in Trinidad breeds yr-round with rainy season peak May–Oct[175].
Status and habitat: Common and widespread resident in brushy pastures, clearings, cultivated areas, forest borders, and other partly open areas in humid regions. Has greatly profited from deforestation, esp. at higher els. Partially replaced in dry and arid zones by Groove-billed Ani, in swampy riverine habitats by Greater Ani[200].
Range: To 2400m n of Orinoco (sight to 2600m, Mérida); to 1200m s of Orinoco. Throughout incl. Islas Mar-

garita and Patos. S Florida. W Indies and sw Costa Rica to w Ecuador and n Argentina.

Groove-billed Ani   Illus. p. 353
Crotophaga sulcirostris   Garrapatero Curtidor
Identification: 12″ (30.5cm). 58g. Black bill laterally compressed, *culmen somewhat curved forming smooth unbroken arc with forehead*. Upper mandible has a few inconspic. grooves running parallel to culmen. Eyes dark. Plumage flat black, foreparts somewhat scaled. Tail very long, loose jointed, and rounded.
Sim. species: Easily confused with Smooth-billed Ani and most readily separated by voice. Smooth-billed is larger and has distinct curved hump on bill (obvious notch where bill meets forehead, as opposed to smooth curved line from forehead onto bill of Groove-billed). Up close look for inconspic. grooves on bill of Groove-billed. Note that young Smooth-billeds usually lack hump on bill.
Voice: Commonest call a forceful, hissing *kiSSSSSyou* (or *peZZZZZuu*), high pitched, very unlike that of Smooth-billed Ani. Also a 2–noted *tee-ul* and various little whistles and clucking sounds, singly or repeated.
Behavior: Much like that of Smooth-billed Ani but less often sits in open in full sun (D. Ascanio). Nests communally with several ♂♂ and ♀♀ building single nest; lay joint clutch of eggs, share incubation and feeding; nonbreeding "helpers" also may attend; also breed in monogamous prs.[79]; Jul–Nov breeding, w Guárico[734].
Status and habitat: Common resident in scrubby vegetation, waste areas, semiopen ranchland, and overgrown or neglected pastures, mainly in dry to arid zones; uncommon and local in llanos. In transitional dry to moist areas occurs with Smooth-billed Ani, but replaced by it in humid regions.

Range: To 750m n of Orinoco; to 200m s of Orinoco. Throughout s to nw Amazonas (Pto. Ayacucho; Río Capuana) and Orinoco region of n Bolívar e to Ciudad

Bolívar (*sulcirostris*). Sw US to w Peru, rarely n Chile; e of Andes in Venez., Guyana, and n Argentina. Aruba to Trinidad.

Tapera

Much like *Dromococcyx* but smaller; bill compressed; plumage striped; graduated tail narrow, long upper tail coverts reach only to middle of tail; alula ("wrist") feathers unusually long.

Striped Cuckoo   PLATE 23
Tapera naevia   Saucé

Identification: 11″ (28cm). 50g. Recalls an overgrown, long-tailed sparrow. Eyes reddish brown to yellowish gray. *Crown and short bushy crest chestnut streaked black, upperparts pale brown streaked black and buff* (incl. upper tail coverts which are over half the length of tail), narrow white eyebrow; chestnut cheeks and *narrow "whisker" line*; below white, throat and chest tinged buff; long graduated tail grayish below narrowly tipped white. Imm.: upperparts dotted buff, throat and chest faintly barred dusky and buff.

Sim. species: Recalls Pavonine and Pheasant cuckoos but both are *much darker and scaly* (not streaked) *above* and with broader white-tipped tails, solid chestnut crowns; Pheasant Cuckoo also has spotted chest.

Voice: Often quite vocal, and songs far-carrying. Commonest song a pure, mellow, minor-keyed whistle, 2d note a half-tone higher than 1st, *wüüüü, weeee*; sometimes expanded to 3 or up to 7 notes in ser., always with last 2 quicker, and next to last a half-tone higher. Onomatopoeic Venez. transcriptions incl., *saucé; tres pesos*, and *tres pesos pide*.

Behavior: Hd. far more than seen. A solitary bird that usually calls from semiexposed perch atop a bush, fence post, or tree, but voice is ventriloquial. Otherwise secretive and skulking, usually occurring alone, on or near gd. and in dense cover. Runs rapidly on gd. and often stops to posture with crest raises, wing droops, and alula flexes as though afflicted with a nervous tic (body movements may flush immobile prey?). Even when singing, long crown feathers, forming *short bushy crest*, are often raised and lowered in an expressive manner, and black alula feathers at bend of wing (like "false wings") are mechanically flexed as though sending a semaphore message. Breeding is parasitic; favors spp. with domed nests such as spinetails, thornbirds, wrens, marsh-tyrants, *Myiozetetes* flycatchers, and Black-striped Sparrow[706]; pale blue to white egg,

small for size of bird; aggressive juvs. kill host nestmates[419]; Sep breeding, w Guárico[734].

Status and habitat: Fairly common resident in scrubby or open areas with scattered trees, thickets, and bushes; also clearings and partially opened areas, overgrown pastures in humid forested regions (where local), and early successional growth on river isls. (Río Orinoco). **Range:** To 2500m n of Orinoco (mostly below 1200m); to 1300m s of Orinoco. Throughout n of Orinoco and in nw Amazonas; locally in n and e Bolívar, Isla Margarita (*naevia*). S Mexico to sw Ecuador, e Bolivia, and c Argentina. Trinidad.

Dromococcyx

Only 5 prs. of tail feathers (?); upper tail coverts unusually long (almost as long as tail); thin neck, small head, and ample tail impart odd visage.

Pheasant Cuckoo   PLATE 23
Dromococcyx phasianellus   Cuco Faisán

Identification: 15″ (38cm). 87g. Eyes reddish brown; bill black above, grayish yellow below, rather long and narrow. *Small head and narrow neck* impart reptilian appearance. *Crown and slight bushy nuchal crest chestnut bordered by narrow white eyebrow; back and tail dark brown*, the feathers *scaled white*, throat whitish bordered by narrow dusky malar line; foreneck and chest grayish buff *sprinkled with dusky spots*; lower underparts white; graduated tail (feathers very wide) broad and fanlike, the feathers gray turning dusky distally and tipped white. Up close note upper tail coverts nearly as long as tail. In hand shows white bar across primaries (like a nightjar). Juv.: gray rather than buff below.

Sim. species: Easily confused with Pavonine Cuckoo which is smaller and *darker above* (dusky black, not brown), has buff (not white) eyebrow, and *lacks* spotted necklace. Striped Cuckoo also smaller, has striped crown, is *much paler and streaky* (not scaled) *above*, and lacks necklace.

Voice: Closely resembles call of Pavonine Cuckoo (and short call of Striped Cuckoo). Usually a 3–note, whistled *pü-püü-wernmr*, last note quavering; less freq. a 4–note *pa, püh, pe-pee*.

Behavior: Like others of genus, furtive and difficult to see; even frequency and extent of vocalizing are unpredictable. Usually found ca. 1–6m up, occas. higher, esp. when calling or excited, but typically remains in thick cover. Flies quickly from one thicket or wooded patch to another, sometimes crossing small open spaces with rather exaggerated "high lifts" of wings, also with tail spread. Eats large insects, incl. grasshoppers and cicadas, and small lizards[706]. A brood parasite, it lays in open nests more than covered nests; 1 long, narrow, dull white egg with wreath of scattered rufous on large end[425].

Status and habitat: Rare or uncommon and very local resident in thickets and dense vegetation along dry to moist forest borders and second-growth woodland; occas. inside forest. In Venez. favors drier regions and lower els. than allied Pavonine Cuckoo, and less numerous than that sp. but may be locally fairly common, i.e., many recs. from Turiamo area (ca. 200m el.), n Aragua.

Range: To ca. 400m. Spottily throughout n of Orinoco. Rec. in w Zulia in Ríos Negro and Yasa (*rufigularis*), base of Coastal Cordillera from Carabobo and Aragua (both slopes of PN Henri Pittier; Ocumare de la Costa), s to e Portuguesa (Turén), Cojedes (e of El Pao), and s Guárico; nw Sucre (Cumaná) and nw and e Bolívar at San Félix, Upata, and El Dorado (*phasianellus*). S Mexico locally to n Bolivia, ne Argentina, and se Brazil.
Note: Perhaps monotypic.

Pavonine Cuckoo   PLATE 23
Dromococcyx pavoninus   Cuco Pavón
Identification: 12″ (30.5cm). 54g. Above, incl. tail, virtually identical to Pheasant Cuckoo but somewhat darker. *Upperparts dusky*, the feathers everywhere *tipped gray* (*looks scaled*), usually 1 narrow white wing bar; crown and slight bushy nuchal crest chestnut; conspic. eyering and long postocular stripe *buff* (not white), rather *diffuse* malar line and cheeks dusky chestnut; throat whitish, *sides of neck and breast unspotted rich buff* (not gray buff) turning white on lower underparts. As in Pheasant Cuckoo, upper tail coverts very long, covering much of tail; mouth lining orange.
Sim. species: Will usually be noted first by voice (see) which is surest way to distinguish this wary sp. from Pheasant Cuckoo. See Striped Cuckoo.
Voice: In Coastal Cordillera and Andes sings irreg. from late Jan to end of May or Jun (occas. Nov–Dec). Song a flat, whistled *püü pee, püü-pe'pe*, 1st and 3d notes lowest, rest a half-tone higher. Cf. Pheasant Cuckoo which typically sings 3- (or occas. 4-) note song that usually ends with long quaver.
Behavior: Sly, sneaky, and solitary in low or mid.-level vegetation. Most vocal mornings, evenings, and at night but with little reg. except early in rainy season. Sings with large twitching alula feathers extended, tail down and rooster-tail of rump feathers puffed (like "broken back") as sits on concealed horizontal perch ca. 3–9m up inside dense cover. Often flies with curious high-winged, almost butterflylike motion, with slow mechanical wing beats (wings seem almost to touch above back and are held there momentarily) and slightly spread tail. Food apparently sim. to that of Pheasant Cuckoo. A brood parasite, esp. on smaller spp., i.e., antbirds and flycatchers, with bag or purse-like nest; eggs white; nestling apparently kills young of host parents[148].

Status and habitat: Uncommon to locally fairly common resident (by voice) in viny areas and thickets along moist to humid forest borders and in dense patches of second-growth vegetation in moist and humid zones; likes to perch beneath or in dense mats of vines. Reg. found in dry to moist second-growth vegetation near Rancho Grande, e.g., km 14,17–20, 24, 32, 33, and 36 on Marcay-Ocumare Rd. Vocal mainly early rainy season in forest-edge thickets above La Azulita, Mérida. In Venez. dist. very spotty but more widespread and numerous than Pheasant Cuckoo.

Range: 400–1950m n of Orinoco; 350–900m s of Orinoco. Spottily recorded in upper Río Negro, w Zulia (*perijanus*); both slopes of Andes in Mérida (sight, La Azulita; sight, San Isidro Rd.; subsp.?); both slopes of Coastal Cordillera in Aragua and Miranda (sight, Maitana and San José de Los Altos—C. Parrish); Interior Cordillera in Miranda (sight, PN Guatopo—C. Sharp); s Amazonas (Sierra Paraima; Putaco; Río Siapa) and s Bolívar e to Sierra de Lema (several sightings) and Paurai-tepui (*pavoninus*). Nw and s Venez. e across the Guianas, e and s Brazil, e Ecuador, e Peru, and ne Bolivia to Paraguay.
Note: Perhaps monotypic[148].

Rufous-winged Ground-Cuckoo   PLATE 23
Neomorphus rufipennis   Pájaro Váquiro
Identification: 20″ (51cm). *Large terrestrial forest cuckoo*. Eyes reddish brown, *extensive bare ocular area orange red*; heavy, slightly decurved bill blackish, tip gray blue. Entire head and upperparts purplish black with strong greenish gloss, bushy crest usually laid flat, inner flight feathers rufous (not very obvious in field), throat gray scaled dusky, *chest purplish black sharply set off from pale smoky brown breast and belly*. Long broad tail and large powerful legs.
Sim. species: Running on gd. this sp. could be mistaken for a chachalaca or small guan, but those spp. are usually in trees. Note cuckoo's "divided" underparts, heavier bill and crest, and up close, bare facial skin.
Voice: Territorial call a loud forceful *whOOu* with dovelike quality but clearer and usually louder. May be given as walks on forest floor or when perched 0.5–3m up on branch or log. Max. calling rate ca. once every 5–10 sec for up to several min. Low guttural *gr'r'r* and loud bill-snapping at army ants and in agonistic encounters.
Behavior: This large forest cuckoo, essentially a forest-dwelling "roadrunner," runs rapidly but may fly up to a perch if frightened. Reg. follows army ants and roving

bands of White-lipped Peccaries. First indication of its presence is often its loud bill-snapping. May also follow beneath groups of small monkeys (e.g., *Saguinus*) taking disturbed insects and fallen fruit. Sometimes wary, at other times can be approached very closely, but generally difficult to locate and see. Forages singly but lives in prs. which range over large areas.

Status and habitat: Rare and local resident in humid lowland forest. Normally in low density.

Range: To 1100m. Locally throughout Amazonas and Bolívar. Venez., Guyana, and n Brazil.

Opisthocomidae: Hoatzin

Guacharacas de Agua o Chenchenas

This peculiar Neotropical species was once thought to be allied to galliformes or cuckoos, but biochemical evidence now suggests that its closest relatives are African turacos. Hoatzins feed mostly on tender leaves, and these are stored in a large specialized crop which, when filled, makes balance and flight difficult. As a result this species often seems awkward and clumsy. Perhaps because of the bacterial fermentation of leaves in its crop, the Hoatzin has an unpleasant odor which is also present in the flesh, making it almost unpalatable. The young are hatched naked and remain in the nest for a long time, eventually acquiring 2 successive coats of down. At hatching they possess a pair of claws on each wing. When frightened, the young are able to drop into the water below, swim to shore, and clamber back into bushes or the nest using their wing claws, bill, and feet. The claws and swimming ability are lost in a few weeks.

Hoatzin   PLATE 15
Opisthocomus hoazin   Guacharaca de Agua o Chenchena

Identification: 24–26″ (61–66cm). 820g. *Long, frazzled "punk haircut," crest and glaring red eyes* impart *prehistoric* appearance. Rather long neck. Large bare ocular area bright blue. Above bronzy olive brown *liberally streaked buff on hindneck and back; broad buff shoulder patch and wing bars;* long rounded tail dark brown *broadly tipped buff;* crest, foreneck and breast creamy buff, *flight feathers and lower underparts chestnut.*

Voice: At slightest disturbance gives loud reedy hissing and blowing sounds as if exhaling loudly. Also guttural grunting notes, *caa-haak,* which at a distance sound more like a mammal or amphibian than a bird.

Behavior: Sedentary and sluggish, invariably found in colonies in thickets or on low to mid.-level branches near or over water, although may roost in uppermost branches. Often sits partially or completely in open when resting, but if disturbed retreats deeper and higher into vegetation, often crashing noisily into foliage and branches as it flaps and hops awkwardly to safety, then pauses to peer back suspiciously. Flies heavily with laborious wing flapping and short glides to cross small openings. Eats mainly young leaves and buds (esp. leaves of legumes) digested in large crop aided by active microbes and bacteria[213]. When not breeding gathers in groups of 20–30 or more; when breeding forms monogamous prs. or cooperative units of 1 pr. and 1 to several offspring helpers[715,783]. Frail stick nest a platform 2–8m up over water; breeds May–Nov in Venez. llanos[214,524].

Status and habitat: Forested riverbanks, oxbow lagoons, and vegetation-choked borders of swampy forest. Very common locally in gallery forest vegetation along rivers and streams in llanos; uncommon and spotty in distrib. s of Orinoco; rare or absent along blackwater rivers.

Range: To ca. 200m. W Apure and Barinas e through Cojedes and Guárico (Anzoátegui?); to se Sucre, ne Monagas, Delta Amacuro, both sides of lower and mid. Orinoco (upriver at least to Caicara), and locally in Amazonas (Río Ventuari; Río Casiquiare; near Sierra de la Neblina). Se Colombia to n Bolivia, Amaz. Brazil, and the Guianas.

STRIGIFORMES

Tytonidae: Barn Owls

Lechuzas de Campanario

Barn Owls form a small family found virtually world-wide. Most of the approximately 17 species are Old World in distribution except for 1 in Hispaniola. They are similar to typical owls in most respects but differ in their heart-shaped faces and long legs. Barn owls also have completely feathered legs, bristles on their toes, and a pectinate (comblike structure) on their middle claw, as do herons. Mainly nocturnal, they are relentless hunters of small rodents and have proved a great benefit to those engaged in agriculture. They show strong fidelity to nest sites. Females are slightly larger than males. More species of barn owls, including some very large ones, are found in the fossil record than are living today.

Barn Owl   PLATE 24
Tyto alba   Lechuza de Campanario
Identification: 14.5″ (37cm). 470g. *Med.-sized, "ghostly pale" owl* with no ear-tufts. Eyes dark brown; bill pinkish white, legs long. Above tawny orange densely mottled gray and dotted black and white; *heart-shaped facial disk white to dark buff rimmed black*, underparts usually buff (*contempta*) to white (*hellmayri*) but color notably variable; a few small dark spots on underparts. In flight from below looks mostly white.
Sim. species: See Striped Owl, Short-eared Owl, and Great and Common potoos, all of which are rather pale and share same habitat.
Voice: Variety of fairly loud hisses, snores, and scraping sounds; does not hoot. Most freq. a rough shriek and dry scraping hiss are hd. as bird flies overhead in darkness. At nest a loud bill-snapping and raspy sounds.
Behavior: Mostly nocturnal although occas. abroad at twilight. Often hunts from fence posts or other fairly low perches. A renowned "mouse catcher," it also takes other small prey incl. insects and sleeping birds. Roosts by day in tree hole or building. Usually 2–4 (occas. more) elongate white eggs; nest with minimum of twigs or trash, in caves, cliffs, abandoned building, church towers, and hollow trees.
Status and habitat: Local resident. Gallery forest borders, light woodland, semiopen areas with scattered trees, and in towns and around human habitations, old buildings, etc., where it often roosts and nests. Not in heavily wooded areas. Seen most often, and prob. most numerous, in llanos. A pr. nested for yrs (usually ca. Jan–Mar) in a tree cavity ca. 6m up and a few meters from dining room at Hato Cedral in w Apure.

Range: To 1500m (prob. higher). Maracaibo Basin, Zulia, and w slope of Andes in Táchira, Mérida, Trujillo (recs?), and Lara (*contempta*); locally elsewhere s to se Bolívar (no Amazonas recs.); Isla Margarita (*hellmayri*). In New World from s Canada to Tierra del Fuego; elsewhere virtually worldwide (more than 30 subspp.) except arctic and antarctic regions and some oceanic isls.

Strigidae: Typical Owls
Lechuzas, Mochuelos, Pavitas, Curucucúes

Owls are nocturnal birds of prey, although a few species hunt partly or primarily by day. They are most notable for their large heads and forward-looking eyes set in round feathered faces. Unlike potoos and nightjars, the eyes of owls do not reflect much light in a beam at night. Their vision is very acute (day or night), but their large eyes are almost fixed in their orbits, and to compensate owls are able to rotate their heads about 270 degrees. Owls also have very large, parabola-shaped outer ear canals and extremely acute hearing which enables them to locate their prey very precisely by sound. Their soft plumage gives them a silent and buoyant flight. Like other raptors, owls have strong hooked bills and strong raptorial feet and claws but with 2 toes pointing forward and 2 backward. Owls locate their prey by sight and sound. Prey is predominately small vertebrates and insects and is swallowed whole; the bones, fur, and other matter are later regurgitated in the form of pellets. Owls breed in monogamous pairs and do not normally build a nest, instead nesting in tree holes or old nests of other birds; a few species occasionally nest on the ground. Eggs are white, and the clutch size varies with food supply. Incubation begins when the first egg is laid, thus nestlings differ in size. Several Venezuelan owls, as is true elsewhere in humid tropical regions, are infrequently seen and poorly known.

Otus

Small owls with large heads; with or without ear-tufts; longish wings reach almost to tail tips; prey heavily on insects.

Foothill Screech-Owl   PLATE 24
Otus roraimae   Curucucú de Piedemonte
Identification: 8.5″ (22cm). 105g. Eyes orange yellow; bill greenish yellow. Small owl with rather inconspic. ear-tufts, *no obvious facial markings or streaks or marks above.* Plumage brown finely vermiculated black, head, neck, and chest often tinged rufous; *a few of upper wing coverts with large round white spots;* facial disk brown somewhat vermiculated dusky, underparts white heavily and finely vermiculated brown with a few dark vertical shaft streaks; flanks and thighs narrowly barred brown. Primaries rufescent brown with numerous black-bordered white bars (best seen in hand). Rufous phase: uniform rufous above with *a few white spots on scapulars;* below mostly rufous finely and densely vermiculated with white, belly whitish.
Sim. species: Tropical Screech-Owl has black-rimmed face and distinct cross-hatched streaks on breast.
Voice: Normal song (900m, Sierra de Lema, Bolívar) a quavering or dribbling toadlike trill, *wu'u'u'u'u'u'u' u'u'u'u'u'u'u . . .* , ca. 3–6 sec, at rate of 10–12 notes/sec (R. Behrstock recording); song sim. at Barinitas, Barinas; also sim. (lasting 4–5 sec) in n Aragua, or may drop a half-tone in middle of trill (Hilty). Song ventrilo-

quial; calling birds difficult to locate. Song typically much faster than that of Tawny-bellied Screech-Owl, but in lowlands s of Orinoco some songs of these 2 spp. are very sim. and sp. limits difficult to define.
Behavior: A small nocturnal *Otus* that sometimes does not decoy well to taped playback and is difficult to see. In Guyana perched mostly at med. to high levels in forest (M. B. Robbins); in PN Henri Pittier has been seen repeatedly at mid. levels or slightly lower.
Status and habitat: Uncommon resident although prob. much underrecorded. Humid lowland and premontane forest and older second-growth woodland. Large no. of recs. from PN Henri Pittier, mostly 350–1050m (a few lower or higher), and can be hd. there most of yr.

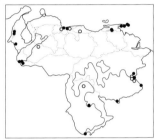

Range: 300–1100m n of Orinoco; 200–1800m s Orinoco. Spottily in mts. of w Zulia (Río Negro; Catatumbo); e base of Andes from Táchira to Barinas (voice, 1995, Barinitas); n cordilleras in Carabobo, Aragua, and Miranda (sight, PN Guatopo—C. Parrish); mts. of Sucre and n Monagas (*napensis*); Amazonas (Cerros Duida and de la Neblina); e Bolívar on or near tepuis (*roraimae*). E base of Andes from Colombia to n Argentina. Mts. of Guyana.
Note 1: Birds from tepuis may be a separate sp.
Note 2: Formerly incl. Guatemalan Screech-Owl, *O. guatemalae* (long trill song) of Mexico to Costa Rica; and Choco Screech-Owl, *O. centralis* (short trill song) of Costa Rica to w Ecuador[242,541]; nw Peru? Sp. limits not fully defined.

Tropical Screech-Owl PLATE 24
Otus choliba   Curucucú Común
Identification: 8.2″ (21cm). 135g. *Eyes yellow.* Small but prom. ear-tufts. Above buffy brown finely vermiculated gray and dusky, a few blackish shaft streaks on back, more on crown; *prom. row of white spots on scapulars* and a few on wing coverts; eyebrows and facial disk buffy white, face rimmed dark chestnut; underparts mixed gray and buffy white with a few narrow dark streaks crossed by several short black horizontal streaks (distinctive cross-hatched appearance). Birds from s Amazonas (*duidae*) are slightly larger, much darker, with crown, hindneck, and upperparts sooty blackish (some almost blackish throughout); chest sooty brown, face and lower underparts gray; underparts coarsely streaked black and narrowly crosshatched enclosing numerous squarish pale spots (looks "ocellated").
Sim. species: In most areas the commonest small owl. Combination of black facial rim and crosshatching below is distinctive. See other *Otus.*

Voice: Often vocal just after dusk and again shortly before dawn. Song a short, tremulous, and whistled trill followed by 1–3 abrupt, accented notes at end, *pprrrr-rrr büü! bük!*, with numerous variations at end, or ending notes omitted. Also a ser. of tremulous *chu'r'ro* notes. When annoyed a complaining *taduú-taduú-taduú-taduú* as flies off.
Behavior: Nocturnal. Typically forages alone, mostly fairly low, but may roost in prs. in a cavity or on an open branch from low to fairly high, usually in thick vegetation. Takes wide range of small prey from insects and arthropods to bats, occas. birds. Nest in almost any kind of cavity, even an open fence post or old bird nest; nest rather low; 1–3 white eggs; Apr–Jun in n Venez.
Status and habitat: Widespread resident in dry to humid regions. Most numerous in light woodland, tall second growth, forest borders, and trees in clearing, gardens, around buildings, ranches, and urban areas in lowlands and foothills, often well into mts. Less numerous in areas of extensive lowland forest; local and at low density in gallery forest in llanos. On Cerro de la Neblina (*duidae*) hd. in dense *Brocchinia*/bamboo scrub forest and high-el. pitcher-plant swamps[801].

Range: To 2400m. Zulia and Falcón e to Anzoátegui; Cerro El Copey, Isla Margarita (*margaritae*); rest of Venez. except s Amazonas (*crucigerus*); s Amazonas on Cerros Duida and de la Neblina (*duidae*). Costa Rica to n Argentina, Paraguay, and s Brazil.
Note: Highland *duidae* (voice differs) may be a separate sp.

Rufescent Screech-Owl PLATE 24
Otus ingens   Curucucú Pálido
Identification: 10″ (25cm). 175g. Large *Otus* with small ear-tufts and reddish *brown to yellowish brown eyes.* Plumage in general rather *uniform rufous to dark brown.* Above vermiculated and mottled blackish, flight feathers barred buff; a few inconspic. white spots on scapulars; usually with pale eyebrows; no dark facial rim; below buff with *a few large vertical streaks and numerous fine cross-hatch markings* (much less distinct than in Tropical Screech-Owl). Some birds are almost uniform rufous below.
Sim. species: Sim. to Tropical Screech-Owl but larger with brown eyes, no dark facial rim, and less white in scapulars.
Voice: Song of ♂ (Lara and w Mérida) somewhat variable but typically a rather short ser. of 8–20 tooting whistles, *hu hu, hu-hu huhuhuhuhuhu*, on same pitch, last half much faster or accelerating. ♀ sim. but ca.

half an octave higher in pitch. Song apparently sim. elsewhere[177].
Behavior: Apparently much like that of Tropical Screech-Owl. Usually seen perched at mid. levels or lower in forest.
Status and habitat: Not well known. Resident in humid and wet premontane forest. Found with some reg. in higher els. of PN Henri Pittier; 3 netted ca. 1800m, Pico Guacamaya (near Portachuelo Pass), Aragua, 17–19 Mar 1977 (J. Fitzpatrick and J. Weske); also found near Choroní Pass, Aragua, Jan 1985 (C. Parrish). Elsewhere recs. few and widely scattered.

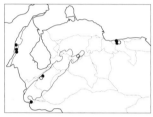

Range: 1000–1700m. Sierra de Perijá (upper Río Negro), Zulia; spottily in Andes in se Táchira, w Mérida (La Azulita), prob. Lara (tapes, this sp.?, PN Yacambú—R. Behrstock); Coastal Cordillera in Aragua (*venezuelanus*). Colombia s in Andes to n Bolivia.

Tawny-bellied Screech-Owl   PLATE 24
Otus watsonii   Curucucú Orejudo
Identification: 9″ (23cm). 130g. Small dark owl with short ear-tufts that are inconspic. or often project rearward. *Eyes yellowish brown to amber.* Color somewhat variable. Above essentially uniform dusky brown to dark tawny, *ear-tufts and facial rim black, below tawny buff with a few dark shaft streaks on breast;* throat and chest finely and obscurely barred dusky, lower breast and belly with a few fine cross-hatched bars (best seen in hand). Rufous-colored birds may show a few large buff spots on wing coverts and tertials. Very dark individuals are virtually unmarked or show only a few narrow black streaks below.
Sim. species: Almost always darker than Tropical Screech-Owl and lacks that sp.'s pale eyebrows and distinct cross-hatched pattern on breast. Tawny-bellied usually shows no shoulder spots. Also see Vermiculated Screech-Owl.
Voice: Song at dawn (Km 87, San Isidro, e Bolívar) a fast quavering or toadlike trill, swelling then fading, 'u'u'u'u'u'u'u'u'U'U'U'U'U'u'u' . . . , lasting ca. 10–15 sec at rate of ca. 9–10 notes/sec (R. Behrstock recording). Some songs (esp. at dusk) are slower, ca. 8 notes/ sec., even lower pitched, and last up to 30 sec. Song closely resembles that of Foothill Screech-Owl (see), but natural songs longer (usually) and slower, and often start softly, increase in volume, then fade at end. Notes have a slight "echo" or pulsing quality, making singer very difficult to locate.
Behavior: Sim. to Tropical Screech-Owl but occurs mainly inside forest and generally more difficult to see. Usually perches from about eye level to mid. level, and when calling apt to remain on same perch for long periods of time.

Status and habitat: Fairly common to common resident inside humid terra firme and várzea forest in lowlands s of Orinoco; also at forest borders, and sometimes in small clearings or around buildings if there are trees. Highland pop. (same subsp.?) in w Venez. is essentially unknown in life.

Range: 2000–2100m n of Orinoco; to 300m s of Orinoco. W Zulia (upper Río Negro drainage) and s Táchira (Río Chiquito); throughout Amazonas and Bolívar (*watsonii*). E Colombia to n Bolivia, Amaz. Brazil, and the Guianas.
Note: Prob. more than 1 sp.[301]; subsp. *usta* of e Peru, s Amaz. Brazil, and Bolivia often raised to full sp. status. Vocal differences across broad extralimital lowland range are marked, with birds in s part of range having slowest songs. Fast songs (Venez. and the Guianas) approach those of Foothill Screech-Owl, *O. roraimae*, but song differences may represent a cline. Highland birds also may be a separate sp. (voice unknown).

White-throated Screech-Owl   PLATE 24
Otus albogularis   Curucucú Gargantiblanco
Identification: 9.5–10.5″ (24–27cm). 185g (1 ♀). Largest *Otus* in Venez. Eyes yellow. Above dark dusky brown to rufescent brown finely dotted and vermiculated buff and white (no scapular spots) with *contrasting white throat and barely protruding ear-tufts;* dark facial disk bordered above by pale forehead and eyebrows; breast dark brown, rather sharply set off from light tawny buff lower breast and belly *(has distinct 2-toned look);* a few bold white-bordered black streaks on breast.
Sim. species: An *Otus* of high els. Note white throat (if visible). All other small Venez. owls are more or less uniform in color below (not 2-toned). See Rufescent Screech-Owl.
Voice: Song (♂?) a rhythmic tooting *pu pu púdu-púdu-púdu-púdu-púdu* . . . , ca. 15 couplets at 5/sec; or *pu pu púdu-púdu-púdu . . . du-du-du.* Song of ♀ (?) sim. but higher pitched. Both may sing simultaneously, 1 starting, then the other joining in rollicking chorus ending with only 2d bird singing at end[242].
Behavior: Sim. to other *Otus.*
Status and habitat: Local or low-density (prob. overlooked) resident of high-el. humid and wet, epiphyte-laden forest, wooded borders, and clearings with trees. More than half of 19 specimens (Colección Phelps) were taken above 2750m; only 1 below 1900m. Relatively common in Ecuador and Peru (M. B. Robbins).

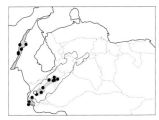

Range: 1300–3100m. Sierra de Perijá (Río Negro), Zulia (*obscurus*); Páramo de Tamá, Táchira (*albogularis?*); Andes of n Táchira and Mérida (*meridensis*). Colombia s in Andes to n Bolivia.

Great Horned Owl PLATE 25
Bubo virginianus Lechuzón Orejudo
Identification: 19–22″ (48–56cm). 1.2kg. Largest owl in country. *Prom. ear-tufts; yellow eyes.* Above dark brown mottled gray and buff, facial disk buffy white rimmed black, narrow white throat (not always visible) bordered black below; *underparts whitish to buff to ochraceous narrowly and evenly barred black* (bars somewhat V shaped), and with a few black shaft streaks.
Sim. species: Found in same habitat as Striped Owl which has bold stripes. Stygian Owl has dark eyes and dark plumage; Short-eared Owl has much smaller, rudimentary ear-tufts and striped underparts.
Voice: Call a deep, mellow ser. of hoots, *whoo-whoo . . . whoo, whoo-whoo*, or other variations, with considerable carrying power. Occas. only a single hoot. Mated prs. may give shrieking cries at nest or to each other.
Behavior: Often out at dusk where seen silhouetted on a high perch against fading light. Formidable in appearance and a powerful solitary hunter, it flies with surprisingly rapid wing beats for so large a bird. Takes a wide variety of prey, esp. med.-sized mammals, even other owls, and occas. insects. Nest in tall tree, broken palm, opened-up tree cavity, or old raptor nest; 2–3 (sometimes more) white eggs. Fledged young 30 Apr, Guárico[369].
Status and habitat: Local. Resident mainly in semi-open to mostly open areas with scattered trees, groves of trees or palms, gallery forest borders, and trees around ranch buildings in lowlands. Favors drier, more seasonal areas. Unreported from paramo in Venez., but elsewhere in Andes often in open areas above treeline. Fairly common and widespread in llanos; during day often roosts around human habitations.

Range: To 1800m (higher?). Recs. spotty. Maracaibo Basin, Zulia, Andes in Mérida and in Lara; e of Andes from Apure and Cojedes to Monagas; Delta Amacuro[343]; n Amazonas (Pto. Ayacucho); Bolívar along Río Orinoco (*nacurutu*), se Bolívar near Santa Elena de Uairén (1 found dead, 1996; subsp.?). N Amer. s to s Peru and s Brazil but local or absent from forested lowlands in tropical regions.
Note: Taxonomy follows König et al.[301]. Small austral birds (Bolivia southward) prob. a separate sp.

Glaucidium

Small; no ear-tufts; narrow triangular black spots ("false eyes") on back of head; rounded wings; longish tail; some spp. have 2 color phases.

Andean Pygmy-Owl PLATE 24
Glaucidium jardinii Pavita Andina
Identification: 6″ (15cm). 62g. *Eyes yellow.* Small, dark, "earless" owl of high Andes. Brown (normal) phase: mainly dark chocolate brown *spotted white above*; crown profusely dotted white, facial disk brownish rimmed by short gray eyebrows; 2 black "false eyes" on back of head*; short tail with 3–4 narrow white to buff white bars visible; throat whitish, *sides of throat, chest, and upper breast dull dark brown somewhat spotted and barred white*, sides and flanks more or less spotted and barred dark brown, rest of underparts whitish *coarsely streaked dusky brown*. Rufous phase (rare): *all dark rufous above and below*; somewhat mottled rufous buff above; breast washed chestnut and vaguely streaked black; tail with ca. 8 equal-width black and rufous bars. A few bird have mixed brown and rufous plumage.
Sim. species: Ferruginous Pygmy-Owl of lower els. is sim. but grayish brown to rufous (not dark brown), has streaked sides and flanks (no spots or bars below), and finer, more streaky dots on crown; dots on crown of Andean Pygmy-Owl are larger, bolder, and more discrete, not streaky.
Voice: Advertising call a little tooting ser. of 10–30 or so evenly spaced (occas. slightly irreg. spaced) *poop* notes at rate of ca. 3/sec, sim. to call of Ferruginous Pygmy-Owl but slightly higher pitched. When excited a ser. of short purring trills, *purr'r'up, purr'r'up, . . . ,* often followed by tooting notes. Less vocal than Ferruginous Pygmy-Owl.
Behavior: Like other *Glaucidium*, active and may call day or night but most often in morning or evening. Typically perches high, often well out in dense foliage on a canopy branch where it watches carefully, then launches attacks on small birds (a favorite target) with swift, maneuverable dashes but does not pursue them. Also eats insects. Small size makes it difficult to spot, but whenever one is discovered it is mobbed unmercifully by canopy birds such as flowerpiercers, tanagers, and hummingbirds. Flicks tail from side to side when agitated or after alighting. Flight is rapid and bounding. Nest in tree cavity.
Status and habitat: Uncommon and perhaps local resident (easily overlooked unless calling). Canopy of humid and wet montane forest, and forest borders; occas. in tall isolated trees in highland pastures but

rarely far from forest. Found with some reg. in n Táchira; also PN Guaramacal, Trujillo (sight/tapes).

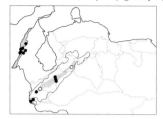

Range: 2000–4000m. Sierra de Perijá, Zulia; Andes of Táchira, Mérida, and Trujillo. Andes of Colombia to n Peru.
Note: Birds of C Amer. and those s of n Peru now considered separate spp.[553].

Ferruginous Pygmy-Owl   PLATE 24
Glaucidium brasilianum   Pavita Ferruginea
Identification: 6.5" (16.5cm). 70g. Eyes yellow. Small, "earless" owl of lower els. Two color phases: *grayish brown above or rufous above*, both somewhat spotted white, esp. on shoulders and tertials; *crown with fine streaky buff to white dots*; 2 oblong black "false eyes" on back of head; *underparts whitish streaked brown or rufous, heaviest on sides and flanks*. Tail as in Andean Pygmy-Owl *but longer*, showing 3 narrow white bars and white tip (in hand also a broken white band at base of tail). A few birds have 1 additional white tail bar. Rufous birds more heavily and broadly streaked below; tail has ca. 12 narrow, equal-width buff and rufous bars. Rufous birds commoner than gray.
Sim. species: At higher el. see Andean Pygmy-Owl. Also see rare Amazonian Pygmy-Owl.
Voice: Song, reg. hd. at dusk, before daybreak, or during day, usually stimulates an extreme mobbing reaction in small birds of dry and arid habitats; song a long-sustained ser., *poik, poik, oik, oik, oik, oik* . . . (up to 50 or more notes), at rate of ca. 2–2.5/sec; some songs end with a few *chur'r'up* notes. Sometimes song starts with a few quick, inflected notes that descend slightly then slide into a prolonged ser.; easily imitated by whistling. When excited a short ser. of purring or trilling *chir'r'up* notes.
Behavior: An aggressive predator on small birds up to ca. its own size, also reptiles, other small vertebrates, and insects. Attacks in swift, maneuverable ambushes. Hunts day or night, but most activity is crepuscular, and everywhere mobbed unmercifully by many small birds whenever it is spotted. Responds strongly to whistled imitations of its call, often flying in almost immediately, flicking tail in agitation and glaring intently in all directions. Flight is fast and slightly bounding. Breeding Mar–Jul, Anzoátegui[187]; Apr–May, Guárico[369,734]. Nest in tree cavity or old woodpecker hole 3–12m up; 2–5 white eggs[175].
Status and habitat: Resident in a wide variety of dry to fairly humid habitats incl. arid scrub with cactus, dry forest, scrubby semiopen areas with trees and thickets, and locally in tall moist to moderately humid forest. Commonest in arid regions, much less numerous and local in moist and humid regions; local s of Orinoco

where mainly at mid. els. on slopes of tepuis. Generally scarce or avoids unbroken lowland forest.

Range: To ca. 1000m (hd. to 1900m, Aragua). Throughout (Zulia?) n of Orinoco (*phalaenoides*); n and c Amazonas (*duidae*); extreme s Amazonas (*ucayalae*); Bolívar (*olivaceum*); Isla Margarita (*margaritae*). Sw US to n Chile, c Argentina, and Uruguay.
Note: Arrangement of subspp.[148] varies.

Amazonian Pygmy-Owl
Glaucidium hardyi   Pavita Amazónica
Identification: 5.5" (14cm). Small "earless" owl. Eyes yellow. *Head grayish brown dotted with white*; 2 small black ovals on hindcrown form "false eyes"; rest of upperparts brownish with a few small white spots and markings on wing coverts; tail blackish with *ca. 3 narrow white bars visible and pale tip*; underparts whitish with dusky rufous smudges and broad blurry streaks on chest and sides. Imm.: no white dots on crown.
Sim. species: Much like gray brown phase of Ferruginous Pygmy-Owl but smaller and with crown dotted (not streaked). Note very different voice.
Voice: Song, often hd. during day (in Peru), a soft, descending, and rather high-pitched trill of 10–20 notes given in ca. 2 sec. Call may not immediately bring to mind that of an owl.
Behavior: In se Peru and Bolivia occurs at mid. levels or higher in tall lowland forest and is active and vocal both day and night, but difficult to see.
Status and habitat: A newly described sp.[267,300,771]. One specimen (originally identified as *G. minutissimum*) with tape-recording, 28 Apr 1967, between El Palmar and Río Grande, e Bolívar (P. Schwartz); recent tape-recordings (bird not seen) on Sierra de Lema, Bolívar[294]. Elsewhere found in tall humid forest in lowlands and foothills. Prob. more widespread than the few Venez. recs. suggest.

Range: To 850m. E Bolívar (Río Grande, Sierra de Lema). E Peru, e Bolivia and w and c Amaz. Brazil; Guyana; Suriname (tape).

Note: Formerly incl. in Least Pygmy-Owl (*G. minutissimum*).

Burrowing Owl   PLATE 24

Athene cunicularia   Mochuelo de Hoyo

Identification: 8.5″ (22cm). 155g. *Long-legged, terrestrial owl*. Eyes yellow; no ear-tufts. Above pale brown *profusely spotted buff and white*, tail very short (barely visible), *prom. white eyebrows (impart a "startled" look)*; below mostly buffy white with mottled brown chest band (sometimes interrupted in middle), lower underparts somewhat coarsely barred brown. Birds from offshore isls. are palest above, those from llanos darkest.

Sim. species: Not likely confused in daylight. At night cf. much larger Striped and Short-eared owls, both with ear-tufts.

Voice: Rather quiet. At dawn or dusk a soft *coo-cooo*. Alarm or scold at nest a rather harsh *QUEE! qua'qua' qua'qua*, sometimes over and over.

Behavior: Diurnal, but most active mornings and evenings. During day perches on gd., mound of dirt, fence post, or other low place; stares intently with glaring yellow eyes and furrowed brow, and occas. flies off short distances in undulating flight. Pounces directly, or hovers and pounces on small vertebrates and some arthropods. Tends to form loose colonies of up to 10 or even 20 monogamous prs. in favorable areas. Nest, dug by ads., a burrow in gd.; 2–11 white eggs that stain darker; breeds Dec–Apr (dry season) in w Apure. ♂ feeds ♀ during incubation. Older juvs. assemble above gd. around nest hole and may stare or invert head upside down in comical manner.

Status and habitat: Fairly common resident locally in grasslands and open dry to arid scrub zones. Most easily seen in arid zones of nw (e.g., Paraguaná and Goajira pens.), on some of large ranches in llanos (e.g., Hato Cedral and Hato El Frio in Apure), and around Maturín, Monagas.

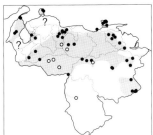

Range: To 1000m. Locally throughout from Zulia to Sucre; n Amazonas (s to mouth of Río Ventuari— K. Zimmer and D. Wolf) and generally in Bolívar s to Santa Elena de Uairén (*minor*); llanos of Apure, Barinas, and Cojedes (*apurensis*); Isla Margarita, Borracha, and Cubagua (*brachyptera*). Breeds locally in w N Amer. (wintering rarely s to Panama), s Florida, W Indies, and open parts of S Amer.

Note: Often placed in genus *Speotyto*. Subsp. *minor* sometimes incl. in *brachyptera*[301].

Lophostrix

Med. size; unusually long white ear-tufts.

Crested Owl   PLATE 25

Lophostrix cristata   Lechuza Copetona

Identification: 16″ (41cm). 545g. *Long white eyebrows and prom. partially white ear-tufts (when erect) impart commanding appearance*. Eyes yellow. Above rufescent (color somewhat variable), 1 or more rows of white spots on wing coverts; primaries barred dark brown and buff, facial disk buff; brown chest *"divided"* somewhat from tawny lower underparts (no streaks). In hand, finely vermiculated dusky above and below.

Sim. species: Unstreaked underparts and "hornlike" ear-tufts are the marks, but except when roosting, ear-tufts are laid back rather flat along side of head and are not conspic.

Voice: Call a short, low-pitched, froglike *k'k'k'kkurrr!* that accelerates into a growling purr; ends abruptly. At a distance sounds like a soft *grrrrr!* repeated ca. once every 5 sec at max. calling rate. Often does not call until 1–2 hrs after dark, then sporadically throughout night.

Behavior: Strictly nocturnal. Roosts from about eye-level to 8m up inside forest, alone or in prs. which sit close together with large white ear-tufts pointed vertically. Although it roosts low, this owl hunts and calls from perches much higher, usually within canopy or subcanopy, then often difficult to see because it is so high overhead. In Costa Rica food items incl. mostly large insects[706]. Tree cavity nest reported in Guyana[789].

Status and habitat: Uncommon to fairly common resident s of Orinoco in tall humid terra firme (várzea?) forest and tall second-growth woodland; infreq. along forest borders but can be called to borders. Density of calling birds (occas. 4–5 can be hd. at once) suggests territories are not large and pops. locally high, e.g., at Junglaven, Amazonas. Prob. more widespread n of Orinoco than the few recs. suggest.

Range: To ca. 300m. S Maracaibo Basin in Zulia (Misión Tucuco) and nw Táchira; Coastal Cordillera in Rancho Grande, Aragua (*wedeli*); Amazonas (sightings in Pto. Ayacucho, Junglaven, and Cerro de la Neblina); n Bolívar in lower Río Caura (Pto. Cabello; Caño La Urbana), and sight/tape at Río Grande (*cristata*). S Mexico locally to Bolivia, Amaz. Brazil, and the Guianas.

Pulsatrix

Fairly large, robust, forest owls with bold spectacles and broad, dark chest band; legs feathered to toes; juvs. mostly white.

Spectacled Owl   PLATE 25
Pulsatrix perspicillata   Lechuzón de Anteojos
Identification: 18″ (46cm). 850g. Large with *bold white "spectacles"* that extend back across eyebrows; eyes yellow (may reflect dull ruby at night). No ear-tufts. Head and upperparts dusky black, rearparts paler; narrow white throat band; *broad blackish chest band*; rest of underparts buff (varies from light to dark buff), tail short (looks "bob-tailed" in flight). Juv.: *mostly white with large heart-shaped black mask*, blackish flight feathers and dusky tail with white-tip. Imm.: as in ad. but paler; head whitish with darker ad. markings faintly indicated; chest band paler and incomplete.
Sim. species: This large, boldly patterned owl with white collar and black bow tie should be unmistakable. At high el. see smaller Buff-fronted Owl. Other large lowland owls are barred below or have prom. ear-tufts.
Voice: Rumbling bass voice, unlike any other in Venez., a ser. of deep, resonant hoots, *BOO Boo boo boo boo*, descending, growing softer and faster; ♂♂ and ♀♀ may give antiphonal duet, ♂ (?) starts with deep chuckling *WHU-Whu-whu-who*u, ♀ (?) follows immediately (or overlaps end of previous song) with higher pitched and laughing *HA-HA-Ha-ha*, then 1st bird finishes with *whu-whu-whu-ha*, sometimes over and over at short intervals, suggesting maniacal laughter. May call any hr of night, and vocal on moonlit or dark nights. Juv. gives a clear *kuUUa* (begging?), rising then falling in pitch.
Behavior: A nocturnal owl that is active immediately after dusk. Roosts at low to moderate hts., sometimes down nearly to eye level, but hunts from higher perches or in canopy inside forest. Takes a wide variety of prey incl. large insects, small mammals, even small owls (seen with captured *Otus* owl). Nest in unlined tree cavity; 2 white eggs; Nov nestlings, Hato Cedral, Apure (D. Ascanio).
Status and habitat: Fairly common low-density resident of mature dry and moist forest, riparian woodland, gallery forest, and humid lowland forest. In dry areas and in gallery forest found where there are at least some large mature trees, e.g., *Pithecellobium* and *Anacardium*. Widespread across llanos and in forested areas s of Orinoco.

Range: To 900m n of Orinoco (hd. to 1000m); to 1450m s of Orinoco. Locally throughout (*perspicillata*); no recs. from arid Carib. regions. S Mexico to w Ecuador, nw Argentina, Paraguay, and s Brazil. Trinidad.

Strix

Med. to fairly large in size; "earless"; eyes dark; some vocalizations quite sim. among various spp. Most spp. (incl. all those in Venez.) placed in *Ciccaba* by earlier authors. Taxonomy follows several sources[148, 430, 604, 772].

Black-and-white Owl   PLATE 25
Strix nigrolineata   Lechuza Blanquinegra
Identification: 17″ (43cm). 400g. Eyes dark. *Head and facial disk black, eyebrows and vague rim around face speckled white*, rest of upperparts blackish brown, a few white bars on inner flight feathers; broad nuchal collar and *underparts white narrowly and evenly barred black*, thighs black finely barred white, tail black with 4 narrow white bars and white tip.
Sim. species: Likely confused only with slightly smaller and much darker Black-banded Owl of s of Orinoco. Latter is *narrowly barred with white on entire upperparts* and is *black narrowly barred white below* (reverse of Black-and-white Owl). Limited hybridization may occur in overlap zone (P. Schwartz).
Voice: Two very different calls, both much like those of next 2 spp: a high-pitched, dry scream, rising then falling, catlike and strained as though only air is being expelled. Territorial or advertising call a deep, resonant, and deliberate *hu, hu, hu, HOO-ah* with variations; when agitated a longer ser. of slow *húwah* notes and a single loud deep *whoou* at intervals (P. Schwartz recording).
Behavior: Nocturnal, monogamous, and sedentary. In Guatemala roosts ca. 14m up (3.5–26m), generally much higher than Mottled Owl, and often with vines overhanging roost perch. Very large home range territory (100 to > 400ha); feeds on insects, esp. scarab beetles, and bats. Nest, very high (16–26m up) in emergent tree, is a small space (no construction) within epiphytic orchid or bromeliad (not in cavity); 1 white egg[192]. In PN Guatopo has been observed hunting (insects?) around outdoor lights at night.
Status and habitat: Resident in moist and humid forest, along forest borders, and in older second-growth woodland in lowland and hilly terrain. Perhaps local; known mainly from 3 areas (Sierra de Perijá, n cordilleras, and Delta Amacuro), but surely more widespread. Replaced s of Orinoco by Black-banded Owl.

Range: To 900m[60]. Base of Sierra de Perijá (several locs.), Zulia; n mts. of Carabobo (Pantanemo; sight, Palmichal[60]), Aragua (Rancho Grande), Distr. Federal (Pto. La Cruz), Miranda (Santa Lucia; sight, PN Guatopo), n Cojedes and Guárico; Delta Amacuro (Tucupita). S Mexico to e Venez. and nw Peru.

Black-banded Owl
PLATE 25
Strix huhula Lechuza Negra
Identification: 14″ (36cm). 385g. No ear-tufts; eyes brown; bill yellowish. Almost a black-and-white "negative" of previous sp. *Above black with numerous finely etched white bars*; face black indistinctly outlined by freckly white rim, *below black finely and densely barred white on throat and chest, more evenly on lower underparts*; tail black with 3 narrow white bars and white tip.
Sim. species: See Black-and-white Owl.
Voice: Very sim. to preceding sp., and the two will respond to tape playback of each other's vocalizations. An ascending, catlike scream, *whoeeruh*, followed after a short pause by a loud *whoou*; also a deliberate, deep, resonant *hu, hu, hu, HUUU*, with variations (P. Schwartz recording).
Behavior: As in Black-and-white Owl. Nocturnal. Usually stays high in trees and flies high over forest openings.
Status and habitat: Known only from a small no. of scattered locs. in Venez., but prob. more numerous than the few recs. suggest. Resident in humid terra firme and várzea forest and forest borders in lowlands. Reg. found in Río Grande area, ne Bolívar. Unrec. in s Bolívar.

Range: To ca. 300m. Prob. throughout Amazonas (Cerro Guanari, Río Casiquiare); n Bolívar in lower Río Caura; and ne Bolívar at El Callao, Río Grande, and upper Río Cuyuní (tape) (*huhula*). Colombia s to e Peru, Bolivia, n Argentina, Amaz. Brazil, and the Guianas.

Mottled Owl
PLATE 25
Strix virgata Lechuza Colilarga
Identification: 13″ (33cm). 260g. *Eyes dark.* No ear-tufts. Variable in color over broad range. *Facial disk brown* with buff to white eyebrows and rims. Upperparts generally dark wood brown finely mottled buff, scapulars spotted buff to white, flight feathers with 4 large buff bars and numerous smaller ones, *underparts entirely tawny buff coarsely streaked dark brown*, tail black with 4 buff white to grayish white bars and pale tip. Some individuals blackish brown on throat and

chest and tawny buff on lower underparts (underparts look 2-toned), but all have a few coarse streaks. Or rather different (se Bolívar): above dark rufescent brown, below rich tawny buff finely barred dark rufous brown, *no obvious coarse streaking*; facial disk dark rufous boldly outlined white, tail with 5–6 *broad* pale brown bands (*macconnelli*).
Sim. species: Variable and sometimes confusing. At high els. see Rufous-banded Owl. Combination of dark eyes and face and coarse streaking below helpful (except *macconnelli*).
Voice: Commonest call a deep, resonant, almost gruff *whoOOOou*, singly, doubled, trebled, or occas. 5–6 or more in a slow ser.; some vocalizations quite sim. to those of 2 previous spp. Also a dry, catlike scream, *wueeiiiier*. Generally more vocal than others of genus.
Behavior: Nocturnal, monogamous, and sedentary. In Guatemala prs. or families often roost together ca. 5m up (0.5–18m) on a horizontal branch or on a vine in dense vegetation. Hunt inside forest or along wooded border on small permanent territory of ca. 22ha (cf. Black-and-white Owl). Preys on insects and small rodents. Nest in cavity 8–17m up in live tree; only ♀ incubates; 2 (avg.) white eggs hatch asynchronously[192].
Status and habitat: Commoner and more widespread than other *Strix* in Venez. Resident in humid forest, forest borders, second-growth woodland, and disturbed or partially settled areas; sometimes quite close around human dwellings. N of Orinoco most recs. are in hilly terrain, foothills, or low els. in mts.

Range: To 1900m n of Orinoco; to ca. 1500m s of Orinoco. Sierra de Perijá, Zulia; both slopes of Andes from Táchira to nw Lara; se Falcón (hd., La Misión—P. Boesman), Yaracuy, and n cordilleras from Carabobo to Sucre, e Monagas, and Delta Amacuro (*virgata*); w and c Amazonas (Caño Paria, tape, Jun 1995; Cerro Parú) and se Bolívar near Auyán-tepui and Cerro Roraima (*macconnelli*). W Mexico to w Ecuador, n Argentina, and Paraguay. Trinidad.

Rufous-banded Owl
PLATE 25
Strix albitarsis Lechuza Patiblanca
Identification: 14.5″ (37cm). Med.-sized highland owl with *dark eyes and no ear-tufts.* Upperparts dark brown coarsely barred and spotted tawny; *conspic. eyebrows and lores buffy white*, facial disk dusky chestnut, *chest dark brown to chestnut mottled and barred buff* (forms broad ill-defined chest band) contrasting with paler underparts ocellated with *large squarish silver spots*; tail dark brown with 4 dark buff bars and narrow buff tip. Juv.: plain buffy brown with dusky mask.

Sim. species: See Mottled Owl which is usually at lower el., not so spotted above or below, and has less prom. facial pattern.

Voice: Very sim. to long songs of Black-banded and Black-and-white owls, a deep, deliberate, resonant *hu, hu hu hu HOOOa*, often repeated every 8–11 sec at max. calling rate (P. Schwartz recording). Differs from above spp. mainly in rhythm, e.g., pause after 1st note, next 3 quicker, last prolonged and strongly emphasized.

Behavior: Nocturnal. Roosts by day at low to moderate hts., sometimes on open branch where conspic. At night has been seen on a variety of mostly med. to high perches in trees and on electric poles adj. to forest. Seems most active just after dusk and before dawn.

Status and habitat: Fairly common resident (by voice) in humid and wet mossy forest (cloud forest), forest borders, and patches of second growth or scattered trees near or adj. to forest.

Range: 2000–3000m. Sierra de Perijá, Zulia; Andes of n Táchira (prob. s Táchira), Mérida, and Trujillo n to Páramo Cendé. Colombia s in mts. to w Peru and Bolivia.

Note: Spelling of *albitarsis* follows del Hoyo[148].

Asio

Close-set eyes and ear-tufts; coarse streaking, esp. below; barking calls.

Striped Owl   PLATE 24
Asio clamator   Lechuza Listada

Identification: 15″ (38cm). 430g. Boldly striped owl of grasslands. Prom. ear-tufts. Eyes dark. *Facial disk white to buff rimmed black all around*; upperparts mostly buff streaked blackish, wings and tail buffy gray barred and mottled brown; *below buffy white with very bold coarse black streaks*. Some individuals much darker, deep tawny above and below.

Sim. species: Likely confused only with rare Stygian Owl which has yellow eyes, darker underparts, and is not conspic. streaked. Also cf. Short-eared Owl which has tiny ears, yellow eyes, and *usually* darker underparts.

Voice: Infreq. hd. calls incl. a loud, semiwhistled *wheeyoo* and a ser. of barking or yapping hoots, *ow, ow, ow, . . .* , like bark of a small dog (P. Schwartz recording). At predawn roost (se Sucre) several soft low hoots (D. Rose).

Behavior: Strictly nocturnal. Generally hunts alone from atop a fence post, small isolated tree, or brushy area and usually does not perch very high, but may roost in prs. high in tall tree. Nest on gd. or low mound; 2–4 eggs in Suriname[253].

Status and habitat: Nonforest owl. Uncommon to fairly common resident; perhaps local (often difficult to find). Semiopen grasslands mixed with scattered trees, brush, and dry gallery forest borders; also sometimes over marshes, even open areas in urban zones (e.g., 1 seen at Universidad de Simon Bolívar, 8 May 1974—C. Parrish) or around habitations (pr. roosting in yard at Guaraunos, Sucre, Mar 1998). Most readily found in open areas of llanos, e.g., Hato El Frio, but occurs at low density even there.

Range: To 1000m. Nw, w, and s Zulia (Río Yasa; w of Maracaibo—C. Parrish; 1 dead on road near Río Catatumbo, 20 Mar 1981—R. Ridgely and A. Keith) e to nw Lara; generally e of Andes from w Apure (sight), Portuguesa, Carabobo, and coastal mts. e to e Sucre (sight), Monagas (Maturín), and n Bolívar (lower Río Caura, sight—J. Pierson; Ciudad Bolívar) s to Auyán-tepui (*clamator*); prob. throughout Gran Sabana. Se Mexico locally to n Argentina and Uruguay.

Note: Has been placed in genus *Rhinoptynx*[403] and *Pseudoscops*[441]; plumage and vocalizations closest to *Asio*[148].

Stygian Owl   PLATE 25
Asio stygius   Lechuza Estigia

Identification: 17″ (43cm). 675g. *Dark with prom., close-set ear-tufts* (conspic. when alert but often lowered at rest). Yellow eyes. Above dark chocolate brown with a few buff markings on crown and back; *facial disk blackish, patch on forehead whitish*, eyebrows and facial rim freckled grayish white; below mixed buff and white and *coarsely streaked dark brown, streaks with distinctive broad cross-bars giving underparts a rather "spotted" or herringbone look*.

Sim. species: Told by very dark appearance, yellow eyes set in dark face, and herringbone-shaped streaks below; up close note inward curving, closely spaced ear-tufts. See Striped and Short-eared owls.

Voice: Infreq. a single, emphatic *woof* or *wupf* at 4- to 5-sec intervals, often deceptively soft; also a short scream, *rre-ehhr* or *mehrr* (by ♀). In display ♂ claps wing tips together below body as flies[268]; well-spaced hoots may be doubled[179].

Behavior: Nocturnal. Little known in Venez., but in Mexico roosts and calls from mid. to upper levels of trees[268].

Status and habitat: Very rare. Known from 4 widely separated regions with contrasting habitats incl. partially forested mts., edge of dry deciduous forest in llanos, and mixed savanna and forest in w Amazonia. Broad span of locs. and els. (in Venez.) is enigmatic.

Range: 200–2000m n of Orinoco; to 250m s of Orinoco. Sierra de Perijá (Pie Nudo); e slope of Andes in Trujillo (Niquitao; Los Palmares), Cojedes (sight, Hato Piñero, 20–21 Jan 1989—D. Wolf, K. Zimmer), and w and c Amazonas at San Fernando de Atabapo and Río Ocamo (*robustus*). S Texas (once); nw Mexico to Nicaragua; Colombia to Guyana and locally s to Argentina. Greater Antilles.

Short-eared Owl   PLATE 24
Asio flammeus   Lechuza Orejicorta
Identification: 13–14″ (33–36cm). 350g. Partially diurnal owl with inconspic. ear-tufts. Dark "eye sockets" accentuate yellow eyes and buffy face. Upperparts brown striped and mottled tawny, below buff to tawny *coarsely streaked blackish on chest*, faintly on breast. In flight from above or below shows *conspic. black wrist patch* and *large pale buff patch at base of flight feathers*.
Sim. species: Striped Owl is boldly striped on *entire* underparts; Stygian Owl is much darker.
Voice: Seldom hd. except when breeding. Gives a ser. of 6–10 short, barking hoots[91], a catlike mewing, and high-pitched *cri cri cri cri* in nest defense[69]. Near Caracas a harsh, scratchy buzz, *jjjjjjeeeaa* (P. Schwartz recording).
Behavior: An open-country owl that is partially diurnal. Hunts by flying rather low with characteristic springy, mothlike flight on slightly crooked wings, then pounces on prey. Quarters back and forth like a harrier. May be abroad during day but seen mainly at dusk or after dark, singly, in 2s or occas. in loosely assoc. groups of 4–6. Reported feeding on frogs in Jun and Jul[186]. Perches on gd., fence posts, or other low sites. Breeding unrec. in Venez.
Status and habitat: Uncommon and very local resident (?) mainly over savanna and damp or marshy areas; all Venez. recs. Jun–Sep. Groups of 4–6 over savanna in Jun, Jul, and Sep near Cantaura, Anzoátegui[186]; Jun 1994–1995 at Hato Cedral, w Apure (D. Ascanio).

Range: To 200m. S Carabobo; Apure (sight, Hato Cedral; Pto. Páez); and Cantaura, Anzoátegui (*pallidicaudus*). Holoarctic breeder. In New World breeds in N Amer., Hawaii, Galápagos Isls.,W Indies, and locally in S Amer. s to Tierra del Fuego. N birds winter s to Mexico.
Note: Subsp. *pallidicaudus*[403] synonymized with *bogotensis* by some [148].

Buff-fronted Owl   PLATE 24
Aegolius harrisii   Curucucú Barriga Amarilla
Identification: 9″ (23cm). 130g. Rare owl of high els. Eyes greenish yellow to amber. Forehead and facial disk yellowish buff, separated by blackish eyebrows that angle upward toward ear-tufts; facial disk rimmed black; rearcrown black, otherwise above dark chocolate brown, *wings spotted white*, broad nuchal collar and *unmarked underparts tawny buff*, tail dark brown with 2 spotted white bands and spotted tip.
Sim. species: A small, compact owl, mostly blackish above and buff below, with short tail and large head. Nothing really like it at high el. See White-throated Screech-Owl.
Voice: Variety of vocalizations reported. On Cerro de la Neblina a relatively high-pitched, evenly spaced ser. of 5–6 notes repeated over and over with short pauses between each series[801]. In Andes (not Venez.) a 3- to 15-sec, extremely fast, somewhat irreg. trill (ca. 9 notes/sec), slightly fluctuating in pitch[179]. In se Brazil a quavering, monotonous ser. *ku-ku-ku . . . 4–20* sec in length, building to slight crescendo; also a single hooting *oouuu*[721].
Behavior: Nocturnal but otherwise unknown in Venez. In Brazil and n Argentina nests in cavities in stubs, palm trunks, etc. Stomach contents and pellets incl. rodent hair and insect parts.
Status and habitat: Resident but apparently very local. Tall humid forest on Cerro de la Neblina where as many as 5 could be hd. simultaneously between ca. 1800 and 2000m el.[801]; 1 in mist-net at night on open rocky area of Auyán-tepui[26]; prob. on most large tepuis. Other recs. are from semiopen highland areas, both humid and relatively dry. In Ecuador taken in second growth adj. to undisturbed mt. forest.

Range: 1000–3800m n of Orinoco; 1800–2000m s of Orinoco. Andes in Mérida (3 specimens from Páramo de la Culata; 1 from unknown loc.), Coastal Cordillera in Distr. Federal (El Junquito); s of Orinoco in Bolívar (Auyán-tepui) and Cerro de la Neblina in Amazonas (*harrisii*). Colombia s spottily in mts. to Peru; nw and ne Brazil spottily to Uruguay, n Argentina, and nw Paraguay.

Steatornithidae: Oilbird
Guácharo

The Oilbird is distantly related to nightjars and to a lesser extent to potoos, but it has been separated from both lineages for a long time[86]. It is characterized by a strong, hooked bill, long rictal bristles, weak feet placed far forward on the body, and a long, stiff tail. It is the only nocturnal fruit-eating bird in the world. Oilbirds roost by day in caves and feed at night on fruit plucked in flight and swallowed whole; the seeds are later regurgitated either in flight through the forest or when the birds return to their caves. Oilbirds are important disseminators of seeds of certain species of forest trees, but large piles of seeds also accumulate and rot beneath their roosts and nests in caves. Oilbirds are capable of navigation by a rather crude echo location (lower pitched than that used by bats), but once outside caves, fruit is apparently located by smell, or in nonaromatic fruits such as palms, by sight[677,687]. One of the largest colonies in the world, near Caripe in eastern Venezuela, is protected within Venezuela's national park system, but extensive deforestation outside this small park, and traditional nonbreeding-season foraging areas that are often far from the breeding caves, threatens the integrity of this and other large colonies, as well as some smaller colonies.

Oilbird
Illus. below, PLATE 25
Steatornis caripensis Guácharo
Identification: 18″ (46cm). 400g. Looks like an enormous nightjar. Strong hooked bill; large dark eyes (reflect red); prom. rictal bristles. *Above rufous brown, below paler more cinnamon*, crown with a few white dots; *wing coverts, primaries, and outer tail feathers with a few back-encircled* white spots (bar-shaped on tail). Long graduated tail crossed by several obscure narrow black bars; in flight note *long and rather narrow wings*.
Sim. species: Like an overgrown nightjar, but habits, vocalizations, and white-dotted plumage unique.
Voice: Noisy, esp. as birds exit caves at dusk or when disturbed inside caves. A variety of screams, snarls, and snoring sounds. Inside caves, and when foraging, give a slow stream of clicks (audible to humans) which are used for navigation by echo location. In flight when foraging outside caves, a rough, raspy, *krr-krr*, prob. for contact[672].

Behavior: Nocturnal and frugivorous. Oilbirds are gregarious, gathering in large nos. in caves or occas. in dark recesses in ravines or on cliffs, where they rest by day and fly out at night, often many kms, to feed on fruits taken during a short, surprisingly aerobatic hover. Eat mostly large-seeded fruits of Lauraceae, Palmaceae, and Burseraceae. If fruit abundance is seasonal, a postbreeding migration occurs (annual or because of deforestation?). Nest in darkness in cave, occas. on shady cliff outside cave. Nest a rim or mound of regurgitated seeds on cave ledge; nests often very close together; 2–4 eggs, white but staining brown, laid at 2- to 6-day intervals. Young grow slowly but when fledge in 3–4 months weigh 50% more than ads.[672,677,687]; breed mostly late Mar–end of Jul at Caripe, n Monagas, then feeding most heavily on Lauraceae[558].
Status and habitat: Resident and sometimes short-distance migrant. Colonies vary from a few prs. to 1000s depending on size of cave, suitable ledges and space for nests, and food. Largest colony (estimated 10,000–18,000 birds) is at PN Cueva del Guácharo, Caripe, Monagas[77,78]. Of 54 colonies reported by Bosque[73] in Venez., 7 (6 in nc region) have vanished in recent yrs mostly because of deforestation and loss of food. Birds also captured at 19 other localities. Only marine (seacoast) cave colony is in e Sucre. Most important area for Oilbirds is n Monagas where 21 caves are known. One colony recently found near top of Cerro Roraima, 2600m, Feb 2000 (D. Ascanio) is highest in Venez. Postbreeders wander widely, even into urban areas.

Range: To 2000m n of Orinoco; to 2600m s of Orinoco. Sierra de Perijá, Zulia (many caves)[96], Andes of n Táchira (specimen), Mérida, and s Lara; sw Portuguesa (specimen), c Falcón, s Yaracuy, Coastal Cordillera of Aragua (specimens), Distr. Federal (no extant colonies) and Miranda; Interior Cordillera in n Cojedes (former colony at Cueva de las Murracas); ne Anzoátegui (2 colonies near Guanta), Sucre, n Monagas (many caves[70,73]); Amazonas (no known colonies but rec. at Río Cataniapo and Cerros Duida and de la Neblina); Bolívar (throughout from Auyán-tepui and base of Sierre de Lema southward). E Panama; Colombia s mostly in Andes to Bolivia; Guyana; Trinidad. Prob. n Brazil.

Oilbird in cave

CAPRIMULGIFORMES

Nyctibiidae: Potoos

Nictibios

Potoos are a small, uniquely Neotropical family of soli-tary and nocturnal birds. Most are so poorly known that they seem more fiction than substance, their gruff or wailing cries ghostly chimeras of the dim nocturnal world they inhabit. Potoos have enormous eyes and mouths and in general resemble nightjars, as they have very cryptic plumage, but they differ from them in, among other things, their vertical perching posture, larger size, and absence of rictal bristles. Their diet is made up mostly or entirely of insects, mainly large night-flying ones captured by sallying to air. Moths are believed to compose a large portion of the diet. Nest sites, as far as known, are depressions or knotholes on branches or stubs where 1 egg is laid; no nest is built. Recent evidence suggests that this ancient family may comprise more species than are presently recognized, and possibly more genera as well, as genetic distances between species are very large[86].

Nyctibius

Rest immobile and camouflaged on stub or branch in-side forest, in isolated tree, or occas. on post in open terrain during day and very difficult to spot. Large head; enormously wide bill with hook at tip; large eyes; narrow slit in upper eyelid, a unique anatomical feature, enables them to see even when eyelids are closed; feathers of foreparts bristle- or hairlike; in hand show powder-down patch on side of rump; ♀♀ slightly heavier than ♂♂.

Great Potoo   PLATE 25
Nyctibius grandis   Nictibio Grande
Identification: 20″ (51cm). 450–640g. *Large and ghostly pale.* Enormous, dark, liquid brown eyes re-flect orange at night. Plumage color variable but *al-most always much paler than Common Potoo.* Whitish to grayish white to (infreq.) mixed brown, buff, and gray, and everywhere *finely marbled and reticulated with black*; shoulders usually darker than rest of plum-age, often with irreg. black patch at bend of wing, sometimes also at base of primaries; a few inconspic. blackish spots on center of chest; long broad tail (9.5″, 24cm) grayish white with *9–10 narrow gray bars* (6–7 show in field), *each crisply bordered black*, pattern di-agnostic but hard to see at a distance in field. May show a scapular band of black mixed rusty and gray-ish white (imm.?).
Sim. species: Much larger than other potoos, but this not always obvious in field. Typically *much whiter* than any other potoo; even darkest individuals are paler than Common Potoo. Long-tailed Potoo is almost as long (although much more of length is tail) but always quite dark. If in doubt, look for *distinctive* black-edged tail bars.

Voice: Call a fairly loud, gruff *BUAAaa*, descending somewhat (at a distance like retching sound of human), given at well-spaced intervals. If disturbed also a low *wuu* or ser. of guttural barking notes. Most vocal on moonlit nights.
Behavior: As in others of genus, rests immobile by day on high, upward projecting limb or stub in tree crown, occas. lower or along side of trunk, and is usually over-looked. When alarmed slowly tilts head upward to more closely mimic a dead snag. Shortly after dusk flies out to a fairly high (rarely down to eye level) open stub and sits very upright, watches alertly with freq. head movements, then sallies after large flying in-sects, or occas. flies around high in seemingly aimless manner but with deep, powerful wing beats, at which time it may capture flying insects. May use same day roost for months. W Guárico nest, Apr; another with 1-wk-old chick (W. Mader); prob. breeds Mar–Jul or Aug; 1 egg, white with dark markings[789].
Status and habitat: Fairly common but low-density res-ident along gallery forest borders and in scattered trees across llanos; also borders of dry to humid forest, and near clearings and treefalls (where there is space to sally at night) inside forest. True numbers are best revealed by driving rural roads after dark and watch-ing for reflective eyeshine with powerful spotlight.

Range: To 800m. Locally throughout s to c Amazonas and c Bolívar (*grandis*). Se Mexico to n Bolivia and s Brazil.

Long-tailed Potoo   PLATE 25
Nyctibius aethereus   Nictibio Colilargo
Identification: 19″ (48cm). 440g. *Large with long gradu-ated tail, 10″ (25cm), over half length of bird. Mainly dark rufescent brown* densely marbled blackish, *crown darker*, fairly distinct dusky malar; wings with several large black bars across primaries (not conspic.); below dark cinnamon buff, paler than above and thickly marbled and freckled dark brown, usually a few inconspic. small black spots in center of chest; *tail cinnamon brown with up to 6 rather large but obscure or ill-defined dusky bands showing beyond wings*
Sim. species: Most like Common Potoo in plumage, but sp. is much smaller, usually paler, lacks long and strongly graduated tail, and has more bands on tail. *Much darker* and longer-tailed than Great Potoo and lacks its distinctive tail markings. Although all po-toos may occur in forest, this is the one most likely to be seen *inside* tall humid forest.
Voice: Advertising call a slow, smooth, and not very loud *waa-ouuu*, 1st part descending, rest ascending

with rebounding yo-yo effect; given at intervals of 30 sec to several min. When disturbed a low, gruff *ruf, ruf, ruf, ruf, ruf*, as if muttering to itself. A local Spanish name, *Raul*, is onomatopoeic.

Behavior: Much as in Great Potoo. Usually roosts low, but at least 4m up, and inside forest, often on side of slender trunk where there is an angled bend. Forages from an open stub at mid. hts. inside forest, usually around a small opening.

Status and habitat: So far as known an uncommon and local resident of humid lowland forest. The small no. of recs. are widely scattered, but this sp. is prob. much underreported and may eventually be found more or less throughout humid lowland forest s of Orinoco. Known from specimens from Bolívar (lower Río Caura; Río Grande; El Dorado); sight recs. at Junglaven, n Amazonas (numerous observers since 1992)[833].

Range: To 200m. N Amazonas; n and e Bolívar s to Río Cuyuní and upper Río Caroní (*longicaudatus*). The Guianas and Colombia (e and w of Andes) s to e Peru, Bolivia, Amaz. and se Brazil, and Paraguay.

Common Potoo
PLATE 25

Nyctibius griseus Nictibio Grisáceo

Identification: 13–15″ (33–38cm). 185g. Med.-sized potoo. Eyes reflect amber or orange. Overall *grayish to dark brown* finely marbled and etched with buff and black and sometimes cinnamon, crown usually dusky; below sim. but more freckled buff and black and usually somewhat streaked; *variable-sized necklace of black spots on chest* (occas. virtually absent); from above tail evenly but rather obscurely banded dusky and grayish white (shows ca. 7–8 bars). Note that overall plumage color is quite variable but falls more or less into 2 phases, grayish or brownish.

Sim. species: Usually looks rather dirty and dark in field and, in direct comparison, much smaller than Great Potoo (experience helps) and usually darker. Lacks large-headed and *broad-headed* "look" of Great Potoo. Common's grayish tail bands are marbled with dusky and *lack* crisp black-edged pattern of much larger, paler Great Potoo with which it is most likely confused, but note that a pale Common Potoo is almost as pale as a dark Great Potoo. Both show black necklace of spotting on chest (usually more prom. in Common). Also cf. Long-tailed Potoo which also is larger, *normally* darker and more rufescent brown (beware of very dark Common Potoos), and with large, wedge-shaped tail.

Voice: Song, given at night, esp. on moonlit nights, is one of most hauntingly beautiful sounds of Amer. trop-

ics—a marvelously apparitional ser. of up to 8 melancholy and wailing or lamenting phrases, each descending, loud at first, and gradually dropping in pitch in sliding steps as fades in volume, *BU-OU, BU-ou, bu-ou, bu-oo, bu-oo, bu-aw,* . . . In some parts of sp.'s range song is attributed to a sloth by rural people.

Behavior: Much as in Great Potoo (see) but sometimes roosts quite low, even down to eye-level and occas. in open on tops of fence posts, etc. After dark takes prom. exposed perch, usually low, less often high, from which it makes freq. sallies to air for large flying insects. One white egg with lilac spots; on slight bare depression on bend of limb; 33-day incubation; 47-day fledging time; at first, young fed by regurgitation[650].

Status and habitat: Fairly common resident in dry to humid forest borders, lighter woodland, woodlots, gallery forest borders, and scattered trees in open or semi-open areas. Both terra firme and várzea areas. Perhaps most numerous, or at least most often seen, in llanos, where nos. best revealed by listening for calls or looking for eyeshine with a spotlight after dark.

Range: To 1800m n of Orinoco; to 1100m s of Orinoco. Sw Táchira (*panamensis*); rest of Venez. n and s of Orinoco (*griseus*). Costa Rica s to n Argentina, Paraguay, and n Uruguay.

Note: Called Gray Potoo by some. Formerly incl. birds from n C Amer. and Carib. Subsp. *panamensis* weakly defined.

Andean Potoo
PLATE 25

Nyctibius maculosus Nictibio Aliblanco

Identification: 15″ (38cm). Rare highland potoo. Size of Common Potoo but overall *very dark brown to brownish black* barred and mottled buff above, rather heavily mottled black below; crown blackish; *white median and greater wing coverts form conspic. whitish band across upper wing*. In hand, under tail coverts white narrowly streaked and tipped black (contrast sharply with dark tail).

Sim. species: From any other potoo by white wing band. Note montane distrib.

Voice: Advertising call (Ecuador and Peru) a nasal, slightly rising *waaaaAAAa*, recalling Long-tailed Potoo but higher pitched. Also a slow, hollow *wok wok wok* (aggression or when disturbed).

Behavior: In Peru roosts by day on stub or limb of *Cecropia* or other fairly large tree; moves to more exposed low to high stub just after dusk where it sits very upright and sallies for flying insects (presum. mostly moths). Calls from several song perches.

Status and habitat: Known from 1 specimen at Boca de Monte (2400m), ne Táchira, in wet montane forest; 1 sight rec.[297] at 2300m, 13 Jan 1993 near Páramo de Tamá.

Range: 2300–2400m. Ne Táchira; s Táchira (sight). Colombia (1800 and 2000m) s in Andes to Ecuador, Peru, and Bolivia (2800m).

Note 1: White-winged Potoo (*N. leucopterus*) of Amaz. Brazil (Manaus area) to Bahía was taken on e side of Essequibo River in Guyana in 1996 (R. Ridgely) and prob. occurs in e Venez. Overall much like Andean Potoo (prom. white shoulder patches) but decidedly smaller. Song in Brazil a long, downslurred, and rather low-pitched whistle, *sweeeeeeuuuuuu*, almost like falling bomb, easily imitated (A. Whittaker).

Note 2: Rufous Potoo (*N. bracteatus*), also taken at same locality in Guyana (R. Ridgely), may occur in e Venez. Very small (10″, 25cm), mostly rufous with irreg. necklace of black spotting across neck. Lower part of young to old second growth in clearings, river edges, and tall humid forest. Song a bouncy ser. of fairly rapid, *Otus*-like notes, *WUU, Poo, poo-poo'poo 'poo . . .*, ca. 15 notes (2.1 sec), slightly accelerating toward end and diminishing in volume (A. Whittaker recording).

Caprimulgidae: Nighthawks and Nightjars

Aguaitacaminos

Members of this virtually cosmopolitan family are often better known by their voices than by sight. Many are rarely seen by day unless accidentally flushed from cover. The Venezuelan species divide naturally into 2 groups: the nighthawks with long, pointed wings and vespertine habits; and true nightjars, with shorter, rounded wings, longer tails, and more nocturnal habits. All have small bills, remarkably wide, gaping mouths, conspicuous rictal bristles, and a little comb-like structure on the nail of the middle toe. The plumage is soft and lax, as in all nocturnal birds, and always cryptically patterned; some birds are so similar they are difficult to distinguish by plumage pattern. The feet are extremely weak, and the birds usually settle directly on the ground or lengthwise on a branch, or at most shuffle only a short distance on foot. Nighthawks forage actively, diving and twisting in rapid aerial pursuit of insects, whereas nightjars sally from stationary perches, mostly on or near the ground and close to cover, or wander around in short, low flights.

Lurocalis

Differ from *Chordeiles* nighthawks in longer, more scimitar-shaped wings not obviously held bent at wrist in flight, *very short tail*, and pale patch on scapulars and inner secondaries.

Short-tailed Nighthawk   PLATE 26
Lurocalis semitorquatus   Aguaitacamino de Cola Corta
Identification: 8.2″ (21cm). 75g. *Short, square tail and long, pointed, all-dark wings* (at rest wings extend well beyond tail). In flight somewhat batlike. Above dusky thickly speckled rufous buff, scapulars and tertials marbled light gray and dusky *forming conspic. pale patch*; some birds also show variable amt. of gray in plumage (esp. on shoulders); band across throat white (inconspic. in field), breast more or less mottled and barred dusky and grayish white, *lower underparts dark rufous.* Tail narrowly tipped white; from above tail crossed by 7–8 very narrow rusty bands (best seen in hand). Or sim. but entire lower underparts densely barred black and rufous (*schaeferi*).
Sim. species: Very like Rufous-bellied Nighthawk but *smaller* and rufous of lower underparts less conspic. Rufous-bellied Nighthawk has extensive rufous markings on underparts; *schaeferi* also differs in rufous lower underparts extensively barred black. Cf. vocalizations.
Voice: Call in ne Peru a ser. of 2–5 rather high, reedy notes, *whueet-whueet-whueet-whueet* (or froglike *quiik, quiik . . .*), each note inflected upward, as birds forage over clearings at dusk. Advertising (or territorial) call in ne Argentina a short, liquid *tuu-it* over and over.
Behavior: A bit more crepuscular than *Chordeiles*, usually not appearing until almost dark. Single birds or prs. (never groups) fly fast and stiff-winged with erratic changes of direction and occas. short glides with wings held slightly below horizontal; in flight usually weave between (not above) rain forest canopy trees. Reg. circle well up over clearings and along forest edges, but occas. dip low over an opening, stream, or oxbow lake. Rest lengthwise on canopy limbs during daylight hours. One egg; laid in depression on bare limb 6–18m up; whitish speckled brown and gray, heavier around middle and large end[121].
Status and habitat: Apparently resident (*semitorquatus*) and migrant (?) from austral regions (*nattereri*). Generally in low density (overlooked?) but prob. throughout in humid lowland forest, forest borders, and over small forest clearings and lagoons. Subsp. *nat-*

tereri, rec. from lowlands to 1100m (Rancho Grande), is prob. a migrant. Subsp. *schaeferi*, rec. only at Rancho Grande (between 1100 and 1150m), is apparently resident.

Range: To 1150m n of Orinoco; to 1000m s of Orinoco. S Zulia, w Portuguesa, Carabobo, Aragua, Dist. Federal, s Amazonas, and se Bolívar (*semitorquatus*); austral breeders (presum.) in n Aragua (Rancho Grande), Delta Amacuro, and ne Bolívar at Río Grande (*nattereri*); n Aragua at Rancho Grande (*schaeferi*). Sight recs. from Carabobo, Miranda, se Sucre (Guaraunos), e Monagas (Caño Colorado), Amazonas (virtually throughout), and Bolívar in lower Río Caura and upper Río Cuyuní (subsp.?). Se Mexico locally to nw Argentina and Uruguay. Austral birds migratory.
Note: Earlier authors often incl. *L. rufiventris* (Rufous-bellied Nighthawk) with present sp., calling enlarged sp. Semicollared Nighthawk[403]. Subsp. *nattereri*, breeding from Amazonia s to Uruguay, may be a separate sp. Taxonomic status of *schaeferi* uncertain.

Rufous-bellied Nighthawk   PLATE 26
Lurocalis rufiventris   Aguaitacamino Ventrirrufo
Identification: 9–10″ (23–25cm). *Larger* than previous sp. Very short tail; long, pointed, all-dark wings. Above like previous sp. Plumage dusky, thickly speckled rufous, buff, and gray, scapulars and tertials paler forming pale patch; band across throat white; underparts dusky, freckled and barred rufous, *lower breast and belly more or less unmarked rufous*. In hand some birds show a few inconspic. black bars on underparts.
Sim. species: See Short-tailed Nighthawk which differs most obviously in its mainly lowland distrib.
Voice: Call in Ecuador, a few times at dusk or dawn, a rather high *wuck* (or *tork*); also a slow 5- to 6-note *qua, QUEE, QUee, qua, qua*, last 2–3 notes dropping in pitch[412]; also a short *weeop* (sim. to *wuck* note above).
Behavior: Much as in Short-tailed Nighthawk. Most likely seen alone or in prs. flying rapidly and erratically through treetops or fairly high over small openings at dusk. Roosts lengthwise by day on high limb in forest tree.
Status and habitat: Apparently resident in humid and wet montane forest, forest borders, and over small clearings. Rare or uncommon (prob. somewhat overlooked); there are only a few recs. from Venez.

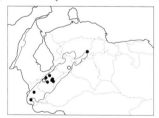

Range: 1400–1800m. Andes from s Táchira (Río Chiquito) and Mérida (San Jacinto) to n Lara at Cabudare. Andes from Colombia to s Bolivia.
Note: Has been considered a subsp. of Short-tailed Nighthawk[10,403].

Chordeiles

Long, pointed wings usually held somewhat bent at wrist in flight; at rest wings reach to about tail tip or beyond (cf. *Caprimulgus*); slightly forked tail; bill very short and wide; few or no rictal bristles; eyes large and dark; feet very small. Feed at dusk and dawn during long aerial sorties lasting 30 min or more; show minor sexual dimorphism.

Least Nighthawk   PLATE 26
Chordeiles pusillus   Aguaitacamino Menudo
Identification: 6.3″ (16cm). *Smallest nighthawk.* Above brown heavily mottled and flecked rufous and gray; *single bold white band across 4 outer primaries of wing* (♂ and ♀); throat white, chest dark brown spotted buff, breast to upper belly narrowly and evenly banded gray and dark brown, under tail coverts white, tail tipped white (except outermost pr. of feathers) but tipping inconspic. In flight note *pale* (buff to white) *trailing edge to inner flight feathers* (conspic. from above). Or above darker; lower underparts, *including vent*, entirely barred (*esmeraldae*).
Sim. species: Much like Lesser Nighthawk but smaller, white wing band even closer to tip, and with *white on rear edge of wing* (watch carefully); up close look for white crissum on n subsp.
Voice: Rather quiet. Low *churr* and weak, nasal *beep* or *week* in flight. Infreq. hd. song, from gd. or while perched in bush, a fast *cur-cur-cur-curry* (or *chu-chu-chu-chu-chuEE*), often given over and over rapidly (P. Schwartz recording).
Behavior: Occurs alone, in scattered prs., or small loosely assoc. groups flying fairly low over grasslands at dawn and dusk. Crepuscular and does not appear until nearly dark. Flight is buoyant, quick, and erratic with many sudden shifts of direction. Sleeps by day under savanna shrubs, occas. on tree branches.
Status and habitat: Fairly common to common resident in scattered savannas across e and s part of country; prob. vagrant n to Carabobo. Easily found in grassland between Upata and Tumeremo in ne Bolívar, grassy hills at s end of Gran Sabana, and savannas of w Amazonia.

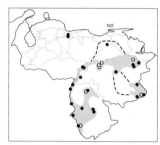

Range: To 1000m. N of Orinoco in s Carabobo (El Paíto near Valencia) and Anzoátegui (Cantaura); prob. s Monagas; throughout grasslands of Bolívar and n Amazonas (*septentrionalis*); c and s Amazonas from Samariapo southward (*esmeraldae*). E Colombia, Guyana, and ne and s Brazil.

Lesser Nighthawk PLATE 26
Chordeiles acutipennis Aguaitacamino Chiquito
Identification: 7.5″ (19cm). 47g. Widespread. Long,
pointed wings with *prom. white band nearer tip than
bend of wing (♀ has buffy white band).* Both size and
wing length notably variable. Above gray thickly mottled and vermiculated with black, white, and buff; narrowly barred tail fairly long and notched. ♂ *has prom.
white subterminal band (esp. conspic. from below) on
all but central tail feathers*; broad band across throat
white (buff—♀); chest mottled brown and buff, *rest of
underparts narrowly and evenly banded brown and
buff.* In hand white wing band approx. 65mm from tip
vs. 95–105 in Common Nighthawk. At rest wings reach
to tail tip (not beyond); white wing bar often partially
exposed behind tertials.
Sim. species: Easily confused with slightly larger Common Nighthawk which has white wing band positioned about equal distance between bend and tip of
wing (not nearer tip), is more extensively barred
below, and has *white* (not buff) and brown barring
below. Both sexes of Common Nighthawk have *white*
wing bands and white subterminal tail bands, but this
most helpful in hand. Also cf. Least Nighthawk. When
flushed off roads at night looks much like several other
nightjars, esp. Little Nightjar, but that sp. is smaller,
lacks ♂ nighthawk's white subterminal tail band, and
is unbarred below.
Voice: Lacks nasal *peent* of Common Nighthawk and
does not "power dive." Infreq. a "winnowing" call in
flight. On gd. a low, nasal, rail-like ser. of *chuck* notes
and a long-sustained, toadlike, dribbling trill.
Behavior: Both this sp. and Common Nighthawk fly
buoyantly with light easy wing strokes alternating with
quicker erratic strokes. Both spp. are crepuscular in
foraging but are occas. abroad by day as well, feeding
over open areas. Lesser flies low, sometimes swerving
perilously close to gd. On migration (no migrants yet
reported in Venez.) normally flies quite high in loosely
assoc. groups. Roosts by day in thickets, small trees, or
close to cover on gd.; after short period of foraging activity at dusk often sits on roads at night, and in spotlight, flushes straight up showing white band at or near
tip of tail. In Costa Rica (Venez.?) reported to sometimes nest and roost in loose colonies[706]. ♂♂ chase
and display to ♀♀ while in flight. Mostly in loose
groups of 10–20 between May and Oct, ne Anzoátegui[186]. Nest on flat-topped boulder in Orinoco region; 2
vinaceous buff eggs marked and dotted grayish[115].
Status and behavior: Uncommon to fairly common resident (some seasonal movements) in a variety of drier,
more open lowland habitats, incl. mangroves,
beaches, saline lagoons, desert scrub, grasslands, and
gallery forests. Thus far only a resident subsp. is reported, but migrants from n (*texensis*), lower C Amer.
(*micromeris*), and austral region (*aequatorialis*) are
possible.
Range: To 1200m n of Orinoco; to 500m s of Orinoco.
Throughout (at least locally) incl. Isla Margarita and
Cayo Sal (*acutipennis*). Sw US to n Bolivia, Paraguay,
and s Brazil. N breeders winter s to nw Colombia.

Common Nighthawk PLATE 26
Chordeiles minor Aguaitacamino Migratorio
Identification: 9″ (23cm). 63g. Very sim. to previous
sp. but larger. Above grayish thickly mottled and vermiculated gray and white; broad throat band white
(buff—♀), rest of underparts narrowly barred dark
brown and white; *prom. white wing band nearer base
of flight feathers than tip*; both sexes have white subterminal tail band. At rest wings project beyond tail;
white wing bar mostly hidden beneath tertials.
Sim. species: See Lesser Nighthawk and much smaller
Least Nighthawk.
Voice: Seldom vocal in Venez. Call a nasal *peent* in
flight. Loud booming sound, produced by vibration of
primaries (?) as dives, is given only on N Amer. breeding gds.
Behavior: Sim. to that of Lesser Nighthawk. Rests on
gd. or more often (?) lengthwise on tree limb during
day. Usually flies quite high, unlike Lesser Nighthawk,
but both fly high in migration. In ne Peru small migrating groups of 8–15 have been seen in early morning
hrs rapidly working southward while foraging low over
rain forest canopy for flying insects. Crepuscular but
also occas. abroad on cloudy days as well.
Status and habitat: Uncommon or rare resident (perhaps underreported). May migrate through Andean
passes in nos. in relatively short period of time during
n spring and fall migratory periods. Only recs. are
10–12 seen over Hotel Los Frailes, Mérida (3000m) at
dawn 25 Apr 1995; another Apr group over city of Mérida (R. Ridgely); and 2 specimens taken 22 Apr at Lagunillas, Mérida.

Range: 1000–3000m (prob. 0–3600m). Andes of
Mérida (*minor*). Breeds from Canada to c Panama;
winters in s S Amer. s to Argentina. Trinidad and
Curaçao.
Note: Other subspp. possible[559].

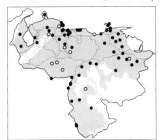

Sand-colored Nighthawk
Chordeiles rupestris   Aguaitacamino Blanco

PLATE 26

Identification: 8″ (20.3cm). *Pale and boldly marked in flight.* Above sandy buff mottled and vermiculated with black, gray, and white, below all white, variable amt. of sandy brown mottling and barring on chest; *outer 4 flight feathers black, rest white tipped black,* wing linings white, central 2 prs. of tail feathers like back, *rest white broadly tipped black,* outermost brown at base.

Sim. species: Contrasting pattern is diagnostic. See much larger and bulkier Nacunda Nighthawk.

Voice: Generally rather quiet but has remarkably wide array of vocalizations for a nighthawk. At intervals throughout night, either perched or during short flights, utters a soft purring trill, a lower, growling *gr'r'ow,* and a sputtering, bubbly *put-put-put-put-put* (chasing?); territorial song a guttural trilling followed by several soft notes, e.g., *gur'r'r'a'a'a'a-pü-pü-püü;* also various other soft notes. Groups foraging at dusk are usually silent. Soft calls hd. mainly around roosts and nests on sandbars.

Behavior: Groups sleep by day on river sandbars, directly on sand, on beached driftwood, or in nearby thickets. At dusk depart in loosely assoc. groups of a few individuals to many dozens that typically fly off together in bounding flight to a distant river bend or oxbow where they forage together, coursing rapidly back and forth at various hts. Occas. even swoop around streetlights in small Amaz. villages. Forage very actively for 15–30 min at dusk, thereafter active only periodically during night, mostly in short fluttery flights around sandbars in vicinity of roost or nest site. Flight is shifting but not as erratic as in Common and Lesser nighthawks; smoother, deeper, oddly mechanical flapping may bring to mind a tern or shorebird. Nests on sandbars during low water period (prob. Dec–Apr), often with terns and skimmers; 2 buff eggs tinged bluish olive and with dark scrawls and spots.

Status and habitat: Sandbars along rivers and over nearby oxbow lagoons, airports and villages in mid. and upper Río Orinoco, and upper Río Negro drainage. Local and much less numerous in Venez. than in w Amazonia. Breeding status needs confirmation; migratory movements (local?) occur during periods of high water.

Range: To 200m. Nc Amazonas southward (*rupestris*). Se Colombia to ne Bolivia and w Amaz. Brazil.

Nyctiprogne

Small and dark with no wing markings; small bill; no rictal bristles; wings reach to tail tips as in *Chordeiles;* gregarious.

Band-tailed Nighthawk
Nyctiprogne leucopyga   Aguaitacamino Coliblanco

PLATE 26

Identification: 6.5–7″ (16.5–18cm). 24g. Slender, pointed, *all-dark wings. Small dark nighthawk with narrow white band across underside of tail* (inconspic. but shows when illuminated from below). Above dark gray brown speckled and vermiculated gray and buff, a few black spots on scapulars; narrow, inconspic. white band across throat; chest vermiculated brown and buff, rest of underparts barred gray and brown. Birds from llanos (*pallida*) are palest (gray brown) in color, those southward in Amazonas darker; *latifasciata* from Casiquiare region almost black above.

Sim. species: Only other nighthawks with all-dark wings are Short-tailed and Rufous-bellied, both much larger and with proportionately longer, broader wings, very short tails, and much faster, more stiff-winged flight. If in doubt, illuminate underside of tail as bird flies overhead at dusk and look for diagnostic band beneath tail.

Voice: Territorial song at dusk from gd. or low perch a low, nasal, froglike *qurk-ta-ta-ta-ta-ta-ta-ta-ta* . . (2–10 *ta* notes), up to 1 phrase/sec, but delivery often irreg.; also a simpler repeated *churk* . . *churk* . . *qurk* . . (ca. 10 notes in 16 sec) or *werk-CHURK.* In flight occas. dives aggressively (only ♂♂?) at others, uttering a soft *jerk* or *neerk* at conclusion of shallow dive.

Behavior: More strictly crepuscular or nocturnal than *Chordeiles* nighthawks, and not likely to be seen until almost nightfall (never abroad during daylight). Forages in groups of 5–100 or more from low to fairly high over rivers, lagoons, and sometimes land, but usually not far from water. Rather quiet when foraging. Most active for 30 min or so just at nightfall. When foraging alternates quick flurries of wing beats with short, teetery glides or sudden swerves in distinctive "gear-changing" flight. By day roosts in little groups in thickets along riverbanks or near other bodies of water.

Status and habitat: Fairly common to locally abundant resident across most of llanos, and along major rivers s of Orinoco. Ponds, streams, and small to large rivers.

Range: To 200m. W Apure (Guasdualito), w Barinas and Portuguesa (Guanare) e to se Monagas (Barrancas); n Bolívar s to La Paragua (*pallida*); throughout

Amazonas (*exigua*). Guyana, French Guiana, and e Colombia s to e Peru (sight), ne Bolivia, and Amaz. Brazil.

Note: Subsp. *latifasciata* may occur in extreme sw Venez.[148].

Podager

Large; long, blunt-tipped wings; broad bill; rictal bristles short and stiff; crepuscular; migratory.

Nacunda Nighthawk
PLATE 26

Podager nacunda   Aguaitacamino Barriga Blanca

Identification: 11–13″ (28–33cm). 165g. Largest nighthawk. *Wings broad, somewhat rounded at tip.* Prom. *white band across black primaries*; *under wing coverts white*. Upperparts buffy brown handsomely reticulated and freckled dark brown and yellowish buff in finely textured pattern; tail with a few narrow dusky bands (inconspic.), all but central feathers with narrow subterminal black band and *large white tip* (lacking—♀); broad band across chest mottled buff and brown, *throat, lower breast, and belly white*. Plumage overall varies slightly from rufescent to grayish.

Sim. species: Large and boldly patterned, but these often not obvious after dark. No other Neotropical caprimulgid is so large. Note mostly white underparts. Cf. smaller Sand-colored Nighthawk which is more extensively white below and lacks white wing band.

Voice: Rarely vocalizes when foraging. Flushes with low *chuck*. Sings from gd., a low stuttering trill *dur'du'du'du . . .* , slow and irreg. in tempo.

Behavior: Crepuscular. High-flying, widely scattered individuals or small loosely assoc. groups appear over open areas or along rivers just before dusk. Infreq. in large groups (prob. migrants). Flight is leisurely, buoyant, reminiscent of a gigantic moth (or Short-eared Owl), as bird holds wings bent down and flies without freq. swerving of smaller nighthawks. By day rests on sandbars or in grassy fields, fully exposed to sun, often in loose groups. Feeds on flying insects at dusk or just after dark. By 1–2 hr after nightfall, again usually at rest along roadsides or in open fields. In Trinidad, 3 nests on gd., Apr; 1–2 eggs, cream blotched and lined rich brown at larger end[175].

Status and habitat: Resident and austral migrant (?); shows marked seasonal variation in nos. Scarce and local in llanos in dry season (Jan–Apr) but common to abundant May–Oct, when many are presum. austral migrants (*nacunda*) which may be slightly larger and darker (?) than resident *minor*. Abundance varies as

follows: 80–100 on ca. 10-km road at Hato Cedral, Apure, 26 Jun 1993, peaking at nearly 300 in Jul; 30–35 at end of Dec 1993; 2–3 in Mar (Hilty and D. Ascanio). Concentrations up to 500 in Jun in ne Anzoátegui[186]. Open areas in dry to humid regions but often local, with birds concentrating in favorable areas.

Range: To 200m n of Orinoco; to 900m (Santa Elena de Uairén) s of Orinoco. Locally throughout (*minor*). E Colombia and the Guianas to s Argentina and Uruguay. Trinidad and Tobago.

Nyctidromus

Like *Caprimulgus* but with bare tarsi; longer tailed than New World *Caprimulgus*.

Pauraque
PLATE 27

Nyctidromus albicollis   Aguaitacamino Común

Identification: 11″ (28cm). 54g. *Long* tail (extends far beyond wings); rounded wings and well-marked shoulder pattern. ♂: crown gray, *cheeks chestnut* (a good mark), *back usually grayish* mottled black and buff, *2 rows of large buff-encircled black spots on scapulars*; *prom. white band across blackish primaries conspic. in flight*; throat white, rest of underparts buff more or less barred blackish. Long tail shows much white from below and *long white stripe near outer edge of tail from above* (conspic. as flushes and spreads tail), outermost pr. of tail feathers dusky. ♀: smaller; wing band buff; tail all dark with buff white tip on tail corners. Rufous phase (uncommon): *crown and upperparts strongly rufous* mottled black and buff. Most rufous birds are from w Zulia, s Táchira, s Apure, and s of Orinoco. In flight note broad, rounded wings and long tail.

Sim. species: Learn this common, widespread sp. well. It is larger, darker (except infreq. seen rufous phase), and more boldly marked than allies. Look for chestnut cheeks, row of scapular spots, wing bands, and ♂'s flashy white tail pattern. See White-tailed and Spot-tailed nightjars; at higher els., Band-winged Nightjar.

Voice: Quite vocal, esp. in dry season when breeding. Call a loud, whistled *cuu-wheéeer-o* (last note faint); at dusk warms up with longer *cuu, cuu, cuu, cuu-wheéeer* or sometimes just *cuu* notes. Calls somewhat variable, even those given by same bird. Most vocal at dusk and predawn. Flushes with soft *whit*.

Behavior: At dusk moves to small opening, roadside, or track where sits on gd. or low perch and sallies out for flying insects at night, esp. just after dusk, returning directly to same spot, or sometimes makes low, rambling sorties before returning to same spot or moving on to another. May be active again for short period just before dawn. By day rests immobile on carpet of leaf litter in wooded area where very difficult to see. May bob head (like doing push-ups) when nervous. When surprised, ♂♂ flush up with "startling" flurry of white patches, bound ahead with a few quick wing strokes and zigzagging flight, then abruptly settle out of sight behind log or trunk and "disappear." Mar and May nests, upper Orinoco; 2 vinaceous buff eggs spotted and marked vinaceous brown; nest a leafy depression on gd. in forest[115].

Status and habitat: Commonest and most widespread nightjar in Venez. and the one most often flushed from partly wooded roadsides at night. Common resident in a wide variety of habitats from dry woodland and gallery forest to tall humid forest borders, second-growth woodland, thickets, and shrubby areas. Generally hides in woodland by day and emerges into openings *in or near* woodlands by night. True nos. are best revealed through its call. Some limited seasonal movements may occur, esp. in low-lying regions of llanos.

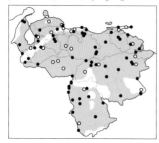

Range: To 1400m n of Orinoco; to 1000m s of Orinoco. Throughout (*albicollis*). S Texas and Mexico to n Argentina and s Brazil.

Caprimulgus

Longish tails; rounded wings that usually do not reach to tip of tail when bird is at rest; prom. rictal bristles; rather solitary; Venez. spp. mostly resident; in hand note feathered tarsi and pectinate mid. toe.

Chuck-will's-widow   PLATE 27
Caprimulgus carolinensis   Aguaitacamino Americano
Identification: 11.5″ (29cm). 115g. Very large. *Virtually identical to Rufous Nightjar except for grayish* (not rufous) tinge to *crown*, and minor differences in tail pattern. In hand both sexes have lateral filaments on rictal bristles (lateral filaments lacking in Rufous Nightjar). Both spp. show irreg. ser. of blotchy black spots running down back and on scapulars, 1 distinctive *beadlike row of small buff white spots at tip of lesser upper wing coverts* (form narrow, pale band), and rufous and black barring at base of primaries (no bold band). The 2 spp. are probably not safely separated in field except by voice (and Chuck not known to sing in Venez.). In hand ♂ Chuck has almost entire distal half of inner web of outer 3 tail feathers white (from below, tail looks mostly white; from above, shows as narrow white stripes *in spread* tail) and narrower black tail bars. ♀ (no white in tail) has buff-tipped tail. Cf. Rufous Nightjar which has less extensive buff white (not pure white) on inner webs of outer tail feathers.
Sim. species: Several ♀♀ nightjars also lack prom. wing bands but are smaller, much less rufous (cf. ♀♀ of Lyre-tailed, Little and Blackish, and Ladder-tailed nightjars).
Voice: Essentially silent on wintering gds. On breeding gds. (not Venez.) says its name, a loud, rhythmic, and rolling *chuk, WILL-WID-o*, often incessantly on moonlit nights.

Behavior: By day sits on leaves on gd. in woodland and is almost never seen unless flushed. By night sallies out, often in long rambling sorties, after prey. One taken at edge of a road in Aragua had a bat (*Rynchonycteris naso*) in its stomach[336].
Status and habitat: Rare n winter resident known from 2 recs.: 1 ♀ 9 Sep 1939, Lourdes, Mérida[15], and 1 ♀ 30 Dec 1971, Los Castillos, Turagua, Aragua, 500m[336]; both specimens are from moist forest borders in foothill or mt. terrain.

Range: 500–1700m (doubtless lower). Mérida and Aragua. Breeds in se US; winters in Florida, Greater Antilles, and C Amer. to w Colombia (1000–2600m).

Rufous Nightjar   PLATE 27
Caprimulgus rufus   Aguaitacamino Rufo
Identification: 11.5″ (29cm). 95g. *Very much like* Chuck-will's-widow. *A large, robust, mostly rufous-looking nightjar* (incl. crown). Top of head and back with numerous irreg. black blotchy streaks and spots; line of small black spots across scapulars; beadlike row of small buff spots at tip of greater wing coverts; tail from above with numerous rather obscure black bars; from below *3 outer tail feathers have large oval buffy white patches on terminal third of inner web* (difficult to see in field); narrow inconsp. buff-white collar across lower throat; chest blackish mottled and vermiculated rufous, lower underparts buffy white scaled black;
Sim. species: See Chuck-will's-widow.
Voice: Song, persistently repeated for short period during early breeding season, an energetic, rhythmic *chuck, wick-wick-WEEoo*, 1st note weak, *wick* notes higher pitched and hurried. Reminiscent of song of Chuck-will's-widow but faster and higher pitched; like Chuck, usually sings from a perch 4–20m up. So far reported singing late Dec–early May n of Orinoco; mid Oct–early May s of Orinoco (many observers).
Behavior: Nocturnal and rarely seen except when calling. Does not sit on roads at night. Sallies out, usually well above gd., in rather extended rambling sorties for flying prey. Forages mostly from perches that are 1 to several meters above gd. In Colombia 2 creamy white eggs with vague blotches of light brown and dull lilac on bare gd. under thicket or in partial open[750]; 4 nests Feb–May, Trinidad[175].
Status and habitat: Resident in fairly dry to humid forest, semiopen to open woodland, second growth, and forest borders. Fairly common (by voice) locally. Seasonal movements possible but unproved; brief and/or irreg. calling periods complicate status verification. S Brazil and Argentina pops. (*rutilus*) are migratory and could reach Venez. during austral winter[551].

Range: To 900m n of Orinoco; to ca. 300m s of Orinoco. Sierra de Perijá and s Maracaibo Basin, Zulia; Andes in w Mérida, Apure (Río Burguita), and n Lara; hd. in se Falcón (Cerro Misión[60]); n cordilleras from Carabobo[60] to Aragua, Distr. Federal, and Miranda (incl. tape, PN Guatopo, Mar 1981—C. Parrish); mts. of Sucre (*minimus*); n Amazonas (s to Río Ventuari) and n Bolívar (lower Río Caura; Río Caroní) e to La Urbana; El Palmar (*rufus*); Delta Amacuro[343]. Costa Rica to n Argentina, s Brazil, and the Guianas.
Note: Taxonomy follows Robbins and Parker[551].

Blackish Nightjar   PLATE 27
Caprimulgus nigrescens   Aguaitacamino Negruzco
Identification: 8.2″ (21cm). 37g. *Small*, short-winged, *rather short-tailed*, chunky, and *very blackish. Wings reach to or almost to tail tips.* ♂: above *blackish* faintly freckled rufous and gray, *below dusky black more or less uniformly and finely barred gray and buff;* faint buff-dotted eyebrow broadest behind eyes; shoulders finely mottled gray; wing coverts with 3 rows of buff dots on tips; *tertials freckled grayish* (show as vague *grayish patch*); inconspic. narrow white throat collar (may show only as small patch on each side of throat). In flight from above shows a small white bar on primaries (spot on inner web of 2d, 3d, and 4th primaries from tip); small but conspic. white tip on outer tail feathers (outermost pr. all dark). ♀: differs in *no white in wings or tail.* Note: In both sexes there is much variation in amt. and intensity of barring below.
Sim. species: Both sexes look very dark in the field and show little or no obvious white. Roraiman Nightjar is very sim. but slightly larger, even blacker, and *occurs at higher el. with no known el. range overlap.* ♂ Roraiman Nightjar also differs in having *prom. white wing bands* and more coarsely and irreg. barred underparts that *change to mostly buff on belly and undertail coverts.* ♀ Blackish doubtfully separable from ♀ Roraiman in field, but note underparts carefully. Chest of Roraiman is mostly black with only a few irreg. gray buff bars, but becomes more coarsely barred and *mostly buff on belly* (not all narrowly and evenly barred). Other points to note are ♀ Roraiman's white tail tipping (lacking in ♀ Blackish, small and obscure in ♂ Blackish) and rufous shoulder spotting. In tepuis, also cf. Band-winged Nightjar which occurs at higher el. and prob. does not overlap. ♂ differs in bold white bands in wings and white tail corners; ♀ Band-winged quite sim. to ♀ Blackish but is larger and sparsely spotted on chest (♀ Blackish is evenly banded). Note that ♀♀ of both spp. lack white tail tipping (*unlike* ♀ Roraiman).

Voice: Notably quiet. Call when foraging or disturbed a soft, liquid *pret!* or *peet!* (like bubble bursting). Also a low *churk, wert,* throaty but weak and given infreq. Song(?), usually only 1 or a few times just after dusk, a ser. of 3–4 soft, purring (froglike) trills, *puurrt . . puurrt . . puurrt,* at rate of 1/sec or slower. At a distance recalls rising call of Pauraque but softer. No loud rhythmic song.
Behavior: Rather confiding and very quiet. Forages alone. Just after dark and for short period before dawn forages actively by sitting on gd. in small forest openings, at edge of rock outcrop, a road, or on log (up to ca. 3m up) projecting out over forest clearings or streams, and sallying out mostly 3–15m for flying insects, or making little sorties back and forth in vicinity of perch, then returning to same place. By day rests alone or occas. 2–3 together, often partially or fully exposed on gd. or log near forest edge, or on large black rock outcrops and boulders. Roost sites reused. One egg on gd. in open, sparsely vegetated area; light pinkish buff blotched dark brown and lilac[185,253]; egg and fledged juv. Nov–early Dec, Suriname.
Status and habitat: Resident. Prob. locally fairly common but often difficult to find. Rocky outcrops, large rocks in rivers, humid forest borders, and small clearings and burns in forested areas. Most numerous in and around rock outcrops, and prob. absent from tracts of unbroken lowland forest.

Range: To 1100m. Amazonas and Bolívar (no recs. in ne Bolívar). E Colombia and the Guianas locally to n Bolivia and Amaz. Brazil.

Band-winged Nightjar   PLATE 27
Caprimulgus longirostris   Aguaitacamino Serrano
Identification: 8.5″ (22cm), 40g. Or in tepuis 9.5″ (24cm), 54g (1♀). Dark *highland* nightjar. *Tail moderately long.* Upperparts black mottled and obscurely barred buff and gray; very indistinct grayish eyebrow; *nuchal collar rufous,* narrow collar on throat white, underparts dusky speckled buffy white on chest, more barred on lower underparts; primaries dusky with *prom. white wing band* formed by white spot on 4 outermost primaries; tail from below blackish with 1 narrow median white band and *broad white terminal band* on all but central tail feathers; tail from above barred dusky and gray with *prom. white tail corners* (conspic. as flushes). ♀: sim. but eyebrow lacking, wing band and throat collar buff, tail dusky narrowly barred buff (no white). Or in tepuis: *larger,* and both sexes blacker above and below; crown only lightly speckled with buff; underparts *sparsely spotted with*

large buff and white spots and obscurely barred buff on lower breast and belly (*roraimae*).
Sim. species: In Andes the only nightjar with conspic. white (or buff) wing band that is likely at high els. In foothills and lower elevations, esp. in n cordilleras, may overlap with Pauraque (larger, longer-tailed, chestnut cheeks, prom. shoulder spots), Little Nightjar (very small), and White-tailed Nightjar (pale above, ♂ extensively white below). In Andes cf. ♀ to ♀ Lyre-tailed Nightjar. In tepui region *roraimae* easily confused with Roraiman and Blackish nightjars (see).
Voice: Song (n of Orinoco) recalls that of White-tailed Nightjar, a high thin *seeeeerp* or *seeEEEeert* (emphasis varies), squeezed out, rising then downslurred in pitch, ca. 1/2 sec (sometimes predawn calling rate faster); also has same wing whir and wing-clap displays. Also a high, thin *chee-wit-chee-wit-chee-wit* in flight. In display ♂ flies over ♀, spreads tail, and produces a whirring sound with wings. Typically sings only for a short period just after dusk and for 30 min or so at predawn.
Behavior: Nocturnal. Perches on gd. or on exposed rocks, boulders, cliffs, rocky roadcuts, rock walls, or to 15m up in trees from which ♂ sings and sallies for flying insects. Also makes long, rambling, aerial sorties, apparently after flying insect prey. Reg. sits on roads at night. By day rests alone or in prs. under a bush or thicket, or in partly concealed spot on roadcut or roadbank. Eggs 1–2 white to pinkish with small spots; on gd. or bare rock[121,589].
Status and habitat: Fairly common and widespread resident in grassy clearings, open slopes, roadcuts, humid forest borders (esp. along roads), and at lower els. in paramo.

Range: 900–3200m n of Orinoco; 1300–2300m s of Orinoco. Sierra de Perijá, Zulia; Andes from Táchira, Mérida, and nw Barinas to Lara; n cordilleras from w Yaracuy and Carabobo to Distr. Federal and se Miranda (Cerro Negro); mts. of Sucre and n Monagas at Cerro Negro (*ruficervix*); tepuis of n and s Amazonas (Guanay to Cerro de la Neblina) and tepuis of Gran Sabana (Roraima; Uei; Ptari; Sororopán; Uaipán; Auyán-tepui) in se Bolívar (*roraimae*). Andes of Colombia to Chile. Guyana; se Brazil, Uruguay, and s Argentina.
Note: Birds from Sucre and Monagas may represent an undescribed subsp. (K. C. Parkes). Subsp. *roraimae*, from tepuis, may be a separate sp. (voice unknown).

Roraiman Nightjar   PLATE 27
Caprimulgus whitelyi   Aguaitacamino de los Tepuis
Identification: 8.8″ (22.4cm). Med.-sized, *dark* nightjar. *Tail somewhat short*; wings reach nearly to tail tip. ♂: above *very black*; wing coverts with several fairly large white terminal spots; *distinct white band across 2–3 outer primaries* (occas. also a vestigial white spot on outermost primary); narrow white throat collar; chest black with a few gray markings, progressively more heavily barred gray and buff rearward, *crissum mostly buff* with only a few coarse black bars; tail black (in hand a few obscure buff bars on outer pr. of feathers), *2d and 3d pr. (from outermost) with large white spots on tip of inner web* (as in Blackish Nightjar) which should be conspic. from below (but not from above). ♀: sim. but *shoulder spots rufous or nearly lacking, no white wing band* (in hand 1 narrow, obscure rufous band), throat buff, white tail spots smaller than in ♂.
Sim. species: Both sexes of *roraimae* race of Band-winged Nightjar are quite sim. but differ as follows: (1) slightly larger in size and tail longer (ca. 1″, 25mm longer), (2) *narrow rufous nuchal collar* (lacking in both ♂ and ♀ Roraiman), (3) *chest spotted* (Roraiman has chest with *some irreg. barring but no spotting*), (4) blackish tail has *all grayish mottled with buff and as wide or wider (usually) than black*, giving tail a more mottled and less distinctly barred appearance (Roraiman has black tail with *distinct grayish bars that are almost always narrower than black*), (5) usually only 1 row of buff to white spots on wing coverts (vs. *usually 2–3 rows* on Roraiman), (6) in hand ♂ Band-winged has *all 3 outermost tail feathers with large ovoid white spot* forming incomplete white tail band (outermost tail feather *all dark in Roraiman*, next 2 with ovoid white spots on inner web but spot smaller than in Band-winged; ♀ Band-winged lacks white in tail, ♀ Roraiman has only small tail spots), and (7) Band-winged has white spot near base of tail feather that forms small median band *from below* (lacking in Roraiman). At lower els. cf. Blackish Nightjar.
Voice: Call (possibly this sp.?), in Feb, a high, thin *seeeeeEER*, louder and ascending at end (reverse of Band-winged Nightjar from Andes) on Cerro Roraima (D. Ascanio recording).
Status and habitat: Rare or local. Only 8 specimens (Coleccíon Phelps). Recs. clustered in Río Marajano (Cerro Jaua) and Cerro Urutaní region suggest this sp. is most numerous in southernmost tepuis. Behavior unknown.

Range: ENDEMIC. 1280–1800m. Known only from Cerro Duida, Amazonas; and Cerro Jaua, Ptari-tepui,

Cerro Urutaní, and Cerro Roraima in Bolívar. Prob. adj. Brazil and Guyana (no recs.).

White-tailed Nightjar PLATE 27
Caprimulgus cayennensis Aguaitacamino Rastrojero
Identification: 8.5″ (22 cm). 35g. *Fairly small and pale with slender proportions.* ♂ very pale; ♀ plainer and darker, esp. below. ♂: above usually gray, crown mottled with black, rest of upperparts mottled and streaked blackish and buff; prom. *cinnamon nuchal collar*; 2 rows of round white spots on wing coverts; *white band across primaries* (conspic. in flight); *below very pale,* throat white, chest buff mottled and scaled brown, *rest of underparts whitish, tail fairly long, from below all white* with single curved black bar across middle (mainly visible in hand), tail from above gray irreg. barred blackish. As flushes shows narrow white streaks in tail (white inner webs show from above). ♀: above mottled like ♂ but brownish, *prom. cinnamon nuchal collar*; flight feathers with narrow rufous bar (inconspic. in field), below mostly mottled and spotted buff, more barred on lower underparts (no white on throat or belly), tail like upperparts (no white). In both sexes plumage of foreparts varies from gray (commoner) to slightly rufescent.
Sim. species: ♂'s small size, cinnamon nuchal collar, and overall pale coloration, esp. below, are helpful. If in doubt, watch for white wing band (as flushes) and white undertail (sometimes visible in flight as bird forages). ♀ most like ♀ of Little and Spot-tailed nightjars but can be told by combination of cinnamon nuchal collar (also present on ♀ Little) and absence of white on throat. Also told from ♀ Little by larger, size longer tail (in hand, tail 120 vs. 90mm), and less spotting on shoulders. Also see larger ♀ Ladder-tailed Nightjar.
Voice: Song, from gd. or to 2m up in grass or dry weeds, a high, thin, drawn out *spit-cheeeeuua*, 1st note faint, last rising then falling. At peak of breeding may call steadily for several hrs after dusk. ♂ in flight display makes a wing-clapping *knock-knock* sound, striking wings together, followed by an audible wing-whir (P. Schwartz recording). *Tic-tic* when flushed; *see-see* occas. in flight[175].
Behavior: Like others of genus, nocturnal and solitary. Rests on gd. during day beneath small shrub, thicket, or in grassy or weedy place, and leaves after dark. Unlike many *Caprimulgus* which sally and return to same spot, this sp. often forages by engaging in long, gamboling flights low over open grassland, wandering or weaving (almost as though floating) around for several min, apparently capturing flying insects. Also sallies and returns to perch or gd. Nest (May) on gd., Orinoco region, 2 pale vinaceous buff eggs marked lilac and rufous brown, esp. at larger end[115]; breeding, Trinidad and Tobago, Feb–Jun[175].
Status and habitat: Fairly common to locally common resident in grassland, scrubby ranch country, grassy or eroded and degraded foothills with scattered bushes and thickets, and tall weedy areas around lagoons. Tends to concentrate in favorable areas, esp. in large, grassy fields away from woodland and in tall weeds around lagoons. This sp. and Least, Lesser, and Nacunda nighthawks are only caprimulgids in Venez.

likely to be encountered in large open areas well away from woodlands.

Range: To 1200m n of Orinoco (sight to 1600m[60]); to 1600m s of Orinoco. Paraguaná Pen. and adj. coast of Falcón (*insularis*); locally in Zulia and rest of Venez. s to n Amazonas and se Bolívar (*cayennensis*). Costa Rica to the Guianas and n Brazil. Aruba to Trinidad and Tobago; Lesser Antilles.

Spot-tailed Nightjar PLATE 27
Caprimulgus maculicaudus Aguaitacamino Cola Pintada
Identification: 8″ (20.3cm). 31g. Handsome nightjar. Small and much *buffier above and below than allies; no white band on wings. Crown blackish,* ocular area and cheeks dusky (blackish "eye sockets"); conspic. *pale rufous buff to whitish eyebrow broader behind eye where finely barred gray, narrow rufous nuchal collar.* Rest of upperparts mottled gray and rufescent buff, wing coverts with *ca. 4 rows of prom. buffy white spots,* upper throat dingy buff white, rest of underparts tawny; squarish dusky area on sides of neck; dusky chest *coarsely scaled and spotted buff and white,* lower underparts dark buff, vaguely scaled. Central tail feathers like back but with numerous small black bars, rest of tail *black tipped white.* Tail from below dusky with broad white terminal band and 2 rows of white spots. ♀: terminal tail band dingy gray (inconspic.), undertail with more spots.
Sim. species: ♂ told from any other nightjar by combination of broad white tail band (conspic. in flight) *and no white wing band;* up close note contrasty facial pattern and nuchal collar. ♀ much like ♀ White-tailed and Little nightjars, but note black crown, prom. long eyebrow, strong face pattern (dusky cheeks and ocular), and obvious spotting on chest.
Voice: Song a high, thin *pit-suueét,* rising at end, not loud but far carrying; nearest songs of Band-winged and White-tailed nightjars. Often given over and over at rate of 1/1–3 sec but only for short period when breeding (Mar?). In e Bolivia, when breeding (Oct), calls almost nonstop for hrs starting just after dusk.
Behavior: As in others of genus. Solitary or in loosely assoc. prs. in Venez. Hides by day in thickets, grass, or patches of woodland. Sings from gd. or a few meters up in grass, tree, or shrub, but often remains somewhat hidden when singing. Sallies short distances for flying insects, or flies low and slow over grasslands in prolonged weaving sorties. Clutch of 2 (loc.?); eggs buff to pink marked dark at larger end[121].

Status and habitat: Very local but perhaps under-recorded (only sporadically vocal?). Scrubby, degraded areas of mixed grass and brush, burned savanna with scrubby *Curatella* trees, edges of marshes (in *Thalia* spp.). Fairly common in open zones in lower Río Caura (R. Behrstock), s of city of Barinas, and locally in wetter, southerly parts of llanos; 1 in Nov, Hato Masaguaral, Guárico[734]; tape-recorded and seen 5 and 6 Jan 1998, Hato Cedral, w Apure; 1 taped 10 Mar 1998 in wet bushy pastures ca. 20km ne of Tucupita, Delta Amacuro; several hd. 21 and 22 Mar 2000 in pastures ne of El Palmar, ne Bolívar[259].

Range: To 200m (higher?). W Barinas, w Apure (sight), sw Guárico (sight), Miranda (loc.?), Monagas (Caripito), Delta Amacuro (tape); s of Orinoco in Amazonas (San Juan de Manapiare; El Carmen) and n Bolívar (La Paragua; seen, lower Río Caura; hd., El Palmar). Sw Mexico very locally to n Bolivia and the Guianas; se Brazil.

Little Nightjar
PLATE 27

Caprimulgus parvulus   Aguaitacamino Pálido

Identification: 8″ (20.3cm). 38g. *Small and grayish; tail short (wings reach to or almost to tail tips)*. ♂: crown gray streaked black; narrow inconspic. cinnamon nuchal collar; wing coverts and back gray mottled and streaked black and buff, 2 rows of small white spots across wing coverts; *large white band across blackish primaries*; throat white sharply set off from fine barring *and spotting on dark brown breast*; 2 central tail feathers like back, rest with large *conspic. white tip* (from below forms almost solid white band). ♀: like ♂ (incl. hint of cinnamon nuchal collar) but crown duskier, wing covert spots buff (not white), throat buffy white (lacks contrast of ♂), *wing band buff, and no white tail tips*.

Sim. species: ♂ told from others by combination of small size, white throat, wing bands, white tail tips, and *short tail*. But beware resting Lesser Nighthawks which show somewhat sim. pattern as flush from roadsides at night. Lesser has longer, more pointed wings (hard to see in spotlight), *heavily barred underparts*, and subterminal (not terminal) tail band. At rest tail of other nightjars, e.g., White-tailed Nightjar and Pauraque, extends beyond or far beyond wing tips. ♀: confusingly like several others but note small size, *short tail*, and absence of prom. head markings. (Cf. ♀ Spot-tailed Nightjar which has blackish crown and long pale eyebrow; also ♀ White-tailed which has buff wing band and prom. spotted shoulders.)

Voice: Sings for only a *short* period early in breeding season. Memorable song consists of a few short notes followed by a fast, bubbly roll, *pĭk-you gobble-gobble-gobble*, at short intervals. Notes are complex yet delicate, almost dainty as if dancing in silvery spaces of light on moonfilled nights. It is an eerily fascinating serenade, coming as if from an unearthly spirit that has been set loose among us, toying with us, ever tantalizing yet unattainable. Hd. mainly late Apr–early May in n Venez. (C. Parrish).

Behavior: Rests alone by day on leaf litter in woodlands and emerges at dusk to forage in small open areas at woodland edge. Sits on gd., often along a roadside, or a few meters above gd. on branch or broken horizontal stub, where sings and sallies for flying prey. Often returns to same or nearby spot after a sally. Most active in 1st hr after dark. Flushes with flurry of fast wing beats.

Status and habitat: Uncommon to locally fairly common resident (easily overlooked unless calling). Borders of dry to humid forest, gallery forest, and shrubby thickets and wooded areas in grassland; lowlands, esp. slightly hilly regions.

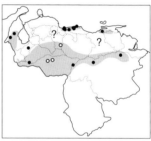

Range: To 1000m. W Zulia; Coastal Cordillera in Aragua, Distr. Federal and Miranda (prob. Carabobo and Interior Cordillera), and locally from w Apure (San Camilo; sight, Hatos Cedral and El Frio) and s Cojedes (sight, Hato Piñero) e to w Sucre (Embalse de Turumiquire) and ne Bolívar at Upata (*heterurus*). N Colombia; ne Peru; Brazil s of the Amazon to Bolivia, c Argentina, and Uruguay.

Note: Birds of e Peru, s Brazil, and Argentina are surely a separate sp. (song very different).

Hydropsalis

Much like *Caprimulgus* but ♂ with decidedly longer, double-notched or "trident-shapd" tail.

Ladder-tailed Nightjar
PLATE 27

Hydropsalis climacocerca   Aguaitacamino Grisáceo

Identification: ♂ 11″ (28cm). ♀ 8″ (20.3cm). 45g (♂). Pale and slender. *Long tail*; long, bluntly rounded wings. ♂: above sandy grayish brown streaked and vermiculated black, throat white merging into grayish brown breast finely barred and spotted buff; *conspic. white wing band across blackish primaries*; tail long and double-notched (central and outer pr. of feathers longer than rest), *from above shows broad slash of white on either side with dark outermost web*, from below mostly white with a few broad angular black bars (the "ladder") across basal half. ♀: same lanky, long-tailed shape as ♂ but with faint cinnamon wing band, *no white in tail*, and buffier underparts; tail notching less pronounced. Or (both sexes) more prom. barred gray and black on tail (from above); lower underparts entirely barred (*schomburgki*).

Sim. species: Boldly patterned ♂ unmistakable. ♀ best told by slender shape and riverbank habitat. Cf. ♀ White-tailed Nightjar.

Voice: Rather quiet. Flushes with soft *chewit*; song a slow ser. of rather sharp *tsick!* notes, not often hd.

Behavior: Nocturnal. Sallies out over water short to med. distances (mostly <20m) from sandbars, driftwood, or low stubs along river edge for flying insects. By day sleeps in driftwood piles, cane, thickets on sandbars, or on adjoining riverbanks. Breeds on river isls. and sandbars during low water; 2 olive eggs speckled dark in scrape in sand.

Status and habitat: Uncommon to fairly common resident on or near sandbars along rivers and river isls., and along edges of old oxbow lagoons, occas. forested streams.

Range: To 350m. Amazonas from Orinoco (San Fernando de Atabapo) and lower Río Ventuari (Las Carmelitas) southward; Bolívar in middle and upper Río Caura from Salta Pará southward (*climacocerca*); Bolívar on Río Paragua and Río Supamo s of El Manteco southward (*schomburgki*). E Colombia to n Bolivia, Amaz. Brazil, and the Guianas.

Uropsalis

Resemble *Caprimulgus* but outermost pr. of tail feathers greatly elongated, outer web reduced, inner very broad; sexes differ, esp. in tail length.

Lyre-tailed Nightjar   PLATE 27
Uropsalis lyra   Aguaitacamino Cola de Lira
Identification: ♂ 33" (84cm), ♀ 10" (25cm). 71g. ♂: *unmistakable with long graceful tail ribbons*. Mostly brownish black with *cinnamon rufous collar*, extensive rufous mottling on wings; *underparts blackish brown narrowly barred black and mottled rufous*. Long tail (28", 71cm) black, inner web edged white and tips white, each feather curving out, then inward lyre-shaped near tip. Tail (without streamers) shows ca. 6 narrow gray white bars from below. ♀: sim. to ♂ but tail normal, *blackish barred rufous on all but central pr.*

of feathers; *crown grayish* mixed or marbled blackish; *cinnamon rufous nuchal collar*, scapular areas and shoulders mottled rufous buff; a few large buff rufous spots on wing coverts; primaries notched rufous. At rest *tail extends well beyond wing tips*.

Sim. species: ♂ with long tail unmistakable. Molting ♂ (no long streamers) is overall quite dark (incl. crown, contra ♀); note dense underparts barring. Both sexes of Band-winged Nightjar show prom. wing bands. Cf. ♀ with slightly smaller ♀ Band-winged Nightjar which has buff wing bands, dark crown (no gray), and lacks ♀ Lyre-tailed's rufous nuchal collar.

Voice: Advertising song a melodious ser. of 5–9 rolling *wéeou-tee* (or *liver-pool*) phrases, each a little higher pitched and stronger or more urgent than preceding. Courtship song (in Colombia) during flight display a rapid *weep weep weep weepupup*; also in flight or perched a *weep weep weep* and rapid, sharp *chip-chip-chip* (W. McKay and P. Gertler).

Behavior: Nocturnal. ♂♂ sally into small forest clearings, over streams, or roads, usually from a perch several meters up, or occas. from gd. at edge of road. A sally may be brief or involve a long aerial sortie before bird returns to same (usually) or different perch. ♂♂ roost by day on slender vines against rock cliffs, cave entrances, beneath bridges, etc., but usually where overhanging vegetation partly conceals them. They are faithful to roost sites for months, even yrs, if unmolested, and sit with long tail straight down, closed or slightly parted and wafting lightly in breeze. In courtship 1 to several ♂♂ circle in small clearings and call and chase 1 or more ♀♀ that join flight (P. Gertler and W. McKay). Nest with 2 eggs in Mar, young in Apr, Altamira, Barinas (D. Ascanio).

Status and habitat: Uncommon and local resident in or near openings in humid and wet premontane and montane forest, almost always where there is a vegetation-covered rocky cliff, ravine, cave, or bridge. Known from 6 specimen locs. in Mérida (all at high els.); recent sight recs. at lower els. incl.: ♂ at 900m near Las Delicias, s Táchira, 21 Jan 1993 and on subsequent occasions (Hilty and J. Rojas); ♂ at 1000m near La Soledad, nw Barinas, 1994 (G. Rodríguez and others); ♂ on San Isidro Rd., nw Barinas[60], 21 Feb 1993; ♀ at 780m on bridge near Altamira, Barinas[259]

Range: 2500–3000m (sight to 780m). Andes of s Táchira (sight, Las Delicias); both slopes in Mérida (*lyra*). Colombia s in Andes to nw Argentina.

APODIFORMES

Apodidae: Swifts

Vencejos

Swifts are a worldwide family of aerial, insect-eating birds with by far the greatest number of species living in tropical latitudes. They superficially resemble swallows but differ in having a more robust body, shorter and stiffer tail, and straighter, faster flight on swept-back wings. Swifts (and hummingbirds) are unique in being able to rotate their wings from the base, a feature that permits the wing to remain fully extended and to derive power on both upstroke and downstroke. Swifts also are notable for their large eyes and very short, weak feet with a reversible fourth toe. Their plumage is compact and predominantly shades of brown and black. Juveniles and immatures look either like adults or are duller and occasionally have pale edging on some feathers. Swifts represent perhaps the ultimate avian adaptation to an aerial existence, feeding, mating, and spending their entire day on the wing. They alight only when roosting or at their nests, at which time they cling to streamside cliffs or enter hollow trees, holes in cliffs, or human-made equivalents such as chimneys. When at rest they cling to a vertical surface aided by sharp claws and all 4 toes pointing forward. Swifts are found over a wide variety of habitats from sea level to high in the mountains and include resident, nomadic, and migratory species; some may undertake daily vertical migrations that also have a seasonal component. Nests of some are semicircular saucers of twigs glued together, whereas those of others are masses of plant floss and feathers glued into a feltlike consistency. Eggs are white. Nestling periods are long, but when young swifts leave the nest they are capable of strong flight. There are, broadly speaking, three groups of swifts in Venezuela: large species in the genera *Streptoprocne* and *Cypseloides*; small to medium-sized species in *Chaetura*; and those with forked tails usually held closed in a needlelike point and/or with prominent white markings as in *Aeronautes*, *Panyptila*, and *Tachornis*. The status and distribution of several Venezuelan swifts are poorly known, and the great similarity of plumages, as well as plumage change with feather wear and soiling, often make field identification unreliable. The generic placement of some taxa is disputed.

Streptoprocne

Large, powerful swifts; robust bodies; squarish to shallowly forked tail; no protruding tail spines.

White-collared Swift   PLATE 28
Streptoprocne zonaris   Vencejo Grande
Identification: 8″ (20.3cm). 90g. Largest swift in Venez. Sooty black with *conspic. white collar encircling neck* (broadest across chest), *tail very slightly forked*. Imm.: sim. but collar vaguely indicated as scaly gray band

across chest and nape, usually lacking on sides of neck.
Sim. species: Size, white collar, and slightly notched tail are the marks.
Voice: Can be noisy when in large milling groups. Flights calls are screeches and thin chittering notes which at a distance sound like parrotlets or small parakeets. Sometimes flocks call in synchrony, producing a pulsating *ss'ree, ss'ree, ss'ree . . .* ; flocks descending at high speed down mt. valleys produce an impressive swooshing rush of air, often accompanied by high chittering.
Behavior: A large, robust, highly social swift that almost always seems to be in varying-sized flocks. Under favorable conditions milling groups of 100s, even 1000s, ride thermals to great hts. on stiff, outspread wings. Flight is deceptively fast and powerful with deep, steady, and fluid wing beats. Stomachs of 2 ♂♂ filled with flying ants of 4 genera[33]. Forage low or high, and often range far from roosting and nesting sites which are on cliffs or rocks behind waterfalls. Typically fly through mist and spray of waterfall to reach roost or nest site. Shallow half-saucer nest of mud, moss, and liverworts on wet rock ledge in dark area; 2 white eggs[381,589].
Status and habitat: Common resident in foothills and mts. and wanders far out into adj. lowlands to forage. Flies over forest, partially open, or completely open terrain. Does not occur (or not reg.) over parts of llanos remote from mts.; rare or infreq. over arid regions of nw. Very large colonies occur on some tepuis, and flocks often fly over summits.

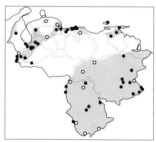

Range: To 3000m n of Orinoco; to 2400m (sight to 2600m) s of Orinoco. Sierra de Perijá, Zulia, and Andes from Táchira n to Lara (*subtropicalis*); in or near mts. throughout rest of country and on Isla Margarita (*albicincta*); n cordilleras (*minor*?). Mexico to n Argentina and s Brazil. Greater Antilles; Trinidad; a few recs. in s US (Texas to Florida).

Cypseloides

Med. large, blackish swifts, some with contrasting collars, but back, wings, and rump always uniform (no contrast), unlike *Chaetura*; no protruding tail spines; tail square to shallowly forked; wings broader and straighter than in *Chaetura*; ♀♀ slightly smaller than ♂♂; glide with wings set at angle below body. Some merge *Cypseloides* in *Streptoprocne*[380].

Chestnut-collared Swift

PLATE 28

Cypseloides rutilus Vencejo Cuellirrojo

Identification: 5–5.3″ (12.7–13.5cm). 20g. Larger, blacker, and longer-tailed than allied *Chaetura*. ♂: blackish brown *incl. upper throat*; *prom. chestnut collar encircles neck and broadens across lower throat and upper chest*. ♀: uniform blackish brown; in hand may show hint of rufous chestnut collar, or sometimes chestnut vaguely indicated on nape or across chest, or more often completely lacking.

Sim. species: In flocks search for diagnostic collar of ♂♂. ♀, best told by presence of ♂, is rarely separable with certainty in field from Spot-fronted and White-chinned swifts. Overlap accidental with very sim. Tepui Swift, although they may meet in lowlands n of tepuis and s of mts. of Sucre and Monagas. ♂ Tepui Swift has *entire throat* and chest chestnut. ♀♀ of the two prob. not separable with certainty in field.

Voice: High-pitched buzzes, *bzt-bzt-bzt* . . . , and longer buzzy rattles *bjjjj . . bjjjj . .*, without exuberant staccato trills and outbursts of *Chaetura* swifts. In general, vocalizations buzzier than those of *Chaetura*.

Behavior: Usually seen in small unmixed groups, less often with other spp. of swifts, perhaps because this sp. tends to forage (fly) higher than *Chaetura* swifts, but reg. assoc. with other swifts at dusk, esp. White-collared, with which Chestnut-collared may roost. Deceptively powerful flight is fluid and leisurely as stiff-winged beats alternate with glides. Glides with wings held below horizontal. Stomach contents of 2 ♂♂ were flying ♀♀ ants[33]. Nest always in damp shady place, usually near water and on a vertical rock surface of cliff, cave entrance, bridge culvert, etc.; saucer or truncated cone of moss, soft plant material, and mud; nest may be reused. In Trinidad breeds mainly May–Aug.; 2 broods/season common; 2 white eggs[128,175,676].

Status and habitat: Uncommon and local resident in foothills and mts. Forages over humid montane forest, partially open or open terrain, often over villages and towns. No long-distance migrants reported (C. Collins).

Range: 600–2200m. Andes from Táchira to Lara; n cordilleras from Yaracuy and Carabobo e to Sucre (*rutilus*). Mexico locally to Guyana and Andes s to Bolivia. Trinidad.

Tepui Swift

PLATE 28

Cypseloides phelpsi Vencejo de los Tepuis

Identification: 5.5–6.3″ (14–16cm). 23g. Se. ♂: blackish brown with *broad orange chestnut collar encircling* neck and extending onto *sides of head, throat, and upper breast*. Tail relatively *long* (62–66mm) and decidedly forked. ♀: sim. but chestnut collar paler and somewhat mixed brown (variable) on throat and chest.

Sim. species: Looks blackish in field and *always* looks long-tailed. In its range easily confused with slightly smaller White-chinned Swift which is shorter, virtually square tail and *looks all black* (in field). In Andes and mts. of north see slightly smaller Chestnut-collared Swift which is shorter-winged, shorter-tailed, browner, and has dark chin and upper throat; ♀ generally has little or no collar.

Voice: Often quiet when foraging. In flocks a squeak followed by a trill and short squeals, *squeek, tititititititititi squi, squi, squi, squi* . . (C. Parrish); also a slow ser. of reedy or hissing *tic* notes.

Behavior: A powerful, long-winged swift that flies fast and is usually seen in single-sp. flocks of 10–20 or so, sometimes accompanying White-collared Swifts. Flies quite high and straight on long-distance commutes; at other times forages over treetops or skims low over grasslands, wheeling rapidly back and forth for several min in a small area before moving on. When foraging, flurries of rapid, stiff wing beats are typically followed by knifelike glides and swerving arcs with wings held down sharply below horizontal. Notably unpredictable in occurrence, groups apparently ranging widely from lowlands to highlands. Roost near water on tepui cliffs. One nest, 3 Mar 1982, in rock grotto on summit of Cerro Roraima at 2600m; cup attached to nearly vertical wall (C. Parrish); usually (?) nests in colonies.

Status and habitat: Uncommon and erratic resident over lowland rainforest, humid and wet montane forest, grasslands (esp. Gran Sabana), and around cliffs and summits of high tepuis. Several unconfirmed sight recs. (possibly this sp.) near Camturama, Amazonas, Río Grande, e Bolívar, and a specimen from Rancho Grande Aragua, suggest this sp. may occas. wander far from tepuis.

Range: 200–2200m; sight to 2600m. Amazonas on Cerros Yapacana, Duida, Parima, Tapirapeco (sight), and de la Neblina; s Bolívar in Upper Río Caura (Meseta de Jaua) and on tepuis of Gran Sabana, incl. upper Río Caroní (Auyán-tepui; Uei-tepui) and Cerro Urutaní; sight recs. at Sierra de Lema and Cerro Roraima; once (specimen) at Rancho Grande, Aragua. Nw Guyana (Merumé Mts; Roraima) and n Brazil.

White-chinned Swift
PLATE 28
Cypseloides cryptus   Vencejo Castaño
Identification: 5.5″ (14cm). 19g. *Fairly large, uniformly dark swift with broad wings and short square tail.* Entirely sooty brown, a little paler below but with *no contrast on plumage.* ♂ has *small white* (occas. buff) *chin patch* (rarely or never discernible in field); whitish chin reduced or lacking in ♀; both sexes may show grayish scaling on sides of forehead. In hand, tail proportionally shorter (41–49mm) and tarsus longer (15–16mm) than in other *Cypseloides.* Imm. and some ♀♀ show white feather tipping on belly and under tail coverts. Imm.: lacks white on chin and may have pale brownish forehead.
Sim. species: Probably rarely identified safely in field. Up close white chin of ♂ is diagnostic; ♀ and imm. Chestnut-collared Swift are slightly smaller and, on avg., a bit longer tailed (this prob. of limited use in field). Also see ♀ Tepui Swift, Spot-fronted Swift (blacker), and Black Swift (as yet unreported in Venez.).
Behavior: A small group in e Bolívar foraged mostly high over partly open terrain. Prob. rarely or never in large groups except to roost. In Costa Rica roosts and apparently nests alone or in loose groups behind waterfalls on steep-sided gorges or cliffs, or where water drips over cliffs. May forage with larger swifts; flight is heavy and direct with rapid, rather batlike wing beats. Nest of mud and plant material attached to wet, vertical rock surface; 1 egg[706].
Status and habitat: Known only from a few widely scattered localities. Resident or migrant? There are 3 or 4 specimens from Rancho Grande (killed flying into windows), 2 taken at night[33] on 20 and 21 Apr 1946; sight recs. (presum. this sp.) from se Bolívar incl. a large roost near Quebrada Jaspe (J. Ayaragueña); up to 16 late in afternoon 4 Jul 1994 n of Santa Elena de Uairén, Bolívar.

Range: To 2000m. Foothills of e Táchira (Burgua) and Aragua (Rancho Grande); s of Orinoco in Bolívar (Cerro Pijiguaos; Auyán-tepui; Ptari-tepui; Sororopán-tepui; sight recs. in se Bolívar). Locally from Belize to Guyana and s in mts. to Peru.
Note: Black Swift (*C. niger*) is unrec. but likely; 7″ (18cm). 56g. Notably *large, uniformly blackish* swift with *slightly forked tail*; in hand or up close note narrow pale gray ("frosty") forehead. ♀ sometimes has white barring on lower underparts; tail shallowly forked. Difficult to separate conclusively from White-chinned Swift in field, but in hand tail longer (48–55 vs. 41–49mm). Specimens required for confirmation.

Has been collected in Guyana, reliably reported in Trinidad, and doubtless occurs, at least as seasonal migrant, in Venez., esp. Oct–Apr. Breeds in w N Amer., W Indies, possibly s to Costa Rica.

Spot-fronted Swift
PLATE 28
Cypseloides cherriei   Vencejo Cuatro Ojos
Identification: 5.3″ (13.5cm). 22g. Rarely identifiable with certainty in field. Small, dark, and with *short square tail. Uniform dark sooty brown above and below*; prom. (esp. in hand) *white loral patch* ("false eyespots"); usually a short white postocular spot and sometimes a frosty white chin (white markings can be present on *either* sex). Imm.: white spots and markings around eyes and on chin reduced or lacking; may show white feather edging on lower underparts[706].
Sim. species: Note relatively large size, absolutely uniform plumage (*no contrast or notably short tail*), and up close in field, white "eyespots."
Behavior: In Costa Rica believed to mostly forage singly or in prs., or occas. with Chestnut-collared Swift, but flight is heavier and more direct than in that sp. Eats flying ants[384,706]. Most specimens at Rancho Grande Biol. Station, Aragua, are of disorientated birds killed flying into lighted windows just after dark on foggy nights. May forage higher and return to roost later than other resident swifts; 2 nests found 15 Jul 1976 and 4 Aug 1977; attached to near-vertical rock face; 2.5–5m above small stream (1 nest near waterfall) below Rancho Grande Biol. Station; conical nest a mass of soft plant material, moss, and filmy ferns; 1 white egg; ads. roost at unused nests, arriving after dark, i.e., between 7:22 and 7:50 P.M[131].
Status and habitat: Very rare resident but perhaps in part overlooked. There are at least 15 specimens from Rancho Grande (9 taken 26 Feb–Jun 1948)[33]; others in Mar, Apr, May, and Nov); and a small no. of sightings Jun, Jul, and Aug. One rec. from Colombia[260], 5 from Costa Rica[706]. Over humid montane forest.

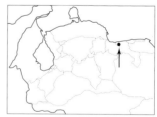

Range: 900–1100m. Aragua (Rancho Grande Biol. Station). Costa Rica (Pacific slope) and Colombia (n end of E Andes).

Chaetura

Med.-sized swifts; usually with contrasting upper tail coverts and/or tail; throat often paler than breast; feather wear and soiling of plumage complicate identification; tail with protruding spines (visible in hand); many confusingly sim. spp. (in field and in hand); voice and flight profile often helpful aids in identification. Fly stiff-winged with snappy, almost twittery wing beats. Nest a semicircular, stick saucer glued with saliva to inside of hollow tree, chimney, or cliff; few nests reported for Venez.

As a 1st step in identification of *Chaetura* swifts in the field, note 3 broad size classes (in Venez.): (1) Large (Chimney, Chapman's, and Ashy-tailed swifts); (2) Med. but with obviously short tail (Short-tailed Swift); and (3) Small (Band-rumped, Gray-rumped, and Vaux's swifts).

Chimney Swift
Chaetura pelagica   Vencejo de Chimenea
Identification: 5–5.5" (12.7–14cm). 24g. *Large* and robust for genus. *In field virtually identical to Ashy-tailed Swift*. Also much like Chapman's Swift but head, wings, and back dusky black (not glossy blue black), back *gradually* shading to dark grayish brown on rump and upper tail coverts; tail smoky gray brown (*in only moderate contrast to back*); *throat whitish gray*, gradually becoming darker on breast and sooty brown on belly.
Sim. species: See Ashy-tailed Swift. Like Chapman's and Ashy-tailed swifts, difficult or impossible to identify with any confidence in field in Venez. Chapman's averages smaller and is glossier and more contrasty above than Chimney and *lacks* latter's *very pale* throat. Also cf. Gray-rumped and Vaux's swifts.
Voice: Rapid ser. of chips and twitters, louder and perhaps not as high pitched as in most others of genus.
Behavior: Aerial. Stiff twittery flight and appearance much like others of genus. Likely to be seen in flocks, esp. associating with migrating swallows (esp. Barn, Bank, and Cliff) and Purple Martins that pass over Andean passes on migration.
Status and habitat: Only 1 specimen (Nov, at Burgua, e Táchira), but possibly a common southward transient over Andean passes in Oct.; northbound transients unreported. Sight recs of 6 birds, prob. this sp., flying over Mucubají Pass, 3600m, 25 Oct 1981 (C. Parrish).

Range: 350m (sight to 3600m). Andes of e Táchira; Mérida (sight). Breeds in N Amer.; winters in w Amaz. Brazil and w Peru.

Chapman's Swift   PLATE 28
Chaetura chapmani   Vencejo de Chapman
Identification: 5" (12.7cm). 22g. Slightly larger than others of genus and *notably dark*. Head, back, and wings *glossy blue black*, *rump and long upper tail coverts* (almost covering tail) *grayish brown to brown, contrasting somewhat with back*, but some individuals show very little contrast; throat grayish brown gradually turning to dark smoky brown on lower underparts.

Sim. species: Not easily identified with confidence. Compared to other *Chaetura* swifts, darker, glossier above, and more uniform above and below (relatively weak contrast on rump and throat). Chimney Swift, a rarely identified n migrant in Venez., and Ashy-tailed Swift are sim. in size but paler with contrasting throats and shorter tails. Resident subsp. of Vaux's Swift is decidedly smaller with contrasting gray rump and *distinctly pale* throat, but beware possible n migrant subsp. of Vaux's which approaches Chapman's in size. Gray-rumped Swift has *sharply contrasting, obviously gray* rump and grayish underparts. Also cf. larger *Cypseloides* swifts which are very uniform above and below.
Voice: When foraging a characteristic, squeezed *che'e'e'e'e'e'd*, often merged into ticking notes sim. to those of others in genus.
Behavior: Forages over lowland and foothill terrain, and prob. reg. associates with other *Chaetura* swifts, esp. Short-tailed and Gray-rumped. Apr nest in Trinidad; nest typical of genus; on vertical rock surface with nests of Short-tailed Swifts[129]; surely also nests in hollow trees.
Status and habitat: Rare and infreq. reported, partly because of difficulty of unambiguous identification in field. Recs. n of Orinoco are from humid forested hill or mountainous terrain; those s of Orinoco are from humid forested lowlands.

Range: To 600m n of Orinoco; to 200m s of Orinoco. Range uncertain. Specimens from w Zulia (Las Alturitas), n Aragua, Sucre (Irapa), nw and sw Amazonas at Caño Cuao, Río Sipapo, and San Carlos de Río Negro, and ne Monagas at Río Guarapiche (*chapmani*); unverified sight recs. elsewhere in Amazonas and from Bolívar (lower Río Caura; near Las Claritas); prob. throughout Amazonas and Bolívar. C Panama spottily e to the Guianas; e Peru; ne Brazil. Trinidad. Distrib. imperfectly known.
Note: A banded specimen taken 11 Jul 1975 in Aragua and originally identified as Chapman's Swift[103] may be Vaux's Swift (*C. vauxi andrei*).

Ashy-tailed Swift   PLATE 28
Chaetura meridionalis   Vencejo de Tormenta
Identification: 5–5.5" (12.7–14cm). 20g. Austral migrant essentially identical to Chimney Swift. *Rather short tailed*. Head and mantle sooty blackish brown becoming *paler dull brown on lower back, rump, and tail*; primaries glossed greenish (all imms., and ads. in fresh plumage), ads. in worn plumage show steel blue gloss

on primaries; *chin whitish, upper throat light brown* usually contrasting strongly with dark brown breast and belly (but much variation in underparts color, and some birds have chin and throat only slightly paler than breast and belly).

Sim. species: Not reliably separable in field from Chimney Swift. In hand 9th primary is 3–8mm longer than 10th vs. both about same length in Chimney Swift; Ashy-tailed also has, on avg., longer tarsi and shorter culmen[380]. Chapman's Swift, also barely separable, is *glossier and bluer* above. Voices may eventually prove helpful.

Voice: Calls from austral *meridionalis*[109] may be slower and lower pitched than those of other *Chaetura*.

Behavior: As in other *Chaetura*, apparently often assoc. with others of genus, esp. Band-rumped and Gray-rumped swifts.

Status and habitat: In Venez. known from only 1 specimen taken 13 Sep at Rancho Grande, Aragua (USNM), apparently a postbreeding austral migrant. The few specimen recs. of austral migrants in n S Amer. and Panama have been taken mostly in Aug. To be looked for approx. early May–Sep. Sp. is common on s breeding gds,. but there are very few postbreeding recs. anywhere.

Range: 900m. N Aragua (*meridionalis*). Breeds in e and s Brazil, Paraguay, and ne Argentina; migrants (specimens) as far n as Panama (Aug), n Colombia (Aug), Suriname (Aug), and n Brazil (6 May at Mucajal, Roraima).

Note: Previously incl. subsp. *andrei*, a smaller form now considered a subsp. of Vaux's Swift, *C. vauxi*[380]. Austral-breeding *meridionalis*, together with *andrei*, were formerly called Ashy-tailed Swift. This English name is here applied only to migratory austral pop. *meridionalis* which also has been called Sick's Swift[380].

Short-tailed Swift   PLATE 28
Chaetura brachyura   Vencejo de Cola Corta
Identification: 4–4.3″ (10.2–10.9cm). 20g. Dark with *strongly contrasting pale rear end* and *very short tail.* Head, wings, and back dull sooty blue black, *rump and long upper tail coverts which completely cover tail contrasting pale ashy brown*; underparts, *incl. throat*, more or less uniform dull dark brown, under tail coverts paler. In flight looks stub tailed with broad *paddlelike wings*; secondaries long and bulging and tend to be separated from body by distinctive gap.

Sim. species: Uniformly dark plumage and *very pale rear end* are good marks, but even more helpful are heavy set proportions, essentially tail-less appearance,

broad wings (esp. secondaries), and floppy, almost batlike, flight unlike that of any other *Chaetura*.

Voice: Rapid twittering much like others in genus.

Behavior: Like other *Chaetura*, often in small flocks and sometimes with other spp. of swifts. Typically rather slow flying (compared with others of genus), a few floppy wing beats alternating with short glides, and usually flies rather high. In display small groups of 3–4 fly in tight formation, chasing round and round while calling excitedly. Roost and nest mostly in tree cavities. Nest typical of genus.

Status and habitat: Common resident over humid forest or partially forested terrain s of Orinoco; less numerous and local n of Orinoco where most often over wooded or partially wooded areas. Wander's widely, occas. over desert scrub, rarely over open llanos.

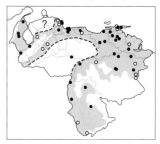

Range: To 900m. Throughout n of Orinoco from Zulia to Delta Amacuro (largely absent from llanos); n Amazons s to San Fernando de Atabapo; n Bolívar from Caicara s to lower Río Paragua and upper Río Cuyuní (*brachyura*); s Amazonas (*cinereocauda?*). C Panama, Colombia to nw Peru, and e of Andes s to n Bolivia and c Brazil.

Note: Assignment of subspp. uncertain.

Vaux's Swift   PLATE 28
Chaetura vauxi   Vencejo de Lomo Marrón
Identification: 4.2–4.4″ (10.7–11.2cm). 18g. *Notably small* swift. Head, back, and wings *dull dusky black*, lower back, rump, and *long* upper tail coverts grayish brown *weakly contrasting* with back; short dusky tail covered by paler upper tail coverts; throat *very pale brownish gray* contrasting with sooty brown breast and belly. Or sim. but larger (ca. 4.7″, 12cm); n migrant (*ridgwayi*).

Sim. species: Good clues are small size compared to other *Chaetura* swifts and overall rather dark appearance (no strong contrast above). Note that throat is *markedly paler* than rest of underparts. In hand, back may show vague greenish gloss (esp. in fresh plumage). Possible presence of larger n temperate migrant forms could complicate identification as they approach size of Chapman's Swift but tend to look *paler throated* and are never as glossy above. Cf. also Gray-rumped Swift which has longer tail and obviously gray rump; also see larger Ashy-tailed Swift.

Voice: In Costa Rica reported to be more varied than those of other *Chaetura*: a thin chipping; high-pitched, rippling chatters; sibilant squeaking and buzzy notes[706].

Behavior: Prs. or groups up to 30 or so regularly fly with other swifts. Flight is fast, a flurry of stiff, buzzy wing beats alternating with jerky, unsteady glides. Display flights involve 2–3 birds sailing with wings held in deep V. Twig cup nest glued with saliva to vertical surface such as hollow tree, crevice in cliff, or other dark area.

Status and habitat: Fairly common yr-round resident in n cordilleras. Larger migrant *C. v. ridgeway* from N Amer. likely (Oct–Apr) but as yet unreported (M. Lentino). Forages over open, semiopen, or forested terrain in foothills and mts., occas. adj. lowlands, and reg. on coast, esp. over towns. There are 5 specimens of Vaux's Swift (all previously identified as Ashytailed Swift, *C. a. andrei*) from 3 localities (Caicara, Bolívar; Altagracia de Orituco, Guárico; and San Félix, Sucre) in lowlands[380] and 2 additional sites in Bolívar (Upata; Cerro Tomasote in Sierra de Imataca)[486]. All of these specimens of *andrei* are essentially identical to *C. vauxi aphanes* (see Note) in plumage and in culmen, wing, and tarsal length (see below).

Range: To 1800m. N mts. from Yaracuy (Boquerón), se Falcón (sight, Cerro Misión), Carabobo, Aragua, Distr. Federal, Miranda, and n Guárico e to ne Anzoátegui, Sucre (San Félix), and n Monagas (Caripe); locally along Orinoco in Bolívar (Caicara to Altagracia); also Upata and Cerro Tomasote (*andrei*). Breeds locally from Alaska (some gaps) s to e Panama; n birds winter from c Mexico to Panama.

Note: Taxonomy of this sp. is controversial. Present arrangement follows Marín[380], merging subsp. *C. vauxi aphanes* with *C. v. andrei* and placing *andrei* with Vaux's Swift. However, M. Lentino (unpubl.) believes subsp. *andrei* is not synonymous with *C. vauxi aphanes*, and furthermore, that Venez. forms of Vaux's Swift represent a sp. separate from N Amer. birds.

Band-rumped Swift PLATE 28
Chaetura spinicauda Vencejo Lomiblanco
Identification: 4.5″ (11.5cm). 15g. *Slender with rather long tail and narrow wings.* Above blue black (not glossy) with *narrow, sharply defined grayish white band across upper tail coverts; throat grayish white* contrasting with dark brown breast and belly.
Sim. species: About same size as several other *Chaetura* but looks smaller because of *slender* proportions. With a good look, easily recognized by narrow and distinctive whitish band across upper tail coverts (under favorable conditions band looks very bright, as though "lit up") and by contrasting pale throat.
Voice: Rapid chittering *chsink* notes in flight, weaker and thinner than those of Short-tailed Swift.

Behavior: A slender, speedy little swift most often found in scattered flocks of varying sizes, typically also with other spp. of swifts. Forage high over forest canopy and cover large areas during midday, but late in afternoon or after a rain groups descend low over clearings and roads, sometimes energetically circling back and forth at almost eye level for prolonged periods of time. On sunny afternoons may circle low and splash to bathe or drink from streams. Nest typical of genus.
Status and habitat: Resident. One of commonest *Chaetura* swifts of e and s lowlands. Almost always over humid lowland or foothill forest or forest clearings; does not range far up into mts.

Range: To 1000m. Base of Paria Pen., Sucre s through Delta Amacuro, and generally in Bolívar (*latirostris*); Amazonas (*spinicauda*). Costa Rica to w Colombia, the Guianas, and n Brazil.
Note: Ranges of subspp. uncertain.

Gray-rumped Swift PLATE 28
Chaetura cinereiventris Vencejo Ceniciento
Identification: 4.4–4.6″ (11.2–11.7cm). 15g. Small blackish *Chaetura* with long, *obviously gray* tail; the 4 subspp. hardly differ at all. Head, wings, and back dusky blue black slightly glossed and *contrasting sharply with gray rump and upper tail coverts*; tail blue black (not glossy) protruding slightly beyond gray upper tail coverts; *underparts dark dusky gray,* only slightly paler on throat; under tail coverts blackish. Or sim. but throat more or less dark gray like rest of underparts (*guianensis*). Or sim. but rump a little less contrasty (*sclateri*).
Sim. species: Everywhere told by *contrasting rump* which looks obviously *gray;* also note grayish tone to underparts (with or without paler throat). Band-rumped Swift has narrow, sharply defined whitish band across rump. Also cf. Ashy-tailed Swift. Others, e.g., Vaux's, and Chapman's have less contrasting "brownish" rear ends; Vaux's also has shorter tail.
Voice: Bursts of rapid chittering; also slower ser. of twittering notes.
Behavior: Typically in groups, often with other *Chaetura* spp. Flight is fast, twittery, and rather direct, usually high over forest. In late afternoons, esp. after rains which force flying insects down, reg. circle low over openings and roads. On sunny afternoons groups also may circle low and, one by one, dip down in flight to splash or drink from streams and rivers. Nest typical of genus.
Status and habitat: Widespread and common resident. N of Orinoco usually over humid forested foot-

hill or mt. terrain. S of Orinoco over hills and slopes of tepuis, and in lowlands. Sight recs. in lowlands at Hato Las Nieves, nw Bolívar, 11–14 Feb 1988 (R. Ridgely and Hilty), and numerous sightings between kms 30 and 85 s of Río Cuyuní, e Bolívar, suggest sp. is underrecorded in lowlands.

Range: To 1400m. Andes of Táchira and Mérida (*schistacea*); Trujillo and Lara (?); mts. of Yaracuy and n cordilleras from Carabobo to Sucre (prob. Monagas); Isla Margarita (*lawrencei*); Amazonas (prob. throughout), but recs. only from sw Amazonas at Yavita-Pimichín and Río Casiquiare (*sclateri*); generally in Bolívar from Hato Las Nieves (sight), Río Paragua, Auyán-tepui, upper Río Cuyuní (sight), and Gran Sabana southward (*guianensis*); possibly ne Bolívar in Sierra de Imatacca. Ne Nicaragua to nw Panama; Colombia and w Ecuador e to the Guianas and n Brazil; n Argentina and se Brazil. Lesser Antilles; Grenada.

Aeronautes

Slender shape; long, slender tail with shallow cleft; slender, pointed wings; rather boldly marked plumage; speedy, twittering flight.

White-tipped Swift   PLATE 28
Aeronautes montivagus   Vencejo Montañés
Identification: 5″ (12.7cm). 19g. Streamlined shape with fairly long, slightly forked tail (no spines). ♂: above entirely glossy brownish black, tertials and *tail tipped white* (white tips sometimes lacking because of wear), *throat and chest white to grayish white*, rest of underparts dark chocolate brown with *small white patch on flanks*, this often extending across belly as *narrow but distinct band*; sometimes also an irreg. median white line from chest to belly. ♀: paler dingy brown, esp. below; usually no white tail tips; throat mottled brown and white, belly band reduced or lacking.
Sim. species: Distinctively patterned and likely confused only with a palm-swift or Lesser Swallow-tailed Swift, all of which occur mostly in lowlands. Lesser Swallow-tailed differs in longer, deeply forked tail (usually held closed in pinpoint), no white tail tips, complete white neck collar, and in foraging and flying alone or in prs. (never in large flocks).
Voice: Distinctive, ratchetlike, buzzing call, *j-j-j-j-j´j´j´ j´j´j´J´J´J´J´J´j´j´j´j´j´j-j-j*, accelerates, loudest in middle, then fades and slows; some calls last several sec, others briefer. Given in flight, even inside nest. Also staccato chipping.

Behavior: Gregarious and usually seen in fast-flying noisy flocks of 10–30 individuals or more. Fly mostly at low to moderate hts. over mt. terrain, esp. in steep valleys and canyons. Nest Feb–Jul, Rancho Grande Biol. Station, Aragua, in holes in building.
Status and habitat: Resident breeder but local, and away from nest colonies often encountered sporadically, perhaps because groups wander widely. At Rancho Grande, Aragua, breeds during 1st half of yr; scarce or absent there latter half of yr. Scattered sight recs. in Andes (Petrolea, Táchira, 22 Jan 1993—Hilty; 15km w of Mérida, 18 Feb 1978; above Barinitas, Barinas, 20 Jan 1975—P. Alden; near Las Cruces, Mérida, Feb 1988—J. Pierson) suggest sp. is underrecorded or erratic there. Mostly occurs in foothills and mts.

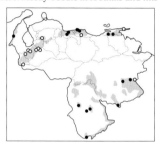

Range: 800–2600m n of Orinoco; ca. 500–1900m s of Orinoco. Sierra de Perijá, Zulia; Andes in se Táchira and Mérida; sight in nw Barinas; sight in PN Dinira, Trujillo/Lara border[60]; n mts. from Carabobo to Distr. Federal and Miranda (sight, PN Guatopo); mts. of Sucre and n Monagas (*montivagus*); s of Orinoco in Amazonas (Cerro Yapacana to Cerro de la Neblina); Bolívar from Auyán-tepui and Sierra de Lema s to Cerro Urutaní; prob. throughout tepuis of Bolívar and Amazonas (*tatei*). Andes from Colombia to Bolivia; Guyana (sight); n Brazil.

Panyptila

Slender and graceful with long, thin wings and long, streamlined tail narrowing to a point; tail deeply forked, and double-pointed when spread; bold, piebald plumage.

Lesser Swallow-tailed Swift   PLATE 28
Panyptila cayennensis   Vencejito Collar Blanco
Identification: 5″ (12.7cm). 18g. *Bold black and white pattern and long deeply forked tail usually held closed in a point*. Above glossy black, tertials and inner flight feathers narrowly edged white, *throat and chest white*, the white extending up onto sides of head and neck; *narrow white nuchal collar* encircles neck; otherwise black below; *white patch on each side of flanks* (visible in flight from above or below). Up close (or in hand) note tiny white spot on each side of forehead; base of outer web of outer tail feather grayish white.
Sim. species: Most likely confused only with White-tipped Swift, a montane sp. (little or no range overlap) with squarish tail and duller plumage.

Voice: Weak chittery notes but not often hd., perhaps because sp. is usually so high overhead.

Behavior: Usually seen in prs., occas. alone (never in flocks of its own); sometimes loosely assoc. with other spp. of swifts (*Chaetura*), but usually flies and forages well above them. Consistently forages higher than any other swift in Venez. except much larger White-collared Swift. Flies in leisurely manner, often in fairly straight lines or in large circles, with tail closed or occas. opened briefly as executes smooth, well-controlled turns, but when actively foraging flies in very jerky, erratic manner with many zigzags and sudden shifts of direction. Fast wing beats alternate with short glides with wings held slightly down. Long tubular nest of plant down, etc., with free-hanging bottom, attached to trunk, branch, or cliff; entrance at bottom; 2–3 white eggs; nest also used for roosting.

Status and habitat: Widespread resident but uncommon and local in occurrence. Everywhere seems to occur in low density, mainly over humid lowland and foothill forest or partly forested terrain. Known from a small no. of specimens, but many sight recs. almost throughout country[259].

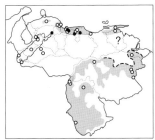

Range: To 1000m. Base and both slopes of Andes in Táchira, Mérida, w Barinas (sight recs.), and nw Trujillo (sight, Paramito); in or near n mts. from c and e Falcón (sight, Sierra de San Luis and Tucacas), Aragua, and Miranda e to nw Anzoátegui (sight, Cerro Tucusito), Sucre and Monagas (sight); n Bolívar (sight, lower Río Caura, Río Grande, and upper Río Cuyuní); n Amazonas sightings at Pto. Ayacucho and Junglaven (*cayennensis*). S Mexico locally to n Bolivia, Amaz. Brazil, and the Guianas; se Brazil. Trinidad and Tobago.

Tachornis

Dingy plumage; slender profile with long, narrow wings; long, deeply forked tail; legs feathered to toes; usually assoc. with palms (esp. moriche palms) and savannas.

Pygmy Palm-Swift   PLATE 28
Tachornis furcata   Vencejo Enano

Identification: 4″ (10.2cm). Looks like miniature Neotropical Palm-Swift. *Deeply forked tail usually held closed in long point.* Above entirely brownish black, below grayish brown grizzled with ashy white on throat and median underparts; belly dirty whitish. Up close or in hand note whitish base of outer tail feather and grayish white edges on tertials. Or sim. but blacker above and throat whiter (*nigrodorsalis*).

Sim. species: Within its limited range not likely confused. Neotropical Palm-Swift (no known overlap) is larger, paler (esp. below where extensively mottled dirty white), and lacks white at outer base of tail.

Voice: Call around nest colony a buzzy *bee, beez, beez, beez-be-be-be*'be'be, accelerating and trailing off. Inside nest a churring *chu-rr-rr-rr*.

Behavior: A small (although hardly "pygmy") swift with pointed tail and fast, twittery flight. Usually in small groups of 3–9, occas. more, that fly rather high with much zigzaging and abrupt veering as they mill in circles. Forked tail is normally held closed but momentarily spread wide during sharp turns. Like other "palm" swifts, uses mainly palms for roosting and nesting. Seven nests with young 4 Feb 2001, Caja Seca, Trujillo, in 3 royal palms (*Roystonea*); 20- to 25-cm-long nest, mostly of feathers (i.e., chickens, parrots), a shapless cylinder with hole at downward end, glued near tip of palm frond.

Status and habitat: Most easily found circling over towns, esp. where there are palms, but also reg. seen away from settled areas where occurs over forest and partially open terrain. Also over forested ridges in foothills. Most recs. are from s and e rim of Maracaibo Basin. Readily seen over towns of El Vigía, Mérida, and La Fria, Táchira.

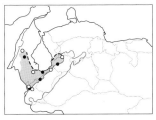

Range: To 500m (sight/photo to 800m at Seboruco, Táchira, 22–23 Jan 1975—P. Alden). S half of Maracaibo Basin n to Las Alturitas and Machiques on w, and nw Táchira, w Mérida, and w Trujillo on e side of basin (*nigrodorsalis*); n to Betijoque, Trujillo (sight at Ceibana—C. Collins), on e side of basin (*furcata*). Colombia (Norte de Santander).

Note: Previously placed in genus *Micropanyptila*.

Neotropical Palm-Swift   PLATE 28
Tachornis squamata   Vencejo Tijereta

Identification: 5.2″ (13.2cm). 11g. Rather pale, dingy, emaciated-looking little swift with *long, deeply forked tail* usually held closed in a point. Above dull grayish brown, the feathers pale-edged giving a slight scaly appearance; below pale dull grayish brown, *entire central underparts extensively grizzled whitish*, under tail coverts dusky fringed and scaled white (*squamata*). Or sim. but darker, somewhat glossed blue black above, underparts slightly darker, more grayish brown (*semota*).

Sim. species: Dull but not likely confused if seen well. Narrow wings, long and pointed tail, and habit of circling over open areas, esp. where there are palms, are good clues. Over Maracaibo Basin see Pygmy Palm-Swift.

Voice: Buzzing or ticking *d-z-z-z-z-z-z-z* and trilling *trrrreeeeee* in flight.

Behavior: Occurs alone, in prs., or in small, loose groups that circle at low to moderate hts. over savannas. Flight is fast, a bit erratic, and notably stiff winged with rapid, almost vibrating, wing beats often interrupted by short sails with wings held below horizontal a bit as bird veers to right, then left. Roosts and nests in hanging dead fronds of moriche palms (*Mauritia*) and almost everywhere closely assoc. with this palm. Enters and exits hidden nest in blink of an eye. Glues J-shaped nest of plant material and feathers inside a pleated hanging dead frond; nest chamber in hook at bottom of J.

Status and habitat: Common and widespread resident over white sandy soil savannas and wet savanna with scattered groves of moriche palms. Uncommon and local n of Orinoco; very local in llanos (few moriche palms) but present yr-round at Hato Masaguaral, Guárico[734]. Distrib. coincides with that of moriche palms which are most numerous in wet savanna and swampy areas (often with standing water) in lowland forest; less numerous over lowland forest.

Range: To 300m n of Orinoco; to 1000m s of Orinoco. Se Falcón at La Misión (sight); and e of Andes from Apure, Barinas, and Cojedes e to Sucre, Monagas, and Delta Amacuro; n Amazonas and throughout Bolívar (*squamata*); s Apure along Río Meta and sw Amazonas (*semota*). E Colombia to e Peru, n Bolivia, Amaz. Brazil, and the Guianas. Trinidad.
Note: Has been placed in genus *Reinarda*; often called Fork-tailed Palm-Swift[403].

Trochilidae: Hummingbirds

Colibries, Tucusitos, Chupaflores

Hummingbirds are a large, exclusively American family. Members range from southern Alaska to Tierra del Fuego, but their greatest diversity and abundance occur within a few degrees of the equator. In tropical latitudes they are found in all land habitats from sea level to just below snowline, and amazingly, they comprise a much larger proportion of the avifauna in high, cold elevations near treeline than they do in the warm lowlands. Hummingbirds include some of the smallest birds in the world, those with the fewest feathers, the fastest metabolism, and the fastest wing beats (up to 80/sec), attributes that relate to their specialization on nectar. Many species have glittering, iridescent, almost gemlike plumage that results from the structural interference of light striking the feathers rather than from pigments. Consequently, their colors often appear to

change with the angle of light and may appear black in poor light. The wings of hummingbirds are uniquely capable of rotating through an angle of 180°, permitting the birds great maneuverability, from stationary hovering to backward flight, and power on both upstroke and downstroke wing beats.

Hummingbirds are important pollinators of flowers and take large quantities of nectar. Most also eat many small insects, their main source of protein. High-elevation and high-latitude species regularly become torpid at night, lowering their body temperature to just above ambient temperature to conserve energy. Flowers specialized for hummingbird pollination often are tubular and red, with floral tubes that fit the length and shape of the hummingbird's bill. Foraging strategies range from mostly dull-colored species that trap-line scattered nectar resources and rarely or never defend them to colorful, highly aggressive species in which both the male and female attempt to exclude all other individuals from patches of flowers. Territories often are extremely fluid, changing almost hour to hour at some trees, and many species are highly mobile, regularly migrating short to long distances in search of nectar resources.

Breeding systems are varied. In genera such as *Phaethornis* and *Colibri*, males form leks and sing to attract females. In other species, males sing alone, advertising from mating territories at flowers or away from them, and also away from other males. *Glaucis* defend territories for one or more females, but as far as known, in all hummingbirds nesting duties are carried out by the females and all species lay 2 white eggs. *Glaucis*, *Threnetes*, *Phaethornis*, and a few others suspend fiber nests with a dangling tail from beneath a *Heliconia*, palm leaf, or bridge culvert; most others, except *Aglaiocercus*, build simple downy cups. The young are fed by regurgitation.

In the following descriptions all glittering colors (which often appear black in the field) are indicated, and wing colors are usually not mentioned as they are brownish black in most cases. Two measurements are given: body length from forehead to tail tip, and bill length. The two combined give total length. Taxonomy follows several current sources[54,148,194,261].

Glaucis

Long, decurved bill and flat crown; appearance and behavior much as in *Phaethornis* but tail normal (no long central tail feathers) and rounded.

Rufous-breasted Hermit   PLATE 32
Glaucis hirsuta   Ermitaño Pecho Canela
Identification: 4.2″ (10.7cm). 7g. Bill decurved (1.3″, 33mm), lower mandible yellow. ♂: above bronzy green, faint dusky mask through eyes; below dull rufous, central pr. of tail feathers bronzy green tipped white, *rest rufous with dusky subterminal band and white tips*. Or very dull and pale below with short dusky malar mark (*affinis*). ♀: duller, esp. below.
Sim. species: Recalls a larger hermit (*Phaethornis*), but note rusty underparts, rufous in tail, and *absence* of projecting white tail tips. Pale-tailed Barbthroat differs

in bold throat pattern, black chest, and mostly whitish (not rufous) undertail. Also see much larger ♀♀ of *Topaza*.

Voice: Flight call a shrill, squeaky *tseep*; territorial call in Trinidad a 5-syllabled *chee-chee-CHee-chee-chee*, rising then falling, and often answered immediately by ♀ in courtship duet[664]; sim. ser. of 3–5 *seet* notes in Venez. in reg. or irreg. ser.

Behavior: Usually seen singly in undergrowth, esp. around thickets of broad-leaved, herbaceous plants such as *Heliconia* and gingers. Trap-lines scattered flowers and spends much time gleaning small insects and spiders from foliage, spiderwebs, etc. Like *Phaethornis*, curious and will often pause close by momentarily to look over a quiet observer. ♂♂ sing alone and do not form group leks. Nest, 1–3m up, a fiber and lichen-covered cup of broad-leaved, fastened beneath *Heliconia* leaf or palm frond tip. In Trinidad nesting areas with 1–3 ♀♀ along a stream or roadside are defended by 1 ♂ but ♂ does not participate in nesting[664].

Status and habitat: Common resident in undergrowth and thickets, esp. around patches of *Heliconia*, *Costus* (gingers), bananas, etc., along streams, roadsides, overgrown coffee and cacao plantations, and humid forest borders and light gaps; occas. mangroves. Local migratory movements into thorn forest during May–Oct rainy season in w Sucre[393].

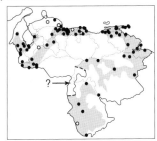

Range: To 1000m n of Orinoco; to 600m s of Orinoco. Maracaibo Basin of Zulia and w base of Andes from Táchira n to Mene Grande, Trujillo; e base of Andes from Táchira to Lara; mts. of Falcón (sight, Sierra de San Luis) and Yaracuy, and n cordilleras from Carabobo e to Sucre, Monagas, and Delta Amacuro; Amazonas s to Cerro Duida; Bolívar e to upper Río Caura (*affinis*); rest of Amazonas and Bolívar (*hirsuta*). C Panama to n Bolivia, s Brazil, and the Guianas. Trinidad and Tobago; Grenada.

Threnetes

Long decurved bill; bold pattern on throat and chest, otherwise dull plumage (no glitter); tail rounded but not elongated as in *Phaethornis* (no long central tail feathers); behavior much as in *Phaethornis*.

Band-tailed Barbthroat   PLATE 32
Threnetes ruckeri   Tucuso de Barba
Identification: 4″ (10.2cm). 5g. Bill long (1.2″, 30mm), slightly decurved. Looks like a paler, faded version of Pale-tailed Barbthroat (no range overlap). Above shining green tinged copper, cheeks and subloral area

dusky, *throat black bordered on sides by short white malar stripe and below by dull orange rufous band*, otherwise *pale smoky gray below*; tail dark greenish black with *narrow white tips and basal third of all but central feathers white*.

Sim. species: Diagonal bands of white in tail are unique in w lowlands. In Andes see Mountain Velvetbreast; s of Orinoco Pale-tailed Barbthroat.

Voice: Song a high, forced *TSEEP, tic'tic'seet'ser-it* repeated every 5 sec or so[61]; also a fast, almost trilled ser. lasting ca. 4–5 sec; starts buzzy but ends with squeaky notes run together.

Behavior: Recalls that of hermits (*Phaethornis*) but shows less curiosity toward an observer. Forages by trap-lining flowers in undergrowth, esp. *Heliconia* and ginger (*Costus*) and is seldom seen much above eye level. In Costa Rica reported to pierce long-tubed flowers, esp. *Calathea*, to reach nectar; gleans for insects in thickets[706]. ♂♂ sing and display from low perches (loose groups?), persistently wagging tails downward as they sing. Nest a thin, loosely woven cup of rootlets and vegetable hair fastened with cobweb to underside of *Heliconia* leaf, etc. ♀ incubates head up facing leaf, as in *Phaethornis*[651].

Status and habitat: Resident in dense thickets and *Heliconia* patches in young second growth and overgrown forest borders (usually not inside mature forest); also neglected banana plantations; lowlands and foothills. Often along streams or other high-sunlight habitats where *Heliconia* is abundant.

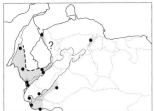

Range: To 300m. Maracaibo Basin, Zulia, nw Táchira, and w Mérida; e base of Andes in e Táchira, w Apure and w Barinas n to Reserva Forestal Ticoporo (*venezuelensis*); possibly Yaracuy (Quebrada El Charal). Guatemala to w Ecuador.

Pale-tailed Barbthroat   PLATE 32
Threnetes niger   Garganta Lanza Coliblanca
Identification: 4″ (10.2cm). 5.6g. Bill somewhat decurved (1.2″, 30mm), black, basal half of lower mandible yellowish gray. ♂: upperparts and central pr. of tail feathers, and base of several inner prs., shining green, *rest of tail from above mostly white with black subterminal band*, the outer feathers with progressively more black on outer edges (from below tail shows broad V of white with dark corners and under tail coverts); patch through eyes dusky, *large white malar stripe encloses black upper throat and narrow but distinct bright rufous throat band*; broad *blackish chest band* becomes dingy gray on belly and under tail coverts. ♀: paler below with grayish throat and buff-tinged belly.

Sim. species: Tail pattern (broad diagonal V of white, esp. prom. from below) and bold throat pattern unique. See Rufous-breasted Hermit; w of Andes, Band-tailed Barbthroat.

Voice: Song in Guyana a brief, high *zit-zit-zeri*, varying to *zer-zee-zer-zeri*, given 2–15 times/min; flight call a hermitlike *seep*[664].

Behavior: Much like that of Band-tailed Barbthroat.

Status and habitat: Uncommon resident (easily overlooked) in thickets and *Heliconia* patches in young second growth and overgrown forest borders; spottily inside cluttered, mature forest with vines, dense thickets, and *Heliconia*. Favors stream borders and other patches of high-sunlight habitat with dense thickets.

Range: To 1000m. Throughout Amazonas and Bolívar (*leucurus*). E Colombia to n Bolivia, e Brazil, and the Guianas.

Note: Specific name *niger* has priority over *leucurus*[148].

Phaethornis

Widespread, mostly lowland hummers of forest understory; long, decurved bill; base of lower mandible red or yellow; crown rather flat; pale facial stripes enclose dusky mask, 2 central tail feathers elongated, tipped white; dull colors predominate in plumage (no glitter); solitary habits; often sit with slightly raised bill and drooped wings; displaying ♂♂ frantically wiggle tail up and down and give squeaky song, sometimes slowly rise up and hover over display perch; closely assoc. with *Heliconia*; conical nest suspended beneath a large leaf; 8 large and 5 med. to small spp. in Venez.; numerous recent taxonomic revisions[148,261,262].

Green Hermit   PLATE 32
Phaethornis guy   Ermitaño Verde

Identification: 5.3" (13.5cm). 6.3g. Bill long and decurved (1.6", 41mm), all but tip of lower mandible reddish. *A large dark hermit.* ♂: mainly dark green above with blue green rump (look for contrast in field), sooty green below; center of underparts gray, face mask dusky; streak *behind eye, malar, and long central throat stripe bright buff;* tail much graduated, central pr. of tail feathers very long and *broadly tipped white.* ♀: like ♂ but usually duller, more sooty gray below; bill and central tail feathers avg. longer. Or sim. but both sexes duller above and 0.25" (6mm) smaller (*apicalis*).

Sim. species: Much darker, esp. below, than any other hermit in its range. See Sooty-capped Hermit. No other large, dark hummers of forest interior have long, white, central tail feathers.

Voice: Flight call a nasal *zurk*; surprisingly loud song by ♂♂ on lek a monotonously repeated *sweerp* or *sweek* note (sometimes 2-noted), repeated ca. 1/sec

for up to several mins, more nasal and metallic than corresponding calls of Western Long-tailed Hermit.

Behavior: Much as in Western Long-tailed Hermit. Often feeds at *Heliconia* and ginger (*Costus*) flowers, but also reg. ascends into canopy to feed at flowering epiphytes. Nest as in others of genus. ♂♂ sing at leks in understory[665]. Breeds Nov–Jul, mostly Jan–Apr, Trinidad[175].

Status and habitat: Uncommon and local resident in humid forest and forest borders, esp. where there is an abundance of *Heliconia* and ginger (*Costus*) in foothills and mts. of w; common in highlands of Sucre and Monagas, and esp. numerous in forested areas with moderate disturbance, i.e., around Caripe, n Monagas.

Range: To 1500m (mostly above ca. 300m). Disjunct. W Zulia (foothills), w base of Andes in Táchira and Mérida; e base in Táchira, and Lara at Cabudare (*apicalis*); mts. of Sucre and n Monagas (*guy*). Costa Rica s in mts. to se Peru.

White-bearded Hermit   PLATE 32
Phaethornis hispidus   Ermitaño Barbiblanco

Identification: 5" (12.7cm). 4.9g. Long, decurved bill, longest in ♂ (1.2–1.4", 30–36mm), lower mandible yellow tipped black. *Large, gray-looking hermit.* Widespread in lower-el. forests of w and s. Above bronzy *grayish green, rump somewhat grayer* (gray-fringed feather edges), dusky face mask bordered by *prom. white postocular and malar; broad and conspic. white central throat stripe;* underparts *grayish* slightly tinged brown, belly whitish. Tail dull dark green (base contrasts with paler upperparts) with broad dusky subterminal band and narrow white tips, 2 central tail feathers very long and tipped white.

Sim. species: Overall *grayish* appearance and prom. white face and throat stripes are diagnostic. See esp. Eastern Long-tailed, Great-billed, Sooty-capped, and Pale-bellied hermits, none of which has such prom. facial markings and grayish plumage.

Voice: Song of ♂ at lek a single *czweet*, over and over at rate of almost 2/sec.

Behavior: Much as in Eastern Long-tailed Hermit but usually does not approach so closely to an observer, and usually found more along forest borders, not flying through forest interior.

Status and habitat: Common resident in humid forest borders, thickets, light gaps, overgrown plantations, and dense young second growth. Favors thickets and more overgrown habitats than Long-tailed Hermit.

Range: To 800m n of Orinoco; to 1000m s of Orinoco. W base of Andes in Táchira (Oropé); e base from Táchira to nw Barinas; generally in Amazonas; nw

Bolívar (lower Río Caura s to Salto Pará) and se Bolívar (Santa Elena de Uairén). Prob. more widespread in Bolívar. E Colombia to n Bolivia and w Amaz. Brazil.

Western Long-tailed Hermit

Phaethornis longirostris Ermitaño Picolargo
Identification: 5.3″ (13.5cm). 5.5g. Long, decurved bill, ♂ 1.7″ (43mm), ♀ 1.4″ (36mm), lower mandible red tipped black. Only in extreme w Venez. *Looks "brownish."* Above dull brownish green, rump tinged buff, feathers scaled dusky; dusky face mask bordered above and below by buff line; *central throat stripe dull buff, rest of underparts dull grayish buff,* graduated tail dull green with dusky subterminal band and narrow whitish tips; *central pr. of tail feathers greatly elongated and broadly tipped white.*
Sim. species: See Pale-bellied Hermit which is slightly smaller, overall shorter billed, and almost whitish below (not grayish buff). In e and s Venez. see Eastern Long-tailed and Great-billed hermits.
Voice: Flight call a high, squeaky *sweep* or *tseeip;* in aggressive interactions a descending, accelerating ser. of 3–5 piercing whistles; advertising song of ♂ a single squeaky, buzzy, or grating note (varies between leks or between ♂♂ within a lek), monotonously, ca. 1/sec[706].
Behavior: Sim. to Eastern Long-tailed Hermit.
Status and habitat: Known from a small no. of mostly foothill recs. in w Zulia.

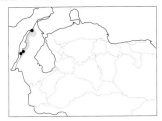

Range: To 1300m. Sierra de Perijá, Zulia (*susurrus*). Se Mexico to n Colombia.
Note: Previously considered a subsp. of Long-tailed Hermit, *P. superciliosus;* taxonomy follows Hinkelmann[261] and Ridgely and Greenfield[541].

Eastern Long-tailed Hermit   PLATE 32

Phaethornis superciliosus Ermitaño Guayanés
Identification: 5.3″ (13.5cm). 4–6.5g. Long, decurved bill, ♂ 1.7″ (43mm), ♀ 1.4″ (36mm), lower mandible red tipped black. *Looks "brownish."* Widespread s of Orinoco. Above dull brownish green, rump tinged buff, feathers scaled dusky; face mask dusky bordered above and below by buff line; *central throat stripe dull buff* (most pronounced in ♀, often lacking in ♂), *underparts dull grayish buff;* graduated tail dull green with dusky subterminal band and narrow whitish tips; *central pr. of tail feathers greatly elongated and broadly tipped white.*
Sim. species: A large, overall brown-looking (not gray or green) hermit. White-bearded Hermit has more prom. white facial stripes and looks *gray* overall (esp. below). Straight-billed Hermit is buffier with straight (not decurved) bill. Sooty-capped Hermit has contrasting coppery rufous rump and longer, flashier white tail tips. Great-billed Hermit is extremely sim. but larger (weight and length) with chest grayer (lacks obvious buff tinge), under tail coverts dark buff like belly (not whitish), and usually lacks distinct gular stripe. Also note minimal range overlap.
Voice: ♂ on song perch a sharp, forceful *tsuk . tsuk . tsuk .,* ca. 2/sec, pulsating and penetrating, often for several min with scarcely a pause.
Behavior: Impish and curious. This quintessential trapliner of widely scattered flowers in forest understory is perpetually on the go but quick to pause momentarily for a "once-over" of human observers, esp. those wearing red clothing items, as well as any other potential new nectar resource along its route. Pauses a few secs to feed at isolated flowers with high nectar rewards (*Heliconia,* gingers, passionflowers, and other vines), then darts off with a squeak and wiggle of tail. Foraging beats may be nearly 1 km in length; also gleans spiders and insects from foliage, bare twigs, and spiderwebs. ♂♂ gather in traditional singing assemblies (leks) where up to several dozen sit on perches at eye level or lower and sing persistently for much of yr. Thick-walled, cone-shaped nest with dangling fiber tail is attached beneath *Heliconia,* palm, or other large leaf; 2 white eggs; ♀ incubates with head up facing leaf cup.
Status and habitat: Common resident in undergrowth of moist and humid forest, at forest borders, and in second-growth woodland in lowlands.

Range: To 1300m. Amazonas s to Río Ventuari; ne Bolívar in lower Caura Valley (*saturatior*); Amazonas s of Ventuari (except Río Negro region) and rest of Bolívar (*superciliosus*). The Guianas, n Brazil (e of Rio Negro) e to mouth of the Amazon; both banks of Amazon from Rio Tapajós eastward.
Note: Taxonomy follows Hinkelmann[261]. Subsp. *saturatior* prob. synonymous with *superciliosus.*

Great-billed Hermit
Phaethornis malaris Ermitaño Picogrande
Identification: 5.5″ (14cm). 7.5–10g. Plumage essentially identical to Long-tailed Hermit but *chest grayer*, lower underparts darker (dark buff, not whitish), and throat streaking more prom., esp. in ♀♀. In field the 2 spp. are best told by distrib.; in hand note differences in measurements. Most individuals of Great-billed Hermit (*insolitus* subsp.) can be separated from Long-tailed Hermits (*superciliosus* subsp.) by their longer wing-cord length (62.5–66 vs. 57–62mm). Bill lengths overlap broadly (38–45.5 vs. 35–42mm) but avg. longer in Great-billed Hermit. Tail lengths almost completely overlap[261].
Sim. species: See Eastern Long-tailed Hermit.
Behavior: Sim. to Eastern Long-tailed Hermit. Occupied nests Aug–Dec, French Guiana[752].
Status and habitat: Known from only a few recs. on extreme sw border of Amazonas. As yet not definitely known to overlap with Eastern Long-tailed Hermit, but overlap seems likely. The 2 spp. are, for the most part, ecological replacements and are often kept separate by rivers[261].

Range: Extreme sw Amazonas at Yavita-Pimichín; confluence of Ríos Casiquiare and Negro; San Carlos de Río Negro; and El Carmen (*insolitus*). Se Colombia, e Ecuador, e Peru, n Bolivia, and nw Brazil; e Suriname, French Guiana, and adj. Brazil.
Note: Has been variously regarded as a subsp. of Long-tailed Hermit, *P. superciliosus*[403], or a full sp.[253,261].

Straight-billed Hermit   PLATE 32
Phaethornis bourcieri Ermitaño Picorrecto
Identification: 4.8″ (12.2cm). 4.3g. *Only Venez. hermit with virtually straight bill* (1.3″, 33mm). Above dull bronzy green with brownish tinge, short buff postocular, and buff white malar stripe; underparts grayish buff with faintly indicated buff central throat stripe; tail dull bronze green with dusky subterminal band and narrow white tips, *elongated central pr. tipped white*. Or smaller (4.6″, 11.7cm), grayer below; throat stripe paler and less distinct (*bourcieri*).
Sim. species: Cf. other large hermits, none of which have a straight bill.
Voice: Typical flight call (Sierra de Lema) a bubbly, trebled *ble'ble'ble!*, uttered very quickly (almost a trill) as bird flies through forest, less often a doubled *blee'-bleep!*, occas. only a single *bleep*. In Suriname (Brownsberg) flight call is consistently the doubled phrase. Song of ♂ in e Ecuador a high, tinkling *téez-e-téez-e-tee*, over and over; rather insectlike[411].

Behavior: As in Eastern Long-tailed Hermit. ♂♂ hold small singing territories, perch 1–4m up, wiggle tails up and down as they sing, and always seem to be in a rush as they fly rapidly through forest understory from one flower or flower patch to another. Usually legitimate pollinators but occas. steal nectar by probing outside base of flower corollas. Reg. visit flowering plants low along forest borders. BC birds, Jan, Río Casiquiare[185].
Status and habitat: Common resident in wet foothills of Sierra de Lema, e Bolívar (up to ca. 1200m); fairly common in adj. humid lowland forests of upper Río Cuyuní where overlaps with Long-tailed Hermit, but apparently less numerous (or locally absent?) in moist or scrubby poor-soil forests in lowlands, e.g., those in white sandy areas. Possibly absent from portions of s Bolívar.

Range: To 1600m. N Amazonas s to Río Ventuari; Bolívar from middle Río Caura (Cerro Tabaro), lower Río Paragua (Cerro Guaiquinima), and Río Cuyuní southward (*whitelyi*); s Amazonas from Cerro Duida and Río Guainía (Yavita-Pimichín trail) southward (*bourcieri*). E Colombia to e Ecuador, ne Peru, n Amaz. Brazil (mostly n of the Amazon), and the Guianas.

Pale-bellied Hermit   PLATE 32
Phaethornis anthophilus Ermitaño Carinegro
Identification: 4.8″ (12.2cm). 4.6g. Bill slightly decurved (1.4″, 36mm), lower mandible *orange red* tipped black. Fairly large *gray and brown* hermit of drier woodlands n of Orinoco. Above *brownish* tinged green, sometimes with indistinct dusky barring on rump; *prom. blackish face mask* enclosed by dull buffy white postocular and malar stripe; *throat mottled dusky* (no central throat stripe), *rest of underparts grayish* turning buffy white on belly; tail dull green basally with broad dusky subterminal band and whitish tips; 2 long white-tipped central tail feathers.
Sim. species: Blackish mask and very pale underparts are the marks, but see Western Long-tailed Hermit. Also cf. White-bearded and Sooty-capped hermits. Reddish (not yellow) on lower mandible separates Pale-bellied from White-bearded Hermit.
Behavior: Sim. to Eastern Long-tailed Hermit. Usually seen low inside forest. Often at *Heliconia* flowers. Breeding Oct–Feb and Apr; gonadal condition indicates Apr–Jun breeding also possible[148].
Status and habitat: Fairly common to common resident in dry and moist forest, light woodland, plantations, and mangroves; often common in gallery forest

in llanos, small nos. in mesic riparian woodland in arid zones. No other hermit in Venez. occurs in such dry habitats.

Range: To 1200m. Maracaibo Basin, Zulia, and w base of Andes n to Trujillo; e Falcón, n cordilleras from Yaracuy and Carabobo e to Monagas (no Sucre recs.); entire e base of Andes and e of them in Apure, Barinas, Portuguesa, and sightings in s Cojedes and Guárico (*anthophilus*)[560]. C Panama and n Colombia[702].

Sooty-capped Hermit   PLATE 32
Phaethornis augusti   Limpiacasa
Identification: 5.2″ (13.2cm). 5.3g. Long, decurved bill (1.4″, 36mm), base of lower mandible red. *The most curious and animated of genus.* Above grayish brown, rump and upper tail coverts *bright cinnamon rufous*; blackish face mask bordered by white postocular stripe and white malar; central throat stripe white, otherwise pale brownish gray below; center pr. of tail feathers bronze green with *very long white tips*, rest of tail dusky broadly tipped white.
Sim. species: Cinnamon rufous rump and long, white central tail feathers (shows more white than any other hermit) are the marks. N of Orinoco see Pale-bellied Hermit; s of Orinoco, Eastern Long-tailed and Straight-billed hermits; in both areas, White-bearded Hermit.
Voice: Song a very high, insistent *tseeo-tseeo, sis-sis-sis*, repeated rapidly over and over (ca. 40 songs/min) from a few low, permanent song perches; constantly wags tail downward as sings. Alone or in small groups.
Behavior: The "darling" of hermits. Trap-lines mostly low flowers and is exceptionally curious and confiding, sometimes darting up to hover in a most charming manner in an observer's face, then dancing off with a squeak and wiggle of long white tail, or pausing again a few meters away for a 2d look. Readily enters open windows and doors of homes, vehicles, etc., fights with itself in front of mirrors, gleans tiny insects and spiders from bare twigs, foliage, and spiderwebs, and darts here and there in a perpetual rush. ♂♂ sing in scattered leks like others of genus. Usual cone-shaped *Phaethornis* nest with dangling tail attached beneath large leaf, under roadbank overhang, or in small bridge culvert. Breeding reported late Dec–Apr (prob. longer) in Aragua.
Status and habitat: Common resident locally in undergrowth and borders of dry to moist forest, plantations, and older second growth, much less common and perhaps local in humid woodland. S of Orinoco also in gallery forest and morichales (*Mauritia* palms) where sometimes fairly common (i.e., Santa Elena de Uairén), but

avoids humid forest. Common and easy to see on dry s slope of PN Henri Pittier, Aragua.

Range: 450–2500m n of Orinoco; 200–1600m s of Orinoco. Sierra de Perijá, Zulia, both slopes of Andes from Táchira n to s Lara, mts. of c and se Falcón, Yaracuy, and n cordilleras from Carabobo e to Paria Pen. of Sucre (*augusti*); n and c Amazonas (Cerro Guanay; Cerro Yapacana; Serranía Maigualide); locally in foothills of nw and e Bolívar (*incanescens*). Ne Colombia to Guyana; prob. n Brazil.

Rupurumi Hermit   PLATE 32
Phaethornis rupurumii   Ermitañito Gargantifusco
Identification: 3.6″ (9.1cm). 3.7g. Bill decurved (1″, 25mm), basal half of lower mandible yellow. *Med.-sized* hermit found only s of Orinoco. Above dull *coppery green* (often looks brownish), upper tail coverts tinged rufous *but with little or no contrast with back*; face and cheeks dusky with bordering buff postocular and malar stripes; *throat mottled with black* (often not obvious in field), *rest of underparts dingy gray*, sometimes with a hint of buff (belly palest), central tail feathers greenish, rest dusky, inner ones tipped white, outer ones tipped buff, 2 central feathers with somewhat elongated white tips (feathers not as long as in previous sp.).
Sim. species: Very sim. Little Hermit, which Rupurumi might meet or overlap in ne Bolívar, usually has buffier, more contrasting rump, buffier underparts, and most subspp. show much less dusky on throat. Gray-chinned Hermit is distinctly greener above (no copper), has gray chin (not very conspic. in field), and is dull cinnamon rufous (not grayish) below. Also cf. smaller, brighter Reddish Hermit.
Voice: ♂♂ gather in small groups with members often scattered in thin dry vine tangles and saplings at forest edge, perch *very low* (mostly 0.5–1.3m up) to sing. Song in lower Río Caura a high, squeaky *SEET, SEET, se'se'se'se'se'yrt*, descending, over and over at rate of 1 song every 2 sec or less for up to several min. In nw Amazonas ♂♂ sang a very squeaky but rather different *etza-squetza, etza-e-yank*, not descending, but songs in both areas end in odd, low note (not squeaky). Song dialect differences worth investigation.
Behavior: Sim. to Little Hermit. Often perches quite low when singing; leks observed have typically had 10 or fewer singing ♂♂.
Status and habitat: Resident in humid forest, forest borders, and dense second growth.
Range: To 500m. N and c Amazonas s to Cerro Yapacana; generally across n Bolívar s to lower Río Paragua

and Auyán-tepui (*rupurumii*). E Colombia, Guyana, n Amaz. Brazil.

Note: Formerly called Dusky-throated Hermit, *P. squalidus*[403], a name now applied to pop. in se Brazil[148].

Reddish Hermit   PLATE 32
Phaethornis ruber   Ermitaño Rufo
Identification: 3″ (7.6cm). 2g. Bill decurved (1″, 25mm), base of lower mandible yellow. *Tiny rufous-colored hermit* found s of Orinoco. ♂: above coppery green, *rump rufous*, postocular buffy white, cheeks dusky, *chin and underparts cinnamon to deep rufous with narrow black belt across mid. breast*; tail dusky bronze, inner feathers narrowly tipped buff, outer ones rufous, central pr. longest, broadly tipped buffy white (protrude somewhat). ♀: paler below, black belt ill defined or absent.
Sim. species: Tiniest and brightest rufous of hermits. Carefully cf. this sp. with larger Rupurumi and Gray-chinned hermits.
Voice: Advertising song in lek (Río Grande) a single *seep* (or *seeit*) steadily repeated 4–6 times, then grows faint or hesitates for a note or 2 before starting anew, the performance continuing for several min. In Delta Amacuro a longer *UU-Z-see-we*, over and over (local or geographical variation or variation between individuals or song groups within leks?). As flies off often sings (context?) a rapidly accelerating, downscale *tzeet . . tzeet, tzeet, tzet-tzet-tzee'tze'tz'ti'ti'ti'i*, ending as bubbly trill (Hilty); also a display song of soft whistles while hovering[61].
Behavior: Usually seen singly, trap-lining for nectar at low flowers or gleaning for insects from understory foliage, spiderwebs, etc., but also reg. up into forest mid. story. Flight is weaving and beelike, as though floating through forest. ♂♂ gather in leks and sing much of each day (yr-round except during molt); perch 0.5–2.5m up on slender twigs in forest understory and wiggle tails up and down rapidly as sing. Song bouts last less than 1 min to several mins and are freq. interrupted by departures as ♂♂ go off to forage briefly. Cone-shaped nest a miniature of larger *Phaethornis* nests; fastened beneath low palm frond tip[446]; 2 BC ♂♂ 2 Jan, Pto. Ayacucho, Amazonas[185].
Status and habitat: Fairly common to common resident in understory of humid terra firme and várzea forest, shady forest borders, small forest openings, and second growth of various ages; lowlands and foothills.
Range: To 1100m. Amazonas s to Río Casiquiare, n Bolívar in lower Río Caura, Río Paragua, and Delta Amacuro (*episcopus*); sight recs. in se sucre (Guara-

unos, 1998–Hilty) and ne Monagas[58] (prob. *episcopus*); s Amazonas and rest of Bolívar (*nigricinctus*). Se Colombia to n Bolivia, s Brazil, and the Guianas.

Gray-chinned Hermit   PLATE 32
Phaethornis griseogularis   Ermitañito Barbigrís
Identification: 3″ (7.6cm). 2g. Bill decurved (1″, 25mm), base of lower mandible yellow. *Tiny cinnamon-colored hermit of Andean foothills and sw Amazonas. Above greenish* with moderately contrasting *rufous rump*; cheeks dusky, postocular and malar stripe buff, underparts pale dull cinnamon ochre, *chin gray* (diagnostic but not conspic.) *and unstreaked.* Narrow black belt across breast very ill defined or absent (both sexes).
Sim. species: Differs subtly from very sim. ♀ of Reddish Hermit in greenish back (no copper), slightly longer white tail tips (best noted in hand), *gray* chin (not whitish to pale cinnamon), and unstreaked throat. ♂ Reddish Hermit has tiny black breast belt and is obviously brighter below. Stripe-throated Hermit, which overlaps in Andean foothills, is slightly larger, more bronzy to coppery above (not so obviously green), overall paler and duller (esp. below), and *throat often mottled or speckled dusky* (not all uniform gray).
Behavior: Much like other small members of genus. See Reddish Hermit.
Status and habitat: Resident inside or at edge of humid forest and at low flowers along roadsides and forest borders. Mainly foothills n of Orinoco and hilly terrain and slopes of tepuis s of Orinoco. Easily confused with Reddish Hermit and prob. often overlooked.

Range: 300–1700m n of Orinoco; 650–1700m s of Orinoco. Sierra de Perijá, Zulia; w base of Andes in Táchira and w Mérida; e base of Andes from s Táchira n to nw Barinas; s Amazonas (Cerro Duida s to Cerro de la Neblina); se Bolívar on Cerro Roraima (*griseogu-*

laris). E Colombia to e Ecuador, ne Peru, and nw Brazil; prob. Guyana.

Little Hermit
Phaethornis longuemareus Ermitañito Pequeño
Identification: 3.3″ (8.4cm). 3g. Bill decurved (1″, 25mm), base of lower mandible yellow. Above bronzy coppery green with somewhat contrasting pale rufous rump; cheeks dusky with buff postocular and fainter buff malar stripe; *below rich cinnamon buff, throat usually speckled or spotted dusky.*
Sim. species: Easily confused with Rupurumi Hermit of s of Orinoco which may meet or overlap in range. Dusky-throated is larger, shows almost no contrast above, and is *gray* below. Also see Gray-chinned and Reddish hermits, both smaller and much more cinnamon rufous below.
Voice: Much geographical variation in song pattern; even subgroups within leks may sing different songs. Typical song is high, squeaky, and complex, repeated over and over with scarcely a break for a min or more from 1 or several low, permanent song perches "owned" by singer in forest or dense second-growth understory[680].
Behavior: Sim. to that of Stripe-throated Hermit.
Status and habitat: Uncommon to fairly common in humid forest, esp. along forest borders and openings where there are dense thickets or patches of flowering *Heliconia.*

Range: To 100m n of Orinoco; to 500m s of Orinoco. Coastal se Sucre (Boca Grande) s to Delta Amacuro (*longuemareus*); nw and ne Bolívar at Pijiguaos and Cerro Tomasote in Sierra de Imataca (*imatacae*). The Guianas and ne Brazil.
Note: Taxonomy follows Hinkelmann and Schuchmann[263]. Subsp. *imatacae* prob. not valid. Disjunct pop. in nw Bolívar needs reevaluation.

Stripe-throated Hermit   PLATE 32
Phaethornis striigularis Ermitañito Gargantirrayado
Identification: 3.3″ (8.4cm). 3g. Bill decurved (1″, 25mm), base of lower mandible yellow. Mainly in w and n Venez. Considerable racial variation. Above bronzy coppery green with moderately contrasting pale rufous rump; cheeks dusky with buff postocular and fainter buff malar stripe; *below dull cinnamon buff, throat usually speckled or spotted dusky.* Or paler and usually no dusky on throat (*ignobilis*).
Sim. species: Gray-chinned Hermit is smaller and overall brighter rufous to buffy rufous below. Does not overlap any other small hermit, but in ne Venez. see Little Hermit.
Voice: ♂ at lek sings a very high, thin, and squeaking 3-part song, i.e., *chup-sit-sik*, monotonously repeated. Groups of ♂♂ within a lek have songs that differ slightly from other subgroups of ♂♂ in same lek; 10- to 15-min. song bouts alternate with 2- to 3-min absences[800]. Territorial song a short, descending ser. of high, thin notes.
Behavior: Like other *Phaethornis*, a solitary bird that trap-lines scattered nectar resources and gleans spiders and small insects from leaves, twigs, and spiderwebs in understory. An audible whirr of wings is often first indication of its presence, but unlike Reddish Hermit, flight is abrupt and darting rather than floating and beelike. ♂♂ gather at traditional song assembles (leks) and sing for much of yr; song perches located in deep shade in thickets, and same sites used for yrs. Little cone-shaped nest with dangling tail usually fastened beneath low palm-frond tip[639].
Status and habitat: Fairly common resident in a variety of moist to humid habitats incl. mature forest, light woodland, overgrown plantations, and esp. second growth and thickets along woodland borders. Often readily found on drier s slope of PN Henri Pittier.

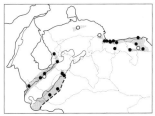

Range: To 1300m. Zulia e of Lago de Maracaibo, and adj. nw Táchira and w Mérida (*striigularis*); both slopes of rest of Andes from e Táchira to Trujillo (prob. Lara), sightings in c and se Falcón[60]; n cordilleras from Carabobo to Miranda and Distr. Federal (*ignobilis*). S Mexico to nw Ecuador and n Colombia.
Note: Previously considered a subspecies of Little Hermit, *P. longuemareus*[403]; taxonomy follows Hinkelmann and Schuchmann[263].

Doryfera

Med. sized; unusually long, thin, straight bill; colors dark and subdued, but frontlet glittering.

Green-fronted Lancebill   PLATE 30
Doryfera ludovicae Pico Lanza Frentiverde
Identification: 4.1″ (10.4cm). 5.7g. *Bill even longer than in previous sp.* (1.3–1.4″, 33–36mm), thin, and *straight*. Much like respective sexes of Blue-fronted Lancebill. ♂: *frontlet glittering green*, rest of crown reddish copper, back bronzy green with blue green tinge on rump; below sooty gray vaguely glossed green; rounded blue black tail vaguely tipped gray on outer corners. ♀: overall duller than ♂; crown bronzy green. In both sexes *head often looks brownish*, contrasting rearcrown color not often apparent.

Sim. species: Given a good look, not likely confused as no other all-dark Andean hummer in Venez. has such a long, thin bill. Cf. Violet-fronted Brilliant, larger *Coeligena* spp., and pufflegs.

Voice: Forages with 2- to 3-note bursts of squeaky, staccato notes[413].

Behavior: Often sits with bill pointed upward. Mostly a trap-liner of flowers in mid. levels of forest, occas. to canopy. Esp. fond of clumps of flowers with long, pendent corolla tubes (Ericaceae and mistletoe), where it hovers without clinging. In Costa Rica ♂♂ have been reported behaving territorially around favorable flower clumps. Cup nest of treefern scales, mosses, and cobwebs attached to rootlets and sunk in moss on rock ledge in dark ravine[260,706].

Status and habitat: Uncommon or rare resident of wet, mossy, montane forest. Almost all Venez. recs. (below) are within 20km of city of Mérida.

Range: 1600–2200m. Mérida (Los Nevados; Mérida, Echicera; Sierra Montañas)(*ludovicae*); possible sight in e Trujillo at PN Guaramacal[60]. Costa Rica; e Panama; Colombia s in Andes to Bolivia.

Note: New spelling of *ludovicae*[148].

Blue-fronted Lancebill   PLATE 30

Doryfera johannae   Pico Lanza Frentiazul

Identification: 3.9″ (9.9cm). 3.7g. Bill rather long (1.0–1.2″, 25–30mm), thin, and very straight. A *dark-looking* hummer in field. ♂: forehead glittering (glowing) violet blue, *rearcrown and nape distinctly reddish copper*, otherwise coppery green above with *upper tail coverts tinged greenish blue*; underparts dark sooty greenish black; *tail rounded*, blue black. ♀: paler than ♂, shining blue green forehead (no glitter); below sooty brownish gray, tail corners minutely tipped gray.

Sim. species: Should be readily told by dark plumage and long, straight bill. In Andes see next sp.

Voice: A few thin, dry, chitting notes while foraging.

Behavior: Rather quiet and unassuming. Usually sits with bill pointed upward. Forages mostly low but ranges up to mid. levels. Favors long, tubular, downward- to horizontally-projecting flowers (e.g., Ericaceae, Gesneriaceae, Rubiaceae) which it trap-lines by hovering without clinging. Esp. fond of flowering vines and often seen around viny tree trunks and cluttered viny areas. Also reg. flycatches tiny flying insects at low to moderate hts. Occas. attempts to defend patches of flowers. Moss and cobweb nest a cylinder suspended from rock overhang in cave; nest cup at top[668].

Status and habitat: Uncommon to locally or seasonally common resident (easily overlooked). Humid and wet forest (mossy cloud forest) and forest borders,

esp. in areas with stunted trees and cluttered, mossy vegetation. Most numerous above ca. 900m. A large no. were taken Feb and Mar at ca. 1365m on Cerro Urutaní (Colección Phelps).

Range: 280–1800m. Tepuis of Amazonas and Bolívar (*guianensis*). Guyana and n Brazil (Roraima); Andes of Colombia to Peru.

Campylopterus

Large; bill strong, usually a bit decurved near tip. ♂♂ of most spp. have shaft of outermost 2 primaries greatly thickened, esp. in middle, and bent at angle (the "sabre"); most spp. in highlands (except Graybreasted Sabrewing).

Gray-breasted Sabrewing   PLATE 30

Campylopterus largipennis   Ala de Sable Gris

Identification: 5″ (12.7cm). 7.6g. Bill slightly decurved (1.2″, 30mm). Shining green above, *uniform gray below*; tail large and rounded, 2 central feathers green, *rest blue black broadly tipped white* (prom. white tail corners). Wings notably long, reaching to or almost to tip of tail. Sexes sim.

Sim. species: Gray underparts might bring to mind a large ♀ hummer, e.g., ♀ Fork-tailed Hummingbird. Large size, ample rounded tail, and white tail corners are unique in lowland habitats where this sp. occurs.

Voice: Rapid stream of loud *chip* notes while foraging.

Behavior: Usually forages at low to mid. levels but occas. ascends to canopy for short periods to forage or mob owls. Often perches in open at forest borders where territorial, aggressively chasing intruding conspecifics or other hummers. Feeds at a variety of flowers and vines incl. *Costus* spp. (Zingiberaceae), and will come to feeders. ♂♂ sing alone or gather in small, loosely assoc. groups. In Brazil, tall, cup-shaped nest on horizontal branch low over water[565].

Status and habitat: Uncommon to fairly common resident in humid forest borders, older second-growth

woodland, overgrown clearings in forested areas, and along forested streambanks in várzea and terra firme regions. Usually not inside unbroken forest.
Range: To 1200m. Throughout Amazonas, Bolívar, and s Delta Amacuro (*largipennis*). E Colombia to n Bolivia, Amaz. and e Brazil, and the Guianas.

Rufous-breasted Sabrewing   PLATE 30
Campylopterus hyperythrus   Ala de Sable Rufo
Identification: 4.1″ (10.4cm). Only in tepuis of se Bolívar. Bill rather short (0.8″, 20mm), slightly decurved, base of lower mandible flesh color. Above coppery green (somewhat glittering) with reddish tinge, *below entirely rufous*, central tail feathers reddish bronze, *outer 3 prs. rufous* (from below, tail looks all rufous). Sexes sim.
Sim. species: Unique in tepuis, but see Buff-breasted Sabrewing. In adj. lowlands see Rufous-breasted Hermit (no known overlap).
Voice: When foraging, a weak, nasal *sqeeek* with strained quality.
Behavior: Single birds are often seen at clumps of low roadside flowers but reg. ascend to canopy to flowering trees or epiphytes. Generally behaves as a territorialist; when several gather at canopy flowers, they aggressively fight and chase conspecifics and other hummers, but also may permit some spp. (e.g., Bananaquit) to feed. Shows strong fidelity to small resource patches, sometimes staying for wks if resources last.
Status and habitat: Wet forest borders on slopes of tepuis, esp. disturbed areas at borders of stunted, mossy, melastome- and *Clusia*-dominated forest and tepuisummit scrub. Fairly common resident, but nos. fluctuate dramatically (seasonal or local?); most common on Sierra de Lema at 1300–1450m, and Cerro Roraima at 2000m.

Range: 1200–2600m. Tepuis of Gran Sabana from Auyán-tepui and Sierra de Lema s to Chimantá-tepui, Cerro Roraima, and Uei-tepui. Guyana; n Brazil.
Note: Has been considered conspecific with Buff-breasted Sabrewing (*C. duidae*)[467].

Buff-breasted Sabrewing   PLATE 31
Campylopterus duidae   Ala de Sable Anteado
Identification: 4″ (10.2cm). 6.3g. Bill stout, *somewhat decurved* (0.9″, 23mm). Only in tepuis of Amazonas and sw Bolívar. Above glittering coppery green, below dingy sooty brown *washed buff on sides, belly, and under tail coverts*; tail bronzy green, *outer 3 prs. of feathers broadly tipped buff, outermost pr. mostly buff*. Sexes sim.

Sim. species: Unique in range, but in adj. lowlands see Rufous-breasted Hermit.
Status and habitat: Very common (large no. of specimens) on many higher and largely inaccessible tepuis in s part of country. Resident in humid and wet borders of dense, low, mossy forest. Appears to be an ecological replacement sp. of Rufous-breasted Hermit.

Range: 1200–2400m. Mts. of Amazonas (Cerros Yavi, Parú, Guanay, Camani, Huachamacari, Marahuaca, Tamacuari, Duida, and de la Neblina) and adj. Bolívar on Cerro Jaua (*duidae*); Cerro Guanacoco, Bolívar (subsp.?); c Bolívar on Cerro Guaiquinima in Río Paragua (*guaiquinimae*). N Brazil (Cerro de la Neblina).

White-tailed Sabrewing   PLATE 30
Campylopterus ensipennis   Ala de Sable Verde
Identification: 4.7″ (12cm). 10g. Bill slightly decurved (1″, 25mm). Only in mts. of ne. ♂: above glittering green, *throat glittering violet blue*, rest of underparts glittering green, central pr. of tail feathers green, rest blue black with outer 3 prs. mostly white (only black at base). ♀: throat patch small and dull blue, rest of underparts duller and uniform green or gray mixed green.
Sim. species: Only hummer in mts. of Sucre and Monagas with prom. white patches in tail, but when perched white not always visible (esp. from above), then can be mistaken for Green Violetear.
Voice: Song a slightly bisyllabic *tzchink*, over and over at ca. 1 note/sec or less, loud for size of bird.
Behavior: Solitary ♂♂ perch on an open twig ca. 2–6m up inside forest and sing persistently, then fly off to forage mostly at low to moderate-ht. flowers (e.g., *Bombax*, Acanthaceae). In light woodland perch and forage higher and commonly in canopy of large flowering *Inga* trees with territorial hummers such as violetears, Golden-tailed Sapphire, and Copper-rumped Hummingbird. Freq. return to thin, bare, "home" perch which changes from day to day as do size of defended territory and foraging ht. Also trap-lines small, dispersed flower resources, e.g., *Palicourea* (C. H. Perrin; Hilty); in Tobago 2 cup nests were large, mostly moss, saddled on horizontal branch in fork and at end of hanging twig, 1.7–2.5m up[148].
Status and habitat: Locally common resident of coffee plantations, forest borders, and light woodland; much less numerous inside humid montane forest. Readily seen in coffee plantations on slopes around Caripe and Cerro Negro, esp. from 1000 to 1600m. Common in coffee, *Heliconia* patches, and second growth in lower els. of PN Paria, Sucre. Because of sp.'s small range, deforestation could become a threat.

Range: 700–1850m. Mts. of Sucre, ne Anzoátegui, and n Monagas. Tobago.

Lazuline Sabrewing   PLATE 30
Campylopterus falcatus   Ala de Sable Pechivioleta
Identification: 5″ (12.7cm). 7.6g. Heavy, black, *decurved* bill (1.1″, 28mm). Large montane hummer with *mostly dark rufous tail*. ♂: above dark shining green, *throat, chest, and center of breast glittering violet blue*, belly green, under tail coverts rufous, *tail dark rufous, 4 central tail feathers broadly tipped greenish black*, outer pr. narrowly edged black. ♀: duller above and below; small patch of glittering blue green on throat; rest of underparts mixed grayish and green, 4 central tail feathers dark green, *rest mostly rufous* narrowly tipped black.
Sim. species: Violet-chested Hummingbird is superficially sim. but lacks rufous in tail. Velvet-fronted Brilliant has short, straight bill and no rufous in tail. At low els. cf. ♀ with Rufous-breasted Hermit.
Voice: Widely scattered ♂♂ sing from rather open, med.-ht. perches; loud, chattery, and sputtery but variable song may continue more or less without interruption for several min, *chik, it, chik, it splek, chat, seet, chik, seet, chik, it, chik, it,* . . . with variations. In w Mérida 1 ♂ sang a chattery but more patterned *sweep, tsit, tsuet, tsit* . . . over and over (1st and 3d notes rising); another a simple *pik-check* over and over in long ser.; yet another a patterned *tsup tsuk sit*. Abrupt notes recall song of Sparkling Violetear.
Behavior: A solitary hummer that mostly feeds at flowers at low to med. hts, usually staying in shade and near or inside cover. Forages by trap-lining or by guarding small patches of flowers, but also occas. gathers in canopy of large flowering trees (esp. *Erythrina*) with other hummers, esp. in dry season.
Status and habitat: Uncommon resident in humid forest, shrubby forest borders, disturbed areas, and gardens.

Range: 900–3000m (most recs. 1200–2300m). Sierra de Perijá, Zulia, Andes from s Táchira n to s Lara, mts. of Yaracuy, and n cordilleras from Carabobo to Distr. Federal and s Miranda. Andes of Colombia and Ecuador.

Florisuga

Large size; strong bill; bold white pattern in plumage; upper tail coverts nearly reach tip of tail.

White-necked Jacobin   PLATES 29, 31
Florisuga mellivora   Colibrí Nuca Blanca
Identification: 4″ (10.2cm). 6.5–7.5g. Heavy bill (0.8″, 20mm) slightly decurved. Large hummer with prom. white tail. ♂: above shining green with usually conspic. *white nape band*; head, throat, and chest glistening blue narrowly boarded green below; *lower breast and belly snowy white, tail white narrowly tipped black*, center of tail from above dark green (long, dark upper tail coverts reach tip of tail). ♀ notably variable: (1) like ♂ or duller and with tail more broadly tipped and edged black, occas. with rufous malar; or (2) above all green, below finely scaled greenish and gray, belly white, under tail coverts steel blue *broadly tipped (scaled) white*, tail like above; or (3) like 2 but with some blue on throat, underparts sooty and *belly and under tail coverts heavily scaled grayish white*.
Sim. species: Combination of white nape, belly, and tail distinctive. If ♀ is in doubt, note scaled under tail coverts. Cf. Black-eared Fairy.
Voice: Weak *tsitt* notes whole foraging.
Behavior: A large hummer that occurs alone or congregates with other hummers at large canopy flowering trees, i.e., *Inga, Erythrina, Guararibea* (incl. *Matisia*), *Vochysia, Bauhinia*, where it is aggressive at patches of flowers and reg. bullies smaller spp. or steals nectar from flowers guarded by them. It does not usually hold territories at flowering trees, however. Away from large flowering trees forages at various hts. but usually quite high, and is reg. seen hovering ("helicoptering") for tiny insects out in open areas at treetop ht., above forest, or over a stream. ♂♂ perform spectacular swooping and diving displays with broadly fanned tail. Nests in c Panama (Jan–Jul) and Costa Rica were downy cups plastered atop broad leaves or palm fronds, 1–3m up, often near forest streams[706,818].
Status and habitat: Uncommon to locally common resident (up to ca. 12 may gather at a large flowering tree) in moderately dry to humid forest borders, clearings, plantations, and cultivated and other disturbed areas with tall flowering trees; also in crown of canopy and emergent trees in humid lowland forest.

Range: To 1600m. Throughout hill and mt. terrain n of Orinoco; generally in Amazonas and Bolívar (*mellivora*). S Mexico to Bolivia, c Brazil, and the Guianas. Trinidad and Tobago.

Colibri

Colored, erectile ear patches end in short violet tuft; ample, rounded tail; short to med.-length bill; montane in distribution.

Brown Violetear   PLATE 30
Colibri delphinae   Colibrí Orejivioleta Marrón
Identification: 4.5″ (11.4cm). 7g. Bill fairly short (0.6–0.7″, 15–18mm) and straight. Large brown hummer of lower mt. regions. ♂: mainly dull sooty brown, grayer below, with *contrasting orange rufous rump* (somewhat scaled dusky); blue violet ear patch and glittering green central throat separated by indistinct whitish loral area and malar stripe; ample tail olive brown with *prom. dusky subterminal band*. ♀: throat patch smaller. Young birds may show much orangish barring on upperparts.
Sim. species: Nothing quite like it. Note orangish rump, short bill, dark ear patch, and persistent song.
Voice: Song typically 4–7 loud *chit* or *jit* notes, ca. 2/sec, often uttered incessantly with scarcely a break; *tu'tut* in flight. Singing persistently Dec–Apr (longer?) in Andes and se Bolívar.
Behavior: ♂♂ form loosely assoc. leks that contain a few to dozens of singing birds scattered over large areas. Sing from relatively open perch within canopy. Gather in nos. at large flowering trees, esp. *Inga* and *Erythrina*, where feed, argue over resources, and behave aggressively, sometimes also territorially; less freq. at low flowers; also at epiphytes (Marcgraviaceae), vines (*Gurania*), and various shrubs[148]. Reg. hawk insects low over small forested streams and perch on boulders in streams. In Trinidad, nest a small cup of plant down saddled over twig 1–2m up[175].
Status and habitat: Rare to common resident. Nos. fluctuate dramatically and unpredictably (?) month to month and yr to yr. Canopy of humid montane forest, tall second growth and coffee plantations with high shady canopy. Periodically abundant Dec–Mar with 100s of ♂♂ singing on territories in Sierra de Lema, Bolívar. Also locally common Dec–Apr in flowering *Erythrina* in Andes, but with few birds singing. Uncommon to rare in n cordilleras.

Range: 300–2000m n of Orinoco; 750–2000m s of Orinoco. Locally throughout mts. n and s of Orinoco. The Guianas and Colombia s in Andes to Bolivia; e Brazil (Bahía). Trinidad.

Green Violetear   PLATE 30
Colibri thalassinus   Colibrí Orejivioleta Verde
Identification: 3.9″ (9.9cm). 5.9g. Bill slightly decurved (0.8″, 20mm). Above and below shining green to coppery green, throat and chest glittery green; *glittering violet ear patch* ends in small pointed tuft; tail shining olive green above, bluish green below; prom. *dusky subterminal tail band* (from above or below). Or greener above (ne Venez.).
Sim. species: Sparkling Violetear is larger with glittery blue chest and dark "chin strap." Overall, Sparkling Violetear is less numerous than Green Violetear, and commoner at higher els.
Voice: Much geographical (or individual?) variation in song. In w Mérida endlessly repeats a short, rough rattle followed by a squeaky note, *b'r'r'r't-steek!*, at brief intervals. In e Mérida (San Isidro Rd.) a double-noted *chak-chit . . . chak-chit . . .* over and over monotonously from a high, bare, treetop twig; in Aragua *Pt'bzzz-ET!* As with Sparkling Violetear, voice notably ventriloquial, and singer often difficult to locate despite singing from high, open, bare perch. Sings persistently during dry season in Andes.
Behavior: A widespread highland hummingbird that is usually aggressive and territorial at flowers but may switch to trap-lining at high els. Feeds at almost any ht. from eye level to canopy, but reg. gathers in large argumentative groups with other hummers in canopy flowering trees, esp. *Inga* and *Erythrina*, where they constantly fight to dominate sections of flowers in canopy.
Status and habitat: Common resident and short-distance migrant. Shows marked seasonal movements, and may disappear from some areas for months. Openings in humid forest, forest borders, older second-growth woodland, plantations, and lighter woodland. Most numerous at higher els. and in more heavily forested zones (e.g., Universidad de Los Andes forest, Mérida; San Isidro Rd.) in early wet season, May–Aug; commoner in coffee zone and other lower, more open woodland during long dry season, Dec–Apr.

Range: 900–3000m (sight to 600m, Barinas). Sierra de Perijá, Zulia, Andes from s Táchira to nw Lara, mts. of c Falcón (Sierra de San Luis), Yaracuy, and n cordilleras e to Distr. Federal and Miranda; Sucre and n Monagas (*cyanotus*). S Mexico s in mts. to Bolivia.
Note: Subsp. *kerdeli* of Sucre and Monagas synonomized with *cyanotus*[148].

Sparkling Violetear   PLATE 30
Colibri coruscans   Colibrí Orejivioleta Grande
Identification: 4.8″ (12.2cm). 7.9g. Large hummer of high mts. Bill slightly decurved (1″, 25mm). Above

shining dark green; *prom. glittering violet ear-tufts extend forward and meet beneath base of bill*; throat and lower underparts glittering green, *patch of blue in center of breast*; tail blue green (bluish below) with *conspic. dusky subterminal band*. Or sim. but tail bluer (*germanus*).

Sim. species: Large size (not always apparent) and blue on underparts separate this sp. from Green Violetear. Up close note dark "chin strap."

Voice: Monotonously repeated song, from bare treetop twig, resembles some dialects of Green Violetear; typically 2–7 dry *chit* notes in a rather irreg., jerky ser. (no. of notes in each song variable), e.g., *chit-chit . . chit-chit-chit-chit chit-chit . . chit-chit-chit . . chit-chit . .* and so on, with only a brief pause (as though it misses a beat now and then) between song phrases. Cf. more complex song of Green Violetear.

Behavior: A territorial and pugnacious hummer that jealously guards nectar resources. Feeds at flowers from low to high, incl. *Castilleja, Centropogon, Clusia, Eucalyptus, Guzmania,* and *Siphocampylus*; also hawks insects. Regularly gathers in nos. at large flowering trees, esp. *Inga* and *Erythrina*, where it argues incessantly and is dominant over most other hummers. In aggression flares ear-tufts ("mouse ears") at conspecifics. Advertises from an exposed, bare twig that is usually high. In display flies up vertically a few meters, then sings, closes wings, spreads tail, and plunges back to perch[162]. Breeding Jul–Oct in Venez.; cup nest of soft plant material, decorated on outside with lichen and saddled over twig[148].

Status and habitat: Resident in highland forest borders, pastures with scattered tall trees, parks, gardens, and settled areas. One of few hummers to use eucalyptus trees (now widely planted in montane areas). A characteristic hummingbird of semiopen highlands but less numerous in Venez. than southward in Andes. Generally found at higher el. than allied Green Violetear, although the two overlap broadly in some areas.

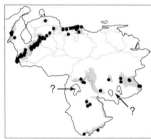

Range: 600–3600m (most rec. above 1500m) n of Orinoco; 1200–2400m s of Orinoco. Sierra de Perijá, Zulia; Andes from s Táchira to s Lara, and mts. from Falcón and Yaracuy e to Distr. Federal, Miranda, and n Guárico (*coruscans*); tepuis of Amazonas s to Cerro de la Neblina; s Bolívar from Cerro Guaiquinima and tepuis of Gran Sabana southward (*germanus*). Colombia s in Andes to n Argentina; n Brazil.

Note: Subsp. *rostratus* of Amazonas synonomized with *germanus*[148].

Anthracothorax

Large; robust proportions; stout, slightly decurved bill; ♂♂ with shining plumage; ♀♀ white below with black central stripe.

Green-throated Mango   PLATE 31

Anthracothorax viridigula   Mango Gargantiverde

Identification: 4″ (10.2cm). 9g. Bill stout, slightly decurved (1.1″, 28mm). ♂: above glittering coppery green with *reddish tinge, esp. on rump*; throat brilliant shining green (no black), large velvety black stripe down mid. line of breast and belly; sides green, tail like others of genus, central feathers black, *outer ones dark wine red* narrowly tipped black. ♀: above sim. to ♂ but with *much more glittering reddish copper on upperparts* (even on crown); outer ♂ but outer feathers narrowly tipped white, *below white with conspic. black stripe down mid. line of underparts*; sides of breast green with strong reddish copper tinge (hard to see in field).

Sim. species: ♂ told from any other ♂ mango by *all-green throat.* ♀ much like others of genus, but crown, upperparts, and sides of breast strongly tinged reddish copper (esp. distinctive in hand).

Voice: Rapid staccato ser. of pebbly notes while hovering at flowers.

Behavior: Sim. to more widespread Black-throated Mango, and like that sp., often hovers ("helicopters") fairly high and out in open for tiny flying insects. Gathers at native and introd. flowering trees, e.g., *Erythrina, Tabebuia, Cordia, Spathodea*, with other hummers and may be aggressive and territorial. In Suriname, open lichen-encrusted nest fully exposed on bare horizontal limb[148,253].

Status and habitat: Resident in mangroves, swamp forest, partially wooded areas, and humid forest borders of coastal plain from Sucre to Delta Amacuro. May occur with Black-throated Mango. Several sight recs. of ♂♂ at Finca Vuelta Larga (near Guaraunos), se Sucre (Mar 13–14, 1998—Hilty, D. Rose, S. Rose, C. Schumacher) suggest sp. is at least seasonally fairly common in Gulf of Paria region.

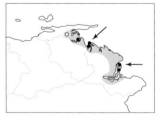

Range: To 50m (near sea level). Se Sucre (sight) s to s Delta Amacuro at Misión San Francisco de Guayo. The Guianas and ne Brazil (to Maranhão). Trinidad.

Green-breasted Mango   PLATE 30

Anthracothorax prevostii   Mango Pechiverde

Identification: 4″ (10.2cm). 6.8g. Bill stout, slightly decurved (1″, 25mm). Locally distributed. ♂: very like ♂ Black-throated Mango but black of throat confined to *relatively narrow central stripe from bill to mid. breast*;

chin and sides of throat to chest shining green. ♀: almost identical to ♀ Black-throated Mango (see) but *upperparts extensively reddish copper*. In Caracas area both sexes have under tail color bluish to blue violet (not maroon).

Sim. species: See other mangos, esp. Black-throated. ♀ mangos are virtually inseparable in field; ♂♂ also often inseparable because they appear all "black." Distrib. of black and green on underparts of ♂ mangos is key, but this can be quite difficult to see.

Voice: In Costa Rica a liquid *tsup* or *tseep*; aggressive note *pzzt!* ♂'s song a buzzy, "zingy" *kazick-kazee*, usually rapidly repeated 3–4 times[706]. A buzzy, twangy song of short phrases, rapidly repeated 3–4 times from high perch in isolated tree[148].

Behavior: Sim. to Black-throated Mango.

Status and habitat: Recs. very spotty and localized. Open forest borders, cultivated areas, parks, gardens, and urban areas. Distrib. and status of this bird are poorly known in Venez.; possibly often overlooked.

Range: To 900m. Known from nw Zulia (Río Anaure), Lara (Guárico), Carabobo, Distr. Federal, n Guárico, c Anzoátegui, and w and e Sucre (*viridicordatus*). E Mexico to w Panama; w Ecuador; ne Peru. Carib. isls.

Black-throated Mango
PLATE 30

Anthracothorax nigricollis   Mango Pechinegro

Identification: 4″ (10.2cm). 7.2g. Bill stout, slightly decurved (0.9″, 23mm). Widespread. ♂: above bright shining green, *entire throat and chest flat black* (no glitter), the black extending narrowly down central underparts to belly; borders of throat and chest blue green, sides and flanks shining green, central tail feathers blackish, outer ones dark wine red tipped black (the wine red hard to see except when tail flicked open). ♀: above shining coppery green, below *white with black stripe down mid. line of underparts*, sides of breast green, tail as in ♂.

Sim. species: ♂ told from other ♂ mangos by all-black throat and chest (often difficult to verify). ♂ Green-throated has no black, ♂ Green-breasted has black mainly confined to center of throat and chest. ♀♀s of the 3 spp. doubtfully separable in field, but (in hand) ♀ Black-throated is only one with essentially *no coppery red* color on upperparts.

Voice: Song *hsl-hsl-hsl-hsl* . . . ,7 sibilant notes[694]; call a sharp, incisive *twick* or *tiuck*[175].

Behavior: Notably insectivorous and best known for habit of hovering ("helicoptering") for flying gnats in open areas high over streams or openings. Also gathers in nos. with other hummers at large native or introd. canopy flowering trees, e.g. *Inga, Erythrina, Tabebuia, Spathodea*. Often dominant but typically not as aggressive or territorial as other spp. ♂♂ sing solitarily (no leks) from scattered tall trees. Shallow cup nest of plant down with a few bits of lichen or bark; usually high on leafless or sparsely foliaged branch[706]; breeds Jan–Jul in Trinidad[175].

Status and habitat: Uncommon to locally common resident (at least seasonally) in forest borders, shrubby clearings, cultivated areas, parks, and gardens in fairly dry to humid regions. ♀-plumaged birds often outnumber ♂♂. Local or seasonal movements occur.

Range: To 1400m n of Orinoco; to 900m s of Orinoco. Throughout, but few recs. in c Venez. W Panama to Bolivia, ne Argentina, s Brazil, and the Guianas. Trinidad and Tobago.

Avocettula

Bill short with tip recurved; rounded tail; closely allied to *Anthracothorax*.

Fiery-tailed Awlbill
PLATE 31

Avocettula recurvirostris   Colibrí Pico Lezna

Identification: 3″ (7.6cm). 4.2g. Bill short (0.6″, 15mm), *upturned at tip*. Maxilla serrated. ♂: above shining green, throat and chest glittering green; *black patch down mid. line of breast to belly*; 4 central tail feathers dark olive green, rest dull coppery purple, outer feathers (from below) reddish copper (in good light). ♀: above like ♂, *below white with black stripe down mid. line of throat and breast*; sides of breast coppery green; tail dark green, outer feathers steel blue narrowly tipped white.

Sim. species: In limited range in Venez. not likely confused if seen well, but note that *both ♂ and ♀ are virtual miniatures of Green-throated Mango*. Also see larger Black-throated Mango; and cf. ♂ with ♂ Blue-tailed Emerald.

Behavior: In Suriname has been reported feeding at flowers of *Clusia* and *Dioclea* growing on rocky quartzite outcrops, a hot, arid microhabitat with mostly scrubby vegetation. Function of upturned and serrated bill is unknown. Breeding evidence Sep–Dec, Suriname; very small cup nest saddled on thick horizontal branch of tall shrub, 5–12m up[148].

Status and habitat: Known from 1 old specimen in Venez. from Cerro Roraima[118] and 1 ♀ seen 28 Feb 1988 at Río Grande, ne Bolívar[259]. To be looked for in forest borders and scrubby vegetation on or around rock outcrops in se Bolívar.

Range: To ca. 1200m. E Bolívar (Cerro Roraima; sight, Río Grande). The Guianas (local), ne Brazil; e Ecuador (once).
Note: Recently placed in genus *Anthracothorax*[148]; plumage and nest sim. but bill and body size differ.

Chrysolampis

Monotypic genus; conical or wedge-shaped head; short, rounded tail; sexes differ.

Ruby-topaz Hummingbird   PLATE 29
Chrysolampis mosquitus   Tucusito Rubí
Identification: 3.2″ (8.1cm). 3.9g. Bill very short (0.4″, 10mm) and slightly decurved; feathers of forehead grow out over base of bill imparting *conical appearance to head*. ♂: *usually looks blackish in field; crown and nape glowing ruby red* (feathers often ruffed) but usually not black, narrow black band from eyes to nape; *throat glittering fiery orange* (or yellow or green depending on light), back and underparts sooty blackish brown; *tail rufous narrowly tipped black*. ♀: very different; above shining coppery green, below *pale smoky gray*; central tail feathers like back, *rest mostly rufous with black subterminal band and narrow white tips* (rufous shows best when hovering). Imm. ♂: like ♀ but darker below, usually with small glittering orange patch on throat; may show smudged brownish belt or median stripe on breast.
Sim. species: Dingy ♀ easily confused. Note unusual head shape and look for rufous in outer tail. Bill of ♀ averages longer than that of ♂.
Voice: Song in Brazil a very high, thin, double-sounding *tliii, tliii, tliii*, . . . from high song perch[565].
Behavior: Most often seen alone at low to high flowers, but sometimes several gather with other hummers in canopy of large flowering trees, esp. *Erythrina*, where they attempt to guard little patches of flowers. They are routinely chased by larger, more aggressive hummers, esp. *Amazilia*, and prob. obtain part of their nectar by filching from within territories of other hummers. When perched ♂♂ often hold crown feathers ruffed and tail spread. In pretty display ♂ revolves rapidly around ♀ and widely fans tail and raises crown feathers.
Status and habitat: Local and highly migratory, but movements need documentation. Dry to moist woodland, scrubby or disturbed areas, gallery forest borders, gardens, and mangroves. Favors drier areas with strong seasonal rainfall. Common most or all yr (at

least Jan–Aug or Sep) at Guaraunos, Sucre; rec. only Aug–Nov at Hato Masaguaral, Guárico[734], but in small nos. at flowering trees throughout Dec–Mar dry season in Cojedes and Apure (Hilty); moves into dry thorn forest (breeding?) during May–Oct rainy season in w Sucre[395]; rec. in Jun at Caicara, nw Bolívar. Some individuals may migrate between Venez. and Trinidad, as well as to and from offshore Venez. isls.

Range: To 1300m n of Orinoco; to 1350m s of Orinoco. Throughout s to n Amazonas (s to Samariapo; San Juan de Manapiare) and s Bolívar (Cerro Urutaní); Islas Los Roques, La Orchila, La Tortuga, La Blanquilla, Los Hermanos, Los Frailes, Los Testigos, Margarita, Coche, Tortuguilla de Sotavento, and Cayo Sal. Colombia to the Guianas, c and s Brazil, and ne Bolivia. Aruba. Trinidad and Tobago.

Topaza

Large hummers; bill thick at base, slightly drooped near tip; fiery plumage; sexes differ; ♂ with 2 long, crossed tail streamers.

Crimson Topaz   PLATE 31
Topaza pella   Topacio Candela Colicanelo
Identification: ♂ 7.5″ (19cm), 12.5g. ♀ 6″ (15cm). Bill thick, tip slightly bent down (0.9″, 23mm). *Very large dark hummer*. ♂: head and neck velvety black turning *fiery reddish copper on back* and glittering gold on upper tail coverts; large gorget glittering emerald to topaz depending on light, squarish across bottom; *rest of underparts glittering dark ruby red, under wing coverts and inner secondaries rufous*, 2 central tail feathers bronze green, next pr. blackish purple, *protruding 2.5″ (6.4cm) beyond rest of tail and crossing each other inward*, rest of tail rufous chestnut (tail from below mostly rufous chestnut). ♀: above shining dark green, below golden green (no glitter), feathers of throat contrasting *dull coppery rufous scaled gray* (show as dull rufous throat patch), *under wing coverts rufous*, tail rather rounded, 4 central feathers dark green turning blackish distally and protruding lancelike a short distance beyond rest of tail; outer tail feathers rufous chestnut. Imm. ♂: like ♀ or with patches of glitter below; tail streamers often lacking. Both sexes have white leg tufts.
Sim. species: Unique in its range but usually looks black and disappointing. Note hulking size, rufous underwings (both sexes), rufous in outer tail. Only infreq. does one see incredible fire in plumage. Not known to

overlap range of next sp. Cf. ♀ (rufous throat patch) with Gould's Jewelfront.
Voice: Loud, persistent chatter or ser. of chips when foraging. In e Bolívar solitary ♂♂ hd. singing Dec–Mar; song, much as in Fiery Topaz, an irreg. ser. of loud, chattery, *chip* notes, typically given more or less continually (with short feeding breaks) throughout day.
Behavior: Feeds at flowers, vines, and epiphytes at almost any ht. from eye level to canopy, and occas. at large mass-flowering trees, but most often at high flowering vines. Guards favorite "patches" of flowers, and both sexes also spend much time foraging by hovering ("helicoptering") for tiny insects high in forest openings or low over shady forested streams. Hovers with very erect posture, tail feathers of ♂ often not crossed when hovering. In e Venez. widely scattered ♂♂ sing alone from a few slender horizontal branches in crown of a mid.-level or subcanopy tree inside or at edge of forest. In Amapá, Brazil, groups of 2–3 ♂♂ sing from fairly low perches over streams (K. Zimmer). Suriname nests reported May and Sep[253].
Status and habitat: Uncommon resident in humid and wet lowland and foothill forest, along forest borders, small shady forest streams, and small clearings and treefalls inside forest. Marked local (?) pop. shifts make this sp. unpredictable to locate.

Range: To 500m. E Bolívar from upper Río Caura (Salta Maijía), lower Río Paragua, and Sierra de Imataca (Río Grande) s to Brazilian border (*pella*). The Guianas and ne Brazil; e Ecuador.

Fiery Topaz   PLATE 31
Topaza pyra   Topacio Candela Colimorado
Identification: ♂ 7.5″ (19cm). ♀ 6″ (15cm). 11.8g. ♂: much like ♂ Crimson Topaz but differs in several minor ways; tail all black *incl. outer tail feathers* (not rufous). In hand (or under ideal conditions in field): black of head continues as narrow black band around gorget ("hooded" effect); gorget smaller and rounded at bottom (square in Crimson Topaz); upper and under tail coverts emerald green (not golden green), breast brighter and fiery red (not dark ruby), inner flight feathers dusky (not rufous); legs tufts black (not white). ♀: much like ♀ Crimson Topaz, incl. rufous throat; differs mainly in *only outer web of outer tail feather buffy rufous* (not outer 3 prs. of feathers rufous).
Sim. species: In field look carefully at outer tail feathers of either sex, your best bet to separate this sp. with any certainty from Crimson Topaz (♂ Fiery Topaz has

no rufous, and ♀ Fiery has tail only narrowly edged rufous). There is as yet no known range overlap between the two in Venez. Cf. ♀ (rufous throat patch) to Gould's Jewelfront which has crescent of orange rufous across chest (esp. prom. in ♂).
Voice: Advertising song a loud, rapid ser. of ticking or smacking chip notes, single, doubled, trebled, or in short, rapid bursts (up to 20 notes), *tsak . . tsu-tsu . . tsa'tsa'tsa'tsa'tsa'tsa'tsa'tsa'tsa'tsa . . . tsak . . . tsak'tsak'tsak . . .* ; highly variable or irreg. sequence is characteristic (C. Parrish recording).
Behavior: Much like Crimson Topaz. Two nests in e Ecuador, small lichen-covered cups on limbs low over water[260].
Status and habitat: Resident in humid sandy-belt forest. The few Venez. recs. are from rocky, cerro-dotted, blackwater regions, esp. along small streams and around waterfalls.

Range: To 300m. C Amazonas from upper Río Asisa (Sabana) s to Caño Pimichín and Cerro de la Neblina. Se Colombia to ne Peru and nw Brazil.
Note: By some treated as a subsp. of Fiery Topaz, *T. pella*[148].

Violet-headed Hummingbird   PLATE 29
Klais guimeti   Tucusito Cabeza Azul
Identification: 3.1″ (7.9cm). 2.8g. Bill short (0.5″, 13mm) and straight. *Very small with prom. white spot behind eyes.* ♂: *entire head and throat blue violet* (bluish in some light), otherwise shining green above, grayish below, greenish on sides; tail green with dusky subterminal band and *narrow grayish tips* on outer feathers. ♀: above shining green (crown vaguely tinged bluish), below gray, tail as in ♂ but with *narrow to broad grayish white tips*.
Sim. species: Both sexes told by small size and conspic. white spot behind eye.
Voice: Sharp, rapid *tsitt* notes or pebbly twitter when foraging. ♂♂ sing alone or in loosely assoc. leks, tirelessly repeating a high, insectlike *pit-seet* or more patterned *tset-it, tset-it, tset-it-sii-sii-sii* or rhythmic *tsid-di-up, tsid-di-up*, over and over at rate of ca. 2 songs/3 sec from bare open twig 4–20m up but usually fairly high.
Behavior: Single birds forage at low to moderate hts., mostly at small, low nectar reward (or insect-pollinated) flowering shrubs and bushes along forest edge. Sometimes interact with other hummers at larger bushes where behave mostly as filchers of nectar within territories of larger spp., or hold small territories of their own. Also visit flowers in large canopy trees (e.g.,

Inga), glean up and down vines, trunks, and foliage, and occas. hawk insects. Flight somewhat weaving and beelike. In Costa Rica, little cup nest low, sometimes several close together, often on vine over stream[629].

Status and habitat: Uncommon and seasonal resident to more open areas inside or along borders of dry to humid forest, shrubby areas, coffee plantations, and second-growth borders. Mostly in foothills, but erratic and unpredictable in occurrence. Watch for this sp. in dry season in drier forest above Maracay and Choroní, Aragua, and near Barinitas, nw Barinas.

Range: 150–1900m (mostly 400–1300m). Ne end of Sierra de Perijá, Zulia, e base of Andes from Táchira n to nw Barinas (Barinitas); mts. of c and se Falcón (Sierra de San Luis; Cerro Misión), Yaracuy, and n cordilleras from Carabobo to Miranda and se Sucre (*guimeti*). N Honduras locally to n Bolivia and w Brazil.
Note: Placed in genus *Abeillia* by some[148].

Lophornis

Tiny hummers with whitish rump band; ♂♂ usually ornate with crests and/or long neck plumes; ♀♀ dull and confusing, but all have black-tipped red bills.

Tufted Coquette   PLATE 29
Lophornis ornatus   Coqueta Abanico Canela
Identification: 2.6″ (6.6cm). 2.3g. ♂ wears "muffler." Bill (0.4″, 10mm) *red with black tip*. ♂: *long bushy rufous crest*; back coppery green with *buffy white rump band*; forehead and throat glittering green; *long rufous plumes with black-dotted tips spring from sides of neck*, rest of underparts green, tail golden rufous, outer feathers edged and tipped rufous. ♀: narrow *frontlet rufous*, crown and upperparts green with *buff to white rump band; throat and chest rufous*, rest of underparts dull rufous, much paler than throat and mixed green on sides; tail bronze green with dusky subterminal band; base of tail rufous, tips buffy white. Imm. ♂: as in ♀ but throat whitish to buff finely dotted blackish.
Sim. species: Not known to overlap ♂ Spangled Coquette which has black-dotted crest and lacks "neck muffler." ♀ Spangled has more rufous on crown, none on throat. Also cf. ♀ to ♀ Festive Coquette, ♀ Black-bellied Thorntail, and ♀ Racket-tailed Coquette.
Behavior: Like other *Lophornis*, seems to wander widely. Forages at almost any ht. from low at shrubs to canopy of large mass-flowering trees where filches nectar from flowers within territories of larger, aggressive hummers. Also feeds at many small low flowers that

have low rewards of nectar, or are too small to be used by larger hummers (e.g., *Lantana*, *Stachytarpheta*). Hovers with steady movements and tail cocked up. Flight is rather slow and beelike, almost as if floating, as bird weaves among foliage, visiting flowers and gleaning small arthropods from foliage or bark.
Status and habitat: Uncommon and erratic resident or seasonal resident (visitor?) to many areas; distrib. spotty. Some movement of birds between Venez. and Trinidad likely. Forest borders, gallery forest, and disturbed areas in dry to humid lowland and foothill regions; more recs. from humid areas.

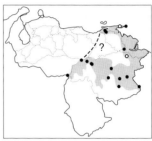

Range: To 950m n of Orinoco; to 700m s of Orinoco. Sucre s to Delta Amacuro; se Apure (Pto. Páez) and n Bolívar from opposite mouth of Río Meta, lower Río Caura, and Río Grande area (sight, 1 ♂, 28–29 Mar 1981—R. Ridgely and others) s to Gran Sabana (Auyán-tepui; Cerro Roraima). The Guianas, ne Brazil. Trinidad.

Spangled Coquette   PLATES 29, 31
Lophornis stictolophus   Coqueta Coronada
Identification: 2.6″ (6.6cm). Short bill (0.4″, 10mm), red with black tip. ♂: *bushy rufous crest dotted black*, upperparts golden green, lower back reddish copper, rump band *buffy white*, throat glittering green (often looks black in field), rest of underparts olive green, tail bronzy rufous (strongly olive in Sierra de Perijá) with dusky subterminal band and rufous tips. ♀: above like ♂ but no crest; *forehead to midcrown rufous*, below mostly buff mixed green, *throat heavily speckled blackish* (chest sometimes dusky), tail dark olive with *dusky subterminal band and rufous base and tips*.
Sim. species: See Tufted Coquette; also Amethyst Woodstar (white flank patches but no white rump).
Behavior: Most often seen in canopy of large flowering trees in foothills where apt to be mistaken for a large bee because of its floating flight (looks as if it is suspended by a string). Usually perches high and at perimeter of canopy foliage. Filches nectar from flowers guarded by larger hummers until chased away, and often gleans tiny insects and spiders by working along bare twigs from low to high. As in all coquettes and thorntails, rump band is conspic. in flight, but beware large hummingbird moths which also show white band on rear abdomen and mimic behavior of very small hummingbirds.
Status and habitat: Uncommon to seasonally fairly common resident in humid foothill forest, esp. at forest borders, but recs. spotty; doubtless wanders widely. Often attracted to brushlike flowers of *Inga*,

Calliandra, and other Mimosoideae. At least in Andes, commoner (more often seen) in early wet season (May–Aug).

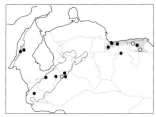

Range: To 1300m. Sierra de Perijá (upper Río Negro), Zulia; w side of Andes in Mérida; e side from ne Táchira n to nw Barinas; n cordilleras from Carabobo and Aragua e to Distr. Federal (sight, 1 ♂, San José de Los Altos, Caracas, 11 Nov 1978—C. Parrish) and s Miranda (Santa Lucía; sight, Dec 1978, PN Guatopo). Colombia s locally in mts. to Peru.

Festive Coquette   PLATES 29, 31
Lophornis chalybeus   Coqueta Abanico Puntiblanco
Identification: 2.9″ (7.4cm). 3g. Bill short (0.5″, 13mm). ♂: *long flaring cheek tufts green finely dotted white*, frontlet and small patch behind eyes glittering green, otherwise dark green above and below; throat glittering green; *narrow white rump band*; upper tail coverts and tail dark reddish bronze. ♀: above coppery green with *narrow buff white rump band*; tail dark olive with dusky subterminal band, *outer feathers narrowly tipped grayish white*, throat spotted green and white, *malar area paler*, rest of underparts mottled buff, green, and black. In hand ♀ has violet-tinged upper tail coverts. Or upper tail coverts and tail reddish copper (*verreauxii*).
Sim. species: ♂ like ♂ Peacock Coquette but crown darker, neck streamers dotted white (not spotted black), and throat all green (not black). ♀ easily confused with ♀ Black-bellied Thorntail and ♀ Racket-tailed Coquette, but both of those have prom. white malar patch.
Behavior: As in other *Lophornis*. Has been seen perched alone at mid. hts. in flowering *Inga* along a small forested creek and at large canopy flowering trees.
Status and habitat: Poorly known in Venez. Humid forest borders. Most recs. are from lower Río Caura region (incl. 7 specimens in Colección Phelps); also taken in mixed white sandy soil scrub forest and savanna in upper Río Caroní. Only Amazonas rec. is a ♂

at flowering vines along Camani Creek, 3 Jan 1993, on mid. Río Ventuari.
Range: To 500m (prob. higher). N Bolívar along lower and mid. Río Caura from Río Mato s to Salto Pará (*klagesi*); upper Río Caroní on Caño Pácara (*verreauxii*); n Amazonas (subsp.?); 1 ♂ (sight) at San Francisco de Yuruaní, se Bolívar (prob. *verreauxii*). Colombia to n Bolivia and n and e Amaz. Brazil.

Peacock Coquette   PLATE 29
Lophornis pavoninus   Coqueta de los Tepuis
Identification: 3.2″ (8.1cm). Short black bill (0.4″, 10mm). *Larger than other coquettes.* ♂: very ornate; crown glittering green (in hand shows narrow violet line down center of forehead), *long flaring green cheek tufts with large black subterminal spot on each feather* (tufts normally held downward, pressed against sides of throat and neck), otherwise shining green above and below; throat black, *rump band white*, upper tail coverts purplish (in hand), tail dark bronzy green. ♀: above entirely shining green, *below dull white coarsely streaked greenish and black*, outer tail feathers narrowly tipped gray.
Sim. species: ♂ unique in tepui highlands, but at lower els. see ♂ Festive Coquette which has green (not black) throat and white-dotted cheek tufts. ♀'s streaks are unique.
Behavior: Usually seen at forest edges where feeds at many flowering shrubs and vines from eye level to canopy. Also filches nectar within territories of larger hummers at canopy flowering trees and is reg. harassed by them. Gleans insects by moving vertically up and down trunks and foliage. Hovers with tail cocked up; slow floating and weaving flight (recalls a large bee) is like that of other coquettes. Up to 5 have been noted together in favorable areas with flowering trees.
Status and habitat: Uncommon and erratic seasonal resident on slopes of tepuis. Very humid and wet forest, forest borders, and older second growth. Migratory or nomadic with sharp pop. shifts on Sierra de Lema, at times numerous (esp. rainy periods), at other times absent. Some movements appear sex related (breeding?) with mainly ♂- or ♀-plumaged birds present.

Range: 500–2000m. Amazonas from Cerros Yavi and Sipapo s to Cerro Duida; Bolívar on Cerro Guaiquinima, and Río Paragua s to Chimantá-tepui and Cerro Urutaní at sw end of Gran Sabana (*duidae*); e Bolívar on Sierra de Lema, Ptari-tepui, and Cerro Roraima (*pavoninus*). Prob. on most tepuis. Guyana.
Note: Subsp. *punctigula* synonymized with *pavoninus*[148].

Popelairia and *Discosura*

Resemble *Lophornis*; tiny with short, straight bill; whitish rump band; both sexes have large white flank patch; ♂♂ have wirelike tails (outer feathers a bare shaft); *Discosura* differs from *Popelairia* mainly in ♂ having bare outer tail-feather shaft greatly elongated and ending in large racket tip. Some merge *Popelairia* into *Discosura*[148].

Black-bellied Thorntail   PLATE 29
Popelairia langsdorffi   Coqueta Cola de Lira
Identification: ♂ 4.8″ (12.2cm). ♀ 2.6″ (6.6cm). 3g. Bill short (0.4″, 10mm). *♂: has wirelike, 3″ (76mm) long outer tail feathers*; crown, throat, and chest glittering green, otherwise above shining green; rump tinged coppery, *narrow white rump band; breast and belly black*, sides somewhat mixed green, *prom. white flank patch* shows in flight; *outer tail feathers dusky brown, very long and pointed* (shafts white and bare for much of length), inner tail feathers very short, bluish. ♀: very different; above shining green, *narrow white rump band*; below mottled green and black with *large white malar patch and white flank patch*; tail deeply forked but feathers not wirelike, dusky bronze basally, bluish subterminally with whitish tips.
Sim. species: Note tiny size (most of ♂'s length is tail). Cf. ♂ to ♂ Racket-tailed Coquette. ♀ told from ♀ Festive Coquette by white malar patch, blackish throat, and white flank patch (both have white rump bands). ♀ prob. not safely told from ♀ Racket-tailed Coquette in field, but latter has buffy white belly and grayish (not dusky) tail (both have whitish tail tips).
Behavior: One or 2 gather with other hummingbirds in canopy of large flowering trees, e.g., *Inga*, *Calliandra*, *Mimosa*, *Vochysia*, and Compositae, where they prob. mostly filch nectar within territories of larger spp., which often chase them. Slow, weaving flight and steady hovering with tail cocked up are sim. to *Lophornis*. In display ♂ darts back and forth in front of and over ♀ while rapidly opening and closing tail and producing a loud cracking sound. Downy cup on horizontal branch up to 10m up[565].
Status and habitat: Prob. fairly common (difficult to see and easily overlooked) in flowering trees in canopy of tall lowland rain forest. Few Venez. recs., but there are 10 specimens from Río Guainía in adj. Colombia (AMNH); 3 ♂♂ and 3 ♀♀ were seen 11–15 Aug 1985 near San Carlos de Río Negro (C. Parrish). Pops. doubtless highly dynamic; unconfirmed sight recs. n to Junglaven, Amazonas.

Range: To 300m. Amazonas at confluence of Ríos Casiquiare and Guainía (*melanosternon*). Se Colombia to n Bolivia and Amaz. and se Brazil.

Racket-tailed Coquette   PLATES 29, 31
Discosura longicauda   Coqueta Cola Raqueta
Identification: ♂ 4″ (10.2cm). ♀ 2.7″ (6.9cm). 3.4g. Bill short (0.4″, 10mm). ♂: unique; head, throat, and chest glittering green, back plain green with *buffy white rump band*; lower breast and belly golden copper, *conspic. white flank patch*; tail brownish purple, long (2″, 51mm), and deeply forked, *distal half of outermost pr. of feathers bare and ending in large round racket*. ♀: very different; above plain green with *buffy white rump band*; black throat bordered by *large white malar patch*, breast green, belly buffy white, *prom. white flank patch* in flight; tail fairly long, deeply forked, dark gray basally, purplish subterminally, outer feathers tipped white.
Sim. species: See Black-bellied Thorntail and Festive Coquette.
Behavior: Usually seen high in canopy of large massflowering trees where it gathers with other hummers. Filches nectar from territories of larger hummers at these trees and is often chased or harassed by larger spp. Flight is slow, weaving, and beelike. Often perches in open on a high bare twig at edge of canopy.
Status and habitat: Uncommon to rare seasonal resident in canopy of humid lowland forest and high along forest borders. Prob. commoner than the few recs. indicate. Nos. fluctuate widely, presum. with abundance of canopy-flowering trees, and very unpredictable in occurrence. Numerous sight recs. Feb–Aug at Río Grande, ne Bolívar; also 3 ♂♂, 2 ♀♀ seen 17 Feb 1982, km 102, Sierra de Lema[259]. Several sight recs. of ♀♀, possibly this sp., at Junglaven, Amazonas.

Range: To 200m (sight to 400m). C and w Amazonas (Nericagua on Orinoco; Cerro Yapacana); Bolívar (no specimens); sightings at Río Grande and Sierra de Lema. The Guianas and e Brazil s to Bahía.

Chlorestes

Resembles *Chlorostilbon* and *Amazilia* but tail rounded; ♂ unusually glittery below; sexes differ. *Chlorestes* merged into *Chlorostilbon* by some[148].

Blue-chinned Sapphire
PLATE 29
Chlorestes notatus Colibrí Verdecito

Identification: 3.5″ (8.9cm). 3.8g. Bill virtually straight (0.7″, 18mm), lower mandible mostly pinkish red tipped black. ♂: above shining bronzy green, underparts *very glittery green, chin, throat, and chest with strong glittery blue tinge* (blue can be hard to see in field), *tail rounded, blue black*. ♀: above shining green, throat and chest gray thickly spotted green, rest of underparts mixed green and grayish white, under tail coverts green, *tail as in ♂*.
Sim. species: *Easily confused*. Note rounded tail (both sexes) and ♂'s glittery bluish underparts. See Glittering-throated Emerald, Copper-rumped Hummingbird, ♂ Blue-tailed Emerald, ♂ Red-billed Emerald (deserts), and Shining-green Hummingbird, all with *forked* tails. Cf. ♀ to ♀ Golden-tailed Sapphire and ♀♀ of White-chested, Versicolored, and Plain-bellied emeralds.
Voice: Song in Trinidad a high metallic *sssooo-sssooo-sssooo*, repeated 3–5 times in ca. 3 sec[175].
Behavior: In good light a "sparkling" hummingbird, although often not seen to advantage. Typically seen alone, perched at low to moderate hts. on open twigs in shade, or occas. at small flowering trees with other hummers where it attempts to hold feeding territories. In dry season in n Venez. also reg. gathers in crowns of large flowering *Erythrina* trees with other hummers. In Trinidad, breeding Feb–Jun; nest a large, deep cup of plant down decorated with lichen and saddled on horizontal branch 2–5m up[175].
Status and habitat: Uncommon to fairly common resident (seldom very numerous) and spotty in occurrence in humid second-growth woodland, forest borders, coffee plantations, shrubby areas, and gardens. Perhaps at least locally (or seasonally) common in n Bolívar (many specimens Nov–Apr).

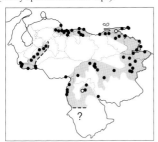

Range: To 1000m n of Orinoco; to 700m s of Orinoco. E base of Andes from Táchira to Portuguesa; in or near n cordilleras from e Falcón and Yaracuy e to Sucre and Delta Amacuro; n and c Amazonas (s to Mondu-apo and Kabadisocaña), and Bolívar s to mid. Río Caura (Salta Pará) and lower Río Cuyuní (*notatus*). Se Colombia, ne Peru, n Amaz. Brazil, and the Guianas; se Brazil. Trinidad.

Chlorostilbon

Widespread and confusing group; ♂♂ small and green; crown and underparts glittery; short tail slightly forked; all ♂♂ fairly sim.; ♀♀ very sim. to each other

(inseparable in field, almost so in hand) and very unlike ♂♂.

Blue-tailed Emerald
PLATES 29, 31
Chlorostilbon mellisugus Esmeralda Coliazul

Identification: 2.9″ (7.4cm). 2.6g. Widespread. Straight black bill (0.5″, 13mm). ♂: very glittery; *crown and underparts glittering green*, lower throat often tinged blue, back shining green, *tail forked, steel blue*. Or sim. but crown tinged golden green (*subfurcatus*); or crown *very glittery golden green*, back tinged reddish copper (*duidae*). ♀: above shining green, below plain light gray with short whitish postocular mark and dusky cheeks; *tail all steel blue*, outer 2–3 prs. of feathers with grayish white tips. In both sexes wings reach *almost* to tip of rather short tail.
Sim. species: ♂'s marks are small size, glittery appearance, and forked steel blue tail. Cf. other *Chlorostilbon*, almost all of which could overlap range of this sp. Also see ♂♂ of Blue-chinned Sapphire and Copper-rumped and Shining-green hummingbirds. ♀ very like other *Chlorostilbon* but tail all steel blue (others have some green in tail, or shorter tails). Also cf. White-chested, Versicolored, and Plain-bellied emeralds.
Voice: Weak, metallic *tsip*; song a short chippery twitter given by ♂ from low open perch.
Behavior: Feeds alone at flowers, usually at low or moderate hts.; occas. 1 or several gather at flowering trees with other mostly larger hummers. Trap-lines scattered resources and reg. visits patches of small, short-tubed, and predom. insect-pollinated flowers which have low nectar rewards, e.g., shrubs and vines such as *Lantana* and *Hibiscus*, or trees such as *Tamarindus*, *Acacia*, and *Cordia*[148]. Occas. steals nectar from holes around bases of flowers with long corollas. Despite small size, flight is straight and darting (not weaving and beelike).
Status and habitat: Fairly common to common resident in a wide variety of habitats incl. dry scrub, gallery forest borders, shrubby or semiopen areas with trees, weedy pastures, cultivated areas, and gardens. S of Orinoco also in moderately humid forest borders and savanna with scattered bushes. Nos. fluctuate seasonally in some areas. Migrates into thorn forest during May–Oct rainy season in w Sucre[395]; present almost yr-round at Hato Masaguaral, Guárico[734].

Range: To 1200m n of Orinoco; to 1850m s of Orinoco. Throughout (except area of next 2 subspp.) incl. Isla. Margarita (*caribaeus*); n Bolívar s to Río Cuyuní (*subfurcatus*); s Bolívar (prob. *subfurcatus*); 1100–1800m on Cerro Duida, Amazonas (*duidae*). Colombia[703] and Ecuador e to the Guianas and Amaz. Brazil. Trinidad.

Red-billed Emerald   PLATE 31
Chlorostilbon gibsoni   Esmeralda Pico Rojo
Identification: 3″ (7.6cm). 2.8g. Bill straight (0.5″, 13mm), lower mandible *bright red tipped black* (♂) *or basally red* (♀). ♂: mainly green; crown glittering golden green, back shining green, underparts incl. under tail coverts intensely glittering green, tail forked, blue black (no blue below), slightly longer than in previous sp. ♀: much like others of genus; above shining green, below plain gray, short white postocular mark; cheeks dusky, *central pr. of tail feathers dark blue green, rest of tail dark green, the feathers dusky green distally, outer feathers narrowly tipped gray white.*
Sim. species: ♂ is only small, very green hummer with mostly red lower mandible; also note its *desert* habitat. ♀ doubtfully separable in field from ♀ Blue-tailed Emerald, but outer tail feathers green (best seen in hand). Also see other *Chlorostilbon* emeralds.
Behavior: Much like that of Blue-tailed Emerald (see). Trap-lines scattered resources or forages at patches of small, mostly insect-pollinated flowers with low nectar rewards that are largely ignored by other hummers. Usually seen perched or feeding rather low.
Status and habitat: Uncommon, local, and erratic in dry and arid regions incl. desert scrub, abused or scrubby areas, and parks and gardens where there are flowers. Pops. highly mobile.

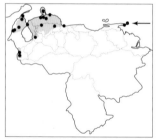

Range: To 1300m. Nw end of Maracaibo Basin and e base of Sierra de Perijá, Zulia; nw base of Andes in Trujillo (Mendoza) and generally in w and c Falcón, n Lara, Yaracuy, and Carabobo (Pto. Cabello); nw and extreme ne Sucre and n Monagas (*nitens*); w base of Andes in nw Táchira (*chrysogaster*). N Colombia.
Note: Distrib. and sp. limits need clarification. Subsp. in w Trujillo uncertain.

Coppery Emerald   PLATE 31
Chlorostilbon russatus   Esmeralda Bronceada
Identification: 3″ (7.6cm). Bill straight (0.6″, 15mm). Only in Sierra de Perijá. ♂: crown glittery green, *rest of upperparts incl. tail coppery green with strong reddish copper tinge,* tail from below bronzy golden green, underparts glittering green to golden green. ♀: above *coppery green,* below pale gray; short white postocular mark; cheeks dusky; *central tail feathers greenish copper,* rest with vague dusky purple subterminal band, outer prs. narrowly tipped grayish white.

Sim. species: So far as known the only *Chlorostilbon* in its range, and much more coppery above than any other.
Behavior: In Colombia feeds at small flowers at low to moderate hts. Flight is darting and direct (not weaving).
Status and habitat: Essentially unknown in Venez. Shrubby forest borders, overgrown roadsides, and cultivated areas in Colombia.

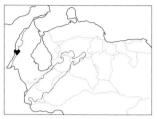

Range: 1100–1200m. Sierra de Perijá (upper Río Negro), w Zulia. Ne Colombia.

Narrow-tailed Emerald   PLATES 29, 31
Chlorostilbon stenura   Esmeralda Cola de Alambre
Identification: 2.8″ (7cm). Bill black (0.6″, 15cm). Uncommon and only at high els. *At rest wings reach to end of tail.* ♂: *crown glittering green* (no gold or copper tinge), rest of upperparts shining green with slight copper tinge, underparts bright glittering green, tail *very short, slightly forked, the feathers green, outer 3 prs. of tail feathers very narrow and pointed ("spiky"),* rest progressively wider, central pr. almost normal width (6mm at tip). ♀: much like others of genus; green above with dusky cheeks and gray underparts; *tail green* with dusky subterminal band (from above), outer 2–3 prs. of feathers with grayish white tips; tail feathers normal (outermost pr. slightly narrowed). In hand, tail of ♂ Short-tailed Emerald 18–24mm (avg. 21.6) vs. 23–24mm (avg. 23.6) for ♂ Narrow-tailed Emerald.
Sim. species: ♂, when hovering and tail is spread, shows distinctive, narrow spiky outer tail feathers (only 2mm wide near tip vs. 6–7mm for Blue-tailed Emerald), but this usually difficult to see in field (easy to verify in hand). Also cf. ♂ to ♂ Short-tailed Emerald which has even shorter tail; at n end of Andes see ♂ Green-tailed Emerald. ♀ essentially indistinguishable in field from most others of genus.
Behavior: Much as in Blue-tailed Emerald (see).
Status and habitat: Infreq. encountered and seldom identified with confidence in field. True status, because of identification problems, is unknown. Apparently humid montane forest borders. Occurs almost en-

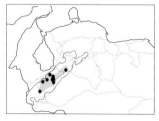

tirely above el. range of Short-tailed Emerald, with only minimal overlap between ca. 1950 and 2200m where the two may occur together interspecifically.

Range: 1950–3000m. Both slopes of Andes in n Táchira and Mérida; e slope in se Trujillo at Guamito (*stenura*). Ne Colombia.

Note: See Note under Green-tailed Emerald (*C. alice*) which is likely only a subsp. of Narrow-tailed Emerald (*C. stenura*).

Green-tailed Emerald
PLATE 31
Chlorostilbon alice   Esmeralda Coliverde
Identification: 2.8″ (7.1cm). Bill short (0.5″, 13mm). ♂: head and neck glittering golden green, back shining green with reddish copper tinge; *underparts very coppery green*, tail short, *olive green* (or purplish olive—Sucre), slightly forked, the outer 3 prs. of feathers *narrow and spikelike* (hard to see in field), the rest progressively wider, central ones normal (Trujillo and Lara). Or sim. but tail feathers all more or less normal width (Falcón to Sucre). ♀: much like others of genus (shining green above, gray below with white postocular streak and dusky cheeks) but tail is short and dark green with dusky subterminal band, outer 2 prs. of feathers with *large prom. gray-white tips*; central pr. *all green*. In both sexes wings reach to tip of tail or slightly beyond. In hand, tail avgs. 20.4mm (♂'s tail 20mm, ♀'s 21.7), even shorter than in Short-tailed Emerald.
Sim. species: ♂ told from ♂ Blue-tailed Emerald by green tail; ♀ from ♀ Blue-tailed by *all-green central tail feathers*, rest green with contrasting dark subterminal tail band, and *large amt. of white* on tail corners. In mts. of Lara and Trujillo, where may overlap Narrow-tailed Emerald, ♂ doubtfully separable in field but tail dark reddish olive, back with distinct reddish copper tinge, and head and underparts with gold tinge (tails very sim.). ♀ essentially identical to ♀ Narrow-tailed Emerald but pale tail tips more prom. Also see Short-tailed Emerald.
Voice: Thin, high, soft chittering while foraging.
Behavior: A "filcher" of nectar within territories of other hummers (e.g., Copper-rumped Hummingbird); also a reg. trap-liner of patches of mostly low nectar reward flowers low along roadsides and in small clearings. Usually seen alone, rarely at large mass-flowering trees.
Status and habitat: Fairly common resident seasonally, but shows marked pop. movements and generally irreg. and unpredictable. At low els. found in dry to moderately humid forest borders, gardens, and cultivated areas with trees. At high els., where less common, also in humid wooded borders.

Range: ENDEMIC. 750–1800m. N end of Andes in Trujillo (below Páramo Misisí; Guamito) and Lara; Falcón (Sierra de San Luis), mts. of Yaracuy, and n cordilleras of Carabobo, Aragua, Distr. Federal, and Miranda (e to Cerro Golfo Triste); mts. of Sucre (except Paria Pen.) s to n Monagas at Caripe.

Note: Narrow-tailed Emerald (*C. stenura*) differs from Green-tailed Emerald primarily in having very narrow outer tail feathers, but in zone of overlap between the two spp. in Andes of Trujillo Green-tailed also has narrow outer tail feathers and is practically indistinguishable from Narrow-tailed which apparently occurs mainly at higher els. and southward in Andes. In all likelihood the two are not separate spp. and Narrow-tailed Emerald is only a race of Green-tailed Emerald (K. Parkes).

Short-tailed Emerald
PLATE 31
Chlorostilbon poortmani   Esmeralda Cola Corta
Identification: 2.7″ (6.9cm). Bill short (0.6″, 15mm). ♂: essentially identical in plumage to ♂ Narrow-tailed Emerald *and usually not separable in field, but tail slightly shorter* (see that sp.), *tail feathers of normal width* (outer ones *not* narrow and spikelike) and dark olive green (contrast somewhat with upper tail coverts). At rest wing tips extend slightly beyond tail (ca. 2–3mm), but this can be difficult to verify and differs only slightly from Narrow-tailed Emerald. In hand the 2 spp. are easily distinguished by shape of tail feathers. ♀: essentially identical to ♀ of Narrow-tailed Emerald and not separable in field except possibly by slightly shorter tail length (*wing tips reach 1–2mm beyond tail in resting Short-tailed Emerald*) and, in some individuals, back and tail tinged reddish copper. In hand all tail feathers normal (not narrow and spiky).
Sim. species: In most of range likely confused only with Narrow-tailed and Blue-tailed emeralds. At n end of Andes also see very sim. Green-tailed Emerald. Field observers should realize that many *Chlorostilbon* hummers they see in Andes will remain unidentified.
Behavior: Usually seen alone foraging and perching rather low (0.5–5m up) at little patches of roadside flowers, or in flower gardens around habitations. Favors horizontal or upright flowers, but also feeds at hanging blossoms (i.e., *Macleania*). Trap-lines and prob. also filches and uses low nectar reward flowers. Flies with weaving, floating movements, more like that of coquettes and woodstars than other *Chlorostilbon*. Cup nest with decorated exterior; May–Jun breeding reported[148].
Status and habitat: Uncommon to fairly common (possibly more numerous but hard to identify in field or in

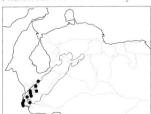

hand) in shrubby pastures, thickets along roadsides, and other partially deforested areas. Usually not far from humid montane forest borders. Most specimens (except an anomalous rec. from Páramo de Tamá) are from els. *below* range of Narrow-tailed Emerald. Seasonal el. movements may account for wide scatter of recs. above and below "normal" range in Andes.
Range: Mostly 800–2200m (once to 150m in w Mérida; once to 300m in nw Táchira; once to 2800m at Páramo de Tamá, Táchira). Both slopes of Andes in Táchira and w slope in Mérida (El Vigía; Zea; Guaraque) (*poortmani*). Ne Colombia.

Thalurania

Slightly decurved bill; tail deeply forked (♂) or slightly forked (♀); sexes very different.

Violet-crowned Woodnymph
Thalurania colombica Tucusito Coronado
Identification: ♂ 4″ (10.2cm), 4.5g. ♀ 3.3″ (8.4cm), 4–4.5g. Bill slightly decurved (0.8″, 20mm). ♂: like ♂ Fork-tailed Woodnymph but *forecrown glittering violet blue* to purplish. ♀: as in ♀ Fork-tailed Woodnymph but throat and chest dingy grayish white, lower breast and belly brownish gray in contrast to throat and chest (2-toned effect).
Sim. species: ♀ superficially like several other ♀ hummers but from any by "divided" 2-toned underparts. In e and s Venez. see Fork-tailed Woodnymph (no range overlap).
Voice: High, dry, fast *kip* or *kyip*, often repeated; aggressive note a dry, scratchy *chut-t-t*[706].
Behavior: Much as in Fork-tailed Woodnymph. Compact, downy cup nest of treefern scales, plant down, and cobwebs on horizontal twig 1–5m up (usually low) inside forest or at edge; breeds Feb–May or Jun in Costa Rica[706]; Mar–Jul or later in n Colombia.
Status and habitat: Common resident inside humid and wet forest and at forest borders in foothill and lower montane els., smaller nos. in lowlands. Relatively sedentary; but postbreeding upslope movements reported in Costa Rica[706].

Range: To 2000m (most recs. 500–1700m). Sierra de Perijá, Zulia, humid portions of Maracaibo Basin, and both slopes of Andes from n Táchira n to nw Lara (Cerro El Cerrón) and se Lara at Terepaima (*colombica*); se Táchira on Cerro El Teleo (*rostrifera*). E Guatemala to n Colombia.
Note: Taxonomy of *Thalurania* reviewed in AOU Check-list[10]. Subsp. *rostrifera* doubtfully distinct.

Fork-tailed Woodnymph   PLATE 29
Thalurania furcata Tucusito Moradito
Identification: ♂ 4″ (10.2cm), 4.6g. ♀ 3.3″ (8.4cm), 4.1g. Bill slightly decurved (0.8″, 20mm). ♂: usually looks very dark; above dark green incl. forecrown; shoulder patch violet blue, *throat and chest glittering (glowing) green, rest of underparts purple to violet blue* (belly blue to violet n of Orinoco, mostly purple s of Orinoco), tail notably long, blue black, and deeply forked. ♀: very different; above green, cheeks vaguely darker; below dingy grayish white, *tail shining green, all but central pr. of feathers with dusky subterminal band and conspic. gray-white tips.*
Sim. species: ♂'s dark plumage and deeply forked tail are distinctive; look for "purple" belly. ♀ easily confused. All ♀ *Chlorostilbon* emeralds are smaller with prom. dusky cheeks. Also cf. ♀ to several *Amazilia*, esp. White-chested, Versicolored, and Plain-bellied emeralds. S of Orinoco see larger Gray-breasted Sabrewing which has much bigger tail and more prom. white tail corners.
Voice: Song a variable ser. of 2–6 pulsing notes in irreg. pattern, e.g., *sii-sii . sii-sii-sii-sii . sii-sii-sii . . .*, insectlike[61].
Behavior: Solitary, territorial, and moderately aggressive sp., usually seen in lower or mid. strata inside forest, less often along forest borders. Feeds at a variety of small flowering shrubs, esp. Rubiaceae (i.e., *Syphilis*, *Psychotria*, and *Hamelia*), also epiphytes, vines (*Combretum*), and large herbs. ♂♂ may guard small patches of flowers or flowering shrubs inside forest, glean insects and spiders from foliage and twigs, or trap-line flowers. ♀♀ more often trap-line or filch nectar resources and are less territorial. Both occas. visit large canopy flowering trees with other hummers but usually do not maintain foraging territories there.
Status and habitat: Common in a variety of humid lowland forest and edge situations and in smaller nos. into foothills. Pops. relatively sedentary.

Range: To 1200m n of Orinoco; to 1900m s of Orinoco. Mts. of ne Anzoátegui, Sucre, and n Monagas (*refulgens*); se Sucre s to Delta Amacuro; generally in Bolívar and ne Amazonas (*fissilis*); rest of Amazonas (*orenocensis*). E of Andes from e Colombia to e Bolivia, ne Argentina, and the Guianas.

Lepidopyga

Much like *Amazilia* but bill slightly decurved, plumage uniform green; scrub, edge, young second growth, and arid habitats.

Shining-green Hummingbird

PLATE 29

Lepidopyga goudoti   Tucusito Pico Curvo

Identification: 3.6″ (9.1cm). 4g. Bill slightly decurved (0.7″, 18mm), lower mandible pinkish tipped black (not conspic.). ♂: above shining green, head and underparts glittering golden green, chin bluish (or bluish green and somewhat glittering in Andes); *tail distinctly forked*, central feathers bronze green like back, rest of tail blue black. ♀: above shining bronze green like ♂, *below dingy white thickly speckled green, sides green,* belly grayish white, tail as in ♂ but less forked.

Sim. species: Easily confused. ♂ closely resembles smaller *Chlorostilbon* emeralds (see esp. Blue-tailed, Green-tailed, and Red-billed); Blue-chinned Sapphire has rounded tail; other sim. spp. (several *Amazilia*) have rufous on upper or under tail coverts (see esp. Steely-vented and Copper-rumped). ♀ has even fewer distinctive marks than ♂ but fewer sim. spp. in range. Cf. esp. ♀ Golden-tailed Sapphire (whiter below, golden rufous tail), ♀ Violet-headed Hummingbird (much smaller), and ♀ White-chinned Sapphire (contrasting reddish copper rump, blue black tail).

Voice: Song a thin, waiflike *twee-dee*, 2d note higher; reminiscent of song of Green-bellied Hummingbird but shorter.

Behavior: Often behaves as a territorialist, defending small patches of low nectar reward flowers at low to moderate hts. Occas. gathers with others at large flowering trees. Spends much time gleaning tiny insects and spiders from twigs, branches, and undersides of foliage, and hawks tiny flying insects. Oct–Mar breeding (Colombia), small cup nest of pale plant down and cobwebs and decorated on outside, 1–1.5m up[148].

Status and habitat: Fairly common to common resident in open dry to moderately humid forest borders, drier woodland, shrubby or partially cleared areas with trees, dry scrub, and degraded vegetation. As with hummers of drier habitats, shows marked seasonal movements. Commonest in dry and arid habitats near sea level in Zulia; scarce and local or irreg. in humid zones in mts.

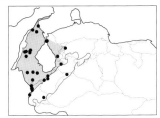

Range: To 1300m (mostly below 300m; once to 1600m?). Nw end of Sierra de Perijá, and ne Zulia e of Maracaibo Basin (*zuliae*); sw Zulia, nw Táchira n along w base of Andes to nw Trujillo and nw Lara (Quebrada Arriba); 1 specimen (error or vagrant?) reportedly from e slope of Andes in nw Barinas (*phaeochroa*); 1 in nw Táchira (?). N Colombia.

Hylocharis

Straight bill broad at base, mostly bright red with black tip; ♀♀ duller than ♂♂.

Rufous-throated Sapphire

PLATE 29

Hylocharis sapphirina   Zafiro Gargantirrufo

Identification: 3.5″ (8.9cm). 4.1g. Bill straight (0.6″, 15mm), *entirely bright red with black tip* (or only lower mandible red—♀). ♂: above dark shining green, *chin and small area around bill rufous* (rufous usually conspic.), throat glittering dark blue (usually looks black), rest of underparts green, *under tail coverts rufous*, central tail feathers purplish copper, *rest chestnut edged black.* ♀: above shining green, *chin rufous*, rest of underparts whitish more or less spotted blue on throat and green on rest of underparts; *under tail coverts rufous, tail as in ♂ but outer feathers tipped pale gray.* Imm ♂: much like ♀ but no rufous on under tail coverts. Some imms. may lack rufous on chin.

Sim. species: ♂'s red bill and rufous chin are distinctive if seen, but both marks less distinctive on ♀. Cf. Golden-tailed Sapphire which may overlap in extreme ne; also ♀ White-chinned Sapphire which lacks rufous on chin and under tail coverts.

Voice: Song a *high* ser. of 4–7 pinging notes, *sping! . . sping! . . sping! . . .*, ca. 4 notes in 2 sec, repeated every few sec[61].

Behavior: Sometimes feeds low at flowering shrubs or vines at forest edges but more often seen perched high. Occurs alone at scattered canopy flowers and freq. gathers with other hummers at large canopy flowering trees. Typically aggressive and territorial. Hawks and gleans insects and has been seen hovering in front of orchids, perhaps to take insects. Reported feeding at flowers of Leguminosae, Rutaceae, Rubiaceae, Myrtaceae, Loranthaceae, Passifloraceae, and Bromeliaceae. In Brazil, cup nest of plant fiber; lined with soft seed down, often decorated on outside with lichens; on horizontal branch 3–10m up[148].

Status and habitat: Uncommon resident (overlooked?) along humid forest borders and in canopy of lowland forest; also shrubby clearings, tall trees in forest clearings, and occas. in drier, more open areas with scrubby trees. Unpredictable in occurrence, apparently because of marked seasonal movements.

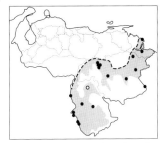

Range: To ca. 500m (once to 1850m, Cerro Roraima). N Delta Amacuro and s generally in Amazonas and Bolívar. E Colombia to ne Bolivia, ne Argentina, Amaz. Brazil (n Amazonas?), and the Guianas. Se Brazil.

White-chinned Sapphire

PLATE 29

Hylocharis cyanus   Zafiro Cabecimorado

Identification: 3.5″ (8.9cm). 3.6g. Bill straight (0.6″, 15mm), *blood red with black tip* (or only lower mandible red—♀). ♂: head, throat, and chest dark violet

blue (usually looks black), rest of upperparts dark green, *upper tail coverts reddish copper contrasting sharply with forked blue black tail*; chin with a few tiny white feathers (amt. of white varies; many individuals have almost none), rest of underparts dark green, under tail coverts steel blue. ♀: above green, *upper tail coverts reddish copper contrasting with forked steel blue tail, outer tail feathers tipped gray*; below grayish white thickly speckled blue on throat and green on breast; belly and *under tail coverts mostly gray* (some birds mostly gray below, mottled green on sides).
Sim. species: ♂'s marks are red bill and contrasting coppery rump band; white chin (only a few feathers) is diagnostic but can rarely be seen in field and is not always present. Cf. more confusing ♀ to ♀ Rufous-throated Sapphire which has rufous chin and under tail coverts. Also cf. ♀ Golden-tailed Sapphire which has golden rufous tail. ♀ Shining-green Hummingbird and several emeralds (White-chested and Versicolored) are superficially sim., as is smaller ♀ Violet-headed Hummingbird.
Voice: ♂♂ advertise from solitary song perches. Song a high, insectlike ser. of squeaking phrases, *ca-seék . . .* or *tweeh-chit . . .* or other variation, given at rate of 2–3 phrases/sec for 30 sec to several mins from a fairly high, bare twig, usually in a rather open area in or beneath tree crown.
Behavior: Takes nectar at a wide variety of flowering trees, shrubs, and vines from near eye level to treetops by hovering at flowers. Reg. gathers with other hummers in canopy of large flowering trees where bickers constantly in attempts to maintain territories with flowers. Also occas. hawks and gleans tiny insects. Small cup nest of plant fibers, cobwebs, and lichen on horizontal branch 1.5–4m up[148].
Status and habitat: Fairly common resident and short-distance migrant. Pops. highly dynamic, being locally numerous one month, absent the next. Moist to humid forest, borders of forest, second growth, and light or disturbed woodland; also gallery forest in drier regions. Generally *spotty and local* n of Orinoco.

Range: To 600m n of Orinoco; to 1250m s of Orinoco. Maracaibo Basin, Zulia, w base of Andes from n Táchira n to Trujillo (Mendoza); e base of Andes in Táchira, Barinas, and Portuguesa; Coastal Cordillera in n Aragua (sight)[596] and Distr. Federal; Sucre and ne Monagas (sight)[58]; Delta Amacuro[343]; throughout Amazonas and Bolívar (*viridiventris*). E Colombia to n Bolivia, Amaz. Brazil, and the Guianas; se Brazil.

Chrysuronia

Strong sexual dimorphism with ♂♂ very bright, ♀♀ dull; size and proportions otherwise much as in *Amazilia*.

Golden-tailed Sapphire   PLATE 29
Chrysuronia oenone   Colibrí Cola de Oro
Identification: 3.7" (9.4cm). ♂ 5.3g. ♀ 4.8g. Bill slightly decurved (0.8", 20mm), black, lower mandible reddish. ♂: *head and throat glittering blue* (but usually looks black in field), back shining green, upper tail coverts reddish copper, *tail golden copper* (usually looks pale rufous in field), very slightly forked (rounded when spread), breast and belly green, under tail coverts gray brown. ♀: very different; head and upperparts shining green, upper tail coverts reddish copper, *tail golden copper* (usually looks rufous like that of ♂) outer feathers narrowly tipped gray, *underparts white speckled greenish along sides of throat, chest, and breast*; under tail coverts gray brown. Imm. ♂: like ♀ but usually with flecks of blue on throat.
Sim. species: ♂ often looks mostly blackish in field. Watch for rufous tail (either sex). ♀ from below is dingy and confusing. ♀ Shining-green Hummingbird is greener below with dark tail. In w part of range cf. ♀ Rufous-tailed Hummingbird which is more or less green below (disked green on lower underparts); also cf. Glittering-throated Emerald, White-chinned Sapphire, and ♀ White-vented Plumeleteer.
Voice: Song rather variable (each individual may have distinct repertoire) but often begins and ends with high squeak note. In Andes solitary ♂♂ perch on bare twig in treetop and sing a high-pitched, squeaky, and jerky song, i.e., *PEEK! pa-ta-la-peek-TEEK . . pa-ta-la-peek-TEEK*, or less patterned *pzeek, pazeek-TEEK-zeek* or more squeaky *cheek, ta'cher-E'keek ta-chee'E-keek . . .* and so on, sometimes without a clear break.
Behavior: In dry season gathers in nos. at large canopy flowering trees where both sexes spend much of time bickering and chasing other hummers in attempt to maintain small feeding territories with flowers. At other times rather solitary at flowers (i.e., *Palicourea*) from low along roadsides and light gaps inside forest to high in canopy. ♂♂ more likely to hold territories, ♀♀ more often trap-line. Both also hawk and glean tiny insects. ♂♂ sing most in early rainy season, May–Jul, either alone or in small loose groups.
Status and habitat: Common resident in humid forest borders, second growth, light woodland, coffee and cacao plantations, parks, and gardens, mostly in foothills and mts. In dry season one of commonest hum-

mers at flowering *Erythrina* trees in Andes and n cordilleras. Large and abrupt seasonal migration s over Portachuelo Pass, Aragua, in Nov, northward in Apr–May to breed (M. Lentino). Seasonal movements elsewhere need documentation.
Range: To 1500m. Sierra de Perijá, Zulia; both sides of Andes from Táchira n to nw Lara; and generally in mts. from c Falcón and Yaracuy e to Sucre and n Monagas (*oenone*). Colombia to n Bolivia and Amaz. Brazil. Trinidad.

Polytmus

Decurved bill; rounded tail; pale green plumage often with white in tail; grasslands or open areas.

White-tailed Goldenthroat   PLATE 29
Polytmus guainumbi   Colibrí Gargantidorado
Identification: 3.8″ (9.7cm). 4.4g (1 ♀). Bill decurved (0.9″, 23mm), lower mandible pinkish. ♂: above *faded golden green*, crown tinged brownish, *cheeks dusky bordered above and below by white line*, underparts golden green (brighter than above), *tail very rounded, green with conspic. white tips; outermost feathers white at base* (shows in flight), outer web of outer tail feather white. ♀: like ♂ but somewhat spotted and mixed green and white below.
Sim. species: In open fields where it occurs, likely confused only with Green-tailed Goldenthroat which is smaller and shows *no white* in tail. Tepui Goldenthroat, mainly at higher el., is larger with black bill and much more white at base of tail.
Voice: Surprisingly loud, sharp *spit! . . spit!, spit! . . . spit! . . .* and so on in rapid, excited ser. while foraging.
Behavior: Chiefly a solitary trap-liner of scattered flowers or patches of low, inconspic. flowers and small flowering shrubs, where it hovers (does not cling) to feed. Also feeds extensively on tiny insects and spiders gleaned from foliage, twigs, stems, and tall grass. Occas. at a small *Erythrina* tree but not in groups at large flowering trees. Breeds Jun–Aug, Trinidad[175]; in w Guárico Oct–Nov[734]; cone-shaped, plant-down nest low in grass, weeds, or bushes, sometimes over water and usually rather exposed[175].
Status and habitat: Locally fairly common resident (some seasonal movement) in damp or marshy grass, dry weedy pastures and roadsides, and brushy gallery forest borders. Commonest in damp grass with a few shrubs, esp. in vicinity of water. One of only hummers (along with Blue-tailed Emerald or other *Polytmus*) likely in dry, mostly open savanna.

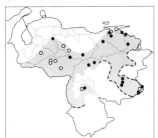

Range: To 200m n of Orinoco; to 1500m s of Orinoco. Generally e of Andes from w Apure, Barinas, and s Cojedes (sightings) e to e Sucre, Monagas, and Delta Amacuro; grasslands of Bolívar s to s end of Gran Sabana; Amazonas s to San Juan de Manapiare (*guainumbi*); 1 rec. from Dist. Federal may be an error. E Colombia to the Guianas and n Brazil (n of the Amazon); se Peru and e Bolivia to n Argentina; e Brazil. Trinidad.

Tepui Goldenthroat   PLATE 29
Polytmus milleri   Colibrí de los Tepuis
Identification: 4.3″ (10.9cm). 4.1–6.1g. Bill blackish, somewhat decurved (0.9″, 23mm). *Large hummingbird.* ♂: above coppery green, below pale (faded) golden green; white mark behind eye; *tail green (darker than upperparts), very rounded, prom. tipped white; basal third of outer tail feathers white* (conspic. in flight, less so when perched), under tail coverts green tipped white. ♀: like ♂ but underparts thickly spotted green and white, lower underparts grayish.
Sim. species: See White-tailed and Green-tailed goldenthroats, which occur mostly at lower el. (overlap locally in tepuis).
Voice: Loud ser. of *tsit* or *tizzie* notes while foraging.
Behavior: Like other *Polytmus*, mainly a solitary traplininer of grassy and scrubby areas where it spends much time hawking insects and feeding at small, isolated, and often inconspic. clumps of low scattered flowers. Stays low, does not reg. perch exposed to view, and because it often trap-lines flowers, is typically seen only briefly and can require patience to locate. Reported at flowers of low-growing, almost gd.-level plants, also Ericaceae, Myrtaceae, and Gesneriaceae. Cone-shaped nest lined with plant-down fibers and decorated with lichens and leaf bits; on small exposed fork of shrub, 0.5–1m up[148].
Status and habitat: Fairly common resident locally but shows marked seasonal movements. Dense, woody, heathlike savanna (e.g., vicinity of Monumento del Soldado Pionero in Gran Sabana), grassy areas with scattered shrubs, brushy gallery forest borders, and morichales. Esp. fond of thickets and isolated patches of shrubs in Gran Sabana. In general, replaces White-tailed Goldenthroat in higher el. savanna in tepui region. Most numerous in rainy season on Gran Sabana and above 1800m on Cerro Roraima (D. Ascanio).

Range: ENDEMIC. 300–2200m. Amazonas on Cerro Duida (elsewhere in Amazonas?); c and s Bolívar on Auyán-tepui, Cerro Jaua, Ptari-tepui, and Gran Sabana s to Cerro Roraima (prob. throughout from Auyán-tepui and Cerro Jaua eastward?). Prob. Guyana and Brazil.

Green-tailed Goldenthroat   PLATE 29
Polytmus theresiae   Garganta de Oro Coliverde
Identification: 3.4″ (8.6cm). 3.8g. Bill somewhat decurved (0.8″, 20mm), lower mandible pinkish tipped dusky. *Smallest of genus.* ♂: above bronzy green, below pale (faded) golden green, sometimes with some white showing through here and there; *short white mark behind eyes*; cheeks dusky, *belly and under tail coverts white or mostly white mixed green*; tail rounded, all bright green, extreme base of outer feathers white. ♀: like ♂ but *underparts white thickly spangled green, outer tail feathers tipped white*.
Sim. species: Often not easily told in field from larger White-tailed Goldenthroat. Look for latter's *white tail tips* and prom. white at base of tail. Also see Tepui Goldenthroat which mostly occurs at higher els.
Voice: Double note, *twit-twit*, and a long whinnying ser., *ting-ting-ting* . . . of up to 10 notes[694].
Behavior: Generally sim. to White-tailed Goldenthroat. Both sexes usually trap-line nectar resources and spend large amts. of time hawking and gleaning tiny insects.
Status and habitat: Uncommon to fairly common resident locally in brushy edges of sandy-belt forest and dry savanna with scattered bushes. Unlike allied White-tailed Goldenthroat, shows no particular affinity for water.

Range: To 300m. Nw Amazonas (sight, Pto. Ayacucho) s to Cerro Duida and Río Negro (*leucorrhous*); only lower Orinoco rec. is 1 taken in 1988 (M. Lentino) at Isla Cocuica (Caño Macareo), Delta Amacuro (*theresiae*). E Colombia to the Guianas, ne Peru, and spottily in Amaz. Brazil.

Leucippus

Med.-sized, dull-plumaged hummers; mostly specialists of arid, scrubby, transitional, or marginal habitats (incl. young river isls.); slightly decurved bill.

Buffy Hummingbird   PLATE 29
Leucippus fallax   Colibrí Anteado
Identification: 3.5″ (8.9cm). Bill slightly decurved (0.8″, 20mm), dusky with pinkish lower mandible. *Drab hummer of arid scrub. Prom. black eyes*; narrow whitish eyering broader behind eye. Overall has *pale, faded appearance.* ♂: above dull faded green, *underparts pale cinnamon* becoming white on belly; tail

rounded, central tail feathers dull green, rest dull green with dusky subterminal band and *conspic. white tips*. ♀: sim. but even dingier. Or both sexes sim. but paler (*richmondi*).
Sim. species: Unique in arid habitats.
Voice: Sings alone or sometimes a few ♂♂ sing from nearby perches (leks?). Variable songs, given from a low or high perch, incl. a sharp, lip-smacking *tsik, tsuk-tic-suk, tsik-sik,* . . . often long sustained; or *tslik, slweeit* over and over; or *calúp, cheek, calúp cheek, eee-chevy chevy* . . . ; or *chaVEET!, chit, chaVEET! chat.* . . . Much individual variation in song; ♂♂ may have unique repertoires but share song patterns.
Behavior: A characteristic hummer of arid desert scrub. Usually solitary and aggressive, defending patches of flowers, e.g., agave, Cactaceae, and *Stachytarpheta.* Also takes juice and flesh of *Armatocereus* cactus fruit; when nectar or fruit is unavailable, feeds heavily on insects[395]. Typically confiding; forages rather low and mostly perches low. In display ♂♂ climb high, then arc downward in semipendulum, producing winnowing sound (mechanical) and calling *tz'-chip, tz'chip, tz'chip.* . . . *brr-brr-brr* as descend through bottom of dive. Nest is usual hummingbird cup saddled on branch 0.6–2m up[395].
Status and habitat: Resident and short-distance migrant; pops. highly dynamic. Common in xerophytic areas incl. cactus and thorn scrub, thorny woodland, dry forest, and mangroves. Numerous in rainy May–Jul months around Coro; abundant near Cerro Santa Ana on Paraguaná Pen. in Feb and generally the commonest hummer in deserts of n Falcón (Hilty). In nw Sucre breeds in coastal arid thorn scrub May–Sep (occas. to Nov) rainy season and migrates inland into taller thorn forest during late Nov–mid Apr dry season. Other hummers move into thorn forest during rainy season when Buffys are absent[395].

Range: To 550m (prob. higher). Nw Zulia e through c Falcón (*cervina*); Lara (s to El Tocuyo) e through arid n base of Coastal Cordillera from Carabobo (Pto. Cabello) to Distr. Federal at Macuto (*fallax*); ne Anzoátegui and nw Sucre; Islas Margarita, Coche, Cubagua, La Tortuga, and Chimana Grande (*richmondi*). Ne Colombia.

Amazilia

Large genus; avg. hummers in many respects (e.g., size, proportions, and med.-length, virtually straight bill); sexes sim. (or nearly so); lack ornate plumage; widespread, often common; a good "yardstick" genus useful for comparison with other genera. Recently separated into 4 genera, *Agyrtia, Polyerata, Saucerottia,* and *Amazilia,* based on minor differences in morphology and plumage[148].

White-chested Emerald
PLATES 29, 31

Amazilia chionopectus   Diamante Colidorado
Identification: 3.5″ (8.9cm). 4.7g. Bill *black*, almost straight (0.7″, 18mm). Crown and sides of head glittering green, rest of upperparts shining coppery green becoming *reddish copper on upper tail coverts; below white, sides of throat and breast green, sometimes the speckling extending toward center of breast;* tail dull bronze green to dull olive, outer feathers with dark subterminal band (visible from above or below).
Sim. species: See Versicolored and Plain-bellied emeralds and ♀ Golden-tailed Sapphire.
Voice: Song a high, buzzy, and squeaky *chu'lénk* or *chu'le'e'e*, several times in reg. or irreg. ser. (Hilty); a rather low, rough *ja-ja-ja-ja—gee jit*, a bit harsh and buzzy[61].
Behavior: A modest-looking hummer that feeds mostly low at scattered forest-edge flowers of vines and shrubs, trap-lines inside forest, or visits mass-flowering canopy trees (i.e., *Inga*). Not notably aggressive. Will visit feeders.
Status and habitat: Resident. Uncommon to seasonally common (nos. highly variable) along humid forest borders, disturbed areas, mangroves, scattered trees in open areas, even weedy fields.

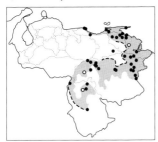

Range: To 100m n of Orinoco; to 500m s of Orinoco (sight to 950m, Sierra de Lema). E Miranda e through Anzoátegui to Sucre, Monagas, and Delta Amacuro; s of Orinoco in n Amazonas (s to San Juan de Manapiare; once to Río Cunucunuma near Cerro Duida); generally in n Bolívar from lower Río Caura, lower Río Paragua, and Sierra de Imataca s to upper Río Cuyuní (*chionopectus*). The Guianas. Trinidad.
Note: Has been placed in genus *Agyrtia*[148].

Plain-bellied Emerald
PLATE 31

Amazilia leucogaster   Diamante Ventriblanco
Identification: 3.5″ (8.9cm). 4.6g. Bill dusky (0.9″, 23mm), *lower mandible pinkish tipped black. Plain little hummer* of ne lowlands. Above shining golden green to coppery green, back, rump, and upper tail coverts shot with bronzy rufous; head, sides of throat, and sides of breast glittering green, flanks green, *central throat and median underparts pure white, sharply set off from green sides of throat;* incomplete greenish band across chest; central tail feathers bronze green,

rest blue black (tail looks *very dark* in field). ♀'s outer tail feathers tipped gray.
Sim. species: White-chested Emerald is very sim. but has all-black bill, contrasting reddish copper band across lower rump, and dusky subterminal band across tail. Both spp. often show irreg. amt. of dusky green extending toward center of chest. Also cf. Versicolored and Glittering-throated emeralds.
Behavior: Solitary and territorial, much like others of genus. Feeds at various hts. but often fairly low. Elsewhere has been reported at a wide variety of flowers. In Suriname visits flowering *Erythrina* in coffee plantations along coast. Reg. hawks and gleans tiny insects. Small cup nest on horizontal branch of *Avicennia* mangrove, 0.6m above water[253].
Status and habitat: Humid forest borders, mangroves (esp. *Avicennia*), second growth, and partially cleared areas; also grass and thickets near large morichales (*Mauritia* palms). Known only from a small no. of specimens; only Monagas rec. is 1 seen at Caño Colorado, 5 Mar 1994 (P. Boesman).

Range: To 250m. E Monagas (sight) s to Delta Amacuro (Pedernales; Capure; Isla Tobeida; Tobejuba) (*leucogaster*). The Guianas and n Brazil.
Note: By some placed in genus *Polyerata*[148]. One rec. from El Trueño, nc Bolívar, may be an error.

Versicolored Emerald
PLATES 29, 31

Amazilia versicolor   Diamante de Capucha Azul
Identification: 3.3″ (8.4cm). 4.1g. Bill black with *mostly pink lower mandible* (0.7″, 18mm). *Head and neck glittering blue green to pale green,* sides of head dull green, rest of upperparts shining bronzy green, *below white, sides of throat and breast somewhat spotted green,* tail dull bronzy olive with dusky subterminal band and narrow pale gray tip. Or *crown, sides of head and neck, and spots on sides of breast glittering blue (hollandi).* Some birds n of Ventuari (*milleri*) also *tinged bluish on head, neck, and sides.*
Sim. species: Very sim. White-chested Emerald has *all-black bill,* reddish copper band across lower rump, and all-green head (no blue). In hand, tail brighter bronzy green (not dull olive). Also see Plain-bellied and rare Sapphire-spangled emeralds.
Behavior: Much as other *Amazilia.* Several gather and argue with other spp. at large canopy flowering trees, esp. *Inga, Vochysia,* and *Calliandra,* or scatter and defend small patches of low flowers (i.e., *Buddleja*) along shrubby borders. Reported feeding from a wide variety of flowers, esp. those with open inflorescenses or short corollas. Also reg. hawks and gleans

tiny insects. Nest in Brazil a plant-down cup like others of genus; mostly 1–6m up[148].
Status and habitat: Locally common resident but nos. show strong seasonal fluctuations. Humid forest borders, shrubby semiopen areas, and savannas with open woodland or scattered trees. Scarce Dec and Jan (dry months) near Pto. Ayacucho, but common Jun–Jul (rainy months).

Range: To 1700m (most recs. below 700m). Generally in s and e Apure (Río Meta), nw Bolívar, and n Amazonas s to Río Ventuari and Yavita-Pimichín (*milleri*); Amazonas s of Río Ventuari (except where occupied by previous subsp.); s Amazonas and n Bolívar e to Sierra de Imataca and s to Paurai-tepui (*hollandi*). E Colombia and the Guianas s to n Amaz. Brazil; n Bolivia e across ne Argentina to se Brazil.
Note: By some placed in genus *Agyrtia*[148].

Glittering-throated Emerald   PLATE 29
Amazilia fimbriata   Diamante Gargantiverde
Identification: 3.3″ (8.4cm). 5g. Bill straight (0.7″, 18mm) to slightly decurved near tip; black with lower mandible pinkish red tipped black. *Widespread, dingy-looking hummer* with *prom. black eyes* and narrow white eyering (or at least conspic. white spot behind eyes). ♂: above bronzy green (head rather pale green), throat glittering green (not conspic.), sides green, *belly white extending as a narrow wedge of white up center of underparts to mid. breast*; tail bronzy green; or central tail feathers blackish (*obscuricauda*, *fimbriata*). ♀: duller; *wedge of white extends to base of throat which is disked green.*
Sim. species: Despite its name, a dull, undistinguished hummingbird. Best mark is narrow wedge of white up central and lower underparts. ♀♀ are esp. dingy and faded looking. See ♀ Blue-chinned Sapphire, White-chested Emerald, Versicolored Emerald, and ♀ Shining-green Hummingbird.
Voice: Song a buzzy, pulsating *tsing . . tsing . . tsing . . .*, very penetrating (insectlike); in flight or territorial defense a high, thin *tsiii, tsiii, tsii-tii-ti'ti'ti'ti'tititititi*, descending and trilled at end.
Behavior: Like most others of genus, territorial and aggressive and often gathers in nos. in canopy of large flowering trees, e.g., *Inga, Erythrina, Vochysia*, etc. Otherwise feeds at almost any ht. on a wide variety of native and introd. flowers of trees, shrubs (e.g., *Lantana* in urban areas), vines, and herbs; also trap-lines nectar and often hawks and gleans tiny insects. Reg. sits in open on relatively conspic. perches. Lichen-covered cup nest on twig fork, branch, or *Cecropia* petiole,

1–4m up; Jan and May–Nov nests[115,186]; 2 nests, Feb, e Venez. (Hilty); yr-round breeding in Suriname[253].
Status and habitat: Widespread and common resident along dry to humid forest borders, gallery forest borders, shrubby second growth, scattered trees in partially open areas, and parks, gardens, and around habitations. Abundant in vicinity of Tucupita, Delta Amacuro. Everywhere it occurs, generally one of commonest hummers.

Range: To 1300m. Virtually throughout except Zulia. E. Falcón, e Lara, and Carabobo e to Sucre, Monagas, Delta Amacuro, and n Bolívar (*elegantissima*); e Táchira, w Apure, Portuguesa, and Cojedes to sw Guárico (*obscuricauda*); n and c Amazonas (s to San Fernando de Atapabo but prob. throughout); ne Bolívar from Sierra de Imataca southward (*fimbriata*). E of Andes from Colombia and the Guianas to s Bolivia and s Brazil.
Note 1: By some placed in genus *Polyerata*[148].
Note 2: Subsp. *obscuricauda* not separable from *fimbriata*[148].
Note 3: Indigo-capped Hummingbird, *A. cyanifrons*, of Colombian Andes could occur in Táchira. ♂ mainly green with deep indigo blue crown, brownish rump, and slightly forked blue black tail. ♀ duller. Open woodland, shrubby clearings, and cultivated areas.
Note 4: Táchira Emerald, *A. distans*[403], is now believed to be a hybrid *Hylocharis cyanus* x *A. fimbriata*[220,782]. 3.3″ (8.4cm). Bill black, lower mandible swollen at base, reddish tipped black. Much like Glittering-throated Emerald but *forecrown glittering blue* turning darker shining blue green on hindcrown; sides of neck to breast glittering blue (not green), throat green spotted and scaled white, *belly grayish* (not white), this extending up central underparts somewhat; 1 ♂ specimen from Burgua (300m), se Táchira, 17 Jul 1954; unverified sightings near San Juan de Colon.

Sapphire-spangled Emerald   PLATE 31
Amazilia lactea   Diamante Pechizafiro
Identification: 3.5″ (8.9cm). 4–4.6g. Bill black (0.7″, 18mm), lower mandible pink tipped black. Few records. Above bronzy green, *throat glittering violet blue (feathers pale-edged so often looks dull gray to sooty gray), white central underparts extending as broad line to belly and under tail coverts*, sides green, central tail feathers bronzy green becoming darker near tip, rest blue black.
Sim. species: Rather dull and confusing. Recalls Glittering-throated Emerald as both have white median underparts. Note Sapphire-spangled's scaly blue throat. Also cf. White-chested Emerald (reddish cop-

per upper tail coverts), Versicolored Emerald (bluish crown), and ♀ White-chinned and Golden-chinned sapphires (both spotted with green below).
Behavior: Poorly known in Venez. Elsewhere much as in other *Amazilia*. In se Peru often forages rather low at disturbed vegetation.
Status and habitat: Humid forest; river borders, and second growth. In Venez. known only from a small no. of specimens, mostly from slopes of Auyán-tepui, near Río Paragua, and headwaters of upper Río Caura.

Range: 300–1400m (most recs. 1100–1400m). C and s Bolívar from Auyán-tepui (1100m) and lower and mid. Río Paragua (several localities) s to Cerro Sarisariñama on Meseta de Jaua at 1400m (*zimmeri*). Spottily in e Peru, n Bolivia, and e Brazil.
Note: By some placed in genus *Polyerata*[148].

Steely-vented Hummingbird   PLATE 29
Amazilia saucerrottei   Amazilia Verde-Azul
Identification: 3.5″ (8.9cm). 4.5g. Bill black (0.7″, 18mm), lower mandible pinkish, tip dusky. *Only* in Andes and Sierra de Perijá. Above dark shining green, *narrow band of reddish copper across upper tail coverts*, below glittering green, *under tail coverts steel blue edged pale gray*, tail slightly forked, blue black. Or sim. but tail brighter blue (*warscewiczi*).
Sim. species: *Often confused* with Copper-rumped Hummingbird which has brownish to rufous under tail coverts and *usually* (but not always) much more brownish to copper color on rump and upper tail coverts. Note that, for the most part, the 2 spp. do not overlap in range. Also see ♂ White-chinned Sapphire, Shining-green and Green-bellied hummingbirds, and smaller Blue-tailed Emerald.
Voice: When excited a rapid ser. of *chit* notes, descending and trilled. Song in Costa Rica a buzzy, squeaky *bzz WEEP-wup*[706].
Behavior: Occurs alone at scattered low flowers or gathers in nos. with other spp. at large flowering trees such as *Erythrina* and *Inga* during Jan–Apr dry season, where pugnacious and territorial. Feeds heavily at *Heliconia* flowers in early wet season in Barinas; also at flowers of many other trees, shrubs, vines, epiphytes, and herbs. Occas. punctures bases of long corollas (esp. Rubiaceae) to steal nectar. Reg. hawks and gleans tiny insects. ♂ ♂ sing alone (no leks) from open perch. In Costa Rica, downy cup nest heavily decorated with lichens, 2–7m up[706].
Status and habitat: Common resident, but nos. vary seasonally. Dry to humid forest borders, coffee

plantations, lighter woodland, shrubby areas, and gardens.

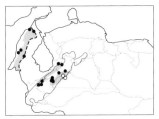

Range: Mostly 400–1500m (recorded 60–3000?m). Sierra de Perijá, Zulia (*warscewiczi*); both slopes of Andes in Mérida and Trujillo (*braccata*); e slope (many sight recs.) in nw Barinas (*braccata?*). Nicaragua and Costa Rica; Colombia.
Note: By some placed in genus *Saucerottia*[148].

Copper-rumped Hummingbird   PLATE 29
Amazilia tobaci   Amazilia Bronceada Coliazul
Identification: 3.4″ (8.6cm). 4.7g. Bill dusky (0.7″, 18mm), lower mandible pinkish tipped dusky. Plumage notably variable. Above generally dark shining green, lower back and rump bronzy brown to smoky cinnamon brown, underparts glittering green, *under tail coverts bronzy brown to rufous brown* (all subspp.), tail forked, very dark shining blue. Or sim. but back reddish copper, brighter than above (*caudata, aliciae*); or generally darker, upperparts green, almost no copper on rump (*monticola*); or rump and upper tail coverts vaguely tinged grayish (*caurensis*).
Sim. species: In area of overlap much like Steely-vented Hummingbird, but Copper-rumped has *rufous to brown under tail coverts* (never blue black) and *usually* more extensive rufous brown on tail coverts and rump (reddish copper of Steely-vented always confined only to narrow band on upper tail coverts). Also see Green-bellied Hummingbird.
Voice: Song a high, thin *air-ree-ca* (last note much lower) with delicate, almost mischievous quality, as if emanating from an elf or pixie, sometimes several in succession. Variations incl. *eet . . spit, de-de-wit* (*de* notes very high pitched); rapid chipping when foraging.
Behavior: A feisty and familiar little hummer. Pugnacious and territorial and more likely to be seen around hotels, flower gardens, and residential areas in Coastal Cordillera than any other hummingbird. Very aggressive; may dominate hummer spp. larger than itself, and even attacks wasps and bees. Feeds high or low at a wide range of flowers of trees (e.g., *Inga, Calliandra, Erythrina, Tabebuia*), shrubs, vines, and herbs, both native and introd. Hovers and hawks flying insects, and gleans from bark, twigs, foliage, and spiderwebs. Downy cup nest on twig or branch, usually not too high.
In Trinidad breeding reported Oct–Jul but mainly Jan–Mar[175].
Status and habitat: Common and widespread in some of most densely settled parts of country, incl. Caracas. Found in parks, gardens, residential areas, almost anywhere there are suitable flowers; fairly dry to humid zones. Also coffee plantations, humid forest borders,

second growth, and partially cleared and bushy areas. Rec. only sporadically (absent Mar; May–Jul; Oct) at Hato Masaguaral, Guárico[734]. Migrates into thorn forest May–Oct rainy season (to breed?) in w Sucre[395].

Range: To 1800m n of Orinoco; to 1700m s of Orinoco. Foothills of c Falcón, Lara (w to Cerro El Cerrón), and Yaracuy (*monticola*); n cordilleras from Carabobo to Miranda; w of Andes in w Táchira (Seboruco) and w Mérida (La Azulita); e of Andes from e Táchira (Petrolea; Burgua), w Apure, nw Barinas, Portuguesa, Cojedes, and Guárico to se Anzoátegui (*feliciae*); mts. of Sucre, Monagas, and Isla Patos (*caudata*); Isla Margarita (*aliciae*); nc Amazonas (s to Cerros Sipapo, Yavi, and Camani) and much of Bolívar s to Cerro Roraima (*caurensis*). Trinidad and Tobago.
Note: By some placed in genus *Saucerottia*[148].

Green-bellied Hummingbird   PLATE 29
Amazilia viridigaster   Amazilia Colimorada
Identification: 3.5″ (8.9cm). 3.8g. Bill black (0.7″, 18mm), lower mandible pinkish with dusky tip. Above and below mainly shining green, *lower back, rump, and upper tail coverts dull smoky brown*, belly dull bronzy brown, *under tail coverts reddish brown* (all subspp.), *tail dark bronzy purple to reddish bronze* (usually looks dark in field).
Sim. species: Within limited Venez. range, 2-toned appearance (green foreparts, smoky brown to dusky rearparts) is distinctive. See Steely-vented and Shining-green hummingbirds and Golden-tailed and White-chinned sapphires.
Voice: Dainty song, almost a mirror image of song of Copper-rumped Hummingbird, a high, thin, pixielike *dee-de-teet* (last note much higher), sometimes repeated several times in rapid succession; also gives numerous variations.
Behavior: Like most other *Amazilia*, rather pugnacious and territorial. Feeds alone at small patches of low roadside flowers of shrubs, vines, and herbs, or gathers with other hummers in small to large flowering trees incl. *Inga, Erythrina*, and *Quararibea* in w Táchira.

Status and habitat: Resident in humid forest borders, light open woodland, second growth, and coffee plantations. There are strong seasonal fluctuations in nos. Fairly common Jan–Feb in e Táchira (near Petrolea).
Range: 200–2100m. W slope of Andes in Táchira and sw Mérida; e slope in Táchira and Barinas n to Santa Bárbara (*iodura*). E Colombia (e slope of Andes).
Note: Formerly incl. Copper-tailed Hummingbird (*A. cupreicauda*). By some placed in genus *Saucerottia*[148].

Copper-tailed Hummingbird
Amazilia cupreicauda   Amazilia Colibronceada
Identification: 3.5″ (8.9cm). 3.8g. Bill black (0.7″, 18mm), lower mandible pinkish with dusky tip. Essentially sim. to Green-bellied Hummingbird but *tail mostly rufous* turning bronzy violet near tip (more rufous in *cupreicauda*).
Sim. species: Two-toned appearance (green foreparts and rufous tail) distinctive. See White-chinned Sapphire.
Behavior: On Cerro de la Neblina only observed inside forest, often gleaning insects from bromeliads. Territorial and usually solitary at patches of flowers low along roadsides on Sierra de Lema. Guyana nest 21 Feb; 3m up in small tree[670].
Status and habitat: Resident in humid forest and forest borders on Sierra de Lema (1400m) where nos. erratic and inconsistent from yr to yr, esp. from Dec to Mar; more numerous Jun–Jul (Hilty). One of commonest birds in humid forest, Dec–Apr, at 750m on Cerro de la Neblina, but only scattered individuals at 1250, 1400, and 1800m[801].

Range: 60–2000m (most recs. above 750m). S Amazonas on Cerro Duida (*duidae*), Sierra de Unturán, and Cerro de la Neblina (*laireti*); c and s Bolívar from mid. Río Caura (Salto Pará) and Río Cuyuní (El Dorado) southward (*cupreicauda*). Tepuis from nw Brazil to w Guyana (Cerro Roraima).
Note: Previously regarded as a subsp. of Green-bellied Hummingbird (*A. viridigaster*)[403]. By some placed in genus *Saucerottia*[148].

Rufous-tailed Hummingbird   PLATE 29
Amazilia tzacatl   Amazilia Colirrufa
Identification: 3.6″ (9.1cm). 5g. Bill straight (0.8″, 20mm), *lower mandible mostly pink* tipped dusky. Only in w Venez. ♂: above green with slightly forked, *all dark rufous tail*; throat and chest glittering green (often not very bright), lower underparts dingy gray mixed green. ♀: throat and chest duller, little or no glitter.

Sim. species: Note *distrib.* of this bird. Rufous tail is distinctive given a good look, but cf. Green-bellied Hummingbird (barely overlaps) which is all dark below and has darker tail. Also cf. ♂ and ♀ Golden-tailed Sapphire, both with golden rufous tail.

Voice: Song in w Mérida colorless, lisping 2-noted *tseee-tseet*; 2d note slightly stronger; repeated every 5 sec. for up to several minutes. Call a low *chup* or *chut*, sometimes in ser.[706].

Behavior: A generalist that feeds at a wide variety of mostly low flowers, but also gathers with other hummers in large canopy flowering trees (e.g., *Inga, Erythrina*). Typically very aggressive and territorial at rich nectar resources and bickers almost constantly with other hummers as it guards a favorite patch of flowers. Also hawks tiny insects and gleans from bark, twigs, foliage, and spiderwebs. A characteristic bird of gardens, dooryards, and cultivated areas. Downy cup much like others of genus; often decorated with lichen and moss; in Costa Rica nests 1–6m up on slender, horizontal, and fairly open twig; yr-round breeding with dry-season peak[706].

Status and habitat: Fairly common to common resident in a variety of disturbed and regrowth habitats incl. coffee plantations, gardens, bushy second growth, and openings along moist to humid forest borders. Numerous in vicinity of La Azulita, Mérida.

Range: To 1700m. Sierra de Perijá, s Zulia, and w side of Andes from Táchira n to Zulia (Mene Grande) and c Lara at El Tocuyo and Carora (*tzacatl*). Ne Mexico to w Ecuador.

Note: By some placed in genus *Saucerottia*[148].

Chalybura

Large hummers; slightly decurved bill; large ample tail; sexes differ; ♂♂ with long silky white under tail coverts.

White-vented Plumeleteer   PLATE 29
Chalybura buffonii   Colibrí Grande Colinegro
Identification: ♂ 4.5" (11.4cm), 6.8g. ♀ 4.2" (10.7cm), 6.4g. Bill slightly decurved (1", 25mm), dusky. *Large.* ♂: above shining green, throat and chest glittering green, duller on rest of underparts; plumelike *under tail coverts puffy and silky white* (conspic.), *long ample forked tail mostly blue black* (central pr. of feathers dark olive). ♀: shining green above; *uniform gray below with conspic. puffy white under tail coverts*; tail dark green, shorter than in ♂, all but central pr. with wide dusky subterminal band and narrow gray tips to outer feathers.

Sim. species: White under tail coverts a good mark in either sex. Cf. ♀ to ♀ woodnymphs, ♀ Golden-tailed

Sapphire, ♀ White-necked Jacobin (dull ones), and smaller ♀ *Chlorostilbon* emeralds.

Behavior: Usually seen singly in lower story of woodland or along shady borders where feeds at scattered flowers by trap-lining, esp. shrubs such as *Hamelia, Palicourea, Malvaviscus*, and *Aphelandra*. Often behaves aggressively and holds territories at patches of flowers such as *Heliconia*. Gathers with other hummers at large canopy flowering trees where, because of its size, it can dominate other spp., but is not esp. territorial there, and often does not attend or remain there consistently. Reg. gleans tiny insects and spiders from foliage and twigs, occas. hawks. Breeds Mar–Jul in Colombia[260].

Status and habitat: Common resident in light open woodland, forest borders, coffee plantations, and shrubby clearings in humid foothills and mts. Some local migratory movements occur, and may concentrate near large flowering trees in dry season.

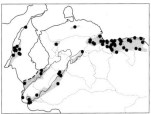

Range: To 1400m. Sierra de Perijá, Zulia, e to w Mérida (*buffoni*); both slopes of rest of Andes from Táchira to nw Lara, locally in Falcón (Sierra de San Luis), mts. of Yaracuy and n cordilleras from Carabobo to Miranda and n Guárico (*aeneicauda*). W Panama to w Ecuador.

Note: Subsp. *interior* synonymized with *buffonii*[148].

Adelomyia

Monotypic genus; small, plain, brownish hummer with hermitlike face pattern and inconspic. habits; rounded tail; forest understory; only in Andes.

Speckled Hummingbird   PLATE 29
Adelomyia melanogenys   Colibrí Serrano Gargantiazul
Identification: 3.3" (8.4cm). 3.8g. Bill short (0.5", 13mm). A hermit look-alike. Above dull bronze green tinged brown, *conspic. blackish cheek patch* bordered above by white postocular; underparts dirty white tinged buff, throat inconspic. speckled dusky, sides brownish, tail dusky brown tipped buff (or tipped whitish—*melanogenys*). Or central underparts whitish (*aeneosticta*).

Sim. species: Despite its name, throat speckling hard to see. Duller and browner than most hummers and often mistaken for a hermit (*Phaethornis*) hummingbird or a ♀ or imm. See larger Brown Violetear.

Voice: When foraging, a rapid, pebbly *dt'dk*, over and over, sometimes lengthened into rattley trills; perched birds give sim. but longer stuttering rattles, *td'd'd'd'd'd*, sometimes over and over for several min. One song a high chittery trill followed by a few exceedingly high, thin notes; also an irreg. ser. of very high, thin *seet* notes, ca. 2/sec; a 3d song type (?) a bubbly, squeezed ser. of high, thin notes that run upscale, slowing dramatically, i.e., *bu'bu'bu'te'te'ti'ti'ti'ti'ti'tic-tic-seea-seea,*

seea seea. Context of various songs needs investigation.

Behavior: A rather solitary little hummer, usually encountered low along shady roadside shrubbery or low inside forest. Mostly a trap-liner of nectar resource, esp. flowers of Gesneriaceae, Rubiaceae, and Ericaceae. Hovers or occas. clings when feeding at flowers; probes short-tubed flowers directly or steals nectar from holes along outer base of long-corolla flowers, e.g., *Passiflora, Fuchsia,* and some bromeliads. Does not gather with other hummers at flowering trees. Hanging nest beneath fern leaves[179].

Status and habitat: Common resident at mid. montane els. in humid and wet forest (cloud forest) and along forest borders. Shows only minor seasonal movements.

Range: 900–2500m. Sierra de Perijá, Zulia; Andes of Táchira n to s Lara (*melanogenys*); c Falcón (Sierra de San Luis), mts. of Yaracuy, and n cordilleras of Carabobo, Aragua, Distr. Federal, and Miranda (*aeneosticta*). Colombia s in Andes to nw Argentina.

Note: Subsp. *debellardiana* synonymized with *melanogenys*[148].

Heliodoxa

Large and robust; dark plumage; heavy bill straight or slightly decurved; feathers extend out over base of upper mandible giving conical or "*tapered*" shape to head; small white spot behind eyes; long wings reach almost to tail tip; tail longish, forked; most spp. sexually dimorphic; Venez. spp. mostly in highlands.

Gould's Jewelfront   PLATE 31
Heliodoxa aurescens   Colibrí Cuellicastaño

Identification: 4.5″ (11.4cm). 6g. Only s Amazonas. Bill straight (0.8″, 20mm) with feathers extending out over base of upper mandible and contributing to "coneheaded" shape. ♂: upperparts mainly green with narrow median line of violet up forecrown (rarely visible in field); chin black, throat glittering green, *broad crescent across chest orange rufous,* otherwise green below; central tail feathers green, *outer ones rufous chestnut tipped and edged bronze green.* ♀: much duller; differs in no median forecrown stripe; malar buff, throat buff spotted green, and narrow tip to outer tail feathers buff (best seen in hand).

Sim. species: Nothing sim. in its range. Either sex told by orange rufous chest band and rufous outer tail.

Behavior: A large but inconspic. hummer of shady forest interior. Not strongly aggressive or territorial; often trap-lines flowers at low to moderate hts. but also is reg. in canopy of large flowering trees (e.g., *Guararibea*) where seems to feed by "crashing" territories of smaller spp. Also hawks tiny insects and gleans foliage

in small open areas, becoming esp. active around mixed-spp. flocks.

Status and habitat: Uncommon resident in humid terra firme and várzea forest and white sandy soil forests in lowlands and foothills. There are several recs. (sight and specimens) in vicinity of San Carlos de Río Negro in sw Amazonas.

Range: To 1000m. C and s Amazonas (upper Río Asisa southward), c Bolívar (Auyán-tepui); se Bolívar (sight, 1 and 3 Jan 1980, 23 and 24km sw of Santa Elena de Uairén—C. Parrish). Se Colombia to n Bolivia and w Amaz. Brazil.

Note: Previously placed in genus *Polyplancta*[193].

Violet-fronted Brilliant   PLATE 30
Heliodoxa leadbeateri   Colibrí Frentiazul

Identification: ♂ 5″ (12.7cm), 7.9g. ♀ 4.3″ (10.9cm), 6.7g. Bill straight to slightly drooped at tip (0.9″, 23mm). Large, dark hummer. *Forehead slopes smoothly out toward bill.* ♂: above dark shining green with *glittering violet forecrown* (hard to see in field); *gorget and chest glittering green,* lower underparts dark green, *tail long and deeply forked,* central feathers bronzy olive, rest blackish. ♀: above dark green, forecrown glittering green; small white postocular spot, cheeks dusky, bordered below by rather *short white malar stripe (sometimes indistinct); throat white thickly disked green,* rest of underparts more or less mottled green with some white showing through; belly tinged buff; tail as in ♂, outer feathers narrowly tipped white. Or underparts tinged buff (*parvula*). Imm.: like ♀ but with large buff malar; underparts white heavily spotted green.

Sim. species: ♂ recalls ♂ Fork-tailed Woodnymph but latter is smaller with purple shoulders and belly. See Green-fronted Lancebill. ♀ easily confused with ♀ Violet-chested Hummingbird but latter is heavily mottled buff below and has distinctly decurved bill. Also cf. Lazuline Sabrewing.

Voice: Song an energetic ser. of low-pitched *chup* notes, singly, in couplets, or up to 6 in irreg. ser., often long sustained.

Behavior: Solitary, mostly 1–10m up inside forest or in small openings at forest edge. Trap-lines scattered flowers and aggressively defends small patches of nectar-rich flowers, mostly at low to med. hts. in forest, infreq. in canopy. Reg. hawks insects. Does not gather in groups at flowering trees but readily visits (trap-line) artificial feeders at forest edge (e.g., at Rancho Grande Biol. Station).

Status and habitat: Uncommon to locally fairly common resident (easily overlooked) in humid and wet forest (cloud forest), forest edges, older second growth, and shady coffee plantations.

Range: 500–2250m. Sierra de Perijá, Zulia; Andes from s Táchira to nw Lara at Cerro El Cerrón and se Lara at Hacienda Terrepaima (*parvula*); Falcón (Sierra de San Luis), mts. of Yaracuy, and n cordilleras from Carabobo to Distr. Federal and Miranda (*leadbeateri*). Colombia s in mts. to n Bolivia.

Velvet-browed Brilliant   PLATE 30
Heliodoxa xanthogonys   Colibrí Frentiverde
Identification: 4.2″ (10.7cm). 6.4g. Bill almost straight (0.8″, 20mm). *Dark*. ♂: crown black with narrow inconspic. glittering green stripe and prom. white postocular spot; rest of upperparts dark shining green, *gorget and chest glittering green* with small violet blue central patch; lower underparts dark green, *tail forked, blackish*. ♀: above dark shining green, cheeks dusky; white postocular spot and *narrow, sometimes ill-defined white malar stripe; underparts white thickly spotted dark green*, center of belly tinged buff, tail forked, blackish with narrow white tips on outer feathers. Imm.: like ♀ but with large buff malar.
Sim. species: Blue-fronted Lancebill, also dark, has long, needle bill and rounded tail. No other hummer in tepuis is so dark.
Voice: Occas. a nasal *squank* in flight.
Behavior: Forages alone, trap-lining flowers or attempting to guard small patches of flowers. Occas. 2–3 gather at flowering shrubs, vines (esp. Ericaceae), and epiphytes high in canopy or low along roadsides, where argue and behave territorially. Inside forest usually low at scattered vines. At times mostly ♂♂ or mostly ♀♀ are seen, suggesting sexes, at least seasonally, use different resources.
Status and habitat: Seasonally common resident in wet premontane forest and forest borders on tepuis. Usually above 1200m. Marked seasonal shifts of pop.

Range: 700–2000m (mostly 1200–1800m). Cerros throughout Amazonas; se Bolívar from Auyán-tepui and Sierra de Lema southward. W Guyana and adj. n Brazil.

Hylonympha

Much like *Thalurania* but with long, deeply forked tail (shorter in ♀).

Scissor-tailed Hummingbird   PLATE 31
Hylonympha macrocerca   Colibrí Tijereta
Identification: ♂ 7.5″ (19cm). ♀ 4.5″ (11.4cm). Bill black, slightly decurved (0.9″, 23mm). *Large, darkbodied, and long-tailed hummer*. ♂: forecrown glittering purple, rest of upperparts dark shining green, gorget and chest glittering green, lower underparts dark green, tail black, *very long* (5.1″, 13cm), *deeply forked*, at rest the long outer pr. of tail feathers often cross slightly. ♀: very different; above shining dark green, *below white thickly spotted green*, lower breast and belly buff, *tail long and deeply forked* (but not nearly as long as ♂'s), dark greenish black becoming steely blue black near tip; *outer web of outer pr. of tail feather cinnamon buff, subterminal band black*.
Sim. species: ♂ recalls ♂ Venezuelan Sylph but lacks its metallic violet and blue tail colors. ♀ Venezuelan Sylph lacks buff on lower underparts and outer tail. Also cf. ♀ Fork-tailed Woodnymph.
Voice: Song a short, pulsating burst, *tsi-tsi-tsip*, repeated every 2–3 sec by ♂ perched on bare twig; call a single penetrating *tsink!* at ca. 2-sec intervals.
Behavior: A rather solitary hummingbird. ♂♂ are most often seen perched on bare horizontal twigs in open lower or mid. story (ca. 3–13m up) inside forest. ♀♀ are more often seen low along forest borders and in second growth where they reg. fed at *Heliconia* and *Costus* flowers by hovering or clinging when feeding. Both feed at a variety of small flowers, incl. flowering bromeliads; also glean tiny insects from bark and leaves. ♂♂, at least seasonally, may behave more as territorialists, ♀♀ more as trap-liners.
Status and habitat: Fairly common resident inside and along borders of humid and wet forest, and esp. in overgrown or neglected coffee plantations and clearings where there are large *Heliconia* patches. Relatively sedentary. Almost entire pop. is found within small and poorly protected PN Península de Paria, where still relatively numerous but vulnerable.

Range: ENDEMIC. 900–1200m (Cerro Humo); 520–920m in areas eastward. Paria Pen. of Sucre from Cerros Azul, Humo, and Terrón de Azúcar eastward.

Sternoclyta

Large; recalls *Heliodoxa* but bill heavier and slightly decurved.

Violet-chested Hummingbird   PLATE 30
Sternoclyta cyanopectus   Colibrí Pechiazul
Identification: 4.5″ (11.4cm). ♂ 8.8g; ♀ 9.5g. *Bill long, notably stout, and somewhat decurved* (1.2″, 30mm). A large, robust hummer. ♂: upperparts shining green, gorget glittering green, *broad crescent across chest glittering violet*, rest of underparts dull green to gray green, tail forked, bronzy green, outer feathers tipped buffy white. ♀: above green like ♂; short white submalar streak (sometimes indistinct); underparts gray densely spotted green, rather sharply separated from rufescent buff flanks and belly; *outer tail feathers prom. tipped white.*
Sim. species: Both sexes of Lazuline Sabrewing show much rufous in tail. Smaller ♂ Violet-fronted Brilliant has almost straight bill and only small glittery patch on chest (not large crescent). ♀ recalls ♀ Golden-tailed Starfrontlet, but note latter's long, straight bill and mostly golden rufous tail. In Andes also see Buff-tailed Coronet.
Voice: Song a ser. of sharp notes, *chit! . . chit! . . chit! . . .*, ca. 1/sec or slightly faster for 10–20 sec or longer. Loud, staccato chips when feeding. In n Aragua 1 bird sang a few *chip* and *weet* notes mixed with short squeaky trills.
Behavior: Solitary and territorial, nearly always seen at low flowers; rarely ascends into canopy and does not gather with other hummers at mass-flowering trees. Often perches for long periods of time near a favorite patch of flowers which are usually jealously defended.
Status and habitat: Local. Resident in humid and wet premontane forest, esp. around patches of *Heliconia* growing in landslides or in treefalls inside forest; also along forest borders and in overgrown coffee plantations. Often seen near Rancho Grande Biol. Station, Aragua; unaccountably scarce and local in Andes.

Range: ENDEMIC. 700–2000m (occas. lower). Andes from n Táchira n to se Lara; n cordilleras from Yaracuy e to Distr. Federal and Miranda at Cerro Negro.

Lafresnaya

Monotypic; sexes differ; long, strongly decurved bill; white in tail; high mts.

Mountain Velvetbreast   PLATE 30
Lafresnaya lafresnayi   Colibrí Terciopelo
Identification: 3.8″ (9.7cm). 5.3g. Thin bill decidedly *decurved* (1″, 25mm, slightly longer in ♀). Dark with mostly white tail. ♂: above shining dark green, below glittering dark green, center of breast and belly velvety black, under tail coverts white tipped green, *central tail feathers dark green, rest white broadly tipped black.* ♀: above dark green, crown dusky brown, below

white thickly spotted green, sides shining green, *tail as in ♂*. Or sim. but white areas of both sexes tinged creamy buff (*tamae*). In all forms ♀♀ are shorter billed but longer winged than ♂♂.
Sim. species: Blocks of white in tail are distinctive. Cf. Collared Inca and Buff-tailed Coronet, both also with white or buff in tail. Inca has long straight bill and white chest band; coronet has buff under wing coverts, buff tertials, shorter straight bill, and different underparts.
Behavior: ♂♂ freq. hold foraging territories; ♀♀ more often trap-line. Both feed by hovering mostly low at flowers with long corolla tubes that fit their curved bills. ♀♀ reported feeding at flowers of *Castilleja, Pentadenia, Siphocampylus*, and *Simbolanthus*; ♂♂ at *Palicourea* and *Castilleja* in Colombia[692]; also noted at *Centropogon* flowers. Both sexes reg. hawk and glean tiny insects. Tail often flicked open as hover. Crown freq. dusted with pollen. Bulky cup nest in dense vegetation, 1–3m up[148].
Status and habitat: Uncommon and local resident in humid and wet montane forest, forest borders, and along streamsides. Occas. in clearing at Universidad de Los Andes forest, w Mérida. Local and seasonal movements need documentation.

Range: 2200–3100m (prob. occas. lower). Sierra de Perijá, Zulia (*lafresnayi*); s Táchira (*tamae*); n Táchira and Mérida n to s Trujillo at Guamito (*greenewalti*). Andes of Colombia to w Bolivia.
Note: Subsp. *tamae* not recognized[148].

Coeligena

Large, fast-flying highland hummers; unusually long, straight, needlelike bill; most with small white spot behind eyes; when feeding usually hover without clinging; mostly trap-line low to medium-ht. flowers, less often guard them; perch with bill angled slightly upward; most spp. relatively sedentary.

Bronzy Inca   PLATE 30
Coeligena coeligena   Colibrí Inca Bronceado
Identification: 4.5″ (11.4cm). 8g. Bill very long and straight (1.3″, 33mm). Large and brown. ♂: *above brown strongly tinged reddish wine to reddish copper*, crown tinged grayish, rump tinged greenish, below largely dull brown, *throat dirty white streaked and spotted dusky*, under tail coverts coppery rufous edged gray, tail large (slightly forked), bronzy brown. Or entire upperparts coppery brown with greenish tinge (*zuliana, columbiana*).
Sim. species: Note long straight bill. See Brown Violetear. No other large hummer is so brown.
Voice: Song a high, short *tsit-sit-it-it*, thinner at end; foraging call a high *szeet . . . zeet, zeet . . zeet . .*, irreg.

Behavior: Primarily a trap-liner of flowers in mid. or lower story inside or at edge of forest. Occas. hawks insects in open areas, and often active in vicinity of mixed-spp. flocks. Fond of long, tubular red flowers of *Cavendishia, Fuchsia, Bomarea,* etc.; also seen at flowers of *Heliconia, Siphocampylus, Heliconia,* and bananas. In Colombia, cup nest 1m up on sapling inside forest[540].

Status and habitat: Fairly common resident although shows marked seasonal shifts in abundance (esp. in Coastal Cordillera of Aragua). Humid and wet montane forest and forest borders., occas. open woodland and coffee plantations. Distrib. possibly local or disjunct (no recs. in Mérida?).

Range: 1000–2300m. Sierra de Perijá, Zulia (*zuliana*); Andes of Táchira, nw Barinas, Trujillo (sight, PN Guaramacal), and Lara (*columbiana*); Sierra de San Luis, Falcón (*zuloagae*); mts. of Yaracuy (Sierra de Aroa); n cordilleras from Carabobo e to Distr. Federal and Miranda (*coeligena*). Colombia s in Andes to Bolivia.
Note: Subsp. *zuloagae* doubtfully distinct.

Collared Inca
Coeligena torquata   Colibrí Inca Acollarado
Identification: 4.5″ (11.4cm). 7.1g. Bill very long (1.3″, 33mm), straight or with slight upturn. ♂: above and below mainly bright shining green, crown, throat, and neck glittery green, crown with narrow violet blue stripe, *broad white triangular-shaped collar across chest*; tail slightly forked, *central pr. of tail feathers green, rest white broadly tipped bronzy green.* ♀: like ♂ but shining green, throat buff disked green, wide white chest band as in ♂, lower underparts grayish densely spotted and mottled green. Or sim. but both sexes *black* faintly glossed green; ♂ (in hand) shows small violet central crown patch. ♀: throat grayish disked dark green (*tamae*).
Sim. species: Either sex easily told by broad white chest band and flashing white tail. Birds in s Táchira look black, those northward green. See Mountain Velvetbreast and Buff-tailed Coronet.
Voice: Soft, low, reedy whistle, *tu-tee,* and longer ser. of rather low-pitched piping whistles, *pip, pip . . ,* and soft *spit* when foraging; excited birds give chattery mix of whistles and soft notes.
Behavior: Principally a solitary trap-liner of low flowers. Occas. maintains vigil over a patch of flowers or visits and remains at a large canopy flowering tree, esp. *Inga,* where it behaves territorially but is not highly aggressive. Darts and flashes among low forest shrubbery and along steep, wet, vegetation-choked roadbanks. Likes to hover at length beneath pendent flowers with long straight corollas and probe directly upward into them, esp. vines, climbers, and shrubs

PLATE 30

such as Ericaceae, *Cavendishia,* and *Fuchsia.* Rarely clings when feeding. Incas are attracted to mixed-spp. flocks, and this sp. is often seen foraging and buzzing around actively in their midst. Cup-shaped plant fiber nest heavily decorated on outside is well hidden under ferns or cliff vegetation[148].
Status and habitat: Fairly common resident in humid and wet forest (cloud forest) and shrubby forest borders. Most numerous in wet forest above ca. 1800m, on avg. at slightly higher el. and in wetter forest than Bronzy Inca. No marked seasonal movements.

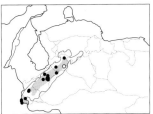

Range: 1500–3000m. Andes of s Táchira (*torquata*); Andes of n Táchira (Zumbador) and Mérida n to ne Trujillo at Cuevas de Carache and Los Palmares (*conradii*). Andes of Colombia to c Peru.

Golden-bellied Starfrontlet
Coeligena bonapartei   Colibrí Inca Ventridorado
Identification: 4.5″ (11.4cm). 6.5g. *Large, dark hummer with golden rufous belly.* Bill very *long* (1.3″, 33mm), straight or with slight upturn. ♂: frontlet glittering green, crown blackish, back golden green becoming *greenish copper on rump; buffy rufous tertial patch* (conspic. band in flight); throat and breast glittering green, small central throat patch violet, *belly intensely glittering coppery gold to reddish gold,* tail slightly forked, bronze green. ♀: like ♂ but duller, frontlet plain green; *no buff tertial patch; throat plain buff,* breast buff densely spotted green, lower underparts unspotted coppery gold.
Sim. species: Look for long bill and golden belly. Golden-tailed Starfrontlet, Buff-tailed Coronet, and ♀ Violet-chested Hummingbird do not overlap.
Behavior: Presum. sim. to Golden-tailed Starfrontlet. In Colombia reported feeding on nectar of *Bomarea, Cavendishia, Fuchsia, Macleonia, Mutisia,* and *Palicourea* and behaving as a trap-liner. Also hawks tiny insects and gleans from plant surfaces[148].
Status and habitat: Status unknown; there are only a few specimens from Perijá region. Humid forest and forest edge.

Range: 1400–3200m. Sierra de Perijá (Cerros Tetarí and Viruela), Zulia (*consita*). Ne Colombia.

Golden-tailed Starfrontlet PLATE 30
Coeligena eos Colibrí Inca Alirrufo

Identification: 4.5″ (11.4cm). 6.6g. *Large, dark green hummer with golden rufous rearparts.* Bill long (1.2″, 30mm), straight or with slight upturn. ♂: frontlet glittering green, crown blackish, back golden green turning *greenish copper on rump*; tertial patch *buffy rufous* (conspic. in flight); throat and breast glittering green, small central throat patch violet, *lower breast and belly glittering coppery gold*, tail slightly forked, *pale rufous* tipped bronze green. ♀: like ♂ but duller, esp. below; *lacks* glittering frontlet and *lacks* buff tertial patch; throat buffy rufous spotted green, chest densely spotted green.

Sim. species: ♂'s "divided" appearance—dark foreparts, golden rufous rearparts—is distinctive. ♀ might recall Buff-tailed Coronet but latter has buff tertial band, mostly green underparts, and creamy buff tail. ♀ also recalls ♀ Violet-chested Hummingbird but bill straight, not decurved. In Sierra de Perijá see Golden-bellied Starfrontlet.

Behavior: Usually found at low to med. hts. where hovers (does not cling) and probes upward, often almost vertically, into long corolla tubes of flowers for nectar from Ericaceae, *Centropogon*, *Fuchsia*, and other spp. Mainly a trap-liner of flowers, but occas. behaves as a territorialist although not highly aggressive. This hyperactive sp. always seems to be on the go, readily mobbing small owls, catching flying insects by helicoptering in open spaces, gleaning from foliage, and moving very actively amidst mixed-spp. flocks.

Status and habitat: Locally fairly common resident. Wet mossy montane forest and forest borders; distrib. spotty. Look for it on Pregonero Rd. in n Táchira and in PN Guaramacal, Trujillo. Migrates upward May or Jun to ? during rainy season.

Range: ENDEMIC. 1400–3200m. Andes from n Táchira, Mérida, nw Barinas, Trujillo (Páramo Cendé), and s Lara (Páramo Nariz).

Note: Formerly considered a subsp. of Golden-bellied Starfrontlet (*C. bonapartei*). Taxonomy follows del Hoyo et al.[148].

Blue-throated Starfrontlet PLATE 30
Coeligena helianthea Colibrí Inca Ventrivioleta

Identification: 4.6″ (11.7cm). 8.2g. Bill notably long (1.4″, 36mm), straight or slightly upturned. In field bird looks very dark with patches of glittering or glowing color. ♂: generally velvety black glossed green, frontlet glittering green, *rump glittering aquamarine*, throat patch glittering violet blue (glows), *belly glittering rosy lilac*, tail slightly forked, greenish black. ♀: above greenish black, *rump glittering aquamarine*, underparts

buffy cinnamon spotted green on chest; *belly spotted glittering rosy pink*.

Sim. species: ♂ is breathtaking in good light but usually looks all dark. Blue green rump and rosy belly are diagnostic for either sex. Golden-bellied Starfrontlet has rearparts mostly golden rufous. In Tamá area cf. Great Sapphirewing.

Behavior: Like others of genus, mainly a trap-liner of flowers. Usually seen alone, mostly at low to med. hts. inside forest or at small forest opening, and freq. active around mixed-spp. flocks. Occas. hawks or gleans tiny insects. In Colombia reported feeding at *Cavendishia, Symbolanthus, Tropaeolum,* and *Passiflora*[692], also *Fuchsia, Bomarea,* and several Ericaceae[148,387].

Status and habitat: Uncommon to fairly common resident inside humid and wet montane forest and in small forest openings. In Colombia also found on shrubby slopes, and in flower gardens and hedges in cultivated and urban areas, habitats more open than where this sp. has been found in Venez. Unreported but likely in Sierra de Perijá, Zulia.

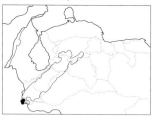

Range: 2400–3000m (sight to 2300m, s Táchira). S Táchira (*tamae*). Ne Colombia.

Ensifera

Large and mainly green; long bill unique; closely allied to *Coeligena* but bill much longer.

Sword-billed Hummingbird PLATE 31
Ensifera ensifera Colibrí Pico Espada

Identification: 5.5″ (14cm). 12g. *Bill extraordinarily long,* up to 4″ (102mm) in ♂, 4.5″ (114mm) in ♀, and slightly upturned. *Unmistakable.* ♂: crown coppery green, rest of upperparts dark shining green, throat dusky, otherwise shining green below; tail forked, bronzy green. ♀: above sim. to ♂, below grayish white, throat spotted green, rest of underparts heavily mixed with green, outermost tail feathers pale-edged.

Voice: Occas. a low, slightly trilled *trr.*

Behavior: Most often seen in flight as it streaks overhead all too quickly. A solitary sp. that forages in mid. or upper levels in trees; pauses momentarily to hover beneath flowers with long pendant corollas, e.g., *Aetanthus, Brugmansia, Datura, Salpichroa, Passiflora,* and *Fuchsia,* which it characteristically probes upward from below, then continues on to distant flowers in large trap-lining circuits. Or occas. sits beneath patches of nectar-rich flowers and feeds at them freq. Also infreq. visits small, short corolla tube flowers. At rest sits with bill pointed upward. Usually perches partially hidden in foliage, less often in open. Occas. hawks insects in flight. Long-distance flights between flowers and habit of perching out of sight generally make this sp. difficult to see. In Ecuador, mossy cup nest among rootlet fibers, usually high; 1 inside occupied hut in paramo[565].

Status and habitat: Uncommon and local resident in wet montane forest, borders of forest, and shrubby areas. Migrates upward to higher els. during wet season (ca. May–Oct) to breed, then often in flower gardens, hedgerows, and elfin woodland in lower edge of paramo, and much easier to find. Descends to lower els. during dry season.

Range: 2200–3000m (lower?). S Táchira (Cerro Las Copas), n Táchira[259], and n in Andes to Mérida, Trujillo, and s Lara at Páramo La Nariz. Colombia to n Bolivia.

[Great Sapphirewing]
Pterophanes cyanopterus Alizafiro Grande
Identification: 6.4″ (16.3cm). 9.8g. Very large. Bill straight (1.2″, 30mm) and rather heavy. ♂: *dark shining blue green above and below*; underparts strongly bluish; *upper and under wing coverts and inner webs of primaries shining blue*, long tail (2.7″, 69mm) *deeply forked*, outer feathers greenish black. ♀: above shining green, forecrown dusky gray, *wing coverts blue* as in ♂ but primaries with much less blue; *underparts cinnamon rufous*; sides and under tail coverts disked green; *deeply forked* tail greenish black edged grayish white.
Sim. species: Large size and slow wing beats are distinctive. In both sexes wings flash blue as bird hovers. ♀ recalls ♀ Golden-tailed and ♀ Blue-throated starfrontlets, but from either by larger size, more rufous on underparts, blue on wings, and forked tail.
Behavior: A spectacular and unmistakable hummingbird, usually seen hovering with slow, batlike wing beats. Forages at flowers at low to moderate hts., either by hovering, clinging momentarily, or perching. Usually solitary and territorial but also trap-lines scattered flowers and is freq. attracted to mixed-spp. flocks of highland tanagers, flowerpiercers, and warblers. Tends to perch on high, prom. bare twigs in early morning. Cup-shaped nest suspended from root or fern, usually below vegetation; 2–4m up[148].

Status and habitat: Known from 1 ♂ seen 6 Apr 1980 at 3150m on Páramo de Tamá (C. Parrish). Occurs in adj. Norte de Santander, Colombia. Paramo and stunted treeline vegetation.
Range: S Táchira (sight) (prob. *cyanopterus*). Colombia s in Andes to Bolivia.

Buff-tailed Coronet   PLATE 30
Boissonneaua flavescens Colibrí Cabecidorado
Identification: 4.5″ (11.4cm). 8g. *Bill short* (0.6″, 15mm). ♂: above dark shining green, head somewhat glittery, below green, belly spotted green and buff, *inner web of tertials and under wing coverts rufous buff* (tertials show as conspic. patch in flight); 2 central tail feathers bronzy green, *rest buff with dusky tip*.
Sim. species: Good marks are buff under wing coverts, buff tertial patch, and pale outer tail feathers. Mountain Velvetbreast lacks buff underwings and is smaller with decurved bill; ♂ also differs in black central breast. Also cf. Collared Inca and Golden-tailed Starfrontlet, both with long bill and different plumage.
Voice: Song a ser. of rapid, sharp *chip* notes[404]; ♂♂ may form small, loose leks.
Behavior: Often behaves territorially at flowers. Feeds mostly at mid. hts. Also hawks insects in long sallies and hovering bouts[692], and occas. gathers with other hummingbirds at canopy flowering trees where keeps mainly inside canopy. Habitually clings to flowers when feeding, holding wings up in a V, and also holds wings up momentarily upon alighting as do others of genus. Reported feeding on nectar of flowers of *Cavendishia, Disterigma, Palicourea*, and hummer-adapted melastome *Huilaea*[179]. In Colombia downy cup nest 4m up, near tip of slender branch[260].
Status and habitat: Uncommon and apparently very local; resident or prob. only a seasonal visitor to many areas. Humid and wet montane forest and along shrubby forest borders. Seen in disturbed forest above Betania, Táchira, in early Jan (C. Parrish).

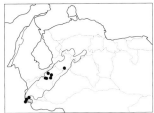

Range: 2100–3600m (once to 4200m?). Andes from s Táchira n to Mérida and se Trujillo at Guamito (*flavescens*). Andes of Colombia to w Ecuador.

Heliangelus

Fairly short, straight bill; ample tail; ♂♂ with glittering gorget; all Venez. spp. with broad pale crescent across chest; ♀♀ with rusty spotted throats; usually with broad pale crescent on chest; hold wings up momentarily upon alighting; only highlands.

Orange-throated Sunangel PLATE 30
Heliangelus mavors　Angel del Sol Cuelliocre
Identification: 3.7" (9.4cm). 4.2g. Bill short (0.6",
15mm), tail rather large and square. ♂: above shining
dark green, narrow frontlet and *throat glittering orange, broad rufous buff crescent across chest;* breast
green mixed buff, belly mostly rufous buff, tail dark
bronzy olive, outer feathers narrowly tipped whitish
(inconspic.). ♀: sim. but duller below; throat buff spotted green; buff chest band faintly indicated, lower underparts mostly rufous buff.
Sim. species: From any other sunangel by *buff* (not
white) pectoral band and orange throat (which often
looks black). See smaller ♀ Tyrian Metaltail.
Voice: When foraging a soft trill lasting several sec,
often a good clue to its presence.
Behavior: Solitary, aggressive, and territorial at
patches of short-tubed flowers mostly low (1–8m up)
along forest borders. Holds wings up in V for a moment upon alighting and in aggressive encounters,
and flicks them up when excited. Seems equally adept
at hovering at flowers or clinging to them when feeding, but almost always clings or perches when a substrate is available. Often active around mixed-spp.
flocks of passerines and readily mobs small owls.
Status and habitat: Common resident in humid and
wet forest, shrubby forest borders, roadsides, pastures
with scattered bushes and trees, and shrub zone into
lower paramo. Marked seasonal migration to lower
els. during rainy season, ca. late May–Oct or Nov? (the
reverse of many highland hummers in Venez.), then
numerous as low as ca. 1500m (e.g., San Isidro Rd., nw
Barinas—Hilty; Anzoátegui, Lara), and 1600m at La
Azulita, Mérida.

Range: 1500–3200m. Andes from n Táchira n to s Lara
(Páramo de Las Rosas; Anzoátegui); s Lara at PN Yacambú (sight). Ne Colombia.

Longuemare's Sunangel PLATE 30
Heliangelus clarisse　Angel del Sol Amatista
Identification: 3.7" (9.4cm). 5.3g. Bill short (0.7",
18mm). *Plumage dark.* ♂: narrow frontlet *glittering
blue;* crown velvety black (or purplish—*violiceps*);
rest of upperparts dark green; prom. white postocular
spot; *gorget glittering pinkish purple; broad crescent-
shaped white pectoral band* bordered below by narrow
glittering band of green across breast, rest of underparts dark shining green mixed gray, under tail coverts
white; tail long and ample, dark bronzy green to black-
ish, outer feathers blackish with tiny white tips (inconspic.). Or sim. but band of green across breast shining
(not glittery); under tail coverts buff (*spencei*). ♀: like

♂ but no glitter on frontlet; throat and underparts duller, throat often with white feather bases showing.
Sim. species: Note med. (not small) size and broad
white chest collar. In Mérida see Orange-throated Sunangel which is usually found *outside* forest.
Voice: When foraging, *spencei* gives a short, low-
pitched, cricketlike trill, *tre'e'e'e'e*[61], very sim. to that of
Orange-throated Sunangel. One vocalization of *verdiscutus* a single, upward-inflected *tsit . . tsit . . tsit . .* ca.
2/sec[61].
Behavior: Behaves as a territorialist along forest edges
where patches of low flowers are plentiful (i.e., hemi-
epiphytic Ericaceae such as *Psammisia*), but inside forest mainly a trap-liner of scattered flowers of vines, epiphytes, and shrubs such as *Palicourea*, mainly in lower
levels of forest, occas. higher. Hovers or clings to flowers when feeding and occas. hawks insects in short sallies from a low perch. Typically holds wings up in V
when clinging to flowers or alighting. Like many highland hummers, often stimulated by passage of mixed-
spp. flocks and forages actively in their midst. 11 BC
birds, May–Aug, Sierra de Perijá and ne Colombia[260].
Jun nest (*spencei*), 2 white eggs; downy cup atop
small root exposed beneath overhang on steep roadbank, 2200m, PN Sierra de Nevada, Mérida.
Status and habitat: Common resident along shrubby
forest borders, bushy pastures, and openings inside forest; 50+ specimens from Sierra de Perijá, 30+ from s Táchira (Colección Phelps). Abundant Jan–Feb along
roadsides and trails above Cerro Las Copas (ca. 2200–
2300m) in upper Río Quinimarí Valley. Isolate *spencei*
of Mérida much less common and *more confined to forest interior,* often seen near Mucuy entrance to PN
Sierra de Nevada (2100–2300m), Mérida.

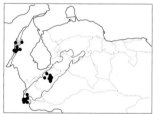

Range: 1800–3100m. Sierra de Perijá, Zulia (*violiceps*);
s Táchira (*verdiscutus*); Andes of c Mérida from Los
Nevados n to Páramo Conejos, and La Carbonera e to
Quintero (*spencei*). Venez. and ne Colombia.
Note: Excludes Amethyst-throated Sunangel (*H. Ame-
thysticollis*) of Ecuador to w Bolivia. Subspp. *violiceps*
and *verdiscutus* previously regarded as subsp. of
Amethyst-throated Sunangel[148]. Subsp. *spencei* previously regarded as a separate sp., Mérida Sunangel[403].

Eriocnemis

Straight bill; portions of plumage highly metallic and
glittery (among most glittering of all hummers); large
white leg puffs (1 sp. with black leg puffs) impart
charming "booted" look; mainly shrubby areas and forest borders at high els. and treeline.

Coppery-bellied Puffleg
PLATE 30
Eriocnemis cupreoventris   Colibrí Pantalón Cobrizo
Identification: 3.8″ (9.7cm). 5.6g. Bill straight (0.8″, 20mm). Scarce. Above shining golden green, *rump glittering emerald green contrasting with prom. forked blue black tail*; underparts glittering golden green becoming *reddish copper on lower breast and belly, large white leg puffs* (conspic.); under tail coverts *intensely glittering dark blue* (glow even in poor light). Sexes alike.
Sim. species: Leg puffs and copper on breast are best marks. Glowing Puffleg also has glittery rump and contrasting dark tail but is slightly smaller and lacks coppery color on breast.
Behavior: Usually seen alone, keeping low as it hovers or clings to feed at flowers with long corolla tubes. Active and aggressive, often darting in and out of shrubbery and vigorously chasing intruders. Like others of genus, holds or flicks up wings momentarily upon alighting. In Colombia reported at flowers of *Cavendishia* and *Palicourea*[692] and Ericaceae (*Pernettya*). Often hawks tiny insects.
Status and habitat: Uncommon or rare resident in wet stunted woodland and in thickets and shrubbery near treeline. Not well known in Venez. Some seasonal el. movement likely.

Range: 2800–3000m. S Táchira (Páramo de Tamá; Cerro El Retiro) n to c Mérida (near Mérida; Páramo La Fria; Páramo Conejos). Ne Colombia.

Glowing Puffleg
PLATE 30
Eriocnemis vestitus   Colibrí Pantalón Verde
Identification: 3.5″ (8.9cm). 4.5g. Bill straight (0.8″, 20mm). Another scarce puffleg with breathtaking colors. ♂: above dark shining green, *rump glittering metallic emerald contrasting with strongly forked black tail; below uniformly dark glittering green*, small violet throat patch; *large and conspic. white leg puffs*; intensely *glittering purple under tail coverts* (glow even in shade). ♀: above like ♂, rump not so glittery, more golden green like back; *throat buff densely speckled green*, small glittering blue central patch and ill-defined buff malar (usually), rest of underparts green mixed buff on breast, white on belly; *large white leg puffs; under tail coverts glittering purple.*
Sim. species: ♂ resembles Golden-breasted Puffleg, and in both spp. brilliant, metallic-looking upper tail coverts contrast sharply with dark tail. ♀ might recall ♀ Tyrian Metaltail as both have buff to rufous throats, but note puffleg's speckled, unkept-looking underparts, leg puffs, and forked blue black tail.
Behavior: Rather inconspic. little hummer that usually stays low (seldom more than ca. 3m up), darts out mo-

mentarily to feed by hovering, perching, or clinging at small tubular flowers on periphery of shrubs (esp. spp. of Ericaceae and Rubiaceae), then just as quickly disappears behind a nearby bush and perches out of sight. Often holds wings up in V momentarily as alights. Behaves as territorialist and guards flowers, or as generalist (or trap-liner), then not guarding or visiting them freq.
Status and habitat: Very local in wet montane forest borders, openings in shrubby highland pastures, along hedgerows, and at interface of mossy elfin woodland and paramo. Uncommon to fairly common near treeline in vicinity of Páramo de Tamá. Also along shrubby roadsides below Páramo Batallón, n Táchira. Specimens are from 2 locs. in Táchira; 6 in Mérida, most recent a ♀ taken 14 Sep 1972 at Mucuchíes; 1 seen 7 Mar 2000 at ca. 2600m in PN Guaramacal, Trujillo (S. Thal, Hilty, D. Ascanio, and others).

Range: 2700–3600m (sight, 2600m, Trujillo). S Táchira n to n Mérida at Páramo La Culata; Páramo Escorial and Mucuchíes (*vestitus*); sight, e Trujillo (subsp.?). Colombia and e Ecuador.

Ocreatus

Monotypic Andean genus; tiny and slender; short bill; leg puffs as in *Eriocnemis*; ♂ has racket-tips to outer tail feathers.

Booted Racket-tail
PLATE 31
Ocreatus underwoodii   Colibrí Cola de Hoja
Identification: ♂ 5″ (12.7cm) incl. tail. ♀ 3″ (7.6cm). 3g. Bill very short (0.5″, 13mm). ♂: unmistakable; above shining green, throat and chest glittering green, rest of underparts shining green, *large conspic. white leg puffs*; central tail feathers green, rest blue black, outermost dusky, *greatly elongated* (3.5″, 8.9cm) *with long bare shaft and large blue black racket-tip.* ♀: tiny and very different; above bright shining green, *below creamy white to white somewhat spotted green; small but conspic. white leg puffs*; under tail coverts buff, tail normal but rather long and deeply forked, dark green with dusky subterminal band, *large grayish white tips on outer feathers.*
Sim. species: Either sex could be mistaken for a puffleg, but both pufflegs occur at higher els. Look for ♂'s remarkable tail, not always easy to see against dark foliage. Note ♀'s tiny size, spotted underparts, and forked tail with bold white tips. See ♀ Purple-backed Thornbill.
Voice: Song a short, thin, bubbly trill, single or doubled (shown), e.g., *tiiiiiieeeeetiiiiiieeee*, each phrase descending[61]; weak twittering when feeding.

Behavior: Flight is weaving and beelike, and at 1st glance this hummer may look more like a large insect than a bird. Hovers or occas. clings to blossoms as trap-lines scattered resources, filches nectar within territories of larger spp., or feeds at low nectar reward, insect-pollinated flowers (e.g., *Impatiens*) at roadsides. ♂♂ and ♀♀ also feed at clusters of flowering shrubs or trees, also at low shrubs in open areas inside forest, and commonly at canopy mass-flowering trees with other spp. of hummers. Esp. fond of *Inga* and *Calliandra* (brushlike inflorescence) flowers; other food plants incl. various Rubiaceae, *Clusia*, *Cavendishia*, and Bromeliaceae. ♂'s delightful, 3-part display, with white "boots" exposed, involves (1) short, horizontal, arcing flights, (2) hovering with tail vertical, and (3) hovering and snapping tail downward repeatedly with audible sound[574].

Status and habitat: Uncommon to seasonally fairly common resident in humid and wet forest borders, second-growth woodland, and well-lit areas inside forest; occas. isolated trees in highland pastures. Shows marked local and seasonal movements.

Range: 850–3000m (most recs. below 2300m). Sierra de Perijá, Zulia, Andes from s Táchira n to e Lara (Terrepaima; Cabudare); Sierra de San Luis, Falcón (*discifer*); n cordilleras from Yaracuy and Carabobo to Distr. Federal and Miranda (*polystictus*). Colombia to n Bolivia.

[Green-tailed Trainbearer]
Lesbia nuna   Colibrí Coludo Verde
Identification: ♂ to 6.5″ (16.5cm), 3.6g. ♀ 4.3″ (10.9cm). *Bill short* (0.4″, 10mm). Presence in Venez. doubtful. ♂: bright shining green, gorget glittering green; *long, narrow, deeply forked tail* (to 4.5″, 114mm) emerald green, outer pr. of tail feathers dusky. ♀: above bright green, *below white thickly spotted green*; narrow tail like ♂'s but shorter (to 3.5″, 89mm).
Voice: High, short, buzzy *bzzzt* in flight.
Status and habitat: HYPOTHETICAL. No modern evidence of its occurrence in Venez. Only record is 1 specimen in British Museum labeled "Sierra Nevada de Mérida," presumably taken by Goering in 1874. Locality may be mislabeled. Subparamo and bushes in highlands.
Range: Presumably Mérida region (*gouldii*) but more likely to be seen in Táchira. In Colombia 2200–2800m. Colombia (n to Tunja, Boyacá) s in Andes to n Bolivia.
Note: Black-tailed Trainbearer (*L. victoriae*) seems more likely to occur in Venez. than Green-tailed; known from as close as Pamplona, Norte de Santander, Colombia. ♂ resembles Green-tailed but larger

(to 10″, 25cm), duller, lower underparts spotted green and buff, tail very long (to 6.5″, 16.5cm), forked, black, all but outermost pr. of feathers tipped bronze green. ♀ above bronze green, below buffy white spotted green, tail like ♂'s but shorter (to 3.5″, 8.9cm). In both sexes tail is broader than in Green-tailed Trainbearer.

Purple-backed Thornbill   PLATE 30
Ramphomicron microrhynchum   Colibrí Pico Espina
Identification: 3.4″ (8.6cm). 3.5g. *Tiny bill* (0.25″, 6mm) *is shortest of all hummingbirds.* ♂: *upperparts entirely shining purple*, gorget glittering green bordered black, rest of underparts dull green; rather long ample tail deeply forked, purplish black. ♀: above bright green, upper tail coverts bronzy rufous, *below buffy white thickly spotted green*, buffiest on throat and under tail coverts; tail strongly forked, dusky glossed purple, *outer feathers with large white tips.* Some (most?) ♀♀ show irreg. *white stripe up rump and lower back.*
Sim. species: ♂ is only Venez. hummer with purple above. ♀ much like ♀ Booted Racket-tail and ♀ Green-tailed Trainbearer but usually shows white stripe up back. Note racket-tail's white leg puffs, trainbearer's longer *green* tail.
Voice: Alarm(?) *ti, ti, ti, ti . . .* , long sustained; song sim. but shrill and weaker[565].
Behavior: Forages from low to high but commonly gathers with other hummingbirds in canopy of large mass-flowering trees where hovers (rarely clings) when feeding at flowers and behaves as a filcher of nectar from territories of larger spp. Flight is floating and beelike. Also feeds heavily on insects in flowers and by gleaning from foliage or by hawking. Seasonally may rely heavily on insects. Nectar plants incl. *Echeveria*, *Castilleja*, *Draba*, and various Ericaceae (*Pernettya*, *Cavendishia*, etc.). In display ♂ traces shallow arcs back and forth in front of ♀, this sometimes accompanied by loud cracking or clapping sounds.
Status and habitat: Very uncommon and local resident; there is marked seasonal migration to higher el. in wet season. Humid and wet forest borders and semi-open to open highland terrain with shrubs, woodlots, scattered trees, and paramo with *Espeletia*. Usually found where there are a few taller trees. Only a few specimens and sight recs. in Venez.: lowest rec. is 1 on 19 Jan 1991, Universidad de Los Andes forest, w Mérida, 2200m—Hilty, K. Zimmer); several in Jun 1999 at Hotel Los Frailes, ne Mérida (D. Ascanio).

Range: 2500–3000m (sight to 2200m). S Táchira in vicinity of Páramo de Tamá; c Mérida (*andicolum*). Colombia s in Andes to n Bolivia.

Metallura

Small to med. size; bill short; tail ample and with metallic gloss (both sexes); ♀♀ duller, often spotted below; some have rufous on throat.

Tyrian Metaltail   PLATE 30
Metallura tyrianthina   Colibrí Verde Colirrojo
Identification: 3.2″ (8.1cm). 3.9g. Bill short (0.4″, 10mm). ♂: above dark bronzy green; *small gorget glittering green*, rest of underparts dark dull green, tail large, somewhat forked, color highly variable depending on light, *usually golden purplish red* (or darker more golden maroon—*chloropogon*). ♀: above like ♂; *throat and chest buffy rufous somewhat speckled green*, rest of underparts buffy white with variable amt. of green spotting.
Sim. species: Learn this sp. well (both sexes) as it is common throughout high els. of n and w Venez. ♂ is very dark. Look for combination of short bill, ample tail, and glittery green gorget. ♀'s mark is rufous throat. See ♀ pufflegs and Orange-throated Sunangel. In Sierra de Perijá see ♀ Perijá Metaltail.
Voice: Song a weak, lispy *seek, sick, see, si, see, seek, sip see* . . ; when excited stuttering trills interspersed with squeaky notes, *tdrrrt, tdrrrt ti-see-see, tdrrrt ti-see-see, prrrt ti-see-see* . . . ; when foraging a rough trill slowing to a ser. of high notes, i.e., *ts'ts'ts'ts'ts'ts'see'see-seek-seek*, descending slightly.
Behavior: Confiding little hummer usually seen low at flowers in shrubby borders and roadsides. Clings when feeding at some flowers, hovers at others. Aggressive (esp. ♂♂) and tends to guard small patches of flowers, although some flowers used by this sp. are low nectar reward, and short-tubed or flat flowers ignored by larger hummers. Food plants incl. *Escallonia, Eugenia, Gaultheria,* and *Palicourea.* Jul nest in cavelike rock niche in Colombia; pendent mass of moss and fibers; small nest chamber partially roofed with moss; ♀ defends small nest territory and adj. flowers[667,692]; 12 BC birds, Apr–Aug, n Colombia[260].
Status and habitat: Common to abundant resident along humid and wet forest borders, overgrown clearings, and shrubby areas, but seldom far from forest. At upper end of range also in elfin woodland and patches of shrubs in paramo. Shows strong seasonal movements, some evidently sex related, as at times mainly ♂♂ or ♀♀ are seen. In general ♀-plumaged birds outnumber adult ♂♂.

Range: 1700–3800m (prob. lower). Sierra de Perijá, Zulia (*districta*); s Táchira (*tyrianthina*); n Táchira n through Andes to Trujillo/Lara border at Páramo de Las Rosas (*oreopola*); Coastal Cordillera in Aragua,

Distr. Federal, and Miranda (*chloropogon*). Colombia s in mts. to Bolivia.

Perijá Metaltail
Metallura iracunda   Colibrí de Perijá
Identification: 4″ (10.2cm). Bill short (0.4″, 10mm). *Large blackish hummer with wine red tail.* ♂: above dull black faintly glossed reddish to coppery to greenish (varies with light), forecrown dark green, *gorget glittering green*, rest of underparts dark brownish black; *long ample tail rather squarish, glistening wine red.* ♀: above dark golden green, *throat cinnamon rufous with a few green spots*, rest of underparts buffy white mixed and spotted dusky brown, esp. on belly (only a few spots on breast); tail as in ♂.
Sim. species: In restricted range likely confused only with Tyrian Metaltail which is much smaller and greenish (not mainly black); ♀ told from ♀ Tyrian by much larger size, also somewhat more uniform underparts.
Status and habitat: Little known but apparently fairly common locally (many specimens). Partially open areas with stunted forest and bushy terrain near treeline, scattered recs. lower. Cerro Pintado is predom. elfin forest and *Swallenochloa* bamboo. A large ser. was taken at 3000–3100m, late Jun–Jul, Sierra de Perijá, and close to Colombia (Colección Phelps). Seasonal el. movements may account for low-el. recs. Despite tiny range, not likely threatened.

Range: 1850–3200m. Sierra de Perijá (Cerros Tres Tetas, Viruela, and Pintado), Zulia. Sierra de Perijá, Colombia.

Chalcostigma

Small group of high-Andean hummers; short bill; long, broad tail; colorful gorget and/or forecrown stripe.

Bronze-tailed Thornbill   PLATE 30
Chalcostigma heteropogon   Pico Espina Bronceado
Identification: 5″ (12.7cm). 5g. *Bill very short (0.5″, 13mm) for size of bird.* Tail large. ♂: above mostly bronzy green, *rump contrasting reddish copper*, forehead and *long gorget stripe glittering green* tipped rosy magenta and ending in a point on chest, rest of underparts bronzy brown, *tail long and ample*, brownish tinged green, slightly forked. ♀: sim. to ♂ but gorget stripe spotted green, no rosy tips.
Sim. species: Note restricted range. At treeline, a large, *long-tailed*, bronzy hummer with contrasting rump and short bill is likely to be this sp. See much smaller Purple-backed Thornbill and paler Bearded Helmetcrest.
Behavior: Occurs singly, feeding at flowers by clinging briefly at each. Aggressive and territorial; guards favor-

ite patches of flowers but also trap-lines widely scattered nectar resources, and at least seasonally, feeds heavily on insects. Does not gather in flowering trees. Food plants incl. *Bartisa*, *Rubus*, *Brachyotum*, and various Ericaceae[148]. Rests in shrubs or on or beneath rock outcrops. Hovers with rather slow wing beats. Prob. rainy season breeder.

Status and habitat: Resident in patches of stunted woodland and shrubs at upper end of montane forest and adj. paramo; often in bushes around cliffs and rocky outcrops. Some seasonal or irreg. el. movement likely. Perhaps locally numerous (several specimens from tiny Venez. range).

Range: 3000–3275m. S Táchira on Páramo de Tamá. Ne Colombia.

Oxypogon

Monotypic; tiny bill; large tail, dull colors; high els.; 4 isolated subspp.

Bearded Helmetcrest   PLATE 31
Oxypogon guerinii   Chivito de los Páramos
Identification: 4.5″ (11.4cm). 4.8g. Bill very short (0.4″, 10mm) for size of bird. ♂: above bronzy green with *long pointed and sometimes slightly bifurcated black crest and shaggy (goatlike) black and white beard*, latter with glittering green stripe; *sides of head blackish forming large triangular patch*; broad white nuchal collar encircles neck and extends downward onto breast, rest of underparts dingy grayish green; decidedly long ample tail slightly forked, the central feathers olive green, outer ones dusky. In hand shafts of tail feathers white. ♀: like ♂ but duller, no crest or beard, lower underparts dull white thickly spotted greenish brown.
Sim. species: At treeline or higher, a large, pale hummer with long tail and blackish triangle on sides of head will be this sp. Cf. Tyrian Metaltail and Orange-throated Sunangel.
Voice: In rainy season ♂♂ sing persistently from tops of shrubs, a simple, high *peek . . . peek . . . peek . . .* for several min without interruption.
Behavior: Usually alone at low flowering bushes or herbs, but several may gather at favorable sites just below paramo in dry season (e.g., in garlic onion fields). Often perches atop large boulders, and occas. walks on gd. where it makes short hovering jumps for insects, or flies in little bounding leaps between short gd.-level flowers. Also feeds heavily on tiny insects picked from flowers of *Espeletia*. Reg. clings to flowers when feeding, and bounds (seems to jump like a little goat, hence Spanish name) from one clump to another, then flies off in spurts and glides, with freq. and

erratic course changes and undulations, to a favorite resting site in a little gorge or canyon. Nectar plants incl. *Siphocampylus*, *Castilleja*, *Draba*, *Espeletia*, and *Echeveria*. Nests in rainy season (ca. Jun–Oct); unusually thick, insulated nest cup of *Espeletia* plant down on rocky cliff, steep bank near water, or in *Espeletia* in paramo.

Status and habitat: Resident. Seasonally very common in open paramo; esp. numerous (e.g., Páramo del Pico Águila) during rainy season when breeding; at other times of yr descends to paramo-forest ecotone near treeline; very few remain in high paramo during dry months. One seen at 2800m, 19 Jan 1993, Páramo Zumbador, n Táchira, is lowest rec.; prob. also in s Táchira (subsp. *guerinii* occurs in adj. Andes of Colombia).

Range: 3600–4500m (sight to 2800m). Andes of n Táchira (sight), Mérida, and Trujillo n to Teta de Niquitao (*lindenii*). Spottily in Andes of n and c Colombia.

Aglaiocercus

Marked sexual dimorphism; ♂♂ with long, metallic-colored tail; ♀♀ with much shorter tail; bill rather short; highlands.

Long-tailed Sylph   PLATE 31
Aglaiocercus kingi   Colibrí Coludo Azul
Identification: ♂ 7–8″ (18–20.3cm), 5.5g. ♀ 3.8″ (9.7cm), 4.5g. Bill short (0.5″, 13cm). ♂: above shining dark green with *glittering green forecrown*; below incl. throat dull green; *tail deeply forked, the outer feathers very long* (up to 6″, 15cm), *brilliant metallic* violet blue, tips more bluish (colors vary with angle of light); or central and outer tail feathers violet blue tinged green at tip (*caudatus*). ♀: very different; *forecrown glittering blue green*, rest of upperparts shining green, *throat white* freckled green, *breast cinnamon rufous*; sides and belly greenish.
Sim. species: Electrifying ♂ unique in w Venez. Bright ♀ often mistaken for ♂ of another sp., but combination of blue forecrown, white throat, and rufous breast unique. See Venezuelan Sylph.
Voice: When foraging a harsh, buzzy *jit* in slow ser.; or in fast bursts, *jit-jit* or *jit-jit-jit*. Song a buzzy, pebbly *bzzzt! bzzzt! . . .* , ca. 1 note/sec.
Behavior: Solitary ♂♂ and ♀♀ are territorial and defend small flowering shrubs or patches of flowers low inside or at edge of forest, but also trap-line scattered flowers. Also occas. visit large flowering trees where other hummers are present, but usually not very territorial or dominant there. Hover or cling when feeding at flowers. Usually a legitimate pollinator but occas. steals nectar by poking holes in outside base of corol-

las. ♂♂ aggressively chase other ♂♂ (display?) with widely spread tail, sometimes several together, ascending high over forest. Bulky hanging nest with dangling tail and side entrance to cup[565] recalls nest of *Phaethornis*.

Status and habitat: Common and widespread resident at treefalls or clearings inside humid and wet forest, forest borders, older second-growth woodland, and in clearings, gardens, and coffee plantations. Local or seasonal movements are limited.

Range: 900–2500m (rarely to 3000m?). Sierra de Perijá, Zulia; Andes from s Táchira n to Lara (*caudatus*); Sierra de San Luis, Falcón; n cordilleras from Yaracuy and Carabobo e to Distr. Federal and Miranda (*margarethae*). Andes of Colombia to Bolivia.
Note: Formerly incl. subsp. *berlepschi*, now a separate sp.[575].

Venezuelan Sylph

Aglaiocercus berlepschi   Colibrí Coludo de Venezuela
Identification: ♂ 7–8″ (18–20.3cm), 5.5g. ♀ 3.8″ (9.7cm), 4.5g. Bill short (0.5″, 13cm). ♂: sim. to Long-tailed Sylph, differing in slightly larger size, violet blue gorget, and central tail feathers more extensively *blue to deep violet tinged green* (*berlepschi*). ♀: very different; upperparts and tail much as in ♀ Long-tailed Sylph incl. blue crown and white tail tips; *below mainly white (no rufous) spotted green on throat and breast*; sides and flanks bronzy green.
Sim. species: Cf. both sexes of Fork-tailed Woodnymph. Also see Long-tailed Sylph and Scissor-tailed Hummingbird, neither known to overlap in range.
Behavior: As in Long-tailed Sylph.
Status and habitat: Humid and wet forest, forest borders, older second-growth woodland, and coffee plantations. Deforestation is extensive within sp.'s small range. Formerly common on Cerro Negro, Monagas, where known from a large ser. of specimens.

Range: ENDEMIC. 1450–1800m. Mts. of w and c Sucre (Cerro Turumiquire to Cerro Papelón) and n Monagas at Cerro Negro.
Note: Now considered separate from Long-tailed Sylph, *A. kingi*[575].

Wedge-billed Hummingbird   PLATE 29

Schistes geoffroyi   Colibrí Pico de Cuña
Identification: 3.3″ (8.4cm). 4g. *Bill short* (0.5″, 13mm), rather broad at base and sharp pointed. ♂: above shining green, *rear crown and rump contrasting reddish copper*, sides of head black bordered above by *long white postocular stripe*; gorget glittering green, rest of underparts green with small glittering blue to violet patch on each side of chest and larger *white pectoral patch below*; tail rounded, central feathers shining green, outer ones blue green with *dark subterminal band and conspic. white tips.* ♀: gorget duller and shining green or mixed with white; violet tufts smaller.
Sim. species: Despite its name, bill shape not conspic. in field. Speckled Hummingbird is much browner and lacks colorful underparts. Copper-rumped, Steely-vented, and Green-bellied hummingbirds all have contrasting brownish rumps but no head pattern.
Voice: Advertising song, from low, open perch inside forest, a high, sibilant *sink . . . sink . . . sink . . .* , ca. 1 note/sec or faster.
Behavior: Solitary and usually seen inside forest in understory or in shady ravines, less freq. in sunny areas along forest borders. Feeds at a variety of mostly low tubular flowers by hovering or less often while clinging. A notorious nectar thief, it reg. pierces a hole in outside base of long-tubed flowers (e.g., *Fuchsia, Centropogon, Cavendishia, Palicourea*) with sharp-pointed bill and steals nectar without effecting pollination. Mostly traplines flowers; not at canopy flowering trees.
Status and habitat: Very uncommon and local resident inside humid and wet forest (cloud forest) and along shrubby forest borders. Erratic and unpredictable; local or seasonal el. movements likely. Sight rec., La Soledad, 21 Nov 1982 (C. Parrish); and San Isidro Rd., 11 Mar 2000 (D. Ascanio, Hilty) are 1st in nw Barinas.

Range: 1000–1800m (sight to 475m). Sierra de Perijá, Zulia; spottily in Andes of s Táchira, w Mérida, nw Barinas (sight), and se Lara; mts. of Yaracuy and Coastal Cordillera in Carabobo, Aragua (to 475m on n slope), and Distr. Federal (*geoffroyi*). Mts. from Colombia to Bolivia.
Note: Has been placed in genus *Augastes*[148].

Black-eared Fairy   PLATE 31

Heliothryx aurita   Colibrí Hada Orejazul
Identification: ♂ 4.1″ (10.4cm), 4.7g. ♀ larger, 4.7″ (12cm), 5.4g. Bill straight (♀ 0.7″, 18mm; slightly shorter in ♂) with *sharp point*. ♂: above bright shining green, crown glittering green; black ear patch tipped violet blue (tips rarely visible in field), *underparts immaculate white, tail rounded, 4 central tail feathers blue black, rest white.* ♀: sim. but 4 central tail feathers ca.

0.5″ (13mm), *longer* than those of ♂; throat often finely speckled gray brown; in hand, tail coverts conceal dark band at base of white outer tail feathers.
Sim. species: White-necked Jacobin has blue head, white nape band, and dark throat and chest. Fairy's behavior (see below) is distinctive.
Voice: Tiny squeaks and *tsit* notes while foraging.
Behavior: A very active, impish hummer, darting quickly from flower to flower, repeatedly opening and closing flashy tail, suddenly flying up to hover momentarily in open, then as quickly dashing away. Reg. hovers ("helicopters") like *Anthracothorax*, dancing in charming, graceful manner in high open areas for tiny flying insects; spends much time (more than most hummers) gleaning from foliage and is a solitary trapliner of nectar; feeds from eye level to treetops but more often at mid. levels or higher, esp. inside forest. Often pierces holes at base of flower corollas to steal nectar. Does not gather at large flowering trees with others. Hovers lightly with notably erect body posture and holds tail cocked jauntily up as it hovers. In display ♂, with ear-tufts expanded, hovers up and down and side to side before ♀, then both make spinning ascent to new perch and ♂ may continue hovering. Downy cup nest covered with lichens; 10m up[565].
Status and habitat: Fairly common resident in humid lowland forest, shady forest borders, and treefalls. Most numerous in white sandy soil regions with blackwater rivers. Reg. up to ca. 1000m in tepui foothills. No strong local or seasonal movements.

Range: To 950m n of Orinoco; to 1300m s of Orinoco. E Sucre and n Monagas; throughout Amazonas and Bolívar (*aurita*). E Colombia to n Bolivia, Amaz. Brazil, and the Guianas; se Brazil.

Long-billed Starthroat   PLATE 30
Heliomaster longirostris   Colibrí Estrella Picolargo
Identification: 4″ (10.2cm). 6.8g. *Bill very long and straight* (1.3–1.4″, 33–36mm). ♂: *forecrown glittering aquamarine*, rest of upperparts bronze green, usually with ill-defined blaze of white up center of rump; *gorget magenta* bordered on sides by white malar stripe; rest of underparts dull grayish, sides and breast tinged green, tail bronze green, outermost feathers tipped white. ♀: crown bronzy like back, gorget variable, duller and irreg. in shape or only flecked with color, or only with dusky spots; tail more broadly tipped white. Imm. birds have buff malars.
Sim. species: Long bill is diagnostic. Cf. ♀ to Gray-breasted Sabrewing and ♀ White-vented Plumeleteer, both with shorter, somewhat decurved bills.

Voice: Dry *tsik* notes while foraging; when excited, faster twittering notes.
Behavior: Will most often be seen alone on a high, open perch, esp. on slender bare twigs. Feeds at small patches of scattered flowers from low to high but predom. high. Reg. hawks tiny insects high in open areas. Visits large mass-flowering canopy trees with other hummers but is not strongly territorial. Will visit feeders. In Costa Rica, nest usually on exposed horizontal branch 5–12m up, often in dead tree[651].
Status and habitat: Thinly spread and unpredictable in occurrence. Forest borders, open second-growth woodland, gallery forest, partially open or cultivated areas with scattered trees and woodlots, and areas of mixed forest and savanna in fairly dry to humid regions. Nowhere very common, but there are more specimens from Sucre than elsewhere; numerous sight recs. on both slopes of Coastal Cordillera in Aragua.

Range: To 800m n of Orinoco; to 1200m s of Orinoco. Sw Zulia; e Falcón and somewhat spottily throughout rest of Venez. (*longirostris*); no recs. from c Venez. (llanos) or s Amazonas. S Mexico to nw Peru; e of Andes s to Bolivia, c Brazil, and the Guianas.

Calliphlox and *Chaetocercus*

Tiny size; fairly long, straight bills; forked or bilobed tails (central feathers often rudimentary). ♂♂ differ trivially in color of body plumage, color and shape of gorget, and color and shape of tail and are reported to assume ♀-like eclipse plumage for part of yr. ♀♀ often not separable in field. In hand told by tail pattern, sometimes also by slight differences in color of underparts. Originally the following 3 spp. were placed in separate genera based on minor differences in tail structure. Present taxonomy merges *Acestrura* into *Chaetocercus*[148].

Amethyst Woodstar   PLATE 29
Calliphlox amethystina   Tucusito Amatista
Identification: ♂ 2.8″ (7cm), ♀ 2.6″ (6.6cm). 2.7g. Bill straight, fairly long for size of bird (0.6″, 15mm). ♂: above dark green, *gorget glittering rosy magenta extending onto sides of neck*; narrow white postocular stripe connects (usually) to *broad white crescent across chest*; rest of underparts gray mixed green; *conspic. white flank patch* (obvious in flight); tail deeply forked, dusky, the outer feathers long, narrow, and pointed. ♀: above like ♂; *throat dingy white*, cheeks dusky brown, a few rosy spots on throat; broad whitish crescent across chest (usually fairly distinct); *breast and belly cinnamon rufous; conspic. white flank*

patches; tail shorter than in ♂, squarish, *central feathers green, rest dusky tipped buffy white to buff*. Note that ♀'s white throat and cinnamon lower underparts impart "divided" look.

Sim. species: In Andean foothills might rarely overlap with Rufous-shafted Woodstar. Cf. the two closely: ♂ Rufous-shafted differs in lighter green upperparts (in direct comparison) and rufous in tail; ♀ Rufous-shafted more uniformly pale cinnamon below (not with contrasting dingy white throat), and outer tail feathers rufous with broad black subterminal band and rufous tips (not all dark with rufous tips).

Behavior: Perches and forages from shrub to canopy hts., but most often seen perched high on slender bare twig in open. As in other small-bodied hummers, flight is floating and beelike with wing beats up to 80/sec. Forages solitarily at scattered small native or introd. flowers or gathers with other hummers at mass-flowering trees, esp. legumes and trees with brushlike inflorescences (e.g., *Inga* and *Calliandra*), where mostly a filcher of nectar within territories of others. In display ♂ arcs back and forth like a pendulum, calls, and produces a presumed mechanical sound. Near Belém, Brazil, tiny cup nest saddled on limb 15m up in open tree at forest edge; 2 nestlings (R. Ridgely; H. Sick).

Status and habitat: Turns up in a wide variety of places, but everywhere *very local or seasonal*; nowhere very numerous. Canopy of tall humid forest, forest borders, gallery forest, partially open or disturbed areas with trees and bushes, and drier mixed savanna and scrub forest. Lowlands and foothills. Very seasonal and/or irreg. n of Orinoco; rec. Aug, Oct, and Dec–Jan, Guárico[734]. Many more recs. s of Orinoco.

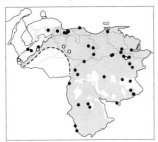

Range: To 1000m n of Orinoco; to 1500m s of Orinoco. Andes of w Mérida (La Azulita), e side of Andes locally from Táchira to Lara; Yaracuy and n cordilleras in Carabobo, Aragua, and Distr. Federal; locally in llanos from w Barinas to Sucre and Delta Amacuro; generally in Amazonas and Bolívar. E Colombia to the Guianas, n Bolivia, ne Argentina, and e Brazil.

Gorgeted Woodstar
PLATES 29, 31

Chaetocercus heliodor   Estrella Cuellirrojo

Identification: ♂ 2.5″ (6.4cm). ♀ 2.3″ (5.8cm). Bill straight (0.5″, 13mm), fairly long for size of bird. ♂: *above dark shining green, gorget purplish, elongated into protruding tufts on sides of neck* and bordered below by broad white pectoral band extending up on sides of neck as narrow white line to behind eye; breast grayish turning green on sides and belly; large white flank patch behind wing (conspic. in flight); tail

rather short, *deeply forked*, blackish. ♀: above dark green, upper tail coverts rufous; *below all buffy cinnamon becoming rufous on lower breast and belly*; dusky ear patch; broad buffy white pectoral band (faintly indicated) extends up sides of neck as narrow line to behind eye; *tail normal (not deeply forked), entirely cinnamon rufous with small black subterminal band*.

Sim. species: ♂ from ♂ Amethyst Woodstar by flaring gorget and shorter tail. Also see ♂ Rufous-shafted Woodstar. ♀ from ♀ Amethyst or ♀ Rufous-shafted by *mostly cinnamon rufous tail* (Amethyst has dark tail with only tips buff; Rufous-shafted has dark central tail feathers and rufous outer ones).

Behavior: Will most often be seen hovering beelike, as if suspended by a string, in front of a large flowering tree, or perched alone on a high bare twig to which it may return freq. between feeding bouts, or from which it may dash off in pursuit of rivals. Feeds at low nectar reward flowers and filches nectar from flowers within territories guarded by larger hummers. Reg. chased by larger hummers.

Status and habitat: Resident and seasonal migrant in humid and wet forest, along forest borders, shady coffee plantations, and disturbed areas and pastures with scattered trees. Infreq. seen and recs. spotty, doubtless because of seasonal movements. To be watched for at els. lower than given below: sight recs. of ♀♀, presum. this sp., w Mérida, 17 Jun 1994, nw Barinas (1500m), 20 Jan 1994 (Hilty), and 28 Nov 1995 (R. Schofield; G. Rodríguez); in Colombia down to 1200m (occas. to 500m).

Range: 2200–3000m (sight to 1500m). Andes of Mérida (*heliodor*). Mts. of e Panama; Andes of Colombia and nw Ecuador.

Note: Subsp. *meridae* synonymized with nominate *heliodor*[217]. Formerly placed in *Acestrura*[148].

Rufous-shafted Woodstar
PLATE 29

Chaetocercus jourdanii   Tucusito Garganta Rosa

Identification: 2.8″ (7cm). Bill straight (0.5″, 13mm). ♂: above shining green, *gorget rosy magenta* (or purple—*jourdanii*), *the sides rounded* and bordered below by broad white pectoral band that extends up as narrow white line to behind eyes, rest of underparts green; *large white flank patch behind wing* (conspic. as hovers); tail deeply forked, *base and shafts rufous* (hard to see in field). ♀: above like ♂; dusky ear patch; *below buffy white* with faintly indicated pale crescent across chest that extends up as narrow line to behind eye; ill-defined dusky breast band; *central tail feathers dark green*, outer 3 prs. rufous with dusky subterminal band; all tail feathers with buff rufous tips.

Sim. species: ♂ closely resembles ♂ Gorgeted Woodstar. Best field mark is rounded sides to gorget (not flared back to point); in direct comparison in hand (perhaps in field) plumage is paler green (Gorgeted tinged blue green), tail longer and with rufous shafts and base. ♀ from ♀ Gorgeted or Amethyst by bicolored tail (dark central feathers, rufous outer ones). **Voice:** ♂♂ sing a thin, lisping 3- to 4-note *tssit, tssit, tssit, tssit* from treetop (C. Parrish).

Behavior: Foraging strategy sim. to that of others of genus. Most often seen perched high on an open twig or hovering beelike in front of a large flowering tree; also at low to mid.-story flowering shrubs inside or at edge of forest. Like other tiny hummers, often filches nectar from patches of flowers guarded by larger hummers, or forages at flowers too small (too little nectar) to be used by larger spp.

Status and habitat: Uncommon to occas. fairly common. Humid and wet forest and forest borders, older second-growth woodland, flower gardens, and partially cleared areas near forest. Most recs. 900–2500m (those at 3000m need verification). Erratic in occurrence; marked seasonal movements to lower el. (reg. to 900m) during rainy season (May–Nov) but also erratically high or low in other months. Seen occas. Jan–Mar in mts. near Colonia Tovar, Aragua; near Rancho Grande Biol. Station in Jun (rainy season).

Range: 900–3000m. Sierra de Perijá, Zulia; Andes from s Táchira to s Lara (*andinus*); Sierra de San Luis, Falcón, and n cordilleras from Yaracuy to Distr. Federal (*rosae*); mts. of Sucre and n Monagas (*jourdanii*). Ne Colombia. Trinidad.

TROGONIFORMES

Trogonidae: Trogons

Sorocuaces, Viudas, Quetzales

Trogons are found predominantly in tropical latitudes. They are believed to have originated in the Old World but are numerous in the New World as well, reaching greatest abundance in humid lowland forests of the Neotropics[169]. They have beautiful, often glossy or metallic colors; quetzals, in particular, are renowned for their brilliant colors and are considered by many to be among the most beautiful birds in the world. In general trogons comprise a rather uniform group of birds, almost all of which are characterized by large eyes, short thick bills, long, strongly graduated, and square-tipped tails held down, small weak feet with 2 toes for-

ward and 2 back, and very upright posture. They feed on insects and fruit usually taken on the wing during a swoop and brief stall or hover before dropping away to a new perch. Nests are in natural cavities or woodpecker holes, or are excavated in wasp, termite, or arboreal ant nests or in soft rotten stubs. Young males resemble females and usually do not acquire definite adult plumage for more than a year.

Pharomachrus

Glistening plumage; greatly elongated upper wing coverts extend below wing; upper tail coverts as long as or longer than tail. ♀: upper wing coverts and upper tail coverts shorter than in ♂; narrow buff edges on primaries (in hand); nest in tree cavities; most highly frugivorous of family.

Crested Quetzal   PLATE 32
Pharomachrus antisianus   Quetzal Coliblanco
Identification: 13″ (33cm). ♂: *bill yellow*; eyes and eyering red. *Short fuzzy green crest projects over bill*; head and upperparts glistening golden green, long wing coverts droop over wings; glistening emerald upper tail coverts project 1″ (25mm) beyond tail; throat and upper breast green, *lower breast and belly brilliant red, 3 outer tail feathers white* (tail all white from below), rest black but usually hidden except occas. as narrow black band showing below tail tip. ♀: *head dull brown*, otherwise above like ♂, scapulars and upper tail coverts shorter (latter do not reach quite to tail tip), throat to mid. breast greenish brown, belly pinkish red, tail black (from below) with *3 outer feathers barred white on outer web and tipped white*. At rest outer edge of tail shows barring.

Sim. species: ♂ told from ♂ Golden-headed Quetzal by white undertail and red eyes, ♀ by barring on tail from below (not all-black tail). Up close note different head color (brown, not golden bronze), but variable light angles often make head color unreliable as a field character. Also see Masked Trogon.

Voice: Song a slow, melancholy ser. of ca. 4–5 whistled *tay, taAAaaao* phrases; easily imitated; a loud cackling when excited.

Behavior: Much as in Golden-headed Quetzal. Solitary birds or prs. spend long periods of time sitting quietly in upper levels of cloud forest trees. Several may gather at fruiting trees, esp. Lauraceae (i.e., *Persea* and *Ocotea*), and spend much of time there, or return freq. to these trees. Feed mostly on relatively large, high-fat fruits taken during short upward sally followed by brief hover or stall as fruit is grasped. Occas. take insects,

small vertebrates or invertebrates, but these mostly fed to young. Flight is fast and undulating, propelling bird through forest in a hurtling manner.

Status and habitat: Uncommon and very low-density resident inside montane wet forest (cloud forest). Local or seasonal el. movement in response to fruit abundance needs documentation. Not as numerous as Golden-headed Quetzal.

Range: 1200–3000m (most recs. below 2700m). Sierra de Perijá, Zulia; Andes from s Táchira n to s Lara (Anzoátegui). Colombia s in mts. to Bolivia.

White-tipped Quetzal   PLATE 34

Pharomachrus fulgidus   Quetzal Dorado

Identification: 13″ (33cm). 165g. ♂: *bill butter yellow*; eyes dark red; small rounded frontal crest. *Upperparts glistening golden green*, long green scapular feathers extending down over wing coverts; throat and chest green; *breast and belly brilliant red*; long upper tail coverts extend slightly beyond central tail feathers; tail black (concealed from above by green upper tail coverts), distal half of 3 *outer feathers white (tail appears almost all white from below)*, flight feathers black. ♀: bill coppery gray, head and upperparts green, chest greenish, breast dull greenish brown turning red on belly; tail dusky black, *distal half of outer 3 feathers barred and tipped white*; no crest and no elongated wing or tail coverts.

Sim. species: Only quetzal in its range. See Collared Trogon.

Voice: Often vocal, esp. Dec–Apr; advertising call a far-carrying, melancholy ser. of slow whistles, *WHOOOOOou, ca'who, WHOOOOOou, ca'who . . .*, (4–6 phrases) without pause. In a common variation *whOOou, ca'who, ca'who, ca'who . . .* (2–several times); or sometimes reversed, e.g., *who, caWHOOou*; or shortened to *caWHOOou* several times. Also loud cackling and rattling calls when excited or disturbed.

Behavior: Much as in Crested and Golden-headed quetzals but more vocal, esp. in early dry season. Also notably gregarious; at times ♂♂ and ♀♀ gather in noisy groups of 4–10 prior to breeding. Perch very upright and sway back and forth slightly as call. Cavity nest dug in rotten tree stub.

Status and habitat: Fairly common resident in humid and wet montane forest (mossy cloud forest), occas. forest borders and tall second growth. Readily found in PN Henri Pittier when vocalizing.

Range: 900–1950m (prob. occas. lower). N cordilleras from w Yaracuy to Aragua (incl. Cerro Golfo Triste)

and Miranda (e to Curupao); mts. of ne Anzoátegui, Sucre, and n Monagas (*fulgidus*); no recs. in Distr. Federal. Ne Colombia.

Golden-headed Quetzal   PLATES 32, 34

Pharomachrus auriceps   Viuda de La Montaña

Identification: 13″ (33cm). Easily confused with Crested Quetzal. ♂: like ♂ Crested Quetzal but crest smaller, eyes dark, head golden bronze (not emerald green), and *underside of tail solid black* (no white). ♀: like ♀ Crested Quetzal but *tail all black* (no white barring), head dusky green with *reddish copper tinge* (not dull flat brown of Crested Quetzal).

Sim. species: Also see Masked Trogon.

Voice: Song a slow, mournful, whistled *cuu-CUUuua*, typically repeated 2–5 times, faster when excited. Also a cackling *kaauuh, ka'ka'ka'ka'ka-ka-ka* as in other quetzals.

Behavior: Solitary birds, prs., or less often groups of 3–6 sit very erect from forest mid. level to canopy. Eat mostly large fruits, esp. of Lauraceae (*Nectandra, Ocotea, Persea*, etc.) and Burseraceae, which are snatched in flight as birds hover-stall momentarily at end of short, upward-swooping sally. Small nos. of arthropods are fed to young. When not feeding, sit quietly and inconspic. on horizontal subcanopy branch and periodically regurgitate large seeds of recently swallowed fruit. Undulating flight is fast and powerful, with wings closing after a few flaps as birds hurtle through forest. Freq. seen with Crested Quetzal at fruiting trees. Cavity nest in rotten stub; 2 grayish blue eggs[589].

Status and habitat: Uncommon resident in wet montane forest, esp. mossy cloud forest, occas. forest borders, and older second-growth woodland. Like other quetzals, difficult to find unless vocalizing. Seasonal movement to lower els. may occur during May–Oct rainy season.

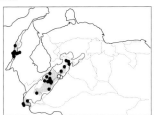

Range: 2000–3100m (sight to 1500m, nw Barinas). Sierra de Perijá, Zulia; Andes from Táchira n to ne Trujillo at Cuevas de Carache (*hargitti*). Colombia s in Andes to n Bolivia.

Pavonine Quetzal   PLATE 34

Pharomachrus pavoninus   Viuda Pico Rojo

Identification: 13″ (33cm). Only quetzal in Amazonas. Bill orange red (♂) or dusky yellow with reddish base (♀). ♂: much like Crested Quetzal. *Small fuzzy crest, head, and upperparts glistening emerald green, lower breast, belly, and under tail coverts brilliant red, tail solid black* (no white), green upper tail coverts reach to but usually not beyond tail. ♀: head olive green (not glistening), upperparts green, throat and chest dull green,

lower breast and belly coffee brown, *under tail coverts stained red*, tail slaty, *outer 2–3 prs. of feathers with a few white bars on outer web* (bars mostly near tip).
Sim. species: See Black-tailed Trogon which is smaller, duller, and lacks long projecting wing coverts.
Voice: Advertising or territorial song a far-carrying but slow ser. of 4–6 long, descending whistles, each followed by an emphatic *chok* note: *wheeeeeear, chok!.. wheeeeeear, chok!,* . . . ; very slow and melancholy. Loud cackling when disturbed. Sometimes rather noisy, calling for 1 hr or more at dawn as moves through forest.
Behavior: Usually found alone or in prs. in canopy of tall forest. Mostly independent of mixed-spp. flocks. Feeds by short outward- and upward-swooping sallies that end in momentary hover-stall during which a large fruit is snatched. Otherwise sits erect and quiet and, unless calling, easily overlooked. Prs. range over very large (up to 1km²) territories.
Status and habitat: Uncommon resident in humid terra firme forest in lowlands. Generally in low density, perhaps also local. Only quetzal in lowlands.

Range: To 700m. S Amazonas (Cerro Duida southward) and sw Bolívar from Salto Guaiquinima southward (*pavoninus*). Se Colombia to n Bolivia and w Amaz. Brazil.

Trogon

Heavy bill hooked at tip; large eyes; short wings; long, graduated, square-tipped tail; ♂♂ have metallic colors, black faces (not always obvious), some with vermiculated gray and black shoulder patches. ♀♀: duller and field identification confusing; most spp. lack vermiculated shoulder patches; larger spp. eat more fruit and fewer insects than smaller spp.; often dig own nest cavity.

Black-tailed Trogon   PLATE 32
Trogon melanurus Sorocuá Cola Negra
Identification: 11″ (28cm), 104g; or in Zulia 12″ (30cm), 115g. Found mostly s of Orinoco. *Bill and narrow eyering orange red* (♂) or yellowish with black culmen and no eyering (♀). *Large trogon.* ♂: above, incl. tail, dark glossy greenish blue, rump bluish, face and throat black, chest green bordered below by narrow white chest band; *lower underparts bright red; tail uniform black below*. Or dark bottle green above, little or no blue (*macrourus*). ♀: upperparts, head, and throat slate gray, wings and tail darker, shoulders sometimes with a little gray and black vermiculation, *chest light*

gray, belly red, tail as in ♂ or with some obscure white barring on outer web and tip of outer feathers. Imms. may show whitish barring on outer tail feathers.
Sim. species: Smaller Collared Trogon shows white barring and tipping on undertail; ♀ is brown (not gray) above. At higher el. see Masked Trogon; in s Amazonas, larger Pavonine Quetzal.
Voice: ♂'s song a long ser. of rather low-pitched, inflected whistles, *waaoo, wahoo,* . . . (or *cuuh, cuuh* . . .), delivered much more slowly than songs of most trogons. Alarm or disturbance (?) a low, chuckling *cluk 'cluk'cluk'cluk*.
Behavior: Usually found alone or in loosely assoc. prs. but occas. gathers in noisy calling groups of 6 or more. Stays mostly in forest mid. story or higher, perches very upright, sometimes slowly rolling head side to side to peer upward, then sallies outward and upward short distances, hovers or stalls momentarily, and snatches arthropod prey from foliage (occas. twigs) or grabs fruit. Mixed fruit/arthropod diet strongly biased toward fruit. As in others of family, flight is undulating and headlong. Nests in holes in trees or in termite nests; 2–3 bluish white eggs[651].
Status and habitat: Uncommon to fairly common resident in humid lowland and foothill forest and tall second-growth woodland; reg. along forest borders and in clearings with scattered trees.

Range: To 100m n of Orinoco; to 1000m s of Orinoco. Nw Zulia (*macroura*); nw Amazonas along Orinoco (Caño Capuana) and generally s of Río Ventuari; Bolívar from lower Río Caura, Río Paragua, and Sierra de Imataca s locally to Gran Sabana (*melanurus*). C Panama to the Guianas, n Bolivia, and s Brazil.

Amazonian White-tailed Trogon   PLATE 32
Trogon viridis Sorocuá Cola Blanca
Identification: 11.5″ (29cm). 82g. *Large trogon.* ♂: *bill greenish ivory; prom. eyering blue white.* Head, throat, and chest shining violet blue, face and shoulders black, back glistening deep green, rump peacock blue (inconspic. in field), *lower breast and belly bright yellow*, closed tail greenish black above, *white below* (outer 3 prs. of feathers black basally with large white tips); in flight large white tips conspic. ♀: bill dusky above, blue gray below; *eyering blue white, complete or somewhat broken*. Plumage mostly dark gray, shoulders vermiculated (etched) black and white, *lower breast and belly orange yellow*, underside of tail black, tips and outer webs of *outer 3 tail feathers white*.
Sim. species: ♂ differs from any other "yellow-bellied" trogon by combination of mostly white undertail and

unbroken blue white eyering. ♀ very like ♀ of either sp. of violaceous trogon but noticeably larger with more prom. blue eyering that is complete or nearly so, and no white on chest. If in doubt, look for nearby ♂. Also see Black-throated Trogon.

Voice: ♂♂ give at least 2 song types: a slow song (ca. 2.5 notes/sec) mostly in areas of overlap with Amazonian Violaceous Trogon, e.g., Río Grande; elsewhere, esp. in drier forest where Amazonian Violaceous does not occur, sings both slow and fast songs, the latter (ca. 4 notes/sec) sim. to those of Amazonian Violaceous Trogon. Fast song typically starts hesitantly, then gains speed and confidence, *caaop, caaop, caao-cao-ca-ca-ca-ca-ca-ca-ca-ca-ca-ca.*

Behavior: Usually seen alone or in prs., both with and away from mixed-spp. flocks. Typically sluggish and unsuspicious, perching erect on open mid.-level branches and slowly turning head to peer around at nearby foliage. Occas. sallies short distances, swooping up in sally-stall or fluttery hover to snatch fruit or grab a caterpillar or katydid from a leaf. Mixed fruit/arthropod diet more heavily biased toward fruit than that of smaller spp. of *Trogon*[532]. Like most others of genus, ♂♂ and ♀♀ periodically gather in loosely assoc. but very excitable groups to call. Hurtle through forest with dipping headlong flight. Dig nest cavity in termite nest or rotten stub.

Status and habitat: Most numerous and freq. seen trogon in Venez. Resident in tall humid forest, forest borders, and second-growth woodland of various ages. Commonest in humid areas, less numerous in dry forest.

Range: To 800m n of Orinoco; to 1300m s of Orinoco. E base of Andes from Táchira to n Portuguesa; Coastal Cordillera in Distr. Federal and Miranda (Cerro Negro); Sucre, Monagas, Delta Amacuro, and generally in Amazonas and Bolívar (*viridis*). E Colombia s to c Bolivia, s Brazil, and the Guianas.

Note: Birds from c Panama to w Ecuador now considered a separate sp.[541].

Collared Trogon
Trogon collaris   Sorocuá Acollarado
PLATE 32

Identification: 10.5″ (27cm). 60g. ♂: *bill yellow*; narrow eyering red. Above dark glossy green, shoulders vermiculated gray and black, face and throat black, chest dark green bordered below by narrow white band; *breast and belly red*, tail green above with black band at tip, *from below outer 3 prs. of feathers narrowly and evenly barred black and white and broadly tipped white.* ♀: bill dusky above, blue gray below; prom. bro-

ken eyering whitish. Green of ♂ replaced by soft coffee brown; face and throat black, narrow or obscure white chest band; breast and belly pinkish to red, *tail from above dark rufous with black band at tip,* from below vermiculated gray and white (looks grayish in field), 3 outer prs. of feathers with narrow black subterminal band and broad white tip (forms 3 bands).

Sim. species: In Andes see Masked Trogon; s of Orinoco see Masked and Black-tailed trogons. In all areas, Masked Trogon occurs mostly at higher el.

Voice: Commonest song of ♂ a soft, melancholy *cu'd, cu, cu, cu, cu* (no. of *cu* notes variable but usually ca. 4); also soft *purr* notes, a descending trill, and *churr* over and over when disturbed as bird quickly raises tail.

Behavior: Rather quiet, easily overlooked, usually found alone or in prs. from understory to subcanopy. Reg. with mixed-spp. flocks. Notably unsuspicious and often can be closely approached. Sits quietly, then makes sudden short to fairly long sallies out and up for fruit, or to foliage to snatch caterpillers and other invertebrates. Flight is headlong and dipping as in others of genus. Nest in cavity in rotten stub.

Status and habitat: Fairly common to common resident in humid and wet foothill and mt. forest and tall second-growth woodland in n Venez.; locally down to sea level in moist riparian woodland in dry zones (e.g., Chuao, Aragua); s of Orinoco uncommon and local in humid lowland and foothill forest. At higher els. in Andes and tepuis replaced by allied Masked Trogon.

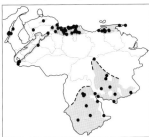

Range: To 2300m (mostly 300–1900m) n of Orinoco; to 1200m s of Orinoco. Sierra de Perijá, Zulia; Andes n to nw Lara; Falcón (Sierra de San Luis); sight, La Misión), mts. of Yaracuy, n cordilleras from Carabobo e through Distr. Federal, Miranda, and n Guárico; mts. of Sucre and n Monagas (*exoptatus*); c and s Amazonas (mid. Río Ventuari southward); Bolívar, mainly in w and s (*collaris*). S Mexico to Bolivia, se Brazil; Guyana; Suriname. Trinidad and Tobago.

Masked Trogon
Trogon personatus   Sorocuá Enmascarado
PLATE 32

Identification: 10.5″ (27cm). 56g. Looks like Collared Trogon with a "make-over." ♂: *bill all yellow; bold eyering orange red.* Above glossy green, shoulders vermiculated gray and white, black *face and throat sharply defined against green chest; narrow white chest band; lower breast and belly red,* tail bronzy green above with black tip, *from below outer 3 prs. of feathers black finely barred white* (at a distance barring blurred) *and broadly tipped white.* Or back strongly tinged reddish bronze (*duidae*); or back golden green (*ptaritepui*). ♀: much like ♀ Collared Trogon but differs in *all-yellow bill* (not dusky upper mandible), *sharper and more conspic. black mask and throat*, and underside of tail *finely and distinctly barred* black and white (not vermiculated gray).

Sim. species: ♂ closely resembles ♂ Collared Trogon, but much finer undertail barring blurs gray at a distance and stands in sharp contrast to large, "blocky white" tail tips; overall foreparts more crisply defined.

Voice: ♂'s song ca. 4–10 slow, soft, cooing notes, *cuu, cuu, cuu, cuu*, or longer *wu whu-whu-whu-whu-whu-hu-hu-hu*, louder in middle. When disturbed a softly squeezed *purrr*, much like Collared Trogon.

Behavior: Sim. to Collared Trogon. A rather quiet trogon of forest mid. levels or lower. Often associates with mixed-spp. flocks. Cavity nest in rotten tree stub; 2 white eggs in Colombia[260].

Status and habitat: Fairly common resident in humid and wet montane forest and along forest borders. Generally occurs above range of Collared Trogon (limited overlap where prob. interspecifically territorial).

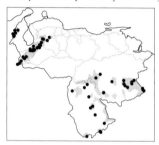

Range: 1500–3000m n of Orinoco; 700–1850m s of Orinoco. Sierra de Perijá, Zulia; Andes from s Táchira to s Lara (*personatus*); mts. of Amazonas; nw Bolívar near lower Río Caura (*duidae*); c and s Bolívar in mid. Rio Paragua (Cerro Guaiquinima) and se tepuis of Auyán, Aprada, Chimantá, Uei, and Roraima (*roraimae*); se Bolívar on Sierra de Lema, Kabanayén, Ptari-tepui, and Uaipán-tepui (*ptaritepui*). Highlands of Colombia s to Bolivia; Guyana and adj. n Brazil.

Black-throated Trogon   PLATE 32
Trogon rufus   Sorocuá Amarillo

Identification: 9.5″ (24cm). 54g. ♂: *bill yellowish green*; eyering yellow orange. Face and throat black, otherwise *head, chest, and upperparts glistening green*, shoulders vermiculated gray and black, narrow pectoral band white, *breast and belly yellow*, tail from above olive green with black tip, from below *3 outer feathers evenly barred black and white and broadly tipped white* (forms 3 bands). Or tail from above golden bronze (*amazonicus*); or reddish bronze (*sulphureus*). ♀: upper mandible dusky, lower yellowish green; broken eyering whitish. *Head, upperparts, throat, and chest brown*, lores blackish, irreg. pectoral band white, *breast and belly yellow, tail from above rufous tipped black*, below like ♂.

Sim. species: ♂ is only "yellow-bellied" trogon with obviously green head and upperparts; also note gray shoulder patch. Cf. ♂ Amazonian Violaceous Trogon

and larger Amazonian White-tailed Trogon. ♀'s yellow belly and brown (not gray) head and upperparts are unique.

Voice: Song of ♂ a slow, evenly spaced ser. of ca. 2–4 *cuk* or *cuh* notes, at rate of 1/sec or slower; also a low, churring *trrr*, much as in other *Trogon*.

Behavior: Sim. to others of genus (see Amazonian White-tailed Trogon). Mid. story or lower, and often in understory. Notably confiding. Occas. at army ant swarms. Nest in cavity 1–4m up[630].

Status and habitat: Uncommon resident in humid lowland forest and older second-growth woodland.

Range: To 900m. C Amazonas from Pto. Yapacana to Río Casiquiare (*sulphureus*); w Amazonas from San Fernando de Atabapo s to Yavita-Pimichín trail and upper Orinoco (*amazonicus*); generally in Bolívar (*rufus*). Honduras to w Ecuador; e of Andes s to n Bolivia, Amaz. Brazil, and the Guianas; se Brazil, e Paraguay, and nw Argentina.

Note: Subspp. *sulphureus* and *amazonicus* doubtfully distinct.

Northern Violaceous Trogon
Trogon caligatus   Sorocuá Violáceo Norteño

Identification: 9″ (23cm). 42g. *The 2 violaceous trogons are the smallest trogons in Venez.* ♂: bill greenish white, *eyering bright orange yellow. Head and chest shining dark blue*, throat and chest black, rest of upperparts dark bottle green to blue green, *shoulder patch finely vermiculated gray and black*, narrow pectoral band white, *breast and belly yellow*, tail from above dark green tipped black, from below barred narrowly barred black and white and broadly tipped white. ♀: upper mandible dusky, lower pale; *broken whitish eyering*. Mostly dark gray, shoulder patch as in ♂; usually with irreg. white chest band (or patch); lower underparts yellow, tail as in ♂ but only outer web of outer 3 prs. of feathers barred and tipped white.

Sim. species: See Amazonian White-tailed Trogon. Other trogons in range have red bellies.

Voice: Song (nw Barinas) a rather fast ser. of downslurred whistled notes, *cuh-cuh-cuh . . . .*, at steady rate (no acceleration) of ca. 3/sec and 7–20 or more notes.

Behavior: Sim. to Amazonian Violaceous Trogon. In Costa Rica 10 cavity nests dug in wasp nests; also in arboreal ant or termite nest or rotten stub high in tree; 2–3 eggs[706]; nest 2–30m up.

Status and habitat: Fairly common resident in Perijá foothills and along e base of Andes. Humid forest borders, treefalls, shady coffee plantations, and clearings with scattered trees; less often inside tall lowland forest.

Range: To 1200m. Sierra de Perijá, Zulia; Andes from s Táchira to w Trujillo, nw Barinas, and nw Cojedes at Río San Carlos (*caligatus*). E Mexico to nw Peru.

Amazonian Violaceous Trogon   PLATE 32
Trogon violaceus   Sorocuá Violáceo Amazónico
Identification: 9″ (23cm). 42g. *Small trogon. ♂ and ♀ essentially identical to respective sexes of previous sp.* Or sim. but ♂ with head slightly glossed purplish blue rather than dark blue (*crissalis*).
Sim. species: Combination of bluish head, yellow eye-ring, and small size separate ♂ from other ♂ "yellow-bellied" trogons. ♀ very like ♀ Amazonian White-tailed Trogon but *smaller* and eyering broken.
Voice: Song up to 15, occas. to ca. 35, rather soft *cow* or *cuh* notes, faster (at least 2/sec up to nearly 4/sec) and higher pitched than that of Black-tailed Trogon; about same speed and pitch as "fast" songs of Amazonian White-tailed Trogon but steadier and without acceleration of that sp. Some w Amaz. pops. (Venez.?) of this sp. show marked variation in song speed, acceleration, etc.
Behavior: Much like others of genus (see Amazonian White-tailed Trogon) but takes proportionately more insects and less fruit than larger White-tailed and Black-tailed trogons[532]. Sallies mostly from perches at med. hts. or higher. Early in yr (or throughout yr?) ♂♂ gather in noisy, exuberant, loosely assoc. groups which call and fly back and forth in apparent attempt to compete for ♀♀ which also may join activity.
Status and habitat: Uncommon and local. Upper levels and canopy of humid lowland forest. Sight recs. extend range to n Monagas[596].

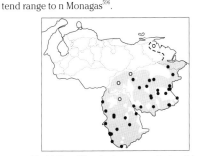

Range: To 1200m. W and s Amazonas (*crissalis*); ne Amazonas and generally in Bolívar (*violaceus*); sightings, n Monagas[58]. Se Colombia s to Bolivia, Amaz. Brazil, and the Guianas. Trinidad.
Note: Birds from s Mexico to nw Peru and w Venez. regarded as a separate sp.[541].

CORACIIFORMES

Cerylidae: Pied and Green Kingfishers
Martines Pescadores

This worldwide assemblage was formerly united under 1 family, with all members generally characterized by large heads, short necks, robust bodies, and short, weak feet. Recent DNA-DNA hybridization studies suggest the assemblage should be regarded as 3 separate families[604], with the Cerylidae being confined to the New World, Africa, and south and east Asia, and the 2 other groups, Wood Kingfishers (Halcyonidae) and Small Kingfishers (Alcedinidae), confined to various parts of the Old World. New World species have disproportionately long heavy bills, and their 2 forward-pointing toes are joined for about a third of their length. New World kingfishers live near water and eat fish taken by diving. Nests are burrows in banks, and usually overlook water, except in American Pygmy Kingfisher. White or buff eggs are laid at the end of the unlined burrow.

Ringed Kingfisher   Illus. p. 442
Megaceryle torquata   Martín Pescador Grande
Identification: 15″ (38cm). 300g. Bill large (3″, 76mm) and heavy, mainly dusky gray with large dull orangish patch near base of lower mandible. A big, tousle-headed kingfisher. ♂: *above powdery gray blue*, supraloral spot, throat, and sides of neck white (white almost encircles neck), *rest of underparts rufous chestnut, under tail covert white*, central tail feathers like back, rest blackish, outer web of outer ones narrowly barred white. In flight *shows large white patch at base of primaries*. ♀: sim. but with blue gray chest band bordered partially below with white, rest of underparts rufous chestnut incl. under tail coverts. Juv.: brownish chest band and extensive white flecking on wings.
Sim. species: Largest kingfisher in Venez. Only Belted Kingfisher is so blue.
Voice: Flight call a loud, rough *klek*, often repeated; a rapid ser. of *klek* notes forming a loud rattle is given in alarm or when disturbed, often in flight.
Behavior: Noisy and apt to protest with loud agitated rattle when flushed. Usually hunts alone, but occurs in loosely assoc. pairs and is often seen flying fairly high overhead with deep, somewhat uneven wing beats and unsteady flight while commuting between watercourses. Spends most of time on perch watching water, then dives, usually without hovering, for fish. On avg. hunts from higher perch (5–10m up) than other kingfishers and eats larger fish, mostly in 50–150mm range, near Leticia, Colombia (J. V. Remsen). Nest in unlined chamber at end of long burrow in bank, mostly Jan–Apr, when water levels are low and fish more concentrated; 3–5 eggs. Forms loose colonies of 4–5 prs. in favorable areas; more than 100 prs. reported in a colony in upper Orinoco[115].
Status and habitat: Common resident along most bodies of freshwater, also brackish and salt water and in

mangroves along coast. Local abundance varies markedly. Large nos. along gallery forest streams in llanos and small muddy streams s of Orinoco; scarce or uncommon along blackwater streams. Some seasonal movements occur as water levels rise and fall, e.g., only Jul–Jan (wet season) at Hato Masaguaral, Guárico[734].

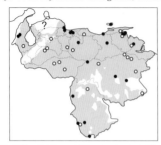

Range: To 500m (sight to 1400m in Andes). Throughout incl. Isla Margarita (*torquata*). S Texas (rare) and Mexico to Tierra del Fuego. Lesser Antilles. Trinidad.

Belted Kingfisher
Illus. below

Megaceryle alcyon   Martín Pescador Migratorio
Identification: 12″ (30.5cm). 150g. Bill 2″ (51mm), proportionately smaller than that of its tropical relatives. Prom. ragged crest. ♂: *head and upperparts pale blue gray*, throat and sides of neck white (almost encircles neck), *underparts white with single gray chest band*; flight feathers and outer tail feathers blackish narrowly barred white. ♀: sim. but with *rufous chest band* extending down sides and flanks (reverse of other kingfishers).
Sim. species: Above sim. to Ringed Kingfisher but decidedly smaller and not all rufous below. All other Venez. kingfishers are greenish above.
Voice: Loud, wooden rattle, perched or in flight; higher pitched and not as coarse as that of Ringed Kingfisher.
Behavior: Usually seen alone in Venez. Perches on branches or cliffs over water and watches carefully, then flies out, often hovers several meters up over water, and dives for fish. Wing beats uneven and flight unsteady as in larger Ringed Kingfisher.
Status and habitat: Generally scarce and uncommon migrant and winter resident from the north, Oct–Apr, mostly in mangroves and near coast; rare inland.

Range: To 450m. Coastal Falcón, Carabobo (Lago de Valencia), coastal Aragua, and Delta Amacuro; Islas Los Testigos; (sight); also Islas Margarita, La Tortuga, La Blanquilla, and Los Roques. Prob. sparingly along entire coast. Possible sight recs. from w Apure (Hato Cedral) and s Cojedes (Hato Piñero). Breeds in N Amer.; winters from coastal Alaska and British Columbia to Carib., occas. to Colombia; Guyana (sight); Galápagos Isls.

Amazon Kingfisher
PLATE 33

Chloroceryle amazona   Martín Pescador Matraquero
Identification: 11″ (28cm). 110g. Bill 2.7″ (69mm). Largest "green" kingfisher; *bill unusually large for size of bird*. Crested. ♂: above *dark oily green* with white cheeks extending back to form collar; below white with short moustachial streak and broad rufous chestnut band across chest; flanks spotted dark green, tail dark green, outer feathers blackish narrowly barred white, *flight feathers unspotted* (or with a few small inconspic. white notches on inner remiges). ♀: sim. but chestnut band replaced by incomplete (usually) dark green chest band.
Sim. species: Often confused with *much smaller* Green Kingfisher which shows prom. white spotting and barring on wings and esp. on tail in flight. Green-and-rufous Kingfisher has *no white* on collar or underparts.
Voice: Song a loud, rapid stream of shrill *tew* or *qew* notes (up to 20 or more) gradually descending in pitch; in flight a dull *chak*; song used mainly during encounters or disputes with conspecifics or with other kingfishers.
Behavior: Scattered individuals perch mostly 1–7m up (higher than perches used by Green Kingfisher, lower than Ringed Kingfisher) on rather exposed snags,

Belted Kingfisher (left, female),
Ringed Kingfisher (right, female)

bridges, etc., in vicinity of fast, slow, or static water. Spend long periods of time watching water, then fly out and plunge for fish. Occas. hover before diving, more often dive without hovering. In se Colombia take fish in 37–112mm range (J. V. Remsen). Flight smoother, faster, lower, and more direct than Ringed and Belted kingfishers. Breeds in holes dug 1.6m or so into stream banks during periods of low water; 3–4 white eggs[626].

Status and habitat: Generally commonest and most conspic. kingfisher in Venez. Resident along banks of streams, rivers, and lagoons with fresh and brackish water, mainly where trees provide abundance of suitable perches. Scarce on open banks of large rivers, but common around lake and lagoon edges with scattered bushes. Common in lowlands, in decreasing nos. along faster-flowing streams in foothills. Seasonal movements occur in response to changing water levels, e.g., rec. only Jul–Feb (irreg.) at Hato Masaguaral, Guárico[734].

Range: To 2500m (most recs. below 600m) n of Orinoco; to 500m s of Orinoco. Throughout (*amazona*). Mexico to n Argentina. Trinidad and Tobago.

Green Kingfisher   PLATE 33
Chloroceryle americana Martín Pescador Pequeño

Identification: 7.5″ (19cm). 27g. Bill 1.6″ (41mm). Miniature of Amazon Kingfisher. ♂: above dark oily green, *wings thickly spotted white*; *white collar encircles neck*; below white with short dark malar streak; broad band across chest rich chestnut, sides and flanks coarsely spotted dark green, central tail feathers dark green, rest blackish with *numerous white spotted bars (tail flashes much white in flight)*. ♀: above like ♂, below buffy white with green chest band and 2d spotted band across mid. breast that continues as coarse V-shaped spots down flanks.

Sim. species: Amazon Kingfisher lacks prom. white in wings and *esp. in tail*. If in doubt, flush bird. Because of small size, easily confused with Pygmy Kingfisher which is even smaller and *all rufous below* (no white on throat or collar). Also cf. larger Green-and-rufous Kingfisher.

Voice: Flight call a low pebbly *tsuut*, usually repeated 2–3 times with stuttering or clicking quality. Song a rapid descending ser. of *tsu* notes, sim. to Amazon Kingfisher but faster and less harsh.

Behavior: Scattered individuals perch mostly 1–3m up on branches or twigs overhanging water, or in vegetation along stream banks or lake edges. Watch for prey and usually plunge without hovering. In se Colombia eat fish mostly in 30–56mm range (J. V. Remsen). Fast

buzzy flight is straight and usually close to water. Nest in creekside burrow usually hidden by overhanging vegetation; 3–5 eggs[789].

Status and habitat: Common resident along banks of small to mid.-sized streams and around edges of lakes and ponds bordered by shrubbery and trees. Likes shady streamsides but does not require completely closed canopy overhead; also mangroves and in small nos. along fast-flowing mt. streams in foothills. Seasonal movements occur in llanos, perhaps elsewhere.

Range: To 1000m. Throughout n of Orinoco (*bottomeana*)[19]; s of Orinoco (*americana*). Sw US to n Chile and c Argentina.

Green-and-rufous Kingfisher   PLATE 33
Chloroceryle inda Martín Pescador Selvático

Identification: 9″ (23cm). 52g. Bill 1.9″ (48mm). *Large edition of Pygmy Kingfisher.* ♂: above shiny dark oily green, wings with sprinkling of small white dots, outer tail feathers with a few dotlike bars; *broad orange buff collar across sides of neck and cheeks extends back as tuft to nape*; underparts entirely buffy orange, paler on sides of neck. ♀: sim. but with narrow band of green feathers dotted or barred buff to white across chest.

Sim. species: Entirely "green and rufous." Shows *no white* on neck or underparts. Much smaller Pygmy Kingfisher has white belly, no white spotting on wings or tail. All other kingfishers have white in plumage above and below.

Voice: In flight a strident, buzzy *bzyoot* or *bzyuut*, as if electrical energy in call. Infreq. hd. song a loud descending ser. of *tew* notes rather like others of genus, given from streamside cover or when perched well back inside forest.

Behavior: Usually seen alone with members of prs. typically well separated. Perches ca. 1–3m up in brushy vegetation or in tangles overhanging water, or other shady places, and watches quietly for fish, then plunges directly into water without hovering. Rarely sits in open. Flies fast, low, and arrowlike, rapidly crossing streams or lagoons and usually plunges into shady vegetation and disappears before stopping.

Status and habitat: Relatively common resident but difficult to see. Favors small, narrow, and shaded streams covered by forest canopy, flooded várzea where water flows back inside forest, and swampy areas with permanent standing and shaded water. Also in mangroves where sometimes quite common (e.g., coastal se Sucre).

Range: To 400m. N base of Coastal Cordillera in Aragua (prob. elsewhere on coast); generally e of Andes

from w Apure, w Barinas, and Cojedes to se Sucre, Monagas, and Delta Amacuro; throughout s of Orinoco (*inda*). Nicaragua to w Ecuador; e of Andes s to n Bolivia and s Brazil.

American Pygmy Kingfisher   PLATE 33
Chloroceryle aenea   Martín Pescador Pigmeo
Identification: 5–5.5″ (12.7–14cm). 15g. *Size of a sparrow*. Bill 1.2″ (30mm). ♂: *above entirely dark oily green* (no white spots), orange rufous collar extends back across cheeks to nape; throat pale orange rufous, rest of underparts rufous chestnut, *central belly and under tail coverts white*. ♀: sim. but with narrow green and white band across chest.
Sim. species: Often confused with much larger Green-and-rufous Kingfisher and Green Kingfisher.
Voice: Perched or in flight an abrupt buzzy *jeeeet* or bisyllabic *jejeet!* Also weak flat ticking notes.
Behavior: A solitary and inconspic. little bird of shady watercourses. Sometimes very confiding. Perches mostly 1–2.5m up and in cover (seldom sits fully in open along riverbanks) where splashes, without hovering, for small fish (8–37mm range in se Colombia—J. V. Remsen) and perhaps occas. other aquatic prey. Sometimes dives repeatedly at short intervals. Flies fast with buzzy wing beats and often difficult for human eye to follow; often nods head and flicks tail. Nest a burrow in bank, roots of fallen tree, etc., not necessarily near water; 3–4 white eggs.
Status and habitat: Widespread and locally fairly common resident but infreq. seen. Thick shrubbery along banks of small wooded streams, forest pools, shrub-bordered lagoons, and flooded várzea forest; often common in mangroves (e.g., se Sucre).

Range: To 400m. S Zulia (Río Catatumbo) spottily e to se Sucre and Delta Amacuro (no recs. from arid nw); throughout s of Orinoco (*aenea*). S Mexico to w Ecuador, n Bolivia, s Brazil, and the Guianas. Trinidad.
Note: Formerly called Pygmy Kingfisher.

Momotidae: Motmots
Pájaro León

Motmots are a small Neotropical family, most diverse in northern Middle America. Most species have long, racket-tipped tails that are often swung side to side. The racket tips on the tail apparently develop as a result of weak attachment of the feather barbs which then break off during preening or abrasion. Birds lacking racket tips or with only 1 feather with a racket tip may be seen at certain times of the year. Motmots' voices are varied, ranging from low, owl-like hoots to longer, melodious modulations. They are rather sluggish birds of forest or lighter woodland. Most eat fruit supplemented by smaller amounts of arthropod and occas. small vertebrate prey. Motmots are usually most active at dawn and late in the afternoon. Nests, as far as known, are unlined burrows dug by both sexes; the 2–5 white eggs are incubated by both sexes.

Momotus

Bill heavy, upper and lower mandible with serrated cutting edge; long graduated tail with racket tips (most spp.).

Blue-crowned Motmot   PLATE 34
Momotus momota   Pájaro León
Identification: 16″ (41cm); or 18″ (46cm) in 2 southernmost subspp. 135g (*momota*). Tail extremely graduated; 2 central feathers very long (10″, 254mm) with bare subterminal shaft and racket tip (all subspp.), outermost pr. short (2.5″, 64mm). *Upperparts generally dark grass green* (or with chestnut nuchal collar—*momota*), distal half of tail and rackets blue; round black *central crown patch ("wears a yarmulka")* surrounded by azure blue band in front, deep violet blue behind; *black mask extends to point on ear coverts* where bordered above and below by narrow azure line; underparts dull olive green with caramel tinge on throat. Or below mostly caramel, throat and chest tinged olive (*subrufescens*); or as in *subrufescens* but lower underparts darker (*osgoodi*). All races show 2–3 bold black droplike spots on center of chest.
Voice: At dawn mainly gives a low, owl-like *oüü-doot*; when disturbed also a low, rolling *h'o'o'o'o'r'r*, sometimes 2–4 birds call more or less simultaneously. One of earliest dawn vocalizations. In n deserts of Falcón most vocal early in rainy season, May–Jul.
Behavior: Usually in loosely assoc. prs. that perch low to fairly high but within foliage; typically perch higher when calling. Sit very still, or if disturbed slowly swing tail side to side in mechanical manner, but otherwise surprisingly furtive and hard to see despite large size. Forage mostly at dawn and dusk by sallying rapidly to foliage, branches, or gd. for vertebrate and invertebrate prey and fruit. At least in humid areas eat more fruit than animal matter. Sit quietly for long periods during day. Nest and sometimes roost at end of long, often curved burrow dug in bank; 3–4 eggs; dry season nests in Costa Rica[641].
Status and habitat: Resident in a wide range of habitats but local and sometimes absent (or in very low

density) in seemingly suitable areas. Moist ravines in desert scrub in n Falcón; dry to humid lowland forest, old second-growth woodland, gallery forest, plantations, and cultivated areas.

Range: To 600m n of Orinoco; to 1200m s of Orinoco. N Perijá region, Zulia, w Lara, c and e Falcón (sight), and Carabobo e to Aragua (*subrufescens*); c Perijá region, c and s Zulia, nw Táchira, and w Mérida (*osgoodi*); e base of Andes in se Táchira, w Apure, and w Barinas (*microstephanus*); throughout Amazonas, Bolívar, and s Delta Amacuro (*momota*). E Mexico to nw Peru, nw Argentina, Paraguay, and se Brazil. Trinidad and Tobago.

PICIFORMES

Galbulidae: Jacamars

Barranqueros y Tucusos Montañeros

Jacamars are a highly distinctive group of New World birds found from southern Mexico to northern Argentina. They are best known for their shimmering, metallic green plumage, slender, tapered bodies, and long, pointed tails, but a few species have short tails and are predominantly brown or chestnut. Almost all of them have long, pointed, and slender bills, and in appearance, as well as in their habit of sallying rapidly and aerobatically for flying insects, they recall Old World bee-eaters (Meropidae). Jacamars are mainly birds of wooded or partially wooded terrain at low elevations; only 1 species (in Colombia and Ecuador) is confined to the highlands. As far as known, all species nest in holes in termitaries or in burrows dug by both sexes in banks or sloping ground. Their 2–4 eggs are white. Young jacamars are covered with down when they hatch.

Brachygalba

Bill long and thin; tail short and squarish (not graduated); plumage predom. brown, belly pale; often perch high or in open.

Pale-headed Jacamar   PLATE 33
Brachygalba goeringi   Barranquero Acollarado
Identification: 7″ (18cm). *Bill unusually long (1.8″, 46mm); tail short (2.3″, 58mm). Eyes dark. Head pale "faded" brown*, crown often with a little coarse black

streaking; cheeks dusky, back, wings, and tail dark greenish to bluish black (somewhat glossy), throat white, band across chest continuing down flanks light brown, *central underparts white crossed by short chestnut band across lower breast*.
Sim. species: Unique in range. S of Orinoco see Brown Jacamar.
Voice: Call a high, thin *weet*, singly or in a ser.; song, from high perch, an accelerating ser. ending in a fast trill, *weet, weet weet t'weet-t'weet-t'weet'ti'ti'ti't't't* by ad. ♂ and ♀[646]; both may sing simultaneously, turning heads side to side rapidly and vibrating tails up and down.
Behavior: Almost always seen sitting on a high bare branch where there is good visibility. Constantly moves head in nervous, jerky manner as watches for flying insects, incl. butterflies and dragonflies, then sallies in big aerobatic loops and returns, often to same perch. Almost always in prs. or family groups up to 6 or so, rarely alone. Sometimes all perch in same tree, even lining up in various directions on same branch to sing. Show some fondness for leguminous trees.
Status and habitat: Resident locally in gallery forest along small to large rivers in llanos but commonest along large rivers with mature forest (e.g., Río Apure); locally in acacia-dominated desert scrub bordering dry arroyos in c Lara, and in partially open shade trees over coffee in foothills (e.g., near Barinitas, Barinas). In all areas family groups tend to cluster in colonies along riverine woodland.

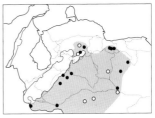

Range: To 1100m. Locally in c Lara (nw of Barquisimeto), and e of Andes from w Apure and nw Barinas e to s Carabobo, Aragua (Rancho Grande?), n Guárico (El Sombrero), and e Apure. Ne Colombia.

Brown Jacamar   PLATE 33
Brachygalba lugubris   Barranquero Castaño
Identification: 7″ (18cm). 16g. *Bill very long (1.9″, 48mm); tail short (2.3″, 58mm); eyes pale blue* (dark—imm.). Above brown, wings and tail glossed blackish brown, below mostly brown, *throat and chin tinged whitish, center of lower breast and belly white*. Or sim. but head tinged rufescent, belly buffy white (*obscuriceps*); or more rufescent brown below, belly fulvous (*fulviventris*).
Sim. species: See Pale-headed Jacamar (no known overlap).
Voice: Song a high, bouncy, and accelerating *plee, plee, plee-plee-plee'ple'ple'pe'pe'e'e'e*, recalling Pale-headed Jacamar. Call a thin *perEET*, sharply rising.
Behavior: Usually in prs. or loosely assoc. groups (families?) of up to 6–7 (occas. more) that perch low to fairly high, occas. even on snags above forest canopy.

Sit upright and watch alertly with rapid head movements, then make long looping sallies out into large open spaces for flying insects. Typically sally farther than previous sp. Often confiding and perch in relatively open trees such as *Cecropia*, where easily seen. **Status and habitat:** Fairly common but local resident of borders of scrubby white sandy soil forest, savanna tree isls., gallery forest borders, river-isl. vegetation, scattered trees and shrubs in clearings and forest borders. Dry to moist regions. Often on snags at edge of forest or woodland. Most numerous in dry/moist forest regions of e Bolívar and along gallery forest borders in Gran Sabana.

Range: To 1500m. N Amazonas (San Juan de Manapiare) southward (*obscuriceps*); nw Bolívar on lower Río Caura (*fulviventris*); rest of Bolívar from Cuidad Bolívar, Upata, and Guasipati southward; s Anzoátegui on Río Cañafistola (*lugubris*). E Colombia and the Guianas s to Bolivia and s Brazil.

Galbula

Long, thin bill somewhat broadened at base; tail often long, much graduated, rounded at tip; plumage highly iridescent.

Yellow-billed Jacamar   PLATE 33
Galbula albirostris   Barranquero Pico Amarillo
Identification: 7.5″ (19cm). 21g. Bill long (1.5″, 38mm), *upper mandible yellow, lower yellow tipped black.* Lores, eyering, and feet bright yellow. ♂: above shining iridescent green, crown green glossed reddish violet, throat white, rest of underparts rufous chestnut, 2 central tail feathers green, rest bronzy rufous (tail all rufous from below). Or sim. but darker, more chestnut below (*chalcocephala*). ♀: throat buff, underparts paler.
Sim. species: See Green-tailed and Rufous-tailed jacamars, both with dark bills.
Voice: Quieter than others of genus. Song, rather like other *Galbula* but faster, a high accelerating *peea-pee-pee-te-t-t-'t't't't't'tttt'r*; also sharp nasal *peek* notes.
Behavior: Single birds or prs. often sit from ca. eye level to 10m up inside tall forest, esp. on large looping vines, in treefalls, or in other somewhat open sites in forest where they watch alertly and sally in rapid loops for flying insects.
Status and habitat: Uncommon resident inside humid terra firme and várzea forest.

Range: To 1300m. W and c Amazonas from Ríos Sipapo and Ventuari southward (*chalcocephala*); Bolívar from lower Río Caura, Río Paragua, and Sierra de Imataca southward (*albirostris*). E Colombia and e Peru e to the Guianas and ne Brazil.

Rufous-tailed Jacamar   PLATE 33
Galbula ruficauda   Tucuso Barranquero
Identification: 10″ (25cm). 23g. Bill long (2″, 51mm), blackish. Or smaller (both sexes), 9″ (23cm), bill shorter (*brevirostris*). ♂: entire upperparts metallic green (back iridescent and shot with gold), sides of head dusky, throat white, pectoral band iridescent golden green, lower underparts rufous chestnut, *2 central tail feathers metallic green* (longer than others), *rest rufous; from below tail all rufous.* ♀: throat buff, underparts usually paler (*ruficauda*). Or both sexes as in *ruficauda* but back and tail reddish copper to golden copper (*pallens*).
Sim. species: S of Orinoco see Green-tailed Jacamar.
Voice: Call a sharp, nasal *peeap.* Freq. hd. song (some variation) a rather high, thin, and complaining *peeo, peeo, peea-pee-pee-pe-pe-pe-pe-pe-e-e-'e'e'eee*, accelerating into trill at end.
Behavior: As in most other spp. of genus, single birds or prs. sit mostly 1–5m up in treefalls or small openings or beneath overhanging cover. Perch very upright and alert with bill pointing upward. Move head rapidly and watch carefully, then sally fast in aerobatic loops for flying insects incl. dragonflies, butterflies, and bees, and return to a favorite perch. Nest a short burrow dug in bank or in termitary; 2–4 white eggs spotted cinnamon[638,646]; Aug–Sep breeding, w Guárico[734].
Status and habitat: Common and widespread resident n of Orinoco in desert scrub, tropical dry and moist forest, gallery forest, shrubby forest borders, and mangroves. Thrives in a wide variety of dry to moist habitats if there is suitable cover and a treefall or small

opening for sallying. Mostly replaced in humid zones s of Orinoco by Green-tailed Jacamar.
Range: To 850m n of Orinoco; to 400m s of Orinoco. Extreme nw Zulia at edge of Goajira Pen. (*pallens*); Zulia s of Lago de Maracaibo, nw Táchira, and w Mérida (*brevirostris*); rest of Venez. n of Orinoco, incl. s Delta Amacuro; drier northernmost Bolívar at Caicara and Río Cuchivero e to Upata and vicinity of El Palmar (*ruficauda*). S Mexico to nw Ecuador and the Guianas; Bolivia to se Brazil.

Green-tailed Jacamar   PLATE 33
Galbula galbula   Tucuso de Bosque Coliverde
Identification: 8.2″ (21cm). 23g. Bill long (2″, 51mm), blackish. ♂: entire upperparts metallic green (back iridescent and shot with reddish gold), chin black, throat white, broad pectoral band coppery green (very iridescent), lower underparts chestnut, *tail iridescent bluish green above, dusky green below* (dark gray in poor light), somewhat *shorter than others of genus* (3.5″, 89mm), rounded at tip. ♀: throat cinnamon buff, pectoral band often mixed with chestnut.
Sim. species: Rufous-tailed Jacamar has decidedly *longer* tail which is *rufous* below. Also cf. Yellow-billed and Bronzy jacamars.
Voice: Song sim. to those of other *Galbula* (esp. Rufous-tailed Jacamar), a long, thin, accelerating ser. of high notes, *peea . . pee, pee,pee-pee-pee-pe-pe'pe' pe'p'p'e'e'e'e'e'e'e*, with complaining quality, ending in trill. Also, often a slow *peeer . . peeer . . peeer . . ser.* that may or may not accelerate but does not end in trill and is rather like song of Paradise Jacamar.
Behavior: As in Rufous-tailed Jacamar. Single birds or prs. sit mostly 1–8m up in little open places, watch alertly with rapid head movements and bill pointed up, and sally out several meters in aerobatic loops for flying insects and return to perch.
Status and habitat: Fairly common to common resident in shrubby borders of humid lowland forest, treefalls and openings inside forest, and gallery forest. Generally found in more humid zones than allied Rufous-tailed Jacamar; the two do not overlap widely.

Range: To 450m. S Delta Amacuro (Curiapo); throughout Amazonas and Bolívar. E Colombia to the Guianas and n and c Brazil.

Bronzy Jacamar   PLATE 33
Galbula leucogastra   Barranquero Dorado
Identification: 8.5″ (22cm). 16g. Bill long (1.5″, 38mm), unusually thin for genus. Rather dark. ♂: *upperparts metallic bronzy blue green*, crown tinged bluish, back

shot with iridescent reddish violet and bronzy gold (can look quite dappled), *throat white*, broad pectoral band (not always complete) bronzy green (iridescent and shot with reddish copper), *belly white* heavily mixed dark gray on sides; tail from above dull dark bluish green, from below dusky, the outer feathers narrowly pale-tipped. ♀: throat buffy white, back and chest duller.
Sim. species: A small, dark-colored jacamar (note habits and habitat) with white throat and belly. See Brown and Green-tailed jacamars.
Voice: Song a slow ser. of 4–5 high, thin *peer* notes (recalls that of Paradise Jacamar but lacks initial pauses). Also, in n Amazonas, both sexes give a slow ticking trill over and over, *t-t-r-r-r-d-d-deet, tadeet, tadeet, tadeet.*
Behavior: Single birds or prs. perch from ca. eye level to subcanopy hts. but are more often high along forest borders. Watch actively and then chase flying insects in looping sallies. Nest a hole dug in termitary.
Status and habitat: Uncommon resident along borders of humid terra firme and várzea forest, esp. borders of scrubby forest, tree isls. in savanna, and forest clearings and treefalls. In all areas almost always assoc. with wooded habitats on white sandy soils.

Range: To 900m. Nw Bolívar (sight, Hato Las Nieves), and n Amazonas from Ríos Ventuari and Asisa southward (*leucogastra*). Se Colombia to e Peru, c Amaz. Brazil, and the Guianas.

Paradise Jacamar   PLATE 33
Galbula dea   Barranquero Colilargo
Identification: 12″ (30.5cm). 30g. Long, thin bill (2.1″, 53mm) and long, pointed tail impart "pointed-at-both-ends" look. *Mostly shining metallic blue black with white throat.* In good light note brown-tinged crown and bronze green gloss on wings. In hand base of inner webs of inner flight feathers white. Or sim. but slightly smaller, 11″ (28cm) (*brunneiceps*).
Sim. species: Looks black at a distance. Note white throat, distinctive shape, and habit of sitting high in canopy.
Voice: Song in Amazonas a high, thin ser. of notes that begin slowly then accelerate slightly, *PEEap . . PEEap . . peeap, peaa, peea, pee-pee-pe'pe'pe*; in e Bolívar also a long, slow ser. of *peea* notes that descend slightly but do not accelerate. Also high *peeap* notes singly.
Behavior: No other jacamar in Venez. normally occurs so high in canopy or perches in open as much as this sp. Single birds, prs., or occas. 3 perch on high bare snags where they have commanding view, or occas. perch a little lower along borders. Sit alert, watching in-

tently with restless head movements, and sally out in swift pursuit of large flying insects incl. bees, wasps, and cicadas. Often sally actively as mixed-spp. flocks pass by. Dig nest cavity in high arboreal termitary. **Status and habitat:** Locally common resident (easily overlooked) in humid lowland forest incl. white sandy soil forest and borders, and scattered trees or high stubs in clearings and second growth. Behavior and foraging microhabitat somewhat convergent with Swallow-winged Puffbird[92].

Range: To 1100m. Throughout Amazonas (*brunneiceps*); Bolívar from upper Río Caura (Río Canaracuni), upper Río Paragua, and Sierra de Imataca southward (*dea*). E Colombia to n Bolivia, Amaz. Brazil, and the Guianas.

Jacamerops

Larger and more robust than *Galbula*; bill very heavy; tail graduated; plumage iridescent.

Great Jacamar   PLATE 33
Jacamerops aureus   Barranquero Grande
Identification: 12″ (30.5cm). 64g. Heavy bodied. *Thick, slightly decurved black bill.* ♂: above metallic golden green, back strongly glossed reddish copper, upper throat dusky green, *lower throat white, rest of underparts deep rufous*, tail from below dull gray (in hand outer feathers tinged blue green). Or back golden green, crown bluish (*aureus*). ♂: throat and underparts cinnamon rufous (paler than ♂).
Sim. species: Largest, heaviest jacamar. Note stout bill and all-rufous underparts with no chest band.
Voice: Not very vocal. Advertising song, typically hd. only at long intervals from high in canopy, a long, slow wolf whistle, rising a little then falling, trailing off, and melancholy, *weeeeeeeeewhuuuuu* (inhale, exhale). During interactions with conspecifics (mates?) a soft, nasal, rising *naaaaaa* (context?). A nasal whining or catlike meowing *waaaaeEEeer* and quavering *whe-e-e-u-u-r*, often followed by bill-snapping, may signal aggression.
Behavior: More sluggish than other jacamars. Long periods of quiet but alert observance from perch at mid.-level to subcanopy hts. inside forest are interrupted by occas. sallies to foliage for large arthropod prey (other?). Sits very erect with tail down, often virtually unmoving except for occas. slow turning of head. Usually alone or in well-separated prs. that are sometimes stimulated to activity by passage of mixed-spp. flocks, but does not follow them.
Status and habitat: Resident. Uncommon and easily overlooked as it neither moves nor vocalizes much

and remains fairly high overhead in humid lowland forest; infreq. high along a forest border or in tall, old, second-growth woodland.

Range: To 500m (once to 800m). Generally in Amazonas; Bolívar from lower Río Caura to its headwaters, and upper Río Paragua (*ridgwayi*); ne Bolívar from Sierra de Imataca to upper Río Cuyuní (*aureus*). Costa Rica to n Bolivia, Amaz. Brazil, and the Guianas.

Bucconidae: Puffbirds
Juan Bobos

Puffbirds are a small New World family with members ranging from southern Mexico to southern Brazil but with greatest diversity in the Amazon Basin. As their name suggests, they are rather heavily built and rotund with large heads, short necks, short, weak legs, and lax "puffy" plumage. The bill has a cleft hook at the tip and varies from rather slender and decurved to large and heavy. Most puffbirds are classic "sit-and-wait" strategists that sit lethargically for long periods of time, then sally for relatively large prey, usually invertebrates or small vertebrates. A few species occasionally sally for fruit. This "lazy" foraging behavior has earned them the Spanish name of *bobo*, or "dummy." Except for *Monasa* and *Hypnelus*, most are unobtrusive and rather quiet, singing only a few times at or before dawn. Nests as far as known are dug in arboreal termitaries; a few species dig burrows in the ground. The 2–3 white eggs are incubated by both parents.

Notharchus

Large headed; heavy bill; long, stiff rictal bristles; tail rounded, slightly graduated, short relative to size of bird.

White-necked Puffbird   PLATE 33
Notharchus macrorhynchos   Juan Bobo
Identification: 10″ (25cm). 95g. *Massive hooked black bill.* ♂: upperparts black with *broad* (or very narrow—*macrorhynchus*) *white forehead*; *broad white nuchal collar*, sides of head and underparts white; broad black breast band; sides and flanks blackish somewhat barred or scaled with white on some birds. ♀: white of underparts obscurely tinged buff.
Sim. species: Most likely confused with *smaller* Pied Puffbird which has long but narrow white eyebrow, white on wings, and large white tail tips (from below). Very rare Brown-banded Puffbird has brown breast band, barred lower underparts, and white on underside of tail.

Voice: Song (mid morning) in Río Grande, Bolívar, a long ser. of rapid *pree* whistles (ca. 30 in 8 sec) on same pitch. At dawn (Iquitos, Peru) a long, nasal, frog-like trill, *prrrrrrrr* . . . (up to 15–20 sec), on same pitch, given once every 2–5 min and by both sexes.
Behavior: Often perches alone on high sunlit snags in early morning, and on less exposed but open branches or snags (e.g., in a tall *Cecropia* tree) later in day. Individuals tend to remain well separated from mates. Sit quietly with only occas. head movement for long periods, then sally abruptly to foliage or branches for large prey such as hard-shelled beetles and small vertebrates, and may return to original perch to "soften" prey by beating it against a branch before eating. Occas. found quite low around army ants. Both sexes excavate nest hole in arboreal termite nest, usually fairly high.
Status and habitat: Widespread and fairly common resident but easily overlooked. Dry, moist, and humid lowland forest and forest borders, tall second-growth woodland, and scattered trees in clearings; also gallery forest. In dry regions confined mostly to riparian areas where there are large trees.

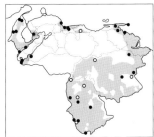

Range: To 1200m. W Venez. e to e base of Andes (except arid nw); e Falcón, n Cordilleras from Carabobo to Miranda; Sucre, Monagas, and n Delta Amacuro; generally in Amazonas; w and c Bolívar (*hyperrhynchus*); s Delta Amacuro s through e Bolívar (Sierra de Imataca) to n end of Gran Sabana (*macrorhynchos*). S Mexico to n Bolivia, Paraguay, and s Brazil.

Brown-banded Puffbird   PLATE 33
Notharchus ordii   Juan de La Selva
Identification: 8″ (20.3cm). 52g. Rare. Heavy hooked black bill. Upperparts black with narrow white forehead; flight feathers tinged brown, underparts white with *narrow black band across chest and broader brown band below*; sides heavily mixed and barred brown and white; tail *from above blackish, from below basal half* (mostly inner webs) *and narrow tips whitish*.
Sim. species: See larger White-necked Puffbird. Smaller Pied Puffbird lacks brown band and has long white eyebrow.
Voice: Song in Brazil a loud, energetic, rhythmic duet, *KUEEP! KUEEP, kee-kee-kee-kee-kee, quaaa, kée-kée-quaaa, kée-kée-quaa, kée-kée-quaa* . . . (up to 15 sec), with 1 bird giving higher *KUEEP* and *kee* calls, 2d the lower *quaa* notes. Song clear and emphatic with "wild, free-spirited" quality. Contact note a soft nasal *yank* (K. Zimmer recordings).
Behavior: Sim. to allied White-necked Puffbird. Members of a pr. tend to remain well separated and perch

high on snags that are usually partly screened by foliage. Sit quietly for long periods of time, then sally abruptly to foliage or branches for large arthropods and prob. small vertebrates. Both members of a pr. assist in excavation of nest cavity in high termite nest. Pr. excavating nest 31 Dec 1990–2 Jan 1991, Junglaven, Amazonas (B. Masters, R. Komuniecki, Hilty, K. Zimmer).
Status and habitat: Known from only a few specimens in widely scattered locs. Canopy of seasonally flooded scrubby várzea forest on white sandy soil adj. to tall terra firme forest. Sightings in e Peru, e Bolivia, and w Brazil are from canopy of terra firme forest; once in Mato Grosso, Brazil, from stunted deciduous forest on a rocky outcrop[833]. Reasons for its rarity are unknown.

Range: To 300m. Throughout Amazonas (sight, mid. Río Ventuari) incl. upper Río Asisa; Cerro Yapacana; Cerro Duida; San Carlos de Río Negro; Cerro de la Neblina). E Peru, e Bolivia, and w and c Amaz. Brazil.

Pied Puffbird   PLATE 33
Notharchus tectus   Juancito Negro
Identification: 6.5″ (16.5cm). 27g. Looks like miniature White-necked Puffbird. Above black; glossy blue black crown sprinkled with *white dots* (like a little starry night) visible up close; *long, narrow white eyebrow*; *white patch on inner flight feathers*; below white with broad black pectoral band; flanks mixed black and white, *tail feathers from below show median white band and broad white tips*.
Sim. species: Despite much smaller size, easily confused with White-necked Puffbird. Note Pied's black forehead, white eyebrow, spotted crown, and white on wings. Cf. Brown-banded Puffbird.
Voice: Often hd. but easily overlooked song, from high overhead, a long, high-pitched, rhythmic *peed-peed-peed-peed-it, peed-it, peed-it, peed-it, peea, pee, pee, pee*, with some variation, but always shrill and usually falling in pitch at end. May be repeated several times with only slight pause between songs. Recalls songs of Tropical Gnatcatcher of Amazonas.
Behavior: Singly or in prs. with members well separated, or sometimes sitting in same or adj. tree. Usually overlooked as it spends most of time in shady canopy or subcanopy of forest where it sits quietly, then at long intervals sallies out to foliage or branch surfaces for large prey. In early morning and late afternoon may sit in open on a high snag overlooking forest or a partially wooded clearing, or on a mid.-level perch in an open tree such as *Cecropia*, and this is when most likely to be seen. Tends to change perches more often than larger members of genus and also more vocal. Digs nest cavity in termitary 4m up or higher.

Status and habitat: Resident in humid terra firme forest, forest borders, tall second-growth woodland, and clearings with scattered trees in lowlands and foothills.

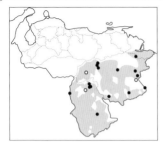

Range: To 1000m. Generally in Amazonas and Bolívar (*tectus*). Costa Rica to w Ecuador, ne Bolivia, Amaz. Brazil, and the Guianas.

Bucco

Smaller than most *Notharchus* (except Pied Puffbird); predom. brown (not black); often with bold pattern on head and chest; bill strong, wide at base, sharply hooked at tip; prom. rictal bristles; tail fairly short, narrow, and slightly to very graduated.

Chestnut-capped Puffbird   PLATE 33
Bucco macrodactylus   Burrito Cabecirrojo
Identification: 6.5″ (16.5cm). 25g. Eyes dark red. *Crown dark reddish chestnut*, otherwise dark brown above (somewhat scaly) with narrow *white frontlet and eyebrow*; nuchal collar cinnamon, *sides of head black bordered below by narrow white line*; upper throat buff, broad black pectoral band bordered below by white on chest, rest of underparts buffy brown densely vermiculated and scaled black. Tail much graduated (outer feathers half length of inner ones).
Sim. species: Viewed from behind, Spotted Puffbird is confusingly sim., but look for its orange rufous forehead and throat and bold spotlike bars below. Collared Puffbird has orange bill, rufous head, and is more often in canopy.
Voice: Usually quiet. Song in Peru a ser. of abrupt, slightly ascending notes ending in twitter, *pup pup pep pep peep peep peep pip pip pip pip pip piz*[444], not loud and mainly at or prior to dawn. Song also described as a plaintive ser. of elaenia-like *wee-a* notes, rising slightly (T. Parker).
Behavior: Usually seen perched alone ca. 1–6m up (occas. higher) on partially concealed or open branches at edge of dense shrubbery, and often near or over water. Like others of genus, sits quietly for long periods, then sallies out various distances, mostly to foliage, for large arthropod prey and small vertebrates. In se Peru, pr. digging nest cavity in arboreal termitary ca. 2.5m up.
Status and habitat: Uncommon resident (overlooked?) in shrubby edges of várzea and swampy or low-lying forest, shrubby streamsides, and flooded young second growth, less often humid forest borders. Everywhere shows affinity for water. Lowlands and foothills.

Range: To 550m. Nw Amazonas (Caño Capuana) and Río Ventuari (Río Asisa) s to San Carlos de Río Negro and Cerro de la Neblina (*macrodactylus*); extreme e Amazonas on upper Río Ventuari; Bolívar in lower Río Caura, upper Río Paragua, and Río Yurán (?). (*caurensis*). E Colombia to e Peru, w Brazil, and n Bolivia.

Spotted Puffbird   PLATE 33
Bucco tamatia   Burrito Moteado
Identification: 7″ (18cm). 35g. Eyes dark red. *Forecrown orange rufous*, rest of upperparts brown, the feathers pale edged (looks faintly scaled); narrow cinnamon nuchal collar; sides of head dusky gray bordered below by narrow white line and large black triangular malar patch; *throat orange rufous, rest of underparts white with coarse, scalelike black spots.*
Sim. species: From behind easily confused with Chestnut-capped Puffbird. No other puffbird is so boldly spotted below.
Voice: Does not sing much. Typically gives only a few songs in dim predawn, a soft but rather long-sustained *puwéep, puwéep . . .* , weak and plaintive, almost hesitant at first, then gradually increasing a little in strength as if bird gains confidence (up to 30 notes in 15 sec). Softly whistled *puwéep* (varied to *jooee* or *joowéep*) notes may gradually change to more strongly inflected, whistled *pu'chooee* at end.
Behavior: Much like others of genus. Usually sits alone (but mate often nearby) and unmoving on a shady perch 2–8m up. At dawn occas. on a more exposed perch at edge of a shrubby creek or woodland. Long periods of inactivity are interrupted by abrupt sallies to foliage or bark for large prey. 5 BC birds Mar–Apr, upper Orinoco[185].
Status and habitat: Uncommon resident but easily overlooked and prob. more numerous than small no. of recs. suggest. So far known mostly from 2 rather different forest habitats: in Amazonas in shrubby forest borders along small rivers, streams, and shady forest-

covered várzea creeks, and in Bolívar, along borders of terra firme forest on sandy or red (lateritic) soils. Majority of Venez. recs. are from small streams near Orinoco in n Amazonas.

Range: To 700m (once to 1400m, Cerro Duida). N Amazonas (vicinity of Cerro Yavi and Samariapo) s to Cerros Yapacana and Duida and San Carlos de Río Negro (sight, 1985—C. Parrish); s Delta Amacuro (Río Amacuro); Bolívar from Río Paragua (near Cerro Guaiquinima) and upper Río Cuyuní s to upper Río Caroní at Cerro Arebuchi (*tamatia*). E Colombia to n Bolivia, Amaz. Brazil, and the Guianas.

Collared Puffbird
PLATE 33

Bucco capensis   Musiú

Identification: 7.5″ (19cm). 51g. *Bill and feet bright red orange*; eyes orange to yellow; eyering orange. Entire head to below eyes orange rufous (crown with fine black barring—*dugandi*), rest of upperparts rufous chestnut finely etched with wavy black lines; *throat white* extending back as narrow buff nuchal collar; *large black pectoral band* also continues around hindneck; rest of underparts buffy white, tail rufous, crossed by 8–9 black bars.

Sim. species: See other *Bucco* puffbirds. Bright red orange bill and rufous head (no black markings) are the marks.

Voice: Song, usually given only a few times at dawn or predawn, a rhythmic and briskly whistled *cua-wíll*, *cua-wíll* . . . , up to 6 phrases or more, with quality of a *Caprimulgus* nightjar; after playback an urgent, rolling *kur'r'r'r'r'r*, *cua-wíll*; songs are weak and difficult to track down.

Behavior: As with all *Bucco*, stoic and difficult to locate. Usually found sitting alone from eye level to subcanopy inside forest. Sits upright and motionless for long periods of time, then sallies out rapidly to foliage or bark for large prey incl. beetles. Sometimes joins or follows mixed-spp. flocks for short periods, then more active, flying short distances and changing perches freq. Can be remarkably unsuspicious, allowing observer to approach closely, or walk past, without moving. Territories appear to be small, with prs. faithful to sites for yrs. In French Guiana, excavating nest cavity in arboreal termitary, Oct[752].

Status and habitat: Uncommon to fairly common resident (usually overlooked) in humid terra firme forest. Doubtless more numerous than the few recs. suggest.

Range: To 1000m. N and w Amazonas s to Yavita-Pimichín and Cerro de la Neblina (*dugandi*); Bolívar from lower Río Caura, Río Paragua, and Sierra de Imataca

(Río Grande) southward (*capensis*). E Colombia to e Peru, w and c Amaz. Brazil, and the Guianas.

Hypnelus

Size, behavior, and vocalizations recall allied *Bucco*, but larger; slightly graduated tail; mostly drier, more open areas.

Russet-throated Puffbird
PLATES 33, 34

Hypnelus ruficollis   Bobito

Identification: 8.5″ (22cm). 50g. Bill heavy and black; eyes yellow; tail narrow. Subspp. differ appreciably. ♂: *above mostly brown*, wing coverts tipped white, rest of upperparts with obscure pale spotting and mottling; narrow buffy white forehead continues through eyes to form *large white cheek patch* and narrow white nuchal collar; *underparts buff with 2 black chest bands* (lower one narrow, sometimes incomplete), some birds show incomplete 3d band; sides mottled dusky brown (*bicinctus, stoicus*). Or only 1 chest band (all 4 subspp. w of Andes e to Paraguaná Pen.); throat deep rufous, rest of underparts buff (*ruficollis, coloratus*); or throat deep rufous, rest of underparts whitish faintly tinged buff (*decolor*).

Sim. species: Only puffbird in arid habitats. In humid zones see Moustached Puffbird (no chest bands) and Spotted Puffbird.

Voice: Song, hd. mainly at dawn, by 1 bird or in unsynchronized duet with mate, a long ser. of rhythmic *woduk* notes (up to 20 sec), accelerating, growing louder, then abruptly slowing and ending with only 1 bird *wo-duk*ing; also occas. a high, insectlike *seeeeep*.

Behavior: Overall more conspic. and active than allied *Bucco* puffbirds. Usually in prs. that may sit close together when singing, but otherwise individuals usually are well separated from each other; occas. families or several together. Sit quietly and watch for long periods, usually from a rather open, horizontal branch 1–8m up, then sally to branch, trunk, foliage, or gd. for large prey, e.g., grasshoppers, lizards, anoles, etc. Dig nest cavity in arboreal termitary, or use old clay nest of hornero; 3 eggs; Aug–Sep breeding, Guárico[734].

Status and habitat: Fairly common resident in arid scrub, dry forest, gallery forest, scrubby areas with trees, and mangroves; locally common (invading) in partially opened-up forest or woodland in moist to humid regions such as s Maracaibo Basin and Delta Amacuro. Everywhere favors dry areas or where rainfall is strongly seasonal.

Range: To 700m. Paraguaná Pen. of Falcón (*decolor*); ne coastal Zulia (Quisiro) e to Dabajuro in w Falcón

(*striaticollis*); nw Zulia at base of Goajira Pen. e to Río Aurare in ne Zulia (s of *striaticollis*); base of Sierra de Perijá in nw Zulia, e of Lago de Maracaibo at Mene Grande (*ruficollis*); s Zulia s of Lago de Maracaibo, nw Táchira, w Mérida, and w Trujillo (*coloratus*); generally in e Falcón, Lara, and e of Andes to Sucre, Delta Amacuro, and s of Orinoco in n Amazonas (Caño Cataniapo; San Juan de Manapiare; sight, mouth of Río Ventuari—K. Zimmer; D. Wolf) and n Bolívar s to Caicara, lower Río Caura, and Río Grande (*bicinctus*); Isla Margarita (*stoicus*). Ne Colombia.

Note 1: Birds from e of Andes in Venez. and in e Colombia, *H. bicinctus* (Two-banded Puffbird), have been considered a separate sp. from single-banded birds of Maracaibo area. Double-banded *bicinctus* and single-banded *ruficollis* hybridize in Maracaibo area of Venez. and Catatumbo region of Colombia.

Note 2: *Hypnelus* has been merged with *Bucco*[136].

Malacoptila

Size and behavior sim. to *Bucco*, but plumage streaky; bill thinner, slightly decurved, not strongly hooked; long rictal bristles; nest in burrow in gd.

White-chested Puffbird   PLATE 33
Malacoptila fusca   Bolio Pechiblanco
Identification: 7" (18cm). 39g. Slightly decurved *bill dull orange, culmen and tip black. Head, neck, and upperparts blackish broadly streaked with buff*, lores and moustachial streak white, underparts dirty white broadly streaked brown, paler and less crisp than above; *narrow crescent of white across chest*; tail brown above, gray below, much graduated.
Sim. species: Only heavily streaked puffbird s of Orinoco.
Voice: High, thin *seeeeee*; song a ser. of high, thin *seeeee* notes, more inflected at end; rather like others of genus.
Behavior: Much like other *Malacoptila*. Perches alone and unmoving, mostly 1–6m up inside or at edge of forest. At long intervals sallies for large prey incl. spiders, orthopterans, and Lepidoptera larvae[253].
Status and habitat: Uncommon or rare resident; prob. more numerous than the few recs. suggest (easily overlooked). Humid terra firme, low-lying transition, and várzea forests.

Range: To 200m. C Amazonas (Pto. Yapacana; sight, confluence of Ríos Orinoco and Ventuari) s to Río Negro at El Carmen (*venezuelae*). E Colombia to e Peru, w Amaz. Brazil, and the Guianas.

Moustached Puffbird   PLATE 33
Malacoptila mystacalis   Bolio de Bigote
Identification: 8.5" (22cm). 50g. Bill blue gray, culmen and tip dusky. Eyes orange red. "Walrus faced." *Elongated forehead feathers* (usually depressed but can be erected like a shield), *lores, and elongated tufts of feathers on chin and malar area white* (the "moustache"), otherwise head and upperparts cinnamon brown, somewhat scaled with whitish, *central throat and broad chest band orange rufous*, rest of underparts white clouded and streaked brown.
Sim. species: Nothing like it in its range. S of Orinoco see White-chested Puffbird.
Voice: Like others of genus, usually sings only a few times early in morning, often before sunrise. Song an extremely high, thin, rather slow *teeez, teeez, teez, teez teez teez teez teez* (10–30 or more notes in 5–10 sec), sometimes the ser. slightly irreg. or accelerating. Song weak and easily overlooked.
Behavior: Well-separated members of prs. usually perch quietly and motionless for long periods, mostly 1–7m up, and are typically very lethargic, almost "stupidly" tame. Watch carefully and at long intervals sally to foliage, trunks, or gd. for prey items that are large for size of bird, e.g., large insects, small vertebrates, then often return to same perch. Change perches with sudden darting flight. Occas. attracted to army ant swarms or join mixed-spp. flocks. Nest a burrow in bank or sloping gd.; collar of small sticks at entrance.
Status and habitat: Fairly common but easily overlooked resident in moist, humid, and wet foothill and montane forest, incl. low-el. cloud forest, esp. where dense and cluttered, and in forest borders and disturbed areas; also moist wooded ravines in dry zones (e.g., tongues of riparian forest extending downslope to Maracay, Aragua).

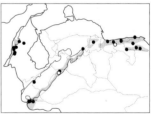

Range: 450–2000m. Sierra de Perijá, Zulia, spottily in Andes from e Táchira, w Mérida, and nw Barinas to se Lara (s of Cabudare); mts. of Yaracuy and n cordilleras from Carabobo e to Distr. Federal and se Miranda at Cerro Negro (*mystacalis*). W and N Colombia.

Nonnula

Shape and behavior sim. to *Bucco*, but much smaller; plumage subdued.

Rusty-breasted Nunlet   PLATE 33
Nonnula rubecula   Juan Feo
Identification: 5.5" (14cm). 19g. *Bill large and long, slightly decurved*, upper mandible dusky, lower mostly blue gray. In body shape a miniature of its larger relatives. Crown brownish gray, sides of head and rest of

upperparts dull brown, loral patch and *narrow eyering dull white, throat and breast bright cinnamon* (varying to faintly tinged cinnamon), sides olive brown, central lower underparts buffy white.

Sim. species: Nothing sim. in its range. Note large bill and head, short tail, and lack of strong markings.

Voice: Song a slow ser. of rather high-pitched whistles, *wheer, wheer, wheer....* , up to 20 notes or more; hd. mainly at dawn or a few times at dusk.

Behavior: An appealing but rather bland little bird whose small size and habit of sitting quietly for some time, then abruptly darting away to a nearby perch, makes it difficult to spot. Occurs alone or in prs. that perch several meters apart inside well-lighted forest mid. levels or lower, occas. in canopy when singing. May briefly assoc. with mixed-spp. flocks, then typically more active when in their midst. Usually rather unsuspicious; when disturbed or nervous flicks tail to one side.

Status and habitat: Easily overlooked resident (learn voice) in humid lowland forest, esp. in areas with large vine tangles. Found mainly in tall forest on red to yellowish soils (not white sandy soils). Fairly common at Junglaven on mid. Río Ventuari.

Range: To 300m. Nw Amazonas (Caño Cataniapo) s to Río Casiquiare (*duidae*); s Amazonas s of Río Casiquiare (*interfluvialis*). Se Colombia, se Peru, Amaz. Brazil, and the Guianas; se Brazil, Paraguay, and ne Argentina; Suriname.

Monasa

Mainly blackish slate with long ample tail; proportions "normal," not as chunky and large-headed as in other puffbird genera; bill large, heavy, slightly decurved, red orange (or slender and yellow in 1 sp.); conspic.

Black Nunbird PLATE 34
Monasa atra Pico de Lacre

Identification: 11″ (28cm). 85g. *Large coral red bill*; culmen somewhat decurved. *Plumage mainly slate gray*, head and tail blackish, *lesser wing coverts white*; greater and median wing coverts narrowly edged white; under wing coverts white.

Sim. species: In s Amazonas see White-fronted Nunbird.

Voice: Sings a noisy, rollicking chorus of loud phrases, *wheer-pt't'r'e'a'r . . .* or *bring-your-be'e'e'e'r*, over and over for up to 15 sec or so, faster and more frantic at end, given singly or by groups with members singing in a jumbled "round."

Behavior: Lethargic and conspic. Forages alone, in loosely assoc. prs., or sometimes several together. Joins understory or canopy mixed-spp. flocks where watches carefully for large insects and small vertebrates. Sits very upright and quiet at low to mid. levels on fairly open branch, then sallies rapidly to foliage or to gd. More active than *Bucco*, and often changes perch fairly freq. Quick to signal danger with loud alarm call. Flies with a few quick wing beats, then a short sail. Like most others of genus, a freq. commensal beneath troops of monkeys which it follows, watching for prey dislodged by primates' activities. Breeding prs. may have helpers, and reg. socialize with conspecifics. Sometimes up to 6 (genetically related?) perch in a line on a high horizontal branch in late afternoon and sing a chorus. Nest a burrow in gd., usually on sloping terrain; small collar of sticks placed at entrance.

Status and habitat: Common resident in humid terra firme forest borders, second growth, várzea forest borders, and river edges, locally inside forest. Partly replaced in sw Amazonas by White-fronted Nunbird.

Range: To 1050m. Ne Monagas (sight)[58] s to s Delta Amacuro (Piacoa) and generally in Amazonas and Bolívar. E Colombia (sight) to the Guianas.

White-fronted Nunbird PLATE 34
Monasa morphoeus Monja

Identification: 10″ (25cm). 73g. *Large coral red bill*; culmen somewhat decurved. *Forehead and chin white*, the feathers puffy, area surrounding forehead and chin blackish, rest of plumage slate gray, tail blackish; under wing coverts gray.

Sim. species: Black Nunbird has white on shoulders, none on head. Does not overlap widely with Black Nunbird.

Voice: Loud rollicking chorus, *dreary, dreary, dreary, . . .* often ending with more frantic *dreary-me, dreary-me . . .* over and over for up to 15–20 sec, by singles, prs., or groups in unsynchronized "rounds." When disturbed a soft dipping *peeo'ddd?*, trilled at end. Freq. hd. alarm a ser. of 4 or more rapid, urgent whistles, *wuEEeo-wuEEeo-wuEEeo-wuEEeo . . .* , the ser. rising a little in pitch, and nearly identical to alarm given by capuchin (*Cebus*) monkeys.

Behavior: Sim. to Black Nunbird but found mainly high in forest canopy, not along borders and in second growth, hence much harder to see. Reg. with canopy mixed-spp. flocks and a flock sentinel that is quick to sound alarm to approaching danger. Food incl. beetles, mantids, and cicadas[801]. Burrow nest ca. 0.8–1.4m long, excavated into level or sloping gd.; small twig

and leaf collar around entrance; 2–3 eggs in enlarged leaf-lined terminal chamber; nestlings fed by parents and helpers[651].
Status and habitat: Fairly common resident inside humid terra firme forest; at Cerro de la Neblina also reported at edge of river and in forest clearings[801]. Generally replaced along forest borders and in second growth by Black Nunbird.

Range: To 200m (prob. higher). W Amazonas from vicinity of San Fernando de Atabapo and Yavita southward (*peruana*). Se Honduras to n Bolivia, and se Brazil.

Swallow-winged Puffbird   PLATE 33
Chelidoptera tenebrosa   Aguantasol
Identification: 6.5″ (16.5cm). 35g. Broad black bill somewhat decurved (not hooked). *Chunky with broad wings and short, wide tail.* Large "blocky" or squarish head. Mainly slaty blue black with *white rump* (hard to see when perched), gray upper breast turning cinnamon rufous on belly; *under tail coverts white.* Long wings reach almost to tail tip.
Sim. species: Plump silhouette high atop canopy recalls a martin, purpletuft, or even flycatcher. Despite name, wings are short and rounded, not swallowlike, and look almost batlike when bird flies. Watch for rufous belly and white rump as bird sallies.
Voice: Rather quiet, occas. a plaintive piping *pi pu* or slight *pit-wit-wit*[620] or harsh squeaky *tzeet.*
Behavior: Solitary birds or more often prs. or groups of 3–6 perch on highest bare twigs in treetops along forest borders or in clearings and make long aerial sorties for flying insects. Fly outward and upward in fast direct pursuit and return with slower undulating flight, usually ending in a little upward swoop to perch. Single birds or little groups also may be seen perched on gd. on sandy banks where they nest. Dig sloping burrow into level sandy gd. or into sandy bank, roadcut, etc.; Jan–Jun nests, Orinoco region[115] (Hilty); 2 white eggs.
Status and habitat: Common resident in humid terra firme and várzea forest borders, savanna woodland, sandy riverbanks, and gallery forests s of Orinoco. Most numerous in white sandy soil areas, i.e., w Amazonas. Scarce and local n of Orinoco.
Range: To 400m n of Orinoco; to 1000m s of Orinoco. Maracaibo Basin, Zulia, w Mérida, and w Trujillo; e Falcón (Cuare; sight, Tucacas); e base of Andes from se Táchira and Portuguesa (Guanare) very locally e to Sucre, ne Monagas (sight, Caño Colorado), and Delta Amacuro; throughout Amazonas and Bolívar (*tene-*

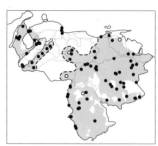

brosa). Colombia to n Bolivia, s Brazil, and the Guianas.

Ramphastidae: New World Barbets and Toucans

Toucans and barbets have traditionally been placed in separate families, toucans being confined to the New World and barbets part of a large pantropical family with most species in the Old World. New World barbets now have been show to be much more closely related to toucans than to Old World barbets[312,511]. The present arrangement unites New World barbets and toucans into 1 family with 3 subfamilies, the Capitoninae for most New World barbets, Semnornithinae for Prong-billed Barbet, and Ramphastinae for toucans.

Capitoninae: Barbets

Capitanes

Barbets are chunky birds with short necks, short tarsi, and heavy bills surrounded by prominent rictal bristles. The 3 Venezuelan species are brightly colored arboreal residents of humid forest. They usually are seen in prs. and eat a mixed diet of fruit and insects. As far as known they roost and nest in natural tree cavities or dig holes in soft wood. Their eggs are white and laid at the bottom of an unlined nest cavity.

Black-spotted Barbet   PLATE 34
Capito niger   Capitán Turero
Identification: 7.5″ (19cm). 55g. Heavy blackish bill, base of lower mandible grayish. ♂: sim. to Gilded Barbet but *forecrown crimson*, crown yellow tinged brown, upperparts streaking lemon yellow, *throat bright red, underparts bright yellow, almost completely unspotted.* ♀: *forecrown and throat bright red*, sides of head streaked yellow (not solid black), breast and belly pale yellow densely spotted black; rest of upperparts as in ♂.
Sim. species: See Gilded Barbet, both sexes of which differ in orange (not red) throat color; ♀♀ of both spp. are heavily spotted below.
Voice: Quiet and infreq. hd. (unlike Gilded Barbet). Song is slow, low pitched, and *Geotrygon*-like in quality, faint at first, then stronger and rhythmic, *wu, woot, wú-woot, wú-woot, wú-woot, wú-woot, wú-woot,* ca. 7–8 sec, may be repeated a few times at 20- to 40-sec intervals; slow and with emphasis on 1st note of each pr.

Behavior: Much like that of Gilded Barbet. Prs. occur high in canopy, often with mixed-spp. flocks, where they search for fruit and arthropods.

Status and habitat: Fairly common resident in tall humid terra firme and várzea forest, and along forest borders. Readily found in lowland forest near Sierra de Lema.

Range: To 200m (prob. higher). E Bolívar from Sierra de Imataca s to upper Río Cuyuní (sight, El Dorado; Carabobo; base of Sierra de Lema). The Guianas and ne Brazil e of Rio Branco and n of the Amazon.
Note: Taxonomy follows Haffer[237].

Gilded Barbet   PLATE 34
Capito auratus   Capitán Dorado
Identification: 7.5″ (19cm). 62g. Heavy blackish bill. *Streaked and spotted.* ♂: crown brownish gold ("old gold"), sides of head and upperparts black with *long yellow eyestripe continuing as yellow scapular stripe forming broad V on back*; spotted yellow wing band and yellow-tipped tertials; lower back and rump somewhat streaked olive yellow, *throat bright orange, rest of underparts yellow, sides and flanks spotted black.* ♀: sim. but upperparts streaked yellow and brownish gold; sides of head black streaked yellow, *underparts heavily spotted black.* Or along Río Negro, ♂ has orange red throat, forecrown mixed gold and red (*transilens*).
Sim. species: In e Bolívar see Black-spotted Barbet, ♂ of which differs in forecrown and throat bright red (not orange) and underparts unspotted. ♀♀ of both spp. are heavily spotted below; ♀ Gilded has orange (not red) throat.
Voice: Song (both sexes) a ser. of low-pitched, hollow, froglike notes, *oo-doot . . oo-doot . oo-doot, o'doot-o'doot-'doot-doot,* or sim. variation (e.g., *knee-deep . .*), 2d note of each pr. emphasized (unlike Black-spotted Barbet), softer at end. Ventriloquial and difficult to locate.
Behavior: Prs. accompany mixed-spp. flocks in forest canopy where they eat mixed diet of fruit and arthropods but often feed heavily on fruit taken by reaching out or down. Also hop and peer a bit sluggishly in foliage, and reach or acrobatically hang head downward to check curled dead leaves for arthropods. Occas. come quite low to fruiting shrubs inside forest or along borders. Dig nest cavity in rotten stub, usually fairly high.
Status and habitat: Common resident in tall humid terra firme and várzea forest and forest borders; scarce in scrubby white sandy soil forest.

Range: To 1600m. Sw Amazonas along Río Negro (*transilens*); rest of Amazonas and w Bolívar e through Caura Valley to Río Paragua and upper Río Caroní (*aurantiicinctus*). Se Colombia to n Bolivia, and w Amaz. Brazil e to Rio Branco.
Note: Formerly considered a subsp. of Black-spotted Barbet[237].

Red-headed Barbet   PLATE 34
Eubucco bourcierii   Capitán Cabecirrojo
Identification: 6.5″ (16.5cm). 34g. Heavy, sharp-pointed, greenish yellow bill; short tail. ♂: *unmistakable; head and neck bright red*; rest of upperparts bright grass green, lores and chin black; narrow white nuchal collar; lower underparts diffusely streaked yellow and green. ♀: very different; frontlet black turning *blue on forecrown* and ochracea orange on crown; *sides of head blue*, rest of *upperparts grass green*, underparts yellow with orange red stained crescent across chest; sides and belly *diffusely streaked* dark green.
Sim. species: ♀ has confusing pattern, but note long, sharp-pointed bill, blue and yellow on head, and streaky underparts.
Voice: A very quiet barbet. Infreq. hd. song a soft note followed by a low, mellow, and rolling trill, *huu,* . . *d'd'd'd'd'd'd'd'd'd,* melodious, ventriloquial, and not far carrying; lasts ca. 1.5 sec.
Behavior: Prs. persistently follow mixed-spp. flocks and actively clamber among branches and foliage from low to high but mostly in mid. story or higher as they search for fruit and arthropod prey. Often seen taking fruit, esp. *Ficus*, melastomes, etc., and habitually search large, curled, hanging dead leaves for insects, often by hanging head downward. Nest in Costa Rica a cavity ca. 1–3m up in fence post or rotting stub; 2–3 eggs, Mar–Jun[706].
Status and habitat: Fairly common (local?) resident in humid and wet forest, forest borders, and tall second-growth woodland.

Range: 1000–1500m (prob. higher). E slope of Andes from se Táchira n to se Lara at Cabudare and Tere-paima (*bourcierii*). Costa Rica to w Ecuador and ne Peru.

Ramphastinae: Toucans

Picos de Frasco, Piapocos, Diostedés, Tucanes, Tilingos

Toucans are quintessential standard-bearers of tropical birds—indeed, it is probably the image of a toucan that comes to mind most often when tropical birds are mentioned. As a group they are colorful and unusual and confined to the New World tropics from Mexico to northern Argentina. Toucans have enormously large colorful bills that are mostly filled with air spaces and are very light in weight despite their size. They also have fringed tongues and the ability to fold their tails flat over their back, which they do when roosting. Superficially they recall hornbills (Bucerotidae) of the Old World, but the 2 groups are not related and share only a few ecological similarities. Toucans occur in a wide variety of forested or wooded regions and feed mostly on fruit and only infrequently take small invertebrate and vertebrate prey. All species nest in holes, the larger species in natural cavities, the smaller toucans in woodpecker holes. Recent evidence has show that toucans are closely related to New World barbets, and the 2 groups are now placed in subfamilies in the same family.

Bill lengths of ♂ toucans avg. longer than those of resp. ♀♀. Larger values given in text are close to upper limit for ♂♂; smaller values are near lower limit for ♀♀. Bill lengths of some individuals may fall outside of maximum and minimum bill lengths given.

Aulacorhynchus

Long, narrow, and strongly graduated tail rounded at tip; plumage mainly green, often with bluish "eye shadow" around eyes; bill decurved, cutting edge of maxilla serrated (widely spaced teeth); spp. differ mainly in bill color and pattern, tail pattern, body size, and occas. rump color; most have narrow white line around base of bill (except Groove-billed Toucanet); bill of ♂♂ longer (up to 1″, 25mm) than that of ♀♀; song fairly sim. in pattern in all spp.; eat mostly fruit, infreq. vertebrate or invertebrate matter; montane in distrib.

Emerald Toucanet   PLATE 34
Aulacorhynchus prasinus   Pico de Frasco
Gargantiblanco
Identification: 15″ (38cm). 165g. Bill 2.25–2.75″ (57–70mm), mostly black with *broad yellow culmen* (upper third of bill), base bordered white (conspic.). Mainly green with blue ocular area; throat white, *under tail coverts chestnut, tail dull bluish, all the feathers broadly tipped chestnut*.

Sim. species: From Yellow-billed Toucanet by chestnut under tail coverts, chestnut tail tips, and much less yellow on bill. Yellow-billed Toucanet is commoner at lower el. In Sierra de Perijá see Crimson-rumped Toucanet.
Voice: Song a guttural, grinding *gŕa-val, gŕa-val, gŕa-val* ... varied to *roouk, roouk, roouk* ... (sexual difference?) at almost 2/sec. Compared to Yellow-billed and Groove-billed toucanets, song is lower pitched, more guttural, and froglike. Also croaks and odd notes in alarm or aggression.
Behavior: Much like Groove-billed Toucanet. Nest in old woodpecker hole or natural cavity in tree at almost any ht.; 3–4 eggs.
Status and habitat: Common resident in humid and wet forest, forest borders, and second-growth woodland, occas. in tree-bordered pastures and other semi-open areas. Mostly replaced at lower els. by allied Yellow-billed Toucanet, but the 2 spp. overlap, esp. at ca. 1700–1900m.

Range: 1700–3100m (possibly lower). Sierra de Perijá, Zulia; Andes from Táchira to s Lara (*albivitta*). C Mexico s in mts. to n Bolivia.

Groove-billed Toucanet   PLATE 34
Aulacorhynchus sulcatus   Pico de Frasco Esmeralda
Identification: 14″ (36cm). 173g. Bill 2.25–3″ (57–76mm), *most of upper mandible incl. tip dull dark red (looks blackish in field)*, base of lower mandible dark red narrowly outlined white, rest of bill blackish. *Plumage mainly green*, brighter below; feathered ocular area blue (blue "eye shadow"), area at base of lower mandible blue, *throat pale gray*, tail narrow, graduated, tip tinged blue. An inconspic. "pinched-in" area immediately below and parallel to culmen (the "groove") extends about half way to tip of bill and may be visible up close.
Sim. species: Other toucanets in range show yellow on bill (see Note below).
Voice: Song a nasal, reedy ser. of notes (just over 2/sec), *raank, raank,* ... continuing for 30 sec or more, with tail cocked and head and forebody jerked up with one note, down with next. A 2d song type is lower pitched and more grinding. On Paria Pen. songs average slightly faster, almost 3 notes/sec.
Behavior: Prs. or small groups forage from lower story to canopy but more often fairly high. Like other *Aulacorhynchus*, can be active, noisy, even inquisitive at times, or quiet and stealthy. Groups may slip single file "following the leader" through upper levels of forest, their presence betrayed only by sound of rapid wing beats on short flights overhead (short rounded wings with high wing loading), or they may quietly "shadow"

mixed-spp. flocks of small birds. Eat mostly fruit and re-gurgitate large seeds. Nest in old woodpecker hole or natural cavity.

Status and habitat: Generally a common resident in humid and wet forest (cloud forest), forest borders, and older second-growth woodland; also occas. wanders into drier woodland at lower els. Migratory movements downslope in rainy season reported in Coastal Cordillera and n Monagas (D. Ascanio).

Range: ENDEMIC. 300–2000m (occas. to sea level). Mts. of c Falcón (Sierra de San Luis); se Falcón (?); nw Lara (Cerro El Cerrón), and Yaracuy e through n cordilleras to Distr. Federal, s Carabobo (Cerro Platillón), and s Miranda (Cerro Negro) on Guárico border (*sulcatus*); mts. of ne Anzoátegui, n Monagas, and Paria Pen., Sucre (*erythrognathus*).

Note: Overlaps and interbreeds locally with Yellow-billed Toucanet in isolated mts. of nw Lara, and on isolated Cerro Platillón on Carabobo/Guárico border. In both areas bill characters are intermed. between the 2 spp.[581].

Yellow-billed Toucanet   PLATE 34
Aulacorhynchus calorhynchus   Pico de Frasco Andino

Identification: 14″ (36cm). Bill 2.1–3″ (53–76mm), base black, *broad culmen and most of upper mandible yellow*, lower mandible black, *base and tip yellow* (bill looks extensively yellow in field); narrow white border along base of bill. Plumage mainly green, feathered ocular area blue, throat pale gray, *tail from above dull blue to blue green*.

Sim. species: Much like Groove-billed Toucanet but smooth, ungrooved bill extensively yellow (not dark reddish black) and entire tail strongly bluish. Widespread Emerald Toucanet has yellow mainly along culmen, chestnut tail tips, and chestnut under tail coverts.

Voice: Song and other vocalizations practically identical to those of Groove-billed Toucanet[581]; a slightly upward-inflected, nasal *raank*, at just over 2 notes/sec. Higher pitched, more nasal, and faster than song of Emerald Toucanet.

Behavior: Much as in Groove-billed Toucanet.

Status and habitat: Uncommon to fairly common resident in humid and wet forest, forest edges, and second-growth woodland, incl. coffee plantations. Overall occurs at lower el. than allied Emerald Toucanet (lowest sight rec., 900m, Río Quinimarí, Táchira, 26–27 Mar 1999—Hilty), but the two overlap in many areas.

Range: 1200–1900m (sight to 900m). Sierra de Perijá, Zulia, both slopes of Andes from Táchira to extreme nw Lara (Cerros El Cerrón and El Cogollal), and in s

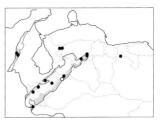

Carabobo (Cerro Platillón). N Colombia (Santa Marta Mts.).

Note: All birds on Cerro Platillón, Carabobo/Guárico border, and Cerros El Cerrón and El Cogollal, nw Lara, show bill characters intermed. between red-billed *A. sulcatus* and yellow-billed *A. calorhynchus*, and Yellow-billed Toucanet has been regarded as a subsp. of Groove-billed Toucanet[236,581].

Chestnut-tipped Toucanet   PLATE 34
Aulacorhynchus derbianus   Pico de Frasco Guayanés

Identification: 15″ (38cm). 145g. Bill 2.2–2.6″ (56–66mm), mostly black; bill *tip, upper half of upper mandible*, and base of upper and lower mandible *dark red*; narrow white border surrounds base of bill. Plumage mainly green (chest tinged bluish—*whitelianus*) with narrow feathered blue gray ocular ring and pale gray throat; *2 central tail feathers* (or *4—whitelianus*) *broadly tipped chestnut*.

Sim. species: The only "green" toucan s of Orinoco. See Guianan Toucanet.

Voice: Song a low, grunting *grank, graank, graank . . .*, a little more than 1 note/sec; recalls others of genus but slower.

Behavior: Not as vocal or gregarious as its Andean allies and usually seen singly or in quiet and unobtrusive prs. inside forest from lower story to subcanopy. Easily overlooked because of habit of sitting quietly for extended periods. Sometimes loosely assoc. with mixed-spp. flocks. Reg. visits fruiting melastome shrubs.

Status and habitat: Uncommon resident (perhaps overlooked) in wet premontane and montane forest. Local or seasonal el. movements (Sierra de Lema) need documentation.

Range: 800–1800m (once to 2400m near summit of Cerro Roraima). Throughout mts. of Amazonas; nw Bolívar on Cerro El Negro in upper Río Cuchivero and Cerro Tabaro in upper Río Nicharé (*duidae*); Bolívar on Sierra de Lema, Cerro Guaiquinima, and cerros of Gran Sabana (*whitelianus*). Adj. Guyana and n Brazil; Andes from s Colombia to n Bolivia.

Crimson-rumped Toucanet   PLATE 34
Aulacorhynchus haematopygus   Pico de Frasco
Lomirrojo
Identification: 17″ (43cm). 215g. *Notably larger than others of genus.* Bill 3.25–3.75″ (83–95mm), *mostly dark maroon red,* culmen blackish, lower mandible blackish tinged dark red, broad white band at base of bill. Plumage mostly green, *incl. throat,* with inconspic. bluish belt across breast; blue at base of bill and around eyes; *rump red* (hard to see); tail blue green above, blue gray below, *broadly tipped chestnut.*
Sim. species: Found only with smaller Yellow-billed Toucanet which has gray throat and much yellow (not dark red) on bill.
Voice: Song a nasal, monotonously repeated *cuah, cuah . . . ,* ca. 2/sec (Hilty); a *gahk, huahk, hoak, gahk . . .* beginning with bark, ending in growl[236].
Behavior: Sim. to Groove-billed Toucanet.
Status and habitat: Resident in humid and wet forest, forest borders, second-growth woodland, and adj. tree-lined pastures. Most numerous (more specimens) at lower els.

Range: 1200–2200m. Sierra de Perijá, Zulia; se Táchira (Cerro Las Copas; sight, 480m, Río Frio[60]) (*haematopygus*). Andes of Colombia (800–2100m) and w Ecuador.

Selenidera

Small toucans; homogeneous in appearance; rather short bill and tail; ♂♂ mostly black with golden ear-tufts; ♀♀ gray or chestnut below; inconspic.; mainly frugivorous.

Guianan Toucanet   PLATE 35
Selenidera culik   Tucancito Pico Negro
Identification: 13″ (33cm). 145g. Bill 2.5–3″ (64–76mm), mostly black, *base of upper mandible and basal half of lower mandible dark red.* Bare skin around eyes green to blue green, bluish behind eyes. ♂: *head and underparts black with long conspic. golden yellow tufts ex-tending from below eyes across cheeks,* small yellow band around back of neck; otherwise above dark olive green, belly mixed gray and yellow, under tail coverts red. ♀: rather different; crown black, nape chestnut, *conspic. golden ear-tufts,* otherwise dark olive above; *underparts iron gray* (vaguely freckled white), belly mixed olive and yellow, under tail coverts red, tail tips chestnut.
Sim. species: Tawny-tufted Toucanet has more color-ful red bill; ♀ also told by chestnut underparts. Occurs mainly e of range of Tawny-tufted Toucanet.
Voice: Commonest call (cry) a high falsetto *kaaaaaaiii iii,* rising, often accompanied by a ser. of rapid, gut-

tural bill rattles, *trrr-trrr-trrr. . . .* Infreq. hd. song a slow ser. of low, guttural, froglike *arrouk* notes, ca. 15 in 10 sec, given as bird flips forward with bill down and tail up on 1st note, then backward with bill up on next note, effect being that of a little mechanical toy rocking stiffly back and forth.
Behavior: This sp.'s seriocomic antics and eccentricity when singing belies its otherwise furtive behavior. Al-most always occurs in prs., although typically only 1 bird is seen because members are usually somewhat separated. Forages mostly in mid. story or subcanopy, less often in canopy, and sometimes loosely assoc. with mixed-spp. flocks. Often makes audible wing noise during short flights within canopy, but this sp. gives impression of deliberate, calculating move-ments, and this, coupled with infreq. vocalizations, makes it difficult to locate. Two, even 3, prs. may inter-act briefly, usually accompanied by much calling and posturing. Often feeds on *Cecropia* catkins.
Status and habitat: Uncommon resident (easily over-looked) in humid terra firme forest and forest borders in lowlands and foothills.

Range: To 900m. Se Bolívar from upper Río Cuyuní s to tepuis around Gran Sabana (sw to Chimantá-tepui; Paurai-tepui). The Guianas and ne Brazil.

Tawny-tufted Toucanet   PLATE 35
Selenidera nattereri   Tucancito Pico Rojo
Identification: 13″ (33cm). 160g. Bill rather short (2–2.5″, 51–64mm), thick, and *colorful, mostly dull red with yellowish culmen, large blue patch near base of bill, and irreg. pale blue spots on maxilla.* Bare skin around eyes pale blue, behind eyes yellow. Head, neck, and underparts glossy black, *long conspic. golden tuft extends from below eyes across cheeks and has lengthened tawny tips;* upperparts dark olive green, flank tufts yellow (not always visible in field), lower underparts chestnut, under tail coverts red, tail tips chestnut. ♀: sim. but *head, neck, and underparts chestnut.*
Sim. species: See Guianan Toucanet.
Voice: Song much like others of genus, a low, froglike ser. of ca. 9 nasal notes, each inflected and almost swallowed, *jeüülp, jeüülp . . . ,* slightly more than 1/sec, given as bird rocks ("see-saws") back and forth with bill down and tail up.
Behavior: Has been seen alone and in prs., mostly from mid. story to subcanopy of tall forest at Jungla-ven, where inconspic. and easily overlooked except for occas. bouts of calling or when visiting a fruiting tree. As in others of genus, 2 or even 3 prs. occas. inter-

act temporarily, usually accompanied by much calling and posturing. May occur at lower density than others of genus (A. Whittaker).
Status and habitat: Poorly known resident. A low-density and easily overlooked sp. of tall humid terra firme forest (red and yellowish soils) at Junglaven, in mid. Río Ventuari. In n Brazil known from low sandy soil forest (campina) as well as tall terra firme forest on poor soils (A. Whittaker).

Range: To 300m. Throughout Amazonas from mid. Río Ventuari (sight), Cerro Yapacana, base of Cerro Duida, San Carlos de Río Negro, and Cerro de la Neblina; s Bolívar in headwaters of Río Paragua (on a tributary of lower Río Carún); possibly lower Río Caura. E Colombia to the Guianas and n Brazil.

Pteroglossus

Med.-sized toucans; slender; dark green to black with red rump; bare colored skin around eyes; cutting edge of long, slightly decurved bill strongly "toothed"; tail long, narrow, strongly graduated. Best told by bill pattern, no. of bands (or lack of) on underparts, and size; roost and nest in tree holes; calls rather sim. in all spp.; bill up to 1" (25mm) longer in ♂ than ♀; almost completely frugivorous.

Collared Araçari   PLATE 35
Pteroglossus torquatus   Tilingo Acollarado
Identification: 16" (41cm). 225g. Bill 3.5–4.5" (89–114mm), *upper mandible mostly ivory yellow*, base of culmen, "teeth," and *lower mandible blackish*; base of bill outlined yellowish white. Eyes yellow with dark spot behind pupil; *bare ocular area red*. Head, neck, and chest black, upperparts dark greenish black with red rump and inconspic. chestnut nuchal collar; *breast yellow* somewhat stained red, large black spot on breast, *single band mixed black and red across upper belly*.
Sim. species: Only araçari in its range.
Voice: Freq. hd. call, often repeated several times at short intervals when excited, a high-pitched, sneezing *pít'sick!* or *kít'sick!*
Behavior: Sim. to others of genus (see Black-necked Araçari). Roosts and nests in old woodpecker hole or natural cavity in live tree or rotten stub, usually fairly high; 3 white eggs. In Costa Rica up to 4 ads. may attend nest[706].
Status and habitat: Moderately common resident (now *very local*) in remaining patches of humid lowland forest and tall second-growth woodland; also tall

trees in partially cleared pastures. Reg. in vicinity of Cerro Misión, e Falcón, and reported from several other areas in e Falcón. Some seasonal movements may occur[571]. Nos. in decline with deforestation.

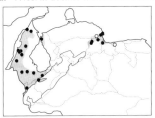

Range: To 1000m (most recs. below 500m). W and s Zulia and w base of Andes in Táchira and Mérida; locally in e Falcón, Yaracuy, and Carabobo (*nuchalis*) once (sight)[486] e to n Aragua at Rancho Grande; but no recent evidence of its presence there. S Mexico to Colombia.

Black-necked Araçari   PLATE 35
Pteroglossus aracari   Tilingo Cuellinegro
Identification: 18" (46cm). 250g. Bill 4.0–4.5" (102–114mm), *culmen black, rest of upper mandible ivory with smudgy black "teeth" marks, lower mandible black*, base of bill outlined white. Eyes dark brown, *orbital skin slate gray*. Upperparts dark slaty olive with red rump; head, neck, and chest black, rest of underparts yellow; *single red band across lower breast*.
Sim. species: From Green and Many-banded araçaris by single red breast band. Also note bill pattern. Ivory-billed Araçari has fused red and black band and *red skin behind eyes*.
Voice: Call a loud, sharp *Kís'sick!* (or *k'sink!*) with reedy quality, often repeated several times at short intervals when members of a group are about to fly. Used as contact call and alarm.
Behavior: Like others of genus, rather gregarious and noisy, often traveling in groups of up to 12 that rest in open trees, follow each other in single file across clearings and into fruiting trees. Keep mostly in upper levels of forest, fly with flurry of rapid wing beats interspersed with short glides; roost communally in large tree cavity or old woodpecker hole. Nest in tree hole; breeding prs. may be assisted by helpers; nest with young, 28 Aug, nw Monagas[186].
Status and habitat: Common and widespread resident in humid lowland forest, forest borders, and scattered trees in clearings in e Bolívar and Delta Amacuro; less numerous and local in ne Venez.

Range: To 550m. Ne Anzoátegui (Bergantín), Sucre, Monagas, Delta Amacuro, and generally in n and e Bolívar from lower Río Caura, Río Paragua, and Sierra de Imataca s through Gran Sabana (*roraimae*). The Guianas and e Brazil.
Note: Subsp. *roraimae* incl. in *atricollis* by some[559].

Many-banded Araçari   PLATE 35
Pteroglossus pluricinctus   Tilingo Multibandeado
Identification: 18″ (46cm). 230g. Bill 4–5″ (102–127mm), *upper mandible yellowish ivory* (to orangish ivory) *with black culmen*; lower mandible black; base of bill outlined yellow ivory. Eyes yellow; *bare skin around eyes lime green to gray green* (pale blue at base of Andes), *red* behind eyes. Upperparts, head, and chest black, wings dark olive green, rump red; *below yellow with 2 black "belts,"* the lower one bordered below with red.
Sim. species: No other araçari is "double-belted" below. See Black-necked, Ivory-billed, and Green araçaris.
Voice: Recalls others of genus, a sharp, metallic *squéénk* (often doubled) or more bisyllabic *ca-síck*. In aggression, a ser. of guttural rattles, *gu'r'r'r'r*, and bill-clacking.
Behavior: Sim. to others of genus. See Black-necked Araçari.
Status and habitat: Uncommon to fairly common resident in humid terra firme and várzea forest in lowlands, also forest borders, occas. gallery forest and lighter woodland in sandy soil zones, and coffee plantations and broken forest in foothills at base of Andes.

Range: To 300m n of Orinoco (sight to 600m); to 900m s of Orinoco. E base of Andes from e Táchira n to nw Barinas; generally in Amazonas and across s Bolívar e to Río Paragua and Paurai-tepui. E Colombia to ne Peru and nw Brazil.

Ivory-billed Araçari   PLATE 35
Pteroglossus azara   Tilingo Pico Amarillo
Identification: 15″ (38cm). 136g. Bill 3–4″ (76–102mm), *entirely ivory* with 8–10 small blackish "teeth" on cutting edge of upper mandible (inconspic. in field). Bare skin around eyes blue gray, behind eyes red. Crown black, sides of head, neck, and throat dark maroon chestnut (usually look black in field), rest of upperparts dark greenish black with red rump; *broad red chest band bordered below by black band*, rest of underparts yellow.
Sim. species: From all other araçaris by almost uniform ivory (bone-colored) bill. Also note fused red and black breast band.

Voice: Call a sharp, forced *skleék* or *kís-sik*, often several times; high pitched and much like several others of genus. Also various yelps and strident screeches unlike other *Pteroglossus*.
Behavior: As in other araçaris. BC birds Jan–mid Apr, w Amazonas[185].
Status and habitat: Fairly common resident in humid terra firme forest and borders, sandy-belt forest, gallery forest, and savanna woodland.

Range: To 350m. Throughout Amazonas; w Bolívar e to upper Río Paragua (*flavirostris*). E Colombia, e Ecuador, ne Peru (n of the Amazon), and n Amaz. Brazil.
Note: Previously called *P. flavirostris*[403].

Green Araçari   PLATE 35
Pteroglossus viridis   Tilingo Limón
Identification: 13.5″ (34cm). 135g. *Much smaller than others of genus and with no breast bands.* Bill 2.5–3.5″ (64–89mm), upper half of upper mandible yellow, lower half reddish ochre turning blackish distally; lower mandible mostly black; band around base of bill orange red. Bare ocular skin pale blue to lime green in front, *red behind.* Head, neck, and chest black, rest of upperparts dark olive green, rump red; *underparts yellow with no bands.* ♀: sim. but head maroon black.
Sim. species: Small size and *unbanded* underparts are the marks.
Behavior: Sim. to others of genus (see Black-necked Araçari). Roosts communally in tree cavity or hole in rotten stub; nest in tree cavity.
Status and habitat: Fairly common resident (local?) in humid terra firme and várzea forest and forest borders. Favors tall diverse forest on rich soils and is rare or absent in scrubby white sandy soil forest. No specimens in Amazonas, but numerous sightings in vicinity of Pto. Ayacucho, Junglaven[833], and mouth of Río Ventuari at Alechiven (1998—K. Zimmer). Relatively common and doubtless more widespread.

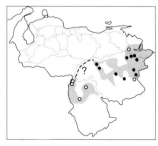

Range: To 600m. N Amazonas (sighting); s Delta Amacuro (Piacoa); Bolívar from lower Río Caura e to Sierra de Imataca and s to Gran Sabana (*viridis*). The Guianas and n Brazil (prob. e Colombia).

Andigena

Colorful with long, graduated tail; unusually long flank feathers soft and lax; bill toothed; highland forests.

Black-billed Mountain-Toucan   PLATE 35
Andigena nigrirostris   Tucán Azul
Identification: 20″ (51cm). *Bill* 3.2–4.2″ (81–107mm), *all black*, and smooth. Bare skin around eyes powder blue in front, yellow behind. *Very colorful.* Crown and nape black, *rest of upperparts dark brownish mustard*, rump light yellow, wings and tail dark blue gray, tail tipped chestnut, *cheeks, sides of neck, and throat white, rest of underparts pale blue*, thighs chestnut, under tail coverts red.
Sim. species: See Black-mandibled Toucan which has yellow bib and all-black upperparts.
Voice: Territorial song a loud, mechanical, nasal-sounding *tuuaaAAT*, rising; a little more than 1/sec; tinny sounding with strong harmonics and sometimes repeated for up to a min or more. Also a rapid ser. of guttural, wooden bill rattles like stork bill-clapping (C. Parrish). May call from open perch or within canopy foliage.
Behavior: Prs. or families, occas. groups up to 6–8, forage in canopy or upper levels of trees and are generally less vocal and less conspic. than lowland toucans. Wander or forage over large areas.
Status and habitat: Very local resident. Wet montane forest, occas. forest borders. Most recent recs. are from vicinity of Páramo de Tamá, Táchira. Seasonal el. movements occur in Peru (Venez.?).

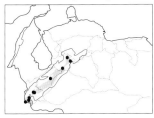

Range: 1800–2700m. Andes of Táchira, Mérida, and s and ne Trujillo from El Rincón to Páramo Cendé (*nigrirostris*). Prob. Lara. Colombia and ne Ecuador.

Ramphastos

Large and conspic.; mostly black with red under tail coverts; long, narrow, square-tipped tail; enormous colorful bill (the quintessential "Fruit Loops"). Two subgroups differ in bill shape, body size, and vocalizations: (1) smaller keel- or channel-billed spp. (Keel-billed, Citron-throated, Channel-billed) with shallow groove ("channel") on upper mandible and *croaking song* and (2) larger, "smooth-billed" spp. (Black-mandibled, White-throated) with *yelping song* (Spanish name *Diostedé* is onomatopoeic). Nowhere in

Venez. are more than 2 spp. sympatric, usually 1 from each group (a "croaker" and a "yelper"). Hybridization between some spp. prs. is extensive, and spp. limits of these taxa uncertain; diet almost entirely fruit; bill notably larger in ♂. Taxonomy follows Haffer[236] in part.

Keel-billed Toucan   PLATE 35
Ramphastos sulfuratus   Piapoco Pico Verde
Identification: 19″ (48cm). 405g. Bill 4.5–6″ (114–152mm), colorful, *mostly pea green with red tip, broad orange smudge on upper mandible*, bluish patch on lower mandible. Bare skin around eyes pale green. Plumage mostly black with yellow rump and red under tail coverts; *throat and chest bright yellow* bordered narrowly below by red.
Sim. species: Colorful green and orange bill unique. See Citron-throated and Black-mandibled toucans.
Voice: Song a ser. of rapidly repeated croaking notes, *crrik, crrik, crrik, . . . ,* at rate of ca. 16 notes/10 sec, sim. to song of Citron-throated Toucan but much faster. Swings bill upward and to side with each note.
Behavior: Sim. to that of others of keel-/channel-billed group (see Channel-billed Toucan). Troop about in prs., families, or occas. in loose groups up to 12, sometimes ranging out into isolated trees away from forest. Nest in large natural cavity at almost any ht. but usually fairly high in tree.
Status and habitat: Resident in tall dry to humid forest, forest borders, and lighter woodland. Some short-distance migratory movement likely. Deforestation now extensive within sp.'s limited Venez. range.

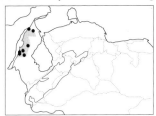

Range: To 450m. Nw end of Sierra de Perijá (Cerro Alto del Cedro s to Río Cogollo), Zulia (*brevicarinatus*). S Mexico to n Colombia.

Citron-throated Toucan   PLATE 35
Ramphastos citreolaemus   Diostedé Garganticitrón
Identification: 19″ (48cm). Bill 4.5–6″ (114–152mm), mostly black, broad *base of upper mandible yellow*, narrow culmen greenish yellow becoming yellow near tip; base of lower mandible blue green. Bare skin around eyes light blue. Plumage black with *yellow rump* and red under tail coverts; *throat and chest pale lemon yellow (often almost white)*, bordered below by inconspic. narrow red band.
Sim. species: Nearest is Black-mandibled Toucan which has prom. bicolored bill, bright yellow throat, and is mostly at higher el. Also see Keel-billed Toucan; e of Andes, Channel-billed Toucan.
Voice: Song a ser. of froglike, croaking *creé-op* notes at ca. 1/sec[236], like others of keel-/channel-billed group, given as bill is swung up then down.

Behavior: Sim. to others of keel-/channel-billed group (see Channel-billed Toucan). Occurs in prs., 3s, or small groups that stay well up in tall trees.
Status and habitat: Resident. Uncommon to rare and declining. Tall humid lowland and foothill forest. Much of forested habit in s Maracaibo Basin and adj. foothills where this bird occurs has now been destroyed. Pr. seen Mar 1999 in foothills above La Fria, Táchira.

Range: To 500m. W side of Maracaibo Basin from Río Negro, Zulia, e around Lago de Maracaibo to Táchira, w Mérida, and Trujillo (Betijoque). N Colombia.
Note: Considered a subsp. of Channel-billed Toucan (*R. vitellinus*) by Haffer[236]; the two are isolated geographically.

Channel-billed Toucan (includes Yellow-ridged Toucan)   PLATE 35
Ramphastos vitellinus   Diostedé Pico Acanalado
Identification: 19″ (48cm). 350g. Bill 3.5–5.5″ (89–140mm), black with *tip, ridge, and base of upper mandible yellow* (*culminatus*); or bill *all black* (occas. small yellow tip) with *bright blue band on base of bill* (*vitellinus*). Facial skin bright baby blue. Plumage mainly black; *throat and chest white* bordered by narrow red line; *rump yellow, under tail coverts red* (*culminatus*). Or *lower throat rich buttery yellow* bordered below by narrow to fairly wide red chest band; *rump* and under tail coverts red (*vitellinus*). Birds along e base of Andes and in s Amazonas n to near Río Ventuari generally have *pure white bibs*, inconspic. red chest band, and yellow ridge on bill. N and e from Ventuari and upper Orinoco to upper Río Caura *bibs contain varying amts. of yellow or orange*; bill pattern variable (culmen partially or all black), rump varies from yellow to orange to red. E of lower Río Caura *bibs are mostly orange yellow*; red chest band broader and more prom., rump red, and bill solid black, typical of pure Channel-billed phenotype (*vitellinus*). In hand *vitellinus* has shorter bill and longer tail.
Sim. species: See larger White-throated Toucan which always has white bib and differs vocally.
Voice: Song a froglike, croaking ser. of bisyllabic notes, *creéop, creéop, creéop, . . . ,* phrases at ca. 1/sec, given while perched in treetop; at faster rate or at a distance phrases sound monosyllabic.
Behavior: Usually in prs. or small groups that stay fairly high in trees, but on avg. somewhat lower than larger "smooth-billed" forms of genus (e.g., White-throated Toucan). Hops around and uses long bill to pluck hard-to-reach fruits and berries. Because of long, projecting bill, looks top heavy in flight. Typical flight is undulating and weak, a few quick flaps then a glide on

set wings. On long flights seems to loose more altitude during glides than it regains flapping. Calling birds perch in open on high bare limbs in treetops and throw heads back and swing bills side to side with each note in comically animated fashion. Nest high in unlined tree cavity.
Status and habitat: Relatively common resident in tall, humid, lowland forest s of Orinoco; also along forest borders and isolated trees in clearings. Uncommon and local along e base of Andes.

Range: To 1700m n of Orinoco; to ca. 300m s of Orinoco (or to 1100m, *vitellinus*). E base of Andes from Táchira to nw Barinas and cerros of nw Lara; generally s of Orinoco in Amazonas (*culminatus*); generally in Bolívar and n of Orinoco in e Sucre, e Monagas, and Delta Amacuro (*vitellinus*). E Colombia to n Bolivia and w Amaz. Brazil (*culminatus*); the Guianas and e Brazil; Trinidad (*vitellinus*).
Note: Incl. Yellow-ridged Toucan (*R. culminatus*) of w Amazonia, formerly considered a separate sp. Hybridization between the 2 spp. is extensive across a zone in upper Orinoco-Río Negro region of Venez. and in Brazil. Pure *vitellinus* occurs in e Venez. w to lower Río Caroní, Paragua, and Caura. Hybrid phenotypes 1st appear in upper watersheds of these rivers, and westward in upper Río Orinoco they become very variable[236].

Black-mandibled Toucan   PLATE 35
Ramphastos ambiguus   Diostedé Pico Negro
Identification: 24″ (61cm). Bill 5.5–7″ (140–178mm), *bicolored; most of upper mandible yellow; wedge at base of upper and most of lower mandible black*. Bare skin around eyes yellow green. Plumage mostly black, mantle often tinged maroon, *rump white*, under tail coverts red, *throat and chest bright yellow*, bordered below by inconspic. line of red.
Sim. species: Nearest is Citron-throated Toucan which has much more black on bill, pale yellow bib, white rump, and is mostly in lowlands (not mts.). Also see Keel-billed Toucan.
Voice: Loud whistled song a rhythmic ser. of yelping notes, *keeyós, ta-dáy* or *keeyós, ta-dáy, ta-dáy*, with gull-like quality (or like small dog in distance), often continued for several min. Bill and tail are jerked up sharply with 1st note which is usually followed by the single note, couplet, or less often a pr. of couplets.
Behavior: Sim. to other "smooth-billed" members of genus (see White-throated Toucan).
Status and habitat: Resident in canopy of humid and wet premontane and montane forest and in tall trees in clearings. Most recs. are from Sierra de Perijá and

Andes where sp. survives in low nos. Now rare in n cordilleras and perhaps locally extirpated. Once in PN Guatopo, Nov 1984 (C. Parrish), otherwise few recent recs.? Seasonal or local el. movements occur.

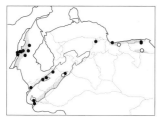

Range: 100–1800m. Sierra de Perijá, Zulia, w base of Andes in Táchira and Mérida, e base from se Táchira to nw Barinas, mts. of Yaracuy, and locally in n cordilleras of Carabobo, Aragua (old sightings on n slope?), and coastal and interior mts. of Miranda (*abbreviatus*). Colombia to e Peru.
Note 1: Has been regarded as conspecific with *R. swainsoni* of C Amer. and w Colombia[236].
Note 2: Subsp. *abbreviatus* prob. not worthy of recognition.

White-throated Toucan (includes Cuvier's and Red-billed Toucans) PLATE 35
Ramphastos tucanus Piapoco de Garganta Blanca
Identification: 24″ (61cm). 600g. Bill 5.5–7″ (140–178mm), *mostly black*, tip of bill, ridge, and base of upper mandible yellow, base of lower mandible light blue (*cuvieri*); or sim. but *black areas of bill replaced by reddish chestnut* (*tucanus*); or sim. but black areas of bill with varying-sized patches of reddish chestnut, esp. on upper mandible (hybrids in zones of intergradation). Bare skin around eyes light blue to aquamarine. Plumage mostly black with *throat and chest white* bordered below by inconspic. line of red; *rump chrome yellow, under tail coverts red.*
Sim. species: Easily confused with either subsp. (or any of numerous hybrid intergrades) of Channel-billed Toucan. In Amazonas pure "yellow-ridged" forms of Channel-billed Toucan (with white chests) are almost identical to White-throated Toucan but are smaller and have *yellow* (not red) rumps and different voices. Birds with yellow on chest are almost always Channel-billed. In e Bolívar (where pops. are more genetically stable) Channel-billed can usually be told by all-black bill (not reddish chestnut) and yellow on chest. In all areas voice is best clue.
Voice: Song a loud, rhythmic ser. of whistled yelps, *eeot! hue! hue*!, last syllable sometimes omitted, given from treetop perch, often over and over for several min, esp. in early morning and late evening. Can be very noisy with several birds calling simultaneously from nearby trees. Cf. very different croaking songs of Channel-billed Toucan.
Behavior: Much as in all "smooth-billed" members of genus. Usually in prs. or small groups which troop around fairly high in trees or in canopy; eat a variety of fruit, rarely invertebrate or small vertebrate prey or eggs and nestlings. Perch higher, on avg., than smaller channel-/keel-billed members of genus. Look top

heavy in flight because of long projecting bill. Flight is undulating, a few quick flaps then a glide on set wings, and so weak birds often seem barely able to reach distant trees or cross large rivers (they always do). Calling birds perch exposed in high treetop snags and bob and throw heads from side to side with each yelp. Nest in cavity in live tree or in old woodpecker hole in dead stub.
Status and habitat: Common resident in humid lowland terra firme and várzea forest, along forest and river borders, and in scattered tall trees in clearings.

Range: To 500m n of Orinoco; to 1100m s of Orinoco. Throughout Amazonas (*cuvieri*); e Sucre, e Monagas, Delta Amacuro, and Bolívar; once (hybrid?) at confluence of Ríos Negro and Casiquiare, Amazonas; e base of Andes from Táchira n to nw Barinas (*tucanus*). E Colombia to n Bolivia and w Amaz. Brazil (*cuvieri*); ne Colombia to the Guianas and e Brazil (*tucanus*).
Note 1: Incl. Cuvier's Toucan (*R. cuvieri*). The 2 forms hybridize extensively in a wide north-south belt across Amazonas s to Manaus, Brazil[236].
Note 2: Orange-billed Toucan (*R. aurantiirostris*) not a valid taxa[584].

Picidae: Woodpeckers and Piculets
Telegrafistas y Carpinteros

Woodpeckers are a familiar group of birds of virtually worldwide distribution. They are best known for their ability to cling upright to trunks and limbs, for drilling holes into wood to secure food, and for their ability to "drum" by hammering their bill rapidly on wood. Not surprisingly, woodpeckers show several unique anatomical adaptations, including strong, chisel-like bills and barb-tipped tongues that can be greatly extended to "harpoon" hard-to-reach wood-boring insects. Additionally, a liquid-filled capsule encases their brain, preventing severe trauma during drumming and drilling. Except for piculets and Old World wyrnecks, most woodpeckers have an unusually stiff tail that is used for support when they climb. In Venezuela several woodpeckers eat some fruit; others at least partly specialize in raiding arboreal ant or termite colonies, and some occasionally sally for flying insects. All Venezuelan species depend on trees for food, shelter, and nests, but a few Andean species south of Venezuela are primarily terrestrial and live in grasslands above treeline. All Venezuelan woodpeckers hollow out cavities and lay white eggs; 1 species is loosely colonial.

Two publications provide worldwide coverage of woodpeckers[603,820].

Picumnus

Tiny; ♂♂'s crown feathers stiff, dotted yellow, orange, or red; ♀♀'s usually dotted white. In all spp. tail short, stiff, and not used for support; tail black, inner webs of 2 central feathers white, and part of outer edge of outer 2 prs. white. Tail not described in following text. New World spp. fall into 2 broad song groups: (1) spp. that sing a long descending trill or (2) spp. that sing a slow descending ser. of ca. 2–6 notes (occas. more). All spp. in both groups give irreg. calls of 1–several notes when foraging; all spp. drum. Taxonomy complex and in need of study.

Golden-spangled Piculet PLATE 37
Picumnus exilis   Telegrafista Verdoso
Identification: 3.5″ (8.9cm). 9.3g. Crown black, forecrown narrowly streaked orange red, rest of crown dotted white (or all dotted white—♀), upperparts pale olive brown, *feathers of shoulders and back with dusky centers and yellowish margins giving spotted or barred appearance*; below dull yellowish white, *throat finely scaled and rest of underparts very narrowly banded dusky*. Some individuals more spotted than barred on lower breast and belly (contrasts with barring on chest).
Sim. species: No other piculet in Venez. is so narrowly and distinctly barred throughout underparts. See Black-spotted Piculet.
Voice: When foraging a high, thin 2-noted (occas. 3–4) *seeeek, seeeek*, varied to *seeeee . . . seee se-se*; penetrating but not loud. Song 5–8 high, thin *seek* or *tseet* notes, the ser. descending slightly in pitch.
Behavior: Prs. or families of 3–5 are active, hanging sideways and hitching along sides of small branches and twigs, or occas. creeping like a nuthatch (*Sitta*) or hopping through dense vine tangles as they follow mixed-spp. flocks. Often spend up to several min drilling 1 or more little holes in a dead twig or small rotten branch. Forage at almost any ht. from eye level to subcanopy. Easily overlooked (listen for song) because of small size. Tiny round nest hole sim. to those of others of genus.
Status and habitat: Fairly common resident inside and along borders of humid forest, at treefalls and other forest openings, and in older second growth.

Range: To 1900m. S Delta Amacuro and e Bolívar from Sierra de Imataca s to Río Paragua and Río Cuyuní (*clarus*); rest of Bolívar and throughout Amazonas (*un-*

dulatus). E Colombia (specimens?) to the Guianas and n and e Brazil.
Note: Subsp. *salvini* (ne Venez.) not recognized. Orinoco Piculet (*P. pumilus*) probably occurs in nw Amazonas (known from w bank of Orinoco at Maipures, Colombia, s to Vaupés). Much like Golden-spangled Piculet but upperparts uniform olive (no scaling or spotting). The two could be conspecific.

Black-dotted Piculet Illus. below
Picumnus nigropunctatus   Telegrafista Punteado
Identification: 3.5″ (8.9cm). Crown black, forecrown narrowly streaked scarlet, rearcrown conspic. dotted white (or all dotted white—♀). Upperparts pale olive brown with faint yellow tinge; shoulders and back somewhat spotted dusky; *underparts clear pale yellow* (occas. buffy white to almost white) finely and faintly barred dusky on throat and *distinctly but sparsely dotted black* (small spots) *on lower underparts*. Some birds show only a few black spots on lower breast and have belly unmarked pale yellow; birds from se Sucre occas. have some fine barring extending onto chest.
Sim. species: Combination of a few scattered black dots on *distinctly yellow* lower underparts is usually diagnostic, but birds with scaly throats and pale or whitish underparts look much like Scaled Piculet; note latter's scaled and dingy white (not yellow) lower underparts.
Voice: Song 2 to several extremely high, thin notes, each slightly lower than the preceding; *tseeet, tseeet, tseee*, etc.; this also used as contact call (?). When foraging may sing a few times in succession, then not again for several min.
Behavior: Members of prs. often forage alone or are well separated from each other, and occas. follow mixed-spp. flocks along forest borders. Occur from eye level to upper levels in trees where hitch sideways

Black-dotted Piculet

along branches, and pause to peck and drill in rotten wood and broken stub and twig ends.

Status and habitat: Resident in swampy forest, forest borders, woodlots, bushy or overgrown pastures, and tree-lined fence rows; everywhere favors swampy or low-lying areas near water. Although known only from ca. 15 specimens, it is common s of Guaraunos in se Sucre, at Caño Colorado, e Monagas (many sightings), and in vicinity of Tucupita, Delta Amacuro. Prob. also in mangroves.

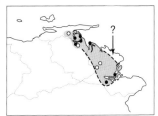

Range: ENDEMIC. To 100m. Se Sucre (La Brea, Guaraunos) to s Delta Amacuro at Merejina and Misión Araguaimujo.

Scaled Piculet

PLATE 37

Picumnus squamulatus   Telegrafista Escamado

Identification: 3.5″ (8.9cm). 11g. Plumage varies geographically. ♂: crown blackish dotted orange to red in front, white behind (or dots yellowish behind—*lovejoyi*; or all dotted white—♀). Plumage pale sandy brown above, dirty white below and *conspic. scaled dusky all over*, inner remiges edged olive yellow. Or lighter and grayer, more crisply scaled below (*lovejoyi*); or *whitest and least scaled* below, some almost unmarked below (*apurensis*); or tinged yellow below (*obsoletus*).

Sim. species: From White-bellied Piculet by *smaller size*, smaller bill, and scaling throughout underparts, but note that in area of overlap (s Apure) a careful look is needed to separate the 2 spp. In s Apure Scaled also is whitish below and shows little scaling on underparts. In mts. of s Táchira see Olivaceous Piculet.

Voice: Commonest song a high, thin *seeek. . seeek . . seeek . . seeek. . seeek*, sometimes a few more shorter, faster notes at end, the whole sequence falling in pitch and sometimes accelerating slightly. Contact note a brief *seek* 1–3 times. In disputes a high, twittering *te'd'd'd'tsee-tsee-tsee*.

Behavior: Occurs alone or more often in loosely assoc. prs., and reg. with mixed-spp. flocks. Hops or hitches sideways along small branches and twigs and in vine tangles, mostly 2–8m up. Pauses now and then to peck vigorously, esp. on twig-sized dead wood and little stub ends. Notably territorial, with prs. or families reg. engaging in vigorous and prolonged boundary disputes with neighbors. Nest in small hole excavated in rotten or soft live wood of branch or stub. May and Sep breeding, w Guárico[734].

Status and habitat: Common and widespread resident in dry and moist forest, gallery forest, light woodland, and shrubby or disturbed areas. Small nos. in humid forest borders. Replaced in desert scrub of nw by Chestnut Piculet.

Range: To 1800m (mostly below 1000m). Base of Sierra de Perijá, nw Zulia (*lovejoyi*); sw Apure e across Guárico and Anzoátegui (*apurensis*); rest of Venez. n of Orinoco from ne Zulia and Falcón e to w Sucre and Monagas (*rohli*); ne Sucre (*obsoletus*) sightings in ne Bolívar at El Palmar may be this sp. or White-bellied Piculet. Ne Colombia.

White-bellied Piculet

PLATE 37

Picumnus spilogaster   Telegrafista Pálido

Identification: 3.8–4″ (9.7–10.2cm). 13.2g. *Relatively large piculet*; bill heavy. Crown black, *forecrown broadly streaked scarlet*, hindcrown dotted white (or crown all dotted white—♀). In both sexes white dots may show as white patch on rearcrown. Upperparts pale grayish brown, shoulders and back faintly to obviously scaled light buff, inner remiges prom. edged yellowish buff; *below dull white to buff white* indistinctly scaled dusky on throat and chest; *lower underparts white, unmarked*.

Sim. species: Scaled Piculet is almost always more scaly below and usually more scaly above. Note White-bellied's larger size, heavy bill, contrasting red and black cap (♂), cleaner whiter appearance below, and limited range. Black-dotted Piculet is distinctly smaller, usually yellowish below, and always with a few black dots (look carefully).

Voice: Song a long (ca. 3 sec), thin, descending trill (unusually long for genus), *ti'eeeeeeeeeeeeeeeeeeeeee eeee*, slightly downscale. In dispute high *ti* notes and short trills. Also a short, fast drumroll.

Behavior: As in others of genus, single birds or prs. actively hop along limbs and through tangles, usually keeping fairly high in trees, where freq. pause to peck and hammer away at twigs and rotten stub ends. Usually independent of mixed-spp. flocks.

Status and habitat: Resident in tall semideciduous gallery forest and wooded borders in Apure; tall humid forest borders, second growth with scattered tall trees, and swampy borders in Delta Amacuro. Uncommon

and perhaps spotty in distrib. In all areas shows a fondness for swampy, low-lying areas.
Range: To 100m. S Apure (Pto. Páez; sight, Hato Los Indios[259]) and e along Orinoco in Bolívar (Altagracia; Caicara) to Delta Amacuro (Misión Araguaimujo; sight, Tucupita[259]) (*orinocensis*). The Guianas and ne Brazil.

Olivaceous Piculet PLATE 37
Picumnus olivaceus Telegrafista Oliva
Identification: 3.5″ (8.9cm). 10.6g. Crown black spotted bright orange in front, white behind (or all dotted white—♀), rest of upperparts pale grayish olive, inner remiges edged yellow olive, *below pale yellowish olive rather obscurely streaked dusky*. Or throat and chest finely barred and washed brownish *contrasting with dusky streaks on yellowish white lower underparts* (*tachirensis*).
Sim. species: Overlaps only with Scaled Piculet which is conspic. scaled all over.
Voice: Song a high, thin, slightly descending trill, *teeeeeee-e-e-e-e*; high, thin *seet* contact notes.
Behavior: Sim. to Scaled Piculet. In Costa Rica, nest a shallow cavity with small 1″ (25mm) diameter hole excavated by both sexes in rotten post, or dead or soft live wood of branch, ca. 1–9m up; 2–3 eggs[706].
Status and habitat: Uncommon resident in moist to humid forest borders, light woodland, and shrubby clearings; mostly foothills and low to mid. el. slopes of Andes.

Range: 800–2300m. Sierra de Perijá, Zulia (*eisenmanni*); both slopes of Andes in Táchira (*tachirensis*); w Mérida (sight, La Azulita)[60]. Guatemala to w Ecuador.

Chestnut Piculet PLATE 37
Picumnus cinnamomeus Telegrafista Castaño
Identification: 4″ (10.2cm). ♂: *mostly bright rufous chestnut*; forehead creamy white, rest of crown black dotted bright yellow. Or sim. but hindcrown spotted white, plumage paler, more cinnamon rufous (*cinnamomeus*). Or forehead tawny rufous, overall dark chestnut (*venezuelensis*). ♀: sim. but crown black, hindcrown spotted white. Or entire crown spotted with white (*perijanus*).
Sim. species: Chestnut plumage is unique.
Voice: Song, infreq. hd. but occas. given several times in a few min, a single extremely high, thin trill (almost insectlike), *t'ï'ï'ï'ï'ï'ï'ï'ï'ï'ï'ï'ï'ï'ï'ï'ï*, ca. 1.5 sec, diminishing toward end. Inaudible at any distance. Also, when foraging a well-spaced ser. of 3–6 notes, *eeeesk. . . eeesk . . . eeesk . . .* on same pitch. Short drumroll is very fast; sometimes drumming given as a ser. of short bursts.

Behavior: Active, hitching sideways or creeping over small branches and twigs somewhat like a *Xenops*, or hopping through thorny thickets or vines, always without using tail for support. Drills into rotten twigs or broken twig ends and may be encountered at almost any ht. Typically in loosely assoc. prs. or little "families" of 3–4 that also may accompany mixed-spp. flocks. Like all piculets, rather inconspic. because of small size and weak vocalizations, but usually not too difficult to see. Nest in small hole excavated by both sexes; Dec. breeding, n Colombia.
Status and habitat: Uncommon to fairly common resident in arid and semiarid scrub, dry forest, scrubby woodland, and mangroves. Esp. favors dense and slightly taller thorny vegetation along "washes" in desert regions. Locally into moist woodland in s Maracaibo Basin.

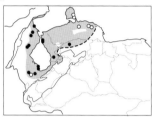

Range: To 100m. Nw Zulia on Goajira Pen. (*cinnamomeus*); nw and ne of Lago de Maracaibo, Zulia, nw Lara, and w and c Falcón e to Cuare (*perijanus?*); rest of s Maracaibo Basin in Zulia (*venezuelensis*). Ne Colombia.
Note: Subsp. *larensis*[17] not recognized.

Chrysoptilus

Monotypic genus; fairly long bill; tail stiff and flat (not concave); unlike in allied *Colaptes*, vocalizations weak. Sometimes merged with *Colaptes*[603].

Spot-breasted Woodpecker PLATE 36
Chrysoptilus punctigula Carpintero Pechipunteado
Identification: 8″ (20.3cm). 65g. ♂: forecrown stained black, rest of crown crimson, *sides of head white* bordered by red malar stripe; *upperparts yellow olive barred black*, rump yellow barred black, throat freckled black and white, *chest tawny yellow turning bright yellow on lower underparts; breast liberally dotted black*. ♀: sim. but only nape red; no red malar.
Sim. species: Superficially much like Golden-olive Woodpecker which is unbarred above (incl. tail), *densely banded* below (no yellow), and found mostly at higher el.
Voice: "Sings through its nose." Infreq. a brisk, very nasal *wic-wic-wic . . .* (ca. 8–10 notes), weak and on same pitch. Also *whew*, a trebled *ta-wick*, and flicker-like *week-a, week-a . . .* in greeting[603].
Behavior: Single birds or prs. occur alone and generally do not attract attention to themselves despite occurring in partially open areas. Chisel or drill into trunks and limbs and occas. drop to gd. for ants. Nest a cavity excavated in fence post, low stub, etc. May–Aug breeding, Guárico[734].

Status and habitat: Uncommon resident in gallery forest borders, light woodland, ranchland with scattered trees, seasonally flooded second growth, and mangroves. S of Orinoco in várzea borders and *Cecropia*-dominated river-edge vegetation. Typically a local and low-density sp.

Range: To 600m n of Orinoco (sight to 1450m, Miranda); to 150m s of Orinoco. S of Lago de Maracaibo in s Zulia, nw Táchira, w Trujillo (Mene Grande), and e Zulia (*zuliae*); generally e of Andes from Táchira, Portuguesa, Carabobo, Aragua (Maracay), and e Miranda to w Sucre (Cumaná), Monagas, and Delta Amacuro; along Orinoco in n Bolívar (Caicara to Ciudad Bolívar); nw Amazonas s to Isla Ratón (*punctipectus*). C Panama to n Bolivia, c Amaz. Brazil, and the Guianas.

Piculus

Tropical genus; med. sized; straight chisel bill not esp. long; typically with red on crown; also red malar (♂♂); bold whitish or yellowish cheek patch or subauricular line; most spp. barred or banded below; not as vocal as *Colaptes*; most spp. drum infreq.

Crimson-mantled Woodpecker   PLATE 36
Piculus rivolii Carpintero Candela
Identification: 10″ (25cm). 86g. *Spectacular*. ♂: above *almost entirely bright scarlet*, crown with a few black stains, rump yellow barred black, tail black, *sides of head white* bordered below by red malar; throat and upper breast black scaled and freckled white, chest often stained red, *rest of underparts bright yellow somewhat scalloped and spotted black on breast*. ♀: forecrown and malar stripe black.
Sim. species: Occurs above range of most woodpeckers, and none has such striking red upperparts. See Golden-olive Woodpecker; in s Táchira cf. Yellow-vented Woodpecker.
Voice: Usually quiet. Calls incl. *ky-ky-ky-ky* . . . ; a rolling *churr-r-r-, ka-weEP, ka-weEP, . . .* ; territorial song a long ser. of *wik* notes[179]. Also a short, metallic rattle like that of a flicker (*Colaptes*); rarely drums.
Behavior: Single birds or prs. forage at almost any ht. but more often well up in trees. Reg. follow mixed-spp. flocks. Hop along limbs, vines, trunks, and stubs as probe, peck, and glean, as well as chisel in rotten wood, check broken stub ends, flake off pieces of bark or moss on epiphyte-laden surfaces. In paramo work over *Espeletia* trunks and flowers and hop on gd.
Status and habitat: Uncommon resident in humid and wet mossy forest and borders, shrubby clearings, stunted treeline woodland, and lower zones of paramo.

Range: 1800–3700m (most recs. 2400–3200m). Sierra de Perijá, Zulia (*zuliensis*)[17]; Andes of s Táchira (*rivolii*); n Táchira and Mérida n to ne Trujillo at Páramo Cendé (*meridae*). Colombia s in Andes to n Bolivia.

Golden-olive Woodpecker   PLATE 36
Piculus rubiginosus Carpintero Dorado Verde
Identification: 8.5″ (22cm). 68g. ♂: forecrown gray, rest of crown red, *sides of head white* bordered below by red malar; otherwise *upperparts uniform golden olive* (incl. tail), throat dark gray freckled with white, *breast and belly narrowly and evenly barred yellow and dark olive*, belly yellower. Or sim. but darker above (old mustard color), much darker below, yellow barring very narrow (*deltanus, guianae, viridissimus*). Andean birds may show prom. pale eyering. ♀: only nape red; no red malar.
Sim. species: See Spot-breasted and Golden-green woodpeckers.
Voice: Commonest call a loud *GREEP!* at long intervals; prs. countercall with long rattle (like Golden-collared Woodpecker).
Behavior: Usually alone or in prs. from fairly low to subcanopy hts. Taps and chisels on upright and bare or mostly bare branches, vines, and trunks, less often gleans and probes; occas. eats fruit and may feed fruit (e.g., *Cecropia* catkins) to fledglings. Often in mixed-spp. flocks. Cavity nest excavated ca. 1.2–18m up in tree; 2–4 eggs[706].
Status and habitat: Fairly common resident in humid and wet premontane and montane forest, esp. around openings, forest borders, second-growth woodland, and scattered trees in clearings. Very local in lowlands, mainly in humid forests of e Venez. (e.g., e of Río Grande).

Range: Mostly 700–2300m (once to 2800m) n of Orinoco; 700–2100m s of Orinoco but locally in lowlands to sea level (Delta Amacuro, nw Bolívar). Sierra de Perijá, Zulia; Andes from Táchira to Lara, mts. of n Falcón, Yaracuy, and n cordilleras e to Miranda (*meridensis*); mts. of ne Anzoátegui, Sucre, and Monagas (*rubigino-*

sus); s Delta Amacuro at Caño Tipuro (*deltanus*); lowlands and hills of Serranía de Imataca s to upper Río Cuyuní in ne Bolívar; generally in foothills and tepuis of Amazonas and Bolívar (*guianae*); summit of Auyántepui (*viridissimus*). Mexico to w Panama; Colombia to nw Argentina; Guyana; Suriname; Trinidad.

Yellow-throated Woodpecker   PLATE 36
Piculus flavigula   Carpintero Cuelliamarillo
Identification: 8″ (20.3cm). 54g. Bold, colorful head; neck thin. ♂: crown, nape, and moustachial streak crimson (no red moustache—*magnus*), *throat, sides of neck, and sides of head golden yellow,* rest of upperparts and tail uniform golden olive, *below dark olive boldly and coarsely scalloped white.* ♀: sim. but crown dark yellow, only nape red; no moustache.
Sim. species: In either sex note yellow which almost encircles head, and bold scallops below. See ♀ Golden-green Woodpecker which has sides of head olive and long narrow malar line.
Voice: Notably quiet. Infreq. a nasal, almost reptilian, hissing *jsssssssssssss,* ca. 2–2.5 sec (or like air escaping from a tire) given once or twice. Also occas. a clear *queea, queea* or ser. of *kee* notes.
Behavior: Single birds or prs. habitually follow mixedspp. flocks, mostly at mid.-forest to canopy hts. inside forest but occas. down to eye level. Climb trunks and branches and tap and drill into bark and wood and feed heavily on ants and termits at times. In se Colombia ♂ digging nest cavity, 15 Nov, 2m above water[260].
Status and habitat: Fairly common resident (easily overlooked) in tall humid terra firme and várzea forest in lowlands; rarely in isolated trees in clearings. Distrib. somewhat local as favors forests growing on richer soils (scarce in scrubby white sandy soil forests).

Range: To 700m. Throughout Amazonas (*magnus*); Bolívar from lower Río Caura and Sierra de Imataca southward (*flavigula*). Se Colombia to n Peru, n Brazil, and the Guianas; se Brazil.

Golden-green Woodpecker   PLATE 36
Piculus chrysochloros   Carpintero Dorado
Identification: 9″ (23cm), 83g in Amazonas. Or 8″ (20.3cm) w of Andes. Two distinctive subspp. Slightly crested. *Eyes blue.* ♂: crown and nape crimson, sides of head and upperparts incl. tail olive; *long narrow yellow moustache line from nostril to neck* bordered below by short red malar streak; yellow throat freckled and barred olive, *rest of underparts finely and evenly banded olive and yellowish white.* In flight basal half of flight

feathers *rufous* (from below). ♀: sim. but *crown and nape dark olive,* no red malar streak, throat barred (*capistratus*). Or ♂ sim. but back and wings yellowish olive, throat uniform yellow, underparts banded olive and buffy yellow. ♀ rather different from ♀ of s subsp: crown and nape dark yellow, throat yellow and unbarred) (*xanthochloros*).
Sim. species: All races told by long, narrow moustachial line; up close note blue eyes. See Yellow-throated Woodpecker.
Voice: Rarely vocalizes. In Ecuador a shrill *shreeyr,* sometimes doubled or tripled[541].
Behavior: Single birds or well-separated members of prs. are usually with mixed-spp. flocks in forest mid. levels or higher but occas. down to eye level. Glean bark surfaces and drill into soft, rotten stubs, feed heavily on ants and termites. An unusually quiet sp.
Status and habitat: Uncommon resident in humid terra firme and várzea forest and forest edges; also in extensive mature gallery forests in llanos (e.g., Hato Piñero). Prob. most numerous (at least formerly) in humid forested parts of Maracaibo Basin.

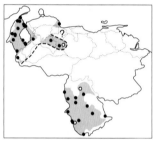

Range: To 450m n of Orinoco; to 650m (sight to 900m) s of Orinoco. Maracaibo Basin, Zulia, and nw Táchira to Trujillo (Mendoza); e base of Andes in Táchira (San Cristobal), Portuguesa, and s Cojedes; e Falcón at Tucacas (*xanthochloros*); nw Amazonas from San Fernando de Atapabo southward (*capistratus*); possibly ne Bolívar and s Delta Amacuro(?). E Panama to the Guianas, se Bolivia, and n Argentina.
Note 1: By some placed in genus *Chrysoptilus.*
Note 2: Perhaps 2 spp. involved.

Celeus

Most spp. chestnut colored (a few spp. creamy to yellowish); shaggy rear-pointing crest imparts hammerheaded appearance; greenish yellow bill; foraging behavior often novel, incl. gleaning bark surface, attacking termite colonies, and eating fruit.

Chestnut Woodpecker   PLATE 36
Celeus elegans   Carpintero Castaño
Identification: 11″ (28cm). 127g. Large, chestnut, and unbarred. *Bill greenish yellow.* Prom. rear-pointing crest ("hammerhead" shape) dark chestnut. Plumage mainly *uniform chestnut above and below,* red malar patch (no red—♀), wings and tail black; *rump and flanks contrasting ochre yellow* (occas. pale cinnamon); under wing coverts and flight feathers (from below) creamy yellow barred black. Or crest cinna-

mon to buffy yellow, shoulders obscurely barred (*hellmayri*).

Sim. species: Shares buffy yellow rump and black tail with smaller Scale-breasted Woodpecker but latter is barred above and below. Also cf. Waved and Ringed woodpeckers.

Voice: In all areas a raspy *whEEjer* or hoarse *whAACH-up* (rising, falling), often several in rapid succession. Sometimes very noisy during disputes. Both sexes give short drumroll.

Behavior: Single birds, prs., families or occas. up to 6 generally forage in mid. story of forest but also higher or lower and reg. follow understory or mid.-level mixed-spp. flocks. Climb larger trunks and limbs where glean from bark, or chip or pry off tiny pieces of bark for hidden prey; occas. open arboreal termite nests and at times feed heavily on fruit (esp. *Clusia* spp.). Trinidad nests Apr–May; hole dug in dead stub or trunk; 3 eggs[175].

Status and habitat: Fairly common resident in humid terra firme and várzea forest, sometimes lighter woodland and forest borders. Mostly foothills and mts. in ne Venez., but widespread at sea level in Delta Amacuro and in lowlands s of Orinoco.

Range: To 1000m n of Orinoco; to 1100m s of Orinoco. Nw Anzoátegui and Sucre s to n Bolívar on lower Río Paragua and Sierra de Imataca (*hellmayri*); ne Monagas s coastally through Delta Amacuro (*deltanus*); throughout Amazonas; Bolívar from lower Río Caura e to upper Río Paragua and Gran Sabana (*jumana*); E Colombia to n and Amaz. Brazil and the Guianas. Trinidad.

Scale-breasted Woodpecker PLATE 36
Celeus grammicus   Carpintero Rojizo
Identification: 9″ (23cm). 67g. Looks like a small edition of Chestnut Woodpecker. Bill creamy yellow. Head and body mainly chestnut with *pale yellow rump and black unbarred tail*; upperparts barred black, throat virtually unbarred, *breast heavily scalloped black*, belly and *crissum unbarred*; red malar patch (no red malar—♀). In flight under wing coverts yellow, flight feathers (from below) cinnamon obscurely barred black. Amt. of barring varies from heavy to only narrow wavy black lines (less in ♀). In some areas (esp. upper Río Caura and upper Río Cuyuní) birds are *almost solid black on chest and breast*, and overall much darker chestnut.

Sim. species: Easily confused with Chestnut Woodpecker which is larger and essentially unbarred above and below. Also much like smaller Waved Wood-

pecker which differs most obviously in contrasting pale head, barred rump and tail, and distinctly barred flight feathers (above and below). Cf. very dark birds with Ringed Woodpecker which always has sharply contrasting pale head.

Voice: Commonest call a nasal *currey-kuu* (or *carry home*), 1st note clear and sliding upward, 2d hoarse and dropping; call essentially identical to that of Waved Woodpecker. Also a scratchy *reêkup*, sometimes repeatedly (like weak version of call of Chestnut Woodpecker); when disturbed a reedy, downscale *KUEE kuaa-kua-kua* (somewhat like that of Cream-colored Woodpecker). Vocalizations generally resemble those of other *Celeus*, esp. Waved and Chestnut woodpeckers. Both sexes drum.

Behavior: Much as in Chestnut Woodpecker but generally found higher in forest and less conspic. Mainly in subcanopy or canopy, esp. on med.-sized to large trunks and canopy limbs where chisels or gleans from bark surfaces, sometimes gleans ants from bark surfaces, and follows canopy mixed-spp. flocks. Several BC birds Mar–May, upper Orinoco[185].

Status and habitat: Fairly common resident in humid terra firme and várzea forest in lowlands, and in foothills of tepuis. Not known to occur with Waved Woodpecker (see Note under that sp.).

Range: To 900m. Throughout Amazonas; Bolívar from lower Río Caura to its headwaters, mid. Río Paragua (Cerro Guaiquinima) and mid. Río Caroní (Auyántepui) southward (*grammicus*). E Colombia to n Bolivia, w Amaz. Brazil, and s of the Amazon e to Río Tapajós. French Guiana.

Waved Woodpecker PLATE 36
Celeus undatus   Carpintero Ondulado
Identification: 8.2″ (21cm). 64g. Bushy crest imparts hammerheaded appearance. Densely barred all over. Bill greenish yellow. *Head and throat contrasting pale cinnamon rufous* with fine dotlike black bars, *rest of upperparts incl. rump dark buffy rufous coarsely barred with wavy black bars*; malar patch red (no red patch— ♀), entire underparts, incl. crissum, pale rufous heavily barred black varying to almost solid black on chest; *tail dark rufous heavily barred and tipped black*, under wing coverts yellow, primaries (from below) rufous boldly and heavily barred black.

Sim. species: Pale head and coarse barring on rump (like back), flight feathers, and tail are the marks. Some individuals are very dark below. See Chestnut and Ringed woodpeckers. Not known to occur with Scale-breasted Woodpecker.

Voice: Freq. hd. territorial call a nasal *currey-kuu* (rises then falls) identical to that of Scale-breasted Woodpecker; at long intervals a loud, rough *WHAACH-cha*, 1 or several times in succession (sim. to Scale-breasted and Chestnut woodpeckers). Both sexes drum. Also a loud, metallic *pring! pring!*, up to 4 notes.

Behavior: Single birds or prs., occas. families, are inconspic. as follow mixed-spp. flocks in upper levels and canopy of tall forest and are often on large trunks and upright branches. Chisel or glean from bark surfaces. Both sexes dig nest hole and feed young by regurgitation; 2 eggs[253].

Status and habitat: Uncommon to fairly common resident locally in humid lowland forest, forest borders, and tall trees in clearings; swampy forest and mangroves in Delta Amacuro.

Range: To 500m. E Sucre (e to Cristóbal Colon); ne Bolívar (Sierra de Imataca and Nuria) s to Sierra de Lema and upper Río Cuyuní (*undatus*); e Delta Amacuro at Caño Guayo near mouth of Orinoco (*amacurensis*). The Guianas and ne Brazil.

Note: Waved Woodpecker may prove to be conspecific with Scaled-breasted Woodpecker (M. B. Robbins).

Cream-colored Woodpecker   PLATE 36
Celeus flavus   Carpintero Amarillo

Identification: 10.5″ (27cm). 105g. Unmistakable *chamois-colored* woodpecker with unkept bushy crest. Prom. black eyes; yellowish bill. *Plumage mainly cream color to buffy yellow*; wing coverts dusky brown to chestnut with varying amts. of creamy yellow edging (in some birds entire wing incl. coverts mainly chestnut); *inner flight feathers dusky rufous to chestnut*, outer ones brownish black; eyering and *tail jet black*; malar patch red (no red—♀); in flight under wing coverts dark rufous. Or sim. but shoulders and most of wing coverts creamy yellow like body, inner flight feathers pale rufous, only outer flight feathers dusky; under wing coverts cinnamon (*semicinnamomeus*).

Voice: Territorial call a ser. of loud, clear, ringing whistles, *Püeer, püEEer, püerr, püerr* (up to 7 notes), usually 2d note highest and stronger, last 2–3 notes descending in pitch (or sometimes 1st 2–3 notes stronger); cf. rather sim. call of Ringed Woodpecker. Call (territorial challenge?) sim. to Chestnut Woodpecker's but higher, less hoarse; a loud, reedy *WhEEjah!*, often doubled or repeated over and over by prs. or groups of birds.

Behavior: This unforgettable woodpecker, in piña colada couture, may be found alone, in prs., or sometimes in loosely assoc. groups up to 6, and is often noisy and conspic. when in groups. Follows mixed-

spp. flocks or forages independently of them about equally, mostly in mid. and upper levels in trees but occas. quite low. Chips and flakes off bark, drills into soft wood and opens arboreal ant nests, (apparently widespread behavior), and eats fruit, esp. *Clusia* arils.

Status and habitat: Resident in humid várzea forest, seasonally flooded gallery forest (in llanos), and swampy or low-lying second-growth woodland and borders; locally in terra firme forest (mainly s of Orinoco). Common in se Sucre, e Monagas, and Delta Amacuro. Elsewhere uncommon and spotty. Many sight recs. in gallery forests of w Apure (Hato Cedral, Hato El Frio).

Range: To 200m (higher?). W Apure (sightings w to Río Caicara) e to n and w Amazonas; lower Río Caura in Bolívar (*flavus*); e Sucre and e Monagas s through Delta Amacuro to ne Bolívar (*semicinnamomeus*). E Colombia to n Bolivia, Amaz. Brazil, and the Guianas; se Brazil.

Ringed Woodpecker   PLATE 36
Celeus torquatus   Carpintero Pechinegro

Identification: 11″ (28cm). 120g. Two plumage types. Barred form (Amazonas): *crested head and throat pale cinnamon rufous*, rest of upperparts rufous chestnut (darker than head), *entire back and wings heavily barred black*; red malar patch (no red—♀); *broad black band on chest and upper breast extends to sides of neck* (does not encircle neck); lower underparts yellow buff *barred black*, tail chestnut barred black. In flight, primaries barred black and chestnut. Unbarred form (mostly e of Río Caura): general plumage sim. but mantle extensively black (band encircles neck), lower underparts cinnamon buff, and *essentially unbarred above and below* (or with a few black bars on shoulders). ♀ of both forms barred above.

Sim. species: Heavily barred Amazonas birds resemble dark-chested individuals of Scale-breasted Woodpecker but differ in pale head, chestnut (not yellow) rump, and barred tail. *Note that at a distance barring is inconspic.* Also cf. smaller Waved Woodpecker.

Voice: Territorial call a loud ringing *KLEE! KLEE! KLEE! KLEE!* on same pitch, usually given a few times mainly at dawn. Typically long intervals between calls. Both sexes drum.

Behavior: Most often seen singly with members of prs. widely separated, and much more away from mixed-spp. flocks than with them. Forage from mid. levels to high in forest, even in canopy of emergent trees. Territories are notably large and calling birds are apt to fly long distances through forest. Chisel small holes in bark or wood, also eat ants, termites, and occas. fruit.

Status and habitat: Uncommon and thinly spread resident in humid terra firme and várzea forest and along forest borders; most numerous in white sandy soil forests of w Amazonas; rare and local e of Río Caura.

Range: To 500m. Throughout Amazonas (*occidentalis*); n Bolívar from lower Río Caura s to Chimantátepui in w Gran Sabana; s Delta Amacuro (*torquatus*); sight recs. to n Monagas (Río Caripe—D. Ascanio; Caño Colorado[58]). Se Colombia to n Bolivia, w and c Amaz. Brazil, and the Guianas; locally in e Brazil.

Dryocopus

Much like *Campephilus* but plumage and vocalizations differ; tail relatively long (concave from above); central tail feathers with long tips.

Lineated Woodpecker   PLATE 36
Dryocopus lineatus Carpintero Real Barbirrayado
Identification: 13.5″ (34cm). 200g. Large. *Bill dusky;* eyes yellow to white. *Crown, long pointed crest, and malar streak crimson,* sides of head and upperparts black, long *narrow* white stripe from nostril runs under eyes and down sides of neck; *conspic. white stripe on each side of back* (stripes do *not* converge in V on back); throat black freckled white, rest of underparts buff white heavily banded black. In flight under wing coverts white. ♀: sim. but forehead and malar black.
Sim. species: Either sex easily confused with ♀ Crimson-crested Woodpecker. Note latter's *broad* (not narrow) white band across face, converging white stripes on back (forming V), and pale bill.
Voice: Call (territorial and pr. communication) a loud *weeka-weeka-weeka-weeka;* also a loud *kip! whu'r'r'r,* drum a slow roll of ca. 5–8 taps (cf. *Campephilus*); also tap with single blows.
Behavior: Alone or in prs. at almost any ht. hitching up large live or decaying stubs, trunks, and limbs. Taps and chisels, often for extended periods of time, on bark surfaces, esp. on dead wood, and scales or pulls off loose dead bark. Also seen eating *Azteca* ants and larvae from *Cecropia* trees; occas. takes fruit. Like most large woodpeckers, rather wary. Flight undulating. In Costa Rica excavates large nest cavity 3–30m up in dead wood; 3–4 eggs[647].
Status and habitat: Widespread and fairly common resident in moist and humid forest borders, plantations, lighter woodland, and clearings with scattered large trees; lowlands and foothills, a few higher in mts.
Range: To 1200m. Maracaibo Basin of Zulia, nw Táchira, and w Mérida; e base of Andes from Táchira n

to w Barinas (*nuperus*); rest of Venez. n of Orinoco incl. Delta Amacuro; all of Amazonas s to Cerro de la Neblina; generally in Bolívar (*lineatus*). Mexico to nw Peru, n Argentina, Paraguay, and se Brazil.

Melanerpes

Med. size; bold head pattern but no malar mark; bill fairly long and circular; typically social.

Yellow-tufted Woodpecker   PLATE 36
Melanerpes cruentatus Carpintero Negro
Identification: 8″ (20.3m). 58g. *Clownlike face.* Eyes yellow. *Crown markings differ.* Mostly glossy black with poppy red central crown patch (no red—♀) and *conspic. bare yellowish white eyering continuing rearward as golden tufts* that join on nape; rump white, *center of lower breast and belly poppy red, sides and flanks barred black and white* (Amazonas and s Bolívar). Or sim. but with *no golden postocular stripe or nape band* on either sex (n and c Amazonas and n Bolívar); or with no postocular band, or only partial brow and band (e base of Andes).
Sim. species: Only small, mainly black woodpecker in its range.
Voice: Noisy. Gives a variety of loud, raucous *r-r-raack'up* calls, often with much wing spreading and bowing; calls generally sim. to those of allied Acorn Woodpecker (*M. formicivorus*) of N Amer. to Colombia.
Behavior: The harlequins of the forest canopy, these very social, almost happy-go-lucky birds are usually in groups of ca. 3–8 that are part of larger, loosely assoc. colonies around clearings or openings in forest canopy. They are quite conspic. as they cling to high dead trunks and stubs, completely omnivorous in diet, and apt to drill into dead wood, sally to air for insects, and peck and eat fruit of all sizes, as well as seeds, esp. arils of *Clusia*. Nesting is loosely communal with 1–

several nests and helpers (offspring from previous generations) at nest cavities in tall dead stubs or trunks[601].
Status and habitat: Common resident in humid terra firme and várzea forest, along forest borders, and esp. in scattered tall dead trees in clearings; coffee plantations in Andean foothills. A few large dead trees or high stubs are requirements.
Range: To 1200m. E base of Andes from Táchira and Apure n to nw Barinas; generally in Amazonas; Bolívar from lower Río Caura, lower Río Paragua, and Sierra de Imataca southward (*extensus*). E Colombia to n Bolivia, Amaz. Brazil, and the Guianas.
Note: Geographical distrib. of head patterns (with or without headbands) is inconsistent; in some areas both variants occur together. The two were formerly considered separate spp. Subsp. *extensus* prob. not worthy of recognition.

Red-crowned Woodpecker   PLATE 36
Melanerpes rubricapillus   Carpintero Habado
Identification: 8″ (20.3cm). 48g. "Zebra-backed" but otherwise dingy and undistinguished. Narrow frontlet yellowish to white, *large circular crown patch red, nape also usually with some red or orange; back and wings black barred white*; rump white, underparts pale dull grayish brown, center of belly red (hard to see); tail black, central and outer feathers barred with white. Or only central crown patch red, central belly orange yellow (*paraguanae*). ♀: head dingy gray brown like underparts; with or without some red, orange, or yellow on nape, sometimes also on forehead (*rubricapillus*). Or ♀ usually with no color on forehead or nape (*paraguanae*).
Sim. species: No other Venez. woodpecker has black-and-white barred back.
Voice: Noisy. Numerous rough, rattling calls incl. *trrrr* or *churr'r;* mate may answer with longer grating *kr'r'a'a'a'a'a'a'a'a*. Both sexes drum.
Behavior: A conspic. woodpecker of semiopen areas. Occurs alone or in prs. from eye level to tree canopy. Chisels off bark and drills into wood, inspects broken branch ends, and often eats fruit incl. *Cecropia*. Nest cavity hollowed out in large cactus, fence post, softer live or dead wood; often quite high; 2 eggs, Mar–Jun breeding, w Guárico[734].
Status and habitat: Common resident in a broad range of disturbed and natural habitats from very arid to moist, and a recent invader into partly deforested humid zones. Desert scrub, dry forest, humid forest borders, plantations, cultivated and urban areas with trees, parks, gardens, and mangroves. Commonest and

most freq. seen woodpecker in n Venez. Spreading through e Bolívar with deforestation.
Range: To 1900m n of Orinoco; to 500m s of Orinoco. Coastal nw and ne Zulia, nw Lara, and w and c Falcón (*paraguanae*); rest of Venez. n of Orinoco incl. Delta Amacuro; nw Amazonas s to Río Cataniapo (spreading southward), n Bolívar s to Río Cuchivero, lower Río Caura, La Paragua, and upper Río Cuyuní at base of Sierra de Lema (sight recs.); Islas Margarita and Patos (*rubricapillus*). Sw Costa Rica to the Guianas.

Veniliornis

Small; bill fairly short and straight; upperparts "old mustard" to brownish; most spp. (except Smoky-brown Woodpecker) coarsely to narrowly banded below; lowland and montane regions.

Smoky-brown Woodpecker   PLATE 36
Veniliornis fumigatus   Carpintero Ahumado
Identification: 6.5″ (16.5cm). 37g. Small. *Entirely uniform dark smoky brown with red crown* (brown—♀), sides of head often somewhat paler, tail dusky. In flight, under wing coverts and underwings coarsely notched dusky and white (looks "checkered").
Sim. species: Only small, all-brown woodpecker in mts. Others are barred below or show facial patterns. See Red-rumped Woodpecker.
Voice: Short *chuck*; rough, nasal rattle (loud for size of bird) very sim. to rattle of Golden-olive Woodpecker; during aggression a wheezy, sucking *whicker*[404].
Behavior: An inconspic. and unassuming little woodpecker that forages quietly from eye level to subcanopy but most often in forest mid. story. Freq. follows mixed-spp. flocks. Climbs trunks and branches and taps and drills into wood. Small nest cavity dug in soft wood of fence post, trunk, or stub, 1.5–8m up; 4 eggs, Feb–May, Costa Rica[706].
Status and habitat: Fairly common resident in humid montane forest, older second growth, coffee plantations, and light woodland.

Range: 800–2900m. Sierra de Perijá, Zulia, Andes from Táchira n to Lara, mts. of Yaracuy, and n cordilleras e to Distr. Federal and Miranda; mts. of ne Anzoátegui, Sucre, and n Monagas (*reichenbachi*). E Mexico s in mts. to n Argentina.

Little Woodpecker   PLATE 36
Veniliornis passerinus   Carpintero Oliváceo
Identification: 6″ (15cm). 31g. *Small and plain*. Crown and nape red, forecrown and sides of head brownish

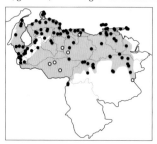

olive with broad but *rather ill-defined dull whitish malar band*, rest of upperparts bright yellowish olive, sometimes wing coverts inconspic. dotted yellowish white and sometimes with a few red stains (best seen in hand); tail dusky with or without some obscure whitish to yellowish bars on outer feathers; underparts dull grayish olive narrowly barred white, underwings (incl. under wing coverts) coarsely barred with white (may show in flight). Or sim. but darker, more olive below (*fidelis*). ♀: no red on crown or nape; outer tail feathers coarsely barred.

Sim. species: Much like Red-stained and Golden-collared woodpeckers but even smaller. Can usually be told from either by ill-defined grayish white eyebrow and malar and lack of yellow on nuchal collar. Compared to Golden-collared Woodpecker, paler with rather "out-of-focus" appearance to barring on underparts.

Voice: Occas. a coarse, wooden rattle; when excited a ser. of *wicka* notes.

Behavior: Occurs alone or in scattered prs. from low to fairly high in trees; sometimes accompanies mixed-spp. flocks along river edges but more often independent of them. Taps and drills industriously into trunks, branches, saplings, rotten stubs, even tall cane and coarse grass stems.

Status and habitat: Fairly common resident along edges of humid terra firme and várzea forest, gallery forest, edges of low-lying woodland, and esp. in seasonally flooded second growth, *Cecropia* saplings, and cane on riverbanks and river isls.; mangroves at mouth of Orinoco. In Amazon Basin restricted mainly to disturbed river edge and river-isl. vegetation (cf. other *Veniliornis*).

Range: To 1200m n of Orinoco; to 400m s of Orinoco. E Táchira and w Apure n to nw Barinas (Barinitas) and e Trujillo (Boconó); e along Río Meta of s Apure to Orinoco and vicinity of Caño Cataniapo, nw Amazonas (*fidelis*); Orinoco in n Bolívar (Caicara) and s Guárico e to Delta Amacuro (*modestus*). E Colombia to n Bolivia, n Argentina, s Brazil, and the Guianas.

Golden-collared Woodpecker   PLATE 36
Veniliornis cassini   Carpintero Cebra
Identification: 7″ (18cm). 35g. *Small.* Crown red bordered behind by *distinct yellow nuchal band*, rest of upperparts bright yellowish olive; *wing coverts always with a few small (often inconspic.) buffy yellow dots*; tail dusky somewhat barred pale olive (more obvious from below); *underparts blackish narrowly banded buffy white*; under wing coverts and flight feathers

(from below) coarsely and boldly barred dusky and white. ♀: sim. but crown dusky olive (no red); nuchal collar and buffy yellow dots on wing coverts as in ♂.

Sim. species: Often impossible to separate from Red-stained Woodpecker in field. Both sexes of Red-stained *lack* yellow dots on wing coverts, and golden collar is less prom. *or absent* (about half of birds lack collar); also note that Red-stained Woodpecker's red shoulder stains are vague, often barely discernible even in hand and not a consistently reliable field mark. Up close (or in hand) Red-stained's underparts barring is olive (not blackish). Also cf. Little Woodpecker.

Voice: In w Amazonas and e Bolívar gives a weak nasal rattle, *drr'r'r'r'r'r'r'r'r'r'r*, rather high pitched, lasting ca. 2 sec (cf. call of next sp.). Prs. greet with rattle calls and raised wings.

Behavior: Alone or in prs. on trunks and branches from forest mid. level to canopy. Reg. with canopy mixed-spp. flocks where quietly climbs trunks and limbs and drills small holes for wood-boring insects.

Status and habitat: Fairly common to common resident in tall humid lowland forest, along forest borders, and in scattered trees in forest clearing. Mainly terra firme forest. Much more widespread than Red-stained Woodpecker; both have been found together e of Pto. Ayacucho, Amazonas.

Range: To 1500m. Mostly e half of Amazonas s to Cerro de la Neblina; generally in Bolívar and w Delta Amacuro; sight to ne Monagas[58]. The Guianas and n Brazil; doubtless also e Colombia.

Red-stained Woodpecker
Veniliornis affinis   Carpintero Barreteado
Identification: 7″ (18cm). 34g. Crown red, *sometimes* bordered behind by narrow yellow nuchal collar (lacking or faint in at least half of all individuals), rest of upperparts bronzy yellowish olive ("old mustard"), *wing coverts unspotted but vaguely stained red* (usually indistinct), *below dark olive* banded white, tail dusky, obscurely barred (mostly from below).

Sim. species: See Golden-collared Woodpecker which has prom. yellow nuchal collar and *always* shows some faint yellow dots on wing coverts (amt. variable but usually visible up close in field). Little Woodpecker has whitish malar and is usually not found inside tall forest.

Voice: Call a rather slow, nasal *kee, kee, kee, kee, kee, kee* (no. of notes varies), very sim. to flight call of Bat Falcon.

Behavior: Single birds or prs. often follow canopy mixed-spp. flocks where they climb trunks and branches from mid. level into canopy and drill for wood-boring insects.

Status and habitat: Uncommon resident, but perhaps often overlooked because inconspic. in field and difficult to distinguish from Golden-collared Woodpecker. Humid terra firme (várzea?) forest, wooded borders, and scattered trees in forest clearings in lowlands.

Range: To 500m. Generally in w half of Amazonas e to vicinity of Cerro Duida, Río Mavaca, and Cerro de la Neblina (*orenocensis*). E Colombia to n Bolivia and Amaz. and se Brazil.

Red-rumped Woodpecker   PLATE 36

Veniliornis kirkii   Carpintero Rabadilla Roja
Identification: 6.5″ (16.5cm). 28g. Much like preceding 3 spp. but only one with *red rump*. Crown red, narrow nuchal band yellow, rest of upperparts bright yellow olive with *red rump and upper tail coverts* (often concealed in field), shoulders usually with a few inconspic. buffy white dots, below grayish olive narrowly and evenly banded white, tail blackish somewhat barred olive (visible mostly from below). ♀: crown grayish brown, nape only tinged yellow.

Sim. species: Most widespread member of genus in Venez. and *only one* there with red rump, although *red often concealed* by wings.

Voice: Distinctive, often hd. call a high, tinny *ca-lick*, singly or repeated several times quickly; also a short drum.

Behavior: A rather inconspic. little bird, easily overlooked except for its freq. calling. Single birds or prs. follow mixed-spp. flocks through woodland and stay mostly in mid. levels or higher in trees. Drill into bark or soft wood. In Trinidad 3 nests, Dec–Apr, 3–7.5m up; 2 eggs[175].

Status and habitat: Fairly common to common resident in dry to moist habitats incl. gallery forest, lighter and drier woodland, plantations, second growth, parks, gardens, cultivated areas, and mangroves; s of

Orinoco much less numerous and restricted to humid mt. forests on slopes of tepuis near Gran Sabana and above range of other *Veniliornis*.

Range: To 1000m n of Orinoco; 1400–1750m s of Orinoco. Generally from Zulia, Falcón (except arid zones), e Táchira, and w Barinas e to Anzoátegui and n Monagas (*continentalis*); e Sucre (*kirkii*); nw Amazonas (Cerro Sipapo; Yutage) and slopes surrounding Gran Sabana from Sierra de Lema (many sight recs.) to Uei-tepui and Cerro Roraima (*monticola*). Costa Rica to w Ecuador. Trinidad and Tobago. Prob. sw Guyana and n Brazil.

Yellow-vented Woodpecker   PLATE 36

Veniliornis dignus   Carpintero Barriga Amarilla
Identification: 7″ (18cm). 38g. Mts. of s Táchira. Crown and nape red, *sides of head blackish with narrow whitish stripe above and below eye*; upperparts yellowish olive (bright mustard) somewhat stained red on mantle; wing coverts sometimes with a few inconspic. white dots (not always present), throat and breast dark grayish olive narrowly and evenly banded white; *unbarred belly sulphur yellow*, tail dusky black, outer feathers barred yellowish olive. ♀: crown dusky; narrow fringe of red on nape.

Sim. species: Note strong facial pattern, unbarred yellow belly, and restricted distrib. in Venez. See Red-rumped Woodpecker.

Voice: Rather quiet; occas. a weak nasal rattle much like others of genus, but higher pitched and markedly faster than rattle of Crimson-mantled Woodpecker with which it shares habitat.

Behavior: Single birds or prs. regularly follow mixed-spp. flocks through forest understory or mid. level, sometimes ranging into canopy, where they are rather unassuming and attract little attention. Hitch along smaller branches, often on underside or in mossy areas, and are apt to tap or drill quietly for long periods without moving.

Status and habitat: Wet upper montane forest (high cloud forest). Known only from 2 specimens in Venez. Scarce in adj. E Andes of Colombia but fairly common westward at els. of 1200–2700m[260].

Range: 1800m. S Táchira in upper Río Chiquito (Hacienda Providencia) (*abdominalis*). Colombia s in Andes to Peru.

Campephilus

Large size; long, straight bill with chisel tip; large crest; tail stiff and concave (from above); all with pale wing patch; young fed by regurgitation.

Crimson-crested Woodpecker   PLATE 36
Campephilus melanoleucos   Carpintero Real Pico Amarillo
Identification: 14″ (36cm). 250g. Eyes yellowish white; *bill pale* (or dusky—w of Andes). ♂: *entire head and crest bright red with white patch surrounding bill* (or with narrow black line above white and extending back to eyes—*melanoleucus*); black and white spot on rear cheek; otherwise neck and upperparts black, *narrow white line down each side of neck continues down each side of back and converges in a conspic. V*; breast and belly barred buff and black; under wing coverts white. ♀: sim. but forehead and front of crest black; neck stripe continues forward as *broad white band below eye to bill* (white almost encloses bill).
Sim. species: ♀ best told from either sex of Lineated Woodpecker by *very broad* (not narrow) *white band across face.* Also note converging white back stripes (not widely separated as in Lineated). Cf. ♂ to Red-necked Woodpecker.
Voice: Contact call or greeting a loud, reedy *CHEESE 'SIK!* Loud, abrupt drum *always* 3–5 rapid taps (but at a distance, drumroll reverberation sounds almost like heavy double tap).
Behavior: Single birds, prs., or occas. groups (families?) up to 5 can be quiet or noisy. Fairly conspic. but almost always wary as climb trunks and large limbs from near gd. to subcanopy. Chisel forcefully into wood, esp. large dead trees and stubs, for wood-boring larvae. Flight is rapid and strongly undulating. Dig large, slightly oval nest hole, usually high in rotten stub or soft wood of live trunk; 2 eggs.
Status and habitat: Widespread and fairly common resident in humid and wet forest, tall second growth, wooded borders, plantations, and isolated trees in clearings; requires presence of large dead trees and limbs; where overlaps with Red-necked Woodpecker, latter occurs inside tall rain forest, Crimson-crested in borders, clearings, and lighter woodland.

Range: To 2000m (mostly below 1500m) n of Orinoco; to 950m s of Orinoco. Zulia w and s of Lago de Maracaibo, nw Táchira, and w Mérida (*malherbii*); ne Zulia and generally e across Venez. to Sucre and Delta Amacuro; throughout Amazonas and Bolívar (*melanoleucos*). Panama to n Argentina and the Guianas. Trinidad.

Red-necked Woodpecker   PLATE 36
Campephilus rubricollis   Carpintero Pescuecirrojo
Identification: 14″ (36cm). 205g. Large. Bill ivory; eyes yellowish white. ♂: *entire head, crest, neck, and chest bright red*, small black and white spot on rear cheek,

rest of upperparts solid black (no white on neck or back), *lower underparts rufous chestnut*; under wing coverts and *basal half of flight feathers rufous chestnut* (conspic. in flight, esp. from below). ♀: sim. but with *conspic. wedge of white* bordered narrowly with black extending from forehead, bill, and chin back to point on rear cheeks.
Sim. species: Told from any other large woodpecker by rufous chestnut underparts; ♀ also by white slash across face.
Voice: Call a reedy, mushy *chiss-sik!* over and over when excited, much like that of Crimson-crested Woodpecker. Drum a loud, quick, double tap, *du'dut*; at a distance the 2 taps almost merge. Cf. 3- to 5-tap drum of Crimson-crested and even longer drum of Lineated Woodpecker.
Behavior: Usually in prs. although members are often well separated. Foraging territories are large. Climb mostly live trunks from eye level to high in canopy, but often remain fairly low, chisel bark surfaces, and drill into large rotten stubs. Like most big woodpeckers, rather suspicious, usually keeping on back sides of trunks and peering around with wary eye. Flight is hurtling, strongly undulating, and somewhat noisy on stiff wing feathers. Dig oval nest cavity, usually high.
Status and habitat: Fairly common low-density resident that is sometimes not met with freq. (listen for drum). Tall humid terra firme forest, occas. forest borders, gallery forest, and trees in clearings in sandy soil forest, as well as richer yellow- and red-soil forests. Prob. also várzea forest but dominant in upland forests, esp. in sandy soil areas.

Range: To 1600m. Throughout Amazonas, Bolívar, and s Delta Amacuro (*rubricollis*). E Colombia to n Bolivia, Amaz. Brazil, and the Guianas.

Powerful Woodpecker   PLATE 36
Campephilus pollens   Carpintero Gigante
Identification: 14.5″ (37cm). Large and robust. *Bill black*; eyes yellow. ♂: *large crest bright red*, otherwise upperparts, head, throat, and chest black with broad white stripe from bill continuing below eyes and down sides of neck; 2 white stripes ("suspenders") on either side of back converge to form broad white V above *conspic. buff white rump*; lower underparts deep buff coarsely barred black. Flight feathers boldly barred black and white on inner webs (visible from below) and with *prom. white tips*. ♀: like ♂ but *crest all black*.
Sim. species: ♀ is only large, *all* "black and white" woodpecker in Venez. ♂ most resembles ♀ of Crimson-crested Woodpecker but note all-red crest

(no black on forehead), white rump, and barred and white-tipped flight feathers (none of this necessarily easy to see in field). In small area of overlap, ♀ Crimson-crested has pale (not jet black) bill. Also cf. ♂ and ♀ Lineated Woodpecker.

Voice: Call a loud, crying *KEEaah*, a loud abrupt *KEEaah-ah-ah-ah*, very reedy and strained, and piercing *EE-EE-aa-aa-a*. Calls somewhat reminiscent of equivalent vocalizations of other *Campephilus*, esp. Magellanic Woodpecker (*C. magellanicus*) of s S Amer. Drum a loud, double tap, 1st tap stronger, 2d almost an echo.

Behavior: A large, heavily built woodpecker usually found inside mature humid and wet mt. forest where it climbs up large trunks and limbs from understory (sometimes quite low) to subcanopy. Vigorously chisels on trunks, presum. for wood-boring insects and larvae. Rather wary.

Status and habitat: Resident in humid and wet upper montane forest. Known from at least 9 specimens from 2 relatively small areas where, at least formerly, perhaps not uncommon.

Range: 1800–2250m. Mts. of s Táchira in upper Río Chiquito (Hacienda La Providencia) and near Páramo de Tamá (*pollens*). Andes of Colombia to Peru.

PASSERIFORMES

The Furnariidae and Dendrocolaptidae are here treated as separate families[10]. The 2 groups have been considered subfamilies within an enlarged Furnariidae family by some authors[606].

Furnariidae: Horneros, Spinetails, and Foliage-gleaners

Albañiles, Güitíos, Raspa Hojas, etc.

The furnariids are a large, diverse group of New World birds that reaches greatest diversity in the south temperate New World and Andes. Their numbers gradually decrease northward, and none is found north of Mexico. In Venezuela they may be found in practically every major terrestrial habitat from the lowlands to the paramo, with more species found south of the Orinoco than elsewhere. Despite their diversity they are not, as a group, very familiar or easy to see, nor are they colorful. Most are shades of dull brown, gray, and rufous. Nevertheless, furnariids are behaviorally one of the most interesting groups of birds in the New World.

Their food consists of insects or invertebrates taken in a variety of ways, often indicated (although not necessarily correctly) by their English names, e.g., foliage-gleaner, leaftosser, treehunter. Names of others may suggest a physical attribute, e.g., spinetail, thistletail, barbtail, tuftedcheek. Nests are varied and remarkable, and regardless of the solution, all nests made by furnariids are enclosed or covered. They range from smooth mud domes of horneros (named for the resemblance of the nest to a rounded mud oven) to large, covered, stick basket nests of canasteros and thornbirds. Others nest in burrows which they dig or in hollow tree cavities and rotten stubs. Songs are trills, rattles, or short whistles, generally not complex and not especially musical. Recent analysis of Furnariidae nest architecture supports some traditional phylogenetic groupings in the family[467,768] as well as some novel groupings[837].

Cinclodes

Rather large, plain furnariids; *Turdus*-like in shape; bill stout, almost straight or slightly decurved; bold buff or white wing band; pale tail corners; spp. mainly in high Andes or austral plains and seacoasts.

Bar-winged Cinclodes   PLATE 38
Cinclodes fuscus   Meneacola

Identification: 7″ (18cm). 32g. Thrushlike. Above mostly dull pale brown, crown darker with *prom. whitish eyestripe* and dusky cheeks; wings dusky with *cinnamon rufous patch across base of flight feathers* (shows as conspic. band in flight), lesser wing coverts edged light cinnamon; throat whitish obscurely scaled dusky, rest of underparts whitish more or less washed buff to light brown, center of belly white; tail brown, outer 3 feathers edged and tipped cinnamon rufous.

Sim. species: Nothing else sim. in paramo where it occurs. See Paramo Pipit.

Voice: Song a short (ca. 2-sec), fast, rattley trill, *tetet't't 't't't't't't*, often ascending, and accompanied by upraised wing flapping; call a sharp *pfip!* often doubled or trebled.

Behavior: Terrestrial, either alone or in loosely allied prs. Stands alert on rocks, gd., or in grass, hops or runs rapidly on gd., then stops with tail cocked at jaunty angle and flicks wings and kicks up tail. Gleans arthropods from gd., damp places, edges of small pools or lagoons, etc., or occas. probes in grass and soil. Nest (prob. rainy season) in rocky outcrop, hole in bank, wall, building, etc., often near stream; 3 white eggs in Chile[280].

Status and habitat: Fairly common to common resident. Grassy, shrubby, and barren or rocky paramo. At lower els. (e.g., 3500–3600m) found esp. near streams, rivulets, damp meadows, edges of lagoons, and muddy places, generally not far from water. At 4000m and higher tends to be more numerous and more widely distrib. across a variety of paramo vegetation types (often rocky areas with little grass) and less restricted to vicinity of water[778]. Recently found on Páramo de Tamá, extreme s Táchira[97].

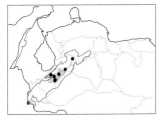

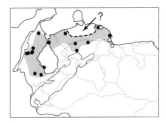

Range: 3250–5000m. S Táchira on Páramo de Tamá (*oreobates*); c Mérida n to s Lara at Páramo de Las Rosas (*heterurus*); no recs. in n Táchira. Colombia s in Andes to Tierra del Fuego; s birds migratory, reaching n to Uruguay and s Brazil.

Furnarius

Smaller than *Cinclodes*; chunky with short tail and long legs; loud, clattering song; unique, ovenlike nest of mud.

Caribbean Hornero   PLATE 39
Furnarius longirostris   Albañil
Identification: 6.5″ (16.5cm). 44g. *Chunky and short-tailed with long, pale, brownish pink legs; long slender bill paler toward tip. Eyes dark. Above bright cinnamon rufous, crown light gray to grayish brownish; long eye-stripe buff to white;* primaries dusky with broad basal band of rufous showing in flight, throat and belly white, rest of underparts washed cinnamon.
Sim. species: Bright cinnamon rufous plumage and terrestrial habitats should easily identify this bird in dry habitats where it occurs.
Voice: Song a loud, fast, clattering or rattling ser. that accelerates then slows at end, on same pitch or slightly dropping at end (ca. 4 sec), *clee'clee'clee-clee-clee* . . . , often answered by another bird; song, after playback, accelerates into steady clattering rattle; call a loud, descending *cheeop*.
Behavior: Usually seen singly, occas. in loosely assoc. prs. that forage on gd. Walks jauntily ("goose-steps") with exaggerated sense of importance as it searches for arthropods, sometimes by flipping over leaves. Often walks in open on quiet country roads and occas. follows army ant swarms. May hop up through tangled vegetation or perch in trees but usually not too high above gd. Unique nest a smooth ovenlike dome of mud (diameter 8–10″, 20–25cm) saddled over horizontal branch or fork; narrow, vertically elongated side entrance spirals inward (right- or left-handed) near bottom; usually 2 white eggs.
Status and habitat: Fairly common resident in dry to moist semiopen areas, ranchland with patches of trees and brush, and dry deciduous forest and borders. Needs damp or muddy places to gather mud for nest, but otherwise shows no special affinity for water or muddy creek banks (unlike allies in Amazonia). Distrib. spotty; some seasonal movements possible in e Falcón. Perhaps spreading with opening of dry forest (D. Ascanio).
Range: ENDEMIC. To 600m. S Zulia (*endoecus*); base of Sierra de Perijá in nw Zulia, w Falcón, and nw Lara

(*longirostris*); sightings in se Falcón, n Yaracuy, and nw Carabobo at San Pablo (prob. *longirostris*). Carib. Colombia.
Note 1: Usually considered a subsp. of Pale-legged Hornero (*F. leucopus*) of Amazonia, but song, habitat, and size differ.
Note 2: Pale-legged Hornero occurs in w Guyana close to se Venez. border and may occur in se Venez.

Leptasthenura

Streaky; tiny bill; long, narrow, double-spiked tail strongly graduated; high Andes or cold austral habitats, esp. dry regions.

Andean Tit-Spinetail   PLATE 38
Leptasthenura andicola   Sietecolas
Identification: 6.5″ (16.5cm). *Stubby black bill and unusually long, double-pointed ("spiky"), black tail.* Crown densely streaked black and chestnut ("dark cap"), forehead and narrow but prom. eyestripe white, rest of *upperparts dusky brown thickly streaked white,* wings dusky, *underparts thickly streaked blackish and white;* graduated tail dusky, central pr. of feathers very long and tapering to 2 points, outer feathers edged white.
Sim. species: Note *capped* appearance and overall streaky plumage. Streak-backed Canastero is brownish with different shape; also cf. ♀ Plumbeous Sierra-Finch which has thick bill and "normal" tail.
Voice: When foraging gives high, thin, tinkling *ti* and *tic* notes. Song a longer tinkling trill that descends a little; when excited, bursts of flat chattery trills over and over, e.g., *tmrn-tm-tmrn-tmrn-tr-tm*- . . . in irreg. sequence.
Behavior: Not esp. shy but usually stays hidden, creeping around from near gd. to 3m up (usually below 1.5m) in scantiest of dense low bushes and grassy vegetation in paramo. Forages actively, hopping on branches, hanging upside down, or reaching out to examine foliage, twigs, and flowers for tiny insects. Usually flies low and quickly to adj. shrubs. Sometimes loosely assoc. with other paramo spp. such as thistletails, sierra-finches, and seedeaters. Nest, late Jul, Páramo San Antonio, a thick, grassy, football-shaped oven with

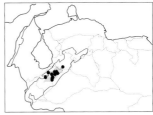

side entrance (USNM); concealed in grass, rocks, on gd., or a few meters up in brush; 2 white eggs.
Status and habitat: Fairly common resident in paramo with *Espeletia* spp. (Compositae) and scattered woody shrubs; also brushy ravines, stunted shrubby *Polylepis sericea* woodland and scrub, and *Stevia lucida* shrubs in paramo/woodland ecotone[778]. Readily found near Páramo del Águila, Mérida.
Range: 3400–4400m. Andes of c Mérida and s Trujillo (*certhia*); Táchira (recs.?). Colombia s in Andes to Bolivia.

Synallaxis

Slender with short wings; usually with med.-length to very long double-pointed, graduated tail; rufous shoulders (wing coverts), sometimes also rufous cap or tail; varying amt. of black (sometimes semiconcealed) on throat; thicket dwelling; difficult to see but easily told by song (learn voices), in most spp. a 2–noted song repeated over and over. Nest a globular ball of sticks with long tubular entrance on side.

Azara's Spinetail   PLATE 43
Synallaxis azarae   Güitío de Azara
Identification: 7″ (18cm). 17g. Only in mts. Forehead brownish gray, otherwise above olive brown with *contrasting rufous crown and shoulders; long* (4.5″, 114mm) *pointed rufous tail*; throat whitish, rest of underparts pale gray tinged brown on chest and sides; short basal feathers on throat black (when feathers raised, throat patch looks black or mixed black and white). Juv.: little or no rufous on crown and shoulders.
Sim. species: Best told by *long* rufous tail, voice, and elevation. Pale-breasted Spinetail is paler below with brownish (not rufous) tail and is mainly in lowlands (not mts.).
Voice: Usual call, often incessantly repeated early in morning, a nasal *be-quick!* or *pip-squeak!* (or *mac-white!*), 2d syllable emphatically rising (recalls Rufous Spinetail).
Behavior: A skulker in thickets and vine tangles and hd. far more than seen, but at dawn may sit partly exposed to sing. Creeps and hops around inside dense vegetation and seldom rises more than ca. 4m up. Usually in prs. and not with mixed-spp. flocks. Globular stick nest with long (0.3–0.4m) entry tube; low in tangled vegetation; 2 white eggs[404]; 1 nest, Feb, Mitisús, Mérida.
Status and habitat: Common and widespread Andean resident in overgrown pastures, bushy roadsides, shrubby areas with bracken ferns, and thickets at edge of cloud forest.

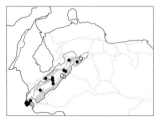

Range: 1600–2300m (sight to 1400m). Andes of Táchira, Mérida, nw Barinas, Trujillo, and se Lara at Guárico (*elegantior*). Colombia s in Andes to n Argentina.
Note: Some regard *elegantior* (Venez. to n Peru) as a separate sp.[179]

McConnell's Spinetail   PLATE 38
Synallaxis macconnelli   Güitío de Bosque
Identification: 6.5″ (16.5cm). 20g. *Dark*. Above dark olive brown with *entire crown, shoulders, and part of wings rufous, tail rufous chestnut, notably short for genus* (ca. 2.8″, 71mm), throat blackish somewhat mixed grayish white, *rest of underparts dark olive brown*. Or pale olivaceous brown (*yavii*).
Sim. species: In its restricted range in Venez. generally at higher el. than others of genus with which it might be confused, although in the Guianas it occurs in lowlands. Cf. lowland Plain-crowned Spinetail with all-grayish brown head (no rufous) and Pale-breasted Spinetail which has longer brown tail and is much paler below. Also see Tepui Spinetail, an arboreal sp.
Voice: Territorial song, unlike others of genus, a low, gravelly, churring *trtrtrtrtr-dek!*, last note brief; sometimes with introductory *churr* note. Song is weak and does not carry far, but typically repeated over and over at short intervals.
Behavior: A skulker in thickets and tangled low vegetation and usually difficult to see, although sometimes sings from a low semiexposed perch at dawn. Like others of genus, usually in prs. Does not follow mixed-spp. flocks, but sometimes more vocal and active as flocks pass nearby. Nest in Brazil a globular ball of sticks with side entrance tube, 3–4m up in shrub (S. Whittaker).
Status and habitat: Uncommon and local resident. Easily overlooked (listen for song) in thickets and dense vegetation at edge of mature, humid, and wet forest on slopes of tepuis. Fairly common along roadside in upper Sierra de Lema.

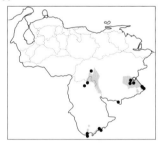

Range: 1000–1900m. N Amazonas on Cerro Yavi (*yavii*); ne Amazonas on Cerro Camani; nw Bolívar on Cerro El Negro (*macconnelli*); tepuis of Gran Sabana from Sororopán-tepui and Ptari-tepui s to Cerro Roraima and Uei-tepui (*griseipectus*); s Amazonas on Cerro de la Neblina (1 specimen from Brazilian side); Cerro Tamacuari. The Guianas and ne Brazil.
Note: Formerly united with Dusky Spinetail (*S. moesta*) of s Colombia to n Peru and Cabanis' Spinetail (*S. cabanisi*) of s Peru and Bolivia.

Pale-breasted Spinetail
PLATE 38

Synallaxis albescens   Güitío Gargantiblanco
Identification: 6.5″ (16.5cm). 15g. Widespread and common. Plumage somewhat variable (often looks rather faded). In general forehead and sides of head pale dull brown, rest of upperparts dingy olive brown with *contrasting rufous crown (rufous begins above eyes) and shoulders*; inconspic. broken grayish eyering; tail dull brown, not esp. long for genus; throat whitish (concealed base of throat feathers black), rest of underparts dingy white somewhat tinged brown to buffy brown on breast and sides. Or sim. but forecrown and sides of head grayish; chest strongly tinged grayish (*josephinae*).
Sim. species: Most likely confused with Azara's Spinetail which has rufous (not brown) tail and is usually found at higher el. S of Orinoco see Plain-crowned and McConnell's spinetails.
Voice: Worth learning. Incessantly repeated song, given yr-round, an emphatic, buzzy *wáit'here*, 1st syllable strongest, 2d falling. Excited birds give ser. of chattery notes.
Behavior: Hd. far more than seen. Prs. are furtive and adept at keeping out of sight. May sing from concealment, but in early morning will sing from a partially exposed position atop a low shrub. Otherwise hops around inside thickets and shrubs, and stays close to gd. and out of sight. Globular nest of coarse sticks has tubular side entrance up to 12″ (30.5cm) long; low in bush; 2 greenish white eggs; Jun–Oct nests, w Apure[137].
Status and habitat: Common resident in grassy and bushy old-field habitats, waste areas, overgrown roadsides, sometimes marshy areas with scattered shrubs; also early-succession vegetation on riverbanks and river isls., and scrubby vegetation in dry and arid regions (e.g., Paraguaná Pen.). Replaced in mts. by Azara's Spinetail.

Range: To 1700m (most recs. much lower). Throughout; s Amazonas (?). Coastal nw Zulia to w Falcón and Lara (*perpallida*); rest of Zulia, nw Táchira, and w Mérida e through Falcón, Yaracuy, and Carabobo to Miranda (*occipitalis*); e base of Andes e to Anzoátegui, Sucre, Monagas, extreme n Amazonas, and n Bolívar (*trinitatis*); c Amazonas (s to Cerro Duida), c and s Bolívar from La Paragua and Cerro El Perro (Río Paragua) to Gran Sabana, and s Delta Amacuro at Misión Araguaimujo (*josephinae*); Isla Margarita and Cubagua (*nesiotis*). Sw Costa Rica to c Argentina. Trinidad.
Note: Subsp. *insignis* (s Apure) also recognized by some[559].

unnamed spinetail

Synallaxis sp. nov.
Identification: 6.2″ (15.7cm). 13.5g. Very like Pale-breasted Spinetail. *Eyes pale brownish yellow. Forecrown and sides of head gray, midcrown and hindcrown rufous*, ill-defined grayish white eyebrow extends to just behind eye; back light brown, flight feathers and tail med. brown, slightly darker than back; *bend of wing and wing coverts rufous*, throat whitish, base of throat feathers black (show black when feathers raised), chest and upper breast pale gray, center of lower breast and belly white, sides and flanks tinged brownish, under tail coverts buffy brown. Tail 75–83mm.
Sim. species: Differs from Pale-breasted Spinetail as follows: *eyes pale brownish yellow*, forecrown and sides of head grayish (not pale dull brownish), *faint grayish white eyeline*; upperparts, wings, and tail slightly *paler brown*. Tail length sim. to that of Pale-breasted Spinetail (avg. for genus).
Voice: Song, nearest White-bellied Spinetail (*S. propinqua*) of Amazon drainage, a quick, chipper *quip! pip-pip-pip-pip*, varied to *quip! pip-pip-pip-pip-pip-pip'pr'r'r'r 'r'r'r*, with trill at end.
Behavior: Much like Pale-breasted Spinetail, and occurs interspecifically with it on Orinoco river isls. Skulks and hops in thickets; keeps mostly 0.5–3m up and out of sight, but may sing from partially exposed position at edge of shrub.
Status and habitat: Discovered by Hilty 23 Jun 1996 on Orinoco river isl. ca. 3km upriver from Camturama Lodge. Subsequently 7 collected there 12–13 May 1999 by M. Lentino, D. Ascanio, R. Rivero, and I. Carreño. Presently known only from several isls. downstream to vicinity of Pto. Ayacucho. Thickets and dense shrubs on semipermanent rocky isls. or rocky and sandy isls. Occurs with Pale-breasted Spinetail, Lesser Wagtail-Tyrant, Riverside Black-Tyrant, and other spp. typical of young vegetation on river isls.

Range: To 200m. Nw Amazonas (isls. of mid. Orinoco). Venez. and adj. Colombia.

Plain-crowned Spinetail
PLATE 38

Synallaxis gujanensis   Güitío Espinoso
Identification: 6.3″ (16cm). 22g. *Head grayish brown* becoming more olive brown on back; *wings and tail rufous*, lores and throat whitish, rest of underparts dull buffy white; chest and sides tinged olive brown.
Sim. species: Unlike most others of genus, has *no rufous* on head. Rusty-backed Spinetail is all rufous

above and nearly always in seasonally flooded areas or near water.

Voice: Territorial song a rather abrupt, scolding *KEW!* . . . *huaa*, with distinct pause between notes; 1st note stronger and higher. As in most *Synallaxis*, often answered by mate.

Behavior: Very skulking. Occurs in prs. but with members often somewhat separated as they forage on or near gd. or to ca. 2m up but remain in contact with freq. calls. Spend about half their time foraging on gd. where move with springy hops and tail cocked up. Not with mixed-spp. flocks. Nest, as in other *Synallaxis*, in shrub or low bushy tree; 2–3 eggs; in Suriname, nest often parasitized by Striped Cuckoo[253].

Status and habitat: Resident. Young second growth in clearings and pastures, shrubby or neglected native gardens, bushy forest borders, and young regrowth vegetation along várzea forest borders, riverbanks, river isls., etc. Fairly common locally in e Bolívar; recs. few and widely scattered in Amazonas.

Range: To 550m. Se Monagas, Delta Amacuro, nw Amazonas and throughout Bolívar (*gujanensis*). E Colombia to n Bolivia, s Brazil, and the Guianas.

Stripe-breasted Spinetail   PLATE 38
Synallaxis cinnamomea   Güitío Canelo

Identification: 5.5″ (14cm). 16g. Dark plumage. Tail rather short for a *Synallaxis*. Above dull dark brown with short ochraceous buff eyebrow; shoulders and wings rufous chestnut, tail chestnut brown, upper throat and malar area white faintly to heavily dotted or streaked black, *rest of underparts ochraceous buff narrowly but thickly streaked dusky*. Or sim. but decidedly paler (*aveledoi*); or sim. but darker (*striatipectus*) or whiter and throat less streaky (*bolivari*).

Sim. species: No other *Synallaxis* is streaked below. See much larger Guttulated and Lineated foliage-gleaners; s of Orinoco, Speckled Spinetail; in ne mts., White-throated Barbtail.

Voice: Song a nasal and rather high-pitched *keep, going?*, 1st note higher, 2d dropping then rising with bouncy inflection; also a soft, whining *peeeur*. Most vocal early in rainy season, at other times song is sporadic.

Behavior: Easily overlooked. Single birds or prs. hop on gd. or skulk to ca. 2m up in thickets. Scratch and toss leaf litter on gd., often remaining in 1 place for some time, or peer in and glean prey from foliage a little above gd. In Paria Pen. forage with small mixed-spp. flocks containing Slaty Antwrens and Three-striped Warblers. When excited raise throat feathers to

form conspic. white patch (like inverted V of white). Nest and eggs as in Pale-breasted Spinetail; breeding recs. scattered throughout yr in Trinidad[175].

Status and habitat: Resident locally in thickets, low vine tangles, and treefalls inside or at edge of humid forest or overgrown coffee plantations; occas. dry deciduous foothills forest (e.g., coastal Aragua) or bushy pastures with ferns, but not far from forest. Very common (ca. 900m) in mts. of Paria Pen., much less numerous and local in Andes.

Range: 250–2000m (most recs. above 700m). Sierra de Perijá, Zulia (*cinnamomea*); Andes from n Táchira (prob. s Táchira) to Lara; mts. of n Falcón (*aveledoi*); e Falcón (Mirimire), Yaracuy, and n cordilleras from Carabobo to Miranda and n Guárico at Cerro Platillón (*bolivari*); mts. of Anzoátegui and w Sucre (*striatipectus*); Paria Pen. of Sucre (*pariae*). E Andes of Colombia (both slopes). Trinidad and Tobago.

Rufous Spinetail
Synallaxis unirufa   Güitío Rufo

Identification: 7″ (18cm). 18g. Long, narrow, double-pointed tail. *Almost completely bright rufous with black bill and conspic. black lores.* Upperparts bright chestnut rufous, below paler, long narrow tail rufous. Throat feathers black basally (black not visible unless feathers are raised, i.e., in aggressive encounters). Or forehead and underparts paler, more cinnamon, with faint pale eyebrow and no black on throat (*munoztebari*).

Sim. species: Overlaps sim.-looking Rufous Wren in mts. of Perijá and s Táchira. Wren is chunkier with "normal" tail and narrow black barring on wings and tail, sometimes buff patch on forehead. In Coastal Cordillera (no range overlap) see Black-throated Spinetail.

Voice: Hd. far more than seen. Commonest call a rather loud, nasal, almost scolding *queeeik* or *quee-queéik*, varied to *quee-quee-quéeik*, upslurred; some vocalizations closely resemble those of Azara's Spinetail (but not those of Black-throated Spinetail with which it was formerly considered conspecific). Alarm a low *churr*.

Behavior: Prs. or families forage alone or occas. around mixed-spp. flocks passing overhead. Hop and clamber mostly 0.2–4m up (not on gd.) in cluttered undergrowth, ferns, and saplings and are quite good at skulking and keeping out of sight. Pick and glean mostly small insect prey from foliage.

Status and habitat: Uncommon to fairly common resident (by voice). Undergrowth of mossy forest, humid and wet forest borders, and older second growth. Often in *Chusquea* bamboo.

Range: 1700–3200m (rarely down to 1300m). Sierra de Perijá, Zulia (*munoztebari*); Andes from s Táchira to ne Trujillo at Páramo Cendé (*meridana*). Andes from Colombia to s Peru.
Note: See taxonomic Note under next sp.

Black-throated Spinetail   PLATE 38
Synallaxis castanea   Güitío Gargantinegro
Identification: 7.2″ (18.3cm). *Only in Coastal Cordillera*. Sim. to Rufous Spinetail but slightly paler and with contrasting black throat. *Completely bright rufous with black bill and lores and narrow black throat* (black *always* visible on throat). In hand, tail slightly longer, 92–108mm vs. 83–100; (ca. 3.9″ vs. 3.4); 8 rather than 10 tail feathers; and tail feather tips less pointed[770].
Sim. species: Nothing sim. in its small range.
Voice: Call a loud *ki-kík*! or rhythmic *kik-kik-kik* or sim. variation, sometimes up to 6 notes (cf. 2- to 3-note calls of Rufous Spinetail); some calls resemble those of Caracas Tapaculo. Vocal mainly early in morning.
Behavior: Sim. to Rufous Spinetail but in general less skulking and easier to see, and often moves out into shrubbery along edges of roadsides. Breeds Apr–Jul, n Venez.[571]
Status and habitat: Fairly common resident in cluttered undergrowth of humid to wet forest, and esp. in shrubby thickets along forest borders. At higher els. sometimes in *Chusquea* bamboo. Readily found in many areas of Coastal Cordillera.

Range: ENDEMIC. 1300–2200m. Coastal Cordillera in Aragua, Distr. Federal, and Miranda (e to vicinity of Caracas).
Note: Has been regarded as a subsp. of Rufous Spinetail (*S. unirufa*)[403] or as a separate sp.[770]

Ruddy Spinetail   PLATE 38
Synallaxis rutilans   Güitío Rojizo
Identification: 6″ (15cm). 17g. Mainly dark reddish brown above with *contrasting black lores and small black throat patch*; forehead, sides of head, and underparts dark rufous chestnut becoming brownish on belly; wings dusky chestnut, tail blackish, double pointed, rather short for genus.

Sim. species: Range does not overlap any sim. allies. See Southern Nightingale-Wren.
Voice: Call (territorial song) a loud, insistent *bîk-waaa* (or *chîk-wup*), over and over by both sexes. Phrase is often doubled.
Behavior: Usually in loosely assoc. prs. that forage by hopping in leaf litter or tangles on or near gd. Skulk in undergrowth and remain out of sight, but may move a little higher (1–2m up) when calling, although seldom in view for more than a moment. Infreq. follow mixed-spp. flocks. BC birds, Apr, Amazonas[185]. Nest as in other *Synallaxis*; 3–4 eggs[506].
Status and habitat: Uncommon to locally fairly common resident (prs. tend to be widely spaced) inside humid terra firme forest on reddish (lateritic) or yellowish soils (not white sandy soil) in lowlands and foothills of tepuis; usually not at forest borders or openings. Readily found near Junglaven, Amazonas.

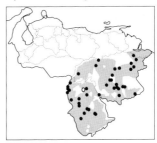

Range: To 1200m. Throughout Amazonas and Bolívar (*dissors*). E Colombia s to n Bolivia, Amaz. Brazil, and the Guianas.

White-whiskered Spinetail   PLATE 38
Synallaxis candei   Güitío Barbiblanco
Identification: 6.5″ (16.5cm). 15g. Striking spinetail of nw deserts. *Mostly bright cinnamon rufous above* with grayish crown, rufous postocular streak, and blackish lores and cheeks; *bold white chin continues as broad white whisker stripe; central throat black*, underparts cinnamon turning white on center of abdomen, tips of flight feathers and *outer 3d of tail blackish*.
Sim. species: No other spinetail in Venez. is so boldly and handsomely marked. Range overlaps Yellow-throated Spinetail, which is usually near water, and Pale-breasted Spinetail.
Voice: Commonest call (territorial song) a hard, nasal *a-DIT-DIT-du*, 1st and last notes weak. Call a nasal *paa pip!* When disturbed or alarmed a longer, nasal, scolding *paa-pip pu pip-a pip pip'pip'pip'pip*; mate also may call more or less simultaneously. Nasal *naaaa* and *keeea* alarm.
Behavior: Individuals, sometimes fairly well separated from a mate, do much of feeding on gd. (unlike many others of genus), hopping actively, often in jerky zig-zags to right then to left, with tail cocked and flicked downward; sometimes forage on fairly open gd. but almost always with vegetation (e.g., spreading acacias) overhead, and also readily go 1–2m up in trees and tangles. In favorable areas territories are quite small and pops. high. Bulky stick nest much like that of other *Synallaxis*. Reported breeding in rainy months,

Oct–Jan on Paraguaná Pen.; 3–4 eggs, turquoise blue to pale greenish[74].

Status and habitat: Fairly common to common resident in desert scrub vegetation, thorn and cactus woodland, salt flats with scattered bushes, and mangrove borders. Often along dry washes (arroyos) with acacia, terrestrial bromeliads, and scrubby vegetation. Readily found in desert scrub around Coro, Falcón, and n and w of Barquisimeto, Lara.

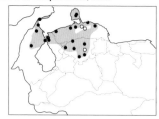

Range: To 1100m. Nw Zulia e to e Falcón (Cuari) and s to vicinity of Barquisimeto and El Tocuyo, Lara (*venezuelensis*). N Colombia.

Note 1: By some placed in genus *Poecilurus*, but vocalizations nearer *Synallaxis* spinetails (e.g., Black-throated Spinetail).

Note 2: Hoary-throated Spinetail, *S. kollari*, of extreme n Brazil (n Roraima) may occur in se Bolívar. Much like White-whiskered Spinetail, it differs in brownish crown, grayish cheeks, all-rufous tail, and "whiskers" mixed black and white. Little known in life, it has recently been found in seasonally flooded forest along Rio Tacutu near Conceiçao do Maú, Brazil[545].

Hellmayrea

Sim. to *Synallaxis* but tail short; vocalizations differ; formerly placed in *Synallaxis* but closer to *Cranioleuca*[82].

White-browed Spinetail   PLATE 38
Hellmayrea gularis   Güitío Paramero

Identification: 5" (12.7cm). 13g. *Tail quite short (2.4",* 61mm), double pointed. High temperate and treeline forest. Above warm rufous brown, tail brighter rufous, *sharp white eyebrow* (conspic.), white chin and upper throat; rest of underparts cinnamon brown (or smoky gray brown—*brunneidorsalis*), outer tail feathers very pointed. Bill black above, pinkish yellow below.

Sim. species: Short tail imparts wrenlike appearance. Mountain Wren has buff eyebrow (no white) and is usually high in trees. Gray-breasted Wood-Wren has black and white streaked cheeks and gray underparts. Also cf. Rufous Spinetail.

Voice: Not often hd. except at dawn. Song in n Táchira a short, buzzy, and accelerating *zit, zit, zit, zit-zit-zit-zit 'zit'i'i'i'iii-zit-zit*, last 2 notes rising. In Trujillo sim. buzzy song accelerates then slows to a chippy ser. at end, *tz tz-tztztztz'tz'tz'ti'ti'tic'tic tic, tic*. When foraging a sharp *chip!* or *chreek!*; also a low, nasal, descending *trrrrrr rrr* (sometimes preceded by a *chip*) and short chitter.

Behavior: Usually seen singly or in loosely assoc. prs., occas. with mixed-spp. flocks but more often independent of them. Quiet and unobtrusive but not particularly shy and sometimes relatively easy to see. Behave

wrenlike as hop in gd.-level mossy tangles, up in vines and mossy branches, or hitch and hop up sides of trunks. Peer, hop, even hang upside down occas., as glean mostly from leaf surfaces, incl. bamboo, and probe moss and curled dead leaves; mainly gd. to 4m up.

Status and habitat: Fairly common but prob. local resident in thickets and dense tangles in mossy montane forest with *Chusquea* bamboo, esp. in stunted high-el. forest at or near treeline/paramo ecotone. Favors very wet treeline habitats.

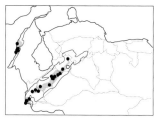

Range: 2300–3200m. Sierra de Perijá, Zulia (*brunneidorsalis*); Andes of s Táchira (*gularis*); n Táchira n through Mérida to ne Trujillo at Cuevas de Carache (*cinereiventris*). Andes of Colombia to c Peru.

Certhiaxis

Lowlands; near water or in marshes; mainly rufous and white; much like *Cranioleuca* but bill longer and thinner; churring or rattling song very different.

Yellow-chinned Spinetail   PLATE 38
Certhiaxis cinnamomea   Güaití de Agua

Identification: 6" (15cm). 15g. *Widespread in marshy areas. Above bright reddish brown* with grayish brown forecrown, *dusky lores*, and ill-defined whitish eyebrow; *underparts mostly dull white* tinged grayish to buff on breast; small chin spot pale yellow (usually only a few *inconspic.* yellow feathers); flight feathers tipped dusky. Or sim. but forecrown grayish (*marabina*); or forecrown reddish brown like rest of upperparts (*orenocensis*); or upperparts pale cinnamon rufous (*cinnamomea*).

Sim. species: A small "bicolored" spinetail, essentially rufous above, whitish below, in marshy areas or near water, is likely this sp. Yellow is hard to see. Also cf. Rusty-backed Spinetail which is much dingier below and usually up in bushes and trees (not in grass).

Voice: Calls freq. throughout day. Loud song a harsh churring rattle, sometimes in duet by ♂ and ♀, becoming louder at first, then settling down and slowing slightly, and remarkably like songs of *Laterallus* rails of sim. habitat. Also gives a ser. of ticking notes (like winding an old watch); occas. a sharp *chip*.

Behavior: Forages alone or in loosely assoc. prs. by hopping on gd. or in grass and bushes, often much in open where easy to see, and rarely more than 3m up. Sometimes picks prey from water's surface using long bill. Apr–Oct nests, w Apure and Guárico[137,734]; bulky globular nest of thorny *Mimosa* twigs (usually) and grass; long entrance tube on side; low in bush or tangle; usually over (or near) water; 3–4 greenish white

eggs; in Trinidad and Suriname often parasitized by Striped Cuckoo[175,253].
Status and habitat: Common resident in marsh grass and adj. bare gd. at edges of ponds and lagoons, grassy, water-filled drainage ditches, scattered bushes in marshes, and edges of mangroves.

Range: To 500m. Maracaibo Basin, Zulia, nw Táchira, w Mérida, and w Trujillo (*marabina*); rest of w Venez. from Falcón, Lara, and n Apure e to Aragua and Guárico (*valenciana*); s Apure, se Guárico, n Amazonas (Caño Platanal), and n Bolívar e to s Sucre and Delta Amacuro (*orenocensis*); n Anzoátegui and n Sucre (*cinnamomea*). N Colombia and locally e of Andes to c Argentina and the Guianas. Trinidad.
Note: Previously called Yellow-throated Spinetail[403].

Cranioleuca

Differ from *Synallaxis* in shorter, more graduated tail (but still double pointed), *arboreal* habits, and song. Tail tips often quite stiff; plumage dull and homogeneous (most spp.); clamber in high canopy foliage or creep over limbs like small foliage-gleaners (not low in thickets like *Synallaxis*); songs of most are rapid ser. of descending chipping notes.

Crested Spinetail   PLATE 38
Cranioleuca subcristata   Güitío Copetón
Identification: 5.5" (14cm). 14g. Dull colored; little or no crest evident in field. *Bill pinkish.* Crown narrowly and faintly streaked black, the feathers elongated, otherwise upperparts pale olive brown with *contrasting rufous wings, rufous tail, and indistinct pale eyestripe*; flight feathers dusky, underparts pale olivaceous brown, paler on throat. In hand, under wing coverts orange rufous.
Sim. species: Despite name, does not look "crested." Pale bill, pale eyebrow, and contrasting rufous wings and tail are good marks for this dull bird which is usually high in trees. No other spinetail in its range is so arboreal.
Voice: Often hd. song of 3–4 high, bouncy notes accelerating into a short, attenuating trill, *pzeep, pzeep, pzeep, pee'pe'e'e'e*, is thin, chattery, and sim. to those of many others in genus; also gives a short, slow rattle and sharp *tsink*!
Behavior: Single birds or prs. often assoc. with mixed-spp. flocks and are relatively easy to see. Hop actively along branches, up among vines, and out into foliage, sometimes twisting back and forth as they go, mainly in mid. levels of vegetation or higher. Breed Jan–Jun,

Rancho Grande[571]; pensile globular dome of grass and moss suspended near end of high branch; entrance hole at bottom; 2 nests Feb–Mar, ne Mérida.
Status and habitat: Common resident in moist and humid forest, forest borders, tall second growth, plantations, and overgrown areas in Coastal Cordillera; less numerous and local in Andes. Mainly foothills and lower montane regions; very locally (mainly Maracaibo region) in lowlands.

Range: 50–1950m (mostly above 400m). Maracaibo Basin in s Zulia and w Trujillo; e slope of Andes from Barinas n to Lara, spottily in Falcón (Sierra de San Luis; sight, Cerro Misión), mts. of Yaracuy, Coastal Cordillera from Carabobo to Miranda; Interior Cordillera on Aragua/Guárico border at Cerro Platillón; mts. of ne Anzoátegui, Sucre and n Monagas (*subcristata*); e base of Andes in Táchira and Apure (*fuscivertex*). A rec. from Guasdualito (50m), w Apure, may be an error. Ne Colombia.

Streak-capped Spinetail
Cranioleuca hellmayri   Güitío Cabecirrayado
Identification: 6" (15cm). Much like Crested Spinetail but *crown chestnut streaked black and sharply contrasting with olive brown back*; short whitish postocular stripe; wings and tail rufous; throat dingy whitish, rest of underparts pale smoky gray.
Sim. species: Much like Crested Spinetail but crown chestnut (not olive brown).
Voice: In Colombia monotonously repeats a weak, high-pitched trill over and over, *ti ti't't'tttt*.
Behavior: Arboreal, mainly 5m to subcanopy ht. In Santa Marta Mts., Colombia, prs. or families follow mixed-spp. flocks where actively glean from foliage of trees, shrubs, and vines and probe cracks in bark and epiphytes. Nest a pendulous ball of grass and leaves (T. B. Johnson).
Status and habitat: Known from 1 ♀ from Sierra de Perijá[363]. Humid montane forest and forest borders.

Range: 700m. Sierra de Perijá (Río Palmar), Zulia. Santa Marta Mts. (1600–3000m), Colombia.

Tepui Spinetail   PLATE 38
Cranioleuca demissa   Güitío de Pantepui
Identification: 5.5″ (14cm). 15g. Slopes of tepuis. Bill dusky, paler at base of mandible. *Crown rufous chestnut*, forehead and rather *weak eyestripe gray*, otherwise olive brown above with contrasting *rufous shoulders, wings, and tail*; underparts light smoky gray, throat slightly freckled dusky.
Sim. species: Only one of its genus in tepuis. More likely mistaken for a small foliage-gleaner, but all are larger, much heavier-billed, and none has contrasting rufous cap. Cf. McConnell's Spinetail.
Voice: Song recalls that of other *Cranioleuca*, a high, bouncy, and thin *TEE TEE'Te ti ti'ti'ti'ti'ti'i'i'i*, accelerating and downscale throughout. Alarm, or when disturbed, a short, rough rattle over and over.
Behavior: Single birds or prs. are usually seen with mixed-spp. flocks that contain other furnariids, Roraiman Antwrens, Tepui Whitestarts, and tanagers. Forages like other *Cranioleuca*, mostly from mid. level to canopy hts., by hopping up through vines and foliage, or sometimes clambering around trunks. Occas. may hitch up viny trunks almost creeperlike. Active and rather easy to see. Nest a bulky, globular-shaped, semipendulous mass of moss.
Status and habitat: Fairly common resident in humid and wet forest and forest borders; also gallery forest and patches of mature woodland in Gran Sabana. Can be seen on Sierra de Lema.

Range: 1100–2450m. Amazonas on Cerros Parú, Duida, and de la Neblina; throughout tepuis of Bolívar except range of next subsp. (*demissa*); Amazonas on Cerro Gimé; Bolívar on Cerros Tabaro and Guaiquinima (*cardonai*). Guyana (Mt. Ayanganna) and n Brazil on Cerro Roraima.

Rusty-backed Spinetail   PLATE 38
Cranioleuca vulpina   Güitío de Cejas Blancas
Identification: 5.8″ (14.7cm). 16g. *Above mostly uniform reddish brown*, crown darker, wings and tail slightly more rufous, *narrow eyestripe dingy white*, sides of head smoky gray brown with suggestion of dusky streaking, underparts dingy smoky grayish brown, throat paler, faintly freckled dusky.
Sim. species: Even more uniform above than Yellow-chinned Spinetail and darker and dingier below (Yellow-chinned has distinct dusky lores and whitish underparts). Both spp. show strong fondness for water, but *note habitat differences*. Crested Spinetail (foothills and mts.) has brownish head and back.

Voice: Sings solo or more often duets (not antiphonal). Typically 1 bird abruptly initiates a song and is immediately joined by mate, both giving loud, chuckling ser. of nasal notes, gradually descending *kuee-kuee-kuee-kuee-quaa-quaa-qua-quaquaquaquaquaqua* (up to 3 sec); song usually given only at rather long intervals. Sometimes only mutter a few *kuee-kweek* notes while foraging.
Behavior: Prs. or little families stay fairly close together as they hop short distances on vines, in tangles, and in shrubby vegetation, mostly 1–7m up, where they glean from bark, leaf petioles, and live or dead foliage. Inconspic. but not shy. May forage actively with small mixed-spp. flocks containing woodcreepers, flycatchers, and greenlets, but usually do not follow them far. Nest a mass of grass wedged in sapling or partly submerged bush with entrance near bottom (no entrance tube); 2 white eggs[115]; Jun–Jul nests (3), w Apure[137].
Status and habitat: Fairly common resident n of Orinoco in gallery forest, seasonally flooded second growth, and shrubby vegetation overhanging banks of rivers and small streams in llanos; s of Orinoco in shrubby borders of várzea forest along rivers, streams, and oxbows.

Range: To 200m. W Apure (*apurensis*); rest of Apure, Portuguesa (Río Guanare), s Cojedes (sight), Amazonas (s to Putaco near Río Mavaca), sw Guárico (Camaguán), and along Orinoco in Bolívar to Delta Amacuro (*alopecias*). Guyana; n Brazil in lower Rio Negro and upper Rio Branco; s of Amazonia in e Bolivia and e Brazil.
Note: Formerly incl. birds of Amazon river isls. from Peru to e Brazil[831].

Speckled Spinetail   PLATE 38
Cranioleuca gutturata   Güitío Pechipunteado
Identification: 5.5″ (14cm). 14g. Rather dark-looking in field. Eyes yellow. Mostly dark olive brown above with *contrasting dark chestnut crown* and narrow deep buff eyebrow; shoulders, wings, and tail rufous chestnut, small chin spot buffy white, *sides of head and rest of underparts buffy white thickly speckled dusky*. Tail is among shortest of genus.
Sim. species: No other spinetail s of Orinoco is so speckled (in n mts. see Stripe-breasted Spinetail) *but cf. rare Orinoco Softtail*. General appearance (incl. shortish tail) might suggest a wren or xenops.
Voice: Song a *very* high-pitched, thin *seeeeee, seeeeee* (sometimes 3–4 notes), easily overlooked. Often sings while foraging with mixed-spp. flocks.
Behavior: One or 2 reg. accompany mixed-spp. flocks from eye level to subcanopy where they actively hop

along branches and in viny tangles and poke, like wrens, into dead leaf clusters and debris, or glean from foliage and twigs. In e Ecuador cone-shaped nest a mass of moss 10″ (25cm) long beneath branch and tapering to entrance hole at bottom (R. Ridgely).

Status and habitat: Uncommon resident inside várzea forest, low-lying transition forest (between flooded and high ground), and poorly drained terra firme forest; also around small, viny forest openings in terra firme forest.

Range: To 750m. Amazonas; Bolívar in lower Río Caura and upper Río Caroní (*hyposticta*). E Colombia to n Bolivia, Amaz. Brazil, Suriname, and French Guiana.
Note: Subsp. *hyposticta* perhaps not recognizable[541].

Schizoeaca

Mostly at or above treeline; long, strongly graduated tail, the feathers ragged, attenuated, much decomposed near end; head wrenlike, some spp. with eyerings or superciliaries; most with colored chin patch; songs are usually short, accelerating (or slowing) chattery trills; taxonomy uncertain, possibly up to 8 allopatric spp.

Ochre-browed Thistletail
PLATE 38
Schizoeaca coryi Piscuiz Frentiocre
Identification: 7″ (18cm). 17g. Tail rather long (but much shorter than in others of genus), feathers pointed, somewhat frayed. Upperparts dull brown, *forehead and fairly prom. superciliary orange rufous*, sides of head and chin duller orange rufous, rest of underparts plain grayish brown, tail dingy brown, the outer feathers dull rufous.
Sim. species: In sp.'s limited high-el. range, see Streak-backed Canastero which is streaked above and shows band of rufous in wings as it flushes. Also cf. Andean Tit-Spinetail.
Voice: Rather quiet. Commonest call a high-pitched, nasal *meeeow*; also a high, nasal *peeeap* (like mouse squeak) when foraging; in alarm or disturbance a high, flat *PEE'd'deet*. Infreq. hd. song a flat, rattling trill, fast then slowing, *pipipi'pi'pi'pi'pi-pi-pi-pi pi pi pi pt pt* (ca. 1.5 sec).
Behavior: Single birds or scattered prs. are inconspic., often difficult to approach closely, and hard to see. Stay mostly in shrubs where actively hop and wiggle through shrubbery and pop in and out of view as glean (very small arthropod prey?) from twigs and tiny leaves. Also sometimes hop on gd. beneath shrubs,

and occas. perch at edge of bush (usually not in open on top), but mostly keep out of sight. Occur alone or sometimes loosely assoc. with a few other paramo spp. such as Andean Tit-Spinetail, Plain-colored Seedeater, and Plumbeous Sierra-Finch.
Status and habitat: Locally common resident but patchy in distrib. in paramo. Dense shrubs at treeline (esp. with *Hypericum* spp.), low *Polylepis sericea* and *Stevia lucida* in shrubby paramo[778], and grassy paramo mixed with *Espeletia*. Commonest at very high els. (e.g., above ca. 3500m). An accessible pop. occurs at ca. 4000m on Páramo del Águila, Mérida.

Range: ENDEMIC. 2800–4100m (once to 2300m). Andes of n Táchira (above Pregonero), Mérida, and Trujillo n to Páramo Cendé on Lara border.

White-chinned Thistletail
Schizoeaca fuliginosa Piscuiz Barbiblanco
Identification: 7.5″ (19cm). 18g. Only s Táchira. Long central tail feathers frayed and ragged-looking. Eyes *grayish white*. Above warm rufous brown, crown darker; *sharp white eyering* and rather obscure but long narrow gray superciliary; underparts *uniform light gray* with small white chin patch, upper throat lightly freckled gray.
Sim. species: Few other spp. in treeline shrubs have such a long, unkept-looking tail. See Perijá and Ochre-browed thistletails, Streak-backed Canastero, and Andean Tit-Spinetail.
Voice: High, sharp, and penetrating *tik*, sometimes rapidly repeated. Song, by both sexes, recalls that of Streak-backed Canastero but longer: a high accelerating and rattlely trill that rises slightly in pitch, ca. 2 sec, *tik, tik, te te'te'tr't't't'r'r'rrrr.*
Behavior: Individuals or prs. are often well separated and not shy but nevertheless can be difficult to see well as they hop and wiggle actively and glean and work over twigs and foliage in dense bushes and shrubs. Often cock or kick up tail, esp. when alarmed, and make short weak flights between shrubs. In E Andes of Colombia a moss, grass, and frailejón down nest was 5″ (13cm) up in grass; 2 white eggs (W. McKay); BC birds, late Mar, Venez.[778]

Status and habitat: Resident in dense, shrubby, elfin forest borders and tangled tall grass, ferns, and bushes at treeline. Mostly a sp. of treeline/paramo ecotone vegetation.
Range: 3000–3300m. S Táchira on Páramo de Tamá and Páramo Cristo (*fuliginosa*). Colombia to n Peru.

Perijá Thistletail   PLATE 43
Schizoeaca perijana   Piscuiz de Perijá
Identification: 8–8.5″ (20.3–22cm). Only in Sierra de Perijá. Tail even longer (ca. 4.6″ vs. 3.4; 116mm vs. 85) than in previous sp.; the feathers more frayed, central feathers reduced to little more than shafts. Upperparts plain grayish brown with *narrow whitish eyering* and faint grayish white superciliary; *small tawny orange chin patch*, rest of throat gray faintly freckled dusky, breast uniform light grayish brown, belly paler, grayish white.
Sim. species: No other thistletail known to overlap its range. See Streak-backed Canastero.
Voice and Behavior: Unknown but probably much like others of genus.
Status and habitat: First described from specimens taken late Jun and early Jul 1974 on Venez. side of Sierra de Perijá[497], but M. A. Carriker took 9 in Jul 1942 (USNM) from nw slope of Cerro Pintado in adj. Colombia. Elfin woodland and low shrubby or mossy vegetation at treeline.

Range: 3000m (up to 3400m in Colombia). Known only from near summit ridge of Sierra de Perijá (9°59′ N, 72°58′ W) on Venez.-Colombia border. Adj. Colombia.

Asthenes

Dull plumage; open or semiopen rocky or grassy areas in paramo, puna, and Patagonian steppes; terrestrial; most with orangish throat patch, rufous wing stripe, and rufous or pale outer web to outer tail feathers; nest usually a large, mostly stick basket, hence "canastero."

Streak-backed Canastero   PLATE 38
Asthenes wyatti   Güitío Coludo
Identification: 6.5″ (16.5cm). Streak backed. Bill fairly long and thin. Above grayish brown *heavily streaked blackish*; short buff eyebrow; flight feathers dusky with *broad rufous band across base* (conspic. in flight), *chin patch orange rufous*, rest of underparts dingy grayish buff, *tail dusky, the outer 3 feathers mostly rufous* (distinctive in flight), tail quite rounded, not unusually long, the feathers very pointed.
Sim. species: Looks dingy and brown on gd. If in doubt, flush bird and look for distinctive wing and tail

pattern. Páramo Pipit has white outer tail feathers; ♀ Plumbeous Sierra-Finch has thick bill and streaks all over. Also see Andean Tit-Spinetail.
Voice: Song a short, flat, rapidly accelerating trill, ca. 1 sec, that rises a little in pitch (sim. to that of many *Asthenes*), *wu'u'ur'ur'd'd'd'd*!
Behavior: Single birds or well separated members of prs. are furtive and semiterrestrial. Run rapidly between bushes, tufts of grass, or rocks, or hop up in shrubs to forage or sing. Peer, glean, or peck in grass, or leap upward to snap insects. Sing from exposed or partly exposed position in top of low bush. Typically flush off low over grass and shrubs, then quickly dive into cover and "freeze" or run. Often flick up slightly cocked trail. In Peru, gd.-level nest a small grassy sphere with side entrance (K. Zyskowski; 2–3 creamy white eggs[163].
Status and habitat: Locally common resident (can be difficult to see) in open paramo with *Espeletia* and scattered low shrubs. Somewhat local, perhaps reflecting irreg. distribution of suitable paramo vegetation. Readily found in vicinity of Páramo del Águila, Mérida (ca. 4000m); less numerous at Páramo Mucubají, Mérida (ca. 3600m).

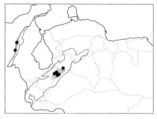

Range: 3600–4100m. Sierra de Perijá, Zulia (*perijanus*); Andes of Mérida (Páramo de Mucuchíes, Laguna Grande, etc.) and Trujillo at Niquitao (*mucuchiesi*). Santa Marta Mts., Colombia, and Andes s to s Peru.

Thripophaga

Broad, rounded tail feathers with no projecting spines (hence the name "softtail"); prob. not closely related to others of genus.

Orinoco Softtail   PLATE 38
Thripophaga cherriei   Rabiblando del Orinoco
Identification: 6.3″ (16cm). Very local. *Eyes dark red.* Mostly warm brown above with *narrow buff eyeline*; shoulders, wings, upper tail coverts, and tail dark rufous, fairly prom. *tawny chin patch* becomes *bright rufous chestnut on upper throat*; sides of head and rest of underparts olive brown with *narrow buff streaks to mid. breast*; under wing coverts tawny orange, tail rounded, not long. In hand, tail feathers notably rounded at tips with no protruding spines.
Sim. species: Most likely confused only with Speckled Spinetail which has underparts buff thickly spotted dusky (not olive brown streaked buff) and longer bill. Look for softtail's orangish throat patch.
Status and habitat: Known from 1 specimen taken 5 Feb 1890 (AMNH); and 23 taken 15 Mar–7 Apr 1970 by G. Pérez, all from a single site in w Amazonas. Consid-

ered fairly common in shrubby understory vegetation along streamsides and in adj. floodplain (várzea) forest (G. Pérez).

Range: ENDEMIC. 120m. Río Capuana, nw Amazonas, Venez.

Phacellodomus

Plain, dull, and unremarkable in appearance; rounded tail lacks spines; open to partly open areas; enormous stick nests; sp.-level taxonomy controversial.

Plain Thornbird   PLATE 38
Phacellodomus inornatus   Güaití
Identification: 6″ (15cm). 24g. *Very plain*. Bill rather stout, slightly decurved, base of mandible yellowish. Mostly dull faded brown above; faintly indicated eyeline and all of underparts dirty buff white, throat paler; tail somewhat rounded, not stiff or "spined."
Sim. species: Dull, nondescript bird that might bring to mind a large wren. Note habits, habitat, and virtual absence of field marks. Tail longer than that of most wrens.
Voice: Song a bright, chippery ser. of loud *chit* or *chee* notes delivered energetically and with mate often enthusiastically joining; accelerates a little, then gradually slows and drops slightly in pitch. Sometimes freq. repeated.
Behavior: Usually seen in prs. or family groups which forage by hopping and gleaning fairly actively, almost wrenlike, on outer ends of branches of large trees, in shrubbery, or on gd. or around base of large trunks. Active and industrious as they sing and forage and almost obsessively gather large thorny or thornless twigs to build or repair their enormous stick nests which may reach 2m in length. Young return to roost in nest for up to 16 months and provide some "help" to ads. Cylindrical, hanging nests, with multiple chambers, are conspic. at ends of spreading branches of majestic old samán (*Pithecellobium*) trees and are a characteristic sight to travelers across llanos. Nests may last for yrs, with some trees containing as many as 5 nests (but only 1 active pr.). Lower nest chambers may be appropriated (often forcibly) by other birds, e.g., Cattle Tyrants, Stripe-backed Wrens, Troupials, and Saffron Finches, obliging thornbird prs. to add new nest chambers (nests may contain up to 4 separate chambers), but nesting with associates may confer greater nesting success. Nests are largest in areas where Troupials reg. pirate nest chambers; 3 white eggs; occas. parasitized by Striped Cuckoos[349,648,649,738]; Jul–Nov breeding, Hato Masaguaral, Guárico[734].

Status and habitat: Common resident in trees around ranch houses, gallery forest borders, dry disturbed areas with scattered trees, and bushes; smaller nos. in moist and humid forest borders.

Range: To 950m. Yaracuy, Carabobo, and se Falcón (sight/tape) e through n foothills to Miranda (*inornatus*); rest of Venez. e of Andes and n of Orinoco from w Apure, Barinas, and Portuguesa e to Sucre and Monagas (*castilloi*)[500]; Delta Amacuro (sight, Tucupita) (*castilloi?*). E Colombia.
Note: Some unite all widely disjunct forms (Marañón Valley, Peru; e Brazil; and e Bolivia to s Brazil and nw Argentina) into a single sp., Plain-fronted Thornbird, *P. rufifrons*[403]; or Common Thornbird[545]. Taxonomy here follows Sibley and Monroe[606], the English name more recent sources[541,545].

Pseudocolaptes

Large, arboreal furnariid; prom. elongated cheek tufts; no obviously protruding barbs on tail; bill of ♀ longer and more decurved than that of ♂.

Streaked Tuftedcheek   PLATE 39
Pseudocolaptes boissonneautii   Cotí Blanco
Identification: 8.5″ (22cm). 48g. Large, unmistakable, buffy brown furnariid with conspic. white "*ear muffs*." Crown dusky narrowly streaked buff, long thin eyebrow buff, rest of upperparts reddish brown somewhat more broadly streaked buff, wing coverts more or less edged rufous forming 2 bars; *rump and long tail contrasting rufous; throat white, the feathers much lengthened onto sides of head forming conspic. flaring white tufts*; chest whitish scaled dusky, gradually changing to bright cinnamon on lower underparts. Or chest less scaled, lower underparts duller (*striaticeps*).
Sim. species: No other sp. has such conspic. white cheeks.
Voice: Not very vocal. Call a dry *chut*; song 1–2 sharp notes accelerating into a fast trill that slows, abruptly so at end, *chut, chut ch'eeeee'e'e'e-e-e*; also freq. gives *chut* notes between songs (P. Schwartz recording); a loud, sharp *stick!* or longer *squik! squik! squik!* ser. when alarmed or disturbed. May sing a few times at dawn or when prs. meet during territory disputes.
Behavior: An arboreal bromeliad specialist. Probes and rummages energetically and noisily in crevices and accumulated leaves and debris in and around base of bromeliads, often propping itself with tail or climbing inside them; also clambers in loose-jointed manner along branches to probe moss and other epi-

phytes, mostly at canopy hts. down into mid. levels, where takes arthropods, caterpillars, and small frogs. Freq. hidden as forages, but falling debris may give away its presence. A reg. member of mixed-spp. flocks (although not all mts. flocks have a pr.) and seldom seen away from them. Nest in tree cavity; eggs white[589]; in allied Buffy Tuftedcheek (*P. lawrencii*) of Panama and Costa Rica, nest a platform of tree-fern scales in cavity[647].

Status and habitat: Uncommon resident in humid and wet montane forest, esp. tall, mossy, epiphyte-laden forest; abundance of arboreal bromeliads is a requirement. Also elfin woodland at treeline.

Range: 1450–3000m. Sierra de Perijá, Zulia; Andes of Táchira, Mérida (nw Barinas?), and Trujillo (*meridae*); s Lara(?); mts. of Yaracuy and Coastal Cordillera from Carabobo to Distr. Federal and Miranda; Interior Cordillera at Cerro Golfo Triste, Aragua (*striaticeps*). Colombia s in Andes to n Bolivia.

Berlepschia

Monotypic; sharp-pointed bill long, slender, and straight; ridge of culmen narrow; wings rather pointed; tail rounded, graduated, the feathers pointed and barbed.

Point-tailed Palmcreeper   PLATE 39
Berlepschia rikeri   Cotí de Palmeras

Identification: 8.5″ (22cm). 37g. *Confined to Moriche Palms. Entire head, neck, and underparts black profusely streaked white* (narrowly on head, coarsely on breast); back, wings, and rounded tail rich rufous chestnut, primaries black.

Voice: Territorial song, usually hd. only a few times at dawn and dusk, a *loud, ringing*, and nasal *kreek!-kreek!-kreek!* . . . ; 20–30 or more notes in 5–7 sec, with hard, almost metallic quality, often answered almost immediately by mate which sings slightly out of sync (duet?). In response to playback also sing a higher pitched, shorter, and softer *kee-kee-kee-kee-kee-kee-ke-ke ki ki ki ki ki*, slowing at end (ca. 3 sec), often over and over with short break. Disturbed or angry birds give nasal *nar* or *daar* and short reedy rattle, *tr-r-r-r*. May sing while hanging upside down beneath frond.

Behavior: An enigmatic bird that spends most of its time hidden in top of moriche palms. Forages by clambering around mostly on underside of fronds where it is esp. adept at clinging upside down beneath fronds. Occas. pauses to peer carefully or reach out for arthropod prey with its long bill; takes prey items (arthropods) from frond pleats and near base of frond. Typically sings only a few times early in morning or at dusk, otherwise difficult to detect except through tape

playback. Prs., or occas. 3 (helpers?), or families up to 4, tend to be widely separated from others and do not assoc. with mixed-spp. flocks. After playback, prs. often react strongly, flying in immediately from long distances, singing loudly and holding "frozen" postures for lengthy periods. Nest undescribed.

Status and habitat: An ultra habitat-specialist, in Venez. found only in varying-sized stands of moriche palms in wet or boggy grassland (sometimes fewer than 12 trees are sufficient to harbor a pr.) and in widely scattered patches of moriche palms in swampy areas inside forest. Local and not found in all groves of moriche palms, e.g., unrec. at s end of Gran Sabana; local in e Monagas (sight, Morichal Largo, 1994—J. Kingery and P. Snetsinger; hd. n of Morichal Largo, 8 Mar 1998); doubtless in Delta Amacuro. Near Manaus, Brazil, also reported in other spp. of palms (A. Whittaker).

Range: To 200m. Known from nw, c, and sw Amazonas (sight s of Pto. Ayacucho; Cerro Duida; tape, San Carlos de Río Negro—C. Parrish); n Bolívar in Río Caura and Canaima (sightings); s Monagas (sightings, Morichal Largo). Se Colombia and e Ecuador to n Bolivia and w Amaz. Brazil. Guyana and Suriname.

Margarornis

Small and dark; tail feathers with stiff projecting spines; creeperlike behavior.

Pearled Treerunner   PLATE 38
Margarornis squamiger   Subepalo Perlado

Identification: 6″ (15cm). 17g. *Creeperlike with handsome pattern.* Mostly bright reddish chestnut above with brownish crown and *long white eyebrow;* cheeks dusky, throat white to yellowish white, rest of underparts olive brown *thickly sprinkled with bold, "pearl-like," yellowish white spots, each ringed in black;* tail stiff and spine-tipped.

Sim. species: Striking and not likely confused if seen well. Hitching along beneath shady limbs, resembles a small woodcreeper, but none is so bright rufous above. See Montane Woodcreeper; at slightly lower els., Spotted Barbtail which is much darker (eyebrow and spotting dark buff), and Rusty-winged Barbtail, also darker, duller, and lacking crisp drop-shaped spotting.

Voice: Quiet. Infreq. a high, thin *tik.* Song a ser. of sim. *tik* notes given as *high-pitched,* short, fast trill over and over; sometimes trill is longer, ca. 1.5 sec.

Behavior: Single birds, prs., or occas. 3–4 follow mixed-spp. flocks and are rarely seen away from them. Forage mainly by hitching up small trunks and out along underside of mossy (occas. bare) limbs in jerky manner of a creeper, but tail usually not used as a prop. Occas. hang paridlike, or even hop and twist along smaller branches and twigs like a foliage-gleaner. Mainly forage from forest mid. levels up into canopy where active, confiding, and easy to see but unobtrusive. Nest a mossy ball with side entrance; eggs white[589].

Status and habitat: Fairly common resident in humid and wet montane forest, esp. in stunted, mossy, epiphyte-laden forest in upper montane els., and forest borders and patches of woodland and *Polylepis* at treeline. Most numerous in Táchira, less so northward. Most recs. above ca. 2300m; local and only in wettest forest at lower els.

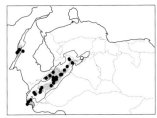

Range: 1800–3200m. Sierra de Perijá, Zulia; Andes from s Táchira and Mérida to ne Trujillo at Páramo Cendé (*perlatus*); sight rec. in s Lara (PN Yacambú, Dec 2000—C. Sharpe). Colombia s in Andes to Bolivia.

Roraimia

Much like *Premnoplex* and perhaps best incl. within it; differs most obviously in plumage.

Roraiman Barbtail   PLATE 38
Roraimia adusta   Pijuí Pechirrayado

Identification: 5.7″ (14.5cm). Only in tepuis. Upperparts dark chestnut, crown dark brown bordered by bright rufous chestnut postocular stripe extending broadly across nape; *prom. blackish mask bordered below by immaculate white throat*, rest of underparts buffy white broadly streaked or flammulated dark brown, under tail coverts rufous. Outermost tail feathers very pointed. Or slightly darker and vaguely scaled dusky above (*obscurodorsalis*).

Sim. species: No other barbtail in tepuis. See larger Tepui Foliage-gleaner.

Voice: Very quiet. Rarely hd. song a slow, metallic ser. of scraping notes, *tlink, sink, sink, tslink . . . ink*, 2d and 3d notes lower pitched (D. Ascanio tape).

Behavior: An easily overlooked sp. usually seen singly, occas. prs., and mostly when with mixed-spp. flocks. Spends most of time climbing up lower part of small moss- and epiphyte-laden trunks and vines. Hitches up in zigzag or twisting manner, or clambers and creeps around, often encircling trunks as it ascends. Stays mostly 1–6m up, and as soon as it emerges into more open mid. level of forest is apt to drop off trunk and back into denser cover near forest floor. Nest unknown.

Status and habitat: Uncommon and hard-to-find resident in wet and cluttered mossy forest and dense melastome-dominated second-growth forest. On Sierra de Lema (1450m) only a few mixed-spp. flocks con-

tain a pr. of these birds. But common in low-canopied scrub vegetation at 1800m and higher on Cerro Roraima (D. Ascanio).

Range: 1000–2500m (usually above 1300m on Sierra de Lema). Cerro Sipapo, nw Amazonas (*obscurodorsalis*); Cerros Duida, Huachamacari, and Parú, c and s Amazonas (*duidae*); Cerro Jaua, sw Bolívar (*mayri*); tepuis and cerros of rest of Bolívar (*adusta*). W Guyana and adj. Brazil.

Note: Previously placed in *Premnoplex*[564].

Premnoplex

Small and dark; prom. barbs project beyond stiffened tail (hence "barbtail"); outer pr. of tail feathers pointed; hitch or clamber around on trunks and limbs.

Spotted Barbtail   PLATE 38
Premnoplex brunnescens   Fafao Punteado

Identification: 5.5″ (14cm). 17g. *Dark*. Forest understory. Above dark mummy brown with dusky tail; short, dark buff eyestripe; throat tawny ochraceous, rest of underparts dark brown *densely covered with large drop-shaped buff spots encircled in black*. Or throat above tawny ochraceous (*rostratus*).

Sim. species: Darker and smaller than other barbtails and foliage-gleaners and only one with *blackish* tail. Cf. Rusty-winged Barbtail (little overlap in Venez.). Pearled Treerunner is bright rufous above and usually at higher el. Several foliage-gleaners and treehunters are much larger and streaked (not spotted). In mts. of ne replaced by White-throated Barbtail.

Voice: Call a high, sibilant *pseEK!* Infreq. hd. song a high, thin *eep eep eep ti'ti'ti'tititi*, accelerating somewhat. In Ecuador a flat, thin trill, *ti ti'ti'ti'ti'ti'ti'ti'ti'ti 'ti'i'i*, slowing a little at end[412].

Behavior: Alone or in prs., mostly 1–6m up in dark understory, occas. higher, where quiet and inconspic. as climbs lower part of trunks and low limbs, hitching up mechanically, usually without tail support. Tends to climb in zigzag lines on both trunks and limbs. More often away from understory mixed-spp. flocks than

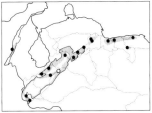

with them. Mossy, ball nest with short entrance tunnel embedded in nest; wedged in crevice between logs, bark, or rocks; or in Ecuador suspended from rock or underside of log[381]; 2 white eggs[644].

Status and habitat: Uncommon resident (easily overlooked) in dark, cluttered understory of wet and mossy mt. forest.

Range: 1000–2500m. Sierra de Perijá, Zulia; Andes of s Táchira and Mérida (*brunnescens*); nw Barinas (sightings, prob. *brunnescens*); n Trujillo at Cuevas de Carache (subsp.?); Lara (Cabudare) and n cordilleras from Yaracuy to Aragua and e and s Miranda (*rostratus*). Costa Rica s in mts. to Bolivia.

White-throated Barbtail   PLATE 43
Premnoplex tatei   Fafao Gargantiblanco
Identification: 5.7″ (14.5cm). Mts. of ne. Much like Spotted Barbtail but underparts streaking bolder, even more profuse, and white (not ochraceous buff). Bill slightly decurved, black (thicker than that of Spotted Barbtail). Dark rufescent brown above with short blackish tail, *short buffy white eyebrow* and streaking on sides of neck; a few buff streaks on mantle; *throat, chest, and central underparts buffy white to white thickly scalloped dusky*, forming coarse and profusely spotted pattern; flanks and belly dark brown with a few narrow buffy white shaft streaks. Tail graduated, strongly barbed. Or sim. but throat more or less unmarked buffy white, underparts paler brown (*tatei*).
Sim. species: No other barbtail occurs in mts. of ne, but there easily confused with much commoner Stripe-breasted Spinetail which has reddish brown (not black) tail, more or less uniformly buff and brown streaked underparts, and no prom. scalloping on throat and chest. In Andes see Spotted Barbtail.
Voice: On Cerro Negro a brisk, almost bubbly ser. of rather low, soft, reedy whistles, *we-whúr, we-whúr, we-heét . . .* , varied to *be-be-búr, be-be-búr . . .* or *pi, pr-pr-pr-prip!* . . . in long ser. when excited.
Behavior: Found alone, in prs., or little family groups. Behaves somewhat wrenlike, clambering and hopping around on or near gd. to ca. 2m up in undergrowth or on logs. Difficult to see because of dense and often mossy vegetation it inhabits.
Status and habitat: Uncommon to fairly common resident (at least formerly) but possibly very local. Now rare or absent from some seemingly suitable areas. Thick, cluttered understory of wet, mossy forest, esp. where dominated by small palms and Araceae. Cerro Negro pop. (1400–1700m el.), not reported for nearly 50 yr, was rediscovered 27 Aug 1994[60,259]. Rare or absent at Las Melenas entrance of PN Paria.

Range: ENDEMIC. 1500–2410m in ne Anzoátegui, s Sucre, and n Monagas on Cerro Negro (*tatei*); n Sucre

on Paria Pen. (1100–1200m on Cerro Humo; 800–885m on Cerro Azul) (*pariae*).
Note: Has been considered a subsp. of Spotted Barbtail[467].

Premnornis

Closely allied to *Premnoplex* and often merged with it, but *lacks* barbs on tail (English name incorrect) and behavior differs.

Rusty-winged Barbtail   PLATE 38
Premnornis guttuligera   Subepalo Punteado
Identification: 5.7″ (14.5cm). 16g. Looks like a *small* foliage-gleaner. Mostly brown above with *buff eyestripe and streaks on hindneck* and a few narrow streaks on mantle; *wings and tail rufous*, wing coverts usually narrowly tipped buff forming 2 indistinct bars; throat buffy white, *sides of head, neck, and rest of underparts brown with extensive broad buff-scalloped streaking*. Tail stiff but no prom. barbs.
Sim. species: Spotted Barbtail is uniformly dark above *incl. tail* (Rusty-winged Barbtail has *rufous* tail) and less profusely streaked below. Lineated Foliage-gleaner is larger, more streaked above, and streaking much more in lines. Also see even larger treehunters.
Voice: Rather quiet. Infreq. calls incl. a sharp, incisive *tseet!* and softer, slightly buzzy *zeet-zeet*. Song a high, thin, bouncy trill, *tsip'tsip'ti'ti'ti'ti'ti'ti'i'i'i'i'i'i*, ca. 1.25 sec[412].
Behavior: Usually seen singly, most often with mixed-spp. flocks in lower story of forest. Behavior recalls a foliage-gleaner (not a *Premnoplex*) as it actively clambers round in tangles, checks clumps of dead leaves, spreads tail, and hops, even clings sideways to branches as it forages, rarely using tail for support.
Status and habitat: Uncommon resident in wet, mossy, montane forest. Most Venez. recs. are from vicinity of Río Chiquito in s Táchira; also can be found on forested pass (1800m) between Bramón and Las Delicias, Táchira.

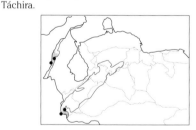

Range: 1800–2900m. Sierra de Perijá, Zulia (only 2000–2200m), and s Táchira (*venezuelana*). Colombia s in Andes to s Peru.

Syndactyla

Occur mostly in understory of mt. forest; bill straight to slightly upturned, *rather short*; usually streaked below, some spp. also streaked above; difficult to see; rough, ratchetlike songs.

Lineated Foliage-gleaner   PLATE 39

Syndactyla subalaris   Tico-Tico Estriado

Identification: 7″ (18cm). 33g. Only in Andes. Above mostly brown, crown and nape blackish (also mantle—*olivacea*) with *fine shaftlike buffy white streaking* becoming broader on back; wings and rump dark brown, tail rufous chestnut, *throat plain unstreaked buff,* rest of *underparts olive brown with narrow rows of crisp buffy white streaks.*

Sim. species: Distinctly streaked in long narrow lines above and below, except for contrasting unmarked throat. Note that streaks continue to lower back. Flammulated and Striped treehunters are sim. but larger, longer-tailed, and have broader streaking.

Voice: Call a harsh, scratchy *jzert* or *jert.* Song 6–10 harsh, scratchy *bzert* notes that start slowly, accelerate a little, then end abruptly, i.e., *bzert, bzert, jzut, jzut-jj-jj-jj.* Call much like that of Guttulated and Tepui foliagegleaners.

Behavior: An active and sometimes noisy bird but difficult to see as it hops along low limbs and inspects smaller branches, twigs, and esp. dead leaf clusters, also clumps of moss and piles of dead leaves and trash that accumulate in branch forks and vine tangles, for a variety of arthropods. Alone or in prs. and more often seen with understory mixed-spp. flocks than away from them. Nest unknown.

Status and habitat: Uncommon and local resident in humid forest, occas. forest borders. Most recs. are from s Táchira; rare northward.

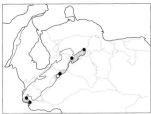

Range: 800–2000m. S Táchira in Río Chiquito Valley (*olivacea*); e slope of Andes from nw Barinas (Altamira) n to Lara at Cabudare (*striolata*). Costa Rica s in mts. to s Peru.

Guttulated Foliage-gleaner   PLATE 43

Syndactyla guttulata   Tico-Tico Goteado

Identification: 7.5″ (19cm). 36g. Much like Lineated Foliage-gleaner but larger, more robust, and *bill thick,* culmen virtually straight, *distal half of lower mandible strongly upturned.* Above dark brown with *prom. tawny buff eyebrow;* crown faintly dotted buff (no streaks); *mantle streaked buff,* rump and tail rufous chestnut; center of throat plain buff, *sides of throat and rest of underparts olive brown broadly streaked buff* (streaks extend onto belly).

Sim. species: No other foliage-gleaner in this sp.'s small range is so streaked. Larger Streak-capped Treehunter looks gray capped with much narrower, less obvious streaking.

Voice: Hd. far more than seen and sometimes not esp. vocal. A rough *chak* as forages; also a rough, sandpapery *raach;* song a harsh ratchetlike and accelerating *cjak . . . cjak . . czak'czak'zak'zak' zak'za'za'za,* some-

times followed by a few more notes at end. May sing only once or a few times at dawn; only at long, irreg. intervals during day.

Behavior: Single birds or well-separated members of prs. are fairly rapid moving and energetic as they follow understory mixed-spp. flocks, esp. those containing Slaty Antwrens, Three-striped Warblers, and Common Bush-Tanagers, or forage alone, mostly 0.2–5m up, occas. much higher, in dense tangles and mossy clutter where keep out of sight and difficult to see. Often hang (even upside down) or cling, tail down, to sides of branches to flake off bark or, with can-openerlike motion, use chisel-shaped bill tip as fulcrum to pry open or split small rotten twigs and branches. Also reg. check curled dead leaves and bases of bromeliads, and occas. at army ant swarms[259]. Territories appear to be at least as large or larger than flocks they follow. Nest, presum. this sp., of twigs placed in cavity in building wall[769].

Status and habitat: Uncommon to fairly common resident in understory of wet premontane forest (cloud forest). Somewhat local. Most readily found near biological station of PN Henri Pittier, Aragua.

Range: ENDEMIC. 900–2100m. C Falcón (sight, Sierra de San Luis)[60]; mts. of Yaracuy (Sierra de Aroa), Coastal Cordillera from Carabobo to Distr. Federal; Interior Cordillera in s Aragua at Cerro Golfo Triste (*guttulata*); mts. of e Anzoátegui (Cerro El Peonía), Sucre, and n Monagas (*pallida*).

Anabacerthia

Small size; mostly montane; forest mid. levels or higher[456]; aside from small amt. of streaking, much like *Philydor,* often rather conspic.

Montane Foliage-gleaner   PLATE 39

Anabacerthia striaticollis   Tico-Tico Pico de Cuña

Identification: 6.5″ (16.5cm). 24g. Widespread and common in mts. Above mostly olivaceous brown to slightly rufescent brown, crown grayer with *prom. buffy white eyering and postocular streak;* dusky cheeks faintly streaked buff, *tail contrasting bright rufous,* throat dull white faintly mottled dusky (looks essentially unmarked in field), rest of underparts pale olivaceous buff with a few vague dusky streaks on chest. Or grayer below (*venezuelana*).

Sim. species: A plain foliage-gleaner with conspic. eyering and postocular and rufous tail. More contrasty Buff-fronted Foliage-gleaner has gray crown and obvious ochre eyebrow and throat. Others of its kind in mts. are heavily streaked.

Voice: A coarse, raspy *chit!* or *skip!* While foraging, notes often doubled (recall those of Streak-capped Treehunter); song a rapid ser. of same rough *chuk* notes, rather staccato.
Behavior: More conspic. and much more easily seen than most foliage-gleaners. Single birds or prs. are conspic. and almost always seem to be on the move as they follow mixed-spp. flocks. Hop rather jerkily, with tail down (but flicked up with each hop), along branches or up through vine tangles, wrestle with hanging dead leaves, or methodically scrutinize partially moss-covered branches, bare twigs, twig tips, or foliage, and occas. check small bromeliads in forest mid. levels or slightly higher or occas. down almost to eye level. Capture a variety of arthropods; prob. occas. small vertebrates. Andean birds seem to be more dedicated dead-leaf searchers than those of Coastal Cordillera. One nest in broken trunk of *Bactris* palm[769]; 2 white eggs[573]; Colombia nest in open-top tree stub cavity; lined with lichen and moss (T. McNish).
Status and habitat: Commonest foliage-gleaner in mts. Resident in humid and wet premontane and montane forest and forest borders. Lack of competing foliage-gleaners (mt. spp. are mostly in understory) may contribute to unusually broad range of foraging substrates and behaviors.

Range: 900–2300m. Sierra de Perijá, Zulia (*perijana*); w side of Andes in Mérida; e side from Táchira to nw Barinas, Trujillo, and Lara (*striaticollis*); mts. of Yaracuy and Coastal Cordillera from Carabobo e to Distr. Federal; Interior Cordillera in Aragua and Miranda (*venezuelana*). Colombia s in Andes to n Bolivia.
Note: Prob. best placed in genus *Philydor*.

Hyloctistes

Longish bill and proportions recall *Philydor*, but plumage more like that of *Syndactyla*.

Eastern Striped Woodhaunter   PLATE 39
Hyloctistes subulatus   Tico-Tico Rayado
Identification: 7.5″ (19cm). 33g. Poorly marked and confusing. Above incl. wings dark brown, crown dusky with rather ill-defined buff eyebrow and *narrow shaft streaks extending to mantle* (not broadly over back), *tail contrasting rufous*, indistinct pale streaking on sides of head; throat and underparts yellowish buffy brown with *blurry* ("flammulated") *dusky streaking on sides of neck, chest, and breast* (only faintly on throat). Or more distinctly streaked on crown, throat, and underparts (*lemae*).
Sim. species: Confusing because markings lack sharp focus. However, no other foliage-gleaners s of Orinoco

are streaked. Rufous-tailed Foliage-gleaner is paler overall, shows only vague streaking on sides of neck and sometimes chest. See smaller Speckled Spinetail ("speckled" below with unmarked crown) and rare Orinoco Softtail. Several woodcreepers are superficially sim., but note different habits.
Voice: Song in lowlands of e Bolívar 2–3 rough whistles followed by a rattle, *chaw, cheee, t'r'r'r'r'r'r'r'r*, given at short intervals mainly at dawn. Song on Sierra de Lema (1000m) a slow, plaintive *kalEEp-cleer*, 1st note higher and falsetto, over and over. A few favorite dawn-song perches are used repeatedly.
Behavior: Single birds or widely spaced members of prs. are found mostly in mid. levels or lower (4–20m up) in forest, but occas. higher when with mixed-spp. flocks containing antshrikes, antwrens, other foliage-gleaners, flycatchers, and shrike-tanagers. Prs. defend large territories and are active but rather furtive, or often hidden, as hop and rummage in tangles, epiphytes (esp. Araceae), and probe into accumulations of dead leaves and trash, usually near trunks, for a variety of arthropods and caterpillars, occas. small vertebrates. In Colombia, platform nest of compound-leaf rachises in burrow; 2 young, 15 Feb (N. Wheelwright).
Status and habitat: Uncommon resident (hard to see and prob. overlooked) in vines, epiphytes, and thicker vegetation around trunks and large limbs in humid and wet forest in lowlands.

Range: To 1000m (most recs. below 600m). C and s Amazonas from Río Asisa southward; c and s Bolívar in headwaters of Ríos Caura, Paragua, and Cuyuní (*subulatus*); se Bolívar on Sierra de Lema (*lemae*). Se Colombia to n Bolivia and Amaz. Brazil; prob. Guyana.
Note: Taxonomy follows Ridgely and Greenfield[541]. Subsp. *subulatus* prob. a separate sp. (K. Zimmer).

Philydor

Slender and rather long-tailed; med. to small size with conspic. eyebrows; little or no streaking; pointed tail feathers; some in canopy, others lower in forest; active; chattering songs; nest in holes in snags or banks.

Chestnut-winged Foliage-gleaner   PLATE 39
Philydor erythropterus   Tico-Tico Alicastaño
Identification: 7″ (18cm). 30g. Grayish olive above with contrasting *rufous chestnut wings and tail*; lores and *throat bright yellowish ochre*; long eyebrow buff, cheeks dusky somewhat streaked buff and bordered on lower edge by indistinct dusky malar; remaining underparts buffy gray with yellowish tinge on breast.

Sim. species: From other foliage-gleaners by chestnut wings. See Buff-fronted, Rufous-rumped, and Rufous-tailed foliage-gleaners.

Voice: Song a very fast buzzy trill that descends slightly, *jiiiiiiiiiiiiiiiiiiie*, about 2 sec, moderate in pitch, often repeated at short intervals but usually given only for a short while at dawn or in early morning hrs.

Behavior: May be alone at dawn, but single birds or prs. soon join mixed-spp. flocks in canopy or emergent rain forest trees and during day are seldom seen away from them. Move actively, hopping along branches and twigs where search mostly foliage in high outer branches, or occas. glean from twigs. Also habitually check hanging, curled, dead leaves by stretching up, or hanging downward, to peer inside. Nest unknown.

Status and habitat: Resident. Tall humid terra firme forest; in w Amazonia also extensively in tall várzea forest. Few specimens from Venez.

Range: To 900m. E Amazonas (Simarawochi near Sierra Parima) and s Bolívar in upper Río Caura and upper Río Caroní (Paurai-tepui) southward (*erythropterus*). E Colombia s to n Bolivia, w Amaz. Brazil, and s of the Amazon to its mouth.

Note: Subsp. *erythropterus* prob. not valid.

Cinnamon-rumped Foliage-gleaner   PLATE 39
Philydor pyrrhodes   Tico-Tico Rabadilla Acanelada

Identification: 6.7" (17cm). 27g. Distinctive but difficult to see. Dark olive brown above with *blackish wings and bright cinnamon rufous rump and tail*; eyebrow and entire underparts *bright ochre*. Bill black.

Sim. species: Blackish wings are the key. Also note habitat. Other foliage-gleaners, e.g., Buff-fronted, Rufous-tailed, and Chestnut-winged, have sim. head patterns (long buff to tawny eyebrows) and rufous tails but lack slaty black wings.

Voice: Remarkable but infreq. hd. song of ♂ a long, buzzy trill, varying from ca. 4 to 15 sec in length, rising slowly in pitch to a crescendo, then abruptly lower at end, *duuuuuuuuuuuUUUUUUEEEEEEEEEETduuuuu*. Song varies somewhat; generally recalls song of White-crowned Spadebill but much longer and louder. Harsh *chek* call.

Behavior: Usually alone or in prs. and more often away from mixed-spp. flocks than with them. Actively clambers over or hangs from tips of palm fronds, arums, *Heliconia*, and other large leaves in understory or rummages in accumulations of dead leaves and debris, mostly rather low (ca. 0.5–8m up) and in thick cover. Typically shy and difficult to observe. Nest unknown.

Status and habitat: Uncommon and very local resident in humid terra firme forest, esp. low-lying areas,

along streams, and in várzea and older second growth; in all areas favors palm-dominated understory.

Range: To 500m. Throughout Amazonas; w Bolívar from lower Río Caura se to Río Carapo, mid. Río Paragua, and upper Río Caroní (Chimantá-tepui); Caño Manamo, Delta Amacuro (sight/tape, 1994). E Colombia to n Bolivia, Amaz. Brazil, and the Guianas.

Rufous-tailed Foliage-gleaner   PLATE 39
Philydor ruficaudatus   Tico-Tico Rabirrufo

Identification: 7" (18cm). 32g. Above olive brown *incl. wings and rump* with *contrasting rufous tail*; *long eyestripe yellowish buff*, underparts dull yellowish olive, throat paler, *chest with some indistinct streaky olive flammulations*.

Sim. species: Combination of brownish body with bright rufous tail is usually diagnostic. Most other foliage-gleaners have rufous or slaty wings, contrasting cap, or are larger and more robust. See Olive-backed and Buff-throated foliage-gleaners and Note below.

Voice: Song in sw Brazil a loud, clattery *ke-ke-ke-kee-kee-kee-kee-. . . ke-ke-ke-ke-ke*, on same pitch, accelerating slightly at start, slowing a bit at end, ca. 25 notes in 3.5 sec; also a more variable *wt-pt-pt, wit-wit-wit, d'd 'd'd'd'd'd'd* (K. Zimmer recording).

Behavior: Singles or prs. are persistent members of canopy or upper-level mixed-spp. flocks and are seldom encountered away from flocks. Actively hop along high outer branches and in vines and glean from live leaves or check curled, hanging dead leaves at mid. levels or higher. Nest unknown.

Status and habitat: Fairly common resident in tall humid terra firme forest in lowlands and lower slopes of tepuis; also in várzea forest.

Range: To 1300m. C Amazonas from Cerro Duida southward (*ruficaudatus*); n Amazonas and nw Bolívar (Río Cuchivero) e through lower Caura Valley (sight, J. Pierson) and c Bolívar (Auyán-tepui; Ptari-tepui; Paurai-tepui) southward (*flavipectus*). E Colombia to n Bolivia, Amaz. Brazil, and the Guianas.

Note: Rufous-rumped Foliage-gleaner (*P. erythrocercus*) is known from adj. Guyana and occurs very close to Venez. border. Very like Rufous-tailed Foliage-gleaner, differing in having both *rump and upper tail coverts rufous* like tail, and underparts uniform (no faint streaking or mottling on chest), both marks difficult to distinguish in field; also differs in slightly bolder, brighter buff eyebrow and slightly brighter, cleaner-looking plumage. Call a squeezed out *squik!* Forages in lower or mid. story, in vine tangles, often on dead leaves, and closer to trunk than Rufous-tailed (K. Zimmer).

Buff-fronted Foliage-gleaner   PLATE 39
Philydor rufus   Tico-Tico Rojizo
Identification: 7.5″ (19cm). 31g. Rather long tailed. Two widely separated pops. in Venez. *Forehead and long prom. eyestripe buff* (or ochraceous—*cuchiverus*), *crown gray* contrasting with brown back; wings mostly rufous, tail pale rufous brown, line behind eye dusky, *sides of head and underparts ochraceous buff*, brightest on throat.
Sim. species: Only foliage-gleaner in Venez. with obviously *gray* crown; more ochraceous below than most. Also note forehead and eyebrow. In mts. of n Venez. often with Montane Foliage-gleaner which is browner and has "spectacles."
Voice: Infreq. hd. song, in n Venez., mainly a few times in early morning, a loose coarse rattle (20 notes in 3 sec) that rises then falls slightly.
Behavior: Prs. or single birds are active and energetic and usually seen with mixed-spp. flocks from forest mid. level to canopy. Hop along branches, bouncing and twisting first to one side then to other as they peer at live foliage, curled dead leaves, and rummage in vines and accumulated leaves and debris in tangles. In n Venez. habitually search suspended dead leaves, sometimes by hanging upside down and tugging at them to dislodge hidden prey. Nest in a burrow in steep bank; occas. a hole in wall or tree cavity; 2 white eggs[573].
Status and habitat: Fairly common resident in n Venez. in humid and wet montane forest and older second-growth woodland. In s Venez., so far as known, only found in tall, humid forest on slopes of 2 tepuis. In Venez. occurs only in mts., unlike in some other parts of range.

Range: 900–1800m n of Orinoco; 1000–1300m s of Orinoco. C Falcón (sight, Sierra de San Luis)[60]; se Lara (Guárico); mts. of Yaracuy and Coastal Cordillera from Carabobo e to Miranda (*columbianus*); n Amazonas (Cerro Calentura) and nw Bolívar on Cerro El

Negro (*cuchiverus*). Costa Rica and w Panama; Colombia s in Andes and adj. lowlands to Bolivia; se Brazil and ne Argentina.

Automolus

Resemble *Philydor* but usually considerably larger, more robust, and heavier-billed; dull; but most with contrasting pale throat and rufous tail; most spp. have loud 1- or 2-note calls and longer song; usually below eye level in lower story of lowland forest[456]; nest in burrow dug in bank.

Tepui Foliage-gleaner   PLATE 39
Automolus roraimae   Tico-Tico Gargantiblanco
Identification: 7″ (18cm). 27g. Endemic to tepuis. Bill blackish above, yellowish flesh at base of lower mandible. Eyes dark. Above dark brown, crown darker with *long whitish eyestripe and blackish cheeks*; upper tail coverts and tail *contrasting* rufous chestnut, *throat white to rich yellowish cream* contrasting with cinnamon brown breast and belly. Or underparts paler more grayish olive (*paraquensis*); or throat buff, rest of underparts tinged rufescent (*duidae*); or overall paler than other subspp. (*urutani*).
Sim. species: Occurs at higher el. than most other foliage-gleaners, and none has such contrasty facial pattern. See Rufous-tailed, Olive-backed, and Buff-throated foliage-gleaners.
Voice: Rough calls and song closely resemble those of Guttulated and other *Syndactyla* foliage-gleaners. When foraging, harsh *tzik* and *chezk* notes; song a long, rough, guttural ser. that rises and accelerates, *tzik . . . chek . . tzik . . jjza-jjza-jjza-jza ja'ja'ja'ja*, the *jjza* ser. very harsh.
Behavior: Single birds, prs., or families forage with mixed-spp. flocks or away from them about equally, keeping mostly low (0.5–8m up) in tangled, cluttered undergrowth where difficult to see. Less freq. clamber around in vine tangles into mid. levels. Movements rather slow and deliberate as they check curled dead leaf blades of palm fronds on which this sp. partly specializes; also peer at other dead leaves, branches, live foliage, and moss, and occas. reach down or hang upside down to examine foliage or bark surfaces. Prey items incl. katydids. Nest unknown.
Status and habitat: Resident in tall, humid, and wet premontane forest and in scrubby, melastome-dominated, mossy forest and tall dense second growth. Uncommon and local in Sierra de Lema at ca.

1450m but common in low-canopied scrub at 1800m and higher on Cerro Roraima (D. Ascanio).
Range: 1300–2500m. Amazonas on Cerro Sipapo (*paraquensis*); Amazonas on Cerros Parú, Yaví, Gimé, Duida, and de la Neblina (*duidae*); sw Bolívar on Cerros Jaua and Urutaní (*urutani*); tepuis surrounding Gran Sabana (*roraimae*). Adj. mts. of n Brazil; prob. w Guyana.
Note 1: Originally described in *Philydor*, later transferred to *Automolus*[401,403,467], but almost certainly not an *Automolus*. Plumage recalls *Philydor*, but voice very sim. to *Syndactyla* and to *Anabaxenops*. Taxonomic re-evaluation needed.
Note 2: Two specimens, originally regarded as a separate sp., Neblina Foliage-gleaner (*P. hylobius*)[403], are juv. (darker, more tawny ochraceous eyebrow and underparts) Tepui Foliage-gleaners[156].
Note 3: Previously called White-throated Foliage-gleaner[403].

Olive-backed Foliage-gleaner   PLATE 39
Automolus infuscatus   Tico-Tico Gorra Aceituna
Identification: 7.5″ (19cm). 31g. *Above uniform dark brown* with contrasting rufous upper tail coverts and tail; faintly indicated narrow buff superciliary and weak eyering; dusky cheeks somewhat mottled buff, *conspic. dull white throat* contrasts with pale dingy brownish gray breast, more brownish on abdomen.
Sim. species: Much like Buff-throated Foliage-gleaner which has more conspic. eyering, buff (not white) throat, and darker underparts. Listen for vocalizations which are very different. Smaller, more svelte Rufous-tailed Foliage-gleaner shows yellowish tones to face and throat, much brighter eyestripe, and is nearly always higher in forest.
Voice: Call, esp. when disturbed, a loud *chĭk-wuk*, 2d note lower pitched, rather like call of some *Synallaxis*, and given over and over; song a loud staccato chatter, *du'du'du'du'du'du'du'du'du'du*, of varying length, and very like that of Chestnut-crowned Foliage-gleaner.
Behavior: Typical of genus. Actively hops and clambers around in low vegetation and vines, mostly 1–4m up in undergrowth, where it rummages in debris and accumulations of dead leaves. Usually in prs., occas. several, and reg. with understory mixed-spp. flocks. In e Ecuador breeding birds or prs. do not show strong fidelity to territories, with much seasonal or postbreeding wandering (P. English). Nest of compound-leaf rachises in burrow; 2 white eggs[752].
Status and habitat: Uncommon to fairly common resident locally in humid terra firme forest in lowlands.

Range: To 1100m. Amazonas, and w and c Bolívar e to Cerro Paurai-tepui (*badius*); ne Bolívar from Altiplanicie de Nuria s to upper Río Cuyuní (*cervicalis*). Se Colombia to se Peru, Amaz. Brazil, and the Guianas.

Buff-throated Foliage-gleaner   PLATE 39
Automolus ochrolaemus   Tico-Tico Gargantianteado
Identification: 7.5″ (19cm). 32g. Plain olive brown above with *conspic. buff eyering* and less distinct postocular streak; sides of head vaguely streaked buff, upper tail coverts and tail rufous chestnut (not in strong contrast to back), *throat light buff*, remaining underparts buffy brown; a few vague blurry buff streaks on chest (hard to see in field).
Sim. species: Most likely confused with Olive-backed Foliage-gleaner which has white throat and shows only faint eyering and postocular stripe. Up close note Buff-throated's faint underparts streaking. The two are most easily told by voice (see). Also cf. Rufous-tailed, Chestnut-crowned, and at higher els., Tepui foliage-gleaners.
Voice: Loud song 4–6 nasal notes that slow a little and drop sharply in pitch, *KEE Kee krr kr ka*, 1st notes louder and urgent, sometimes over and over. A buzzy *durrr* when disturbed.
Behavior: Tends to stay out of sight as it actively peers and pokes in debris and dead leaves and hops and twists along low branches or through tangles from near gd. to 5m up. Alone or in prs. and sometimes with mixed-spp. flocks. Presence is most often betrayed by loud song hd. mainly at dawn or dusk. In Costa Rica, nest of compound-leaf rachises at end of burrow 18–30″ (45–76cm) deep dug in bank; 2–3 white eggs[647].
Status and habitat: Uncommon to fairly common resident in tangled undergrowth, treefalls, and creekside shrubbery in humid terra firme and várzea forest, and second-growth woodland.

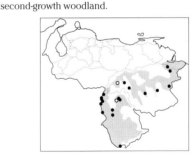

Range: To 1000. Throughout Amazonas; nw Bolívar, Auyán-tepui, and Sierra de Imataca s prob. to Brazilian border (*turdinus*). Mexico to w Ecuador; e Colombia to n Bolivia, Amaz. Brazil, and the Guianas.

Chestnut-crowned Foliage-gleaner   PLATE 39
Automolus rufipileatus   Tico-Tico Gorra Castaña
Identification: 7.8″ (19.8cm). 34g. Large and dark. *Eyes orange yellow*. Blackish bill not as heavy as in others of genus. *Crown chestnut* contrasting somewhat with *uniform reddish brown upperparts*; rump and tail rufous chestnut, underparts pale buffy brown, lightest on throat.
Sim. species: Resembles several other *Automolus* foliage-gleaners, esp. Ruddy, Buff-throated, and Olive-

backed. Look for yellowish eyes, and note habitat and voice.

Voice: Song a loud, nasal rattle, *d'd'd'd'd'd'd'd'd'd'd 'd'd'a*, descending slightly; hd. mostly at dawn when given over and over at short intervals. Very like song of Olive-backed Foliage-gleaner.

Behavior: As in other *Automolus*, single birds or well-separated members of prs. are active as they rummage in thickets, clumps of dead leaves, etc., in lower growth, but very skulking and wary and usually difficult to see. Sometimes with mixed-spp. flocks but also often forage alone. 2 BC ♂♂, Feb, Amazonas[185]. Nest unknown.

Status and habitat: Resident. Dense undergrowth in várzea and riverine forest, esp. in young second growth and wet or swampy thickets along rivers or in poorly drained areas. Although characteristic of dense flood-plain vegetation over much of broad range, also in stream valleys in well-drained hilly terrain in se Bolívar. Sight recs. in n Amazonas (Alechiven on lower Río Ventuari, 1998—K. Zimmer and D. Wolf) and ne and sw of Santa Elena de Uairén, Bolívar (Jun 1994—Hilty) extend range of this underrecorded sp.

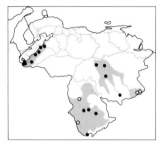

Range: To 550m (sight to 950m). E base of Andes from se Táchira to nw Barinas (Barinitas); c and s Amazonas (sight, lower Río Ventuari; Cerro Duida), Bolívar in lower and mid. Río Caura, headwaters of Río Paragua, and sightings in se Bolívar (*consobrinus*). E Colombia to n Bolivia, part of Amaz. Brazil, and the Guianas.

Ruddy Foliage-gleaner

Automolus rubiginosus   Tico-Tico Garganticastaño
Identification: 7.5″ (19cm). 40g. *Overall very dark.* Upperparts incl. wings dark earthy brown, *tail blackish chestnut, throat dark cinnamon rufous* (some individuals paler, more tawny), contrasting with dark buffy brown underparts; sides and belly dark brown.
Sim. species: A uniformly dark foliage-gleaner with paler contrasting throat. Chestnut-crowned Foliage-gleaner is dark but has conspic. yellow eyes and chestnut crown and tail. Tawny-throated and Short-billed leaftossers are smaller with longer bills and shorter tails.
Voice: In all areas an odd nasal and whining *keeaaah* that ascends, often steadily repeated. Hd. mostly at dawn.
Behavior: Usually seen alone, with members of prs. remaining well separated. Forages very low, mostly 0.1–3m up in forest undergrowth, where actively checks clumps of leaves and other accumulations of debris in vine tangles and thick vegetation, and occas. forages on gd. Seldom follows mixed-spp. flocks and generally

furtive and difficult to see. Almost always noted first by voice. Rootlet and plant-fiber nest at end of long burrow in steep bank; 2 white eggs[381,563].

Status and habitat: Uncommon and local resident in humid and wet terra firme and várzea forest, second growth of various ages, and shrubby forest borders.

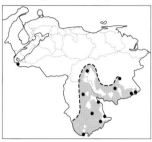

Range: To 1300m. W Apure (upper Río Arauca); e and s Amazonas (Río Asisa southward); nw Bolívar (Cerro El Negro) and across s Bolívar from upper Río Paragua and Auyán-tepui s to Paurai-tepui and Santa Elena de Uairén (*venezuelanus*). C Mexico spottily to w Ecuador, n Bolivia, extreme nw Brazil, and the Guianas.
Note: Prob. more than 1 sp. over vast range.

Thripadectes

Larger and more robust than *Automolus*; heavy black bill; large, rounded tail with no spines; plumage streaked. Nest at end of burrow dug in bank.

Flammulated Treehunter   PLATE 39

Thripadectes flammulatus   Trepapalo Rojizo
Identification: 9.5″ (24cm). 52g. Looks like a larger and more contrasty version of Striped Treehunter. Bill not esp. heavy for size of bird. *Blackish above and below; upperparts narrowly streaked buff, and underparts and crissum broadly and boldly streaked buff,* wings brownish chestnut, rump and tail chestnut. Or sim. but with essentially unstreaked buff throat (*bricenoi*).
Sim. species: Largest and most boldly streaked treehunter. No other in Venez. is so boldly patterned, but see much smaller Striped Treehunter and Lineated Foliage-gleaner, both of lower els.
Voice: Rarely hd. song a slow rattle, *t-a-a'a'a'a'a'a'a'a 'a'a-a-a*, even in tempo or slightly increasing, occas. slowing at end; rather low pitched, lasting 1.5–2 sec; a sharp *chek* when foraging[545].
Behavior: Forages actively by probing and rummaging in debris and tangles from near gd. to ca. 2m up in forest; usually alone and independent of mixed-spp. flocks.

Furtive and difficult to see. In Colombia, nest of root-lets in burrow; white eggs[589].
Status and habitat: Rare (few Venez. recs.) and local resident near treeline. Undergrowth and tangles in wet, mossy, upper montane forest and in dense borders, mossy trunks, and *Chusquea* bamboo.
Range: 2700–3000m. Andes of Mérida near Páramos Culata, Conejos, and Escorial (*bricenoi*); s Táchira on Cerro Las Copas (*flammulatus*). Colombia s in Andes to n Peru.

Striped Treehunter   PLATE 39
Thripadectes holostictus   Trepapalo Listado
Identification: 8″ (20.3cm). 44g. Closely resembles larger Flammulated Treehunter. *Upperparts blackish conspic. streaked buff*, rump, *wings, and tail rufous chestnut*, below differs from previous sp. in having throat and chest buff streaked dusky, *breast mostly buffy brown only narrowly and weakly streaked buff* (Flammulated's entire underparts are broadly and boldly streaked). Juv.: blacker below, hence more sim. to Flammulated Treehunter, but more scaled (less streaked).
Sim. species: Intermed. in size between larger Flammulated Treehunter and smaller Lineated Foliage-gleaner. More slender foliage-gleaner has brown (not rufous) wings, narrow buff postocular stripe, more linear streaking, and unmarked buff throat.
Voice: Call a fast, flycatcherlike *kl'li'li'li'li'li'li'lip!* Song a lower-pitched, staccato rattle that slows toward end, ca. 1.2 sec.
Behavior: Sim. to Flammulated Treehunter and like it furtive and difficult to see, but occurs at lower els. Nest in Peru in burrow in steep bank or vegetation-covered roadcut[573].
Status and habitat: Resident in tangled, mossy undergrowth and thickets in wet montane forest, often in *Chusquea* bamboo.

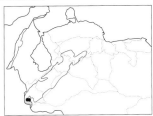

Range: 1800–2000m. S Táchira at Hacienda La Providencia in upper Río Chiquito (*holostictus*). Colombia s in Andes to n Bolivia.

Streak-capped Treehunter   PLATE 39
Thripadectes virgaticeps   Trepapalo Pechirrayado
Identification: 8.5″ (22cm). 45g. Less streaked than others of genus. *Crown and nape dusky gray* with a few fine whitish shaft streaks; cheeks dusky *finely streaked pale gray*, rest of upperparts *virtually unstreaked* rufescent brown, rump and tail chestnut, *throat and chest bright tawny ochraceous, throat rather weakly streaked and scaled dusky* (very little streaking on chest), rest of underparts essentially unstreaked warm cinnamon brown.

Sim. species: Lacks strong markings. Note large size, *decidedly grayish crown and face*, and bright throat. Others with which it occurs are either heavily streaked, e.g., Striped Treehunter, Lineated and Guttulated foliage-gleaners, or entirely unstreaked, e.g., Montane and Buff-fronted foliage-gleaners.
Voice: Song a loud, raspy (angry quality) *reep-reep-reep-reep* (4–7 notes) every 5 sec. Alarm a strident and penetrating *st'R'E'E'E'K!* Also a sharp note doubled or tripled, *st-duk!*, and sharp *SKIP!* note.
Behavior: Alone or in well-separated prs. that are generally furtive and hard to see. Sometimes with mixed-spp. flocks containing warblers, bush-tanagers, and foliage-gleaners, where hop along limbs and peer and probe into moss, vine tangles, and clumps of debris, mostly 0.5–5m up in dense undergrowth. Platform nest of rootlets at end of burrow, often near top of steep bank and beneath overhang; 2 white eggs[382].
Status and habitat: Uncommon and local resident in mossy undergrowth of humid and wet montane forest and tangled or shrubby forest borders. Occurs at lower els. than other *Thripadectes*. More numerous in Colombia.

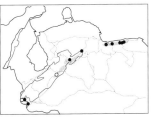

Range: 1250–2150m. S Táchira (*tachirensis*); se Lara (Anzoátegui; Cabudare); Coastal Cordillera from Carabobo to Distr. Federal (*klagesi*). Colombia s in Andes to e and w Ecuador.

Xenops

Distinctive group with narrow (laterally compressed), slightly upturned bill (most spp.); most also show white crescentic malar stripe; all show rufous wing stripe; hitch sideways along bare twigs; do not use tail for support; lower levels to forest canopy; nest in small holes they excavate in soft wood.

Streaked Xenops   PLATE 43
Xenops rutilans   Pico Lezna Rayado
Identification: 4.8″ (12.2cm). 12.6g. Bill stubby, lower mandible upturned at tip. *Short crescentic white malar stripe.* Above brown, cap dusky sharply streaked buff, the *streaks spreading onto mantle and upper back*; short dingy white eyeline; wings blackish with *broad diagonal cinnamon band across base of flight feathers* (conspic. in flight); tail rufous with 2 narrow vertical black bands (*black often hidden in field*) formed by black inner webs of a few inner tail feathers, throat white, essentially unstreaked, rest of underparts olive brown rather *narrowly streaked white*.
Sim. species: Most likely confused with Plain Xenops which lacks streaking. S of Orinoco see Slender-billed Xenops, a lowland bird (no overlap).

Voice: Song a short chattery ser. of 5–6 shrill metallic *zeet* notes; accelerates and rises slightly, then slows and descends.

Behavior: Like most others in genus, gleans slender bare twigs and vines and broken twig ends, usually by hanging beneath or on side of them and hitching along sideways, occas. pausing to peck vigorously at soft wood or pry off small pieces of bark. Usually in prs., occas. 3s, which tend to stay close together as they follow mixed-spp. flocks. Forage mostly in forest mid. levels or subcanopy, although also sometimes lower. Pr. excavating hole 8m up in rotten stub, Feb, n Aragua (Hilty); in Trinidad, 2.4–3m up in tree cavity; nest platform of leaf petioles and root fibers; 2–3 white eggs[39].

Status and habitat: Fairly common resident in humid and wet foothill and mt. forest, forest borders, and tall second growth. A few scattered lowland recs. (Portuguesa, Guárico, and Anzoátegui) suggest it may occur *very locally* in lowlands (further verification desirable).

Range: Mainly 700–2200m (rarely to sea level). Sierra de Perijá, Zulia, and Andes of s Táchira (*perijanus*); Andes from Mérida to Lara, mts. of Yaracuy, n cordilleras from Carabobo to Miranda, and mts. of ne Anzoátegui, Sucre, and n Monagas (*heterurus*). Costa Rica s in mts. to n Argentina; Brazil s of the Amazon to e Bolivia and ne Argentina. Trinidad.

Slender-billed Xenops   PLATE 38
Xenops tenuirostris   Pico Lezna Menor
Identification: 4.5″ (11.4cm). 9.3g. Bill rather *thin and sharp pointed* (lower mandible slightly upturned, but this rarely apparent in field). *Short white malar stripe.* Overall very like Streaked Xenops (no range overlap), differing in fainter streaking on underparts (streaks faint or virtually absent on lower breast and belly of Slender-billed) and more black showing in tail (2 vertical black bands usually visible in field; inconspic. on tail of Streaked).
Sim. species: Rufous-tailed Xenops lacks white malar, has all-rufous tail, and has streakier but paler underparts (none of this easy to verify in field). Plain Xenops lacks streaks. N of Orinoco see nearly identical Streaked Xenops.
Voice: Song in e Ecuador a rather metallic but colorless *ch-ch-chit-chit-chee-chee-chit-chit-chit-chit*, 10–12 notes (<2 sec) on same pitch (K. Zimmer recording).
Behavior: In e Peru rather like others of genus but almost always high in canopy with mixed-spp. flocks. Foraging movements perhaps less stereotyped than in other *Xenops* as it gleans bare slender twigs, often by

hanging beneath or on side of them and hitching along sideways; also hitches along or briefly climbs like a creeper, and wiggles and hops in vine tangles and foliage like a tiny foliage-gleaner. Usually in prs., members of which remain fairly close together. Nest and eggs unknown.

Status and habitat: Resident in tall humid forest in lowlands. Prob. fairly common, but few specimen recs. and difficult to identify with certainty because it is usually so high in canopy. In Brazil may show some preference for várzea and riverine forest[545].

Range: To 200m (prob. higher). Nw Amazonas at Caño Cataniapo (*tenuirostris*); rest of Amazonas, and lower Río Caura in Bolívar (*acutirostris*); se Bolívar on Sierra de Lema (several sightings). E Colombia to n Bolivia, Amaz. Brazil, and the Guianas.

Plain Xenops   PLATE 38
Xenops minutus   Pico Lezna Pechirrayado
Identification: 4.8″ (12.2cm). 11.8g. Lower mandible upturned. *Least streaked of genus* (amt. of streaking varies). Above uniform brown with short buff eyeline and *white crescentic-shaped malar stripe*; wings blackish with *broad cinnamon band across base of flight feathers* (conspic. in flight), tail rufous with 2 narrow vertical black lines; throat whitish, rest of underparts brownish olive, a faint indication of buff streaks on chest. Or sim. but crown finely streaked, sometimes faintly on mantle, chest obviously streaked (*ruficaudus, remoratus*).
Sim. species: Generally the only xenops in *lowlands* n of Orinoco, and only one anywhere that has *unstreaked back*. In field others look streaked *above and esp. below*, but in ne Venez. and s of Orinoco cf. lightly streaked birds carefully, esp. in montane areas (e.g., Sucre and Monagas), with Streaked Xenops. Also cf. Wedge-billed Woodcreeper.
Voice: Song a short, fast, chittery trill, accelerating then slowing and descending at end, *fit fit fit-ft'ft'ft'f'f'f'f'f 'f'fi'i'i*, or *chit, chit, chi-ch'ch'e'e'e'e'i'i'i*, ca. 1.5 sec. Soft *chit* notes when foraging. Also (n Amazonas) a slower (but brisk), slightly descending *fist, fist-fist-fist*.
Behavior: Sim. to others of genus but forages lower, mostly in forest mid. levels or lower and often at little more than eye level. Nest a small hole 1.5–9m up in rotten limb or trunk; lined with shredded fibers; 2 white eggs[706].
Status and habitat: Fairly common to common resident in dry to moist forest, forest borders, lighter woodland, plantations, and viny second growth. Found in lighter woodland and drier regions than other *Xenops*

and overall much commoner than any other *Xenops*, although it is less numerous s of Orinoco. Overlaps in range, to some extent, with all 3 other *Xenops* in Venez. but is infreq. found together with any of them.

Range: To 2200m (usually below 1500m). Nw Zulia (*olivaceus*); s Zulia, nw Táchira, w Mérida, w Lara, and generally e of Andes to e Miranda (*neglectus*); Sucre, Monagas, and Delta Amacuro; Amazonas, except Río Negro region, and Bolívar except the se (*ruficaudus*); s Amazonas along Río Negro and upper Río Orinoco (*remoratus*). Se Mexico to ne Argentina and se Brazil.

Rufous-tailed Xenops   PLATE 38
Xenops milleri   Pico Lezna Rabirrufo
Identification: 4.2″ (10.7cm). 12g. *Bill thin and straight* (not upturned). *No malar stripe.* Crown dusky finely and crisply streaked buff, small indistinct whitish eyeline; back brown streaked pale buff, wings blackish with *broad diagonal cinnamon band across base of flight feathers* (conspic. in flight), rump and *tail all rufous* (no black in tail), underparts more or less streaked brownish olive and light buff.
Sim. species: Only xenops *lacking crescentic white malar stripe* (plain faced) and only one with *solid rufous tail* (neither mark particularly easy to verify in field). Bill shape best verified in hand. Rufous-tailed is more streaked above, paler below, than any other (but this also best seen in direct comparison). See esp. Slender-billed Xenops.
Voice: Song near Manaus, Brazil, a forceful, bouncy *chit-chit, chit, chuEET, chuEET, chuEET, chueet, chueet, chueet, chue ee*, loudest and rising slightly in middle but fading to inconclusive end (K. Zimmer recording).
Behavior: Typical of genus. Clings to side of small bare twigs and hitches or sidles along, staying mostly perpendicular to twig axis, and often constantly turning from side to side, or pausing to peck at rotten tip of a twig, or to flake off small piece of bark for tiny arthropod prey. Usually with mixed-spp. flocks containing

tanagers, greenlets, antwrens, and woodcreepers in canopy of tall forest. In Brazil, nest cavity in arboreal termitary (A. Whittaker).
Status and habitat: Doubtless more numerous than the few recs. suggest, as this sp. stays very high and is difficult to distinguish with confidence from other *Xenops*. Resident in canopy of tall humid terra firme forest in lowlands, and in tall sandy soil forest.
Range: To 400m. C and s Amazonas and s Bolívar in upper Río Paragua and upper Río Caroní. E Colombia s to n Bolivia and e across Amaz. Brazil and the Guianas.

Sclerurus

Dark, semiterrestrial birds of humid lowland and foothill forest; all very sim., with short legs; short, black, stiffened tails; and most spp. with long slender bills deftly employed (like tweezers) to rapidly toss leaves; all have pale, contrasting throats; dig long nest tunnel into bank.

Tawny-throated Leaftosser   PLATE 39
Sclerurus mexicanus   Raspa Hoja Pechirrojizo
Identification: 6.3″ (16cm). 24g. Bill long (0.8″, 20mm), slender, straight or slightly drooped near tip. Above rich dark brown with rufous chestnut rump and black tail; *throat and chest rich tawny rufous* turning dark brown on rest of underparts.
Sim. species: Gray-throated Leaftosser has whitish throat and rufous chest, but leaftossers often face away from observer so this can be difficult to see. In se cf. Short-billed and Black-tailed leaftossers.
Voice: Song, hd. mostly at dawn, 4–5 thin, slurred, and descending whistles, *pseeer-pseeer-pseer-psee-pse*[706], sometimes ending in excited chatter; alarm call a loud, sharp, chipmunklike *squeek!* as in other *Sclerurus*.
Behavior: Sim. to Gray-throated Leaftosser. Nest of compound-leaf rachises at end of burrow in bank or steep slope; 2 white eggs[752].
Status and habitat: Uncommon and local resident in moist places on or near floor of humid and wet forest, mostly foothills and lower slopes. To be watched for in Andes; sight, presum. this sp, nw Barinas[60].

Range: 1450–2000m? n of Orinoco; 300–1100m s of Orinoco. Sierra de Perijá (Cerro Mashirampé), Zulia; n and c Amazonas (Cerros Guanay and Duida); c Bolívar from Cerro Guaiquinima and Auyán-tepui southward (?) (*andinus*). Se Mexico locally (large gap in c Amazonia) to n Bolivia and se Brazil.

Gray-throated Leaftosser
PLATE 39

Sclerurus albigularis   Raspa Hoja Gargantigris

Identification: 6.5" (16.5cm). 38g. Bill long (0.8", 20mm), slender, and straight to slightly upturned. Rich dark brown above with rufous chestnut rump and black tail; *throat grayish white* contrasting with *band of rufous brown on chest* and grayish to olive brown lower underparts.

Sim. species: Whitish throat and dark chest band are key marks. Over most of Venez. range the only *Sclerurus* present. Overlaps Tawny-throated in Sierra de Perijá.

Voice: Song, hd. mainly at dawn and usually given from a low branch 1–3m up, a loud, ringing *túee, túee, túee, tweéep*, rising a little and each note strongly inflected upward; occas. a longer, more complex version with more notes, changing to rattley trill at end. In conflict *chuee-chuee-chuee che'e'e'e'e'e'e*, much faster than song, and last part a high-pitched rattle. Loud *squick!* alarm like others of genus.

Behavior: Like other *Sclerurus*, a furtive, largely terrestrial forest bird, usually seen when it flushes ahead with a sharp call. Hops, not walks, in jerky mechanical manner on gd. or logs. Forages by tossing aside dead leaves (hence its name), then looks for prey items beneath leaves, often spending several min in same place. Also digs or probes soft earth beneath leaves. Solitary or in well-separated 2s and not with mixed-spp. flocks. In Colombia and Trinidad, nest platform of compound-leaf rachises at end of short curving burrow in slope or bank; 2 white eggs; nests in rainy latter half of year[39,750].

Status and habitat: Fairly common resident locally (easily overlooked unless singing) in moist places and ravines in humid and wet forest, mostly in foothills and lower mt. slopes.

Range: 450–1500m (up to 2200m in Sierra de Perijá; above 800m on Paria Pen.). Sierra de Perijá, Zulia (*kunanensis*); s Táchira; nw Lara (Cerro El Cogollal) and se Lara; mts. of Yaracuy and n cordilleras from Carabobo to Miranda; ne Anzoátegui, Sucre, and n Monagas (*albigularis*). Costa Rica and w Panama; Colombia s in mts. locally to n Bolivia; sw Brazil; extreme ne Bolivia. Trinidad.

Short-billed Leaftosser

Sclerurus rufigularis   Raspa Hoja Pechianteado

Identification: 6" (15cm). 22g. Bill *short* for genus (0.6", 15mm), virtually straight. Above rich dark brown with rufous chestnut rump and blackish tail; *throat tawny to pale tawny ochraceous*, turning dark brown on breast and belly. May show faint cinnamon buff lores and eyebrow.

Sim. species: Very like Tawny-throated Leaftosser, differing mainly in shorter, straighter bill; also paler, buffier throat, sometimes a vague pale eyebrow (only overlap in se Bolívar). Black-tailed Leaftosser is slightly larger, also has longer bill, whitish chin (sw subsp. also faintly scaled dusky on throat); in hand, rump less contrasting with back.

Voice: Primary song in sw Brazil 3–5 high, forceful, metallic whistles, *TZEET, SEEer, Seeer, seea*, descending, with halting, lazy delivery, sometimes preceded by brief introductory note; sharp *squeak* alarm (K. Zimmer recording).

Behavior: Sim. to others of genus, incl. nest (see Gray-throated Leaftosser).

Status and habitat: Resident on or near floor of humid terra firme forest in lowlands and foothills. Widespread in vicinity of cerros of se Bolívar with more specimens from vicinity of Cerro Guaiquinima than elsewhere. Most numerous and widely distrib. *Sclerurus* in s Venez.

Range: To 900m. Amazonas from Cerro Parú southward; Bolívar from lower Río Caura, mid. Río Paragua (Cerro Guaiquinima), and upper Río Caroní southward (*fulvigularis*). Se Colombia to ne Peru, extreme ne Bolivia, c Amaz. Brazil, and the Guianas.

Black-tailed Leaftosser
PLATE 39

Sclerurus caudacutus   Raspa Hoja Rabiagudo

Identification: 7" (18cm). 42g. Bill long (0.8", 20mm) and slender, lower mandible slightly upturned. Above dark brown, forecrown and upper tail coverts tinged reddish brown, tail blackish, *chin whitish, throat tawny ochraceous* turning reddish brown on chest and dark brown on lower underparts. Or overall darker brown, chin *and throat whitish faintly scaled dusky* (*brunneus*).

Sim. species: Slightly larger than others of genus and, in its range, only one with white on chin (or also throat), but this very hard to see in field. Longer bill may separate it from Short-billed Leaftosser; white on chin and slight upturn to bill may separate it from Tawny-throated Leaftosser.

Voice: Song accelerates then slows and fades, *queet, queet, queet-queet-queet'queet'ke'he'he'keke'queet 'queet-que-queet*, loud and emphatic (P. Schwartz recording); or often a bright, descending *PEEK, PEEK, Peek, peek, pee pic pic*, variable in speed and length. Like other *Sclerurus*, sings a few songs from low branch mainly at dawn or dusk. Alarm a loud *squeek!* much like others of genus.

Behavior: Sim. to others of genus (see Gray-throated Leaftosser). Nest, Brazil and Peru, a platform of compound-leaf rachises in burrow; 2 white eggs[506] (K. Zyskowski).

Status and habitat: Uncommon to fairly common resident locally (easily overlooked) on or near shady floor of humid terra firme forest in lowlands and foothills. Often around old logs. Most recs. are in hilly terrain or at lower els. in tepuis incl. vicinity of Cerro Guaiquinima.

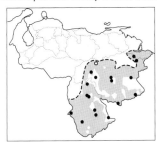

Range: To 1100m. N, c, and se Amazonas and locally throughout Bolívar (*insignis*); sw Amazonas along Yavita-Pimichín trail (*brunneus*). Se Colombia to n Bolivia, Amaz. Brazil, and the Guianas; se Brazil.

Lochmias

Monotypic; tail somewhat rounded, stiffened, with short, hairlike spines projecting from it; semiterrestrial; found near water; possibly allied to *Sclerurus* or *Margarornis* (K. Zyskowski).

Sharp-tailed Streamcreeper   PLATE 39
Lochmias nematura   Macuquiño
Identification: 5.7″ (14.5cm). 23g. Mt. streams and stream banks. Bill fairly long, slender, slightly decurved. Above rich dark brown slightly tinged reddish; short, faint eyebrow dotted black and white, tail blackish, throat white scaled dusky, *rest of underparts brown thickly spotted white*. Or sim. but larger (6″, 15cm), bill slightly longer, legs black, no eyebrow, and *less spotted* on sides and flanks (*sororia*).
Sim. species: Spotted Barbtail has buff (not white) spots, longer tail, and different habits. Streamcreeper's shape (long bill, short tail) and behavior recall a leaftosser.
Voice: Not very vocal. Song on Sierra de Lema, Bolívar, a fairly hard, chattery rattle, a little hesitant at first then accelerating slightly, *pit, pit-pit-pit'pt'pt'pt'pt'pt'pt'pt* . . . . ., flat and low pitched, ca. 3–3.5 sec; at dawn may be repeated a few times at short intervals.
Behavior: Semiterrestrial. Hops furtively in dense *Heliconia* and *Calathea* thickets, vine tangles, and vegetation at edge of rushing mt. streams, or on boulders and vegetation-covered or mossy rocks out in streams, where it flicks or tosses leaves and probes and pecks rather like a leaftosser. Usually quiet, sluggish, and solitary or in well-spaced 2s; when flushes, flies in jerky, erratic manner. Breeds May–Jun in Rancho Grande, Aragua[571]; nest in Brazil a densely woven ball of bamboo leaves and rootlets at end of burrow in bank; 2 white eggs[205] (K. Zyskowski).
Status and habitat: Rare and local resident of mts. of n Venez.; more numerous and widespread resident s of Orinoco, but nowhere common. Humid and wet mt. forest where confined to vicinity of stream banks and damp shady ravines with water. Occas. along stream (850m) below Rancho Grande Biol. Station, Aragua.

Range: 850–1300m n of Orinoco; 1000–2500m s of Orinoco. Sierra de Aroa, Yaracuy (1300m), n Aragua, and Distr. Federal (*sororia*); s Amazonas (Río Mavaca; Río Ocamo; Cerro de la Neblina); Bolívar in lower Río Caura (Cerro Tabaro) and more northerly tepuis of Chimantá, Sororopán, Aprada, and Auyán-tepui (*chimantae*); tepuis of s Bolívar on Cerro Jaua, Cerro Cuquenán, Cerro Roraima, and Uei-tepui (*castanonota*); Sierra de Lema (sight, subsp.?). E Panama s in mts. to nw Bolivia; lowlands and mts. of se Brazil, e Paraguay, ne Argentina, and Uruguay.

Dendrocolaptidae: Woodcreepers

Trepadores

Woodcreepers are a rather homogeneous group of scansorial bark-foragers found from northern Mexico to Argentina. The family is closely related to ovenbirds, especially the Philidorinae ovenbirds, and has been treated as a subfamily within the Furnariidae by some recent authors[606]. Woodcreepers are remarkably uniform in plumage, a factor that contributes to the difficulty of identifying them in the field and properly cataloguing subspecies in museums[376]. They are, however, diverse in bill shape. Bills range from short and wedge-shaped to long and sicklelike. All species have long, stiff tail feathers with projecting and downcurving spines that aid in support during climbing. Members of several genera, especially *Dendrocincla*, *Dendrocolaptes*, and *Xiphorhynchus*, frequently follow army ants. Woodcreepers' songs, often long rattling or wailing trills, are a major component of dawn and dusk choruses in many localities. Nests are in cavities, the eggs are white, and both sexes (except in *Dendrocincla* and *Sittasomus*) help with all aspects of breeding.

Dendrocincla

Med. size; slender, med.-long bill; tail longish and stiff; plumage virtually unmarked above and below, crown feathers often somewhat ruffed; mainly lowlands, although 1 sp. reaches treeline; some follow army ants.

Tyrannine Woodcreeper
Dendrocincla tyrannina   Trepador Paramero
Identification: 10″ (25cm). 60g. Bill (1.3″, 33mm) blackish. Largest *unstreaked* woodcreeper. *Almost entirely warm brown, wings and tail rufous chestnut*, throat pale brown, crown with a few faint shaft streaks (mainly visible in hand), throat and chest with a few indistinct shaft streaks.

Sim. species: Only essentially unstreaked woodcreeper at high el. Plain-brown and Ruddy woodcreepers are smaller and occur at lower el.

Voice: Song a *long*, slightly accelerating ser. that starts hesitantly with a few wooden notes gradually increasing in tempo to a frenzied rattle, then slowing and winding down right at end, lasting 10–16 sec, occas. more; alarm a high, tremulous *tr'E'E'E'E'A* in Ecuador[412,413].

Behavior: A relatively quiet and inconspic. sp. that has been encountered singly, often with mixed-spp. flocks, where it climbs lower part of trunks or out on lower limbs. Nest undescribed.

Status and habitat: Resident inside humid and wet upper montane forest. A poorly known sp., generally considered to be rare and local; however, at least 6 specimens were taken at Hacienda La Providencia in upper Río Chiquito during Feb and Mar of 1955–1956 (Colección Phelps) at els. of 1800–2300m.

Range: 1800–2800m. N Táchira on Páramo Zumbador; s Táchira in upper Río Chiquito (Cerro Las Copas) and Cerro El Teteo (*hellmayri*). Colombia s locally in Andes to s Peru.

Plain-brown Woodcreeper   PLATE 37
Dendrocincla fuliginosa   Trepador Marrón

Identification: 8.5″ (22cm). 37g. Common and widespread. Bill straight (1″, 25mm), dusky to greenish above, pale below; *eyes brown* (all subspp.). Or 9″ (23cm), bill all blackish (*fuliginosa*). Crown often obviously "ruffed." *Plumage mostly plain brown* (more olivaceous brown in w part of range), throat paler, flight feathers and tail rufous chestnut, *cheeks grayish*, and *usually with indistinct dusky malar mark*. Or larger, cheeks paler gray; dark buff postocular line; more distinct dusky malar; chin *buffy white* with a few darker shaft streaks (*fuliginosa*). Juv.: whitish mottling on throat and chest.

Sim. species: As name implies, mostly plain brown and devoid of good field marks. Note weak facial pattern; this varies geographically and is most obvious in e Bolívar where birds also show *distinct whitish chin*. Very sim. White-chinned Woodcreeper (see) is more uniform with darker, "smoky" look and no pattern on cheeks. In w Venez. see Ruddy Woodcreeper, at very high els. Tyrannine Woodcreeper; also Smoky-brown Woodpecker.

Voice: Infreq. hd. song a rapid ser. of notes running downscale, *ke-te-te-te-tu-tu-tu-tu-tue-tue-tue-tue-chu-chu-chu-chu-chew-chew*. Over army ants, and occas. away from ants, its prolix song is a chattery, "pot-boiling" ser. rising and falling, and given over and over for up to several min with no evident break in song. Call of *fuliginosa* a loud *stick!*

Behavior: Reg. follows army ants where noisy groups of 3–6, occas. up to 12, are active, boldly sallying in forest lower levels for fleeing prey, flicking wings and moving from trunk to trunk. In presence of professional ant-following antbirds or larger woodcreepers, tends to stay higher on trunks (up to 10m up) and much more an arboreal generalist than allied White-chinned Woodcreeper[803]. Takes prey from trunks, vines, air, live foliage, and epiphytes, only occas. from gd. Away from ant swarms usually forages alone or in prs., where climbs trunks, mostly keeping in lower levels of forest, occas. ascending to lower canopy. Orthopterans and beetles are largest part of diet in w Amazonia[110,805]. Leaf-lined nest in broken end of palm, stub, trunk, or cavity 1–9m up; 2 white eggs; late Apr–Aug, Costa Rica and Trinidad[175,706].

Status and habitat: Fairly common resident over a wide range of habitats from dry deciduous forest to tall humid forest, cocoa plantations, and second-growth woodland in lowlands and foothills. Less numerous (or locally absent) in gallery forests of interior; not in desert scrub or coastal thorn woodland.

Range: To 1800m (most recs. below 1300m). Throughout. W Zulia and Andes of Táchira and Mérida (*lafresnayei*); Trujillo (subsp.?); n mts. from n Falcón (Sierra de San Luis) and w Lara to Paria Pen., and llanos of Guárico and Monagas (*meruloides*); w llanos in Táchira, Apure, Barinas, Cojedes, and Portuguesa (*barinensis*); Delta Amacuro (*deltana*); s of Orinoco in Amazonas and nw Bolívar (*phaeochroa*); e Bolívar from Altiplanicie de Nuria s to Cerro Roraima (*fuliginosa*). Honduras to w Ecuador; e of Andes s to Bolivia, Amaz. Brazil e to Maranhão; ne Brazil (Pernambuco and Alagoas); the Guianas.

White-chinned Woodcreeper   PLATE 37
Dendrocincla merula   Trepador Barbiblanco

Identification: 8.2″ (21cm). 44g. *Bill all dusky above, yellowish green below*, slightly shorter (0.9″, 23mm) and thinner than that of Plain-brown Woodcreeper. *Eyes brown* (all areas in Venez.). Closely resembles Plain-brown Woodcreeper, and they are most alike in areas where they overlap (Amazonas race of Plain-brown also has pale chin). White-chinned overall is slightly smaller and *darker above and below*, with *uniform* brown head (absolutely no head markings, and lacking *Plain-brown's grayish cheeks and dusky malar*); rather indistinct pale gray loral spot; sharply *contrasting, narrow white median chin and upper throat patch*; rufous chestnut of wings and tail only in slight contrast to back (contrast more obvious in Plain-brown).

Sim. species: White-chinned Woodcreeper overall has rather *uniform smoky brown appearance*, darker than Plain-brown Woodcreeper. Other woodcreepers are streaked.
Voice: Song in Venez. unknown; near Manaus, Brazil, a clipped, descending *kue, kue, kue, ku, ku, ku, ku, ku,* slowing at end; alarm or disturbance an irreg. ser. of rough rattles, *shu-shu, shu-shu-shu-shu, shu-shu-shu . . . ,* like rattle of Pale-breasted Thrush but long sustained[246].
Behavior: Even more of an obligate army ant follower than Plain-brown Woodcreeper and rarely or never found foraging away from them. Dominates Plain-brown Woodcreeper at swarms, and unlike that sp., usually alone or in prs. and mainly a gd. forager. Clings or hops low over ants, mostly less than 1m up on saplings or trunks, and darts to gd. (ca. 90% of prey attempts) for prey incl. esp. spiders (21% of diet), soft-bodied orthopterans and roaches, and some beetles. In general quicker and much more timid and difficult to see than Plain-brown[809]. Two BC birds, Mar–Apr, upper Orinoco[185]. Nest unknown.
Status and habitat: Scarce and perhaps also local resident inside humid terra firme forest, incl. sandy soil forests.

Range: To 300m. Throughout Amazonas (Caño Catani-apo southward); n Bolívar in Río Nicharé, lower Río Caura, and mid. Río Paragua (vicinity of Cerro El Perro at Río Pacaraque) (*bartletti*). Se Colombia to n Bolivia, Amaz. Brazil, and the Guianas.
Note: N birds (incl. *bartletti*) are prob. a separate sp. from pale-eyed birds of Amazon Basin.

Ruddy Woodcreeper   PLATE 37
Dendrocincla homochroa   Trepador Rojizo
Identification: 8″ (20.3cm). 42g. Bill straight (0.9″, 23mm). Uniform dark rufescent brown with chestnut crown (contrasts somewhat with back) and paler, more tawny throat.
Sim. species: Darker and more uniform than any other in its range. Plain-brown Woodcreeper is dull olivaceous brown with grayish cheeks and dark malar. At high els. see larger Tyrannine Woodcreeper.
Voice: Rarely hd. song, in Costa Rica, a ser. of ca. 12 or more *wheet* notes at leisurely pace, slowing at end and much like that of Buff-throated Woodcreeper (B. Spencer recording); sharp squeaky *kink* or *quink*; descending, nasal, scratchy *deeeeah*, often with quaver or roll at end; *squeeirr!* or prolonged *churr*[706].
Behavior: Another woodcreeper that reg. follows army ants. Clings upright to vertical trunks or saplings and sallies to leaves, bark, or gd. for fleeing arthropod

prey; away from ants climbs and searches bark surfaces on lower part of trunks and limbs. Usually solitary but occas. 2–3 at army ant swarms; infreq. with mixed-spp. flocks. Nest in Costa Rica in hollow palm trunk or cavity, 0.6–5m up; 2 eggs, Apr–Jun[706].
Status and habitat: Resident in humid forest or partially cleared forested areas in foothills. Fairly common (many specimens) formerly, but in decline; forest destruction is extensive within its small Venez. range.

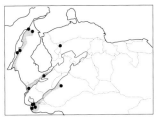

Range: To 1250m (most recs. below 450m). Base of Sierra de Perijá, Zulia, w slope of Andes in Táchira, Mérida (no recs. from Trujillo), and nw Lara (Cerro El Cogollal); e base of Andes in Táchira, Apure, and w Barinas at Ciudad Bolívar (*meridionalis*). S Mexico to Colombia.

Deconychura

Dull; med. sized; lack extensive streaking; recognized by short, relatively thin bill and longish tail.

Long-tailed Woodcreeper   PLATE 37
Deconychura longicauda   Trepador Colilargo
Identification: 8–8.5″ (20.3–22cm). 27g. Bill straight (0.8–0.9″, 20–23mm). ♂ larger than ♀. *Rather slender appearance accentuated by longish tail.* Above mainly brown, crown and nape with a few obscure buff shaft streaks and *narrow pale buff postocular mark*; wings and tail rufous chestnut, *tail proportionately longer than in other genera*, throat dull buffy white faintly streaked dusky and *somewhat spotted with buff on throat and chest* (streaking and spotting inconspic.); rest of underparts olivaceous brown, chest and breast with a few long pale shaft streaks (overall looks more streaked than spotted below).
Sim. species: See Spot-throated Woodcreeper. At any distance does not show obvious streaking or spotting on underparts (markings confined mostly to throat and chest) so can look like a Plain-brown Woodcreeper with longish tail and short bill, or even like a Wedge-billed Woodcreeper.
Voice: Dramatic song a slow, descending ser. of 6–12 whistles, *PEEE . . peee . . peuu puu tuu tuu tuu tu*; alarm (or disturbance) a hard, fast ser. of low trills, *trrr-trrr- . . . ,* over and over at ca. 3/sec.
Behavior: Usually seen singly or in loosely assoc. prs. with mixed-spp. flocks. Forages mostly at low to mid. hts. in forest by hitching up trunks and out on limbs. In e Peru typically rather quiet, although occas. sings while foraging. Does not follow army ants. Cavity nest lined with dry leaves, 9m up in broken, open-top stub; 3 eggs, Apr[790].

Status and habitat: Uncommon and perhaps local resident in humid terra firme forest. In se Peru, also low-lying or várzea forest.

Range: To 400m. C and s Amazonas from upper Río Metacuni southward; Bolívar from lower Río Caura and mid. Río Paragua (Cerro Guaiquinima) southward (*connectens*). Se Colombia to n Bolivia, Amaz. Brazil, and the Guianas.

Spot-throated Woodcreeper   PLATE 43
Deconychura stictolaema   Trepador Pechipunteado
Identification: 7.5–8″ (19–20.3cm). 18g. *Bill notably short* (0.6–0.7″, 15–18mm), *straight, and thin*. Looks like a small, short-tailed, and short-billed version of Long-tailed Woodcreeper. Differs most obviously from that sp. by *shorter bill*, also by slightly smaller size (but note some size overlap possible). Plumage differs from Long-tailed Woodcreeper as follows: virtually unstreaked crown, rufous rump (hard to see in field), throat with more buff spotting (but spots virtually confined to throat with only a few extending onto chest), and virtual absence of streaking on breast.
Sim. species: Easily confused with several other woodcreepers. See esp. Plain-brown, Wedge-billed, and Ocellated woodcreepers. Most *Xiphorhynchus* woodcreepers are more obviously streaked.
Voice: Infreq. hd. song in ne Peru a rather fast, penetrating (or vibrating) ser. of notes on same pitch, *wuee-ee-ee-EE-EE-EE-ee-ee-ee-ee-e-e*, shrill and loudest in middle, then trailing off; brings to mind a small antbird (P. Donahue recording).
Behavior: Quiet and easily overlooked, usually foraging with mixed-spp. flocks in lower story of forest. Behavior in general sim. to that of Long-tailed Woodcreeper[545].
Status and habitat: Known from only 4 localities in Amazonas; inside humid lowland forest.

Range: To 200m. C and s Amazonas at Cerro Yapacana, Yavita, Capibara on Río Casiquiare, and Cerro

de la Neblina (*secunda*). Se Colombia, e Ecuador, and ne Peru e across c Amaz. Brazil. Guyana; French Guiana.

Glyphorynchus

Monotypic; small and widespread; short stubby bill flattened at tip; longish tail rounded with projecting spiny tips that are unusually long and downcurved.

Wedge-billed Woodcreeper   PLATE 37
Glyphorynchus spirurus   Trepador Pico de Cuña
Identification: 5.5″ (14cm). 14g. *Smallest woodcreeper. Short conical bill.* Mainly dull brown with *short buff eyebrow*; lower back, rump, and tail rufous, throat light to dark buff, rest of underparts olivaceous brown, throat somewhat spotted dusky, breast with chevron-shaped buff spots spreading over chest and upper breast, a few less obvious buff shaft streaks on lower underparts. In flight shows *prom. buff wing band across base of flight feathers* (from below).
Sim. species: Note diminutive size and stubby bill. Olivaceous Woodcreeper is nearly as small but unmarked and has "divided" look with grayish foreparts, rufous rearparts. In Amazonas see Spot-throated Woodcreeper which is larger and has thin (not conical) bill. *Xenops* have sim. size, shape, and wing band but different behavior.
Voice: Call a weak, sneezing *chief!* or *chief beef!*; song in e Bolívar a fussy little ser. of notes, squeezed out and rising up scale, *too-e, too-e, tu-tu-tu-tue 'tue 'twu 'tweetwee.* Song varies geographically.
Behavior: A rather inconspic. and unassuming little bird that seems to spend most of its time twitching nervously and myopically climbing lower part of large tree trunks. Occurs alone or in prs. and with mixed-spp. flocks or independent of them about equally. Forages by mechanically hitching up trunks (much less often limbs) like a little windup toy and pecking at or flaking off tiny bits of bark (esp. of trees with fine scaly bark) for minute hidden food items. Occas. hitches downward in reverse for short distances. Nest a shallow cup of rootlets in tree or stub cavity, furrow of trunk, etc., gd. level to 20m up; 2 white eggs[706].
Status and habitat: Common to very common resident in humid and wet terra firme and várzea forest and shady second-growth woodland; occas. trees in clearings. True nos. are often better revealed by mist-nets.

Range: To 1800m. Sierra de Perijá, Zulia, and very locally in Andes in s Táchira, w Mérida, nw Barinas, and se Lara at Cabudare (*integratus*); Amazonas (except extreme south) e across s Bolívar (*rufigularis*); s Amazonas on Cerro de la Neblina (*coronobscurus*); ne Bolívar from Altiplanicie de Nuria and Río Grande s to Ptari-tepui and Gran Sabana (*spirurus*); Sucre s to Delta Amacuro (*amacurensis*). S Mexico to w Ecuador, n Bolivia, Amaz. and e Brazil, and the Guianas.

Sittasomus

Small size; pointed bill; tail rounded; plain, unmarked plumage.

Olivaceous Woodcreeper   PLATE 37
Sittasomus griseicapillus   Trepador Verdón
Identification: 6″ (15cm). 13g. Short, thin bill. *Head, neck, and underparts uniform olivaceous gray*, back olive brown, lower back, rump, flight feathers, and tail rufous. In flight shows *conspic. buff band across base of flight feathers* (band shows only from below). Some birds from Anzoátegui are slightly tinged yellowish buff on head and underparts.
Sim. species: Only Wedge-billed Woodcreeper, which has short stubby bill, eyebrow, and spots on throat and chest, is so small. In flight conspic. buff wing band recalls Swainson's Thrush.
Voice: Song a thin ser. of little piping notes that rapidly run up scale then down again (as if outlining a "normal distribution" on bell-shaped probability curve), e.g., *wu-wu-wu-we-we-we-ee-ee-e-e-e-ee-ee-we-we-we-wu-wu-wu*. Typically given only at intervals of several min.
Behavior: Another rather unassuming little woodcreeper that goes quietly about its business of incessantly climbing straight up trunks and large limbs. Usually forages solitarily, less often in prs. Reg. follows mixed-spp. flocks but also found independent of them about equally. Fairly conspic. and easy to see as rapidly hitches up mostly large smooth trunks and limbs in jerky fashion. Typically climbs from lower story to subcanopy before flying down to base of another trunk to repeat process. Has habit of occas. sallying out short distance to air in quick, erratic pursuit of small flushed prey. Nest, in Costa Rica, dry leaves in crevice 12m up in palm stub[644]; 3 white eggs in Tobago[573].
Status and habitat: Common and widespread resident in moist and humid forest, forest edge, and shady old second-growth woodland and plantations. Favors rather open forest.

Range: To 2300m n of Orinoco; to 1600m s of Orinoco. Sierra de Perijá, Zulia (*perijanus*); s Táchira (*tachirensis*); locally n on both slopes of Andes n to nw Lara; c and se Falcón, mts. of Yaracuy and n cordilleras e to

Sucre and n Monagas (*griseus*); w and s Amazonas (*amazonus*); n and c Amazonas and generally in Bolívar (*axillaris*). Mexico to n Argentina and se Brazil.
Note: Single sp. of *Sittasomus* currently recognized consists of several vocally and morphologically distinct taxa.

Nasica

Large and with long neck; long, decurved bill.

Long-billed Woodcreeper   PLATE 37, Illus. below
Nasica longirostris   Trepador Pescuecilargo
Identification: 14″ (36cm). 87g. Long, thin neck, small head, and *long, slightly decurved bill* impart sinister, almost "reptilian" appearance. Bill to 2.8″ (71mm), pinkish cream in color. Crown and back of neck blackish brown finely streaked buff, postocular streak white, rest of upperparts reddish chestnut incl. rather long tail; *throat white in contrast to crown and back of neck*; rest of underparts brown with large black-edged, lance-shaped white streaks spreading over most of underparts.
Sim. species: Shape, long bill, and bold plumage unmistakable.
Voice: Song a long, slow ser. of loud wailing or lamenting whistles, *whoooOOOooo, whoooOOOooo, whoooOOOooo* . . . (up to ca. 6 whistles, each rising a bit in middle); Limpkin-like and easily imitated. Apt to call only a few times before falling quiet.
Behavior: Single birds or prs. forage on trunks and large limbs in forest canopy, occas. lower, where they take prey such as small reptiles, amphibians, and spi-

Long-billed Woodcreeper

ders (incl. tarantulas) from bromeliads, tree cavities, and epiphytes. Also probe cracks and crevices in bark. Reg. follow mixed-spp. flocks. Decoy well to whistled imitations of song but remain high and typically wary. Nest, in Ecuador, hole 4m up in small tree in clearing (R. Ridgely); imms. Jan and May, Pto. Ayacucho[185].

Status and habitat: Fairly common resident in várzea forest and swampy and low-lying forest along streams and rivers; also *locally* in terra firme forest on richer soils (rarely white sandy soil forest), e.g., Junglaven and Camani lodges. Not as confined to várzea forest as in Amaz. Peru and Brazil.

Range: To 200m (prob. slightly higher). Generally in w Amazonas. E Colombia to Bolivia, Amaz. Brazil, and French Guiana.

Dendrexetastes

Large and robust; strong, thick bill; rather uniform plumage; more active and agile than allies.

Cinnamon-throated Woodcreeper   PLATE 43
Dendrexetastes rufigula   Trepador Garganta Canela
Identification: 9.5″ (24cm). 70g. *Heavy straight bill pale horn gray.* Above plain brown tinged grayish, below pale brown, throat buff; chest with *fairly prom. necklace of drop-shaped white streaks edged black*; sometimes with a few blackish bars on belly and under tail coverts; wings rufous brown (weak contrast with body); rump and *tail dull rufous.*
Sim. species: Stout bill, necklace, and uniform plumage are the marks. Barred and Black-banded woodcreepers look uniform at a distance; Barred has reddish bill; Black-banded has finely streaked head. Also cf. Plain-brown and White-chinned woodcreepers, both with whitish chins (in area of overlap), and both often at army ants.
Voice: Song in Venez. and Suriname, one of 1st hd. at dawn and last at dusk, a fast, ripping, "rubber-lipped" ser. of *tew* notes louder and accelerating, then diminishing slightly in volume, but more or less on same pitch; song flatter and *not obviously* slowing much at end (contra birds in sw Amazonia). Song is evocative, haunting, and wild-sounding as if singer is possessed or tormented.
Behavior: Unusual for a woodcreeper. Single birds or well-separated prs. climb large smooth trunks and limbs and reg. travel with canopy mixed-spp. flocks, but often hitch far out canopy limbs and into outer foliage. There they may actively hop and clamber about in live outer foliage like a foliage-gleaner (*Philydor*),

peer into leaf clusters, hang upside down to glean foliage, even palm fronds, and often feed on fruit located in terminal clusters. In Peru, nest of dry leaves in tree cavity or thatch of roof; 2 white eggs (K. Zyskowski).
Status and habitat: Uncommon resident in humid lowland terra firme forest. In Venez. known only from Sierra de Imataca (Río Grande); numerous sight recs. (since late 1970s); 1 specimen (Colección Phelps)[259]. In w Amazonia found in várzea forest, disturbed areas, and river isls.

Range: To 300m. Ne Bolívar (Río Grande) and s Delta Amacuro (*rufigula*). Se Colombia to n Bolivia, Amaz. Brazil, and the Guianas.
Note: Song, duller plumage, and grayish bill rather unlike subspp. in w Amazonia.

Hylexetastes

Very large; heavy bodied; strong, dark red bill; overall much like *Dendrocolaptes*[810].

Red-billed Woodcreeper   PLATE 37
Hylexetastes perrotii   Trepador Pico Rojo
Identification: 11.5″ (29cm). 115g. *Bill heavy, slightly decurved,* and dark red (1.5″, 38mm). *Large, rare woodcreeper* of e rain forests. Above mainly brown, crown darker and with *contrasting dull whitish lores and ill-defined whitish stripe below and behind eyes;* wings and tail rufous chestnut, *throat whitish,* otherwise olive brown below; *belly usually narrowly barred black* (inconspic.), under tail coverts ochraceous narrowly barred black.
Sim. species: A very large, essentially unmarked woodcreeper with heavy reddish bill and whitish face pattern. Beware Amazonian Barred Woodcreeper, which also is large, has reddish bill, and often looks very uniform in field (bars hard to see), but it lacks strong facial pattern. Strong-billed and Black-banded woodcreepers are dark billed and streaked on head and underparts.
Voice: Song in Brazil is several loud, piercing whistles inflected upward[810].
Behavior: In Brazil found singly or in prs. from understory to canopy, also at army ant swarms and with mixed-spp. flocks. When at ant swarms stays very low and, because of size, easily dominates other spp. In French Guiana, nest in dead tree cavity[751].
Status and habitat: In Venez. known from 1 specimen from Río Yurán, a tributary of upper Río Cuyuní; and 1 sight rec. n of Sierra de Lema (D. Stejskal). Rare in tall humid forest.

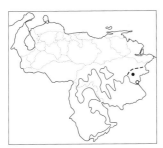

Range: To 200m. Extreme e Bolívar in upper Río Cuyuní drainage (*perrotii*). The Guianas and ne Brazil s to the Amazon.

Xiphocolaptes

Largest woodcreeper in Venez.; very heavy bodied; long, heavy, and decurved bill; separate highland and lowland pops.

Strong-billed Woodcreeper   PLATE 37
Xiphocolaptes promeropirhynchus   Trepador Pico Negro
Identification: 12″ (30.5cm). 120g. Plumage somewhat variable. Unusually long bill (1.5–1.8″, 38–46mm) heavy, *blackish, slightly decurved*. Crown blackish, crown and head narrowly streaked buff and with *rather ill-defined buff postocular stripe*, rest of upperparts brown, wings and tail rufous chestnut; throat *whitish with obscure buffy white stripe below eyes and prom. dusky malar*, remaining underparts brown rather broadly streaked buffy white, center of belly and under tail coverts finely barred black (barring inconspic. and difficult to see in field, sometimes virtually absent). Or sim. but finely streaked above, little or no barring on lower underparts (*procerus*). Or belly somewhat rufescent, *bill straighter, pale horn color* (*orenocensis, neblinae, tenebrosus*).
Sim. species: Extraordinarily large size and long, heavy bill are usually a tip-off. Easily confused with Blackbanded Woodcreeper, but note that sp.'s smaller size, shorter, straight black bill, no dusky malar, and if close, distinct barring on sides and flanks (bars can be hard to see in field). Buff-throated Woodcreeper lacks strong facial pattern (no black malar), and its bill is thinner. Also see Red-billed and Barred woodcreepers.
Voice: At dawn and dusk a slow ser. of 4–5 paired and rhythmic whistles, 2d note of each pr. lower than preceding, and entire ser. descending in pitch, e.g., *WEE-uut, WE-uut, We-uuh, we-uuh, we-uuh*; also occas. a catlike *meow* and various unmusical lisping notes.
Behavior: Occurs alone or in scattered prs., sometimes with mixed-spp. flocks. Foraging behavior notably versatile; climbs trunks and med. to large limbs, rummages in bromeliads and accumulated litter in trees, follows army ants, and occas. drops to gd. where clambers over roots and flips over leaves. At high els. at least partially a bromeliad specialist. One BC bird, May, upper Orinoco[185].
Status and habitat: Rare to uncommon resident in humid and wet forest in foothills and mts., incl. cloud

forest, occas. moist forest (n base of Coastal Cordillera) n of Orinoco; mainly lowlands s of Orinoco where less numerous.

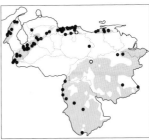

Range: 400–2800m n of Orinoco (scattered recs. lower); lowlands to 1800m s of Orinoco. Sierra de Perijá, Zulia; Andes of Táchira, Mérida, and Trujillo (*promeropirhynchus*); nw Zulia, n Mérida, Lara, mts. of Yaracuy, n cordilleras from Carabobo to Miranda, e Guárico (Santa María de Ipire), and ne mts. in Anzoátegui (Barcelona), Sucre, and n Monagas (*procerus*); ne Bolívar near El Palmar (prob. *procerus*); lowlands of most of Amazonas (*orenocensis*); Cerro de la Neblina, Amazonas (*neblinae*); se Bolívar on Cerros Chimantá and Roraima (*tenebrosus*); sight recs. from lower Río Caura at Maripa (P. Boesman). Mexico s (mostly in mts.) to Bolivia and e through c Amaz. Brazil to the Guianas.
Note: Highland and lowland forms may represent separate spp. Some recognize subsp. *sanctaemartae* in Sierra de Perijá[559].

Dendrocolaptes

Moderately large; bill heavy but straight, a little short for size of bird; plumage pattern usually incl. barring; crown often obviously ruffed; "sleek-headed" birds are prob. dominant ♀♀, "ruffed-crown" birds subordinate ♂♂[812]; tail rounded.

Northern Barred-Woodcreeper
Dendrocolaptes sanctithomae   Trepador Barreteado Centroamericano
Identification: 11″ (28cm). 69g. Long, heavy bill almost straight (1.5″, 38mm), *brownish black*. Crown often ruffed. *Head, back, and underparts pale brown evenly barred dusky*, barring often faint on shoulders and upperparts; wings, rump, and tail rufous chestnut.
Sim. species: From Cocoa, Black-banded, and Strong-billed woodcreepers by extensive barring.
Voice: Song a slow, melancholy *huuuwit, . . huuwit, huuwit, huwit, huwit* (ca. 4–6 notes), sometimes last note or 2 louder; when excited a longer, more urgent, and faster ser., *huey, huey, . . . huuuey, huuuey . . . tuue, tue, tue*, rising then falling. Cf. very different song of Amaz. birds. Call a reedy *pfew*.
Behavior: Sim. to Amazonian Barred-Woodcreeper. In Costa Rica, nest in hollow palm stub or natural cavity, 1–6m up; nest lined with bits of bark and leaves; 2 white eggs, May–Jul[706].
Status and habitat: Resident in humid lowland forest, old second growth, and light woodland. Has limited

distrib. in Venez. and known from rather small no. of specimens.

Range: To 450m. Sierra de Perijá, Zulia, and s around Lago de Maracaibo to w Mérida (*punctipectus*). S Mexico to nw Ecuador.
Note: Taxonomy follows Marantz[376].

Amazonian Barred-Woodcreeper   PLATE 37
Dendrocolaptes certhia   Trepador Barreteado Amazónico
Identification: 11" (28cm). 69g. Long, heavy, reddish bill almost straight (1.5", 38mm). Crown often ruffed. Sim. to Northern Barred-Woodcreeper but differs in paler, more buffy brown plumage, *much less conspic. barring*, and *distinctly reddish bill*.
Sim. species: Barring difficult to see on this sp. Look for red bill. Very rare Red-billed Woodcreeper, even larger, is only other with such obviously reddish bill. Also cf. Black-banded Woodcreeper which is streaked on foreparts, has black bill, and barring only on lower underparts. Buff-throated Woodcreeper has longer pale bill. Strong-billed Woodcreeper is larger, heavier-billed, and streaky.
Voice: Like others in genus, sings mostly in predawn and at dusk. Song in Amazonas a rather high-pitched, descending whinny with wild laughing quality, *whee-whee-EE-EE-Ee-ee-ee-ee-eu eu eu*, fading at end, closely resembling song of Black-banded Woodcreeper. Also various rough nasal notes and snarls at army ant swarms. Songs vary somewhat geographically.
Behavior: Single birds or prs. (infreq. more) forage mostly at army ant swarms but also away from them with mixed-spp. flocks or alone. Forage 1–10m up (but mostly low) over ants by clinging to or hitching up larger trunks, then dropping to gd. or sallying to foliage or trunks to capture fleeing arthropod prey or occas. small vertebrates. Sometimes rather inactive and may cling motionless to trunks, as if dazed, for extended periods. Away from ants more apt. to forage in mid. story, or even higher, in forest, occas. climbing

large limbs into canopy where take prey from bark surfaces, crevices, and epiphytes[447]. Nine BC birds, Apr, upper Orinoco[185]; in Brazil, nest in tree cavity; 1 white egg[506].
Status and habitat: Uncommon to fairly common resident in humid terra firme forest and tall second-growth woodland; occas. along forest borders or in low-lying floodplain forests.
Range: To 1400m. Throughout Amazonas, Bolívar, and s Delta Amacuro (*certhia*). E Colombia to n Bolivia, Amaz. Brazil, and the Guianas; se Brazil.
Note: Taxonomy follows Marantz[376].

Black-banded Woodcreeper   PLATE 37
Dendrocolaptes picumnus   Trepador Tanguero
Identification: 10" (25cm). 76g. *Bill heavy, essentially straight* (1.4", 36mm), *black*. Crown often ruffed. *Crown and sides of head dusky brown* contrasting with broad but rather indistinct pale buff eyebrow; throat pale buffy white lightly streaked dusky, mantle and breast brown heavily streaked pale buff, *lower breast to crissum brown narrowly and evenly barred black* (hard to see unless close), wings and tail rufous chestnut. In n mts. from Falcón to Sucre less barred below (*seilerni*); in e lowlands belly barring extensive and more prom. (*picumnus*).
Sim. species: Looks like small edition of Strong-billed Woodcreeper and easily confused with it. In general less robust, bill shorter, lower mandible straight (not decurved slightly), no obvious pale stripe below eyes or dark malar, and barring more extensive on lower underparts. In hand Black-banded has sharper, black-edged streaking on chest (not buffy and somewhat diffuse), and streaks on throat. Also see both Barred and Red-billed woodcreepers.
Voice: In Amazonas, at dawn and dusk, a long, whinnying ser. of 15–20 *whin* notes (in 4–5 sec) that accelerate slightly then gradually slow down but remain more or less on same pitch (Amazonian Barred-Woodcreeper's song is sim. but slower and has fewer notes). Day song a shorter, descending whinny, *whi'ii'ii'ii'i'i'i'i'i'i*. Also various rattles, squeals, and snarling sounds. Alarm a growling-squeak *chauhhh-eesk*[812]. Birds in n cordilleras sing a sim. quavering dawn and dusk song.
Behavior: Single birds, prs., or several commonly forage fairly low over army ants, where wait or hitch slowly up large vertical trunks, then mostly sally out to logs or gd. for wide size-range of mostly arthropod prey. Individuals or prs. also forage alone or with mixed-spp. flocks of insectivores from mid. levels to canopy where take prey from bark and often sally. Sleek-headed birds (presum. ♀♀) help ruff-headed mates in disputes and trespass a little on neighbors' areas, and both sexes sing near roost sites at dawn and dusk. Nest in tree cavity; 2 white eggs[812].
Status and habitat: Uncommon resident (seems nowhere very numerous) in humid forest, occas. along forest borders, in nearby isolated trees in clearings, and locally in dry and moist forest in Coastal Cordillera.
Range: 400–2700m n of Orinoco; to 500m s of Orinoco. Sierra de Perijá, Zulia, and Andes of Táchira, Mérida, nw Barinas, and sightings in e Trujillo at PN Guaramacal (*multistrigatus*); mts. of Falcón (Sierra de San Luis) and n cordilleras from Yaracuy to Aragua, and mts. of

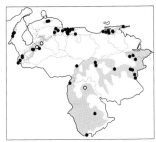

Anzoátegui, Sucre, and n Monagas (*seilerni*); spottily in Amazonas and Bolívar (*picumnus*). Costa Rica to Bolivia, w and n Amaz. Brazil, and the Guianas.

Xiphorhynchus

Confusing group with many spp. *difficult* to separate; med. size; med. to longish bills straight or slightly decurved, heavier than *Lepidocolaptes*; plumage streaked or spotted; mostly lowlands; taxonomy of several spp. not well understood; note carefully foraging sites: overlap in diet between spp. greater than overlap in foraging substrates and/or habitats.

Straight-billed Woodcreeper   PLATES 37, 43
Xiphorhynchus picus   Trepador Subesube
Identification: 8″ (20.3cm). 35g. *Bill straight and pointed* (1–1.2″, 25–30mm), *chalky white* in north, dull *pinkish white* in south. Widespread and variable (9 subspp. in Venez.). N subspp. (Lago de Maracaibo to Sucre) generally bright rufous above; *contrasting dusky crown with buffy white streaklike spots extending just to upper edge of mantle*; ill-defined whitish postocular stripe; wings and tail rufous chestnut, *sides of head, foreneck, and throat chalky white vaguely scaled dusky*, a few broad lancelike streaks splashed onto chest become narrower on upper breast. Or sim. but somewhat darker above and below; throat and foreneck with less white and more streaked and marked dusky (*deltanus, duidae*).
Sim. species: N birds easily told by extensive chalky white of throat and foreneck, and in all areas by very pale, straight, chisel-like bill and *streaks on head which end abruptly at edge of contrasting rufous mantle*. Striped Woodcreeper is very sim. to s birds but its bill is darker, thinner, and less chisel-like, plumage duller olivaceous brown (not so rufous), and *body entirely streaked above incl. mantle and back and more streaked below* (Straight-billed streaked only to upper mantle and more scaly below). In far s cf. Ocellated Woodcreeper.
Voice: In coastal areas (Falcón) gives impressive, although relatively brief, dawn chorus in dry season (yr-round?); also sings freq. during day. Song a rather high-pitched, nasal, and fast ser. of whistles, run together, *we-re-re-re-re-re-re-re-re-eh-eh, eh, uh*, on same pitch or descending and slowing slightly, sometimes last note or 2 ascending. Dusk song often longer and more drawn out. Song sim. in nw Amazonas.
Behavior: Single birds or prs. follow mixed-spp. flocks or forage independently of them. N of Orinoco usually rather conspic. as climb smaller trunks and limbs at low to mid. hts., often at about eye level; check bro-

ken stub ends and cracks and fissures in bark for arthropod prey. Nest of bark flakes, fairly low in broken stub, or cavity in tree or cactus; 2–3 white eggs; Apr–Aug breeding[115,119,186,734].
Status and habitat: Resident n of Orinoco in mangroves, gallery forests, and a variety of habitats ranging from desert scrub, dry forest, and dry open woodland to partially cleared humid areas with scattered trees; s of Orinoco in várzea, scrubby sandy-belt woodland, and adj. humid forest edges (not inside tall rain forest). Common in arid zones, progressively less numerous and more habitat-restricted in humid zones.

Range: To 1400m n of Orinoco; to 200m s of Orinoco. Throughout s to c Amazonas and n Bolívar. Extreme n Zulia e to e side of mouth of Lago de Maracaibo (*picirostris*); rest of Zulia, nw Táchira, and w Mérida (*saturatior*); w Falcón e to Paraguaná Pen. and n Lara (*paraguanae*); e Falcón and Carabobo e to Miranda (*choicus*); e base of Andes e to Sucre and along s bank of Orinoco in n Bolívar e to Altagracia (*phalara*); both banks of Orinoco from Ciudad Bolívar to Barrancas, Monagas (*picus*); Delta Amacuro (*deltanus*); Amazonas s to Cerro Duida and nw Bolívar in Río Cuchivero (*duidae*); Isla Margarita (*longirostris*). C Panama to n Bolivia, Amaz. Brazil, and the Guianas. Trinidad.
Note: Zimmer's Woodcreeper (*X. necopinus*) could occur in s Amazonas (specimens from upper Rio Negro, Brazil). Very like nominate Straight-billed and best told by different song, a short, fast trill, *tr'r'r'r'r'r'r'r 'r'r'r*, nasal and descending slightly in pitch (A. Whittaker recording).

Striped Woodcreeper   PLATE 37
Xiphorhynchus obsoletus   Trepador Loco
Identification: 8″ (20.3cm). 31g. Bill virtually straight (0.8–1″, 20–25mm), pale grayish, duskier on maxilla (not as pale or as long as in Straight-billed Woodcreeper). *Looks obviously striped above and below*. Mostly dull brown; crown dusky, *large drop-shaped buff streaks on crown extend over entire mantle and back*; rump, wings, and tail rufous chestnut, throat buff, this spreading onto chest and vaguely scaled dusky, rest of underparts olive brown with *numerous broad and conspic. whitish buff streaks extending to belly*. Or markings on throat and chest more scalelike (*caicarae*).
Sim. species: Most likely confused with s races of Straight-billed Woodcreeper. Smaller Lineated Woodcreeper is unstreaked above, has thin, decurved bill, and is high in canopy. Ocellated Woodcreeper has almost unstreaked back and distinctly scaled ("ocellated") throat and chest. Chestnut-rumped Wood-

creeper is larger, darker, streaked fulvous, and has longer, black bill.

Voice: Abrupt song a loud, emphatic, almost explosive rattle-trill, descending somewhat then sharply rising, *tr'e'e'a'a'a'e'e'e'e'eP!* Given a few times at dawn, only at long intervals during day.

Behavior: Single birds or prs. act much like Straight-billed Woodcreepers but typically forage even lower, mainly 0.1–6m up, where climb mostly small to med.-size trunks and limbs. Often cling beneath limbs. Generally more active than Straight-billed and more often in or near thick cover where harder to see and perhaps also shyer. BC birds, Feb–May, Nov, Amazonas[185]; in Suriname, nest in holes in palm stubs of arboreal termite nests; 2 white eggs[253].

Status and habitat: Uncommon to locally common resident in swampy or várzea forest, seasonally flooded gallery forest, and forested creek banks. Usually not far from water or wet, low-lying wooded areas. Relatively numerous along Orinoco and Río Ventuari in Amazonas.

Range: To 500m. E base of Andes from Táchira and Barinas e to s Cojedes (sight) and w across Apure to Orinoco; generally in Amazonas; Bolívar from lower Río Caura e to upper Río Caroní and Río Cuyuní (*notatus*); n Bolívar along the Orinoco from Caicara e to Altagracia (*caicarae*); Delta Amacuro (*obsoletus*); e Monagas at Río Guarapiche (subsp.?). E Colombia to n Bolivia, Amaz. Brazil, and the Guianas.

Ocellated Woodcreeper

Xiphorhynchus ocellatus   Trepador de Ocelos
Identification: 8″ (20.3cm). 35g. Bill (1.1–1.2″, 28–30mm) blackish above, pale below, thinner than in previous 2 spp. Mainly brown; crown dusky with numerous drop-shaped buff streaks, a few fine shaftlike streaks (lines) extend onto mantle (but these almost invisible in field, so *back looks unmarked at any distance)*; wings, rump, and tail rufous chestnut, throat buff faintly scaled dusky, *feathers of lower throat and chest buff roundly scalloped dusky* (distinctly scaled appearance), *rest of underparts brown and virtually unmarked*.

Sim. species: Easily confused. Fine scaling on throat and chest and essentially unmarked back and breast are good marks. In general a little less robust than previous 2 spp. Straight-billed Woodcreeper is brighter rufous with heavier pale bill and more streaked underparts. Striped Woodcreeper is boldly striped above *and* below. Very sim. Lineated Woodcreeper is almost always in canopy and has numerous crisp, linelike streaks on underparts. Also see larger and longer-billed Buff-throated and Chestnut-rumped woodcreepers.

Voice: Song in e Peru an angry or scolding ser. of hard, nasal, unmusical notes, often followed by 1–2 sharp notes and a downslurred whining sound, *qeek-qeek-qeek-qeek-qeek-qeek, CHIK! CHIK! neeea*, given rapidly. The 1st ser. or the sharp and whining notes at end are also given separately (T. Parker recording). Less vocal than most others of genus.

Behavior: Found singly or more often in loosely assoc. prs. in lower part of forest where a freq. member of lower story mixed-spp. flocks. Climb trunks or limbs and often work in tangles and cluttered areas where examine accumulations of leaves and moss for arthropod prey. Generally rather inconspic.

Status and habitat: Resident in interior of humid terra firme forest; prob. also low-lying forest transitional to várzea. There are only a small no. of specimens from Venez.

Range: To 200m. Sw Amazonas from San Fernando de Atabapo, Yavita-Pimichín trail, and Río Casiquiare southward (*ocellatus*). Se Colombia to Bolivia, w Amaz. Brazil, and along the Amazon to its mouth.
Note: Subsp. *lineatocapillus* (s Venez.) recognized by some[560].

Chestnut-rumped Woodcreeper   PLATE 37

Xiphorhynchus pardalotus   Trepador Silbador
Identification: 9″ (23cm). 37g. Bill blackish, fairly long (1.2–1.3″, 30–33mm), not esp. heavy, lower mandible almost straight. *Notably dark-looking woodcreeper.* Above brown, crown dusky, crown and sides of head with narrow buff streaks *continuing to lower back as long, drop-shaped, black-edged buff streaks*; rump, wings, and tail rufous chestnut; *throat dark cinnamon buff*, somewhat streaked dusky on lower throat, *rest of underparts dull dark brown densely and conspic. streaked fulvous* (streaks rather narrow).

Sim. species: Confusingly sim. to several others of genus. Overlaps both subspp. of Buff-throated Woodcreeper s of Orinoco, and these are, unfortunately, the races most closely resembling Chestnut-rumped. In addition to different vocalizations and habits (see below), Chestnut-rumped is *smaller* with shorter, straighter, *all-black* bill, upperparts streaked to rump (not to upper or mid. back), *underparts darker (esp. throat) with deep fulvous streaking dark and narrow* (not buffy white, broad, and spreading across chest). Buff-throated's larger size often helpful; both spp. are "rufous rumped," so rump color not helpful. Above, Chestnut-rumped is nearest Striped Woodcreeper but differs in black bill, darker plumage, and much darker (fulvous not buffy white) stripes above and below; the two prob. *do not* overlap in habitat.

Voice: Not as vocal as Buff-throated Woodcreeper. Song, most often hd. a few times at dawn and dusk, infreq. during day, a sharp, smacking ser. accelerating upward slightly, *chup!* . . *chup! chit chit-chit chee che-che-che-ee*, low pitched; or short, sharp *chup!* . . *chup! chup-cha*; longer songs may descend and slow at end; call a sharp, stuttered *duk* or *stuk-stuk* (like call of Ruddy Tody-Flycatcher but louder).

Behavior: Single birds or prs. wander alone or more often follow mixed-spp. flocks, esp. those containing *Thamnomanes* antshrikes and *Myrmotherula* antwrens. Typically rather inconspic. and forage very low, climbing on base and lower part of trunks, often starting almost on forest floor, and moving up into lower mid. level of forest; also hitch up limbs where examine mostly bark surfaces and fissures in bark, less often accumulations of suspended leaves (cf. Buff-throated Woodcreeper). Typically wary and stay in darker, more shady areas of forest than allies. In French Guiana, nest of bark flakes in tree cavity; 1 white egg[752].

Status and habitat: Uncommon to fairly common resident (easily overlooked) inside humid and wet lowland and hill forest and at forest borders. Ranges well up onto lower slopes of tepuis. Most numerous in high rainfall areas, e.g., e Bolívar.

Range: To 1800m. Throughout Amazonas (Caño Catataniapo southward) and Bolívar (*caurensis*). The Guianas and ne Brazil n of the Amazon; extreme e Colombia (recs.?).

Buff-throated Woodcreeper
PLATE 37

Xiphorhynchus guttatus Trepador Pegón

Identification: 10.5–11" (27–28cm). 64g. Bill long (1.4", 36mm), narrow, and distinctly decurved. Much like Cocoa Woodcreeper (formerly incl. with this sp.) but distinctly larger, bill all pale horn (*guttatoides*) or dusky above and pale below (*polystictus*); streaking on underparts broader (almost flammulated), darker (cinnamon buff), and with small but definite amt. of streaking on mantle.

Sim. species: See Cocoa and Chestnut-rumped woodcreepers. Also cf. Straight-billed, Striped, and Ocellated woodcreepers, all decidedly smaller with shorter, essentially straight, almost daggerlike bills. Black-banded Woodcreeper has more massive bill, finer streaking below, and barring on flanks and lower underparts. Even larger Strong-billed Woodcreeper has enormous bill and conspic. dusky malar.

Voice: Has a variety of vocalizations, and prob. in all areas has more than 1 day song. Dawn and dusk song (Río Grande) a rhythmic *chév-re, chév-re, chév-re, chév-re, chév-re*, downscale (recalls song of Strong-

billed Woodcreeper). Day song in Río Grande a fast ser. of whistles that accelerate then gradually slow, *dui-dui-kui'kui'kui'kui'kui'kui'ku'u'u'ut, ut*. Also gives (Amazonas and prob. throughout) a long, leisurely, almost lamenting ser. of accelerating notes that rise a little in middle then slow and descend, *tep, tep, tep teep-twee-tweep-tweep-tweep-teep-teep-tee-tee-toe-toe-toe*. Call or contact a loud, smacking *pyeero*, often hd. at dusk.

Behavior: Usually encountered singly or less often in loosely assoc. prs., either with mixed-spp. flocks or independent of them about equally. Hitches up sides of trunks and limbs, often starting at fairly low to moderate hts. and continuing up into more open subcanopy where it is fairly conspic. and more easily seen than some others of genus. Searches crevices and fissures in bark, and epiphytic growth, but much of prey is taken from accumulations of suspended dead leaves. Orthopterans and beetles are largest components of diet in e Peru and n Bolivia[110]. Sometimes at army ant swarms although not as freq. as *Dendrocincla*. Nest in crevice in tree or stump, usually not high; eggs white[573,752].

Status and habitat: Fairly common to common resident in humid terra firme and várzea forest, forest borders, and second-growth woodland. Generally the commonest and most freq. seen woodcreepers of Orinoco.

Range: To 500m. N Amazonas (s to Samariapo), Bolívar, sw Anzoátegui (Río Zuata), and Delta Amacuro (*polystictus*); w and s Amazonas (*guttatoides*). Se Colombia to e Bolivia, Amaz. Brazil, and the Guianas; se Brazil.

Note: See taxonomic Note under Cocoa Woodcreeper.

Cocoa Woodcreeper

Xiphorhynchus susurrans Trepador Chillón

Identification: 9" (23cm). 45g. Bill long (1.3", 33mm), somewhat decurved, *dusky above, pale below*. *Common widespread woodcreeper of n Venez*. All taxa formerly incl. in Buff-throated Woodcreeper. Mainly warm brown, crown dusky with *small, drop-shaped buff spots extending onto nape and with a few marks onto mantle* (or some birds essentially unmarked on mantle, esp. in n cordillera); rump, wings, and tail rufous chestnut, throat pale buff, rest of *underparts brown, broadly and conspic. streaked buff*. Or sim. but *bill all black and slightly longer*; lower throat and chest scaled dusky (not so obviously streaked), breast somewhat spotted buffy white, center of lower underparts vaguely barred (*jardinei* and *susurrans*).

Sim. species: Over most of range readily recognized by combination of fairly large size, streaky underparts, and long, narrow, somewhat decurved bill. Note that

amt. of streaking on back (n coastal birds have almost none) and *bill color* vary geographically. There is *little or no overlap* in range with Buff-throated Woodcreeper of mainly s of Orinoco. At higher els. see Olive-backed Woodcreeper which looks distinctly "spotted." Also see smaller, thinner-billed Streak-headed Woodcreeper. Larger Black-banded Woodcreeper has heavier, straighter, all-black bill, narrower streaks, and barred lower underparts. In gallery woodland of llanos cf. Striped Woodcreeper.
Voice: Most songs closely resemble those of Buff-throated Woodcreeper of s of Orinoco but dawn song and calls differ. Typical dawn song, in n cordillera, accelerates then slows and descends slightly, *tu-wee, tuwee, tuwee, Wee Wee, Wee, wert, wert, wert, wert, wert, wer,* with variations. Also, dawn or day, a clear, whistled *peer-peer-peer-peer-peer-peer-peerp*, downscale. Fast song of birds from Paria Pen. (*jardinei*) is thinner and more or less on same pitch; *jardinei* also sings a slow song (fewer notes) rather like other races and a loud, slow, 3-noted call (song?) that descends.
Behavior: Sim. to Buff-throated Woodcreeper. In n cordillera (Aragua) freq. found with other woodcreepers at army ant swarms. Nest of bark, wood chips, and leaf bits in tree hole or end of broken stub; 2 white eggs[39,175].
Status and habitat: Widespread and usually common resident in moist and humid forest, forest borders, shady second-growth woodland, and coffee and cocoa plantations in lowlands and foothills.

Range: To 1800m. Maracaibo Basin, Zulia; nw Táchira, n end of Andes in Lara, mts. of Falcón, and e of Andes from Táchira, Apure, Barinas, Portuguesa, and Yaracuy to n Guárico and Miranda (*nanus*); ne Anzoátegui to e Sucre (Paria Pen.) and n Monagas (*jardinei*); se Sucre (*susurrans*); Isla Margarita (*margaritae*). Guatemala to n Colombia. Trinidad.
Note: All subspp. formerly united with Buff-throated Woodcreeper, *X. guttatus*[403]; recently separated based on differences in size and voice[545]. Subsp. *demonstratus* (nw Táchira) synonymous with *nanus*[559].

Olive-backed Woodcreeper   PLATE 37
Xiphorhynchus triangularis   Trepador Lomiaceituno
Identification: 9" (23cm). 41g. Bill long (1.2", 30mm), slightly decurved, dusky above, bluish gray below. *Distinctive spotted appearance.* Mostly olive brown, crown duskier and finely spotted buffy white, *fairly prom. buffy white eyering* and vague whitish postocular mark; rest of upperparts with only a few faint spotlike streaks extending to mid. back (looks essentially unmarked in field), wings and tail brownish rufous, throat dirty buffy

white scaled dusky, *rest of underparts olive brown prom. spotted buffy white.*
Sim. species: No other woodcreeper in Venez. highlands looks so spotted below. Note obvious pale eyering.
Voice: Infreq. hd. call a sharp, penetrating, and slurred *wEEeeeeu.* "Loudsong" a hard *we we we-we-we-we-we-WE-WE-We-we wa*, accelerating then slowing[412]. Faintsong a weak, nasal *quee, quee QUEE-que'e'e'e*, accelerating into slow trill at end, often over and over.
Behavior: Quiet and inconspic., seen singly or in prs. and usually with mixed-spp. flocks. Diligently climbs moss- or partly moss-covered trunks of various sizes, and larger mossy limbs. Forages much more by inspecting moss than bare wood surfaces; ranges from understory to subcanopy, but more often at mid. level or higher.
Status and habitat: Uncommon to locally fairly common resident (inconspic.) inside humid and wet forest (cloud forest), infreq. forest borders.

Range: 1000–2500m. Sierra de Perijá, Zulia; Andes of Táchira and Mérida (*triangularis*); Andes of Trujillo and se Lara; mts. of Yaracuy and n cordilleras e to Miranda and Distr. Federal (*hylodromus*). Colombia s in Andes to n Bolivia.

Lepidocolaptes

Rather small and slender; thin, decurved bill; crisp linear streaking below (also above in some spp.); 3 Venez. spp. largely allopatric in distrib.

Streak-headed Woodcreeper   PLATE 37
Lepidocolaptes souleyetii   Trepadorcito Listado
Identification: 7.5–8" (19–20.3cm). 23g. *Slender, reddish bill slightly decurved* (1", 25mm). *Overall has pale, "faded" appearance.* Crown and nape dusky finely streaked buff, sides of head somewhat streaked with buffy white, back light reddish brown sometimes also with a few buff streaks; wings, rump, and tail rufous, throat buffy white, rest of underparts brown *broadly and distinctly streaked with dusky-edged whitish streaks.*
Sim. species: In n Venez. a slender and streaky little woodcreeper of dry or light woodland is likely to be this sp. Look for thin, reddish bill (cf. Straight-billed Woodcreeper). In se Bolívar cf. closely with Lineated Woodcreeper which has dark bill (not reddish), darker upperparts, plain or dotted (not streaked) crown, and is usually inside forest.
Voice: Song a high-pitched, thin, flat trill, *p'e'e'e'e'e'e 'eeeeaaa*, rapid and descending throughout, ca. 2–2.5 sec. Alarm a short, flat rattle-trill.
Behavior: Occurs singly or in loosely assoc. prs. that are most likely to be seen alone in lightly wooded

areas; also sometimes with mixed-spp. flocks containing woodpeckers, other woodcreepers, small flycatchers, and greenlets. Climbs trunks from low to high and hitches out beneath high limbs to search bare bark surfaces and tiny crevices. Nest in hole or broken stub, lined with pieces of bark; Jun–Jul breeding, Guárico and Anzoátegui[186,734]; 2 white eggs[39].

Status and habitat: Common and widespread resident along forest borders, gallery forests, light open woodland, plantations, and cleared areas with scattered trees, mostly in dry to moist regions. Replaced in tall humid forest by Lineated Woodcreeper.

Range: To 1600m n of Orinoco; to 1100m s of Orinoco. W base of Andes in Táchira and Mérida; e base in Táchira and w Barinas (*lineaticeps*); rest of Venez. n of Orinoco and s of it in n and c Bolívar (Río Cuchivero to El Palmar) s to Río Paragua (*littoralis*); Bolívar at s end of Gran Sabana (*uaireni*). Mexico to nw Peru and e to extreme n Brazil (n Roraima); Guyana (sight). Trinidad.

Montane Woodcreeper PLATE 37
Lepidocolaptes lacrymiger Trepador Gamusita
Identification: 7.5″ (19cm). Slender, grayish horn bill (1″, 25mm) slightly decurved. *Brighter, more sharply focused streaking than previous sp.* Above rufescent brown, crown dusky finely spotted buff white; ill-defined whitish postocular stripe, rest of upperparts unstreaked; throat whitish somewhat scaled dusky, rest of underparts light brown with *long, sharply defined black-edged white streaks* forming bold and linear pattern of streaking.
Sim. species: Occurs above range of Streak-headed Woodcreeper. Sometimes with larger, more robust Olive-backed Woodcreeper which is distinctly spotted on head and underparts.
Voice: Unlike many woodcreepers, rather quiet. Infreq. hd. song (also unlike allies and not loud) a thin, high-pitched, and chattery *swit-swit-swit-swiz-swiz'is 'is'it'it't't't*, accelerating at end. More likely mistaken for a *Terenura* antwren or *Thraupis* tanager. Song a little smoother in n cordilleras.
Behavior: Single birds or prs. are almost always seen following mixed-spp. flocks in upper levels and canopy of forest where they climb trunks and spend much time hitching along beneath mossy or partly bare limbs. Probe beneath and glean from moss and lichens, also less freq. from bark surfaces, small cracks, and fissures for arthropod prey. Nest in natural cavity or cranny in tree, or in old woodpecker hole, low to high; white eggs[260,573].

Status and habitat: Common resident in humid and wet montane forest (cloud forest) and stunted forest almost up to treeline; also forest borders and tall second growth. Some seasonal movements to lower els., esp. in rainy months.

Range: 900–2900m (most recs. above 1500m). Sierra de Perijá, Zulia; Andes from Táchira n to se Lara (*lacrymiger*); Coastal Cordillera from Carabobo to Distr. Federal and Miranda; mts. of sw Sucre on Cerro Papelón (*lafresnayi*). Mts. of Colombia s to Bolivia.
Note: Formerly called Spot-crowned Woodcreeper, *L. affinis*; does not incl. birds of C Amer.[10,545]

Lineated Woodcreeper PLATE 43
Lepidocolaptes albolineatus Trepadorcito Goteado
Identification: 7″ (18cm). 24g. Slender, decurved bill (0.9″, 23mm). Small and sharply patterned below. *Above plain brown*, crown dusky brown finely spotted buffy white (or slightly larger, crown unspotted—*duidae*); wings, rump, and tail somewhat rufous; throat dull white, rest of underparts grayish brown with *numerous narrow black-edged whitish streaks* forming conspic. and distinct linear pattern of streaking.
Sim. species: In field looks uniform brown above (dots on crown difficult to see; or lacking in south). Note small size, thin bill, and canopy habitat. In e Bolívar cf. Streak-headed Woodcreeper which is *very sim.* but paler above with streaky crown and upper back, reddish bill, and fondness for dry open woodland. Cf. larger, heavier-billed Striped, Straight-billed, and Ocellated woodcreepers.
Voice: Two song types: birds of w Amazonas sing a rapid, nasal, and descending *pe-pee-pee-pee-peer-peer-peer-pear*, high and thin in quality. In e Bolívar (*albolineatus*) sings a faster but *chattery* ser. of notes (ca. 20 notes in 2 sec) that rises slightly then falls in pitch, and is much lower in pitch than song of w birds. In all areas songs given at rather long intervals.
Behavior: Single birds or prs. are most often seen with canopy mixed-spp. flocks where they climb trunks and

limbs and hitch along underside of limbs high in canopy of tall forest. Often work quite far out beneath limbs where peer and pick at bark or chip or flake off tiny pieces of bark. Nest in tree cavity in French Guiana[752].

Status and habitat: Fairly common resident but easily overlooked, except for occas. song, in tall humid terra firme forest in Amazonas; prob. also várzea forest; generally less numerous in e Bolívar.

Range: To 1300m. Throughout Amazonas; w and s Bolívar from lower Río Caura (sight) to headwaters of Río Caroní (*duidae*); ne Bolívar from Sierra de Imataca (Río Grande) and Río Yuruán (tributary of mid. Río Cuyuní) s to base of Sierra de Lema at El Venamo (*albolineatus*); ne Monagas (sight, Caño Colorado)[60]. The Guianas to e Ecuador, e Peru, n Bolivia, and Amaz. Brazil (doubtless also se Colombia).

Note: Amaz. subspp. incl. *duidae*, and Guianan subspp. incl. *albolineatus* prob. represent separate spp.

Campylorhamphus

Long, thin, strikingly decurved bill; streaked plumage quite sim. in all spp.; mostly allopatric in distribution.

Red-billed Scythebill   PLATE 37
Campylorhamphus trochilirostris   Trepador Pico de Garfio

Identification: 9″ (23cm). 36g. *Very long, narrow bill* (cord 2.4″, 61mm) *reddish and sickle shaped*. Above light reddish brown, crown duskier, head and upperparts to mid. back narrowly but sharply streaked buff, rump, wings, and tail rufous chestnut contrasting with back; below plain brown, throat and breast streaked buff, more broadly than on upperparts (streaks sometimes dusky edged).

Sim. species: Most widespread scythebill in Venez. and the one most likely to be seen. Rare Brown-billed Scythebill has shorter, reddish brown bill and darker plumage. S of Orinoco see Curve-billed Scythebill, a darker bird in every aspect, less streaked above (streaks narrow, obscure, and extending only to mantle, not to mid. back), head streaking fine, and underparts somewhat spotted (spotlike streaks).

Voice: Dawn song (Portuguesa), almost continually for 5–10 min in dry season, a rapid, descending whinny, *we'he'he'he'he'he'he'e'e'e'e'e*; at dawn in n Aragua a loud, fast, sharply rising rattle, *stri'i'i'i'i'i'TI'I'K!*, emphatic and sometimes doubled. Both rising and descending songs sometimes given by same individual (context?).

Behavior: Typically rather wary and not apt to remain in view for long. Single birds or prs. forage alone or follow mixed-spp. flocks about equally. Like other woodcreepers climb trunks and limbs at almost all hts., but sometimes, esp. in dry forest, spend much of time very low, even on or near gd. Probe with long bill into holes and crevices in trees, stubs, and fallen logs; occas. peer at and probe into bromeliads or other epiphytic growth. Prey incl. many soft-bodied items such as spiders. Nest in cavity or broken stub or stump; eggs white[589].

Status and habitat: Fairly common resident in wide variety of wooded habitats incl. dry deciduous forest, gal-

lery forest, open woodlots, forest borders, and humid and wet premontane forest, even mossy cloud forest. Most numerous in gallery forest in llanos and in wet mt. forests of n cordilleras.

Range: To 2000m n of Orinoco; to 950m s of Orinoco. Throughout n of Orinoco from Zulia to Sucre (incl. Paria Pen.), n Monagas, sw Anzoátegui and s to Orinoco; n Bolívar locally to headwaters of Río Caura, Río Paragua, and Río Caroní at Hato Santa Teresa (*venezuelensis*). N Colombia to n Brazil; w Ecuador and nw Peru; locally across Amaz. Brazil to n Argentina.

Curve-billed Scythebill   PLATE 37
Campylorhamphus procurvoides   Trepador Pico de Hoz

Identification: 8.5″ (22cm). 30g. Very long, narrow bill (cord 2.4″, 61mm), *about same color and length* as in Red-billed Scythebill. Plumage much like Red-billed Scythebill but darker. Above uniform dark reddish brown, head to upper mantle (not to mid. back) finely streaked buff (at any distance looks unmarked), below dark reddish brown with *narrow spotlike buff streaks* to upper belly; generally looks more spotted, esp. on throat, less obviously streaked, and overall markings not as distinct as in Red-billed Scythebill.

Sim. species: In range overlaps only Red-billed Scythebill, but the two do not share same habitats (deforestation may bring them in contact).

Voice: Song, a few times briefly at dawn, a melancholy and lamenting *kuweee, kuwee, kwee wee-wee-we-we-we*, on same pitch, accelerating fractionally, and ending abruptly (P. Schwartz recording).

Behavior: An inconspic. bird of mid. levels in rain forest interior where usually seen with mixed-spp. flocks. Hitches creeperlike, mostly up small to med.-sized trunks and more or less upright limbs and checks crevices and broken ends of twigs and stubs. Like others of genus, wary and often hard to see.

Status and habitat: Uncommon resident (easily overlooked) in tall humid and wet terra firme forest in low-

lands and foothills. Found with some reg. in Río Grande region of ne Bolívar.
Range: To 450m (sight to 900m, Sierra de Lema—J. Pierson; D. Ascanio; Hilty). S Amazonas from Yavita-Pimichín and Río Casiquiare southward; ne Bolívar from Sierra de Imataca s to upper Río Cuyuní (*sanus*); ne Monagas (sight, Caño Colorado[60]). Se Colombia, ne Peru, Amaz. Brazil, and the Guianas.

Brown-billed Scythebill
Campylorhamphus pusillus   Trepador Piquicurvado
Identification: 8.5–9" (22–23cm). 40g. Very long, narrow bill (cord 2", 51mm) *reddish brown to dusky brown, often paler at base.* Plumage much like Red-billed Scythebill but darker, overall dark wood brown, narrowly streaked rich buff to mid. of back and upper belly.
Sim. species: Best told by range (little or no overlap with Red-billed Scythebill); Brown-billed has duller bill (not reddish), often pale at base. In hand, plumage darker and streaking darker and without dusky edges.
Voice: Seldom hd. song somewhat variable but typically a tremulous, almost wailing *twee-twee-weo-WEO-WEO-weo-weo-weo-wee-we-we-we*, loudest in middle, successive songs often more or less connected by soft *twe* and *we* notes or little trills.
Behavior: In Colombia 1–2 reg. follow mixed-spp. flocks and climb trunks and hitch out on mossy undersides of branches to probe crevices, moss, epiphytes, base of palm fronds, etc., in mid. strata or subcanopy, occas. lower. Usually not on bare trunks or limbs. Like other scythebills, rather wary and often difficult to see well.
Status and habitat: Resident in humid and wet forest, esp. mossy forest, occas. forest borders and older second growth. Prob. uncommon; at least 12 or more specimens from its small range in Venez.

Range: 1800–2175m. Sierra de Perijá, Zulia, and Andes of s Táchira in Río Chiquito (*tachirensis*). Costa Rica and Panama; W Colombia to n Peru.

Thamnophilidae: Typical Antbirds

Hormigueros

Antbirds are a large and diverse family of suboscine passeriforms found only in the Neotropics. They reach their greatest diversity in the Amazonian region, with only a few species occurring as far north as southern Mexico and as far south as northern Argentina. Recent biochemical evidence[604] has shown that the original

Formicariidae family is actually composed of 2 fairly discrete groups best placed in separate families. They are the Thamnophilidae, a primarily arboreal group of antbirds, and the Formicariidae, a mainly terrestrial group. The 2 families also differ in degree of sexual dimorphism, which is marked in most Thamnophilidae but not in the Formicariidae. Thamnophilidae occur primarily in lowland and premontane forests, with few occurring much above middle elevations in the Andes; several Formicariidae live at very high elevations, a few even above treeline. Despite their name, relatively few antbirds are persistently associated with ants, and none regularly feeds on ants. A small number of species, mainly in the genera *Percnostola*, *Myrmeciza*, *Pithys*, *Gymnopithys*, *Hylophylax*, *Phaenostictus*, and *Phlegopsis*, follow army ants, mainly the ant *Eciton burchelli*. The birds use the raiding ant swarms as beaters, capturing prey flushed by the ants which forage on or near the forest floor. All members of the family, whether they are specialized army ant followers or not, feed on arthropods. The English names of many genera, e.g., antshrikes, antwrens, antvireos, suggest their similarity to groups of north temperate latitude birds familiar to the people naming them, but these names are not necessarily accurate reflections of the birds' behavior. The calls of antbirds are generally simple and unvarying, a reflection of their primitive syringeal anatomy compared to oscine songbirds. Nevertheless, the songs are often loud and distinctive and usually given by both sexes, and they are often the only indication of a bird's presence. Nests are varied, often simple suspended baskets; a few are pensile pouches or are in cavities. Much of what is known about antbirds in life is due to the pioneering studies of E. O. Willis[804,806] and references in the following species accounts.

Cymbilaimus

Large and robust; heavy bill; finely barred plumage.

Fasciated Antshrike   PLATE 40
Cymbilaimus lineatus   Hormiguerote Barreteado
Identification: 7" (18cm). 37g. Robust body; heavy, hooked, mostly black bill; eyes ruby red. ♂: above *black finely barred* (etched) *all over with white*, crown black (or with a few white bars on forehead—*intermedius*); barring slightly broader on breast and belly. ♀: above incl. tail black finely barred buff, crown chestnut, underparts buff finely and evenly barred black.
Sim. species: ♂ Barred Antshrike is much more coarsely barred (looks whiter) and not found inside tall forest; ♀ Barred Antshrike is unstreaked except for sides of head.
Voice: Song a slow ser. of 4–6 soft resonant whistles, *cüwe-cüwe-cüwe-cüwe-cüwe*, notably ventriloquial. Alarm a short, hard, staccato rattle.
Behavior: A rather aloof sp. that tends to remain sequestered in vine tangles in forest mid. levels or higher, but occas. much lower and will rarely even chase flushed prey to gd. Usually in prs. which remain somewhat apart from one another. Movements are rather deliberate as they hop and peer in foliage for

large arthropods. Generally remain within vines or cover where easily overlooked unless singing or noted with mixed-spp. flocks. Rarely at army ants. Loosely woven nest 2–8m up; fastened by rim to a sapling; 2 creamy white eggs spotted dark brown and lilac[651,790].
Status and habitat: Uncommon to fairly common resident high in vine-tangled forest borders or vines around treefalls inside forest; also second-growth woodland and dense foliage along streams.

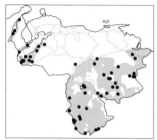

Range: To 1300m. Base of Sierra de Perijá, Zulia, w base of Andes in Táchira and Mérida; e base from Táchira n to nw Barinas and Portuguesa; throughout Amazonas and w Bolívar (*intermedius*); e Bolívar (*lineatus*). Se Honduras to n Bolivia, Amaz. Brazil, and the Guianas.
Note: Subsp. *brangeri* of Sierra de Perijá[18] not recognized.

Frederickena

Large; strong bill; robust proportions with fairly short tail; flat nuchal crest not obvious; tail rounded, graduated; low density and infreq. seen.

Black-throated Antshrike   PLATE 40
Frederickena viridis   Hormiguero Rayado Copetón
Identification: 8.5″ (22cm). 73g. Big, robust antshrike with long, flat crest. Heavy, mostly black bill; eyes ruby red (both sexes). ♂: *crown, throat, and chest black*, rest of body slate gray, small concealed white interscapular patch; tail faintly barred white. ♀: crown chestnut, back and wings bright reddish brown, tail black barred whitish, *forehead, sides of head, and entire underparts finely and evenly barred black and white*. Imm. ♂: like ♀ above but rufous gradually replaced by slate gray.
Sim. species: ♂ recalls several other "gray" antbirds but is much larger and darker than any. Cf. ♀ to ♀ Fasciated Antshrike which is barred *above* and below, and to smaller ♂ Barred Antshrike.
Voice: ♂'s song a slow, almost hypnotic ser. of clear, insistent whistles, *peeeur, peeeur, peeur . . .* , at a steady pace (ca. 12 notes in 7 sec), sometimes growing a little stronger as it goes along. ♀'s song sim. but slightly higher pitched. Alarm a low growling *churr*.
Behavior: A shy, skulking bird that stays in forest undergrowth and hops and peers in foliage in deliberate fashion. Lives in prs. that are often widely separated from neighboring prs. (or territories may be large). As in most antshrikes, tail is pounded downward with each note as bird sings. Occas. at army ant swarms.

Nest an open basket in fork of twiggy branch low in shrub; 2 creamy white eggs with purplish hairlines and spots[253] (A. Whittaker).
Status and habitat: Rare and local resident in humid and wet terra firme forest in lowlands; esp. near small, vine-tangled forest openings, or around older treefalls filled with vines, saplings, and regrowth vegetation. Has been found along road from San Isidro (El 88) w to Río Cuyuní in e Bolívar.

Range: To 500m. E Bolívar from lower Río Caura, mid. Río Paragua (Cerro Guaiquinima), and Sierra de Imataca s to upper Río Paragua (Salto Maijía) and Río Caroní headwaters; upper Río Cuyuní (sight). The Guianas and ne Brazil n of the Amazon.

Taraba

Monotypic genus; widespread; fairly long, heavy bill; tail rounded and strongly graduated; bicolored plumage; shrubby areas.

Great Antshrike   PLATE 40
Taraba major   Batara Mayor
Identification: 8″ (20.3cm). 56g. *Eyes fire red* (both sexes); heavy, hooked, black bill; slight crest. ♂: above jet black with white tipping on wing coverts forming about 3 bars; concealed white interscapular patch; tail solid black, primaries usually edged white (*granadensis*). Or all tail feathers barred with white, underparts incl. crissum immaculate white (*semifasciata*). Or central pr. of tail feathers solid black, rest coarsely barred with white; crissum grayish white (*duidae*). ♀: bright rufous chestnut above incl. tail; lores and cheeks tinged dusky, underparts white, flanks and belly tinged reddish brown; crissum dull cinnamon brown. Or crissum bright cinnamon (*semifasciata*).
Sim. species: In both sexes distinctive "bicolored" appearance and brilliant red eyes (like red "plastic" buttons) are unique.
Voice: Song, by both sexes, a long, accelerating ("bouncing ball") ser. of nasal chuckling notes, *Cuk, Cuk, cuk, cuk, cuk-cuk-cuk-cukcukcukcukcucucu-waaa*, snarled note at end is usually characteristic but varies in intensity and emphasis and is occas. left off. Also various low growls, *cah* notes, and a throaty alarm rattle.
Behavior: Usually in prs. that are not esp. furtive but hop around rather deliberately in low vine tangles and thickets and generally keep out of sight. Peer and peck for fairly large arthropod prey from mostly live foliage and twigs and occas. take small vertebrates. Sing from

within cover. Not with mixed-spp. flocks; infreq. at army ants. Bulky open cup nest suspended by rim, 1.5–2.5m up in thicket; 2 eggs, dull white to cream marked with dark brown spots and lilac streaks[647].
Status and habitat: Fairly common resident in overgrown clearings, young second growth, and bushes and thickets in moist to humid forest borders, locally in dry (but not arid) regions.

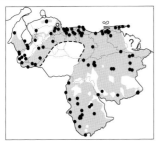

Range: To 1900m (mostly below 1500m). Throughout. Maracaibo Basin, Zulia; e of Andes from e Táchira, w Apure, Barinas, and c and se Falcón (Sierra de San Luis) e to ne Miranda (*granadensis*); se Miranda and Guárico e to Sucre (Paria Pen.), Monagas, Delta Amacuro, and generally in Amazonas and Bolívar (*semifasciata*); up to 2200m in s Amazonas (Cerro de la Neblina) and sw Bolívar on Cerro Jaua (*duidae*). S Mexico to n Argentina and se Brazil.

Sakesphorus

Usually show prom. crest (small crest in some spp.); bold black and white plumage patterns; drier regions or edge habitat in Venez.

Black-crested Antshrike
PLATE 40
Sakesphorus canadensis   Hormiguero Copetón
Identification: 6.2″ (15.7cm). 24g. *Conspic. bushy crest.* ♂: entire *head, neck, and chest black tapering to a point on lower breast*; narrow *whitish nuchal collar extends down sides of neck* to grayish lower underparts; back reddish brown, wings black, wing coverts spotted and edged white forming 3 bars; inner flight feathers edged white; tail black, the feathers tipped and edged white (*intermedius*). Or sim. but face and throat frosted with white and sides, flanks, and lower underparts white (*pulchellus*). Or overall paler, back grayish brown, crest black, rest of head, neck, and breast heavily mixed white, flanks and lower underparts white (*phainoleucus*). ♀: bushy *crest rufous chestnut*; sides of head buff speckled black, rest of upperparts light brown, wings black, wing coverts spotted and edged white forming 3 bars; *tail blackish* tipped and edged white; underparts buff, palest on throat and belly; *varying amt. of ill-defined black streaking on chest and breast* (*intermedius*). Or sim. but upperparts bright cinnamon rufous; below bright cinnamon only lightly streaked (*puchellus*).
Sim. species: Either sex is nearest Black-backed Antshrike which is much less numerous and confined to dry zones of nw.

Voice: Often hd. song, by both sexes (higher in ♀), an accelerating and ascending ser. of bouncy nasal notes, *cuew, cuew-cue-cue-cue-cut-cut-cu'cu'cu'cu 'cuét*. Songs of w races (*phainoleucus; pulchellus*) sim. but may end with 2–3 lower-pitched snarl notes at end (D. Ascanio).
Behavior: Prs. or families peer and hop about in thickets and bushes or ascend into canopy of dry, deciduous woodland. Inconspic. but not difficult to see. Often with small mixed-spp. flocks of antwrens, flycatchers, and greenlets. Thin-walled cup nest suspended by rim to low fork; 2 white eggs spotted reddish brown; breeding Jun–Sep, Orinoco region[115]; Jul, Guárico[734].
Status and habitat: Common resident in dry to moist regions. Scrubby or brushy vegetation in desert scrub, semiarid vegetation, dry deciduous woodland, gallery forests, and mangroves; also forest borders (esp. vine tangles) in humid regions. May occur with Black-backed Antshrike in dry areas, but that sp. favors denser, more viny areas.

Range: To ca. 800m. Locally throughout except s Amazonia. Goajira Pen. of nw Zulia e across Falcón and n Lara (*phainoleucus*); w and s Zulia southward (*pulchellus*); e Zulia (subsp.?); e base of Andes from e Táchira, w Apure, Barinas, and e Falcón e to Miranda, and s to n Amazonas (s to Pto. Yapacana) and nw Bolívar to Santa Elena de Uairén (*intermedius*); e Anzoátegui to e Sucre, Monagas, and Delta Amacuro (*trinitatis*); s Amazonas along Río Casiquiare (*fumosus*). N Colombia to n Brazil and the Guianas; very locally in se Colombia, ne Peru, and sw Brazil. Trinidad.
Note: Subsp. *paraguanae* is synonym for *phainoleucus*[467].

Black-backed Antshrike
PLATE 40
Sakesphorus melanonotus   Hormiguero Espalda Negra
Identification: 6.3″ (16cm). 25g. Small, flattish crest. Bill black. ♂: *entire head and upperparts black* (concealed white interscapular patch in both sexes), 3 white wing bars, prom. white-edged tertials and white edgings on upper tail coverts; tail tipped and edged white, *below black, flanks and belly white*, under tail coverts tipped white. ♀: slightly crested crown *dusky* edged brown, *prom. buff eyering*; back light brown, wings coverts with *3 buff bars*, flight feathers blackish heavily edged buff, *tail dull rufous*, sides of head and underparts dull buff, faint *dusky mottling on chest*.
Sim. species: ♂ most likely confused with Black-crested Antshrike which is much more crested and has white collar and extensive white on underparts. ♀ Black-crested has *prom.* rufous crest (not small dusky

brown crest) and blackish tail. Note ♀ Black-backed's prom. eyering.

Voice: Unlike other antshrikes, a laconic and sotto voce singer. Territorial song a single soft *cuua*, also a short, nasal roll, *qurrrrr*. Also gives a short nasal *caaaaa*, a nasal grunting, rolled *gur'r'a*, and soft nasal *cahunk*? (or *ca-who*?).

Behavior: A rather grave and prosaic sp. that is quiet, slow moving, and inconspic. Prs. act heavy-gaited and lethargic as they hop methodically ca. 0.2–6m up in tangled and scrubby woodland and peer at foliage for arthropods, and may drop to gd., even hop on gd., and occas. follow army ants. Territories are rather small. Tail held down and constantly flicked downward, then slowly raised. Fairly conspic. open cup nest of course material suspended in small fork 0.6m up, Mar (R. Ridgely); breeds Mar–Jul, n Colombia[260].

Status and habitat: Uncommon and local resident (narrow habitat requirements) in dense vines in dry to moist, low-canopied (<10m) dry forest and cut-over or disturbed woodland in arid to dry regions. Dense vines are key. Good places to find sp. are e end of PN Morrocoy and e foothills of Sierra de San Luis, Falcón.

Range: To 1300m (most recs. below 500m). Nw Zulia s to Río Palmar and e locally in arid regions to e Miranda (Cabo Codera), s Lara (vicinity of Barquisimeto), and Yaracuy; s on e side of Maracaibo Basin to Táchira (Ureña). Coastal and ne Colombia (s to Norte de Santander).

Thamnophilus

Heavy but fairly short bill with prom. hook at tip; sexes differ, ♂♂ mostly black and/or dark gray or with barring, ♀♀ paler, often brownish; obscure to prom. bushy crest; wings squarish; mostly lower strata inside or at edge of dry to humid forest.

Barred Antshrike   PLATE 40
Thamnophilus doliatus   Pavita Hormiguera Común
Identification: 6.5″ (16.5cm). 25g. Eyes yellow. Rather bushy, disheveled crest (both sexes). ♂ wears "prisoner's garb" of black and white bars. ♂: crown black, base of central feathers white, sides of head streaked, and rest of *upperparts coarsely barred black and white*, underparts white coarsely barred black. ♀: crown chestnut, upperparts bright to dark rufous, *sides of head and nape streaked blackish and buff*, breast uniform cinnamon, palest on throat. Or sim. but ♂ blacker (white barring much narrower than black), ♀ darker above and below (*nigrescens*).
Sim. species: In most of Venez. ♂ is unique, but in Sierra de Perijá see very sim. ♂ Bar-crested Antshrike. ♀

recalls ♀ Black-crested Antshrike but has no white on wings, no streaking below, and tail all rufous (not blackish). ♀ Bar-crested Antshrike is barred below.

Voice: Freq. hd. song, by both sexes, a nasal, accelerating *hu, hu hu hu, hu'hu'hu'u'u'u-wank*, usually accompanied by varying amts. of display (below); occas. a nasal, strained *cuee, ueee, ueee*, upscale; a low growl, *graaaaa*, is typical of genus.

Behavior: A "colorful" personality and a perennial favorite. Like the class "clown," ♂ rapidly bobs and bows stiffly with crest raised and tail held depressed, spread and vibrating with each note as he sings his chuckling song. ♀♀ answer with less swagger and animation. Prs. maintain relatively small territories, forage mostly 1–6m up, and tend to keep out of sight. Hop heavily within vegetation and peer and glean for large arthropods which they take from leaves and twigs like most other antshrikes; occas. follow army ants. Deep, thin-walled, open cup or bag nest of fibers suspended by rim from fork 1–9m up; 2 white eggs spotted dark brown or gray[790]; 1 nest in May, w Apure[137].

Status and habitat: Widespread and common resident in shrubby forest borders, overgrown clearings, thickets, and other successional vegetation. Rarely or never inside mature humid forest, unlike on isl. of Tobago. Found in dry and humid regions.

Range: To 2000m (most recs. below 1250m). Maracaibo region of Zulia and adj. Táchira and w Mérida (*nigrescens*); rest of Venez. s to s Amazonas (San Carlos de Río Negro), and n Bolívar e to Ciudad Bolívar; Isla Margarita (*fraterculus*); ne Bolívar from lower Río Paragua to Delta Amacuro (*doliatus*). S Mexico to w Peru, n Argentina, and se Brazil. Trinidad and Tobago.

Bar-crested Antshrike
Thamnophilus multistriatus   Pavita Hormiguera Coronipintada
Identification: 6.5″ (16.5cm). 28g. ♂: very sim. to ♂ Barred Antshrike but less crested; small *crest black conspic. barred white* (not black with white at base of crest), *upperparts blacker* with narrow white bars (but in area of overlap both spp. have narrow white barring), *tail* ca. 0.5″ (13mm) *longer and with more* (8–9 vs. 4–5) *narrow white bars*. ♀: above mostly rufous chestnut (darker than ♀ Barred Antshrike), sides of head and throat black streaked white, *rest of underparts narrowly barred black and white*, flanks and belly tinged rufous.
Sim. species: ♂ nearly identical to ♂ Barred Antshrike and best told by accompanying ♀ which is barred (not plain below).

Voice: Much like Barred Antshrike but lazier and with marked acceleration at end; typically 6–10 notes, *dü, dü dü dü du du-du-da'da.*

Behavior: Sim. to Barred Antshrike although more often seen higher in trees. Breeding evidence Mar–Jun, Colombia[260].

Status and habitat: In Colombia, where locally a fairly common resident, found in shrubby borders of dry to humid forest and in clearings, parks, and cultivated areas with thickets and trees. Generally replaced at lower els. by Barred Antshrike. Limited distrib. in Venez. and no recent recs. (1 specimen taken 1951).

Range: 1650m. Known only from upper Río Negro (Cerro Jamayaujaina), Sierra de Perijá, Zulia (*oecotonophilus*). Interandean valleys of Colombia (400–2200m; mainly above 900m).

Blackish-gray Antshrike PLATE 41
Thamnophilus nigrocinereus Choca Cenicienta

Identification: 6.5" (16.5cm). 27g. Strong, hooked bill; eyes reddish brown. ♂: crown black, back slaty mixed black with concealed white interscapular patch; wings black with narrow white fringing on scapulars and wing coverts forming several bars (at least 2 prom. ones); flight feathers narrowly edge white, tail black *narrowly tipped white*, sides of head and underparts uniform gray. ♀: crown to below eyes slate gray (darkest on crown), *back, wings, and tail uniform dark rufescent brown* (wing coverts faintly edged cinnamon but essentially no bars or edgings), *underparts orange rufous*, paler and browner on belly.

Sim. species: ♂ resembles several other essentially "black and gray" antbirds and is most easily told by presence of ♀ or by voice, but it is *only large antbird with white fringing (rather than spots) on wing coverts.* ♂ White-shouldered Antshrike and Caura Antbird are blacker and have only small white dots on wing coverts. ♂♂ of Eastern Slaty- and Amazonian antshrikes are *much paler gray* overall (Amazonian has all-gray head) and have bolder white markings on wings and tail. Also cf. ♂ Spot-winged Antshrike. ♀ most resembles ♀ Caura Antbird, but note essentially uniform brown wings (no spots).

Voice: Song a low, nasal, and hollow *keeook. . keok, keok-ku-ku-ku'ku'ku*, accelerating and descending slightly in pitch; trogonlike. Calls incl. a low, complaining *caw* and churring growl, *ur-r-r-r-r-r.*

Behavior: Prs. lead rather quiet and inconspic. lives in undergrowth vegetation, staying mostly at about eye level or a little higher as they hop, with deliberate movements, and peer about in foliage much like others of genus. Occas. move down near or on gd. Incon-

spic. but not esp. secretive, and rarely with small mixed-spp. flocks. Mar breeding, upper Orinoco[185].

Status and habitat: Fairly common resident very locally in scrubby, low-canopied, white sandy soil forest or woodland (canopy 4–10m), esp. in zones that are seasonally flooded, and in gallery forest along seasonally flooded creeks; also sometimes in moderate to dense scrub in nonflooded regions, less often at edges of taller lateritic (red) soil forests.

Range: To 200m (once to 400m at Piedra del Cucuy, sw Amazonas). Locally throughout w Amazonas; lower Río Caura, Bolívar (*cinereoniger*). E Colombia and Río Negro and lower Amazon Basin of Brazil.

White-shouldered Antshrike PLATE 41
Thamnophilus aethiops Choca Lomiblanca

Identification: 6.2" (15.7cm). 26g. Heavy bill; eyes reddish brown (always?). ♂: almost entirely dark gray with black crown, wings, and tail; *several rows of small white dots on wing coverts*, bend of wing white (no white interscapular patch in Venez. subsp.). ♀: *above uniformly dark rufous chestnut* (no markings on wings or tail, no interscapular patch), below paler somewhat more orange chestnut.

Sim. species: Both sexes easily mistaken, but ♂ is darker and has less prom. white shoulder dots than any antshrike or antbird in Venez.; ♀ is uniform and shows no markings. Cf. esp. both sexes of large and habitat-restricted Caura Antbird, also Blackish-gray and Amazonian antshrikes, Eastern Slaty-Antshrike, and Spot-winged Antbird.

Voice: Song a low, steady ser. of ca. 6 *very nasal* notes, *aunk, unk, unk, . . .* (ca. 3 notes/sec), trogonlike. Also a nasal *ahh* or *raah*, typical of genus.

Behavior: A rather solitary antshrike, typically skulking and at times can be devilishly cunning in its ability to remain out of sight. Usually found alone or in prs. in tangled or dense patches of vegetation, mostly 1–6m up, in forest understory. Does not follow mixed-spp. flocks. Peers and hops with deliberate movements much like others of genus.

Status and habitat: Uncommon and local resident (widely separated prs.) in vine tangles and esp. around older treefalls or light gaps inside tall humid forest, and along shrubby forest borders. Elsewhere (s of the Amazon in Brazil) reg. in bamboo-filled light gaps (K. Zimmer).

Range: To 400m (once to 860m, Cerro Jaua, sw Bolívar). Generally in Amazonas; n Bolívar from lower Río Caura and Río Paragua e to Río Caroní headwaters at Icabarú (*polionotus*). Extreme e Colombia to ne

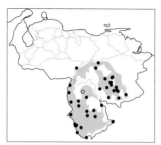

Peru, n Bolivia, and Amaz. Brazil (mostly s of the Amazon).

Mouse-colored Antshrike PLATE 41
Thamnophilus murinus Pavita Gris
Identification: 5.5″ (14cm). 18g. Dull and undistinguished. Eyes grayish brown. ♂: above gray with *brownish-tinged flight feathers*; small concealed white interscapular patch; wing coverts narrowly tipped buffy white forming *2 rather faint dotted bars*; underparts light gray, paler almost whitish on throat and belly and tinged brownish on flanks; tail sometimes obscurely tipped white. ♀: above brown with *weakly contrasting chestnut crown and tail*; wings dull reddish brown; 2 faint buff-dotted wing bars; underparts olivaceous buff, throat paler, sides washed brownish.
Sim. species: Confusing because it is so plain. Look for ♂'s brownish wings and faint buff-dotted bars and ♀'s chestnut crown and faint (not conspic.) wing dots. ♀♀ of Eastern Slaty- and Spot-winged antshrikes have bolder wing markings.
Voice: Song a nasal, unhurried *ank, ank, ank, ank, ank, ank-ánkaa* (cadence and quality of taunting or mocking by children), the strongly accented and slightly hurried next-to-last note characteristic; overall has lazy quality.
Behavior: Rather unremarkable in appearance and behavior. Generally occurs in prs. that wander alone or more often follow mixed-spp. flocks in thicker part of low to lower mid. story of forest. Hop and peer rather methodically in foliage, reach out and snatch prey, or occas. flutter or lunge for fleeing arthropods much as do other *Thamnophilus* antshrikes. Less suspicious that some of its allies and normally not too difficult to see.
Status and habitat: Uncommon to locally fairly common resident in humid forest and sometimes at forest borders; most numerous in sandy soil forests.

Range: To 1300m. Throughout Amazonas and Bolívar (*murinus*). Se Colombia to s Peru (prob. n Bolivia), w and n Amaz. Brazil, and the Guianas.

Western Slaty-Antshrike
Thamnophilus atrinucha Tiojorita Pintada
Identification: 6″ (15cm). 22g. Eyes brown. ♂: virtually identical to ♂ Eastern Slaty-Antshrike but sides of head somewhat grizzled dusky (not esp. conspic.), white markings on wings and tail often somewhat bolder. ♀: much like ♀ Eastern Slaty-Antshrike but sides of head slightly grizzled like ♂'s; crown and tail dull reddish brown only in slight contrast to brownish back, and markings on wings and tail buff (not mostly white). Birds from base of Sierra de Perijá are blacker, esp. on head, than those along w base of Andes.
Sim. species: Nothing sim. in its range. E of Andes see Eastern Slaty- and Amazonian antshrikes.
Voice: Song is ca. 10–30 accelerating, whistled *hu* or *du* notes ending in distinctive nasal *dwenk* note; calls incl. a loud *ank gr-r-r-r-r* and nasal *cah* and *cah-cah*.
Behavior: Sim. to Guianan Slaty-Antshrike but in general a little more conspic. and easier to see. Forages in low and mid. levels of forest, is often assoc. with mixed-spp. flocks, and occas. follows army ant swarms. Pumps tail downward with each note as it sings. Prob. breeds in all but wettest months; thin-walled cup nest of dark fibers attached by rim to fork 1–4m up; 2 white eggs spotted shades of brown[647].
Status and habitat: Fairly common resident in humid forest, shrubby forest borders, and shady second-growth woodland. Habitat now very fragmented by deforestation.

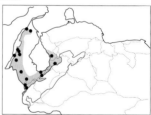

Range: To 1000m. Base of Sierra de Perijá and s Maracaibo Basin; e Zulia s to w Mérida and nw Táchira (*atrinucha*). Guatemala to sw Ecuador.
Note: Previously considered a subsp. of next sp.[275]. Subsp. *subcinereus* not recognized[275].

Guianan Slaty-Antshrike PLATE 41
Thamnophilus punctatus Tiojorita Punteada
Identification: 6″ (15cm). 20.5g. Eyes brown. ♂: body mainly gray, paler below with *black cap*; back mixed black and with usually concealed white interscapular patch; wings black with *white at bend of wing and several spotted white wing bars*; *flight feathers* (esp. inner ones) *edged white*; upper tail coverts and *tail black, both conspic. tipped white*. ♀: above olivaceous brown with *contrasting chestnut crown*; usually concealed white interscapular patch; wing coverts dusky, flight feathers and tail reddish brown, *all feathers marked with white as in* ♂ (inner flight feathers edged buff);

underparts buff, paler more buffy white on throat, brownish on sides.

Sim. species: ♂ closely resembles several other "gray and black" antshrikes (see esp. Blackish-gray, Amazonian, and Pearly antshrikes) but can be told from any by combination of *black* cap, overall *pale gray* plumage, and *bold* white markings. In e Bolívar *paraensis* race of Amazonian Antshrike has black cap and is almost identical to ♂ Guianan Slaty-Antshrike, and there the two prob. best told by presence of respective ♀ or by voice. W of Andes see next sp. ♀ resembles ♀ Mouse-colored Antshrike, but note bold wing markings.

Voice: Song in ne Bolívar a nasal and leisurely ser. of ca. 9–10 notes (1st few lengthened) that gradually accelerate and rise in pitch, *oank, oank, ank, ank, ank, ank-ank-ankank*, with bouncy effect but lacking distinct nasal note at end (cf. Western Slaty-Antshrike). Song overall most like that of Black-crested Antshrike (K. Zimmer). Also gives a nasal *caw* sim. to that of many other *Thamnophilus*.

Behavior: Rather inconspic. but not shy; usually found in scattered prs. at low or mid. levels in forested areas. May follow mixed-spp. flocks but more often independent of them. Movements are deliberate as hop from branch to branch, or up vines near trunks, peering slowly and gleaning or lunging, or occas. fluttering clumsily for mostly arthropod prey. Often pound tail down as forage. Vibrate tail to "beat" of song.

Status and habitat: Fairly common resident, at least locally, in dry to moderately humid forest, mostly in or near shrubby borders, in drier or partly deciduous forest, gallery forest, and bushy second growth. Less numerous inside humid forest, then usually near openings, treefalls, or other well-lit locations. Seems most numerous in poorer or sandier soil forests.

Range: To 1500m. E base of Andes in Táchira, Apure, and nw Barinas n to Barinitas (*interpositus*); e Sucre (Paria Pen.; Guanoco) s to Delta Amacuro, and throughout Amazonas and Bolívar (*punctatus*). Se Colombia to e Peru, Amaz. Brazil, and the Guianas.
Note: Formerly incl. Western Slaty-Antshrike (*T. atrinucha*)[275].

Amazonian Antshrike   PLATE 41
Thamnophilus amazonicus   Choca Gorro Gris
Identification: 5.7" (14.5cm). 17g. ♂: essentially identical to ♂ Eastern Slaty-Antshrike but with *head uniform gray* (no black cap) and overall slightly smaller (*cinereiceps*). Or slightly larger (6", 15cm), crown black, and essentially indistinguishable from Eastern Slaty-Antshrike on

plumage characteristics (*paraensis*). ♀ in all areas very unlike Eastern Slaty-Antshrike; *crown rufous chestnut becoming orange rufous on rest of head, neck, and underparts* and in sharp contrast to *white lower breast and belly*; back olive brown, otherwise wings and tail dusky marked with white as in ♂. Or crown orange rufous like underparts, belly buff (*paraensis*).
Sim. species: See Eastern Slaty-Antshrike. In s Amazonas, Pearly Antshrike.
Voice: ♂'s song a fairly rapid, trogonlike ser. of rolling notes that accelerate and grow louder in middle, then slow and diminish at end, lasting ca. 3.5 sec. Slightly spread tail vibrates downward with each note. ♀'s song sim. but slightly higher pitched.
Behavior: Prs. range mostly from about eye level to 10m up, sometimes even higher, keeping mostly inside forest, occas. at edge. Usually not too difficult to see as hop rather deliberately on small branches and vines and peer carefully at foliage. Forage with understory mixed-spp. flocks or independent of them.
Status and habitat: Common resident locally (*cinereiceps*) in várzea forest and stunted várzea forest scrub on white sandy soil and sandy alluvial soils; less numerous and local in adj. terra firme forests on lateritic soils. S of the Amazon in Brazil shows strong affinity for bamboo (A. Whittaker).

Range: To 400m (once to 1300m on Cerro Yapacana). Amazonas (*cinereiceps*); e Bolívar in upper Río Cuyuní and near Ptari-tepui in upper Río Carrao (*paraensis*). E Colombia, to n Bolivia, Amaz. Brazil, and the Guianas.

Streak-backed Antshrike   PLATE 41
Thamnophilus insignis   Choca Insigne
Identification: 6.7" (17cm). 26g. *Only in tepuis.* ♂: much like Eastern Slaty- and Amazonian antshrikes but larger, slightly darker, and white markings even bolder. *Crown black with some white showing on nape*; back mixed black and gray, with white of interscapular patch often visible; upper tail coverts gray tipped white, wings and tail black with *white markings* as in ♂♂ of Eastern Slaty- and Amazonian antshrikes; sides of head and *underparts uniform dark gray*. ♀: much like ♂ but forecrown barred gray and white, *crown rich chestnut with fringe of white showing on nape*. Or slightly smaller (6.3", 16cm), forehead of ♀ black (*nigrofrontalis*).
Sim. species: Occurs mostly *above* range of other sim.-appearing "gray and black" antshrikes, all of which are smaller and lack white on nape. If in doubt, note chestnut crown of ♀.

Voice: Sings a few times at dawn but generally less vocal than most *Thamnophilus*. Song of ♂ a slowly accelerating, very nasal *cunk, cuk cuk-cu-cu-cu-cu-cu-cu 'cu'cu'cucurank* (recalls that of numerous other *Thamnophilus*). Higher-pitched *rank* at end is characteristic. ♀ sings a sim. but higher-pitched song.

Behavior: Usually in prs. that are rather sedate, quiet, and easily overlooked. Forage mostly alone or occas. with mixed-spp. flocks in forest mid. levels or lower, or in canopy of low, stunted forest, where hop with slow, deliberate movements and peer at foliage for arthropods. Generally rather inconspic. although not shy. ♂♂ and ♀♀ threaten rivals in "face-offs" at territory boundaries by raising their crests, and nape, and interscapular feathers (both white), drooping wings, and spreading and lowering tail, showing bold array of white markings, all the while singing and pivoting back and forth in comical and mechanical manner.

Status and habitat: Uncommon to locally common resident. Humid and wet forest borders (mossy forest), dense stunted melastome- and *Clusia*-dominated second growth on white sand, gallery forest and tree isls. in Gran Sabana, and dense stands of *Bonnetia* high on tepuis. There are large nos. of specimens from slopes of some tepuis in s Bolívar, e.g., Aprada, Chimantá, Jaua, Uaipán, and Uei.

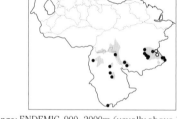

Range: ENDEMIC. 900–2000m (usually above 1200m). Cerro Sipapo, Amazonas (*nigrofrontalis*); tepuis of rest of Amazonas s to Cerro de la Neblina; tepuis of s Bolívar (*insignis*). Prob. adj. Guyana and n Brazil.

Megastictus

Sim. to *Thamnophilus* but bill and body proportions more slender; no interscapular patch; boldly spotted wing and tail markings.

Pearly Antshrike   PLATE 41
Megastictus margaritatus   Hormiguero Margarita
Identification: 5.5″ (14cm). 19.5g. Scarce and local. *Eyes white to grayish white*; bill not as heavy as in *Thamnophilus*. ♂: head and upperparts mostly bluish gray (no white interscapular), wings and tail blackish with *unusually large white terminal spots on wing coverts (form several boldly spotted bars), inner flight feathers, tertials, upper tail coverts, and tail tips*; underparts gray, paler than above and palest on throat. ♀: brown above with brownish olive crown; wings and tail brownish black *marked like ♂ but with buff spots*; underparts bright yellow buff, paler on throat.

Sim. species: Pattern of both sexes recalls that of several other antshrikes (esp. Eastern Slaty- and Amazonian antshrikes) but none has such large, bold white spotting. Esp. note large, white-spotted tertials (other antshrikes have white-edged tertials).

Voice: Distinctive 2-part song is 2–4 whistled introductory notes followed by much longer ser. of rough, grating notes, *whee? whee? whee? jrr-jrr-jrr-jrr-jrr-jrr* (G. Rosenberg). Commonest call, by foraging birds, a ser. of upward-inflected notes, *wink, wink, wink . . .* , ca. 5–20 notes at 2/sec or less (K. Zimmer).

Behavior: Prs. or groups of 3–4 (families?) are unobtrusive but not esp. wary, and often quiet as they hop up through open low to mid.-story branches 4–10m up. Forage somewhat like *Thamnomanes* antshrikes, often making short sallies to foliage (K. Zimmer), also peer and glean in foliage. May change perches fairly quickly, mainly by short hops. Often flick tail up and down rapidly as forage.

Status and habitat: Apparently an uncommon resident inside humid terra firme forest in lowlands. Known from relatively few specimens in Venez. In nw Brazil (Manaus to Sao Gabriel) commonest in sandy soil regions (K. Zimmer).

Range: To 400m. S Amazonas (Yavita-Pimichín and vicinity of Cerro Duida) southward; Bolívar in headwaters of Río Caura and Río Paragua (Caño Espuma; Río Carún). Se Colombia to e Ecuador, ne Peru, and nw Brazil; sc Amaz. Brazil.

Pygiptila

Chunkier, shorter-tailed, and more compact (but primaries longer) than *Thamnophilus*.

Spot-winged Antshrike   PLATE 41
Pygiptila stellaris   Choca Alipunteada
Identification: 5.5″ (14cm). 23g. *Chunky and short-tailed* (tail ca. 1.4–1.6″, 36–41mm). Bill large and long for size of bird. ♂: mostly dark blue gray with *black crown and nape* (black sometimes spreading onto back), concealed white interscapular patch, wings and tail blackish, wing coverts tipped white forming *several small but distinctive dotted bars*; underparts dark blue gray, palest on throat. ♀: forehead, lores, and sides of head olivaceous buff, otherwise blue gray above; shoulders (no dots) and esp. *primaries rufous brown*, underparts dull clay buff, palest on throat and tinged olive brown on sides.

Sim. species: Has large-headed, broad-shouldered, and short-tailed appearance. Look for it with mixed-

spp. flocks in forest canopy where it might recall an overgrown antwren. ♂'s blackish crown and wing dots and ♀'s contrasting rufous brown wings are good marks.
Voice: When foraging with mixed-spp. flocks often gives a sharp, forceful *tzuck!* and *tchack!* and descending *zheeer* or combined into a sharp *tzuck-zheeer* (K. Zimmer). Unusual song a ser. of ca. 4–6 (varies from 1 to 10) short, vibrating trills, each trill culminating in a rising whistle, *t-t-t-TEEER!* . . *t-t-t-TEEER!* . . with 1- to 2-sec pause between trills. Sometimes songs will be given over and over for several min with only short pauses between each song.
Behavior: Almost always seen in prs., or occas. families, accompanying mixed-spp. flocks in canopy or subcanopy of tall forest. Hustles energetically along high branches and peers into live outer foliage, leans forward and downward to snatch or lunge for prey, and occas. checks curled dead leaves. Generally maintains horizontal posture and presents squat, short-legged stance. Nest in Peru was 11m up in crown of small tree (C. Munn).
Status and habitat: Fairly common to common resident (but easily overlooked) inside or along edges of tall humid terra firme forest in lowlands; less numerous in canopy of várzea forest.

Range: To 700m (most recs. below 400m). Generally in Amazonas; w and s Bolívar from lower Río Caura, mid. Río Paragua (Salto Guaiquinima), and headwaters of Río Caroní on Río Icabarú southward (*occipitalis*); lower Río Cuyuní near El Dorado (sight, Mar 1999) (prob. *occipitalis*). Se Colombia to n Bolivia, Amaz. Brazil, and the Guianas.

Russet Antshrike   PLATE 40
Thamnistes anabatinus   Hormiguero Bermejo
Identification: 6" (15cm). 21g. Robust, short-tailed antshrike of w Táchira foothills. Bill heavy and hooked. ♂: above olivaceous brown, crown tinged rufescent; *long buff eyebrow; wings rufescent brown, tail rufous*, sides of head and underparts mostly dull ochraceous, brightest on throat; sides and belly washed olive brown, concealed orange rufous interscapular patch. ♀: sim. but no interscapular patch.
Sim. species: Looks more like a foliage-gleaner than an antshrike. Note stocky shape, heavy hooked bill, and very limited distrib. in Venez. Buff-fronted Foliage-gleaner has gray crown, lankier shape, and long, narrow tail. Also see Montane Foliage-gleaner.
Song: Infreq. hd. song (in Colombia) a moderately high-pitched *peeu, peeu-peeu-peeu-peeu-peeu*, also a

high, sibilant *peet-seep*, varied to *peet-se-seet-sip*, not hd. often but occas. repeated persistently. Vocalizations more like those of some tanagers than an antbird. In Costa Rica song described as a simple *chew, chew-chew-chew-chew-chew-chip* (K. Zimmer).
Behavior: Single birds or prs. forage in forest mid. levels or higher and are much more often seen with mixed-spp. flocks than away from them. Forage actively, mostly by peering and gleaning in outer foliage of small branches. Generally fairly easy to see. Nest a vireolike cup high in tree[647].
Status and habitat: Humid foothill forest; in Colombia along forest borders and rather open second growth. Prob. a rare resident in Venez. as it is known only from 1 locality.

Range: 1250m (0–1500m in Colombia but mainly foothills). Cerro El Teteo, se Táchira (*gularis*). S Mexico to se Ecuador; se Colombia along base of mts. to n Bolivia.

Dysithamnus

Resemble *Thamnomanes* but chunkier, shorter tailed, and large headed; posture horizontal; glean from foliage (no sallying); mostly in foothills (unlike *Thamnomanes*).

Plain Antvireo   PLATE 40
Dysithamnus mentalis   Burujara Pequeña
Identification: 4.5" (11.4cm). 13.5g. Large-headed, short-tailed little bird somewhat resembling genus *Vireo* in shape and behavior. ♂: above gray to olive gray with darker crown and *contrasting dusky cheeks*; wing coverts blackish with *3 narrow white wing bars*, flight feathers tinged brownish, small white interscapular patch; underparts white mottled and clouded with gray on breast and slightly washed buff (pale yellow—*viridis*) on belly. Or sim. but *much darker gray* above and below, only slightly paler on throat and belly, no buff yellow wash on belly (*spodionotus*). Or dark like *spodionota* but throat and belly whitish (*ptaritepui*). ♀: *rufous crown and nape bordered by prom. white eyering* and dusky mottling on cheeks, otherwise above grayish olive tinged brownish, faint whitish- to buff-edged wing coverts; below white clouded gray, palest on throat, faintly yellow (strongly yellow—*viridis*) on belly. Or sim. but brown above, buffy brown below with whitish central throat and median underparts (*spodionotus, ptaritepui*).
Sim. species: Rather variable and undistinguished. Aside from shape, ♂ is pale below with distinctive dusky cheeks; note ♀'s rufous crown and eyering. Spinetails are more slender and longer-tailed; antwrens smaller, thinner-billed, and more active.

Voice: Song a short accelerating roll that is soft, bouncy, and downscale, *buu, bu bu-bu-bu'bu'u'u'u'u*, like a "small" *Thamnophilus* but higher pitched and subdued. Two common calls incl. a weak nasal *naa* over and over and a soft, querulous, ascending (slides upward) *bu-u-u-u-u-et?* (K. Zimmer recording).
Behavior: As name implies, a plain little bird, but seen often enough to merit learning well. Usually in prs. or families that forage alone or follow small understory mixed-spp. flocks. Unobtrusive and rather sluggish (like *Vireo*), they hop along branches and peer and glean in foliage or hover momentarily beneath leaves. Deep, thin-walled, open cup attached by rim to fork 0.6–2m up in bush; nest often decorated with bits of moss; 2 whitish eggs blotched purplish brown[647].
Status and habitat: Fairly common resident in humid forest and shrubby or viny forest borders; mostly foothills and lower slopes.

Range: 450–2200m (locally to sea level). Throughout in mts. Sierra de Perijá, Zulia, both slopes of Andes in Táchira, and e slope in Barinas (*viridis*); n in Andes (subsp.?); Lara (incl. nw at Cerro El Cerrón), c Falcón (Sierra de San Luis)[60]; n mts. from Yaracuy and Carabobo e to Paria Pen., Sucre (*cumbreanus*); se Sucre and Monagas (subsp?); ne Bolívar from Sierra de Imataca to upper Río Cuyuní (*andrei*); s Bolívar on Ptaritepui and Sororopán-tepui (*ptaritepui*); tepuis of Amazonas and rest of Bolívar from Río Cuchivero and lower Río Caura to Gran Sabana (*spodionotus*). Se Mexico s (mostly in mts.) to w Ecuador, n Argentina, and s Brazil.
Note: Subsp. *semicinereus* (Sierra de Perijá) not recognized.

Venezuelan Antvireo   PLATE 41
Dysithamnus tucuyensis   Burujara Plomiza
Identification: 5″ (12.7cm). 20g. ♂: mostly slate gray, darker on throat and chest; bend of wing white, wing coverts blackish with 2 narrow white-dotted wing bars and indistinct white scapular dots. In hand may show faint white shaft streaking on chest and breast. ♀: *crown bright reddish chestnut, rest of upperparts reddish brown, sides of head and entire underparts gray broadly and profusely streaked whitish*, flanks tinged brown.
Sim. species: ♂ might be mistaken for Plain Antvireo but is larger and uniformly dark above and below; also see smaller ♂ Slaty Antwren. ♀'s heavily streaked underparts are unique.
Voice: Song a soft, breezy ser. of whistles that descend in pitch, *weee, wheer, wheer, whuu, were*; not often hd.

Behavior: Prs. or occas. up to 4 forage quietly and inconspic., mostly 0.5–6m up in forest understory, and are usually with small mixed-spp. flocks, esp. those containing Slaty Antwrens, Plain Antvireos, and Three-striped Warblers. Like allied Plain Antvireo, often hops up upright branches, palm fronds, and petioles of large leaves, or out along slender branches where peers amidst foliage, and sometimes hops somewhat sideways. Forages quietly with deliberate but steady movements and rather horizontal posture with tail held down and head slightly hunched. Behavior overall much like that of Plain Antvireo (Hilty), but on avg. may forage lower than that sp., even occas. dropping to leaf litter on forest floor for prey (K. Zimmer).
Status and habitat: Rare to locally fairly common (easily overlooked) resident inside humid and wet premontane forest and around cluttered treefalls, landslides, and viny forest borders. Most readily found near Rancho Grande Biol. Station, Aragua; now rare near Caripe.

Range: ENDEMIC. 800–1900m. Andes of s Lara (Bucarito); c Falcón (sight) in Sierra de San Luis[60]; Coastal Cordillera (no. recs. in Interior Cordillera) from Yaracuy and Carabobo to Distr. Federal (Pico Avila) and Miranda; mts. of n Monagas (Caripe).
Note: Originally described in *Dysithamnus* but incorrectly transferred to *Thamnomanes*[401]; then called Plumbeous Antshrike, *T. plumbeus tucuyensis*[403]. Here treated as a sp. distinct from *leucostictus* of Colombia (e slope of E Andes in Meta) and e Ecuador, and from birds of se Brazil[545].

Thamnomanes

♂♂ uniform gray in plumage; ♀♀ usually somewhat 2-toned below. Rather long tailed and long winged (unlike allied *Dysithamnus*); no crest; bill wider and tarsi shorter than in allies; perch erect and sally to foliage. Important as sentinels in mixed-spp. flocks[422,576].

Dusky-throated Antshrike   PLATE 41
Thamnomanes ardesiacus   Burujara Pizarreña
Identification: 5.5″ (14cm). 17g. Rather long tailed and flycatcherlike in behavior. ♂: *dark bluish gray*, somewhat paler below, with *contrasting black chin and throat* (this not always easy to see in field), tail sometimes faintly tipped white (best seen in hand); small white interscapular patch. ♀: dull olive brown above, somewhat mottled grayish on face, sometimes with vague pale eyering; wings and tail slightly rufescent, *below mostly ochraceous buff with pale, almost whitish*

throat (throat not in strong contrast with breast) and gray-tinged chest.

Sim. species: ♂ Cinereous Antshrike lacks black throat and has slightly longer tail. ♀ Cinereous has grayish chest contrasting sharply with bright cinnamon rufous lower underparts. ♀ superficially sim. to several ♀ antwrens but much larger.

Voice: Song a sharply ascending ser. of coarse, raspy whistles, *jaaw, jaaw, jaw, jay, juu, ju, ju j-j-j*, accelerating and somewhat attenuated at end before ending abruptly; sharp calls incl. an incisive *skéeap!* (louder and sharper than corresponding call of Cinereous Antshrike) and buzzy *juueeer* (like snarl of *Gymnopithys*); also a flat *week-week, week* rather like call of Cinereous Antshrike but lacking that sp.'s loud rattle, and generally quieter.

Behavior: Sits mostly 1–5m up in understory, somewhat erect like sallying flycatchers, although not as upright as Cinereous Antshrike. Employs a sally-gleaning "sit-and-wait" foraging strategy (but usually doesn't wait too long!) followed by relatively long prey-capture sallies to bark or foliage or occas. to air. Prs. or families are normally with mixed-spp. flocks. On avg. stays lower in understory than Cinereous Antshrike, not as noisy and not as critical to mixed flock cohesion as that sp., but sentinel behavior is useful. Occas. at army ants. In se Peru nests in 1st half of rainy season (Aug–Jan); vireolike nest 0.5–2m up in fork of small sapling; often festooned with dead leaves; 2 pinkish white eggs spotted reddish brown (C. Munn).

Status and habitat: Uncommon to fairly common resident inside humid terra firme and várzea forest.

Range: To 1100m. Generally in Amazonas and Bolívar n to c Delta Amacuro (*obidensis*). Se Colombia to n Bolivia and Brazil mostly n of the Amazon e to the Guianas.

Cinereous Antshrike PLATES 41, 43
Thamnomanes caesius Choca Guayanesa
Identification: 5.5″ (14cm). 16g. Rather long tailed and flycatcherlike in behavior. ♂: *uniform dark bluish gray*, wings and tail slightly darker; small concealed white interscapular patch. ♀: plain olivaceous brown above; white interscapular patch; throat pale gray becoming pale brownish gray on chest *and sharply separated from bright orange rufous* of mid. breast and belly; under wing coverts rufous.

Sim. species: See Dusky-throated Antshrike. ♀ Cinereous's bright, "divided" underparts are diagnostic.

Voice: Soliloquy of low, whistled *wert-wert* phrases, often interrupted by loud, staccato rattles, *d'd'd'd'd'd*,

is a good indicator of presence of this sp. in understory mixed-spp. flock. Call (contact?) an often repeated, whistled *tuee, tuee* . . . ; less often hd. song is several slow wheezy whistles accelerating into rapid bubbly trill fading at end, *squeet . . squeet, wheet, wheet, whee, wheesp wheesp whes whes we we we e-e-e-u-u-u-r*, lasting ca. 6 sec.

Behavior: Noisy and excitable and a key member in cohesion and maintenance of mixed-spp. flocks in forest understory. Because it sits more in open than other spp., valuable as a sentinel, and few understory rain forest flocks form or move as a collective unit without 1 or a pr. of these birds present. Sit quite erect on slender horizontal perches 2–12m up, or move lower over army ants which they occas. follow. Following a short wait, sally to twigs or foliage for insects (occas. to air), and often return to same or nearby perch much as do some flycatchers. An energetic sp. found in prs. or families; some flocks contain 4–5 of these birds. Breeds in 1st part of rainy season in s Peru; open cup nest 0.5–3m up in fern-covered fork of sapling; 2 pinkish white eggs blotched reddish brown[37] (C. Munn).

Status and habitat: Common and widespread resident inside humid terra firme and várzea forest in lowlands.

Range: To 850m. Throughout Amazonas; n Bolívar from lower Río Caura and Sierra de Imataca and Nuria southward (*glaucus*). Se Colombia, e Ecuador, and n Peru e across n and c Amaz. Brazil to the Guianas; coastal e Brazil.

Myrmotherula
Almost certainly not a monophyletic group; small; short tail; rather long, thin bill; ♀♀ of many spp. are confusing and difficult to identify; near gd. to canopy. Three groups based on ♂ plumages: (1) mostly striped black and white, (2) predom. brown and buff with or without chestnut rumps, and (3) mainly gray and black with or without black throat and white-tipped wing coverts. Groups 2 and 3 are often important components of mixed-spp. flocks.

Pygmy Antwren PLATE 40
Myrmotherula brachyura Hormiguerito Pigmeo
Identification: 3.3″ (8.4cm). 6.9g. *Tiny and virtually tailless.* ♂: crown, sides of head, and upperparts black *coarsely streaked white*, wings black with 2 white bars and white edgings, tail all black, *throat white* bordered by narrow black malar line (malar only slightly set off from black streaking on sides of head), *remaining underparts clear yellow somewhat streaked black on sides*

of chest; white interscapular patch. ♀: sim. but crown and nape streaked orange buff, *throat and breast broadly suffused cinnamon buff*, chest somewhat streaked blackish.
Sim. species: Closely resembles Yellow-throated Antwren but throat white (not yellow) and known area of overlap in Amazonas is small.
Voice: Song a short accelerating ("bouncing ball") ser. of notes on same pitch, *peeup, peeup-peeup-pee-pee-ee-e-e'e'e'eeee*. Contact note in e Bolívar a slow *cheer-cheer* (or *peer-peer*), the note characteristically doubled.
Behavior: Prs. forage from mid. levels to canopy of tall forest or occas. lower along shrubby forest borders. Sometimes join mixed-spp. flocks where restlessly flick wings and hop and glean actively in foliage. Territories believed to be quite small so prs. typically do not follow flocks far (K. Zimmer). Bulky nest ca. 6m up, se Colombia[260].
Status and habitat: Common resident in humid terra firme and várzea forest in lowlands, esp. fairly high along shrubby forest and viny streamside borders, and in tall second-growth woodland. Characteristic of canopy and subcanopy forest light-gaps (K. Zimmer).

Range: To 950m (most recs. below 500m). N Amazonas (Caño Capuana) southward; n Bolívar from lower Río Caura and Sierra de Imataca and s Delta Amacuro at Misión Araguaimujo southward (*brachyura*). Panama and w Colombia (where perhaps a separate sp.); se Colombia to n Bolivia, Amaz. Brazil, and the Guianas.

Yellow-throated Antwren
PLATE 43
Myrmotherula ambigua Hormiguerito Gargantiamarillo
Identification: 3.4″ (8.6cm). 6g. Closely resembles Pygmy Antwren. ♂ differs in having *underparts entirely yellow* (no white throat). In hand, streaking of mantle (and interscapular patch) somewhat yellowish (not white). ♀: essentially identical to ♀ Pygmy Antwren and prob. indistinguishable in field. In hand, throat yellowish (not white), sides of breast buffier, crown streaking perhaps darker.
Sim. species: See Pygmy Antwren. In hand Yellow-throated Antwren has slightly longer bill than Pygmy (12–12.5 vs. 10.5–11.5mm) and longer tail (21–24 vs. 17–19mm)[398].
Voice: Slow ser. of ca. 10–15 thin, high-pitched whistles delivered steadily, *weeeu, weeeu, weeeu, . . .* (or *peeeu, peeeu, peeeu . . .*), less than 2 notes/sec, all on same pitch (C. Parrish recording).
Behavior: An inconspic. little bird of high forest canopy where usually found with mixed-spp. flocks. Rest-

less and active as peers and gleans in outer foliage (C. Parrish). Also often in vine tangles and masses of philodendrons high on main trunks of canopy trees; normally more than 15m up, but reg. lower at forest edges (K. Zimmer).
Status and habitat: Tall humid terra firme forest in lowlands; most numerous in areas of poor or white sandy soil. Known from just a few specimen localities in s Amazonas; also sight recs. in Aug 1985 at San Carlos de Río Negro, Amazonas (C. Parrish), but prob. often overlooked. May occur in extreme s Bolívar; recent specimens from Río Mucujaí, 60 km w of Río Branco, by D. Stotz in adj. Brazil[545].

Range: To 200m (prob. higher). Amazonas from base of Cerro Duida s to confluence of Ríos Casiquiare, Negro, and Guainía; San Carlos de Río Negro and Cerro de la Neblina. Adj. e Colombia and nw Brazil.

Guianan Streaked-Antwren
PLATE 40
Myrmotherula surinamensis Hormiguerito Rayado de Las Guayanas
Identification: 3.8″ (9.7cm). 8.3g. ♂: *above black boldly streaked white*, wings black with 2 white wing bars and white-edged flight feathers; white interscapular patch; *underparts white narrowly streaked black to mid. breast*, tail with small white tips (mostly visible from below). ♀: sim. to ♂ but *entire head and neck orange rufous with fine black streaking mainly on rear-crown and nape*; throat and chest washed pale orangish buff and *unstreaked* or (in Venez.) usually with band of fine streaks on breast; malar mark absent or thin; central lower underparts whitish.
Sim. species: See very sim. Amazonian Streaked-Antwren; also Cherrie's and Pygmy antwrens.
Voice: Song (upper Río Cuyuní) a bubbly ser. of ca. 6–8 notes that quickly rise and fall (recalls that of Amazonian Streaked-Antwren but faster and more notes), i.e., *tu-tu-HEE-HEE-hay-hay-ha* (*tu* notes on same pitch or rising, *HEE* notes highest, last 3 falling in pitch), entire phrase typically repeated 4–8 times in rapid succession (no pause). Song bout itself may be given over and over more or less simultaneously by both sexes. Other vocalizations, also given *by both sexes*, incl. a vibrating trill of ca. 50 notes/2.5 sec. Also a short, breezy *weet-weet-weet-weet* and faster, rattling (3–5 notes) *tu-tu-tu-tu-tu*. Contact call a soft, nasal *nay-who* (recalls that of several other *Myrmotherula*).
Behavior: Prs. constantly flick wings and fidget as they hop in vines and foliage and glean actively, often reaching out to pick small arthropods from foliage and twigs. Prs. often stay rather close together and relatively low, mostly 1.5–6m up, and usually are not too

difficult to see. Generally not with mixed-spp. flocks but may be active in vicinity of other edge and thicket dwellers, e.g., Buff-breasted Wrens and Silver-beaked Tanagers.
Status and habitat: Uncommon and local resident in e Bolívar in dense vines and overgrown second growth, esp. along small streams and shrubby humid forest borders.

Range: To 400m. Nw Amazonas (Caño Capuana, San Fernando de Atabapo) and mid. Río Ventuari (Las Carmelitas; sight, Junglaven) s to Río Casiquiare and Cerro de la Neblina; n Bolívar from lower Río Caura, Río Paragua, and Sierra de Imataca (Río Grande) southward; Delta Amacuro at Misión Araguaimujo. The Guianas and n Amaz. Brazil n of the Amazon and e of Rio Negro.
Note: Using plumage characters of Isler et al.[277], M. Lentino and R. Restall identified ♀♀ in the Colección Phelps of this sp. and of Amazonian Streaked-Antwren from near San Fernando de Atabapo, Amazonas, the only site in Venez. where the two are known to overlap.

Amazonian Streaked-Antwren
Myrmotherula multostriata Hormiguerito Rayado de Amazonas
Identification: 3.7″ (9.4cm). 8.5g. ♂ and ♀ essentially identical to respective sexes of Guianan Streaked-Antwren. In hand ♀ differs from ♀ Guianan in whitish throat bordered by *thin black malar line*; chest washed orangish buff, throat and chest finely streaked and dotted black, some blurry streaking continuing down to flanks, central lower underparts whitish.
Sim. species: See Guianan Streaked-Antwren which is separable by voice, minor differences in ♀ plumages, and in most areas, range.
Voice: Vibrating "loudsong" of ca. 40 notes/2.5 sec. is given only (?) by ♂[277]. Territorial song, by both sexes in e Peru (same in Venez.?), *way hey HEE, hay-aa*, rises then falls in large slow steps with mid. note highest; re-

calls song of Guianan Streaked-Antwren but simpler and with altered pattern. In n Amazonas a fairly loud, nasal *nyEE-here* (rising, falling) while foraging; also a kittenlike meowing, *ny-a-a-a*, like short rattle.
Behavior: As in Guianan Streaked-Antwren.
Status and habitat: Uncommon and local resident of large patches of dense river-edge vines and thickets, esp in humid várzea forest regions.
Range: To 200m. Nw Amazonas along upper Orinoco (San Fernando de Atabapo). E Colombia to se Peru and Amaz. Brazil s of the Amazon (locally n of Amazon in vicinity of lower Río Negro).
Note: Taxonomy revised[277].

Cherrie's Antwren
PLATE 43
Myrmotherula cherriei Hormiguerito de Igapó
Identification: 4.1″ (10.4cm). 8g. Much like Guianan Streaked-Antwren but longer tailed (27–30 vs. 23–25mm). ♂: differs in having underparts *much more coarsely streaked black* (black streaks about as wide as white) and *streaks continuing to belly*; no white interscapular patch. ♀: resembles ♀ Guianan Streaked-Antwren but crown paler buff and more extensively streaked (*entire crown light buff coarsely streaked black*; sides of head finely streaked black), underparts *entirely buff* (no white on belly), black malar stripe broad (not thin or absent), throat dotted black, *chest and mid. breast more heavily and boldly streaked black* (conspic. in field), and tail longer and more prom. tipped white. In most of area of overlap, ♀ Guianan Streaked-Antwren is essentially unstreaked below. In hand Cherrie's Antwren has slightly longer, heavier bill than Guianan Streaked-Antwren (9.4–10.3 vs. 8.7–9.7mm), *decidedly longer tail* (above), and no white interscapular patch[277].
Voice: Song, given less freq. than that of many antwrens, a fast, ascending rattle, *trdddddddddddddddd*, unmusical and with hard, flat quality; call a flat, dull *tsuu*.
Behavior: Prs. freq. follow small mixed-spp. flocks containing antshrikes, antwrens, greenlets, wrens, and honeycreepers (K. Zimmer) but also forage away from flocks, and generally stay low, mostly 0.2–6m up in shrubs and thickets. Hop actively and glean insects from foliage; usually relatively easy to see.
Status and habitat: Fairly common resident locally. Occurs mainly in 2 habitats: (1) seasonally flooded, low-canopied, and fairly dense scrub forest on white sandy soil and (2) thickets and palm-filled borders of low-canopied seasonally flooded gallery forest along small creeks in regions of savanna. Rarely, has also been seen in low bushes in white sandy soil savanna adj. to dense seasonally flooded forest.

Range: To 550m. Throughout Amazonas (except se). E Colombia and adj. nw Brazil in upper Rio Negro drainage.

Rufous-bellied Antwren
PLATE 40

Myrmotherula guttata Hormiguerito Vientre Rufo

Identification: 3.9″ (9.9cm). 9.7g. Tail short. ♂: head to lower back entirely gray, rump brown, wing-coverts black with *2 boldly spotted buff bars; tertials with large bold buff spots;* upper tail coverts and tail tipped buff; concealed white interscapular patch; throat to mid. breast gray, lower underparts cinnamon rufous. ♀: *bold wing and tail markings* like ♂ but gray of upperparts replaced by *brown;* throat grayish white turning pale olivaceous brown on breast.

Sim. species: ♂ and ♀ told from any other antwren by conspic. wing markings and *large spots on tertials.* Also note rather "divided" appearance of ♂'s plumage—gray foreparts, rufous brown rearparts.

Voice: Commonest call (contact?) a *harsh, grating,* and low-pitched *j'r'r* or *j'r'r'r'r* rattle (length varies), typically repeated 3–4 times in irreg., agitated ser.; when foraging also gives a thin, rattley trill (recalls that of White-browed Antbird). Song a high, penetrating ser. of whistles on same pitch or slightly rising, *wheeee, wheeee, wheee, whee, whee, . . . ,* ca. 10–20 notes, delivered slowly (2 notes/sec or slower) but sometimes a little faster and more urgent toward end.

Behavior: Usually in prs., occas. single birds or 3s, that stay very low, usually within 2m of gd., and inside forest. Typically somewhat retiring, and easily overlooked in dim understory light. Often cling to side of small vertical saplings as hop in undergrowth or flit short distances between saplings. Forage away from understory mixed-spp. flocks, less often with them, also occas. around army ant swarms.

Status and habitat: Uncommon to locally fairly common resident inside humid terra firme forest in lowlands; sometimes also in damp, low-lying areas inside forest.

Range: To 700m. E and s Amazonas (Río Asisa; Cerro Duida; Yavita-Pimichín s to Cerro de la Neblina; many sightings at Junglaven); n Bolívar from lower Río Caura, mid. Río Paragua (Salto Guaiquinima), and Sierra de Imataca southward. The Guianas and n Brazil; prob. extreme e Colombia.

Brown-bellied Antwren
PLATE 40

Myrmotherula gutturalis Hormiguerito Espalda Marrón

Identification: 4.4″ (11.2cm). 9g. Tail longer than allies. Eyes yellow to whitish (♂); dark? (♀). ♂: looks

♀-plumaged; above olivaceous brown, wings and tail reddish brown, *wing coverts with 2 rows of small buffy white dots forming inconspic. dotted bars;* no interscapular patch; *throat checkered black and white,* breast gray turning brown on lower underparts. ♀: above dull olivaceous brown, wings and tail reddish brown, wing coverts with tiny buff dots on tips; *throat and chest ochraceous* turning buffy brown on rest of underparts.

Sim. species: ♂ shares checkered throat only with Stipple-throated Antwren but has back and rump plain brown (not rufous) and is overall duller and browner; the two are not known to overlap in range. Dull ♀, which looks like many other ♀ *Myrmotherula,* is prob. best told by overall brownish plumage and tiny, buff-dotted wing bars; in both sexes note distinctive habit of hanging from dead leaves. See ♀♀ of White-flanked and Long-winged antwrens.

Voice: Song a thin, chattery trill (ca. 2 sec), quite high pitched, with hint of a squeak at onset, typically rising a little then descending, i.e., *pe-e-e-e-e-ee-ee-ee-e-e-e-u.* Various soft, high, metallic notes while foraging. Recalls song of Stipple-throated Antwren. ♂♂ in agonistic display, often lasting many min, face each other with wings drooped, bill raised, and checkered throat flared as give repeated harsh, buzzy calls (K. Zimmer).

Behavior: Prs. or families persistently follow *Thamnomanes*-led mixed-spp. flocks in lower and mid. levels of forest but sometimes move up into subcanopy. This dead-leaf foraging specialist is restless and active as persistently inspects hanging curled dead leaves and leaf litter accumulated in branch forks by reaching downward, or by clinging upside-down from leaf tip. Also occas. checks or hangs from tips of live leaves. This sp., along with White-flanked and Long-winged antwrens, comprises the trio of antwrens commonest in lower story mixed-spp. flocks in e Venez.

Status and habitat: Uncommon to fairly common resident inside mature humid and wet forest in lowlands and foothills.

Range: To 1000m. Extreme e Venez. from Sierra de Imataca and upper Río Cuyuní southward. The Guianas and ne Brazil n of the Amazon.

Stipple-throated Antwren
PLATE 40

Myrmotherula haematonota Hormiguerito Espalda Rufa

Identification: 4.2″ (10.7cm). 8.8g. Bill shorter and thicker than in previous sp. Eyes usually dark (sometimes pale). ♂: upperparts and tail brown, *lower back and rump rufous,* shoulders somewhat dusky with *3 rows of white spotted bars* (lower row sometimes buff), throat checkered black and white, breast iron gray, flanks and belly brown. No interscapular patch. ♀: above much like ♂ incl. *rufous lower back and rump*; wing coverts tipped buff forming 3 spotted bars, underparts uniform ochraceous buff.

Sim. species: ♂ and ♀ recall respective sexes of Brown-bellied Antwren, but both easily told by rufous lower back and rump. Range overlap between the two is minimal. Also cf. ♀♀ of White-flanked and Long-winged antwrens.

Voice: Song a high, metallic trill, *ti'ti'ti'e'e'e'e'ee'ee'ee 'ee'e'e'e'e'ei'ei'ei*, ascending slightly then slowly descending (ca. 20–25 whistled notes in 2–2.5 sec). Recalls trill of *Picumnus* but lower pitched and much shriller.

Behavior: A dead-leaf specialist. Prs. or families are restless and active but difficult to see or follow, as they move rapidly through forest understory, almost always with mixed-spp. flocks that contain woodcreepers, antshrikes, and other antwrens. Spend most of time examining curled hanging dead leaves or piles of dead leaves suspended in branch forks, often by hanging from beneath tips of dead leaves. Less often search through live foliage.

Status and habitat: Uncommon and easily overlooked resident in lower story of humid terra firme forest. Prs. occur in some, but apparently not all, mixed-spp. flocks near Junglaven.

Range: To 1300m. Amazonas generally, and e across Bolívar from Río Nicharé, lower Río Caura, Auyán-tepui, and Paurai-tepui southward (*pyrrhonota*). Se Colombia and e Ecuador to n Bolivia and w Amaz. Brazil.
Note: Rufous-tailed Antwren (*M. erythrura*) may occur in sw Amazonas (found in adj. Colombia and Brazil). ♂ much like ♂ Stipple-throated Antwren but tail also rufous (not esp. conspic. in field), forehead, sides of head, and underparts light gray (often with some faint black stippling on throat), abdomen brownish. ♀ much like ♀ Stipple-throated but with brighter ochraceous throat and rufous tail.

White-flanked Antwren
PLATE 40

Myrmotherula axillaris   Hormiguerito Costados Blancos

Identification: 4.2″ (10.7cm). 8.1g. Two distinctive forms. (1) ♂: entirely black above and below, bend of wing white, wing coverts with 2 rows of small white dots forming dotted bars; *feathers of axillaries and flanks unusually long, silky, and white*, often partially or completely concealed (watch for conspic. flash of white as wings are flicked). (2) Or sim. but upperparts gray, only throat and chest black, lower underparts gray (*axillaris*). ♀: above brown with 2 rows of faintly

indicated buff dots on wing coverts; buffy below with paler buffy to whitish throat; conspic. white flank tufts as in ♂. Or darker brown above, esp. on back, wings, and tail (*axillaris*).

Sim. species: Either sex and either race of this widespread sp. easily told from any other antwren by strobe-like white flashes of flank tufts which are exposed as wings are flicked.

Voice: Call or contact note in Amazonas a nasal, 2-noted, and often hd. *naa-who* (*melaena*); call or contact note in Bolívar (e of Río Caura) a single note; alarm a dry, rattling *trrrrrr*. Song in Amazonas (both sexes) 6–10 wheezy whistles, 2/sec, descending throughout, *phee, peh, peh-peh-peh-puu-puu-pua*.

Behavior: Prs. or families are persistent followers of mixed-spp. flocks containing woodcreepers, antshrikes, and other antwrens. Forage mainly in understory to mid. strata in forest. Active and restless, and constantly seem to flick wings to expose white flank patches, like little winking lights, as they glean from foliage, hop in vine tangles, and occas. check curled dead leaves. Nest (C Amer.) a deep, dead-leaf cup, lined and fastened by black rhizomorph fibers; attached by rim to fork 0.2–4m up, always with 1 or several large leaves overhanging nest; 2 white eggs speckled reddish brown in wreath mostly at larger end[706,818].

Status and habitat: Common resident in humid lowland forest and older second-growth woodland. One of most numerous antwrens in lowland forests s of Orinoco.

Range: To 1000m. Sierra de Perijá, Zulia (Río Aricuaisa), and w base of Andes from Táchira n to w Trujillo; e slope in e Táchira, w Apure, and w Barinas; w and c Amazonas s to Cerro de la Neblina; w Bolívar e to upper Río Cuchivero (*melaena*); e Amazonas, rest of Bolívar, and s Delta Amacuro (Sacupana) n to Río Guarapiche, ne Monagas (*axillaris*). Honduras to n Bolivia, Amaz. Brazil, and the Guianas; coastal e and se Brazil.
Note: Voice and plumage differences suggest the 2 forms may be separate spp.

Slaty Antwren
PLATE 40

Myrmotherula schisticolor   Hormiguerito Apizarrado

Identification: 4″ (10.2cm). 8.8g. ♂: mostly blackish slate, slightly paler below; *throat black spreading onto upper breast* (not in strong contrast to slaty gray lower underparts); wing coverts black, *2 white-dotted wing bars* (sometimes a 3d dotted bar shows), flight feathers tinged brown, tail obscurely tipped white (not a field mark). ♀: dull and confusing; above uniformly *plain* *gray*, wings and tail tinged brownish (coverts essentially unmarked), *throat ochre* becoming dirty ochraceous brown on breast and belly.

Sim. species: ♂ is nearest ♂ Long-winged Antwren found only s of Orinoco. In foothill range ♂ might be confused with much larger Venezuelan Antvireo. ♀ looks much like several other ♀ antwrens, but none overlap in Slaty's limited foothill range in Venez. Note uniformly gray upperparts, rather dark and rich ochraceous color below. Behavior and habits are also good clues.

Voice: When foraging often gives a soft, nasal, meowing *nyeeet*, rather low pitched and squeezed out; a nasal, twisting *myaa-a*; and short *tee-up*. Infreq. hd. song a rather high, forced ser. of 2–3 slow whistles on same pitch, *swEEErt, swEEErt, swEEErt* (Hilty); or sometimes little whistled notes strung together in long ser. of identical notes (K. Zimmer).

Behavior: Prs. or little parties of 3–4 work rather quietly and unobtrusively through undergrowth, mostly 0.5–4m up, often accompanying Three-striped Warblers, bush-tanagers, and others, and glean insects mostly from foliage. Peer beneath live or curled hanging dead leaves and may hang downward or cling beneath foliage. Nest a deep, thin-walled, black fiber cup suspended from low horizontal fork; 2 eggs, white to cream blotched and spotted dark[647].

Status and habitat: Fairly common to common (easily overlooked) resident in shady interior of moist to wet premontane and montane forest and older second-growth woodland; mainly foothills and lower mt. els.; rarely to near sea level; small nos. in dry foothill forest, i.e., n slope of PN Henri Pittier.

Range: 20–2250m (mostly 350–2000m). Sierra de Perijá, Zulia, both slopes of Andes from s Táchira to nw Lara (Cerros Cogollal and El Cerrón), mts. of Falcón (sight, Sierra de San Luis) and Yaracuy, n cordilleras from Carabobo to Distr. Federal and Miranda, and mts. of ne Anzoátegui, Sucre, and n Monagas (*sanctaemartae*). S Mexico s in mts. to s Peru.

Long-winged Antwren   PLATE 43
Myrmotherula longipennis   Hormiguerito Alilargo
Identification: 4.2″ (10.7cm). 8.5g. ♂: much like Slaty Antwren but slightly paler; mostly dark gray, paler below, with *contrasting black patch on throat and central chest* (black extends only to mid. chest); bend of wings white, wing coverts black *fringed* (not spotted) *white forming 3 narrow bars*, tail *narrowly* (but distinctly) *tipped white*; usually concealed white interscapular patch. ♀: upperparts uniform brown; concealed white interscapular patch; *wings tinged*

rufescent; wing coverts essentially unmarked or obscurely tipped buff, throat and faintly suggested eyering *whitish, chest strongly buff* turning brownish on breast and *whitish on mid. belly*; no tail tipping.

Sim. species: Both sexes easily confused as they occur with several sim. congeners. ♂ Gray Antwren is paler gray and has no black throat patch; ♂ Plain-winged occurs mostly at els. above Long-winged and has no white on wing coverts or tail tip. Also cf. ♂ White-flanked Antwren. ♀ Gray Antwren is decidedly paler, more blue gray above, and paler almost uniform cinnamon below; ♀ Plain-winged is more rufescent above (looks darker), lacks white belly. Look for flashing white patches on ♀ White-flanked.

Voice: Song a ser. of 5–6 soft whistles, *weary-weary-weary-weary-weary* (or *jewie, jewie . .*), a little buzzy or raspy, on same pitch or slightly rising. Call a nasal, reedy, and somewhat horse *néw-newt* (2–4 notes) or *náa-new*. Song and call resemble respective vocalizations of White-flanked Antwren.

Behavior: Prs. or families are reg. members of mixed-spp. flocks in understory or mid. levels of lowland rain forest. Actively glean in foliage, typically moving rapidly out into terminal leaves (unlike Gray and White-flanked antwrens) and reg. hover momentarily in front of or beneath leaves for small arthropod prey. Disputing ♂♂ threaten with exposed and raised white interscapular patch and raised wings. Like White-flanked Antwrens, almost constantly flick or twitch wings up slightly, but movement not as exaggerated as in that sp. (cf. Gray Antwren). In se Peru open cup nest in branch fork 2–6m up in leafy sapling (C. Munn).

Status and habitat: Uncommon to locally fairly common resident in lower levels of humid terra firme and várzea forest in lowlands and lower slopes of tepuis.

Range: To 1300m (mostly below 900m). C and s Amazonas (Río Asisa southward) and e through n Bolívar from lower Río Caura and Sierra de Imataca southward (*longipennis*). Se Colombia and e Ecuador to n Bolivia, Amaz. Brazil, and the Guianas.

Plain-winged Antwren   PLATE 40
Myrmotherula behni   Hormiguerito de Ala Limpia
Identification: 3.8″ (9.7cm). 7.9g. Rather short tailed. ♂: uniform slate gray above and below, *wing coverts and tail tips unmarked*, throat black spreading down central underparts to mid. breast or lower (black can be hard to see). ♀: above rufescent brown (or olive brown—*yavii*), wing coverts and tail unmarked; faintly indicated eyering and throat whitish contrasting with light brown underparts (or paler olive buff—*yavii*).

Sim. species: Generally occurs above range of other *Myrmotherula* antwrens. ♂ is only *Myrmotherula* with complete absence of white on wing coverts *and* tail. Cf. Long-winged and Gray antwrens, and larger Plain Antvireo. ♀ is darker, more rufescent above, and dingier and browner (not ochraceous) below than ♀♀ of any of above spp.

Voice: Call a high, forced *pszzyeek* (bisyllabic) and softer, 2-noted *tyou-tyou* (B. Whitney recording); *keeeur-ker*[545] is prob. a different transcription of this 2-noted call. Mobs or scolds with head lowered as gives short *wree-wree-wree* with bill open wide.

Behavior: Rather quiet prs. glean in understory foliage, mostly 2–10m up, and are usually seen with understory mixed-spp. flocks, esp. those with Two-banded Warblers. Also forage in lower levels beneath large canopy mixed-spp. flocks.

Status and habitat: Resident in tall humid and wet premontane forest on slopes of tepuis. Fairly common, at least locally, with numerous specimens from many tepuis (see range), but otherwise remains a rather poorly known and underreported sp. Known distrib. is spotty within larger tepui mts. Sierra de Lema may be most accessible place to see it in Venez.; there is 1 specimen from km 125 and numerous sight recs. between ca. km 111 and 130 where fairly common in understory of tall mature forest (not stunted melastome forests).

Range: 1000–1800m (sight recs. to ca. 950m). Amazonas on Cerros Yavi, Calentura, Parú, and de la Neblina, and upper Río Ocamo; nw Bolívar on Cerro Tabaro (upper Río Nicharé) and Cerro El Negro in upper Río Cuchivero (*yavii*); Cerro Camani, upper Río Ventuari (*camanii*); s and e Bolívar in Sierra Uainama (Cerro Urutaní), Sierra de Lema and Cerro Roraima at Arabopó (*inornata*). Locally in e Colombia, n Brazil, and Guyana.

Gray Antwren
PLATE 40

Myrmotherula menetriesii Hormiguerito Gargantigris
Identification: 3.8″ (9.7cm). 8.9g. Short tailed. ♂: *no black throat patch*; above uniform blue gray, below pale blue gray, wing coverts *black fringed white* forming 2 white bars (usually a 3d short bar), tail narrowly tipped white (can be hard to see in field). ♀: pale bluish gray above; wings and tail tinged olive brown and unmarked; faintly indicated eyering and throat buff white, rest of underparts rather bright ochraceous, sides and belly duller. Or sim. but ♂ and ♀ darker blue gray (*cinereiventris*).
Sim. species: ♂ is only "gray" *Myrmotherula* in Venez. that *lacks* black throat patch, but juv. ♂♂ of others

may show little or no black on throat. Cf. ♂ Long-winged and Plain-winged antwrens. ♀ much like ♀♀ of other "gray" antwrens (esp. White-flanked, Long-winged, and Plain-winged) but *decidedly* paler gray above and brighter ochraceous below.

Voice: Commonest call by both sexes, when foraging, a soft, rattlelike *pit'ty-pit'ty-pew* or *pew-pit'ty-pit'ty*, varied to *pew-peeu-pe'de'deet!;* also occas. a more complex, jumbled call, esp. in response to tape playback (K. Zimmer). Freq. hd. song a weak, wavering ser. of ca. 10–12 *reee* or *weeet* whistles that slowly rise in pitch and sometimes accelerate slightly.

Behavior: Usually in prs., sometimes several (families?), accompanying mixed-spp. flocks through forest mid. levels or higher. Apt to forage higher than most understory flock members (e.g., *Thamnomanes*) but a little lower than true canopy spp. Active and restless as flick or twitch tail to side (also sometimes flick wings) and hop and glean in vines and foliage of large trees. Nest, mostly of dead leaves wrapped and suspended in fork, 4–10m up; Feb nest, Junglaven, Amazonas.

Status and habitat: Fairly common to common resident, mainly in humid terra firme forest, and high around treefalls and forest openings.

Range: To 1000m. Throughout Amazonas; e across Bolívar from lower Río Caura and upper Río Paragua se to Cerro Paurai-tepui (*pallida*); rest of e Bolívar n and e of previous subsp. from lower Río Paragua, Sierra de Imataca, and s Delta Amacuro s (*cinereiventris*). Se Colombia and e Ecuador to n Bolivia, Amaz. Brazil, and the Guianas.

Note: Recs. from Cerro Turumiquire (FMNH) and Yacua, Sucre (USNM) need verification.

Herpsilochmus

Long tails and bold black-and-white patterns bring to mind a gnatcatcher; crown black (♂) or black mixed with rufous or white (♀); most with prom. white superciliary, white wing bars, and white tail tips; high in canopy; ♂♂ usually more difficult to identify than ♀♀.

Spot-tailed Antwren
PLATE 43

Herpsilochmus sticturus Tiluchi Rabipunteado
Identification: 4.3″ (10.9cm). 9.3g. ♂: *crown all black* with *long white eyebrow* and black postocular; back dark gray mixed black; semiconcealed interscapular patch white; wings black with 2 large white-spotted wing bars; flight feathers edged white; *below gray*, paler on throat and center of belly, black tail with prom. white tips, central feathers with 2–3 white spots on inner webs forming spotlike bars (visible from

above). ♀: above like ♂ but *crown black with long narrow streaks of dark rufous (hard to see in field)*, below grayish white faintly tinged buffy olive throughout.
Sim. species: See very sim. ♂ Todd's Antwren which differs mainly in small amt. of white (dotting and mottling) on forehead. ♀ told from ♀ Todd's by rufous (not white) streaking in crown. At higher els. see Roraiman Antwren; w of Río Caura, Spot-backed Antwren.
Voice: Song a stuttering ser. that starts slowly then accelerates slightly, *chwnk chwnk, chwnk, chi chi-chi'ch'ch'ch'ch'ch'ch'ch'ch*, on same pitch; song has a hard, nasal, staccato edge and is overall much like song of Pygmy Antwren. Cf. song of Roraiman Antwren.
Behavior: Sim. to that of Todd's Antwren. The two occur together in forest canopy, even in same mixed-spp. flocks.
Status and habitat: Uncommon to fairly common (perhaps local) resident in moist and humid terra firme forest in lowlands. May range into slightly drier forest than Todd's Antwren (fairly common in canopy of tall moist forest only a few km s of El Dorado).

Range: To 300m (prob. higher). N Bolívar from lower Río Caura (Maripa) and e Bolívar from Anacoco s to Río Cuyuní region (*sticturus*). The Guianas and adj. ne Brazil.
Note: Some incl. Dugand's Antwren (*H. dugandi*) of w Amazonia with this sp. Songs nearly identical.

Todd's Antwren   PLATE 40
Herpsilochmus stictocephalus   Tiluchí de las Tierras Bajas
Identification: 4.5″ (11.4cm). 9.6g. Closely resembles Spot-tailed Antwren. In field *only reliable mark separating ♂ Todd's from ♂ Spot-tailed is presence of some white dotting on forehead* (may form small whitish patch); and *note vocal differences.* In hand some of following also may be helpful: Todd's has back slightly paler, semiconcealed white interscapular patch has *almost no black, underparts white* tinged pale gray on chest and sides (not almost uniform gray below); tail slightly longer (ca. 45 vs. 40mm), and white central tail spots and tips larger. ♀: like ♂ but *black crown entirely dotted white* (much more conspic. than in ♂), throat and chest buff, palest on throat, and rather sharply set off from whitish lower underparts.
Sim. species: In Venez. overlaps Spot-tailed (not but Spot-backed) Antwren which is less common and, despite its name, has less prom. tail spots than Todd's. In field ♂♂ of the two are best told by presence of a ♀ or by voice; or *given a very good look*, by presence of tiny amt. of white dotting on forehead of Todd's (all black

in ♂ Spot-tailed). ♀ Spot-tailed has rufous (not white) crown streaks, but this also can be difficult to verify in field.
Voice: ♂'s song a fairly rapid, descending whinny of about 12 notes, *we'he'he-e-e-e-e-e-e-a*, soft, laugh-like, and much higher pitched than song of Spot-tailed Antwren. Song of ♀ sim. but slightly higher pitched.
Behavior: Prs. keep very high and in outer foliage of forest canopy trees where they are difficult to see well. Both this sp. and Spot-tailed Antwren faithfully follow canopy mixed-spp. flocks, and the 2 spp. may occur together in these flocks (commonly so in adj. Guyana, fide M. B. Robbins), but they also occas. forage away from canopy flocks. Hop fairly actively and peer and glean in high foliage, mostly for arthropods which they take by pecking or lunging.
Status and habitat: Fairly common but easily overlooked resident in tall humid terra firme forest. Mainly lowlands.

Range: To 300m. Extreme e Bolívar from Sierra de Imataca s to Río Yuruán, upper Río Cuyuní, and base of Cerro Venamo. The Guianas and adj. extreme n Brazil (once).

Spot-backed Antwren   PLATE 40
Herpsilochmus dorsimaculatus   Tiluchí Espalda Manchada
Identification: 4.5″ (11.4cm). 9.5g. ♂ much like ♂ Spot-tailed Antwren, and ranges narrowly overlap along lower and mid. Río Caura. ♂ Spot-backed is slightly larger, *back distinctly streaked and spotted with black*, tail longer (ca. 50 vs. 40mm), and underparts whiter (shows grayish wash only on chest and sides). ♀: additionally differs in forecrown black with a few *tawny spots (not obvious in field)*, rest of crown black *conspic. dotted white*, and *throat and chest much brighter and more extensively buff* (contrasts with white lower underparts).
Sim. species: Either sex easily confused with Spot-tailed Antwren and most reliably told by voice. In most of Amazonas prob. overlaps no other *Herpsilochmus* except rather different Rufous-winged Antwren. In tepuis see Roraiman Antwren.
Voice: Song, often over and over at short intervals, a short (2 sec), rubbery-lipped, fast trill rising slightly then falling, with last notes more distinct, *eeeeeieieieieieieeeeeeeeeeee'e'e'r*, notably soft, ventriloquial (has quality of song of White-browed Antbird).
Behavior: Sim. to that of Todd's Antwren, although perhaps not always so high in forest. Like all lowland *Herpsilochmus*, forages mostly amidst foliage where usually difficult to see.

Status and habitat: Uncommon resident in canopy and vine-tangled borders or high around old treefalls in terra firme and várzea forest. Near Junglaven has been found most often in várzea forest.

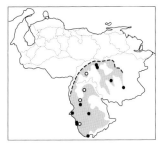

Range: To 400m. N Amazonas (Yapacana; sightings, Junglaven) southward; nw Bolívar from Hato Las Nieves (sight, K. Zimmer) and lower Río Caura, Cerro Guaiquinima (falls), and upper Río Caroní (Caño Apácara) southward. Extreme e Colombia s in Rio Negro drainage of Brazil to near Manaus.

Roraiman Antwren
PLATE 40
Herpsilochmus roraimae Tiluchi del Roraima
Identification: 5″ (12.7cm). Another sp. closely resembling the previous 3 spp. but occurring at higher els. with little or no overlap. Roraiman Antwren differs from all 3 in *decidedly larger size and longer tail* (it is largest *Herpsilochmus* in Venez.), tail with *more rows of spotlike bars* (at least 5 visible) crossing both webs of central tail feathers (from above, spots occur in prs.). Also note rather *extensive black streaking on back* (unlike Todd's Antwren). ♀: additionally differs from other ♀♀ (except Todd's) in black crown entirely dotted white (no rufous or tawny) and light buff wash across chest; from ♀ Todd's principally by larger size, black streaking on center of back, and decidedly longer tail with more rows of spots.
Voice: Song a hard, fast, and staccato ser. of ca. 20 nasal notes (in 2.5 sec) that are slightly louder in middle then decelerate toward end; *ch che'che'che'che'che'che'che'che'che ch ch ch*. Recalls songs of Spot-tailed Antwren but *slows* (not accelerates) toward end. As in others of genus, tail vibrates with each note as bird sings.
Behavior: Single birds, prs., or occas. several (families?) follow canopy mixed-spp. flocks and are relatively active as they search mainly tops of leaves of high outer foliage. Peer quickly, then glean or lunge for arthropod prey or occas. quickly flutter short distances into air for flushed prey.

Status and habitat: Resident in humid and wet premontane forest and forest edges on slopes of tepuis. Common on Sierra de Lema; apparently more numerous (many more specimens) on cerros of Bolívar (esp. in se Bolívar) than in Amazonas.
Range: 900–2000m. Cerros of Amazonas (Cerro Parú; Cerro Duida, upper Río Ocamo and Río Siapa; Cerro de la Neblina); nw Bolívar from Cerros Tabaro and Guaiquinima southward (*kathleenae*); se Bolívar from Aprada-tepui, Auyán-tepui, and Sierra de Lema southward (*roraimae*). N Brazil (Neblina) and Guyana (Mt. Twek-quay).

Rufous-winged Antwren
PLATE 40
Herpsilochmus rufimarginatus Tiluchi Alirrufo
Identification: 4.5″ (11.4cm). 10.4g. Crown and narrow line through eyes black, *long superciliary white*; back gray mixed black in center, wing coverts with 2 broad white bars; *primaries and most of secondaries bright rufous chestnut*, innermost secondaries edged white, throat white, *rest of underparts pale yellow*; rounded tail blackish broadly tipped white. ♀: sim. but *crown chestnut*, back brownish olive.
Sim. species: Patch of rufous chestnut on wings and yellowish underparts easily separate this from any other *Herpsilochmus*, but like others of genus, often difficult to see well.
Voice: Song, by both sexes (higher pitched in ♀), a smoothly accelerating, gravelly sounding *here-hip-pip-pip-pip-pi'pi'pi'pi'pi'pi'pi* or *kuu, ku ku ku-ku-ku'ku' ku'we'e'e'e'e'djjt, djjt*, bouncy (like a little bouncing ball), descending somewhat, and with rough note at end; tail is depressed, partially fanned, and vibrates to "beat" of song (Hilty). Foraging birds repeat a single nasal *kelp* (like pianissimo Barred Forest-Falcon) and nasal, descending rattle, *wa'a'a'a* (K. Zimmer recording).
Behavior: Prs. stay mostly in foliage of canopy where they are difficult to see. Forage alone or with mixed-spp. flocks, actively gleaning in foliage and occas. hover-gleaning for arthropod prey.
Status and habitat: Fairly common but somewhat local resident in fairly wide range of dry to moist (semideciduous) forest, esp. in north, as well as tall humid forest, viny forest borders, and foliage with pinnately compound leaves (legumes). N of Orinoco mostly in hilly terrain or foothills (e.g., n slope PN Henri Pittier). S of Orinoco in dry to humid forest in lowlands and foothills.

Range: To 1000m. Sierra de Perijá, Zulia, w base of Andes in Mérida and Trujillo, e base locally from Táchira to Portuguesa (Turén); se Falcón (sight, La

Misión), n cordilleras from Carabobo to Distr. Federal and se Miranda (sight, PN Guatopo); n Monagas (Caripe); spottily in n and c Amazonas and n Bolívar from lower Río Caura and Sierra de Imataca s to lower Río Caroní (La Paragua) and lower Río Cuyuní (*frater*). E Panama to ne Argentina and Guyana.

Formicivora

Scrub (not forest); sexes very different; ♂♂ darker *below* than above; long fringy band of white on sides.

Northern White-fringed Antwren   PLATE 40
Formicivora intermedia   Coicorita
Identification: 5″ (12.7cm). 9.4g. ♂: above smoky brown, wings black with single broad white bar and extensive white dotting on coverts; black sides of head and underparts separated by *broad white superciliary continuing as stripe down sides of neck and chest and widening on sides and flanks* (where feathers unusually long); tail slightly rounded, tipped white. Or with back dusky brown (*fumosa*) or back reddish brown (*orenocensis*). ♀: somewhat variable; above generally like ♂; sides of head grayish, below dirty white to buff with variable amt. of dusky streaking and mottling on chest. Or coarsely spotted black on breast (*fumosa*). Or back reddish brown, underparts white more extensively streaked black (*orenocensis*).
Sim. species: ♂'s pattern (darker below than above) unusual; long white "racing" stripe bordering black underparts is unmistakable. ♀ told by combination of eyebrow, wing and breast markings, and habitat.
Voice: Vocalizations soft and unusual. Both sexes of all subspp. give single whistled *tu* and mushy, bisyllabic *chúret*. Song a weak little pianissimo phrase, slightly descending, *juup, tu-du-du-du-du-du* (inhale, exhale); song (or call?) a ser. of 2–5 soft syncopated notes, *ju-ju . . . ju-ju-ju-ju. . . . ju-ju-ju . . .* , in little Morse code patterns, often long continuing or followed by soft trill.
Behavior: Prs. forage from near gd. to ca. 5m up, hopping in deliberate fashion, gleaning small arthropods from foliage and small twigs, and wagging partly spread tail from side to side. Often lean down to peer at sides of branches. Freq. with small mixed-spp. flocks containing flycatchers, gnatcatchers, greenlets, wrens, and grassquits. Not shy but can be hard to see clearly in dense vegetation where they live. Nest a thinly woven grass cup suspended by rim from fork; 2 grayish white eggs spotted lilac and blotched brown.
Status and habitat: Common resident in dry to semi-arid scrub and brushland, dry forest, thickets along dry forest borders, gallery forest borders, and edges of mangroves (but generally not in very arid scrub).
Range: To 1600m (once to 2000m; usually well below 1000m). Maracaibo Basin of Zulia, Táchira, Mérida, and Trujillo (*fumosa*); rest of drier Venez. n of Orinoco e to Sucre and w Monagas; Isla Margarita (*intermedia*); n Amazonas s to Caño Cataniapo) e across n Bolívar to Sierra de Imataca, lower Río Cuyuní, and locally in s Anzoátegui; Delta Amacuro (several sight recs.) and c Monagas (*orenocensis*). N Colombia (incl. c Andean valleys). Chacachare Isl. (off Trinidad); Tobago.

Note: Previously considered a subsp. of Southern White-fringed Antwren (*F. grisea*)[403,545].

Southern White-fringed Antwren   PLATE 40
Formicivora grisea   Coicorita del Sur
Identification: 5″ (12.7cm). 9.4g. ♂: essentially sim. to Northern White-fringed Antwren. ♀: above generally like ♂ but duller; sides of head grayish, *eyebrow and underparts bright cinnamon rufous.*
Sim. species: Cf. Northern White-fringed Antwren (no known range overlap).
Voice: Vocalizations very unlike Northern White-fringed Antwren. Song (San Carlos de Río Negro and Suriname) a rather low, husky *chuup, chuup, chuup . . .* (ca. 50 notes in 13 sec), often repeated 2–3 times with little more than a 1-sec pause between songs; lower pitched than Northern White-fringed Antwren (above), and reedy; also ca. 10–20 low, coarse notes, *qlip-qlip-qlip . . .* , 3/sec; and liquid *queek, chuup* (C. Parrish recording).
Behavior: Sim. to that of Northern White-fringed Antwren.
Status and habitat: Fairly common resident in thickets and bushes in white sandy soil savannas, borders of low-canopied scrub woodland, tree isls. in savanna, and scattered bushes on rocky outcrops. In Venez. closely tied to scrubby bushes on white sandy soil.

Range: To 300m. W Amazonas from Samariapo, San Fernando de Atabapo, and vicinity of Cerro Yapacana s to Caño Casiquiare and Río Negro (*rufiventris*). E Colombia and n Brazil e to the Guianas, extreme e Amaz. Brazil, and sc Brazil (s of the Amazon) w to e Bolivia; se Brazil.
Note: Previous authors incl. Northern White-fringed Antwren (*F. intermedia*) with present sp., under the name White-fringed Antwren[403,545].

Drymophila

Extensively streaked and spotted; long ample tail strongly graduated; fond of bamboo; sexes differ slightly.

Long-tailed Antbird
PLATE 40
Drymophila caudata   Hormiguerito Cuclillo
Identification: 6″ (15cm). 12g. *Long tailed and streaky.*
♂: *head and upperparts heavily streaked black and white*, rump rufous, wing coverts black with 2 white-fringed wing bars; underparts white finely streaked black on throat, chest, and sides; *flanks, belly, and under tail coverts bright tawny orange; long graduated tail dusky boldly tipped white.* ♀: sim. but crown and nape streaked dark rufous and black, back olive and black; overall duller, much more narrowly and sparsely streaked black, breast tinged buff, flanks and belly dull cinnamon buff.
Sim. species: More likely mistaken for a wren or furnariid than an antbird. Note streaked foreparts, orange rufous rearparts, bold white tail tips, and habitat.
Voice: Song is unusual for an antbird; typically given as an unsynchronized duet, ♂ singing 2 clear rhythmic notes then 2 wheezy, asthmatic phrases, *chuet, chuet, pa-FJEEE-jit, pa-FJEEE-jit* (FJEEE part higher pitched and louder), ♀ chiming in with soft descending *tu, tu, tu, to, to,* about half way through ♂'s song.
Behavior: Prs., occas. families, act like wrens as they hop in dense bamboo and shrubby tangles from eye level to subcanopy; may forage very low, almost down to gd., and reg. cling to side of vertical stems. Peer carefully, then lunge out to peck mostly arthropod prey. Sing freq. and not esp. shy, but tend to remain in cover and can be difficult to see.
Status and habitat: Resident. Somewhat local (microhabitat is patchy) in moist to humid second growth and shrubby forest with native or introd. (Asian) bamboo; also away from bamboo in vine tangles, forest borders, and overgrown coffee plantations. Unlike most others of genus, not restricted to bamboo, although most freq. found in it. Common in disturbed areas on Paria Pen.; much more local in Andes and n cordilleras.

Range: 500–1800m. Sierra de Perijá, Zulia (*aristeguietana*); spottily in Andes from sw Mérida to nw Lara (Cerro El Cogollal) and se Lara (Cabudare); Sierra de San Luis, Falcón; mts. of Yaracuy; and n cordilleras from Carabobo to Distr. Federal and Miranda; mts. of Sucre and n Monagas (*klagesi*). Colombia s locally in mts. to n Bolivia.

Terenura

Small and warblerlike; thin bill, slender body, moderately long tail; most with orange-rufous rump or back patch; forest canopy.

Rufous-rumped Antwren
PLATE 43
Terenura callinota   Hormiguerito Rabadilla Rufa
Identification: 4.2″ (10.7cm). 7g. Warblerlike. ♂: *crown and narrow line through eyes black; long white eyestripe*; back olive with concealed rufous interscapular patch; *contrasting orange-rufous rump*; bend of wing yellow (often concealed), wing coverts black with 2 yellowish white wing bars; below grayish white, belly tinged pale yellow, tail grayish. ♀: sim. but crown and wing coverts olive like back.
Sim. species: Rufous-winged Antwren is superficially sim. but larger and with rufous wing patch but no rufous on rump. Note behavioral differences.
Voice: Thin, high song a rapid 2–part trill, starting slowly then accelerating into chippery staccato trill, *sue-see-wee-st'e'e'e'e'e'e'e'e*. Recalls song of Tennessee Warbler.
Behavior: A nervous and energetic little sprite, usually found singly or in prs. in canopy mixed-spp. flocks, esp. those containing woodcreepers, flycatchers, and other small insectivores. Gleans in high foliage for insects in restless, warblerlike manner, moving rapidly and occas. hanging upside down or downward. Combination of small size, habit of staying high in canopy foliage, and infreq. singing make this sp. difficult to locate or see. Raises and spreads rufous interscapular patch (looks "puffbacked") in agonistic display toward conspecific.
Status and habitat: Known from only 1 specimen in Venez. and small no. of sight recs., but prob. much more numerous, at least locally, than these few recs. suggest as it is easily overlooked. Canopy of humid and wet mt. forest (cloud forest) and at forest borders. Sight recs. in w Barinas as follows: single birds 6 and 8 Aug, 28 Dec 1982, and 13 Oct 1983, 5.1km sw of La Soledad, nw Barinas (C. Parrish); 4 seen 23 Apr 1995, San Isidro Rd., nw Barinas (R. Ridgely); 1 seen above La Azulita, Mérida, at ca. 1850m on 20 Jun 1993 and 1 on 19 Jun 1994[259].

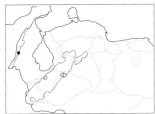

Range: 1450m (sight recs. 1450–1900m). Sierra de Perijá at Cerro Pejochaina, Zulia (*venezuelana*); w slope of Andes in w Mérida (sight); e slope of Andes in nw Barinas (subsp.?). Costa Rica and Panama; Colombia s in mts. to s Peru; s Guyana and adj. Suriname.

Ash-winged Antwren   PLATE 40
Terenura spodioptila   Hormiguerito Piojito
Identification: 4.2″ (10.7cm). 6.5g. ♂: crown and narrow line through eyes black, *long grayish eyestripe*; upperparts olive gray with *rufous back and orange-rufous rump*; bend of wing and under wing coverts yellowish white, wing coverts blackish with *2 white wing bars*; underparts pale gray, throat whitish. ♀: sim. but crown and back brownish turning *rufous on rump*, indistinct buff eyebrow; throat and breast tinged grayish brown, belly faintly yellow. Juv: duller and yellower below.
Sim. species: Usually high overhead in forest canopy where distinctive markings are difficult to see, then easily mistaken for a greenlet (none have wing bars) or warbler. Watch for rufous back and rump.
Voice: Song, as in others of genus, a high-pitched, bouncy ser. of emphatic notes that accelerate into a fast, chippy trill, *tsip, tsee tsee tse te'ti'ti'ti'ti'tititi*. Recalls song of Tennessee Warbler.
Behavior: A busy and energetic little denizen of high-canopy foliage, always heard far more than seen. Single birds or more often prs. are persistent members of canopy mixed-spp. flocks where they actively glean from terminal foliage and habitually cling upside down to leaves like greenlets. Small size and habit of foraging very high make them difficult to see. During aggressive encounters raise and puff out rufous back feathers in spectacular "puffback" display.
Status and habitat: Fairly common (easily overlooked) resident in tall humid and wet forest in lowlands and foothills.

Range: To 1100m. Throughout Amazonas; Bolívar (lower Río Caura; Sierra de Imataca) and s Delta Amacuro southward (*spodioptila*). E Colombia to the Guianas and n Brazil e of Rio Negro and n of the Amazon.

Cercomacra

Fairly thin bill; slim body and fairly long, graduated tail (cf. *Myrmeciza*); gray to blackish to jet ♂♂ all much alike; ♀♀ ochraceous to dark rufous below (except Jet Antbird); the various spp. inhabit canopy vines, shrubby forest edges, thickets near water, or bamboo; retiring habits.

Gray Antbird   PLATE 43
Cercomacra cinerascens   Hormiguero Gris
Identification: 6.3″ (16cm). 18g. Tail rather long. ♂: *plain gray*, slightly paler below; wing coverts faintly dotted white forming obscure bars (inconspic., some-

times absent), concealed white interscapular patch (often small or lacking); *rounded, graduated tail broadly tipped dull white* (white visible from below). ♀: dull olivaceous brown above; rump and tail grayer, wing coverts sometimes with small whitish dots; *forehead and underparts dull ochraceous* washed olive, a little brighter on throat and central underparts; tail as in ♂.
Sim. species: Unlike most others of genus, found only in canopy or subcanopy. ♂ much like ♂ Dusky Antbird but tail spots larger (vestigial in Dusky). Cf. Spot-winged Antshrike, also in canopy. ♀ is a "plain Jane," best told by large tail spots (from below) and voice.
Voice: Usual song (in Venez.) a mushy rising and falling *crook-shank, . . .* repeated slowly several times, often the only clue to bird's presence; also a nasal *kua-dík . . .* 5–6 times (like reverse of previous call). Also a faster, rhythmic *kéep-it-up . . .* ser. of phrases repeated several times, usually (always?) antiphonal with both sexes participating.
Behavior: A notorious skulker that barricades itself inside enormous vine tangles high in rain forest subcanopy and usually refuses to leave them, hence difficult to see. Almost always in prs. Moves around rather quietly in vines as pecks or gleans mostly from leaves. Does not follow mixed-spp. flocks, but often more vocal and active when flocks pass nearby.
Status and habitat: Fairly common to common (by voice) resident in dense treetop vine tangles inside terra firme and várzea forest and at forest borders in lowlands.

Range: To 900m. Throughout Amazonas; w Bolívar from lower Río Caura e to Río Paragua and headwaters of Río Caroní (*cinerascens*); ne Bolívar and s Delta Amacuro from Sierra de Imataca s to upper Río Cuyuní (*immaculata*). E Colombia and e Ecuador to n Bolivia, Amaz. Brazil, and the Guianas.

Dusky Antbird   PLATE 41
Cercomacra tyrannina   Hormiguero Tirano
Identification: 5.7″ (14.5cm). 16g. Much like Gray Antbird. ♂: plain gray above, paler gray below; wing coverts blackish narrowly but distinctly tipped white forming 2 rather weak bars and white fringes on lesser upper wing coverts; semiconcealed white interscapular patch; tail vaguely tipped white (white often missing through wear). Or plain gray to dusky gray above, gray below, conspic. white wing bars and narrow white scalloping on lesser coverts (*saturatior*). ♀: brown above; crown tinged gray, semiconcealed white interscapular patch; wing coverts faintly tipped

buff, below rather bright orangish tawny. Or above darker; below incl. cheeks darker, more chestnut rufous (*saturatior*).

Sim. species: More common than others with which it is likely confused. Both sexes of Spot-winged Antbird have distinctly "spotted" wing coverts (not fringed). Gray Antbird is sim. but a canopy dweller. Also cf. larger White-shouldered and Blackish-gray antshrikes.

Voice: Often hd. song is usually an unsynchronized duet. ♂ begins with rather loose rattlely ser. of whistles that starts slowly, then accelerates rapidly and rises in pitch, *pu pu pe pi'pi'pi̇!*, and ♀ joins in (usually) with jerky, and rather different, *juut-ut'juut-ut'juut-ut'juut-ut*. When disturbed a low-pitched, tight buzz, *drrrrr*.

Behavior: Rather drab and unassuming prs. usually stay within a few meters of gd. where they are frequently hd. but somewhat retiring; tend to remain hidden in thickets, and may require some work to see well. Seldom follow army ants or mixed flocks. Hop deliberately and peer at foliage and twigs for arthropod prey. Nest in Costa Rica a deep hanging pouch with oblique entrance at top; hung from fork of slender, drooping branch or vine, 0.6–3m up; 2 eggs, white spotted reddish brown, heavier at large end[706].

Status and habitat: Fairly common to common resident. Shrubby borders of humid forest, second-growth woodland, and thickets in clearings.

Range: To 1800m (mostly below 1200m). Maracaibo Basin of Zulia, w base of Andes n to Mérida and e base n to Río Guanare, Portuguesa (*vicina*); Amazonas and nw Bolívar (*tyrannina*); s and e Bolívar (*saturatior*); s Monagas (Uverito) and Delta Amacuro (subsp.?). Se Mexico to w Ecuador, Amaz. Brazil n of the Amazon, and the Guianas.

Note: Taxonomy revised[47,219]. Newly described Willis' Antbird (*C. laeta*) from lower Amazonia and ne Brazil is known up Rio Negro to San Gabriel de Cachoeira and may occur in s Venez. Both sexes much like respective sexes of Dusky Antbird. Song a bright, clear, almost bubbly *pee'dánk, pee'dánk . . .* , ca. 4 phrases (A. Whittaker recording).

Jet Antbird
PLATE 41

Cercomacra nigricans Hormiguerito Negro

Identification: 6″ (15cm). 17g. ♂: mainly jet black with *2 prom. white wing bars*; white at bend of wing (inconspic.), white fringing on upper wing coverts and concealed white interscapular patch; tail graduated, *broadly tipped white*. ♀: above dark gray, white wing and tail markings like ♂; below slaty gray *densely freckled and streaked white* on throat and breast. Imm ♂:

may show some narrow white streaking below. Imm ♀: tinged brown above, whitish below spotted gray on throat and breast.

Sim. species: ♂ is blackest and most boldly marked of genus in Venez. ♀ told from others by whitish streaking below. In coastal mt. forests see Venezuelan Antvireo (no known overlap).

Voice: Freq. hd. song is often only clue to this sp.'s presence. ♂♂ sing solos or duets with ♀♀. ♂'s song a rather harsh and halting *chék-off, chék-off, chék-off, chék-off* (swallows last note of each phrase); ♀ overlaps ♂'s last syllable of each phrase with rhythmic, gravelly *karump, karump, karump, karump*; result is a syncopated and antiphonal *chék-kor-rump, chék-kor-rump . . .* ; or ♀ sings between phrases of ♂ (no overlap of notes), producing a rhythmic and complex 4-syllable effect.

Behavior: Prs. stay together and skulk in dense low shrubbery where they are difficult to see. Remain in foliage as hop short distances and glean arthropod prey from leaves or twigs. Do not follow mixed-spp. flocks and rarely at army ant swarms.

Status and habitat: Locally common resident of shrubby areas, viny young second growth, and overgrown pastures; at Hato Cedral, w Apure, found in dense, viny, low-canopied (<8m), and seasonally inundated scrub forest (D. Ascanio). In most areas shows affinity for water or wet, low-lying areas where there are dense thickets and vines.

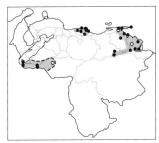

Range: To 600m (most recs. below 400m). Disjunct range. Sw Táchira and adj. w Apure (incl. Hato Cedral); foothills of n cordilleras in Distr. Federal and Miranda; e Sucre, e Monagas, and Orinoco from s Anzoátegui (Soledad) to Delta Amacuro. Panama to sw Ecuador.

Note: Río Branco Antbird (*C. carbonaria*) of n Brazil along Rio Branco and lower Rio Mucujaí, and s Guyana (sight), may occur in se Bolívar. ♂ essentially identical to ♂ Jet Antbird. ♀ above slate gray, throat white streaked dark gray, rest of underparts pale ochraceous. Thickets in gallery forest; calls incl. *pook-pook-pook . . .* and faster, syncopated *kikuk, kikuk, kikuk . . .* , both up to 20 notes[545].

Myrmoborus

Chunky and short-tailed; rather long, pale, blue gray legs; ♂♂ mostly gray and black; ♀♀ brown, buff, and white; undergrowth; songs rather sim.; tail pounded downward.

White-browed Antbird   PLATE 44
Myrmoborus leucophrys   Hormiguero Bejuquero
Identification: 5.4″ (13.7cm). 20g. ♂: *forehead and long, broad eyebrow white*, sides of head and throat black, otherwise dark blue gray above and below (black of throat merges with gray chest; no markings on wings). Or black throat sharply set off from dark gray of rest of underparts (*angustirostris*). ♀: *forehead and long eyebrow cinnamon bordered below by black mask*; crown and upperparts brown with 3 narrow and rather inconspic. buff-dotted wing bars; below white, flanks and belly olive brown.
Sim. species: Conspicuous eyebrows (white in ♂, cinnamon in ♀) are good marks. In addition, ♂ told from ♂ Black-faced Antbird by absence of wing bars; ♀ Black-faced has bold buff bars, white throat contrasting with mostly buff underparts.
Voice: Sings mainly at dawn; song of ♂ and ♀ a long, rapid stream of quavering notes (ca. 30 in 2.5–3 sec) run together, *pe'ee'ee'ee'. . . . eer*, and that descend slowly. Alarm a thin, tinny rattle; sharp *skip!* when disturbed.
Behavior: Prs. keep mostly out of sight in understory; drop to gd. from low perch or move 0.2–4m up around treefalls or in thick undergrowth where hop, then lunge or sally short distances for arthropods. Often cling to sides of vertical stems. Follow army ants if swarms move through their territories, otherwise prs. are usually alone. Easily overlooked except for persistent early morning song.
Status and habitat: Common resident in a wide range of edge, treefall, and disturbed habitats in humid terra firme and várzea forest, white sandy soil várzea scrub, and humid foothill forest; locally in patches of dense vegetation in dry forest (e.g., w of El Palmar, Bolívar). All territories incl. some patches of fairly thick vegetation, also often *Heliconia*.

Range: To 1000m (most recs. below ca. 600m). E base of Andes from Táchira and w Apure to nw Barinas (*erythrophrys*); sightings n to se Lara (Jun 1999, PN Yacambú—D. Ascanio); generally in Amazonas, Bolívar, and s Delta Amacuro (*angustirostris*). E Colombia s (gap in w Amazonia?) to n Bolivia, Amaz. Brazil, and the Guianas.

Black-faced Antbird   PLATE 44
Myrmoborus myotherinus   Hormiguero Ratonero
Identification: 5″ (12.7cm). 21.5g. Eyes dark red. ♂: a paler version of previous sp. *Narrow* grayish white forehead and eyebrow; sides of head and throat black, crown and upperparts blue gray, *wing coverts black*

with 3 narrow white bars; concealed white interscapular patch; underparts *pale* gray. ♀: distinctive; dark brown above with *buff forehead, narrow buff eyebrow, and several bright buff wing bars*; cheeks black, *throat white* bordered by vague necklace of black on chest, *otherwise contrasting bright orange buff below*.
Sim. species: Look for ♂'s black face and wing bars. ♀ brighter below than most. See White-browed Antbird.
Voice: Song a loud, nasal ser. of ca. 12 notes, *je-jee-jee-jee-Jee-Jee-Jee-jee-jee-je-je*, loudest in middle, then slowing and slightly descending near end; alarm a sharp, low-pitched *péeap*.
Behavior: Usually in prs. that either use horizontal perches or cling to side of vertical stems with equal facility. Stay mostly 0.2–4m up in forest undergrowth where hop rather deliberately, peer carefully, and lunge out to foliage or drop to gd. for arthropod prey. Occas. at army ant swarms. Generally easier to see than others of genus, sometimes remarkably unsuspicious.
Status and habitat: Resident inside humid terra firme forest, old second growth, and transitional (occas. seasonally flooded) forest. Scarce and uncommon in lower Río Caura, but there are many specimens from s Amazonas and s Bolívar (Salto Maijía in upper Río Paragua) where prob. fairly common.

Range: To 900m. E Amazonas from headwaters of Río Ventuari (Kabadisocaña) southward; Bolívar from lower Río Caura (Cerro Primavera), Río Paragua (Salto Guaiquinima), and upper Río Caroní (Icabarú) southward (*elegans*). Se Colombia to n Bolivia and w and s Amaz. Brazil.

Hypocnemis

Rather large headed, short tailed, and streaky; vocal in lower growth at forest borders.

Warbling Antbird   PLATE 40
Hypocnemis cantator   Hormiguero Cantarín
Identification: 4.7″ (12cm). 13g. Small and streaked; tail fairly short. ♂: *head black with long white eyestripe and narrow white streak on median crown; black line through eyes; sides of neck and back streaked black and white* and olive; wing coverts black spotted white; 2 white-dotted wing bars; flight feathers and tail brown, throat and breast white tinged yellow and rather finely mottled and streaked black (amt. of streaking variable but heaviest on sides of chest); *flanks and belly bright orange rufous*. Or darker and richer in color, throat and breast white, flanks and

belly deep rufous, chest more heavily streaked black (*notaea*). ♀: sim. but duller, crown and back tinged brown; wing bars dotted buff.
Sim. species: Streaky appearance might recall some wrens or warblers. Also somewhat like *Herpsilochmus* antwrens, but they occur mainly high in *canopy*. In mts. (no overlap) cf. Long-tailed Antbird.
Voice: Often hd. song a lazy, descending, and buzzy *tew, tew-tzew-tzew-tur pur paw*, husky, rough, almost snarling at end, up to 12 notes; ♀ often answers with sim. but higher pitched and shorter version before ♂ finishes. Contact call (or?) a soft, slightly wheezy, complaining *wur-tew* or *wur-tew-tew* (1st note lower), often over and over, while foraging. Songs of subsp. *notaea* are sim. but higher pitched, cleaner (much less buzzy), and faster.
Behavior: Rather passive and sedate, usually seen in prs. wandering alone in lower story of forest or a little higher, occas. assoc. with mixed-spp. flocks, or follow army ant swarms. Rather sedentary and not too difficult to see, they hop and peer in foliage and vines, sometimes fairly actively, and peck at or sally to mostly overhead foliage or occas. lunge or chase fleeing insect prey.
Status and habitat: Fairly common to common resident in vines and dense vegetation around treefalls and at edges of terra firme and várzea forest, shrubby borders of savanna woodland, and taller second growth; occas. wanders inside forest. Also in thickets along creeks and swampy or wet areas. Lowlands and foothills; most recs. of *notaea* are in foothills.

Range: To 1200m. Throughout Amazonas and s Bolívar e to headwaters of Río Caroní (*flavescens*); n Bolívar from lower Río Caura (El Cambur) e to Río Cuyuní and Gran Sabana (*notaea*). E Colombia to n Bolivia, Amaz. Brazil, and the Guianas.

Hypocnemoides

Small, chunky, and gray; long bill; long upper tail coverts cover most of short tail; always near water.

Black-chinned Antbird   PLATE 41
Hypocnemoides melanopogon   Hormiguero Barbinegro
Identification: 4.8″ (12.2cm). 14g. Plump with *short tail and long, slender black bill*. Eyes light gray. ♂: dark gray, slightly paler below, with *black throat patch*; wing coverts black with several narrow fringing white bars; *tail feathers narrowly but conspic. tipped white*. Or much paler gray below, whitish on mid. breast and

belly, black throat patch smaller (*occidentalis*). ♀: above like ♂, below white heavily clouded gray on throat, chest, and sides. Or white of underparts more spotted with gray (*occidentalis*).
Sim. species: ♂ resembles several other small "gray" antbirds, esp. Long-winged Antwren and Black-throated Antbird, but told by short tail with distinct white tips, and esp. *note habitat differences*. Also see rare ♂ Yapacana Antbird. ♀ recalls ♂ Silvered Antbird but much smaller and with different proportions.
Voice: Song by both ♂ and ♀ an accelerating *psheep psheep eep ep-ep-e-e-'e'e'e'weep-wee'-jeep-jeep*, slowing, descending slightly, and raspy at end; alarm a double sounding *péechup*.
Behavior: Usually in prs., occas. noisy groups (families?), and generally fairly easy to see. Like Silvered Antbird, restricted to edges of watercourses, but this sp. stays mostly 0.1–2m up over water and perches on horizontal limbs or clings to side of sapling with equal ease. Hops through streamside vegetation, occas. on gd., and gleans from twigs or foliage near water, lunges for prey, or sallies short distances to foliage. Also reported making looping sallies from low branch out to water surface (K. Zimmer). BC bird, May, Pto. Ayacucho[185].
Status and habitat: Resident in swamps, borders of creeks and streams, lake edges and seasonally inundated (várzea) forest. Almost always near water; sometimes along temporarily dry watercourses. Fairly common in w Amazonas, local in e Bolívar. Specimens and sight recs. extend range to n Monagas[60] (R. Ridgely) and se Sucre[596].

Range: To 400m (sight to 950m, Santa Elena de Uairén). Se Sucre (Caño La Brea), and e Monagas (Río Guarapiche); s to Delta Amacuro; sw Guárico (Río Zuata) nw Bolívar from lower Río Caura and La Paragua s to Gran Sabana (*melanopogon*); throughout Amazonas and s Bolívar e to headwaters of Río Caroní at Icabarú (*occidentalis*). E Colombia, ne Ecuador, and n Peru (n of the Amazon) e to the Guianas and Amaz. Brazil (mostly n of the Amazon).

Hylophylax

Small and plump; moderately wide, flattish (flycatcher-like) bill; short, roundish tail; ornate markings on back; humid forest undergrowth; freq. follow army ants.

Spot-backed Antbird
PLATE 44

Hylophylax naevia Hormiguero Espalda Punteada

Identification: 4.8″ (12.2cm). 13g. Very small with rather long, flattish bill. Legs pinkish; eyes brownish to gray. ♂: crown grayish brown, *cheeks and sides of head dark gray*, back brown, semiconcealed white interscapular patch; *center of back black with large round buff spots*; wing coverts black spotted buff to white forming 3 bars; tertials black tipped buff, rounded tail reddish brown with subterminal black band and buff tips; *throat black* otherwise *white below with bold black-streaked necklace on chest*; flanks and belly cinnamon buff. ♀: above much like ♂; throat white bordered by broad black malar line, *rest of underparts buff with black necklace*.

Sim. species: See Dot-backed and Banded antbirds.

Voice: Song a soft, high-pitched, and rhythmic *pfée-be, pfée-be, PFEE-BE, pfée-be, pfée-be, pfeee-be*, growing louder in middle then fading. A buzzy *chirr'r* in mild alarm; and sharp *peéea*.

Behavior: An attractive but inconspic. little bird of forest understory that forages at army ant swarms or away from them about equally. Individuals or prs. perch mostly 0.5–3m up on branches and vines in undergrowth, or cling to side of vertical saplings. Drop to gd. or sally rapidly to foliage and twigs for prey. Tail flicked up in alarm. Hold mostly "classical" permanent territories defended by both sexes which sing and bicker loudly at conspecifics near boundaries.

Status and habitat: Uncommon to fairly common resident (easily overlooked) in understory of humid terra firme forest, also low-lying transitional forest and occas. várzea forest.

Range: To 1100m. N Amazonas (Caño Cataniapo) s to Cerro de la Neblina; Bolívar from lower Río Caura, mid. Río Paragua (Salto Guaiquinima), and extreme upper Río Cuyuní near Guyana border (Camborere) southward (*naevia*). Se Colombia to n Bolivia, Amaz. Brazil, and the Guianas.

Note: Subsp. *consobrina* not recognized[489].

Dot-backed Antbird
PLATE 44

Hylophylax punctulata Hormiguero Punteado

Identification: 4.5″ (11.4cm). 11g. Closely resembles much commoner Spot-backed Antbird but tail even shorter (ca. 30–33 vs. 38–45mm), legs gray (not pinkish), and eyes dark. Both sexes differ in being grayer above, with *cheeks and sides of head white to whitish* (not dark gray), *white* (not buff) *spots covering entire back, rump, and upper tail coverts*; tail black (not reddish brown with black subterminal band), *lower underparts all white* (little or no cinnamon buff on flanks). ♂

and ♀ Dot-backed are sim., differing only in throat of ♂ solid black, throat of ♀ white with broad black border on sides forming malar stripe.

Sim. species: Note that differences in color and extent of spotting on back between Spot-backed and Dot-backed antbirds are *difficult to unambiguously distinguish* in field. The two are most easily separated by song. Also cf. Banded Antbird.

Voice: Song a loud, briskly whistled *whee-pEEo*, over and over; when excited sings same but faster. Not as vocal as Spot-backed Antbird.

Behavior: Sim. to Spot-backed Antbird but perches and forages lower, mostly less than 2m up (occas. higher in response to playback). Occurs in prs., generally alone and not with mixed-spp. flocks or army ant swarms. Usually remains in dense low vegetation where difficult to see.

Status and habitat: Uncommon and local resident in thick vegetation and dense stands of saplings along streambanks in humid várzea forest or low-lying swampy or transitional forest. Shows strong preference for vicinity of small streams. Most Venez. recs. are clustered in a few areas in Amazonas.

Range: To 300m. Amazonas from lower and mid. Río Ventuari (Sabana; Las Carmelitas; sight, Junglaven, 1998—K. Zimmer) southward; w Bolívar in lower and middle Río Caura (*punctulata*). E Colombia (1 rec.); e Ecuador s to n Bolivia and w Amaz. and n Brazil.

Scale-backed Antbird
PLATE 41

Hylophylax poecilinota Hormiguero Lomo Escamado

Identification: 5″ (12.7cm). 18g. Large dark eyes. ♂: head, upper back, and underparts gray, mid. back and wings black, wing coverts, back, and rump broadly fringed ("scaled") with white; semiconcealed white interscapular patch; tail black with row of large white spots near center and narrow white tip. ♀: scaled like ♂, but the 2 subspp. *differ markedly from each other*. Across most of s Venez. back brown to reddish brown, wing coverts, back, and rump heavily scaled buff to pale cinnamon, *crown and sides of head orange rufous*, chin buff, *rest of underparts light gray*. Or scaling white, head and *entire* underparts orange rufous (*duidae*).

Sim. species: No other small antbird is so heavily scaled above.

Voice: Song is ca. 5–10 or more slow, slightly quavering whistles, *pureeeee, pureeeeee, pureeeeee . . .* , each about a quarter- to half-tone higher in pitch than the preceding; sim. to songs of Rufous-bellied Antwren and Banded Antbird.

Behavior: A faithful but rather quiet and low-key attendant of army ant swarms. Often driven into subordinate peripheral positions at swarms by larger, more aggressive obligate followers[811]. Also often forages away from ant swarms, alone or in prs., mostly 0.5–3m up in understory. Adept at clinging to side of vertical saplings and stems from which sallies to gd., low foliage, or twig and bark surfaces for arthropod prey. Flicks tail up when excited or alarmed, and often remarkably unsuspicious.

Status and habitat: Fairly common resident in open undergrowth of humid terra firme forest, less often low-lying swampy or várzea forest. Most numerous in white sandy soil forests of upper Orinoco and Río Negro region.

Range: To 1300m. N and c Amazonas s to Caño Usate and se side of Cerro Duida; Bolívar from lower Río Caura, mid. Río Paragua (Cerro Guaiquinima), and Sierra de Imataca southward (*poecilinota*); w and s Amazonas from San Fernando de Atabapo and w side of Cerro Duida southward (*duidae*). E Colombia to n Bolivia, Amaz. Brazil, and the Guianas.
Note: Differences in plumage suggest more than 1 sp. involved.

Dichrozona

Monotypic genus; small and cute; long bill, bobbed tail, and bold plumage.

Banded Antbird   PLATE 44
Dichrozona cincta   Hormiguerito Bandeado
Identification: 4″ (10.2cm). 16g. Small with long, thin bill and short (0.9″, 23mm) tail. ♂: crown and mantle reddish brown, lower back and rump black, rump crossed by *narrow white band* (conspic. in flight), unusually long black wing coverts with *2 wide buff bars* (upper bar often whitish), flight feathers dusky brown, tail dusky, *outer feathers white*, ill-defined eyebrow and sides of head grayish white, underparts immaculate white with *bold black-spotted necklace across chest*. ♀: wing bars and rump buff, less spotted below.
Sim. species: Pattern recalls Spot-backed and Dot-backed antbirds but told from ♂ of either by white throat; from ♂ or ♀ of either by conspic. white rump band which is more or less continuous with lower wing bar (imparts odd appearance) and by white outer tail feathers often conspic. in flight. Also cf. Wing-banded Wren and Collared Gnatwren.
Voice: Startled or alarmed foraging birds (nw Brazil) give a brief, thin rattle (rather soft), shorter *tchirr*, and querulous *keewit* (K. Zimmer). Song (se Peru) a distinctive ser. of 12 or more high, thin, and drawn-out notes, *psszueeé, psszueeé, . . .*, delivered slowly, ascending fractionally, and with slight buzz or insectlike quality. Sings a few times at dawn but otherwise usually rather quiet.
Behavior: Has an almost reptilian aspect to its behavior. Usually found alone or in prs. walking slowly on forest floor, but more apt to sing from atop a log or slightly elevated perch. Often slowly wiggles or twitches tail from side to side, also spreads tail exposing ribbon of white on outer tail edges as it walks. Does not follow mixed-spp. flocks.
Status and habitat: Resident in interior of shady but relatively open terra firme forest. Few recs. in Venez. Elsewhere sp. has large territories, or prs. are well separated and occur in low density.

Range: To 200m. Sw Amazonas (Yavita-Pimichín trail); doubtless southward (*cincta*). Se Colombia and e Ecuador to n Bolivia and w Amaz. Brazil.

Schistocichla

Small and uniform group of antbirds united by color patterns (♂♂ gray with white wing dots, ♀♀ orange rufous below with buff wing dots). Differ from *Percnostola* (where formerly placed) by rounder heads (no long crest feathers) and wing coverts with spots (not fringed with white or buff). Both genera close to *Myrmeciza*.

Spot-winged Antbird   PLATE 41
Schistocichla leucostigma   Hormiguero Alipunteado
Identification: 5.7″ (14.5cm). 24g. Two rather different forms (prob. at least 2 or more distinct spp.). *Long legs pinkish* (*infuscata, leucostigma*) or *legs dark gray* (all other subspp.). ♂: above dark gray (no white interscapular patch) with *contrasting pale gray underparts*; *2 rows of small white dots on wing coverts* form rather inconspic. dotted bars; flanks and belly tinged olive. Or sim. but underparts almost as dark as upperparts (*subplumbea, obscura, saturata*). Or also with shorter bill (*saturata*). ♀: *crown and sides of head gray* contrasting with dark reddish brown back and *orange rufous underparts*; wing coverts dusky with *small but conspic. buff-dotted bars*; tail dusky. Or ♀ sim. but sides of head brownish olive (*infuscata*). Or sim. but darker overall (*subplumbea, obscura, saturata*).
Sim. species: ♂ much like Caura Antbird but smaller and, in area of overlap, distinctly 2-toned (darker above than below). ♀ Caura Antbird is much larger than ♀ Spot-winged and not so long-legged.

Voice: Song of lowland birds (Las Claritas, Bolívar) a long, flat, rattling trill, last half slightly louder, then diminishing at end, *jee-e-e-e-e-e-e-ee-ee-ee-ea* . . . (ca. 25–35 notes in 2–3 sec), 1st note or 2 distinct, rest vibrating at more or less same pitch and speed. A soft *chirr* when distributed; louder, sharp *stick-stick* in alarm. Song of highland subsp. in adj. Guyana quite different (M. Robbins).
Behavior: Usually in prs. which are somewhat furtive and difficult to see. Hop low through undergrowth, on logs, or on gd., and occas. cling to vertical saplings and stems. Infreq. around army ant swarms. Forage mostly within ca. 1m of gd., moving or hopping slowly, peering carefully, then pecking arthropods from leaf litter, twigs, and live leaves.
Status and habitat: Fairly common resident in se Bolívar (many specimens and sightings). Dense undergrowth or in regrowth around treefalls inside humid terra firme forest, also damp places inside forest, esp. near small streams.

Range: To 400m in se Táchira; to 1500m s of Orinoco. Extreme sw Táchira (*subplumbea*); n Amazonas at Junglaven[833]; s Amazonas from Río Casiquiare southward (*infuscata*); se Bolívar in upper Río Cuyuní and base of Sierra de Lema (*leucostigma*); upper Sierra de Lema and vicinity of Gran Sabana on Cerros Ptari, Sororopán, Chimantá, Aprada, Uaipán, and Uei-tepui (*obscura*); base of Cerro Roraima (*saturata*). E Colombia to n Bolivia, Amaz. Brazil, and the Guianas.
Note: Often placed in *Percnostola*[403] but by some in *Schistocichla*[545,827]. Subspp. *obscura* and *saturata*, of tepui highlands, have dark legs and a different song and are prob. a separate sp. from pink-legged birds in lowlands.

Caura Antbird   PLATE 43
Schistocichla caurensis   Hormiguerote Alipunteado
Identification: 7.5″ (19cm). 39g. *Large*. Bill long, heavy, and black; eyes reddish brown (3.4″, 86mm); legs dark gray. ♂: *uniform blackish slate* above and below; *2 rows of white dots on wing coverts* form dotted bars. ♀: crown, sides of head, and cheeks dark gray, rest of upperparts reddish brown, wing coverts dusky with *2 prom. buff-spotted bars*; *underparts rufous chestnut*, flanks and belly tinged brownish, tail dusky.
Sim. species: Much like ♂ White-shouldered Antshrike which has black crown and more white dots on wing coverts. Also cf. ♂ to dark-legged subspp. of Spot-winged Antbird which are smaller but have longer legs (minimum range overlap); and to pinkish-legged subspp. of ♂ Spot-winged Antbird. ♀ essentially a larger,

heavier-billed edition of ♀ Spot-winged Antbird but darker below.
Voice: Song a slow ser. of shrill, slightly buzzy notes (strongly modulated), *JEEP . . JEEP, JEET, JEET-jee-jee-jit-jit-jaa-jaa*, descending throughout; recalls song of Black-chinned Antbird but much slower. Bicker and scold with variety of snarls, *jeea* and *jeer*, and rough chattering *plee-ap* (K. Zimmer recording).
Behavior: Occurs in quiet prs. on or near gd. on boulder-strewn hillsides. Hops on roots and in accumulated litter and tangles at base of or beneath large boulders, or on gd. in shady places where spends long periods of time tossing leaves before moving a little. Very little song in early Mar (K. Zimmer).
Status and habitat: Fairly common but *very local* resident of forested, boulder-strewn foothills and lower slopes of tepuis. Presence of many *large* boulders and rock outcrops in humid forest may be key. Local or patchy distrib. reflects microhabitat requirements.

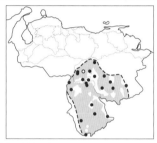

Range: 100–1300m (most recs. in foothills above 300m). Spottily in Amazonas (hills); extreme nw Bolívar (Serranía de Pijiguaos), e locally throughout Río Caura drainage and e to upper Río Caroní at Cerro Chimantá. Extreme nw Brazil (Rio Padauiri).
Note: The 2 subspp., *australis* (Amazonas, nw Bolívar) and *caurensis* (Río Caura eastward), do not differ appreciably and are not worthy of recognition.

Clytoctantes

Deep, laterally compressed and upturned bill; long hindclaw (hallux); distrib. of spp. highly disjunct.

Recurve-billed Bushbird   PLATE 42
Clytoctantes alixii   Hormiguero Pico de Hoz
Identification: 6.3″ (16cm). Scarce resident of Perijá region. Black bill deep but very thin, *bladelike and strongly upturned*; tail quite short; legs and feet large and strong. ♂: slate gray with *lores, foreface, throat, and most of breast black*; wing coverts faintly dotted white; small concealed white interscapular patch. ♀: *above chestnut*, wings darker, wing coverts faintly dotted buff, tail dusky, *underparts rich reddish chestnut*; interscapular patch as in ♂.
Sim. species: Unmistakable if seen well. No other antbird in Venez. has such an unusual bill.
Voice: In Colombia a ♀ gave a chirring *ke'e'e'ew*, recalling that of Ocellated Antbird[816].
Behavior: Poorly known. A secretive sp. seen once at an army ant swarm in Colombia[260]. Has been seen pecking at dead stems, then ripping them apart with

quick upward movements of bladelike bill and peer-ing into cut gashes in stems, apparently for insects[816].
Status and habitat: Poorly known. Small no. of speci-mens from Venez., most taken in early 1950s, the most recent in 1965, all come from upper Río Negro Valley of Zulia. In Colombia has been found in dense, almost impenetrable stands of young second growth, and in dense shrubbery along forest borders.

Range: 300(?)–1200m. E slope of Sierra de Perijá (upper Río Negro Valley) at Cerro Ayapa; El Escon-dido (1075m); La Sabana (1200m); 7km downstream from La Sabana; Panapicho (300m); near village of Ranchería Julián (= Barranquilla, 960m) ca. 15km nw of Machiques in Ríos Apón and Macoita valleys. N Colombia.

Sclateria

Long, thin, narrow bill; wings and tail rounded; non-scutate tarsi; sexes differ; always near water.

Silvered Antbird   PLATE 41
Sclateria naevia   Hormiguero Trepador
Identification: 6″ (15cm). 20g. Bill long and slender. Legs long and *grayish pink*. Two distinctive forms. ♂ of *argentata* (n and c Amazonas): dark gray above; wing coverts dusky with 2 rows of small white dots; below white, sides of chest and breast blurry gray-white ob-scurely mottled and scalloped gray. ♀ of *argentata*: dark brown above with 2 rows of small buffy rufous dots on wing coverts; central underparts white, *sides of head and neck and sides of body cinnamon rufous.* Or (rest of s Venez.) sim. to respective sexes above but ♂ with throat and underparts white *broadly and exten-sively streaked gray* (less on throat), ♀ with *extensive gray brown streaking below.* ♀ *diaphora* (Río Caura) has throat white, breast washed tawny ochraceous, and lower underparts reddish brown somewhat streaked paler. Birds in e Sucre (*naevia*) have short whitish eyebrows and are more spotted and scaled below than other races.
Sim. species: Despite differences in underparts of sub-spp., all are easily recognized by long, thin bill, long, pale legs, and habitat. ♀ Black-chinned Antbird recalls ♂ *argentata* (the two are found together in same habi-tat), but latter has black throat and fringed (not dot-ted) white wing coverts. Also cf. rare Yapacana Ant-bird which is strikingly sim. to ♂ *argentata* but not so mottled on sides.
Voice: In all areas song of both sexes is 1–2 brief, intro-ductory notes accelerating into a loud, ringing cre-scendo that swells in volume then gradually dimin-ishes, *tweep, twep, tip-tip-tip-tí-tí-ti-ti-ti-TI-TI-TI-TI-TI-ti-*

ti-ti-ti-ti-i-i-i (ca. 4 sec). Alarm a loud *chip* or *chit-it*; bub-bly *pup'pup* muttered while foraging.
Behavior: An easily overlooked sp. that works edges of oozy watercourses. Occas. sings loudly but keeps mostly under cover as hops with deliberate move-ments and picks small spiders and insects from water's surface or leaf litter with deft little stabs. Usually in prs., although members are often well separated. Holds long linear territories along water's edge. Also hops on gd., on leaf litter, and on twigs just above and at edge of water. Not with mixed-spp. flocks, nor esp. furtive, but sometimes difficult to see well. May cock tail or flick it from side to side when alarmed.
Status and habitat: Resident of shady undergrowth or overhanging vegetation along banks of streams, rivers, lagoons, and oxbows in terra firme or várzea forest, and wet areas with standing water in várzea and swampy forest. Very common in Delta Amacuro and in swampy areas of e Sucre; much more local and less numerous southward.

Range: To 500m. Generally in Amazonas (*argentata*); n Bolívar in lower Río Caura and Río Mocho (*diaphora*); rest of Bolívar and Delta Amacuro n to se Sucre (*nae-via*). Se Colombia to n Bolivia, Amaz. Brazil, and the Guianas.

Percnostola

Two spp. of uncertain taxonomic affinity; 1 or both possibly allied to *Myrmeciza*; pound tail downward like that genus.

Black-headed Antbird   PLATE 41
Percnostola rufifrons   Hormiguero Cabecinegro
Identification: 5.7″ (14.5cm). 25g. Eyes gray. Bill black (♂) or with mandible grayish (♀) and rather heavy. Feathers of crown lengthened (longer in ♂) forming shaggy crest, but crest usually *not* raised or much evi-dent in field. ♂: dark gray with black crown and throat but neither in strong contrast to rest of plumage, wing coverts black with at least 3 narrow white-fringed wing bars; *no interscapular patch* (either sex). ♀: very differ-ent; crown dull rufous chestnut, upperparts dark gray-ish brown, wing coverts dusky with *broad dark buff fringes forming 3 distinct bars*; *throat and chest cinna-mon rufous* contrasting with paler, more ochraceous belly; flanks olivaceous.
Sim. species: ♂ superficially like several others in fam-ily, incl. larger White-shouldered and Blackish-gray antshrikes (neither have black throats) and smaller ♂ Black-chinned Antbird which has short, white-tipped

tail and is usually near water. Note ♀'s buff bars and distinctly 2-toned underparts. Cf. esp. ♀ Spot-winged and Black-throated antbirds and larger ♀ Caura antbird.

Voice: Song of ♂ and ♀ (from Vaupés, Colombia) a loud, whistled *pa, peer-peer-peer-peer-peer-pear-pear*, slightly dropping in pitch near end. Call a hard *kuip* sim. to others of genus in w Amazonia.

Behavior: Usually found in loosely assoc. prs. which stay low in understory and hop in thicker foliage or move in ser. of wing-assisted hops and flights through more open forest understory. Sometimes drop to gd., and reg. around army ant swarms where they are subordinate to more aggressive obligate army ant following birds. Not particularly difficult to see, and sometimes surprisingly unsuspicious.

Status and habitat: Resident in interior of humid terra firme forest where shows some affinity for thick growth around treefalls or in other dense vegetation. Fairly common (numerous specimens) in s Amazonas.

Range: To 350m. S Amazonas from Yavita-Pimichín trail and Cerro Duida southward (*minor*). Adj. e Colombia and nw Brazil; ne Peru (very small range).
Note: Subsp. *minor* has been considered a separate sp., Amazonas Antbird[99], but voices and plumages are practically identical to nominate subsp. (Hilty; M. Isler and P. Isler).

Myrmeciza

Most ♂♂ predom. blackish (some exceptions); bill, tail, and body size more or less avg. for antbirds; almost certainly not a monophyletic group; may comprise at least 3 separate genera.

Yapacana Antbird   PLATE 43
Myrmeciza disjuncta   Hormiguero del Yapacana
Identification: 5.3″ (13.5cm). 14–15g (1 ♀). *Bill long and slender*, base of lower mandible pinkish; *legs pinkish gray*. ♂: dark gray with blackish wings; wing coverts with *2 rows of small white dots* forming dotlike bars; concealed white interscapular patch; *below white tinged pale gray, sides and belly gray*; rather short black tail faintly tipped white (inconspic.). ♀: sim. above but lacks wing dots; below uniform ochraceous buff, throat paler.
Sim. species: Remarkably like *argentata* race of Silvered Antbird which is somewhat larger and proportionately even longer billed (ca. 20 vs. 16 mm), sides of body mottled and scalloped gray, and always near water. ♀ Silvered has buff wing dots and white median underparts. ♀ also closely resembles ♀ Black-chinned

Antbird which has shorter bill, broader white tail tips, and is always near water. Also cf. ♀ with ♀ Black-throated Antbird which has grayish face, brown (not gray) back, and extensive buff dots on wing coverts.
Voice: Song of ♂ a rather loud, buzzy *kzzzzzzzzzZZZ ZZZ, ki-ki-kzzzzip*; may be repeated several times in succession; ♀'s song sim. but usually a shorter single buzz, i.e., *kzzzzZZZZ* (K. Zimmer recording). Song unusual and very unlike that of other Venez. antbirds.
Behavior: A semiterrestrial species of dense vegetation. Remains close to gd. and is extremely difficult to see (habitat virtually impenetrable) but occas. moves out along trail edges in early morning. Hops through vegetation or jumps up to snatch prey from beneath leaves, or hops on gd. where tosses leaves; once seen on gd. at an army ant swarm[832].
Status and habitat: An extreme habitat specialist. Known from only 11 specimens (9 in Venez.) but a common resident very locally (24 prs. in 1350-m transect) in undergrowth of dense, seasonally flooded, scrubby savanna woodland with bamboo, dense mats of sawgrass, and other impenetrable and spiny vegetation at PN Yapacana, s bank of lower Río Ventuari[832]. In very low canopy (0.5–6m), seasonally saturated white sandy soil "shrubby campina" in PN Jáu, Roraima, Brazil[66].

Range: 100m. C and s Amazonas at Pto. Yapacana; Caño San Miguel; Cerro de la Neblina; sightings near mouth of Río Ventuari[832]; and San Carlos-Solano trail, Amazonas, in 1985 (C. Parrish). E Colombia; n Brazil (Rio Branco).
Note: Prob. does not belong in genus *Myrmeciza*.

White-bellied Antbird   PLATE 41
Myrmeciza longipes   Hormiguero Vientriblanco
Identification: 6″ (15cm). 26g. Long pinkish gray legs; inconspic. bluish eyering. ♂: *above mostly bright rufous chestnut*, crown duller, long gray eyebrow continuing down behind cheeks; *face, throat, and chest black* sharply set off from *white median underparts*; flanks cinnamon, concealed interscapular patch white. Or sim. but with 2 rows of black dots on wing coverts (black-dotted bars), black of chest turning iron gray on breast and rufous on flanks and belly, center of lower underparts pale (*griseipectus*). ♀: *above bright rufous* like ♂ but crown brownish; gray forehead and eyebrow enclose dusky *cheeks*; wing coverts with small black dots: *below ochraceous with white throat and white central lower underparts*. Or black spotting on wing coverts more prom., throat and chest darker (*griseipectus*).

Sim. species: Bright rufous upperparts should identify either sex of this rather widespread bird.

Voice: Often hd. song a bright, ringing crescendo of 15–25 loud, rapid *jeer* notes (recalls Canyon Wren, *Catherpes mexicanus*, of N Amer.), descending, trailing off, and ending in a few *chew* notes on same pitch. Alarm a single downslurred *jeeeeeer*.

Behavior: Prs., occas. singles, are usually found hopping on or near gd. where they forage by pausing to flip leaves over or push leaves aside to search for hidden arthropods. Occas. follow army ants; in Panama various kinds of ants are reg. eaten[790]. Sometimes surprisingly unsuspicious, at other times retiring and difficult to see. BC ♀, May, upper Orinoco[185].

Status and habitat: Fairly common to locally very common resident (by voice) in undergrowth of dry deciduous forest, moist semideciduous forest, shrubby second growth; gallery forest in llanos; s of Orinoco also in humid forest, there usually in treefall thickets or shrubby forest borders where may be interspecifically territorial with Black-throated Antbird. Very common in PN Morrocoy, Falcón.

Range: To 1300m (once to 2300m?). Nw Zulia from Goajira Pen. s to Río Palmar (*panamensis*); rest of Maracaibo Basin, n Lara, Falcón (incl. sightings, Sierra de San Luis), and generally e of Andes across n part of llanos to Sucre (*longipes*); n Monagas s to Delta Amacuro, n and c Amazonas (s to Río Asisa; sight, mouth of Río Ventuari); nw and ne Bolívar s to Cerro El Negro and upper Río Cuyuní (*griseipectus*). Panama to n Brazil (Roraima; mouth of the Amazon), w Guyana, and French Guiana. Trinidad.

Ferruginous-backed Antbird   PLATE 43
Myrmeciza ferruginea   Hormiguero Lomirrufo
Identification: 6″ (15cm). 26g. Conspic. *bare blue ocular area*. Legs bluish gray. ♂: *above mostly bright chestnut*, wing coverts black with *2 bold buff bars*, often a hint of a 3d white bar; *sides of head, throat, and chest black* bordered behind by white postocular stripe extending down sides of neck to sides of breast; lower breast grayish white, flanks and belly rufous brown. ♀: sim. but with small white throat patch.

Sim. species: An elegant and beautifully patterned little antbird, not likely confused if seen well. Note restricted range in Venez.

Voice: Song a high, tinkling ser. of rhythmic couplets with some variation in pattern, typically *ti-WHEEty, WHEEty, WHEEty, WHEEty, whee*, falling a little in pitch, often faster when excited; occas. a rapid *te-de'de'de'de'de-de-de* (like accelerated main song with rhythm lost). Song recalls that of Spot-backed Antbird.

Alarm a thin, dry rattle sim. to that of many other *Myrmeciza* but higher pitched.

Behavior: Occurs in prs. but individuals are often well separated from each other. Walks lightly, and with head bobbing, over fallen leaves on rain forest floor, or less often hops up on perches to 1.5m up in understory. Picks arthropod prey from leaf litter. Sings from fallen logs or from gd., sometimes singing as it walks. Typically rather unsuspicious and decoys well to tape playback. In Suriname, open cup nest of dead leaves lined with fine rootlets, on gd.; creamy eggs with purplish horizontal lines that may broaden toward large end[253].

Status and habitat: Common resident in shady interior of tall, hilly, humid forest in lowlands of Río Grande.

Range: To 300m. Ne Bolívar in Sierra de Imataca (*ferruginea*). The Guianas and ne Amaz. Brazil (mostly n of the Amazon).

Black-throated Antbird   PLATE 41
Myrmeciza atrothorax   Hormiguero Gargantinegro
Identification: 5.5″ (14cm). 16g. Small and dark with slender bill. Eyes reddish brown. ♂: dark *umber brown above*; wing coverts dusky with numerous *small white dots* on shoulders forming at least 3 white-dotted wing bars; *tail dusky*, forehead and sides of head dark gray, *throat and chest black* becoming dark brownish gray on lower underparts. ♀: above like ♂ but with wings browner, dots on wing coverts buff; *throat white turning orange rufous on breast*, paler on belly. Concealed white interscapular patch (both sexes).

Sim. species: See Gray-bellied Antbird. ♀ much like ♀ Spot-winged, Caura, and Black-headed antbirds, but all are larger and lack whitish throats.

Voice: Song a rather loud, high-pitched, forced *pe'pee pee-pee-pee-pee-peep*, unmusical and slightly ascending at end. Sharp, noisy *PSEEyap!* when disturbed; also *chip* and flat rattle, *chip-chip't't't't*;

Behavior: Prs. or families are often noisy and excitable, and easily aroused to state of agitation. Call noisily as they flick wings and tails, fidget excitedly, pivot back and forth on low perches, and hop and skulk on or near gd. or to ca. 3m up in grassy thickets. Despite noisy habits, very clever at keeping out of view. Use horizontal or diagonal perches, but not adept at clinging to vertical saplings as do many others of genus. Not reg. around army ant swarms.

Status and habitat: A common resident of *grassy thickets* along humid forest borders, well-lit treefalls inside forest, grassy savanna forest borders, grass and thickets in mauritia palm swamps, and thickets at edges of low-lying or riverine forest.

Range: To 1600m (most recs. below 1200m). Throughout Amazonas and Bolívar (few recs. in ne); s Delta Amacuro at mouth of Río Amacuro (*atrothorax*). Se Colombia to n Bolivia, Amaz. Brazil, and the Guianas.

Gray-bellied Antbird   PLATE 41
Myrmeciza pelzelni   Hormiguero Vientre Gris
Identification: 5" (12.7cm). 26g(?)(1 ♀). Eyes reddish brown. Bill slender. ♂: *looks much like ♂ Black-throated Antbird but with shorter tail.* Crown dark brownish gray, *back, wings, and tail reddish brown*, wing coverts blackish with *2 rows of large buff spots*; tips of tertials (sometimes inner secondaries) also with large buff tips; sides of head and neck mottled gray and white; *throat to center of breast black* surrounded by gray across lower breast, this somewhat mixed whitish on sides of chest and breast; belly and lower underparts brown. ♀: above much like ♂; *throat and chest white, feathers of mid. breast heavily margined black giving scaled appearance*, lower underparts olive brown. No interscapular patch (either sex).
Sim. species: ♂ told from ♂ Black-throated Antbird by *reddish brown* (not dark umber brown) upperparts, shorter rufescent (not dusky) tail (length ca. 53 vs. 64mm), large buff spots on wing coverts (not small white ones), buff spots on tertials, and grayish white sides of head continuing to sides of breast. Note that despite name, neither sex of Gray-bellied Antbird has *obviously* gray belly. ♀'s band of blackish scaling on mostly white underparts is unique.
Voice: Song ca. 12–15 high, shrill, slightly buzzy, and penetrating whistles, *shree, shree, shree, shree . . . . shrEE, shREE, SHREE*, the ser. growing somewhat louder, more insistent, and increasing slightly in pitch toward end; each song ca. 4–4.5 sec, with 5-sec pause between songs (recalls song of Scale-backed Antbird but faster). In agonistic response or alarm, both sexes give a low, rubber-lipped rattle, spit out (K. Zimmer recording).
Behavior: Prs. are highly territorial. Walk in deliberate manner over forest floor or occas. on logs or fallen branches, much in manner of Ferruginous-backed Antbird (or N Amer.–breeding Ovenbird), and pick arthropods from leaf litter or glean from moss-covered bases of understory saplings, bases of terrestrial bromeliads, or surface of mossy logs (K. Zimmer).
Status and habitat: Not well known. Specimens are from undergrowth of humid forest; 2 near Cerro de la Neblina were "in [humid] forest with sapling-sized trees and dense undergrowth"[801]. In upper Rio Negro of Brazil found in a variety of sandy soil habitats from

tall forest with fairly open understory to dense low-canopied "campina" woodland on pure white sandy soil with abundance of terrestrial bromeliads. Where taller forest is occupied, most trees are relatively thin (sapling sized) and uniformly and densely distrib. (K. Zimmer).

Range: To 200m. S Amazonas from Río Casiquiare southward. E Colombia and nw Brazil.

Immaculate Antbird   PLATE 41
Myrmeciza immaculata   Hormiguerote Inmaculado
Identification: 7.3" (18.5cm). 44g. *Prom. bare ocular skin pale blue in front of eyes, whitish behind.* ♂: uniform sooty black, bend of wing white, *tail long and ample.* ♀: face, cheeks, and chin blackish, otherwise *rich dark brown*, tail dusky, ocular skin as in ♂.
Sim. species: Easily told by large size and bare ocular skin as there are no others like it in Andes. See Dull-mantled Antbird; in se Táchira may meet Spot-winged Antbird which has white wing dots.
Voice: Song a fast ser. of 8–10 strong whistled *peep* notes, slowing at end; loud *chirk* call resembles that of a *Turdus* thrush.
Behavior: Prs. or families reg. cling to side of vertical saplings and stems and move with wing-assisted hops through undergrowth; peer, peck, and keep mostly out of sight. Often follow army ant swarms in foothills. At higher els., where swarms are scarce and widely scattered, prs. are more often encountered away from ants. When excited or singing vigorously, pound slightly spread tail downward vigorously.
Status and habitat: Local. Resident inside and at shrubby borders of humid and wet foothill and premontane forest, and older second-growth woodland. Freq. seen along San Isidro Rd. (1450m) in nw Barinas.

Range: 950–1700m. Sierra de Perijá (headwaters of Ríos Apón and Negro), Zulia, and w slope of Andes from Táchira n to Mérida at La Azulita (*brunnea*); e slope of Andes from Táchira n to nw Barinas (sight) and e Lara at Cabudare (*immaculata*). Costa Rica to w Ecuador and n Colombia.

Dull-mantled Antbird PLATE 41
Myrmeciza laemosticta Hormiguero Pechinegro
Identification: 5.5″ (14cm). 25g. Eyes dark red. ♂:
head to lower breast iron gray, throat blackish, flanks
and lower underparts reddish brown, upperparts incl.
tail reddish brown, wing coverts brownish becoming
black subterminally and tipped white forming *2 dotted
bars;* concealed white interscapular patch. ♀: sim. but
throat and upper chest black *narrowly but heavily
scaled or barred white,* wing dots buff.
Sim. species: In limited range in Venez. there are few
others like it. See. Immaculate Antbird which is all
black (all dark brown—♀) with bluish white ocular
area.
Voice: Song in Panama a rather thin, weak *beet, beet,
beet-beet-beet-beet,* dropping a bit at end and not far
carrying; ♀ may follow with slightly softer *beet-beet
chutu* (R. Ridgely). In Costa Rica described as a lilting
ser. of 3–4 clear, high whistles, then 3–5 more, usually
on lower pitch, *twee twee twee, tyew-tyew-tyew-tyew*[706].
Behavior: In Panama and Colombia single birds or prs.
use horizontal perches or often cling to side of vertical
saplings as they move with short jumps and wing-
assisted hops through undergrowth, mostly keeping
under cover. Peck and sally for arthropod prey, check
accumulations of litter, and occas. drop to gd. May
also attend army ant swarms.
Status and habitat: Resident in humid and wet forest,
esp. in shady ravines and streamsides in foothills and
steep forested terrain. There are a no. of specimens
from near small settlement of Barranquilla in w Zulia;
a few from Las Mesas, Táchira; 1 from La Azulita, w
Mérida. These areas are now heavily deforested.

Range: 400–1100m. Sierra de Perijá (Cerro Ayapa; Barranquilla) in w Zulia, and w base of Andes in w Mérida
and e base at Las Mesas, Táchira (*palliata*). Costa Rica
to w Venez.
Note: Subsp. *venezuelae* merged with *palliata*[552] but
Venez. birds are paler and differ in other minor ways.

Pithys

Prom. facial tufts; only other member of genus (1 specimen) is unknown in life and perhaps a hybrid[545].

White-plumed Antbird PLATE 44
Pithys albifrons Hormiguero Plumón Blanco
Identification: 5″ (12.7cm). 21g. Unmistakable. *Long
pointed white tufts on forehead form 2 "horns," and
long white tuft on chin forms "goatee."* Head and throat
black with short white eyeline (no eyeline—*peruviana*),
back and wings dark blue gray, *nuchal collar, underparts, rump, and tail chestnut,* legs orange yellow.

Voice: Mild alarm (esp. over army ants) a ser. of soft to
fairly loud *chirr* notes; high-intensity alarm and in aggressive encounters a sharp *STIK!-STIK!,* varying from 1
to 3 notes. A thin, descending *seeeeea,* sometimes repeated at short intervals or with other notes interspersed, is perhaps a song but apparently there is no
loud territorial song.
Behavior: A well-known obligate army ant follower
and seldom seen away from them. Often the most numerous sp. at swarms with up to 12 or more in attendance, but typically wary and difficult to see, fleeing to
dense cover at 1st sign of danger where skulks and
gives chirring alarm notes. May return to swarm when
danger is past, or leave to forage at another ant swarm,
but readily "habituates" to quiet human observers and
within 1 hr or so will allow a close approach. Typically
stays low over ants where clings to sides of slender, vertical saplings and stems, bounces rapidly from one to
another, and darts to gd., foliage, or branches for fleeing arthropod prey. Two nests (Suriname and Guyana)
sunk in dead leaves 30–40cm up in spiny crown of
small palm; 2 rosy white eggs speckled brownish[273,807];
8 BC birds Mar–Apr, upper Orinoco[185].
Status and habitat: Fairly common resident inside
humid and wet terra firme forest and mature second-
growth woodland in lowlands; follows army ants to forest borders.

Range: To 500m in s Táchira (*peruviana*); to 1350m s
of Orinoco. Se Táchira and w Apure (Las Bonitas);
throughout Amazonas and Bolívar (*albifrons*). E Colombia to e Peru, Amaz. Brazil n of the Amazon, and
the Guianas.

Gymnopithys

Chunky and short-tailed; strong legs; bare ocular area;
obligate army ant followers in rainforest.

Rufous-throated Antbird PLATE 44
Gymnopithys rufigula Hormiguero Gargantirrufo
Identification: 5.5″ (14cm). 27g. Large pale blue orbital ring. Legs pinkish. Above uniform warm brown
with blackish lores and cheeks; concealed white interscapular patch (cinnamon in ♀), *throat bright buff*
edged chestnut and turning ochraceous on breast and
brownish on sides and flanks. Or sim. but forehead
black, *throat and sides of face rufous chestnut* turning
rich ochraceous buff on chest and brown on lower underparts (*pallida*).
Sim. species: Unlikely to be confused. Bare orbital ring
imparts startled, "wide-eyed" look. Note contrasting
throat and habits.

Voice: Repertoire of about 12 vocalizations, most given when attending army ant swarms, are sim., in part, to those of White-plumed Antbird and incl. a low ser. of soft *chirr* notes in mild alarm; and sharp, staccato, *stit-tit!* and *stit-it-it!* in high-intensity alarm. However, this sp. has a loud primary song, a high, whinnylike ser. of notes that quickly rise and fall, *we-whe-whee-HE-He-he'hu'we'we;* recalls that of allied Bicolored Antbird (*G. bicolor*) of w Amazonia.

Behavior: A professional army ant follower, seldom seen away from raiding swarms of *Eciton* army ants except when traveling low through forest from one swarm to another. Prs. or bickering groups up to 20 gather at army ant swarms, usually along with other spp. such as White-plumed Antbird and Plain-brown Woodcreeper. Flee at slightest hint of danger to skulk and chirr in dense undergrowth, but return when danger is past, and "habituate" quickly to quiet observers. Typically cling ca. 0.2–2m up on side of vertical stems and saplings and watch intently, pivot, and then rapidly drop to gd., or sally to nearby foliage or branches for prey escaping ant. In allied Bicolored Antbird (and presum. also this sp.), territories are fluid, with sphere of dominance strongest near nests but weakening with birds less aggressive and less dominant as trespass across neighbors' territories to distant swarms.

Status and habitat: Fairly common resident in undergrowth inside humid terra firme forest; follows army ants to forest edge but avoids openings and loathe even to cross narrow roads or streams. Distrib. in forest not uniform (corresponds to whereabouts of army ant swarms) and can be difficult to locate.

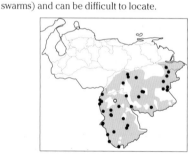

Range: To 900m. Sw Amazonas on upper Río Guainía and Río Atabapo near Yavita-Pimichín (*pallidigula*); rest of Amazonas and Bolívar e to Sierra de Imataca and s to upper Río Cuyuní and Sierra de Lema (*pallida*). The Guianas and ne Brazil e of Rio Negro.
Note I: Nominate *rufigula* apparently reported in error from upper Río Cuyuní[403].
Note 2: Bicolored Antbird (*G. bicolor*) of lower C Amer., nw and e Colombia, and nw Brazil s to Peru may occur in sw Amazonas (in e Colombia occurs very near Venez. border). Above uniform rufous brown with conspic. bare blue ocular ring; malar, lower cheeks, and auriculars blackish; throat and median underparts white; sides of neck and breast brown. An obligate army ant follower.

Phlegopsis

Pr. of large obligate army ant followers; bare red ocular skin; ornate plumage.

Reddish-winged Bare-eye   PLATE 42
Phlegopsis erythroptera   Hormiguero Ojipelado
Identification: 7.3″ (18.5cm). 49g. *Large bare ocular area bright red* (or small red patch behind eye—♀). ♂: mostly black, feathers of *wing coverts and entire back conspic. fringed white* (looks scaled), *2 rufous wing bars; broad rufous band across flight feathers forms 3d bar.* ♀: quite different; above dark rufescent brown, wings and tail black, *2 bold buff bars on wing coverts, a 3d buff band across flight feathers;* throat pale orange rufous turning dark rufous on breast, brownish on belly.
Sim. species: ♂ unmistakable. Cf. ♀ with ♀ Scale-backed Antbird which is much smaller and lacks bold buff wing bands. Also see Wing-banded Antbird.
Voice: Song ca. 4–6 hoarse whistles, *whee-wheerp . wheerp . . wheeur . . . wheeur,* the ser. descending, slowing, and becoming buzzy. When alarmed or excited a loud, sharp, metallic *pchiirr* with buzzy quality.
Behavior: A spectacular-looking but wary obligate army ant swarm follower of rain forest understory. Follows mainly the ant *Eciton burchelli.* Usually found in prs. or disputing families which are dominant over almost all other antbirds at army ant swarms. Perch on low horizontal branches or tree buttresses, or cling to vertical stems and saplings, and drop to gd. from perches less than 1m up, or toss leaves for prey[814]. Like many army ant followers, initially wary and difficult to see but habituate somewhat to patient observers.
Status and habitat: Resident in undergrowth of humid terra firme forest. Generally much less numerous than smaller ant-following antbirds with which it is found; only a minority of army ant swarms will have 1 or a pr. of these birds in attendance. In Venez. known from only a few specimens.

Range: To 300m. S Amazonas from Yavita-Pimichín trail (La Cruz) and Río Mavaca s to Cerro de la Neblina (*erythroptera*). Se Colombia to e Ecuador, ne Peru, n Bolivia, and w Amaz. Brazil.

Myrmornis

Unusual rotund shape with long bill and stub tail; tertials long and broad; despite appearance, not closely related to formicariid antbirds. Vocally allied to Thamnophilines, perhaps nearest *Hylophylax* or *Myrmeciza*[586]; nest location and egg color also unlike formicariids.

Wing-banded Antbird   PLATE 42
Myrmornis torquata   Pollito de Selvas
Identification: 6.5″ (16.5cm). 46g. Bill long; tail very short, carried erect. *Short legs* greenish yellow; bare orbital skin blue. ♂: above dull chestnut faintly scaled

dusky; wings blackish with *several tawny buff bars and broad band near tip of flight feathers; throat and chest black* bordered all around, incl. behind eye, by irreg. area of vermiculated black and white; remaining underparts gray, crissum rufous chestnut; concealed white interscapular patch. ♀: sim. but throat and chest rufous, only cheeks black; interscapular patch smaller. **Sim. species:** An oddly proportioned gd. dweller unlike anthrushes or antpittas and easily told from either by bold buff bars on wings. Cf. Black-faced and Rufous-capped antthrushes, Black-throated Antbird, and much smaller Banded Antbird.
Voice: Song, hd. mainly at dawn, a fairly loud ser. of 10–14 whistled and strongly inflected *préea* notes (each note rising than falling sharply), evenly spaced, the whole ser. gradually rising and lasting up to 4 sec; when alarmed a rough *churr*. Most vocal in rainy season.
Behavior: Prs. are relatively unsuspicious and mostly terrestrial, often foraging quite close together on gd. Hop (not walk as do antthrushes) on forest floor, probing in leaf litter and flicking or pushing aside leaves with bill (usually do not seize leaf), sometimes almost disappearing beneath leaves. Not attracted to army ant swarms. If alarmed may mount a perch to eye level or higher and flick wings. Usually sing from perch 1–3m up. A nest in French Guiana was suspended within a branch fork 2m up in sapling; creamy white eggs with violet brown streaks and spots, esp. at larger end; in Fr. Guiana breeds in rainy Mar–Oct period, peak Sep–Oct[751].
Status and habitat: Very local resident on floor of humid and wet forest in lowlands and lower slopes of tepuis. Venez. recs. are mainly from areas of high rainfall and on forested slopes in hilly regions. Formerly fairly numerous in tall forest near Río Grande, ne Bolívar, but area now heavily deforested.

Range: To 1200m. C and s Amazonas (Cerro Parú) southward; Bolívar from lower Río Caura and Sierra de Imataca southward (*torquata*). Disjunct pops. in Panama and adj. n Colombia; extreme e Colombia to the Guianas and e Brazil; extreme s Colombia and adj. e Ecuador and n Peru.

Formicariidae: Ground Antbirds

Hormigueros de Tierra

This family was formerly united with typical Thamnophiline antbirds in the enlarged family Formicariidae. Evidence from DNA studies[604] indicates a closer relationship between ground antbirds and tapaculos and gnateaters than with Thamnophiline antbirds. As

their name implies, the ground antbirds are terrestrial or semiterrestrial when foraging, although they may sing from a slightly elevated perch. Antthrushes mostly walk, whereas antpittas tend to hop when moving on the ground. Almost all species are various shades of brown, buff, chestnut, and black, some also with streaking and barring in their plumage. The calls of many ground antbirds are loud, sometimes unusual, and often the only indication of a bird's presence, as most are difficult to observe. They reach their greatest diversity in the Andes where a series of species replace each other with increasing elevation up to or even above treeline. Nests for many species remain undescribed.

Rufous-capped Antthrush   PLATE 42
Formicarius colma   Pollito Hormiguero

Identification: 7″ (18cm). 47g. Looks like a small forest rail. Jaunty with short cocked tail. ♂: forehead black, *rest of crown bright rufous chestnut*, back plain brown, tail dusky, *throat, sides of head, and upper breast black*, this gradually becoming sooty gray brown on lower underparts; cinnamon band on primaries (from below only). ♀: sim. but throat white usually with variable amt. of black speckling (younger ♀♀?), or throat all black (older ♀♀?). Juv: face and throat tinged rusty.
Sim. species: See Black-faced Antthrush.
Voice: Song an erie quavering glissando that falters and drops slightly in pitch at first, then slowly and steadily rises to end, *wu-u-u-u-er-er-u-u-u-u-u-u-u-u-u-u-u-u-u-u* (ca. 4 sec). Pitch and speed of song vary geographically (Hilty). At dusk and also as alarm, a loud, sharp *KEET!* (K. Zimmer).
Behavior: Generally like others of genus. Largely terrestrial and usually seen walking lightly and alertly, with tail cocked and head bobbing, over forest floor, pecking here and there or pausing to flick aside leaves. Often follows army ants, keeping mostly at periphery. Sings from gd. or a perch up to ca. 4m up and, unlike Black-faced Antthrush, freq. flies in directly to an eye-level perch, rather than walking, in response to imitation of its song.
Status and habitat: Uncommon resident (low density and hard to see) in humid lowland forest, primarily terra firme, less often transitional forest or várzea. Does not overlap widely in Venez. with allied Black-faced Antthrush, but latter in Venez. seems to occupy a broader range of forest types; elsewhere the pattern varies[713]. Reg. seen at Junglaven, Amazonas, where in absence of Black-faced Antthrush, occurs in both terra firme and várzea forest.

Range: To 1100m (Auyán-tepui). Amazonas (except where next subsp. occurs); Delta Amacuro[343] and

Bolívar from lower Río Caura and Sierra de Imataca southward (*colma*); c Amazonas on Cerro Yapacana and Isla Temblador (100km w of Cerro Duida) southward in upper Orinoco (*nigrifrons*). Se Colombia to n Bolivia, Amaz. and se Brazil, and the Guianas.

Black-faced Antthrush
PLATE 42

Formicarius analis   Gallito Hormiguero

Identification: 7–7.5" (18–19cm). 59g. Looks like a small rail as it walks on forest floor. *Short cocked tail* imparts dapper appearance. Bare bluish white ocular patch widest in front and behind eyes. Upperparts brown turning reddish brown on upper tail coverts and dusky on tail; *forepart of cheeks and throat black*, narrow postocular and small patch on rearcheek and sides of neck cinnamon to rufous (*griseoventris*); or cinnamon (*crissalis*); or dark brown like rest of head (*saturatus*). Rest of underparts smoky gray tinged olive, under tail coverts chestnut. Sexes sim.

Sim. species: In s Táchira see Rufous-breasted Antthrush which has dark rufous crown and breast. S of Orinoco see Rufous-capped Antthrush which has most of crown bright rufous chestnut, is much more extensively black below. All *Formicarius* are easily identified by voice, and their presence is almost always first noted by voice.

Voice: One of *the* characteristic sounds of lowland and foothill rain forests. Territorial call a loud, emphatic whistle followed, after a brief pause, by 2–10 or more whistles, the 2d slighter higher pitched, the rest descending in pitch and sometimes slowing up in tempo, *WHU!; wŭ-wŭ*, varying to *WHU!; wŭwŭwŭwŭwŭwŭ-wŭ wŭ*. In some areas mostly only long or short songs are hd. In n Aragua (Rancho Grande) *typically gives long song at dawn* (up to 20 notes or more) but *sings short songs* (4–5 notes) *during day*. When disturbed a loud *churlip!* over and over; this also often given at dusk.

Behavior: A fetching little bird with self-assured demeanor. Like others of genus, terrestrial and usually seen alone, walking briskly and jauntily with twitching tail cocked up and head bobbing forward jerkily as bird moves across forest floor like a little crake. Freq. stops to peck here and there or to flip aside a leaf. Sometimes pauses for longer periods of time to vigorously flick aside leaves as searches for mostly arthropod prey. Also a reg. attendant at army and swarms where keeps mostly at periphery of swarms. Somewhat retiring but usually responds well to a whistled imitation of its song. Nest a leafy cup less than 4m up in cavity or hollow stump; 2 white eggs[647].

Status and habitat: Common resident (by voice) in humid terra firme and várzea forest and taller second-growth woodland in lowlands, foothills, and lower mt. slopes. Curiously absent from Amazonas.

Range: To 1700m n of Orinoco; to 800m s of Orinoco. Sierra de Perijá, Zulia, and w base of Andes in Táchira, Mérida, Trujillo, and Zulia (Mene Grande) (*griseoventris*); e base n to Lara; c and e Falcón (Mirimire; sightings, Sierra de San Luis); mts. of Yaracuy n to Distr. Federal and se Miranda; Sucre s to c Monagas (*saturatus*); e Bolívar from Sierra de Imataca s to Gran Sabana at Cerro Roraima (*cris-*

salis). Hondurus to n Bolivia, Amaz. Brazil (absent from nc Brazil), and the Guianas. Trinidad.

Note: Different song types predom. regionally, but much individual variation exists across vast range. Formerly incl. Mexican Antthrush (*F. moniliger*) of Mexico to n Hondurus[266]; possibly up to 3 spp. involved[606].

Rufous-breasted Antthrush
PLATE 42

Formicarius rufipectus   Hormiguero Pechirrojo

Identification: 7.5" (19cm). 78g. A chestnut replica of Black-faced Antthrush. Narrow bare bluish ocular area widest in front and behind eye. Forecrown black, *rest of crown and nape dark chestnut*, lores, sides of head, and throat black *contrasting with rufous chestnut underparts*; back and wings dark olive brown, upper tail coverts chestnut, tail blackish. ♀: crown mainly black, rearcrown dark chestnut. In both sexes bill heavier and longer and tail somewhat longer than in Black-faced Antthrush.

Sim. species: In limited range in Venez. confusion likely only with Black-faced Antthrush which lacks rufous chestnut on crown and breast and has very different voice.

Voice: Song a flat insipid *üü, üü* whistle (quality of Striped Cuckoo), 2d note on same pitch or a quarter-tone higher than 1st; at dawn often steadily repeated at 10- to 20-sec intervals.

Behavior: Like others of genus, walks, with head bobbing forward and tail cocked, on floor of forest but is much more difficult to see than allies, perhaps in part because of dense habitat in which it lives. Alone or in prs. but individuals usually well separated.

Status and habitat: Fairly common resident (by voice) locally in wet montane forest and dense, older second-growth woodland; also occas. in dense thickets at forest edge. Reg. hd. near forested summit between Bramón and Las Delicias, s Táchira; several specimens from Hacienda Providencia in upper Río Chiquito Valley.

Range: 1100–2200m. Sierra de Perijá, Zulia (Kunana; Pejochaina), and s Táchira (*lasallei*). Costa Rica to Colombia, w and e Ecuador, and c Peru.

Chamaeza

Plump and short-tailed; bill small for size of bird; legs not esp. long; all spp. terrestrial and walk (not hop); boldly streaked or scalloped below; often hd. but inconspic. on floor of humid forest.

Schwartz's Antthrush   PLATE 42
Chamaeza turdina   Hormiguero Mazamorrero
Identification: 7.5″ (19cm). Looks like a "short-tailed" thrush. Short bill and partially cocked tail. Legs dusky. Above reddish brown, brighter on rump; buff loral spot continues as *prom white supra- and postocular stripe;* throat essentially unmarked white, rest of underparts almost pure white (no buff even on crissum), the feathers rather arrowhead-shaped and broadly edged dark brown forming *bold angular scalloping,* esp. heavy across upper breast. Sexes sim.
Sim. species: Closely resembles Short-tailed Antthrush and in field the two are almost always separated by their very different voices and by elevation (Short-tailed occurs lower). In hand or up close, note Schwartz's slightly smaller size, dark legs, smaller bill, overall darker plumage, unmarked tail, and more scalloped (less streaked) and more heavily marked breast.
Voice: Two song types: (1) a remarkably long ser. of whistled *cu* notes (ca. 2–3/sec for up to 50 sec) *without pause,* the ser. gaining slightly in volume, tempo, and pitch as it goes along; (2) a loud abrupt and descending ser. of *cuu* or *cuk* notes that slow and wind down into a laughlike ser. of notes that stop abruptly or gradually merge into song type 1. After either song sometimes gives a short ser. of chuckling notes at end, e.g., ... *cu-cu-cu, towak, wak, wak, wak.* Alarm a loud, abrupt *ble'blink!*
Behavior: A forest recluse, apt to give away its presence by its loud song but otherwise retiring, and often perversely ingenious at remaining out of sight. Lives in widely scattered prs. on forest floor where it walks with alert air and jaunty steps, threading its way among clutter and debris, and often twitching short, cocked tail downward as it goes. Usually forages alone, flicking aside leaves as it walks. Sings from gd., pausing momentarily as it walks, or sometimes mounts a log or slightly elevated perch 1–4m up to sing. Prs. are sedentary and maintain permanent territories which they occupy for yrs.
Status and habitat: Fairly common resident but often thinly spread and local in humid and wet montane forest. Territories usually rather widely scattered, but each contains some thickets and tangled or cluttered understory vegetation. Mainly found above range of Short-tailed Antthrush (limited overlap at ca. 1100–

1500m) and prob. interspecifically territorial where they occur together.
Range: 1500–2100m (sight to 1100m, Aragua). Yaracuy (Sierra de Aroa); Coastal Cordillera from Carabobo to n Miranda at Izcaragua (*chionogaster*). Colombia (local).
Note: Previously called Rufous-tailed Antthrush, *C. ruficauda*[403], a name now applied to birds in se Brazil. N birds have been called Schwartz's Antpitta[817] and Scalloped Antpitta[545].

Short-tailed Antthrush   PLATE 42
Chamaeza campanisona   Hormiguero Cuascá
Identification: 8″ (20.3cm). 85g. Looks like a "short-tailed" thrush. Small bill, lower mandible pale; legs pale grayish pink; partially cocked tail. Above olive brown with buff loral spot; *prom. white supra- and postocular stripe;* tail with black subterminal band and narrow buffy white tips (hard to see in field); *below white to buffy white, rather boldly and coarsely streaked blackish* from lower edge of throat to upper belly. Or sim. but with richer deep buff wash on chest, contrasting pale buff throat, and lower underparts also somewhat scaled, approaching that of previous sp. (*yavii, huachamacarii, obscura*).
Sim. species: As name implies, tail is short, averaging ca. 50mm vs. 70mm in Schwartz's Antthrush, but this not esp. helpful in field. Best known by voice.
Voice: Distinctive song in Coastal Cordillera and Andes a ventriloquial, trogonlike ser. of ca. 10 slowly accelerating and rising *whoo* notes followed by abruptly slowing and falling ser. of inflected *woop* notes; alarm note a sharp *quoak.* Song of birds on Sierra de Lema (*obscura*) is sim. but decidedly faster, esp. 1st half, and with more notes, the whole ser. tending to roll or slide along rapidly. Most vocal early in rainy season (ca. Apr–Aug) both n and s of Orinoco, then a freq. voice.
Behavior: Much like allied Schwartz's Antthrush. Prs. may maintain permanent territories but seem more apt to wander than Schwartz's and are hence less predictable to locate.
Status and habitat: Fairly common resident locally in moist and humid premontane forest. In Coastal Cordillera ranges locally downward into moist forest, even humid ravines in dry forest, and is largely replaced in wet forest above ca. 1100–1500m by Schwartz's Antthrush. S of Orinoco mainly humid forest on lower slopes of tepuis.

Range: 400–1850m (mostly below 1500m). W slope of Andes from Táchira to nw Lara (Cerro El Cerrón), e slope in se Lara; hills of c Falcón (sight, Sierra de San

Luis[60]); mts of Yaracuy and n cordilleras from Carabobo e to Distr. Federal and Miranda (*venezuelana*); s
of Orinoco on Cerro Yavi, Amazonas (*yavii*); Cerros
Huachamacari, Amazonas (*huachamacarii*); Cerros Calentura and de la Neblina, Amazonas, and Bolívar on
Cerro El Negro, Cerro Tabaro, and tepuis of Gran Sabana incl. Sierra de Lema and Cerro Urutaní (*obscura*); Cerro Roraima (*fulvescens*). E Colombia s in mts.
to Bolivia; Guyana; se Brazil and adj. e Paraguay and
ne Argentina.

Grallaria

Plump, rotund, and long legged (an "egg on legs"); terrestrial and run, or walk quickly, or hop with springy
bounds; tail short, almost vestigial; mostly clothed in attractive but somber shades of brown, buff, and black,
some also with extensive barring, streaking, and intri-
cate reticulated markings on plumage; typically furtive
and hd. far more than seen; greatest diversity in humid
mt. forests; live in prs.; sexes sim.

Great Antpitta   PLATE 42
Grallaria excelsa Hormiguero Tororoi Excelso
Identification: 9.5–10″ (24–25cm). 218–266g (allied
Giant Antpitta, *G. gigantea*). *Rare, oversized antpitta of
mid. montane els. Bill large and heavy,* upper mandible
black, lower grayish horn. Forehead brown with *midcrown to nape contrasting gray* (faintly scaled black),
rest of upperparts olive brown, central throat buffy
white; rather obscure blackish submalar bordered
above by narrow area of buffy white; lores, sides of
head and neck, and entire underparts ochraceous
boldly and coarsely scalloped with wavy black lines;
under tail coverts unbarred bright tawny ochre.
Sim. species: *Closely* resembles Undulated Antpitta,
and field identification based on visual characters
problematic. Undulated is smaller (but this may not be
obvious in field), has more distinct blackish malar,
less contrasting gray crown, and proportionally
smaller bill. Voice and known distrib. may be helpful
but not conclusive. In hand, tarsus of Great Antpitta
avgs. longer (ca. 61–66 vs. 57–61mm) and bill longer
(ca. 32–34 vs. 26–31mm).
Voice: Song nearly identical to that of Giant Antpitta;
in PN Yacambú, Lara, a long (4–6 sec), low-pitched,
rubber-lipped trill, *br'r'r'r'r'r'r'* . . . *r'r'r'r'r'ub*, of 14–20
notes/sec, with barely perceptible rise in pitch and
tempo and *abrupt* ending (Hilty). This song is essentially identical to that of Undulated Antpitta, but rate of
delivery does not decrease at end of each song-bout as
it invariably does in Undulated; also a low, hollow *du-
du-du-du*[196,413]. Songs sim. to this have been recorded in
PN Yacambú at els. more appropriate for Great Antpitta than Undulated Antpitta[60,61].
Behavior: Apparently sim. to others of genus. Hops on
floor of wet montane forest. Stomach contents of Giant
Antpitta were bits of giant earthworms and remains of
a beetle[196]. In Ecuador Giant Antpitta has been seen in
a pasture adj. to forest, and singing from perches 3–5m
up inside forest[196].
Status and habitat: Uncertain. Only recent recs. (sightings) are in PN Yacambú (D. Willis; Hilty; D. Ascanio).

Last specimens taken in Sierra de Perijá on 8 and 18
Mar 1952. Several specimens originally attributed to
this sp. (i.e., Llano Rucio, Mérida; El Valle, Mérida; Páramo Aricagua) are now believed to be Undulated Antpitta. All verified specimens are from cluttered understory of humid and wet montane forest (cloud forest)
at intermed. els. and *mostly at lower els.* than those of
Undulated Antpitta.

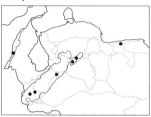

Range: ENDEMIC. 1700–2300m. Known definitely from
Sierra de Perijá, Zulia (Pejochaina); n Táchira (Queni-
quea; Boca de Monte); Trujillo/Mérida border (La
Cuchilla); and Lara at Guárico (prob. PN Yacambú)
(*excelsa*); Aragua (near Colonia Tovar) in Coastal Cor-
dillera (*phelpsi*)[196].
Note: Great Antpitta is perhaps conspecific with Giant
Antpitta (*G. gigantea*) of Colombia and Ecuador.

Undulated Antpitta   PLATE 43
Grallaria squamigera Hormiguero Tororoi Ondulado
Identification: 8–8.5″ (20.3–22cm); 112–149g. Large
montane antpitta very sim. to Great Antpitta (the two
prob. not reliably separated by sight in field). Bill fairly
heavy. *Midcrown to nape gray,* forehead and rest of upperparts olive brown, the feathers faintly scaled dusky,
lores buffy white; central throat white bordered by
rather prom. blackish submalar stripe; sides of head
and underparts *ochraceous boldly scalloped with wavy
black lines*; under tail coverts unbarred bright tawny
ochre. In hand note that forehead has a few buff shaft
streaks (absent in Great Antpitta).
Sim. species: See Great Antpitta which, as far as
known, occurs mostly at lower el. (some overlap).
Voice: Song a low, hollow, rapidly vibrating ("rubber-
lipped") ser. of notes, *hühühühühühühühü'hü'hü hü*;, rising a little at end and with last several notes slowing
and more distinct; has quality of a frog or a screech-
owl (*Otus*), and like latter, often hd. in dim light of
predawn.
Behavior: A large, mostly terrestrial bird, almost always encountered alone on leafy floor of forest. Shy
and retiring but sometimes ventures into grassy openings or onto open forest trails in early morning or into
areas with low filtered light. Moves with big springy
hops interrupted by abrupt pauses to stand bolt upright and stare, or vigorously flick aside a few leaves.
Sings from gd. or atop logs.
Status and habitat: Locally fairly common resident inside wet montane forest. Favors fairly dense mossy forest
from fairly short to tall. Several hd., mid. Apr, near Laguna Mucubají, ca. 3400m (P. Boesman); a common
voice at dawn above 2400m in PN Guaramacal, Trujillo.
Range: 2000–3300m (hd. to 3400m). Andes from s Táchira (Páramo de Tamá) n through Mérida to se Tru-

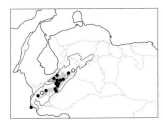

jillo at Teta de Niquitao (*squamigera*); and e Trujillo (sight/tape) at PN Guaramacal (prob. *squamigera*). Colombia to n Bolivia.

Variegated Antpitta

Grallaria varia   Hormiguero Tororoi Cabecinegro
Identification: 8″ (20.3cm). 118g. Large, somewhat streaky antpitta in lowlands s of Orinoco. Bill dark gray above; paler below, pinkish at base. Olive brown above with *midcrown to nape gray*, feathers of crown and upperparts narrowly edged blackish and somewhat pale-centered giving "scaly" or vaguely streaked look (shaft streaks) to plumage; lores and *prom. submalar stripe buffy*; cheeks, throat, and chest rufous brown, the feathers with pale centers forming vague streaks; *partially concealed patch of white on central chest, lower underparts pale buffy ochraceous indistinctly streaked light buff and dusky*.
Sim. species: Occurs mainly below range of foothill-inhabiting Scaled Antpitta which is very sim. but slightly smaller, lacks pale shaft streaking above, has weakly defined transverse band across base of throat (rather than patch), and lower underparts darker, more tawny (not buff). In hand, tarsus of Scaled is shorter (42–43 vs. 47–51mm).
Voice: Song in Suriname a low-pitched, sonorous ser. of hooting notes, *whü whü whü whüü-WHUU-WHUU WHü whü*, ca. 2.5 sec; accelerating a little and swelling to a crescendo, then fading slightly and ending abruptly. Song has penetrating, vibrating quality and can be hd. long distances in forest (difficult to track down). Often sings for extended periods at dusk.
Behavior: Like others of genus, a large, mostly terrestrial bird that is shy and difficult to see. Most active during predawn and dusk periods when light levels are low. Forages alone by hopping on forest floor, pausing occas. to flick aside leaves. Usually stays in or near cover, but sings from atop a log or sometimes a fairly open branch several meters up. Dec nest (Suriname) a shallow cup of rootlets and moss in crevice 1m up in trunk of large tree; 2 turquoise eggs[253].

Status and habitat: Resident inside tall humid terra firme forest at low els., prob. also lower-lying transitional forest. Everywhere seems to occur in low density, but prob. more vocal (and more easily detected) in rainy season when few observers are afield.
Range: To 640m (Sierra Parima). S Amazonas from Río Casiquiare (Caño Atamoni) s to Sierra Parima and Cerro de la Neblina (*cinereiceps*); ne Bolívar (1 ♂ taken 25 Jun 1965) at Río Grande (*varia?*). Guianas and e Amaz. Brazil; coastal e and se Brazil.

Scaled Antpitta   PLATE 42

Grallaria guatimalensis   Hormiguero Tororoi Escamado
Identification: 7″ (18cm). 95g. Or slightly smaller (*regulus*), ca. 6.5″, (16.5cm). Plumage varies geographically. Above olive brown, *midcrown to nape gray*, all of *feathers of upperparts narrowly edged dusky* giving "scaly" look, sides of head and throat dark brown, lores and *broad buff malar stripe almost meet an ill-defined transverse buff crescent across lower throat*; chest brown turning *bright orange ochraceous on flanks and lower underparts*; feathers of throat to mid. breast with numerous pale shaft streaks forming whitish streaks (*regulus*); or sim. but gray confined to nape (*carmelitae*); or larger and darker, esp. below with little or no whitish streaking; bill larger and heavier (*roraimae*).
Sim. species: S of Orinoco see Variegated Antpitta which usually occurs only in lowlands and has much paler lower underparts. In s Táchira see very sim. Táchira Antpitta. Also cf. Plain-backed Antpitta which is almost uniform brown with whitish throat and prom. dusky malar.
Voice: Song a quavering, "rubber-lipped" vibrato of low, hollow notes that gradually slide up scale, *uuuuu uuuuouououohuhuhu*, and end abruptly; ca. 4 sec. Sings mostly at dawn and dusk.
Behavior: Like others of genus, forages by hoping on gd., but sings from log or horizontal perch ca. 1–2m up, or occas. much higher (up to 15m up). Generally secretive and difficult to see. When flushed, flies off low and fast, often a considerable distance.
Status and habitat: Resident. Widespread but spotty and local. Humid and wet foothill and mt. forest, esp. in ravines and damp valleys with cluttered undergrowth and dense vegetation. Sometimes survives in small patches of forest. Prob. throughout tepuis s of Orinoco.

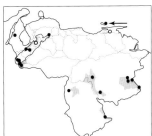

Range: 350–2400m n of Orinoco; 650–2000m s of Orinoco. Sierra de Perija, Zulia (*carmelitae*); spottily on both slopes of Andes from s Táchira, w Apure (El

Nula), and Mérida n to c Trujillo (tape, Sabaneta), and se Lara at Cabudare (*regulus*); tape, Sucre-Monagas border on Cerro Negro[259](subsp.?); n and s Amazonas (Cerro Sipapo; Sierra Parima), n Bolívar in lower Río Caura (Cerro Tabaro) and its headwaters at Cerro Jaua; upper Río Cuyuní on Sierra de Lema (many observers), Ptari-tepui, and Cerro Roraima (*roraimae*). Cerro El Copey (ca. 800m), Isla Margarita (*schwartzii*). Mts. of c Mexico to Bolivia and n Brazil. Trinidad.

Táchira Antpitta   PLATE 43
Grallaria chthonia   Hormiguero Tororoi Tachirense
Identification: 6–6.5″ (15–16.5cm). Known from only 1 locality in s Táchira. Very sim. to Scaled Antpitta and *prob. not reliably separable by sight in field*. Táchira Antpitta is slightly *smaller* and browner above; also differs in *breast buff becoming pale whitish buff on belly* (not rich orange ochraceous), and *breast and flanks faintly but distinctly scaled or barred gray*. In hand, throat slightly darker, more dusky brown (not reddish brown); tarsal length sim. to Scaled Antpitta; bill slightly longer (22–23 vs. 19mm) and more slender.
Sim. species: In addition to Scaled Antpitta, see Undulated and Great antpittas, both much larger and boldly scalloped below.
Behavior: Behavior and voice prob. sim. to that of Scaled Antpitta which it closely resembles. The 2 spp. may be el. replacements as recs. of Scaled Antpitta in Táchira are from lower els. (350–1250 vs. 1800–2100m), or Táchira Antpitta may be only a subsp. of Scaled.
Status and habitat: Known from 4 specimens taken Feb 1955 and Mar 1956 at Hacienda La Providencia, s Táchira[792], and not found since then. Undergrowth of thick, mossy forest (cloud forest). This area currently suffers from much deforestation. Status unknown but possibly threatened.

Range: ENDEMIC. 1800–2100m. S Táchira (upper Río Chiquito).

Plain-backed Antpitta   PLATE 42
Grallaria haplonota   Hormiguero Torero
Identification: 6.7″ (17cm). 85g. N cordilleras. *Uniform olive brown above* with crown slightly tinged gray, upper tail coverts rufescent, lores and *throat whitish bordered by distinct dusky submalar and buffy white malar*, chest olive brown turning buffy ochraceous on lower underparts. Or underparts darker, belly dark rufous (*pariae*).
Sim. species: See Scaled Antpitta which has dark throat and always looks somewhat streaked and scaled (not uniform).
Voice: Song a slow, measured ser. of ca. 5–9 low, hollow notes rising slightly in middle, *wü, wüü, wüü,*

whüü whüü, wüü wü. Sings repeatedly for short period at dawn, during day in late dry and early rainy season. When foraging a soft *whoou*, slightly higher pitched than song.
Behavior: Like others of genus, usually on or near gd. Typically shy and retiring, staying in cover of thick undergrowth, but occas. quite unsuspicious, hopping in open on forest floor. Moves across forest floor by bounding along kangaroo-like with springy hops and a few quick steps. Forages with quick stabbing motions of bill to dig in soft gd. for earthworms (apparently an important part of diet), but stops every few sec to stand bolt upright and stare. Sings from gd. or a perch up to 2m up.
Status and habitat: Locally common resident but usually difficult to see. Undergrowth of humid and wet forest (cloud forest), esp. around thick cluttered areas and treefalls. A common voice in vicinity of Rancho Grande Biol. Station, Aragua, and at Palmichal, Carabobo.

Range: 900–1950m. N end of Andes in Lara (Bucarito); mts. of Yaracuy, and n cordilleras from Carabobo to Miranda e to Carupano and PN Guatopo (*haplonota*); Cerros Humo and Azul on Paria Pen., Sucre (*pariae*). Mts. of e and w Ecuador; prob. w Colombia.

Chestnut-crowned Antpitta   PLATE 42
Grallaria ruficapilla   Hormiguero Compadre
Identification: 7.5–8″ (19–20.3mm). 72g. Large and widespread. Legs pale blue gray. *Crown, sides of head to below eyes, and nape bright cinnamon rufous* in sharp contrast to olive brown upperparts; *large puffy snowy white throat*; remaining underparts white *broadly streaked dusky olive*, heaviest on sides and flanks.
Sim. species: One of commonest highland antpittas. Not likely confused if seen well. Cf. differently shaped *Chamaeza* antthrushes which are sim. only in being streaked below.
Voice: Often hd. song 3 clear whistles, *püe, paaw, puuee*, 1st highest, 2d lowest, 3d slurred up. An onomatopoeic local name is *compra pan* ("buy bread"); other local names, *compadre* and *seco estoy*, are also onomatopoeic; also a startlingly loud, downslurred whistle, *püéeeeeu*, hd. much more in some areas than others, i.e., Mucuy area of PN Sierra Nevada where hd. almost to exclusion of 3-noted song.
Behavior: Like others of genus, largely terrestrial and usually alone, although occas. prs. are seen together, sometimes even quite close. Hops or uses a hopping-running gait when moving quickly, stopping freq. in

abrupt, upright manner to stare. When foraging, often *runs* a few steps, stops bolt upright, then pecks quickly and vigorously at leaf litter, but does not toss leaves. May spend long periods of time foraging in small area. Noted eating earthworms. Behavior typically furtive and retiring but often comes readily to whistled imitation of song. During predawn half-light may leave cover to bound, with springy hops, across roads or into small clearings to forage. A nest in Colombia was a mass of dead leaves, roots, and moss some ht. above gd.[589].

Status and habitat: Widespread and common resident. One of most consistently vocal *Grallaria*, but distrib. complex. At lower els. and in absence of other large *Grallaria* occurs in treefalls, second growth, *and* inside mature humid and wet forest, e.g., Mucuy area of PN Sierra Nevada; at higher els. and in presence of other *Grallaria* found mostly in forest edges, treefalls, landslide gaps, or second growth of various ages. Readily hd., and can be seen with patience, in forests above Colonia Tovar, Aragua.

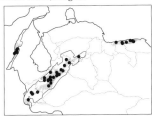

Range: 1300–3000m (tape to 3450m, Laguna Negra, Mérida—P. Boesman). Sierra de Perijá, Zulia (*perijana*); Andes of s Táchira n to ne Trujillo at Páramos Misisí and Cendé (*nigrolineata*); Andes of Lara (Cubiro), and Coastal Cordillera in Aragua, Distr. Federal, and Miranda (*avilae*). Colombia to e and w Peru.

Gray-naped Antpitta   PLATE 42
Grallaria griseonucha   Hormiguero de Nuca Gris
Identification: 6.3″ (16cm). Upperparts reddish brown with *prom. gray band extending back from eyes across rearcrown and nape*; underparts rich rufous. Or sim. but upperparts olive brown (*tachirae*).
Sim. species: Nearest is Rufous Antpitta, but that sp. is not known to occur n of Táchira Depression.
Voice: Two song types. Primary song a rapid rising ser. of low whistled notes, last 2–3 loudest, *wü, wü-wü-wú wu'wU'WU*, with hollow quality, delivered quickly and ending abruptly. Also a single whistled *whüüt?* at long intervals, or combined into 2s, 3s, or 4s in irreg. Morse code–like ser. that may continue for several min.
Behavior: Much like others of genus. Usually alone, hopping or run-hopping on or near gd. or to ca. 4m up, occas. much higher, when calling. May call for long periods from same perch, then hop or fly down to gd. Usually remains inside shrubbery, but not esp. shy or difficult to see once inside thickets it haunts. Shakes body as sings; squats slightly near conclusion of song.
Status and habitat: Locally fairly common to common resident by voice in dense vegetation in treefalls, landslides, cluttered areas, and along borders of wet, mossy forest; usually not inside open forest. Up to 10

hd. near summit of PN Guaramacal, Trujillo, 11 Feb 1998 (Hilty and D. Ascanio).

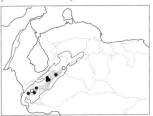

Range: ENDEMIC. 2300–2800m. Andes of n Táchira (*tachirae*); Andes of Mérida and e Trujillo (tape) n to PN Guaramacal (*griseonucha*).

Rufous Antpitta   PLATE 42
Grallaria rufula   Hormiguero Pichón Rufo
Identification: 5.5″ (14cm). 38g. *Uniform rich rufous above*, slightly paler rufous below becoming paler, more tawny rufous on belly; dark buff loral spot and narrow buff eyering. Or slightly larger (5.7″, 14.5cm) and *very different*: above *plain olive brown* with dusky crescent encircling forepart of eye; narrow indistinct whitish eyering; underparts drab buff to whitish brown, paler on throat; center of belly whitish; no rufous in plumage (*saltuensis*). In hand, tarsus of *saltuensis* longer (45–46 vs. 41–42mm).
Sim. species: A small, uniform antpitta likely confused only with even smaller Rusty-breasted or Slate-crowned antpittas, both of which show bolder facial markings and some white below.
Voice: Song in Colombia, and prob. Táchira, a short, flat, 2- or 3-noted *tüü, titee*, or *tüü, tüük*, last phrase a quarter-tone lower in pitch; at any distance song sounds 2-noted. Also, in Ecuador, a series of *tu* notes run together rapidly in a 1- to 4-sec.-long trill[541]. Song of birds in Sierra de Perijá unknown.
Behavior: Like others of genus, retiring and difficult to see. Single birds, prs., or well-separated members of prs. hop or run-hop on gd. when foraging but hop up onto branches and in vegetation to ca. 2m up when disturbed or calling. May hop into small openings in dim predawn light. In Ecuador, steep-walled, grass-stem cup nest 0.75m up in cavity on side of large moss-covered stump; 1 turquoise egg[793].
Status and habitat: Resident in thick shrubbery and bamboo at edge of mossy montane forest; also in treefalls, dense second growth with saplings, and overgrown areas. Often in damp places.

Range: 2000–3100m. Sierra de Perijá, Zulia (*saltuensis*); s Táchira in upper Río Chiquito, Páramo de Tamá, and Cerro El Teteo (*rufula*). Colombia s in Andes to Bolivia.

Note: Birds from Sierra de Perijá (*saltuensis*) differ in plumage and size from those elsewhere and are prob. a separate sp.

Hylopezus

Rather small, plump, and stub-tailed; bill proportionately small; streaked or spotted underparts; bright ochraceous under wing coverts; most with prom. eyering or loral spot and pinkish legs; lowland rain forests.

Spotted Antpitta   PLATE 42
Hylopezus macularius   Hormiguero Pichón Punteado
Identification: 5.5″ (14cm). 48g. Unusually large dark eyes surrounded by *prom. buff eyering and loral spot.* Crown and nape gray, rest of upperparts uniform pale olive brown with 2 faint buff-tipped wing bars; *throat snowy white* with narrow black malar line; conspic. *black necklace across buff-washed chest*; lower underparts white, flanks and belly cinnamon; under wing coverts ochraceous, black patch bordered ochraceous at base of primaries forms wing band visible mainly in flight. Or sim. but back browner (*diversus*).
Sim. species: A strikingly patterned antpitta, unlikely to be confused if seen well. Thrush-like Antpitta is superficially sim. but lacks bold facial pattern, and streaking on underparts is subdued. Cf. smaller Spot-backed Antbird.
Voice: Song in e Bolívar a low, rhythmically whistled *wü-whoo, wü-whee-whee*, 1st and 3d notes lower in pitch; has breezy, hollow, and reedy quality, unmistakable once hd. and not likely overlooked. Sings mostly at dawn and esp. late in evening. For brief but unpredictable periods of a few days or wks (advertising or breeding?) may sing throughout day. Alarm a guttural *cu-cu-cu-cu*. Song of birds in s Amazonas unknown. In ne Peru (same subsp.?) a more musical *kuhlo-kuhlo-kuhlo, klu, klu*[545].
Behavior: An endearing little bird with expressive manner. Moves with rapid, springy hops or occas. short run-hops across forest floor, then pauses in stiff upright position and may fluff out feathers, or bend over to quickly flick aside leaves. Sings from gd. or more often a slightly elevated perch, typically a large vine or diagonal branch 0.2–1.5m up. May sing for several min without moving from song perch. With each song, head is raised slightly and a little bare pink skin may be visible as throat expands and contracts during song. Like most antpittas, typically rather shy and difficult to see although generally less so than many *Grallaria*, and occas. rather easily seen.

Status and habitat: Uncommon and apparently very local resident (prs. widely scattered) inside tall humid lowland forest. Song periods may be brief, resulting in under-reporting of nos.
Range: To 500m. C Amazonas (Pto. Yapacana; vicinity of Cerro Duida; Río Casiquiare) southward (*diversus*); e Bolívar in Sierra de Imataca (*macularius*); base of Sierra de Lema (sightings/tape, km 80, 84, and 88) in e Bolívar (prob. *macularius*). Se Colombia and ne Peru e to the Guianas, mouth of the Amazon, and ne Brazil.
Note: Songs of subspp. differ over broad range. Possibly more than 1 sp. involved.

Myrmothera

Plumage and song recall *Grallaria*, but smaller than most, bill thinner; blurry streaked underparts recall *Hylopezus*; terrestrial; humid forest.

Thrush-like Antpitta   PLATE 42
Myrmothera campanisona   Hormiguero Campanero
Identification: 6″ (15cm). 47g. *Resembles a tail-less thrush.* Uniform warm brown above with buffy white loral patch and buff postocular ring enclosing rear half of eye; below dull white with some *blurry brown streaking on chest and breast*; flanks tinged gray.
Sim. species: See Spotted Antpitta; at high els., Tepui Antpitta.
Voice: Song, at intervals throughout day, a short ser. of 5–6 hollow, resonant whistles, *wüh wüh WUH Wüh wü*, increasing in volume then fading at end. Often remains on slightly elevated perch and sings for long periods of time without moving. Also, freq. a short, breathy, almost musical little rattle, *rururururu' ru'ru*, slowing slightly at end, trogonlike, and hd. more often late in afternoon (K. Zimmer recording). Often sings from same thicket for days or weeks on end.
Behavior: Shy and furtive, and almost Machiavellian in its uncanny ability to remain hidden inside dense treefall tangles. Often hd., however, and sings at various times throughout day. Hops on gd. or ascends to ca. 1.5m up in vegetation, and if pressed, likely to fall silent or slip away unseen. Lives in prs. that are quite sedentary; 3 nests early Dec–late Jan in French Guiana; shallow cup nest 0.25–0.6m up in rosette of small palm or herbaceous plant; 2 bluish green eggs with dark brown markings around larger end[751].
Status and habitat: Resident. Primarily an antpitta of dense young regrowth in treefalls and in stands of dense saplings, clutter and shrubbery in openings inside or at edge of terra firme, or low-lying transitional

forest, or along streams. Locally fairly common. In some areas singing birds are widely scattered, a reflection, perhaps, of suitable treefall microhabitat.
Range: To 800m. C and s Amazonas from San Fernando de Atapabo and vicinity of Cerro Duida southward (*dissors*); Bolívar from Sierra de Imataca (Río Grande) s to Sierra de Lema (*campanisona*). Se Colombia to extreme n Bolivia, n Amaz. Brazil, and the Guianas.

Tepui Antpitta   PLATE 43
Myrmothera simplex   Hormiguero de los Tepuis
Identification: 6.3″ (16cm). 54g. Above reddish brown with *grayish loral patch* and narrow grayish buff eyering (much wider behind eyes), *throat white contrasting with broad brownish chest band* (or band olive brown—*duidae*; or chest band grayish washed olive brown—*simplex*); rest of underparts dull grayish white tinged gray to olive gray on flanks; legs pinkish. All subspp. rather sim.; *simplex* and *pacaraimae* have slightly paler, grayer, and less extensive chest bands.
Sim. species: Few others in its tepui range. Broad chest band is unique. In foothills see Thrush-like Antpitta; at higher els., Scaled Antpitta.
Voice: Song 6–7 (occas. more) low-pitched, deliberately paced, hollow notes, *whu-whu-whu-WU-hu-hu*, 1st ones rising slightly in pitch and increasing in volume, last 2–3 on same pitch. Recalls song of Thrush-like Antpitta. Also gives a low, hollow rattle-trill.
Behavior: Like others of genus, stays mostly hidden in clutter of mossy forest undergrowth, esp. around old treefalls and fallen mossy limbs, where hard to see. Hops on forest floor, or alternates hopping with a few running steps. Sings from near gd. to ca. 3m up. Sometimes surprisingly fearless and curious, at other times devilishly difficult even to glimpse.
Status and habitat: Resident in mossy premontane forest and melastome-dominated second growth on slopes of tepuis. Fairly common by voice on Sierra de Lema, but prs. are typically widely separated.

Range: 600–2400m (mostly above 1200m). Mts. of Amazonas from Cerros Yavi and Sipapo s to Sierra de Unturán and Cerro de la Neblina (*duidae*); se Amazonas (Río Ocamo) and s Bolívar on Paurai-tepui and Cerro Urutaní; in Sierra Pacaraima (*pacaraimae*); nw and c Bolívar on Cerros Tabaro, Guaiquinima, and Sarisariñama and Meseta de Jaua (*guaiquinimae*); cerros of Gran Sabana from Auyán-tepui and Sierra de Lema s to Cerro Roraima and Brazilian border (*simplex*). Adj. n Brazil. Prob. Guyana.
Note: Previously called Brown-breasted Antpitta[403].

Grallaricula

Like a small edition of *Grallaria*; bill short and narrow; rictal bristles prom.; typically found in lower strata of forest, not on gd.; live in prs.; sexes sim; several spp. notably rare and local.

Rusty-breasted Antpitta   PLATE 42
Grallaricula ferrugineipectus   Ponchito Pechicastaño
Identification: 4″ (10.2cm). 16g. Plump and virtually tail-less. Long legs. Above olive brown with crown essentially concolor with back (or at most vaguely tinged gray), *conspic. buffy white loral patch and eye-ring* (widest in front and behind eye) separated by dusky crescent in front of eyes; throat orange rufous, *narrow whitish crescent across upper chest*, rest of underparts orange rufous, center of lower breast and belly white. Or crown rufous chestnut, underparts darker, white crescent on chest less conspic. (*rara*).
Sim. species: Much like Slate-crowned Antpitta but no gray crown; neither sp. likely to be found unless singing, and songs very different.
Voice: Sings persistently May–Aug (early rainy season), infreq. in dry season; song *twa-twa-twa-twa-twa-twa-qwe-qwe-qwe-qwe-qwe-qwe-qwi-qua-qua*, with *qwe* notes higher pitched and louder; a sad, liquid *quierk* or doubled *quiu-quiu* alarm.
Behavior: Like others of genus, usually seen alone. Lives in sedentary prs. with members usually well separated. Stays low inside shady forest, esp. near thickets and vine tangles. Typically perches 1–3m up on mossy limbs, and sallies out rapidly to foliage (sally-strike) or drops to gd. briefly, mostly for arthropods. Often surprisingly unsuspicious, but combination of sudden movements and generally low ambient light where sp. lives makes it difficult to see. Breeding begins late May; shallow twig cup ca. 1m up; 2 pale greenish or grayish eggs marked with shades of brown[577].
Status and habitat: Fairly common to common resident (by voice) but easily overlooked. Humid premontane and montane forest and tall second-growth woodland, esp. in or near large vine tangles and understory clutter. One seen 15km w of Turgua, Miranda, 24 Sep 1984 (C. Parrish) is one of easternmost recs.

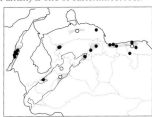

Range: 250–2200m (usually above 800m). Sierra de Perijá, Zulia (*rara*); Andes from Mérida (La Azulita) and nw Barinas (sight/tape, San Isidro Rd.) n through Trujillo to se Lara (Cabudare) and cerros of nw Lara; mts. of c and e Falcón and Yaracuy, and n cordilleras e to Distr. Federal and Miranda (*ferrugineipectus*). Colombia (Santa Marta Mts. and E Andes); Andes of Peru and nw Bolivia.
Note: Birds of Peru and Bolivia perhaps a separate sp.[545].

Slate-crowned Antpitta

PLATE 42

Grallaricula nana   Ponchito Enano

Identification: 4.3″ (10.9cm). 20g. Much like previous sp. Above olive brown with entire *crown and nape contrasting gray; prom. buff loral patch and eyering* separated by dusky crescent in front of eye; *below deep ferruginous*, paler on throat and with *narrow whitish crescent at base of throat;* center of belly whitish. Or lower mandible yellowish flesh, upperparts paler; throat pale rufous, breast darker chestnut (forms broad dark band), belly pale (*cumanensis, pariae*).

Sim. species: In most of range decidedly darker below than Rusty-breasted Antpitta and with gray crown and more prom. loral patch; in Sierra de Perijá (where Rusty-breasted is also dark below) told by *contrasting* crown and voice. Rare Hooded Antpitta is pale gray below.

Voice: Distinctive song, sim. in all mt. areas n of Orinoco, a rapid ser. of fifelike or piping notes that run up scale a little, then continue in long arcing descent, *we'e'e'ti'ti'ti'ti'ti'ti'ti'ti'ti'ti'te'te'e'e'e* (ca. 30 notes in 3 sec); fairly high pitched and ventriloquial making bird difficult to locate. Usually sings from perch several meters up. Sings at least Jan–Jul but most vocal early in wet season. Song of birds in Bolívar unknown.

Behavior: Sedentary and difficult to see. Single birds perch and move with wing-assisted hops mostly 0.5–3m up inside forest, but may sing from much higher perch, often partially in open. Reg. drop to forest floor and hop, then stop abruptly like a *Catharus* thrush[458]; from low perches peer and peck from surface of mossy trunks and limbs, or sally rapidly to nearby leaf or to gd. for arthropod prey.

Status and habitat: Fairly common to common resident (by voice) in all mt. areas n of Orinoco. Inside wet and mossy montane forest (cloud forest), esp where there is much clutter and vegetation in understory. Occurs mostly above el. range of Rusty-breasted Antpitta.

Range: 700–2800m. Disjunct range. Andes of Táchira and Mérida n to ne Trujillo at Cuevas de Carache (*nana*); Coastal Cordillera in Aragua and Distr. Federal (*olivascens*); Cerro Tucucito on Miranda/Anzoátegui border (sight, C. Parrish) (prob. *olivascens*); mts. of Anzoátegui, w Sucre, and n Monagas (*cumanensis*); e Sucre on Cerros Humo and Azul on Paria Pen. (*pariae*); se Bolívar on cerros of Gran Sabana from Ptari-tepui to Cerros Cuquenán and Roraima (*kukenamensis*). Colombia s in Andes to extreme n Peru.

Scallop-breasted Antpitta

PLATE 42

Grallaricula loricata   Ponchito Pechiescamado

Identification: 4.2″ (10.7cm). Only in mts. of n Venez. Above brown with bright chestnut crown and nape; prom. buff *loral patch and narrow buff eyering* (widest in front of and behind eye); throat buff bordered by dusky whisker (submalar) and buff malar; narrow, partially concealed white crescent at base of throat; *rest of underparts white heavily scalloped black*, belly white.

Sim. species: Looks like a miniature Chestnut-crowned Antpitta, but small size precludes confusion.

Voice: Unknown. Perhaps song very seasonal.

Behavior: An enigmatic little bird that, on rare occas., pops up into view to stare but seems to rarely vocalize. Sightings well above Rancho Grande Biol. Station have been of solitary birds perching at or below eye level (but not on gd.) inside forest (C. Parrish). One near Choroní Pass perched by clinging to side of vertical vine at eye level (K. Zimmer).

Status and habitat: Rare or possibly quite local; few recs. and certainly not often seen. May occur at els. slightly higher than those visited by most observers. Undergrowth of wet mossy forest (cloud forest).

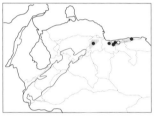

Range: ENDEMIC. 1440–2100m (sight rec. to 1200m, Rancho Grande—C. Parrish). Mts. of Yaracuy (Sierra de Aroa) and Coastal Cordillera in Carabobo, Aragua (Rancho Grande; Cumbre de Choroní), and Distr. Federal (Silla de Caracas).

Hooded Antpitta

PLATE 42

Grallaricula cucullata   Ponchito Cabecicastaño

Identification: 4″ (10.2cm). Mts. of s Táchira. *Bill orange. Entire head and nape rufous chestnut*, throat slightly paler, back olive brown, wings and tail tinged reddish brown, narrow white crescent across top of chest, *rest of underparts pale smoky olive gray*, center of belly whitish.

Sim. species: No other small *Grallaricula* has orange bill and contrasting rufous head.

Behavior: Like others of genus, usually seen hopping through undergrowth from near gd. to about eye level. Often rocks body side to side while holding head and

legs stationary[260] as do some larger antpittas. Three BC birds, May–Sep, Colombia[127].

Status and habitat: Few records in Venez. Perhaps rare and local but prob. also overlooked. Inside understory of wet montane forest. To be looked for at lower els. in PN Tamá.

Range: 1800–2550m. S Táchira in upper Río Chiquito at Hacienda La Providencia (*venezuelana*); sight, w Apure (2550m), upper Río Oirá, 19 Sep 1983 (C. Parrish) near border of Táchira (prob. *venezuelana*). Colombia.

[Conopophagidae: Gnateaters]

Chupadientes

Chestnut-belted Gnateater (*Conopophaga aurita*), not reported in Venez., may occur along its e border with Guyana and in extreme s Amazonas. 4.5″ (11.4cm). ♂: crown brown, *forehead, sides of head, and throat black* forming broad black mask ending in *small silvery postocular tuft*, otherwise brown, darker above, center of belly white, bill black, legs pale blue. Solitary and inconspic. on low perches inside humid lowland forest. Call (nw Peru) a weak, rustling *chief;* also a short, flat *chat'up, chat'up* . . . , in irreg. delivery (Hilty). Song in Manaus, Brazil, a dry, chattery rattle or slow trill, ca. 30–40 notes in 2.5 sec (K. Zimmer recording).

Rhinocryptidae: Tapaculos

Tapaculos

This New World family is most diverse in the southern third of South America. A few species range northward, mostly in the mountains, to Costa Rica. They are most closely related to antbirds but differ from them in, among other things, a cocked tail and movable flap or operculum covering the nostrils. Tapaculos are terrestrial or semiterrestrial insectivores that run or hop. Flights are short and weak and usually consist of little more than wing-assisted hops. Some austral species occur in dry open country, but all Venezuelan species inhabit humid mountain forest. Nests, as far as known, are globular balls in burrows, banks, crevices, or tree cavities and are always well concealed. Most Venezuelan species belong to the genus *Scytalopus*, a group of wrenlike birds characterized by narrow, laterally compressed bills, a high, thin culmen, and dusky or blackish plumage. The various species are difficult to distinguish even in the hand, and their taxonomy is still poorly understood—indeed even the number of species is still unknown. Recent biochemical evidence[604] demonstrates that tapaculos are most closely related to gnateaters (Conopophagidae) and to ground antbirds (Formicariidae). The name *tapaculo* is derived from the Spanish word meaning "to cover your posterior," a reference to their habit of holding the tail cocked up[139].

Scytalopus

Mouselike behavior (often known as "feathered mice"); tail usually cocked, but relaxed when foraging; most are dark gray to blackish; plumages differ little between spp.; hop in dark mossy tangles on or near gd.; weak flight; complex geographical variation and secretive habits complicate taxonomy and field observation; no. of spp. in genus uncertain, but usually no more than 2 spp. occur together; zones of overlap between spp. are usually narrow compared to their respective el. distrib.; songs and scold notes prob. most reliable indicators of spp. limits; juv. and imm. plumages of all spp. rich reddish brown with varying amt. of darker barring. Present taxonomy[303] subject to revision.

Unicolored Tapaculo PLATE 53

Scytalopus unicolor   Pájaro Ratón Unicolor

Identification: 4.8″ (12.2cm). 18g. Wrenlike with short cocked tail. Sexes sim. ♂: *uniform blackish slate* above and below (no barring). ♀: sim. but paler and with brown flanks either uniform or obscurely barred.

Sim. species: Blackish ad. *much darker* than any other *Scytalopus* in Venez. except Northern White-crowned Tapaculo which has white crown spot and brown rearparts.

Voice: Song above Bramón, Táchira (1800m), a notably *low-pitched* and *nasal* or hollow ser. of *unk* notes, ca. 1/sec, but occas. given at ca. 2/sec, for up to 1 min. Above Betania, Táchira (2200m), a slow, nasal, paired ser. of whistles, *cueep-cueep, cueep-cueep* . . . , ca. 1 couplet/sec, typically long sustained; after playback a single *cueep* over and over.

Behavior: Hops on or near gd. and usually stays somewhat concealed in shrubby vegetation, but occas. ascends to ca. 2m up in tangles and mossy thickets. Not shy, but because it seems to be continually on the move and stays in dark recesses, can be difficult to see well. Usually alone, or members of prs. well separated.

Status and habitat: Resident. Occurs in thickets in small forest openings or at forest edges; also in stands of dense saplings and in forest edge shrubbery with briars, sedges, and ferns in highland pastures.

Range: 1800–2200m (prob. higher and lower). Andes of Táchira and c Mérida (*latrans*). Colombia s in Andes to n Peru.

Note 1: The present taxonomic arrangement follows Krabbe and Schulenberg[303] uniting all subspp. from Venez. to n Peru into a single sp.

Note 2: Ash-colored Tapaculo (*Myiornis senilis*) undoubtedly occurs in Venez. as it is known from Tamá region in adj. Colombia. Rather long tailed, 5.5″ (14cm), uniform gray, paler below, belly tinged cinnamon. Juv. cinnamon rufous above; buffy ochraceous below; wing coverts, tertials, and tail faintly barred dusky. Unusual song (Ecuador) is variable, typically a low, nasal *chup* . . . . . *chup* . . . *chup* . . *chup-chup* . .

ché-chup-chup . . ché-ché-a-chup, chĩk-a-da-dup, chĩk-a-da-dup, che-e-e-te-te-te-tetetetetEEEEEEEeeer, terr, galloping phrases in middle, squealing trill at end (ca. 10 sec), or any part of song singly.

Northern White-crowned Tapaculo
PLATE 53

Scytalopus atratus   Pájaro Ratón de Corona Blanca
Identification: 4.8″ (12.2cm). 23g. ♂: dark slaty gray above and below; throat slightly paler, *prom. white central crown spot;* flanks and crissum dark brown obscurely barred black. ♀: sim. but *white crown patch usually reduced, occas. lacking,* paler gray, esp. below; breast somewhat mottled with white.
Sim. species: ♂ almost as dark as Unicolored Tapaculo but always shows white crown patch. ♀♀ (and younger birds?) lacking white in crown are much like Brown-rumped Tapaculo, then best told by voice.
Voice: Song in s Táchira and nw Barinas a rather slow ser. of low, nasal notes, *keyouk, keyouk* . . . , ca. 2 to 3/sec for 10–20 sec or more.
Behavior: Secretive mouselike behavior much like others of genus. Almost always seen alone.
Status and habitat: Fairly common resident (by voice) in s Táchira, perhaps local on e slope of Andes where recorded only in nw Barinas (1450m) on San Isidro Rd. (1st rec. 15 Jan 1991)[259]; several subsequently[596]. Shrubby undergrowth, treefalls, and overgrown roadbanks in humid and wet montane forest; also dense undergrowth and borders of second-growth woodland and coffee plantations.

Range: 1150–1900m. Río Negro region of Sierra de Perijá, Zulia, and Andes of s Táchira (*nigricans*); sightings, nw Barinas (subsp.?). Colombia to s Peru.
Note: Previously called Rufous-vented Tapaculo, *S. femoralis*[403], a taxa now split into 4 Andean spp. ranging s to w Bolivia[303,541].

Mérida Tapaculo
PLATE 53

Scytalopus meridanus   Pájaro Ratón de Mérida
Identification: 4.8″ (12.2cm). 20g. ♂: above *dark gray*, rump and upper tail coverts brown *obscurely barred dusky,* below dark gray, *flanks, belly, and crissum cinnamon brown barred dusky;* most birds show vague whitish mottling on breast. ♀: sim. but paler above, much paler below, usually with whitish mottling on breast; belly tinged pale tawny rufous, rump and flanks barred as in ♂. Some birds (Santo Domingo, Mérida) show very little barring.
Sim. species: ♂ like ♂ Northern White-crowned Tapaculo but a little paler gray below and no white crown spot. ♀ closely resembles ♀ Northern White-crowned Tapaculo (those without crown spots) and in field

prob. best told by voice. Rufous-rumped Tapaculo is always smaller and shorter-billed, generally paler gray below, and with little or no barring.
Voice: Songs are fast, med.-pitched trills, sometimes only 1–2 sec in length, or up to 10–15 sec, at rate of 8–20 notes/sec (PN Guaramacal, ca. 2400m). Loud, almost squeaky (alarm?) *knee-deep!* sometimes followed by slowly accelerating *tidip, tidip, tidip, tidip. . .* of bisyllabic notes (PN Yacambú, ca. 1700m); also a squealing rattle, *sque'e'e'E'E'E'e'e'e'd'd'd.* Birds (this sp.?) have been hd. giving slower songs of 6–8 notes/sec in n Táchira. Songs described here may involve more than 1 sp.
Behavior: Usually seen singly, occas. in prs., in dense vegetation where run or scurry on gd. or move with short wing-assisted hops, mostly less than 1m up. In favorable areas territories are small but vigorously maintained by these cunning little warriors. Secretive habits and dense or mossy vegetation make them difficult to see, but they are often fearless of quiet observers and will approach closely to tape playback, even hopping over an observer's shoes.
Status and habitat: Resident. Dense thickets, tangled undergrowth on floor of humid and wet forest, tall second-growth woodland, and along bushy forest borders. A specimen (AMNH) from 4000m el. in Merida has been referred to this sp., but vocal data and further comparisons are needed[303]. Reports of a *Scytalopus* sp. from Sierra de San Luis, Falcón, may refer to this sp. or to Caracas Tapaculo.

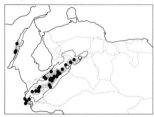

Range: 1600–3300m (possibly to 4000m). Sierra de Perijá, Zulia; Andes from s Táchira n through Mérida and Trujillo to Páramo Cendé on Trujillo/Lara border; PN Yacambú, s Lara (sight/tape—many observers). Colombia (prob. C and E Andes).
Note: Formerly called Brown-rumped Tapaculo, *S. latebricola*[403], a taxa now split into 4 spp. ranging from n Venez. and Colombia's Santa Marta Mts. s to Ecuador[303]. Venez. spp. incl. Caracas and Mérida tapaculos.

Caracas Tapaculo
PLATE 53

Scytalopus caracae   Pájaro Ratón de Caracas
Identification: 4.8″ (12.2cm). Above dark gray with brownish rump and upper tail coverts; underparts gray becoming dark cinnamon brown on flanks and belly; *brownish rearparts rather weakly barred black* (barring not conspic. in field).
Sim. species: No other *Scytalopus* in its range.
Voice: Very noisy with vocalizations unlike others of genus. Song a loud, rhythmic *ka KICK-ka-ca*, over and over, with emphatic angry quality. Also various squeals and short nasal notes.
Behavior: Mouselike. Scurries around on forest floor, perpetually in a rush, hopping through mossy clutter

and brush piles as quickly as a mouse, pausing here and there to poke head up and stare, just as quickly darting on. Nearly always seen singly, occas. in prs. Not with mixed-spp. flocks but often active, moving about and calling more when a flock is overhead. **Status and habitat:** Common to locally very common resident on floor of humid and wet mossy forest (cloud forest) and in dense shrubbery at edge of forest openings and on roadbanks.

Range: ENDEMIC. 1200–2140m; sight/tape to 2400m, Pico Oriental (D. Ascanio). Coastal Cordillera in Aragua, Distr. Federal, and Miranda; Cerro Turumiquire in Cordillera de Caripe of w Sucre.
Note: Formerly regarded as a subsp. of Brown-rumped Tapaculo (*S. latebricola*). Present taxonomy follows Krabbe and Schulenberg[303]. See taxonomic note under Mérida Tapaculo.

Rufous-rumped Tapaculo
PLATE 43
Scytalopus griseicollis   Pájaro Ratón Oscuro
Identification: 4–4.3″ (10.2–10.9cm). *Small and short-tailed; short, thin bill; found near treeline.* Head and foreparts *pale gray,* slightly darker on crown; *rump and flanks sharply contrasting cinnamon rufous and unbarred,* center of belly whitish.
Sim. species: *Palest gray* of any *Scytalopus* in Venez. Note contrasting rearparts, lack of barring, and treeline habitat. Cf. Unicolored Tapaculo which is slaty black (not pale gray). Mérida Tapaculo shows *less contrasting rearparts* (esp. ♀) and has barred flanks.
Voice: Unknown.
Behavior: Presum. sim. to others of genus. May be easier to see than other *Scytalopus* because of more open treeline habitat it occupies.
Status and habitat: Poorly known. Small no. of Venez. specimens have been taken in Trujillo and on Trujillo/Lara border. Low stunted woodland, shrubs, and grass at treeline.

Range: 2800–3200m (to 2500m?). S Trujillo (Guamito; Teta de Niquitao) and n Trujillo/Lara border at Cuevas

de Carache and Páramo de Las Rosas (*fuscicauda*). Ne Colombia (E Andes from Bogotá northward).
Note: Taxonomy follows Krabbe and Schulenberg[303]. *S. griseicollis* is now considered 1 of numerous spp. That were formerly united under name Andean Tapaculo (*S. magellanicus*)[403]. Closely resembles nominate *griseicollis* subsp. of ne Colombia and, at least until voice is known, regarded as a subsp. of that form[303].

Ocellated Tapaculo
PLATE 42
Acropternis orthonyx   Gran Pájaro Ratón
Identification: 8.5″ (22cm). 91g. Spectacular but reclusive bird of high Andes. *Large and unmistakable.* Short, black, triangular-shaped bill with wide, flat culmen extending onto forehead (like a small shield); long, straight hindclaw (1″, 25mm) and long tail. *Plumage mostly bright reddish chestnut thickly sprinkled with black-encircled white spots;* forehead, face, throat, and rump unspotted bright rufous, wings and tail dusky black, tail rounded. Sexes sim.
Voice: Song, by both sexes, a loud, far-carrying whistle, *quEEEow,* mostly at dawn when typically repeated for 1 min or more at slightly less than 1 note/sec; when disturbed or challenging a conspecific, a strident whistled *kueee!* and jaylike *KEEa* varied to *phEEEeo!* may be often repeated several times in succession.
Behavior: Well-separated members of prs. are sedentary but shy and difficult to see except by tape playback. Hop heavily on or near gd. or low through undergrowth vegetation, almost always keeping beneath bamboo, but can move quickly and stealthily at times. Forage by scratching with both feet at once, typically scratching 2–3 times, pausing to inspect disturbed gd. after each scratch, then moving a short distance with bounding hop or 2 and repeating process. At favorable spots may scratch for several min in same place, almost burying themselves in a hole. Sing (whistle) from gd. as they move, or from stationary perch up to 3m up, extending neck and bill upward with each whistle.
Status and habitat: Resident. Fairly common *very locally* on floor of wet upper montane forest with *Chusquea* bamboo; also occas. in rather open patches of semi-isolated, stunted second growth with bamboo at treeline. Based on calling birds, distrib. is patchy, consisting of small, non-randomly distributed pops. (colonies?) prospering in narrow microhabitat limits. Some bamboo seems to be a requirement. Generally does not thrive in patchy or small and fragmented forests.

Range: 2250–3300m. Andes from s Táchira (Cerro Las Copas) n through Mérida to Trujillo/Lara border at Páramo La Nariz (*orthonyx*). Andes of Colombia, Ecuador, and extreme n Peru.

Tyrannidae: Tyrant Flycatchers
Atrapamoscas

Tyrant Flycatchers are found from the Arctic to Tierra del Fuego but reach their greatest diversity in warmer tropical regions. They occur in almost every habitat from the seacoast to snowline and are diverse in appearance and behavior. Many species that breed in north and south temperate regions are migratory, and several of them occur in Venezuela as nonbreeding residents during the north and south temperate winters. Unlike most temperate breeding species which are arboreal and sally to the air for insects, flycatchers found in tropical latitudes include species that are terrestrial, some of which run rapidly on the ground, and arboreal species that sally to foliage, glean foliage like vireos, or eat mostly fruit. Field identification of the many similar species can be very difficult, and some knowledge of shapes, voices, and habits of the various genera is essential. Breeding systems and male participation at the nest vary, but monogamy predominates. In a few genera, including *Lophotriccus*, *Pipromorpha*, and possibly *Laniocera*, males remain on display leks much of the time and breeding is polygamous. Nest sites range from the ground to cliffs and the forest canopy; nest shape varies greatly, some being simple open cups, others closed domes or elaborately suspended nests such as those of *Onychorhynchus*, *Rhynchocyclus*, and others. A few, notably *Myiarchus*, are cavity nesters; *Legatus* pirates nests from other birds. The present family has been separated into as many as four subfamilies (Elaeniinae, Fluvicolinae, Tyranninae, and Tityrinae)[467]. Some authors, most notably Sibley and Ahlquist[604] and Prum[513,514], argue for different arrangements, including an enlarged family that combines flycatchers, cotingas, and manakins under a single umbrella family. It should be emphasized that the taxonomy of many groups in the Tyrannidae, as well as the inclusion of some species formerly placed with cotingas or manakins, remains controversial[309] and that the present arrangement will almost certainly undergo change. The terminology of foraging behavior generally follows Fitzpatrick[176].

Phyllomyias

Diverse, confusing genus with numerous recent taxonomic revisions[545,758]; short bill, most (but not all) with well-marked wing bars; generally lack crisp yellow wing edgings of *Zimmerius*; med.-length tail typically narrow, held down or only slightly cocked.

White-fronted Tyrannulet   PLATE 48
Phyllomyias zeledoni   Atrapamoscas de Piernas Asperas

Identification: 4.5″ (11.4cm). 10.7g. Rare and local. Eyes light reddish brown. Bill horn above, *pinkish orange below*, culmen more curved than in other tyrannulets, otherwise rather narrow. *Crown grayish* contrasting slightly with olive upperparts (or mainly forecrown and midcrown gray—*viridiceps*), *2 narrow pale yellowish wing bars*; inner flight feathers and tertials prom. edged yellow, outer primaries plain dusky;

sharp white eyebrow from nostril to slightly beyond eye is distinctly broadest in front of eye and curved and narrow over eye; narrow loral line dusky; sides of head grizzled grayish and white, throat grayish white, *chest somewhat flammulated yellowish olive* forming vague blurry streaks; belly clear yellow. Or sim. but slightly duller yellow below (Andes). In field, "rough legs" (spiny tarsi) are visible with telescope.
Sim. species: Difficult to identify with confidence. Looks like a small Yellow-olive Flatbill with narrow (not wide) bill. Also easily confused with Southern Beardless-Tyrannulet and Yellow-crowned, Venezuelan, Golden-faced, and Brown-capped tyrannulets, all of which show ill-defined eyebrow; also cf. Sooty-headed Tyrannulet (no wing bars). Look for White-fronted's grayish crown, distinctive eyebrow shape, gray-flecked face, and yellowish wing bars; also note el. at which it occurs. Lacks dusky cheek patch of *Leptopogon* and *Pogonotriccus* flycatchers.
Voice: Song, in Mar in Trujillo, a ser. of ca. 8–10 high, slightly buzzy notes, *PEEza, PEEza* . . . (ca. 9 notes in 4 sec), quite forceful, on same pitch; bill opened wide. Song given at fairly short intervals, or once a min or less; also *PEEza*, singly at intervals of 2–3 sec.
Behavior: Usually seen alone, or singly with mixed-spp. flocks containing foliage-gleaners, other flycatchers, wood-warblers, and tanagers. Stays mostly in mid. levels or higher with mixed-spp. flocks, but may forage quite low (down almost to eye level) away from them. Rather sedentary and will spend long periods of time in one tree, often sitting quite still as it pauses to cock head and peer around. Flits up and briefly hover-gleans from beneath foliage, occas. perch-gleans for tiny insects. Posture more horizontal (like *Zimmerius*) than upright, but tail held level with body or only slightly cocked.
Status and habitat: Very uncommon and local (only a few specimens). Resident in borders of humid and wet forest, second-growth woodland, and scattered trees in clearings in foothills and mts. Recent sightings are from vicinity of Rancho Grande Biol. Station (900–1000m); above Choroní, Aragua, at 475m; and above Boconó, Trujillo (1800m), in PN Guaramacal (Hilty and D. Ascanio).

Range: 475–1800m. Sierra de Perijá (1640m) on Cerro Pejochaina (*wetmorei*); e slope of Andes above Boconó, Trujillo (sight); Coastal Cordillera in c Carabobo (Aguacatal) and Aragua (Rancho Grande; s of Choroní), nw Miranda at Hacienda Izcaragua, and Interior Cordillera in sw Miranda at Santa Lucía (*viridiceps*); Cerro Chimantá (1300m), se Bolívar (*bunites*).

Spottily in mts. of Costa Rica, Panama, Colombia, Ecuador, and Peru.
Note: Sometimes placed in genus *Acrochordopus* and merged with Rough-legged Tyrannulet (*P. burmeisteri*) of s S Amer. Both do differ from all other tyrannulets in having spiny tarsi, but voices of n and s forms very different.

Sooty-headed Tyrannulet
PLATE 46
Phyllomyias griseiceps   Atrapamoscas Cabecigris
Identification: 4.4″ (11.2cm). 7.6g. Eyes dark; slight crest; *exceptionally short bill.* Crown dusky brown to dusky gray, upperparts dull olive brown, *wings and tail unmarked dusky brown with no bars or edgings* (birds from Paria Pen. may show bars and edgings, esp. in fresh plumage), short, inconspic. white eyebrow; throat and sides of head somewhat grizzled grayish white, chest clouded olive, lower underparts pale yellow.
Sim. species: Plain, essentially unmarked tyrannulet with *tiny bill* (6–7mm) and distinctive voice. Note *lack of any wing bars or edgings*; also crown dark and sooty (hence name), but this alone not esp. distinctive. Cf. esp. Southern Beardless-Tyrannulet, Mouse-colored Tyrannulet, and spp. of *Zimmerius* and *Tolmomyias*, all of which have wing bars and/or edgings. Greenish Elaenia is larger, longer-tailed, and shows some wing edgings (but no bars).
Voice: Advertising song from exposed treetop perch a snappy, rhythmic *whit! wheet-wheet-wheéuu*, often given after a long pause (no. of *wheet* notes varies from 1 to 3); also a slightly trilled *tee'p'p'pip*. Song patterns vary geographically, those in se Bolívar differing most, a *wheet, whit, w'r'r'r*, last part disintegrating into rolled trill.
Behavior: Usually alone or in prs. in outermost mid. level or canopy foliage where sallies out and up various distances, sometimes 1m or more to hover-glean from beneath leaves. Also occas. perch-gleans, flits short distances like a kinglet (*Regulus*), and reg. eats small berries. Independent of mixed-spp. flocks, or occas. with them. Nest a small lichen-encrusted cup in small fork of dead branch 13m up in nw Ecuador (R. Ridgely).
Status and habitat: Locally common resident but *easily overlooked* (need to know song); distrib. somewhat spotty. Treetops in moist and humid forest borders, cacao and coffee plantations, tree-scattered clearings, and broken forest.

Range: To 1300m n of Orinoco; to 460m s of Orinoco. W and e Zulia, spottily in Andes from Táchira n to Lara, se Falcón (sight), mts. of Yaracuy, and n cordille-

ras from Carabobo to Distr. Federal and s Miranda at Cerro Negro; Anzoátegui, Sucre, and Monagas (*cristatus*); se Amazonas on Cerros Parima and de la Neblina; nw Bolívar from Hato Las Nieves (sight), lower Río Caura (sight, Maripa, Jan 1990—J. Pierson, D. Stejskal), lower Río Paragua and Sierra de Imataca s to Brazilian border (*pallidiceps*). E Panama locally to w Ecuador and c Peru; Guyana; Suriname (tape); e Brazil (spotty).

Urich's Tyrannulet
PLATE 46
Phyllomyias urichi   Atrapamoscas de Paria
Identification: 4.7″ (12cm). 7–8g. *Small bill*; no crest. *Above bright olive, crown grayish weakly contrasting with dusky*; wings and tail dusky, *2 conspic. whitish to yellowish white wing bars* and edgings; inconspic. yellowish white supraloral mark and eyering; *sides of head clean yellowish white* (no obvious dusky patches, no grizzled pattern); throat yellowish white, rest of underparts pale yellow, chest tinged (slightly flammulated) olive.
Sim. species: A little larger than several allies, and known range is very restricted (but perhaps overlooked elsewhere). Note small bill, weakly contrasting crown, wing bars, and absence of markings on sides of head. There are potentially a large no. of small flycatchers in mts. of ne Venez. with which this sp. could be confused. Cf. esp. Southern Beardless-Tyrannulet, Forest Elaenia, Yellow-olive and Zimmer's flatbills; Sooty-crowned, Yellow-crowned, and Golden-faced tyrannulets; and Pale-tipped Inezia.
Status and habitat: Known from 4 localities incl. 4 specimens from Quebrada Bonita, Anzoátegui (3 from Caripe, Monagas), all presumably from forested terrain. Deforestation and habitat degradation in these areas are extensive. No recent recs.

Range: ENDEMIC. 900–1100m. Mts. of ne Anzoátegui (Quebrada Bonita), Sucre (Los Palmales, Villaroel), and n Monagas (Caripe).
Note: Very sim. to Reiser's Tyrannulet (*P. reiseri*) of se Brazil and by some considered an isolated geographic pop. of it[710]. Also formerly considered conspecific with more widespread Greenish Tyrannulet (*P. virescens*) of Guyana and e Brazil w to Argentina and Bolivia. Song of Greenish Tyrannulet is known[100]; song of isolated *urichi* in Venez. is unknown.

[Ashy-headed Tyrannulet]
Phyllomyias cinereiceps   Atrapamoscas Cabecicenizo
Identification: 4″ (10.2cm). Short bill; dark red eyes. *Above pale olive green with contrasting blue gray crown*; narrow lores and eyering white, sides of head pale greenish yellow with *prom. black crescent on ear*

coverts; wings dusky with 2 yellowish white wing bars and yellowish white edgings on inner flight feathers; below bright yellow flammulated olive on throat and breast (*looks faintly and finely streaked*).
Sim. species: Plumage overall much like that of Marble-faced and Variegated bristle-tyrants; also larger Slaty-capped Flycatcher but note contrasting blue gray crown, greenish yellow on sides of head, and fine streaking on clean yellow underparts.
Behavior: Single birds or prs. follow mixed-spp. flocks in upper levels of forest. Sit upright, change perches quickly, or flit up and hover-glean tiny prey from foliage.
Status and habitat: Known from 3 sight recs., all above Bramón in s Táchira. First, in 1988, with tape-recording (Cornell Library of Nat. Sounds) by B. Whitney; 2 others near Matamula, 1700–1900m, 21–22 Dec 1996 (P. Boesman). Closest Colombian recs. are from w slope of E Andes in Norte de Santander.

Range: S Táchira. Spottily in Andes from Colombia (1400–2700m) to s Peru.

Black-capped Tyrannulet   PLATE 46
Phyllomyias nigrocapillus   Atrapamoscas Gorra Negra
Identification: 4.4″ (11.2cm). *Short bill and tail. Crown blackish* contrasting with dark olive green upperparts; *narrow white eyestripe; wing coverts black with 2 yellowish white bars* (spotted bars); inner flight feathers and tertials edged yellowish buff, throat grayish, *rest of underparts rich yellow*, chest heavily washed olive. Or sim. but cap dusky brown (*aureus*).
Sim. species: Occurs with Tawny-rumped Tyrannulet, *Mecocerculus* tyrannulets, and bristle-tyrants, but none has combination of blackish cap, black wing coverts with boldly spotted wing bars, and deep yellow underparts.
Voice: Call a clear, high *peeeeep*, unflycatcher-like, often persistently repeated.
Behavior: Restless and kingletlike as fidgets, flicks wings, pivots on branches, and gleans in outer foliage and branches from lower mid. level to canopy; occas. hangs from a leaf or hover-gleans insects from foliage, but does not sally. Occas. takes small berries, mostly by hovering. One or 2 faithfully accompany mixed-spp. flocks where perch rather horizontally with tail slightly cocked.
Status and habitat: Uncommon to fairly common resident in tall humid and wet montane forest, at forest edges, and in small parklike areas or pastures with trees in forested areas.
Range: 1800–3000m (sight to 1500m, May 1999, PN Yacambú—R. Ridgely). S Táchira (*nigrocapillus*); Andes

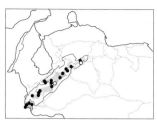

of n Táchira, Mérida, Trujillo, and s Lara n to Cubiro (*aureus*). Andes from Colombia to s Peru.
Note: Previously placed in genus *Tyranniscus*.

Tawny-rumped Tyrannulet   PLATE 48
Phyllomyias uropygialis   Atrapamoscas de Rabadilla Leonada
Identification: 4″ (10.2cm). 8.7g. Slight peaked crest. *Narrow stubby bill*; tail often cocked. Crown sooty brown with narrow gray supraloral line; back dark brown, wings blackish with *2 bold buff bars*; inner flight feathers and tertials edged buff, *rump and upper tail coverts tawny to tawny cinnamon* (diagnostic but rump normally hidden by wings), *face and throat gray*, throat vaguely streaked dusky, chest buffy olive turning buffy white on belly.
Sim. species: Overall rather dingy and "small headed" in appearance. Best marks (if rump is not seen) are dark upperparts, buff wing bars, and lack of yellow below. See Black-capped, Venezuelan, White-banded, and White-throated tyrannulets.
Voice: Song, mostly early in morning, high and forceful but rather weak, *tzeep, TEASE-you* (or *tzeep, ZEE-u*), sometimes given over and over at short intervals. Most vocal in early rainy season.
Behavior: Single birds or prs. occur alone or sometimes follow mixed-spp. flocks containing warblers, flowerpiercers, tanagers, and brush-finches. Perch with fairly upright posture and stay mostly in canopy or in higher part of shrubs where forage by short upward sallies to underside of foliage to hover-glean tiny arthropods. Usually rather easy to see.
Status and habitat: Resident but possibly some seasonal movement. Scattered shrubs, thickets, and patches of stunted trees in highland pastures, bushy ravines, and semiopen areas up to treeline; also borders of wet montane forest with bamboo. Found with some reg. in treeline shrubbery (3000m) near Hotel Los Frailes, Mérida (mid 1980s onward). Sight recs. at Pregonero, Táchira, 2350m, Jan 1995, and near Santo Domingo, Mérida, 2800m (Hilty); Parque Alberto Carnavalli, near Apartaderos, Mérida, 2650m, Jan 1990 (J. Pierson, D. Stejskal).

Range: 3100m (sight recs. 2350–3000m). N Táchira (sight), w Mérida (Páramo La Negra), and ne Mérida (numerous sightings). Colombia locally s in Andes to w Bolivia.
Note: Formerly placed in genus *Tyranniscus*.

Zimmerius

Sharp gilded edgings on all wing coverts (but no wing bars) and flight feathers; stubby bill; *narrow* cocked tail and horizontal posture; mainly eat berries; most spp. in highlands. As in some other genera of small flycatchers, ♂♂ have longer tail (ca. 10mm longer) than ♀♀. Formerly placed in *Tyranniscus*[757].

Golden-faced Tyrannulet PLATE 46
Zimmerius chrysops   Atrapamoscas Caridorado
Identification: 4.3″ (10.9cm). 10.5g. Eyes dark. Overall rather dull. Above plain olive, *sharp narrow yellow edgings on wing coverts and flight feathers (no bars); narrow frontlet, eyebrow, and usually also face and chin washed yellow* (not esp. conspic. except up close), throat yellowish white turning dull grayish white on lower underparts.
Sim. species: Confusion most likely with Venezuelan Tyrannulet which is larger and more distinctly marked (dark crown, no yellow on face); both only in mts. Also see White-fronted, Black-capped, and Tawny-rumped tyrannulets.
Voice: One of *the* characteristic sounds from canopy of mid.-el. highland forests; a querulous, inflected *hueer?*; also, esp. at dawn, a distinctive *teer-tif;* a plaintive *chu-de-de'e'e* and slow, drowsy *cheeee . . cheeee . . cheeee . . .* (4–5 notes) rather like that of Venezuelan Tyrannulet; in aerial chase (display?) a loud, rattling wing flutter.
Behavior: Perky and active as perches horizontally with tail slightly cocked. Flutters or hover-gleans to trunk and limb surfaces or to outer canopy foliage, esp. for mistletoe berries, occas. berries of other epiphytes. Single birds or prs. are encountered low to high and about as often alone as with mixed-spp. flocks. Usually fairly conspic., often perching atop outer canopy foliage. Dome-shaped nest with side entrance; tucked into hanging moss 8–12m up. In Colombia, breeding prolonged, at least Apr–Nov[260].
Status and habitat: Common resident in humid montane forest, forest borders, coffee plantations, and light second-growth woodland. Replaced at higher els. by next sp.

Range: 450–2400m (most numerous 500–1500m, occas. to near sea level). Sierra de Perijá, Zulia; w slope of Andes from Táchira n to w Trujillo (Escuque); e slope n to nw Barinas, Trujillo (Boconó), and se Lara at Anzoátegui and Terepaima (*chrysops*); mts. of ne Anzoátegui, Sucre (Paria Pen.), and n Monagas at Caripe (*cumanensis*). Colombia s in Andes to n Peru.

Venezuelan Tyrannulet PLATE 46
Zimmerius improbus   Atrapamoscas de Serranías
Identification: 5″ (12.7cm). 10.9g. Eyes dark. *Bold facial pattern and cocked tail.* Crown sooty brown (or dark gray—*petersi*) contrasting with olive back; *conspic. white spectacles and supraloral mark* start at nostrils; lores black, spot below eye whitish, *wing coverts and flight feathers crisply edged yellow (no wing bars)*, below whitish, chest and sides tinged gray, belly faintly yellowish.
Sim. species: Golden-faced Tyrannulet is uniform above (no contrasting dark crown) and has subdued facial pattern washed yellow (yellow not obvious at a distance). Both spp. share distinctive yellow wing edging. Also see White-fronted, Black-capped, and Tawny-rumped tyrannulets.
Voice: In Mérida 2–5 sad, halting, slightly descending whistles, each note fractionally lower than previous, *wheeeeaa, ... wheeeeaa, . . .* etc., notes often hurried at end. Or sing duet, 1 bird giving single *wheeeeeea* whistle, 2d answering with 3–4 *wheeeeeea* whistles. Also a buzzy *szzzzz.*
Behavior: Single birds or prs. are lively and active as forage alone or with mixed-spp. flocks. Often perch in open on outer edge of foliage in tree crowns, or stand on leaves, where typically show horizontal posture, cocked tail, and feet spread apart. Hover-glean and flutter in foliage for small berries, esp. mistletoe, and a few insects. Domed, ball-shaped nest with side entrance in clump of hanging moss; eye level to fairly high.
Status and habitat: Common resident in humid forest and wooded borders, lighter woodland, and clearings with scattered trees. In Andes found mainly above range of Golden-faced Tyrannulet. In n mts., where that sp. does not occur, found at lower els.

Range: 1800–3000m in Sierra de Perijá; 800–3000m in Andes; 400–2000m in Coastal Cordillera. Sierra de Perijá, Zulia, and s Táchira (*tamae*); w slope of Andes n to Mérida, e slope from Táchira to nw Barinas (*improbus*); Trujillo (subsp.?); s Lara e through mts. of Yaracuy and Carabobo to Distr. Federal and Miranda (*petersi*). N Colombia.

Note: Previously called Paltry Tyrannulet[403], a name now applied to birds in C Amer.

Slender-footed Tyrannulet   PLATE 46
Zimmerius gracilipes   Atrapamoscas Patifino
Identification: 4" (10.2cm). 7.5g. Eyes light gray. *Tail cocked.* Canopy of rain forest. Crown gray, upperparts dark olive, *wing coverts and flight feathers sharply edged yellow* (no bars), *short inconspic. whitish eyebrow;* loral area somewhat grayish, below dull grayish white, breast and sides with olive yellow tinge.
Sim. species: Easily confused. Look for rather indistinct facial pattern and sharply etched yellow wing edgings. Yellow-crowned Tyrannulet has grayish face and conspic. white wing bars; *Tolmomyias* flatbills are larger with wing bars and wide flat bills. Forest Elaenia, also larger, has spotted wing bars and longer tail not unusually cocked. White-lored Tyrannulet has more prom. white eyebrow and bold, white-spotted wing bars.
Voice: Day song a short, soft, querulous *chu, chu-chu'RE?*, rising sharply at end. Contact call a short, soft, rising *pureet*, rather melodious. Dawn song in Suriname a short, hard whistle, *tuu, de'de*, 1st note descending, last 2 higher, typically 2–4 in a ser. then a slight pause, repeated over and over.
Behavior: An inconspic. but lively little bird of rain forest canopy and crown of emergent trees. Occurs alone or in prs. and often with mixed-spp. flocks. Feeds mainly on mistletoe berries taken while perched or in short fluttery hovers; also hover-gleans and flits short distances to foliage for small insects in canopy. Rounded ball-shaped nest with side entrance; 2 dull white eggs spotted chestnut and lilac at larger end[37].
Status and habitat: Fairly common to common resident (easily overlooked) in humid terra firme and várzea forest, forest borders, and clearings with scattered trees. Lowlands and slopes of tepuis.

Range: To 2000m (mostly below 1000m). Throughout Amazonas; Bolívar from lower Río Caura, upper Río Paragua, and Cerro Roraima south (*gracilipes*); ne Bolívar from Sierra de Imataca s to Auyán-tepui, lower Río Paragua (La Paragua), and Sierra de Lema (*acer*). Se Colombia to n Bolivia, Amaz. Brazil, and the Guianas.
Note: Birds of higher els. in Guyana may be vocally distinct from those in lowlands (M. B. Robbins).

Ornithion

Small and short-tailed; bill long and heavy for size of bird; notable for prom. eyebrow and wing bars; forest canopy and edges; inconspic. except for song.

Brown-capped Tyrannulet   PLATE 46
Ornithion brunneicapillum   Atrapamoscas Gorro Pardo
Identification: 3.3" (8.4cm). 7.1g. Chunky and stubtailed. Bill *long and thick;* tail short. Crown brown contrasting with olive upperparts; *broad eyebrow from nostril narrows to point behind eye; wings unmarked brown* (no bars or edgings), tail brown, below bright yellow, chest and sides faintly washed olive.
Sim. species: An inconspic. but well-marked tyrannulet told by heavy bill, prom. eyebrow, unmarked wings, and stubby tail (25–29mm). More extensively yellow below than most other tyrannulets. See Sootyheaded (no bars) and Mouse-colored tyrannulets; also Southern Beardless-Tyrannulet.
Voice: Song in Barinas 4–6 downscale whistles, *PEE, pih-pey-peer-pear;* in n Aragua a melancholy *plee, te-de-du-dueet*, descending, then ascending at end.
Behavior: Inconspic. and easily overlooked. Hops and perch-gleans with active vireolike movements in outer twigs and foliage and at various hts., but usually fairly high in forest, lower along edges. Occas. inspects hanging dead leaves or hangs upside down, mostly for arthropod prey. Often with mixed-spp. flocks. Nests in Panama[790] and Ecuador (R. Ridgely) crude flat saucers of twigs, leaf petioles, and bark; 3.5–12m up on small fork.
Status and habitat: Resident. Uncommon and local (recs. spotty) but prob. often overlooked. Humid lowland and foothill forest, older second growth, light open woodland, and coffee plantations. Seen with some reg. on e slope of Andes near Barinitas; only w-slope rec. is I seen Jan 1983, Río Perdido, La Azulita (C. Parrish).

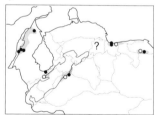

Range: To 1200m. Base of Sierra de Perijá, w Zulia, w slope of Andes in Mérida, e slope in nw Barinas; n cordilleras in Carabobo, Aragua (sightings, Ocumare de La Costa), and s Miranda on Cerro Negro (*dilutum*). Costa Rica to nw Ecuador.
Note: Considered distinct from Yellow-bellied Tyrannulet (*O. semiflavum*) of s Mexico to n Costa Rica[707].

White-lored Tyrannulet   PLATE 46
Ornithion inerme   Atrapamoscas de Cejas Blancas
Identification: 3.6" (9.1cm). 6.1g. Rather long, thick bill. *Prom. white eyebrows meet over top of bill, become very narrow over and behind eyes;* faint whitish eyering; crown grayish becoming olive on back; wings dusky with *2 bold white-dotted wing bars;* sides of head, throat, and chest dull gray, lower underparts pale yellow.
Sim. species: Usually found by voice. Once located, easily told by *spotted* wing bars and large eyebrow; tail

longer (1.3–1.5″, 32–39mm) than in previous sp. Cf. Slender-footed Tyrannulet and *Tolmomyias* flatbills.

Voice: Song a high, metallic, and ringing *sree-de-de-de*; when excited a faster, longer *swee'di-di-di-di-d'd'd'd 'd'ddd*, ending in metallic accelerating trill that attenuates somewhat. Song fairly loud, penetrating, and often persistently repeated.

Behavior: Occurs singly or in prs. Typically remains high in canopy where seldom detected except by persistent call, and even then can be difficult to locate and even harder to see well. Occas. found lower, rarely even down to eye level. Wanders alone or with mixed-spp. flocks. Forages actively, mostly by perch-gleaning, occas. flitting short distances in foliage for small arthropod prey.

Status and habitat: Fairly common resident (easily overlooked except for voice) in canopy of tall humid forest in lowlands and foothills; occas. lower along forest and streamside borders; gallery forest in s Gran Sabana.

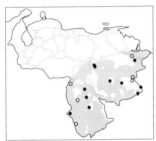

Range: To 950m (sight/tape to 1200m, Sierra de Lema). Throughout Amazonas; Bolívar from lower Río Caura and Sierra de Imataca southward. Se Colombia to n Bolivia, Amaz. Brazil, and the Guianas; se Brazil.

Southern Beardless-Tyrannulet   PLATE 46
Camptostoma obsoletum   Atrapamoscas Lampiño

Identification: 4″ (10.2cm). 7.3g. *Small and plain but with pert, animated behavior.* "Peaked" crest; short bill (base of lower mandible orangish pink); distinct "sleepy-eyed look" (small eyes) and *short* (ca. 1.5″, 38mm), *usually cocked tail.* Above dull gray brown to grayish olive brown, *crown browner;* short, vaguely indicated whitish eyebrow; narrow inconspic. whitish eyering; *2 dull white wing bars;* dingy white edgings on tertials; throat grayish turning to dull yellowish olive on chest; belly clear pale yellow.

Sim. species: As name implies, essentially "beardless," as are several other genera of small flycatchers, but this not a field mark. On this widespread bird look for contrasting darker crown, slight bushy crest, whitish wing bars, and cocked tail which help separate it from many other look-alikes. Other features incl. "small-eyed" look, shortish tail, horizontal posture, and vireo-like movements. Cf. Mouse-colored, Slender-billed, and Sooty-headed tyrannulets; also Pale-tipped Inezia and, in ne, see rare Urich's Tyrannulet.

Voice: Often hd. call a plaintive *peeeeee-tee*, much like 2-note calls of Pale-tipped Inezia and Mouse-colored Tyrannulet, but with 1st note long-dawn. Day song ca. 4–8 clear, melancholy whistles, falling in pitch, *pLEE, plee, plee, pee pe pe*, rather slow.

Behavior: Single birds or prs. forage mostly independently of mixed-spp. flocks by hopping and peering among partly open twigs or foliage from shrub to sub-canopy hts. Hop or occas. flit short distances and change perches freq. but overall seem a little sluggish, almost vireolike, as they mostly perch-glean or pluck insects and small invertebrate prey from adjacent substrates. Rarely sally to air and infreq. eat small berries. Readily mob and fuss when Ferruginous Pygmy-Owls vocalize. Nest a small globular ball with side entrance, located in a wide variety of cryptic locations, usually fairly high; 2 eggs white finely dotted cinnamon in wreath. Breeding Dec–Feb, Hato Masaguaral, Guárico[734].

Status and habitat: Common resident in a wide variety of habitats from dry scrubby vegetation to shrubbery along borders of humid and wet forest, also clearings and gardens. Everywhere assoc. with shrubby or edge vegetation.

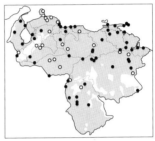

Range: To 1000m. Zulia, nw Táchira, and Lara (*pusillum*); Falcón, Yaracuy, and rest of Venez. n of Orinoco; Amazonas s to Río Ventuari, Bolívar, and Isla Patos (*venezuelae*); Amazonas s of Río Ventuari (*napaeum*). Sw Costa Rica to n Argentina and se Brazil.

Mouse-colored Tyrannulet   PLATE 46
Phaeomyias murina   Atrapamoscas Color Ratón

Identification: 5″ (12.7cm). 9.8g. Plain and nondescript with *flat-headed, long-tailed* appearance. Bill dusky, lower mandible pinkish at base. Above plain mouse brown, *long grayish white eyebrow from nostril to well behind eye; 2 broad dull buff wing bars;* strong buffy white tertial edgings; sides of head grayish tinged brown, throat grayish white turning to grayish olive on chest; lower underparts dull white, usually with faint yellow tinge.

Sim. species: Easily confused but distinctive once *shape*, plumage, and vocal characteristics are learned. Note *flat-headed* appearance, long tail (55–64mm) often held down, long dingy eyebrow, and buff (in Venez.) wing bars. Southern Beardless-Tyrannulet is smaller, perkier, has slight bushy crest, and usually holds tail cocked. Slender-billed Tyrannulet is also slightly crested, more "yellow-bellied," and has *short* (not long) eyebrow. Fuscous Flycatcher is larger, even longer tailed, has more conspic. wing bars, and *retiring* habits. Also cf. Pale-tipped Inezia and Pale-eyed Pygmy-Tyrant.

Voice: Prs. occas. give lively duets reminiscent of Yellow Tyrannulet (K. Zimmer); when foraging, a hard, nasal rattle, *td td'd'd'd'd'd*, and nasal *tee tep* often followed by rattle; either of these and other short notes *often answered immediately* by mate. Cf. *tee tep* call with very sim. call (listen carefully) of Pale-tipped Inezia which doubles or trebles 2d note. Dawn song a long, energetic, almost bubbly *tu-tu-tu-tu-tu . . tu-tu-Tu-Te-Teep!* . . ser., rambling on with no clear break for several min, gradually changes to more complex *tu-tu-tu-Te-Tee-Tr'trp!* (last part louder, roll at end), over and over.

Behavior: Despite burden of its name, a lively and engaging little bird. Single birds or prs. forage alone or occas. assoc. temporarily with mixed-spp. flocks. Prs. usually stay relatively close together when foraging, hopping actively or flitting short distances. Perch-glean tiny insects from foliage or sally short distances (0.1–0.5m) and hover-glean from foliage, or snap insects, without hovering, from a leaf; also occas. take berries. Often forage in legume (Leguminosae) trees. Small feather-lined grass nest; to 6m up in tree fork[253]; 2 pale cream or white eggs[379]; breeds May–Oct, n Colombia[260].

Status and habitat: Common and widespread resident in arid scrub, borders of dry and moist woodland, waste areas, gardens, and semiopen areas with shrubs and woodland. Fond of *Acacia* and other scrubby, partly open trees. Uncommon and local in humid areas.

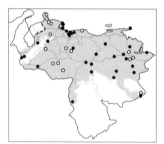

Range: To 1900m n of Orinoco; to 950m s of Orinoco. Throughout except s Amazonas (*incompta*). W Panama s to nw Argentina, Paraguay, and s Brazil; sw Ecuador and nw Peru. Trinidad.

Tyrannulus

Shares yellow crown patch with larger *Myiopagis* elaenias; also resembles *Zimmerius* tyrannulets but bill and tail shorter than members of either genus; widespread, not inside forest. Tail of ♂ longer than that of ♀.

Yellow-crowned Tyrannulet   PLATE 46
Tyrannulus elatus   Atrapamoscas Copete Amarillo
Identification: 4.2″ (10.7cm). 7.5g. Small and plump; *very short bill; rounded head*. Above olive brown; crown brown; large but usually concealed golden yellow crown patch (both sexes) is occas. flared in dramatic manner; short, indistinct whitish eyebrow; wings and short tail dusky, *2 conspic. white wing bars* and broad white tertial edgings; *throat, chest, and sides of face light gray*, breast washed olive, lower underparts pale yellow. In fresh plumage tail narrowly pale-tipped.

Sim. species: *Hd. far more than seen* (learn voice). Best marks are distinct grayish face, stubby bill, and bold

wing bars. Looks like miniature Forest Elaenia but plumper, rounder headed, and much shorter billed. When diagnostic crown patch is concealed (it usually is) may look much like Southern Beardless-Tyrannulet or Sooty-headed (no wing bars) or White-fronted tyrannulets. Also cf. *Zimmerius* tyrannulets, all with crisp yellow edgings but no bars.

Voice: Commonest advertising call a brief little "wolf whistle," *wee, wheer* or *pree teer*, 1st note rising, 2d falling; persistently given at intervals, even in heat of day. A Spanish name, *de día*, is derived from call[403].

Behavior: Often hd. although inconspic. and sometimes hard to see. Sits alone, sometimes very quietly for long periods, mostly in tops of small trees in gardens and clearings, or in top of emergent trees in rain forest canopy. Flits short distances upward to hover-glean, sometimes hovers for several sec, to obtain a variety of small berries, also tiny insects. Not with mixed-spp. flocks, and unlike *Zimmerius* and *Phyllomyias* does not carry short tail cocked. Nest in Panama a shallow cup of fine material 8–10m up (E. Eisenmann; R. Ridgely); 2 eggs, cream color; breeds at least Mar–Aug, n Colombia[260].

Status and habitat: Common resident (need to know call) in light woodland, forest borders, shrubby clearings, and gardens. Often in small trees (e.g., citrus) around human dwellings. Also crown of canopy and emergent trees in tall humid terra firme and várzea forest.

Range: To 1200m. Maracaibo Basin, Zulia, and adj. nw Táchira, w Mérida, and w Trujillo, e base of Andes in Táchira, Apure, and Barinas n to Santa Bárbara; mts. of Sucre (*panamensis*); e Monagas (sight/tape, 1994—P. Boesman) and Delta Amacuro; generally s of Orinoco in Amazonas and Bolívar (*elatus*). Costa Rica to w Ecuador; n Colombia and e of Andes to n Bolivia, Amaz. Brazil, and the Guianas.
Note: Neither subsp. recognized by some[467].

Myiopagis

Recall *Elaenia* but smaller, usually darker capped, and in general a less well-defined group; crown patch white or yellow and normally concealed (unlike *Elaenia*); tail long for size of bird; mostly forest or woodland dwellers; generally inconspic.

Gray Elaenia   PLATE 45
Myiopagis caniceps   Bobito Gris
Identification: 5″ (12.7cm). 10.3g. Little or no crest. Bill rather heavy and thick for genus. *Sexes differ.* ♂: above *all gray* with small concealed *white* crown

patch; *wings black, 2 bold white wing bars*, inner flight feathers narrowly and tertials broadly edged white, *below pale gray turning white on belly.* ♀: rather different; *crown gray concealing bright yellow crown patch*, otherwise *bright olive above; wings black with 2 yellowish wing bars*; inner remiges narrowly edged and tertials broadly edged pale yellow, throat gray, chest yellowish olive, belly yellow.

Sim. species: Mostly gray ♂ looks like a becard, esp. Cinereous Becard, but is smaller and more slender. ♀ much like Forest and Yellow-crowned elaenias but with cleaner, crisper pattern, blacker wings, and no streaking below (streaking characteristic of Forest Elaenia). Note habitat differences (Yellow-crowned Elaenia occurs low inside swamp forest). Also cf. Slender-footed Tyrannulet and *Tolmomyias* flatbills, none of which have such contrasting black wings.

Voice: Song a high, fast, penetrating ser. of whistled notes, *e-e-p-p-p-pepepepe. . . . pepepepupupupu* (ca. 40 notes in 3 sec), slightly descending; when excited a snappy *ee-ee-ee-pit-chew, pit-chew, pee-chew* (K. Zimmer recordings).

Behavior: Single birds or prs. behave like other *Myiopagis*. Perch rather erect, sometimes with tail slightly cocked, and glean or occas. hover-glean in high outer canopy foliage. Most often seen with canopy mixed-spp. flocks.

Status and habitat: There are only a small no. of recs., but surely overlooked (need to know voice). Treetops in humid terra firme and várzea forest in lowlands. Apparently resident; rec. in most months in n Amazonas, but austral migrants may augment resident breeding pop.

Range: To 1200m n of Orinoco; to 300m s of Orinoco. Sierra de Perijá (Río Negro), Zulia (where prob. a migrant); Amazonas s to Yavita-Pimichín (prob. throughout); Bolívar from lower Río Caura to upper Río Paragua (*cinerea*). E Panama to w Ecuador; e of Andes to nw Argentina and se Brazil; sw Guyana; French Guyana (absent from much of the Guianas and e Brazil).
Note: Prob. does not belong with *Myiopagis*.

Forest Elaenia   PLATE 45
Myiopagis gaimardii   Bobito de Selva
Identification: 5″ (12.7cm). 12.2g. Rather "flat headed" with longish tail. Eyes dark; bill relatively narrow, *pinkish at base of lower mandible; little or no crest.* Crown brown (darker than back) with *weakly indicated whitish eyebrow*; concealed white to yellowish white coronal patch, rest of upperparts dull brownish olive, wings dusky with *2 spotted yellowish wing bars*; flight feathers and tertials edged yellow, *sides of head gray-*

ish (somewhat grizzled), throat grayish white, breast yellowish with *suggestion of olive streaking*, belly pale yellow.

Sim. species: Often confused. Learn its voice. Greenish Elaenia lacks wing bars, Yellow-crowned Elaenia is unstreaked below and has *very different voice*; all *Tolmomyias* have wider, flatter bills; also cf. Mouse-colored and Slender-footed tyrannulets and Southern Beardless-Tyrannulet.

Voice: Advertising call, one of *the* common vocalizations in many lowland forests of Venez., is a short *pill' drEET!*, 2d part slightly buzzy and rising, typically given at long intervals. When disturbed *pa-Beér!* and 1–4 soft, reedy *tweeer* notes. Infreq. hd. dawn song a short, complex ser. of notes.

Behavior: An inconspic. little bird found alone or in prs. in forest mid. story or higher. Sits moderately upright, sometimes with tail slightly cocked. Often not very active, changing perches infreq. by flitting short distances. Forages by perch-gleaning or sallying short distances and hover-gleaning from foliage for small arthropods and berries. Follows mixed-spp. flocks or is independent of them about equally. Cup nest 3–5m up (prob. usually higher); like that of Yellow-bellied Elaenia but unlined; 2 eggs, pale cream marked deep red-brown and lavender at larger end[175].

Status and habitat: Common resident (need to known voice) in moist and humid lowland forest and tall second-growth woodland, along forest borders, and high around treefalls. Despite name, territories almost always incl. a treefall or bit of edge habitat.

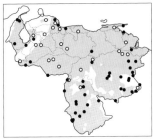

Range: To 1500m (most recs. below 1000m). Throughout (except arid zones) n of Orinoco (*bogotensis*); generally in Amazonas, Bolívar, and Delta Amacuro (*guianensis*). C Panama to n Bolivia, Amaz. Brazil, and the Guianas. Trinidad.

Yellow-crowned Elaenia   PLATE 48
Myiopagis flavivertex   Bobito Corona Amarilla
Identification: 5″ (12.7cm). 12g. Eyes dark; bill narrow, pinkish at base of lower mandible; little or no crest. Much like Forest Elaenia, incl. wing bars, but largely concealed *crown patch bright yellow* (not white), upperparts darker, *throat and chest darker more grayish olive* (not grayish white), and *breast with no hint of blurry streaking*; sides of head brownish olive (not gray).

Sim. species: See Greenish Elaenia (no wing bars), ♀ Gray Elaenia, and *Tolmomyias* flatbills, all with different proportions and behavior. Also cf. Saffron-crested Tyrant-Manakin which lacks wing bars and is not in swampy forest.

Voice: Call, often only at long intervals, an abrupt, explosive *WEECHECHe'e'e*, loud for such a small bird but trailing off quickly into short rattle.

Behavior: Occurs alone or in scattered prs. in lower story of swampy forest where sits rather upright and immobile, occas. sallying short distances to foliage. Usually not with mixed-spp. flocks.

Status and habitat: Uncommon and local (easily overlooked) except for infreq. call in shady várzea and swamp forest in sandy soil areas of Amazonas; common in e Monagas and Delta Amacuro in várzea and swamp forest on richer alluvial soils.

Range: To 200m. Nw and c Amazonas from Platanillal (sight/tape) and Caño Capuana s to Río Casiquiare; ne Monagas (sight, Caño Colorado[58]) s through Delta Amacuro. Very locally in e Ecuador, n Peru, and extreme w Brazil; the Guianas and the Amazon drainage from its mouth to Rio Juruá, Brazil.

Greenish Elaenia   PLATE 45
Myiopagis viridicata   Bobito Verdoso
Identification: 5.2″ (13.2cm). 12.8g. Or (*zuliae*) 5.8″ (14.7cm). Eyes dark; base of lower mandible pinkish. Above olive, crown tinged gray, *narrow and faintly indicated eyestripe* and concealed yellow crown patch; wing coverts narrowly edged yellowish (*no obvious wing bars*), flight feathers and tertials edged yellowish, throat grayish, chest yellow flammulated with gray (looks vaguely mottled or streaked), lower breast and belly clear pale yellow.

Sim. species: Looks a lot like Forest Elaenia but shows no wing bars (Forest always with wing bars), has yellow (not white) crown patch, and face cleaner (lacks slightly "grizzled" gray of Forest). Cf. *Tolmomyias* flatbills, all of which have broader bills and more prom. edgings on wing coverts and flight feathers. Also cf. Northern Scrub-Flycatcher.

Voice: Commonest call a harsh, buzzy *jeeeet!* (almost 2-parted); or *squeewzit* and shorter *skzeet* (K. Zimmer). In Costa Rica, dawn song *peer-ee, peer-pee, peer-peer-pee*, persistently repeated[633].

Behavior: Usually found singly, sometimes accompanying small mixed-spp. flocks in lower or mid. levels of shady open woodland where perch-gleans from foliage and twigs or visits fruiting trees and shrubs. Sits rather erect but otherwise inconspic. and undistinguished. Small, loosely woven cup nest ca. 6m up in fork; 2 eggs whitish, blotched and marked lilac and brown, most heavily at larger end[562].

Status and habitat: Prob. resident, but pops. from C Amer. and s S Amer. are migratory, and these also may

occur in Venez. Uncommon (easily overlooked) in light woodland, gallery forest, and clearings with scattered trees, esp. in dry viny areas. Common in n Sierra de Perijá with large no. of specimens taken Jul–early Aug (a few in early Mar).

Range: To 1000m n of Orinoco; to 300m s of Orinoco. Sierra de Perijá, Zulia (*zuliae*); w base of Andes in Táchira at Seboruco (*accola*), e base from Táchira, Barinas, Portuguesa, and e Lara to Anzoátegui, and in n cordilleras from Carabobo to Sucre; n Amazonas (s to San Fernando de Atabapo and Las Carmelitas); nw Bolívar from Caicara, Ciudad Bolívar, and El Callao s to Río Paragua (*restricta*); Delta Amacuro[343]. Mexico to n Argentina and se Brazil.

Note: Possibly more than 1 sp. involved.

Elaenia

To most observers, the various spp. of *Elaenia* are Tweedledum and Tweedledee, notable for being notoriously difficult to separate in field, esp. if not vocalizing; most are slightly to prom. crested but small headed with small roundish bills; whitish wing bars (2 or 3); yellowish or whitish bellies; often whitish patch in crown; tail longish, square; typical of shrubby or semiopen areas. In hand note virtual lack of rictal bristles. Present taxonomy follows Lanyon[321].

Great Elaenia   PLATE 45
Elaenia dayi   Bobito Gigante
Identification: 8″ (20.3cm). Tepuis. *Large*; *notably long tail*; *uniformly dark above*. Head roundish (usually little or no crest; occas. slight bushy crest); bill small, base of mandible flesh. Upperparts incl. tail dark smoky brown (no concealed white in crown); dark color of crown extends to below eyes; prom. but *narrow broken whitish eyering*; 2 dull dirty whitish wing bars; tertials narrowly edged white, underparts grayish olive, throat paler, lower breast and belly vaguely tinged yellow.

Sim. species: Recalls Black-billed Thrush, but note small bill, wing bars, trimmer and more upright posture, and tendency of all elaenias to look small headed. Also see resident race of Swainson's Flycatcher which has very dark head and tail contrasting with paler back (elaenia much more uniform), a longer, heavier bill, and more uniform light gray throat and chest (note that resident race of Swainson's Flycatcher does not have strongly contrasting yellow belly, hence looks more like elaenia).

Voice: Call an odd, rather loud, somewhat variable *SQUEE'ch'ch'ch-cheet-cheet*, 1st note high, mid. part

rattling; sometimes call is abbreviated (D. Ascanio recording).
Behavior: Single birds or prs. perch in mid. or upper parts of small trees, at times in open, at other times mostly out of view inside shrubbery. Browse in foliage and eat fruit. Usually not with mixed-spp. flocks.
Status and habitat: Resident. On Gran Sabana found in shrubs, small trees, and patches of stunted savanna woodland. At higher els. in humid forest and forest borders; mossy *Bonnetia* forest on Cerro Chimantá. Fairly numerous at higher els. with many specimens from 2000m and higher on Cerros Huachamacari, Roraima, and Cuquenán. At lower end of range (e.g., on Gran Sabana) rare and difficult to find. Most numerous in rainy season at els. above ca. 2000m on Cerro Roraima (D. Ascanio).

Range: ENDEMIC. 300–2600m (most recs. above 1800m). Amazonas on Cerros Parú, Huachamacari, Marahuaca, and Duida; Bolívar on Meseta de Jaua (*tyleri*); Bolívar on Auyán-tepui above 1850m (*auyantepui*); cerros of Gran Sabana incl. vicinity of Sierra de Lema (sightings), and Cerros Ptari, Chimantá, Cuquenán, and Roraima (*dayi*). Prob. Guyana.

Yellow-bellied Elaenia
PLATE 45

Elaenia flavogaster Bobito Copetón Vientre Amarillo
Identification: 6.5″ (16.5cm). 24g. Small headed; *prom. upstanding crest usually bushy and parted in middle to reveal white crown patch.* Olive brown above; inconspic. whitish eyering; *2 prom. white wing bars* and edgings; pale gray throat clouded grayish olive on chest and sides; lower underparts pale yellow (faint in some individuals). Some examples from Delta Amacuro are browner above, grayer below, only faintly yellow on belly.
Sim. species: *Commonest and most familiar elaenia in Venez.,* but despite its name not especially "yellow bellied." Best told by prom. "divided" crest which almost always shows white. Learn voice and distinctive profile. See Lesser, Small-billed, and Plain-crested elaenias.
Voice: Often hd. call a wheezy, asthmatic *breeeeer.* Prs. often sing simultaneously (duet?), 1 a hoarse, buzzy *brueezz* over and over, then 2d *bree bee-bee* or sim. repeatedly, the effect of both together that of a confused, poorly choreographed performance. Dawn song a leisurely and buzzy *spud-deeer, spud-deeer-dzz, spud-deeer, . . .* over and over[633].
Behavior: Lively, garrulous, and easily aroused to a state of confused noisy excitement. Browses in shrubbery for berries and insects, hover-gleans for berries,

and occas. sallies short distances for flying insects. Occurs singly, in prs., or sometimes several together at fruiting shrubs and usually perched at least partly in open. Nest a feather-lined grass cup adorned with bark and lichens; 2 eggs, pale salmon with reddish brown spots around larger end[633]; May–Sep nests, ne Colombia[63]; building, 22 Mar, ne Bolívar.
Status and habitat: Common resident in dry to humid semiopen areas; shrubs, thickets, woodland borders, parks, gardens, sometimes numerous even in towns, but often scarce or absent in seemingly suitable areas in forested zones.

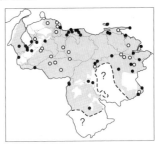

Range: To 1750m. Throughout incl. Islas Margarita and Patos (*flavogaster*); no recs. s of Cerro Duida in s Amazonas. S Mexico to n Argentina (absent from much of w and c Amazonia) and se Brazil; the Guianas; Trinidad and Tobago.
Note: Large Elaenia (*E. spectabilis*), an austral migrant (breeds from n Argentina and e Bolivia across s Brazil) to most of Amazonia, prob. occurs seasonally in s Amazonas. Recalls Yellow-bellied Elaenia but larger (7″, 18cm), crest smaller, less bifurcated (smaller, rounder head), little or no white showing in crown, and usually with *3 distinct whitish wing bars.* Shrubby areas.

Lesser Elaenia
PLATE 48

Elaenia chiriquensis Bobito Copetón Moño Blanco
Identification: 5.5″ (14cm). 13g. Dull, confusing, and almost devoid of good field marks. *Rather prom. crest* (often held flat so rearcrown looks somewhat "squared off"); *small semiconcealed white patch in crown usually visible, at least from back of head.* Above grayish brown with narrow whitish eyering (not prom.); 2 whitish wing bars; flight feathers and tertials edged dull white; below pale dingy gray on throat and chest, lower underparts white tinged yellow.
Sim. species: Plain with "faded or worn" appearance. Best told by elimination of other sim. spp., *and by voice,* rather than specific characters. Cf. larger Yellow-bellied Elaenia which has more prom. bifurcated crest; Plain-crested with small rear-projecting crest and no white in crown; Small-billed with rounded head and white eyering; also Mountain Elaenia and, in tepuis, Sierran Elaenia.
Voice: Commonest call (nw Bolívar) a clear, whistled *weEEa* (K. Zimmer recording); sim. in Amazonas and Aragua; other calls, all softer and more plaintive (less hoarse) than Yellow-bellied Elaenia's, incl. a short, slightly buzzy *beer'ta,* 1st note descending; a *chí-bur* or *jwebü,* a longer *freeeee* (much like Yellow-bellied Elaenia), and softer *weeb* or *beezb*[545].

Behavior: Rather like Yellow-bellied Elaenia but not as noisy or conspic. Prs. sit fairly erect when calling, more horizontal when foraging by perch-gleaning in foliage. Usually seen at about eye level or somewhat higher and tend to remain partially out of sight in foliage. In Costa Rica, small feather-lined cup ca. 1–4m up in bush or tree; 2 eggs (rarely 1), dull white with spots of brown in a wreath at larger end; ♀ may sing while incubating[633].

Status and habitat: Uncommon and local resident in lowlands and foothills; in a few areas fairly common (e.g., near Pto. Ayacucho). Open to semiopen areas, incl. overgrown pastures, cultivated land with bushy fence rows, and open or waste areas with scattered trees. Pops. from C Amer. and s South Amer. are migratory, and both may occur in Venez. Seasonal movements and/or changes in nos. poorly known.

Range: To 3000m n of Orinoco (most recs. below 1900m); to 2200m s of Orinoco. Throughout in open areas s to s Amazonas and Bolívar (*albivertex*) but few recs. in llanos. Costa Rica to n Argentina and s Brazil.
Note 1: Caribbean Elaenia (*E. martinica*) breeds on many small isls. in Caribbean incl. Neatherlands Antilles off coast of Venez. Could occur on mainland Venez. or offshore isls. Much like Lesser Elaenia but crest larger, white crown patch larger.
Note 2: White-crested Elaenia (*E. albiceps*), breeding in Andes from s Colombia to Tierra del Fuego, occurs widely across Amazonia as a migrant and prob. occurs in s Amazonas. Much like Small-billed Elaenia but almost always shows much white in small crest; less obvious eyering; throat and breast pale gray tinged olive on sides; belly whitish.

Sierran Elaenia   PLATE 45
Elaenia pallatangae   Bobito de los Tepuis
Identification: 5.8″ (14.7cm). 17g. *Tepuis.* Slightly crested; *semiconcealed white crown patch usually visible.* Above dark olive brown, narrow yellowish white eyering; wings dusky with *2 whitish bars*; inner flight feathers edged yellowish; tertials broadly edged white, below yellowish heavily washed olive on throat, chest, and sides; *center of breast and belly clear yellow.*
Sim. species: Only elaenia in wet forest borders of tepui highlands. Darker and more yellowish than allies. Cf. Yellow-bellied, Lesser, and Plain-crested, all of which are paler and occur in brushy or semiopen areas.
Voice: Call a simple *pfeEEu* most resembling that of Mountain Elaenia.

Behavior: Rather like others of genus. Often with mixed-spp. flocks where it takes small berries (esp. melastomes) and perch-gleans in foliage from eye level to tops of moderate-sized trees. Cup nest 1m up in fork in bush, Peru[725].
Status and habitat: Fairly common resident in humid and wet forest borders, esp. in areas of stunted or scrubby forest around edges of rocky openings, and borders of melastome-dominated regrowth. Foothills and slopes of tepuis.

Range: 950–2400m. Sierra de la Neblina (*davidwillardi*); cerros of rest of Amazonas and Bolívar incl. Sierra de Lema (*olivina*). Andes of c Colombia s to Bolivia; Guyana.

Small-billed Elaenia   PLATE 45
Elaenia parvirostris   Bobito Copetón Pico Corto
Identification: 5.8″ (14.7cm). 15.5g. *Rounded head* (no crest), *prom. whitish eyering.* Grayer and with more "clean-cut" appearance than other elaenias in Venez. Bill roundish, slightly pinkish tinged, not obviously shorter or smaller than those of others of genus. Above olivaceous with concealed white crown patch; *2 dull white wing bars* and hint of a 3d; flight feathers and tertials edged yellowish green; sides of head, throat, and breast light gray, chest tinged brownish olive, *lower underparts white*, sometimes with vague yellow tinge.
Sim. species: Note *seasonal presence* in Venez. Overall is nearest Mountain Elaenia which more or less lacks eyering, is generally more olive, has strong yellow-olive tinge to underparts, and is strictly confined to mts. Plain-crested, Yellow-bellied, and Lesser elaenias all look obviously crested.
Voice: Rather quiet in Venez. Commonest calls in Brazil a mellow *pew*, sometimes lengthened to *peewhew*; a hard *kup*; and when excited, more complex, burry calls (K. Zimmer).
Behavior: Scattered single birds or small, loosely assoc. groups occur in low shrubbery where they perch-glean from foliage and eat small berries. Relatively quiet and inconspic. in Venez. Often somewhat nervous acting and skittish in Venez.
Status and habitat: Uncommon to locally fairly common austral migrant, early Apr–late Sep, to savanna with scattered bushes and trees, gallery forest borders, shrubby clearings, and gardens. Specimen recs. 3 Apr–29 Sep; sight recs. 2 Mar 2000, Maracay (Hilty) and 20 Mar 1979, San José de Los Altos, Miranda (C. Parrish); May–Sep, Hato Masaguaral, Guárico[734]. There are more recs. from llanos, esp. Guárico and w Amazonas, than elsewhere.

Range: To 1250m. Open areas throughout incl. Isla Margarita; no recs. w of Andes. Breeds from e Bolivia, Paraguay, s Brazil, and n Argentina southward; winters (austral winter) e of Andes n to n S Amer. Trinidad; rarely Netherlands Antilles.

Plain-crested Elaenia   PLATE 48
Elaenia cristata   Bobito Crestiapagado
Identification: 5.7" (14.5cm). 18g. *Head somewhat crested*; crest tends to project rearward but is often partly raised; *no white crown patch*. Most of lower mandible pinkish, tip grayish horn. Above dull brown with slight olive tinge; 2 whitish wing bars; narrow whitish wing edgings; throat and chest grayish white tinged olive (esp. on chest which may occas. show hint of smudgy streaking), lower underparts white *tinged yellowish*.
Sim. species: A *dull* and undistinguished elaenia. *Note habitat and crest shape. Study all birds carefully to verify absence of white in crown.* Lesser Elaenia is sim. but has white (mostly concealed) in crown; Small-billed Elaenia has prom. white eyering, narrow streak of concealed white in crown (white rarely visible in field), and no crest. Also Cf. Yellow-bellied and Rufous-crowned elaenias.
Voice: Whistled dawn song over and over a short, rapid roll, *cheV'a'rear*, last part buzzy (or *CHEE'beer-ip*, the *beer* note descending and buzzy); call a soft, melodious *wee*. Day song a low, gravelly, but snappy *peeu*, *peeu, p'pr'pr're'bit, pi'pi'pi* (3-parted). Easily overlooked calls incl. a short, squeezed *wee-he-he-he-e* (rattle quality); occas. a low *wheesp* or *wheeb*; also *dsooty-EEo*, rising then falling.
Behavior: Most often seen alone or in scattered prs. in or near tops of shrubs or in small scrubby trees. Generally fairly conspic. and easy to see, but like many elaenias can be wary. Forages mostly by perch-gleaning or fluttery hovers to foliage for berries and a few insects.
Status and habitat: Resident. Uncommon to fairly common locally in parklike savannas dotted with scattered

bushes and small trees (esp. *Curatella* and *Brysonima*) and in dry brushy and scrubby areas in lowlands and foothills.
Range: To ca. 400m n of Orinoco; to 1350m s of Orinoco. Nw Lara (Cerro El Cerrón) and generally e of Andes from s Apure (Cararabo), w Barinas, and n Aragua to Monagas and Delta Amacuro; s of Orinoco in Amazonas; throughout Bolívar except range of next subsp. (*cristata*); Kabanayén near Ptari-tepui at 1200m (*alticola*). The Guianas and e Brazil; e Colombia (no recs.?).

Mountain Elaenia   PLATE 48
Elaenia frantzii   Bobito Copetón Montañero
Identification: 5.5" (14cm). 17g. *Head rounded (no crest); no white in crown*; bill short; weakly indicated *narrow eyering yellowish*. Above uniform olive brown, wings dusky with 2 dirty whitish bars; flight feathers narrowly edged yellowish, tertials broadly edged white, throat, chest, and sides grayish olive, belly yellowish white.
Sim. species: Dingy and undistinguished. Overall looks dull *yellowish olive* (less brown than allies). Note round uncrested head, wing bars, weak eyering, and Andean habitat. Cf. Small-billed Elaenia which occurs mostly in lowlands. Lesser and Yellow-bellied elaenias have white in crown; Plain-crested has obvious flat crest.
Voice: Dawn song a breezy *WEeu-tic* over and over. Other vocalizations, both at dawn and during day, incl. a clear *peeeer* and *pfeeit! ch'weer* notes as well as a relatively short, buzzy *freeeer*.
Behavior: Rather like Yellow-bellied Elaenia but not as noisy and animated. Single birds or prs. perch-glean in foliage and occas. sally to air but depend heavily on small berries and fruits and sometimes gather in nos. at favorable trees or shrubs. Marked local and seasonal pop. shifts are prob. in response to changes in fruit abundance. Occas. with mixed-spp. flocks at forest borders. Small, firm, moss-covered cup nest usually lined with feathers; 2–17m up in a variety of tree locations; 2 dull white or pale buff eggs with brown spots forming wreath at larger end[644]; Feb nest, PN Guaramacal, Trujillo.
Status and habitat: Common in highland pastures with scattered trees, shrubby areas, lighter woodland, and forest borders. Local or seasonal movements need documentation.

Range: 1700–2250m in Sierra de Perijá, Zulia (*browni*); 1200–2900m in Andes from Táchira n to cerros of nw Lara; n Falcón (Sierra de San Luis); mts. of Yaracuy, and Coastal Cordillera from Carabobo to

Distr. Federal; Miranda (?); Interior Cordillera on Cara-bobo/Guárico border at Cerro Platillón; mts. of w Sucre, and n Monagas on Cerro Negro (*pudica*). Guatemala to Colombia.

Rufous-crowned Elaenia
PLATE 45

Elaenia ruficeps   Bobito Copetón Moño Rojo

Identification: 5.7" (14.5cm). 19g. Short rearward projecting crest with *usually visible rufous patch on rear-crown* (less prom. in ♀) forms *distinct peak* or "bump" toward back of head. *Upperparts dark olive brown*, wings dusky; 2 dirty white wing bars; flight feathers edged yellow olive, tertials edged whitish, below *dull pale yellow with indistinct blurry streaking from throat to lower breast*; tail shorter than in others of genus.

Sim. species: Only elaenia with rufous crown patch (look carefully). Note "bump" toward rear of head (even if crest laid flat), strong hint of streaking below, overall darker plumage than other elaenias. Occurs in same habitat as Plain-crested Elaenia.

Voice: Song at San Carlos de Río Negro a loose, mushy rattle, squeezed out, *chu'd'd'd'u!* (or *rr-rr'rd'd'dt*), low pitched and ending abruptly; song is odd, mechanical-sounding, and often given only at intervals of several min. (C. Parrish recording).

Behavior: Single birds or prs. perch at edges or on top of shrubs and small trees to sing. Perch-glean in foliage and generally less conspic. than most elaenias.

Status and habitat: Uncommon resident in open or semiopen areas with scattered bushes, stunted trees, edges of forest isls., and scrubby forest in savanna regions. *Mainly* sandy soil and white sand regions.

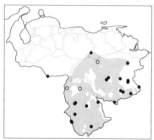

Range: To 1400m. S Meta along Río Meta; sw Anzoátegui (Barrancas); throughout Amazonas and Bolívar. Distrib. spotty. E Colombia; the Guianas; locally in n and c Brazil.

Slaty Elaenia
PLATE 45

Elaenia strepera   Bobito Escandaloso

Identification: 6" (15cm). 19g. *Mainly dark gray with white belly*. Bill flatter and wider than in others of genus; no crest; white crown patch usually concealed. ♂: above *uniform dark gray*, wings and tail brownish, 2 dull white wing bars and poorly indicated whitish edgings on remiges; below paler gray than above; *center of belly and crissum white*. ♀: sim. but tinged olive above; wing bars and edgings more evident; underparts paler olive gray, belly tinged yellow. Imm: buff to whitish wing bars and edgings; whitish on throat; breast vaguely streaked dusky and dirty white. Wings long for genus.

Sim. species: Recalls Smoke-colored Pewee or Olive-sided Flycatcher more than an elaenia. Told from these, or any elaenia, by overall uniform dark plumage and white belly.

Voice: Quiet on wintering gds. Song when breeding (prob. rarely if ever hd. in Venez.) a short, rough, accelerating *uh, uh-u'h'hhh?* with dry reedy quality like a locust.

Behavior: Rather inconspic., usually found alone and independent of mixed-spp. flocks. Sits erect and quiet for periods of time on fairly open twigs at mid. hts. along forest borders, then may fly off some distance. Perch-gleans or hover-gleans berries and insects.

Status and habitat: Austral migrant. Only a few Venez. recs.; apparently rare and local. Specimens taken 4 Aug–5 Sep. Sightings of single birds on 11 Sep 1985, PN Guatopo, Miranda (C. Parrish); 4 Mar 1998 near Las Claritas, e Bolívar (M. Fritz and Hilty); and 8 Mar 1998, Río Grande, ne Bolívar (M. Fritz, S. Rose, D. Rose, Hilty).

Range: To 900m. Rec. in Carabobo (Sierra de Cara-bobo), Guárico (Altagracia de Orituco), Sucre (Cristobal Colon), Monagas (Caripe), nw Bolívar (Pijiguaos), and ne Bolívar (Upata; El Callao); sight recs. in Miranda and ne Bolívar. Breeds on e slope of Andes in s Bolivia and nw Argentina; migrates/winters across w Amazonia n to e Colombia and Venez.[377].

Sublegatus

Small genus; spp. limits controversial; *very short*, all-dark bill wider than in *Myiopagis*; no white crown patch.

Northern Scrub-Flycatcher
PLATE 45

Sublegatus arenarum   Atrapamoscas de Arbustales

Identification: 5.7" (14.5cm). 13g. Trim and dapper and looks like a small *Myiarchus*. *Stubby black bill*; slight crest. Upperparts grayish brown, short indistinct eyeline whitish, *2 dull whitish wing bars*; tertials broadly edged dull brownish white to buff; *contrasting dusky tail* (broader near tip); throat and chest pale gray, *sharply "divided"* from clear yellow lower underparts.

Sim. species: Cf. carefully with next sp.; they were formerly considered same sp. Also, several elaenias, e.g., Yellow-bellied, Lesser, and Small-billed, are superficially sim. but lack eyebrow, contrasting dark tail, and "divided" look to underparts; up close most elaenia have pink at base of mandible. *Myiarchus* flycatchers are larger with longer, heavier bills. Also cf. Southern Beardless-Tyrannulet, Mouse-colored Tyrannulet, and Fuscous Flycatcher.

Voice: Generally rather quiet. Calls incl. an abrupt *pweEEe!* and *peEEap!* given singly or doubled; occas. a 4-noted call (e Falcón); on Islas Los Roques only single-note calls have been hd. (D. Ascanio). Birds in sw Portuguesa (this sp. or *orinocensis* subsp. of Amazonian Scrub-Flycatcher) give a brisk, whistled *phew!-dit* at 10- to 20-sec intervals shortly after dawn; in w Apure a single *pfweE* or *weEEe* at well-spaced intervals during midday.

Behavior: A rather quiet and inconspic. bird that sits alone, alert and fairly upright in thickets, in shade of a small tree, or sometimes in open along fences, etc. Typically perches quite low, holds tail down, and sallies short distances to air or to foliage, or occas. perchgleans on foliage and twigs. Also eats small berries from shrubs or cactus by hover-gleaning for them. Cup nest 2–6m up; 2 creamy white eggs with wreath of dark brown at larger end[175].

Status and habitat: Fairly common resident in dry to arid regions of Carib. lowlands. Desert scrub, dry brush along washes, deciduous thorn woodland, and mangroves. Easily found around Coro, Falcón.

Range: To 600m. Zulia, Falcón, and n Lara e to Sucre; e of Andes rec. from Portuguesa e to Monagas; n Bolívar in lower Río Caura (but see Note below); Islas Margarita and Patos (*glaber*); Islas Los Roques (*pallens*); La Tortuga (*tortugensis*). Costa Rica to n Colombia and n Guianas; Trinidad; Netherlands Antilles.

Note 1: Formerly incl. next sp., the entire complex called Scrub Flycatcher, *S. modestus*[467]. Taxonomic split based mainly on vocal differences[545].

Note 2: Recs. from e of Andes from Apure to Monagas and s to lower Río Caura and lower Orinoco area need reevaluation.

Amazonian Scrub-Flycatcher

Sublegatus obscurior   Atrapamoscas del Dosel
Identification: 5.5″ (14cm). 14g. Generally resembles previous sp. but slightly smaller and *decidedly darker, dingier, and more extensively gray below*; belly whitish only vaguely tinged buffy yellow (does not contrast strongly with gray of chest).

Sim. species: In most areas this and previous sp. are slightly separated by range, but they overlap in ne Venez. where care must be taken. In direct comparison they look rather different, with this sp. being much darker and "muddier" below and without much contrast between gray and yellow. Also note voice, habitat, and text under previous sp.

Voice: Song in e Ecuador a rather sweet *chwedeé . . . chwedeé . . . chwedeé . . .*, often continuing for several min without pause[545].

Behavior: Much as in Northern Scrub-Flycatcher.

Status and habitat: Uncommon resident in scrubby vegetation, dry open woodland, and savanna with scattered low bushes and trees, e.g., *Curatella* and *Brysonima* (*orinocensis*); presum. austral or s migrant *obscurior* known only from 1 rec.

Range: To 460m. S Guárico, sw Anzoátegui, and along Orinoco from mouth of Río Apure to Ciudad Bolívar; n Bolívar from Río Cuchivero e to Río Paragua and upper Cuyuní (*orinocensis*); s Bolívar (Cerro Guaiquinima) (*obscurior*). Se Colombia e Ecuador and e Peru, to n Bolivia, Amaz. Brazil, and the Guianas.

Note: Present taxonomy follows several sources[467,545,757], treating this sp., Northern Scrub-Flycatcher, and Southern Scrub-Flycatcher (*S. modestus*) of s of Amazon basin, as separate spp. All were formerly united under Short-billed Flycatcher[403]. Scrub-inhabitating *orinocensis* of lower Orinoco valley and n Guyana may represent yet an additional sp. (M. B. Robbins).

Mecocerculus

Andean group; flattish bill; bold wing bars and eyestripes; small black patch at base of flight feathers; size, tail length (generally fairly long), posture, and behavior vary; White-throated Tyrannulet is least typical of genus.

White-banded Tyrannulet   PLATE 46

Mecocerculus stictopterus   Atrapamoscas Ligero Rabiblanco
Identification: 5″ (12.7cm). 10.7g. Small, thin bill. *Crown gray contrasting* with olive brown upperparts, *long broad white eyebrow*; wing coverts black, *2 wide white wing bars*; outer flight feathers and tertials edged whitish, inner flight feathers edged bright ochre; throat and chest light gray, lower underparts white tinged yellow, *tail from below looks mostly dull white* (outer 2 feathers mostly dull buff white).

Sim. species: Bold eyebrow, wing bars, and contrasting crown are the marks for this clean-cut and distinctive-looking flycatcher. Note horizontal posture. Cf. White-throated Tyrannulet which has puffy white throat, vertical posture, and long droopy tail, and White-tailed Tyrannulet (see Note).

Voice: Utters sharp staccato notes, occas. a rapid trill, ascending then descending, *t't'i'i'iiiiiiiiiiiiii'i'i'i'i, tik, tik!*, punctuated by 1–2 sharp notes at end.
Behavior: Prs. or little parties of 3–5 forage with mixed-spp. flocks, chattering noisily and occas. chasing each other as they hop rapidly up through foliage in restless, warblerlike manner with body held quite horizontal. Sally or leap up *short* distances to underside of leaves or lunge out in short sallies and snatch prey from above or below leaves; also occas. perch-glean and reg. hang paridlike. Occur mainly in mid. level to canopy of trees but occas. quiet low in forest-edge thickets or in stunted forest.
Status and habitat: Fairly common resident in humid and wet montane forest, mossy elfin woodland, and borders.

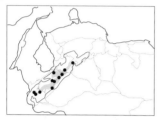

Range: 1900–3050m. Andes of n Táchira, Mérida, and Trujillo n to Páramo Cendé on Lara border (*albocaudatus*). Colombia s in Andes to n Bolivia.
Note: White-tailed Tyrannulet (*M. poecilocerus*) is known from Norte de Santander, Colombia, and may occur in s Táchira. Recalls White-banded Tyrannulet but smaller, rump *greenish yellow*; tail shorter and mostly white from below (outer 2 feathers white).

Sulphur-bellied Tyrannulet
Mecocerculus minor   Atrapamoscas Ligero Menor
Identification: 4.7″ (12cm). Bill thin, base of lower mandible pale. Overall shape much like White-banded Tyrannulet. Crown dark olive gray, back dark olive; *narrow white superciliary* and dusky loral patch; wing coverts dusky with *2 prom. buff bars* and yellow buff edgings; below olive yellow turning *bright suphur yellow on lower breast and belly*.
Sim. species: From other *Mecocerculus* by buff bars and yellow underparts. See Variegated Bristle-Tyrant with different posture, prom. facial markings.
Voice: In Ecuador a rapid *weeka* or *wedup* and slightly descending, nasal *week week week week* (ca. 1 sec) then, after a brief pause, sometimes a final, higher *week* at end[412].
Behavior: Forages singly or in prs., often with mixed-spp. flocks; like most others of genus, perches rather horizontally[545].

Status and habitat: Rare. Known only from 2 specimens in Venez. In Ecuador primarily along forest edges and in nearby second growth and clearings with scattered trees; possibly increasing in nos.[545].
Range: To 1800m. S Táchira in upper Río Chiquito at Hacienda La Providencia. Colombia s locally in Andes to c Peru.

White-throated Tyrannulet   PLATE 46
Mecocerculus leucophrys   Atrapamoscas Ligero Frentiblanco
Identification: 5.5″ (14cm). 10.1g. Small black bill. *Puffy white throat* imparts rather large-headed appearance. *Long droopy tail* (longer in ♂). Note geographical variation. Above brown, crown darker, short indistinct white eyebrow; *2 white wing bars*; tertials edged white, *puffy white throat contrasts* with light brown breast; belly whitish. Or sim. but above darker brown, wing bars buff, breast dark olive (*roraimae*). Or breast dark brownish olive (*parui*).
Sim. species: Told everywhere by conspic. puffy white throat, upright posture, and long, droopy, but expressive tail. Cf. other *Mecocerculus*.
Voice: Typically quite vocal as forages, uttering a variety of soft, sputtering *pri'i'it* and *pur'r'r'r't-prit* calls; also *pit-pit-pit*, spit out, and other soft notes. At dawn an excited *ch'd'dik, ch'd'dik, ch'd'dik, chéw* with variations[541].
Behavior: One of *the* characteristic montane forest birds throughout Andes. Prs. or groups of 3–5 are usually assoc. with mixed-spp. flocks, perch rather erect with tails down, and dart short distances upward to foliage, often hover-gleaning beneath leaves. Also often myopically work over bushes and trees by gleaning, flitting, and hanging paridlike. Forage from low to high but more freq. in upper levels and canopy in or along borders of forest, but at almost any ht. in elfin woodland. Often fly in characteristic jerky, undulating manner with tail down and semispread when moving between nearby trees or shrubs. Small open cup nest 2m up in tree; breeds Jan or Feb–Aug in Colombia[260].
Status and habitat: Very common resident in a wide variety of montane habitats incl. humid and wet forest, forest borders, overgrown pastures, and elfin woodland at treeline. Some seasonal el. movements occur, with birds moving to lower els. early in wet season, e.g., down to 1350m in PN Henri Pittier.

Range: 1350–3700m n of Orinoco; 1300–2450m s of Orinoco. Sierra de Perijá, Zulia, Andes of Táchira n to s Lara (*gularis*); Coastal Cordillera from Yaracuy and Carabobo to Distr. Federal and Miranda (*palliditergum*); mts. of w Sucre and n Monagas (*nigriceps*);

Amazonas on Cerro Parú (*parui*); Amazonas on Cerros Huachamacari, Yavi, Duida, and de la Neblina (*roraimae*); Bolívar on Meseta de Jaua, Cerro Guaiquinima, Auyán-tepui, and cerros of Gran Sabana e and s to Cerro Roraima and Uei-tepui (*chapmani*)[152]. Colombia s in Andes to nw Argentina.

Serpophaga

Plumage mostly gray and white; bill and legs black; short to longish tail; concealed white crown patch (♂ and ♀); some spp. perch-glean actively in foliage, others (assoc. with water) sally to air.

River Tyrannulet
Serpophaga hypoleuca   Atrapamoscas de Ríos
Identification: 4.2″ (10.7cm). Small, slender, and long-tailed. *Elongated crown feathers (flat crest) and sides of head to eyes grayish black*, concealed crown patch white, upperparts gray tinged brown, wings and narrow tail dusky brown with *no obvious bars or edgings*; throat and lower underparts white, *chest and sides light gray*, bill and legs black.
Sim. species: More likely mistaken for a gnatcatcher than another flycatcher. Torrent Tyrannulet, superficially sim., is only in mts.
Voice: Thin, weak *see-blik!* or *pit-chiik!* and *tsit* while foraging. Prs. in territorial defense sing chattery duet, *p'dit-p'dit-p'dit!*, or rapid, bubbly *pik-up, pik-up, . . .*; also a sputtery, rattling *chip-skéep! prf f f f f f ft 'ft 'ft'-chip! chip!*, 2d note highest.
Behavior: Occurs alone or more often in scattered prs. that are active and somewhat gnatcatcherlike as they hop, mostly 0.3–5m up in shrubs and young river-edge vegetation, cock heads to peer, then perch-glean from foliage or occas. sally short distances to air. Forage with rather horizontal posture (tail flat, not cocked), but at rest more upright. Typically restless, somewhat wary, and after a few min apt to fly off some distance to new site. Jun nest (D. Ascanio); late Jul fledgling and 13 Oct nest, Hato El Frio, Apure; tight, fine grass and spiderweb nest, feather lined; 0.5m up in semi-woody herb in dry pasture; 2 unmarked dull buff white eggs[137].
Status and habitat: Uncommon and local. Resident but possibly some seasonal movements. Patches of thorny bushes, or thorny vegetation mixed with tall weeds and open spaces, esp. around watercourses and lagoons in llanos; young successional vegetation on river isls. in Orinoco. Reg., but easily overlooked, at Hato Cedral and Hato El Frio, w Apure.

Range: To 200m. W Apure (sightings), Río Meta, and Río Apure, and along the mid. and lower Orinoco from nw Amazonas (river isls. near Pto. Ayacucho) e to Ciudad Bolívar and s Anzoátegui (*venezuelana*). The Amazon and its tributaries in se Colombia, e Ecuador, n Bolivia, and Amaz. Brazil.

Torrent Tyrannulet   PLATE 46
Serpophaga cinerea   Atrapamoscas de Torrentes
Identification: 4.5″ (11.4cm). 8g. Plump and short-tailed. *Crown and sides of head black, wings black* with 2 white wing bars and white-edged tertials; *tail black* narrowly tipped white, back, rump, and underparts pale gray, belly whitish. Concealed white crown patch (sometimes lacking in ♀).
Sim. species: Not likely confused. Occurs on boulders in rushing mt. streams, a habitat it shares with White-capped Dipper, Black Phoebe, and Torrent Duck.
Voice: Loud, sharp, freq. repeated *seek* note audible above stream noise. Song a high, thin *seek! ti'ti'ti'ti'ti'ti*, last part trilled, sometimes hesitant or irreg. In Costa Rica, song a duet of repeated *chip* notes; at dawn sim. but faster[633].
Behavior: A characteristic bird of rushing mt. streams. Sprightly and alert prs., well separated or sometimes sitting close together, patrol small sections of rocky streams and are usually seen sitting on a boulder in middle of stream or on low branch overhanging water. Often flick up tails and sally in little circles to surface of rocks, nearby vegetation, or to air (low or sometimes almost straight up) for flying insects. Occas. venture short distances into adj. pastures. Moss-covered, feather-lined nest 1–4m up on branch over water; 2 pale buff, unmarked eggs[633]; Feb nest, PN Guaramacal, Trujillo.
Status and habitat: Common resident along boulder-filled mt. streams, esp. small, narrow streams, and around highland lagoons. Most numerous along rushing mt. streams at mid. els.; nos. decline sharply at lower els. where river gradient slows.

Range: 1500–2200m (sight recs. to 3000m). Sierra de Perijá, Zulia; and Andes of Táchira, Mérida, and Trujillo (*cinerea*). Highlands of Costa Rica and w Panama; Andes from Colombia to Bolivia.

Inezia

Diverse-appearing group united more by skull and syringeal characters than by external characteristics; rather narrow bill; med. to longish tail; little or no crest; tail slightly cocked; rather horizontal posture; possibly not monophyletic.

Pale-tipped Inezia
PLATE 46
Inezia caudata   Inezia Coluda
Identification: 4.7″ (12cm). 8.4g. Narrow but *longish* black bill. *Eyes yellowish white to grayish white* (or pale gray ?—*caudata*). Uncrested. Above dull grayish brown with *prom. white "spectacles"* from nostrils to around eyes; dusky loral spot; wings dusky, 2 narrow white wing bars, *longish dusky tail edged and tipped white* (white conspic. up close), chin whitish, rest of underparts yellow, lower throat and chest faintly tinged buff. Or sim. but lower throat and chest distinctly tinged buff (*caudata*).
Sim. species: Best marks are clean-cut head pattern with "spectacles," white wing bars, and distinctive tail. From Amazonian Inezia by pale eyes. Also cf. Southern Beardless-Tyrannulet and Mouse-colored and Slender-billed tyrannulets.
Voice: Often quite vocal. Commonest day song (*intermedia*) a rather loud *TEEP! tedede*, or *Teep, tee'r'r*, last part falling and doubled or trebled (cf. Mouse-colored Tyrannulet); or longer, descending *TEEP! tee-de-dear*. Alternate song varies but typically a rather long, lazy, descending ser. of high, clear notes, e.g., *peep, pe-de-de-de-deer, deer, deer, deer*, or sim. variation (reminiscent of Southern Beardless-Tyrannulet), given singly, or more or less simultaneously as duet by members of a pr. Dawn song sim. to day song but faster and repeated over and over; contact call *chew* (singly or several in ser.) and *pit*; vocalizations of *caudata* sim. to next sp. but duet and alternate songs not yet reported[834].
Behavior: Single birds or prs. hop, with tail slightly cocked and often flicked up, as perch-glean from twigs and green leaves or sally outward short distances and hover-glean from beneath foliage. In llanos often forage quite low (esp. when away from mixed-spp. flocks) in tall dry weeds, shrubby areas, and woodland, and may drop to gd. Also forage up into mid. level or higher in woodland with mixed-spp. flocks. Often advertise presence by freq. vocalizations. In gallery forests occur with small mixed-spp. flocks, or away from them, about equally. Thin neat cup nest suspended from fork, 2.5m up or higher.
Status and habitat: Resident. Common in dry and moist woodland, gallery forest, and scrubby or weedy areas with bushes and trees. Shows some fondness for vicinity of seasonally flooded areas. Often in mangroves in the Guianas (*caudata*).

Range: To 400m. Maracaibo Basin of Zulia, Táchira, Trujillo, and Falcón (absent from very arid zones), and e of Andes from Portuguesa and Cojedes generally e to ne Anzoátegui, and Sucre (?), (*intermedia*); Apure, n

Bolívar, incl. lower Río Caura, s Guárico, and s Monagas at Barrancas (*caudata*); prob. Delta Amacuro. N Colombia to the Guianas (mostly coastal); n Brazil (upper Rio Branco e to Amapá).
Note: Taxonomy recently revised[834]. Formerly Pale-tipped Tyrannulet in part[403].

Amazonian Inezia
Inezia subflava   Inezia Oscura
Identification: 4.7″ (12cm). Sim. to previous sp. and not separable in field by plumage characters. Ads. separable (?) by eye color and always by voice. In hand, bill longer, legs shorter, and chest washed olive (not buff); *eyes usually brown* (not pale), but juvs. of both spp. may have dark eyes.
Sim. species: See Pale-tipped Inezia.
Voice: Very unlike Pale-tipped Inezia. "Loudsong," given at intervals throughout day, a dry rattle, 0.5–2 sec, on same pitch. Duet song of ♂ a short *pee-chew*; that of ♀ a faster 2- to 3-syllable *kutup* or *kutterup*; songs often sung as a rhythmic duet, e.g., *pee-chew, kutterup, pee-chew, kutterup . . .* for several sec; or occas. either song given singly. Contact call *pik*. After playback also *pee . . chew-chew-chew-chew-chew* (5 or more *chew* notes).
Behavior: Sim. to previous sp. but perches and forages rather low, often only 1–3m up and usually near water.
Status and habitat: Uncommon resident, perhaps also local. Shrubby vegetation along forest-bordered stream banks, rivers, and lakes. Swamp, várzea, or low-lying forest areas. Shows strong affinity for water, esp. around small openings with bushes.

Range: To 200m. Amazonas from Caño Cuao and mid. Río Ventuari (sight/tape, Junglaven) southward (*obscura*). E Colombia, Brazil along Rio Negro and the Amazon e to Rio Xingú, and s locally in ne Bolivia.
Note: Following Zimmer and Whittaker[834], Amazonian Inezia is now considered 1 of 2 spp. that formerly comprised Pale-tipped Tyrannulet[403].

Slender-billed Inezia
PLATE 46
Inezia tenuirostris   Atrapamoscas de Pico Tenue
Identification: 3.6″ (9.1cm). *Small and nondescript.* Bill short and narrow. Crown and upperparts olive brown; *narrow white eyline* from base of bill to beyond eyes; *2 narrow white wing bars*; tertials edged dull white, throat dirty grayish white, breast dirty yellowish white clouded olive, *belly clear pale yellow*. In hand, tail narrowly edged and tipped white.
Sim. species: The quintessential dull brown tyrannulet. Best told by combination of small size, eyeline,

whitish wing bars, yellow belly, and trilled song. Southern Beardless-Tyrannulet is larger and more crested; Mouse-colored Tyrannulet has longer eyebrow, long tail, no yellow below; also see Pale-tipped Inezia.
Voice: Song a flat, insipid trill, *tleeeeeeee'e'e'e'e'e'e'e'e* (ca. 2 sec), thin and slightly descending or attenuated at end.
Behavior: A modest if somewhat fidgety inhabitant of n deserts. Prs. move with horizontal posture and tail slightly cocked. Usually forage alone, keeping mostly 1–5m up in *Acacia* and scrub vegetation where they are active and agile hover-gleaners from foliage; also often perch-glean like vireos. Typically confiding and sedentary, but quickly come to mob owls.
Status and habitat: Common resident in desert scrub and other xerophytic vegetation, low dry woodland, and edges of mangroves. Esp. fond of *Acacia* spp. and commonest in extremely arid scrub, e.g., Paraguaná Pen.

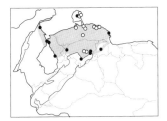

Range: To 800m. Nw Zulia e across Falcón to Boca del Tocuyo (sight), and s to s Lara at Barquisimeto. Ne Colombia.
Note: Previously called Slender-billed Tyrannulet[403].

Yellow Tyrannulet   PLATE 46
Capsiempis flaveola   Atrapamoscas Amarillo
Identification: 4.5″ (11.4cm). 7.9g. *Small yellowish flycatcher with rounded head and drooped tail long relative to body*; bill rather thick. Short narrow eyebrow *whitish* (occas. yellowish white), otherwise above yellowish olive; wings dusky brown with *2 pale yellowish to whitish wing bars* and faint yellowish edgings; tertials broadly edged dull white, *entire underparts bright yellow*. Or paler, more faded yellowish brown overall (*leucophrys*). In hand note dull whitish nasal plumes (both races).
Sim. species: No other small tyrannulet looks so yellowish overall. See larger Ochre-lored Flatbill which has wide bill and orangish loral spot.
Voice: May sing alone, but most often prs. perform lively, sputtering, simultaneous duets, a rhythmic *pít-tic-keek* (*pretty-cake*) spit out, repeated rapidly 10 times or more when excited (apparently both sing same phrase?); also at intervals a soft nasal trill, *trrrrrrrr*, reminiscent of a toad. When foraging soft *pee-tee* or *pee-teetee* notes.
Behavior: Prs. or family groups of 3–4 are vocal and chattery as they perch-glean mostly 1–8m up in foliage, flutter short distances (<0.5m), or hover-glean for insects and a few small berries. Generally not with mixed-spp. flocks. Posture rather horizontal when foraging but more upright at rest. Tend to remain out of sight in foliage but notably territorial and respond

strongly to tape playback. Nest an open cup with moss on outside; 3–7m up in small tree or shrub; 2 white eggs[633].
Status and habitat: Fairly common resident in thickets and shrubby borders of dry to humid forest, gallery forest, streamside vegetation, and bushy overgrown clearing.

Range: To 600m n of Orinoco; to 300m s of Orinoco. E base of Sierra de Perijá, Zulia, e to nw Táchira, w Mérida, sw Lara (*leucophrys*); e Falcón and generally (except arid areas) across rest of Venez. n of Orinoco e to Delta Amacuro; throughout Amazonas s to Cerro de la Neblina; Bolívar s to lower Río Caura, lower Río Paragua (La Paragua), and upper Río Cuyuní at base of Sierra de Lema (*cerulus*); prob. throughout s Bolívar. Nicaragua to the Guianas and n Brazil; se Brazil; spottily in s Peru, n Bolivia, and w Brazil.
Note: Taxonomic placement uncertain. Placed in *Phylloscartes*[757] or believed allied with *Phaeomyias*[317] but vocally nearest Amazonian Inezia[834].

Stigmatura

Long wagging tail with bold markings; broad wing band; duet songs; inhabit shrubby or scrubby semi-open edges.

Lesser Wagtail-Tyrant
Stigmatura napensis   Rabicano Menor
Identification: 5.2″ (13.2cm). Short bill. *Long, graduated, and expressive tail*. Above grayish olive; eyestripe and weak eyering pale yellow; wing edgings and *2 wing bars yellowish white*, 1 forming large pale slash; underparts light yellow, breast tinged olive, *tail blackish, all but central feathers broadly tipped white* and with broad yellowish white base.
Sim. species: Nothing remotely like it in its limited "river isl." habitat. Note spectacles, wing bars, and unusually long, rounded, white-tipped tail which is often cocked up.
Voice: When foraging a soft, whistled *wheéert?*; also *weeeEE!* and harsh, scolding rattle, *sque'e'e'e*, descending slightly. Territorial song a rollicking duet by mated pair; one sings *pfew! skew*, the other a rattle, *d'u'u*, the phrases alternating in rapid succession, i.e., *pfew!, skew'du'u'u, skew'd'u'u, pfew! skew'd'u'u, skew-'d'u'u . . .* and so on, repeated several times in frantic burst of energy.
Behavior: A charming and sprightly little bird, usually found in prs. or families that perch-glean actively in foliage and also make short aerial sallies as they hop

1–5m up in bushes and grass. Constantly jerk tails up to sharp angle above back, sometimes also slightly spread tail (but do not "wag" it). Usually fairly easy to observe although typically do not remain long in open and move in and out of foliage quickly. Territories can be very small and vigorously defended.

Status and habitat: First seen and taped 23 Jun 1996 (3 pairs) by Hilty et al. on a small Orinoco river isl. ca. 3–4km upriver from Camturama Lodge, Amazonas[259], and several specimens taken 13 May 1999 (M. Lentino and D. Ascanio). A specialists of young regenerating and bushy vegetation on river isls. In w Amazon Basin found mainly in early-succession vegetation on sandy river isls., esp. in shrubby *Tessaria* (Compositae) trees, or mixed with *Salix* (Salicaceae), tall grass, bushes, saplings, and small *Cecropia* trees.

Range: To 200m. Nw Amazonas on Orinoco river isls. near Pto Ayacucho (subsp.?). Brazil (the Amazon from mouth of Rio Tapajós to ne Rio Negro) to ne Peru and e Ecuador (upper Río Napo); Brazil on lower Rio Madeira and Rio Juruá; ne Brazil (Pernambuco and w and c Bahia).

Uromyias

Flat crest; stubby bill; notably long tail; high Andes.

Agile Tit-Tyrant   PLATE 45

Uromyias agilis   Atrapamoscas Agil
Identification: 5″ (12.7cm). *Bill stubby*, lower mandible orange tipped black. Central crown feathers long and black forming short flat crest; *prom. broad white eyebrow*, rest of head brownish narrowly streaked grayish white, back brown *streaked dusky*, wings dusky (no bars), tertials edged white, throat and breast grayish white streaked black, lower underparts unmarked creamy to yellowish; *notably long graduated tail* (3″, 76mm), outer pr. of tail feathers edged white.
Sim. species: No other small flycatcher in high Andes of Venez. is so heavily streaked. Note short bill, prom. eyebrow, and long tail. Habits and habitat are helpful clues.
Voice: Song a shrill chattery trill, sometimes followed by a little hic-up at end, e.g., *t't't't't't't't't't't'r'e'e'e, spew-it!*, or either separately. A soft *chip* and snappy, bisyllabic *speuuwit!* while foraging. Some trills descend in pitch.
Behavior: Prs. or little groups (families?) of up to 6 reg. follow mixed-spp. flocks and are fairly easy to see. Perch rather upright with tail depressed, flit to different perch freq., perch-glean from foliage or more often

dart up or straight out, striking leaves and snatching prey with scarcely a pause, mostly at low to mid. hts. (1–6m up).

Status and habitat: Uncommon resident in lower growth and borders of wet montane forest, almost always where there is *Chusquea* bamboo. Smaller nos. range up into elfin woodland at treeline.

Range: 2300–2600m. N Táchira (Páramo Zumbador and La Negra; sight, Páramo Batallón), s and c Mérida (Mucuchíes). Colombia s in Andes to s Ecuador.

Bearded Tachuri   PLATE 46

Polystictus pectoralis   Atrapamoscas Piojito
Identification: 3.8″ (9.7cm). 12g. *Tiny buff-colored flycatcher of tall grass.* ♂: *head slaty black*, crown feathers long forming shaggy crest somewhat streaked whitish; narrow white supraloral line; lores black, *throat to lower cheeks grizzled black and white* ("salt and pepper"), otherwise reddish brown above; wing coverts dusky with 2 vague rufous buff wing bars and tertial edgings; *below yellowish buff*, belly whitish. ♀: paler above, crown grayish streaked black, *throat whitish, rest of underparts bright yellowish buff.*
Sim. species: ♂ unique. ♀ recalls Tawny-crowned Pygmy-Tyrant which is grayish white (not yellow buff) below.
Voice: Usually quiet. Morning flight song in Brazil a rising *tee-tee-tee-teet* followed by short grasshopperlike wing-buzz at peak of 20- to 100-m flight to 10m above grass and bushes. During day also sings same song (without wing-buzz) from perch in low bush. Also gives this same song every 3 sec in near darkness of predawn as flies in circles. When foraging a short *pee-wee* as tail is jerked up; short rattle, *chup-chup-seet-seet*, and *peewee* notes with fledglings[459].
Behavior: An inconspic. little grassland bird with odd behavior. Usually seen alone, much less often 2 together, perching in tall grass and weeds or in tops of bushes. Flushes from grass, flies low in erratic or zigzag lines for short distance, and drops into grass, sometimes pausing momentarily before disappearing into cover. Perch-gleans within grass and also forages by clinging to grass stems, sometimes using long legs to grasp 2 separated stems, then flitting out in grass to hover-glean or snap small insects from grass or other vegetation. Pr. formation not proved, and possibly ♂♂ display while only ♀♀ care for 2 fledglings. Small 200-m-diameter territories[459].
Status and habitat: Rare and declining. Resident *very locally* in tall dry grass or grass mixed with scattered shrubs; also dense heathlike areas of tall grass and low woody growth (e.g., n end of Gran Sabana). Four recent recs. (1995–2001) are from Gran Sabana (Hilty;

D. Ascanio; F. Thompson); 2 more (Nov 1997, 1998) are from tall grass and weeds near Río Caicara, Hato Cedral (D. Ascanio). May wander seasonally or emigrate seasonally or periodically to areas of suitable tall grass. Threatened by burning and overgrazing which destroys tall dry grass this sp. requires.

Range: 1300m (sightings to 1450m). Local in grasslands of w Barinas and w Apure; s Carabobo (El Paito); sw Monagas (El Merey; Uverito); n Amazonas (El Platanal); n Bolívar (Caicara; lower Río Caura at Maripa); and se Bolívar in Gran Sabana (sightings[259]) s to Acopán-tepui, Santa Elena de Uairén, and Cerro Roraima (*brevipennis*); a rec. from Chiguara, Mérida, is prob. in error. Colombia very locally to s Guyana and Suriname; e Bolivia and s Brazil to n Argentina and Uruguay.

Pseudocolopteryx

Reed and marsh dwellers mainly in austral region; thin bill; plumage sim. in all spp.; several with flattish crests; retiring; often migratory; small cup nest in fork of shrub or tree in marsh.

Crested Doradito
Pseudocolopteryx sclateri   Doradito Copetón
Identification: 4″ (10.2cm). Thin, narrow, warblerlike bill. *Long shaggy crest feathers blackish* edged yellowish white (crest looks streaked, often held somewhat depressed), semiconcealed yellow crown stripe; *cheeks dusky,* otherwise pale olive above somewhat streaked dusky on back, 2 dull whitish wing bars and dull whitish tertial edges; *underparts bright chrome yellow.* In hand note unusually long, sharp hallux (rear) nail.
Sim. species: Nothing really sim. in marshes and reeds. See Pale-tipped Inezia, ♀ Bearded Tachuri, Tawny-crowned Pygmy-Tyrant, and Common Tody-Flycatcher.
Voice: Song in Trinidad a squeaky *tsik-tsik-tsee-lee*; call a high, thin, soft *sik*[545].
Behavior: Usually seen singly, in prs., or in little family groups of up to 4 that hop around perch-gleaning in marshy vegetation or tall weeds and grass where they are inconspic. and sometimes difficult to see. Occas. cling to side of sedge or reed stems, or sit up in view for short periods. Ads. with begging juv., Jun, e Falcón.
Status and habitat: Rare and local. Marshes and tall grass and weeds (esp. *Polygum,* water hyacinth, and rushes) in or near water. First recs. (5 specimens) 29 Aug and 25 Sep 1982 by R. Ramirez at Las Coquizas

(Río Hueque) and San José de la Costa, Falcón; several found Dec 1982 at Embalse de Tacarigua, Falcón (R. Ramirez); 16 ads. and juvs. there late 1984 (C. Parrish and A. Altman), none in early 1985 with flood water levels. Juvs. molting into ad. plumage Aug–Sep 1982; juvs. Jan–Feb 1983 and Jul 1983, and fledglings Oct 1984, suggest 3 yr of sustained breeding (M. Lentino). Perhaps an opportunistic breeder exploiting suitable ephemeral habitats. Refound Jun 1994 at Embalse de Tacarigua[259]. Only recs. away from Falcón are 1 seen 19 Jul 1983 at Hato Cedral (R. W. Andrews fide C. Parrish) and a juv. collected near PN Henri Pittier (Laguna de Turiamo), Aragua.

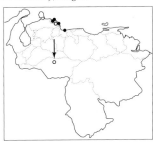

Range: To 200m. E Falcón, n Aragua, and w Apure (once). Scattered recs. in Trinidad (breeding), Guyana, Bolivia (once), and from e Paraguay and s Brazil s to s of Buenos Aires.

Euscarthmus

Short tail; short rounded wings; narrow pointed bill.

Tawny-crowned Pygmy-Tyrant   PLATE 46
Euscarthmus meloryphus   Atrapamoscas Copete Castaño
Identification: 4″ (10.2cm). 7.3g. Plain little flycatcher of dry, weedy thickets. Thin bill; lower mandible yellow. *Slight peaked crest. Large black eyes contrast with "faded" dull brown upperparts, faintly buff-tinged face, and buff white lores;* semiconcealed rufous crown patch; indistinct whitish eyering; *wings essentially unmarked* (or with 2 faint cinnamon wing bars); throat whitish, chest tinged brownish, belly faintly yellow.
Sim. species: Note *big dark eyes,* slight crest, unmarked wings, and small bill. Scrub Greenlet is even plainer with pale bill, often pale eyes, and olive upperparts. Slender-billed Tyrannulet has wing bars and weak eyestripe. Also see Pale-tipped Inezia.
Voice: Advertising song an abrupt, dry, stuttering *ple'bik!*, lengthened to *ple-plit'erick,* locustlike, sometimes over and over. irreg. even throughout heat of day.
Behavior: Usually seen singly, and when singing often stubbornly refuses to leave thick cover. When foraging, hops short distances and perch-gleans from foliage or flits like a little vireo in thickets and weeds, mostly within 0.5–2m up., sometimes virtually on gd. and difficult to see. Often clings to side of vertical stems. Does not assoc. with mixed-spp. flocks. Density of singing birds (all ♂♂?) in some weedy areas is remarkably high, suggesting local (or colonial?) distrib.

and *small* territories. Four BC birds Oct–Nov, Cúcuta, Colombia[260]. In Ecuador, thin dry cup nest suspended 0.5–1.7m up in bush; 2 yellowish white eggs with lilac and buff spots, often visible through nest[379].
Status and habitat: Resident. Common very locally in dry weedy fields, waste areas, and dry to arid scrub vegetation. Mainly dry to arid regions, esp. where there are tall dry weeds and scrubby bushes. A good colonizer of dry disturbed areas.

Range: To 1000m. N and w Zulia, nw Táchira (Ureña), Falcón, n Lara s to Barquisimeto, and Coastal Cordillera of Carabobo, Aragua, and Distr. Federal; Anzoátegui, Sucre (e to Los Mangos), and Monagas; n Bolívar from Ciudad Bolívar to Tumeremo (*paulus*). Disjunct. N Colombia and Venez.; w Ecuador and nw Peru; e Bolivia and Paraguay to e Brazil, Argentina and Uruguay.

Mionectes

Longish, slender bill; few or no rictal bristles; forest understory; mostly frugivorous; often flick up a wing over back. Incls. spp. formerly in *Pipromorpha*.

Olive-striped Flycatcher   PLATE 46
Mionectes olivaceus   Atrapamoscas Frutero Rayado
Identification: 5.2″ (13.2cm). 13g. Small, streaky, nervous-acting flycatcher usually seen at fruiting trees and shrubs. Thin bill. Crown, sides of head, and upperparts dark greenish olive, *prom. white spot behind eyes*; wings brownish with no obvious bars (or with weakly indicated buff bars—*meridae*), flight feathers narrowly edged yellowish green, underparts dull yellow *narrowly and profusely streaked olive on sides of head, throat, and breast* and becoming clear yellow on belly.
Sim. species: Occurs only in mts. where should be easily recognized by streaky underparts and conspic. white postocular spot. Cf. much smaller Scale-crested Pygmy-Tyrant.
Voice: Not very vocal. Loosely assoc. groups of displaying ♂♂ utter a high, almost hissing *tse-tse-tse-tse* at short intervals, the ser. ventriloquial and rising and falling slightly. Silent or occas. a high, thin *seeee* when foraging.
Behavior: A solitary and rather reclusive little flycatcher, most apt to be seen flicking wings in agitated manner as it visits small fruiting trees. Eats insects, but more than half of diet is small berries and arils (esp. *Clusia* and *Trema*) taken with deft hover; also executes upward hover-gleans for insects beneath foliage or clings momentarily to leaves. Often active around mixed-spp. flocks, and esp. when other birds visit fruit-

ing trees. At rest in undergrowth often nods head and looks from side to side in curiously reptilian manner, and may flick up a wing like *Leptopogon*. In Trinidad 2 nests believed to be of this sp. were globular with side entrance (no dangling tail), suspended from roots; 3 white eggs[39]; or placed beside vertical cliff, bank, or base of tree in Costa Rica[706].
Status and habitat: Common and widespread resident although easily overlooked. Shady humid forest, along forest borders, and in second-growth woodland. Mistnests reveal its true abundance. In Coastal Cordillera there are downslope migratory movements during rainy Aug–Nov months (D. Ascanio and M. Lentino).

Range: 150–3000m (mostly 900–2300m). Sierra de Perijá, Zulia; Andes from s Táchira and Barinas n to nw Lara (Cerro El Cerrón), se Lara (Cabudare), and Sierra de San Luis, Falcón (*meridae*); mts. of Yaracuy, n cordilleras from Carabobo to Distr. Federal and Miranda se to Cerro Negro, and mts. of Sucre e to Paria Pen., and in Monagas (*venezuelensis*). Costa Rica s in mts. to n Bolivia.

Ochre-bellied Flycatcher   PLATE 46
Mionectes oleagineus   Atrapamoscas Frutero Aceitunado
Identification: 5″ (12.7cm). 11g. Rather slender and small-headed; bill narrow, lower mandible pinkish basally; mouth lining yellow. Above dull greenish olive ("tarnished" copper), wings and tail brownish, *2 ochraceous buff wing bars* (often rather indistinct) and narrow wing edgings; *tertials with fairly well marked buff edges*; sides of head, throat, and underparts dull grayish olive, *lower breast and belly tawny ochraceous*. Or sim. but grayer above and on chest (*abdominalis*). Or sim. but wing bars faint (*intensa* and *dorsalis*).
Sim. species: Note thin bill, "burnt orange" lower underparts, and wing-raising habit. See very sim. McConnell's Flycatcher. Ruddy-tailed Flycatcher and Cinnamon Neopipo are much smaller, both with tiny bill and mostly rufous wings, rump, and tail. Also see larger ♀ Cinereous Antshrike.
Voice: ♂♂ sing persistently from slender, horizontal perches 2–6m up and freq. flick up one wing or the other and raise short crest. Song a variable ser. of *chup*, *up*, and *char* notes. At normal speed sounds like ser. of chirps, twitters, and little sneezing *choo* and *pitchóo* notes[786,819].
Behavior: A quirky-acting little understory flycatcher that is solitary and inconspic. Eats mostly fruit by sallying up short distances to hover-glean, e.g., arils of *Clusia* and berries of *Psychotria*. Also hover-gleans

small quantities of insects, and occas. joins mixed-spp. flocks for short periods of time (less often with flocks than next sp.). Freq. flicks up 1 wing in a "salute." ♂♂ sing persistently and display alone or in leks with variable dispersion of ♂♂ and complex repertoire of displays. ♂♂ own small (<1ha) territories, or behave as subordinate satellite ♂♂ on territories of others (and often eventually replace original owner), or behave as floaters with no territory. When ♀ visits, ♂ increases song and wing-flick rate, follows ♀, and displays by (1) hopping rapidly between perches and calling, (2) performing slow, arcing, flutter-flights with body held vertical, or (3) rising up in "hover" flight and returning to same or near perch[671,786]. Pyriform-shape, side-entrance nest usually moss covered; suspended from root or vine or under stream bank; 2–3 white eggs[790]; only ♀ attends nest[633].

Status and habitat: Common and widespread resident inside humid forest, second-growth woodland, and esp. near forest streams in lowlands and lower slopes of tepuis. Where it occurs with McConnell's Flycatcher (slopes of tepuis), McConnell's occurs inside tall mature forest, Ochre-bellied more along forest edges, second growth, and lighter woodland.

Range: To 1400m n of Orinoco; to 1800m s of Orinoco. Zulia (except arid zones), nw Táchira, w Mérida, and w Trujillo at Betijoque (*parcus*); n cordilleras in Distr. Federal and Miranda e to Cerro Negro (*abdominalis*); mts. of ne Anzoátegui, Sucre and n Monagas s across Delta Amacuro (*pallidiventris*); e base of Andes in Táchira n to Portuguesa; n and w Amazonas s across lower Río Ventuari to Río Negro, and nw Bolívar in lower Río Caura (*chloronotus*); Amazonas in upper Río Ventuari and rest of Bolívar (*intensus*); 1450–1850m on Cerros Chimantá and Roraima (*dorsalis*). S Mexico to w Ecuador, n Bolivia, Amaz. Brazil, and the Guianas; se Brazil.

Note: Previously placed in genus *Pipromorpha*[403].

McConnell's Flycatcher PLATE 48

Mionectes macconnelli Atrapamoscas Frutero Meridional

Identification: 5" (12.7cm). 12g. Very sim. to Ochre-bellied Flycatcher and not always safely told in field. Note difference in el. distrib.: Ochre-bellied is *mainly in lowlands*, McConnell's (in Venez.) mainly on slopes of tepuis and at higher els. McConnell's differs in *complete absence of wing bars*, but bars often indistinct on Ochre-bellied, and note that the 2 subspp. of Ochre-bellied with faintest wing bars are in area of overlap with McConnell's. McConnell's also shows *no visible*

edging on tertials in field but note that, in hand, hidden inner edges of tertials are narrowly edged buff. In hand, mouth lining blackish (yellowish in Ochre-bellied Flycatcher).

Voice: Displaying ♂♂ in Brazil sing near gd. to 2m up (lower than Ochre-bellied Flycatcher), often near base of buttressed tree, where they give ser. of rough *Turdus*-like *wiib* notes, sometimes varied with odd nasal *rin-tin-tin-tin-tin* . . . (up to 3/sec), very unlike song of Ochre-bellied Flycatcher[819]. On Sierra de Lema Bolívar, a metallic, rattling *tic . . chik . . . chíd'd'lick'chíd'-d'lick'chíd'd'lick'-chíd'd'lick . . tic*; given rapidly, the phrases run together, sounding as if given by 2 birds.

Behavior: Sim. to that of Ochre-bellied Flycatcher. Reg. follows small mixed-spp. flocks in forest interior. Forages 1–25m up (on avg. much higher than Ochre-bellied), both near or far from forest streams; sweeps head back and forth, then sallies for small berries and insects. When perched often flicks up 1 wing as do others of genus. Displays are short fluttering and hovering flights, at times by 2 birds. Displays in sim. locality each day, usually 50–100m from neighboring ♂♂; leks tend to follow creeks. Oven-shaped nests hang over small forest streams; 3 white eggs; young grow very slowly; breeds Jan–Mar, peak of rainy season near Manaus, Brazil[819].

Status and habitat: Resident. Uncommon to fairly common inside tall humid forest in foothills and slopes of tepuis. Most recs. 700–1700m.

Range: 700–2000m (once to 450m in Sierra de Imataca). Amazonas on Cerros Duida and de la Neblina (*mercedesfosterae*); rest of tepuis of Amazonas incl. Cerros Camani, Sipapo, and Yavi and upper Río Siapa; tepuis of Bolívar except ne (*roraimae*); ne Bolívar (*macconnelli*). The Guianas and ne Brazil; se Peru and n Bolivia.

Note: Previously placed in genus *Pipromorpha*[403].

Leptopogon

Superficially like *Pogonotriccus* (grizzled face, dusky crescent on rear of cheek) but larger, longer-tailed, and longer, heavier bill; perch very upright; often quickly lift 1 wing up over back; lower levels inside forest; small spine at base of 1st primary on underwing.

Slaty-capped Flycatcher PLATE 46

Leptopogon superciliaris Levanta Alas Gorro Gris

Identification: 5.5" (14cm). 12.6g. Eyes grayish. *Bill fairly long*, narrow, and black, base of lower mandible pinkish. *Crown dark gray*, indistinct grayish white eyeline; lores and sides of head grizzled gray and white with small dusky spot below eyes and *crescentic black patch on rear cheeks*, otherwise olive above; wings dusky, *2 prom.* "*spotted*" *yellowish white wing bars*; flight feathers edged pale yellow, tertials broadly edged and tipped yellowish white, throat and breast yellowish vaguely flammulated olive, lower breast and belly clear yellow.

Sim. species: Easily confused with Marble-faced and Venezuelan bristle-tyrants which are smaller (not always obvious). Look for Slaty-capped's longer, heavier bill, longer tail, and wing bars which are distinctly spotted (bars formed by 2 rows of spots). Note that bars are yellowish in all 3 spp. At lower els. see Sepia-capped Flycatcher which is darker with rufous brown crown.

Voice: Freq. utters abrupt sneezing *Ah'chew* (or *hit'you*) as forages; also a little downscale *tt-t-e-e-e* trill and sharp, emphatic *skEET'de'e'e'e'er!*

Behavior: As in *Phylloscartes*, *Mionectes*, and several other genera of small flycatchers, freq. flicks up a wing when at rest. Single birds or prs. perch upright in low or mid. story, sally outward or slightly upward short distances (<2m) to underside of foliage where take small arthropod prey by hover-gleaning, or more often snap prey from leaf during momentary pause (no hovering) before continuing on to new perch. Occas. take small fruit. Mostly forage with mixed-spp. flocks. Much more conspic. than allied Sepia-capped Flycatcher which replaces it at lower els. Semiglobular nest with side entrance, sometimes a visor; suspended from log, root, or edge of earth bank; 2 white eggs[39,633]; 2 nests Feb–Mar, n Aragua.

Status and habitat: Common resident in humid forest, second-growth woodland, bushy coffee plantations, and along wooded borders. Mainly foothills and lower slopes.

Range: 400–2000m. Sierra de Perijá, Zulia, Andes from Táchira to e Lara (Cabudare), and generally in mts. from Falcón and Yaracuy e to Sucre and n Monagas (*venezuelensis*); extreme e Sucre at Cristobal Colon (*pariae*). Costa Rica s in mts. to n Bolivia.

Sepia-capped Flycatcher   PLATE 46
Leptopogon amaurocephalus   Levanta Alas Gorro Sepia
Identification: 5.5″ (14cm). 11.4g. Closely resembles Slaty-capped Flycatcher (range overlap minimal) but facial area buffy white grizzled dusky (not gray and white), crown dark reddish brown, and wing bars buff (not yellowish white). Or sim but darker above; wing bars and edgings more yellowish (*obscuritergum*).

Sim. species: See Slaty-capped Flycatcher.
Voice: Call a harsh, almost explosive *SKET'a'a'j'j'j* or *SKET'd'd'r'r'r*, last part chattery and vibrating. Also a sim. but softer, descending rattle.
Behavior: Sim. to that of Slaty-capped Flycatcher but less conspic. and less often at forest borders. When perched, often flicks up one wing then other, as if saluting. Single birds or prs. are often with mixed-spp. flocks. Forage from eye level to mid. level in forest, executing short sallies straight out or slightly upward to underside of foliage to hover-glean or occas. sally-strike and then continue to new perch. Eat mostly small arthropods, occas. berries. Active and change perches freq. Nest a round, side-entrance ball suspended from roots, beneath logs, or under stream bank; 1–3 white eggs[409].
Status and habitat: Uncommon resident in understory of moist and humid forest and light second-growth woodland; locally in gallery forest in llanos (mainly perimeter of llanos); along e base of Andes also in coffee plantations, disturbed woodland, and ravines. Replaced above ca. 800m by Slaty-capped Flycatcher. S of Orinoco (Slaty-capped Flycatcher absent) occurs at higher els. than n of Orinoco and mainly in interior of humid and wet forest on slopes of tepuis.

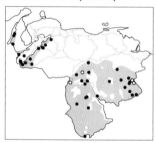

Range: 100–600m n of Orinoco; to 1600m s of Orinoco. Ne base of Sierra de Perijá, Zulia (*diversus*); w base of Andes in Táchira, e base n to Portuguesa (Acarigua); c Amazonas on Cerro Yapacana; nw Bolívar at Pijiguaos and Sta. Rosalía (*orinocensis*); lowlands of nw Amazonas (sightings, Dec 1993, Pto. Ayacucho), cerros of n Amazonas (Calentura; Guanay; Yavi; Parú) and upper Río Ventuari s to s Amazonas (Cerros Duida and de la Neblina); Bolívar from upper Río Cuchivero, Río Paragua, Sierra de Lema (sightings), and Gran Sabana s to Santa Elena de Uairén (*obscuritergum*). Mexico to the Guianas; s Amazonia (absent from n Amazonia) to n Argentina and se Brazil.

Rufous-breasted Flycatcher   PLATE 46
Leptopogon rufipectus   Levanta Alas Carirrufo
Identification: 5.2″ (13.2cm). 13.3g. Eyes brown; bill black. *Crown gray* contrasting with olive green upperparts; *lores, sides of head, throat, and chest rich rufous sharply separated from clear yellow lower breast and belly*; sides of head grizzled dusky, rear cheeks with dusky crescent patch; wings dusky, *2 spotted buffy rufous wing bars*; flight feathers edged yellowish buff, *tertials broadly edged yellowish white* (conspic. in field), tail reddish brown.
Sim. species: Rufous face, throat, and chest sharply separated from yellow lower underparts diagnostic. Cf.

Variegated Bristle-Tyrant, which is smaller and uniform yellow below (no "divided" underparts), and Cinnamon Flycatcher.
Voice: Advertising call 1–5 loud, abrupt, squeaky *spiK!* notes, like squeeze toy, typically given only at long intervals (1 min or more).
Behavior: Single birds or prs. call noisily but rather infreq. as follow mixed-spp. flocks in forest mid. levels, sit upright on small open branches and vines which afford good view, sally out to hover-glean prey from foliage, and then drop away to new perch. Occas. lift or flick up a wing. Often wait 30 sec to 1 min on a perch before moving.
Status and habitat: Resident. Fairly common locally in humid and wet mossy forest. Many specimens from Hacienda La Providencia; seen fairly reg. near pass between Bramón and Las Delicias but not as numerous or conspic. as allied Slaty-capped Flycatcher.

Range: 1800–2700m. S Táchira in upper Río Chiquito, Páramo de Tamá, and pass above Bramón (*venezuelanus*). Colombia s locally in Andes to extreme n Peru.

Phylloscartes

Large but well-defined group; slender bill; slender body and long, narrow, cocked tail; perch more horizontally than upright; mostly humid forest canopy; majority in mts. or s of Amazon Basin; often with restricted ranges; in hand note short, plushlike, white nasal plumes that contrast with dark forehead. Previously some have incl. genus *Pogonotriccus* in *Phylloscartes*[545,757].

Black-fronted Tyrannulet
PLATE 46
Phylloscartes nigrifrons Atrapamoscas Frentinegro
Identification: 5″ (12.7cm). Tepuis only. *Long slender tail held cocked. Narrow forehead and loral line black* (impart distinct frown to face), small white spot (nasal plumes) at base of bill; narrow white eyebrow mark; crown gray, sides of head mixed gray and white and *bordered behind by narrow, distinct black crescent*; back olive, wing coverts black, *2 narrow but crisp yellowish white wing bars*; flight feathers and tail dusky edged olive green, *underparts light gray* vaguely mottled gray and white on throat and chest; belly tinged yellowish.
Sim. species: In restricted range cf. Slender-footed and White-lored tyrannulets, both of which lack distinctive head pattern. Also cf. Chapman's Bristle-Tyrant which has different posture and behavior.
Voice: Infreq. hd. song a long (2-3 sec), very thin trill, last half slightly descending (D. Ascanio); also, when foraging, a thin, sharp *tsuk-cheez-tr'r'r'r'r'r'r'r'r'r'r'*, 2d note highest, last a rattlelike trill, as tail is vibrated.

Call, when foraging, *chek-chek-ch'leet!*, last part slightly trilled.
Behavior: Prs. or family groups up to 6 forage mostly at low- to mid.-forest levels, occas. higher, and are usually with mixed-spp. flocks containing greenlets, tanagers, and arboreal spp. of antwrens and spinetails. Active and sprightly as sally or flit upward short distances to hover-glean, mostly from beneath leaves, then quickly move on to new perch. Jauntily cocked tail is often flicked down slightly as birds forage. Occas. raise or flick up 1 wing (as in *Leptopogon*, etc.) as if afflicted by a tic.
Status and habitat: Resident in humid and wet premontane forest, forest borders, occas. also dense melastome-dominated second growth. Fairly common on Sierra de Lema, e Bolívar.

Range: ENDEMIC. 900–1800m. Cerros of Amazonas (s to Cerro de la Neblina) and Bolívar. Doubtless in adj. Brazil and Guyana.
Note: Olive-green Tyrannulet (*P. virescens*) of the Guianas to vicinity of Manaus, Brazil, may occur in e Venez. 4.8″ (12.2cm). Slender and rather long tailed; uniform olive above with 2 prom. yellow wing bars and edgings on flight feathers, fairly conspic. yellow eyering; vague dusky mottling on pale cheeks; below pale yellow, whitish on throat, clouded olive on chest. Canopy of humid lowland forest.

Rufous-browed Tyrannulet
Phylloscartes superciliaris Atrapamoscas Frentirrufo
Identification: 4.8″ (12.2cm). 7.5g. Sierra de Perijá. Slender bill; narrow cocked tail. *Narrow frontlet, supraloral line, and eyering rufous* (impart frowning expression), crown and nape dark gray, *cheeks white encircled by narrow oval of black* (black broadest at rear of cheeks), otherwise olive green above; wing coverts blackish (no bars), inner flight feathers edged bright yellow green, underparts pale gray turning whitish on belly (sometimes belly tinged yellowish). In hand note short white nasal plumes (in field look for tiny white spot near upper base of bill).
Sim. species: Unique in limited range. In Coastal Cordillera see Rufous-lored Tyrannulet.
Voice: Rather noisy. In Costa Rica a lively arresting *swick* or *squeet*, a breathy emphatic *pisseet* or sharp *swee-swee-swee*[706].
Behavior: A sprightly and active little flycatcher, often chattery as it works through canopy and upper levels of forest, occas. lower along edges and gaps. Hops and flits in foliage, darts up to outermost foliage of tree crown to snap prey from beneath leaves or occas. to take small berries (*Miconia*, *Trema*). Usually in prs. or

family groups, and often with mixed-spp. flocks. Believed to breed Mar–May or Jun in Costa Rica[706].
Status and habitat: In Costa Rica found in forest and forest borders in humid and wet foothill and lower montane forest. Collection locs. in Venez. are in sim. habitat. Apparently relatively common (known from a fair no. of specimens) within its limited range in Venez.

Range: 1650–2000m. Sierra de Perijá in upper Río Negro (Cerros Pejochaina, Yin-taina, and Jurustaco), of w Zulia (*griseocapillus*). Costa Rica and Panama; very locally in Colombia (w slope of e Andes in Santander) and e slope of Andes in Ecuador.

Rufous-lored Tyrannulet   PLATE 46
Phylloscartes flaviventris   Atrapamoscas Cerdoso Vientre
Identification: 4.8″ (12.2cm). Thin bill. *Long, narrow tail held cocked.* Distinctive *"dark-faced"* appearance. *Rufous supraloral line and eyering* continue as short yellowish superciliary; cheeks mixed buffy yellow and black with *prom. black crescent on rear cheeks*; above dark olive, wing coverts blackish with *2 conspic. yellow wing bars*; flight feathers edged greenish yellow; *below bright yellow.*
Sim. species: Often with Venezuelan and Marble-faced bristle-tyrants, but note differences in posture (bristle-tyrants perch upright with tail down) and sallying behavior; neither bristle-tyrant has rufous on face.
Voice: Fussy call, while foraging, a high, thin, and jangling *teep-teep-teep* (1–4 notes) given quickly; also a sputtery, jangling *te'te'skeek!*
Behavior: Prs. or families of 3–4 forage in mid. or upper levels of trees, usually with mixed-spp. flocks. Active and sprightly, flitting from twig to twig, then abruptly darting outward or upward short distances to hover-glean small prey from beneath leaves or from sides of hanging leaves. Also occas. glean from leaves while perched. With rather horizontal posture, long and habitually cocked tail, and restless movements, behavior may bring to mind a gnatcatcher.
Status and habitat: Uncommon to fairly common but inconspic. resident in humid and wet forest (cloud forest) and along forest borders. Most numerous in Coastal Cordillera, esp. around Rancho Grande and Maracay-Choroní Rd.
Range: ENDEMIC. 300–1000m (prob. higher). Mts. of Yaracuy; Coastal Cordillera of w Carabobo (sight, Palmichal) e to Aragua and Distr. Federal; Interior Cordillera in Miranda at Cerro Negro; and sight, PN Guatopo (C. Parrish).
Note 1: Formerly placed in genus *Pogonotriccus* and called Yellow-bellied Bristle-Tyrant, *P. flaviventris*. Pos-

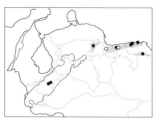

ture, behavior, and morphological characters are consistent with *Phylloscartes*.
Note 2: Specimens reported at 2 localities in Mérida (Mérida; Egido) are prob. in error[178,249].

Pogonotriccus

Bill slender and relatively short (like *Phylloscartes*), but posture more upright; tail not cocked; mid. levels of humid montane forest; forage by upward hover-gleaning; freq. flick up 1 wing ("wing lift"); merged into *Phylloscartes* by some, but morphological characters and behavior suggest retaining this well-defined group in *Pogonotriccus*.

Chapman's Bristle-Tyrant   PLATE 46
Pogonotriccus chapmani   Atrapamoscas Escurridizo
Identification: 4.7″ (12cm). 7–8g. Tepuis. Crown *and* upperparts dull olive, crown slighter darker; *ill-defined whitish eyebrow*; dusky lores; facial area somewhat grizzled gray and white; *black crescentic patch at rear of cheeks*; wing coverts dusky with *2 conspic. buff wing bars*; tertials broadly edged pale buff (form small spots at tip), throat and breast clouded olive yellow turning clear pale yellow on belly. Or above paler, more yellowish olive (*duidae*).
Sim. species: Best marks are conspic. wing bars, eyeline, uniform upperparts (crown and back same color), and distinctive upright posture when perched. Sepia-capped Flycatcher is larger, has proportionately longer bill and tail and dark rufous brown crown. Also see Black-fronted and Slender-footed tyrannulets and Roraiman Flycatcher.
Behavior: Prs. stay fairly close together and follow mixed-spp. flocks through forest understory or mid.-story levels. Sit erect and watch, then flit out short distances, mostly to underside of foliage to capture small arthropods by hover-gleaning momentarily before dropping away to new perch. Freq. lift or flick up 1 wing as do others of genus.
Status and habitat: Resident inside tall humid and wet forest (esp. mossy forest) on slopes of tepuis. Rare and

local on Sierra de Lema, but judging from no. of specimens, much more numerous on many tepuis westward, e.g., Aprada, Chimantá, Parú, Ptari, and Sipapo. **Range:** ENDEMIC. 1000–2000m. S Amazonas on Cerros Duida and de la Neblina and upper Río Ocamo (*duidae*); n Amazonas on Cerros Sipapo and Parú; nw Bolívar on Cerro Tabaro (Río Nicharé), sw Bolívar (Cerro Jaua), Río Paragua drainage (Cerro Guaiquinima), and se Bolívar on tepuis of Gran Sabana from Ptari and Sierra de Lema (sight) s to Sorocopán, Uaipán, Aprada, Chimantá, Acopán, Roraima, and Urutaní (*chapmani*); unrec. on Auyán-tepui. Doubtless in adj. Brazil and Guyana.

Variegated Bristle-Tyrant
Pogonotriccus poecilotis Atrapamoscas Andino
Identification: 4.5″ (11.4cm). 8g. Restricted to Andes. Lower mandible *orange to orange yellow*. *Crown and nape gray*, sides of head and indistinct eyeline somewhat grizzled grayish and white; *conspic. dusky crescentic patch behind eyes*, otherwise upperparts olive, wing coverts dusky, *2 broad conspic. buff wing bars*; flight feathers narrowly edged yellowish green, underparts pale yellow. Or crown blackish gray, contrasting more with back (*pifanoi*).
Sim. species: Bold wing bars and orange on bill are the marks. Marble-faced Bristle-Tyrant has *blackish bill*, *indistinct dull yellowish wing bars*, and occurs mostly at lower els. Also cf. larger Slaty-capped Flycatcher which has "spotted" yellowish bars; and smaller Black-capped Tyrannulet which is much darker and with blackish crown.
Voice: Clear, thin *whee-see* on 1 pitch[404]; in Ecuador a tanager-like *tsit*, often repeated several times, sometimes extended into a *tsit-tsit-tsit-ts-ts-ts-tseweeeét*[541].
Behavior: Single birds or prs. follow mixed-spp. flocks in forest mid. levels or higher and are likely to draw attention to themselves by habit of freq. flicking or lifting up one wing then the other. Perch quite upright and execute short, fast, looping sally-strikes outward and upward to underside of leaves.
Status and habitat: Fairly common resident very locally in humid and wet montane forest (cloud forest). Distrib. in Venez. notably local. Sight recs. amplify its range: near Las Delicias, Táchira, 1800m, 9 Apr 1980 (C. Parrish), and 22 Jan 1996 (Hilty); e slope of Andes in nw Barinas (sw of La Soledad) 10 Apr 1982, and 6 separate dates there in Sep and Nov 1982 (C. Parrish); San Isidro Rd., nw Barinas (numerous recs.).

Range: 1500–2300m. Sierra de Perijá, Zulia (*pifanoi*); w slope of Andes in Mérida; e slope in Táchira (incl. Río Chiquito), nw Barinas (sight), and s Lara at Guárico (*poecilotis*). Colombia s in Andes to s Peru.

Marble-faced Bristle-Tyrant
PLATE 46
Pogonotriccus ophthalmicus Atrapamoscas Carimarmóreo
Identification: 4.7″ (12cm). 11g. Bill short and blackish, base of lower mandible slightly paler. Crown dark gray contrasting with olive back; facial area grizzled grayish white (vaguely yellowish on cheeks), *prom. black crescent enclosing rear of cheeks*; *wing coverts dull dusky brown, 2 dull and rather indistinct wing bars*; inner flight feathers edged greenish yellow, tertials broadly tipped yellowish, upper throat dingy grayish white, rest of underparts yellowish, breast washed olive.
Sim. species: In n mts. most likely confused with Venezuelan Bristle-Tyrant, but note *dull* (not black) wing coverts and *indistinct wing bars*. Larger Slaty-capped Flycatcher has longer, heavier bill, longer, tail, and *spotted* wing bars. Also see Sepia-capped Flycatcher; in Andes, Variegated Bristle-Tyrant and Venezuelan Tyrannulet.
Voice: Contact call, when foraging, a brief *ju-E!* (double-sounding but run together); song a bubbly trill descending slightly then ascending, and beginning or ending (or both) with same doubled notes (above), *ju-E, pit'pe'e'e'e'e'a'a'a'e'e'e'e'e'pit'pit . . ju-E.* Calls and song very sim. to those of Venezuelan Bristle-Tyrant.
Behavior: Prs. or small parties reg. follow mixed-spp. flocks in forest mid. levels or lower, occas. in subcanopy. Sit very upright and scan rapidly and alertly, then make sudden little acrobatic sallies, mostly to underside of foliage for small prey which is typically snapped with only a slight pause in flight. Sometimes surprisingly fearless of humans, and often lift or flick up 1 wing as if sending a semaphore signal. Mossy cup nest ca. 18m up on slender forked branch in Colombia[260].
Status and habitat: Common resident in humid and wet mt. forests; characteristic of mossy premontane forest (cloud forest) of n cordilleras.

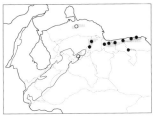

Range: 800–1700m. Mts. of Yaracuy, and Coastal Cordillera in Carabobo, Aragua, and Distr. Federal; Interior Cordillera in s Aragua at Cerro Golfo Triste (*purus*); sightings in mts. of c Falcón and s Lara[60]. Colombia s in Andes to n Bolivia.

Venezuelan Bristle-Tyrant
PLATE 46
Pogonotriccus venezuelanus Atrapamoscas Cerdoso Venezolano
Identification: 4.5″ (11.4cm). 9g. Much like Marble-faced Bristle-Tyrant but fractionally smaller; base of lower mandible *pale and pinkish*. Best told in field by *black wing coverts* (not dull dusky brown) with *distinct (not faint and blurry) yellowish white wing bars*. In di-

rect comparison *throat* and underparts more uniformly yellow.

Sim. species: See Marble-faced Bristle-Tyrant.

Voice: Soft double-noted call *che'dip*; song a fast trill, *ch'e'e'e'e'd'd'd'd'd'e'e'eWEEP!*, descending then ascending. Both vocalizations much like those of Marble-faced Bristle-Tyrant.

Behavior: Sim. to that of Marble-faced Bristle-Tyrant, and the 2 spp. are reg. found together in the same mixed-spp. flocks. Some flocks, however, may have only 1 of the 2 spp.

Status and habitat: Fairly common resident in humid and wet premontane and montane forest (cloud forest) and at forest openings.

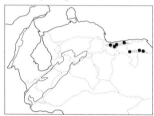

Range: ENDEMIC. 950–1400m. Coastal Cordillera from Carabobo e to Distr. Federal, and Interior Cordillera in s Aragua (Cerro Golfo Triste) and s Miranda (Cerro Negro).

Corythopis

Terrestrial flycatchers of humid lowland forest; long legs; formerly placed, together with gnateaters, in Conopophagidae; side-entrance nest a moss-covered, oven-shaped ball on forest floor.

Ringed Antpipit   PLATE 49
Corythopis torquata   Chupadiente

Identification: 5.5″ (14cm). 14g. Somewhat pipit-like in shape and appearance. Eyes gray. Bill rather long and narrow, black above, pinkish to yellowish below; legs pink. Crown and sides of head gray, otherwise uniform dark brown above; *underparts pure white with bold black necklace across chest more or less coalescing at top to form chest band*; flanks and undertail coverts gray; tail rather short. Imm: chest streaking brown.

Sim. species: As bird walks away in dim light of rain forest floor, distinctive markings may not be readily apparent. Cf. Ovenbird and Northern Waterthrush, both more extensively streaked below. Ovenbird has prom. eyering and orange crown stripe. Also cf. Spotted, Dotbacked, and Banded antbirds and larger Spotted Antpitta.

Voice: Song, often hd. repeatedly for short period at dawn, a shrill, whistled *peeur-prayer* uttered quickly; 1st note descends, 2d rebounds. There is some geographical variation in song. Singing may be somewhat seasonal.

Behavior: Habit of walking on gd., horizontal posture, and freq. teetering and head bobbing might bring to mind a pipit, hence this sp.'s name. It is otherwise utterly different, being confined to inside of forest. Often first noted by freq. bill-snapping (note rather whimsi-

cal Spanish name), esp. when disturbed and when foraging. Walks with springy gait on gd., or perches on low branches or fallen logs, and sallies or makes wing-assisted leaps upward to underside of low foliage for arthropods. Does not follow mixed-spp. flocks and is rarely around army ant swarms. Forages over fairly large territories, and at least at dawn, calls reg. as it moves considerable distances through forest. Not esp. shy, but habit of remaining on the move can make it difficult to watch. Mossy, covered (ovenlike) nest on forest floor; 2 pinkish eggs with darker mottling[449].

Status and habitat: Uncommon to fairly common resident in humid terra firme forest in lowlands and lower slopes of tepuis; occas. in low-lying areas subject to brief inundation. Possibly somewhat local.

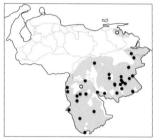

Range: To 1400m. Throughout Amazonas and Bolívar (*anthoides*); sighting (presum. this sp.) n to Caño Colorado, Monagas[297]. Se Colombia to n Bolivia, Amaz. Brazil, and the Guianas.

Myiornis

Tiny; virtually tail-less; large head and bill; trashy hanging nest with tiny porch and entrance on side; syringeal anatomy close to *Hemitriccus*[323].

Short-tailed Pygmy-Tyrant   PLATE 46
Myiornis ecaudatus   Pico Chato Pigmeo Descolado

Identification: 2.7″ (6.9cm). 4.2g. *Smallest* passerine. Tail (18mm) barely extends beyond coverts; bill unusually long for size of bird. Head gray with blackish lores and *white supraloral line and eyering* ("spectacles"); back bright olive green, wings and tail black (no bars), inner flight feathers edged yellow, *underparts white* smudged olive on chest and sides; belly tinged yellow.

Sim. species: Almost a miniature of Slate-headed Tody-Flycatcher, but the two are not likely to be confused because of habitat differences. Slate-headed is larger, longer-tailed, has prom. yellow wing bars, and occurs low in thickets. In most cases, the pygmy-tyrant is much more likely to be mistaken for a large beetle or insect, esp. in flight, than another bird.

Voice: Song a high-pitched ser. of up to ca. 15 *c'r'e'eek* notes, at first hesitant, then accelerating and descending slightly; also *cre'e'e'e*, *k'e'e'e'e*, 2d note lower, over and over, or either separately, all much like a cricket or small frog. Unlikely to be recognized as a bird vocalization. Chirplike squeaks sim. to that of a well-rosined bird squeaker. Also a soft, purring ser. of trilled notes, much lower in pitch.

Behavior: Difficult to see because of small size, easily overlooked voice, and abrupt movements which are hard to follow. Sits quietly, mostly in mid.-forest levels, for varying periods of time, then darts out to snap off an insect from underside of foliage and continue a short distance to new perch, or more often takes prey by extended hover-gleaning from beneath leaves. May sally to air in little weaving circles, then looks much like a large bee. Movements overall are mechanical and insectlike. Nest rather large (for size of bird); moss and fiber ball with side entrance; suspended from twig 1–8m up; 2 white eggs with brownish to cinnamon spots in wreath at larger end and scattered else-where[391,790]; early Jan nest, nw Amazonas.
Status and habitat: Fairly common but easily over-looked resident in tall humid forest, occas. light open woodland, around treefalls, and tall trees in clearings. Recs. spotty n of Orinoco.

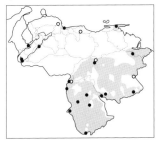

Range: To 500m n of Orinoco; to 900m s of Orinoco. W slope of Andes in Mérida, e slope n to Barinas (Barini-tas); se Falcón (sight, Cerro Misión[60]); n base of Coastal Cordillera in Carabobo, Interior Cordillera in Miranda at PN Guatopo (sight, 20 Feb 1983—C. Par-rish); se Sucre; ne Monagas (sight[58]); Delta Amacuro[343]; and generally in Amazonas and Bolívar (*miserabilis*). Costa Rica to n Bolivia, Amaz. Brazil (mostly absent n of the Amazon), and the Guianas. Trinidad.

Lophotriccus

Small size; most spp. with shaggy crest of elongated feathers that usually lies flat; some have unusually loud calls for size of bird.

Scale-crested Pygmy-Tyrant   PLATE 46
Lophotriccus pileatus   Pico Chato de Penacho
Identification: 4″ (10.2cm). 7.4g. Only in n mts. Tiny with *yellow eyes and broad ample crest of rufous-edged black feathers*; crest can be raised and spread fanlike, imparting comically fierce appearance. Crest usually laid flat, but visible as it normally projects beyond rear-crown. Upperparts olive green, wings and tail dusky, wings with 2 weakly indicated yellowish bars; flight feathers and tail edged olive, *underparts yellowish white with blurry olive gray streaking on throat and breast.*
Sim. species: Confusion likely only with larger, un-crested Olive-striped Flycatcher.
Voice: Surprisingly loud for so small a bird, a metallic ser. of *preet* or *pic* or *trik* notes, sometimes accelerating or rising in pitch; or sometimes a quick ser. that slows.

Also a soft *purrrr*. Vocalizes at intervals throughout day.
Behavior: A tiny flycatcher with fierce countenance, but inconspic. and rarely noted unless calling, and even then can be difficult to spot. Rather solitary; sits from ca. eye level to lower mid. story, often on fairly open twigs, scans about, then abruptly darts out or up in sally-strike to foliage; occas. hover-gleans from fo-liage. Most active when a mixed-spp. flock is nearby. ♂♂ may gather in loosely assoc. leks ("exploded" leks) where they advertise themselves by calling. Pen-sile globular nest with side entrance, visor, and long, thin, dangling tail; attached to twig a few meters up; attended by ♀[644].
Status and habitat: Fairly common to common resi-dent in humid and wet forest and tall older second growth. Foothills and lower slopes.

Range: Mostly 450–2000m (rarely to nearly sea level). Sierra de Perijá, Zulia, Andes from Táchira to cerros of nw Lara, Yaracuy, c and e Falcón (sightings, Sierra de San Luis), and n cordilleras from e Carabobo to Distr. Federal, s Aragua, and s Miranda; mts. of nw Anzoáte-gui (*santaeluciae*). Costa Rica s in mts. to s Peru.
Note: Double-banded Pygmy-Tyrant (*L. vitiosus*) of se Colombia, n Brazil, and the Guianas, could occur in s or e Venez. Much like Scale-crested Pygmy-Tyrant but crown feathers gray (not rufous).

Helmeted Pygmy-Tyrant   PLATE 46
Lophotriccus galeatus   Atrapamoscas Pigmeo de Casquete
Identification: 4″ (10.2cm). 6.6g. Tiny. Eyes yellowish to orangish white; basal half of lower mandible pink. Above olive with narrow and *elongated crest feathers black edged olive*, wings and tail dusky, the feathers narrowly edged olive, 2 faint olive wing bars; *below whitish narrowly and rather indistinctly streaked gray.*
Sim. species: Much like White-eyed Tody-Tyrant which is larger, has bold yellow wing bars, olive crown, and yellowish underparts (Helmeted shows virtually no yel-low below). Also see Snethlage's and Pearly-vented tody-tyrants.
Voice: Recalls that of Scale-crested Pygmy-Tyrant, a loud ser. of 4–10 *pik* or *trik* notes, or often in longer irreg. sequence, sometimes accelerating or rising slightly in pitch; also 2–3 quick *pik* notes followed by short, rising, rattlelike notes. Calls irreg. throughout day but sometimes only at long intervals.
Behavior: Hd. far more than seen. Solitary birds (♂♂?) reg. call from mid. levels inside or near edge of forest and are prob. members of dispersed leks. For-

age by darting up short distances to strike at underside of foliage, and snatch prey without hovering, mostly in mid.-forest levels or slightly lower. Occas. with mixed-spp. flocks. Nest a pendent pouch suspended from small twig; visored entrance low on side; 2–3 white eggs[253].

Status and habitat: Common and widespread resident in terra firme and várzea forest in lowlands and foothills of tepuis; most numerous in slighter drier, scrubbier forest of white sandy soil regions.

Range: To 1100m. E Sucre, ne Monagas, Delta Amacuro, and generally in Amazonas and Bolívar. Se Colombia to the Guianas and ne Brazil.
Note: Previously placed in genus *Lophotriccus*[467]; or *Colopteryx* because of narrow crest feathers and vestigial outer 3 primaries[400,403].

Pale-eyed Pygmy-Tyrant   PLATE 46
Lophotriccus pilaris   Atrapamoscas Pigmeo Ojiblanco
Identification: 3.8″ (9.7cm). 6g. Small, dingy flycatcher characteristic of drier habitats. *Eyes yellowish white* (dark—juv.). Bill flat (but not wide), basal half to two-thirds pinkish. *Upperparts entirely olive green incl.* crown; wing and tail feathers dusky edged yellowish olive, *2 dull yellowish white wings bars*; below dull white *obscurely streaked and smudged gray on throat and upper breast* (amt. of streaking varies). In hand peculiar wing diagnostic: outer 4 primaries very short and narrow. Or sim. but crown gray, lores and ocular area tinged rufous (*griseiceps*).
Sim. species: Easily confused with slightly larger Pearly-vented Tody-Tyrant which has longer bill and *brownish* (not olive) upperparts; also note different vocalizations, up close orangish (not whitish) eyes. Shares dry woodlands with several other superficially sim. tyrannulets, i.e., see Slender-billed and Pale-tipped inezias and Yellow-olive Flatbill; also Southern Beardless-Tyrannulet.
Voice: Dry *tic* notes and rapid nasal trills (sings through its "nose") of varying length; notes and trills often combined, e.g., *tic-ttttttttttt*. Some calls weak, others surprisingly loud for size of bird.
Behavior: Active but rather inconspic., seen singly or in prs. and sometimes with mixed-spp. flocks containing greenlets and other small flycatchers. Flits out or up short distances in sally-strikes to foliage, or more often to hover-glean momentarily beneath leaves, usually from about eye level to subcanopy hts. Nest (Jun–Jul in llanos) often very close to gd.; a suspended, woven fiber bag with little porch covering small side entrance.

Status and habitat: Common resident in arid scrub, dry and moist (deciduous and semideciduous) forest, light woodland, and gallery forest.

Range: To ca. 1000m n of Orinoco (to 1700m in Sierra de Perijá); to 300m s of Orinoco. Nw Zulia s across Maracaibo Basin to nw Táchira (*pilaris*); dry areas throughout rest of Venez. n of Orinoco (*venezuelensis*); n Amazonas s to Pto. Ayacucho, s Guárico, and across n Bolívar to lower Río Paragua (La Paragua) and Tumeremo; Delta Amacuro (*griseiceps*). W Panama to Guyana.
Note: Often placed in genus *Atalotriccus*[403,467].

Hemitriccus

Small, mostly nondescript flycatchers widespread in Neotropics; bills fairly long, flat, and narrow (not as long and flat as in *Todirostrum*); eyes usually white, yellow, or orange; taxonomically confusing group; now incls. several genera formerly considered separate, i.e., *Idioptilon*, *Snethlagea*[757]; ♂♂ larger than ♀♀.

Pearly-vented Tody-Tyrant   PLATE 46
Hemitriccus margaritaceiventer   Pico Chato Vientre Perla
Identification: 4.4″ (11.2cm). 8.4g. Small, drab tody-tyrant of dry or scrubby habitats. Bill fairly long; *eyes "bloodshot" orange to pale yellow* (duller—imm.). *Above plain grayish brown*; lores and inconspic. eyering dull whitish, wings and tail dusky with yellowish olive edgings; 2 fairly prom. buff white wing bars; underparts dull white with *some indistinct blurry gray brown streaking on throat and breast*; belly and flanks pearly to silky white, the flank feathers long. Or s of Orinoco, *darker* and rather different: above sooty brown, sometimes with faint olive tinge; wing bars obscure, lower underparts ochraceous buff, bill reddish (*duidae*). Or like *duidae* but paler (*breweri*, *auyantepui*).
Sim. species: Most likely confused with Pale-eyed Pygmy-Tyrant which is *always olive above* (not brownish) and in e has grayish crown; also note Pale-eyed's smaller size, *shorter* bill, pale eyes, yellowish tinge (usually) to belly, and different vocalizations.
Voice: N of Orinoco a brief *pik* or *tuk* and *sput-spik!*; a short, rising *tuk-tuk-tu-tu're'et*; in Gran Sabana a thin, fast, and downscale *stick, tic-tic-ter'r'r'r'r'r'r'r'r'r'r* or sim. variation, and single *stick* and *tuk* notes.
Behavior: Inconspic. but usually not too difficult to see. Occurs alone or in scattered prs. that hop deliberately among small twigs and foliage and pause every few sec to look upward at leaves and twigs. Perch-

glean, lunge out, flit up to sally-strike at leaves, and occas. sally short distances to air. Forage from near gd. to ca. 6m up (canopy of high bushes) but mostly eye level or lower. Nest a globular bag with side entrance near top; suspended from drooping twig; 1–3 dull white eggs sparsely speckled rusty at large end[750]. Breeds May–Jun in ne Colombia[260].

Status and habitat: Fairly common resident in thickets, arid scrub, and dry deciduous woodland, occas. moist woodland borders. Dense heathlike scrub at n end of Gran Sabana.

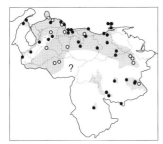

Range: To 1000m n of Orinoco; ca. 1000–2000m s of Orinoco. Nw Zulia from Goajira Pen. s to nw Táchira, Trujillo, Falcón, Lara, Yaracuy, n cordilleras from Carabobo to Sucre, and inland generally e of Andes and n of Orinoco, and Isla Margarita (*impiger*); Amazonas on Cerro Duida (*duidae*); Cerro Jaua (*breweri*); se Bolívar from Cerro Guaiquinima and Auyán-tepui s to Sierra de Lema (many sight recs.) and Cerros Sororopán and Urutaní (*auyantepui*). N and c Colombia; s of Amazon Basin from s Peru, e Bolivia, and n Argentina to e Brazil.

Note 1: Formerly placed in genus *Idioptilon*.
Note 2: Birds s of Orinoco perhaps a separate sp.
Note 3: Pelzeln's Tody-Tyrant (*H. inornatus*) of Manaus area n to nw Brazil (Rio Icana, upper Rio Negro) may occur ins Venez. Very like Pearly-vented Tody-Tyrant but slightly smaller with whitish (not yellowish to buff) wing bars, whitish to pale gray eyes, and more brownish upperparts. Best told by low-pitched, insectlike song, *tid-dip, tid, te'de*, given quickly, with scraping quality; canopy of stunted or tall woodland in white sandy soil regions (K. Zimmer).

White-eyed Tody-Tyrant

Hemitriccus zosterops   Pico Chato Ojiblanco
Identification: 4.4″ (11.2cm). 7.9g. Eyes yellowish to gray to reddish brown (not white); base of lower mandible pale, tip black. *Above olive green* (sometimes with vague whitish supraloral), *2 yellowish wing bars;* flight feathers edged olive yellow, *throat grayish white finely streaked olive,* breast tinged yellowish and narrowly and indistinctly streaked olive, lower underparts clear pale yellow; tail slightly longer (46–51mm) than in others of genus.

Sim. species: A plain-looking, "olive-colored" little flycatcher. Note streaky appearance of underparts, habitat, and voice. Generally yellower below than others with which it might be confused. Cf. Helmeted Pygmy-Tyrant, Pearly-vented Tody-Tyrant, Forest Elaenia, and very rare Snethlage's Tody-Tyrant. Others are unstreaked below

(i.e., Mouse-colored Tyrannulet and Southern Beardless-Tyrannulet). Also cf. *Tolmomyias* flatbills.
Voice: In se Ecuador a dry insectlike *tic* or longer ser.; *tic, tic, tic, tidididididt,* accelerating into trill; often repeated at intervals throughout day[545].
Behavior: Usually seen singly, perched ca. 4–10m up, often on fairly open twigs, but can be difficult to spot as sometimes not very active. Occas. with mixed-spp. flocks but much more often independent of them. Sally-strikes short distances outward and upward, sometimes with slight pause as prey is snapped from beneath leaves, but usually does not hover-glean.
Status and habitat: Resident inside tall humid terra firme and transitional or low-lying forest in lowlands.

Range: To 200m. C Amazonas from Cerro Yapacana, Cerro Duida, and Yavita-Pimichín s to Cerro de la Neblina (*zosterops*). Se Colombia, e Ecuador, n Peru, n Brazil n of the Amazon (absent from most of Rio Negro and Rio Branco region), and the Guianas.
Note: Does not incl. birds of s of the Amazon[545].

Snethlage's Tody-Tyrant

Hemitriccus minor   Pico Chato de Cola Angosta
Identification: 4″ (10.2cm). 7g. Eyes buff white. Bill unusually flattened, but culmen also slightly arched or decurved (lower mandible thick near tip). Above olive green (no whitish supraloral), *2 yellowish wing bars;* flight feathers edged greenish yellow; underparts incl. *throat pale yellowish, throat, breast, and flanks finely and indistinctly streaked grayish olive,* only center of belly unstreaked. Some individuals are mainly white (not yellow) below. In hand, bill wider at base and shorter than that of White-eyed Tody-Tyrant; nostrils round and conspic. (narrow, slitlike, and parallel to culmen in White-eyed); crown feathers longer than in other *Hemitriccus*[545]. *Tail rather short* (28–36mm).
Sim. species: Closely resembles White-eyed Tody-Tyrant (habitat differs). Presently misunderstood; field marks (i.e., eye color, bill shape, nostrils, absence of supraloral mark, more uniform underparts) may be subject to revision. If specimens are correctly identified, tail length differences (Snethlage's has shorter tail) may prove definitive. Also cf. Pearly-vented Tody-Tyrant which is brownish above (esp. near Cerro Duidae), Helmeted Pygmy-Tyrant which is crested, and Pale-eyed Pygmy-Tyrant which prob. does not overlap in range.
Voice: Song in Rio Negro, Brazil, a ser. of 3 or more gravelly trills, with or without introductory *pik* notes, and with gaps between trills about as long as trills (K. Zimmer).

Behavior: Poorly known. In Brazil found singly or in prs., mostly 3–8m up and independent of mixed-spp. flocks. Inconspic. and seldom noted unless calling[545]. **Status and habitat:** Known from 4 specimens: a ♂ on 2 Feb 1946 from Río Padauiri, Amazonas; a ♀ on 6 May 1947 at Pto. Yapacana; a ♀ on 21 Feb 1972 at San Carlos de Río Negro; and a ♀ on 2 Apr 1983 at Río Cunucunuma (near Cerro Duida), Amazonas. All specimens need reconfirmation in light of recent taxonomic work. In Brazil found in vine tangles around light gaps and along edges of humid forest.

Range: To 220m. C and s Amazonas from Pto. Yapacana s to vicinity of Cerro Duida, Río Casiquiare, and San Carlos de Río Negro (*pallens*). C Amaz. Brazil.
Note 1: Formerly placed in genus *Snethlagea*.
Note 2: Boat-billed Tody-Tyrant (*H. josephinae*) of the Guianas (w to Supenaam River, Guyana) may occur in e Venez. Eyes *reddish brown*. Above olive (*no trace of bars or edgings*), narrow lores and postocular area gray, underparts pale yellow, throat grayish white. Bill not unusually large or heavy for genus. Vine tangles, esp. at gaps and edges, mid. levels in humid forest. Dry, descending *pic-pic-pic*[160].

Black-throated Tody-Tyrant   PLATE 46
Hemitriccus granadensis   Pico Chato Gargantinegro
Identification: 4″ (10.2cm). 7.9g. Looks "bare faced." Eyes reddish brown. *Lores and large, circular orbital area buff to buffy white,* crown and upperparts bright olive green, wings and tail dusky (no bars) edged olive green, *upper throat, sides of neck, and forepart of cheeks black,* lower throat and breast light gray becoming silky white on belly; flanks tinged yellowish. Or sim. but ocular area white; eyes (always?) yellowish white to orange (*intensus*).
Sim. species: Easily told by large, "bald-looking" face and black across throat and neck. Note lack of wing bars and habitat.
Voice: In Colombia a short, gravelly stutter, *dut't't dut't't*; a froglike *tip-buuuuu* and sharp *pik, peet peet*; also a low wing-whirring in flight as in others of genus.
Behavior: Rather quiet and inactive much of time. Sits ca. 1–8m up, occas. higher, and not shy but unobtrusive and easily overlooked. Vocalizes and forages most actively when mixed-spp. flocks pass nearby. Stays mostly in thick vegetation, hops and peers with deliberate movements, then darts out or up in sally-strike to foliage to snap small arthropod prey, and without pause continues to new perch.
Status and habitat: Resident around light gaps and in shrubby borders of humid and wet forest, and in

shrubby second-growth woodland. Known from many specimens in Sierra de Perijá; locally fairly common in s Táchira where known from nearly 20 specimens from Río Chiquito and Tamá region. Only a few specimens from Coastal Cordillera, mostly from Distr. Federal at El Junquito and No León.

Range: 1800–3000m. Sierra de Perijá, Zulia; s Táchira in Río Chiquito (*intensus*); s Táchira on Páramo de Tamá (*andinus*); Coastal Cordillera in Distr. Federal (*federalis*); sight, Pico Guacamaya, Aragua, ca. 1800m, 2 Dec 1978 (C. Parrish). Locally in mts. from Colombia to n Bolivia.

Black-chested Tyrant   PLATE 46
Taeniotriccus andrei   Atrapamoscas Pechinegro
Identification: 4.7″ (12cm). 9.4g. Rare. Plumage unmistakable. Eyes dark. ♂: *forehead, sides of head, and throat rufous chestnut* (concealed rufous band across nape), otherwise *black above* incl. *long bushy crest* (feathers usually laid flat over crown); *bold slash of yellow across base of flight feathers* continues rearward as yellow stripe down tertials (forms inverted L of yellow); *broad black chest band*; belly gray tinged yellow. ♀: sim. but back and tail olive brown, chest band olive gray.
Status and habitat: Poorly known in life. Most Venez. specimens are from swampy mangrove- and palm-dominated tidal forests far out in Orinoco Delta (9 from Misión Araguaimujo). In Brazil, on e bank of lower Rio Xingú, occas. observed in bamboo-dominated understory in terra firme forest, and rank understory of *Cecropia*-dominated second growth near river[545]. There is a publ. rec. of 1 seen 13 Mar 1995, Caño Colorado, Monagas, 7–8m up in bamboo mixed with second growth in flooded forest[296].

Range: To 350m. N Bolívar in lower and mid. Río Caura (La Prisión; Salto Pará), upper Río Paragua (Río Carún), and Delta Amacuro (Misión Araguaimujo; Isla del Tigre) (*andrei*); possibly e Monagas (sight). Ne Brazil (ne Amazonas; n Roraima) and e Brazil (s of the Amazon).
Note: Has been placed in genus *Poecilotriccus*[323,467,757].

Poecilotriccus

Plump; bill narrower and slightly shorter (most spp.) than in *Todirostrum*; short, narrow tail not cocked; thicket dwellers; mostly weak 1- to 2-note calls and low-pitched trills; incls. some spp. formerly placed in *Todirostrum*[323].

Ruddy Tody-Flycatcher PLATE 46
Poecilotriccus russatum Titirijí Bermejo
Identification: 4″ (10.2cm). Bill shorter (10–11mm) than in others of genus; eyes dark. *Forehead and facial area rich dark cinnamon rufous*, slightly paler on throat and chest; crown *contrasting sooty black* (gray in ♀), upperparts dark olive, *2 cinnamon rufous wing bars*; inner remiges edged greenish yellow, lower underparts gray, flanks tinged brown.
Sim. species: Unique in limited range. Note variation in intensity of color on foreparts (some birds notably dark).
Voice: Call a weak, dull *tsuk, sick, tr'r'r'r'r'r'r'r*, sometimes followed by 2–3 more short bursts of trills; or any of the 3 above vocalizations separately. When disturbed other variations, i.e., *chip-t'b'r'r'r'r, squeeeeo, t'b'r'r* with squeak in middle. Overall, songs recall those of Slate-headed Tody-Flycatcher.
Behavior: Prs. lead quiet and reclusive lives in dense thickets. In general behave much like Slate-headed Tody-Flycatcher but can be even more skulking. Stay mostly 0.1–2m up and are inconspic. and hard to see, but with patience these charming little birds can be enticed into view although they are not apt to remain long in 1 place. Usually not with mixed-spp. flocks.
Status and habitat: Resident in dense thickets at borders of humid and wet (mossy) forest and older second growth. Fairly common (easily overlooked) at edges of stunted, melastome-dominated woodland on Sierra de Lema.

Range: 1300–2500m. Se Bolívar on tepuis of Gran Sabana from Auyán-tepui and Sierra de Lema (sightings) s to Cerros Aprada, Chimantá, Ptari, Sororopán, Uei, Roraima, and Cuquenán. Brazil (Uei-tepui); Guyana.
Note 1: Formerly placed in genus *Todirostrum*[403]; now transferred to *Poecilotriccus*[323].
Note 2: Rusty-fronted Tody-Flycatcher (*P. latirostre*), widespread across w and c Amazonia (as close as Mitú, in se Colombia), may occur in s Amazonas. *Forehead and face rusty buff*, crown brownish gray, upperparts olive; 2 ochraceous wing bars; below grayish white. Skulks in dense thickets in clearings and at forest edge.

Slate-headed Tody-Flycatcher PLATE 46
Poecilotriccus sylvia Titirijí Cabecicenizo
Identification: 4″ (10.2cm). 7.2g. Bill fairly long; eyes usually dark (occas. gray, yellow, or whitish). Crown and nape gray with *conspic. white supraloral line and broken eyering* ("spectacles"), back olive, wings blackish, *2 bold yellow wing bars*; inner flight feathers edged yellow, upper throat whitish, *lower throat and breast gray* becoming white on belly.
Sim. species: See Short-tailed and Pale-eyed pygmy-tyrants, neither of which inhabits thickets.
Voice: Advertisement calls incl. a soft, gravelly *trup* or *trup grrrr*, varying to *tik trrrrrr;* nasal froglike *grrrrrr* also is given singly. When excited *tíc-a-turrr*. All vocalizations insect- or froglike.
Behavior: Easily overlooked except for soft calls. Prs. stay well concealed and usually fairly close together inside thickets and shrubbery and are prob. always audible (if not visible) to each other. Hop around mostly 0.1–4m up, peer at foliage, and flit upward in sally-strike to snap prey beneath leaves with scarcely a pause and continue on to new perch. Not shy but may require patience to see. Pendent, pear-shaped nest with side entrance sim. to that of Common Tody-Flycatcher; low in thicket; 2 creamy white eggs dotted and spotted brown at larger end[115].
Status and habitat: Locally common resident in dense thickets along forest borders, shrubby young second growth, and overgrown roadsides and pastures. Dry to humid regions (commoner in moist and humid regions); prob. throughout n of Orinoco but recs. spotty.

Range: To 1000m. Maracaibo Basin of Zulia, nw Táchira n to w Trujillo; Lara, e Falcón, and generally e of Andes to Aragua and w Guárico; se Sucre (sight), ne Monagas (Caño Colorado[60]), and Delta Amacuro at Piacoa[60]; n Amazonas (sight, Junglaven) and n Bolívar from La Urbana and Caicara e to upper Río Cuyuní at Venamo (*griseolum*). S Mexico to the Guianas and spottily to ne Brazil.
Note: Formerly placed in *Todirostrum*. Taxonomy follows Lanyon[323].

Rufous-crowned Tody-Flycatcher PLATE 46
Poecilotriccus ruficeps Pico Chato de Corona Rufa
Identification: 3.8″ (9.7cm). 6.6g. Plump with large puffy head; bill long and narrow except at base; large, dark eyes. *Crown rufous bordered behind by narrow black line and then by broad gray nape;* supraloral spot and cheeks buff, *cheeks bordered behind and below by black which extends forward, forming large black patch on each side of throat;* otherwise bright olive above;

wings and tail blackish, wings with 2 buffy yellow wing bars and bright yellow edgings; chin somewhat smudged rufous, lower throat and chest buffy white bordered below by band of olive mixed black, breast and belly yellow.

Sim. species: Bold head pattern unmistakable. Cf. White-throated Spadebill and rare Yellow-breasted Spadebill.

Voice: Low-pitched, flat *chak, chak*; gravelly *stick' di'dik*; abrupt *pip'pmrrr* (like shuffling deck of cards); stuttering *pa'treer-pît-pît-pît* or sim. variation; and thin trill. When excited stuttering trills are mixed with squeaking *squEEeo* notes and prs. may countercall in loose duet. Vocalizations soft, easily overlooked, and usually given only at well-spaced intervals.

Behavior: Another reclusive little flycatcher that will seldom be noted except for its occas. weak calls uttered from concealment. Live in quiet prs. or families that stay close together and mostly out of sight 0.5–3m up in thickets and low shrubbery. Dart out or upward in sally-strike (without stopping) to snap small prey from underside of foliage and continue to new perch. Movements abrupt and difficult to follow, although birds occas. perch briefly in semiopen at edge of foliage.

Status and habitat: Resident in shrubby roadside thickets, borders of wet montane forest, and bushy highland pastures. Known from only 3 main locs., specimens from s Táchira and n Mérida (N. K. Johnson); and sight recs. from PN Guaramacal, Trujillo, by numerous observers[60,259].

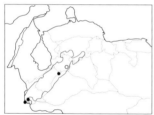

Range: 1800–2900m. S Táchira in Río Chiquito and Páramo de Tamá (*ruficeps*); n Mérida at La Cuchilla and in e Trujillo (*melanomystax*). Colombia s in Andes to extreme n Peru.

Todirostrum

Large, diverse genus comprising 2 distinct assemblages: (1) inhabitants of gardens, parks, and low to mid.-level shrubbery in edge situations and (2) forest-edge inhabitants in canopy or subcanopy; both groups with bright, high-pitched, piping notes. Many spp. colorful; *narrow cocked tails* (shortest in canopy spp.); long legs; eye color, in some spp., variable and as yet not correlated with age, sex, or geographical loc.; unusual bill long, flat, and rather wide, broadest in canopy-dwelling Black-headed and Painted todyflycatchers; longest and narrowest in desert-dwelling Maracaibo Tody-Flycatcher. Formerly incl. several spp. now placed in *Poecilotriccus*.

Spotted Tody-Flycatcher   PLATE 46
Todirostrum maculatum   Titirijí Manchado

Identification: 4″ (10.2cm). 7.2g. Eyes usually *yellowish orange* (occas. gray or brown). Crown sooty black with white loral line and a few whitish central crown streaks (often concealed), hindcrown gray; upperparts olive, wings dusky, *wing coverts and flight feathers heavily edged yellow* (but wing bars obscure or ill defined), throat white finely streaked and dotted black, rest of underparts yellow, breast and sides densely streaked black.

Sim. species: Note restricted range in Venez. See canopy-dwelling Painted Tody-Flycatcher.

Voice: Advertisement song a loud (esp. for so small a bird), bright ser. of up to 12 *PIP!* or *PEK!* notes (ca. 2/ sec), often answered immediately by mate in slightly out-of-sync duet.

Behavior: Found in loosely assoc. prs. that range from eye level to fairly high in trees. Sprightly in behavior and often quite bold and fearless, but overall seem less animated than Common Tody-Flycatcher. Usually not too difficult to see as they occur in both fairly dense vegetation and well-lit open parts of trees. Not with mixed-spp. flocks. Trashy-looking, pensile nest with hanging tail and side entrance hole is sim. to others of genus; often placed near wasp's nest; 2 white eggs with reddish dots[253].

Status and habitat: Resident in shrubby second growth along rivers, and borders of mangroves. Most often in mangroves in Venez. Also young river-edge or river-isl. vegetation and young *Cecropia* mixed with grass and openings.

Range: To 100m. E Sucre, ne Monagas, and Delta Amacuro (*amacurense*)[166]. Se Colombia to n Bolivia, Amazon Basin, and the Guianas.

Common Tody-Flycatcher   PLATE 46
Todirostrum cinereum   Titirijí Lomicenizo

Identification: 4″ (10.2cm). 6.8g. Commonest *Todirostrum* in Venez. Eyes usually yellowish to white (dark in younger birds?). *Forecrown and sides of head black shading to gray on hindcrown and back*; wings black with prom. yellow edgings on wing coverts and flight feathers; tail rounded (strongly graduated) and black, outer feathers narrowly tipped white, *underparts entirely bright yellow*.

Sim. species: See Maracaibo Tody-Flycatcher. Black-headed Tody-Flycatcher has white throat and all-black head.

Voice: Often quite vocal. A single bright *peept!*, sometimes doubled or trebled or in long ser. of up to 12, e.g., *p-peept! p-peept!* . . . , surprisingly loud for so small a bird. A trilled *te'e'e'e'e't!*, singly or several in longer ser., recalls that of Tropical Kingbird.

Behavior: A droll little bird with almost perpetually cocked, wagging tail. Hops and flutters about, pauses to look up, draws a bead on small insects, then darts up lightening quick in a sally-strike to snap them from beneath leaves. Also occas. sallies briefly to air. Usually in prs. from about eye level upward to canopy of smaller trees (not in canopy of tall trees). In common display hitches sideways along or up a branch with tail slightly spread, cocked straight up over back, and shivering (J. Fitzpatrick). Nest a trashy little bag suspended from twig; side entrance and long dangling tail complete disguise; usually low (1–5m up, occas. much higher); 2–3 white eggs; breeding May–Oct (Jun peak), w Apure and w Guárico[137,734]; 2 nests Jan–late Mar, w Apure; 2 late Mar, ne Bolívar.

Status and habitat: Common resident in all kinds of shrubby areas, thickets, gardens, cultivated areas, overgrown clearings, and forest edges. Ranges into dry (but not arid) regions; increasingly uncommon and local s of Orinoco and absent from heavily forested regions of s Amazonas. Replaced in desert scrub of c Falcón by Maracaibo Tody-Flycatcher.

Maracaibo Tody-Flycatcher

Range: To 1650m n of Orinoco; to 1300m s of Orinoco. Generally n of Orinoco except arid nw Zulia e to c Falcón; n Amazonas s to Río Ventuari and San Fernando de Atabapo; Bolívar s to lower Río Caura, lower Río Paragua (La Paragua), and s end of Gran Sabana at Santa Elena de Uairén (*cinereum*). S Mexico to nw Peru, n Bolivia, and se Brazil (absent from most of Amazonia).

Maracaibo Tody-Flycatcher   Illus. above
Todirostrum viridanum   Titirijí de Maracaibo

Identification: 4″ (10.2cm). Pale, desert-dwelling ally of Common Tody-Flycatcher. *Bill long*, black above, pinkish below; eyes dark (occas. yellowish white; age?). Forecrown black turning light gray on hindcrown, back *pale olive*; *narrow supraloral mark and semiconcealed coronal mark yellowish white*, wings blackish *broadly edged buffy yellow*, inner flight feathers broadly edged dull whitish, blackish tail notably short with rounded corners is tipped *and edged* white (unlike Common Tody-Flycatcher, tail not strongly graduated; outer feathers only 4 mm shorter than central ones); underparts pale yellow, flanks tinged ochraceous.

Sim. species: Easily confused with Common Tody-Flycatcher but usually shows white markings above lores and on crown, has broader wing edgings, is paler and "faded looking" above and below, and has longer bill (14–16 vs. 12–13mm) and shorter, more squarish tail (ca. 27–33mm vs. 34–38mm) *with white edges*.

Voice: Advertising song ca. 6 sharp *seek!* notes in a ser.; much like Black-headed Tody-Flycatcher.

Behavior: Generally sim. to that of Common Tody-Flycatcher. Occurs in prs. at about eye level or a little higher in scrub vegetation. Usually rather easy to see.

Status and habitat: Fairly common resident in arid desert scrub and low thorny vegetation, esp. around Coro; commonest in plant associations of *Acacia, Cercidium, Cardon,* and *Opuntia*. Replaced (with minor overlap) by Common Tody-Flycatcher in dry to moist regions of slightly higher rainfall and more mesic vegetation.

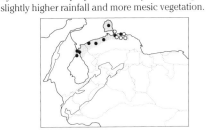

Range: ENDEMIC. To 200m. Coastal Zulia from near Maracaibo e through n Falcón to vicinity of Piritú; sight e to Tocoporo.

Note: Previously considered a subsp. of Common Tody-Flycatcher[403] or a separate sp.[167,545].

Painted Tody-Flycatcher   PLATE 46
Todirostrum pictum   Titirijí Pintado
Identification: 4″ (10.2cm). 6.8g. Eyes dark (always?); bill long. Much like previous sp. *but lacks broad golden yellow postocular stripe. Head black with short white supraloral mark,* broad white malar, and black moustache (submalar); back bright olive yellow, wings and tail blackish, wings with 2 yellow wing bars and crisp yellow edgings; *upper throat white,* otherwise yellow below with *broad necklace of black streaks on sides of throat, across chest, and down sides of breast.*
Sim. species: See Common Tody-Flycatcher.
Voice: Call a double-sounding *chevik.* Song a ser. of 8–12 bright, emphatic *peek!* notes, ca. 2/sec, sometimes accelerated slightly when excited. Vocalizations piercing and surprisingly loud for so small a bird.
Behavior: Single birds or well-separated prs. stay mostly in high outer foliage of canopy trees, hop with cocked tail and peer upward, then dart up suddenly in sally-strike to snap small prey from beneath nearby leaves. Small size and habit of keeping in high foliage make them inconspic. and difficult to locate. Seldom with mixed-spp. flocks. Trashy pendent nest like others of genus but usually quite high.
Status and habitat: Fairly common resident, but few specimens and easily overlooked except for voice. High canopy of tall humid terra firme and várzea forest, esp. along forest borders, tall second growth, and in clearings with scattered tall trees. Also canopy of tall tropical dry forest in ne Bolívar.

Range: To 400m. Throughout Amazonas; s and e Bolívar (*pictum*). The Guianas and ne Brazil (e of Rio Negro).
Note: Yellow-browed Tody-Flycatcher (*T. chrysocrotaphum guttatum*) of se Colombia southward may occur in extreme sw Venez.; no verifiable recs. for Venez. (contra Meyer de Schauensee and Phelps[403]). 4″ (10.2cm). Vocalizations, behavior, and plumage much like Painted Tody-Flycatcher but with broad yellow postocular stripe and *unmarked* yellow underparts.

Black-headed Tody-Flycatcher   PLATE 46
Todirostrum nigriceps   Titirijí Cabecinegro
Identification: 4″ (10.2cm). 6.4g. Dark eyes; long, flat bill; rather *short* tail; some individuals with narrow white supraloral mark. *Entire crown to below eyes glossy black* sharply contrasting with bright olive yellow back; wings and tail blackish, wings with 2 yellow wing bars and crisp yellow edgings; *throat white,* otherwise bright yellow below.

Sim. species: Confusion likely only with Common Tody-Flycatcher which has longer tail, lacks contrasting crown and back (only forecrown black; gray rearcrown merges into olive of back), and has all yellow underparts.
Voice: Advertising call sim. to those of Yellow-browed (in Note) and Painted tody-flycatchers, a bright *peep!*, singly or doubled; song a brisk ser. of up to 12 notes. Calls throughout day but often only at long intervals.
Behavior: Sim. to Common Tody-Flycatcher but occurs mainly in upper mid. level in canopy of forest (not low) and stays mostly inside outer perimeter of foliage where easily overlooked except for loud call. Pendent trashy ball nest with side entrance, downy lining, and dangling tail sim. to other *Todirostrum*; usually fairly high.
Status and habitat: Uncommon and apparently local resident in Andes in humid forest borders, secondgrowth woodland, coffee plantations, and thinned woodland with scattered high trees. Mainly near mts. or in foothills. There are many more specimens from Perijá region than Andes, but sp. can usually be found near Barinitas on e slope of Andes.

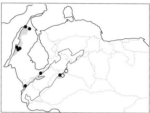

Range: To 1000m. Sierra de Perijá, Zulia; w base of Andes in nw Táchira and w Mérida; e base in nw Barinas and sw Portuguesa (sight, Tucupido Dam)[60]. Costa Rica to w Ecuador.

Ramphotrigon

Resemble *Rhynchocyclus* but bill not as wide; nest in tree cavities (all spp.?); prob. more closely related to *Myiarchus* than to other flatbills[319].

Bamboo Flatbill   PLATE 45
Ramphotrigon megacephala   Pico Chato Cabezón
Identification: 5.2″ (13.2cm). 14g. Slightly heavy headed. Bill flat, *not unusually wide.* Above olive, crown dusky with *narrow whitish eyestripe broadest over lores* and curving over eyes; wings and tail dusky, wing coverts with *2 prom. buff to cinnamon buff wing bars;* flight feathers and tail edged olive yellow, *throat and chest grayish olive with a few faint smudgy yellow streaks;* lower underparts clear yellow.
Sim. species: Overall rather dingy and undistinguished. Best keys are bamboo habitat, distinctive voice, and eyebrow. *Rhynchocyclus* flatbills are larger; *Tolmomyias* flatbills are unstreaked below.
Voice: Easily overlooked advertising call a soft *wheé-whoo* (or *bam-boo*), an inhale-exhale sound, 1st note slightly higher pitched. Call hd. at intervals throughout day. Typically a pause of 5–10 sec between each call. Also a more complex song briefly at dawn.

Behavior: Rather solitary, quiet, and inconspic. in forest understory to mid. story (mostly 3–10m). Usually closely assoc. with bamboo and much more often independent of mixed-spp. flocks than with them. Perches very upright without moving, sallies straight out or up a short distance to hover-glean prey from foliage, then drops away to new perch.

Status and habitat: Uncommon and local resident in bamboo inside or at edge of humid forest. In n Venez. also in patches of introd. Asian bamboo in disturbed or neglected plantations, e.g., along Río Trilla near Turiamo-Cumboto junction in Aragua, where first noted 2 Jan 1985 (A. Altman and C. Parrish); and above Choroní, Aragua, Jan 1996 (G. Rodríguez).

Range: To 600m. W base of Andes in w Trujillo (Betijoque); e base of Andes in w Apure (Las Bonitas) and w Barinas (Ciudad Bolivia); ne Yaracuy (Taría), and Coastal Cordillera (sightings) in n Aragua (*venezuelensis*); s Amazonas on upper Río Siapa at 540m (*pectoralis*). Disjunct range. N and se Colombia to e Ecuador; se Peru, n Bolivia, and sw Brazil; n Argentina, se Paraguay, and se Brazil.
Note: Called Large-headed Flatbill by previous authors.

Rufous-tailed Flatbill   PLATE 45
Ramphotrigon ruficauda   Pico Chato Barbirrufo
Identification: 6″ (15cm). 18g. Large headed. Bill flat and fairly wide. Above dark olive, crown tinged grayish; inconspic. whitish supraloral line and pale eyering; wings dusky with *wing coverts, 2 prom. wing bars, and broad edging on flight feathers bright rufous, tail entirely rufous,* underparts grayish olive indistinctly streaked and flammulated yellow on throat and breast, central belly yellow, under tail coverts rufous.
Sim. species: No other rain forest flycatcher has such extensive rufous wing markings *and* all-rufous tail.
Voice: Not esp. vocal. Melancholy song a *softly* whistled, drawn-out *weeeaaaweeee*, sometimes followed by brief low note; whole phrase sags a bit in pitch in middle and has wheezy quality; also a more hesitant *püüeeeaaaeeeer* that seems to rise slightly in undulating manner. Cf. song of Dusky-capped Flycatcher.
Behavior: Members of a pr., either well separated or sometimes close together, perch in mid. story or understory in more open parts of forest. Sit quietly for long periods, sometimes slowly rolling heads as if slightly dizzy, then suddenly flying outward and upward and, with brief fluttery hover, snatch prey from foliage and drop away to new perch. More often away from mixed-spp. flocks than in them.

Status and habitat: Uncommon to fairly common resident but spottily distrib. in open interior of humid terra firme and várzea forest in lowlands.

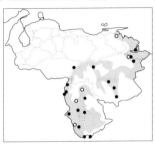

Range: To 500m. Ne Monagas (sight[58]), Delta Amacuro (Caño Merejina), and generally in Amazonas and Bolívar. Se Colombia to n Bolivia, Amaz. Brazil, and the Guianas.

Rhynchocyclus

Large headed; *notably broad,* flat bill; duller plumage and larger size than *Tolmomyias.*

Olivaceous Flatbill   PLATE 45
Rhynchocyclus olivaceus   Pico Chato Aceitunado
Identification: 6″ (15cm). 19.7g. Large headed. *Unusually broad flat bill* dusky above, pinkish gray below. Upperparts dark olive with *fairly distinct whitish eyering* ("wide-eyed" look), wings and tail brown, wing coverts and flight feathers edged yellow olive, *2 poorly marked yellowish wing bars; below olive flammulated with yellow.* Or sim. but flight feathers edged olive buff to buff, underparts grayish olive (*guianensis*).
Sim. species: Generally larger and bulkier than others with which it is likely confused. See Olive-striped Flycatcher, Bamboo Flatbill, and *Tolmomyias* flatbills. In Táchira cf. rare Fulvous-breasted Flatbill.
Voice: Song in n Venez. 5–7 nasal, upslurred notes, *tree-tree-tree-tree-e-e-e*, ascending and faster at end (J. Fitzpatrick), hd. mainly at dawn. Call a loud, explosive, slightly buzzy *pFWEET!*, sometimes several times in succession.
Behavior: Lethargic and usually acts a little dazed. Alone or more often with forest bird flocks. Sits quietly, looking about in mid. story or lower. Perches very erect, turns head slowly, mostly staring upward, and darts out quickly to foliage or twig to snap up arthropods, then drops away to new perch (seldom sallies to air). Bulky, pear-shaped nest usually with downward-projecting entrance spout at side of bottom (shape of *Tolmomyias* nest but larger and material coarser); 2–7m up, often used as dormitory[633].
Status and habitat: Uncommon resident in tall humid terra firme forest and older second-growth woodland; prob. also várzea forest s of Orinoco.
Range: To 1000m n of Orinoco; to 500m s of Orinoco. Base of Sierra de Perijá, Zulia, and w base of Andes in Táchira, Mérida, and e Zulia (Mene Grande); e base from Táchira n to se Lara (sight, PN Yacambú, Jun 1999—R. Ridgely; D. Ascanio); mts. of Yaracuy, se Falcón (Sierra de Chichiriviche), and Coastal Cordillera

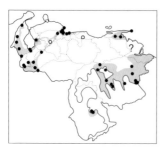

from Carabobo e to Aragua (*flavus*); Paria Pen., Sucre and Río Caripe, n Monagas (*jelambianus*); se Sucre; c Amazonas (Cerro Duida), southward(?); throughout Bolívar (*guianensis*). Panama to n Bolivia, Amaz. Brazil, and the Guianas; coastal e Brazil.

Fulvous-breasted Flatbill

Rhynchocyclus fulvipectus   Pico Chato Pechifulvo
Identification: 6″ (15cm). 26g. Large headed. Broad flat bill pale below. Upperparts dark olive with faint pale eyering; wings dusky brown, *wing coverts heavily edged tawny buff* (no bars), flight feathers edged yellowish olive, *throat and chest dull tawny ochre*, lower underparts yellowish washed olive on breast and flanks.
Sim. species: Best told from other *Rhynchocyclus* flatbills by tawny buff on wing coverts and distinctive color on underparts.
Voice: In Ecuador a wheezy and upslurred *zhreepp*[541].
Behavior: Sim. to that of Olivaceous Flatbill. Likely to be found with mixed-spp. flocks in lower levels of forest.
Status and habitat: Rare resident in humid to wet montane forest. Known only from Hacienda La Providencia (1 ♂, 19 Feb 1956).

Range: 1800m. S Táchira in Río Chiquito. Colombia spottily s in Andes to Bolivia.

Tolmomyias

Broad flat bill (but not as broad as in *Platyrinchus* and *Rhynchocyclus*); rictal bristles not well developed; arboreal; forage using upward strike or upward hover-glean method; inconspic.; yellow wing bars and edgings; some have songs with sim. temporal pattern; nests are beautifully woven hanging bags (often of black fibers) with curved, downward-pointing entrance spout; some spp. place nests near wasp nests. Spp. notoriously difficult to identify by sight and always most reliably told by voice; taxonomy not well understood; several unrecognized spp. likely in genus; previous English names incl. flatbill and flycatcher.

Yellow-olive Flatbill   PLATE 45

Tolmomyias sulphurescens   Pico Chato Sulfuroso
Identification: 5.6″ (14.2cm). 15.2g. Eyes light brown to gray (all subspp.); bill blackish above, pale gray to flesh below. *Largest and most widespread of genus. Two rather distinct types, but head often looks ruffed in both forms.* In n and w: *crown olive (only vaguely tinged gray), only in rather weak contrast to bright olive upperparts*; rather indistinct whitish supraloral line and faint eyering; wings and tail dusky, wings with 2 yellowish bars and crisp yellowish edgings to all flight feathers; throat pale olive gray, rest of underparts sulphur yellow with strong olive wash on breast. Birds from s Táchira (*confusus*) and Amazonas and s Bolívar (*duidae*): sim. but with *darker, more strongly grayish-tinged crowns* and gray-tinged underparts.
Sim. species: Much like Zimmer's Flatbill (see); also cf. smaller Gray-crowned and Ochre-lored flatbills. Forest Elaenia has short, narrow bill, obscure streaking below, and slender shape. Also see Slender-footed Tyrannulet.
Voice: Complex. More than 1 sp. doubtless involved. Birds n of Orinoco (n Monagas) give nasal, buzzy *ps . ps . . . psst . . . psst . . . PSST*; in n Aragua a sim. buzzy *bzz. . . . bzzz . . . bzzzzzz, bzzzzzz*. Birds s of Orinoco typically give sharp 2-noted ser., *spik!. . . . . spik!*, with pause of 1–3 sec between notes, or several *spik!* notes in long irreg. sequence. In all areas there is often a long pause (up to several min) between songs. Most vocalizations somewhat resemble those of Zimmer's Flatbill but are more staccato and much less nasal.
Behavior: Single birds or prs. follow mixed-spp. flocks or forage alone about equally. Perch more at lower hts. and forage more upright than others of genus and with tail straight to slightly cocked. Foraging is slow and deliberate, with a pause as bird peers carefully, then moves to a new perch or flits at foliage or sallies short distances (up to ca. 2m) to snap prey in upward strike or during brief hover-glean to underside of leaf, then normally continues to new perch. Also occas. perch-gleans or chases disturbed insects and eats small berries. Nest a pear-shaped bag of black, hairlike fibers; short, downward-facing entrance tube at side of bottom; 2–7m up, often suspended in open over road, stream, etc.; reg. built near a wasp's nest; 2–3 creamy white eggs with slight rufous tinge and brown speckles. Nest also used as dormitory[633]; in n Colombia most breeding Jan–Jun.
Status and habitat: Fairly common resident in a wide variety of dry to humid habitats, incl. light open woodland, gallery forest, shady plantations, and semiopen areas with scattered trees and woodlots. S of Orinoco mainly along forest borders, small clearings, and river edges or on river isls. (not inside tall mature forest). Reaches max. abundance in drier woodlands in n part of country.
Range: To 1900m n of Orinoco; to 1500m s of Orinoco. W Zulia, n Táchira, and generally n of Orinoco except where next subsp. occurs (*exortivus*); w base of Andes in Táchira and e base in w Apure (*confusus*); Delta Amacuro and n Bolívar from Caicara, Río Cuchivero, lower Río Caura, lower Río Paragua, and Sierra de Imataca s to upper Río Cuyuní (*cherriei*); Amazonas gener-

ally, and Bolívar s of previous subsp. (*duidae*). S Mexico to n Argentina and se Brazil.
Note: Marked regional differences in vocalizations, plumage, and eye color over vast range suggest several spp. are involved.

Zimmer's Flatbill

Tolmomyias assimilis   Pico Chato Aliamarillo
Identification: 5.3″ (13.5cm). 14.5g. Only s of Orinoco. Eyes brown; bill blackish above, paler brownish or grayish below. Very sim. to larger Yellow-olive Flatbill and smaller Gray-crowned Flatbill; Zimmer's is essentially intermed. between the two. *This trio represents one of the most confusing field identification challenges in Venez.* Furthermore, in area of overlap (s of Orinoco), subspp. of Yellow-olive are most sim. to Zimmer's. Latter best told from Yellow-olive by *pale spot* ("speculum") at base of primaries (produced by broader pale yellow edges at base of outer 3 or 4 primaries), but this difficult to see in field. Also note *smaller size* (a good clue if seen well), *differences in voice, habitat* (Zimmer's occurs inside mature forest, Yellow-olive mostly at forest edges and in more open areas), and *differences in posture* (see Behavior). In hand Zimmer's has 10th (outer) primary longer than 4th (reverse in Yellow-olive); most (but not all) individuals of the 2 spp. separate by flattened wing cord (62–66mm in Zimmer's vs. 65–70mm in Yellow-olive). Almost equally sim. Gray-crowned Flatbill is incrementally *smaller* still, has *grayest crown* (usually in sharp contrast to olive back), orangish lower mandible (all areas?), and lacks, or has faintly indicated, pale wing speculum. *Learn voices* (below). In hand, wing cord (flat) of Gray-crowned is 55–60mm (apparently no overlap with Yellow-olive and Zimmer's).
Voice: "Sings through its nose." Song a ser. of 3–5 notes, *very nasal and buzzy*, given in leisurely but emphatic manner, *znuu . . . . znuu . znuuu-znuuu*, varied to *znuu . . . . znuu . . znuuu . znuuu-PIK!*, the ser. accelerating somewhat at end. Typically a lengthy pause (up to several min) between songs.
Behavior: A little more active and sprightly than Yellow-olive Flatbill. Usually seen amid foliage in mid. to subcanopy levels of forest, and often accompanies small mixed flocks. Foraging behavior otherwise much like Yellow-olive Flatbill, but posture more horizontal and tail often cocked up slightly. Perches fairly close to foliage from which it mounts short upward strikes or upward hover-gleans for small prey. In allied Yellow-margined Flatbill, retort-shaped nest of black fibers much like that of Yellow-olive Flatbill but much higher, 9–21m up; usually near wasp's nest[706].

Status and habitat: Uncommon to fairly common resident (doubtless underrecorded because of identification problems) in humid terra firme and várzea forest, and at forest edges; lowlands and lower slopes of tepuis. More a forest bird than Yellow-olive Flatbill. Majority of canopy mixed-spp. flocks at Junglaven and San Carlos de Río Negro in Amazonas contain a pr. of these birds (Hilty; C. Parrish).

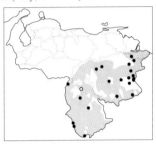

Range: To 1200m. Generally in Amazonas; n Bolívar in lower Río Caura (*neglectus*); rest of Bolívar from Río Paragua (Guaiquinima) and Sierra de Imataca southward (*examinatus*). Se Colombia to n Bolivia, Amaz. Brazil, and the Guianas.
Note: Previously called Yellow-margined Flycatcher[403]; that name now applied only to taxa of C Amer. and w of Andes[541].

Gray-crowned Flatbill   PLATE 45

Tolmomyias poliocephalus   Pico Chato de Corona Gris
Identification: 4.7″ (12cm). 11g. Eyes brown (always?); bill blackish, lower mandible orangish to flesh (all areas?). *Closely resembles* Yellow-olive and Zimmer's flatbills but *smaller. Crown and nape gray contrasting with olive back*; small whitish supraloral mark (sometimes a faintly indicated whitish eyering), wings blackish, wing coverts and flight feathers sharply edged yellow, base of primaries sometimes with faint pale patch; throat grayish yellow, breast yellow washed olive, center of lower underparts yellow.
Sim. species: Smaller and with more distinctly contrasting gray crown than Zimmer's Flatbill (see); the two often occur together. Also see Yellow-olive Flatbill.
Voice: Song in all areas a leisurely and slightly husky ser. of whistles, *teeawe . . . . teeawe . . teeawe . teeawe*, with variations, the ser. often growing stronger and accelerating. At dawn often repeats song over and over with scarcely a break for several min. Song of *sclateri* (the Guianas; e Venez.?) rather different, a flatter, piping, fifelike ser. of 3–6 slow, shrill whistles, *pfee . . pfee*, *. . . ,* last 3 notes often higher pitched; each ser. often more or less merged with next.
Behavior: Single birds or prs. forage at mid. levels or higher and are often high in crown of canopy and emergent trees where they flit to foliage in upward strikes or hover-glean small insects. Almost always seen with insectivorous canopy mixed-spp. flocks. Nest a pendent pouch much like others of genus; 2–25m up; often near wasp's nest; 2 creamy white eggs with small reddish spots and blotches[253].
Status and habitat: Common resident but easily overlooked in canopy of humid terra firme and várzea forest.

Range: To ca. 1000m. N Amazonas s to vicinity of Río Ventuari, and generally across Bolívar and Delta Amacuro (*klagesi*); c Amazonas from near Cerro Duida southward (*poliocephalus*). Se Colombia to n Bolivia, Amaz. Brazil, and the Guianas; coastal e Brazil.

Ochre-lored Flatbill PLATE 45
Tolmomyias flaviventris Pico Chato Amarillento
Identification: 5" (12.7cm). 11.3g. Conspic. dark eyes; broad flat bill. *Above, incl. crown, bright yellowish olive, supraloral spot and narrow eyering ochraceous orange* (visible up close), wings and tail dusky, wings with 2 yellowish wing bars and yellow edgings; *below bright yellow with ochre wash on throat and chest*, the ochre sometimes extending onto sides of head. Amaz. birds (*dissors*) are slightly smaller, 4.8" (12.2cm).
Sim. species: From others of genus by uniform upperparts (crown concolor with back) and brighter yellow underparts. Also note prom. black eyes (set off against yellowish olive sides of head).
Voice: Sim. in all 3 subspp. Often hd. song 3–5 rather loud, penetrating whistles, *sweeEP! . . . . sweeEP! . . . . . . sweeEP!*, with pause of 1–several sec between notes. Call a single *sweeEP!*
Behavior: Single birds or prs. stay mostly inside upper levels of trees and are inconspic. despite freq. vocalizations. Sometimes with mixed-spp. flocks, although often in lightly wooded regions where few flocks form. Generally less active than most others of genus. Sit fairly erect and quiet and watch, then change perches or sally out to hover-glean prey from twigs or beneath foliage, and drop away to new perch. Also, often take prey in upward sally-strike without hovering. Pensile nest as in others of genus but of pale rootlets (not black); usually suspended on slender twig near wasp nest; 2–3 creamy white eggs with a few dark brown spots at larger end[250]; in n Colombia 19 nests, Apr–Jun[750]; breeding May–Sep, Apure and Guárico[137,734].
Status and habitat: Common resident (by voice) in dry to moist forest, woodland borders, light woodland, shrubby areas, and gallery forest across n Venez. Commonest in dry, strongly seasonal areas, less numerous and local in humid regions of Amazonas and Bolívar where confined mainly to open sandy soil savanna woodland and borders.
Range: To 900m. Nw Venez. from Zulia to Miranda and w of Andes s to Táchira (*aurulentus*); rest of Venez. n of Orinoco, Delta Amacuro, and c and e Bolívar (*collingwoodi*); nw Bolívar, and Amazonas s to vicinity of Cerro Duida (*dissors*), prob. also s Amazonas. E Panama (sight) and e Ecuador e to the Guianas and n Brazil. Trinidad and Tobago.

Note: Previously called Yellow-breasted Flycatcher[403]; birds from s Peru to s Brazil now considered a separate sp., Olive-faced Flatbill, *T. viridiceps*[28].

Platyrinchus

Tiny; chunky; stub tailed; bill extraordinarily wide and flat (wider than long); unusually large eyes; large blocky head; sudden darting movements; forage by upward strikes, "scooping" prey from beneath foliage; inconspic. in understory; hummingbird-like nest cup in low branch fork.

White-crested Spadebill PLATE 46
Platyrinchus platyrhynchos Pico Chato Cabecigris
Identification: 4.2" (10.7cm). 13g. Largest spadebill; bill broadest (12mm) of genus; very short tail. *No obvious facial pattern. Crown dark gray*, with paler gray sides of head, whitish supraloral spot, large semiconcealed white coronal patch (smaller—♀), and contrasting russet brown back; wings and tail dusky (no wings bars), throat white, *rest of underparts bright ochraceous*; legs pinkish yellow.
Sim. species: Nearest is Cinnamon-crested Spadebill which is smaller, lacks gray crown, and has weakly defined face pattern. Other spadebills show strong face pattern.
Voice: Commonest vocalization (call or alarm?) a sharp *skip!* or *pEEip!* rather like that of a leaftosser (*Sclerurus*), sometimes repeated at 3- to 5-sec intervals. Less often hd. song a thin, buzzy trill that runs up scale quickly, then back down, *pr're're'e'e'e'e'E'E'E'R'r'r'r' 'r'r'r'r*, sometimes with sharp squeak note at end.
Behavior: Prs. are found mostly 2–5m up in fairly open forest understory. Like other spadebills, sit immobile, then move suddenly to new perch 1–several m away, but generally easier to see than smaller allies because of larger size and habit of perching more in open above dense understory vegetation. Dart out rapidly in sally-strike to snap ("scoop") small arthropods from be-

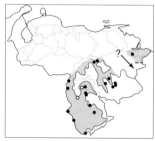

neath leaves and continue without pause to new perch. Do not follow mixed-spp. flocks but may call and move actively in their midst.

Status and habitat: Uncommon to locally fairly common resident in open understory of humid terra firme forest. Most numerous in sandy soil forests.

Range: To 300m. Throughout Amazonas; Bolívar from lower Río Caura, mid. Río Paragua (Cerro Guaiquinima), and Sierra de Imataca southward (*platyrhynchos*). E Colombia s to n Bolivia, Amaz. Brazil, and the Guianas.

Yellow-throated Spadebill   PLATE 46
Platyrinchus flavigularis   Pico Chato Gargantiamarillo
Identification: 4" (10.2cm). Andes. Bill black above, pale below, proportionately broadest (11mm) of genus; stubby tail. *No eyering or face pattern. Crown and nape reddish brown* contrasting with grayish olive upperparts; semiconcealed white coronal patch; wings and tail dusky (no wing bars), *underparts sulphur yellow, breast tinged olive.*

Sim. species: Larger than others of genus with which it occurs.

Voice: Call a sharp *peeeyr* repeated slowly at intervals of 4–5 sec[545].

Behavior: Poorly known in Venez. but elsewhere apparently much like others of genus (see White-throated Spadebill).

Status and habitat: Local resident in undergrowth of humid and wet montane forest. Recs. very spotty but perhaps, in part, overlooked. Nine specimens (Colección Phelps) from Cerro Pejochaina, w Zulia (incl. 5 in one day at 1800–1900m) suggest sp. is at least locally fairly common.

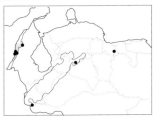

Range: 1250–2100m. Sierra de Perijá, Zulia; Andes of se Táchira (Cerro El Teteo, 1250m) and se Lara at Guárico (*vividus*); Coastal Cordillera at El Trompillo, Carabobo (subsp.?). Colombia s in Andes to s Peru.
Note: El Trompillo locality rec. needs verification.

Cinnamon-crested Spadebill
Platyrinchus saturatus   Pico Chato Copete Acanelado
Identification: 3.6" (9.1cm). 10.8g. Tiny Amaz. spadebill lacking *facial pattern*; blackish bill, stubby tail. Above uniform dark reddish brown, fairly prom. dusky patch at base of primaries; mostly concealed orange rufous coronal stripe (smaller—♀), *inconspic. buffy white eyering and loral spot; otherwise sides of head brown and unmarked; throat white* contrasting with brownish chest and sides; central lower underparts yellowish white.

Sim. species: From commoner Golden-crowned Spadebill by rufous tone to upperparts, essentially unmarked

face, and white throat contrasting with dark chest and sides.

Voice: Song s of the Amazon a low-pitched, 3- to 6-note *ka-knee-knee-knee-knee* in little, slow, rattlelike or pulsating bursts (K. Zimmer recording); call in e Bolívar a sharp, nasal *squik!*; rising, or more double-sounding *squik-ik!*, latter recalls White-throated Spadebill.

Behavior: Much like others of genus (see White-throated Spadebill) and difficult to see. Favors dense stands of saplings and bushy undergrowth where perches very low, mostly below ca. 1.5m up, occas. to 3m. Periods of immobility are interrupted by abrupt darting flights when changing perches or in sally-strikes to scoop off insects from beneath leaves. Has been noted in understory mixed-spp. flocks (K. Zimmer).

Status and habitat: Uncommon or rare resident (difficult to find) in understory of humid terra firme forest, esp. where their are many small saplings.

Range: To 900m. Throughout Amazonas; n Bolívar from Pijiguaos, lower Río Caura, mid. Río Paragua (Cerro Guaiquinima), and upper Río Cuyuní watershed southward (*saturatus*). E Colombia and e Ecuador to the Guianas and n Brazil; sw Brazil in Rondônia.

White-throated Spadebill   PLATE 46
Platyrinchus mystaceus   Pico Chato Gargantiblanco
Identification: 3.8" (9.7cm). 9.3g. Tiny; broad blackish bill; stubby tail; *rather bold facial pattern.* Crown and upperparts brown, semiconcealed golden crown patch (smaller—♀), *prom. buffy white eyering and buff line drooping behind eyes; cheeks buff bordered in front by elongated blackish patch below eyes* (forms broad "sideburns"), and behind by another *curving blackish patch enclosing rear of ear coverts; throat white,* rest of underparts yellowish white with faint ochre wash on breast. Or sim. but much brighter ochre below (*duidae, ventralis*). Or crown grayish, overall paler; almost whitish below (*imatacae*).

Sim. species: Nothing like it in mts. Golden-crowned Spadebill, only s of Orinoco, has sim. face pattern but differs in black-edged crown patch and dingy yellow (not contrasting white) throat.

Voice: Most often hd. call a short, sharp *squeep!* or *skip!*, often doubled or given in excited, irreg. ser. Song a high, thin trill, *pe'e'e'e'e'e'e'e'e'e'eet,* rising slightly then descending. A flight display with manakin-like wing-whir is also reported[541].

Behavior: Occurs in prs. but members usually remain well separated. Perch immobile and inconspic., ca. 0.3–5m up, often for long periods. Occas. dart short to med. distances in sally-strikes to undersides of leaves for small insects which they scoop off with audible bill-snap and continue without pausing to new perch. Flights are abrupt and fast—in "blink of an eye"—making these birds difficult to follow when they fly, esp. in dim. understory light. May join understory mixed-spp. flocks, esp. in gallery forest in llanos, but more often seen independent of flocks. Move and sally at faster rate in presence of flocks. In Costa Rica breed Mar–May; smoothly formed black, fiber-lined, cone-like cup 1–3m up; 2 white eggs, yellow faintly tinged with rufous wreath[706].

Status and habitat: Fairly common and widespread resident in understory of dry and moist forest, incl. gallery forest, in lowlands and foothills; smaller nos. in humid and wet forest in mts. Sometimes in tangled or bushy areas along forest borders. Easily overlooked.

Range: To 1800m. Sierra de Perijá, Zulia (*perijanus*); e Táchira (*neglectus*); w base of Andes in Trujillo (Mendoza); hills of Falcón (except arid zones) and generally from Lara and Yaracuy e through mts. to ne Anzoátegui, Sucre, and Monagas; e base of Andes from w Barinas (Calderas) e to n Guárico; n Bolívar from Caicara e to Delta Amacuro (*insularis*); n and c Amazonas on Cerros Yavi and Duida; Roraiman region of Bolívar on Gran Sabana (*duidae*); extreme s Amazonas on Cerro de la Neblina (*ventralis*); ne Bolívar on Sierra de Imataca (*imatacae*); Cerros Ptari, Sororopán, and Aprada (*ptaritepui*). E Costa Rica to ne Argentina, se Brazil; Guyana; French Guiana.
Note: Prob. more than 1 sp. over broad range. Some subspp. possibly invalid.

Golden-crowned Spadebill   PLATE 46
Platyrinchus coronatus   Pico Chato Corona Dorada
Identification: 3.5″ (8.9cm). 8.5g. *Smallest* spadebill. Wide bill blackish above, pale yellowish below. *Strong facial pattern*. Olive above with *broad orange rufous crown bordered black*; partially concealed golden yellow crown stripe (♂ only); prom. buffy white eyering and yellowish line drooping behind eyes; cheeks yellowish *bordered in front by elongated blackish patch below eye* (forms broad "sideburns"), and behind by another *curving blackish patch enclosing rear of cheeks*; throat yellowish white, rest of underparts pale yellow with vaguely streaked grayish olive wash on breast.
Sim. species: Much like White-throated Spadebill (see); also cf. Cinnamon-crested Spadebill which *lacks* facial pattern.
Voice: Freq. hd. song a weak, insectlike, and high-pitched trill, *se'e'e'e'e'e'r'r'r'r'e'e'ep*, descending

slightly in middle, then ascending briefly at end, sometimes with 1–3 sharp *pip* notes at end; barely audible at any distance and easily overlooked. In short flight display between perches makes ser. of audible wing-whirs.
Behavior: Usually noted first by voice. Like White-throated Spadebill, inconspic. and easily overlooked despite fact that it perches higher, mostly 1–5m up, and in more open understory of forest. Single birds, prs., or families (ad. pr. with offspring) sit immobile but alert, often for long periods, then dart out in upward sally-strikes short to long distances (up to ca. 10m) to foliage or new perch. In Costa Rica freq. with understory mixed-spp. flocks (K. Zimmer). Nest cup like that of a hummingbird but bulkier; 1–2m up in fork of sapling; 2–3 whitish or creamy buff eggs blotched various shades of brown[633].
Status and habitat: Fairly common resident, but seemingly much more numerous in some areas than others. Humid terra firme and várzea forest in lowlands and foothills.

Range: To 1500m. N Amazonas from Pto. Ayacucho (sight), Caño Cuao, and Cerros Parú and Yapacana southward (*coronatus*); generally in Bolívar from lower Río Caura, Río Paragua (Salto Guaiquinima), and Sierra de Imataca southward (*gumia*); Delta Amacuro[343]. Honduras to w Ecuador; se Colombia to n Bolivia, Amaz. Brazil (to mouth of the Amazon), and the Guianas.

Onychorhynchus

Spectacular crest; bill long, wide, fairly flat, and hooked; unusually long rictal bristles (as long as bill) and short legs; long, slender, loose (not woven) pensile nest with side entrance to shallow enclosed chamber.

Northern Royal-Flycatcher
Onychorhynchus mexicanus   Atrapamoscas Real Centroamericano
Identification: 6.8″ (17.3cm). 21g. Rather undistinguished except on rare occas. when spectacular crest is partially exposed. Closed crest projecting behind head, together with rather long, wide bill, imparts distinctive "hammerheaded" appearance. Fully expanded crest of ♂ (a 180° fan perpendicular to axis of body) bright scarlet with numerous black dots and large glossy steel-blue tips (same but crest orange yellow—♀ and imm.). Legs yellowish. Upperparts brown, wing coverts with numerous buff dots on tips; *rump*

and tail bright cinnamon, throat buffy white, rest of underparts bright buff more or less freckled or indistinctly barred brownish olive. Imm.: more extensively barred.
Sim. species: Long bill, hammerheaded appearance, and cinnamon tail are the marks. Spectacular crest seldom seen to advantage.
Voice: Unusually quiet, infreq. a long ser. of nasal *cur-lip* notes, at rate of ca. 1 every 2 sec or so; recalls a *Galbula* jacamar.
Behavior: Occurs in prs. but usually seen alone. Birds are inconspic. as wait quietly but alertly, then sally med. distances to foliage and snap prey without hovering. Usually independent of mixed-spp. flocks or occas. in or beneath them. Occur mainly in understory, rarely to subcanopy. Function of remarkable crest uncertain as it is rarely seen expanded, but prob. functions in courtship and aggressive encounters[218]. Under natural conditions may raise crest when preening, in agonistic display toward another ♂, and in head-swaying display to mate as ♂ turns head from side to side, fans tail, and quivers wings. When handled, mist-netted birds typically expose crest and twist head side to side. Remarkable nest a long (1–2m!) and loose (not woven) pensile structure with side entrance to shallow nest chamber; attached to slender branch or vine 2.5–6m up over shady stream; 2 eggs, dark reddish brown at larger end, paler at small end; nestlings barred[633].
Status and habitat: Uncommon and local resident in shady lower levels of moist and humid forest, forest borders, gallery forest, and older second growth, esp. near streams. Most numerous in areas where rainfall is not too high (i.e., Perijá foothills).

Range: To 2000m (most recs. below 1400m). Base of Sierra de Perijá, Zulia, w slope of Andes in w Mérida (sight, El Vigía) and Trujillo (Betijoque); e slope at Barinitas, nw Barinas (*fraterculus*). S Mexico to n Colombia.
Note: Formerly regarded as a subsp. of Royal Flycatcher (*O. coronatus*) complex from s Mexico to Amazonia.

Amazonian Royal-Flycatcher   PLATE 45
Onychorhynchus coronatus   Atrapamoscas Real Amazónico
Identification: 6.3″ (16cm). 13g. Sim. to Northern Royal-Flycatcher but *tail darker, more rufous* (not bright cinnamon); lower back with fine buff and black barring; underparts more distinctly barred, belly darker buff (*coronatus, castelnaudi*). Imm.: more heavily barred.

Sim. species: Often looks rather plain. Long bill, rufous tail, and "hammerheaded" appearance are unique. N of Orinoco see Northern Royal-Flycatcher.
Voice: Two-syllable *curr-lep* (slurred up) is sim. to that of Northern Royal-Flycatcher.
Behavior: As in Northern Royal-Flycatcher.
Status and habitat: Uncommon to rare in humid lowland forest. May show some affinity for várzea forest, swampy terrain, and vicinity of water. Mixed mangrove and palm swamps in Delta Amacuro.

Range: To 1000m s of Orinoco. Sucre on Paria Pen. and s to Delta Amacuro; locally throughout Bolívar, and Amazonas from Río Ventuari s to Cerro Duida (*coronatus*); s Amazonas near mouth of Río Casiquiare, and Sierra Imerí (*castelnaudi*). Amaz. Brazil and the Guianas.
Note: Does not incl. various nw and e forms, now all considered separate spp.[545].

Neopipo

Poorly known; formerly considered a manakin (Pipridae) but prob. most closely related to *Myiophobus* flycatchers[406]; no rictal bristles.

Cinnamon Neopipo   PLATE 44
Neopipo cinnamomea   Atrapamoscas Canelo
Identification: 3.6″ (9.1cm). 7g. Small with large blackish eyes. Narrow black bill, base of lower mandible orange; *legs dusky gray. Crown, sides of head, and mantle dull gray turning bright cinnamon rufous on rump and tail*; concealed golden yellow coronal stripe (smaller, sometimes duller rufous—♀), flight feathers dusky edged rufous, throat buffy white, rest of underparts cinnamon.
Sim. species: Resembles much commoner Ruddy-tailed Flycatcher so closely the two are prob. often overlooked. Note this sp. has *dark* (not yellowish) legs, narrow rounded bill, lacks rictal bristles (conspic. up close in Ruddy-tailed), and has more uniform underparts, and usually concealed yellow crown stripe. This sp. also is shorter tailed and appears more round headed and hunched.
Voice: Song a sprightly ser. of ca. 12–14 little piping notes (like a piccolo but flat), *pee . . pa pee . . fe-FEE-fee-feaa-feaa-feaa-feaa-feaa*, 2d note lowest, 5th highest, rest gradually downscale, delivered slowly and lasting ca. 5–6 sec. Might recall song of Southern Nightingale-Wren but more "allegro" or up tempo (K. Zimmer recording). Call a short, slightly wheezy *pfEEeo*, rising then falling (A. Whittaker).

Behavior: Still poorly known. Occurs in forest mid. levels or higher.
Status and habitat: Generally scarce or local throughout range. Most rec. are from white sandy soil forests in terra firme regions. Perhaps often overlooked (confusion with *Terenotriccus*). Recently found in a no. of places in white sandy soil forests in vicinity of Manaus and Rio Negro, Brazil (A. Whittaker).

Range: To 200m. C and s Amazonas from Cerro Yapacana to Cerro de la Neblina (*cinnamomea*); taped and seen (Mar 2002) near Las Claritas, Bolívar (Hilty and D. Ascanio). E Colombia (near Venez. border) to e Ecuador (few recs.), e Peru, and Amaz. Brazil; locally in the Guianas.
Note: Previously called Cinnamon Manakin[403], Cinnamon Tyrant[406], and Cinnamon Tyrant-Manakin[545]; often placed with manakins.

Terenotriccus

Small; aerobatic; rather wide bill enclosed by basket of long rictal bristles; most closely related to *Myiobius*[322].

Ruddy-tailed Flycatcher   PLATE 46
Terenotriccus erythrurus   Atrapamoscas Colicastaño
Identification: ♂ 4″ (10.2cm), 7g. ♀ slightly smaller, 6g. *Unusually large black eyes*; short bill, slight crest; *yellowish legs.* Head and mantle olive gray turning *bright cinnamon on rump and rufous on tail*; inner flight feathers edged rufous (no wing bars), narrow white eyering (faint); throat dingy white, rest of underparts pale cinnamon. Or sim. but throat grayish (*erythrurus*); or chest darker with tawny wash (*flavigularis*).
Sim. species: Remarkably like Cinnamon Neopipo which is *even smaller* and *shorter-tailed* (in hand, tail 32–37 vs. 39–46mm for Ruddy-tailed Flycatcher), and duller and more uniformly cinnamon below. Neopipo's posture and shape differ: neopipo perches more horizontally (not upright), has narrow and rounded (not broad) bill, rounded head (no crest), concealed yellow coronal patch (absent in Ruddy-tailed), and lacks eyering. Up close note Ruddy-tailed's yellowish legs (dusky blue gray in neopipo). In hand note *absence* of rictal bristles. Also cf. Ochre-bellied Flycatcher; in mts., Cinnamon Flycatcher.
Voice: Calls at intervals throughout day, esp. when foraging, a high, thin (rather faint) *teeu-TEEP!* (2d note much higher) that brings to mind a hummingbird vocalization. Song a clear and penetrating, but not very loud, ser. of 6–7 high, thin whistles, 1st 2–3 louder, the

rest accelerating and descending in pitch, *keeek, keek, eek-eek-eek-eek-eek*, insectlike; in common variation song slowly rises then falls, *wi, wi, wi, keeek . . keek, keek keek keek.*
Behavior: Usually alone or in well-separated prs. that sit bolt upright on thin open twigs in mid. levels of forest. More often independent of mixed-spp. flocks than with them. Movements abrupt and quick and incl. freq. perch changes, aerobatic chasing of small flying prey, esp. Homoptera (leafhoppers), taken in air or from foliage, and in extended hover-gleaning from leaves, twigs, even trunks. At rest occas. flicks up both wings at once. Panama nest a pear-shaped pouch of dark fibers and leaf fragments with visor-covered entrance on side near bottom; suspended from vine or twig 2–6m up; 2 white eggs blotched dark brown mostly around larger end[633]; breeds Feb–Aug, nw Colombia[260].
Status and habitat: Fairly common to common resident (easily overlooked) inside humid terra firme and várzea forest and tall second growth in lowlands, decreasing nos. in mts. (sight recs. to 1000m, Portachuelo Pass, Aragua, 27 Nov 1975—C. Parrish; 4 Mar 1977—C. Parrish; 11 Mar 1977—J. V. Remsen, J. Fitzpatrick, C. Parrish).

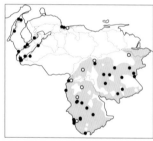

Range: To 600m (sightings to 1000m). Sierra de Perijá, Zulia, w base of Andes in Táchira, Mérida, and Trujillo; e base from Táchira n to nw Barinas; Coastal Cordillera in Carabobo and sightings (presum. this subsp.) in Aragua (*fulvigularis*); generally in Amazonas; Bolívar from lower Río Caura e to mid. and upper Río Paragua and Río Caroní (*venezuelensis*); lower Río Paragua, Auyán-tepui, and upper Río Cuyuní (*erythrurus*); sightings n to Río Grande in Sierra de Imataca. S Mexico to n Bolivia, Amaz. Brazil, and the Guianas.
Note: Placed in *Myiobius* by some[606]; the 2 genera differ markedly in voice, behavior, and morphology.

Myiobius

Distinctive yellow rump and black tail; large black eyes; long rictal bristles enclose bill like a basket; highly aerobatic but not esp. vocal; inside dry to humid forest; tail-fanning behavior recalls Old World fantails (*Ripidura*).

Whiskered Flycatcher   PLATE 45
Myiobius barbatus   Atrapamoscas Barbudo
Identification: 5″ (12.7cm). 11g. Large black eyes. *Conspic. lemon yellow rump contrasts with rounded black tail*, otherwise olive green above with usually con-

cealed yellow coronal stripe (small or lacking—♀), faint yellowish white eyering; wings unmarked, throat dirty white, *chest pale grayish olive to brownish gray with slight tawny buff wash that contrasts with yellow lower underparts.*
Sim. species: Easily confused with next 2 spp., but note carefully their ranges (there is little overlap). See esp. Black-tailed Flycatcher.
Behavior: An ever-nervous and vivacious bit of feathered energy. Look for singles or prs. in midst of mixed-spp. flocks where animated, active, and whitestart-(*Myioborus-*) like foraging behavior is easily spotted. Unusual "flush and chase" feeding strategy puts them in almost constant motion, fanning and closing tail, drooping wings, and pivoting and posturing on perches, or clinging momentarily to sides of trunks, before executing short aerobatic sallies in pursuit of flushed insects. Perch with very horizontal posture, mostly ca. 3–15m up in open low to mid.-story level, display bright rump patch, and posture with impunity (posturing startles insect prey) as they forage. Allied Sulphur-rumped Flycatcher (*M. sulphureipygius*) of C Amer. builds messy bell-shaped nest with entrance on side at bottom; suspended from branch 2–14m up, often over stream; 2 white eggs speckled dark brown[633].
Status and habitat: Uncommon to fairly common resident in humid terra firme forest and low-lying forest along streams in lowlands and foothills. Replaced in dry forest by Black-tailed Flycatcher; in mts. of w by Tawny-breasted Flycatcher.

Range: To 1600m (most recs. below 900m). Amazonas from upper Río Ventuari southward; n Bolívar (lower Río Caura, Río Paragua, Sierra de Imataca) and s Delta Amacuro s to Cerro Roraima (*barbatus*). Se Colombia to n Bolivia, Amaz. Brazil, and the Guianas; coastal e and se Brazil.
Note: Previously called Sulphur-rumped Flycatcher[403]; that name now applies to birds w of Andes[10].

Black-tailed Flycatcher

Myiobius atricaudus   Atrapamoscas Colinegro
Identification: 5" (12.7cm). 10g. Large black eyes. Closely resembles Whiskered Flycatcher and like it has *conspic. lemon yellow rump and somewhat rounded black tail.* Above olive green (slightly paler than Whiskered Flycatcher), concealed yellow coronal patch (small—♀), throat buffy white, *broad chest band tawny buff to grayish buff* (a little darker than previous sp.), the buff extending down sides onto flanks, rest of underparts yellow.

Sim. species: Overlaps minimally with Whiskered Flycatcher in e Venez., but both are very sim. Habitat differences helpful (Black-tailed favors drier woodland); chest band (buff on both spp.) is slightly darker and extends down sides on Black-tailed. *Does not* overlap Tawny-breasted Flycatcher.
Voice: Very quiet. Occas. soft *tsit* note while foraging.
Behavior: Basically sim. to Whiskered Flycatcher but somewhat less acrobatic, not drooping wings and fanning tail as much. Most often seen with mixed-spp. flocks. Nest-site loc. and egg color differ. In c Panama, 8 nests Jun–Jul; like Sulphur-rumped Flycatcher (*M. sulphureipygius*) of C Amer. but all suspended over water; 2 dull peach-colored eggs with faint wreath of darker marks at larger end[229].
Status and habitat: Resident in dry to moist forest and shrubby second growth; also humid forest borders, esp. near water. Replaced in interior of humid forest by better-known Whiskered Flycatcher. Prob. more widespread in drier forests of n Bolívar than small no. of recs. suggest. One seen Feb 1993 ca. 10km w of El Palmar, Bolívar.

Range: To 200m. N Bolívar in vicinity of Orinoco from Caicara e to San Felix, Upata, El Palmar (sightings), and near border of Delta Amacuro (*modestus*). Costa Rica to nw Peru; e Ecuador, e Peru, and Amaz. Brazil s of the Amazon; se Brazil.

Tawny-breasted Flycatcher   PLATE 45

Myiobius villosus   Atrapamoscas Peludo
Identification: 5.5" (14cm). 13g. Prom. black eyes. *Conspic. lemon yellow rump contrasts with rounded black tail* as in previous 2 spp. Above dusky olive, usually concealed yellow crown patch (rufous—♀), throat dirty whitish; *broad breast band and sides deep tawny ochraceous to tawny brown,* central belly yellow.
Sim. species: Easily confused with smaller and paler (in Venez.) Whiskered and Black-tailed flycatchers, but those 2 spp. not known to overlap it in range. Tawny-breasted is richer and darker below.
Voice: Typically quiet. A sharp, almost explosive *espīt!* recalls note of Sulfur-rumped Flycatcher (*M. sulphurei-pygius*) of C Amer.
Behavior: Sim. to that of Whiskered Flycatcher.
Status and habitat: Rare or uncommon and local resident in lower levels of humid and wet mt. forest, esp. near streams and usually not far from water. Few recs. in Venez. A montane replacement of Whiskered Flycatcher.
Range: 960–1900m. Sierra de Perijá, Zulia; se Táchira (Río Chiquito; Cerro El Teteo) and w base of Andes in

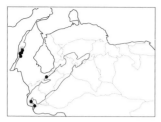

Mérida (*schaeferi*). Colombia s locally in Andes to n Bolivia.

Myiophobus

Small; recall *Empidonax* but darker; concealed coronal stripes; many are rare, local, poorly known, and inconspic.; genus possibly polyphyletic[320,545].

Flavescent Flycatcher   PLATE 45
Myiophobus flavicans   Atrapamoscas Amarilloso
Identification: 5″ (12.7cm). 10.2g. Shape and posture suggest an *Empidonax*. Olive above with *fairly prom. supraloral line and broken yellowish eyering*; concealed yellow coronal patch (absent—♀); wings and tail dusky brown, 2 weakly marked cinnamon buff wing bars; olive edgings on flight feathers and tertials; underparts yellowish flammulated olive on chest giving *vaguely streaked* appearance. Or sim. but yellower below, less olive (*caripensis*).
Sim. species: Eyering and buff wing bars are good marks. Wing bars buffier and underparts yellower than in any migrant *Empidonax*. In mts. s of Orinoco see Roraiman Flycatcher.
Voice: Infreq. a sharp *tsink*. Song, mostly at dawn (?), a fast rhythmic ser. of 5–8 *Kawhik* notes[541].
Behavior: Single birds or prs. perch erect in understory or mid. story where they are quiet and inconspic. More often away from mixed-spp. flocks than with them. Sally short distances to foliage, occas. to air. Cup nest of twigs, tiny vines, and feather lining in Colombia[260].
Status and habitat: Fairly common resident in humid and wet forest and forest borders. Most numerous in wetter forests. Seen with some reg. near Choroní Pass, PN Henri Pittier.

Range: 900–2300m (usually above 1300m). Sierra de Perijá, Zulia, and s Táchira (*perijanus*); n Táchira, Andes of Mérida and Barinas (sight recs.) n to Lara; mts. of Yaracuy and n cordilleras from Carabobo e to Distr. Federal and Miranda at Cerro Negro (*venezuelanus*); w Sucre, and n Monagas on Cerro Negro (*caripensis*). Colombia s in Andes to c Peru.

Roraiman Flycatcher   PLATE 45
Myiophobus roraimae   Atrapamoscas del Roraima
Identification: 5.3″ (13.5cm). 13g. Shape and posture suggest an *Empidonax*. Bill black, lower mandible dull orange yellow. Above dark olive, inconspic. broken eyering yellowish white; concealed orange rufous crown patch (absent—♀), wings and tail dusky brown, *2 broad and conspic. rufous wing bars; flight feathers* (esp. inner ones) *broadly edged rufous*; underparts yellowish white heavily washed olive on breast; center of belly yellowish.
Sim. species: In limited range most likely confused with a migrant *Empidonax*, but none has rufous wing bars and edgings. Cf. Chapman's Bristle-Tyrant.
Voice: Unknown.
Behavior: An inconspic. little flycatcher that perches rather erect and quiet in understory or mid. story of forest and sallies short distances to foliage for small arthropod prey. Usually alone and not with mixed-spp. flocks.
Status and habitat: Resident in humid and wet forest on tepuis. Fairly common to common (large no. of specimens) at moderate els. on many higher tepuis (e.g., Aprada, Chimantá, Guaiquinima, Gimé, Parú, Ptari, Urutaní, Yavi), esp. between 1300 and 1800m; rare on Sierra de Lema which may lack sufficient el. to sustain sp. In some Andean areas (not Venez.) reported from sandy or impoverished-soil forests[545].

Range: 900–2000m (to 550m on Brazilian side of Cerro de la Neblina). S Amazonas on Cerro de la Neblina (*sadiecoatsae*); cerros of rest of Amazonas; nw Bolívar in mid. Río Caura (Cerro Tabaro); generally on tepuis of se Bolívar (*roraimae*). W Guyana; Brazil (Cerro de la Neblina); very locally in e Colombia and Andes of Ecuador and Peru.

Bran-colored Flycatcher   PLATE 45
Myiophobus fasciatus   Atrapamoscas Pechirrayado
Identification: 5″ (12.7cm). 10.5g. Widespread and inconspic. Somewhat like *Empidonax* in shape and posture. *Above reddish brown* with short yellowish white supraloral line and inconspic. broken eyering; semiconcealed yellow crown stripe (faint or absent—♀); wings and tail dark brown, *2 large prom. buffy white wing bars*, and faint whitish edgings; below dirty eggshell white with conspic. blurry brown streaks on breast; center of belly tinged yellow.
Sim. species: Distinctive reddish brown upperparts (color of "bran flakes") and streaky breast are the marks. ♀ Vermilion Flycatcher is larger, lacks wing bars, and tends to perch in open. No *Empidonax* is so streaked below.

Voice: Dawn song a husky, whistled *tep, chew-e*, over and over, mid. note lowest and after slight pause. At odd intervals during day a short, squeezed *wee'he 'he'he'e*, nasal, almost rattlelike; occas. a low *wheesp* or *wheeb*.

Behavior: Members of prs. are usually well separated and almost always encountered singly. Perch fairly low and mostly out of view in bushy areas in pastures or along forest borders. Often twitch wings rapidly and look around in nervous manner, sitting a moment, then abruptly disappearing. Perch erect and flit and perch-glean in foliage or sally to air for insects. Also take berries from small fruiting trees. Woven, vireolike cup nest fastened by rim to low horizontal fork; 2 eggs, cream with a few rusty spots at larger end[589].

Status and behavior: Common resident but somewhat local. Bushy overgrown pastures, shrubby forest borders and fence rows, thickets, brush in waste areas, and early-successional vegetation along rivers and on river isls.; dry to humid regions (but not arid). Benefits from shrubby regrowth following deforestation.

Range: To 1700m n of Orinoco; to 1200m s of Orinoco. Prob. throughout. Sierra de Perijá, Zulia; Andes from Táchira and Barinas to Lara; lowlands and mts. from Yaracuy and Carabobo to Sucre, Isla Patos, and Monagas; e Bolívar from Sierra de Imataca to Brazil border; s Amazonas (*fasciatus*); scattered sight recs. in e Falcón, Apure, Cojedes, Guárico, and n Amazonas (sight, river isl. near Pto. Ayacucho, Jun 1996). Sw Costa Rica locally to n Chile, n Argentina, and s Brazil (absent from much of c Amazonia); the Guianas (local).

Pyrrhomyias

Widespread Andean sp.; mainly rufous; allied to much larger *Hirundinea*[320,760].

Cinnamon Flycatcher   PLATE 45
Pyrrhomyias cinnamomea   Atrapamoscas Acanelado
Identification: 5″ (12.7cm). 10.8g. *Small dark rufous flycatcher of Andes and n mts.* Bill very short. *Above dark cinnamon rufous*, crown rufous chestnut with concealed golden yellow crown patch (both sexes); wings and tail dusky, *2 rufous wing bars*; *rufous patch on inner flight feathers*; tail edged dark rufous, underparts almost entirely cinnamon rufous, belly paler. Or tail more extensively edged rufous, underparts dark rufous (*pariae*). Or entirely dark olive above, tail dusky brown with no rufous (*pyrrhoptera*).
Sim. species: Only small, mostly rufous flycatcher in mts. See larger Cliff Flycatcher. In s Táchira see Rufous-breasted Flycatcher which has rufous extending up

onto side of face and neck, sharply "divided" underparts, and different behavior (often flicks up a wing).
Voice: Often hd. call a dull, low-pitched ("flatulent") little rattle, *pti-i-i-i*, spit out rather abruptly; also a stuttering *pit, pit-pit-pit-it* and a few *chip, tsip*, and *pit* notes. No dawn song.

Behavior: A charming and rather conspic. little bird that perches up with confident, self-assured manner. Often remarkably confiding. Sits erect and alert, 3–15m up, then energetically executes saucy little sallies short distances (mostly <2m) to air, rarely to foliage, and returns abruptly, as if restrained by a leash, to same perch. Highly sedentary on small, relatively permanent territories. May forage actively in presence of mixed-spp. flocks but does not reg. assoc. with or follow them. Moss and lichen cup nest on rock ledge, in crevice of rocks or bark, fallen log, etc., at least 1–5m up; 2 white eggs blotched reddish brown. In n cordilleras breeding starts Apr–May[133,170].

Status and habitat: Common resident flycatcher in highlands. Humid and wet forest borders, small forest openings, older second growth, and forest-bordered roadsides, almost always where there is small opening for sallying.

Range: 700–2900m. Sierra de Perijá, Zulia, and s Táchira (*pyrrhoptera*); Andes of n Táchira n to Lara, mts. of Yaracuy, n cordilleras from Carabobo e to e Miranda (*vieillotioides*); mts. of ne Anzoátegui, w and c Sucre, and n Monagas (*spadix*); Paria Pen., Sucre on Cerros Humo and Azul (*pariae*). Colombia s in Andes to nw Argentina.

Contopus

Rather undistinguished small to midsized flycatchers; crested (some more than others); relatively broad bill and long wings; no obvious eyering; dull or poorly defined wing bars; perch in open and sally for flying insects; several migratory spp. breed in N Amer.; field identification of some spp. difficult or unreliable without voice.

Tropical Pewee   PLATES 45, 47
Contopus cinereus   Pibí Cenizo
Identification: 5.5″ (14cm). 12g. Bill dusky above, yellowish below; *smaller and shorter-winged* than migrant *Contopus* pewees (primaries extend a third or less of tail length vs. ca. half in migrant *Contopus*). Upperparts dull grayish brown, *crown slightly darker, loral spot grayish to whitish* (not conspic. and sometimes faint), wings dusky, wing coverts and inner flight feathers pale-edged, wing bars blurry or absent, underparts

whitish, faint smoky olive wash on breast and sides, center of belly yellowish white.

Sim. species: Much like migrant wood-pewees and sometimes not safely told in field except by voice (all *Contopus* call freq.). In general Tropical Pewee is a bit smaller, trimmer, apparent tail length looks longer (because of short primary extension), crown darker, and lores usually show pale spot. In hand Tropical's 10th (outermost) primary feather is shorter than 6th (in wood-pewees it is longer) and wing shorter (65–77 vs. 77–91mm in wood-pewees)[543]. Also much like migrant *Empidonax* flycatchers which are about same size, but note pewee's less distinct wing bars, grayer color, loral spot, and voice. Pewees tend to perch up in more conspic. positions; *Empidonax* usually remain more within foliage.

Voice: Often hd. call a short, slightly trilled *tre'e'e'e* or *tir'r'r'ip* or sim. variation. Also a sharp rising *fweet!*; at dawn may sing ser. of rising *weet* notes.

Behavior: Single birds or prs. are rather sedentary and not apt to call attention to themselves as they perch erect and alert at mid. levels or lower, usually in fairly open areas at or near edge of forest. Sally med. to long distances out to air for insects and then return to same perch, often vibrating tail briefly as they land. Rarely with mixed-spp. flocks. Lichen-covered cup nest 3–14m up on fairly exposed horizontal branch or in more upright fork; 3 dull white eggs spotted brown and lilac, mostly at larger end[633].

Status and habitat: Fairly common resident along moist and humid forest edges, lighter woodland, plantations, shrubby clearings with scattered trees, and gallery forest, mostly in or near mts. or hilly regions. Most numerous in areas of moderate to low rainfall.

Range: To 1900m. Widespread in n Venez. from Zulia, Falcón, and in or near n cordilleras from Táchira, Portuguesa, s Cojedes, n Guárico, e to Sucre and Monagas; s Amazonas on Río Siapa (*bogotensis*); n Bolívar at Altagracia (*surinamensis*). S Mexico locally to n Argentina, Paraguay, s Brazil (not Amazonia), and the Guianas. Trinidad.

Eastern Wood-Pewee   PLATE 47
Contopus virens   Pibí Oriental
Identification: 6″ (15cm). 14g. Slight crest. Lower mandible *typically* dull pale yellow with dark tip. Dark grayish olive above (*no eyering*); wings and tail dusky with *2 distinct light gray wing bars* (buffy on young birds); below whitish, breast and sides tinged grayish olive, belly sometimes with faint yellowish wash, esp. young birds.

Sim. species: Very like Western Wood-Pewee (see) and prob. impossible to distinguish with certainty except by voice (both spp. call freq. on nonbreeding gds.). Willow, Alder, and Acadian flycatchers best told by prom. eyerings (wood-pewees lack eyerings), but Willow Flycatcher (occas. Alder) also often lacks eyering and also may have indistinct wing bars. In general, compared to migrant wood-pewees, these *Empidonax* are browner or greener (less gray), rounder headed, shorter billed, and shorter winged (wing tips barely extend beyond base of tail but reach a third to half way to tail tip in migrant wood-pewees). Also cf. larger migrant Olive-sided Flycatcher. Among resident spp. carefully cf. smaller Tropical Pewee.

Voice: Often vocal on wintering gds. and during both migration periods. Song a plaintive slurred *peeeawee*, drawn out; also a shorter whistled *peeeur*.

Behavior: Usually found alone perched quite erect and alert at mid. levels or higher in trees. Perches on small, partly open branches in or beneath canopy where reg. sallies out long distances to air for flying insects and returns to same perch. Not with mixed-spp. flocks. Holds feeding territories; this perhaps the reason for freq. vocalizations.

Status and habitat: Locally fairly common migrant and nonbreeding winter resident from n, rec. 13 Sep–23 Apr. Tall river-edge and gallery-forest trees, esp. where *Anacardium* (wild cashews) are numerous, and in plantations and parklike areas. Seems most numerous along e base of Andes in tall riparian forest along rivers emerging from Andes, where sometimes several can be found in small area.

Range: To 1300m n of Orinoco; to ca. 700m s of Orinoco. Sierra de Perijá, Zulia; Andes from Táchira n to Lara, Sierra de San Luis, Falcón, and Coastal Cordillera in Carabobo, Aragua, and Distr. Federal (sight, Caracas—R. Ridgely); n Amazonas (San Juan de Maniapure) and nw Bolívar on Cerro El Negro; sight/tape, Río Grande, Bolívar, Jan 1996; Delta Amacuro[343]. Breeds in e N Amer.; winters mainly in n and w S Amer. from Colombia to n Bolivia and w Brazil.

Western Wood-Pewee
Contopus sordidulus   Pibí Occidental
Identification: 6″ (15cm). 13.2g. Plumage practically identical to that of Eastern Wood-Pewee, and *the two are usually not reliably separated on nonbreeding gds. except by voice* (but both are often quite vocal on nonbreeding gds.). On avg., in fresh plumage Western Wood-Pewee is slightly darker and browner (less gray, never olive); breast band darker, browner, and more

continuous across breast; under wing coverts grayish (not white), and typically half or more of lower mandible is *dusky* (only tip in Eastern). Postbreeding arrivals on nonbreeding gds. (prior to molt) are especially drab and may not even be separable in hand as wing formulas are sim. Young of both spp. show fairly distinct pale wing bars.

Sim. species: See Eastern Wood-Pewee.

Voice: Commonest call a hoarse, nasal *phreeer* with burry quality very unlike usual call of Eastern Wood-Pewee, but Eastern occas. gives burry or hoarse call rather like that of Western Wood-Pewee.

Behavior: Sim. to that of Eastern Wood-Pewee.

Status and habitat: Uncertain. Migrant and nonbreeding winter resident from north, rec. only 6 Feb–17 Apr (no fall migrant recs?). Forest borders in humid regions. There are only a few specimens from Venez., but sp. is prob. more numerous and widespread than these suggest.

Range: To ca. 1000m. S Amazonas from Misión Parima (02°46′ N, 64°19′ W) s to Cerro de la Neblina (*veliei*); once on Sierra de Lema (km 125), e Bolívar (presum. *saturatus*). Breeds in w N Amer.; winters mostly in w S Amer. s to n Bolivia (once Argentina?).

Smoke-colored Pewee   PLATE 47
Contopus fumigatus   Pibí Ahumado

Identification: 6.7″ (17cm). 18.2g. "Peaked" crest; lower mandible yellowish. *Uniform dark gray above and below*; wings and tail dusky, underparts slightly paler, esp. belly. Imm.: whitish edgings on wings. Or in tepuis slightly smaller (6.5″, 16.5cm), darker (dark slaty gray), and wings blacker (*duidae*).

Sim. species: Nearest is Olive-sided Flycatcher in size and coloration, but note that sp.'s "unbuttoned vest" and whitish flank tufts often protruding behind wings.

Voice: Dawn song in n Aragua a spirited, whistled *whueer!* or more variable *whueer, whu-u'whuet!* over and over last 3 notes quick and rising. Call everywhere (dawn and during day) a loud *pip! pip! pip!*, often incessantly.

Behavior: Usually seen alone perched erect on high, bare twig from which it has commanding view. Sallies out long distances for flying insects and usually returns to same perch. Vibrates tail as it alights. Usually more vocal and active as mixed-spp. flocks pass through its territory. Open-cup moss- and lichen-covered nest saddled over horizontal branch, usually high.

Status and habitat: Common resident in humid mt. forest, forest borders, and clearings with scattered trees near forest.

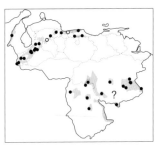

Range: Ca. 500–2800m n of Orinoco; 900–1900m s of Orinoco. Sierra de Perijá, Zulia; Andes from s Táchira to Lara at Cabudare (*ardosiacus*); mts. of Yaracuy, n cordilleras from Carabobo to Miranda (*cineraceus*); mts. of n and c Amazonas and Bolívar (*duidae*). Andes from Colombia to n Argentina. Guyana.

Note: Now considered a separate sp. from birds of C Amer., and from Mexico and sw United States[10,541]. Formerly all were called Greater Pewee, *C. fumigatus*.

Olive-sided Flycatcher   PLATE 47
Contopus cooperi   Pibí Boreal

Identification: 7″ (18cm). 32g. Bill fairly broad, lower mandible orangish; *rather stout, large-headed flycatcher with small peaked crest, long slender wings, and relatively short tail*. Mainly dark brownish olive with faintly indicated grayish wing bars and edgings; throat and median underparts creamy white, sides and flanks extensively dark olive, almost meeting across chest or sometimes forming ill-defined chest band ("unbuttoned or partially buttoned vest"); *large puffy white patch sometimes protrudes as conspic. tuft behind wing* (tuft not always visible).

Sim. species: Resembles an overgrown wood-pewee but chunkier, shorter-tailed, and with darker sides, more prom. white throat, and fainter wing bars. Look for white flank tufts protruding behind rear of wing. Greater Pewee is all dark gray.

Voice: On wintering gds. not esp. vocal but at times gives a fast, whistled *pip-pip-pip*, much like Smoke-colored Pewee. Before or during n migration may give full song, a loud, rhythmic, whistled *hic, three-beers*.

Behavior: Single birds perch on high exposed dead branches or snags from which they sally out long distances to air for flying insects and usually return to same perch. Maintain solitary, nonbreeding territories on wintering gds. where they often can be found on same perches for wks on end. Do not assoc. with mixed-spp. flocks.

Status and habitat: Uncommon and local. Migrant and nonbreeding winter resident from the north, mid Oct–mid Apr; latest rec. is 12 Apr at Rancho Grande, Aragua[33]. Moist and humid forest, wooded borders, and clearings with scattered trees. Mostly humid zones in foothills and mts.
Range: 400–2200m (sight recs. to 200m). Mts. of n Venez. from Zulia and Táchira to Sucre and Monagas; s Amazonas (once on Cerro de la Neblina); sight recs. in e Bolívar (18 Oct 1993, Sierra de Lema—P. Coopmans); 2 seen Jan 1996, Río Grande, 200m. Breeds in n and w N Amer. e to the Guianas; winters mostly in mts. of n and w S Amer. Trinidad.
Note: Specific name *cooperi* has priority over long-used *borealis*[22].

Empidonax

Uniform in appearance; notoriously confusing group of primarily N Amer. breeders; most show pale eyering, all show pale wing bars and tertial edgings, dull brownish to olive upperparts, and whitish to dull yellow underparts; plumage differs slightly with age and molt (mainly brightness of wing bars and body plumage); field marks are relative and voice is key; open cup nests.

Alder Flycatcher
Empidonax alnorum and
Willow Flycatcher
Empidonax traillii   Atrapamoscas Pálido
Identification: 5.5″ (14cm). 12–13g. These 2 N Amer. breeding migrants are usually not distinguishable on wintering gds. unless calling, nor in hand, and are here treated and mapped together. Bill dusky, lower mandible usually entirely pale. Upperparts brownish to grayish strongly washed olive, narrow whitish eyering fairly prom. to absent; wings dusky brown, *2 fairly well marked* (usually) *pale buff to dull whitish wing bars* (dullest on older returning migrants), throat whitish (moderate contrast with gray-tinged face), breast grayish to brownish olive, belly yellowish to whitish (yellower in young birds).
Sim. species: Very sim. to Acadian Flycatcher and best told by voice. All 3 spp. reg. give call notes, but not song, on wintering gds. Acadian avgs. greener above, yellower below, and tends to have more prom. eyering; in all cases, field identification should be reinforced by confirmation of vocal differences (see under Voice). In hand, Acadian has difference between longest and 6th (5th from outside) primary of more than 6mm, Alder and Willow *usually* less than 6mm. Euler's Flycatcher, also very sim., best told by buffier wing bars, much shorter primary extension, and vocalizations. Fuscous Flycatcher is larger with long, narrow eyebrow, buff wing bars, and notably long tail. Also see *Contopus* pewees.
Voice: Usual call of more southerly breeding Willow Flycatcher a short, dry *whit!*; that of more northerly breeding Alder Flycatcher a soft *pit* or *pip*. Full songs of these 2 siblings are rarely hd. on wintering gds., although partial to full songs may be hd. during northward passage; Willow sings *FEtz-bew!* with 1st note emphasized, Alder a burry *freeBEeo* with 2d note emphasized.

Behavior: Wintering birds in Venez. usually hold small individual territories where they are inconspic., sally to air from low perches, and forage mostly independently of mixed-spp. flocks. *Empidonax* often flick tails downward (unlike pewees which may vibrate tail upon alighting).
Status and habitat: Migrant and nonbreeding winter residents from north, 30 Aug–13 Feb (prob. remain later), to shrubby forest borders and open moist and humid forest. Known from small no. of recs. mostly from w part of Venez. Status of the 2 siblings unclear because of identification problems. Since the 2 spp. are separable in the field solely on basis of voice and thus cannot be distinguished in Venez. in most cases, they are mapped together here. Most S Amer. birds may be Alder Flycatchers, whereas Willow Flycatchers may occur mostly in C Amer.

Range: To 550m (doubtless much higher). Sierra de Perijá and s end of Maracaibo Basin, Zulia, w base of Andes in Táchira, Mérida, and Trujillo (Mendoza); se Lara, c and e Falcón (Coro; Mirimire), n Aragua, and e of Andes in w Apure (Guasdualito). Breed in N Amer.; winter from s Mexico to Panama and mostly in mountainous w half of S Amer. s to n Argentina.

Acadian Flycatcher
Empidonax virescens   Atrapamoscas Copete Verde
Identification: 5.5″ (14cm). 12.9g. Rather large flat bill (largest bill of genus), lower mandible pinkish yellow; long wings extend half length of tail (primary extension among longest of genus). *Uniformly greenish olive* above, pale lores; *whitish eyering conspic. but narrow* (sometimes faint), 2 pale *buff* wing bars and buff tertial edgings, throat usually whitish, rest of underparts dull white with brownish olive wash on breast, distinct yellowish tinge on flanks and lower underparts.
Sim. species: See Alder and Willow flycatchers. Acadian looks greenish tinged above and pale below, but as a rule not safely told from Alder and Willow except by voice. *Contopus* pewees are larger and bulkier, differ in shape (crested, longer winged), and have less obvious wing bars, usually little evident eyering. On wintering gds. Acadian almost always safely told only by voice.
Voice: Often hd. call a fairly loud *wheep!* or *fweep!*, rather unlike that of Willow or Alder flycatchers.
Behavior: Usually found alone at moderate ht. in wooded regions where sallies to air or foliage and bark surfaces for insects and often returns to same perch. Mostly independent of mixed-spp. flocks. Rather lethargic. Does not flick wings or tail much; often perches with wings slightly drooped[290].

Status and habitat: Uncommon migrant and non-breeding winter resident from the north, Nov–Mar, to forest borders, shady plantations, and second-growth woodland. Almost certainly more numerous than small no. of recs. indicates. Found reg. in Río Quinimarí (ca. 1000m) of se Táchira.

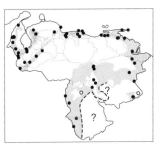

Range: 600–1200m (prob. lower and higher). Sierra de Perijá, Zulia, nw Táchira n to w Trujillo (Betijoque); se Táchira (sight). Breeds in e N Amer.; winters from Costa Rica to Colombia (to 2600m) and s Ecuador.

Lathrotriccus

Inconspic. forest dwellers; resemble *Empidonax* but anatomical details differ[325].

Euler's Flycatcher   PLATE 45
Lathrotriccus euleri   Atrapamoscas de Sotobosque
Identification: 5″ (12.7cm). 11g. Rather flat bill dark above, pale below. *Crown and upperparts brown*, obscure whitish supraloral line; faint narrow eyering; wings dusky, *2 pale buff wing bars*; inner flight feathers edged pale buff, underparts pale dull yellowish, paler on throat, washed olive on breast and sides; belly yellowish. Or slightly paler and grayer overall (*bolivianus*). Austral migrants (browner above, whiter below; rufous-tinged wing bars) unrec. but possible.
Sim. species: Dull and confusing. Looks like a migrant *Empidonax* but browner and with buff wing bars. Best clue is distinctive voice. In hand (field?) wings shorter and rounder than in *Empidonax*. Also cf. Tropical Pewee and Fuscous Flycatcher.
Voice: Song an abrupt, almost explosive *FEEU! pe'pe 'pe'p'p*, 1st note loudest, last notes run together, buzzy and downscale.
Behavior: Rather quiet and inconspic., except for occas. loud call. Usually seen alone and perched fairly erect in lower story of forest. Sallies out to foliage and may return to same perch a few times before moving on (not as faithful to perch as *Empidonax* and *Contopus*). Generally independent of mixed-spp. flocks. Nest a soft, black-fiber-lined cup in fork or over knothole; 1–2m up; 2–3 eggs, cream with reddish brown spots and blotches, chiefly at larger end[175].
Status and habitat: Uncommon to locally fairly common resident in moist and humid forest, open forest borders, and mature second-growth woodland. Lowlands and foothills, but distrib. somewhat spotty. Found reg. above Maracay in drier vegetation along Choroní Rd.
Range: To 1500m n of Orinoco; to 1000m s of Orinoco. Maracaibo Basin, w and e Falcón, and generally in

Andes and n cordilleras e to Anzoátegui, Sucre, Monagas, and Delta Amacuro; nw Bolívar (Cerro Tabaro; lower Río Caura) e to Sierra de Imataca and Río Cuyuní (*flaviventris*); Amazonas e to se Bolívar (*bolivianus*). Andes s to n Argentina; Amazon Basin s of the Amazon to n Argentina and Uruguay; locally in the Guianas.
Note: Formerly placed in *Empidonax*[325]. Subsp. *lawrencei* synonymized with *flaviventris*.

Fuscous Flycatcher   PLATE 45
Cnemotriccus fuscatus   Atrapamoscas Fusco
Identification: 5.7″ (14.5cm). 11.9g. Rather dingy, inconspic. flycatcher with *flattish* head, *long, thin eyeline, and unusually long tail* (65–72mm); bill rather long and thin; base of lower mandible pale. Prom. blackish eyes. Above plain brown with *long, narrow, dull white eyebrow* (slight curve over eyes imparts frown); *2 broad buff wing bars* (bright to dull) and buff edgings on inner flight feathers; throat dirty white, breast brownish gray, belly pale yellow. Or dark brown above (*fuscatior*); or rufescent brown above, belly whitish (*duidae*).
Sim. species: Shape, eyebrow, and wing bars are best marks. Recalls both *Empidonax* and Euler's Flycatcher but larger, much longer tailed. Mouse-colored Tyrannulet is paler, has less distinct eyebrow, whitish wing bars (most races), shorter tail, and different habits. Also cf. pewees.
Voice: Soft, easily overlooked song in Apure a low-pitched, slightly buzzy *jaw-jew-jew-jew jew*, quick but slowing at end; at dawn a shorter rolling *pü-breeer-breeer*. Call a short, abrupt *feétz-beeu*; in se Sucre a strong, reedy *pfEEO!* and *pfeeu-pfeeu-pfeea*. At dawn birds of c and s Amazonas (*duidae*) give clear whistled *chueeeeeEEEEchueeET!*, rising (last note slightly higher); or *chueeEEE!*; and softer *chuEEEEchee*, over and over, very unlike n forms (K. Zimmer recording).
Behavior: A modest little flycatcher of retiring manners. Single birds or well-separated prs. are inconspic. as perch low (0.1–3m up) and quietly in undergrowth and sally short distances to foliage, often hovering momentarily beneath a leaf, or sallying down to gd. Posture rather horizontal. Stay in shady areas inside or beneath cover where easily overlooked except for occas. song. Rarely venture into open, and most subspp. show affinity for low-lying or swampy places near water. Seldom with mixed-spp. flocks. Trinidad nest a black-fiber-lined twig and bark cup 3m up in fork; 3 white eggs with black markings, chiefly around larger end[175].
Status and habitat: Uncommon to fairly common resident in a fairly wide variety of habitats incl. thickets

inside or at edge of dry to humid forest, along borders of gallery forest, thickets along várzea forest creeks, and in dense vegetation on river isls. (e.g., in Orinoco).

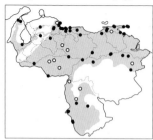

Range: To 900m n of Orinoco (most recs. below 500m); to 250m s of Orinoco. W Apure (*fuscatior*); rest of Venez. n of Orinoco; n Bolívar from mouth of Río Apure (Caicara) e to Delta Amacuro and lower Río Cuyuní (*cabanisi*); c and s Amazonas from Cerro Yapacana southward (*duidae*); several sight recs. in nw Amazonas (subsp.?). N Colombia and e of Andes s to n Argentina and s Brazil.
Note: Variation in song, plumage, and habits suggests more than 1 sp. Subsp. *duidae* in particular is prob. a separate sp. (A. Whittaker).

Sayornis

Mainly n temperate latitudes; relatively narrow bill; longish tail; erect posture; well-formed cup nest.

Black Phoebe   PLATE 48
Sayornis nigricans   Tigüin de Agua
Identification: 7″ (18cm). 18g. Unmistakable. *Entirely sooty black with white belly*; 2 white wing bars; inner flight feathers broadly edged white, long tail notched at tip and narrowly edged white; bill and legs blackish. ♀: duller.
Voice: Bright, rising *peeert* and other shrill notes. Infreq. given flight song a ser. of trills mixed with thin scraping notes, i.e., *t't't't-esk-u, t't't't, esk-u, psip, esk-u, t't't't* . . . and so on as flutters almost vertically, then earthward to a perch. May continue song, accompanied by raising and spreading wings and tail, when perched.
Behavior: Confiding, sometimes almost fearless. Prs. perch on boulders in streams or on buildings, utility lines, fences, and other exposed places, usually near water. Sally to near surface of water, to gd., or occas. to air and often return to same perch. Freq. dip tail upon alighting or when perched. Cup nest of mud pellets and grass on rocky ledge, crevice, under bridge or eave; in vicinity of water; 2–3 white eggs, sometimes with brown spots.
Status and habitat: Common resident in semiopen areas along streams and around shores of small ponds and lakes, mainly in foothills and mts. (rarely to sea level). Often around human habitations if there is moving water.
Range: To 3000m (mostly 200–2500m). Throughout mts. of n from Zulia, Falcón, and Táchira to Anzoátegui, Sucre, and Monagas (*angustirostris*). W N Amer. s

in mts. to nw Argentina. Austral breeders migratory n to Colombia.
Note: Extent of white edging on wings and amt. of white on belly are clinal, with least white on wings and most white on belly in N Amer. birds, reverse in S. Amer.

Pyrocephalus

Monotypic genus; widespread; n temperate and austral pops. migratory; unusual among tyrannids for sexual dimorphism.

Vermilion Flycatcher   PLATE 45
Pyrocephalus rubinus   Atrapamoscas Sangre de Toro
Identification: 5.5″ (14cm). 14g. Slight crest. ♂ unmistakable; *crown and entire underparts brilliant crimson*; stripe through eyes, rearcrown, and upperparts sooty black. ♀: very different; above ashy brown, wings and tail darker, throat and breast whitish, *breast with variable amt. of dusky streaking, flanks and lower underparts strawberry*, belly sometimes whitish. Imm ♂: above like ♀; below all white broadly streaked dusky, small amts. of pink in patches (or none at all) on crown and underparts. Austral birds (as yet unrec. in Venez. but likely) sim., but ♀♀ *lack* pink; dark streaking extends over belly.
Sim. species: ♀ and imm. often confused. Note combination of crest, erect posture, streaks, and strawberry tinge on lower underparts. See Bran-colored Flycatcher and ♀ *Knipolegus* tyrants.
Voice: Call a high, metallic *peep!* or 3–4 slightly trilled notes. ♂ sings a high, tinkling song in predawn darkness, *titi'tr'e'e'E*, over and over. In delightful flight display, at intervals throughout day, rarely even at night, ♂ climbs steeply but slowly on fluttery wings and begins singing ser. of tinkling trills which continue as wings are raised in V and bird flutters slowly earthward. In alarm (e.g., hawk overhead) ♂♂ may fly up, circle, and rapidly repeat this same trill.
Behavior: A small black and red bird perched on a fence, bush, or low open branch beneath an isolated tree is likely to be this sp. Known as *Hijo del Sol* ("Son of the Sun") to many Spanish speakers, this celebrated little jewel often seems almost out of place among the dry, scrubby places it frequents. Single birds or scattered prs. are notably confiding but keep to themselves. Sally to gd., often pouncing with brief flutter, for insects, less often sally to air. Open lichen and grass cup nest suspended or saddled in low fork; 2–3 white eggs with large red brown spots; Mar–Nov breeding, Apure to Anzoátegui[137,186,734].

Status and habitat: Common and widespread resident in dry to moist open or semiopen country with trees and scrubby vegetation, esp. in parklike areas, hotel gds., also borders of deciduous woodlands and desert scrub.

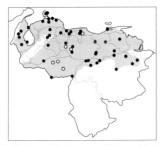

Range: To 800m n of Orinoco; to 500m s of Orinoco. Throughout in semiopen areas n of Orinoco and in n Bolívar (*saturatus*). Sw US to s Argentina and n Chile. Galápagos Isls.
Note: Austral breeding migrants (*P. r. rubinus*) reach s Colombia and possibly s Venez. ♂ as above. ♀ white heavily streaked dusky below (no strawberry wash); yellow crissum.

Ochthoeca

Mainly open or semiopen highlands or shrubby stream borders; short, thin bill; long rictal bristles; chunky shape; narrow tail; most have long eyebrow.

Blackish Chat-Tyrant   PLATE 45
Ochthoeca nigrita   Pitajo Negro
Identification: 4.6" (11.7cm). Andean streamsides. Entirely slaty black with *large elongated white supraloral spot* ("false eye") ending at top of each eye.
Sim. species: Should not be confused, but see Black Phoebe. White "eyespots" are conspic. In s Táchira see Slaty-backed Chat-Tyrant.
Voice: Infreq. gives rather loud, buzzy whistle, abrupt and slightly descending.
Behavior: Single birds or well-separated members of prs. perch low, sometimes partly in open, where they sally out in loops for flying insects and often return to same perch. Generally occur in dense streamside vegetation where they are easily overlooked except for fairly loud calls which can be hd. above roar of water. Sedentary and not with mixed-spp. flocks.
Status and habitat: Uncommon and local resident in dense shrubbery along steep-gradient mt. streams or in nearby humid and wet forest borders. Has been seen occas. at upper end of San Isidro Rd. (1500m), nw Bari-

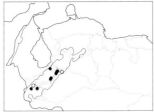

nas, and along shrub-bordered streams above La Grita (ca. 2100m), n Táchira.
Range: ENDEMIC. 1900–2900m (sightings to 1500m). N Táchira (Páramo Zumbador) to n Mérida and nw Barinas (sightings).
Note: Previously considered a subsp. of Slaty-backed Chat-Tyrant (*O. cinnamomeiventris*)[403].

Slaty-backed Chat-Tyrant
Ochthoeca cinnamomeiventris   Pitajo Espalda Negra
Identification: 4.8" (12.2cm). 11.9g. Streamsides in s Táchira. Head, upperparts, and throat slaty black; *large elongated white supraloral spot* ("false eye") ends at top of each eye; lower *breast and belly rich dark chestnut.*
Sim. species: Unlikely confused, but see Black Phoebe which has white on wings but not on head. In n Táchira and Mérida see Blackish Chat-Tyrant.
Voice: Infreq. hd. advertising call a loud, burry whistle, *sweeeeeea,* rising slightly then falling. Easily hd. above noise of rushing mt. streams. In Ecuador dawn song this same phrase followed by 3–4 *tseét* notes[541].
Behavior: Sim. to Blackish Chat-Tyrant.
Status and habitat: Locally fairly common resident of bushy forest borders or shrubbery near mt. streams. Numerous specimens from vicinity of Cerro Las Copas. Wooded streamsides with patches of thick vegetation are key.

Range: 1800–2800m. S Táchira in Río Chiquito and Cerro Las Copas (*cinnamomeiventris*). Colombia s in Andes to n Bolivia.
Note: See Note under Blackish Chat-Tyrant.

Rufous-breasted Chat-Tyrant   PLATE 45
Ochthoeca rufipectoralis   Pitajo Pechirrufo
Identification: 5.2" (13.2cm). 12g. Chunky and large-headed. Short, thin bill. Above warm brown, crown grayish brown, *forehead and long narrow eyebrow white,* wings and tail dusky, *1 bold cinnamon rufous wing bar* (sometimes 2 rufous bars visible); tail narrowly edged white; underparts grayish white with *broad cinnamon rufous breast band.*
Sim. species: Eyebrow and broad breast band are best marks. See Brown-backed Chat-Tyrant.
Voice: Song in Colombia an abrupt *ch-brrr, ch-brrr, ch-brrr;* also clucking notes[360]; a faint *cleeoo* and rapid ser. of *pt* notes ending with 2 *cleeoo* notes.
Behavior: Usually in rather lively but quiet prs. or families of 3–4 that stay close together in mid. to upper part of stunted trees and treeline shrubs. Perch upright with alert attitude, in open or semiopen, and with tail down. Move from tree to tree in short bouncy flights. Sally to foliage, often hovering adroitly to take small in-

sects; less often sally to air. May follow mixed-spp. flocks or forage independently of them about equally. In Colombia, moss cup nest on rock ledge, and sheltered by stunted trees[750].
Status and behavior: Fairly common resident (many specimens) of high-el. humid and wet forest, stunted forest, and shrubby slopes near treeline. Much more a woodland bird than Brown-backed Chat-Tyrant.

Range: 2750–3100m. Sierra de Perijá, Zulia (*rubicundula*). Colombia s in Andes to n Bolivia.

Brown-backed Chat-Tyrant   PLATE 45
Ochthoeca fumicolor   Pitajo Ahumado
Identification: 6″ (15cm). 17g. Flat headed; short, thin bill. Two distinct races. Above brown with *long bright rufous eyebrow*; wings and tail dusky, *2 prom. rufous wing bars* (lower one usually broadest), throat grayish, *rest of underparts bright rufous*, center of belly and under tail coverts whitish, tail conspic. edged white. Or sim. but *long eyebrow whitish*, throat grayish, rest of underparts smoky olive brown, center of belly and under tail coverts buff to clay (*fumicolor*).
Sim. species: Cf. Rufous-breasted Chat-Tyrant which has well-defined breast band.
Voice: Rather quiet. Occas. a soft *prip!* when foraging; perched a clear, whistled *kleeeip*. At dawn (ne Mérida) prs. sing a fast, rhythmic duet, *plee, plít'ter'téw, plít'ter'téw* . . . , chattery, up to 12 phrases slowing at end; song variations (always duets?) incl. *cháp'pa-cháp'pa* or *cháp'it'dip!*; also other soft notes sung while perched or in flight.
Behavior: Single birds or scattered prs. are conspic. as take prom. perches on top or side of shrubs and bushes, perch erect with tail down, and sally out varying distances to gd., foliage, or air for small insect prey. After prey capture sometime return to same bush or more often continue to another, typically moving considerable distance. Fur-lined cup nest, 18 Mar, low in an *Espeletia*[778]. Eggs in Colombia white with a few rusty spots[580].
Status and habitat: Common resident in fairly open high-el. habitats incl. stunted trees, bushes, and thickets at treeline, shrub-bordered pastures, *Polylepis* woodland at or above treeline, and open paramo with

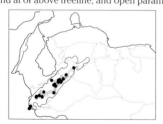

Espeletia. Some seasonal or local el. movements occur as it is occas. found in wooded borders well below treeline.
Range: 2200–4200m (most recs. above 2700m). Andes of s Táchira on Páramo de Tamá (*fumicolor*); Andes of n Táchira and Mérida n to Trujillo/Lara border at Páramo Cendé (*superciliosa*). Colombia s in Andes to n Bolivia.
Note: Birds n and s of Táchira Depression could be separate spp.[545].

Yellow-bellied Chat-Tyrant   PLATE 45
Ochthoeca diadema   Pitajo Diadema
Identification: 4.8″ (12.2cm). Large headed; short, thin bill. Above dark olive, crown darker; broad *bright yellow* forehead (occas. ochre yellow) *continues as long narrow yellow eyebrow*; lores blackish, wings and tail dull grayish brown (essentially unmarked), throat and center of belly bright yellow, rest of underparts yellowish olive. Or back rufescent brown, wing bars rufous, broad rufous edgings on wings (*rubellula*).
Sim. species: Combination of chunky shape, yellow on underparts, and long yellow eyestripe diagnostic; also note habitat. Cf. Rufous-breasted Chat-Tyrant, Citrine Warbler, and Superciliaried and Oleaginous hemispinguses, all with white or yellow eyebrows and different habits.
Voice: Dawn song in n Táchira a fast, thin, and delicate little trill (ca. 1.5 sec) that ascends slightly, *chiiiiiiii-iiiiiiiit* (or *prrrreeeeeeeee*), like fingers running up a comb. Song typically given only a few times at first light. Day song (infreq. hd.) in Trujillo a longer (2 sec), thin trill that sags slightly in middle, *chiiiiiiiiaaaaaaaa iiiiiiii*, then ascends at end; also a much longer trill (4.2 sec), *pppprrrreeeeeeeeeeeeeeeaa*, that slowly rises then drops slightly at end. In conflict a rising trill followed immediately by slower descending trill, over and over, *preeeeeeeeee'sku'u'u'u*, and other sharp bickering notes. In all areas sings mainly for a short time at dawn.
Behavior: A quiet and retiring bird that stays out of public eye. Single birds or well-separated prs. perch fairly erect, mostly 0.5–5m up in mossy forest understory, flick tail up, and sally short distances to take insect prey from foliage with audible snap; also sally to twigs, occas. to gd. Sometimes surprisingly fearless, but typically inconspic. in thick shadowy undergrowth this sp. haunts. Active around mixed-spp. flocks but does not follow them. Descriptions of nest type are conflicting; 4 creamy white eggs, apparently in mossy cup on bank[589].
Status and habitat: Fairly common resident but easily overlooked. Inside humid and wet mossy forest (cloud forest); often near forest borders, but normally not out in open.
Range: 2100–3050m. Sierra de Perijá, Zulia (*rubellula*); Andes of s Táchira (*diadema*) and n Táchira, Mérida, and Trujillo n to Cuevas de Carache (*meridana*); 1950–ca. 2200m in Coastal Cordillera of Aragua and Distr. Federal (*tovarensis*). Colombia s in Andes to n Bolivia.
Note 1: Generic placement controversial[189,320,545].
Note 2: Crowned Chat-Tyrant (*O. frontalis*) of Andes from ne Colombia (Norte de Santander) to Bolivia

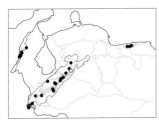

could occur in s Táchira. Dark brown above (no bars); *prom. white forehead and long white eyebrow*; underparts dark gray; under tail coverts rufous buff. Undergrowth of stunted treeline shrubbery.

Ochthornis

Short, thin, flattish bill; tail squarish; drab plumage; riverine habits.

Drab Water-Tyrant   PLATE 45
Ochthornis littoralis   Atrapamoscas Ribereño
Identification: 5.3″ (13.5cm). 13.4g. Nondescript. *Never far from banks of large rivers.* Mainly *pale sandy brown*, crown browner with weakly indicated whitish supraloral line, dusky loral mark, and whitish chin and belly; wings and tail dusky brown, rump pale (color of dry sand).
Sim. species: A drab little bird with dark and contrasting wings and tail. Riverbank habitat a good clue. See Fuscous Flycatcher.
Voice: Rather quiet but occas. a soft *squEEEa*. Prs. also give lively, sputtering duets of a few fast but variable phrases changing to ca. 4–6 rhythmic phrases . . . *WHEE'te'dek, WHEE'te'dek* . . . accompanied by wing fluttering (K. Zimmer).
Behavior: Always near water. Single birds or more often prs. are inconspic. as perch on exposed roots and vines overhanging or protruding from bare, steepcut riverbanks, or on sticks and brush piles near water's edge. Typically flush in front of passing boats and fly ahead 50–100m, low along water's edge, before stopping in open again. Sally short distances to air or gd., or close to surface of water for insects. When rivers flood their banks, water-tyrants move (migrate) vertically with water level and continue to perch low (0.2–1m up) over water, on snags and bushes. In se Peru, open cup nest of grass, rootlets, and mud 3m up on riverbank ledge; dry season.
Status and habitat: Usually common but sometimes rather thinly spread resident along steep eroded banks of large rivers, esp. where snags, exposed roots, and

driftwood are present; not grassy riverbanks and rarely along small shady forest streams.
Range: To 600m. Throughout Amazonas and Bolívar (but not ne Bolívar); possible sight rec. in ne Monagas[58]. Se Colombia to n Bolivia and w and c Amaz. Brazil; s Guyana; French Guiana and extreme ne Brazil.

Myiotheretes

Forested or open Andean highlands; notable for cinnamon or rufous patches in wings (sometimes also tail); fairly long bill; short legs; strong fliers.

Smoky Bush-Tyrant   PLATE 47
Myiotheretes fumigatus   Atrapamoscas Terrestre
Identification: 8″ (20.3cm). Large dark tyrannid of high Andes. *At rest nondescript and somewhat thrushlike.* Uniform dark smoky brown with whitish mottling on throat; wings and tail dusky; *under wing coverts and base of inner margins of flight feathers cinnamon rufous* (conspic. only in flight), under tail coverts dingy buff. Or with obscure grayish white eyebrow, under tail coverts brownish (*olivaceus*).
Sim. species: In flight dark plumage and flashing rufous wings are diagnostic. Cf. Streak-throated Bush-Tyrant and Cliff Flycatcher, both paler and with rufous in wings and tail. Also cf. Black-billed Thrush.
Voice: Dawn song a long-sustained but halting ser. of clear, whistled notes, *cheea, cheea, cheea, chuEE*, or more often singer alternates 3- and 4-noted phrases, *chura, chura, chEEea . chura, chura, chura cheEEea*, with scarcely a break between songs. One of earliest predawn singers. During day occas. a soft downslurred whistle, *peeeee* (recalls that of Dusky-capped Flycatcher). Infreq. a soft, 3-noted, slurred whistle, falling then rising.
Behavior: Prs. sit alert and erect on open limbs in canopy and keep partly obscured by foliage, or much less often perch in open on high bare snags (latter mainly at dawn). Sally-glean outward various distances to take prey from foliage or limbs, less often hawk prey in long swoops to air or down to near gd. May join mixed-spp. flocks but most often independent of them.
Status and habitat: Uncommon and local resident in canopy of humid and wet forest and forest borders. Usually well below treeline; replaced at higher el. and in more open areas by Streak-throated Bush-Tyrant. Found reg. at ca. 2200–2400m in PN Guaramacal, Trujillo.

Range: 2200–3600m. Sierra de Perijá, Zulia, and Andes of s Táchira (*olivaceus*); Andes of n Táchira, Mérida, and Trujillo n to Cuevas de Carache and Páramo Cendé (*lugubris*). Colombia s in Andes to s Peru.

Streak-throated Bush-Tyrant   PLATE 47

Myiotheretes striaticollis   Atrapamoscas Chifla Perro
Identification: 9″ (23cm). 64g. Large. Relatively heavy bill. Short legs. Above plain brown; obscure frosty supraloral mark; wings and tail dusky, *under wing coverts, base of inner webs of flight feathers, and all but central pr. of tail feathers cinnamon tipped black* (conspic. blocks of cinnamon in flight), *throat white streaked dusky*, rest of underparts cinnamon.
Sim. species: From a distance brings to mind a thrush, but note short-legged stance. Watch for striking cinnamon color in wings and tail. In forested areas see Smoky Bush-Tyrant and Cliff Flycatcher.
Voice: Often hd. call a loud, clear whistle, *peeeeee*, slightly rising and unmistakably humanlike in quality. Also a strident, whistled *stee-deek!* (quality of *Tyrannus*). Territorial and advertisement call 2–4 loud humanlike whistles (like placing fingers in mouth to whistle), *püEEET . . wuuu . . eee*, varied to *püEEET . . wüEET . . . sueet . . peeu* (ca. 5 sec). Spanish name ("dog whistler") reflects these latter vocalizations.
Behavior: Usually alone or in well-scattered prs. that sit in open on high perches, incl. overhead wires or tops of bushes, and sally long distances in swooping forays to air or gd. for arthropods and small vertebrates. Freq. return to same perch. When perched often dip tail down and sideways in sweeping motion. Nestlings in trashy cup nest under bridge, early Mar, Mitisús, Mérida.
Status and behavior: Uncommon resident in open pastures or cleared areas with a few scattered trees and bushes, overgrown landslides, and around buildings and habitations (e.g., Hotel Los Frailes, Mérida); locally up into lower paramo. Avoids very wet and very dry regions; some seasonal el. movement likely. Replaced inside humid montane forest by Smoky Bush-Tyrant.

Range: 2100–3100m (prob. higher). Sierra de Perijá, Zulia; Andes of Táchira and Mérida (*striaticollis*). Colombia s in Andes to nw Argentina.

Hirundinea

Long, pointed, swallowlike wings; longish tail; *unusually short legs*; bill broad; rictal bristles short; most closely related to smaller *Pyrrhomyias*; inhabits cliffs and large rock outcrops.

Cliff Flycatcher   PLATE 47

Hirundinea ferruginea   Atrapamoscas de Precipicios
Identification: 7.3″ (18.5cm). 21g. Unmistakable in cliff habitat. Bill rather long and wide at base; wings long. Above incl. wings and tail sooty brown; *large rufous patch at base of flight feathers* (inner webs of most flight feathers) *and all but central pr. of tail feathers rufous broadly tipped dusky* (conspic. in flight), narrow frontlet, orbital area, and cheeks freckled black and white ("salt and pepper" look), chin gray, rest of underparts dull rufous. Or wings and tail sooty black essentially without rufous (*ferruginea*).
Voice: Dawn song a rapid, high, tinny *kit-ti-LEE* over and over. Day calls sim. (single phrase) or a high-pitched, insistent *killy, killy . . .* or *kaleé, kaleé . . .* and other noisy variations, all nasal, metallic, and ringing. Some calls resemble those of American Kestrel and Bat Falcon; vocalizations throughout vast range are sim.
Behavior: Prs. or families perch on large, exposed rock faces or cliffs or on plants that have gained purchase in crevices on cliffs. Conspic. as chatter noisily and sally long distances in buoyant, swallowlike flight for flying insects. Often abruptly execute "about-face" on perch and are typically rather excitable and restless, although notably fearless of humans. Near nest ads. perform distraction displays. Grass and moss cup nest in crevice or ledge on cliff, roadcut, esp. on quartzite cerros and mesas s of Orinoco.
Status and habitat: Local. Resident, confined to cliffs, rock canyon faces, roadcuts, and rock quarries. First reported in Venez. Andes 12km w of Barinitas on 26 Jul 1969 (P. Alden) and 26 Nov 1982 at La Fundación, w of Pregonero, Táchira (C. Parrish); many subsequent recs. Not yet found in highland towns or around buildings as in s part of range but perhaps spreading. More widespread s of Orinoco.

Range: Disjunct. 1000–2500m n of Orinoco (sight recs. to 750m); 100–1900m s of Orinoco. Sierra de Perijá, Zulia; nw Barinas (*sclateri*); sight, ne Táchira (subsp.?); cerros of Amazonas s to San Carlos de Río Negro (sight); cerros of Bolívar (*ferruginea*). Mts. from Colombia to Cuzco, Peru; mts. of n Bolivia to c Argentina; cerros of e Colombia and the Guianas; e Bolivia to se Brazil, e Paraguay, ne Argentina, and Uruguay. Austral birds migratory.

Knipolegus

Most spp. in s S Amer.; sexually dimorphic (♂♂ often black with conspic. blue gray bills); notably quiet; ♂♂ give aerial displays (vertical sallies) accompanied by weak clicking and buzzing vocalizations at peak of flight; open cup nests low in trees or shrubs.

Rufous-tailed Tyrant PLATE 45
Knipolegus poecilurus Viudita de las Serranías
Identification: 6" (15cm). 14.6g. *Eyes red.* Bill fairly
long. Above brownish gray, wings darker with *2 broad
buffy gray wing bars*; inner flight feathers edged buff,
under wing coverts cinnamon, tail dusky, *all but central pr. broadly edged cinnamon* (conspic. in flight),
outermost pr. all cinnamon, throat and belly pale buff,
breast olive gray sometimes indistinctly streaked buff.
Or sim. but wing markings fainter and whitish, underparts duller and grayer, tail with only hint of cinnamon
edging (*salvini*). Or wings essentially unmarked; no
cinnamon on tail (*paraquensis*).
Sim. species: Red eyes and rufous in tail are diagnostic
in Andes. Tepui races duller, darker, and confusing.
Note shape and erect posture which might recall a
Contopus pewee or ♀ Vermilion Flycatcher, also buffy
throat and habit of sitting up in open. Up close look for
red eyes which are duller than in Andean birds.
Voice: Call in se Bolívar a short, metallic trill, *triiit.*
Behavior: Recalls that of a phoebe. Perches fairly upright and usually exposed on shrubs, lower part of
trees, or on fences, or higher along forest edges. Often
lifts tail then slowly lowers it. Sallies to air for insects or
drops briefly to gd. Alone or in prs. and seldom
around mixed-spp. flocks.
Status and habitat: Uncommon and local resident
both n and s of Orinoco. Humid and wet, semiopen,
montane areas. Mature or second-growth forest borders and bushy pastures with scattered trees. S of Orinoco in openings in dense melastome-dominated and
stunted second growth on white sandy soils of Sierra
de Lema (1350m).

Range: 1000–2000m n of Orinoco; 900–2400m s of Orinoco. Sierra de Perijá (*poecilurus*); Andes of n Táchira
(no s Táchira recs.?), Mérida, and nw Barinas (sight,
San Isidro Rd.); Coastal Cordillera in Distr. Federal; Interior Cordillera on Cerro Platillón, Aragua/Carabobo
border (*venezuelanus*); nw Amazonas on Cerro Sipapo (*paraquensis*); c and s Amazonas (Cerros Yapacana; Duida; de la Neblina; Sierra de Unturán) and s
Bolívar from Meseta de Jaua and Sierra de Lema southward (*salvini*). Locally in Andes from Colombia to n
Bolivia. W Guyana.

Riverside Tyrant PLATE 48
Knipolegus orenocensis Viudita Ribereña
Identification: 6" (15cm). 19.3g. *Thickish bill pale blue
gray tipped black*; eyes dark. Somewhat "puff headed"
in appearance. ♂: overall dull slaty black, flight feathers brownish, lower back and lower underparts tinged

grayish; slight bushy or peaked crest; tail somewhat
rounded. ♀: much paler, uniform ashy gray tinged
olive, head slightly darker. Juv.: much like ♀, indistinct
buff streaking below.
Sim. species: Slight crest and erect posture suggest a
phoebe. Cf. ♂ with ♂ Amazonian Black-Tyrant which
is smaller, glossy black, and along shady streamsides
or inside low-canopied várzea forest. Also see much
smaller Black Manakin. ♀ nearest ♀ Amazonian Black-
Tyrant but larger and with little or no streaking below,
and always note habitat differences.
Voice: Soft, musical *peEEo* with downward inflection.
In e Brazil (*sclateri*) has jump display sim. to many others of genus; ♂ darts up a few meters into air and
makes mechanical (or vocal?) clicking sound as it
drops back to perch[545].
Behavior: Single birds or prs. perch mostly 0.5–4m up
in grass and shrubs, sometimes in open on top where
conspic., but more often partially in cover. Sally out or
down to grass or foliage or drop to gd. for prey. Often
flick tail up. At times wary and difficult to approach
closely.
Status and habitat: Local resident. Early-succession
vegetation on seasonally flooded river isls., esp. in
areas with tall grass mixed with shrubs, patches of *Tessaria* (Compositae), and young *Cecropia* saplings.
Found with some reg. on river isls. in vicinity of Pto.
Ayacucho. Scattered sight recs. (and video) Nov–Mar
in marshes at Hato Cedral, w Apure (D. Ascanio).

Range: To 150m. Lower Río Apure (San Fernando de
Apure), and Orinoco from vicinity of Pto. Ayacucho
(sight[259]) and mouth of Río Meta (Pto. Páez) to se Anzoátegui at Soledad (*orenocensis*); sight, w Apure at
Hato Cedral (prob. *orenocensis*). Extreme e Colombia
(Meta); the Amazon and larger tributaries from se Ecuador (Río Napo) to e Brazil.

Amazonian Black-Tyrant PLATE 48
Knipolegus poecilocercus Atrapamoscas Remoloncito
Identification: 5" (12.7cm). 14g. *Stout bill blue gray
tipped black* (♂), or bill brownish (♀). *Unusually large
dark eyes* (esp. ♀). Sexes very different. ♂: *entirely
glossy blue black*, primaries faintly tinged brownish. ♀:
looks a little bull headed; tail short; upperparts brown,
lores and inconspic. eyering grayish white; *2 broad
buff wing bars* and buff edgings; *upper tail coverts cinnamon rufous, tail broadly edged cinnamon rufous* (all
feathers), under wing coverts white, underparts
creamy buff, *breast and sides with some coarse blurry
brown streaks* coalescing to form incomplete dark
band across chest; belly pale yellowish. In both sexes

wing extension very short; rictal bristles conspic; in hand outer 3 primaries very narrow.

Sim. species: ♂ very sim. to ♂ Black Manakin, but manakin occurs in scrubby white sandy soil woodlands (not assoc. with water or várzea forest). ♂ manakin has somewhat more *rounded* head and slightly shorter, thicker bill with culmen more decurved near tip, almost no rictal bristles, and different behavior (see). ♀ tyrant recalls Bran-colored Flycatcher, ♀ Vermilion Flycatcher, and larger Riverside Tyrant, but all lack rufous on upper tail coverts and tail.

Voice: Solitary and unusually quiet. Even advertising song of displaying ♂♂ is a faint, unremarkable clicking, *tic-dik*, or vaguely trebled *see-sa'lick*, or more buzzy *bzzEEa* hardly audible more than a few meters away. Display calls are given as ♂ jumps vertically ca. 0.2–0.3m into air and calls as he flips forward and drops back to display perch, which is usually a thick, horizontal vine 1–1.5m up inside shady open várzea forest. ♂♂ posture (aggression?) with head and tail lowered and wings fanning as follow other ♂♂ through low creekside shrubbery.

Behavior: Inconspic. and usually solitary; sits mostly at or below eye level in shady and often vine-tangled places, usually not too far from water, and sallies or flits out to foliage, down to water surface, or to gd. Posture is rather horizontal and movements abrupt and manakinlike. Aside from jump display, ♂♂ do little to attract attention to themselves. Because of displays, ♂♂ are seen more often than ♀♀, but latter are sometimes loosely assoc. with other várzea birds, e.g., antshrikes and antwrens in mixed-spp. flocks. Nest an untidy ball (side entrance?) of moss and grass in branch fork 1m up at edge of small forest stream in nw Brazil[260]; 2 ♀♀ with nest material, mid Feb, Hato Cedral.

Status and habitat: Locally common resident in interior of swampy or seasonally flooded, low-canopied várzea forest, esp. along sluggish forest streams where there are numerous large vines. Proximity of water a requirement, and likes moderately open understory with large looping vines.

Range: To 200m. W Apure (upper Río Arauca; sightings, Hato Cedral[259]); and n and c Amazonas (recs. spotty). E Colombia (local) to Guyana; Rio Negro drainage of Brazil; e Ecuador; ne Peru along the Amazon and a few tributaries e to e Brazil.

Note: Formerly placed in genus *Phaeotriccus*[403].

Satrapa

Distinctive yellow and olive bird of open terrain; austral birds migratory; recalls a kingbird but not closely related to other tyrannids.

Yellow-browed Tyrant   PLATE 47
Satrapa icterophrys   Atrapamoscas Cejas Amarillas

Identification: 6.3″ (16cm). 20g. Rather short, narrow bill. Short legs. Above olive green, crown tinged dusky olive, *long conspic. yellow eyestripe* and blackish mask; wings blackish with gray edgings (2 rather indistinct wing bars); tail blackish, slightly notched and narrowly edged white; *underparts bright yellow*, chest tinged olive.

Sim. species: Most likely confused with one of the numerous *Myiozetetes* or kiskadee-type flycatchers or Cattle Tyrant, but none has yellow eyestripe.

Behavior: Usually seen alone, less often in prs. Perches erect and more or less in open on side or top of larger trees. Sallies to air or more often to trunks and branches where may pause, fluttering momentarily, to snatch prey. Building open cup nest, 17 Aug; fledged young 21 Sep, Hato El Frio, Apure[137]; building nest, Jun, Hato Cedral, w Apure (G. Rodríguez).

Status and habitat: Uncommon and local breeding resident of gallery forest borders, open areas with scattered trees (e.g., around ranch buildings in llanos), and pastures with shrubs or little groves of trees. Often around wet or marshy areas. Fairly common (prs.) in Jan near Tucupita, Delta Amacuro. Breeds sparingly in llanos. Presence of austral migrants seems unlikely, but there are more recs. during austral winter months (wet season) than at other times of yr. Possibly some local or seasonal movements within Venez.

Range: To 500m n of Orinoco; to 150m along Orinoco. W Apure (sight), s Cojedes (sight), and s Carabobo e to Delta Amacuro, and n Bolívar (Las Bonitas; sight, lower Río Caura at Maripa). E Bolivia and e and s Brazil s to e Argentina and Uruguay; northbound austral migrants reach Amazon River.

Colonia

Elongated central tail feathers; widespread in forested regions; no close allies.

Long-tailed Tyrant   PLATE 48
Colonia colonus   Atrapamoscas Coludo

Identification: ♂ 11″ (28mm), ♀ 8″ (20.3cm). 18g. Unmistakable. *Central pr. of tail feathers very long* (up to

5″, 13cm in ♂); bill wide, short, and swallowlike. ♂: entirely brownish black with *conspic. white forehead and eyebrow* and "frosty" grayish white crown mixed with black; stripe (variable in size) of white down center of back and rump. ♀: sim. but tail shorter, crown duller, belly grayish mottled with white.

Voice: Commonly hd. call a soft, rising *wheeet* (recalls Barn Swallow) as flicks tail up; also a longer *twee-ta, twee-ta, twee-ta . . .* , softly.

Behavior: These vivacious little tyrants are conspic. and confiding as they perch up fairly high in open on exposed dead snags or trunks and flick striking tail streamers up and down and call. They are quite sedentary and maintain small territories around a favorite snag or trunk which serves for nesting and foraging; rarely venture far away. Feed heavily on bees, also other flying insects captured in short- to med.-distance sallies to air, and faithfully return to same perch. Nest a mat of compound-leaf rachises in cavity in dead stub or burned trunk; eggs white.

Status and habitat: Common resident but somewhat local; presence of suitable dead stub with cavity, and nearby colonies of bees, are requirements. Small clearings, forest borders, or other openings in humid forested regions.

Range: To 350m (prob. higher). S Amazonas (Cerro de la Neblina); Bolívar from lower Río Caura (sight, Maripa), Río Paragua, and Sierra de Imataca (Río Grande) s to upper Río Cuyuní (*poecilonotus*). Honduras to w Ecuador; the Guianas; e base of Andes from Colombia to n Bolivia and e across s Brazil to ne Argentina and se Brazil.

Machetornis

Semiterrestrial flycatcher; wings short (esp. outermost primary) and rounded; "looks" and sounds much like a kingbird (*Tyrannus*), but uncertain taxonomic affinity suggests similarity due to convergence[318,320].

Cattle Tyrant   PLATE 47
Machetornis rixosus   Atrapamoscas Jinete
Identification: 8″ (20.3cm). 33g. *Kingbird-like with red eyes and long legs for running.* Bill thin. Above pale sandy brown to caramel brown, usually concealed fiery scarlet crown patch (both sexes), *narrow dusky mask; underparts* (and under wing coverts) *bright yellow;* broad but dingy tail tips (visible mainly on underside of tail) contrasting yellowish cinnamon. ♀: may show buff wash on throat and chest.

Sim. species: Recalls a kingbird (e.g., Tropical Kingbird) but shape and behavior, esp. habit of remaining on gd. or of riding on backs of animals, should make identification easy.

Voice: Calls resemble those of Tropical Kingbird but are higher, thinner, and squeakier. Dawn song, also like Tropical Kingbird's but higher pitched, is a short, trilled *t'te'te'ree!*, over and over. At dusk may give a more complex, sustained, rising and falling ser. of squeaky *tic* notes and short trills.

Behavior: Prs. or families are unusual in that they are mainly terrestrial when foraging; otherwise sit up on top of bushes, lower branches of trees, or rooftops. Run rapidly on long legs, follow cattle, horses, capybaras, etc.; often ride on their backs, drop off to capture disturbed prey, and immediately return. Occas. sally to air from elevated perch. When resting usually seek elevated perch in bush, tree, or atop building. Appropriate abandoned thornbird nests or build bulky, grass ball nest well above gd.; 3 creamy buff eggs heavily marked shades of chestnut[425]; breeding Jun–Oct, Guárico[137,734].

Status and habitat: Common and widespread resident in open or semiopen terrain, cattle pastures, agricultural land, and around ranch buildings; usually where there are a few scattered bushes but not wooded areas. Favors drier regions. Some dispersal or local movements occur (1 seen 14 Feb 1998 at 3600m above Apartaderos, Mérida).

Range: Mostly below 300m; occas. to 1000m (vagrant higher). Throughout in semiopen areas n of Orinoco; Delta Amacuro and n Bolívar from Caicara and lower Río Caura e to El Palmar (*flavigularis*). Panama (vagrant) and n Colombia; e Bolivia to e Brazil and s to e Argentina and Uruguay.

Note: Subsp. *obscurodorsalis* of s Cojedes, Barinas, and w Apure not recognized.

Fluvicola

Small; pied plumage; maxilla sharply hooked at tip; prom. rictal bristles; tail slightly rounded; active; always near water.

Pied Water-Tyrant   PLATE 48
Fluvicola pica   Viudita Acuática
Identification: 5.3″ (13.5cm). 13g. *Chunky little black-and-white flycatcher usually seen in open marshy areas.* ♂: *mainly white; rearcrown, wings, and tail black*, back mixed black and white, tertials and tail narrowly tipped white. ♀: sim, but rearcrown and back mixed

brownish. Imm.: much duller and with black replaced by brown, but retains pattern of ad.

Sim. species: See ♀ White-headed Marsh-Tyrant.

Voice: Call a short, nasal *dreéap!*, sometimes accompanied by a little vertical jump of ca. 1m; most often hd. at dawn or dusk. Also a soft *pick* like bubble bursting. Song (?) a slightly buzzy *choo-wer* over and over.

Behavior: Usually alone or in scattered prs. that are tame and conspic. Perch low in emergent vegetation over water or on gd. at water's edge. Reach out, flutter or hover to pick prey from gd. or water (rarely sally to air), run and dart short distances on gd., or leap upward from gd. for flying prey. Freq. spread tail and constantly flick tail downward. In general much more active and perky than White-headed Marsh-Tyrant. Holds a territory only during breeding season[332]. Oval-shaped nest a ball of dried grass, plant down, and leaves with feather lining and side entrance; at end of branch in bush, low and near water (usually over water late in wet season); 2–3 white eggs with a few brown spots at larger end[175]; breeds Apr–Nov, Guárico[734], Jun–Aug peak[137].

Status and habitat: Common resident around freshwater marshes and ponds. Seldom far from water.

Range: To 450m. Throughout n Venez.; Amazonas s to mouth of Río Ventuari; n Bolívar from lower Río Caura and Sierra de Imataca s to Brazilian border at Icabarú (*pica*). Panama to the Guianas and ne Brazil; e Ecuador (once). Trinidad.

Arundinicola

Chunky little "chocolate and vanilla" dweller of marshes; fairly heavy billed for a small flycatcher; prom. rictal bristles; tail slightly rounded; outermost primary short, next abnormally narrow; related to *Fluvicola*.

White-headed Marsh-Tyrant   PLATE 48
Arundinicola leucocephala   Atrapamoscas Duende

Identification: 5″ (12.7cm). 14g. Large headed; slight crest. ♂: unmistakable; *dark chocolate brown* ("bitter chocolate") *with white head*; lower mandible dull orange yellow. In hand outermost primary very short and curved; next narrow and pointed. ♀: above pale ashy gray brown, wings dusky, tail black, *forecrown, sides of head, and underparts dull eggshell white*; chest often smudged gray; *prom. blackish eyes* (contrast with pale face); base of bill dull orangish.

Sim. species: ♀ nearest imm. Pied Water-Tyrant which has suggestion of ad. plumage, although much duller

and browner, and always has contrasting rearcrown and whitish rump. Also note differences in posture and habits.

Voice: Usually quiet; occas. a high, sharp *sedik!*

Behavior: A conspic. but sedentary little flycatcher, almost always seen perched upright on top of marsh vegetation or on a low snag near or over water. Occurs in prs., but ♂♂ are seen far more than ♀♀, in part because contrasting plumage of ♂♂ makes them more conspic. Sally short distances to air or briefly drop to gd. for insect prey, then immediately return to elevated perch. Fly low, sometimes considerable distances, to new perch. Jun–Nov breeding in Guárico[734] and Apure[137]; ball nest like that of Pied Water-Tyrant but with "porch" concealing entrance; 2–4 creamy white eggs.

Status and habitat: Common resident around freshwater marshes, ponds, and damp grass in llanos; marshy areas along larger rivers. Most numerous in llanos; generally local elsewhere.

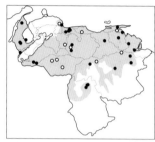

Range: To 450m. N of Orinoco (arid nw?); s of Orinoco in n and c Amazonas (s to Caño Parucito; San Juan de Manaipare) and n Bolívar s to Río Cuchivero, La Paragua, and El Callao. N Colombia; e of Andes (except sw Amazonia) s to ne Argentina and se Brazil; the Guianas. Trinidad.

Attila

Large head; heavy hooked bill; prom. rictal bristles; vocal but notably inconspic.; wooded regions; as far as known, nest an open mossy cup wedged in branch fork, crevice, rocky outcrop, base of bromeliad, etc., often rather low. Formerly placed in Cotingidae.

Bright-rumped Attila   PLATE 49
Attila spadiceus   Atrapamoscas Quieto Polimorfo

Identification: 7.5″ (19cm). 31.4g. Widespread. *Plumage variable but always with 2 wing bars, and rump contrasting with back* (rump often difficult to see in field). Large headed; long, heavy, hooked bill; lower mandible pinkish tipped dusky; eyes orangish (usually) to brownish. Typical plumage: *olive above with contrasting yellow rump*; wings dusky, *2 grayish white to rufous-tinged wing bars*; throat and breast olive narrowly streaked yellow; belly whitish, tail dull rufous. Plumage limits: a very small proportion of individuals are mainly gray or mainly bright rufous, but all have 2 dingy wing bars, contrasting yellow rump (not much contrast in rufous birds), and tend to be streaked yellowish or whitish below.

Sim. species: Range of variability in this sp. is confusing, but note that most individuals look more or less as described under "typical plumage" above. This is only attila with *prom. wing bars*, and only one that usually looks *obviously streaked below*. See other attilas.
Voice: Hd. far more than seen. Main song a loud, emphatically whistled *whée-tit, whée-tit, whée-tit, whée-tit, wheeuu*, gradually ascending in pitch then last note lower and downslurred; also separately, or alternated with above, *weed we-to, weed, we-to, weed wee-to, we're took*[818], swelling and rising then sliding off at end. There are numerous variations, esp. at dawn, but the 2-noted *whee-tit* or *beed-it* or 3-noted *weed, we-to* phrases are characteristic. A loud, angry rattle, *di-di-di-di!*, when alarmed or disturbed.
Behavior: Recalling their namesake somewhat, attilas are solitary, inclined to bully or behave aggressively, and attract attention to themselves with persistent singing. They are often reluctant to move when singing, however, hence difficult to see. Often act sluggish, and are sometimes with mixed-spp. flocks but more often independent of them. Forage at almost any ht. but mostly in forest mid. levels or a little higher, where they peer carefully, sometimes up to 20–30 sec before moving, then sally or lunge short distances, or flutter to foliage and branches for larger insects and fruit. Cup nest often fairly low in fork, mossy rock outcrop, tree crevice or cavity, etc.; 3–4 pale buff eggs coarsely marked reddish brown, esp. at larger end.
Status and habitat: Fairly common resident in humid forest, forest borders, tall second-growth woodland, and clearings with tall trees. Occas. in large gallery forests in w llanos (sight/tape, Bruzual, Apure, 7 Aug 1998—D. Ascanio).

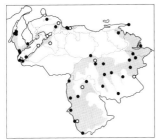

Range: To 2100m n of Orinoco; to 400m s of Orinoco. Maracaibo Basin, Zulia, and w base of Andes in Táchira (*parvirostris*), e base in Táchira and w Apure; mts. of se Lara, c and se Falcón[60], and Yaracuy; Coastal Cordillera of Carabobo (sight) and Aragua; Sucre (Paria Pen.), ne Monagas, and Delta Amacuro; generally in Amazonas and Bolívar (*spadiceus*). Mexico to w Ecuador, n Bolivia, Amaz. Brazil, and the Guianas; coastal se Brazil. Trinidad.

Rufous-tailed Attila
Attila phoenicurus Atrapamoscas Quieto Rabicastaño
Identification: 7" (18cm). 34.5g. Rare. Small attila. *Bill mostly dark, shorter* and rounder than in others of genus. *Head (to just below eyes) and nape smoky gray sharply contrasting with dark rufous upperparts*; upper tail coverts and tail slightly paler rufous (no obvious

contrast), primaries blackish *contrasting with rufous tertials; chin whitish*, throat and underparts cinnamon rufous (paler than above), chest strongly tinged dark rufous forming broad but indistinct dark band.
Sim. species: Much like Citron-bellied Attila (see) which has decidedly longer bill, grayish white throat (not just gray crown and sides of head), lacks strong contrast between head and back, and is duller above with contrasting rump. Bright-rumped Attila has wing bars and yellow rump; rufous morph of Bright-rumped Attila usually does not have contrasting gray head.
Voice: On breeding gds. in s Brazil a loud *whee? whee? whee-bit?* over and over[545].
Status and habitat: Austral migrant. Known in Venez. from 1 ♀ (USNM) from Cerro Yapacana, Amazonas. In Brazil occurs in mid. to upper levels inside humid forest.

Range: Ca. 150m. C Amazonas. Breeds in se Brazil; migrants reported May–Oct across c Amaz. Brazil; n Bolivia (once); Paraguay (once).
Note: Formerly placed in genus *Pseudattila*.

Citron-bellied Attila   PLATE 49
Attila citriniventris Atrapamoscas Quieto Vientre Citrino
Identification: 7" (18cm). 35g. Bill dusky, *lower mandible pinkish tipped dusky*. Rather short tailed. *Entire head gray* (foreface obscurely streaked dusky, but this scarcely evident in field) *becoming grayish white on chin and throat*; back contrasting olive rufous turning *pale cinnamon rufous on rump*; primaries dusky, otherwise wings and tail dull rufous with *no wing bars*; breast tawny cinnamon tinged and indistinctly streaked olive, belly bright ochre yellow.
Sim. species: Easily confused. Much like Rufous-tailed Attila which has shorter, mostly dark bill, rufous (not grayish white) throat, and little or no contrast between rump and tail; Rufous-tailed's more contrasting chest band also may be helpful. Bright-rumped Attila has *wing bars*, yellow on rump (always), and grayer-headed individuals look obviously streaked on head and underparts. Cinnamon Attila is all rufous (not gray).
Voice: Like other *Attila*, often a persistent singer. Song a loud, rapidly whistled, and slightly rising *whee-whee-wheewheewu*, last note lower. Much like song of Bright-rumped Attila but shorter (some songs only 4–5 notes), and all notes (except last pr.) single, not doubled. Also a flat *whee-whee-whee-whee-whee* on same pitch. In response to tape playback, songs lengthened to 10 notes or more (C. Parrish recording, San Carlos de Río Negro). Cf. song of Bright-rumped Attila.
Behavior: As in Bright-rumped Attila.

Status and habitat: Known from small no. of recs. from humid terra firme forest in lowland Amazonas. Perhaps overlooked because of confusion (song and plumage) with other *Attila*.

Range: To 500m. C and s Amazonas (Cerro Yapacana to Salto Huá). E Ecuador, ne Peru, nw Brazil, and e Colombia (1 sight rec.).

Cinnamon Attila   PLATE 49
Attila cinnamomeus   Atrapamoscas Quieto Acanelado
Identification: 8″ (20.3cm). 38g. Bill black; eyes reddish brown. Tail longer than in others of genus. *Mostly deep rufous above with no wing bars and no contrast on rump*; below paler, more cinnamon rufous, wings coverts dusky broadly edged rufous (look mainly rufous), primaries blackish.
Sim. species: Rufous morphs of Bright-rumped Attila always have contrasting yellow rump, *wing bars* (whitish to rufous), and tend to be streaky below. Citron-bellied Attila is very sim. from below, but note gray head and pale rump. Also cf. Rufous-tailed Attila which has top and sides of head gray.
Voice: Like others of genus, notably vocal. Commonest call a loud, somewhat drowsy whistle, *püpuEEEeeeear*, rising in middle then descending, raptor-like and often given over and over. Song a loud, whistled *weary weary weary weer-ry*, ascending and rather like that of Bright-rumped Attila. Also a slow, reedy ser. of 3–several ascending whistles with hesitant delivery, e.g., *püü whee whee* (last 2 notes on same pitch), or *who, hee, whee*, over and over in various patterns.
Behavior: Occurs in prs., although most often seen singly and generally independent of mixed-spp. flocks. Forages in mid. levels of forest but reg. descends quite low. Sluggish as hops with tail down and peers carefully in foliage, then lunges or flutters for large arthropods, occas. fruit. Overall easier to see than others of genus and sometimes remarkably unsuspicious. Suri-

name nest a stick cup with finer material; wedged in crevice at base of bromeliad, etc.; 3 eggs salmon pink with purplish spots and reddish brown markings[253].
Status and habitat: Fairly common to common resident very locally; swamp and várzea forest, esp. around old lakes, flooded oxbows, sluggish streams, and low-lying forest and palm swamps in river deltas.
Range: To 400m. Se Sucre, ne Monagas, and Delta Amacuro; sightings in se Táchira on Río Sarare[60]; locally in n Amazonas (Pto. Ayacucho; Cerro Duida; Junglaven, sighting) southward; extreme s Bolívar along Río Icabarú. E Colombia to n Bolivia, Amaz. Brazil, and the Guianas.

Rhytipterna

Hooked bill; prom. rictal bristles; rather long tail; prob. closely related to *Myiarchus*[319]; nests unknown.

Grayish Mourner   PLATE 50
Rhytipterna simplex   Plañidera Amazónica
Identification: 8″ (20.3cm). 33g. Bill black, base of lower mandible pinkish; eyes dark red to reddish brown. *Very plain in appearance.* Uniform gray above and below; primaries faintly tinged brownish, underparts with slight olive tinge, belly paler with faint yellow olive tinge. Feathers of hindcrown rather long imparting slightly "flat-headed" look. Imm. may have narrow fulvous edges on wings and tail.
Sim. species: Often not safely told from slightly larger Screaming Piha except by voice; both call freq. Piha is somewhat larger and more robust (difficult to judge in absence of direct comparison) with rounder head shape and stouter, all-dark bill. Eye color differences (redder in mourner, grayer in piha) and mourner's more yellowish-tinged underparts may be helpful in some circumstances. Mourner is freq. with mixed-spp. flocks, piha rarely or never with them.
Voice: Unusual song, hd. for short period at dawn, a rapid, rising ser. of notes followed by abrupt sneezing note at end, *kululululululululu-plip!*, sometimes given several times at short intervals. Variations incl. a slower rising ser. with fewer notes, and *pflew* note several times.
Behavior: Rather inconspic. and quiet (except at dawn), usually seen alone, less often prs. or families. Perch from forest mid. level to subcanopy, sit quietly, them sally out varying distances to snatch insects from foliage. Also occas. take fruit. Seen with canopy mixed-spp. flocks or away from them about equally.

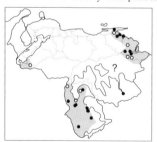

Status and habitat: Fairly common resident (easily overlooked unless calling) in humid terra firme forest, less often várzea forest. Generally most numerous in sandy soil forests.
Range: To 1300m. Throughout Amazonas, Bolívar, and Delta Amacuro (*frederici*); sight/tape in ne Monagas at Caño Colorado[58] and Río Caripe (D. Ascanio). E Colombia s to n Bolivia, Amaz. Brazil, and the Guianas; se Brazil.

Pale-bellied Mourner   PLATE 48
Rhytipterna immunda   Plañidera Pálida
Identification: 7.5″ (19cm). 28g. Looks like a slender, faded *Myiarchus*. *Bill short* (compared to *Myiarchus*), *narrow, and all blackish.* Upperparts dull grayish brown, crown to eyes slightly darker, upper tail coverts and tail browner, wings dusky brown, 2 indistinct grayish wing bars; *primaries and tail narrowly edged rufous*, tertials edged grayish white; throat and chest pale gray, rest of underparts pale dull yellow, *flanks* (and sometimes belly) *tinged buff to light rufous*. In hand, bill width (at nostrils) 5.6–6.4 vs. 7.1–8.7mm in Short-crested Flycatcher[315].
Sim. species: Often misidentified as a *Myiarchus*. See resident Short-crested, Brown-crested, and migrant Swainson's flycatchers. Differs from *Myiarchus* in less upright posture, more slender, short-legged proportions, grayer and more rounded head (no crest), larger eyes, and sluggish behavior.
Voice: At dawn or occas. later in morning in n Amazonas a clear, whistled *duuuuu-WEETyou* (K. Zimmer) or slightly longer, notably drowsy *püü, wee weeEEEa*, over and over.
Behavior: Single birds or prs. perch from eye level to fairly high in bushes and trees. Rather quiet and difficult to see, they sing mostly from inside scrubby vegetation and usually within 5m of gd., occas. much higher. Peer about slowly like other mourners, and reg. sally short distances to hover-glean insects or fruit. Have been seen in mixed-spp. flocks with antshrikes, antwrens, small flycatchers, gnatcatchers, and greenlets.
Status and habitat: No specimens. Uncommon to locally fairly common resident of savanna woodland and borders in white sandy soil areas and scrubby low-canopied várzea woodland[833]. First taped 31 Dec 1990 (K. Zimmer and Hilty), identification confirmed Mar 1992 (K. Zimmer and R. Ridgely), and again Feb–Mar 1993 (tape and photo) near Junglaven Lodge; also taped at Alechiven Lodge at mouth of Río Ventuari, Feb 1998 (K. Zimmer).

Range: 300m. N Amazonas in lower and mid. Río Ventuari (tapes and photos). E Colombia to the Guianas and locally s to n Matto Grosso, Brazil.

Sirystes

Related to *Myiarchus*, and like them nest in tree cavities, but plumage more contrasting.

Eastern Sirystes   PLATE 47
Sirystes sibilator   Atrapamoscas de Rabadilla Blanca
Identification: 7.2″ (18.3cm). 32g. Shape much like *Myiarchus*. Distinctive black, gray, and white plumage reminiscent of a becard. Bushy headed. *Crown and sides of head to below eyes black*, back mottled gray and brown, *rump white*, wings black, wing coverts edged gray, primaries conspic. edged white; *rather long square tail black*; throat and chest pale gray turning white on breast and belly. Thighs brownish (usually concealed by flank feathers). Sexes sim.
Sim. species: High in canopy easily confused with a *Myiarchus* or a becard, but none has white rump. Also cf. Fork-tailed Flycatcher, Eastern Kingbird, and Black-capped and White-winged becards.
Voice: Noisy and energetic whistles from treetops; *wheer whît-it* or *wheer whît* or *wheer, pe-pe-pe* or sim. variation, often over and over in excited manner. Alarm sim. but faster and longer, *wheeer, pi'pi'pi'pi 'pi'pi*.
Behavior: Proportions and behavior, incl. habit of raising slight bushy crest and nodding head, recall a *Myiarchus*. Single birds or prs. perch rather erect and alert in canopy and are found with mixed-spp. flocks or independent of them about equally. Often rather noisy but otherwise easily overlooked. Seem to forage or wander over large areas. Sally to twigs more than foliage to snap prey during brief fluttering hover (outward hover-gleaning), or occas. without hovering. Prey is mostly fairly large arthropods.
Status and habitat: Resident. Canopy of humid foothill forest and forest borders. Known in Venez. from only a small no. of specimens. In Amaz. Peru most numerous in várzea forest.

Range: 300–550m. E base of Andes in se Táchira (Santo Domingo; Burgua), w Apure (El Nula), Barinas (Barinas; Rio Masparro), and Portuguesa (Río Tucupido) (*albocinereus*). E Colombia, most of w Amazonia e to se Brazil; the Guianas.
Note: Formerly incl. Western Sirystes (*S. albogriseus*) of Panama to w Ecuador[541].

Myiarchus

Another widespread, homogenous-looking group whose members, in appearance, are Tweedledum and Tweedledee, all notoriously difficult to distinguish; all slightly crested; bill slightly hooked; differences in appearance are minor, e.g., bill shape and size, head color, edgings on wings and tail; vocalizations are key to defining spp. limits in genus[316], hence voices often critical to field identification; note that imms. of almost all spp. show rufous edging on flight feathers, sometimes also wing coverts and tail; a few spp. migratory; nearly all forage by outward hover-gleaning for fairly large arthropod prey; trashy (usually) nest in tree cavity, crevice in building, etc.

Dusky-capped Flycatcher   PLATE 48
Myiarchus tuberculifer   Atrapamoscas Gorra Negruzco
Identification: 7" (18cm). 19.4g. *Smallest Myiarchus in* Venez. *Bill rather thin, all blackish. Somewhat bushy crested. Crown sooty brownish black contrasting with dull dark olive upperparts*; wing coverts edged dull grayish white to yellowish white, primaries usually faintly edged cinnamon rufous (inconspic.), tertials edged dull yellowish white, *tail dark brown with no rufous edgings*; throat and breast light gray, belly clear yellow. Or sim. but back paler and tinged gray (*pallidus*).
Sim. species: Aside from distinctive vocalizations, the small size, contrasting bushy crown, and absence of rufous in tail are best marks for this widespread, relatively easy-to-identify *Myiarchus*.
Voice: Most freq. call a plaintive, drawn-out whistle, *puuueeea*, dropping slightly at end; also a soft, brief *whit*. Sometimes a rapid ser. of short whistles; dawn song consists of plaintive whistles alternated with *huit* notes[316]. Often a whistled *wheee-peer* or *wheee-peer-br'br* over and over when excited.
Behavior: Alone or in prs. and reg. with mixed-spp. flocks, but everywhere rather quiet (calls are soft) and unobtrusive. Usually stays well up in more open mid. level or canopy of trees where characteristically bobs head as it looks around. Sallies out to foliage or small branches and hover-gleans arthropods, less often sallies to air or gd. Breeds Mar–Jun; cavity nest as in others of genus[316].
Status and habitat: Has widest el. distrib. of any *Myiarchus*, and occurs in a wide range of habitats. Resident in dry, moist, or humid forest, along forest borders, at openings inside tall mature forest (where stays mainly

in canopy), in a variety of second-growth habitats, and in coffee plantations, wooded streamsides, and mangroves. Fairly common, but more numerous in second growth or disturbed habitats than in tall forest. Generally scarce and local in llanos.
Range: To 2000m n of Orinoco; to 1300m s of Orinoco. Throughout n of Orinoco incl. Islas Los Roques, Los Testigos, and Margarita (*pallidus*); Amazonas, Bolívar, and Delta Amacuro (*tuberculifer*). Sw US to nw Argentina, Amaz. Brazil, and the Guianas; locally in se Brazil. Trinidad.

Swainson's Flycatcher   PLATE 48
Myiarchus swainsoni   Atrapamoscas de Cresta Oscura
Identification: 7.5" (19cm). 24g. Two races. Resident (*phaeonotus*): *bill dusky*; upperparts dark brown tinged olive with *contrasting sooty black crown* (extending to just below eyes) *and sooty black tail*; wing coverts and flight feathers weakly edged dull grayish white (not conspic.); throat and breast pale gray, belly *faintly yellow to dull white* (little contrast between breast and belly and almost no color on either). Austral migrant (*swainsoni*): very different; *bill reddish* (esp. lower mandible); *upperparts incl. crown dull faded brown faintly tinged olive* (crown not in contrast with back), tail slightly darker brown, throat and breast pale gray, belly pale whitish yellow.
Sim. species: Resident race is nearest Short-crested Flycatcher, but dusky on that sp.'s crown does not extend to below eyes, and belly much brighter yellow. Dusky-capped Flycatcher is a bit smaller, more contrasty, and also has much brighter yellow belly (resident Swainson's can look almost white-bellied). Also cf. Great Elaenia, larger and uniformly dark above. Migrant race (commoner s of Orinoco) *looks faded and pale* compared to other *Myiarchus*; if in doubt, look for its *reddish bill*. Also cf. Pale-bellied Mourner.
Voice: Resident birds give a soft *phreeer*, often followed by several whistled *hic, prit*, and *preer* notes. Song of austral birds (s Brazil) a loud *pút-it-here* or *pút-it* or *here-pút it*[40]; commonest call of austral birds a soft, whistled *how* (K. Zimmer).
Behavior: Rather like Brown-crested Flycatcher. Resident birds occur alone or in prs., typically independent of mixed-spp. flocks. Austral migrants are most often found in forest canopy and with canopy mixed-spp. flocks.
Status and habitat: Resident birds (only s of Orinoco) are uncommon and local in humid forest borders, lighter sandy soil woodland, mangroves (Delta Amacuro), and patches of scrubby trees in Gran Sabana.

Austral migrant and nonbreeding winter resident birds from s latitudes, rec. 26 Mar–8 Sep to humid terra firme and várzea forest and forest borders, are fairly common s of Orinoco; spotty n of Orinoco.
Range: To 300m (austral migrants); to 1800m (resident birds) on tepuis. Throughout Amazonas, Bolívar, and Delta Amacuro (resident *phaeonotus*); Lara and Cojedes e and s to Orinoco; generally in Amazonas and Bolívar (austral migrant *swainsoni*). E Colombia to c Argentina, Uruguay, and the Guianas; Trinidad.
Note: Subsp. *fumosus* of se Venez. recognized by some[559].

Short-crested Flycatcher
PLATE 48
Myiarchus ferox Atrapamoscas Garrochero Chico
Identification: 7.4″ (18.9cm). 24g. Bill blackish (slightly paler in old birds). Above dark brown, *darker on crown*; wing coverts edged dull white (2 indistinct bars), primaries narrowly and tertials broadly edged dull white, *tail dark brown* (no rufous edges) and *darker than back*; throat and breast gray contrasting with pale yellow belly (*ferox*). Or bill paler, more dusky horn (sometimes base of lower mandible pale), *plumage overall paler and faded with back tinged olive*; in fresh plumage may show faint rufous brown edges on upper tail coverts and tail; underparts duller, more faded than in *ferox* (*brunnescens*).
Sim. species: Darker, more contrasty s subsp. (*ferox*) is nearest resident race of Swainson's Flycatcher (see); more northerly and westerly *brunnescens* almost identical in plumage to Venezuelan and Panama flycatchers and best told by voice and range. Brown-crested Flycatcher has much heavier bill, bushier and paler brown crest, and *usually* shows rufous on *both* wings and tail (rufous often hard to see).
Voice: Commonest vocalization, by far, is dawn and day song; at dawn a short, soft, purring (or rolling) trill, *turrrt* or *prrrt*, lasting ca. 1 sec, at rate of 1/3–4 sec; day song identical but given at irreg. rate and intervals. To intruding conspecifics also utters all of the following: short, mostly 2-noted hiccup (*huit*) notes; short, slightly descending whistle (rasp-whistle)[316]; and *distinctive*, but infreq. hd. whinny-rattle, *WHE-E-e-e-e-e-e*, slightly downscale, lasting 2 to 4 sec, which may be used in territorial disputes.
Behavior: Much as in others of genus. Single birds or prs. perch rather upright from about eye level to mid. level in vegetation, watch carefully, and sally or lunge short distances and flutter momentarily to pick off prey from foliage or branches. Typically sedentary and independent of mixed-spp. flocks. Tree-cavity nest often lined with cast-off snake skin; 2 creamy white eggs with band of reddish spots around larger end[253]; breeds Mar–May[316].
Status and habitat: Fairly common resident s of Orinoco in humid forest borders, clearings, and second growth along riverbanks. Spotty and less numerous in llanos, where most recs. are from Apure. Overlaps Venezuelan Flycatcher to small extent in e Venez.
Range: To 500m n of Orinoco; to 1000m s of Orinoco. E Táchira, w and e Apure, w Barinas (Barinas), Portuguesa (Guanare), and Guárico (El Sombrero) s to nw Amazonas and nw Bolívar incl. Caicara and Altagracia

(*brunnescens*); Amazons s of Río Ventuari, rest of Bolívar, Delta Amacuro (mouth of Río Amacuro), Monagas, and e Sucre (*ferox*). E of Andes from e Colombia to n Argentina, se Brazil, and the Guianas.
Note: The 2 subspp. (above) intergrade extensively, and many birds are not separable[316].

Venezuelan Flycatcher
PLATE 48
Myiarchus venezuelensis Atrapamoscas de Venezuela
Identification: 7.5″ (19cm). 24.4g. Bill heavy, blackish (little or no pinkish at base of lower mandible). In all respects plumage virtually identical to *brunnescens* race of Short-crested Flycatcher and to Panama Flycatcher, and almost certainly *not separable in field from either except by voice and range*. Note that Venezuelan Flycatcher overlaps Short-crested Flycatcher only locally in extreme e Venez., and Panama Flycatcher occurs only around Maracaibo Basin. Venezuelan and Panama flycatchers show a bit of narrow rufous to cinnamon yellow edging on outer web of all but outermost tail feathers (usually visible only in hand; rarely in field). Venezuelan also much like Brown-crested Flycatcher (bill of both very sim. in size; latter usually with pinkish at base), but in fresh plumage *wing covert edgings of Venezuelan grayer and more distinct*, forming 2 fairly well marked gray bars; primaries usually edged grayish buff (not distinctly rufous as in Brown-crested). Note Brown-crested's bushier-headed appearance and slightly paler, more uniform brownish upperparts (Venezuelan has *darker and grayer tinge to head and neck* and olive tinge to back).
Voice: Less vocal than Brown-crested Flycatcher. Dawn song a repeated ser. of plaintive whistles (no *huit* notes) at intervals of 1–several sec; day song sim. but given much less freq. Gives repeated hiccup calls, rasps, rasp-whistles (no rolls or *huit* notes) to intruding conspecifics; also a whistled *wheer-r-r* much like that of Dusky-capped Flycatcher. No purring trill as in Short-crested Flycatcher[316].
Behavior: Sim. to Brown-crested Flycatcher (see). Breeds Apr–May, perhaps Mar–Jun; nest undocumented[316].
Status and habitat: Uncommon and local resident but underreported because of identification difficulty. Dry and moist forest (deciduous or semideciduous), forest borders, gallery forest, and scrubby or brushy second growth with scattered taller trees. Can be found with reg. in Turiamo-Ocumare area of Aragua, e end of Sierra de San Luis, Falcón; also near Upata, e Bolívar.
Range: To ca. 500m. Nw Zulia (Alto del Cedro) e to e Lara (near Barquisimeto), Falcón, Yaracuy, n base of

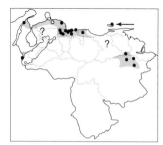

Coastal Cordillera in Carabobo, Aragua, and Distr. Federal (e to Pto. La Cruz); Interior Cordillera in Miranda (Santa Lucía) and n Cojedes (?); ne Bolívar (El Callao; Upata; El Palmar; El Manteco); Isla Margarita. Tobago.

Panama Flycatcher   PLATE 48
Myiarchus panamensis   Atrapamoscas de Panamá
Identification: 7.5″ (19cm). 28g. *Confined to Maracaibo Basin.* Virtually identical in plumage to *brunnescens* race of Short-crested Flycatcher but bill slightly longer and heavier; bill usually blackish, occas. paler at base, rarely grayish brown throughout. Range slightly overlaps Venezuelan Flycatcher which is prob. not separable in field except by voice; Venezuelan perhaps can be told by *grayer, more prom. wing bars* (fresh plumage). Panama also overlaps larger, bushier-crested Brown-crested Flycatcher and smaller Dusky-capped Flycatcher. In mts. cf. Pale-edged Flycatcher.
Voice: Softer and not as sharp as that of Brown-crested or Great Crested flycatchers. Day call a short, slowly modulated whistle at infreq. intervals, sometimes in prs. or in rapid ser. which may grade into modified *huit* notes or short rolls (trills); dawn song a ser. of isolated, short, slowly modulated whistles (vibrato) identical to those given by foraging birds during daylight hr; notes given at 2- to 3-sec intervals[316]. In Panama, dawn song described as a fast, whistled *tséedew* or *wheedee-dew*; also semiwhistled, twittering *tee, deedeedeedeedeedee* with variations, and soft, clear whistled *whee* and *prrrt* notes[543].
Behavior: Much like Short-crested Flycatcher (see). Breeds late Mar–early Jun; nest a natural cavity; lining as in others of genus[316].
Status and habitat: Uncommon resident. Open dry, moist, and humid woodland and borders, brushy pastures, and scrubby semiopen areas. Also (at least in Colombia) in mangroves.

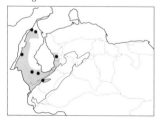

Range: To 150m. Nw Zulia (Carrasquero; Los Motilones; Río Guasare), s Zulia (Santa Bárbara; Encontrados), Mérida (El Vigía), and ne Zulia at Mene

Grande (*panamensis*). Panama and n Colombia (up to 500m).
Note: *Panamensis* formerly regarded as a subsp. of Short-crested Flycatcher.

Pale-edged Flycatcher   PLATE 48
Myiarchus cephalotes   Atrapamoscas Montañero Juí
Identification: 7.5″ (19cm). 20g. Overall one of sleekest, most sharply patterned *Myiarchus* in Venez. Bill rather thin. Above olive brown, crown slightly darker (but *little or no obvious contrast*, and crown *not* dusky), wing coverts edged grayish to buffy white forming 2 fairly evident wing bars; inner flight feathers sharply edged whitish, *tail brown* (like back) *crisply bordered on sides with white* (white may not extend quite to tip); throat and breast light gray, belly clear yellow.
Sim. species: Clean white tail edges are the key. Cf. esp. Dusky-capped Flycatcher which always has contrasting dusky crown and no white tail edges. Other *Myiarchus* overlap minimally (or not at all), only in foothills.
Voice: Commonest call (prob. contact) during day a clear, emphatic *fweee!* or *PEEa*; also a spirited but plaintive whistled *wheep, pip-peer-peer-peer*, 2d note brief (Hilty). Responds to conspecifics with repeated rasp notes, rasp-whistles, and ser. of slightly descending whistles, but no trilled rolls (also no hiccup notes in Venez.); dawn song a ser. of clear, piercing whistles (same as contact call during day) but given continually at intervals of 5 sec or more[316].
Behavior: Alone or in prs., mostly 2–10m up around forest borders and openings, sometimes with mixed-spp. flocks. Sallies out to hover-glean from foliage and branches, occas. sallies to air. Rather quiet, unobtrusive habits seldom attract much attention. Mar–Apr nests, E Andes of Colombia.
Status and habitat: Uncommon to fairly common resident in moist and humid forest borders, forest openings, and lighter woodland. Readily seen on s side of pass between Maracay and Choroní.

Range: 1400–2100m (prob. slightly lower). Andes of Trujillo and Lara, Coastal Cordillera in Aragua and Distr. Federal (prob. Miranda); Interior Cordillera on n Guárico/Aragua border (Cerro Platillón); mts. of Sucre and n Monagas (*caribbaeus*). Colombia s in Andes to Bolivia.
Note: Subsp. *caribbaeus* vocally somewhat divergent from birds of Colombia southward[316].

Brown-crested Flycatcher   PLATE 48
Myiarchus tyrannulus   Atrapamoscas Garrochero Colirrufo
Identification: 8″ (20.3cm). 30g. *Bill heavy*, black above, *base of lower mandible usually pinkish.* Rather bushy crown dull brown contrasting slightly with paler brown back; wing coverts edged dull grayish white forming 2 dull wing bars; *primaries edged rufous* (reduced or disappearing with wear), secondaries edged dull grayish white; *inner webs of all but central pr. of tail feathers largely rufous* (tail looks quite rufous from below, but *rufous may not be visible from above*); throat to mid. breast pale gray, rest of underparts pale yellow. Birds from offshore isls. are paler above and below (look distinctly "faded" compared to mainland races).
Sim. species: In all areas note *heavy bill*, slightly crested look, and prom. rufous edgings on wings and tail (esp. underside). Only Great Crested Flycatcher is as large and heavy-billed, and it is darker above, much more richly colored below. No other Venez. *Myiarchus* has rufous edging on *both* wings and tail (often hard to see) but beware birds in worn plumage (rufous faint or absent) and juvs. of all spp., all of which show rufous edgings. Also cf. Venezuelan and Panama flycatchers.
Voice: Often noisy. Commonest call a sharp, inflected *whît*; also a rolling *pr-pr'r'r't!*, often repeated 2–3 times in succession when excited. No long whistled notes[316]; dawn song a whistled roll, *WHEE'p'peer*, over and over.
Behavior: Single birds or prs. are usually rather conspic. as perch in open at eye level or higher in well-lit foliage of bushes and trees. Typically alert, they occas. nod heads and forage by sallying out and hover-gleaning prey from foliage or snatching it in sally-strike without pausing; occas. sally to air or drop to gd. Nest mainly in tree cavities, stubs, etc.; nest often lined with cast-off snake skin; 2–3 creamy white eggs heavily marked dark purple and lavender, esp. at larger end[175].
Status and habitat: Common and widespread resident in arid scrub, dry and moist woodland, gallery forest, humid forest borders, scrubby disturbed vegetation, and mangroves.

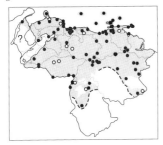

Range: To 1100m n of Orinoco; to 300m s of Orinoco. Throughout s to c Amazonas (vicinity of Cerro Yapacana); Bolívar s to lower Río Caura, lower Río Paragua (La Paragua), and lower Río Cuyuní at El Dorado; Islas Margarita, Los Testigos, Los Frailes, La Tortuga, and Patos (*tyrannulus*); Islas Los Roques (*brevipennis*); La

Blanquilla (*blanquillae*). Sw US to n Costa Rica; n Colombia to n Argentina and se Brazil (not w Amazonia); the Guianas; Netherlands Antilles; Trinidad.
Note: Subspp. *blanquillae* and *brevipennis* not recognized by some[559].

Great Crested Flycatcher   PLATE 48
Myiarchus crinitus   Atrapamoscas Copetón
Identification: 8″ (20.3cm). 34g. N temperate migrant. Most distinctively marked *Myiarchus* in Venez. Resembles Brown-crested Flycatcher but bill even heavier; upperparts darker, more olive brown incl. crown (crown not brown); *tail even more rufous* (looks completely rufous from below because entire inner web of all but central pr. of tail feathers is rufous); and throat to mid. breast darker gray in *sharp contrast* to richer yellow lower underparts. Note that rufous tail edges usually show from above on this sp.
Sim. species: No other *Myiarchus* in Venez. shows so much rufous on both wings and tail, or has such rich contrasting underparts.
Voice: Loud, rising *wheeep!* freq. hd. on wintering gds. Throaty rolling ser. of *prrrip* notes (commonly hd. on temperate breeding gds.) seldom given in Venez.
Behavior: Rather inconspic. and not often seen on wintering gds. Most often found singly around fruiting trees and shrubs.
Status and habitat: Uncommon migrant and winter resident from the north, mid Oct–end of Mar. Humid forest borders, second growth, plantations, and lighter woodland. Reg. seen in coffee plantations of s Táchira.

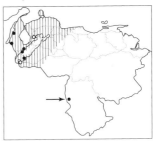

Range: To 1200m. Sierra de Perijá, Zulia, w base of Andes in w Mérida and w Trujillo (sight near Río Jirajara); e base in Táchira (Las Mesas; sight, Petrolero, 19 Jan 1995); once at San Fernando de Atapabo, Amazonas. Breeds in e N Amer.; winters from s US to Colombia; n Ecuador (sight recs.).

Pitangus and *Philohydor*

Two moderately large flycatchers with black-and-white striped heads and bright yellow underparts; maxilla hooked at tip; tail square; tarsus short. Both very sim. in appearance, and both formerly placed in *Pitangus*; syringeal anatomy and nest structure differ[318].

Great Kiskadee   PLATE 47
Pitangus sulphuratus   Cristofué
Identification: 8.5″ (22cm). 63g. Broad shouldered and short tailed. *Heavy, straight black bill.* Black crown

encircled by broad white band; concealed crown patch yellow, sides of head black, often with tiny yellow rictal mark, otherwise brown above; *wings and tail edged rufous* (or with only narrow rufous edges on wings, almost none on tail—*trinitatis*), throat white, rest of underparts bright yellow.

Sim. species: From Boat-billed Flycatcher by brown (not olive) back, rufous in wings and tail (but this variable and with little rufous in birds of e and s Venez.), and smaller, *straight* bill. Also cf. Lesser Kiskadee and smaller *Myiozetetes* flycatchers.

Voice: Soon familiar to every traveler or resident. Gives a variety of loud, exuberant calls. Most familiar is *KISS-ka-DEE* (hence English name), often shortened to *ka-DEE!* Spanish name, *Cristofué* (and *Ben-te-ví* in Portuguese), is onomatopoeic also.

Behavior: Very much a public character. Brash, noisy, and irascible, conspic. almost wherever it occurs. Alone or in prs., usually not groups, that often perch rather low, freq. near water. Aggressive and notably opportunistic when feeding, kiskadees eat almost anything from insects and small vertebrates to fish and occas. fruit. Nest a large, untidy ball of grass with side entrance (a few open cups reported); wedged into high branch fork, utility-pole brace, etc.; 2–4 eggs cream with a few dark reddish brown markings at larger end; breeding Mar–Sep, Guárico[734]; 1 nest, late Mar, ne Bolívar.

Status and habitat: Resident. Common and ubiquitous around habitations, clearings, cultivated areas, even in trees overlooking boulevards in large cities, also gallery-forest borders and lighter woodland. Shows fondness for water. In forested areas confined mainly to river and lake borders. Dry to humid areas, also riparian woodland in arid regions. As yet, no recs. in s Amazonas and sw Bolívar.

Range: To 1600m (occas. higher) n of Orinoco; to 500m s of Orinoco. N of Orinoco from Zulia to Sucre, w Monagas, and w Delta Amacuro; n Amazonas s to mouth of Río Ventuari; n Bolívar along Orinoco e to about Ciudad Guyana (*rufipennis*); Isla Patos, e Sucre, e Monagas, Delta Amacuro, rest of n Amazonas (s to Las Carmelitas), rest of n Bolívar s to lower Río Caura and mid. Río Paragua; e Bolívar from Sierra de Imataca to Santa Elena de Uairén (*trinitatis*). S Texas and Mexico to c Argentina. Trinidad.

Lesser Kiskadee   PLATE 47
Philohydor lictor   Pecho Amarillo Orillero
Identification: 7″ (18cm). 25g. Sim. to Great Kiskadee (esp. browner-winged and browner-tailed *trinitatis*

subsp.) but *always near water*. Best told by smaller size, more slender body (lacks Great Kiskadee's robust, muscular look), *proportionately longer and much narrower bill*, and faint rufous edgings on wings and tail. Rufous edgings prom. in imms. Note habitat and esp. diagnostic calls.

Sim. species: Best mark is long bill on this bird, which otherwise resembles several other flycatchers with typical "kiskadee" head pattern. Esp. cf. Rusty-margined, Social, and White-bearded flycatchers.

Voice: Commonest call, very unlike that of Great Kiskadee, a wheezy, slightly buzzy *SQUEEEZE, Me-Ba'by!*, sometimes repeated several times in succession, or a shorter *SQUEEEZE, me!* (or *SQUEE-be*). Other calls incl. an excited chattery greeting, *ca-déde* varying to *ca-déde-er*, with much wing fluttering and raising of crown feathers; also various squealing calls much like those of Great Kiskadee.

Behavior: Generally quieter and more sedate than allied Great Kiskadee. Prs. or families of 3–4 perch low, usually less than 3m up, over water. Sally to vegetation or surface of water, occas. drop to gd. along shore, and unlike Great Kiskadee, are not pugnacious and aggressive. Nest an open cup of grass or coarse material on stump or in low shrub; usually over water[656]; 2–3 creamy eggs spotted violet at larger end[253]; breeding Jun–Oct, w Apure[137].

Status and habitat: Rarely far from water. Resident. Shores of wooded lagoons, ponds, sluggish streams, and mangrove borders, where perches in shrubby vegetation, and on fallen dead limbs protruding from water. Common along streams and lagoons in llanos, esp. where there are overhanging branches and vegetation in water; less numerous and local s of Orinoco. Shares habitat with Great Kiskadee but not along bare, open riverbanks where Great also occurs. No recs. (?) for s Amazonas and s Bolívar.

Range: To 350m (sight, 1300, Lara). Generally s to n Amazonas (San Fernando de Atabapo); n Bolívar s to lower Río Caura, lower Río Paragua, and lower Río Cuyuní (El Dorado); Delta Amacuro (*lictor*). Panama to n Bolivia, Amaz. and sc Brazil, and the Guianas; coastal e Brazil.

Megarynchus

Broad, heavy bill; tarsus short; plumage much like Great Kiskadee but anatomically closer to *Tyrannopsis*[318].

Boat-billed Flycatcher
PLATE 47

Megarynchus pitangua   Atrapamoscas Picón

Identification: 9" (23cm). 62g. *Kiskadee-like. Oversized black bill with distinctly decurved culmen.* Tail rather short. Crown and sides of head blackish with concealed yellow (to orange rufous) coronal stripe and *broad white eyebrows almost completely encircling crown* (touch on nape); back brownish *olive*, wings brown with *no rufous edging* (faint rufous edging on imm. birds), throat white, otherwise bright yellow below.

Sim. species: Often confused with Great Kiskadee. Pay attention to bill differences. Boat-billed Flycatcher has very large bill (like a "swollen nose") with obvious decurve to culmen. Also note definite olive tinge to back and absence of rufous in wings. Smaller Lesser Kiskadee is usually low and near water.

Voice: Noisy with irritating, unpleasant (to human ears) vocalizations. Most freq. call a nasal, grating, and mocking *nya-nya-nya-nya* as bobs head. Also a quavering *kwée'le*. In disputes an even louder, more insistent, squealing *squEE'lee'lee* and *squ'E'E'le'le'le* over and over. Some vocalizations recall those of Great Kiskadee. Dawn song a slightly reedy *whée-dic* over and over at 1/sec.

Behavior: Prs. usually perch fairly high, most often on interior branches of rather open trees (esp. *Cecropia*) where they are not as conspic. as Great Kiskadee. Occas. perch in open on top or sides of larger trees. Sally varying distances (usually not too far) to foliage or bark surfaces to snap prey in sally-strike without pausing, or sometimes flutter momentarily for a variety of large arthropods, small vertebrates, and fruit. Perch or hover to take fruit. Shallow cup nest 6–30m up; 2–3 whitish eggs thickly speckled brown and pale lilac[623].

Status and habitat: Fairly common resident in dry, moist, and humid forest borders, light woodland, plantations, and second growth with scattered trees. Often found in tall trees along riparian woodland in dry areas. Widespread but less numerous than Great Kiskadee, and prefers more wooded surroundings.

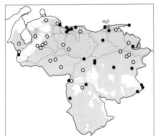

Range: To ca. 1900m (mostly below 1000m). Generally n of Orinoco incl. Delta Amacuro and s to c Amazonas (s to San Fernando de Atabapo); southward?; n Bolívar s to lower Río Caura, lower Río Paragua, and Brazilian border at Santa Elena de Uairén; Isla Patos (*pitangua*). Mexico to ne Argentina and se Brazil. Trinidad.

Phelpsia

Recently erected genus[16]. Much like *Myiozetetes* but with different proportions (tiny bill, large head); different vocalizations; open cup nest.

White-bearded Flycatcher
PLATE 47

Phelpsia inornata   Atrapamoscas Barbiblanco

Identification: 7" (18cm). 29g. Only in llanos. *Large puffy head accentuates stubby bill.* Crown and sides of head brownish black (no concealed coronal patch), *long white eyebrows touch on nape*; upperparts olive brown, primaries narrowly edged yellowish; *puffy white throat*, rest of underparts bright yellow.

Sim. species: Despite remarkable resemblance to Rusty-margined and Social flycatchers, this sp. easily told by distinctive "puff-headed" appearance (throat also puffy) and almost ridiculously short bill. Note rufous wing edgings on Rusty-margined; duller dusky head and prom. buff wing edgings on Social. If in doubt, listen for distinctive duets.

Voice: Commonest call, a sharp, rising *churup*, serves as loc. call; ser. of *churup* notes in alarm[735]. Vigorous (antiphonal?) duet a staccato, hammering *CHEE'ter, CHEE'ter, CHEE'ter . . .* (up to 12 couplets by each member of pr.) given early in morning but only a few times and at long intervals. Duets, always given by prs. sitting close together, are accompanied by much excited bowing of body and energetic bursts of wing flapping.

Behavior: Found in prs., or if in 3s, one is a nonbreeding helper that assists in nesting. Perch at various hts., and overall quieter and much more inconspic. than allied *Myiozetetes*, but prs. are quick to duet in territorial defense, then usually perch high in open and display and call loudly. Often sally to gd. for prey, also to grass or low vegetation; less often sally to air or leaves; infreq. eat small fruits. Breed Mar–Aug; small, open cup nest on high, horizontal branch fork; 2 eggs, white with a few dark dots and blotches at larger end[735].

Status and habitat: Fairly common low-profile resident of ranchland with scattered trees, around habitations, groves of trees, and in lighter wooded borders and gallery forest. Often in trees around ranch buildings where most readily located by listening for vocalizations at dawn. Very common at Hato Los Indios (Río Capanaparo), se Apure.

Range: ENDEMIC. To 450m. Llanos from s base of coastal mts. in Carabobo (Valencia), Miranda (Santa Lucia, Curupao), and ne Anzoátegui (Barcelona) s to w Apure (El Amparo) and n Bolívar (Caicara; near Las

Bonitas); Delta Amacuro (tape, 4km s of Macareito, 13 Jan 1997—Hilty). Doubtless ne Colombia.
Note: Originally placed in *Myiozetetes* then *Conopias*; now *Phelpsia*[318,735].

Myiozetetes

Short bill; white throat; most are look-alikes with "kiskadee" plumage pattern; white eyestripe does not quite encircle crown; widespread, but some spp. have curious range gaps; others migratory; often forage by aerial hawking, but facultatively use almost all other tyrannid foraging methods[176]; as far as known, messy dry grass nest a ball with side entrance, fairly high and conspic., wedged in branch fork, building, etc.; occas. pirate nests from other spp.

Social Flycatcher   PLATE 47
Myiozetetes similis   Pitirre Copete Rojo
Identification: 7″ (18cm). 24g. Short black bill. Concealed *red* coronal stripe. Pale and rather faded looking. *Crown and cheeks dull dusky*, back strongly *tinged olive*; grayish white wing edgings on wing coverts usually form 2 dull wing bars, flight feathers edged grayish white, tertials broadly edged grayish buff (*columbianus*). Or much like Rusty-margined Flycatcher: crown and cheeks *blackish* with long white eyestripe that *does not meet on nape; back brownish olive*, wing coverts, primaries, and tertials narrowly edged pale olive buff to cinnamon buff (no wing bars); throat white, rest of underparts yellow (*similis*). Juv. (all races): broad cinnamon edges on feathers of wings and tail.
Sim. species: See Rusty-margined and White-bearded flycatchers. Lesser Kiskadee has *much longer* bill.
Voice: Commonest call a sharp *chiit*, often doubled or in rapid ser. Pr. or groups give high, rolling *chi't't't'i'i'i 'i'i'r* over and over in high-energy bursts, often mixed with *chiit* and other notes. Some calls closely resemble those of Rusty-margined Flycatcher.
Behavior: Prs. or family groups are lively, excitable, and often noisy but lack brash chutzpah of larger Great Kiskadee. Perch conspicuously in open on sides or top of small to large trees and sally to foliage or to air, also perch-glean and reg. drop to gd., then return to same or nearby perch. Gather around fruiting trees and shrubs, and take small berries with quick hoverglean. Like Rusty-margined Flycatcher, often very active at dusk, sallying up repeatedly for small flying insects. Sometimes fly with noisy wing fluttering (display?). Domed nest with side entrance; wedged in fork of branch, often over water or near bee, wasp, or stinging ant nest (occas. in cavities that are stuffed with grass); usually 3 eggs, whitish finely spotted shades of brown mostly at larger end[790]. Breeding May–Jul, Hato Masaguaral, Guárico[734].
Status and habitat: Common resident and migrant (short or long distance?) in shrubby clearings, forest borders, gardens, and residential areas in moist to humid zones. More often around dwellings and in urban areas than Rusty-margined Flycatcher. Breeding resident in most of c and w Venez, but largely absent from llanos in rainy season (ca. Jun–Oct); scarce, *absent*, or only seasonal (ca. Apr–Nov?) in much of e

Venez. (e.g., largely absent from Río Grande s to Santa Elena de Uairén). Nos. variable in nw Amazonas (more in Jun than Dec–Feb?). Migratory movements and seasonal status (i.e., movement out of llanos and into Amazonia during rainy season?) need documentation. Between Mar and Oct some birds may be migrants from s of Venez.

Range: To 1500m n of Orinoco; to 500m (sight recs. to 900m) s of Orinoco. Locally throughout s to n Amazonas (scarce in llanos), n Bolívar along Orinoco, and from Sierra de Imataca s to upper Río Caroní, but not extreme east (*columbianus*); rest of Amazonas, and Bolívar e to Río Paragua (*similis*). Mexico to ne Argentina and se Brazil; no Guyana recs.

Rusty-margined Flycatcher   PLATE 47
Myiozetetes cayanensis   Atrapamoscas Pecho Amarillo
Identification: 7″ (18cm). 26g. Short black bill. Concealed golden yellow coronal stripe. *Crown and sides of head black contrasting sharply with long white eyebrows which do not meet on rearcrown; back brown, primaries narrowly edged rufous* (often not conspic.), throat white, rest of underparts bright yellow. Or back tinged olive (*hellmayri*). Or with broader rufous wing edgings and prom. rufous edgings on tail (*rufipennis*). Imm. (all races): broad cinnamon rufous wing and tail edgings.
Sim. species: Most often confused with Social Flycatcher which differs in several subtle ways. Social (*columbianus*) has *faded dusky* (not contrasting black) cheeks, *olive* back (most Rusty-margineds are brown backed), pale buff edgings on wing coverts (form 2 illdefined wing bars), and broad buff-edged tertials. But cf. carefully darker *similis* subsp. of Social in s Venez. which has blackish cheeks and crown and obscure wing edgings. Note also that some vocalizations of these 2 spp. are very different, others quite sim. In hand the two are easily separated by different crownpatch color. Also see White-bearded and Gray-capped flycatchers.
Voice: Call a long-drawn, plaintive *peeeeeeea* with thin complaining or sad quality; when excited a loud, emphatic *puuuuureeeEET-EET-EET!*, varied to *tuWEET, cheat! cheat! cheat! cheat!* Greets with excited, rolling *TU-U-REE* over and over, erect posture, and wing flapping; also a rapid rolling ser. of *qa-wit* notes and *tis-u* and various other notes. Dawn song *fweee* over and over, occas. with short couplet or other note added.
Behavior: Usually in prs. or sociable little families that behave much like Social Flycatchers, but there is a gentle, ineffable melancholy to demeanor of Rusty-

margineds. Sit in open at almost any ht. from eye level or lower up to treetops, and forage by sallying to gd., to foliage, or to air for insects. Also take small berries by hover-gleaning and rapid hover-snatches. Sometimes fly with noisy wing fluttering (display?). At dusk families often sit on open perches, call repeatedly, and make short upward sallies over and over in a last intense burst of activity for flying insects before retiring. Large, messy, domed nest of dried grass with side entrance; wedged near end of branch where conspic. Breeding Mar–Aug, Hato Masaguaral, Guárico[734].

Status and habitat: Common resident in forest borders, river edges, gallery forests, and all kinds of cultivated and disturbed areas with trees. In some areas numerous in residential areas, parks, and gardens; shows some fondness for vicinity of water. Dry (not arid) to humid regions. Less numerous and local s of Orinoco where nos. may fluctuate seasonally and status (resident or migrant?) of some pops. unclear.

Range: To 1900m n of Orinoco; to 1000m s of Orinoco (prob. higher). Maracaibo Basin, Zulia, and w slope of Andes from Táchira to w Lara (*hellmayri*); rest of Venez. n of Orinoco (*rufipennis*); Amazonas, Bolívar, and Delta Amacuro (*cayanensis*). W Panama to se Brazil (absent from w Amazonia) and the Guianas.

Gray-capped Flycatcher PLATE 47
Myiozetetes granadensis Pispirillo Copete Gris
Identification: 7" (18cm). 28g. Small black bill. Head smoky gray with dusky mask across eyes and ear coverts; *white forehead extends rearward as short narrow white eyebrow* (often rather indistinct) *just to eyes*; concealed crown patch red tipped yellow (absent—♀), upperparts olive, wings and tail brown, wing edgings yellowish olive, throat dull white, rest of underparts yellow.
Sim. species: Mostly gray head and short eyebrow are the marks. Rusty-margined and Social flycatchers have bolder black-and-white striped heads. Smaller Dusky-chested Flycatcher lacks head pattern and has dark smudgy chest band. Tropical Kingbird and Sulphury Flycatcher, both larger and rangier in appearance, also lack eyebrow.
Voice: Sharp nasal *kip!*, also *kip, kip, kip-it!*, and a variety of other notes, some much like those of Social Flycatcher but sharper and more nasal.
Behavior: Rather like Social Flycatcher but not as excitable. Prs. or family groups may call noisily as sit exposed on tops of bushes or tall trees. Perch from eye level to treetops but often rather low around edge of clearings and near habitations where sally short to med. distances to air or occas. to foliage for insects

and a few berries. Nest sim. to that of Rusty-margined Flycatcher and sometimes close to it; mostly 1.5–8m up; 4 eggs, dull white speckled and blotched darker colors in wreath[706].
Status and habitat: Local in Venez. Resident in humid forest borders and shrubby clearings with scattered tall trees.

Range: To 550m. C and s Amazonas (vicinity of Cerro Duida and upper Río Ventuari at Kabadisocaña southward); Bolívar from lower Río Caura to upper Río Paragua at Río Carún (*obscurior*). Honduras to w Ecuador; se Colombia and nw Brazil s to n Bolivia.

Dusky-chested Flycatcher PLATE 47
Myiozetetes luteiventris Pispirillo Cresta Anaranjada
Identification: 6" (15cm). 16.5g. Stubby bill. *Entire head and upperparts dark brown* (no head markings, no wing edgings) with concealed orange yellow coronal patch (absent—♀), median throat whitish vaguely streaked or mixed gray, rest of underparts rich yellow, upper *breast heavily smudged and flammulated olive* (looks streaky); feathers of crown rather long; tail square.
Sim. species: Shape recalls *Myiozetetes* but plumage mimics that of Sulphury Flycatcher. No other *Myiozetetes* has unmarked head and smudgy streaking on chest.
Voice: Distinctive meowing calls incl. a whining *meeow*, softer *neea*, and when excited a rapid *neea-ne-wît!*, last recalling Gray-capped Flycatcher but more nasal and whining. Sometimes noisy for short periods.
Behavior: Sociable but darkly attired prs. or families lead modest lives high in forest canopy where they wander widely and would go largely unnoticed but for freq. hd. meowing calls. This sp. perches erect on twigs or stands on top of leaves, mostly high in crown of trees. Typically sits fully exposed unlike *Conopias* flycatchers and sallies short distance to foliage, less often to air, for insects. More often independent of mixed-spp. flocks than with them, but reg. with other birds at fruiting trees and shrubs, where may drop much lower and eagerly hover-glean small berries or reach for them from a perch. May spend long periods of time around a favorite fruiting tree. Often flicks up tail as it calls or alights, and sometimes jerks up head and tail when calling.
Status and habitat: A low-density resident in shrubby forest edges or high in canopy of humid terra firme forest; occas. in partially cleared areas with scattered trees. Usually not found in scrubby white sandy soil forests but in forests on more fertile soils in sandy belt areas. Uncommon and local but more numerous than

the few recs. suggest (need to know voice). Known from numerous sight recs. (Jun 1995–1996) in vicinity of Pto. Ayacucho, Amazonas (Hilty), and Junglaven (many observers).

Range: To 350m. N Amazonas (sight); n Bolívar in lower Río Caura (sightings) and c Bolívar on Río Paragua (*luteiventris*). Disjunct range. Se Colombia to extreme n Bolivia, w and c Amaz. Brazil, and the Guianas.
Note: By some placed in genus *Tyrannopsis*[403]; by others in *Myiozetetes*[318,467,545].

Conopias

Related to *Myiozetetes*; rather long heavy bill; claw of mid. toe unusually long (note habits); most spp. lack concealed crown patch; humid forest canopy; grass or fiber nest in tree cavity or old oropendola or cacique nest.

Lemon-browed Flycatcher   PLATE 47
Conopias cinchoneti   Pecho Amarillo de la Selva Nublada
Identification: 6.3″ (16cm). Upperparts and sides of head dark olive, wings and tail browner, forehead grayish yellow *continuing as long broad yellow eyebrows that almost meet on nape; throat and underparts bright yellow*.
Sim. species: No other kiskadee look-alike (see esp. *Myiozetetes* and *Conopias*) has broad yellow eyebrows. Distinctive habits and voice also are good clues.
Voice: Often rather noisy, giving high, quavering *pa'treeeer* or *pa'treeer-pa'treeer-pa'treeer* with peculiar nasal and complaining quality; distinctive once learned.
Behavior: Sim. to that of Yellow-throated Flycatcher. Almost always seen in sociable prs. or families of 3–5, bobbing heads and perching in open on top of canopy, although sometimes can be difficult to locate. Like to perch on small open twigs above canopy or stand directly on leaves. Sally up short distances for flying insects or sally-hover to foliage.
Status and habitat: Notably local resident in steep, humid, and wet mt. forest (cloud forest) and treetops at forest borders. Many sight recs. in nw Barinas (no specimens); lowest rec. a sighting below La Azulita, w Mérida, 450m, Dec 1998 (P. Coopmans).
Range: 950–2150m (sightings to 450m). Sierra de Perijá, Zulia, w slope of Andes in w Mérida (La Azulita) and w Trujillo at Escuque (*icterophrys*); e slope of Andes in nw Barinas (sight recs.). Colombia s in Andes to s Peru.

Yellow-throated Flycatcher   PLATE 47
Conopias parva   Atrapamoscas Diadema
Identification: 6.5″ (16.5cm). 21g. Bill fairly long. Black crown completely encircled by *broad white forehead and eyebrow* (form ring around crown); concealed crown patch yellow; rest of upperparts olive, wings and tail dusky, underparts entirely bright yellow.
Sim. species: Microhabitat and habits much like those of Three-striped Flycatcher. Yellow-throated's white "ring" is *broad* but can be difficult to see as this sp. often sits high in canopy and then doesn't look much different about *Myiozetetes* flycatchers which have smaller bills and white throats.
Voice: Often rather vocal; call a rapid, querulous, almost trilled *quee'le'le*, usually repeated several times.
Behavior: Single birds, prs., or families stay fairly close together, perch exposed on small twigs or stand on leaves on top of canopy foliage and rarely come low even at borders. Change perches freq., bob heads, and utter quavering calls. Sally short distances to foliage or twigs for insects which are snatched during brief hover. Also sally to air for flying insects and occas. take fruit. Join mixed-spp. flocks but do not seem to follow them, and are at least equally often independent of them. Nest in hole or crevice, stuffed with grass, usually high; 2 eggs glossed cream and streaked and blotched dark forming ring at large end[253].
Status and habitat: Uncommon to locally common resident in canopy of humid forest or at forest borders in lowlands and foothills. Perhaps local. Almost daily 8–18 Aug 1985, San Carlos de Río Negro, sw Amazonas (C. Parrish); reg. in foothills of Sierra de Lema, Bolívar.

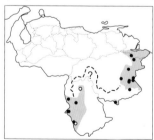

Range: To 1300m. W Amazonas from San Fernando de Atabapo and Cerro Yapacana s to San Carlos de Río Negro; e Bolívar from Sierra de Imataca s to Gran Sabana (*parva*). E Colombia, ne Brazil, and the Guianas; scattered recs. in e Ecuador, e Peru, and w Brazil.

Note: Here placed in *Conopias* and regarded as a sp. separate from White-ringed Flycatcher (*C. albovittata*) of C Amer. and nw S Amer.[318,545]

Three-striped Flycatcher
Conopias trivirgata   Atrapamoscas Trilistado
Identification: 5.5″ (14cm). Few recs. in Venez. Smallest of genus. Bill fairly long and narrow. Crown and cheeks dusky brown (no concealed coronal patch), *long narrow white superciliary* starting at base of bill completely encircles crown (but not across forehead); *back olive contrasting sharply with blackish wings and tail*; underparts bright lemon yellow, chest faintly tinged olive.
Sim. species: Looks like a small edition of more widespread Yellow-throated Flycatcher but with duller crown and less extensive eyestripe (Yellow-throated has white eyestripe over forehead), and back much paler than wings (wings show strong contrast). Also cf. Social and Rusty-margined flycatchers, both larger and with white throats.
Voice: Most freq. call (se Peru) a rather thick, low-pitched *chu-burr*, often over and over almost simultaneously by a pr.
Behavior: Prs. or family groups stay in crown of high trees and almost always perch in outer foliage or stand exposed on tops of leaves. Sally short distances into air or to foliage for insects. Occur with mixed-spp. flocks or away from them about equally. Because of habit of remaining very high, easily overlooked except for freq. calling.
Status and habitat: Known from 1 specimen from Taracunina, Bolívar (04°15′ N, 64°35′ W), uppermost Río Caura, and a sight rec. in 1992 at Canaima, s Bolívar (P. Coopmans). Canopy of humid forest.

Range: 950m. S Bolívar (*berlepschi*). Range spotty and disjunct. E Peru; n Bolivia; e Amaz. Brazil; e Paraguay and ne Argentina to se Brazil.

Myiodynastes

Large, hulking flycatchers; long, heavy bill; prom. black moustache; rufous in tail; loud, unpleasant-sounding vocalizations; related to *Conopias*.

Streaked Flycatcher   PLATE 47
Myiodynastes maculatus   Gran Atrapamoscas Listado
Identification: 8.5″ (22cm). 43g. Large bill, lower mandible pinkish tipped dusky. Resident races: above mainly dusky brown streaked pale brown; concealed yellow crown patch; *wing coverts and primaries edged*

cinnamon rufous, tertials edged yellowish white, upper tail coverts and *tail heavily edged rufous*, central feathers dusky; *broad eyebrow yellowish white*; blackish patch through eyes bordered below by whitish lower cheeks and *dusky moustachial streak*; underparts (incl. chin) dull white to pale yellow faintly streaked dark brown on throat, broadly on breast and flanks, lower underparts dull white, crissum tinged yellow. Austral migrant: above *boldly streaked black (not brownish)*, wing coverts and primaries edged whitish, upper tail coverts and *tail mostly dusky black with narrow rufous edgings*; underparts white *sharply and extensively streaked black*.
Sim. species: Austral migrants more boldly and crisply streaked blackish than dull, "faded-looking" residents. See smaller Variegated and Piratic flycatchers.
Voice: Resident birds give a loud *sqUEE-zik!*, often doubled; a penetrating *teep!* and *chup*. Dawn and dusk song (Jun, w Apure) a quick, rhythmic *WEET, wiggle-your-feet!* over and over without pause.
Behavior: Sometimes noisy and conspic. (esp. resident subspp.) but in general not as engaging as some of allies. Can occur at almost any ht. but more often perches at mid. levels or a little higher and on rather open perches within a tree. May sit quietly for lengthy periods of time. Occurs alone or in prs., sometimes with mixed-spp. flocks. Takes large arthropods by short sallies to foliage or branches, also freq. eats fruit. Austral migrants heavily frugivorous (more so than resident forms?). Nest in tree cavity or broken stub filled with twigs and fine material; occas. open cup in palm, under eave, etc.; 2–3 whitish eggs heavily marked red or lilac[175,633]; breeding Mar–Apr, Hato Masaguaral, Guárico[734].
Status and habitat: Fairly common resident n of Orinoco in light woodland, second growth, clearings with scattered trees, forest borders, and mangroves. Most numerous in dry open forest. S of Orinoco mainly forest borders, river-edge várzea, and river isls. Some local movement of resident subspp. occurs[186], incl. birds wandering to high els. Austral migrants rec. 1 Mar–2 Sep, mainly s of Orinoco.

Range: To 2000m (resident subspp.); to 300m (austral migrant). Generally w of Andes w Falcón (e to Curimagua), and e base of Andes from Táchira to Portuguesa (*difficilis*); rest of Venez. n of Orinoco; Amazonas and Bolívar; Isla Margarita (*tobagensis*); Amazonas, Bolívar, and spottily n of Orinoco (austral breeding *solitarius*). E Mexico to c Argentina and se Brazil. Trinidad and Tobago. Nonbreeding n C Amer. birds (*insolens*) winter s to Panama and n S Amer. but are

unreported in Venez.; s breeders (*solitarius*) from n Bolivia and c Brazil s to Argentina winter e of Andes n to
n S Amer.

Golden-crowned Flycatcher   PLATE 47
Myiodynastes chrysocephalus   Atrapamoscas Corona
Dorada
Identification: 8.5″ (22cm). 37g. Large heavy bill. Resembles a dull-plumaged kiskadee. Crown dusky with
usually concealed golden yellow crown patch; *long
white eyebrow bordered by dusky stripe through eyes*;
lower cheeks and throat buffy white separated by
*broad, dusky, and slightly out-of-focus moustachial
stripe*; back dull brownish olive, *wings and tail dusky
heavily edged rufous*, chin whitish, *throat and chest buff
obscurely streaked olive*, lower underparts yellow.
Sim. species: Great Kiskadee and Boat-billed Flycatcher lack dusky malar and breast streaking, and
their plumage is much brighter and more sharply focused. Streaked Flycatcher has no yellow on underparts. Also see smaller Lemon-browed, Variegated,
and Piratic flycatchers.
Voice: Often noisy, persistently repeating a loud, forceful *skEEZZ-u* (like squeezing a rubber bath toy).
Behavior: Single birds or prs. sit slightly hunched,
often nodding heads and calling loudly from open or
partly open perch in canopy or a little lower. Freq. attract attention to themselves with loud, angry calls, but
at other times behave in calm, pacific manner. Hover
for or hawk insects and fruit in tree crowns. May
briefly join mixed-spp. flocks, but more often independent of them. Moss cup nest on cliff, crevice, rocky
roadcut, hole in bank, or tree cavity; 2 eggs, dull
cream finely spotted reddish brown.
Status and habitat: Fairly common resident in humid
and wet forest borders, around old landslides, treefalls, or along roadsides, occas. scattered trees in highland pastures but near forest. Some seasonal movements may occur; erratic and scarce Jan–Mar in
Andes, noisy and conspic. Jun–Jul. An ecological replacement of Streaked Flycatcher in cloud forest.

Range: 600–2300m. Throughout mts. of n Venez. from
Zulia, Táchira, and c Falcón (Sierra de San Luis) to
Sucre and n Monagas (*cinerascens*). E Panama s in
mts. to nw Argentina.

Legatus

Short billed and short legged; tail square; no crest; resembles *Empidonomus* but syrinx more like *Myiozetetes*[318]; robs nests of other birds, esp. large icterids,

Piratic Flycatcher   PLATE 47
Legatus leucophaius   Atrapamoscas Ladrón
Identification: 6″ (15cm). 23g. *Bill short and broad.*
Above plain brown with *no streaks on back*; *wings virtually unmarked*, flight feathers narrowly edged whitish, concealed yellow crown patch; *long whitish eyebrow*; *dusky mask across sides of head*; whitish malar
and narrow dusky submalar; below dull white, breast
and sides with blurry brown streaking; suggestion of rufous edging on upper tail coverts and tail feathers in
some birds.
Sim. species: Variegated Flycatcher is larger, has
longer bill, streaked back, prom. rufous edgings on
tail, and streaking on underparts is usually more
sharply focused (resident birds duller).
Voice: Song, hd. mostly 1st half of yr and often tirelessly repeated throughout day, a clear upslurred whistle, *weeEEE?*, sometimes followed after distinct pause
of 1–2 sec by tremulous, rising whistle, *wiririre?*; some
individuals usually incl. 2d whistle, others mostly omit
it. Also rarely give (context?) froglike *reek-reek-reek-
. . .* (ca. 15 notes in 3 sec), recalling song of Scrub
Greenlet.
Behavior: A little bird with chutzpah. Perches high
and usually in open where it sings all day, pausing
only to fly off and gorge quickly on fruits before returning to singing post a few min later. Ads. are almost entirely frugivorous (quick feeding may be an adaptation
aiding piratical behavior) but feed insects to young. As
name implies, prs. pirate domed or pendent nests of
various birds (caciques, oropendolas, orioles, becards, *Tolmomyias* flatbills, and others) by sheer persis-
tence, constantly harassing rightful owners. Some
evicted birds are 10 times the weight of these flycatchers. Many oropendola or cacique colonies have a pr.
of these birds. Mar and Aug breeding, Guárico[734]; Feb
breeding in Barinas, Mar in e Bolívar (Hilty); 2–3 gray
brown eggs with dark brown scrawls[790]. Eggs of appropriated nest always thrown out.
Status and habitat: Locally fairly common. Resident
and/or migrant in moist and humid forest borders,
clearings with scattered trees, partially deforested
areas, second growth, lighter woodland, and plantations. Nos. prob. augmented by influx of migrants from
C Amer. from ca. late Sep–early Jan (period of absence in Panama[417]); most numerous Mar–Jun (later?)
in vicinity of Rancho Grande; mostly absent (?) from
Andes in rainy season. Seasonal abundance and
breeding need documentation; austral migrants also
possible.

Range: To 1000m n of Orinoco; to 600m s of Orinoco.
Locally (or seasonally?) n of Orinoco but mainly in or

near mts. (and not arid regions); throughout Amazonas and Bolívar (*leucophaius*). Se Mexico to n Argentina and se Brazil.

Empidonomus and Griseotyrannus

Short rictal bristles; slender body; short legs; longish tail; the 2 genera formerly united; Crowned Slaty Flycatcher now placed in *Griseotyrannus* based on differences in syringeal anatomy[318].

Variegated Flycatcher
PLATE 47

Empidonomus varius Atrapamoscas Veteado

Identification: 7″ (18cm). 25g. Basal half of lower mandible pinkish. Resident and migrant races both much like Piratic Flycatcher (incl. concealed yellow crown patch) but larger with longer bill; *more or less streaked back*; *more prom. wing edgings*, and *rump and tail feathers broadly edged rufous*. Migrant race (*varius*): larger (7.5″, 19cm) with proportionately longer wings, longer tail, and *more heavily and distinctly streaked underparts* (streaking blacker and crisper than on resident birds). Some resident birds show only vague streaking below.

Sim. species: Resembles smaller and more compact Piratic Flycatcher, also larger, much heavier-billed Streaked Flycatcher.

Voice: Unusually quiet. Rarely a thin *zuree* or *zreeetee*[694] or *seeu*, high pitched, sibilant, and inaudible at any distance.

Behavior: An erratic, enigmatic bird, seemingly without demesne or domain, likely to turn up in a variety of unpredictable places. Usually seen alone, perched up fairly erect on edge of a large shrub, tree, or other prom. place, sometimes high but on avg. lower than Piratic Flycatcher. Sallies to air or flutters and hovers in front of foliage for insects and small fruit. Austral migrants perhaps more frugivorous than residents (?). Occas. with mixed-spp. flocks in forest canopy, but more often independent of them. Not yet reported breeding in Venez.

Status and habitat: Uncommon to fairly common presumed resident (*rufinus*); common austral migrant (*varius*). Tall humid forest canopy, forest borders, lighter woodland, and shrubby clearings with scattered trees. Nos. greatly augmented by influx of austral migrants mid Mar–mid Sep (once to 26 Oct at Seboruco, Táchira), esp. in more heavily forested areas s of Orinoco.

Range: To 1900m n of Orinoco; to 1300m s of Orinoco. E base of Andes in Barinas and Portuguesa, e Falcón (Mirimire), n cordilleras from Aragua (Rancho

Grande), Distr. Federal, and Guárico e to Sucre and Delta Amacuro; throughout Amazonas and Bolívar (resident *rufinus*); locally from w Táchira, e Lara, and Yaracuy e to Sucre and s to Orinoco; throughout Amazonas and Bolívar (migrant *varius*). E Colombia and the Guianas to c Argentina and Uruguay. Trinidad. S breeders (*varius*) reach Colombia, Venez., the Guianas, and Trinidad during austral winter; accidental in e N Amer.

Note: Resident and larger austral migrant birds may be separate spp.

Crowned Slaty Flycatcher
PLATE 47

Griseotyrannus aurantioatrocristatus Atrapamoscas Copete Negro y Amarillo

Identification: 7″ (18cm). 27g. Dull and rather flat headed. Tail longish. *Crown black* (concealed yellow coronal patch) *contrasting with dull smoky brown upperparts* (no edgings); sides of head (to above eyes) and entire underparts dingy brownish gray, paler and with faint buffy brown wash on belly.

Sim. species: Slender shape and longish tail recall a *Myiarchus*. Note contrasting black crown, unmarked uniform gray underparts, and habit of perching high in open at edge of forest.

Voice: Usually silent in Venez. In Argentina a high, thin *pseeet*; song a thin, buzzy, rising *be-bee-beee-beeez*.

Behavior: On Venez. wintering grounds occurs singly. Perches in tops of canopy and emergent rain forest trees and sallies to air for flying insects. Does not assoc. with mixed-spp. flocks.

Status and habitat: Known from only 3 specimens in Venez.: 2 from Río Ocamo, Amazonas, at 150m; and 1 ♀ on 1 Feb 1950, Portachuelo Pass, Aragua (where surely accidental). Also sight recs.: 8 seen 8–18 Aug 1985, San Carlos de Río Negro, sw Amazonas (C. Parrish); 1 at 2500m, Feb 2000, above Santo Domingo, Mérida (D. Ascanio and others). Prob. a fairly common austral migrant to s Amazonas; accidental n of Orinoco. Canopy of tall humid forest; vagrant to tall trees in open areas.

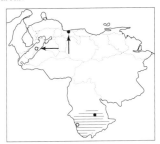

Range: To ca. 1050m (once to 2500m). S Amazonas; n Aragua (*aurantioatrocristatus*); ne Mérida (sight). Breeds from e Brazil (s of the Amazon) and n Bolivia to c Argentina and Uruguay; austral birds migrate into w Amazonia reaching s Colombia, s Venez., and Guyana.

Note: Formerly placed in genus *Empidonomus*.

Tyrannopsis

Resembles Tropical Kingbird but anatomically closest to *Megarynchus*[318]; open cup nest (like *Megarynchus* and *Tyrannus*) in moriche palm.

Sulphury Flycatcher   PLATE 47
Tyrannopsis sulphurea   Atrapamoscas Sulfuroso
Identification: 8″ (20.3cm). 54g. Looks like a *small, dark Tropical Kingbird with short bill* and short, square tail. Crown dusky gray with concealed golden yellow crown patch and dark brownish olive upperparts; wings plain dark brown; *broad dusky facial area; center of throat white enclosed by blurry dark gray streaking on sides of throat; chest tinged olive* (somewhat streaky at sides), rest of underparts bright yellow.
Sim. species: From either Tropical or White-throated kingbirds by dark, indistinctly streaked area surrounding throat; also note short bill, rounder head, overall darker, more brownish-tinged upperparts, and habits. Dusky-chested Flycatcher is smaller, dark capped, and with more extensive smudgy streaking on breast.
Voice: Long periods of quiet are interrupted by abrupt, high-energy outbursts of strident, almost electrified screeches, *zhrEEEEEEEE!, zhr-zhrEEEEEEEEE!*, as prs. rapidly countercall in fast repartee (like electric bug-zappers). Song a sim.-sounding, high-pitched, penetrating ser. of blurred trills, *zhr'dek . . . zhr'r'r'e'k. . . . zhr' dek'dek . . .*, like pulses of electric energy. Some vocalizations recall those of Gray Kingbird.
Behavior: Prs. almost always hang around in vicinity of crowns of moriche palms but can be quiet and inconspic. Perch erect, sally to air for insects, or fly off, sometimes long distances, to fruit tree to hover momentarily and grab small fruits (seen eating *Virola* arils). Nest a cup of sticks at base of fronds of moriche palm; 2 eggs creamy buff blotched brown and pale violet[175].
Status and habitat: A moriche palm (*Mauritia flexuosa*) specialist, although sometimes found away from it along forest borders. Uncommon and local resident even in moriches. Occas. in or around small towns if there are moriches nearby. Highest els. are sight recs. in moriche groves near Santa Elena de Uairén, se Bolívar, 1 Jan 1980 (C. Parrish) and 1 Mar 1998 (Hilty and others).

Range: To 500m (sight to 900m). Very locally in se Sucre (Guaraunos), n and e Monagas[60], se Monagas, Delta Amacuro, spottily throughout Amazonas and Bolívar. E Colombia to n Bolivia, Amaz. and s Brazil, and the Guianas. Trinidad.

Tyrannus

Tyrannical, aggressive, and despotic near nest sites; erect, alert posture; quintessential "flycatching" behavior (aerial hawkers); perch in open; sexes alike; wings pointed, outer primaries incised at tip; open cup nest in tree or shrub.

Tropical Kingbird   PLATE 47
Tyrannus melancholicus   Pitirre Chicharrero
Identification: 8.5″ (22cm). 39g. Widespread and conspic. Fairly heavy bill; narrow base to notched tail. *Head gray* with dusky mask through eyes; concealed orange crown patch, *back grayish olive*, wings and slightly forked tail dusky brown, *throat pale gray turning olive on chest and bright yellow on breast and belly.* Imm.: overall paler, esp. on head; very young birds have faint rusty scaling on wing coverts, pale edges to primaries, whitish throat.
Sim. species: This bird is so common that its shape and appearance should be memorized as a "yardstick" against which to cf. many other spp. Cf. esp. Sulphury Flycatcher and very sim. White-throated Kingbird.
Voice: Sometimes rather noisy. Excitable prs. give a variety of high twittering *tre'e'e'e'e'eip* trills, often during short flight or as they alight, the trilling often accompanied by raised, vibrating wings. Dawn song, one of 1st to be hd. in wee hrs, a more complex rising trill.
Behavior: The paradigm for genus. Perches up erect in open atop a tree, on a wire, or other high exposed place. Watches alertly and sallies med. or long distances to air, often in dramatic sweeps, for flying insects, occas. also sallies to gd., foliage, or water, and may pursue wily prey in agile flight. Hovers well. Notably pugnacious and is esp. intolerant of large marauding intruders such as toucans, caracaras, and hawks which it chases vigorously. Nest a rather frail cup usually saddled in fork 5–15m up; 2–3 creamy white eggs boldly spotted and streaked reddish brown; breeding Apr–Nov, w Apure[137].
Status and habitat: Common and widespread resident in all kinds of habitats from dry woodland borders to humid rain forest borders, urban areas, clearings, gardens, and roadsides. Nos. augmented by austral migrants Mar–Oct (esp. obvious in humid zones of e and s Venez.). Increasing in nos. with deforestation.

Range: To 2200m (vagrant to 3000m). Throughout n of Orinoco, Delta Amacuro, and along s bank of Orinoco in nw Bolívar (*satrapa*); Amazonas and rest of Bolívar (*melancholicus*). Sw US to w Peru and c Argentina.

Aruba, Bonaire, and Curaçao; Trinidad and Tobago; Grenada. N and s pops. migratory.
Note: Subsp. *chloronotus*[403] is invalid[467].

White-throated Kingbird   PLATE 47
Tyrannus albogularis   Pitirre Gargantiblanco
Identification: 8.2″ (21cm). 38g. Local. Very sim. to Tropical Kingbird, differing mainly in *paler gray head* (looks almost whitish in field) with *sharply contrasting blackish mask*; *pure white throat turning bright yellow on rest of underparts with no obvious olive chest band separating throat from breast* as in Tropical Kingbird (or sometimes shows tinge of olive); *back lighter and brighter olive green.* Proportions slimmer and slightly longer tailed than Tropical Kingbird, features which enhance White-throated's more contrasty pattern.
Sim. species: *Easily confused* with Tropical Kingbird which sometimes looks quite pale headed, esp. imms. Note White-throated's clean white throat, virtual absence of olive on chest, more conspic. dusky mask, and more olive green back. Overall White-throated is *crisper, cleaner cut, and more contrasty*, lacking Tropical's typical "gray" look, but beware fresh-plumaged Tropicals which may be rather bright. A good rule is if there is any doubt, it is Tropical Kingbird. Also note vocal differences and distrib.
Voice: Most vocalizations recall those of Tropical Kingbird but are higher, thinner, and delivered faster, hence sound squeaky. Common advertising or territorial call from perch a shrill, trilled *tic . . tic . . tic'i'i'i'i'i 'i'i'i'i*; sometimes sings a long irreg. ser. of *tic* notes and *ti'i'i'i'i'i'i'i'i'i'i* trills for up to several min.
Behavior: In general aspect much like more widespread Tropical Kingbird, although shows some preference for vicinity of water or damp grasslands, and unlike Tropical Kingbird, generally does not perch very high and is not as aggressive. Likes to perch in open on fence wires or exposed on trees and shrubs where it sallies to air for flying insects. Postbreeding birds may occur in a variety of places, even settled areas, around villages, etc., and may occur with Tropical Kingbirds.
Status and habitat: Uncommon in vicinity of Santa Elena de Uairén where almost certainly a yr-round resident and presumed breeder in small (seasonally varying?) nos., although breeding not yet proved. Elsewhere a rare and local vagrant or austral or s Amaz. migrant (?). Possibly overlooked and may prove to be more widespread. Sight recs. from San Fernando de Yuruaní, se Bolívar, 7 Mar 1982 (C. Parrish); Pto. Ayacucho, Amazonas, 18 Feb 1994 (K. Zimmer) and 2 there

17 Jun 1996; 1 on 1 Jul 1994 at El Palmar[259]; possibly Delta Amacuro[343].
Range: To 900m. Nw Amazonas (sight); Sucre (specimen?); ne Bolívar (sight), and se Bolívar (Santa Elena de Uairén). The Guianas to e Bolivia and s Brazil. Austral birds migrate across w Amazonia reaching e Peru, e Ecuador, and se Colombia; s Venez. (?).

Gray Kingbird   PLATE 47
Tyrannus dominicensis   Pitirre Gris
Identification: 9″ (23cm). 47g. Large headed; heavy black bill. *Above gray with conspic. black mask through eyes*; concealed orange yellow crown patch; wings and slightly forked tail dusky, wing coverts and primaries edged whitish (no bars), *underparts white* with gray tinge on chest. Juv.: sim. but with rusty edges on wing coverts, rump, and tail.
Sim. species: Slightly smaller Tropical Kingbird is olive above and mostly yellow below. Gray Kingbird's silhouette is sim. to Tropical Kingbird's but with noticeably larger head, heavier bill, and overall more robust proportions. See Eastern Kingbird.
Voice: Often rather noisy, uttering shrill, chattery *pitch-chir'r'r'e*, slightly trilled.
Behavior: Typically alone, less often prs. or loosely assoc. groups. Spends most of time on conspic. perch atop a bush, fence, or utility wire where makes long sweeping sallies for flying insects and watches for intruders such as caracaras. Notably pugnacious; nesting birds readily attack birds and mammals, large and small. Occas. hover-gleans for fruit. Apr nest, sw Guárico[734]; fledged juvs, Feb, w Apure (Hilty); Apr–Jul breeding, w Apure[137]; breeding also reported at Ciudad Bolívar[489]; thin cup nest of coarse twigs and grass in bush or tree; 3 eggs pinkish blotched brown.
Status and habitat: Very local breeding resident, the few recs. mainly from c llanos. Also locally a fairly common nonbreeding winter resident from W Indies (bulk of recs. Sep–mid Apr) to drier open or semiopen areas with scattered bushes and trees, in ranchland, parks, towns, and borders of mangroves. Most numerous near coast and on offshore isls. Trans-Carib. migrants (*vorax*) likely but unrec.

Range: To 1700m (most recs. much lower). Throughout n of Orinoco; s to nw Amazonas, n Bolívar near Orinoco, and Delta Amacuro; Islas Margarita, Las Aves, Los Roques, La Orchila, La Tortuga, and La Blanquilla (*dominicensis*). Breeds in coastal se US, W Indies, isls. off Venez. (incl. Netherland Antilles), Venez., (prob. Colombia), Trinidad and Tobago. Winters in W Indies,

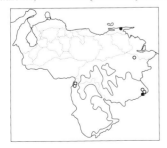

Panama, n Colombia, n Venez., n Brazil (rarely), and the Guianas.

Eastern Kingbird
Tyrannus tyrannus   Pitirre Americano
Identification: 8″ (20.3cm). 42g. *Upperparts and head to below eyes blackish;* concealed fiery orange crown stripe; *underparts snowy white; tail* (often fanned in flight) *black with conspic. white terminal band.*
Sim. species: White tail band is good mark. Gray Kingbird is gray above (not black) and lacks white tail band; also note heavier bill. Eastern Sirystes has gray throat and chest, white rump, and no white tail band. Also cf. imm. Fork-tailed Flycatcher.
Voice: Very quiet during migration and on wintering gds.
Behavior: Prs. are noisy, pugnacious, and very intolerant of their own or other spp. on n breeding gds., but their behavior is completely opposite during migration and on wintering gds. There, in a transformation worthy of Jekyll and Hyde, they are curiously silent, travel in compact, erratically behaving flocks of varying sizes that wheel, change direction abruptly, descend en mass on fruiting trees, esp. *Ficus*, along major rivers, and are subordinate to all of their tropical relatives. Occas. a few accompany flocks of Fork-tailed Flycatchers. In Venez. mostly likely seen as single straggling migrants.
Status and habitat: Rare passage migrant. Known from 5 specimens from 3 locs. (below) and small no. of scattered sight recs. as follows: 2 well-worn individuals seen 18 Jan 1974, 4km n of Tucacas, Falcón (P. Alden); singles seen 19 Aug 1990, Isla Margarita, 4 Apr 1992, Cumboto, Aragua (P. Boesman); and 1 Mar 1997, Hato Cedral, Apure (D. Fisher). Can occur in almost any habitat from forest to mostly open areas. Most migratory movement in this sp. is apparently w of Venez.

Range: To 1700m. Mérida; Bolívar (3 specimens, Cerro Roraima, 10–17 Mar 1950); sightings in e Falcón, Aragua, w Apure, Isla Margarita, and Islas Los Roques (specimen 2 Nov 1973). Breeds in N Amer.; winters in w Amazonia s to s Bolivia and n Argentina; scattered recs. in coastal Peru, Chile, Guyana, e Brazil, and Falkland Isls.

Fork-tailed Flycatcher   PLATE 48
Tyrannus savana   Atrapamoscas Tijereta
Identification: ♂ 15″ (38cm). ♀ 11″ (28cm). 31.5g (*savanna*), 28g (*monachus*). *Long, deeply forked tail* (shorter in ♀♀ and young birds). *Crown, nape, and sides of head to below eyes black,* concealed coronal

stripe yellow; back light gray, wings dusky, wing coverts narrowly edged light gray, tail black, basal half of outer web of outer tail feathers white; *underparts entirely white.* Or sim. but back dark gray (*savana*). Imm. and molting ads. lack long outer tail feathers; imm. also has *brownish cap,* duller wings, and brown-tinged back. In hand the 3 subspp. in Venez. may be told by degree of emargination of outer 3 primaries (most obvious on ad. ♂♂): bluntest tip and least emargination (resident *sanctaemartae*); deeply notched with thick tip (*monachus* of C Amer. and nw S Amer.); and deeply notched with thin tip (s migrant *savana*).
Sim. species: Long-tailed birds distinctive. Short-tailed birds recall Eastern Kingbird, Gray Kingbird, and even Eastern Sirystes but almost always with some "fork" evident in tail.
Voice: Not very vocal. Thin tittering; rapid ser. of *tic* notes; high *jeek.*
Behavior: Occur in prs. when breeding, but migratory or wandering birds occur alone or in small to large flocks. Typically perch in open on fence or top of bush or small tree and sally-hawk to air for insects or occas. sally to gd. or water. May congregate in nos. at fruiting trees where hover-glean and flutter for small berries. Migratory birds are apt to turn up almost anywhere, even atop canopy of tall humid forest. During austral summer large nos. appear in Venez., esp. short-tailed, brown-capped imms., and gradually amass in spectacular nos. of up to 5000–10,000 or more locally at roosts in mangroves, in llanos, and on river isls. in Orinoco. Roosting groups scatter long distances each morning to feed. Peak nos. in late Sep in ne Anzoátegui[186]. Nest a shallow plant-material cup 1–10m up; 3 glossy white eggs irreg. marked chocolate and lilac[790]; Oct nests, w Apure[137].
Status and habitat: Ranchland, savanna, and drier semiopen areas with scattered trees; also along rivers and river isls. in forested regions, and mangroves. A few resident birds (*sanctaemartae*), mostly in nw Zulia, are augmented by large nos. of austral migrants (*savana*) present mainly early Mar–mid Oct, with a few groups arriving by 1st wk of Feb (flocks up to 80 at Hato Los Indios); recs. for C Amer. breeders (*monachus*) are scattered throughout yr, and some of these birds may breed in Venez.

Range: To 1600m. Throughout incl. Islas Margarita, Los Testigos, and Patos. Resident in nw Zulia on Goajira Pen. (*sanctaemartae*); resident and migrant (*monachus*) and austral-breeding migrant (*savana*) throughout. Breeds from Mexico to Panama (some migrants reach n S Amer.); also locally from Colombia to s Suriname; lower Amaz. Brazil; n Bolivia and s Brazil to c Argentina. Austral migrants reported over most of continent; a few overshoot to W Indies and e N Amer. **Note:** Has also been placed in genus *Muscivora*.

Genera Incertae Sedis

Species in the genera *Schiffornis*, *Piprites*, *Lipaugus*, *Laniocera*, *Xenopsaris*, *Pachyramphus*, *Platypsaris*, and *Tityra* are here placed at the end of the Tyrannidae, recognizing that they appear to be tyrannoid but of uncertain affinity[10,309,513,604]. In the past the genera *Schiffornis* and *Piprites* have been placed in Pipridae (Manakins), the others in Cotingidae (Cotingas).

Schiffornis

Dull plumage; stout shape; rounded crown and large, dark, staring eyes; forest understory; formerly placed with manakins; now believed allied to *Laniocera* and *Laniisoma* mourners and to *Pachyramphus*, *Xenopsaris*, and *Iodopleura* in a group intermed. between flycatchers, manakins, and cotingas[518].

Thrush-like Schiffornis   PLATE 44
Schiffornis turdinus   Silbador Paraulata
Identification: 6.5″ (16.5cm). 29g. *Plain. Large, dark, dreamy-looking eyes and faintly indicated pale eyering*; distinctly rounded head. Mainly uniform olive brown above; wings and tail dull brown, below slightly paler olive brown than above. W birds (*stenorhynchus*) more rufous brown above, esp. on wings; throat and chest brown tinged yellowish contrasting somewhat with grayish olive lower underparts (imparts "divided" look to underparts).
Sim. species: A confusing bird that might bring to mind a short-tailed, dull brown thrush, although shape and behavior are somewhat manakinlike. Wide-eyed, round-headed look (rather vacant stare) is helpful once learned, as are stocky proportions and *lack* of distinct markings. See Várzea Schiffornis. Several ♀ manakins are equally nondescript but are all much smaller and usually "greener."
Voice: Distinctive territorial song, usually at intervals of 1—several min apart, varies geographically, roughly corresponding to subspecific differences, but always easily recognizable. Typically a clear, sweet 3-to 4-note whistle, halting after 1st note, 2d note high, last note sharply inflected upward, e.g., in Amazonas *weeeeee .. PREE, a-weET!*
Behavior: A solitary and retiring bird of forest understory that is hd. occas. but not often seen. Best known by voice, it is difficult to track down. Perches normally, or clings 1–2m up to side of vertical stems or saplings, and peers slowly about, often looking a little dazed. Makes short sallies to foliage for insect prey and visits small fruiting trees in understory. Seldom encountered with mixed-spp. flocks. Nest in Costa Rica a bulky leaf-lined cup of skeletal leaves and fine rootlets; 0.5–1.5m up in palm stump or lodged against palm trunk; 2 pale buff eggs marked with dark brown and lilac gray in wreath at larger end[647].

Status and habitat: Fairly common resident (based on voice) in humid and wet forest and tall second-growth woodland in lowlands and foothills of Orinoco. Local n of Orinoco.

Range: To 1800m n of Orinoco (most recs. much lower); to 800m s of Orinoco (hd. to 1450m, Sierra de Lema). Zulia, e and w base of Andes from Táchira and Barinas to Lara; e Falcón (Tellería; hd., Cerro Misión) and Yaracuy to Aragua (*stenorhynchus*); Miranda (?); throughout Amazonas (*amazonus*); Bolívar and Delta Amacuro (*olivaceus*). Se Mexico to n Bolivia, Amaz. Brazil, and the Guianas; coastal e Brazil.
Note: Previously called Thrush-like Manakin[403].

Várzea Schiffornis   PLATE 44
Schiffornis major   Silbador Mayor
Identification: 6″ (15cm). 30g. Swampy forest. Large blackish eyes. *Crown and sides of head gray*, otherwise above reddish brown, flight feathers dusky, *upper tail coverts and tail bright cinnamon rufous*, throat dull gray turning yellowish cinnamon on breast; lower underparts pale cinnamon.
Sim. species: Overall more or less cinnamon rufous. Look for contrasting grayish crown. Bright enough and large enough to be confused with Cinnamon Attila and esp. Citron-bellied Attila, but both are even larger and have longer, hooked bills. Note vocal differences. Also cf. duller Thrush-like Schiffornis.
Voice: Advertising song recalls that of Thrush-like Schiffornis but longer and more complex, a long, slow ser. of slurred whistles, somewhat syncopated, *twoweeo*, *tweeEET, teeu-dewEE, tweeEET . . . teeu . . . dewEET . . . teeu . . . dewEET*, last 2 phrases coming after pauses of ca. 2–3 sec; most vocal at dawn and dusk.
Behavior: Sim. to Thrush-like Schiffornis which replaces it in terra firma and upland forest, but unlike that sp., sometimes seen in prs. Perches in understory, usually acts stolid and sluggish, as if a little dazed.

Status and habitat: Known from only a small no. of recs. in Venez. Inhabits várzea forest understory, esp. along creeks and stream banks (rarely far from water) and sim. swampy or low-lying forest or forest borders subject to freq. inundation. This habitat is not extensive in Venez., perhaps accounting for apparently local distrib. of this sp.
Range: To 200m. W Amazonas from Caño Capuana southward (*duidae*). Se Colombia to n Bolivia and w and c Amaz. Brazil.
Note: Previously called Greater Manakin[403] and Várzea Mourner[545].

Piprites

Another genus of uncertain taxonomic affinity; chunky, short tailed, round headed, and large eyed; plumage rather becardlike.

Wing-barred Piprites   PLATE 44
Piprites chloris   Quejoso de Ala Barreteada
Identification: 5" (12.7cm). 14.8g. Marked racial variation. Mostly bright olive green above with narrow yellow forehead and lores and *bright yellow eyering* ("spectacles"); *nape gray*; wing coverts dusky with *single conspic. yellow wing bar* and a 2d (upper) inconspic. bar; tertials broadly edged yellow to white, tail dusky, *throat yellow*, otherwise light gray below; under tail coverts yellowish. Or sim. but underparts mostly yellow, chest clouded olive (*perijanus* and *tschudii*); tail tipped yellowish white (*perijanus*). Sexes sim.
Sim. species: Usually located by voice. Although formerly considered a manakin, looks like almost anything but a manakin, and is more likely to be mistaken for another flycatcher, becard, or vireo, esp. Yellow-throated Vireo, which has bold white wing bars. Note *plump proportions, large rounded head,* and *notably large blackish eyes.* Bill and tail are rather short compared to most flycatchers.
Voice: Infreq. hd. advertising song, usually given at rather long intervals (from 30 sec to several min), a clear, slightly nasal, and leisurely ser. of whistles, *quee, quee quee queedle-le quee, quee?* or sim. variation. Warbled phrase in middle, and slight hesitation of notes at beginning and end, are typical. Overall has quality of a shorebird, e.g., a curlew. Singing is markedly seasonal at Rancho Grande Biol. Station, Aragua, with much more vocalization in early rainy season (May–Jun).
Behavior: Hd. far more than seen. Almost always seen singly and often with mixed-spp. flocks in mid. or upper levels of forest. Behavior is placid, sluggish, almost vacuous (becardlike), perching semiupright, changing perches after a few moments, or sallying short distances, esp. upward to hover-glean insects from foliage. Occas. takes small berries. Generally remains in upper foliage where inconspic. Flies abruptly and quickly when moving in or between trees, hence difficult to follow by eye.
Status and habitat: Resident in a fairly broad range of humid lowland and premontane forest and older second growth ranging from sandy-belt woodland and tall forest in lowlands to wet montane forest (cloud forest) in mts.

Range: 350–2000m n of Orinoco; to 1700m s of Orinoco. Sierra de Perijá, Zulia, and se Táchira (*perijanus*); Coastal Cordillera in Carabobo and Aragua; Paria Pen., Sucre; n and c Amazonas (s to Cerro Duida), and n Bolívar from lower Río Caura (sight) and Sierra de Imataca southward (*chlorion*); s Amazonas s to Sierra Imerí at Salto de Húa (*tschudii*). N Colombia and generally e of Andes in forested regions s to n Bolivia and Amaz. Brazil; ne Argentina, e Paraguay, and adj. se Brazil.
Note: Often called Wing-barred Manakin[403].

Lipaugus

Dull-colored forest spp.; *Turdus*-like shape but tail longer; tarsi short; tail moderately long; bill fairly broad at base; some rictal bristles; sexes sim. (most spp.); some notably vocal; taxonomic placement uncertain.

Screaming Piha   PLATE 50
Lipaugus vociferans   Minero
Identification: 10" (25cm). 80g. *Turdus*-sized, all-gray bird. *Entirely gray,* slightly paler on throat and belly; flight feathers and tail tinged brownish, underparts vaguely tinged olive; mouth lining orange (visible as calls); eyes dark grayish. Imm.: tinged rufous on upper wing coverts and flight feathers. Sexes sim.
Sim. species: Much like Grayish Mourner and often not easily told in field except by voice. Mourner is somewhat smaller, thinner-billed, and more uniform below (throat not paler than breast). Perhaps also told by reddish brown (not dark grayish) eyes. Mourner is often with mixed-spp. flocks, piha rarely or never with them. In hand note olive-tinged underparts.
Voice: One of *the* sounds of rain forest s of Orinoco. Loud advertising call is 1–4 low, growling whistles followed by whip-cracking and explosive, ringing cry, *wuur . . . wuur . . . wuEEo, WHEE-you!* Sometimes warms up with just the low *wuur* or *weuur* growls; during peak periods of calling may give only a *wuE, WHEE-you!* phrase (cf. very different calls of Grayish Mourner). ♂♂ call much of day and virtually yr-round. Limited song cooperation between nearby ♂♂ ensures that singers do not overlap songs.
Behavior: Incontestably unique. ♂♂ gather in well-separated display arenas (leks) in mid. story or lower inside forest, where each ♂ maintains a little territory ca. 40–60m from its nearest competitor in lek and attempts to attract ♀♀ by sheer vocal power and song energy ("yelling matches"). Head is jerked backward vio-

lently during each song, but otherwise ♂♂ sit relatively immobile on calling perches and can be difficult to locate. Leks contain 3–25 or more ♂♂, occas. 2–3 times that many. ♂♂ spend at least 75% of time on calling perches and leave only briefly to visit fruiting trees, then return. Ads. eat almost entirely fruit taken during short upward fluttering hover or sally-stall. Do not follow mixed-spp. flocks. Nest a tiny stick platform 7m or so up in small tree and completely concealed by sitting ♀[689].

Status and habitat: Common and widespread resident in humid terra firme and várzea forest in lowlands, smaller nos. into tepui foothills. Unrec. but likely in e Monagas.

Range: To 1400m (most recs. below ca. 900m). Se Sucre (Guanoco), s Delta Amacuro[343], and generally in Amazonas and Bolívar. E Colombia s to n Bolivia, Amaz. Brazil, and the Guianas; coastal e Brazil (Pernambuco to Espírito Santo).

Rose-collared Piha   PLATE 50
Lipaugus streptophorus   Minero Collar Rosado
Identification: 8.5″ (22cm). E tepuis. ♂: mainly gray, slightly paler below, esp. on belly, with *pinkish magenta collar* (completely encircling neck) *and crissum*. ♀ and imm.: *all gray* with *cinnamon rufous* crissum. Birds with collars mixed rose and buff are imm. ♂♂.
Sim. species: ♂ unmistakable. ♀ from Screaming Piha and Grayish Mourner by cinnamon rufous crissum.
Voice: Generally rather quiet. Infreq. at dawn or at long intervals during day calls a few times. Song a clear, whistled *sueeet-suEEEeeeeoo*, sliding up then down, reminiscent of Screaming Piha but much softer and drawn out. More often gives single *swEEEeeu*; rising whistled *preEE!*; or longer, rising *SWEEEEEET!* Occas. soft *wee* notes when foraging.
Behavior: More staid and pacific than allied Screaming Piha of lowlands. Single birds or more often prs. or little families of 3–5 visit fruiting trees (esp. melastomes) or sit on high bare stubs partially or completely in open for short periods of time. Otherwise mostly remain quiet and inside canopy where easily overlooked. Also, unlike Screaming Piha this sp. seems to form prs., not leks, and forages on insects as well as fruit. Reg. in small melastome trees where sallies up to hover or flutter for berries, which are mashed before eating.
Status and habitat: Uncommon and perhaps local on Sierra de Lema (insufficient el.?). Humid and wet premontane forest and forest borders on slopes of tepuis and dense older, melastome-dominated second

growth. Known from large ser. of specimens from Ptari-tepui (esp. 1350–1750m) and Aprada-tepui where perhaps more numerous.

Range: 1000–1800m (most recs. above ca. 1300m). Mts. of se Bolívar on Sierra de Lema, Ptari-tepui, Aprada-tepui, Acopán-tepui, Uei-tepui, and Cerro Roraima. Tepuis of adj. Guyana and Brazil.
Note: Dusky Piha (*L. fuscocinereus*) occurs in Colombia very close to Táchira border and may occur in Venez. Large (12.5″, 32cm), long tailed, plain gray. Occurs in leks in upper levels of humid montane forest; loud *whee-a-wheee* call recalls that of other *Lipaugus*.

Laniocera

Bill rather small for size of bird and not hooked; few rictal bristles; rather long tail; 2 allopatric spp. (1 in Venez.); traditionally placed close to *Rhytipterna* (songs and behavior very sim.) in Tyrannidae but now believed closer to *Schiffornis* or Cotingidae[518].

Cinereous Mourner   PLATE 50
Laniocera hypopyrra   Plañidera Cinérea
Identification: 8.2″ (21cm). 46g. Rather thrushlike in appearance. Rounded bill and head. Mainly gray, slightly paler below, primaries tinged brownish, *2 rows of large cinnamon buff spots form "spotted" wing bars*; tertials and tail tipped cinnamon buff (spots small and inconspic.), orange rufous pectoral tufts (often hidden); sometimes a few black-tipped orange buff spots on breast and crissum. ♀: pectoral tufts pale lemon yellow.
Sim. species: No other med.-sized gray bird of lowland forests has bold cinnamon buff wing bars. Other "orangish" markings are variable in extent and generally not conspic. in field. See Grayish Mourner and Screaming Piha. Imm. mourners, pihas, and thrushes usually have *extensive* rusty scaling and spotting below.
Voice: Song 10–15 high, thin, and slurred *seee-a-way* phrases delivered with drowsy, hypnotic quality. First phrase is often more long drawn, *cheeeeee, a-wee*, then bird settles into singsong rhythm. Song, sometimes given tirelessly even during heat of day but typically with lengthy pause between songs, is far carrying but has ventriloquial quality. To the uninitiated will likely be passed off as a distant insect or amphibian.
Behavior: An understated and easily overlooked sp. ♂♂ are inconspic. as sing alone from semiopen perches or vines in forest mid. levels or lower (down almost to eye level) and are often loosely assoc. into small leks of 2–4 individuals although singers always

keep well apart, perhaps barely within earshot. Feed on fruit and insects by sallying to leaves and often briefly fluttering or hovering to make prey captures. Occas. assoc. with understory mixed-spp. flocks, although infreq. seen away from singing perches.
Status and habitat: Uncommon and local (leks widely scattered) resident in tall humid terra firme forest, esp. on sloping terrain or near ravines.

Range: To 500m. Se Sucre (Caño La Brea) s through ne Monagas to Delta Amacuro; generally in Amazonas, and n Bolívar from lower Río Caura, lower Río Paragua, and Río Grande (Sierra de Imataca) southward. Se Colombia s to n Bolivia, Amaz. Brazil, and the Guianas; coastal e Brazil (isolated pop.).

Xenopsaris

No rictal bristles; resembles a small *Pachyramphus* becard; differs in lack of strong sexual dimorphism, smaller size, and open cup nest; in hand also in tarsal scutellation and short, pointed 9th primary.

White-naped Xenopsaris   PLATE 49
Xenopsaris albinucha   Jipato de Nuca Blanca
Identification: 5″ (12.7cm). 10.2g. Large headed with rather stout black bill. ♂: *crown glossy blue black with conspic. white lores*; grayish white nape band (not always conspic.); *back grayish brown*, wings and tail dusky brown, *wing coverts and inner flight feathers edged white*, sides of head, neck, and *underparts white*, chest with faint tinge of gray, outer web of outer pr. of tail feathers white. ♀: slightly duller; crown tinged brown. Imm.: upperparts tinged brown (esp. crown), nape grayish, belly yellowish.
Sim. species: Whitish nuchal collar is narrow and not esp. prom. in field. Overall remarkably like ♂ Cinereous Becard but smaller, more or less *pure white below* (not gray), and with distinct *brownish tinge* to back, wings, and tail and *white edging on inner flight feathers*.
Voice: Dainty little song, hd. most often during rainy season, a high, thin, hesitant *teep, tre'e'e'e'a . . eea . . wu'u'u'e'e'e-e-e-e-e-p*, 1st trill rising then falling, last trill long, quavering, and rising. Song not far carrying. Sometimes only partial songs are given, or song pattern is varied. Typically there is long interval between songs, but may be hd. at any time during day.
Behavior: Usually seen alone or in prs. with members well separated. Often sits quietly, hence easily overlooked. Perches rather erect and upright with crown flat. Sits mostly in outer foliage of trees and sallies

short distances (0.5–1.5m) to hover-glean from tops of leaves, or sally-strike leaves without pausing. Occas. actively and aerobatically chases fleeing prey; reg. descends low, even to gd. briefly, to snatch prey. Cup nest in branch fork 10–15m up (prob. also lower); Jun–Sep, w Apure[137]; Jul nest, Hato El Frio, Apure (D. Ascanio).
Status and habitat: Uncommon and local resident. Most readily found in isolated groves of trees around ranch buildings (e.g., Hato Cedral, Hato El Frio) in llanos. Also drier gallery-forest borders, brushy areas, and scattered trees in open or mostly open terrain. Only a small no. of specimens from Venez. Sight recs. extend range to near San Félix, w Falcón, 18 Mar 1981 (R. Ridgely and A. Keith); and 1 ca. 15km sw of El Palmar, 3 Jul 1993 (Hilty and G. Rodríguez); 1 near El Dorado, e Bolívar, 1988 (Hilty).

Range: To 550m. Ne Lara (n of Barquisimeto at El Cují) and w Falcón (sight); w Apure e to Anzoátegui and across n Bolívar (Caicara; La Prisión; Ciudad Bolívar; Upata; sight, El Palmar[259]) (*minor*); sightings s to lower Río Cuyuní. Range disjunct. Ne Brazil (state of Roraima); Guyana; e Brazil to n Bolivia and c Argentina. Prob. e Colombia.
Note: Taxonomic status uncertain.

Pachyramphus

Large headed; heavy billed; strongly graduated and fairly short tail in most spp.; 9th primary of all ♂♂ half length of 10th (outermost), incised near tip (but not double-pointed as in *Platypsaris*); most spp. sexually dimorphic; typically sluggish, arboreal, and not very conspic.; large globular nest with entrance hole on side or near bottom; nest usually wedged in fork. Has been placed in both Cotingidae and Tyrannidae, but perhaps nearest *Schiffornis*[518].

Green-backed Becard   PLATE 49
Pachyramphus viridis   Cabezón Gargantigris
Identification: 6″ (15cm). 21g. ♂: *crown glossy black*, lores whitish, narrow eyering yellowish, sides of head (almost encircling neck) grayish olive, rest of upperparts *bright olive green*, flight feathers blackish edged olive, below grayish white with *broad olive yellow pectoral band*. ♀: sim. but *crown olive* like back, *lesser wing coverts rufous* (small patch at bend of wing only on ♀), pectoral band obscure.
Sim. species: Should be easily identified. In Andes (no overlap) see ♀ Barred Becard.

Voice: Song of ♂ a soft crescendo of whistled notes, *trididideédeédeédeé*, rather musical[545]. Call a high, nasal *q-wink, q-qink* . . . , rather thin, delicate, and rising, up to 12 times.

Behavior: Alone or in rather inconspic. prs., members of which are often well separated. Hop sluggishly in relatively open upper part of trees, pausing often to peer carefully, then reach or more often sally short distances and hover-glean insects from surface of foliage. Foraging behavior recalls that of Barred Becard, and like it, Green-backed often accompanies mixed-spp. flocks. Rather large messy ball nest like others of genus.

Status and habitat: Uncommon and local resident. Favors tall moist to humid forest, light woodland, and shrubby borders; shows preference for moist forest, i.e., around El Dorado, Bolívar; also locally in humid forest on slopes of tepuis (Sierra de Lema), esp. where forest is broken or opened.

Range: To 1000m. E Bolívar from Sierra de Imataca s to Ptari-tepui, Paurai-tepui, and Cerro Roraima (*griseigularis*). Disjunct. Guyana; near mouth of the Amazon, Brazil; e Bolivia, n Argentina, and Uruguay to e and se Brazil.

Barred Becard   PLATE 49
Pachyramphus versicolor   Cabezón Veteado

Identification: 5″ (12.7cm). 17g. Only in Andes. ♂: *crown and upperparts glossy black*, rump gray (usually concealed), scapular band, wing coverts, and inner flight feathers broadly edged white, lores and narrow eyering whitish yellow, throat, sides of head to above eyes, and neck pale greenish yellow obscurely barred dusky, *rest of underparts pale gray barred dusky*. ♀: crown gray, back olive, *wing coverts and inner remiges heavily edged rufous*, sides of head and neck and underparts pale greenish yellow *barred dark gray*, belly grayish white.

Sim. species: Either sex by chunky shape, stout bill, and barred underparts which are inconspic. at a distance. Note contrasting rufous on ♀'s wings.

Voice: Song of ♂ a plaintive, rising *we-pi-pi-ti´ti´tre´ tre´ree*, soft and melodious, sometimes falling at end. Hd. most often in early morning. Call a soft, whistled *tu-duu*.

Behavior: Prs. behave a little sluggishly but are nevertheless a little more active than others of genus. They are reg. members of mixed-spp. flocks in forest mid. levels or higher where they perch fairly upright, peer carefully, hop along branches like vireos, or fly short distances, then sally out to foliage to hover-glean ar-

thropods or to take small fruits. Large globular nest of moss and vines has entrance near bottom; 2–10m up; 1 egg (Costa Rica) white spotted and lined cinnamon and brown at large end[706].

Status and habitat: Uncommon to fairly common resident in humid and wet montane forest, forest borders, and light open woodland. Never seems very numerous.

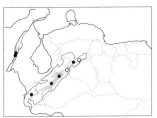

Range: 2000–2900m. Sierra de Perijá, Zulia; Andes from n Táchira (Zumbador) n on e slope of Andes to se Lara (Anzoátegui) (*versicolor*). Mts. of Costa Rica and w Panama; Colombia s in mts. to n Bolivia.

[Glossy-backed Becard]
Pachyramphus surinamus   Cabezón Brillante

Identification: 5.2″ (13.2cm). 20g. ♂: above glossy black with some white on scapulars; below pure white. ♀: *crown chestnut* dotted black and *contrasting with light gray mantle*; rump white, wings and tail black, wing feathers edged rufous, tail edged whitish buff; sides of head dusky, *underparts white*.

Voice: Dawn song, from high semiconcealed canopy perch, a soft, sweet *wuweet, weet-weet-weet-weet* (quality of Rose-breasted Chat) of ca. 5–9 notes, repeated at intervals of 5–9 sec; contact calls when foraging *kweeé, kew-kew-kew* (up to 5 *kew* notes); when agitated a longer, thin ser. of notes, *wee, tee-tee-te-ti-ti-ti-ti´ti´ti´ti*, faster and trilled at end (A. Whittaker recordings).

Behavior: In Brazil members of prs. usually stay well separated in small to large canopy and emergent-level mixed-spp. flocks. Move at rather deliberate pace with short hops or flights (0.5–10m) and peer and pick, or hover-glean (rarely sally) for insects and occas. fruit, mostly in thick leaf clusters in high outer branches, or on bare horizontal branches. Territories are large (more than 100ha), and birds may fly long distances from one emergent tree to another. Mostly forage higher than allied Black-capped Becard. Brazil nests reported Jul–Oct (dry season); suspended ball nest with side entrance; 25–30m up, usually near wasp or bee nest[450,796,797].

Status and habitat: No specimens; 1 sight rec. (with verified tape-recording) in Venez., ca. 21km s on Maripa-Trincheras Rd., lower Río Caura, 9 Feb 1992 (J. Pierson and D. Stejskal). In Brazil in emergent trees, high canopy, and subcanopy of tall humid forest, and at forest borders[797]. Easily overlooked (need to know voice) because of great ht. at which this forest sp. usually occurs.
Range: 200m. Lower Río Caura, Bolívar (sight). Locally in the Guianas and lower Amaz. Brazil (mostly n of the Amazon and e of Rio Negro); 25km w of Tefé at Alvaräes (sight).

White-winged Becard   PLATE 49
Pachyramphus polychopterus   Cabezón Aliblanco
Identification: 6″ (15cm). 19.5g. *Widespread.* ♂: crown glossy blue black, rest of upperparts black with gray rump and *prom. white scapular bar*, wing coverts edged and tipped white forming *2 white bars*, inner remiges edged white, *sides of head and underparts dark gray*; graduated *tail black broadly tipped white* (from below tail tips show as prs. of white spots). ♀: crown and sides of head brownish gray with dusky lores, whitish supraloral line and *prom. broken white eyering*; back light brown, wings dusky with *broad cinnamon buff edgings on scapulars, wing coverts, and inner remiges*; underparts pale yellow washed gray on breast; tail black broadly tipped cinnamon buff (looks spotted from below), outer web of outermost pr. of tail feathers buff. Or ♂ *jet black below* (not dark gray), ♀ *grayish olive above* (not light brown) in Amazonas (*nigriventris*) and e Táchira (subsp.?).
Sim. species: ♂ is *much blacker below* than any other *Pachyramphus* in Venez. (see Black-capped and Black-and-white becards). Also cf. ♂ to ♂ White-shouldered Tanager. ♀ recognized as a becard by large-headed, heavy-billed look; note broken eyering and prom. wing edgings; ♀ lacks "fancy" head pattern of ♀ Black-and-white and ♀ Black-capped becards.
Voice: Song a soft, warbled *teeur, tur-tur-tur-turtur?* or sim. variation; also a weak *tew te tu tu tu*, falling slightly in pitch. Both sexes sing.
Behavior: Single birds or prs. perch rather upright, move a little sluggishly, and follow bird flocks in mid. or upper levels of wooded regions, or forage independently of them in more open second growth. Peer carefully, then sally and flutter short distances for large insects, caterpillers, and some fruit. Nest a large grassy ball with side entrance; wedged (not suspended) in outer fork of fairly high branch; 3–4 pale gray eggs mottled brown; ♀ incubates; Aug–Sep nests, w Apure[137].

Status and habitat: Common and widespread resident. Moist to humid regions in forest borders, second-growth woodland, riparian and gallery forests, plantations, clearings with scattered trees, and borders of mangroves. Most widespread becard in Venez. Two ♂♂ killed at lighted windows at night, Rancho Grande Biol. Station, Aragua, 18 and 23 Apr, prob. represent local migratory movements[33].
Range: To 1900m. Throughout Venez. except Duida region (*tristis*); Amazonas near Cerro Duida (*nigriventris*) southward; se Táchira (subsp.?). Guatemala to e Argentina and Uruguay (austral birds migratory). Trinidad and Tobago.

Black-capped Becard   PLATE 49
Pachyramphus marginatus   Cabezón de Cachucha Negra
Identification: 5.3″ (13.5cm). 18g. *Mainly lowland rainforests s of Orinoco.* ♂: crown glossy blue black, *back mixed black and gray*, wings black, scapulars, wing coverts, and inner remiges heavily edged white; tail graduated, black broadly tipped white; *gray supraloral stripe* meets over bill; sides of head, nape, and underparts gray. ♀: *crown chestnut*, lores dusky; prom. *broken white eyering*, otherwise grayish olive above; wings black, wing coverts and inner remiges edged ochraceous buff, tail black edged and broadly tipped cinnamon buff, below grayish olive tinged yellow.
Sim. species: ♂ is *smaller* and *much paler gray below* than ♂ White-winged Becard; up close note *gray* supraloral line (lacking in latter). ♀ from ♀ White-winged by *chestnut* crown. Also cf. Black-and-white Becard which does not overlap.
Voice: Songs somewhat variable, but all have soft, melancholy quality; a musical and pleasing *tewtewtew-teé, dew-dew* or *twee-twee-tee-eet, dear-dear*, notes running upscale, last 2 lower; or sometimes a thin accelerating trill, *tre-tre'tre-e-e-e-it*, last note slightly lower. One or 2 lower notes at end are characteristic. At dawn a soft, delicate, and shorter *tew, tew-tweet!*, rising sharply at end.
Behavior: Prs. are reg. members of canopy mixed-spp. flocks, but because they remain so high are easily overlooked. Like other becards, act a little sluggish as peer carefully, then flutter or sally for insects or fruit in canopy.
Status and habitat: Fairly common resident inside tall humid forest and older second-growth woodland. Replaced by White-winged Becard along forest borders and in more disturbed areas.

Range: To 1000m. Throughout Amazonas and Bolívar (*nanus*). Se Colombia to n Bolivia, Amaz. Brazil, and the Guianas; coastal e Brazil.

Note: A rec. from Carabobo by Hellmayr[256] is a misidentification (M. Lentino).

Black-and-white Becard   PLATE 49
Pachyramphus albogriseus   Cabezón Blanco y Negro

Identification: 5.5″ (14cm). 18.5g. Only in mts. of n and w. *Boldly patterned*. ♂: glossy blue black cap in sharp contrast to *unstreaked* gray back and nape; *narrow white supraloral mark meets over bill*; wings and tail jet black, wing coverts edged white forming *2 prom. white bars*; flight feathers and tertials boldly edged white; rounded (graduated) tail broadly tipped white, sides of head and underparts medium gray. ♀: *chestnut crown sharply encircled by black line*; *narrow white eyeline and broken eyering*; back grayish olive, wings black with broad buffy cinnamon edgings; rounded tail black tipped buff, central feathers brown, sides of head light gray, throat and breast pale grayish olive faintly tinged yellow, lower underparts clear light yellow.

Sim. species: ♂ from other confusing "black-and-white" becards (esp. lowland Black-capped Becard) by unstreaked back, *lack* of white on scapulars, and broader white edgings on wing coverts and flight feathers; up close white supraloral mark is diagnostic; in hand, tail longer (55–65 vs. 48–55mm). Cinereous Becard is unstreaked above but lacks bold wing markings and is much paler below. Also see *much darker* ♂ White-winged Becard. ♀ from sim. allies by ornate head pattern.

Voice: Song (with minor variations) a short, musically warbled *t'you, t'you-duEET?* varied to *chu-chu, chu-E?* or briefer *chu-u-rE?*, typically rising abruptly at end. Song is soft and tender, usually given only at infreq. intervals.

Behavior: A demure, soft-spoken little bird. Like allied Black-capped Becard, occurs mainly high inside forest where often follows mixed-spp. flocks and is inconspic. and easily overlooked except for occas. song. After each perch change, sits still, peers upward, then executes short fluttery sallies upward to foliage or twigs for arthropods and occas. berries, or moves on. Nest in Costa Rica a globular mass of dead leaves, moss, and vine bits, with bottom entrance; built into vertical fork near tip of branch in subcanopy or at forest edge, 7–20m up[706].

Status and habitat: Fairly common but local resident in humid and wet foothill and lower montane forest

and occas. along forest borders. Fairly common and readily found in PN Henri Pittier, Aragua.

Range: 1200–2200m (sight to 900m, Aragua). Sierra de Perijá, Zulia (*coronatus*); Andes from s Táchira n through Mérida and nw Barinas (sight) to nw Lara (Cerro El Cerrón); mts. of Yaracuy, and Coastal Cordillera in Carabobo, Aragua, and Distr. Federal; mts. of Sucre (*albogriseus*); Miranda(?). Andes of Colombia (very local) s to s Peru.

Cinereous Becard   PLATE 49
Pachyramphus rufus   Cabezón Cinéreo

Identification: 5.5″ (14cm). 18.5g. ♂: above mainly pearl gray with *glossy black crown, prom. grayish white lores and narrow frontlet*; flight feathers and tail dusky, wing coverts and inner remiges narrowly edged white, below white tinged gray on breast. ♀: very different; *bright cinnamon rufous above, more chestnut on crown, lores gray, lower primary coverts black* (form contrasting patch at base of flight feathers), primaries dusky edged rufous, underparts whitish tinged orange buff on chest. Juv. ♂: like ♀ but crown dusky gray.

Sim. species: ♂ is nearest White-naped Xenopsaris but is larger, grayer above and below (not brownish above, white below), and with much more prom. white lores. Also see ♂ Black-and-white and Black-capped becards, both of which are unlikely to overlap present sp. much in range. ♀ much like Cinnamon Becard but whiter below, esp. throat and belly. Look for conspic. black patch formed by primary coverts (much less obvious in ♀ Cinnamon Becard). When in prs., combination of gray ♂ and rufous ♀ is helpful.

Voice: Large repertoire of songs. Both sexes sing sweetly whistled, strongly inflected *tuweé-tuweé-tuweé-tuweé-tuwé-wee*, more or less on same pitch, and thin, dainty trill, *tuwe'e'e'e'e'e'e'e*, that rises sharply. Also sing longer accelerating and rising trill that slows and descends at end, *we de-de-de-de-de-de'DE'DE'De'di'dididi*. Song (Delta Amacuro) a slightly hoarse *we-p-pe-pe-pe-pe-pe-pe-PE-WE-o*, running up scale. All songs sound melancholy. Calls incl. a high, metallic *eeeeE*, rising slightly at end, and buzzy *breez-det*.

Behavior: Usually in prs. that stay fairly high in trees where they move sluggishly, but tend to change perches freq. as they peer slowly and perch-glean in foliage for caterpillers and other arthropods, or sally up and snatch prey, with little or no pause, from beneath leaves, or search for small fruits and berries. Sometimes with mixed-spp. flocks along woodland borders, but more often independent of them. Inconspic. and easily overlooked except for occas. vocalizations. Bulky globular nest with side entrance; wedged high in branch fork; Jun nest, Chuao, Aragua (Hilty); 2–5 eggs, vinaceous brown with dark spots, often in ring at large end[253].

Status and habitat: Uncommon to fairly common locally. Resident in dry to moist areas incl. open woodland, forest borders, riparian woodland, shrubby second growth, pastures with scattered trees, plantations, mangroves, and other lightly wooded areas. Everywhere in rather low density.

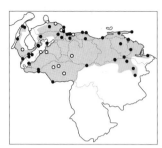

Range: To 1300m. Generally n of Orinoco; Delta Amacuro, s bank of Orinoco in Bolívar from Caicara to Ciudad Bolívar, and s to Upata, El Palmar (sight), and lower Río Cuyuní at El Dorado (*rufus*). Panama and n Colombia to the Guianas, n Brazil, and Amazon Basin s to ne Peru (e Ecuador?).

Chestnut-crowned Becard   PLATE 49
Pachyramphus castaneus   Cabezón Castaño
Identification: 5.7″ (14.5cm). 17.3g. Sexes sim. Above mostly dark rufous, crown darker and more chestnut, lores dusky, supraloral line buff, *narrow gray band from behind eyes encircles crown*; primaries dusky, sides of head and underparts pale cinnamon buff, more whitish on throat and belly. Or overall darker, crown dusky chestnut (*parui*).
Sim. species: Gray nuchal band is the mark. Cf. otherwise very sim. ♀ Cinereous and ♀ Cinnamon becards.
Voice: Song a soft, lamenting *deeeeu, deeu-dee-de-de*, thin, melodic, descending, and delivered at leisurely pace. No. of notes at end variable. Much like song of Cinnamon Becard.
Behavior: Single birds or prs. are confiding and tend to perch on relatively open inner branches, but otherwise do little to call attention to themselves except for dainty song which is given at infreq. intervals. Sluggish behavior and freq. head nodding much like others of genus. Stay mostly in mid. or upper levels of trees, perch-glean or sally short distances to strike or hover-glean for large insects, caterpillers, and occas. berries. More often away from mixed-spp. flocks than with them. Large untidy nest of grass and fibers has downward-facing entrance low on side; wedged in fairly high outer branch of tree.
Status and habitat: Fairly common to locally common resident in a variety of light woodland habitats incl. dry to humid forest borders, second growth, riparian forest, coffee plantations, and clearings with scattered trees.
Range: To 1700m. N end of Andes in Lara (Cabudare), Falcón (Sierra de San Luis), foothills of Yaracuy, and e

through n cordilleras to Anzoátegui, Sucre, and n Monagas (*intermedius*); Amazonas on Cerro Parú (*parui*); se Bolívar near Santa Elena de Uairén (*saturatus*). Se Colombia to n Bolivia and e across Amaz. Brazil; e Paraguay, ne Argentina, and se Brazil.

Cinnamon Becard   PLATE 49
Pachyramphus cinnamomeus   Cabezón Canelo
Identification: 5.5″ (14cm). 17g. *Only w of Andes.* Above mainly cinnamon rufous with blackish lores and gray supraloral line; primary coverts rufous like back, primaries dusky edged rufous, below pale cinnamon, throat whitish, chest and sides of neck tinged orangish buff. ♀: sim. but slightly paler, almost whitish below.
Sim. species: Easily confused with ♀♀ of several other becards. See ♀ Cinereous and ♀ One-colored. Both sexes of more widespread Chestnut-crowned Becard have gray nape bands.
Voice: Often hd. song a sweet, mellow *tee, deer-dear-dear-dear*, falling in pitch and trailing off at end. Much like song of Chestnut-crowned Becard but delivered a little more briskly.
Behavior: Sim. to Chestnut-crowned Becard. Takes wide range of arthropod prey and small berries mostly by short sallies to foliage or twigs. Large, trashy ball nest with side entrance, typical of genus; wedged fairly high in fork and near end of branch; 3 olive gray eggs spotted and streaked olive brown around larger end[785].
Status and habitat: Resident in humid forest borders and light second growth and open woodland. Easily found around La Azulita, Mérida.

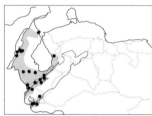

Range: To 1200m. S Maracaibo Basin of Zulia (n to Mene Grande), nw Táchira, and w Mérida (*magdalenae*); prob. w Trujillo; e slope of Andes in s Táchira (several locs.) (*badius*). Se Mexico to sw Ecuador.

Platypsaris

Sim. to *Pachyramphus* but larger; bill larger, head bushier, tail longer, nest placement (below) and voices differ; in hand 9th primary half length of 10th (outermost), incised at tip forming double point; ♂♂ blackish to gray and with no white, ♀♀ all or mostly rufous; nests, as far as known, are messy globular balls attached or suspended (not wedged) at tip of branch fork; side entrance. Sometimes incl. in *Pachyramphus*[10,403,683].

Pink-throated Becard   PLATE 49
Platypsaris minor   Pico Grueso Gargantirrosado
Identification: 6.5″ (16.5cm). 37g. Blackish bill heavy and shrikelike. ♂: above entirely black, below slate gray with *large rose pink crescent across lower throat* (sometimes hard to see in field). ♀: very different;

crown and back dark gray *contrasting with rufous rump, wings, and tail*; supraloral spot, sides of head, neck, and *entire underparts buffy cinnamon*. Subad. ♂: like ♀ but with varying amts. of black on body; wings and tail rufous; some with pink on throat.

Sim. species: ♂ unique. ♀ from ♀ Chestnut-crowned Becard by larger size, contrasting dark gray crown and back. Also cf. several attilas, esp. rare Citron-bellied which has gray head.

Voice: Usually quiet. Infreq. hd. call a clear, rising whistle, *tuuuueeeE*, sometimes also a few high *tic* notes.

Behavior: Single birds or prs., occas. families, usually follow mixed-spp. flocks at mid. level to canopy hts. in tall forest. Perch rather upright, peer sluggishly, freq. bob head, and occas. sally upward short distances to foliage for large insects, or for fruit taken during sally-stall. Typically make only 1 or a few perch changes within a tree, then fly off some distance to new foraging site, hence often difficult to follow or observe for any length of time.

Status and habitat: Uncommon resident (easily overlooked) in humid forest and forest borders. Prob. more widespread than small no. of recs. suggests.

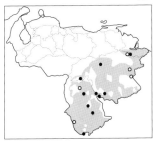

Range: To 800m. Amazonas (recs. spotty); n Bolívar from lower Río Caura and Sierra de Imataca (Río Grande) s to upper Río Cuyuní near Km 88 (sight). Se Colombia to n Bolivia, Amaz. Brazil, and the Guianas.

One-colored Becard
Platypsaris homochrous   Pico Grueso Gris
Identification: 6.5″ (16.5cm). 35g. Blackish bill *heavy and shrikelike. Plumage 2-toned* (darker above) in both sexes. ♂: above *entirely blackish slate*, crown, wings, and tail darker, *underparts uniform med. gray* (paler than above). ♀: above uniform cinnamon rufous, outer flight feathers dusky, *underparts cinnamon buff, paler almost whitish on throat and center of belly.*

Sim. species: ♂ is only all-black becard in Maracaibo area. See ♂ White-winged Becard which shows white on wings and tail. Easily confused ♀ much like either sex of Cinnamon Becard but larger and with heavier bill; note Cinnamon's darker and more chestnut crown, *contrasting dusky lores* (hard to see), and usually brighter underparts (One-colored has pale throat and belly). ♀ Cinereous Becard is smaller and whitish below.

Voice: Loud, sharp, and chattering *ske-e-et'et'itTT, tseer, tsrip* or sim. variation in Colombia.

Behavior: Much like Pink-throated Becard but found in lighter, more open woodland.

Status and habitat: Resident. Dry, moist, and humid forest borders and light woodland. Known from relatively small no. of recs. in Venez.

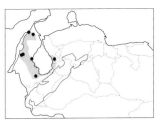

Range: To ca. 500m. Base of Sierra de Perijá and both sides of Maracaibo Basin (ne to Mene Grande), Zulia (*canescens*). C Panama to nw Peru.

Tityra

Chunky, short tailed, and predom. white; mostly frugivorous; 2 spp. with bare facial skin; cavity nesters; 9th primary very short (as in becards), outermost normal. Taxonomy not resolved. Here provisionally placed in Tyrannidae[10] but may belong in Cotingidae.

Black-crowned Tityra   PLATE 49
Tityra inquisitor   Bacaco Pequeño
Identification: 7.5″ (19cm). 40g. Bill blackish. ♂ is *only tityra with no red on face.* ♂: *crown to below eyes black*, otherwise mostly white tinged pearl on back; wings and tail black. ♀: sim. but forehead tinged buff, *sides of heady rusty*, back dingy gray more or less streaked brownish black.

Sim. species: ♂ easily told by solid black cap (no red); ♀'s contrasting rusty cheeks are diagnostic. See Black-tailed and Masked tityras.

Voice: Usually quiet. Occas., perched or in flight, an odd nasal grunting, *uurnt* or *uurnt-uurnt*, with buzzy quality.

Behavior: Rather antisocial prs. or families perch in canopy, often in open on exposed limbs, where they may remain for some time. Ads. eat fruit (mostly large, relatively nutritious fruits) and capture some insects for their young, but act sluggish and do not seem to spend much time foraging. Fly fast and straight, and like other tityras, behave aggressively toward other birds and are almost never with mixed-spp. flocks. Nest a cavity in stub; lined with leaves and small twigs. Breeding May–Aug, sw Guárico[734].

Status and habitat: Fairly common but locally distrib. resident in borders of tall humid forest, mature second growth, river edges, and isolated tall trees in clearings.

Largely or completely absent from arid regions of nw and from w half of llanos.
Range: To 1100m. Locally n of Orinoco, but not in arid regions or llanos. S Maracaibo Basin, Zulia, w slope of Andes n to Trujillo, e slope from se Táchira and w Apure to nw Barinas (sight); se Falcón[60]; n cordilleras in Carabobo, Aragua, and Guárico e to Sucre; Amazonas; n Bolívar in lower Río Caura, Río Paragua, Sierra de Imataca, and upper Río Cuyuní (*erythrogenys*). Colombia to ne Argentina, se Brazil (absent from n Amazon Basin), and the Guianas.

Black-tailed Tityra   PLATE 49
Tityra cayana   Bacaco Benedictino
Identification: 8.5″ (22cm). 69g. *Bill red tipped black (both sexes), lores and orbital area red.* ♂: above mainly silvery white with *black crown* extending to below eyes; wings and *tail black*, inner flight feathers silvery gray, underparts white. ♀: sim. but above dingy gray finely streaked brown, *crown dusky brown*, underparts with *conspic. linelike dusky streaks on breast.*
Sim. species: ♂ much like ♂ Masked Tityra but crown all black (not just narrow black area surrounding bare red skin). ♀ Masked Tityra is unstreaked below. Also cf. Black-crowned Tityra which lacks red.
Voice: Not very vocal. Occas. a nasal, buzzy *neebit-neebit*, sometimes 3 notes. Also a nasal, grunting *weenk, weenk, weenk, weenk.*
Behavior: Usually in prs. or loose groups that do not assoc. with other birds. Perch in canopy, often in open on high, bare limb. Fly straight and fast between destinations, and as in other tityras, ads. eat almost entirely fruit but feed some insects to young. Nest in high natural cavity, woodpecker hole, or broken stub; lined with leaves and small twigs.
Status and habitat: Fairly common resident of humid forest or partially forested habitats, esp. at forest borders, scattered large trees in clearings, along rivers, plantations, and light woodland. Not arid regions.

Range: To 1100m. Throughout, but n of Orinoco mainly near mts. (*cayana*). E of Andes from Colombia to ne Argentina, se Brazil, and the Guianas.

Masked Tityra   PLATE 49
Tityra semifasciata   Bacaco de Antifaz
Identification: 8.3″ (21.1cm). 77g. *Bill red tipped black; bare ocular area and lores red* (both sexes). ♂: *forecrown* (but not midcrown or rearcrown) *and narrow area surrounding face black*; plumage otherwise *mainly white*; upperparts tinged pearl gray, wings black, tertials grayish white; tail black, base and *broad tip white.*

♀: like ♂ but *entire crown smoky brown* (no black mask enclosing red), back dull grayish, underparts *unstreaked* dingy grayish brown.
Sim. species: Both sexes are nearest Black-tailed Tityra. ♂ from other tityras by white crown (black only around ocular area), ♀ by combination of red face and *unstreaked* underparts. Cf. Black-crowned Tityra.
Voice: Infreq. hd. call a nasal, bisyllabic grunting, *guránk*, or *gurank-gureek*, 1–several times, usually with 2d note a little higher.
Behavior: Rather antisocial prs. or families of 3–4 are most often seen in fruiting trees or hanging around high, bare stub, esp. if there is a cavity they can usurp for nesting. Typically behave in aggressive or bullying manner toward other birds. Highly arboreal and mostly frugivorous; pluck fruit while perched, and occas. hover or make short sallies that end in flutter or pause to snatch prey from foliage. Also hop lethargically along large limbs and occas. take small lizards or pursue insect prey. In Costa Rica reported to take many arillate fruits[706]. Nest in hole in high stub; 2 dark buff eggs heavily marked brown and black; ♀ incubates[647].
Status and habitat: Generally a fairly common to common resident in tall moist to humid forest borders and clearings with a few scattered tall trees; also (more easily overlooked) around high open limbs and stubs inside forest.

Range: To 1800m (most recs. in foothills or higher). Sierra de Perijá, Zulia, Andes from Táchira to Lara; mts. of Yaracuy and n cordilleras from Carabobo to Distr. Federal and Miranda (*columbiana*). N Mexico to w Ecuador; extreme se Colombia and e Ecuador to n Bolivia and Amaz. Brazil (mostly s of the Amazon); French Guiana.

Cotingidae: Cotingas
Cotingas, Graniceras

This heterogeneous group of New World birds is most closely allied to the tyrant-flycatchers and to manakins and is considered by many to be only a subfamily within the enlarged Tyrannidae[606]. Several groups formerly placed in separate families, including the Sharpbill (Oxyruncidae) and cocks-of-the-rock (Rupicolidae), are now placed in Cotingidae[604,605]. Others traditionally placed in Cotingidae, e.g., *Lipaugus* and *Laniocera*, now appear more closely allied with flycatchers and have been placed near the end of that family as genera incertae sedis. Still other genera, e.g.,

Laniisoma and *Iodopleura*, seem to share characters with *Schiffornis*[513,518] and also may not be true cotingas. Almost half the cotinga genera are monotypic; others are so unusual that their relationship, if any, to others in the family is uncertain. As a group they are essentially arboreal forest or forest-edge dwellers, and almost all of them eat some fruit—several eat almost entirely fruit. Otherwise they share few anatomical or behavioral characteristics and count among their members some of the most beautiful birds on the continent as well as some of the most bizarre in appearance or behavior. Breeding varies from monogamous in a few species to polygamous in lek-forming species. Nests are usually shallow, flimsy saucers or cups; in many species the females perform all nesting duties. Much information on their remarkable breeding and mating systems and their complex relationships with fruiting trees has been accumulated by A. F. Skutch[647], B. K. Snow[661,662], and D. W. Snow[687,689].

Oxyruncus

Plump and spotted; very sharp-pointed bill; outermost primary emarginate (as in many flycatchers), slightly "saw edged" (hooked barbs); tail square, 10 feathers; highly disjunct distrib.; has been placed in its own family (Oxyruncidae)[10]; or with Cotingidae[513,604,605].

Sharpbill   PLATE 50
Oxyruncus cristatus   Picoagudo
Identification: 6.7" (17cm). 35–42g. *Sharp, conical bill; eyes orange red to yellow.* Rather plump. *Both sexes with black-bordered flame scarlet central crown stripe* flattened as partly concealed crest; otherwise upperparts bright olive green, 2 faintly indicated (scalloped) yellowish wing bars; flight feathers black, tertials broadly edged yellow, feathers of squarish black tail edged olive, *sides of head, neck, and throat grayish white finely scaled black, entire underparts white thickly scalloped and spotted black,* belly white or vaguely tinged yellowish.
Sim. species: Pointed bill, orange eyes, and spotted underparts are the marks for this unusual bird. Cf. Spotted and Speckled tanagers.
Voice: Song, often given only at long intervals, a long-drawn, buzzy trill that descends slightly, *bzeeeeeee uuuuu'u'u'a'a'a.* ♂♂ sing alone or in loosely assoc. lek when advertising and call 2–3 times/min.
Behavior: A rather inconspic. bird of high forest canopy. Reg. follows mixed-spp. flocks containing flycatchers, greenlets, warblers, and tanagers and is seldom seen away from them unless singing. Single birds or prs. move in deliberate fashion, hop in foliage, peer carefully, turn and cock heads, then lunge and grasp arthropod prey. Freq. wedge bill into rolled leaves or partly open arils using pry-gape tactic[708] and often hang upside down from leaf to extract arthropod prey. Substantial proportion of diet is fruit, incl. surprisingly large ones. Red crest exposed during agonistic encounters with same or other spp. Feb nest on Sierra de Lema; hummingbird-like open cup of plant down molded into feltlike consistency; in open at tip of high, exposed *Cecropia* branch.

Status and habitat: Resident in humid and wet forest on slopes of tepuis (mainly se Bolívar). Possibly local. Most readily found between ca. 800 and 1200m on Sierra de Lema.

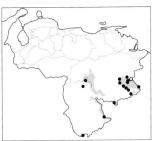

Range: 500–1800m. Extreme n Amazonas (Cerro Calentura; Alto Caño Parucito) and s Amazonas (Sierra Parima; Cerro de la Neblina); tepuis of se Bolívar (Auyán-tepui; Sierra de Lema s to Chimantá-and Paurai-tepuis and Cerro Urutaní) (*phelpsi*); se Bolívar on Cerro Roraima (*hypoglaucus*). Costa Rica; Panama; the Guianas; scattered recs. or small pops. in e Peru, n Bolivia, ne Argentina, and Brazil.

Ampelion

Two high-Andean spp. (1 in Venez.); heavyset proportions; long, full crest; thick gray bill; allied to plantcutters[313].

Red-crested Cotinga   PLATE 50
Ampelion rubrocristatus   Cotinga Cresta Roja
Identification: 8.5" (22cm). 66g. Short, thick, *chalky white bill tipped black; eyes red.* Mainly *dark gray,* head, throat, wings, and tail blackish, long, narrow chestnut maroon crest usually laid flat on rearcrown and nape (hence hard to see), rarely spread in spectacular fan shape; rump and lower belly streaked white, large white spot on inner web of all but central tail feathers forms *white central band* visible from below at rest (above and below in flight). Imm: crest reduced or lacking, body brownish, somewhat streaked whitish above, yellowish white below.
Sim. species: Nothing really like it in Andean treeline zone it inhabits. See Great Thrush.
Voice: Very quiet. Occas. a peculiar froglike trill or chatter, *tmrnrrr,* perched or in flight, and a low, guttural *gr-grrt.*
Behavior: A plump bird of stolid demeanor. This cotinga is fond of sitting exposed and upright at top of a bush or high bare tree branch where it remains motionless but alert for extended periods of time and, in so doing, gives every impression of surfeited idleness. Seen singly, in prs., or in little groups up to ca. 6 that seem a trifle sluggish as they eat fruit which they take while perched or in short sally, and occas. sally clumsily for flying insects. Bow rapidly, flip tail up, and raise and spread spectacular crest ("wild hairdo") during agonistic and courtship encounters between 2 or more birds. Wings rattle in flight. Bolivia nest 1.6m up in small tree; twig-and-lichen cup stained red, apparently from berries; 1 nestling[776].

Status and habitat: Resident. Less numerous in Venez. than southward. Humid and wet montane forest, forest borders, patches of secondary woodland, and cultivated areas with hedgerows, scattered trees, and bushes. May range up into isolated patches of *Polylepis* and other shrubs above normal treeline.

Range: 2500–3250m. Sierra de Perijá, Zulia; Andes from Táchira to ne Trujillo (Páramo Cendé and Páramo Jabón) at Lara border. Colombia s in mts. to Bolivia.

Pipreola

Plump and short-tailed; bill and legs usually red to red orange; wings rounded; plumage mostly green and yellow (except Red-banded Fruiteater); sexes differ somewhat; sluggish behavior; extremely high-pitched calls; inconspic. in humid and wet mt. forests.

Barred Fruiteater   PLATE 50
Pipreola arcuata   Granicera Requintilla
Identification: 8.5″ (22cm). 120g. *Large* highland fruiteater. Eyes dark red (usually); bill dark plum red; *legs bright red*. ♂: *entire head to chest black*, otherwise pale yellow below *thickly and evenly barred black*; above dark olive green, greater wing coverts and tertials mostly black with large pale yellow tips, the *yellowish tertial spots esp. large and conspic.*; band of pale yellow and black barring across tips of upper tail coverts; tail with black subterminal band and narrow yellowish tip. ♀: sim. but head to chest dark olive green.
Sim. species: Large size, bold tertial spots, and barring on underparts are the marks. Also note row of spots on wing coverts. No other fruiteater in Venez. has such bright red legs. See smaller Green-and-black Fruiteater.
Voice: Advertising song an extremely high, thin, almost hissing *s-seeeeeeeeeeeeeaaaaaee* (ca. 2.5 sec) that descends throughout, then usually with slight rise at end; or song may rise slightly then descend with or without slight uptick at end, i.e., *si-si-si-iiiiEEEse-eeeeeeeeeett*. Song lacks long ser. of *tic* notes that precedes song of Green-and-black Fruiteater.
Behavior: Like others of genus. A big, rotund, and sluggish personage. Bouts of relatively active foraging for fruit in forest mid. level or higher, esp. early in morning, are followed by long periods of inactivity as bird sits upright and perfectly still, or sits and turns head slowly to watch. Alone, in prs., or 3–4 together, sometimes with Green-and-black Fruiteaters. More often independent of mixed-spp. flocks than with them.
Status and habitat: Uncommon resident in wet, mossy, montane forest (cloud forest) and forest borders. Narrowly overlaps upper range limit of Green-

and-black Fruiteater but mostly found above that sp. and generally less numerous. Found reg. above ca. 2300m (slightly lower in wet season) in PN Guaramacal, Trujillo, and in forest above Zumbador, n Táchira. Some downslope movement in wet season may occur.

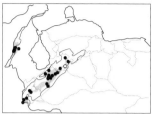

Range: 1800–3100m. Sierra de Perijá, Zulia; Andes from Táchira to Trujillo/Lara border at Páramo Cendé (*arcuata*). Colombia s in Andes to Bolivia.

Green-and-black Fruiteater   PLATE 50
Pipreola riefferii   Granicera Verdecita
Identification: 7.7″ (19.5cm). 50g. Bill and legs orange red; eyes dark. ♂: above moss green, *head, throat, and chest black bordered by yellow band around chest and up onto sides of neck*; lower underparts yellow somewhat mixed green on sides; tertials dusky *narrowly tipped white*. ♀: sim. but *head to upper breast green like back*, yellow border less distinct; *lower underparts with blurry green streaks*.
Sim. species: ♂ or ♀ *from rear* (and they often seem to be turned away) resembles respective sex of Barred Fruiteater, but note that sp.'s "spotted" wing coverts and more obvious spotting on tertials. ♂ or ♀ Handsome Fruiteater, *from behind*, shows 3–4 prom. roundish white spots on tertials. ♀ additionally, *from front*, told by green "hood and bib" and lack of barring below. ♀ Golden-breasted Fruiteater is entirely streaked below (no hood or bib).
Voice: Often hd. song an extremely high-pitched, sibilant (almost hissing) *tic-tic-ti-ti-ti-tiseeeeeeeeeeeeeeeeeaa*, up to 5 sec, descending and dying away, last notes usually run together. Song usually does not rise at end. Also a fast *ti-tsi-tsi-tsi-tsi-tsi-tsi-tsi-* . . . ; both vocalizations easily mistaken for an insect.
Behavior: A portly and sluggish resident of misty cloud forests. Dressed in leaf green, prs. or occas. loosely assoc. family groups of 3–6 perch quietly and unobtrusively for long periods, or hop lethargically, or sometimes fairly actively for brief periods, as they quietly search for fruit in small trees and shrubs, but often remain in small area. Range from about eye level to subcanopy, occas. into canopy, and are often with mixed-spp. flocks which they may follow short distances. Take fruit by reaching while perched, less often in clumsy hover. Often rather unsuspicious. Two nests in Colombia, rootlet-lined moss cups 1–2m up at forest edge; 2 eggs, cream with wreath of fine red brown dots on larger end, fewer elsewhere[404].
Status and habitat: Fairly common to common but inconspic. resident in Andes in humid and wet mossy forest (cloud forest), forest borders, second-growth woodland, and occas. small patches of trees away from forest; less common in Coastal Cordillera where

occurs mostly above range of Handsome Fruiteater and in wetter forest than Golden-breasted Fruiteater. In Andes mostly replaced at high els. by Barred Fruiteater.

Range: 1800–3050m in Andes (sight recs. to 1450m); 1750–2150m (occas. to ca. 1100m) in Coastal Cordillera. Sierra de Perijá, Zulia, and s Táchira (*riefferii*); n Táchira to n Trujillo and se Lara (sight recs., PN Yacambú); Coastal Cordillera in Aragua, Distr. Federal, and Miranda e to near Petare (*melanolaema*). Colombia s in Andes to c Peru.

Golden-breasted Fruiteater   PLATE 50
Pipreola aureopectus   Granicera Pechidorada
Identification: 6.8″ (17.3cm). 46g. Eyes yellowish white to yellow orange; bill orange red; legs gray green. ♂: above incl. sides of head bright grass green, lores and chin greenish black, *tertials narrowly tipped white, throat and center of breast bright yellow*, center of belly lemon yellow, sides of body green, somewhat mottled on flanks. Or sim. but yellow of throat and upper breast less extensive (*aureopectus*). ♀: bright grass green above with narrow white tips on tertials, *below yellow heavily streaked* (flammulated) *green*, yellower on throat and belly.
Sim. species: ♂ lacks black hood, ♀ is entirely streaked below; both are much brighter green than Green-and-black Fruiteater. Both sexes of Handsome Fruiteater have *large, roundish*, white tertial spots.
Voice: Song (ca. 3 sec) a high, sibilant *pseEEEeeeeeeeeaaaeeeEET tic! tic!*, rising quickly then slowly descending and finally ascending again, last notes after a short pause. Or sometimes a slightly abbreviated *seeeeeEEE!*, not loud but stronger and more forceful at end, and sim. in quality (but not pattern) to that of other *Pipreola*.
Behavior: Most often seen in prs. that stay in mid. strata of forest or a little higher. Like other *Pipreola*, look a bit pudgy and act sluggish, even clumsy, as they hop around in search of small fruits and berries. Often with mixed-spp. flocks, or are stimulated to forage as flocks pass through.
Status and habitat: Fairly common resident of humid premontane and montane forest. Of the 3 spp. of fruiteaters in n cordilleras, this one favors slighter drier forest (avoids or is least numerous in foggy zones) at *intermed.* els., hence is most readily found on s slope of mts. in PN Henri Pittier at els. of ca. 1300–1500m. Green-and-black Fruiteater is more numerous at higher and wetter els., Handsome Fruiteater at lower els.
Range: 1700–3100m in Sierra de Perijá, Zulia; 1000–2300m in Andes from s Táchira to cerros of nw Lara (*aureopectus*); 800–2050m in Coastal Cordillera of Car-

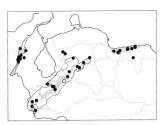

abobo, Aragua, and Distr. Federal; Interior Cordillera on Cerro Golfo Triste, Aragua (*festiva*); prob. Miranda (no recs.). Ne and w Colombia.

Handsome Fruiteater   PLATE 50
Pipreola formosa   Granicera Hermosa
Identification: 6.3″ (16cm). 43g. Eyes orange yellow (occas. dark; young?); bill orange red, legs olive. ♂: entire head and throat black contrasting with bright green upperparts, *3 large roundish white spots on tertials; chest fiery orange red* turning yellow on rest of underparts; flanks greenish. ♀: throat and upperparts bright grassy green, *2–3 bold white spots on tips of tertials*, small orange to yellow crescent across chest, *breast to belly yellow finely barred and spotted green*. Or throat also spotted and barred green, chest scarlet (*rubidior*).
Sim. species: ♂'s orange red chest patch and ♀'s barring are unique, but perhaps best marks are bold round tertial spots. In Coastal Cordillera occurs with Green-and-black and Golden-breasted fruiteaters; in mts. of ne unique.
Voice: High, thin *pik* and high, thin *ti'ti'ti'ti'ti'ti'ti'ti* . . . ; song on Cerro Negro, Monagas, a high *peeEEE eeeeeee'e'e'e*, louder near start but smooth, slowing at end, and not varying much in pitch.
Behavior: Usually found alone or in prs. or 3s sitting quietly from ca. eye level to 10m up inside forest where peers carefully, then moves a short distance every 20–30 sec or so. May join mixed-spp. flocks as they pass through, but usually does not move far with them. Eats mostly small fruits and berries, either while perched or in short upward sally to grasp them while momentarily hovering heavily. Often remarkably tame and impassive, allowing close approach.
Status and habitat: Fairly common resident of Coastal Cordillera but can be difficult to locate because of sedentary habits. Moderately humid to wet and mossy premontane and montane forest (cloud forest). Common in mts. of Paria Pen. and esp. on Cerro Negro, Monagas. There are sight recs. (no specimens) from Sierra de San

Luis, Falcón, the 1st on 11 Dec. 1978 (C. Parrish); easternmost rec. in coastal mts. is 1 seen on Cerro Tucusito, nw Anzoátegui, 3 Mar 1981 (C. Parrish). **Range:** ENDEMIC. 800–2200m. Sierra de San Luis, Falcón (sightings); mts. of Yaracuy, Coastal Cordillera from Carabobo to Distr. Federal and Miranda, Interior Cordillera in s Aragua (Cerro Golfo Triste), Miranda at Cerro Negro (*formosa*); sightings in adj. hills of nw Anzoátegui (prob. *formosa*); ne Anzoátegui, w Sucre, and n Monagas on Cerro Negro (*rubidior*); Cerros Humo and Azul, Paria Pen., Sucre (*pariae*).

Red-banded Fruiteater   PLATE 50
Pipreola whitelyi   Granicera Degollada
Identification: 6.8″ (17.3cm). Only in tepuis. Eyes orange red (♂), yellowish (♀); *bill and legs coral red*, duller in ♀. ♂: mostly gray green above with tawny buff eyebrow; cheeks rusty, wings and tail rufescent brown, *below gray with conspic. coral red crescent across chest* turning tawny and extending up sides of neck toward eyebrow; crissum ochre. ♀: above rather like ♂ but duller, *below yellowish white sharply streaked with black*.
Sim. species: ♂ unique. ♀ recalls Sharpbill and smaller Speckled and Spotted tanagers, but note plump shape, facial pattern, and streaks (not spots). Also cf. ♀ Bearded and White bellbirds, both much larger and lacking fruiteater's facial pattern.
Voice: Call, by both sexes, a high, thin trill (almost a hiss) that drops initially then ascends smoothly throughout, *tseeaaaaeeeeeeeeee* (pattern nearest Golden-breasted Fruiteater), lasting 2–3 sec. Does not vocalize often; also high, thin *ti* notes, often about 6 in ser., when excited.
Behavior: Like others of genus, deliberate of movement and easily overlooked. Found most often at low to mid. levels inside forest, occas. at forest edge, infreq. quite high in canopy. Single birds sometimes assoc. with mixed-spp. flocks, esp. those containing tanagers, but are just as often encountered alone or in prs. at fruiting trees and shrubs. Even when moving and foraging in fruiting trees this sp. is surprisingly inconspic.
Status and habitat: A difficult-to-locate, low-density resident of humid and wet montane forest, esp. mossy forest and dense, stunted, melastome-dominated second growth. Many specimens from Cerro Ptari, where perhaps most numerous. A majority of specimens from all tepuis are from els. slightly higher than those that can be reached by road on Sierra de Lema.

Range: 1300–2100m. Se Bolívar on tepuis of Gran Sabana from Cerro Ptari and Sierra de Lema s to Cerros

Chimantá, Cuquenan, and Roraima (*kathleenae*); 1800–2250m on Cerro Roraima (*whitelyi*). Guyana.

Ampelioides

Monotypic genus; recalls *Pipreola* fruiteaters but plumage pattern more complex, soft parts not colorful, and voice very different; ♀ more boldly marked below than ♂.

Scaled Fruiteater   PLATE 50
Ampelioides tschudii   Come Fruta Talabartero
Identification: 8″ (20.3cm). 80g. *Patchy and scaly looking. Plump and short-tailed.* Eyes yellow; bill black above, bluish olive below; legs lead gray. ♂: *head to below eyes glossy black, lores and stripe from base of bill to below eyes yellowish white and joining pale yellow nuchal collar*, above black heavily scaled olive yellow, wings black, lesser wing coverts scaled olive, greater ones entirely olive forming broad band; throat white scaled dusky, *below yellowish white heavily scaled olive*, short tail mostly olive, outer feathers black, narrow tips whitish. ♀: sim. but head olive, underparts scaling dusky and *more boldly patterned*.
Sim. species: Shape and eye-catching pattern unique. Limited distrib. in Venez.
Voice: Territorial or advertising song a loud, raptorlike whistle, rising in pitch and volume then fading, *wheeeEEEEaaa*, sometimes given at short intervals. Much lower in pitch than *Pipreola* fruiteaters. In Colombia calling period is very seasonal.
Behavior: An enigmatic sp., unpredictable in occurrence. Usually solitary or in prs., less often in groups of 3–4. Hop deliberately along moss- and bromeliad-covered limbs in mid. story or canopy where eat mostly fruit. Generally more active and wary than *Pipreola*, and harder to see, but also may sit quietly for long periods. Freq. with canopy mixed-spp. flocks. Wings may produce noisy rattling sound in flight (♂♂ only?).
Status and habitat: Uncommon or rare, perhaps also local. Seasonal or irreg. movements likely. Wet montane forest (cloud forest). Only a few specimens from Venez. (most from Sierra de Perijá).

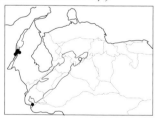

Range: 1250–2000m. Río Negro region of Sierra de Perijá (Cerro Pejochaina), Zulia; se Táchira (Cerro El Teteo); sight, se Lara at PN Yacambú, Jan 1999 (J. Langham). Locally in Andes of Colombia to n Bolivia.

Iodopleura

Tiny and chunky; stubby bill; short, square tail; long wings; taxonomically perhaps nearest *Schiffornis*[518].

White-browed Purpletuft   PLATE 49
Iodopleura isabellae   Cotinguita Frente Blanca
Identification: 4.5″ (11.4cm). 20g. Small and rotund
but with notably long wings. Above sooty brownish
black, cap darker and glossed black; *white rump band*;
*bold white crescent in front of eyes; broad white postoc-
ular stripe*; central underparts white, sides of body
sooty brown, glossy purple flank tufts long and silky
(hard to see except in display), most of lower underparts heavily mottled and coarsely barred with brown,
under wing coverts and base of primaries white (in
flight from below), long silky white under tail coverts.
♀: sim. but no purple.
Sim. species: Size, bold face pattern, and habits distinctive. See Dusky Purpletuft.
Voice: Quiet and infreq. hd., but has a variety of calls,
all weak, the most freq. being a soft, high, trilled
tre'e'e'd and a thin but shrill and rising *eeeEE* or *tueeEE*
over and over; also ser. of soft trills, *sr'r'r—sr'r'r—sr'r'r*;
high, weak *jee-jee-jee*; and thin, high, rattling *ti-ti'ti-ti-ti-
ti-ti* as greeting (or threat?).
Behavior: This sp. is most apt to be seen in early morning and late afternoon, typically in prs. or little parties
up to ca. 6 birds that sit bolt upright in open on top of
tall rain forest trees. May sit there quietly for several
min before flying off to another treetop, or repeatedly
sally out and upward short distance to air for flying insects. Also eat much fruit, incl. mistletoe berries, usually taken during brief hover, occas. while perched. Regurgitate seeds of many of fruits they eat, and occas.
may even descend quite low along forest borders. Prs.
or groups are unpredictable in occurrence and may
wander over large areas of rain forest canopy. Tiny
hummingbird-like cup nest atop high branch in Brazil
(R. Ridgely).
Status and habitat: Uncommon but doubtless often
overlooked. Treetops in humid terra firme and várzea
forest, incl. white sandy soil forest and forest edges.
Seen in Amazonas with some reg. e of Pto. Ayacucho
and at Junglaven.

Range: To 200m (prob. higher). Throughout lowland
Amazonas from Pto. Ayacucho (sight[508]), Junglaven
(sight), and San Fernando de Atabapo southward (*isabellae*). Se Colombia to n Bolivia and Amaz. Brazil (n
of the Amazon only w of Rio Negro).

Dusky Purpletuft
Iodopleura fusca   Cotinguita Fusca
Identification: 4.5″ (11.4cm). 15.5g. Small and rotund.
Above black, *rump white*, below dark sooty brown
glossed purple on flanks (hard to see in field), *center
of lower breast and belly white*, unusually elongated

white under tail coverts almost as long as tail; white
patch at base of primaries (in flight from below). ♀:
sim. but no purple.
Sim. species: White-browed Purpletuft not known to
overlap in range. Also cf. Swallow-winged Puffbird.
Voice: Soft trilled and high, thin notes sim. to those of
White-browed Purpletuft.
Behavior: Sim. to White-browed Purpletuft. Prs. or 3–4
sit in open atop canopy and emergent trees and occas.
sally short distances to air for flying insects, or eat fruit.
Status and habitat: Known in Venez. from 2 specimens from Río Icabarú. Also sight recs. of pr. with
fledgling 19km s of El Dorado, Feb 1993 (J. Pierson);
and prs. at Río Grande bridge, Sierra de Imataca, most
recent 22 Mar 2000 (D. Ascanio; Hilty). Canopy of tall
humid forest and along forest edges.

Range: To 500m. Se Bolívar (Río Icabarú); sightings in
ne and e Bolívar (Río Grande; El Dorado). The Guianas and ne Brazil.
Note: Possibly conspecific with White-browed Purpletuft, but no interbreeding known.

Andean Laniisoma   PLATE 50
Laniisoma buckleyi   Cotinga Pirari
Identification: 6.8″ (17.3cm). 48g. Bill black above,
gray green below, slightly hooked; legs olive green. ♂:
crown to below eyes black, rest of upperparts bright
olive green, *underparts golden yellow with a few scalelike bars on sides of throat, breast, and flanks*. ♀: sim.
but head olive green like back; underparts more scaly.
Imm.: like ♀ but with large rufous spots on tips of wing
coverts. Juv.: very different; mostly cinnamon with
black feather tipping; wing coverts olive green, underparts whitish somewhat barred dusky, lower underparts cinnamon.
Sim. species: Cf. Green-and-black and Golden-
breasted fruiteaters, both larger, found at higher el.,
and without barring below (but superficially sim. from
behind). ♀ Barred Becard is smaller, pale yellow
below, has rufous patch in wings, and is at higher els.
Voice: Call in Peru a high-pitched, sibilant, and insectlike *psiiiiiiiieeeee*, often repeated persistently but at
long intervals in morning or early afternoon by ♂♂
perched in subcanopy[457].
Behavior: Unknown in Venez. Elsewhere a solitary,
sluggish, and inconspic. bird, easily overlooked (need
to know voice). Occurs from low to high inside forest
and has been reported eating melastome berries[685]
and insects.
Status and habitat: Apparently rare. Known in Venez.
from 1 specimen, Mar 1941, Barinas, and 5 specimens,

Jul–Nov, 1954, se Táchira. Humid foothill forest. No recent observations.

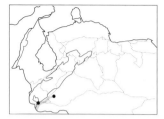

Range: 200–530m (600m in Colombia; to 1800m in e Peru). E base of Andes in Táchira (Burgua) and Barinas at Santa Bárbara (*venezuelensis*). Disjunct range. Base of Andes in e Colombia (1 rec.); e Ecuador and e Peru; Bolivia.
Note: Previously called Shrike-like Cotinga[403] and Elegant Mourner[545]. Does not incl. birds of se Brazil (*L. elegans*).

Cotinga

Plump; med. size; fairly long winged and short tailed; short, wide bill; short legs; ♂♂ notable for brilliant, almost "electric" colors (structural color); some spp. allopatric in distrib.; ♂♂ notably silent vocally, but outer primaries somewhat attenuated in some spp. to produce mechanical trilling sounds; ♀♀ utter monosyllabic ser. of notes in threat display; ♀ performs all nesting duties; small, frail, stick platform nest high in canopy is completely covered by ♀.

Purple-breasted Cotinga   PLATE 50
Cotinga cotinga   Cotinga Pechimorada
Identification: 7" (18cm). 54g. Dovelike shape. Small black bill; *large* black eyes. ♂: *glistening dark violet blue*, wings and rather short tail black, *throat to lower breast dark wine purple*. ♀: very different; above dusky brown *heavily scaled whitish*, below buff, the feathers with dusky brown centers and whitish edges (*looks heavily spotted and scaled*), chin and crissum unmarked; under wing coverts dull cinnamon.
Sim. species: ♂ not likely confused. ♀ nearest ♀ Spangled Cotinga but much darker and more heavily spotted and scaled.
Voice: Usually silent. Rarely a high, plaintive, complaining *preeeeeeer*, like call of Dusky-capped Flycatcher, over and over; easily overlooked. ♂'s wings produce snap and whirring in flight.
Behavior: ♂♂ of this brilliant sp. often perch up on open bare limbs in tops of tall trees in early morning or late afternoon, then fly off some distance and out of view into forest canopy. Spend most of day in canopy where relatively inactive. ♀♀ (and imm. ♂♂) also perch up in open but typically for briefer periods of time. Individuals or several may gather for brief periods at fruiting trees, alone or with other spp. of birds but not with mixed-spp. flocks. Reach or sally-stall for fruit. Fight is fast and strongly undulating with distinctive "bob-tailed" silhouette.
Status and habitat: Rare to uncommon resident (doubtless often overlooked) in canopy and at edge of humid forest and tall trees in clearings. May show preference for sandy soil forests.

Range: To 600m. S Amazonas (Yavita-Pimichín southward); e Bolívar from Sierra de Imataca (Río Grande) s to Auyán-tepui and Sierra de Lema. Extreme e Colombia to the Guianas and ne Brazil.

Blue Cotinga
Cotinga nattererii   Cotinga Azul
Identification: 7.2" (18.3cm). *Plump, dovelike shape* with small black bill and *large* black eyes. ♂: *glistening turquoise blue* with black feather bases showing through here and there; *dark wine red throat and* mid. belly; wings black, flight feathers edged blue, tail rather short and black. ♀: very different; above drab dusky brown, the feathers scaled buffy white, below buffy brown *more or less scaled and spotted dark brown throughout* (feathers dark centered) *except on throat*; belly and *under wing coverts cinnamon* (sometimes conspic. in flight).
Sim. species: Brilliant ♂ unmistakable but often looks black against sky or in poor light. ♀ shows more contrast between upper- and underparts than others of genus (none known to overlap); scaly appearance recalls a juv. *Turdus* thrush, but note plump, small-headed shape and large eyes.
Voice: No known vocalization. ♂'s wings produce trilling whistle in flight.
Behavior: In Colombia often perches high and exposed on bare branch above canopy where erect dovelike posture is characteristic. Several may gather at fruiting trees, but otherwise solitary and sluggish, perching quietly and inconspic. for long periods in canopy. Ad. diet is wholly fruit taken by brief fluttering hover or hover-stall. Tiny nest on horizontal limb 30m up; nest torn apart after use; site may be reused in succeeding yr; nestling covered with white natal down.

Status and habitat: Known from 1 ♀ taken 30 Oct 1956 in w Mérida, and 1 ♀ seen 25 Jan 1973, 10km n of San Juan de Colon, Táchira (P. Alden). Humid forest.
Range: To 100m. W base of Andes in nw Táchira (sight) and Mérida (Santa Elena). C Panama to nw Ecuador.

Spangled Cotinga
PLATE 50

Cotinga cayana   Cotinga Gargantimorada
Identification: 8″ (20.3cm). 65g. Small black bill. Eyes black. ♂: *brilliant, shiny (enamel-like), turquoise blue,* entire body with *patches of black feather bases showing through,* wings and tail black, throat dark wine red. ♀: very different; above dark grayish brown, the feathers edged pale buffy white giving rather scaled appearance; below sim. but *paler,* the *scaling rather obscure,* throat uniform grayish, under wing coverts *dull* cinnamon brown (as in other ♀ *Cotinga*). Imm. ♂: like ♀ but with patches of blue showing.
Sim. species: ♂ unique in range. ♀ is somewhat scaly and unkept looking but overall *much paler* and more uniform (less spotted or scaled) than ♀ Purple-throated Cotinga. ♀ Pompadour Cotinga is *uniform* brownish gray.
Voice: ♂♂ infreq. give low *booo,* soft and easily overlooked from exposed perch above canopy (A. Whittaker). In flight wings (always?) produce whining or whistlelike trill which is louder in display flights as ♂♂ fly downward and outward for 40m or so, then brake suddenly and return[689].
Behavior: Several ♂♂ in loose, dispersed lek (♂♂ often several hundred meters apart) typically sit erect and immobile atop highest emergent rain forest trees in early morning, also less persistently in late afternoon, when low sun angle illuminates their brilliant plumage to max. advantage. Occupy same sites day after day (seasonal?) in display of pure, dazzling color (no song or dance routine). During midday both sexes spend long periods of time alone, sitting quietly inside canopy, or occas. fly off to visit fruiting trees. Flight is slightly undulating. Diet of ads. is almost wholly fruit, usually taken during brief fluttery hover or hover-stall. Tiny frail stick nest completely covered by ♀.
Status and habitat: Fairly common resident in humid terra firme and várzea forest, gallery forest, and forest isls. in sandy-belt soil regions. Some local or seasonal movements occur (need documentation).

Range: To 500m. Se Táchira (Burgua); generally in Amazonas, and Bolívar (few recs. in lower and mid. Río Paragua) n to se Delta Amacuro at Joburé. E Colombia to n Bolivia, Amaz. Brazil, and the Guianas.

Xipholena

Plump and short-tailed; glistening plumage; flight feathers mostly white; long, stiffened upper wing coverts (2 of 3 spp.) partly cover flight feathers.

Pompadour Cotinga
PLATE 50

Xipholena punicea   Cotinga Vino Tinto
Identification: 8″ (20.3cm). 65g. *Eyes white to yellowish white* (both sexes). ♂: *glistening wine red* (in hand, feathers white at base) *with white flight feathers* narrowly tipped black; elongated and stiff greater wing coverts wine red with white shafts partly covering flight feathers. ♀: very different; mainly grayish, paler below; throat and belly grayish white, wings and tail dusky, *greater wing coverts and inner flight feathers broadly edged white.* Imm: like ♀ but eyes dark.
Sim. species: Gorgeous ♂ cannot be confused, even in flight, when rapidly fanned white wings twinkle transparently against dark foliage. Plump ♀ looks like a large, gray, short-tailed thrush. Note white eyes and white wing edgings.
Voice: Normally silent. Rarely a sudden, loud, froglike croak with rattlelike quality[30], also described as hollow mechanical rattle[545].
Behavior: Usually seen alone. Early in morning and late in afternoon ♂♂, and to lesser extent ♀♀, take exposed perch on high bare stub or branch above canopy where they may sit for several min or sometimes much longer. Otherwise, during day perch quietly and inconspic. in canopy or occas. fly off to fill up at fruiting trees. Generally not with mixed-spp. flocks, but occas. several may be present in fruiting trees. Fly high over clearings in strong undulating flight with white wings alternately fanned rapidly then closed tightly for an instant. Mostly silent display may involve ritualized slow chasing between 2–4 ♂♂ in treetops, perhaps to determine dominance; unlike in other group-displaying cotingas, site may shift over a wide area rather than remain fixed at 1 locality. ♀♀ watch but do not participate in these chases[682]. A Mar nest in Guyana was ca. 20m up in bamboo at edge of clearing; frail open nest of curly wood tendrils; 1 blunt greenish gray egg, spotted and blotched drab, denser at large end; incubating ♀ entirely conceals small nest. Breeding may be prolonged[689].
Status and habitat: Uncommon to fairly common resident in sandy soil forests, esp. white sand areas of mixed savanna and woodland or gallery forest. Less numerous or more local in tall humid forest on richer soils. Generally occurs in rather low density but often

seen in vicinity of Km 84–98 on El Dorado–Santa
Elena de Uairén Rd. in e Bolívar.
Range: To 1300m. Throughout Amazonas; Bolívar
from lower Río Caura (Río Mato), mid. Río Paragua,
and Sierra de Imataca (Río Grande) southward. E Colombia e to the Guianas and n and c Amaz. Brazil.

Procnias

Unusually wide gape; ♂♂ decorated with long wattles
and notable for powerful vocalizations because of
highly modified syringeal cartilage and muscles; drab
♀♀ attend shallow stick nest.

Bearded Bellbird   PLATE 50
Procnias averano   Campanero Herrero
Identification: ♂ 11.5″ (29cm), 180g. ♀ 10.5″ (27cm),
125g. ♂: *mainly silvery white, head warm brown* (feathers dense and fuzzy), *wings and tail black*, bare throat
covered with numerous stringy, black, mosslike wattles giving unkept, almost grotesquely "bearded" appearance. Bare pink patch on side of tibia exposed
during display. ♀ (no "beard"): *crown and sides of
head dusky olive contrasting with olive green upperparts*; back and wings somewhat dappled dusky gray;
throat and breast bright *greenish yellow* flammulated
dark olive (yellow streaking on underparts broader
and more obvious than olive streaking); crissum pale
yellow.
Sim. species: ♂ might be mistaken for a ♂ tityra. ♀,
barely separable from ♀ White Bellbird, is smaller, has
darker head that contrasts with upperparts (♀ White
Bellbird is concolor above), and chest more extensively yellowish streaked. In hand ♀ Bearded has
slightly longer tail (93–97 vs. approx. 85–87mm) and
longer bill (ca. 17–18 vs. 15–16mm).
Voice: ♂ has 3 different calls, all assoc. with advertising from display perch: (1) loud, dull *bock!* (or *bok!*),
like hammer pounding on iron, at intervals of a few
sec; (2) metallic, hammer-on-anvil ser., *tonk, tonk,
tonk* . . . ; and (3) loud and more musical, *tic-tock, tic-
tock, tic-tock* . . . ; simultaneous with each *tic* note a
high, ringing *eeee* (like a harmonic or echo) is given.
♀ essentially silent. In Coastal Cordillera ♂♂ vocal
mainly Mar–Jul; in e and se Bolívar vocal at least Dec–
Aug (prob. longer).
Behavior: Polygamous ♂♂ spend most of each day
calling on permanent territories, either advertising
from exposed perches above canopy or giving other
calls and ritualized displays within canopy or in forest
mid. levels. Calls are ventriloquial, making birds difficult to locate. Ads. and young eat mostly large protein-
rich drupes of Lauraceae and Burseraceae, also small
berries. Large seeds regurgitated unharmed. ♀♀ are infreq. seen except when feeding at fruiting trees. All nesting done by ♀; inconspic. twig platform 3–15m up; 1
light tan egg mottled brown; long (33-day) fledging
period[661].
Status and habitat: Uncommon and local resident in
moist and humid forest in foothill and lower mt. els.
Readily hd. (often hard to see) at start of rainy season
in foothills on n slope PN Henri Pittier (200–500m).
Some seasonal movements may occur n of Orinoco;
pops. s of Orinoco appear to be resident.

Range: 350–1600m n of Orinoco (sightings lower);
700–1500m s of Orinoco. Nw end of Sierra de Perijá
(Alto del Cedro), Zulia; Andes of se and nw Lara (sightings, PN Yacambú; Cerro El Cogollal), Falcón (Sierra
de San Luis), mts. of Yaracuy, Coastal Cordillera in Carabobo and n Aragua; n Sucre s to n Monagas (Casu-
aré); s Amazonas (Cerro de la Neblina); Bolívar in
upper Río Caura (Manina), and tepuis of Gran Sabana
from Sierra de Lema and Acopán-tepui s to Cerros Urutaní and Roraima, and Uei-tepui (*carnobarba*). Ne Colombia locally to Guyana and ne Brazil. Trinidad.

White Bellbird   PLATE 51
Procnias alba   Pájaro Campanero
Identification: ♂ 11.5″ (29cm), 210g. ♀ 10.5″ (27cm).
Bill and eyes black. ♂: *entirely white*; 1 long black wattle extends from base of upper mandible down over
right side of bill. ♀: very like ♀ Bearded Bellbird but
crown olive green more or less concolor with back;
sides of head tinged dusky, and throat and underparts
heavily flammulated yellow and olive green, streaking
fine on throat, more blurry and coarse on breast and
belly (overall looks rather olive). Other minor differences (see under Bearded Bellbird) are prob. best
noted in hand.
Sim. species: ♂ is only all-white bird in rain forest canopy, but cf. ♂ Bearded Bellbird and tityras. ♀ much
like ♀ Bearded Bellbird (see).
Voice: Two distinctive vocalizations. First, with 2 variations, a loud *kong-kay* like 2 sharp blows on a cracked
bell, given with head held immobile; a louder version
is produced with head angled right for 1st note, then
swung forcefully to left for 2d note while wattle is simultaneously flipped temporarily to left side of bill[687].
Second call a more musical, droning *duaaaaaaaaa . .
deeeeee*, almost hypnotic, last part fainter and like
echo of 1st part. Both calls are ventriloquial. Second
call, most bell-like of any member of genus, may be
one to which bellbirds owe their name. Vocal at least
Dec–Jul in se Bolívar, with birds most vocal during latter half of this period.
Behavior: ♂♂ are solitary and polygamous but tend to
concentrate loosely into groups of a few individuals
(leks are large, perhaps several km²) widely separated
from other leks. ♂♂ spend most of each day calling
from a few permanent advertising perches in canopy,
also reg. from 1 or more exposed bare branches above
canopy where they are much more conspic. ♀♀ remain in forest canopy and are infreq. encountered except at fruiting trees. Diet of ads. and young is mostly
large protein-rich fruit of Lauraceae and Burseraceae.
Large seeds are regurgitated.

Status and habitat: Quite local in tall humid lowland forest and lower slopes of tepuis where broadly overlaps Bearded Bellbird, but main pop. centered at slightly lower el. In se Venez. there is upslope migratory movement ca. Dec–Jun or Jul (when ♂♂ call and presum. breed) and downslope movement into adj. lowland forest during latter half of year, at which time sp. is quiet and difficult to find.

Range: 450–1100m (sight recs. 100–1450m). S Amazonas (Cerro de la Neblina); e Bolívar from Sierra de Imataca (Río Grande) and Auyán-tepui s across lowlands and tepuis of Gran Sabana to Cerro Urutaní, Paurai-tepui, and Cerro Roraima. The Guianas; scattered recs. and isol. pops. in ne Brazil (lower Rio Negro to se Pará); vagrant to Trinidad.

Gymnoderus

Bare head with loose skin imparts ghoulish, vulturine look; powder down in plumage gives unusual powdery gray "bloom" to feathers; no known close relatives.

Bare-necked Fruitcrow   PLATE 51
Gymnoderus foetidus   Pavita Pescuecipelada
Identification: ♂ 15″ (38cm), 345g. ♀ 14″ (36cm), 220g. *Vulturine in appearance (esp. head).* Bill blue gray tipped black. ♂: *mainly black,* feathers of crown, face, and upper throat short, dense, and velvetlike; rest of sides of head, neck, and lower throat bare, the loose skin forming many lappets and folds; *wings silvery gray above,* dull dusky blue gray below; *in flight upper wing surface flashes silvery white.* ♀: sim. to ♂ but dark grayish, esp. below; *upper wing surface dark gray more or less like back* (shows some whitish edgings), facial skin less folded and wrinkled, underparts with some pale scaly edging on feathers. Imm.: like ♀ but more scaled.
Sim. species: Robust shape accentuated by thin, bare neck and small head diagnostic. In flight cf. ♀ Amazonian Umbrellabird.
Voice: No vocalizations known.
Behavior: A large, odd-looking frugivor, most often seen alone flying high over rivers or forest where deep, loose, wing strokes, like swimming "breast-stroke," and flashing pale upper wing surface (♂) are characteristic. Less often seen perched in fruiting tree or high along forested river edge. Rarely (in Venez.) in loosely assoc. migratory or wandering groups up to 20 or so in forest or flying high overhead. Typically rather wary. Displaying ♂♂ fly between trees and aggressively supplant each other or engage in slow chasing flights through canopy. Feed on fruit, esp. figs and Lauraceae

fruits. Nest (Brazil and se Peru) small cryptic platform of lichens and tendrils on horizontal branch; 15–20m up; near lake in Peru; hidden by incubating ♀; 1 egg; no ♂ present at nest[42,689].
Status and habitat: Uncommon resident and seasonal wanderer or short-distance migrant in várzea and terra firme forest and forest borders. Most often seen along large rivers and on river isls.

Range: To 150m (sightings to ca. 200m). Nw Bolívar (Isla Bachaco; sight, Hato Las Nieves—D. Ascanio); w and c Amazonas from Orinoco and lower and mid. Río Ventuari (Las Carmelitas; sightings, Junglaven) southward (no recs. on Río Negro). Se Colombia s to n Bolivia, Amaz. Brazil (mostly s of the Amazon), and the Guianas.

Querula

Heavy bill and black plumage recall crows of n temperate latitudes; no obvious close relatives.

Purple-throated Fruitcrow   PLATE 51
Querula purpurata   Pájaro Toro
Identification: ♂ 11.5″ (29cm), 102g. ♀ 10.5″ (27cm), 98g. *Chunky; legs unusually short and weak;* bill blue gray, wide. ♂: entirely flat black with *glistening magenta throat* (fanned into broad gorget in display). ♀: entirely flat black.
Sim. species: ♂'s dark magenta throat can be hard to see. Behavior, distinctive silhouette, bounding flight, and calls are diagnostic.
Voice: Noisy. Groups give a variety of low mellow whistles, incl. slow, rising *ooouuua* and *weeoooowhuu (ooo* part sliding lower then rising), both often given over and over. Also various harsh notes.
Behavior: A notably bold and curious (territorial?) sp., easily attracted with even a poor imitation of its whistles. Travels in prs. or more often small restless groups of 3–6 in canopy, attracting much attention with repeated calls and swooping and bounding flight as they wander over large areas of forest. Freq. shake tail side to side, esp. when excited. Ads. eat mainly fruit plucked in flight at terminus of upward swoop and momentary stall or flutter. Nest a flat, flimsy platform high on exposed fork of branch tip 10–20m up or higher; attended by communal groups (helpers?) of 3–4 ads.; 1 dark olive egg thickly marked dark brown; long (32–33 days) fledging period despite being fed mostly insects[681].
Status and habitat: Fairly common to common resident in humid forest and tall second-growth woodland on rich alluvial soils. Less numerous in white sandy soil forests.

Range: To 500m. S Amazonas (Cerro Duida; Río Ocamo); Bolívar from lower Río Caura, Río Paragua, and Sierra de Imataca southward. Costa Rica to w Ecuador; se Colombia to n Bolivia, Amaz. Brazil (mostly s of the Amazon), ne Brazil, and the Guianas.

Haematoderus

Another cotinga genus of uncertain relationship; large; heavy billed; crimson feathers unusually long and stiff.

[Crimson Fruitcrow]
Haematoderus militaris   Pájaro Torero Militar
Identification: 14″ (36cm). Dark red bill. ♂: *mostly glistening crimson* (incl. bushy crest sometimes evident); wings and tail dusky brown. ♀: head, neck, and underparts *rosy red* (feathers not stiff like ♂'s), back, wings, and tail dark brown. Imm. (?): gray below with variable amt. of red (or mostly red with varying amts. of gray).
Sim. species: Easily confused with Guianan or Black-necked red-cotingas (see), which are remarkably sim. in pattern but much smaller and lack massive head and bulk of fruitcrow.
Voice: Generally quiet. Gives short, low-pitched, owl-like hoot, sometimes doubled or repeated at irreg. intervals[48]; or loud *bok* (A. Whittaker).
Behavior: Usually seen alone on favorite high limb (esp. ♂♂) in shaded canopy or subcanopy of emergent rain forest tree where may sit quietly for long periods of time. Forages alone, occas. in groups up to 3–4. Despite name, as yet known to take mainly (or only?) arthropods and invertebrates (Orthopterans and Coleoptera). Flight is undulating. In slow, silent display (during midmorning hr) ♂ flies upward, on shallow wing beats, to ca. 30m above treetops, then descends slowly with wings open in V, tail spread, and body feathers puffed, and at treetop ht. glides in spiral into forest. Display may be repeated several times. Nest a tiny platform of rootlets on high branch fork[795].

Status and habitat: Known from 1 sight rec. of a ♀ in forest at 140m, 13 Feb 1984, at base of Cerro de la Neblina[801]. Nearest rec. is in vicinity of Manaus, Brazil. Everywhere rare or in low density. Some seasonal movements may occur. Photo or specimen verification desirable.
Range: Extreme s Amazonas. The Guianas and ne Brazil mainly n of the Amazon w to Manaus; once in Rondônia.

Pyroderus

Large; bill heavy but proportionately not as broad as in *Querula*; throat feathers of ♂ shiny; large, strong legs and feet.

Red-ruffed Fruitcrow   PLATE 51
Pyroderus scutatus   Pájaro Torero
Identification: ♂ 17″ (43cm), 420g. ♀ 15″ (38cm), 325g. Bill pale blue gray (♂) or dusky (♀). Rather short tailed, large headed, and robust. ♂: mainly black; *broad gorget of orange feathers tipped dark red* (has "crinkled" look); breast with variable amt. of chestnut mottling. Or sim. but breast and belly chestnut, thighs and crissum black (*orenocensis*). ♀: throat duller orange but still "crinkled."
Sim. species: Should be easily recognized. Large icterids, e.g., oropendolas and caciques, have yellow in tail or red on rump.
Voice: Usually quiet. ♂♂, at lek in tree or group of trees, display with low, resonant, and double-sounding boom, *ooo-m, ooo-m, ooo-m* . . (has electronic quality), 2d part louder. Given esp. as other ♂♂ or ♀♀ arrive. ♂♂ also gives "twangy" call between bouts of booming.
Behavior: Usually seen alone at various hts. inside forest, or in Andes occas. loosely assoc. with Andean Cocks-of-the-rock, caciques, and oropendolas at fruiting trees. Eat mainly (entirely?) fruit. Flight is labored and undulating. Fly through, not above, forest, and sometimes rather unwary, even curious. In spectacular but rarely observed display 7–8 ♂♂ gather before sunrise at traditional display sites for ca. 1 hr. In close proximity and each on favorite perch ca. 6m up, they bend forward and call, then flare bib as they straighten up, sometimes also quiver wings. ♂♂ may chase each other and tend to look downward (for ♀♀?) continually[689]. Small stick nest a flat platform high on slender branch; 1 egg (more?) pale buff blotched and spotted reddish brown and lilac[589].
Status and habitat: Rare or uncommon (very local) resident in wet montane forest (cloud forest) and forest borders in Andes, and in tropical dry forest and tropical moist forest in lowlands of ne Bolívar. Now increasingly rare and local with loss of habitat, esp. in Coastal Cordillera and dry forests w of El Palmar (latter rapidly being destroyed for cattle pastures).
Range: 1200–1900m n of Orinoco; 50–500m s of Orinoco. Sierra de Perijá, Zulia; Andes of Táchira n through Mérida and nw Barinas, Trujillo (recs.?), Lara (sight, PN Yacambú); mts. of Yaracuy and Coastal Cordillera in Carabobo, Aragua, and Distr. Federal (*granadensis*); ne Bolívar from Upata e to Sierra de Imataca (incl. El Palmar; Guasipati; El Callao) and s to lower

Río Cuyuní near El Dorado (*orenocensis*). Andes of Colombia, nw Ecuador (rare), and Peru; Guyana; se Brazil, e Paraguay, and ne Argentina.

Cephalopterus

Large with black plumage; stiff expanded crest (the "umbrella"); long feathered wattle hangs from neck (shorter in ♀) in S Amer. spp.; large, strong legs and feet; trachea has 2 expanded parts.

Amazonian Umbrellabird   PLATE 51
Cephalopterus ornatus   Pájaro Paraguas
Identification: ♂ 20″ (51cm). ♀ 16.5″ (42cm), 380g. Eyes white; bill very heavy, blackish. Has wild, slightly disheveled, Valkyrian countenance. ♂: entirely lustrous black with umbrella-shaped crest somewhat recurved over bill (feathers arising from forecrown stiff with white shafts); long expandable and feathered wattle, 3–4″ (7.6–10.2cm) long, hangs from throat (but often held against body and not very conspic. in field). ♀: crest less exaggerated (more pointed); wattle shorter; plumage duller.
Sim. species: In bounding flight prob. most likely mistaken for a large woodpecker (*Dryocopus* or *Campephilus*), but note that umbrellabird's crest (both sexes) is permanently erect, even in flight. Smaller Purple-throated Fruitcrow lacks crest and has different habits.
Voice: Usually silent. Displaying ♂♂ lean forward with grating sound as air sacs are filled, then utter low booming as thrust head forward. Both sexes occas. give soft guttural *churr* and *go-whgogogo* 1–several times[689].
Behavior: An alert and wary sp., often excessively so, that seldom permits observer to approach closely. Most often seen alone, occas. several together in large open trees or in deeply undulating, woodpeckerlike flight across large rivers. Move with heavy jaylike hops on open limbs in canopy or subcanopy and may sit for short periods of time in open. Feed mostly on fruit. Groups of 2–5 ♂♂ may display on high open branches in early morning. At intervals lean forward with crest and wattle expanded and utter low booming calls like distant bull (hence a freq. Spanish name), this sometimes accompanied by ritualized chasing[545]. Flat twig nest high or low on forked branch; 1 buff brown egg with dark brown and lilac marks and spots[608].
Status and habitat: Uncommon resident along borders of terra firme and esp. várzea forest along large rivers, lakes, and river isls. Most readily seen when perched in *Cecropia* trees along rivers.
Range: To 200m. Nw Amazonas (San Borja Falls) above mouth of Río Meta; n Amazonas mainly along

Orinoco and Río Ventuari s to Pto. Yapacana (*ornatus*); prob. also rivers of s Amazonas. Se Colombia s to n Bolivia, w and c Amaz. Brazil, and s Guyana.

Perissocephalus

Related to umbrellabirds and fruitcrows; unusually broad, rounded wings; unique vocalizations.

Capuchinbird   PLATE 51
Perissocephalus tricolor   Pájaro Capuchino
Identification: 14″ (36cm). ♂ 360g, ♀ 320g. Large, curious-looking bird with bob-tail, *bald blue gray head*, and heavy bill. *Mainly cinnamon brown*, darker on rump, reddish chestnut on belly; *under tail coverts orange rufous*, the feathers long, curled, and capable of being raised and puffed out like globular orangish "taillights" on either side of tail during display; wings and tail blackish, under wing coverts white. ♀: under tail covert feathers not lengthened.
Sim. species: Bald head imparts peculiar small-headed, hump-shouldered appearance to this unforgettable bird which looks as if it might have flown straight from the pages of a Grimms' Fairy Tale. Cf. ♀ Guianan Cock-of-the-rock, also brown and with peculiar misshapen appearance.
Voice: Remarkable display song a loud, far-carrying, growling *grrraaaaaaaaooooooooooooo*, much like sound of a distant chain saw, and up close often preceded by hissing sound, as if bird is inhaling. Not forgotten once hd. Also *wark* as forages; *rack* in alarm[662]. Calling somewhat cooperative as nearby birds tend to avoid overlapping long display songs.
Behavior: Ads. eat much fruit, also some arthropods. Feed on a wide variety of fruits but esp. spp. of Lauraceae, seasonally also on palms. Forage alone, mostly in canopy or lower along forest borders. Take fruit by making short upward and rather slow sallies ending in brief "stall." Often sit quietly in shady canopy and regurgitate seeds following short feeding bouts. ♂♂ gather in permanent leks of 4–15 or more. During day members are dispersed but within hearing distance (some perhaps also in visual contact). At dawn 12 or more gather at traditional site in canopy of 1 or a few large, adjoining forest trees and call, display, and fly back and forth vigorously for up to 1 hr before dispersing. In remarkable display ♂♂ lean forward to produce "inhaling air sound," then begin *grrr* portion of call and pull themselves up very erect as continue the *aaaaaaa*, expand a ruff of neck feathers (emphasizes bald head), cock tail sharply, fluff out 2 orange rufous puff-balls on either side of base of tail (like "tail-

lights"), and with bill pointing downward slightly, finish the long *oooooooooo* of "chain saw" call. Occas. call at dusk. ♀♀ (in Guyana) incubate 1 egg (2?) on tiny platform of *Eugenia* twigs, 4–6m up. Slow molt may last from Apr to Dec in Guyana[662].
Status and habitat: Resident. Leks are widely separated in tall humid forest in lowlands, but individuals wander far into forested tepui foothills. Song and display at least Dec–Jul or Aug (longer?) in e Bolívar; strong display Jan–Mar.

Range: To 1400m. S Amazonas from vicinity of Cerro Duida and Yavita-Pimichín trail s; e Bolívar from Cerro Guaiquinima, Auyán-tepui, and Sierra de Imataca (Río Grande) s across Gran Sabana. The Guianas and ne Brazil (n of the Amazon).

Phoenicircus

Two beautiful and unusual spp.; ♀♀ larger than ♂♂; short wings; ♂♂ loosely assoc. in leks; 7th primary of ♂ deeply emarginate near tips and extremely narrow (normal in ♀); taxonomic assignment uncertain, possibly allied with manakins.

Guianan Red-Cotinga PLATE 51
Phoenicircus carnifex Cotinga Roja
Identification: ♂ 8.5" (22cm), 82g. ♀ 9.5" (24cm), 95g. Eyes dark brown; bill horn color, lower mandible orange; legs pinkish flesh. ♂: stunning; *long flat crest glistening crimson, rest of head, throat, and back lustrous blackish maroon*, wing coverts, inner flight feathers, and tertials dark rufous; *breast, belly, rump, and tail scarlet*, tail broadly tipped rufous. ♀: like ♂ but much duller; *crown raspberry red*, back and wings brownish olive, tail dull rufous, throat and chest pinkish tinged brown, lower underparts rose red.
Sim. species: Only other predom. "red-and-black" birds of sim. size in its range are Silver-beaked Tanager and Red-and-black Grosbeak. ♀ Guianan Cock-of-the-rock is much larger, darker, and mainly brown.
Voice: Advertising call, at dawn, a loud *pee-chew-eet*. In display flights between perches ♂♂ produce mechanical trilling sound (like rapidly calling crickets) with modified 7th primary[689]; also a high-pitched whistle as ♂ swoops onto perch at end of display flight. In alarm or disturbance both sexes give *wheep*, singly or in long ser. Rarely a loud, 2-part wing-buzz[756].
Behavior: A "tongue of flames" in forest, but despite brilliant colors, not very conspic., somewhat wary, and hardly ever seen often enough. Entirely frugivorous, and unless calling and located at a lek, likely seen

only at fruit trees. Takes fruit while perched or in flight with swooping snatch, stall, or hover, mostly in understory or a little higher, either alone or sometimes several birds together in fruit tree, but not with mixed-spp. flocks. In Suriname displays in leks approx. Dec–May (later?), with ca. 8 ♂♂ which call noisily 8–12m up in understory or lower mid. strata, almost exclusively during 1st 1–2 hr after first light; rarely later. ♂♂ on lek are in auditory but not necessarily visual contact. Displays consist of calling and freq. flights between about 12 perches[756]. Typically perch bent slightly forward with short wings drooped, tail down, and brilliant rump exposed.
Status and habitat: Rare and very local. Resident inside humid and wet lowland forest. Leks are widely separated, and few have been found. In Guyana sp. is, at least locally, fairly common (M. B. Robbins). Small no. of sight recs. between km 84 and 89 on road s of El Dorado (D. Ascanio; H. Cleve; D. Stejskal; Hilty) and at Río Grande in the Sierra de Imataca.

Range: To 250m. E Bolívar in vicinity of upper Río Cuyuní (Carabobo); Río Grande (sight). The Guianas and ne Brazil.

Black-necked Red-Cotinga PLATE 51
Phoenicircus nigricollis Cotinga Roja Pescuecinegra
Identification: ♂ 8.5" (22cm), 93g. ♀ 9.5" (24cm), 103g. Stunning. Eyes dark brown; bill yellow ochre; legs pinkish red. ♂: *long flat crest glistening crimson*, rest of head, neck, back, and wings deep velvety black, flight feathers dark brown, rump and tail crimson, *tail broadly tipped black*; throat black, *rest of underparts glistening red*. ♀: pattern sim. to ♂ but crown and tail dull rufous, tail tipped brown; black areas replaced by brown, lower underparts dull rose red.
Sim. species: Neither sex likely mistaken if seen clearly. ♂ is one of most beautiful birds in Venez.
Voice: Perched birds advertise with loud, explosive, and harsh *SKREEA!* (or *SQUIIK!*), metallic and accompanied by head bobbing. Brief *skree* calls sometimes given at end of display flights. Trilling whistle (cricket-like) is produced by modified wing feathers during flight.
Behavior: Unknown in Venez. A small and wary but richly colored frugivor of forest interior. ♂♂ call, with varying levels of commitment (seasonal?), for short period early in morning but relatively little or not at all during remainder of day. In ne Peru groups of 6–10 or more ♂♂ display in lower mid. level of forest on permanent, largely exclusive, nonresource-based territories that are circular or elliptical and as much as 30–

60m in max. diameter. Each ♂ advertises and displays from 3–5 favorite perches which are often horizontal sections of looping lianas. ♂♂ maintain auditory contact but are prob. not visible to each other most of time. ♀♀ apparently do all nesting activities. **Status and habitat:** Rare and local. Interior of humid terra firme forest. Known from only 2 localities in Venez.

Range: To 200m. Sw Amazonas along Río Negro (El Carmen) and at Cerro de la Neblina. Se Colombia, e Ecuador, ne Peru, and c Amaz. Brazil e to Rios Negro and Tapajós.

Rupicola

Icons of beauty, notable for their brilliant colors, uniquely truncated tertials, and fanlike crests; 2 spp. long placed in separate family, Rupicolidae; now usually in Cotingidae, despite being somewhat manakin-like in behavior; only the Guianan sp. has been studied in any detail; large moss and mud nest glued to inaccessible place on cliff; attended only by ♀.

Andean Cock-of-the-rock   PLATE 51
Rupicola peruviana   Gallito de las Sierras
Identification: 12″ (30.5cm). ♂ 270g, ♀ 220g. Large, chunky, brilliantly colored bird of Andes. Bill orange red. Eyes yellow and placed high on side of head. ♂: *shocking fluorescent orange red* with permanently erect disklike crest nearly covering bill; *wings and tail jet black, tertials pearl gray*, unusually broad and truncated. In hand outermost primary narrow and emarginate for nearly half its length. ♀: foreparts dark cinnamon brown, more dull orangish brown on rear body; inner flight feathers and tertials grayish brown; *crest small*; bill and legs dusky; eyes bluish white. Imm. ♂: like ♀; eyes pale yellow mixed amber.
Sim. species: In flight unforgettable ♂ is ball of flames fanned by jet wings. ♀ sometimes confused because it is so unlike ♂. Note ♀'s large size, chunky shape, and small, lumpy crest.
Voice: ♂♂ are noisy at leks, otherwise only occas. a loud nasal *raank*, when disturbed. Advertising calls incl. a long, low-pitched, and harsh *jummrreE!* (or *oeeeeE!*), long ser. of rough, nasal *urr-ur-ur-ur-ur*. . . . notes, and when ♀♀ are present at lek, ♂♂ give clucking chant, *kip-kip-kip* . . . , which may continue for several min.
Behavior: Polygamous ♂♂ spend early mornings and late afternoons during long breeding season calling

and displaying from leks which are usually on sides of steep forested ravines. Matinee performances are usually less vigorous, but some display and activity may occur throughout day at leks. Up to 15 or more ♂♂ gather in forest mid. levels (not on gd. as in Guianan Cock-of-the-rock) and carry out ser. of head-bobbing and bowing displays and arching "push-ups," sometimes accompanied by a few slow wing flaps or abrupt "about-face" movements, all the while uttering loud crowing vocalizations. Display is frantic when ♀♀ approach. Typically suspicious and hard to approach, but less so when feeding at fruiting trees (mostly mornings and evenings) where sally up (sally-stall) and snatch large fruits. Ads. mostly frugivorous on high-protein fruits of Lauraceae, Annonaceae, and Rubiaceae, but fruits of at least 14 other plant families reported in diet. Young fed much animal matter[367]. Nest built and attended by ♀; mud cup plastered to inaccessible spot on cave entrance or beneath sheltered rock or boulder outcrop; usually fairly close to, occas. far (1km or more) from, lek; 2 eggs[41].
Status and habitat: Very local. Resident in steep humid and wet forested ravines. Usually near streams and always with large rocky outcrops or overhangs nearby. In Venez. first discovered in Táchira in Feb 1969 by P. Schwartz and so far known from only 1 other loc. in Venez. (upper San Isidro Valley, nw Barinas), an unprotected area.

Range: Ca. 1000–1550m. Andes of s Táchira (Cerro El Teteo at 1000m), nw Barinas in upper San Isidro Valley (*aequatorialis*); also "Mérida" without specific loc. (British Museum of Natural History); possibly Trujillo (?). Andes of Colombia (500–2400m) s to Bolivia.

Guianan Cock-of-the-rock   PLATE 51
Rupicola rupicola   Gallito de las Rocas
Identification: 11″ (28cm). ♂ 210g, ♀ 190g. Tepuis and s lowlands. Slightly smaller but even more gaudy than its Andean relative. Eyes orange (♂) or bluish white to dull yellow (♀). ♂: *intense orange with flat, wheel-like frontal crest completely covering bill*, crest outlined by narrow subterminal line of maroon (like Roman helmet); wings black; *white speculum on inner flight feathers* (conspic. in flight); tertials black, edged and tipped white, unusually broad and truncated at tip, and outer webs lengthened into long curly and springy orange filaments; rufflelike orange upper tail coverts cover most of short black tail. ♀: more or less uniform dusky brown with *small lumpline crest*.
Sim. species: Dull, rather misshapen ♀ told by chunky shape and small crest. See ♀ Guianan Red-Cotinga and Capuchinbird.

Voice: Can be noisy at display arena. Commonest call at or away from display arena a loud, crowing *GET-REAL*, 2d note somewhat drawn out. Foraging ♂♂ give nasal, drawn-out *qaaaOWW* at long intervals; during aggressive interactions low wavering caws, gabbling, and various rough notes. ♀ rarely gives high, plaintive *quEEeo* and *quaao*.

Behavior: Despite ♂'s brilliant colors, not as conspic. as one might imagine, and most easily located by voice, esp. near a display arena. Polygamous ♂♂ spend much of each day at communal lek, either perched above arena where they freq. squabble with other ♂♂ over ownership of small display territories, or in silent and static posturing at gd.-level courts owned and cleared of leaves and debris by each ♂. Only performances of dominant ♂♂ are greeted with éclat by ♀♀ who chose ♂♂ for mating, thus a select few ♂♂ garner most copulations[753,754]. Otherwise ♂♂ are usually in mid. strata of forest or in canopy of fruiting trees. Flight is strong, fast, and direct. Large leks may contain 40–50 ♂♂, but most are much smaller (size limited by availability of nest sites for ♀♀). Nest a mud-and-moss cup plastered to vertical rock wall, inside shallow rock cave, etc.; 2 eggs; ♀ attends all nest duties. In e Bolívar display peaks Nov–Apr.

Status and habitat: Fairly common but local resident around rocky outcrops and isolated cerros in tepui region. Key, everywhere, is presence of suitable rocky areas (cliffs, boulders, etc.) for safe nest sites. Can be seen at numerous localities along "escalera" of Sierra de Lema, e Bolívar.

Range: To 2000m. Throughout Amazonas; nw Bolívar e to Río Cuyuní and Gran Sabana. E Colombia to the Guianas and n Brazil.

Pipridae: Manakins

Saltarines

Manakins are a rather diverse family with all members found in the Neotropics. They are most numerous and diverse in the Amazonian region with a few species found at lower elevations in the Andes and other mountainous regions. These small forest birds are characterized by short roundish bills, short tails, chunky shape, large eyes, and the middle toe partially joined to an adjacent toe. They move suddenly and abruptly, and unlike most passerines, they do not hop along branches. Males of most genera are bright and contrastingly patterned, whereas females are dull greenish. Members of *Pipra, Dixiphia, Lepidothrix, Chiro-*

xiphia, Manacus, and a few other genera are well known for their remarkable displays, often performed at a communal lek. There the males—the boys of la dolce vita—give advertising calls and perform often complex repertoires of stereotyped movements accompanied by bizarre mechanical as well as vocal sounds, all with great élan and aimed at attracting females for mating. In these genera females perform all nesting activities. Manakins as currently recognized, however, are a polyphyletic group[512,513,518]. Three genera previously placed with manakins, *Neopipo, Schiffornis,* and *Piprites,* are now believed to be closer to tyrannids, and several other genera currently included in the family do not appear to be true manakins. In particular, *Tyranneutes* and *Neopelma* do not seem to share a close relationship with any manakins and are in many respects also rather tyrannid-like[684]; they have no elaborate display, no sexual dimorphism, and no bright plumage.

Chloropipo

Inconspic.; longish tail; mostly montane; prob. best merged with *Xenopipo*[514]; nesting and displays poorly known.

Olive Manakin   PLATE 44
Chloropipo uniformis   Saltarín Uniforme
Identification: 5.3″ (13.5cm). Large dark eyes; dusky legs; short dark bill. *Uniform dark olive above and below;* throat paler, lower breast and belly pale and tinged yellowish. Faint *yellowish eyering.* Under wing coverts whitish (not easily seen in field). Overall chunky with rather long tail (for a manakin); long wings extend well out onto tail. Sexes sim.

Sim. species: On tepui slopes easily confused with ♀ Scarlet-horned Manakin which is a bit smaller, has brownish orange (not dusky) legs, shorter wings (much shorter primary extension), and slight tufts on rearcrown. Also cf. allied ♀ Black Manakin of lowland scrub habitats.

Voice: Infreq. hd. advertising call a clear, rising whistle, *preeeeeeeeEE*, penetrating but not loud, typically given only at long intervals. Rising whistle occas. preceded by a few low, stuttery *stu-tu-tu-tu-tu* notes given quickly, or a short *chip* note.

Behavior: A notably solitary manakin that perches inside shady forest at mid. levels or lower. Reg. comes out along forest borders to feed on small fruits and berries (e.g., melastomes), esp. when *Tangara* tanagers, thrushes, and other manakins are present, but does not follow mixed-spp. flocks. Overall quiet, inconspic., and does not attract much attention to itself. Often reacts strongly to tape playbacks and may defend a resource-based territory.

Status and habitat: Fairly common but easily overlooked resident of humid and wet mossy forest, stunted melastome-dominated second growth, and wooded borders on slopes of tepuis. Commonest in regions with many melastomes. Some seasonal el. movement likely.

Range: 800–2100m (possible sighting to 450m). Amazonas on Cerros Duida and Sipapo (*duidae*); s Bolívar

from upper Río Caura (Cerro Jaua), Auyán-tepui, and Sierra de Lema southward (*uniformis*). Adj. Guyana and n Brazil (Cerro Uei).

Golden-winged Manakin
PLATE 44

Masius chrysopterus   Saltarín Alidorado
Identification: 4.3″ (10.9cm). 12g. Legs raspberry to purplish brown; tail longer (both sexes) than in most small manakins. ♂: mostly jet black; *feathers of fore-crown golden yellow, curling forward to form flat crest over bill*; rest of central crown golden yellow, the feathers flattened into quill-like shafts and tipped orange forming stiff, flat crest; elongated black feathers on sides of crown form small inconspic. "horns"; *median throat and larger patch on lower throat yellow; most of underwings, incl. inner webs of flight feathers, and inner webs of most tail feathers bright yellow* (yellow in wings conspic. in flight; concealed at rest; yellow in tail seldom visible). ♀: olive above, paler olive below; *median throat, larger area on lower throat, and belly pale olive yellow.* Imm. ♂: like ♀, but older birds may show some yellow on crest and brighter yellow on throat; subads. mottled with black.
Sim. species: ♂ is ornate, but this not always evident in field (at rest looks mainly black). ♀ usually shows enough of distinctive yellow pattern on throat (like ♂ but duller) to be easily recognized; note unusual leg color and longish tail.
Voice: Notably quiet. Occas. a blurred and slightly trilled *teeeeee* from mid. level or canopy perch. Weak advertising call is soft and not far carrying, a low, nasal, grunting *nurrt*, varied to *tseet-nurrt*, from display arena 2–11m up; also, in display flight, a thin *see* lasting 1–3 sec. Avg. 4–6 display calls/min[693].
Behavior: Striking in appearance but inconspic. in behavior and easily overlooked. ♂♂ slip quietly through low or mid.-story levels of cloud forest and sally for small fruits and berries, esp. Melastomataceae, either alone or briefly assoc. with mixed tanager flocks in subcanopy. ♂♂ advertise up to 80% of day from variety of perches within a 30-to 40-m-diameter or smaller, individual, and spatially separated territory (at least at peak of breeding), but despite large amt. of display time, they are not conspic. to human observers. Displays in s Colombia and Ecuador, like those of *Corapipo*, are centered over mossy log or tree buttress where (1) ♂ calls, makes stereotyped approach flights from downhill obliquely down to a log, lands, gives 2-noted call and quick "rebound jump" with call (effect is 3-noted *pk-k-ker*) and (2) perches on log, "freezes" in chin-down tail-up display for 1–20 sec, and/or per-

forms silent, mechanical, side-to-side bowing display with head low and "horns" raised. Mating may occur after rebound jump[516,693]. ♀♀ sally and hover mostly for small fruit and are inconspic. and infreq. seen. Imm. "floaters" disperse widely. Nest a small mossy cup suspended in low fork.
Status and habitat: Uncommon resident in humid and wet forest (cloud forest) and tall second growth, and at fruiting trees along forest borders. Recs. rather scattered in Andes, but sp. is easily overlooked. Found with some reg. in nw Barinas (San Isidro Rd.) and PN Guaramacal, Trujillo.

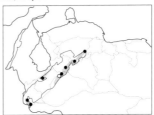

Range: 1000–2100m. W slope of Andes in w Mérida (La Azulita); e slope of Andes in se Táchira, nw Barinas (Calderas; sight, San Isidro Rd.), e Trujillo (Boconó), and s Lara at Cabudare and Guárico (*chrysopterus*). Colombia s in Andes to n Peru.

Machaeropterus

Very small; unusual color patterns; spp. mostly allopatric; ♂♂ of all spp. with abnormally thickened, twisted inner flight feathers.

Striped Manakin
PLATE 44

Machaeropterus regulus   Saltarín Rayado
Identification: 3.7″ (9.4cm). 9.4g. Tiny. Eyes dark orange; legs pinkish gray. ♂: *crown and nape bright glistening red*, the feathers lengthened to form flat crest, otherwise bright olive green above; inner webs of inner flight feathers white (hard to see in field), throat whitish, *rest of underparts reddish chestnut striped and stained pinkish and white*, breast stained crimson. Or breast with a few crimson streaks, rump tinged yellowish (*obscurostriatus*). Or with chest stained yellow forming band (*aureopectus*). ♀: above olive, throat dingy white, breast and sides pale yellowish olive indistinctly streaked whitish and pink (brighter on sides), belly yellowish.
Sim. species: Easily confused with Fiery-capped Manakin (see).
Voice: Commonest call (Andes and Amazonas) of ♂♂ on advertising perches a soft, sharply enunciated *pit-sink*, steadily at ca. 15- to 30-sec intervals. Normally call from a no. of different perches ca. 8–15m up, but may remain on each for several min before moving.
Behavior: An inconspic. bird that perches in forest mid. levels or lower, often without moving for extended periods of time. Even when calling can be difficult to track down. ♂♂ advertise in small dispersed leks with individuals well separated but prob. within earshot. Spend long periods of time giving soft advertising call, then fly off for a few min to fill up on berries at

nearby tree or shrub. When ♂ gains attention of ♀ he then apparently makes repeated short vertical jumps with vibrating wings and insectlike buzzes[235]; in ne Ecuador, in presence of ♀, a ♂ made sharp buzzing sounds as it revolved rapidly around a slender horizontal twig[647]. In Brazil 2 ♂♂ perch together, 1 flips to hanging position and rapidly rotates to and fro while producing whirring sound[610].

Status and habitat: Resident. Fairly common very locally, with many specimens from Río Negro in Zulia; Las Mesas in ne Táchira; and Barinitas and Altamira in Barinas. Humid forest, old second growth, and fruiting trees along forest borders. N of Orinoco mainly in foothills and lower Andean slopes. Very local in lowlands and hilly terrain s of Orinoco (pops. widely scattered or overlooked?).

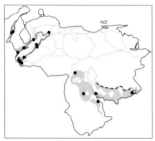

Range: 100–1200m (most recs. above 300m). Base of Sierra de Perijá, s Maracaibo Basin, Zulia, and w base of Andes in Táchira; e slope from se Táchira to nw Barinas (*zulianus*); w slope at El Vigía, Mérida, n to Trujillo at Betijoque (*obscurostriatus*); c Amazonas (La Sabana; Kabadisocaña; Simarawochi); nw and se Bolívar (Pijiguaos; Cerro Paurai) (*aureopectus*); sight rec. 15km w of Santa Elena de Uairén (C. Parrish) (subsp.?). W Colombia; e Colombia to n Peru, nw Amaz. Brazil, and Guyana (rare); se Brazil (last possibly a separate sp.).

Fiery-capped Manakin   PLATE 44
Machaeropterus pyrocephalus   Saltarín Cabeciencendido

Identification: 3.7″ (9.4cm). 9.8g. Eyes dark reddish orange; legs purplish pink. Short tail. ♂: *crown and nape glistening golden yellow*, small red central crown stripe (not conspic.); back rosy rufous, wing coverts olive, flight feathers dusky, inner webs of inner flight feathers and under wing coverts white (not conspic.); sides of head olive, *underparts pale pinkish white streaked rosy brown*. ♀: above uniform bright olive, throat grayish, breast yellowish olive turning pale yellow on belly, and both *breast and belly flammulated with olive* (looks vaguely streaked). Imm. ♂: like ♀ but usually with small amt. of golden yellow on forecrown.

Sim. species: At first glance, ♂ is superficially sim. to ♂ Striped Manakin. Latter has solid red crown (never shows yellow), all-olive back (not rosy rufous), more heavily striped underparts, and in area of overlap, a yellow-stained chest band. ♀ Striped Manakin is very sim. to ♀ Fiery-capped but paler and streakier below, and streaking pinkish (not olive). No other ♀ manakins are streaked below.

Voice: Advertising call a high, delicate, and soft *tiink*, often given no more than once or twice a min; easily mistaken for a little frog (quality of small bell); sometimes slightly drawn out.

Behavior: ♂♂ advertise from several slender horizontal perches in forest mid. level (ca. 10–15m up), but calls, even if recognized, are hard to pinpoint to source. ♂♂ are usually loosely assoc. in a lek (exploded lek), the individuals being within earshot but prob. not within sight of each other. Some ♂♂ (low ranking?) may advertise from solitary locs. In Brazil (elsewhere?) displaying ♂♂ perch alone or in prs., 1 hanging downward and rotating so rapidly side to side it blurrs; also produces a loud *zsssss* sound, apparently from large secondaries[610]. Fly (display?) with noisy wing beats. Away from display areas seen mainly during brief visits to fruiting trees and shrubs, esp. melastomes. ♀ on nest 14 Mar, lower Río Caura; leafy cup nest suspended from sapling fork, 1m up; eggs dull white streaked and mottled brown[80].

Status and habitat: Very local (overlooked?) resident. Humid lowland forest, tall second growth, and forest borders. Reasons for sp.'s very local occurrence in Venez. are unknown. There are a few small, widely scattered leks along Maripa–Trincheras road s of Caño Urbano. Only Amazonas rec. is 1 subad. ♂ (yellow in crown) seen repeatedly 15 Jun 1995 in fruiting *Miconia* sp. ca. 20km e of Pto. Ayacucho[259].

Range: 100–200m. Bolívar in lower Río Caura from Maripa to Prisión and in mid. Río Paragua (Cerro El Perro; Piedra Pintada) (*pallidiceps*); nw Amazonas (sight). Se Peru e across sc Brazil; ne Brazil (Roraima).

Xenopipo

Lowlands; longish tail; closely allied to *Chloropipo* but smaller, sexually dimorphic, and more vocal.

Black Manakin   PLATE 44
Xenopipo atronitens   Saltarín Negro

Identification: 5″ (12.7cm). 16g. Fairly *long tailed* for a manakin. Eyes and legs dark. ♂ has *bluish gray bill tipped black*. ♂: entirely glossy blue black above and below; flight feathers and tail tinged brownish. ♀: dark olive above, slightly paler below, lower breast and belly tinged yellowish.

Sim. species: ♂ remarkably like ♂ Amazonian Black-Tyrant. Normally the 2 spp. are in different habitats, but in some areas even habitats are juxtaposed, in which case behavior and voice are best clues. In hand manakin told by partially fused outer 2 toes. Manakin's longish tail might otherwise recall a tanager (e.g., larger Red-shouldered Tanager) or finch. ♀ more uniformly dark than other manakins with which it occurs; ♀ White-bearded Manakin has orangish legs; ♀ Golden-headed Manakin is smaller and much paler. ♀ nearly identical to either sex of Olive Manakin of upper tepui slopes (little overlap) but slightly smaller. ♀ also recalls a tyrannulet or small flycatcher, but note lack of wing edgings and rounder head.

Voice: Often rather quiet, but when excited or displaying can be noisy, giving a variety of loud, sharp calls incl. *skee! kep-kep-kep-kep*, sometimes rough 1st note omitted; rattle trill, *tr'r'r'r'r'r'r'r'r'r*, and sharp notes.

Behavior: Rather uncharacteristic of family. Feeds alone, or 2 or 3 may gather with other birds at small fruiting trees. Sometimes with small mixed-spp. flocks in scrubby vegetation. Display limited chiefly to calling and chasing rivals or ♀♀. No special perches or display areas used[610].

Status and habitat: Fairly common resident in scrubby savanna forest, scrub woodland, and low-canopied and stunted várzea forest, almost always in white sandy soil regions.

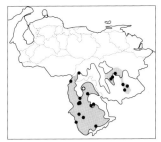

Range: To 1200m (most recs. below 700m). Spottily throughout Amazonas and c and s Bolívar in sandy soil regions. Extreme e Colombia to the Guianas and n Brazil (e of Rio Negro); small isolated pops. in e Peru and ne Bolivia.

Manacus

Small and chunky; ♂♂ with long, puffed throat feathers; ♀♀ dull olive, legs usually orange; ♂♂ perform complex mechanical snapping displays accompanied by jumps and whistles, all near gd.; these are "classic" manakin displays familiar to most visitors to Neotropics.

White-bearded Manakin　　　　PLATE 44
Manacus manacus　Saltarín Maraquero

Identification: 4.2″ (10.7cm). 16.5g. *Legs rich orange* (both sexes). ♂: *mainly black and white.* Crown, back, wings, and tail black, *broad white collar encircles neck; entire underparts white*, rump gray, belly tinged gray; feathers of throat lengthened to form long beard which can be extended straight forward and spread like fan. Or sim. but gray areas of plumage darker (*umbrosus, manacus*). ♀: dull olive above and below, throat tinged grayish, belly more olive yellow.

Sim. species: ♀ much like ♀ *Chiroxiphia* manakins but smaller and chunkier and lacks ♀ Lance-tailed's spikes. ♀ told from other ♀ manakins by orange legs.

Voice: Freq. call a soft, trilled *peerr*; in display *chwee* and excited *pee-you*[674]; also loud and vigorous firecracker-like snaps and "Bronx cheer" rolls produced mechanically with wings.

Behavior: One of noisiest and best-known lek-forming manakins, and likely the 1st to come to mind at mention of family. ♂♂ gather in tight groups of ca. 10–20, sometimes more, but can be difficult to see unless "habituated" to humans. Display yr-round but abate somewhat during late-yr molt. Each ♂ "owns" a small "court" on forest floor where it cleans gd. of leaves and debris and performs 6 kinds of displays, all with panache and flare. Gd.-level displays take place between 2 or more vertical saplings in a court, other displays are 1–2m up. Dazzling, high-energy repertoire incls. to-and-fro jumps between saplings; explosive wing-snapping jumps (the "firecrackers") between bases of adj. saplings; sliding down pole (sapling); and rapid wing "fanning" while perched. Calling, snapping, and display approach pandemonium upon arrival of a ♀. Mating is promiscuous, but ♀ chooses. Away from lek sally rapidly for fruit and a few insects in understory, and ♂♂ sometimes move in loose groups as forage, pausing periodically to snap wings. Wings of ♂♂ produce dry rustling in flight. Nest a flimsy shallow cup suspended from low fork, often near stream; 2 eggs, dull white with brown streaks mainly at larger end[674].

Status and habitat: Resident locally in dense second growth, shrubby forest borders, gallery forest, overgrown plantations, and tall forest in humid regions. S of Orinoco often in shrubby borders of white sandy soil forest. In most areas, thick cover with numerous small saplings for jump displays are a requirement, whether inside or at edge of forest.

Range: To 750m n of Orinoco; to 1000m s of Orinoco. Sierra de Perijá, Zulia, w slope of Andes in Táchira, Mérida, and Trujillo; e slope in Táchira, Apure, and Barinas (n to Barinitas and Altamira); s of Orinoco in n Amazonas; nw Bolívar e through lower Río Caura, mid. Río Paragua (Salto Uraima), and s Gran Sabana (Santa Elena de Uairén) southward (*interior*); c Amazonas on Cerro Yapacana, lower Río Ventuari, and Río Asisa (*umbrosus*); s Amazonas near Río Casiquiare (*manacus*). Sw Colombia and w Ecuador; n and e Colombia s to ne Peru, n Bolivia, Amaz. Brazil, and the Guianas; isol. pops. in ne Argentina, e Paraguay, and se and coastal e Brazil.

Corapipo

Two small black-and-white spp.; allopatric; long silky white throat feathers; rather elaborate displays.

White-throated Manakin
PLATE 44

Corapipo gutturalis   Saltarín Gargantiblanco

Identification: 3.7″ (9.4cm). 8.3g. Tiny. Eyes and legs dark. ♂: glossy blue black above, deep black below; *throat and central chest white* extending to point on upper breast; inner webs of inner primaries white (hard to see even in flight), tail short; bill dusky, lower mandible whitish pink. ♀: above bright olive, below dingy white to grayish white, broad area across chest and sides smudged olive. Imm. ♂: like ♀ but throat and chest white; older birds may have blackish mask or blackish mottling above and below.

Sim. species: ♀ much paler (whitish) below than any ally; note dull legs and lack of yellow on belly.

Voice: Contact call (when foraging) a high, wiry, and bouncy *tseeu* or *tseeu, tseee* or *tseeu, tsee-tsee*, 1st or sometimes all notes slightly trilled; 1st note descends, rest higher pitched. Remarkably like call of Ruddy-tailed Flycatcher.

Behavior: Highly energetic, exceedingly quick, and often difficult to see. Found at low to mid. hts. inside forest, occas. with mixed-spp. flocks. Like most manakins, divides time between displays and brief visits to fruiting trees and shrubs. Display repertoire complex. Territorial ♂♂ display over large fallen logs in simple "exploded" lek (♂♂ well separated) with much visiting between ♂♂, or in "detached" or mobile leks with several ♂♂ at a log. In presence of ♀ a calling ♂ flies to log, lands facing away, jumps over ♀ and alights (again facing away) with popping wing snap, performs "wing-shiver" display as slides (rapid steps) backward toward ♀ which touches ♂'s wing to accept. ♂ then repeats ritualized flight display, drops to log, and jumps to waiting ♀. ♂♂ display to each other in less complex variation of above sequence but with white throat patch facing intruding ♂. Also a slow-wing "butterfly" flight toward log is reported. In favorable areas several leks may be situated only a few hundred meters apart[510,731]. In above-canopy flight display, ♂ flies with puffed throat, gives ca. 8 high *seeee* notes (in 9 sec) and wing snap at end[140].

Status and habitat: Uncommon to locally fairly common resident in humid hilly or foothill forest, occas. forest borders. Mainly hilly terrain and lower slopes of tepuis. Recs. spotty in Amazonas.

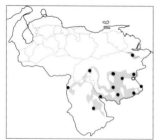

Range: 200–1100m. N Amazonas (Cerro Sipapo); nw Bolívar (Cerro El Negro) e through upper Río Caura, upper Río Paragua, and upper Río Cuyuní southward; nw Bolívar in Sierra de Imataca s locally to Brazil border. The Guianas and ne Brazil (e of Rio Negro).

White-ruffed Manakin

Corapipo leucorrhoa   Saltarín Buchiblanco

Identification: 3.8″ (9.7cm). 12.5g. Tiny. Dark eyes and legs. ♂: mainly glossy blue black; *throat white*, the feathers long, silky, and extending onto sides of neck to form large fan-shaped ruff. ♀: above pale olive green, *throat gray*, breast yellowish olive turning *pale yellow on belly*. Imm. ♂: like ad. ♀ but throat paler gray or mixed white; 2d-yr birds gain blackish mask and white throat.

Sim. species: ♀ from ♀ Golden-headed and ♀ White-crowned manakins by gray throat and yellowish belly; ♀ White-bearded Manakin is larger and has orange legs. ♀ Striped Manakin usually shows vague streaking below and pinkish on flanks.

Voice: Call a high, thin, insectlike *s-e-e-e-e-e-e*, slightly trilled (sounds blurred); in flight display a twangy *seet' t't'u-u-u.*

Behavior: Single birds, 2s, or small loose groups containing both sexes and imms. forage in forest mid. levels or lower. In C Amer. (*altera*) wander widely and migrate to higher els. during nonbreeding period. ♂♂ gather in small leks, usually near old fallen log around which displays are centered. ♂♂ alternately fly toward log in slow bouncing and fluttering flight with puffed out plumage and ruff spread (like bouncing black and white ball) or fly swiftly and directly at log as they give dull wing snap and sometimes a few shrill cries[644]. Displays of *leucorrhoa* (Venez.) presum. sim. Shallow cup nest suspended from fork in lower or mid. story of forest; 2 eggs, whitish heavily marked with brown[706].

Status and habitat: Very local resident. Humid to wet foothill forest, mature second growth, and small fruiting trees at borders.

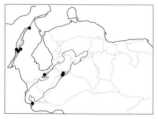

Range: To 1200m. Sierra de Perijá, Zulia, w slope of Andes in Mérida (Santa Elena); e slope in se Táchira (Cerro El Teteo) and nw Barinas in vicinity of Altamira (*leucorrhoa*). Se Honduras to n Colombia.

Chiroxiphia

Large; ♂♂ in Venez. share sim. black plumage with blue back and crimson cap; differ in length of central tail feathers; all have complex cooperative displays.

Lance-tailed Manakin
PLATE 44

Chiroxiphia lanceolata   Saltarín Cola de Lanza o Benitaro

Identification: 5.3″ (13.5cm). 17.5g. Legs orange (♂) or pale yellowish orange (♀). Two spiky central tail feathers project ca. 0.5″ (13mm) in ♂, less in ♀. ♂: *deep velvety black with glistening crimson central crown patch* (lengthened feathers project rearward forming short, flat, double-pointed crest); *back and* *shoulders bright sky blue.* ♀: olive above incl. wings and tail; underparts dingy grayish olive, paler on throat and tinged yellow on belly. Imm. ♂: olive like ♀ but with crimson crown patch.

Sim. species: ♂ much like next sp., but no known range overlap. ♀ is nearest ♀ White-bearded Manakin but larger, paler, longer tailed, and legs paler.

Voice: ♂♂ advertise with loud, whistled *toe-LEE-dough* ("Toledo"), *curry-ho,* and mellow *toe-curry-ho;* also a single mellow *kow;* nasal, gurgling snarl, *tuuuoo.* In full display a nasal, buzzy, and froglike *na-a-a-a-a-a-a* continuously. A local name, *Benitaro,* suggests main advertising call.

Behavior: This sp. is often hd. but can be frustratingly difficult to see displaying. Several ♂♂ gather in loosely assoc. groups in understory or lower mid. story during breeding season (cease activity in latter part of rainy season) and spend much of time calling, interrupted by short visits to nearby fruiting trees such as *Trema* and melastomes. Two, occas. 3, ♂♂ cooperate to perform display (unlike most spp. where ♂♂ are noncooperative rivals, e.g., *Pipra* and *Manacus*). Both ♂♂ take equal part in joint performance which is usually close to gd. and over a fallen log surrounded by dense cover. Displays incl. side-by-side calling, ♂♂ alternately jumping up and down, and short to-and-fro flights. Only dominant ♂ mates; subordinates may remain as apprentices for yrs. ♀♀ visit displaying ♂♂ to mate, otherwise lead quiet, inconspic. lives and undertake all nesting activities alone. Small shallow cup nest of fibers attached to low horizontal fork; 2 cream to brownish white eggs spotted reddish brown and lilac in wreath around larger end[238].

Status and habitat: Common resident in dry deciduous and moist semideciduous forest, dry secondary woodland, and overgrown areas around plantations.

Range: To ca. 1200m (once to 1700m). Base of Sierra de Perijá, Zulia, and nw Táchira (Ureña) n to ne Zulia (Mene Grande); nw Lara, c and e Falcón, Yaracuy, Portuguesa (Acarigua), and s Cojedes e across n Venez. to Sucre and n Monagas (Maturín). Isla Margarita (to 900m). Costa Rica to n Colombia.

Blue-backed Manakin
Chiroxiphia pareola   Saltarín Lomo Azul

Identification: 5" (12.7cm). 19g. *Legs orange* (♂) or *pale orange* (♀). ♂: much like Lance-tailed Manakin but *no projecting central tail feathers;* blue of back slightly darker, underparts slightly paler. ♀: very like ♀ Lance-tailed but tail normal; lower underparts strongly tinged yellow. Imm. ♂: olive with red cap.

Sim. species: ♂ not likely confused (no overlap with Lance-tailed Manakin). ♀ is nearest ♀ Black Manakin which is longer tailed and has dark (not yellowish orange) legs. ♀ White-bearded Manakin is smaller, chunky, and has bright orange legs.

Voice: Most vocal in rainy season. In ne Bolívar displaying ♂♂ advertise with rising whistled *queenk!* and clear whistled *wheet-weet!* Also give *clock-clock-clock* and nasal *naaaaaaa* (latter much like a vocalization of Lance-tailed Manakin).

Behavior: Overall much like Lance-tailed Manakin, and like it can be devilishly hard to see. Blue-backed's vocalizations are mostly unlike Lance-tailed's, but displays are rather sim. except that instead of alternate jumping, ♂ Blue-backeds perform a more elaborate and complex cartwheeling jump where dominant ♂ leaps backward over subordinate which simultaneously slides forward and, in turn, leaps backward over dominant bird, and so on, in dizzying but spectacular vortex of activity. This ♂-♂ cooperation (as opposed to competing rivals) and complexity of performance is one of most highly evolved displays in W Hemisphere[181,678]. ♀♀ approach dominant ♂ (of the two) to mate but otherwise lead solitary and inconspic. lives and perform all nesting activities. Subordinate "apprentice" ♂♂ may wait yrs to replace a dominate ♂.

Status and habitat: Fairly common resident very locally in dry deciduous forest, moist semideciduous forest, and bushy second growth. Not humid forest. Can be found locally in dry forests e of El Palmar and se of Tumeremo.

Range: To 500m. Ne Bolívar from near Ciudad Bolívar (Río Candelarita) and Sierra de Imataca s to lower Río Paraguay (La Paragua) and lower Río Cuyuní (*pareola*). S Colombia (base of Andes) to e Peru, Amaz. Brazil (mostly s of the Amazon), ne Brazil, and the Guianas; e Brazil. Tobago.

Note: Prob. more than 1 sp. Vocalizations differ across range.

Pipra, Dixiphia, and *Lepidothrix*

Tiny, short tailed, and fubsy; ad. ♂♂ usually boldly patterned, ♀♀ plain and olive; imm. ♂♂ resemble ♀♀ but soon acquire color on head, and eyes often paler; some display in leks, others alone; complex displays, usually well up in trees, may incl. vocal and mechanical sounds; as far as known, nest a small cup suspended from fork; nest attended only by ♀. Several spp. formerly placed in *Pipra* have recently been moved to separate genera *Dixiphia* and *Lepidothrix* based on syringeal anatomy[514].

Wire-tailed Manakin
PLATE 44

Pipra filicauda   Saltarín Cola de Hilo

Identification: 4.5″ (11.4cm). 15g. *Eyes white.* Legs dark. ♂: *crown, nape, and edge of mantle glistening scarlet*, rest of upperparts black, inner flight feathers with band of white (visible in flight), *forehead, sides of head, and underparts bright yellow*; bare shafts of inner tail feathers project as long wirelike filaments curving outward and downward at least 1.5″ (38mm) beyond tail (look carefully to see in field). ♀: uniform olive above, paler and more yellow olive below; throat palest, *belly light yellow; tail filaments as in ♂ but shorter.*

Sim. species: ♀ from allies by large size, *white eyes,* and *yellowish* belly. Tail filaments relatively easy to see if bird is close.

Voice: Advertising call, sometimes given only at long intervals, a nasal, descending, and attenuated *eeeeeeeu,* with peculiar hard quality; in display a *klok* or *kloop,* apparently with wings[587].

Behavior: Often rather quiet, and unless calling likely seen only at fruiting trees (esp. at *Ficus*) where sallies and hovers for berries. ♂♂ gather in groups and display in forest or woodland understory, but either sex may occur at almost any ht., incl. canopy, when feeding at fruiting trees. Leks often rather diffuse with ♂♂, or groups of ♂♂, some distance apart and each with several display perches; ♂♂ perform alone or with a ♂ partner. Mostly silent displays incl. lateral side-jumps or little slides forward and backward on branch; slow butterflylike flapping while perched or in flight and accompanied by a *klok* at end of swooping landing; also commonly a side-to-side pivoting (or about-face) with body feathers much erected, wings drooped, head low, and tail filaments raised, at which point bird looks like a little hedgehog! At height of display, ♂'s filaments tickle face of ♀[587] in rare example of tactile display.

Status and behavior: Local. Resident in low-lying or swampy gallery forest, tall second growth, light open woodland, and coffee and cacao plantations. S of Orinoco mainly várzea forest or low-lying areas. In all habitats usually not far from water.

Range: To 1000m n of Orinoco; to 300m s of Orinoco. Zulia (except arid n), w base of Andes from Táchira to ne Zulia (Mene Grande) and s Lara (Bucarito); e base from Táchira to nw Barinas; mts. of Yaracuy and n cordilleras from Carabobo to Distr. Federal and Miranda (no recs. in Falcón); llanos of w Apure (sight, Hato Cedral) through Portuguesa to s Cojedes (sightings); throughout w Amazonas (*filicauda*). N and e Colombia, e Ecuador, ne Peru, and adj. nw Brazil.

Crimson-hooded Manakin
PLATE 44

Pipra aureola   Saltarín Cabecianaranjado

Identification: 4.5″ (11.4cm). 16g. Mainly swamps of ne. *Eyes white* (both sexes). ♂: *head and mantle glistening red*, otherwise black above; band of white on inner remiges (visible in flight), *forehead, sides of head, and throat bright orange, throat feathers stained crimson, breast crimson,* belly mixed red and black, flanks black, thighs yellow. ♀: above uniform dull olive, *throat dull ochre,* breast mostly grayish olive faintly tinged yellowish ochre, center of belly dull ochre. Some ♀♀ (and imm. ♂♂) show a few flecks and stains of red and orange on underparts.

Sim. species: ♂ won't be confused. ♀ told by large size, white eyes, and dull ochre throat, sometimes by flecks of color on underparts. Cf. ♀ White-bearded Manakin and smaller ♀ Golden-headed Manakin.

Voice: Advertising call a nasal, penetrating *neeeeeer* (or *eeeeeeeuu*) that descends at end; usually answered immed. (like an echo) by a neighboring ♂, or ♂♂, and very sim. to that of Wire-tailed Manakin. In display a soft *eeer-teet.*

Behavior: Stylish ♂♂ gather with others in loosely assoc. leks in shady woodland interior where they spend most of yr advertising and displaying from little horizontal branches 2–5m up. Details of displays prob. resemble those of Wire-tailed Manakin but are not studied. ♂♂ often visit each other on display perches and may display to each other when ♀♀ are absent. Like Wire-tailed Manakin, will travel some distance through forest to feed at fruiting *Ficus* trees, or will visit isolated fruit trees outside forest. ♀ performs all nesting activities.

Status and habitat: Local resident in swamp forest and tangled low-lying forest or woodland near water; also in dry to moist semideciduous woodland in hilly areas, esp. with vine tangles and *Attalea* palms, but usually near swampy or poorly drained forest. Readily found on Finca Vuelta Larga (s of Guaraunos), se Sucre. In w Guyana occurs in higher el. but poorly drained forest at base of tepuis (M. B. Robbins); in Amapá, Brazil, also in white sandy "campina" forest (A. Whittaker).

Range: To 150m (at 1200m near Cerro Roraima). Se Sucre (lowlands w to El Pilar), e Monagas and Delta Amacuro; Bolívar near Cerro Roraima (*aureola*). Coastal regions of the Guianas e to mouth of the Amazon; along lower Amazon w to Manaus, Brazil.

Scarlet-horned Manakin
PLATE 44

Pipra cornuta   Saltarín Encopetado

Identification: 5" (12.7cm). 25g. Found only in tepuis. *Eyes white* (ad. ♂) or dark (♀ and imm.). Bill pale (♂) or *dark* (♀); legs pinkish to pale brownish orange. ♂: deep black with *glistening red head, feathers of rearcrown lengthened to form 2 prom. tufts which project diagonally outward and slightly upward* (not flattened rearward); thighs red. ♀: above dull olive tinged gray, rearcrown with slight tufts; underparts olive gray (paler than above), throat and belly vaguely tinged yellowish. In both sexes *tail proportionally longer than in others of genus*. Imm. ♂: like ♀ but bill paler.

Sim. species: ♀ dull and undistinguished. Note pale legs (usually), slight tuft on rearcrown, short wings, and longish tail. Cf. esp. Olive Manakin; also ♀ White-bearded Manakin.

Voice: Advertisement sound an abrupt crackling or rough-sounding *P'R'ROP!* (like electric bug-zapper) produced by *rapid* vibration of wings, this typically followed by short forward leap. Calls incl. a rather squeaky, metallic *squee-ke-Slick!* and audible bill-snap, latter apparently part of display repertoire; also a more abbreviated *ee'Slick!* and *Skip!*

Behavior: Groups of 3–20 or more ♂♂ form leks and display from traditional perches mostly 2–8m up, occas. much higher. Eat fruit, esp. melastome berries, which they take at any ht. Display at least Nov–Jun or Jul (yr-round?), but intensity and duration vary greatly (usually much activity Jan–Mar). Typically a ♂ performs 3–5 displays, then leaves dance perch for 10–15 sec before returning. In commonest display, a "sliding backward" display, ♂ abruptly jumps forward 6–10" (15–25cm) on perch and produces harsh crackling sound (usually), then seems to slide or "float" backward with steps too fast to see to starting point. This often repeated several times in rapid succession, or sometimes jump-slide sequence is reversed. In presence of ♀ a ♂ "slides" backward toward ♀ and twitches tail up and down, tickling side of ♀'s body in a show of élan[688]. Away from display arenas ♂♂ and ♀♀ sally and hover for berries (esp. melastomes) or sit quietly in lower levels of forest.

Status and habitat: Fairly common to common resident, but leks of ♂♂ often widely scattered. Humid and wet premontane forest and forest borders. ♂♂ often concentrate in leks in areas of dense old second growth or areas with abundance of slender saplings.

Range: 500–1800m. Throughout tepuis of Amazonas (Cerros Yavi and Sipapo s to Cerro de la Neblina); mts. from nw Bolívar (upper Río Cuchivero), Río Caura, and Sierra de Lema s to Uei-tepui. Adj. Guyana and n Brazil (Roraima).

Golden-headed Manakin
PLATE 44

Pipra erythrocephala   Saltarín Cabecidorado

Identification: 3.7" (9.4cm). 12.5g. Eyes white (ad. ♂) or gray to dark brown (♀ and imm.). *Bill yellowish to grayish white*; legs pale or flesh. ♂: jet black with *glistening golden yellow crown and nape*; thighs red (sometimes mixed white); red or white hard to see except in display. ♀: above plain olive, below paler olive gray turning yellowish white on belly. In hand outer primaries emarginate and very pointed (both sexes). Imm. ♂: like ♀, but older ones acquire pale eyes.

Sim. species: ♀'s best marks are pale bill and legs; ♀ also duller and dingier than ♀ Blue-crowned Manakin. ♀ White-crowned Manakin has contrasting gray crown, red eyes. ♀ *Coropipo* have dusky bills and legs, almost no yellow tinge on bellies. Other sim. ♀ manakins are larger or have orangish legs.

Voice: Displaying ♂♂ are noisy, uttering sharp, dry, chipping and trilling notes. Advertising call a clear *pu*; when more excited a trill and 1 or more final notes added, *pu-prrrrr-pt*, varied to *pir-pir-prrrrr-pt-pt!*[675].

Behavior: An endearing little performer, and not as hard to see as many allies. ♂♂ gather in permanent leks of 6–15, occas. many more, each ♂ occupying horizontal perches ca. 10–20m up, mostly in adj. trees, and display almost yr-round to attract attention of ♀♀. One common display is a sharp buzz accompanied by rapid backward slide along horizontal perch. In another dramatic display, so fast it is difficult to see, ♂♂ fly out 20–40m or so and return very fast in swooping S-shaped flight, giving accelerating ser. of buzzy *kew* notes and swooping up to display perch. Ads. are mostly frugivorous and visit a wide variety of fruiting trees, esp. Melastomataceae, from understory to canopy; berries plucked during short hover. ♀ builds thinly woven cup nest fastened to horizontal fork ca. 1–10m up; 2 pale greenish yellow eggs thickly spotted and streaked brown in wreath at large end[675].

Status and habitat: Resident in upper levels of humid forest and open second-growth woodland, and in fruiting trees and shrubs along forest borders. Also gallery forest in Gran Sabana. Uncommon and local in hilly terrain and lower mt. els. n of Orinoco; generally common to locally abundant s of Orinoco, esp. in sandy-belt forests of Amazonas.

Range: 100–1700m n of Orinoco; to 2000m s of Orinoco (mostly below 1000m in both regions). Sierra de Perijá, Zulia, w slope of Andes from Mérida (La Azu-

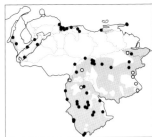

lita) to Trujillo (Betijoque), e slope from n Táchira to nw Barinas; n cordilleras from w Carabobo (Palmichal) to Distr. Federal and Miranda; w Sucre e through Paria Pen.; Delta Amacuro[343] and generally in Amazonas and Bolívar (*erythrocephala*). E Panama, n Colombia; e of Andes s to n Peru, Brazil n of the Amazon, and the Guianas. Trinidad.

White-crowned Manakin   PLATE 44
Dixiphia pipra   Saltarín Cabeciblanco
Identification: 3.8″ (9.7cm). 11.7g. *Eyes red* (brighter or more conspic. in ♀). ♂: deep black with *snow white crown and nape* (the feathers long and silky). ♀: *crown and sides of head gray contrasting with plain olive upperparts*; below pale dull gray, breast and sides tinged olive. Or above bright olive, underparts pale olive weakly tinged yellowish (*coracina*).
Sim. species: ♂ unique (but cf. ♂ Golden-crowned Manakin). ♀'s red eyes and contrasting gray head make her relatively easy to identify (for a ♀ manakin).
Voice: Advertising song a rather short, slightly buzzy trill, *jeeeeeeeeee*, given ca. twice a min from advertising perches 2–6m up.
Behavior: Typically ca. 4–12 territorial ♂♂ are well spaced within a dispersed lek, where they sit quietly, call occas., and are much more audible than visible to their nearest rivals which may be more than 100m away. The few displays are quick to-and-fro flights between perches, an about-face, a shallow S-curve swooping flight, and in presence of ♀, a slow, flapping, butterflylike flight[673]. ♀♀ and ♀-plumaged birds are usually seen at small fruiting trees in understory where they sally and hover for small berries and occas. assoc. briefly with understory mixed-spp. flocks.
Status and habitat: S of Orinoco a fairly common resident in lowlands and foothills, although visually seldom very numerous (mist-nets reveal its true numbers). Interior of tall humid forest, white sandy soil forest, and reg. in savanna tree isls. and palm-dominated várzea scrub in sandy soil areas. Very local in nw Venez. where found only in foothill and mt. regions.

Range: 800–1600m in nw Venez.; near sea level in Sucre; to 1100m s of Orinoco (to 1500m on Brazilian side of Cerro de la Neblina). Sierra de Perijá, Zulia; e base of Andes from se Táchira (Cerro El Teteo) to se Lara at Cabudare (*coracina*); se Sucre (Guanoco) to Delta Amacuro, and throughout Amazonas and Bolívar (*pipra*). Costa Rica to w Ecuador; e of Andes from Colombia to e Peru, Amaz. Brazil, and the Guianas; coastal e Brazil.

Note: Prob. more than 1 sp. Previously placed in genus *Pipra*. Taxonomy follows Prum[514].

Blue-crowned Manakin   PLATE 44
Lepidothrix coronata   Saltarín Corona Azul
Identification: 3.7″ (9.4cm). 9.4g. Chunky and short-tailed. ♂: deep black with *glistening azure blue crown and nape*. ♀: *above bright grassy green*, throat paler and tinged grayish, breast pale olive green turning *pale yellow on belly*. Imm. ♂: like ♀ but with blue crown, sometimes also with black mottling on body.
Sim. species: ♂ likely confused only with ♂ White-crowned Manakin which has more extensive white (not blue) crown continuing to nape. ♀ has *brightest and greenest* upperparts of any small manakin.
Voice: ♂'s often hd. advertising call, from horizontal display twigs 2–6m up, a low, slightly hoarse *tho-wiik . . . tho-wiik . . tho-wiik, tho-wiik*, slow and at same speed or accelerating slightly (quality of each phrase much like that of Dwarf Tyrant-Manakin). Also, at intervals, a soft trill, *treereereeree*, by both sexes and imms. Imm. ♂♂ may call from established perches.
Behavior: Not as noisy or conspic. as some *Pipra*. Displaying ♂♂ sing alone or gather in dispersed leks in forest interior with individuals in lek scattered over wide area. Call from a few slender advertising perches 2–6m up (occas. higher). Calling periods are interrupted by short visits to small understory fruiting trees where they quickly fill up on small berries. ♀♀ and imms. are freq. seen with mixed-spp. flocks in forest understory. Nest in Costa Rica a tiny, shallow fiber cup attached by rim to branch fork 0.5–2m up inside forest; 2 dull white to pale gray eggs, heavily mottled with brown or rufous brown, esp. in wreath[706].
Status and habitat: Locally common resident inside humid forest in lowlands and on lower slopes of tepuis.

Range: To 1200m. Generally in Amazonas; Bolívar from upper Río Cuchivero, lower Río Caura, lower Río Paragua, and Gran Sabana (Ptari-tepui) southward (*carbonata*). Costa Rica to w Ecuador (prob. a separate sp.); se Colombia to n Bolivia and w Amaz. Brazil (e to Rio Negro and Madeira).
Note: Previously placed in genus *Pipra*. Taxonomy follows Prum[514].

Orange-bellied Manakin   PLATE 44
Lepidothrix suavissima   Saltarín Frentiblanco
Identification: 3.6″ (9.1cm). 11g. Tiny. *Eyes dark*. ♂: unmistakable if seen well; velvety black with *snow white*

forehead and glistening azure blue rump (hard to see in field); large rounded patch of *deep chrome yellow on lower breast and belly partly divided by median black line*; flanks olive. ♀: forehead blue gray, *upperparts bright grassy green, crown and rump tinged bluish* (rump more emerald blue), below yellowish olive, paler on throat and turning *bright deep yellow on lower breast and belly*. Imm ♂: like ♀; older imms. show patches of black.
Sim. species: ♀ Blue-crowned Manakin, mainly at low els., lacks bluish tinge above and is not so contrasting yellow on belly. ♀ superficially recalls a ♀ euphonia (e.g., ♀ Plumbeous and White-lored) but smaller, thinner-billed, and with more contrasting underparts.
Voice: Primary advertising call, which is weak and not apt to attract much attention from human observers, is a short, nasal, slightly rising *aank*, much like a small frog or distant bark of small dog. ♂♂ also give rapid warbling or fluttery ser. of 7–8 piping notes that rise and fall in pitch and emphasis, i.e., *whee-pee-pee-pi-pi-pe-pee*, varied to quavering *wu WE WE wa we we wit* (on Sierra de Lema), sometimes accompanied by flashing out wings 1–2 times. Also may alternate *aank* call with short, slow trill, *pr'r'r'r* (like Short-crested Flycatcher). Countersinging ♂♂ give piping call[515].
Behavior: Both sexes are usually encountered singly during visits to small understory fruiting trees and shrubs where they quickly hover for a few berries and small fruits as do other small manakins, and then disappear. Often forage more actively when mixed-spp. flocks move through. Otherwise displaying ♂♂ are solitary and sit on isolated little perches 2–8m up. Some ♂♂ may be within hearing distance of other ♂♂ (exploded lek), but most (in Sierra de Lema) appear to be solitary. Although often sit quietly, ♂♂ seem perpetually poised for bursts of high-energy display.
Status and habitat: Locally a fairly common resident (easily overlooked) inside humid and wet forest and shrubby forest borders in foothills and lower slopes of tepuis; very locally also in hilly lowlands, e.g., Río Grande (250m) near Sierra de Imataca (sightings, 28–29 Mar 1981—R. Ridgely, K. Berlin, M. Kleinbaum; and 13 Feb 1993—Hilty) and at ca. 300m at base of Sierra de Lema (many observers).

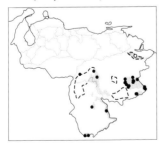

Range: 500–1800m (sight recs. to 250m). C Amazonas from Cerro Duida southward; locally in nw Bolívar (Pijiguaos; Cerro El Negro), ne Bolívar (sight, Sierra de Imataca), and generally on tepuis of se Bolívar (Auyán-tepui, Ptari-tepui, and Sierra de Lema southward). N Brazil; n Guyana.

Note: Usually placed in genus *Pipra.* Here considered a separate sp. from lowland White-fronted Manakin (*L. serena*) of the Guianas and ne Brazil[509,514,515]. Has been called Tepui Manakin[607].

Heterocercus

Four allopatric spp. (1 in Venez.); rather flycatcher-like; dark olive above, chestnut below; unusually long wings (esp. in ♂♂); gorget of long silky feathers; tail highly graduated, 2 outer prs. of feathers short and narrow, rest pointed and angular at tip (or tail forked and normal in some). Prob. related to *Pipra* (R. Prum); small cup nest suspended from low forked branch.

Yellow-crested Manakin   PLATE 44
Heterocercus flavivertex   Saltarín Gargantiplateado
Identification: 5.5″ (14cm). 22g. *Svelte and long tailed for a manakin.* ♂: above deep olive green with concealed orange yellow crown patch; sides of head dark gray, *throat silky white*, feathers lengthened and flared forming small tuft on each side of neck; *chest dark chestnut*, sides olive fading to pale chestnut on belly; tail rather short and forked. ♀: no crown patch, *throat gray, rest of underparts dull cinnamon buff.* Imm. or subad. ♂: like ♀ (but may be sexually active).
Sim. species: ♂ easily recognized. ♀ from other ♀ manakins by contrasting gray throat and larger size.
Voice: Perched ♂♂ utter a high, thin, and slightly trilled *t-t-t-t-t-t-t*; advertising call an explosive *speeeeeeeeEEEEEits-spit-cheeeeeeeeu* (rises, stutters or hiccups, then falls in pitch), often several times in succession; or sometimes just a short *speeeee* (abbreviated advertisement). In flight display, prob. directed at intruding ♂♂, a loud, angry *klee, klee, klee, . . . , . . .* (3–15 notes), chattery and dropping slightly in pitch with each note. Other less freq. hd. vocalizations are described[517].
Behavior: A quiet bird given to sudden bursts of energetic display and foraging. ♂♂ vigorously defend small, isolated, nonresourse-based territories by sitting alone at eye level or higher (2–5m up) on established display perches in fairly open forest understory. May remain silent, sitting erect and immobile for 5–10 min or more, then irrupt with loud, explosive advertisement call but scarcely a hint of body movement. Occas. fly off to fill up on fruit from small or large tree and return. Also reg. sally-glean for arthropods. Periodically undertake energetic flight displays as call loudly and fly rapidly through forest, prob. in aggressive pursuit of competitor ♂♂. Several courtship displays incl. a unique tail-shiver display where ♂ bends forward, flares gorget, raises and spreads tail, and quivers body and tail for a sec. ♂ also performs above-canopy flight display, and a flight display apparently accompanied by mechanical *whoosh* sound. When not engaged in display, usually seen alone in lower levels of forest, sometimes briefly with mixed-spp. flocks. In n Amazonas breeds Feb–May; 1 nest 2m up over water[517].
Status and habitat: Locally fairly common resident in low, scrubby, and damp woodland, stunted sandy soil várzea, and riparian and gallery forest. In all areas

mainly in dense, scrubby, and usually seasonally flooded and low-canopied forest or woodland on sandy or white sandy soils. Readily found in vicinity of Camani and Junglaven lodges in n Amazonas.

Range: To 300m. Extreme se Apure (Pto. Páez) and throughout w and c Amazonas. E Colombia and n Brazil (mainly Rio Negro).
Note: English name follows Ridgely and Tudor[545].

Tyranneutes

Genus with 2 drab spp.; ♂♂ widely scattered, sometimes a few within hearing of each other when calling; flycatcherlike, and relationship to other manakins uncertain; extremely short tail; wings pointed, primaries much longer than secondaries.

Dwarf Tyrant-Manakin   PLATE 44
Tyranneutes stolzmanni   Saltarín Enano
Identification: 3.3″ (8.4cm). 7.2g. Dingy and flycatcherlike. *Eyes gray to yellowish or orangish white.* Bill rather large. Upperparts uniform dull olive (no concealed coronal patch), throat and breast olive gray, breast slightly darker and obscurely smudged and streaked with yellowish white, belly clear pale yellow. When excited can raise *very short* frontal crest. Tail of ♂ quite short (22–29mm), tail of ♀ also short but slightly longer than that of ♂; sexes otherwise sim.
Sim. species: Looks like a tiny flycatcher or, like its name, a *tiny* manakin. This drab, featureless little bird is usually located by voice. Several ♀ or ♀-plumaged imm. ♂ manakins are dull olive and resemble it but are larger, most also dark eyed (older imm. ♂♂ of some spp. may be light eyed). Most small flycatchers, e.g., White-eyed Tody-Tyrant and Helmeted Pygmy-Tyrant, have wing markings. In e Bolívar see Tiny Tyrant-Manakin.
Voice: Advertising call (song) a simple, slightly hoarse *tjur-heet!* (or *du-veet!*), monotonously repeated every 5 sec or so. Recalls advertising call of Blue-crowned Manakin, but latter always given in a ser., not singly. Also, in s Peru, a short, nasal *new, nuw-nuw-nuw*, 1st note slightly higher.
Behavior: Inconspic. and seldom noticed unless calling, but notably vocal. ♂♂ are solitary, but sometimes 2–3 are stationed close enough to be within hearing distance of each other. Each calls tirelessly throughout most of day from a few favorite bare horizontal twigs 3–15m up that are always more or less in open mid. level part of a tree inside forest. Nevertheless, sit very still and can be difficult to spot. Usually feed alone, tak-

ing small fruits and berries at all hts., sometimes going high into canopy to feed. Display performed above forest canopy has been seen, but context is unknown.
Status and habitat: Fairly common to common resident by voice inside humid terra firme forest; occas. várzea forest. Very common in white sandy soil forests of Amazonas.

Range: To 300m. Throughout Amazonas; nw Bolívar from lower Río Caura and mid. Río Paragua (Cerro Guaiquinima) se to upper Río Caroní. Se Colombia to n Bolivia and Amaz. Brazil (not ne Brazil e of Rio Negro).

Tiny Tyrant-Manakin   PLATE 44
Tyranneutes virescens   Saltarín Aceituno
Identification: 3.2″ (8.1cm). 7g. Closely resembles Dwarf Tyrant-Manakin and about same size. *Eyes brown.* Above dull olive with concealed golden yellow coronal patch (smaller—♀), below much like Dwarf Tyrant-Manakin but belly paler, tail even shorter (18–24mm), tail of ♀ longer than that of ♂.
Sim. species: See Dwarf Tyrant-Manakin.
Voice: Advertising call, over and over at short intervals throughout day, a warbled, melancholy-sounding *weedle-de-dee* (or *Nicky the Greek* or *chuckle-de-dee*); much more vocal during drier 1st half of yr.
Behavior: Recalls Dwarf Tyrant-Manakin. A solitary little bird—a true "loner"—that spends most of day perched on open horizontal twig in slender tree. Rarely 2–4 ♂♂ are positioned within hearing distance of each other. ♂♂ sit from a little above eye level to forest mid. level and call almost continually (86% of day, or ca. 6000 calls/day!) during long breeding season. Almost all advertising is done from a few favorite twig perches in 2–3 nearby trees. Eat mostly fruit, but occas. sally up from song perch to foliage to hover-glean an insect. Displays incl. (1) slow floating flight between perches, or a short jump-float with fanning wings, yellow crest erected like coxcomb, legs dan-

gling, and body vertical, and (2) sideways peering display while perched[673].
Status and habitat: Uncommon and perhaps local resident (e Venez. is at extreme w edge of range) in humid terra firme forest incl. sandy soil forests. Found with some reg. near Río Grande, e Bolívar.
Range: To ca. 500m. E Bolívar from Sierra de Imataca (Río Grande) s to Auyán-tepui; extreme s Bolívar (hd. 25km w of El Pauji, 18 Feb 1990). The Guianas and ne Brazil (e of lower Rio Negro).

Neopelma

Small genus (only 1 sp. in Venez.); drab plumage; sexes sim.; ♂♂ display and sing alone, or 2–3 may be within earshot of each other; bill slightly hooked; prom. rictal bristles; closely allied to tyrant-flycatchers.

Saffron-crested Tyrant-Manakin   PLATE 44
Neopelma chrysocephalum   Saltarín Corona de Oro
Identification: 5.3″ (13.5cm). 16g. Flycatcherlike with slightly "hammer-headed" shape. Bill and tail rather long (compared to other manakins) eyes yellowish white to orangish. Above olive green, wings and tail tinged brownish (*no edgings*); crown and sides of head dusky olive gray; wide *semiconcealed golden yellow central crown stripe* forms slight flattish crest at rear of head (yellow usually visible but can be hard to see); sides of head and throat dull olive gray turning grayish olive on chest and *contrasting soft yellow on lower breast and belly*.
Sim. species: Much more likely to be mistaken for a flycatcher (which it prob. is) than a manakin. Note somewhat chunky shape, horizontal posture, up close orange to yellow eyes. Absence of wing bars separates it from many flycatchers, but see esp. Greenish and Forest elaenias, both of which show some pale wing edgings (Forest Elaenia has wing bars). Also see smaller Dwarf Tyrant-Manakin.
Voice: Loud, nasal song recalls an insect more than a bird; a twangy *jewee-jewEE-JEWEE-JEwee-jewee* with quality of Jew's harp or mouth bow, occas. shortened to 3–4 notes, i.e., *jeewie, jew nu-nu*; or (in aggressive challenge?) reversed to *buuu, jewy, jewy, jew*, followed by ser. of loud *squik!* notes for up to 1 min. Songs are often given persistently and at short intervals but are ventriloquial, and calling birds can be difficult to track down. Occas., when 2 ♂♂ sit together, a ser. of 20–30 short whistled *wheen!* notes, more if the two are countercalling. Also a sharp sneezing *kwip* 1–3 times in alarm.
Behavior: Solitary in lower, more open parts of scrubby or sandy soil woodland. Hover-gleans small fruits from understory trees and takes insects with short sally-strikes to foliage incl. hanging leaves. Simple displays are given by solitary ♂♂ with each ♂ well separated but prob. within hearing distance of another. Or sometimes 2 ♂♂ sit 1–2m apart and whistle at each other. ♂'s advertising display is a short upward jump with raised and spread crest as it gives twanging call. No special perch used; displays mostly from 3 to 20m up[142,673].

Status and habitat: Uncommon resident in white sandy soil forests and scrubby forest isls. mixed with savanna. Prob. more numerous than the few recs. suggest; sight recs. (with tape) e of Samariapo 16 Jun 1995 (Hilty) and at Junglaven[60] extend range across n Amazonas.

Range: To 700m. Locally throughout Amazonas (specimen recs. from Yavita-Pimichín southward); Bolívar from upper Río Caura (Río Carapo), mid. Paragua (Cerro Torono) and Río Caroní (Auyán-tepui) southward. Extreme e Colombia e to the Guianas and n Brazil.

Vireonidae: Vireos and Greenlets

Verderones, Chivíes

Members of this small New World family of 9-primaried oscines are best known for their dull plumage and repetitive songs which are often repeatedly endlessly. All vireos are arboreal and eat insects; some also are quite frugivorous, at least seasonally. Vireos live in forest or dry scrub and build open cup nests suspended by the rim from a branch fork. Except for the genus *Vireo*, they are nonmigratory.

Cyclarhis

Heavyset; heavy, hooked bill; rather sluggish; arboreal; hd. more than seen.

Rufous-browed Peppershrike   PLATE 55
Cyclarhis gujanensis   Sirirí
Identification: 6″ (15cm). 28g. Bull-headed with "shrikelike" bill; orange eyes and pinkish legs. Crown and nape gray, *forehead and broad eyebrow rufous*, rest of upperparts bright olive, cheeks and upper throat light gray, lower throat, chest, and sides bright greenish yellow (or bright yellow—*flavipectus*), rest of underparts pale gray to whitish. Or head darker and grayer; rufous eyebrow and forehead very narrow; overall darker (*gujanensis*).
Sim. species: Plumage recalls that of Green-backed Becard but ♂ of that sp. has black cap. ♀ becard has olive head (no rufous eyebrow); up close note peppershrike's eye and leg color.
Voice: Often hd. song is a good one to learn. Each bird sings at least 2–6 song variations[260], typically a rather hurried, semimusical, and whistled phrase of 5–7 notes, e.g., *Do you wash every week?*[644]. A popular Spanish rendition is *Hay viene forestero*.

Behavior: Hd. far more often than seen. Sings most of yr but sluggish, arboreal behavior and habit of staying in foliage make it hard to see. Reg. follows mixed-spp. flocks along forest edges, otherwise usually alone or in well-scattered prs. in upper levels of trees where takes moderately large arthropods, mostly from foliage. Thin-walled grass nest cup usually high; 2–3 pinkish white eggs spotted and blotched brown[175]; May nest, Orinoco region[115].

Status and habitat: Common and widespread resident n of Orinoco in dry to moist woodland and borders, scrubby or degraded areas, and around clearings with scattered trees; locally along humid forest borders following partial deforestation. Vagrant to 3000m (once, 14 Feb 1998, Hotel Los Frailes, Mérida—D. Ascanio). S of Orinoco in humid forest borders and locally in humid and wet premontane forest on slopes of tepuis (e.g., Sierra de Lema).

Range: To 1950m n of Orinoco (sight to 3000m); to 1600m s of Orinoco. E end of Paria Pen., Sucre (*flavipectus*); rest of Venez. s to n Amazonas, n Bolívar, and Delta Amacuro (*parvus*); s Amazonas and c and s Bolívar (*gujanensis*). Mexico to c Argentina. Trinidad.

Vireolanius

Much like *Cyclarhis* in shape and size; plumage mostly green and yellow; formerly placed in separate family; also sometimes placed in genus *Smaragdolanius*.

Yellow-browed Shrike-Vireo   PLATE 55
Vireolanius eximius   Sirirí Real Gorro Azul
Identification: 5.5″ (14cm). Rather chunky and short-tailed. *Bill heavy, strongly hooked.* Crown blue, *otherwise bright grass green above with long yellow eyestripe from nostrils to far behind eyes*; supraloral line dusky, spot below eyes and throat yellow, rest of underparts yellowish green. ♀: slightly duller; crown mixed green and blue.
Sim. species: Note *restricted* Venez. range. ♀ Green Honeycreeper is much slimmer and all green; Blue-naped Chlorophonia is smaller with much shorter bill.
Voice: Song in e Panama a 3- to 4-note whistled phrase, *peer-peer-peer*, often over and over throughout day[543].
Behavior: Unknown in Venez. Elsewhere a sluggish bird of high canopy foliage. Difficult to see. Reg. with mixed-spp. flocks.
Status and habitat: Prob. fairly common resident in foothills of Sierra de Perijá (many specimens from Barranquilla, Zulia) and in se Táchira (also a no. of specimens).

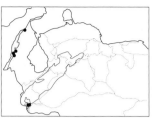

Range: 350–1250m (once to 1700m). E slope of Sierra de Perijá, Zulia, from Cerro Alto del Cedro southward; e Táchira (Burgua; Cerro El Teteo) at se base of Andes (*eximius*). E Panama and n Colombia.
Note: Perhaps only a subsp. of Green Shrike-Vireo (*V. pulchellus*) of C Amer.

Slaty-capped Shrike-Vireo   PLATE 55
Vireolanius leucotis   Sirirí Real Orejiblanco
Identification: 6″ (15cm). 25g. Rather chunky and short-tailed. *Bill heavy, strongly hooked. Eyes lime green*; legs gray. Crown dark gray, narrow yellow forehead and *long yellow eyestripe extend to nape*; sides of head dark gray with yellow spot below eye, broad white stripe across cheeks; narrow black malar line, otherwise above olive green; below bright chrome yellow turning greenish yellow on flanks and belly.
Sim. species: Strong facial pattern and lime green eyes impart fierce expression. Cf. Rufous-browed Peppershrike.
Voice: Song, often monotonously repeated while foraging, a high whistle, *eeear* or *deeear*, at rate of ca. 1/sec for up to several min without pause. Occas. a soft *whit* note. May sing for a long time then fall silent for prolonged period. Song much like that of Brown-headed and Tawny-crowned greenlets.
Behavior: Fierce countenance belies a rather modest life high amidst canopy foliage. Single birds or prs. are seldom seen except when with large canopy mixed-spp. flocks where they hop with moderate-paced movements through high outer foliage. Peer carefully at leaves, esp. undersides, and occas. hang from leaf, as they work steadily along outer branches. Take a variety of arthropods, esp. green caterpillers. Mostly stay well up in canopy, infreq. down to mid. level. They are tireless singers, but habit of remaining high in foliage makes them difficult to see.
Status and habitat: Uncommon to fairly common resident (need to know song) in canopy of humid and wet forest and along forest borders. More often seen in foothills and lower tepui slopes than in lowland forest areas.

Range: 200–1300m. N Amazonas s to Cerro Duida (prob. throughout); Bolívar in lower and mid. Río Caura, and generally from mid. Río Paragua (Cerro Guaiquinima) and Sierra de Imataca southward (*leucotis*). W Colombia and nw Ecuador; se Colombia to e Bolivia, Amaz. Brazil (mostly s of the Amazon), extreme e Brazil, and the Guianas.

Vireo

Dull plumaged; heavy bill; rather sluggish behavior; arboreal; attract attention with monotonous, often-repeated songs; majority are migratory at least in part; delicate cup nest suspended from high fork.

Red-eyed Vireo   PLATE 55
Vireo olivaceus   Julián Chiví Ojirrojo
Identification: 5.8″ (14.7cm). 15.5g. Eyes red (n migrants) or reddish brown (resident and austral migrants). Above dull olive green, *crown and nape gray*; *eyestripe white sharply bordered above by narrow black line and below by blackish streak through eyes*; underparts white to grayish white, crissum faintly tinged yellow (some individuals show little or no yellow). Or usually shows yellowish olive tinge on sides and flanks and *definite yellow tinge on crissum* (*vividior*). Or little or no tinge on flanks; yellow-tinged crissum mainly on freshly molted autumn and imm. birds (*olivaceus*).
Sim. species: Nearest is Yellow-green Vireo which has blurred (not crisp) facial pattern, brighter upperparts, more yellow on sides and flanks, and *contrasting yellowish crissum* (Red-eyed has little or no yellow). From Black-whiskered Vireo by lack of "whisker," but beware molting or wet Red-eyed which may appear to show faint whisker. In mts. cf. Brown-capped Vireo. In hand some red-eyed groups can be separated as follows: n migrant Red-eyed (*olivaceus*) has longest wing with outermost (9th) primary usually longer than 6th, and always longer than 5th; austral migrant Red-eyed (*chivi*) has outermost usually shorter than 5th, always shorter than 6th; Yellow-green Vireo is intermed., outermost usually shorter than 6th, sometimes equal to 6th, or occas. as short as 5th[827].
Voice: N Amer. breeders (*olivaceus*) and apparently also austral breeders (*chivi*) are silent and do not sing on wintering gds. and rarely in migration. Resident *vividior* songs recall those of N Amer. birds, but phrases are shorter and choppier, *hear me . . . see-me . . . che-ve . . .*, and so on in long "preachy" discourse. Also cf. song of Yellow-green Vireo.
Behavior: Single birds or prs. forage in deliberate, unhurried manner, peering in canopy or upper-level foliage, singing as they go and, in almost casual manner, pausing now and then to reach forward for caterpillar or other small prey. Despite seemingly insouciant manner, they usually keep on the move and are often with mixed-spp. flocks, esp. in lowland forest where they may forage high in canopy and emergent trees. Resident birds may eat some small berries; migrants reported (in Panama) to feed heavily on fruit. Nest a well-formed, thin fiber cup suspended from fork; 2 white eggs spotted blackish mostly at larger end.

Status and habitat: Common resident (many specimens; *vividior*) throughout in dry to humid forest, forest borders, and light woodland. Common transient and uncommon (?) to fairly common winter resident from the north (*olivaceus*), 3 Sep–12 Apr, with distinct increase in no. of recs. in Oct and Mar/early Apr (very fat transients in early Apr at Rancho Grande Biol. Station); Oct recs. are predom. from Andes through which many n temperate breeding migrants may pass on s migration. Recs. of *olivaceus* in general are mainly from w half of country. Uncommon (?) austral winter resident (*chivi*) Mar–Aug to forest and forest borders s of Orinoco. There is only small no. of specimens of *chivi* from Venez. Recorded (subsp.?) at Hato Masaguaral, Guárico, only Mar–Nov[734]. Seasonal movements and breeding areas or periods of residency of the various subspp. need furthur confirmation. Rec. from Islas Los Roques[347] may be N Amer. migrant. Highest rec. (prob. *olivaceus*) is a sighting from Los Frailes, Mérida[60].

Range: To 1900m (sight to 3000m). Throughout incl. Islas Margarita and Patos (resident *vividior*). To 1650m throughout (N Amer. breeding *olivaceus*); Islas Los Roques (subsp.?). S of Orinoco in Amazonas and Bolívar (austral breeding *chivi*). Breeds from N Amer. to n Argentina; N Amer. breeders winter s mostly into Amazon Basin; austral birds winter n into Amazon Basin and s Venezuela.
Note: *V. chivi* (Chivi Vireo) is sometimes considered a separate sp. Present taxonomy follows Johnson and Zink[282].

Yellow-green Vireo   PLATE 55
Vireo flavoviridis   Vireo Ventriamarillo
Identification: 5.8″ (14.7cm). 18g. Much like Red-eyed Vireo and *not always safely separated in field*. On typical individuals look for duller gray crown, little or no evident black lines bordering eyestripe, *brighter and more yellow olive upperparts*, and brighter and more extensive *yellow* on sides, flanks, and *under tail coverts*; also yellowish tinge on cheeks and sides of neck, and yellow (not dingy white) underwing coverts.
Sim. species: See Red-eyed Vireo.
Voice: Rarely sings on wintering gds. Songs (C Amer.) are sim. to those of n temperate breeding Red-eyed Vireo but shorter, less musical, and faster.
Behavior: Sim. to Red-eyed Vireo.
Status and habitat: Presently known only from 1 specimen but doubtless overlooked because of difficulty of separating this sp. from various subspp. of Red-eyed Vireo (difficult in field *and* in hand). Perhaps a rare

transient. Sightings, presumed this sp., from Aragua and elsewhere need confirmation.

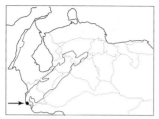

Range: S Táchira (once at Páramo de Tamá). Breeds in C Amer.[417] and possibly nw Colombia (Jan–Sep), spending nonbreeding season in nw S Amer. (mostly w and s of Venez.).

Black-whiskered Vireo   PLATE 55
Vireo altiloquus   Julián Chiví Bigotinegro
Identification: 6″ (15cm). 19g. Eyes dark red. Much like Red-eyed Vireo but with slightly longer, heavier bill and *narrow black malar streak* (variable). Overall duller and less distinctly patterned than Red-eyed Vireo. Crown dull gray, *only slightly contrasting* with dull olive back; dark red eyes; white eyestripe bordered above and below by narrow black line; underparts grayish white tinged yellow on sides, flanks, and over tail coverts. Or sim. but whiter below (*bonairensis*).
Sim. species: See under Red-eyed Vireo.
Voice: N migrants apparently do not sing on wintering gds. Resident offshore isl. birds sing typically 3-parted *whip, Tom-Kelly* recalling song of Red-eyed Vireo but faster and more clipped.
Behavior: Sim. to Red-eyed Vireo.
Status and habitat: Resident in dry to scrubby woodland on offshore isls.; vagrant or transient inland in small nos. from W Indies to moist and humid forest borders. N migrants (specimens) recorded 16 Sep–24 Oct and 5 Mar–19 Apr; sight recs. to 25 Apr at Hotel Los Frailes (3000m), Mérida (R. Ridgely). No overwinter recs.?; 1 captured (very fat) and 2 seen 19 Apr at Rancho Grande Biol. Station, Aragua[33].

Range: To 240m (offshore isls.); to 2000m (specimens on mainland); sight to 3000m. Breeds on Islas Los Roques and Margarita (*bonairensis*); migrant from W Indies to w half of country (mainly Andes) and s of Orinoco (*altiloquus*); once on upper Río Cuyuní (*barbatulus*). Breeds from s Florida and W Indies to Bonaire

and Curaçao. Scattered winter recs. to ne Peru, Amaz. Brazil, and the Guianas. Trinidad.

Brown-capped Vireo   PLATE 55
Vireo leucophrys   Julián Chiví de Gorro Marrón
Identification: 5″ (12.7cm). 12g. Lower mandible mostly pinkish. *Prom. black eyes* set off by pale sides of head. *Crown rich dark brown* contrasting with olive brown upperparts; prom. but slightly blurry *white eyebrow*; *throat whitish, rest of underparts clear light yellow*.
Sim. species: Only *Vireo* with distinctly *brown* cap; note conspic. "beady" black eyes, small size, and yellow underparts. Several greenlets (*Hylophilus*) have brown crowns, but all are smaller, thin-billed, and unlikely to overlap in range.
Voice: Both song and call much like that of allied Warbling Vireo (*V. gilvus*) of N Amer., although Brown-capped Vireo does not sing so persistently. Song a silky, rippling, and somewhat hurried little refrain, *here you sée me hear me sing so swéet*, all the notes run together and with emphatic rising inflection at end. Call a buzzy *zreeee*, sometimes 2–4 times.
Behavior: An unprepossessing little bird of mt. forests, more often a voice than a visible presence. Single birds or prs. are reg. members of upper-story or canopy mixed-spp. flocks where they actively glean small insects and caterpillers from foliage; occas. take small fruits. Seem to sing almost unconsciously, as if in a reverie, as they go along.
Status and habitat: Common resident in humid and wet forest, tall second growth, coffee plantations, and wooded borders.

Range: 700–2500m. Sierra de Perijá, Zulia; Andes from Táchira to Lara; mts. of Falcón (Sierra de San Luis) and Yaracuy, n cordilleras, and mts. of e Sucre and n Monagas (*mirandae*). Mts. from s Mexico to e Panama; Andes from Colombia to n Bolivia.
Note: Taxonomy follows AOU checklist[10], treating *leucophrys* as separate sp. from N Amer. breeding Warbling Vireo (*V. gilvus*). Songs and calls of the two are very sim.

Yellow-throated Vireo   PLATE 55
Vireo flavifrons   Vireo Gargantiamarillo
Identification: 5.5″ (14cm). 18g. Head and back yellowish olive with *bold yellow lores and eyering* ("spectacles"); rump gray, wings and tail dusky, *2 prom. white wing bars*; white edgings on inner flight feathers; throat and chest bright yellow sharply set off from white belly.

Sim. species: Note vireo's bold spectacles, wing bars, and clean-cut appearance. Wing-barred Manakin is duller; lacks vireo's yellow throat and chest and contrasting white lower underparts.

Voice: Occas. sings on wintering gds., giving brief versions of full song. Rich pleasing song composed of short 2- to 3-note phrases with distinct husky quality.

Behavior: Usually seen singly on wintering gds., either wandering alone or sometimes accompanying mixed-spp. flocks. Moves slowly and deliberately as hops and peers in foliage, mostly in upper levels of trees, occas. lower.

Status and habitat: Uncommon migrant and nonbreeding resident from N Amer., recorded 22 Nov–3 Mar (prob. occurs both earlier and later) to moist and humid forest borders, riparian woodland, old second growth, and coffee plantations. Several sight recs. augment range incl. birds seen 22 Dec 1980, Turiamo, Aragua (A. Altman); 5 Dec 1992, Rancho Grande, Aragua (P. Boesman); 5 Feb 1995 and 24 Feb 1996, Río Boconoito (100m), Portuguesa (Hilty).

Range: 800–1800m (sightings to 100m). Andes in s and n Táchira, w Mérida, sw Portuguesa (sight), and Lara; Coastal Cordillera in Aragua (sight) and Dist. Federal (sight); mts. of n Sucre (Cerro Papelón). Breeds in e N Amer.; winters in C Amer., a few to Colombia. Curaçao; Trinidad and Tobago.

Hylophilus

Small and warblerlike; rather slender, pointed bill; arboreal; many spp. freq. cling upside down from leaf tips when foraging. Three broad subgroups (with exceptions): Group 1: Generally have pale eyes; somewhat thicker, more conical bill; simple repetitive song; inhabit mostly scrub or forest edges, and mostly in prs. Incls. Scrub, Gray-chested, Lemon-chested, Ashyheaded, Brown-headed, and Tepui greenlets, although Tepui's song differs. Group 2: Usually have dark eyes; thinner, warblerlike bill; complex song; occur in forest canopy, sometimes in groups. Incls. Golden-fronted, Dusky-capped, Buff-cheeked, and Rufous-naped greenlets. Group 3: Tawny-crowned Greenlet of humid forest understory with song unlike any of above; eyes light or dark. *Hylophilus* prob. comprises more than 1 genus.

Scrub Greenlet   PLATE 55
Hylophilus flavipes   Verderón Patipálido
Identification: 4.5″ (11.4cm). 10.5g. Quintessential little brown bird. *Bill and legs pinkish; eyes white or dark*

(in w Venez. pale-eyed birds seem to predom.; in c and e regions dark-eyed birds predom.). Or eye color may be related to age (?). Above pale brownish olive (looks "faded"), flight feathers edged yellowish olive (no bars), below dull dirty white to grayish white, vaguely buff-tinged on breast; sometimes a hint of yellowish on flanks and under tail coverts. Or sim. but slightly brighter; throat whitish, chest tinged buff, underparts tinged yellowish (*acuticauda*). Imm.: dark eyes (always?).

Sim. species: Dull and lacking good marks. Note pinkish bill, faded appearance of plumage, and white eyes (if present). Dry scrubby habitat and distrib. (mostly n of Orinoco) eliminate most allies. Cf. Golden-fronted Greenlet which has brownish forecrown and is always yellower below.

Voice: Often hd. song a penetrating ser., *turee, turee, turee . . .* , of 4–20 or more notes (usually ca. 10 notes but avg. longer in s Venez.). Song speed varies (geographical or individual?). Nasal scold, *nyaa-nyaa-nyaa . . .* , sim. to many others of genus.

Behavior: A drab little thespian of mostly scrubby habitats. Single birds, prs., or families forage alone or sometimes assoc. with small mixed-spp. flocks that contain flycatchers and other insectivores. Mostly forage 2–8m up where move deliberately to fairly rapidly, gleaning small arthropod prey from foliage and reg. hanging upside down from leaf tips to inspect undersides of live leaves or curled dead leaves. Nest (Tobago) a deep cup of fine grass and other plant material suspended from fork a few meters up; 3 eggs, white lightly spotted with brown[175].

Status and habitat: Common resident in desert scrub, dry to moist forest (deciduous to semideciduous) borders, gallery forest, and esp. dry, degraded scrubby areas with regenerating trees.

Range: To 1200m n of Orinoco; to 500m s of Orinoco. W and s Maracaibo region, w base of Andes n to Mérida and e base n to w Barinas and w Portuguesa (*galbanus*); n Zulia e to Sucre, rest of Venez. n of Orinoco, n Bolívar along Orinoco (Caicara) and s to lower Río Paragua (La Paragua) and Río Cuyuní at El Dorado; Isla Margarita (*acuticauda*). Costa Rica to Colombia; Tobago.

Gray-chested Greenlet   PLATE 55
Hylophilus semicinereus   Verderón Cabeza Verde
Identification: 4.7″ (12cm). 13g. Bill dusky above, pinkish below; *eyes whitish to gray*. Above olive green, rearcrown grayish (not in strong contrast), *below gray* vaguely tinged brown; *sides of chest* (occas. most of

chest) *greenish yellow*, flanks and under tail coverts faintly tinged greenish yellow.

Sim. species: Another undistinguished greenlet. Best marks are pale eyes and more or less uniformly dull gray underparts. Look for olive yellow tinge on sides of chest. Cf. esp. Brown-headed and Buff-cheeked greenlets. Lemon-chested and Ashy-headed greenlets, both with broad yellow breast bands, doubtfully overlap in range.

Voice: Song recalls that of Scrub Greenlet; 1 slightly down-slurred note repeated 20 times or more, *peeer, peeer, peeer, peeer* . . . , ca. 1 note/sec.

Behavior: Much like other *Hylophilus*. Usually found with mixed-spp. flocks high in canopy, esp. in vines or along borders of forest, where stays mostly in outer foliage and searches leaves or hangs from leaf tips to glean small insects.

Status and habitat: Uncommon and possibly local resident (need to know voice) of humid forest, scrubby várzea, and tall second growth, esp. in sandy soil areas where forest is lower canopied or somewhat scrubby.

Range: To 350m. N Amazonas (San Fernando de Atabapo; sight/tape Junglaven) southward; c Bolívar along mid. Río Paragua (Cerro Guaiquinima) and its upper tributaries (*viridiceps*); prob. upper Río Caura. E Colombia (photo in Meta); nw, c, and e Amaz. Brazil, extreme ne Bolivia (PN Noel Kempff), and French Guiana.

Lemon-chested Greenlet   PLATE 55
Hylophilus thoracicus   Verderón Vientre Gris
Identification: 4.8″ (12.2cm). 12.5g. Bill dark above, pinkish below; legs pinkish gray; *eyes whitish to orangish yellow* (sometimes brown—juv.?). Rearcrown and nape gray contrasting somewhat with bright olive green upperparts; *broad greenish yellow pectoral band* sharply divides gray throat and lower underparts.

Sim. species: Very sim. Ashy-headed Greenlet has entirely gray head (often not too obvious in field) and more diffuse yellow underparts. If in doubt, note differences in song *and habitat*. Tepui Greenlet (mostly above range of Lemon-chested) has *gray* (not olive) wings. Also cf. Buff-cheeked Greenlet.

Voice: Song a bright, penetrating ser. of ca. 6–10 notes (ca. 3/sec) on same pitch, *chewee-chewee-chewee* . . . (or *reebe-reebe-reebe* . . .), sometimes growing louder as song progresses. May sing persistently for variable length of time.

Behavior: Single birds or prs. often follow mixed-spp. flocks, esp. along forest borders, but also forage independently of them. May occur in same canopy flocks

with allied Buff-cheeked Greenlet. Prs. are typically very territorial. Forage actively at mid. levels or higher in forest, and like many others of genus, often hang upside down from tips of leaves near outer edge of canopy.

Status and habitat: Locally fairly common resident in moist and humid forest, tall second growth, and wooded borders. Known only from terra firme forest in Venez.

Range: To 700m (sight/tape to 900m, Sierra de Lema). N Bolívar from lower and mid. Río Caura and Sierra de Imataca s to upper Río Cuyuní (*griseiventris*). Se Colombia, e Peru, n Bolivia, and s Amaz. Brazil e narrowly to extreme ne Brazil and the Guianas; se Brazil.

Ashy-headed Greenlet   PLATE 55
Hylophilus pectoralis   Verderón Cabecigris
Identification: 4.7″ (12cm). 11.5g. *Eyes dark* (pale orangish brown); legs grayish pink. *Top and sides of head and nape brownish gray*, rest of upperparts olive green, upper throat pale gray, *lower throat to mid. breast and sides and flanks greenish yellow*, center of lower underparts pale gray.

Sim. species: Much like Lemon-chested Greenlet but entire head and nape gray (not just nape), and yellow of underparts extensive, washing over entire breast and flanks (not a sharply defined band across chest). In tepui mts. see Tepui Greenlet.

Voice: In Suriname sings persistently, a brisk *churée-churée-churée* . . . , ca. 8–10 notes in 2–2.5 sec, much like song of Scrub Greenlet and usually with diagnostic slightly trilled note at end.

Behavior: In Suriname usually seen singly or in prs., and occas. with small mixed-spp. flocks along lighter woodland borders. Stays mostly in upper levels of trees, occas. down almost to eye level. Nest in Suriname a shallow, open, thin cup (eggs visible from below) suspended from fork; 2 eggs, white with small black blotches mostly at larger end; breeds late Dec–Jun in Suriname[253].

Status and habitat: Known from 1 specimen, 29 Jan 1965, from mangroves near mouth of Río Amacuro,

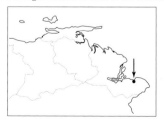

Delta Amacuro. In the Guianas relatively numerous in mangroves and on sandy coastal plain in open borders of moderately humid forest, light woodland, and areas with shrubs and scattered trees.
Range: Once at sea level in se Delta Amacuro. The Guianas and e Brazil s to nw Bolivia.

Brown-headed Greenlet   PLATE 55
Hylophilus brunneiceps   Verderón Cabecicastaño
Identification: 4.5″ (11.4cm). 9.6g. *Plain* and *confusing*. Bill dark above, pinkish below; *eyes gray to whitish* (or reddish brown in juv.?); legs flesh pink. *Head brown to slightly rufescent brown* in weak contrast with olive upperparts; flight feathers inconspic. edged yellowish, *below mainly gray* faintly tinged brownish on throat and chest; flanks and under tail coverts yellowish.
Sim. species: Learn song. This dull-plumaged bird is devoid of good field marks and easily confused. *Overall looks "grayer" below than any other greenlet* (e.g., Gray-chested Greenlet). Very sim. Dusky-capped Greenlet is dingier and browner above and yellowish (not gray) below. Buff-cheeked Greenlet, also very sim., has grayish crown, buffy facial area, and contrasting whitish belly.
Voice: Territorial song a loud, slow *seeeeaarn, seeeeaarn, seeeeaarn . . .* (or *peeeern, peeeern, peeeern, . . .*), each note inflected downward; given at rate of ca. 1 note/sec or less, and on same pitch (recalls song of Slaty-capped Shrike-Vireo). After playback a ser. of twitters, then 4–5 soft notes and a louder, descending *swe'swe'swe'swe'swe'swe'peer-peer-peer-PEEERN PEEERN PEEERN*[633]; when excited (agitated?) a faster, ringing *ree-ree-ree . . .* varying from 10 to 50 notes/song at ca. 3 notes/sec, over and over at short intervals, much like Scrub Greenlet's song.
Behavior: An active little bird that forages 5–12m up in leafy areas. Lives in prs. or families and is sometimes with mixed-spp. flocks. Takes small insects and caterpillars by habitually hanging upside down from leaf tips or clumps of leaves at ends of branches; occas. also sally-hovers to underside of leaves.
Status and habitat: Uncommon resident of savanna woodland and scrubby low-canopied forest in sandy soil blackwater areas, and borders of tall várzea forest and stream borders.

Range: To 200m (prob. higher). N Amazonas (Samariapo; sightings, Junglaven) s to Cerro de la Neblina and Sierra de Unturán (*brunneiceps*). E Colombia and adj. Rio Negro drainage of nw Brazil.

Tepui Greenlet   PLATE 55
Hylophilus sclateri   Verderón de los Tepuis
Identification: 4.7″ (12cm). Only in tepuis. Bill pinkish dusky above, pinkish below; legs gray; *eyes gray to white*. Entire head and cheeks gray, crown darker, lores buffy, *back olive green contrasting with gray wings and tail*; throat whitish, *chest yellow* (forms band) turning greenish yellow on sides and flanks, central lower underparts white. ♀: less distinct chest band. Chest band slightly darker yellow in birds from Amazonas. Juv.: eyes dark.
Sim. species: This is another greenlet with broad yellow pectoral band (see Lemon-chested and Ashy-headed) but occurs at higher els. From allies by contrasting gray wings and tail. Others more or less lack yellow pectoral band, i.e., Gray-chested, Brown-headed, and Buff-cheeked greenlets.
Voice: Song a short, clear, whistled *suuWEEEeeuu*, rising then falling quickly, often over and over; unlike any other in genus; also a nasal, downslurred scold.
Behavior: Prs. or several are reg. members of canopy or upper-level mixed-spp. flocks, esp. those that contain other spp. endemic to tepui region. Restless and active as forage mostly high in outer foliage, reg. peering at top of leaves and also often hanging upside down to outer leaves to glean small insects. May forage much lower along forest borders.
Status and habitat: Common resident in humid and wet montane forest and forest borders. Easily seen on Sierra de Lema where reg. occurs down to ca. 900m (lower than most tepui endemics).

Range: 600–2000m. Amazonas (Cerros Camani, Calentura, Sipapo, Duida, Parú, and de la Neblina); nw Bolívar (Cerro El Negro) and throughout tepuis of se Bolívar from Cerro Guaiquinima and Auyán-tepui southward. Adj. sw Guyana and n Brazil (Roraima).

Golden-fronted Greenlet   PLATE 55
Hylophilus aurantiifrons   Verderón Luisucho
Identification: 4.7″ (12cm). 9.1g. Bill dark above, pinkish below. *Beady black eyes*. Forehead cinnamon gold turning *light reddish brown on crown and nape*, rest of upperparts bright olive green, *sides of head and neck buff*, throat whitish, *breast and belly pale yellow*, chest washed buff, under tail coverts brighter yellow than chest. Or crown darker reddish brown, pale yellow below (*helvinus*).
Sim. species: Despite name, crown looks dull rufous to caramel brown (not golden). Generally lacks strong markings, but pale buff face contributes to conspic. *"black-eyed"* look. Told from Scrub Greenlet by dark eyes (but Scrub may have dark eyes, esp. in area of

overlap), brownish cap, and yellowish underparts. If
in doubt, note very different vocalizations.
Voice: Song, esp. during 1st half of yr, a short, quick,
semimusical *de-wichy-de-whéter*, often over and over;
recalls a N Amer. parulid.
Behavior: Travels in lively and chattery prs. or families
of 3–6, often with mixed-spp. flocks but also forages independently of them. Gleans and flutters actively in
mid. to upper levels of trees, and like many other *Hylophilus*, often hangs upside down from tips of outer
leaves to search for insects. Deep leaf-stem and grass
cup suspended from lateral fork or vine 1.6–10m up; 3
white eggs sparsely dotted brown, often parasitized by
Shiny Cowbird[175].
Status and habitat: Common resident in rather wide
variety of vegetation types incl. forest borders, gallery
forest, tall second growth, plantations, and occas. gardens in dry to humid zones. Generally in moister areas
than Scrub Greenlet (some overlap), but usually not inside tall humid or wet forest except in humid terra firme
and várzea forest of e Monagas (e.g., Caño Colorado)
where it is abundant and only *Hylophilus* present.

Range: To 1900m. W Maracaibo Basin, Zulia, e to w
base of Andes in Táchira and Mérida (*helvinus*); rest
of n Venez. e to Paria Pen., Sucre, and s to se Delta
Amacuro (Isla Burojoida) (*saturatus*). C Panama and
Colombia; Trinidad.

Dusky-capped Greenlet   PLATE 55
Hylophilus hypoxanthus   Verderón Gorra Fusca
Identification: 4.7″ (12cm). Bill dark above, pinkish
below. *Eyes dark. Crown and sides of head warm
brown*, back olive tinged brownish; wings and tail
olive, flight feathers inconspic. edged olive yellow, median throat whitish, *rest of underparts incl. under tail coverts clear pale yellow*; sides of head and chest washed
buff; from below tail rather yellowish (pale yellow
feather edges).
Sim. species: Only Amaz. greenlet with all-yellow underparts. Brown-headed (sim. in appearance) and
Gray-chested greenlets are mainly gray below; latter
also has white eyes.
Voice: Complex song (in ne Peru) a snappy 4-syllabled
whitchy-whEET-wEEu (last 2 notes strongly emphasized), varied to *pü-whitchy-wEEu*, the 2 songs often
more or less alternated by same singer. Song resembles that of Buff-cheeked Greenlet.
Behavior: Single birds or prs. are usually seen following mixed-spp. flocks from mid. levels to high in forest
canopy where they are very active and always on the

go. Sing constantly when foraging, and their lively
songs often will be first indication of presence of a
mixed-spp. flock nearby. Often hang upside down
from tip of outer leaves to glean small insects and
caterpillars.
Status and habitat: Resident in humid terra firme and
várzea forest. Known from only a few recs. (specimens
and sightings), but prob. fairly common. Easily overlooked (need to know song).

Range: To 200m (prob. higher). W Amazonas from San
Fernando de Atabapo s to confluence of Ríos Guainía
and Casiquiare (*hypoxanthus*). Se Colombia to n Bolivia and Amaz. Brazil.

Buff-cheeked Greenlet   PLATE 55
Hylophilus muscicapinus   Verderón Atrapamoscas
Identification: 4.7″ (12cm). 11g. *Dull and confusing*
and not as distinctive as its name might suggest. Bill
dark above, pinkish below; eyes brown (occas. gray?).
Crown and nape gray, rest of upperparts olive, *forehead and cheeks buff, this extending onto sides of neck
and as buff wash across chest*; throat whitish, lower underparts whitish, under tail coverts faintly tinged
yellow.
Sim. species: *Learn incessantly repeated song*, and
look for grayish crown and buff on face and chest
(hard to see as this bird is usually high in canopy).
Other greenlets in its range have yellow breast bands
(Ashy-headed, Lemon-chested, and Tepui) or are
more or less uniformly yellow below (Dusky-capped)
or gray below (Brown-headed).
Voice: Song a snappy, parulid-like *whitchy-ta-whEEu*
(or *split-your-Ear*), over and over. Most vocal Dec–May
in e Bolívar, with marked Jun–Jul drop-off in song activity.
Behavior: Prs. or little parties are persistent members
of canopy mixed-spp. flocks. Behavior sim. to other
dark-eyed *Hylophilus* that inhabit forest canopy. For-

age in high outer foliage and often hang upside down from tips of leaves to inspect undersurfaces for insects. Loud song is often first indication of presence of a canopy mixed-spp. flock approaching. In tall lowland forest of e Bolívar may occur in mixed-spp. flocks with Lemon-chested Greenlet; on slopes of tepuis occurs with Tepui Greenlet.

Status and habitat: Common resident in humid terra firme and várzea forest in lowlands and foothills. Less numerous in tall moist forest (e.g., near lower Río Cuyuní). Easily overlooked except for song.

Range: To 1100m. Forested areas throughout Amazonas and Bolívar (*muscicapinus*). The Guianas and ne and e Amaz. Brazil.

Rufous-naped Greenlet   PLATE 55
Hylophilus semibrunneus   Verderón Gorro Castaño
Identification: 4.7″ (12cm). 11.4g. Bill dark above, flesh pink below, a bit heavier than others of genus. *Eyes brown. Crown, nape, and rear cheeks dark rufous* contrasting with olive green upperparts (mantle tinged reddish brown), *lores, facial area, and cheeks grayish white*, throat white, rest of underparts yellowish white, *chest and sides of neck tinged cinnamon* (forms diffuse cinnamon pectoral band), under tail coverts clear pale yellow.

Sim. species: Confusion most likely with Golden-fronted Greenlet which *lacks* strong rufous crown and has more uniform underparts (no cinnamon pectoral band). Also see Scrub Greenlet which is much paler.

Voice: In Colombia, weak song a fast, complex *wa-chee-ra-dit'it*, rising somewhat in pitch.

Behavior: Like other dark-eyed *Hylophilus*. In Colombia forages actively in leaves in forest mid. levels or subcanopy and is often with mixed-spp. flocks. Likes to hang upside down from leaf tips to glean insects.

Status and habitat: Humid montane forest and forest borders. There are numerous specimens, esp. from ne end of Sierra de Perijá.

Range: 450–2000m. Sierra de Perijá, Zulia (Cerro Alto del Cedro to upper Río Negro drainage at Barranquilla and Cerro Mashirampé). Colombia and n Ecuador.

Tawny-crowned Greenlet   PLATE 55
Hylophilus ochraceiceps   Verderón Frente Rufa
Identification: 4.5″ (11.4cm). 10.5g. Eyes pale or brown (*ferrugineifrons*) or brown (*luteifrons*). *Forehead tawny rufous* changing to rufous on crown and brownish olive on nape and rest of upperparts; wings and esp. *tail tinged brownish yellow*; throat dull whitish, rest of underparts dingy yellowish gray, breast and sides vaguely streaked with wash of olive. Or *forehead*

dull buffy yellow, crown tinged olive and *not* strongly contrasting with back; underparts slightly buffier (*luteifrons*).

Sim. species: Dingy and easily confused but almost invariably noted first by distinctive vocalizations. Crown not always tawny (despite name), but look for *some contrast* between forecrown (whether dark tawny or yellowish tinged) and back. Other greenlets with which it could be confused (e.g., Brown-headed, Buff-cheeked, Dusky-capped) occur in canopy, not understory. Cf. ♀ Plain Antvireo which has white eyering, more contrasting rufous crown, faint wing bars, heavier hooked bill, and very different behavior. Several ♀ antwrens (*Myrmotherula*) are superficially sim. but lack contrasting forehead and have heavier bills.

Voice: Song a penetrating and ventriloquial whistle, *teeeeeeuuuu* (often sounds somewhat 2-parted, and last part may descend slightly), repeated over and over ca. once every 2.5 sec. Recalls song of Slaty-capped Shrike-Vireo but slower, and of Collared Gnatwren. Often gives nasal scolding *naaa*, a good clue.

Behavior: Single birds or prs. reg. forage in lower strata *inside* forest, most often with mixed-spp. flocks that contain ant-tanagers, antshrikes, and antwrens, but also occas. independent of them. Like others of genus, active and often hangs upside down from tips of live leaves to look for small arthropod prey. Sings freq., but high-pitched song is difficult to track down. In Costa Rica, nest a sturdy fiber cup partly covered with moss; suspended from horizontal fork 2–7m up; 2 eggs[633].

Status and habitat: Fairly common resident (easily overlooked) in lower levels inside humid terra firme and transitional forest in lowlands. Rare or absent in scrubby sandy belt forests.

Range: To 1600m. Generally in Amazonas; Bolívar from lower Río Caura, upper Río Paragua, Auyán-tepui, and upper Río Cuyuní (Sierra de Lema) s to s Gran Sabana (*ferrugineifrons*); ne Bolívar in region of Sierra de Imataca and at Cerro Roraima (*luteifrons*). Se Mexico to w Ecuador; se Colombia to n Bolivia, Amaz. Brazil, and the Guianas.

Note: Birds of C Amer. may be a separate sp.

Corvidae: Jays

Urracas, Querrequerres

Members of this family are found virtually worldwide but reach their greatest diversity in north temperate regions. No typical crows (*Corvus*) occur south of Nicaragua. Jays, by contrast, occur widely across South America, but there are only a few species and they compose a relatively insignificant component of the overall avifauna. Both groups are a veritable rogues' gallery of winged opportunists, renown for their clever behavior and intelligence. Tropical jays are arboreal and essentially omnivores. Most wander in groups at various heights through open woodland or along forest borders. As far as known they build large, twiggy, cup nests in shrubs or trees. The habits and nesting behavior of jays in Venezuela are poorly known, but elsewhere jays have proved to be fascinating subjects with complex social organization. For worldwide coverage see Madge and Burn[372].

Black-collared Jay

PLATE 23

Cyanolyca armillata   Urraca o Urraca Negricollareja
Identification: 12.5″ (32cm). 100g. Slender and long-tailed. Andes. Mostly intense deep blue (or deep purplish blue—*meridana*), crown and nape milky blue, *forehead and mask through eyes velvety black continuing down sides of neck as narrow black band and black collar beneath throat*; throat bright royal blue, underside of wings black, underside of long tail black.
Sim. species: Only "blue" jay in Venez. Andes. Often looks blackish, esp. in poor light.
Voice: Fine, large repertoire of clicks, smacks, guttural notes, and "falsetto" sounds, some loud, others soft. A call may be repeated several times or interspersed with others as if at random, sometimes with considerable pause between sounds. Examples include *grr . . . EEp . . . gurr . . . smack-smack-smack-smack*; also *jeet!, skeet!*, mushy *chaak!* and loud piercing *eek!-eek!-EEK!* varied to *chzak-eek!*, and metallic *tnk! tnk!* as travel through forest.
Behavior: Prs. or varying-sized groups travel alone, sometimes quietly, at other times calling noisily. May assoc. with mixed-spp. flocks, esp. those with larger spp. such as caciques, Hooded Mountain-Tanagers, and Crimson-mantled Woodpeckers, and typically range over large areas. Stay mostly in higher part of trees where they pause to peer carefully and then, with a few large bounding hops, move quickly up through trees. Although curious, can be sly and adept at keeping out of sight.
Status and habitat: Uncommon resident of tall humid and wet upper montane forest and stunted or dwarf forest close to treeline. Found with some reg. above ca. 2200m in PN Guaramacal, Trujillo, but easily overlooked unless calling.

Range: 1600–3200m. Andes of s Táchira (*armillata*); Andes of n Táchira, Mérida, and Trujillo (*meridana*). Colombia s in Andes to n Ecuador.

Note: Black-collared birds of Venez. to n Ecuador (*armillata*) formerly united with white-collared birds (*viridicyana*) of Peru and Bolivia.

Cyanocorax

Large, robust, and boldly patterned; usually with much white in plumage; prom. bristlelike feathers on forehead; noisy, social, and remain together, prob. in related groups; mainly in lowlands.

Violaceous Jay

PLATE 23

Cyanocorax violaceus   Corobero
Identification: 14″ (36cm). 260g. Slight crest. *Eyes dark. Usually looks dull in field. Head, throat, and chest black*, nape milky blue white turning dull powdery to smoky violet blue on rest of plumage; *wings and tail uniform dark purplish blue*, underwings black.
Sim. species: Looks much like rare Azure-naped Jay, but that sp. has most of crown whitish, narrow white tail tips, white crissum, and faded, "washed out" appearance; up close also note *yellow eyes*. Azure-naped also has browner upperparts and duller underparts, but this not always obvious in field. Cayenne Jay is mostly white below.
Voice: Bounces up and down and screams a loud, raspy *PEEOUGH!* and *JEEeer!*, both calls falling in pitch, often over and over; also a loud, flat *clop-clop-clop-clop* and variety of other odd sounds.
Behavior: Troops about in rather noisy, seemingly undisciplined groups of its own, up to 12 or more that tend to stay on the move and wander over large areas. Stay mainly in canopy, and like most jays, are curious but can be stealthy and inconspic., and sometimes difficult to see well. Mob readily and are great opportunists, taking fruit, small vertebrates, arthropods, and eggs. Bulky nest, Apr, Orinoco area; 9m up; 5 bluish white eggs thickly speckled shades of brown[115].
Status and habitat: Uncommon to locally fairly common resident in dry to humid forest borders, gallery forest, savanna woodland, and along riverbanks s of Orinoco; degraded dry woodland and xerophytic scrub in n Anzoátegui. Does not penetrate much inside terra firme forest. Uncommon along e base of Andes and in e llanos. Few recs. in extreme s Amazonas.

Range: To 400m (sight to 500m, nw Barinas). E base of Andes from Táchira and w Apure n to Portuguesa (Guanare); locally through Guárico to s Anzoátegui; throughout Amazonas; nw Bolívar from Río Cuchivero and lower and mid. Río Caura e to Río Paragua (*violaceus*); sightings in Sierra de Imataca (subsp.?); n and ne Anzoátegui at Barcelona and Píritu (*pallidus*). E Colombia s to n Bolivia, w Amaz. Brazil, and sw Guyana.

Azure-naped Jay
Cyanocorax heilprini   Piarro Nuca Celeste
Identification: 14″ (36cm). *Eyes yellowish white. Forecrown, sides of head, throat, and chest black*, forecrown feathers bushy and dense forming short frontal crest; *midcrown to nape milky blue* white; short pale blue malar stripe (inconspic.), back, wings, and tail faded dull brownish violet, *tail with relatively narrow white tip*; rest of underparts dull dark violet blue, *center of belly and crissum white*.
Sim. species: Easily confused with common and widespread Violaceous Jay (see). Best marks are yellow eyes, whitish crown, and white tail tips. Note faded, "washed out" appearance.
Voice: Scolds and mobs with great variety of calls incl. nasal, honking *duk-duk*; harsh, descending *JEEoop*; smooth, abrupt *keop*; liquid *puk*; rapid *je-je-je*; and staccato clicking (K. Zimmer recording). Vocalizations generally resemble those of Cayenne Jay. Lacks harsh descending call of Violaceous Jay.
Behavior: Little known. As in other *Cyanocorax*, groups wander widely.
Status and habitat: Very local resident of sandy-belt forest edges, second growth, and light savanna woodland. Known from only a small no. of specimens.

Range: To 200m. W Amazonas from Samariapo, mouth of Río Ventuari (sight), and Pto. Yapacana s to Yavita-Pimichín and San Carlos de Río Negro. E Colombia and adj. nw Brazil.

Black-chested Jay   PLATE 23
Cyanocorax affinis   Urraca Cosquiol
Identification: 14″ (36cm). 210g. *Eyes yellow* (ad.). *Head, throat, and chest black*, feathers of forecrown dense and stiff; small spot of royal blue above and below eyes; short inconspic. blue malar mark; back dull brownish violet, wings and tail more dusky violet blue, *lower breast, belly, and broad tail tips white*. Imm.: black foreparts replaced by brown; eyes dark.
Sim. species: Overlaps (minimally) only with very different Inca Jay. In e Venez. see Cayenne Jay.
Voice: Commonest call a loud *kyoop!*, often doubled; a reedy, rising *wreenk!* and various guttural clicks and rattles.
Behavior: Usually in groups of 3–8, occas. more, that are active as they roam over large areas. As with many jays, tend to move unobtrusively and stealthily from tree to tree, often keeping rather low, typically a few

flaps and a glide, but occas. loud contact calls are apt to betray their presence. Quick to mob, and opportunistic when foraging, ranging from near gd. (occas. dropping to gd.) to well up in trees. Nest a bowl of coarse sticks with fine twig lining, in branch fork; 11 nests, Apr–May, n Colombia; 3–5 eggs, pale buff or brownish white heavily spotted and blotched olive brown[750].
Status and habitat: Uncommon to locally fairly common resident in dry to moist forest, riparian woodland, bushy pastures with scattered trees, and scrubby regrowth and cut-over areas; locally along borders of humid woodland. In n Falcón primarily in low, moist semideciduous woodland on hills 150–300m or so above sea level (not in sea level arid scrub); readily found in e foothills of Sierra de San Luis.

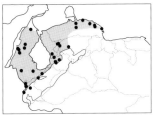

Range: To 1700m. Sierra de Perijá, Zulia, locally in Maracaibo Basin, w base of Andes from Táchira and Mérida to Trujillo, w and n Lara, and c and e Falcón e to Boca del Tocuyo (*affinis*). Costa Rica to Colombia.

Cayenne Jay   PLATE 23
Cyanocorax cayanus   Piarro Nuca Blanca
Identification: 13.5″ (34cm). 175g. *Eyes icy blue white.* Most of head, throat, and chest black, feathers of forecrown stiff and dense; spot of azure blue above and below eyes; short triangular blue-white malar mark; *hindcrown, nape, and underparts white*, back brownish violet, wings and tail dull dusky violet blue, *tail broadly tipped white*.
Sim. species: Extensive white in plumage is diagnostic. Violaceous Jay, which only partially overlaps it in range, looks drab and uniform by comparison.
Voice: A variety of vocalizations; commonest is a loud *keep! Yop!* or either note separately, also a loud, downslurred *KEEOOP!*, ringing *kup-kup-kup* (sometimes only 2 notes), and harsh *kriit!*
Behavior: Families or groups of up to 12 or more range widely, with members slipping silently, almost stealthily, through mid. or lower levels of forest, at other times straggling along while calling noisily. Groups mob

readily. Breeding is cooperative (ads. have 1–3 helpers), and members become quiet and secretive when nesting; large stick nest, 2–5m up, often in isolated tree apart from forest, i.e., citrus trees near human dwellings; up to 4 eggs; breed Jan–Mar, e Bolívar.
Status and habitat: Fairly common to common (somewhat local) resident in humid and wet lowland forest, along forest borders, and in clearings with scattered trees.
Range: To 1100m. N and e Bolívar from lower Río Caura, lower and mid. Río Paragua (s to Cerro Guaiquinima), lower Río Caroní (Pt. Ordaz), and Sierra de Imataca s to upper Río Cuyuní and s end of Gran Sabana at Parai-tepui; s Delta Amacuro. The Guianas and ne Brazil.

Inca Jay   PLATE 23
Cyanocorax yncas   Querrequerre
Identification: 12″ (30.5cm). 84g. *Unmistakable "green and yellow" jay of n mts.* Eyes yellow. Plushy velvet-blue forecrown feathers form short crest; midcrown white, hindcrown blue, *most of sides of head, and throat and chest black*, small blue spot over eye; large blue malar stripe, *otherwise green above and yellow below, outer 4 prs. of tail feathers yellow* (conspic. in flight); tail graduated.
Sim. species: Nothing like it. Generally not found with Black-collared Jay.
Voice: Noisy. Commonest call a rather high, nasal *quin-quin-quin* or *quin-gun-gun*; has a wide variety of other vocalizations incl. *clee-op* (often trebled); dry, ticking *jeer*; glottal *T'dle, T'dle*; lip-smacking notes; etc.
Behavior: Active groups of 3–9, occas. more, roam over large permanent territories, often crossing gaps or flying single file from tree to tree. Usually fairly conspicuous and noisy but quieter when foraging and become very quiet and secretive when nesting. Range from high to low in trees where take a wide variety of arthropods, small vertebrates, and occas. fruit. Nest in Colombia a shallow, loosely woven basket 4–10m up; 4 bluish white eggs densely blotched brownish; each flock has a dominant breeding pr. and 1 or more helpers[6].
Status and habitat: Uncommon to locally common resident in humid montane forest and esp. tall open second growth, wooded borders, and coffee plantations. Generally most numerous in wooded hill or mt. areas with considerable habitat disturbance; local and erratic in lowlands. Seasonal or local el. movements (i.e., in Coastal Cordillera) need documentation.

Range: Mostly 200–2800m (occas. to sea level). Sierra de Perijá, Zulia; Andes from s Táchira to s Lara (*andico-*

lus); mts. of nw Lara, Falcón (Sierra de San Luis), and Yaracuy e through n cordilleras to Sucre and n Monagas (Caripe); locally in llanos of n Guárico and Anzoátegui (*guatimalensis*). Andes from Colombia to Bolivia.
Note: Previously called Green Jay[403], a name now applied to C Amer. birds. Subsp. *cyanodorsalis* replaced by *andicolus*[489].

Hirundinidae: Martins and Swallows
Golondrinas

Swallows and martins share a long and affectionate relationship with humans. Virtually worldwide in distribution, they have lived in close proximity to people since recorded history. Characterized by streamlined bodies, long, pointed wings, and wide gapes, they are graceful and accomplished in flight and spend much of their lives in the air. Unlike in swifts, the flight of swallows is buoyant and maneuverable, and they frequently perch on wires, branches, or roofs. Resident and north temperate breeding migrants occur in Venezuela, and it is possible that a few austral breeders also reach Venezuela. Most members of this family are gregarious at least seasonally, and some gather in large roosting and feeding flocks. Nests of resident species are usually placed in cavities or holes, and unlike north temperate breeding species they seldom use artificial nest boxes. The taxonomic limits of several genera are poorly defined. Worldwide coverage of the family can be found in a recent publication[763].

Progne

Large with fairly long, slightly forked tail; sexes alike or different; rather gregarious; taxonomy of some groups unclear and identification difficult; here incls. *Phaeoprogne*[598] which differs in brown plumage and solitary nesting habits.

Brown-chested Martin   PLATE 52
Progne tapera   Golondrina de Río
Identification: 7″ (18cm). 32g (*tapera*). *Above light brown*, wings and tail darker (up close, feathers slightly pale-edged), throat dirty white, merging into smudgy *grayish brown chest band*; lower breast and belly white, *under tail coverts snowy white, the feathers long, often conspic. fluffed, and visible on either side of tail from above* (resident subsp. *tapera*). Or *larger*, 7.5″ (19cm), throat pure white, chest band darker, more sharply demarcated and with *irreg. vertical line of droplike brown spots down center of chest* (austral migrant *fusca*).
Sim. species: Easily confused with both Bank and Rough-winged swallows, although both are smaller and latter also lacks chest band. Size difference is usually apparent. If in doubt, *look for martin's diagnostic protruding white under tail coverts.* Also beware various imm. martins and swallows, almost all of which show some blue-green in plumage.
Voice: Calls and rich gurgling song (resident *tapera*) much like that of Purple Martin, e.g., *jureee'e't, rejur'r'r, wee-chup-jure'e'e'e'e* . . . and so on (*jure'e'e*

rises, *rejur'r'r* falls); also a rough, buzzy *j'jrt-j'jrt-j'jrt-j'jrt* and many other notes.

Behavior: Resident birds scatter over open terrain and nest singly in stubs or cavities. Flight is easy and graceful, and foraging is rather low, almost never high; often seen resting on fence wires, little stubs, bushes, driftwood piles, or snags. Austral migrants typically spend much time resting or loafing in large flocks of 100s to 1000s. Prs. nest solitarily in holes in stubs, etc., sometimes around water. In parts of range (Venez.?) make use of old hornero (*Furnaris*) nests and cavities in termite nests; 1 nest in May, w Apure[525].

Status and habitat: Breeding resident and nonbreeding austral winter resident to clearings and all kinds of open or semiopen areas incl. riverbanks, sandbars, savanna with scattered trees, and around habitations. Both subspp. fond of water and often forage low over rivers. Resident (*tapera*) breeds in small nos. but is not numerous. Austral migrant (*fusca*), rec. 30 Mar–7 Oct, is widespread in lowlands (seen as high as 1900m, La Mucuy, Mérida, May 1996—R. Ridgely); spotty in occurrence n of Orinoco but many recs. of large flocks in n cordilleras; up to 1000 or more seen late each evening migrating n over Portachuelo Pass, Aragua, 28 Jul–31 Aug with minimum of 17,000 during the month[33]; locally abundant s of Orinoco with large concentrations (100s to 1000s) massing on electric wires, bare trees at edges of savanna, and on river isls. in nw Amazonas.

Range: To 1000m (*tapera*); to 400m, sight to 1900m (*fusca*). Locally throughout (*tapera*); prob. throughout but no recs. from Sucre, Delta Amacuro, and Bolívar (*fusca*). Colombia and the Guianas s to c Argentina. Panama (*fusca*); Trinidad.

Note: Formerly placed in genus *Phaeoprogne*. Resident and migrant forms may be separate spp.

Gray-breasted Martin
PLATE 52
Progne chalybea   Golondrina Urbana

Identification: 7″ (18cm). 39g. ♂: *upperparts glossy dark blue*, throat to mid. breast grayish brown sometimes with a little blue gloss; *lower underparts white* (no obvious. streaking but sometimes with a few narrow black shaft streaks). ♀: sim. but no blue gloss on chest; feathers of throat and chest often faintly pale-edged, scaly, and merging with dingy white to buffy white lower underparts and with little or no streaking (resident *chalybea*). Or sim but ♂ and ♀ larger (7.5″, 19cm), longer tailed (73–95 vs. 56–69mm), and underparts slightly paler (austral migrant *macrorhamphus*).

Sim. species: Commonest and most widespread martin in Venez., and the one with *least* difference between sexes. Learn this species well for comparison with others, incl. 1 or more species that are sim. but as yet little rec. in Venez. (below). ♀ Purple Martin has pale forehead and pale nape band; ♂ Purple and ♂ Southern martins (see Note) are all dark below; ♀ Southern Martin is dark and scaly below. Also watch for individuals with sharply demarcated white bellies which may be Caribbean Martins.

Voice: Rich, gurgling, bubbling song given in flight and when perched.

Behavior: A social martin, often seen in loose flocks of varying sizes in towns and urban areas. Away from human habitation most likely to be seen in prs. that nest in holes in snags, natural cavities, also in eaves or cavities in buildings. Flight is graceful and leisurely, and this sp. often flies quite high (unlike Brown-chested Martin). Nest a cup of loose sticks and stems. Courtship and pr. formation in Mar in ne Bolívar (Hilty); Jun fledglings, w Apure[137].

Status and habitat: Widespread and common resident almost throughout country, although nos. vary seasonally, suggesting local migratory movements (or austral migrants). Several 1000 in mass movement s over Portachuelo Pass, Aragua, 18–26 Jul[33]. When not breeding may gather in large roosting aggregations (e.g., 1000s in El Palmar Plaza, Bolívar, Jan–late Feb). Austral-breeding *macrorhamphus* is known from 1 specimen 18 Apr on Caño Casiquiare (El Merey), Amazonas; another (?) in Oct. Austral migrants common in Suriname[253]. Unidentified martin, possibly this sp., at 2400m on Pico Oriental, Coastal Cordillera, Sep 2000 (D. Ascanio).

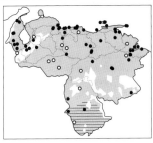

Range: To 1200m. Throughout incl. isls. of La Borracha, Margarita, and Patos (*chalybea*); austral migrant recorded on Río Casiquiare, Amazonas (*macrorhamphus*). Breeds from Mexico to Bolivia and c Argentina; the Guianas. Curaçao; Trinidad. Austral migrants winter n to Curaçao, Suriname, and n Brazil.

Note: Subsp. *domestica* synonymous with *macrorhamphus*[559].

Purple Martin
PLATE 52
Progne subis   Golondrina de Iglesias

Identification: 7.3″ (18.5cm). 47g. ♂: dark *glossy* midnight blue above and below. ♀: above brown faintly glossed dark blue on crown and back; narrow *brownish gray forehead*; inconspic. *narrow grayish white collar on rear of neck*; below grayish brown somewhat scaled grayish on throat and chest and becoming whitish on lower breast and belly; lower underparts with a few dark shaft streaks.

Sim. species: See Gray-breasted, Southern, and Caribbean martins; also cf. Cuban Martin (see Note).

Voice: Rich gurgling and bubbling notes in flight and while perched.
Behavior: Seen singly or in small to large flocks in flight over semiopen or open terrain from lowlands to high mt. passes.
Status and habitat: Very local but seasonally abundant transient from the north with specimens 10 Sep–11 Oct and 18–19 Apr. Sight recs. of small to large nos. over Mucubají Pass, Mérida, as follows: up to 150/hr 15 Aug 1997 and 400/hr 16 Aug 1997 at max. rate[297]; from 2 to 190 (in 2 hr) 20–21 Oct 1979 and 25 Oct 1981 (C. Parrish). Scattered individuals or small groups (all this sp.?) late Jan to mid Feb in Miranda; 1 ♂ and 3 ♀♀ (plus other unidentified martins) 11 Feb 1980, San José de Los Altos, Miranda (C. Parrish); and 1 ad. ♂ (presum. this sp.) 5 Feb 1997, Hato Cedral, Apure (Hilty) may represent overwintering birds or early northbound migrants. Large movement of this sp. over Mucubají Pass needs better documentation; movements over other mt. passes (e.g., Táchira) may occur.

Range: To 3600m. Prob. throughout. Rec. in Zulia, Mérida, Portuguesa, nw Bolívar (lower Río Caura), and s Amazonas; sight recs. in Mérida, Apure, Aragua, Miranda, and Islas Las Aves (*subis*). Breeds in N Amer.; migrates (recs. spotty) through C Amer. (over Carib.?), wintering locally in S Amer., mostly in s Brazil, a few to n Argentina. Other N Amer. breeding subspp. (*hesperia* and *arboricola*) also may migrate through n S Amer. (wintering areas unknown).
Note: Cuban Martin (*P. cryptoleuca*) migrates away from Cuba during n winter months; specimens taken in Curaçao. ♂ like ♂ Purple Martin but with a few white feathers on belly; ♀ very like ♀ Gray-breasted Martin. Specimen confirmation would be required for verification in Venez.

[Caribbean Martin]
Progne dominicensis   Golondrina Caribeña
Identification: 7.3″ (18.5cm). 40g. Known only from sight recs. ♂: glossy blue black with *sharply separated white lower breast, belly, and crissum*. ♀: patterned like ♂ but duller, grayish brown below and on flanks. In both sexes *tail longer and more deeply notched* than in most other *Progne* (except Southern Martin).
Sim. species: ♂ is only all-dark martin with sharply demarcated white lower breast and belly. ♀'s pattern echos that of ♂. Cf. ♂ closely with ♂ Purple Martin and austral-breeding Southern Martin; ♀ with ♀ Gray-breasted Martin which is slightly smaller and with less sharply separated pale lower underparts.

Behavior: In Tobago notably social and often seen flying fairly high over forested or semiopen terrain.
Status and habitat: Breeds as close as Tobago (where common). So far known in Venez. only from several seen (presum. this sp.) Jan–Feb, late 1970s, San José de Los Altos, Miranda (C. Parrish). Rec. Jan–Oct (breeds approx. Apr–Jul) in Tobago[175]. Specimen documentation needed.

Range: Breeds from Jamaica e through most of W Indies and s to Tobago, rarely Bermuda. Guyana (sight).

[Southern Martin]   PLATE 52
Progne elegans   Golondrina Negra
Identification: 7–8″ (18–20.3cm). ♂: essentially identical to ♂ Purple Martin: entirely glossy blue black; *tail more deeply forked* than in Purple Martin (imparts longer-tailed look). ♀ and imm.: dusky blue black above and not strongly glossed; below dusky brown incl. belly, with rather *coarse pale edging*, esp. on lower underparts (unkempt, scaled appearance). Some ♀♀ are almost uniformly dark below (in any plumage much darker than ♀ Purple Martin).
Status and habitat: Known in Venez. from 1 sight rec. 28 Jul 1975 of an "all dark" martin near La Bajada (n of Tucacas), Falcón (C. Parrish), very prob. this austral migrant sp. Specimen verification required. There is a Jul specimen from Obaldía, San Blas, Panama, and several Apr–Jul sight recs., presumably this sp., in Panama[543]; Jul sight recs. from Rio Vaupés in Brazil[400]; sight recs. from Leticia, Colombia[260]; at least 8 specimens of *elegans* (May–Aug) from Suriname[253].

Range: Sea level. E Falcón (n of Tucacas). Breeds in Bolivia, s Brazil, Paraguay, Argentina, and Uruguay; austral migrant n to ne Peru and nw Brazil, rarely to Panama, Colombia, and Suriname.
Note: Does not incl. resident Peruvian Martin (*P. murphyi*) of coastal Peru and Chile or resident Galápagos Martin (*P. modesta*) of Galápagos Isls.

Tachycineta

Rather small with clean-cut plumage; dark above, white below; slightly to deeply forked tail; several with white rumps, varying amts. of white on tertials and/or secondaries; often assoc. with water.

White-winged Swallow   PLATE 52
Tachycineta albiventer   Golondrina de Agua
Identification: 5.2″ (13.2cm). 17g. Dark glossy blue to bluish green above; *inner flight feathers, tertials, and greater wing coverts broadly edged white* forming white patch variable in size but *conspic.* at rest or in flight; *rump and underparts immaculate white*. A few birds show faint white supraloral mark; some individuals in worn plumage show *very little* white edging on wing. Imm.: like ad. but brownish above with white rump; little or no white on wings.
Sim. species: No other Venez. swallow shows white in wings. Cf. Black-collared Swallow which is all dark above with long forked tail and narrow black band across chest.
Voice: Soft, slightly buzzy *twe'e'e'd* in flight or perched. In occas. predawn performance in dark gives long-sustained ser. of metallic, scraping *jee-reek* notes, ca. 1/sec, as flies back and forth low over water.
Behavior: A confiding little swallow, found along almost all major rivers and larger lakes. Single birds, prs., or groups up to 12, occas. more, are usually seen flying low over water, or perched on bare snags or stubs over or near water. Flies more in zigzags than in circles, and seldom strays far from bodies of water. Nests Feb–Apr, Orinoco region; grass and feathers in hole in stub, eave, crevice between boulders, cliff, etc.; 4 white eggs[115].
Status and habitat: Common and widespread resident over rivers, lakes, and estuarine areas.

Range: To 450m. Throughout incl. Isla Margarita. N Colombia and e of Andes s to n Argentina, se Brazil, and the Guianas.

[Tree Swallow]
Tachycineta bicolor   Golondrina Bicolor
Identification: 5.3″ (13.5cm). 20g. Accidental. *Dark glossy bluish green above* (bluer when breeding), wings blackish, *tertials narrowly edged white*, underparts immaculate white. ♀: slightly duller. Imm.: grayish brown above, dingy white below with indistinct brownish breast band.
Sim. species: White-winged Swallow has white in wings and white rump; also cf. Blue-and-white Swallow, differing mainly in smaller size, black under tail coverts, and overall bluer (not greenish) tinge to upperparts. Also cf. ads. and imms. of Brown-bellied and Pale-footed swallows, both only at high els.
Behavior: As in others of genus.
Status and habitat: Known only from sight recs. in mangrove and estuarine lagoons w of Chichiriviche, Falcón, as follows: ca. 25 seen 25 Feb 1972 (P. Alden); more than 200 seen and photographed 15 Jan 1976 (P. Alden); ca. 15 seen 6 and 7 Mar 1976 (C. Parrish).

Range: Sea level at Chichiriviche, Falcón (sightings). Breeds in N Amer.; winters s to Bahamas, Greater Antilles, Honduras, and Nicaragua, occas. to Canal Zone of Panama; scattered recs. in Colombia, Trinidad, and Guyana.

Notiochelidon

Small group of S Amer. swallows; dark above; notched tail; dark crissum; pale feet; buzzy calls; some members have been placed in genus *Pygochelidon*.

Brown-bellied Swallow   PLATE 52
Notiochelidon murina   Golondrina de Vientre Castaño
Identification: 5.5″ (14cm). 12.5g. *Large, dark swallow of Andes*. Above dark glossy bluish green, wings and tail dusky brown, *underparts dull smoky brown*, under tail coverts dusky bluish, *tail rather long and deeply forked*. ♀: duller. Imm.: sooty brown above, dull grayish white below; throat dark brown.
Sim. species: A large, all-dark swallow near treeline is likely to be this one. Note deeply forked tail. Juv. Blue-and-white Swallows are smaller, and even dingy ones are not so dark below.
Behavior: Flies mostly in small flocks of 6–30 or so, sometimes flying back and forth quite near gd., at other times circling very high. Flight is buoyant, fluid, and fairly rapid, typically in large circles as groups forage through an area then move on. Quieter and much less vocal than allies. Small colonies nest in cavities in cliffs, roadcuts, or eaves of buildings; Sep–Oct, Colombia[260].
Status and habitat: Resident, but some local or seasonal migratory movements occur (need documentation). Numerous in early wet-season months of Jun–Jul in Mérida and other Andean areas; less numerous and local in Dec–Apr dry season. Reliably found in vicinity of Laguna Mucubají most of yr, but day-to-day movements erratic. Milling flocks up to 300 in upper Río Quinimarí (1900m), 26 Mar 1999, may have been pushed to lower el. by bad weather at higher els.

Range: 2200–3000m (sight recs. 1900–3600m). Sierra de Perijá (Cerro Viruela), Zulia; Andes from s Táchira n to s Trujillo at Niquitao (*meridensis*). Colombia in Santa Marta Mts. and Andes s to Bolivia.
Note: Has been placed in genus *Pygochelidon*[508].

Blue-and-white Swallow   PLATE 52
Notiochelidon cyanoleuca   Golondrina Azul y Blanco
Identification: 4.7″ (12cm). 10.5g. Above dark glossy blue, *underparts immaculate white*, under wing coverts smoky blue black; flanks and under tail coverts blackish (*cyanoleuca*). Or *larger* (5.3″, 13.5cm), under wing coverts whitish mottled and tinged pale brown (diagnostic in hand), black on under tail coverts less extensive (*patagonica*): Imm.: above brown; faint pinkish brown tinge on throat, stronger dark brown tinge on chest.
Sim. species: Ad. likely confused only with Pale-footed Swallow (see). Dull brownish imms. very like imm. Pale-footed Swallows and prob. best told by combination of voice and habitat. Also cf. Rough-winged Swallow which has pale rump, and migrant Bank Swallow.
Voice: Song an energetic, buzzy, and not very musical trill, *tizi'zi'zi'zi'tzz-tzz-tzz-tzzi-zzi-zzi-zzi-zzi-zzzz* (like grease in hot skillet), or *tizzzzzzzzzzzziiiiiiiiii*, often long sustained or repeated over and over with scarcely a pause between songs. Sings alone or in groups lined up on wires. Thin, slightly buzzy *tzee* in flight.
Behavior: Widespread and familiar in Andes where typically seen in small chatty groups that tirelessly circle back and forth at low to moderate hts. Flight is leisurely, more in circles and loops than in lines (cf. Pale-footed Swallow). Readily nests and forages in close proximity to humans, and its cheerful comings and goings are much enjoyed. Nests singly or in colonies as space permits, in eaves, crevices, cliffs, drain pipes, or holes dug in banks; 2–4 white eggs; some breeding may occur all yr[762].

Status and habitat: Common resident around human habitations and in almost all villages and towns in Andes and n cordilleras (*cyanoleuca*) where has profited greatly from deforestation and settlement. In tepuis look for colonies around roadcuts or on cliffs. Marked seasonal or local el. movements occur among resident birds. Flocks of 60 on 16 Jul and of 34 on 4 Aug flying over Portachuelo Pass were not birds from local colonies[33]. Irreg. Jul–Feb at Hato Masaguaral, Guárico[734]. Austral migrants (*patagonica*) reported Jun–Aug, mainly in lowlands or foothills, not mts.
Range: To 2500m (resident birds mainly in foothills from ca. 400m or higher). Resident throughout in mts. (*cyanoleuca*); Zulia, Táchira, Apure, Carabobo, Distr. Federal, Miranda, Anzoátegui, and Sucre (austral migrant *patagonica*). Breeds from Costa Rica to Tierra del Fuego; mts. of Guyana. Austral migrants reported n to Panama, Colombia, Venez., the Guianas, and Trinidad; rarely to Nicaragua and Mexico.

Pale-footed Swallow   PLATE 52
Notiochelidon flavipes   Golondrina de Patas Pálidas
Identification: 4.5″ (11.4cm). 9.4g. Local over high-el. forests. Almost identical to resident subsp. of Blue-and-white Swallow but *smaller* with *throat and chest smoky pinkish brown to cinnamon; sides and flanks more extensively sooty to blackish* (looks black in field).
Sim. species: Likely to be overlooked because so closely resembles slightly larger Blue-and-white Swallow. The two are sometimes together in mixed-spp. flocks, but Pale-footed is almost always near or over forest and, on avg., occurs at higher els. Dingy cinnamon throat (a distinctive difference in hand) often hard to see in field. Note *small* size (useful in direct field comparison), *dark* flanks, and esp. *distinctive trilled vocalizations*. Pale-footed tends to fly faster and straighter, more in lines than circles.
Voice: Flight calls incl. a crisp, crackling *tszeet* and soft, trilled *tr'e'e'e'e'e'd*, both very unlike thin, buzzy notes of Blue-and-white Swallow.
Behavior: Small flocks of 4–15, rarely up to 50 or more, fly rapidly back and forth low over forest, small clearings, and roads. Flight is energetic and erratic, often with incessant backtracking. Perch on bare exposed twigs or branches of tall trees. Occas. with Blue-and-white Swallows but more often independent of them.
Status and habitat: Local. Known from 2 specimens[338,567] and increasing no. of sight records. First noted by K. Kaufman at Universidad de Los Andes forest, Mérida, Aug 1985 (subsequent recs. there by many observers); ca. 35 seen much lower (1550m) on 29 Jan 1994, San Isidro Rd., nw Barinas[259]; since 1992 at PN

Guaramacal, Trujillo (many observers). Venez. recs. avg. lower in el. than those southward in Andes. **Range:** 2200–2400m (sight to 1550m). Andes from s Táchira (Betania) n to Trujillo (Páramo La Cristalina near Boconó); sight on Trujillo/Lara border in Humocaro/Alto Río Carache area[60]. Andes from Colombia to Bolivia.

Atticora

Black-and-white swallows with sleek, glossy plumage; long, deeply forked tail; usually near or over water.

White-banded Swallow PLATE 52
Atticora fasciata Golondrina Cintura Blanca
Identification: 6″ (15cm). 13g. Entirely glossy blue black above and below with *broad white band across breast; tail long and deeply forked* (usually held closed in a point). Imm.: brownish; breast band broader but less distinct.
Sim. species: At a glance could be confused with Black-collared Swallow if latter's white underparts (sometimes not too evident) are missed.
Voice: Often utters harsh buzzy *bzrrrt* in flight.
Behavior: Usually in small groups energetically zigzagging or circling back and forth rather low over water, or perching in tight little groups on boulders or on small stubs protruding above water. Flush off abruptly, scattering over water with darting, almost batlike flight. Occas. fly fairly high, and may assoc. with Black-collared Swallows. Breed in small colonies; dig nest holes in riverbanks during low-water periods.
Status and habitat: Common resident along clear ("muddy") and blackwater rivers. In blackwater regions, where commoner, prefers vicinity of rocky rapids and falls on larger rivers. Almost always in vicinity of running water, rarely over lakes; occas. over forested clearings away from water.

Range: To 700m. Generally in Amazonas, Bolívar, and Delta Amacuro. E Colombia to n Bolivia, Amaz. Brazil, and the Guianas.

Black-collared Swallow PLATE 52
Atticora melanoleuca Golondrina Collar Negro
Identification: 6″ (15cm). 10.8g. Rapids and rocky rivers. Glossy blue black above, *snowy white below with narrow black breast band* and black under tail coverts. Imm.: above brown; white of throat and breast tinged brown.
Sim. species: Black breast band is diagnostic but sometimes hard to see, then much like Blue-and-white Swal-

low but note latter's shorter tail (not pointed). See White-banded Swallow. Also cf. imm. with imms. of Bank, Barn, and White-thighed swallows.
Voice: Call a buzzy *jtt*.
Behavior: Small, loosely assoc. groups fly in lazy, graceful circles low over water or quite high over rivers, rocky outcrops, and adj. forest. Freq. forage with other swallows, esp. White-banded. Rest on boulders and snags in rivers. May gather in large flocks, occas. up to 80 or so, and circle high overhead after rainshowers. Feb–Mar nests of dry grass and feathers; ca. 2m above water; crevices in large rock or hole in riverbank; 3 white eggs[115,185].
Status and habitat: Uncommon to locally fairly common resident along larger blackwater rivers, mainly where there are boulders, rock outcrops, and rapids (areas where blackflies are numerous); spotty and local away from blackwater areas. Some seasonal or irreg. movements occur, e.g., few or absent at Camturama, nw Amazonas, in Jun (high water) but common Dec–Mar (low water).

Range: To 300m. Generally in w and c Amazonas and e along Orinoco to Delta Amacuro; n Bolívar s to Río Cuchivero, lower Río Caura, mid. Río Paragua (Salto Auraima), and lower Río Cuyuní (sightings). Locally from e Colombia to the Guianas and n Brazil (Guianan Shield area); blackwater areas s of the Amazon in Brazil and spottily s to ne Argentina.

White-thighed Swallow PLATE 52
Neochelidon tibialis Golondrina Muslos Blancos
Identification: 4.5″ (11.4cm). 9.8g. Tiny and batlike. *Above mostly brownish black* slightly glossed bluish on crown and back; *rump paler, underparts entirely smoky brown, leg tufts white* (inconspic. in field), crissum blackish, tail prom. forked.
Sim. species: Leg tufts are diagnostic but difficult to see. Better marks are diminutive size, dark plumage, and slightly paler rump. No other *swallow* in its range is so dark above and below. Cf. larger Rough-winged Swallow.
Voice: In Colombia a soft, slightly trilled *pe'e'e'e'd*.
Behavior: Prs., families, or small groups are confiding as they fly rather low and buoyantly with erratic batlike movements, more in circles than in lines. Often perch close together on low to high bare twigs or branches. Nest of dry grass in hole in bank (?) or hole in dead stub.
Status and habitat: Humid forest borders and small openings (treefalls, landslides, or clearings) in forested regions. There are a no. of specimens from

upper Río Paragua drainage. Most recs. are from s Amazonas and Bolívar; elsewhere rare and local. A pr. seen at 950m in forested terrain 24km w of Santa Elena de Uairén on 1 Jan 1980 is highest rec. (C. Parrish).

Range: To 900m (sight 950m). Nw, c, and s Amazonas; Bolívar from mid. Río Caroní (Auyán-tepui) s to extreme upper Río Paragua at Salto Maisa and Cerro Paurai (*griseiventris*); w of Santa Elena de Uairén (sight). Panama and w Colombia.

Southern Rough-winged Swallow   PLATE 52
Stelgidopteryx ruficollis   Golondrina Ala de Sierra
Identification: 5.3″ (13.5cm). 15g. Widespread and common. Above plain brown, *notably darker on forecrown, wings, and tail; rump light brown to whitish usually contrasting with darker back and tail*; tertials edged white, *throat cinnamon buff*, breast pale ashy brown becoming *pale yellowish* to whitish on belly (palest in very worn plumage); tail almost square. At rest note *slight peaked crown* and wings that extend to tip of tail or beyond. In hand longest under tail covert feathers show broad dusky band and narrow white tip; outer web of outer primary serrate (the "rough wing").
Sim. species: Easily told in flight (in most cases) by *pale rump*, but often confused when perched. Good marks at rest are dark forecrown, slight crest, buff throat, and long, dark wings. In flight *larger* Brown-chested Martin shows white on either side of base of tail, and concolor rump (but some Rough-wings show little contrast on rump). Also see Bank and Tawny-headed swallows; in far s cf. smaller, darker White-thighed Swallow.
Voice: Call a slightly buzzed, upslurred *sureee*.
Behavior: Single birds, prs., or small groups are found throughout open areas. Flight somewhat erratic but more in lines than in circles as birds course back and forth at low to moderate ht. Individuals or prs. often perch up prom. on bare twig or wire. Nest in small holes in banks along roadsides, riverbanks, etc., alone or in loose colonies.; 4 white eggs.
Status and habitat: Common resident in open terrain and clearings in forested regions. Perhaps because it often nests on riverbanks, seems more numerous around water.
Range: To 1600m. Generally throughout (*aequalis*) but mostly absent from llanos. Breeds from Costa Rica generally to n Argentina and Uruguay. Widespread Amaz. resident and austral migrant *ruficollis* is known from Colombia and Suriname[559] and is likely in Venez.
Note: Northern Rough-winged Swallow (*S. serripennis*) is unrec. but known as close as Bonaire, Aruba, and Curaçao. Breeds s to Costa Rica and winters to

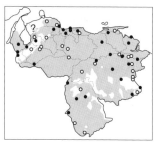

Panama. Differs in having rump uniform with back (not pale) and overall more uniform plumage above and below.

Tawny-headed Swallow   PLATE 52
Alopochelidon fucata   Golondrina Cabecitostada
Identification: 4.7″ (12cm). 14g. Small, pale swallow. *Forehead, eyebrow, and hindcrown tawny rufous,* crown dusky with the feathers edged tawny, upperparts pale grayish brown, rump paler (feathers pale-edged), wings and short, almost square, tail dark brown, *throat and chest pale buffy rufous* (much paler than head), lower underparts dull white. Juv.: paler, feathers of upperparts heavily pale-edged and scaly; rufous of head more buff.
Sim. species: Looks much like a small Southern Rough-winged Swallow, and some Tawny-headeds show slightly pale rump. Note *small* size and *pale* coloration. Diagnostic head color, sometimes hard to see, is most visible as bird flies *toward* observer.
Voice: Soft trilled *treeeeb* in flight.
Behavior: Flies in prs. or small loose groups, sometimes up to 20 or more, back and forth in lazy and swoopy little circles over grasslands. Colonies keep to themselves and are seldom with other swallows, although migrating Barn Swallows fly with them during passage. Grass and feather-lined nest at end of long hole in bank in Brazil[40].
Status and habitat: Very local in colonies over grasslands and other open or semiopen areas. Sometimes near water but shows no preference for it. Most numerous on Gran Sabana (esp. between ca. km 200 and 220) where resident and presumably breeds. Presence away from Gran Sabana spotty and perhaps seasonal, or vagrant (i.e., Coastal Cordillera; sight recs. May and Aug 1994, Represa Guamo, Monagas—P. Boesman, H. Laidlow, B. Finch; Hilty).
Range: To 1600m (most recs. above 450m). Coastal Cordillera in Aragua, Miranda, and Distr. Federal; w Sucre (Cumaná); n Monagas (sight, Represa Guamo),

s Amazonas (Cerro de la Neblina), and e Bolívar (Sierra de Imataca; throughout Gran Sabana s to Santa Elena de Uairén). E Bolivia and s Brazil to n Argentina; scattered recs. in Colombia, Peru, and n Brazil (Roraima).

Note: Placed in genus *Stelgidopteryx* by some[598].

Bank Swallow (Sand Martin) PLATE 52
Riparia riparia Golondrina Parda

Identification: 4.7″ (12cm). 11g. *Miniature of Brown-chested Martin but with shorter tail.* Above uniform brown, wings and slightly forked tail darker; underparts eggshell white with *contrasting narrow brown chest band* (often hard to see in field); inner remiges and tertials narrowly edged white.

Sim. species: Brown-chested Martin is much larger, longer-tailed, and in flight from above, note white showing on either side of base of tail; in addition austral migrants (*fusca*) have sprinkling of dark spotting vertically down chest. Some imm. swallows also have suggestion of brown band across chest. Also cf. larger imm. Barn Swallow.

Voice: Occas. a dry, chattery *trr-trr-trr* in flight.

Behavior: Single birds or a few scattered individuals can nearly always be seen with large groups of Barn Swallows, esp. in llanos. Also may be found in small to large groups, esp. when migrating. Small size and fluttery or erratic flight set them apart from other swallows.

Status and habitat: Migrant from N Amer. in large nos. Sep–Oct; widespread as transient and nonbreeding n winter resident across llanos and elsewhere in small nos. with large concentrations in Guárico (P. Alden). N migration Apr–early May apparently more diffuse. Many funnel through mt. passes during s passage (i.e., 100/hr passing Laguna Mucubají on 14 Sep 1994; several 100 with other swallows 25 and 27 Oct 1996, Laguna Mucubají[207]. Late dates for northbound migrants incl. sight recs. on 26 Apr 1983, Hato Masaguaral, Guárico (B. Thomas); 30 Apr 1966 at Encontrados, Zulia (R. Ridgely and others); and "until May" in Amazonas[115]. Small nos. move n over Gran Sabana, latest date 18 Apr, se Bolívar[207]. Mainly open terrain, ranchland, and grassy areas.

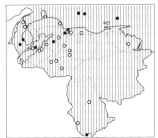

Range: To 3600m. Throughout, but most recs. are n of Orinoco; offshore isls. of Los Roques, La Orchila, and Los Testigos (*riparia*). Breeds in N Hemisphere and locally in tropical portions of Old World. In New World winters mainly in S Amer. s to Patagonia.

Note: Known in Old World as Sand Martin. New and Old World birds may be separate spp.[606].

Barn Swallow PLATE 52
Hirundo rustica Golondrina de Horquilla

Identification: 6″ (15cm). 17g. Ad. has bicolored underwing and long, "swallowlike," *deeply forked tail.* ♂: upperparts glossy blue black, *forehead and throat dark rufous,* rest of underparts cinnamon buff separated from throat by often incomplete black line; *tail with row of small white spots on inner webs* (form broad "chevron" of white on underside of tail). ♀: sim. but underparts whitish; tail shorter. Imm.: duller above, little or no rufous on forehead; throat tinged buff, *rest of underparts whitish,* tail short with very little fork.

Sim. species: Fork-tailed ads. with rusty underparts are distinctive, but most are duller on "wintering" gds. Imm. birds are usually whitish below, lack forked tail, and can easily be confused with migrant Cliff and Bank swallows. Barn Swallow always has dark forehead, usually some gloss to upperparts, and up close look for white in tail.

Voice: Rather quiet on wintering gds.; occas. a soft, rising *tweet.* Fast chattery song hd. mainly when breeding.

Behavior: An industrious bird that flies with the grace of a ballerina. Readily follows cattle, machinery, or anything that stirs up flying insects; can occur almost anywhere, but is usually seen in open terrain where it may occur alone, in small groups, or in immense flocks. Flies low and fast, swooping and fluttering around buildings or tirelessly coursing back and forth in zigzag lines across open fields. Usually quiet on wintering gds.

Status and habitat: Common to abundant passage migrant and nonbreeding n winter resident. Rec. in all months but mainly present early Sep–late Apr with vagrants over-summering. Open terrain, ranchland, and grassy fields. Particularly fond of burned or recently harvested sugarcane fields.

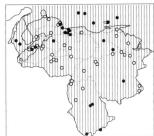

Range: To 3600m. Throughout incl. isls. of Las Aves, Los Roques, La Orchila, Los Testigos, La Tortuga, and Margarita (*erythrogaster*). Breeds in N Amer., Europe, Asia, and N Africa; locally in Argentina[386]. N Amer. breeding birds winter s locally throughout S Amer.; also Aruba to Trinidad and Tobago. Wintering range of austral breeders unknown.

Cliff Swallow
Petrochelidon pyrrhonota Golondrina Risquera

Identification: 5.3″ (13.5cm). 21g. *Buff white forehead* and narrow buff nuchal collar contrast with dark glossy blue cap and *chestnut throat and sides of head;* central throat blackish; back dusky blue with a few narrow white streaks, *rump buff contrasting with short,* *square, blackish tail*; lower underparts white. Juv.: above drab brown, vaguely indicated buff nuchal collar and *dull tawny rump*; below dingy ashy brown mixed buff, belly paler; some also with dark buff throat.

Sim. species: Ad. best told by pale forehead, buff rump, and squarish tail. Note pale "collared" look. Juv. dull and confusing but usually with enough of ad. pattern to be recognized. See Barn Swallow.

Behavior: Most often seen as passage migrant in varying-sized flocks. Often assoc. with other swallows.

Status and habitat: Common southbound transient very locally in Andes, mainly Aug–Oct; 1 seen 13 Apr 1992 at La Yé, Apure (P. Boesman) is only spring rec. During southward migration many funnel through high mt. passes, i.e., 100s/day over Laguna Mucubají, Mérida, 15–16 Aug 1997; and more than 100/min passing over Laguna Mucubají 25–27 Oct 1997 at max. rate[297]; 100s moving down Santo Domingo Valley below Mucubají, Mérida, 23 Oct 1993 (P. Coopmans); up to 32/hr over Páramo Mucubají, Mérida, 25 Oct 1981 (C. Parrish); 2 seen 30 Oct 1991 at Mantecal, Apure (C. Parrish), is latest southward date. Open grassy terrain, ranchland, and agricultural areas. No overwintering recs.

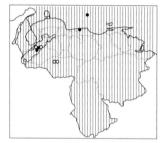

Range: To 3600m. Known from Mérida, Apure (sight), Distr. Federal, and Isla La Orchila (*pyrrhonota*); doubtless throughout w half of country. Breeds in N Amer.; winters mostly in s S Amer.; Guyana (sight).
Note: Generic taxonomy follows Sheldon and Winkler[598].

Troglodytidae: Wrens

Cucaracheros

Wren are found primarily in the New World, with the greatest number of species in Central and tropical South America. Only 1 species occurs in the Old World. As a group they are rather small, chunky, and thin-billed birds with cocked tails and predominantly brown plumage, often with darker barring on the wings and tail. Most are active, fidgety "busybodies" but nevertheless quite skulking in behavior. A great many are gifted singers, especially members of the genera *Thryothorus* and *Cyphorhinus* (the "song" wrens). Mated pairs of *Thryothorus* wrens and some others are notable for their amazingly precise antiphonal duets. Most wrens build domed nests and some also build "dummy" nests which may serve as dormitories. Breeding systems are monogamous or polygamous, and in some species one or more "helpers," usu-

ally young of previous generations, assist with nesting duties. Wrens, especially in Venezuela, are notable for the amount of geographical variation in their plumage.

Black-capped Donacobius   PLATE 48
Donacobius atricapillus   Cucarachero de Agua
Identification: 8.5″ (22cm). 33g. Slender and long-tailed. *Eyes golden yellow*. Top and sides of head black becoming dark chocolate brown on back; white patch in primaries (conspic. in flight); long black tail graduated and boldly tipped white, rump and underparts deep creamy buff with a few narrow black bars etched on flanks; both sexes have small patch of bare orange skin (visible when singing) on sides of neck.

Sim. species: Hard to mistake in its marshy domicile. Cf. Bicolored Wren.

Voice: Has large repertoire of whistled calls, many of them components of loud antiphonal duets accompanied by tail-wagging displays performed by mated prs. perched in open atop marsh grass or shrubs. Typically duet is slow ser. of loud, liquid notes, *whot-whot-whot-whot-whot* (or *whick-whick* . . .), as mate (♀?) utters scratchy *jeeeeer, jeeeeer, jeeeeer* . . . over and over. In a variation 1st bird utters a rough *jeeeer*, 2d a musical *kuEEa*.

Behavior: These engaging jesters of the marsh, boldly panoplied in black and cream, never fail to charm audiences with their remarkable, seemingly impromptu performances of display and song from atop bushtop stages. These proclamations, however, are earnest announcements of territorial ownership. This sp. is most often found in prs., occas. in 3s, that are noisy and conspic. when they perch up exposed in marsh grass or shrubs around grass-bordered lagoons, but they forage lower and mostly out of sight in marsh grass. Fly low, straight, and rather slow (despite fast wing beats) between tall bushes in marshes. In striking display prs. sit in open, side by side or one a little above the other, and bob heads and wag partly spread tails side to side asynchronously while singing loud duet. Nests in llanos reported May–Jun; deep bulky cup in tall grass near or over water; 3 eggs densely mottled reddish brown[646]; cooperative breeding also reported[292].

Status and habitat: Fairly common resident but spotty and local in distrib. Found in grassy marshes, grassy borders of lakes and rivers, and vegetation-choked lagoons and oxbows. Not as numerous in Venez. as in Amazon Basin.

Range: To 750m n of Orinoco; to 200m s of Orinoco (sight to 950m). Generally n of Orinoco incl. Delta Amacuro; Amazonas s to Río Ventuari; n Bolívar s to

lower Río Caura and lower Río Cuyuní (El Dorado); spottily s to Santa Elena de Uairén on Brazilian border (*atricapillus*). E Panama, n Colombia, and e of Andes s to ne Argentina and the Guianas.
Note: Formerly placed in Mimidae.

Campylorhynchus

Large wrens, usually with strongly contrasting plumage patterns; long, thin bill; long tail; prs. or in small social units; vocalizations unmusical; large messy nest a globe with side entrance; social behavior well documented[507,519].

Bicolored Wren
PLATE 53
Campylorhynchus griseus Cucarachero Currucuchú
Identification: 8.5″ (22cm). 43g. Large. Eyes dark. Crown, nape, and line through eyes dusky brown, *long eyebrow white*, rest of upperparts contrasting reddish brown, inner flight feathers and tertials obscurely barred blackish, long and ample tail dark brown finely barred black, all but central tail feathers with *broad white subterminal band* (looks white-tipped); *underparts white*. Or no barring on wings or tail (*albicilius*). Or upperparts grayish brown, no barring (*pallidus, griseus*).
Sim. species: Best marks are large size, eyebrows, and white underparts. Cf. Black-capped Donacobius which has yellow eyes, no eyebrow, and creamy underparts. Also Tropical Mockingbird.
Voice: Noisy. Calls incl. a loud *awk-chook* and guttural *óok-a-chuk* in n Lara. Often sings duets; animated prs. (in Apure) sit side by side in opposite directions, spread and depress tails, droop wings, ruff back feathers, and pivot back and forth as sing loud, throaty, rhythmic *Oh-chuck, Awk-a-chuck* or strangling *AW-chuck—walk* several times; scold with loud, harsh *rud* notes. Geographical differences in song dialects are marked. Birds of Falcón (*albicilius*), in particular, sing different songs from birds of llanos (*minor*).
Behavior: These are bold, inquisitive wrens, not the least bit shy, and fond of living in close proximity to human dwellings. Snoopy prs. or families hop deliberately, peering and pecking in seriocomic fashion in crannies and crevices, clambering over limbs, palm fronds, in brush piles, along guttering of buildings, at almost any ht. from gd., where they spend considerable time, to high in trees. Nesting prs. often are assisted by 1–2 helpers, presum. offspring of previous generation. May appropriate large abandoned nests of other spp. such as *Pitangus* and *Myiozetetes* for their own use, or build grassy domed nest; 3–5 buff to cinna-

mon eggs thickly speckled brown. Jan–Mar nesting, ne Anzoátegui and n Bolívar[186] (Hilty); May–Aug breeding, Hato Masaguaral, Guárico[734].
Status and habitat: Common resident in arid and semi-arid desert scrub with cactus and in dry woodland; less numerous in coffee plantations, light woodland, villages, and cultivated areas with trees in moist and humid regions. Local in llanos where most often seen around ranch buildings. In some areas, i.e., n end of Andes in Lara and Trujillo, and in Sucre, ranges well up into mts.
Range: To 1600m n of Orinoco; to 500m (sight recs. to 950m) s of Orinoco. Base of Sierra de Perijá and Maracaibo Basin, Zulia, e through Falcón, Lara, and w Trujillo (*albicilius*); rest of Venez. e of Andes and n of Orinoco, Delta Amacuro, and n Bolívar from Río Cuchivero and lower Río Caura e to Sierra de Imataca, Nuria, and lower Río Cuyuní (La Bomba); se Bolívar at Santa Elena de Uairén (*minor*); nw Amazonas (Pto. Ayacucho) ne along Orinoco to Altagracia, Bolívar (*griseus*); n Amazonas from Caño Cataniapo and Caño Parucito se to Río Manapiare (*pallidus*). Colombia to Guyana and extreme n Brazil (Roraima).

Stripe-backed Wren
PLATE 53
Campylorhynchus nuchalis Cucarachero Chocorocoy
Identification: 7″ (18cm). 25g. Eyes yellowish white; bill chalky horn. Crown dingy white (pale brown—*nuchalis*) dotted and scaled dusky, *broad white eyebrow; back dull white striped black*, mantle tinged brownish buff, *wings and tail black coarsely barred white*; underparts dull eggshell white *coarsely spotted black*.
Sim. species: Only Venez. wren striped above and barred below. Cf. ♂ Barred Antshrike.
Voice: Territorial songs are duets given by dominant pr., or sometimes by several birds at once in unsynchronized chorus. Scratchy and unpleasant duet a rapidly repeated *zhewît-here* or *arrowak-gero-kíck* or sim. variation, often with syncopation or "beat." Foraging birds give slow ser. of sharp *klip* notes and many harsh guttural and clucking notes.
Behavior: A social sp., easy to see but does not seem quite as comfortable in vicinity of people as Bicolored Wren. Lives in groups of 2–10 (usually 2–3) with 20–40 groups composing a loosely assoc. colony. Each group is polyandrous and cooperative with a dominant ♂ and ♀ and subordinate "helper" ♂♂ unrelated to dominant ♀. Or dominant pr. in group is monogamous if "helper" sons are related to dominant ♀. Stay mostly high in trees where actively hop along large limbs and inspect bark and leaf surfaces. Groups defend all-purpose terrritories of 1–4ha. Appropriate abandoned nests of other birds such as thornbirds, kiskadees, and *Myiozetetes* flycatchers, or build domed grass and stick nest 2–10m up in legume tree; breed Apr–Sep; 4 white eggs[507,734].
Status and habitat: Uncommon to locally common resident. Dry, moist, and occas. humid woodland borders, gallery forest, and scattered trees in cultivated areas, parks, and gardens. Usually not found with Bicolored Wren (interspecifically territorial?). Quite local at Hato Cedral in w Apure but abundant at Hato Los Indios in e Apure.

Range: To 800m (sight) n of Orinoco; to 100m s of Orinoco. Se Lara (sightings, vicinity of Barquisimeto), Falcón (sight, La Misión), Yaracuy, coastal Carabobo, Aragua, Distr. Federal, Miranda, and s to n Guárico (*brevipennis*); Apure, Barinas, Portuguesa, and Cojedes e to se Guárico, n Anzoátegui, w Sucre, and along Orinoco from se Apure (Pto. Páez) and n Bolívar (Caicara; lower Río Caura) to w Monagas (many sightings) and Delta Amacuro (*nuchalis*). N Colombia.

Cinnycerthia

Large size; short bill; ample tail; relatively unmarked rufous plumage; montane; notably social.

Rufous Wren   PLATE 53
Cinnycerthia unirufa   Cucarachero Bayo
Identification: 7″ (18cm). *Uniform bright rufous with contrasting black lores*; wings and tail faintly barred black or often with no barring present (*chakei*). Or sim. but paler, more cinnamon rufous, primaries dusky with faint blackish barring (*unirufa*). Both subspp. frequently show *pale powdery buff to pale grayish forehead and crown*, or sometimes only forehead pale (commoner in ♂♂ and much commoner in *unirufa*). Eyes gray brown (both subspp.).
Sim. species: Rufous Spinetail has remarkably sim. plumage but utterly different shape (long double-pointed tail) and vocalizations.
Voice: A gifted and innovative singer. Mobs with loud harsh *geeea* and *jeer*, calls incl. sharp *tsip* and *tsap*. Songs (solo or antiphonal duets) are rather slow, flute-like, and repetitive, e.g., *wuu-tweedie, wuu-tweedie, wu-weedie-weedie-weedie-weedie*; or *ee-o, t-e-e-e-e-e-e-e-e-e*; sometimes a rolling *tódaly-tóadly-tódaly . . .* rapidly up to 15 times or more.
Behavior: A bird of dense cloud forests, difficult to see but curious, and often approaches to mob noisily. Families or groups, sometimes up to 12 or more, follow mixed-spp. flocks and are often dominant sp. in them, but also forage independently of mixed flocks.

Forage from near gd. to a few meters up in dense vegetation where rummage in accumulations of dead leaves, peer and glean in foliage, and generally keep out of sight.
Status and habitat: Common resident in cluttered undergrowth of humid and wet mossy forest, forest borders, and dense tangles, esp. with bamboo, occas. in shrubbery and stunted woodland up to treeline.
Range: 1800–3100m (most recs. above 2200m). Sierra de Perijá (upper Río Negro), Zulia (*chakei*); s Táchira at Páramo de Tamá and Río Chiquito (*unirufa*). Colombia s in Andes to n Peru.

Cistothorus

Small; streaked back; cocked tail; grass or marshes; taxonomic status of various forms needs revision.

Grass Wren   PLATE 53
Cistothorus platensis   Cucarachero Sabanero o de Ciénaga
Identification: 4″ (10.2cm). 11g. *Tiny with cocked tail.* Upperparts brown; weak eyebrow buff (often obscure); *center of back blackish narrowly streaked white*, wings and stubby tail plain finely barred black; rump essentially unbarred plain brown, underparts dull white, sides and flanks tinged brown, or sometimes eyebrow essentially absent; rump unbarred or occas. obscurely barred dusky, and throat and chest whiter (*alticola*). Or slightly larger; above reddish brown, streaks broader, short eyebrow (mostly a postocular) buff, wings and tail coarsely barred black, barring on rump obscure or absent; sides of head and throat pale buff, most of rest of underparts warm buff (whiter on median breast), flanks and belly unbarred cinnamon (*tamae*).
Sim. species: Note that birds from Páramo de Tamá are much rufescent above and much more extensively buff to cinnamon below than the other 2 subspp. Both subspp. differ from Mérida Wren (overlap minimal) in having *essentially unstreaked crown and unbarred rump*, eyebrow obscure and *buff* or entirely lacking (Mérida Wren has strong white eyestripe), and *wing and tail barring much finer*. Also see larger House Wren.
Voice: Much geographical variation in song structure between pops. A composer[305] with individuals typically singing many songs, the more complex ones given as antiphonal duets. In Páramo de Tamá a rather long-sustained, complex ser. of clucking notes, churrs, chattery rattles, and buzzes ending in trill, i.e., *cheh, cheh, cheh, ti-ti-ti, prrr-titititi . . .* and so on (C. Parrish); a ser. of ca. 5 phrases, each on a different pitch, *tu-tu-tu-tu, tee-tee-tee, ter-ter-ter, tsee-ee-ee-ee . . .* etc. (P. Schwartz recording).
Behavior: A wee little wren that spends most of its time close to gd. in wet grass, flushes weakly with fluttering wings, and soon tumbles down into grass again. Prs. are usually part of small, loose colonies. Often sings from exposed perches but otherwise creeps and hops on or near gd. and in tall sedgy grass or wet tangles at base of a bush where difficult to observe or flush. In Chile, large, ball-shaped, grass nest concealed in grass and on or near gd.; 4–6 white eggs[280].

Status and habitat: Resident very locally in wet grassy and sedgy areas (marshes?) with or without a few scattered bushes, in mts. Only lowland recs. are 2 ♂♂ from Uverito, se Monagas (dry grass?). Most colonies isolated and widely scattered.

Range: 900–3300m (ca. 50m in se Monagas). Andes of s Táchira on Páramo de Tamá (*tamae*); Sierra de Perijá, Zulia; Andes of Mérida and s Lara, Coastal Cordillera in Carabobo, Aragua, Distr. Federal, and Miranda (sight, PN Macarao); border of Sucre and Monagas at Cerro Negro; se Monagas at Uverito; se Bolívar (Kabanayén to Cerro Roraima and Santa Elena de Uairén) on Gran Sabana (*alticola*). N Amer. locally to se Brazil and Argentina; Falkland Isls.
Note: Here regarded as conspecific with N Amer. birds (*stellaris* group) which are usually called Sedge Wren. The 2 groups are so different vocally they are almost surely separate spp.[10]

Mérida Wren
PLATE 53
Cistothorus meridae   Cucarachero Triguero
Identification: 4.2″ (10.7cm). Much like Grass Wren. *Tiny with short, cocked tail.* Crown rich brown faintly streaked dusky; *long eyebrow* white, *sides of neck and upperparts coarsely streaked dusky and white* (much more than in Grass Wren), wings, rump, and tail dark brown *coarsely barred buff*, underparts dull white *extensively barred buff and blackish on sides and flanks.*
Sim. species: From Grass Wren by bold eyestripe, *extensive* streaking above, and barring on sides and flanks; also easily told by voice and, to a lesser extent, habitat.
Voice: Prs. have large repertoires mostly consisting of delightfully energetic, bubbly duets, some antiphonal. In one variation a bird sings 1–2 *tic* notes and long scolding buzz, the other a buzzy glissando that rises and falls; in another variation a bird repeats a clicking buzz over and over, the other a spirited bubbly ser. of notes. Scold with low buzz. Prs. are "composers" and display much individual and geographic variation in song repertoires between pops. on different paramos.
Behavior: These charming little birds are usually found in prs. that stay low to gd. and scurry about in paramo vegetation and grass and, unless singing, are inconspic. and easily overlooked. As in others of genus, flight is feeble and buzzy, and they seldom fly far. Prs. usually perch close together when singing, and 1 or both members readily ascend to top of an *Espeletia* or shrub for short energetic song bouts, but they are not persistent singers. Vigorously defend terri-

tories, often coming from long distances to song play-back. Forage on or near gd. for arthropod prey.
Status and habitat: Uncommon to fairly common but somewhat local resident of treeline shrub zone and open paramo. Favors damper, richer, more floristically diverse paramo slopes, esp. where *Espeletia* and other shrubs are tall; may require *Espeletia* in territory. Reg. on Páramo Batallón, n Táchira, and Páramo del Águila, Mérida.

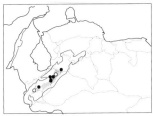

Range: ENDEMIC. 3000–4100m. Andes of n Táchira (sightings)[259], Mérida (numerous areas in paramo), and s Trujillo (Teta de Niquitao).
Note: Previously called Páramo Wren[403] and Mérida Wren[544].

Thryothorus

Large genus; med.-sized to largish wrens; mostly Neotropical in distrib.; usually with black-and-white streaked cheeks; skulk in thickets; sing antiphonal duets; globular or football-shaped nest with side entrance.

Whiskered Wren
PLATE 53
Thryothorus mystacalis   Cucarachero Bigotudo
Identification: 6.5″ (16.5cm). 29g. Large highland wren. *Crown to upper mantle dark gray contrasting with reddish brown wings and back*; tail uniform rufous (no barring); *long white eyestripe*; sides of head gray narrowly streaked white and bordered below by buff white malar and *prom. black submalar streak* (the "whisker"); throat buffy white, chest buffy gray, lower underparts buff, somewhat browner on flanks. Or tail buffy brown barred black; throat white (*consobrinus*). Juv.: much duller, foreparts mainly gray; whisker faintly indicated; rearparts dull rufous.
Sim. species: Best marks are large size (for a *Thryothorus*), 2-toned upperparts, and black whisker stripe. Overlaps Rufous-and-white Wren, smaller Gray-breasted Wood-Wren, Rufous-breasted Wren, and marginally Buff-breasted Wren, last mainly at lower els.
Voice: Songs, mostly given as antiphonal duets by prs., are variable but easily recognizable as there is a smooth, liquid quality to phrases which are delivered rather slowly, often with fairly long pauses between songs; e.g., an antiphonal *WE-O, co, cream-o-wheat!* Also a liquid and bubbly *wit-wit-wit* and *whick-wit-wit*.
Behavior: A gifted songster, but as in others of genus, prs. are given to excessive skulking in thickets and usually are difficult to see well and always hd. far more than seen. Do not follow mixed-spp. flocks but are often active and may move higher in vegetation in

their presence. Nest a fibrous ball with side entrance; 0.3m up in ferns[33]; breeding late Dec–Feb, n Aragua.
Status and habitat: Fairly common resident by voice in dense thickets, vine tangles, and ferns along forest borders, around overgrown treefalls inside forest, or in other shrubby areas.

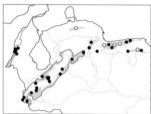

Range: 600–2400m. Andes of s Táchira (*tachirensis*); Sierra de Perijá (Río Negro), Zulia; Andes of Mérida, nw Barinas, and Trujillo n to s Lara (*consobrinus*); c Falcón (Sierra de San Luis), mts. of Yaracuy, and n Cojedes (Cerro Azul) e through n cordilleras to Distr. Federal and Cerro Negro, Miranda (*ruficaudatus*). Colombia s in mts. to s Ecuador.
Note: Previously called Moustached Wren[403], a name now used for birds in Peru, Bolivia, and Brazil s of the Amazon.

Coraya Wren   PLATE 53
Thryothorus coraya   Cucarachero de Lluvias
Identification: 5.7″ (14.5cm). 17g. Rather dark wren. *Crown and sides of head black, the black curving downward onto sides of neck*; narrow white eyebrow; several narrow white stripes on cheeks and short, vertical white mark at rear of cheeks; upperparts dark reddish brown, wings blackish, tail brown barred black, *median throat white bordered on sides by broad black malar*, breast ochraceous buff, lower underparts brown to reddish brown (*ridgwayi, obscurus*). Or crown reddish brown, underparts darker, more tawny buff (*obscurus*). Or crown more or less like back, breast pale gray (*caurensis*). Or nearest *ridgwayi* but paler above and on lower underparts (*barrowcloughiana*).
Sim. species: Everywhere darker and with blacker face than allies (e Bolívar birds are darkest of all). Note distinctive vocalizations of e birds.
Voice: As in others of genus, most songs are antiphonal duets initiated by 1 member of a pr. and completed by the other. On slopes of Sierra de Lema (1000m) in extreme e Bolívar prs. sing a loud, musical, slurred song, e.g., *seeeEEEyou, ear-ear-ear-ear* with variations (last 4 notes by 2d bird), always perfectly synchronized. In Amazonas gives loud liquid duets and also several other vocalizations, incl. buzzy *jeer jeer*, often followed by rapid *wop-wop-wop-wop*; these last 2 vocalizations apparently not given by birds of e Bolívar. Everywhere songs lack rich mellow quality of those of Whiskered Wren.
Behavior: As in most members of genus, prs. stay fairly close together, keep mostly out of view in dense thickets, and sing freq. to keep track of each other. Sometimes join mixed-spp. flocks but do not follow them, then move a little higher in vine tangles, even into mid. strata occas., where easier to see. Forage by pecking and gleaning from foliage and small branches.

Status and habitat: Várzea and terra firme forest in lowlands and lower tepui slopes in Amazonas. Locally in both lowlands and highlands of Bolívar. Fairly common resident in foothills and slopes of humid and wet premontane forest on Sierra de Lema of e Bolívar, but curiously rare (or absent?) in adj. lowlands.

Range: To ca. 1850m (a few recs. to 2400m on summits of tepuis). Lowlands of Amazonas s of Río Ventuari; Bolívar from lower Río Caura e through mid. Río Paragua (Cerro Guaiquinima) to upper Río Caroní (*caurensis*); Río Amacuro in s Delta Amacuro and e Bolívar from upper Río Cuyuní to n Gran Sabana (*ridgwayi*); se Bolívar on Cerros Roraima and Cúquenan (*barrowcloughiana*)[19]; Bolívar on Auyán-tepui (*obscurus*). E Colombia, e Ecuador, e Peru, and extreme nw Brazil e to the Guianas and e Amaz. Brazil (absent from c Amaz. Brazil).
Note: Plumage and vocal differences between lowland and highland birds suggest there is more than 1 sp.

Rufous-breasted Wren   PLATE 53
Thryothorus rutilus   Cucarachero Pechicastaño
Identification: 5.5″ (14cm). 16g. Above uniform warm brown, crown tinged rufous, tail barred black (wings unbarred), narrow eyebrow white, *lores, sides of head, neck, and throat thickly freckled black and white* ("salt and pepper") in sharp contrast to *deep rufous breast*; center of belly white. Or paler, crown and upperparts uniform gray brown; pale cinnamon rufous breast somewhat speckled black (*laetus*).
Sim. species: Speckled face and throat and contrasting breast are diagnostic. Cf. Buff-breasted and Whiskered wrens.
Voice: Vigorous, antiphonal songs recalls those of Buff-breasted Wren but are higher pitched, flatter (less musical), and notable for many slurred notes, typically a rollicking phrase delivered in lively vivace tempo, repeated 2–3 times, e.g., *too-see-HEEear to-see, too-see-HEEear to-see*, then song changes. Call a rising *tipbreeeeze*, like running fingers up a comb.
Behavior: A puckish, energetic sp. found in prs. or families that forage from lower growth to ca. 10m up, somewhat higher than others of genus and consequently sometimes easier to see. Glean in foliage, often examine curled dead leaves, or hop up vines near trunks, typically searching in thorough, methodical manner. Share habitat, to some extent, with Rufous-and-white and Buff-breasted wrens. Grassy domed nest typical of genus; 1–5m up in vine tangle, curled dead *Cecropia* leaf, etc.; 2–3 white eggs spotted brown, more heavily at large end[633]; Feb nest, PN Morrocoy, Falcón.

Status and habitat: Fairly common to common resident by voice in scrubby thickets, vine tangles, and borders of dry semideciduous forest, moist forest, and lighter woodland, esp. in foothills.

Range: To 1700m. Sierra de Perijá, Zulia (*laetus*); nw Táchira (*intensus*); foothills of both slopes of Andes from Táchira and Barinas n to cerros of nw Lara, n Portuguesa (Turén), mts. of c and e Falcón, Yaracuy, n cordilleras e to Miranda, and mts. of Sucre and Monagas s to Maturín (*rutilus*). Costa Rica to c Panama; n Colombia.

Buff-breasted Wren   PLATE 53
Thryothorus leucotis   Cucarachero Flanquileonado
Identification: 5.6″ (14.2cm). 15.5g. Widespread. Above uniform warm brown with *prom. white eyebrow; cheeks whitish narrowly streaked black*, wings and tail finely barred black, throat white *becoming buff on breast, cinnamon buff on sides and crissum*, whitish on central belly. Or darker above and below (*zuliensis*). Or paler, grayish brown above, buffy white to almost pure white below (*hypoleucus*). Or sim. but *slightly smaller* (5.2″, 13.2cm) (*venezuelanus, hypoleucus, albipectus*).
Sim. species: Not as well marked as many allies and may almost recall an overgrown House Wren, but that sp. has no cheek stripes. Rufous-and-white Wren is larger and all white below; Whiskered Wren is larger with gray crown and black whisker. Also cf. Rufous-breasted Wren.
Voice: Often hd. call a loud, incisive *pssEET-CHOO!* Songs, given singly or more often by prs. singing high-energy antiphonal duets, resemble those of many others of genus; typically a musical but rather loose, slack-jawed *amelia-choke, amelia-choke . . .* or rapidly repeated *tseEE-now, don't give'me'CHURT now, . .* or sim. variation. Simpler songs often repeated many times, complex ones less repetitive. Birds from Delta Amacuro (*albipectus*) have very different call, a slow, musical *ee-yurk, ee-yurk* (almost always doubled) over and over; scold very buzzy; songs recall those of other races but flatter and less energetic.
Behavior: Active and inquisitive like others of genus and also can be a little hard to see. Prs. stay mostly 0.2–5 m up in thickets but occas. go to gd. to forage. Actively hop and glean in foliage and work over piles of accumulated leaves and trash in vines and branches for arthropods. Globular nest has side entrance near top; 2–3 white eggs, spotted brown and lilac, esp. at larger end[260].
Status and habitat: Common resident in bushy thickets along forest borders, streams, and clearings from re-

gions of dry deciduous woodland to borders of humid forest, várzea, and mangrove swamps. In all areas shows some affinity for water, esp. s of Orinoco. Abundant in mixed mangrove and flooded palm (*Manicaria*) forest of Delta Amacuro (few or no competing congeners); absent from extreme ne Venez.

Range: To 750m n of Orinoco; to 950m s of Orinoco. W and s part of Maracaibo Basin, and w base of Andes in nw Táchira and w Mérida (*zuliensis*); n and e part of Maracaibo Basin e through Trujillo, Lara, Falcón, Yaracuy, and e base of Andes from Barinas, Portuguesa, and Cojedes to Carabobo and Aragua (*venezuelanus*); rest of n Venez. e to s Anzoátegui and ne Bolívar at Cuidad Bolívar (*hypoleucus*); se Monagas, Delta Amacuro, and n and e Bolívar from lower Río Caura s to Gran Sabana (*albipectus*); extreme sw Barinas, s Táchira, w and s Apure, nw Bolívar (Río Cuchivero), and Amazonas s to Río Casiquiare and Caño Parucito (*bogotensis*); s Amazonas (subsp.?). E Panama, n Colombia, and generally e of Andes s to n Bolivia and s Brazil.

Rufous-and-white Wren   PLATE 53
Thryothorus rufalbus   Cucarachero Rojizo
Identification: 6″ (15cm). 22g. Large. *Above mostly bright reddish brown*, wings and tail narrowly barred black, *long eyestripe white*, sides of head streaked black and white, *underparts white*, sides and flanks tinged gray brown, under tail coverts coarsely barred black and white. Or crown and underparts tinged grayish (*minlosi*).
Sim. species: A big, bright rufous wren with white median underparts. See Buff-breasted and Rufous-and-white wrens.
Voice: Like no other in genus. Typically a ser. of variable but extremely melodic, hooting whistles; a common variation of many is 4–5 low-pitched, slow, bouncing whistles preceded and descending in pitch, e.g., *weee, boo boo boo boo whît*. ♂ and ♀ may duet (not antiphonal), one bird singing a ser. of melodious hoots, other a soft, purring *ou-ou-ou-ouuu'u'u'u'u'u*, slowing, descending, and trailing off. Whatever the variation, not forgotten once hd.
Behavior: A rather furtive wren than seems deliberate and calculating in its movements and is usually hard to see. Certainly hd. more often than seen. Individuals or prs. forage by hopping on or near gd., peering in foliage, or inspecting piles of debris in tree forks to ca. 6m up. Not with mixed-spp. flocks. Grassy, globular-shaped nest with side entrance near top.
Status and habitat: Fairly common resident in undergrowth, tangles, and borders of dry deciduous to moist

semideciduous forest, lighter woodland, coffee plantations, and gallery forest; locally into wooded humid
zones. In extreme ne Monagas (Caño Colorado),
where no other *Thryothorus* wren occurs, also *inside*
tall humid várzea forest.

Range: To 1500m. Sierra de Perijá and Maracaibo
Basin; w base of Andes from Táchira to Trujillo; e base
of Andes in s Táchira, Apure, Barinas, Portuguesa, and
Cojedes (*minlosi*); rest of n Venez. from Falcón (Sierra
de San Luis eastward), Lara (recs.?), Trujillo, and Yaracuy e through n cordilleras to Sucre and n Monagas; s
in llanos of e Guárico and s Anzoátegui (*cumanensis*).
Se Mexico to Colombia.

Troglodytes

Small; dull plumaged; cocked tail; montane forest (except widespread House Wren); cunning behavior.

House Wren   PLATE 53
Troglodytes aedon   Cucarachero Común
Identification: 4.5″ (11.4cm). 12g. Plain brown to grayish brown with *faintly indicated buffy white eyebrow*;
wings and tail with narrow dark barring, below dull
white to buffy white, palest on throat and belly, buffiest on breast and sides.
Sim. species: Common and worth learning well as a
comparison with other spp. A small brown and buff
wren lacking prom. marks. Behavior and song are
good clues. Cf. larger Plain Thornbird.
Voice: Song a spirited ser. of bubbling, gurgling, and
chattering notes given yr-round. Individuals have large
song repertoires, and there is much geographical and
individual variation, but most songs are easily recognizable and do not differ greatly from those of n temperate birds.
Behavior: A cheerful and industrious little bird that
usually lives in prs. in company of people and also in
natural environments. Lively, irascible, often confiding, and seemingly possessed of insatiable curiosity, it
carries tail cocked, scolds readily, and actively hops
along fence rows, in shrubbery, thickets, trees, and
around dwellings. May breed yr-round in some areas.;
Jul and Oct, Guárico[734]. Globular nest of coarse grass
and twigs is lined with feathers; in cranny, building,
low shrubbery, even on gd.; 3–5 eggs whitish densely
marked brown. Some polygamy occurs.
Status and habitat: Uncommon to common resident
in almost all open or semiopen habitats from lowlands
to treeline or higher, and along rivers and small clearings in forested regions, but not inside tall forest. Most

numerous around human habitations, but use of DDT
in antimalarial campaigns before 1980s greatly reduced nos. of this endearing little bird[403].

Range: To 2600m (sightings to 3600m) n of Orinoco; to
1700m s of Orinoco. Generally in Zulia and Andes
from s Táchira, Mérida, and nw Barinas to Trujillo and
Lara (*effutitus*); rest of Venez. (*albicans*). Canada to
Tierra del Fuego; Trinidad and Tobago; Lesser Antilles.
Note: Some authors recognize more than 1 sp.[10].
Subsp. *effutitus* has priority over *striatulus*[489].

Mountain Wren   PLATE 53
Troglodytes solstitialis   Cucarachero Paramero
Identification: 4.2″ (10.7cm). 12.5g. Looks like a
smaller, more rufous edition of House Wren. Above rufous brown with *broad buff eyebrow*; wings and *short
tail* narrowly barred dusky; *sides of head, neck, and
breast rich buff*, throat slightly paler, belly whitish,
under tail coverts brownish barred dusky.
Sim. species: More rufous than a House Wren and with
distinctive, broad buff eyebrow and even shorter tail;
also note smaller size and different habitat. S of Orinoco see Tepui Wren.
Voice: Vocalizations rather weak and easily overlooked. Call a flat, descending trill, often given repeatedly for several min. Musical tinkling song, like small
wind chime or breaking of fine glass, *wiss'lee'ree*, or
longer phrase.
Behavior: Not as bold or curious as allied House
Wren, nor is it found in company of humans. This is an
active, fidgety sp. like its allies, but it is much quieter,
staying in or close to cover, and always well up in trees
and vines, often at mid. levels or higher. Reg. seen hopping around large vine-covered trunks or along inner
part of large mossy limbs. Except for calls and songs,
which are not loud, inconspic. and easily overlooked.
Bulky domed nest sim. to that of House Wren; 2 white
eggs.
Status and habitat: Fairly common resident in humid
and wet montane forest, esp. eye level or higher on
trunks around forest openings and borders. Most nu-

merous in regions with some forest disturbance, e.g., Universidad de Los Andes forest in w Mérida.
Range: 1700–3300m. Sierra de Perijá, Zulia; Andes from s Táchira to s Lara (*solitarius*). Andes of Colombia to n Argentina.

Tepui Wren   PLATE 53
Troglodytes rufulus   Cucarachero de Pantepui
Identification: 4.8″ (12.2cm), 16g. Or 4.5″ (11.4cm) (*marahuacae*). Tepuis. *Remarkable for extensive geographical variation in plumage between scattered pops.* Overall much like Mountain Wren but larger and more intensely colored. Above rich chestnut brown, *eyebrow deep ochraceous buff*, wings and tail narrowly barred black, cheeks washed ochraceous, median underparts whitish to light gray, sides brownish, flanks and lower underparts rich brown. Or *median underparts dark rich brown* (*wetmorei, marahuacae*). Or median underparts grayish white, sides and flanks bright rufous brown (*rufulus, fulvigularis*).
Sim. species: All subspp. show prom. eyestripe, more contrasting underparts, and brighter or more richly colored upperparts than House Wren.
Voice: Song on Cerro Roraima a ser. of high, thin, silvery notes delivered in slow, choppy manner, *slick . . seeleet, . . seet . . slick . . t'slik . . slick . . seeleet . .*, like little metallic musical scrapes of a violin being tuned, or a rosined bird squeaker; reminiscent of song of Mountain Wren. Song may continue for several min (D. Ascanio recording).
Behavior: Like its allies, active and fidgety, also tame and confiding. Occurs singly or in prs. low in undergrowth, or on gd. where it hops quickly over mossy rocks, logs, and leaf litter (D. Ascanio).
Status and habitat: Resident and common at least locally. Humid and wet forest, shrubby forest edges, and bushes in open rocky areas. Known from large no. of specimens taken by collectors on tepui expeditions; common above ca. 2200m on Cerro Roraima. Occurs lower on Cerro Sipapo (to 1000m), Cerro Sarisariñama (to 1100m), and Parú-tepui (to 1300m) than elsewhere; highest el. is from summit of Cerro Roraima. Not reported on Sierra de Lema which may lack sufficient el. to sustain a pop.

Range: 1000–2800m (most recs. 1600–2400m). Virtually throughout on tepuis of Amazonas and s half of Bolívar. N Amazonas on Cerros Sipapo, Guanay, and Yavi (*yavii*); c Amazonas on Cerro Marahuaca (*marahuacae*)[499]; c Amazonas on Cerros Duida, Parú, and Huachamacari; sw Bolívar on Cerros Jaua and Sarisariñama (*duidae*); s Amazonas on Cerro de la Neblina

(*wetmorei*); se Bolívar on Auyán-tepui, Ptari-tepui, Chimantá-tepui, and Sororopán-tepui (*fulvigularis*); Cerro Roraima and Uei-tepui (*rufulus*). N Brazil (Roraima). Doubtless Guyana.

Henicorhina

Small; short, cocked tail; slender bill; boldly streaked face; fidget in forest undergrowth.

White-breasted Wood-Wren   PLATE 53
Henicorhina leucosticta   Cucarachero Selvático del Sur
Identification: 4.2″ (10.7cm). 15g. Lowland counterpart of Gray-breasted Wood-Wren. *Crown black with prom. white eyebrow; sides of head black streaked white*, back rufous chestnut, wings and tail dark brown barred black, *throat and breast immaculate white*, sides of breast grayish rufous, flanks and lower underparts brown.
Sim. species: See Gray-breasted Wood-Wren of higher els.
Voice: A "composer" whose energetic songs are richer, shorter, and even more varied than those of Gray-breasted Wood-Wren; common variations, usually repeated several times, incl. *cheery-cheery-chéee* and *we-per-chee, purty-choo* and *GEEeear-hurry-hurry* and *sKEEET, purty-purty-purty*, and so on; also rattling trills; *chut* call and *churr* scold.
Behavior: Like Gray-breasted Wood-Wren, hd. more than seen and always seems to be on the go. Perky, inquisitive, and usually seen alone or in prs. hopping on fallen logs, in thick tangled cover, treefalls, or on or near forest floor. Never flies far before ducking into a treefall or woodpile from which it may peer out suspiciously, then scampers away quick as a mouse, only to reappear again a short distance away. Not easy to see but usually will come out to look over observers with patience. Sometimes around army ant swarms. Globular nest with side entrance; usually close to gd.; 2 white eggs; also builds dormitory nests.
Status and habitat: Fairly common resident in humid and wet lowland and foothill forest, esp. in cluttered areas and around logs. Found at lower els. than Gray-breasted Wood-Wren (ranges do not meet in Venez.).

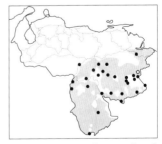

Range: To 1800m. Amazonas (few recs. in w Amazonas) and Bolívar (*leucosticta*). S Mexico to w Ecuador; e Colombia to ne Peru, extreme n Brazil, and the Guianas.

Gray-breasted Wood-Wren   PLATE 53
Henicorhina leucophrys   Cucarachero Selvático
Identification: 4.4″ (11.2cm). 16.7g. Andes and Coastal
Cordillera. Cocked tail very short. Crown dark brown
with *conspic. white eyebrow; cheeks black streaked
white;* upperparts dark reddish brown, wings and tail
faintly barred black, throat white, *breast gray,* flanks
and lower underparts rufous brown. Or throat more or
less streaked with black (*meridana, tamae*).
Sim. species: See allied White-breasted Wood-Wren
(no overlap).
Voice: Sings antiphonal duets and solos yr-round. Distinctive and musical songs vary geographically and locally. Also, prs. are "composers" and tend to develop
their own unique repertoires. Typically songs are loud,
energetic, and rhythmic, e.g., *put-on-your-nightie, put-
on-your-nightie . . .* , often rapidly repeated many times,
or a shorter *you're witty, stee, you're witty stee . . .* or
worth-a-penny, worth-a-penny . . . ; songs longer and
more complex than those of allied White-breasted
Wood-Wren. When disturbed a gravelly *churr.*
Behavior: Prs. of these charming, if hyperactive, little
busybodies always seem to be on the go, hoping
through dark tangled undergrowth, scurrying here and
there, and poking into debris. Adept at staying out of
sight, they are hd. far more than seen but sometimes
are inquisitive and come readily to look over patient
observers or those with tape playback of bird's own
song. Often active as mixed-spp. flocks pass by.
Strongly territorial and sedentary. Food is small arthropods. Globular nest with downward-facing entrance;
concealed low in undergrowth; 2 white eggs.
Status and habitat: Common resident in thickets in
damp, mossy undergrowth of humid and wet montane
forest, shrubby forest borders, and treefalls and tangles
in second-growth woodland.

Range: 900–3000m. Sierra de Perijá, Zulia (*manas-
tarae*); Andes of s Táchira (*tamae*); Andes of n Táchira, Mérida, and Trujillo (*meridana*); mts. of Sierra
de San Luis, Falcón (*sanluisensis*); Andes of Lara, mts.
of Yaracuy, and n cordilleras from Carabobo to Miranda (*venezuelensis*). Mexico s in mts. to n Bolivia.

Cyphorhinus

Bill with high ridged culmen; wings and tail rounded;
furtive on or near forest floor; marvelously complex
and/or melodious songs.

Musician Wren   PLATE 53
Cyphorhinus arada   Violinero
Identification: 5″ (12.7cm). 21g. Bill thick for a wren,
culmen high. Bare ocular skin dull blue (inconspic.).

Crown chestnut, *nuchal collar blackish streaked white,*
rest of upperparts dark brown, wings and tail finely
barred black (seldom visible in field), *throat and chest
orange rufous* contrasting with buff brown lower
breast; darker on flanks and belly. Or center of lower
breast and belly buffy white (*aradus*).
Sim. species: See Wing-banded and Flutist wrens and
Southern Nightingale-Wren, none of which have bare
blue ocular ring or chestnut underparts.
Voice: An inspired singer that gives memorable virtu-
oso song performances singly or in duet. One bird
sings more high notes, the other more guttural notes.
Song is unusually complex, typically composed of several guttural *churr* notes or pot-boiling sounds interrupted by abrupt switches to melodic, flutelike, whistled phrases that may be repeated several times before
changing again, all the while with occas. guttural
churring notes inserted; phrases are notable for jumps
of an octave or more in pitch between notes, e.g., *grr,
E-O-pu-ho-who-E . . grr-grr, pu-E-O-who-ho . . grr, E-pur-
E-O-Le-ho . . . chik-grr . . . E-O, who-E-ho, Le-ho . . .* and
so on (*E* and *Le* notes much higher and flutelike).
Birds from atop Sierra de Lema (1400m) sing less complex songs.
Behavior: These celebrated singers are sly and clever
minstrels of dim forest understory. They move like
woodland spirits, a bit fidgety but quick and cunning,
tantalizing with their intermittent fragments of marvelous song, but unlikely to reveal themselves for more
than a moment. Prs. or families hop on or near gd.,
cling to side of vertical saplings, perch on buttresses or
logs, or poke under fallen leaves, and occas. follow
army ants. Usually wary and difficult to observe without tape playback, and even then may come in to look
over an observer quickly, then move off, all the while
giving occas. low churring calls. Vase-shaped leaf nest
with tubular entrance saddled over small, low branch;
2 white eggs[37].
Status and habitat: Fairly common resident (a sp. that
never seems common enough) inside humid terra
firme and low-lying or várzea forest.

Range: To 1000m (sight/tape to 1400m, Sierra de
Lema). E Bolívar from Sierra de Imataca s to n Gran Sa-
bana and upper Río Caroní at Río Tirica (*urbanoi*); se
Bolívar near Cerro Roraima (*arada*). Se Colombia to n
Bolivia, Amaz. Brazil (not upper Rio Negro region),
and the Guianas.
Note: Subsp. is *arada*, not *aradus*[256,401].

Microcerculus

Unusually long bill, short tail, and rather long legs; dark colors; feathers of lower underparts long, lax, and soft; forest undergrowth.

Southern Nightingale-Wren   PLATE 53
Microcerculus marginatus   Cucarachero Ruiseñor
Identification: 4.3" (10.9cm). 20.5g. Dark with stubby, cocked tail. Above dark wood brown, wings and tail unbarred, *throat to center of belly white* with *variable* amt. of irreg. brownish scaling and barring on sides, varying from almost none to fine brown scaling across most of chest to belly; lower underparts dark brown (*marginatus*). Or sim. but overall darker below with throat white faintly scaled brown, breast to center of belly white to grayish white narrowly and profusely scalloped brown (*squamulatus*). Juv.: sim. but throat and chest grayish, rest of underparts dark brown.
Sim. species: Almost always located first by distinctive voice, hence not likely confused. See White-breasted Wood-Wren, ♀ Banded Antbird, and larger ♀ Silvered Antbird.
Voice: Learn song as this sp. is hd. far more than it is seen. Song (n Venez.) 2–4 quick whistles, rising at first, then ser. descends, at first rapidly, then abruptly slowing and becoming very long drawn, with each succeeding note barely a quarter-tone lower in pitch than the preceding, and notes coming at much longer intervals (up to 10 sec apart at end), i.e., *we-ee-EEE!-EEt eee, eee . . . eee . . . . eee . . . . . eee . . . . eee . . .* and so on for up to 1 min or more.
Behavior: A furtive, inconspic. bird that scurries across forest floor or through dark tangles and debris a little above forest floor. Walks well, and almost constantly teeters rear end, as if it is mounted on springs. Members of prs. are very territorial but usually remain well separated from each other and do not assoc. with mixed-spp. flocks.
Status and habitat: Common resident in undergrowth of humid and wet forest; n of Orinoco mainly in wooded ravines in foothills and lower mt. els.

Range: To 1700m n of Orinoco (most recs. above ca. 200m); to 200m s of Orinoco. Sierra de Perijá, Zulia; both slopes of Andes from n Táchira, Mérida, and nw Barinas (sight) to Lara; Sierra de San Luis, Falcón[60], hills of se Falcón (sight), mts. of Yaracuy, and n cordillera from Carabobo to Miranda and Distr. Federal (*squamulatus*); se Táchira and w Apure; sw Amazonas on Yavita-Pimichín trail (*marginatus*). Costa Rica to w

Ecuador and n Colombia; se Colombia to n Bolivia and Amaz. Brazil (mostly s of the Amazon).
Note: By some called Scaly-breasted Wren[10]. Song differences in S Amer. birds suggests more than 1 sp. is involved.

Wing-banded Wren   PLATE 53
Microcerculus bambla   Cucarachero Bandeado
Identification: 4.5" (11.4cm). 19g. Tail very short. Above dark wood brown, wings dusky with *1 bold white wing bar* (sometimes also a faintly indicated upper bar); below gray, flanks and lower underparts dark reddish brown with little or no barring. Or lower underparts narrowly barred dusky (*bambla*).
Sim. species: Only wren in Venez. with 1 bold wing bar. See Banded Antbird.
Voice: Unusual song (quality of Southern Nightingale-Wren), in extreme e Venez., 6–7 well-spaced, piercing whistles accelerating into long, slowly descending and quavering glissando, trailing off, *eee . . . . . ee . . . ee . . ee . ee-e-e-e-e-e-e-e-e-e-e-e-e-e-e-e-e-e-e*. Sometimes song is shorter and seems to rise slightly.
Behavior: Much like Southern Nightingale Wren. A furtive wren of undergrowth or floor of forest interior.
Status and habitat: Uncommon resident of humid forest. Most recs. of this sp. in Venez. are from hilly terrain and foothills or lower slopes around cerros and tepuis (above ca. 250m). Notably local in Venez.

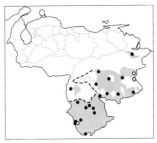

Range: 150–1500m. Nw Amazonas from Cerros Sipapo, Yapacana, and Duidas to Cerro de la Neblina; nw Bolívar from Río Nicharé, mid. and upper Río Caura, and Río Paragua (Cerro Guaiquinima; Salto Maisa), and headwaters of Río Caura at Parai-tepui (*caurensis*); Sierra de Imataca (Río Grande); mid. Río Caroní at Auyán-tepui (*bambla*); sight and tape recs. on upper Río Cuyuní, 72–73km s of El Dorado (17 Dec 1978—Hilty; Feb 1992—K. Zimmer), presum. *bambla*. The Guianas and ne Brazil; e Ecuador (mostly foothills); e Peru (mostly foothills).

Flutist Wren   PLATE 53
Microcerculus ustulatus   Cucarachero Flautista
Identification: 4.5" (11.4cm). 22g. Unmarked brown wren with voice like a piccolo. Tail short. Almost *entirely dark chestnut brown*, throat paler and more buffy brown, plumage unbarred. Or a few vague spots and bars on chest, pale scaling on center of lower breast and belly (*duidae, lunatipectus*). Juv.: much obscure dark barring below.
Sim. species: A plain, uniformly dark little wren, nearest Southern Nightingale-Wren in appearance but even

darker below (Nightingale is whitish on throat). Also
see Tepui Wren which shows prom. buff eyebrow.
Voice: Hd. far more than seen. Lovely flutelike song a
ser. of whistles, often very humanlike, and highly variable (a "composer"). Songs are typically slow and mel-
ancholic, i.e., *wee, püü, wee püü, tee, tee, tee, tee, tee*
(1st and 3d note highest, *tee* notes slowly ascending).
In another common variation, 1st note highest, next 2
on same pitch, last 2 drop a half to full tone and slow
noticeably (as if bird loses interest in singing), i.e., *tee,
düü, düü, daw, daw*. In many songs a few patterned
notes are followed by long ser. of notes that trail off
downscale.
Behavior: Very sim. to that of Southern Nightingale-
Wren. A solitary, territorial and cunning little elf that
scurries around on dimly lit forest floor, scampering
into dark tangles then reappearing mouselike from another exit, or hopping through mossy tangles and bouldery recesses a little above forest floor. Typically
walks, rather than hops, on forest floor. Picks, gleans,
and probes for a variety of arthropods. Territorial prs.
are usually well separated.
Status and habitat: Fairly common resident in cluttered understory or on floor of humid and wet forest,
esp. mossy forest on slopes of cerros and tepuis.

Range: 850–2100m (most recs. 900–1500m). Cerros
throughout Amazonas; w Bolívar in Río Caura watershed (*duidae*); c Bolívar along Río Paragua to headwaters of Río Caroní (*lunatipectus*); e Bolívar from Sierra
de Lema s through tepuis of Gran Sabana (*obscurus*);
se Bolívar on Cerros Roraima and Cuquenán (*ustulatus*). W Guyana and n Brazil (Roraima).

Cinclidae: Dippers

Pájaros de Agua

The dippers are a small passerine family of semi-
aquatic birds. They are distributed discontinuously
with 3 species in the New World and 2 in the Old
World. Dippers have large feet, dense plumage,
(young also with dense down), a musty odor, an exceptionally large oil gland, a moveable nostril covering, and a well-developed nictitating membrane.
Chunky in shape and hardy by nature, dippers are restricted to cold, fast-flowing streams where they feed
on a variety of aquatic life. Some species, but not
those in South America, readily swim underwater or
walk on the bottom of streams.

White-capped Dipper   PLATE 48
Cinclus leucocephalus   Pájaro de Agua
Identification: 6.5″ (16.5cm). 44g. *Bold pattern*. Plump
with short tail. *Crown, nape, and patch on upper back
white*, rest of upperparts sooty brownish black, *underparts white*, flanks, thighs, and under tail coverts chocolate brown.
Sim. species: Unmistakable. Shares its mt. streams with
Torrent Duck, Torrent Tyrannulet, and Black Phoebe.
Voice: Song a prolonged loud trill. Flight call a loud,
buzzy *stre'e'e'e'e'd* (or *zre'e'e'e'e'd*), like high-voltage
electricity, readily hd. even above rushing streams.
Behavior: Single birds or loosely assoc. prs. bob up
and down on boulders at water's edge, often amidst
spray of swirling mt. torrents, as they forage by rapidly
picking tiny aquatic prey from water or wet rock surfaces. Fly fast and low, with buzzy wing beats, as they
patrol linear riverine territories. May wade in water,
dip bills or occas. heads into water, and have been
noted floating briefly on water surface, but do not go
underwater or swim underwater as does American Dipper (*C. mexicanus*). Sometimes repeatedly flex wings
downward in peculiar mechanical manner. Large,
mossy, domed nest in streamside crevice, rock ledge,
or under bridge; 2 eggs; Feb–Mar (2 nests), Mérida.
Status and habitat: Fairly common resident but sometimes difficult to locate. Restricted to bouldery, rushing mt. streams. Densities of less than 1 to ca. 2 prs./km
of stream are normal. Readily found in upper Río
Santo Domingo, Mérida.

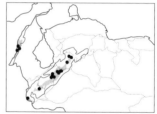

Range: 2000–2600m (sight recs. 1600–3000m; prob.
lower). Sierra de Perijá, Zulia; Andes from s Táchira
and Mérida to Trujillo/Lara border at Páramo de Las
Rosas (*leuconotus*). Colombia s in Andes to Bolivia.

Polioptilidae: Gnatwrens and Gnatcatchers

Chiritos

The taxonomic position of gnatcatchers and gnatwrens remains controversial. Some include them in the
Sylviidae as the only New World members of a primarily Old World family. Others place both genera in the
subfamily Polioptilinae, including them with thrushes
(Turdinae), Old World warblers (Sylviinae), and other
species in the enlarged family Muscicapidae[606]. They
are treated here as a small New World family of their
own[597]. Both groups are insectivorous and somewhat
wrenlike in general behavior. Gnatcatchers are
sprightly, hyperactive little birds, mainly gray and
white, and they live in the upper levels of foliage of
woodland or shrubland. Gnatwrens also are very ac-

tive little birds, but they are mainly brown and white and live in the lower growth of heavy forest or higher in vine tangles. Nests of all genera, as far as known, are small, well-formed cups.

Collared Gnatwren PLATE 53
Microbates collaris Chirito Acollarado
Identification: 4.3″ (10.9cm). 10.3g. *Slender* little bird with long, thin bill and short, usually cocked tail. Above brown, crown darker, wings tinged rufescent, sides of head grayish white, *prom. eyebrow white; black line behind eyes*; long black malar stripe; underparts whitish with *broad black bar across center of chest*; flanks and belly olive brown.
Sim. species: A strikingly patterned little bird that should be easily told by boldly striped head and black chest band. See Banded, Spot-breasted, and Dot-backed antbirds.
Voice: Song a high, thin, drawn-out *eeeeeea* repeated every 4–5 sec for long periods. At a distance sounds very like song of Slaty-capped Shrike-Vireo and of Tawny-crowned Greenlet. Scolds with harsh *jipp*.
Behavior: A perky and animated little bird that constantly wags cocked tail and is often curious but generally difficult to see. Sallies to gd., flits to foliage, or more often stretches neck out to pick or glean from leaves or poke into curled dead leaves as it works through lower vines and tangled undergrowth. Prs. or families and sometimes with mixed flocks. Bulky cup nest of dead leaves near forest floor; 2 white eggs with a few dark spots[448].
Status and habitat: Uncommon to locally common resident, by voice, in undergrowth of humid terra firme forest. Most numerous in southernmost Amazonas (e.g., Yavita-Pimichín) and Bolívar (Cerro Guaiquinima to headwaters of Río Paragua).

Range: To 900m. Amazonas from vicinity of Cerro Duida southward (*collaris*); Bolívar along mid. and upper Río Paragua and Paurai-tepui and Chimantá-tepui in upper Río Caroní (*paraguensis*). Se Colombia, e Ecuador, se Peru, Amaz. Brazil n of the Amazon, and the Guianas.

Long-billed Gnatwren PLATE 53
Ramphocaenus melanurus Chirito Picón
Identification: 5.2″ (13.2cm). 9.1g. Extraordinarily "emaciated-looking" little bird with very long, thin bill and rather long, animated blackish tail. Above grayish brown, *sides of head and sides of underparts mostly cinnamon buff*, throat white (but base of throat feathers black), chest dull buff somewhat smudged dusky;

graduated tail dusky, *all but central feathers broadly tipped white*. Or mainly dull white below; sides of head and flanks tinged buff (*trinitatis*). Or above more rufescent brown, sides of head brighter ochraceous buff, below grayish white, chest and sides gray, no white tail tips, bill shorter (*albiventris*).
Sim. species: *Looks like a little "stick" bird*. No wren has such a long bill. Tropical Gnatcatcher is whitish with black cap. Also cf. Collared Gnatwren which is only in forest undergrowth.
Voice: In n Venez. commonest song a slow, dry rattle, *tdr'dr'dr'dr'dr'dr'dr'dr'dr*. S of Orinoco (nw Amazonas) sim. but smoother (not rattling) and faster. Also petulant meowing notes. Songs vary geographically.
Behavior: A droll little bird that seems to be all bill and legs and wiggling cocked-up tail is likely to be this sp. Prs. or families call to each other and extend necks and needle bills to pick small arthropod prey from leaves and twigs, or investigate curled, hanging dead leaves, as they actively and quickly work through vine tangles and dense foliage ca. 2–10m up. Forage with mixed-spp. flocks or independently of them. Often difficult to see. Grassy cup nest with hairlike, black fiber lining; 2 white eggs spotted reddish brown mostly at larger end[646].
Status and habitat: Fairly common to common resident in high vine tangles in moist to humid forest borders, light woodland, shrubby areas, and treefalls and openings inside terra firme and várzea forest. Locally fairly common in dry forest (e.g., PN Morrocoy). Large arboreal vine tangles are key in all habitats.

Range: To 1700m n of Orinoco; to 1000m s of Orinoco. Virtually throughout, except llanos. Base of Sierra de Perijá and adj. w Zulia (*sanctaemartae*); e Zulia, w base of Andes, Falcón, Lara, and generally e of Andes from Apure and Yaracuy to Anzoátegui, Sucre, and n Monagas (*trinitatis*); Delta Amacuro (subsp.?); Amazonas and Bolívar e to Río Paragua (La Paragua), headwaters of Río Caroní, and s Gran Sabana at Santa Elena de Uairén (*duidae*); e Bolívar from Sierra de Imataca to Auyán-tepui, Sierra de Lema, and n Gran Sabana (*albiventris*). S Mexico to n Bolivia, Amaz. Brazil, and the Guianas; coastal e and se Brazil. Trinidad.

Polioptila

Slender; longish, pointed bill; mostly blue gray; ♂♂ often with black caps; tail long, narrow, graduated, and cocked up; active and fidgety.

Tropical Gnatcatcher   PLATE 53
Polioptila plumbea   Chirito de Chaparrales
Identification: 5" (12.7cm). 6.8g. ♂: *crown, nape, and sides of head down to eyes glossy black* contrasting with pale blue gray back; wings and tail black, inner flight feathers edged white, *rounded tail black, outer feathers white*, lores and underparts white (lores black—*innotata*), breast and sides tinged gray. ♀: like ♂ but cap blue gray like back, narrow eyering white (inconspic.); flight feathers tinged brownish.
Sim. species: ♀ recalls Bicolored Conebill, a mangrove sp. that lacks gnatcatcher's sprightly behavior. Also cf. larger, chunkier Hooded Tanager. Rare Guianan Gnatcatcher is most sim. of all (esp. to ♀) but has *gray sides of head and underparts* and *contrasting* white belly.
Voice: Call a petulant, mewing *meeuuuu* and buzzy *gezzzzzz*. Song varies geographically; in n Falcón a brisk, whistled *wees-wees-wees . . .* , ca. 6–10 notes on same pitch; in gallery forest in w Apure a lively *sweet-sweet-see-su-sweet-sweet-sweet-suweet-suweet*, descending slightly in middle then ascending, each note inflected; in savanna woodland in nw Amazonas sim. but slightly higher pitched, faster, and more obviously descending then ascending.
Behavior: A saucy little birdlet with fidgety habits and constantly twitching, cocked tail. Prs. glean or hover-glean small insects from terminal twigs or leaves by hopping lightly and quickly along upper limbs of smaller trees (esp. dry areas) or in outer canopy foliage in humid forest borders. Often notably fearless. Reg. follow insectivorous bird flocks but also forage away from them. In Costa Rica, dainty moss and lichen cup nest saddled on limb ca. 2–8m up; 2–3 white eggs speckled with brown[706].
Status and habitat: Common and widespread resident of desert scrub, *Acacia* woodland, light dry woodland, and shrubby areas; also in moist and humid forest canopy where nos. decrease sharply. Abundant in arid Paraguaná Pen., n Falcón.

Range: To 1200m. Generally n of Orinoco (except where next subsp. occurs); Isla Margarita (*plumbiceps*); Delta Amacuro (recs.?); s Apure, w Amazonas, and n Bolívar (*innotata*). Mexico to w and e Peru, Amaz. (mostly n of the Amazon) and e Brazil, and the Guianas.
Note: Birds of C Amer. and w of Andes are prob. a separate sp.; vocal differences suggest more than 1 sp. also likely e of Andes.

Guianan Gnatcatcher   PLATE 53
Polioptila guianensis   Chirito Brujito
Identification: 4.3" (10.9cm). 5.2g. Local. ♂: *overall mostly dark gray with sharply contrasting white belly and crissum*; lores and narrow eyering white, flight feathers black (*no white edging*), tail mostly black, only outer pr. of feathers white, next pr. partly white. ♀: sim. but facial area and throat paler gray.
Sim. species: Likely confused only with Tropical Gnatcatcher (see).
Voice: Song in nw Brazil typically a high, thin, insistent *sii-sii-sii . . .* of ca. 8–15 notes in 1–2 sec, rather weak but often given over and over at short intervals (A. Whittaker recording).
Behavior: In Brazil forages high in canopy of terra firme forest where very active in outer foliage and branches and usually with mixed-spp. flocks (A. Whittaker).
Status and habitat: Rare or uncommon resident, restricted to white sandy soil forest. Few recs.: 2 prs. seen 16–19 Dec 1979 near San Carlos de Río Negro (C. Parrish). To be looked for in extreme se Bolívar.

Range: To 150m. Sw Amazonas where known from vicinity of Cerro Duida (Río Pescado), mouth of Río Casiquiare, Yavita-Pimichín, San Carlos de Río Negro; and near Cerro de la Neblina[801] (*facilis*). Disjunct pops. in extreme nw Brazil (upper Rio Negro); sw, c, and lower Amaz. Brazil; the Guianas.

Turdidae: Solitaires and Thrushes
Paraulatas

Thrushes form a large worldwide family most numerous in the Old World. Sometimes considered only a subfamily of the large, mostly Old World Muscicapidae family[606], they nevertheless form a rather homogenous group morphologically. Among them are some of the finest songbirds in the world. Thrushes eat a variety of fruit and animal matter, and they often forage on the ground. The various species of *Turdus* are the largest and best-known Venezuelan thrushes. *Catharus* and *Myadestes* are shy woodland dwellers, more typical of montane areas; although less often seen, some species in these 2 genera are notable for their beautiful flutelike songs.

Myadestes

Short, broad bill; short legs; rather long tail; highly arboreal (unlike *Turdus*); nest on steep bank, in stump, etc.

Andean Solitaire   PLATE 54
Myadestes ralloides   Paraulata Cotarita
Identification: 7" (18cm). 28.5g. Eyes dark. Short bill dusky above, yellowish below. *Upperparts rufescent brown*, more rufous on rump; *head and underparts entirely iron gray*; whitish band at base of inner flight feathers visible in flight (not at rest), tail dark brown *tipped white*, outermost pr. with wedge of white on inner web. Imm.: mostly rufescent brown heavily spotted ochraceous; crown and underparts more dusky.
Sim. species: A rather slender, long-tailed, gray and brown bird sitting erect and immobile inside montane forests is likely to be this sp. Note wing stripe and white tail tips as it flies.
Voice: Lovely, lilting song is usually first indication of this sp.'s presence; clear halting phrases, of pipelike purity, are often separated by extended pauses, *lee-day . . . lur-lur . . . see-see . . . eee-ooo, ee-oh-lay . . . lur-lur-lur*, and so on. Birds from s Táchira are most melodic of all, their intermittent phrases pouring forth with ineffably pure, ethereal tones. Rarely witnessed flight song, as flies out over mt. forest, a jumble of musical notes sim. to slow song but greatly accelerated (recalls song of some *Atlapetes* brush-finches).
Behavior: A shy and unobtrusive bird that sits motionless and erect in mid.-story foliage or lower. Tends to slip away quietly if an observer intrudes, and would doubtless often be overlooked except for freq. hd. song. Usually not with mixed-spp. flocks but reg. visits small fruiting trees (i.e., Melastomataceae), esp. when other spp. are present or when a mixed-spp. flock is present. Mossy cup nest on bank or log; 2 dull white eggs speckled reddish brown at larger end; in Colombia, breeding Mar–Aug.
Status and habitat: Common resident (by voice) in humid and wet montane forest (cloud forest) and in taller, older second-growth woodland.

Range: 900–2800m (accidental to 4500m). Sierra de Perijá, Zulia; Andes from s Táchira n to se Lara; Sierra de San Luis, Falcón[60]; prob. Yaracuy (no recs.?) and Coastal Cordillera in Carabobo, Aragua, n Miranda (tapes, PN Macarao), and Distr. Federal (*venezuelensis*). Colombia s in Andes to Bolivia.

Cichlopsis

By some placed in *Myadestes*[403,467], but differ in rufescent plumage, more horizontal posture, unmusical song, and nest in fork of branch[544].

Rufous-brown Solitaire   PLATE 54
Cichlopsis leucogenys   Paraulata Gargantianaranjada
Identification: 8.2" (21cm). 45g (1 ♀). Slender, long-tailed, and small-billed; short legs. Bill blackish above, yellow orange below; narrow inconspic. yellow eye-ring (♂) or no eyering (♀). *Mainly uniform warm brown*, tail rufescent brown, outer feathers edged paler rufous, *median throat rufous* (often inconspic.), sides of throat slightly dusky, center of lower breast and belly pale grayish brown, *under tail coverts pale orange rufous*.
Sim. species: Lacks good field marks. ♀ *Turdus* thrushes are larger, bulkier (not slender and long-tailed), have streaked throats, and *lack* contrasting under tail coverts. Try to see solitaire's diagnostic orange central throat.
Voice: Singing may be very seasonal (mostly rainy season?). Songs are typically short, varied, and complex, often loud but more squeaky and chattery than musical; a few melodic and squeaky notes mixed with chips, short buzzes, and trills in rapid sequence, given at short intervals. Sings mainly early in morning. Song recalls that of Yellow-legged Thrush; to n observers it will recall a mimid (Mimidae) thrush, i.e., a thrasher (*Toxostoma*) or catbird (*Dumatella*). Call a high, vanishingly thin *eeeeee*, often given at 3- to 5-sec intervals for a min or more; reminiscent of a fruiteater vocalization.
Behavior: An inconspic., solitary bird of forest interior. Sits more horizontally than others of genus, mostly at mid. levels or higher, and alternates quiet periods with bouts of active foraging at fruiting trees and shrubs (esp. Melastomataceae), esp. when mixed-spp. flocks containing tanagers, manakins, and other fruit-eating spp. are present. Reaches for fruit while perched or sallies up short distances to snatch it in sally-stall. Cup nest in fork of branch in Brazil[544].
Status and habitat: Rare to uncommon resident but occas. quite common for short periods of time, and some short-distance seasonal or el. movements likely. Humid and wet mossy forest and dense second growth on slopes of tepuis; often in fruiting melastomes along forest borders.

Range: 900–1450m (sight to 400m, 26 Nov 1980—R. Webster). Se Bolívar (mts. of Gran Sabana) from

Auyán-tepui, Ptari-tepui, and Sierra de Lema s to Paurai-tepui and Cerro Roraima (*gularis*). Disjunct. Sw Colombia; e Peru; Guyana; Suriname; coastal se Brazil.

Catharus

Migratory and resident spp.; former dull plumaged, latter with colorful orange bills, eyerings (some), and legs; mostly furtive and inconspic.; large cup nest near gd.

Slaty-backed Nightingale-Thrush   PLATE 54
Catharus fuscater   Paraulata Apizarrada
Identification: 7″ (18cm). 38g. *Bill and legs yellow orange*. Eyes white. *Crown and sides of head black* with narrow orange eyering (not too conspic.); *rest of upperparts slate gray*, underparts pale gray, center of lower breast and belly yellowish white to white.
Sim. species: Most likely confused with Spotted Nightingale-Thrush (see). Pale-eyed Thrush is larger, entirely lustrous black, and usually not in dense undergrowth.
Voice: Song a dreamy, mesmerizing ser. of low, flutelike phrases, at a distance much like an old squeaky porch swing, e.g., *eer-lee* or *ur-eee-lee*, phrases halting and hypnotic, as if disembodied from bird and floating eerily through forest. Call a catlike *meow*. Song infreq. hd. in dry season but throughout day in early wet season in Mérida.
Behavior: Like many of its allies, this is a shy denizen of cloud forest understory, and as an observer approaches, a singing bird inevitably drifts farther away, the conjurer of such solemn and serene notes seemingly never quite within reach. Forages alone on forest floor, picking at or vigorously flipping leaves, then pausing to watch carefully. Often eats earthworms. In Venez. and elsewhere reg. follows small swarms of highland army ants (*Labidus*) and is more readily seen then that at almost any other time. May hop on gd. into small forest openings or road edge in predawn. Nest in Costa Rica a cup lined with black rhizomorphs, with moss on outside; 0.5–3m up in bush; 2 eggs, blue green thickly spotted and blotched rufous chestnut[101,706].
Status and habitat: Locally common resident in humid and wet mossy forest. Common above Mucuy at PN Sierra Nevada. True nos. are best revealed in Jun when song is at a peak. Possibly interspecifically territorial with Spotted Nightingale-Thrush as the two do not seem to occur together.

Range: 1500–2900m. Sierra de Perijá, Zulia; Andes of s Táchira n through Mérida, nw Barinas, Trujillo, and se

Lara (*fuscater*). Costa Rica and Panama; locally in Andes from Colombia to n Bolivia.

Spotted Nightingale-Thrush   PLATE 54
Catharus dryas   Paraulata Ruiseñor
Identification: 7″ (18cm). 38g. Bill and legs orange; narrow eyering orange yellow. *Crown and sides of head black* contrasting with olive upperparts; *below pale apricot yellow spotted dusky on throat and breast*; flanks grayish, under tail coverts white (specimens fade to gray above, white below).
Sim. species: Nearest is Slaty-backed Nightingale-Thrush, but it is pale gray below with unspotted yellowish belly.
Voice: Rich liquid song phrases of this sp. have same inspirational and elevating character that marks so many of its allies' songs. Song is pure, flutelike, and intermittent, *cholo-chu . . . ee-o . . . tuEEo . . . lur-we, clo-EE-o . . .* , and other short whistled phrases, occas. odd guttural notes; overall a little choppy and hurried; many phrases strongly reminiscent of Wood Thrush (*Hylocichla mustelina*) of N Amer. (P. Schwartz recording).
Behavior: Another nightingale-thrush that is almost diabolically shy and difficult to see, certainly hd. far more than seen. Singers always seem to keep just ahead and out of sight of an advancing observer, their ineffably pure, ethereal tones forever receding. Stay in undergrowth, forage alone by hopping on gd., alternately picking at or tossing leaves, then abruptly raising up to look around alertly as do many others of genus.
Status and habitat: Very local resident (overlooked?) in lower levels of humid and mossy forest, esp. in damp ravines and along forested streams. Distrib. unaccountably spotty. The few sight recs. are scattered on w slope in Mérida (above La Azulita, Jan 1974—M. Gochfeld and M. Kleinbaum; Universidad de Los Andes forest, 23 Mar 1981—R. Ridgely and A. Keith); e slope in nw Barinas at La Soledad (Feb 1991—P. Boesman); and San Isidro Rd. (tapes 1998; sight 11 Mar 2000).

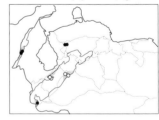

Range: 900–2200m. Sierra de Perijá, Zulia (upper Río Negro on Cerro Pejochaina; Kunana); w slope of Andes in Mérida (sight) and nw Lara (Cerros El Cerrón and El Cogollal); e slope of Andes on Cerro El Teteo in se Táchira, and sightings/tapes in nw Barinas (*maculatus*). S Mexico to Honduras; Colombia s locally in Andes to n Argentina.

Orange-billed Nightingale-Thrush   PLATE 54
Catharus aurantiirostris   Mirlo Pico Anaranjado
Identification: 6.5″ (16.5cm). 27g. Bill and legs bright orange; conspic. orange eyering. Above warm rufescent brown, underparts plain gray, paler and whitish

on throat and belly (*barbaritoi*, *birchalli*). Or paler, olive brown above (*aurantiirostris*).

Sim. species: From other brown-backed thrushes (*Catharus* and *Turdus*) by conspic. orange bill, eyering, and legs.

Voice: Despite this sp.'s name, its songs are squeaky, unmusical, and somewhat variable. There are numerous geographical dialects, and individuals sing several different songs, typically a rather jerky, sputtering *spits, BE-ja-a-FILbert*, some songs shorter. Call a nasal, scolding *ra-a-a-a*.

Behavior: Usually seen alone, occas. in prs., skulking near gd. and within confines of thickets where timid and difficult to see. Hops on gd., flicks aside a leaf, then raises head up quickly to watch as if fearful its actions might have attracted attention. Sings from a mostly concealed perch near gd. to ca. 2m up (higher after playback). Does not follow mixed-spp. flocks. Bulky, thick-walled, grass and moss nest cup, 1–3m up in dense shrub or thicket; 2 pale blue eggs somewhat spotted brownish[706,779]. In Colombia, breeding Mar–Jul[260].

Status and habitat: Fairly common but locally distrib. resident. Thickets in dry semideciduous to moist evergreen forest borders, overgrown pastures and fence rows, coffee plantations, even shrubby areas in towns and around habitations (e.g., in Colonia Tovar, Aragua, and in city of Mérida).

Range: 800–2900m. Sierra de Perijá, Zulia (*barbaritoi*); Andes from s Táchira n to Mérida, Trujillo, and nw and se Lara (Cerro El Cerrón); Falcón (Sierra de San Luis); Coastal Cordillera from Carabobo to Distr. Federal and Miranda; Interior Cordillera in Guárico at Cerro Platillón (*aurantiirostris*); mts. of ne Anzoátegui, Sucre, and n Monagas (*birchalli*). N Mexico to w Panama; Colombia; Trinidad.

Gray-cheeked Thrush

PLATE 54

Catharus minimus   Paraulata de Cara Gris

Identification: 7″ (18cm). 32g. Closely resembles Swainson's Thrush but shows at most only an indistinct and incomplete whitish loral area and eyering. Upperparts are dull olivaceous brown (occas. warm brown), *cheeks usually grayish* (often hard to see), below dull white, lower throat and chest tinged buff (less than on Swainson's) and thickly speckled dark brown, sides and flanks tinged grayish. Overall Gray-cheeked is duller, grayer, and colder-looking, but not all birds may be reliably separated in field.

Sim. species: In addition to commoner Swainson's Thrush, cf. with Veery. Veery is more rufescent above,

less speckled below (speckling confined to throat and upper chest), and grayish on sides and flanks.

Voice: Call a weak *queeah*, not often hd. Rarely or never sings on wintering gds.

Behavior: A shy bird that usually stays in dense cover and, unlike Swainson's Thrush, forages in damp shady areas, mostly on gd. and alone or only loosely assoc. with conspecifics. Seldom seen in fruiting trees.

Status and habitat: Fairly common but infreq. seen migrant and nonbreeding n winter resident, rec. 12 Oct–2 May in a wide variety of wooded regions. Can turn up almost anywhere in migration. Most recs. are from Andes (presum. migrants) and from s of Orinoco where large nos. appear to be n winter residents; 3 in migration, late evening of Apr 22, Rancho Grande Biol. Station, Aragua[33].

Range: To 3000m n of Orinoco; to 1500m s of Orinoco. Throughout (*minimus*). Breeds in N Amer. and ne Siberia; winters mostly in n S Amer. s to Ecuador, n Peru, Brazil n of the Amazon; Guyana; Suriname (sight). Trinidad; Curaçao.

Note: Bicknell's Thrush (*C. bicknelli*), now regarded as a sp. distinct from Gray-cheeked Thrush, breeds in ne N Amer.; winters in Carib.; could occur in Venez. (no S Amer. recs.), but there is no reliable way to separate the 2 spp. in field. Confirmation would require a specimen.

Swainson's Thrush

PLATE 54

Catharus ustulatus   Paraulata Lomiaceituna

Identification: 7″ (18cm). 28g. Upperparts uniform olive brown, *lores and usually conspic. eyering pale buff*, cheeks buffy brown, underparts dull white with *buff tinge and dusky spotting and speckling on lower throat and chest*.

Sim. species: Best marks are large eyering and buff cheeks. Imm. Swainson's in Oct and Nov may show little evident eyering, then easily confused with Gray-cheeked Thrush (see); in hand Swainson's has shorter wing than Gray-cheeked (88–105 vs. 97–109mm). Also cf. Veery.

Voice: Soft *whit* note. Short, weak versions of its beautiful, flutelike, upward spiraling song can be hd. sporadically by late Mar before migration.

Behavior: A timid bird that behaves as if perpetually fearful, and apt to flee at the slightest movement. Occurs alone, or occas. several are loosely assoc. at fruiting trees and shrubs where they stare wide-eyed, then bolt for cover after hurriedly fluttering for a few berries, or gobbling *Cecropia* catkins. Although mainly frugivorous, sometimes accompany mixed-spp. flocks,

mostly in mid. story or lower, but generally staying well above gd. Before n migration become highly frugivorous, concentrating in nos. around favorable fruiting trees.
Status and habitat: Fairly common transient and uncommon nonbreeding winter resident from N Amer., rec. 25 Oct–29 Mar (doubtless occurs later) to humid forest, light woodland, second growth, and shady coffee plantations in mts. of w half of country. True nos., esp. during migratory build-ups, are better revealed through mist-netting. Commoner in disturbed areas than inside mature humid forest. No recs. in *lowlands* n of Orinoco, but likely there during migration. Recs. few and scattered s of Orinoco.

Range: 800–2300m n of Orinoco; to 150m s of Orinoco. Mts. of w from Zulia, Táchira, Mérida, nw Barinas, and Falcón to Yaracuy, Aragua, and Miranda; Distr. Federal?; Amazonas (San Fernando de Atabapo; Cerro Duida; Cerro de la Neblina); Bolívar s to Cerro Roraima (*swainsoni*). Breeds in N Amer.; winters mainly in w S Amer. from Colombia and Venez. to nw Argentina; a few from Mexico to Panama and W Indies.

Veery   PLATE 54
Catharus fuscescens   Paraulata Cachetona
Identification: 7″ (18cm). 30g. Large dark eyes. *Above warm rufescent brown*, lores grayish, faint narrow eyering grayish (inconspic. or often absent), *throat and chest buffy white rather indistinctly speckled brown* (spots smaller, fewer, and more confined to upper chest than in Swainson's Thrush); sides and flanks mostly silky grayish white, center of lower breast and belly whitish.
Sim. species: Much like Swainson's and Gray-cheeked thrushes but more rufescent above than either. Also from Swainson's by grayer underparts, esp. sides and flanks, different face pattern (no obvious eyering), and fainter speckling. See Gray-cheeked Thrush.
Voice: May give a short *few* call but does not sing during n migration in S Amer.
Behavior: Shy and seldom seen on migration or wintering gds.
Status and habitat: Prob. an uncommon migrant and nonbreeding winter resident from N Amer., rec. 16 Oct–19 Apr from a wide range of localities but rather small no. of recs. Gd. or undergrowth in forest or wooded regions. Migratory routes and wintering range are not well known; prob. winters from s Venez. southward; 1 very fat migrant taken 19 Apr, Rancho Grande Biol. Station, Aragua[33]. Subsp. *salicicola* is known from Portuguesa, Carabobo, and Sucre; subsp. *fuliginosa* (breeding mainly in se Canada) is unrec.

Range: To 900m n of Orinoco; to 1050m s of Orinoco. Prob. throughout (*fuscescens* and *salicicola*). Rec. in Andes of n Táchira, Mérida, Trujillo, and se Lara; Portuguesa, se Falcón (sight)[60]; Coastal Cordillera in Carabobo, Aragua, Miranda[741], and mts. of Sucre; spottily in Amazonas and Bolívar. Breeds in N Amer.; transient in C Amer. and W Indies; winters mainly in nw S Amer. from Colombia and Guyana to e Peru (once), n Bolivia, and Amaz. Brazil.

Platycichla

Much like *Turdus*, and perhaps best merged into that genus, but slightly smaller; ♂ plumage predom. black or blackish, ♀ brownish; songs complex but not very melodious.

Yellow-legged Thrush   PLATE 54
Platycichla flavipes   Paraulata Negra
Identification: 8.5″ (22cm). 57g. Eyes dark (both sexes). ♂: *bill, narrow eyering, and legs bright yellow*. Head to mid. breast, wings, and tail black; *back, rump, flanks, and belly dark gray*. ♀: above plain olive brown with *narrow yellow eyering*; throat grayish white rather vaguely streaked dusky, rest of underparts pale brownish buff, *center of belly whitish*, under wing coverts bright buff; legs dull yellowish, bill usually dusky, culmen yellow. Or ♂ more extensively black below, ♀ sim. but dark brown above, gray brown below (*melanopleura*).
Sim. species: ♂ from ♂ Pale-eyed Thrush by dark eyes and gray back and lower underparts (gray *not obvious* at a distance). ♀ from ♀ Pale-eyed by streaked throat, yellow eyering, dark (not pale to grayish) eyes, and buffy white belly (not gray). Up close note ♀ Yellow-legged's more olive-tinged back (not uniform brownish). Also cf. Black-hooded Thrush.
Voice: Semimusical song is long, rambling, and highly individualistic. Song may continue for an hr with only short indefinite breaks. Some (all?) individuals incl. mimetic phrases of other birds, and each sings a unique set of song phrases, often remarkably different from others; some birds sing mostly squeaky songs, some musical, others with many mimic phrases (vocal copying of songs often poor). Typically songs contain some high, sputtering *sweet to-weeea-speét* and *swet to-weeea* phrases. Songs usually thinner, scratchier, and without freq. high-low jumps of songs of Pale-eyed Thrush. Sings mostly during 1st half of year.
Behavior: Single ♂♂ take high perch within open, well-lit canopy when singing; otherwise individuals or prs. may occur at almost any ht. Feed mostly at fruiting

trees and shrubs, only infreq. on gd. Like many Neotropical thrushes, can be wary and difficult to approach. In Trinidad breeds Mar–Jul; shallow moss-
covered, partially mud cup nest on bank or rock face;
2 eggs pale blue to greenish blue marked with reddish
brown; Mar–Jul[175].

Status and habitat: Fairly common resident. Some migratory movements may occur (details not known).
Fewer recs. late Jul–Nov; migratory flock of 24 northward through Portachuelo Pass[33] on 16 Aug 1945.
Humid forest borders, light open woodland, coffee
plantations, and second growth. Often sings from high
in eucalyptus (not native) in lightly settled areas.

Range: 480–2500m n of Orinoco; 1000–1800m s of Orinoco; 100–900m on Isla Margarita. S Zulia(?); Andes
from s Táchira, Mérida, nw Barinas, and Trujillo to nw
Lara (Cerros El Cogollal and El Cerrón); Falcón (Sierra
de San Luis), mts. of Yaracuy, n cordilleras from Carabobo to Distr. Federal and e Miranda; nw Bolívar
(Cerro Tabaro) in Río Caura; cerros of se Bolívar from
mid. Río Paragua (Cerro Guaiquinima), mid. Río
Caroní (Auyán-tepui) and Sierra de Lema southward
(*venezuelensis*); Cerro Roraima (*polionota*); mts. of ne
in Anzoátegui, Sucre, n Monagas, and Isla Margarita
(*melanopleura*). Ne Colombia; se Brazil, ne Argentina,
and e Paraguay.

Pale-eyed Thrush
PLATE 54
Platycichla leucops   Paraulata Ojiblanca
Identification: 8″ (20.3cm). 66g. ♂: *bill and legs orange
yellow; eyes bluish white*; otherwise *entirely lustrous
black*. ♀: dull dark brown above (no olive tinge), sides
of head and underparts pale brown becoming *grayish
buff on lower breast and belly*; sides tinged rufescent;
under wing coverts cinnamon rufous; bill dusky, legs
dull yellowish brown, eyes grayish, dark in juv.
Sim. species: ♂ from any other "black" thrush in
Venez. by *white eyes*. ♀ paler than ♀ Yellow-legged
Thrush and usually found inside humid forest. ♀
Glossy-blacked Thrush is larger, darker, and usually
streaky on throat.
Voice: An excellent songster. Song a long and choppy
but musical ser., *wheer-o-weet, chup-e, ez-t, e-ta, ti't,
eez, cheur-ez-weet, EE skee, weewee . . . .*, unusually varied and complex, with many high, thin notes (high-
low jumps are characteristic). *Often mimics other spp.*,
mixing their songs with its own. Recalls song of
Yellow-legged Thrush but much more musical. Song
hd. mainly May–Jun in Aragua and Lara.
Behavior: Usually irrationally shy and difficult to see.
Occurs alone or in prs., feeds in fruiting trees, esp.
when other birds are present, and prob. also forages

on gd. inside forest. Otherwise usually seen in forest
mid. levels or lower, although sings from subcanopy.
Not with mixed-spp. flocks.

Status and habitat: Rare to uncommon and perhaps
also local resident in humid and wet montane forest,
esp. mossy forest and old second-growth woodland.
Some seasonal movements may occur; all specimen
recs. are late Nov–late Jun (except 1 rec. on 1 Aug,
Ptari-tepui). Rare or absent on Sierra de Lema mid
Dec–early Mar (Hilty), but several seen 30 Mar–3 Apr
at 1300–1400m (R. Ridgely).

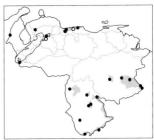

Range: 900–1850m n of Orinoco; 1100–1800m s of Orinoco. Sierra de Perijá, Zulia (once); Andes of s Táchira n to nw Lara (Cerro El Cogollal) and se Lara
(Cubiro; sight, PN Yacambú); Coastal Cordillera in Carabobo, Aragua, and Miranda; spottily in Amazonas
(Cerros Parú and Sipapo to Cerros Duida, Tamacuarí,
and de la Neblina); mts. of se Bolívar (Cerro Guaiquinima and Auyán-tepui; Sierra de Lema s to Cerro
Roraima and Uei-tepui). Mts. of adj. Guyana and Brazil
(Roraima); Andes from s Colombia to Bolivia.

Turdus

Familiar, almost worldwide genus; strong legs; squarish tail; occur in many habitats; well-known songsters;
sturdy cup nest, often partly of mud.

Great Thrush
PLATE 54
Turdus fuscater   Paraulata Morera
Identification: 13″ (33cm). 140g. *Large, dingy brownish gray thrush.* Bill and legs yellow orange. ♂: above
uniform dark grayish brown with blackish lores and
narrow orange eyering; *wings and tail dusky black*, underparts pale brownish gray, palest on belly. Or paler
and grayer above and below, belly pale buffy gray
(*clarus*). ♀ and imm.: paler, esp. below; eyering faint
or absent.
Sim. species: Much *larger* and paler (grayish to sooty
rather than black) than other "black" thrushes. In flight
so large it may bring to mind a small *Accipiter* as it
swoops into a ravine.
Voice: Rich, varied song given mostly in predawn darkness is leisurely ser. of loud, thick whistles, e.g., *so
clear-e, so clear-e, so clear-he* and so on, often mixed
with nasal *nwee-nwee* and a few high-pitched notes or
dry trills. After a few phrases, song drifts to new
phrases in slow, fluidlike transition. During day often
rather noisy, giving robinlike *sée-ert*, loud *kuet-kuet-
kuet-kuet*, waxwing-like *eeeee*, and loud *cheeyop*.
Behavior: A widespread and familiar bird throughout
Andean highlands. Single birds, prs., or families are

conspic. and often noisy as they hop on gd., roads, or in other open areas, visit fruiting trees and shrubs, and often perch in open. Nest (Apr) a large bulky cup low in shrub; 2 eggs blue spotted darker chiefly at larger end[589,778].

Status and habitat: Very common resident in cultivated areas, farmyards, partially opened areas, borders of humid and wet forest, and lower zones of paramo. Requires a few shrubs or trees or bushy ravine in its territory, but quickly colonizes clearings in high montane forest and thrives in presence of people. Has profited from deforestation, and doubtless much more numerous now than formerly.

Range: 1600–4200m. Sierra de Perijá, Zulia (*clarus*); Andes of s Táchira n through Mérida, Trujillo, and se Lara (*gigas*). Colombia s in Andes to Bolivia.

Glossy-black Thrush
PLATE 54
Turdus serranus   Paraulata Ciote

Identification: 10″ (25cm). 73g. ♂: *bill and legs orange yellow*, otherwise *entirely glossy black with narrow orange eyering* (usually fairly conspic.) and dark eyes. ♀: dark brown above with *narrow dull orange yellow eyering (not conspic.)*; tail dusky; underparts dark olive brown (or sooty gray—*cumanensis*) only slightly paler than above, throat somewhat streaked black (or essentially unstreaked—*atrosericeus*); under wing converts orange ochraceous (duller—*cumanensis*); bill dull yellowish, legs brownish yellow; eyes dark.

Sim. species: ♂ Great Thrush is obviously larger and dingier than ♂ Glossy-black. ♀ is *darkest* of ♀ thrushes in Venez. Under ideal conditions ♀ told from ♀ Yellow-legged, Pale-legged, and Black-hooded thrushes by combination of eyering (Pale-eyed has little or no evident eyering) and *darker and more uniform underparts* (belly not obviously paler).

Voice: Unmusical song a rapidly mumbled *te-do-de-de-do-deet*, all notes run together, rather shrill, gradually rising throughout, and monotonously repeated at short intervals. In predawn darkness sings nonstop for 30 min or more, then abruptly falls silent after sunrise. Day song sim. but apparently seasonal and given only for short period when breeding.

Behavior: Often rather shy and hard to see well, despite persistent singing at dawn. Inconspic. as forages on gd., sometimes hopping into open along roads at dawn. Reg. visits fruiting trees where briefly assoc. with other spp. Otherwise usually alone or in prs. and usually not with mixed-spp. flocks. Mossy cup nest on low vine, etc.; 2 pale blue eggs spotted purple and light brown. Colombia breeding, Mar–Oct[260].

Status and habitat: Locally common resident in humid and wet montane forest. Small migratory movements may occur; flock of 10–12 in open area of forest

on Cerro Negro, Sucre, 26 Aug 1994 (Hilty and P. Boesman). Up to 2400m on Cerro Oriental in Coastal Cordillera (D. Ascanio).

Range: 950–2900m. S Táchira on Páramo de Tamá (*fuscobrunneus*); Sierra de Perijá, Zulia, Andes from n Táchira (recs.?) to Lara; mts. of Yaracuy and Coastal Cordillera in Carabobo, Aragua, Distr. Federal, and Miranda (*atrosericeus*); mts. of ne Anzoátegui, Sucre, and n Monagas (*cumanensis*). Andes of Colombia to n Argentina.

Black-hooded Thrush
PLATE 54
Turdus olivater   Paraulata Cabecinegra

Identification: 9.5″ (24cm). 70g (*olivater*), 85g (*kemptoni*). Shows considerable geographical variation. ♂: *bill, eyering, and legs yellow; entire head, throat, and chest black* (form "hood"), otherwise olive brown above; wings and tail dusky black, underparts vary from olive gray to olive brown to ochraceous (*olivater, roraimae*). Or throat and chest somewhat smudged and streaked black (not sharply defined bib), lower underparts bright buffy brown (*duidae*). Or as in *duidae* but brighter buff below (*kemptoni*). Or back darker, more slaty olive (*paraquensis*). ♀: sim. to ♂ but black foreparts replaced by *brown*, throat and chest somewhat darker than lower underparts (a faint suggestion of ♂'s "hood"); bill dusky or vaguely yellowish, *little or no eyering*; legs yellowish brown; plumage overall mostly buffy brown. Or above dark brown, throat more or less streaked blackish, upper breast grayish, lower breast and belly bright tawny (*roraimae*).

Sim. species: ♂'s hood is distinctive. ♀ very sim. to ♀ Glossy-black Thrush and esp. to ♀ Pale-eyed Thrush. ♀ Glossy-black is darker and more uniform; ♀ Pale-eyed is smaller, darker, lacks ♀ Black-hooded's slight "hooded" look of dark chest, and usually (?) has duskier bill. Black-billed Thrush is grayer and has whitish belly.

Voice: Song a full-bodied, *Turdus*-like caroling, *TEEur .. turee .. todee .. churdur .. turwere .. turee ..* and so on, the phrases warbled, typically bi- or trisyllabic and all rather sim.; pauses between phrases often separated by high, thin *ee'ee* notes.

Behavior: Usually alone, but several may gather briefly with other spp. at fruiting trees, esp. melastomes. Sing from forest mid. levels to canopy but forage on gd., flipping leaves, much as do other *Turdus*, and often around army ant swarms. Mossy cup nest may be low; 2 pale blue eggs spotted purple and light brown; breeding Jan–Jul, ne Colombia[260].

Status and habitat: Uncommon resident (possibly short-distance migrant?). Humid forest and second-growth woodland, occas. along wooded borders. Uncommon to locally common s of Orinoco in sim. or wetter habitat. In all areas there are sharp seasonal and/or local swings in pop. nos.

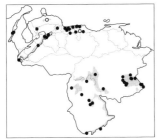

Range: 800–1950m n of Orinoco; 950–2600m s of Orinoco. Sierra de Perijá, Zulia; Andes of s Táchira n through Mérida, nw Barinas, Trujillo, and Lara; mts. of n Falcón (Sierra de San Luis[60]) and Yaracuy, n cordilleras from Carabobo and n Guárico to Miranda (*olivater*); n Amazonas on Cerros Yavi, Parú, Huachmacare, and Duida; nw Bolívar on Cerro Tabaro (*duidae*); n Amazonas on Cerro Sipapo (*paraquensis*); s Amazonas on Cerro de la Neblina (*kemptoni*); se Bolívar on Sierra de Lema and cerros of Gran Sabana (*roraimae*). Mts. of Colombia; adj. Guyana and n Brazil; Suriname (once).

Chestnut-bellied Thrush   PLATE 54
Turdus fulviventris   Paraulata Vientre Castaño
Identification: 10″ (25cm). Bill yellowish; narrow eyering orange; legs dull pale yellow. ♂: *entire head and throat black*, throat narrowly streaked whitish, back dark gray, wings and tail dusky, chest light gray forming *distinct broad band; breast and belly rich ferruginous*, crissum grayish brown. ♀: sim. but duller.
Sim. species: Only *Turdus* in Venez. with ferruginous underparts. Gray chest band is fairly conspic. Those familiar with American Robin (*T. migratorius*) of N Amer. will note a striking resemblance.
Voice: Does not sing as much as most *Turdus*. Song a notably variable ser. of choppy phrases, somewhat *Turdus*-like but with many trills and buzzes, *che'e'e-chert chee-rt-ee e'r'r'r, chu-wurt, titi, t't't, eet* . . . (P. Schwartz recording). Call a wooden *peent*.
Behavior: Found alone or in scattered prs. ♂♂ sing from forest canopy, but both sexes spend much time foraging on gd. inside forest where they toss or flip leaves aside with bill, often spending several min at a site before moving a short distance and repeating process. May eat some fruit but are rarely seen in fruiting trees with other spp. or with mixed-spp. flocks.
Status and habitat: Uncommon resident, seemingly nowhere very numerous. Humid montane forest and forest borders; occas. in lighter second-growth woodland. Some local and/or seasonal el. movements may occur (nos. unaccountably erratic?). Generally easier to find in early part of rainy season, May–Jul, when more singing occurs.
Range: 1300–2700m. Sierra de Perijá, Zulia; Andes of s Táchira n through Mérida, nw Barinas (sightings), and to n Trujillo (Carache; Páramo Las Rosas). Andes of Colombia to n Peru.

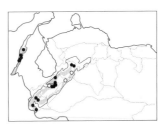

Note: Clay-colored Thrush (*T. grayi*) occurs virtually to border of Venez. in Goajira Pen., Colombia. Above dull olive brown, below uniform pale buffy brown with a few inconspic. dusky streaks on throat. Occurs in cultivated areas with scattered trees and around habitations, esp. in drier zones.

Bare-eyed Thrush   PLATE 54
Turdus nudigenis   Paraulata Ojo de Candil
Identification: 9″ (23cm). 60g. Large, *bare, orange yellow ocular ring conspic.* Bill yellowish, basal half dusky. Above uniform grayish brown tinged olive, throat whitish streaked dusky, breast pale clay brown (paler than above), belly and crissum white. Eyering present even in juv.
Sim. species: From any other *Turdus* by conspic. bare ocular ring.
Voice: Song a melodious caroling, even more musical than that of many other *Turdus*, but many high notes and phrases, *clee-er . . weer-o . . ee . . wur-eer, wureer . .* and so on. Distinctive call a nasal, meowing *cue-erree* sliding up sharply.
Behavior: Rather solitary and mostly arboreal, though readily forages on gd. like others *Turdus*. Tends to be inconspic. but is often in flowering or fruiting trees, and on lawns and gardens in residential areas. Jul–Sep breeding, Guárico[734]; May–Jun in Orinoco region; nest is usual *Turdus* cup of mud and plant material; 2–4 pale blue green eggs blotched russet[186].
Status and habitat: Common resident. Gallery forest borders, coffee plantations, and semiopen areas with scattered groves of trees; also parks, gardens, and urban areas where there are trees and bushy areas. Generally less numerous and much less conspic. than Pale-breasted Thrush.

Range: To 1800m n of Orinoco (mostly below 800m); to 950m s of Orinoco. C and se Falcón (sight, Churuguara and La Misión), both slopes of Andes from s Táchira to w Trujillo, n cordilleras from Yaracuy and Carabobo to Sucre, and generally e of Andes to Delta Amacuro[343]; nw Amazonas (s to Isla Ratón); n Bolívar s to lower Río Caura (Maripa; El Cambur), lower Río Paragua and from Sierra de Imataca s to Cerro Roraima and Santa Elena de Uairen; Islas Margarita and Patos (*nudigenis*). E Colombia to the Guianas and extreme ne Brazil. Trinidad and Tobago; Lesser Antilles.

Black-billed Thrush
PLATE 54
Turdus ignobilis   Paraulata Pico Negro
Identification: 9" (23cm). 57g. *Dull with all-black bill* (no eyering). Andean birds: above *dull brown* (no contrast), throat white narrowly streaked dusky; small, rather ill-defined whitish crescent below throat (inconspic.), otherwise pale brown below, center of breast, belly, and crissum dull white, under wing coverts faintly washed buff (not conspic.). S of Orinoco: rather different; above uniform *dark grayish brown, below mostly dull gray* (or brown—*murinus*), median throat white streaked dusky (white inconspic.), center of lower underparts dirty white. Underwings as above.
Sim. species: Lacks good marks. Moreover, birds s of Orinoco (esp. in Amazonas) are darker overall, grayer below, and hardly look like same sp. Everywhere best told by black bill, dingy white lower underparts, and general absence of marks. See Pale-vented, Pale-breasted, Lawrence's, and Cocoa thrushes; also Palm Tanager.
Voice: Song in n cordilleras a rather slow caroling *churre, churre, ee, TE-0-we, churre . . .* and so on with pleasing, relaxed phrases; some individuals sing very repetitive phrases; call in w Mérida a loud *pfeea!* or *wEEa!* In se Venez. songs are sim. but may rise and fall in more distinct and repetitive pattern. In general songs recall those of American Robin (*T. migratorius*). Calls s of Orinoco (Sierra de Lema) include nasal, rising *queek!*; soft *prip* (like *Catharus* thrush); when disturbed a rather loud *Quee-kipper-kipper-kipper* as flies off low into forest, this call sim. to that given by some other *Turdus* thrushes.
Behavior: Sim. to that of other *Turdus*. Occurs alone or in prs. and mostly independent of mixed-spp. flocks. Often forages by hopping on gd., usually near or in forest, and reg. visits fruiting trees and shrubs, esp. melastomes. Has habit of constantly flicking tail downward. Generally not shy and relatively easy to see. Often perches on open mid.-level branch.
Status and habitat: Uncommon to locally fairly common resident. Light woodland, tall second growth, disturbed areas, coffee plantations, even parks and gardens n of Orinoco. Humid forest borders on slopes of tepuis s of Orinoco. Generally less numerous in Venez. (esp. n of Orinoco) than in Colombia. Coarse cup nest, usually with mud, low in bush, tree, or stump; 2 blue eggs heavily marked brown.

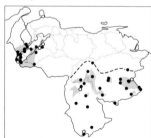

Range: To 1600m n of Orinoco; 700–1950m s of Orinoco. W base of Andes in Táchira, Mérida, and Zulia, e base from s Táchira and w Apure (Guasdualito) n to Mérida and nw Barinas (*debilis*); Amazonas on slopes of Cerros Duida and Yapacana (*arthuri*); Amazonas on Cerros Yavi, Guanay, Camani, Parú, and Duida, Sierra de Unturán, and Cerro de la Neblina; Bolívar in lower and upper Río Caura, mid. Río Paragua (Cerro Guaiquinima), and cerros of Gran Sabana from Auyántepui and Sierra de Lema southward (*murinus*). Guyana and Suriname; Colombia s in Andes and lowlands to n Bolivia and w and c Amaz. Brazil.

Lawrence's Thrush
PLATE 54
Turdus lawrencii   Paraulata Imitadora
Identification: 8.5" (22cm). 73g. *Bright yellow bill* and *conspic. yellow eyering* (♂); or dusky bill and narrow yellow eyering (♀ and imm.). ♂: above uniform rich dark brown, throat white heavily and coarsely streaked dusky (shows more dusky than white), no whitish crescent below throat, rest of underparts dull brown to olivaceous brown, *center of belly and crissum white*; under wing coverts orange cinnamon (visible in hand). ♀: dull and paler above and below; white of underparts often tinged buff.
Sim. species: ♂'s best marks are conspic. yellow bill and eyering and white crissum, but best of all is unusual song. ♀ much like Black-billed Thrush (*debilis*) but with *buffy tone* (not grayish) to underparts. ♀ also much like *orinocensis* race of Cocoa Thrush, esp. below, but duller and lacks warm rufescent tones of *orinocensis*; in hand latter has inner flight feathers edged cinnamon. Also cf. White-necked Thrush.
Voice: One of best mimics in New World. Individuals effortlessly copy songs, or often only parts of songs, and calls of dozens of local birds, as well as frogs and insects, with almost flawless accuracy. Song is a loud, deliberate ser. of vocal imitations with short pauses and occas. non-mimetic phrases of its own, the ser. often continuing uninterrupted for 30 min or more from a high perch. Each singer has unique repertoire. It is a good bet that aside from characteristic non-mimetic phrases, a stream of vocalizations of gd.-dwelling birds emanating from canopy are being given by this fascinating bird. Calls incl. a shrill *kuk-peer!*, plaintive *perwheee*, abrupt *weecheee*, and loud *peep peep peep!*
Behavior: ♂♂ sing from reg. song perches day after day from forest mid. level to high canopy where they are difficult to locate even when singing, almost impossible when silent. Occas. accompany mixed-spp. flocks. Forage quietly and unobtrusively on gd. where flip over leaves like many others of genus, or visit fruiting trees and shrubs at almost any ht. May have atypical thrush mating system, either promiscuous or polygynous, as song appears directed toward ♀♀, not territorial defense[245].
Status and habitat: Rare (small no. of specimens) and local resident in Venez. Humid terra firme forest incl. sandy soil forest. In e Peru mainly várzea and transition forest. Sight recs. as follows: 1 on 3 Aug 1982, 10km w of Santa Elena de Uairén, Bolívar (C. Parrish); 1 on 18 Jan 1991, w of El Paují, Bolívar (Hilty).

Range: To 1200m. S Amazonas along Río Negro (El Carmen) and Cerro de la Neblina; Bolívar in upper Río Paragua (Salto Capurí; Caño Antabari), upper Río Caroní (sightings), and Cerro Roraima. Se Colombia to n Bolivia and w Amaz. and nw Brazil.

Pale-breasted Thrush
PLATE 54

Turdus leucomelas Paraulata Montañera

Identification: 9″ (23cm). 62g. Bill dusky to greenish dusky. *Gray head contrasts with pale olive brown upperparts*; wings sometimes tinged russet; throat white streaked dusky, breast and flanks pale grayish brown, center of lower breast, belly, and crissum white. Under wing coverts and inner webs of all but outermost flight feathers cinnamon (usually not conspic. in field).

Sim. species: From all other sim. spp. by gray head *contrasting* with back. Black-billed Thrush is uniform above and below; Cocoa and Pale-vented thrushes are rufescent above and below.

Voice: Song a pleasant caroling reminiscent of American Robin (*T. migratorius*) but more complex; phrases *hereit, hereit, tuwee* or *tuwee, tuwee* are prom.; call a raspy, harsh *reep reep reep* and rough *jig jig*. Sings mainly Dec–Jul.

Behavior: This well-known thrush, at home in backyards, gardens, and woodlands throughout settled areas, hardly needs introduction. Sings from mid. or upper levels of trees but forages on gd. by hopping on lawns, roadsides, etc., like others of genus. Reg. visits fruiting trees and shrubs, and is often out hopping along roadsides well before first light. Nest a moss and rootlet cup in shrub, tree, or on building; 2–3 bluish green eggs spotted reddish brown; breeding Jul–Aug, Guárico and ne Anzoátegui[186,734], but prob. most of yr.

Status and habitat: Common and widespread resident in moderately dry, moist, and humid forest borders, light or disturbed woodland, second growth, plantations, parks, and cultivated areas. Equally at home in urban and rural settings. One of commonest birds

around habitations in n Venez. (e.g., Caracas and Maracay).

Range: To 2000m n of Orinoco; to 1900m s of Orinoco. Generally n of Orinoco and s of it in Amazonas s to Cerro Yapacana; n Bolívar from Caicara and Sierra de Imataca s to Gran Sabana at Santa Elena de Uairén (*albiventer*). N Colombia e through Guianas and e and se Brazil to ne Bolivia and ne Argentina; isolated pop. in San Martín, Peru.

Cocoa Thrush
PLATE 54

Turdus fumigatus Paraulata Acanelada

Identification: 9″ (23cm). 61g. Bill dusky. Mostly bright reddish brown. *Above uniform rich rufescent brown, below warm cinnamon brown*, throat dull white indistinctly and narrowly streaked dusky, center of belly and under tail coverts slightly paler. Or overall even brighter, richer cinnamon brown (*fumigatus*). Or decidedly darker and browner above, whitish on belly and crissum. All races show variation in color, esp. on underparts, with some individuals much paler than others (but always darkest in *orinocensis*). In hand note bright cinnamon orange under wing coverts and inner flight feather edging.

Sim. species: Brighter and more uniformly reddish brown than any other *Turdus* in Venez. Cf. darker *orinocensis* subsp. with Pale-breasted Thrush.

Voice: Song (*fumigatus*) a long musical caroling with numerous slurred phrases, the whole gliding smoothly along within narrow range of pitches, *pree-er, churry, churry, o-ee-o, lulu, o-E-er, cheer-er, wu-e, wu-e, E-a-o-eeo, te-a, te-a, e-o-to-e, cheer-o, o-ee-, urr, wu-EE-er, toe-ee-tu-tu, o-ee-o* . . . and so on (listen for often-repeated *o-ee-o* phrases). Or song choppy, some phrases squeaky, and overall less musical (*orinocensis*). In all races, not as vocal as some *Turdus*; most vocal 1st half of yr.

Behavior: Alone or in prs. Sings from mid. levels or higher in trees, forages mostly on gd. by hopping then pausing to peer carefully or to flip leaves with bill. Also reg. in fruiting trees. Inconspic. and somewhat retiring in forested regions but much less so in cultivated and urban areas. Has habit of shivering tail upon alighting. Bulky plant and mud cup nest to 5m up on trunk, stump, or niche in bank; 2–4 eggs, pale greenish blue marked with pale reddish brown[691].

Status and habitat: Resident. Uncommon to fairly common locally n of Orinoco in cultivated areas, light woodland, parks, gardens, and cocoa and coffee plantations. Local in gallery forest in llanos and spotty in terra firme and várzea forests s of Orinoco; fairly numerous in e Bolívar (tall várzea) on upper Río Cuyuní.

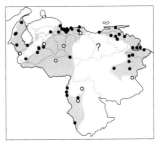

Range: To 1800m n of Orinoco; to 500m s of Orinoco. Base of Sierra de Perijá and s of Lago de Maracaibo, Zulia, w base of Andes in Táchira; e Lara, Yaracuy, and generally e of Andes (except e base) to Sucre and n Monagas at Caripe (*aquilonalis*); Delta Amacuro; Bolívar from lower Río Paragua to Sierra de Imataca and upper Río Cuyuní (*fumigatus*); e base of Andes in se Táchira, w Apure, and w Barinas (n to Barinitas), and w Amazonas s to Río Casiquiare (*orinocensis*). E Colombia to the Guianas, ne and e central Brazil; coastal e Brazil. Trinidad; part of Lesser Antilles.
Note: Hauxwell's Thrush (*T. hauxwelli*) of w and c Amaz. Brazil may meet Cocoa Thrush close to border of sw Venez. The two are possibly conspecific; Hauxwell's is less rufescent above, more olivaceous brown below.

White-necked Thrush   PLATE 54
Turdus albicollis   Paraulata Chote
Identification: 9″ (23cm). 50g. Dark thrush. Bill blackish; narrow yellow eyering (inconspic.). *Above dark brown incl. sides of head*; throat white *heavily and coarsely streaked black* (white barely visible) and *bordered below by narrow crescent of white on upper chest, rest of underparts light gray* turning white on central belly and crissum.
Sim. species: Looks dark headed with narrow, inconspic. white crescent across chest. Pale gray breast and sides also are good marks. Various races of Black-billed Thrush are all darker and more uniform below (white crescent beneath throat ill defined).
Voice: Song, in same mold as many *Turdus*, is melodious, but slower, lazier, and with what seems to be monotonously little variation: *churrwerr . . eeerr . . weeerr . . eerr'e . .* ; the paired, sing-song phrases are hypnotic. Despite monotony of song, paired (low-high) phrases are not identical to each other (listen carefully). Alarm a rough *jjig-wig* or *jjig-wig-wig*.
Behavior: More secretive and harder to see than most *Turdus* but does reg. hop out on bare gd. in openings at edge of forested roadsides or in trails early in morning. Sings from elevated perch in lower or mid. story of forest but forages on forest floor, visits fruiting trees and shrubs in forest mid. levels or lower, and is reg. around army ant swarms. Does not follow mixed-spp. flocks. In some areas sought as a cagebird for its pleasing song.
Status and habitat: Uncommon to locally fairly common resident in humid and wet forest and forest edges, mainly in foothills or mts. n of Orinoco. Widespread in terra firme and várzea forest in lowlands s of Orinoco. Look for it at dawn on roadsides around Rancho Grande Biol. Station, Aragua.

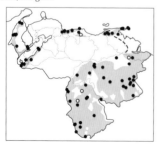

Range: To 1900m n of Orinoco; to 1600m s of Orinoco. Sierra de Perijá, Zulia; w base of Andes in Mérida (prob. Táchira); e base in Táchira, w Apure, and nw Barinas; Coastal Cordillera in e Carabobo, Aragua, Distr. Federal, and Miranda; mts. of ne Anzoátegui n Monagas, and Sucre (*phaeopygoides*); generally in Amazonas and Bolívar (*phaeopygus*). N Colombia and the Guianas to w and c Brazil and nw Argentina; coastal e and se Brazil to ne Argentina and e Paraguay. Trinidad and Tobago.
Note: Subsp. *minuscula* incl. within *phaeopygoides*[467].

Mimidae: Mockingbirds and Thrashers
Paraulatas Llaneras y Zorzales

Mockingbirds and thrashers are a small New World family now believed to be most closely related to starlings (Sturnidae). They are beloved for their cheerful songs and, in the case of some mockingbirds, their powers of vocal mimicry. Otherwise they are rather slender and long-tailed with dull and undistinguished plumage. The family is mostly insectivorous, but fruit is also eaten. Nests are usually bulky open cups.

Tropical Mockingbird   PLATE 48
Mimus gilvus   Paraulata Llanera
Identification: 10″ (25cm). 54g. *Slender and long-tailed*. Eyes *yellow*. Pale smoky gray above with *long chalky white eyestripe* and black patch through eyes; wings blackish; coverts edged whitish forming 2 indistinct wing bars (no white wing patch); flight feathers edged white; *tail blackish, much rounded, all but central feathers broadly tipped white*; underparts dull eggshell white. Imm.: duller and browner; eyes dark.
Sim. species: A conspic., long-tailed, gray bird of semi-open dry country is likely to be this sp. Shape recalls Bicolored Wren, but that sp. is much darker above, with blackish crown and rufescent upperparts.
Voice: An energetic and inspired singer. Song a long, rambling, musical ser. of choppy notes and phrases, some repeated, some not; e.g., *you're a chéater . . dirty-dirty . . cheater . . chipa-chipa . .* and so on; reminiscent of Northern Mockingbird (*M. polyglottos*) but huskier, and unlike it, seems not to mimic other birds. Alarm a loud *jeeop!*
Behavior: Like various allies, something of a buffoon, alternatively behaving as a singer, aggressor, and buoyant clown. Often seen perched in open on electric lines, atop tall cactuses, or in other conspic. places. Occurs in prs. which are aggressive around nest sites and quick to mob small owls. Often forages on gd. where it runs quickly and stops abruptly with long tail held up. Like Northern Mockingbird, frequently "wing lifts." Eats insects, even small vertebrates, and a variety of small fruits and berries. Nest a twiggy bowl in bush or shrub; 2–3 eggs; pale greenish blue with rusty spots at larger end[589]; breeding Mar–Apr, w Guárico[734]; late Jan–Sep, ne Anzoátegui[186].
Status and habitat: Common in towns, ranchland, and other drier open areas with scattered shrubbery. Commonest in arid regions dominated by *Acacia*, cactus, and thorn scrub. Abundant on Paraguaná Pen. and deserts of n Falcón.

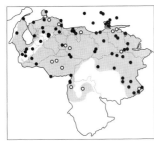

Range: To 2200m n of Orinoco; to 1300m s of Orinoco. Generally s to n Amazonas (Pto. Ayacucho; sight, Samariapo; Junglaven), n Bolívar (s to La Paragua), and se Bolívar (Paurai-tepui; Santa Elena de Uairén); Islas Los Testigos, Los Frailes, Margarita, Coche, and Cubagua (*melanopterus*); La Orchila, La Tortuga, Tortuguilla, La Blanquilla, and La Horquilla on Los Hermanos (*rostratus*); Los Roques(?). S Mexico to Honduras; introd. in Panama; nw Ecuador; Colombia to the Guianas and extreme n Brazil; coastal e Brazil. Trinidad and Tobago. Many Carib. isls.

Note: Chalk-browed Mockingbird (*M. saturninus*) may eventually be found in se Bolívar, as it is known from isolated pops. in adj. n Brazil and the Guianas. Much like Tropical Mockingbird but brownish (not gray) and usually somewhat streaky above; white eyebrow prom.; underparts often a bit dingy and brownish and with vague streaking on flanks. Song typical of genus, sometimes with a few mimetic phrases.

Pearly-eyed Thrasher

Margarops fuscatus   Zorzal   PLATE 48

Identification: 11″ (28cm). 75g. *No recent recs. on Venez.* isls. Bill yellowish pink tipped dusky, slightly decurved; *eyes pale yellow.* Above dull grayish brown somewhat mottled dusky, inner flight feathers and tertials edged white, *long tail tipped white* (narrowly above, broadly below); *underparts white coarsely streaked and scaled brown.*

Sim. species: Looks like a large, dull, long-tailed thrush.

Voice: Song in Lesser Antilles a slow, choppy ser. of rising and falling notes, musical but husky.

Status and habitat: Dense scrub and dry woodland. Not found on Isla Horquilla (in Los Hermanos) since 1908 and presumed extinct there (*bonairensis*). Reasons for its disappearance are unknown.

Range: Formerly Isla Horquilla in Los Hermanos isls. Bonaire; Curaçao (once); Bahamas, Puerto Rico, Lesser Antilles.

Motacillidae: Pipits and Wagtails

Camineros y Miracielitos

A few wagtails breed or are vagrant to North America. Otherwise, the only New World motacillids are pipits. One Venezuelan species inhabits the cold paramo high above the Andean treeline, the other is found in grasslands of central and southern Venezuela. Pipits are terrestrial birds. All of them have a flight song and are mainly insectivorous.

Anthus

Streaky and brown; notched tail; white outer tail feathers; thin bill and long hindclaw; almost all spp. very sim. in appearance, often with vague eyering.

Yellowish Pipit   PLATE 65

Anthus lutescens   Caminero

Identification: 5.3″ (13.5cm). 14g. Small pipit. Rather slender, delicate proportions. *Bill thin*, dusky above, pale below; legs pinkish. *Upperparts buffy brown heavily streaked blackish* (streaking coarse on back), narrow eyering and underparts buff; *conspic. necklace of dusky streaks across chest*; lower underparts tinged yellow, tail dusky brown, *2 outer prs. of feathers white* (conspic. in flight). Birds in worn plumage are paler, often whitish below.

Sim. species: Thin bill and white outer tail feathers separate it from any sparrow-plumaged emberizid. Above treeline see larger Páramo Pipit.

Voice: Peculiar, buzzy song is delivered from gd., or more often in long-sustained ser. in flight. Typically flies upward then "parachutes" earthward with wings spread and raised, as sings a few high twittery notes followed by long, nasal, descending buzz, *tsit'sit'sit'tiz-bzzzzzzeeeeeeeeuuuu*, the performance often repeated over and over as bird circles high overhead. Not uncommonly 3–4 singers may be aloft simultaneously. Flush with brief *chit-chit*.

Behavior: A bird of open grasslands that walks or runs quickly through grass, crouches if alarmed, and is difficult to see unless flushed. Flight is swooping, and when flushed, bird usually flies up very high and goes far away before alighting. Does not gather in flocks but is loosely colonial, perhaps because of restricted nature of habitat. Ovenlike nest in short grass; Jun, Anzoátegui[186]; May, Sep, and Oct breeding, w Apure[137].

Status and habitat: Locally common resident in grasslands and open fields where grass is *very short*, also along bare or nearly bare lake borders if grass is present nearby.

Range: To 200m n of Orinoco; to 1300m s of Orinoco. Generally e of Andes from Apure, Barinas, and s Carabobo (El Paito) e to e Monagas and Delta Amacuro; n Amazonas (San Juan de Manapiare; prob. elsewhere); n Bolívar in lower Río Caura (many sightings) and s locally through Gran Sabana (*lutescens*). E Colombia locally to the Guianas and extreme e and s Brazil; e Bolivia and s to c Argentina. Coastal Peru and n Chile (where doubtless a separate sp.); Panama.

Páramo Pipit   PLATE 65
Anthus bogotensis   Miracielito
Identification: 6" (15cm). 26g. Bill thin; legs pinkish. *Above buffy brown broadly streaked dusky brown*; narrow eyering whitish, underparts *more or less uniform deep buff with a few dusky streaks and spots across chest* forming narrow, ill-defined necklace, sometimes also a few markings on sides; tail dark brown, *outer 2 prs. of feathers mostly buffy white* (both subspp.).
Sim. species: From any canastero or streaked emberizid, i.e., ♀ Plumbeous Sierra-Finch, ♀ Plain-colored Seedeater, by combination of rather long, thin bill, white outer tail feathers, and *rich buff* underparts (streaking on underparts not conspic. in field). Also cf. Grassland and Stripe-tailed yellow-finches, both usually at lower els.
Voice: Flushes with dry *chit-chit*. Flight song, delivered with wings held up stiffly over back like many other pipits and skylarks, is a long, nasal, wheezy buzz followed by high, chattery notes, *nyeeeezzzzzzzzz, dziit-it, dziit-it, chit-it-it-it'it'it*. Also sings from top of rock or shrub, delivering sim. or less complex song; in n Táchira, while perched, a lively, jumbled song with note quality of *Carduelis* siskin.
Behavior: Occurs alone, in prs., or in loosely assoc. groups of 6 or more in favorable areas. Like others of genus, runs through grass, crouches if alarmed, and usually seen only when flushed, then flies off with strongly undulating flight, sometimes circling and landing close at hand, at other times flying off long distances. Believed breeding, late Mar, nw Venez.[778]; small groups Jan–Feb, prs. in Jun, Mérida.
Status and habitat: Locally fairly common resident but sometimes hard to find; paramo and fields and pastures at or above treeline. Favors flatter, more open, grassy areas, esp. drier sites. Some seasonal or local el. movements may occur. Reliably found near Laguna Mucubají (3600m) and Páramo del Águila (4000m), Mérida.; seen/taped on Páramo Batallón, n Táchira, 19 Jan 1996.

Range: 2200–4100m. Andes of s Táchira on Páramo de Tamá (*bogotensis*); n Táchira (sight), Mérida, and Trujillo n to Páramo Cendé (*meridae*). Colombia s locally in Andes to n Argentina.

Bombycillidae: Waxwings
Alas de Cera

Three mainly north temperate and Eurasian species. They are gregarious, eat mainly fruit and a few insects, and are noted for their sleek, well-groomed appearance and waxy red tips on secondaries, hence their name.

Cedar Waxwing   PLATE 48
Bombycilla cedrorum   Ala de Cera
Identification: 7" (18cm). 32g. Accidental. Sleek cinnamon brown with *clean-cut black mask and pointed crest*; mask outlined in white, chin black, wings and tail gray, red tips on secondaries; *broad yellow band on tail tips*; belly yellowish.
Voice: High, thin, lisping *eeeeee*, slightly quavering, over and over.
Behavior: In temperate latitudes gregarious, flying and feeding in tight flocks at fruiting trees. Also sally clumsily for insects. Prob. small straggling flocks to n S Amer.
Status and habitat: Accidental in Venez. Only rec. is 1 bird taken on Cerro Pejochaina (1650m), Sierra de Perijá, Zulia[20].

Range: Breeds in N Amer.; winters s in decreasing nos. to c Panama, Greater Antilles, and Colombia (once). [The vast 9-primaried passeriform groups including parulids, thraupids, cardinalids, icterids, and emberizids were placed into a single magafamily by Sibley and Monroe[606], but each is here regarded as a separate family following the AOU checklist[10].]

Parulidae: Wood-Warblers
Reinitas, Candelitas, Canarios de Mangle

This family comprises 2 main groups in South America: residents and those that migrate to North America to breed. The resident species include 4 genera: (1) yellowthroats (*Geothlypis*—1 species), which resemble their northern allies; (2) whitestarts (*Myioborus*), an active and highly arboreal group of montane species; (3) chats (*Granatellus*), a small Neotropical genus with only 1 species in Venez.; and (4) *Basileuterus*, a large group, many of which have striped heads and occur mostly in lower levels of humid forest where they often follow mixed-species flocks. Many *Basileuterus* warblers differ little from *Hemispingus* tanagers, a fact that highlights the close relationship of the 2 families. More than half of all wood-warblers in Venezuela are long-distance migrants that breed in temperate North

America east of the Rockies. They include the genera *Vermivora, Parula, Dendroica, Mniotilta, Setophaga, Protonotaria, Helmitheros, Limnothlypis, Seiurus, Oporornis, Geothlypis* (1 species), and *Wilsonia*. They are for the most part smaller, more delicately proportioned, more active, and more colorful than their resident counterparts. They forage by gleaning insects from leaves, and a few also take nectar or hop or walk on the ground. Many of them are sexually dimorphic. Immature plumages often differ as well, and in South America more individuals are seen in immature or nonbreeding plumage than in adult breeding plumage. Their sprightly songs, given so freely in the breeding season, are almost never heard in Venezuela, although weak chip notes are frequently uttered. Territorial songs, therefore, are not described for these migrant species.

Vermivora

Small with thin, sharp-pointed bill; plain plumage; sexes sim.; some spp. fond of nectar; very sim. to *Parula*; prob. not monophyletic.

[Blue-winged Warbler]
Vermivora pinus   Reinita Aliazul
Identification: 4.5″ (11.4cm). 8.5g. ♂: most of head and entire underparts bright yellow with short black line through eye; hindcrown and upperparts olive green; wings grayish with *2 bold white wing bars*; large white spots on tail corners visible from below. ♀: duller.
Sim. species: Wing bars, black eyeline, and all-yellow underparts are key marks. Cf. Golden-winged Warbler and imm. Yellow Warbler.
Status and habitat: Accidental. Known from 1 bird netted and photographed in Oct near Turiamo, n Aragua, by J. Fitzpatrick and D. Williard.

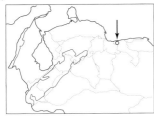

Range: Once in n Aragua. Breeds in e US; winters from s Mexico to Nicaragua, rarely to e Panama and Colombia; also in Greater Antilles e to St. John Isl. (sight).

Golden-winged Warbler   PLATE 55
Vermivora chrysoptera   Reinita Alidorada
Identification: 4.5″ (11.4cm). 8.2g. ♂: gray above with *yellow forecrown and large yellow patch on wing coverts*; *bold black mask* bordered white; *throat black*, rest of underparts white. ♀: black of face replaced by dusky gray, crown and upperparts duller. White tail corners conspic. from below in both sexes. Occas. hybridizes with Blue-winged Warbler, producing 2 phenotypes: (1) Brewster's Warbler, usually result of "pure" Golden-winged × "pure" Blue-winged cross, and (2) Lawrence's Warbler, usually result of a 2d-

generation backcross. Brewster's looks like a Blue-winged but is all or mostly white below, usually with yellow forecrown and yellow (or occas. white) wing bars. Lawrence's (rarer of the two) looks like a Golden-winged but has yellow head stripes, yellow underparts, and white wing bars (see Note).
Sim. species: ♂'s mask, black throat, and large yellow wing patch unique.
Duller ♀ shows enough of ♂'s pattern for recognition.
Behavior: Single birds are usually seen accompanying mixed-spp. flocks. Actively glean from foliage at wide range of hts. from near gd. to canopy but generally fairly high. Also reg. check curled, suspended dead leaves. Often somewhat difficult to see.
Status and habitat: Uncommon transient and nonbreeding n winter resident, early Oct (Sep?)–late Mar (specimens 6 Oct–29 Mar), to humid montane forest, forest borders, second-growth woodland, and coffee plantations. Earliest sighting is 1 seen 4 Oct[297]. ♀-plumaged birds commoner at lower els. Rare or vagrant to tepuis (1 on 26 Nov 1980, Sierra de Lema, 1400m—R. Webster and E. Copper); once in e Sucre at Las Melenas, 13 Mar 1998 (Hilty, S. Rose, D. Rose, C. Schumacher).

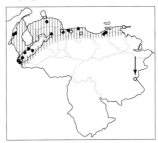

Range: 950–2400m (once to 3000m; sight to 800m). Sierra de Perijá, Zulia; Andes from s Táchira to s Lara, mts. of Falcón (Sierra de San Luis), Coastal Cordillera from Carabobo and Aragua e to ne Anzoátegui and w and e Sucre (sight); se Bolívar (sight). Breeds in e N Amer.; winters from Guatemala to Colombia.
Note: Records of Lawrence's Warbler phenotype incl. 1 specimen from upper Río Chiquito, s Táchira; 1 seen at Universidad de Los Andes forest, Mérida, Jan 1994 (J. Coons and R. Webster); 1 there Feb 1995 (R. Behrstock), another 19 Nov 1996 above La Azulita, Mérida[297]. Brewster's Warbler phenotype unrec.[723].

Tennessee Warbler   PLATE 55
Vermivora peregrina   Reinita Gorro Gris
Identification: 4.7″ (12cm). 9.1g. *Thin, sharp-pointed bill*. Breeding-plumage ♂: *crown gray contrasting with bright greenish olive upperparts*; eyestripe and underparts white, obscure dusky streak through eyes; usually a tinge of olive yellow on flanks. Breeding-plumage ♀: duller, crown less gray (less contrast with back), below tinged olive yellow, esp. on chest and sides. Imm.: mainly dull greenish olive above, *often with trace of 1 whitish wing bar*, crown faintly gray, *narrow eyestripe yellowish white*, underparts dingy yellowish white, sides and flanks tinged olive, *under tail coverts white*. By Jan–Feb many are in ad. plumage.
Sim. species: Dull and nondescript. Good marks for ad. and imm. are *thin* straight bill, contrasting gray

cap, pale eyestripe, and white under tail coverts. Look for faint wing bar on imm. only. Cf. esp. Scrub and Golden-fronted greenlets and ♀ Bicolored, Chestnut-vented, and White-eared conebills.
Behavior: A dull-plumaged, unobtrusive sp. that may be found with mixed-spp. flocks or away from them. Most often seen in flowering trees, esp. *Erythrina*, with hummingbirds, honeycreepers, and euphonias where often sips nectar and may have face stained reddish to dark orange from pollen. Also gleans in foliage and occas. checks small hanging dead leaves; eye level to canopy. In early Mar gathers in premigratory groups up to 20 or more along wooded e foothills of Andes.
Status and habitat: Transient and nonbreeding n winter resident, mid Sep–mid Apr (specimens to 13 Apr), to coffee plantations, light open woodland, and forest borders in moist to humid regions, mostly in foothills and mts., occas. in lowlands. Common in Táchira; somewhat less numerous n through Andes but becomes much commoner as premigratory groups work n through foothills; uncommon in Coastal Cordillera.

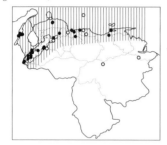

Range: Mostly 600–2200m (sight recs. sea level to 3000m). Throughout n mts. from Zulia, Táchira, and Falcón to Sucre; Islas Los Roques (sight); once (sight) in lower Río Caura, Bolívar[60]; once to Río Grande, e Bolívar. Breeds in n N Amer.; winters mainly from Guatemala to Colombia and w Venez.; occas. to n Ecuador; French Guiana (3 recs.).

Parula

Small; short, pale bill; olive patch in center of bluish back; buzzy songs.

Northern Parula

Parula americana   Reinita Americana
Identification: 4.5″ (11.4cm). 8.3g. Accidental. Tiny; relatively short tailed. Above blue gray with dusky line through eyes; *conspic. broken white eyering*; large patch on mantle olive green, wings and tail dusky blue, *2 bold white wing bars*; throat and breast yellow, chest crossed by narrow band of black somewhat mixed chestnut that joins a patch of blue gray on sides of chest; lower underparts white. ♀: no chest band.
Sim. species: Superficially much like Tropical Parula which *lacks* broken eyering and ♂'s chest bands.
Status and habitat: Accidental. Known from 3 specimens. An unsexed bird 25 Oct 1969 and a ♂ on 23 Oct 1973, both on Islas Los Roques (Colección Phelps); 1 taken 27 Nov 1984 near Adícora, Paraguaná Pen., Falcón[75].

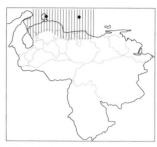

Range: To 50m. N Falcón and Islas Los Roques. Breeds in e N Amer.; winters in W Indies and C Amer. s to Costa Rica; rarely Panama. Curaçao; Tobago.

Tropical Parula   PLATE 56
Parula pitiayumi   Reinita Montañera
Identification: 4.5″ (11.4cm). 6.9g. ♂: *above blue gray with black mask through eyes; no white eyering* or markings around eyes; wings dusky blue, *2 "spotted" white wing bars*; below bright yellow, chest stained orange forming broad band; lower underparts white, outer 2–3 prs. of tail feathers with large white spot near tip of inner webs. ♀: duller, no black mask; chest band obscure.
Sim. species: Either sex from Northern Parula by absence of eyering; ♂ also by presence of black mask. ♂ lacks Northern's narrow dark chest bands.
Voice: Song typically an energetic, buzzy *tsuey-twuey-twuey-tu-tu-tu-ti-ti'ti'ti'ti'ti'zip* that accelerates and rises. In common variation, 2–3 short buzzes are followed by rising trill, then 1 or more buzzy notes. Songs recall those of Northern Parula.
Behavior: Usually seen singly or in prs. along wooded borders, often with mixed-spp. flocks. Stays fairly high up in trees and gleans actively in foliage. Sometimes sings persistently. Dome-shaped nest with side entrance usually high and in epiphytes or moss; 2 white eggs marked chestnut[175].
Status and habitat: Fairly common to locally common resident in forest borders, light woodland, and coffee plantations in moist to humid regions, mostly in foothills and highlands. Once to 3000m, 14 Feb 1998, Hotel Los Frailes, Mérida (Hilty and D. Ascanio).

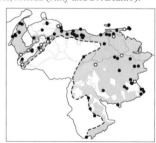

Range: To 2500m n of Orinoco (vagrant higher); to 2000m s of Orinoco. Throughout montane regions (locally in lowlands) from Zulia and Táchira e to Sucre, Monagas, and Delta Amacuro[343], and s through Guárico to n Bolívar (*elegans*); mts. of Amazonas and Bolívar (*roraimae*). Texas to n Argentina and the Guianas. Trinidad; Tobago.

Dendroica

Small, prim, and delicate; many with gay patterns and kaleidoscopic colors; bill sharp-pointed; tail square; arboreal; most spp. breed in N Amer. and are highly migratory; a few are resident in Carib.

Yellow Warbler   PLATE 56
Dendroica aestiva   Reinita Amarilla
Identification: 4.5″ (11.4cm). 9g. N migrant. ♂: mainly *bright canary yellow*, hindcrown and back slightly tinged olive, wings and tail dusky broadly edged yellow (*tail all yellow from below*), underparts bright yellow, *breast with variable amt. of rusty streaking* (sometimes faint). ♀ and imm.: mainly yellow, brighter below, rusty breast streaking faint or usually absent, wings and tail dusky broadly edged dull yellow (tail yellow below).
Sim. species: ♂ distinctive. ♀ and imm. easily confused with imm. and ♀ Bicolored, Chestnut-vented, and White-eared conebills, but warbler always has all-yellow undertail, and usually more prom. black eye. ♀ of Golden and Mangrove warblers doubtfully separable in field; both have shorter primary extension and thinner bills.
Voice: Call a loud, flat *tsip*; no song in Venez.
Behavior: Restless and active, like a dancing sunbeam, continually on the go, gleaning, hover-gleaning, and flitting in foliage and shrubbery. Forages at almost any ht. from eye level to treetop. Usually independent of mixed-spp. flocks.
Status and habitat: Fairly common to common transient and n winter resident, mid–late Sep (once 26 Aug) to 10 Apr (prob. later), to all kinds of dry, moist, and humid semiopen areas in lowlands, esp. tree-lined streams, groves of trees around ranch buildings, and shrubby second growth in more humid zones. Very common in disturbed woodlands and overgrown plantations around Tucupita, Delta Amacuro; less numerous s of Orinoco.

Range: To ca. 1000m; sight to 3000m[60]. Throughout s to c Amazonas (once to Cerro de la Neblina) and n Bolívar (*aestiva*); doubtless offshore isls.; also reported n of Orinoco (*morcomi*[500], *amnicola*). Breeds in N Amer.; winters s to n Bolivia (rarely), c Brazil, the Guianas, Trinidad and Tobago.
Note: Taxonomic references[85,144,298,436].

Golden Warbler   PLATE 56
Dendroica petechia   Canario de Oro
Identification: 4.5″ (11.4cm). 9g. ♂: *crown chestnut*, sides of head yellow, throat and breast yellow *streaked chestnut* (*cienagae*). Or crown chestnut, otherwise more or less as in nearctic migrants (*aurifrons, rufopileata, obscura*). ♀ and imm. of all resident races: essentially sim. to nearctic migrant Yellow Warbler; mainly yellow (no rusty on head), brighter below, rusty breast streaking faint or usually absent, wings and tail dusky broadly edged dull yellow (tail yellow below). ♀ differs from ♀ Yellow Warbler in shorter wing (primary) extension and thinner bill.
Sim. species: See under Yellow Warbler.
Voice: Songs in Falcón recall those of n migratory birds but shorter, typically a few bright, fast notes, then 2 emphatic notes, i.e., *e'sa, e'sa, swEEa-swEEa*. Loud *tsip* call commonly when foraging.
Behavior: Sim. to Yellow Warbler.
Status and habitat: Resident and generally restricted to vicinity of mangroves. Fairly common on many offshore isls.

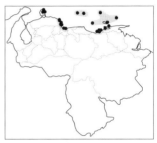

Range: To ca. 100m. Coastal e Falcón (Paraguaná Pen. e to Tucacas) and adj. offshore isls., coastal Carabobo and Aragua (*cienagae*); coastal Anzoátegui and w Sucre; isls. in Bay of Guanta; Islas Tortuga, Las Tortuguillas, and Píritu (*aurifrons*); Islas Margarita, Cubagua, La Blanquilla, and Los Testigos (*rufopileata*); Los Roques, Las Aves, and La Orchila (*obscura*). Also breeds from Florida keys (local) and Bahamas s throughout W Indies to Grenadines and Barbados; Isla San Andrés; Providencia; Cozumel.
Note: Taxonomy follows recent studies[85,144,298].

Mangrove Warbler   PLATE 56
Dendroica erithachorides   Canario de Mangle
Identification: 4.5″ (11.4cm). 9g. ♂: like ♂ migrant Yellow Warbler but *entire head and breast chestnut* (*chrysendeta*). Or head mostly chestnut, sides of head tinged chestnut, breast chestnut streaked yellow (*paraguanae*). ♀: essentially identical to ♀ Yellow Warbler but note shorter primary extension and thinner bill.
Behavior: Sim. to Yellow Warbler.
Status and habitat: Resident and generally restricted to vicinity of mangroves. Locally quite common in nw Zulia. Resident birds usually not found with Bicolored Conebill (competitive exclusion?).
Range: To ca. 100m. Goajira Pen. and Punta de Mangle, Zulia (*chrysendeta*); Paraguaná Pen. at Adicora(?), Falcón (*paraguanae*). Baja California s on Pacific coast to w Panama; coastal nw Colombia to n

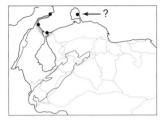

Peru; Cocos Isl.; Escudo, Coiba, Pearl, and Galápagos Isls.; locally on Gulf Coast of C Amer. from Mexico to Colombia.
Note: Taxonomy follows recent studies[85,144,298].

Chestnut-sided Warbler
Dendroica pensylvanica   Reinita Lados Castaños
Identification: 4.5″ (11.4cm). 9g. Prim with smartly cocked tail. Nonbreeding plumage and imm: *above bright olive green with conspic. white eyering*; wings and tail dusky, 2 prom. yellowish white wing bars; below white, palest on lower underparts; ads. usually show some chestnut on sides. Breeding ad.: *crown bright yellow*; back olive streaked black, 2 yellowish wing bars; broad black line through eyes; *cheeks and underparts white, vertical black line below eye continues as broad chestnut streak on sides and flanks*.
Sim. species: Imm. is brighter olive above and whiter below than any other migrant warbler. Note eyering and cocked tail.
Voice: Often a simple flat *chip*; no song in Venez.
Behavior: Single birds have been seen alone and with mixed-spp. flocks at mid. levels or lower along wooded edges.
Status and habitat: Rare. Known from 2 specimens: 1 ♂ 15 Apr 1954, Ocumare de la Costa (200m); and 1 (unsexed) 20 Oct 1973 on Isla Namusqui in Islas Los Roques. At least 8 subsequent sight recs. from n Aragua (Rancho Grande Biol. Station; Choroní; Ocumare de La Costa, Turiamo), 1 from n Miranda, all early Jan to 27 Mar (various observers)[259]. Dry deciduous to humid forest borders, plantations, and second growth along streams.

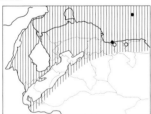

Range: To 200m (sight to 1000m). Aragua and Islas Los Roques; Miranda (sighting). Breeds in e N Amer.; winters mostly from Guatemala to Panama; scattered recs. in Colombia, nw Ecuador, and Netherlands Antilles.

[Magnolia Warbler]
Dendroica magnolia   Reinita Manchada
Identification: 5″ (12.7cm). 8.7g. Nonbreeding-plumage ♂: dull olive above with grayish head and white spectacles; back olive streaked black, 2 white wing bars; *yellowish rump; broad white band* on either side of

blackish tail; *below yellow with spotlike black streaks on breast*. Nonbreeding-plumage ♀: duller with less yellow below; less streaking. Breeding-plumage ♂: much brighter; *bold black mask*, narrow postocular stripe white, crown gray, back black; *large white patch on wing coverts*; underparts yellow with *bold black necklace across chest and coarse streaking on breast and sides*. Breeding-plumage ♀: much like nonbreeding-plumage ♂. Imm.: nearest nonbreeding ♀ but few or no black streaks below.
Sim. species: In any plumage, combination of yellow rump, white tail bars, and black streaks on yellow underparts distinctive.
Status and habitat: Accidental. Only rec. is 1 ♂ (imm.?) taken 2km s of Ocumare de La Costa, Aragua, 31 Dec 1970 by A. R. Phillips and W. J. Schaldach, Jr. (Colección PROFAUNA).

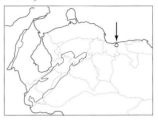

Range: Once in n Aragua. Breeds in e N Amer.; winters from c Mexico to e Panama; scattered recs. in Colombia and Barbados; sightings in Trinidad and Tobago.

Cape May Warbler
Dendroica tigrina   Reinita Atigrada
Identification: 5″ (12.7cm). 11g. In all plumages note *yellow patch on neck* (duller in ♀ and imm.) and *yellow rump*. Breeding-plumage ♂: above olive green to gray green, *large white patch on wing coverts; rump yellow*, crown blackish, *cheeks chestnut* mostly enclosed by yellow *which broadens to large yellow patch on sides of neck*; below yellow variably but *often heavily streaked black*. Breeding-plumage ♀: like breeding-plumage ♂ but duller; above all dingy gray green vaguely streaked dusky; 2 faint whitish bars; *sides of head yellow enclosing faint olive cheek patch*, lower underparts white. Imm. ♂: like ad. ♀ but with large white patch on wing coverts. Imm. ♀: even duller, grayer above, dingy white to yellowish white streaked dusky below; no white patch on wing coverts.
Sim. species: Blackburnian Warbler has more prom. eyebrow; yellow or orange is confined to throat; and never any yellow on rump. Also see Black-throated Green Warbler.
Status and habitat: Rare migrant from N Amer. Known from 8 specimens: 1 on 30 Oct 1973, Isla Los Roques (Isla Namusqui); 6 from Isla La Orchila, 22–29 Oct 1974.; and 1 ♀ 10km w of Chichiriviche, Falcón[341]. Several sight recs. incl. 2 ♂♂ (photographed) 13 Mar 1970, Acarigua, Portuguesa (P. Alden); 1 seen, Caracas, Feb 1975 (M. L. Goodwin and R. Restall); 1 on 1 Jan 1976 and 1 on 6 Jan 1976, El Junko Country Club, Distr. Federal (P. Alden, R. Arbib, and M. L. Goodwin). Rare on mainland. Gardens, cultivated areas, and flowering trees, esp. *Erythrina*.

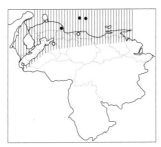

Range: To 1000m (sight). Falcón; Islas Los Roques and La Orchila; sightings in Portuguesa and Distr. Federal. Breeds in e N Amer.; winters mainly in W Indies s to Netherlands Antilles; scattered recs. s to Panama, Colombia, Trinidad and Tobago.

Black-throated Blue Warbler
Dendroica caerulescens   Reinita Azul y Negra
Identification: 5″ (12.7cm). 10g. Only warbler with *white spot at base of primaries*. ♂ unique: dull blue above with distinctive white spot near base of primaries; *sides of head, throat, chest, and sides black, center of breast and lower underparts white*. ♀: above olive brown, *narrow eyestripe and partial eyering whitish; cheeks dusky; small whitish spot on primaries* (sometimes faint or absent), dull yellowish brown to buff below.
Sim. species: Good points on ♀ are facial markings and unique wing spot (if present). ♀ otherwise might be mistaken for a ♀ conebill or dacnis.
Status and habitat: Very rare migrant from N Amer. Known from 1 specimen, 18 Nov 1968 on Cerro Platillón, n Guárico; sight recs. of 1 on 27 Oct 1937, Ocumare de La Costa, Aragua (A. Wetmore); 1 ♂ seen (at window at night), 21 Apr, Rancho Grande Biol. Station, Aragua[33].

Range: To 1900m. N Guárico (*caerulescens*); n Aragua (sight). Breeds in e N Amer.; winters mostly in Greater Antilles; scattered recs. s to s C Amer., Colombia, Netherlands Antilles, and Trinidad.

Yellow-rumped Warbler
Dendroica coronata   Reinita Coronada
Identification: 5–5.5″ (12.7–14cm). 12.5g. Nonbreeding plumage: above dull brownish with dusky streaks on back; 2 wing bars whitish; *conspic. yellow rump*; white patch in tail corners; throat white, rest of underparts dingy white somewhat streaked brownish on breast and sides, *usually with conspic. yellow patch on sides* of chest. Breeding-plumage ♂: much brighter, dark blue gray above streaked black, forecrown and mask black; yellow coronal patch; narrow white eye-

line; 2 white wings bars; *conspic. yellow rump*; underparts white with black chest, *yellow patch on sides*, and black streaking on sides of breast. W form (Audubon's) has yellow throat (usually a trace even in imm. birds). Breeding-plumage ♀: sim. but duller; less black on underparts.
Sim. species: Yellow rump and yellow patch at sides of chest should be diagnostic in any plumage.
Status and habitat: Accidental: 1 ♀ (*coronata*) taken 30 Apr 1965, mouth of Río Amacuro, Delta Amacuro. At least 2 sight recs. of w form (*auduboni*): imm./partial ad. w form with flecks of yellow on throat 19 Jan 1988, Hotel Los Frailes (3000m), Mérida[259]; and same bird (presum.) seen again 19 Mar 1988 at same loc. (M. Van Beirs). No other recs. of w form in S Amer.

Range: Delta Amacuro and Mérida (sightings). Breeds in Canada and ne US; winters through US s to Mexico and Greater Antilles, erratically to Panama.

Black-throated Green Warbler
Dendroica virens   Reinita Gorginegra
Identification: 5″ (12.7cm). 9g. Imm.: above olive green, wings dusky, 2 white wing bars, *sides of head incl. eyestripe yellow, cheeks usually with faint olive ear patch*; below whitish with varying amts. of blackish on chest and streaky black on sides. Ad. ♂: brighter and sharper with solid black throat and chest; sides streaked black. Ad. ♀: duller; less black on chest; throat white.
Sim. species: Note "yellow-faced" appearance in all plumages. Cf. Blackburnian and Cape May warblers.
Status and habitat: Rare transient and nonbreeding winter resident from N Amer., early Nov–late Feb (sight). Known from 1 ♀ taken 11 Nov 1968 at Punta de Mangle, nw Zulia, and another in Aragua (unknown el.)[462]. More than 20 sight recs. (numerous observers) in mts. of Mérida (to 2200m), s Lara, Aragua, Miranda, and e Sucre (twice in mts. of Paria Pen.); at least 12 of these sightings are from n Aragua.

Range: Sea level (1 specimen); 900–2200m (sight recs.). Zulia; N mts. from Mérida and Lara to Sucre. Breeds in e N Amer.; migrates to C Amer. and W Indies; rarely to n Colombia, Netherlands Antilles, and Trinidad.

[Palm Warbler]
Dendroica palmarum   Reinita de Palmeras
Identification: 5.5″ (14cm). 10.5g. Nonbreeding ad. and imm.: above drab grayish, rump slightly olive, *narrow eyering whitish*, dusky line through eyes; underparts dingy whitish, breast and sides somewhat streaked dusky rufous, *under tail coverts yellow*. Breeding ad.: *dark rufous crown*; prom. *yellowish to white eyestripe* and *smudgy blackish line through eyes*; upperparts brown, indistinctly streaked dusky on back; wings with faint pale edges, underparts whitish, throat and crissum yellow, breast with *blurry dark rufous streaking (palmarum)*. Or sim. but *underparts all yellow*, breast with blurry streaks (*hypochrysea*).
Sim. species: Dark rufous cap and yellow throat are distinctive, as is habit of constantly dipping tail downward.
Status and habitat: Accidental; 1 ad. (*palmarum* form) seen and photographed 29 Jun 1995, Laguna Mucubají (3600m), Mérida[560].

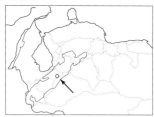

Range: Mérida (once). Breeds in n N Amer. Winters from e US seaboard and Gulf Coast to ne Nicaragua and Greater Antilles (e to Virgin Isls.); scattered recs. to Costa Rica, e Panama, and Netherlands Antilles.

Bay-breasted Warbler   PLATE 55
Dendroica castanea   Reinita Pecho Bayo
Identification: 5″ (12.7cm). 10.8g. Imm.: very like nonbreeding Blackpoll Warbler, differing in underparts usually tinged *buff* incl. under tail coverts, instead of underparts tinged olive with long white under tail coverts; *legs and feet blackish* (rarely an imm. has pale legs); ads. often with traces of chestnut on sides. Breeding-plumage ♂: crown, throat, chest, and sides chestnut, face black bordered behind by large buff neck patch; 2 white wing bars; lower underparts pale buff. Breeding-plumage ♀: sim. to imm. but darker and more heavily streaked; upperparts dusky, underparts buff with varying amts. of chestnut on sides. Nonbreeding-plumage ad.: like ♀ but chestnut reduced.
Sim. species: See Blackpoll Warbler. Breeding-plumage Bay-breasted rarely seen in Venez.
Behavior: Rather quiet and unassuming, usually seen singly and often with mixed-spp. flocks. Forages from about eye level to canopy (usually mid. levels or higher), bobbing rear end and slightly elevated tail as it moves restlessly. Often eats small berries.
Status and habitat: Fairly common transient and nonbreeding winter resident from n, 29 Oct–18 Mar; sight

recs. to 22 Apr, Rancho Grande Biol. Station, Aragua[33]; and 24 Apr 1996, Hotel Los Frailes, Mérida (R. Ridgely). Forest edges, light woodland, and coffee plantations, mostly at lower els. in Andes. Most numerous on w slope of Andes, fewer on e slope; nos. rapidly decline eastward in n cordilleras. Once in llanos at Hato Piñero, Cojedes, 12 Jan 1991 (Hilty and K. Zimmer); easternmost rec. is 1 at Río Grande, e Bolívar (C. Parrish).

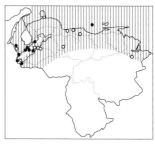

Range: To 3600m (most recs. 100–1500m). Lowlands and mts. of Zulia; Andes of Táchira, Mérida, and Trujillo (no recs. in Lara, Falcón, or Yaracuy?); nw Barinas (sightings); n cordilleras in Aragua; Miranda (sightings); Cojedes (sight[259]); e Bolívar (sight); Isla Tortuga (specimen). Breeds in n N Amer.; migrates through C Amer. and W Indies; winters s to Panama and nw S Amer.; Guyana (sight). Trinidad (a few sightings).

Blackpoll Warbler   PLATE 55
Dendroica striata   Reinita Rayada
Identification: 5″ (12.7cm). 10.5g. *Legs pinkish yellow.* Nonbreeding plumage: above dull grayish olive narrowly streaked black on crown and back; wings and tail dusky; *2 white wing bars*; below dull yellowish olive *indistinctly streaked dusky on sides*; lower underparts and unusually long under tail coverts white. Imm.: sim. but duller, streaking often obscure. Breeding-plumage ♂: *solid black crown* and black malar enclose large *white cheek patch*, rest of upperparts gray streaked black; below white streaked black on sides. Breeding-plumage ♀: like nonbreeding-plumage birds but brighter and more sharply streaked below.
Sim. species: Nonbreeding birds (esp. imms.) very like imm. Bay-breasted Warbler, told by white crissum (usually buff in Bay-breasted), more olive tone to underparts, and more breast streaking (imm. Bay-breasted usually lacks streaking below), but best marks are Blackpoll's *pale legs and feet* (usually blackish in Bay-breasted, but imm. birds occas. have pale legs). Soles of feet always pale in Blackpoll, never in Bay-breasted. Also see Black-and-white Warbler.
Voice: Occas. flat *chip* when foraging is much like that of Yellow Warbler; no song in Venez.
Behavior: Usually seen singly, presum. on winter territories, accompanying mixed-spp. flocks in canopy of tall forest or occas. lower in vine-tangled streamside borders. A large percentage of canopy flocks s of Orinoco will contain 1 or 2 of these birds. Constantly dips tail down as actively gleans insects from foliage, less often from twigs, in high outer part of trees; also occas. takes small berries.
Status and habitat: Transient and nonbreeding n winter resident, late Sep–mid May (specimens 27 Sep–9

May), sight to 16 May (D. Ascanio). Migrants can show up in almost any wooded habitat, but recs. n of Orinoco and esp. from coastal mts. are clustered during migratory periods (Sep–Nov and Apr–May); 50–60 seen 21 Apr–5 May (peak of 42 on 22 Apr) at Rancho Grande Biol. Station, Aragua[33]. Only small nos. overwinter at base of Andes and n cordilleras, but a fairly common to common wintering bird s of Orinoco in tall humid terra firme and várzea forest, occas. scattered small to large trees in clearings. Birds molting into partial breeding plumage may be seen by late Mar.

Range: To ca. 1000m (wintering birds); to 3000m and prob. higher (migrants). Throughout; also Islas Las Aves, Los Roques, La Orchila, and Margarita, Isla de Aves, and islets off e coast of Falcón. Breeds in n N Amer.; migrates through W Indies, Trinidad and Tobago; winters mostly in w Amazonia s to n Bolivia, c Brazil, and the Guianas; scattered recs. to s Chile and Uruguay.

Blackburnian Warbler   PLATE 55
Dendroica fusca   Reinita Gargantianaranjada
Identification: 5" (12.7cm). 8.5g. *Pumpkin orange throat patch* in most plumages. Breeding-plumage ♂: above black with a few white stripes on back, *large white patch on wing coverts*; patch on forecrown, *broad eyestripe, and sides of neck to chest fiery orange (brightest on throat) and enclosing large triangular black patch through eyes*; below white, sides streaked black; white near outer corners of tail. ♀ and imm.: above dull olive streaked dusky, 2 white wing bars, *facial pattern, underparts, and tail like* ♂ *but duller*, fiery orange replaced by pumpkin (pale yellow in imm.). Imm. ♂♂ are darker above than imm. ♀♀.
Sim. species: Told in any plumage by yellow to orange throat and eyestripe which wraps around angular black patch through eyes. See Cape May Warbler. Bright ♂♂ much in evidence 1–2 months before n migration.
Voice: Infreq. a thin *chip* note; no song in Venez.
Behavior: Occurs singly or occas. several together in loosely assoc. pre- or postmigratory groups. Spends most of n winter period on solitary nonbreeding territory. Forages alone or more often follows mixed-spp. flocks where moves actively in mid.- or upper-level foliage. Perch-gleans or hover-gleans tiny insects from live leaves or curled dead leaves, occas. chases flushed prey in brief sallies.
Status and habitat: Transient and nonbreeding n winter resident, mid Aug–late Apr (specimens 12 Aug–26 Apr); latest sight recs. 25 Apr 1996 at Hotel Los Frailes, Mérida, and 29 Apr 1996 at La Azulita, Mérida (R.

Ridgely and others). Humid and wet montane forest, woodland borders, coffee plantations, and partially cleared areas. Common and widespread in mts. n of Orinoco; uncommon in mts. s of Orinoco. Ad. ♂♂ commonest at higher els. and in more mature forest, ♀♀ and imms. commoner at lower els., in coffee plantations and lighter or disturbed woodland. Most numerous n winter resident warbler in Venez. Andes and only one reg. wintering above ca. 2000m.

Range: Mostly 800–3100m n of Orinoco; 1000–2800m s of Orinoco (occas. to sea level in both areas). N mts. from Zulia and Táchira to Anzoátegui and Sucre; Delta Amacuro (once); scattered recs. on cerros of Amazonas and in se Bolívar to Gran Sabana; Islas Los Roques, La Orchila, and Los Frailes. Breeds in e N Amer.; migrates through C Amer. and Greater Antilles; winters mostly in mts. of nw S Amer. s to n Bolivia; Guyana (sight).

Cerulean Warbler   PLATE 55
Dendroica cerulea   Reinita Cerúlea
Identification: 4.5" (11.4cm). 8.5g. Ad. ♂: *above dull cerulean blue*, wings dusky, *2 white wing bars*; back streaked black; *below white with narrow black band across chest* and dusky streaking on sides. ♀ and imm.: dingy pale olive green above with *blue gray tinge to crown and nape*; narrow *yellowish white eyebrow*; *2 large white wing bars*; below dull yellowish white turning white on lower underparts; *breast and sides usually tinged buff and with suggestion of darker blurry streaking*.
Sim. species: ♀ and imm. are easily confused. Good points are odd blue gray tinge to crown, pale eyestripe, and obscure streaking on buff-tinged breast.
Voice: Occas. a weak *chip*; no song in Venez.
Behavior: Single birds hold small nonbreeding territories during their seasonal residency and are quiet and relatively inconspic. as they follow mixed-spp. flocks containing flycatchers, warblers, and tanagers. Actively glean and hover-glean in foliage, mostly at mid. levels or slightly higher. In early Mar gather in premigratory groups of up to 12 or more, sometimes also with groups of Tennessee Warblers, along wooded e foothills of Andes.
Status and habitat: Uncommon to fairly common transient and nonbreeding n winter resident. Specimens mid Oct–early Mar (sight recs. 3 Oct–16 Mar—C. Sharpe; Hilty) in Aragua and nw Barinas. Humid premontane forest and esp. forest borders, shady coffee plantations, and light woodland. Essentially a bird of foothills and lower els. of Andes and n cordilleras. ♀♀ and ♀-plumaged birds predominate at lower els. (e.g.,

ca. 500–800m), ♂♂ higher. Most numerous in Coastal Cordillera and in Andes of Mérida and Táchira; both sexes much more numerous on e slope of Andes than w slope. A sp. in decline; formerly much more numerous[787].

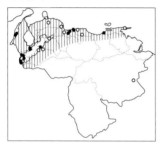

Range: To 1900m. Mts. from Zulia, Táchira, and Falcón (sight) e to w Sucre (Los Altos); once in se Bolívar on Sierra de Lema[259]. Breeds in e US, migrates through C Amer. and Greater Antilles; winters mostly in Andes s to n Bolivia.

Mniotilta and Setophaga

Two N Amer. breeding genera, both perhaps best merged with *Dendroica*.

Black-and-white Warbler   PLATE 55
Mniotilta varia   Reinita Trepadora
Identification: 5″ (12.7cm). 10g. Ad. ♂: *streaked black and white above and below*; cheeks and median throat black, center of breast and belly unstreaked white. ♀ and imm.: *above sim. to* ♂; *eyebrow and face white*, cheeks smudged gray, underparts white with a little black streaking on sides.
Sim. species: ♂ is nearest breeding ♂ Blackpoll Warbler but latter has *solid* black cap and *unstreaked* white cheeks. ♀ from ♀ Blackpoll by stronger black and white marking above (Blackpoll is tinged olive above).
Behavior: Single birds hold little nonbreeding wintering territories and usually follow mixed-spp. flocks. Forage by hitching creeperlike along mostly large, bare trunks and limbs, from lower mid. levels to subcanopy, and peer rapidly first to one side then the other as glean insects from bark surfaces.
Status and habitat: Uncommon to fairly common transient and nonbreeding n winter resident, early Sep–early Apr, to humid montane forest, light woodland, coffee plantations, and second growth.

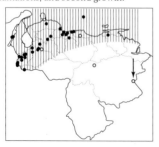

Range: To 2500m (most recs. 400–2200m). N mts. from Zulia, Táchira, and Falcón e to Distr. Federal and Sucre (Cerro Papelón); Isla La Orchila; sight recs. in n Bolívar (lower Río Caura)[297] and Sierra de Lema (at least 2 sightings). Breeds in e N Amer.; winters from s US to w Ecuador, n Peru (sightings), W Indies, and Trinidad.

American Redstart   PLATE 56
Setophaga ruticilla   Candelita Migratoria
Identification: 5″ (12.7cm). 8.5g. Ad. ♂: glossy black with *bright orange wing band, orange patch on sides of chest, and orange sides of base of tail*; belly white. Ad. ♀: above grayish olive, head grayer, white spectacles; below whitish; *markings on wings, chest, and tail like breeding* ♂ *but yellow*. Imm. ♂: like ♀ but slightly browner above, buffier below, *pectoral patch orangish*; prior to n migration 2d-yr birds may show a few black feathers on head. Ad. ♂ plumage not acquired until after 1st breeding season. Imm. ♀: like ad. ♀ but small amt. of yellow on wings and chest.
Sim. species: Wing, tail, and chest pattern unique in any plumage.
Voice: Flat *chit*; no song in Venez.
Behavior: Extremely active and hyperenergetic, constantly fanning tail and drooping wings as it executes short, highly aerobatic sallies for flushed insects or gleans from bark and foliage. Forages in mid. or upper story, reg. following mixed-spp. flocks, or when alone, more often low around light gaps and openings. Prob. holds winter territories.
Status and habitat: Fairly common transient and nonbreeding n winter resident, late Aug–early May (sight recs. 13 Aug–30 May) in lowlands and lower els. in mts. Migrants reach n cordilleras of Aragua in nos. during 1st week of Sep[33]. Moist to humid forest borders, coffee plantations, lighter woodland, and shrubby areas; also mangroves. ♀♀ and young ♂♂ commoner in foothills and lower els. and in younger vegetation; ad. ♂♂ more numerous at higher els. or in older, more mature woodland. Widespread in a variety of habitats but seldom numerous.

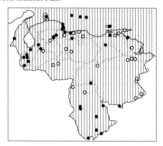

Range: To 3000 n of Orinoco (most recs. below 2000m); once to 3600m[60]; to 1800m s of Orinoco. Throughout incl. Islas Los Roques, La Orchila, Las Aves, and Margarita. Breeds in N Amer.; winters from s Florida, W Indies, and C Amer. to s Peru, n Amaz. Brazil, and the Guianas.

Prothonotary Warbler PLATE 56
Protonotaria citrea Reinita Protonotaria
Identification: 5.5″ (14cm). 12.5g. Plump and short-tailed (looks larger than it really is). ♂: *entire head and most of underparts bright golden yellow*, head punctuated by prom. black eyes; lower underparts immaculate white; back olive, wings and tail blue gray, tail shows white near tips (mostly from below). ♀: duller; head less golden.
Sim. species: Golden foreparts and blue gray wings are the marks. See ♀ Hooded Warbler and Yellow Warbler; orioles are larger, all with black wings and tail.
Status and habitat: Fairly common to common nonbreeding winter resident from N Amer. Specimen recs. 26 Sep–8 Mar. Mangroves, a few in adj. riparian or moist woodland, semiopen cattleland with patches of trees, and desert scrub. Mainly near coast, scattered recs. inland, e.g., 1 at 3000m, Hotel Los Frailes, ne Mérida, Nov 1990 (G. Rodríguez); 1 seen twice at Hato Cedral Feb 1998[259]; 1 at Junglaven, n Amazonas (J. Langham); 1 on 3 Mar 1993, Caurama Lodge, lower Río Caura, n Bolívar (J. Kingery and R. Behrstock[259]); 1 seen 6 Sep and 7 Mar, Rancho Grande Biol. Station, Aragua[33].

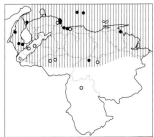

Range: To 3000m (most recs. below 200m). W and s Zulia and coast e to Sucre; Islas Los Roques and La Orchila; sight recs. inland in se Falcón, Mérida, w Apure, and n Amazonas; n Bolívar (specimen and sight). Breeds in e US; winters from Mexico to n Colombia, scattered recs. e to Trinidad and Tobago, Guyana, and Suriname; French Guiana (sight).

Worm-eating Warbler
Helmitheros vermivorus Reinita Gusanera
Identification: 5″ (12.7cm). 13g. *Crown boldly striped black and buff*, otherwise above brownish olive; sides of head, throat, and chest rich buff to ochre buff, lower underparts dingy buffy white. Sexes and age classes sim.
Sim. species: Pattern recalls Three-striped Warbler, but that sp. has much duller head stripes, more olive upperparts (not brownish), and is dingy whitish below.

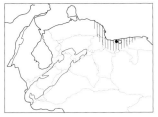

Behavior: Spends most of time in lower strata of forest, close to gd. or hopping on forest floor. On wintering gds. behaves mainly as a dead-leaf specialist, gleaning from hanging and curled dead leaves.
Status and habitat: Very rare. Known from 1 ♀ taken 19 Oct 1981 at Rancho Grande (PN Henri Pittier), Aragua[341]. One sight rec. in early Mar 1998, n of Portachuelo Pass, Aragua (J. Rowlett).
Range: N Aragua (twice). Breeds in s Canada and e US; winters from s Mexico to Panama and Greater Antilles e to Virgin Isls.

[Swainson's Warbler]
Limnothlypis swainsonii Canario de Swainson
Identification: 5.3″ (13.5cm). Dull brownish warbler with fairly *long straight bill* (culmen straight, distal part of lower mandible angled up slightly); *flattened forehead. Crown rich brown*, rest of upperparts duller brown; *long eyestripe dull whitish* with dark brown line through eyes; *underparts dull white* to whitish faintly tinged pale yellow, sides and flanks often tinged grayish brown. No sex or age differences in plumage.
Sim. species: Nearest is Worm-eating Warbler which has contrasting head stripes. Also see Northern Waterthrush.
Status and habitat: Known from a publ. sight rec. of 1 seen 2 Feb 1994 in shady undergrowth of a 23-ha grove of white mangroves (*Laguncularia racemosa*) on Ana Maria Campos Pen. (10°48′ N, 71°32′ W) e of Maracaibo, Zulia[105]. Terrestrial; walks on gd.; flips over leaves.

Range: N Zulia (once). Breeds in se US; winters locally in W Indies (esp. Greater Antilles), a few e to Virgin Isls. and Bermuda. Casual in Bahamas; also Yucatán Pen., Mexico, and Belize s to Swan Isl., Honduras.

Seiurus

Somewhat pipitlike in appearance; longish legs; dull plumage; strong eyebrow; underparts streaked; semiterrestrial and walk on gd.; large for parulids; Ovenbird differs in several respects from waterthrushes and may belong in a separate genus.

Ovenbird
Seiurus aurocapillus Reinita Hornera
Identification: 5″ (12.7cm). 18g. Plump and short-tailed with rather "wide-eyed" look. Above olive brown with *conspic. white eyering* and orange coronal stripe bordered black on sides; *below white heavily streaked black on breast and sides*. Legs pinkish.
Sim. species: Shape and size of a waterthrush but told from either by coronal stripe, eyering (waterthrushes have eyestripes), and usually by habitat.

Behavior: Solitary, quiet, and prob. often overlooked. Walks on forest floor, often teetering rear end somewhat. **Status and habitat:** Rare. Three specimens: 1 on 22 Oct 1938 at Cerro Santa Ana, Paraguaná; 1 ♂ on 27 Oct 1974 at Isla La Orchila; and 1 ♀ taken 9 Sep 1964 at Portachuelo Pass, Aragua. Sight recs. as follows: 1 on 19 Apr and 2 on 22 Apr (at windows at night), Rancho Grande Biol. Station, Aragua[33]; 1 on 25 Nov 1982, San Isidro Rd., nw Barinas (C. Parrish); and 1 near Portachuelo Pass, Feb 1990 (J. Pierson). Can occur as a transient or rare nonbreeding winter resident in almost any wooded habitat. (incl. desert scrub). To be watched for on floor of moist to humid forest and light woodland.

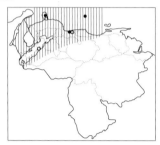

Range: To 1000m. Known from Falcón, Aragua, and Isla La Orchila; sighting in nw Barinas and Aragua. Breeds in e N Amer.; winters mostly in C Amer. and W Indies, small nos. s to n Colombia, Netherlands Antilles, Trinidad and Tobago.

Northern Waterthrush   PLATE 56
Seiurus noveboracensis   Reinita de Charcos
Identification: 5.5″ (14cm). 15.5g. Long, dull pink legs. Above olive brown; *long creamy eyebrow slightly narrower behind eye*; below uniform yellowish to creamy white *densely streaked dark brown*, incl. fine dotlike streaking (usually) on throat. Some birds have eyestripe and underparts almost white.
Sim. species: See rare Louisiana Waterthrush; also Riverside Warbler and Ovenbird.
Voice: Loud metallic *chink* advertises winter territory; occas. sings weakly just before migration.
Behavior: A terrestrial bird that is fond of watercourses and damp wooded areas. Walks on gd. or on logs with mincing steps and almost constant teetering up and down as if its rear end were attached to springs. Forages by picking up dead leaves and tossing them aside. May migrate in loosely assoc. groups but otherwise a solitary bird with both sexes holding and defending individual foraging territories for up to 6 months (approx. Oct–late Apr) in Venez. Winter territories average 1000–2500m² (ca. 20% of size of breeding territory) but are occas. much larger or smaller. Survivors return yr after yr to same winter territories. Arriving transients may remain for days or wks in an area before moving to permanent territories (onset of dry season may reduce food and force birds to move), thus contributing to some fluidity of overall pop.[578]
Status and habitat: Common transient and nonbreeding winter resident from N Amer., mid Sep–mid May (max. spread of dates 5 Sep–ca. 20 May, rarely Jun). Southbound transients arrive in large nos. mid Sep–

early Nov; northward movement is diffuse and subdued, mostly mid Apr–early May[578]. Mangroves, sluggish stream borders, forest- or woodland-bordered pools, damp low-lying areas in forest, and wooded urban areas (e.g., Botanical Gardens in Caracas). In all areas requires access to water (but not necessarily in its territory).

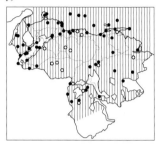

Range: To 2100m (mostly below 1500m); to 900m s of Orinoco. Throughout s to c Amazonas and s Bolívar; also Islas Los Roques, La Orchila, La Tortuga, Los Testigos, Las Aves, and Margarita. Breeds in n N Amer.; winters from s US southward, mostly in n S Amer. s to Ecuador, n Brazil, the Guianas; Trinidad and Tobago.

Louisiana Waterthrush
Seiurus motacilla   Reinita de Luisiana
Identification: 5.7″ (14.5cm). 19g. Very sim. to Northern Waterthrush but *bill heavier* (diagnostic with experience), *eyestripe whiter and broader*, esp. behind eyes; throat unstreaked (usually hard to see) with only dusky moustachial streak on sides (Northern Waterthrush has central throat dotted white), and *underparts white with contrasting rich buff flanks*; legs pinkish.
Sim. species: Easily confused with Northern Waterthrush (above). Also cf. Riverside Warbler and Ovenbird.
Behavior: Much like Northern Waterthrush. A solitary sp. that walks on gd., bobs rear end, and sulks in damp shady areas.
Status and habitat: Rare migrant from N Amer. Known from 3 specimens: 24 Oct 1940, Cubiro, Lara; 14 Feb 1973, 35km s of Cabudare, Lara; and 1 ♀ on 11 Sep 1964, Portachuelo Pass, Aragua. At least 3 sight recs., presum. this sp., in nw Barinas on San Isidro Rd. (C. Parrish; C. Boesman; D. Stejskal). Likes running water in damp wooded areas; unlike Northern Waterthrush, seldom in mangroves.

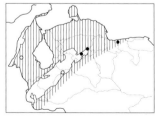

Range: Ca. 500–1800m. N mts. in Lara and Aragua; sight recs. in w Zulia (22 Feb 2000—C. Sharpe) and nw Barinas. Breeds in e US; winters mostly in C Amer. and W Indies, rarely to Colombia and Netherlands Antilles.

Oporornis

Olive above, all or partly yellow below; several with gray to brownish bib and eyerings or spectacles; always unstreaked; larger, more pot-bellied than most parulids.

Kentucky Warbler   PLATE 56
Oporornis formosus   Reinita Hermosa
Identification: 5″ (12.7cm). 14g. ♂: above olive green with blackish forecrown, *yellow spectacles, and broad black "sideburns" extending from below eyes to sides of neck*; underparts bright yellow. ♀: black on face and neck scaly and less extensive. Imm.: may show no black.
Sim. species: Facial pattern of ♀ and imm. Canada Warbler can look quite sim. Note Canada's gray (not olive) upperparts. Also cf. ♂ yellowthroats which have black on face but lack yellow spectacles.
Behavior: Quiet and easily overlooked. Forages by hopping on gd. or 1–2m up in low growth inside shady forest. Does not follow mixed-spp. flocks. In Panama reg. follows army ant swarms.
Status and habitat: Rare transient and very rare non-breeding winter resident from n, rec. (specimens) 8 Oct–10 Mar, in mts. of nw. Largest no. of specimens from Sierra de Perijá where may be uncommon to locally fairly common. Understory or gd. in moist to humid forest or secondary woodland. Sight recs. of 1 on 12–13 Jan 1983, Encontrados, Zulia (R. Fairbanks and S. Gautlett); 1 ♂ seen 21 Mar 1996, km 132, Sierra de Lema, Bolívar (R. Taylor and others) is easternmost rec.

Range: To 1200m. Sierra de Perijá, Zulia; w slope of Andes in Táchira, Mérida, and Trujillo; e base in w Portuguesa (Hacienda Marquesena); s base of Coastal Cordillera in Aragua (Maracay); Islas La Orchila and Los Roques (Isla Namusqui); sightings in s Zulia and se Bolívar. Breeds in e US; winters mostly from s Mexico to Panama, a few to n Colombia and Netherlands Antilles.

Connecticut Warbler
Oporornis agilis   Reinita de Connecticut
Identification: 5.5″ (14cm). 12g. *All plumages have conspic. unbroken white eyering.* ♂: olive green above with *entire head, throat, and chest gray, palest on throat*; crown sometimes with faint brown tinge; lower underparts dull yellow; long under tail coverts reach nearly to tail tip. ♀: sim. but *hood paler with obvious brownish tinge*, palest on throat. Imm.: much like ♀ but hood even browner, upperparts brownish olive. In all plumages note *rather long and slender* ("stretched")

shape sim. to that of a waterthrush, and tail projecting only slightly beyond under tail coverts.
Sim. species: Likely confused only with Mourning Warbler, although ad. ♂♂ should be easily separated (♂ Mourning has broken eyering and black bib). ♀ and imm. *cannot be told with certainty from ♀ and imm. Mourning on basis of eyering alone* because a few Mournings have complete or almost complete eyerings. In addition to eyering (almost always *narrower* in Mourning), note Connecticut's longer, more slender, and more horizontal shape (more like a waterthrush). Other minor differences, best noted in hand, include Connecticut's duller yellow underparts, overall browner hood, slightly larger size, and long under tail coverts which extend nearly to tail tip. In hand Connecticut's wing avgs. longer (64–77 vs. 55–67mm), and sp. can always be told by wing length minus tail length equal to 19mm or more[324].
Behavior: A retiring and elusive skulker in tall grass and thickets where solitary and silent. Spends much time *walking* on gd. where easily overlooked, but occas. flushes into a bush where may sit motionless and stare intently for a moment before flitting off to some dark recess.
Status and habitat: Uncommon to rare transient from north. Specimen recs. 23 Sep–31 Oct and late Apr–8 May; latest sighting is 9 May. There is concentrated southward passage in Oct and northward passage late Apr–early May, e.g., 8 specimens taken 18–28 Oct 1973 on Isla Namusqui in Los Roques; and sight recs. of a no. of individuals 25–28 Apr 1984 at Hato Masaguaral, Guárico, and Los Anaucos, Miranda[741]; 2 at Rancho Grande Biol. Station, Aragua, 29 Apr and 2 May[33]; and 1 on 24–25 Apr 1996 at Hotel Los Frailes, Mérida (R. Ridgely). A specimen from Rancho Grand, dated 13 Jul 1961 (Coleccíon PROFAUNA), is prob. mislabeled. Main migratory movement appears to be over passes in Andes and Coastal Cordillera to Amazonia. Parks, gardens, or almost any habitat with trees and shrubbery.

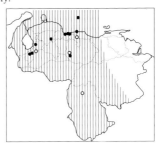

Range: To 4200m (Teleférico, Mérida). Andes of Mérida, Trujillo, and Lara (Terepaima), mts. of Carabobo, Aragua, and Distr. Fed.; llanos of Guárico (Hato Flores Moradas; sight, Masaguaral); Miranda (sight); n Amazonas (sight, Junglaven)[833]; Islas Los Roques. Breeds in n N Amer.; migrates through W Indies; winters mostly in w Amazonia s to s Peru and Mato Grosso, Brazil; French Guiana (sight).

Mourning Warbler

PLATE 56

Oporornis philadelphia   Reinita Enlutada

Identification: 5″ (12.7cm). 11.5g. ♂ wears black crepe bib. ♂: above olive green with *all-gray head (no eyering)* and crinkly *black lower throat*, underparts bright yellow. ♀: duller with *pale gray or brownish-tinged head*; throat paler gray. Imm.: typically has *broken white eyering*, ♀ usually lacks eyering but there is much variation; a few may show narrow but complete eyering. In all plumages note rather rounded or pot-bellied shape and upright posture.

Sim. species: Ad. ♂ with crepelike black bib and lack of eyering should be easily recognized, but cf. Connecticut Warbler. All imms. or ♀♀ *lacking* eyerings or with *broken* eyerings should be separable from Connecticut Warbler which *always* has complete eyering. For any individual with complete eyering, see under Connecticut Warbler and note different shapes of these 2 spp. Mourning is *shaped* more like most other warblers, Connecticut more like a waterthrush.

Behavior: A solitary sp. that skulks in tall grass and thickets and hops on or near gd. but is normally not too difficult to see. Often readily pops into view to squeaking noises. Not with mixed-spp. flocks.

Status and habitat: Transient and nonbreeding winter resident from the north, mid Oct–mid Mar (specimens); latest sightings are 3 birds seen 9 Apr, Rancho Grande Biol. Station, Aragua[33]; 1 on 12 Apr 1998[60]; 1 ♀ 23 Apr 1996, Altamira, Barinas, another ♀ 29 Apr 1996 near La Azulita, Mérida (R. Ridgely). Small grassy clearings with bushes and thickets, and grassy and shrubby forest borders in humid montane regions. Fairly common locally, mainly in foothills and lower mt. els.; normally not any distance away from mts.

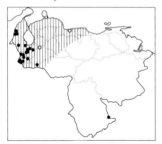

Range: 100–1900m; sight to 3000m[60]. Sierra de Perijá and s Maracaibo Basin, Zulia; both slopes of Andes of Táchira and Mérida, adj. w Apure (Guasdualito) and nw Barinas (sightings); n Aragua (sightings, PN Henri Pittier); once (accidental) in s Amazonas (Sierra Parima). Breeds in n N Amer.; migrates through C Amer.; winters from Nicaragua to n Ecuador.

Geothlypis

Widespread; ♂♂ with black mask, both sexes with yellow bib or all-yellow underparts; wet thickets and damp grass; center of diversity in Mexico.

Common Yellowthroat

Geothlypis trichas   Reinita Gargantiamarilla

Identification: 5″ (12.7cm). 9.5g. ♂: above olive with *broad black mask across forehead, face, and cheeks is bordered above by line of white* to pale gray; throat and breast yellow fading to white on center of belly; flanks tinged brownish, crissum yellow. ♀: *head mostly olive* (no mask) like rest of upperparts; faint whitish eyering; *throat yellow* turning dirty whitish on breast and belly, brownish on sides and flanks. Imm.: like ♀ but brownish (not olive) above.

Sim. species: ♂ from ♂ Masked Yellowthroat by white line over top of mask; olive (not gray) forecrown. ♀ from ♀ Masked by yellow confined mainly to throat (not almost all yellow below).

Status and habitat: Known from 1 old specimen from uncertain locality, possibly in Mérida Andes. Difficult to see; may be overlooked as it skulks in tall damp grass and grassy areas with bushes.

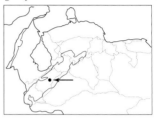

Range: Breeds in N Amer. and Mexico; winters from s US to Panama and in W Indies; rare in Colombia; Netherlands Antilles.

Masked Yellowthroat

PLATE 56

Geothlypis aequinoctialis   Reinita Equinoccial

Identification: 5.2″ (13.2cm). 13g. ♂: *broad black mask with forecrown and area above mask gray*, rest of upperparts olive green; underparts bright yellow, sides of body olive green. ♀: sim. but sides of head olive (no black mask), crown and sometimes cheeks tinged gray (variable and gray often absent), faint yellowish lores and eyering; underparts mostly yellow, flanks olive.

Sim. species: ♂ is nearest ♂ Common Yellowthroat, but latter has white line bordering top of mask. ♀♀ that lack gray are much like ♀ Common Yellowthroat but more extensively yellow below. Also Cf. Flavescent Warbler and smaller ♀ Crested Doradito.

Voice: Song a complex, musical *tee-chee-chee teeche weet teecheweet* (P. Schwartz recording); call a husky *chup*.

Behavior: An engaging and winsome little bird with a black domino and yellow underparts. Like others of genus, a skulker in grass and bushes but often pops up, nervously twitching, to scold or chatter, and may suddenly burst into vigorous song. After a few songs, proclaimed from atop a small bush, most often scurries off into thick vegetation. Alone or in prs. Often eats small caterpillars. Does not assoc. with other birds. Nest in Trinidad a deep grassy cup placed low; 2 white eggs marked brown and lilac[175].

Status and habitat: Fairly common but local resident in wet bushy and grassy fields, damp thickets along woodland borders, marshes, and sometimes tall damp grass in open savanna. Shows fondness for thickets and water or damp areas. Uncommon in llanos.

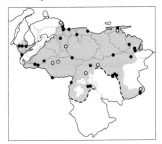

Range: To 900m. W Zulia, Táchira, and e Falcón (sight) and generally e of Andes e to Sucre and Delta Amacuro; n Amazonas (Pto. Ayacucho; *El Platanal*); Bolívar from lower Río Caura e to vicinity of Ciudad Bolívar and El Palmar; s locally to Santa Elena de Uairén (*aequinoctialis*). Colombia and the Guianas s to w Peru, n Argentina, and Uruguay.

Hooded Warbler

Wilsonia citrina   Reinita de Capucha
Identification: 5″ (12.7cm). 10.5g. ♂: *black crown, hindneck, throat, and chest (the "hood") surround bright yellow forehead and face*; otherwise olive green above and bright yellow below; outer tail feathers white on inner web (tail shows white from below). ♀ and imm.: ♂'s black hood replaced by a few dusky feathers outlining top and rear of yellow face (or top and rear of face rather sharply outlined only with olive), throat and underparts mostly yellow, otherwise like ♂ incl. white in tail.
Sim. species: ♀ told from ♀ Prothonotary Warbler by yellow face outlined olive to dusky (a hint of "hood"), olive (not blue gray) wings and tail, and yellow under tail coverts. Also see ♀ Yellow Warbler.
Status and habitat: Rare. Known from 4 specimens: 1 from Punta de Mangle, Zulia, 10 Nov 1968; 2 from Islas Los Roques (Isla Namusqui) 18 and 26 Oct 1974; 1 from Isla La Orchila 28 Oct 1974; and a sight rec. 27 Mar 1977, Cueva del Guano, Falcón (G. Orians and C. Bosque).

Range: To 50m. Nw Zulia and Falcón (sight); Islas Los Roques and La Orchila. Breeds in e US; winters mainly in C Amer., scattered recs. to Colombia, Netherlands Antilles, and Trinidad.

Canada Warbler   PLATE 56

Wilsonia canadensis   Reinita Canadiense
Identification: 5″ (12.7cm). 9.5g. *Above uniform gray with yellow spectacles;* forehead and area below eyes black; *underparts bright yellow with dainty black necklace of streaks across chest;* under tail coverts white. ♀ and imm.: somewhat duller but usually with traces of black necklace on chest (lacking in some imms.); no black on face.
Sim. species: Look for necklace; imms. without it can be told by yellow spectacles and uniform gray upperparts.
Voice: Faint *chip* note; no song in Venez.
Behavior: Usually seen singly with mixed-spp. flocks, less often away from flocks. Inconspic. despite active and sprightly behavior. Sallies short distances to foliage or air and gleans insects from foliage, mostly rather low inside forest. Often flicks tail.
Status and habitat: Transient and nonbreeding n winter resident, late Oct–early Mar (prob. later) to humid and wet montane forest (esp. inside forest) and older second-growth woodland. Fairly common in mts. of s Táchira; in diminishing nos. n through Andes and Coastal Cordillera to Aragua; rare (few specimens or sightings) in tepuis. A ♂ seen 25 Jan 1990 on Cerro Humo, Paria Pen., Sucre, is northeasternmost rec. (C. Sharpe).

Range: 800–2100m n of Orinoco; ca. 1000–1400m s of Orinoco. Sierra de Perijá, Zulia, and Andes of Táchira and Mérida; nw Barinas (sight); Coastal Cordillera in Carabobo, Aragua and s Miranda; e Sucre (sight[297]); n Amazonas and se Bolívar (Sierra de Lema). Breeds in N Amer.; migrates mostly through C Amer., winters mainly in nw S Amer. s to s Peru, rarely to n Brazil (Roraima).

Myioborus

Widespread, familiar; very active, arboreal; all in highlands; many are el. or geographical replacements of each other; flash white in habitually spread and rounded tail; prom. rictal bristles; differ primarily in head patterns; spp. limits often unclear; called "redstarts" by most previous authors.

Slate-throated Whitestart   PLATE 56

Myioborus miniatus   Candelita Gargantipizarra
Identification: 5.5″ (14cm). 10g. *Upperparts, head, and neck dark gray turning blackish on throat* (barely contrasting with head), central crown patch chestnut, breast and belly bright yellow, under tail coverts

white; rounded tail dark gray, *outer tail feathers white.* Or breast and belly lemon yellow (*pallidiventris*). Or narrow inconspic. tawny wash on chest (*verticalis*).
Sim. species: Most widespread *Myioborus* whitestart and the *only one* with dark throat. Occurs at least locally with several other spp. of *Myioborus* in Venez., but often found at lower els.
Voice: Lively song a short and rather colorless little warble, *sit-see-see-see-seet*, of 4–5 notes run together.
Behavior: This quintessential "fantail" is an endearing if harum-scarum little imp that employs a flush-and-chase foraging strategy resulting in bouts of hyperactivity interspersed with periods of relative calm. Single birds or prs. constantly pivot and posture with wings half-spread and drooped, and tail cocked and fanned, as they hop along branches, dart to side of trunks, and whirl and dash in little aerobatic loops and sudden lunges, all apparently with aim of flushing small prey which they chase down. Often follow mixed-spp. flocks but also forage independently of them. Bold pattern and saucy behavior, almost a "catch-me-if-you can" invitation, are employed in and out of mixed-spp. flocks but prob. more consistently when traveling with mixed-spp. flocks. Rootlet and leaf cup nest with roof, tucked into crevice in steep bank or stump; 2–3 eggs. In n Aragua 8 nests late Mar–early Jun[132].
Status and habitat: Widespread and common resident of humid and wet forest in mts. In Andes mostly replaced at higher els. by allied White-fronted Whitestart, but the two reg. overlap narrowly at mid.-montane els. On cerros s of Orinoco occurs widely with Tepui Whitestart, in n Amazonas with White-faced Whitestart.

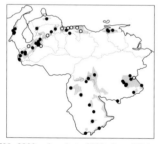

Range: 700–2300m (rarely to 3000m) n of Orinoco; 600–1800m s of Orinoco. Sierra de Perijá, Zulia; Andes from s Táchira to Trujillo (*ballux*); mts. of Lara, Falcón, and Yaracuy e through n cordilleras to w Sucre (not Paria) and n Monagas (*pallidiventris*); throughout cerros of Amazonas, nw Bolívar (Cerro Tabaro), and tepuis of Gran Sabana from Ptari-tepui and Sierra de Lema s to Paurai-tepui and Cerro Roraima (*verticalis*). N Mexico (rarely sw US) to Panama; Andes from Colombia to s Bolivia; tepuis of n Brazil and Guyana.

Golden-fronted Whitestart   PLATE 56
Myioborus ornatus   Candelita Copetiamarilla
Identification: 5.5″ (14cm). *Crown, most of head, and underparts bright lemon yellow; frontlet, ocular area, and chin white;* rearcrown, nape, sides of neck, and mottling on sides of chest black, rest of upperparts dark gray; under tail coverts and *outer 2 tail feathers white.*

Sim. species: In its limited range the only whitestart with white face and yellow forecrown. At lower els. see Slate-throated Whitestart.
Voice: Song in s Táchira a high-pitched, rapid, rambling, and somewhat repetitious stream of notes, *wee which-a-wee, sa-weeEEsa wee, weE sa-wee, weEsa weet . . .* for up to 15 sec; sharp *tsip* while foraging.
Behavior: Sim. to previous sp. but often in groups of 4–6 or more (families?), foraging alone or with mixed-spp. flocks containing other warblers, tanagers, and flowerpiercers. Ranges from understory to subcanopy but usually fairly high, and often exceedingly active, habitually fanning tail and drooping and half-spreading wings (more so than White-fronted Whitestart) as sallies in aerobatic little loops for fleeing insects, clinging sideways to vertical trunks, and staying constantly on the go.
Status and habitat: Common resident in mid.-montane humid and wet forest, forest borders, and stunted woodland up almost to treeline. Readily found in forest (mostly above *Podocarpus* zone) on trail from Betánia to Páramo de Tamá.

Range: 2100–3000m. Highlands of s Táchira s of Río Uribante (*ornatus*). Andes of Colombia.

White-fronted Whitestart   PLATE 56
Myioborus albifrons   Candelita Frentiblanca
Identification: 5.5″ (14cm). Andes. *Crown black with orange rufous central patch* (varies in size); *frontlet, foreface, and ocular area white,* rest of upperparts dark gray; tail black, outer 2 prs. of feathers white; throat and chest yellow tinged tawny, breast and belly bright lemon yellow, under tail coverts white. Imm.: sim. but white of frontlet, lores, and eyering narrow and reduced. Juv.: no white on face; throat and chest yellow mottled with gray.
Sim. species: Occurs mostly above range of Slate-throated Whitestart. White mask of ad. is diagnostic.
Voice: Song, often hd. at dawn, a cheerful, lively, rambling ser., *swit,swit,wesee,wasee,tsee,tsee,ree,ree,ree, sit,pee,pee,swit,swit . . .* and so on, rising and falling in pitch and often continuing for nearly 30 sec. In duets, mate (♀?) joins after a few sec with ser. of high, sibilant *tzee* notes that may continue after mate finishes.
Behavior: Sim. to most others of genus. Employs a flush-and-chase foraging strategy, resulting in hyperactive bouts of foraging interspersed with periods of relative calm. When foraging, fans cocked tail, droops semispread wings, and pivots and darts about, hops along high or low branches, clings to trunks and vines, and aerobatically dashes after fleeing prey in short sallies or in whirling downward-spiraling chases. Usually in prs. which are conspic., confiding, and reg. members of mixed-spp. flocks.

Status and habitat: Fairly common resident at high els. in wet, mossy, epiphyte-laden forest, along forest borders, and in scattered trees in clearings. At lower els. overlaps with Slate-throated Whitestart, the two sometimes in same mixed-spp. flocks.

Range: ENDEMIC. 2200–3200m. Andes of n Táchira (Páramo Zumbador), Mérida, and Trujillo n to Páramo Cendé near Lara border.
Note: Possibly conspecific with Golden-fronted Whitestart (*M. ornatus*) of Colombia and Spectacled Whitestart (*M. melanocephalus*) of Andes s of Colombia.

Paria Whitestart
PLATE 56
Myioborus pariae Candelita de Paria
Identification: 5″ (12.7cm). Very like Tepui Whitestart but with yellow spectacles. *Large chestnut crown patch; narrow yellow loral line and yellow eyering form spectacles*; rest of upperparts dark gray; underparts incl. throat entirely bright lemon yellow, tail dusky, under tail coverts and outer tail feathers white.
Sim. species: See Slate-throated Whitestart (no overlap) which has dark throat and no yellow on face.
Voice: Bright, lively song may rise in middle and is almost always louder, more insistent, and rising at end, e.g., *wheetsa-wheetsa-wheetsa-wesee, tezsa-sweet-see-ZEE-ZEET*; songs somewhat variable (individuals may sing more than 1 song type) and often complex with mix of high and low notes. Song recalls that of White-fronted Whitestart.
Behavior: Sim. to other *Myioborus* (see Slate-throated Whitestart) but somewhat less aerobatic and animated. Ranges from about eye level to mid. level in forest, occas. higher. Has most often been observed singly or in prs., occas. with small mixed-spp. flocks.
Status and habitat: Resident. Uncommon around treefalls and openings inside humid forest, along forest borders, and in second growth and coffee plantations above villages of Manacal and Las Melenas at edge of PN Península de Paria; all specimen recs. also at edge of or within PN Península de Paria (only 37,500ha). Only 1 specimen from Cerro Azul; surveys from Jun–Sep 1988 on Cerro El Olvido turned up only 1 bird[127]. A threatened sp.

Range: ENDEMIC. 800–1150m; sightings to 685m. Paria Pen., Sucre (Cerros Humo, Azul, and El Olvido, and adj. ridges).
Note: Previously called Yellow-faced Redstart[403].

Tepui Whitestart
PLATE 56
Myioborus castaneocapillus Candelita Gorjeadora
Identification: 5.3″ (13.5cm). 11g. *Crown chestnut* with faintly indicated white supraloral line and inconspic. broken white eyering; sides of head and upperparts dark smoky brownish gray; *underparts entirely bright lemon yellow*, under tail coverts and *outer tail feathers white*. Or with supraloral line and broken eyering white varying from prom. to inconspic.; underparts deep cadmium yellow (*duidae*).
Sim. species: Easily confused with Slate-throated Whitestart which often is with it in mixed-spp. flocks but has dark throat. Both spp. have chestnut crown patch, but Tepui Whitestart's is much larger.
Voice: Weak, infreq. hd song (Sierra de Lema) a long, thin, sibilant (almost hissing) crescendo, slowly rising, *tszzzzzzzzeeeeeeee*, high pitched, varied to *tsis-tsis-tsis-sis-sis-se-se-sesesesseeeee*. Less often gives rather slow, warbling trill, colorless and more like others of genus.
Behavior: Usually seen in prs. that are faithful members of mixed-spp. flocks. Behavior recalls that of others of genus (see White-fronted Whitestart) but this sp. seems to forage over broader vertical range in forest than Andean allies. Somewhat less animated and less energetic than Slate-throated Whitestart. Freq. cocks and fans tail but less often engages in exaggerated wing spreading as it forages.
Status and habitat: Common resident in humid and wet forest, tall second growth, and wooded borders on slopes of tepuis.

Range: 1250–2200m. N and c Amazonas on Cerros Parú, Huachamacari, and Duida; s Bolívar on Cerro Jaua (*duidae*); s Amazonas on Cerro de la Neblina (*maguirei*); tepuis of e Bolívar from Auyán-tepui and Sierra de Lema southward (*castaneocapillus*). S Guyana and n Brazil.
Note: Previously called Brown-capped Redstart[403]. That name now applies to birds resident in Andes of Bolivia and nw Argentina.

Guaiquinima Whitestart
PLATE 56
Myioborus cardonai Candelita de Cardona
Identification: 5.3″ (13.5cm). *Crown velvety black* (no chestnut), sides of head dark gray with faint white supraloral mark and *white spectacles* (sometimes also chin white), rest of upperparts dark gray, *below en-*

tirely deep cadium orange, tail black, under tail coverts and *outer tail feathers white.*
Sim. species: Does not occur with any other whitestart.
Status and habitat: Known from large ser. of specimens from upper-el. forests on Cerro Guaiquinima where prob. fairly common. Total area of habitat on slopes of Cerro Guaiquinima (el. 1800m) is relatively small. Nothing is known of this bird in life.

Range: ENDEMIC. 1200–1700m. Cerro Guaiquinima, c Bolívar.
Note: Previously called Saffron-breasted Redstart[403]. Prob. best treated as a subsp. of White-faced Whitestart (*M. albifacies*), and both may be subspp. of Tepui Whitestart (*M. castaneocapillus*)[544].

White-faced Whitestart   PLATE 56
Myioborus albifacies   Candelita Cara Blanca
Identification: 5.3″ (13.5cm). *Crown and nape velvety black, ocular area and sides of head white*, otherwise sides of head and upperparts dark gray, *underparts entirely deep cadmium yellow to deep orange*, tail dark gray, under tail coverts and outer tail feathers white.
Sim. species: Occurs only with Slate-throated Whitestart which has dark throat and no white on face. Also cf. Guaiquinima and Tepui whitestarts.
Status and habitat: Known from only 3 tepuis in n Amazonas but from a substantial no. of specimens, so prob. fairly numerous. Almost nothing is known of bird in life, but presum. it is much like others of genus. Greatest no. of specimens are from Cerro Sipapo, and at lower els. there (900–1600m) than elsewhere (1700–2250m).

Range: ENDEMIC. 900–2250m. N Amazonas on Cerros Sipapo, Yavi, and Guanay.
Note: Possibly conspecific with Guaiquinima Whitestart (*M. cardonaí*). Facial color, chief difference between them, is notably plastic in many spp. of *Myioborus*[544]. Except for black crowns, both forms also are much like Tepui Whitestart (*M. castaneocapillus*). All 3 pops. are isolated on separate tepuis.

Basileuterus

Large genus; closely allied to *Hemispingus* tanagers; typically show striped crown or long eyestripe; larger, heavier bodied, and heavier billed than migratory genera such as *Dendroica* and *Vermivora*; tail rounded; most have pale legs; mainly forest and woodland undergrowth; most diverse in Andes.

Black-crested Warbler   PLATE 56
Basileuterus nigrocristatus   Chiví Guicherito
Identification: 5.5″ (14cm). 14g. Sharply defined stripes on forepart of head. Olive above with *black central forecrown stripe* (the feathers long but not raised to form a crest), *eyebrows bright yellow, lores and short line through eyes black*; underparts bright golden yellow, sides and lower underparts tinged olive, tail rounded.
Sim. species: Flavescent (prob. no overlap) and Citrine warblers have olive (not black) head stripes. Also see Superciliaried Hemispingus.
Voice: Call a loud, sharp *chit*. Loud, energetic song, hd. mostly in early morning, a few sharp, sputtering notes accelerating gradually into fast, rattling ser. that rises, *tsuk, . tsuk, tsweet tweet-tueet-ueet'ueet'eet'et 'et'et't't't*; sometimes repeated over and over at short intervals.
Behavior: Prs. are energetic and excitable but tend to skulk in thickets and other low growth and are sometimes rather difficult to see. Forage actively, hopping and peering in foliage and keeping mostly out of sight, but occas. pop in and out of view briefly. Reg. follow mixed-spp. flocks. Grassy cup nest on bank or mound of moss on gd.; eggs thickly spotted and blotched red brown[589].
Status and habitat: Fairly common to common resident in dense shrubbery along forest borders, young second growth in highland pastures, and stunted forest up to treeline. In all areas fond of *Chusquea* bamboo.

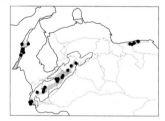

Range: 2000–3100m in Andes; 1800–2200m in Coastal Cordillera (sight to 2580m, Cerro Oriental—D. Ascanio). Sierra de Perijá, Zulia; Andes from s Táchira to ne Trujillo on Lara border; Coastal Cordillera in Aragua, Distr. Federal, and Miranda. Andes from Colombia to c Peru.

Citrine Warbler   PLATE 56
Basileuterus luteoviridis   Chiví Cetrino
Identification: 5.5″ (14cm). 16.5g. Dull and undistinguished. *Legs yellowish brown*. Above dull dark olive, *short yellow eyestripe* narrows and extends to above eye or just slightly beyond; lores dusky, *below dull golden yellow*, sides, flanks, and lower underparts heavily tinged olive, chest with slight olive tinge.

Sim. species: Often not safely told from Superciliaried Hemispingus in field. Citrine Warbler has *broader but shorter eyestripe*, is marginally richer yellow below (in direct comparison), and has *yellowish brown* (not slate horn) *legs* and distinctly *rounded* (not squarish) tail. Hemispingus shows small blackish patch at base of primaries (primary coverts), is yellower below eyes, duskier behind eyes, and sometimes shows faint dusky mottling on throat. Also cf. Black-crested Warbler and Oleaginous Hemispingus.

Voice: Gives complex duet, one bird chattering rapidly, other giving a ser. of high, thin or squeaky notes (P. Schwartz recording). Solo songs are somewhat variable, typically short, fast, chattery trills followed by 2 or more distinct and emphatic notes at end, e.g., *ch'ch 'chu'u' chu-cheet!* varied to *te'e'e'ee te teet!*; or longer sputtery ser. that accelerates into trill then slows; slightly buzzy *psit* notes when foraging.

Behavior: An active, energetic warbler, most often seen in prs. or families accompanying mixed-spp. flocks composed of flycatcher, tanagers, and other warblers. Works sedulously through lower foliage gleaning insects from leaves and keeping mostly out of sight.

Status and habitat: Resident in humid and wet montane forest and dense, shrubby forest borders. Most numerous at high els. in s Táchira, e.g., above 2700m at Cerro El Retiro, Cerro Las Copas, and Páramo de Tamá.

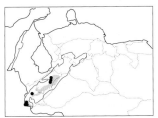

Range: 2400–3000m. Andes of s Táchira n to c Mérida at La Culata (*luteoviridis*). Andes of Colombia s to Bolivia.

Flavescent Warbler
PLATE 56
Basileuterus flaveolus   Chiví Amarillento
Identification: 5.5" (14cm). 13g. Semiterrestrial. Bill dusky; legs straw to dull dusky yellow. Above bright olive with *short narrow yellow eyestripe*; blackish loral stripe; *entire underparts bright golden yellow*, sides and flanks lightly tinged olive.

Sim. species: Much like Citrine Warbler and Superciliaried Hemispingus, both of which occur at higher els. Cf. smaller ♀ Yellow, ♀ Masked, ♀ Prothonotary, and rare ♀ Hooded warblers.

Voice: Song is sharp, jerky, and delivered quickly, *ek, Ease-a Ease-a, E, chéu-chéu-chéu*, or *seeka-seeka-SEETA, cheu-cheu-cheu*, or sim. var., 1st ser. often abbreviated, last 3 *cheu* notes characteristic but sometimes abbreviated. Some songs recall those of Riverside Warbler.

Behavior: A modest and rather retiring warbler that forages on or near gd. by hopping or walking, but usually sings from perch a little above gd. Commonly keeps in rather thick cover and would be little noticed but for

occas. bursts of loud song. Sometimes with mixed-spp. flocks; tends to flick or sweep partly spread tail from side to side like Riverside Warbler. Covered leaf and fiber nest on gd.; side entrance, 3 eggs[260].

Status and habitat: Fairly common resident (easily overlooked) in dry semideciduous and moist evergreen forest, light woodland, and dry, scrubby second growth, mainly in foothill or hilly terrain. Fairly common at low els. on both slopes of PN Henri Pittier and in dry forests on Sierra de Chichiriviche. Common in scrubby foothill vegetation of w Táchira.

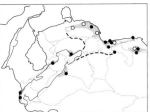

Range: 250–1200m (sight recs. almost to sea level). W base of Andes in Táchira and Trujillo; c and e Falcón (sight, Sierra de San Luis; Mirimire), and n cordilleras from Carabobo and n Guárico to Distr. Federal and e Miranda; sw Portuguesa. Ne Colombia; e Bolivia, e and s Brazil, and n Paraguay; Guyana.

Note 1: S birds may be a separate sp.
Note 2: Placed in genus *Phaeothlypis* by some[81].

Three-striped Warbler
PLATE 56
Basileuterus tristriatus   Chiví Tres Rayas
Identification: 5" (12.7cm). 12g. Drab plumaged. Above grayish olive, *crown and sides of head dull buff with 2 broad blackish coronal stripes, blackish loral stripe*, and dusky patch on rear cheek narrowing and curving forward beneath eye (encloses buff spot below eye); *underparts dingy yellowish white*, flanks tinged olive, belly more buff (*bessereri*). Or dark olive above with bold coronal and facial markings (*auricularis*); or drab with *virtually no dusky markings* on sides of head (*meridanus*); or crown and sides of head olive, underparts heavily tinged olive (*pariae*).

Sim. species: Despite geographical variation, easily recognized by combination of head markings and dull underparts (no bright yellow). Note that Andean birds, the drabbest of group, essentially lack markings on sides of head. Oleaginous Hemispingus is much more uniform looking, *lacks* broad pale central crown stripe, and is generally darker below. Also Cf. Golden-crowned Warbler.

Voice: Incessant call, while foraging, a high, reedy *chee-wéep*. Song an unmusical, agitated chipping, mid. part descending, last part ascending, *tsit tsit tsit ee-tse-te'ti'ti'ti'ti'ti'chi-chi-chi-e-e-ez-ez*.

Behavior: Travels in little parties, lively and excitable as work through lower-story vegetation in ebullient, chattery manner, peering at foliage, gleaning, sally-fluttering short distances to undersides of leaves, chipping noisily, and flicking tails up with every move. Reg. members of mixed-spp. flocks, esp. with Common Bush-Tanagers, but also travel independently. Nest a cup (domed?) on gd. (or a little above?); 2 eggs.

Status and habitat: Common resident in undergrowth of humid and wet forest and older second growth in foothills and mts.

Range: 800–2700m (most recs. below 2300m). Sierra de Perijá, Zulia, and Andes of s Táchira (*auricularis*); Andes of n Táchira, Mérida, and nw Barinas (sight) n to s Lara (*meridanus*); mts. of nw Lara, Yaracuy, and e through n cordilleras to s Sucre and n Monagas (*bessereri*); Sucre on Paria Pen. (*pariae*). Costa Rica, Panama, and Andes from Colombia to n Bolivia.

Roraiman Warbler   PLATE 56
Basileuterus roraimae   Chiví de Los Tepuis
Identification: 5.5″ (14cm). 14.5g. Notably dark appearance. Upperparts dark olive green, *2 long black coronal stripes enclose orange rufous central crown stripe* (often not conspic.); eyestripe yellowish in front of eye and becoming yellowish olive behind eye; short dusky stripe through eye (often inconspic.); faint broken yellow eyering; throat and underparts bright yellow, chest and sides heavily tinged olive.
Sim. species: Not unlike Golden-crowned Warbler which is smaller, overall *much paler and gray* (not olive) *above*, and has grayish eyestripe (not yellow to olive), grayish on sides of head, and more uniform yellow underparts.
Voice: Song a ser. of bouncy *tic* notes rapidly accelerating and ending in smooth rising buzz, *tis, tis-tis-tic'tic 'tic't't't'z'zzzzzzzZZZZE*, overall resembling dawn song of Russet-crowned Warbler; also a more choppy, stuttering *tis, tis tis my wish-wish-to'go'wee'wee!*, accelerating and rising somewhat. Songs sometimes given over and over in quick succession. Sings mainly early in morning.
Behavior: Frequents shady borders and thickets and tends to remain out of view. Prs. or families of 3–4 forage fairly low, mostly 2–10m up inside forest. Occur alone or join mixed-spp. flocks and move up into forest mid. level or even a little higher. Often flick tail

downward as actively hop along branches and twigs and peer at foliage.
Status and habitat: Resident in humid forest and thick vegetation along forest borders. Shows no special affinity for bamboo in Venez. Fairly common within narrow band at ca. 800–1100m on Sierra de Lema, Bolívar.
Range: 800–1800m. Most cerros of Amazonas and Bolívar (no recs. Cerro Guanay, Amazonas, or Meseta de Jaua, Bolívar). Adj. Guyana and extreme n Brazil.
Note: Previously considered a subsp. of Two-banded Warbler (*B. bivittatus*) of se Peru to nw Argentina[403].

Golden-crowned Warbler   PLATE 56
Basileuterus culicivorus   Chiví Silbador
Identification: 5″ (12.7cm). 10g. *Upperparts gray, 2 prom. black coronal stripes*, and semiconcealed yellow to orange rufous median coronal stripe; *eyebrow grayish white*, lores and line through eye blackish, small whitish spot below eye; sides of head buffy gray, *underparts entirely bright golden yellow*. Or coronal stripe yellow, upperparts paler gray (*indignus*). Or upperparts grayish olive (*olivascens*). Or upperparts brownish olive (*segrex*); legs pale yellowish brown.
Sim. species: Widespread and overall with crisper, more clean-cut pattern than others of genus. See esp. Flavescent, Three-striped, Two-banded, Gray-throated, and Gray-headed warblers. Note restricted ranges of several of these spp.
Voice: High, thin, chattery song, *pits-seet-seet-seet-seet* or *seet-seet-seet-seet-SEET-sit* or sim., stronger toward end. Constantly gives chipping *pits* and buzzy *vreet* while foraging.
Behavior: Prs. or little families behave in bright and lively manner and are usually rather easy to see as they chatter, constantly flick up slightly cocked tails, and glean from foliage in understory down almost to gd. Often with mixed-spp. flocks where their constant vocalizations may serve to stimulate flock activity. Nest a grass, rootlet, and fiber dome with side entrance; low on bank or on forest floor; 2–4 white eggs marked reddish brown mainly at larger end[175,706].
Status and habitat: Fairly common resident in moist semideciduous to humid evergreen forest, light woodland, coffee plantations, and shady areas with thickets and patches of dense vegetation. Mainly in foothills and lower mt. slopes.

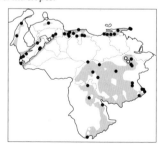

Range: To 2100m (most recs. 200–1700m) n of Orinoco; to 1750m s of Orinoco (mostly above 300m). Sierra de Perijá, Zulia (*indignus*); Andes from s Táchira to Lara, mts. of Falcón (Sierra de San Luis), Yaracuy, and e through n cordilleras to Distr. Federal and Miranda (*cabanisi*); mts. of ne Anzoátegui, Sucre, and n Monagas (*olivascens*); mts. of e Amazonas e through Bolívar (*segrex*). W Mexico to w Panama; n Colombia spottily to s Guyana and n Brazil; e Brazil to n Bolivia, n Argentina, and Uruguay. Trinidad.

Rufous-capped Warbler   PLATE 56
Basileuterus rufifrons   Chiví Corona Castaña
Identification: 5" (12.7cm). 11g. Dainty and clean-cut. Above bright olive green, *crown and cheeks rufous chestnut separated by long narrow white eyestripe*; blackish loral stripe bordered below by whitish area extending back beneath eye (forms small white patch below eye), *underparts bright golden yellow.*
Sim. species: Chestnut on crown and cheeks diagnostic; also note very restricted range in Venez.
Voice: Song in Colombia a fast, energetic *tis-tis weecha weecha beEEcher* with variations, but emphatic *beEEcher* or *reEEcha* at ending is characteristic.
Behavior: A bright, chipper little warbler with jaunty cocked-up tail. Usually seen in loosely assoc. prs. that stay in thickets or other low vegetation, but often inquisitive and relatively easy to see. In Costa Rica, oven-shaped nest on gd; concealed near rock, log, or bush; 1–3 white eggs finely speckled cinnamon, mostly at larger end[644].
Status and habitat: Resident. In Colombia found in tangles and thickets in moist semideciduous and humid evergreen woodland, second growth, and coffee plantations. Known from only 1 region (several specimens) in Venez.

Range: 1000m. Sierra de Perijá in Río Apón (Barranquilla) and Ríos Cogollo and Palmar, Zulia (*mesochrysus*). S Mexico to Colombia.
Note: Taxonomy follows AOU checklist[10].

Gray-headed Warbler   PLATE 56
Basileuterus griseiceps   Chiví Cabecigrís
Identification: 5.5" (14cm). Only in mts. of ne. *Crown, nape, and sides of head to below eyes dark gray; short white supraloral streak*; chin white, usually a little whitish mottling on cheeks; rest of upperparts olive green; *underparts deep yellow*, flanks tinged olive; legs dull yellowish orange.
Sim. species: Only "gray-headed" *Basileuterus* in its limited range. Cf. Golden-crowned and Three-striped warblers, both with conspic. crown stripes.
Voice: Prs. apparently sing duets (not antiphonal), ♂(?) a lively, surprisingly loud, slurred ser. of mostly 2- to 3-note phrases, *we-chee-cHEEeer, wee-EE, wee-chEE-cheEEEar, wee-chEE-chEAT!, whueet, wee-chEE-cheEEa* . . . and so on, or may pause momentarily after

several phrases. Simultaneously ♀(?) gives emphatic ser. of *chack* notes in rather irreg. sequence. Soft *tsank* contact call.
Behavior: Like other *Basileuterus*, seems sedate, even shy compared with more energetic and animated n migratory kin. Prs. or families are moderately active but stay low, mostly 1–4m up, close together and in dense vegetation when foraging, or move somewhat higher when accompanying small mixed-spp. flocks which may incl. spinetails, barbtails, tanagers, and brush-finches. Gleans from upper leaf surfaces, or less often reaches below or hangs almost upside down to search beneath leaves. Also gleans from twigs, broken twig ends, and occas. at curled hanging dead leaves. Breeding May–Jul[62]; fledglings in Aug.
Status and habitat: Rare and threatened. Resident. Apparently dependent on mature humid forest with undisturbed understory, although occas. found in fingers of semidegraded forest in coffee plantations. Known from 42 specimens taken between 1898 and 1963, all but 3 from Cerro Negro and vicinity of Cerro Turumiquire. Thereafter known from only 1 sighting, presum. this sp. (ca. Jun 1987), until a few prs. were relocated on Cerro Negro, Sucre/Monagas border, in 1993, and subsequently seen by several observers[62]. Possible sightings e of Teresén (= 17km e of Caripe) in Los Cumbres de San Bonifacio need confirmation. Status of sp. in Serranía de Turumiquire is unknown.

Range: ENDEMIC. 1200–2440m. Slopes of Cerro Negro (1400–1600m) on Sucre/Monagas border; Serranía de Turumiquire (1525–2440m); 1 rec. from San Antonio, Sucre; 2 recs. from Cerro Peonía on Sucre/Monagas/Anzoátegui border.

Gray-throated Warbler   PLATE 56
Basileuterus cinereicollis   Chiví Gargantigrís
Identification: 5.5" (14cm). Looks very dark in field. Above dark olive, *crown and sides of head dark gray*, 2 poorly indicated black coronal stripes and semiconcealed lemon yellow coronal patch; *upper throat whitish turning gray on sides of throat, chest, and upper breast*; rest of underparts pale yellow *sharply cut off* from gray of upper breast; flanks tinged olive.
Sim. species: Note "dark-headed" appearance and sharply "divided" underparts; crown patch often not visible. Rather sim. to Russet-crowned Warbler which occurs largely at higher els. (overlap?). Also see Golden-crowned Warbler which has prom. crown stripes and no gray below, and duller Three-striped Warbler.
Voice: Infreq. hd. song (Jun–?) is 3–6 *high-pitched* wispy notes, *sa see-see-sa-SEE!* or *swee-swee-se-SEET!*, or longer *we, we-E-E-a-WEEK!* (last notes run together).

Song pattern variable but always weak and insignificant (easily overlooked), typically with last note stronger and higher pitched or rising.

Behavior: A poorly known and infreq. seen bird of dense undergrowth where it keeps low (mostly 1–5m up) and is usually retiring and difficult to see. Apparently not with mixed-spp. flocks.

Status and habitat: Rare and/or local resident. Humid premontane forest and forest borders, esp. on steep slopes with tangled vegetation, and vine-covered and overgrown landslides and treefalls. Can be found along roadside a few km above La Azulita, Mérida[259].

Range: 1100–2100m. Sierra de Perijá (*zuliensis*); w slope of Andes in Táchira and Mérida (*cinereicollis*); once on e slope in extreme s Táchira (subsp.?). Both slopes of e Andes in Colombia.

Note: Subsp. name *pallidulus* now applied only to birds on w slope (Colombian side) of Sierra de Perijá[19].

Russet-crowned Warbler   PLATE 56
Basileuterus coronatus   Chiví Corona Anaranjada

Identification: 5.7″ (14.5cm). 16g. Rather *large, dark, montane warbler. Above dark olive, entire head iron gray, narrow orange rufous coronal patch bordered by 2 fairly prom. black coronal stripes and black stripe through eyes*; throat and upper chest pale gray (paler than head), rest of underparts deep yellow, chest, sides, and flanks heavily tinged olive.

Sim. species: Gray-throated Warbler has inconspic. yellow coronal patch (not orange), *shows little or no evidence of* crown stripes, and has gray extending to mid. breast and *sharply separated* from yellow underparts. Golden-crowned Warbler is gray above and much paler. Both spp. occur mostly at lower els. Also cf. Black-crested Warbler.

Voice: One of earliest singers at dawn, often hd. at first hint of light. Song a few sputtery notes followed by smoothly rising glissando, *teet, tut't't'u'u'treeeeeeEE* or *tzinkle tzinkle tzinkle zuuurreeeeEE*, at short intervals, given by 1 bird, or more or less simultaneously or alternately by ♂ and ♀. Prs. also sing antiphonal duets, ♂'s song ending in rising note, ♀'s falling at end (P. Schwartz). Typically sing only for a short period at dawn, rarely during day. Call when disturbed a pulsating, low-pitched *pl-b* or *pl-b-b*.

Behavior: This rather large, dark, quiet warbler will not come out to meet an observer but can be engaging enough to those that penetrate dim forest retreats where it lives. Prs. or families often follow mixed-spp. flocks but stay mostly in shady lower levels inside forest where they are inconspic. Forage fairly actively, esp. by hopping up around large vine-covered trunks, and also sally-glean short distances to leaves, or hop and peer in foliage. Not esp. difficult to see but some-

what retiring and cautious, infreq. allowing close approach. Nest, prob. domed type of genus, in a bank; white eggs spotted cinnamon[589].

Status and habitat: Fairly common resident inside humid and wet forest, older second-growth woodland, and to forest edges, but not usually in open at edges.

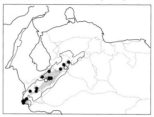

Range: 1800–2800m. Andes of Táchira, Mérida, and Trujillo n to Páramo Cendé (*regulus*). Andes from Colombia to n Bolivia.

Riverside Warbler   PLATE 56
Basileuterus rivularis   Chiví de Ríos

Identification: 5.5″ (14cm). 12.5g. Above incl. rump and tail olivaceous brown, crown sooty gray, *eyebrow and sides of head cinnamon*, dusky stripe through eye, below white tinged cinnamon buff on chest, sides, and lower underparts.

Sim. species: Behavior recalls a waterthrush but appearance quite different. Note terrestrial behavior and habit of energetically sweeping fanned tail back and forth.

Voice: Song loud and ringing, an accelerating crescendo of *tseeu* notes ending with a few slower, distinct, and loud *chew* notes, easily hd. above sound of rushing streams, e.g., *tseeu, tseeu, teeu tee tee chu-chu-chu-chu-chu-CHU-CHEW-CHEW-CHEW* (ca. 20–25 notes).

Behavior: A coy, semiterrestrial songster, hd. far more than seen. Hops, or sometimes hop-walks with springy steps, at edges of puddles or streams and sweeps broadly fanned tail from side to side but does not bob like a waterthrush. Sings from gd., a log, or other low perch. When pressed, repeatedly flushes ahead short distances with loud *chip* or, with a coquettish glance backward, retreats altogether from view into some shady recess. Nest of allied Buff-rumped Warbler (*B. fulvicauda*) a grass and rootlet oven with side entrance; on bank near stream; 2 dull white eggs speckled rusty with dense ring at larger end.

Status and habitat: Fairly common resident along forest streams, shady roadside puddles, and other damp places with standing water. Sometimes a short distance inside forest, but seldom any distance from water.

Range: To 1100m. Ne Monagas (sightings) and Delta Amacuro; throughout Amazonas and Bolívar (*mesoleuca*). Range highly disjunct. The Guianas and ne Brazil; e base of Andes in Bolivia; n Mato Grosso, Brazil; se Brazil, e Paraguay, and ne Argentina.

Note: By some placed in genus *Phaeothlypis*[10]. Has been considered conspecific with Buff-rumped Warbler (*B. fulvicauda*) of w Amazonia and C Amer.; they may meet in sw Amazonas. Buff-rumped differs in rump and basal half of tail buff.

Granatellus

Large for a warbler; rose on underparts; long, slightly rounded tail; heavy bill; only S Amer. representative of small, mainly C Amer. group.

Rose-breasted Chat   PLATE 56
Granatellus pelzelni   Reinita Pechirroja
Identification: 5″ (12.7cm). 11.5g. Bill fairly thick, dark gray above, bluish gray below. ♂: crown and sides of head black; *short white postocular*, rearcrown and rest of upperparts dark slate blue, tail black, throat white narrowly bordered by black; *breast and central underparts pinkish rose*, sides and flanks white. ♀: dark blue gray above, tail dusky, forehead, eyebrow, sides of head, and underparts cinnamon buff, paler on throat and belly, *under tail coverts tinged pinkish rose.*
Sim. species: ♀ not as distinctive as ♂ but easily told by conspic. pink under tail coverts.
Voice: Usual song a loud, clear, whistled *wheet-wheet-wheet-wheet-wheet* of up to ca. 8 notes; occas. rhythm of notes varied slightly. Call, when foraging or moving, a distinctive nasal *tank* or *tank-tank.*
Behavior: A rather quiet and reserved chat, quite unlike eccentric and seriocomic Yellow-breasted Chat (*Icteria virens*) of N Amer. which is, at best, only distantly related. This sp. lives in rather loosely assoc. prs. that typically forage from forest mid. levels to subcanopy, only occas. lower along forest borders, and everywhere stay mostly in or near big vine tangles. Restless and almost always on the go; tail held slightly cocked and spread, and constantly flicked up and wings usually slightly drooped (foraging technique?) as peer in foliage or lunge for insects. Freq. follow mixed-spp. flocks. Despite bold plumage, rather retiring and often tantalizingly difficult to see.
Status and habitat: Uncommon to fairly common resident. Local in high vines inside moist semideciduous to humid evergreen forest, and at forest borders; likes massive vine tangles in ancient treefall scars.

Range: To 850m. Throughout Amazonas and Bolívar (*pelzelni*). The Guianas and e and c Brazil. Prob. e Colombia.

Thraupidae: Tanagers
Verdines, Tangaras, Fruteros, Azulejos

Tanagers comprise a large polyphyletic group of birds with various members most closely related to warblers, honeycreepers, and emberizid and cardinalid finches[89,299]. Several genera traditionally included with tanagers, i.e., *Piranga*, *Chlorophonia*, and *Euphonia*, are most closely related to the cardinalids and are not true tanagers, whereas several other genera, traditionally included with emberizids, are almost certainly most closely related to tanagers, i.e., *Saltator*, *Tiaris*, *Volatinia*, *Sporophila*, and *Haplospiza*[299]. Some tanagers are small, delicate, and thin-billed, much like tropical warblers; others are large, robust, and heavy-billed like saltators and some finches. Tanagers are primarily Neotropical in distribution and are found in virtually all forested habitats from the lowlands to treeline but are most numerous in humid forest at low to middle elevations in tropical latitudes. Tanagers are best known for their colorful plumages; some rank among the most beautiful small birds in the world. A few, however, are drab and retiring. Most species eat a mixed diet of fruit and insects. With some notable exceptions, most tanagers are poor songsters that sing thin, squeaky, unmusical songs. Most species build open cup nests of grass and fibers; a few build globe-shaped nests with side entrances.

Coereba

Widespread; short, decurved, pointed bill; large domed nest unlike other honeycreepers or tanagers; more than 30 described races attest to unique plasticity of plumage characters and adaptability.

Bananaquit   PLATE 59
Coereba flaveola   Reinita Común
Identification: 4″ (10.2cm). 9g. Warblerlike but short tailed. *Thin, sharp-pointed bill is slightly decurved.* Above brownish gray to slaty black; crown and sides of head blackish, *long conspic. white eyestripe; rump yellow;* small white spot at base of primaries (absent in *guianensis*, *roraimae*, *minima*; obscure in *intermedia*); throat pale gray, *rest of underparts bright yellow*, under tail coverts white. Or *entirely dull black*, sometimes belly tinged olive (*laurae*). Or foreparts *black*, wings and tail dusky, back and lower underparts dark olive (*lowii*). Or like *lowii* but smaller (*melanornis*).
Sim. species: Best marks are long white eyebrows, wing spot (if present), distinctive bill, and gray and yellow underparts.
Voice: A persistent if unaccomplished singer. Song is unmusical, usually a rapid ser. of shrill buzzes and hissing *chip* notes, often incessantly repeated. There is much geographical variation in song patterns, and each individual also sings several different songs.
Behavior: An energetic little scrap of feathers, most likely to be seen alone singing from high open twig or

moving rapidly, almost frantically, among clusters of flowers and sipping nectar. Probes open corollas, brushlike inflorescenses, or pokes holes in bases of long tubular flowers with equal facility. Also eats or pierces small berries for juice and reg. steals protein corpuscles from leaf axils of *Cecropia* trees. Strong, short legs permit it to cling or hang upside down with ease while feeding. Follows mixed-spp. flocks in forested areas but more often independent of them. Around habitations may become tame and fearless, boldly entering homes or restaurants if bowls of sugar are available. In Colombia breeding reported yr-round; Apr–Aug, Guárico[734]; Apr, ne Anzoátegui[186]. Both sexes, alone or in cooperation, build "dummy" or dormitory nests and breeding nests; oval grassy ball with side entrance; ♀ incubates 2–3 buff white eggs thickly dotted reddish brown, esp. at larger end[624].

Status and habitat: Resident in canopy or edge of humid forest, tall second growth, open woodland, plantations, urban and cultivated areas, farms, gardens, or wherever there is abundance of native or non-native flowers. Very common in coastal areas, esp. in Sucre and n Monagas where abundant; much less numerous or locally absent in tall humid forest s of Orinoco.

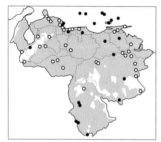

Range: To 2000m. Throughout. Lowlands from e Zulia to Sucre and s to Orinoco, except where next 3 subspp. occur (*luteola*); Perijá and Maracaibo region, Zulia, and w base of Andes in Táchira and Mérida (*obscura*); w slope of Andes (above *obscura*) in Táchira and Mérida (*montana*); n Bolívar from Río Cuchivero to Delta Amacuro and Río Mánamo on border with se Monagas (*bolivari*); nw Bolívar in lower Río Caura from Suapuré to La Prisión (*guianensis*); nw Amazonas at Pto. Ayacucho and Caño Cataniapo (*columbiana*); s Apure along Río Meta, w Amazonas from San Carlos and Sierra Imerí to Río Siapa and e to Gran Sabana (*roraimae*); c Amazonas from Samariapo and Río Ventuari s to Río Casiquiare (*minima*); sw Amazonas at Yavita-Pimichín and Río Guainía to Río Casiquiare (*intermedia*); and offshore isls. of Cayo Sal, Falcón (*melanornis*); Islas Los Roques (*lowii*); Isla La Tortuga (*ferryi*); Isla Los Hermanos and Pto. Real on Islas Los Frailes (*frailensis*); Islas Los Testigos on Testigo Grande and Conejo (*laurae*). Se Mexico generally to ne Argentina. S Florida (rare); W Indies (except Cuba) to Trinidad and Tobago.

Note: Often placed in family of its own, Coerebidae, as only remaining member of family[10]. Also sometimes placed with Parulidae. Bananaquit does differ from all of these groups in various ways[594].

Conirostrum

Small and warblerlike; sharp-pointed bill; 1 group in highlands, another in lowlands; all with gray to bluish upperparts, several with chestnut on underparts or under tail coverts; lowland group (4 spp.) formerly placed in *Ateleodacnis*[467,544].

Chestnut-vented Conebill   PLATE 59
Conirostrum speciosum   Mielerito Azul

Identification: 4″ (10.2cm). 8.4g. Bill sharp pointed, slightly decurved. ♂: above mainly dull grayish blue, paler below; wings dusky edged gray blue, *small white spot at base of primaries; under tail coverts chestnut*. Or slightly darker above, much darker below (looks almost uniform), no white wing spot (*amazonum*). ♀: very different; crown and nape gray blue, lores buff *contrasting* with bright yellow olive upperparts; throat and chest buffy white, lower underparts dull white, flanks tinged buffy olive; under tail coverts buff.

Sim. species: In llanos a small, dull, bluish bird with chestnut under tail coverts will surely be this sp. ♀ best told by attendant ♂. Cf. Tennessee Warbler which has white eyestripe; also see Scrub Greenlet.

Voice: Song a high, thin *tidé, tidé, tidé, tidé, ti'dee'rît* at leisurely pace. High *tic* and *ti* notes when foraging.

Behavior: Prs. or families of 3–5 are active, warblerlike, and full of nervous energy but easily overlooked as forage high in outer foliage. Esp. fond of searching tiny leaflets and axils of doubly-compound foliage of legumes (Leguminosae), busily hustling from one spray of leaflets to next, often hanging upside down to probe and glean with sharp-pointed bill. Occas. also with little mixed-spp. flocks. Nest (Minas Gerais, Brazil) a tiny leaf petiole and fiber cup hidden in curled leaf; 3 bluish green eggs with brown spots[538].

Status and habitat: Uncommon and thinly spread resident in canopy of gallery forest and treetops in scattered groves of large trees (i.e., *Pithecellobium*) in llanos. Generally favors drier, strongly seasonal areas. Only recs. s of Orinoco are sightings sw of El Palmar, Jan 1998 (D. Ascanio) and a pr. in semideciduous gallery forest ca. 10km w of Tumeremo, Bolívar, 6 Mar 1998[259].

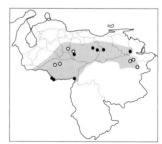

Range: To ca. 200m. W Apure and s Cojedes (sightings) e to Guárico, Anzoátegui, and s Monagas at Barrancas (*guaricola*); s Apure along Río Meta (*amazonum*); ne Bolívar from El Palmar to Tumeremo (sightings, subsp.?). Range disjunct. Locally in the Guianas; e Ecuador (once); e Peru (mainly river isls.) and Brazil s of the Amazon to n Argentina.

White-eared Conebill PLATE 59
Conirostrum leucogenys Mielerito Orejiblanco
Identification: 3.8″ (9.7cm). 7g. Small and short-tailed.
♂: above mainly dark bluish gray with *shiny black crown and nape*; conspic. *white ear patch* and narrow white rump band (usually not conspic.); wings and tail blackish, underparts gray tinged blue, center of belly white, *under tail coverts chestnut.* ♀: very different; dull bluish gray above with whitish rump; *eyebrow, sides of head, and underparts yellowish buff*, breast tinged olive, belly yellowish.
Sim. species: ♂'s black crown and white cheeks are diagnostic. ♀, best told by attendant ♂, recalls dull ♀ Bicolored Conebill but has thinner bill, pale rump (hard to see), and is more yellowish below. Also cf. Tennessee Warbler.
Voice: Song is a high, thin, tinkling ser. of notes, *tsingle, tséet-e-tséet*, or sim. variation, usually short, occas. longer, to ca. 1.5 sec, complex, unmusical, and often slowing or fading at end. Often sung persistently but easily overlooked.
Behavior: Much as in Chestnut-vented Conebill. Lively prs. or little parties of 3–5 sedulously glean minute prey in high outer foliage of legumes and other tall trees with compound or pinnately compound leaves. Often hang upside down from leaves. Sip nectar from *Erythrina* flowers, esp. in dry season, then may come lower or to small trees, but otherwise remain high and are easily overlooked. Sometimes with small mixed-spp. flocks.
Status and habitat: Uncommon to locally fairly common resident in dry to moist (semideciduous) open woodland, wooded borders, cacao plantations, gallery forests, and scattered tall spreading legumes in pastures. Also in moist-humid transition forest, esp. where there are large legume trees (e.g., foothills of Coastal Cordillera above Ocumare de La Costa, Aragua).

Range: To ca. 800m (once to 1300m at Curimagua, Falcón). Perijá region, Zulia, and w base of Andes in Táchira, Mérida, and Trujillo (*cyanochrous*); e Zulia to e Falcón (prob. n Lara), Yaracuy, Carabobo, and n Aragua (*leucogenys*). E Panama and Colombia.

Bicolored Conebill PLATE 59
Conirostrum bicolor Mielero Manglero
Identification: 4.5″ (11.4cm). 11g. *Eyes dull red; legs pinkish*; bill dark above, pinkish below, thicker than others of genus. ♂: *above dull gray blue*, flight feathers dusky edged dull blue, loral area, face, and underparts pale buffy gray, buffiest on lower underparts. ♀: like ♂ but duller. Imm.: above dull grayish olive (many birds tinged yellowish olive), *face and underparts pale buffy*

yellow somewhat washed olive on sides; center of belly whitish.
Sim. species: Easily confused, esp. duller ♀♀ and imms. Nearest are ♀ and imm. Yellow, Mangrove, and Golden warblers which have dark eyes, dusky legs, and *all-yellow* undertail. Also see Tennessee Warbler and ♀ Hooded Tanager. Not known to overlap with other *Conirostrum* in Venez.
Voice: Infreq. hd. song a high-pitched, squeaky, and somewhat buzzy *pfits, t'wit'wit'wit'chit* or sim. variation. Recalls songs of Bananaquit. Soft calls, when foraging, incl. a high, sibilant *tsik*, also *pit-sik* and *few-it-sip.*
Behavior: Prs. or families busily glean for small arthropods in foliage and twigs of mangroves. Keep in mid. to upper levels of foliage, occas. down to eye level, as peer and probe into tight clusters of small leaves. Usually not with mixed-spp. flocks. Easily attracted to squeaking noises and will often closely approach observer. Small compact nest a deep cup of grass mixed with feathers, 0.3–4m up in fork of mangrove branch; 2 pale buff eggs with dark brown blotches mainly at larger end; in Trinidad often parasitized by Shiny Cowbird[175]; breeding Feb–May, Goajira, Colombia. May breed in imm. plumage[544].
Status and habitat: Fairly common to common resident in mangroves, and in Venez. rarely any distance away from them. May be interspecifically territorial with Mangrove and Golden warblers.

Range: Sea level. Locally on coast from nw Zulia to Sucre and Delta Amacuro; Isla Margarita and Tobeida; islets off e Falcón (*bicolor*). Coastal n Colombia e to the Guianas and spottily on coast of Brazil s to São Paulo; mouth of the Amazon upriver to e Peru and e Ecuador (river isls. and shore). Trinidad.

Rufous-browed Conebill PLATE 57
Conirostrum rufum Mielero Rufo
Identification: 5″ (12.7cm). 11g. *Forehead chestnut, lores and cheeks dusky, otherwise upperparts blue gray, wings and tail darker, occas. 1 faint whitish wing bar; tertials narrowly edged white, underparts ferruginous.*
Sim. species: Rusty Flowerpiercer is much paler below with blackish face mask and hooked bill. Also cf. larger Blue-backed Conebill which has blue back, and Rufous-chested Tanager.
Voice: High-pitched, fast, complex ser. of squeaky notes. Recalls song of Blue-backed Conebill.
Behavior: In Colombia much like Blue-backed Conebill. Mostly encountered in prs., less often in small groups. Sometimes follow mixed-spp. flocks that con-

tain small flycatchers, flowerpiercers, and tanagers. In Colombia breeding reported Aug–Sep.

Status and habitat: In Venez. 1st reported (4 specimens) 30 Aug–1 Sep 1978 at top of Cerro El Retiro, Táchira. In Colombia uncommon to fairly common in bushy or shrubby areas (not forest) and stunted trees up to treeline.

Range: 2800m. Mts. of s Táchira. Colombia in Santa Marta Mts. and E Andes (2650–3300m).

Blue-backed Conebill   PLATE 57
Conirostrum sitticolor   Mielero Purpúreo
Identification: 5″ (12.7cm). 10.4g. Sharp-pointed, conical bill. Head, throat, and chest black, inconspic. blue postocular stripe joins *cobalt blue back*; wings and tail blackish, *lower underparts ferruginous*, sharply separated from black of chest. Or no blue postocular stripe (*sitticolor*), or eyebrow faint, underparts paler, more rufous (*pallidus*).
Sim. species: Brightest of conebills and more likely mistaken for a flowerpiercer or tanager. Cf. Mérida and Rusty flowerpiercers, Slaty-backed Tanager, and Plushcap, none of which has blue back. Also see Rufous-browed Conebill which barely reaches Venez.
Voice: Song, mostly given in early morning, a high-pitched, complex, bubbly jumble of chipping and twittering notes rather like that of *Diglossa* spp. and some other *Conirostrum*, e.g., a rapid *chipapita-chipapita, jeet, chipapita. . . .*, repetitious and somewhat musical; up to 6 sec in length and may be given over and over with only a 1- to 2-sec pause between songs.
Behavior: An active sp., nearly always seen in mixed-spp. flocks with warblers, flowerpiercers, and tanagers. Mainly insectivorous and a quintessential "gleaner" of minutia from dense leaf whorls, leaf axils, and twig and leaf surfaces. Has habit of hopping around and perching right out in open on upper surface of dense canopy foliage, both when foraging and singing. Often stretches up, in paridlike manner, to peer down between tight leaf clusters.
Status and habitat: Uncommon to fairly common resident in humid and wet, high montane forest and forest borders up to treeline.

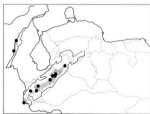

Range: 2550–3500m (numerous sightings to 2300m in n Táchira). Sierra de Perijá (Cerro Viruela southward), Zulia (*pallidus*); s Táchira (*sitticolor*); n Táchira, Mérida, and Trujillo n to Páramo Cristalina-Boconó (*intermedium*). Colombia s in Andes to n Bolivia.

Capped Conebill   PLATE 57
Conirostrum albifrons   Mielerito Gorra Blanca
Identification: 5″ (12.7cm). 10g. ♂: *forecrown glossy blue* inconspic. streaked with white, *otherwise mostly slaty black*, shoulders, back, and rump glossed ultramarine blue (but usually looks black in field). Or sim. but *crown snow white (albifrons)*. ♀: *crown glossy blue, nape gray*, otherwise bright olive above; brighter yellow olive on rump; wings and tail edged olive yellow, sides of head and underparts gray tinged blue and becoming yellowish olive on belly. Or sim. but more extensively yellow olive below (*albifrons*).
Sim. species: ♂♂ with white caps unmistakable. Those with blue caps (look closely) easily mistaken for any of the all-dark flowerpiercers. ♀ brings to mind ♀ Blue Dacnis of lower el. but has duller upperparts. Also cf. Tennessee Warbler.
Voice: Dawn song (*albifrons*) a high, leisurely *wee-see-wee-see-wee-see-weez*, 1st note stronger; varies to *swee-ty, swee-ty, swee-ty, tit'til'tit*, last part trilled. *Chit* notes while foraging.
Behavior: Prs. are reg. members of mixed-spp. flocks containing furnariids, warblers, flowerpiercers, and tanagers in upper levels or canopy of woodland. Actively move along branches with peculiar creeping gait that is accentuated by habit of constantly flicking tail up as they go. Like others of genus, forage mostly by picking and gleaning insects from leaves, leaf axils, and bud tips in high outer foliage. Reg. hang upside down to glean.
Status and habitat: Resident in humid and mossy montane forest, along forest borders, and in tall second growth. Fairly numerous in highlands of s Táchira, uncommon or rare in Coastal Cordillera.

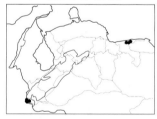

Range: 2200–3000m in s Táchira; 1850–2000m in Coastal Cordillera. Andes of s Táchira (*albifrons*); Coastal Cordillera in Aragua (Colonia Tovar) and Distr. Federal (*cyanonotum*); prob. also adj. Miranda. Colombia s in Andes to s Bolivia.

Schistochlamys

Thick, saltator-like bill; relatively long, *rounded* tail; under wing coverts white; semiopen terrain.

Black-faced Tanager

PLATE 62

Schistochlamys melanopis   Tangara de Cara Negra

Identification: 7.5″ (19cm). 33g. Bill short and heavy, blue gray tipped black; eyes dark red. *Forecrown, face, throat, and center of chest black*, otherwise above uniform gray, below slightly paler gray, center of belly whitish; outer tail feathers narrowly tipped white (fresh plumage). Imm.: very different; above yellowish olive with *broken yellow eyering*; bill, lores, and cheeks somewhat dusky, underparts pale olive strongly tinged yellow, paler and yellower on lower underparts; tail rounded (unlike ads.), sometimes vaguely pale-tipped. Older imms. acquire black on face while still olive. May breed in imm. plumage.

Sim. species: Ad. not likely confused, but imm. (if apart from ad., and it often is), with rather thick, dusky bill, brings to mind a finch or imm. saltator, although none is so uniform. Look for eyering, yellowish belly, and rounded tail.

Voice: Song a rambling, whistled *swéet, ríght here for mé*, repeated 3–4 times in succession. Also occas. a rather weak *tee-tseet-tseet-tseet* or more rambling, disconnected ser. Infreq. call note a sharp *swik*.

Behavior: Usually in prs. or 3s that perch up in open on tops of bushes or small trees, then fly off low and far away to another shrub, or browse alone for fruits and berries (have been seen eating very hot peppers) and a few insects. In Venez. rarely or never with mixed-spp. flocks and generally a bit wary. Grassy open cup nest low and near open area; 2 eggs grayish to yellowish white thickly covered with dark brown spots and blotches[252].

Status and habitat: Uncommon to locally fairly common resident of sandy soil savannas, esp. freq. burned areas dotted with fire-resistant bushes and small trees (*Curatella, Brysonima*, etc.). Invades deforested, almost completely denuded grassy foothills and lower slopes of Andes and n cordilleras (e.g., slopes above La Victoria, Aragua). Absent or local in low, more extensively inundated parts of llanos. N of Orinoco more numerous in open foothill and montane locations than in lowlands.

Range: To 1800m. N of Orinoco found in or near mts. from Zulia to w Sucre and Monagas; s of Orinoco in open terrain throughout (*aterrima*). Colombia to the Guianas, e and s Brazil (mostly absent from Amazonia) to e Peru.

Cissopis and *Lamprospiza*

Large, long-tailed, black-and-white tanagers which somewhat resemble each other (taxonomically related?); both with short, heavy bill; *Lamprospiza* unrec. but likely in Venez.; humid forest areas.

Magpie Tanager

PLATE 62

Cissopis leveriana   Moriche Blanco

Identification: 10.5″ (27cm). 71g. *Large, boldly patterned, piebald bird with yellow eyes and long tail.* Bill short and thick, upper mandible strongly decurved and hooked at tip. Head, mantle, throat, and chest glossy blue black, the feathers of chest long, lancelike, and *extending as ragged points onto white of back, shoulders, and breast*; wings and tail black, inner flight feathers broadly edged white, *tail graduated and broadly tipped white*.

Voice: Most often hd. are metallic *chek* calls. Infreq. hd. song an unmusical but exuberant ser. of jerky whistles, chatters, and squeaky notes, e.g., *t-t-t, chu-chu tweéte, chuchu-tweéti* or sim. variation, often repeated a no. of times.

Behavior: Noisy and conspic. prs. or families, occas. single birds, bring to mind jays in appearance and behavior as they hop up through shrubbery, call sharply, and fly in rather slow, steady, and direct flight from tree to tree in clearings. Often sit up in open on isolated shrub or tree for extended periods of time. Forage at almost any ht. but more often at low to med. hts. for fruit and a few insects that seem to be taken almost incidentally. Generally independent of other spp. although occas. with mixed flocks along forest borders or in forest canopy. Cup nest of twigs, grass, and other plant material on fork and concealed in foliage 3.5m up[274].

Status and habitat: Common resident in shrubby and regenerating clearings in humid forest, irreg. and cutover second growth, and river edge várzea. Disperses through top of forest canopy. Sight recs. on w side of Andes n to Valera, Trujillo, 17 Feb 1978 (P. Alden), and on e slope n to PN Yacambú, Lara, early 1990s (P. Boesman; Hilty) may be range expansions following deforestation.

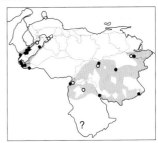

Range: To 2000m (usually much lower) n of Orinoco; to 950m s of Andes. W base of Andes in Táchira, Mérida, and Trujillo (sight); e base of Andes locally in Táchira, w Apure, nw Barinas, and se Lara (sight); Amazonas s to Río Ventuari; Bolívar from lower Río Caura, Río Paragua, and Sierra de Imataca southward (*leveriana*). E Colombia to n Bolivia and the Guianas (not c and e Amaz. Brazil); se Brazil, e Paraguay, and ne Argentina.

Note: Red-billed Pied-Tanager (*Lamprospiza melano-leuca*) of the Guianas to e Peru could occur in e Venez. 7" (18cm). 34g. Bill red. Throat, chest, and upperparts black; oblique black line from sides of chest up to throat, otherwise white (♀ mostly gray above). Top of rain forest canopy. Imm. sim. but bill dark, plumage duller.

White-capped Tanager   PLATE 58
Sericossypha albocristata   Cuaresmero
Identification: 9.5" (24cm). 114g. Spectacular jaylike tanager. ♂: *lores and crown snow white, throat and chest ruby red*, otherwise deep velvety black, wings glossed blue black. In hand feathers of forehead and lores short, dense, and plushy. ♀: sim. but throat dark violet carmine (usually looks black in field). Imm.: all black with white crown.
Sim. species: Behavior and large size might recall a jay rather than a tanager. Snowy crown is unmistakable.
Voice: Almost certainly hd. long before seen. Members of groups constantly utter a loud *PEEEAAP!* or *PEEEAR!*, often preceded or followed by sharp, shrieking *KEEP!* or *KIP!* notes as wander through forest. Call, which sounds like extremely loud peeping of a baby chicken, is responsible for the name "Pájaro Pollo" in Colombia.
Behavior: In Colombia noisy and wide-ranging flocks of 4–8, occas. up to 20, wander over immense areas, often flying rapidly from treetop to treetop, pausing only a few moments before continuing. Flock members peer, posture, and cock tails in exaggerated, jaylike fashion as they boldly leap up through trees and search for insects and fruit, then rapidly fly on, sometimes moving 100s of meters before pausing.
Status and habitat: Humid and mossy high montane forest and forest borders. Rare, unpredictable (local?), and low-density resident at n end of range in Venez.

Range: 1800–3000m. S Táchira in vicinity of Páramo de Tamá. Colombia very spottily s to c Peru.
Note: Taxonomic placement controversial[414].

Chlorospingus

Rather chunky; bill stouter than *Hemispingus*; several spp. or subspp. with pale eyes and postocular spots; mostly rather dull plumage (olive, gray, and dull yellow); often "nuclear" and conspic. in mixed-spp. flocks; all spp. montane.

Common Bush-Tanager   PLATE 57
Chlorospingus ophthalmicus   Tangara Líder
Identification: 5.5" (14cm). 18.5g. Geographically variable[440]. Eyes usually white to yellowish white to brownish white. *Head to below eyes dark brown to dark olive*,

eyering and *prom. postocular spot white* (all subspp.), otherwise above olive green, throat white to buff faintly *speckled* dusky; *broad dull olive yellow chest band often tinged ochraceous*; lower breast and belly grayish white, flanks and under tail coverts olive yellow. Or head sooty black, throat whitish thickly freckled black (*venezuelanus*). Juv.: eyes brown.
Sim. species: In all areas look for pale eyes and postocular spot. W Andean birds from Lara s are prettier and more boldly marked than birds of e slope and coastal mts. Confusion most likely with Ashy-throated Bush-Tanager of s Táchira.
Voice: Call notes incl. buzzy *tzit* over and over, longer and trilled *ts'i'i'i'i'i't*, and *chup*. Dawn song a long, monotonic *chup, chup, chup. . . . ,* 1 note/sec for up to several min.
Behavior: Bush-tanager are active, social birds, always on the go and given to constant vocalizing. They are, in short, staunch and steady companions, not flashy, but reliable, trustworthy associates. It is this suite of "Goldilocks characteristics," perhaps, which make them ideal catalysts for the development and cohesion of mixed-spp. flocks. They form prs. when breeding but otherwise roam about in groups of 3–10 or even more, and few montane mixed-spp. flocks develop without these birds. Call and chatter constantly, and actively and alertly hop on branches and up through foliage from understory to subcanopy. Notably active and opportunistic when foraging; eat fruit, sip nectar by mashing flower ovaries or eating small flowers, and take insects by peering at foliage and twigs; little seems to escape their eyes. Bulky cup nest of fibers, leaves, and rootlets embedded on steep, mossy bank or in epiphytes to 16m up; 2 white eggs spotted cinnamon and brown mostly at large end[644].
Status and habitat: Generally a common and widespread resident in humid and wet premontane and montane forest, tall second-growth woodland, and bushy forest borders.

Range: 900–3000m (most recs. 1000–2300m). Sierra de Perijá, Zulia (*ponsi*); s Táchira and w Mérida n to c Lara (*venezuelanus*); e Mérida, e Trujillo, and extreme nw Lara at Cerro El Cerrón; n cordilleras from Carabobo to Distr. Federal and Miranda se to Cerro Negro (*jacqueti*); Sierra de San Luis, Falcón, and mts. of Yaracuy (*falconensis*). Mts. from s Mexico to nw Argentina.

Ashy-throated Bush-Tanager   PLATE 57
Chlorospingus canigularis   Tangara Líder de Los Andes
Identification: 5.5" (14cm). 18g. Eyes dark reddish brown (no white postocular spot). *Top and sides of head gray*, cheeks slightly darker, rest of upperparts olive green, throat and underparts *uniform* light gray with *sharply defined yellow chest band*, sides and

flanks olive, under tail coverts yellow. Bill more slender than in others of genus.

Sim. species: Much like Common Bush-Tanager but always has dark eyes and lacks latter's bold white postocular spot (Common Bush-Tanager has "white-eyed" look); also note narrower, more sharply defined chest band; up close look for unspotted throat (spotted in Common Bush-Tanager), *gray* crown (not black), and dark cheeks.

Voice: Thin chipping and rapid chittering notes when foraging. Song in Peru may be a high *seet* accelerated into rapid, chittery trill, descending then rising to abrupt end[274].

Behavior: Prs. or families are usually seen with mixed-spp. flocks. Tend to remain in forest mid. levels but reg. ascend into subcanopy. Relatively active as hop along bare limbs and out into foliage. Most prey (arthropods) is taken from foliage by gleaning, reaching out, or occas. in short sally to a leaf. Eat less fruit than allied Common Bush-Tanager.

Status and habitat: Uncommon to locally fairly common resident in humid and wet montane forest and forest borders in upper Río Chiquito (now much deforestation) and Cerro El Teteo. Seen with some reg. near Mata Mula pass (1700–1800m) between Bramón and Las Delicias, and in upper Río Quinimarí.

Range: 1250–2000m; sight to 2150m[60]. S Táchira (*canigularis*). Costa Rica; w Panama (sight); Colombia s in Andes to s Peru.

Cnemoscopus

A sp. allied to *Chlorospingus* and *Hemispingus* but larger; bill heavier and pink; legs and tail longer; only high in Andes.

Gray-hooded Bush-Tanager   PLATE 57
Cnemoscopus rubrirostris   Tangara de Pico Rojo
Identification: 6.5″ (16.5cm). 21g. *Bill pink and conical*; legs pinkish brown. Above olive green, head, throat, and chest gray, throat and chest paler and sharply separated from bright yellow lower underparts.

Sim. species: Pink bill, gray hood, and tail-wagging habits are distinctive. Cf. Gray-capped Hemispingus and ♀ Capped Conebill.

Voice: Call a high, sharp *swit*; song a high, squeaky jumble of sputtering notes that end in downward-inflected *sweee*[274].

Behavior: Usually seen in prs. or groups of 3–8 following mixed-spp. flocks of warblers, tanagers, and conebills. Forage in canopy or subcanopy, mainly on limbs, by starting in interior of trees and working outward into terminal foliage, all the while moving with curious hopping or walking gait and teetering body slightly

like a Tree Pipit (*Anthus trivialis*) and flicking tail upward. Eat a variety of fruit but mainly search foliage, and seem more insectivorous than allied *Chlorospingus* bush-tanagers.

Status and habitat: Fairly common resident in humid and wet montane forest, occas. along forest borders. Readily seen in steep forests above Betania on trail to Páramo de Tamá. In some areas (Venez.?) may show fondness for native *Alnus*[544].

Range: 2300–3000m. S Táchira on Páramo de Tamá and upper Río Chiquito (*rubrirostris*). Colombia s locally in Andes to s Peru.

Hemispingus

Mostly a rather dull, confusing group of high-Andean tanagers; some very like *Basileuterus* warblers; most have striped heads; bill thin to fairly strong; almost always in groups; in several spp. groups sing simultaneously; some spp. poorly known in life.

Black-capped Hemispingus   PLATE 57
Hemispingus atropileus   Buscador Gorro Negro
Identification: 6.5″ (16.5cm). 22g. *Crown and sides of head black, long narrow eyestripe buffy white*; rest of upperparts olive green; below ochre yellow, sides and flanks heavily tinged olive.

Sim. species: Head pattern resembles Slaty-backed Hemispingus but underparts ochre (not bright ferruginous); Superciliaried Hemispingus and Citrine Warbler have duller head stripes (no black). Also cf. Black-headed Hemispingus.

Voice: High, hissing *tsit* and high-pitched, lively chittering or squeaking notes when foraging, these often accelerated into trills. Dawn song in Peru 3–5 rich *chew* notes alternated with 6–9 high *zeeet* notes, from exposed treetop perch[274].

Behavior: Fast-moving prs. or groups up to 5–6 are active and act much like *Basileuterus* warblers as they move rapidly and glean in foliage of bushes and bamboo (*Chusquea*) from near gd. to ca. 6m up. Travel with or lead mixed-spp. flocks containing warblers, tanagers, brush-finches, and other mostly insectivorous spp., but tend to stay in understory. Also forage independently of flocks and eat some fruit. Not shy but can be difficult to see well as they usually stay in fairly dense vegetation. In Peru cup nest of leaves and stems; pale rose eggs with numerous reddish gray spots and streaks randomly or nearer large end[725].

Status and habitat: Fairly common resident (limited distrib. in Venez.) in wet, high, montane forest, dense forest borders, and treeline elfin forest where there is bamboo (*Chusquea*). Seldom away from bamboo.

Can be found at upper end of trail from Betania to Páramo de Tamá.

Range: 2300–3000m. S Táchira in upper Río Chiquito valley and vicinity of Páramo de Tamá (*atropileus*). Colombia s in Andes to s Peru.

Superciliaried Hemispingus   PLATE 57
Hemispingus superciliaris   Buscador Cejas Amarillas
Identification: 5.5″ (14cm). 14g. Bill fairly thin; *legs dusky gray.* Above entirely uniform olive green with *long narrow yellow eyestripe* from nostril to far behind eyes; lores and sides of head dusky; faint yellowish line below eyes, *prom. blackish triangular patch at base of flight feathers* (formed by greater primary coverts); below clear pale yellow, brightest on breast and belly, throat vaguely mottled dusky; chest, sides, and flanks tinged olive.
Sim. species: Very sim. to Citrine Warbler and perhaps often not safely separated in field. Warbler has pale (not dark) legs. Also look for warbler's broader and *shorter* eyebrow that ends above or just beyond eyes; faint whitish chin and rounded tail. Warbler also *lacks* yellow area below eyes, generally lacks dusky area behind eyes, lacks dark patch at base of primaries, lacks dusky mottling on throat, and is slightly richer yellow below (in direct comparison). Note that almost all of these differences are subtle and not discernible on all birds in field. Some individuals may go unidentified. Also cf. Oleaginous Hemispingus.
Voice: At dawn sings 3- to 4-sec bursts of hard *tsit* notes that accelerate to form loose rattle-trills, then slow at end, usually given simultaneously by prs., sometimes 3 or 4 birds in wavelike crescendo[274].
Behavior: Forages higher than Black-capped Hemispingus but also down to eye level or lower, esp. along forest borders and roadsides. Prs. or noisy, chittering groups of 3–20 usually forage with mixed-spp. flocks containing small flycatchers, wrens, tanagers, and conebills. Very active, restlessly peering and hopping in foliage, occas. hanging downward to glean insects from top and bottom of live leaves. May take a few (?) small berries and seeds. Sometimes forage out into rather open trees (i.e., in *Alnus*) and generally fairly easy to see.

Status and habitat: Fairly common to common resident in humid and wet montane forest, bushy forest borders, and second growth.
Range: 1900–3600m (mostly 2100–3200m). Andes of n Táchira, Mérida, and Trujillo n to Páramo Cendé (*chrysophrys*); prob. s Táchira. Colombia s in Andes to Bolivia (birds of c Peru and Bolivia prob. a separate sp.).

Oleaginous Hemispingus   PLATE 57
Hemispingus frontalis   Buscador Oleaginoso
Identification: 6″ (15cm). 17g. Drab. Upperparts dull olive; *long narrow buff eyebrow* (paler behind eye); sides of head dusky olive; throat ochraceous, rest of underparts dull olive tinged ochre. Or brighter olive above, eyebrow greenish ochre, usually more ochraceous below (*flavidorsalis*). Or more ochraceous to buffy ochraceous below (*iteratus, hanieli*).
Sim. species: A dull-looking bird. Long *narrow* eyebrow is only good mark. See Three-striped Warbler. Three other sim. spp., Citrine Warbler and Superciliaried and Black-capped hemispinguses, occur mostly at higher els.
Voice: Rather quiet. Soft *chit* notes while foraging. Song, given by dueting prs., trios, or *quartets* of foraging birds in early morning, is sung more or less simultaneously by group at ca. 15-sec intervals. When 1 bird (always the same?) starts, others immediately join with identical songs which sound slightly out of sync, producing vibrating chorus lasting ca. 5 sec, with each bird singing chattery stream of high-pitched, chipping notes, *chipa'chipa'chip-chit'chit'chit'chit'it'it'it . . .*, accelerating then slowing[259].
Behavior: Forages in compact groups of ca. 4–8 that accompany, or are sometimes most numerous sp. in, understory mixed flocks. An industrious, dead-leaf specialist, working through undergrowth or slightly higher, esp. in viny cluttered areas, flying short distances then hopping up branches in rather jerky manner while constantly flicking tail and peering at foliage. Most often flies or hops directly to clumps of curled, hanging dead leaves which it inspects carefully by clinging, hanging upside down, or stretching down to peer into curled leaves.
Status and habitat: Fairly common resident but easily overlooked in viny undergrowth of humid and wet montane forest and in tall, older second-growth forest.

Range: 1600–2900m (sight to 1400m). Sierra de Perijá, Zulia (*flavidorsalis*); Andes of s Táchira n through Mérida and Trujillo to Lara border at Páramo de Las Rosas (*ignobilis*); Coastal Cordillera in Aragua (prob. Distr. Federal) and Miranda (*hanieli*); mts. of Sucre and n Monagas (*iteratus*). Andes from Colombia to Bolivia.

Note: Plumages of Venez. subspp. differ somewhat from races southward[544], but vocalizations and behavior seem similar.

Gray-capped Hemispingus   PLATE 57
Hemispingus reyi   Buscador Rey
Identification: 6″ (15cm). *Crown to bottom of eyes gray* ("hooded" appearance), contrasting with olive green back and upperparts; below dull yellow, sides and flanks tinged olive.
Sim. species: Note contrasting cap. Other *Hemispingus* in its limited range have eyestripes. Also cf. Citrine Warbler.
Voice: Sharp, insistent *tee chew chew* (P. Schwartz recording) or *stit-sit, seet!* may be song. When foraging, buzzy *bzit* notes; also a high, thin *seep*, longer *seeeep*, and thin chittering notes.
Behavior: Prs., or sometimes large groups up to 20 or more, forage with mixed-spp. flocks where they may be most numerous sp. Methodically examine leaf surfaces, esp. of bamboo, by peering, reaching, and occas. hanging downward as work over foliage, and take prey most often from tops of foliage surfaces. Stay mainly in lower levels (2–8m up) of forest and usually fairly easy to see, often coming out to edge of forest along roadsides.
Status and habitat: Fairly common resident in wet, mossy, montane forest and forest borders with *Chusquea* bamboo. Almost always in or near bamboo. Behavior and habits overall much as in Black-capped Hemispingus of s Táchira.

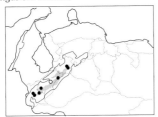

Range: ENDEMIC. 2300–3000m (sightings to 2150m, PN Guaramacal). Andes of n Táchira, Mérida, and Trujillo n to Páramo Misisí near Lara border.

Black-eared Hemispingus   PLATE 57
Hemispingus melanotis   Buscador Orejinegro
Identification: 6″ (15cm). 16g. *Crown and nape gray, sides of head black* forming mask; inconspic. white supraloral mark sometimes extending back as narrow eyebrow; inconspic. white spot on lower eyelid; wings and tail brownish, *underparts cinnamon buff*, brightest on throat, whitish on belly; sides tinged brown.
Sim. species: Combination of black mask and cinnamon underparts are the marks. See Oleaginous and Black-capped hemispinguses and Black-crested Warbler.
Behavior: Prs. often follow mixed-spp. flocks and forage from understory to mid. levels, occas. into subcanopy, but more often low along forest borders. Hop actively through foliage, glean or pick insects from leaves, and often check whorls of dead bamboo leaves.

Status and habitat: Resident in humid and wet forest and along forest borders. Known from rather small no. of recs. in Venez.

Range: 1800–2800m. S Táchira near Páramo de Tamá and in upper Río Chiquito at Hacienda La Providencia and Cerro El Retiro (*melanotis*). Colombia s spottily in Andes to n Bolivia.

Slaty-backed Hemispingus   PLATE 57
Hemispingus goeringi   Buscador Lomipizarra
Identification: 6″ (15cm). Bold pattern. *Crown and sides of head jet black* with *long conspic. white eyebrows* that start just in front of eyes; upperparts slate gray, *below rich orange rufous*, brownish on belly; *unusually long heavy tarsi and large feet*; bill notably short; tail rather short.
Sim. species: At a glance might be mistaken for Plushcap which has yellow forehead and lacks eyebrows; or Blue-backed Conebill which has blue back and black throat. In s Táchira see Black-eared Hemispingus.
Voice: Song, hd. a few times at dawn and often as a duet by pr., an energetic ser. of rapid staccato notes with *plink* notes throughout; may continue uninterrupted for a min or more.
Behavior: Most often in prs. but also singly or occas. in groups (families?) up to 5, and often with mixed-spp. flocks that contain warblers, flowerpiercers, conebills, and tanagers. Stays low (gd. to ca. 5m up) and in dense cover, appearing momentarily, then disappearing or fluttering jerkily across open space or road and quickly diving into cover. At dawn may forage alone or in prs. in small open areas at edge of forest by hopping on gd. or in grass. Reaches out or up for prey, and often jumps upward with little "springy" leaps to pick prey from beneath leaves.
Status and habitat: Uncommon and easily overlooked resident in wet upper montane forest, esp. in dense shrubby borders and stunted vegetation. Often in or near bamboo (requirement?). Seen with some reg. at upper els. above La Mucuy, PN Sierra Nevada, Mérida[127], and freq. Jan–Mar 1993–1999, at 2300–2500m, near Páramo Batallón on Mérida/Táchira border (Hilty; R. Hannikman). Doubtless has declined as a result of deforestation and forest fragmentation.

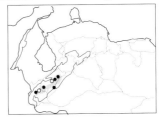

Range: ENDEMIC. 2600–3200m (sightings to 2300m, n Táchira). N Táchira (Páramo Zumbador; sight, Páramo Batallón); s half of Mérida (Páramo La Negra; Páramo Escorial; Páramo Aricagua; Mucuchíes; sight, above La Mucuy).

Black-headed Hemispingus   PLATE 57
Hemispingus verticalis   Buscador Cabecinegro
Identification: 6″ (15cm). 13g. Small *Hemispingus*. Thin, warblerlike bill. White eyes impart oddly disconcerting appearance. *Head, throat, and sides of neck black, median crown stripe sandy brown*, rest of upperparts gray, wings and tail blackish; below pale gray, center of lower underparts tinged whitish. Imm.: eyes dark.
Sim. species: Pattern and color suggest a small *Atlapetes* brush-finch or warbler rather than a tanager. Black on sides of head is somewhat rounded behind, giving impression of a large black disc on each side of head.
Voice: Song a 5- to 15-sec burst of squeaky, twittering notes mixed with stream of higher-pitched thin *seet* or *steet* notes, apparently given by 2 or more birds. Squeaky notes may cease for intervals of 10–12 sec before another song is initiated, but high *seet* notes continue at slower rate[274].
Behavior: A restless and fast-moving little bird usually found in prs., families, or small groups up to ca. 5 that assoc. with mixed-spp. flocks of furnariids, conebills, tanagers, and brush-finches. Forages in bamboo and upper foliage of bushes and small trees, esp. in crowns where foliage is dense and stiff. *Walks* on tops of leaves and gleans insects from upper leaf surfaces, petioles, and leaf axils, and eats a few small berries.
Status and habitat: Resident in wet, dense, upper montane forest, elfin woodland, and stunted shrubbery near treeline, often where there are gaps and openings in vegetation. Known from only a few recs. in Venez.

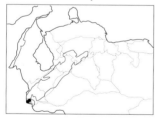

Range: 2800–3000m (prob. higher). S Táchira on Páramo de Tamá and Cerro El Retiro. Colombia s in Andes to n Peru.

Thlypopsis

Small, active, and warblerlike; rather thin bill; contrasting orange or rufous head; all montane except 1 sp.

Orange-headed Tanager   PLATE 58
Thlypopsis sordida   Frutero de Sombrero
Identification: 5.5″ (14cm). 17g. Short, yellowish bill. *Entire head orange rufous becoming yellow on lores and throat*; otherwise above gray tinged brown, below pale gray, central lower underparts whitish. ♀: *crown*

pale olive yellow, back darker and more yellow olive, *lores, ocular area, sides of head, throat, and chest yellowish*, lower underparts yellowish white, sides and flanks tinged buffy olive; faint buff olive wash on breast. Imm.: above olive, crown yellowish, sides of head, throat, and chest yellow becoming paler and clouded olive on rest of underparts.
Sim. species: Only "orange-headed" bird along Orinoco. Note ♀'s pale bill and yellow face.
Voice: Gives high, thin *seet* or *sit* calls. Territorial song (Peru and Bolivia) by 2 birds, possibly in duet, *seet seet t-t-t-t-t-t-t-t-d-dit*, 1st 2 notes higher pitched than chitter that follows[274].
Behavior: Prs. or little groups of 3–4 are active, almost warblerlike, as hop in foliage and peer and glean for insects, or occas. hover or flutter, mostly from eye level to tops of shrubs and small trees. Occas. eat small berries. Open cup nest in Argentina was 2m up; 2 bluish white eggs with brown and light cinnamon markings[159].
Status and habitat: Resident in small nos. in shrubby vegetation and trees on river isls., and in river-created second growth along banks of Orinoco. Perhaps local.

Range: To 100m (sight to 200m). Riverbanks and isls. of Orinoco from nw Amazonas (sight 30km s of Pto. Ayacucho[259]) and n Bolívar e to se Anzoátegui and vicinity of Ciudad Bolívar (*orinocensis*). Disjunct. Se Colombia and e Ecuador to n Argentina and Brazil s of the Amazon.

Fulvous-headed Tanager   PLATE 58
Thlypopsis fulviceps   Frutero Cabecileonado
Identification: 5″ (12.7cm). 11.7g. *Small gray bird with chestnut head*. Bill relatively short. ♂: *head and throat chestnut*, paler on throat; *rest of upperparts olive gray, breast and sides light gray*; central lower underparts white; flanks tinged olive gray. Or above darker gray, under tail coverts buff (*obscuriceps*). ♀: sim. but throat paler.
Sim. species: No other montane sp. has such sharply defined chestnut head and throat.
Voice: Calls are insignificant, high *tsit* and *chik* notes. Territorial song, rarely hd., a high *chi chi cht-cht-tit-t-t-t-t-t-t*, accelerating and trailing off (P. Schwartz recording).
Behavior: One or 2 birds, occas. up to ca. 5 (families?), are reg. assoc. with mixed-spp. flocks in canopy inside forest or often much lower along forest borders. Very active as search for insects, mostly on leaves of various sizes, by perch-gleaning, reaching downward from perch, clinging sideways or upside down to

leaves, pulling or tugging to extract prey, and often probing curled and hanging dead leaves. Also often eat small berries, esp. of Melastomataceae.

Status and habitat: Uncommon to locally fairly common resident in canopy vines and shrubby, vine-tangled borders of moist to humid forest, second-growth woodland, and shrubby gardens in urban areas (i.e., Caracas). Most numerous in moist to semi-humid forest (e.g., s slope of Coastal Cordillera below Rancho Grande Biol. Station, Aragua), nos. decreasing sharply in more humid zones. Distrib. somewhat spotty, perhaps because of narrow habitat preferences.

Range: 800–1900m. Sierra de Perijá, Zulia (*obscuriceps*); w slope of Andes in Táchira and Mérida; e slope from ne Táchira to n end of Andes in Lara (*meridensis*); n cordilleras from Carabobo and n Guárico to Distr. Federal and Miranda; mts. of ne Anzoátegui, w Sucre, and n Monagas (*fulviceps*). Ne Colombia (Sierra de Perijá and Norte de Santander).

Hemithraupis

Small, warblerlike tanagers; bill thin; ♂♂ brightly patterned, ♀♀ duller.

Guira Tanager   PLATE 59
Hemithraupis guira   Pintasilgo Buchinegro
Identification: 5.5″ (14cm). 12g. *Looks like a small oriole.* Bill thin, warblerlike, and orange (both sexes). ♂: *black face and throat outlined all around with bright yellow*; crown and upperparts bright yellowish olive, rump orange rufous turning yellowish on upper tail coverts (usually concealed by wings); *broad chest patch tawny turning lemon yellow on center of breast*; sides and belly gray, crissum yellow. ♀: bright yellowish olive above with *inconspic. yellow eyestripe and eyering*; rump yellowish, wings and tail dusky narrowly edged yellow, sides of head and underparts pale yellow, brighter yellow on throat, chest, and under tail coverts; center of breast and belly whitish, *sides* (and sometimes lower breast and belly) *grayish*.
Sim. species: Dull warblerlike ♀ easily confused. ♀ Yellow-backed Tanager *lacks* eyestripe, is darker and greener above, brighter and more uniform yellow below (some races), and has olive (not gray) flanks; up close note yellow wing edgings. ♀ Yellow Warbler is brighter yellow above, *lacks* eyestripe, eyering (entire side of head yellow), and gray sides, and has yellow undertail. Various ♀ euphonias also are somewhat sim., but all have thicker bills.

Voice: Song of ♂ in n Aragua 6–7 sharp, incisive notes, *sa-sit-sit-sit-sit-sit* (rather weak); also a ser. of rapid squeaking and chipping notes reminiscent of Bananaquit.
Behavior: Prs. or more often little family groups forage alone or with upper-level or canopy mixed-spp. flocks dominated by insectivores. Active and warblerlike in high outermost foliage as they hop, bend down, hang, or flutter to inspect top and bottom surfaces of leaves or peer beneath twigs, and occas. eat small fruits. In Paraguay a flimsy cup nest of plant fibers and lichen in high fork; white eggs sprinkled cinnamon brown on larger end[44].
Status and habitat: Fairly common locally. Resident in canopy of dry, moist, and moderately humid forest, tall second growth or open woodland, shady coffee and cacao plantations, and scattered trees in clearings. Seldom numerous but turns up in a wide variety of mostly "edge" habitats and light woodland.

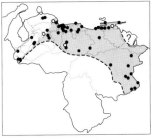

Range: To 1450m. W base of Andes from Táchira (Seboruco) to Trujillo (Betijoque); e base from e Táchira to Portuguesa and s Lara (Cabudare); Falcón (Sierra de San Luis); prob. Yaracuy; generally in n cordilleras from Carabobo and Aragua e to Sucre and n Monagas, and from Cojedes to Anzoátegui; e Bolívar from lower Río Paragua and Sierra de Imataca s to Río Cuyuní (*nigrigula*); rest of se Bolívar s to Brazilian border (*roraimae*). Colombia and w Ecuador; the Guianas, ne Brazil, and generally from se Colombia and Brazil s of the Amazon s to n Argentina.

Yellow-backed Tanager   PLATE 59
Hemithraupis flavicollis   Pintasilgo Buchidorado
Identification: 5″ (12.7cm). 12g. Bill thin; blackish above, pale below. ♂: head (to below eyes) and upperparts black, white spot on wings (usually), *lower back and rump bright yellow*; throat, belly, and under tail coverts bright yellow, breast to upper belly grayish white, upper breast indistinctly scaled black. ♀: above olive green, wing coverts and flight feathers edged yellow, rump tinged yellow; *underparts entirely yellow, throat and crissum brighter yellow*, sides clouded olive.
Sim. species: ♀ very sim. to ♀ Guira Tanager but underparts all yellow.
Voice: When foraging a high *tsick* and *tut* and *tyoo tsick*[274]; song in Brazil, *si, si, si, si . . .* , insectlike[611].
Behavior: Prs. or families actively glean in high outer foliage of canopy and reg. follow mixed-spp. flocks containing both insectivores and frugivores. Glean from foliage mostly by reaching or hanging downward, occas. fluttering or hovering, or sallying short distances to air. Also eat some fruit.

Status and habitat: Fairly common resident in humid terra firme and várzea forest and forest borders. In forests of n Amazonas a pr. occurs with almost every large canopy flock.

Range: To 950m. Bolívar in Río Cuyuní (*aurigularis*); generally in Amazonas and rest of Bolívar (*hellmayri*). Disjunct range. N Colombia; e Colombia to the Guianas and ne Brazil; se Colombia to n Bolivia and s central Brazil; coastal se Brazil.

Hooded Tanager   PLATE 59
Nemosia pileata   Frutero de Coronita
Identification: 5.3″ (13.5cm). 16g. Chunky and short-tailed. *Eyes and legs bright yellow.* ♂: *crown, sides of head, and neck extending to sides of chest black*, short supraloral line white, rest of upperparts porcelain blue, flight feathers black edged dull gray blue; *underparts immaculate white.* ♀: like ♂ but head gray blue like back, throat and chest tinged buff, no black on sides of chest.
Sim. species: ♀ could be mistaken for Bicolored Conebill, but note yellow eyes and legs and whitish lores; conebill is duller below. Also see ♀ White-eared Conebill and Tropical Gnatcatcher.
Voice: Mostly high-pitched, lisped *tic* and *sip* notes. Dawn song a high, insistent *tsip-tsip ti-CHEW ti-CHEW* or variant[274]; when excited *tic, tic-ttttttttttttttttt* and other chips and trills.
Behavior: Prs., families, or little groups up to 6 forage in single-sp. groups or are occas. loosely assoc. with a few other spp. Stay mostly on rather substantial open branches (much less on twigs) in open trees where hop along rather deliberately, almost vireolike, peering at bark surfaces or leaf petioles and gleaning and picking insects. Occas. glean or hover around leaves, only infreq. eat fruit. Most often seen in *Cecropia* and Leguminosae trees where they attract attention to themselves with occas. outbursts of chipping and twittering. Thin cup nest bound to branch with spiderwebs; 2 bluish eggs spotted brown or lilac gray[274]; Oct fledglings[137].
Status and habitat: Seems nowhere very numerous. Resident in moist semideciduous and humid evergreen woodland, mostly in semiopen situations, pastures with scattered open trees, along woodland borders, and in irreg. second growth, often in vicinity of water. May also occur at edge of mangroves and in *Cecropia* trees on river isls. Some seasonal movements may occur in llanos (P. Coopmans).
Range: To 600m. Maracaibo Basin, Zulia, w Lara, se Falcón (sight, Morrocoy area), spottily in n cordilleras of Carabobo, Aragua, and Distr. Federal, and locally e

of Andes from w Apure and s Cojedes (sightings, Hato Piñero) e to Anzoátegui and Delta Amacuro; ne Bolívar s to El Palmar (*hypoleuca*); and s to Tumeremo (sight). N Colombia to the Guianas and ne Brazil; w Amazonia s of the Amazon to n Argentina and se Brazil.

Rosy Thrush-Tanager   PLATE 62
Rhodinocichla rosea   Frutero Paraulata
Identification: 8″ (20.3cm). 42g. Bill rather long and thin. ♂: above dark slaty gray, wings tinged brownish, *long eyebrow* (narrow behind eye), *bend of wing, and entire underparts bright begonia rose*, flanks broadly grayish brown. Or sim. but supraloral spot (no eyebrow) carmine rose (*beebei*). ♀: like ♂ but rose replaced by orange cinnamon, incl. eyebrow which becomes narrow and white behind eye; center of belly white, under tail coverts rufous.
Voice: Song a loud, clear, musical ser. of choppy but forceful phrases, *cholo, cheela, cholo, cheela, chela* . . . , hd. esp. during 1st half of yr; may also alternate phrases, i.e., *tor-CHIL-o, waCHEer, tor-CHIL-o* . . . ; song given by ♂ and ♀ separately and antiphonally. When foraging, occas. a ringing, jaylike *eeoo* and short, dry *tur-ta'tup* (latter resembles call of Tawny-crowned Pygmy-Tyrant).
Behavior: A lovely bird with an enchanting song, but a notorious skulker and often difficult to see, even with patience. Partially terrestrial; lives in prs. that forage on gd. where they spend long periods of time flipping or throwing leaves to side with bill, sometimes almost disappearing inside piles of leaves, then hopping a short distance and repeating process. Eat insects, seeds, and fruits. Sing from perch mostly 1–6m up but always within cover. Coarse twig cup nest lined with rachises of acacialike shrubs, sometimes black fungal rhizomorphs; ca. 1m up in thicket; 2–3 eggs, white or pale blue with black markings forming wreath at large end[199,706].
Status and habitat: Resident in thickets and tangled undergrowth in dry deciduous woodland, moist semideciduous woodland, and locally into humid premontane forest borders and bushy second growth. Mainly foothills and lower slopes. Decidedly local (narrow microhabitat tolerance) but sometimes surprisingly common, even in wooded areas in city limits of Caracas (e.g., Urbanización San José; Hotel Tamanaco), also fairly common in e foothills of Sierra de San Luis and locally elsewhere. Southeasternmost recs. are 5 hd. and seen at San Francisco de Macaira, n Guárico, 1 Mar 1981 (C. Parrish).
Range: 450–1450m (sight to 100m). Base of Sierra de Perijá, Zulia (*beebei*); c and e Falcón (Sierra de San

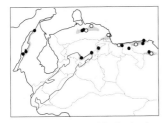

Luis to PN Morrocoy); n base of Andes in s Lara (El Tocuyo), mts. of Yaracuy, and n cordilleras from Carabobo to Distr. Federal and se Miranda at Cerro Negro;
sight, ne Guárico (*rosea*). W Mexico; w Costa Rica and
Panama; locally in Colombia.

Mitrospingus

Two spp. (1 in Venez.); large, notably dull; bill fairly
short; wings and tail rounded; differ markedly in
behavior.

Olive-backed Tanager   PLATE 62
Mitrospingus oleagineus   Frutero Aceituno
Identification: 7.7″ (19.5cm). Drab and undistinguished.
*Eyes gray. Forehead, sides of head, and throat dark
gray,* upperparts dark olive, wings and tail dusky gray
brown; rest of underparts olive yellow, brighter and yellower on center of breast.
Sim. species: Has few good marks, but nothing really
sim. in tepui foothills where it occurs. See smaller ♀
White-shouldered Tanager with all-gray head.
Voice: Easily overlooked song a short *zweee-eet?* or
zwee-er-eet?, often over and over at intervals of 1–3
sec. Two or 3 may sing at same time[274]. A high, thin
seeep; thin, drawn-out, and rising *seeeeeek;* and buzzy
pzzzzz, pzzzzz . . while foraging; thin, ticking *tic'tic'tic
. .* contact notes.
Behavior: This rather large, sluggish, dull-plumaged
tanager with quiet manners moves about in single-sp.
groups of 5–20 or more, and also is often with mixed-
spp. flocks. Typically forage rather quietly through understory or lower mid. story of forest but are nevertheless a keystone sp. in formation and maintenance of
some understory flocks in tepuis. Forage methodically,
mostly by hopping and peering at foliage, reaching up
to snap insect prey, occas. lunging in heavy, semiacro-
batic manner to grasp mostly insect prey. Also snatch
prey from foliage during short clumsy sallies. Some
fruit eaten, esp. melastome berries.
Status and habitat: Humid and wet forest and forest
borders on slopes of tepuis. Common resident on Si-

erra de Lema in mature forest and dense, stunted, melastome-dominated second growth on white sandy soil.
Range: 900–1800m. Gran Sabana from Ptari-tepui and
Sierra de Lema s to Chimantá-tepui, Sororopán-tepui,
and Aprada-tepui (*obscuripectus*); vicinity of Cerro Roraima (*oleagineus*). Guyana and n Brazil (Uei-tepui).

Eucometis

"Gray and yellow" with stout bill; prom. but short rictal
bristles; slight hook on maxilla; wings and tail
rounded.

Gray-headed Tanager   PLATE 62
Eucometis penicillata   Bachaquero
Identification: 7.3″ (18.5cm). 29g. *Short bushy crest on
rearcrown. Entire head gray,* throat pale gray, rest of upperparts olive yellow, *underparts bright cadium yellow,*
chest tinged tawny. Or throat tinged olive (*cristata*); or
throat whitish turning gray on chest (*penicillata*).
Sim. species: ♀ White-shouldered Tanager is smaller,
duller, and usually much higher up in vegetation (not
near gd.).
Voice: Sharp *stet* and *chip* call notes. Alarm in se Colombia *schip!* In n Aragua sings a high, buzzy *pzzzt-
buzzt-buzzt-fzzzt*; song in Panama a more varied musical sputter, *eat eat meat chop, 'safurry chew, 'safurry
chew* or the like[818].
Behavior: N of Orinoco single birds, prs., or several
faithfully attend army ant swarms but also forage away
from them, mostly for insects, in lower levels (1–10m
up) of forest and light woodland. Often flick tail open
and hold crest up slightly as perch upright or horizontal over ants. In Amazonia seldom with army ants but
may assoc. with mixed-spp. flocks. In all areas retiring,
staying mostly in thick or shady vegetation and not apt
to remain long in open. Eat mostly insects, also small
amt. of fruit. Nest 0.6–3m up, often in spiny palm near
forest edge; thin-walled cup of fibers and rootlets; 1–3
eggs vary in color, dirty white, gray, bluish gray to pinkish buff heavily mottled brown[624].
Status and habitat: Fairly common but somewhat
local resident in a wide range of habitats incl. interior
of open humid lowland and premontane forest, coffee
plantations, and lighter second-growth woodland; also
gallery forest and riparian woodland in fairly dry
regions.

Range: To 1200m. Sierra de Perijá, Zulia; w base of
Andes in Táchira and Mérida; e base from Táchira and
w Apure n to Portuguesa (near Tucupido) (*cristata*); c
and e Falcón (sight, Sierra de San Luis; Mirimire; Chichiriviche) and se Lara e through n cordilleras to Distr.

Federal and se Miranda at Acarigua and Tacarigua (*affinis*); nw Amazonas at Caño Capuana (120m; 2 specimens) opposite mouth of Río Vichada (*penicillata*). Se Mexico to the Guianas and s Brazil (absent from nw Brazil); Paraguay (sight).

Lanio

Bold black and tawny pattern; slender with long tail; bill rather long with tooth and hook (but not esp. shrikelike); prom. rictal bristles; rain forest canopy.

Fulvous Shrike-Tanager   PLATE 62
Lanio fulvus   Frutero Dentado
Identification: 7″ (18cm). 24g. ♂: *head, throat, wings, and tail black*, otherwise *body mostly dark burnt orange*, rump and large patch on chest tawny ochre, under tail coverts tawny ochre; under wing coverts white (often conspic. in flight); in hand a few concealed white feathers on lesser upper wing coverts; rump slightly mottled black. ♀: very different; head brownish gray turning *rufescent brown on back; rump and tail rufous brown*; throat pale brownish to buffy gray turning ochraceous olive on breast and *rufescent to tawny ochraceous on lower breast and belly*.
Sim. species: Dull, easily confused ♀ much like ♀ Flame-crested Tanager but larger, heavier-billed, and with breast contrasting with belly (not more or less uniform ochraceous buff below). ♀ Fulvous-crested Tanager has spectacles, olive upperparts, and paler underparts. Also cf. ♀ Cinereous and Dusky-throated antshrikes.
Voice: Noisy. Freq. utters loud, sharp, descending *TSUU!* which promotes cohesion of canopy mixed-spp. flocks. Alarm call (and false alarm call) also a descending *TSUU!* but *repeated rapidly* several times (twice normal rate) and with strong harmonic structure. Nonalarm notes delivered at half the rate of alarms and descend through twice the frequency range. Song, at dawn, a high, forced *tzee-a, tzee-a, tzee-a*.
Behavior: A canopy mixed-spp. flock sentinel that is almost always at center of flock activity. Single birds or separated prs. sit rather upright on relatively open mid.-level or subcanopy perches and alertly watch activities of other birds, mostly above them, waiting for their varied activities to dislodge or flush prey which shrike-tanagers then chase down in rapid, flycatcher-like sallies. Also occas. sally to foliage or branches. Because of their open perch position and visibility, these shrike-tanagers are almost always 1st members of flock to sound alarm at approaching danger[421].

Status and habitat: Fairly common to common resident in tall humid terra firme and várzea forest, and at forest borders in lowlands and lower slopes of tepuis.
Range: 350–950m n of Orinoco; to 1300m s of Orinoco. Se Táchira at Burgua and Cerro El Teteo (*peruvianus*); n Amazonas (Cerro Parú) southward; Bolívar from upper Río Caura, mid. Río Paragua (Cerro Guaiquinima), and Sierra de Imataca (Río Grande) s to Brazilian border (*fulvus*). E base of Andes in Colombia and generally n of the Amazon from se Colombia, e Ecuador, and ne Peru to the Guianas.

Rufous-crested Tanager   PLATE 58
Creurgops verticalis   Frutero Crestirrufo
Identification: 6″ (15cm). 24g. Tail fairly long; *bill rather heavy.* ♂: crown, sides of head to below eyes, and upperparts dull blue gray; partly concealed rufous crown stripe narrowly bordered black; *underparts orangish cinnamon.* ♀: no crown stripe; underparts paler.
Sim. species: Pattern recalls Black-eared Hemispingus but lacks that sp.'s black cheeks. Rusty Flowerpiercer is much smaller, bill thinner. Also see Plushcap. At lower els. cf. Fawn-breasted Tanager.
Behavior: Usually in prs. that assoc. with mixed-spp. flocks containing warblers, conebills, and tanagers. Eats some fruit but primarily an insectivorous sp. that hops along bare or mossy limbs in canopy and works out into terminal foliage where it probes, pecks, and reaches out or up, or hangs downward to glean insects from leaves. Active and energetic but not as restless as smaller *Hemispingus* and *Tangara*.
Status and habitat: Known from only a few recs. in Venez. Resident in humid montane forest.

Range: 1800m. S Táchira in upper Río Chiquito Valley (Hacienda La Providencia). Colombia s in Andes to c Peru.

Tachyphonus

Rather slender, thin-billed, and long-tailed; ♂♂ mostly black with white on shoulders and/or under wing coverts; velvetlike feathers on forehead; ♀♀ olive to brown; imm. ♂♂ like ♀♀ but with black patches and mottling; widespread, mostly lowlands.

White-lined Tanager   PLATE 62
Tachyphonus rufus   Chocolatero
Identification: 7.3″ (18.5cm). 33g. Despite name, there is no white line. Bill mostly blue gray, rather conical and pointed. ♂: *entirely lustrous black* slightly glossed bluish, bend of wing and under wing coverts white (conspic. in flight but no white visible at rest). ♀: very

different; *entirely uniform brownish rufous,* slightly paler below. Imm. ♂: like ♀; older birds show patches of black in plumage.

Sim. species: Often confused. ♂ flashes conspic. white under wing coverts in flight and looks much like ♂ Red-shouldered Tanager but larger (the two rarely overlap). ♂ White-shouldered Tanager, a forest bird, has *large* white shoulder patches; also see ♂ Shiny Cowbird. ♀ looks like various ♀ becards, but note thin bill. If in doubt, look for attendant mate as they are usually in prs. (in no other is ♂ all black, ♀ all rufous), and note habitat.

Voice: Sings infreq. Song, sometimes given in flight, a bouncy, chattery *chuEE, chuit, chuit-chuit-chuit* and so on, 1st syllable strongest. In e Mérida a soft, tentative *cheewank, wink, cheewank, wink, cheewank . . . ,* 1st note falling, 2d rising, in leisurely hypnotic cadence.

Behavior: Almost always in closely assoc. prs. that stay rather low in bushy clearings. Often pop up into open briefly before flying off, ♂ or ♀ following its mate in low flight across an opening. Usually independent of mixed-spp. flocks. Hop and peer in foliage like others of genus and take small fruits which are usually mashed before eating. Also eat papayas and other fruits in gardens, and glean and pick insects from leaves, make short sallies to air, and reg. drop to gd. for insects. In all areas tend to stay out of sight when foraging. Bulky leaf, tendril, and rootlet cup nest 1.2–6m up in shrub, tree, or banana plant; 2 eggs white to light purplish with darker markings; breeding Mar–May, Orinoco region[115,706].

Status and habitat: Common and widespread resident, mainly in humid foothill and montane areas n of Orinoco. Shrubby clearings, forest borders, cultivated areas, plantations, and gardens. Few recs. in llanos.

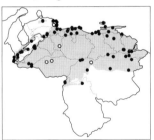

Range: To 1600m n of Orinoco; to 800m s of Orinoco. Throughout (except arid nw) s to n Amazonas (Pto. Ayacucho, Cerro Yavi), n Bolívar s to Río Cuchivero and lower Río Cuyuní at El Dorado; Isla Margarita. Costa Rica to nw Ecuador; spottily in s Ecuador and Peru; n Colombia e to the Guianas and s in e Brazil (not w and c Amazonia) to n Argentina.

Flame-crested Tanager   PLATE 62
Tachyphonus cristatus   Frutero Cresta Rojiza
Identification: 6.5″ (16.5cm). 19g. ♂: mostly black with *broad, flat crest bright red* (or *orange—intercedens*) bordered buff; narrow inconspic. rump and small patch on *upper throat yellowish buff;* bend of wing and under wing coverts white (concealed but often conspic. as flicks wings). ♀: very different; forehead and sides of

head gray, center of crown and mantle rufescent, *lower back and tail rich rufescent brown;* throat light buffy gray to whitish, *rest of underparts contrasting bright ochraceous buff.* Or mostly yellowish brown tinged olive above, almost uniform ochraceous below (*intercedens*).

Sim. species: ♂'s crest diagnostic (esp. red subsp. in Amazonas) if visible; otherwise best told from ♂ Fulvous-crested Tanager by buff throat spot; up close note latter's white pectoral tuft and esp. the tawny flank patch. ♀ nearest ♀ Fulvous Shrike-Tanager (see); ♀ Fulvous-crested Tanager differs in gray head, olive (not rufescent brown) upperparts, an eyering, and buff to yellowish underparts.

Voice: Thin *seeep* while foraging[260]; also *chet*[274]; insignificant *chat, tseh, tseh, tseh, tsititi*[611].

Behavior: A vivacious, high-energy bird, usually seen foraging rapidly with fast-moving canopy mixed-spp. flocks in which it is a "core" member. Occurs in prs. (most canopy flocks have a pr. of these birds), occas. little families, that hop along slender canopy branches and energetically peer in high outer foliage. Glean and flutter in foliage, occas. reach or hang downward to capture insects. Also eat berries and small fruits, then sometimes descend lower at forest borders. Not an easy bird to observe at length.

Status and habitat: Fairly common to common resident in humid terra firme forest, old second-growth woodland, and at forest borders.

Range: To 1400m. Throughout Amazonas; Bolívar from lower Río Caura, mid. Río Paragua, and upper Río Caroní (Paurai-tepui) southward (*orinocensis*); e Bolívar from Sierra de Imataca southward (*intercedens*). Se Colombia to ne Bolivia, Amaz. Brazil, and the Guianas; coastal se Brazil.

Fulvous-crested Tanager   PLATE 62
Tachyphonus surinamus   Frutero Crestileonado
Identification: 6.5″ (16.5cm). 23g. Bill thinner than Flame-crested Tanager's. ♂: mostly black with *short, flat, yellow buff crest* (often partly concealed) and buff rump; bend of wing, under wing coverts, and *usually visible pectoral tufts white;* protruding flank patch tawny. ♀: very different; *crown and sides of head gray;* fairly conspic. *broken yellowish eyering;* rest of upperparts dark olive; below buffy white, chest and sides tinged grayish, belly and under tail coverts *contrasting ochraceous.* Or underparts buffier, belly and crissum bright ochraceous (*brevipes*).

Sim. species: See Flame-crested Tanager. Cf. ♀ with ♀ Fulvous Shrike-Tanager and ♀ Flame-crested Tanager.

Voice: In nw Bolívar infreq. hd. song(?) an extremely high, sibilant, almost hissing *sieeeee-siiiiiiiii* (2d part higher), sometimes with additional *sii* at end. High, weak *steep* note, high *tseek-tseek-tseek*, and buzzy rattle while foraging.

Behavior: Like so many of genus, energetic, nervous acting, and often seems to be constantly fidgeting and flicking wings. Prs. or families follow mixed-spp. flocks in forest mid. levels, less freq. in high canopy where Flame-crested Tanager occurs, and partial to shrubby forest edges or natural breaks in forest. Often at eye level or lower along forest borders and in bushes at edges of rocky outcrops. ♂♂ flick wings when excited, exposing white flank patch momentarily (like a little winking light). Eat small fruit and peer and flutter in foliage for insects. Not easy to observe at length.

Status and habitat: Uncommon to locally fairly common resident in humid terra firme forest, shrubby forest edges, and esp. sandy soil forest, scrubby sandy soil woodland, and wooded borders at edges of rocky outcrops.

Range: To 1400m. Se Sucre, e Monagas, and Delta Amacuro; n Amazonas s to Cerros Parú and Duida, and generally in Bolívar (*surinamus*); s Amazonas from Yavita-Pimichín to Cerro de la Neblina (*brevipes*). Se Colombia to e Peru, Amaz. Brazil, and the Guianas.

Red-shouldered Tanager   PLATE 62
Tachyphonus phoenicius   Frutero Hombros Rojos

Identification: 6.3″ (16cm). 21g. Bill thin for genus. ♂: entirely glossy blue black, *small area at bend of wing white tipped red* (red usually concealed; sometimes visible as bird flies), under wing coverts white. ♀: very different; above dark brownish gray, *head to below eyes and neck darker with dusky mask*; *contrasting white throat*; chest and sides light gray, rest of underparts creamy white. Juv.: like ♀ but streaked dusky below.

Sim. species: ♂ much like ♂ White-lined Tanager but smaller (incl. bill), glossier, and in different habitat. Red shoulder spot diagnostic if seen (usually concealed when bird is perched). ♀'s best marks are dark head ("hooded" effect) and contrasting whitish throat.

Voice: Call notes incl. high, thin, insignificant *chup*, *cheup*, and *tsit*.

Behavior: Single birds, prs., or families are often restless and nervous acting as wander alone in bushy savanna, or less often with small mixed-spp. bird parties in scrubby woodland or borders. Hop and flit mostly 1–6m up in dense, leathery foliage of savanna bushes for insects and small fruits. Can be wary and difficult

to approach. Grassy cup nest in grass on gd. in Suriname; 1–2 eggs, grayish spotted and entirely blotched chocolate brown at larger end[253].

Status and habitat: Uncommon to locally common resident in white sandy soil savanna with scattered high bushes, thickets, and patches of light woodland; also scrubby savanna openings in white sandy soil.forested regions, and around rocky outcrops.

Range: To 2000m. Generally in Amazonas; nw Bolívar (Río Cuchivero) e to mid. Río Paragua (Cerro Guaiquinima), mid. Río Caroní (Auyán-tepui), and Sierra de Lema southward. E Colombia to the Guianas and extreme n Brazil; ne Peru; c Brazil (s of the Amazon).

White-shouldered Tanager   PLATE 62
Tachyphonus luctuosus   Frutero Negro

Identification: 5.5″ (14cm). 14g. ♂: entirely lustrous black with *conspic. white shoulder patch* (lesser and median upper wing coverts); white under wing coverts. ♀ very different; *crown and sides of head gray, throat grayish white*, otherwise yellowish olive above and light yellow below; chest and sides tinged olive.

Sim. species: ♂ often confused with ♂ White-lined Tanager which shows, at most, a little white only at bend of closed wing (not a shoulder patch) and is found in different habitat. ♀ almost a miniature of Gray-headed Tanager and *often misidentified as latter;* aside from smaller size, note uncrested head and different habits and habitat. Also cf. both sexes of Red-shouldered Tanager.

Voice: Rather insignificant calls incl. high-pitched, sharp, almost hissing *tseer*. Song a thin, high *seet-seet-seet* (sometimes 4 notes) or briefer *seet-seet* (easily overlooked).

Behavior: An active, energetic sp. that likes mid.-story forest vine tangles. Prs. or families are normally core members of mixed-spp. flocks, where forage from lower mid. levels to subcanopy, and prs. may travel and forage alternately with understory or canopy mixed-spp. flocks. Mostly hop or flit short distances in foliage and vines and actively snatch insect prey from upper leaf surfaces by lunges, flutter-chases, or short sallies. Also take small amts. of fruit. In threat display to competitors, ♂♂ puff up shoulder feathers in bold display of white. Trinidad nest a deep open cup 1–1.5m up; 3 eggs, rich buff to pale cream blotched reddish brown[39].

Status and habitat: Common resident in tall humid forest, esp. in dense foliage and vine tangles above treefalls and small openings in forest, also forest borders and older second growth.

Range: To 900m n of Orinoco; to 1100m s of Orinoco. Maracaibo region of Zulia and w base of Andes in Táchira, Mérida, and Zulia n to Mene Grande (*panamensis*); e base of Andes from e Táchira to w Barinas and nw Cojedes (Río San Carlos); n and e Sucre s to Delta Amacuro; generally in Amazonas (sw?) and Bolívar (*luctuosus*); extreme n and e Sucre (*flaviventris*). Honduras to e Bolivia, Amaz. Brazil, and the Guianas. Trinidad.

Habia

Dull plumage but with varying amts. of rose red in plumage (or yellow to ochre—♀♀); heavy bill; often follow army ants; almost certainly most closely related to S Amer. cardinalid finches (cardinals, grosbeaks) and not true tanagers[299].

Red-crowned Ant-Tanager   PLATE 62
Habia rubica   Cardenal Hormiguero
Identification: 7″ (18cm). ♂ 34g, ♀ 31g. ♂: above dusky red, *throat and chest bright rosy red* contrasting with duller pinkish red to brownish red lower underparts; semiconcealed *red coronal stripe* narrowly bordered black (both red and black inconspic.). ♀: above olive brown, *central crown patch tawny orange, throat pale ochraceous buff* contrasting with pale buffy brown underparts; under tail coverts ochraceous buff. Or both sexes paler above and below (*crissalis*).
Sim. species: Best marks are crown stripe, contrasting throat, and rough calls. Cf. ♀ Crimson-backed and White-lined tanagers.
Voice: Contact and scolding calls are rough, grating *chak* or *chat* notes. Dawn song (by ♂ mainly when breeding) and day song patterns vary geographically. Typically up to six 2- to 4-syllable phrases whistled slowly and sweetly, e.g., in w Barinas *tjee, dear-dear-dear*, 1st note harsh, rest melancholy and trailing off. Day songs simpler. "Faint" (soft) songs reported in Belize and Costa Rica.
Behavior: A rather shy but curious tanager of forest understory, almost always noted first by its rough grating calls. Territorial prs. or families mob noisily, fuss at borders, and are often with understory mixed-spp. flocks. Forage mostly 1–5m up, occas. much higher, by hopping up through undergrowth vegetation, peering at leaves and twigs, and picking insects directly off leaf or bark surfaces. Insect or arthropod prey is often larger than tanager's bill. Also take some fruit. Reg. follow army ants in C Amer. and Trinidad but rarely in S Amer. Despite noisy behavior, adept at staying out of

view and can be devilishly hard to see well. In C. Amer., shallow, thin, fiber and rootlet cup nest fastened by rim, mostly 1–4m up in bush; 2–3 eggs, white or bluish with pale cinnamon spots forming wreath at larger end[791,802].
Status and habitat: Undergrowth inside humid forest, esp. in ravines, near streams, or where vegetation is thicker. Fairly common resident, at least formerly, in foothills of Maracaibo region (large no. of specimens), but deforestation now extensive in this region. Subsp. *mesopotamia* only known from type loc. on Río Yuruán, a tributary of Río Cuyuní.

Range: 350–1400m n of Orinoco; to 100m s of Orinoco. Entire base of Sierra de Perijá, Zulia (*perijana*); w base of Andes from Mérida n to cerros of nw Lara; e base in Táchira n to se Lara (*coccinea*); mts. of ne Anzoátegui, n Monagas and Sucre (*crissalis*); e Bolívar on Río Yuruán near El Dorado (*mesopotamia*). W and e Mexico to n Colombia and Trinidad; se Colombia to n Bolivia and Amaz. Brazil mostly s of the Amazon; se Brazil.

Piranga

Thick-set proportions; heavy bill; ♂♂ with some red; ♀♀ olive and yellow (most spp.); relatively minor element in tropical avifaunas, several are migratory spp. that breed in N Amer.; almost certainly most closely allied to *Pheucticus* grosbeaks (Cardinalidae) and not to tanagers[299].

Highland Hepatic-Tanager   PLATE 58
Piranga lutea   Cardenal Montañero
Identification: 7″ (18cm). 30g. *Bicolored bill dusky horn above, paler below*. ♂: *mostly rosy brick red*, darker above, rosiest on belly, *lores grayish*. Or darker above and below (*haemalea*). ♀: above yellow olive, *lores gray*; underparts thick yellow, sides and flanks tinged olive. Or sim. but darker; underparts more obviously tinged olive (*haemalea*). In ♂ and ♀ of both races, cheeks are only vaguely darker than upperparts (unlike N Amer. breeding Northern Hepatic-Tanager [*P. hepatica*]).
Sim. species: Either sex easily confused with Summer Tanager. ♂ Summer is brighter and rosier with bill usually creamy yellowish (not grayish); ♀ Summer is greener above, brighter yellow below, and bill also paler. But Summer's bill (both sexes) often a bit dusky on "wintering" gds., and Highland Hepatic-Tanager's bill not as dusky as Northern Hepatic-Tanager's (see Note); more reliable is *bicolored bill color* of Highland Hepatic-Tanager (Summer's bill always more or less

uniform above and below). Up close Highland Hepatic-Tanager's *dusky gray* lores are diagnostic (both sexes).
Voice: Most often hd. call a simple *chup*, also used in alarm. Sweet, musical, but repetitious song (PN Henri Pittier) a leisurely and choppy ser. of throaty phrases, rising and falling, e.g., *wueep, purty, churdik, wudik, purty, wordik, chueet, breep, cheet,* or shorter *whip, chew'wip, worry, jury, keép-fit.* Song length varies, typically ca. 4–8 phrases; dawn song sim. but longer and with only slight pauses between songs.
Behavior: Single birds or prs. are "loners," often slightly apart from forest and only infreq. with mixed-spp. flocks. Hop sluggishly and peer in canopy and mid.-level foliage, sally awkwardly to air, or flutter for variety of often large insect prey; also eat fruits, seeds, and nectar. Crude grass and fine rootlet cup (C Amer. and Colombia) on bank or 6–12m up on high branch or vertical trunk; 2–3 eggs, white or blue to greenish spotted with gray, violet, or brown[706,750].
Status and habitat: Uncommon (low density) resident of moist to humid forest borders, light woodland, plantations, and open second growth. Readily found in moist wooded ravines just above Maracay on lower Choroní Rd. (ca. 500–800m); in general most numerous at ca. 700–1500m.

Range: 450–2050m n of Orinoco; 800–1800m s of Orinoco. Sierra de Perijá, Zulia; Andes from s Táchira to Lara; mts. of Falcón (Sierra de San Luis) and Yaracay e to Sucre and n Monagas (*faceta*); tepuis of Amazonas and Bolívar (*haemalea*). Mts. of Costa Rica to Bolivia; tepuis from n Brazil to Guyana and Suriname. Trinidad.
Note: Taxonomy follows Burns[90]. Does not incl. Northern Hepatic-Tanager (*P. hepatica*) of w US to Nicaragua or Lowland Hepatic-Tanager (*P. flava*) of the Guianas, e Brazil, and n Argentina. Some also consider Blood-red Tanager (*P. haemalea*) of tepuis to Suriname a separate sp.[81,253].

Summer Tanager   PLATE 58
Piranga rubra   Cardenal Migratorio
Identification: 7" (18cm). 28g. *Bill yellowish* (usually) to pale grayish horn. ♂: all *bright rosy red*, somewhat darker above (but not as dark or "liver-colored" as Highland Hepatic-Tanager); flight feathers dusky edged rosy red. ♀: much like ♀ Highland Hepatic-Tanager; above yellow olive, below light yellow (somewhat paler than ♀ Highland Hepatic-Tanager) with *very little olive wash on breast and sides* (strongly olive in ♀ Highland Hepatic-Tanager). Subad. ♂ like ♀ but with patches of red (sometimes looks very mottled).

Sim. species: See Highland Hepatic-Tanager.
Voice: Rarely sings in Venez. but often gives distinctive, staccato *TIC-a-tup* call.
Behavior: Seen singly in rather open mid.-level part of canopy of trees in lightly wooded areas. Commonly executes quick, short sallies after flying insects, incl. many bees and wasps, which it catches mostly in crown of rather open trees. Also hops with slow deliberate movements and peers at foliage or bark, or flutter-gleans for static arthropod prey, and eats varying quantities of fruit (seasonal?). Sometimes peripherally assoc. with mixed-spp. flocks.
Status and habitat: Fairly common nonbreeding n winter resident, 18 Sep–10 May (mostly mid Oct–end of Mar), to rather open habitats incl. humid forest borders, clearings with scattered trees, coffee plantations, and thinned or open woodland. Most recs. n and s of Orinoco are in or near foothills or in mts., only a small no. from humid lowland forest, very few in llanos.

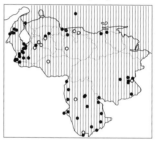

Range: To 3050m. Throughout, mainly in mts. n and s of Orinoco (*rubra*). Breeds in US and n Mexico; winters from Mexico to n Bolivia, w Amaz. Brazil, Guyana, Suriname; French Guiana (a few recs.); Chile (once). Netherlands Antilles; Trinidad.

Scarlet Tanager
Piranga olivacea   Cardenal Migratorio Alinegro
Identification: 6.5" (16.5cm). 35g. Breeding-plumage ♂: seen mainly in Jan–Apr, before and during n migration; *mostly bright scarlet; wings and tail black*, thighs black; inner web of inner flight feathers white (rarely visible in field). Nonbreeding ♂: most likely seen during arrival from n breeding gds.; above olive, below greenish yellow, *wings and tail black*. Molting ♂: like nonbreeding ♂ but mottled red and green. 1st-yr ♂: like ♀ or more orangish red. ♀: above olive green, below pale yellow, chest and sides clouded olive, *wings and tail dusky* (not jet black), young birds rarely with faint pale wing bars.
Sim. species: In any plumage unmarked black wings and tail (either sex) are good marks. Cf. Summer Tanager and Highland Hepatic-Tanager which do not have contrasting black wings and tail.
Voice: On wintering gds. in ne Peru occas. gives abrupt *chi-burr* call.
Behavior: In ne Peru wintering birds are usually seen alone, mostly in mid. or upper levels of rather open trees in clearings near forest. Sally rapidly to air or foliage for insects, mostly within tree crown, and take some insect prey by perch-gleaning.
Status and habitat: Rare passage migrant from N Amer. At least 4 specimens taken 18–31 Oct; 1 sight

rec. 15 Apr 1980, above Ocumare de La Costa, Aragua (C. Summerhayes). Humid forest on mainland; arid scrub on offshore isls. In ne Peru in clearings and second growth with scattered tall open trees, and on river isls.

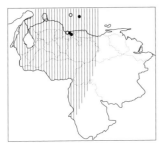

Range: To 630m (surely higher). Aragua (El Limón; below Rancho Grande; sight, Ocumare de La Costa); 2 specimens from Islas Los Roques (Isla Namusqui and Madríz-Qui); Isla de Aves (sight). Breeds in N Amer.; migrates through C Amer. and W Indies; winters mostly in nw S Amer., esp. in w Amazonia; Guyana (sight).

White-winged Tanager   PLATE 58
Piranga leucoptera   Cardenal Guamero
Identification: 5.5″ (14cm). 17g. ♂: *bright poppy red* with black lores, wings, and tail; *2 broad white wing bars*; thighs black. ♀: head and rump olive yellow, lores black, back olive, *wings and tail dusky, 2 broad white wing bars; underparts rich buttery yellow*, throat and chest faintly tinged orange, sides tinged olive. Imm. ♂: like ♀ but more orange red on throat and chest.
Sim. species: Only "red" or "yellowish" tanager in Venez. with conspic. white wing bars. Cf. migratory Scarlet Tanager.
Voice: Freq. hd. calls are often first indication of this sp.'s presence. Distinctive *pit-sweet!* or *pit-sweet-sweet!*, the *seet* notes musical and rising; also various sharp *weet* and *chip* notes; song a thin, wiry *e-seé-se-whEET*.
Behavior: Prs. or chattery groups of 3–6 call freq.; usually forage in semiopen on top or outer edge of canopy foliage, either alone or with mixed-spp. flocks, and are fairly easy to see. Forage somewhat above other spp. Peer and flutter in high outer twigs and foliage, look under small branches in manner of some *Tangara*, and take fruit, incl. melastome berries and *Heliocarpus* (Tilaceae) seeds. Small cup nest 14m up on mossy branch; built by ♀[706].
Status and habitat: Fairly common resident in a wide range of habitats, but in all of them essentially a bird of high edges. Canopy of humid montane forest, tall second growth woodland, coffee plantations, and drier, more seasonal mt. forest, esp. drier areas where forest is broken or disturbed. In mature forest uses top of canopy as a "horizontal" edge.
Range: 650–2100m n of Orinoco; 1000–1800m s of Orinoco. Sierra de Perijá, Zulia; Andes from Táchira to nw Lara (Cerro El Cerrón); mts. from Falcón (Sierra de San Luis) and Yaracuy e to Sucre and n Monagas; nw Bolívar (Cerro Tabaro); se Bolívar from Ptari-tepui and Sierra de Lema (sightings) s across tepuis of Gran Sa-

bana to Cerro Roraima and Uei-tepui (*venezuelae*). E Mexico locally s in mts. to Bolivia.

Ramphocelus

Lower mandible swollen at base, chalky to silvery white, esp. prom. in ♂♂; plumage of ♂'s head and neck short, dense, and velvety; ♂♂ are black, blackish maroon, or glistening crimson, ♀♀ much duller; notably social; edge habitats or near water; ♂♂ of some spp. very beautiful; taxonomy reviewed by Hackett[234].

Silver-beaked Tanager   PLATE 62
Ramphocelus carbo   Pico de Plata
Identification: 7″ (18cm). 25g. ♀-plumaged birds predominate. Bill black above; *lower mandible swollen at base, shining silvery white* tipped black (♂); much duller, less swollen (♀). ♂: *head and underparts velvety blackish crimson*, brightest and glistening on throat and chest, rest of upperparts blackish tinged dark crimson; wings and tail dusky. Or sim. but ♂ with throat and chest dark crimson *contrasting* with black lower underparts; above blackish, little or no crimson tinge (*capitalis*). ♀ and imm. ♂: dull dark reddish brown, brighter on rump; *below dull brick red to dark pinkish brown*. Or sim. but plain brown above, paler brown below, only tinge of rufescence on belly (*carbo*).
Sim. species: ♂ is stunning in good light but often looks blackish; can always be told by white on bill. ♀ easily confused with several other brownish ♀ tanagers and finches but usually shows paler lower mandible and has brick red underparts. Cf. ♀ White-lined Tanager; n and w of Andes see ♀ Crimson-backed Tanager.
Voice: Commonest call a loud, metallic *chank*. Dawn song (occas. later in day) an energetic but rather repetitive ser. of phrases without much richness, *tu tu tweep, chip-tup tweep, tu tu tweep, chip, sput, seek . . .* and so on. Some individuals sing leisurely, even simpler, repetitive *spit weet, sput, wheer . . .* over and over.
Behavior: Naturalists will quickly make the acquaintance of noisy, engaging, and omnipresent groups of these birds. They travel in bands of 4–10, occas. more, trooping noisily about in undergrowth along forest borders or in gardens and clearings. Groups may briefly join mixed-spp. flocks along borders. Prs. do not seem to defend territories against conspecifics. Often act quite nervous, with much agitated flicking of wings and tail as peer in foliage for fruit and insects. About half of diet is fruit, esp. melastomes berries, which are usually mashed. Hop rapidly and heavily in foliage and chase disturbed and fleeing insect prey. Occas.

eat flowers (for nectar?) or drink nectar. Duller ♀♀ and imms. outnumber ad.-plumaged ♂♂. Bulky cup nest ca. 1–3m up (occas. higher) in bush; 1–3 eggs, greenish to bluish with darker markings; nests may be close together, occas. reused[646]; breeding reported Apr–May.

Status and habitat: Common resident in bushy forest borders, overgrown clearings, second growth, and around habitations. Mostly humid areas. Scarce or locally absent in llanos, e.g., unrec. at Hato Masaguaral, Guárico[734].

Range: To 1900m n of Orinoco; to 1250m s of Orinoco. Falcón (w to Sierra de San Luis) e through n cordilleras to Miranda and s through e Lara, Cojedes, Portuguesa, Barinas, and Apure (*venezuelensis*); ne Anzoátegui, Sucre, Monagas, and Delta Amacuro (*capitalis*); se Sucre at Guanoco (*magnirostris*); throughout Amazonas and Bolívar (*carbo*). E Colombia to Paraguay, Brazil, and the Guianas. Trinidad.

Crimson-backed Tanager   PLATE 62
Ramphocelus dimidiatus   Sangre de Toro Encendido
Identification: 7″ (18cm). 28g. ♀-plumaged birds predominate. Bill blackish above, *base of lower mandible swollen, silvery white* (♂) or duller (♀). ♂: head, throat, chest, and back dark velvety crimson, *rump bright red*, wings and tail deep black, *breast, sides, and flanks crimson*, center of belly and thighs black. ♀: head and throat sooty contrasting with dark red to brownish red (brick red) underparts; otherwise back dusky maroon, *rump contrasting dark red*; wings and tail dusky.
Sim. species: Good marks for either sex are red rump and red or reddish lower underparts. E of Andes see Silver-beaked Tanager. Cf. Red-crowned Ant-Tanager.
Voice: Call much like that of Silver-beaked Tanager, a nasal *chank* while foraging. Dawn and day song in nw Táchira a long, slow ser. of rather clipped single or double notes, *reet, skréa, seek, reé-a, séea, bz-weet, wit-weet, fzeet, reéza, bzeep, skeéa* . . . , slightly buzzy, notes rising and falling, for up to several min without a clear break.
Behavior: Sim. to Silver-beaked Tanager. Almost always conspic. and noisy and in groups of its own that troop about in undergrowth or mid. levels along wooded borders. Hop and peer heavily in foliage for fruit and insects. May gather in large nos. to roost, e.g., more than 50 in citrus grove at La Fria, Táchira, in mid Jan. Cup nest low in shrub; 2 blue eggs finely spotted dark[750].
Status and habitat: Fairly common to common resident in shrubby clearings, cultivated areas, gardens,

and moist to humid forest borders. Smaller nos. in dry, scrubby second growth (i.e., above Ureña, Táchira).

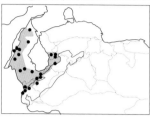

Range: To 1300m. Nw and e Zulia and Maracaibo region s to nw Táchira, w Mérida, and w Trujillo (*dimidiatus*). W Panama and n Colombia.

Thraupis

Widespread, common, and conspic.; among most familiar of all tanagers; villages, gardens, and forest edges; colors mostly subdued; bill rather heavy.

Blue-gray Tanager   PLATE 61
Thraupis episcopus   Azulejo de Jardín
Identification: 7″ (18cm). 35g. *Head, neck, and underparts pale powdery blue gray contrasting with darker and bluer back*; shoulders (lesser and median upper wing coverts) deep cobalt blue, wings dusky broadly edged bright blue, tail dull bluish edged bright blue. Or shoulders lavender blue (*nesophilus*). Or shoulders cobalt blue, lesser upper wing coverts and 1 wing bar white (*mediana*). Imm.: much duller.
Sim. species: Adults always have *head paler than back*. Drabber Palm Tanager is sim. in many respects but rear half of wing contrasting black. Along n coastal region and in llanos cf. very sim. Glaucous Tanager.
Voice: Commonest calls are rising *seeeee* and dry, strained *tsuup*, sometimes followed by a few twittery notes. Song, by both sexes, a complex ser. of squeaky and twittering notes with variable pattern, typically mixed with strained *tsuee* and *tsuup* notes. Quite sim. to that of Palm Tanager.
Behavior: The noisy, conspic. "Azulejo" is one of Venez.'s most familiar birds in settled areas. A sociable sp., it lives in prs. but may form single-sp. groups at times, and several may roost together. Also briefly joins mixed-spp. flocks, and readily goes to fruiting trees with other spp. Foraging behavior is versatile, as peers head down along branches, scans foliage, sallies clumsily to air, takes a variety of fruit, and nectar from flowers, and damages papaya and other fruits in gardens. Usually stays well up in trees or shrubbery. Nest 3–20m up; thick deep cup in branch fork, crevice in building, even in nests of other spp. such as thornbirds; 1–3 eggs, whitish to grayish green with brown or darker markings; breeding May–Jul, Guárico[734]; prob. most of yr.
Status and habitat: Common and widespread resident in broad spectrum of essentially nonforest habitats incl. all kinds of settled areas, plantations, city parks, gardens, young to old second growth, and forest borders in dry to humid regions. Everywhere thrives in human-altered habitats. Partly to mostly replaced in arid zones along Carib. coast by Glaucous Tanager.

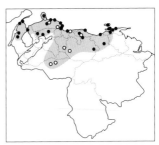

Range: To 2200m n of Orinoco; to 1700m s of Orinoco. Throughout n of Orinoco except area of next subsp. (*cana*); lowlands of e Sucre, e Monagas, Delta Amacuro; n Amazonas and throughout Bolívar except lower Río Caura (*nesophilus*); lower Río Caura and Amazonas s of Río Ventuari (*mediana*). Se Mexico to n Bolivia, Amaz. Brazil, and the Guianas. Trinidad and Tobago. Introd. to Lima, Peru.

Glaucous Tanager

PLATE 61

Thraupis glaucocolpa Azulejo Verdeviche
Identification: 6.7″ (17cm). 33g. Head and upperparts pale smoky gray, back slightly tinged bluish and *more or less concolor with head*; wings dusky, coverts and *flight feathers edged pale aquamarine*, greener in ♀ and imm.; small *blackish triangle at base of flight feathers*; underparts gray, breast and sides faintly tinged bluish green, *belly white*.
Sim. species: Very sim. to Blue-gray Tanager and easily overlooked among this usually more numerous relative (but Glaucous predominates in drier coastal areas). Glaucous always has "sooty" look. Told from Blue-gray by concolor head and back, conspic. black patch at base of outer flight feathers, sharply contrasting white belly, and generally aqua-green (not blue gray) flight feathers; also note Glaucous's larger bill. Beware imm. Blue-grays which have head and back almost concolor; then look for blackish wing spot and white belly.
Voice: Song, unlike allied Blue-gray Tanager, a pulsating ser. of remarkably high-pitched notes that swell in volume as song progresses, *e-e-e-ee-ee-eee-eee-see-SEE-SEE-SEE*, infreq. hd. but much more at beginning of rainy season. Infreq. call a high, thin, almost sweet *sweEEeeeee*, descending at end, singly at intervals of 10 sec or so.
Behavior: Lives in shadow of much more well known cousin, Blue-gray Tanager, and is generally less sociable, less conspic., less numerous, and much less widespread than that sp. Single birds or prs. stay mostly well up in trees and generally behave like others of genus (see Blue-gray Tanager). May usurp nests of thornbirds[648] or steal material from Bananaquit (and other spp.?) for nesting; breeding Apr–Jul, Anzoátegui[186]; Aug, Guárico[734].
Status and habitat: Fairly common resident locally in dry and arid zones. Deciduous woodland, dry scrubby and thorny vegetation, plantations, and gardens near coast. Local in llanos where found mostly in groves of large trees, esp. around ranch buildings. In e Falcón nos. seem to increase markedly during May–Jul onset of rains; seasonal movements may occur.

Range: To 800m. Entire Carib. coast from n Zulia to Sucre and s to n Lara, sw Apure (sightings, Hato Cedral; Hato El Frio), c Guárico, and c Anzoátegui. Ne Colombia.

Palm Tanager

PLATE 61

Thraupis palmarum Azulejo de Palmeras
Identification: 7.5″ (19cm). 36g. Drab in color but plumage shiny. Mostly smoky grayish olive with brownish to yellowish tinge; *crown* (or at least forecrown) *distinctly tinged yellowish*, wing coverts and base of flight feathers dull grayish olive, *rear half of wings dusky black* (folded wings form black triangle), tail dusky, ♂ often with bluish tinge to breast. Or sim. but breast tinged smoky violet gray (*atripennis*). ♀ (both races): generally paler with slight yellowish tinge above and below.
Sim. species: Shape and behavior much like better-known Blue-gray Tanager, and often with it, but in any light can be told by black rear half of wings (conspic. in flight or at rest). Also cf. various thrushes, e.g., Pale-breasted and Black-billed, all larger.
Voice: Squeaky song a fast stream of sputtering and clear notes, all at about same speed. Much like song of Blue-gray Tanager but slightly less musical; lacks strained *tsuee* notes characteristic of Blue-gray's song.
Behavior: Much like that of Blue-gray Tanager and sometimes with it, but less an urban bird and often in treetops in forested regions. Rather social, occurring in prs., also often in small noisy groups, and occas. up to 12 gather in bare treetops. Foraging behavior, like that of Blue-gray Tanager, is notably versatile. Readily clings to tips of palm fronds, hangs upside down beneath frond tips, eats fruit and flower petals, and gleans and sallies for insects, taking about equal amts. of fruit and insect matter. In Costa Rica, neat cup nest of grass, dry leaf strips, palm fibers, etc., in palm, leaf cluster, epiphyte, cavity, or crevice, even building, 6–30m up; 2 eggs, pale bluish heavily spotted brown and pale lilac[706].

Status and habitat: Common resident in populated areas, cultivated regions with scattered trees, second growth, and forest edges. Also reg. in top of forest canopy which it uses as "horizontal" edge. Fairly dry to humid regions. Esp. numerous in scrubby patches of woodland and gallery forest borders in Gran Sabana (where few Blue-gray Tanagers occur).
Range: To 1450m. Maracaibo Basin and w base of Andes in Táchira and Mérida (*atripennis*); rest of Venez.; Islas Margarita and Patos (*melanoptera*). S Nicaragua to se Brazil and the Guianas.

Blue-capped Tanager   PLATE 58
Thraupis cyanocephala   Azulejo Montañero
Identification: 7″ (18cm). 36g. Plumage varies geographically. *Above bright yellow olive, head and entire underparts shining cornflower blue*, thighs yellow, under tail coverts olive yellow; bend of wing and *under wing coverts bright yellow (olivicyanea)*. Or sim. but underparts dark gray, under tail coverts bright yellow like thighs (*auricrissa, hypophaea*). Or only crown blue, sides of head dusky (form mask), malar line freckled whitish, underparts plain gray, thighs and under tail coverts contrasting olive yellow (*subcinerea, buesingi*).
Sim. species: Nothing quite like it despite considerable plumage variation. Blue cap and yellow under tail coverts are good marks in all races. Note yellow under wing coverts as it flies.
Voice: Not esp. vocal. Song a twittery, unmusical jumble of notes somewhat resembling that of Blue-gray Tanager, e.g., a strained *tsuee-tsuee-tee-ee-ee-seet*.
Behavior: A handsome tanager but so common and so fond of trashy, disturbed habitats that it seldom commands much admiration from observers. Prs. or up to 8 or more follow mixed-spp. flocks along forest borders, esp. those containing *Tangara* and other tanagers, or wander alone or gather briefly with other spp. at fruiting trees. Mostly stay fairly high in trees where they are active, conspic., and easy to see. Feed heavily on fruit, sometimes descending low to fruiting shrubs. Also take a few insects from foliage or in clumsy sallies to air. Open cup nest 8m up in fork of limb; 2 pale greenish blue eggs marked brown[175].
Status and habitat: Common to locally very common resident in patches of second-growth woodland, shrubby forest borders, highland pastures with scattered trees, and tree-lined fence rows. Most numerous above ca. 1800m.

Range: 1300–2800m (to 800m on Paria Pen.). Sierra de Perijá, Zulia; Andes of s Táchira n through Mérida and Trujillo (*auricrissa*); Páramo de Las Rosas, s Lara (*hypo-*

phaea); Coastal Cordillera in Aragua, Distr. Federal, and Miranda (*olivicyanea*); Paria Pen., Sucre (*buesingi*); mts. of s Sucre and n Monagas (*subcinerea*). Colombia s in Andes to n Bolivia. Trinidad.

Blue-backed Tanager   PLATE 61
Cyanicterus cyanicterus   Frutero Lomiazul
Identification: 6.7″ (17cm). 34g. Long, heavy bill with decurved culmen blackish; legs bright orange; eyes red orange to dark red. *Upperparts, head, throat, and chest deep cadet blue*, more violet blue on throat and chest; lores black, *breast and lower underparts bright yellow*, thighs dark blue. ♀ paler than ♂: above cerulean blue tinged greenish, lores, *sides of head, and throat deep buffy yellow becoming bright yellow on lower underparts*.
Sim. species: Unique in its range. Color pattern nearer a mountain-tanager than anything in lowlands.
Voice: Can be quite noisy, both sexes giving high-pitched, loud, and *penetrating*, mostly 2- or 3-note calls (songs?) while perched or in flight, *keeee, kuuu* or *keeee, ksuuu-ksuuu*, or various combinations, occas. up to 5 notes in ser.
Behavior: A scarce and poorly known bird, encountered only *high* in forest canopy. Usually in prs. and often with mixed-spp. flocks, but apt to leave them behind because of its habit of flying straight off to some distant high treetop, all the while calling loudly, then apt to return again within 10–15 min. Forages by hopping along open branches in canopy. Foraging territories appear to be very large as prs. wander widely and are notoriously erratic and unpredictable.
Status and habitat: Rare to uncommon and local (low density) resident of tall humid forest in lowlands and foothills, and at forest borders; occas. in isolated trees (esp. *Cecropia*) in forest clearings. Can be found along road from km 88 (San Isidro) w to upper Río Cuyuní; also at km 73 along El Dorado–Santa Elena Rd.

Range: To 200m. E Bolívar (Río Yuruán near El Dorado; sight recs. s to base of Sierra de Lema). The Guianas and ne Brazil (near Manaus).
Note: Taxonomic placement uncertain.

Buthraupis

Large tanagers of high els.; bold patterns, yellow underparts.

Hooded Mountain-Tanager   PLATE 58
Buthraupis montana   Cachaquito Gigante
Identification: 9″ (23cm). 96g. *Eyes bright red. Head, neck, and upper throat black* (the "hood"), nape and

rest of upperparts cornflower blue, wings and tail dusky tinged greenish, *below bright golden yellow*, narrow band on lower flanks blue, *thighs black (gigas)*. Or sim. but flight feathers and tail narrowly edged olive; upperparts with faint olive tinge (*venezuelana*).
Sim. species: Easily recognized by hulking size, black head, blue upperparts, and red eyes; black thighs are conspic. in field. See Black-chested Mountain-Tanager.
Voice: Groups, sometimes stimulated by extraneous noises, simultaneously give loud bursts of squealing notes. Also, when foraging, *weeck* and *toot* notes, or *toot-weeck* phrases, often rapidly; also weak *ti* notes singly or in rapid ser. In flight display, ♂ (?) flies out high in large 100-m circle above forest and sings rapid, exuberant *chip'ut-chip'ut-chip-ut* . . . until it dives back into forest.
Behavior: A large, gaudy, social tanager of high cloud forests. Usually in conspic. groups of 3–10, occas. more, that roam over large areas. Flocks move along steep forested slopes or canyons, the members often crossing considerable gaps with each flight, and stragglers hurrying along to keep up with faster-moving members. Also often in loosely assoc. mixed flocks of 2–8 with mountain-caciques, Black-collared Jays, and Crimson-mantled Woodpeckers where forage rapidly. Away from these mixed flocks, or with mixed-spp. flocks of smaller birds, forage in slower methodical manner, mostly on branches 1″ (25mm) in diameter or larger. Hop up through outer canopy limbs, lean down to inspect sides of branches and foliage, and esp. lichens on branches, also eat many small berries and fruit.
Status and habitat: Fairly common (low density) resident in humid and wet montane forest and tall second-growth woodland. Despite restricted range in Venez., known from substantial no. of specimens.

Range: 1800–3000m. Sierra de Perijá, Zulia (*venezuelana*)[17]; s Táchira (*gigas*). Andes of Colombia s to Bolivia.

Black-chested Mountain-Tanager   PLATE 58
Buthraupis eximia   Cachaquito Rabadilla Azul
Identification: 8″ (20.3cm). 63g. Bill short and thick; eyes dark. *Crown, nape, and rump dark blue, back rich moss green*, wings and tail black, lesser wing coverts blue, rest of wing coverts and inner flight feathers heavily edged moss green, *sides of head, throat, and chest black*, breast and belly golden yellow, thighs yellow (base of feathers black).
Sim. species: From above looks very dark, hence may recall larger Hooded Tanager but that sp. is almost entirely yellow below (no black on lower throat or chest).

Voice: Long, complex song a repetitive *tititi-turri-tititi-tee-ter-turry* . . . up to 30 sec; *seep* and *chip* notes while foraging[274].
Behavior: Another large, boldly marked tanager of cold, damp treeline forests but somewhat more reserved in manner, less social, and less often seen than Hooded Mountain-Tanager. In Colombia prs. or more often groups of 3–6 forage alone or with mixed flocks, and like other large *Buthraupis*, typically roam over large areas. Move quietly through upper part of trees where they hop rather heavily along mossy limbs, pause to peer downward, and sometimes hop out into open tops of stunted vegetation. Have been noted taking mostly fruit.
Status and habitat: Mossy and wet upper montane forest, forest borders, and elfin woodland at or near treeline. An uncommon (low density) resident that barely reaches border of Venez.

Range: 2800–3000m. S Táchira near Páramo de Tamá, and Cerro El Retiro in upper Río Chiquito Valley (*eximia*). Andes of Colombia, Ecuador, and extreme n Peru.

Anisognathus

Small genus; bold, colorful plumage patterns; bill rather short and thick; highly frugivorous; typical of high, wet Andean forests and borders.

Scarlet-bellied Mountain-Tanager   PLATE 58
Anisognathus igniventris   Cachaquito Vientre Rojo
Identification: 7.5″ (19cm). 34g. Unmistakable. Rich velvety black with triangular red patch on neck; *glistening sky blue shoulders and rump* (blue rump usually visible only in flight); *mid. breast to belly scarlet*; thighs and under tail coverts mixed black and scarlet. Imm.: underparts orange red; juv. has scarlet breast mixed tawny.
Voice: Sings more than others of genus. At dawn, or at long intervals during day, a tinkling (like little bells) jumble of rapid, complex, rising and falling notes mixed with lower-pitched nasal notes, almost like cranking an old engine. Sings from concealed or semi-open perch.
Behavior: Prs. or loosely assoc. groups up to 8 or more forage alone, or join mixed tanager and finch flocks in forest or along forest borders. Forage from low to high and may sit relatively immobile for a moment, then hop jaylike up through foliage. Eat mostly fruit, gulped or mashed, supplemented by insects. Flight somewhat undulating.
Status and habitat: Uncommon to locally fairly common resident. Wet and mossy forest, dense forest borders, treeline elfin forest, and hedgerows or bushes in

high pastures. Some seasonal or nomadic el. movements may occur.

Range: 2700–3000m (sight to 2380m, near Betania, 19 Jan 1995). S Táchira in vicinity of Páramo de Tamá, and upper Río Chiquito Valley at Cerro El Retiro (*lunulatus*). Andes from Colombia to c Bolivia.

Lacrimose Mountain-Tanager PLATE 58
Anisognathus lacrymosus Cachaquito Vientre Dorado
Identification: 7″ (18cm). 31g. Above slaty, blacker on crown and sides of head; *small yellow spot below eye* (the "tear") and larger triangular-shaped yellow spot on rearcheek; wings narrowly edged blue (inconspic.), *median throat and all of underparts yellow to tawny yellow*, yellower on lower breast and belly. Or forecrown and sides of head dark yellow olive, back dusky bluish gray, underparts darker (*tamae*). Or like *tamae* but paler, esp. on back (*pallididorsalis*).
Sim. species: In high mt. forests easily told by yellow "tears" on sides of head and bright mustard yellow underparts.
Voice: High, thin *see* or *seeek* notes while foraging; also short bursts of staccato chipping (2–8 notes) over and over. Short song (?) *ee-chut-chut-ee*, over and over, esp. when excited.
Behavior: An affable, easy-to-see tanager, often notably confiding. Prs. or small groups are fairly conspic. and habitually fraternize with fast-moving mixed-spp. flocks containing flycatchers, finches, and other tanagers, but also forage away from them, peering around in leisurely manner. Range from eye level to subcanopy, hop rather heavily in foliage, take mostly fruit, and also glean insects from leaves or occas. sally awkwardly for flying insects. May pause to rest quietly in open or semiopen on low or high open branch, sometimes remaining there for several min.
Status and habitat: Common resident in humid forest, shrubby forest borders, and at high els., in stunted mossy forest up to treeline.

Range: 1800–3200m. Sierra de Perijá, Zulia (*pallididorsalis*); sw Táchira on Páramo de Tamá (*tamae*); n Táchira, Mérida, and Trujillo n to Páramos Cendé and Misisí (*melanops*). Andes of Colombia s to s Peru.

Blue-winged Mountain-Tanager PLATE 58
Anisognathus somptuosus Cachaquito Primavera
Identification: 7″ (18cm). 42g. Head to below eyes black; back, wings, and tail black, *large patch on central and rear crown golden yellow*, lower back tinged greenish (inconspic. in field); shoulders violet blue, flight feathers and tail broadly edged bright blue (forms conspic. blue patch on wings), *underparts bright golden yellow*. Or back and rump moss green (*victorini*). Or back greenish black (*virididorsalis*).
Sim. species: Unmistakable if seen well. In Andes see Lacrimose Mountain-Tanager.
Voice: Generally rather quiet. Song a rapid, high-pitched, almost twittering *ti-ti-ti-ti ti'ti'ti'TI'TI'TI'ti'ti'ti'ti 'ti'ti'ti ti ti*; a little louder and faster in middle. When foraging soft *tic* notes, or short bursts of *tic* notes, sometimes extended into little trills.
Behavior: Conspic. but rather independent-minded prs. or groups of 3–10 forage at various hts. from quite low to occas. high in canopy, and inside or at edge of forest. These are energetic birds that forage actively, but in a distinctive, stereotyped manner, typically run-hopping along slender, bare branches, working out fairly quickly to terminal foliage clusters where pause or hop deliberately and spend up to 30 sec peering around carefully, stretching up, leaning down, occas. pecking or lunging short distance for prey, then flying to another branch and repeating process. Also reg. check hanging dead leaves for insects and eat small fruits and berries. Little parties forage alone or join mixed-spp. flocks containing warblers and tanagers but freq. strike out on their own in unpredictable or erratic forays.
Status and habitat: Fairly common resident in humid and wet forest, forest borders, and tall second-growth woodland in n cordilleras. Readily come to trays of fruit presented at Rancho Grande Biol. Station, Aragua.

Range: 900–2100m. S Táchira in upper Río Chiquito Valley (*victorini*); Coastal Cordillera from Yaracuy to Distr. Federal and Miranda (*venezuelanus*); Interior Cordillera at Cerro Golfo Triste, s Aragua (*virididorsalis*). Colombia s in Andes to c Bolivia.
Note: Formerly *A. flavinucha*[559].

Iridosornis

Small genus; notable for exceptionally rich, almost glowing color in plumage; rather puff-headed; small, short bill; only high els. in Andes.

Golden-crowned Tanager
PLATE 58

Iridosornis rufivertex Frutero Cabecidorado

Identification: 7″ (18cm). 23g. Bill conical and short. Inky black head and throat surround *large round patch of glowing golden yellow* on crown (feathers long and silky), *otherwise intense deep purplish blue*, wings and tail black edged greenish to purplish blue; *belly and under tail coverts chestnut*.

Sim. species: A stunning bird, but in poor light extraordinarily rich colors may look blackish. Cf. smaller, all-blue Masked Flowerpiercer, and Plushcap which is all rusty below.

Voice: Rather quiet. High *tsip* or *tsick* notes while foraging, and occas. high, thin *seeeep*.

Behavior: Unknown in Venez. Elsewhere a dark, quiet dweller of dense elfin woodland whose comings and goings seem veiled in secrecy. Single birds, prs., or families move rapidly with mixed-spp. flocks containing flowerpiercers, conebills, and other tanagers, or forage alone, mostly 0.5–5m up inside or at edge of dense low forest. Fly quickly across small openings, dive into cover, and usually keep out of sight, or momentarily appear in open as hop along slender bare or mossy branches to search for insects and fruit. Most insects taken from leaf surfaces.

Status and habitat: In Venez., where at extreme n end of range, known from only a few recs. Occurs in thick shrubbery and borders of low, dense, mossy elfin forest near treeline.

Range: 2800–3000m. S Táchira in vicinity of Páramo de Tamá, and upper Río Chiquito at Cerro El Retiro (*rufivertex*); ne Mérida (?). Andes of Colombia to n Ecuador.

Dubusia

Bill thinner and longer (in proportion to size of bird) than in larger *Buthraupis* which it recalls in plumage; vocalizations unusual.

Buff-breasted Mountain-Tanager
PLATE 58

Dubusia taeniata Cachaquito Montañero

Identification: 7.5″ (19cm). 37g. Entire head, nape, throat, and chest black; *long, broad eyebrow of frosty blue freckles and streaks*; rest of upperparts dark blue; *narrow inconspic. chest band buff*, breast and belly bright yellow, under tail coverts buff.

Sim. species: Superficially like a no. of mountain-tanagers but from any by frosty eyebrow. Despite name, buff chest band not conspic.

Voice: Song, sometimes repeated over and over at short intervals for a few min early in morning, a loud, whistled *pheeeee-bay*, 2d note lower, or slurred lower.

Behavior: Usually hd. before seen. Single birds or prs. follow mixed-spp. flocks or wander alone over large areas. Hop along limbs and peer at moss and foliage. Forage from eye level to treetops but more often fairly low. Usually remain at least partially concealed in foliage, but now and then sit up in open on bushtop for a few moments. Eat many kinds of small fruits and berries incl. mistletoe, and search mossy branches for insects.

Status and habitat: Uncommon and local resident in wet, mossy montane forest, wooded borders, and patches of elfin woodland up to treeline. Most numerous in zones of stunted forest near treeline. Somewhat erratic or unpredictable in occurrence, perhaps because foraging territories are large.

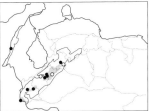

Range: 2000–3000m. Sierra de Perijá, Zulia; Andes of Táchira, Mérida, and Trujillo n to Páramo Misisí (*taeniata*). Colombia s in mts. to s Peru.

Note: Has been placed in genus *Delothraupis*.

Pipraeidea

Monotypic genus with no obviously close allies; wide bill; long wings.

Fawn-breasted Tanager
PLATE 58

Pipraeidea melanonota Chachaquito

Identification: 5.5″ (14cm). 20.5g. *Eyes fire red*. Rather wide, swallowlike bill with small hook on tip. *Crown and nape sky blue, forehead and broad mask black*; otherwise dark dusky blue above; rump sky blue (like crown), underparts uniform fawn buff. ♀: sim. but duller, crown smoky gray blue. In both sexes, wings long and tail short relative to body size.

Sim. species: Should be easily identified. Rusty Flowerpiercer lacks contrasting head pattern and red eyes.

Voice: Infreq. hd. song a ser. of high *see* or *sweee* notes, varying from a few notes given slowly to 12 or more notes uttered very fast like pulsating trill.

Behavior: May recall that of both *Tersina* and *Tangara*. Something of a "loner" but sometimes also assoc. with mixed-spp. flocks. Seems curiously detached, flighty at times, and may display tendency toward nomadism. Often hops along large limbs and perch-gleans, occas. sallies up and hovers briefly beneath leaf, or sallies to air for flying insects; also at almost any ht. in fruiting trees and shrubs. Flight is swift and fluid, and apt to fly off some distance before alighting. Nests are high and concealed in epiphytes and moss.

Status and habitat: Uncommon to fairly common resident but thinly spread in bushy pastures, cultivated areas with large trees, and along forest borders and clearings with scattered trees. Essentially a forest-edge tanager. Recent sight recs. at els. much lower than specimen recs. may be range expansions with deforestation. Low recs. incl. 5 seen at ca. 400m, 1 Mar 1981, Morros de Macaira, Guárico (C. Parrish); pr. at ca. 550m, 10 Jan 1988 near La Victoria, Aragua; and 1 at ca. 1200m, 5 Feb 1994, near Bramón, Táchira. Birds from Amazonas resident (?).

Range: 1500–2500m (sight recs. to 400m) n of Orinoco; 950–2100m s of Orinoco. W slope of Andes from s Táchira to nw Lara (Cerro El Cogollal); e slope from se Táchira to se Lara (sight); Coastal Cordillera from Carabobo to Distr. Federal, Interior Cordillera in s Miranda and n Guárico (sight, San Francisco de Macaira—C. Parrish); mts. of w Sucre; mts. of n and s Amazonas on Cerro Yavi; Cerro Taracuniña in Sierra Parima (*venezuelensis*); se Bolívar (?). Andes from Colombia to n Argentina; se Brazil to e Paraguay, e Argentina, and Uruguay.

Euphonia

Small, fubsy, and short tailed; short, thick bill; sexes usually differ. Broadly composed of 3 groups: (1) ♂♂ with standard black and yellow pattern; ♀♀ dull; penetrating *beem-beem* whistle or (some spp.) also use vocal mimicry; (2) ♂♂ mostly shiny blue black (no yellow on head); ♀♀ dull; low harsh rattle calls; and (3) both sexes with dull ♀-type plumage (♀♀ dullest); songs complex and chattery. Identification of ♀♀ of all groups difficult. Mistletoe an important food for many spp. As far as known, build domed fiber and moss nest with side entrance; almost certainly not related to tanagers and may be either a separate radiation or related to carduelee finches[299].

Golden-rumped Euphonia   PLATE 61
Euphonia cyanocephala   Curruñatá Corona Azul
Identification: 4.5″ (11.4cm). 14g. ♂: *crown and nape sky blue* contrasting with steely blue black (to purplish black) upperparts; *rump golden yellow*; narrow frontlet, sides of head, and throat black, rest of underparts buttery orange yellow. ♀: *frontlet orange rufous, crown and nape light blue*, otherwise olive green above and olive yellow below, brightest on belly (some ♀♀ are gray-tinged below with only faint yellow).
Sim. species: ♀ from ♀ Chestnut-breasted Chlorophonia by rufous forehead, brighter blue cap, and duller, more uniform underparts. ♂ should be unmistakable, but see Chestnut-breasted Chlorophonia.
Voice: Song, lasting up to 10 sec, a fast, complex stream of twittery and squeaky notes mixed with low-pitched *chup* notes. Call a soft, whistled *cheeer*, slightly

descending, much like call of Blue-naped Chlorophonia but lower pitched.
Behavior: Prs. or little groups spend much of time in large clumps of fruiting mistletoe in canopy of trees where they are rather quiet, or give soft calls and keep mostly to themselves. Occas. joined by other euphonias in mistletoe, and only infreq. or incidentally assoc. with mixed-spp. flocks. May wander locally (prob. widely) when not breeding. Globular grass and moss nest with side entrance; 2 eggs, cream marked brown and black mostly at larger end[175]; 3 nests, Jan–Feb, Aragua and Trujillo; on high roadcut bank and 4–8m up in trees.
Status and habitat: Uncommon to fairly common resident in humid forest borders, second-growth woodland, disturbed or partially open areas, and shady coffee plantations, mainly in mts. Unpredictable and erratic in occurrence; commonest in s Táchira.

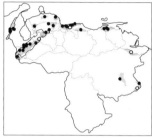

Range: Mostly 600–2500m (occas. to sea level) n of Orinoco; 500–1500m s of Orinoco. Sierra de Perijá, Zulia; Andes and n mts. from Táchira, Lara, and Falcón (incl. Sierra de San Luis) e to Sucre and n Monagas; se Bolívar on Cerro Roraima and Uaipán-tepui (*intermedia*); Santa Elaena de Uairén (sight); n Amazonas[833] (?). Colombia s in mts. to n Bolivia; s Guyana and Suriname; e Paraguay, ne Argentina, and se Brazil; Trinidad.
Note: Formerly Blue-hooded Euphonia[403]; now split into 3 spp.[10].

Thick-billed Euphonia   PLATE 61
Euphonia laniirostris   Curruñatá Piquigordo
Identification: 4.5″ (11.4cm). 13.5g. True to name, bill is thicker than in most others of genus (limited use in field). ♂: *forecrown patch yellow* (extends back to behind eye), rest of crown, sides of head, and upperparts glossy blue black; *below entirely yellow* (incl. throat and under tail coverts); oval on inner web of outer 2 prs. of tail feathers white (visible from below). ♀: above *uniform olive* (no yellow on forehead), lores gray, sides and flanks olive yellow, *center of throat and center of lower breast and belly bright yellow*, chest strongly tinged olive. Imm. ♂: like ♀ but with yellow forecrown and *wedge-shaped blackish mask*, sometimes also with a little black on wings. In hand, cutting edge of upper mandible *and* tip of lower mandible slightly recurved.
Sim. species: In most of range only dark-backed ♂ euphonia with *all-yellow underparts* (not black throat). In ne cf. ♂ Violaceous Euphonia which has smaller yellow forehead patch and rich orange yellow throat and chest. ♀ Violaceous *prob. inseparable* from ♀ Thick-

billed in field but above darker olive yellow and below more uniform olive yellow (range overlap minimal); ♀ told from ♀ Trinidad Euphonia by yellow (not gray) median underparts and larger size; ♀ Orange-bellied Euphonia has orange or yellow forehead, gray nape, and mostly buffy gray underparts with contrasting yellow olive sides; ♀ White-vented Euphonia has white lower underparts. *With all ♀ euphonias, always look for accompanying ♂.*
Voice: Both sexes, but esp. ♂♂, give wide variety of calls, incl. loud, sharp, whistled *preet!*, harsh, buzzy rattle, *tzi'i'i'i'i't*, and many semimusical phrases; also an excellent mimic with wide repertoire, esp. of alarm and contact notes[416,529]. Song a long rambling ser. of original and mimicked notes of other birds.
Behavior: Single birds or prs. wander alone or at various times assoc. with mixed-spp. flocks or groups of other euphonias. Forage from mid. hts. to tree crown, most often rather high, for small fruits, esp. mistletoe. Globular side entrance nest typical of genus; 2–4 white eggs thickly speckled reddish brown[750].
Status and habitat: Fairly common resident in woodlots, clearings with trees, forest borders, gallery forest, second-growth woodland, plantations, cultivated areas, and trees around habitation. Relatively dry to humid regions.

Range: To 1900m. Sierra de Perijá, Zulia, base and both slopes of Andes from s Táchira to nw Lara, c and e Falcón, and generally in hills and mts. from Yaracuy to Sucre and n Monagas; s locally to c Apure, and Guárico at Hato Masaguaral (*crassirostris*). Costa Rica to e Bolivia and c Brazil; Trinidad.

Violaceous Euphonia   PLATE 61
Euphonia violacea   Curruñatá Capa Negra
Identification: 4.5″ (11.4cm). 14g. This sp. and Thick-billed Euphonia are *only ♂ euphonias in Venez. with no black on throat.* ♂: forehead yellow (does not quite extend back to eyes), sides of head and upperparts steely blue black, *below entirely deep buttery yellow* (orange yellow on throat and chest), belly yellow; undertail as in Thick-billed Euphonia. ♀: *above uniform dark olive green,* below mostly olive yellow, central throat and breast yellowish turning deep yellow on center of lower underparts.
Sim. species: See Thick-billed Euphonia which may overlap in Sucre and n Monagas. Identification of ♀ (in absence of ♂) can be tricky. *Absolutely uniform upperparts* (no yellowish on forecrown) and absence of any gray eliminate several ♀ euphonias (Orange-bellied, Purple-throated, White-lored, and Plumbe-

ous), and absence of white or rufous belly eliminates White-vented and Rufous-bellied. ♀ nearly identical to ♀ Thick-billed but latter has less olive tinge on underparts.
Voice: Song a spluttering, rambling ser. of relatively distinct phrases that alternate abruptly between buzzy trills, chattery notes, musical or harsh notes, and imitations of other birds. Buzzes, chattery notes, and short trills are characteristic.
Behavior: Sim. to other *Euphonia*. Generally forages fairly high. Eats by gulping or mashing, mostly small berries incl. mistletoe, bromeliads, epiphytic cactus, and catkins of *Piper* and *Cecropia*. Single birds, prs., or small groups wander alone, occas. follow mixed-spp. flocks along forest borders, or join mixed groups of euphonias at mistletoe. One or several sometimes take prom. perch on high, open, bare twig or branch to rest. Nest typical of genus; 3–5 dull white eggs with various reddish markings at larger end[539].
Status and habitat: Common resident in canopy of humid forest, forest borders, second-growth woodland, shrubby clearings with taller trees, and trees around habitations.

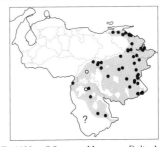

Range: To 1100m. S Sucre, e Monagas, Delta Amacuro, n and e Amazonas s to Río Ocamo (Misión Ocamo) and Cerro Duida; generally in Bolívar (*rodwayi*). Guianas s across e Amaz. Brazil to e Paraguay, ne Argentina, and se Brazil. Trinidad.
Note: Subsp. *rodwayi* prob. synonymous with *violacea.*

Orange-bellied Euphonia   PLATE 61
Euphonia xanthogaster   Curruñatá Azulejo
Identification: 4.3″ (10.9cm). 13g. ♂: *forecrown to just behind eyes rufous chestnut;* rest of head, throat, and upperparts steely blue black; *below deep orange yellow;* inner web of outer pr. of tail feathers white, next pr. with white oval on inner web. Or *forecrown deep chestnut;* underparts darker, stained "burnt" orange (*badissima*); or *forecrown yellow faintly tinged rufous* (*brevirostris*). ♀: *forecrown chestnut, hindcrown gray contrasting with dark olive back;* throat and chest dingy olive gray turning buffy clay on lower underparts; sides and flanks tinged olive yellow. Or throat and chest more yellowish olive (*brevirostris*).
Sim. species: ♂♂ of races with chestnut forecrown are easily told. Others most like ♂ Purple-throated Euphonia but dark orange yellow (not bright yellow) below. Also cf. ♂ Trinidad Euphonia. ♀ told from any other ♀ by combination of some rufous on forecrown (all races) and distinctive gray nape.

Voice: Call a nasal, gravelly *nay nay* or complaining *chee dee* (2–4 notes); song a rambling disconnected *deeu deeu . . . deet deet deet . . . jew jew . . . chu chu chu . . . jew, ju-du-du-du . . .* and so on. Elsewhere in broad range (outside Venez.) has several rather different vocalizations (and some forms may be separate spp.).

Behavior: Prs. or families follow canopy or understory mixed-spp. flocks, esp. those that contain other fruit-eating birds. Also join groups of birds at fruiting trees. Eat mostly fruit, esp. berries of *Miconia* spp., fruits of arums (Araceae), mistletoe, *Cecropia*, and many small fruits taken from understory to canopy, but more often at low to moderate hts. Occas. sally or hover to capture insects and spiders from webs. Nest typical of genus; 4 eggs, cream color with dark spots[482]. In w Colombia, breeding Nov–Apr.

Status and habitat: Common resident in humid and wet forest (esp. cloud forest), forest borders, and second-growth woodland.

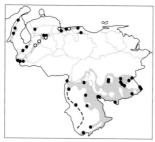

Range: 350–2250m (mostly 900–1800m). Sierra de Perijá, Zulia; Andes of s Táchira, Mérida, nw Barinas, Trujillo, and Lara (*badissima*); n cordilleras from Carabobo (prob. Yaracuy) e to Dist. Federal and Miranda (*exsul*); generally on most cerros of Amazonas; cerros of Bolívar from upper Río Caura (Maniña; Cerro Taracuniña), mid. Río Paragua (Cerro Guaiquinima), Auyán-tepui, and upper Río Cuyuní (Sierra de Lema) southward (*brevirostris*). E Panama s in Andes to Bolivia; lowlands of w Amazonia e to Guyana; se Brazil.
Note: Subsp. *lecroyana*[19] synonymous with *badissima*[559].

White-vented Euphonia   PLATE 61
Euphonia minuta   Curruñatá Menudito
Identification: 3.7″ (9.4cm). 10g. *Small.* ♂: patch on forehead yellow (does not extend back to eyes); rest of head, throat, and upperparts steely blue black; below bright yellow, central belly and *under tail coverts white*; inner web of outer 3 prs. of tail feathers mostly white. ♀: above entirely yellow olive, *throat gray* sharply contrasting with bright olive yellow breast, sides, and flanks; *center of lower underparts grayish white*.
Sim. species: Either sex from all other *Euphonia* by white or mostly white belly and under tail coverts. Note small size and ♂'s small yellow forehead patch.
Voice: Call a single (usually) sharp *veet*, also a sputtery *wee-chu*. Song is surprisingly loud and forceful, a shrill, semipatterned ser. of sharp and staccato notes, *tu VEEVEET, ch VEET, cheewit, chewit, . . . VEET . . . ch-VEET, tsik, veEE, vic-squik, veEE, squik-squik, veEE . . .*

and so on, the loud *VEET* and *veEE* notes characteristic; may repeat same phrase several times.
Behavior: A bird of rain forest canopy and treetops. Single birds, prs., or little groups, sometimes composed mostly of ♂ ♂ or mostly ♀-plumaged birds, follow mixed-spp. flocks or spend long periods of time in large clumps of high mistletoe. May wander over large areas. Eat mostly fruit, esp. mistletoe, and a few insects. Often wag or twitch partly spread tail to side. Nest in Costa Rica 3–18m up; a mossy ball with side entrance; in epiphytes or on mossy limb; 3–5 white eggs blotched and spotted brown[651].
Status and habitat: Fairly common resident but sometimes hard to identify (remains so high in forest) in humid lowland terra firme and várzea forest and along forest borders and scattered giant trees in clearings.

Range: To 500m n of Orinoco; to 900m s of Orinoco. Se base of Andes in Táchira (Burgua); e Sucre (Guanoco) s to Delta Amacuro; throughout Amazonas; Bolívar from lower Río Caura, Río Paragua, and Sierra de Imataca (Río Grande) southward (*minuta*). S Mexico s locally to e Bolivia, Amaz. Brazil, and the Guianas.

Trinidad Euphonia   PLATE 61
Euphonia trinitatis   Curruñatá Saucito
Identification: 3.8″ (9.7cm). 11g. Small. ♂: *prom. yellow forecrown patch extends well behind eyes*; rest of head, throat, and upperparts steely blue black; below bright yellow *incl. under tail coverts*; inner web of outer 2 tail feathers mostly white (except tip). ♀: above olive; throat, belly, and under tail coverts dull yellow, *breast and upper belly light gray*, sides tinged yellowish olive. Imm.: forecrown yellow, upperparts olive; below like ad. ♂ but much duller, throat often mottled with black.
Sim. species: Over most of range ♂ easily told by large yellow crown patch, *dark throat* (cf. Thick-billed and Violaceous euphonias), and *all-bright-yellow* lower underparts. ♂ Orange-bellied Euphonia has rufous forehead and darker underparts. Good marks for ♀ are small size (Thick-billed and Violaceous both larger and heavier-billed) and light gray on center of breast and belly. ♀ Trinidad lacks gray nape of ♀ Orange-bellied. S of Orinoco and se base of Andes meets nearly identical Purple-throated Euphonia (see).
Voice: Notably vocal but sometimes difficult to locate. Commonest calls are a clear, whistled *tee, dee* (on same pitch) and *duu-dee* (1st note lower), both virtually identical to those of Purple-throated Euphonia. Song a short jumble of musical and scratchy unmusical notes mostly unaccented. Song and calls often alternated[274].

Behavior: Often seen in prs. or little groups of 3–8 of varying composition, sometimes mostly ♂♂, sometimes mostly ♀-plumaged birds. Wander widely, feed on many small fruits and berries, esp. mistletoe berries, also glean small insects from twigs, spiderwebs, etc. Perch on high, bare, semiexposed branches to call. Usually independent of mixed-spp. flocks. Nest typical of genus; 1.4–12m up; 3–4 eggs pale cream or white marked with brown[175]; Apr nest, Orinoco area[115].
Status and habitat: Common resident in dry to moist forest, gallery forest, light woodland, forest borders, partially cleared or cultivated areas, and scrubby vegetation. Locally into humid regions along s border of range where meets and is replaced by Purple-throated Euphonia. Highest el recs. are sightings at 1200m in Sierra de San Luis, Falcón, 1992 (J. Pierson); and 1450m, San José de Los Altos, Miranda, Aug–Sep 1999 (G. Rodríguez).

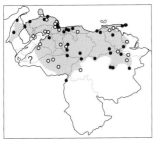

Range: To 600m (sight to 1450m) n of Orinoco; to 300m s of Orinoco. Throughout n of Orinoco; n Amazonas s to vicinity of Pto. Ayacucho; n Bolívar s to lower Río Caura, Río Paragua (La Paragua), and El Dorado. N Colombia; Trinidad.
Note: Possibly not a distinct sp. from Purple-throated Euphonia, but the two have apparently been taken at same loc. in several places (see Note below).

Purple-throated Euphonia
PLATE 61
Euphonia chlorotica   Curruñatá Azuquero
Identification: 4″ (10.2cm). 11g. *Virtually identical to slightly smaller Trinidad Euphonia*. ♂: glossed purplish (rather than bluish) on upperparts and throat, and yellow of crown slightly less extensive, extending to just behind eyes. ♀: very like ♀ Trinidad Euphonia, and prob. not separable in field, but upperparts olive with *faint grayish tinge*; median underparts perhaps slightly less extensively gray. Imms. of both spp. are dull greenish yellow below and prob. inseparable. Generally the two are best told by their mostly separate ranges which meet or overlap only slightly (as far as presently known) mostly just s of Orinoco.
Sim. species: Aside from ♂ Trinidad, ♂ likely confused only with ♂ of rare Finsch's Euphonia which is darker and burnt orange below. All other ♀ euphonias s of Orinoco have gray or white somewhere on head or underparts, except larger ♀ Violaceous.
Voice: Commonest call a plaintive, whistled *tee, dee*, 2d note on same pitch or slightly higher and essentially identical to that of Trinidad Euphonia. When excited a rising, whistled *wheeet!*
Behavior: Much as in Trinidad Euphonia.

Status and habitat: Fairly common resident of relatively seasonal moist forest (n Bolívar), humid forest, wooded borders, and gallery forest. Also scrubby savanna woodland in white sandy soil areas. Overall favors more humid and heavily forested regions than allied Trinidad Euphonia.

Range: To 300m n of Orinoco; to 900m s of Orinoco. Se base of Andes in Táchira (Santo Domingo) and w Apure (Guasdualito); generally s of Orinoco in Amazonas and Bolívar (*cynophora*)[467]; possibly Caicara de Maturín, Monagas[186]. E Colombia s to n Argentina (absent from much of Amazon Basin).
Note: Perhaps not a sp. distinct from Trinidad Euphonia[544]. Specimens of both taken in se Táchira and w Apure; at or near Pto. Ayacucho (incl. Caño Cataniapo), Amazonas; and at Caicara, Bolívar.

Finsch's Euphonia
PLATE 61
Euphonia finschi   Curruñatá Guayanés
Identification: 4″ (10.2cm). 10–11g. ♂: *yellow forecrown patch extends just to eyes*; rest of head, throat, and upperparts steely blue black; *base of inner webs of flight feathers white* (prom. in flight); *breast and lower underparts rich burnt orange* (darkest from mid. breast to belly); *no white in tail*. ♀: above olive, *forecrown slightly yellowish*, faint dusky area through eye; *below entirely olive yellow* becoming plain yellow on center of belly. In hand, bill rather short and thin for genus.
Sim. species: ♂ much like ♂ Purple-throated Euphonia but underparts are dark ochraceous orange; in flight *note white in wing* (like "white propeller"). ♀ very like ♀ Violaceous Euphonia but smaller and thinner-billed. ♀ from ♀ Purple-throated by yellowish forecrown; from ♀ Trinidad by absence of gray on underparts. Look for accompanying ♂♂.
Voice: Call a clear, whistled *dee-dee* (2–4 notes), much like Purple-throated and Trinidad euphonias but given a bit more slowly. Also a plaintive *beeee*.
Behavior: Prs. or little groups (families?), often consisting of several ♀-plumaged birds and 1 ad. ♂, are active as wander along gallery-forest borders and call and chatter from treetops, or fly off swiftly in bounding flight to visit distant fruiting trees and shrubs. As in many others of genus, 1 or several often perch together on high, bare twigs and call. Noted eating mistletoe berries.
Status and habitat: Known from 1 specimen in extreme se Venez. (1200m) at Arabopó near Cerro Roraima; relatively common e in the Guianas. Sight recs. of 4 birds seen and tape-recorded 28 Feb 1994 and 18 Feb 1995 and early Mar 1998 ca. 16km ne of Santa Elena de Uairén (900m)[259].

Range: 900–1200m. Se Bolívar near Santa Elena de Uairén. N Brazil (n Roraima), c Guyana, Suriname, and French Guiana.

Rufous-bellied Euphonia   PLATE 61
Euphonia rufiventris   Fruterito Vientre Rufo
Identification: 4.5″ (11.4cm). 14g. Rather heavy bill. ♂: *has no yellow on head*; entire upperparts, head, throat, and chest steely blue black; *lower breast and belly deep tawny rufous*; small inconspic. yellowish patch on sides of chest; no white in tail. ♀: dark olive above with grayish nape; median underparts gray; chin, sides of throat, and breast olive yellow; *belly and under tail coverts dark rufous*.
Sim. species: ♂'s all-dark head and dark rufous belly are diagnostic. ♀ from any other ♀ euphonia in Venez. by dark rufous lower underparts.
Voice: Often hd. call a low-pitched, harsh rattle, *j'a'a'a'a, j'a'a'a'a, j'a'a'a'a* (2–6 notes), with gravelly quality. At a distance might be mistaken for a cicada. Possible duet song is reported[274].
Behavior: Prs. wander alone or follow mixed-spp. flocks in forest canopy and high in emergent trees. Feed heavily on mistletoe berries and fruits of bromeliads and other epiphytes but only infreq. assoc. with other euphonias at mistletoe. Typically mash fruit before swallowing.
Status and habitat: Common resident but easily overlooked except for voice. Tall humid forest, occas. along forest borders.

Range: To 1100m. Throughout Amazonas; Bolívar from lower Río Caura, mid. Río Paragua, and Sierra de Imataca (sight, Río Grande) southward (*carnegiei*)[154]. Se Colombia to e Bolivia and w and c Amaz. Brazil.

Golden-sided Euphonia   PLATE 61
Euphonia cayennensis   Fruterito de Hombros Dorados
Identification: 4.5″ (11.4cm). 13.5g. ♂: all glossy, steely blue black with usually *conspic. golden yellow*

pectoral tuft (sometimes stained rufous). ♀: above dark olive green, crown tinged brown, chin, sides of throat, sides of breast, and flanks olive yellow, center of throat and breast gray, *belly and under tail coverts gray*.
Sim. species: Striking ♂ unique. ♀ much like ♀ Rufous-bellied Euphonia but lower underparts grayish (not dark rufous). ♀ is only euphonia with *all of central underparts* gray.
Voice: Call almost identical to that of Rufous-bellied Euphonia, a low, harsh, and gravelly *j'a'a'a'a*, repeated 2–6 times, sometimes quickly. Also gives longer, buzzy rattle, *bjjjjjjjjjjjjjjjjjjjjjjj*, ca. 2 sec; and higher, softer, and nasal *ruee-e-et* run together, rather like that of several other *Euphonia*. Possible duet of whistles is reported[274].
Behavior: Sim. to that of Rufous-bellied Euphonia. Usually seen singly or in prs. that wander alone, assoc. with other euphonias or with mixed-spp. flocks in canopy or upper levels of rain forest. Occas. drops quite low. Often slowly twitches tail to one side, or side to side. Nests in Brazil are domed and typical of genus; often low; also remodel abandoned nests of other spp.; 3–5 eggs, whitish with a few red spots[660].
Status and habitat: Rather few recs. Resident in humid forest, along forest borders, and in savanna woodland. Distrib. spotty in Venez. Found with some freq. in vicinity of Río Grande.

Range: To 1100m. Ne Bolívar from Sierra de Imataca (Río Grande) s to Auyán-tepui, and Cerro Roraima. The Guianas and ne Brazil.

Plumbeous Euphonia   PLATE 61
Euphonia plumbea   Fruterito Plomizo
Identification: 3.8″ (9.7cm). 9 g. Rather dull plumaged. ♂: *has no yellow on forehead*; entire upperparts, head, throat, and chest bluish gray; mid. breast to crissum rich cadium yellow, sides and flanks mottled blue gray. ♀: *pattern sim. to* ♂ but head dull gray, rest of upperparts dark olive, throat and chest pale gray, lower underparts olive yellow, brightest on center of breast and belly.
Sim. species: Pattern of ♂ recalls that of Rufous-bellied Euphonia but latter much darker (dark steel blue, not grayish) above and darker below. ♀ is nearest ♀ White-lored Euphonia but lacks white loral patch and has gray chest. Also see ♀ White-vented Euphonia.
Voice: Commonest call a high, clear *dee-dee* or *dee, dee-dee*, with notes on same pitch; much like that of Trinidad and Purple-throated euphonias but 1st note of those 2 spp. often lower pitched. Song in n Amazonas a squeaky, jumbled *o'fiddle-de-wEET!*, uttered

quickly; song (P. Schwartz recording) *WEET sweeta-swee-swee*, jumbled and often mixed with call notes[274].
Behavior: Usually seen in prs., occas. small groups or families, also with other euphonias, in tops of bushes and trees. Feed on small fruits and berries and often fly off swiftly across open savanna to distant trees or shrubs.
Status and habitat: Uncommon to locally common resident in scrubby open woodland, savanna forest borders, bushes in savanna, and scrub vegetation around edges of large rock outcrops in white sandy soil regions. Occas. in borders of tall humid forest. May wander over large areas and is somewhat erratic and unpredictable (seasonal?) in occurrence.

Range: To 1000m. Amazonas (vicinity of Río Ventuari) southward; spottily (patches of savanna) across c, s and ne Bolívar. N Brazil (Rio Negro; Amapá), Guyana; Suriname; French Guiana (once).

White-lored Euphonia
PLATE 61
Euphonia chrysopasta   Fruterito de Lores Blancos
Identification: 4.5″ (11.4cm). 14g. *Bill rather thick* and grayish, lower mandible slightly upturned. ♂: looks ♀-plumaged; above bronzy olive with *strong blue gray tinge* ("powdery" look); *oval-shaped white loral patch, white chin*, and white narrowly across frontlet; below olive yellow becoming clear yellow on center of belly. ♀: above much like ♂, incl. whitish loral area; crown and nape grayer, sides of head yellowish olive, *underparts mostly gray*, sides, flanks, and under tail coverts yellow olive.
Sim. species: Dull plumaged but nonetheless distinctive with whitish loral patch. Despite its old name (see Note), belly not in strong contrast to rest of underparts. ♀ grayer below than others of genus. Up close note thickish, slightly "crooked-looking" bill ("crooked" grin). Cf. ♀ Golden-sided and Rufous-bellied euphonias.
Voice: Commonest call *spitz wéet!* over and over, and sharp, smacking *spitz!*; ♂'s jumbled song of *chit, sit, spitz, wéek*, and other notes sputters on, e.g., *P-pfits'et cheéu . . sit, fits . . pa'fits-a-whew!* . . . , some songs more or less patterned. ♂ sings from high bare twig in open.
Behavior: Single birds, prs., or little gangs of 6 or so are often chatty and noisy as feed or loaf in high clumps of mistletoe or in fruiting trees. Irreg. also with canopy mixed-spp. flocks where stay quite high and often search slender bare twigs for insects. Infreq. descend low along forest borders to fruiting shrubs. ♂♂ spread and twitch tail to one side, and sometimes pump rear body up and down while singing. Football-shaped, side-entrance nest typical of genus; 5–10m up.

Status and habitat: Common resident in canopy and at borders of tall humid terra firme and várzea forest, esp. where there are large clumps of canopy mistletoe; also in scattered trees in clearings.

Range: To 900m. Throughout Amazonas, Bolívar incl. Sierra de Imataca, and s Delta Amacuro (*nitida*). Se Colombia to n Bolivia, Amaz. Brazil, and the Guianas.
Note: Earlier called Golden-bellied Euphonia[403].

Chlorophonia

Plumper and shorter-tailed than *Euphonia*; bill short, broadening at base; plumage mostly bright emerald green, dense and glistening on head; frugivorous; stomach rudimentary; mostly montane; often remain hidden in foliage, hence less conspic. than *Euphonia*; large mossy globular nest with side-entrance hole; young fed by regurgitation; almost certainly not tanagers, and represent either separate lineage or are closely related to cardueline finches[299].

Blue-naped Chlorophonia
PLATE 60
Chlorophonia cyanea   Verdín Montañero
Identification: 4.5″ (11.4cm). 14.5g. ♂: *entire head, throat, and chest bright emerald green, sharply separated from yellow breast and lower underparts*; narrow frontlet yellow, *ocular ring blue, broad nuchal collar blue*, otherwise green above; *rump bright blue*. Or back mixed blue (*roraimae*). Or no yellow forehead, back mixed blue (*longipennis*). ♀: duller; forehead yellowish, no blue ocular ring; blue nuchal collar like ♂ but rump green like back; green throat merges into olive yellow breast and belly. Or no yellow on forehead (*longipennis*).
Sim. species: Other ♂ chlorophonias and euphonias have yellow (not blue) rumps. Look for ♂'s blue eyering and nape. ♀ rather like ♀ Chestnut-breasted Chlorophonia but crown green (not dark blue). ♀ smaller and brighter green than imm. Bay-headed and Rufous-cheeked tanagers.
Voice: Often gives low *chaak* and soft, pleading *pleee* when foraging or before flight (latter much like that of Golden-rumped Euphonia); also a nasal *peent* and short, gravelly rattle.
Behavior: These dainty, jewel-like birdlets occur in prs. or more often timid little groups of 3–12. Often act sluggish and spend long periods of time sitting in clumps of fruiting mistletoe high in canopy. Ads. eat almost entirely fruit, esp. mistletoe berries, and are sometimes with mixed-spp. flocks containing *Tangara*, or with feeding aggregations of birds in fruiting trees where they gorge on tiny *Miconia* spp. (Melastomataceae) berries.

Status and habitat: Uncommon to fairly common resident but easily overlooked because of soft calls and habit of not moving around much. Humid and wet forest, forest borders, tall second-growth woodland, and scattered trees with mistletoe in highland pastures. Some seasonal or irreg. movements occur.

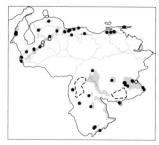

Range: 700–2500m n of Orinoco; 500–1800m s of Orinoco. Sierra de Perijá, Zulia; Andes from s Táchira to s Lara (*longipennis*); cerros of nw Lara (Cerro El Cogollal); mts. of c Falcón, Yaracuy, and cordilleras e to Distr. Federal and se Miranda (*frontalis*); ne Anzoátegui, Sucre, and n Monagas (*minuscula*); throughout cerros of Amazonas and Bolívar (*roraimae*). Andes from Colombia to Bolivia; tepuis of Venez. and Guyana; e Paraguay, ne Argentina, and se Brazil.

Chestnut-breasted Chlorophonia   PLATE 60
Chlorophonia pyrrhophrys   Verdín Vientre Castaño
Identification: 4.6″ (11.7cm). 17g. ♂: colorful; *crown deep blue* bordered by short black line behind eye and cobalt blue nape band; rest of upperparts rich mossy green, rump bright yellow, frontlet, *sides of head, throat, and chest bright emerald green* bordered below by narrow black line; *broad chestnut median stripe from mid. breast to under tail coverts*; sides and flanks yellow. ♀: pattern recalls that of ♂, *incl. blue crown*, but lacks yellow rump; green foreparts duller; lower underparts predom. olive yellow. Bill wider and deeper than in Blue-naped Chlorophonia.
Sim. species: ♂ shares blue crown and yellow rump with Golden-rumped Euphonia, but plumage otherwise very different. ♀ recalls ♀ Golden-rumped Euphonia (see). Also cf. Blue-naped Chlorophonia.
Voice: Commonest call a soft, nasal *neck-nuur* over and over. Song a long, rambling *tut-tut-tut too-dée too-dée . . .* or *na-deár, na-deár . . . to-d'leép*, with variations (P. Schwartz recording); contact note a nasal, downslurred whistle, *teeeur*, sweet but penetrating in quality (like that of Venezuelan Tyrannulet and Golden-rumped Euphonia).
Behavior: Prs. or small groups occur mainly in canopy or upper levels of epiphyte-laden trees in highland forests, mostly alone but occas. with mixed-spp. flocks. Feed mostly on berries of mistletoe, often spending long periods of time in large epiphytic clumps; also eat berries of Ericaceae and occas. peer at twigs, epiphytes, and moss for small insects. Nest typical of genus; 1 was 6m up on roadbank (unusual site?) in Mar (R. Ridgely). Young fed by regurgitation as in other *Chlorophonia*.
Status and habitat: Uncommon and somewhat local resident. Tall epiphyte-burdened montane forest

(cloud forest), forest borders, and older second growth. Reg. found at lower els. in PN Guaramacal, Trujillo, and Mucuy entrance to PN Sierra Nevada, Mérida.

Range: 1800–3000m. Sierra de Perijá, Zulia; Andes of Táchira, Mérida, and Trujillo n to Páramo Misisí. Andes from Colombia to c Peru.

Chlorochrysa

Rich glistening green plumage (♂♂); resemble allied *Tangara* and usually with them; differ in voice, behavior, heavier tarsus (often hang upside down), and longer, proportionately thinner bill; sexes also obviously different, unlike *Tangara*.

[Orange-eared Tanager]   PLATE 58
Chlorochrysa calliparaea   Tangara Orejianaranja
Identification: 5″ (12.7cm). 17g. Known only from sight records. ♂: *shining emerald green* above with small orange crown spot and *orange rump band*; throat *black with prom. dark orange spot on sides of neck (the "ears")*; breast and sides rich emerald green, central lower underparts blue green; black bases to green feathers often showing through here and there. ♀: sim. but *much duller* with dull grayish throat; smaller dark orange spot on neck.
Sim. species: With good look, ♂ not likely confused. Look for dark throat and orange neck spot; rump band often noticeable in flight. ♀ more likely confused; look for gray throat and *orange rump band*; also cf. ♀ with other mostly "green" Andean spp. incl. ♀ Green Honeycreeper, imm. Bay-headed Tanager, ♀ Swallow Tanager, and ♀ chlorophonias.
Voice: Call a high-pitched, wheezy *seeep*.
Behavior: Stunning emerald of this bird is not often seen to full advantage. Single birds, prs., or families of 3 are persistent members of mixed-spp. flocks with other tanagers where they forage from lower mid. levels to subcanopy. Active and fast moving; forage mostly by peering at undersides of leaves, either by reaching up, stretching, or hanging downward, or often by hanging from leaf tips in outer foliage. Eat small fruits but take proportionately fewer than allied *Tangara*, and overall faster moving and spend correspondingly more time searching for insects than *Tangara*.
Status and habitat: No specimens but many sight recs.: 1st seen 9 Jan 1987, San Isidro Rd., nw Barinas[259]; subsequently seen by many observers. No other Venez. recs. but surely more widespread within narrow el. band. Resident in wet forest (cloud forest) and forest edge.

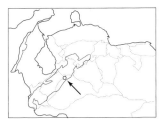

Range: 1450m (900–1800m in Colombia). Nw Barinas (prob. *bourcieri*). Colombia (upper Magdalena Valley; e slope of E Andes from w Caquetá southward) s to n Bolivia.

Tangara

Large, widespread genus (most spp. of any genus on continent); typically colorful and complex plumage patterns; forest canopy and edge; partially frugivorous; feed heavily on berries of melastomes (esp. *Miconia*) and *Cecropia*; up to 8–9 may coexist sympatrically; niche partitioning is mainly by different insect-searching techniques. Sp. diversity often high in lowland rain forest but even higher in Andes; replaced at very high els. by larger *Anisognathus*, *Iridosornis*, and *Buthraupis*. Vocal efforts minimal; weak songs infreq. hd., undescribed in some spp.; most prob. breed in rainy season, late Apr–Oct in Venez.

Golden Tanager   PLATE 60
Tangara arthus   Tangara Dorada
Identification: 5.2″ (13.2cm). 22g. Two very different races in Venez. *Head golden yellow* with narrow black area surrounding bill and black *"trapezoid-shaped" patch on ear coverts*; otherwise golden yellow above; back streaked black, wings and tail black, flight feathers edged green, underparts yellow, *broad chestnut band across breast and down sides to under tail coverts* (*arthus*). Or sim. but *all golden yellow below* (no chestnut), yellow slightly paler (*aurulenta*).
Sim. species: Not likely confused if seen well. Cf. Saffron-crowned Tanager; in s Táchira see Flame-faced Tanager.
Voice: Freq. a slightly buzzy *seet* while foraging; also staccato chipping notes.
Behavior: A speedy little "golden" bird of cloud forests. Behavior is typical of the group of *Tangara* that forage by quickly and systematically working along branches, leaning over and peering "head down," first on one side then on other, to check sides and under surfaces of branches for insects. Progress outward along branches in little spurts and pauses, then seem to quickly lose interest and move on. This sp. gleans insects mostly from partly mossy branches (usually not twigs or foliage) at mid.-level to canopy hts. in interior of trees. Also occas. hangs from vines to search bark or moss substrates. About half of diet is fruit, esp. berries of melastomes, and single birds, prs., or up to nearly 12 may be with mixed-spp. flocks or temporary feeding aggregations at fruiting trees. One breeding rec. in Mar; in Colombia, breeding Apr–Oct[260].

Status and habitat: Common resident in humid and wet forest (cloud forest) and forest borders. No recs. (?) in s Táchira yet.

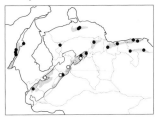

Range: 700–2000m. Sierra de Perijá, Zulia (*aurulenta*); s Táchira (subsp. *sclateri?*); both slopes of Andes from n Táchira to cerros of nw Lara, mts. of Yaracuy and Falcón (Sierra de San Luis), and n cordilleras from Carabobo to Miranda (*arthus*). Colombia s in Andes to n Bolivia.

Saffron-crowned Tanager   PLATE 60
Tangara xanthocephala   Tangara Corona Amarilla
Identification: 5.2″ (13.2cm). 19g. "Wears a golden helmet." *Entire crown, nape, and sides of head glistening golden yellow*, throat and small mask black; inconspic. nuchal collar black, *body mostly glistening opalescent blue green* (color varies with light), back streaked black, wings and tail black edged bluish green, *center of breast and lower underparts buffy cinnamon*. Juv.: mostly dingy grayish; yellow of head faintly indicated.
Sim. species: Over most of range yellow head and bluish body should be diagnostic, but cf. sim. head patterns of Golden and Flame-faced tanagers.
Voice: Contact note when foraging a high *tsit*, when excited a rapid stream of *tsit* notes. Song (?) a short ser. of high squeaky notes.
Behavior: Like many others of genus, may be seen singly, in prs., or in groups up to 10 or so and usually with mixed-spp. flocks containing other *Tangara*. All of them often feed in fruiting trees, esp. melastomes (*Miconia* spp.) and *Cecropia* trees. When searching for insects, behavior is typical of *Tangara* that forage by peering "head down," first along one side of branch then along other. Customarily stay well out on smaller, mostly bare branches, even onto twigs, less often in leafy terminal foliage except to eat berries. Usually stay high and more along forest borders and in tall second growth than inside forest.
Status and habitat: Fairly common resident in humid and wet montane forest (cloud forest), forest edges, and second-growth woodland. Most numerous in upper half of el. range where reg. assoc. with Beryl-spangled, Golden, and Black-capped tanagers.

Range: 1800–2300m (sightings to 1450m). Sierra de Perijá, Zulia; Andes from s Táchira n to s Lara (*venusta*). Colombia s in Andes to Bolivia.

Flame-faced Tanager   PLATE 60
Tangara parzudakii   Tangara Cara de Fuego
Identification: 5.5″ (14cm). 28g. Only in s Táchira. Lores, ocular area, throat, and broad bar extending back from bottom of throat to ear coverts black; *forecrown and cheeks red orange*, hindcrown, nape, and sides of neck glistening yellow, *back, wings, and tail black, shoulders, rump, and underparts glistening silvery opalescent green*; center of belly and under tail coverts cinnamon buff.
Sim. species: Pattern confusingly like Saffron-crowned Tanager, but they barely overlap in Venez. Key marks are red face, black back, and opal on shoulders and underparts.
Voice: *Seeet* call rather like that of Golden Tanager; also a high, sharp chittering.
Behavior: Much like Golden Tanager but forages for insects on mossier limbs. Moves outward quickly and systematically along inner branches, leaning down first on one side then on other to inspect moss and lichens, esp. hanging clumps, but seldom searches leaves. Sometimes also hangs upside down for several sec to check moss clumps. Usually with canopy mixed-spp. flocks that contain other *Tangara* tanagers, and like them, eats a wide variety of small fruits and berries.
Status and habitat: Resident in wet montane forest (cloud forest), also forest borders and tall second growth. Few recs. in Venez. where occurs at northernmost tip of range.

Range: 1900m (mostly 1600–2500m in Colombia). S Táchira (Hacienda La Providencia in upper Río Chiquito) (*parzudakii*). Colombia s in Andes to e Peru.

Rufous-cheeked Tanager   PLATE 60
Tangara rufigenis   Tangara Mejillas Rufas
Identification: 5″ (12.7cm). 17.4g. Only in Coastal Cordillera. ♂: *lores and cheeks rufous* (form small mask), otherwise above mostly smoky bluish green (shining in good light), rump bluish, wings and tail blackish, wing coverts broadly edged blue green, flight feathers edged cinnamon brown; *underparts shining bluish green, center of belly and under tail coverts cinnamon rufous*. Imm.: much duller but usually with hint of rufous.
Sim. species: For a *Tangara* rather undistinguished. Rufous cheeks and rufous lower underparts are the marks. Imm. Bay-headed Tanager has brownish-tinged head. ♀ Black-headed Tanager has dusky crown and obscure chest streaking.

Behavior: A lively and active little bird that searches outer foliage like a Speckled Tanager. Single birds or prs., rarely up to ca. 8, follow mixed-spp. flocks containing other *Tangara*. Rapidly searches for insects by moving out along small terminal limbs and peering at twigs and esp. at foliage in restless, almost warblerlike fashion. Feeds heavily on small berries, esp. of melastomes. Mostly in mid. or upper levels of trees but descends to eye level at small fruiting trees along forest borders. Not an easy bird to observe at length.
Status and habitat: Uncommon resident in wet premontane and montane forest and along forest borders, esp. in disturbed or landslide areas where there is an abundance of melastome trees and shrubs (esp. *Miconia* spp.). May move downslope in rainy season (May–Sep?).

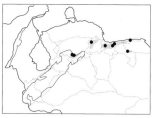

Range: ENDEMIC. 900–2050m. Andes of s Lara (El Tocuyo, Bucarito); mts. of Yaracuy, Coastal Cordillera from Carabobo to Distr. Federal (vicinity of Caracas), and Interior Cordillera in s Aragua (Cerro Golfo Triste).

Beryl-spangled Tanager   PLATE 60
Tangara nigroviridis   Tangara Mariposa
Identification: 5″ (12.7cm). 17.5g. Spotted and dappled. *Crown, nape, and cheeks bluish opal* (or greenish opal or yellowish opal depending on light), small but conspic. *black mask through eyes*; upper back black, rump pale turquoise, wing coverts and flight feathers edged dark blue, sides of neck and *underparts black spotted and dappled with opalescent blue*; belly opal. Or sim. but flight feathers edged bluish green, underparts slightly lighter and brighter blue (*lozanoana*). Juv.: dull brownish gray somewhat spotted dusky.
Sim. species: A dark, heavily spotted tanager that could be confused with ♂ Black-capped Tanager, although latter has black crown and only a little black scaling on chest.
Voice: High-pitched *sit* and *chit* notes, singly or in excited bursts, much like many others of genus. Song a high, thin *see, sit sit, see see, tzle'tzle'tzeet*, weak, easily overlooked, and not hd. often.
Behavior: Typical of group of *Tangara* that forage by peering "head down" along branches, but this sp. searches mostly very small, bare, outer branches and twigs, esp. those that hang down; occas. also examines moss tufts on twigs, even ends of bare twigs. Looks first on one side, then a hop or 2, and peers or hangs down beneath other side in highly stereotyped maneuver. When not checking beneath small dead twigs, likely to be seen foraging for berries in melastome trees (esp. *Miconia* spp.). Prs. or lively groups of 3–25, occas. even more, forage from eye level to canopy with mixed-spp. flocks that normally contain other *Tangara* spp.

Status and habitat: Commonest and most widespread *Tangara* in Venez. Resident in humid and wet montane forest and forest borders, shrubby second-growth woodland, and overgrown areas. Most numerous in shrubby edges and light woodland where fruiting melastome trees are abundant, esp. at ca. 1500–2200m.

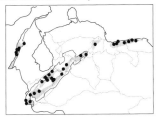

Range: 1250–2500m (a few recs. to 3000m). Sierra de Perijá, Zulia; Andes from s Táchira to se Lara (*lozanoana*); mts. of Yaracuy and Coastal Cordillera from Carabobo to Distr. Federal and Miranda at Hacienda Izcaragua (*cyanescens*). Andes of Colombia to n Bolivia.
Note: Subsp. *lozanoana*[19] differs little from *cyanescens*.

Blue-and-black Tanager
PLATE 60
Tangara vassorii   Tangara Piquirón
Identification: 5″ (12.7cm). 18g. Mostly dark blue. Bill unusually short for genus; eyes dark. ♂: *shining dark cobalt blue* with small black mask; *wings and tail black*, shoulders and single wing bar (inconspic.) dark cobalt blue. ♀: duller.
Sim. species: Looks very dark in field (dark blue does not contrast much with black) and can easily be confused with any of "blue" or "black" flowerpiercers. See esp. Masked, Bluish, Glossy, and Black flowerpiercers. Note Masked Flowerpiercer's hooked bill and red eyes. Also cf. ♂ Capped Conebill.
Voice: Infreq. hd. song a high, thin *tsiit, tsiit tsiit tsiit*, forceful but not loud. Also rapid *tsit* and *chip* notes while foraging.
Behavior: Prs. or lively groups of up to ca. 6 are usually seen with mixed-spp. flocks, esp. at fruiting melastome trees and shrubs, and almost always seem to be on the move. Insect foraging behavior not as stereotyped as in many others of genus. Typically hop and peer in outer foliage, mostly for fruit, or less often peer, with head down, underneath small bare limbs and twigs a few times, before rapidly moving on. Also occas. inspect leaves, small bromeliads, or hang upside down to examine various substrates. Diet prob. incl. much more fruit than insect matter.
Status and habitat: Fairly common resident in broken humid and wet montane forest, forest borders, and older melastome-dominated second growth in pas-

tures. No other *Tangara* is reg. found at els. as high as this sp., (commonest at 2200–2600m), and it normally assoc. with *Anisognathus*, *Diglossa*, and *Conirostrum* more than with other *Tangara*. Small seasonal el. movements likely.
Range: 1800–3200m (most recs. above 2000m). Andes of s Táchira n through Mérida to ne Trujillo on Páramos Cendé and Misisí (*vassorii*). Colombia s in mts. to Bolivia.

Black-capped Tanager
PLATE 60
Tangara heinei   Tangara Gorro Negro
Identification: 5.3″ (13.5cm). 19.4g. ♂: *crown and nape black*, rest of upperparts shining silvery gray blue, wings and tail darker; *sides of head, neck, and throat pale aquamarine*, feathers of chest dark-edged giving scaled or streaked effect; rest of underparts dull gray blue. ♀: dull and very different; crown dark greenish gray, *rest of upperparts pale green*, flight feathers blackish *broadly edged pale green* (forms patch of green on wing), *sides of head, throat, and chest pale silvery green*, chest somewhat streaked and freckled black, rest of underparts gray, flanks bright olive green.
Sim. species: ♂ is nearest Beryl-spangled Tanager (see). ♀ is "patchwork quilt" of generally subdued colors, and overall much like ♀ Black-headed Tanager; latter differs in blue-tinged (not pale green) wing edges, mottled gray (not silvery green) throat, and distinctly yellowish (not greenish) sides of lower underparts.
Voice: Song, given while perched or occas. in flight, a long (up to 10 sec), oddly mechanical-sounding and very fast *t'kling-t'kling-t'kling . . .* , not loud but with ringing quality (as if 2 birds are singing). One of few *Tangara* that sings freq.
Behavior: More of a "loner" than other *Tangara*. Single birds, prs., or families of 3–4 often wander alone, or may assoc. for short periods of time with mixed-spp. flocks or temporary feeding groups of tanagers in fruiting trees and shrubs. Eat much fruit, esp. melastome berries. Forage for insects with stereotypical movements of many *Tangara* (see Beryl-spangled Tanager) by leaning down to peer at sides of mainly horizontal and bare to partially mossy twigs and branches, but "lean-over" movements briefer, shallower, and overall less diligent. Also hop and peer in foliage, and occas. hang from vines. Nest a grassy cup decorated with moss; 1–2.3m up[274], prob. also higher; breeding Jan–Sep, Colombia[260].
Status and habitat: Uncommon to locally fairly common resident in humid and wet forest edges, shrubby clearings and pastures, and older second-growth woodland; usually not inside forest. Seldom very nu-

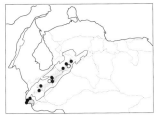

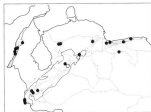

merous; some seasonal el. movements in Coastal Cordillera with birds occurring at lower els. (as low as 1000m at Rancho Grande Biol. Station, Aragua) during early months of rainy season.
Range: 1250–2800m (sightings to 1000m). Sierra de Perijá, Zulia, Andes from Táchira to mts. of se Lara (Cubiro) and nw Lara (Cerros El Cogollal and El Cerrón), mts. of Yaracuy and n cordilleras from Carabobo and n Guárico to Distr. Federal (no recs. in Miranda?). Andes of Colombia to n Ecuador.

Black-headed Tanager   PLATE 60
Tangara cyanoptera   Tangara Copino
Identification: 5.5″ (14cm). 18.5g. ♂: *head and throat black*, rest of body entirely shining yellowish to greenish opal, usually with faint dusky mottling on chest; wings and tail black, flight feathers heavily edged *deep blue* forming large patch (often hard to see in field). ♀: *crown, mantle, and shoulders gray blue*, lower back pale green, flight feathers narrowly edged blue green; *sides of head, and throat to mid. breast dingy white mottled gray, lower underparts pale yellow*, brightest on flanks. Or ♂ dull dark opalescent somewhat mottled with black below; *wings and tail solid black* (no edgings); ♀ darker above; rump and lower underparts yellower (*whitelyi*).
Sim. species: ♂ recalls ♂ Burnished-buff Tanager, but latter only has black mask (not entire head black). Drab ♀ is nearest ♀ Black-capped Tanager; also beware young Burnished-buff Tanagers which are rather featureless (hence like ♀ Black-headed).
Voice: High buzzy or lispy notes while foraging. Song (*cyanoptera*) a high, thin, *weeu weeu, weeu* (D. Ascanio).
Behavior: Usually seen singly or in prs. or families, infreq. more. Occur alone, with mixed-spp. flocks, and with various spp. at fruiting trees. Stay mainly in canopy or fairly high. Search for insects with rather generalized behavior that incl. hopping quickly and peering at foliage and twigs, brief flutters or lunges, and occas. rather shallow "lean-down" movements to check sides of branches or tufts of *Usnea*. Overall a bit of a dilettante at insect foraging. Open cup nest, 10m up, Feb, PN Guaramacal, Trujillo.
Status and habitat: Uncommon to locally fairly common resident in moist to moderately humid woodland, mainly along open borders, scattered trees in clearings, plantations, and lighter woodland. S of Orinoco in humid and wet forest, and stunted, mossy, melastome-dominated second growth on tepuis (not lowlands).

Range: 450–2200m (mostly above 800m) n of Orinoco; 1100–2250m s of Orinoco. Sierra de Perijá, Zulia; Andes from Táchira to nw Lara (Cerro El Cerrón), mts. of Falcón and Yaracuy, and n cordilleras e to Sucre and n Monagas (*cyanoptera*); cerros of Amazonas (Parú, Yavi, and Sipapo s to Duida and de la Neblina), sw Bolívar (Cerro Jaua; Sarisariñama); tepuis of se Bolívar from Auyán-tepui and Sierra de Lema southward (*whitelyi*). N Colombia; mts. of adj. n Brazil and w Guyana.
Note: The 2 forms may be separate spp.

Burnished-buff Tanager   PLATE 60
Tangara cayana   Tangara Monjita
Identification: 5.5″ (14cm). 19g. *Plumage color varies with light.* Crown rufous varying to coppery or golden rufous with light angle, *mask through eyes and cheeks black*, otherwise glistening "burnished buff" (greenish gold to straw gold) above; wings and tail dusky heavily edged pale greenish blue; below mostly shiny buff, some birds also with violet gray tinge on throat and median underparts (intensity of violet gray varies). ♀ and imm.: much duller, smoky buff tinged gray above, dingy grayish buff below. Imms. can look *greenish*.
Sim. species: Potentially confusing because of highly iridescent plumage which varies dramatically in color depending on light angle. Look for rufous cap and black mask, and note habitat.
Voice: Call a buzzy *tzzit*. Infreq. hd. song a rather long, echolike (or pulsating), buzzing trill, *sizza'sizza'sizza* . . . (10 or more notes in ca. 2–3 sec), like 2 birds singing at once. Reminiscent of song of Black-capped Tanager.
Behavior: Usually seen alone or in prs. or occas. 3s, often whizzing by to some distant tree, where hops and peers in foliage or occas. looks down a few times to inspect sides of twigs and small branches for insects. Overall seems to eat mostly berries and small fruits, and a dilettante at insect foraging. An "open-situation" tanager and not with mixed-spp. flocks (none in areas it frequents) but joins other spp. at fruiting trees and often travels across large open areas to patches of scrub or isolated fruiting trees and shrubs. Breeding Dec–Apr, Orinoco region; open cup nest rather low in scrubby tree in savanna; 2 dirty white eggs finely speckled dark, more at large end[115]; May nests, w Apure[525].
Status and habitat: Common resident in drier open habitats, ranchland, gallery and savanna woodland borders, and scrubby wasteland. Reg. in gardens and in trees around ranch buildings in llanos.

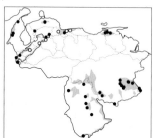

Range: To 2500m n of Orinoco (most recs. below ca. 1000m); to 1800m s of Orinoco. Virtually throughout in open or semiopen areas (*cayana*); no recs. in s Amazonas. E Colombia to the Guianas and ne Brazil; e and c Brazil and e Bolivia s to Paraguay and ne Argentina. **Note:** Scrub Tanager (*T. vitriolina*) of interandean Colombian valleys is spreading with deforestation and may occur in sw Venez. Resembles Burnished-buff Tanager; mostly dull silvery green with rufous crown, black mask, buff belly and crissum. Scrub, waste, and disturbed areas, foothills and mts.

Blue-necked Tanager   PLATE 60
Tangara cyanicollis   Tangara Rey
Identification: 5″ (12.7cm). 17g. Mostly black with *contrasting turquoise blue head turning deep purplish blue on throat*; lores black; *shoulders and rump glistening silvery green to burnished gold* depending on light; inner flight feathers and tail feathers edged silver green. Imm.: much duller, often mostly brown, older birds mottled black but still with brownish head.
Sim. species: Spectacular and not likely confused. S of Orinoco see Masked Tanager which has superficially sim. pattern but white belly.
Voice: Weak chips and a *seep*.
Behavior: A charming and lively little sp., usually seen in prs. or families of 3–4 along forest borders or lightly wooded areas but not inside forest. Loaf on relatively open branches at various hts., usually fairly high, where occas. sally clumsily to air or pick insects from nearby foliage, then fly off to fill up at fruiting trees and shrubs. Diet is mostly fruit, about half of which is *Miconia* berries, also *Cecropia* catkins and many other fruits. Along forest borders sometimes with mixed flocks but not reg. assoc. with them. In Colombia breeds Jan–Aug; mossy cup nest at moderate ht. in tree in clearing; Feb nest, PN Guaramacal, Trujillo.
Status and habitat: Uncommon to fairly common resident in semiopen situations incl. bushy pastures, humid forest borders, coffee plantations, and lighter woodland. Perhaps spreading with deforestation.

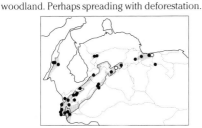

Range: 100–2100m (most recs. 300–1700m). Sierra de Perijá, Zulia; Andes from s Táchira n on both slopes to cerros of nw Lara (El Cogollal and Cerrón); mts. of Yaracuy, Coastal Cordillera in Carabobo, and Aragua e to PN Henri Pittier (sightings); Interior Cordillera on Cerro Platillón, n Guárico (*hannahiae*). Colombia s in Andes to n Bolivia; s central Brazil.

Masked Tanager   PLATE 60
Tangara nigrocincta   Tangara Pechinegra
Identification: 5″ (12.7cm). 17g. Has faded, "*washed out*" appearance. *Head pale lavender blue*, small black

mask; cheeks tinged greenish; *otherwise mostly black above and below*; shoulders and rump bright blue, wing coverts and flight feathers broadly edged pale silvery green, *center of lower breast and belly white.* ♀: duller, black on breast edged dusky gray.
Sim. species: Turquoise Tanager lacks contrasting pale head and has yellow (not white) belly.
Voice: Bursts of high, staccato ticking notes have hard, gravelly quality. Song a weak complex of jumbled notes followed by a very high-pitched buzzy or sibilant trill, not far carrying.
Behavior: Another "open-situation" *Tangara* that behaves much like Blue-necked Tanager. Usually in prs. or little families that spend much time sitting on bare perches in open. Occas. execute rather clumsy little short-distance sallies to air for flying insects, or fly off to fill up on small berries at fruiting trees and shrubs. Perch high but may come quite low to *Miconia* and other melastomes shrubs. Usually not with mixed-spp. flocks but reg. gather with other small birds at fruiting trees and shrubs.
Status and habitat: Uncommon resident around borders of humid forest, in shrubby clearings with scattered trees, and in various stages of second growth. Rather uncommon and local.

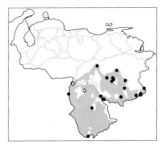

Range: To 950m. Throughout Amazonas; Bolívar from Río Cuchivero, lower Río Caura, and lower Río Paragua (La Paragua) s to Gran Sabana (Auyán-tepui) and Brazilian border. Guyana, nw Brazil, and e Colombia s in an arc to n Bolivia and c Brazil.

Turquoise Tanager   PLATE 60
Tangara mexicana   Tangara Turquesa
Identification: 5.5″ (14cm). 20g. At a distance looks mostly black with yellow belly. Up close a "patchwork quilt" of blues and blacks. *Above mostly black* with small turquoise blue patch on shoulder and blue rump; forecrown, sides of head (incl. above eyes), throat, chest, and sides dull cobalt blue somewhat spangled black on chest, heavily mottled with black on sides and flanks; *center of mid. breast to crissum pale yellow.*
Sim. species: Name of this dark-looking tanager is misleading. Opal-rumped Tanager also looks very dark, esp. from below, but note contrasting chestnut belly. Also see Masked Tanager and rare White-bellied Dacnis.
Voice: Rapid streams of high, chipping *tic* notes, sometimes trilled, esp. as groups take flight; higher pitched than in many *Tangara*.

Behavior: A sp. that lives in excitable and twittery little groups of 3–10 or so that seem to lose interest in whatever they are doing after a short time, then rush off headlong on a new adventure. Travel mostly in single-sp. groups, visit fruiting trees and shrubs, esp. *Miconia* and *Cecropia*, search in perfunctory manner for insects by "leaning down" to peer at sides or under surfaces of rather high open, often dead branches or twigs, also occas. search foliage, check flowers, or sally awkwardly to air. Then fly off across open space to loaf in top of a tall bare tree. Sometimes briefly with mixed-spp. flocks but more often in independent groups of their own. Small, open cup nest fairly high; 3 grayish green eggs marked brown. Helpers also may feed young[175,690].

Status and habitat: Fairly common resident in humid forest borders, second-growth woodland, river isls., *Cecropia* trees, and scattered tall trees in clearings. Scarce in areas of extensive forest, i.e., s Amazonas, and tepuis of Bolívar.

Range: To 1000m (mostly below 500m); to 2000m on Cerro de la Neblina. Sucre (incl. Paria Pen.) and n Monagas s to Delta Amacuro; generally in Amazonas and Bolívar (*media*). E Colombia to n Bolivia, Amaz. Brazil, and the Guianas; coastal se Brazil. Trinidad.

Opal-rumped Tanager
PLATE 60

Tangara velia   Tanagrella

Identification: 5.5″ (14cm). 20g. *Looks mostly black with chestnut belly.* Above deep black, *rump glistening yellowish opal,* wing coverts and flight feathers edged brilliant deep blue; forecrown, sides of head, and throat deep blue, irreg. black band across bottom of throat (inconspic. in field), rest of underparts deep glistening blue, *center of lower breast to crissum chestnut.*

Sim. species: Most likely confused only with Turquoise Tanager which has yellow lower underparts. Also cf. Masked Tanager and Rufous-bellied Euphonia.

Voice: High, thin, rapid bursts of *sit* or *sis* notes, often about 5–6 notes, while foraging. Weak little song of high, thin notes quickly rises in pitch then descends, *tiz-tiz-tiz-ti'ti-ti-ti-E'E-ti-ti-ti-tz.*

Behavior: Prs. or small groups follow canopy mixed-spp. flocks for short periods, or go with faster-moving tanager-honeycreeper groups to fruiting trees or to high canopy or emergent trees. Search for insects by peering "head down" beneath mostly high limbs in methodical, almost mechanical manner, looking first on one side of branch then on other, or check epiphytes and debris on large limbs in canopy or subcanopy. Occas. hitch around large canopy limbs and trunks almost like Black-and-white Warbler. Does not often de-

scend low to fruiting shrubs along forest borders (unlike some *Tangara*), and single birds or 2–3 reg. perch on high open branches above emergent treetops early in morning. Noted bathing in large bromeliads.

Status and habitat: Uncommon resident (prob. often overlooked) in tall lowland forest, forest borders, and treetops in clearings. Most numerous in areas of high rainfall.

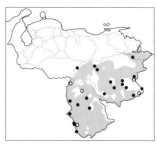

Range: To 1200m (mostly below 500m). Generally in Amazonas (no specimens but numerous sight recs. n of Río Ventuari); Bolívar from lower Río Caura (Suapuré), Río Paragua at Cerro Guaiquinima (*iridina*); Sierra de Imataca (Río Grande) southward (*iridina* or *velia*). Se Colombia to n Bolivia, Amaz. Brazil, and the Guianas; coastal se Brazil.

Paradise Tanager
PLATE 60

Tangara chilensis   Siete Colores

Identification: 5.5″ (14cm). 20.5g. Gaudy "harlequin" pattern. *Head scaly apple green* (feathers short and stiff) with black eyering; rest of upperparts mostly black, *rump scarlet, upper tail coverts golden yellow,* narrow turquoise slash across shoulders; throat purplish, rest of underparts *turquoise blue,* center of lower breast, belly, and under tail coverts black.

Voice: Rapid, high-pitched chipping usually signals this sp.'s approach. Calls include *chak* and rising *zeet,* singly, together, or in irreg. ser. Dawn song *chak-zeet* over and over, ca. 1 phrase/2 sec[274]. Day song (in se Peru) *tsip seeea-wee* over and over.

Behavior: This is an ebullient, mercurial sort of bird usually seen in chippy, high-energy groups of 4–20 or more that swarm rapidly through high canopy or emergent tree crowns, forage restlessly for a few min, then are apt to quickly fly off to some distant high tree. Often assoc. with mixed-spp. flocks, even lead them briefly, but their frantic, capricious pace is usually too fast and erratic for prolonged assoc. with other spp. except Green-and-gold Tanagers and a few other tanagers and honeycreepers. Like many *Tangara,* eat berries and small fruits and mostly stay high, but may briefly descend low to fruiting shrubs. Go through motions of searching bare canopy and subcanopy branches for insects by peering beneath first one side then other; also hop and peer in outer foliage, inspect bromeliads and other epiphytic canopy plants but seem to loose interest quickly, and before long the entire bubbly group is flying off on some errand. Flocking shows some seasonality; largest flocks Dec–Apr; fewest or none Jun–? in e Venez. when prob. nesting. In Peru, little cup nest, built mostly by ♀, high (30+m) in small outer fork[161].

Status and habitat: Common resident (seasonal fluctuations) in humid terra firme and várzea forest, forest borders, and treetops in clearings.

Range: To 1450m. Throughout Amazonas; Bolívar from lower Río Caura, mid. Río Paragua (Cerro Guaiquinima), mid. Río Caroní (Auyán-tepui), and upper Río Cuyuní s to Brazilian border (*coelicolor*). E Colombia to n Bolivia, Amaz. Brazil, and the Guianas.

Green-and-gold Tanager   PLATE 60
Tangara schrankii   Tangara Carinegra
Identification: 5″ (12.7cm). 19g. Mostly green and yellow. ♂: *forehead, ocular ring, and squarish patch behind eyes black, crown glistening yellow,* back bright green streaked black, rump yellow, wings and tail black edged green, outer flight feathers edged blue; *below green, center of underparts bright yellow.* ♀: sim. but duller; crown green, rump yellowish green.
Sim. species: From other mostly "green" tanagers by yellow crown and bold black facial pattern. Cf. Yellow-bellied and rare Dotted tanagers.
Voice: Thin *chit* notes.
Behavior: An habitual associate of Paradise Tanager (although not vice versa). Prs., or more often small groups up to 8 or so, forage with mixed-spp. flocks high in canopy but are apt to fly off with rapidly moving groups of honeycreepers, dacnises, and *Tangara* tanagers, leaving slower flocking spp. behind. Visit many kinds of fruiting trees, often in assoc. with other frugivores. Search for insects mostly by "lean-down" method employed by many highland tanagers, mechanically inspecting sides and undersurfaces of mostly bare branches and limbs and continuing out into small terminal twigs and foliage to glean from leaves. Forage mostly in canopy, but occas. will come quite low at edge or even inside forest with understory flocks. In Peru a cup nest was 2m up at base of 1st frond on small palm[274].
Status and habitat: Uncommon resident in tall humid forest, forest borders, and second growth. Easternmost

rec. is 1 seen 1 Jan 1980, 24km w of Santa Elena de Uairén (C. Parrish). Known from only small no. of recs. in Venez.; common southward in Amaz. Brazil.
Range: To 900m. Extreme e Amazonas (upper Río Ventuari at Kabadisocaña) s to Cerro de la Neblina; Bolívar in uppermost Río Caura, upper Río Paragua, and upper Río Caroní at Cerro Paurai (*venezuelana*); sight, Santa Elena de Uairén. Se Colombia to n Bolivia and w Amaz. Brazil (mostly s of the Amazon).

Spotted Tanager   PLATE 60
Tangara punctata   Tangara de Mejillas Gris
Identification: 5″ (12.7cm). 15g. Above mostly bright green thickly spotted and scaled black, *forehead, foreface, and throat strongly tinged bluish gray,* wings and tail black broadly edged green, central underparts white thickly spotted black, *sides and flanks yellowish green spotted black,* center of lower breast, belly, and under tail coverts yellowish white, more or less unspotted.
Sim. species: Often confused with Speckled Tanager (see) of mainly highlands; Spotted Tanager, more a lowland sp., is much less numerous on slopes of tepuis. Also see Yellow-bellied Tanager.
Behavior: Much like Speckled Tanager. Single birds, prs., or families wander alone or join mixed-spp. flocks. Usually forage in forest canopy but drop lower to fruiting shrubs at openings and often join temporary feeding groups at fruiting trees. Otherwise mainly a "foliage" *Tangara* that spends its time searching for insects high in outer foliage, esp. on terminal twigs and small leaves. Active and restless as peers, stretches to look up or down, or hangs downward in foliage.
Status and habitat: Uncommon resident in canopy of humid forest, forest borders, tall second growth, and scattered trees in clearings. Mainly lowlands and foothills or lower slopes of tepuis. Replaced at higher els. in tepuis by Speckled Tanager.

Range: To 1600m (most recs. below 1100m). N Amazonas (incl. Cerros Parú, Sipapo, and Duida) s to Cerro de la Neblina; locally throughout Bolívar from Río Cuchivero and Sierra de Imataca s to Brazilian border (*punctata*). The Guianas and ne Brazil n and s of the Amazon.

Speckled Tanager   PLATE 60
Tangara guttata   Tangara Pintada
Identification: 5.2″ (13.2cm). 18g. Crown greenish yellow, rest of upperparts bright green, both spotted black; lores black, *forehead, foreface, short eyestripe, and orbital area yellow*; wings and tail black *edged pale blue*; *underparts white thickly spotted black*, center

of belly and flanks unspotted yellowish green. Or sim. but less yellow on head (*bogotensis*).

Sim. species: Confusingly sim. to Spotted Tanager which has greener head, *grayish face and throat*, less white on underparts (sides and flanks are yellowish green), and *green-edged* wings. Note that Speckled Tanager (in area of overlap) looks quite "yellow headed" and is largely confined to mts. In tepuis cf. Yellow-bellied Tanager; in s lowlands, Dotted Tanager.

Voice: High-pitched chipping notes, often in rapid stream as bird takes flight.

Behavior: Twittery prs. or little groups are often assoc. with mixed-spp. flocks in upper levels or canopy of forest. Reg. join temporary groups at fruiting trees and shrubs, esp. at melastomes, *Trema* (Ulmaceae), and Euphorbiaceae, where sometimes drop down to eye level. May range over fairly large areas during course of a day. Insect-foraging behavior is energetic and typical of *Tangara* that rapidly search in high foliage and twigs near tips of branches. Often rather acrobatic as scramble out through foliage, peer up, lean out or down, hang downward, or cling beneath leaves to check leaf undersurfaces[669]. In Costa Rica, compact fiber cup nest (no moss) 3–8m up on leafy branch at forest edge; 2 white eggs heavily mottled brown; 3 ads. reported at a nest[624,706].

Status and habitat: Common resident in humid forest borders, shrubby second growth with tall trees, shady coffee plantations, and light woodland. Everywhere found mainly in foothills and lower slopes, unlike Spotted Tanager which is more widespread in lowlands. The two overlap widely in el. distrib. but are infreq. found together.

Range: 400–2000m. Sierra de Perijá, Zulia, Andes from s Táchira n to s Lara (*bogotensis*); mts. of Falcón (Sierra de San Luis) and Yaracuy, and n cordilleras from Carabobo and Aragua e to Sucre and n Monagas; cerros of Amazonas s to Cerro de la Neblina; w Bolívar from Río Cuchivero to Río Paragua (*chrysophrys*); cerros of Gran Sabana from Auyán-tepui and Sierra de Lema (sightings) southward (*guttata*). Costa Rica to Colombia; Trinidad.

Yellow-bellied Tanager
PLATE 60

Tangara xanthogastra Tangara Vientre Amarillo

Identification: 4.7″ (12cm). 15g. *Mostly bright emerald green*, slightly yellowish green below; *upperparts, throat, and breast spotted black*, wings and tail dusky *broadly edged green*, wing coverts and inner remiges edged bluish green, center of lower breast, belly, and under tail coverts *bright yellow* (*xanthogastra*). Or 5″

(12.7cm); sim. but slightly larger; inconspic. narrow yellow eyering (*phelpsi*).

Sim. species: Easily confused. Speckled Tanager has yellow face and white underparts. Spotted Tanager has gray face and throat and green-edged wings. Dotted Tanager is essentially unspotted above and below. Note differences in el. distrib. of these birds.

Voice: Weak *chit* and *seet* notes like others of genus.

Behavior: Single birds, prs., or fidgety little groups are reg. members of canopy mixed-spp. flocks, esp. those composed mostly of fast-moving dacnises, honeycreepers, and other *Tangara* tanagers. Also join temporary groups at fruiting trees and shrubs and may come quite low along forest borders, esp. to feed on *Miconia* berries and other melastomes. Insect-searching behavior is rather generalized and incls. lean-down branch searching (see under Golden Tanager) and acrobatic searching in outer twigs and foliage (see Speckled Tanager). Early in morning often sits up on high prom. perch above canopy for short periods of time.

Status and habitat: Uncommon and thinly spread resident in humid lowlands (*xanthogastra*); locally common on humid slopes of tepuis (*phelpsi*). Canopy of forest, older second growth, and shrubby forest borders. Highland *phelpsi* common in mossy, melastome-dominated second growth on sandy soils of Sierra de Lema.

Range: To 750m (*xanthogastra*); ca. 1000–1800m (*phelpsi*). Cerros of n and s Amazonas (Yavi, Sipapo, de la Neblina), lower Río Caura (Río Nicharé), and cerros of Gran Sabana from Auyán-tepui, Ptari-tepui, and Sierra de Lema (sightings) southward (*phelpsi*); headwaters of Río Ventuari (Kabadisocaña) and Río Asisa, ne Amazonas, and s Bolívar in mid. Río Caura and upper Río Paragua (*xanthogastra*). Se Colombia to n Bolivia, s Amaz. Brazil, and Guyana.

Note: Possibly 2 spp. involved.

Dotted Tanager
PLATE 60

Tangara varia Tangara Manchada

Identification: 4.5″ (11.4cm). 10g. Small and essentially unmarked. ♂: *mostly bright green*, lores black, *wings and tail black broadly edged dull blue* (wings look bluish in field), throat and chest somewhat dotted black (also with black bases of feathers showing through occas.). ♀: sim. but underparts essentially unspotted and paler, more greenish yellow; wing edgings greenish.

Sim. species: Easily confused with imms. and ads. of several other small *Tangara*. Be *especially careful* with imms. of Bay-headed, Green-and-gold, Yellow-bellied,

Speckled, and Spotted tanagers; and with ads. of last 3 as well. Imms. of all of above may lack spotting. Best marks for this difficult bird are its small size, blue on wings (♂ only), and *lack* of yellow below; also dots on chest (♂ only), but these are *hard to see in field*. ♀ looks quite uniform green overall (cf. ♀ Blue Dacnis which has bluish head and pink legs).
Behavior: Poorly known. Found with mixed-spp. flocks from mid. levels to canopy of trees. Searches small branches and foliage for insects and fruit[808]. Near Manaus, Brazil, noted only singly or in prs.[544].
Status and habitat: Resident. Humid forest and forest edges, prob. also second growth and scattered trees in clearings. May be fairly common in s Amazonas judging from no. of specimens from vicinity of El Carmen and San Carlos de Río Negro. Very few recs. from n Amazonas or s Bolívar.

Range: To 300m. N Amazonas (Caño Cuao; Samariapo) s to Río Negro drainage; s Bolívar in headwaters of Río Paragua (Salto María Espuma). Guyana; Suriname (1 old rec.); French Guiana (a few recs.); n Brazil in Rios Negro and Tapajós drainages (elsewhere?).

Bay-headed Tanager   PLATE 60
Tangara gyrola   Tangara Cabeza de Lacre
Identification: 5.5″ (14cm). 19.5g. *Head brick red*, rest of upperparts grass green, narrow golden nuchal collar (some races also with faint gold burnish on shoulders); below entirely green, thighs rufous. Or lower throat and median breast to belly blue (*gyrola*); or all blue below, under tail coverts green (*parva*). Imm.: much duller but usually with some brownish head color faintly indicated.
Sim. species: Contrasting "bay" head and mostly green body are the marks. Dull juv. and imm. birds easily confused with ♀ Green Honeycreeper, but note tanager's thicker, blunter bill. Imm. Rufous-cheeked Tanager usually has rufous on cheeks and under tail coverts.
Voice: Freq. call a thin, buzzy, nasal *seeaawee*, dropping in pitch then rebounding. Song in Trinidad *see, seee, seee, tsou, tsooy*, last 2 notes lower[175].
Behavior: Single birds, prs., or families follow mixed-spp. flocks at mid. level to canopy hts. Move along branches in little spurts and pauses, habitually peering "head down" in rather perfunctory and mechanical manner beneath mostly live bare limbs, occas. dead branches (less often mossy limbs and small terminal twigs) in deliberate, stereotyped manner of many forest-dwelling *Tangara*. Also eat small fruits and berries (60–70% of diet) from many trees and shrubs, esp.

melastomes, *Cecropia*, and *Ficus*[274,669]. In Costa Rica, mossy open cup nest 2–8m up, concealed in foliage; freq. in isolated tree in clearing, or crown of sapling; 2 dull white eggs speckled brown, esp. in wreath at larger end[624]; in Colombia breeds at least Mar–Nov.
Status and habitat: Common resident in humid and wet forest, forest borders, and second-growth woodland, even scattered trees in clearings. N of Orinoco mainly in foothills and mts. Some minor seasonal or local el. movements occur, prob. in response to fruit availability.

Range: To 1800m (mostly above 300m) n of Orinoco; to 1600m s of Orinoco. Sierra de Perijá, Zulia; base and both slopes of Andes from s Táchira n through w Barinas, w Portuguesa, and Lara; mts. of c and se Falcón, mts. of Yaracuy, and n cordilleras from Carabobo and n Guárico e to Distr. Federal and Miranda (*toddi*); mts. of ne Anzoátegui, Sucre, and n Monagas (*viridissima*); n and c Amazonas (mostly on cerros) and from nw Bolívar e across lower Río Caura, mid. Río Paragua, and Sierra de Imataca (Río Grande) southward (*gyrola*); s Amazonas along Río Negro (*parva*). Costa Rica to n Bolivia, Amaz. Brazil, and the Guianas.

Dacnis

Small and restless; sharp-pointed, conical bills; eyes often colorful (both sexes), but sexes otherwise very different; mostly humid forest canopy; some spp. rare or overlooked.

Blue Dacnis   PLATE 59
Dacnis cayana   Mielero Turquesa
Identification: 5″ (12.7cm). 13g. Eyes dark red; *legs pink*; conical bill short, straight, and pointed, pinkish at base. ♂: *mainly glistening turquoise blue; small mask, central throat patch, upper back, wings, and tail black*, wings broadly edged blue. ♀ very different; above *bright grass green*, paler below; *crown and sides of head grayish blue*, throat gray, flight feathers edged dusky. Imm. ♂: like ♀; head may be bluer.
Sim. species: Much commoner than any other dacnis or honeycreeper in Venez. Cf. ♂ Black-faced Dacnis and ♂ *Cyanerpes* honeycreepers. ♀'s blue head and green body should be distinctive; in mts. see ♀ Capped Conebill.
Voice: High-pitched *tsit* notes; song (?) of similar lispy note over and over.
Behavior: Occurs singly, in prs., or families of 3–4 (not large groups) that forage in restless, nervous manner with mixed-spp. flocks from mid. levels to high can-

opy, or briefly join feeding aggregations at fruiting trees. Spend majority of time searching for insects on leaves and leaf petioles, esp. at insect-damaged leaves[223], and smaller amt. of time feeding on small fruits, berries, and occas. nectar. Deep, pouchlike cup of fine fibers and compacted seed down suspended from fork, 5m or more up; 2 whitish eggs with dark marks[635].

Status and habitat: Generally a common and widespread resident in canopy of terra firme and várzea forest, along forest borders, tall second-growth woodland, and shrubby clearings with scattered trees; also gallery forest. Lowlands and foothills. Absent from dry areas of n Zulia, Falcón, and llanos.

Range: To 1200m n of Orinoco; to 1400m s of Orinoco. Base of Sierra de Perijá and c and s Maracaibo lowlands of Zulia, w and e base of Andes from s Táchira n to Lara, n Venez. from se Falcón, Yaracuy, and n Guárico to Sucre and Monagas, Delta Amacuro, and generally s of Orinoco (*cayana*). Honduras to Bolivia, n Argentina, se Brazil, and the Guianas. Trinidad.

Black-faced Dacnis   PLATE 59
Dacnis lineata   Mielero Celeste
Identification: 4.5″ (11.4cm). *Eyes golden yellow* (duller—♀); bill conical and sharp pointed. ♂: *mostly glistening turquoise blue with broad black mask continuing to hindneck and upper back*; wings and tail black with turquoise band across most of upper half of wing; *center of belly and under tail coverts white.* ♀: very different; above *brown*, flight feathers and tail dark brown; under wing coverts white; below pale brown to pale olive brown fading to *buffy white or whitish on center of lower underparts.*
Sim. species: ♂ recalls more widespread Blue Dacnis, but note golden eyes, blue throat, and white belly. Nondescript ♀ best told by attendant ♂. Good marks are thin bill, yellow eyes, and pale belly. Cf. esp. ♀ Yellow-bellied and White-bellied dacnises, both tinged yellowish below.
Voice: High-pitched, insignificant *tzit* notes.
Behavior: Single birds, prs., or rarely groups up to 6–12 follow mixed-spp. flocks, join temporary feeding aggregations of other dacnises, honeycreepers, and tanagers at fruiting trees, or occas. forage independently of other birds. Found mainly in canopy where peer, reach, and hover-glean in outer foliage and reg. visit trees for small fruits. Often eat *Cecropia* catkins. Like others of genus, active and restless and relatively easy to see.
Status and habitat: Uncommon resident in humid forest, forest borders, dense to open second-growth wood-

land, and scattered tall trees in forest clearings; occas gallery forest. Recs. rather spotty.

Range: To 450m n of Orinoco; to 1300m s of Orinoco. Se Táchira (Burgua); Amazonas (most recs. s of Río Ventuari); Bolívar generally from Serranía Pijiguaos, lower Río Caura, lower Río Paragua, and Río Cuyuní southward (*lineata*). N Colombia; se Colombia to n Bolivia, Amaz. Brazil, and the Guianas.

Yellow-bellied Dacnis   PLATE 59
Dacnis flaviventer   Mielero Vientre Amarillo
Identification: 4.5″ (11.4cm). 13g. *Eyes red* (♂ and ♀); short, *sharp-pointed*, conical bill. ♂: crown moss green (hard to see color in field), otherwise sides of head and upperparts black; *scapular stripe and rump bright yellow; center of upper throat black, rest of underparts bright chrome yellow.* ♀: above olive brown, wings and tail dusky brown, *below dull pale yellowish* heavily washed olive gray on throat, chest, and sides; belly pale buff to creamy yellow.
Sim. species: ♂ unmistakable if seen well, although might bring to mind a Bananaquit. ♀'s best mark is red eye (surprisingly conspic. even at a distance). ♀ Black-faced Dacnis has yellow eyes, brown back (no olive), and whitish belly (not yellow). ♀ White-bellied Dacnis is sim. but has dark eyes.
Voice: High, buzzy *zreet* and *zeet* notes.
Behavior: Sim. to that of Black-faced Dacnis but mostly seen alone or in prs. Usually keeps high, briefly assoc. with tanagers and honeycreepers at fruiting trees, less often with permanent mixed-spp. flocks, and gleans in foliage. Like others of genus, restless and high-strung but occas. perches quietly on high open twig for a few min.
Status and habitat: Uncommon resident in canopy of humid terra firme and várzea forest, along forest borders, and in disturbed areas with tall trees and shrubby second growth. Known from only a small no. of recs. in Venez.

Range: To 350m. N Amazonas from vicinity of Río Ventuari (San Fernando de Atabapo, San Juan de Manaipare) southward (but only a few recs. s of Río Ventuari); Bolívar from lower Río Caura and upper Río Paragua southward. Se Colombia to n Bolivia and w and c Amaz. Brazil.

White-bellied Dacnis   PLATE 59
Dacnis albiventris   Mielero Vientre Blanco
Identification: 4.3″ (10.9cm). 11g. Very rare. *Eyes golden yellow* (♂) or *pale brown to grayish brown* (♀). Bill among shortest in genus, conical and pointed. Tail short. ♂: mostly intense cobalt blue, wings and tail blackish heavily edged blue; *angular black mask through lores and eyes* curves downward to point below and behind eyes; mid. breast and lower underparts white, sharply and squarely cut off from blue of chest; flanks somewhat clouded and mottled bluish. ♀: above plain dull brown incl. sides of head to below eyes; lores slightly darker (foreface and sides of throat have slight scaly look up close); lower back, rump, and upper tail coverts strongly tinged olive; *median underparts dull yellowish*, sides of throat, breast, flanks, and crissum clouded grayish brown; flight feathers and tail dusky brown. Imm. ♂: like ♀ but flight feathers contrasting blackish; older imm. ♂♂ also acquire grayish yellow eyes and whitish bellies, thus taking on "look" of ad. ♂.
Sim. species: ♂ is darker, more intense blue, and less patterned than Black-faced Dacnis. Also cf. Turquoise Tanager (larger and more mottled) and Hooded Tanager (all white below). ♀ much like ♀ Yellow-bellied Dacnis, and unless eye color is seen, prob. not safely told except when accompanied by ad. ♂. Points to look for are browner head and upperparts (no olive tinge) and more uniformly dull yellow median underparts. Also see ♀ Black-faced Dacnis (yellow eyes).
Voice: In flight a soft, silky *seeeee*.
Behavior: Poorly known. Prs. or little groups of 3–10 containing ♂♂, ♀♀, and imms. follow fast-moving flocks of *Tangara* tanagers and dacnises high in forest canopy and in tops of emergent trees. Groups glean for insects in high outer foliage, rapidly inspecting small leaves, esp. leaflets of pinnately compound leaves, or hang upside down from leaves, then fly off in straggling little groups to distant emergent trees. Flocks also wander alone and descend lower along forest edges to visit fruiting melastome trees (*Miconia*) where there are manakins, tanagers, and other fruit-eating birds.
Status and habitat: Rare. Tall humid terra firme forest and forest borders in lowlands. Two specimens in

Venez.: 1 near Cerro Duida, another at El Carmen on Río Negro. Sight recs. as follows: 1 ♂, Junglaven, 13 May 1992 (R. Behrstock and B. Finch); 9–10 near El Gavilán (e of Pto. Ayacucho), 15 Jun 1995[259]. Possibly overlooked because of seminomadism and treetop habits.
Range: To 200m. Amazonas (scattered recs.). Se Colombia (3 recs., only 1 from definite loc.), e Ecuador, ne Peru, and w Amaz. Brazil mostly n of the Amazon.

Chlorophanes

Larger, and bill stouter than in *Cyanerpes* or *Dacnis*; partly nectivorous.

Green Honeycreeper   PLATE 59
Chlorophanes spiza   Mielero Verde
Identification: 5.5″ (14cm). 17g. *Sharp-pointed, slightly decurved bill bright yellow* with black on culmen (duller in ♀). ♂: *top and sides of head black*, otherwise *entirely glistening aquamarine*, a little bluer below; flight feathers blackish edged blue green. ♀: bright grass green above, yellowish green below, paler on throat. Or throat and central lower underparts yellowish (*subtropicalis*). Imm. ♂: like ♀; older imms. mottled green and turquoise.
Sim. species: ♀'s best mark is bill shape. Dull imm. Bay-headed Tanager has heavier, blunter bill, less uniformly green plumage (usually traces of pattern on head or wings). Rufous-cheeked Tanager is also duller with rufous on cheeks and crissum.
Voice: Mostly high *psit* or *tseet* notes.
Behavior: A restless, nervous-acting bird that flicks wings anxiously, seems to constantly look up to check for danger, and often behaves aggressively toward other spp. Single birds, prs., or families follow mixed-spp. flocks containing other canopy tanagers and honeycreepers or join them briefly at fruiting trees. Forage in mid. levels or higher in forest. Eat much fruit (more than 60% of diet) incl. *Miconia* berries and *Cecropia* catkins, sip nectar (ca. 20% of diet), esp. from large cup-shaped flowers of balsa (*Ochroma*), glean insects from twigs and leaves (ca. 15% of diet), and occas. sally to air for flying insects. Shallow leaf, fiber, and horsehair cup nest built by ♀; fastened to fork with spiderweb, 3–12m up; 2 white eggs with wreath of brown spots at larger end[635].
Status and habitat: Fairly common resident in humid forest, second-growth woodland, and wooded borders in lowlands and foothills, smaller nos. into highlands. Unlike *Cyanerpes* honeycreepers, rather sedentary.

Range: To 1250m n of Orinoco; to 1400m s of Orinoco. Sierra de Perijá, Zulia, and w base of Andes from Táchira to Trujillo (*subtropicalis*); e base of Andes from Táchira to nw Barinas and s Lara (sightings, PN Yacambú); n cordilleras from Carabobo and Aragua e to Paria Pen., Sucre; throughout Amazonas and w and s Bolívar (*spiza*). S Mexico to e Bolivia, Amaz. Brazil, and the Guianas; coastal se Brazil. Trinidad.

Cyanerpes

Long, thin, decurved bill; colorful legs; long wings and short tail; ♂♂ usually brilliant purplish blue, ♀♀ greenish; often in groups; sometimes heavily nectivorous; reg. migrate short distances; canopy of dry to humid forest.

Short-billed Honeycreeper   PLATE 59
Cyanerpes nitidus   Copeicillo Pico Corto
Identification: 4″ (10.2cm). 9g. *Bill short* (0.4″, 10mm), slightly decurved (lower mandible almost straight); legs pinkish red (♂) or pale pink (♀). ♂: mainly glistening blue, paler below; lores, ocular area, *center of throat, and broader area spreading across chest black*; wings, *under wing coverts*, tail, and center of belly black. ♀: above bright grass green *incl. sides of head*; lores blackish, *short blue malar stripe* (inconspic.), throat buff, rest of underparts greenish flammulated with white, belly pale buff; *under wing coverts buffy white*.
Sim. species: ♂ from ♂ Red-legged Honeycreeper by black throat, short bill, and *pinkish* (not red) legs; note Red-legged's azure crown, black back, and *yellow* under wing coverts. ♂ Purple Honeycreeper differs in longer bill, small black throat patch (cut off at bottom of throat), and lemon yellow legs. ♀ from ♀ Red-legged Honeycreeper by short bill, blue malar stripe, and buffy white (not yellow) under wing coverts. ♀ also easily confused with ♀ Purple Honeycreeper, but latter has longer bill, cinnamon forehead, lores, and sides of head (not greenish), and greenish gray (not pale pink) legs.
Behavior: Sim. to other *Cyanerpes* and often with them, although generally less numerous and less often seen. Singly or in prs. with mixed-spp. flocks in forest canopy, or with tanager-honeycreeper groups in fruiting trees where take small berries and glean insects from foliage or branches. Amt. of nectar feeding unknown. Unlike some others of genus, almost never in single-sp. groups.
Status and habitat: Fairly common resident in tall humid forest and forest edges in sandy soil forests,

e.g., Junglaven on Río Ventuari. Elsewhere uncommon with recs. widely scattered.
Range: To 400m (prob. higher). Throughout Amazonas; nw Bolívar from Río Nicharé, lower Río Caura, mid. Río Paragua (Cerro Guaiquinima), and upper Río Caroní southward. E of Andes from se Colombia to ne Peru and nw Amaz. Brazil; Guyana.

Purple Honeycreeper   PLATE 59
Cyanerpes caeruleus   Copeicillo Violáceo
Identification: 4.5″ (11.4cm). 12g. Bill long, slender, and decurved. *Legs bright lemon yellow;* tail short. ♂: all glistening purplish blue; *small mask; throat* (but not chest), *wings, tail, and belly black; under wing coverts black*. ♀: above bright grass green; *lores cinnamon, sides of head freckled cinnamon*, narrow blue malar stripe (inconspic. in field); *throat cinnamon, rest of underparts yellowish buff streaked green*, sometimes with a little blue mixed on sides; under wing coverts dull yellowish white. In both sexes bill of *caeruleus* longer than that of *microrhynchus* (18–23 vs. 15–17mm).
Sim. species: ♂ from any other honeycreeper in Venez. by bright lemon yellow legs; see Short-billed Honeycreeper. ♀ from ♀ Short-billed Honeycreeper by much longer bill and cinnamon on lores and sides of head. Also cf. Red-legged Honeycreeper.
Voice: High, lisping *zzree* notes.
Behavior: Prs., family groups, or sometimes large single-sp. groups forage and travel alone or more often assoc. with mixed-spp. flocks (12 or more may forage with large mixed-spp. flocks) where they are usually in canopy but occas. come low along borders. Drink nectar, take a variety of mostly small berries (melastomes; *Trema*) and arils (*Clusia*) which they extract with their long bills as soon as open, and spend much time searching branch and twig surfaces for insects, less time on foliage or sallying to air. Nest a small moss cup lined with rootlets; mostly 2–3m up (prob. often higher); 2 white eggs with dark blotchy markings[175].
Status and habitat: Fairly common resident (abundance varies seasonally) in canopy and borders of humid forest and old shrubby second growth. More closely tied to *humid* areas than Red-legged Honeycreeper.

Range: To 1500m n of Orinoco; to 1800m s of Orinoco. W and s Zulia, w base of Andes in Táchira and Mérida, and e base from Táchira n to se Lara; n and w Amazonas s to Brazil (*microrhynchus*); n Falcón (sight, Sierra de San Luis); n cordilleras from w Carabobo e to Sucre, e Monagas, and Delta Amacuro; e Amazonas and generally in Bolívar (*caeruleus*). E Panama to nw

Ecuador; se Colombia to e Bolivia, Amaz. Brazil, and the Guianas. Trinidad.

Red-legged Honeycreeper   PLATE 59
Cyanerpes cyaneus   Tucuso de Montaña
Identification: 4.8″ (12.2cm). 14g. *Bill long, slender, and decurved; legs bright red* (dull red to pinkish—♀).
♂: mostly glistening purple blue, *crown azure*, small mask, *upper back*, wings, tail, and center of belly black; under wing linings bright yellow. ♀: above olive green *incl. forehead, lores, and sides of head*; below grayish to pale yellow with rather blurry olive streaking; under wing coverts pale yellow. In both sexes bill longest in *eximius*, shortest in *dispar* (18.5–23 vs. 13.5–15.5mm); most variable in *cyaneus* (16–25mm); in all races bill shape varies from almost straight to very decurved. Total body lengths vary in sim. fashion. Imm. ♂: like ♀ but soon acquires mostly black wings, advanced ones with patches of blue. Postbreeding ♂: molts into "eclipse" type plumage (rare among Neotropical birds) which resembles ♀ but with black back, wings, and tail.
Sim. species: ♂ by azure crown, black back (no black on throat), and bright red legs; in flight by yellow under wing coverts. ♀ by plain olive face (no buff, no blue malar stripe) and yellow under wing coverts. See Short-billed Honeycreeper.
Voice: At dawn a weak ser. of unmusical *tsip* and *chat* notes; high, wheezy, ascending *shree*; perched or in flight constant *tsip* notes.
Behavior: Normally restless and energetic. In pairs when breeding, otherwise in varying-sized, single-sp. groups up to 15 or so that follow mixed-spp. flocks or fly off long distances independent of them, or pause to rest on high exposed twigs or hide in high vine tangles. Forage mostly in canopy or forest mid. levels for small berries and arils, or puncture holes in large fruits. Glean insects from branch surfaces, occas. foliage, and reg. flutter or sally for flying insects. Also feed to varying extent on nectar. Around habitations readily come to tables with fruit. Thin-walled fiber cup nest suspended by rim from twig 3–15m up in tree or shrub; 2 white eggs speckled light brown mostly around larger end[624].
Status and habitat: Locally or seasonally common in dry to humid forest borders, second-growth shrubbery, clearings, lighter woodland, and plantations (esp. coffee and cacao). Generally found in drier areas than Purple Honeycreeper. Resident, but shows marked local/seasonal migratory movements which need documentation.

Range: To 1500m n of Orinoco; to 2000m s of Orinoco. W Zulia, scattered recs. on both sides of Andes and adj. Portuguesa; mts. of c Falcón and Yaracuy, and e through n cordilleras from Carabobo to Sucre; Isla Margarita (*eximius*); c Monagas, Delta Amacuro, and Bolívar (*cyaneus*); throughout Amazonas (*dispar*). E Mexico to n Bolivia, Amaz. Brazil, and the Guianas; coastal se Brazil. Trinidad and Tobago.

Diglossopis

Large, blue, forest-based flowerpiercers; bill not as strongly modified as in *Diglossa*; frilled tongue unlike that of *Diglossa*; diet predom. fruit; placed in *Diglossa* by most earlier authors but shared nectar-feeding adaptations perhaps result of convergence rather than common ancestry[57].

Bluish Flowerpiercer   PLATE 57
Diglossopis caerulescens   Roba Néctar Azulado
Identification: 5.5″ (14cm). 13g. *Eyes dark red* (often dull red); *bill rather thin, only slightly upturned* (even less in ♀). ♂: *frontlet and loral area black* forming small mask, otherwise above *dull gray blue*, slightly paler on throat and chest and turning grayish white tinged blue on lower breast and belly. ♀: upperparts duller.
Sim. species: Dull and often looks blackish in poor light, then easily confused with other "dark" flowerpiercers. Most like Masked Flowerpiercer which has same general pattern but is larger, brighter blue (but imms. much like adult Bluish Flowerpiercer), and *always with larger* black mask (not just loral area) and usually with brighter red eyes. Best mark for separating imms. of these 2 spp. is *size of black mask*.
Voice: Often hd. call a hard, metallic *tiink*, distinctive and a good clue to sp.'s presence. Song a few slow, high notes, then an accelerating shower of chattery, staccato notes (may vary geographically or individually?) that cascade from treetop, e.g., *eeeEET, esa-eet, eat'tsu-ti'tip-ta-leep'ta-lip'chlip, chee-ep, cheelip'liz'si . . .* and so on, often descending somewhat in pitch and ending in fussy, tittering jumble; varies from 2 sec to long sustained.
Behavior: Usually seen singly or in prs., and with mixed-spp. flocks containing warblers, tanagers, and other flowerpiercers. Ranges from forest mid. levels to canopy. Feeds heavily on small berries (esp. *Miconia* spp.), gleans insects from foliage and twigs, but spends less time puncturing flowers for nectar than smaller *Diglossa*. Dry grass, fern, and moss cup nest in bush; eggs pale greenish blue blotched and spotted reddish brown mainly at larger end[580]; Feb nest with 2 eggs; on steep mossy road bank, Trujillo.

Status and habitat: Common resident in humid and wet montane forest, tall second growth, and borders in Coastal Cordillera; less numerous in Andes. Some seasonal movements likely.
Range: 1600–3200m in Andes; 1400–2100m in n mts. Sierra de Perijá, Zulia (*ginesi*); Andes from s Táchira n through Mérida and n Trujillo to Páramo Cendé (*saturata*); Coastal Cordillera in Carabobo, Aragua, and Distr. Federal (*caerulescens*). Colombia s in Andes to n Bolivia.

Masked Flowerpiercer   PLATE 57
Diglossopis cyanea   Roba Néctar de Antifaz
Identification: 6″ (15cm). 17g. *Bright red eyes.* Bill strongly hooked and upturned. *Forehead, lores, chin, and sides of head black* (black encircles eyes, forming "mask"), otherwise entirely rich deep blue. ♀: slightly duller and tinged gray below. Imm.: duller, more gray blue, esp. below; belly and crissum feathers edged whitish.
Sim. species: Largest and brightest blue flowerpiercer in Venez. Cf. esp. imm. with ad. and imm. Bluish Flowerpiercer and Capped Conebill. Overlaps only with Bluish Flowerpiercer in Venez.
Voice: Song, hd. all yr, is high and wirey, 2–3 thin *zeet* notes, then rapid, increasingly complex ser. of tinkling and twittering notes, descending somewhat in pitch and often ending in 2 thin but distinct *zeet* or *seet* notes; each bird may sing slightly different song, or several different songs?; the 2–3 introductory notes, distinctive in this sp., seem to be lacking in other *Diglossa* songs in Venez.
Behavior: Solitary, in prs., or in small groups (families) up to ca. 4, usually with mixed-spp. flocks of tanagers where actively forage at almost any ht. but mostly at mid. levels or higher. Feed heavily on small fruits and berries, may occas. pierce flowers for nectar or fruits for juice, but overall much more frugivorous than smaller *Diglossa* allies. May also glean or sally for small insects. Seasonal or periodic migratory movements occur, mostly between higher and lower els., with groups of 20–30 moving together (25 moving upslope along San Isidro Rd. at 1450m in nw Barinas in Jun). Seasonal movements need documentation. Cup nest of grass and moss; feather lined; eggs as in previous sp.[589].
Status and habitat: Generally a common resident in all kinds of humid and wet montane forest, along forest borders, shrubby areas, and roadside borders up to treeline.

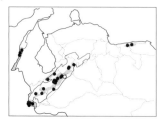

Range: 1800–3200m (sightings to 1450m) in Andes; 1800–2200m in Coastal Cordillera. Upper Río Negro in Sierra de Perijá, Zulia (*obscura*); Andes of s Táchira n

to Mérida, nw Barinas (sight), and ne Trujillo at Páramo Cendé (*cyanea*); Coastal Cordillera in Aragua and Distr. Federal (*tovarensis*); prob. Miranda. Colombia s in Andes to Bolivia.
Note: Possibly more than 1 sp. (songs different in s part of range).

Diglossa

Small and hyperactive; slightly upturned bill, upper mandible longer than lower and sharply hooked at tip; lower mandible sharp pointed; tongue shaped like upside-down U with brush tip; often heavily nectivorous; only in mts., but some spp. undertake vertical migrations; several usually sympatric. Incl. 2 broad subgroups: (1) large, mostly black, high-el. spp. that are highly aggressive and feed heavily on nectar and some fruit and (2) small, timid, sexually dimorphic spp. that feed on nectar and insects (little or no fruit). Taxonomy controversial[233]; placed in Emberizidae by some[10], here retained in Thraupidae[467]. *Diglossopis* often merged into *Diglossa*.

Greater Flowerpiercer   PLATE 57
Diglossa major   Roba Néctar de Los Tepuis
Identification: 6.8″ (17.3m). *Large flowerpiercer*, bill notably *thick* at base, strongly hooked; eyes reddish brown. *Black mask over forehead, lores, ocular area, and chin; narrow white malar*, otherwise mainly bluish slate *finely streaked silvery blue all over* (inconspic.); *under tail coverts chestnut*; tail rather long (*gilliardi*). Or fine streaking mainly on upperparts (*chimantae, major*). Or streaking obscure above and below (*disjuncta*). Imm.: dusky brown above, gray brown streaked dirty white below; white malar stripe freckled black, under tail coverts chestnut.
Sim. species: Only flowerpiercer in its range. Cf. dark-looking ♂ Purple Honeycreeper.
Voice: Unusual song, given singly or in complex duet, consists of burst of notes more or less repeated over and over, entire song occas. lasting 30 sec to several min. In duets, one bird sings harsh or flat, low-pitched notes, the other high, tinkling notes, combined effect a fast, sputtery, chattery ser. of notes alternating with high, squeaky, tinkling notes, all of which rise and fall slightly in pitch. Not very musical; recalls pulsating bursts of static on a cheap radio.
Behavior: An active sp. that freq. flicks wings as it pierces flowers or probes directly into short flower corollas (where a valid pollinator) for nectar, esp. of arboreal bromeliad flowers. Forages from eye level to canopy, more often high. Sometimes with mixed-spp. flocks of tanagers, warblers, and thrushes. Cup nest of grass and twigs, presumed this sp., between rocks under overhang; less than 0.4m up[198].
Status and habitat: Humid and wet upper-el. forest, forest borders, stunted cloud forest, and dense, mossy second growth. Uncommon and local on Sierra de Lema (1400–1500m), esp. in stunted, melastome-dominated, second-growth forest on white sandy soil. Shows marked local/seasonal movements (at least at lower els.); much commoner in rainy season on Sierra de Lema (D. Ascanio). Common to abundant on Cerro

Roraima above 2000m (C. Parrish); in general most recs. on all tepuis are above ca. 1800m.

Range: 1400–2850m. Tepuis on Gran Sabana in se Bolívar. Auyán-tepui (*gilliardi*); Ptari-tepui, Sororopán-tepui, Uaipán-tepui, Aprada-tepui, and Acopán-tepui (*disjuncta*); Chimantá-tepui (*chimantae*); Cerro Roraima, Cerro Cuquenán, and Uei-tepui (*major*); Sierra de Lema (subsp.?). N Brazil; prob. Guyana.

Scaled Flowerpiercer
PLATE 57

Diglossa duidae   Roba Néctar del Duida

Identification: 5.5″ (14cm). 16g. Tepuis of Amazonas. Bill upturned, strongly hooked; eyes reddish brown. Above grayish black, head darker (no mask); small blue gray shoulder patch not in strong contrast to upperparts; *throat and chest blackish turning dark gray on breast, somewhat spotted or scaled with pale gray on belly*; under tail coverts mixed gray and whitish. Or with black mainly on throat (*hitchcocki, georgebarrowcloughi*). Juv.: above dull dusky gray (no bluish) with blackish crown; below uniform med. gray; greater and median wing coverts white-tipped forming wing bars (all subspp.?).

Sim. species: Dark and rather uniform-looking flowerpiercer with no strong contrast to plumage. No other *Diglossa* in its remote, isolated range.

Status and habitat: Essentially unknown in life but apparently numerous as it is known from large no. of specimens from several tepuis. Lowest el. recs. are from Cerro Sipapo (1400–1800m); highest from Cerros Marahuaca and de la Neblina.

Range: 1400–2600m. N Amazonas on Cerros Guanay, Yavi, and Sipapo (*hitchcocki*); Sierra de la Neblina (*georgebarrowcloughi*)[153]; c and s Amazonas on Cerros Parú, Huachamacari, Duida, and Marahuaca; sw Bolívar on Cerro Sarisariñama and Meseta de Jaua (*duidae*). N Brazil (Cerro de la Neblina).

Glossy Flowerpiercer
PLATE 57

Diglossa lafresnayii   Roba Néctar Lustroso

Identification: 5.7″ (14.5cm). 16g. Bill strongly upturned and sharply hooked at tip; lower mandible pale gray. Plumage entirely glossy black above; small but *conspic. triangular-shaped blue gray shoulder patch*; underparts flat black.

Sim. species: Over most of range in Venez. easily recognized as it is only "all-black" flowerpiercer. In s Táchira occurs with very sim. Black Flowerpiercer (see), and there the two are often not separable in field. Also cf. ♂ White-sided Flowerpiercer which may not show white until it flicks wings.

Voice: Song an exuberant stream of rapid chattering and chipping notes, *chit'chat'chip'chap'chip'chip 'cheet'chit . . .* and so on for up to 1 min or more; colorless, rather directionless, and rising and falling with no clear pattern; some songs more repetitive with galloping pattern to notes. Sometimes sung more or less simultaneously as a duet by pr. (antiphonal?).

Behavior: Usually sings from top of shrub but otherwise restless, rather furtive, and often difficult to see well. Hops quickly and secretively through thick vegetation, occas. popping up into view momentarily to pierce flower for nectar, or to dart after flying insect, then disappearing again quick as a wink. Keeps low as crosses open spaces quickly and dives into cover. Prs. defend territories when breeding, but when not breeding each bird vigorously defends individual territory against other conspecifics and other nectar feeders. Reg. forages with mixed-spp. flocks, but also away from them.

Status and habitat: Fairly common in shrubby thickets and stunted mossy forest borders at treeline, and in wet forest borders, overgrown pastures, hedgerows, and flower gardens at lower el. Largely replaced in drier areas by Mérida Flowerpiercer.

Range: 2000–3500m. Throughout Andes of Táchira, Mérida, and Trujillo n to Páramo Misisí, and Páramo de las Rosas on Lara border (*lafresnayii*). Andes of Colombia and Ecuador; n Peru (Cajamarca).

Black Flowerpiercer
PLATE 57

Diglossa humeralis   Roba Néctar Negro y Gris

Identification: 5.4″ (13.7cm). 12g. Bill strongly upturned and sharply hooked at tip. Very sim. to previous sp. but slightly smaller. Above glossy black, rump dark gray (not conspic. in field or in hand), small but *conspic. triangular-shaped shoulder patch blue gray*; underparts flat black. Imm.: grayish brown, indistinctly streaked dusky; below paler and more prom. streaked.

Sim. species: *Practically inseparable* from Glossy Flowerpiercer in field, but note that only Glossy Flower-

piercer is found n of Táchira Depression in Andes and only Black Flowerpiercer is found in Sierra de Perijá. But both occur together in s Táchira; there many will remain unidentified. Some points to note are Black's slightly smaller size, shorter bill (9–10 vs. 10–12mm), *gray rump* (not much contrast), and perhaps slightly less glossy plumage and grayer shoulder patch.
Voice: Sputtering and twittering song sim. to that of Glossy Flowerpiercer but even faster (F. Vuilleumier).
Behavior: Sim. to Glossy Flowerpiercer but less often follows mixed-spp. flocks. Like Glossy, forms prs. to breed, but otherwise individuals aggressively defend solitary territories with flowers against conspecifics and other nectar feeders such as hummingbirds during nonbreeding season. Nesting prs. are hostile toward other prs. of same sp.[420] In Ecuador a rootlet and moss cup nest suspended from thorns on edges of a swordlike aloe leaf; 0.8m up; 2 bluish eggs speckled with rufous[209].
Status and habitat: Resident. Stunted humid and wet elfin forest, shrubby borders, and wooded ravines, mostly at or near treeline.

Range: 2175–3300m (most recs. above 2700m). Sierra de Perijá, Zulia (*nocticolor*); extreme s Táchira on Páramo de Tamá (*humeralis*).
Note: Previously treated as race of Carbonated Flowerpiercer (*D. carbonaria*), along with next sp.

Mérida Flowerpiercer
PLATE 57
Diglossa gloriosa Roba Néctar de Mérida
Identification: 5.3″ (13.5cm). 11g. Deep black (not glossy) with *small, triangular, blue gray shoulder patch*; faint blue gray eyebrow and rump (both usually inconspic.); *mid. breast, belly, and under tail coverts chestnut, flanks gray* (not always conspic. in field); may show traces of rufous malar stripe. Imm.: dusky brown above; dark brown streaked buff on throat and chest; rusty buff somewhat streaked dusky on lower underparts.
Sim. species: Gray shoulders and chestnut belly are the marks. Rusty Flowerpiercer lacks shoulder patch and is much paler below. Larger Blue-backed Conebill is brighter with blue back. Glossy Flowerpiercer is all black below.
Behavior: Sim. to Glossy and Black flowerpiercers but not nearly as furtive, this sp. is often quite easy to see despite nervous, high-strung behavior. Usually alone or in prs. working quickly through patches of flowers, piercing one after another in rapid succession. Prs. aggressively defend joint feeding territories when breeding and maintain individual territories when not breeding. May follow mixed-spp. flocks but more often independent of them. Nest, prob. this sp., deep grass and moss cup atop bank; Apr[778].

Status and habitat: Common resident in cultivated areas with bushy hedgerows, flower gardens, and in patches of stunted woodland and shrubbery from treeline to far above it. Favors dry and rather open highland valleys; much less numerous or absent in wet montane forest.

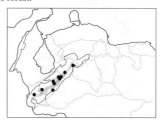

Range: ENDEMIC. 2500–4150m. Andes of n Táchira, Mérida, and Trujillo n to Páramo Cendé on Lara border.
Note: Formerly a subsp. of Coal-black Flowerpiercer (*D. carbonaria*) which was split into 3 spp.[777] or 4 spp.[216].

White-sided Flowerpiercer
PLATE 57
Diglossa albilatera Roba Néctar de Lados Blancos
Identification: 4.8″ (12.2cm). 10g. Bill slightly upturned and hooked at tip. ♂: entirely blackish slate; *under wing coverts and partly concealed tufts on sides of breast white* (conspic. as bird flicks wings or flies). Or plumage grayer (*federalis*). ♀: above olive brown, throat and chest rich buffy brown to tawny, flanks buffy olive, central lower underparts white; *under wing coverts and lengthened tufts on sides of breast white as in* ♂; occas. shows 1 faint whitish wing bar. Imm.: like ♀ but indistinctly streaked dusky below.
Sim. species: Either sex easily told by white tufts protruding beneath wings (if in doubt, watch for wing flicks).
Voice: Song 1–2 high, shrill notes followed by lower-pitched rattle-trill of even pitch and strength, *SWEE-ti 'ti'ti'ti't'ti'ti'ti'ti'ti'ti'ti'ti*, entire song lasting just over 1 sec. In n cordilleras typically a high, thin, tinny trill descending slightly, then a flat rattle, *tititititititititititittte'te 'te'te'te'te'te*. When disturbed a flat buzzy trill, much faster than song and sometimes rising slightly in pitch.
Behavior: A small sp., in behavior most sim. to Slaty and Venezuelan flowerpiercers. Single birds or prs. are restless and hyperactive as they constantly flick wings and display little flashes of white with each flick. Move somewhat furtively along dense forest borders. Occur from eye level to canopy but mostly at mid. levels where pierce flower corollas for nectar, going from one to another in rapid succession. Esp. fond of flowering vines and trees. Occas. sally short distances for insects. Occur with mixed-spp. flocks or away from them about equally. Cup nest of moss, grass, and lichens 1m up in bamboo; eggs, in Colombia, greenish blue thickly marked reddish brown around larger end[589].
Status and habitat: Fairly common resident along humid forest borders, esp. where there are many shrubs and vines, and around openings or treefalls in forest; also cultivated areas and highland gardens. More numerous at lower els. (ca. 1800–2400m) than other *Diglossa*.

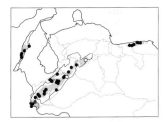

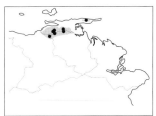

Range: 1600–3200m. Sierra de Perijá, Zulia; Andes from s Táchira n to Mérida and paramos of n Trujillo/s Lara border (*albilatera*); PN Yacambú (sight), Lara; Coastal Cordillera (sightings up to 2400m, Pico Oriental–D. Ascanio) in Aragua and Distr. Federal (*federalis*); prob. adj. Miranda. Andes from Colombia to s Peru.

Venezuelan Flowerpiercer
PLATE 57

Diglossa venezuelensis   Roba Néctar de Venezuela

Identification: 5″ (12.7cm). Much like White-sided Flowerpiercer (no range overlap) but slightly larger. ♂ differs from ♂ White-sided in plumage *all black* (not dark gray), white pectoral tufts and wing linings smaller. ♀: *head dark yellowish olive*, otherwise above like ♀ White-sided Flowerpiercer but slightly darker; below darker, throat and chest dull dark yellowish olive turning brownish olive on lower underparts; *white pectoral tufts and wing linings* as above.

Sim. species: Overlaps only Rusty Flowerpiercer, ♂ of which is cinnamon below; both sexes *lack* white pectoral tufts (but white tufts not very obvious on Venezuelan Flowerpiercer). Cf. ♀ to Golden-fronted Greenlet and ♀ Guira Tanager.

Voice: Song on Cerro Negro a complex but somewhat repetitive ser. of soft, low-pitched notes uttered rapidly, the whole ser. lasting up to ca. 25 sec, chattery and rising and falling several times; recalls Greater Flowerpiercer but softer and lacks that sp.'s energy and speed[61].

Behavior: A nervous, hyperactive bird much like others of genus. Takes nectar by piercing flowers at almost any ht. (most recs. are at mid. hts.) but also often quite low, even foraging near gd. in *Heliconia* thickets. Occurs singly or in prs. and generally not with mixed-spp. flocks.

Status and habitat: Resident in humid forest borders, young to advanced second growth, and shrubby areas adj. to forest. Apparently fairly common formerly as it is known from rather large no. of specimens incl. 17 taken late Jan–Feb 1963 on Cerro Turumiquire, Sucre. A few recent sight recs. from near Melenas at se edge of PN Península de Paria[127] and on Cerro Negro[127], most recent being 1 ♀-plumaged bird photographed[62] in Apr 1994. Status of this sp. on Cerro Turumiquire, a region now converted primarily to shade coffee plantations, is unknown. Deforestation is extensive within small, narrow el. range of this seriously threatened bird.

Range: ENDEMIC. 1525–2450m in Cordillera de Caripe; 1675–1775m on Cerro Negro; sight recs. at ca. 885m at Melenas on Paria Pen., Sucre. Paria Pen. (Cerro Humo), Sucre; mts. of sw Sucre from e slope of

Cerro Peonía e to Cerro Turumiquire on Sucre/Monagas border; Cerro Negro on Sucre and Monagas border.

Note: This sp. closely allied to widespread White-sided Flowerpiercer.

Rusty Flowerpiercer
PLATE 57

Diglossa sittoides   Roba Néctar Payador

Identification: 4.7″ (12cm). 9g. Small with sharply hooked, upturned bill. ♂: above blue gray; narrow *blackish mask on forehead, lores, and sides of head*; below *entirely cinnamon*; flight feathers and tail dusky. ♀: above olive brown, usually with 2 *faint* yellowish wing bars; tertials pale edged; facial area often tinged yellowish; underparts olive tinged pale yellow to whitish, often with *ill-defined dusky streaking*; central lower underparts unstreaked. Or slightly paler above and below (*coelestis*); or both sexes darker above and below, head almost blackish (*mandeli*). Imm. and subad. ♂: like ♀ or with varying amts. of cinnamon on underparts.

Sim. species: No other *Diglossa* in Venez. is so "bicolored." See Mérida Flowerpiercer; also Rufous-browed and Blue-backed conebills.

Voice: Call a sharp *cheek*[274].

Behavior: Usually seen singly or in prs., only incidentally in mixed-spp. flocks. Quick and active, feeding heavily on nectar obtained by piercing bases of flower corollas. Also sally actively for small flying insects. Around favorable patches of flowers, individuals or prs. may attempt to hold feeding territories but are timid and reg. harassed by larger flowerpiercers and hummingbirds which they avoid by darting into dense vegetation or by leaving area. Individuals may wander over relatively large areas. Unlike larger allies, do not feed much (if at all) on fruit. Deep cup nest; 2 gray to blue eggs with obscure gray spots[274].

Status and habitat: Generally in low density or very locally fairly common. Resident in shrubby areas along forest and woodland borders, coffee plantations, and flowering shrubs and hedgerows around habitations, even in large urban areas. Not inside mature forest.

Range: 800–2500m (most recs. ca. 1200–2000m). Sierra de Perijá, Zulia (*coelestis*); Andes from s Táchira and w Barinas to se and nw Lara (*dorbignyi*); mts. of Yaracuy and Coastal Cordillera from Carabobo to Distr. Federal and Miranda; Interior Cordillera on Cerro Azul, n Cojedes, and Cerro Golfo Triste, s Aragua (*hyperythra*); Cerro Turumiquire, Sucre (*mandeli*); no recs. (?) on Paria Pen. Colombia s in Andes to nw Argentina.

Tersina

Has been placed in separate family, Tersinidae[401]. Differs from other tanagers in broad, flat bill, long swallowlike wings, and short, weak tarsi; aerial insect feeder; eats large fruits; nomadic or migratory habits; hole nester; gregarious.

Swallow Tanager   PLATE 60
Tersina viridis   Azulejo Golondrina
Identification: 6″ (15cm). 29g. *Rather plump*; bill flat, wider than long; *tail short*. ♂: *shining turquoise blue, forehead, lores, ocular area, and throat black*; flight feathers and tail black broadly edged blue, flanks barred black, *center of lower breast to crissum white*. ♀: pattern sim. but *mostly dull green*, facial area and throat mottled brownish gray, center of lower underparts buffy yellow; *flanks yellow barred dark green*.
Sim. species: ♂'s blue color and habit of perching high in open might recall ♂ Spangled Cotinga. ♀ recalls several "greenish" tanagers, but note barred flanks and chunky shape.
Voice: Commonest call a high, slightly buzzy *tzeet*, distinctive once learned; ♂'s squeaky, twittering song recalls that of Blue-gray Tanager.
Behavior: Gregarious, and esp. so when not breeding, then gathering in varying-sized groups of 5–100 or more. Flight is strong and swift. Typically sit in open on high bare branches. Eat much fruit, esp. Lauraceae, by reaching or hanging downward or hovering[569], and sally for flying insects. As breeding approaches, ♂♂ display to each other and to ♀♀ with exaggerated bowing, bobbing, and chasing. Prs. breed singly or in loose colonies; cavity in buildings, bridges, wall, or dug by ♀ in bank or roadcut; 2–3 white eggs[569,750].
Status and habitat: Resident, short-distance migrant, and nomad. Moist and humid lowland and premontane forest, second growth, and wooded borders. Locally in dry semideciduous forest. Common breeder across n hills and cordilleras, incl. PN Henri Pittier, Feb–late Jul; absent rest of yr. S of Orinoco erratic, mainly Jul–Feb but nos. inconsistent suggesting nomadism. In Andes occurrence erratic and movements not well documented. In all nonbreeding areas prob. partially nomadic. Two migratory flocks of ca. 75 and 125 respectively, and several groups of 20 or more in bare trees over coffee on Cerro Negro, Sucre, 25 Aug 1994[259]; 3 on 18 Nov 1978, Serranía de Chichiriviche, Falcón, were prob. nomads (C. Parrish). Prob. throughout, at least as nomad.
Range: To 1800m n of Orinoco; to 1050m s of Orinoco. Sierra de Perijá, Zulia; w slope of Andes from nw Táchira (La Fria) n to Trujillo (sight); e slope from s Táchira to w Barinas and Portuguesa (Acarigua); e Fal-

cón (sight, Serranía de Chichiriviche), n cordilleras from Carabobo and n Guárico (Cerro Platillón) to Distr. Federal and e Miranda; mts. of Sucre and n Monagas; nonbreeding migrant (?) locally across Amazonas and Bolívar (*occidentalis*). E Panama to n Argentina, se Brazil (austral birds migratory), and the Guianas. Trinidad.

Plushcap   PLATE 58
Catamblyrhynchus diadema   Cabecipeludo
Identification: 5.5″ (14cm). 16g. Short, black bill thick and swollen. *Forecrown golden yellow*, the feathers extremely dense, stiff, and plushy (hence name); hindcrown, nape, and line over eyes black, rest of upperparts blue gray; *sides of head and underparts chestnut*; tail rounded, the feathers (in hand) pointed, outer web very narrow. Imm.: above olive gray, paler below; throat and chest somewhat streaked dusky, lower underparts tinged rufescent.
Sim. species: Plushcap's basic plumage—blue gray above and chestnut below—is shared by numerous highland tanagers and emberizids. See Blue-backed Conebill, Slaty-backed Hemispingus, and Rufous-crested Tanager, none of which has yellow forecrown. Also see Golden-crowned Tanager, rare in Venez.
Voice: Soft, high, undistinctive *chip* notes when foraging. Infreq. hd. song, in Peru, a monotone of unmusical *chip* notes and twitters, 15–60 sec in length; reminiscent of song of several *Hemispingus* tanagers (T. Parker) or of a hummingbird.
Behavior: One or 2, or occas. families, follow mixed-spp. flocks containing warblers, conebills, tanagers, and brush-finches and are seldom seen away from flocks. Primarily a foraging specialist on *Chusquea* bamboo, this sp. actively hops up curving bamboo stems or clings or twists around sideways paridlike to peer and then push bill into whorls of foliage at stem internodes. Food is apparently small insects and some plant material. Nest undescribed. Forages mainly in lower half of forest (1–6m up) and always seems to be on the move, seldom remaining in view for more than a few moments.
Status and habitat: Uncommon resident of wet mossy montane forest, dense forest borders, and elfin woodland, wherever there is *Chusquea* bamboo.
Range: 2300–2900m in Andes; 1800–2200m (prob. higher) in Coastal Cordillera. Sierra de Perijá, Zulia; Andes from s Táchira to se Trujillo at Cerro Teta de Niquitao (*diadema*); Coastal Cordillera in Aragua and Distr. Federal (*federalis*); prob. Miranda. Colombia s in Andes to nw Argentina.

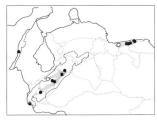

Note 1: Systematic position of this bird is uncertain. Has been placed in its own family, Catamblyrhynchidae; in a subfamily within Emberizidae; or in Thraupidae. **Note 2:** Called Plush-capped Finch by most earlier authors.

Cardinalidae: Cardinals, Grosbeaks, and Saltators

Picogordos, Lechoseros, y Cardenales

This is a small group of South American finches, along with others in North America, that are closely related to emberizid finches and to tanagers. Included here are several species of grosbeaks, saltators, and cardinals. New evidence suggests that *Habia* and *Piranga* tanagers, as well as euphonias and chlorophonias, probably belong here, whereas saltators do not[299].

Saltator

Large and heavy-billed; culmen somewhat decurved; many with olive or grayish upperparts, often with eyestripe and black malar or border on pale throat; most spp. frugivorous; almost certainly more closely related to tanagers than to cardinalids[299].

Southern Grayish Saltator — PLATE 63

Saltator coerulescens   Lechosero Ajicero
Identification: 8″ (20.3cm). 55g. *Head and upperparts mostly gray*, flight feathers tinged olive green, *short eyebrow white*, median throat whitish bordered by *black malar stripe*; underparts mostly pale gray tinged buff, belly and under tail coverts buff. Or upperparts and breast more olive gray (*olivascens*).
Sim. species: Both Buff-throated and Streaked saltators have olive (not obviously gray) backs. Also cf. ♀ Shiny Cowbird with more pointed bill and uniform underparts.
Voice: Songs vary geographically and individually. In Falcón, a loud, musical *wee chop cheeEEeer* (mid. note drops). In w Apure a halting or jerky ser. of emphatic phrases, *yur-FEET! your SEAT! tduur* or sim. variation, somewhat musical. In common variation ♂ sings *feétz-your wheét*, ♀ answers with sim. *whit, yu, wheet*. Prs. also duet (not antiphonal) in territorial defense, one giving loud *SPEAK YOUR, pit-pit-pit-pit, CHEAP Your . . .* and so on while mate sings high, choppy, chattering notes. Or prs. may give loosely antiphonal duets, one bird singing 3–4 notes, other a longer ser., then 1st bird finishing song. Call a forced, almost squeaky *tseet!*
Behavior: These are noisy, boisterous birds, at times bubbly and effervescent as they sing and chase one an-

other back and forth, but at other times unobtrusive, even a bit furtive, as they slip around quietly and keep under cover. Usually in prs. or groups that incl. prs. and helpers. Territorial and forage alone in bushy or disturbed areas, usually staying well up in vegetation. Ads. feed almost entirely on fruit, flowers, and buds or young leaves, infreq. insects; more insects fed to young. Bulky stick and grass cup nest, 1.8–4m up and well hidden in dense shrubbery; 2–3 pale blue eggs with fine black lines at larger end[706,750]; breeding in May, Guárico; Sep fledglings, w Apure[137,734].
Status and habitat: Common resident in dry scrub, deciduous woodland, and gallery forest borders in n Venez.; humid forest borders, second-growth thickets, and bushy pastures elsewhere. No recs. s of Río Ventuari, Amazonas, or s Bolívar.

Range: To 850m n of Orinoco; to 300m s of Orinoco. Widespread s to nw Amazonas (to Río Ventuari), n Bolívar (Ciudad Bolívar; lower Río Paragua), Sierra de Imataca and Delta Amacuro (*brewsteri*); se Bolívar at base of Cerro Roraima (*olivascens*). Nw Mexico to n Argentina and Uruguay.
Note: Perhaps a separate sp. from birds of C Amer. and w of Andes; there are a no. of distinct vocal groups e of Andes as well.

Buff-throated Saltator — PLATE 63

Saltator maximus   Picurero
Identification: 8″ (20.3cm). 42g. *Upperparts bright olive green*; sides of head and most of underparts gray, *short eyebrow white*; central throat mostly buff (upper throat whitish) bordered on sides by *broad black malar stripe*; center of belly and under tail coverts ochraceous to cinnamon buff.
Sim. species: Despite name, buff throat stripe is inconspic. and only partly buff. Cf. Southern Grayish Saltator which is *obviously gray* (not olive green) above and lacks buff on throat. Also see Streaked Saltator.
Voice: A fine singer with pleasing, if repetitious, caroling song recalling that of several *Turdus* thrushes. Typically a rather soft *cheete-lewert, weete-wert, sweetle-e-er, e-te-were . . .* and so on. Sometimes sings softly ("faint song") as if singing to itself. Call a thin, strained squeak.
Behavior: A bird of quiet manners and a sweet song. Usually seen singly or in prs., sometimes with mixed-spp. flocks. Forages at almost any ht. but usually well up in trees, for fruit, flowers, buds, nectar from mashed flowers, and tender new leaves, rarely insects. Can be rather wary, and typically remains partially hidden or in shady areas. Coarse leaf, twig, and weed nest cup,

usually low; 2 pale blue eggs with ring of marks around larger end[750]; Jun and Aug nests, n Colombia. **Status and habitat:** Common resident in humid forest borders, shrubby second growth, lighter woodland, and plantations, even urban areas where there is shrubbery and tree cover. N of Orinoco found primarily in or near mts. and replaced in dry and scrubby areas by Streaked Saltator. S of Orinoco widespread in both lowlands and foothills.

Range: To 1650m n of Orinoco; to 1400m s of Orinoco. Perijá region of Zulia, w and e base of Andes, c and se Falcón (Sierra de San Luis; sight, Cerro Misión), n cordilleras from Yaracuy to Distr. Federal and Miranda, and nw end of llanos in Portuguesa (Ospino) and Cojedes (sight, Hato Piñero); throughout Amazonas and Bolívar; mouth of Río Amacuro in Delta Amacuro (*maximus*). Mexico to nw Peru, n Bolivia, Amaz. Brazil; the Guianas; se Brazil.

Streaked Saltator   PLATE 63
Saltator striatipectus   Lechosero Pechirrayado
Identification: 7.5″ (19cm). 36g. Thick bill blackish narrowly tipped yellow. *Above olive green,* head grayer with *short white eyebrow*; rump grayish, below whitish *broadly streaked dusky,* median throat and belly unstreaked, breast sometimes with buff tinge.
Sim. species: Combination of size and streaking below diagnostic. Southern Grayish Saltator is gray (not olive green) above; Buff-throated Saltator has black malar and unstreaked underparts.
Voice: Often hd. song a lazy and musically whistled *o-chúck, chuk-weEEeaaar* or a repeated *chuck weEEear;* or *chur WEET chuck wEEer* or sim. variation. Call a loud *quick.*
Behavior: May sing from fairly high perches in early morning, but otherwise can be rather inconspic. as browses at various hts. from ca. eye level to well up in trees. Occurs alone, in prs., or in families, and like others of genus, almost wholly frugivorous, eating a large variety of fruits, also flower petals and flower parts. Cup nest 0.6–6m up in vines or thicket; 2 eggs[624], pale greenish blue with band of black lines around larger end[589].
Status and habitat: Fairly common to common resident in dry to moist (but not arid) regions. Forest borders, bushy pastures, gardens, light woodland, scrubby second growth, and waste areas, usually in or near foothills or lower montane els. A sp. that has profited from deforestation.
Range: To 2000m (most recs. below 1600m). S Zulia, w and e base of Andes n to se Lara (PN Yacambú); Fal-

cón (incl. Sierra de San Luis), and generally from Yaracuy and n Portuguesa e through n cordilleras to Sucre, n Monagas, and n Guárico; Isla Patos (*perstriatus*). Costa Rica to w Peru.
Note: Formerly *S. albicollis.* Does not incl. Lesser Antillean Saltator (*S. albicollis*), now considered a separate sp.[10,593]

Orinocan Saltator   PLATE 63
Saltator orenocensis   Lechosero Pechiblanco
Identification: 7.5″ (19cm). 35g. Above dark gray, *crown, sides of head, and neck extending to chest black with long conspic. white eyestripe*; small white spot at base of mandible, median throat and breast white, *rest of underparts bright cinnamon buff,* brightest on sides, flanks, and under tail coverts. Or sim. but more extensively buff below (*rufescens*).
Sim. species: Bold head pattern and rich buff underparts are striking and not likely confused.
Voice: Loud, exuberant song mainly hd. at dawn by 1 bird, or more often as lively duet (antiphonal?) by pr., or occas. trio, perching close together on high exposed twig. In n Falcón song a spirited, rollicking *chup'ep FEETS er'chup, chup'er FEETS er'chup . . .* and so on (*FEETS* note much higher pitched), the other a rapid chatter. Birds in w Apure (and elsewhere in llanos) sing different songs.
Behavior: Prs. or trios forage alone, mostly for fruit and flowers (eat flower petals or mash them for nectar), rarely insects. Stay well up in trees and can be conspic. when singing, but otherwise unobtrusive as browse in foliage. Readily mob small owls and snakes. Prs. or trios are typically very territorial and come quickly and sing excitedly following an imitation of their song. Breeding, May in Guárico, Jul in w Apure[137,734].
Status and habitat: Fairly common resident in dry regions. Dry deciduous woodland and mesic vegetation along dry washes and creeks in arid regions of n Fal-

cón; gallery forest borders, brush, and scrubby vegetation in llanos.

Range: To 600m. Sw and e Zulia, e to n Lara and c Falcón (*rufescens*); e of Andes from Cojedes and w Apure e through Guárico and Anzoátegui to w Sucre and s Monagas (Barrancas); s bank of Orinoco in n Bolívar (Caicara; Ciudad Bolívar; sight, Pto. Ordaz) and s Delta Amacuro at Piacoa (*orenocensis*). Ne Colombia.

Note: Geographic differences in songs need investigation.

Slate-colored Grosbeak   PLATE 63
Saltator grossus   Picogordo Gargantiblanco

Identification: 7.5″ (19cm). 44g. *Thick coral red bill.* ♂: *mostly dark bluish slate,* central throat white, lores, sides of head, and narrow band surrounding throat black. ♀: sim. but lacks black around face and throat; paler gray below. Imm.: like ♀ but duller; no white on throat.

Sim. species: Best marks are "hot pink" bill and slaty plumage. Small white throat often hard to see.

Voice: Song recalls that of a peppershrike but much richer, a loud, full-bodied whistle, *wHEchit, cheechEEEr, tur-cHEit* or *prEEtuur, püü-TREEit* or *Three-more-BEEErs* or sim. variation; usually 2–3 or more song types are alternated by each individual; often sings a "faint song," a soft version of preceding songs. Calls incl. a cardinal-like *peek* and nasal whine.

Behavior: Prs. are strongly territorial, but except for occas. song or call are not apt to attract attention to themselves. Wander over large territories as forage mostly for fruit (seeds?) and some arthropod prey in mid. or upper levels inside forest, only occas. low at edges. Single birds or prs. often join mixed-spp. flocks but are not core members.

Status and habitat: Fairly common resident in humid terra firme and várzea forest, esp. in high vine tangles; also forest borders and tall second growth. Most numerous in areas of high rainfall.

Range: To 1300m. Generally in Amazonas and Bolívar (*grossus*). Honduras to n Bolivia, Amaz. Brazil, and the Guianas.

Note: Often placed in genus *Pitylus*[403]. Taxonomy follows recent authors[10,149,726].

Red-and-black Grosbeak   PLATE 63
Periporphyrus erythromelas   Picogordo Rojinegro

Identification: 8″ (20.3cm). 48g. Exceptionally thick blackish bill. ♂: *entire head and throat black,* otherwise *ox-blood red above; nuchal collar and underparts brighter spectrum red* turning rosy on lower underparts.

♀: *head and throat black* (like ♂), upperparts olive green, underparts olive yellow becoming yellow on belly. Imm.: like ♀ but more olive.

Sim. species: ♀ recalls Yellow-green Grosbeak but larger, bill much more massive, and entire head (not just foreface) black. ♂ not likely mistaken if seen well, but see ♂ Guianan Red-Cotinga.

Voice: Calls incl. a high-pitched, sharp *spink!* and *psack!* Song, by both ♂ and ♀, an exceptionally sweet, syrupy ser. of halting phrases that slide up and down, *UuureEE, ss'PEeeeuu, reet-here . . . UuureEEcheer, preEEer, psek! . . . Pseet cheer REeechur, rEEar . . .* and so on; given slowly with pauses. Song typically composed of variations built around 2–3 standard phrases.

Behavior: This large, strong grosbeak occurs in prs. or families in shady lower levels of forest, or occas. ascends into subcanopy or down to eye level. Feeds at scattered low-density fruit resources (not large fruiting trees), and infreq. noted except for occas. sharp note or fragment of its sweet song which is hd. mainly in morning hrs. Tends to remain on the move and can be wary and difficult to approach or follow. Forages and moves independently of mixed-spp. flocks and ranges widely on notably large territory.

Status and habitat: Resident. Rare to very uncommon inside mature humid lowland rain forest. Difficult to locate and not reg. encountered in Venez. Look for it in Río Grande Forest Reserve and in lowland forests n of Sierra de Lema.

Range: To 1000m. E Bolívar and s Delta Amacuro from Sierra de Imataca (Río Grande) s locally to upper Río Cuyuní (sight recs.); Cerro Roraima (1000m). The Guianas e to e Brazil around mouth of the Amazon.

Pheucticus

Large and robust with very heavy bill; all have black wings with large white wing spots; taxonomy reviewed[505].

Southern Yellow-Grosbeak   PLATE 63
Pheucticus chrysogaster   Picogordo Amarillo

Identification: 8″ (20.3cm). 65g. Thick bill blackish above, pale below with dusky tip. ♂: *mostly bright golden yellow,* back streaked black, *wings black, 2 broad white wing bars; patch at base of flight feathers and large spots on tips of inner flight feathers white;* tail black, under tail coverts and inner webs of outer tail feathers white. ♀: sim. but duller, upperparts more olive yellow; rearcrown as well as back streaked black; wings and tail brownish.

Sim. species: Looks like an oriole in flight, but note extensive white in wings. Cf. Yellow-backed Oriole which has black throat. Also see Black-backed Grosbeak which is all black above.

Voice: Call a high, metallic *eek* like others of genus. Rich, mellow song a liquid ser. of slow phrases reminiscent of a *Turdus* thrush but fuller and smoother. Each bird has large repertoire of song types.

Behavior: Acts sluggish, almost dazed at times, as perches quietly and looks around. Alone or in prs., low to high but usually fairly high when foraging and singing. Takes arthropod prey from foliage and eats many kinds of fruits and seeds. Often perches in open and may allow close approach.

Status and habitat: Uncommon and *very local* resident. Humid forest borders, bushy clearings, and hedgerows in cultivated highlands.

Range: 950–2000m. Sierra de Perijá (upper Río Negro), Zulia; n end of Andes in Lara (Cubiro; Cabudare); Coastal Cordillera in Aragua, Distr. Federal, and Miranda; Interior Cordillera in Aragua; mts. of s Sucre and n Monagas on Cerros Turumiquire and Negro (*laubmanni*). S Colombia s in Andes to s Peru.

Note: Taxonomy of "yellow-grosbeaks" uncertain. S Amer. birds are here regarded as distinct from Mexican Yellow-Grosbeak (*P. chrysopeplus*) of Mexico and Black-thighed Grosbeak (*P. tibialis*) of Costa Rica and Panama[10,541,544].

Black-backed Grosbeak   PLATE 63
Pheucticus aureoventris   Picogordo Pechinegro

Identification: 8″ (20.3cm). Thick, dusky gray blue bill. Upperparts, head, throat, and chest black, rump and *rest of underparts bright yellow, 2 broad white wing bars and prom. white patch at base of flight feathers; outer 3 prs. of tail feathers broadly tipped white.* ♀: sim. but upperparts brownish black more or less mottled with yellow, wings and tail with less white, underparts yellow, throat and breast heavily spotted and mottled with black.

Sim. species: Southern Yellow-Grosbeak has all-yellow head and upperparts; smaller ♂ Rose-breasted Grosbeak is rose and white below. ♀'s plumage pattern less distinct but always with much more black than in Southern Yellow-Grosbeak.

Voice: Rich, mellow song and sharp *keek!* or *eek!* note much like that of other *Pheucticus*.

Behavior: Single birds or prs. usually forage alone and are generally independent of mixed-spp. flocks, although occas. 3 or 4 may occur together in fruiting

tree. Feed at almost any ht., even on gd., but sing from perch high in tree. Generally easy to see.

Status and habitat: Uncommon or rare resident of dry to arid montane valleys with scrubby woodland, tree-lined borders, and shrubs. Scarcity and restricted distrib. in Venez. prob. due to limited dry (rainshadow) habitat in highland valleys. Known from upper Río Chama at San Jacinto; La Pedregosa; and Páramo del Morro. Some migratory movement possible.

Range: Ca. 1450–2500m. Andes of c Mérida (*meridensis*). Colombia s in Andes to n Argentina; lowlands of e Bolivia, sw Brazil, and Paraguay.

Rose-breasted Grosbeak   PLATE 63
Pheucticus ludovicianus   Picogordo Degollado

Identification: 7.5″ (19cm). 42g. *Thick, chalky white bill* (♂); duller (♀). Breeding-plumage ♂ (prior to n migration): head, throat, and upperparts black with *white rump; large white patches on wing coverts, white patch at base of flight feathers, and white spots on tertials*; rest of underparts white with *large rose red triangle on chest.* Nonbreeding ♂: sim. but above mottled brownish, a few buff streaks on head, incl. narrow buff eyeline and coronal stripe; underparts flecked brown with traces of rose. ♀ and imm.: mainly dark brown streaked dusky above; *prom. white eyestripe and coronal stripe*; cheeks dark brown, wing bars buffy white, tertials buff-tipped; throat whitish, *breast and sides buffy white with numerous rather short narrow blackish streaks.*

Sim. species: ♂ unmistakable if rose breast is seen. In flight flashing "black and white" wing pattern might recall ♂ Black-and-white Seedeater. ♀'s best marks are heavy bill, robust shape, striped head, dark cheeks, and fine streaking below.

Voice: Occas. a high, metallic *eek* like other *Pheucticus*. Little or no song in Venez.

Behavior: Returning migrants arrive singly and wander alone or in small loose group of 2–5 to fruiting trees where they eat many seeds and fruits. Largely independent of mixed-spp. flocks. During nonbreeding months of residency gradually join with others of their kind, forming loosely assoc. but increasingly larger and apparently seminomadic groups. By Mar or Apr restless-acting groups of 20–40 perch in semiopen prior to moving northward.

Status and habitat: Very uncommon fall transient; increasingly numerous nonbreeding n winter resident and spring transient (mid Oct–mid Apr), most numerous after Dec. Dry to humid forest borders, tall second growth, and light woodland in foothills and mts. Largest no. of specimens from Sierra de Perijá and

Andes of Táchira and Mérida with decreasing nos. east-ward through coastal mts. (but many sight recs. from vicinity of Caracas). Vagrants likely almost anywhere.

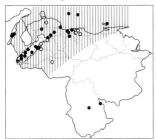

Range: To 2000m (most mainland recs. above ca. 600m, occas. lower). Sierra de Perijá, Zulia; Andes from s Táchira to Lara; Sierra de San Luis, Falcón (sight); mts. of Yaracuy and n cordilleras from Cara-bobo to Distr. Federal, Miranda, and nw Guárico; c Amazonas (once on Cerro Duida; once in Sierra Par-ima on Upper Río Metacuni); Islas Los Roques (once on Isla Namusqui); Isla de Aves (once); Isla Margarita (*ludovicianus*). Breeds in N Amer.; migrates through C Amer. and W Indies; winters from Mexico to Colombia and Venez., rarely to c Peru; Guyana (once).

Cyanocompsa

Med.-sized grosbeaks; heavy bill; plumage dark blue (♂) or brown (♀); undergrowth of forest or scrub; inconspic.

Blue-black Grosbeak   PLATE 64
Cyanocompsa cyanoides   Picogordo Azul
Identification: 6.3″ (16cm). 25g. Notably *heavy, black-ish bill* conical and pointed; culmen straight. ♂: *mostly dark blackish blue*; lores and cheeks blackish; *fore-head, faintly indicated eyebrow, and small shoulder patch bright blue* (inconspic.). Or overall bluer; fore-head, eyebrow, spot at lower base of bill, and small shoulder patch azure blue (*rothschildii*). ♀: *uniform dark brown* with slight rufescent tinge.
Sim. species: See Ultramarine Grosbeak.
Voice: Often hd. song by ♂ (occas. ♀) in Coastal Cor-dillera a few slow introductory notes, then a rich musi-cal jumble of descending notes. Songs in Andes and s of Orinoco differ somewhat. Call, esp. when disturbed or nervous, a sharp, metallic *chink* or *chink-chink*, often accompanied by sweeping upflick of tail.
Behavior: This sp. is hd. far more than seen. Prs. often remain rather close together as they move through thick, shady undergrowth and keep out of sight. Sing from concealed locations and rarely perch exposed or more than a few meters up. Forage independently of other birds, mostly for scattered, low-density fruit and occas. insects. May crush and eat many seeds (?). Cup nest varies in size; fine twigs, rootlets, and fungal rhizo-morphs, 0.4–5m up in spiny palm, tree fern, or shrub; 2 bluish white eggs with wreath of reddish brown dots at larger end[624,709]; breeding evidence Feb–Oct, Colombia[260].

Status and habitat: Resident. Often common in thick-ets and dense vegetation in humid forest, second growth, shrubby forest borders, and overgrown planta-tions in lowlands and foothills. Not away from humid areas.

Range: To 1400m n of Orinoco; to 1000m s of Orinoco. Base of Sierra de Perijá, Zulia, both slopes of Andes from Táchira n to Mérida and Barinas (prob. Lara); Yaracuy, se Falcón, and n cordilleras from Carabobo to Distr. Federal and se Miranda at Cerro Negro (*cya-noides*); Sucre, n Monagas, Delta Amacuro, and gener-ally in Amazonas and Bolívar (*rothschildii*). S Mexico to nw Peru, n Bolivia, Amaz. Brazil, and the Guianas.

Ultramarine Grosbeak   PLATE 64
Cyanocompsa brissonii   Picogordo Guaro
Identification: 6″ (15cm). 23g. Heavy blackish bill. ♂: much like Blue-black Grosbeak but slightly smaller; bill shorter, thicker, more swollen, and with decurved culmen; in area of overlap also differs in *forehead, short eyebrow, spot at base of bill, and small shoulder patch contrasting azure blue* (much brighter than in Blue-black Grosbeak), and rump contrasting light blue (not concolor with back). ♀: resembles ♀ Blue-black but slightly smaller and much paler brown; above warm snuff brown, *below cinnamon to pale buffy brown, paler than above.*
Voice: Song somewhat like that of Blue-black Gros-beak but higher pitched and faster; a rich ser. of rising and falling warbles, *wee-se-weep wee-so-weeep wee see wee-so-weeep*, without Blue-black's slow introduc-tory phrases; overall recalls N Amer.–breeding Blue Grosbeak (*Guiraca caerulea*). Sharp, metallic *pik* call unlike that of Blue-black Grosbeak.
Behavior: Has skulking habits like allied Blue-black Grosbeak and perhaps more wary, but lives in drier and less dense habitat so sometimes a little easier to glimpse. Usually in prs. that are almost always within ca. 4m of gd., either close together or well separated but independent of other birds.
Status and habitat: Uncommon to locally fairly com-mon resident in arid and semiarid desert scrub, dry for-est borders, dry scrub, thickets, and shrubby borders in agricultural areas.
Range: To 1600m (most recs. below 900m). C Falcón (vicinity of Sierra de San Luis; Coro), n base of Andes in s Lara (Cubiro; PN Yacambú), and arid zones at base of n cordilleras from Carabobo to Miranda and n Guárico (Cerro Platillón; Altagracia de Orituco); w

Sucre s to c Monagas (*minor*). Sw Colombia (local); e Bolivia and e Brazil s to n Argentina and Uruguay.
Note: Formerly *C. cyanea*[403]. Also placed in genus *Passerina*[712].

Caryothraustes

Two spp. (1 in Venez.), smaller in size and bill not as heavy as in other grosbeaks; both olive yellow with black on face; lowland rain forests.

Yellow-green Grosbeak   PLATE 63
Caryothraustes canadensis   Picogordo Verde
Identification: 6.7″ (17cm). 33g. Thick blackish bill pale gray at base. *Mostly bright olive yellow with black lores, foreface, and upper throat*; wings and tail darker, underparts bright primuline yellow tinged olive on chest, sides, and flanks.
Sim. species: Confusion likely only with larger ♀ Red-and-black Grosbeak which has all-black head and much larger bill.
Voice: When foraging, loud, buzzy rattle, *b'z'z'et!* and loud, often-repeated *teach-yerp!* with rising then falling inflection. Dawn song a rather lively but monotonously repeated *chap, chap cheeweep . . .* with scarcely a pause.
Behavior: Troops about in noisy prs. or flocks of up to 12 or more, from mid. level to forest canopy. Usually not too difficult to see. Follow mixed-spp. flocks, or more often groups forage independently of them. Sing from within canopy or occas. while perched in open on bare branch above canopy. Groups of up to 16 have been noted at dusk, suggesting they may roost in close proximity. Feed on fruit and some insects.
Status and habitat: Uncommon to locally common resident in humid forest and forest borders in lowlands and tepui foothills. Most numerous in areas of high rainfall, least numerous in white sandy soil forests.

Range: To 1000m. Locally throughout Amazonas and Bolívar (*canadensis*). E Colombia to the Guianas, ne and e Brazil.

Paroaria

Short, stout bill; red on head; gray to blackish upperparts; white below; mostly in open areas, often near water.

Red-capped Cardinal   PLATE 65
Paroaria gularis   Cardenal Bandera Alemana
Identification: 6.5″ (16.5cm). 22g. Eyes orange to red (ad.). Bill black above, pinkish below. Slight nuchal crest. *Head, throat, and center of chest coming to a point on breast glistening crimson*, lores and *broad postocular band black*; rest of upperparts black; partial collar on sides of neck white, rest of underparts white. Or sim. but lower throat and center of chest black (*gularis*). Imm.: upperparts brownish, crown dark brown, face, throat, and pointed bib reaching to breast paler buffy brown, lower underparts dirty white; eyes dark.
Sim. species: Ads. unmistakable, but brown-headed imms. often confused. Imm.'s pattern echos that of ad. but duller. If in doubt, look for presence of ads., a few of which are usually with groups of imms.
Voice: Generally rather quiet. Song a clear, sweet *suweet-chú*, rising, falling, repeated at short intervals; call a soft *chuép*.
Behavior: All visitors to llanos soon make the acquaintance of this friendly and conspic. little bird with its old "German flag" colors, hence Spanish name. Singly, in prs., or in families, often near water where forage independently by inspecting bare sticks and twigs, hopping on bare or muddy gd., on floating vegetation, or in shrubbery, then fly off low to rest in nearby shrub. Away from water forage well up in large spreading trees such as *Pithecellobium* by hopping along large limbs and picking and gleaning insects from bark. Around ranch houses readily attracted to feeders with rice and fruit and may gather in large nos. Nest a thin, neatly formed rootlet cup low in marsh; 2–3 greenish white eggs with brown and mauve patches [115]; breeding Jun–Nov, Guárico[734].
Status and habitat: Common to abundant resident in llanos, found in virtually all open or semiopen habitats with even a few shrubs or trees, and esp. in vicinity of water. Commonest passerine at Hato Los Indios, e Apure. In forested regions s of Orinoco much less numerous and less conspic., there mainly along riverbanks and around oxbows lakes.

Range: To 300m. W Apure, Barinas, Portuguesa, and Cojedes e to Anzoátegui, Monagas, and Delta Amacuro; n Bolívar s to lower Río Caura and lower Río Cuyuní (*nigrogenis*); nw Amazonas in vicinity of Pto. Ayacucho (many sightings; subsp.?); Amazonas s of Río Ventuari; upper Río Paragua of s Bolívar (*gularis*). E Colombia and the Guianas s to n Bolivia and Amaz. Brazil (except nc Brazil). Trinidad.

Cardinalis

Unusually thick, conical bill; smart, upstanding crest; ♂ and ♀ plumages mirror those of Northern Cardinal (*C. cardinalis*).

Vermilion Cardinal   PLATE 65
Cardinalis phoeniceus   Cardenal Coriano
Identification: 7.5″ (19cm). Thick bill pale gray tipped dusky. Long pointed crest held vertical. ♂: *bright rose red* with black chin; wings and tail red tinged brownish. ♀: head gray, also with *long pointed red crest*; back pale grayish brown, *tail tinged red*, chin black, sides of head and malar area whitish mixed gray, *rest of underparts cinnamon buff.*
Sim. species: Sexes very different, but no other sp. in desert has such a thick bill and long red crest.
Voice: Unfortunately not as persistent a singer as allied Northern Cardinal (*C. cardinalis*). Lovely song is reminiscent of that sp. although slower and sweeter, a loud, whistled *cheer . . o-weet . . toweet, toweet, toweet,* or *swit-sweeet . . chee-chEEo . . swit-sweet . . chee-chEEo cheeu . . tsuu* or other sim. variation, given in rather halting manner; more often hd. is loud, smacking *chip* note. Most vocal early in rainy season (May–Jul).
Behavior: A glimpse of red in desert is likely to be this bird. Erect "ramrod" straight posture, esp. when singing, and long vertical crest impart commanding appearance. Often perches in open on high open branch over *Acacia* canopy when singing, otherwise hops about in low vegetation or on gd. and usually keeps out of sight, although readily detected by sharp chipping notes as forages. Usually alone or in scattered prs., but occas. groups of 5–6 are encountered. Readily mobs small owls.
Status and habitat: Fairly common resident in thorny desert scrub, hot dry *Acacia* woodland, and other low xerophytic vegetation. Readily found in desert scrub around city of Coro, Falcón, and nw of Barquisimeto, Lara, but seems not to occur in areas with even slightly higher rainfall.

Range: To 150m. Extreme nw Zulia (Paraguaipoa) e to e Falcón (w of Mirimire) and s locally to se Lara at Barquisimeto; ne Anzoátegui, w Sucre (w end of Araya Pen. and vicinity of Golfo de Cariaco e to Carupano); Isla Margarita. Ne Colombia.

Indigo Bunting   PLATE 64
Passerina cyanea   Azulillo
Identification: 5″ (12.7cm). 13.5g. *Accidental*. Bill short and thick. Breeding-plumage ♂: mainly *bright methyl blue; head and foreparts purplish blue*, wings and tail dusky heavily edged blue. Nonbreeding-plumage ♂ and imm.: rich brown above, pale brownish white below, *usually with some blue on wings and tail*; bluish may show beneath buff feather edges on underparts. ♀: warm brown above with *indistinct buff wing bars*; below brownish white *diffusely streaked dusky* on breast and sides, throat and belly whitish; ♀ may show tinge of blue on wings, very young birds faint whitish wing bars.
Sim. species: Breeding ♂ unmistakable (unlikely in Venez.). Confusing ♀ and imms. resemble ♀ Blue-black Grassquit but paler (esp. throat and belly), bill thicker, and breast streaking diffuse (not crisp).
Status and habitat: Known from 1 specimen, Dec 1950, at ca. 1000m, La Sabana (Ayapa), Sierra de Perijá, Zulia (Colección Pons, Caracas).

Range: W Zulia. Breeds in N Amer.; migrates and winters from Mexico, Florida, and W Indies to Panama, rarely Colombia; Netherlands Antilles; Trinidad (once).

Dickcissel   PLATE 65
Spiza americana   Arrocero Americano
Identification: 6″ (15cm). 26g. Looks like a small meadowlark but acts like a finch. Bill conical and pointed. Breeding-plumage ♂: *head grayish with yellow eyestripe; shoulders rufous chestnut*, rest of upperparts light brown streaked dusky; throat white; narrow black malar meets *V-shaped black bib on chest; breast yellow*, lower underparts whitish, sides gray. Nonbreeding ♂: duller, less yellow; bib reduced or lacking. ♀: even duller than nonbreeding ♂; above all brown streaked blackish, *faint yellow eyebrow*; chestnut on shoulders reduced; throat white bordered by *narrow blackish malar; patch of yellow on chest, some dusky streaking and smudging on sides*, lower underparts dingy whitish.
Sim. species: Best marks for ♀ and nonbreeding ♂ are rusty shoulders, streaky, sparrowlike appearance, and habit of gathering in flocks. See Bobolink, Grassland and Yellow-browed sparrows, and imm. Saffron and Stripe-tailed yellow-finches.

Voice: Often hd. call, esp. in flight, a husky *jeet*, and other chattery notes. Large flocks are noisy. Does not sing on wintering gds.

Behavior: Formerly wintering groups scattered widely in small flocks over grasslands, but now they concentrate in immense flocks in rice-growing areas where they roost and feed. Stream out in long, stringy flocks during day to rice fields where they are a serious economic problem to rice growers. Flocks may wander widely in search of food. Planting rice in roadside ditches, and clearing brush from around rice fields (to which flocks flee when attacked by Peregrine Falcons, Merlins, and harriers), has helped disperse flocks (G. Basili).

Status and habitat: Abundant but very local nonbreeding winter resident from N Amer., Nov–Apr (rarely to Jun). Gathers in immense flocks, some up to a quarter of a million birds (flocks of 5000–25,000 or so are reg.), which roost or concentrate in scattered rice-growing areas, mainly in Portuguesa and w Guárico, and move from field to field. Formerly large nos. passed through Portachuelo Pass to rice fields near Maracay. Much of world population now winters in c Venez., and habit (in part recently evolved) of gathering in enormous flocks to feed in rice fields brings this sp. into economic conflict with agriculture (G. Basili).

Range: To 600m (sight to 1000m, Portachuelo Pass). Throughout n of Orinoco e to Anzoátegui (Monagas?) and s to n Amazonas and n Bolívar; Islas Los Roques. Breeds in N Amer.; migrates mostly through Mid. Amer.; winters from Mexico to Colombia, irreg. to Trinidad, rarely n Brazil (Roraima) and the Guianas.

Emberizidae: Emberizid Finches

Canarios, Espigueros, Semilleros, Tordillos

The emberizid finches comprise a poorly defined family most closely related to tanagers (Thraupidae) and cardinalid finches (Cardinalidae). Some recent authors have combined them with other 9-primaried oscines, including vireos, warblers, tanagers, grosbeaks, and icterids, into 1 large, unwieldly family. The Emberizidae are here retained in a more traditional arrangement, recognizing that many taxonomic issues remain unresolved. Indeed, recent evident suggests that several emberizid genera, especially *Tiaris*, *Volatinia*, and *Sporophila*, as well as *Haplospiza*, are more closely related to tanagers than to other emberizids[299]. There are many Old World members of this group and even

more in the New World. Various species occur from the Arctic to Tierra del Fuego and from high mountains to tropical lowlands. In Venezuela there is about an equal number of species in lowland and highland regions. Many occur in open or semiopen areas (e.g., *Oryzoborus*, *Sporophila*, *Sicalis*, *Phrygilus*, *Ammodramus*, and *Emberizoides*), but members of other genera such as *Arremon*, *Atlapetes*, and *Haplospiza* occur primarily inside forest. Most Emberizidae have rather thick or conical bills useful for crushing seeds. Venezuelan members of this family are most often found on or near the ground or in the tops of bushes or low vegetation. Members of *Oryzoborus* and *Sporophila* and a few other species are superb singers. Nests vary from simple open cups of fibers and rootlets to football-shaped domed nests with side entrances. Young are fed directly or, in the case of seedeaters and grassquits, by regurgitation.

Blue-black Grassquit   PLATE 64
Volatinia jacarina   Semillero Chirrí

Identification: 4″ (10.2cm). 9.3g. Slender, sharp-pointed, and conical blackish bill smaller than in *Sporophila*. Tail rounded. ♂: *glossy blue black*; small white patch at bend of wing (often visible when perched) and white under wing coverts (conspic. in flight). ♀: above brown; wings and tail dusky brown broadly edged buffy brown; below whitish buff to buffy brown, *breast and flanks streaked dusky*. Imm. ♂: sim. to ♀ but darker above. Subad. ♂ (occas. breeds): like ♀ but with *blue black patches and mottling* on plumage. ♀♀, imms., and subad. ♂♂ usually greatly outnumber birds in ad. ♂♂ plumage.

Sim. species: ♂'s *glossy* blue black plumage and ♀'s streaks are diagnostic. No *Sporophila* is all glossy blue black or streaked below. Note slender conical bill. Seed-finches are much larger. Also cf. Sooty and Black-faced grassquits.

Voice: From low perch ♂♂ tireless repeat short, buzzy *duézz-uu* or *bís'zeeer*, usually accompanied by short, vertical jump with spread tail. ♂♂ sing all yr.

Behavior: A familiar little bird of open country, most likely seen when small, loose groups, often with other seedeaters, flush up nervously from grass and waste areas into bushy fencerows or shrubbery. When breeding, territorial ♂♂ spend much time on low perches or fence wires, endlessly performing curious little jump displays which sometimes almost turn into somersaults and are accompanied by an anemic, buzzy song. Jump display reportedly used in pr. formation

and in greater projection of sound for breeding-territory maintenance[4,799]. Feed mostly on seeds taken from gd. Tiny, thin-walled cup nest low in grass or bush; 2–3 eggs, white or bluish heavily speckled with brown, more at thicker end[706]; breeding, Jul and Nov, Hato Masaguaral, Guárico[734]; Apr–Aug, n Colombia.
Status and habitat: Very common and widespread resident in grassy and weedy clearings, waste areas, dry bushy pastures, and other semiopen country, mainly in lowlands. Xerophytic to humid areas but most numerous in dry zones. Some seasonal wandering.
Range: To 2000m. Prob. throughout; Isla Margarita (*splendens*). S Mexico to w Peru, n Chile, Argentina, s Brazil, and the Guianas. Trinidad; Grenada.

Tiaris

Resemble *Sporophila* but both sexes dull plumaged (except yellow-faced Grassquit); bill shape unusual, upper mandible angled downward from nostril (but culmen otherwise almost straight); bill narrower, more pointed than in *Sporophila*; tail rather short; favor dry areas; globe-shaped nest with side entrance (unlike *Sporophila*).

Sooty Grassquit   PLATE 64
Tiaris fuliginosa   Tordillo Ahumado
Identification: 4.5″ (11.4cm). 13g. Bill dusky, gape pinkish (♂) or yellowish (♀). ♂: *dull sooty black with olive tinge, esp. on back*; lower underparts tinged grayish brown. ♀: drab; above dull olive brown, slightly brighter and more buff below and turning dingy whitish on center of belly.
Sim. species: Ad. ♂ Blue-black Grassquit is always glossy blue black (not dull sooty) and shows white under wing (watch in flight); even imm. ♂ Blue-blacks are never as dull and uniform as this sp. ♀ nearly identical to ♀ Black-faced Grassquit, and the two prob. cannot safely be told in field except by attendant ♂ (note drier habitat favored by Black-faced). ♀ Sooty is slightly larger and darker, esp. below. Dull-colored Grassquit also is very sim. (both sexes) to ♀ but overall paler, esp. below, sometimes also with bicolored bill.
Voice: Song recalls that of Black-faced Grassquit but shorter, a thin, wiry *ezz'u'da'leé*, slurred together quickly; has peculiar buzzy ("grease on hot skillet") quality. Call *chee*.
Behavior: Most often seen singly or in prs., occas. in small loose groups, from near gd. to mid. levels in trees but usually fairly low. Nest a flimsy globe of grass and rootlets, large side entrance; on gd., stump, bank, or to 9m up in tree; 2–4 white eggs with brown markings, esp at larger end; May and Jul–Dec breeding, Trinidad[175].
Status and habitat: Not well known. Eruptive and nomadic, wandering to grassy and regenerating burned areas and moist to humid forest edges (the other 2 non-yellow *Tiaris* in Venez. favor drier areas). Unpredictable in occurrence but periodically numerous with ♂♂ singing only short distances apart along roadsides, e.g., on s slope of PN Henri Pittier. Some movements may be seasonal; 1 specimen (1200m) from

tepui region. Highest rec. is 1 at 2300m, PN Guaramacal, Trujillo (D. Ascanio, J. del Hoyo, J. Sargatal).

Range: 800–1700m (sight recs. at 500 and 2300m). Disjunct range. Sierra de Perijá (Río Negro), Zulia; e slope of Andes in nw Barinas (Calderas), e Trujillo (sight), and n end of Andes in se Lara (Cabudare); e Falcón, locally in Coastal Cordillera of Carabobo, Aragua, and Distr. Federal; sw Sucre (several areas near Cumanacoa); base of Cerro Roraima, e Bolívar. Colombia (only 1 verifiable rec.); s Guyana; e Bolivia (1 rec.); Mato Grosso, Brazil (2 recs.), se Brazil; Trinidad.
Note: Subspp. *zuliae* and *fumosa* not recognized[27].

Black-faced Grassquit   PLATE 64
Tiaris bicolor   Tordillo Común
Identification: 4″ (10.2cm). 10.5g. Bill dusky above, paler below, *gape pinkish* (♂) or bill pale (♀). ♂: *above dull olive; forecrown, sides of head, throat, and breast deep sooty black* shading to gray on belly; flanks tinged olive. Or black only to mid. breast (*tortugensis*). ♀: above *dull pale olive gray*, paler olive gray below becoming dingy whitish on center of belly. In both sexes culmen distinctly decurved, imparting "bent" look to bill.
Sim. species: ♂'s blackish foreparts and olive rearparts give "bicolored" look that is diagnostic. Cf. Sooty Grassquit which is all black, and Dull-colored Grassquit which is much paler with 2-toned bill. ♀ doubtfully separable from ♀ Sooty Grassquit but smaller, overall grayer (not brown), and center of belly whiter. The 2 spp. partly separate by habitat.
Voice: Song a buzzy *tse-tsee-tsee-tsizzle-tsizzle-tsizzle* or shorter, or thin *tsit'l, tzil'ti, ti'teet* or sim. variation from perch or in short display flight as ♂ holds up and rapidly vibrates wings and floats earthward.
Behavior: A confiding little bird of dry waste areas that often makes itself at home in vicinity of humans. Almost any lawn, patch of scrub, or neglected area will do. Lives in rather quiet prs. or families, forages for seeds on gd. or by perching on grass and weed stems, also eats buds and a few insects. Hops boldly on gd., is easy to see, and seeks shelter in dry thickets. ♂♂ sing from semiopen perches a few meters up. Along with other spp., readily mobs pygmy-owls. Grassy dome-shaped nest with side entrance; usually low, occas. high; 2–3 whitish eggs marked pale red brown at larger end; breeding Aug–Jan, Trinidad[175].
Status and habitat: Fairly common resident in dry to arid scrub, grass and weeds along borders of dry scrubby woodland, and patches of brush and grass in

urban areas (e.g., Caracas). Mainly dry areas; not far into humid zones.

Range: To 850m. Coast from nw Zulia to w Sucre (e to Carupano), inland to w and s Lara; very locally s to w Mérida and n Portuguesa (Acarigua); Islas Margarita, Coche, and Cubagua (*omissa*); La Blanquilla and Los Hermanos (*johnstonei*); La Tortuga (*tortugensis*). Colombia to Trinidad and Tobago; W Indies.

Yellow-faced Grassquit   PLATE 64

Tiaris olivacea   Tordillo Coloradito

Identification: 4.2″ (10.7cm). 9.5g. ♂: forecrown, sides of head, and underparts to mid. breast deep black, *short eyebrow and throat patch butter yellow*, otherwise olive above; lower underparts grayish olive. ♀ and imm. ♂: sim. but dull olive replaces black on head and breast; yellow markings faintly indicated (sometimes virtually absent in ♀).

Sim. species: Facial markings are the key but often faint in ♀. Note limited range in Venez. ♀ is more olive than most ♀ *Sporophila*.

Voice: Song a ser. of weak, buzzy trills, *ttttt-tee*, almost insectlike, sometimes given by ♂ during short, fluttery flights between shrubs, or with fluttering wings while perched in front of ♀.

Behavior: Usually in scattered prs. or families and easy to see. Infreq. several may assoc. loosely with other seedeaters and grassquits. Forage on gd. or by clinging to grass stems for seeds, or glean in low shrubbery for seeds, berries, and occas. insects. Flight is short and weak. Football-shaped nest with side entrance; low in shrub or grass; 2–3 white eggs spotted brown at larger end[589].

Status and habitat: Local resident in semiopen areas in foothills and cooler mid.-montane els. Grassy and bushy pastures, roadsides, shrubbery, and settled areas. Most recs. are from s Táchira (i.e., vicinity of Bramón, Villa Páez, and Betania); rare n to Mérida.

Range: 450–2300m. S Táchira n to sw Mérida (Mesa Bolívar) and ne Táchira at Las Mesas (*pusilla*). E Mexico to Colombia; Greater Antilles.

Dull-colored Grassquit   PLATE 64

Tiaris obscura   Tordillo Pardo

Identification: 4.3″ (10.9cm). 11g. Bill slender (compared to *Sporophila*) and conical. Bill often bicolored with *upper mandible dusky, lower pale* (esp. ♀♀), but more than half of all ♂♂ have bill mostly dark, only underside pale (subsp. *haplochroma* only). Sexes sim.: above grayish brown, wings browner, below uniform brownish gray, often with buff tinge to flanks and under tail coverts.

Sim. species: Very sim. to ♀ and juv. Sooty Grassquit but duller brown (less buff). ♂♂ are hen-plumaged, hence this sp. easily overlooked. Look for 2-toned bill, a key mark (but not all birds show it). Bill is a little more slender and conical than in *Sporophila*; also note that bills of some ♀ *Sporophila* and both sexes of Sooty Grassquit can look bicolored. Watch for flocks of pure ♀-plumaged birds, singing ♂♂, or prs. of dull-plumaged birds. In other seedeater and grassquit flocks there are almost always a few ad.-plumaged ♂♂ present.

Voice: Song a short, sizzling *tzeedle'tzee* or *is'sis'tl'zee*, fast, buzzy, and with quality of hot grease in a pan; recalls that of Sooty Grassquit.

Behavior: Usually seen alone, in prs., or a few in loosely assoc. groups. In some areas (Venez.?) also with other seedeaters. Like others of genus feeds on gd. or in grass and weeds, and sings from low perch. Ovoid, globular nest like others of genus (P. Schwartz); BC birds, Jun–Sep, n Colombia.

Status and habitat: Very spotty and unpredictable in occurrence. Dry to moist woodland borders, dry brushy ravines, and abused or neglected areas with tall grass and brush. At times relatively numerous. Seasonally or periodically a common breeding bird above Maracay on dry, lower-el. slopes of PN Henri Pittier (C. Parrish; tapes—P. Schwartz). May wander locally or seasonally, but movements not well known.

Range: 400–2000m (most recs. above 700m). Andes of Táchira and w Mérida; Yaracuy (once); n cordilleras in Carabobo, Aragua, Distr. Federal, and Miranda; sight rec. at San Francisco de Macaira, n Guárico, 1 Mar 1981 (C. Parrish); sw Sucre (Santa María in Cerro Turumiquire) and Río Cocollar, n Monagas (*haplochroma*). Colombia s locally, mostly in mts., to n Argentina.

Note: Earlier placed in *Sporophila* and called Dull-colored Seedeater[403]; then transferred to *Tiaris*[27].

Dolospingus

Like *Sporophila* but larger; bill longer and conical.

White-naped Seedeater

PLATE 64

Dolospingus fringilloides Semillero Nuca Blanca

Identification: 5.2″ (13.2cm). Sharp-pointed, conical bill pale (♂) or dusky (♀). Tail rather long. ♂: upperparts, head, and upper throat black; small white patch on nape (inconspic. in field); *1 broad white wing bar* (often a partial dotted 2d bar), small white spot at base of flight feathers and whitish rump; *below white with narrow white band extending up on sides of neck almost to back of nape*; chest and sides mottled blackish. ♀: uniform warm cinnamon brown above and below, paler on throat; center of lower breast and belly buffy white.

Sim. species: ♂ looks rather like ♂ Wing-barred Seedeater but larger and with bill that is larger, *longer*, more conical, and pale. More confusing ♀ best told from *Sporophila* allies by larger size and heavier, cone-shaped bill. ♀ Lesser Seed-Finch has white under wing coverts and is not so pale on belly; ♀ Blue-black Grosbeak is larger.

Voice: Song at San Carlos de Río Negro (and Vaupés, Colombia) a loud, fast, musical *ne-ne-ne, te-te-te, ge-ge-ge, jii-jii-jii, tuE tuE tuE*; in a common variation, *te'e'e'se, te'e'e'se, chuEE-chuEE-chuEE-chuEE, jreet-jreet-jreet* or sim. Songs typically composed of 3–4 sets of paired or triplet notes with abrupt changes between each pr. or triplet. Some songs contain only triplets, others are more varied, e.g., *te'e'se-te'e'se, tuee-tuee, threey-threey-threey*. Call a sharp *tzink!*

Behavior: Single birds or prs. occur alone from near gd. to 4m up in wet thickets. More wary than *Sporophila* and usually not assoc. with other seed-eating birds.

Status and habitat: Damp or wet openings inside white sandy soil forest, or wet openings along savanna/forest interfaces, esp. where there is abundant large-leafed herbaceous foliage and terrestrial Araceae. Patchy distrib. perhaps related to narrow microhabitat requirements.

Range: To 200m. C and s Amazonas from Cerros Yapacana and Duida s to Río Casiquiare (Caño San Miguel) and San Carlos de Río Negro (sight, Apr 1985—C. Parrish). E Colombia (Vaupés); upper Rio Negro, Brazil; s Guyana (M. B. Robbins).

Oryzoborus

Closely related to *Sporophila* but larger; bill massive for size of bird, broad at base; ♂'s plumage mostly black; ♀'s dark brown; not gregarious; thin grass cup nest low in bush.

Lesser Seed-Finch

PLATE 64

Oryzoborus angolensis Semillero Vientricastaño

Identification: 5″ (12.7cm). 13.5g. Heavy black bill. ♂: upperparts, head, throat, and chest glossy black, line from *mid. breast to crissum dark chestnut*; bend of wing, small wing speculum (usually), and *under wing coverts white*. ♀: warm brown above, buffy brown below, darker on chest and turning pale cinnamon buff on belly; under wing coverts white.

Sim. species: ♂'s best mark is chestnut on breast and belly but this sometimes hard to see; note heavy black bill and white underwings as it flies. ♀ from ♀ *Sporophila* by *much heavier*, "squared-off" bill (culmen not as obviously decurved) and larger size. Other ♀ *Oryzoborus* are even larger, with more massive bills. Both sexes have habit of flicking wings rapidly, showing little strobelike flashes of white on underwings, a good hint. Also cf. ♂ to ♂ Orchard Oriole and ♀ Silver-beaked Tanager.

Voice: An unusually fine singer. Song a long, sweet ser. of whistled notes changing about midway to faster, chattery notes that fade; 1st part recalls song of Indigo Bunting, *techu, techu chu chi techu chu chi . . .* and so on, often with trills at end. Also performs flight songs.

Behavior: This cheerful songster of shrubby forest clearings sings from prom. perches atop bushes, freq. moving from one to another, but otherwise keeps low in shrubby vegetation and mostly out of sight. Lives in prs., but most often sexes keep apart and it is singing ♂ that is seen. Forage independently of other birds, occas. with seedeaters or grassquits. Glean grass seeds mostly by clinging to long stems that bend over, also by perching on adj. stronger stems and reaching out, by hovering in front of grass tips, or by hopping on gd. for seeds.

Status and habitat: Resident in shrubby and grassy forest borders and regenerating clearings in humid regions. N of Orinoco rather local, mainly near or in foothills, with sporadic (seasonal?) recs. around periphery of llanos. Common in e Bolívar. Often sought as cagebird for its fine song, a practice that has contributed to its decline locally.

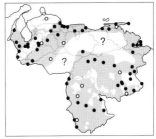

Range: To 1200m n of Orinoco; to 1400m s of Orinoco. Sierra de Perijá, Zulia, both slopes of Andes from s Táchira to Lara; Sierra de San Luis, Falcón (sight); n cordilleras in Carabobo, Aragua, and Miranda; spottily in w Apure, Portuguesa, nw and s Cojedes (San Carlos; sight, Hato Piñero); s Guárico (Santa Rita); Sucre s to Delta Amacuro and throughout Amazonas and Bolívar (*angolensis*). Se Mexico to ne Argentina, se Brazil, and the Guianas. Trinidad.

Note: Subsp. *torridus* invalid[438]. Some consider all-dark birds of C Amer. to w Ecuador (Thick-billed Seed-Finch, *O. funereus*) a separate sp. from chestnut-bellied birds (*angolensis* group) of e of Andes. The 2 forms interbreed in Santa Marta area and upper Magdalena Valley, Colombia[401,437], and songs are sim. throughout[544]. Some suggest merging *Oryzoborus* into *Sporophila*[438,609].

Large-billed Seed-Finch
PLATE 64

Oryzoborus crassirostris   Semillero Picón

Identification: 5.7″ (14.5cm). 20g. Both ♂ and ♀ very sim. to respective sexes of Great-billed Seed-Finch and perhaps not safely separated in field. *Bill smooth and chalky white* (♂) or black (♀), massive and "squared off" but not quite as large as in Great-billed Seed-Finch. Possibly can be separated from that sp. in field by smaller size, proportionately smaller bill, and smooth, shiny bill texture (not dull with linelike striations). In some areas it is prob. safe to separate the 2 spp. by range (see Range). In hand Large-billed can be identified by its shorter tail (53–59 vs. 61–72mm) and smaller bill dimensions (culmen ca. 13–15 vs. 16–17mm; depth at nostril 14 vs. 17mm; and max. width 12 vs. 16mm). ♀ overall is *paler* brown below than Great-billed Seed-Finch, but this most readily apparent only in direct comparison.

Voice: ♂ is a persistent singer with loud, musical song resembling that of Lesser Seed-Finch but more repetitious. Also performs complex flight song.

Behavior: Unlike *Sporophila*, usually solitary or in prs., and more wary and difficult to see. Occas. gathers in small nomadic groups up to 25 or so that may be accompanied by a few *Sporophila*. Territorial ♂♂ sing from prom. spot atop small to large shrub, typically sing a few songs, then fly to new perch. Eat grass seeds by perching on stem or more often by perching on adj. stronger stem that will support bird's weight, and reaching for seeds. Also hop on gd. for grass seeds.

Status and habitat: Widespread but *very spotty breeding* resident. When not breeding, prob. nomadic or a short-distance migrant (movements need documentation). Semiopen areas incl. grassy borders of dry forest, ranchland with scattered bushes and patches of tall grass, and (esp. in Delta Amacuro) in low-lying, seasonally flooded areas with bushes, trees, and grass. In w Guárico rec. Jul–Nov (late rainy season) with Nov breeding[734]. Flock of 24 seen in tall grass 8 Feb 1998, Cerro Misión, Falcón (Hilty and D. Ascanio).

Range: To 500m n of Orinoco; to 200m s of Orinoco. S end of Maracaibo Basin, Zulia, w base of Andes in Mérida and Trujillo, e base in Táchira; se Falcón (sightings, Cerro Misión), Coastal Cordillera in n Carabobo

and n Aragua (Cata); spottily in Portuguesa, Cojedes, w Guárico, ne Monagas (sightings, P. Boesman), Delta Amacuro, and n Amazonas; n Bolívar from near Caicara e to Sierra de Imataca (*crassirostris*); se Bolívar (sight, Santa Elena de Uairén). N Colombia and e of Andes s to ne Peru, Brazil n of the Amazon, and the Guianas.

Great-billed Seed-Finch
PLATE 64

Oryzoborus maximiliani   Semillero Picón Grande

Identification: 6.3″ (16cm). 25g. *Massive* (almost grotesquely large) *chalky white bill is dull and somewhat rough or bonelike in texture* (♂); or bill black (♀). ♂: entirely glossy blue black, *speculum* (spot) *at base of flight feathers, bend of wing, and under wing coverts white.* ♀: above brown tinged yellowish olive, bend of wing and under wing coverts white (no speculum), underparts dark buffy brown with faint rufescent tinge, belly paler. Subad. ♂: like ♀ but with patches of black.

Sim. species: Very like Large-billed Seed-Finch and perhaps often not safely told in field (see under that sp.), but up close note rough texture of bill. Unusually large bill separates it from *Sporophila*. No other Venez. seedeater or finch has, for its size, a bill of comparable dimension. Cf. larger *Cyanocompsa* grosbeaks.

Voice: Loud, complex songs composed mostly of sweet musical notes, trills, and short rattles; usually begin with 2–3 musical whistled notes, then a rattle-trill, then musical notes, and so on in long complex fashion. ♂♂ sing many different songs, but all songs generally contain more trills and rattles than those of other *Oryzoborus*. ♂♂ singing persistently Aug–Sep, Delta Amacuro. Typically fly to new perch after singing only 1–2 songs. Subad. ♂♂ sing and may breed in mixed plumage.

Behavior: Seen in loosely assoc. prs. when breeding, otherwise sexes usually remain apart and generally do not form flocks of their own or assoc. much with other seedeaters. Eat seeds, alighting on grass stems which often bend to gd. under bird's considerable weight, or by perching on adj. stronger perch and reaching out to seed heads.

Status and habitat: *Very local* in wet pastures, tall grass along rivers and lakes, emergent shrubbery in marshes, and mixed wet grass and shrubbery along swampy forest borders. Prob. resident; common and widespread in Delta Amacuro with many ad. and subad. territorial ♂♂ singing along Caño Mánamo n of Tucupita in late Aug. Specimens Nov and Jan–Mar, Delta Amacuro and se Sucre.

Range: To ca. 100m. Se Sucre (Guaraunos), n Bolívar along Orinoco (Caicara; lower Río Caura at Maripa),

and Delta Amacuro (*magnirostris*). Disjunct distrib. Pacific Colombia, w and e Ecuador, se Peru; n Bolivia; s and se Brazil; the Guianas (spotty) e to mouth of the Amazon.
Note: Taxonomy complex and controversial[544].

Sporophila

Widespread genus; *short, thick bill with distinctly decurved culmen* (unlike *Oryzoborus* and *Dolospingus*); ♂♂ may have bold black, white, gray, tawny, or rufous patterns; ♀♀ dull brown, all very sim. and difficult to identify; many spp. nomadic or migratory (seasonal movements not documented); excellent songsters and widely trapped for cagebird trade; ♀-plumaged birds usually greatly outnumber breeding plumage ♂♂; open cup nest of grass and rootlets.

Gray Seedeater   PLATE 64
Sporophila intermedia   Espiguero Pico de Plata
Identification: 4.2″ (10.7cm). 12g. Sim. to Slate-colored Seedeater but *bill yellowish pink to brownish pink* (♂) or blackish (♀); legs dark. ♂: overall plain gray (*much paler* than Slate-colored), *usually with no white neck spot* (but occas. present), and *never with white wing bar* (but this often lacking in Slate-colored). Up close note more swollen bill with *decidedly decurved culmen*. ♀: sim. to and prob. inseparable from ♀ Slate-colored Seedeater, and from most other dark-billed ♀ *Sporophila*; above warm brown tinged tawny, face tinged buff, throat and chest clay to dark cinnamon becoming paler whitish buff on lower underparts. Imm. ♂: like ♀; older birds (>1 yr) progressively more gray.
Sim. species: See Slate-colored Seedeater. In hand Gray is separated from Slate-colored by greater depth of upper mandible (4.5 vs. 3mm), shorter wing (<60 vs. ≥60mm), longer tarsus (≥15 vs. ≤14mm)[398]. Also see Plumbeous Seedeater.
Voice: Song a spirited ser. of musical twitters, chips, and trills usually beginning *chu chu chu-wee . . .*, much richer, more varied, and lower pitched than that of Slate-colored Seedeater. Some or all ♂♂ incorporate mimetic phrases and songs, or partial songs, of many other birds into their own rambling songs. Accuracy and extent of vocal copying by ♂♂ vary.
Behavior: When breeding, ♂♂ scatter on territories and sing from prom. perches atop shrubs, trees, or fence rows. At other times ♂♂ and ♀♀ gather in small, rather nervous and skittish flocks composed mostly of ♀-plumaged birds that feed on gd. in semiopen areas or settle into tall grass, perch on grass stems, and eat seeds directly from ends of grass stems. Unlike other *Sporophila* in Venez., also eat insects, at least in dry season, by foraging on large tree limbs (esp. *Pithecellobium*) or by fluttering for flying insects; also noted drinking nectar. Breeding May or Jun–Oct, longer than in most *Sporophila*. This is only seedeater in Venez. that is not exclusively a seed-eating bird, and its catholic diet and long breeding season may permit yr-round residency, unique among *Sporophila*[137,743] (R. Restall). Thin cup nest 2–7m up in bush or small tree; 2–3 eggs creamy, marked dark brown[175].
Status and habitat: Very common resident in a wide variety of partly open, dry to humid habitats, incl. gallery forest borders, bushy pastures, fence rows, parks, gardens, grassy waste areas in urban and rural regions, wooded borders, and young second growth. This is *the* "gray" seedeater most likely to be seen anywhere, and only *Sporophila* in Venez. that is not nomadic or migratory. At Hato Masaguaral, Guárico, the only *Sporophila* present yr-round[734,743].

Range: To 1200m n of Orinoco; to 300m s of Orinoco. Throughout s to sw Amazonas, Bolívar (except sw), and Delta Amacuro (*intermedia*). Colombia to Guyana. Trinidad (now rare).
Note: About 20% of all individuals have varying amts. of white on rump, white edging on wing coverts, some white on neck, and slightly smaller bill. This pop. could represent a cryptic sp., Ring-necked Seedeater (*S. insularis*)[559].

Slate-colored Seedeater   PLATE 64
Sporophila schistacea   Espiguero Apizarrado
Identification: 4.2″ (10.7cm). 11g. *Bill yellowish* (♂) or horn gray (♀); culmen almost straight to slightly decurved; legs pale gray (?). ♂: *dark gray*, darker on wings and tail, slightly paler below; *center of breast white, belly and under tail coverts whitish*; small white wing speculum; *usually at least a partial white wing bar* (or faintly indicated by a few white tips on median wing coverts); *small inconspic. white spot on side of neck* (occas. lacking in young ♂♂). ♀: above pale olive brown, chest and throat paler with weak tawny wash on chest, set off somewhat from pale dirty white lower underparts. In hand note peculiar bill shape: depth of upper mandible (maxilla) much shallower than that of lower mandible.
Sim. species: ♂ often confused with ♂ of much commoner and more widespread Gray Seedeater which has pinkish yellow bill, is paler gray (often hard to judge in field), and usually does not show white wing bar (may occas. show neck spot). ♂ Plumbeous Seedeater has blackish bill. ♀ prob. inseparable from ♀ of Gray or from other darker-billed ♀ *Sporophila*, but note faint tawny wash on chest. ♀ Gray Seedeater has blacker bill.
Voice: Song a high, sibilant, rapid *zit, zit, ze'z'z'z'z'ze 'ze'tuwee-tuwee-tuwee*, with variations. Song is loud, vigorous, parulid-like, and much less musical than songs of Gray Seedeater (P. Schwartz recording). Song given perched or in fluttery display flights.
Behavior: An enigmatic species that seems to be irruptive and nomadic, appearing in small groups to breed where bamboo and grass seed are maturing and abundant, then disappearing. In Costa Rica (prob. elsewhere) seldom breeds in same place in consecutive

yrs, wanders widely, occurs singly or in prs. or occas. little groups, and is most likely to be seen perched fairly high in trees or bamboo. Forages in bamboo, other grasses, or on gd. Jun nests, mid. Orinoco region (Caicara); thin-walled rootlet and horsehair cup 2–4m up in small tree or spiny palm; 3 grayish white eggs dotted and blotched darker[115]; Panama nests 4–5m up in thorny vine or bamboo, Feb and Jun–Sep; ♂♂ defend small territories; apparently monogamous prs. not formed as ♀♀ incubate eggs and feed young unassisted; ♀ feeds some insects to nestlings[706,722].

Status and habitat: Rare, unpredictable, and poorly known. Breeding assoc. with patches of seeding bamboo and perhaps other grasses; also attracted to regenerating burned areas with large crops of grass seeds. Recs. widely scattered. Light woodland, bamboo, bushy clearings, and young second growth.

Range: To 1000m. Sierra de Perijá (once at 2000m), Zulia; Andes of w Mérida; n Aragua (sight, PN Henri Pittier—P. Schwartz and C. Parrish); w Sucre, e Monagas, and Delta Amacuro; n Bolívar (Caicara, La Unión) and scattered recs. in se Bolívar at Ptari-tepui, Cerro Roraima, Maijia Salto (*longipennis*). Locally from s Mexico to nw Ecuador; Guyana (sight); Suriname; Brazil at mouth of the Amazon; very locally along e base of Andes from e Colombia to n Bolivia.

Plumbeous Seedeater   PLATE 64
Sporophila plumbea Espiguero Plomizo
Identification: 4.3″ (10.9cm). 11.5g. Bill blackish (♂) or horn gray above, base of lower mandible yellowish green (♀); bill in both sexes *not as heavy or decurved as in Gray Seedeater.* ♂: above dark gray, paler on lower back and rump; wings and tail dusky, small white wing speculum; below pale gray, *chin and small subloral area whitish* (conspic. in field), lower breast and belly whitish. ♀: above brownish tinged olive, below pale buff tinged gray (looks dirty), under tail coverts dull whitish. Imm. ♂: like ♀; older birds (>1 yr) progressively more gray. ♀♀ (perhaps younger birds) tinged yellowish below. Tail shorter than in Gray Seedeater.

Sim. species: ♂ from any other seedeater by combination of black bill and whitish malar area. ♀ from other ♀ *Sporophila* by partially "bicolored" bill (usually) and generally duller plumage with more olive and grayish tones (not rich buffy brown), but is prob. not safely told from them (in most cases) in field.

Voice: Song hd. Jun–Jul, se Venez., a long ser. of loud, vigorous, clear phrases, *queet ut, heet ut-ut, heet uh chut-et, chue-et, tu'et tu'et, cheet cheet, s'few s'few*

s'few, 'wáit-ter, queet, ut* and so on, with variation in sequence (P. Schwartz recording).

Behavior: ♂♂ sing from scattered low bushes during breeding season. At other times both sexes gather in small flocks, or mingle with other seedeaters and yellow-finches, and feed on grass seeds by perching on bending stems, or by hoping on gd. ♀-plumage birds usually outnumber adult ♂♂.

Status and habitat: Permanent or seasonal resident in damp or low-lying savanna, partially flooded areas with scattered bushes, and gallery forest borders. Sometimes in patches of heathlike scrub in savanna well away from water. Local; seldom numerous. Many more recs. (sightings and specimens) from s Bolívar than elsewhere. Most recs. n of Orinoco may represent nomadic or migratory birds.

Range: To 1100m n of Orinoco; to 1400m s of Orinoco. Sierra de Perijá (Kunana), Zulia; s Apure along Río Meta (Cararabo), s Carabobo (El Trompillo); Aragua (?); locally in s Amazonas; generally in Bolívar but most recs. are in nw, ne, and se (*whiteleyana*); 1 ♀ from Los Altos, Sucre, needs verification; 1 ♀ specimen from Serranía de Imataca, ne Bolívar, is prob. Gray Seedeater. Colombia to the Guianas and mouth of the Amazon; e Bolivia and s central Brazil s to Paraguay and ne Argentina.

Wing-barred Seedeater   PLATE 64
Sporophila americana Espiguero Variable
Identification: 4.3″ (10.9cm). 11g. Bill thickest of genus in Venez. Bill black (♂) or dark (♀). ♂: above glossy black with *narrow white nape band, 1 white wing bar,* and usually a 2d faintly indicated bar; rump gray, underparts grayish white extending up narrowly on sides of neck; *narrow black chest band often interrupted* or occas. lacking; sides and flanks mottled gray. ♀: above dark olive brown, below pale buffy olive brown, chin and belly whitish.

Sim. species: Lined and Lesson's seedeaters have prom. white malar patches and black on throat. ♀ has darkest upperparts of any *Sporophila* in Venez. but still best known by attendant ♂ (see Table 1). Other "black-and-white" seedeaters do not overlap in range.

Voice: Song of allied Variable Seedeater (*S. corvina*) in Panama a musical, warbled *chee-a chee-aweet, o-wee, tweet o-wee toche tiche*[228]. Song given perched or during little fluttering flight display with back feathers ruffed.

Behavior: Prs. or small flocks cling to grass stems to feed on seeds or flush up and scatter to nearby shrubbery. Also eat small berries and occas. insects. Nest in

Panama (Variable Seedeater) a neat grass and rootlet cup near gd. to 8m up in grass, bush, or small tree; 2 eggs, pale gray speckled and blotched dark gray and brown[228].

Status and habitat: Scarce and local resident (seasonal?) in grassy and shrubby areas, bushy roadsides, waste areas, mangroves, and marshy or periodically inundated vegetation. Known only from small no. of recs. (Sep, Nov, Jan, Feb) in ne Venez.

Range: To 50m (near sea level). Se Sucre (Tunapuí) s through e Monagas to n and e Delta Amacuro (*americana*). The Guianas to mouth of the Amazon and upriver to lower Río Negro.

Note: Does not incl. Caquetá Seedeater (*S. murallae*) of se Colombia to se Peru and w Amaz. Brazil or Variable Seedeater (*S. corvina*) of s C Amer. and nw S Amer.[704]. Some unite all taxa, incl. birds of n C Amer., under the name Variable Seedeater (*S. americana*)[10,439].

Lined Seedeater   PLATE 64
Sporophila lineola   Espiguero Bigotudo

Identification: 4.5″ (11.4cm). 9.3g. Thick blackish bill (♂) or *mostly pale yellowish bill* (♀). ♂: *above glossy black with white coronal stripe*; white spot at base of primaries (size varies) and white rump band (amt. of white varies); *throat black bordered by broad oval-shaped white malar stripe*; rest of underparts white. ♀: above olive brown, throat, chest, and flanks rich yellowish buff contrasting with *rather sharply defined buffy white center of breast, belly, and under tail coverts.*

Sim. species: ♂ much like ♂ Lesson's Seedeater (see); ♀ indistinguishable from Lesson's (see Table 1). In ne see Wing-barred Seedeater.

Voice: Typical song of ♂ a few short, chattery notes followed by a rattle, *jit, jit, jit, jit'd'd'd'd'd'd*; reg. sings in Venez. Cf. song of Lesson's Seedeater.

Behavior: A charming little bird that occurs singly or in small, scattered, loosely assoc. groups. Wanders to areas of tall grass with seeds where it alights and flutters near ends of slender grass stems which bend under bird's weight as it reaches down for seeds. Feeds mainly by perching on grass stems, seldom on gd. ♂♂ often sing in Venez., but as yet not known to breed[583].

Status and habitat: Uncommon to locally fairly common nonbreeding migrant from e Brazil to semiopen grassy areas with bushes and trees, flooded pastures, borders of gallery forest and mangroves, and occas. drier areas. Present in Venez. approx. late May–early Dec; a few arrive earlier or linger later[583]. Note that Lesson's Seedeater breeds in Venez. at same time of yr that Lined is present as nonbreeding seasonal resi-

dent. Highest recs. are 7 at km 123 (1450m), 10 Jul 1997, Sierra de Lema, Bolívar[596]. Esp. numerous in w end of llanos from Cojedes to w Apure (D. Ascanio).

Range: To ca. 500m (sightings to 1450m). Nw Táchira (La Fria); no recs. in Zulia, w or c Falcón, or Lara; e of Andes from Táchira, Apure, Barinas, Portuguesa, and Carabobo e to Sucre, Monagas, and Delta Amacuro[343]; scattered recs. in w Amazonas and n Bolívar (*lineola*). Two breeding pops.: one breeds from e Bolivia and s Brazil (Rondônia, Matto Grosso, and Goiás) to n Argentina and migrates and winters n across w and c Amazonia to se Colombia and upper Río Negro in nw Brazil (*restricta*) but is unrec. in Venez. A 2d pop. breeding in e Brazil, possibly n to s Suriname, migrates nw through the Guianas to Venez. All Venez. birds are apparently from this latter pop. To be watched for as a breeder in extreme se Venez.

Lesson's Seedeater   PLATE 64
Sporophila bouvronides   Bengalí

Identification: 4.5″ (11.4cm). 9.6g. ♂: much like ♂ Lined Seedeater but *no white coronal stripe* (or only indicated by a few white dots; *white malar patch much smaller* (forms narrow white oval across lower cheeks) and *sides and flanks heavily mottled with black*. ♀: indistinguishable from ♀ Lined Seedeater. Some ♂♂ in ♀ plumage (hen type) are sexually mature and known to breed.

Sim. species: ♂ Lesson's looks "*blacker headed*" because of smaller white malar and no white coronal stripe. ♀ Lesson's and Lined seedeaters are only ♀ *Sporophila* in Venez. with combination of mostly yellowish bill and unstreaked back, but the two cannot be told apart in field (Table 1). See either sex of Wing-barred Seedeater, and larger Black-and-white and White-naped seedeaters.

Voice: A persistent singer early in rainy season, May–Aug. Song a short, rubbery trill followed by abrupt *tu-weet* at end; or sometimes a few *tic* notes followed by a trill, then either a pause or more *tic* notes. Sometimes just a single short rattle, *drdrdrdrdrdr*, with no notes at end.

Behavior: Upon arrival ♂♂ claim small territories and sing constantly from perches that are usually fairly high. Breed in prs., and after breeding gather in vary-ing-sized flocks and scatter throughout grassy areas. Eat grass seeds, mainly by perching on grass stems (not a gd. forager) that often bend nearly to gd. beneath bird's weight. Frail grass and black-fiber-lined cup near gd. to 10m up; 2–3 whitish eggs with dark markings[175].

Status and habitat: Breeding resident May–early Nov with scattered individuals earlier or later; Apr–end of Sep in ne Anzoátegui[186]. Common in gallery forest borders, pastures, grassy clearings, and other disturbed semiopen areas with bushes and trees. Abundant breeder along Río Boconoito, sw Portuguesa, in Jun. Present Aug–Nov at Hato Masaguaral, Guárico[734]. Largely or entirely absent Dec–Apr (dry season) when presum. migrates s into w and c Amazonia; details of movements not fully understood[583].

Range: To 900m n of Orinoco; to 500m s of Orinoco. Widespread s to w Amazonas and n Bolívar. Breeds from n Colombia to the Guianas; migrates s to se Colombia, e Peru, and w Brazil.

Black-and-white Seedeater
PLATE 64
Sporophila luctuosa   Espiguero Negriblanco
Identification: 4.5″ (11.4cm). 12.5g. Bill bluish white above, grayish below (♂) or blackish (♀). ♂: mostly glossy black with *white lower breast, belly, and under tail coverts; large white wing speculum.* ♀: above olive brown, below dull buffy brown, paler than above, and becoming *buffy white on center of lower underparts.*
Sim. species: ♂ is nearest ♂ Yellow-bellied Seedeater but latter *lacks* large white wing speculum and is olive (not black) above. Also cf. ♂♂ of Wing-barred, Lined, and Lesson's seedeaters, all of which show much more white below. ♂ Rose-breasted Grosbeak is much larger. ♀ virtually identical to ♀ Yellow-bellied Seedeater but whitish (not yellowish) on center of belly. ♀ Lesson's and Lined both have more extensively white lower underparts.
Voice: Song a few harsh notes, then melodious phrases, *chaaw, cheee, childedee-chea-chea-chea,* varying to *jaaaw, geee, chutchutchut-jeet* (P. Schwartz recording).
Behavior: Occurs in prs. when breeding, but at other times gathers in varying-sized flocks up to 30 or more that wander to grassy areas and feed on grass seeds. Forage by clinging to grass stems and reaching for

seeds, seldom hop on gd. Do not assoc. much with other seedeaters and grassquits.
Status and habitat: Very local resident. May breed in loose colonies in grassy and bushy areas, pastures, roadsides, and around settled areas. A colony was present above La Azulita, Mérida, but seasonal or periodic nomadism likely (notably nomadic elsewhere).
Range: 900–3100m (once to 240m at La Victoria, w Apure; most recs. 1400–2200m). Andes from s Táchira to ne Trujillo at Páramo Misisí. Mts. of Colombia s to n Bolivia.

Yellow-bellied Seedeater
PLATE 64
Sporophila nigricollis   Espiguero Vientriamarillo
Identification: 4.3″ (10.9cm). 9.6g. Bill light bluish gray (♂) or *dark* (♀). ♂: *crown, sides of head, throat, and chest black* (form hood); otherwise dark olive above; wings and tail brownish; *lower underparts pale creamy yellow to almost white,* flanks often somewhat mottled dusky; some birds have small white wing speculum. ♀: above olive brown, below buffy brown turning *buffy yellow (not whitish) on breast and belly.*
Sim. species: Name is misleading as even brightest ♂♂ are quite pale yellow below; duller ones are whitish. Better marks are black hood and olive upperparts which set ♂ apart from all other Venez. seedeaters. Cf. ♂ Black-and-white Seedeater. ♀ doubtfully separable from other dark-billed *Sporophila*. ♀ Lined and Lesson's Seedeaters have whitish (not buffy yellow) lower underparts; ♀ Black-and-white is slightly larger, belly paler, more whitish (see Table 1).
Voice: Song a short, musical ser. of slurred whistles, *tsu tsu tsu chew-see'see-sa-héet* or sim. variation, last note typically higher and accented. Not as musical as some members of genus.
Behavior: Prs. hold territories and ♂♂ sing from perches in tops of shrubs or well up in trees, but during dry season gather in loosely assoc. groups, sometimes with other seedeaters and grassquits, and wander to grassy areas with good seed crops. Thin, deep, meshlike cup nest low in bush or small tree; 2–3 eggs, pale greenish to buff, thickly spotted brown; breeding, Jun–Nov, Trinidad[3,175].
Status and habitat: Usually a fairly common resident in grassy or shrubby clearings, agricultural areas, roadsides, and woodland and forest borders in moderately dry to humid areas. Some seasonal nomadism (needs documentation).

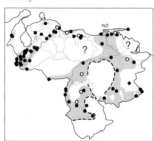

Range: To 2500m n of Orinoco (most recs. below 2000m); to 1400m s of Orinoco. Throughout n of Ori-

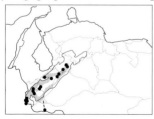

Table I. Identification of female *Sporophila* seedeaters in Venezuela

Species	Size (in)	Bill	Breast/Belly	Upperparts
Largest in size				
Lesson's Seedeater	4.5"	dusky black	contrasting whitish	olive brown
Lined Seedeater	4.5"	dusky black	contrasting whitish	olive brown
Black-and-white Seed-eater	4.5"	dusky black	whitish tinged yellow	olive brown
Intermediate in size				
Wing-barred Seedeater	4.3"	dusky (?)	dull whitish	dark olive brown; darkest brown of all
Yellow-bellied Seedeater	4.3"	dusky	thick buffy yellow	olive brown
Plumbeous Seedeater	4.3"	horn gray above; base of lower mandible yellowish green	buff tinged gray (muddy appearance)	brown tinged olive; the most olive above, grayest below
Gray Seedeater	4.2"	blackish; bill swollen; culmen very curved	whitish	olive brown
Slate-colored Seedeater	4.2"	grayish horn	faint tawny wash on breast	pale olive brown
Smallest in size				
Ruddy-breasted Seed-eater	4"	brownish; base of lower mandible pale pinkish	buff to pale cinnamon	wing coverts and inner flight feathers edged pale buff
Chestnut-bellied Seed-eater	4"	dusky	median underparts paler, washed ochre	inner flight feathers and tail edged pale brown

noco, incl. Delta Amacuro[343], but most recs. in or near foothills or mts.; n and c Amazonas (s to near Cerro Duida); locally throughout Bolívar (*nigricollis*). Costa Rica to Suriname and se Brazil (absent from all of e and c Amazonia).

Ruddy-breasted Seedeater
PLATE 64
Sporophila minuta Espiguero Canelillo
Identification: 4" (10.2cm). 8g. Bill thick, stubby, and black (♂); or brownish, base of lower mandible pinkish or pale (♀). ♂: above incl. sides of head brownish gray, wings and tail dusky, small white speculum at base of primaries (most conspic. in flight); *rump and underparts cinnamon rufous.* ♀: above buffy brown, wing coverts and inner flight feathers edged pale buff, underparts buff to pale dull cinnamon.
Sim. species: ♂ easily recognized by rufous rump and underparts. S of Orinoco cf. Chestnut-bellied Seedeater. ♀ is smaller and buffier than most ♀ *Sporophila* in Venez. but best told by accompanying ad. ♂ (see Table 1).
Voice: Song a variable but fast, lively ser. of musical little whistles and sputters, notes often given in prs. or couplets, i.e., *seet-seet, chew-chew, peet, wheet, spit 'wit-chew, pit-wit,* over and over at short intervals.
Behavior: Found in prs. when breeding, but during rest of yr gathers in varying-sized flocks that mix with other seedeaters and grassquits. May form larger flocks than most other seedeaters and wander more widely.

Forage by hopping on gd., mostly for seeds, or by clinging to grass stems and reaching for seeds. Occas. eat a few small berries and insects. Coarse grassy nest notable for stiff stems projecting above rim; low in grass to 2m up in bush; 2 white eggs spotted several shades of reddish brown[175]; Jun breeding, w Apure[525].
Status and habitat: Common and widespread seasonal resident in open grassy fields, roadsides, semi-open areas with grass and bushes, and gallery forest borders. Nomadic outside breeding season. Present May–Jan at Hato Masaguaral, Guárico[734]. Flocks. of 100 or more near Guaraunos, Sucre, in late Feb.

Range: To 1600m. Throughout (except nw?) n of Orinoco; nw Amazonas s to Cerro Duida; nw and e Bolívar s to Santa Elena de Uairén; Isla Margarita (*minuta*). W Mexico locally to nw Ecuador and e to the Guianas and mouth of the Amazon, Brazil. Trinidad.

Chestnut-bellied Seedeater PLATE 64
Sporophila castaneiventris Espiguero Vientricastaño
Identification: 4″ (10.2cm). 7.7g. Bill dusky. ♂: *mostly bright blue gray,* wings and tail dusky edged blue gray, some birds with small white spot at base of primaries; *median stripe down underparts from chin to tail dark chestnut maroon.* ♀: above olive brown, wing coverts, flight feathers, and tail dusky brown edged pale brown, below brownish buff, *median underparts paler and washed ochraceous.*
Sim. species: ♂ likely confused only with ♂ Ruddy-breasted Seedeater which has rump and *all* of underparts pale rufous. ♀ is smaller than other dark-billed *Sporophila* (except Ruddy-breasted) and more buffy ochraceous below.
Voice: Song a short to sometimes long, rambling ser. of melodic and varied notes with many repeated phrases. Sharp *chéeoo* call.
Behavior: Trim and handsome little ♂ is most likely seen when it perches up to sing in tops of grass or shrubs along riverbanks. Breeds in prs. but at other times gathers in flocks, often with grassquits and other seedeaters, in tall grass along riverbanks. Most of time, ♀-plumaged birds seem to outnumber ♂♂. Take seeds by perching on grass stems and reaching over to seed heads, also forage by hopping on gd. Grassy cup nest may be decorated with plant down; low in bush; 2–3 white eggs thickly spotted brown and lilac and with irreg. black lines[37].
Status and habitat: Few recs. in Venez. (n limit of range). Common and widespread across Amazon Basin where resident in tall grass and shrubbery along riverbanks, lake margins, marshy areas, and grassy clearings around habitations. Prob. relatively minor seasonal movements.

Range: To 200m. Sw Amazonas along Río Negro (1 sight, possibly this sp., on Orinoco isl. s of Pto. Ayacucho)[60]. Se Colombia to n Bolivia, most of Amaz. Brazil (except n central region) and the Guianas.

Catamenia

Small seed-eating finches; mainly high els.; bill thick, but bill shape of the 2 Venez. spp. differs; ♂♂ have chestnut under tail coverts.

Plain-colored Seedeater PLATE 64
Catamenia inornata Semillero Desairado
Identification: 5.4″ (13.7cm). 13.5g. Short, thick, *pinkish bill* (both sexes). ♂: *plain gray* (paler than Páramo Seedeater), back narrowly streaked blackish, below

olive gray turning dirty buffy olive on belly; *under tail coverts dark rufous.* ♀: *above grayish brown narrowly streaked dusky on crown and back;* below pale dull brownish buff, *unstreaked* (or sometimes throat and chest obscurely streaked), and much paler on belly; *under tail coverts rufous.* Imm: buffy brown *heavily streaked above and below* (streaking fine and dense on head), belly dull buff, largely unstreaked, bill dusky; streaking fainter in older or worn-plumage juv. birds.
Sim. species: ♂ from ♂ Páramo Seedeater by much paler and more uniform gray plumage (no blackish foreface) and obviously streaked back. ♀ is paler and grayer than ♀ Páramo Seedeater and more obviously streaked on crown and upperparts. Imms. of the two so sim. they may not always be separable in field; Plain-colored is paler, throat and chest grayer, lower underparts paler. Habits usually differ, and in all plumages note bill differences.
Voice: Somewhat variable, possibly geographical dialects. In ne Colombia typically 2–3 musical notes then 2–4 slow buzzes, *chit ta'ta zreeee, bzzzz, breeee* (last 3 notes inhale, exhale, inhale).
Behavior: A plain-looking little finch of treeless high Andes. Occurs in prs. when breeding, otherwise alone or more often in small scattered groups that are sometimes loosely assoc. with a few other paramo spp. Feed on seeds in bushes or by hopping on gd. in bare, rocky, or short-grass areas; feed heavily on *Espeletia* seeds by perching up on exposed seed clusters. Sing from top of small bush and flush up into small bushes or fly off long distances. In Colombia breeding evidence most of yr[260]. In part a nomad and opportunistic breeder that seeks abundant paramo seed crops, breeding prolifically during favorable yrs.
Status and habitat: Uncommon resident in paramo, highland pastures with or without scattered low bushes, occas. shrubby ravines at or above treeline. Inhabits much more open terrain than allied Páramo Seedeater. Usually numerous following wet yrs with abundant seed crops in paramo. Prob. in all paramos of Táchira and Mérida. Look for it around Páramo del Águila, Mérida.

Range: 3250–4200m. S Táchira on Páramo de Tamá (*minor*); Mérida in vicinity of Páramos Mucuchíes and San Antonio; sightings at Páramo Mucubají and Páramo del Águila (*mucuchiesi*). Colombia s in Andes to n and c Argentina.

Páramo Seedeater PLATE 64
Catamenia homochroa Semillero de las Alturas
Identification: 5.2″ (13.2cm). 14.5g. Conical bill pinkish to yellowish pink (♂) or paler (♀). Bill paler, more

slender and pointed than in other *Catamenia*. ♂: *uniform dark gray, foreface blackish*, underparts slightly paler, belly tinged brownish, *under tail coverts chestnut*. Or sim. but paler, back and tail underparts tinged brownish, a few obscure streaks on back (*duncani*). ♀: upperparts olive brown, head tinged grayish brown, crown and back *faintly streaked dusky*, underparts *unstreaked* warm grayish to buffy brown, more buffy brown on lower underparts; *under tail coverts chestnut*. Or sim. but above rich russet brown, dusky streaking broader, underparts warm brown, usually with some obscure dusky streaking on breast (*duncani*). Imm. (both sexes): brown heavily streaked dusky above and below, belly buff, crissum tinged rufous; older birds gradually become less streaked.
Sim. species: Dark ♂ with yellowish bill, blackish foreface, and chestnut crissum distinctive. ♀ and imm. easily confused with ♀ and imm. Plain-colored Seedeater (see), but they usually have streaky underparts and paler crissum.
Voice: *Tsit-tsit* in flight[179].
Behavior: A quiet and retiring little finch usually seen alone, in prs., or in small groups (families?). Often with mixed-spp. flocks of tanagers, flowerpiercers, and brush-finches. Stay low in shrubbery and hop on gd. for seeds and grit. Timing of breeding possibly assoc. with bamboo (*Chusquea* and *Swallenochloa*) seeding[179].
Status and habitat: Scarce and local in Andes. Dense stunted forest and low shrubby vegetation or second growth up to treeline. Despite name, not in open paramo. In Venez. known mainly from Sierra de Perijá (specimens from several localities) and on or near summits of a few high tepuis in se Bolívar. Based on no. of specimens from Uei-tepui, Cerro Cuquenán, and Cerro Roraima, fairly common from 1900m upward to their summits; 8 seen early Feb on summit of Roraima (D. Ascanio).

Range: 2600–3500m n of Orinoco; 1600–2450m s of Orinoco (sight to 2800m). Sierra de Perijá, Zulia; Mérida on Páramos San Antonio and Nevados (*homochroa*); cerros of Amazonas from Cerro Camani s to Cerro de la Neblina; scattered cerros of s Bolívar incl. Meseta de Jaua, Auyán-tepui, Sororopán-tepui, Uei-tepui, Cerro Cuquenán, and Cerro Roraima (*duncani*). Adj. n Brazil (Cerro de la Neblina); doubtless Guyana. Colombia s locally in Andes to Bolivia.

Phrygilus

Large group of mostly high-Andean finches (only 1 in Venez.); thick conical bill; ♂♂ mainly gray; ♀♀ gray to brownish, some streaky; semiterrestrial in open or bushy terrain.

Plumbeous Sierra-Finch
PLATE 64
Phrygilus unicolor Fringilo Aplomado
Identification: 6″ (15cm). 21g. Blackish bill sharp pointed, conical, and *small* for size of bird; also looks rather small headed. Sexes very different. ♂: *uniform leaden gray*, slightly paler below, faint pale eyering; wings and tail dusky, inner flight feathers narrowly edged whitish (inconspic.). ♀: above brownish, below dull whitish *broadly and profusely streaked dusky above and below*.
Sim. species: ♂ from other "gray" highland finches by larger size, dark plumage, and small bill. Also cf. ♂ Slaty Finch which is smaller and darker. Heavily striped ♀ looks like overgrown sparrow. Cf. imm. *Catamenia*, both paler and *much less streaked*, and imm. Rufous-collared Sparrow which has fine (not coarse) streaking and usually a hint of ad.'s head pattern.
Voice: Infreq. hd. song, from low bush, top of rock, or in flight in E Andes of Colombia, a short, dull buzz, then a chipping rattle. Weak *tsip* notes as flushes.
Behavior: Well-separated individuals, prs., or occas. small, loose groups forage for seeds in paramo by walking on gd. or hopping over rough or rocky terrain. Wait for a close approach before flushing, then often fly off and drop quickly back to cover, or occas. stop and hop up exposed on top of rock or shrub. Often loosely assoc. with other paramo spp. such as thistletails, titspinetails, and seedeaters.
Status and habitat: Fairly common resident in open paramo with or without *Espeletia*, grass around rocky outcrops, pastures, cultivated fields, boggy meadows, and esp. along rivulets and drainage ditches. Commonest at high els. (above ca. 3800m) but entire pops. occas. forced lower during Jul–Sep snowstorms. Look for this sp. around Páramo del Águila, Mérida.

Range: 3000–4500m. Paramos of Mérida and Trujillo n to Páramo Cendé (*nivarius*); s Táchira on Páramo de Tamá (*geospizopsis*); no recs. on paramos of n Táchira. Colombia s in Andes to Tierra del Fuego.
Note: Some recognize only subsp. *nivarius*[467].

Sicalis

Small, predom. "yellow" finches (hence name), most spp. streaked and sparrowlike above (esp. ♀♀ and imms.); bill conical, culmen slightly decurved; tail feathers pointed, outer vane very narrow; numerous age- and sex-related plumages complicate identification.

Saffron Finch   PLATE 65
Sicalis flaveola   Canario de Tejado
Identification: 5.5″ (14cm). 20g. ♂: *head and underparts bright yellow, forecrown to slightly beyond eyes bright orange*, rest of upperparts bright olive yellow (occas. faintly streaked dusky), flight feathers and tail dusky broadly edged olive yellow. ♀: like ♂ but duller; above slightly darker, mantle somewhat streaked. Imm.: sim. to juv. but with *broad band of yellow across chest*. In all plumages under wing coverts and inner webs of flight feathers bright yellow. Juv.: above mostly light brown streaked dusky, rump olive yellow; flight feathers dusky edged bright yellow olive; sides of head gray, underparts grayish white vaguely streaked; under tail coverts yellow.
Sim. species: Commonest *Sicalis* finch and worth learning well. ♂ is brightest of genus. Confusion will most often occur with Orange-fronted Yellow-Finch (see) in s half of llanos. Also see Grassland and Stripe-tailed yellow-finches.
Voice: Song a dry, chattery, rather monotonic ser. of notes, *weezip, weezip, tsit, tsit, weezip, ts-tsit, weezip, weezip, tsik, ta-sik, weezip, tsit* . . . and so on, often for a min or more; rambling and lazy. Call a dry *chit*.
Behavior: A vivacious little finch that loves companionship. Gathers in small to large flocks most of the yr, scatters over bare or open grassy places, hops on gd. to feed on weed and grass seeds, and flushes up to bushes or cover at slightest hint of danger, or lines up on fence wires to rest. Usually does not perch very high. Even when paired to nest, may form loose colonies in favorable areas. A popular cagebird. Nest in burrow in stream banks, cavity in post, tree, etc., or abandoned nest of other bird, e.g., Yellow-chinned Spinetail, thornbird, kiskadee, oriole; 1(?)–4 pale bluish white eggs thickly spotted brown, mostly at large end; breeding, late May, Orinoco region[115]; Jun–Nov, w Guárico and w Apure[137,734].
Status and habitat: Common to abundant resident (some seasonal movements) in ranchland and semi-open areas with scattered bushes and trees; gallery forest borders, shrubby woodland, and lawns and gardens in rural and urban areas. Favors drier areas than Orange-fronted Yellow-Finch, and part of pop. may move out of llanos and into surrounding drier areas during rainiest months.

Range: To 1850m. Throughout n of Orinoco and s to n Amazonas (Pto. Ayacucho; Junglaven) and n Bolívar along Orinoco from Caicara, lower Río Caura, Ciudad Bolívar, and El Palmar e to Delta Amacuro (*flaveola*). N and e Colombia to Guyana; Suriname (?); w Peru; e Bolivia and se Brazil s to c Argentina.

Orange-fronted Yellow-Finch   PLATE 65
Sicalis columbiana   Canario de Sabana
Identification: 5″ (12.7cm). ♂: much like ♂ Saffron Finch *but more olive green; bill slightly heavier and more angular. Forecrown contrasting orange* (does not extend back to eyes) sharply set off from dark yellowish olive crown and upperparts; *lores and narrow eyering blackish*; wings and tail dusky edged yellow, below bright yellow, chest and sides tinged olive. In hand inner webs of flight feathers grayish white (not yellow). ♀: above grayish brown, *head slightly grayer, eyes and narrow eyering blackish* (like bruised or *black eye*); *flight feathers edged yellowish olive*; below pale gray brown, throat and belly whitish, *chest faintly streaked dusky*, crissum yellowish olive, bill dusky above, pale and faintly yellowish below. Legs pinkish flesh in both sexes. ♂ may molt into hen plumage after breeding. Imm.: like ♀ but breast with faint dusky streaks.
Sim. species: ♂ from ♂ Saffron Finch by overall greenish olive (not yellowish) appearance, esp. on upperparts, *narrow and sharply defined orange band on forehead* (not with orange extending back over midcrown), black eyering, and duller yellow underparts. In direct comparison note Orange-fronted's *smaller* size. ♀ from ♀ Saffron by *uniform* plumage (essentially no streaking), dingy (not yellowish) underparts, yellowish olive edging on flight feathers, and "black eye."
Voice: Flight call a soft, trebled *chu-re-reet*, uttered quickly; song a short, chippy ser. of unmusical notes.
Behavior: Prs. or small flocks scatter on gd. in open areas to feed but fly off to tree, shrub, or fence if alarmed. Often assoc. with Saffron Finches. Nest semi-colonially, up to 12 prs. or more in holes in vertical dirt bank in llanos, also hollow limb, crevice in rock wall; grassy cup nest; 4 pale blue eggs speckled brown at larger end; breeding, Jun–Jul[115] (C. Parrish); nest in Nov, fledgling in Jun[137].
Status and habitat: Common resident in wetter southern half of llanos in grassy areas with scattered bushes and trees, along stream banks, and around water holes and ranch buildings. Increasingly common s of Río Apure, there partially replacing Saffron Finch (e.g.,

abundant at Hato Los Indios in se Apure; Saffron scarce there); nos. rapidly decrease n of Río Apure (rare at Hato Piñero, Cojedes). Seasonal movements marked; this sp. is *most numerous* in w Apure in rainy months.

Range: To 300m. E of Andes from s Cojedes (Hato Nuevo; sight, Hato Piñero), s Guárico (Camaguán; Santa Rita), s Monagas, and Delta Amacuro s through Apure to n Amazonas (s to San Fernando de Atabapo and Río Ventuari); n Bolívar s to La Paragua and Upata (*columbiana*). Disjunct. E Colombia; c and e Amaz. Basin near the Amazon; interior e Brazil; ne Peru (once); Trinidad (once).

Stripe-tailed Yellow-Finch   PLATE 65
Sicalis citrina   Canarito

Identification: 4.7″ (12cm). 11.6g. Upperparts dull yellowish olive with *bright yellow forecrown and rump* (both unstreaked), back streaked dusky, wings dusky edged olive yellow; *inner web of outer 2 tail feathers with large white spot near tip* (conspic. from below, not from above even in flight); *sides of head plain olive*, below yellow, chest and sides tinged olive. ♀: dull and streaky; above brown rather obscurely streaked dusky, below *dull yellow thickly streaked dusky on throat, breast, and sides*; wings and tail as in ♂.

Sim. species: Whitish tail spots diagnostic if seen but usually hard to see. Look for ♂'s plain olive face and *unstreaked* yellowish olive crown which separate it from Grassland Yellow-Finch which has yellow eyering and streaked crown. ♀ is only one of genus that is *yellow and streaked below*.

Voice: In n mts. song given in display flight as bird flies up then slowly flutters earthward, a musical *chu'u'u 'u'u'u'u'u'u, zew-tew-tew-you*, chattery notes at end lower pitched. From perch a weak, semimusical warble, somewhat 2-parted, *chi-chew-chew, chewa-chew-chew-chew-chewee-chee*, colorless, mostly on same pitch.

Behavior: Forms prs. when breeding, otherwise usually in small, loosely assoc. flocks of up to 20 or so in grassy areas or along roadsides. Feed on seeds taken mostly from gd.

Status and habitat: Uncommon to fairly common resident very locally. Loose colonies in suitable areas; some seasonal movement or nomadism, and unpredictable in occurrence. Look for it on high, grassy slopes above La Victoria, Aragua.

Range: To 1900m. Spottily in Sierra de Perijá, Zulia, Lara (San Pedro), Coastal Cordillera from Carabobo e

to Distr. Federal and Miranda; c Amazonas at base of Cerro Duida; nw Bolívar (Hato Las Nieves); se Bolívar from lower Río Paragua s to Gran Sabana (*browni*). Ne Colombia locally e to s Guyana and s Suriname; se Peru, spottily in Brazil s of the Amazon; n Argentina.

Grassland Yellow-Finch   PLATE 65
Sicalis luteola   Canario Chirigüe

Identification: 4.7″ (12cm). 13g. ♂: above yellowish olive, *crown and nape finely streaked dusky*, back broadly streaked dusky, rump unstreaked bright olive yellow; *lores, narrow eyering, and ocular area yellow*; wings and tail dusky edged pale brown (no bars), below bright yellow, sides tinged olive. ♀: above pale brown streaked dusky (incl. crown), *supraloral line and eyering yellow* (not as conspic. as in ♂), below dull yellow, sides of head and neck and sides of body strongly tinged olive; some individuals buff on throat and chest (*luteola*). Or sim. but larger, darker olive above and below; crown more heavily streaked, both sexes with *less prom. yellow facial markings*; ♀ has throat and chest dull ochraceous (*bogotensis*).

Sim. species: Easily confused with other yellow-finches, but from any by yellow on lores and around eyes; ♀ additionally by *streaked* crown. ♀ Stripe-tailed has *unstreaked* crown and streaky underparts.

Voice: Song a fast ser. of high chips, buzzes, and trills, given while perched or in display flight high overhead. In display typically flies up high, then flutters earthward slowly as sings. Call, in flight or perched, a short, high, semimusical *kreéez-zip* or *tease-zip*, with complex quality.

Behavior: Occurs singly, in prs., or in small groups which often are nervous and excitable as they perch in short or tall grass, drop to gd. to feed on seeds and insects, and often flush off erratically giving high-pitched chipping notes. Breeding perhaps loosely colonial in suitable areas. Grassy cup nest in tall grass or edge of marsh; 3 pale bluish green eggs speckled brown[115]; Oct nest, w Apure[137].

Status and habitat: Lowland race *luteola* uncommon to locally fairly common resident in open grassland, fields, and edges of marshes. Distrib. uneven and abundance unpredictable; seasonal movements or nomadism likely. Unrec. at Hato Masaguaral, Guárico but reported at adj. Hato Flores Moradas, Guárico. Fairly common (wet and dry season) at Hato Cedral, Apure; flocks of more than 100, Feb 1988, Hato Piñero, Cojedes (J. Pierson).

Range: To 1200m. Ne Falcón; e of Andes from w Apure (sight), w Barinas (sight), and s Cojedes (sight) e

across Guárico to Monagas and nw Bolívar (sightings, Hato Las Nieves, Feb 1991—R. Ridgely and Hilty), ne Bolívar (Upata) and se Bolívar at Cerro Roraima and on Gran Sabana (*luteola*). 2800–3000m in Andes of s Táchira (Páramo de Tamá), n Táchira (El Cobre), and Mérida near Páramo de Conejos (*bogotensis*). E Colombia; c Ecuador; Peru; Guyana and Suriname; mouth of the Amazon; austral breeders in Argentina, Uruguay, and extreme se Brazil migrate n to e Bolivia and s Brazil.

Note: Highland *bogotensis* perhaps a separate sp.

Haplospiza

Small montane finches (1 in Venez.); forest-dwelling, bamboo-seed specialists; bill more slender than in most seed-eating allies; buzzy songs.

Slaty Finch   PLATE 64
Haplospiza rustica   Semillero Apizarrado
Identification: 5" (12.7cm). 16g. *Conical, pointed bill, rather slender for a finch.* ♂: *uniform slate gray,* slightly paler below; wings and tail blackish edged slate gray. ♀: above dark olive brown, wings and tail dusky edged dark rufescent brown; throat dirty white, rest of underparts buffy olive with rather *obscure dusky streaking on breast.*
Sim. species: A good mark for either sex is slender conical bill (culmen straight). See various flowerpiercers and larger, paler ♂ Plumbeous Sierra-Finch, and ♂ Páramo Seedeater. More confusing ♀ is nearest ♀ and imm. Plain-colored and ♀ and imm. Páramo seedeaters, both more or less streaked above and below; note that ♀ Plain-colored and Páramo seedeaters have wash of chestnut on crissum.
Voice: Some ♂♂ sing long, complex songs, others short, complicated bursts of buzzy chips and trills that recall songs of Bananaquit. Whether long or short, songs begin as thin, rapid trills (almost like an electrical hum) that increase in loudness and complexity toward end, i.e., *iiiiiiiiiiiitttttttTTTez'ez'ja'wEEz'let'ti* (may last up to 3.5 sec), at short intervals. All apparently give long, buzzy flight song (twice as long as when perched).
Behavior: A nomadic sp. that seeks patches of mass-seeding *Chusquea* bamboo for breeding. In seeding bamboo ♂♂ immediately set up small territories with ♂♂ singing 50–100m apart; sing incessantly from low, or sometimes very high, exposed bare twigs. Breed during bamboo seeding then vanish when seed crop is exhausted. Infreq. encountered away from seeding bamboo, then usually in lower growth where keep mostly out of sight and forage for grass seeds on or near gd. Elsewhere single birds and small groups have been reported with small mixed-spp. flocks.
Status and habitat: Rare nomadic resident although *very locally* and temporally numerous when concentrates to breed at mass-seeding bamboo in humid and wet montane forest, i.e., many 14–15 Jan 1995 below Páramo Batallón, s Mérida. Also in highland clearings and overgrown pastures. Bamboo seed crops are unpredictable and some seeding die-offs are small (only a few ha), thus, Slaty Finches need large areas of mt.

forest with bamboo for survival. One tepui specimen, and 1 sighting at 2800m Feb 1998, PN Guaramacal, Trujillo (D. Ascanio and others), may be wandering birds.

Range: 2000–2600m (sight to 2800m); 1900–2100m in Coastal Cordillera. Sierra de Perijá, Zulia; Andes of n Táchira and s Mérida (sight, Páramos Zumbador and Batallón); Trujillo (sight); Coastal Cordillera in Aragua and Distr. Federal (*rustica*); prob. Miranda; s Amazonas on Cerro de la Neblina[801]; Bolívar near summit (1850m) of Chimantá-tepui (*arcana*). Mts. from s Mexico to nw Bolivia.

Gray Pileated-Finch   PLATE 65
Coryphospingus pileatus   Granero Cabecita de Fósforo
Identification: 5.3" (13.5cm). 15.5g. Rather thick conical bill. ♂: *above gray; narrow white eyering* accentuates prom. black eyes; *black crown conceals long, flat, flame red crest* (spectacular on rare occas. when exposed); flight feathers and tail dusky, below mostly white, breast grayish white. ♀: sim. but duller and upperparts slightly brownish gray; crown brownish gray (no red crest), *eyering white*, breast tinged and somewhat streaked grayish brown, belly whitish tinged buff.
Sim. species: ♀ lacks good marks, but no other really like her. Look for white eyering. ♀ seedeaters and grassquits are browner; seedeaters also have thicker bills.
Voice: Song, rather infreq. hd., a leisurely ser. of flat, almost vireolike phrases, *tslip tslip tsweet, tslip tslip tsweet* (P. Schwartz recording).
Behavior: A rather quiet, unobtrusive, and not too freq. seen little finch of dry scrubby areas. May be seen alone, less often in prs., families, or 6–8; but most often loosely assoc. with other spp. Forages on or near gd. in dry scrub and thickets for seeds and most insects. Occas. perches in open briefly, and readily mobs small owls. Brilliant red crest of ♂ seldom seen to advantage, but flared in agonistic behavior toward

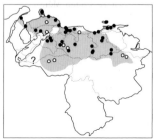

other ♂♂; prob. also in sexual display to ♀. Nesting Mar–Jul.

Status and habitat: Uncommon resident in arid scrub, dry thorn woodland, and gallery-forest borders; occas. thickets in moist areas. Occurs in lowlands, hilly terrain, and foothills but nowhere very numerous. Some local or seasonal movement possible; not found Dec–Jan at Hato Masaguaral, Guárico[734].

Range: To 750m n of Orinoco; to 100m s of Orinoco. N Zulia, Falcón, and n Lara e to Sucre and e of Andes s to Apure and ne Bolívar (Ciudad Bolívar; sight, Upata); Isla Margarita (*brevicaudus*). N and sw Colombia; e Brazil.

Note: Previously called Pileated Finch[403].

Atlapetes

Large genus; mostly montane; midsized finches; bill fairly short and conical; several subgroups in genus (mostly yellow below, mostly white below, etc.); stay rather low in vegetation where inconspic. but not esp. furtive; taxonomic revisions abound[190,531].

Moustached Brush-Finch   PLATE 63
Atlapetes albofrenatus   Atlapetes de Freno Blanco
Identification: 6.8″ (17.3cm). Above bright olive green, *crown and nape cinnamon rufous*, sides of head black; *conspic. white malar stripe* bordered below by narrow black submalar line (inconspic.); chin white, *rest of underparts yellow* heavily clouded olive on sides and flanks.

Sim. species: Generally resembles Rufous-naped Brush-Finch but olive green (not slaty) above, and always shows prom. white malar stripe. In s Táchira see Pale-naped Brush-Finch.

Voice: Song, given a few times in early morning, is variable but typically a few musical notes, e.g., *czeet, czeet, czeet, czeet, tswit-tswit-tswit-tsu-tsu-tsu-tsu-tsu-tsu*, last notes rapid and clattery. Call a high, thin *eeesp*, often trebled.

Behavior: A rather arboreal brush-finch that is often easy to see. Prs. or families are nimble but methodical as peer and hop on mossy trunks, low limbs, and in foliage for arthropod prey, fruits, and berries. Stay mostly 1–10m up and more often independent of mixed-spp. flocks than with them. Fledglings May, Jun (Mérida).

Status and habitat: Fairly common resident in montane habitats ranging from moist to very humid forest and mossy cloud forest. Often in humid forest borders, overgrown clearings, or old second growth, also around treefalls or small open areas inside forest. Lowest el. recs. are near La Azulita, Mérida[60].

Range: 2100–2500m (sight to ca. 1500m). Ne Táchira (Boca del Monte) n to Mérida (*meridae*). Colombia s in E Andes to latitude of Bogotá.

Pale-naped Brush-Finch   PLATE 63
Atlapetes pallidinucha   Atlapetes Nuca Pálida
Identification: 7″ (18cm). 35g. Above slaty gray with *broad cinnamon coronal stripe bordered yellow and turning white on rearcrown and nape*; sides of head black (large mask), short black moustachial line; *underparts yellow*, sides, flanks, and lower underparts clouded grayish olive.

Sim. species: Crown stripe that changes from cinnamon to white is diagnostic. See Northern Rufous-naped and Moustached brush-finches.

Voice: Territorial song, mostly at dawn, a thin, high *tsie . . . tsie weu, tsi . . . tsie weu tsie weu, ti . . . ti wee tsits we weee* or *tsie . . . tsie tsieu*, 1st ser. of *tsi* notes alike or descending, *tsiu* sharply rising. Given in duet. Advertising song *wheet-tew-tew-tew*[179].

Behavior: Much like Rufous-naped Brush-Finch but stays lower and out of sight more. In Colombia prs. are often with mixed-spp. flocks containing flower-piercers, tanagers, and other brush-finches in treeline vegetation; stay low, occas. hop on gd., and pop in and out of view briefly along shrubby edges.

Status and habitat: Resident in bushy forest borders, stunted or shrubby second growth, and dwarf forest up to treeline. Judging from no. of specimens, fairly common on Cerro El Retiro at 2700–2800m.

Range: 2500–3275m. S Táchira on Páramo de Tamá, Cerro El Retiro, and Cerro Las Copas (*pallidinucha*). Andes of Colombia, Ecuador, and n Peru.

Ochre-breasted Brush-Finch   PLATE 63
Atlapetes semirufus   Atlapetes Ajicero
Identification: 7″ (18cm). 28g. Above olive with *entire head, throat, and breast orange rufous*, center of lower underparts yellow, flanks and under tail coverts olive. Or head and underparts paler, chin and center of throat white (*albigula*); or back darker olive gray (*zimmeri*). Juv.: head tinged gray.

Sim. species: No other brush-finch in n Venez. has all orange rufous foreparts.

Voice: Territorial song a short, whistled *wheet, peet, p'tsu-tsu-tsu* or *eeet, wheet, sweet-sweet-sweet*; or shorter *swiit, chew-chew-chew* or sim. variation; typically 1st note rises. In n mts. most vocal early in rainy season.

Behavior: Normally a modest and somewhat retiring bird that keeps out of view in thickets, but at times hops up into open, sings, makes bold advances, and seems undeniably curious. Occurs alone or in prs. or little families that hop on or near gd., pause to vigorously flick leaves aside with bill, or move up into lower foliage to take small fruits and berries. May hop up into open along shrubby borders in early morning, then usually rather easy to see. Only incidentally with mixed-spp. flocks. Juvs. seen Feb–Mar, PN Henri Pittier.

Status and habitat: Fairly common resident in humid to wet forest borders, regrowth vegetation in landslides, and other openings or shrubby areas in montane forest. Most numerous in n cordilleras (Falcón to Monagas); much less numerous in Andes.

Range: 600–2700m (sightings to 500m, Aragua). Nw Táchira at Seboruco (*albigula*); s and ne Táchira (no Mérida recs.) and se Trujillo at Boconó (*zimmeri*); n Trujillo (Páramo Cendé), Lara nw to Cerro El Cerrón, and Falcón on Sierra de San Luis (*benedettii*); mts. of Yaracuy, n cordilleras from Carabobo and n Guárico e to ne Anzoátegui, Sucre, and n Monagas at Caripe (*denisei*). Colombia in E Andes s to Cundinamarca.

Tepui Brush-Finch

PLATE 63

Atlapetes personatus   Atlapetes de Tepuis

Identification: 6.8″ (17.3cm). Much racial variation. *Crown and sides of head chestnut*, otherwise above slaty, chin, throat, and underparts yellow, sides, flanks, and under tail coverts dark olive (*personatus*). Or entire head, chin, and sides of throat chestnut (*collaris*); or head and throat chestnut (*paraquensis, parui, duidae*); or head, throat, and chest chestnut (*jugularis*). Imm.: head mostly yellowish brown (no chestnut), chest mottled brownish.

Sim. species: No other brush-finch occurs with it, but note dramatic geographic variation in amt. of chestnut color on head and underparts. Most observers will see only nominate *personatus*.

Voice: At dawn on Sierra de Lema prs. sing an unmusical *speek! speek! speeu-TEE-tu'tu'* (mid. note loudest and highest); when excited prs. sing simultaneous (not antiphonal) duets, a crescendo of rapid, chattery, forceful *tsit* and *ti* notes ending with 2–4 buzzy notes squeezed out, *ti'ti'ti'ti'ti'ti'ti'ti'tsit'tsit'tsit'tsit'chi'chi'chi 'che'che'chewee-chewee*. Generally rather quiet with only a few exuberant outbursts at dawn.

Behavior: A nimble and puckish bird, often curious and not too shy. Prs. or family groups of 3–4 hop in shrubbery and thickets and cock or flip up tails as they forage alone in early morning hrs, often coming into open at forest borders, occas. even hopping on gd. Sometimes with mixed-spp. flocks, esp. later in morning, but also often independent of them. Forage mostly

below eye level, peering and pecking for insect prey and berries. Most readily seen early in morning but tend to remain out of sight as day lengthens.

Status and habitat: Widespread and common resident of tepuis. Shrubbery along borders of humid and wet forest. On Sierra de Lema common in borders of dense, melastome-dominated, young to old second growth, esp. on white sandy soil.

Range: 1000–2500m. Amazonas on Cerros Yavi, Camani, Guanay, and Sipapo and Sierra de Maigualida (*paraquensis*); Cerro Parú (*parui*); Amazonas on Cerro de la Neblina (*jugularis*); Amazonas on Cerro Duida and upper Río Ocamo; Bolívar on Cerro Guaiquinima, Meseta de Jaua, and Cerro Urutaní (*duidae*); Bolívar on Auyán-tepui (*collaris*); throughout cerros of Gran Sabana from Ptari-tepui, Sierra de Lema (sight), Aprada-tepui, Chimantá-tepui, and Acopán-tepui to Cerros Cuquenán and Roraima (*personatus*). N Brazil (Cerro de la Neblina); Guyana.

Slaty Brush-Finch

PLATE 63

Atlapetes schistaceus   Atlapetes Sombrero de Pelo

Identification: 7″ (18cm). Above slate gray with *rufous chestnut crown and nape*; sides of head blackish bordered below by narrow but conspic. *white malar stripe* and narrow black submalar line; throat grayish white, rest of underparts gray, flanks dark gray. Or sim. but with white loral spot (*tamae*).

Sim. species: In high-Andean shrubbery a mostly slaty to blackish finch with chestnut crown will likely be this sp. See Chestnut-crowned Brush-Finch.

Voice: Often sings persistently for brief period at dawn, typically a short *tsuu, tweet-tweet*, slowly, 1st note downslurred. Prs. also sing poorly coordinated duets (not antiphonal) of high-pitched notes and trills that end with distinctive *chewy-chewy-chewy* or *t'chew, t'chew, t'chew*. Thin *tseet* notes when foraging.

Behavior: A handsome brush-finch, active and relatively easy to see. Prs. or families reg. follow mixed-spp. flocks, stay low in shrubbery or ascend well up

into small dense trees by hopping up through branches. Away from mixed-spp. flocks remain more under cover where may forage very low or on gd. Diet is insects and some fruit. BC birds Apr–Sep, n Colombia.
Status and habitat: Common resident in humid and wet montane forest, esp. in shrubby forest borders, stunted mossy forest, thickets and hedgerows up to treeline, and patches of woody vegetation above treeline.
Range: 2000–3800m. Sierra de Perijá, Zulia (*fumidus*); s Táchira (*tamae*); n Táchira, Mérida, and Trujillo n to Páramo Cendé on Lara border (*castaneifrons*). Colombia s in Andes to n Peru.

Rufous-naped Brush-Finch   PLATE 63
Atlapetes latinuchus   Atlapetes Frentinegro
Identification: 6.5″ (16.5cm). 30g. *Crown and nape rufous chestnut*, forehead and sides of head black (form mask), cheeks gray bordered by dusky malar; rest of upperparts *slate gray* tinged olive, *below yellow*, sides and flanks olive.
Sim. species: Good marks are combination of chestnut crown, slaty back, and yellow underparts. Moustached Brush-Finch is olive above and always has conspic. white malar. In s Táchira see Pale-naped Brush-Finch.
Voice: Song in Colombia, given a few times early in morning, is fast, complicated, and energetic, typically with 3–4 distinct parts, *t't't't't't'ut,weet-weet-weet-tu-tu-few-few-few*, lasting ca. 2–3 sec and with much variation in pattern. Beginning trill is usually characteristic.
Behavior: Sim. to that of Tepui and Slaty brush-finches. Eggs pale buff speckled reddish brown chiefly around larger end[589].
Status and habitat: Resident in shrubby forest borders and second growth. Judging from no. of specimens, common within its limited range in Venez. Replaced in Venez. Andes by allied Slaty Brush-Finch with which it is apparently interspecifically competitive; the two occur in a patchwork of nonoverlapping ranges s through Andes[530].

Range: 1100–2200m. Sierra de Perijá (upper Río Negro), Zulia (*phelpsi*). Colombia s spottily in Andes to n Peru.
Note: Excludes Southern Rufous-naped Brush-Finch (*A. taczanowskii*) of s Peru and Bolivia[190]. Taxonomic status of *phelpsi* not evaluated[190].

Buarremon

Formerly placed in *Atlapetes* but differ in secretive habits and song structure; genetically allied to *Lysurus*; plumage nearer *Arremon* than *Atlapetes*[531].

Chestnut-capped Brush-Finch   PLATE 63
Buarremon brunneinuchus   Atlapetes Gargantillo
Identification: 7.5″ (19cm). 45g. *Crown chestnut narrowly edged golden cinnamon on sides*; forehead and sides of head black with 3 inconspic. white spots across forehead; otherwise dark olive above; conspic. *puffy white throat bordered below by narrow black chest band*, rest of underparts white, sides, flanks, belly, and under tail coverts grayish olive. Or sim. but no black chest band (*allinornatus*).
Sim. species: Several *Atlapetes* have chestnut crowns but none also has black chest band (most subspp.) and white underparts of this attractive bird. See Stripe-headed Brush-Finch which has black-and-gray striped head.
Voice: High, sibilant, almost hissing song in Mérida, *pit-'t'zeet seee, seee, seee, tzu-zeet* or sim.; near upper limit of human hearing; call *seeeep*, almost inaudible except when close.
Behavior: Semiterrestrial and a notorious skulker that is easily overlooked but curious, and may hop up boldly and puff out throat as it looks over a patient and quiet observer. Single birds or prs. are quiet as hop on gd., flick leaves aside with bill, or move low through thick undergrowth. Often active as mixed-spp. flocks pass by. Display to conspecifics with exaggerated head bobbing, throat puffed and forecrown feathers raised. Eat mostly insects, some berries. Coarse, bulky, cup nest with fine lining, low in bush or sapling in forest; 2 eggs, pale bluish white or white[101,706]; breeding evidence, Mar–Aug, n Colombia.
Status and habitat: Fairly common but easily overlooked resident in undergrowth of humid and wet forest and older second-growth woodland. Interspecifically competitive with Stripe-headed Brush-Finch, and in Venez. found at higher els. (above ca. 1800m) than that sp. but also in low els. in its absence (i.e., s Lara). In n cordilleras the two may occur at same els. but appear to be interspecifically territorial or limit each other locally(?).

Range: 1000–3100m in Andes; 1000–2100 in Coastal Cordillera (sight to 2400, Cerro Oriental—D. Ascanio). Sierra de Perijá, Zulia; Andes from s Táchira n through Mérida, Trujillo, and s Lara (*frontalis*); Falcón in Sierra de San Luis (*allinornatus*); mts. of Yaracuy and n cordilleras from Carabobo to Distr. Federal and Miranda on Cerro Negro (*xanthogenys*). Colombia s in mts. to s Peru.
Note 1: *Brunneinuchus* spelling changed[10].
Note 2: Subsp. *xanthogenys* may not be distinguishable from *frontalis*.

Stripe-headed Brush-Finch

PLATE 63

Buarremon torquatus   Corbatico

Identification: 7″ (18cm). 42g. Variation in head pattern rather complex, but in general, birds in Sierra de Perijá and Andes have *all head stripes gray*; birds from n coastal range eastward have *eyestripe whitish*. Upperparts dark olive green, *crown and sides of head black with gray median coronal stripe and long narrow white eyestripes*; below white with narrow black band across chest; lower underparts olive brown; bend of wing yellow (*phaeopleurus*). Or single coronal stripe gray, eyestripes buff to white; *breast band broad (phygas)*; or sim. to *phaeopleurus* but head stripes all gray (*perijanus, larensis*).

Sim. species: No other med.-sized bird with black and gray head stripes occurs with it. At lower els. see Black-striped Sparrow.

Voice: Song recalls that of Chestnut-capped Brush-Finch but shorter. A very high-pitched *zu-zeet, ah-z-teee*. In n Monagas *EE-sit, ezzaweet . . . EE-sit . . . ezzaseet . . . ease-sit . . . tsEE-a-teet . . .* and so on in rather irreg. fashion, often continuing on and on without clear break.

Behavior: Typical of *Buarremon* (and unlike *Atlapetes*), notably furtive and often hard to see. Hops on or near gd. and stays mostly under cover. BC birds Feb–Aug, n Colombia.

Status and habitat: Uncommon to common resident inside humid and wet montane forest. Overlaps locally in several places with Chestnut-capped Brush-Finch (where prob. interspecifically territorial), but more numerous at *lower* els. than that sp. and most numerous in areas where it does not occur at all, i.e., at ca. 1000–1200m around Caripe, Monagas. This is reverse of pattern southward in Andes.

Range: 900–1800. Sierra de Perijá, Zulia (*perijanus*); Andes in n Táchira (both slopes), sw Mérida, nw and se Lara (Cerros El Cogollal and El Cerrón; Cabudare) (*larensis*); Coastal Cordillera in Carabobo, Aragua (Rancho Grande), and Miranda (Curupao), Interior Cordillera from n Guárico (Cerro Platillón) to Aragua on Cerro Golfo Triste (*phaeopleurus*); mts. of ne Anzoátegui, Sucre, and n Monagas (*phygas*). Colombia s in mts. to nw Argentina.

Note: Birds of Mérida Andes s to n Peru may be separate subsp., *assimilis*[476].

Arremon

Resemble *Atlapetes* but smaller; head striped; usually with all or most of bill bright yellow or orange; yellow at bend of wing (all Venez. spp.); lowlands and foot-hills (below range of *Atlapetes*); ball-like, side-entrance nest on gd.; high-pitched songs.

Pectoral Sparrow

PLATE 63

Arremon taciturnus   Tico-Tico

Identification: 6″ (15cm). 24g. Bill black above, yellow below. *Crown and sides of head black with narrow gray coronal stripe and whitish eyestripe* starting above eye; black on sides of neck continues as partial band across chest (forms black patch on each side of chest); back and shoulders olive green, *bend of wing golden yellow* (usually visible), wings and tail dusky brown, underparts white, sides and flanks gray (*axillaris*). Or s of Orinoco, bill solid black, *chest band more or less complete*; eyestripe starts at bill (*taciturnus*). ♀: sim. but tinged buff below; chest band grayish and incomplete or only faintly indicated in both subspp.

Sim. species: Bold pattern unmistakable on this attractive but shy bird. In drier nw see Golden-winged Sparrow (no overlap).

Voice: Insectlike song an extremely high, thin, buzzy *chit-tic-tzzzzzz, tzzzzzz, tzzzzzz* along e base of Andes; s of Orinoco sim. or varied to *tzzz, tzzz, tzzz, zzzzzzzzzz-zzzzit*. Sharp *tzip* call like others of genus.

Behavior: An unobtrusive, semiterrestrial bird found alone or in prs. on or near gd. in shady forest interior. Hops and scratches in forest-floor leaf litter, or perches a little above gd. Likes to sing from atop logs. Retiring and stays out of view, but not a skulker. Grass-and-leaf ball nest with side entrance low in shrub or palm base; 2 whitish eggs finely spotted brown and purple[253].

Status and habitat: Fairly common resident in open undergrowth of humid forest and older second growth; also occas. light woodland and coffee plantations, esp. adjacent to humid wooded ravines.

Range: To 1000m n of Orinoco; to 1500m s of Orinoco. E base of Andes from Táchira, w Apure, and w Barinas n to ne Portuguesa at Turén (*axillaris*); generally in Amazonas and Bolívar (*taciturnus*). E Colombia to the Guianas, se Peru, n Bolivia, and c and e Amaz. Brazil; coastal se Brazil.

Golden-winged Sparrow

PLATE 63

Arremon schlegeli   Maizcuba

Identification: 6″ (15cm). 27g. *Bill bright yellow* (dusky in imm.). *Crown, sides of head, chin, and broad band down sides of neck to edge of chest black* (like a black helmet), mantle light gray, wing coverts and back olive yellow, *bend of wing and upper shoulder bright yellow, wings and tail slate gray*; underparts white, flanks gray. ♀: bill duller, underparts tinged buff.

Sim. species: Nothing like it in dry zones of nw Venez. See Pectoral Sparrow which it almost meets along e base of Andes.
Voice: Infreq. hd and easily overlooked song, from perch a few meters up, a high-pitched, sibilant, weak *zeut, zeut, zeut, zeee,* given a few times early in morning. Singing may be seasonal, with most song in early rainy season.
Behavior: Almost always seen singly or in prs., members either well separated or sometimes foraging close together. Not shy or furtive but easily passed by because of rather unobtrusive and semiterrestrial habits. Tends to remain mostly out of sight as forages by hopping on gd., scratching in leaf litter, or moving through low vegetation (up to ca. 3m up). Eats fruit, seeds, and insects, often spending up to several min in a small area, either in thick or relatively open shady vegetation before moving. Breeds Apr–Sep in Colombia[260]; nest in n Colombia a cup with domed roof; 0.5m up in rock crevice; dead leaves, small twigs, and lining of fine grass; eggs white with pinkish translucence and a few black dots at large end[764].
Status and habitat: Uncommon resident in dry to moist (deciduous to semideciduous) forest borders, scrubby second growth, and dry thickets in wooded ravines and hillsides. Mainly in hilly terrain; nowhere very numerous. Can be found in dry vegetation from edge of El Limón, Maracay, upward where occurs with Black-striped Sparrow (apparently not interspecifically territorial). Reg. at Hotel Trujillo, city of Trujillo, late 1970s (P. Alden; B. Thomas).

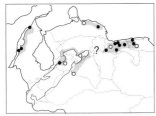

Range: 250–1400m. Sierra de Perijá (Alto del Cedro s to Río Negro), Zulia; w base of Andes in w Trujillo, n end in Lara (sight, Sanare), e base in sw Portuguesa (sight, Boconoito, 1998—D. Ascanio), e Falcón (Mirimire; sight, Guaibacoa); s slope of Coastal Cordillera in Carabobo, Aragua, and Distr. Federal, n Guárico (La Sierra), and Interior Cordillera in s Miranda e to Los Anaucos (*schlegeli*). Ne Colombia.

Arremonops

Sim. to *Arremon* but duller; crown striped; back olive; legs and feet large and strong.

Black-striped Sparrow   PLATE 63
Arremonops conirostris Curtío
Identification: 6.5″ (16.5cm). 30g. *Crown and sides of head gray with 2 black crown stripes and black line through eyes;* upperparts brownish olive, bend of wing yellow; underparts dull white, broad wash of gray on chest and sides; brownish olive on lower underparts. Or upperparts olive, underparts grayer (*umbrinus*).
Sim. species: See Tocuyo Sparrow.

Voice: Songs, hd. mainly at or shortly after dawn, vary geographically; most birds have 2 or more song types. Near Coro, Falcón, a slow, measured *wü . . wee, chivit, chivit, chivit, chivit, chivit.* Typically a few slow or sputtery notes, then a longer, often accelerating ser. of notes that end abruptly. Another common variation, *tsweet-tsweet, tsweet-tseeu, ti-ti-ti-ti,* ends in slow trill. In n Aragua *tur, cheee, tu chup-chup-chup-chup-chup* (no. of *chup* notes variable).
Behavior: A rather retiring, semiterrestrial bird usually seen alone, in prs., or in families (not with mixed-spp. flocks). Forages mostly by hopping on gd. for arthropods and seeds; also jumps up for low fruits and berries or ascends a few meters up in bushes, esp. to sing. Side-entrance nest a bulky domed structure of coarse plant material, near gd. to 1.8m up; 2, rarely 3, white eggs[706]; breeding evidence, Apr–Oct, ne Colombia.
Status and habitat: Fairly common resident in dry to humid regions. Bushy forest and woodland borders, overgrown clearings, shady plantations, and cultivated areas with thickets. Can occur in fairly dry scrubby habitat but replaced in dry and arid zones of c Falcón and n Zulia by Tocuyo Sparrow.

Range: To 1300m n of Orinoco; to 300m s of Orinoco. Sierra de Perijá, Zulia, and w base of Andes in Táchira, Mérida, and Trujillo (*umbrinus*); w Lara, c and e Falcón, and generally from Yaracuy and Carabobo e to mts. of Sucre and Monagas; entire e base of Andes from Táchira and w Apure to Portuguesa, and e across s Cojedes (sightings, Hato Piñero) and w Guárico (Altagracia de Orituco; Hato Masaguaral); n Bolívar from Caicara and Río Cuchivero e to lower Río Paragua at La Paragua (*conirostris*); n Amazonas (sight/tape, Samariapo[259]) (prob. *conirostris*). Honduras to w Ecuador and n Brazil (Roraima).

Tocuyo Sparrow   PLATE 63
Arremonops tocuyensis Curtío del Tocuyo
Identification: 5.2″ (13.2cm). Smaller, paler version of Black-striped Sparrow. Differs mainly in small size, paler upperparts, and crown *dull whitish to whitish clay* (not gray); black crown stripes and eyestripes as in Black-striped Sparrow. Additionally, underparts are more extensively white with buffy gray tinge on chest and buff tinge on belly.
Sim. species: Black-striped Sparrow has less contrasting black and *gray* (not whitish clay) crown stripes. Also note range (minimal overlap) and very different song.
Voice: Not as vocal as allied Black-striped Sparrow. Song, in early morning, a short, sweet *tit, tit'ti'ti'ti 'tsuee tsuee* or *sweeu, sweeu, eeee, tu'tu'tu'tu (eeee*

very high pitched; last phrase a chatter) or *tsuee, tsuee, tzEE, tu-tu-tu*. Song pattern somewhat variable but usually with 3 more or less distinct parts.

Behavior: Much like better known Black-striped Sparrow, but the two overlap only narrowly in range. Semiterrestrial and inconspic. Sings from partially open perches 1–4m up, otherwise stays on or near gd. and mostly out of sight.

Status and habitat: Uncommon and local resident in brushy borders of dry, low-canopied, deciduous woodland and in patches of thorny brush and dry scrub sometimes mixed with tall grass. Occurs in dry to moist regions but usually not very arid desert scrub dominated by *Acacia* and cactus. Occurs very locally w to near Coro, Falcón (e.g., Maicillal), and ne of Barquisimeto, Lara.

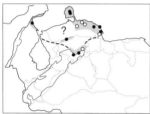

Range: To 1100m (most recs. much lower). Nw Zulia (Paraguaipoa) e locally to e Falcón (Cuare) and s in Lara to n base of Andes (San Miguel; sightings below Sanare). Ne Colombia.

Ammodramus

Flat headed; streaky, rather short, narrow tail; open areas with grass; both Venez. spp. formerly placed in *Myiospiza*.

Grassland Sparrow   PLATE 65
Ammodramus humeralis   Sabanerito de Pajonales
Identification: 5″ (12.7cm). 16g. Plain little sparrow with *grayish face, white eyering, and touch of yellow "makeup" over lores*. Above gray heavily streaked reddish brown, bend of wing yellow (often concealed), wing coverts brown edged buff, flight feathers dusky, *inner ones broadly edged chestnut rufous* (form fairly distinct patch on wings), *narrow white eyering; yellow supraloral spot slightly lengthened, sides of head and neck grayish*, underparts dingy whitish, chest and flanks smudged pale grayish brown. Or darker above (*columbianus*); or sides of head grayer (*humeralis*). Juv.: much buffier, incl. eyebrow; chest streaked dusky; chestnut wing edgings usually present.

Sim. species: Often confused with Yellow-browed Sparrow. Grassland's best marks are its eyering, *gray on head*, and yellow *only* on lores. Also, look for chestnut wing edgings (sometime faint on worn plumage). Up close or in hand, streaking on upperparts is blacker (esp. on crown) and edged chestnut.

Voice: Dainty songs vary somewhat (individual or geographical?). Typically a thin, delicate, musical *tic-JEEE-tic'wazeee*, somewhat buzzy at end, or *ee-beezz, slip-slow-EEE*. Also soft chatters and chips in display, agonistic encounters, and alarm.

Behavior: Most conspic. when sings from top of grass clump, shrub, or fence wire in early morning or evening. Otherwise stays mostly hidden in grass and forages on gd. for grass and weed seeds and a few insects. Runs nimbly between tufts of grass and occas. hops into open areas. Flushes from grass with slightly zigzag flight, flies a short distance, then drops in and difficult to flush again. Territories are small[348]. Open cup nest (or occas. sphere with side entrance); 2–3 white eggs; nests in Jun (6) and Oct (3), w Apure[137].

Status and habitat: A grassland bird. Rather common resident in open and relatively short grassy and weedy areas s of Orinoco and n to about c Apure and s Monagas; uncommon and local northward. In some areas, but not all, occurs with Yellow-browed Sparrow; interactions, if any, between the 2 spp. unknown.

Range: To 1300m n of Orinoco; to 1750m s of Orinoco. Goajira Pen., Zulia (*pallidulus*); e of Andes in Barinas and Portuguesa (*columbianus*); elsewhere throughout in grasslands (*humeralis*). Ne Colombia to the Guianas and s to e and s Brazil, extreme se Peru, e Bolivia, and n Argentina.

Yellow-browed Sparrow   PLATE 65
Ammodramus aurifrons   Sabanerito Frentiamarillo
Identification: 5″ (12.7cm). 14.5g. Above grayish brown streaked blackish brown, *prom. yellow lores and eyebrow* (lower eyelid also yellow), bend of wing yellow; wing coverts and wings dusky edged pale brown (no chestnut edgings); underparts dull whitish smudged light gray on chest and sides. Or darker grayish brown above (*tenebrosus*). Juv.: dull and plain; no yellow eyebrow.

Sim. species: See Grassland Sparrow.

Voice: Song a telephone "busy signal," *tic, zzzzzz, zzzzzz, zzzzzz, tic* note (occas. 2 notes) faint, last 3 buzzes; monotonously repeated even through heat of day.

Behavior: Unlike Grassland Sparrow, this is an assertive and conspic. little bird that hops or scurries rapidly over bare gd., and often allows close approach. Forages for weed and grass seeds and insects, and occas. pauses to sing from gd., or more often takes prom. low perch on stick, bush, or grass to sing. Usually alone or in scattered prs. Breeding May–Oct, w Apure; 2–3 eggs[137].

Status and habitat: Common and widespread resident in open areas with clumps of grass and bushes, around ranch buildings, and semiopen riverbanks and sandbars. In some areas occurs with allied Grassland Sparrow, in other areas only one or the other is found. Nos.

decrease sharply southward toward Orinoco, e.g., very scarce at Hato Los Indios, se Apure; no recs. in nw Amazonas or in lower Río Caura of n Bolívar.

Range: To 300m n of Orinoco; to 200m s of Orinoco. E base of Andes from Táchira, w Apure, Barinas, and s Cojedes (sightings) e to sw Anzoátegui and Delta Amacuro (*apurensis*); sw Amazonas in Río Negro drainage (*tenebrosus*). E Colombia s to n Bolivia, w Amaz. Brazil e (narrowly) to mouth of the Amazon.

Lincoln's Sparrow
Melospiza lincolnii
Identification: 5.5″ (14cm). Above grayish brown streaked dusky; crown dark brown with pale medial line; *sides of head gray* with dark line through eyes and *narrow but prom. white eyering*; below dull whitish, *chest and sides strongly washed buff and finely streaked dusky*; streaks may merge forming vague central chest spot.
Sim. species: In Venez., where there are few other sim. sp., should be recognized by combination of eyering, grayish face, and fine streaking on *contrasting buff chest*.
Status and habitat: Accidental. Known from 1 bird (*lincolnii*) netted at Portachuelo Pass (1000m), PN Henri Pittier, Aragua[559]; no specimen. Tends to skulk in thickets and brushy areas along wooded edges and keeps out of sight. Quiet and inconspic. on wintering gds.

Range: Breeds in n and w N Amer.; winters from s US to Honduras, very infreq. to Costa Rica and w and c Panama.

Zonotrichia

Only S Amer. member of this predom. N Amer. genus; conspic. crown stripes; widespread.

Rufous-collared Sparrow   PLATE 65
Zonotrichia capensis   Correporsuelo
Identification: 5.5–6″ (14–15cm). 20–25g. Slight crest. *Head gray with 2 broad black crown stripes and black-*

ish line through eyes; narrow but *prom. rufous collar*, above rufescent brown streaked black, 2 dull white wing bars; below dingy grayish white with *black patch on sides of chest* (forms incomplete band), sometimes mottled black across chest; sides and flanks grayish brown. Juv.: dingy; densely but *narrowly* streaked above and below; older birds with hint of ad. head pattern. Birds from tepuis are darker and dingier (*roraimae, macconnelli, inaccessibilis*). Or *much larger* (ca. 7″, 18cm); above dark with broad black head stripes; *below mostly gray*, rufous collar extends to black on sides of chest which continues as band of black freckles across chest (*perezchinchillae*). Size varies geographically: birds from coastal mts. and most of tepuis are smallest (ca. 5.5″, 14cm); those from Andes intermediate (6.1″, 15.5cm); those from southernmost tepuis largest, e.g., *inaccessibilis* on Cerro de la Neblina, Amazonas (6.5″, 16.5cm) and *perezchinchillae* on Cerro Marahuaca, Bolívar (6.8–7″, 17.3–18cm).
Sim. species: Common in montane areas and worth learning well. Streaky juvs. may recall ♀ Plumbeous Sierra-Finch or other juv. finches but generally do not stray far from ads.
Voice: Has dozens (perhaps 100s) of geographical song dialects but almost everywhere easily recognized, typically 1–2 slurred whistles with or without trill of varying length at end, e.g., *tee-teeooo, e'e'e'e'e* (2d note slurred lower); or *teeooo, teeeee* and so on.
Behavior: Almost everyone in Andes will be familiar with this friendly and ubiquitous little ward of settled areas and dooryards. It lives in semiopen areas and thrives in company of people. Prs. have small territories and others trespass or form small, loosely assoc. flocks that wander locally. Hop on open gd. and peck for weed and grass seeds, grit, and insects. Mount a rock, shrub, or low open perch to sing, and loaf in low bushes, hedgerows, and small trees. Neat nest cup on gd.; 2–3 pale greenish blue eggs speckled and blotched brown[644]. Some breeding activity likely yr-round.
Status and habitat: Common resident in Andes in agricultural areas, open areas with bushes and scattered trees, hedgerows, parks, gardens, and lawns in rural and urban areas. Often very common in towns; mainly in highlands.

Range: 800–4000m n of Orinoco; mostly 850–2800m s of Orinoco; local at 120–200m in nw Bolívar and nw Amazonas. Sierra de Perijá, Zulia; Andes from s Táchira to s Lara (*costaricensis*); n mts. from c Falcón and Yaracuy e to Sucre (Paria Pen.?) and n Monagas; n Bolívar (120m) at Caicara (*venezuelae*); lowlands of nw Amazonas (Capuana, Pto. Ayacucho), cerros of

Amazonas (except Neblina), Cerro Guaiquinima and Gran Sabana except Cerro Roraima (*roraimae*); summit of Cerro de la Neblina (*inaccessibilis*); sw Bolívar on Cerro Marahuaca on Meseta de Jaua (*perezchinchillae*); summit of Cerro Roraima (*macconnelli*). S Mexico s in mts. to Panama; Andes; e Colombia to the Guianas, and Brazil s to Tierra del Fuego (but absent from most of Amazon Basin).

Note: *Perezchinchillae* perhaps a separate sp.

Emberizoides

Med.-sized finches; streaky; long, highly graduated tail with pointed feathers, central ones twice length of outer ones; savanna and scrub habitats.

Wedge-tailed Grass-Finch   PLATE 65
Emberizoides herbicola   Sabanero Coludo
Identification: 8″ (20.3cm). 25g. *Bill "bicolored," black above, yellow below; unusually long, pointed tail.* Above incl. tail brown to grayish brown, back streaked black, *lores and eyering white;* bend of wing yellow (often concealed), wing coverts and flight feathers edged olive, underparts grayish white, chest and sides smudged brownish. Or sim. but upperparts grayish (not brown), below whiter, breast and crissum tinged buff (*apurensis*).
Sim. species: A large, long-tailed finch that flushes up from open grassland is likely to be this sp. See rare Duida Grass-Finch; also Dickcissel, ♀ Red-breasted Blackbird, and nonbreeding-plumage Bobolink.
Voice: Semimusical song, mostly at dawn, a short, clipped *t'chîĺl'ip* varied to *t-t-chîĺl'ip* (no trills). Song pattern variable (prob. geographical and individual differences). Day songs may be longer and incl. trills.
Behavior: Briefly at dawn, or late in afternoon, this sp. may perch up on a fence post or top of shrub to sing, but otherwise usually in or near tall grass where furtive and difficult to see unless flushed into open. Most often flushes up, flies short distance, then drops into cover again. Single birds or prs. are usually well separated. Run rapidly on gd., and prob. forage mostly on gd. Fledglings, Nov and Jun, w Apure[137].
Status and habitat: Uncommon to fairly common resident (usually more numerous than it appears to be) in *tall* open grassland with or without scattered bushes. True nos. are best revealed by listening for singing birds at dawn. Commonest in grass 1m or more in ht.

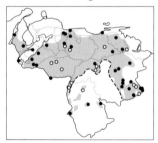

Range: To 1600m n and s of Orinoco. Grasslands throughout except in area of next subsp. (*sphenurus*); e base of Andes from Portuguesa, e Mérida, and Apure

to w Guárico at Calabozo (*apurensis*). Costa Rica locally to the Guianas and mouth of the Amazon in e Brazil; n Bolivia and s Brazil s to n Argentina.

Duida Grass-Finch   PLATE 65
Emberizoides duidae   Sabanero Coludo del Duida
Identification: 8.5″ (22cm). Very sim. to Wedge-tailed Grass-Finch but overall *decidedly darker*. Differs most obviously as follows: slightly *larger size; above darker brown,* esp. on crown and tail which are dusky (not grayish brown to brown), cheeks dusky, chest, flanks, and under tail coverts darker and *distinctly brown* (not lightly smudged brownish).
Behavior: Presum. much like that of Wedge-tailed Grass-Finch.
Status and habitat: Known only from a few specimens from savannas of Cerro Duida. Unknown in life. Occurs mainly above range of Wedge-tailed Grass-Finch.

Range: ENDEMIC. 1300–2000m. Cerro Duida, Amazonas.
Note: Regarded as a full sp.[167], but perhaps only a subsp. of Wedge-tailed Grass-Finch.

Icteridae: American Orioles and Blackbirds
Conotos, Arrendajos, Tordos, Turpiales

Members of this rather heterogeneous family are perhaps best known for their large size, predominantly black plumage, and the beautiful pouch- or stocking-like nests woven by caciques, orioles, and oropendolas. Most species are confined to the American tropics, with a few mostly migratory species breeding in North America or southern South America. Icterids are characterized by strong legs and feet, rather long, sharp-pointed, and conical bills, and a culmen which often extends well up onto the forehead and, in some species, is expanded or bulbous. The sexes are usually similar in resident tropical species, but females often are duller in migratory species. Males tend to be larger, often dramatically so in oropendolas and caciques. Most orioles have musical songs, whereas caciques and oropendolas are notable for their complex, often bizarre vocalizations. Breeding is solitary or colonial, and the colonial species are often polygamous, as are the parasitic cowbirds. Breeding colonies of caciques and oropendolas present one of the most fascinating spectacles in the American tropics, but the complex interworkings of these colonies have been studied in only a few species to date[554,555,556]. Some icterids have profited from human activity and are now conspicuous birds in settled areas; regrettably, others have suffered heavily with settlement. The icterids sometimes have been placed in a subfamily in Emberizidae[606], and some aspects of icterid taxonomy remain unresolved[279,311,314].

Bobolink   PLATE 67
Dolichonyx oryzivorus Tordo Arrocero
Identification: 7″ (18cm). Rather thick conical bill. Tail graduated, feathers pointed and spiky. ♀ and non-breeding ♂: streaky and sparrowlike; *crown striped dusky and buff, upperparts streaked black and buff,* below uniform yellowish buff to buff with a few narrow dusky streaks on flanks and belly; spiky tail *uniform dusky brown.* Breeding ♂: *mostly black; hindcrown and nape yellow buff, scapulars, lower back, and rump white.* ♂♂ molt into breeding plumage ca. Nov–Jan (on austral wintering gds.). In fresh plumage, black feathers almost completely obscured by long buffy tips which are lost with wear. Birds passing through Venez. may be partially black. Full breeding dress usually not acquired until May.
Sim. species: ♀ Red-breasted Blackbird has more heavily streaked underparts usually tinged rosy pink, and shows barred tail. Also see Dickcissel and Wedge-tailed Grass-Finch.
Voice: Flight call a distinctive *peenk.* Song, rarely hd. in migration in Venez., a rapid bubbly ser. of notes.
Behavior: Normally rather gregarious in migration, but in both southward and northward passage may be seen singly, in 2s, 3s, or in flocks. May assoc. with other icterids such as Red-breasted Blackbirds. Feeds heavily on seeds and is fond of rice.
Status and habitat: Fairly common southbound transient from N Amer., late Sep–early Nov, and northbound transient, early Apr–early May. At Hato El Frio, Apure, rec. 27 Sep–1 Nov 1983, with max. of 63 on 17 Oct and 60 on 1 Nov (R. W. Andrews); up to 3000 in rice fields near Calabozo, Guárico, on 16 and 17 Oct 1971 (P. Alden); ca. 50 during 1978 southward passage at Hato Masaguaral, Guárico[734]. Three seen 25 Apr 1996 at 2500m near Santo Domingo, Mérida (R. Ridgely), and 1 at 4000m on 2 May 1992 Páramo del Águila, Mérida[60], suggest some migrate over Andes.

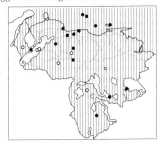

Range: To 500m (sight to 4000m). Recs. scattered from Maracaibo Basin, Zulia (sight), w Mérida, n cordilleras of Carabobo, Aragua, and Distr. Federal; and in Apure, Portuguesa, Guárico, s Amazonas, and Bolívar; Islas Los Roques, La Orchila, La Tortuga, and Margarita. Breeds in e N Amer. Migrates chiefly through W Indies;

winters in s Peru, e Bolivia, s Brazil, Paraguay, and n Argentina.

Agelaius

Small icterids; straight, sharp-pointed bills; ♂♂ black with contrasting color on head or shoulders; ♀♀ heavily streaked; wetlands.

Yellow-hooded Blackbird   PLATE 67
Agelaius icterocephalus Turpial de Agua
Identification: 7″ (18cm). ♂ 36g, ♀ 27g. Bill black, sides of lower mandible involute. ♂: *black with bright yellow head, neck, and chest;* lores and partial eyering black. ♀: above dusky brown obscurely mottled yellowish olive; *eyebrow, throat, and chest yellow,* sides of head dingy yellowish, lower underparts dull olive yellow, brownish on belly. Juv. ♂: like ♀ but gradually acquires black.
Sim. species: ♂ unmistakable. ♀'s pattern recalls that of ♂ but much duller. At a distance in marsh, ♀ is the dull brown bird with yellowish throat and chest.
Voice: Labored, unmusical song (like rusty hinge), *jur-gul-ZLEEE!* (or *took, tooWEEEZ*), 1st note weak, last loud and raspy; recalls song of Red-winged Blackbird (*A. phoeniceus*) of N Amer. Song sometimes followed by short, musical *te-tiddle-de-de-do-dee,* down then up. Call a harsh, low *check.*
Behavior: Rather gregarious and usually loosely colonial even when breeding. When not breeding forms small, or occas. large, flocks that always seem to be in marshes or near water but seasonally may commute many km to distant roost. Perch and forage for insects in reeds and tall grass, generally not on gd. Grass and weed cup nest slung in reeds and tall grass, often in stands of *Thalia*; 3–4 pale blue eggs dotted and scrawled black[175]. Breeding Aug–Nov, Guárico[734]; single nests Jul and Oct, w Apure[137].
Status and habitat: Fairly common to common resident in freshwater marshes, flooded wetlands, and riverbanks, mainly in open country. S of Orinoco mostly along rivers. Marked postbreeding movements in llanos, with birds largely absent during Feb–May dry season (1 transient flock of 45 birds) at Hato Masaguaral, Guárico; flocks up to 600 in wet season[734].

Range: To 600m n of Orinoco; to 250m s of Orinoco. Widespread (near water) n of Orinoco; n Amazonas s to Río Ventuari; n Bolívar in lower Río Caura and s to vicinity of El Palmar and Guasipati (*icterocephalus*). N Colombia to the Guianas, ne Brazil, and the Amazon from its mouth to e Peru.

Sturnella

Grassland birds; incl. spp. originally placed in *Sturnella* which have long thin bills and no sexual dimorphism; now also incls. spp. formerly placed in the genus *Leistes*, ♂♂ of which are mostly red and black, ♀♀ dull and streaky, bills short and thick.

Eastern Meadowlark PLATE 67
Sturnella magna Perdigón
Identification: 9″ (23cm). ♂ 102g, ♀ 76g. Chunky and short-tailed. Long, pointed bill slopes smoothly onto forehead. Above brown streaked blackish and buff; crown striped dull white and blackish; flight feathers and tail narrowly barred blackish; *below yellow with broad black V across chest*; sides, flanks, and belly buff with a few coarse streaks; *white outer tail feathers* flash in flight or when tail is flicked.
Sim. species: In grasslands, where it lives, likely confused only with ♀ Red-breasted Blackbird or ♀ or nonbreeding-plumage ♂ Bobolink. Both lack yellow below.
Voice: Songs resemble those of N Amer. birds but are flatter, more run together, and often with more than 4 slurred whistles. In w Venez. a clear, slurred *cheewaseea, chewa-chorra*. Not as vocal as n counterparts.
Behavior: A rather sedate and composed bird of fields and grasslands. Stretches up to watch carefully, or crouches to avoid detection, but is not a "close sitter" like many open-country birds. If danger approaches, flicks tail in alarm, springs up, and flies off rather leisurely with flurry of shallow wing beats alternating with stiff glides on downcurved wings. Walks jerkily on gd. where forages for insects, but sings from elevated perch such as a post or small bush. Mostly occurs alone or in prs., occas. several in rather loosely composed flocks. Dome-shaped grass nest with side entrance, on gd.; 2 eggs; May and Nov nests, ne Anzoátegui[186]; breeding perhaps prolonged.
Status and habitat: Fairly common resident locally in open grassland from lowlands to paramo. Spreading with deforestation.

Range: 1700–3000m in Andes of Táchira, Mérida, and Trujillo (*meridionalis*). Lowlands to 2000m throughout rest of country except area of next subsp. (*paralios*); ca. 1300m in vicinity of Cerro Roraima, se Bolívar (*praticola*). E N Amer. locally s to the Guianas and n Brazil.
Note: Subsp. *monticola* is a synonym for *praticola*[467].

Red-breasted Blackbird PLATE 67
Sturnella militaris Tordo Pechirrojo
Identification: 7.5″ (19cm). ♂ 48g, ♀ 41g. Bill rather short, deep, and laterally compressed. Breeding ♂: *black with bright red throat and breast*. In fresh plumage feathers heavily buff-edged (black and red mostly obscured), but this quickly wears away by breeding season; tail rather short. ♀: looks like a large streaky sparrow; above heavily streaked pale brown and dusky; *prom. buff eyestripe and median crown stripe*; below buffy brown *streaked dusky, usually with rose tinge on chest*; tail brown *barred* dusky. In hand note long rear (hallux) nail.
Sim. species: See ♀ and nonbreeding ♂ Bobolink and Dickcissel.
Voice: Songs vary geographically, typically 1–3 weak notes and a buzzy trill, e.g., *e-sic-er-LEEEEZZ* or *chert-zleeeeee-e-e-e*, or 1–2 notes and 2 buzzes on different pitches. Calls incl. a hard *pleek* and dry rattle.
Behavior: Recalls a Bobolink more than a meadowlark. A gregarious and semicolonial sp. that forages in grassy pastures and spends much more of its time out of sight than we might wish. One moment a half dozen may be visible, perching up on bushes, fence posts, or in straggling lines on fence wires, even singing, and a moment later they all vanish into tall grass. Forage on gd. for insects, grubs, caterpillers, and some seeds, often remaining out of sight for extended periods. ♂♂ sing from conspic. perches, and during breeding periods fly up into air and sing as they flutter slowly earthward. May breed in loose colonies with ♂♂ defending small territories. Otherwise ♂♂, ♀♀, and imms. are loosely gregarious in small and erratically wandering flocks of their own. Grassy cup nest on or near gd., sometimes with entrance tunnel; 2–4 eggs, deep cream heavily blotched pale reddish brown; often parasitized by Shiny Cowbird[175]; ♂♂ possibly polygamous[253]. Colonies often move and usually do not nest in same area in successive yrs.
Status and habitat: Locally common resident in grassy pastures and rice fields; sometimes in damp areas but usually not marshes. Wander erratically in small postbreeding flocks. Irregular (2–300) at Hato Masaguaral, Guárico, with largest nos. Mar–May, many in imm. (or fresh molt?) plumage[734]. Readily colonize new grassy pastures after forest clearing, e.g., near El Palmar, Bolívar.

Range: To 600m n of Orinoco; to 950m s of Orinoco. S Zulia (Encontrados) e to w Lara and se Falcón (sightings), and generally e of Andes from w Apure, w Barinas, and s Carabobo e to Monagas and Delta Ama-

curo; c and s Amazonas (throughout?); spottily in grasslands of Bolívar. Sw Costa Rica to the Guianas and Amaz. Brazil (absent from most of w Amazonia). Trinidad.
Note: Often placed in genus *Leistes*.

Lampropsar

Plushy forecrown; short bill; rather long, ample tail; some vocalizations sim. to "grackles" of other genera; prob. related to *Macroagelaius*.

Velvet-fronted Grackle   PLATE 66
Lampropsar tanagrinus   Tordo Frente Aterciopelada
Identification: ♂ 8″ (20.3cm), ♀ 7.5″ (19cm). Sexes sim. in size. *Eyes dark; bill black, unusually short, and conical.* Entirely black, upperparts somewhat glossed blue black; wings, tail, and belly plain black. *Tail fairly long, rounded at tip, and flat* (not keeled). In hand, feathers of forehead dense, stiff, and plushlike (like Velcro strip). ♀ slightly duller below.
Sim. species: Smallest "grackle" in Venez. and the one with shortest bill, but best told by combination of habits, habitat, and long-tailed appearance. See Carib Grackle (yellow eyes; short, keel-shaped tail), Shiny Cowbird, and Red-rumped Cacique.
Voice: In flight a *check* and *chak* much like *Quiscalus* grackles; when foraging a higher, semiwhistled *cheziit* and other notes. Musical song, like small musical bells or a wind chime, given at any time but esp. in evening, a rhythmic, gurgling *puk, chur-cal-a-wík!* varied to *chek, chuk, churcal-a-wík!* or shorter *chuk-your-Wheat!*, sometimes with several birds joining chorus. Both sexes sing.
Behavior: Usually in active, conspic. groups of 6–30, occas. more, that troop about noisily or quietly, inside or along edge of forest, usually rather low. Groups settle low in shrubs and trees along lake or stream borders or work through swampy or seasonally flooded forest from eye level to lower canopy where they flick tails up and energetically peer above and below leaves, at terminal twigs, peck from branch tips, even flowers, reach down, or hang from twigs as they go after arthropod prey, and then after a few min, all fly off in chattery, carefree group, singing as they go. In Guyana a nest over small creek[694].
Status and habitat: Fairly common resident very locally in Venez.; interior and edges of várzea forest, low-lying gallery forest, lake edges, forested stream banks, and mangroves. Very common along Caño Colorado in e Monagas.

Range: To 200m. E Sucre, ne Monagas, and throughout Delta Amacuro s to ne Bolívar (Ciudad Bolívar); nw Amazonas at Munduapo (*guianensis*). Guyana and extreme n Brazil (Roraima); se Colombia to n Bolivia and w Amaz. Brazil.

Macroagelaius

Slender; long tailed; short bill; only 2 spp. (1 in Venez.), both with restricted range; some vocalizations recall those of *Quiscalus* and *Lampropsar;* arboreal, forest birds.

Golden-tufted Mountain-Grackle   PLATE 66
Macroagelaius imthurni   Moriche de Los Tepuis
Identification: ♂ 11″ (28cm), ♀ 10″ (25cm). 40g. Bill blackish; eyes dark. *Entirely black* (in hand somewhat glossy blue black); *golden yellow pectoral tufts prom. in flight* (partly or completely concealed at rest), tail rather long, rounded at tip, and flat (not keel shaped). ♀: flat black (lacks gloss of ♂), tail slightly shorter.
Sim. species: Only grackle in forested upper els. of tepui region. Yellow tufts are the mark.
Voice: Song an unusual and melodic combination of tinkling and rusty-gate squeaks, often sung in flight as well as when perched. Some vocalizations antiphonal. ♂♂ sing high *ku-tlée*, ♀♀ join with antiphonal *E-tlit* or other phrase; also 1 or 2 singing subgroups often answer another, than all may join chorus and up to 25 or more fly off together singing cheerful melody of tinkling notes, e.g., *kut . . . ku-tlée, E-tlit . . . kiew! tut . . . skreedle-E-churk . . . jerk-jerk-ET! . . .* and so on in memorable performance. Wings may produce slight whistle (stiff-winged sound) in flight.
Behavior: Troops around in various-sized flocks, sometimes quite large, flying from treetop to treetop in forest, often singing as they go. Groups range over large areas. Fast, shallow wing beats and somewhat spread tail impart rather buzzy aspect to flight. Hop and peer in upper level or canopy foliage, mostly for insects, occas. small berries. Bulky cup nest 12m up; forest edge; 5 ads. fed 3 young; Mar; Sierra de Lema.
Status and habitat: Fairly common resident of wet misty forest and forest borders on slopes of tepuis. Favors tall mature forest; less numerous in stunted melastome-dominated forests on white sandy soil. Usually easily found on Sierra de Lema.

Range: 500–2000m. Scattered in tepuis of n and c Amazonas (Cerros Guanay, Calentura, Yavi, Sipapo, and Duida and upper Río Ocamo); nw Bolívar along Río Cuchivero (Cerro Tabaro), upper Río Caura (Sarisariñama), and generally on tepuis of se Bolívar from Auyán-tepui and Sierra de Lema (sightings) s to Acopán-tepui, Uei-tepui, and Cerro Roraima. Guyana and extreme n Brazil.

Note: Previously called Golden-tufted Grackle[403] and Tepui Mountain-Grackle[279,544].

Quiscalus

Relatively large (♂♂ larger than ♀♀); bill long, slender, culmen flattened at base forming small, rounded frontal plate; frontlet plushy; ♂ carries rounded tail in shape of V, even in flight; ♂♂ strut and parade on gd.

Carib Grackle   PLATE 66
Quiscalus lugubris   Tordito

Identification: ♂ 10.5″ (27cm), 75g. ♀ 8.5″ (22cm), 50g. *Eyes pale yellow* (both sexes); bill black, *slender, and slightly decurved*. ♂: *above glossy purplish blue black* (like "blued steel"), *underparts slightly duller*; wings glossy blue black; tail relatively short (for a grackle), held in distinct V shape. ♀: above dull dark brown; wings and tail dusky, underparts paler brown, throat palest, *tail normal* (not concave). Isl. birds less glossy and slightly smaller.

Sim. species: May meet but not known to overlap to any extent with larger, longer-tailed Great-tailed Grackle. From Shiny Cowbird in pale eyes, grackle bill, and wedge-shaped tail (♂).

Voice: Noisy. Commonest call a loud, ringing, bouncy *queek-queek-queek-queek*, often over and over; also a loud descending *keerr* and other loud ringing, twittering, and chucking calls.

Behavior: Like most grackles, behaves in a bold, noisy, self-confident manner, strutting around with head held high. Forages mostly on gd. Usually seen in boisterous groups that are conspic. around ranch buildings in countryside and in plazas and residential areas in towns where they become practically pensioners of people. ♂♂ seem to spend much of their time parading around on gd., strutting stiffly with raised tail and fluttering wings, beside ♀♀, or pausing to raise head and point bill skyward in characteristic display. Roost in large, noisy flocks in trees with dense foliage, often in towns and city parks. Nest alone or more often in colonies; some polygamy; coarse open cup of mud, dead leaves, and dry grass low to high up. Breed May–Nov, Guárico[734]; 2–4 greenish white eggs with blackish scrawls[175].

Status and habitat: Common but somewhat local resident of llanos, esp. around ranch buildings; also common in towns, plazas, cultivated areas with trees, and mangroves and disturbed areas along coast. Profits from human settlement and may be spreading, esp. in coastal Falcón. Some local seasonal (?) movements in llanos.

Range: To 850m. Coastal Falcón (sight, Coro; Chichiriviche), ne Lara (Matatero) e along coast to Sucre, and generally e of Andes to Delta Amacuro and s to Orinoco and n Bolívar in lower Río Caura (*lugubris*); Islas Margarita and Los Frailes (*insularis*); Los Hermanos (*orquillensis*); Los Testigos (*luminosus*). E Colombia to the Guianas (near coast) and extreme ne Brazil s to mouth of the Amazon. Trinidad and Tobago; vagrant to Bonaire and Aruba. Lesser Antilles.

Great-tailed Grackle   PLATE 66
Quiscalus mexicanus   Galandra

Identification: ♂ 17″ (43cm), 200g. ♀ 13″ (33cm), 110g. *Long, stout bill; eyes yellow* (♂) or yellowish brown (♀). ♂: entirely glossy purplish blue black with *long wedge-shaped tail held up in a V*. ♀: above dark coffee brown with vague buff eyebrow; cheeks darker brown, wings and tail dusky brown; below paler and more buffy brown, palest on throat and turning dark brown on belly and under tail coverts; *tail shorter, less obviously wedge-shaped than in* ♂. 1st-yr birds: like ♀ but eyes dark.

Sim. species: Flat-headed, long-tailed profile should be distinctive in either sex. ♂ Giant Cowbird has flat tail, shorter bill, red eyes, and normally shows a ruff. Greater Ani shares many sim. features (glossy plumage, pale eyes, long tail) but with thicker bent bill and different habits. Also cf. much smaller Shiny Cowbird.

Voice: Noisy. Both sexes have a variety of calls incl. a rough *chak* and sharp ser. of *krit* or *quit* notes given rapidly; ♂ also a shrill, quavering *kuuueeeeeeee*, drawn out.

Behavior: Loosely gregarious although also seen alone. Roosts and nests colonially in trees but forages mostly on gd., esp. in vicinity of water where scavenges anything edible. Thrives in coastal towns and settled areas where generally behaves in a bold and assertive way. ♂♂ strut and swagger as they walk about, and freq. display (also threat) in self-aggrandizing manner by stretching tall with bill pointed to sky. Nest a deep cup of mud and coarse vegetation in trees in parks, around human habitations, along rivers, or in bushes in marshes. In Costa Rica 2–3 eggs bright blue to pale blue gray dotted and scrawled black and brown[644].

Status and habitat: Common local resident along coast of arid nw Zulia. Mangroves, estuaries, semiopen areas with scattered trees, and esp. in towns where congregates in parks, on waterfronts, and around dooryards.

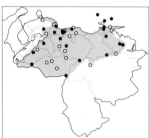

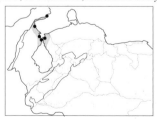

Range: To 100m. Nw Zulia from Goajira Pen. to mouth of Lago de Maracaibo (*peruvianus*). Sw US to nw Peru.

Molothrus

Short, somewhat conical bill extends upward to meet forehead; ♂♂ glossy black (except 1 sp.); ♀♀ duller; brood parasites, ranging from partial to complete.

Shiny Cowbird   PLATE 66
Molothrus bonariensis   Tordo Mirlo
Identification: ♂ 8″ (20.3cm), 45g. ♀ 7.5″ (19cm), 31g. *Eyes dark. Bill short, thick, and conical. Rather small headed.* ♂: mostly blue black glossed purplish; wings and tail shiny blue black with greenish tinge; tail square. ♀: above dingy grayish brown to dull brown; short indistinct pale eyebrow; below much paler grayish brown, wings and tail dusky brown. Juv.: buffier than ♀ and obscurely streaked brown below.
Sim. species: ♂ best told by small-headed, barrel-chested, and short-billed shape. In flight note rather shallow wing beats. Carib Grackle has pale eyes, long bill, and keel-shaped tail. ♀ is dull with few marks and is best known by company she keeps (♂♂ usually nearby), shape, calls, and habits. Cf. ♀ to ♀ Carib Grackle which has longer bill, and Southern Grayish Saltator.
Voice: ♂'s song a musical liquid phrase with a few harsh notes, usually accompanied by puffing up neck feathers.
Behavior: Like most cowbirds, social and most often seen in small loose groups, occas. alone. Forage in open areas on gd. by walking, often with tail slightly cocked, but show no special preference for cattle. Flight is slightly swooping. In display flight ♂ angles upward with rapid, shallow, wing-tip flight. On gd. ♂♂ strut and display in self-aggrandizing manner to ♀♀ which are brood parasites on a large no. of birds, mostly smaller than themselves (known to parasitize more than 160 spp.; in llanos esp. *Fluvicola* and *Arundinicola*). Eggs whitish with variable markings; up to 5 a yr[175]; breeding May–Nov, Hato Masaguaral, Guárico[734].
Status and habitat: Common resident in cultivated areas, pastures, and forest clearings. Occupies a broad spectrum of mostly nonforest or regrowth and disturbed habitats from dry to humid.

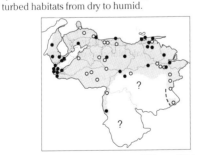

Range: To 1600m n of Orinoco; to 250m s of Orinoco. Widespread s to n Amazonas (s to San Fernando de Atabapo) and n and e Bolívar from Río Guaniamo and lower Río Caura e to El Palmar and s to Santa Elena de Uairén (sight) (*venezuelensis*). Panama to s Chile and s Argentina; Trinidad and Tobago; most of W Indies; se US (spreading).

Giant Cowbird   PLATE 66
Molothrus oryzivora   Tordo Pirata
Identification: ♂ 14″ (36cm), 180g. ♀ 11″ (28cm), 135g. Long tail (esp. ♂), head rather small; bill stout with small black frontal shield. *Eyes red orange to yellow* (♂) or dark (♀). ♂ has distinct "humpbacked" look due to *large ruff of feathers on nape;* overall shiny blue black with purplish gloss; wings and tail glossy blue black. ♀: smaller, plain dull blackish to brownish black (no gloss, no ruff). Juv.: like ♀ but bill sometimes yellowish and eyes pale; feathers pale-edged. Ads. in flight look long-tailed with wedge-shaped, barrel-chested body and rapid, slightly undulating flight, a few flaps, then wings closed tightly.
Sim. species: ♂ is almost as large as Great-tailed Grackle but bill shorter and stouter, ruff conspic., and tail flat, rounded, and shorter. Also see Greater Ani. ♀ best known by distinctive "cowbird" silhouette and intermed. size, considerably larger than Shiny Cowbird, smaller than ♀ Great-tailed Grackle; nearby, frontal shield diagnostic.
Voice: ♂ occas. gives nasal, metallic *neek* or *neck-neck* when foraging. Displaying birds have a remarkable variety of odd, disconnected notes incl. an ascending, screeching *freeeeee;* some notes sound electronic or mechanical.
Behavior: Occur alone, in prs., or in groups of 3–20, occas. even more. Perch high in trees near cacique or oropendola colonies, on which they are obligate brood parasites, but are more often seen flying in direct line high overhead. Feed on gd. by walking around, often along riverbanks or in other open areas, sometimes take fruit with their hosts in trees, follow cattle for disturbed insects, and may perch on backs of cattle. Nesting is parasitic. Eggs laid, by stealth, in nests of oropendolas and caciques which usually attempt to drive ♀♀ away. Up to 6 eggs in 1 nest[175]; egg color, shape, and size vary; bluish eggs in cacique nests, white ones in *Psarocolius* oropendula nests[253]. Details in Smith[655] need documentation.
Status and habitat: Widespread resident but disperses widely and only vagrant or local to many areas. Relatively numerous only s of Orinoco where there are many cacique and oropendola colonies. Borders of humid forest and a variety of partially deforested and semiopen areas in humid regions. Perhaps spreading into Andes with deforestation (1 at 1700m, 13 Feb 1998, Mitisús, Mérida, is highest rec.—Hilty, D. Ascanio).

Range: To 1600m (sight, 1700m). Spottily throughout (few recs. in llanos) n and s of Orinoco (*oryzivora*). Se Mexico to w Ecuador, ne Argentina, and s Brazil; the Guianas. Trinidad and Tobago.
Note: Formerly placed in genus *Scaphidura*[281,310].

Icterus

Slender with long tail; bill sharp pointed and slightly decurved; plumage orange and black, or yellow and black; sexes sim. except n migratory spp.; mostly Mexico to n S Amer.; beautifully woven, hanging nests.

Moriche Oriole   PLATE 66
Icterus chrysocephalus   Moriche
Identification: 8.5″ (22cm). 42g. Bill slender and pointed. Mostly black; *crown, shoulders, rump, and thighs golden yellow*; under wing coverts lemon yellow; base of inner webs of flight feathers edged white (occas. visible in flight).
Sim. species: No other oriole is so black and marked with such distinctive pattern of yellow.
Voice: Sweet, musical song a long, slow, almost detached ser. of rising and falling whistles, *weet, sa-weet, . . say-su-weet, . . he, your-he, sa-lee, ee, su-lee . . your sa-wee, . . jur, sa-lee-ee . . .* and so on, mostly 2- to 3-note phrases, occas. halting but mostly sliding along in long, almost hypnotic, dialogue. Calls incl. a *meow* and gracklelike *chek.*
Behavior: Usually seen alone or in prs., occas. groups up to ca. 5, that wander alone, mostly in treetops along forest borders and in moriche palms. Sometimes with mixed-spp. flocks. Prs. display to each other with elaborate, extended bobbing and bowing. Forage methodically on palm fronds and in other spp. of trees, where often spend long periods of time in a single tree, then fly off considerable distance. Forage by taking short hops, carefully bending down to peer beneath leaves, or stretching up to examine upper surfaces for insects, or visit flowers for nectar. Thin, oriolelike, basket nest fastened beneath palm frond; 1–2 creamy eggs spotted and marked shades of brown, mostly at larger end[37]; building nest, 3m up in dead, hanging moriche palm frond, mid Feb, Canaima.
Status and habitat: Somewhat local and seldom very numerous. Resident in humid forest borders, gallery forest, savanna with scattered trees, and moriche palm groves. Shows affinity for moriche palms but sometimes well away from them. A popular cagebird in some areas.

Range: To 200m n of Orinoco; to 1200m s of Orinoco. Locally in s and e Apure (Cararabo; San Fernando de Apure); se Sucre (Guanoco), e Monagas (Guanipa), Delta Amacuro, and generally in Amazonas and Bolívar. E Colombia to ne Peru, and Amaz. Brazil n of the Amazon e to the Guianas.

Note: Interbreeds and is perhaps conspecific with Epaulet Oriole (*I. cayanensis*) of the Guianas and Brazil s of the Amazon s to c Argentina[467,544].

Baltimore Oriole   PLATE 66
Icterus galbula   Turpial de Baltimore
Identification: 7.5″ (19cm). 34g. ♂: entire head, neck, and most of upperparts black; *shoulders, rump, outer tip of tail, and lower underparts bright chrome orange*; white wing bar and *prom. white edging on flight feathers.* ♀: above brownish olive to brownish gray, wings dusky with *2 white bars*; below yellowish orange with *bright orange wash on breast.* First-yr ♂: like ♀. First-yr ♀: paler below, whitish on throat and belly.
Sim. species: ♂ is more extensively black above than resident orioles (all except Venezuelan Troupial have only a black bib). ♀ is nearest ♀ Orchard Oriole but with strong orange wash on breast (not mainly greenish yellow).
Behavior: Usually seen singly, and like other orioles, spends much of its time in flowering trees, esp. *Erythrina.*
Status and habitat: Very uncommon or rare nonbreeding n winter visitor, mainly early Jan–early Mar (1 specimen 23 Oct 1948 at Los Motilónes, Sierra de Perijá, is only fall rec.). Dates of sightings and specimens, 10 Jan–4 Mar, suggest some birds from lower C Amer. continue wandering eastward, reaching Venez. at a late date. At least 12 sightings, mostly in mts. from Mérida (city of Mérida) and Trujillo to Distr. Fed. and Miranda (incl. PN Guatopo); also once at Sauca Falcón, once at Hato Piñero (numerous observers).

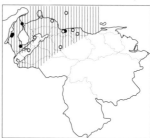

Range: To 500m (sight to 950m in Caracas; to 1500m in Mérida). Specimen recs. in w Zulia (4 locs.) and Aragua (El Limón); sightings in mts. of Mérida, Trujillo, Falcón, Aragua, Distr. Federal, Miranda, Cojedes, and Islas Las Aves. Breeds in e N Amer.; migrates and winters from Mexico to Panama; a few to Colombia, nw Ecuador (once), and Trinidad and Tobago.

Orchard Oriole   PLATE 66
Icterus spurius   Turpial de Huertos
Identification: 6.7″ (17cm). 20g. Small, dark oriole. ♂: mostly black with *breast, belly, shoulders, and rump dark orange chestnut*; 1 white wing bar; *flight feathers edged white.* ♀: above *yellowish olive*, *wing bars* and buffy white edgings; sides of head and underparts greenish yellow. First-yr ♂: like ♀ but with *black bib*; below brighter yellow.
Sim. species: ♂ from any other oriole by dark orange chestnut color (not bright orange or yellow) and small

size. At a glance could be confused with ♀ Silver-beaked Tanager as overall dark coloration of the two is superficially sim.; also cf. ♂ Lesser Seed-Finch. Dingy greenish-looking ♀ is nearest imm. Yellow Oriole but smaller and with 2 whitish wing bars. Combination of strong greenish tinge and black bib will distinguish 1st-yr ♂.

Behavior: In Panama feeds heavily on nectar of *Erythrina* blossoms. To be looked for in sim. trees in Venez.

Status and habitat: Rare nonbreeding winter visitor. Known from 4 specimens from Zulia (La Sierra; Río Aurare; Santa Bárbara del Zulia) and 1 from city of Maracay, Aragua, all taken 9 Jan–9 Feb but reportedly present Sep–Mar[403].

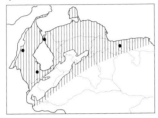

Range: To 400m. W Zulia and Aragua (*spurius*). Breeds in N Amer.; migrates and winters from Mexico s to Panama, sparingly to n Colombia.

Venezuelan Troupial   PLATE 66
Icterus icterus   Turpial Venezolano

Identification: 10.5″ (27cm), 68g in arid nw (*ridgwayi*). 9″ (23cm) in s border of llanos (*metae*). National bird of Venez. Bill blue gray; *yellow eyes* surrounded by large bare blue ocular area extending rearward to point. *Entire head, throat, and chest black, the chest feathers long and pointed forming a shaggy border*; nape, mantle, rump, and rest of underparts bright spectrum orange; back, wings, and tail black, broad slash of white across median wing coverts and on inner flight feathers (*ridgwayi*). Or sim. but smaller, only forecrown, face, and chest black (not whole head), and scapular band spectrum orange mixed white (*metae*). Juv.: paler, more lemon yellow; wings and tail brownish.

Sim. species: Strikingly patterned and not likely confused.

Voice: Often hd. song a loud, musical, and distinctive ser. of slow whistles, *taaw chEER, taaw chEER, . . .* up to 9 times, or *CHEEer toe, CHEEer toe . . .* over and over, varied to *taaw chu chEEEra, taaw chu hEEEra . . .* or other sim. phrase. In all areas, song phrases typically are composed of couplets or triplets whistled over and over.

Behavior: More often than not it is rich, hypnotic song phrases that alert one to presence of this beautiful bird which often perches atop a large columnar cactus or high bare branch to sing. Troupials feed heavily on nectar and spend long periods of time in flowering trees. Also peer for insects and puncture small berries for juice. Occur singly, in prs., or in family groups, and are highly esteemed as cagebirds for their beauty and rich song. Build their own woven nest or appropriate old nests of thornbirds, Great Kiskadee, ca-

ciques, or orioles; 3 white eggs tinged pinkish buff and thickly spotted and marked brown around larger end[115]; breed in wet and dry season (Jun–Jul and Nov–Dec) in n Falcón[350]; Jun–Sep, w Guárico[734].

Status and habitat: Fairly common resident of desert scrub, dry woodland, gallery forest borders, and ranchland with scattered trees. Most numerous in very xerophytic vegetation in n Falcón.

Range: To 1300m n of Orinoco; to 100m s of Orinoco. Coast from Goajira Pen., Zulia, e to Paraguaná Pen. and e Falcón, and s to se Lara (sight, near Barquisimeto); Isla Margarita (*ridgwayi*); generally e of Andes from Carabobo and w Apure e to Sucre and Monagas (Maturín); s bank of Orinoco in Bolívar from Caicara e to Ciudad Bolívar (*icterus*); s Apure at Paragüito and Cararabo along Río Meta (*metae*). N Colombia.
Note: Orange-backed forms, *croconotus* of se Colombia to n Argentina and c Amaz. Brazil, and *jamacaii* (Campo Oriole) of e Brazil, are often treated as subspp. of *I. icterus*. Nest usurpation not reported in these forms.

Yellow-backed Oriole   PLATE 66
Icterus chrysater   Toche

Identification: 8.5″ (22cm). 45g. Sleek, clean-cut oriole. Mainly highlands. Predom. bright golden yellow with contrasting black forehead, ocular area, large bib, wings, and tail. Bib sometimes outlined ochre. ♀ slightly duller.

Sim. species: Only other "yellow-backed" oriole is Yellow Oriole which has *smaller* black bib (*no black on forehead*) and *always* shows at least a faint white wing bar and some white edging on inner flight feathers. Note that Yellow-backed Oriole has *solid black wings* (never shows any white).

Voice: Sweet, pleasing song a loud, clear ser. of almost humanlike whistles, *WEET, wa, WEET, waa, wee wee wa WEET . . wa, WEET* and so on, rising, falling, and delivered at leisurely pace, or varied to more complex *whee, who-hee, who-hee, who-hee, ha-heet, wita-wita-wita*. Sometimes gives detached, jerky ser. of *weet* and *jur-keet* notes, esp. when excited or as flies with exaggerated jerky pumping of tail and rear body. Songs tend to ramble, phrases often repeat, and sometimes pauses or extra notes are added almost as an afterthought.

Behavior: Single birds, prs., or several are conspic. and act like other orioles as hop along upper branches of trees in highland pastures, check flowers, and occas. sing loudly. Usually not with mixed-spp. flocks.

Status and habitat: Fairly common resident. Dry foothills to humid highlands, mainly in semiopen areas, clearings and pastures with scattered trees, forest borders, and coffee plantations. Almost always in foothills or mts., rarely or very locally to lowlands. Has profited from deforestation.

Range: Ca. 500–2800m, occas. lower (once near sea level in Carabobo). Andes from s Táchira n to nw and se Lara; Falcón (Sierra de San Luis); mts. of Yaracuy; n cordilleras from Carabobo to Distr. Federal and se Miranda at Cerro Negro (*giraudii*). Se Mexico to Colombia (not Costa Rica).

Yellow Oriole   PLATE 66
Icterus nigrogularis   Gonzalito
Identification: 8″ (20.3cm). 38g. Resembles Yellow-backed Oriole. Mostly bright yellow; *lores, ocular area, and throat black*; wings and tail black with *1 narrow white wing bar and white edgings on inner flight feathers* (amt. of white varies greatly, sometimes faint and not evident at a distance). In general *trinitatis* shows least white on wings, *helioeides*, with broad white edges, the most.
Sim. species: See Yellow-backed Oriole which is almost always at higher els. (overlaps locally) and always has solid black wings. Also cf. Orange-crowned and Yellow-tailed orioles, both with black backs.
Voice: Doesn't sing as much as most orioles. Song a detached ser. of short musical phrases, *tur-a-leet, tur-sweet, tuur . . . tweet, tweet* and so on; or *swét, weet-weet-weet-pít-tear* or sim. variation; dawn song has added harsh and high-pitched notes (P. Schwartz recording). Occas. a rather sharp *ka-chek* over and over.
Behavior: Roams about in prs. or 3s, or alone. Hops and peers in foliage for insects or visits flowering trees for nectar. Occas. eats or punctures small berries. Eye level to canopy but everywhere conspic. and easy to see. Usual *Icterus* pendent nest, sometimes quite low; 2–3 eggs, white to bluish white, purplish black scrawls at larger end[750]; breeding May–Sep, w Guárico[734].
Status and habitat: Common resident in arid scrub, dry woodland, gallery forest borders, shrubby areas, gardens, and ranchland. Often in flowering trees around habitations. The commonest oriole over most of n Venez. and esp. in llanos. Rare or absent in humid areas.
Range: To 850m (to 1800m in Lara). Widespread e of Andes (w of Andes ?) and n of Orinoco e to Sucre, Monagas, and Delta Amacuro; nw Amazonas (Río Cataniapo; sight, Camturama Lodge); n Bolívar s to lower Río Caura, lower Río Paragua (La Paragua), and Tumeremo (*nigrogularis*); Paria Pen., Sucre, and Isla

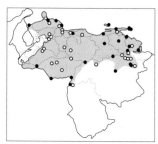

Patos (*trinitatis*); Isla Margarita (*helioeides*). N Colombia to the Guianas and mouth of the Amazon in ne Brazil. Netherlands Antilles; Trinidad and Tobago.

Yellow-tailed Oriole   PLATE 66
Icterus mesomelas   Turpial Cola Amarilla
Identification: 8.5″ (22cm). 40g. Shows much yellow in tail. Mostly bright yellow; lores, ocular region, bib, *upper back*, wings, and central tail feathers black; shoulders and *outer tail feathers yellow* (from below, entire under surface looks yellow). No white on wing.
Sim. species: Only Venez. oriole with conspic. yellow in tail. Black back and yellow in tail easily separate it from Yellow-backed Oriole. Also see Orange-crowned Oriole.
Voice: Distinctive call a loud, whistled *pik-drup* or *pik, pik-drup*, often repeated several times. Song a rich ser. of whistled *chuck, chuck-yeaow* phrases, up to several times per song.
Behavior: Sim. to other orioles. Prs. or families usually forage fairly high. Has habit of jerking tail up and down when flying, giving impression of labored flight. Usual pendent *Icterus* nest 2–4m up; in Guatemala 3 white eggs tinged blue with dark brown blotches around large end, finer dots elsewhere[624].
Status and habitat: Uncommon resident of humid forest borders and second growth. May show some affinity for water as is often in riparian woodland, river borders, and swampy or wetter vegetation.

Range: To 500m. W and s part of Maracaibo Basin, Zulia, e to w base of Andes in Táchira and Mérida (*carrikeri*). Se Mexico to nw Peru.

Orange-crowned Oriole   PLATE 66
Icterus auricapillus   Gonzalito Real
Identification: 7.7″ (19.5cm). 32g. *Crown, nape, rear cheeks, and sides of neck rich red orange to golden orange*; narrow forehead, ocular area, bib, *upper back*, wings, and *tail* black; shoulders (lesser wing coverts), rump, and underparts yellow. Juv.: sim. but much

paler, crown mostly yellowish, back dusky olive, wings sometimes with 2 vague whitish bars.

Sim. species: Fiery orange crown is the key mark, but amt. and intensity of orange vary. Cf. Yellow-tailed, Yellow, and Yellow-backed orioles.

Voice: Song a loud, musical, whistled *werr, chéet-your-kurr;* also a musical but slower, longer, rambling ser.; call a burry and complaining *wheea,* sharp *ze'e't;* occas. when foraging a loud, clear, whistled *krEEEa.*

Behavior: Sim. to that of Yellow Oriole but favors somewhat more humid and wooded regions. Single birds or prs. hop along branches, lean over to peer at foliage, and check flowers for nectar. Stay fairly high. Usually not with mixed-spp. flocks but often with other birds in canopy of flowering trees.

Status and habitat: Uncommon resident in moist to humid forest borders, light woodland, ranchland or semiopen areas with woodlots, palms, or trees along pasture borders. Absent from arid regions; rare or absent in wetter portions of llanos; scarce and irreg. at Hato Masaguaral, Guárico[734]. Over most of range occurs in low density.

Range: To 1900m n of Orinoco; to 300m s of Orinoco. Generally in Zulia, w base of Andes, and locally from Falcón e to Sucre and Monagas; entire e base of Andes, Cojedes, and Guárico; locally along Orinoco in sw Anzoátegui (Río Zuata), Delta Amacuro[343], and n Bolívar (Caicara; Maripa; Caño Maniapure e to Río Paragua; sight, El Palmar). E Panama and n Colombia.

Oriole Blackbird   PLATE 67
Gymnomystax mexicanus   Tordo Maicero
Identification: ♂ 12″ (30.5cm), ♀ 10.5″ (27cm). 94g (unsexed). Large and oriolelike. Bill rather heavy and pointed. *Mostly golden yellow with black back, wings, and fairly long tail;* bare black lores, ocular region, and black malar mark; tail rather long and rounded. Imm. ♂: sim but black on central crown.

Sim. species: Looks like an oversized oriole, esp. in flight. Note large size, absence of bib, and different habits.

Voice: Song is harsh, unmusical, and given perched or in flight, a wheezy, buzzy, *shssveek-shssveek-shssveek* (varies from 1 to 4 notes) sometimes preceded or followed by a few loud, grating *grt* notes.

Behavior: A conspic. bird of semiopen terrain that can turn up in a wide variety of places. Most often encountered in loose flocks of a few individuals up to several dozen. Forage on gd. in grassy pastures and on riverbanks, or perch and loaf up in tall grass or trees, often near water. Freq. first noted by harsh, scraping calls.

Also forage in small groups of 2–8 in creekside vegetation where they hop slowly and peer carefully at leaves. Nest a thick-walled grass and weed cup to 6m up in tree; pale blue eggs marked brown at larger end; breeding Jun–Sep, w Apure and w Guárico[137,645,734]; Mar nest, e Falcón.

Status and habitat: Common resident in llanos. Ranchland, esp. along riverbanks, marshes, lagoons, gallery forest borders, and trees in villages. S of Orinoco mainly on open or semiopen riverbanks and river isls. where there are mud flats, marshes, tall grass, and young second growth. Fairly dry to humid regions, but in all areas shows some preference for vicinity of water.

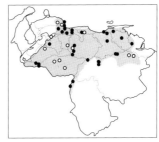

Range: To 1000m (sight to 1400m, PN Yacambú, Lara) n of Orinoco; to 200m s of Orinoco. E Falcón (Boca del Tocuyo), se Lara (sight), Yaracuy, and generally e of Andes from Portuguesa and w Apure e to sw Sucre (Río Cocollar), Monagas, and Delta Amacuro; nw Amazonas (s to Samariapo); n Bolívar s to lower Río Caura and vicinity of El Palmar. Ne Colombia to the Guianas (recs. spotty; none in Suriname); Brazil mostly along the Amazon from its mouth to se Colombia, e Ecuador, and e Peru.

Cacicus

Fairly large, mostly black icterids; patches of red or yellow on wings, rump, and tail; bill whitish, pointed; culmen extends back slightly onto forehead; eyes blue (usually) or white; ♂♂ much larger than ♀♀; most spp. nest colonially (except Solitary Cacique); deep, pouchlike hanging nests.

Yellow-rumped Cacique   PLATE 67
Cacicus cela   Arrendajo Común
Identification: ♂ 11″ (28cm), 104g. ♀ 9″ (23cm), 60g. Bill creamy white. Eyes icy blue. Mostly glossy black, *prom. patch on median wing coverts, lower back, rump, belly, under tail coverts, and basal third of tail rich chrome yellow* (outer tail feathers with more yellow than innermost).

Sim. species: Most likely confused with larger oropendolas which also have yellow on tail. This common, widespread cacique also has yellow on wings, rump, and under tail coverts. In mts. of w see Mountain Cacique; in lowlands s of Orinoco, Red-rumped Cacique.

Voice: Noisy, esp. around breeding colonies. Commonest call a loud, downscale *Sheek . . weer, wrup* or often just last 2 notes, *weer, wrup* (or *worry, bird*); a variety of harsh to melodious calls while foraging. ♂♂ are often excellent mimics and imitate songs and calls of many other birds, even mechanical sounds.

Behavior: Gregarious and conspic., esp. around nesting colonies where there is much noise and commotion with birds coming and going constantly. Forage away from colony, at almost any ht., lower at forest edge, usually higher inside forest. Nesting behavior complex. Young ♂♂ fight with other ♂♂ to gain short-lived dominance (often less than 1 breeding season) at nest colonies of ♀♀ and breed preferentially with older, more successful coteries of ♀♀ that cooperate and link nests together in center of colony to fend off nest predators. Older, déclassé ♂♂ operate as low-ranking satellites near colony; young ♀♀ may be driven from colony or forced to exposed perimeter of colony[555]. Nest in same tree with oropendolas, or more often separately; no. of nests varies from ca. 6 to 75. Nests shorter than oropendola nests, more oblong in shape, and placed much closer together, some interwoven; colonies often near wasps' nests and typically in isolated or "safe" tree (e.g., in a village, on river isl.) away from marauding monkeys and raptors; 5 active colonies, late Feb–Mar, e Bolívar. Many roost on isls. in Río Orinoco.

Status and habitat: Common to very common resident in humid lowlands in almost all kinds of wooded or partially wooded habitats, even in towns and settled areas. Least numerous in dry regions and llanos, most numerous s of Orinoco.

Range: To 1000m n of Orinoco; to 500m s of Orinoco. Widespread n and s of Orinoco (*cela*). W Panama to n Bolivia, Amaz. Brazil, and the Guianas; coastal e Brazil.

Red-rumped Cacique   PLATE 67
Cacicus haemorrhous   Arrendajo Rabadilla Encarnada
Identification: ♂ 10.5″ (27cm), 100g. ♀ 8.5″ (22cm), 69g. Bill creamy greenish white. Eyes icy blue; brownish in young birds. Glossy blue black above and below; *lower back, rump, and upper tail coverts bright red*, but red often concealed by closed wing; tail square. ♀ sim. but not glossy.

Sim. species: The only *"red-rumped" cacique in its range in Venez.* Red can be hard to see unless bird flies. Cf. Yellow-rumped Cacique. Subtropical Cacique, *only* in Andes, is larger, duller, shows less red, and has rounded tail.

Voice: Flight call a reedy *shoowip!;* when foraging gives many odd notes, whistles, and guttural quack. Noisy around nesting colonies.

Behavior: Gregarious and conspic. at breeding colonies but tends to forage alone or in small, loosely assoc. groups away from colony, then less conspic. Reg. with mixed-spp. flocks in mid. levels or higher inside forest or at forest edge. Unlike Yellow-rumped Cacique, chooses mainly trees at forest edge (not isolated trees in clearings) for nest colonies; in Suriname colonies of 20 and 30 nests, early Mar; hanging, stockinglike nest built by ♀; 2 white eggs with reddish and purplish dots and blotches[253].

Status and habitat: Resident in humid forest and forest borders. Most numerous in lower Río Caura and lowlands of e Bolívar from Sierra de Imataca s to base of Sierra de Lema, but everywhere somewhat local and colonies widely spaced. Recs. very spotty in Amazonas.

Range: To 900m. Nw Amazonas (Nericagua; Cerro Sipapo) and sw Amazonas (Río Negro); n Bolívar from Caño Maniapure, lower Río Caura, mid. Río Paragua (Guaiquinima), and Sierra de Imataca southward (*haemorrhous*). Se Colombia to n Bolivia, Amaz. Brazil, and the Guianas; se Brazil, e Paraguay, and ne Argentina.

Subtropical Cacique   PLATE 67
Cacicus uropygialis   Arrendajo de Selva Nublada
Identification: ♂ 11.5″ (29cm), 70g. ♀ 10″ (25cm), 54g. *Bill creamy greenish white*. Eyes icy blue; brownish in young birds. *Plumage black*, glossy above; *red rump* usually concealed except when bird flies; tail rather rounded.

Sim. species: Pale bill and red rump are the marks. See larger Russet-backed Oropendola and Yellow-billed Cacique.

Voice: Rather noisy. Large vocabulary of calls incls. a loud, ringing *qua-qua-qua-quee-quEE-QUEET*; in flight or perched a nasal, bisyllabic *q-ok* that descends; also a liquid *cawik!* and loud *whuit-whuit-whuit-whuit*.

Behavior: Usually seen in varying-sized groups of its own, or with groups of Russet-backed Oropendolas. Groups also may join other large frugivores such as Red-ruffed Fruitcrows and Andean Cocks-of-the-rock in fruiting trees (i.e., *Cecropia*), and reg. accompany mixed-spp. flocks of passerines where hop along branches and peer at foliage from about eye level to canopy. Nest in small colonies (up to ca. 12 nests) in semi-isolated tree over steep ravine.

Status and habitat: Uncommon and local resident in humid and wet montane forest and along forest borders. Readily found (many sight recs., no specimens) on San Isidro Rd., nw Barinas.

Range: 1300–2300m. Sierra de Perijá, Zulia; Andes of s Táchira (upper Río Chiquito) n to nw Barinas. Colombia s locally in Andes to c Peru.
Note: By some considered a subsp. of Scarlet-rumped Cacique (*I. microrhynchus*) of lowland w Nicaragua to w Ecuador; *microrhynchus* itself may comprise 2 spp.[543].

Northern Mountain-Cacique   PLATE 67
Cacicus leucoramphus   Arrendajo Aliamarillo Colinegro
Identification: ♂ 11″ (28cm), ♀ 10″ (25cm). Bill bluish gray, creamy at tip. Eyes icy blue. Mostly silky black *incl. tail; lesser wing coverts, lower back, and rump bright yellow*; head slightly crested (inconspic.).
Sim. species: Nothing really like it in its montane habitat. In lowlands see Yellow-rumped Cacique.
Voice: Can be rather noisy, giving various loud calls when foraging, most freq. a nasal, gull-like *kee-a*, or *peEEea*, and nasal *caa*, both often repeated; also a more jaylike *krek*.
Behavior: This is a large, strong, often noisy bird that reg. accompanies mixed-spp. flocks, esp. those composed of Black-collared Jays, Hooded Mountain-Tanagers, and sometimes Crimson-mantled Woodpeckers, but is otherwise infreq. encountered. Occurs singly or in prs. and actively hops along mid- or upper-level branches, quickly peers at foliage and epiphytic growth, checks bromeliads, then moves on with flock. Typically keeps on the move and is difficult to see for more than short periods of time.
Status and habitat: Resident in humid and wet montane forest. In Venez. known from rather large no. of specimens from Hacienda Providencia (1900–2100m) in upper Río Chiquito of s Táchira, and a few on Cerro Las Copas (2700–2800m).

Range: 1900–2800m. S Táchira (*leucoramphus*). Colombia s in Andes to c Peru.
Note: Does not incl. birds of s Peru and Bolivia, Southern Mountain-Cacique, *C. chrysonotus*[467].

Solitary Cacique   PLATE 67
Cacicus solitarius   Arrendajo Negro Solitario
Identification: ♂ 11″ (28cm), 90g. ♀ 9.5″ (24cm), 80g. Bill *creamy greenish white. Eyes dark. Uniformly silky black* (no gloss), flight feathers tinged brownish black; slight flat crest on rearcrown (usually not apparent in field).
Sim. species: In limited range in Venez. not likely confused. Other med.-sized to large "black" birds of wet shrubby edges in its range incl. anis, White-lined Tanager, Carib Grackle, and Shiny and Giant cowbirds, but none has large whitish bill. No overlap with Yellow-billed or Scarlet-rumped caciques.
Voice: Can be noisy or very quiet and stealthy. A large and varied repertoire of bizarre sounds. In Venez. a kittenlike *mee-er*, liquid *E'yup*, and other short odd notes (P. Schwartz recording). In Amaz. ne Peru a loud, resounding *TSONK!* usually repeated several times, a nasal squishing or mocking *naaaaaah*, and a strange ser. of "electronic" sounds, apparently the main song.
Behavior: True to its name, this sp. is rather solitary and usually alone or in prs. Occas. one is seen following its mate as they fly low across a small stream or clearing. They are great skulkers in thickets but very territorial and come quickly to imitations of their calls. Forage low and out of sight but occas. move higher if vegetation is thick. Eat many large arthropods. Nest a solitary hanging pouch (no colonies), thinner walled than those of other *Cacicus*; usually fairly low, sometimes over water. In Brazil, 2 eggs, vinaceous white sparsely dotted and blotched darker[425].
Status and habitat: Resident. Rank second growth, thickets and grass along borders of rivers and lakes, and at edge of swampy or low-lying forest. There are only a few specimen recs. for Venez.

Range: To 300m; sight to 450m[60]. Se base of Andes in Táchira (Santo Domingo), w Apure (Guasdualito, El Amparo), and w Barinas (Veguita). Se Colombia to n Argentina, Uruguay, and Brazil s of the Rio Amazon (but not se Brazil).
Note: Previously called Solitary Black-Cacique[403].

Yellow-billed Cacique   PLATE 67
Amblycercus holosericeus   Arrendajo Andino
Identification: ♂ 9.5″ (24cm), 70g. ♀ 8.5″ (22cm), 56g. Only in mts. of w and n. *Bill and eyes yellowish white* (both sexes). *Plumage entirely dull black*; feathers of rearcrown lengthened, but slight crest seldom evident in field; narrow white eyering.
Sim. species: Subtropical Cacique is more arboreal and has blue eyes and red rump (often hard to see). Lowland-inhabiting Solitary Cacique differs only in dark eyes, but no known range overlap.

Voice: Often vocal when with mixed-spp. flocks, and always hd. more than seen. ♂ (in w Venez. and Costa Rica) gives 1–several clear whistles, *whew-whew . . . ,* answered at once by *wheeee, churrr* from ♀; also a low, gravelly, grating *gr'ra'ra'ra'ra'ra*[61,624]. In lowland Panama a variety of liquid whistles and long churrs incl. a loud, whistled *pur-wee-pew,* sweet *wreeeeeoo,* harsher *queeyoo,* and ducklike ser. of quacking notes[543].

Behavior: A furtive dweller in dense thickets inside or in shrubbery at edges of high mt. forest where it stays low and skulks even as it follows mixed-spp. flocks that contain flowerpiercers, *Basileuterus* warblers, and tanagers. Usually in prs., but observers will be lucky to glimpse even 1 briefly popping into view or flying low across a shrubby opening. In Costa Rica 2 nests in overgrown cane fields surrounded by thickets; bulky vine and cane-leaf cup 1m up; 1–2 pale blue eggs with wreath of black spots at larger end[624].

Status and habitat: Uncommon resident, perhaps also local. Humid and wet high montane forest and adj. shrubby borders, esp. with *Chusquea* bamboo, also dense second growth with bamboo. Recs. in Venez. are spotty. Seen most reg. at upper end of road between Zumbador and Queniquea in n Táchira.

Range: 1800–3100m. Sierra de Perijá, Zulia, Andes of s and n Táchira and Mérida; 1800–2000m in Coastal Cordillera of Aragua and Distr. Federal (*australis*). Lowlands and foothills from e Mexico to nw Peru; mts. from Colombia to n Bolivia.

Note: Closely allied to and sometimes placed in genus *Cacicus,* but voice, dist., nest, and osteological features of skull differ. Taxonomy of lowland birds of C Amer. and w S Amer., and of isolated highland birds in Peru and Bolivia, uncertain[183,304].

Psarocolius

Among the largest of all passerines, and ♂♂ always much larger than ♀♀; stout, sharp-pointed bill with culmen broad and flattened as it expands onto forehead; tail yellow with black central feathers; unusual display calls of ♂♂ end with forward lunge; gregarious; colonial nesters; long, free-swinging, stockinglike nests in large isolated tree.

Crested Oropendola   PLATE 67
Psarocolius decumanus   Conoto Negro
Identification: ♂ 18″ (46cm), 300g. ♀ 14.5″ (37cm), 180g. *Bill ivory to creamy white.* Eyes icy blue. Inconspic. hairlike crest of 3–4 feathers. Mostly black; rump, flanks, and under tail coverts maroon chestnut (hard

to see in field); tail yellow, central pr. of feathers black.

Sim. species: *Only large blackish oropendola with all-whitish bill.* Cf. much smaller Red-rumped Cacique whose rump is often hidden or hard to see, even in flight.

Voice: Typical song, as ♂ falls forward with wings slightly raised and tail up, is loud, accelerating, and gurgling *st-st-e-e-e-E-E-E-E'WOO! chif, chif, chif, chif,* peculiar 1st ser. like a rusty spring expanding, the *chif* sounds produced by rustling of wings as bird completes display and regains balance; call a low *choke,* in flight and while foraging.

Behavior: More solitary than other *Psarocolius* and apt to be seen alone, flying overhead with steady, purposeful wing beats, or off foraging alone. Also sometimes in small groups of its own or in mixed cacique and oropendola flocks where it peers and hops heavily in upper-level and canopy foliage for large arthropods, fruit, and nectar. May spend large amts. of time in flowering trees such as *Erythrina.* Nesting colonies are usually not large, but as in other oropendolas, are a characteristic sight in many areas as they are almost always located conspic. in a large isolated tree. Sometimes colonies are located near nesting colonies of other spp. of oropendolas. Each nest colony has a dominant ♂ surrounded by subordinates holding territories in nearby trees; mating promiscuous[164]. Trinidad eggs pale green or gray with blackish spots or lines[728].

Status and habitat: Uncommon to fairly common resident in lighter woodland and borders, broken or partially cleared areas, coffee and cacao plantations, and cultivated areas with scattered trees in lowlands and foothills. Mainly moist and humid zones; riparian woodland in dry regions. Primarily a bird of semiopen or opened up areas, it also readily invades humid lowland forest following partial deforestation. Straggler to llanos.

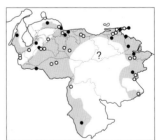

Range: To 1900m n of Orinoco; to 500m s of Orinoco. Prob. throughout (*decumanus*) but few recs. s of Orinoco. Panama to e Bolivia, n Argentina, se Brazil, and the Guianas.

Russet-backed Oropendola   PLATE 67
Psarocolius angustifrons   Conoto Aceituno
Identification: ♂ 18.5″ (47cm), 280g. ♀ 14″ (36cm), 180g. Large, dingy oropendola. Bill dusky horn (*oleagineus*); eyes usually dark. Inconspic. hairlike crest. Mostly rather dingy yellowish olive, *foreface and throat often more yellowish,* back tinged rufous olive and turn-

ing rufous brown on rump; under tail coverts rufous chestnut, *tail mostly yellow*, central pr. of feathers dusky olive, outer pr. olive. Or sim. but *bill orange yellow*, forecrown yellow (*neglectus*).

Sim. species: Occurs only with Crested Oropendola which is mostly black with contrasting ivory bill.

Voice: Songs show much geographical and individual variation, but all sound like greatly amplified water dripping into a pool. In Mérida *Whoop-ko-keék!*, 1st note low, last more than an octave higher, as ♂, with tail up, leans far forward and downward and rustles wings. In Lara (*neglectus*) ♂ sings loud, liquid *ou-oou-ouu'PLOP!*, rising throughout; in Aragua a somewhat sim. *u-pu-pU-POIK!* Call (both sexes) a loud *Schweep!* and softer, rising *wink* or *chwink*.

Behavior: A noisy and social bird that forages, nests, and roosts in groups. Hop and peer actively but heavily in mid.-level or canopy foliage, taking large arthropods, fruit, and nectar, esp. from *Erythrina* blossoms. Open *Inga* pods for pulp around seeds. ♂♂ and ♀♀ forage together, often spending long periods of time in a tree, then all departing more or less together in straggling groups. Fly with steady, rowing, crowlike (*Corvus*) wing beats. Nest colonially, but colonies typically small in Coastal Cordillera (2–8 nests), to 20 or more in Andes. Large, conspic., pendant nest are usually hung from outer limbs of large, isolated trees where they form a familiar sight to travelers. Some colonies are accompanied by Yellow-rumped Cacique nests in same tree. Mating promiscuous. Breeding seasons(s) need documentation; eggs from Antioquia, Colombia, pale pinkish lightly spotted and blotched reddish brown, mostly at larger end[589].

Status and habitat: Uncommon to locally common (e.g., Rancho Grande) in humid and wet forest and forest borders, smaller nos. into light woodland and shady coffee plantations with tall trees. Local in Andes.

Range: 1200–2500m in Andes; 400–2000m in Coastal Cordillera. Sierra de Perijá, Zulia; Andes of s Táchira, c Mérida, and se Lara (*neglectus*); mts. of Yaracuy, and Coastal Cordillera from Carabobo e to Distr. Federal and Miranda; Interior Cordillera in s Aragua (Cerro Golfo Triste) and sightings in s Miranda at PN Guatopo (*oleagineus*). Colombia s in mts., foothills, and lowlands to n Bolivia and w Amaz. Brazil.

Note: Differences in voice and plumage between highland and lowland forms need investigation.

Green Oropendola   PLATE 67
Psarocolius viridis   Conoto Verde
Identification: ♂ 18" (46cm), 375g. ♀ 15" (38cm), 225g. *Bill gray green, outer half tipped bright orange.*

Eyes pale blue. Inconspic. hairlike crest. *Mostly bright yellowish olive*, wings dusky, rump, belly, thighs, and under tail coverts maroon chestnut; *tail mostly bright yellow*, central pr. of feathers blackish olive, outer web of outer pr. olive.

Sim. species: Rather like Olive Oropendola which is larger, has more "divided" appearance (pale in front, dark behind), bare pink cheeks, and black and orange bill. Also see Crested Oropendola.

Voice: Memorable song of displaying ♂♂ a rapid, squealing, and liquid *Qu-Q-Q-q-q-q-q D'D'D'CLOCK*, *agoogoo*, 1st part like a giant spring stretching, then dull sticks knocking, last part a mellow hooting, all produced as ♂ extends neck and falls forward in swoon with raised tail and fluttering wings, only to regain balance just as performance ends. Call *chut-ut*, scratchy *queea*, and other notes.

Behavior: Gregarious and noisy, esp. around nest colonies. Usually seen in loosely assoc. groups foraging in canopy by hopping rather heavily and peering at foliage for arthropods, fruit, and nectar, or commuting to and from nesting colonies. Fly with deep, flexible wing beats as though rowing through air. Nest colonies are conspic.; 3–30 (occas. more) long, pendant nests suspended high and near end of slender branches. In Suriname eggs white with reddish and purplish lines and spots[253].

Status and habitat: Resident in tall humid forest in lowlands and foothills. Common in Río Grande Forest Reserve, esp. in areas where forest is undisturbed or only lightly disturbed. Extensive disturbance favors Crested Oropendola. Generally less numerous southward and westward across Bolívar and Amazonas.

Range: To 1100m. Se Sucre, e Monagas, and Delta Amacuro; c Amazonas from Río Ventuari southward, and generally in Bolívar. Se Colombia, e Ecuador, ne Peru, and Amaz. Brazil e to the Guianas.

Olive Oropendola   PLATE 67
Psarocolius yuracares   Conoto Pico Encarnado
Identification: ♂ 20" (51cm), 360g. ♀ 16" (41cm). Large oropendola. *Bill black, outer half orange red.* Eyes brown; *bare skin on cheeks pink.* Inconspic. hairlike crest. *Looks "divided" with pale foreparts and dark rearparts.* Head, back, throat, and breast olive yellow; lower back, wings, and lower underparts deep chestnut; tail mostly bright yellow, central pr. of feathers olive.

Sim. species: Easily confused with smaller, paler Green Oropendola which lacks "divided" appearance and bare cheeks.

Voice: Loud "song" of ♂ recalls that of Crested Oropendola, a liquid, gurgling, and "expanding" *stek-ek-ek-ek-eh-eh-eh-o'o'GLOOP!*, given as ♂ falls forward on perch and rustles wings up over back. Nasal *raap* and *whrup* calls in flight and when foraging.

Behavior: Much as in Green Oropendola but more of a "loner." Most often seen alone, less often groups of 2–5. Stays high in forest canopy and is often seen flying rather high and long distances over forest canopy. Sometimes with Green Oropendola. Breeding colonies small. Pendant nest in semi-isolated trees.

Status and habitat: Resident in humid lowland forest on red, yellow, or white sandy soils about equally, also in rich floodplain várzea soil forests. Everywhere uncommon and in rather low density.

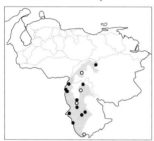

Range: To 200m. Nw Bolívar in vicinity of Cerro Cerbatana (sightings, Hato Las Nieves) and lower Río Caura, and generally in n and w Amazonas (*yuracares*). Se Colombia to n Bolivia and Amaz. Brazil (mostly s of the Amazon).

Note 1: Some treat birds of lower Amaz. Brazil as a separate sp., *P. bifasciatus* (Pará Oropendola).

Note 2: Often placed in genus *Gymnostinops*.

Fringillidae: Cardueline Finches

Jilgueros, Chirulís

The Fringillidae is predominantly an Old World group but includes the cardueline siskins in the New World[467]. Fringillids differ from emberizids in having 10 primaries rather than 9. All New World carduelines are now placed in the genus *Carduelis*; formerly they were placed in the genus *Spinus*.

Carduelis

Small seed-eating finches; short conical bill; ♂♂ boldly patterned, either "hooded" or "capped" or all dark above; bold yellow or white wing band; ♀♀ dull, all quite sim.; gregarious; undulating flight; most members confined to n latitudes or to cooler mt. regions in Neotropics.

Hooded Siskin   PLATE 65
Carduelis magellanica   Jilguero Encapuchado
Identification: 4″ (10.2cm). 11g. *Mostly bright yellow* with black head, wings, and tail. Bill conical, propor-

tionately larger and longer than in Andean Siskin. ♂: *entire head, throat, and upper chest black*, nape and back bright olive yellow, rump bright chrome yellow; *wings black with yellow band* across base of flight feathers; tail black with yellow base; underparts bright yellow. ♀: above dull yellow olive (no black head), rump dull yellow, wings and tail as in ♂ but duller, *underparts entirely pale yellow* with vague olive tinge.

Sim. species: Does not overlap any other siskin in Venez. In mts. of n and w see Andean Siskin, ♀ of which is duller and grayer on breast and yellowish white on belly.

Voice: Soft, sweet *tseeu* call much like other *Carduelis*. Song a long-sustained ser. of twittery notes, often given by prs. or several birds simultaneously.

Behavior: Like others of genus, always seems to be carefree and cheerful. Vivacious, twittery little groups, occas. prs., wander alone over open or shrubby areas, often flying far off in dipping and bounding flight. Feed mostly on small seeds from bushes and small trees, but also readily feed on gd., and may spend considerable periods of time busily feeding before moving on.

Status and habitat: Uncommon, nomadic, and unpredictable in gallery forest borders and grasslands in Gran Sabana. There are 2 specimens presum. from Río Meta where perhaps vagrant.

Range: To 1300m. Apure along Río Meta (Cararabo); se Bolívar from Guayaraca (s side of Auyán-tepui) and Ptari-tepui s to Upuigma-tepui, Uei-tepui, Santa Elena de Uairén, and Cerro Roraima (*longirostris*). Guyana; mts. of s Colombia to n Chile; e Bolivia and e Brazil s to c Argentina.

Red Siskin   PLATE 65
Carduelis cucullata   Cardenalito
Identification: 4″ (10.2cm). ♂: *mostly red* (more orange red below) *with black head and throat* forming hood; *wings black*, shoulders stained red, *broad salmon red band across base of flight feathers*; inner flight feathers edged white; tail black. ♀: above mostly light sandy brown, rump stained reddish, wings as in ♂ but dingier red and black; below grayish white *heavily stained salmon red on sides of breast*.

Sim. species: ♂ unmistakable if seen well (a red version of Hooded Siskin). Cf. ♀ with ♂ Ruddy-breasted Seedeater and ♀ Vermilion Flycatcher.

Voice: Contact calls incl. rough siskinlike *jut*; more commonly a clear, high *ka-lee*, bell-like, 2d note higher.

Behavior: A charming little bird and, like others of genus, very social. Occurs in prs. when breeding, otherwise in small lively groups up to 12 or more, usually high in trees. Nonbreeding groups are seminomadic and wander widely. Breed in moist premontane forest and wander widely into drier el. zones. Some groups may commute daily between higher-el. roosting and lower-el. feeding areas. Feed on a wide variety of dry seeds, small fruits, and berries (e.g., *Urera baccifera*, *Cordia*, *Trixis*, *Eupatorium*, and *Wedelia*) of shrubs, second-growth plants, and canopy trees[124]; also some nectar, and prob. insects. Breed mainly in early wet season, May–early Jul, with smaller nos. breeding Nov–Dec. Nest apparently high in tall tree.

Status and habitat: Now *very rare* and *endangered*. At least formerly resident in moist and humid premontane forests with seasonal, even daily, el. movements into drier semideciduous forest and semiopen areas at lower els. Sadly, excessive and unrelenting trapping for cagebird trade, for export (it produces fertile red or reddish offspring when paired with canaries), and for sport *have driven it to brink of extinction*. Pop. estimates in w and c Venez. range from 600 to 6000; almost certainly extinct in ne Venez.[124,548] and locally extinct over much of its former range in w and c Venez. The locations of recent sight recs. are not shown on the range map or given below.

Range: To 1300m. *Formerly* throughout foothills and mts. of n Venez. from Sierra de Perijá, Zulia, n base of Andes (Mérida, Trujillo, Lara, Portuguesa, w Barinas); c and e Falcón, Yaracuy, and n Guárico e to Distr. Federal and Miranda, and mts. of ne Anzoátegui, Sucre, and n Monagas. Ne Colombia (Norte de Santander); Trinidad (no recs. since 1960); Monos Isl. (extirpated); Gasparee Isl. (no recent recs.). Puerto Rico (introd. or escaped cagebirds); Cuba (introd. or escaped birds).

Andean Siskin   PLATE 65
Carduelis spinescens   Jilguero Andino

Identification: 4.3″ (10.9cm). 11.5g. ♂: above mainly olive green with *sharp black cap*; *wings black with broad yellow band across primaries* (esp. conspic. in flight), inner flight feathers edged white; tail black with yellow base; below olive yellow becoming yellow on lower underparts. ♀: above olive (no black cap), *below dull grayish yellow, paler more yellowish white on lower underparts*; wings and tail as in ♂. Juv.: dark grayish olive above, paler grayish below; wings and tail as in ads.

Sim. species: ♂ easily told by black cap and yellow wing band. ♀ very sim. to other ♀ siskins and prob. not reliably told except by presence of ♂. This sp. overlaps only Yellow-bellied Siskin. ♀ of latter is slightly

larger, darker olive above, and somewhat more 2-toned below (olive throat, yellow belly). Elsewhere cf. ♀ Hooded and ♀ Yellow-faced siskins. Goldfinches have white (not yellow) wing bands.

Voice: Goldfinch-like *tswee* notes in flight. Song a long-sustained, lively ser. of high chips and trills typical of genus.

Behavior: Usually in vivacious and chatty little flocks of its own that perch high in trees, often on tiptop branches, or roam out over open terrain and paramo. Feed at almost any ht. from gd. to treetops, mostly on seeds, esp. of *Espeletia* in paramo, and fly off in undulating flight, the various members cheerfully dipping and bobbing as they go. Occas. loosely assoc. with mixed-spp. flocks. May breed opportunistically and prolifically when there are unusually large seed crops in paramo, e.g., at end of wet season.

Status and habitat: Common but somewhat nomadic and unpredictable resident in woodland borders, highland pastures with scattered trees, cultivated areas, around habitations, esp. where there are pine trees (non-native), and in paramo. One of few native birds that uses non-native pine groves and scattered pine trees, now planted widely in Andes.

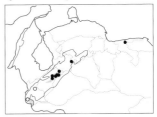

Range: 2700–4100m (sight to 1800m, s and n Táchira). Andes of Táchira (sight), Mérida, and Trujillo n to Páramo Cendé; Coastal Cordillera in Aragua at Colonia Tovar (*spinescens*); prob. Sierra de Perijá, Zulia (recs. on Colombian side). Andes of Colombia and n Ecuador.

Yellow-faced Siskin   PLATE 65
Carduelis yarrellii   Jilguero Cara Amarilla

Identification: 4.3″ (10.9cm). Bright yellow version of Andean Siskin, but no range overlap. Bill *thicker* than in other *Carduelis* in Venez. ♂: *cap black*, otherwise *bright olive yellow above*, sometimes with a little black spotting on back; *rump bright golden yellow*, wings black with yellow band as in others of genus; tail black with yellow base; *sides of head, nape, and underparts bright canary yellow*. ♀: above like ♂ but no black cap; wings and tail as in ♂; *below bright yellow*.

Sim. species: Most like Andean Siskin but occurs only with Yellow-bellied Siskin. ♂ of latter mostly black, but ♀ differs mainly in being dull, not bright yellow, below. ♀ siskins usually occur with ♂♂ which helps clarify potential problems. Also cf. goldfinches which have *white* wing bands.

Status and habitat: An enigma. Prob. not a native sp.; recs. may pertain to escaped cagebirds. Known from 2 localities in se Carabobo, both near Lago de Valencia (Hacienda El Trompillo; 1 unsexed bird 30 Sep 1963 at Hacienda La Araguata, Pirapira, in Colección

PROFAUNA), and a 3d bird (♂) of unknown date and uncertain loc. from "Barquisimeto," Lara. There are no sight recs. In e Brazil found in dry scrub, agricultural areas, second growth, plantations, and urban areas. In Brazil trapped extensively for cage trade, a likely source of Venez.'s birds.

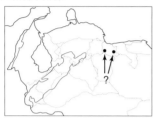

Range: Ca. 400m. Venez. in w Carabobo; possibly Lara (?). Extreme e Brazil, incl. an isolated pop. in interior e Brazil.

Yellow-bellied Siskin   PLATE 65
Carduelis xanthogastra   Jilguero Vientriamarillo
Identification: 4.2″ (10.7cm). 11.5g. Conical bill, upper mandible decurved. ♂: *upperparts, head, and chest black* sharply contrasting with bright yellow lower breast and belly; *1 broad yellow band across base of flight feathers*; basal half of all but central tail feathers yellow. ♀: above entirely dull yellow olive, throat and breast yellow olive *contrasting somewhat with yellow belly* (vague 2-toned pattern suggests that of ♂ but duller), wings and tail as in ♂.
Sim. species: See Andean and Yellow-bellied siskins. Lesser Goldfinch has white wing band.
Voice: Song a fast, bubbly ser. of twitters, buzzy notes, and musical sputterings, almost as if randomly generated; complex and usually with a few high, thin notes mixed with low nasal notes; 5–30 in length.
Behavior: Prs. or small groups wander widely to highland clearings and borders. Feed on tiny seeds at almost any ht. but usually well up in trees, infreq. on gd. More a woodland bird than Lesser Goldfinch, and despite superficial resemblance to that sp., quieter and less animated, lacking merry cheerfulness of goldfinches. In Colombia a little cup nest was 4m up in a *Cupresses* tree; 2 speckled eggs[404].
Status and habitat: Local and erratic resident. Humid forest borders, highland pastures, and clearings with scattered trees. Prob. somewhat nomadic, like others of genus. More recs. from s Táchira than elsewhere.

Range: 800–2200m (to 2800m in s Táchira; sight to 600m, Aragua). Sierra de Perijá, Zulia; Andes in Táchira, Mérida, and Lara (no Trujillo recs.); mts. of Yaracuy and n cordilleras from Carabobo to Aragua and Miranda; Paria Pen. (incl. Cerro Azul), Sucre (*xanthogastra*). Costa Rica and w Panama; mts. of Colombia; s Peru and Bolivia.

Lesser Goldfinch   PLATE 65
Carduelis psaltria   Chirulí
Identification: 4″ (10.2cm). 10g. ♂: *upperparts and sides of head glossy black; below bright yellow; conspic. white patch at base of flight feathers* (band in flight), white edging on tertials. ♀: above olive green, wings and tail dusky; below dull olive yellow becoming bright yellow on belly; wings dusky with white markings as in ♂.
Sim. species: Look for white wing band. All other siskins in Venez. have yellow wing band. Also cf. several ♂ euphonias, all with small yellow caps.
Voice: Clear, descending *peee-ee* and little rattles are often hd. as birds fly. Less often rambling and twittery song of musical and scratchy notes delivered in jerky disconnected fashion.
Behavior: Like all goldfinches, very social and almost always in little groups that seem possessed of a cheerful and carefree manner as they flit in tall roadside weeds, eat tiny seeds, or perch high in trees and sing and converse in twittery voices. Sometimes quite tame. When not breeding, seminomadic and can appear almost anywhere. Forage from gd. to treetops but are often in dry, weedy, or waste areas, spending considerable time at a site, then flushing off in dipping flight with musical calls and grating notes. Compact, thick-walled nest cup 1–8m up; 2–3 white eggs; breeds late wet season in Costa Rica[706].
Status and habitat: Fairly common to common resident in semiopen areas, cultivated fields, hedges, weedy roadsides, waste areas, groves of trees, and gardens. Lowlands and foothills, often in dry areas; no recs. in Zulia; largely absent from llanos.

Range: To 2500m n of Orinoco; to 100m s of Orinoco. In or near both slopes of Andes from Táchira to Lara, c and e Falcón; n cordilleras and Cojedes e to Sucre; scattered recs. s across llanos to Orinoco (Caicara; Altagracia) and ne Bolívar at El Palmar (sight) and Upata (*columbiana*). W US to Panama; Colombia locally to n Peru.

Introduced Species

Rose-ringed Parakeet
Psittacula krameri
Identification: 16.5" (42cm). Mainly bright green with *thick rosy red bill* and *long, almost needlelike pointed tail*; chin and moustachial line black. ♂ has bluish nape bordered below by narrow rose ring encircling hindneck.
Status and habitat: A small colony is resident and breeding in Parque del Este, Caracas. First noted in 1984 (6–8 birds); present pop. estimated at 50–60, half being juvs.[134]. Feed on fruits and seeds in or near park. Competition with native Brown-throated Parakeets for nest holes has been noted.
Range: 900m. Caracas (Parque del Este), Distr. Federal. An Old World sp. found from sub-Saharan Africa to India, se China, and Burma. Introd. locally from Europe to Hong Kong and Singapore. Curaçao in New World.

[Tricolored (Black-headed) Munia]
Lonchura malacca   Monjita
Identification: 4" (10.2cm). Thick gray bill. Chunky with short, wedge-shaped tail. ♂: *head, throat, and chest black*; rest of upperparts brown; breast and sides white, large belly patch black. ♀ and imm.: all dull brown, paler below.
Status and habitat: Ca. 10 seen 18 Jun 1996 in weedy roadside adj. to Guacara (near Valencia), Carabobo, with other unconfirmed sightings in llanos. A freq. cagebird among sellers in Caracas[595].
Range: Native to s India and Sri Lanka. Introd. in Tokyo, Japan, Hong Kong, and Hawaii.

Java Sparrow
Lonchura oryzivora   Alondra
Identification: 6" (15cm). *Massive rosy bill.* Narrow red eyering. Robust body shape. Head and throat black with *large white cheek patch*; rest of upperparts and breast *gray*; flight feathers and tail black, belly dull rusty, crissum white. Imm.: dull gray brown above, grayish white below; white cheeks faintly indicated.
Status and habitat: A popular cagebird, now escaped and established near Acarigua, Portuguesa, along Caracas-Maracay highway, and near Maracay, Aragua.

Rice fields in Acarigua-Barinas area serve as major trapping area for cage trade incl. this sp. A pop. near Caricuao, has been established for several yrs[595]. Specimen confirmation (?).
Range: To ca. 400m. Native to Java and Bali, Indonesia. Introd. into many warmer parts of world incl. s Florida (now extinct) and Puerto Rico.

House Sparrow
Passer domesticus   Gorrión
Identification: 6" (15cm). ♂: *crown gray*; brownish chestnut nape extends to eye; *black bib*, prom. curving white moustachial patch; above streaked reddish brown; 1 white wing bar; rump and lower underparts dull gray brown; bill blackish. ♀: nondescript; above streaked buff like ♂; dingy buff superciliary, dusky postocular; dingy brownish gray and unstreaked below.
Status and habitat: First noted 31 Aug 1996 at La Guaira seaport, Distr. Federal, when a small colony was found in assoc. with native Saffron Finches (D. Ascanio). Subsequently refound Sep 1996 with breeding suspected[595]. A serious pest in many parts of world, often displacing native birds.
Range: W Asia and N Africa. Now virtually worldwide in n temperate latitudes and in many s temperate areas. Established locally in most countries in S Amer., mainly in cooler s latitudes.

Black-headed (Village) Weaver
Ploceus cucullatus
Identification: 5.5" (14cm). Thick conical bill. Eyes red. ♂: mostly *bright yellow with black face and throat* (amt. of black varies with race); scapulars and wing coverts black, coverts and dusky flight feathers heavily edged yellow. ♀: above brownish somewhat streaked dusky; *wing coverts and flight feathers edged bright yellow; eyebrow and most of underparts dingy yellow.* Some races with yellow confined mainly to throat and chest; lower underparts mostly white.
Status and habitat: Up to 10 birds and 30 nests were discovered in early 1999 along edge of Lago de Maracay and near Mariara, Carabobo, by J. Colvee and C. Bosque; 1 ad. ♂ specimen (Coleccíon Phelps).
Range: E Africa. An accidental introduction to Venez.
Note: Sight recs. of Southern Masked Weaver (*P. velatus*) also recently reported in n Venez.[559].

Bibliography

1. Agro, D. J., and R. S. Ridgely. 1998. First record of the Striped Manakin *Machaeropterus regulus* in Guyana. *Bull. Br. Ornithol. Club* 118:122–123.
2. Aguilera P., E. 1982. La comunidad de ibises (Threskiornithidae) en los llanos de Venezuela. *Mem. Soc. Cienc. Nat. La Salle* 48:59–75.
3. Alderton, C. C. 1961. The breeding cycle of the Yellow-bellied Seedeater in Panama. *Condor* 63:390–398.
4. ———. 1963. The breeding behavior of the Blue-black Grassquit. *Condor* 65:154–162.
5. Altman, A., and C. Parrish. 1978. Sight records of Wilson's Phalarope, Ruff, and other shorebirds from Venezuela. *Am. Birds* 32:309–310.
6. Alvarez, H. 1975. The social system of the Green Jay in Colombia. *Living Bird* 14:5–43.
7. Alvarez del Toro, M. 1971. On the biology of the American Finfoot in southern Mexico. *Living Bird* 10:79–88.
8. Amadon, D. 1982. A revision of the sub-buteonine hawks (Accipitridae, Aves). *Am. Mus. Novit.* 2741:1–20.
9. American Ornithologist' Union. 1957. *Check-list of North American Birds.* 5th ed. Lord Baltimore Press, Baltimore, MD.
10. ———. 1998. *Check-list of North American Birds.* 7th ed. American Ornithologists' Union, Washington, D.C.
11. Arnal, H. "Páramo de Piedras Blancas: una reserva biológica." Unpubl. ms.
12. Ascanio E., D., and G. A. Rodríguez. 1995. *Lista de fauna silvestre del Hato El Cedral Santuario de Fauna Matiyure, estado Apure, Venezuela.* 2d ed. Soc. Conservacionista Audubon de Venezuela, Caracas.
13. Aveledo H., R. 1957. Aves de la región del Río Guasare. *Bol. Soc. Venez. Cienc. Nat.* 18:73–100.
14. ———. 1961. Lista de las aves colecionadas en la Estación Biológica de los Andes. *Bol. Soc. Venez. Cienc. Nat.* 22:213–225.
15. ———. 1963. Especie de la familia Caprimulgidae nueva para la avifauna de Venezuela. *Bol. Soc. Venez. Cienc. Nat.* 23:245–246.
16. ———. 1986. *Phelpsia* un nuevo género de aves dedicado a la familia Phelps. *Bol. Soc. Venez. Cienc. Nat.* 40:11–14.
17. Aveledo H., R., and L. A. Pérez, C. 1989. Tres nuevas subespecies de aves (Picidae, Parulidae y Thraupidae) de la Sierra de Perija, Venezuela y lista hipotetica para la avifauna Colombiana de Perija. *Bol. Soc. Venez. Cienc. Nat.* 43:7–25.
18. ———. 1991. Dos nuevas subespecies de aves (Trochilidae y Formicariidae) de la region oriental y occidental de Venezuela. *Bol. Soc. Venez. Cienc. Nat.* 44:15–25.
19. ———. 1994. Descripción de nueve subespecies nuevas y comentarios sobre dos especies de aves de Venezuela. *Bol. Soc. Venez. Cienc. Nat.* 44:229–257.
20. Aveledo H., R., and A. R. Pons. 1952. Aves nuevas y extensiones de distribución a Venezuela. *Novedades Científicas*, Ser. Zool., no. 7:1–25.
21. Bahr, N. 1995. Additions to the list of new species of birds described from 1981 to 1990. *Bull. Br. Ornithol. Club* 115:114–116.
22. Banks, R. C., and M. R. Browning. 1995. Comments on the status of revived old names for some North American birds. *Auk* 112:663–648.
23. Banks, R. C., and C. J. Dove. 1992. The generic name for Crested Caracaras (Aves: Falconidae). *Proc. Biol. Soc. Wash.* 105:420–425.
24. Barrowclough, G. F., and P. Escalante-Pliego. 1990. Notes on the birds of the Sierra de Unturán southern Venezuela. *Bull. Br. Ornithol. Club* 110:167–169.
25. Barrowclough, G. F., P. Escalante-Pliego, R. Aveledos H., and L. A. Pérez-Chinchilla. 1995. An annotated list of the birds of the Cerro Tamacuarí region, Serranía de Tapirapecó, Federal Territory of Amazonas, Venezuela. *Bull. Br. Ornithol. Club* 115:211–219.
26. Barrowclough, G. F., M. Lentino R., and P. R. Sweet. 1997. New records of birds from Auyántepui, estado Bolívar, Venezuela. *Bull. Br. Ornithol. Club* 117:194–198.
27. Bates, J. M. 1997. Distribution and geographical variation in three South American grassquits (Emberizinae, *Tiaris*). *Studies in Neotropical Ornithology Honoring Ted Parker*, Ornithol. Monogr. no. 48:91–110.
28. Bates, J. M., T. A. Parker III, A. P. Caparella, and T. Davis. 1992. Observations on the *campo, cerrado* and forest avifauna of eastern dpto. Santa Cruz, Bolivia, including 21 species new to the country. *Bull. Br. Ornithol. Club* 112:86–98.
29. Beebe, M. B., and W. Beebe. 1910. *Our Search for a Wilderness.* Constable, London.
30. Beebe, W. 1909. An ornithological reconnaissance of northeastern Venezuela. *Zoologica* 1:67–114.
31. ———. 1924. The rarest nests in the tallest grass stems. *Bull. N. Y. Zool. Soc.* 27:114–117.
32. ———. 1925. The Variegated Tinamou, *Crypturellus variegatus variegatus* (Gmelin). *Zoologica* 6:195–227.
33. ———. 1947. Avian migration at Rancho Grande in north central Venezuela. *Ibis* 32:153–168.
34. ———. 1949. *High Jungle.* Duell, Sloan and Pearce, New York.
35. ———. 1950. Home life of the Bat Falcon, *Falco albigularis albigularis* Daudin. *Zoologica* 35:69–86.
36. Beebe, W., and J. Crane. 1947. Ecology of Rancho Grande, a subtropical cloud forest in northern Venezuela. *Zoologica* 32:43–60.

37. Beebe, W., G. I. Hartley, and P. G. Howes. 1917. *Tropical Wild Life in British Guiana.* New York Zoological Soc., New York.

38. Behrstock, R. 1996. Voices of Stripe-backed Bittern *Ixobrychus involucris*, Least Bittern *I. exilis*, and Zigzag Heron *Zebrilus undulatus*, with notes on distribution. *Cotinga* 5:55–61.

39. Belcher, C., and G. D. Smooker. 1934–1937. Birds of the colony of Trinidad and Tobago [6 parts]. *Ibis* (13) 4:572–595. *et seq.*

40. Belton, W. 1985. Birds of Rio Grande do Sul, Brazil. Part 2. Formicariidae through Corvidae. *Bull. Am. Mus. Nat. Hist.* 180:1–241.

41. Benalcazar, C. E., and F. S. Benalcazar. 1984. Historia natural del Gallo de Roca Andino (*Rupicola peruviana sanguinolena*). *Cespedecia* 13:59–92.

42. Berault, E. 1970. The nesting of *Gymnoderus foetidus. Ibis* 112:256.

43. Berry, P. E., B. K. Holst, and K. Yatskievych. 1994. *Flora of the Venezuelan Guayana.* Timber Press, Portland, OR.

44. Bertoni, A. de W. 1918. Apuntes sôbre aves del Paraguay. *Hornero* 1:188–191.

45. Bessinger, S. R., B. T. Thomas, and S. D. Strahl. 1988. Vocalizations, food habits, and nesting biology of the Slender-billed Kite with comparisons to the Snail Kite. *Wilson Bull.* 100:604–616.

46. Betts, B. J., and D. A. Jenni. 1991. Time budgets and the adaptiveness of polyandry in Northern Jacanas. *Wilson Bull.* 103:578–597.

47. Bierregaard, R., M. Cohn-Haft, and D. F. Stotz. 1997. Cryptic biodiversity: an overlooked species and new subspecies of antbird (Aves: Formicariidae) with a revision of *Cercomacra tyrannina* in northeastern South America. *Studies in Neotropical Ornithology Honoring Ted Parker*, Ornithol. Monogr. no. 48:129–145.

48. Bierregaard, R., Jr., D. Stotz, L. Harper, and G. Powell. 1987. Observations on the occurrence and behaviour of the Crimson Fruitcrow *Haematoderus militaris* in central Amazonia. *Bull. Br. Ornithol. Club* 107:134–137.

49. Bird, D. 1994. The field characters of distant Great and Cory's Shearwaters. *Birding World* 7: 279–282.

50. Birkenholz, D. E., and D. E. Jenni. 1964. Observations on the Spotted Rail and Pinnated Bittern in Costa Rica. *Auk* 81:558–559.

51. Bisbal, F. J. 1990. Inventario preliminar de la fauna del Cerro Santa Ana, Península de Paraguaná, estado Falcón, Venezuela. *Acta Cient. Venez.* 41:177–185.

52. _____. 1992. *Inventario preliminar de la fauna de la cuenca del Río Morón, estado Carabobo, Venezuela. (Aves).* Ministerio del Ambiente y de los Recursos Naturales Renovables, Caracas.

53. Blake, E. R. 1977. *Manual of Neotropical Birds.* Vol. 1. University of Chicago Press, Chicago, IL.

54. Bleiweiss, R., J. A. W. Kirsch, and J. C. Matheus. 1997. DNA hybridization evidence for the principal lineages of hummingbirds (Aves: Trochilidae). *Mol. Biol. Evol.* 14:325–343.

55. Blokpoel, H., C. L. Casler, F. Espinoza, G. D. Tessier, and J. R. Lira. 1984. Distribution and numbers of terns in northwestern Venezuela during January–February 1983. *Colon. Waterbirds* 7:111–116.

56. Blydenstein, J. 1967. Tropical savanna vegetation of the llanos of Colombia. *Ecology* 48:1–15.

57. Bock, W. J. 1985. Is *Diglossa* (?Thraupinae) monophyletic? *Neotropical Ornithology*, Ornithol. Monogr. no. 36:319–332.

58. Boesman, P. 1995. Caño Colorado: a lowland tropical forest in north-east Venezuela. *Cotinga* 3: 31–34.

59. _____. 1997. Recent observations of the Rusty-flanked Crake *Laterallus levraudi. Cotinga* 7:39–42.

60. _____. 1998. Some new information on the distribution of Venezuelan birds. *Cotinga* 9:27–39.

61. _____. 1999. *Birds of Venezuela.* Compact disc recording. Bird Songs International, Westernieland, Netherlands.

62. Boesman, P., and J. Curson. 1995. Grey-headed Warbler *Basileuterus griseiceps* in danger of extinction? *Cotinga* 3:35–39.

63. Boggs, G. O. 1961. Notas sobre las aves de "El Centro" en el valle medio del Río Magdalena, Colombia. *Noved. Colombianas* 1:401–423.

64. Bonaccorsi, G. 1998. Nouvelle observation du canard souchet *Anas clypeata* au Venezuela. *Alauda* 66:69.

65. Bond, J. 1961. *Birds of the West Indies.* Houghton Mifflin, Boston, MA.

66. Borges, S. H., and R. A. M. de Almeida. In press. First Brazilian record of the Yapacana Antbird (*Myrmeciza disjunct*) with additional notes on its natural history. *Wilson Bull.*

67. Borrero, J. I. 1952. Apuntes sobre aves Colombianas. *Lozania* 3:1–12.

68. _____. 1960. Notas sobre aves de la Amazonia y Ornioquia Colombianas. *Caldasia* 8:485–514.

69. _____. 1962. Notas varias sobre *Asio flammeus bogotensis. Rev. Biol. Trop.* 10:45–59.

70. Bosque, C. 1978. La distribución del Guácharo, *Steatornis caripensis* (Aves: Steatornithidae) en Venezuela. *Bol. Soc. Venez. Espel.* 9:29–48.

71. _____. 1982. Actividad reproductiva de las aves del ambiente semiárido de la Península de Paraguaná, edo. Falcón. *Acta Cient. Venez.* 33 (Suppl. 1):121.

72. _____. 1983. La utilización de ambientes xerofitos neotropicales por aves migratorieas de Norte América. *Acta Cient. Venez.* 34 (Suppl. 1):135.

73. _____. 1986. Actualizacion de la distribucion del Guácharo (*Steatornis caripensis*) en Venezuela. *Bol. Soc. Venez. Espel.* 22:1–10.

74. Bosque, C., and M. Lentino. 1987a. The nest, eggs, and young of the White-whiskered Spinetail (*Synallaxis* [*Poecilurus*] *candei*). *Wilson Bull.* 99: 104–106.

75. _____. 1987b. The passage of North American migratory land birds through xerophytic habitats on the western coast of Venezuela. *Biotropica* 19: 267–273.

76. Bosque, C., and O. de Parra. 1992. Digestive efficiency and rate of food passage in Oilbird nestlings. *Condor* 94:557–571.

77. Bosque, C., and R. Ramírez. 1988. Post-breeding migration of Oilbirds. *Wilson Bull.* 100:675–677.

78. Bosque, C., R. Ramiréz, and D. Rodríguez. 1995. The diet of the Oilbird in Venezuela. *Ornitol. Neotrop.* 6:67–80.

79. Bowen, B. S., R. R. Koford, and S. L. Vehrencamp. 1989. Dispersal in the communally breeding Groove-billed Ani (*Crotophaga sulcirostris*). *Condor* 91:52–64.

80. Bradshaw, C. G., and G. M. Kirwan. 1995. A description of the nest of Fiery-capped Manakin *Machaeropterus pyrocephalus* from northern Bolívar, Venezuela. *Cotinga* 4:30–31.

81. Braun, M. J., D. W. Finch, M. B. Robbins, and B. K. Schmidt. 2000. *A Field Checklist of the Birds of Guyana*. Smithsonian Inst., Washington, D.C.

82. Braun, M. J., and T. A. Parker III. 1985. Molecular, morphological, and behavioral evidence concerning the taxonomic relationships of "*Synallaxis*" *gularis* and other synallaxines. *Neotropical Ornithology*, Ornithol. Monogr. no. 36:333–346.

83. Brown, L., and D. Amadon. 1968. *Eagles, Hawks and Falcons of the World*. Vols. 1–2. McGraw-Hill, New York.

84. Browning, R. 1989. The correct name for the Olivaceous Cormorant, "Maiague" of Piso (1658). *Wilson Bull.* 101:101–106.

85. ———. 1994. A taxonomic review of *Dendroica petechia* (Yellow Warbler)(Aves: Parulinae). *Proc. Biol. Soc. Wash.* 107:27–51.

86. Brumfield, R. T., D. L. Swofford, and M. J. Braun. 1997. Evolutionary relationships among the potoos (Nyctibiidae) based on isozymes. *Studies in Neotropical Ornithology Honoring Ted Parker*, Ornithol. Monogr. no. 48:129–145.

87. Buchholz, R. 1989. Singing behavior and ornamentation in the Yellow-knobbed Curassow (*Crax daubentoni*). Master's thesis, Univ. of Florida, Gainsville.

88. ———. 1995. The descending whistle display and female visitation rates in the Yellow-knobbed Curassow, *Crax daubentoni*, in Venezuela. *Ornitol. Neotrop.* 6:27–36.

89. Burns, K. J. 1997. Molecular systematics of tanagers (Thraupinae): evolution and biogeography of a diverse radiation of neotropical birds. *Mol. Phylogenet. Evol.* 8:334–348.

90. ———. 1998. Molecular phylogenetics of the genus *Piranga*: implications for biogeography and the evolution of morphology and behavior. *Auk* 115:621–634.

91. Burton, J. A., ed. 1973. *Owls of the World*. E. P. Dutton, New York.

92. ———. 1976. Feeding behavior in the Paradise Jacamar and the Swallow-Wing. *Living Bird* 15:223–238.

93. Busto, B., and C. Ramo. 1982. Datos preliminares sobre la reproducción del Corocoro Rojo (*Eudocimus ruber*) en el llano Venezolano. *Actas VIII Congr. Latinoamericano Zool., Mérida*: 801–805.

94. Caballero, L., A. Wilinski, and A. E. Seijas. 1981. Una nueva especie de ave para Venezuela y dos para el estado Zulia. *Acta Cient. Venez.* 32 (Suppl. 1):80.

95. ———. 1984. Una nueva especie de *Rallus* (Gruiformes: Rallidae) para Venezuela. *Bol. Soc. Venez. Cienc. Nat.* 39:107–110.

96. Calchi, R. 1993. Distribución y estado actual del Guácharo (*Steatornis caripensis*) en el estado Zulia, Venezuela. *El Guácharo* 32:1–49.

97. ———. 1995. Primer registro de *Cinclodes fuscus* (Aves: Furnariidae) para el Páramo de Tamá, frontera Colombo-Venezolana. *Ornitol. Neotrop.* 6: 121–123.

98. Calchi, R., and A. L. Viloria. 1991. Occurrence of the Andean Condor in the Perijá mountains of Venezuela. *Wilson Bull.* 103:720–722.

99. Capparella, P., G. H. Rosenberg, and S. W. Cardiff. 1997. A new subspecies of *Percnostola rufifrons* (Formicariidae) from northeastern amazonian Peru, with a revision of the *rufifrons* complex. *Studies in Neotropical Ornithology Honoring Ted Parker*, Ornithol. Monogr. no. 48:165–170.

100. Cardoso da Silva, J. M. 1996. New data support the specific status of Reiser's Tyrannulet, a central Brazilian endemic. *Bull. Br. Ornithol. Club* 116:109–113.

101. Carriker, M. A., Jr. 1910. An annotated list of the birds of Costa Rica, including Cocos Island. *Ann. Carnegie Mus.* 6:314–915.

102. Casler, C. L. 1992. Bibliografia ornitologica de Venezuela. *Bol. Cent. Invest. Biol.* 26:1–143.

103. ———. 1996. First record of the Great Black-backed Gull (*Larus marinus*) in Venezuela. *Bol. Cent. Invest. Biol.* 30:1–7.

104. Casler, C. L., and E. E. Esté. 1996. Mangrove avifauna of the Peninsula Ana Maria Campos, on the shore of Lake Maracaibo, Venezuela. *Bol. Cent. Invest. Biol.* 30:9–44.

105. ———. 1997. Record of Swainson's Warbler (*Limnothlypis swainsonii*) in northern South America. *Bol. Cent. Invest. Biol.* 31:95–98.

106. Casler, C. L., E. E. Esté, and H. M. Pardo. 1994. Breeding of the Greater Flamingo in western Venezuela. *Colon. Waterbirds* 17:28–34.

107. Casler, C. L., and J. R. Lira. 1979a. El pato negro, *Netta erythrophthalma*, en el estado Portuguesa, Venezuela. *Bol. Cent. Invest. Biol.* 13:33–34.

108. ———. 1979b. Censos poblacionales de aves marinas de la costa occidental del golfo de Venezuela. *Bol. Cent. Invest. Biol.* 13:37–85.

109. Chantler, P., and G. Driessens. 1995. *Swifts: A Guide to the Swifts and Treeswifts of the World*. Pica Press, Sussex, U.K.

110. Chapman, A., and K. Rosenberg. 1991. Diets of four sympatric amazonian woodcreepers (Dendrocolaptidae). *Condor* 93:904–915.

111. Chapman, F. M. 1917. The distribution of bird life in Colombia. *Bull. Am. Mus. Nat. Hist.* 36:1–169.

112. _____. 1929. Descriptions of new birds from Mt. Duida, Venezuela. *Am. Mus. Novit.* 380:1–27.

113. _____. 1931. The upper zonal bird-life of Mts. Roraima and Duida. *Bull. Am. Mus. Nat. Hist.* 63: 1–135.

114. _____. 1939. The upper zonal birds of Mt. Auyan-tepui, Venezuela. *Am. Mus. Novit.* 1051: 1–15.

115. Cherrie, G. K. 1916. A contribution to the ornithology of the Orinoco region. *Brooklyn Inst. Mus. Sci. Bull.* 2:133–374.

116. Chesser, R. T. 1994. Migration in South America, an overview of the austral system. *Bird Conserv. Int.* 4:91–107.

117. _____. 1995. Patterns of seasonal and geographical distribution of austral migrant flycatchers (Tyrannidae) in Bolivia. *Studies in Neotropical Ornithology Honoring Ted Parker*, Ornithol. Monogr. no. 48:171–204.

118. Chubb, C. 1916, 1921. *The Birds of British Guiana.* Vols. 1–2. Quaritch, London.

119. Clark, A. H. 1902. The birds of Margarita Island, Venezuela. *Auk* 19:258–267.

120. _____. 1926. Bird life on Margarita Island, Venezuela. *Sci. Monthly* 22:533–536.

121. Cleere, N., and D. Nurney. 1998. *Nightjars: A Guide to the Nightjars, Frogmouths, Potoos, Oilbirds and Owlet-Nightjars of the World.* Pica Press, Sussex, U.K.

122. Clements, J. F. 1991. *Birds of the World: A Checklist.* Ibis Publ., Vista, CA.

123. _____. 1997. *Birds of the World: A Checklist. Supplements No. 1 and English Name Index.* Ibis Publ., Vista, CA.

124. Coats, S., and W. H. Phelps, Jr. 1985. The Venezuelan Red Siskin: case history of an endangered species. Ornithol. Monogr. 36:977–985.

125. Coats, S., and A. R. Rivero M. 1984. Report on the status and natural history of *Spinus cucullatus* (Aves: Fringillidae) in Venezuela. *Bol. Soc. Venez. Cienc. Nat.* 39:25–64.

126. Collar, N. J., M. J. Crosby, and A. J. Stattersfield. 1994. *Birds to Watch 2: The World List of Threatened Birds.* BirdLife International, Cambridge, U.K.

127. Collar, N. J., L. P. Gonzaga, N. Krabbe, A. Madroño Nieto, L. G. Naranjo, T. A. Parker III, and D. C. Wege. 1992. *Threatened Birds of the Americas: The ICBP/IUCN Red Data Book.* 3d ed., pt. 2. Smithsonian Inst. Press/IUCN, Washington, D.C.

128. Collins, C. T. 1968a. The comparative biology of two species of swifts in Trinidad, West Indies. *Bull. Fla. State Mus. Biol. Sci.* 11:257–320.

129. _____. 1968b. Notes on the biology of Chapman's Swift *Chaetura chapmani. Am. Mus. Novit.* 2320:1–15.

130. _____. 1972. Weights of some birds of north-central Venezuela. *Bull. Br. Ornithol. Club* 92:151–153.

131. _____. 1980. The biology of the Spot-fronted Swift in Venezuela. *Am. Birds* 34:852–855.

132. Collins, C. T., and T. P. Ryan. 1994. Notes on the breeding biology of the Slate-throated Redstart

(*Myioborus miniatus*) in Venezuela. *Ornitol. Neotrop.* 5:125–128.

133. _____. 1995. The biology of the Cinnamon Flycatcher *Pyrrhomyias cinnamomea* in Venezuela. *Ornitol. Neotrop.* 6:19–25.

134. Colvée, J. 1999. First report of the Rose-ringed Parakeet (*Psittacula krameri*) in Venezuela and preliminary observations on its behavior. *Ornitol. Neotrop.* 10:115–117.

135. Cook, R. E. 1974. Origin of the highland avifauna of southern Venezuela. *Syst. Zool.* 23:257–264.

136. Cottrell, G. W. 1968. The genera of puffbirds (Bucconidae). *Breviora* 285:1–5.

137. Cruz, A., and R. W. Andrews. 1989. Observations on the breeding biology of passerines in a seasonally flooded savanna in Venezuela. *Wilson Bull.* 101:62–76.

138. Cuello, J. 1959. Una colección de aves del Río Caura, Venezuela. *Bol. Soc. Venez. Cienc. Nat.* 20: 267–274.

139. Darwin, C. R. 1845. *The Voyage of the Beagle.* Reprint ed., 1955. J. M. Dent and Sons, London.

140. Davis, T. 1982. A flight-song display of White-throated Manakin. *Wilson Bull.* 94:594–595.

141. Davis, T. A. W. 1935. Some nesting notes from the savannas of the Rupununi district, British Guiana. *Ibis* 5:530–537.

142. _____. 1949. Field notes on the Orange-crested Manakin *Neopelma chrysocephalum. Ibis* 91:349–350.

143. Davis, W. E., Jr., P. K. Donahue, and E. G. Perkins. 1980. Observations of the behavior of the Zigzag Heron. *Condor* 82:460–461.

144. DeBenedictis, P. 1997. Yellow Warblers, outside in. *Birding* 29:328–331.

145. Delacour, J. 1923. Notes on the birds of the states of Guárico and Apure in Venezuela. *Ibis* 5: 136–150.

146. _____. 1954, 1956, 1959. *The Waterfowl of the World.* Vols. 1–3. Country Life Ltd., London.

147. Delacour, J., and D. Amadon. 1973. *Curassows and Related Birds.* American Museum of Natural History, New York.

148. del Hoyo, J., A. Elliott, and J. Sargatal, eds. 1992–1999. *Handbook of Birds of the World.* Vols. 1–5. Lynx Editions, Barcelona.

149. Demastes, J. W., and J. V. Remsen, Jr. 1994. The genus *Caryothraustes* (Cardinalinae) is not monophyletic. *Wilson Bull.* 106:733–738.

150. Desenne, P., and S. Strahl. 1991. Trade and the conservation status of the family Psittacidae in Venezuela. *Bird Conserv. Int.* 1:153–169.

151. _____. 1994. Situación poblacional y jerarquización de especies para la conservacion de la familia Psittacidae en Venezuela. Pp. 231–272 in *Biologia y Conservación de Los Psitacidos de Venezuela* (G. Morales, I. Novo, D. Bigio, A. Luy, and F. Rojas-Suaréz, eds.). Gráficas Giavimar, Caracas.

152. Dickerman, R. W. 1985. A new subspecies of *Mecocerculus leucophrys* from Venezuela. *Bull. Br. Ornithol. Club* 105:73–75.

153. _____. 1987. Notes on the plumage of *Diglossa*

duidae with the description of a new subspecies. *Bull. Br. Ornithol. Club* 107:42–43.

154. _____. 1988a. An unnamed subspecies of *Euphonia rufiventris* from Venezuela and northern Brazil. *Bull. Br. Ornithol. Club* 108:20–22.

155. _____. 1988b. A review of the Least Nighthawk *Chordeiles pusillus. Bull. Br. Ornithol. Club* 108: 120–125.

156. Dickerman, R. W., G. F. Barrowclough, P. F. Cannell, W. H. Phelps, Jr., and D. E. Willard. 1986. *Philydor hylobius* Wetmore and Phelps is a synonym of *Automolus roraimae* Hellmayr. *Auk* 103:431–432.

157. Dickerman, R. W., and W. H. Phelps, Jr. 1982. An annotated list of the birds of Cerro Urutaní on the border of estado Bolívar, Venezuela and Territorio Roraima, Brasil. *Am. Mus. Novit.* 2732: 1–20.

158. _____. 1987. Tres nuevas atrapamoscas (Tyrannidae) del Cerro de la Neblina territorio Amazonas, Venezuela. *Bol. Soc. Venez. Cienc. Nat.* 144:27–32.

159. Dinelli, L. 1918. Notas biológicas sobre aves del noreste de la Argentina. *Hornero* 3:253–258.

160. Donahue, P. 1985. Notes on some little known or previously unrecorded birds of Suriname. *Am. Birds* 39:229–230.

161. Donahue, P., and T. Wood. 1992. Observations at a Paradise Tanager nest. *Wilson Bull.* 104:360–361.

162. Dorst. J. 1956. Étude biologique des trochilides des hauts plateaux pérouviens. *L'Oiseau et Rev. Fran. d'Ornith.* 26:165–193.

163. _____. 1963. Note sur la nidification et le comportement acoustique du peune *Asthenes wyatti punensis* (Furnariidés) au Pérou. *L'Oiseau et Rev. Fran. d'Ornith.* 33:1–6.

164. Drury, W. H., Jr. 1962. Breeding activities, especially nest building of the Yellowtail (*Ostinops decumanus*) in Trinidad, West Indies. *Zoologica* 47:39–58.

165. Dunning, J. B., ed. 1993. *CRC Handbook of Avian Body Masses.* CRC Press, Boca Raton, FL.

166. Eisenmann, E., and W. H. Phelps, Jr. 1971. Una nueva subespecie de *Todirostrum maculatum* del delta del Orinoco. *Bol. Soc. Venez. Cienc. Nat.* 29: 186–194.

167. Eisenmann, E., and L. L. Short. 1982. Systematics of the avian genus *Emberizoides* (Emberizidae). *Am. Mus. Novit.* 2740:1–21.

168. English, P., and C. Bodenhorst. 1991. The voice and first nesting records of the Zigzag Heron in Ecuador. *Wilson Bull.* 103:661–664.

169. Espinosa de Los Monteros, A. 1998. Phylogenetic relationships among the trogons. *Auk* 115:937–954.

170. Ewert, D. 1975. Notes on the nests of four avian species from the Coastal Cordillera of Venezuela. *Wilson Bull.* 87:105–106.

171. Feduccia, A. 1973. Evolutionary trends in the neotropical ovenbirds and woodhewers. Ornithol. Monogr. no. 13.

172. Fernández B., A. 1990. Registros de aves del Parque Nacional Henri Pittier. Notas de campo de la Estación Biológica "Alberto Fernández Yépez," de Rancho Grande. *Universidad Central de Venezuela*, Fac. Agronomía, Maracay.

173. Fernández Y., A. 1945a. Fauna y flora Tortuguenses 1. Aves de la Isla la Tortuga. *Mem. Soc. Cienc. Nat. La Salle* 4:29–31.

174. _____. 1945b. Lista parcial de las aves de la Isla Tortuga. *Mem. Soc. Cienc. Nat. La Salle* 4:47–48.

175. ffrench, R. 1991. *A Guide to the Birds of Trinidad and Tobago.* 2d. ed. Comstock Publ., Ithaca, NY.

176. Fitzpatrick, J. W. 1980. Foraging behavior of neotropical tyrant flycatchers. *Condor* 82:43–57.

177. Fitzpatrick, J. W., and J. P. O'Neill. 1986. *Otus petersoni*, a new screech-owl from the eastern Andes with systematic notes on *O. colombianus* and *O. ingens. Wilson Bull.* 98:1–14.

178. Fitzpatrick, J. W., and D. Stotz. 1997. A new species of tyrannulet (*Phylloscartes*) from the andean foothills of Peru and Bolivia. *Studies in Neotropical Ornithology Honoring Ted Parker*, Ornithol. Monogr. no. 48:37–44.

179. Fjeldså, J., and N. Krabbe. 1990. *Birds of the High Andes.* Zoological Museum, Univ. of Copenhagen and Apollo Books, Svendborg, Denmark.

180. Forshaw, J. M. 1973. *Parrots of the World.* Doubleday, New York.

181. Foster, M. S. 1977. Odd couples in manakins: a study of social organization and cooperative breeding in *Chiroxiphia linearis. Am. Nat.* 111: 845–853.

182. Frederick, P. C., and K. L. Bildstein. 1992. Foraging ecology of seven species of neotropical ibises (Threskiornithidae) during the dry season in the llanos of Venezuela. *Wilson Bull.* 104:1–21.

183. Freeman, S., and R. M. Zink. 1995. A phylogenetic study of the blackbirds based on variation in mitochondrial DNA restriction sites. *Syst. Biol.* 44: 409–420.

184. Freese, C. H. 1975. Notes on the nesting of the Double-striped Thick-knee (*Burhinus bistriatus*) in Costa Rica. *Condor* 77:353.

185. Friedmann, H. 1948. Birds collected by the National Geographic Society's expeditions to northern Brazil and southern Venezuela. *Proc. U.S. Nat. Mus.* 97:373–569.

186. Friedman, H., and F. D. Smith. 1950. A contribution to the ornithology of northeastern Venezuela. *Proc. U.S. Nat. Mus.* 100:411–538.

187. _____. 1955. A further contribution to the ornithology of northeastern Venezuela. *Proc. U.S. Natl. Mus.* 104:463–524.

188. Frisch, S., and J. D. Frisch. 1964. *Aves Brasileiras.* Irmãos Vitale, São Paulo, Brazil.

189. García-Moreno, J., P. Arctander, and J. Fjeldså. 1998. Pre-Pleistocene differentiation among chat-tyrants. *Condor* 100:629–640.

190. García-Moreno, J., and J. Fjeldså. 1999. Re-evaluation of species limits in the genus *Atlapetes* based on mtDNA sequence data. *Ibis* 141:199–207.

191. Gentry, A. H. 1993. *A Field Guide to the Families and Genera of Woody Plants of Northwest South*

America (Colombia, Ecuador, Peru). Conservation International, Washington, D.C.

192. Gerhardt, R. P., N. B. González, D. M. Gerhardt, and C. J. Flatten. 1994. Breeding biology and home range of two *Ciccaba* owls. *Wilson. Bull.* 106:629–639.

193. Gerwin, J. A., and R. M. Zink. 1989. Phylogenetic patterns in the genus *Heliodoxa* (Aves: Trochilidae): an allozymic perspective. *Wilson Bull.* 101: 525–544.

194. _____. 1998. Phylogenetic patterns in the Trochilidae. *Auk* 115:105–118.

195. Gill, F. B., F. J. Stokes, and C. C. Stokes. 1974. Observations on the Horned Screamer. *Wilson Bull.* 86:43–50.

196. Gilliard, E. T. 1939. A new race of *Grallaria excelsa* from Venezuela. *Am. Mus. Novit.* 1016:1–3.

197. _____. 1940. Descriptions of seven new birds from Venezuela. *Am. Mus. Novit.* 1071:1–13.

198. _____. 1941. The birds of Mt. Auyán-tepui, Venezuela. *Bull. Am. Mus. Nat. Hist.* 77:439–508.

199. _____. 1959. Notes on some birds of northern Venezuela. *Am. Mus. Novit.* 1927:1–33.

200. Gineo F., S., and S. D. Strahl. 1988. Segregación de habitat de tres especies simpátricas del género *Crotophaga* (*C. ani, C. sulcirostris y C. major*, Cuculidae, Cuculiformes) en los llanos centrales. *Acta Cient. Venez.* 39 (Suppl. 1):65.

201. Ginés, H., and R. Aveledo H. 1958. Aves de cazas de Venezuela. Soc. Cienc. Nat. La Salle Monogr. no. 4.

202. Ginés, H., R. Aveledo H., A. R. Pons, G. Yepez Tamayo, and R. Muñoz-Tebar. 1953. Lista y comentario de las aves colectadas en la región de Perijá. *Mem. Soc. Cienc. Nat. La Salle* 13:145–202.

203. Ginés, H., R. Aveledo H., G. Yepez Tamayo, G. Linares, and J. Poján. 1951. Avifauna de la region de Baruta y Hatillo. *Mem. Soc. Cienc. Nat. La Salle* 11:237–323.

204. Ginés, H., and G. Y. Tamayo. 1960. Aspectos de la naturaleza de las Islas Las Aves, Venezuela. *Mem. Soc. Cienc. Nat. La Salle* 20:5–53.

205. Goeldi, E. A. 1894. Nesting of *Lochmias nematura* and *Phibalura flavirostris*. *Ibis* Ser. 6:484–494.

206. Gómez-Dallmeier, F., and A. T. Cringan. 1989. *Biology, Conservation and Management of Waterfowl in Venezuela*. Editorial Ex Libris, Caracas.

207. Gómez-Dallmeier, F., and M. K. Rylander. 1982. Observations on the feeding ecology and bioenergetics of the White-faced Whistling-Duck in Venezuela. *Wildfowl* 33:17–21.

208. González, J. A. 1996. Kleptoparasitism in mixed-species foraging flocks of wading birds during the late dry season in the llanos of Venezuela. *Colon. Waterbirds* 19:226–231.

209. Goodfellow, W. 1901. Results of an ornithological journey through Colombia and Ecuador. *Ibis* 1901:300–319; 458–480; 699–715.

210. Goodwin, D. 1983. *Pigeons and Doves of the World*. 3d ed. Cornell University Press, Ithaca, NY.

211. Goodwin, M. L. 1997. *Birding in Venezuela*. CGM-Corp., Caracas.

212. Goodwin, M. L., and M. Lentino. 1990. *Bird List of Yacambú National Park, State of Lara, Venezuela*. Soc. Conservacionista Audubon de Venezuela, Caracas.

213. Grajal, A. 1995. Structure and function of the digestive tract of the Hoatzin (*Opisthocomus hoazin*): a folivorous bird with foregut fermentation. *Auk* 112:20–28.

214. Grajal, A., and S. Strahl. 1991. A bird with the guts to eat leaves. *Anim. Kingdom* Aug:48–54.

215. Grant, P. 1997. *Gulls: A Guide to Identification*. 2d. ed. Calton, Staffordshire, U.K.

216. Graves, G. R. 1982. Speciation in the Carbonated Flower-Piercer (*Diglossa brunneiventris*). *Bull. Br. Ornithol. Club* 100:230–232.

217. _____. 1986. Systematics of the gorgeted woodstars (Aves: Trochilidae: *Acestrura*). *Proc. Biol. Soc. Wash.* 99:218–224.

218. _____. 1990. Function of crest displays in royal flycatchers (*Onychorhynchus*). *Condor* 92:522–524.

219. _____. 1997. Colorimetric and morphometric gradients in Colombian populations of Dusky Antbirds (*Cercomacra tyrannina*), with a description of a new species, *Cercomacra parkeri*. *Studies in Neotropical Ornithology Honoring Ted Parker*, Ornithol. Monogr. no. 48:21–44.

220. _____. 1998. Diagnoses of hybrid hummingbirds (Aves: Trochilidae), 5. Probable hybrid origin of *Amazilia distans* Wetmore & Phelps. *Proc. Biol. Soc. Wash.* 111:28–34.

221. Graves, G. R., and D. U. Restrepo. 1989. A new allopatric taxon in the *Hapalopsittaca amazonina* (Psittacidae) superspecies from Colombia. *Wilson Bull.* 101:369–376.

222. Graves, G. R., and R. L. Zusi. 1990. Body weights from the lower Río Xingú, Brazil. *Bull. Br. Ornithol. Club* 110:20–25.

223. Greenberg, R., and J. Gradwohl. 1980. Leaf surface specialization of birds and arthropods in a Panamanian forest. *Oecologia* 46:115–124.

224. Gremone, C., and J. L. Gómez. 1983. Isla de Aves como área de desove de la tortuga verde *Chelonia mydas*. FUDENA, Caracas.

225. Griffiths, C. 1994. Monophyly of the Falconiformes based on syringeal morphology. *Auk* 111: 787–805.

226. _____. 1999. Phylogeny of the Falconidae inferred from molecular and morphological data. *Auk* 116:116–130.

227. Griscom, L. 1937. Leach's Petrel off coast of Venezuela. *Auk* 54:530.

228. Gross, A. O. 1952. Nesting of Hick's Seedeater at Barro Colorado Island, Canal Zone. *Auk* 69:433–446.

229. _____. 1961. Nesting of the Black-tailed Flycatcher on Barro Colorado Island. *Wilson Bull.* 76:248–266.

230. Grub, P. J. 1971. Interpretation of the "Massenerhebung" effect on tropical mountains. *Nature* 229:44–45.

231. Guzman, H. 1986. Feeding areas and relative abundance of the American Flamingo along the coast of Venezuela. *Am. Birds* 40:535–541.

232. Guzman, H., and R. W. Schreiber. 1987. Distribu-

tion and status of Brown Pelicans in Venezuela in 1983. *Wilson Bull.* 99:275–279.

233. Hackett, S. J. 1995. Molecular systematics and zoogeography of flowerpiercers in the *Diglossa baritula* complex. *Auk* 112:156–170.

234. ———. 1996. Molecular phylogenetics and biogeography of tanagers in the genus *Ramphocelus. Molec. Phylogenet. Evol.* 5:368–382.

235. Haffer, J. 1967. On birds from the northern Chocó region, nw Colombia. *Veröff. Zool. Staatssammlung, München* 11:123–149.

236. ———. 1974. *Avian speciation in tropical South America.* Publ. Nuttall Ornithol. Club no. 14.

237. ———. 1997. Contact zones between birds of southern Amazonia. *Studies in Neotropical Ornithology Honoring Ted Parker,* Ornithol. Monogr. no. 48:281–305.

238. Hallinan, T. 1924. Notes on Panama birds. *Auk* 41:304–326.

239. Hancock, J., and H. Elliott. 1978. *Herons of the World.* Harper & Row, New York.

240. Hancock, J., and J. A. Kushlan. 1985. *The Heron Handbook.* Croom Helm, London.

241. Hancock, J., J. A. Kushlan, and M. P. Kahl. 1992. *Storks, Ibises and Spoonbills of the World.* Academic Press, London.

242. Hardy, J. W., B. B. Coffee, Jr., and G. B. Reynard. 1999. *Voices of New World Owls.* ARA Records, Gainesville, FL.

243. Hardy, J. W., and T. A. Parker III. 1985. *Voices of the New World Thrushes.* ARA Records, Gainesville, FL.

244. ———. 1994. *Voices of Neotropical Wood Warblers.* ARA Records, Gainesville, FL.

245. ———. 1997. The nature and probable function of vocal copying in Lawrence's Thrush, *Turdus lawrencii. Studies in Neotropical Ornithology Honoring Ted Parker,* Ornithol. Monogr. no. 48:307–320.

246. Hardy, J. W., T. A. Parker III, and B. Coffee. 1991. *Voices of the Woodcreepers.* ARA Records, Gainesville, FL.

247. Hardy, J. W., J. Vielliard, and R. Straneck. 1993. *Voices of the Tinamous.* ARA Records, Gainesville, FL.

248. Harrison, P. 1985. *Seabirds: An Identification Guide.* Houghton Mifflin, Boston, MA.

249. Hartert, E. 1897. A new species of *Leptotriccus. Bull. Br. Ornithol. Club* 7:5.

250. Haverschmidt, F. 1974a. Notes on the life history of the Yellow-breasted Flycatcher in Surinam. *Wilson Bull.* 80:215–220.

251. ———. 1974b. The occurrence of the Giant Snipe *Gallinago undulata* in Surinam. *Bull. Br. Ornithol. Club* 94:132–134.

252. ———. 1975. More bird records from Suriname. *Bull. Br. Ornithol. Club* 95:74–77.

253. Haverschmidt, F., and G. F. Mees. 1994. *Birds of Suriname.* Rev. ed. Vaco, Paramaribo, Suriname.

254. Hayes, F. E. 1995. Definitions for migrant birds: What is a neotropical migrant? *Auk* 112:521–523.

255. Hayman, P., J. Marchant, and T. Prater. 1986. *Shorebirds: An Identification Guide.* Houghton Mifflin, Boston, MA.

256. Hellmayr, C. E. 1924–1949. Catalogue of Birds of the Americas. *Field Mus. Nat. Hist. Publ. Zool.* Ser., no. 13, pts. 1–11.

257. Hilty, S. L. 1992. Birding the Venezuelan llanos. *Am. Birds* 46:360–369.

258. ———. 1997. Seasonal distribution of birds at a cloud-forest locality, the Anchicayá Valley, in western Colombia. *Studies in Neotropical Ornithology Honoring Ted Parker,* Ornithol. Monogr. no. 48:321–344.

259. ———. 1999. Three bird species new to Venezuela and notes on the behavior and distribution of other poorly known species. *Bull. Br. Ornithol. Club* 119:220–235.

260. Hilty, S. L., and W. L. Brown. 1986. *A Guide to the Birds of Colombia.* Princeton University Press, Princeton, NJ.

261. Hinkelmann, C. 1996a. Systematics and geographical variation in long-tailed hermit hummingbirds, the *Phaethornis superciliosus-longirostrus* species group (Trochilidae), with notes on their biogeography. *Ornitol. Neotrop.* 7:119–148.

262. ———. 1996b. Evidence for natural hybridisation in hermit hummingbirds (*Phaethornis* spp.). *Bull. Br. Ornithol. Club* 116:5–14.

263. Hinkelmann, C., and K.-L. Schuchmann. 1997. Phylogeny of the hermit hummingbirds (Trochilidae: Phaethornithinae). *Studies in Neotrop. Fauna Environ.* 32:142–163.

264. Holdridge, L. R. 1967. *Life Zone Ecology.* Tropical Science Center, San José, Costa Rica.

265. Holman, J. A. 1961. Osteology of living and fossil New World quails (Aves, Galliformes). *Bull. Fla. State Mus. Biol. Sci.* 6:131–233.

266. Howell, S. N. 1994. The specific status of Black-faced Antthrushes in Middle America. *Cotinga* 1: 21–24.

267. Howell, S. N., and M. B. Robbins. 1995. Species limits of the Least Pygmy-Owl (*Glaucidium minutissimum*) complex. *Wilson Bull.* 107:7–25.

268. Howell, S. N. G., and S. Webb. 1995. *A Guide to the Birds of Mexico and Northern Central America.* Oxford University Press, Oxford, U.K.

269. Howell, S. N., and A. Whittaker. 1995. Field identification of Orange-breasted and Bat falcons. *Cotinga* 4:36–43.

270. Hoyos F., J. 1983. *Guia de Arboles de Venezuela.* Soc. Cienc. Nat. La Salle Monogr. no. 32.

271. ———. 1990. Los Arboles de Caracas. 3d ed. Soc. Cienc. Nat. La Salle Monogr. no. 24.

272. Huber, T., and C. Alarcon. 1988. *Mapa de vegetacion de Venezuela.* 1:2,000,000 scale. Ministerio del Ambiente y de los Recursos Naturales Renovables, División de Vegetación, Caracas.

273. Ingels, J. 1980. A nest of the White-plumed Antbird (*Pithy albifrons*) in Suriname. *Auk* 97: 407–408.

274. Isler, M. L., and P. R. Isler. 1987. *The Tanagers: Natural History, Distribution, and Identification.* Smithsonian. Inst. Press, Washington, D.C.

275. Isler, M. L., P. R. Isler, and B. M. Whitney. 1997. Biogeography and systematics of the *Thamnophilus punctatus* (Thamnophilidae) complex. *Studies in Neotropical Ornithology Honoring Ted Parker,* Ornithol. Monogr. no. 48:355–382.

276. ———. 1998. Use of vocalizations to establish species limits in antbirds (Passeriformes: Thamnophilidae). *Auk* 115:577–590.

277. ———. 1999. Species limits in antbirds (Passeriformes: Thamnophilidae): the *Myrmotherula surinamensis* complex. *Auk* 116:83–96.

278. Janzen, D. 1974. Tropical blackwater rivers, animals, and mast fruiting by the Dipterocarpaceae. *Biotropica* 6:69–103.

279. Jaramillo, A., and P. Burke. 1999. *New World Blackbirds: The Icterids.* Princeton University Press, Princeton, NJ.

280. Johnson, A. W. 1965, 1967. *The Birds of Chile and Adjacent Regions of Argentina, Bolivia and Peru.* Vols. 1–2. Platt Estab. Gráficos, Buenos Aires.

281. Johnson, K. P., and S. M. Lanyon. 1999. Molecular systematics of the grackles and allies, and the effect of additional sequence (CYT *B* and ND2). *Auk* 116:759–768.

282. Johnson, N. K., and R. M. Zink. 1985. Genetic evidence for relationships among the Red-eyed, Yellow-green, and Chivi vireos. *Wilson Bull.* 97:421–435.

283. Johnston, R. F. 1961. The genera of American ground doves. *Auk* 78:372–378.

284. Joseph, L. 1992. Notes on the distribution and natural history of the Sun Parakeet *Aratinga solstitialis solstitialis. Ornitol. Neotrop.* 3:17–26.

285. ———. 2000. Beginning an end to 63 years of uncertainty: the neotropical parakeets known as *Pyrrhura picta* and *P. leucotis* comprise more than two species. *Proc. Acad. Nat. Sci. Phila.* 150:279–292.

286. Junge, G. C. A., and K. H. Voous. 1955. The distribution and relationship of *Sterna eurygnatha. Ardea* 43:226–227.

287. Juniper, T., and M. Parr. 1998. *Parrots: A Guide to Parrots of the World.* Pica Press, Sussex, U.K.

288. Kahl, M. P. 1991. Observations on the Jabiru and Maguari storks in Argentina, 1969. *Condor* 73:220–229.

289. Karr, J. P. 1991. Ecological, behavorial and distributional notes on some central Panama birds. *Condor* 73:107–111.

290. Kaufman, K. 1990. *A Field Guide to Advanced Birding.* Houghton Mifflin, Boston, MA.

291. Kilham, L., and P. O'Brien. 1979. Early breeding behavior of Lineated Woodpeckers. *Condor* 81:299–303.

292. Kiltie, R. A., and J. W. Fitzpatrick. 1984. Reproduction and social organization of the Black-capped Donacobius (*Donacobius atricapillus*). *Auk* 101:804–811.

293. King, J. R. 1991. Body weights of some Ecuadorean birds. *Bull. Br. Ornithol. Club* 111:46–49.

294. Kirwan, G. 1996. Records of Amazonian Pygmy-Owl (*Glaucidium hardyi*) from southeast Venezuela. *Cotinga* 5:71–72.

295. ———. 1996. Neotropical notebook. *Cotinga* 6:37.

296. Kirwan, G., N. Bostock, C. Bradshaw, and J. Hornbuckle. 1995. Neotropical notebook. *Cotinga* 4:68.

297. Kirwan, G., and C. Sharpe. 1999. Range extensions and notes on the status of little-known species from Venezuela. *Bull. Br. Ornithol. Club* 119:39–47.

298. Klein, N. K., and W. H. Brown. 1994. Intraspecific molecular phylogeny in the Yellow Warbler (*Dendroica petechia*) and implications for avian biogeography in the West Indies. *Evolution* 48:1914–1932.

299. Klicka, J., K. P. Johnson, and S. M. Lanyon. 2000. New World nine-primaried oscine relationships: constructing a mitochondrial DNA framework. *Auk* 117:321–336.

300. König, G. 1991. Zur Taxonomie und Ökologie der Sperlingskäuze (*Glaucidium* spp.) des Andenraumes. *Okol. Vögel* 13:15–76.

301. König, G., F. Weick, and J.-H. Becking. 1999. *Owls: A Guide to the Owls of the World.* Pica Press, Sussex, U.K.

302. Krabbe, N., G. DeSmet, P. Greenfield, M. Jácome, J. C. Matheus, and F. Sornoza M. 1994. Giant Antpitta *Grallaria gigantea. Cotinga* 2:32–34.

303. Krabbe, N., and T. Schulenberg. 1997. Species limits and natural history of *Scytalopus* tapaculos (Rhinocryptidae), with descriptions of the Ecuadorian taxa, including three new species. *Studies in Neotropical Ornithology Honoring Ted Parker*, Ornithol. Monogr. no. 48:46–88.

304. Kratter, A. 1993. Geographic variation in the Yellow-billed Cacique, *Amblycercus holosericeus*, a partial bamboo specialists. *Condor* 95:641–651.

305. Kroodsma, E. E., W.-C. Liu, E. Goodwin, and P. A. Bedell. 1999. The ecology of song improvisation as illustrated by North American Sedge Wrens. *Auk* 116:373–386.

306. Kushlan, J. A. 1979. Feeding ecology and prey selection in the White Ibis. *Condor* 81:376–389.

307. Kushlan, J. A., J. A. Hancock, and B. Pinowska. 1982. Behavior of Whistling and Capped herons in the seasonal savannas of Venezuela and Argentina. *Condor* 84:255–260.

308. Lancaster, D. A. 1970. Breeding behavior of the Cattle Egret in Colombia. *Living Bird* 9:167–194.

309. Lanyon, S. M. 1985. Molecular perspectives on higher-level relationships in the Tyrannoidea (Aves). *Syst. Zool.* 34:404–418.

310. ———. 1992. Interspecific brood parasitism in blackbirds (Icterinae): a phylogenetic perspective. *Science* 255:77–79.

311. ———. 1994. Polyphyly of the blackbird genus *Agelaius* and the importance of assumptions of monophyly in comparative studies. *Evolution* 48:679–693.

312. Lanyon, S. M., and J. G. Hall. 1994. Reexamination of barbet monophyly using mitochondrial-DNA sequence data. *Auk* 111:389–397.

313. Lanyon, S. M., and W. E. Lanyon. 1988. The systematic position of the plantcutters, *Phytotoma. Auk* 106:422–432.

314. Lanyon, S. M., and K. E. Omland. 1999. A molecular phylogeny of the blackbirds (Icteridae): five lineages revealed by cytochrome-*b* sequence. *Auk* 116:629–639.

315. Lanyon, W. E. 1973. Range and affinity of the Pale-bellied Mourner (*Rhytipterna immunda*). *Auk* 90:672–674.

316. ———. 1978. Revision of the *Myiarchus* flycatchers of South America. *Bull. Am. Mus. Nat. Hist.* 161:429–627.

317. ———. 1984a. The systematic position of the Cocos Flycatcher. *Condor* 86:42–47.

318. ———. 1984b. A phylogeny of the kingbirds and their allies. *Am. Mus. Novit.* 2797:1–28.

319. ———. 1985. A phylogeny of the myiarchine flycatchers. *Neotropical Ornithology*, Ornithol. Monogr. no. 36:360–380.

320. ———. 1986. A phylogeny of the thirty-three genera in the *Empidonax* assemblage of tyrant flycatchers. *Am. Mus. Novit.* 2846:1–64.

321. ———. 1988a. A phylogeny of the thirty-two genera in the *Elaenia* assemblage of tyrant flycatchers. *Am. Mus. Novit.* 1914:1–57.

322. ———. 1988b. The phylogenetic affinities of the flycatcher genera *Myiobius* Darwin and *Terenotriccus* Ridgway. *Am. Mus. Novit.* 2915:1–11.

323. ———. 1988c. A phylogeny of the flatbill and tody-tyrant assemblage of tyrant flycatchers. *Am. Mus. Novit.* 2923:1–41.

324. Lanyon, W. E., and J. Bull. 1967. Identification of Connecticut, Mourning and MacGillivray's Warblers. *Bird Banding* 38:187–194.

325. Lanyon, W. E., and S. M. Lanyon. 1986. Generic status of Euler's Flycatcher: a morphological and biochemical study. *Auk* 103:341–350.

326. Lapham, H. 1970. A study of nesting behavior of *Ortalis ruficauda. Bol. Soc. Venez. Cienc. Nat.* 28:291–329.

327. Lau, P., C. Bosque, and S. Strahl. 1998. Nest predation in relation to nest placement in the Greater Ani (*Crotophaga ani*). *Ornitol. Neotrop.* 9:87–92.

328. Laughlin, R. M. 1952. A nesting of the Double-toothed Kite in Panama. *Condor* 54:137–139.

329. Lazell, J. D. 1967. The ternery on Aves Island in March. *Condor* 69:87–88.

330. LeCroy, M. 1976. Bird observations in Los Roques, Venezuela. *Am. Mus. Novit.* 2599:1–30.

331. Lefebvre, G., B. Poulin, and R. McNeil. 1992a. Abundance, feeding behavior, and body condition of nearctic warblers wintering in Venezuelan mangroves. *Wilson Bull.* 104:400–412.

332. ———. 1992b. Settlement period and function of long-term territory in tropical mangrove passerines. *Condor* 94:83–92.

333. Lehmann, F. C., V. 1943. El genero *Morphnus. Caldasia* 2:165–179.

334. Lehmann, F. C., V, and J. Haffer. 1960. Notas sobre *Buteo albigula* Philippi. *Noved. Colombianas* 1:242–255.

335. Lentino R., M. 1972. Avifauna de la Hacienda El Limón, D. F. (Venezuela). *Mem. Soc. Cienc. Nat. La Salle* 92:73–132.

336. ———. 1978. Extensiones de distribución de ocho especies de aves de Venezuela. *Mem. Soc. Cienc. Nat. La Salle.* 109:113–118.

337. ———. 1986. Estudio de los Flamencos (*Phoenicopterus ruber*) por la costa de Venezuela. *Acta Cient. Venez.* 37 (Suppl. no. 1):103.

338. ———. 1988. *Notiochelidon flavipes* a swallow new to Venezuela. *Bull. Br. Ornithol. Club* 108:70–71.

339. ———. 1989. Avifauna de la laguna de Tacarigua estado Miranda (Venezuela). *Bol. Soc. Venez. Cienc. Nat.* 43:193–212.

340. ———. 1997. Lista actualizada de las aves de Venezuela. Pp. 145–202 in *Vertebrados Actuales y Fósiles de Venezuela* (E. La Marca, ed.). Museo. de Cienciãs y Tecnología de Mérida, Mérida, Venezuela.

341. Lentino R. M., F. J. Bisbal E., A. A. Ospino, and R. A. Rivero. 1984. Nuevos registros y extensiones de distribución para especies de aves en Venezuela. *Bol. Soc. Venez. Cienc. Nat.* 39:111–119.

342. Lentino, R. M., and C. Bosque. 1989. Lista preliminar de la avifauna del Marahuaka. *Acta Terramaris* 1:65–70.

343. Lentino, M., and J. Colvée. 1998. *Lista de las Aves del Estado Delta Amacuro.* Soc. Conservacionista Audubon de Venezuela, Caracas.

344. Lentino, M., and M. L. Goodwin. 1991a. *Lista de las aves del Parque Nacional Morrocoy Refugio de Fauna Silvestre de Cuare y áreas aledañas, estado Falcón, Venezuela.* Soc. Conservacionista Audubon de Venezuela, Caracas.

345. ———. 1991b. *Lista de las aves del Parque Nacional Henri Pittier (Rancho Grande), estado Aragua, Venezuela.* Soc. Conservacionista Audubon de Venezuela, Caracas.

346. Lentino, M., A. L. Luy, and M. L. Goodwin. 1993. *Lista de las Aves del Parque Nacional Guatopo, Estado Miranda, Venezuela.* Soc. Conservacionista Audubon de Venezuela, Caracas.

347. Lentino, M., A. Luy G., and A. R. Bruni. 1994. *Lista de Las Aves del Parque Nacional Archipiélago Los Roques, Venezuela.* Soc. Conservacionista Audubon de Venezuela, Caracas.

348. Lill, A. 1974. Behavior of the Grassland Sparrow and two species of seed-finches. *Auk* 91:35–43.

349. Lindell, C. 1996. Benefits and costs to Plain-fronted Thornbirds (*Phacellodomus rufifrons*) of interactions with avian nest associates. *Auk* 113:565–577.

350. Lindell, C., and C. Bosque. 1999. Notes on the breeding and roosting biology of Troupials (*Icterus icterus*) in Venezuela. *Ornitol. Neotrop.* 10:85–90.

351. Lira, J. R. 1979. *Sterna caspia* (Aves) en Venezuela. *Bol. Cent. Invest. Biol.* 13:99–103.

352. Lira, J. R., and C. L. Casler. 1978. Las poblaciones de aves marinas de la costa Guajira del Golfo de Venezuela. *Acta Cient. Venez.* 29 (Suppl. no. 2):164.

353. ———. 1979a. Aves acuaticas nuevas para el estado Zulia. *Bol. Cent. Invest. Biol.* 13:89–95.

354. ———. 1979b. Dos Laridae (Aves) nuevas para el territorio continental de Venezuela. *Bol. Cent. Invest. Biol.* 13:107–109.

355. ———. 1979c. Observaciones sobre el Gallito Azul, *Porphyrula martinica*, en los arrozales de Portuguesa. *Acta Cient. Venez.* 30 (Suppl. no. 1):43.

356. ———. 1981. La avifauna del Gran Eneal y del área de manglares del Río Limón, la Isla de San Carlos y la Ciénaga de Los Olivitos, estado Zulia. *Acta Cient. Venez.* 32 (Suppl. no. 1):81.

357. ———. 1982. El Gallito Azul (*Porphyrula martinica*). Su presencia en los arrozales de Portuguesa, Venezuela. *Natura* 72:30–33.

358. Livezey, B. C. 1986. A phylogenetic analysis of recent Anseriform genera using morphological characters. *Auk* 103:737–754.

359. ———. 1995. Phylogeny and comparative ecology of stiff-tailed ducks (Anatidae: Oxyurini). *Wilson Bull.* 107:214–234.

360. ———. 1997a. A phylogenetic analysis of modern sheldgeese and sheldducks (Anatidae, Tadornini). *Ibis* 139:51–66.

361. ———. 1997b. A phylogenetic classification of waterfowl (Aves: Anseriformes), including selected fossil species. *Ann. Carnegie Mus.* 66:457–496.

362. Lockwood, M. W. 1999. Possible anywhere, Fork-tailed Flycatcher. *Birding* 31:126–138.

363. López, E. 1991. Cardenalito (*Carduelis cucullata*): extensión de su área de distribución y *Cranioleuca hellmayri*: nueva especie de ave para el país, cuenca del Río Lajas, estado Zulia, *Acta. Cient. Venez.* 42 (Suppl. no. 1):295.

364. López, E., M. Guerrero, J. Toledo, and A. Soler. 1991. Inventario de fauna silvestre en la cuenca media del Río Palmar, estado Zulia. *Acta Cient. Venez.* 42:52.

365. Lord, R., and F. Yunes G. 1986. Colonial breeding of the Eared Dove (*Zenaida auriculata*) in northwestern Venezuela. *Vida Silvestre Neotrop.* 1:62–67.

366. Lowe, P. 1911. *A Naturalist on Desert Islands.* Witherby, London.

367. Luy, A., and D. Bigio E. 1994. Notes on the feeding habits of the Andean Cock-of-the-rock (*Rupicola peruviana*). *Ornitol. Neotrop.* 5:115–116.

368. Mader, W. J. 1979. First nest description for the genus *Micrastur* (forest falcons). *Condor* 81:320.

369. ———. 1981. Notes on nesting raptors in the llanos of Venezuela. *Condor* 83:48–51.

370. ———. 1982. Ecology and breeding habits of the Savanna Hawk in the llanos of Venezuela. *Condor* 84:261–271.

371. Madge, S., and H. Burn. 1988. *Wildfowl: An Identification Guide to the Ducks, Geese and Swans of the World.* Houghton Mifflin, Boston, MA.

372. ———. *Crows and Jays: A Guide to the Crows, Jays and Magpies of the World.* Princeton University Press, Princeton, NJ.

373. Madriz, M. A. 1983. Food habits of the Brazilian Duck in Apure state, Venezuela. *J. Wildl. Manage.* 47:531–533.

374. Madriz, M. A., and F. Gómez-Dallmeier. 1979. Comparación de los ciclos reproductivos de los patos *D. viduata* y *A. brasiliensis* en el llano inundable alto Apure, Venezuela. *Acta Cient. Venez.* 30:43.

375. Maguire, B. 1970. On the flora of the Guyana highland. *Biotropica* 2:85–100.

376. Marantz, C. A. 1997. Geographic variation of plumage patterns in the woodcreeper genus *Dendrocolaptes* (Dendrocolaptidae). *Studies in Neotropical Ornithology Honoring Ted Parker*, Ornithol. Monogr. no. 48:399–443.

377. Marantz, C. A., and J. V. Remsen, Jr. 1991. Seasonal distribution of the Slaty Elaenia, a little known austral migrant of South Ameria. *J. Field Ornithol.* 62:162–172.

378. Marca, E. La. 1997. *Vertebrados de Venezuela.* Museo de Ciencias y Technología de Mérida, Mérida, Venezuela.

379. Marchant. 1960. The breeding of some southwestern Ecuadorian birds. *Ibis* 102:349–382; 584–599.

380. Marín, M. 1997. Species limits and distribution of some New World spine-tailed swifts (*Chaetura* spp.). *Studies in Neotropical Ornithology Honoring Ted Parker*, Ornithol. Monogr. no. 48:431–443.

381. Marín, M., and J. M. Carrión B. 1991. Nests and eggs of some Ecuadorian birds. *Ornitol. Neotrop.* 2:44–46.

382. ———. 1994. Additional notes on nest and eggs of some Ecuadorian birds. *Ornitol. Neotrop.* 5:121–124.

383. Marín, M., and F. G. Stiles. 1992. On the biology of five species of swifts (Apodidae: Cypseloidinae) in Costa Rica. *Proc. West. Found. Vertebr. Zool.* 4:286–351.

384. ———. 1995. Notes on the biology of the Spot-fronted Swift. *Condor* 95:479–483.

385. Marini, M. A., J. C. Motta-Junior, L. A. S. Vasconcellos, and R. B. Cavalcanti. 1997. Avian body masses from the cerrado region of central Brazil. *Ornitol. Neotrop.* 8:93–99.

386. Mayer, E., and W. H. Phelps, Jr. 1967. The origin of the bird fauna of the south Venezuelan highlands. *Bull. Am. Mus. Nat. Hist.* 136:273–327.

387. Mazariegos H., L. A. 2000. *Hummingbirds of Colombia.* Imprelibros, Cali, Colombia.

388. McCracken, K. G., and F. H. Sheldon. 1998. Molecular and osteological heron phylogenies: sources of incongruence. *Auk* 115:127–141.

389. McLoughlin, E., and P. J. K. Burton. 1970. Field notes on the breeding and diet of some South American parrots. *Foreign Birds* 36:169–171; 210–213.

390. McNeil, R. 1982. Winter resident repeats and returns of austral and boreal migrant birds banded in Venezuela. *J. Field Ornithol.* 53:125–132.

391. ———. 1986. Notes on the nesting of the Short-tailed Pygmy-Tyrant (*Myiornis ecaudatus*) in northeastern Venezuela. *Condor* 70:181–182.

392. McNeil, R., B. Limoges, F. Mercier, and J. R. Rodríguez S. 1987. Wilson's Phalarope in South America. *Am. Birds* 41:391.

393. McNeil, R., and J. R. Rodríguez S. 1985. Nest, seasonal movements, and breeding of Buffy Hummingbirds in xeric habitats of northeastern Venezuela. *Wilson Bull.* 97:547–551.

394. McNeil, R., J. R. Rodríguez S., and F. Mercier. 1985a. Winter range expansion of the Long-billed Curlew (*Numenius americanus*) to the South American continent. *Auk* 102:174–175.

395. _____. 1985b. Eastward range expansion of the Marbled Godwit in South America. *Wilson Bull.* 97:2243–2244.

396. Mees, G. F. 1974. Additions to the avifauna of Suriname. *Zool. Meded.* 48:55–67.

397. Mercier, F., R. McNeil, and J. R. Rodríguez S. 1987. First occurrence of Bar-tailed Godwit in South America and status of the Marbled Godwit in northeastern Venezuela. *J. Field Ornithol.* 58: 78–80.

398. Meyer de Schauensee, R. 1948–1952. The birds of the Republic of Colombia. *Caldasia* (pts. 1–5), nos. 22–26:251–1212.

399. _____. 1952. The status of *Sporophila lineola* (Lined Seedeater) and *S. bouvronides* (Lesson's Seedeater). *Proc. Acad. Nat. Sci. Phila.* 104:175–181.

400. _____. 1964. *The Birds of Colombia.* Livingston Publ. Co., Narberth, PA.

401. _____. 1966. *The Species of Birds of South America with Their Distribution.* Livingston Publ. Co., Narberth, PA.

402. _____. 1970. *A Guide to the Birds of South America.* Livingston Publ. Co., Wynnewood, PA.

403. Meyer de Schauensee, R., and W. H. Phelps, Jr. 1978. *A Guide to the Birds of Venezuela.* Princeton University Press, Princeton, NJ.

404. Miller, A. H. 1963. Seasonal activity and ecology of the avifauna of an American equatorial cloud forest. *Univ. Calif. Publ. Zool.* 66:1–74.

405. Ministerio del Ambiente y de los Recursos Naturales Renovables. 1990. *Atlas Escolar de Venezuela.* Servicio Autónomo de Geografía y Cartografía Nacional, Caracas.

406. Mobley, J. A., and R. O. Prum. 1995. Phylogenetic relationships of the Cinnamon Tyrant, *Neopipo cinnamomea*, to the tyrant flycatchers (Tyrannidae). *Condor* 97:650–662.

407. Moffett, G. M., Jr. 1970. A study of nesting Torrent Ducks in the Andes. *Living Bird* 9:5–28.

408. Monroe, B. L., and M. R. Browning. 1992. A reanalysis of *Butorides. Bull. Br. Ornithol. Club* 112: 81–85.

409. Moore, R. T. 1944. Nesting of the Brown-capped Leptopogon in Mexico. *Condor* 46:6–8.

410. Moore, J. V. 1993. *Sounds of La Selva.* Astral Sounds Recording, San Jose, CA.

411. _____. 1994, 1996, 1997. *Ecuador: More Bird Vocalizations from the Lowland Rainforest.* Vols.1–3. Astral Sounds Recording, San Jose, CA.

412. _____. 1997. *The Birds of Cabanas San Isidro.* Vols. 1–2. John V. Moore Nature Recordings, San Jose, CA.

413. Moore, J. V., P. Coopmans, R. S. Ridgely, and M. Lysinger. 1999. *The Birds of Northwest Ecuador. Vol. 1. The Upper Foothills and Subtropics.* Three compact disc recordings. John V. Moore Nature Recordings, San Jose, CA.

414. Morony, J. J., Jr. 1985. Systematic relations of *Sericossypha albocristata* (Thraupinae). *Neotropical Ornithology*, Ornithol. Monogr. no. 36:383–389.

415. Morrison, R. I. G., R. K. Ross, F. Espinosa, and D. Figueroa. 1989. *Atlas of Nearctic Shorebirds on the Coast of South America.* Vols. 1–2. Canadian Wildlife Service Special Publ., Ottawa.

416. Morton, E. 1976. Vocal mimicry in the Thickbilled Euphonia. *Wilson Bull.* 88:485–487.

417. _____. 1977. Intratropical migration in the Yellow-green Vireo and Piratic Flycatcher. *Auk* 94: 97–106.

418. _____. 1979. A comparative survey of avian social systems in northern Venezuelan habitats. Pp. 233–259 in *Vertebrate Ecology in the Northern Neotropics* (J. F. Eisenberg, ed.). Smithsonian Inst. Press, Washington, D.C.

419. Morton, E., and S. M. Farabaugh. 1979. Infanticide and other adaptations of nestling Striped Cuckoos, *Tapera naevia. Ibis* 121:212–213.

420. Moynihan, M. 1963. Interspecific relations between some andean birds. *Ibis* 105:327–339.

421. Munn, C. 1986. Birds that cry wolf. *Nature* 319: 143–145.

422. Munn, C., and J. Terborgh. 1979. Multi-species territoriality in neotropical foraging flocks. *Condor* 81:338–347.

423. Murphy, R. C. 1936. Bird islands of Venezuela. *Geogr. Rev.* 42:551–561.

424. Murphy, W. L. 2001. Noteworthy observations of pelagic seabirds wintering at sea in the southern Caribbean. *Sea Swallow* 50:18–25.

425. Naumburg, E. M. B. 1930. The birds of Matto Grosso, Brazil. *Bull. Am. Mus. Nat. Hist.* 60:1–432.

426. Navarro, R., J. R. Rodríguez S., G. C. Marín, and R. Egáñez. 1984. Nuevos registros de especies de aves para el estado Sucre. *Acta Cient. Venez.* 35 (Suppl. no. 1):483.

427. Nelson, J. B. 1975. Breeding biology of frigatebirds—a comparative review. *Living Bird* 14:113–155.

428. Niño, I. O., and S. D. Strahl. 1991. Estimación de abundancia del Pauji de Copete *Crax daubentoni* en los llanos del estado Guárico, Venezuela. *Acta Cient. Venez.* 42 (Suppl. no. 1):49.

429. Noël de Visscher, M. 1977. A mixed colony of egrets and Magnificent Frigatebirds in Venezuela. *Le Gerfaut* 67:203–233.

430. Norberg, R. Å. 1977. Occurrence and independent evolution of bilateral ear asymmetry in owls and implications in owl taxonomy. *Philos. Trans. Royal Soc. London* 280:375–408.

431. Nottebohm, F., and M. Nottebohm. 1969. The parrots of Bush-Bush. *Anim. Kingdom* 72:19–23.

432. Ogden, J., and B. T. Thomas. 1985. A colonial wading bird survey in the central llanos. *Colon. Waterbirds* 8:23–31.

433. Olivares, A. 1962. Aves de la región sur de la Sierra de la Macarena, Meta, Colombia. *Rev. Acad. Colombiana Cienc. Exactas Fisicas Nat.* 11:305–344.

434. Olsen, K. M., and H. Larsson. 1997. *Skuas and Jaegers: A Guide to the Skuas and Jaegers of the World.* Yale University Press, New Haven, CT.

435. Olson, S. L. 1973. A classification of the Rallidae. *Wilson Bull.* 85:381–416.

436. _____. 1980. Geographic variation in the Yellow Warblers (*Dendroica petechia*: Parulidae) of the

Pacific coast of Middle and South America. *Proc. Biol. Soc. Wash.* 93:473–481.

437. ———. 1981a. Interaction between the two subspecies groups of the seed-finch *Sporophila angolensis* in the Magdalena Valley, Colombia. *Auk* 98: 379–381.

438. ———. 1981b. A revision of the subspecies of *Sporophila* ("*oryzoborus*") *angolensis* (Aves: Emberizinae). *Proc. Biol. Soc. Wash.* 94:101–106.

439. ———. 1981c. The nature of variability in the Variable Seedeater of Panamá (*Sporophila americana*, Emberizinae). *Proc. Biol. Soc. Wash.* 94:380–390.

440. ———. 1983. Geographic variation in *Chlorospingus ophthalmicus* in Colombia and Venezuela (Aves: Thraupidae). *Proc. Biol. Soc. Wash.* 96: 103–109.

441. ———. 1995. The genera of owls in the Asioninae. *Bull. Br. Ornithol. Club* 115:35–39.

442. O'Neill, J. P. 1969. Distributional notes on the birds of Peru including twelve species previously unreported from the republic. *Occas. Pap. Mus. Zool. La. State Univ.* 37:1–11.

443. O'Neill, J. P., and T. A. Parker. 1977. Taxonomy and range of *Pionus* "*seniloides*" in Peru. *Condor* 79:274.

444. O'Neill, J. P., and D. L. Pearson. 1974. Estudio preliminar de las aves de Yarinacocha departamento de Loreto, Peru. *Publ. Mus. Hist. Nat. Javiér Prado Ser. A* (zool.) 25:1–13.

445. Oniki, Y. 1970a. Roosting behavior of three species of woodcreepers (Dendrocolaptidae) in Brazil. *Condor* 72:233.

446. ———. 1970b. Nesting behavior of Reddish Hermits (*Phaethornis ruber*). *Auk* 87:720–728.

447. Oniki, Y., and E. O. Willis. 1972. Studies of ant-following birds north of the eastern Amazon. *Acta Amazonica* 2:127–151.

448. ———. 1979. A nest of the Collared Gnatwren (*Microbates collaris*). *Condor* 81:101–102.

449. ———. 1980. A nest of the Ringed Antpipit (*Corythopis torquata*). *Wilson Bull.* 92:126–127.

450. ———. 1982. Breeding records of birds from Manaus, Brazil. Formicariidae to Pipridae. *Rev. Bras. Biol.* 42:563–569.

451. Osbourne, D. R., and G. R. Bourne. 1977. Breeding behavior and food habits of the Wattled Jacana. *Condor* 79:98–105.

452. Osgood, W. H., and B. Conover. 1922. Game birds from northwestern Venezuela. *Field Mus. Nat. Hist. Publ. Zool.* 12:19–41.

453. Ouellet, H. 1990. Notes on the iris colour in females of two manakins (Pipridae). *Bull. Br. Ornithol. Club* 110:140–141.

454. Palmer, R. S. 1962. *Handbook of North American Birds.* Vol. 1. Yale University Press, New Haven, CT.

455. Parker, M. 1997. Ecology of nesting Laughing Falcons and Bat Falcons in Tikal National Park, Guatemala: foraging and niche breadth. Master's thesis, Boise State Univ., Boise, Idaho.

456. Parker, T. A., III. 1979. An introduction to foliage-gleaner identification. *Continental Birds* 1:32–37.

457. Parker, T. A., III, and S. A. Parker. 1982. Behavioral and distributional notes on some unusual birds of a lower montane cloud forest in Peru. *Bull. Br. Ornithol. Club* 102:63–70.

458. Parker, T. A., III, T. S. Schulenberg, G. R. Graves, and M. J. Braun. 1985. The avifauna of the Huancabamba region, northern Peru. *Neotropical Ornithology*, Ornithol. Monogr. no. 36:169–197.

459. Parker, T. A., III, and E. O. Willis. 1997. Notes on three tiny grassland flycatchers, with comments on the disappearance of South American fire-diversified savannas. *Studies in Neotropical Ornithology Honoring Ted Parker*, Ornithol. Monogr. no. 48:549–555.

460. Paulson, D. R. 1983. Flocking in the Hook-billed Kite. *Auk* 100:749–750.

461. Paynter, R. A., Jr. 1982. *Ornithological Gazetteer of Venezuela.* Museum of Comparative Zoology, Cambridge, MA.

462. ———. 1995. *Nearctic passerine migrants in South America.* Publ. Nuttall Ornithol. Club no. 25.

463. Paynter, R. A., Jr., and M. A. Traylor, Jr. 1981. *Ornithological Gazetteer of Colombia.* Museum of Comparative Zoology, Cambridge, MA.

464. Penard, R. P., and A. P. Penard. 1908. *De Vogels van Guyana.* Vol. 1. Wed. F. P. Penard, Paramaribo, Suriname.

465. Pereira, L. 1982. Localidades de Guácharos en el estado Lara. *El Guácharo* 22:10.

466. Pérez, G., and A. Fernández-Badillo. 1988. El Gallito Azul, *Porphyrula martinica* (Aves: Rallidae), plaga del arroz en Venezuela. *Acta Cient. Venez.* 39 (Suppl. no. 1):216.

467. Peters, J. L. 1931–1986. *Checklist of Birds of the World.* Vols. 1–15. Harvard University Press, Cambridge, MA.

468. Peterson, R. T. 1980. *A Field Guide to the Birds East of the Rockies.* Houghton Mifflin, Boston, MA.

469. Phelps, K. Deery de. 1954. *Aves Venezolanas. Cien de las Más Conocidas.* Creole Petroleum Corp., Caracas.

470. Phelps, W. H. 1938. La expedición del American Museum of Natural History al Monte Auyantepui. *Bol. Soc. Venez. Cienc. Nat.* 4:251–265.

471. ———. 1941. Seventeen new birds from Venezuela. *Am. Mus. Novit.* 1153:1–17.

472. ———. 1944a. *Bulbulcus ibis* in Venezuela. *Auk* 61:656.

473. ———. 1944b. Las aves de Perijá. *Bol. Soc. Venez. Cienc. Nat.* 56:265–338.

474. ———. 1944c. Resumen de las colecciones ornithologicas hechas en Venezuela. *Bol. Soc. Venez. Cienc. Nat.* 61:325–444.

475. ———. 1961. Night migration at 4200 meters in Venezuela. *Auk* 78:93–94.

476. Phelps, W. H., and T. T. Gilliard. 1941. Seventeen new birds from Venezuela. *Am. Mus. Novit.* 1153: 1–17.

477. Phelps, W. H., and W. H. Phelps, Jr. 1948a. Notas sobre aves Venezolanas. *Bol. Soc. Venez. Cienc. Nat.* 11:189–210.

478. _____. 1948b. The discovery of the habitat of Gould's Hummingbird, *Hylonympha macrocerca*. *Auk* 65:62–66.

479. _____. 1950a. Las aves de las islas Los Roques y las Aves y descripción de un nuevo canario de mangle. *Bol. Soc. Venez. Cienc. Nat.* 13:7–30.

480. _____. 1950b. Lista de las aves de Venezuela con su distribución. Parte 2, Passeriformes. *Bol. Soc. Venez. Cienc. Nat.* 12:1–427.

481. _____. 1952. Nine new subspecies of birds from Venezuela. *Proc. Biol. Soc. Wash.* 65:46–54.

482. _____. 1954. Notes on Venezuelan birds and descriptions of six new subspecies. *Proc. Biol. Soc. Wash.* 67:103–113.

483. _____. 1955. Seven new birds from Cerro de la Neblina, Territorio Amazonas, Venezuela. *Proc. Biol. Soc. Wash.* 68:113–124.

484. _____. 1956a. Three new birds from Cerro El Teteo, Venezuela, and extensions of ranges to Venezuela and Colombia. *Proc. Biol. Soc. Wash.* 69:127–134.

485. _____. 1956b. Five new birds from Río Chiquito, Táchira, Venezuela, and two extensions of ranges from Colombia. *Proc. Biol. Soc. Wash.* 69: 157–166.

486. _____. 1958. Lista de las aves de Venezuela con su distribución. Parte 1, No Passeriformes. *Bol. Soc. Venez. Cienc. Nat.* 19:1–317.

487. _____. 1959. Las aves de la Isla La Orchila. *Bol. Soc. Venez. Cienc. Nat.* 20:252–266.

488. _____. 1962. Two new subspecies of birds from Venezuela. *Proc. Biol. Soc. Wash.* 75:199–203.

489. _____. 1963. Lista de las aves de Venezuela con su distribución. Parte 2, Passeriformes. 2d ed. *Bol. Soc. Venez. Cienc. Nat.* 24:1–479.

490. _____. 1965. Lista de las aves del Cerro de la Neblina, Venezuela y notas sobre su descubrimiento y ascenso. *Bol. Soc. Venez. Cienc. Nat.* 26:11–35.

491. Phelps, W. H., Jr. 1945. Las aves de las Islas Los Testigos, Los Frailes y La Tortuga. *Bol. Soc. Venez. Cienc. Nat.* 9:257–283.

492. _____. 1948. Las aves de la Isla La Blanquilla y de Los Morros El Fondeadero y La Horquilla del Archipiélago de Los Hermanos. *Bol. Soc. Venez. Cienc. Nat.* 11:85–118.

493. _____. 1973. Adiciones a las listas de aves de Sur America, Brazil y Venezuela y notas sobre aves Venezolanas. *Bol. Soc. Venez. Cienc. Nat.* 30: 23–40.

494. _____. 1975. Willet breeding in Los Roques archipielago, Venezuela. *Auk* 92:164–165.

495. _____. 1976. Descripción de una raza geográfica de *Crypturellus obsoletus* (Aves: Tinamidae) de los Andes de Venezuela. *Bol. Soc. Venez. Cienc. Nat.* 32:15–22.

496. _____. 1977a. Aves colectadas en las mesetas de Sarisariñama y Jaua durante tres expediciónes al Macizo de Jaua, estado Bolívar. Descripciónes de dos nuevas subspecies. *Bol. Soc. Venez. Cienc. Nat.* 33:15–42.

497. _____. 1977b. Una nueva especie y dos nuevas subespecies de aves (Psittacidae, Furnariidae) de La Sierra de Perijá cerca de la divisoria Colombo-Venezolana. *Bol. Soc. Venez. Cienc. Nat.* 33:45–53.

498. Phelps, W. H., Jr., and R. Aveledo H. 1966. A new subspecies of *Icterus icterus* and other notes on the birds of northern South America. *Am. Mus. Novit.* 2270:1–14.

499. _____. 1984. Dos nuevas subespecies de aves (Troglodytidae, Fringillidae) del Cerro Marahuaca, Territorio Amazonas, Venezuela. *Bol. Soc. Venez. Cienc. Nat.* 39:5–10.

500. _____. 1987. Cinco nuevas subespecies de aves (Rallidae, Trochilidae, Picidae, Furnariidae) y tres extensiones de distribución para Venezuela. *Bol. Soc. Venez. Cienc. Nat.* 41:7–26.

501. _____. 1988. Una nueva subespecie de aves de la familia (Trochilidae) de la Serranía Tapirapeco Territorio Amazonas, Venezuela. *Bol. Soc. Venez. Cienc. Nat.* 42:7–10.

502. Phelps, W. H., Jr., and R. Dickerman. 1980. Cuatro subespecies nuevas de aves (Furnariidae, Formicariidae) de la region de pantepui, estado Bolívar y Territorio Amazonas, Venezuela. *Bol. Soc. Venez. Cienc. Nat.* 33:139–147.

503. Phelps, W. H., Jr., and R. Meyer de Schauensee. 1994. *Una Guía de las Aves de Venezuela*. 2d ed. Ex Libris, Caracas.

504. Phillips, A. R. 1975. Semipalmated Sandpiper: identification, migrations, summer and winter ranges. *Am. Birds* 29:799–806.

505. _____. 1994. A review of the northern *Pheucticus* grosbeaks. *Bull. Br. Ornithol. Club* 114:162–170.

506. Pinto, O. 1953. Sobre a coleção Carlos Estevão de peles, ninhos e ovos das aves de Belém (Pará). *Pap. Avul. Dept. Zool. São Paulo* 11:111–222.

507. Piper, W. H. 1994. Courtship, copulation, nesting behavior and brood parasitism in the Venezuelan Stripe-backed Wren. *Condor* 96:654–671.

508. Poulsen, B. O. 1992. Range extensions of Orange-cheeked Parrot and White-browed Purpletuft in amazonian Venezuela. *Bull. Br. Ornithol. Club* 112: 276–277.

509. _____. 1985.Observations of the White-fronted Manakin (*Pipra serena*) in Suriname. *Auk* 102: 384–387.

510. Prum, R. O. 1986. The displays of the White-throated Manakin *Corapipo gutturalis* in Suriname. *Ibis* 128:91–102.

511. _____. 1988. Phylogenetic interrelationships of the barbets (Aves: Capitonidae) and toucans (Aves: Ramphastidae) based on morphology with comparisons to DNA-DNA hybridization. *Zool. J. Linnean Soc.* 92:313–343.

512. _____. 1990a. Phylogenetic analysis of the evolution of display behavior in the neotropical manakins (Aves: Pipridae). *Ethology* 84:202–231.

513. _____. 1990b. A test of the monophyly of the manakins (Pipridae) and the cotingas (Cotingidae) based on morphology. *Occas. Pap. Mus. Zool. Univ. Mich.* 723:1–44.

514. _____. 1992. Syringeal morphology, phylogeny, and evolution of the neotropical manakins (Aves: Pipridae). *Am. Mus. Novit.* 3043:1–65.

515. _____. 1994. Species status of the White-fronted Manakin, *Lepidothrix serena* (Pipridae) with comments on conservation biology. *Condor* 96:692–702.

516. Prum, R. O., and A. E. Johnson. 1987. Display behavior, foraging ecology, and systematics of the Golden-winged Manakin (*Masius chrysopterus*). *Wilson Bull.* 99:521–539.

517. Prum, R. O., J. D. Kaplan, and J. E. Pierson. 1996. Display behavior and natural history of the Yellow-crowned Manakin (*Heterocercus flavivertex*: Pipridae). *Condor* 98:722–735.

518. Prum, R. O., and W. E. Lanyon. 1989. Monophyly and phylogeny of the *Schiffornis* group (Tyrannoidea). *Condor* 91:444–461.

519. Rabenold, K. N. 1990. *Campylorhynchus* wrens: the ecology of delayed dispersal and cooperation in the Venezuelan savanna. Pp. 159–196 in *Cooperative Breeding in Birds: Long-term Studies of Ecology and Behavior* (P. B. Stacey and W. D. Koenig, eds.). Cambridge University Press, Cambridge, U.K.

520. Raffaele, H. J., J. Wiley, O. Garrido, A. Keith, and J. Raffaele. 1998. *A Guide to the Birds of the West Indies.* Princeton University Press, Princeton, NJ.

521. Ralph, C. P. 1975. Life style of *Coccyzus pumilus*, a tropical cuckoo. *Condor* 77:60–72.

522. Ramia, M. 1967. Tipos de sabanas de los llanos de Venezuela. *Bol. Soc. Venez. Cienc. Nat.* 27:264–288.

523. Ramo, C., and B. Busto. 1982. Notes on the breeding of the Chestnut-bellied Heron (*Agamia agami*) in Venezuela. *Auk* 99:784.

524. _____. 1984a. La Chenchena (*Opisthocomus hoazin*): algunos datos sobre su nidificación en Venezuela. *Biotropica* 16:330–331.

525. _____. 1984b. Nidificación de los Passeriformes en los llanos de Apure (Venezuela). *Biotropica* 16:59–68.

526. _____. 1984c. Observations at a King Vulture (*Sarcoramphus papa*) nest in Venezuela. *Auk* 105:195–196.

527. _____. 1984d. Censo aereo de corocoros (*Eudocimus ruber*) y otras aves acuaticas en Venezuela. *Bol. Soc. Venez. Cienc. Nat.* 39:65–87.

528. _____. 1988. Status of the nesting population of the Scarlet Ibis (*Eudocimus ruber*) in the Venezuelan llanos. *Colon. Waterbirds* 11:311–314.

529. Remsen, J. V., Jr. 1976. Observations of vocal mimicry in the Thick-billed Euphonia. *Wilson Bull.* 88:487–488.

530. Remsen, J. V., Jr., and G. S. Graves IV. 1995a. Distribution patterns and zoogeography of *Atlapetes* brush-finches (Emberizinae) of the Andes. *Auk* 112:210–224.

531. _____. 1995b. Distribution patterns of *Buarremon* brush-finches (Emberizinae) and interspecific competition in andean birds. *Auk* 112:225–236.

532. Remsen, J. V., Jr., M. A. Hyde, and A. Chapman. 1993. The diets of neotropical trogons, motmots, barbets and toucans. *Condor* 95:178–192.

533. Remsen, J. V., Jr., and T. A. Parker III. 1990. Seasonal distribution of the Azure Gallinule (*Porphyrula flavirostris*) with comments on vagrancy in rails and gallinules. *Wilson Bull.* 102:380–399.

534. Remsen, J. V., Jr., and S. K. Robinson. 1990. A classification scheme for foraging behavior of birds in terrestrial habitats. *Studies in Avian Biol.* 12:144–160.

535. República de Venezuela. 1976. *Mapa Ecologica.* 1:2,000,000 scale. Ministerio del Ambiente y de los Recursos Naturales Renovables, Dirección Cartografía Nacional, Caracas.

536. _____. 1995. *Mapa Fisico.* 1:2,000,000 scale. Servicio Autónomo de Geografía y Cartografía Nacional, Caracas.

537. Rettig, N. 1977. In quest of the snatcher. *Audubon Mag.* 79:26–49.

538. Ribon, R., and J. E. Simon. 1997. The nest and eggs of the Chestnut-vented Conebill *Conirostrum speciosum* (Temminck, 1824). *Ornitol. Neotrop.* 8:71–72.

539. Ricklefs, R. E. 1976. Growth rates of birds in the humid New World tropics. *Ibis* 118:179–207.

540. Ridgely, R. S., and S. J. C. Gaulin. 1980. The birds of Finca Merenberg, Huila Department, Colombia. *Condor* 82:379–391.

541. Ridgely, R. S., and P. J. Greenfield. 2001. *The Birds of Ecuador.* Vols. 1–2. Cornell University Press, Ithaca, NY.

542. Ridgely, R. S., P. Greenfield, and M. Guerrero. 1998. *Una Lista Anotada de las Aves de Ecuador Continental.* Fundación Ornithológica del Ecuador, Quito.

543. Ridgely, R. S., and J. Gwynne. 1989. *A Guide to the Birds of Panama with Costa Rica, Nicaragua, and Honduras.* 2d ed. Princeton University Press, Princeton NJ.

544. Ridgely, R. S., and G. Tudor. 1989. *The Birds of South America.* Vol. 1. University of Texas Press, Austin.

545. _____. 1994. *The Birds of South America.* Vol. 2. University of Texas Press, Austin.

546. Ridgway, R. 1912. *A Nomenclature of Colors for Ornithologists.* Little Brown, Boston, MA.

547. Ripley, S. D. 1977. *Rails of the World.* David R. Godine, Boston, MA.

548. Rivero M., A. R. 1983. *El Cardenalito de Venezuela.* Casa Propia, Imprecolor, Barquisimeto.

549. Robbins, M. B., and S. N. G. Howell. 1993. A new species of pygmy-owl (Strigidae: *Glaucidium*) from the eastern Andes. *Wilson Bull.* 107:1–6.

550. Robbins, M. B., N. Krabbe, G. H. Rosenberg, and F. Sonorza M. 1994. Geographic variation in the Andean Siskin *Carduelis spinescens* with comments on its status in Ecuador. *Ornitol. Neotrop.* 5:61–63.

551. Robbins, M. B., and T. A. Parker III. 1997. Voice and taxonomy of *Caprimulgus* (*rufus*) *otiosus* (Caprimulgidae), with a reevaluation of *Caprimulgus*

rufus subspecies. *Studies in Neotropical Ornithology Honoring Ted Parker*, Ornithol. Monogr. no. 48:601–607.

552. Robbins, M. B., and R. S. Ridgely. 1991. *Sipia rosenbergi* (Formicariidae) is a synonym of *Myrmeciza [laemostica] nigricauda*, with comments on the validity of the genus *Sipia*. *Bull. Br. Ornithol. Club* 111:11–18.

553. Robbins, M. B., and F. G. Stiles. 1999. A new species of pygmy-owl (Strigidae: *Glaucidium*) from the Pacific slope of the northern Andes. *Auk* 116: 305–315.

554. Robinson, S. K. 1986a. Social security for birds. *Nat. Hist.* Mar:38–47.

555. ———. 1986b. Competitive and mutualistic interactions among females in a neotropical oriole. *Anim. Behav.* 34:113–122.

556. ———. 1986c. The evolution of social behavior and mating systems in the blackbirds (Icterinae). Pp. 175–200 in *Ecological Aspects of Social Evolution* (D. I. Rubenstein and R. A. Wrangham, eds.). Princeton University Press, Princeton, NJ.

557. ———. 1997. Birds of a Peruvian oxbow lake: populations, resources, predation, and social behavior. *Studies in Neotropical Ornithology Honoring Ted Parker*, Ornithol. Monogr. no. 48:613–639.

558. Roca, R., and P. Gutiérrez. 1991. Fine feathered foresters. *Wild. Conserv.* 94:78–88.

559. Rodner, C., M. Lentino, and R. Restall. 2000. *Checklist of the Birds of Northern South America.* Yale University Press, New Haven, CT.

560. Rodríguez, G., and M. Lentino. 1997. Range expansion and summering of Palm Warbler *Dendroica palmarum* in Venezuela. *Bull. Br. Ornithol. Club*, 117:76–77.

561. Rojas, 1991. Biología reproductiva de la cotorra: *Amazona barbadensis* (Aves: Psittaciformes) en la Peninsula de Macanao, edo. Nueva Esparta. Lic. Biol. thesis, Universidad Central de Venezuela.

562. Rowley, J. S. 1962. Nesting of the birds of Morelos, Mexico. *Condor* 64:253–271.

563. ———. 1966. Breeding records of birds of the Sierra Madre del Sur, Oaxaca, Mexico. *Proc. West. Found. Vertebr. Zool.* 1:107–204.

564. Rudge, D. W., and R. J. Raikow. 1992. The phylogenetic relationships of the *Margarornis* assemblage (Furnariidae). *Condor* 94:760–766.

565. Ruschi, A. 1973. *Beija-flores (Hummingbirds).* Museu de Biologia "Prof. Mello Leitáo," Santa Teresa, Brazil.

566. ———. 1979. *Aves do Brasil.* Editora Rios Ltd., São Paulo.

567. Ryan, T. P., and M. Lentino R. 1995. An additional record of the Pale-footed Swallow *Notiochelidon flavipes* from Venezuela. *Bull. Br. Ornithol. Club* 111:28–29.

568. Sarmiento, G. 1984. *The Ecology of Neotropical Savannas.* Harvard University Press, Cambridge, MA.

569. Schäfer, E. 1953a. Contribution to the life history of the Swallow-Tanager. *Auk* 70:440–460.

570. ———. 1953b. Estudio bioecológico comparativo sobre algunos Cracidae del norte y centro Venezuela. *Bol. Soc. Venez. Cienc. Nat.* 15:30–63.

571. Schäfer, E., and W. H. Phelps. 1954. Las aves del Parque Nacional "Henri Pittier" (Rancho Grande) y sus funciónes ecológicas. *Bol. Soc. Venez. Cienc. Nat.* 16:1–171.

572. Schmitz-Ornés, A. 1998. Group size and nesting in the Rufous-vented Chachalaca (*Ortalis ruficauda*) in north and central Venezuela. *Ornitol. Neotrop.* 9:177–184.

573. Schönwetter, M. 1963, 1974. *Handbuch der Oologie.* Vols. 1–2. Akademie-Verlag, Berlin.

574. Schuchmann, K.-L. 1987. The display of the Booted Racket-tailed Hummingbird *Ocreatus underwoodii*, with notes on the systematic position of the genus. *Bull. Br. Ornithol. Club* 107:20–22.

575. Schuchmann, K.-L., and K. Duffner. 1993. Geographic variation and speciation patterns in the andean hummingbird genus *Aglaicercus* Zimmer 1930. *Mitt. Zool. Mus. Berl.* 69 *Suppl.: Ann. Orn.* 17: 75–92.

576. Schulenberg, T. S. 1983. Foraging behavior, ecomorphology, and systematics of some antshrikes (Formicariidae: *Thamnomanes*). *Wilson Bull.* 95: 505–521.

577. Schwartz, P. 1957. Observaciónes sobre *Grallaricula ferrugineipectus*. *Bol. Soc. Venez. Cienc. Nat.* 18:42–62.

578. ———. 1964a. The Northern Waterthrush in Venezuela. *Living Bird* 3:169–184.

579. ———. 1964b. *Birds Songs from the Tropics.* Vibra El Llano. Vol. 2. LP record. Institut. Neotropical, Caracas.

580. ———. 1968. Notes on two neotropical nightjars, *Caprimulgus anthonyi* and *C. parvulus*. *Condor* 70: 223–227.

581. ———. 1972a. On the taxonomic rank of the Yellow-billed Toucanet. *Bol. Soc. Venez. Cienc. Nat.* 29:459–476.

582. ———. 1972b. *Micrastur gilvicollis*, a valid species sympatric with *M. ruficollis* in Amazonia. *Condor* 74:399–415.

583. ———. 1975. Solved and unsolved problems in the *Sporophila lineola bouvronides* complex. *Ann. Carnegie Mus.* 45:277–285.

584. ———. 1977. Some clarifications about *Ramphastos "aurantiirostris."* *Auk* 94:775–777.

585. Schwartz, P., and M. Lentino. 1984a. Relaciones de los tinamidos Venezolanos del groupo *Crypturellus noctivagus* indicado por su voz (Aves: Tinamidae). Serie Informes Científicos DGSIIA/IC/23, Ministerio del Ambiente y de los Recursos Naturales Renovables, Caracas.

586. ———. 1984b. Estudio sobre la posición sistematica de *Myrmornis torquata* (Aves: Formicariidae). Serie Informes Científicos DGSIIA/IC/23, Ministerio del Ambiente y de los Recursos Naturales Renovables, Caracas.

587. Schwartz, P., and D. W. Snow. 1978. Display and related behavior of the Wire-tailed Manakin. *Living Bird* 17:51–78.

588. Schwerdtfeger, W., ed. 1976. *World Survey of Climatology*. Vol. 12. Elsevier Scientific Publ., Amsterdam.

589. Sclater, P. L., and O. Salvin. 1879. On the birds collected by T. K. Salmon in the state of Antioquia, United States of Colombia. *Proc. Zool. Soc. London* 1879:486–550.

590. Scott, D. A., and M. Carbonell, eds. 1986. *A Directory of Neotropical Wetlands*. International Union Conserv. Nature and Natural Resources, Cambridge, U.K.

591. Seavy, N., and R. P. Gerhardt. 1998. Breeding biology and nestling diet of the Great Black-Hawk. *J. Raptor Res.* 32:175–177.

592. Seavy, N., M. Schulze, D. Whitacre, and M. Vasquez. 1998. Breeding biology and behavior of the Plumbeous Kite. *Wilson Bull.* 110:77–85.

593. Seutin, G., J. Brawn, R. E. Ricklefs, and E. Bermingham. 1993. Genetic distance among populations of a tropical passerine, the Streaked Saltator (*Saltator albicollis*). *Auk* 110:117–126.

594. Seutin, G., N. K. Klein, R. E. Ricklefs, and E. Bermingham. 1994. Historical biogeography of the Bananaquit (*Coereba flaveola*) in the Caribbean region: a mitochondrial DNA assessment. *Evolution* 48:1041–1061.

595. Sharpe, C. J., D. Ascanio-Echeverría, and R. Restell. 1997. Three species of exotic passerine in Venezuela. *Cotinga* 7:43–44.

596. Sharpe, C. J., D. Ascanio-Echeverría, and G. A. Rodríguez. 2001. Further range extensions and noteworthy records for Venezuelan birds. *Bull. Br. Ornithol. Club* 121:50–62.

597. Sheldon, F., and F. B. Gill. 1996. A reconsideration of songbird phylogeny, with emphasis on the evolution of titmice and the sylvioid relatives. *Syst. Biol.* 45:473–495.

598. Sheldon, F., and D. Winkler. 1993. Intergeneric phylogenetic relationships of swallows estimated by DNA-DNA hybridization. *Auk* 110:798–824.

599. Sherman, P. T. 1995a. Breeding biology of White-winged Trumpeters (*Psophia leucoptera*) in Peru. *Auk* 112:285–295.

600. ———. 1995b. Social organizationn of cooperatively polyandrous White-winged Trumpeters (*Psophia leucoptera*). *Auk* 112:296–309.

601. Short, L. L., Jr. 1970. Notes on the habits of some Argentine and Peruvian woodpeckers. *Am. Mus. Novit.* 2413:1–37.

602. ———. 1973. The Green-barred Flicker and Golden-green Woodpecker of South America. *Living Bird* 12:51–54.

603. ———. 1982. *Woodpeckers of the World*. Delaware Mus. Nat. Hist. Monogr. 4.

604. Sibley, C. G., and J. Ahlquist. 1990. *Phylogeny and Classification of Birds: A Study in Molecular Evolution*. Yale University Press, New Haven, CT.

605. Sibley, C. G., S. M. Lanyon, and J. E. Ahlquist. 1984. The relationships of the Sharpbill (*Oxyruncus cristatus*). *Condor* 86:48–52.

606. Sibley, C. G., and B. L. Monroe, Jr. 1990. *Distribution and Taxonomy of Birds of the World*. Yale University Press, New Haven, CT.

607. ———. 1993. *A Supplement to Distribution and Taxonomy of Birds of the World*. Yale University Press, New Haven, CT.

608. Sick, H. 1951. An egg of the Umbrellabird. *Wilson Bull.* 63:338–339.

609. ———. 1963. Hybridization in certain Brazilian Fringillidae (*Sporophila* and *Oryzoborus*). *Proc. 13th Intern. Ornithol. Congr.*, pp. 161–170.

610. ———. 1967. Courtship behavior in manakins (Pipridae), a review. *Living Bird* 6:5–22.

611. ———. 1993. *Birds in Brazil: A Natural History*. Princeton University Press, Princeton, NJ.

612. Silva, J. L. 1999. Notes about the distribution of *Pauxi pauxi* and *Aburria aburri* in Venezuela. *Wilson Bull.* 111:564–569.

613. Silva, J. L., and S. D. Strahl. 1991. Human impact on chachalacas, guans and curassows (Galliformes: Cracidae) in Venezuela. Pp. 37–52 in *Neotropical Wildlife Use and Conservation* (J. G. Robinson and K. H. Redford, eds.). University of Chicago Press, Chicago, IL.

614. Skutch, A. F. 1945a. Incubation and nesting periods of Central American birds. *Auk* 62: 8–37.

615. ———. 1945b. On the habits and nest of the antthrush *Formicarius analis*. *Wilson Bull.* 57:122–128.

616. ———. 1946. Life histories of two Panamanian antbirds. *Condor* 48:16–28.

617. ———. 1947a. A nest of the Sunbittern in Costa Rica. *Wilson Bull.* 59:38.

618. ———. 1947b. Life history of the Marbled Wood-Quail. *Condor* 49:217–232.

619. ———. 1948a. Life history of the Olivaceous Piculet and related forms (*Picumnus aurifrons*). *Ibis* 90:433–449.

620. ———. 1948b. Life history notes on puffbirds. *Wilson Bull.* 60:81–97.

621. ———. 1949. Life history of the Ruddy Quail-Dove. *Condor* 51:3–19.

622. ———. 1950. The nesting seasons of Central American birds in relation to climate and food supply. *Ibis* 92:185–222.

623. ———. 1951. Life history of the Boat-billed Flycatcher. *Auk* 68:30–49.

624. ———. 1954. *Life Histories of Central American Birds*. Vol. 1. Pac. Coast Avifauna no. 31.

625. ———. 1956. A nesting of the Collared Trogon. *Auk* 73:354–366.

626. ———. 1957. Life history of the Amazon Kingfisher. *Condor* 59:217–229.

627. ———. 1958a. Roosting and nesting of aracari toucans. *Condor* 60:201–219.

628. ———. 1958b. Life history of the White-whiskered Softwing (*Malacoptila panamensis*). *Ibis* 100:209–231.

629. ———. 1958c. Life history of the Violet-headed Hummingbird. *Wilson Bull.* 70:5–19.

630. ———. 1959a. Life history of the Black-throated Trogon. *Wilson. Bull.* 71:5–18.

631. ———. 1959b. Life history of the Blue Ground-Dove. *Condor* 61:65–74.

632. ———. 1959c. Life history of the Groove-billed Ani. *Auk* 76:281–317.

633. ———. 1960. *Life Histories of Central American Birds.* Vol. 2. Pac. Coast Avifauna no. 34.

634. ———. 1962a. Life history of the White-tailed Trogon (*Trogon viridis*). *Ibis* 104:301–313.

635. ———. 1962b. Life histories of honeycreepers. *Condor* 64:92–116.

636. ———. 1962c. On the habits of the Queo (*Rhodinocichla rosea*). *Auk* 79:633–639.

637. ———. 1963a. Life history of the Little Tinamou. *Condor* 65:224–231.

638. ———. 1963b. Life history of the Rufous-tailed Jacamar (*Galbula ruficauda*) in Costa Rica. *Ibis* 105:354–368.

639. ———. 1964a. Life histories of hermit hummingbirds. *Auk* 81:5–25.

640. ———. 1964b. Life histories of Central American pigeons. *Wilson Bull.* 76:211–247.

641. ———. 1964c. Life history of the Blue Diademed (Crowned) Motmot. *Ibis* 106:321–332.

642. ———. 1965. Life history notes on two tropical American kites. *Condor* 67:235–246.

643. ———. 1966. Life histories of three tropical cuckoos. *Wilson Bull.* 78:139–165.

644. ———. 1967a. *Life Histories of Central American Highland Birds.* Publ. Nuttall Ornithol. Club no. 7.

645. ———. 1967b. Life history notes on the Orioleblackbird (*Gymnomystax mexicanus*) in Venezuela. *El Hornero* 10:379–388.

646. ———. 1968. The nesting of some Venezuelan birds. *Condor* 70:66–82.

647. ———. 1969a. *Life Histories of Central American Birds.* Vol. 3. Pac. Coast Avifauna no. 35.

648. ———. 1969b. A study of the Rufous-fronted Thornbird and associated birds. Part I. Life history of the Rufous-fronted Thornbird. *Wilson Bull.* 81:5–43.

649. ———. 1969c. A study of the Rufous-fronted Thornbird and associated birds. Part II. Birds which breed in thornbirds' nests. *Wilson Bull.* 81:123–139.

650. ———. 1970. Life history of the Common Potoo. *Living Bird* 9:265–280.

651. ———. 1972. *Studies of Tropical American Birds.* Publ. Nuttall Ornithol. Club no. 10.

652. ———. 1973. *The Life of the Hummingbird.* Crown Publ., New York.

653. ———. 1981. *New Studies of Tropical American Birds.* Publ. Nuttall Ornithol. Club no. 19.

654. Slud, P. 1964. The birds of Costa Rica: distribution and ecology. *Bull. Am. Mus. Nat. Hist.* 128:1–430.

655. Smith, N. G. 1968. On the advantage of being parasitized. *Nature* 219:690–694.

656. Smith, W. J. 1962. The nest of *Pitangus lictor. Auk* 79:108–111.

657. ———. 1971. Behavioral characteristics of serpophagine tyrannids. *Condor* 73:259–286.

658. Smith, W. J., and F. Vuilleumier. 1971. Evolutionary relationships of some South American ground-tyrants. *Bull. Mus. Comp. Zool.* 141:181–232.

659. Smithe, F. B. 1975. *Naturalist's Color Guide and Supplement.* American Museum of Natural History, New York.

660. Snethlage, E. 1935. Beiträge zur Brutbiologie brasilianische Vögel. *J. Ornithol.* 83:1–24; 532–562.

661. Snow, B. K. 1970. A field study of the Bearded Bellbird in Trinidad. *Ibis* 112:299–329.

662. ———. 1972. A field study of the Calfbird *Perissocephalus tricolor. Ibis*:114:139–162.

663. ———. 1973a. The behavior and ecology of hermit hummingbirds in the Kanaku Mountains, Guyana. *Wilson Bull.* 85:163–177.

664. ———. 1973b. Social organization of the Hairy Hermit (*Glaucis hirsuta*). *Ardea* 61:94–105.

665. ———. 1974. Lek behavior and breeding of the Guy's Hermit Hummingbird *Phaethornis guy. Ibis* 116:278–297.

666. ———. 1979. The Oilbirds of Los Tayos. *Wilson Bull.* 91:457–461.

667. ———. 1980. Nest and territoriality of a female Tyrian Metaltail. *Wilson Bull.* 92:508–509.

668. Snow, B. K., and M. Gochfeld. 1977. Field notes on the nests of the Green-fronted Lancebill *Doryfera ludoviciae* and the Blue-fronted Lancebill *Doryfera johannae. Bull. Br. Ornithol. Club* 97:121–125.

669. Snow, B. K., and D. W. Snow. 1971. The feeding ecology of tanagers and honeycreepers in Trinidad. *Auk* 88:291–322.

670. ———. 1974. Breeding of the Green-bellied Hummingbird. *Auk* 91:626.

671. ———. 1979. The Ochre-bellied Flycatcher and the evolution of lek behavior. *Condor* 81:286–292.

672. Snow, D. W. 1961a. Natural history of the Oilbird *Steatornis caripensis* in Trinidad, W. I. General behavior and breeding habits. *Zoologica* 46:27–47.

673. ———. 1961b. The displays of the manakins *Pipra pipra* and *Tyranneutes virescens. Ibis* 103:110–113.

674. ———. 1962a. A field study of the Black and white Manakin, *Manacus manacus*, in Trinidad. *Zoologica* 47:65–104.

675. ———. 1962b. A field study of the Golden-headed Manakin *Pipra erythrocephala* in Trinidad. *Zoologica* 47:183–198.

676. ———. 1962c. Notes on the biology of some Trinidad swifts. *Zoologica* 47:129–139.

677. ———. 1962d. Natural history of the Oilbird *Steatornis caripensis* in Trinidad W. I. II. Population, breeding, ecology and food. *Zoologica* 47:199–221.

678. ———. 1963. The display of the Blue-backed Manakin *Chiroxiphia pareola* in Tobago, West Indies. *Zoologica* 48:167–176.

679. ———. 1964. Beeding seasons and annual cycles of Trinidad land-birds. *Zoologica* 49:1–39.

680. ———. 1968. The singing assemblies of Little Hermits. *Living Bird* 7:47–55.

681. ———. 1971a. Observations on the Purple-throated Fruit-Crow in Guyana. *Living Bird* 10:5–17.

682. ———. 1971b. Display of the Pompadour Cotinga *Xipholena punicea. Ibis* 113:102–104.

683. ———. 1973. The classification of the Cotingidae. *Breviora* 409:1–27.

684. ———. 1975a. The classification of the manakins. *Bull. Br. Ornithol. Club* 95:20–27.

685. ———. 1975b. *Laniisoma elegans* in Peru. *Auk* 92: 583–584.

686. ———. 1976a. The relationship between climate and annual cycles in the Cotingidae. *Ibis* 118: 366–401.

687. ———. 1976b. *The Web of Adaptation: Bird Studies in the American Tropics.* Quadrangle, New York.

688. ———. 1977. The display of the Scarlet-horned Manakin, *Pipra coronuta. Bull. Br. Ornithol. Club* 97:23–27.

689. ———. 1982. *The Cotingas.* Cornell University Press, Ithaca, NY.

690. Snow, D. W., and C. T. Collins. 1962. Social breeding behavior of the Mexican Tanager. *Condor* 64: 161.

691. Snow, D. W., and B. K. Snow. 1963. Breeding and annual cycle of three Trinidad thrushes. *Wilson Bull.* 75:27–41.

692. ———. 1980. Relationships between hummingbirds and flowers in the Andes of Colombia. *Bull. Br. Mus. Nat. Hist.* 38:105–139.

693. ———. 1992. Display of the Golden-winged Manakin *Masius chrysopterus. Bull. Br. Ornithol. Club* 112:264–270.

694. Snyder, D. E. 1966. *The Birds of Guyana.* Peabody Museum, Salem, MA.

695. Stephens, L., and M. A. Traylor, Jr. 1985. *Ornithological Gazetteer of the Guianas.* Museum of Comparative Zoology, Cambridge, MA.

696. Steyermark, J. A., and O. Huber. 1978. *Flora del Avila.* Sociedad Venezolana Ciencias Naturales y Ministerio del Ambiente y de los Recursos Naturales Renovables, Caracas.

697. Stiles, F. G. 1975. Ecology, flowering phenology, and hummingbird pollination of some Costa Rican *Heliconia* species. *Ecology* 56:285–301.

698. ———. 1978. Possible specialization for hummingbird-hunting in the Tiny Hawk. *Auk* 95:550–553.

699. ———. 1981. Notes on the Uniform Crake in Costa Rica. *Wilson Bull.* 93:107–108.

700. ———. 1983. Dos nuevas aves para el estado Apure. *Ecol. Conserv. Ornitol. Latinoamer.* 1:8.

701. ———. 1984. Inventario preliminar de las aves de las selvas nubladas de Monte Zerpa y la Mucuy, Mérida, Venezuela. *Bol. Soc. Venez. Cienc. Nat.* 39:11–23.

702. ———. 1995. Distribución y variación en el Hermitaño Carinegro (*Phaethornis anthophilus*) en Colombia. *Caldasia* 18:119–149.

703. ———. 1996a. A new species of Emerald Hummingbird (Trochilidae, *Chlorostilbon*) from the Sierra de Chiribiquete, southeastern Colombia, with a review of the *C. mellisugus* complex. *Wilson Bull.* 108:1–27.

704. ———. 1996b. When black plus white equals gray: the nature of variation in the Variable Seedeater complex (Emberizinae: *Sporophila*). *Ornitol. Neotrop.* 7:75–107.

705. Stiles, F. G., and D. J. Levey. 1988. The Graybreasted Crake (*Laterallus exilis*) in Costa Rica: vocalizations, distribution, and interactions with White-throated Crakes (*L. albigularis*). *Condor* 90: 607–612.

706. Stiles, F. G., and A. F. Skutch. 1989. *A Guide to the Birds of Costa Rica.* Cornell University Press, Ithaca, NY.

707. Stiles, F. G., and S. Smith. 1980. Notes on bird distribution in Costa Rica. *Brenesia* 17:137–156.

708. Stiles, F. G., and B. Whitney. 1983. Notes on the behavior of the Costa Rican Sharpbill (*Oxyruncus cristatus frater*). *Auk* 100:117–125.

709. Stone, W. 1918. Birds of the Panama Canal Zone, with special reference to a collection made by Lindsey L. Jewell. *Proc. Acad. Nat. Sci. Phila.* 70: 239–280.

710. Stotz, D. F. 1990. The taxonomic status of *Phyllomyias reiseri. Bull. Br. Ornithol. Club* 110:184–187.

711. ———. 1992. Specific status and nomenclature of *Hemitriccus minimus* and *Hemitriccus aenigma. Auk* 109:916–917.

712. Stotz, D. F., J. W. Fitzpatrick, T. A. Parker III, and D. K. Moskovitz. 1996. *Neotropical Birds: Ecology and Conservation.* University of Chicago Press, Chicago, IL.

713. Stouffer, P. C. 1997. Interspecific aggression in *Formicarius* antthrushes? The view from central amazonian Brazil. *Auk* 114:780–785.

714. Strahl, S. D. 1985. Folivoría, dieta, y estrategias alimenticias de la Chenchena (*Opisthocomus hoazin*) en los llanos Venezuela. *Acta Cient. Venez.* 36 (Suppl. no. 1):32.

715. ———. 1988. The social organization and behaviour of the Hoatzin *Opistocomus hoazin* in central Venezuela. *Ibis* 130:483–502.

716. Strahl, S. D., P. A. Desenne, J. L. Jiménez, and I. R. Goldstein. 1991. Behavior and biology of the Hawk-headed Parrot, *Deroptyus accipitrinus*, in southern Venezuela. *Condor* 93:177–180.

717. Strahl, S. D., and A. Grajal. 1991. Conservation of large avian frugivores and the management of neotropical protected areas. *Oryx* 25:50–55.

718. Strahl, S. D., J. L. Silva, and R. Buchholz. 1991. Seasonal habitat use and mating systems of the Yellow-knobbed Curassow, *Crax daubentoni*, and the Rufous-vented Chachalaca, *Ortalis ruficauda*, in central Venezuela. *Acta XX Congr. Int. Ornithol.*

719. ———. 1997. Seasonal habitat use, group behavior, and an apparent polygamous mating system in the Yellow-knobbed Curassow, *Crax daubentoni*. In *The Cracidae: Their Biology and Conservation* (S. D. Strahl, D. Beaujon, D. Brooks, A. Begazo, G. Sedaghatkish, and F. Olmos, eds.). Hancock House, Blaine, WA.

720. Strauch, J. F., Jr. 1975. Observations at a nest of the Black-and-white Hawk-Eagle. *Condor* 77:512.

721. Studer, A., and D. M. Texeira. 1994. Notes on the Buff-fronted Owl *Aegolius harrisii* in Brazil. *Bull. Br. Ornithol. Club* 111:62–63.

722. Stutchbury, B. J., P. R. Martin, and E. S. Morton. 1996. Nesting behavior of the Slate-colored Seedeater (*Sporophila schistacea*) in Panama. *Ornitol. Neotrop.* 7:63–65.

723. Swales, B. H. 1923. *Vermivora leucobronchialis* in Venezuela. *Auk* 40:132–133.

724. Swann, H. K. 1921. Notes on a collection of Accipitres from the Mérida district, w Venezuela. *Auk* 38:357–364.

725. Taczanowski, L. 1884–1886. *Ornithologie du Pérou.* 3 vols. R. Friedlander, Berlin.

726. Tamplin, J. W., J. W. Demastes, and J. V. Remsen, Jr. 1993. Biochemical and morphometric relationships among some members of the Cardinalinae. *Wilson Bull.* 105:93–113.

727. Tannenbaum, B., and P. H. Wrege. 1984a. Breeding synchrony and nesting mortality in Oilbirds breeding in the Cueva del Guácharo. *Bol. Soc. Venez. Cienc. Nat.* 39:121–137.

728. Tashian, R. E. 1957. Nesting behavior of the Crested Oropendola (*Psarocholius decumanus*) in northern Trinidad, British West Indies. *Zoologica* 42:87–98.

729. Taylor, B. 1998. *Rails: A Guide to the Rails, Crakes, Gallinules and Coots of the World.* Pica Press, Sussex, U.K.

730. Teixeira, D. M., and M. E. N. Puga. 1984. Notes on *Coturnicops notata. Condor* 86:342–343.

731. Théry, M. 1990. Display repertoire and social organization of the White-fronted and White-throated manakins. *Wilson Bull.* 102:123–130.

732. Thomas, B. T. 1978. The Dwarf Cuckoo in Venezuela. *Condor* 80:105–106.

733. _____. 1979a. Plumage succession of nestling Maguari Storks. *Bol. Soc. Venez. Cienc. Nat.* 34:239–341.

734. _____. 1979b. The birds of a ranch in the Venezuelan llanos. Pp. 213–232 in *Vertebrate Ecology in the Northern Neotropics* (J. F. Eisenberg, ed.). Smithsonian Inst. Press, Washington, D.C.

735. _____. 1979c. Introduction to the behavior and breeding of the White-bearded Flycatcher *Conopias inornata. Auk:* 96:767–775.

736. _____. 1981. Jabiru nest, nest building, and quintuplets. *Condor* 83:84–85.

737. _____. 1982. Weights of some Venezuelan birds. *Bull. Br. Ornithol. Club* 102:48–52.

738. _____. 1983. The Plain-fronted Thornbird: nest construction, material choice, and nest defense behavior. *Wilson Bull.* 95:106–117.

739. _____. 1987. Spring shorebird migration through central Venezuela. *Wilson Bull.* 99:571–578.

740. _____. 1990. Additional weights of Venezuelan birds. *Bull. Br. Ornithol. Club* 110:48–51.

741. _____. 1993. Birds of a northern Venezuelan secondary-scrub habitat. *Bull. Br. Ornithol. Club* 113: 9–17.

742. _____. 1994. Blue-tailed Emerald Hummingbird (*Chlorostilbon mellisugus*) nesting and nestling development. *Ornitol. Neotrop.* 5:57–60.

743. _____. 1996. Notes on the distribution, body mass, foods and vocal mimicry of the Gray Seedeater (*Sporophila intermedia*). *Ornitol. Neotrop.* 7: 165–169.

744. Thomas, B. T., and J. Ingels. 1995. On the type specimen, type locality, distribution and clutch size of the Sunbittern *Eurypyga helias. Bull. Br. Ornithol. Club* 115:226–228.

745. Thomas, B. T., and S. D. Strahl. 1990. Nesting behavior of Sunbitterns (*Eurypyga helias*) in Venezuela. *Condor* 92:576–581.

746. Thorstrom, R. 1997. A description of nests and behavior of the Gray-headed Kite. *Wilson Bull.* 109:173–177.

747. Thorstrom, R., J. D. Ramos, and J. M. Castillo. 2000. Breeding biology and behavior of the Collared Forest-Falcon (*Micrastur semitorquatus*) in Guatemala. *Ornitol. Neotrop.* 11:1–12.

748. Thorstrom, R., J. D. Ramos, and C. M. Morales. 2000. Breeding biology of Barred Forest-Falcons (*Micrastur ruficollis*) in northeastern Guatemala. *Auk* 117:781–786.

749. Thorstrom, R., C. W. Turley, F. G. Ramirez, and B. A. Gilroy. 1990. Descriptions of nests, eggs and young of the Barred Forest-Falcon (*Micrastur ruficollis*) and of the Collared Forest-Falcon (*M. semitorquatus*). *Condor* 92:237–239.

750. Todd, W. E., and M. A. Carriker, Jr. 1922. The birds of the Santa Marta region of Colombia: a study in altitudinal distribution. *Ann. Carnegie Mus.* 14:3–582.

751. Tostain, O., and J. L. Dujardin. 1988. Nesting of the Wing-banded Antbird and the Thrush-like Antpitta in French Guiana. *Condor* 90:236–239.

752. Tostain, O., J. L. Dujardin, Ch. Erard, and J.-M. Thiollay. 1992. *Oiseaux de Guyane.* Société d'Études Ornithologiques, Maxéville, France.

753. Trail, P. 1985a. A lek's icon. The courtship display of a Guianan Cock-of-the-rock. *Am. Birds* 39: 235–240.

754. _____. 1985b. Territoriality and dominance in the lek-breeding Guianan Cock-of-the-rock. *Nat. Geogr. Res.* 1:112–123.

755. _____. 1987. Predation and antipredation behavior at Guianan Cock-of-the-rock leks. *Auk* 104: 496–507.

756. Trail, P. W., and P. Donahue. 1991. Notes on the behavior and ecology of the red-cotingas (Cotingidae: *Phoenicircus*). *Wilson Bull.* 103:539–551.

757. Traylor, M. A., Jr. 1977. A classification of the tyrant flycatchers (Tyrannidae). *Bull. Mus. Comp. Zool.* 148:129–184.

758. _____. 1982. Notes on tyrant flycatchers (Aves: Tyrannidae). *Fieldiana, Zool.*, new ser. 13:1–22.

759. _____. 1985. Species limits in the *Ochthoeca diadema* species-group (Tyrannidae). *Neotropical Ornithology*, Ornithol. Monogr. no. 36:430–442.

760. Traylor, M. A., Jr., and J. W. Fitzpatrick. 1982. A survey of the tyrant flycatchers. *Living Bird* 19: 7–50.

761. Troth, R. G. 1979. Vegetational types on a ranch in the central llanos of Venezuela. Pp. 17–30 in *Vertebrate Ecology in the Northern Neotropics* (J. F. Eisenberg, ed.). Smithsonian Inst. Press, Washington, D.C.

762. Turner, A. 1983. Food selection and the timing of breeding of the Blue-and-white Swallow *Notiochelidon cyanoleuca* in Venezuela. *Ibis* 125:450–462.

763. Turner, A., and C. Rose. 1989. *A Handbook to the Swallows and Martins of the World.* Christopher Helm, London.

764. Tye, H., and A. Tye. 1992. First description of the

eggs and nest of the Golden-winged Sparrow *Arremon schlegeli*. *Ornitol. Neotrop.* 3:71.

765. Urbina, L., ed. 1992. *Areas Naturales Protegidas de Venezuela*. Serie Aspectos Conceptuales y Metodológicos, DGSPOA/ACM/01.

766. U. S. Board on Geographical Names. 1961. *Venezuela. Gazetteer No. 56*. Office of Geography, Dept. of Interior, Washington, D.C.

767. Vareschi, V. 1970. *Flora de Los Paramos de Venezuela*. Universidad de Los Andes, Mérida.

768. Vaurie, C. 1971. *Classification of the Ovenbirds (Furnariidae)*. Witherby, London.

769. ———. 1980. Taxonomy and geographical distribution of the Furnariidae (Aves, Passeriformes). *Bull. Am. Mus. Nat. Hist.* 166:1–357.

770. Vaurie, C., and P. Schwartz. 1972. Morphology and vocalizations of *Synallaxis unirufa* and *Synallaxis castanea* (Furnariidae, Aves), with comments on other *Synallaxis*. *Am. Mus. Novit.* 2483:1–13.

771. Vielliard, J. 1989. Uma nova espécie de *Glaucidium* (Aves, Strigidae) da Amazônia. *Rev. Bras. Zool.* 6:685–693.

772. Voous, K. H. 1964. Wood owls of the genus *Strix* and *Ciccaba*. *Zool. Meded.* 39:471–478.

773. ———. 1983. *Birds of the Netherlands Antilles*. De Walburg Press, Curaçao.

774. ———. 1986. Striated or Green herons in the south Caribbean islands? *Aus. Naturhist. Mus. Wien* 88/89:101–106.

775. Vuilleumire, F. 1969a. Systematics and evolution in *Diglossa* (Aves: Coerebidae). *Am. Mus. Novit.* 2381:1–44.

776. ———. 1969b. Field notes on some birds from the Bolivian Andes. *Ibis* 111:599–608.

777. ———. 1975. Zoogeography of andean birds: two major barriers; speciation and taxonomy of the *Diglossa carbonaria* superspecies. *Natl. Geogr. Res.* 16:713–731.

778. Vuilleumire, F., and D. N. Ewert. 1978. The distribution of birds in Venezuelan páramos. *Bull. Am. Mus. Nat. Hist.* 162:51–90.

779. Wallace, G. J. 1965. Studies on neotropical thrushes in Colombia. *Publ. Mus. Mich. State Univ. Biol. Ser.* 3:1–47.

780. Wattel, J. 1973. *Geographical differentiation in the genus Accipter*. *Publ. Nuttall Ornithol. Club no. 13*.

781. Wege, D. C., and A. J. Long. 1995. *Key Areas for Threatened Birds in the Neotropics*. BirdLife Conserv. Ser. no. 5. Smithsonian Inst. Press., Washington, D.C.

782. Weller, A. A., and K.-L. Schuchmann. 1997. The hybrid origin of a Venezuelan trochilid, *Amazilia distans* Wetmore & Phelps 1956. *Ornitol. Neotrop.* 8:107–112.

783. Werf, E. A. Van der, and S. D. Strahl. 1990. Effects of unit size and territory defense on communal nest care in the Hoatzin (*Opisthocomus hoazin*). *Auk* 107:626–628.

784. Werf, E. A. Van der, J. S. Zaneveld, and K. H. Voous. 1958. Field observations on the birds of the Islas Las Aves in the southern Caribbean Sea. *Ardea* 46:37–58.

785. West, S. 1976. First description of the eggs of the Cinnamon Becard. *Condor* 78:422–423.

786. Westcott, D. A., and J. N. M. Smith. 1994. Behavior and social organization during the breeding season in *Mionectes oleagineus*, a lekking flycatcher. *Condor* 96:672–683.

787. Wetmore, A. 1939. Observations on the birds of northern Venezuela. *Proc. U.S. Nat. Mus.* 87:173–260.

788. ———. 1965. *Birds of the Republic of Panama. Part 1. Tinamidae (Tinamous) to Rhynchopidae (Skimmers)*. Smithsonian Inst. Press, Washington, D.C.

789. ———. 1968. *Birds of the Republic of Panama. Part 2. Columbidae (Pigeons) to Picidae (Woodpeckers)*. Smithsonian Inst. Press, Washington, D.C.

790. ———. 1972. *Birds of the Republic of Panama. Part 3. Passeriformes: Dendrocolaptidae (Woodcreepers) to Oxyruncidae (Sharpbills)*. Smithsonian Inst. Press, Washington, D.C.

791. Wetmore, A., R. Pasquier, and S. Olson. 1984. *Birds of the Republic of Panama. Part 4. Passeriformes: Suborder Passers, Hirundinidae (Swallows) to Fringillidae (Finches)*. Smithsonian Inst. Press, Washington, D.C.

792. Wetmore, A., and W. H. Phelps. 1956. Further additions to the list of birds of Venezuela. *Proc. Biol. Soc. Wash.* 69:1–12.

793. Whitney, B. M. 1992. A nest and egg of the Rufous Antpitta in Ecuador. *Wilson Bull.* 104:759–760.

794. ———. 1994. A new *Scytalopus* tapaculo (Rhinocryptidae) from Bolivia, with notes on other Bolivian members of the genus and the *magellanicus* complex. *Wilson Bull.* 106:585–614.

795. Whittaker, A. 1993. Notes on the behaviour of the Crimson Fruitcrow *Haematoderus militaris* near Manaus, Brazil, with the first nesting record for this species. *Bull. Br. Ornithol. Club* 113:93–96.

796. ———. 1995. Range extensions and nesting of the Glossy-backed Becard *Pachyramphus surinamus* in central amazonian Brazil. *Bull. Br. Ornithol. Club* 115:45–47.

797. ———. 1998. Observations on the behavior, vocalizations and distribution of the Glossy-backed Beard (*Pachyramphus surinamus*), a poorly-known canopy inhabitant of amazonian rainforests. *Ararajuba* 6:37–41.

798. ———. 2001. Notes on the poorly-known Buckley's Forest-Falcon (*Micrastur buckleyi*) including voice, range and the first Brazilian records. *Bull. Brit. Ornithol. Club* 121:198–207.

799. Wilczynski, W., M. J. Ryan, and E. A. Brenowitz. 1989. The display of the Blue-black Grassquit: the acoustic advantage of getting high. *Ethology* 80:218–222.

800. Wiley, R. H. 1971. Song groups in a singing assembly of Little Hermits. *Condor* 73:28–35.

801. Willard, D. E., M. S. Foster, G. F. Barrowclough, R. W. Dickerman, P. F. Cannell, S. L. Coats, J. L. Cracraft, and J. P. O'Neill. 1991. The birds of Cerro de la Neblina, Territorio Federal Ama-

zonas, Venezuela. *Fieldiana, Zool.*, new ser. 65: 1–80.

802. Willis, E. O. 1961. A study of nesting ant-tanagers in British Honduras. *Condor* 63:479–503.

803. ———. 1966. Interspecific competition and the foraging behavior of the Plain-brown Woodcreeper. *Ecology* 74:667–672.

804. ———. 1967. The behavior of Bicolored Antbirds. *Univ. Calif. Publ. Zool.* 79:1–132.

805. ———. 1972a. The behavior of the Plain-brown Woodcreeper *Dendrocincla fuliginosa. Wilson Bull.* 81:377–420.

806. ———. 1972b. The behavior of Spotted Antbirds. Ornithol. Monogr. no. 10.

807. ———. 1972c. Breeding of the White-plumed Antbird (*Pithys albifrons*). *Auk* 89:192.

808. ———. 1977. Lista preliminar das aves da parte noroeste e áreas vizinhas da Reserva Ducke, Amazonas, Brasil. *Rev. Bras. Biol.* 37:585–601.

809. ———. 1979. Behavior and ecology of two forms of White-chinned Woodcreepeers (*Dendrocincla merula*, Dendrocolaptidae) in Amazonia. *Pap. Avul. Dept. Zool. São Paulo* 33:27–66.

810. ———. 1982a. The behavior of Red-billed Woodcreepers (*Hylexetastes perrotii*). *Rev. Bras. Biol.* 42:655–666.

811. ———. 1982b. The behavior of Scale-backed Antbirds. *Wilson Bull* 94:447–462.

812. ———. 1982c. The behavior of Black-banded Woodcreepers (*Dendrocolaptes picumnus*). *Condor* 84:272–285.

813. ———. 1983. Trans-andean *Xiphorhynchus* (Aves, Dendrocolaptidae) as army ant followers. *Rev. Bras. Biol.* 43:125–131.

814. ———. 1984a. *Phlegopsis erythroptera* (Gould, 1855) and relatives (Aves, Formicariidae) as army ant followers. *Rev. Bras. Zool.* 2:165–170.

815. ———. 1984b. Antshrikes (Formicariidae) as army ant followers. *Pap. Avul. Dept. Zool. São Paulo* 35:177–182.

816. ———. 1988. Behavioral notes, breeding records, and range extensions for Colombian birds. *Rev. Acad. Col. Cienc.* 16:137–150.

817. ———. 1992. Three *Chaemaeza* antthrushes in eastern Brazil (Formicariidae). *Condor* 94:110–116.

818. Willis, E. O., and E. Eisenmann. 1979. A revised list of birds of Barro Colorado Isl. Panama. *Smithson. Contrib. Zool.* 2911–2931.

819. Willis, E. O., D. Wechsler, and Y. Oniki. 1978. On the behavior and nesting of McConnell's Flycatcher (*Pipromorpha macconnelli*): does female rejection lead to male promiscuity? *Auk* 95:1–8.

820. Winkler, H., D. Christie, and D. Nurney. 1995.

Woodpeckers: A Guide to the Woodpeckers, Piculets and Wrynecks of the World. Pica Press, Sussex, U.K.

821. Yépez T., G. 1953. Estudio sobre la region de Perijá y sus habitantes, XI. El Indio y las aves. *Mem. Soc. Cienc. Nat. La Salle* 13(35):141–143.

822. ———. 1957. Aves colectadas por primera vez en Margarita. *Mem. Soc. Cienc. Nat. La Salle* 17:156–159.

823. ———. 1958. Nota sobre las aves de las Islas Coche y Cubagua. *Mem. Soc. Cienc. Nat. La Salle* 18:90–94.

824. ———. 1963–1964. Ornitología de las Islas Margarita, Coche y Cubajua (Venezuela). Pts. 1–4. *Mem. Soc. Cienc. Nat. La Salle* 23:75–112; 167–249; and 24:5–39; 103–162.

825. Young, C. G. 1929. A contribution to the ornithology of the coastland of British Guiana. *Publ. Univ. Zulia*, 12th ser., 5:1–38.

826. Zahl, P. A. 1950. Search for the Scarlet Ibis in Venezuela. *Natl. Geogr. Mag.* 97:633–661.

827. Zimmer, J. T. 1931–1955. Studies of Peruvian birds. *Am. Mus. Novit.* nos. 1–66. 3 vols.

828. Zimmer, J. T., and W. H. Phelps. 1944. New species and subspecies of birds from Venezuela. 1. *Am. Mus. Novit.* 1270:1–16.

829. ———. 1945. New species and subspecies of birds from Venezuela. 2. *Am. Mus. Novit.* 1274: 1–9.

830. ———. 1947. Twenty-three new subspecies of birds from Venezuela and Brazil. *Am. Mus. Novit.* 1312:1–23.

831. Zimmer, K. J. 1997. Species limits in *Cranioleuca vulpina. Studies in Neotropical Ornithology Honoring Ted Parker,* Ornithol. Monogr. no. 48:849–864.

832. ———. 1999. Behavior and vocalizations of the Caura and the Yapacana antbirds. *Wilson Bull.* 111:195–209.

833. Zimmer, K. J., and S. L. Hilty. 1997. Avifauna of a locality in the upper Orinoco drainage of Amazonas, Venezuela. *Studies in Neotropical Ornithology Honoring Ted Parker,* Ornithol. Monogr. no. 48:865–886.

834. Zimmer, K. J., and A. Whittaker. 2000. Species limits in Pale-tipped Tyrannulets (*Inezia*: Tyrannidae). *Wilson Bull.* 112:51–66.

835. Zonfrillo, B. 1977. Re-discovery of the Andean Condor (*Vultur gryphys*) in Venezuela. *Bull. Br. Ornithol. Club* 97:17–18.

836. Zuloaga, G. 1955. The Isla de Aves story. *Geograph. Rev.* 2:172–180.

837. Zyskowski, K., and R. O. Prum. 1999. Phylogenetic analysis of the nest architecture of neotropical ovenbirds (Furnariidae). *Auk* 116:891–911.

Index

English names are printed in roman type; scientific names are in italics. Numbers in bold refer to plate numbers; numbers in italics refer to text illustrations.

PAGE 876 IS BLANK

Speed Index to Commoner Groups

Numbers in bold refer to plate numbers.